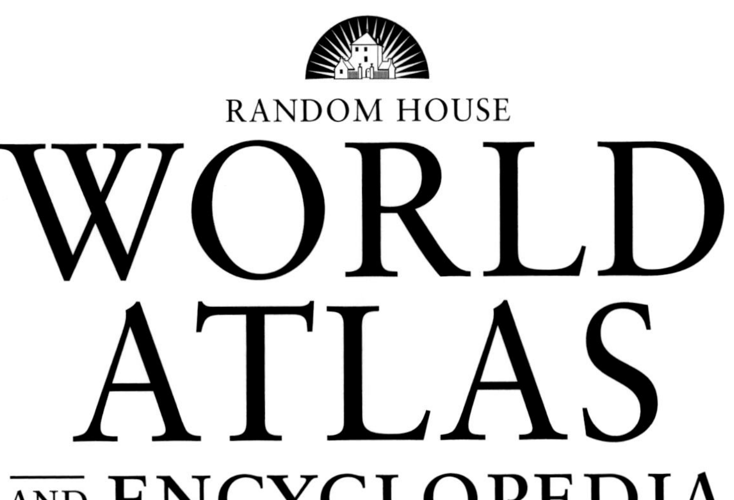

WORLD ATLAS AND ENCYCLOPEDIA

Vector data courtesy of Gräfe and Unser Verlag GmbH, München, Germany
(city-centre maps of Bangkok, Beijing, Cape Town, Jerusalem, Mexico City, Moscow, Singapore, Sydney, Tokyo and Washington D.C.)

The following city maps utilize base data supplied courtesy of MapQuest.com, Inc. (© MapQuest)
(Las Vegas, New Orleans, Orlando)

All satellite images in this section courtesy of NPA Group, Edenbridge, Kent (www.satmaps.com)

 Published in the United States by Random House Reference, an imprint of The Random House Information Group, a division of Random House, Inc., New York, and simultaneously in Canada by Random House of Canada Limited, Toronto.

Please address inquiries about electronic licensing of any products for use on a network, in software or on CD-ROM to the Subsidiary Rights Department, Random House Information Group, fax 212-572-6003.
This book is available at special discounts for bulk purchases for sales promotions or premiums. Special editions, including personalized covers, excerpts of existing books, and corporate imprints, can be created in large quantities for special needs. For more information, write to Random House, Inc., Special Markets/Premium Sales, 1745 Broadway, MD 6-2, New York, NY, 10019 or e-mail specialmarkets@randomhouse.com.

Visit the Random House Reference Web site: www.randomwords.com

Printed in Hong Kong
10 9 8 7 6 5 4 3 2 1

ISBN: 978-0-375-42610-0

RANDOM HOUSE

WORLD ATLAS AND ENCYCLOPEDIA

RANDOM HOUSE REFERENCE

NEW YORK TORONTO LONDON SYDNEY AUCKLAND

Contents

WORLD STATISTICS 8

Europe and Russia 10

Asia 11

Africa 12

Oceania and Antarctica 13

North America 14

South America 15

COUNTRIES OF THE WORLD 16

Afghanistan 17

Albania 18

Algeria 19

Angola 20

Antarctica 21

Argentina 22

Armenia 23

Atlantic Islands 24

- The Azores 24
- Bermuda 24
- Canary Islands 24
- Cape Verde 24
- Falkland Islands 24
- Madeira 24
- St Helena 25
- St Pierre & Miquelon 25
- São Tomé & Principe 25
- Tristan da Cunha 25

Australia 26

Austria 28

Azerbaijan 29

Bahrain 30

Bangladesh 31

Belarus 32

Belgium 33

Belize 34

Benin 35

Bhutan 36

Bolivia 37

Bosnia-Herzegovina 38

Botswana 39

Brazil 40

Bulgaria 42

Burkina Faso 43

Burma (Myanmar) 44

Burundi 45

Cambodia 46

Cameroon 47

Canada 48

Caribbean Islands 50

- Anguilla 50
- Antigua & Barbuda 50
- Aruba 50
- Bahamas 50
- Barbados 51
- Cayman Islands 51
- Dominica 51
- Grenada 52
- Guadeloupe 52
- Martinique 52
- Montserrat 52
- Netherlands Antilles 52
- Puerto Rico 52
- St Kitts & Nevis 52
- St Lucia 52
- St Vincent & The Grenadines 53
- Turks & Caicos Islands 53
- British Virgin Islands 53
- US Virgin Islands 53

Central African Republic 54

Chad 55

Chile 56

China 57

Colombia 60

Congo, Republic of The 61

Congo, Democratic Republic of The 62

Costa Rica 63

Croatia 64

Cuba 65

Cyprus 66

Czech Republic 67

Denmark 68

- Faeroe Islands 69
- Greenland 69

Djibouti 70

Dominican Republic 71

East Timor 72

Ecuador 73

Egypt 74

El Salvador 75

Equatorial Guinea 76

Eritrea 77

Estonia 78

Ethiopia 79

Fiji 80

Finland 81

France 82

French Guiana 84

Gabon 85

Gambia, The 86

Georgia 87

Germany 88

Ghana 90

Greece 91
Guatemala 92
Guinea 93
Guinea-Bissau 94
Guyana 95
Haiti 96
Honduras 97
Hungary 98
Iceland 99
India 100
Indian Ocean Islands 102
Christmas Island 102
Cocos Islands 102
Comoros 102
Maldives 103
Mayotte 103
Réunion 103
Seychelles 103
Indonesia 104
Iran 105
Iraq 106
Ireland 107
Israel 108
Italy 110
Vatican City 111
San Marino 111
Ivory Coast 112
Jamaica 113
Japan 114
Jordan 116
Kazakhstan 117
Kenya 118
Korea, North 119
Korea, South 120
Kuwait 121
Kyrgyzstan 122
Laos 123
Latvia 124
Lebanon 125
Lesotho 126
Liberia 127
Libya 128
Lithuania 129
Luxembourg 130
Macedonia 131
Madagascar 132
Malawi 133
Malaysia 134
Brunei 135
Mali 136
Malta 137
Mauritania 138
Mauritius 139
Mexico 140
Moldova 141
Mongolia 142
Montenegro 143
Morocco 144
Mozambique 145
Namibia 146
Nepal 147
Netherlands 148
New Zealand 149
Nicaragua 150
Niger 151
Nigeria 152
Norway 153
Oman 154
Pacific Ocean Islands 155
American Samoa 155
Cook Islands 155
French Polynesia 155
Guam 155
Kiribati 155
Marshall Islands 155
Micronesia 156
Nauru 156
New Caledonia 156
Niue 157
Norfolk Island 157
Northern Marianas 157
Palau 157
Pitcairn Island 157
Samoa 157
Solomon Islands 157
Tokelau 158
Tonga 158
Tuvalu 158
Vanuatu 158
Wallis & Futuna Islands 158
Pakistan 159
Panama 161
Papua New Guinea 162
Paraguay 163
Peru 164
Philippines 165
Poland 166
Portugal 167
Qatar 168
Romania 169
Russia 170
Rwanda 173
Saudi Arabia 174
Senegal 175
Serbia 176

Sierra Leone 177
Singapore 178
Slovak Republic 179
Slovenia 180
Somalia 181
South Africa 182
Spain 184
Andorra 185
Gibraltar 185
Sri Lanka 186
Sudan 187
Suriname 188
Swaziland 189
Sweden 190
Switzerland 191
Liechtenstein 191
Syria 192
Taiwan 193
Tajikistan 194
Tanzania 195
Thailand 196
Togo 197
Trinidad & Tobago 198
Tunisia 199
Turkey 200
Turkmenistan 201
Uganda 202
Ukraine 203
United Arab Emirates 204
United Kingdom 205
United States 207
Uruguay 210
Uzbekistan 211
Venezuela 212
Vietnam 213
Yemen 214
Zambia 215
Zimbabwe 216
Index and Picture Acknowledgements 217

CITY MAPS 221
Amsterdam 222
Athens 222
Atlanta 223
Baghdad 223
Bangkok 223
Barcelona 224
Beijing 224
Berlin 225
Boston 226
Budapest 227
Buenos Aires 227
Cairo 227
Cape Town 228
Copenhagen 228
Chicago 229
Delhi 230
Dublin 230
Edinburgh 231
Guangzhou 231
Helsinki 231
Hong Kong 232
Istanbul 232
Jakarta 232
Jerusalem 233
Johannesburg 233
Karachi 233
Kolkata 234
Lagos 234
Las Vegas 234
Lima 234
London 235
Lisbon 236
Los Angeles 236
Madrid 237
Manila 237
Melbourne 238
Mexico City 238
Miami 238
Milan 239
Moscow 239
Montreal 240
Mumbai 240
Munich 241
New Orleans 241
New York 242
Orlando 243
Osaka 243
Oslo 243
Paris 244
Prague 245
Rio de Janeiro 245
Rome 246
San Francisco 246
St Petersburg 247
Santiago 247
São Paulo 247
Seoul 247
Shanghai 248
Singapore City 248
Stockholm 249
Sydney 249
Tokyo 250
Tehran 251

Toronto 251
Vienna 252
Warsaw 252
Washington DC 253
Wellington 253

CITY MAP INDEX **254**

SATELLITE IMAGES **264**
Cape Town 264
Chicago 265
Karachi 266
London 267
New York 268
San Francisco 269
Santiago 270
Sydney 271
Tokyo 272

WORLD ATLAS **273**
World Political 274
Arctic Ocean 276
Antarctica 277
Europe Physical 278
Europe Political 279
Scandinavia 280
Ireland 282
Scotland 283
England and Wales 284
British Isles 286
Netherlands, Belgium, Luxembourg 287
Central Europe 288
Eastern Europe and Turkey 290
France 292
Spain and Portugal 293
Italy and the Balkan States 294
Balearics, Canaries, Madeira 296
Malta, Crete, Corfu, Rhodes, Cyprus 297
Asia Physical 298
Asia Political 299
Russia and Central Asia 300
Japan 302
China and the Far East 304
Northern China and Korea 306
Indonesia and the Philippines 308
Mainland South-East Asia 310
South Asia 312
Northern India, Pakistan, Nepal 314
The Middle East 316
The Near East 318
Arabia and the Horn of Africa 319
Africa Physical 320
Africa Political 321
Northern Africa 322
Central and Southern Africa 324
East Africa 326
Southern Africa 328
Australia and Oceania Physical and Political 330
New Zealand 331
Western Australia 332
Eastern Australia 334
Pacific Ocean 336
North America Physical 338
North America Political 339
Canada 340
Western Canada 342
Eastern Canada 344
United States 346
United States West 348
Central and Southern California and Western Washington 350
United States Mid-West and North-East 352
North-Eastern United States 354
United States South 356
Mexico 358
Central America and the West Indies 360
South America Physical 362
South America Political 363
South America North 364
Central South America 366
South America South 368

INDEX TO WORLD MAPS **369**

The World

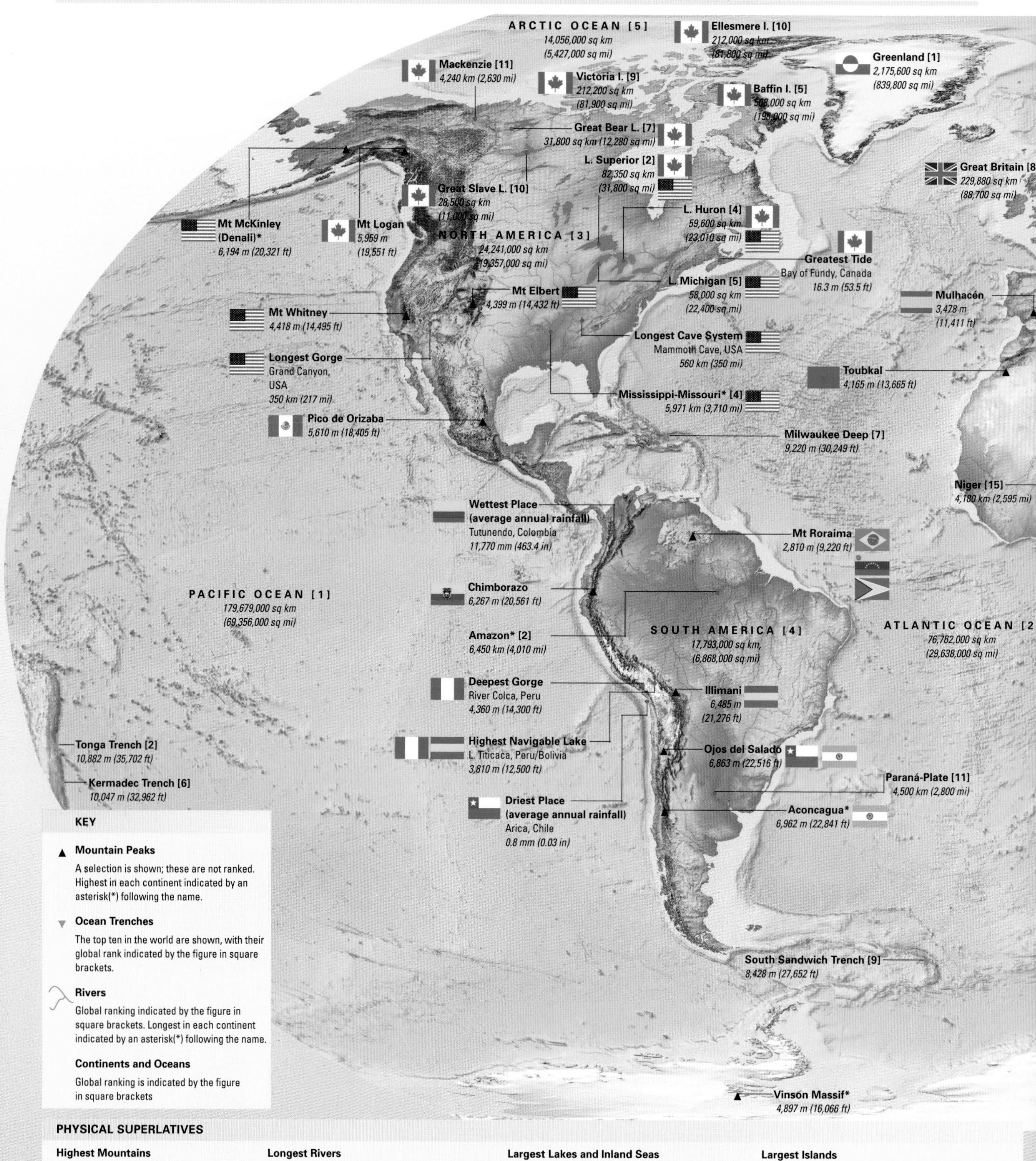

PHYSICAL SUPERLATIVES

Highest Mountains	Longest Rivers	Largest Lakes and Inland Seas	Largest Islands
1 Everest, Asia *8,850 m (29,035 ft)*	1 Nile, Africa *6,670 km (4,140 mi)*	1 Caspian Sea, Asia *371,000 sq km (143,000 sq mi)*	1 Greenland, N. America *2,175,600 sq km (839,800 sq mi)*
2 K2 (Godwin Austen), Asia *8,611 m (28,251 ft)*	2 Amazon, S. America *6,450 km (4,010 mi)*	2 Lake Superior, N. America *82,350 sq km (31,800 sq mi)*	2 New Guinea, Oceania *821,030 sq km (317,000 sq mi)*
3 Kanchenjunga, Asia *8,598 m (28,208 ft)*	3 Yangtze, Asia *6,380 km (3,960 mi)*	3 Lake Victoria, Africa *68,000 sq km (26,000 sq mi)*	3 Borneo, Asia *744,360 sq km (287,400 sq mi)*
4 Lhotse, Asia *8,516 m (27,939 ft)*	4 Mississippi-Missouri, N. America *5,971 km (3,710 mi)*	4 Lake Huron, N. America *59,600 sq km (23,010 sq mi)*	4 Madagascar, Africa *587,040 sq km (226,660 sq mi)*
5 Makalu, Asia *8,481 m (27,824 ft)*	5 Yenisey-Angara, Asia *5,550 km (3,445 mi)*	5 Lake Michigan, N. America *58,000 sq km (22,400 sq mi)*	5 Baffin Island, N. America *508,000 sq km (196,100 sq mi)*
6 Cho Oyu, Asia *8,201 m (26,906 ft)*	6 Huang He, Asia *5,464 km (3,395 mi)*	6 Lake Tanganyika, Africa *33,000 sq km (13,000 sq mi)*	6 Sumatra, Asia *473,600 sq km (182,860 sq mi)*
7 Dhaulagiri, Asia *8,172 m (26,811 ft)*	7 Ob-Irtysh, Asia *5,410 km (3,360 mi)*	7 Great Bear Lake, N. America *31,800 sq km (12,280 sq mi)*	7 Honshu, Asia *230,500 sq km (88,980 sq mi)*
8 Manaslu, Asia *8,156 m (26,758 ft)*	8 Congo, Africa *4,670 km (2,900 mi)*	8 Lake Baikal, Asia *30,500 sq km (11,780 sq mi)*	8 Great Britain, Europe *229,880 sq km (88,700 sq mi)*
9 Nanga Parbat, Asia *8,126 m (26,660 ft)*	9 Mekong, Asia *4,500 km (2,795 mi)*	9 Lake Malawi/Nyasa, Africa *29,600 sq km (11,430 sq mi)*	9 Victoria Island, N. America *212,200 sq km (81,900 sq mi)*
10 Annapurna, Asia *8,078 m (26,502 ft)*	10 Amur, Asia *4,442 km (2,760 mi)*	10 Great Slave Lake, N. America *28,500 sq km (11,000 sq mi)*	10 Ellesmere Island, N. America *212,000 sq km (81,800 sq mi)*

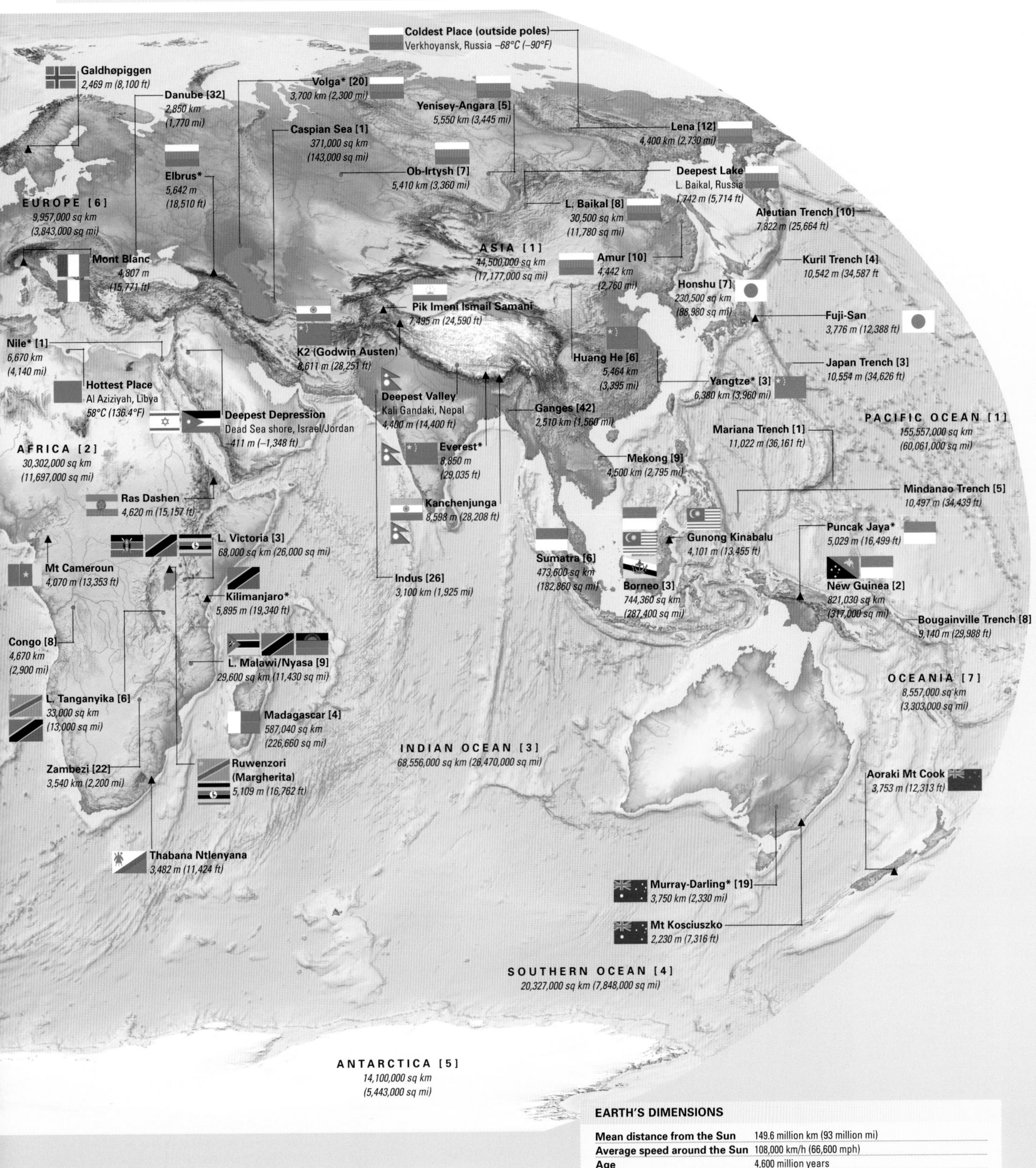

EARTH'S DIMENSIONS

Mean distance from the Sun	149.6 million km (93 million mi)
Average speed around the Sun	108,000 km/h (66,600 mph)
Age	4,600 million years
Mass	5.9×10^{21} tonnes
Density (water = 1)	5.52
Volume	$1,083,230 \times 10^{6}$ cu km ($260,000 \times 10^{6}$ cu mi)
Area	510 million sq km (197 million sq mi)
Land surface	149 million sq km (58 million sq mi) = 29.3% of total area
Water surface	361 million sq km (139 million sq mi) = 70.7% of total area
Equatorial circumference	40,074 km (24,901 mi)
Polar circumference	40,008 km (24,860 mi)
Equatorial diameter	12,756 km (7,926 mi)
Polar diameter	12,714 km (7,900 mi)

INSIDE THE EARTH

Layer	Density (water = 1)	Temperature		State	Thickness	
Crust (continental)	2.8	<500°C	(930°F)	Solid	*c.* 40 km	(*c.* 25 mi)
Crust (oceanic)	2.9	<1,100°C	(2,010°F)	Solid	*c.* 7 km	(*c.* 4 mi)
Upper mantle	4.3	<1,400°C	(2,550°F)	Molten	*c.* 900 km	(*c.* 560 mi)
Lower mantle	5.5	<1,700°C	(3,090°F)	Solid	*c.* 1,900 km	(*c.* 1,180 mi)
Outer core	10.0	<2,300°C	(7,170°F)	Molten	*c.* 2,200 km	(*c.* 1,370 mi)
Inner core	13.5	<5,500°C	(9,930°F)	Solid	*c.* 1,300 km	(*c.* 810 mi)

Europe and Russia

COUNTRIES: AREA

	Country/Territory	Area sq km (thousands)	Area sq mi (thousands)
Largest			
1	Russia	17,075	6,593
2	Ukraine	604	233
3	France	552	213
4	Spain	498	192
5	Sweden	450	174
6	Germany	357	138
7	Finland	338	131
8	Norway	324	125
9	Poland	323	125
10	Italy	301	116
11	United Kingdom	242	93.4
12	Romania	238	92.0
13	Belarus	208	80.2
14	Greece	132	50.9
15	Bulgaria	111	42.8
16	Iceland	103	39.8
17	Serbia & Montenegro*	102	39.4
18	Hungary	93.0	35.9
19	Portugal	88.8	34.3
20	Austria	83.9	32.4
Smallest			
1	Vatican City	0.0004	0.0002
2	Monaco	0.001	0.0004
3	Gibraltar (UK)	0.006	0.002
4	San Marino	0.06	0.02
5	Liechtenstein	0.16	0.06
6	Malta	0.32	0.12
7	Andorra	0.47	0.18
8	Færoe Is. (Denmark)	1.4	0.54
9	Luxembourg	2.6	1.0
10	Slovenia	20.3	7.8

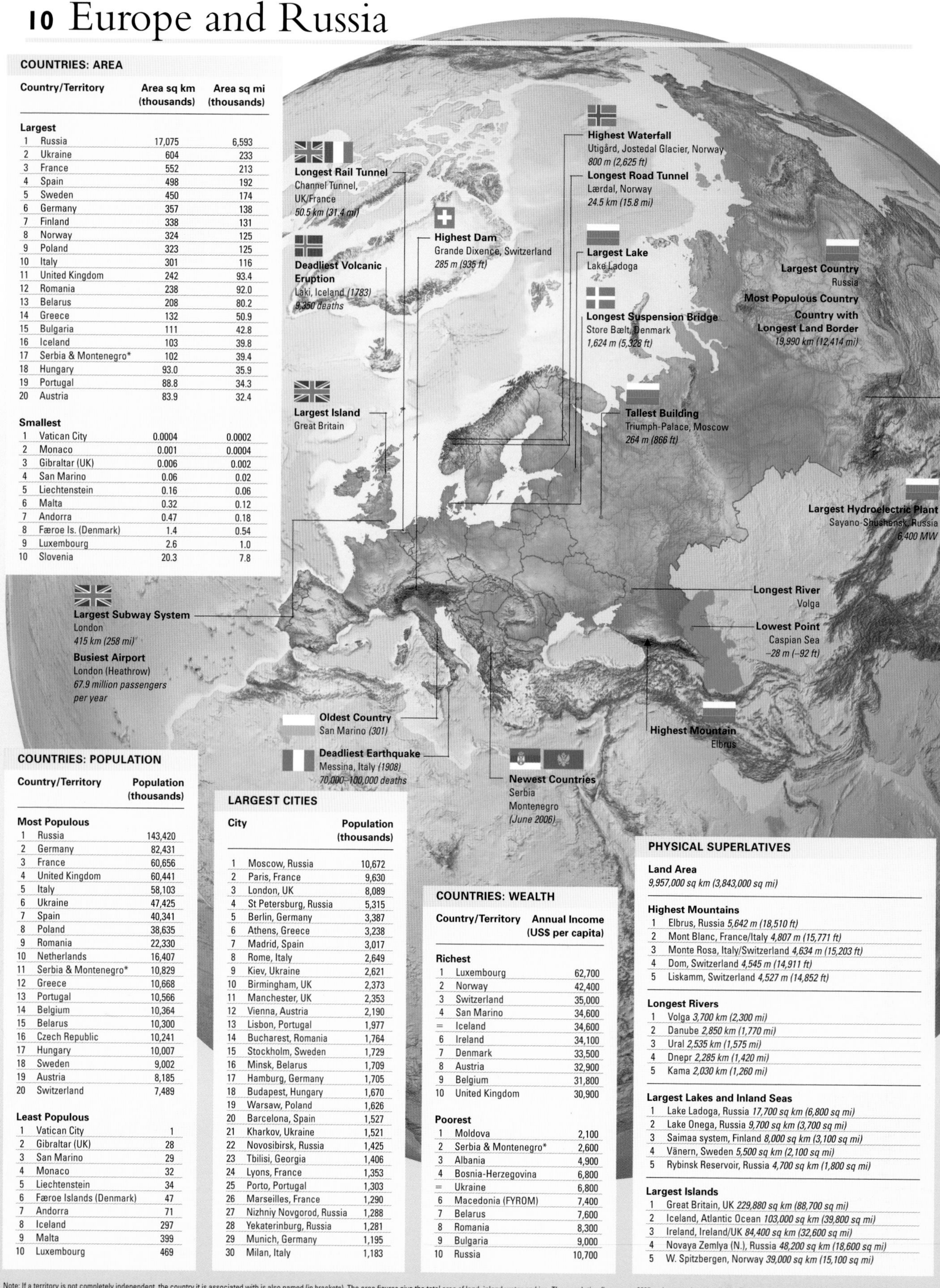

COUNTRIES: POPULATION

	Country/Territory	Population (thousands)
Most Populous		
1	Russia	143,420
2	Germany	82,431
3	France	60,656
4	United Kingdom	60,441
5	Italy	58,103
6	Ukraine	47,425
7	Spain	40,341
8	Poland	38,635
9	Romania	22,330
10	Netherlands	16,407
11	Serbia & Montenegro*	10,829
12	Greece	10,668
13	Portugal	10,566
14	Belgium	10,364
15	Belarus	10,300
16	Czech Republic	10,241
17	Hungary	10,007
18	Sweden	9,002
19	Austria	8,185
20	Switzerland	7,489
Least Populous		
1	Vatican City	1
2	Gibraltar (UK)	28
3	San Marino	29
4	Monaco	32
5	Liechtenstein	34
6	Færoe Islands (Denmark)	47
7	Andorra	71
8	Iceland	297
9	Malta	399
10	Luxembourg	469

LARGEST CITIES

	City	Population (thousands)
1	Moscow, Russia	10,672
2	Paris, France	9,630
3	London, UK	8,089
4	St Petersburg, Russia	5,315
5	Berlin, Germany	3,387
6	Athens, Greece	3,238
7	Madrid, Spain	3,017
8	Rome, Italy	2,649
9	Kiev, Ukraine	2,621
10	Birmingham, UK	2,373
11	Manchester, UK	2,353
12	Vienna, Austria	2,190
13	Lisbon, Portugal	1,977
14	Bucharest, Romania	1,764
15	Stockholm, Sweden	1,729
16	Minsk, Belarus	1,709
17	Hamburg, Germany	1,705
18	Budapest, Hungary	1,670
19	Warsaw, Poland	1,626
20	Barcelona, Spain	1,527
21	Kharkov, Ukraine	1,521
22	Novosibirsk, Russia	1,425
23	Tbilisi, Georgia	1,406
24	Lyons, France	1,353
25	Porto, Portugal	1,303
26	Marseilles, France	1,290
27	Nizhniy Novgorod, Russia	1,288
28	Yekaterinburg, Russia	1,281
29	Munich, Germany	1,195
30	Milan, Italy	1,183

COUNTRIES: WEALTH

	Country/Territory	Annual Income (US$ per capita)
Richest		
1	Luxembourg	62,700
2	Norway	42,400
3	Switzerland	35,000
4	San Marino	34,600
=	Iceland	34,600
6	Ireland	34,100
7	Denmark	33,500
8	Austria	32,900
9	Belgium	31,800
10	United Kingdom	30,900
Poorest		
1	Moldova	2,100
2	Serbia & Montenegro*	2,600
3	Albania	4,900
4	Bosnia-Herzegovina	6,800
=	Ukraine	6,800
6	Macedonia (FYROM)	7,400
7	Belarus	7,600
8	Romania	8,300
9	Bulgaria	9,000
10	Russia	10,700

PHYSICAL SUPERLATIVES

Land Area

9,957,000 sq km (3,843,000 sq mi)

Highest Mountains

1. Elbrus, Russia *5,642 m (18,510 ft)*
2. Mont Blanc, France/Italy *4,807 m (15,771 ft)*
3. Monte Rosa, Italy/Switzerland *4,634 m (15,203 ft)*
4. Dom, Switzerland *4,545 m (14,911 ft)*
5. Liskamm, Switzerland *4,527 m (14,852 ft)*

Longest Rivers

1. Volga *3,700 km (2,300 mi)*
2. Danube *2,850 km (1,770 mi)*
3. Ural *2,535 km (1,575 mi)*
4. Dnepr *2,285 km (1,420 mi)*
5. Kama *2,030 km (1,260 mi)*

Largest Lakes and Inland Seas

1. Lake Ladoga, Russia *17,700 sq km (6,800 sq mi)*
2. Lake Onega, Russia *9,700 sq km (3,700 sq mi)*
3. Saimaa system, Finland *8,000 sq km (3,100 sq mi)*
4. Vänern, Sweden *5,500 sq km (2,100 sq mi)*
5. Rybinsk Reservoir, Russia *4,700 sq km (1,800 sq mi)*

Largest Islands

1. Great Britain, UK *229,880 sq km (88,700 sq mi)*
2. Iceland, Atlantic Ocean *103,000 sq km (39,800 sq mi)*
3. Ireland, Ireland/UK *84,400 sq km (32,600 sq mi)*
4. Novaya Zemlya (N.), Russia *48,200 sq km (18,600 sq mi)*
5. W. Spitzbergen, Norway *39,000 sq km (15,100 sq mi)*

Note: If a territory is not completely independent, the country it is associated with is also named (in brackets). The area figures give the total area of land, inland water and ice. The population figures are 2005 estimates where available. The annual income is the Gross Domestic Product per capita (measured using the purchasing-power parity method, enabling comparisons to be made between countries through their purchasing power) in US dollars; the figures are the latest available, usually 2005 estimates. The city population figures are taken from the most recent census or estimate available, and as far as possible are the population of the metropolitan area or urban agglomeration (for example, greater New York or Paris).

*In June 2006, Serbia and Montenegro formally declared their independence and are now separate sovereign states.

COUNTRIES: AREA

	Country/Territory	Area sq km (thousands)	Area sq mi (thousands)
Largest			
1	China	9,597	3,705
2	India	3,287	1,269
3	Kazakhstan	2,725	1,052
4	Saudi Arabia	2,150	830
5	Indonesia	1,905	735
6	Iran	1,648	636
7	Mongolia	1,567	605
8	Pakistan	796	307
9	Turkey	775	299
10	Burma (= Myanmar)	677	261
11	Afghanistan	652	252
12	Yemen	528	204
13	Thailand	513	198
14	Turkmenistan	488	188
15	Uzbekistan	447	173
16	Iraq	438	169
17	Japan	378	146
18	Vietnam	332	128
19	Malaysia	330	127
20	Oman	310	119
Smallest			
1	Macau (China)	0.02	0.007
2	Maldives	0.30	0.12
3	Gaza Strip (OPT)	0.36	0.14
4	Singapore	0.68	0.26
5	Bahrain	0.69	0.27
6	Hong Kong (China)	1.1	0.42
7	Brunei	5.8	2.2
8	West Bank (OPT)	5.9	2.3
9	Cyprus	9.3	3.6
10	Lebanon	10.4	4.0

COUNTRIES: POPULATION

	Country/Territory	Population (thousands)
Most Populous		
1	China	1,306,314
2	India	1,080,264
3	Indonesia	241,974
4	Pakistan	162,420
5	Bangladesh	144,320
6	Japan	127,417
7	Philippines	87,857
8	Vietnam	83,536
9	Turkey	69,661
10	Iran	68,018
11	Thailand	65,444
12	South Korea	48,423
13	Burma (= Myanmar)	42,909
14	Afghanistan	29,929
15	Nepal	27,677
16	Uzbekistan	26,851
17	Saudi Arabia	26,418
18	Iraq	26,075
19	Malaysia	23,953
20	North Korea	22,912
Least Populous		
1	Maldives	349
2	Brunei	372
3	Macau (China)	449
4	Bahrain	688
5	Cyprus	780
6	Qatar	863
7	East Timor	1,041
8	Gaza Strip (OPT)	1,376
9	Bhutan	2,232
10	Kuwait	2,336

LARGEST CITIES

	City	Population (thousands)
1	Mumbai (Bombay), India	18,336
2	Delhi, India	15,334
3	Kolkata (Calcutta), India	14,299
4	Jakarta, Indonesia	13,194
5	Shanghai, China	12,665
6	Dhaka, Bangladesh	12,560
7	Tokyo, Japan	12,064
8	Karachi, Pakistan	11,819
9	Beijing, China	10,849
10	Manila, Philippines	10,677
11	Seoul, South Korea	9,888
12	Tianjin, China	9,346
13	Istanbul, Turkey	8,953
14	Tehran, Iran	7,352
15	Hong Kong, China	7,182
16	Chennai (Madras), India	6,915
17	Bangkok, Thailand	6,604
18	Bangalore, India	6,532
19	Yokohama, Japan	6,427
20	Lahore, Pakistan	6,373
21	Hyderabad, India	6,145
22	Wuhan, China	6,003
23	Baghdad, Iraq	5,910
24	Riyadh, Saudi Arabia	5,514
25	Ahmedabad, India	5,171
26	Ho Chi Minh City, Vietnam	5,030
27	Chongqing, China	4,975
28	Shenyang, China	4,916
29	Pune, India	4,485
30	Singapore City, Singapore	4,372

COUNTRIES: WEALTH

	Country/Territory	Annual Income (US$ per capita)
Richest		
1	Hong Kong (China)	36,800
2	Japan	30,400
3	Singapore	29,700
4	United Arab Emirates	29,100
5	Taiwan	26,700
6	Qatar	26,000
7	Brunei	23,600
8	Israel	22,200
9	Kuwait	22,100
10	Cyprus	21,600
Poorest		
1	East Timor	400
2	Gaza Strip (OPT)	600
3	Afghanistan	800
=	Yemen	800
5	West Bank (OPT)	1,100
6	Tajikistan	1,200
7	Bhutan	1,400
8	Nepal	1,500
9	North Korea	1,800
=	Burma (= Myanmar)	1,800

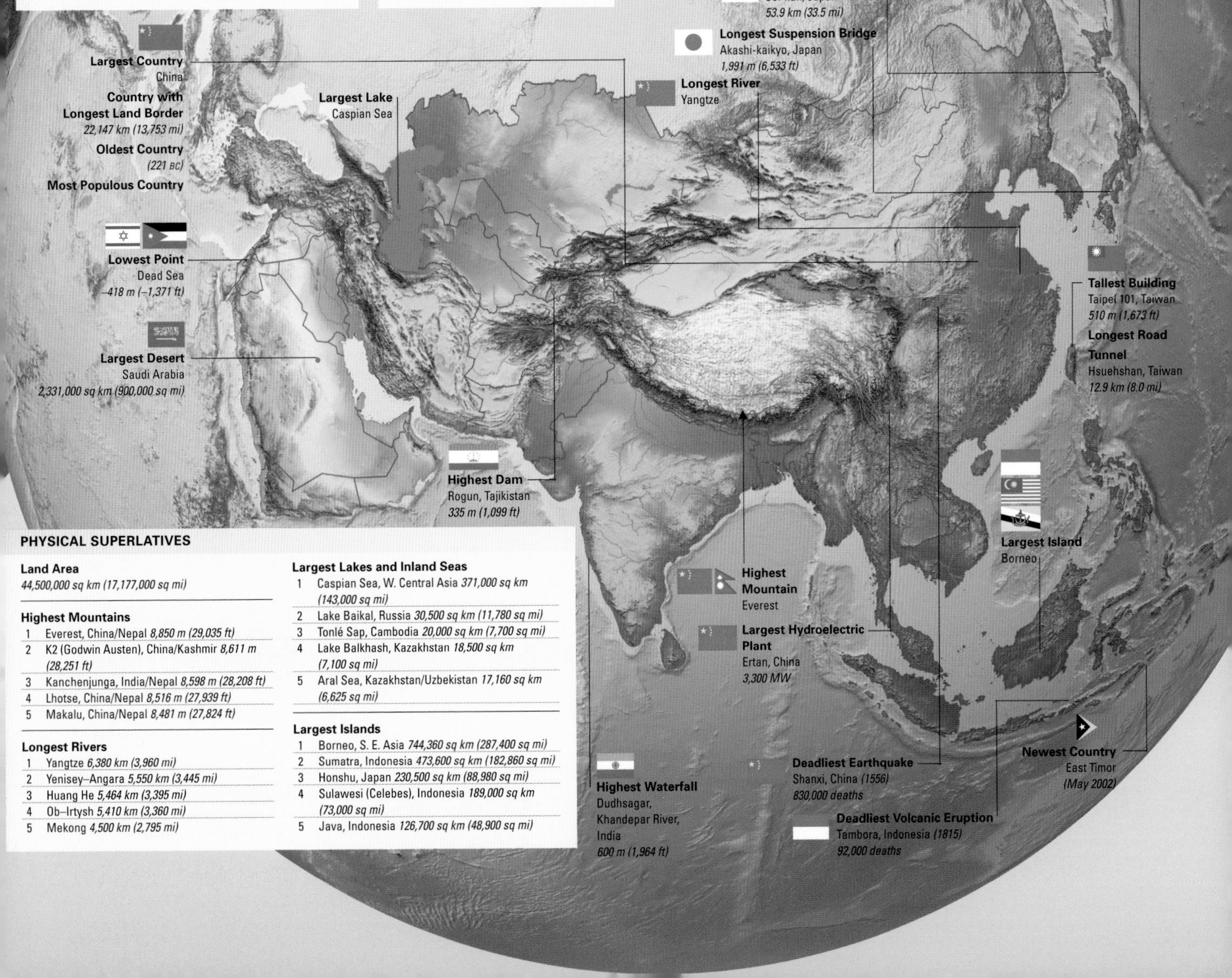

PHYSICAL SUPERLATIVES

Land Area
44,500,000 sq km (17,177,000 sq mi)

Highest Mountains
1. Everest, China/Nepal *8,850 m (29,035 ft)*
2. K2 (Godwin Austen), China/Kashmir *8,611 m (28,251 ft)*
3. Kanchenjunga, India/Nepal *8,598 m (28,208 ft)*
4. Lhotse, China/Nepal *8,516 m (27,939 ft)*
5. Makalu, China/Nepal *8,481 m (27,824 ft)*

Longest Rivers
1. Yangtze *6,380 km (3,960 mi)*
2. Yenisey–Angara *5,550 km (3,445 mi)*
3. Huang He *5,464 km (3,395 mi)*
4. Ob–Irtysh *5,410 km (3,360 mi)*
5. Mekong *4,500 km (2,795 mi)*

Largest Lakes and Inland Seas
1. Caspian Sea, W. Central Asia *371,000 sq km (143,000 sq mi)*
2. Lake Baikal, Russia *30,500 sq km (11,780 sq mi)*
3. Tonlé Sap, Cambodia *20,000 sq km (7,700 sq mi)*
4. Lake Balkhash, Kazakhstan *18,500 sq km (7,100 sq mi)*
5. Aral Sea, Kazakhstan/Uzbekistan *17,160 sq km (6,625 sq mi)*

Largest Islands
1. Borneo, S. E. Asia *744,360 sq km (287,400 sq mi)*
2. Sumatra, Indonesia *473,600 sq km (182,860 sq mi)*
3. Honshu, Japan *230,500 sq km (88,980 sq mi)*
4. Sulawesi (Celebes), Indonesia *189,000 sq km (73,000 sq mi)*
5. Java, Indonesia *126,700 sq km (48,900 sq mi)*

Africa

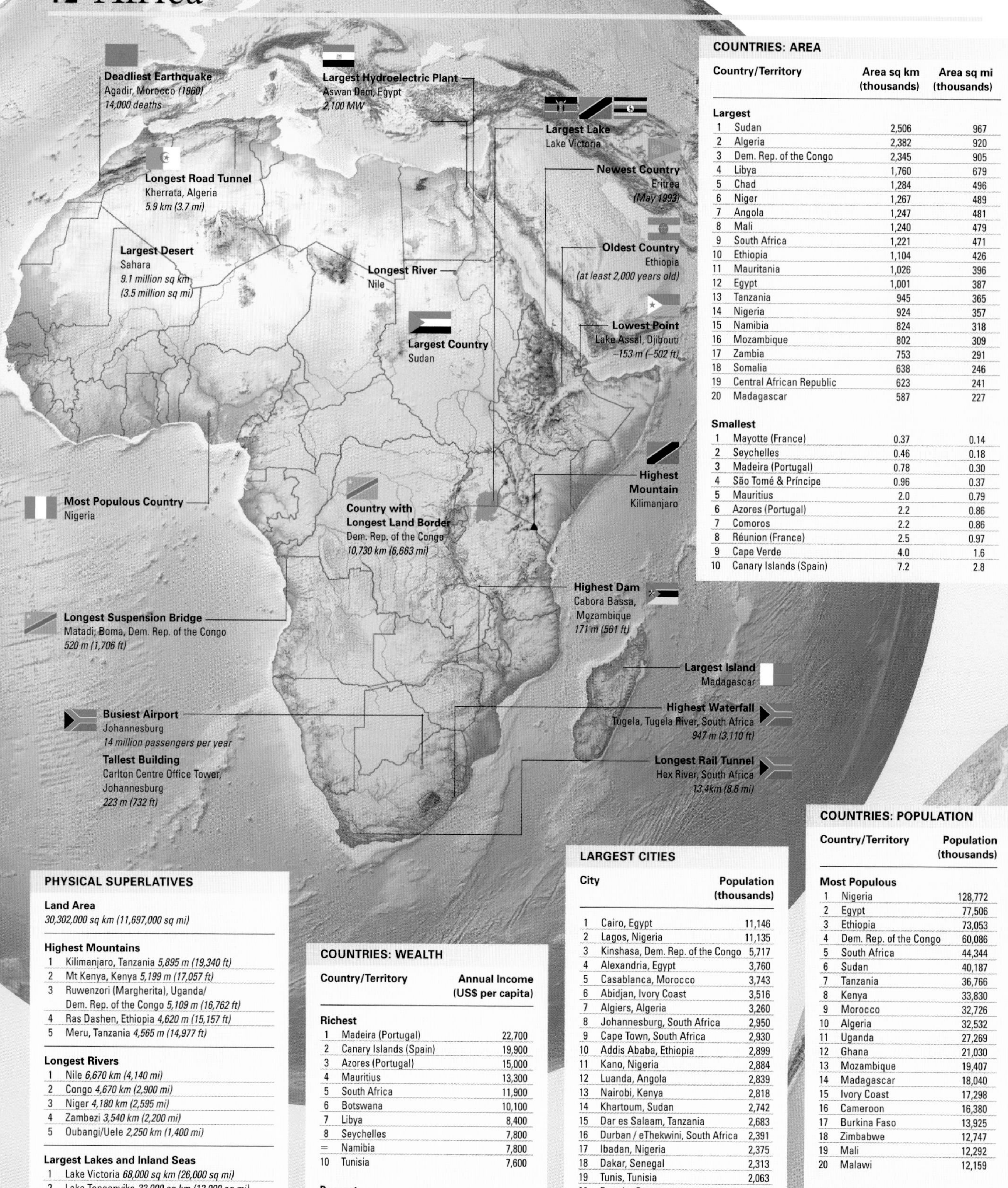

COUNTRIES: AREA

	Country/Territory	Area sq km (thousands)	Area sq mi (thousands)
Largest			
1	Sudan	2,506	967
2	Algeria	2,382	920
3	Dem. Rep. of the Congo	2,345	905
4	Libya	1,760	679
5	Chad	1,284	496
6	Niger	1,267	489
7	Angola	1,247	481
8	Mali	1,240	479
9	South Africa	1,221	471
10	Ethiopia	1,104	426
11	Mauritania	1,026	396
12	Egypt	1,001	387
13	Tanzania	945	365
14	Nigeria	924	357
15	Namibia	824	318
16	Mozambique	802	309
17	Zambia	753	291
18	Somalia	638	246
19	Central African Republic	623	241
20	Madagascar	587	227
Smallest			
1	Mayotte (France)	0.37	0.14
2	Seychelles	0.46	0.18
3	Madeira (Portugal)	0.78	0.30
4	São Tomé & Príncipe	0.96	0.37
5	Mauritius	2.0	0.79
6	Azores (Portugal)	2.2	0.86
7	Comoros	2.2	0.86
8	Réunion (France)	2.5	0.97
9	Cape Verde	4.0	1.6
10	Canary Islands (Spain)	7.2	2.8

PHYSICAL SUPERLATIVES

Land Area
30,302,000 sq km (11,697,000 sq mi)

Highest Mountains
1. Kilimanjaro, Tanzania *5,895 m (19,340 ft)*
2. Mt Kenya, Kenya *5,199 m (17,057 ft)*
3. Ruwenzori (Margherita), Uganda/ Dem. Rep. of the Congo *5,109 m (16,762 ft)*
4. Ras Dashen, Ethiopia *4,620 m (15,157 ft)*
5. Meru, Tanzania *4,565 m (14,977 ft)*

Longest Rivers
1. Nile *6,670 km (4,140 mi)*
2. Congo *4,670 km (2,900 mi)*
3. Niger *4,180 km (2,595 mi)*
4. Zambezi *3,540 km (2,200 mi)*
5. Oubangi/Uele *2,250 km (1,400 mi)*

Largest Lakes and Inland Seas
1. Lake Victoria *68,000 sq km (26,000 sq mi)*
2. Lake Tanganyika *33,000 sq km (13,000 sq mi)*
3. Lake Malawi/Nyasa *29,600 sq km (11,430 sq mi)*
4. Lake Chad *25,000 sq km (9,700 sq mi)*
5. Lake Turkana *8,500 sq km (3,300 sq mi)*

Largest Islands
1. Madagascar *587,040 sq km (226,660 sq mi)*
2. Socotra *3,600 sq km (1,400 sq mi)*
3. Réunion *2,500 sq km (965 sq mi)*
4. Tenerife *2,350 sq km (900 sq mi)*
5. Mauritius *1,865 sq km (720 sq mi)*

COUNTRIES: WEALTH

	Country/Territory	Annual Income (US$ per capita)
Richest		
1	Madeira (Portugal)	22,700
2	Canary Islands (Spain)	19,900
3	Azores (Portugal)	15,000
4	Mauritius	13,300
5	South Africa	11,900
6	Botswana	10,100
7	Libya	8,400
8	Seychelles	7,800
=	Namibia	7,800
10	Tunisia	7,600
Poorest		
1	Comoros	600
=	Malawi	600
=	Somalia	600
4	Burundi	700
=	Liberia	700
=	Tanzania	700
7	Congo	800
=	Dem. Rep. of the Congo	800
=	Ethiopia	800
=	Sierra Leone	800

LARGEST CITIES

	City	Population (thousands)
1	Cairo, Egypt	11,146
2	Lagos, Nigeria	11,135
3	Kinshasa, Dem. Rep. of the Congo	5,717
4	Alexandria, Egypt	3,760
5	Casablanca, Morocco	3,743
6	Abidjan, Ivory Coast	3,516
7	Algiers, Algeria	3,260
8	Johannesburg, South Africa	2,950
9	Cape Town, South Africa	2,930
10	Addis Ababa, Ethiopia	2,899
11	Kano, Nigeria	2,884
12	Luanda, Angola	2,839
13	Nairobi, Kenya	2,818
14	Khartoum, Sudan	2,742
15	Dar es Salaam, Tanzania	2,683
16	Durban / eThekwini, South Africa	2,391
17	Ibadan, Nigeria	2,375
18	Dakar, Senegal	2,313
19	Tunis, Tunisia	2,063
20	Douala, Cameroon	1,980
21	Accra, Ghana	1,970
22	Rabat, Morocco	1,859
23	Antananarivo, Madagascar	1,808
24	Tripoli, Libya	1,733
25	Yaoundé, Cameroon	1,727
26	Pretoria / Tshwane, South Africa	1,590
27	Harare, Zimbabwe	1,527
28	Conakry, Guinea	1,465
29	Lusaka, Zambia	1,450
30	Bamako, Mali	1,379

COUNTRIES: POPULATION

	Country/Territory	Population (thousands)
Most Populous		
1	Nigeria	128,772
2	Egypt	77,506
3	Ethiopia	73,053
4	Dem. Rep. of the Congo	60,086
5	South Africa	44,344
6	Sudan	40,187
7	Tanzania	36,766
8	Kenya	33,830
9	Morocco	32,726
10	Algeria	32,532
11	Uganda	27,269
12	Ghana	21,030
13	Mozambique	19,407
14	Madagascar	18,040
15	Ivory Coast	17,298
16	Cameroon	16,380
17	Burkina Faso	13,925
18	Zimbabwe	12,747
19	Mali	12,292
20	Malawi	12,159
Least Populous		
1	Seychelles	81
2	São Tomé & Príncipe	187
3	Mayotte (France)	194
4	Azores (Portugal)	236
5	Madeira (Portugal)	241
6	Western Sahara	273
7	Cape Verde	418
8	Djibouti	477
9	Equatorial Guinea	536
10	Comoros	671

PHYSICAL SUPERLATIVES

Land Area
8,557,000 sq km (3,303,000 sq mi)

Highest Mountains
1. Puncak Jaya, Indonesia *5,029 m (16,499 ft)*
2. Puncak Trikora, Indonesia *4,730 m (15,518 ft)*
3. Puncak Mandala, Indonesia *4,702 m (15,427 ft)*
4. Mt Wilhelm, Papua New Guinea *4,508 m (14,790 ft)*
5. Mauna Kea, USA (Hawai'i) *4,205 m (13,796 ft)*

Longest Rivers
1. Murray–Darling *3,750 km (2,330 mi)*
2. Darling *3,070 km (1,905 mi)*
3. Murray *2,575 km (1,600 mi)*
4. Murrumbidgee *1,690 km (1,050 mi)*
5. Lachlan *1,370 km (850 mi)*

Largest Lakes and Inland Seas
1. Lake Eyre, Australia *8,900 sq km (3,400 sq mi)*
2. Lake Torrens, Australia *5,800 sq km (2,200 sq mi)*
3. Lake Gairdner, Australia *4,800 sq km (1,900 sq mi)*
4. Lake Mackay, Australia *3,490 sq km (1,380 sq mi)*
5. Lake Amadeus, Australia *1,032 sq km (400 sq mi)*

Largest Islands
1. New Guinea, Indon./Papua NG *821,030 sq km (317,000 sq mi)*
2. New Zealand (S.), Pacific Ocean *150,500 sq km (58,100 sq mi)*
3. New Zealand (N.), Pacific Ocean *114,700 sq km (44,300 sq mi)*
4. Tasmania, Australia *67,800 sq km (26,200 sq mi)*
5. New Britain, Papua NG *37,800 sq km (14,600 sq mi)*

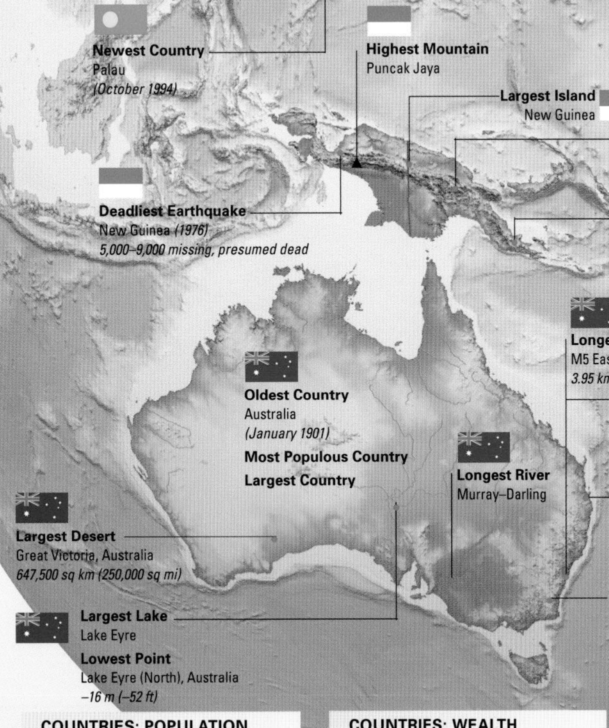

COUNTRIES: AREA

	Country/Territory	Area sq km (thousands)	Area sq mi (thousands)
1	Australia	7,741	2,989
2	Papua New Guinea	463	179
3	New Zealand	271	104
4	Solomon Islands	28.9	11.2
5	New Caledonia (France)	18.6	7.2
6	Fiji Islands	18.3	7.1
7	Vanuatu	12.2	4.7
8	French Polynesia (France)	4.0	1.5
9	Samoa	2.8	1.1
10	Kiribati	0.73	0.28
11	Fed. States of Micronesia	0.70	0.27
12	Tonga	0.65	0.25
13	Guam (US)	0.55	0.21
14	Northern Mariana Islands (US)	0.46	0.18
15	Palau	0.46	0.18
16	Cook Is. (NZ)	0.24	0.09
17	American Samoa (US)	0.20	0.08
18	Wallis & Futuna Islands (France)	0.20	0.08
19	Marshall Islands	0.18	0.07
20	Tuvalu	0.03	0.01
21	Nauru	0.02	0.008

COUNTRIES: POPULATION

	Country/Territory	Population (thousands)
1	Australia	20,090
2	Papua New Guinea	5,545
3	New Zealand	4,035
4	Fiji Islands	893
5	Solomon Islands	538
6	French Polynesia (France)	270
7	New Caledonia (France)	216
8	Vanuatu	206
9	Samoa	177
10	Guam (US)	169
11	Tonga	112
12	Fed. States of Micronesia	108
13	Kiribati	103
14	Northern Mariana Is. (US)	80
15	Marshall Islands	59
16	American Samoa (US)	58
17	Cook Islands (NZ)	21
18	Palau	20
19	Wallis & Futuna Is. (France)	16
20	Nauru	13
21	Tuvalu	12

COUNTRIES: WEALTH

	Country/Territory	Annual Income (US$ per capita)
1	Australia	32,000
2	New Zealand	24,100
3	Guam (US)	21,000
4	French Polynesia (France)	17,500
5	New Caledonia (France)	15,000
6	Northern Mariana Is. (US)	12,500
7	Palau	9,000
8	American Samoa (US)	8,000
9	Fiji Islands	6,000
10	Samoa	5,600
11	Nauru	5,000
12	Cook Islands (NZ)	5,000
13	Wallis & Futuna Is. (France)	3,800
14	Vanuatu	2,900
15	Papua New Guinea	2,400
16	Tonga	2,300
17	Fed. States of Micronesia	2,000
18	Solomon Islands	1,700
19	Marshall Islands	1,600
20	Tuvalu	1,100
21	Kiribati	800

LARGEST CITIES

	City	Population (thousands)
1	Sydney, Australia	4,388
2	Melbourne, Australia	3,663
3	Brisbane, Australia	1,769
4	Perth, Australia	1,484
5	Auckland, New Zealand	1,152
6	Adelaide, Australia	1,137

Antarctica

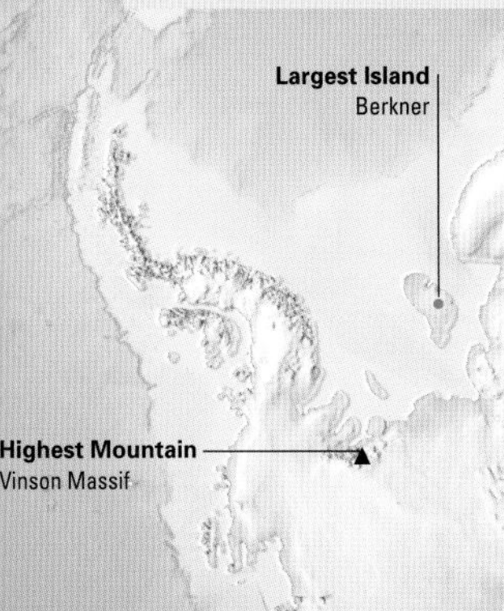

PHYSICAL SUPERLATIVES

Land Area
14,100,000 sq km (5,443,000 sq mi)

Highest Mountains
1. Vinson Massif, W. Antarctica *4,897 m (16,066 ft)*
2. Mt Tyree, W. Antarctica *4,852 m (15,920 ft)*
3. Mt Kirkpatrick, Transantarctic Mountains *4,528 m (14,855 ft)*
4. Mt Markham, Transantarctic Mountains *4,349 m (14,268 ft)*
5. Mt Jackson, Antarctic Peninsula *4,191 m (13,751 ft)*

Largest Islands
1. Berkner, Ronne Ice Shelf *47,920 sq km (18,500 sq mi)*
2. Alexander, Bellingshausen Sea *43,200 sq km (16,630 sq mi)*
3. Thurston, Amundsen Sea *15,700 sq km (6,045 sq mi)*
4. Carney, Amundsen Sea *8,500 sq km (3,275 sq mi)*
5. Roosevelt, Ross Ice Shelf *7,500 sq km (2,890 sq mi)*

North America

Highest Mountain
Mt McKinley (Denali)

Largest Island
Greenland

Largest Lake
Lake Superior

Tallest Building
Sears Tower, Chicago
442 m (1,450 ft)

Longest Road Tunnel
Ted Williams, Boston
4.2 km (2.6 mi)

Longest Rail Tunnel
Mount MacDonald, Canada
14.6 km (9.1 mi)

Largest Country
Canada

Largest Hydroelectric Plant
Grand Coulee, United States
6,809 MW

Largest Subway System
New York,
370 km (230 mi)

Oldest Country
United States
(July 1776)

Highest Waterfall
Yosemite, Yosemite Creek, United States
739 m (2,425 ft)

Most Populous Country
Country with Longest Land Border
12,034 km (7,473 mi)

Busiest Airport
Atlanta (Hartsfield)
85.9 million passengers per year

Newest Country
Antigua & Barbuda
(November 1981)

Lowest Point
Death Valley, United States
–86 m (–282 ft)

Largest Desert
Great Basin, United States
492,100 sq km (190,000 sq mi)

Deadliest Volcanic Eruption
Mt Pelée, Martinique *(1902)*
29,025 deaths

Longest River
Mississippi–Missouri

Highest Dam
Manuel M. Torres, Mexico
261 m (856 ft)

Deadliest Earthquake
Guatemala City, Guatemala *(1976)*
23,000 deaths

COUNTRIES: AREA

	Country/Territory	Area sq km (thousands)	Area sq mi (thousands)
Largest			
1	Canada	9,971	3,850
2	United States of America	9,629	3,718
3	Greenland (Denmark)	2,176	840
4	Mexico	1,958	756
5	Nicaragua	130	50.2
6	Honduras	112	43.3
7	Cuba	111	42.8
8	Guatemala	109	42.0
9	Panama	75.5	29.2
10	Costa Rica	51.1	19.7
11	Dominican Republic	48.5	18.7
12	Haiti	27.8	10.7
13	Belize	23.0	8.9
14	El Salvador	21.0	8.1
15	Bahamas	13.9	5.4
16	Jamaica	11.0	4.2
17	Puerto Rico (US)	8.9	3.4
18	Trinidad & Tobago	5.1	2.0
19	Guadeloupe (France)	1.7	0.66
20	Martinique (France)	1.1	0.43
Smallest			
1	Bermuda (UK)	0.05	0.02
2	Anguilla (UK)	0.10	0.04
3	Montserrat (UK)	0.10	0.04
4	Virgin Islands (UK)	0.15	0.06
5	Aruba (Netherlands)	0.19	0.07
6	Cayman Islands (UK)	0.26	0.10
7	St Kitts & Nevis	0.26	0.10
8	Grenada	0.34	0.13
9	Virgin Islands (US)	0.35	0.13
10	St Vincent & the Grenadines	0.39	0.15

COUNTRIES: POPULATION

	Country/Territory	Population (thousands)
Most Populous		
1	United States of America	295,734
2	Mexico	106,203
3	Canada	32,805
4	Guatemala	14,655
5	Cuba	11,347
6	Dominican Republic	8,950
7	Haiti	8,122
8	Honduras	6,975
9	El Salvador	6,705
10	Nicaragua	5,465
11	Costa Rica	4,016
12	Puerto Rico (US)	3,917
13	Panama	3,039
14	Jamaica	2,732
15	Trinidad & Tobago	1,089
16	Guadeloupe (France)	449
17	Martinique (France)	433
18	Bahamas	302
19	Belize	279
20	Barbados	279
Least Populous		
1	Montserrat (UK)	9
2	Anguilla (UK)	13
3	Turks & Caicos Is. (UK)	21
4	Virgin Islands (UK)	23
5	St Kitts & Nevis	39
6	Cayman Islands (UK)	44
7	Greenland (Denmark)	56
8	Bermuda (UK)	65
9	Dominica	69
10	Antigua & Barbuda	69

LARGEST CITIES

	City	Population (thousands)
1	Mexico City, Mexico	19,013
2	New York, USA	17,800
3	Los Angeles, USA	11,789
4	Chicago, USA	8,308
5	Philadelphia, USA	5,149
6	Toronto, Canada	5,060
7	Miami, USA	4,919
8	Dallas-Fort Worth, USA	4,146
9	Boston, USA	4,032
10	Washington, USA	3,934
11	Guadalajara, Mexico	3,905
12	Detroit, USA	3,903
13	Houston, USA	3,823
14	Monterrey, Mexico	3,517
15	Montréal, Canada	3,511
16	Atlanta, USA	3,500
17	Guatemala City, Guatemala	3,242
18	San Francisco, USA	3,229
19	Phoenix, USA	2,907
20	Seattle, USA	2,712
21	San Diego, USA	2,674
22	Santo Domingo, Dom. Rep.	2,563
23	Minneapolis–St Paul, USA	2,389
24	San Juan, Puerto Rico	2,357
25	Havana, Cuba	2,192
26	Vancouver, Canada	2,125
27	Port-au-Prince, Haiti	2,090
28	St Louis, USA	2,078
29	Baltimore, USA	2,076
30	Tampa–St Petersburg, USA	2,062

PHYSICAL SUPERLATIVES

Land Area
24,241,000 sq km (9,357,000 sq mi)

Highest Mountains
1. Mt McKinley (Denali), USA (Alaska) *6,194 m (20,321 ft)*
2. Mt Logan, Canada *5,959 m (19,551 ft)*
3. Pico de Orizaba, Mexico *5,610 m (18,405 ft)*
4. Mt St Elias, Canada/USA *5,489 m (18,008 ft)*
5. Popocatépetl, Mexico *5,452 m (17,887 ft)*

Longest Rivers
1. Mississippi–Missouri *5,971 km (3,710 mi)*
2. Mackenzie *4,240 km (2,630 mi)*
3. Missouri *4,088 km (2,540 mi)*
4. Mississippi *3,782 km (2,350 mi)*
5. Yukon *3,185 km (1,980 mi)*

Largest Lakes and Inland Seas
1. Lake Superior, Canada/USA *82,350 sq km (31,800 sq mi)*
2. Lake Huron, Canada/USA *59,600 sq km (23,010 sq mi)*
3. Lake Michigan, USA *58,000 sq km (22,400 sq mi)*
4. Great Bear Lake, Canada *31,800 sq km (12,280 sq mi)*
5. Great Slave Lake, Canada *28,500 sq km (11,000 sq mi)*

Largest Islands
1. Greenland, Atlantic Ocean *2,175,600 sq km (839,800 sq mi)*
2. Baffin Island, Canada *508,000 sq km (196,100 sq mi)*
3. Victoria Island, Canada *212,200 sq km (81,900 sq mi)*
4. Ellesmere Island, Canada *212,000 sq km (81,800 sq mi)*
5. Cuba, Caribbean Sea *110,860 sq km (42,800 sq mi)*

COUNTRIES: WEALTH

	Country/Territory	Annual Income (US$ per capita)
Richest		
1	United States of America	41,800
2	Virgin Islands (UK)	38,500
3	Bermuda (UK)	36,000
4	Canada	32,800
5	Cayman Islands (UK)	32,300
6	Aruba (Netherlands)	28,000
7	Greenland (Denmark)	20,000
8	Bahamas	18,800
9	Puerto Rico (US)	18,500
10	Barbados	17,300
Poorest		
1	Haiti	1,600
2	Nicaragua	2,800
3	Honduras	2,900
=	St Vincent & the Grenadines	2,900
5	Cuba	3,300
6	Montserrat (UK)	3,400
7	Jamaica	4,300
=	Guatemala	4,300
9	Grenada	5,000
10	El Salvador	5,100

COUNTRIES: AREA

	Country/Territory	Area sq km (thousands)	Area sq mi (thousands)
1	Brazil	8,514	3,287
2	Argentina	2,780	1,074
3	Peru	1,285	496
4	Colombia	1,139	440
5	Bolivia	1,099	424
6	Venezuela	912	352
7	Chile	757	292
8	Paraguay	407	157
9	Ecuador	284	109
10	Guyana	215	83

COUNTRIES: POPULATION

	Country/Territory	Population (thousands)
1	Brazil	186,113
2	Colombia	42,954
3	Argentina	39,538
4	Peru	27,926
5	Venezuela	25,375
6	Chile	15,981
7	Ecuador	13,364
8	Bolivia	8,858
9	Paraguay	6,348
10	Uruguay	3,416

LARGEST CITIES

	City	Population (thousands)
1	São Paulo, Brazil	18,333
2	Buenos Aires, Argentina	13,349
3	Rio de Janeiro, Brazil	11,469
4	Lima, Peru	8,180
5	Bogotá, Colombia	7,594
6	Santiago, Chile	5,623
7	Belo Horizonte, Brazil	5,304
8	Pôrto Alegre, Brazil	3,795
9	Recife, Brazil	3,527
10	Brasília, Brazil	3,341
11	Salvador, Brazil	3,331
12	Caracas, Venezuela	3,276
13	Fortaleza, Brazil	3,261
14	Medellín, Colombia	3,236
15	Curitiba, Brazil	2,871
16	Campinas, Brazil	2,640
17	Cali, Colombia	2,583
18	Guayaquil, Ecuador	2,387
19	Valencia, Venezuela	2,330
20	Maracaibo, Venezuela	2,182
21	Belém, Brazil	2,097
22	Barranquilla, Colombia	1,918
23	Goiânia, Brazil	1,878
24	Asunción, Paraguay	1,750
25	Manaus, Brazil	1,673
26	Santos, Brazil	1,634
27	Córdoba, Argentina	1,592
28	La Paz, Bolivia	1,533
29	Quito, Ecuador	1,514
30	Montevideo, Uruguay	1,353

PHYSICAL SUPERLATIVES

Land Area
17,793,000 sq km (6,868,000 sq mi)

Highest Mountains
1 Aconcagua, Argentina *6,962 m (22,841 ft)*
2 Bonete, Argentina *6,872 m (22,546 ft)*
3 Ojos del Salado, Argentina/Chile *6,863 m (22,516 ft)*
4 Pissis, Argentina *6,779 m (22,241 ft)*
5 Mercedario, Argentina/Chile *6,770 m (22,211 ft)*

Longest Rivers
1 Amazon *6,450 km (4,010 mi)*
2 Paraná–Plate *4,500 km (2,800 mi)*
3 Purus *3,350 km (2,080 mi)*
4 Madeira *3,200 km (1,990 mi)*
5 São Francisco *2,900 km (1,800 mi)*

Largest Lakes and Inland Seas
1 Lake Titicaca, Bolivia/Peru *8,300 sq km (3,200 sq mi)*
2 Lake Poopo, Bolivia *2,800 sq km (1,100 sq mi)*
3 Lake Mar Chiquita, Argentina *2,000 sq km (780 sq mi)*
4 Lake General Carrera (Buenos Aires), Argentina/Chile *1,850 sq km (720 sq mi)*
5 Lake Argentino, Argentina *1,470 sq km (575 sq mi)*

Largest Islands
1 Tierra del Fuego, Argentine/Chile *47,000 sq km (18,100 sq mi)*
2 Chiloe, Chile *8,400 sq km (3,235 sq mi)*
3 Falkland Is. (East), Atlantic Ocean *6,800 sq km (2,600 sq mi)*
4 Wellington, Chile *5,560 sq km (2,140 sq mi)*
5 Riesco, Chile *5,110 sq km (1,970 sq mi)*

COUNTRIES: WEALTH

	Country/Territory	Annual Income (US$ per capita)
1	Argentina	13,600
2	Chile	11,300
3	Uruguay	10,000
4	Brazil	8,500
5	French Guiana (France)	8,300
6	Colombia	7,100
7	Venezuela	6,400
8	Peru	6,000
9	Paraguay	4,900
10	Suriname	4,700

COUNTRIES OF THE WORLD

KEY

- City or town
- Capital city
- Major airport
- Highest point in country
- International boundary
- Railway
- Road
- River

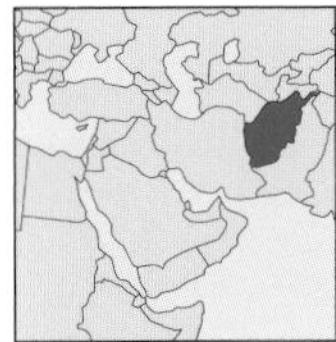

Introduced in January 2002, this flag replaces that of the Mujaheddin ("holy warriors"), who defeated Afghanistan's socialist government but lost power at the end of 2001. The flag is the 19th different design used by the country since 1901.

Area 251,772 sq mi [652,090 sq km]
Population 28,514,000
Capital (population) Kabul (1,565,000)
Government Transitional regime
Ethnic groups Pashtun (Pathan) 44%, Tajik 25%, Hazara 10%, Uzbek 8%, others 8%
Languages Pashtu, Dari/Persian (both official), Uzbek
Religions Islam (Sunni Muslim 84%, Shiite Muslim 15%), others
Currency Afghani = 100 puls
Website www.afghan-web.com

The Islamic Republic of Afghanistan is a landlocked country bordered by Turkmenistan, Uzbekistan, Tajikistan, China, Pakistan, and Iran. The main regions are the northern plains, the central highlands, and the southwestern lowlands.

The central highlands, comprising most of the Hindu Kush and its foothills, with peaks rising to more than 21,000 ft [6,400 m], cover nearly three-quarters of the land. Many Afghans live in the deep valleys of the highlands. The River Kabul flows east to the Khyber Pass border with Pakistan.

Much of the southwest is desert, while the northern plains contain most of the country's limited agricultural land. Grasslands cover much of the north, while the vegetation in the dry south is sparse.

Trees are rare in both regions. But forests of such coniferous trees as pine and fir grow on the higher mountain slopes, with cedars lower down. Alder, ash, juniper, oak, and walnut grow in the mountain valleys.

CLIMATE

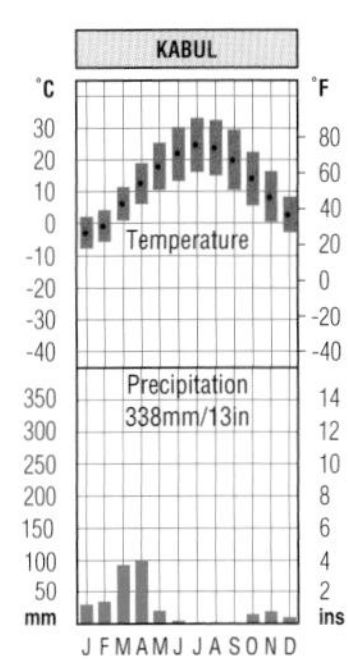

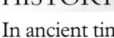

The height of the land and the country's remote position have a great effect on the climate. In winter, northerly winds bring cold, snowy weather in the mountains, but summers are hot and dry. The rainfall decreases to the south with temperatures higher throughout the year.

HISTORY

In ancient times, the area was invaded by Aryans, Persians, Greeks, and Macedonians, and warrior armies from central Asia. Arab armies introduced Islam in the late 7th century. It has always occupied a strategic position, because the Khyber Pass was both the gateway to India and the back door to Russia.

Its modern history began in 1747, when local tribes united for the first time, though a civil war was fought between 1819 and 1835 as factions struggled for power. In 1839, British troops invaded Afghanistan, in an attempt to reduce Russian influence. Over the next 80 years, Britain fought three Anglo-Afghan wars to maintain control over the region. The British finally withdrew in 1921, when Afghanistan became independent.

POLITICS

In 1964, Afghanistan adopted a democratic constitution, but the country's ruler, King Zahir, and the legislature failed to agree on reforms. Muhammad Daoud Khan, the king's cousin, seized power in 1973 and abolished the monarchy. He ruled as president until 1978, when he was killed during a left-wing coup. The new regime's socialist policies conflicted with Islam and provoked a rebellion.

On 25 December 1987, Soviet troops invaded Afghanistan to support the left-wing regime. The Soviet occupation led to a protracted civil war. Various Muslim groups united behind the banner of the Mujaheddin ("holy warriors") to wage a guerrilla campaign, financed by the United States and aided by Pakistan. Soviet forces withdrew in 1989.

By 1992, the Mujaheddin had overthrown the government. The fundamentalist Muslim Taliban ("students") became the dominant group and, by 2000, the Taliban regime controlled 90% of the land.

In October 2001, the Taliban regime refused to hand over Saudi-born Osama bin Laden, the man suspected of masterminding the attacks on New York City and Washington D.C. on September 11, 2001. This led to international action being taken against Afghanistan, with the United States to the fore. The objective was to destroy both bin Laden's terrorist organization, al Qaida, and the Taliban. In November, the Taliban regime collapsed and a coalition government was set up, led by Hamid Karzai, who was sworn into office in 2002. Later that year, more than 1,000 people died in an earthquake in northern Afghanistan.

Despite ongoing conflict, a draft constitution was approved in January 2004. The first democratic elections for president were held in October 2004, won by Hamid Karzai. September 2005 saw parliamentary and provincial elections.

ECONOMY

Afghanistan is one of the world's poorest countries. About 60% of the people are farmers, many of whom are seminomadic herders. Wheat is the chief crop. Natural gas is produced, together with some coal, copper, gold, precious stones, and salt. There are few factories. Exports include karakul skins (which are used to make hats and jackets), carpets, dried fruit, and nuts.

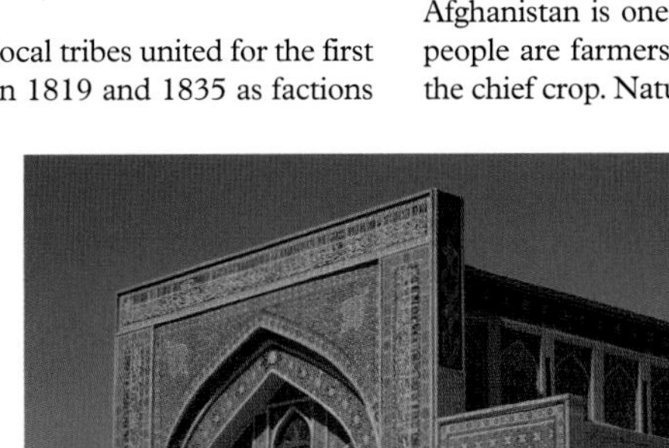

***Great Mosque of Herat**, known as the Majsjid-i-Jami, or the Friday Mosque, built in the 13th century during the Timurid dynasties*

KABUL

Capital of Afghanistan situated on the River Kabul in the eastern part of the country. It is strategically located in a high mountain valley in the Hindu Kush. The city was taken by Genghis Khan in the 13th century. Later it became part of the Mogul Empire, from 1526 to 1738. It has been the capital since 1776 and was occupied by the British during the Afghan Wars in the 19th century. Following the Soviet invasion in 1979, Kabul was the scene of bitter fighting. Unrest continued into the mid-1990s as rival Muslim groups fought for control. Industries include textiles, leather goods, and furniture.

Albania

Albania's official name, Shqiperia, means "Land of the Eagle," and the black double eagle was the emblem of the 15th-century hero Skanderberg. A star placed above the eagle in 1946 was removed in 1992 when a non-Communist government was formed.

Area 11,100 sq mi [28,748 sq km]
Population 3,545,000
Capital (population) Tirana (300,000)
Government Multiparty republic
Ethnic groups Albanian 95%, Greek 3%, Macedonian,Vlachs, Gypsy
Languages Albanian (official)
Religions Many people say they are non-believers; of the believers, 70% follow Islam and 30% follow Christianity (Orthodox 20%, Roman Catholic 10%)
Currency Lek = 100 qindars
Website www.parlament.al

The Republic of Albania lies in the Balkan Peninsula. It faces the Adriatic Sea in the west and is bordered by Serbia and Montenegro, Macedonia and Greece. About 70% of the land is mountainous, with the highest point, Korab, reaching 9,068 ft [2,764 m] on the Macedonian border. Most Albanians live in the west on the coastal lowlands—the main farming region. Albania lies in an earthquake zone and severe earthquakes occur occasionally.

CLIMATE

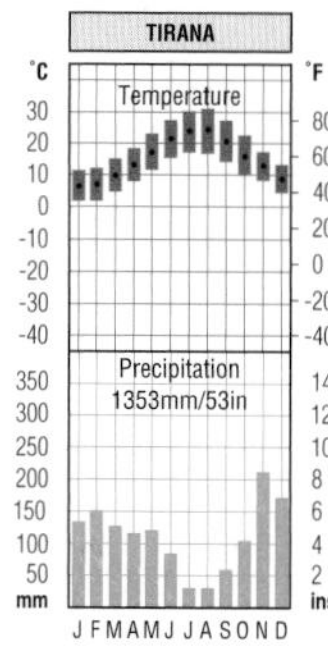

The coastal areas of Albania have a typical Mediterranean climate, with fairly dry, sunny summers and cool, moist winters. The mountains have a severe climate, with heavy winter snow.

HISTORY

Albania was originally part of a region called Illyria. In 167 BC, it became part of the Roman Empire. When the Roman Empire broke up in AD 395, much of Albania became part of the Byzantine Empire. The country was later conquered by Goths, Bulgarians, Slavs, and Normans, although southern Albania remained part of the Byzantine Empire until 1204.

Much of Albania became part of the Serbian Empire in the 14th century and in the 15th century, a leader named Skanderberg, now regarded as a national hero, successfully led the Albanians against the invading Ottoman Turks. But after his death in 1468, the Turks took over the country. Albania was part of the Ottoman Empire until 1912, when Albania declared its independence.

Italy invaded Albania in 1939, but German forces took over the country in 1943. At the end of World War II, an Albanian People's Republic was formed under the Communist leaders who had led the partisans against the Germans. Pursuing a modernization program on rigid Stalinist lines, the regime of Enver Hoxha at various times associated politically and economically with Yugoslavia (to 1948), the Soviet Union (1948–61), and China (1961–77), before following a fiercely independent policy. After Hoxha died in 1985, his successor, Ramiz Alia, continued the dictator's austere policies, but by the end of the decade, even Albania was affected by the sweeping changes in Eastern Europe.

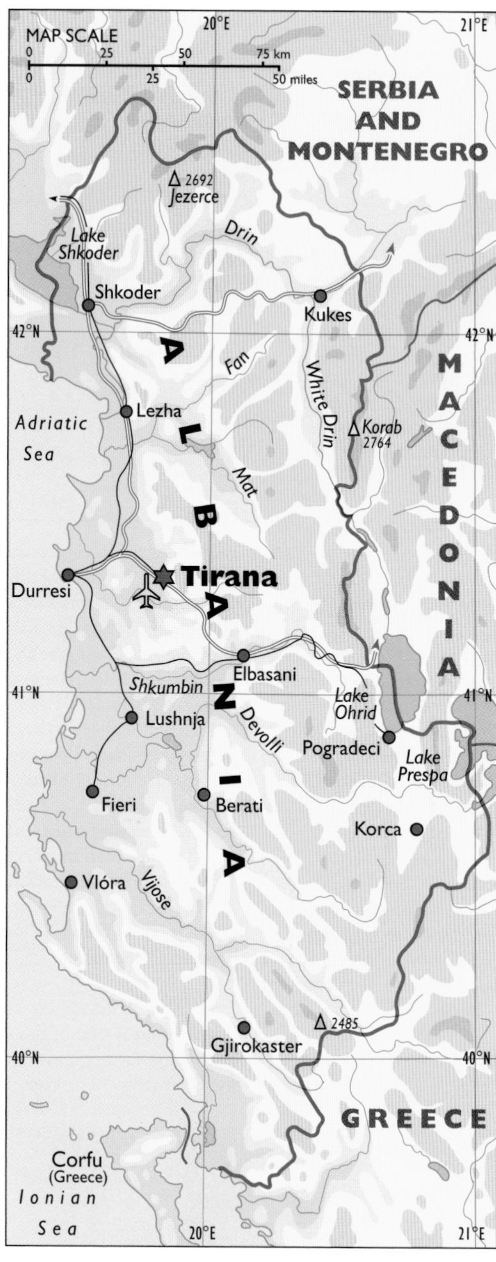

POLITICS

In 1990, the more progressive wing of the Communist Party, led by Ramiz Alia, won the struggle for power. The new government instituted a wide program of reform, including the legalization of religion, the encouragement of foreign investment, the introduction of a free market for peasants' produce, and the establishment of pluralist democracy. The Communists comfortably retained their majority in 1991 elections, but the government was brought down two months later by a general strike. An interim coalition "national salvation" committee took over, but collapsed within six months.

Elections in 1992 finally brought to an end the last Communist regime in Europe when the non-Communist Democratic Party won power. In 1997, amid a financial crisis caused by the collapse of fraudulent pyramid-selling schemes, fresh elections took place. The socialist-led government that took power was reelected in 2001. The stability of the region was threatened when Albanian-speaking Kosovars and Macedonians, many favoring the creation of a Greater Albania, fought with government forces in northwestern Macedonia.

ECONOMY

Albania is Europe's poorest country. Some 62% of the population are employed in agriculture. Major crops include fruits, corn, olives, potatoes, sugar beets, vegetables, and wheat. Livestock farming and the fishing industry are also important.

Private ownership has been encouraged since 1991, but change has been slow. Albania has some minerals, such as chromite, copper, and nickel, which are exported. There is also some oil, brown coal, and hydroelectricity, and a few heavy industries.

TIRANA (TIRANË)

Capital of Albania situated on the banks of the River Ishm in central Albania. Tirana's geographical position on the fertile forested land between the Adriatic and eastern Albania played a major part in its development from settlement to capital city. The city was founded in the early 17th century by the Ottoman Turks and became the capital in 1920. In 1946 the Communists came to power and the industrial sector of the city was developed. Industries include metal goods, agricultural machinery and textiles. Places of interest include Skanderberg Square with the main historical buildings. Also the 18th century Haxhi Ethem Bey Mosque; Art Gallery (Albanian); National Museum of History.

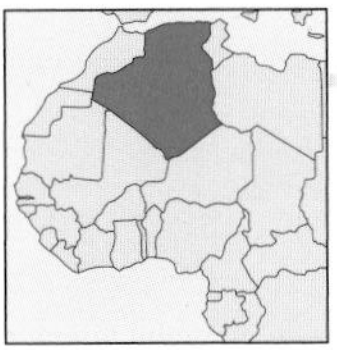

The star and crescent and the color green on Algeria's flag are traditional symbols of the Islamic religion. The liberation movement which fought for independence from French rule from 1954 used this flag. It became the national flag when Algeria became independent in 1962.

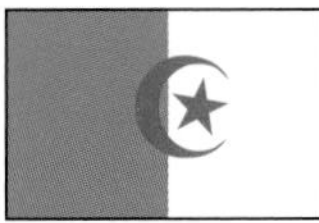

Area 919,590 sq mi [2,381,741 sq km]
Population 32,129,000
Capital (population) Algiers (Alger, 1,722,000)
Government Socialist republic
Ethnic groups Arab-Berber 99%
Languages Arabic and Berber (both official), French
Religions Sunni Muslim 99%
Currency Algerian dinar = 100 centimes
Website www.algeria-un.org

The People's Democratic Republic of Algeria is Africa's second largest country after Sudan. Most Algerians live in the north, on the fertile coastal plains and hill country. South of this region lie high plateaus and ranges of the Atlas Mountains. Four-fifths of Algeria is in the Sahara, the world's largest desert.

CLIMATE

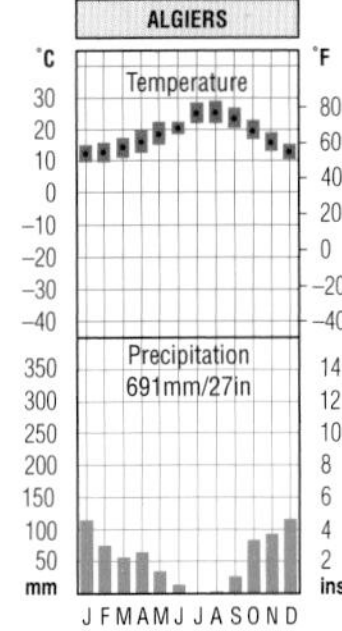

The coast has a Mediterranean climate, with warm and dry summers and mild and moist winters. The northern highlands have warmer summers and colder winters. The arid Sahara is hot by day and cool by night. Annual rainfall is less than 8 in [200 mm].

HISTORY

In early times, the region came under such rulers as the Phoenicians, Carthaginians, Romans, and Vandals. Arabs invaded the area in the AD 600s, converting the local Berbers to Islam and introducing Arabic. Intermarriage has made it difficult to distinguish Arabs from Berbers by ancestry, though Berber dialects are still spoken. A law, effective from July 1998 making Arabic the only language allowed in public life, met with much opposition in Berber-speaking areas.

POLITICS

Algeria experienced French colonial rule and colonization by settlers, finally achieving independence in 1962, following years of bitter warfare between nationalist guerrillas and French armed forces. After independence, the socialist FLN (National Liberation Party) formed a one-party government. Opposition parties were permitted in 1989.

In 1991, a Muslim party, the FIS (Islamic Salvation Front) won an election. The FLN cancelled the election results and declared a state of emergency. Terrorist activities mounted and, between 1991 and 1999, about 100,000 people were killed. A proposal to ban political parties based on religion was approved in a referendum in 1996. In 1999, Abdelaziz Boutflika, the candidate thought to be favored by the army, was elected president. The scale of the violence was reduced. In 2005, the government agreed to accept the demands of the Berber community, including official recognition of the Berber language. In September an amnesty for Islamist guerrillas was approved in a referendum.

ECONOMY

Algeria is a developing country, whose main income is from its two main natural resources, oil and natural gas. Its natural gas reserves are among the world's largest. Oil and natural gas account for around two-thirds of the country's total revenues and more than 90% of the exports. Algeria's crude oil refining capacity is the biggest in Africa. About 16% of the population are employed in agriculture.

***An Algerian** camel train crosses the desert*

ALGIERS

Capital and largest city of Algeria, north Africa's chief port on the Mediterranean. Founded by the Phoenicians, it has been ruled by Romans, Berber Arabs, Turks, and Muslim Barbary pirates. In 1830 the French made Algiers the capital of the colony of Algeria. In World War II it was the headquarters of the Allies and seat of the French provisional government. During the 1950s and 1960s it was a focus for the violent struggle for independence. The old city is based round a 16th-century Turkish citadel. The 11th-century Sidi Abderrahman Mosque is a major destination for pilgrims.

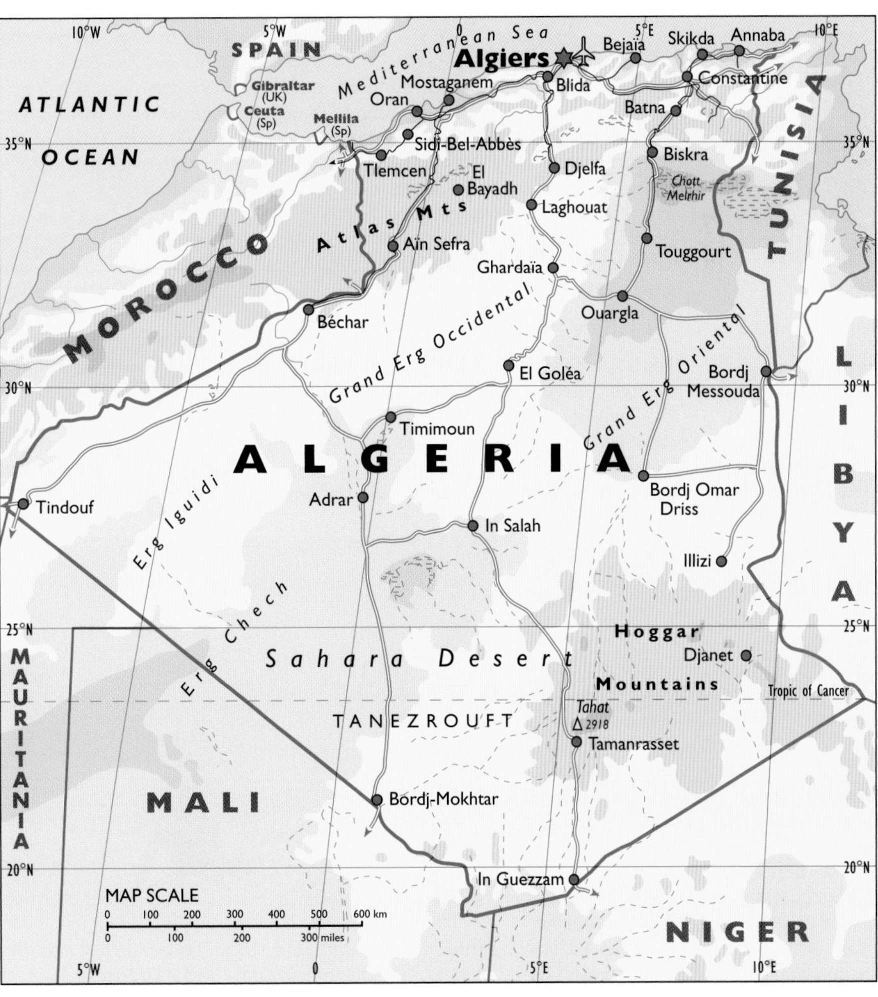

Angola

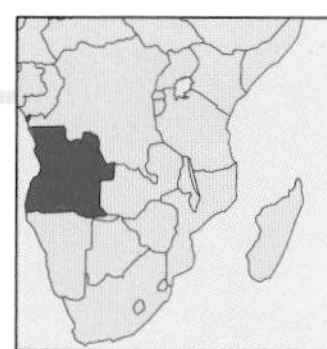

The flag is based on the flag of the MPLA (the Popular Movement for the Liberation of Angola) during the independence struggle. The emblem includes a star symbolizing socialism, one half of a gearwheel to represent industry, and a machete symbolizing agriculture.

Area 481,351 sq mi [1,246,700 sq km]
Population 10.979,000
Capital (population) Luanda (2,250,000)
Government Multiparty republic
Ethnic groups Ovimbundu 37%, Kimbundu 25%, Bakongo 13%, others 25%
Languages Portuguese (official), many others
Religions Traditional beliefs 47%, Roman Catholic 38%, Protestant 15%
Currency Kwanza = 100 lwei
Website www.angola.org

The Republic of Angola is a large country, more than twice the size of France, on the southwestern coast of Africa. The majority of the country is part of the plateau that forms most of southern Africa, with a narrow coastal plain in the west.

Angola has many rivers. In the northeast, several rivers flow northwards to become tributaries of the River Congo, while in the south, some rivers, including the Cubango (Okavango) and the Cuanda, flow southeastwards into inland drainage basins in the interior of Africa.

CLIMATE

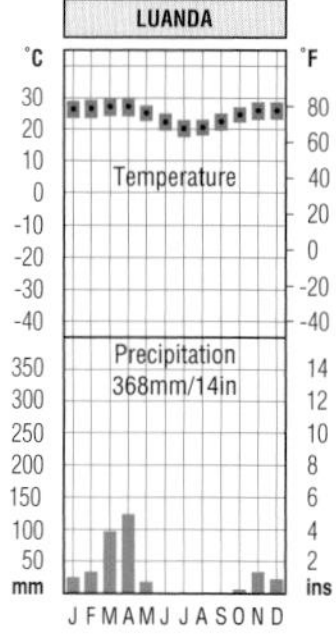

Angola has a tropical climate, with temperatures of over 68°F [20°C] all year round, though upland areas are cooler. The coastal regions are dry, increasingly so to the south of Luanda, but the rainfall increases to the north and east. The rainy season is between November and April. Tropical forests flourish in the north, but the vegetation along the coast is sparse, with semidesert in the south.

HISTORY

Bantu-speaking peoples from the north settled in Angola around 2,000 years ago. In the late 15th century, Portuguese navigators, seeking a route to Asia around Africa, explored the coast and, in the early 16th century, the Portuguese set up bases.

Angola became important as a source of slaves for Brazil, Portugal's huge colony in South America. After the decline of the slave trade, Portuguese settlers began to develop the land. The Portuguese population increased gently in the 20th century.

In the 1950s, local nationalists began to demand independence. In 1956, the MPLA (Popular Movement for the Liberation of Angola) was founded with support from the Mbundu and mestizos (people of African and European descent). The MPLA led a revolt in Luanda in 1961, but it was put down by Portuguese troops.

Other opposition groups developed. In the north, the Kongo set up the FNLA (Front for the Liberation of Angola), while, in 1966, southern peoples, including many Ovimbundu, formed UNITA (National Union for the Total Independence of Angola).

POLITICS

The Portuguese agreed to grant Angola independence in 1975, after which rival nationalist forces began a struggle for power. A long-running civil war developed between the government forces, who received aid from the Soviet Union and Cuba, the FNLA in the north and UNITA in the south. As the war developed, both the FNLA and UNITA turned to the West for support, while UNITA received support from South Africa. FNLA guerrilla activity ended in 1984, but UNITA took control of large areas. Economic progress was hampered not only by the vast spending on defense and security, but also by the MPLA government's austere Marxist policies.

In 1991, a peace accord was agreed and multiparty elections were held, in which the MPLA, which had renounced Marxism-Leninism, won a majority with Jose Eduardo Dos Santos, president since 1979, retaining power. But UNITA's leaders rejected the election result and civil war resumed in 1994. In 1997, the government invited UNITA leader, Jonas Savimbi, to join a coalition but he refused.

Savimbi was killed in action in February 2002, raising hopes of peace and the army and rebels signed a ceasefire to end conflict. Angola then started the lengthy process of rebuilding its devastated infrastructure with thousands of refugees to be resettled and landmines to be cleared.

ECONOMY

Angola is a developing country, where 70% of the people are poor farmers, although agriculture contributes only about 9% of the gross domestic product. The main food crops include cassava, corn, sweet potatoes, and beans, while bananas, coffee, palm products, seed cotton, and sugar cane are grown for export. Cattle are the leading livestock, but sheep and goats are raised in drier areas.

Despite the poverty of most of its people and its low per capita GNP, Angola has much economic potential. It has oil reserves near Luanda and in the enclave of Cabinda, which is separated from Angola by a strip of land belonging to the Democratic Republic of Congo. Oil and mineral fuels are the leading exports.

Other resources include diamonds (the second most important export), copper, and manganese. Angola also has a growing industrial sector. Manufactures include cement, chemicals, processed food, and textiles.

***Oil rig** in Luanda harbor; with the US and China as key customers the oil industry of Angola has been a major boon to the economy*

LUANDA

Capital, chief port, and largest city of Angola, on the Atlantic coast. Luanda was first settled by the Portuguese in 1575. Its economy thrived on the shipment of more than 3 million slaves to Brazil until the abolition of slavery in the 19th century. Today, it exports crops from the province of Luanda.

Antarctica is the fifth-largest continent (larger than Europe or Australasia), covering almost 10% of the world's total land area. Surrounding the South Pole, it is bordered by the Antarctic Ocean and the southern sections of the Atlantic, Pacific, and Indian Oceans. Almost entirely within the Antarctic Circle, it is of great strategic and scientific interest.

No people live there permanently, though scientists frequently stay for short periods to conduct research and exploration. Seven nations lay claim to sectors of it. Covered by an ice-sheet with an average thickness of *c.* 5,900 ft [1,800 m], it contains *c.* 90% of the world's ice and more than 70% of its fresh water and plays a crucial role in the circulation of the atmosphere and ocean, and hence in determining the planetary climate.

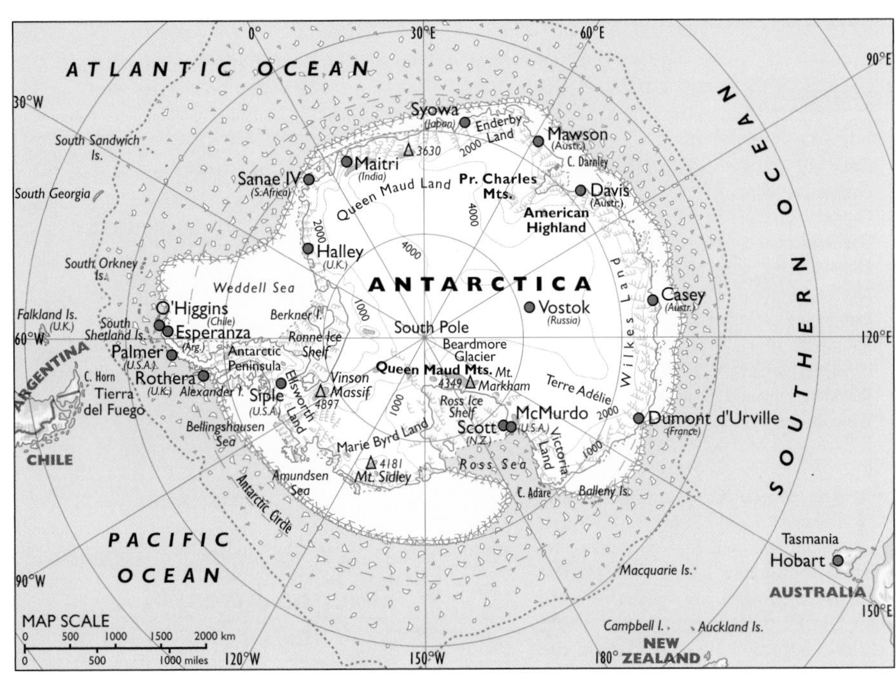

LAND

Resembling an open fan, with the Antarctic Peninsula as a handle, the continent is a snowy desert covering approximately 5.5 million sq mi [14.2 million sq km]. The land is a high plateau with an average elevation of 6,000 ft [1,800 m] and rising to 16,066 ft [4,897 m] in the Vinson Massif. Mountain ranges occur near the coasts.

The interior, or South Polar Plateau, lies beneath *c.* 6,500 ft [2,000 m] of snow, accumulated over tens of thousands of years. Mineral deposits exist in the mountains, but their recovery is not practicable. Coal may be plentiful, but the value of known deposits of copper, nickel, gold, and iron will not repay the expense, both financial and environmental, of their extraction and export.

SEAS AND GLACIERS

Antarctic rivers are frozen, inching towards the sea, and instead of lakes there are large bodies of ice along the coasts. The great Beardmore Glacier creeps down from the South Polar Plateau, and eventually becomes part of the Ross Ice Shelf. The southernmost part of the Atlantic is the portion of the Antarctic Ocean known as the Weddell Sea.

CLIMATE AND VEGETATION

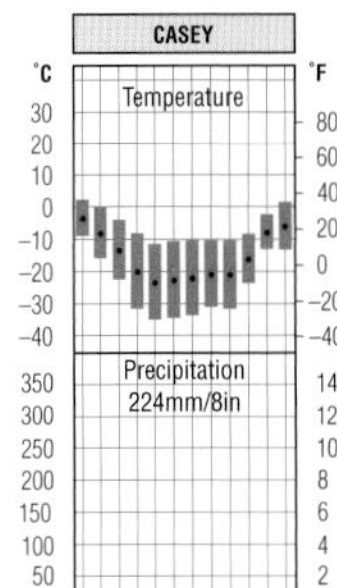

The coldest, windiest, highest (on average), and driest continent. During summer, more solar radiation reaches the surface at the South Pole than is received at the Equator in an equivalent period.

Mostly uninhabitable, Antarctica is cold all year, with only a few coastal areas free from snow or ice in summer (December to February). On most of the continent the temperature remains below freezing, and in August it has been recorded at nearly -130°F [-90°C]. Precipitation is generally 7–15in [18–38cm] of snow a year, but it melts at a slower rate, allowing a buildup over the centuries.

Mosses manage to survive on rocks along the outer rim of the continent. Certain algae grow on the snow, and others appear in pools of fresh water when melting occurs.

HISTORY

Antarctic islands were sighted first in the 18th century, and in 1820 Nathaniel Palmer reached the Antarctic Peninsula. Between 1838 and 1840, US explorer Charles Wilkes discovered enough of the coast to prove that a continent existed, and the English explorer James Clark Ross made coastal maps. Toward the end of the 19th century, exploration of the interior developed into a race for the South Pole. Roald Amundsen reached the Pole on 14 December 1911, a month before Captain Robert Scott. The airplane brought a new era of exploration, and Richard E. Byrd became the best-known of the airborne polar explorers.

ANTARCTIC TREATY

The Antarctic Treaty in 1961 set aside the area for peaceful uses only, guaranteeing freedom of scientific investigation, banning waste disposal and nuclear testing, and suspending the issue of territorial rights. By 1990 the original 12 signatories had grown to 25, with a further 15 nations granted observer status in subsequent deliberations. But the Treaty itself was threatened by wrangles between different countries, government agencies, and international pressure groups.

Finally in July 1991, the belated agreement of the UK and the USA assured unanimity on a new accord to ban all mineral exploration for a further 50 years. This can only be rescinded if all the present signatories, plus a majority of any future adherents, agree. While the treaty has always lacked a formal mechanism for enforcement, it is firmly underwritten by public concern generated by the efforts of environmental pressure groups such as Greenpeace, which has been foremost in the campaign to have Antarctica declared as a "World Park."

The continent appears to be under threat from global warming. Some scientists believe this was the cause of the breakup of ice shelves along the Antarctic peninsula. Rising temperatures have also disturbed the breeding patterns of the Adelie penguins.

Area 5,405,430 sq mi [108,108 sq mi ice-free, 5,297,322 sq mi ice-covered]
14 million sq km [280,000 sq km ice-free, 13.72 million sq km ice-covered]
Government The Antarctic Treaty
Websites www.antarctica.ac.uk; www.aad.gov.au

Paradise Bay *in Antarctica; the bay is home to penguins, seals, and whales*

Argentina

The "celeste" (sky blue) and white stripes were the symbols of independence around the city of Buenos Aires, where an independent government was set up in 1810. It became the national flag in 1816. The gold May Sun was added two years later.

Area 1,073,512 sq mi [2,780,400 sq km]
Population 39,145,000
Capital (population) Buenos Aires (2,965,000)
Government Federal republic
Ethnic groups European 97%, Mestizo, Amerindian
Languages Spanish (official)
Religions Roman Catholic 92%, Protestant 2%, Jewish 2%, others
Currency Peso = 10,000 australs
Website www.sectur.gov.ar

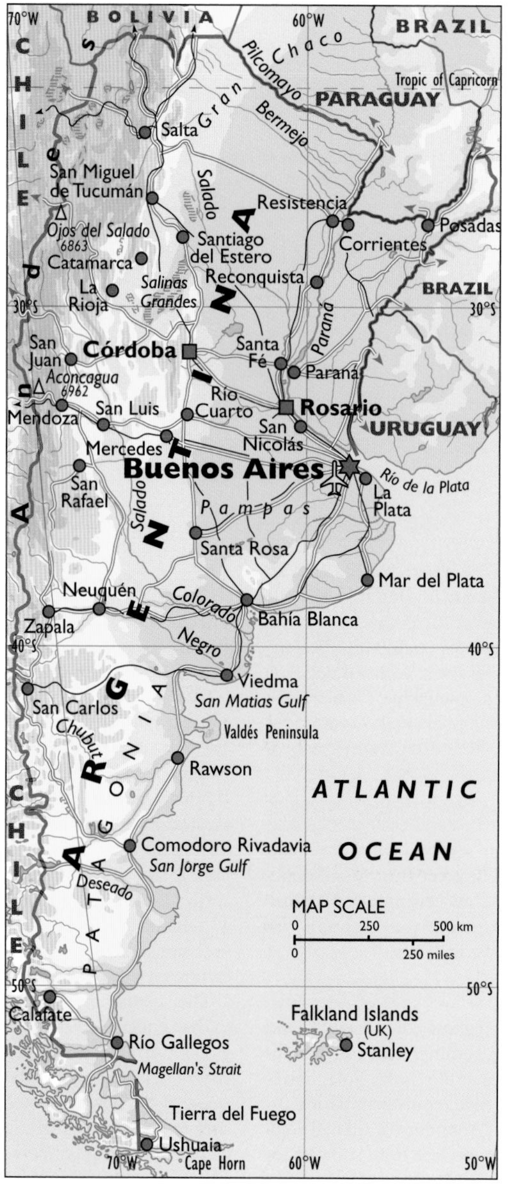

The Argentine Republic is the largest of South America's Spanish-speaking countries. Its western boundary lies in the Andes, with basins, ridges, and peaks of more than 19,685 ft [6,000 m] in the north. South of latitude 27°S, the ridges merge into a single high cordillera, with Aconcagua, at 22,849 ft [6,962 m], the tallest mountain in the western hemisphere.

In the south, the Andes are lower, with glaciers and volcanoes. Eastern Argentina is a series of alluvial plains, from the Andean foothills to the sea. The Gran Chaco in the north slopes down to the Paraná River, from the high desert of the Andean foothills to lowland swamp forest. Between the Paraná and Uruguay rivers is Mesopotamia, a fertile region. Further south are the damp and fertile pampa grasslands. Thereafter, the pampa gives way to the dry, windswept plateaus of Patagonia toward Tierra del Fuego.

CLIMATE

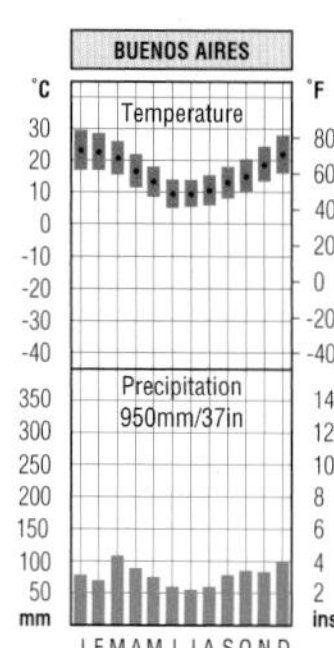

The climate varies from subtropical in the north to temperate in the south. Rainfall is abundant in the northeast, but is lower to the west and south. Patagonia is a dry region, crossed by rivers that rise in the Andes.

HISTORY

Spanish explorers first reached the coast in 1516, landing on the shores of the Rio de la Plata. They were soon followed by others in search of gold and silver. Early prosperity, based on stock raising and farming, combined with stable government, was boosted from 1870 by a massive influx of European immigrants, particularly Italians and Spaniards, for whom Argentina was a viable alternative to the United States. They settled lands recently cleared of Native Americans, often organized by huge land companies.

Development of a good railroad network to the ports, plus steamship services to Europe, and, from 1877, refrigerated vessels, helped to create the strong meat, wool, and wheat economy that carried Argentina into the 20th century. Before the Great Depression in the 1930s, Argentina was one of the world's more prosperous nations.

POLITICS

The collapse in the economy during the Great Depression led to a military coup in 1930. This started a long period of military intervention in the politics of the country.

From 1976, the "dirty war," saw the torture, wrongful imprisonment, and murder ("disappearance") of up to 15,000 people by the military with 2 million people fleeing the country. In 1982, the government, blamed for the poor state of the economy, launched an invasion of the Falkland Islands (Islas Malvinas), which they had claimed since 1820. Britain regained the islands by sending an expeditionary force. After losing the conflict Argentina's President Galtieri resigned. Constitutional government was restored in 1983, though the army remained influential.

In 1999, Argentina and Britain signed an agreement concerning the Falkland Islands, the first since 1982. This meant that Argentines were allowed to visit the Falkland Islands and erect a memorial to their war dead, with Argentina agreeing to allow flights from the Falkland Islands to Chile.

In December 2001, violent protests broke out when the government introduced severe austerity measures, with the peso devalued and policies aimed at restoring the economy announced. The economy finally began to grow again in 2003 and 2004.

ECONOMY

An "upper-middle-income" developing country and one of the richest in South America in terms of natural resources, especially its fertile farmland. The economic base is mainly agricultural. Chief products are beef, corn, and wheat. Sheep are raised in drier parts of the country, while other crops include citrus fruits, cotton, flax, grapes, potatoes, sorghum, sugar cane, sunflower seeds, and tea.

Oilfields in Patagonia and the Piedmont make Argentina almost self-sufficient in oil and natural gas, these are a valuable export.

BUENOS AIRES

Capital of Argentina, on the estuary of the Río de la Plata, 240 km [150 mi] from the Atlantic Ocean. Originally founded by Spain in 1536, it was refounded in 1580 after being destroyed by the indigenous population. It became a separate federal district and capital of Argentina in 1880. Buenos Aires later developed as a commercial center for beef, grain, and dairy products. It is the seat of the National University (1821). The people of Buenos Aires are known as Portenos and are of multinational origins, with Italian and German names actually outnumbering Spanish. The city is renowned for its vibrant nightlife, with people rarely eating before 9pm and indeed many staying out until dawn. Industries include meat processing, flour milling, textiles, metal works, and automobile assembly.

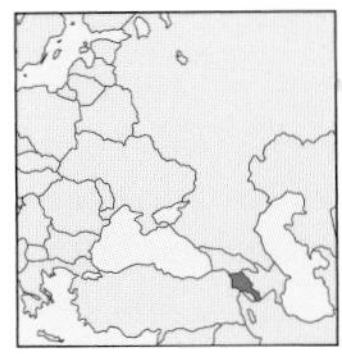

Armenia's flag was first used between 1918 and 1922, when the country was an independent republic. It was readopted on 24 August 1990. The red represents the blood shed in the past, the blue the land of Armenia, and the orange the courage of the people.

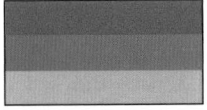

YEREVAN

Capital of Armenia, on the River Razdan, southern Caucasus. One of the world's oldest cities, it was capital of Armenia from as early as the 7th century (though under Persian control). A crucial crossroads for caravan routes between India and Transcaucasia, it is the site of a 16th-century Turkish fortress. It is a traditional winemaking center. Industries include chemicals, plastics, cables, tires, metals, vodka.

Area 11,506 sq mi [29,800 sq km]
Population 2,991,000
Capital (population) Yerevan (1,249,000)
Government Multiparty republic
Ethnic groups Armenian 93%, Russian 2%, Azeri 1%, others (mostly Kurds) 4%
Languages Armenian (official)
Religions Armenian Apostolic 94%
Currency Dram = 100 couma
Website www.armeniaforeignministry.com

The Republic of Armenia is a landlocked country in southwestern Asia. Mostly consisting of a rugged plateau, criss-crossed by long faults. Movements along the faults cause earth tremors and occasionally major earthquakes. Armenia's highest point is Mount Aragats, at 13,149 ft [4,090 m] above sea level. The lowest land is in the northwest, where the capital Yerevan is situated. The largest lake is Ozero (Lake) Sevan.

The vegetation in Armenia ranges from semidesert to grassy steppe, forest, mountain pastures, and treeless tundra at the highest levels. Oak forests are found in the southeast, with beech being the most common tree in the forests of the northeast. Originally it was a much larger kingdom centered on Mount Ararat incorporating present-day northeast Turkey and parts of northwest Iran.

CLIMATE

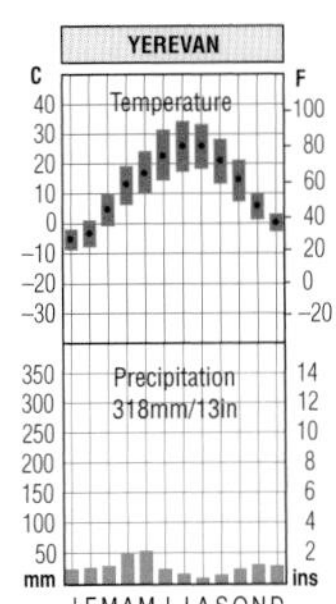

The height of the land, which averages 4,920 ft [1,500 m] gives rise to severe winters and cool summers. The highest peaks are snow-capped, but the total yearly rainfall is low, between 8 and 31 in [200 and 800 mm].

HISTORY

Armenia was an advanced ancient kingdom, considered to be one of the original sites of iron and bronze smelting. A nation was established in the 6th century BC and Alexander the Great expelled the Persians in 330 BC. In 69 BC Armenia was incorporated into the Roman Empire. In AD 303, Armenia became the first country to adopt Christianity as its state religion. From 886 to 1046 Armenia was an independent kingom. From the 11th to 15th centuries the Mongols were the greatest power in the region. By the 16th century Armenia was controlled by the Ottoman Empire. Despite religious discrimination, the Armenians generally prospered under Turkish rule. Eastern Armenia was the battleground between the rival Ottoman and Persian empires. In 1828 Russia acquired Persian Armenia and (with many promises of religious tolerance) many Armenians moved to the Russian-controlled area. In Turkish Armenia, British promises of protection encouraged nationalist movements. The Turkish response was uncompromising killing about 200,000 in 1896 alone. In the Russian sector, a process of Russification was enforced.

During World War I, Armenia was the battleground for the Turkish and Russian armies. Armenians were accused of aiding the Russians and Turkish atrocities intensified. More than 600,000 Armenians were killed by Turkish troops and 1.75 million were deported to Syria and Palestine. The Armenian Autonomous Republic was set up in the area held by Russia in 1918, but the western part of historic Armenia remained in Turkey, and the northwest was held by Iran. In 1920, Armenia became a Communist republic. In 1922, it became, with Azerbaijan and Georgia, part of the Transcaucasian Republic within the Soviet Union. But the three territories became separate Soviet Socialist Republics in 1936. Earthquakes in 1984 and 1988 killed more than 80,000 people and destroyed many cities.

After the breakup of the Soviet Union in 1991, Armenia became an independent republic and joined the Commonwealth of Independent States (CIS).

POLITICS

Armenia has long disputed the status of Nagorno-Karabakh, an area enclosed by Azerbaijan where the majority of the people are Armenians. In 1992, Armenia occupied the territory between its eastern border and Nagorno-Karabakh. A ceasefire in 1994 left Armenia in control of about 20% of Azerbaijan's land area. With Azerbaijan and its ally Turkey blockading its borders, Armenia became increasingly dependent on Iran and Georgia for access to the outside world.

In 1998 Robert Kocharian former leader of Nagorno-Karabakh, became president. In 1999, gunmen stormed parliament and killed the prime minister.

A 9th-century church *stands on Lake Sevan, an alpine freshwater lake near the border with Azerbaijan*

ECONOMY

The World Bank classifies Armenia as a "lower-middle-income" economy. Conflict with Azerbaijan in the early 1990s and the earthquakes have damaged the economy, but since 1992 the government has encouraged free enterprise.

Poverty, corruption, and political assassinations contributed to Armenia losing 20% of its population in the 1990s. The country is highly industrialized with production dominated by mining and chemicals. Copper is the chief metal, but gold, lead, and zinc are also mined. Agriculture is the second-largest sector, with cotton, tobacco, fruit, and rice the main products.

AZORES

The Azores is a group of nine large and several small islands rising from the Mid-Atlantic Ridge in the North Atlantic Ocean. They are mostly mountainous, of relatively recent volcanic origin and lie about 745 mi [1,200 km] west of Lisbon. They have been Portuguese since the mid-15th century. From 1938 until 1978, they were governed as three districts of Portugal, becoming an autonomous region in 1976. Farming and fishing are the main occupations.

Area 868 sq mi [2,247 sq km]
Population 243,000
Capital (population) Ponta Delgada (21,000)
Government Autonomous region of Portugal
Ethnic groups Azorean
Languages Portuguese (official)
Religion Roman Catholic
Currency Euro = 100 cents
Website www.drtacores.pt

BERMUDA

Bermuda comprises some 150 small islands, the coral caps of ancient volcanoes rising from the floor of the North Atlantic Ocean. Uninhabited when discovered in 1503 by the Spaniard Juan Mermúdez, the islands were taken over by the British over a century later, with slaves brought from Virginia. Bermuda is Britain's oldest overseas territory, but has a long tradition of self-government. Tourism is the mainstay of the economy, but the islands are a tax haven for overseas companies.

Area 21 sq mi [53 sq km]
Population 65,000
Capital (population) Hamilton (1,000)
Government Parliamentary British overseas territory with internal self-government
Ethnic groups Black 55%, White 34%, others
Languages English (official), Portuguese
Religion Anglican 23%, Roman Catholic 15%, African Methodist Episcopal 11%, others
Currency Bermudian dollar = 100 cents
Website www.bermudatourism.com

CANARY ISLANDS

The Canary Islands are seven large islands and many small volcanic islands situated off southern Morocco, with the main islands being Fuertaventura, Gran Canaria, Lanzarote, and Tenerife. The climate is subtropical, dry at sea level, wetter in the mountains. Claimed by Portugal in 1341, they were ceded to Spain in 1479 and have been two Spanish provinces since 1927. The statute of autonomy was granted in 1982. Tourism is the most important source of income. Farming and fishing are also key earners.

Area 2,875 sq mi [7,447 sq km]
Population 1,672,689
Capital Santa Cruz (Tenerife), Las Palmas (Gran Canaria)
Government Constitutional monarchy
Ethnic groups Spanish
Languages Spanish (official)
Religion Roman Catholic
Currency Euro = 100 cents
Website www.canarias.org

CAPE VERDE

The Republic of Cape Verde consists of ten large and five small islands, divided into the Barlavento (windward) and Sotavento (leeward) groups. They are volcanic and mainly mountainous, with steep cliffs and rocky headlands. The highest point is on the island of Fogo, an active volcano standing at 9,281 ft [2,829 m]). The climate is tropical, being hot for most of the year and mainly dry at sea level. The higher ground is cooler.

Area 1,557 sq mi [4,033 sq km]
Population 415,000
Capital (population) Praia (95,000)
Government Multiparty republic
Ethnic groups Creole (mulatto) 71%, African 28%
Languages Portuguese and Crioulo
Religion Roman Catholic and Protestant
Currency Cape Verde escudo = 100 centavos
Website www.caboverde.com

Portuguese since the 15th century, Verde included Portuguese Guinea (now Guinea-Bissau) until 1879, when the mainland territory was separated. It was populated with slaves from Africa, and used chiefly as a provisioning station and assembly point for slaves in the trade from West Africa. In 1991, the ruling party was soundly trounced in the country's first multiparty elections by a newly legalized opposition party, the Movement for Democracy (MPD). The former ruling African Independence Party (PAICV) regained power in 2001.

Bananas, beans, coffee, fruit, groundnuts, corn, and sugar cane are grown on the wetter, higher ground, when they are not ruined by endemic droughts. Cape Verde's exports comprise fish and fish preparations and bananas. Economic problems include high unemployment levels and the arrival of thousands of Angolan refugees. Cape Verde became fully independent in 1975.

FALKLAND ISLANDS

The Falkland Islands (Islas Malvinas) lie 480 km [300 mi] to the west of Argentina and consist of two main islands, and more than 200 small ones.

Discovered in 1592 by the English navigator John Davis, the Falklands were first occupied nearly 200 years later by the French (East) and the British (West). The French interest, bought by Spain in 1770, was assumed by Argentina in 1806. The British, who had withdrawn in 1774, returned in 1832. They dispossessed the Argentinian settlers and founded a settlement of their own, one that became a colony in 1892.

In 1982, Argentinian forces invaded the islands, but two months later, after armed conflict and the loss of 255 British and over 1,000 Argentines, the United Kingdom regained possession. In 1999, a formal agreement between Britain and Argentina permitted Argentinians to visit the islands. The majority of the population lives in Stanley and everywhere outside the town is known as the Camp, from the Spanish word for countryside. The economy is dominated by sheep-farming, though an offshore fishery now provides much needed income.

Area 4,700 sq mi [12,173 sq km]
Population 2,967
Capital (population) Stanley (2,000)
Government Overseas British territory
Ethnic groups British
Languages English (official)
Religions Anglican
Currency Falkland pound = 100 pence
Website www.falklandislands.com

MADEIRA

Madeira is the largest of the group of volcanic islands lying 350 mi [550 km] west of the Moroccan coast. Porto Santo, the uninhabited Islas Selvagens (not shown on the map), and the Desertas complete the group. The island of Madeira makes up more than 90% of the total area.

With a warm climate and fertile soils, the Madeira Islands are known for their rich exotic plant life. The abundance of species is all the more surprising because rainfall is confined to the winter months. The present name, meaning "wood," was given by the Portuguese when they first saw the forested islands in 1419. The forests were largely destroyed and a farming industry was established. Spain held the islands between 1580 and 1640, while Britain occupied the islands twice early in the 19th century. Thereafter it came under the rule of Portugal and in 1974 was granted autonomy.

Major crops include bananas, corn, mangoes, oranges, and sugar cane. Grapes are grown to make Madeira wine. Fishing is important, as is tourism. Madeira is also known for its hand embroidery and wickerwork crafted from willow.

Area 307 sq mi [794 sq km]
Population 253,482
Capital (population) Funchal (5,618)
Government Autonomous region of Portugal
Ethnic groups Portuguese
Languages Portuguese (official)
Religions Roman Catholic
Currency Euro = 100 cents
Website www.madeiratourism.org

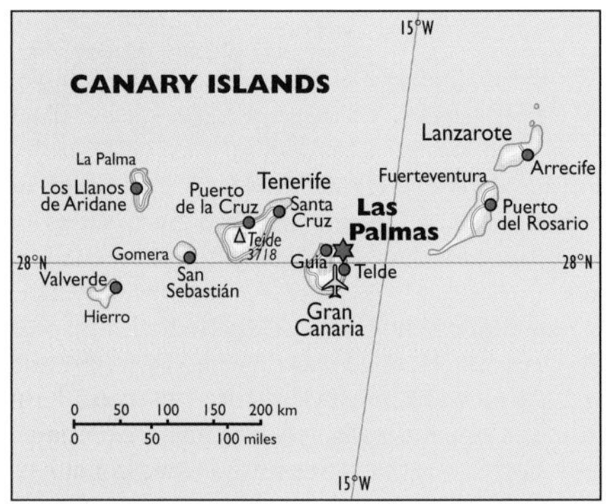

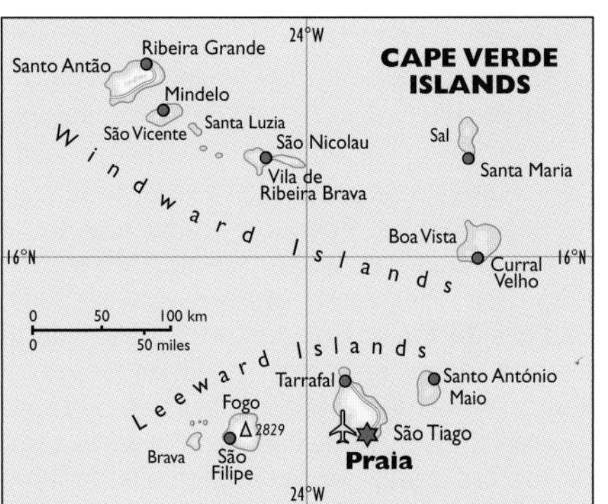

ST PIERRE & MIQUELON

Area 93 sq mi [242 sq km]
Population 7,012
Capital (population)
St Pierre (5,618)
Government Self-governing territorial collectivity of France
Ethnic groups Basques and Bretons
Languages French (official)
Religions Roman Catholic
Currency Euro = 100 cents
Website www2.st-pierre-et-miquelon.info

A group of eight small islands in the Gulf of St Lawrence, south west of Newfoundland, Canada. Miquelon is the largest island. The group was claimed for France in 1535, and since 1985 has been a "territorial collectivity," sending delegates to the French parliament. Fishing is the most important activity, and has led to disputes with Canada.

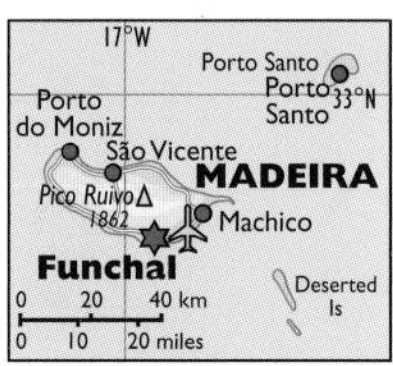

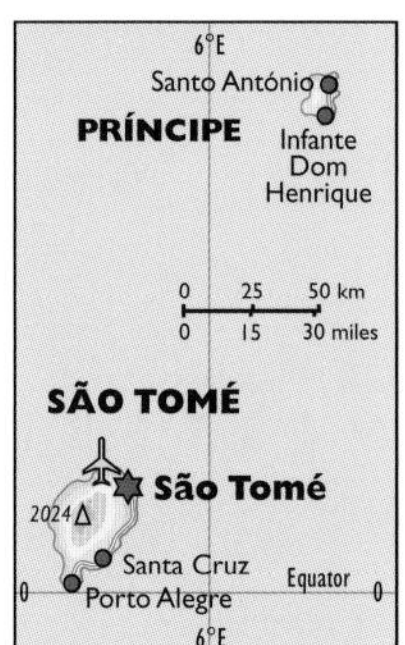

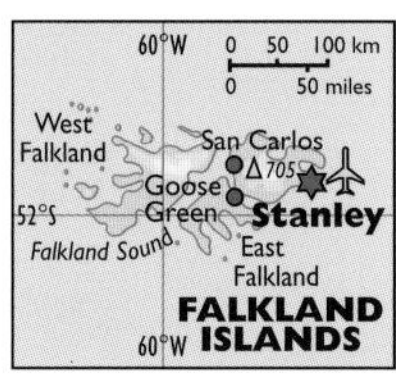

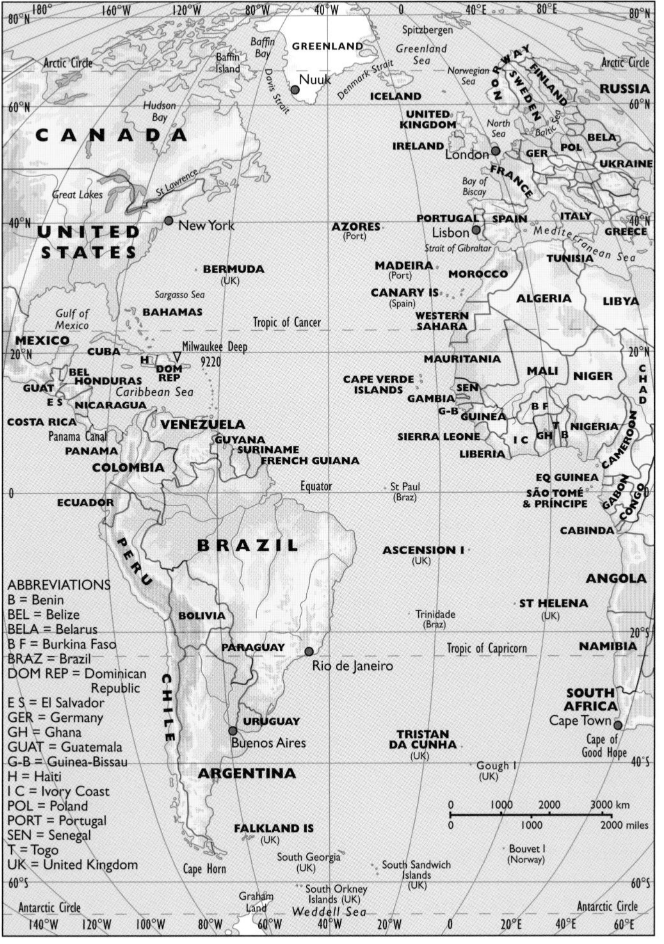

SÃO TOMÉ & PRÍNCIPE

Area 372 sq mi [964 sq km]
Population 187,410
Capital (population)
São Tomé (5,618)
Government Republic
Ethnic groups Mestico, Angolares, Forros, Servicais, Tongas, Europeans (primarily Portuguese)
Languages Portuguese (official)
Religions Roman Catholic
Currency Dobra = 100 céntimos
Website www.saotome.st

In the Gulf of Guinea, 200 mi [300 km] off the west coast of Africa. São Tome is the largest of two volcanic and mountainous islands, the vegetation is mainly tropical rainforest. They were discovered in 1471. The Portuguese established plantations in the late 18th century. The islands became independent in 1975. Cocoa, coffee, bananas, and coconuts are grown on plantations, and their export is the republic's major source of income.

ST HELENA

Area 47 sq mi [122 sq km]
Population 5,000
Capital (population) Jamestown (884)
Government British overseas territory
Ethnic groups Britsih
Languages English (official)
Religion Anglican
Currency Pound sterling = 100 pence
Website www.sainthelena.gov.sh

South Atlantic island, 1,190 mi [1,920 km] from the coast of west Africa Discovered by the Portuguese in 1502, it was captured by the Dutch in 1633 and passed to the British East India Company in 1659. It became a British crown colony in 1834 and is chiefly known as the place of Napoleon I's exile. It is now a UK dependent territory and administrative center for the islands of Ascension and Tristan da Cunha. The main employer on the island is the St Helena government. Its industry includes the servicing of ships and the export of fish and handicrafts.

TRISTAN DA CUNHA

Area 38 sq mi [98 sq km]
Population 273
Capital (population) Edinburgh of the Seven Seas (273)
Government British overseas territory
Ethnic groups British
Languages English (official)
Religions Anglican
Currency Pound sterling = 100 pence
Website www.tristandc.com

Tristan da Cunha is one of a group of four islands in the south Atlantic Ocean, between South Africa and South America. The group was discovered in 1506 by the Portuguese and annexed by Britain in 1816. In 1961, Tristan, suffered a volcanic eruption that caused the evacuation to Britain of the entire population. However one year later the islanders voted overwhelmingly to return to their remote home. It is the world's most isolated settlement and is administered from St Helena.

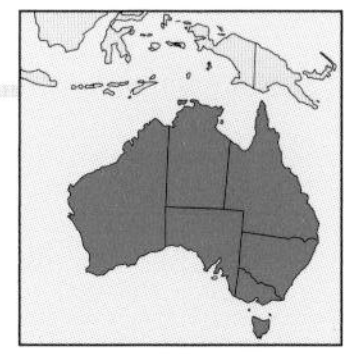

The national flag (above left) was adopted in 1901. It includes the British Union Flag, revealing Australia's historic links with Britain. In 1995, the Australian government put the flag used by the country's Aboriginal people (below left) on the same footing as the national flag.

Australia is the world's sixth-largest country. The huge Western Plateau makes up 66% of its land area, and is mainly flat and dry. Off the coast of northeast Queensland lies the Great Barrier Reef. The Great Dividing Range extends down the entire east coast and into Victoria. The mountains of Tasmania are a southerly extension of the range. The highlands separate the east coastal plains from the Central Lowlands and include Australia's highest peak, Mount Kosciuszko, in New South Wales. The capital, Canberra, lies in the foothills. The southeast lowlands are drained by the Murray and Darling, Australia's two longest rivers. Lake Eyre is the continent's largest lake. It lies on the edge of the Simpson Desert and is a dry salt flat for most of the year. Alice Springs lies in the heart of the continent, close to Ayers Rock (Uluru).

Much of the Western Plateau is desert, although areas of grass and low shrubs are found on its margins. The grasslands of the Central Lowlands are used to raise livestock. The north has areas of savanna and rainforest. In dry areas, acacias are common. Eucalyptus grows in wetter regions.

CLIMATE

Only 10% of Australia has an average annual rainfall greater than 39 in [1,000 mm]. These areas include some of the tropical north (where Darwin is situated), the northeast coast, and the southeast. The coasts are usually warm and many parts of the south and southwest, including Perth, enjoy a Mediterranean climate of dry summers and moist winters. The interior is dry and many rivers are only seasonal.

HISTORY

Native Australians (Aborigines) entered the continent from southeast Asia more than 50,000 years ago. They settled throughout the country and remained isolated from the rest of the world until the first European explorers, the Dutch, arrived in the 17th century. The Dutch did not settle. In 1770 British explorer Captain James Cook reached Botany Bay and claimed the east coast for Great Britain. In 1788 Britain built its first settlement (for convicts) on the site of present-day Sydney. The first free settlers arrived three years later.

In the 19th century, the economy developed rapidly, based on mining and sheep-rearing. At this time the continent was divided into colonies, which later were to become states. In 1901 the states of Queensland, Victoria, Tasmania, New South Wales, South Australia, and Western Australia, federated to create the Commonwealth of Australia. In 1911 the Northern Territory joined the federation. A range of progressive social welfare policies were adopted, such as old-age pensions in 1909. The federal capital was established in 1927 at Canberra, Australian Capital Territory. Australia fought as a member of the Allies in both world wars. The Battle of the Coral Sea in 1942 prevented a full-scale attack on the continent.

POLITICS

Post-1945 Australia steadily realigned itself with its Asian neighbors. Robert Menzies, Australia's longest-serving prime minister, oversaw many economic and social reforms and dispatched Australian troops to the Vietnam War. In 1977 Prime Minister Gough Whitlam was removed from office by the British governor general. He was succeeded by Malcolm Fraser. In 1983 elections, the Labor Party defeated Fraser's Liberal Party, and Bob Hawke became prime minister. His shrewd handling of industrial disputes and economic recession helped him win a record four terms in office. In 1991 Hawke was forced to resign as leader and was succeeded by Paul Keating. Backed by a series of opinion polls, Keating proposed that Australia should become a republic by 2001.

Keating won the 1993 general election and persevered with his free market reforms. In 1996 elections, Keating was defeated by a coalition led by John Howard. In 1998 Howard narrowly secured a second term in office. In a referendum of 1999 Australia voted against becoming a republic. In 2000 Sydney hosted the 28th Summer Olympic Games, nicknamed the "Friendly Games."

The historic maltreatment of Native Australians remains a contentious political issue. In 1993 the government passed the Native Title Act

SYDNEY
Temperature
Precipitation 1181mm/46in

DARWIN
Temperature
Precipitation 1488mm/59in

PERTH
Temperature
Precipitation 881mm/35in

Area 2,988,885 sq mi [7,741,229 sq km]
Population 19,913,000
Capital (population) Canberra (309,000)
Government Federal constitutional monarchy
Ethnic groups Caucasian 92%, Asian 7%, Aboriginal 1%
Languages English (official)
Religions Roman Catholic 26%, Anglican 26%, other Christian 24%, non-Christian24%
Currency Australian dollar = 100 cents
Website www.australia.gov.au

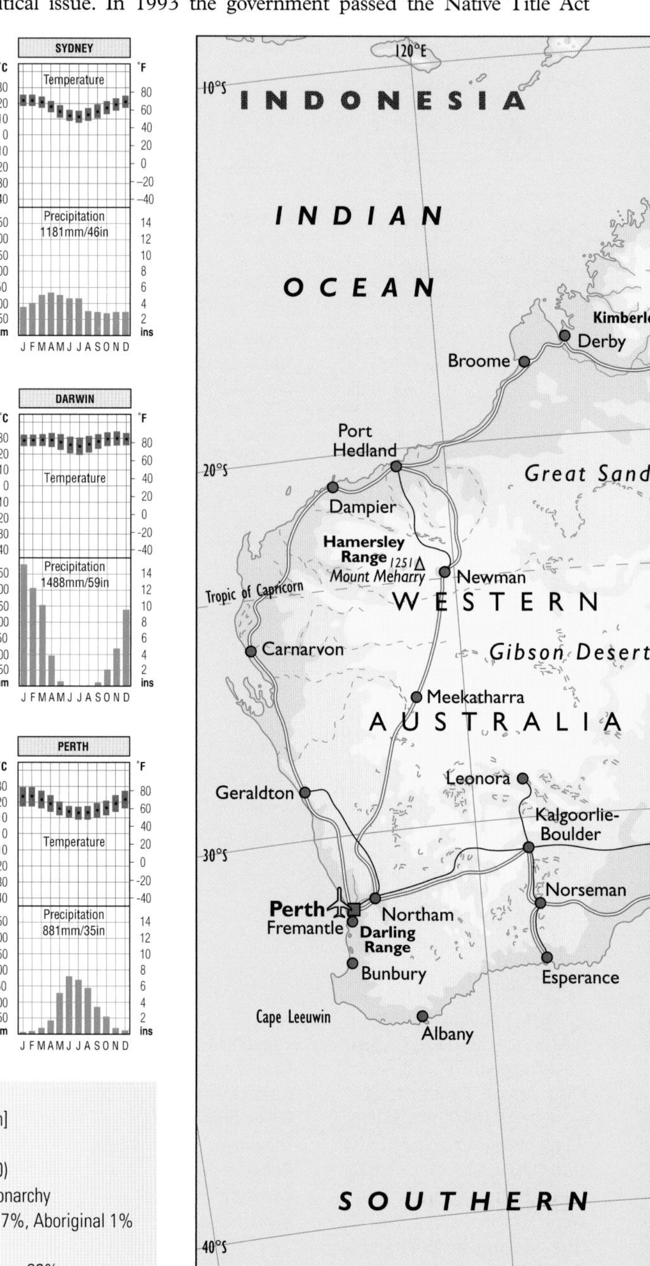

GREAT BARRIER REEF

The world's largest tropical coral reef, in the Coral Sea off the north east coast of Queensland. It was first explored by James Cook in 1770. It forms a natural breakwater and is up to 800 m [2,600 ft] wide. The reef is separated from the mainland by a shallow lagoon, 11–24 km [7–15 mi] wide. At 2,000 km [1,250 mi] in length, with an area of approximately 207,000 sq km [80,000 sq mi] the reef is the largest natural feature on earth. A World Heritage Area since 1981 it is the world's biggest tropical marine reserve. and home to 360 species of hard corals.

which restored to Native Australians land rights over their traditional hunting and sacred areas. In January 2002, eastern Australia suffered devastating bush fires.

Howard secured a fourth term in 2004 elections and vowed to stay leader of the Liberal Party for as long as the members want him.

In recent years Australia has brokered peace deals in the more troubled spots of the Pacific such as Papua New Guinea and the Solomon Islands.

ECONOMY

Australia is a prosperous country. Originally an agrarian economy, although crops grow on only 6% of the land. The country remains a major producer and exporter of farm products, particularly cattle, wheat, and wool. Grapes grown for winemaking are also important. Australia is rich in natural resources and is a major producer of minerals, such as bauxite, coal, copper, diamonds, gold, iron ore, manganese, nickel, silver, tin, tungsten, and zinc. Some oil and natural gas are also produced.

The majority of Australia's imports are manufactured products. They include machinery and other capital goods required by factories. The country has a highly developed manufacturing sector; the major products include consumer goods, notably foodstuffs and household articles. Tourism is a vital industry.

CANBERRA

Capital of Australia on the River Molonglo, Australian Capital Territory, southeastern Australia. Settled in the early 1820s, it was chosen in 1908 as the new site for Australia's capital (succeeding Melbourne). The transfer of all governmental agencies was not completed until after World War II. Canberra has the Australian National University (1946), Royal Australian Mint (1965), Royal Military College, and Stromlo Observatory. The new Parliament House was opened in 1988. Other important buildings include the National Library, National Museum, and National Gallery. Tidbinbilla Nature Reserve is located just outside the city.

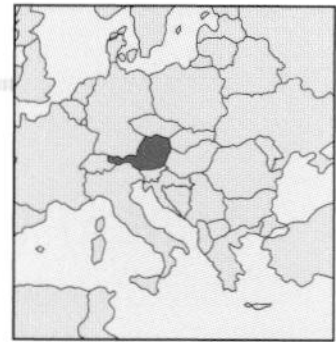

According to legend, the colors on Austria's flag date back to a battle in 1191, during the Third Crusade, when an Austrian duke's tunic was stained with blood, except under his swordbelt, where it remained white. The flag was officially adopted in 1918.

Area 32,378 sq mi [83,859 sq km]
Population 8,175,000
Capital (population) Vienna (1,560,000)
Government Federal republic
Ethnic groups Austrian 90%, Croatian, Slovene, others
Languages German (official)
Religions Roman Catholic 78%, Protestant 5%, Islam and others 17%
Currency Euro = 100 cents
Website www.austria.info

***The picturesque village of Mitteldorf** in the high alpine region of the Tyrol, western Austria, is popular with winter and summer visitors alike*

The Republic of Austria is a landlocked country in the heart of Europe. About three-quarters of the land is mountainous. Northern Austria contains the valley of the River Danube, and the Vienna Basin. This is Austria's main farming region.

Southern Austria contains ranges of the Alps, which rise to their highest point of 12,457 ft [3,797 m] at Grossglockner.

CLIMATE

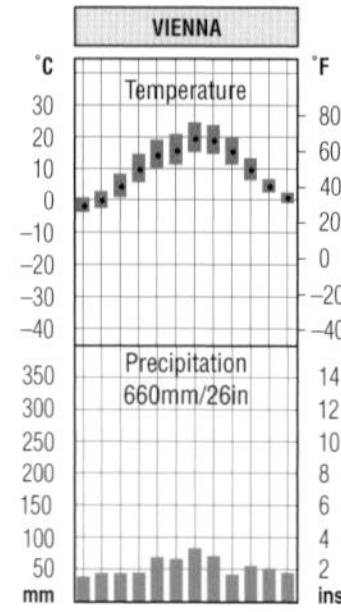

The climate is influenced both by westerly and easterly winds. The moist westerly winds bring rain and snow. They also moderate the temperatures. Dry easterly winds bring very cold weather during the winter and hot weather during the summer.

HISTORY

Following the collapse of the Roman Empire, of which Austria south of the Danube formed a part, the area was invaded and settled by waves of Asian, Germanic and Slav peoples. In the late 8th century, Austria came under the rule of Charlemagne, but in the 10th century, the area was overrun by Magyars.

In 955, the German king Otto I brought Austria under his rule, and in 962 it became part of what later became known as the Holy Roman Empire. German emperors ruled the area until 1806, when the Holy Roman Empire broke up. The Habsburg ruler of the Holy Roman Empire became Emperor Francis I of Austria. In 1867, Austria and Hungary set up the powerful dual monarchy of Austria-Hungary.

Austria-Hungary was allied to Germany in World War I, but the defeated empire collapsed in 1918. Austria's present boundaries derive from the Versailles Treaty, signed in France in June 1919. In 1933, the Christian Socialist Chancellor Engelbert Dollfuss ended parliamentary democracy and ruled as a dictator. He was assassinated in 1934 due to his opposition to the Austrian Nazi Party's aim of uniting Austria and Germany.

The *Anschluss* (union with Germany) was achieved by the German invasion in March 1938. Austria became a province of the Third Reich called Ostmark until the defeat of the Axis powers in 1945.

POLITICS

After World War II, Austria was occupied by the Allies, Britain, France, and the United States and it paid reparations for a 10-year period. After agreeing to be permanently neutral, Austria became an independent federal republic in 1955.

In 1994, two-thirds of the people voted in favor of joining the European Union and the country became a member in 1995. Austria became a center of controversy in 1999, when the extreme right-wing Freedom Party, led by Jörg Haider, who had described Nazi Germany's employment policies as "sound," came second in national elections. In February 2000, a coalition government was formed consisting of equal numbers of ministers from the conservative People's Party, which had come third in the elections, and the Freedom Party. However, the Freedom Party suffered a setback in 2001 when its vote fell in city elections in Vienna.

ECONOMY

Austria is a prosperous country with plenty of hydroelectric power, some oil and natural gas, and reserves of lignite (brown coal). The country's leading economic activity is manufacturing metals and metal products, including iron and steel, vehicles, machinery, machine tools, and ships. Craft industries, making such things as fine glassware, jewelry, and porcelain are also important. Dairy and livestock farming are the leading agricultural activities. Major crops include barley, potatoes, rye, sugar beets, and wheat.

VIENNA (WIEN)

Capital of Austria, on the River Danube. Vienna flourished under the Romans, but after they left in the 5th century it fell to a succession of eastern European invaders. The first Habsburg ruler was installed in 1276. It was the seat of the Holy Roman Empire 1558–1806. Occupied by the French during the Napoleonic Wars, it was later chosen as the site of the Congress of Vienna. Capital of the Austro-Hungarian Empire, it was the cultural and social center of 19th-century Europe under Emperor Franz Joseph. After World War II, it was occupied (1945–55) by joint Soviet-Western forces. Historic buildings include St Stephen's Cathedral (12th-C), the Schönbrunn, and the Hofburg.

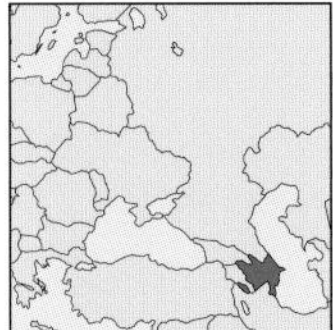

Azerbaijan's flag was adopted in 1991. Light blue is a traditional Turkic color. At the center of the red stripe is a white crescent and star, traditional symbols of Islam. The points of the star represent the eight groups of people in Azerbaijan.

The Republic of Azerbaijan lies in eastern Transcaucasia, bordering the Caspian Sea to the east. The Caucasus Mountains are in the north and include Azerbaijan's highest peak, Mount Bazar-Dyuzi, at 14,652 ft [4,466 m]. Another highland region including the Little Caucasus Mountains and part of the rugged Armenian plateau, lies in the southwest.

Between these regions lies a broad plain drained by the River Kura, its eastern part (south of the capital Baku) lies below sea level. Azerbaijan also includes the Nakhichevan Autonomous Republic on the Iran frontier, an area cut off from the rest of Azerbaijan by Armenian territory.

Forests grow on the mountains, while the lowlands comprise grassy steppe or semidesert.

Area 33,436 sq mi [86,600 sq km]
Population 7,868,000
Capital (population) Baku (1,792,000)
Government Federal multiparty republic
Ethnic groups Azeri 90%, Dagestani 3%, Russian, Armenian, others
Languages Azerbaijani (official), Russian, Armenian
Religions Islam 93%, Russian Orthodox 2%, Armenian Orthodox
Currency Azerbaijani manat = 100 gopik
Website www.president.az

CLIMATE

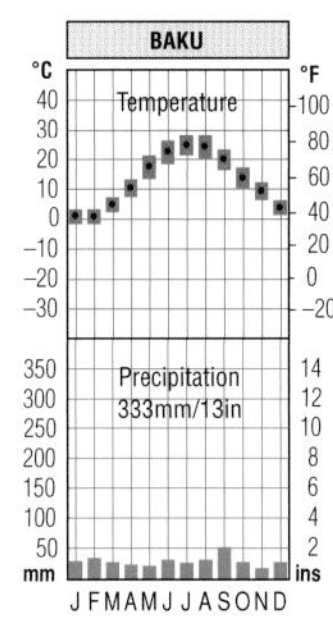

Azerbaijan has hot summers and cool winters. The plains have low rainfall ranging from *c.* 5 to 15 in [130 to 380 mm] a year. The uplands have much higher rainfall as does the subtropical southeast coast.

HISTORY

In ancient times, the area now called Azerbaijan was invaded many times. Arab armies introduced Islam in 642, but most modern Azerbaijanis are descendants of Persians and Turkic peoples who migrated to the area from the east by the 9th century.

Azerbaijan was ruled by the Mongols between the 13th and 15th centuries and then by the Persian Safavid dynasty. By the early 19th century it was under Russian control.

After the Russian Revolution of 1917, attempts were made to form a Transcaucasian Federation made up of Armenia, Azerbaijan, and Georgia. When this failed, Azerbaijanis set up an independent state. But Russian forces occupied the area in 1920. In 1922, the Communists set up a Transcaucasian Republic consisting of Armenia, Azerbaijan, and Georgia, and placed it under Russian control. In 1936, the areas became separate Soviet Socialist Republics within the Soviet Union.

POLITICS

Following the breakup of the Soviet Union in 1991, Azerbaijan became independent. In 1992, Abulfaz Elchibey became president in Azerbaijan's first contested election. In 1993 Elchibey fled and Heydar Aliev, former head of the Communist Party and the KGB in Azerbaijan, assumed the presidency. He was elected later that year and Azerbaijan joined the Commonwealth of Independent States (CIS).

Economic progress was slow, partly because of the conflict with Armenia over the enclave of Nagorno-Karabakh, a region in Azerbaijan where the majority of people are Christian Armenians. A ceasefire in 1994 left Armenia in control of about 20% of Azerbaijan's land area. Talks held in 2001 in an attempt to resolve the dispute proved fruitless and sporadic fighting continues.

In 1998 Aliev was reelected president. In 2001 Azerbaijan joined the Council of Europe. In 2003, Aliev's son Ilham Aliev became president. His government was reelected in 2005, despite charges of fraud.

ECONOMY

In the mid-1990s, the World Bank classified Azerbaijan as a "lower- middle-income" economy. Yet, by the late 1990s, the oil reserves in the Baku area on the Caspian Sea, and in the sea itself, held great promise. Oil extraction and manufacturing, including oil refining and the production of chemicals, machinery, and textiles, are now the most valuable sources of revenue.

Large areas of land are irrigated and crops include cotton, fruit, grains, tea, tobacco, and vegetables. Fishing is still important although the Caspian Sea is becoming increasingly polluted. Private enterprise is now encouraged.

BAKU

Capital of Azerbaijan, a port on the west coast of the Caspian Sea. A trade and craft center in the Middle Ages, Baku prospered under the Shirvan shahs in the 15th century. Commercial oil production began in the 1870s. At the beginning of the 20th century, Baku lay at the center of the world's largest oilfield. Industries include oil processing and equipment, shipbuilding, electrical machinery, chemicals.

Baku *The rigs of this forest of derricks have produced oil for more than a century*

Bahrain

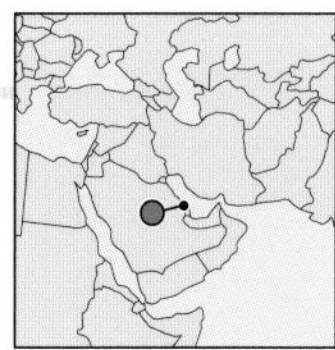

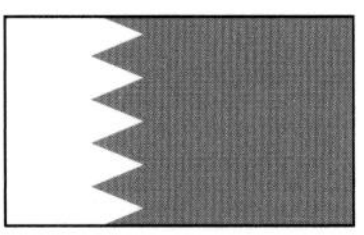

Red and white are traditional colors of the Gulf States. The white historically identified friendly Arab states. The five steps in the serration denote the five Pillars of Islam.

Area 268 sq mi [694 sq km]
Population 678,000
Capital (population) Manama (140,000)
Government Constitutional hereditary monarchy
Ethnic groups Bahraini 62%, others
Languages Arabic, English, Farsi, Urdu
Religions Muslim (Shi'a and Sunni) 81%, Christian 9%, other
Currency Bahraini dinar = 1000 fils
Website www.bahrain.gov.bh

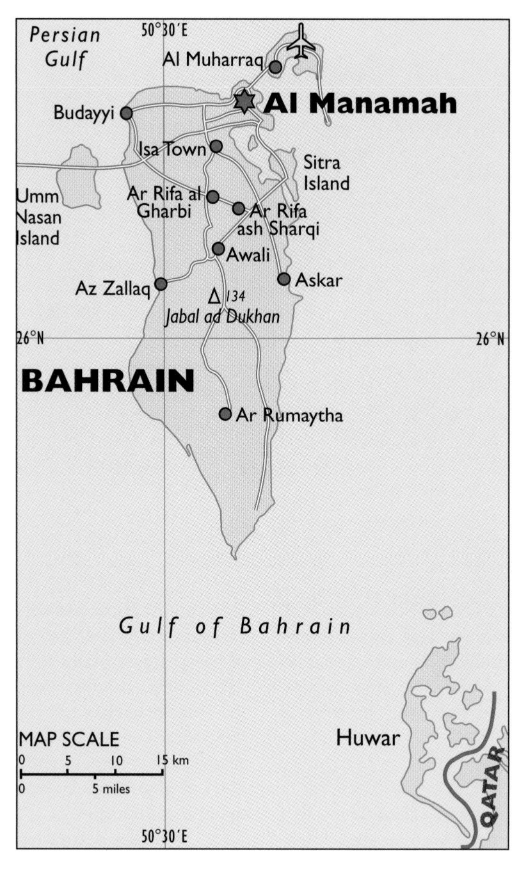

The Kingdom of Bahrain, a former Emirate and now a constitutional hereditary monarchy, is an archipelago consisting of more than 30 islands in the Persian Gulf. The largest of the islands, also called Bahrain, makes up seven-eighths of the country. Causeways link the island of Bahrain to the second largest island of Al Muharraq to the northeast and also to the Arabian peninsula.

Sandy, desert plains make up most of this small, low-lying island country. In the northern coastal areas of Bahrain, freshwater springs provide water for drinking and also for irrigation.

CLIMATE

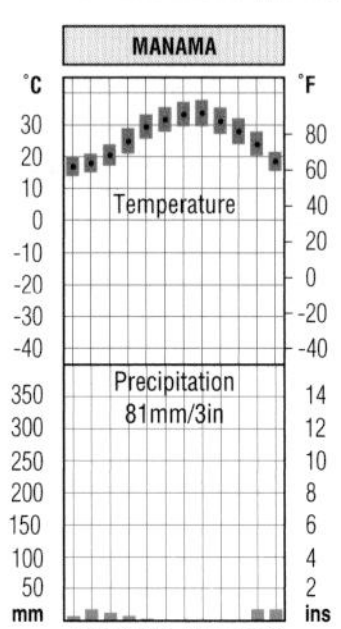

Bahrain has a humid climate. Winters are mild, with temperatures ranging from about 50°F [10°C] to 80°F [27°C]. Summers are hot and humid, with temperatures often soaring to more than 100°F [38°C]. The average annual rainfall is low. Northern Bahrain is the wettest area, with about 3 in [80 mm] a year. The rain occurs mainly in winter and rainfall is almost non-existent in summer months.

HISTORY

Bahrain was part of a trading civilization called Dilmun, which prospered between about 2000 and 1800 BC. This civilization was linked to the Sumerian, Babylonian, and Assyrian civilizations to the north, and with the Indus Valley civilization in what is now Pakistan. Bahrain later came under Islamic Arab influence of the from the 7th century.

Portugal seized the archipelago from its Arab rulers in 1521, but the Persians conquered the islands in 1603, holding them against attacks by the Portuguese and Omanis. However, in 1782, the Al Khalifah Arabs from Saudi Arabia took over the islands and they have ruled ever since.

In the early 19th century, Britain helped Bahrain to prevent annexation by Saudi Arabian invaders. As a result, Bahrain agreed to let Britain take control of its foreign affairs. Bahrain effectively became a British protectorate, though it was not called one. In the 1920s and 1930s, the Bahrainis established welfare systems, which were later funded by revenue from oil, which was discovered in 1932.

Political reforms began in the 1950s and, in 1970, the Emir turned over some of his power to a Council of State, which became a Cabinet. Britain withdrew from the Persian Gulf region in 1971 and Bahrain became fully independent.

POLITICS

Bahrain adopted a new constitution in 1973. This created a National Assembly with 30 elected members. However, relations between the National Assembly and the ruling Al Khalifa family were difficult and the National Assembly was dissolved in 1975. The country was then ruled by the Emir and his cabinet, headed by the prime minister, the Emir's appointee.

MANAMA (AL-MANAMAH)

Capital of Bahrain, on the north coast of Bahrain Island, in the Persian Gulf. It was made a free port in 1958, and a deepwater harbor was built in 1962. It is the country's principal port and commercial center. Industries include oil refining, banking, and boatbuilding.

In February 2002, a new constitution changed the country from an Emirate into a constitutional hereditary monarchy and the ruler Sheikh Hamad bin Isa Al-Khalifa became king. Elections for a new directly elected House of Deputies took place later that year, with women allowed to vote for the first time. The 40-member House of Deputies together with a second chamber, a Shura Council, consisting of experts appointed by the king, made up the National Assembly, Bahrain's first parliament since 1975.

Political problems in recent years have included tensions between the Sunni Muslims and the Shiite majority. During the First Gulf War, Bahrain supported Iraq against Iran and, in 1996, Bahrain accused Iran of supporting an underground Shiite organization. Relations with Iran improved in 2002–4.

The fact that the US Fifth Fleet uses Bahrain as its headquarters in the Persian Gulf has provoked terrorist incidents. Although the people have more freedom than others in the region, opposition groups continue to press for further progress, including greater powers for the elected House of Deputies. The opposition groups organized large public rallies in 2005.

ECONOMY

The people of Bahrain enjoy one of the highest standards of living in the Persian Gulf. The average life expectancy at birth (2005 estimate) is 74 years and free medical services are available. Adult literacy is at 89%.

Bahrain's prosperity is based on oil, although the country lacks major reserves. Petroleum and petroleum products accounted for 68% of the exports in 2002. However, when oil production waned in the 1970s, Bahrain diversified its economy. Its aluminum smelting plant is the Gulf's largest non-oil industrial complex and aluminum, in all forms, accounted for 15% of the exports in 2002. Textiles and clothing accounted for another 8%.

In the late 1990s, industry, commerce, and services employed 79% of the workforce, government 20% and agriculture 1%. Bahrain is a major banking and financial center, and it is home to numerous multinational companies that operate in the Gulf region. In 2003, work began on a complete renovation of the old port of Manama. Construction, fishing, and transport are important and a tourist industry is developing.

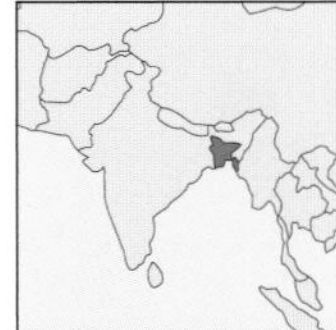

Bangladesh adopted this flag in 1971, following the country's break from Pakistan. The green is said to represent the fertility of the land. The red disk is the sun of independence. It commemorates the blood shed during the struggle for freedom.

Bangladesh

Area 55,598 sq mi 143,998 sq km[]
Population 141,340,000
Capital (population) Dhaka (3,839,000)
Government Multiparty republic
Ethnic groups Bengali 98%, tribal groups
Languages Bangali (official), English
Religions Islam 83%, Hinduism 16%
Currency Taka =100 paisas
Website www.bangladeshonline.com

The People's Republic of Bangladesh is one of the world's most densely populated countries. Apart from the hilly regions in the far northeast and southeast, most of the land is flat and covered by fertile alluvium spread over the land by the Ganges, Brahmaputra and Meghna rivers. These rivers overflow when they are swollen by the annual monsoon rains. Floods also occur along the coast, 357 mi [575 km] long, when tropical cyclones (the name for hurricanes in this region) drive seawater inland. These periodic storms cause great human suffering. The world's most devastating tropical cyclone ever recorded occurred in Bangladesh in 1970, when an estimated 1 million people were killed. Most of Bangladesh is cultivated, but forests cover about 16% of the land. They include bamboo forests in the northeast and mangrove forests in the swampy Sundarbans region in the southwest, which is a sanctuary for the Royal Bengal tiger.

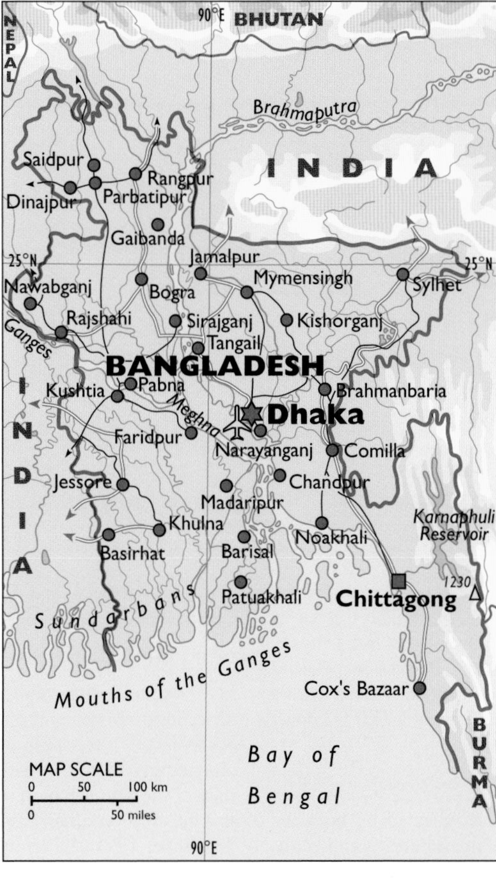

DHAKA (DACCA)

Capital of Bangladesh, a port on the Ganges delta, eastern Bangladesh. Its influence grew as the 17th century Mogul capital of Bengal. In 1765 it came under British control. At independence (1947) it was made capital of the province of East Pakistan. Severely damaged during the war of independence from Pakistan, it became capital of Bangladesh (1971). Sights include the Dakeshwari Temple, Bara Katra Palace (1644) and mosques. It is in the center of the world's largest jute-producing area. Industries include engineering, textiles, printing, glass, chemicals.

CLIMATE

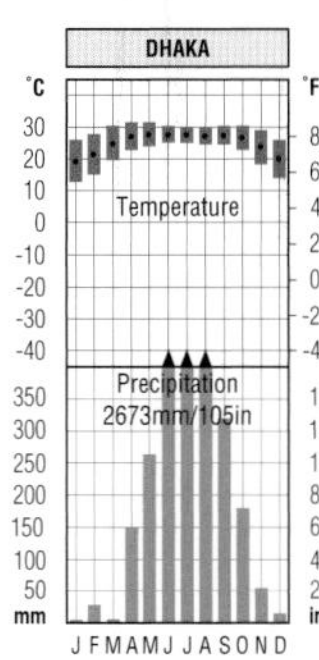

Bangladesh has a tropical monsoon climate. Dry northerly winds blow during the winter, but, in summer, moist winds from the south bring monsoon rains. In 1998, around two-thirds of the entire country was submerged, causing extensive damage. In December 2004, Bangladesh emerged relatively unscathed by the tsunami in the Indian Ocean.

HISTORY

For 300 years after the mid-8th century AD, Buddhist rulers governed eastern Bengal, the area that now makes up Bangladesh. In the 13th century, Muslims from the north extended their rule into Bengal and, in 1576, the area became part of the Muslim Mughal Empire which was ruled by the emperor Akbar. This empire, which also included India, Pakistan and Afghanistan, began to break up in the early 18th century. Europeans, who had first made contact with the area in the 16th century, began to gain influence.

The East India Company, chartered by the English government in 1600 to develop trade in Asia, became the leading trade power in Bengal by the mid-18th century. In 1757, following the defeat of the Nawab of Bengal in the Battle of Plessey, the East India Company effectively ruled Bengal. Discontent with the company led to the Sepoy Rebellion in 1857. In 1958, the British government took over the East India Company and its territory became known as British India.

POLITICS

In 1947, British India was partitioned between the mainly Hindu India and the Muslim Pakistan. Pakistan consisted of two parts, West and East Pakistan, which were separated by about 1,000 mi [1,600 km] of Indian territory. Differences developed between West and East Pakistan, since people in the east felt themselves victims of ethnic and economic discrimination by the Urdu and Punjabi-speaking peoples of the west.

In 1971, resentment turned to war when Bengali irregulars, aided by Indian troops, established the independent nation of "Free Bengal," with Sheikh Mujibur Rahman as head of state. The Sheikh's assassination in 1975—in one of the four military coups in the first 11 years of independence—led finally to a takeover by General Zia Rahman, who created an Islamic state before he, too, was assassinated in 1981. General Ershad took over in a coup in 1982. He resigned as army chief in 1986 to become a civilian president.

By 1990, protests from supporters of his two predecessors toppled Ershad from power and, after the first free parliamentary elections since independence, a coalition government was formed in 1991. Many problems arose in the 1990s, including the increasing strength of Muslim fundamentalism and the consequences of cyclone damage. In 1996, Sheikh Hasina Wajed of the Awami League became prime minister, but, in 1999, she was defeated by Khaleda Zia, leader of the Nationalist Party.

Young Bangladeshi women *in an after-school reading group*

ECONOMY

Bangladesh is one of the world's poorest countries. Its economy depends mainly on agriculture, which employs more than half of the workforce. Rice is the chief crop and Bangladesh is the world's fourth largest producer.

Other important crops include jute, sugar cane, tobacco, and wheat. Jute processing is the leading manufacturing industry and jute is the leading export. Other manufactures include leather, paper, and textiles.

Belarus

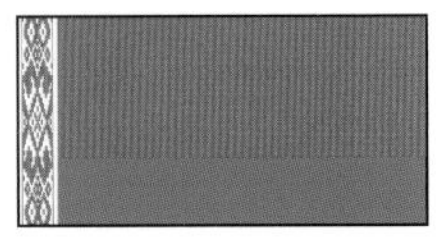

In September 1991, Belarus adopted a red and white flag, replacing the flag used in the Soviet era. In June 1995, following a referendum vote to improve relations with Russia, it was replaced with a design similar to the old flag, but without the hammer and sickle.

Area 80,154 sq mi [207,600 sq km]
Population 10,311,000
Capital (population) Minsk (1,677,000)
Government Multiparty republic
Ethnic groups Belarusian 81%, Russian 11%, Polish, Ukrainian, others
Languages Belarusian, Russian (both official)
Religions Eastern Orthodox 80%, others 20%
Currency Belarusian rouble = 100 kopecks
Website www.mfa.gov.by/eng

***A baker serves customers** at a bakery in Minsk*

The Republic of Belarus is a landlocked country in Eastern Europe, formerly part of the Soviet Union. The land is low-lying and mostly flat. In the south, much of the land is marshy. This area contains Europe's largest marsh and peat bog, the Pripet Marshes.

A hilly region extends rom northeast to southwest and includes the highest point in Belarus, situated near the capital Minsk. This hill reaches a height of 1,122 ft [342 m] above sea level. Over 1,000 lakes, mostly small, dot the landscape. Forests cover large areas. Belarus and Poland jointly control a remnant of virgin forest, which contains a herd of rare wisent (European bison). This is the Belovezha Forest, which is known as the Bialowieza Forest in Poland.

CLIMATE

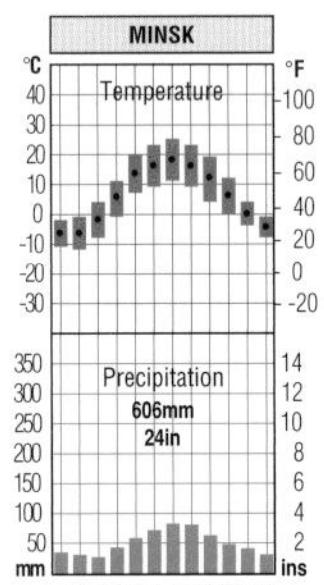

The climate of Belarus is affected by both the moderating influence of the Baltic Sea and continental conditions to the east. The winters are cold and the summers warm.

HISTORY

Slavic people settled in what is now Belarus about 1,500 years ago. In the 9th century, the area became part of the first East Slavic state, Kievan Rus, which became a major European power in the 10th and 11th centuries. Mongol invaders captured the eastern part of Kievan Rus in the 13th century, while Germanic tribes threatened from the west. Belarus allied itself with Lithuania, which also became a powerful state. In 1386, the Lithuanian Grand Duke married the queen of Poland and Lithuanian-Polish kings ruled both countries until 1569, when Lithuania with Belarus merged with Poland. In the 18th century, Russia took most of eastern Poland, including Belarus. Yet the people of Belarus continued to maintain their individuality.

Following the Russian Revolution of 1917, a Communist government replaced tsarist rule in Russia, and, in March 1918, Belarus became an independent, non-Communist republic. Later that year, Russian Communists invaded Belarus, renaming it Byelorussia, a name derived from the Russian *Belaya Rus*, or White Russia. They established a Communist government there in 1919, and in 1922, the country became a founder republic of the Soviet Union. In 1939, Russia occupied what is now western Belarus, which had been part of Poland since 1919. Nazi troops occupied the area between 1941 and 1944, during which one in four citizens died. Byelorussia became a founding member of the United Nations in 1945.

MINSK

Capital of Belarus, on the River Svisloch. Founded *c.* 1060, it was under Lithuanian and Polish rule before becoming part of Russia in 1793. During World War II Minsk was almost completely destroyed and only a few historical buildings were left standing. The city was rebuilt as the showplace city of a modern republic. In 1974 Minsk was awarded the Soviet title of "Hero City" for its sufferings in World War II and speedy reconstruction. In 1991, Minsk became the administrative center of the newly formed CIS. Industries include textiles, machinery, motor vehicles, electronic goods.

POLITICS

In 1990, the Byelorussian parliament declared that its laws took precedence over those of the Soviet Union. On 25 August 1991, many observers were very surprised that this most conservative and Communist-dominated of parliaments declared its independence. This quiet state of the Soviet Union played a supporting role in its deconstruction and the creation of the Commonwealth of Independent States (CIS). In September 1991, the republic changed its name back from the Russian form of Byelorussia to Belarus, its Belarusian form.

The Communists retained control in Belarus after independence. A new constitution introduced in 1994 led to presidential elections that brought Alexander Lukashenko to power. This enabled economic reform to get under way, though the country remained pro-Russian. Lukashenko favored a union with Russia and, in 1999, signed a union treaty committing the countries to setting up a confederal state. However, Russia insisted that a referendum would have to take place before any merger took place. In 2001, Lukashenko was re-elected president amid accusations of electoral fraud. A referendum in 2004 showed overwhelming support for the removal of the two-term limit on Lukashenko's rule Western observers alleged fraud saying that the vote was neither free nor fair.

In 2005 Belarus was listed by the US as Europe's last remaining outpost of tyranny.

ECONOMY

The World Bank classifies Belarus as an "upper-middle-income" economy. Like other former republics of the Soviet Union, it faces many problems in turning from Communism to a free-market economy.

Under Communist rule, many manufacturing industries were set up, making such things as chemicals, trucks, and tractors, machine tools, and textiles. Farming is important and major products include barley, eggs, flax, meat, potatoes, and other vegetables, rye and sugar beet. Leading exports include machinery and transport equipment, chemicals, and food products.

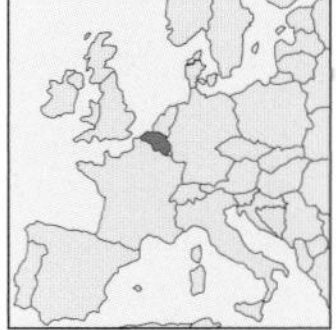

Belgium's national flag was adopted in 1830, when the country won its independence from the Netherlands. The colors came from the arms of the province of Brabant, in central Belgium, which rebelled against Austrian rule in 1787.

The Kingdom of Belgium is a densely populated country in western Europe. Behind the 39 mi [63 km] long coastline on the North Sea, lie its coastal plains. Some low-lying areas, called polders, are protected from the sea by dikes (sea walls).

Central Belgium consists of low plateaus and the only highland region is the Ardennes in the southeast. The Ardennes, reaching a height of 2,277 ft [694 m], consists largely of moorland, peat bogs and woodland. The country's chief rivers are the Schelde, which flows through Tournai, Gent (or Ghent), and Antwerp in the west, and the Sambre and the Meuse, which flow between the central plateau and the Ardennes.

Area 11,787 sq mi [30,528 sq km]
Population 10,348,000
Capital (population) Brussels (136,000)
Government Federal constitutional monarchy
Ethnic groups Belgian 89% (Fleming 58%, Walloon 31%), others
Languages Dutch, French, German (all official)
Religions Roman Catholic 75%, others 25%
Currency Euro = 100 cents
Website www.belgium.be

CLIMATE

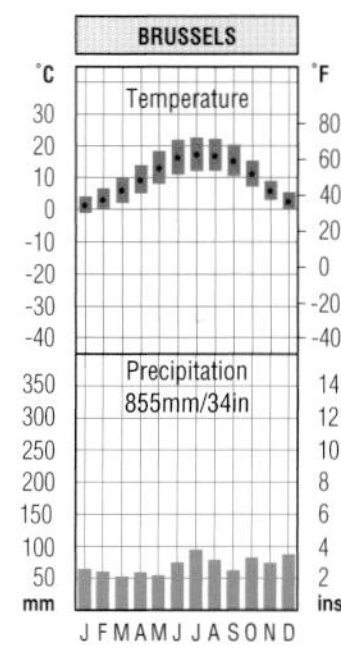

The moderating effects of the sea give much of Belgium a temperate climate, with mild winters and cool summers. Moist winds from the Atlantic Ocean bring significant amounts of rainfall throughout the year, especially in the Ardennes. During January and February, much snow falls in the Ardennes, where temperatures are more extreme. Brussels has mild winters and warm summers.

HISTORY

Due to its strategic position, Belgium has often been called the "cockpit of Europe." In the Middle Ages, the area was split into small states, but, with the Netherlands and Luxembourg, it was united and made prosperous by the dukes of Burgundy in the 14th and 15th centuries. Later, at various times, Belgium came under Austrian, Spanish, and French rule.

From 1815, following the Napoleonic Wars, Belgium and the Netherlands were united as the "Low Countries" but, in 1830, a National Congress proclaimed independence from the Dutch. In 1831, Prince Leopold of Saxe-Coburg became Belgium's king.

The division between Belgium and the Netherlands rested on history rather than geography. Belgium was a mainly Roman Catholic country while the Netherlands was mainly Protestant. Both were neutral in foreign policy, but both were occupied by the Nazis from 1940 until September 1944.

Historic buildings *line a canal in Bruges; the city's name is derived from Bryggja, which means landing stage in Old Norse*

After World War II, Belgium achieved rapid economic progress, first through collaboration with the Netherlands and Luxembourg, which formed a customs union called Benelux, and later as a founder member of what is now the European Union. In 1960, Belgium granted independence to the Belgian Congo (now the Democratic Republic of the Congo) and, in 1962, its supervision of Ruanda-Urundi (now Rwanda and Burundi) was ended.

POLITICS

Belgium has always been an uneasy marriage of two peoples: the majority Flemings, who speak a language closely related to Dutch, and the Walloons, who speak French. The dividing line between the two communities runs east–west, just south of Brussels, although the capital is officially bilingual.

Since the inception of the country, the Flemings have caught up and overtaken the Walloons in cultural influence as well as in numbers. In 1971, the constitution was revised and three economic regions were established: Flanders (Vlaanderen), Wallonia (Wallonie), and Brussels. However, tensions remained.

In 1993, Belgium adopted a federal system of government, with each of the three regions being granted its own regional assembly. Further changes in 2001 gave the regions greater tax-raising powers, plus responsibility for agriculture and the promotion of trade. Elections under this system were held in 1995 and 1999. Since 1995, the Chamber of Deputies has had 150 members, and the Senate 71. The regional assembly of Flanders had 118 deputies, while the assemblies of Brussels and Wallonia had 75 each.

ECONOMY

Belgium is a major trading nation, with a highly developed economy. Almost 75% of its trade is with other EU nations.

With few natural resources it must import a large percentage of the raw materials required for industry. Its main products include chemicals, processed food, and steel. The steelworks lie near to ports because they are powered by petroleum. In 2002, parliament voted to phase out the use of nuclear energy by 2025.

Agriculture employs less than 2% of the people, but Belgian farmers produce most of the food needed by the people. The chief crops are barley and wheat, but the most valuable activities are dairy farming and livestock rearing.

BRUSSELS (BRUXELLES)

Capital of Belgium and of Brabant province, central Belgium. During the Middle Ages, it achieved prosperity through the wool trade and became capital of the Spanish Netherlands. In 1830 it became capital of newly independent Belgium. Places of interest include a 13th-century cathedral, the town hall, splendid art nouveau buildings, and academies of fine arts. The main commercial, financial, cultural, and administrative center of Belgium, it is also the headquarters of the European Union (EU) and of the North Atlantic Treaty Organization (NATO). Industries include textiles, chemicals, electronic equipment, electrical goods, brewing.

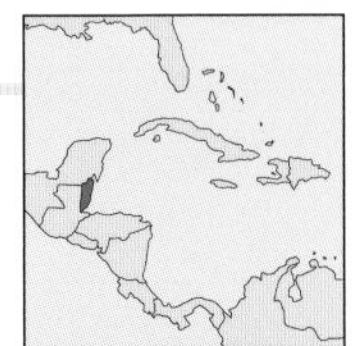

Above the shield is a mahogany tree, beside it stand two woodcutters denoting the two main ethnic groups of Belize. A ring of 50 laurel leaves marks the year 1950, start of the liberation struggle. The country's motto is also shown—Sub umbra floreo (I flourish in the shade).

Area 22,966 sq km [8,867 sq miles]
Population 273,000
Capital (population) Belmopan (8,000)
Government Constitutional monarchy
Ethnic groups Mestizo 49%, Creole 25%, Mayan Indian 11%, Garifuna 6%, others 9%
Languages English (official), Spanish, Creole
Religions Roman Catholic 50%, Protestant 27%, others
Currency Belizean dollar = 100 cents
Website www.belize.gov.bz

Belize is a monarchy whose head of state is Britain's monarch. It lies on the Caribbean Sea in central America. A governor general represents the monarch, while an elected government, headed by a prime minister, rules the country day-to-day.

Behind the swampy coastal plain in the south, the land rises to the low Maya Mountains, which reach 3,675 ft [1,120 m] at Victoria Peak. Northern Belize is mostly low lying and swampy. The main river, the River Belize, flows across the center of the country. Rainforest covers large areas. A barrier reef stretches 185 mi (297 km) along the coast, the longest of its kind in the Western Hemisphere.

CLIMATE

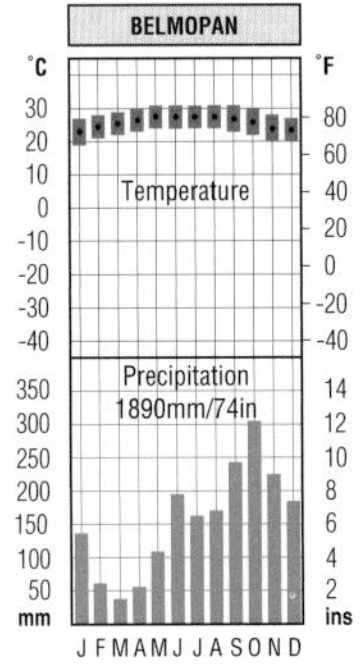

Belize has a humid tropical climate with high temperatures all year. Average rainfall ranges from 52 in [1,300 mm] in the north to over 150 in [3,800 mm] in the south. It is occasionally hit by hurricanes, a storm in 2001 killed 22 and left 12,000 homeless.

HISTORY

Between 300 BC and AD 1000 Belize was part of the Maya Empire. In the 16th century Spain claimed the area but did not settle. The first European settlement was founded by shipwrecked soldiers in 1638. Over the next 150 years Britain gradually took control of Belize and established sugar plantations using slave labor.

In 1862 Belize became the colony of British Honduras. Renamed Belize in 1973 it gained full independence in 1981. Guatemala, which had claimed the area since the early 19th century, opposed Belize's independence and British troops remained to prevent a possible invasion.

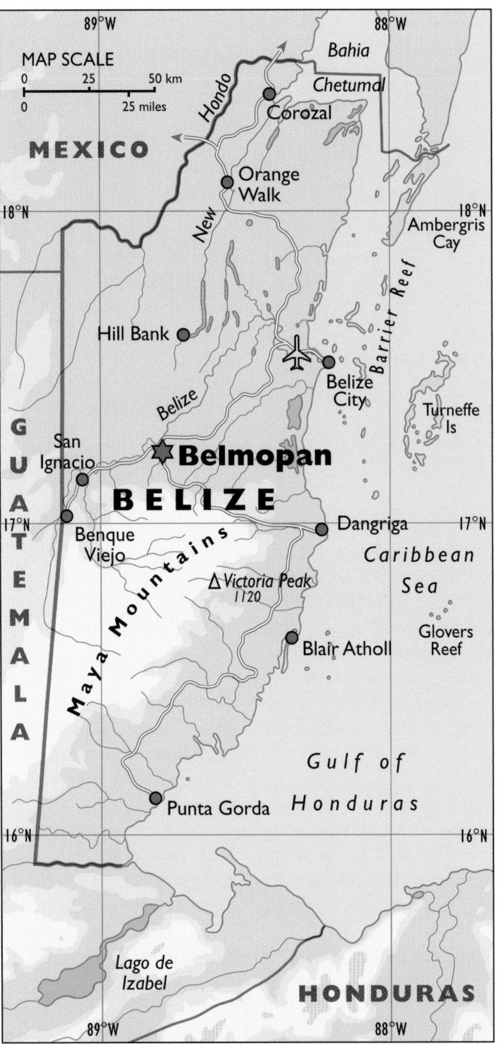

***Mangrove forest and delta** on Caribbean coast of Belize; mangroves are important for providing a habitat for wildlife*

BELMOPAN

Capital of Belize, on the River Belize. It replaced Belize City, 50 mi [80 km] upstream, as capital in 1971, the latter having been largely destroyed by a hurricane in 1961. The building of Belmopan began in 1966 and was completed in 1971. As an inland city temperatures are high in the daytime but much cooler at night. In its center are the National Assembly Building and the majority of central government offices. Residents are mostly government employees and their families. As the city is relatively new, inhabitants originate from other areas of the country, with just a small indigenous population.

POLITICS

In 1983, Guatemala reduced its claim to the southern half of Belize. Improved relations in the early 1990s led Guatemala to recognize Belize's independence and in 1992, Britain agreed to withdraw its troops from the country. Mayan land rights remain a contentious political issue.

High levels of unemployment are a major problem as is a growing involvement in the South American drug trade which has brought with it increasing levels of violent crime

ECONOMY

The World Bank classifies Belize as a "lower-middle-income" developing country. Tourism is the mainstay of the economy and in recent years cruise ships have called there, bringing extra income. Agriculture is still important, with cane sugar the chief commercial crop and export. Other crops include bananas, beans, citrus fruits, corn, and rice. Forestry is of longstanding importance, even featuring on the flag. Fishing is the second biggest earner.

MAYA

Outstanding culture of classic American civilization, occupying south Mexico and north Central America. The civilization divides into three periods. The pre-classic era was from 1000 BC to AD 300. The classic era, when it was at its height, was from the 3rd to the 9th centuries. The Maya built great temple cities. They were skilful potters and weavers and productive farmers. They worshipped gods and ancestors and blood sacrifice was an important element of religion. The post-classic era extended from AD 1000 to 1500 when the Maya civilization declined. Much was destroyed after the Spanish conquest in the 16th century.

The colors on this flag, used by Africa's oldest independent nation, Ethiopia, symbolize African unity. Benin adopted this flag after independence in 1960. A flag with a red (Communist) star replaced it between 1975 and 1990, after which Benin dropped its Communist policies.

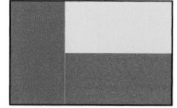

Benin

The Republic of Benin, formerly called Dahomey, is one of Africa's smallest countries. It extends north–south for about 390 mi [620 km]. The coastline on the Bight of Benin, which is about 62 mi [100 km] long, is lined by lagoons. It lacks natural harbors and the harbor at Cotonou, the main port and commercial center, is artificial.

Behind the coastal lagoons is a flat plain. Beyond this plain is a marshy depression, but the land rises to a low plateau in central Benin. The highest land is in the northwest.

Savanna covers most of northern Benin. The north is home to many typical savanna animals, such as buffaloes, elephants, and lions. The north has two national parks, the Penjari and the "W," which Benin shares with Burkina Faso and Niger.

MAP SCALE
0 50 100 km
0 50 miles
NIGER
BURKINA FASO
Niger
Malanville
Alibori
Kandi
Mékrou
Atakora Mountains
635
Natitingou
10°N
Nikki
BENIN
Djougou
Parakou
Bassila
TOGO
NIGERIA
Savalou
Savé
Ouémé
Kétou
Abomey
Pobé
Allada
Porto-Novo
Ouidah
Cotonou
Grand Popo
Bight of Benin

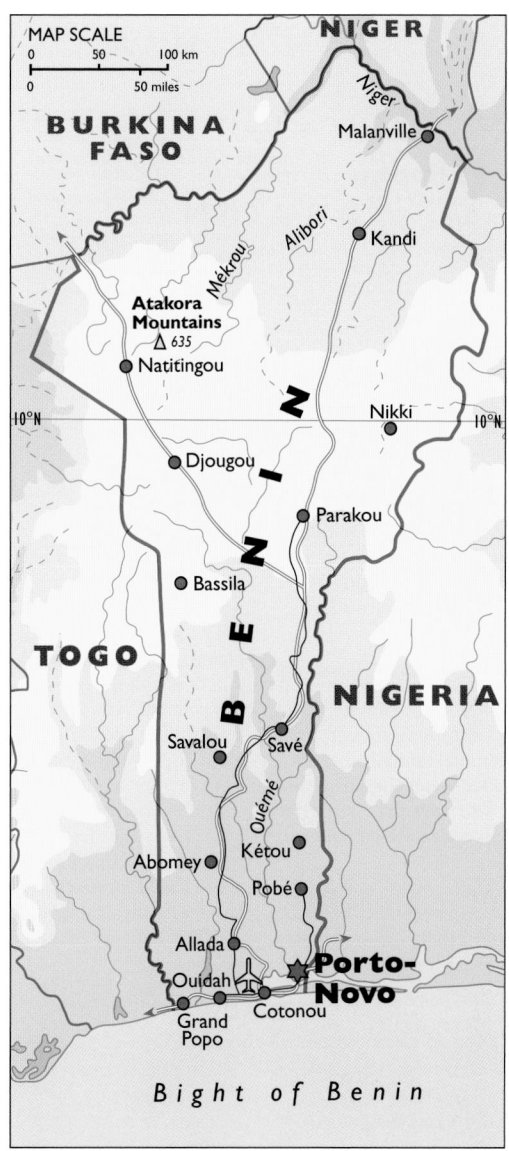

Area 43,483 sq mi [112,622 sq km]
Population 7,250,000
Capital (population) Porto-Novo (233,000)
Government Multiparty republic
Ethnic groups Fon, Adja, Bariba, Yoruba, Fulani
Languages French (official), Fon, Adja, Yoruba
Religions Traditional beliefs 50%, Christianity 30%, Islam 20%
Currency CFA franc = 100 centimes
Website www.gouv.bj/en/

CLIMATE

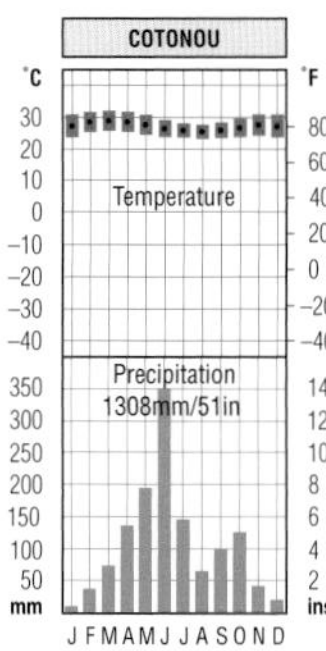

Benin has a hot, wet climate. The average annual temperature on the coast is 77°F [25°C], while the average annual rainfall is 52 in [1,330 mm]. The forested inland plains are wetter than the coast, but the rainfall decreases to the north, which has rainy summer season and a very dry winter.

HISTORY

The ancient kingdom of Dahomey, a prominent West African kingdom that developed in the 15th century, had its capital at Abomey in what is now southwestern Benin. In the 17th century, the kings of Dahomey became involved in supplying slaves to European slave traders, including the Portuguese, who shipped many Dahomeans to the Americas. The shoreline of present-day Benin became part of what was called the Slave Coast. Many slaves were shipped to Brazil. Traces of the culture and religion of the slaves still survive in parts of the Americas, For example, the voodoo cult in Haiti originated in Dahomey.

After slavery was ended in the 19th century, France began to gain influence in the area. Around 1851, France signed a treaty with the kingdom of Dahomey and, in the 1890s, the area, which also included some other small African states, became a French colony. From 1904, they ruled Dahomey as part of a huge region called French West Africa, which also included what are now Burkina Faso, Guinea, Ivory Coast, Mauritania, Mali, Niger, and Senegal. Dahomey became an overseas territory of France in 1946 and a self-governing nation in the French Community in 1958. Full independence was achieved in 1960.

PORTO-NOVO

Capital of Benin, a port on the Gulf of Guinea near the border with Nigeria. Settled by 16th-century Portuguese traders, it later became a shipping point for slaves to America. It was made the country's capital at independence in 1960, but Cotonou is assuming increasing importance. Today it is a market for the surrounding agricultural region.

POLITICS

Dahomey suffered from instability and unrest in the early years of independence. The first president, Hubert Maga, was removed in 1963 in a military coup led by General Christophe Soglo. A presidential council was set up in 1970 and Hubert Maga became one of three rotating presidents. But this regime was overthrown in 1973 by a coup led by Lt-Col Matthieu Kérékou. In 1975, Kérékou announced that the country would be renamed Benin after the powerful state known for its magnificent sculptures in southwestern Nigeria. Benin became a Marxist-Leninist People's Republic and, in 1977, it became a one-party state. This regime, headed by President Kérékou, held power until 1989, when, following the lead of several East European countries in abandoning Communism, Kérékou announced that his country would also abandon Marxism-Leninism and, instead, follow liberal economic policies.

In 1990, a new democratic constitution with a presidential system was introduced. Presidential elections were held in 1991 and Nicéphore Soglo, a former World Bank executive and prime minister, defeated Kérékou. However, in 1996, Kérékou defeated Soglo and returned to power. Kérékou, who was reelected in 2001, worked to restore Benin's fragile economy. Many observers have praised Benin's transition from a Marxist-Leninist state into one of Africa's most stable democracies.

ECONOMY

Benin is a poor developing country. About half of the population depends on agriculture, but farming is largely at subsistence level. The main food crops include beans, cassava, millet, rice, sorghum, and yams. The chief cash crops are cotton, palm oil, and palm kernels. Forestry is also important.

Benin produces some oil, but manufacturing remains on a small scale. It depends heavily upon Nigeria for trade.

Bhutan

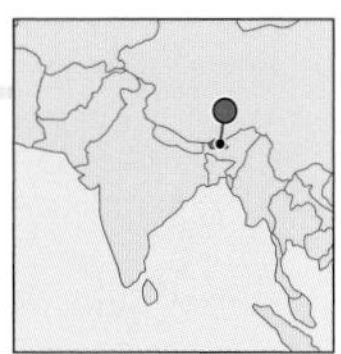

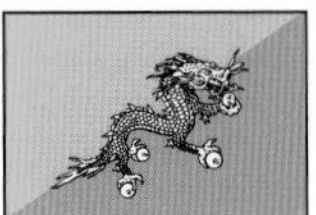

The dragon dates to the 17th century. The jewels in the dragon's claws represent Bhutan's wealth. The white symbolizes purity. The gold represents the secular power of the Druk Gyalpo (Dragon King), and the orange, the spiritual power of Buddhism.

Area 18,147 sq mi [47,000 sq km]
Population 2,186,000
Capital (population) Thimphu (35,000)
Government Constitutional monarchy
Ethnic groups Bhutanese 50%, Nepalese 35%
Languages Dzongkha (official)
Religions Buddhism 75%, Hinduism 25%
Currency Ngultrum = 100 cetrum
Website www.bhutan.gov.bt

The Kingdom of Bhutan is a small, landlocked country in the eastern Himalayas, between India and the Tibetan plateau of China. Southern Bhutan, along the border with India, is the lowest land region, ranging between about 160 and 2,950 ft [50 and 900 m] above sea level. North of the plains is a mountainous region between about 4,920 and 13,940 ft [1,500 and 4,250 m]. The northernmost region lies in the Great Himalayan range, reaching more than 23,950 ft [7,300 m]. Most people live in the fertile valleys of rivers which flow generally from north to south.

CLIMATE

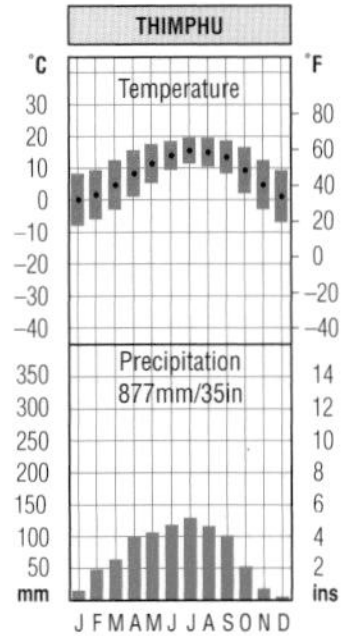

The altitude determines the climate. The southern plains have a subtropical, rainy climate, with an average annual rainfall of around 197 in [5,000 mm]. Dense vegetation covers much of the region, with savanna in the far south. Central Bhutan has a moderate climate, though winters are cold.

HISTORY

Around 1,200 years ago Tibetan invaders settled in the area.

In the early 17th century, Bhutan became a separate state when a Tibetan lama (Buddhist monk), who was both a spiritual and temporal ruler, took power. The country was divided into districts ruled by governors and fort commanders. The 19th century was plagued by civil wars in which rival governors battled for power. In 1907, Bhutan became a monarchy when Ugyen Wangchuk, the powerful governor of Tongsa district, made himself Maharajah (now King) and set up the country's first effective central government. The monarch was hereditary and the Maharajah's successors have ruled the country ever since.

In 1910, Britain took control of Bhutan's foreign affairs in 1910, but it did not interfere in internal affairs. This treaty was renewed with newly independent India in 1949. India also returned some parts of Bhutan which had been annexed by Britain and agreed to help Bhutan develop its economy and, later, its defense.

POLITICS

Bhutan's remote but strategic position cut it off from the outside world for centuries and it only began to open up to outsiders in the 1970s. The roots of reform go back to 1952 when Jigme Dorji Wangchuk succeeded to the throne and a national assembly was established to advise the king. Slavery was abolished in 1958 and, in 1959, Bhutan admitted several thousand refugees after China had annexed Tibet. The first cabinet was set up in 1968.

In 1972, King Jigme Dorji Wangchuk died and was succeeded by his son, Jigme Singye Wangchuk. The new king continued Bhutan's policy of slow modernization. The first foreign tourists were admitted in 1974, although tourism was restricted to people on prepackaged or guided tours. Independent travel was discouraged as Bhutan sought to preserve its majority Buddhist culture. A television service was not introduced until 1999.

The king gave up some of the monarch's absolute powers in 1998, giving up his role as head of the government. Instead, he ruled in conjunction with the government, a National Assembly and a royal advisory council. In 2005, the government published a new draft constitution, which would make Bhutan a democracy with a parliament consisting of two elected houses. The parliament would have the right to impeach the king by a two-thirds vote.

Ethnic conflict has marred Bhutan's recent history. In 1986, a new law came into force making citizenship dependent on length of residence in Bhutan. Many ethnic Nepalis living in the south were made illegal immigrants, while other measures emphasizing Buddhist culture further antagonized the minority Nepalis. This led to violence in 1990, causing many Nepalis to flee. In 2005 the king announced that he would step down in 2008, when democratic elections would be held.

ECONOMY

Bhutan is a poor country. The rugged terrain makes the building of roads and other infrastructure difficult. Agriculture, mainly subsistence farming, cattle rearing, and forestry, accounts for 93% of the workforce. Barley, rice and wheat are the chief food crops. Other products include citrus fruits, dairy products, and con. Industry is small scale, some coal is mined in the south.

The country's economy is closely linked to that of India with nearly 90% of Bhutan's total exports going to India. Bhutan has considerable hydroelectric power potential and electricity is exported to India. However, economic development is hampered by Bhutan's desire to maintain its traditional culture. The controls placed by the government on outside groups have inevitably restricted foreign investment.

THIMPHU

Bhutan's capital is located in the west of the country. The city is modern in age only (established in 1952) as all new buildings are built following traditional designs. Among its sights are the Memorial Chorten (dedicated to the king's late father Jigme Dorji Wangchuck) and the Tashicho Dzong a 350-year-old structure built by Shabdrung Ngawang Namgyal and refurbished in 1961 to house government departments and ministries.

Buddhist monks chanting and drumming *during the Wangdi Tsechu Festival at Wangdue Phodrang Dzong*

This flag, which has been Bolivia's national and merchant flag since 1888, dates back to 1825 when Bolivia became independent. The red stands for Bolivia's animals and the courage of the army, the yellow for its mineral resources, and the green for its agricultural wealth.

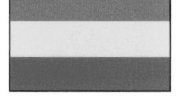

Area 424,162 sq mi [1,098,581 sq km]
Population 8,724,000
Capital (population) La Paz (seat of government, 940,000); Sucre (legal capital/seat of judiciary, 177,000)
Government Multiparty republic
Ethnic groups Mestizo 30%, Quechua 30%, Aymara 25%, White 15%
Languages Spanish, Aymara, Quechua (all official)
Religions Roman Catholic 95%
Currency Boliviano = 100 centavos
Website www.bolivia.com

The Republic of Bolivia is a landlocked country in South America. It can be divided into two regions. The west is dominated by two parallel ranges of the Andes Mountains. The western cordillera forms Bolivia's border with Chile. The eastern range runs through the heart of Bolivia. Between the two, lies the Altiplano. The Altiplano is the most densely populated region of Bolivia and the site of its famous ruins. It includes the seat of government, La Paz, close to Lake Titicaca. Sucre, the legal capital, lies in the Andean foothills.

The east is a relatively unexplored region of lush, tropical rainforest, inhabited mainly by Native South Americans. In the southeast lies the Gran Chaco.

The windswept Altiplano is a grassland region. The semi-arid Gran Chaco is a largely unpopulated vast lowland plain, drained by the River Madeira, a tributary of the Amazon. The region is famous for its quebracho trees which are a major source of tannin.

CLIMATE

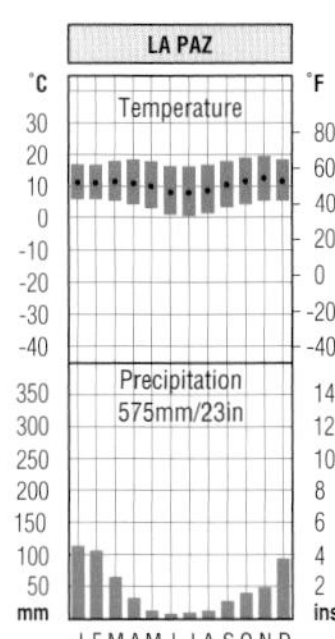

Bolivia's climate varies greatly according the to altitude with the highest Andean peaks permanently covered in snow. In contrast, the eastern plains have a humid tropical climate. The main rainy season takes place between December and February.

HISTORY

American Indians have lived in Bolivia for at least 10,000 years. The main groups today are the Aymara and Quechua people.

When Spanish soldiers arrived in the early 16th century, Bolivia was part of the Inca empire. Following the defeat of the Incas, Spain ruled from 1532 to 1825, when Antonio José de Sucre, one of revolutionary leader Simón Bolívar's generals, defeated the Spaniards.

Since independence, Bolivia has lost much territory to its neighbors. In 1932, Bolivia fought with Paraguay for control of the Gran Chaco region. Bolivia lost and most of this area passed to Paraguay in 1938.

POLITICS

Following the Chaco War, Bolivia entered a long period of instability. It had ten presidents, six of whom were members of the military, between 1936 and 1952, when the Revolutionary Movement replaced the military. The new government launched a series of reforms, which included the breakup of large estates and the granting of land to Amerindian farmers. Another military uprising occurred in 1964, heralding another period of instability.

Elections were held in 1980, but the military again intervened until 1982, when civilian government was restored. Presidential elections were held in 1989, 1993 and 1997, when General Hugo Bánzer Suárez, who had ruled as a dictator in the 1970s, became president. In 2005, Evo Morales, a left-wing Aymaran Indian and peasant leader, was elected president.

LA PAZ

Administrative capital and largest city of Bolivia, in the west of the country. Founded by the Spanish in 1548 on the site of an Inca village, it was one of the centers of revolt in the War of Independence (1809–24). Located at 12,000 ft [3,600 m] in the Andes, it is the world's highest capital city. Industries include chemicals, tanning, flour-milling, electrical equipment, textiles, brewing and distilling.

ECONOMY

Bolivia is one of the poorest countries in South America. It has several natural resources, including tin, silver, and natural gas, but the chief activity is agriculture, which employs 47% of the people. Potatoes, wheat and a grain called quinoa are important crops on the Altiplano, while bananas, cocoa, coffee, and corn are grown at the lower, warmer levels.

Manufacturing is small-scale and the main exports are mineral ores and fossil fuels. Coca, which is used to make cocaine, is exported illegally. In 2002–3, the production of coca plummeted, causing social unrest. In 2004, the people voted in favor of a government plan to export natural gas via a port in Peru.

***Plaza San Francisco** in La Paz, with the 16th century Iglesia de San Francisco in the background*

Bosnia-Herzegovina

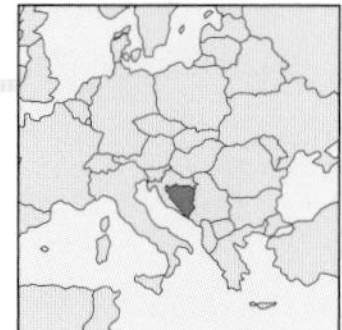

A new flag was adopted in 1998, as the previous flag was thought to be synonymous with the wartime Muslim regime. The blue background and white stars represent the country's links with the EU. The triangle stands for the three ethnic groups in the country.

Area 19,767 sq mi [51,197 sq km]
Population 4,008,000
Capital (population) Sarajevo (529,000)
Government Federal republic
Ethnic groups Bosnian 48%, Serb 37%, Croat 14%
Languages Bosnian, Serbian, Croatian
Religions Islam 40%, Serbian Orthodox 31%, Roman Catholic 15%, others 14%
Currency Convertible marka = 100 convertible pfenniga
Website www.fbihvlada.gov.ba/engleski/

Bosnia-Herzegovina is one of the five republics to emerge from the former Federal People's Republic of Yugoslavia. Much of the country is mountainous or hilly, with an arid limestone plateau in the southwest. The River Sava, which forms most of the northern border with Croatia, is a tributary of the River Danube. Because of the country's shape, the coastline is limited to a short stretch of 13 mi [20 km] on the Adriatic coast.

CLIMATE

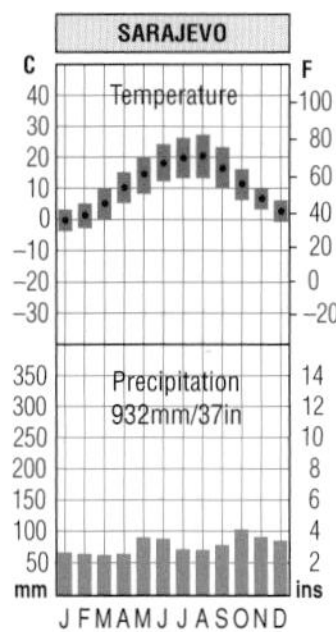

The coast benefits from a Mediterranean climate. Summers are dry and sunny, while winters are moist and mild. Inland, the weather is more severe, with hot, dry summers and bitterly cold, snowy winters. The north experiences the most severe weather.

HISTORY

Slavs settled in the area that is now Bosnia-Herzegovina around 1,400 years ago. In the late 15th century, the area was taken by the Ottoman Turks. In 1878, the dual monarchy of Austria-Hungary gained temporary control over Bosnia-Herzegovina and it formally took over the area in 1908. The assassination of Archduke Franz Ferdinand of Austria-Hungary in Sarajevo, in June 1914, was the catalyst for the start of World War I. In 1918, Bosnia-Herzegovina became part of the Kingdom of the Serbs, Croats, and Slovenes, renamed Yugoslavia in 1929. Germany occupied Yugoslavia during World War II, and Bosnia-Herzegovina came under a puppet regime in Croatia. A Communist government took over in Yugoslavia in 1945, and a new constitution in 1946 made the country a federal state, with Bosnia-Herzegovina as one of its six constituent republics.

Under Communism, Bosnia-Herzegovina was a potentially explosive area due to its mix of Bosnian Muslims, Orthodox Christian Serbs, and Roman Catholic Croats, as well as Albanian, gypsy, and Ukrainian minorities. The ethnic and religious differences started to exert themselves after the death of Yugoslavia's president Josip Broz Tito in 1980, and increasing indications that Communist economic policies were not working.

POLITICS

Free elections were held in 1990 and non-Communists won a majority, with a Muslim, Alija Izetbegovic, as president. In 1991, Croatia and Slovenia declared themselves independent republics and seceded from Yugoslavia. Bosnia-Herzegovina held a referendum on independence in 1992. Most Bosnian Serbs boycotted the vote, but the Muslims and Croats voted in favor and Bosnia-Herzegovina proclaimed its independence. War then broke out.

At first, the Muslim-dominated government allied itself uneasily with the Croat minority, but it was at once under attack by local Serbs, supported by their conationals from beyond Bosnia-Herzegovina's borders. In their "ethnic cleansing" campaign, heavily equipped Serb militias drove poorly-armed Muslims from towns they had long inhabited. By early 1993, the Muslims controlled less than a third of the former federal republic, and even the capital, Sarajevo, became disputed territory, with constant shelling.

The Muslim-Croat alliance rapidly disintegrated and refugees approached the million mark. Tougher economic sanctions on Serbia in April 1993 had little effect on the war in Bosnia. A small UN force attempted to deliver relief supplies to civilians and maintain "safe" Muslim areas to no avail.

In 1995, the warring parties agreed to a solution to the conflict, the Dayton Peace Accord—the dividing of the country into two self-governing provinces, one Bosnian Serb and the other Muslim-Croat, under a central, unified, multiethnic government. A NATO-led force helped stabilize the country, this was replaced in 2004 by a European force when problems were no longer political.

ECONOMY

The economy of Bosnia-Herzegovina, was shattered by the war in the early 1990s. Manufactures include electrical equipment, machinery and transport equipment, and textiles. Farm products include fruits, corn, tobacco, vegetables, and wheat, but the country has to import food.

Old Bridge, Mostar *built in 1566 and destroyed in November 1993, when it was shelled by Bosnian Croat troops; it reopened in 2004*

SARAJEVO

Capital of Bosnia-Herzegovina, on the River Miljacka. It fell to the Turks in 1429, and flourished as a commercial center in the Ottoman Empire. Passing to the Austro-Hungarian Empire in 1878, the city was a center of Serb and Bosnian resistance to Austrian rule. In June 1914 a Serb nationalist assassinated Austrian Archduke Franz Ferdinand in the city, an act that precipitated World War I. In 1991 Sarajevo became the focal point of the civil war between Bosnian-Serb troops and Bosnian government forces. The city lay under prolonged siege, often without water, electricity, or basic medical supplies. After the 1995 Dayton Peace Accord, it in effect became a Bosnian city, though with a reduced population as many Serbs fled.

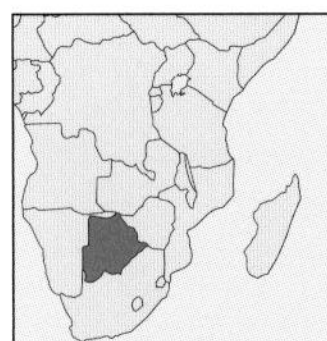

The black-and-white zebra stripe in the center of Botswana's flag symbolizes racial harmony. The blue represents rainwater, because water supply is the most vital need in this dry country. This flag was adopted in 1966, when Botswana became independent from Britain.

The Republic of Botswana is a landlocked country which lies in the heart of southern Africa. The majority of the land is flat or gently rolling, with an average height of about 3,280 ft [1,000 m]. More hilly country lies in the east. The Kalahari, a semidesert area covers much of Botswana.

Most of the south has no permanent streams. But large depressions occur in the north. In one, the Okavango River, which flows from Angola, forms a large delta, an area of swampland. Another depression contains the Makgadikgadi Salt Pans. During floods, the Botletle River drains from the Okavango Swamps into the Makgadikgadi Salt Pans.

ANGOLA
ZAMBIA
Cubango
Caprivi Strip
Zambezi
ZIMBABWE
NAMIBIA
Okavango Delta
Maun
Makgadikgadi Pans
Francistown
Selebi-Pikwe
BOTSWANA
Serowe
Limpopo
Kalahari Desert
Mahalapye
Tropic of Capricorn
Tshane
Molepolole
Gaborone
Otse Mt 1489
Lobatse
Molopo
SOUTH AFRICA
MAP SCALE
0 100 200 300 400 km
0 100 200 miles
20°E 25°E 30°E 20°S 25°S

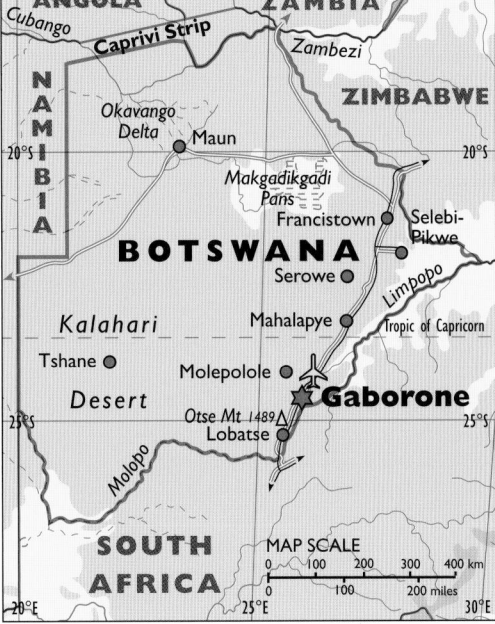

Area 224,606 sq mi [581,730 sq km]
Population 1,562,000
Capital (population) Gaberone (186,000)
Government Multiparty republic
Ethnic groups Tswana (or Setswana) 79%, Kalanga 11%, Basarwa 3%, others
Languages English (official), Setswana
Religions Traditional beliefs 85%, Christianity 15%
Currency Pula = 100 thebe
Website www.gov.bw

CLIMATE

Temperatures are high during the summer which runs from October to April, but the winter months are much cooler. Night-time temperatures in winter sometimes drop below freezing. The average rainfall ranges from over 16 in [400 mm] in the east to less than 8 in [200 mm] in the southwest.

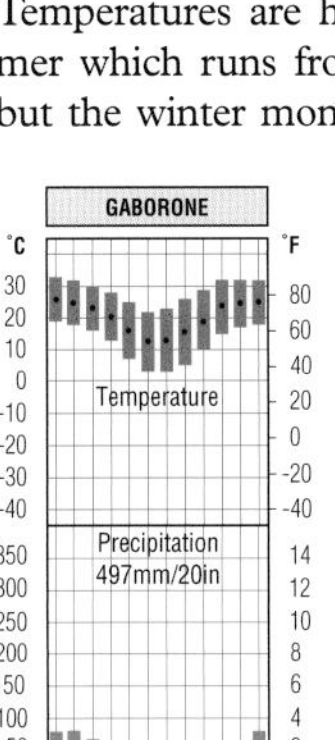

Gaborone, the capital of Botswana, lies in the wetter eastern part of the country, where the majority of the population lives. The rainy season occurs during summer, between the months of November and March. Frosts sometimes occur in parts of the east when the temperature drops below freezing.

HISTORY

The earliest inhabitants of the region were the San, who are also called Bushmen. They had a nomadic way of life, hunting wild animals and collecting plant foods.

The Tswana, who speak a Bantu language, now form the majority of the population. They are cattle owners, who settled in eastern Botswana more than 1,000 years ago. Their arrival led the San to move into the Kalahari region. Today, the San form a tiny minority, most of whom live in permanent settlements and work on cattle ranches.

POLITICS

Britain ruled the area as the Bechuanaland Protectorate between 1885 and 1966. When the country became independent, it adopted the name of Botswana. Since then, unlike many African countries, Botswana has been a stable multiparty democracy.

The economy has undergone a steady process of diversification under successive presidents. Botswana's first president, Sir Seretse Khama, who died in 1980, and his successor, Sir Ketumile Masire, who served from 1980 until 1998, when he retired in favor of Festus Mogae. Despite a severe drought, the economy expanded and the government introduced major social programs. Tourism also grew as huge national parks and reserves were established. However, by the early 2000s, Botswana had the world's highest rate of HIV infection—around one in five of the population had the virus. The average life expectancy fell from 60 to 40 years. Botswana does however have one of Africa's most progressive programs in place to deal with the disease.

ECONOMY

In 1966, Botswana was one of Africa's poorest countries, depending on meat and live cattle for its exports. But the discovery of minerals, including coal, cobalt, copper, and nickel, has helped to diversify the economy. The mining of diamonds at Orapa, started in 1971 and was the chief factor in the transformation of the economy. By 1997, Botswana had become the world's leading producer, overtaking Australia and the Democratic Republic of the Congo. Diamonds accounted for about 74% of Botswana's exports, followed by copper-nickel matte, textiles, and meat products. Another major source of income comes from tourists, the majority of whom come from South Africa, which continues to have a great influence on Botswana.

The development of mining and tourism has reduced the relative importance of farming, though agriculture still employs about one-fifth of the population. The most important type of farming is livestock raising, particularly cattle, which are mostly reared in the wetter east. Crops include beans, corn, millet, sorghum, and vegetables.

Elephant searching for food *in Chobe National Park*

GABORONE

Capital of Botswana, close to the border with South Africa. First settled in the 1890s, it served as the administrative headquarters of the former Bechuanaland Protectorate. In 1966 it became the capital of an independent Botswana.

The green on the flag symbolizes Brazil's rainforests and the yellow diamond its mineral wealth. The blue sphere bears the motto "Order and Progress." The 27 stars, arranged in the pattern of the night sky over Rio de Janeiro, represent the states and the federal district.

The Federative Republic of Brazil is the world's fifth largest country. Structurally, it has two main regions. In the north is the vast Amazon basin, once an inland sea and now drained by a river system that carries one-fifth of the world's running water. The largest area of river plain is in the upper part of the basin, along the frontiers with Bolivia and Peru. Downstream, the flood plain is relatively narrow.

The Brazilian Highlands make up the country's second main region and consist largely of hard crystalline rock dissected into rolling uplands. They include the heartland (Mato Grosso) and the whole western flank of the country from the bulge to the border with Uruguay. The undulating plateau of the northern highlands carries poor soils.

The typical vegetation is thorny scrub which, in the south, merges into wooded savanna. Conditions are better in the south, where rainfall is more reliable. More than 60% of the population lives in the four southern and southeastern states, the most developed part of Brazil, though accounting only for 17% of Brazil's total area.

CLIMATE

Manaus has high temperatures all through the year. The rainfall is heavy, though the period from June to September is drier than the rest of the year. The capital, Brasília, and the city Rio de Janeiro also have tropical climates, with much more marked dry seasons than Manaus. The far south has a temperate climate. The northeastern interior is the driest region, with an average annual rainfall of only 10 in [250 mm] in places. The rainfall is also unreliable and severe droughts are common in this region.

The Amazon basin contains the world's largest rainforests, which the Brazilians call the selvas. The forests contain an enormous variety of plant and animal species. But many species are threatened by loggers and those who wish to exploit the forests. The destruction of the forest is also ruining the lives of the last surviving groups of Amazonian Indians.

Forests grow on the northeastern coasts, but the dry interior has large areas of thorny scrub. The southeast contains fertile farmland and large ranches.

HISTORY

The Portuguese explorer Pedro Alvarez Cabral claimed Brazil for Portugal in 1500. While Spain was occupied in western South America, the first Portuguese colonists settled in the northeast in the 1530s. They were followed by other settlers, missionaries, explorers and prospectors who gradually penetrated the country during the 17th and 18th centuries. They found many groups of Amerindians, some of whom lived seminomadic lives, hunting, fishing, and gathering fruits, while others lived in farming villages, growing cassava and other crops.

The Portuguese enslaved many Amerindians who were used for plantation work, while others were driven into the interior. The Portuguese also introduced about 4 million African slaves, notably in the sugarcane-growing areas in the northeast. For many decades following the early settlements, Brazil was mainly a sugar-producing colony, with most plantations centered on the rich coastal plains of the northeast. These areas later produced cotton, cocoa, rice, and other crops. In the south, colonists penetrated the interior in search of slaves and minerals, especially gold and diamonds. The city of Ouro Preto in Minas Gerais was built and Rio de Janeiro grew as a port for the area.

Initially little more than a group of rival provinces, Brazil began to unite in 1808, when the Portuguese royal court, transferred from Lisbon to Rio de Janeiro. The eldest son of King Joas VI of Portugal was chosen as the "Perpetual Defender" of Brazil by a national congress. In 1822, he proclaimed the independence of the country and was chosen as the constitutional emperor with the title of Pedro I. He became increasingly unpopular and was forced to abdicate in 1831. He was succeeded by his five-year-old son, Pedro II, who officially took office in 1841. Pedro's liberal policies included the gradual abolition of slavery.

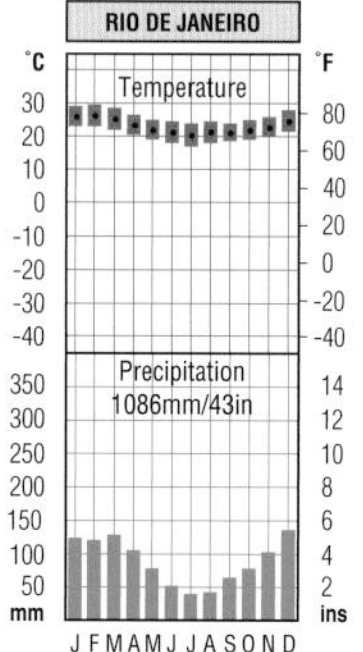

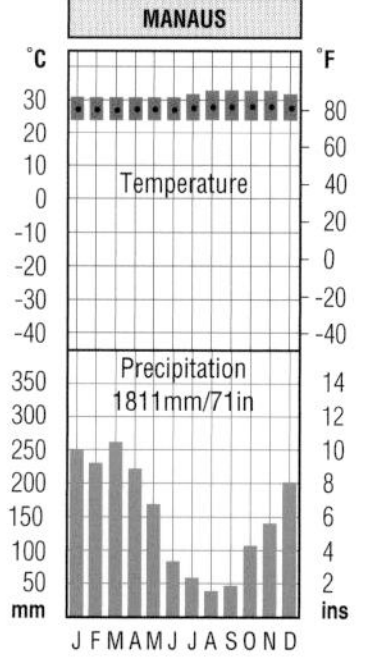

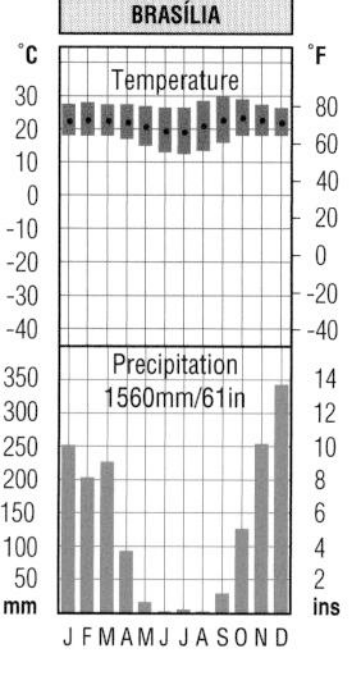

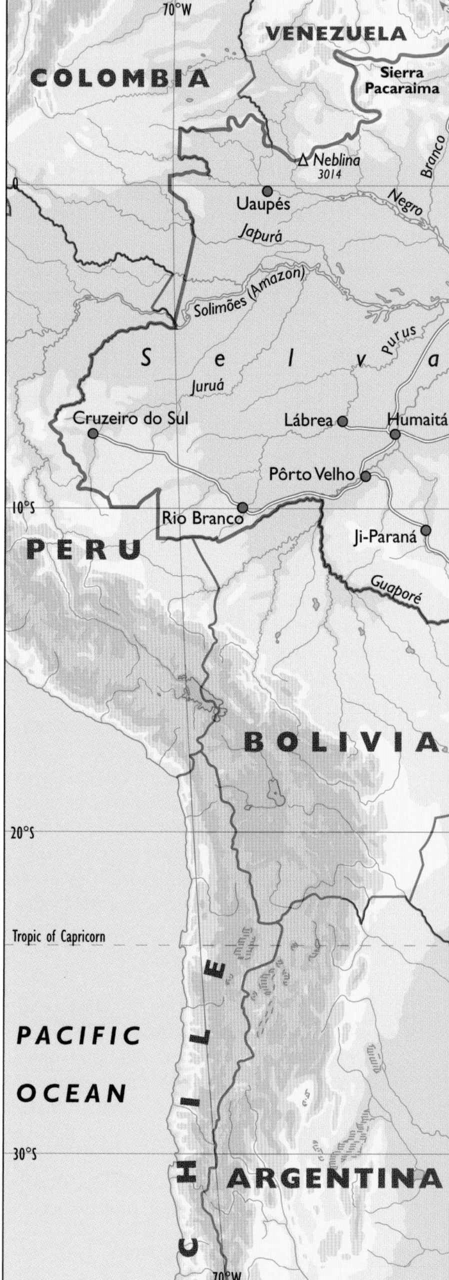

***Aerial view of Rio de Janeiro,** with the Brazilian Highlands in the background and the Christ the Redeemer (Cristo Redentor) statue to the fore; the statue measures 38 m (125 ft)*

During the 19th century, São Paulo state became the center of a huge coffee-growing industry. While the fortunes made in mining helped to develop Rio de Janeiro, profits from coffee were invested in the city of São Paulo. Immigrants from Italy and Germany settled in the south, introducing farming in the fertile valleys, in coexistence with the cattle ranchers and gauchos of the plains. The second half of the 19th century saw the development of the wild rubber industry in the Amazon basin, where the city of Manaus, with its world-famous opera house, served as a center and market. Although Manaus lies 1,000 mi [1,600 km] from the mouth of the Amazon, rubber from the hinterland could be shipped out directly to world markets in ocean-going steamers. Brazil enjoyed a virtual monopoly of the rubber trade until the early 20th century, when Malaya began to compete, later with massive success.

A federal system was adopted for the United States of Brazil in the 1881 constitution and Brazil became a republic in 1889. Until 1930, the country experienced very strong economic expansion and prospered, but social unrest in 1930 resulted in a major revolt. From then on the country was under the control of President Getulio Vargas, who established a strong corporate state similar to that of fascist Italy, although Brazil entered World War II on the side of the Allies. Democracy, often corrupt, prevailed from 1956, 1964 and 1985. In between there were five military presidents of illiberal regimes.

POLITICS

A new constitution came into force in October 1988—the eighth since Brazil became independent from Portugal in 1822. The constitution transferred powers from the president to the congress and paved the way for a return to democracy. In 1989, Fernando Collor de Mello was elected to cut inflation and combat corruption. But he made little progress and in 1992, with inflation soaring, his vice-president, Itamar Franco, took over as president. He served until 1994 when the Social Democrat Fernando Henrique Cardoso, a former finance minister, was elected president.

In elections in 2002, Luiz Inácio Lula da Silva, leader of the left-wing Workers' Party, was elected president. Popularly known as "Lula," he had promised many social reforms. In office, he proved to be a pragmatist, following moderate economic policies. In 2005, his government was damaged by corruption charges.

ECONOMY

Brazil's total volume of production is one of the largest in the world, but many people, including poor farmers and residents of the *favelas* (city slums), do not share in the country's fast economic growth. Widespread poverty, together with high inflation and unemployment, cause political problems.

Industry is the most valuable activity, employing about 20% of the workforce. Brazil is among the world's top producers of bauxite, chrome, diamonds, gold, iron ore, manganese, and tin. Its manufactures include aircraft, automobiles, chemicals, processed food, raw sugar, iron and steel, paper and textiles.

Agriculture employs 28% of workers. Coffee is a major export. Other leading products include bananas, citrus fruits, cocoa, corn, rice, soybeans and sugar cane. Brazil is the top producer of eggs, meat, and milk in South America.

Forestry is a major industry, though the exploitation of the rainforests, with 1.5% to 4% of Brazil's forest being destroyed every year, is a disaster for the entire world.

Area 3,287,338 sq mi [8,514,215 sq km]
Population 184,101,000
Capital (population) Brasilia (2,016,000)
Government Federal republic
Ethnic groups White 55%, Mulatto 38%, Black 6%, others 1%
Languages Portuguese (official)
Religions Roman Catholic 80%
Currency Real = 100 centavos
Website www.turismo.gov.br

BRASÍLIA

Capital city, located in west central Brazil. Although the city was originally planned in 1891, building did not start until 1956. The city was laid out in the shape of an aircraft, and Oscar Niemeyer designed the modernist public buildings. It was inaugurated as the capital in 1960, in order to develop Brazil's interior.

Bulgaria

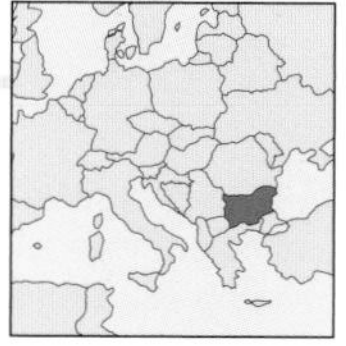

This flag, first adopted in 1878, uses the colors associated with the Slav people. The national emblem, incorporating a lion—a symbol of Bulgaria since the 14th century—was first added to the flag in 1947. It is now added only for official government occasions.

Area 42,823 sq mi [110,912 sq km]
Population 7,518,000
Capital (population) Sofia (1,139,000)
Government Multiparty republic
Ethnic groups Bulgarian 84%, Turkish 9%, Gypsy 5%, Macedonian, Armenian, others
Languages Bulgarian (official), Turkish
Religions Bulgarian Orthodox 83%, Islam 12%, Roman Catholic 2%, others
Currency Lev = 100 stotinki
Website www.government.bg/English

BALKAN MOUNTAINS

Major mountain range of the Balkan Peninsula, extending from eastern Serbia through central Bulgaria to the Black Sea. The range is a continuation of the Carpathian Mountains. It is rich in minerals and forms a climatic barrier for the interior. The highest pass is Shipka Pass, *c.*4,166 ft [1,270 m], and the highest peak is Botev, 7,793 ft [2,375 m].

The Republic of Bulgaria is a country in the Balkan Peninsula, facing the Black Sea in the east. There are two main lowland regions. The Danubian lowlands in the north consists of a plateau that descends to the Danube, which forms much of the boundary with Romania. The other lowland region is the warmer valley of the River Maritsa, where cotton, fruits, grains, rice, tobacco, and vines are grown.

Separating the two lowland areas are the Balkan Mountains (Stara Planina), rising to heights of over 6,500 ft [2,000 m]. North of the capital Sofia (Sofiya), the Balkan Mountains contain rich mineral veins of iron and non-ferrous metals.

In south-facing valleys overlooking the Maritsa Plain, plums, tobacco and vines are grown. A feature of this area is Kazanluk, from which attar of roses is exported worldwide to the cosmetics industry. South and west of the Maritsa Valley are the Rhodope (or Rhodopi) Mountains, which contain lead, zinc and copper ores.

CLIMATE

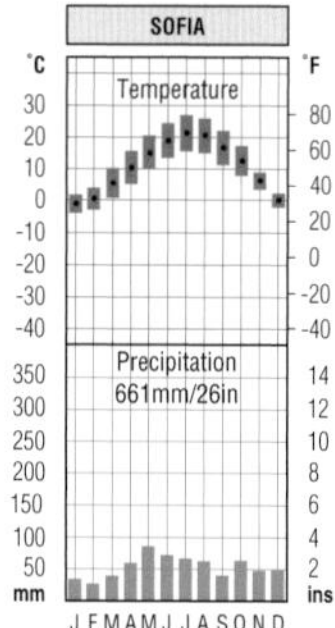

The average temperature in Sofia is 60–70°F (15–21°C) in the summer and 30–40°F (between −1 and 5°C) in the winter. Other regions experience more extreme ranges of temperature but winters are rarely severe.Rainfall is moderate all through the year.

HISTORY

Most of the Bulgarian people are descendants of Slavs and nomadic Bulgar tribes who arrived from the east in the 6th and 7th centuries. A powerful Bulgar kingdom was set up in 681, but the country became part of the Byzantine Empire in the 11th century.

Ottoman Turks ruled Bulgaria from 1396 and ethnic Turks still form a sizeable minority in the country. In 1879, Bulgaria became a monarchy, and in 1908 became fully independent. Bulgaria was an ally of Germany in World War I (1914–18) and again in World War II (1939–45). In 1944, Soviet troops invaded Bulgaria. After the war, the monarchy was abolished and the country became a Communist ally of the Soviet Union.

SOFIA (SOFIJA)

Capital of Bulgaria and Sofia province, in west central Bulgaria, at the foot of the Vitosha Mountains. Known for its hot mineral springs, Sofia was founded by the Romans in the 2nd century AD. From 1018 to 1185, it was ruled by the Byzantine Empire (as Triaditsa). Sofia passed to the second Bulgarian Empire (1186–1382), and then to the Ottoman Empire (1382–1878). In 1877, Sofia was captured by Russia and chosen as the capital of Bulgaria by the Congress of Berlin. Industries include steel, machinery, textiles, rubber, chemicals, metallurgy, leather goods, food processing.

POLITICS

In the period after World War II, and especially under President Zhikov from 1954, Bulgaria became all-too dependent on the Soviet Union. In 1990, the Communist Party held on to power under increasing pressure by ousting Zhikov, renouncing its leading role in the nation's affairs and changing its name to the Socialist Party, before winning the first free elections since the war, albeit unconvincingly and against confused opposition. With improved organization, the Union of Democratic Forces defeated the old guard in the following year and began the task of making the transition to a free-market economy. Subsequent governments faced numerous problems, including inflation, food shortages, rising unemployment, strikes, a large foreign debt, a declining manufacturing industry, increased prices for raw materials, and a potential drop in the expanding tourist industry. In 2001, the former king, Siméon Saxe-Coburg-Gotha, who had left Bulgaria in 1948 when the monarchy was abolished, became prime minister. He left office when his party lost the elections in 2005.

ECONOMY

According to the World Bank, Bulgaria in the 1990s was a "lower-middle-income" developing country. Bulgaria has some deposits of minerals, including brown coal, manganese, and iron ore. Manufacturing is the leading economic activity, though problems arose in the early 1990s, because much industrial technology was outdated. The main products are chemicals, processed foods, metal products, machinery, and textiles. Manufactures are the leading exports. Bulgaria trades mainly with countries in Eastern Europe.

Wheat and corn are the chief crops of Bulgaria. Fruit, oilseeds, tobacco, and vegetables are also important. Livestock farming, particularly the rearing of dairy and beef cattle, sheep, and pigs, is an important source of revenue.

***Rila Monastery,** founded in 10th century it is listed as a UNESCO World Heritage Site*

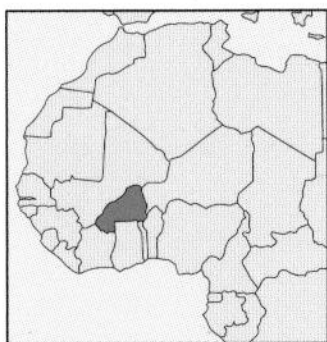

This flag was adopted in 1984, when Upper Volta was renamed Burkino Faso. The red, green and yellow colors used on this flag symbolize the desire for African unity. This is because they are used on the flag of Ethiopia, Africa's oldest independent country.

The Democratic People's Republic of Burkina Faso is a landlocked country, a little larger than the United Kingdom, in West Africa. But Burkina Faso has only one-sixth of the population of the UK. Burkina Faso consists of a plateau, between about 650 and 2,300 ft [300 m–700 m] above sea level. The plateau is cut by several rivers. Most of the rivers flow south into Ghana or east into the River Niger. During droughts, some of the rivers stop flowing, becoming marshes.

The northern part of the country is covered by savanna, consisting of grassland with stunted trees and shrubs. It is part of a region called the Sahel, where the land merges into the Sahara Desert. Overgrazing of the land and deforestation are common problems in the Sahel, causing desertification in many areas of the country.

Area 105,791 sq mi [274,000 sq km]
Population 13,575,000
Capital (population) Ouagadougou (637,000)
Government Multiparty republic
Ethnic groups Mossi 40%, Gurunsi, Senufo, Lobi, Bobo, Mande, Fulani
Languages French (official), Mossi, Fulani
Religions Islam 50%, traditional beliefs 40%, Christianity 10%
Currency CFA franc = 100 centimes
Website www.burkinaembassy-usa.org

Woodlands border the rivers and parts of the southeast region are swampy. The southeast contains the "W" National Park, which Burkina Faso shares with Benin and Niger, and the Arly Park. A third wildlife area is the Po Park situated south of Ouagadougou.

CLIMATE

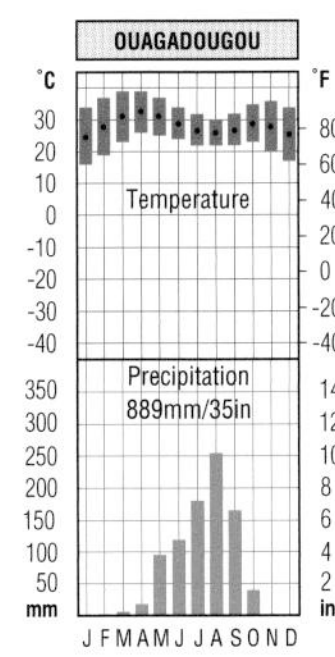

Burkina Faso has three main seasons. From October to February, it is relatively cool and dry. From March to April, it is hot and dry, while it is hot and humid from May to September.

HISTORY

The people of Burkina Faso are divided into two main groups. The Voltaic group includes the Mossi, who form the largest single group, and the Bobo. The other main group is the Mande family. Burkina Faso also contains some Fulani herders and Hausa traders, who are related to the people of northern Nigeria. In early times, the ethnic groups in Burkina Faso were divided into kingdoms and chiefdoms. The leading kingdom, which was ruled by an absolute monarch called the Moro Naba, was that of the Mossi. It has existed since the 13th century. The semi-autonomous states fiercely resisted domination by the larger Mali and Songhai Empires.

The French conquered the Mossi capital of Ouagadougou in 1897 and they made the area a protectorate. In 1919, the area became a French colony called Upper Volta. In 1947, Upper Volta gained semi-autonomy within the French Union, and in 1958 became an autonomous republic within the French Community.

POLITICS

Upper Volta achieved independence in 1960 and adopted a strong presidential form of government. Persistent drought and austerity measures led to a military coup in 1966. Civilian rule partially returned in 1970 but the military, led by Sangoule Lamizana, regained power in 1974. Lamizana became president after elections in 1978, but was overthrown in 1980. Parliament and the constitution were suspended and a series of military regimes ensued. In 1983 Thomas Sankara gained power in a bloody coup.

In 1984, as a symbolic break from the country's colonial past, Sankara changed Upper Volta's name to Burkina Faso "land of the incorruptible." In 1987, Sankara was assassinated and Captain Blaise Campaore seized power. Campaore became president in unopposed elections in 1991. Elections in 1992 were the first multiparty ballots since 1978. In 1998 elections, Campaore gained a landslide victory. More than 7% of the population have HIV, the second highest rate of infection in Africa.

ECONOMY

Burkina Faso is one of the world's 20 poorest countries and has become extremely dependent on foreign aid. Approximately 90% of the people earn their living by farming or by raising livestock. Grazing land covers around 37% of the land and farmland covers around 10%.

Most of Burkina Faso is dry with thin soils. The country's main food crops are beans, corn, millet, rice, and sorghum. Cotton, groundnuts and shea nuts, whose seeds produce a fat used to make cooking oil and soap, are grown for sale abroad. Livestock is also important.

The country has few resources and manufacturing is on a small scale. There are deposits of manganese, zinc, lead, and nickel in the north of the country, but exploitation awaits improvements to the transport system. Many young men work abroad in Ghana and Ivory Coast. The money they send to their families is important to the country's economy.

***Families of alluvial gold diggers** work in precarious conditions on the Yako site, about 100 km away from Ouagadougou*

OUAGADOUGOU

Capital city lying in the center of Burkina Faso. Ouagadougou was founded in the late 11th century as capital of the Mossi empire, it remained the center of Mossi power until captured by the French in 1896. Industries include handicrafts, textiles, food processing, groundnuts, and vegetable oil.

Burma (Myanmar)

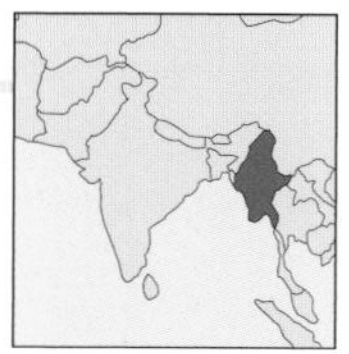

The colors on the flag were adopted in 1948 when Burma gained independence from Britain. The socialist symbol, added in 1974, includes a ring of 14 stars representing the country's 14 states. The gearwheel represents industry, the rice plant agriculture.

Area 261,227 sq mi [676,578 sq km]
Population 42,720,000
Capital (population) Rangoon (2,513,000)
Government Military regime
Ethnic groups Burman 68%, Shan 9%, Karen 7%, Rakhine 4%, Chinese, Indian, Mon
Languages Burmese (official), minority ethnic groups have their own languages
Religions Buddhism 89%, Christianity, Islam
Currency Kyat = 100 pyas
Website www.burmaproject.org

The Union of Burma is now officially known as the Union of Myanmar; its name was changed in 1989. Mountains border the country in the east and west, with the highest mountains in the north. Burma's highest mountain is Hkakabo Razi, which is 19,294 ft [5,881 m] high. Between these ranges is central Burma, which contains the fertile valleys of the Irrawaddy and Sittang rivers. The Irrawaddy delta on the Bay of Bengal is one of the world's leading rice-growing areas. Burma also includes the long Tenasserim coast in the southeast.

CLIMATE

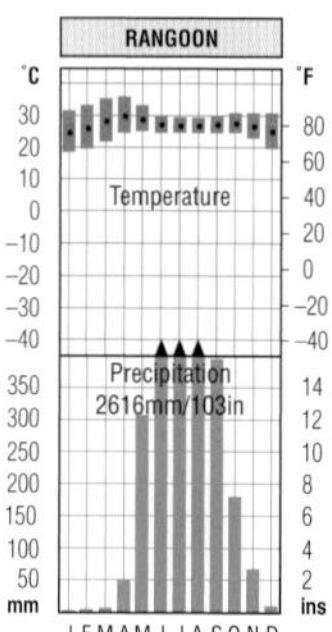

Burma has a tropical monsoon climate. There are three seasons. The rainy season runs from late May to mid-October. A cool, dry season follows, between late October and the middle part of February. The hot season lasts from late February to mid-May, though temperatures remain high during the humid rainy season.

HISTORY

Conflict between the Burmans and Mons dominated Burma's early history. In 1044 the Burman King Anawratha unified the Irrawaddy delta region. In 1287 Kublai Khan conquered the Burman capital, Pagan. Burma was divided: the Shan controlled north Burma, while the resurgent Mons held the south. In the 16th century, the Burmans subjugated the Shan. In 1758 Alaungapaya reunified Burma, defeating the Mons kingdom and establishing the Konbaung dynasty.

Wars with British India marked much of the 19th century. The first war in 1824 resulted in the British gaining the coastal regions of Tenasserim and Arakan. The second war in 1852 saw the British gain control of the Irrawaddy delta. British India annexed Burma in the third war of 1885. In 1937 Burma gained limited self-government. Helped by the Burmese Independent Army, led by Aung San, Japan conquered the country in 1942. The installation of a puppet regime led Aung San to form a resistance movement. In 1947 Aung San was murdered. Burma achieved independence in 1948.

RANGOON (YANGON)

Capital of Burma (Myanmar), a seaport on the Rangoon (Yangon) River. The name Yangon means "end of strife," Rangoon is the anglicized version. The site of a Buddhist shrine, it became capital in 1886, when the British annexed the country. Heavy fighting took place there in World War II between British and Japanese forces. It is the country's chief trade center.

POLITICS

The socialist AFPFL government, led by U Nu, faced secessionist revolts by communists and Karen tribesmen. In 1958 U Nu invited General Ne Win to reestablish order. Civilian rule returned in 1960, but in 1962 Ne Win mounted a successful coup. His military dictatorship faced mass insurgency. In 1974 Ne Win became president. Mass demonstrations forced Ne Win to resign in 1988, but the military retained power under the guise of the State Law and Order Restoration Council (SLORC), led by General Saw Muang. In 1989 the country's name changed to Myanmar. The National League for Democracy (NLD), led by Aung San Suu Kyi, won elections in 1990, but SLORC annulled the result and placed Aung San Suu Kyi under house arrest. In 1997 SLORC became the State Peace and Development Council (SPDC). In 1998, NLD calls for the reconvening of Parliament led to mass detention of political opponents by the SPDC. In 2002 the SPDC released Aung San Suu Kyi from house arrest. She was arrested again in 2003.

In 2004 a United Nations report criticized the regime for holding more than 1,800 political detainees and for its failure to release opposition leader Aung San Suu Kyi from house arrest.

In November 2005 Burma announced that it was moving the seat of government to Pyinmana 250 mi (400 km) north of Rangoon, with immediate effect. Officials would not commit to whether this new site would become the capital with officials saying that everything would be made public at the appropriate time. The reason given for the move was that Pyinmana is in the center of the country

ECONOMY

Agriculture is the main activity, employing 66% of the workforce. The chief crop is rice. Groundnuts, corn, plantains, pulses, seed cotton, sesame seeds, and sugar cane are also produced. Forestry is important and teak is a major product. Fish and shellfish are another industry. The varied natural resources are mostly underdeveloped, but it is famous for its precious stones, especially rubies. Burma is almost self-sufficient in oil and natural gas.

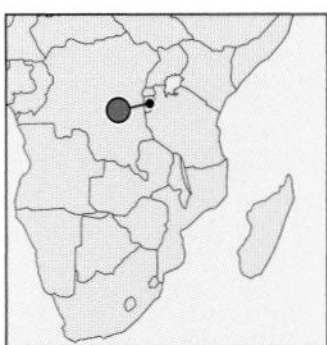

This flag was adopted in 1967 when Burundi became a republic. It has three red stars rimmed in green, symbolizing the nation's motto of "Unité, Travail, Progrès." The green represents hope for the future, the red the struggle for independence, and the white the desire for peace.

Area 10,747 sq mi [27,834 sq km]
Population 6,231,000
Capital (population) Bujumbura (235,000)
Government Republic
Ethnic groups Hutu 85%, Tutsi 14%, Twa (Pygmy)
Languages French, Kirundi (both official)
Religions Roman Catholic 62%, traditional beliefs 23%, Islam 10%, Protestant 5%
Currency Burundi franc = 100 centimes
Website www.burundi-embassy-berlin.com

The Republic of Burundi is a small country in east-central Africa. A section of the Great Rift Valley, lies in the west. It contains part of Lake Tanganyika, whose shoreline is 2,533 ft [772 m] above sea level. East of the Rift Valley is a mountain zone, rising to 8,760 ft [2,670 m]. The land descends to the east in a series of steppe-like plateaus. Burundi forms part of the Nile-Congo watershed and contains the headwaters of the River Kagera, the most remote source of the Nile.

Grassland covers much of Burundi, because much of the original forest has been cleared by farming and overgrazing. New forests are now being planted to halt the loss of soil fertility caused by erosion.

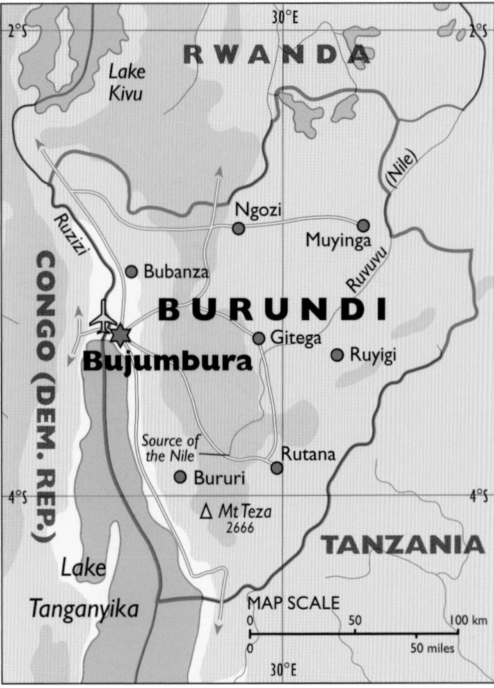

CLIMATE

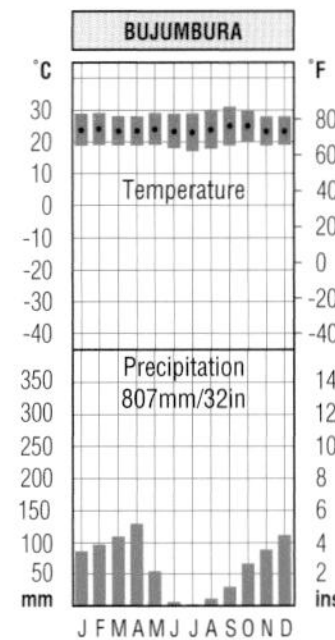

Bujumbura has an average annual temperature of 73°F [23°C]. June to August and December-January are dry, but the rest of the year rainy. The mountains and the central plateaus are distinctly cooler and wetter than the Rift Valley floor, but the rainfall decreases to the east.

HISTORY

The first known inhabitants of the area were the Twa, a pygmy group of hunting and gathering people, who now make up just 1% of the population. Around 1,000 years ago, a Bantu-speaking, iron-using farming people from the west, the Hutu, began to settle, pushing the Twa into remote areas. A third group, the cattle-owning Tutsi from the northeast, arrived around 600 years ago. They gradually took control of the area and, although in the minority, formed the ruling class. The Tutsi created a feudal state, making the Hutu serfs. The explorers Richard Burton and John Hanning Speke visited the area in 1858 in their quest to find the source of the Nile.

A powerful Tutsi kingdom under Mwami (king) Rugamba, that developed in the late 18th century, had broken up by the 1880s. Germany conquered what are now Burundi and Rwanda, in the late 1890s. The area, called Ruanda-Urundi, became part of German East Africa. But after Germany's defeat in World War I, Belgium took control.

In 1961, the people of Urundi voted to become a monarchy under Mwami Mwambutsa IV, who had ruled since 1915, while the people of Ruanda voted to become a republic.

POLITICS

The two territories finally became fully independent as Burundi and Rwanda on July 1, 1962. Since then, Burundi has suffered great conflict caused by ethnic rivalry between the Hutu majority and the Tutsi. Around 300,000 people have perished with many thousands displaced or as refugees. In 1965, Mwambutsa refused to appoint a Hutu prime minister, although the Hutu were in the majority. An attempted coup was brutally put down. In 1966, Mwambutsa was deposed by his son who became Mwami Ntare V, but Tutsi prime minister Michel Micombero deposed Ntare and declared Burundi to be a republic, with himself as president.

Between 1966 and 1972, most Hutu and some Tutsi were removed from high office. This culminated in a rebellion, when between 100,000 and 200,000 mostly Hutu were killed. In 1976, Jean-Baptiste Bagaza, a Tutsi, deposed Micombero. In 1981, Burundi became a one-party state, but Bagaza was deposed in 1987 by a coup led by Pierre Buyoya. Another uprising in 1988 led to the slaughter of thousands of Hutus.

In 1992, a new constitution gave the country a multiparty system and, in 1993, Melchior Ndadaye, a Hutu, beat Buyoya in presidential elections. But supporters of Bagaza assassinated Ndadaye. In 1994, the new president, Cyprien Ntaryamira, a Hutu, was killed in a plane crash, together with the Rwandan president, causing more ethnic violence. In 1996, Buyoya staged another coup and suspended the constitution. In 1999, peace talks began which led, in 2001, to the setting up of a transitional, power-sharing government. However, some Hutu rebel groups refused to sign the ceasefire. In 2003, Domitien Ndayizeye succeeded Buyoya as president, under the power-sharing agreement. In 2004, the disarming of rebels and soldiers began. In 2005, the people voted in favor of the new power-sharing constitution and hopes were high of an end to the conflict.

ECONOMY

Burundi is one of the world's poorest countries. 94% of the people depend on farming, mainly at subsistence level. The main food crops are bananas, beans, cassava, corn, and sweet potatoes. Cattle, goats and sheep are raised and fish is important.

The economy depends on coffee and tea, which account for 90% of foreign exchange earnings, and cotton.

***In-patients prepare food** at the state hospital in Buhiga, Burundi, which is supported by Médecins Sans Frontières*

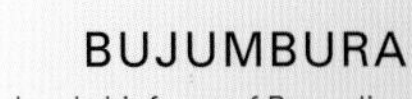

BUJUMBURA

Capital and chief port of Burundi, east -central Africa, at the northeast end of Lake Tanganyika. Founded in 1899 as part of German East Africa, it was the capital of Ruanda-Urundi after World War I and remained capital of Burundi upon independence in 1962.

Cambodia

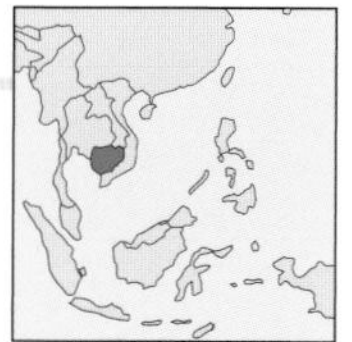

Red is the traditional color of Cambodia. The blue symbolizes the water resources that are so important to the people, three-quarters of whom depend on farming for a living. The silhouette is the historic temple at Angkor Wat.

Area 69,898 sq mi [181,035 sq km]
Population 13,363,000
Capital (population) Phnom Penh (1,000,000)
Government Constitutional monarchy
Ethnic groups Khmer 90%, Vietnamese 5%, Chinese 1%, others
Languages Khmer (official), French, English
Religions Buddhism 95%, others 5%
Currency Riel = 100 sen
Website www.cambodia.gov.kh

The Kingdom of Cambodia is a country in Southeast Asia. Low mountains border the country except in the southeast. But most of Cambodia consists of plains drained by the River Mekong, which enters Cambodia from Laos in the north and exits through Vietnam in the southeast. The northwest contains Tonlé Sap (or Great Lake). In the dry season, this lake drains into the River Mekong. But in the wet season, the level of the Mekong rises and water flows in the opposite direction from the river into Tonlé Sap—the lake then becomes the largest freshwater lake in Asia.

CLIMATE

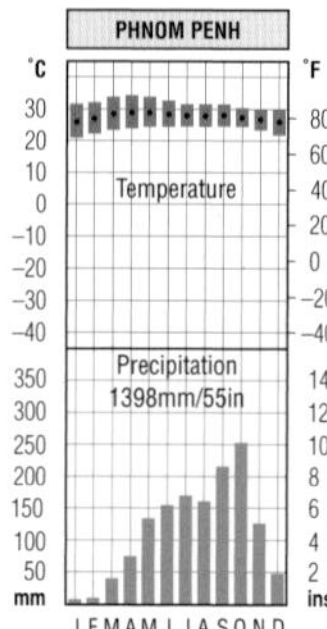

Cambodia has a tropical monsoon climate, with high temperatures all through the year. The dry season, when winds blow from the north or northeast, runs November to April. During the rainy season, May to October, moist winds blow from the south or southeast. The high humidity and heat often make conditions unpleasant. The rainfall is heaviest near the coast, and rather lower inland.

HISTORY

From 802 to 1431, the Hindu-Buddhist Khmer people ruled a great empire. Its zenith came in the reign of Suryavarman II (1113–50), who built the great funerary temple of Angkor Wat. Together with Angkor Thom, the Angkor Wat site contains the world's largest group of religious buildings. The wealth of the kingdom rested on fish from the lake and rice from the flooded lowlands, for which an extensive system of irrigation channels and strong reservoirs was developed. Thai forces captured Angkor in 1431 and forests covered the site. Since its rediscovery in 1860, it has been gradually restored and is now a major tourist attraction.

France ruled the country from 1863 as part of Indochina until it achieved independence in 1954. In a short period of stability during the late 1950s and 1960s, the country developed its small-scale agricultural resources and rubber plantations. It remained predominantly rural, but achieved self-sufficiency in food, with some exports.

PHNOM PENH (PHNUM PÉNH)

Capital of Cambodia, in the south of the country, a port at the confluence of the rivers Mekong and Tonlé Sap. Founded in the 14th century, the city was the capital of the Khmers after 1434. In 1865, it became the capital of Cambodia. Occupied by the Japanese during World War II, it was extensively damaged during the Cambodian civil war. After the Khmer Rouge took power in 1975, the population was drastically reduced when many of its inhabitants were forcibly removed to work in the countryside. Industries include rice milling, brewing, distilling.

POLITICS

In 1969, US planes bombed North Vietnamese targets in Cambodia. In 1970, King Norodom Sihanouk was overthrown and Cambodia became a republic. Under assault from South Vietnamese troops, the Communist Vietnamese withdrew deep into Cambodia. US raids ended in 1973, but fighting continued as Cambodia's Communists in the Khmer Rouge fought against the government. The Khmer Rouge, led by Pol Pot, were victorious in 1975. They began a reign of terror, murdering government officials and educated people. Up to 2 million people were estimated to have been killed. After the overthrow of Pol Pot by Vietnamese forces in 1979, civil war raged between the puppet government of the People's Republic of Kampuchea (Cambodia) and the US-backed government of Democratic Kampuchea, a coalition of Prince Sihanouk, the Khmer Liberation Front, and the Khmer Rouge, who, from 1982, claimed to have abandoned their Communist ideology.

The Silver Pagoda, *Phnom Penh, lies inside the Royal Palace complex. It draws its name from the over 5,000 silver tiles which cover the floor*

Devastated by war and denied almost any aid, Cambodia continued to decline. It was only the withdrawal of Vietnamese troops in 1989, sparking fear of a Khmer Rouge revival, that forced a settlement. In October 1991, a UN-brokered peace plan for elections in 1993 was accepted by all parties. A new constitution was adopted in September 1993, restoring democracy and the monarchy. Sihanouk again became king. However, the Khmer Rouge continued hostilities and were banned in 1994. In 1997, Hu Sen, the second prime minister, engineered a coup against Prince Norodom Ranariddh (Sihanouk's son), the first prime minister Ranariddh went into exile but returned in 1998. Elections in 1998 resulted in victory for Hu Sen, but Ranariddh alleged electoral fraud. A coalition government was formed in December 1998, with Hu Sen as prime minister. In 2001, the government set up a court to try leaders of the Khmer Rouge. In 2004, Sihanouk abdicated due to ill health and was succeeded by his son Prince Norodom Sihamoni.

ECONOMY

Cambodia is a poor country whose economy has been wrecked by war. By 1986, it was only able to supply 80% of its needs. Recovery has been slow. Farming is the main activity and rice, rubber, and corn important. Tourism is increasing—the impressive Angkor temples are a major attraction.

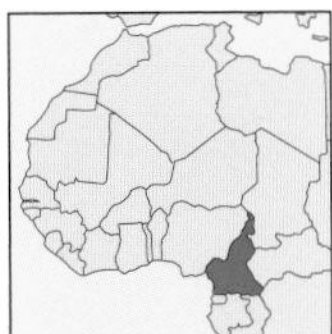

Cameroon uses the colors that appear on the flag of Ethiopia, Africa's oldest independent nation. These colors symbolize African unity. The flag is based on the tricolor adopted in 1957. The design with the yellow liberty star dates from 1975.

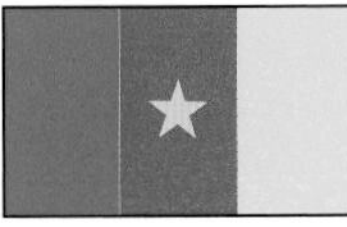

The Republic of Cameroon in West Africa got its name from the Portuguese word *camarões*, or prawns. This name was used by Portuguese explorers who fished for prawns along the coast. Behind the narrow coastal plains on the Gulf of Guinea, the land rises to a series of plateaus. In the north, the land slopes down towards the Lake Chad (Tchad) basin. The mountain region in the southwest of the country includes Mount Cameroon, a volcano that erupts from time to time. The vegetation varies greatly from north to south. The deserts in the north merge into dry and moist savanna in central Cameroon, with dense tropical rainforests in the humid south.

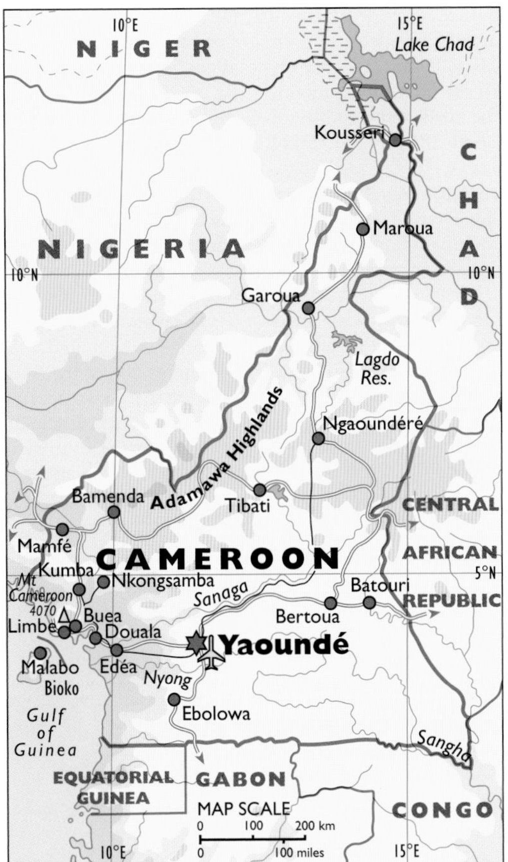

Area 475,442 sq km [183,568 sq mi]
Population 16,064,000
Capital (population) Yaoundé (649,000)
Government Multiparty republic
Ethnic groups Cameroon Highlanders 31%, Bantu 27%, Kirdi 11%, Fulani 10%, others
Languages French and English (both official), many others
Religions Christianity 40%, traditional beliefs 40%, Islam 20%
Currency CFA franc = 100 centimes
Website www.camnet.cm

YAOUNDÉ

Capital of Cameroon, West Africa. Located in beautiful hills on the edge of dense jungle, German traders founded it in 1888. During World War I, it was occupied by Belgian troops, and later acted as capital (1921–60) of French Cameroon. Since independence, it has grown rapidly as a financial and administrative center with strong Western influences. It is the site of the University of Cameroon (1962). The city also serves as a market for the surrounding region, notably in coffee, cacao, and sugar.

CLIMATE

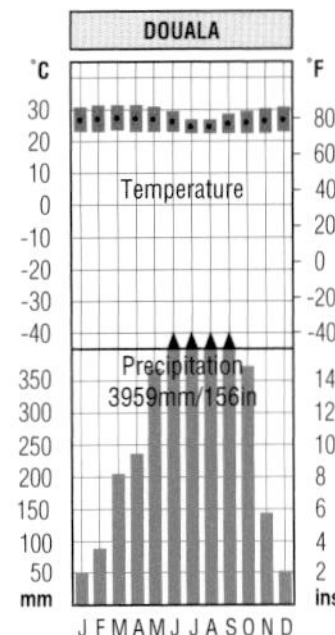

Rainfall is heavy, especially in the highlands. The rainiest months near the coast are June to September. The rainfall decreases to the north and the far north has a hot, dry climate. Temperatures are high on the coast, whereas the inland plateaus are cooler.

HISTORY

Among the early inhabitants of Cameroon were groups of Bantu-speaking people. (There are now more than 160 ethnic groups, each with their own language.) In the late 15th century, Portuguese explorers, who were seeking a sea route to Asia around Africa, reached the Cameroon coast. From the 17th century, southern Cameroon was a center of the slave trade, but slavery was ended in the early 19th century. In 1884, the area became a German protectorate. Germany lost Cameroon during World War I (1914–18). The country was then divided into two parts, one ruled by Britain and the other by France.

POLITICS

In 1960, French Cameroon became the independent Cameroon Republic. In 1961, after a vote in British Cameroon, part of the territory joined the Cameroon Republic to become the Federal Republic of Cameroon. The other part joined Nigeria. In 1972, Cameroon became a unitary state called the United Republic of Cameroon. It adopted the name Republic of Cameroon in 1984, but the country had two official languages. Opposition parties were legalized in 1992, and Paul Biya was elected president in 1993 and 1997. In 1995, partly to placate the English-speaking people, Cameroon became the 52nd member of the Commonwealth. In 2002, the International Court of Justice gave Cameroon sovereignty over the disputed oil-rich Bakassi peninsula, but Nigeria failed to reach the deadline for the handover of the area in 2004.

Presidential elections in 2004 saw Paul Biya win a new seven-year term with more than 70% of the vote. The result was accepted by Commonwealth observers, but opposition parties alleged widespread fraud.

ECONOMY

Like most countries in tropical Africa, Cameroon's economy is based on agriculture, which employs 73% of the people. The chief food crops include cassava, corn, millet, sweet potatoes, and yams.

Cameroon is fortunate in having some oil, the country's chief export, and bauxite. Although Cameroon has few manufacturing and processing industries, its mineral exports and its self-sufficiency in food production make it one of the wealthier countries in tropical Africa. Another important industry is forestry, ranking second among the exports, after oil. Other exports are cocoa, coffee, aluminum, and cotton.

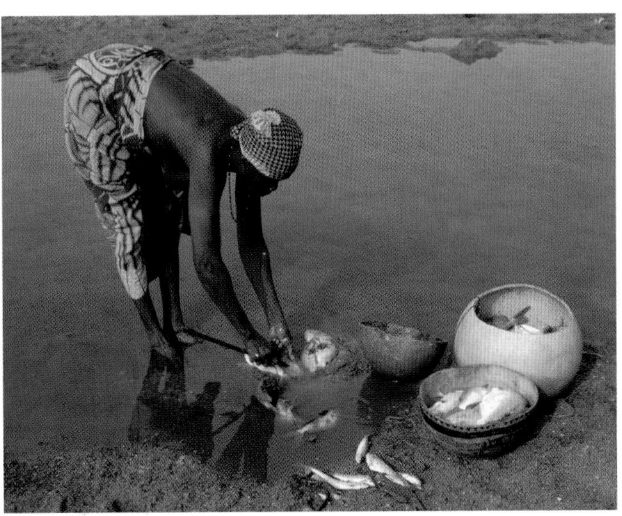

Woman cleaning fish *in Rey Bouba, home of the Mond people, Province du Nord region; the region covers much of the northern half of the country*

Canada

Canada's flag, with its simple 11-pointed maple leaf emblem, was adopted in 1965 after many attempts to find an acceptable design. The old flag, used from 1892, was the British Red Ensign, but this flag became unpopular with Canada's French community.

A vast confederation of ten provinces and three territories, Canada is the world's second largest country after Russia, with an even longer coastline—about 155,000 mi [250,000 km]. It is sparsely populated because it contains vast areas of virtually unoccupied mountains, cold forests, tundra and polar desert in the north and west. About 80% of the population of Canada lives within about 186 mi [300 km] of the southern border.

Forests of cedars, hemlocks and other trees grow on the western mountains, with firs and spruces at the higher levels. The mountain forests provide habitats for bears, deer, and mountain lions, while the sure-footed Rocky Mountain goats and bighorn sheep roam above the tree line (the upper limit of tree growth).

The interior plains were once grassy prairies. While the drier areas are still used for grazing cattle, the wetter areas are used largely for growing wheat and other cereals. North of the prairies are the boreal forests which, in turn merge into the treeless tundra and Arctic wastelands in the far north. The lowlands in southeastern Canada contain forests of deciduous trees, such as beech, hickory, oak, and walnut.

CLIMATE

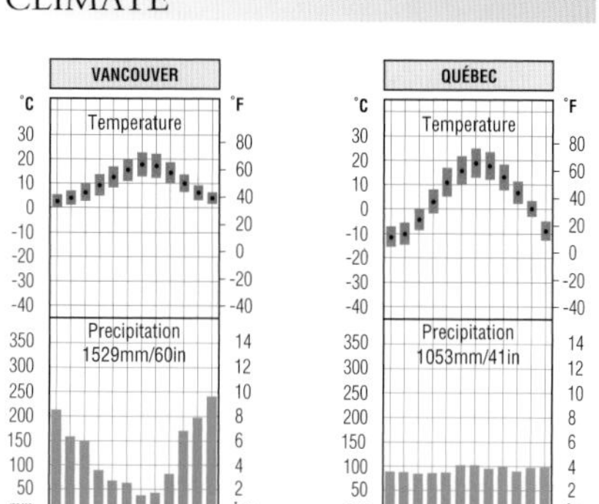

Canada has a cold climate. In winter, temperatures fall below freezing point throughout most of the country. But the southwestern coast has a relatively mild climate. Along the Arctic Circle, the temperatures are, on average, below freezing for seven months a year. By contrast, hot winds from the Gulf of Mexico warm southern Ontario and the St Lawrence River lowlands in summer. As a result, southern Ontario has a frost-free season of nearly six months.

The coasts of British Columbia are wet, with an average annual rainfall of more than 2,500 mm [98 in] in places. The prairies however are arid or semi-arid, with an average annual rainfall of 10 to 20 in [250 mm–500 mm]. The rainfall in southeastern Canada ranges from around 31 in [800 mm] in southern Ontario to about 59 in [1,500 mm] on the coasts of Newfoundland and Nova Scotia. Heavy snow falls in eastern Canada in winter.

Area 3,849,653 sq mi [9,970,610 sq km]
Population 32,508,000
Capital (population) Ottawa (774,000)
Government Federal multiparty constitutional monarchy
Ethnic groups British origin 28%, French origin 23%, other European 15%, Amerindian/Inuit 2%, others
Languages English and French (both official)
Religions Roman Catholic 46%, Protestant 36%, Judaism, Islam, Hinduism
Currency Canadian dollar = 100 cents
Website http://canada.gc.ca

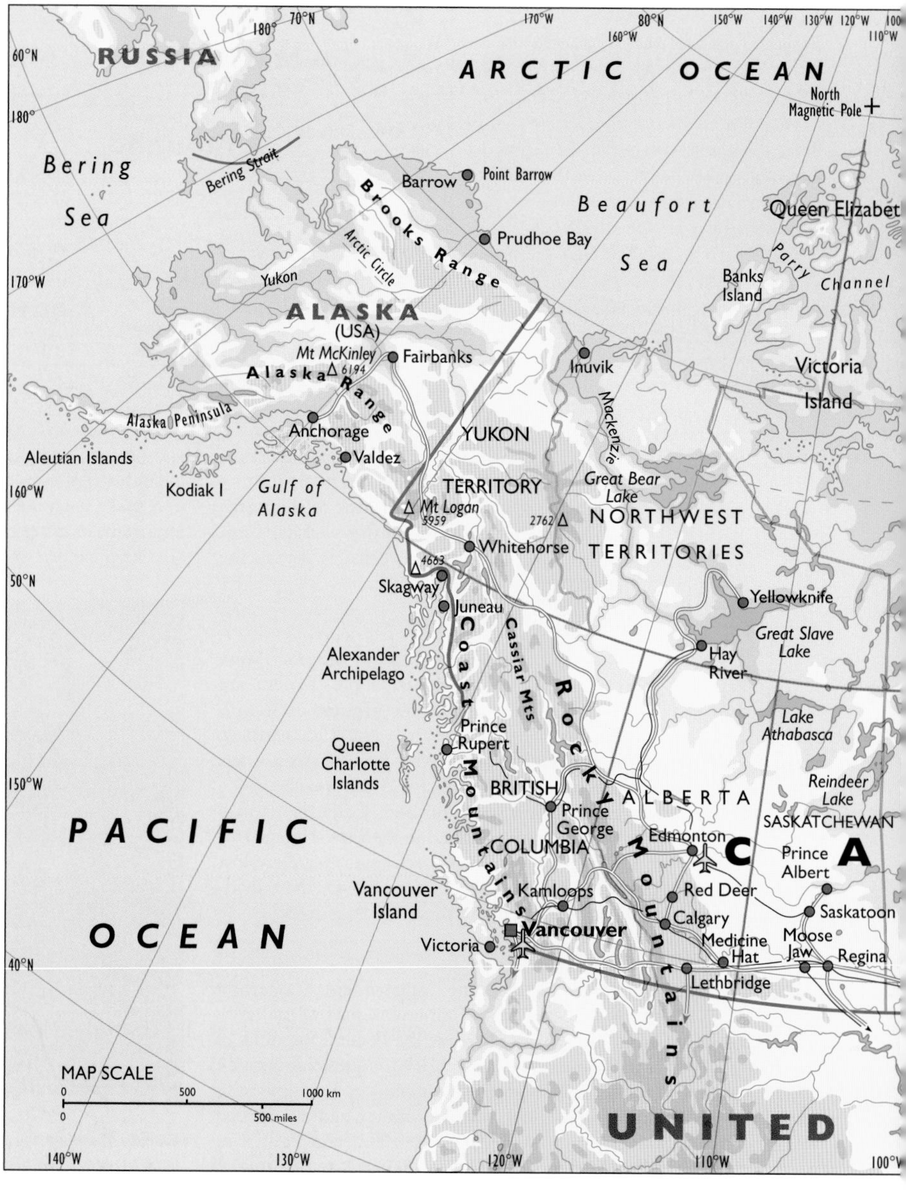

HISTORY

Canada's first people, ancestors of the Native Americans, arrived in North America from Asia around 40,000 years ago. Later arrivals were the Inuit (Eskimos), who also came from Asia. Norse voyagers and fishermen were probably the first to visit Canada, but John Cabot's later discovery of North America in 1497 led to the race to annex lands and wealth, with France and Britain the main contenders.

The creation of the British Commonwealth in 1931 made Canada a sovereign nation under the crown. Canada is now a constitutional monarchy. Under the Constitution Act of 1982, Queen Elizabeth II is head of state and a symbol of the close ties between Canada and Britain. The British monarch is represented by an appointed governor-general, but the country is ruled by a prime minister and an elected, two-chamber parliament.

POLITICS

Canada combines the cabinet system with a federal form of government, with each province having its own government. The federal government can reject any law passed by a provincial legislature, though this seldom happens in practice. The territories are self-governing, but the federal government plays a large part in their administration.

Canada and the United States of America have the largest bilateral trade flow in the world. Economic cooperation was further enhanced in 1993 when Canada, the United States, and Mexico set up NAFTA (North American Free Trade Agreement).

A constant problem facing those who want to maintain the unity of Canada is the persistence of French culture in Québec, which has fuelled a separatist movement seeking to turn the province into an independent French-speaking republic. More than two-thirds of the population of Québec are French speakers. In 1994, the people of Québec voted the separatist Parti Québécois into provincial office. The incoming prime minister announced that independence for Québec would be the subject of a referendum in 1995. In that referendum, 49.4% voted "Yes" (for separation) while 50.5% voted "No."

Provincial elections in 1998 resulted in another victory for the Parti Québécois. But while the separatist party won 75 out of the 125 seats in the provincial assembly, it won only 43% of the popular vote, compared with 44% for the anti-secessionist Liberal Party and 12% for the floating Action Démocratique de Québec. Also significant was a ruling by Canada's highest court that, under Canadian law, Québec does not have the right to secede unilaterally. The court ruled that, should a clear majority of the people in the province vote by "a clear majority" to a "clear question" in favor of independence, the federal government and the other provinces would have to negotiate Québec's secession.

Toronto City Hall, *designed by Finnish architect Viljo Revell, it opened in 1965*

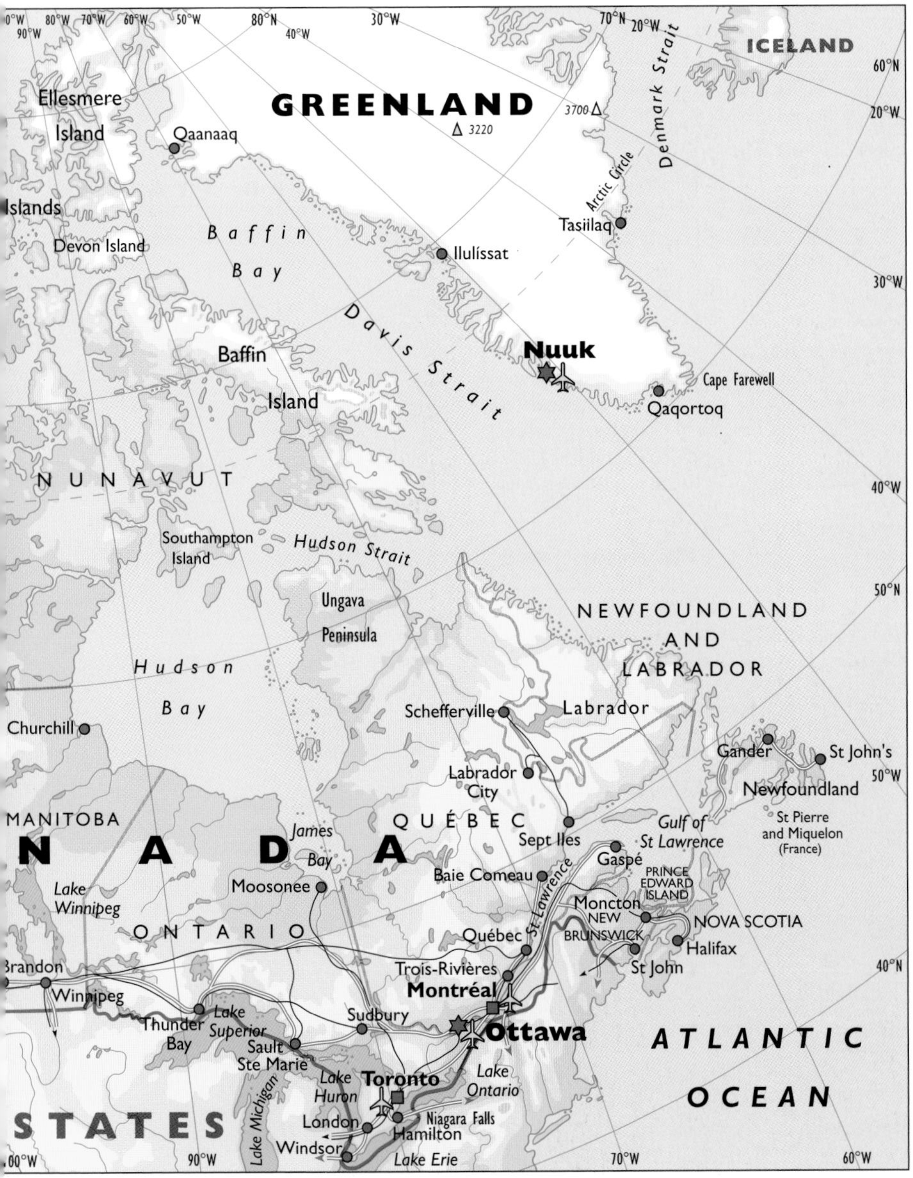

Other problems involve the rights of the aboriginal Native Americans and the Inuit, who together numbered about 470,000 in 1991. In 1999, a new Inuit territory was created. Called Nunavut, it is made up of 64% of the former Northwest Territories, and covers 649,965 sq mi [2,201,400 sq km]. The population in 1991 was about 25,000, 85% of whom were Inuit. Nunavut, whose capital is Iqaluit (formerly Frobisher Bay), will depend on future aid, but its mineral reserves and the prospects of an ecotourist industry hold out promise for the future.

ECONOMY

Canada is a highly developed and prosperous country. Although farmland covers only 8% of the country, Canadian farms are highly productive, Canada is one of the world's leading producers of barley, wheat, meat and milk. Forestry and fishing are other important industries. It is rich in natural resources, especially oil and natural gas. Canada exports minerals, including copper, gold, iron ore, uranium and zinc. Manufacturing is important, mainly in the cities where 79% of the population lives. Canada processes farm and mineral products. It also produces automobiles, chemicals, electronic goods, machinery, paper, and timber products.

Tourism is an important source of income with both winter and summer popular tourist seasons.

OTTAWA

Capital of Canada, in southeast Ontario, on the Ottawa River and the Rideau Canal. Founded in 1826 as Bytown, it acquired its present name in 1854. Queen Victoria chose it as capital of the United Provinces in 1858, and in 1867 it became the national capital of the Dominion of Canada. Industries include glassmaking, printing, publishing, sawmilling, pulp-making, and clocks and watches.

ANGUILLA

Most northerly of the Leeward Islands. Settled in the 17th century by English colonists, it became part of the St. Kitts-Nevis-Anguilla group. Declared independent in 1967, it readopted British colonial status in 1980, and is now a self-governing dependency. The economy of the flat, coral island is based on fishing and tourism.

Area 37 sq mi [96 sq km]
Population 13,000
Capital The Valley (1,169)
Government Overseas territory of the UK
Ethnic groups Black 90%, Mixed 5%, White 3%
Languages English
Religions Anglican 29%, Methodist 24%, Protestant 30%, Roman Catholic 6%
Currency East Caribbean dollar = 100 cents
Website www.anguilla-vacation.com

ANTIGUA & BARBUDA

Part of the Lesser Antilles in the Leeward Islands. Antigua is atypical of the Leeward Islands as it has no rivers or forests. Barbuda, by contrast, is a wooded, low coral atoll. Only 1,400 people live on the game reserve island of Barbuda, where lobster fishing is the main occupation, and none on the rocky island of Redondo. Antigua and Barbuda gained internal self-government in 1967 and independence in 1981. The islands are dependent on tourism.

Area 171 sq mi [442 sq km]
Population 68,000
Capital St. John's (22,634)
Government Constitutional monarchy
Ethnic groups Black, British, others
Languages English, Local dialects
Religions Christian
Currency East Caribbean dollar = 100 cents
Website www.antigua-barbuda.org

ARUBA

Dutch island in the Caribbean, off the coast of northwest Venezuela. First inhabited by Caquetios Indians from the Arawak tribe. It was part of the Netherlands Antilles until 1986. Independence was revoked in 1990, at Aruba's request, and it is now an autonomous part of the Netherlands. Oil refining, phosphates, and tourism are the key earners.

Area 75 sq mi [193 sq km]
Population 71,000
Capital Oranjestad (26,355)
Government Parliamentary democracy
Ethnic groups Mixed White/Caribbean Amerindian 80%
Languages Dutch (official), Papiamento, English, Spanish
Religions Roman Catholic 82%, Protestant 8%
Currency Aruban guilder/florin = 100 cents
Website www.aruba.com

BAHAMAS

Small independent state in the West Indies including over 700 islands, of which 14 serve as the main hub. The largest island is Grand Bahama. Mainly limestone and coral, the rocky terrain provides little chance for agricultural development. Most of the islands are low, flat, and riverless with mangrove swamps. The land is at its highest at Mount Alvernia on Cat Island with a measurement of 206 ft (63 m). The longest known underwater cave and cavern system in the world is situated in Lucayan National Park on Grand Bahama. The climate of the islands is subtropical with temperatures averaging 70–90°F [21–32°C].

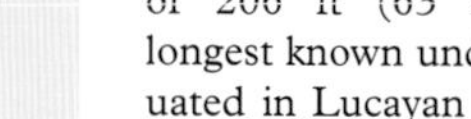

In 1964, Britain granted limited self-government to the Bahamas. They became a Commonwealth in 1969, with independence in 1973. Income is from tourism, fishing, salt, and rum.

Area 5,358 sq mi [13,878 sq km]
Population 297,000
Capital Nassau (210,832)
Government Constitutional parliamentary democracy
Ethnic groups Black 85%, White 12%, others
Languages English (official), Creole
Religions Baptist 35%, Anglican 15%, Roman Catholic 14%, Pentecostal 8%, Church of God 5%, Methodist 4%, others
Currency Bahamian dollar = 100 cents
Website www.bahamas.gov.bs

CARIBBEAN SEA

Extension of the northern Atlantic Ocean linked to the Gulf of Mexico by the Yucatán Channel and to the Pacific Ocean by the Panama Canal. The first European to discover the Caribbean was Columbus in 1492, who named it after the Carib. It soon lay on the route of many Spanish expeditions and became notorious for piracy, particularly after other European powers established colonies in the West Indies. With the opening of the Panama Canal (1914), its strategic importance increased. Area: *c.*1,020,000 sq mi (2.64 million sq km).

***Dutch buildings** in central Oranjestad, Aruba*

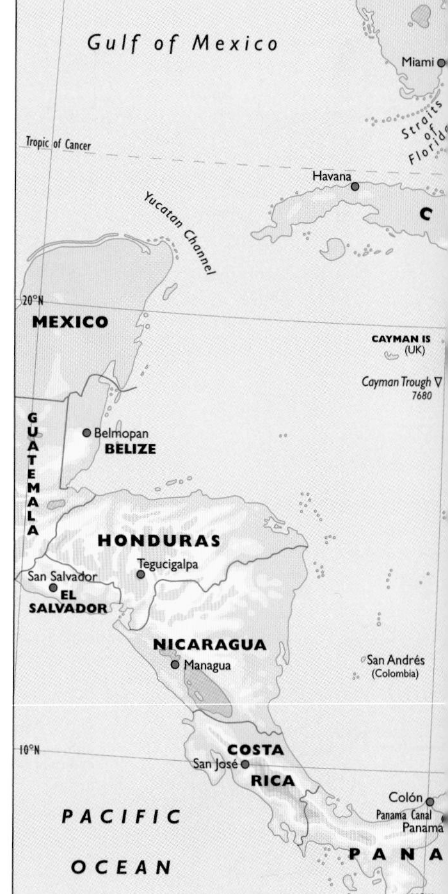

BARBADOS

Island state in the Windward Islands, West Indies. Barbados' warm climate encouraged the growth of its two largest industries: sugar cane and tourism. It was settled by the British in 1627, and dominated by British plantation owners (using African slave labor until the abolition of slavery) for the next 300 years. It gained independence in 1966.

Area 166 sq mi [430 sq km]
Population 277,000
Capital Bridgetown (80,000)
Government Parliamentary democracy
Ethnic groups Black 90%, Asian, White
Languages English
Religions Protestant 67%, Roman Catholic 4%
Currency Barbadian dollar = 100 cents
Website www.barbados.org

CAYMAN ISLANDS

British dependency in the West Indies, comprising Grand Cayman, Little Cayman, and Cayman Brac, 200 mi (325 km) northwest of Jamaica, in the Caribbean Sea. The islands are riverless and the coasts mostly protected by offshore reefs. They were discovered by Columbus in 1503, and ceded to Britain in the 17th century. The islanders voted against independence in 1962. Tourism, international finance, and turtle and shark fishing, are major sources of revenue.

Area 102 sq mi [264 sq km]
Population 42,000
Capital Georgetown (20,600)
Government Overseas territory of the UK
Ethnic groups Mixed 40%, White 20%, Black 20%
Languages English
Religions Protestant, Roman Catholic
Currency Caymanian dollar = 100 cents
Website www.gov.ky

DOMINICA

An independent island nation in the east Caribbean Sea, it is the largest of the Windward Islands. The present population are mainly the descendants of African slaves. Dominica is mountainous and heavily forested, and the climate is tropical. It boasts the Morne Trois Pitons National Park—established in 1975 and declared a World Heritage Site in 1997. The park plays host to the Boiling Lake and the Valley of Desolation as well as many other lakes and waterfalls and is centered on the Morne Trois Pitons volcano which rises to 4,403 ft (1,342 m).

Area 290 sq mi [751 sq km]
Population 70,000
Capital Roseau (20,000)
Government Parliamentary democracy
Ethnic groups Black, Mixed black and European, European, Syrian, Carib Amerindian
Languages English (official), French patois
Religions Roman Catholic 77%, Protestant 15%
Currency East Caribbean dollar = 100 cents
Website www.avirtualdominica.com

Dominica achieved complete independence as a republic within the Commonwealth in 1978. It is one of the poorest Caribbean countries. Agriculture dominates the economy. In recent years the island has benefitted greatly from being the location for Hollywood movies.

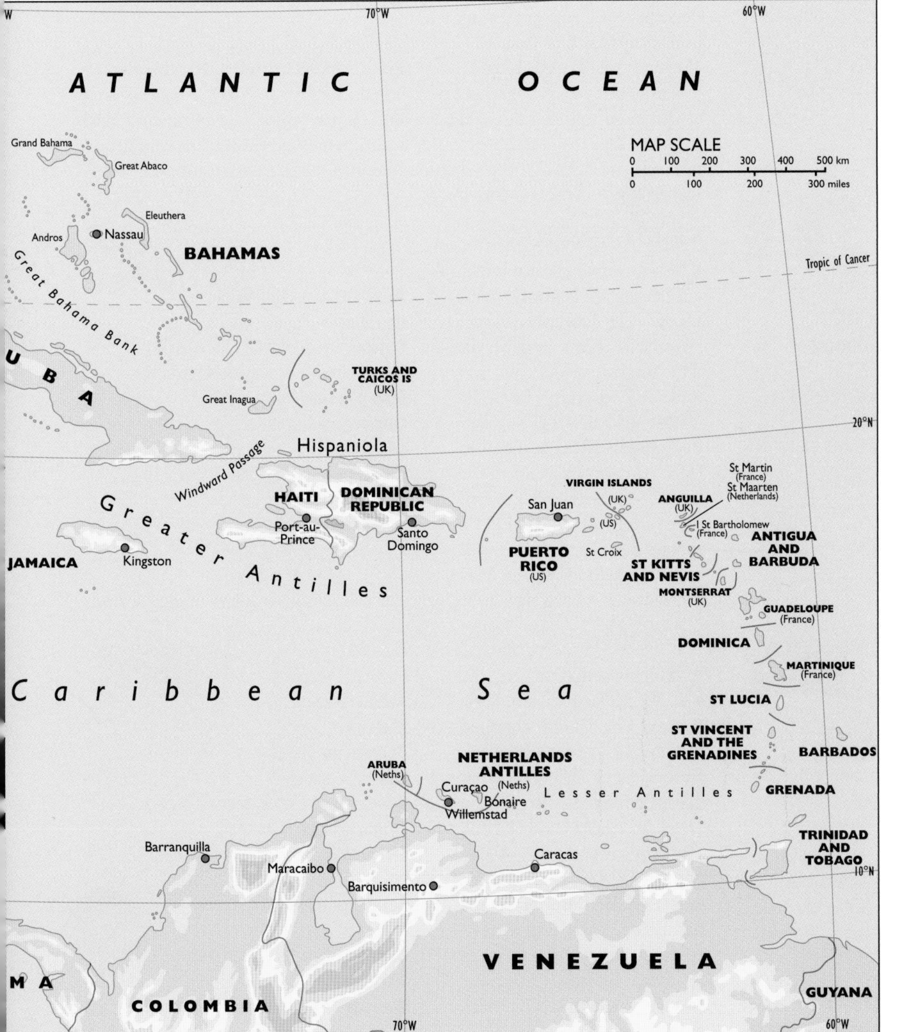

***A cannon rusts** at the ruins of Fort Shirley, overlooking Prince Rupert Bay, Dominica*

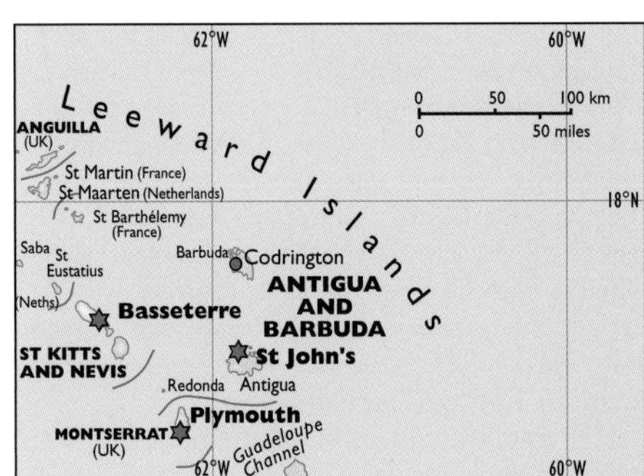

GRENADA

Independent island nation in the southeast Caribbean Sea, the most southerly of the Windward Islands, 100 mi [160 km] north of Venezuela. It consists of Grenada and the smaller islands of the Southern Grenadines dependency. It is volcanic in origin, with a ridge of mountains running north–south. The climate is tropical with occasional hurricanes. The agrarian economy is based on cocoa, bananas, sugar, spices, and citrus fruits. It depends greatly on tourism.

Area 133 sq mi [344 sq km]
Population 101,400
Capital St. George's (8,000)
Government Constitutional monarchy
Ethnic groups Black 82%, others
Languages English (official), French patois
Religions Roman Catholic 53%, Protestant 47%
Currency East Caribbean dollar = 100 cents
Website www.grenadagrenadines.com

GUADELOUPE

French overseas department (since 1946), consisting of the islands of Basse-Terre, Grande-Terre and several smaller islands in the Leeward Islands. The Island of Saint Martin is shared with the Netherlands Antilles.Discovered in 1493 by Columbus and settled by France in 1635. Guadeloupe was briefly held by Britain and Sweden, but reverted to French rule in 1816. The chief crops are sugar cane and bananas. Industries include distilling and tourism.

Area 658 sq mi [1,705 sq km]
Population 440,000
Capital Basse-Terre (14,000)
Government Overseas department of France
Ethnic groups Black or mulatto 90%, White 5%
Languages English (official), Spanish, Creole
Religions Roman Catholic 95%, Hindu and pagan African 4%
Currency Euro = 100 cents
Website www.guadeloupe.pref.gouv.fr

MARTINIQUE

Island in the Windward group of the Lesser Antilles. Martinique was inhabited by Carib Indians until they were displaced by French settlers after 1635. The island became a permanent French possession after the Napoleonic Wars. Of volcanic origin, it is the largest of the Lesser Antilles. In 1902, a volcanic eruption completely destroyed the original capital, St. Pierre.

Area 425 sq mi [1,102 sq km]
Population 426,000
Capital Fort de France (100,000)
Government Overseas department of France
Ethnic groups African and African-White-Indian mixture 90%
Languages French, Creole patois
Religions Roman Catholic 85%, Protestant 10%
Currency Euro = 100 cents
Website www.martinique.org

MONTSERRAT

Montserrat is one of the Leeward Islands in the Lesser Antilles. It is dominated by an active volcano in the Soufrière Hills. The British colonized it in 1632. It formed part of the Leeward Island colony from 1871 until 1956, when it became a separate, dependent territory of the UK. In 1995, a volcanic eruption destroyed the capital, Plymouth, and most of the population fled. Many have since returned. Revenue comes from tourism, offshore finance, and cotton.

Area 40 sq mi [102 sq km]
Population 9,000
Capital Brades Estate (interim)
Government Overseas territory of the UK
Ethnic groups Black, White
Languages English
Religions Christian
Currency East Caribbean dollar = 100 cents
Website www.gov.ms

NETHERLANDS ANTILLES

Group of five main islands (and part of a sixth) in the West Indies. The islands were settled by the Spanish in 1527 and captured by the Dutch in 1634. They were granted internal self-government in 1954. The group includes Aruba, Bonaire, Curaçao, Saba, Saint Eustatius, and the southern half of Saint Maarten. Oil refining, petrochemicals, and tourism provide revenue.

Area 309 sq mi [800 sq km]
Population 216,000
Capital Willemstad (Curacao) (130,000)
Government Autonomous country within the Kingdom of the Netherlands
Ethnic groups Mixed Black 85%, others
Languages Papiamento 65%, English 16%, Dutch 7% (official)
Religions Roman Catholic 72%, others
Currency Netherlands Antillean guilder = 100 cents
Website www.gov.an

PUERTO RICO

The Commonwealth of Puerto Rico is the easternmost island in the Greater Antilles. The land is mountainous, with a narrow coastal plain. The highest point is Cerro de Punta (1,338 m [4,389 ft]). The climate is hot and wet. Ceded by Spain to the US in 1898, Puerto Rico became a self-governing commonwealth in free association with the US after a referendum in 1952. Puerto Ricans are US citizens, but pay no federal taxes, nor do they vote in US congressional or presidential elections. The island is the most industrialized and urbanized in the Caribbean, and manufacturing and tourism are growing industries. Cash crops include bananas, coffee, sugar, tobacco, tropical fruits, vegetables, and spices.

Area 8,959 sq km [3,459 sq mi]
Population 3,916,632
Capital (population) San Juan (433,733)
Government Commonwealth
Ethnic groups White 80%, black 8%, others
Languages Spanish, English
Religions Roman Catholic 85%, others 15%
Currency US dollar = 100 cents
Website www.gotopuertorico.com

ST. KITTS & NEVIS

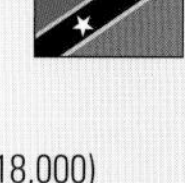

Self-governing state in the Leeward Islands, West Indies. It comprises the islands St. Kitts and Nevis. The English settled in 1623 and the French in 1624. The Treaty of Paris (1783) settled Anglo-French disputes over possession, and the islands gained self-government in 1967. Nevis held a referendum on independence from St. Kitts in May 1998 and is still campaigning. Industries include tourism, sugar, cotton.

Area 101 sq mi [261 sq km]
Population 39,000
Capital Basseterre (St Kitts) (18,000)
Government Constitutional monarchy
Ethnic groups Black
Languages English
Religions Anglican, Roman Catholic
Currency East Caribbean dollar = 100 cents
Website www.stkittsnevis.net

ST. LUCIA

Volcanic island in the Windward group, West Indies. The island changed hands 14 times between France and Britain before being ceded to Britain in 1814. It finally achieved full self-government in 1979. Mountainous (the twin peton peaks are a scenic highlight), lush and forested, its tourist income is growing rapidly, especially from cruise ships. The principal export is bananas.

Area 208 sq mi [539 sq km]
Population 162,000
Capital Castries
Government Parliamentary democracy
Ethnic groups Black 90%
Languages English (official), French patois
Religions Roman Catholic 68%, Protestant
Currency East Caribbean dollar = 100 cents
Website www.stlucia.gov.lc

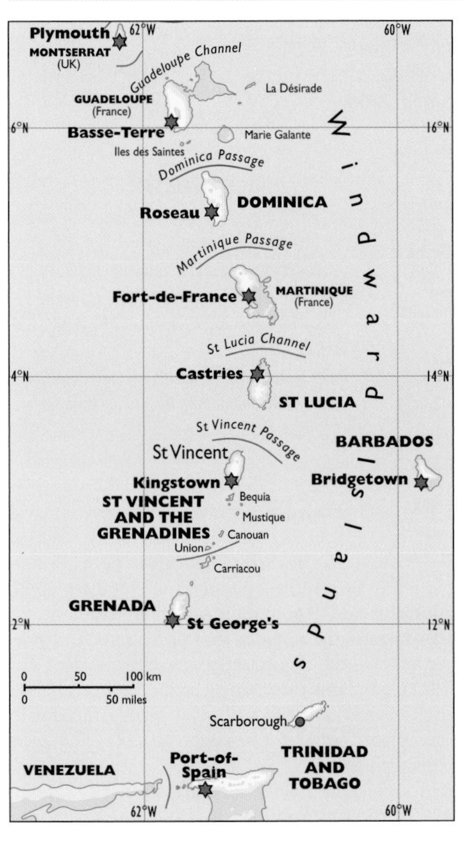

WINDWARD ISLANDS

Southern group of the Lesser Antilles islands, southeast West Indies. They extend from the Leeward Islands to the northeast coast of Venezuela. The principal islands are Martinique, Grenada, Dominica, St. Lucia and St. Vincent and the Grenadines group. The islands, volcanic in origin, are mountainous and forested. Tropical crops are grown, including sugar cane, bananas, spices, limes, and cacao, but tourism is the leading industry. The islands were inhabited by the indigenous Carib until colonization began in the 17th century. The next two centuries witnessed a struggle for control between France and Britain. Britain eventually controlled all the islands, with the exception of Martinique.

ST VINCENT & GRENADINES

Area 150 sq mi [388 sq km]
Population 117,000
Capital Kingstown
Government Parliamentary democracy
Ethnic groups Black 66%, Mixed 19%
Languages English, French patois
Religions Anglican 47%, Methodist 28%, Roman Catholic 13%
Currency East Caribbean dollar = 100 cents
Website www.svgtourism.com

Island state of the Windward Islands, between St Lucia and Grenada comprising the volcanic island of St Vincent and five islands of the Grenadine group, including Mustique. In 1783 the British deported most of the native Carib population, who were replaced by African slave labor. St Vincent was part of the British Windward Islands colony (1880–1958) and of the West Indies Federation (1958–62). It gained self-government in 1969 and full independence in the Commonwealth in 1979.

TURKS & CAICOS

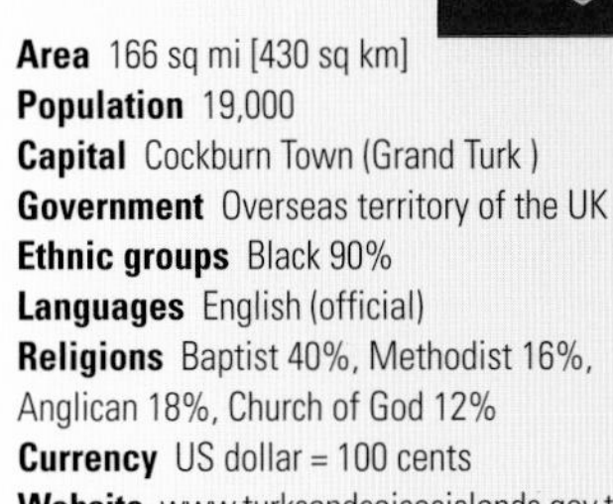
Area 166 sq mi [430 sq km]
Population 19,000
Capital Cockburn Town (Grand Turk)
Government Overseas territory of the UK
Ethnic groups Black 90%
Languages English (official)
Religions Baptist 40%, Methodist 16%, Anglican 18%, Church of God 12%
Currency US dollar = 100 cents
Website www.turksandcaicosislands.gov.tc

Turks and Caicos are two island groups of the British West Indies that include more than 40 islands, eight of which are inhabited. Grand Turk is the capital island and home of the government, while Providenciales is the most developed of the islands and their center of tourism. Discovered in 1512 by Ponce de León, the islands were British from 1766. They were then administered via Jamaica from 1873–1959, and a separate Crown Colony from 1973. Most food products are imported. Exports include salt, sponges, and shellfish. The main sources of income are tourism and offshore banking.

BRITISH VIRGIN ISLANDS

Area 58 sq mi [151 sq km]
Population 22,000
Capital Road Town (Tortola)
Government Overseas territory of the UK
Ethnic groups Black 84%
Languages English (official)
Religions Protestant 86%, Roman Catholic 10%
Currency US dollar = 100 cents
Website www.bvitourism.com

British colony in the West Indies. It is a group of 36 islands, which form part of the Antilles between the Caribbean Sea and the Atlantic Ocean. Tortola is the commercial center and capital island: it is also home to the highest point in the group, Mount Sage—1,709 ft (521 m). First settled in the 17th century, the islands formed part of the Leeward Islands colony until 1956. The chief economic activity is tourism, though construction, rum production, and offshore banking are also important. Livestock farming is the leading form of agriculture.

US VIRGIN ISLANDS

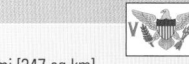

Area 134 sq mi [347 sq km]
Population 125,000
Capital Charlotte Amalie (St Thomas)
Government Unincorporated territory of the US
Ethnic groups Black 76%, White 13%
Languages English 75%, Spanish or Spanish Creole 17%, French or French Creole 7%
Religions Baptist 42%, Roman Catholic 34%
Currency US dollar = 100 cents
Website www.usvi.net

Group of 68 islands in the Lesser Antilles. Chief islands are St Croix, St John and St Thomas. Spanish from 1553, the islands were Danish until 1917, when the USA bought them for US$25 million to protect the northern approaches to the newly completed Panama Canal. The islands' residents are now US citizens. Tourism is the biggest earner, though on St Croix there is an oil refinery and an aluminum plant.

Central African Republic

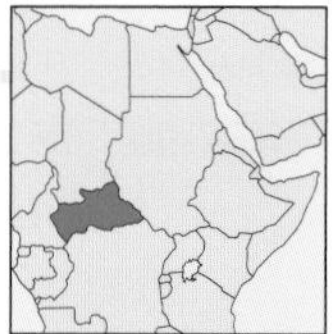

The red, yellow, and green colors on this flag were originally used by Ethiopia, Africa's oldest independent nation. They symbolize African unity. The blue, white, and red recall the flag of France, the country's colonial ruler. This flag was adopted in 1958.

The Central African Republic is a remote landlocked country in central Africa. It lies on a plateau, mostly 1,970–2,620 ft (600–800 m) above sea level, forming a watershed between the headwaters of two river systems. In the south, the rivers flow into the navigable River Ubangi (a tributary of the Congo). The Ubangi and the Bomu form much of its southern border. In the north, most rivers are headwaters of the River Chari, which flows north into Lake Chad.

Wooded savanna covers much of the country, with open grasslands in the north and rainforests in the southwest. The country has many forest and savanna animals, such as buffalo, leopards, lions, and elephants, and many bird species. About 6% of the land is protected in national parks and reserves, but tourism is on a small scale because of the republic's remoteness.

CLIMATE

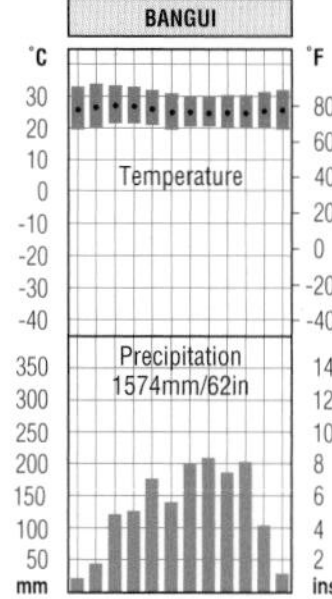

The climate is warm throughout the year, with an average annual rainfall in Bangui totalling 62 in [1,574 mm]. The north is drier, with an average annual rainfall total of about 31 in [800 mm].

HISTORY

Little is known of the country's early history. Between the 16th and 19th centuries, the population was greatly reduced by slavery, and the country is still thinly populated. France first occupied the area in 1887, and in 1894 established the colony of Ubangi-Shari at Bangui. In 1906 the colony was united with Chad, and in 1910 was subsumed into French Equatorial Africa (which included Chad, Congo, and Gabon). Forced-labor rebellions occurred in 1928, 1935 and 1946. During World War II Ubangi-Shari supported the Free French. Post-1945 the colony received representation in the French parliament. In 1958 the colony voted to become a self-governing republic within the French community, and became the Central African Republic.

POLITICS

In 1960 Central African Republic declared independence, but the next six years saw a deterioration in the economy, and increasing government corruption and inefficiency under President David Dacko. It became a one-party state in 1962. In 1966 Colonel Jean Bédel Bokassa assumed power in a bloodless coup. He abrogated the constitution and dissolved the National Assembly.

In 1976 Bokassa transformed the republic into an empire, and proclaimed himself Emperor Bokassa I. The country was renamed the Central African Empire. His rule became increasingly brutal, and in 1979 he was deposed in a French-backed coup led by Dacko. Dacko, faced with continuing unrest, was replaced by André Kolingba in 1981. The army quickly banned all political parties.

The country adopted a new, multiparty constitution in 1991. Elections were held in 1993. An army rebellion in 1996 was finally put down in 1997 with the assistance of French troops. An attempted coup in 2001 was put down, with Libyan help, by President Ange-Félix Patassé, who had served as president since 1993. But a coup in 2003 brought General François Bozize to power and Patassé went into exile in Togo. A new constitution was introduced in 2004, followed by elections in 2005 which were won by General Bozize.

ECONOMY

The World Bank classifies the Central African Republic as a "low-income" developing country. Approximately 10% of the land is cultivated and over 80% of the workforce are engaged in subsistence agriculture. The main food crops are bananas, corn, manioc, millet, and yams. Coffee, cotton, timber, and tobacco are the main cash crops

Diamonds, the only major mineral resource, are the most valuable single export. Manufacturing is on a very small scale. Products include beer, cotton fabrics, footwear, leather, soap, and sawn timber. The Central African Republic's development has been greatly impeded by its remote position, its poor transport system, and its untrained workforce. The country is heavily dependent on aid, especially from France.

BANGUI

Capital of the Central African Republic, on the River Ubangi, near the border with the Democratic Republic of Congo. Founded in 1889 by the French, it is the nation's chief port for international trade. Places of interest include the triumphal arch dedicated to Jean-Bédel Bokassa, the Boganda Museum, and the central market. Industries include textiles, shoes, food processing, beer, and soap.

Area 240,534 sq mi [622,984 sq km]
Population 3,742,000
Capital (population) Bangui (553,000)
Government Multiparty republic
Ethnic groups Baya 33%, Banda 27%, Mandjia 13%, Sara 10%, Mboum 7% Mbaka 4%, others
Languages French (official), Sangho
Religions Traditional beliefs 35%, Protestant 25%, Roman Catholic 25%, Islam 15%
Currency CFA franc = 100 centimes
Website www.banguinet.net

A family of BaAka pygmies, *an indigenous hunter-gatherer group located throughout Cameroon and the Central African Republic, prepare a meal outside their hut*

UBANGI (OUBANGI)

The River Ubangi is a major tributary of the River Congo in central Africa, beginning at the junction of the Mbomou and Uele rivers. The Ubangi defines the boundary between the Central African Republic and the Democratic Republic of the Congo (DRC), passing through Bangui, after which it forms the boundary between the DRC and the Republic of Congo before emptying into the River Congo. It is an important artery for river boats between Bangui and Brazzaville.

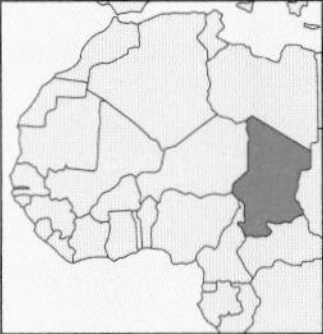

Chad's flag was adopted in 1959 as the country prepared for independence in 1960. The blue represents the sky, the streams in southern Chad, and hope. The yellow symbolizes the sun and the Sahara in the north. The red represents national sacrifice.

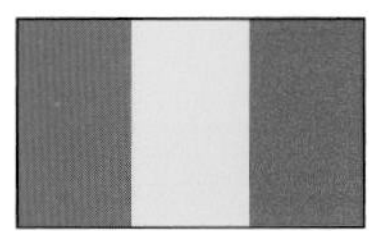

Chad is Africa's fifth largest country. It is more than twice as big as France (the former colonial power). Southern Chad is crossed by rivers that flow into Lake Chad, on the western border with Nigeria. The capital, Ndjamena, lies on the banks of the River Chari. Beyond a large depression (northeast of Lake Chad) are the Tibesti Mountains, which rise steeply from the sands of the Sahara Desert. The mountains contain Chad's highest peak, Emi Koussi, at 11,204 ft [3,415 m]. The far south contains forests, while central Chad is a region of savanna, merging into the dry grasslands of the Sahel. Plants are rare in the northern desert. Droughts are common in north central Chad. Long droughts, overgrazing, and felling for firewood have exposed the Sahel's soil and wind erosion is increasing desertification.

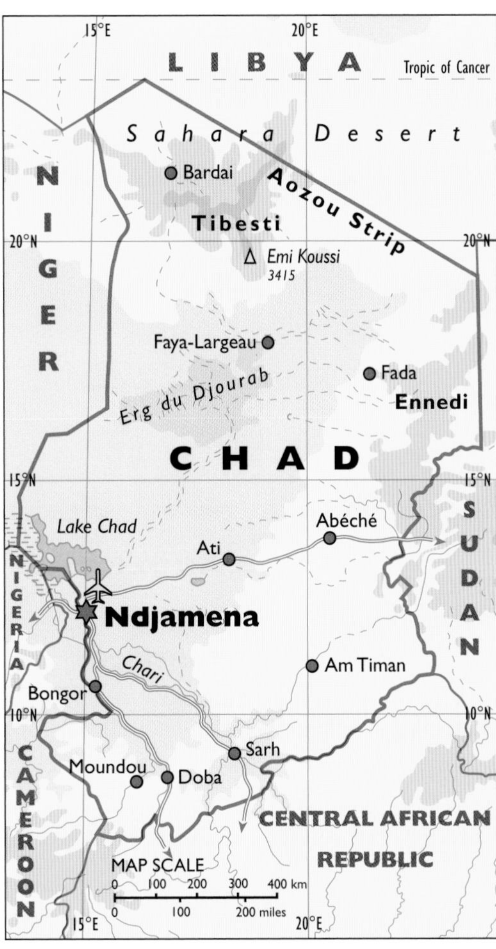

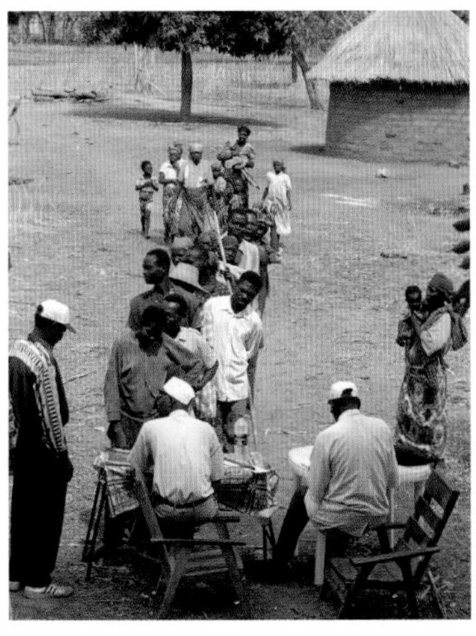

***Villagers register** to be tested for sleeping sickness at Danmadja village*

Area 495,752 sq mi [1,284,000 sq km]
Population 9,539,000
Capital (population) Ndjamena (530,000)
Government Multiparty republic
Ethnic groups 200 distinct groups: mostly Muslim in the north and center; mostly Christian or animist in the south
Languages French and Arabic (both official), many others
Religions Islam 51%, Christianity 35%, animist 7%
Currency CFA franc = 100 centimes
Website www.chadembassy.org

NDJAMENA

Capital of Chad, a port on the River Chari. Founded by the French in 1900, it was known as Fort Lamy until 1973. Ndjamena grew rapidly after independence in 1960. An important market for the surrounding region, which produces livestock, dates, and cereals. The main industry is meat processing.

CLIMATE

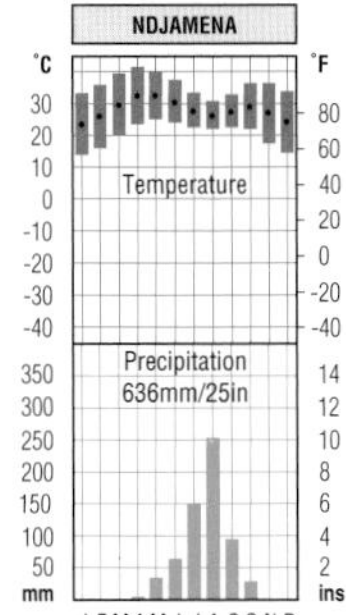

Central Chad has a hot tropical climate. There is a marked dry season from November to April. The south is wetter, with an average annual rainfall of about 39 in [1,000 mm]. Conversely, the hot northern desert has an average annual rainfall of less than 5 in [130 mm].

HISTORY

Chad straddles two, often conflicting worlds: the north, populated by nomadic or semi-nomadic Muslim peoples, such as Arabs and Tuaregs; and the dominant south, where a sedentary population practice Christianity or traditional religions, such as animism. Lake Chad was an important watering point for the trans-Saharan caravans. Around AD 700 North African nomads founded the Kanem Empire. In the 14th century, the kingdom of Bornu expanded to incorporate Kanem. In the late 19th century the region fell to Sudan.

The first major European explorations were by the French in 1890. The French defeated the Sudanese in 1900, and in 1908 Chad became the largest province of French Equatorial Africa. In 1920 it became a separate colony.

POLITICS

In 1958 Chad gained autonomous status within the French Community, and in 1960 achieved full independence. Divisions between north and south rapidly surfaced. In 1965, President François Tombalbaye declared a one-party state and the northern Muslims, led by the Chad National Liberation Front (Frolinat), rebelled. By 1973 the government, helped by the French, quashed the revolt. In 1980 Libya occupied northern Chad. In 1982, two leaders of Frolinat, Hissène Habré and Goukouni Oueddi, formed rival regimes. Splits soon emerged and Libya's bombing of Chad in 1983 led to the deployment of 3,000 French troops. Libyan troops retreated, retaining only the uranium-rich Aozou Strip. A ceasefire took effect in 1987. In 1990, Habré was removed in a coup led by Idriss Déby. In 1994, the Aozou Strip was awarded to Chad. In 1996, a new democratic constitution was adopted and multiparty elections confirmed Déby as president. He was reelected in 2001. In 2002 a peace treaty, signed by the government and the Movement for Democracy and Justice, ended three years of civil war. In 2004–5, Chad forces clashed with pro-Sudanese militia as the conflict in Sudan's Darfur province spilled over the border.

ECONOMY

Chad is one of the world's poorest countries, though its gold, uranium, and oil reserves could be exploited to improve the situation but this has been hampered by a poor infrastructure. Agriculture dominates the economy, more than 80% of the workforce is engaged in farming, mainly at subsistence level. Groundnuts, millet, rice, and sorghum are major crops in the wetter south. The most valuable crop is cotton.

LAKE CHAD (TCHAD)

North-central African lake, mainly in Chad, partly in Nigeria, Cameroon and Niger. The chief tributary is the River Chari. The lake has no outlet. The surface area varies by season from 3,861 to 10,000 sq mi [10,000–26,000 sq km]; maximum depth 25 ft (7.6 m).

Chile

Chile's flag was adopted in 1817. It was designed in that year by an American serving in the Chilean army who was inspired by the US Stars and Stripes. The white represents the snow-capped Andes, the blue the sky, and the red the blood of the nation's patriots.

Area 292,133 sq mi [756,626 sq km]
Population 15,824,000
Capital (population) Santiago (4,789,000)
Government Multiparty republic
Ethnic groups Mestizo 95%, Amerindian 3%
Languages Spanish (official)
Religions Roman Catholic 89%, Protestant 11%
Currency Chilean peso = 100 centavos
Website www.chileangovernment.cl

The Republic of Chile stretches 2,650 mi [4,260 km] from north to south, while the maximum east-west distance is only 270 mi [430 km]. The Andes mountains form Chile's eastern borders with Argentina and Bolivia. Ojos del Salado, at 6,863 m [22,516 f], is the second-highest peak in South America. Easter Island lies 2,200 mi [3,500 km] off Chile's west coast.

Western Chile contains three main land regions. In the north is the sparsely populated Atacama Desert, stretching 1,000 mi [1,600 km] south from the Peruvian border. The Central Valley, which contains the capital, Santiago, Valparaíso, and Concepción, is by far the most densely populated region. In the south, the land has been heavily glaciated, the coastal uplands have been worn into islands, while the inland valleys are arms of the sea.

In the far south, the Strait of Magellan separates the Chilean mainland from Tierra del Fuego. Punta Arenas is the world's southernmost city.

CLIMATE

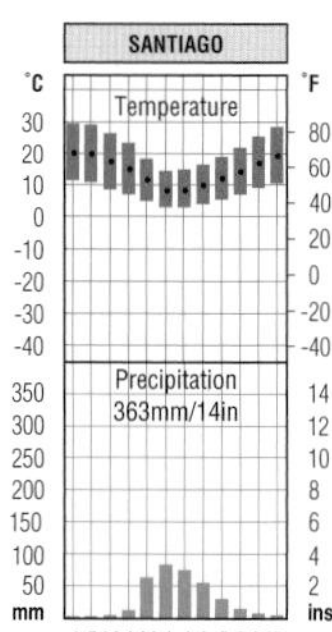

Chile is divided into three main climate zones. The Atacama Desert in the north has an arid climate, but temperatures are moderated by the cold Peru Current. Central Chile has a Mediterranean climate with hot, dry summers and mild, moist winters. The south has a cool and stormy climate prone to alpine conditions.

HISTORY

Amerindian people reached the southern tip of South America at least 8,000 years ago. In 1520, the Portuguese navigator Ferdinand Magellan became the first European to sight Chile. The country became a Spanish colony in the 1540s. Under Spain, the economy in the north was based on mining, while huge ranches, or *haciendas*, were set up in central Chile. After Chile became independent in 1818, mining continued to flourish in the north, while Valparaiso developed as a port exporting produce from central Chile to California and Australia. During a war (1879–83), it gained mineral-rich areas from Peru and Bolivia. Industrial growth, fuelled by revenue from nitrate exports, began in the early 20th century.

SANTIAGO

Capital of Chile, in central region on the River Mapocho, 55 mi [90 km] from the Atlantic coast. Founded in 1541, it was destroyed by an earthquake in 1647. Most of the architecture dates from after 1850. It is the administrative, commercial, and cultural center, accounting for nearly a third of the population.

POLITICS

After World War II, Chile faced economic problems, partly caused by falls in world copper prices. A Christian Democrat was elected president in 1964, but was replaced by Salvador Allende Gossens in 1970. Allende's administration, the world's first democratically elected Marxist government, was overthrown in a CIA-backed coup in 1973. General Augusto Pinochet Ugarte took power as a dictator, banning all political activity in a repressive regime. A new constitution took effect from 1981, allowing for an eventual return to democracy. Elections took place in 1989. President Patrico Aylwin took office in 1990, but Pinochet continued office as commander-in-chief of the armed forces. Eduardo Frei was elected president in 1993 and he was succeeded by a socialist, Ricardo Lagos, who narrowly defeated a conservative candidate in January 2000. In 1999, General Pinochet, who was visiting Britain for medical treatment, was faced with extradition to Spain to answer charges that he had presided over acts of torture when he was Chile's dictator. In 2000, he was allowed to return to Chile where, in 2001, he was found to be too ill to stand trial. New charges were brought against him in 2004 and, in 2005 he was placed under house arrest.

ECONOMY

The World Bank classifies Chile as a "lower-middle-income" developing country. Mining is important. Minerals dominate Chile's exports. The most valuable activity is manufacturing. Products include processed foods, metals, iron and steel, wood products, and textiles.

Agriculture employs 18% of the workforce. The chief crop is wheat. Beans, fruits, corn, and livestock products are also important. Chile's fishing industry is one of the world's largest.

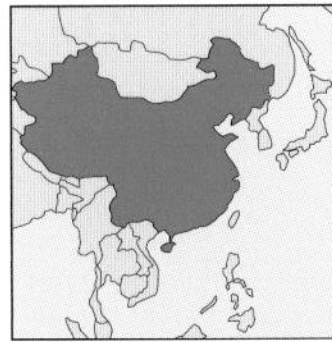

China's flag was adopted in 1949, when the country became a Communist People's Republic. Red is the traditional color of both China and Communism. The large star represents the Communist Party program. The smaller stars symbolize the four main social classes.

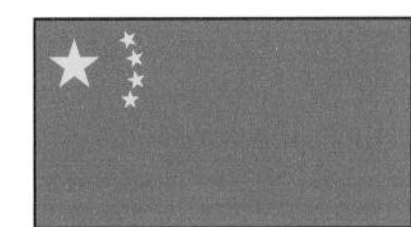

The People's Republic of China is the world's third largest country. Most people live on the eastern coastal plains, in the highlands or the fertile valleys of the rivers Huang He and Yangtze, Asia's longest river, at 3,960 mi [6,380 km].

Western China includes the bleak Tibetan plateau, bounded by the Himalayas. Everest, the world's highest peak, lies on the Nepal-Tibet border. Other ranges include the Tian Shan and Kunlun Shan. China also has deserts, such as the Gobi.

Large areas in the west are covered by sparse grasses or desert. The most luxuriant forests are in the southeast, such as the bamboo forest habitat of the rare giant panda.

CLIMATE

The capital, Beijing, in northeast China, has cold winters and warm summers, with moderate rainfall. Shanghai, in the east-central region, has milder winters and more rain. The southeast region has a wet, subtropical climate. In the west, the climate is more cold and severe.

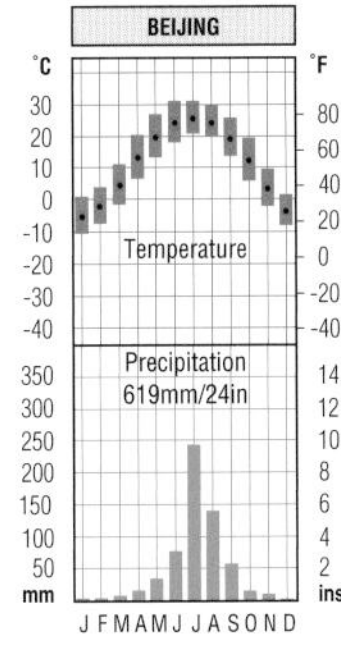

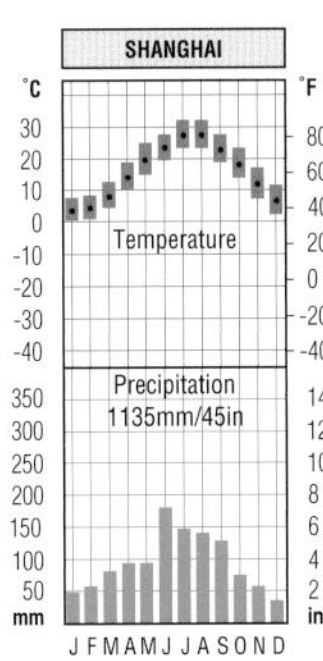

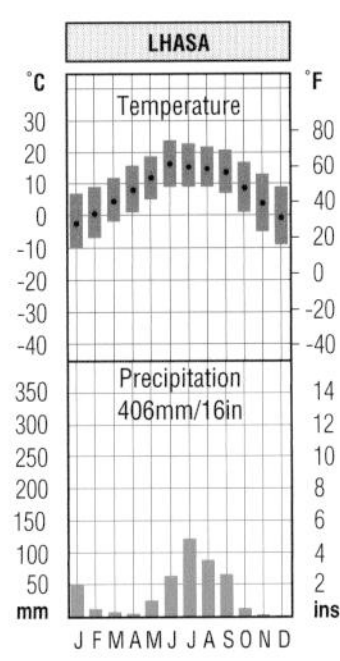

HISTORY

The first documented dynasty was the Shang (1523–1030 BC), when bronze casting was perfected. The Zhou dynasty (1030–221 BC) was the age of Chinese classical literature, in particular Confucious and Lao Tzu. China was unified by Qin Shihuangdi, whose tomb near Xian contains the famous terracotta army. The Qin dynasty (221–206 BC) also built the majority of the Great Wall. The Han dynasty (202 BC–AD 220) developed the Empire, a bureaucracy based on Confucianism, and also introduced Buddhism. China then split into three kingdoms (Wei, Shu, and Wu) and the influence of Buddhism and Taoism grew. The T'ang dynasty from 618–907 was a golden era of artistic achievement, especially in poetry and fine art. Genghis Khan conquered most of China in the 1210s and established the Mongol empire. Kublai Khan founded the Yüan dynasty (1271–1368), an era of dialogue with Europe. The Ming dynasty (1368–1644) reestablished Chinese rule and is famed for its fine porcelain. The Manchu Qing dynasty (1644–1912) began by vastly extending the empire, but the 19th century was marked by foreign interventions, such as the Opium War (1839–42), when Britain occupied Hong Kong. Popular disaffection culminated in the Boxer Rebellion (1900). The last Emperor (Henry Pu Yi) was overthrown in a revolution led by Sun Yat-sen and a republic established (1912).

China rapidly fragmented between a Beijing government supported by warlords, and Sun Yat-sen's nationalist Kuomintang government in Guangzhou. The Communist Party of China initially allied with the Kuomintang. In 1926, the Kuomintang, led by Chiang Kai-shek, emerged victorious and turned on their Communist allies. In 1930 a rival communist government was established, but was uprooted by Kuomintang troops and began the Long March (1934). Japan, taking advantage of the turmoil, established the puppet state of Manchukuo (1932). Chiang was forced to ally with the Communists. Japan launched a full-scale invasion in 1937, and conquered much of north and east China. From 1941 Chinese forces, with Allied support, began to regain territory. At the end of World War II, civil war resumed: nationalists supported by the USA and Communists by Russia. The Communists, with greater popular support, triumphed and the Kuomintang fled to Taiwan.

Area 3,705,387 sq mi [9,596,961 sq km]
Population 1,298,848,000
Capital (population) Beijing (7,362,000)
Government Single-party Communist republic
Ethnic groups Han Chinese 92%, many others
Languages Mandarin Chinese (official)
Religions Atheist (official)
Currency Renminbi yuan = 10 jiao = 100 fen
Website www.china.org.cn/english

BEIJING (PEKING)

Capital of the People's Republic of China, between the Pei and Hun rivers, northeast China. A settlement since 1000 BC, Beijing served as China's capital from 1421 to 1911. After the establishment of the Chinese Republic (1911–12), Beijing remained the political center of China. The seat of government was transferred to Nanking in 1928. Beijing ("northern capital") became known as Pei-p'ing ("northern peace"). Occupied by the Japanese in 1937, it was restored to China in 1945 and came under Communist control in 1949. Its name was restored as capital of the People's Republic. The city comprises two walled sections: the Inner (Tatar) City, including the Forbidden City (imperial palace complex), and the Outer (Chinese) city. Beijing is the political, cultural, educational, financial, and transportation center of China. Heavy industry expanded after the end of the Civil War, and products now include textiles, iron, and steel.

***The Forbidden City in Beijing**—home to the imperial palace during the Ming and Qing dynasties (15th to early 20th century) and now a UNESCO listed World Heritage Site*

POLITICS

Mao Zedong established the People's Republic of China on October 1, 1949. In 1950 China seized Tibet. Domestically, Mao began to collectivize agriculture and nationalize industry. In 1958 the Great Leap Forward planned to revolutionize industrial production. The Cultural Revolution (1966–76) mobilized Chinese youth against bourgeois culture. By 1971 China had a seat on the UN security council and its own nuclear capability. Following Mao's death (1976), a power struggle developed between the Gang of Four and moderates led by Deng Xiaoping; the latter emerged victorious. Deng began a process of modernization, forging closer links with the West. In 1989 a pro-democracy demonstration was crushed in Tiananmen Square. In 1997 Jiang Zemin succeeded Deng as paramount leader and in 2002 was succeeded by Hu Jintao. Providing that the country's leaders continue to follow their pragmatic path, many experts predict a major economic blossoming for China in the 21st century.

ECONOMY

By 2005, China had the world's sixth largest economy. However as its population is almost 1.3 billion China remains a poor country. The government announced in 2004 that it planned to slow down the country's rapid economic growth to help the rural poor, who had become relatively worse off as China's industries expanded.

Agriculture still employs nearly half of the population, but while less than 3% of the country can be cultivated, China has practiced intensive farming for thousands of years and, as a result, is largely self-sufficient in food. However, the threat of floods and drought remain, despite government initiatives in soil conservancy, afforestation, together with irrigation and drainage projects. The crops grown vary according to the climate. The warm southeast has a long growing season and two to three crops can be grown on the same plot of land in a single year. Major crops in the area include rice, tea, and sweet potatoes. In the north, with its cooler climate and shorter growing season, wheat is the chief crop, together with corn and sorghum. Western China is largely arid and barren and crops are grown only around isolated oases. However, nomadic pastoralists, such as the Uighurs in Xinjiang, raise goats, horses and sheep.

China leads the world in the production of rice, sweet potatoes, and wheat. It also ranks among the top five producers of bananas, barley, natural rubber, sesame seed, sorghum, soybeans, sugar cane, and tea. Livestock are also important. China leads the world in producing eggs, goats, horses, and mules. It also ranks among the top five producers of beef and veal, cattle, poultry meat, sheep and wool.

The Badaling section *of the Great Wall is one of the best preserved sections*

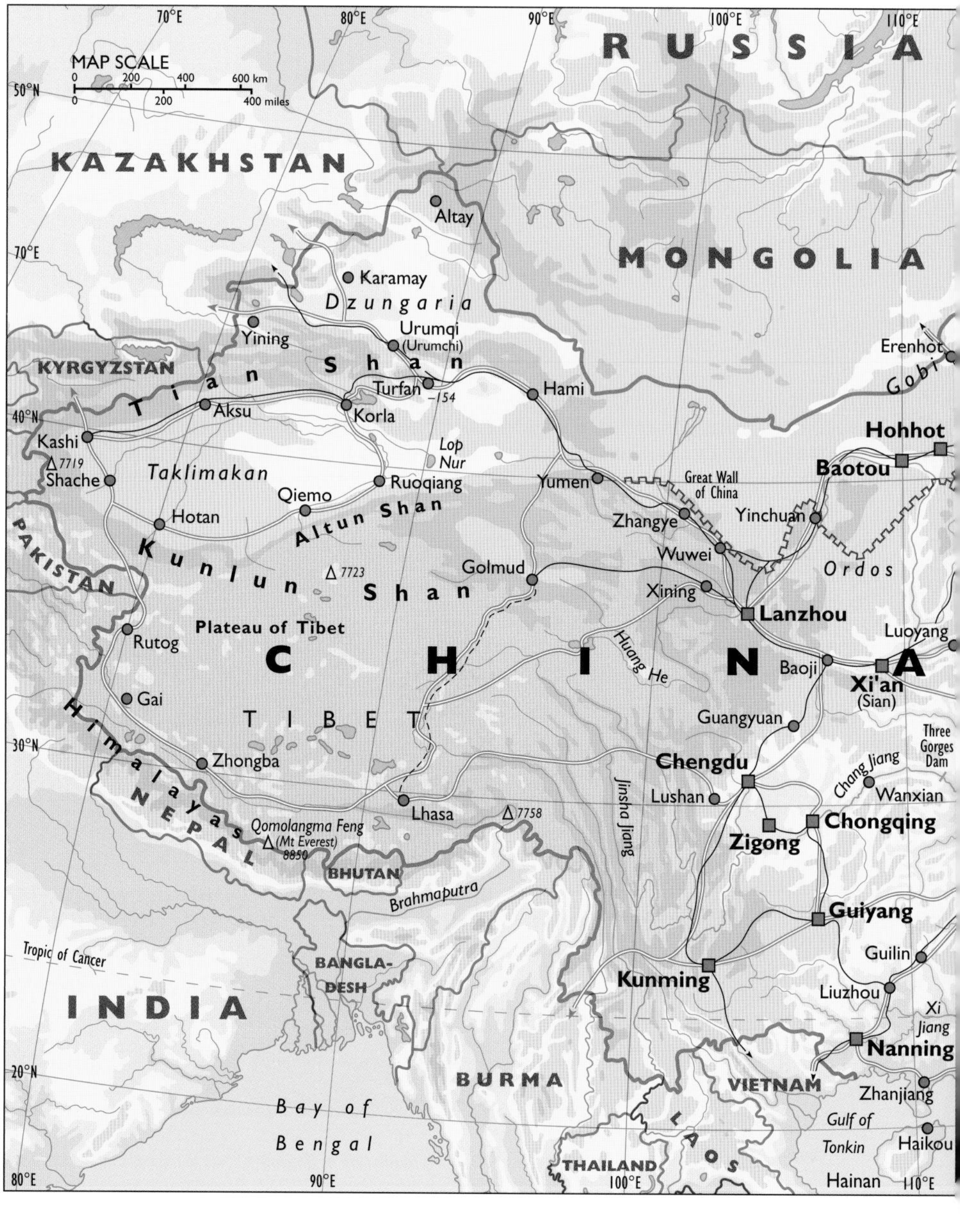

MAP SCALE
0 200 400 600 km
0 200 400 miles
70°E
80°E
90°E
100°E
110°E
50°N
40°N
30°N
20°N
RUSSIA
KAZAKHSTAN
MONGOLIA
KYRGYZSTAN
PAKISTAN
NEPAL
BHUTAN
BANGLA-DESH
INDIA
BURMA
THAILAND
LAOS
VIETNAM
CHINA
TIBET
Altay
Karamay
Dzungaria
Urumqi (Urumchi)
Yining
Tian Shan
Turfan –154
Hami
Aksu
Korla
Kashi
Δ 7719
Shache
Taklimakan
Lop Nur
Qiemo
Ruoqiang
Yumen
Great Wall of China
Hotan
Altun Shan
Kunlun Shan
Δ 7723
Golmud
Zhangye
Wuwei
Xining
Plateau of Tibet
Rutog
Gai
Huang He
Zhongba
Himalayas
Lhasa
Δ 7758
Qomolangma Feng Δ (Mt Everest) 8850
Brahmaputra
Jinsha Jiang
Tropic of Cancer
Bay of Bengal
Erenhot
Gobi
Hohhot
Baotou
Yinchuan
Ordos
Lanzhou
Luoyang
Baoji
Xi'an (Sian)
Guangyuan
Three Gorges Dam
Chengdu
Chang Jiang
Wanxian
Lushan
Chongqing
Zigong
Guiyang
Guilin
Kunming
Liuzhou
Xi Jiang
Nanning
Zhanjiang
Gulf of Tonkin
Haikou
Hainan

MACAU (MACAO)

Former Portuguese overseas province in southeast China, 40 mi [64 km] west of Hong Kong, on the River Pearl estuary; it consists of the 2 sq mi [6 sq km] Macau Peninsula and the islands of Taipa and Colôane. The city of Santa Nome de Deus de Macao (co-extensive with the peninsula) connects via a narrow isthmus to the Chinese province of Guangzhou. Vasco da Gama discovered Macau in 1497, and the Portuguese colonized the island in 1557. In 1849, Portugal declared it a free port. In 1887, the Chinese government recognized Portugal's right of "perpetual occupation." Competition from Hong Kong and the silting of Macau's harbor led to the port's decline at the end of the 19th century. In 1974, Macau became a Chinese province under Portuguese administration. It returned to China in 1999 though China promised that its socialist economic system will not be practiced there. Gambling and tourism are dominant in the economy. Other industries include textiles, electronics, and plastics. Macau has a population of 455,000 of whom 50% are Buddhist and 15% Catholic. Cantonese is spoken by nearly 90% of the population.

Largo do Senado Square, *the main square in Macau and the center for many of the celebrations held throughout the year, especially Chinese New Year, which takes place in late January*

HONG KONG

(XIANGGANG SPECIAL ADMINISTRATIVE REGION)

Former British Crown Colony off the coast of southeast China; the capital is Victoria on Hong Kong Island. Hong Kong comprises: Hong Kong Island, ceded to Britain by China in 1842; the mainland peninsula of Kowloon, acquired in 1860; the New Territories on the mainland, leased for 99 years in 1898; and some 230 islets in the South China Sea. The climate is subtropical, with hot, dry summers. In 1984, the UK and China signed a Joint Declaration in which it was agreed that China would resume sovereignity over Hong Kong in 1997. It also provided that Hong Kong would become a special administrative region, with its existing social and economic structure unchanged for 50 years. It would remain a free port. The last British governor, Chris Patten (1992–97), introduced a legislative council. The handover to China was completed on July 1, 1997, and Chief Executive Tung Chee-hwa was sworn in and a provisional legislative council appointed. Hong Kong is a vital international financial center with a strong manufacturing base.

Hong Kong from Victoria Peak; *the Peak is the highest mountain on Hong Kong Island (1811 ft/552 m) and a key attraction, it can be reached via a funicular tram and is home to the Peak Tower*

Colombia

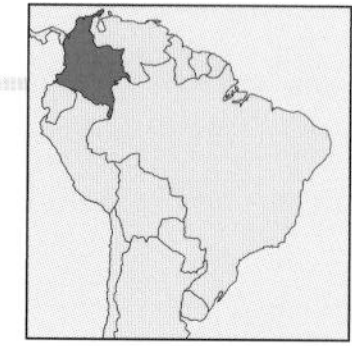

The yellow on Colombia's flag depicts the land, which is separated from the tyranny of Spain by the blue, symbolizing the Atlantic Ocean. The red symbolizes the blood of the people who fought to make the country independent. The flag has been used since 1806.

Area 439,735 sq mi [1,138,914 sq km]
Population 42,311,000
Capital (population) Bogotá (6,545,000)
Government Multiparty republic
Ethnic groups Mestizo 58%, White 20%, Mulatto 14%, Black 4%
Languages Spanish (official)
Religions Roman Catholic 90%
Currency Colombian peso = 100 centavos
Website www.gobiernoenlinea.gov.co/ingles

Colombia is the only South American country to have coastlines on both the Pacific Ocean and the Caribbean Sea. Cartagena is the main Caribbean port. Colombia is dominated by three ranges of the Andean Mountains. On the edge of the western Cordillera lies the city of Cali. The Central Cordillera is a chain of volcanoes that divides the valleys of the rivers Magdalena and Cauca. It includes the city of Medellín. The eastern Cordillera contains the capital, Bogotá, at 9,200 ft [2,800 m]. East of the Andes lie plains drained by headwaters of the Amazon and Orinoco rivers.

Vegetation varies from dense rainforest in the south east to tundra in the snow-capped Andes. Coffee plantations line the western slopes of the eastern Cordillera. The ancient forests of the Caribbean lowlands have mostly been cleared. Savanna (*llanos*) covers the north eastern plains.

CLIMATE

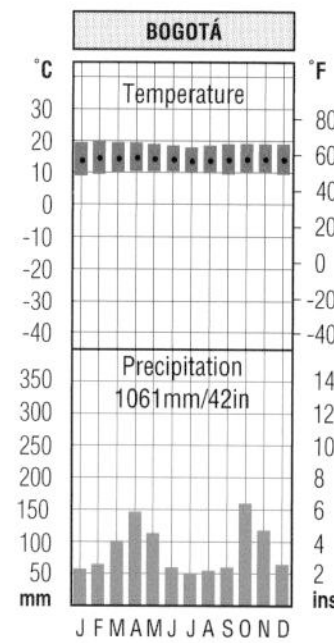

Altitude greatly affects the climate. The Pacific lowlands have a tropical, rainy climate, but Bogotá has mild annual temperatures. The lowlands of the Caribbean and the Magdalena valley both have dry seasons.

HISTORY

The pre-Colombian Chibcha civilization lived undisturbed in the eastern cordillera for thousands of years. In 1525 the Spanish established the first European settlement at Santa Marta. By 1538 conquistador Gonzalo Jiménez de Quesada conquered the Chibcha and established the city of Bogotá. Colombia became part of the New Kingdom of Granada, whose territory also included Ecuador, Panama, and Venezuela.

In 1819 Simón Bolívar defeated the Spanish at Boyacá, and established Greater Colombia. Bolívar became president. In 1830, Ecuador and Venezuela gained independence. In 1885, the Republic of Colombia was formed. Differences between republican and federalist factions proved irreconcilable and the first civil war from 1899–1902 killed nearly 100,000 people. In 1903, aided by the United States, Panama gained independence. The second civil war (La Violencia, 1949–57) was even more bloody.

Coffee plants *in a plantation near Armenia, Colombia; the economy of this area is based heavily on the growing of coffee and bananas*

POLITICS

In 1957 Liberal and Conservative parties formed a National Front Coalition, which held power until 1974. Throughout the 1970s, Colombia's illegal trade in cocaine grew steadily, creating wealthy drug barons. In the 1980s, armed cartels (such as the Cali) destabilized Colombia with frequent assassinations of political and media figures.

A new constitution in 1991 protected human rights. Social Conservative Party (PSC) leader Andrés Pastrana Arango won the 1998 presidential elections and, in an effort to end the 30-year guerrilla war, negotiated with the Revolutionary Armed Forces of Colombia (FARC) and the National Liberation Army (ELN). Pastrana granted FARC a safe haven in southeast Colombia.

In 1999, the worst earthquake in Colombia's history killed more than 1,000 people and left thousands homeless. In 2002 Pastrana declared war on FARC, sending the army into FARC's "safe haven." Alvaro Uribe defeated Pastrana in 2002 presidential elections. Uribe promised even tougher action against terrorism.

ECONOMY

Colombia is a lower-middle income developing country. It is the world's second-largest coffee producer. Other crops include bananas, cocoa, and corn. Colombia also exports coal, oil, emeralds, and gold. In 1997 a collapse in the world coffee and banana markets led to a budget deficit. In 1998 Colombia devalued the peso, triggering the longest strike (20 days) in Colombia's history.

BOGOTÁ

Capital of Colombia, in the center of the country on a fertile plateau. Bogotá was founded in 1538 by the Spanish on the site of a Chibcha Indian settlement. In 1819 it became the capital of Greater Colombia, part of which later formed Colombia. Today, it is a center for culture, education, and finance. Industries include tobacco, sugar, flour, textiles, engineering, and chemicals.

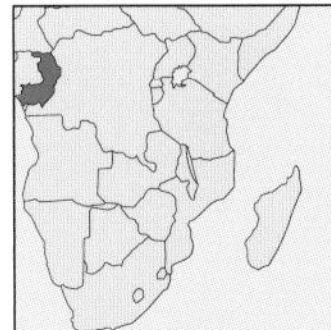

Congo's red flag, with the national emblem of a crossed hoe and mattock (a kind of pick-ax), was dropped in 1990, when the country officially abandoned the Communist policies it had followed since 1970. This new flag was adopted in its place.

The Republic of Congo lies on the River Congo in west-central Africa. The Equator runs through the center of the country. Congo has a narrow coastal plain on which stands its main port, Pointe Noire, which itself lies on the Gulf of Guinea. Behind the plain are forested highlands through which the River Niari has carved a fertile valley. To the east lies Malebo (formerly Stanley) Pool, a large lake where the River Congo widens.

Central Congo consists of luxuriant savanna. Tree species include the valuable okoumé and mahogany. The north contains large swamps in the tributary valleys of the Congo and Ubangi rivers.

BRAZZAVILLE

Capital and largest city of the Congo, West Africa, on the River Congo, below Malebo Pool. Founded in 1880, it was capital of French Equatorial Africa (1910–58) and a base for Free French forces in World War II. It has a university (1972) and a cathedral. It is a major port, connected by rail to the main Atlantic seaport of Pointe-Noire.

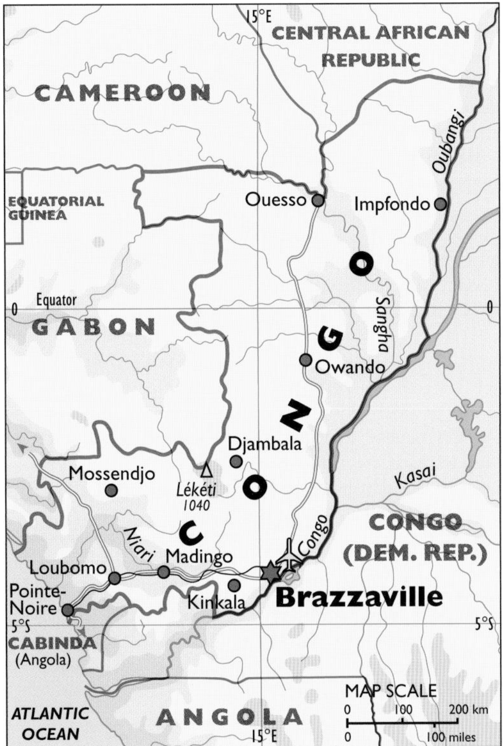

Area 132,046 sq mi [342,000 sq km]
Population 2,998,000
Capital (population) Brazzaville (938,000)
Government Military regime
Ethnic groups Kongo 48%, Sangha 20%, Teke 17%, M'bochi 12%
Languages French (official), many others
Religions Christianity 50%, animist 48%, Islam 2%
Currency CFA franc = 100 centimes
Website www.congo-site.com

CLIMATE

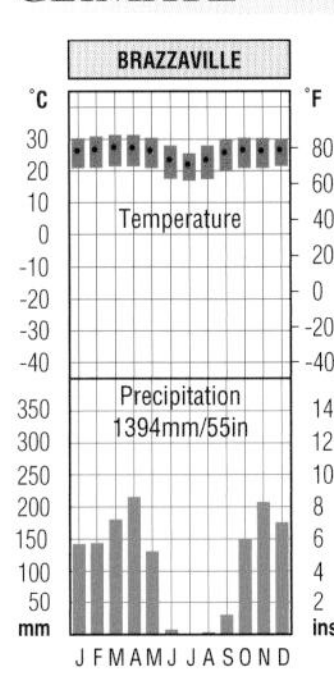

Most of the country has a humid, equatorial climate, with rain throughout the year. Brazzaville has a dry season between June and September. The narrow treeless coastal plain is drier and cooler than the rest of the country, because the cold Benguela current flows northwards along the coast.

HISTORY

The Loango and Bakongo kingdoms dominated the Congo when the first Europeans arrived in 1482. Between the 15th and 18th centuries, part of Congo belonged to the huge Kongo kingdom, whose center lay to the south. Portuguese explorers reached the coast of Congo in the 15th century and the area soon became a trading region, the main commodities being slaves and ivory. The slave trade continued until the 19th century.

European exploration of the interior did not occur until the late 19th century. In 1880 Pierre Savorgnan de Brazza explored the area and it became a French protectorate. It became known as Middle Congo, a country within French Equatorial Africa, which also included Chad, Gabon, and Ubangi-Shari (now called Central African Republic). In 1910 Brazzaville became the capital of French Equatorial Africa. In 1960 the Republic of Congo gained independence.

POLITICS

In 1964 Congo adopted Marxism-Leninism as the state ideology. The military, led by Marien Ngouabi, seized power in 1968. Ngouabi created the Congolese Workers Party (PCT) and was assassinated in 1977. The PCT retained power under Colonel Denis Sassou-Nguesso. In 1990 it renounced Marxism and Sassou-Nguesso was deposed. The Pan-African Union for Social Democracy (UPADS), led by Pascal Lissouba, won multi-party elections in 1992. However, in 1997, Sassou-Nguesso, assisted by his personal militia and also by troops from Angola, launched an uprising which overthrew Lissouba, who fled the country, taking refuge in Burkina Faso. But forces loyal to Lissouba fought back, starting a civil war. Ceasefires were agreed in 1999 and, in 2002, Sassou-Nguesso was elected president, winning 89% of the vote. A peace accord was signed in 2003.

ECONOMY

The World Bank classifies Congo as a "lower-middle-income" developing country. Agriculture is the most important activity, employing about 60% of the workforce. But many farmers function merely at a subsistence level. The chief food crops include bananas, cassava, corn, plantains, rice, and yams, while the leading cash crops include cocoa, coffee, and sugar cane.

Congo's main exports are oil (which makes up 90% of the total) and timber. Manufacturing is relatively unimportant at the moment, hampered as it is by poor transport links. Inland, rivers form the main lines of communication, and Brazzaville is linked to the port of Pointe-Noire by the Congo-Ocean Railway.

Pygmy chimpanzees, Brazzaville; *also known as bonobos, these chimpanzees are said to be man's closest relative and are unique to the Congo Basin; they are now an endangered species and it is feared that they will be hunted to extinction*

Congo (Democratic Republic of)

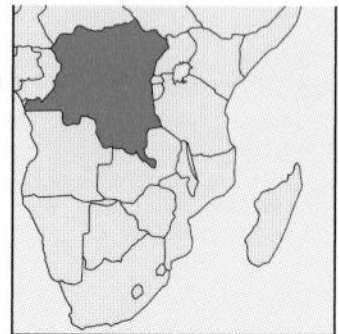

The Democratic Republic of the Congo adopted a new flag in 1997 after Laurent Kabila rose to power. The blue represents the UN's role in securing independence for the country, and the six small stars represent the original provinces of the independent state.

Democratic Republic of Congo is Africa's third-largest country. It is dominated by the River Congo. Northcentral Congo consists of a high plateau. In the east, the plateau rises to 16,762 ft [5,109 m] in the Ruwenzori mountains. Lakes Albert and Edward form much of Congo's border with Uganda. Lake Kivu lies along its border with Rwanda. Lake Tanganyika forms the border with Tanzania. All the lakes lie in an arm of the Great Rift Valley. Dense equatorial rainforests grow in the north, with savanna and swamps in the south.

CLIMATE

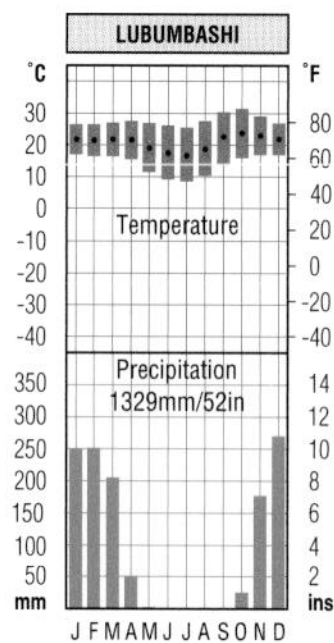

Much of Congo has an equatorial climate with high temperatures and heavy rainfall throughout the year. The south has a more subtropical climate.

HISTORY

From the 14th century, large Bantu kingdoms emerged. In 1482, a Portuguese navigator became the first European to reach the mouth of the River Congo. In the 19th century, ivory and slave traders formed powerful states. Henry Morton Stanley's explorations from 1874–77 established the route of the Congo. In 1878, King Leopold II of Belgium employed Stanley to found colonies along the Congo. In 1885, Leopold established the Congo Free State. His empire grew, and concessionaires gained control of the lucrative rubber trade. In 1908, Belgium established direct control as the colony of Belgian Congo. European companies exploited African labor to develop copper and diamond mines.

POLITICS

In 1960, the Republic of the Congo gained independence and Patrice Lumumba became prime minister. Joseph Mobutu, commander in chief of the Congolese National Army, seized power later that year. Lumumba was imprisoned and later murdered. In 1964, Belgian Congo plunged into civil war and Belgian troops intervened. In 1965, Mobutu proclaimed himself president and began a campaign of "Africanization:" Leopoldville became Kinshasa in 1966; the country and river renamed Zaïre in 1971; Katanga became Shaba in 1972; and Mobutu adopted the name Mobutu Sese Seko. Zaïre became a one-party state. Mobutu was reelected unopposed in 1974 and 1977, finally accepting opposition parties in 1990, though elections were repeatedly deferred. In 1995, millions of Hutus fled from Rwanda into east Zaïre, to escape possible Tutsi reprisals. In 1996 rebels, led by Laurent Kabila, overthrew Mobuto. Zaïre became the Democratic Republic of Congo. In 1998, Congo descended into civil war between government forces, and Tutsi-dominated Congolese Rally for Democracy (RCD). The Lusaka Peace Agreement (1999) brought a ceasefire and 5,500 UN peacekeeping troops, but fighting continued. By 2001 the civil war had claimed more than 2.5 million lives. In 2001, Kabila was assassinated. He was succeeded by his son Joseph Kabila who, under a peace agreement, was installed as interim president of a transitional government in 2003. Unrest continued into 2005 with large swathes of the country still beyond the control of the government.

ECONOMY

Congo is a low-income developing country. It is the world's leading producer of cobalt and the second-largest producer of diamonds. Agriculture employs 71% of the workforce, mainly at subsistence level. Palm oil is the most vital cash crop.

KINSHASA

Capital of Democratic Republic of Congo, Kinshasa is a port on the River Congo and is located directly opposite Brazzaville, the capital of Republic of Congo. Founded in 1881, it replaced Boma as the capital of the Belgian Congo in 1923. Its name was changed in 1966.The city's population is greater than that of the rest of the country put together. It is known for its vibrancy and for being an important center for music. Industries include tanning, chemicals, brewing, and textiles.

Area 905,350 sq mi [2,344,858 sq km]
Population 58,318,000
Capital (population) Kinshasa (4,665,000)
Government Single-party republic
Ethnic groups Over 200; the largest are Mongo, Luba, Kongo, Mangbetu-Azande
Languages French (official), tribal languages
Religions Roman Catholic 50%, Protestant 20%, Islam 10%, others
Currency Congolese franc = 100 centimes
Website www.monuc.org

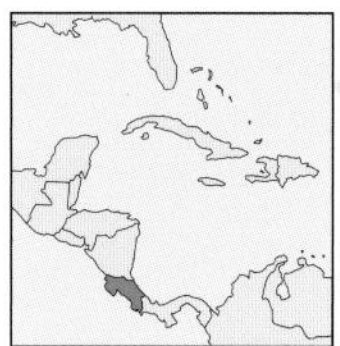

Costa Rica's flag is based on the blue-white-blue pattern of the Central American Federation (1823–39). This Federation consisted of Costa Rica, El Salvador, Guatemala, Honduras and Nicaragua. The red stripe, which was adopted in 1848, reflects the colors of France.

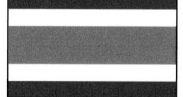

The Republic of Costa Rica in Central America is bordered by Nicaragua to the north and Panama to the south. It has coastlines on both the Pacific Ocean and on the Caribbean Sea. Central Costa Rica consists of mountain ranges and plateaux with many volcanoes. The Meseta Central, where the capital, San José is situated, and the Valle del General in the southeast, have rich, volcanic soils and are the most thickly populated parts of Costa Rica.

The highlands descend to the Caribbean lowlands and the Pacific Coast region, with its low mountain ranges. San José stands at about 1,170 m [3,840 ft] above sea level.

Evergreen forests cover around 50% of Costa Rica. Oaks grow in the highlands, palm trees along the Caribbean coast and mangrove swamps are common on the Pacific coast.

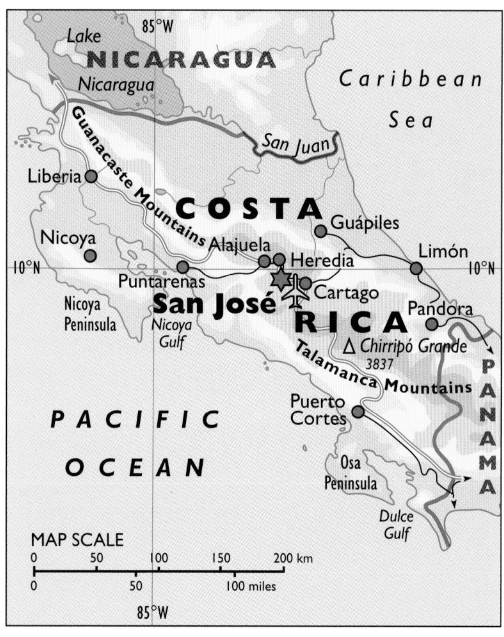

CLIMATE

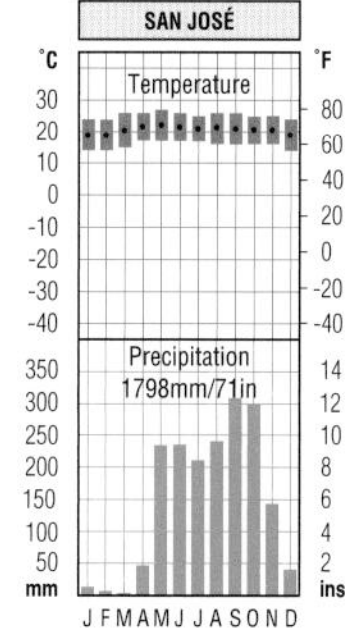

The Meseta Central benefits from a pleasant climate and an average annual temperature of 20°C [68° F], compared with more than 27°C [81° F] on the coast. The coolest months are December and January. The northeast trade winds bring heavy rain to the Caribbean coast. There is only half as much rainfall in the the highlands and on the Pacific coastlands as occurs on the Caribbean coast.

HISTORY

Christopher Columbus reached the Caribbean coast in 1502 and named the land Costa Rica, Spanish for "rich coast." Rumors of treasure attracted many Spaniards to settle in the country from 1561.

Spain ruled the country until 1821, when Spain's Central American colonies broke away to join the Mexican empire in 1822. In 1823, the Central American states broke with Mexico and set up the Central American Federation, the members being Costa Rica, Guatemala, Honduras, Nicaragua, and El Salvador. Later, this large union broke up and Costa Rica became fully independent in 1838. From the late 19th century, Costa Rica experienced a number of revolutions, with both periods of dictatorship and democracy. In 1917–19 General Tinoco formed a dictatorship then in 1948, following a revolt, the armed forces were abolished.

SAN JOSÉ

Capital and largest city of Costa Rica, in central Costa Rica, capital of San José province. Founded around 1736, it succeeded Cartago as capital in 1823, and soon became the center of a prosperous coffee trade. Products include coffee, sugar cane, cacao, vegetables, fruit, tobacco.

Area 19,730 sq mi [51,100 sq km]
Population 3,957,000
Capital (population) San José (337,000)
Government Multiparty republic
Ethnic groups White (including Mestizo) 94%, Black 3%, Amerindian 1%, Chinese 1%, others
Languages Spanish (official), English
Religions Roman Catholic 76%, Evangelical 14%
Currency Costa Rican colón = 100 céntimos
Website www.visitcostarica.com

POLITICS

Jose Figueres Ferrer served as president from 1953 to 1958 and again from 1970 to 1974. In 1987 President Oscar Arias Sanchez was awarded the Nobel Peace Prize for his efforts to end the civil wars in Central America.

In 2002 Abel Pancho won the presidential elections. Costa Rica's image was tarnished in 2004 when three former presidents were imprisoned on charges of corruption. Despite this, Costa Rica is seen as an example of political stability in the region and continues to maintain this without having to resort to armed forces.

ECONOMY

Costa Rica is classified by the World Bank as a "lower-middle-income" developing country. It is one of the most prosperous countries in Central America. There are high educational standards, and a high average life expectancy of 78 years.

Agriculture employs 24% of the workforce. Major crops include coffee, pineapples, bananas, and sugar. Other crops include beans, citrus fruits, cocoa, potatoes, rice, and corn. Cattle ranching is important.

The country's resources include its forests, but it lacks minerals apart from some bauxite and manganese. Manufacturing is increasing with electronics to the fore. It also has hydropower.

Tourism is a fast-growing industry with ecotourism gaining in importance. The United States is Costa Rica's chief trading partner.

Mountain village of Zarcero, *Alajuela in Central Valley, famed for the multiformed topiary of its main square*

Croatia

Croatia adopted a red, white, and blue flag in 1848. Under Communist rule, a red star appeared at the center. In 1990, the red star was replaced by the present coat of arms, which symbolizes the various parts of the country.

Area 21,829 sq mi [56,538 sq km]
Population 4,497,000
Capital (population) Zagreb (779,000)
Government Multiparty republic
Ethnic groups Croat 90%, Serb 5%, others
Languages Croatian 96%
Religions Roman Catholic 88%, Orthodox 4%, Islam 1%, others
Currency Kuna = 100 lipas
Website www.vlada.hr/default.asp?ru=2

The Republic of Croatia was part of Yugoslavia until becoming independent in 1991. The region bordering the Adriatic Sea is called Dalmatia. It includes the coastal ranges, which contain large areas of bare limestone, reaching 6,276 ft [1,913 m] at Mount Troglav. Other highlands lie in the northeast. Most of the rest of the country consists of the fertile Pannonian Plains, which are drained by Croatia's two main rivers, the Drava and the Sava.

CLIMATE

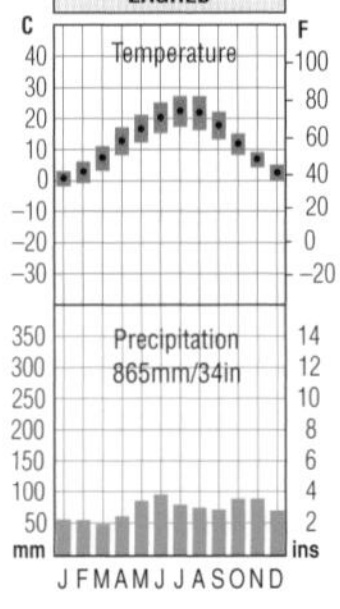

The coastal area has a climate akin to that of the Mediterranean, with hot, dry summers and mild, moist winters. Inland, the climate becomes more continental. Winters are cold, while temperatures often soar to 100°F [38°C] in the summer months.

HISTORY

Slav people settled in the area around 1,400 years ago. In 803, Croatia became part of the Holy Roman Empire. In 1102, the king of Hungary also became king of Croatia, creating a union that lasted 800 years. In 1526, much of Croatia and Hungary came under the Ottoman Turks. At about the same time, the Austrian Habsburgs gained control of the rest of Croatia. In 1699, the Habsburgs drove out the Turks and Croatia again came under Hungarian rule. In 1809, Croatia became part of the Illyrian provinces of Napoleon I of France, but the Habsburgs took over in 1815.

In 1867, Croatia became part of the dual monarchy of Austria-Hungary and in 1868 Croatia signed an agreement with Hungary guaranteeing Croatia some of its historic rights. During World War I, Austria-Hungary fought on the side of the defeated Axis powers, and, in 1918, the empire was broken up. Croatia declared its independence and joined with neighboring states to form the Kingdom of the Serbs, Croats and Slovenes. Serbian domination provoked Croatian opposition. In 1929, the king changed the country's name to Yugoslavia and began to rule as a dictator. He was assassinated in 1934 by a Bulgarian employed by a Croatian terrorist group, provoking more hostility between Croats and Serbs.

Germany occupied Croatia in World War II. After the war, Communists took power in Yugoslavia, with Josip Broz Tito as its leader. After Tito's death in 1980, economic and ethnic rivalries threatened stability. In the early 1990s, Yugoslavia split into five nations. One of them, Croatia, declared itself independent in 1991.

POLITICS

After Serbia supplied arms to Serbs living in Croatia, war broke out between the two republics, causing great damage, large-scale movements of refugees and disruption of the economy, including the vital tourist industry.

In 1992, the United Nations sent a peacekeeping force to Croatia, effectively ending the war with Serbia. However, in 1992, war broke out in Bosnia-Herzegovina and Bosnian Croats occupied parts of the country. In 1994, Croatia helped to end the Croat-Muslim conflict in Bosnia-Herzegovina and, in 1995, after retaking some areas occupied by Serbs, it contributed to the drawing up of the Dayton Peace Accord, which ended the civil war.

Croatia's arch-nationalist president, Franco Tudjman, died in December 1999. In January 2000, Tudjman's Croatian Democratic Union was defeated in a general election by a more liberal, westward-leaning alliance of Social Democrats and Social Liberals. Stipe Mesic, the last head of state of the former Yugoslavia before it disintegrated in 1991, was elected president. In 2000, the government announced that it would prosecute suspected war criminals and cooperate with the war crimes tribunal in The Hague.

ECONOMY

The wars of the early 1990s disrupted Croatia's economy. Tourism on the Dalmatian coast had been a major industry and is making a gradual return. The manufacturing industries provide the chief exports. Manufactures include cement, chemicals, refined oil and oil products, ships, steel, and wood products.

Agriculture is important and major farm products include fruits, livestock, corn, soybeans, sugar beets, and wheat.

Dubrovnik harbor and old city; *built in the 13th century, the town remains unspoilt*

ZAGREB

Capital of Croatia, on the River Sava. Founded in the 11th century, it became capital of the Hungarian province of Croatia and Slavonia during the 14th century. The city was an important center of the 19th-century Croatian nationalist movement. In 1918 it was the meeting place of the Croatian Diet (parliament), which severed all ties with Austria-Hungary. In World War II, Zagreb was the capital of the Axis-controlled, puppet Croatian state. It was wrested from Axis control in 1945, and became capital of the Croatian Republic of Yugoslavia. Following the breakup of Yugoslavia in 1992, Zagreb remained capital of the newly independent state of Croatia. The city has many places of historical interest, including a Gothic cathedral and a Baroque archiepiscopal palace. Zagreb has a university (founded 1669) and an Academy of Arts and Sciences (1861).

Cuba's flag, the "Lone Star" banner, was designed in 1849, but it was not adopted as the national flag until 1901, after Spain had withdrawn from the country. The red triangle represents the Cuban people's bloody struggle for independence.

The Republic of Cuba is the largest island country in the Caribbean Sea. It consists of one large island, Cuba, the Isle ofYouth (Isla de la Juventud) and about 1,600 small islets. Mountains and hills cover about a quarter of Cuba. The highest mountain range, the Sierra Maestra in the southeast, reaches 6,562 ft [2,000 m] above sea level at the Pico Real del Turquino. The rest of the land consists of gently rolling country or coastal plains, crossed by fertile valleys that have been carved by the short, mostly shallow and narrow rivers.

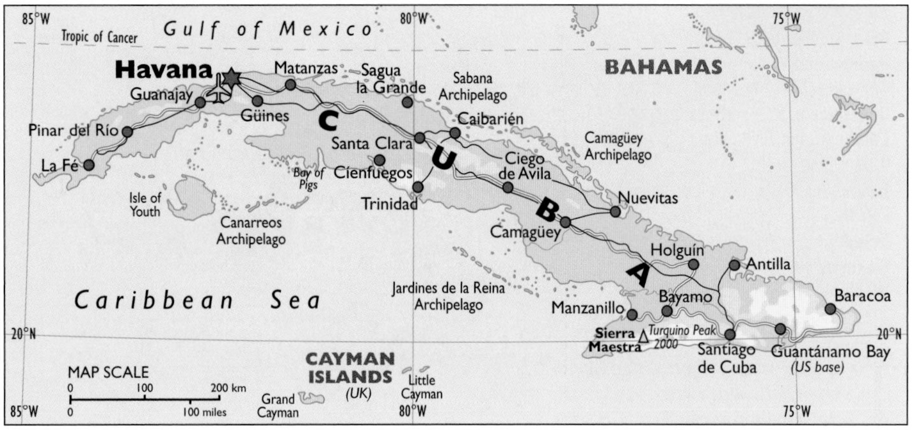

Farmland covers about half of Cuba amnd 66% of this is given over to sugar cane. Pine forests still grow, especially in the south east. Mangrove swamps line some coastal areas.

CLIMATE

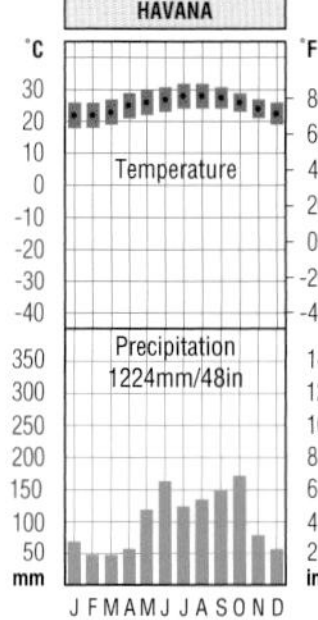

Cuba lies in the tropics, but sea breezes moderate the temperature, warming the land in winter and cooling it in summer.

HISTORY

In 1492 Christopher Columbus discovered the island and Spaniards began to settle there from 1511. Spanish rule ended in 1898, when the United States defeated Spain in the Spanish-American War. The United States ruled Cuba from 1898 until 1902, when the people elected Tomás Estrada Palma as president of the independent Republic of Cuba, though American influence remained strong. In 1933, an army sergeant named Fulgencio Batista seized power and ruled as dictator. However, under a new constitution, he was elected president in 1940, serving until 1944. He again seized power in 1952 and became dictator once more, but, on January 1, 1959, he fled Cuba following the overthrow of his regime by a revolutionary force led by a young lawyer, Fidel Castro. Many Cubans who were opposed to Castro left the country, settling in the United States.

POLITICS

The United States opposed Castro's policies, so he turned to the Soviet Union for assistance. In 1962, the US learned that nuclear missile bases armed by the Soviet Union had been established in Cuba. The US ordered the Soviet Union to remove the missiles and bases. After a few days, during which many people feared that a world war might break out, the Soviet Union agreed to American demands.

Cuba's relations with the Soviet Union remained strong until 1991, when the Soviet Union was broken up. The loss of Soviet aid greatly damaged Cuba's economy and the new situation undermined Castro's considerable social achievements. However, in February 1993, elections showed a high level of support for his left-wing policies. In 1998, hopes of a thaw in relations with the United States were raised when the US government announced that it was lifting the ban on flights to Cuba. The Pope, making his first visit to Cuba, criticized the "unjust and ethically unacceptable" US blockade on Cuba. In 2000, the United States lifted its food embargo on Cuba. The last Russian base in Cuba closed in 2002. In 2004, following a United States crackdown on currency and travel, Cuba declared that US dollars would no longer be accepted as payments for goods and services.

HAVANA (LA HABANA)

Capital of Cuba, on the north west coast. It is the largest city and port in the West Indies. Havana was founded by the Spanish explorer Diego Velázquez in 1515, and moved to its present site in 1519. It became Cuba's capital at the end of the 16th century. Industries include oil refining, textiles, sugar, and cigars.

Area 42,803 sq mi [110,861 sq km]
Population 11,309,000
Capital (population) Havana (2,192,000)
Government Socialist republic
Ethnic groups Mulatto 51%, White 37%, Black 11%
Languages Spanish (official)
Religions Christianity
Currency Cuban peso = 100 centavos
Website www.cubagob.gov.cu/ingles/

ECONOMY

The World Bank classifies Cuba as a "lower-middle-income" country. Sugar cane remains Cuba's outstandingly important cash crop, accounting for more than 60% of the country's exports. It is grown on more than half of the island's cultivated land and Cuba is one of the world's top ten producers of the product. Before 1959, the sugar cane was grown on large estates, many of them owned by US companies. Following the revolution, they were nationalized and the Soviet Union and Eastern European countries replaced the United States as the main market. The other main crop is tobacco, which is grown in the northwest. Cattle raising, milk production, and rice cultivation have also been encouraged to help diversify the economy, and the Castro regime has devoted considerable efforts to improving the quality of rural life, making standards of living more homogeneous throughout the island.

Minerals and concentrates rank second to sugar among Cuba's exports, followed by fish products, tobacco, and tobacco products, including the famous cigars, and citrus fruits. In the 1990s, Cuba sought to increase its trade with Latin America and China. Tourism is a major source of income, but the industry was badly hit following the terrorist attacks on the United States in 2001.

***Vintage cars** line the street near the Capitol building, Havana*

Cyprus

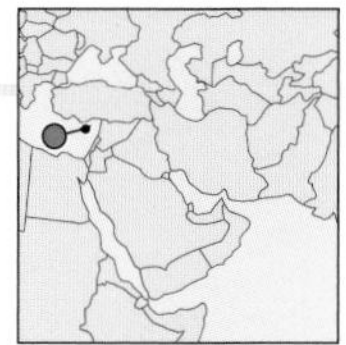

This flag became the official flag when the country became independent from Britain in 1960. It shows an outline map of the island, with two olive branches. Since Cyprus was divided, the separate communities have flown the Greek and Turkish flags.

Area 3,572 sq mi [9,251 sq km]
Population 776,000
Capital (population) Nicosia (198,000)
Government Multiparty republic
Ethnic groups Greek Cypriot 77%, Turkish Cypriot 18%, others
Languages Greek and Turkish (both official), English
Religions Greek Orthodox 78%, Islam 8%
Currency Cypriot pound = 100 cents
Website www.cyprus.gov.cy

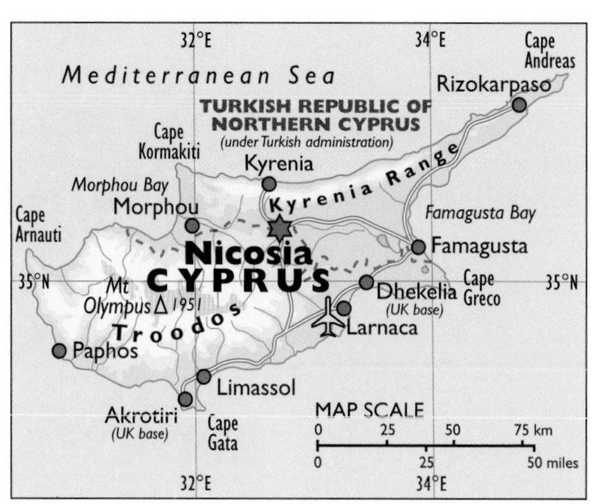

The Republic of Cyprus is an island nation which lies in the northeastern Mediterranean Sea. Geographers regard it as part of Asia, but it resembles southern Europe in many ways. Cyprus has scenic mountain ranges, including the Kyrenia Range in the north and the Troodos Mountains in the south, which rise to 6,401 ft [1,951 m] at Mount Olympus.

The island also contains fertile lowlands used extensively for agriculture, including the broad Mesaoria Plain. Pine forests grow on the mountain slopes.

CLIMATE

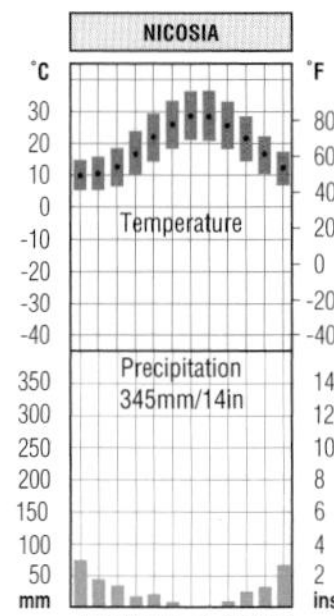

Cyprus experiences hot, dry summers and mild, wet winters. Summers are hotter than those farther west in the Mediterranean as Cyprus lies close to the hot mainland of southwestern Asia.

HISTORY

The history of Cyprus dates back to 7000 BC. Greeks settled on Cyprus around 3,200 years ago. By 1050 BC Cyprus was fully established as a Greek island having embraced the language and culture of Greece. In 333 BC it became part of the empire of Alexander the Great and in 58 BC part of the Roman Empire. From AD 330, the island was under the Byzantine empire.

Cyprus was defeated in 1191 by Richard the Lionheart and the island was sold to the Knights Templar. Catholicism became the official religion. The island was under Venetian control from 1489 and fortifications were added to the towns of Nicosia and Famagusta. In the 1570s, it became part of the Turkish Ottoman Empire and Islam was introduced.

Turkish rule continued until 1878 when Cyprus was leased to Britain although it was still part of the Ottoman Empire. When the Ottomans entered World War I in 1914, on the side of Germany, the island was annexed by Britain. It was proclaimed a Crown colony in 1925.

In the 1950s, Greek Cypriots, who made up four-fifths of the population, led by Greek Orthodox Archbishop Makarios, began a campaign for enosis (union) with Greece. A secret guerrilla force called EOKA attacked the British who exiled Makarios.

POLITICS

Cyprus became an independent country in 1960 with Makarios as president. Britain retained two military bases. The constitution of Cyprus provided for power-sharing between the Greek and Turkish Cypriots. But the constitution proved unworkable and fighting broke out. In 1964 the UN sent in a peace-keeping force.

In 1974, Cypriot forces led by Greek officers overthrew Makarios. This led Turkey to invade northern Cyprus, a territory occupying about 40% of the island. Many Greek Cypriots fled from the north, which, in 1983, was proclaimed an independent state called the Turkish Republic of Northern Cyprus. However, the only country to recognize its status was Turkey. The UN regards Cyprus as a single nation under the Greek-Cypriot government in the south. It is estimated that more than 30,000 Turkish troops are deployed in northern Cyprus. Despite UN-brokered peace negotiations, there are still frequent border clashes between the two communities.

In 2002, the European Union invited Cyprus to become a member. In April 2004, the people voted on a UN plan to reunify the island. The Turkish Cypriots voted in favor of the plan, but the Greek Cypriots voted against. As a result of this, only the south was admitted to membership of the EU on 1 May 2004.

ECONOMY

Cyprus got its name from the Greek word kypros, meaning copper, but little copper remains. The chief minerals are asbestos and chromium. The most valuable activity in Cyprus is tourism.

Industry employs 37% of the workforce and manufactures include cement, clothes, footwear, tiles, and wine. In the early 1990s, the United Nations reclassified Cyprus as a developed rather than developing country, though the economy of the Turkish-Cypriot north lags behind that of the more prosperous Greek-Cypriot south.

Interior of Asinou Church, *Troodos Region; the church is filled with frescoes from the 12th century and is one of the 10 monuments in the area to be listed as a UNESCO World Heritage Site*

NICOSIA (LEVKOSÍA)

Capital of Cyprus, in the center of the island. Known to the ancients as Ledra, the city was later held by Byzantines, French crusaders and Venetians. The Ottoman Turks occupied the city from 1571 to 1878, when it passed to Britain. It is now divided into Greek and Turkish sectors by a UN-maintained "Green Line" and is the only divided city in Europe. Industries include cigarettes, textiles, and footwear.

After independence, on January 1, 1993, the Czech Republic adopted the former flag of Czechoslovakia. It features the red and white of Bohemia in the west, together with the blue of Moravia and Slovakia. Red, white, and blue are the colors of Pan-Slavic liberation.

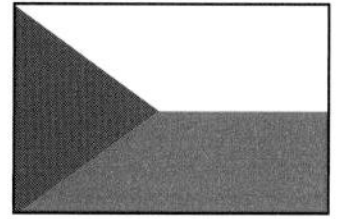

Area 78,866 sq mi [30,450 sq km]
Population 10,246,000
Capital (population) Prague (1,193,000)
Government Multiparty republic
Ethnic groups Czech 81%, Moravian 13%, Slovak 3%, Polish, German, Silesian, Gypsy, Hungarian, Ukrainian
Languages Czech (official)
Religions Atheist 40%, Roman Catholic 39%, Protestant 4%, Orthodox 3%, others
Currency Czech koruna = 100 haler
Website www.czech.cz

The Czech Republic is the western three-fifths of the former country of Czechoslovakia. It contains two regions: Bohemia in the west and Moravia in the east. Mountains border much of the country in the west. The Bohemian basin in the north-center is a fertile lowland region, with Prague, the capital city, as its main center. Highlands cover much of the center of the country, with lowlands in the southeast. Some rivers, such as the Elbe (Labe) and Oder (Odra) flow north into Germany and Poland. In the south, rivers flow into the Danube Basin.

CLIMATE

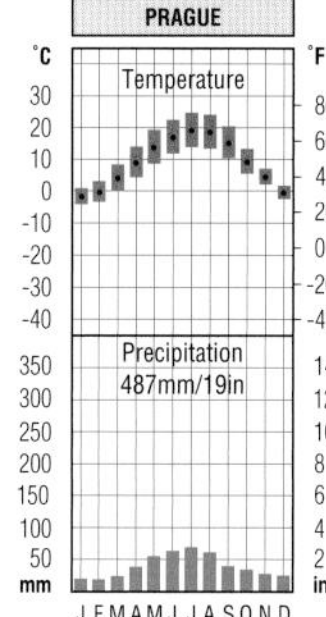

The climate of the Czech Republic is influenced by its landlocked position in east-central Europe. The country experiences a humid continental climate, with warm summers and cold winters. The average rainfall is moderate, with 20 in to 30 in (500 mm–750 mm) annually in lowland areas.

HISTORY

The ancestors of the Czech people began to settle in what is now the Czech Republic around 1,500 years ago. Bohemia, in the west, became important in the 10th century as a kingdom within the Holy Roman Empire. By the 14th century, Prague was one of Europe's major cultural cities. Religious wars in the first half of the 15th century led many Czech people to become Protestants. From 1526, the Roman Catholic Habsburgs from Austria began to rule the area, but, in 1618, a Czech Protestant rebellion started the Thirty Years' War. From 1620, most Czechs were made to convert to Catholicism and adopt German as their language.

Czech nationalism grew throughout the 19th century. During World War I, Czech nationalists advocated the creation of an independent nation. At the end of the war, when Austria-Hungary collapsed, the new republic of Czechoslovakia was founded. The 1920s and 1930s were generally a period of stability and economic progress, but problems arose concerning the country's minority groups. Many Slovaks wanted a greater degree of self-government, while Germans living in Sudetenland, in western Czechoslovakia, were unhappy under Czech rule.

In 1938, Sudetenland was turned over to Germany and, in March 1939, Germany occupied the rest of the country. By 1945, following the Nazi defeat, a coalition government, including Czech Communists, was formed to rule the country. In 1948, Communist leaders seized control and made the country an ally of the Soviet Union in the Cold War. In 1968, the Communist government introduced reforms, which were known as the "Prague spring." However, Russian and other East European troops invaded and suppressed the reform group.

POLITICS

When democratic reforms were introduced in the Soviet Union in the 1980s, the Czechs also demanded change. In 1989, the Federal Assembly elected Václav Havel, a noted playwright and dissident, as the country's president and, in 1990, free elections were held. The smooth transition from Communism to democracy was called the "Velvet Revolution." The road to a free-market economy was not easy, with resulting inflation, falling production, strikes, and unemployment, though tourism has partly made up for some of the economic decline. Political problems also arose when Slovaks began to demand independence. On January 1, 1993, the more statist Slovakia broke away from the free-market Czech Republic. However, the split was generally amicable and border adjustments were negligible. The Czechs and Slovaks maintained a customs union and other economic ties. Meanwhile the Czech government continued to develop ties with Western Europe when it became a member of NATO in 1992. On May 1, 2004 the Czech Republic became a member of the European Union.

ECONOMY

Under Communist rule the Czech Republic became one of the most industrialized parts of Eastern Europe. The country has deposits of coal, uranium, iron ore, magnesite, tin, and zinc. Manufactures include such products as chemicals, iron, steel, and machinery, but the country also has light industries making such things as glassware and textiles for export. Manufacturing employs about 40% of the Czech Republic's entire workforce.

Farming is important. The main crops include barley, fruit, hops for beer-making, corn, potatoes, sugar beets, vegetables, and wheat. Cattle and other livestock are raised. The country was admitted into the Organization for Economic Co-operation and Development (OECD) in 1995.

PRAGUE (PRAHA)

Capital of the Czech Republic, on the River Vltava. Founded in the 9th century, it grew rapidly after Wenceslaus I established a German settlement in 1232. In the 14th century it was the capital of Bohemia. It was the capital of the Czechoslovak Republic (1918–93). Occupied in World War II by the Germans it was liberated by Soviet troops in 1945. Prague was the center of Czech resistance to the Soviet invasion of 1968. Sights include Hradcany Castle and Charles Bridge. An important commercial center, industries include engineering, iron, and steel.

Stare Mesto, Prague; *the beautiful Old Town dates back to the 13th century*

Denmark

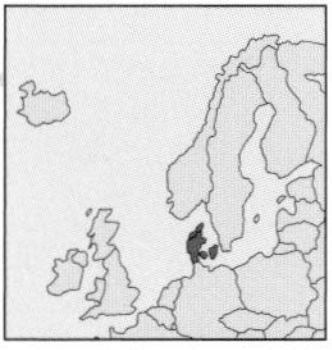

Denmark's flag is called the Dannebrog, or "the spirit of Denmark." It may be the oldest national flag in continuous use. It represents a vision thought to have been seen by the Danish King Waldemar II before the Battle of Lyndanisse, which took place in Estonia in 1219.

Area 16,639 sq mi [43,094 sq km]
Population 5,413,000
Capital (population) Copenhagen (488,000)
Government Parliamentary monarchy
Ethnic groups Scandinavian, Inuit, Faeroese, German
Languages Danish (official), English, Faerose
Religions Evangelical Lutheran 95%
Currency Danish krone = 100 øre
Website http://denmark.dk

The Kingdom of Denmark is the smallest country in Scandinavia. It consists of a peninsula called Jutland (Jylland), which is joined to Germany, and more than 400 islands, 89 of which are inhabited. The land is flat and mostly covered by rocks dropped there by huge ice sheets during the last Ice Age. The highest point in Denmark is on Jutland and is only 568 ft [173 m].

CLIMATE

Denmark has a cool but pleasant climate. During cold spells in the winter The Sound between Sjælland and Sweden may freeze over. Summers are warm. Rainfall occurs throughout the year.

HISTORY

Danish Vikings terrorized much of Western Europe for about 300 years after AD 800. Danish kings ruled England in the 11th century. Control of the entrances to the Baltic Sea contributed to the power of Denmark in the Middle Ages, when the kingdom dominated its neighbors and expanded its territories to include Norway, Iceland, Greenland, and the Faroe Islands. The link with Norway was broken in 1814, and with Iceland in 1944, but Greenland and the Faroes retained connections with Denmark. The granite island of Bornholm, off the southern tip of Sweden, also remains a Danish possession. This island was occupied by Germany in World War II, but it was liberated by the Soviet Union and returned to Denmark in 1946. Denmark was also occupied by Germany in 1940, but it was liberated in 1945. The Danes then set about rebuilding their industries and restoring their economy.

POLITICS

Denmark is a generally comfortable mixture of striking political opposites. The Lutheran tradition and the cradle of Hans Christian Andersen's fairy tales coexist with open attitudes to pornography and one of the highest illegitimacy rates in the West.

The country is one of the "greenest" of the developed nations, with a pioneering Ministry of Pollution. In 1991, it became the first government anywhere to fine industries for emissions of carbon dioxide, the primary "greenhouse" gas.

It joined the North Atlantic Treaty Organization (NATO) in 1949, and in 1973 it joined the European Community (now the European Union). However, it remains one of the European Union's least enthusiastic members and was one of the four countries that did not adopt the euro, the single EU currency, on January 1, 2002. In 1972, in order to join the EC, Denmark had become the first Scandinavian country to break away from the other major economic grouping in Europe, the European Free Trade Association (EFTA), but it continued to cooperate with its five Scandinavian partners through the consultative Nordic Council which was set up in 1953.

The Danes enjoy some of the world's highest living standards, although the cost of welfare provisions was high. The election of a Liberal-Conservative coalition in 2001 led to cutbacks. Under Prime Minister Anders Fogh Rasmussen, who won a second term in 2005, the government also tightened immigration controls, causing criticism by the UN High Commissioner for Refugees.

Denmark granted home rule to the Faeroe Islands in 1948, although in 1998, the government of the Faeroes announced plans for independence. In 1979, home rule was also granted to Greenland, which demonstrated its new-found independence by withdrawing from the European Community in 1985. Denmark is a constitutional monarchy, with a hereditary monarch, and its constitution was amended in 1953 to allow female succession to the throne.

ECONOMY

Denmark has few mineral resources, though there is now some oil and natural gas from the North Sea. It is one of Europe's wealthiest industrial nations. Farming employs only 4% of workers, but it is highly scientific and productive with dairy farming and pig and poultry breeding chief areas.

From a firm agricultural base, Denmark has developed a wide range of industries. Some, including brewing, meat canning, fish processing, pottery, textiles, and furniture making, use Danish products, but others, such as shipbuilding, oil refining, engineering and metal-working, depend on imported raw materials. Copenhagen is the chief industrial center and draws more than a million tourists each year. At the other end of the scale is Legoland, the famous miniature town of plastic bricks, built at Billand, northwest of Vejle in eastern Jutland. It was here that Lego was created before it became the world's best-selling construction toy and a prominent Danish export.

COPENHAGEN (KØBENHAVN)

Capital and chief port of Denmark on east Sjaelland and north Amager Island, in the Øresund. A trading and fishing center by the early 12th century, it became Denmark's capital in 1443. It has a 17th-century stock exchange, the Amalienborg Palace (home of the royal family) and the Christianborgs Palace. Other sights include the Tivoli Amusement Park and the Little Mermaid sculpture. The commercial and cultural center of the nation, it has shipbuilding, chemical, and brewing industries.

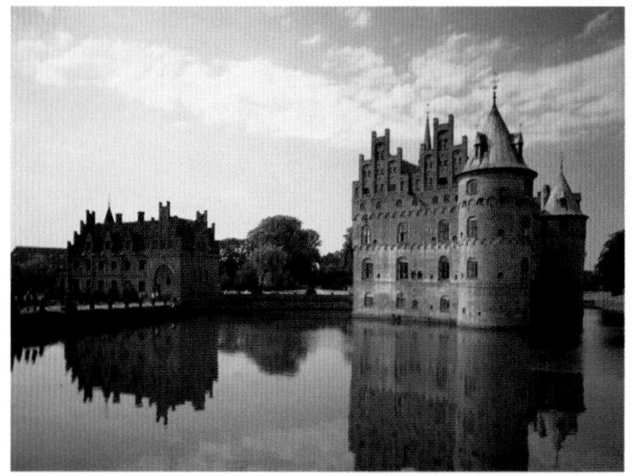

Egeskor Castle, *Fuenen*

FAEROE ISLANDS

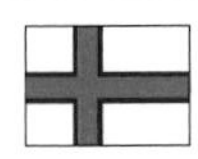
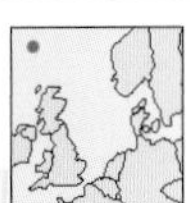

Area 545.3 sq mi [1,399 sq km]
Population 46,962
Capital (population) Torshavn (17,939)
Government Self-governing overseas administrative division of Denmark
Ethnic groups Scandinavian
Languages Faroese, Danish
Religions Evangelical Lutheran
Currency Danish krone = 100 ore
Website www.visit-faroeislands.com

The Faeroe (or Faroe) Islands are an autonomous region of Denmark. Situated in the North Atlantic Ocean between Iceland and the Shetland Islands, the region consists of 18 islands, 17 of which are inhabited. The main islands are Streymoy, on which the capital Tórshavn stands, Vágar, Suduroy, and Sandoy. The islands have rugged coasts with abundant birdlife. Most people live on the small coastal lowlands.

CLIMATE Winters are mild under the influence of the North Atlantic Drift, the extension of the warm Gulf Stream. Summers are cool and the weather is often overcast. Fogs are common and winds are often strong.

HISTORY Irish monks settled on the islands in the 6th century AD, though most of the islanders today are descendants of Vikings. The Faeroe Islands were part of the Kingdom of Norway from the 11th century until 1380. The islands came under Danish control when Norway joined the Kingdom of Denmark. British troops occupied the islands during World War II (1939–45), but they reverted to Danish control after the war.

POLITICS The Danes granted the islands self-government in 1948, making them a self-governing overseas administrative division of Denmark, with Denmark responsible for defence and foreign relations. The islands have their own parliament, consisting of 32 members elected on a proportional basis from the seven constituencies. The parliament elects the leader of the majority group as prime minister. Two members are elected to the Danish parliament.

In 2001, a planned referendum on independence was cancelled when the Danish government stated that it would cut off all financial aid to the islands within four years of independence.

TÓRSHAVN

Capital city in the center of the Faeroe Islands. In 800, Norwegian settlers replaced an Irish settlement on the islands. Tórshavn became the central meeting place. Christianity was introduced in about 1000. The isles came under Norwegian rule in 1035 and under Danish rule in 1816. Tórshavn became the seat of government in 1856. The Faeroese seafishing trade started in Tórshavn. Since 1974 the town has been joined with Kaldbak, Hoyvík, Argir and Kollafjørur.

ECONOMY The people enjoy a high standard of living. Fishing is the main activity and the country has benefited, since the 1990s, from increased production, together with high export prices. Faeroese fishermen have traditionally hunted pilot whales, but animal rights activists have called for the abandonment of the cull.

The government hopes to diversify the economy and explore the prospects of offshore oil and natural gas fields. The islands benefit from a Danish subsidy which accounts for 15% of the GDP. Tourism is also important, along with the production of wool.

GREENLAND

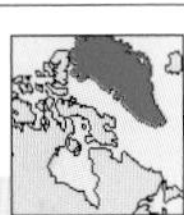

Area 836,330 sq mi [2,166,086 sq km]
Population 56,375
Capital (population) Nuuk (13,400)
Government Self-governing overseas administrative division of Denmark
Ethnic groups Greenlander 88% (Inuit and Greenland-born whites), Danish and others 12%
Languages Greenlandic (East Inuit), Danish, English
Religions Evangelical Lutheran
Currency Danish krone = 100 ore
Website http://dk.nanoq.gl

Situated in the northwest Atlantic Ocean and lying mostly within the Arctic Circle, Greenland is regarded by geographers as the world's largest island. It is almost three times larger than the second largest island, New Guinea.

An ice sheet, the world's second largest after Antarctica, covers more than 85% of its area with an average depth of 5,000 ft [1,500 m]. Settlement is confined to the rocky southwest coast.

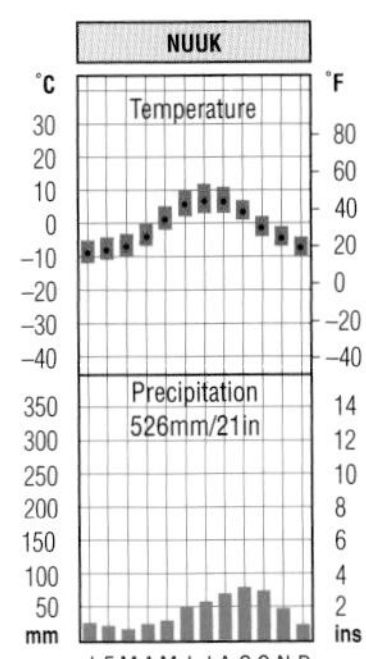

CLIMATE The southwest coast, where the capital Nuuk (Godthåb) is situated, is warmed by Atlantic currents, even so, it has more than seven months with average temperatures below freezing.

HISTORY European discovery of Greenland is credited to Erik the Red, who settled in 982, founding a colony that lasted more than 500 years. Greenland became a Danish possession in 1380 and an integral part of the Danish kingdom in 1953.

POLITICS It was taken into the EC in 1973, despite a majority of Greenlanders voting against this. In 1979, after another referendum, home rule was introduced, with full internal self-government in 1981. In 1985, Greenland withdrew from the EC, halving the Community's land area.

ECONOMY Greenland still relies heavily on Danish aid and Denmark is its main trading partner. The chief rural occupations are sheep-rearing and fishing, with shrimp, prawns, and mollusks being exported. The only major manufacturing industry is fish canning, which has drawn many Inuit to the towns. Few Inuit now follow the traditional life of nomadic hunting.

Most Greenlanders live between the primitive and the modern. Yet a nationalist mood prevails, buoyed by rich fish stocks, lead, and zinc from Uummannaq in the northwest, untapped uranium in the south, and possible oil in the east. In addition, an adventure-orientated tourist industry is expanding. In 1997, the nationalist resurgence led to Greenland making Inuit name forms official.

NUUK (DANISH, GODTHÅB)

Capital and largest town of Greenland, at the mouth of a group of fjords on the southwest coast. Founded in 1721, it is Greenland's oldest Danish settlement. Places of interest include the Greenlandic National Museum and Archives, the Katuaq Cultural Center (with the island's only cinema) and Niels Lynges' House.

Djibouti

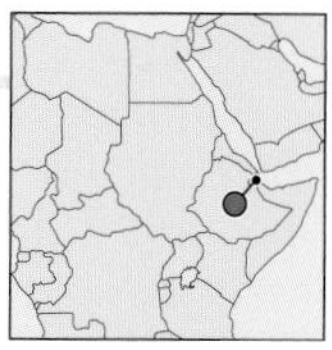

Based on the banner of the African People's League for Independence. Blue is the color of the Issas people and also the sky and the sea. Green is for the Afar people and symbolizes fertile earth. The white triangle signifies peace and equality, the red star is a symbol of unity.

Area 8,958 sq mi [23,200 sq km]
Population 467,000
Capital (population) Djibouti (317,000)
Government Multiparty republic
Ethnic groups Somali 60%, Afar 35%
Languages Arabic and French (both official)
Religions Islam 94%, Christianity 6%
Currency Djiboutian franc = 100 centimes
Website www.presidence.dj

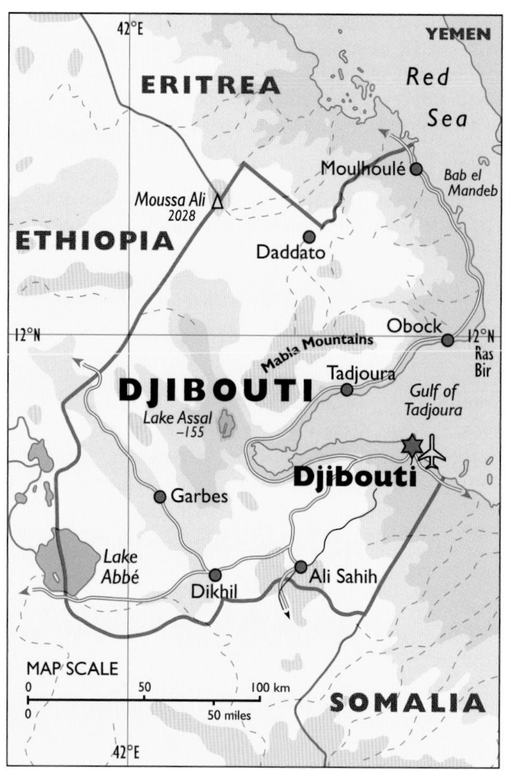

The Republic of Djibouti is a small country on the northeast coast of Africa, the capital is also Djibouti. Djibouti occupies a strategic position around the Gulf of Tadjoura, where the Red Sea meets the Gulf of Aden. Behind the coastal plain lie the Mabla Mountains, rising to Moussa Ali at 6,654 ft [2,028 m]. Djibouti contains the lowest point on the African continent, Lake Assal, at 509 ft [155 m] below sea level.

Nearly 90% of the land is semidesert, and shortage of pasture and water make farming difficult.

CLIMATE

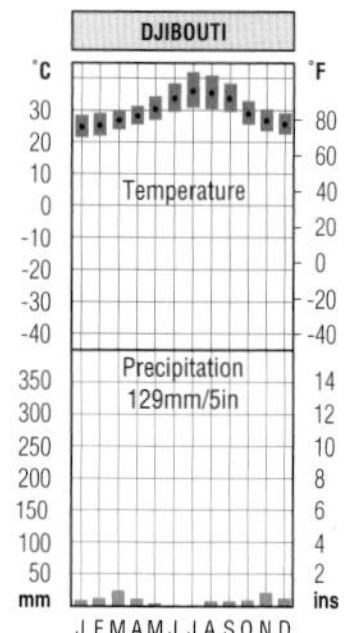

Djibouti has one of the world's hottest and driest climates with summer temperatures regularly exceeding 100°F [42°C]. Average annual rainfall is only 5 in [130 mm]. In the wooded Mabla Mountains, the average annual rainfall reaches 20 in [500 mm].

HISTORY

Islam arrived in the 9th century. The subsequent conversion of the Afars led to conflict with Christian Ethiopians who lived in the interior. By the 19th century, Somalian Issas moved north and occupied much of the Afars' traditional grazing land.

France gained influence in 1862, with its interest centered around Djibouti, the French commercial rival to the port of Aden. French Somaliland was established in 1888.

A referendum in 1967 saw 60% of the electorate vote to retain links with France, though most Issas favored independence. The country was renamed the French Territory of the Afars and Issas.

POLITICS

In 1977 the Republic of Djibouti gained full independence, and Hassan Gouled Aptidon of the Popular Rally for Progress (RPP) was elected president. He declared a one-party state in 1981. Protests against the Issas-dominated regime forced the adoption of a multi-party constitution in 1992. The Front for the Restoration of Unity and Democracy (FRUD), supported primarily by Afars, boycotted 1993 elections, and Aptidon was reelected for a fourth six-year term. FRUD rebels continued an armed campaign for political representation. In 1996, government and FRUD forces signed a peace agreement, recognizing FRUD as a political party.

In 1999, Ismael Omar Gelleh succeeded Aptidon as president in the country's first multiparty presidential elections. He pursues a policy of closer links with France, which still has a strong military presence in Djibouti. In addition it is forging closer ties with the United States, with the only US military base in sub-Saharan Africa stationed there.

ECONOMY

Djibouti is a poor nation, heavily reliant on food imports and revenue from the capital city. A free-trade zone, it has no major resources and manufacturing is on a very small scale. The only important activity is livestock raising, and 50% of the population are pastoral nomads.

Its location at the mouth of the Red Sea is of great economic importance as it serves as a vital transshipment point.

Travertine vents *on Lake Abbé in the southwest of Djibouti on the border with Ethiopia; the vents are formed by a calcium-rich flow from below the lake and they expel unpleasant sulfurous gases; the lake is heavily salted and therefore totally undrinkable*

DJIBOUTI (JIBUTI)

Capital of Djibouti, on the western shore of an isthmus in the Gulf of Tadjoura, northeast Africa. Founded in 1888, it became capital in 1892, and a free port in 1949. Ethiopian emperor Menelik II built a railway from Addis Ababa, and Djibouti became the chief port for handling Ethiopian trade. While Eritrea was federated with Ethiopia (1952–93), it lost this status to the Red Sea port of Assab. Now home to two-thirds of the country's population.

GULF OF ADEN

A body of water that makes up the western arm of the Arabian Sea, meeting the Red Sea at the Babu l-Mandeb strait. The gulf runs in a west–east direction, between Yemen and Somalia, meeting Djibouti at the western end. It is about 560 mi [900 km] long, and 500 km [310 mi] wide at the eastern end, between Ra's Asir of Somalia and the city of al-Mukalla in Yemen.The Gulf of Aden is an important route for commercial shipping.

RED SEA

Narrow arm of the Indian Ocean between northeast Africa and the Arabian Peninsula, connected to the Mediterranean by the Gulf of Suez and the Suez Canal. With the building of vessels too large for the canal and the construction of pipelines, the Red Sea's importance as a trade route has diminished. Its widest point is 200 mi [320 km]. It covers an area of 169,000 sq mi [438,000 sq km].

Blue represents liberty, red stands for blood shed during the struggle for liberation, and the white cross is a symbol of sacrifice. The coat of arms features a Bible open at the Gospel of St. John, symbolizing the Trinitarian movement that led the movement for independence.

Area 18,730 sq mi [48,511 sq km]
Population 8,834,000
Capital (population) Santo Domingo (2,061,000)
Government Multiparty republic
Ethnic groups Mulatto 73%, White 16%, Black 11%
Languages Spanish (official)
Religions Roman Catholic 95%
Currency Dominican peso = 100 centavos
Website www.dominicanrepublic.com

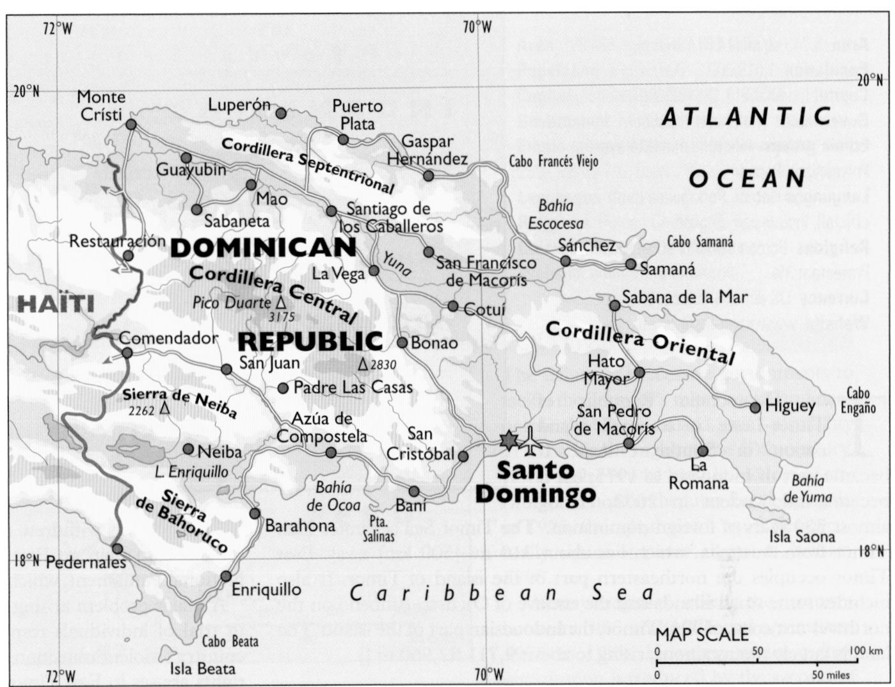

The Dominican Republic is the second largest of the Caribbean nations in both area and population, it shares the island of Hispaniola with Haiti, the Dominican Republic occupying the eastern two-thirds. Of the steep-sided mountains that dominate the island, the country includes the northern Cordillera Septentrional, the huge Cordillera Central, which rises to Pico Duarte, at 10,414 ft [3,175 m] the highest peak in the Caribbean, and the southern Sierra de Baoruco. Between them and to the east lie fertile valleys and lowlands, including the Vega Real and the coastal plains where the main sugar plantations are found.

CLIMATE

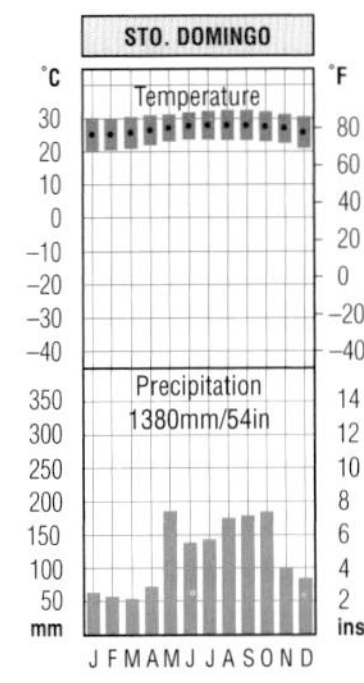

Typical of the Caribbean region, the climate is humid and hot throughout the year close to sea level, while cooler conditions prevail in the mountains. Rainfall is heavy, especially in the northeast.

HISTORY

Christopher Columbus "discovered" the island on December 5, 1492. Its Amerindian population was soon to be decimated. The city of Santo Domingo, now the capital and chief port, was founded by Columbus' brother Bartholomew four years later and is the oldest in the Americas. For a long time a Spanish colony, Hispaniola was initially the centerpiece of their empire, but was later to become a poor relation.

In 1795, it became French, then Spanish again in 1809. But in 1821, when it was called Santo Domingo, it won its independence. Haiti held the territory from 1822 until 1844 when, on restoring sovereignty, it became the Dominican Republic.

Growing American influence culminated in occupation between 1916 and 1924. This was followed by a period of corrupt dictatorship. From 1930 until his assassination in 1961, the country was ruled by Rafael Trujillo, one of Latin America's best-known dictators, who imprisoned or killed many of his opponents. A power struggle developed between the military, the upper class, those who wanted the country to become a democracy, and others who favored making it a Communist regime.

***Boats moored** in Bayahibe Bay, on the southeast coast*

POLITICS

In 1962 Juan Bosch became president, but was ousted in 1963. Bosch supporters tried to seize power in 1965, but were met bystrong military opposition. This led to US military intervention in 1965. In 1966, a new constitution was adopted and Joaquín Balaguer was elected president (1966–78, 1986–96). Elections have been known to be violent and the United States has kept a watchful eye.

Leonel Fernandez was elected president for a second time in 2004. He had campaigned on a ticket that promised to tackle inflation and once in office he introduced austerity measures that included cuts to state spending.

SANTO DOMINGO (formerly CIUDAD TRUJILLO, 1936–61)

Capital and chief port of the Dominican Republic, on the south coast, on the River Ozama. Founded in 1496, it is the oldest continuous European settlement in the Americas. It was the seat of the Spanish viceroys in the early 1500s, and base for the Spaniards' conquering expeditions until it was devastated by an earthquake in 1562. It houses more than a third of the country's population, many of whom work in the sugar industry.

ECONOMY

The World Bank describes the Dominican Republic as a "lower-middle-income" developing country. In the 1990s, industrial growth that exploited the country's huge hydroelectric potential, mining, and tourism has augmented the traditional agricultural economy, though the country is far from politically stable. Agriculture is a major activity. Leading crops include avocados, bananas, beans, mangoes, oranges, plantains, rice, sugar cane, and tobacco.

Gold and nickel are mined. Sugar refining is a major industry, with the bulk of the production exported to the United States. Leading exports are ferronickels, sugar, coffee, cocoa, and gold. Its main trading partner is the United States.

Egypt

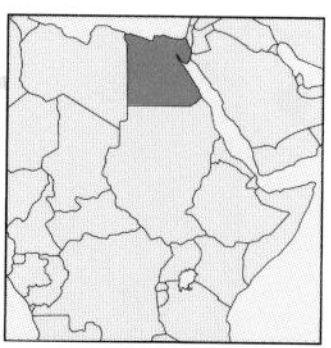

A flag consisting of three bands of red, white and black, the colors of the Pan-Arab movement, was adopted in 1958. The present design has a gold eagle in the center. This symbolizes Saladin, the warrior who led the Arabs in the 12th century.

Area 386,659 sq mi [1,001,449 sq km]
Population 76,117,000
Capital (population) Cairo (6,801,000)
Government Republic
Ethnic groups Egyptians/Bedouins/Berbers 99%
Languages Arabic (official), French, English
Religions Islam (mainly Sunni Muslim) 94%, Christian (mainly Coptic Christian) and others 6%
Currency Egyptian pound = 100 piastres
Website www.egypt.gov.eg/english/default.asp

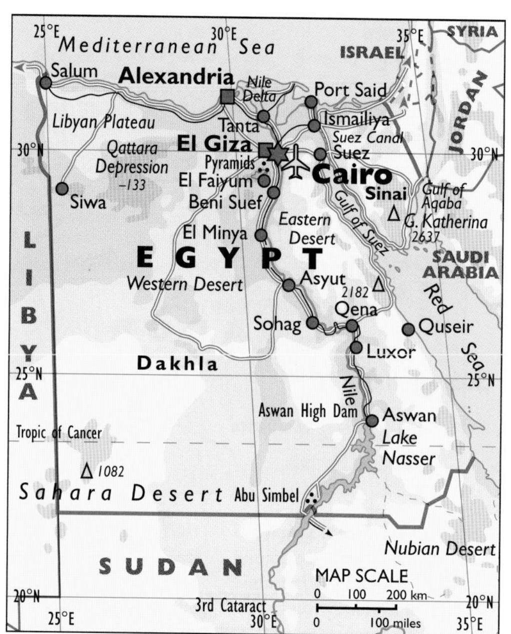

The Arab Republic of Egypt is Africa's second largest country by population after Nigeria. Most of Egypt is desert. Almost all the people live either in the Nile Valley and its fertile delta or along the Suez Canal, the artificial waterway between the Mediterranean and Red seas. This canal shortens the sea journey between the United Kingdom and India by 6,027 mi [9,700 km]. Recent attempts have been made to irrigate parts of the Western Desert.

Apart from the Nile Valley, Egypt has three other main regions. The Western and Eastern deserts are part of the Sahara. The Sinai Peninsula (Es Sina), to the east of the Suez Canal, is very mountainous and contains Egypt's highest peak, Gebel Katherina (8,650 ft [2,637 m]); few people live in this area.

CLIMATE

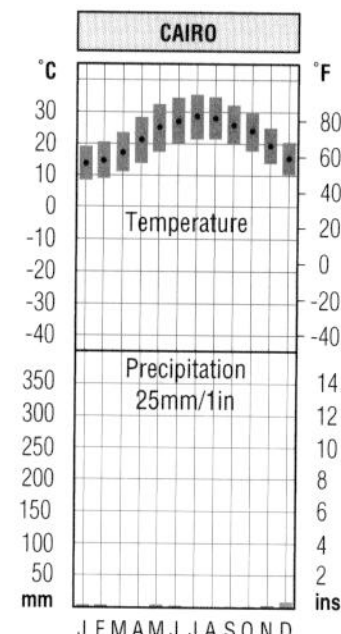

Egypt has a desert climate and is one of the world's sunniest countries. The low rainfall occurs in winter, if at all. Winters are mild, but summers hot. Conditions become unpleasant when hot and dusty winds blow from the deserts into the Nile Valley.

HISTORY

Ancient Egypt, which was founded about 5,000 years ago, was one of the great early civilizations. Throughout the country, pyramids, temples, and richly decorated tombs are memorials to its great achievements. After Ancient Egypt declined, the country came under successive foreign rulers. Arabs occupied Egypt in AD 639–42. They introduced the Arabic language and Islam. Their influence was so great that many Egyptians now regard themselves as Arabs.

Egypt came under British rule in 1882, but it gained partial independence in 1922, becoming a monarchy.

CAIRO (AL-QAHIRAH)

Capital of Egypt and port on the River Nile. The largest city in Africa, Cairo was founded in 969 by the Fatimid dynasty and subsequently fortified by Saladin. Medieval Cairo became capital of the Mamluk empire, but declined under Turkish rule. During the 20th century it grew dramatically in population and area. Nearby are world-famous archaeological sites, the Sphinx and the Pyramids of Giza. Old Cairo is a world heritage site containing over 400 mosques and other fine examples of Islamic art and architecture. Its five universities include the world's oldest, housed in the mosque of Al Azhar (972) and the center of Shiite Koranic study.

POLITICS

In 1952, following a military revolution led by General Muhammad Naguib, the monarchy was abolished and Egypt became a republic. Naguib became president, but he was overthrown in 1954 by Colonel Gamal Abdel Nasser. President Nasser sought to develop Egypt's economy, and he announced a major project to build a new dam at Aswan to provide electricity and water for irrigation. When Britain and the United States failed to provide finance for building the dam, Nasser seized the Suez Canal Company in July 1956. In retaliation, Israel, backed by British and French troops, invaded the Sinai Peninsula and the Suez Canal region. However, under international pressure, they were forced to withdraw. Construction of the Aswan High Dam began in 1960 and it was fully operational by 1968.

In 1967, Egypt lost territory to Israel in the Six-Day War and Nasser tendered his resignation, but the people refused to accept it. After his death in 1970, Nasser was succeeded by his vice-president, Anwar el-Sadat. In 1973, Egypt launched a surprise attack in the Sinai Peninsula, but its troops were finally forced back to the Suez Canal. In 1977, Sadat began a peace process when he visited Israel and addressed the Knesset (Israel's parliament). Finally, in 1979, Egypt and Israel signed a peace treaty under which Egypt regained the Sinai Peninsula. However, extremists opposed contacts with Israel and, in 1981, Sadat was assassinated. He was succeeded as president by Hosni Mubarak.

In the 1990s, attacks on foreign visitors severely damaged tourism, despite efforts to curb the activities of Islamic extremists. In 1997, terrorists killed 58 foreign tourists near Luxor. Unrest continued in the 21st century. In 2005, Mubarak was victorious in the first contested presidential elections, but members of the banned Muslim Brotherhood, standing as independents, made gains in parliament.

ECONOMY

Egypt is Africa's second most industrialized country after South Africa, but remains a developing country. The people are poor, farming employs 34% of the workers. Most *fellahin* (peasants) grow food crops such as beans, corn, rice, sugar cane, and wheat, but cotton is the chief cash crop. Egypt depends increasingly on the Nile. Its waters are seasonal, and control and storage have become essential in the last 100 years. The Aswan High Dam is the greatest Nile dam, and the water behind it in Lake Nasser makes desert reclamation possible. The electricity produced is important for industrial development. Another vital export prospect is natural gas.

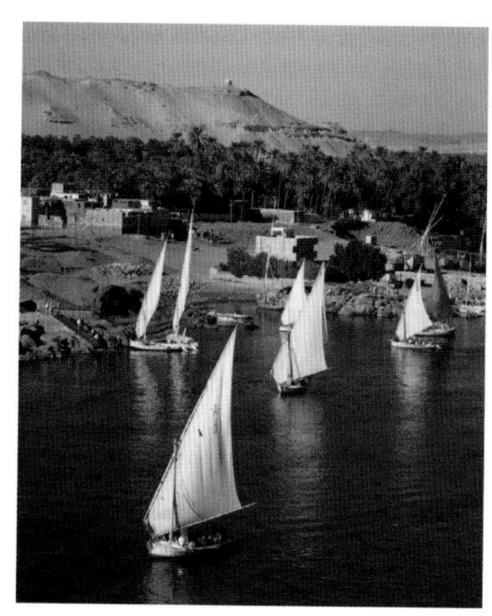

***Feluccas on the Nile** at*
Aswan in southern Egypt

This flag was adopted in 1912, replacing the earlier "Stars and Stripes." The blue and white stripes are featured on the flags of several central American countries which gained their independence from Spain at the same time in 1821.

El Salvador is the smallest and most densely populated country in Central America. It has a narrow coastal plain along the Pacific Ocean. The majority of the interior is mountainous with many extinct volcanic peaks, overlooking a heavily populated central plateau. Earthquakes are common; in 1854, an earthquake destroyed the capital, San Salvador. In October 1986, another earthquake killed 400 people and caused widespread damage.

Grassland and some virgin forests of original oak and pine are found in the highlands. The central plateau and valleys have areas of grass and deciduous woodland, while tropical savanna or forest cover the coastal regions.

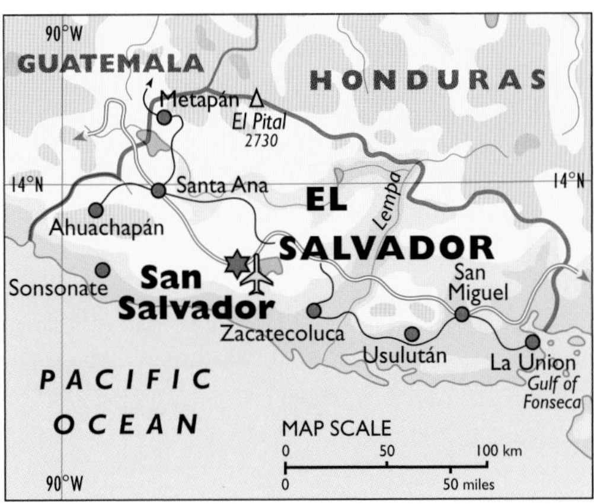

Area 21,041 sq km [8,124 sq mi]
Population 6,588,000
Capital (population) San Salvador (473,000)
Government Republic
Ethnic groups Mestizo 90%, White 9%, Amerindian 1%
Languages Spanish (official)
Religions Roman Catholic 83%
Currency US dollar = 100 cents
Website www.elsalvadorturismo.gob.sv

CLIMATE

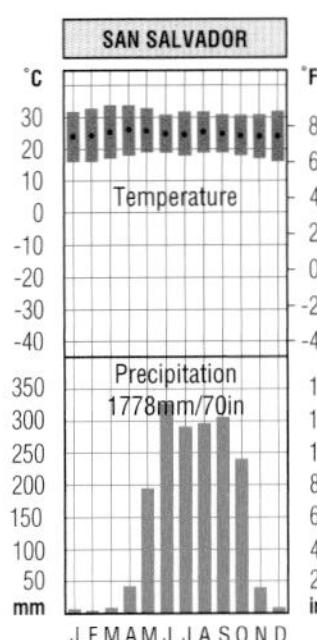

The coast has a hot tropical climate. Inland, the climate is moderated by altitude. The center region has similar temperatures by day, but nights are cooler. Rain falls most afternoons between May and October.

HISTORY

In 1524–26 Spanish explorer Pedro de Alvarado conquered Native American tribes such as the Pipil, and the region became part of the Spanish Viceroyalty of Guatemala. Independence was achieved in 1821, and in 1823 El Salvador joined the Central American Federation. The federation dissolved in 1839.

El Salvador declared independence in 1841, but was continually subject to foreign interference (especially from Guatemala and Nicaragua). It was at this time that El Salvador's coffee plantations developed.

POLITICS

Following a collapse in the world coffee market, Maximiliano Hernández Martínez seized power in a palace coup in 1931. In 1944 a general strike overthrew his brutal dictatorship. After a period of progressive government, a military junta headed by Julio Adalberto Rivera from 1962 to 1967 and Fidel Sánchez Hernández from 1967 to 1972 seized power. Honduras' discriminatory immigration laws exacerbated tension on the border between the two countries. The "Soccer War" of 1969 broke out following an ill-tempered World Cup qualifying match. Within four days, El Salvador captured much of Honduras. A ceasefire occurred and the troops withdrew.

In the 1970s, the repressive National Republican Alliance (ARENA) regime compounded El Salvador's problems of overpopulation, unequal distribution of wealth, and social unrest. Civil war broke out in 1979 between US-backed government forces and the Farabundo Marti National Liberation Front (FMLN). The 12-year war claimed 75,000 lives and caused mass homelessness. A ceasefire held from 1992, and the FMLN became a recognized political party. In 1993 a UN Truth Commission led to the removal of senior army officers for human rights abuses and the decommissioning of FMLN arms. Armando Calderón Sol became president in 1994 elections; Francisco Flores succeeded him in 1999.

In 2001, massive earthquakes killed about 1,200 people and left one million homeless. Tony Saca won 2004 presidential elections to become the fourth successive ARENA president.

ECONOMY

El Salvador is a lower-middle-income developing country. Farmland and pasture account for approximately 60% of land use. El Salvador is the world's 10th largest producer of coffee. Its reliance on the crop caused economic structural imbalance. Sugar and cotton grow on the coastal lowlands. Fishing is important, but manufacturing is on a small scale. The civil war devastated the economy. Between 1993 and 1995, El Salvador received more than US$100 million of credit from the International Monetary Fund.

Volcan Santa Ana *(Ilamatepec); at 7,812 ft (2381 m) Santa Ana is the highest volcano in El Salvador, its last eruption in 2005 killed two and caused the evacuation of thousands*

SAN SALVADOR

Capital and largest city of El Salvador in central El Salvador. Founded in 1524 near the volcano of San Salvador, which rises to 6,184 ft [1,885 m] and last erupted in 1917. The city has frequently been damaged by earthquakes. The main industry is the processing of the coffee which is grown on the rich volcanic soils of the area. Other manufactures include beer, textiles, and tobacco.

Equatorial Guinea

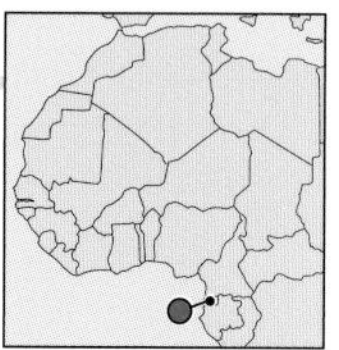

Green is for agriculture, white is peace, and red is for blood shed in the fight for independence. Blue represents the Atlantic. The tree on the coat of arms is the tree under which the 1843 treaty with Spain was signed. The six stars represent the mainland and the five islands.

Area 10,830 sq mi [28,051 sq km]
Population 523,000
Capital (population) Malabo (30,000)
Government Multiparty republic (transitional)
Ethnic groups Bubi (on Bioko), Fang (in Rio Muni)
Languages Spanish and French (both official)
Religions Christianity
Currency CFA franc = 100 centimes
Website www.ceiba-guinea-ecuatorial.org

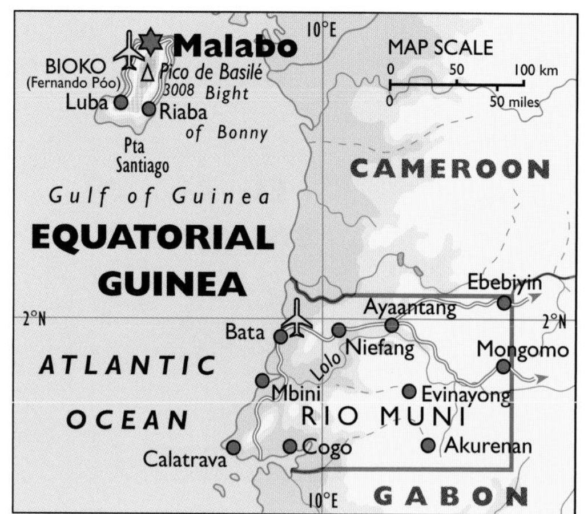

The Republic of Equatorial Guinea is located in west-central Africa and is one of the smallest countries on the African continent. It consists of a mainland territory between Cameroon and Gabon, called Río Muni (Mbini), and five islands in the Bight of Biafra (Bonny), the largest of which is Bioko (Fernando Póo).

Bioko is a volcanic island with fertile soils and a steep rocky coast. Malabo's harbor is part of a submerged volcano. Bioko is mountainous, rising to a height of 9,869 ft [3,008 m] at the Pico de Santa Isabel. It has varied vegetation with trees such as teak, mahogany, oak, walnut, and rosewood, and grasslands at higher levels.

Mainland Río Muni (90% of all land) consists mainly of hills and plateaus behind the coastal plains. Its main river, the Lolo, rises in Gabon. Dense forest covers most of Río Muni and provides a habitat for animals such as lions, gazelles, and elephants.

CLIMATE

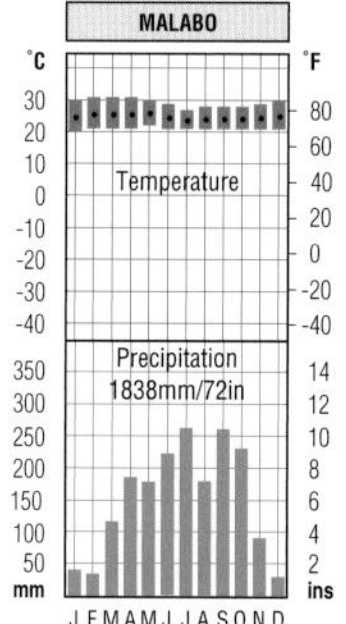

Situated on the equator, Equatorial Guinea has a tropical climate. High temperatures and high humidity are the norm with an average annual temperature of 77° F [25° C]. Bioko has heavy rainfall and there is a dry season from December to February. Río Muni has a similar climate to Bioko, though rainfall diminishes inland.

HISTORY

In 1472 Portuguese navigator Fernão do Pó sighted the largest island of Bioko. In 1778, Portugal ceded the islands and commercial mainland rights to Spain in exchange for some Brazilian territories. Yellow fever hit Spanish settlers on Bioko, and they withdrew in 1781. In 1827, Spain leased bases on Bioko to Britain, and the British settled some freed slaves. Descendants of these former slaves (*Fernandinos*) remain on the island. Spain returned in the mid-19th century and developed plantations on Bioko.

In 1956, the islands became the Overseas Provinces in the Gulf of Guinea. In 1959, the territory was divided into two provinces, Fernando Póo and Río Muni, and named Spanish Guinea. The two territories reunified in 1963 and became the Autonomous Territories of Equatorial Guinea. In 1968 the territory gained independence as the Republic of Equatorial Guinea.

POLITICS

In 1969, as a result of social unrest caused by factors such as ethnic conflict and economic problems, President Francisco Macías Nguema annulled the constitution. A military dictatorship ensued with up to 100,000 refugees fleeing to neighboring countries. Nguema's dictatorship endured from 1968 to 1979 during which time more than 40,000 people were killed.

In 1979, Lieutenant-Colonel Teodoro Obiang Nguema Mbasogo deposed Nguema in a military coup. A 1991 referendum voted to set up a multiparty democracy, consisting of the ruling Equatorial Guinea Democratic Party (PDGE) and ten opposition parties. The main parties and most of the electorate boycotted elections in 1993, and the PDGE formed a government. In 1996 elections, again boycotted by most opposition parties, President Obiang claimed 99% of the vote. Human rights organizations accuse his regime of routine arrests and torture of opponents and the president is seen to control all the political parties.

In 2004 a coup attempt by foreign mercenaries was foiled and the leaders were arrested.

ECONOMY

Equatorial Guinea is a poor country. Agriculture employs around 60% of the people, though many farmers live at subsistence level, making little contribution to the economy. The main food crops are bananas, cassava, and sweet potatoes. The chief cash crop is cocoa, grown on Bioko, though this has been hit by a worldwide dip in cocoa prices.

Oil has been produced off Bioko since 1966. By 2002 it accounted for more than 80% of exports. Despite the rapid expansion of the economy and massive increase in revenue, a UN human rights report stated that 65% of the people still live in "extreme poverty."

The government has promised that agriculture will benefit from the large amounts of revenue gained from oil, but this has yet to materialise. Other natural resources that have yet to be developed include titanium, iron ore, manganese, and uranium. The country has forfeited much aid from the World Bank and the IMF through corruption and mismanagement.

Cocoa *(Theobroma cacao)*

COCOA

Cocoa is the basic ingredient of chocolate. Also a drink obtained from the seeds of the tropical American evergreen tree *Theobroma cacao*. The seeds are crushed and some fatty substances are removed to produce cocoa powder. The cocoa industry is a key employer in Equatorial Guinea. Family Sterculiaceae.

MALABO

Seaport capital of Equatorial Guinea, on Bioko island, in the Gulf of Guinea in west central Africa. Founded in 1827 as a British base to suppress the slave trade, it was known as Santa Isabel until 1973. Malabo stands on the edge of a volcanic crater that acts as a natural harbor. Industries include fish processing, hardwoods, cocoa, coffee.

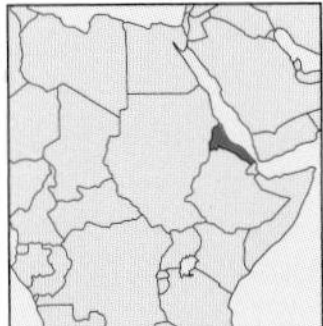

Based on the flag of the EPLF, the red triangle symbolizes blood shed in the fight for freedom, the blue triangle represents the Red Sea, the green triangle stands for agriculture. From 1952–9 Eritrea's flag bore a green wreath and olive branch in the center of a field of United Nations' blue.

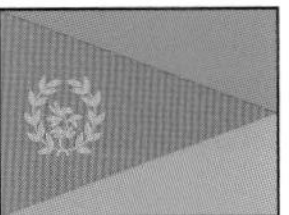

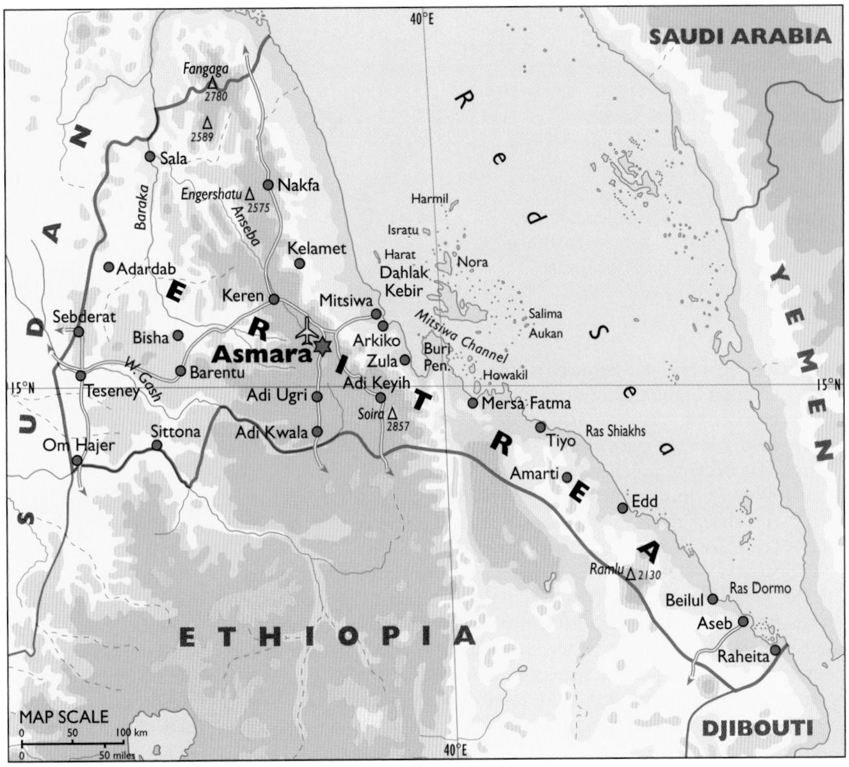

The State of Eritrea occupies a strategic geopolitical position on the Red Sea in northeastern Africa. The coastal plain extends inland between 10 and 40 mil [6–64 km]. Inland are mountains. In the southwest, the mountains descend to the Danakil Desert. This desert contains Eritrea's lowest point at 246 ft [75 m] below sea level.

CLIMATE

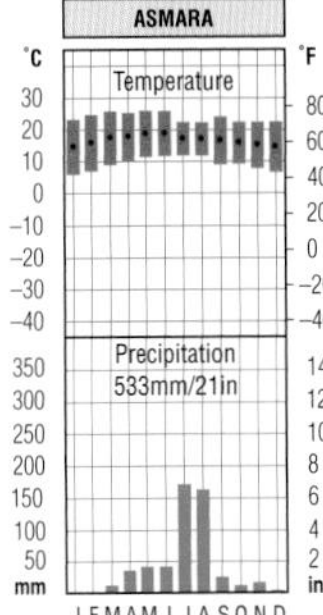

The temperature ranges from 61°F [16°C] in the highlands to 81°F [27°C] on the coastal plain. Rainfall on the coastal plain is between 6 and 10 in [150–250 mm] with up to 24 in [610 mm] in the highlands. The rainy season is from June to September.

HISTORY

The first settlers were from Africa, followed by others from the Arabian peninsula. Between AD 50 and 600, Eritrea was part of the Ethiopian kingdom of Axum. The people of Axum were converted to Christianity in the 4th century, but Muslims gained control of the area in the 7th century, introducing Islam to the coastal areas. Christianity survived inland.

In the 16th century, the Ottoman Empire took over the coastal area. Italy made Eritrea a colony in 1890. In 1935, Italy also conquered Ethiopia. During World War II, a British force drove the Italians out off northeastern Africa. After the war, a British military administration ruled Eritrea.

In 1950, the UN made Eritrea a self-governing part of Ethiopia. Ethiopian rule proved unpopular and, in 1958, Eritrean nationalists formed the Eritrean Liberation Front (ELF). War broke out in 1961 between the ELF and the Ethiopians. In 1962, Ethiopia declared Eritrea to be a province, sparking off a war of independence.

The Eritrean People's Liberation Front (EPLF) was formed in 1970, replacing the ELF as the main anti-Ethiopian organization. In 1974, Ethiopian Emperor Haile Selassie was overthrown and a military government took power. EPLF victories gradually weakened Ethiopia's government and the regime collapsed in 1991. The EPLF then formed a provisional government.

POLITICS

Eritrea declared independence in 1993, with Isaias Afewerki as president. The ruling People's Front for Democracy and Justice is the only party permitted in the country. The government has been criticized for the repression of opposition and closing the private press in 2001. Eritrea's relations with Ethiopia deteriorated in 1998 over a border dispute around the town of Badme, on Eritrea's southwestern border. The conflict erupted into violence when Ethiopia bombed Asmara airport, and Eritrea attacked Mekele in northern Ethiopia. The conflict continued into 2000. A ceasefire was agreed and a peace plan drawn up. UN observers arrived to help find a settlement. In 2001, the two countries agreed to a UN-proposed mediator to demarcate the border. In 2003, the boundary commission ruled that Badme lies in Eritrea. Tension continued and, in late 2005, Eritrea ordered UN peacekeeping troops to leave the country.

Area 45,405 sq mi [117,600 sq km]
Population 4,447,000
Capital (population) Asmara (358,000)
Government Transitional government
Ethnic groups Tigrinya 50%, Tigre and Kunama 40%, Afar 4%, Saho 3% and others
Languages Afar, Arabic, Tigre and Kunama, Tigrinya
Religions Islam, Coptic Christian, Roman Catholic
Currency Nakfa = 100 cents
Website www.shabait.com

ASMARA (ASMERA)

Capital of Eritrea, northeast Africa. Occupied by Italy in 1889 then their colonial capital and main base for the invasion of Ethiopia (1935–6). In the 1950s, the US built Africa's biggest military communications center here. Absorbed by Ethiopia in 1952, it was the main garrison in the fight against independence-seeking Eritrean rebels. In 1993 it became the capital of independent Eritrea.

ECONOMY

One of Africa's poorest countries: half the population lives below the poverty line and life expectancy is 52 years. Since 1993, the economy has been set back by droughts, border conflict, and high population increase. The main activity is farming, mostly at subsistence level. Agriculture employs 80% of the workforce.

St Michael's Catholic Church, *Keren, Anseba province; this Romanesque church is the oldest Catholic church in Eritrea*

Estonia

Estonia's flag was used between 1918 and 1940, when the country was an independent republic. It was readopted June 1988. The blue is said to symbolize the sky, the black Estonia's black soil, and the white the snow that blankets the land in winter.

Area 17,413 sq mi [45,100 sq km]
Population 1,342,000
Capital (population) Tallinn (418,000)
Government Multiparty republic
Ethnic groups Estonian 65%, Russian 28%, Ukranian 2%, Belarusian 2%, Finnish 1%
Languages Estonian (official), Russian
Religions Lutheran, Russian and Estonian Orthodox, Methodist, Baptist, Roman Catholic
Currency Estonian kroon = 100 senti
Website www.riik.ee/en

The Republic of Estonia is the smallest of the three states on the east coast of the Baltic Sea, which were formerly part of the Soviet Union, but became independent in the early 1990s. Estonia consists of a generally flat plain which was covered by ice sheets during the Ice Age. The land is strewn with moraine (rocks deposited by the ice).

The country is dotted with more than 1,500 small lakes. Water, including the large Lake Peipus (Ozero Chudskoye) and the River Narva, makes up much of Estonia's eastern border with Russia. Estonia has more than 800 islands, which together comprise about a tenth of the country. The largest island is Saaremaa (Sarema).

Farmland and pasture account for more than 33% of land use.

CLIMATE

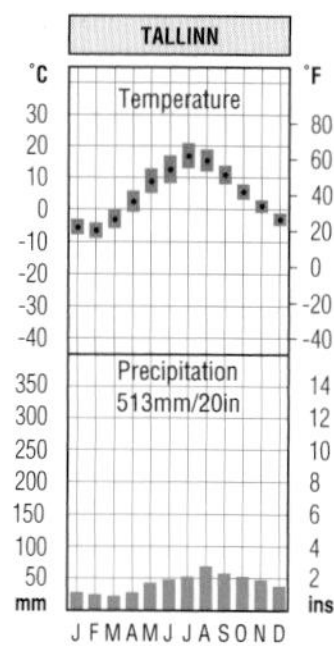

Despite its position to the north, Estonia has a fairly mild climate because of its proximity to the sea. Sea winds tend to warm the land during winter and cool it in summer. Rainfall averages from 19 to 23 in (480–580 mm).

HISTORY

The ancestors of the Estonians, who are related to the Finns, settled in the area several thousand years ago. Divided into several separate states, they were vulnerable to Viking attacks, but in the early 13th century, German crusaders, known as the Teutonic Knights, introduced Christianity. Germany took control of the southern part of Estonia and Denmark took control of the north. The Danes sold the north to the Germans in 1324 and Estonia became part of the Holy Roman Empire.

In 1561, Sweden took over northern Estonia and Poland ruled the south. Sweden controlled the entire country from 1625 until 1721 but, following the victory of Peter the Great over Sweden in the Great Northern War (1700–21), the area became part of the Russian Empire. On 24 February 1918, Estonia declared its independence. A democratic form of government was established in 1919. However, a fascist coup in 1934 ended democratic rule.

POLITICS

In 1939, Germany and the Soviet Union agreed to take over large areas of eastern Europe, and it was agreed that the Soviet Union would take over Estonia. The Soviet Union forcibly annexed the country in 1940. Germany invaded Estonia in 1941, but the Soviet Union regained control in 1944 when the country became the Estonian Soviet Socialist Republic. Many Estonians opposed Soviet rule and were deported to Siberia. About 100,000 Estonians settled in the West.

Resistance to Soviet rule was fuelled in the 1980s when the Soviet leader Mikhail Gorbachev began to introduce reforms and many Estonians called for independence. In 1990, the Estonian parliament declared Soviet rule invalid and called for a gradual transition to full independence. The Soviet Union regarded this action as illegal, but finally the Soviet State Council recognized the Estonian parliament's proclamation of independence in September 1991, shortly before the Soviet Union itself was dissolved in December 1991.

Since independence, Estonia has sought to increase links with Europe. It was admitted to the Council of Europe in 1993; has been a member of the World Trade Organization since 1999, and a member of NATO and the European Union since 2004. But despite the fact that it had the highest standard of living among the 15 former Soviet republics, Estonia has found the change to a free-market economy hard-going.

Other problems facing Estonia include crime, rural under-development and the status of its non-Estonian citizens, including Russians who make up about 30% of the population. In the country's first free elections in 1992, only Estonians were permitted to vote and all Russians were excluded. Tension on this issue continued through the 1990s as dual citizenship was outlawed, while restrictions imposed on Russians applying for Estonian citizenship included having to pass an Estonian language test.

TALLINN

Capital and largest city of Estonia, on the Gulf of Finland, opposite Helsinki. Founded in 1219 by the Danes, it became a member of the Hanseatic League in 1285. It passed to Sweden in 1561, and was ceded to Russia in 1721. Developed in the 19th century for Russia's Baltic Fleet, it remains a major port and industrial center. It was badly damaged in World War II. Tourism is increasing. Industries include machinery, cables, paper.

ECONOMY

Manufacturing is Estonia's most valuable activity. The timber industry is among the most important industries, alongside metal-working, shipbuilding, clothing, textiles, chemicals, and food processing. Food processing is based primarily on extremely efficient dairy farming and pig breeding, but oats, barley, and potatoes are suited to the cool climate and the average soils.

Like the other two Baltic states, Estonia is not rich in natural resources, though its oil shale is an important mineral deposit; enough natural gas is extracted to supply St Petersburg, Russia's second largest city. The leading exports are mineral fuels and chemical products, followed by food, textiles and cloth, and wood and paper products. Finland and Russia are the leading trading partners.

***A street in the Old Town** of Tallinn, with the spire of St. Nicholas Church in the background*

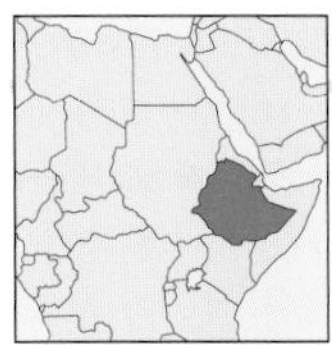

The tricolor flag of Ethiopia first appeared in 1897. The central pentangle was introduced in 1996, and represents the common will of the country's 68 ethnic groups, and the present sequence was adopted in 1914.

ADDIS ABABA (AMHARIC, "NEW FLOWER")

Capital and largest city in Ethiopia, located on a plateau at 8,000 ft [2,440 m] in the highlands of Shewa province. Addis Ababa was made capital of Ethiopia in 1889. It is the headquarters of the African Union (AU). It is the main center for the country's vital coffee trade. Industries include food, tanning, textiles, wood products.

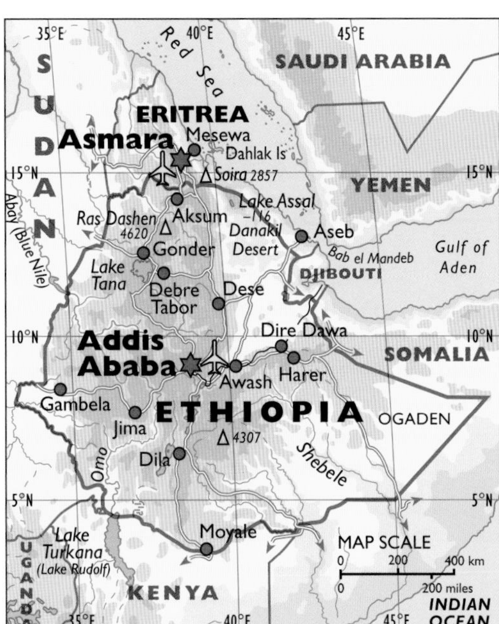

Area 426,370 sq mi [1,104,300 sq km]
Population 67,851,000
Capital (population) Addis Ababa (2,424,000)
Government Federation of nine provinces
Ethnic groups Oromo 40%, Amhara and Tigre 32%, Sidamo 9%, Shankella 6%, Somali 6% , others
Languages Amharic (official), many others
Religions Islam 47%, Ethiopian Orthodox 40%, traditional beliefs 12%
Currency Birr = 100 cents
Website www.mfa.gov.et

Ethiopia is dominated by the Ethiopian Plateau, a block of volcanic mountains. Its average height is 6,000 ft to 8,000 ft [1,800 m to 2,450 m], rising in the north to 15,157ft [4620m], at Ras Dashen. The Great Rift Valley bisects the plateau. The Eastern Highlands include the Somali Plateau and the desert of the Ogaden Plateau. The Western Highlands include the capital, Addis Ababa, the Blue Nile (Abbay), and its source, Lake Tana (Ethiopia's largest lake). The Danakil Desert forms Ethiopia's border with Eritrea.

Grass, farmland, and trees cover most of the highlands. Semidesert and tropical savanna cover parts of the lowlands. Dense rainforest grows in the southwest.

CLIMATE

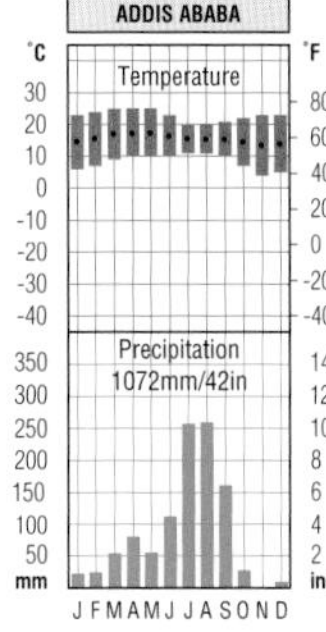

Ethiopia's climate is greatly affected by altitude. Addis Ababa, at 8,000 ft [2,450 m], has an average annual temperature of 68°F [20°C]. Rainfall is generally more than 39 in [1,000 mm], with a rainy season from April to September. The northeastern and southwestern lowlands are extremely hot and arid with less than 20 in [500 mm] rainfall, and frequent droughts.

HISTORY

According to legend, Menelik I, son of King Solomon and the Queen of Sheba, founded Ethiopia in about 1000 BC. In AD 321, the northern kingdom of Axum introduced Coptic Christianity. Judaism flourished in the 6th century. The expansion of Islam led to the isolation of Axum and the kingdom fragmented in the 16th century.

In 1855, Kasa reestablished unity, and proclaimed himself Negus (Emperor) Theodore, thereby founding the modern state. European intervention marked the late 19th century, and Menelik II became emperor with Italian support. He expanded the empire, made Addis Ababa his capital in 1889, and defeated an Italian invasion in 1895. In 1930, Menelik II's grandnephew, Ras Tafari Makonnen, was crowned Emperor Haile Selassie I. In 1935, Italian troops invaded Ethiopia (Abyssinia). In 1936, Italy combined Ethiopia with Somalia and Eritrea to form Italian East Africa. During World War II, British and South African forces recaptured Ethiopia, and Haile Selassie was restored as emperor in 1941.

In 1952, Eritrea federated with Ethiopia. The 1960s witnessed violent demands for Eritrean secession and economic equality. In 1962 Ethiopia annexed Eritrea.

POLITICS

In 1974, following famine in Ethiopia, Haille Selassie was killed. The monarchy was then abolished by the Provisional Military Administrative Council (PMAC). Military rule was repressive, and civil war broke out. The new PMAC leader, Mengistu Mariam, recaptured territory in Eritrea and the Ogaden with Soviet military assistance.

In 1984–5 widespread famine received global news coverage and 10,000 Falashas were airlifted to Israel. In 1987, Mengistu established the People's Democratic Republic of Ethiopia.

In 1991, the Tigrean-based Ethiopian People's Revolutionary Democratic Front (EPRDF) and the Eritrean People's Liberation Front (EPLF) brought down Mengistu. In 1995 the Federal Democratic Republic of Ethiopia was created, with Meles Zenawi as prime minister. A border war with Eritrea occurred in 1998–2000. Elections in 2005 led to protests and a crackdown on the opposition and press.

ECONOMY

Having been afflicted by drought and civil war in the 1970s and 1980s, Ethiopia is now one of the world's poorest countries. Agriculture is the main activity. Unfortunately the heavy reliance on agriculture in a drought-prone country has had dire consequences for the wealth of the nation.

A 2004 UN report stated that Ethiopia remained on the brink of disaster, with spiraling population growth, slow economic growth, and environmental degradation. Coffee is the leading cash crop and export.

***A group of women** return from Lake Tana to Chache and Alua with jugs full of water*

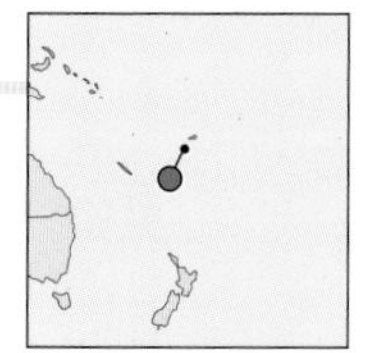

A modified version of the colonial flag, it includes the UK flag and the shield of the coat of arms. The light blue represents the Pacific. Each quarter of the St George cross features a product or symbol of Fiji: sugar cane, coconut palm, bananas, dove of peace, and lion with cocoa pod.

Area 7,056 sq mi [18,274 sq km]
Population 881,000
Capital (population) Suva (70,000)
Government Republic
Ethnic groups Fijian 51% (predominantly Melanesian with a Polynesian admixture), Indian 44%, others
Languages English (official), Fijian, Hindustani
Religions Christian 52% (Methodist 37%, Roman Catholic 9%), Hindu 38%, Muslim 8%, others
Currency Fiji dollar = 100 cents
Website www.fiji.gov.fj

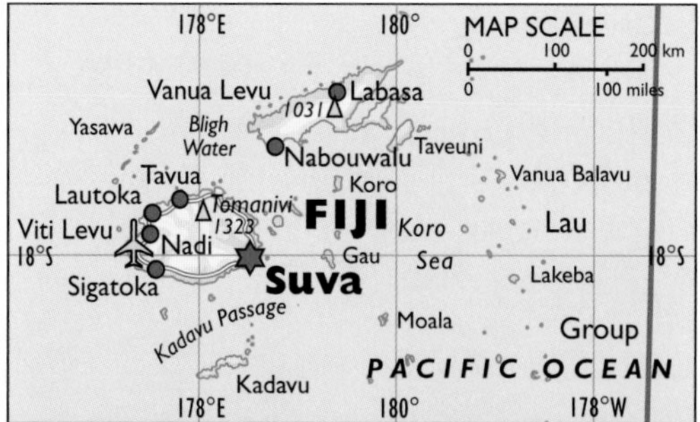

***Palm trees;** coconuts produced by the palm trees of Fiji are of great economic import to the islands*

The Republic of Fiji Islands consists of more than 800 Melanesian islands situated in the South Pacific Ocean. The larger ones are mountainous and volcanic, and they are surrounded by coral reefs. There are also fertile coastal plains and river valleys. The rest of the islands are low, sandy coral atolls.. Easily the biggest islands are Viti Levu (meaning "Big Island"), with the capital Suva on its south coast, and Vanua Levu ("Big Land"), which is just over half the size of the larger island.

Tropical forests cover more than half of the area of the islands.

CLIMATE

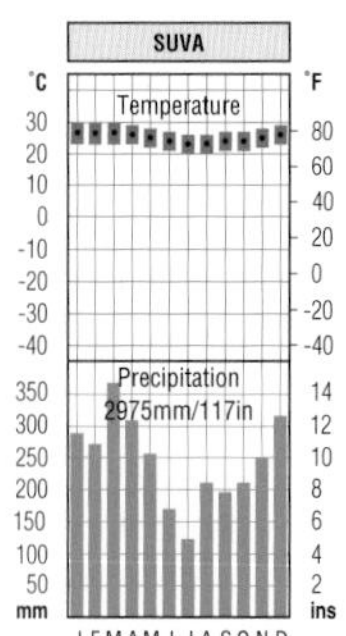

Fiji has a tropical oceanic climate, with southeast trade winds blowing throughout the year, Average temperatures vary between 60°F [16°C] and 90°F [32°C]. The average annual rainfall in Suva is 118 in [3,000 mm]. Heavy rains occur, especially between November and April. Much of the rain comes in short, heavy showers often after a sunny morning. But rains may last all day during the rainy season.

HISTORY

Melanesians, possibly from Indonesia, settled on the islands thousands of years ago, while a small group of Polynesians also reached the islands about 1,900 years ago. In 1643. the Dutch navigator Abel Janszoon Tasman became the first European to reach the islands. The British Captain James Cook arrived on Vatoa, one of the southern islands in 1774. Christian missionaries began to arrive in the 1830s.

Following conflict between various Fijian tribes in the mid-19th century, a local Christian chief named Cacobau, took control of western Fiji after having helped to restore peace there, while another Christian. Ma'afu. controlled the east. In 1871, European settlers named Cacobau king of Fiji and, in 1874, Fiji, at the request of Cacobau and other chiefs, became a British crown colony. In the late 19th century, European traders, missionaries and escaped convicts from Australia also settled in Fiji and, between 1879 and 1916, the British brought in more than 60,000 indentured laborers to work on the sugar plantations.

POLITICS

Fiji finally became independent on 10 October 1970, with Ratu Sir Kamisese Mara as prime minister. Fiji suffers today from its colonial past. Until the late 1980s, the Indian workers and their descendants outnumbered the native Fijians. Mixing between the two groups was minimal and the ethnic Indians were second-class citizens in terms of electoral representation, economic opportunity and land ownership. However, they played an important role in the economy. The constitution adopted on independence was intended to ease racial tension. But, in 1987, two military coups led by Lt-Colonel Sitiveni Rabuka, overthrew the elected (and first) Indian majority government, although it had been led by an ethnic Fijian, Timoci Bavadra. The leaders suspended the constitution and set up a Fijian-dominated republic outside the Commonwealth.

The country returned to civilian rule in 1990. However, in 1992, elections were held under a new constitution guaranteeing Melanesian supremacy and Rabuka became prime minister. However, thousands of ethnic Indians had already emigrated before these elections, taking their valuable skills with them and causing severe economic problems. Fiji was readmitted to the Commonwealth in 1997 after it had introduced a non-discriminatory constitution. Peaceful elections in 1999 led to victory for the Fiji Labor Party, whose leader, an ethnic Indian, Mahendra Chaudhry, became prime minister, defeating Rabuka.

In May 2000, ethnic Fijians, led by businessman George Speight, seized parliament and held the prime minister, his cabinet, and several MPs hostage. They were eventually disarmed and arrested, but Chaudhry was dismissed as prime minister. The army appointed an ethnic Fijian, Laisenia Qarase, leader of the nationalist Fiji United Party, as the new prime minister. His party won the elections in 2001 and the ethnic Indian Fijian Labor Party became the official opposition. Following the 2000 coup, the Commonwealth again expelled Fiji, but it was readmitted in 2002. In 2004, George Speight was sentenced to death but Fiji's president commuted the sentence to life imprisonment. In 2004, Fiji sent soldiers to Iraq for peacekeeping duties.

ECONOMY

Fiji is one of the more developed of the Pacific island states, But agriculture, which employs 70% of the population, remains the mainstay of its economy. Sugar cane, copra, and ginger are the main cash crops, and fish and timber are also exported. Other crops include bananas, cassava, coconuts, sweet potatoes, and rice.

Fiji mines gold, one of the main exports, silver and limestone, but sugar processing makes up one-third of industrial activity. Other manufactures include beer, cement, and cigarettes. Tourism is another important activity, with 300,000 to 400,000 visitors arriving annually. However, ethnic and political tensions have slowed the development of the tourist industry.

The leading markets for Fiji's exports are Australia, the United Kingdom, the United States, and Japan. Imports come from Australia, New Zealand, the United States, and Japan. Fiji is heavily dependent on foreign aid.

SUVA

Seaport on the southeast coast of Viti Levu Island, in the southwest Pacific Ocean, capital of Fiji. It is the manufacturing and trade center of the islands, with an excellent harbor. Exports include tropical fruits, copra, and gold.

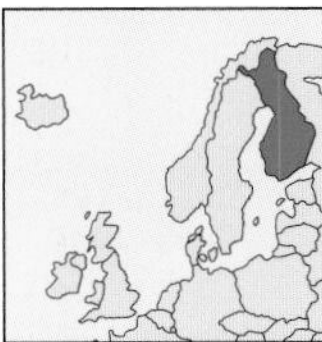

Finland

The flag of Finland was adopted in 1918, after the country had become an independent republic in 1917, following a century of Russian rule. The blue represents Finland's many lakes; the white symbolizes the blanket of snow which masks the land in winter.

The Republic of Finland (Suomi) has four geographical regions. In the south and west, on the Gulfs of Bothnia and Finland, is a low, narrow coastal strip, where most Finns live. The capital and largest city, Helsinki, is here. The Åland Islands lie in the entrance to the Gulf of Bothnia. Most of the interior is a beautiful wooded plateau, with more than 60,000 lakes. The Saimaa area is Europe's largest inland water system. A third of Finland lies within the Arctic Circle; this "land of the midnight sun" is called Lappi (Lapland).

Forests (birch, pine, and spruce) cover 60% of Finland. The vegetation becomes more and more sparse to the north, until it merges into Arctic tundra.

CLIMATE

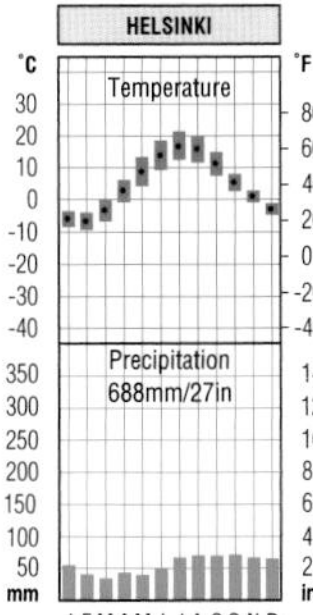

Finland has short, warm summers; Helsinki's July average is 63°F [17°C]. In Lapland, the temperatures are lower, and in June the sun never sets. Winters are long and cold; Helsinki's January average is 21°F [26°C]. The North Atlantic Drift keeps the Arctic coasts free of ice.

HISTORY

In the 8th century, Finnish-speaking settlers forced the Lapps to the north. Between 1150 and 1809, Finland was under Swedish rule. The close links between the countries continue today. Swedish remains an official language in Finland and one of the legacies of this period is a Swedish-speaking minority of 6% of the total population. In some localities on the south and west coasts, Swedish speakers are in the majority and Åland, an island closer to the Swedish coast than to Finland, is a self-governing province. Many towns use both Finnish and Swedish names. For example, Helsinki is Helsingfors, and Turku is Åbo in Swedish. Finnish bears little relation to the Swedish or any other Scandinavian language. It is closest to Magyar, the language of Hungary.

Lutheranism arrived in the 16th century. Wars between Sweden and Russia devastated Finland. Following the Northern War (1700–21), Russia gained much Finnish land. In the Napoleonic Wars, Russia conquered Finland and in 1809, it became an independent grand duchy of the Russian Empire, though the Russian tsar was its grand duke. Nationalist feelings developed during the 19th century, but in 1899 Russia sought to enforce its culture on the Finns. In 1903, the Russian governor suspended the constitution and became dictator, though following much resistance, self-government was restored in 1906. Finland proclaimed its independence in 1917, after the Russian Revolution and the collapse of the Russian Empire and, in 1919, it adopted a republican constitution. During World War I, the Soviet Union declared war on Finland and took the southern part of Karelia, where 12% of the Finnish people lived. Finland allied itself to Germany and Finnish troops regained southern Karelia. But at the end of the war, Russia regained southern Karelia and other parts of Finland. It also had to pay massive reparations to the Soviet Union.

After World War II, Finland pursued a policy of neutralism acceptable to the Soviet Union and this continued into the 1990s until the collapse of the Soviet Union. Finland also strengthened its links with other north European countries and became an associate member of the European Free Trade Association (EFTA) in 1961. Finland became a full member of EFTA in 1986, in a decade when its economy was growing at a faster rate than that of Japan.

HELSINKI

Capital of Finland, in the south of the country, on the Gulf of Finland. Founded in 1550 by Gustavus I (Vasa), it became the capital in 1812. It has two universities (1849, 1908), a cathedral (1852), museums, and art galleries. The commercial and administrative center of the country, it is Finland's largest port. Industries include shipbuilding, engineering, food processing, ceramics, textiles.

Area 130,558 sq mi [338,145 sq km]
Population 5,215,000
Capital (population) Helsinki (549,000)
Government Multiparty republic
Ethnic groups Finnish 93%, Swedish 6%
Languages Finnish and Swedish (both official)
Religions Evangelical Lutheran 89%
Currency Euro = 100 cents
Website www.government.fi

POLITICS

In 1992, along with most of its fellow EFTA members, Finland, which had no longer any need to be neutral, applied for membership of the European Union (EU). In 1994, the Finnish people voted in favor of joining the EU and the country officially joined on January 1, 1995. On January 1, 2002 the euro became Finland's official sole unit of currency. Finland has also discussed the possibility of joining NATO. However, polls since the events of September 11, 2001 suggest that the majority of Finns favor non-alliance.

ECONOMY

Forests are Finland's most valuable resource. Forestry accounts for 35% of exports. The chief manufactures are wood and paper products. Post-1945 the economy has diversified. Engineering, shipbuilding and textile industries have grown. Farming employs only 9% of workforce. The economy has slowly recovered from the recession caused by the collapse of the Soviet bloc.

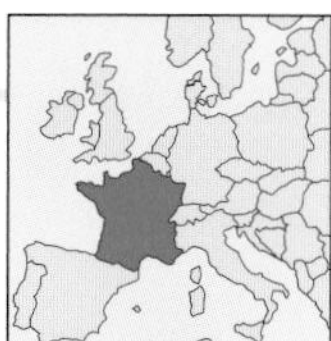

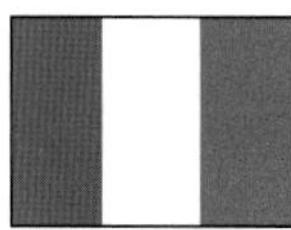

The colors of this flag originated during the French Revolution of 1789. The red and blue are said to represent Paris, while the white represented the monarchy. The present design was adopted in 1794, and is meant to symbolize republican principles.

Area 212,934 sq mi [551,500 sq km]
Population 60,424,000
Capital (population) Paris (2,152,000)
Government Multiparty republic
Ethnic groups Celtic, Latin, Arab, Teutonic, Slavic
Languages French (official)
Religions Roman Catholic 85%, Islam 8%, others
Currency Euro = 100 cents
Website www.elysee.fr

The Republic of France is the largest country in Western Europe. The scenery is extremely varied. The Vosges Mountains overlook the Rhine Valley in the northeast, the Jura Mountains and the Alps form the borders with Switzerland and Italy in the southeast, while the Pyrenees straddle France's border with Spain. The only large highland area entirely within France is the Massif Central between the Rhône-Saône Valley and the basin of Aquitaine. This dramatic area, covering one-sixth of the country, has peaks rising to more than 5,900 ft [1,800 m]. Volcanic activity dating back 10 to 30 million years ago appears in the form of steep-sided volcanic plugs. Brittany (Bretagne) and Normandy (Normande) form a scenic hill region. Fertile lowlands cover most of northern France, including the densely populated Paris Basin. Another major lowland area, the Aquitanian Basin, is in the southwest, while the Rhône-Saône Valley and the Mediterranean lowlands are in the southeast.

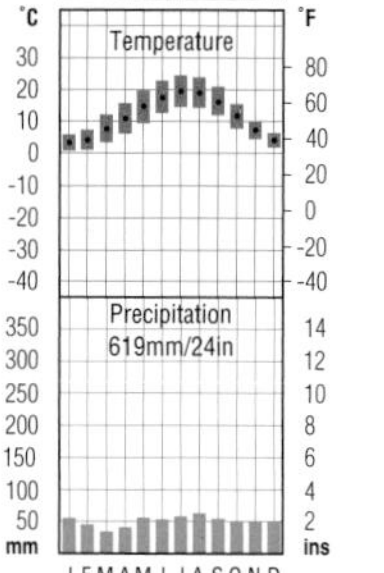

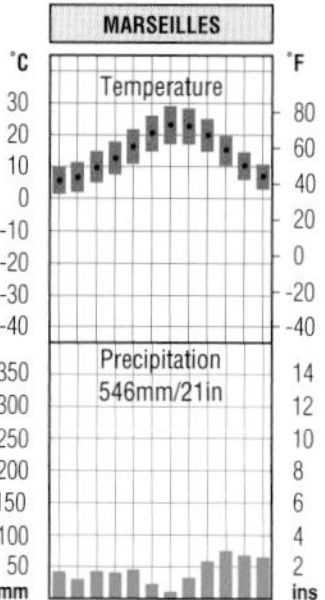

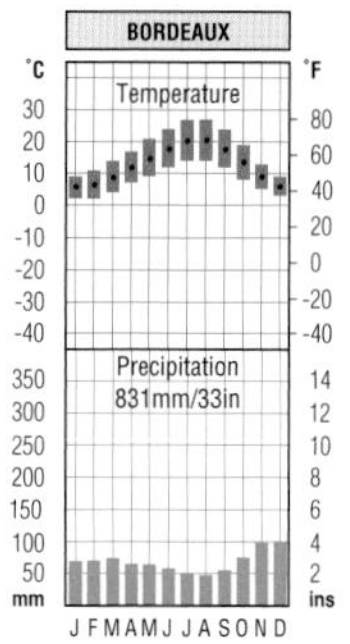

CLIMATE

The climate varies from west to east and from north to south. The west comes under the moderating influence of the Atlantic Ocean, giving generally mild weather. To the east, summers are warmer and winters colder. The climate also becomes warmer as one travels from north to south. The Mediterranean Sea coast experiences hot, dry summers and mild, moist winters. The Alps, Jura, and Pyrenees mountains have snowy winters. Winter sports centers are found in all three areas. Large glaciers occupy high valleys in the Alps.

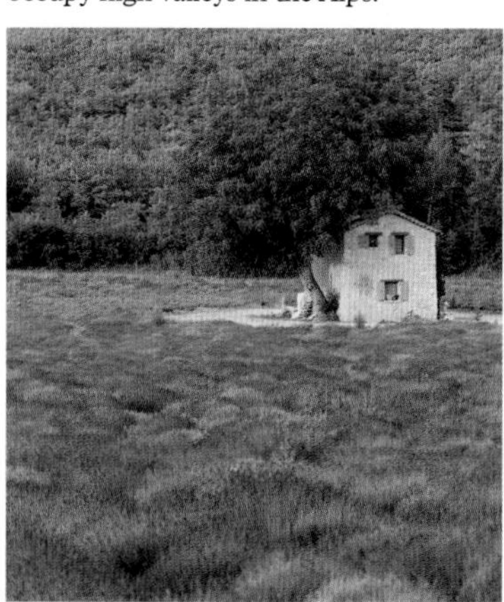

Cottage in field of lavender,
Provence

HISTORY

The Romans conquered France (then called Gaul) in the 50s BC. Roman rule began to decline in the 5th century AD and, in 486, the Frankish realm (as France was by then called) became independent under a Christian king, Clovis. In 800, Charlemagne, who had been king of the Franks since 768, became emperor of the Romans. Through conquest, his empire extended from central Italy to Denmark, and from eastern Germany to the Atlantic Ocean. However, in 843, the empire was divided into three parts and the area of France contracted.

After the Norman invasion of England in 1066, large areas of France came under English rule. By 1453, after the Hundred Years' War, France drove most of the English out. In this war, the French kings lost much power to French nobles, but Louis XI, who reigned from 1461 to 1483, laid the foundations for absolute rule by French kings.

France later became a powerful monarchy, but the French Revolution (1789–99) ended absolute rule by French kings. In 1799 Napoleon Bonaparte took power and fought a series of brilliant military campaigns before his final defeat in 1815. The monarchy was restored until 1848, when the Second Republic was founded. In 1852, Napoleon's nephew became Napoleon III, but the Third Republic was established in 1875.

France was the scene of much fighting during World War I (1914–18) and World War II (1939–45), causing great loss of life and much damage to the economy.

Post-war aid from the United States started a revival in its economy, but Communist-led strikes often crippled production. France also faced growing support for independence movements in its overseas empire. After a bitter war, France withdrew from French Indo-China in 1954 and then faced a long and costly struggle in Algeria, finally ending with Algeria's independence in 1962. The problems in Algeria caused considerable unrest in France in the 1950s and, in 1958, De Gaulle was recalled to power as prime minister. His government prepared a new constitution, establishing the Fifth Republic. It gave the president greater executive powers and reduced the power of parliament. The Electoral College elected De Gaulle as president for a seven-year term.

De Gaulle gave independence to many of its overseas territories and made France a major player in an alliance of western European nations. In 1957, France became a founder member of the European Economic Community (EEC). De Gaulle opposed British membership in 1963, considering that Britain's links with the United States would give it too much influence in Europe's economy, but his popularity waned in the late 1960s when huge student demonstrations and workers' strikes paralyzed the country and he resigned as president in 1969. His successor, Georges Pompidou, changed course in foreign affairs by re-establishing closer contacts with the United States and supporting the entry of Britain into the EEC.

POLITICS

Rapid urban growth has resulted in overcrowding and the growth of poorly built new districts to house immigrants, especially those from Spain and North Africa. The 4 million underprivileged workers from the Maghreb became a major political issue in the 1990s, leading to political successes in some areas for the extreme right. In France, as in most other countries, there also remains a disparity between the richer and the poorer regions. Other problems faced by France include unemployment, pollution, and the growing number of elderly people.

A socialist government under Lionel Jospin was elected in 1997. He increased the minimum wage, shortened the working week, and adopted the euro. However, in 2002 center-right parties won a resounding victory and Jean-Pierre Raffarin replaced Jospin as Prime Minister.

France has a long record of independence in foreign affairs and in 2003 it angered the US and some of its allies in the EU by opposing the invasion of Iraq, arguing that the UN weapons inspectors should be given more time to search for weapons of mass destruction in Iraq. France's stance angered some US congressmen who called for a boycott of French goods. The number of US tourist to France also fell.

PARIS

The capital of France is situated on the River Seine. When the Romans took Paris in 52 BC, it was a small village on the Ile de la Cité on the Seine. Under their rule it became an important administrative center. During the 14th century Paris rebelled against the Crown and declared itself an independent commune. It suffered further civil disorder during the Hundred Years' War. In the 16th century, it underwent fresh expansion, its architecture strongly influenced by the Italian Renaiassance. In the reign of Louis XIII, Cardinal Richelieu established Paris as the cultural and political center of Europe. The French Revolution began in Paris when the Bastille was stormed by crowds in 1789. Under Emperor Napoleon I the city began to assume its present-day form. The work of modernization was continued under Napoleon III, when Baron Haussmann was commissioned to plan the boulevards, bridges and parks. Although occupied during the Franco-Prussian War (1870–71) and again in World War II, Paris was not badly damaged. The city proper consists of the Paris department, Ville de Paris. Its many famous buildings and landmarks include the Eiffel Tower, Arc de Triomphe, the Louvre, Notre Dame, and the Pompidou Center. Paris is an important European cultural, commercial and communications center and is noted for its fashion industry and for the manufacture of luxury articles.

A resounding "no" vote in the referendum on the European constitution in May 2005 led to the resignation of Raffarin and further decline in the relationship between Jacques Chirac and Tony Blair over the UK rebate and Common Agricultural Policy subsidies for French farmers.

ECONOMY

France is one of the world's most developed countries. It has the world's fourth largest economy. Its natural resources include its fertile soil, together with deposits of bauxite, coal, iron ore, oil, and natural gas, and potash. France is one of the world's top manufacturing nations and it has often innovated in bold and imaginative ways. The TGV, Concorde, and hypermarkets are all typical examples. Paris is a world center of fashion industries, but France has many other industrial towns and cities. Major manufactures include aircraft, automobiles, chemicals, electronic products, machinery, metal products, processed food, steel and textiles.

Agriculture employs about 2% of the people, but France is the largest producer of farm products in Western Europe, producing most of the food it needs. Wheat is a leading crop and livestock farming is of major importance. The food-processing industry is well known, especially for its cheeses, such as Brie and Camembert, and its top-quality wines from areas such as Alsace, Bordeaux, Burgundy, Champagne, and the Loire valley. Fishing and forestry are leading industries. France is a popular year-round destination both for its beaches and for its mountains.

MONACO

Area 0.4 sq mi [1 sq km]
Population 32,000
Capital (population) Monaco (30,000)
Government Constitutional monarchy
Religions Roman Catholic 62%, Protestant 30%
Currency Euro = 100 cents
Website www.visitmonaco.com

The tiny Principality of Monaco consists of a narrow strip of coastline and a rocky peninsula on the French Riviera. Like the rest of the Riviera, it has mild, moist winters and dry, sunny summers. Average temperatures range from 50°F [10°C] in January to 75°F [24°C] in July. The average annual rainfall is about 31 in [800 mm].

The Genoese from northern Italy gained control of Monaco in the 12th century and, from 1297, it has been ruled for most of the time by the Genoese Grimaldi family. Monaco attracted little attention until the late 19th century when it developed into a major tourist resort. World attention was focused on Monaco in 1956 when Prince Rainier III of Monaco married the actress Grace Kelly. Their son, Prince Albert, became ruler upon Rainier's death in 2005. The country's wealth comes mainly from banking, finance, gambling and tourism. There are three casinos, a marine museum, a zoo, and botanical gardens. It also stages the Monte Carlo Rally and the Monaco Grand Prix. Manufactures include chemicals, electronic goods and plastics. In 2001, France threatened to break its ties with Monaco unless it revised its legal system and prevented money laundering.

French Guiana

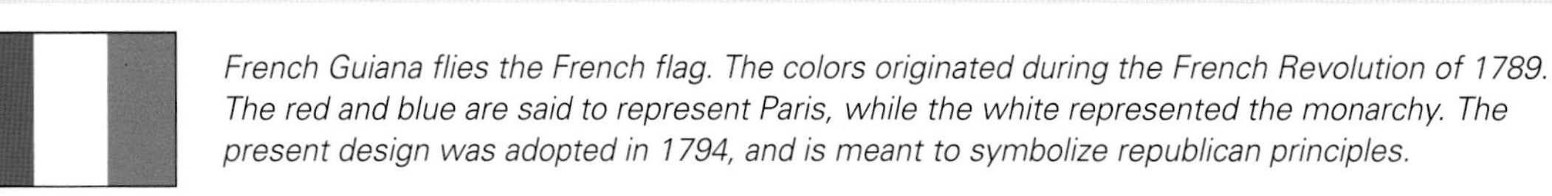

French Guiana flies the French flag. The colors originated during the French Revolution of 1789. The red and blue are said to represent Paris, while the white represented the monarchy. The present design was adopted in 1794, and is meant to symbolize republican principles.

Area 34,749 sq mi [90,000 sq km]
Population 191,000
Capital (population) Cayenne (51,000)
Government Overseas department of France
Ethnic groups Black or Mulatto 66%, East Indian/Chinese and Amerindian 12%, White 12%, others 10%
Languages French (official)
Religions Roman Catholic
Currency Euro = 100 cents
Website www.guyane.pref.gouv.fr

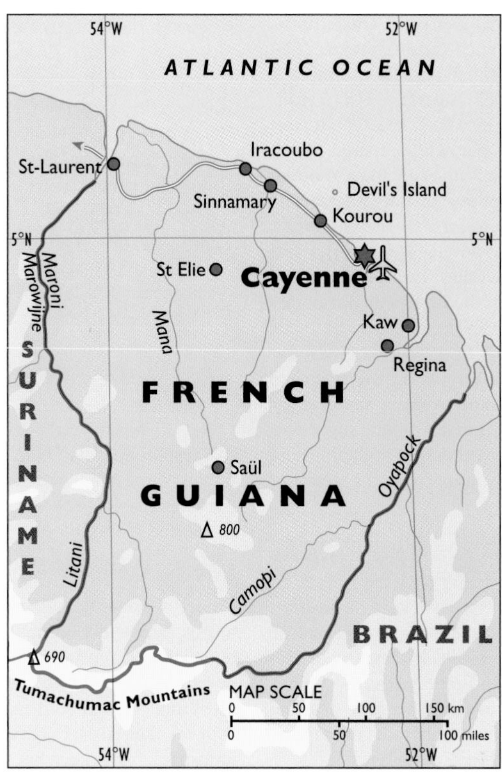

CAYENNE

Capital and chief port of French Guiana, on the Atlantic coast. Founded in 1643 and named after an Indian Chief. Places of interest include the cathedral, the ruined 17th century Fort Cépérou,Hôtel de Ville, and museums of local history.

French Guiana is a French overseas department and the smallest country in mainland South America. The coastal plain is swampy in places, but dry areas are cultivated, particularly near the capital Cayenne. The River Maroni forms the border with Suriname, and the River Oyapock its eastern border with Brazil. Inland lies a plateau, with the low Tumuchumac Mountains in the south. Most of the rivers run north towards the Atlantic Ocean.

Rainforest covers approximately 90% of the land and contains valuable hardwood species. Mangrove swamps line parts of the coast; other areas are covered by tropical savanna.

CLIMATE

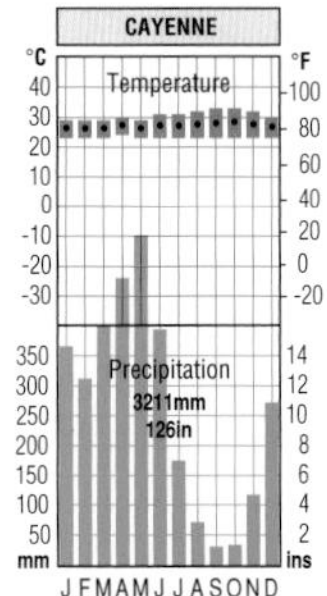

French Guiana has a hot equatorial climate with high temperatures throughout the year. Rainfall is heavy, especially between December and June, but it is dry between August and October. Northeast trade winds blow across the country constantly.

HISTORY

The first people to live in what is now French Guiana were Amerindians. Today only a few of them survive in the interior. The first Europeans to explore the coast arrived in 1500 and they were followed by adventurers seeking El Dorado. The French were the first settlers in 1604 and French merchants founded Cayenne in 1637. The area became a French colony in the late 17th century, with a plantation economy dependent on African slaves. It remained French except for a brief period in the early 19th century. Slavery was abolished in 1848, and Asian laborers were introduced to work the land. From the time of the French Revolution, France used the colony as a penal settlement, and between 1852 and 1945 the country was notorious for the harsh treatment of prisoners. Captain Alfred Dreyfus was imprisoned on Devil's Island.

POLITICS

In 1946, French Guiana became an overseas department of France, and in 1974 it also became an administrative region. An independence movement developed in the 1980s, but most of the people want to retain links with France and continue to obtain financial aid to develop their territory.

ECONOMY

Although it has rich forest and mineral resources, such as bauxite (aluminum ore), French Guiana is a developing country with high unemployment. It depends greatly on France for money to run its services and the government is the country's biggest employer. Since 1975, Kourou has been the European Space Agency's rocket-launching site and has earned money for France by sending communications satellites into space.

The main industries are fishing, forestry, gold mining, and agriculture. Crops include bananas, cassava, rice, and sugar cane. French Guiana's main exports are shrimps, timber, and rosewood essence.

DEVIL'S ISLAND (ÎLE DU DIABLE)

The smallest island of the three Iles du Salut off the coast of French Guiana. A notorious French penal colony from 1852 to 1945 and most famous for the prison and the harsh treatment of its inmates whether they be political prisoners or murderers. Few prisoners made it off the island due to the high levels of disease and escape was almost impossible. The publicity surrounding the case of Captain Alfred Dreyfus in 1894 brought the horrors of this prison to the fore.

The launch of the third Ariane space rocket, *seen from a beach in Kourou, French Guiana*

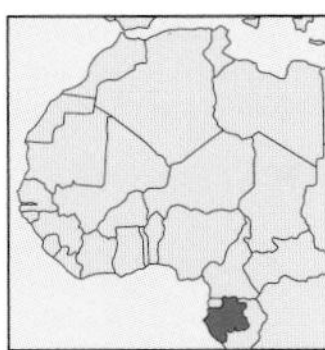

Gabon

Gabon's flag was adopted in 1960 when the country became independent from France. The central yellow stripe symbolizes the Equator which runs through Gabon. The green stands for the country's forests. The blue symbolizes the sea.

RIVER OGOOUÉ (OGOWE)

The main river of Gabon, its basin drains nearly the entire country. Some of its tributaries can be found in Cameroon the Republic of Congo, and Equatorial Guinea. The Ogooué is about 560 mi [900 km] in length, rising in the northwest of the Bateke Plateau. It empties into the Gulf of Guinea, south of Port Gentil. The delta is approximately 62 mi [100 km] long and 2 mi wide. The total waterbasin is 86,431sq mi [223,856 sq km], and is largely made up of forest.

Area 103,347 sq mi [267,668 sq km]
Population 1,355,000
Capital (population) Libreville (362,000)
Government Multiparty republic
Ethnic groups Bantu tribes: Fang, Bandjabi, Bapounou, Eshira, Myene, Nzebi, Obamba and Okande
Languages French (official), Fang, Myene, Nzebi, Bapounou/Eschira, Bandjabi
Religions Christianity 75%, animist, Islam
Currency CFA franc = 100 centimes
Website www.senat.ga

The Gabonese Republic lies on the Equator in west-central Africa. In area, it is a little larger than the United Kingdom, with a coastline 500 mi [800 km] long. Behind the narrow, partly lagoon-lined coastal plain, the land rises to hills, plateaux and mountains divided by deep valleys carved by the River Ogooué and its tributaries.

Dense rainforest covers about 75% of Gabon, with tropical savanna in the east and south. The forests teem with wildlife, and Gabon has several national parks and wildlife reserves.

CLIMATE

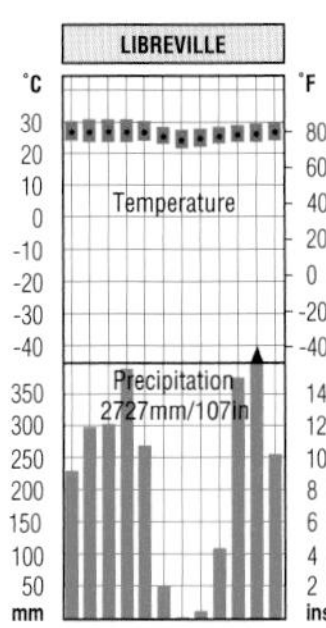

Most of Gabon has an equatorial climate. There are high temperatures and humidity throughout the year. The rainfall is heavy and the skies are often cloudy.

HISTORY

Explorers from Portugal reached the Gabon coast in the 1470s, and the area later became a source of slaves.

In 1839 France established the first European settlement. In 1849 freed slaves founded Libreville. Gabon became a French colony in the 1880s and achieved full independence in 1960.

Léon Mba was Gabon's first president from 1960 to 1967. In 1964, an attempted coup was put down when French troops intervened and crushed the revolt. In 1967, following the death of Léon Mba, Bernard-Albert Bongo, who later renamed himself El Hadj Omar Bongo, became president. He made Gabon a one-party state in 1968.

POLITICS

Free elections took place in 1990. The Gabonese Democratic Party (PDG) won a majority in the National Assembly. President Bongo, of the PDG, won the presidential elections in 1993, although accusations of fraud and corruption led to riots in Libreville. The international community condemned Bongo for his harsh suppression of popular demonstrations. He was re-elected in 1998. In 2003, constitutional changes enabled Bongo to stand as president as many times as he wished. In November 2005 he was again elected president and despite the preemptive protestations of the opposition, the elections were deemed free and fair by international observers.

ECONOMY

Gabon's abundant natural resources include its forests, oil and natural gas deposits near Port Gentil, together with manganese and uranium. These mineral deposits make Gabon one of Africa's wealthier countries.

However, agriculture still employs about 75% of the workforce, most farmers producing little more than they need to support their families. Crops include bananas, cassava, corn, and sugar cane. Cocoa and coffee are grown for export. Other exports include oil, manganese, timber and wood products, and uranium.

LIBREVILLE

Capital and largest city of Gabon, at the mouth of the River Gabon, on the Gulf of Guinea. Founded by the French in 1843, and named Libreville (French for Freetown) in 1849, it was initially a refuge for escaped slaves. The city expanded with the development of the country's minerals and is now also an administrative center. Places of interest include the Musée des Arts et Traditions, the French cultural center, the presidential palace, St. Marie's Cathedral, the Eglise St. Michel with its carved wooden columns, Nkembo, the Arboretum de Sibang, and two cultural villages. Other industries include timber (hardwoods), palm oil, and rubber.

Timber stored at Owendo, *a suburb of Libreville*

Gambia, The

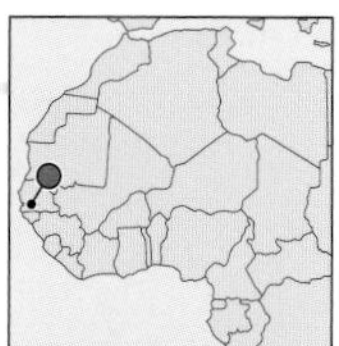

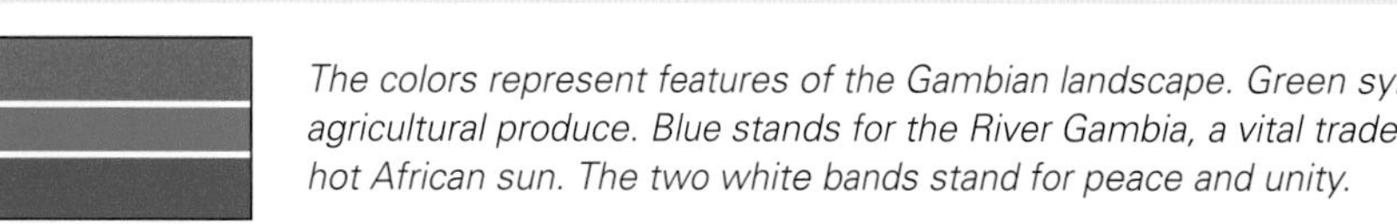

The colors represent features of the Gambian landscape. Green symbolizes the land and agricultural produce. Blue stands for the River Gambia, a vital trade route. Red represents the hot African sun. The two white bands stand for peace and unity.

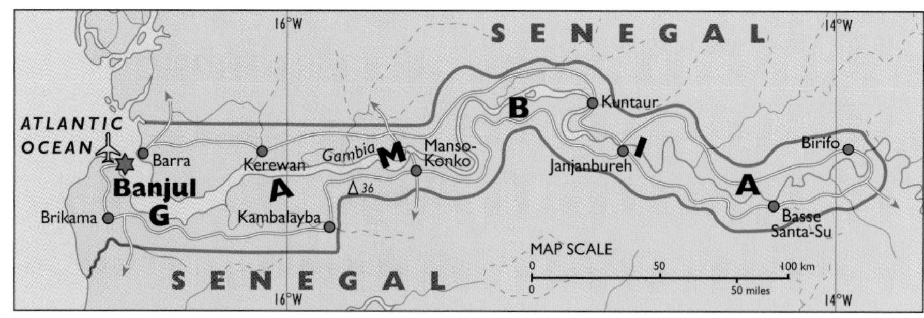

The Republic of the Gambia is the smallest country in mainland Africa. It consists of a narrow strip of land bordering the River Gambia. The Gambia is almost entirely enclosed by Senegal, except along the short Atlantic coastline. The land is flat near the sea.

Mangrove swamps line the river banks. Much tropical savanna has been cleared for farming. The Gambia is rich in wildlife and has six national parks and reserves as well as several forest parks.

CLIMATE

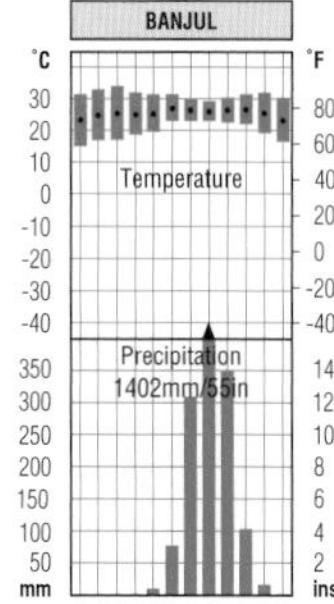

The Gambia has hot and humid summers, but winter temperatures (November to May) drop to around 61°F [16°C]. In the summer, moist winds heading southwest bring rain, which is heaviest on the coast.

HISTORY

Portuguese mariners reached Gambia's coast in 1455, when the area was part of the Mali empire. In the 16th century, Portuguese and English slave traders operated in the area. English traders bought rights to trade on the River Gambia in 1588, and in 1664 the English established a settlement on an island in the river estuary. In 1765, the British founded a colony called Senegambia, which included parts of present-day Gambia and Senegal. In 1783, Britain handed this colony over to France.

During the 1860s and 1870s, Britain and France discussed the exchange of the Gambia for some other French territory. No agreement was reached and Britain made the Gambia a British colony in 1888. It remained under British rule intil it achieved full independence in 1965 with Dawda Jawara as prime minister. In 1970 the Gambia became a republic.

POLITICS

Relations between the French-speaking Senegalese and the English-speaking Gambians form a major political issue. In 1981, an attempted coup in the Gambia was put down with the help of Senegalese troops. In 1982, The Gambia and Senegal set up a defence alliance, called the Confederation of Senegambia, though this alliance was later dissolved in 1989.

In 1992, Jawara was re-elected as president for a fifth term. In July 1994, he was overthrown in a military coup and fled into exile. The coup was led by Yahya Jammeh who was elected president in 1996. His regime faced charges of political repression. In 2001, Jammeh lifted the ban on opposition parties and was reelected, though he is still criticized for impingeing press freedom.

Area 4,361 sq mi [11,295 sq km]
Population 1,547,000
Capital (population) Banjul (42,000)
Government Military regime
Ethnic groups Mandinka 42%, Fula 18%, Wolof 16%, Jola 10%, Serahuli 9%, others
Languages English (official), Mandinka, Wolof, Fula
Religions Islam 90%, Christianity 9%, traditional beliefs 1%
Currency Dalasi = 100 butut
Website www.gambia.gm

ECONOMY

Agriculture is the main activity, employing more than 80% of the workforce. However, the government announced in 2004 that large oil reserves had been discovered. The main food crops include cassava, millet. and sorghum, but groundnuts and groundnut products are the chief exports.

The money sent home by Gambians living abroad is important for the economy. Tourism is a growing industry.

MANGROVE

Common name for any one of 120 species of tropical trees or shrubs found in marine swampy areas. Also known as coastal woodland, tidal forest and mangrove forest.Its stilt-like aerial roots, which arise from the branches and hang down into the water, produce a thick undergrowth, useful in the reclaiming of land along tropical coasts. Even within the same delta the composition of the mangrove can vary substantially according to the conditions of salinity, tidal system and substrate (soil foundation). Some species have roots that rise up out of the water. It grows to a height of 70 ft [20 m].

Batik for sale *outside Gena Bes batik showroom and workshop, Bakau*

BANJUL

Capital of the Gambia, the city lies on St. Mary's Island, where the River Gambia enters the Atlantic Ocean. It was founded as a trading post by the British in 1816 and originally named Bathhurst after Henry Bathurst, the secretary of the British Colonial Office. Banjul is Gambia's chief port and commercial center. The main industry is groundnut processing, though tourism is growing rapidly.

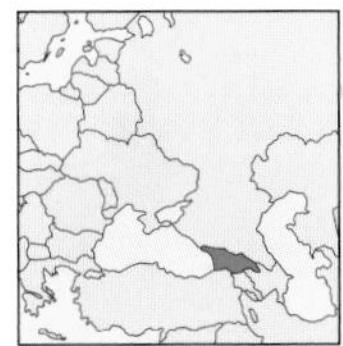

The Republic of Georgia adopted a new flag in 2004. The flag had been in use some 500 years before as that of the medieval Georgian kingdom. It was subsequently used as the official symbol of the political party—United National Movement.

Georgia is located on the borders of Europe and Asia, facing the Black Sea. The land is rugged with the Caucasus Mountains forming its northern border. The highest mountain in this range, Mount Elbrus (18,506 ft [5,642 m]), lies over the border in Russia.

Lower ranges run through southern Georgia, through which pass the borders with Turkey and Armenia. The Black Sea coastal plains are in the west. In the east a low plateau extends into Azerbaijan. The main river in the east is the River Kura, on which the capital Tbilisi stands.

Area 26,911 sq mi [69,700 sq km]
Population 4,694,000
Capital (population) Tbilisi (1,268,000)
Government Multiparty republic
Ethnic groups Georgian 70%, Armenian 8%, Russian 6%, Azeri 6%, Ossetiam 3%, Greek 2%, Abkhaz 2%, others
Languages Georgian (official), Russian
Religions Georgian Orthodox 65%, Islam 11%, Russian Orthodox 10%, Amenian Apostolic 8%
Currency Lari = 100 tetri
Website www.parliament.ge

CLIMATE

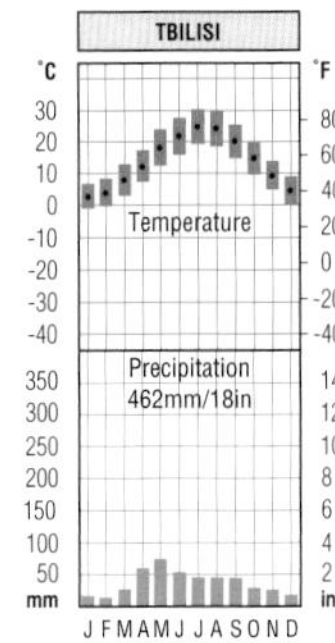

The Black Sea plains have hot summers and mild winters, when the temperature seldom drops below freezing. Rainfall is heavy, but inland Tbilisi has moderate rainfall, with the heaviest rains in the spring and early summer.

HISTORY

The first Georgian state was set up nearly 2,000 years ago and, by the 3rd century BC, most of what is now Georgia was united as a single kingdom. For much of its history, Georgia was ruled by various conquerors. For example, between about 60 BC and the 11th century, the area was ruled successively by Romans, Persians, Byzantines, Arabs, and Seljuk Turks. Christianity was introduced in AD 330 and most Georgians are now members of the Georgian Orthodox Church. Georgia freed itself from foreign rule in the 11th and 12th centuries, but Mongol armies invaded in the 13th century. From the 16th to the 18th centuries, Iran and the Turkish Ottoman Empire struggled for control of the area.

In the late 18th century, Georgia sought the protection of Russia and, by the early 19th century was part of the Russian Empire. After the Russian Revolution of 1917, Georgia declared itself independent and was recognized by the League of Nations. However, Russian troops invaded in 1921, making Georgia part of the Soviet regime. From 1922, Georgia, Armenia, and Azerbaijan were linked, forming the Transcaucasian Republic. But, in 1936, the territories became separate republics within the Soviet Union. Renowned for their longevity, the people of Georgia are famous for producing Josef Stalin, who was born in Gori, 40 mi [65 km] northwest of the capital Tbilisi. Stalin ruled the Soviet Union from 1929 until his death in 1953.

POLITICS

A maverick among the Soviet republics, Georgia was the first to declare its independence after the Baltic states (April 1991) and deferred joining the Commonwealth of Independent States (CIS) until 1993.

In 1991, Zviad Gamsakhurdia, a non-Communist who had been democratically elected president of Georgia in 1990, found himself holed up in Tbilisi's KGB headquarters, under siege from rebel forces. They represented widespread opposition to his government's policies, ranging from the economy to the imprisonment of his opponents. In January 1992, following the breakup of the Soviet Union, Gamsakhurdia fled the country and a military council took power.

Georgia contains three regions of minority peoples: South Ossetia, in north-central Georgia, where civil war broke out in the early 1990s, with nationalists demanding the right to set up their own governments; Abkhazia in the northwest, which proclaimed its sovereignty in 1994 with fierce fighting continuing until the late 1990s; Adjaria (or Adzharia) in the southwest, whose autonomy was recognized in Georgia's constitution in 2000.

In March 1992, Eduard Shevardnadze, former Soviet Foreign Minister, was named head of state and was elected, unopposed, later that year. He was reelected in 1995 and 2000, but Georgia faced mounting problems, which threatened its stability. In 2001, Georgia and Abkhazia signed a peace accord and agreed to the safe return of refugees. In 2002, Russian and Georgian troops attacked Chechen rebels in Pankisi Gorge in northeastern Georgia. US officials believed that Taliban fighters and other Islamic terrorists had also moved into this region. In 2004, Mikhail Saakashvili was elected president, but his authority was challenged by separatists in the three minority regions. 2005 saw an agreement by Russia to withdraw troops from its two remaining bases by the end of 2008.

ECONOMY

Georgia is a developing country. Agriculture is important. Major products include barley, citrus fruits, grapes for wine-making, corn, tea, tobacco, and vegetables. Food processing, and silk- and perfume-making are other important activities. Sheep and cattle are reared.

Barite (barium ore), coal, copper, and manganese are mined, and tourism is a major industry on the Black Sea coast. Georgia's mountains have huge potential for generating hydroelectric power, but most of Georgia's electricity is generated in Russia or Ukraine.

TBILISI (TIFLIS)

Largest city and capital of Georgia, on the upper River Kura. It was founded in the 5th century ad, and ruled successively by the Iranians, Byzantines, Arabs, Mongols, and Turks, before coming under Russian rule in 1801. Tbilisi's importance lies in its location on the trade route between the Black Sea and Caspian Sea. It is now the administrative and economic focus of modern Transcaucasia. Industries include chemicals, petroleum products, locomotives, electrical equipment.

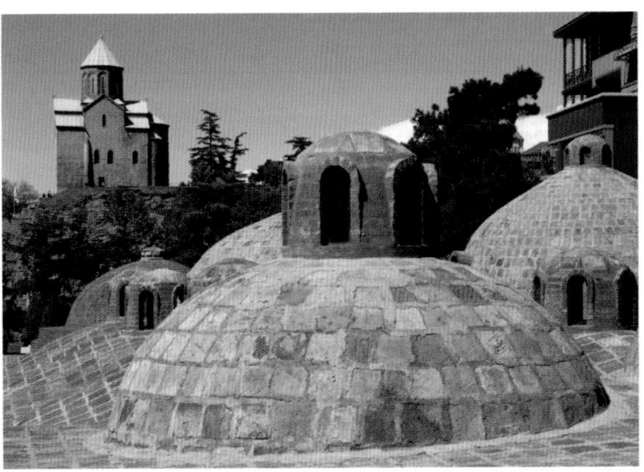

The historic Tbilisi Baths, *housed in subterranean caverns with brick domes*

Ghana's flag has red, green, and yellow bands like the flag of Ethiopia, Africa's oldest independent nation. These colors symbolize African unity. The black star is a symbol of African freedom. Ghana's flag was adopted when the country became independent in 1957.

Area 92,098 sq mi [238,533 sq km]
Population 20,757,000
Capital (population) Accra (949,000)
Government Republic
Ethnic groups Akan 44%, Moshi-Dagomba 16%, Ewe 13%, Ga 8%, Gurma 3%, Yoruba 1%
Languages English (official), Akan, Moshi-Dagomba, Ewe, Ga
Religions Christianity 63%, traditional beliefs 21%, Islam 16%
Currency Cedi = 100 pesewas
Website www.ghana.gov.gh

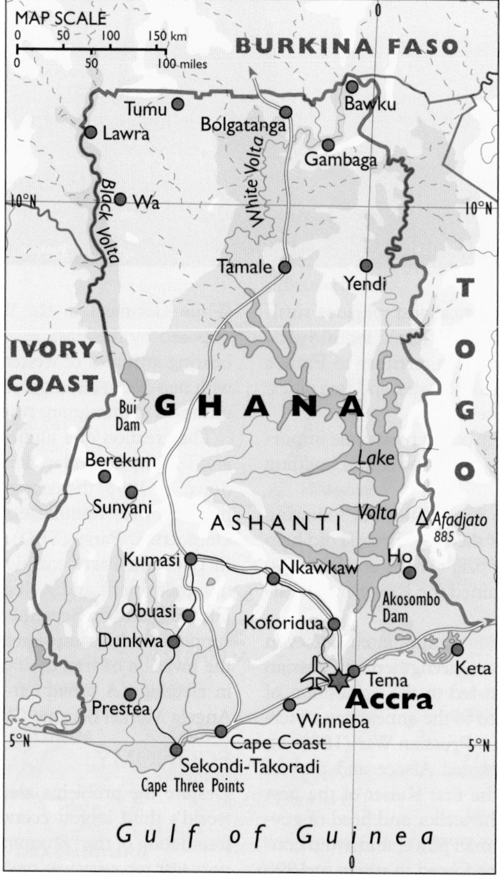

The Republic of Ghana faces the Gulf of Guinea in West Africa. This hot country, just north of the Equator, was formerly called the Gold Coast. Behind the thickly populated southern coastal plains, which are lined with lagoons, lies a plateau region in the southwest.

Northern Ghana is drained by the Black and White Volta Rivers, which flow into Lake Volta. This lake, which has formed behind the Akosombo Dam, is one of the world's largest artificially created lakes.

Rainforests grow in the southwest. To the north, the forests merge into savanna (tropical grassland with some woodland). More open grasslands dominate in the far north.

CLIMATE

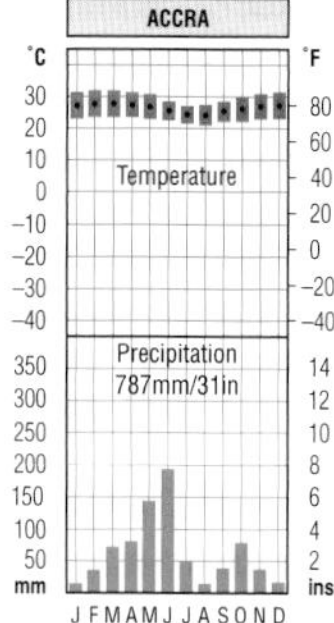

Ghana has a tropical climate. A cool offshore current reduces temperatures on the coast, and the north is hotter. The heaviest rains occur in the southwest. There are marked dry seasons in northern and eastern Ghana.

HISTORY

Ghana was a great African empire which flourished to the northwest of present-day Ghana between the AD 300s and 1000s. Modern Ghana was the first country in the Commonwealth to be ruled by black Africans.

Portuguese explorers reached the area in 1471 and named it the Gold Coast. The area became a center of the slave trade in the 17th century. The slave trade was ended in the 1860s and the British gradually took control of the area. The country became independent in 1957, when it was renamed Ghana.

POLITICS

After independence, attempts were made to develop the economy by creating large state-owned manufacturing industries. But debt and corruption, together with falls in the price of cocoa, the chief export, caused economic problems. This led to instability and frequent coups. In 1981, power was invested in a Provisional National Defense Council, led by Flight-Lieutenant Jerry Rawlings.

The government steadied the economy and introduced several new policies, including the relaxation of government controls. In 1992, a new constitution was introduced which allowed for multiparty elections. Rawlings was reelected later that year, and served until his retirement in 2000. The economy expanded in the 1990s, largely because the government followed World Bank policies. When Rawlings retired, the opposition leader, John Agyekum Kufuor, leader of the New Patriotic Party, was elected president, defeating Rawlings' vice-president. He was reelected in 2004.

ECONOMY

The World Bank classifies Ghana as a "low-income" developing country. Most people are poor and farming employs 59% of the population. Food crops include cassava, groundnuts, corn, millet, plantains, rice and yams. But cocoa is the most valuable export crop. Timber and gold are also exported. Other valuable crops include tobacco, coffee, coconuts, and palm kernels.

Many small factories produce goods, such as beverages, cement, and clothing, for local consumption. The aluminum smelter at Tema, a port near Accra, is the country's largest factory. There are plans to construct around 378 mi [600 km] of pipeline which will form part of the West African Gas Pipeline Project. The aim is to lessen the dependence of electricity production on hydroelectric stations.

The wives of a Nankani chief *use natural pigments and dung to decorate the huts within their compound; one of the women uses an earth-based pigment to paint a frieze of crocodile reliefs*

ACCRA

Capital and largest city of Ghana, on the Gulf of Guinea. Occupied by the Ga people since the 15th century, it became the capital of Britain's Gold Coast colony in 1875. Today it is a major port and economic center and is increasingly popular with tourists. Industries include engineering, timber, textiles, chemicals. The principal export is cacao.

Guinea's flag was adopted when the country became independent from France in 1958. It uses the colors of the flag of Ethiopia, Africa's oldest nation, which symbolize African unity. The red represents work, the yellow justice, and the green solidarity.

The Republic of Guinea, which faces the Atlantic Ocean in West Africa, can be divided into four regions: an alluvial coastal plain, which includes the capital, Conakry; the highland region of the Fouta Djallon, the source of one of Africa's longest rivers, the Niger; the northeast savanna; and the southeast Guinea Highlands, which rise to 5,748 ft [1,752 m] at Mount Nimba.

Mangrove swamps grow along parts of the coast. Inland, the Fouta Djallon is largely open grassland. North eastern Guinea is tropical savanna, with acacia and shea scattered across the grassland. Rainforests of ebony, mahogany, and teak grow in the Guinea Highlands.

Area 94,925 sq mi [245,857 sq km]
Population 9,246,000
Capital (population) Conakry (1,232,000)
Government Multiparty republic
Ethnic groups Peuhl 40%, Malinke 30%, Soussou 20%, others 10%
Languages French (official)
Religions Islam 85%, Christianity 8%, traditional beliefs 7%
Currency Guinean franc = 100 cauris
Website www.guinee.gov.gn

CLIMATE

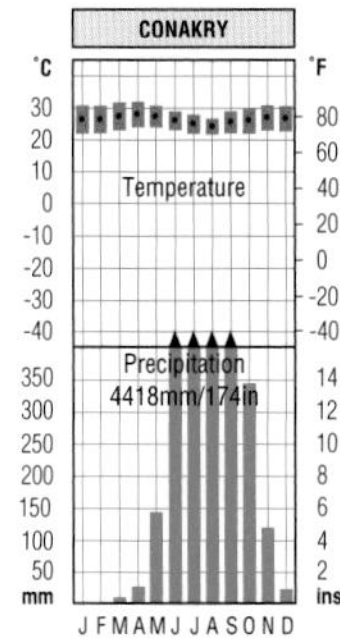

Guinea has a tropical climate. Conakry on the coast has heavy rains during its relatively cool season between May and November. Hot, dry harmattan winds blow southwestwards from the Sahara in the dry season. The Fouta Djalon is cooler than the coast. The driest region is in the northeast. This region and the southeastern highlands have greater temperature variations than on the coast.

HISTORY

The northeast Guinea plains formed part of the medieval Empire of Ghana. The Malinke formed the Mali Empire, which dominated the region in the 12th century. The Songhai Empire supplanted the Malinke in the 15th century.

Portuguese explorers arrived in the mid-15th century and the slave trade began soon afterwards. From the 17th century, other European slave traders became active in Guinea. In the early 18th century, the Fulani embarked on a *jihad* (holy war) and gained control of the Fouta Djallon. Following a series of wars, France won control in the mid-19th century and, in 1891, it made Guinea a French colony. France exploited its bauxite deposits and mining unions developed.

In 1958, Guinea voted to become an independent republic and France severed all aid. Its first president, Sékou Touré (1958–84), adopted a Marxist programme of reform and embraced Pan-Africanism. Opposition parties were banned, and dissent brutally suppressed. In 1970, Portuguese Guinea (now Guinea-Bissau) invaded Guinea. Conakry later acted as the headquarters for independence movements in Guinea-Bissau. A military coup followed Touré's death in 1984, and Colonel Lansana Conté established the Military Committee for National Recovery (CMRN). Conté improved relations with the West and introduced free-enterprise policies.

CONAKRY

Capital city of Guinea, Conakry is located on Tombo Island, in the Atlantic Ocean and is connected to the mainland via a causeway. Founded in 1884 and occupied by French forces in 1887, it is Guinea's largest city. A major port and the administrative and commercial center of Guinea, its economy revolves largely round the port, from where it exports alumina and bananas. Manufactures include food products, automobiles and beverages. The city is noted for its botanical garden. The Marché Madina, one of the largest markets in west Africa, is also worth a visit as are the cathedral and national museum.

POLITICS

Civil unrest forced the introduction of a multiparty system in 1992. Elections in 1993 confirmed Conté as president, amid claims of voting fraud. In February 1996, Conté foiled an attempted military coup. He was reelected in 1998.

By 2000, Guinea was home to about 500,000 refugees from the wars in neighbouring Sierra Leone and Liberia. In 2000, rebel incursions from these countries killed more than 1,000 people, caused massive population displacement, and threatened to destablilize Guinea. Conté was reelected in 2003, though the poll was boycotted by the opposition. His ailing health brings into question whether he will survive the full term. The president survived an assassination attempt in 2005 when shots were fired at his car.

ECONOMY

The World Bank classifies Guinea as a "low-income" developing country. It is the world's second-largest producer of bauxite which accounts for 90% of its exports. Guinea has 25% of the world's known reserves of bauxite.

Other natural resources include diamonds, gold, iron ore, and uranium. Due to the mining industry, the rail and road infrastructure is improving. Agriculture (mainly at subsistence level) employs 78% of the workforce. Major crops include bananas, cassava, coffee, palm kernels, pineapples, rice. and sweet potatoes. Cattle and other livestock are raised in highland areas.

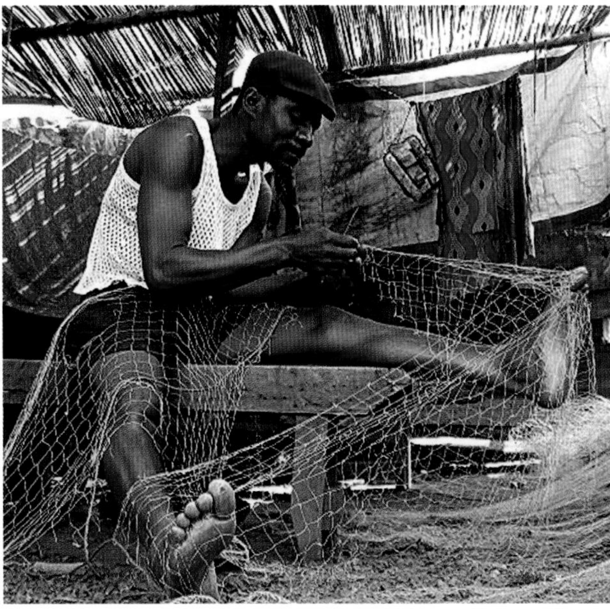

***A Guinean fisherman** repairs a fishing net in Conakry*

Guinea-Bissau

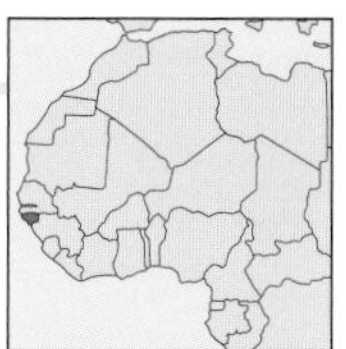

Red symbolizes the blood shed in the liberation struggle; yellow is for the hot African sun; green represents the fertile land and hope for the future. The black star stands for the African continent, paying homage to the flag of Ghana, the first African colony to gain independence.

Area 13,948 sq mi [36,125 sq km]
Population 1,388,000
Capital (population) Bissau (200,000)
Government Interim government
Ethnic groups Balanta 30%, Fula 20%, Manjaca 14%, Mandinga 13%, Papel 7%
Languages Portuguese (official),Crioulo
Religions Traditional beliefs 50%, Islam 45%, Christianity 5%
Currency CFA franc = 100 centimes
Website www.republica-da-guine-bissau.org

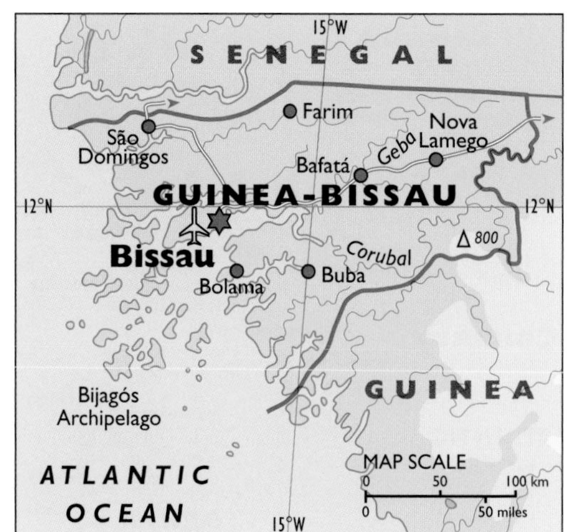

The Republic of Guinea-Bissau is a small country in West Africa. The land is mostly low-lying, with a broad, swampy, coastal plain and many flat offshore islands, including the Bijagós Archipelago. Mangrove forests line the coasts, and dense rainforest covers much of the coastal plain.

CLIMATE

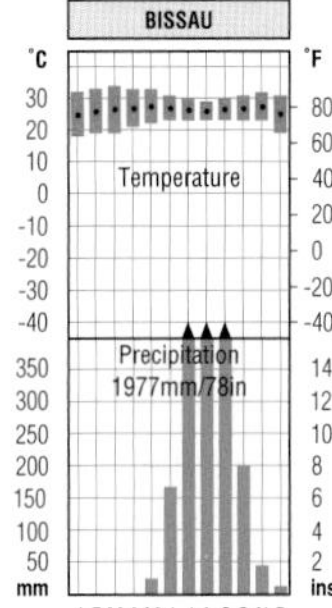

The country has a tropical climate, with its dry season from December to May and its rainy season from June to November.

HISTORY

It was first visited by Portuguese navigators in 1446. From the 17th to the early 19th century, Portugal used the coast as a slave-trading base. Portugal appointed a governor to administer Guinea-Bissau and the Cape Verde Islands in 1836, but in 1879 the territories separated and Guinea-Bissau became a colony, then called Portuguese Guinea. Development was slow, partly because the territory did not attract settlers on the same scale as Portugal's much healthier African colonies of Angola and Mozambique.

In 1956, African nationalists in Portuguese Guinea and Cape Verde founded the African Party for the Independence of Guinea and Cape Verde (PAIGC). Because Portugal seemed determined to hang on to its overseas territories, the PAIGC began a guerrilla war in 1963. By 1968, it held two-thirds of the country. In 1972, a rebel National Assembly, elected by the people in the PAIGC-controlled areas, voted to make the country independent as Guinea-Bissau.

POLITICS

In 1974, it formally achieved independence (followed by Cape Verde in 1975). The independent nation faced many problems arising from its under-developed economy and its lack of trained personnel. Guinea-Bissau's leaders favored union with Cape Verde. This objective was abandoned in 1980, when an army coup, led by Major João Vieira, overthrew the government. The Revolutionary Council which took over opposed unification with Cape Verde; it concentrated on national policies and socialist reforms.

In 1991, the PAIGC voted to introduce a multiparty system. The PAIGC won the 1994 elections, and Vieira was elected president. In 1998 an army rebellion sparked a civil war. The army rebels took power in 1999, but elections were held in 1999–2000. Kumba Ialá became president in 2000 but was overthrown in a coup in 2003. Civilian government was restored in 2004 when parliamentary elections were held.

ECONOMY

Guinea-Bissau is a poor country. Agriculture employs more than 70% of the workforce, but most farming is at subsistence level. Major crops include beans, coconuts, groundnuts, corn, and rice. Fishing is also important.

BIJAGOS ARCHIPELAGO

Formed by the prehistoric delta of the Rio Grande de Buba and the Rio Geba, the Bijagos Archipelago consists of 88 islands and islets spread over 4,000 sq mi [10,000 sq km]. The rainy season brings fresh water into the coastal zone, while coastal currents from north and south meet, making the delta region vulnerable yet biologically rich. Between the islands, extensive mud flats are drained by a network of canals and creeks as the tide recedes. The characteristic vegetation of the islands is the palm groves. The tidal areas form a unique mosaic of mangroves and tidal flats. Hippos have adapted to life in sea water, while otters coexist with manatees, for whom the archipelago forms one of the most important strongholds in the region. Two species of dolphin live here. Reptiles include two species of crocodile and four species of marine turtle, including the green turtle for which the Bijagos Archipelago is the most important breeding site in West Africa. The archipelago is inhabited almost exclusively by the Bijagos ethnic group.

A fisherman *tips his boat over to empty it of water, on a beach of the Bijagos Island*

BISSAU

Capital of Guinea-Bissau, near the mouth of the River Geba, western Africa. Established by the Portuguese as a slave-trading center in 1687, Bissau became a free port in 1869. It replaced Bonama as capital in 1941. The port has recently been improved. Industries include oil processing.

Guyana's flag was adopted in 1966 when the country became independent from Britain. The colors symbolize the people's energy in building a new nation (red), their perseverance (black), minerals (yellow), rivers (white), and agriculture and forests (green).

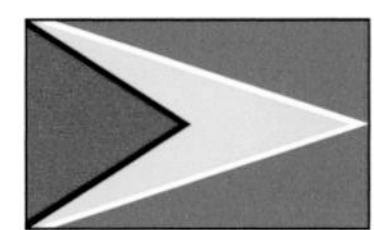

The Co-operative Republic of Guyana borders the Atlantic Ocean. It is the only English-speaking country in mainland South America and. The coastal plain, where the majority lives, is between 2 and 30 mi [3–48 km] wide, much of it below sea level. Dykes prevent flooding. Inland is hilly and forested and this terrain makes up Guyana's largest region. The land rises to 9,219 ft [2,810 m] in the Pakaraima Mountains, part of the Guiana Highlands on Guyana's western border. Other highlands are in the south and southwest. Guyana has impressive waterfalls, such as the King George VI Falls (1,601 ft [488 m], the Great Falls (840 ft [256 m]), and Kaieteur Falls (741 ft [226 m]).

The coastal plain is largely farmed, but wet savanna covers some areas. Inland, rainforests, rich in plant and animal species, cover about 85% of the country. Savanna occurs in the southwest.

CLIMATE

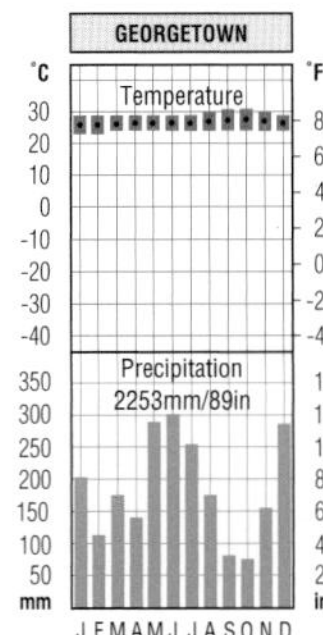

Guyana has a hot, humid equatorial climate. Rainfall ranges from 90 in [2,280 mm] on the coast to 140 in [3,560 mm] in the rainforest region. The rainfall decreases to the west and south.

Area 83,000 sq mi [214,969 sq km]
Population 706,000
Capital (population) Georgetown (150,000)
Government Multiparty republic
Ethnic groups East Indian 50%, Black 36%, Amerindian 7%, others
Languages English (official), Creole, Hindi, Urdu
Religions Christianity 50%, Hinduism 35%, Islam 10%, others
Currency Guyanese dollar = 100 cents
Website www.guyana-tourism.com

HISTORY

The first inhabitants of Guyana were Arawak, Carib and Warrau Amerindians. The Dutch founded a settlement in what is now Guyana in 1581 and, in 1620, the Dutch West India Company began to set up armed bases and to import African slaves to work on the sugar plantations. However, between 1780 and 1813, the territory changed hands between the Dutch, French and British. Britain occupied Guyana in 1814 during the Napoleonic Wars, and, in 1831, Britain founded the colony of British Guiana. After slavery was abolished in 1834, many former slaves set up their own farms with East Indian and Chinese laborers introduced to replace them. Gold was discovered in 1879. In 1889, Venezuela claimed part of the territory, but its claims were overruled by an international arbitration tribunal. In 1953, the left-wing Guyanese Progressive People's Party (PPP) led by East Indian Cheddi Jagan won the elections. Britain then sent in troops and set up an interim administration. The constitution was restored in 1957, when the PPP split into a mostly Indian party, led by Jagan, and another group, led by a black lawyer, Forbes Burnham. Burnham's party, the more moderate People's National Congress (PNC), consisted mainly of the descendants of Africans. In 1961, British Guiana became self-governing, with Jagan as prime minister. Riots, strikes, and racial coflict broke out in the early 1960s. Elections in 1964 were won by the PNC and its ally, the United Force and Burnham became prime minister

GEORGETOWN

Capital and largest city of Guyana, at the mouth of the River Demerara. Founded in 1781 by the British, it was the capital of the united colonies of Essequibo and Demerara and was known as Stabroek during the brief Dutch occupation from 1784. Renamed Georgetown in 1812. Industries: shipbuilding, brewing.

POLITICS

British Guiana became independent as Guyana on 26 May 1966 with Burnham as prime minister. In 1970, Guyana became a republic but remained a member of the Commonwealth. In 1980 Burnham became president and served in that post until his death in 1985. He was succeeded by the prime minister Desmond Hoyte, but, in 1992, the PPP won the elections and Ched di Jagan was elected president. On his death in 1997, he was succeeded by his wife Janet, who herself retired on health grounds in 1999. Her successor, Bharrat Jagdeo, a former finance minister, was reelected in 2001 when the PPP won both the presidential and parliamentary elections. Venezuela continues to claim Guyanese territory west of the Essequibo river, while Suriname is in dispute with Guyana over the headwaters of the Corentyne River, which forms part of the border between the two countries. Guyana also has a long-standing dispute with Suriname over their sea boundary, which runs through a potentially important offshore oilfield.

***Kaieteur Falls** on the Potaro River; the falls have a drop of 741 ft (226 m) and are considered to be amongst the most powerful falls on Earth*

ECONOMY

Guyana is a poor developing country. Its resources include gold, bauxite (aluminum ore), and other minerals, its forests and fertile soils. Agriculture and mining are the chief activities. The leading crops are sugar cane and rice, but citrus fruits, cocoa, coffee, and plantains are also important. Farmers also produce beef, pork, poultry, and dairy products. Fishing and forestry are other activities

Blue represents Haitians of African and French descent. Red represents blood shed in the struggle for independence. The coat of arms features a liberty cap on a royal palm tree and two cannons flanked by flags with a scroll reading l'Union Fait la Force (Strength in Unity).

The Republic of Haiti occupies the western third of Hispaniola, the Caribbean's second largest island. The country's culture is associated with exciting music with strong rhythms and voodoo which is practised by around 80% of the people. The land is mainly rugged, with mountain chains forming peninsulas in the north and south. The highest peak, 8,793 ft [2,680 m] is in Massif de la Selle in the southeast. Between the peninsulas is the Golfe de la Gonâve, which contains the large Isle de la Gonâve. Haiti's long coastline, which extends about 1,100 mi [1,770 km], is deeply indented.

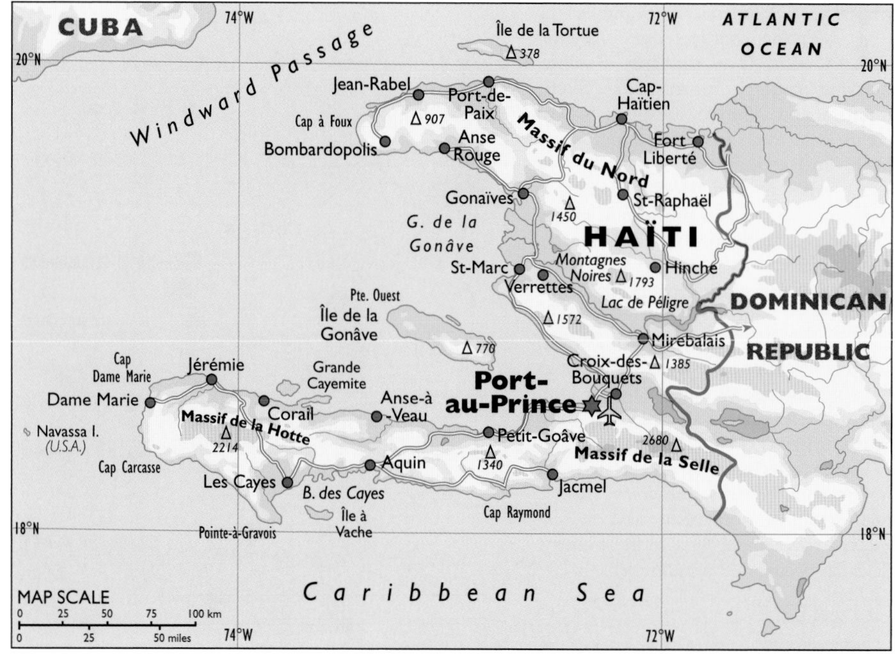

CLIMATE

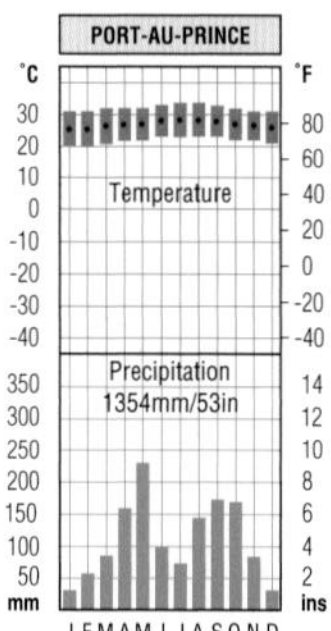

Haiti has a hot, humid tropical climate. Annual rainfall in the northern highlands is about 79 in [2,000 mm], more than twice that of the southern coast. The country is subject to tropical storms, which cause great damage.

Area 10,714 sq mi [27,750 sq km]
Population 7,656,000
Capital (population) Port-au-Prince (917,000)
Government Multiparty republic
Ethnic groups Black 95%, Mulatto/White 5%
Languages French and Creole (both official)
Religions Roman Catholic 80%, Voodoo
Currency Gourde = 100 centimes
Website www.haititourisme.org

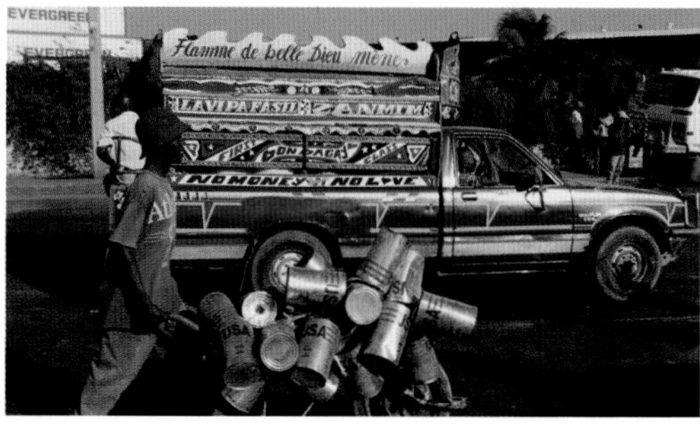

***A young market vendor** hauls a wheelbarrow full of empty tin cans near the Marche des Bossales, Port-au-Prince's main market*

PORT-AU-PRINCE

Capital of Haiti, a port on the southeast shore of the Gulf of Gonâve, on the west coast of Hispaniola. Founded by the French in 1749, Port-au-Prince became the capital of Haiti in 1770. Industries include tobacco, textiles, cement, coffee, sugar.

HISTORY

In 1496, Spain established a settlement at Santo Domingo, now capital of the neighboring Dominican Republic. This was the first European settlement in the Western Hemisphere. The local Arawak Amerindians were annihilated by Spanish settlers in barely 25 years. Spain ceded to the western part of Hispaniola to France in 1697. This area became Haiti. With an economy based on sugar cultivation and forestry, Haiti soon became prosperous.

In 1801, former slave Toussaint Louverture, led a revolt and proclaimed himself governor-general. A French force failed to conquer the interior of Haiti and the country became independent in 1804. Another former slave, Jean-Jacques Dessalines declared himself emperor. In 1915, following conflict between black and mulatto Haitians, the United States invaded the country to protect its interests. The troops withdrew in 1934, although the United States maintained control over the economy until 1947.

In 1956, François Duvalier ("Papa Doc") seized power in a military coup. He was elected president in 1957. Duvalier established a brutal dictatorship. He died in 1971 and his son Jean Claude Duvalier ("Baby Doc") became president. Like his father, Baby Doc used a murderous militia, the Tontons Macoutes, to conduct a reign of terror and maintain rule. In 1986, popular unrest forced Baby Doc to flee and a military regime took over.

POLITICS

The country's first multiparty elections were held in December 1990, the winner was radical Roman Catholic priest, Father Jean-Bertrand Aristide, who promised sweeping reforms. Aristide was reelected in 1994. But he stood down in 1995 and was succeeded by René Préval. Violence and poverty still prevailed and, in 1999, Préval dissolved parliament and declared that he would rule by decree. But in the elections of 2000, Aristide again became president amid accusations of electoral irregularities, surviving an attempted coup in 2001. In 2003, voodoo was recognized as a religion. In 2004, rebels seized several towns and cities in an anti-government uprising. Aristide fled the country, accusing the United States of forcing him into exile. An interim president, Boniface Alexandre, was sworn in as president and an interim government, led by prime minister Gerald Latortue, a former foreign secretary and UN official, took control and a UN peace-keeping force arrived. Floods in May 2004 caused major loss of life in Haiti and the Dominican Republic, while, later that year, Hurricane Jeanne killed nearly 3,000 people in the northwest. In 2005, Hurricane Denis killed at least 45 people. Money-laundering, corruption, and drug-trafficking are rife. Haiti is considered to be the transshipment point for cocaine en route to the United States.

ECONOMY

Haiti is the poorest country in the Western Hemisphere and 80% of the people live below the poverty line. Agriculture is the occupation of two-thirds of the people, but coffee is the only significant cash crop.

Honduras officially adopted its present flag in 1866. It is based on the flag of the Central American Federation, set up in 1823 and consisting of Costa Rica, El Salvador, Guatemala, Honduras, and Nicaragua. Honduras left the Federation in 1838.

The Republic of Honduras is the second largest country in Central America. It has two coastlines. The north Caribbean coast extends for about 375 mim [600 k], its deep offshore waters prompted the Spanish to name the country Honduras (Spanish for "depths"); and a narrow, 50 mi [80 km] long, Pacific outlet to the Gulf of Fonseca. Along the north coast are vast banana plantations. To the east lies the Mosquito Coast. The Cordilleras highlands form 80% of Honduras, and include the capital, Tegucigalpa.

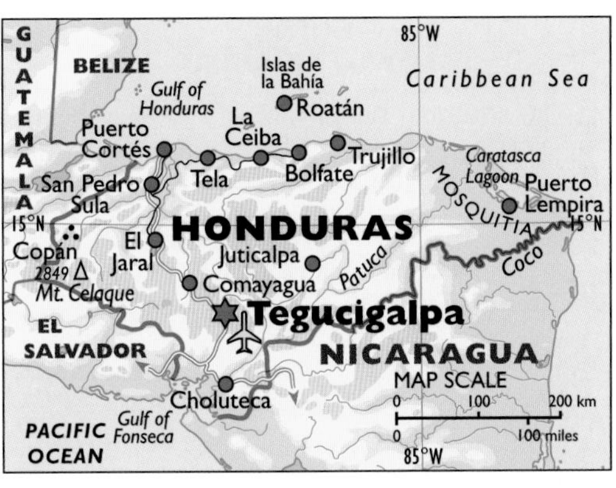

Area 43,277 sq mi [112,088 sq km]
Population 6,824,000
Capital (population) Tegucigalpa (850,000)
Government Republic
Ethnic groups Mestizo 90%, Amerindian 7%, Black (including Black Carib) 2%, White 1%
Languages Spanish (official), Amerindian dialects
Religions Roman Catholic 97%
Currency Honduran lempira = 100 centavos
Website www.letsgohonduras.com

Pine forests cover 75% of Honduras. The northern coastal plains contain rainforest and tropical savanna. The Mosquito Coast contains mangrove swamps and dense forests. Mahogany and rosewood forest grow on lower mountain slopes.

CLIMATE

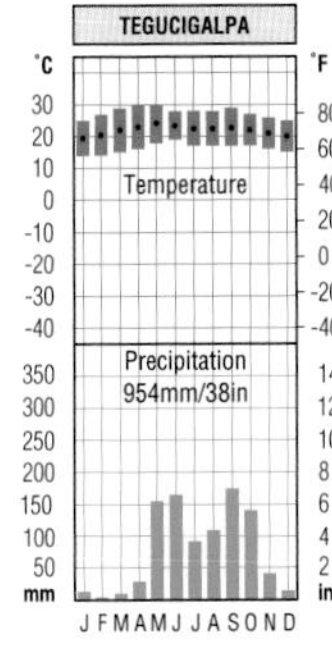

The climate is tropical, though the uplands, where the capital Tegucigalpa is situated, are cooler than the coastal plains. The heaviest rainfall occurs November through May. The coast is often battered by hurricanes. In October 1998, Honduras and Nicaragua were hit by Hurricane Mitch, which caused floods and mudslides.

HISTORY

From AD 400 to 900, the Maya civilization flourished. The Spanish discovered the magnificent ruins at Copán in western Honduras in 1576, but these became covered in dense forest and were only rediscovered in 1839. Columbus sighted the coast in 1502. Pedro de Alvarado founded the first Spanish settlements in 1524. The Spanish gradually subdued the native population and established gold and silver mines.

In 1821 Honduras gained independence, and formed part of the Mexican Empire. From 1823 to 1838, Honduras was a member of the Central American Federation. Throughout the rest of the 19th century, Honduras was subject to continuous political interference, especially from Guatemala. Britain controlled the Mosquito Coast.

In the 1890s, American companies developed plantations in Honduras to grow bananas, which soon became the country's chief source of income. The companies exerted great political influence and the country became known as a "banana republic," a name that was later applied to several other Latin American nations.

After World War II, demands grew for greater national autonomy and workers' rights. A military coup overthrew the Liberal government in 1963. In 1969, Honduras fought the short "Soccer War" with El Salvador. The war was sparked off by the treatment of fans during a World Cup soccer series. Though the real reason was that Honduras had forced Salvadoreans in Honduras to give up land.

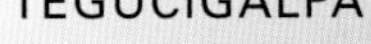

TEGUCIGALPA

Capital and largest city of Honduras, located in the mountainous central Cordilleras. Founded in the 16th century by the Spanish as a silver and gold mining town, it became the national capital in 1880. Industries include sugar, textiles, chemicals, cigarettes.

POLITICS

Civilian government returned in 1982. During the 1980s, Honduras allowed US-backed Contra rebels from Nicaragua to operate in Honduras against Nicaragua's left-wing Sandinista government. Honduras was heavily dependent on US aid. Popular demonstrations against the Contras, led to the declaration of a state of emergency in 1988. A ceasefire was then signed in Nicaragua, after which the Contra bases were closed down.

In 1992 Honduras signed a treaty with El Salvador, settling the disputed border. Liberal Party leader Carlos Flores became president in 1997 elections. In 1998, Hurricane Mitch killed more than 5,500 people and left 14 million people homeless. Human rights organizations estimated that "death squads," often backed by the police, killed more than 1,000 street children in 2000. National Party leader Ricardo Maduro became president in 2001 elections.

ECONOMY

Honduras is the least industrialized country in Central America, and the poorest developing nation in the Americas. It has very few mineral resources, other than silver, lead, and zinc.

Agriculture dominates the economy, forming 78% of exports and employing 38% of the workforce. Bananas and coffee are the leading exports, and corn the principal food crop. Cattle are raised in the mountain valleys and on the southern Pacific plains.

Fishing and forestry are also important. There are vast timber resources. Lack of an adequate transport infrastructure hampers development.

__Stela in the ruins of Copan,__ to the west of Honduras; the great Mayan civilization once thrived in the area and it has been designated a UNESCO World Heritage Site

Hungary

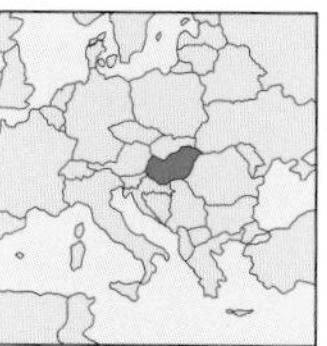

Hungary's flag was adopted in 1919. A state emblem was added in 1949 and removed in 1957. The colors of red, white, and green had been used in the Hungarian arms since the 15th century. The tricolor design became popular during the 1848 rebellion against Habsburg rule.

Area 35,920 sq mi [93,032 sq km]
Population 10,032,000
Capital (population) Budapest (1,819,000)
Government Multiparty republic
Ethnic groups Magyar 90%, Gypsy, German, Serb, Romanian, Slovak
Languages Hungarian (official)
Religions Roman Catholic 68%, Calvinist 20%, Lutheran 5%, others
Currency Forint = 100 fillér
Website www.magyarorszag.hu/angol

The Republic of Hungary is a landlocked country in central Europe. The land is mostly low-lying and drained by the Danube (Duna) and its tributary, the Tisza. Most of the land east of the Danube belongs to a region called the Great Plain (Nagyalföld), which covers about half of Hungary.

West of the Danube is a hilly region, with some low mountains, called Transdanubia. This region contains the country's largest lake, Balaton. In the northwest is a small, fertile and mostly flat region called the Little Plain (Kisalföld).

Much of Hungary's original vegetation has been cleared. Large forests remain in the scenic northeastern highlands

CLIMATE

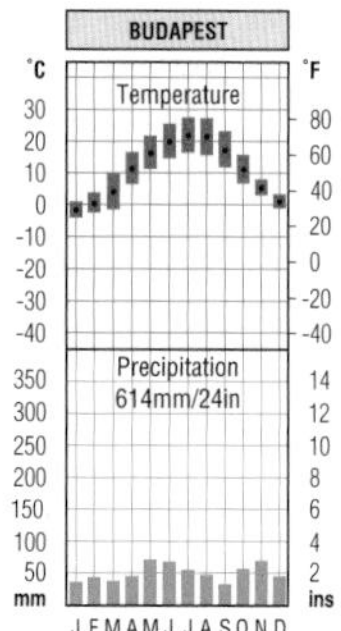

Hungary lies far from the moderating influence of the sea. As a result, summers are warmer and sunnier, and the winters colder than in Western Europe.

HISTORY

Magyars first arrived in the area from the east in the 9th century. In the 11th century, Hungary's first king, Stephen I, made Roman Catholicism the official religion. Hungary became a powerful kingdom, but in 1526 it was defeated by Turkish forces, who later occupied much of Hungary. In the late 17th century, the Austrian Habsburgs conquered Hungary. In 1867, Austria granted Hungary equal status in a "dual monarchy," called Austria-Hungary. In 1914, a Bosnian student killed Archduke Franz Ferdinand, the heir to the Austria-Hungary throne. This led to World War I, when Austria-Hungary fought alongside Germany. Defeat in 1918 led to nearly 70% of its territory being apportioned by the Treaty of Versailles to Czechoslovakia, Yugoslavia and Romania. Some 2.6 million Hungarians live in these countries today.

The government hoped to regain these territories by siding with Hitler's Germany in World War II, but the Germans occupied the country in 1944 and later that year the Red Army invaded. Elections were held in 1945 and, in 1946, the country was declared a republic. Although the smallholders had won a clear majority of the votes in the 1945 elections, the Communists gradually took control even after failing to win a majority of the votes cast in new elections in 1947.

POLITICS

Hungary became a Communist state in 1949, with a constitution based on that of the Soviet Union. The first leader of the Communist government was Mathias Rákosi, who was replaced in 1953 by Imre Nagy. Nagy sought to relax Communist policies and was forced from office in 1955. He was replaced by Rákosi in 1956 and this led to a major uprising in which many Hungarians were killed or imprisoned. Nagy and his coworkers were executed for treason in 1958.

Janos Kádár came to power in the wake of the suppression, but his was a relatively progressive leadership, including an element of political reform and a measure of economic liberalism. However, in the late 1970s, the economic situation worsened and new political parties started to appear.

Kádár resigned in 1989 and the central Committee of the Socialist Workers' Party (the Communist Party) agreed to sweeping reforms, including the introduction of a pluralist system and a democratic parliament, which had formally been little more than a rubber-stamp assembly. The trial of Imre Nagy and his coworkers was declared unlawful and their bodies were reburied with honor in June 1989.

***Szechenyi Baths,** Budapest; early-20th-century neo-Baroque thermal baths*

In 1990, Hungarians voted into office a center-right coalition headed by the Democratic Forum. In 1994, the Hungarian Socialist Party (made up of ex-Communists) won a majority and governed in coalition with the Alliance of Free Democrats. However, in elections in 1998, Victor Orbán, leader of the Fidesz-Hungarian Civic Party, became prime minister. In 2002, the Socialists and the Free Democrat coalition, led by Peter Medgyessy, won a majority in parliament. Hungary became a member of NATO and the EU in 2004.

BUDAPEST

Capital of Hungary, on the River Danube. It was created in 1873 by uniting the towns of Buda (capital of Hungary since the 14th century) and Pest on the opposite bank. It became one of the two capitals of the Austro-Hungarian Empire. In 1918, it was declared capital of an independent Hungary. Budapest was the scene of a popular uprising against the Soviet Union in 1956. The old town contains a remarkable collection of buildings, including Buda Castle, the parliament building, the National Museum, and Roman remains.

ECONOMY

Under communism the economy was transformed from agrarian to industrial. The new factories were owned by the government, as was most of the land. From the late 1980s, the government worked to increase private ownership. This change of policy caused many problems, including inflation and high rates of unemployment.

Manufacturing is the most valuable activity. The major products include aluminum made from local bauxite, chemicals, electrical and electronic goods, processed food, iron and steel, and vehicles. Agriculture remains important, major crops include grapes, corn, potatoes, sugar beets, and wheat.

Iceland's flag dates from 1915. It became the official flag in 1944, when Iceland became fully independent. The flag, which uses Iceland's traditional colors, blue and white, is the same as Norway's flag, except that the blue and red colors are reversed.

The Republic of Iceland, in the North Atlantic Ocean, though deemed part of Europe, is closer to Greenland than Scotland. Iceland sits astride the Mid-Atlantic Ridge, the geological boundary between Europe and North America. The island is slowly getting wider as the ocean is stretched apart by the forces of plate tectonics.

Iceland has around 200 volcanoes and eruptions are frequent. An eruption under the Vatnajökull ice cap in 1996 created a subglacial lake which subsequently burst, causing severe flooding. Geysers and hot springs are other volcanic features. During the thousand years that Iceland has been settled, between 150 and 200 volcanic eruptions have occurred. Ice caps and glaciers cover about one-eighth of the land. The only habitable regions are the coastal lowlands.

Area 39,768 sq mi [103,000 sq km]
Population 294,000
Capital (population) Reykjavik (108,000)
Government Multiparty republic
Ethnic groups Icelandic 97%, Danish 1%
Languages Icelandic (official)
Religions Evangelical Lutheran 87%, other Protestant 4%, Roman Catholic 2%, others
Currency Icelandic króna = 100 aurar
Website www.icetourist.is

Vegetation is sparse or non-existent on 75% of the land. Treeless grassland or bogs cover some areas. Deep fjords fringe the coast.

CLIMATE

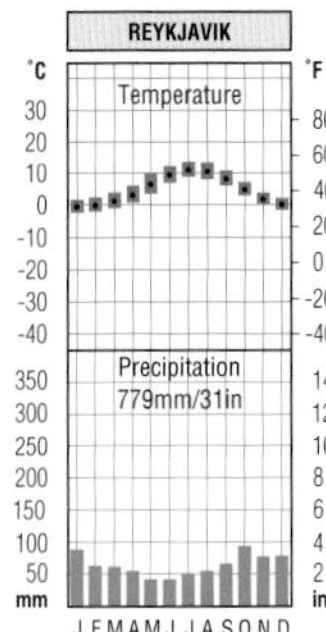

Although it lies far to the north, Iceland's climate is moderated by the warm waters of the Gulf Stream. The port of Reykjavik is ice-free all the year round.

HISTORY

Iceland was colonized by Vikings from Norway in AD 874 and the population grew as more settlers arrived from Norway and from the Viking colonies in the British Isles. In 930, the settlers founded the oldest, and what is thought to be the world's first, parliament (the Althing). One early settler was Erik the Red, a Viking who sailed to Greenland in about 982 and founded another colony there in about 985.

Iceland was an independent country until 1262 when, following a series of civil wars, the Althing recognized the rule of the king of Norway. When Norway united with Denmark in 1380, Iceland came under the rule of Danish kingdoms. Life on Iceland was never easy. The Black Death, which swept the island in 1402, claimed two-thirds of the population, while, in the late 18th century, volcanic eruptions destroyed crops, farmland, and livestock, causing a famine. Then, during the Napoleonic Wars in the early 19th century, food supplies from Europe failed to reach the island and many people starved.

When Norway was separated from Denmark in 1814, Iceland remained under Danish rule. In the late 19th century, the invention of motorized craft, which changed the fishing industry, led to mounting demands for self-government. In 1918, Iceland was acknowledged as a sovereign state, but remained united with Denmark through a common monarch. During World War II, when Germany occupied Denmark, British and American troops landed in Iceland to protect it from invasion by the Germans. Finally, following a referendum in which 97% of the people voted to cut all ties with Denmark, Iceland became a fully independent republic on 17 June 1944.

REYKJAVÍK

Capital of Iceland, a port on the southwest coast. Founded in 870, it was the island's first permanent settlement. It expanded during the 18th century, and became the capital in 1918. During World War II, it served as a British and US air base. Tourism is now important. Industries include food processing, fishing, textiles, metallurgy, printing and publishing, and shipbuilding.

POLITICS

Fishing, on which Iceland's economy is based, is a major political issue. From 1975, Iceland extended its territorial waters to 200 nautical miles, causing skirmishes between Icelandic and British vessels. The issue was resolved in 1977 when Britain agreed not to fish in the disputed waters. Another problem developed in the late 1980s when Iceland reduced the allowable catches in its waters, because overfishing was causing the depletion of fishing stocks, especially of cod. The reduction of the fish catch led to a slowdown in the economy and, eventually, to a recession, though the economy recovered in the mid-1990s when the conservation measures appeared to have been successful. Iceland left the International Whaling Commission in 1992, because of its alleged anti-whaling policy. It rejoined in 2002, but in 2003 undertook its first whale hunt for 15 years, stating that it was a scientific catch to study the impact of whales on fish stocks.

Iceland has no armed forces of its own. However, it joined NATO in 1949 and, under a NATO agreement, the United States maintains a base on the island, which remains a political issue.

ECONOMY

Iceland has few resources other than the fishing grounds which surround it. Fishing and fish processing are major industries which dominate Iceland's overseas trade. Overfishing is an economic problem. Barely 1% of the land is used to grow crops, mainly root vegetables and fodder for livestock, but, 23% of the country is used for grazing sheep and cattle. Iceland is self-sufficient in meat and dairy products. Fruit and vegetables are grown in greenhouses heated by water from hot springs. Manufacturing is important and includes aluminum, cement, clothing, electrical equipment, fertilizers, and processed foods. Geothermal power is a key energy source.

Hallgrimskirkja, Reykjavik; *named after 17th-century hymn writer Hallgrímur Pétursson the church was finally completed in 1986; the statue is of Leifur Eiríksson, the first European to discover America (1000 AD)*

India

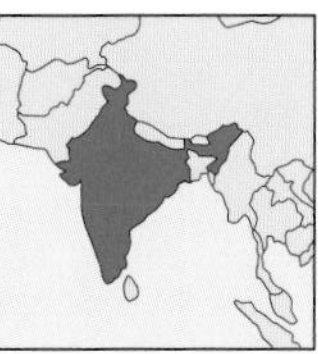

The Indian flag was adopted shortly after the country gained independence from Britain in 1947. The saffron (orange) represents renunciation, the white is for truth and the green symbolizes mankind's relationship with nature. The central wheel represents dynamism and change.

The Republic of India, the world's seventh largest country, extends from high in the Himalayas, through the Tropic of Cancer, to the warm waters of the Indian Ocean at Cape Comorin. India is the world's second most populous nation after China, and the largest democracy. The north contains the mountains and foothills of the Himalayan range. Rivers such as the Brahmaputra and Ganges (Ganga) rise in the Himalayas and flow across the fertile northern plains. Southern India consists of a large plateau called the Deccan which is bordered by two mountain ranges, the Western Ghats and the Eastern Ghats.

The Karakoram Range in the far north has permanently snow-covered peaks. The eastern Ganges delta has mangrove swamps. Between the gulfs of Kutch and Cambay are the deciduous forest habitats of the last of India's wild lions. The Ghats are clad in heavy rainforest.

CLIMATE

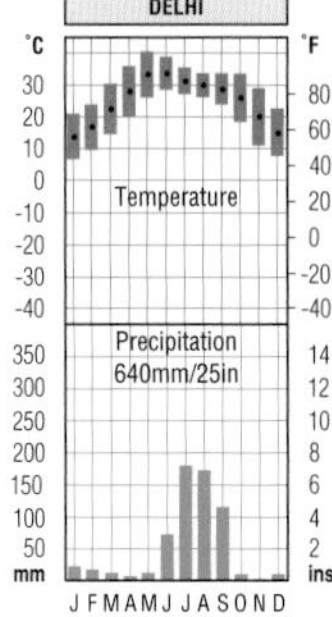

India has three seasons. The weather during the cool season, October to February, is mild in the northern plains, but southern India remains hot, though temperatures are a little lower than for the rest of the year. Temperatures on the northern plains sometimes soar to 120°F [49°C] during the hot season from March to the end of June. Monsoon season starts in the middle of June and continues into September. At this time, moist southeasterly winds from the Indian Ocean bring heavy rains to India. Darjeeling in the northeast has an average annual rainfall of 120 in [3,040 mm], but parts of the Great Indian Desert in the northwest have only 2 in [50 mm] of rain a year. The monsoon rains are essential for India's farmers. If they arrive late, crops may be ruined. If the rainfall is considerably higher than average, floods may cause great destruction.

HISTORY

India's early settlers were scattered across the subcontinent in Stone Age times. The first of its many civilizations began to flourish in the Indus Valley in what is now Pakistan and western India around 4,500 years ago, and in the Ganges Valley from about 1500 BC, when Aryan people arrived in India from central Asia. The earlier, darker-skinned people, the Dravidians, moved southwards, ahead of the Aryans, and their descendants are now the main inhabitants of southern India.

India was the birthplace of several major religions including Hinduism, Buddhism and Sikhism. Islam was introduced from about AD 1000. The Muslim Mughal empire was founded in 1526. From the 17th century Britain began to gain influence and from 1858 to 1947, India was ruled as part of the British empire.

An independence movement began in India after the Sepoy Rebellion (1857–9) and, in 1885, the Indian National Congress was founded. In 1906, Indian Muslims, concerned that Hindus formed the majority of the members of the Indian National Congress, founded the Muslim League. In 1920, Mohandas K. Gandhi, a former lawyer, became leader of the Indian National Congress which soon became a mass movement. Gandhi's policy of non-violent disobedience proved highly effective, and in response Britain began to introduce political reforms. In the 1930s, the Muslim League called for the establishment of a Muslim state, called Pakistan.

In 1947, it was agreed that British India be partitioned into the mainly Hindu India and the Muslim Pakistan. Both countries became independent in August 1947, but the events were marred by mass slaughter as Hindus and Sikhs fled from Pakistan, and Muslims flocked to Pakistan from India. In the boundary disputes and reshuffling of minority populations that followed, some 1 million lives were lost. Since 1947–8, events have done little to promote good relations between the countries.

Taj Mahal, Agra. *Built in 1632–48 by the Emperor Shah Jahan as a tomb for his wife, the white marble building is an outstanding example of Mughal architecture*

NEW DELHI

Capital of India, in the north of the country, on the River Yamuna in Delhi Union Territory. Planned by the British architects Edwin Lutyens and Herbert Baker, it was constructed in 1912–29 to replace Calcutta (now Kolkata) as the capital of British India. Whereas Old Delhi is primarily a commercial center, New Delhi has an administrative function. Places of interest include the Coronation Durbar Site, the Crafts Museum and Humayun's Tomb. Industries include textile production, chemicals, machine tools, plastics, electrical appliances, and traditional crafts.

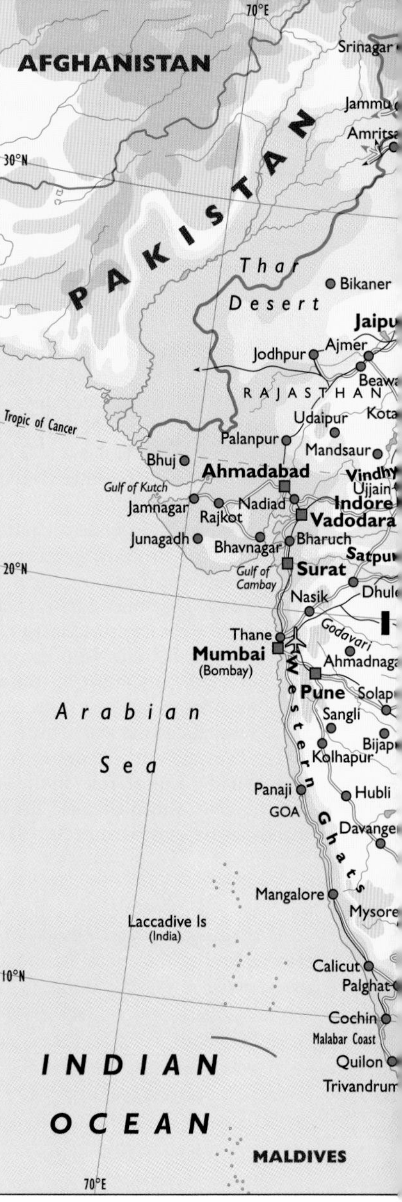

POLITICS

Gandhi was assassinated in 1948 by a Hindu extremist who hated him for his tolerant attitude towards Muslims. The country adopted a new constitution in 1948 making it a democratic republic within the Commonwealth, and elections were held in 1951 and 1952. India's first prime minister was Jawaharlal Nehru. The government sought to develop the economy and raise living standards at home, while, on the international stage, Nehru won great respect for his policy of non-alignment and neutrality. The disputed status of Kashmir was then India's thorniest security problem.

In 1966, Nehru's daughter, Indira Gandhi, took office. Her Congress Party lost support because of food shortages, unemployment, and other problems. In 1971, India helped the people of East Pakistan achieve independence from West Pakistan to become Bangladesh. India tested its first atomic bomb in 1974, but pledged to use nuclear power for peaceful purposes only. In 1977, Mrs Gandhi lost her seat in parliament and her Congress Party was defeated by the Janata Party, a coalition led by Morarji R. Desai. Disputes in the Janata Party led to Desai's resignation in 1979 and, in 1980, Congress-I (the I standing for Indira) won the elections. Mrs Gandhi again became prime minister, but her government faced many problems. One problem was that many Sikhs wanted more control over the Punjab, and Sikh radicals began to commit acts of violence to draw attention to their cause. In 1984, armed Sikhs occupied the sacred Golden Temple, in Amritsar. In response, Indian troops attacked the temple, causing much damage and deaths. In October, 1984, two of Mrs Gandhi's Sikh guards assassinated her. Her son, Rajiv, was chosen to succeed her as prime minister, but, in 1989, Congress lost its majority in parliament and Rajiv resigned as prime minister, then during elections in 1991, he was assassinated by Tamil extremists.

Area 1,269,212 sq mi [3,287,263 sq km]
Population 1,065,071,000
Capital (population) New Delhi (295,000)
Government Multiparty federal republic
Ethnic groups Indo-Aryan (Caucasoid) 72%, Dravidian (Aboriginal) 25%, others (mainly Mongoloid) 3%
Languages Hindi, English,Telugu, Bengali, Marathi, Tamil, Urdu, Gujurati, Malayalam, Kannada, Oriya, Punjabi, Assamese, Kasmiri, Sindhi and Sanskrit (all official)
Religions Hinduism 82%, Islam 12%, Christianity 2%, Sikhism 2%, Buddhism and others
Currency Indian rupee = 100 paisa
Website www.incredibleindia.org

India is a vast country with an enormous diversity of cultures. It has more than a dozen major languages, and many minor languages. Hindi, the national language, and the Dravidian languages of the south (Kannada, Tamil, Telugu, and Malayam) are Indo-European. Sino-Tibetan languages are spoken in the north and east, while smaller groups speak residual languages in forested hill refuges.

Hinduism is all-pervasive and Buddhism is slowly reviving in the country of its origin. Jainism is strong in the merchant towns around Mount Abu in the Aravallis hills north of Ahmadabad. Islam has contributed many mosques and monuments, the Taj Mahal being the best known and India retains a large Muslim minority. The Punjab's militant Sikhs now seek separation. However, India's most intractable problem remains the divided region of Kashmir, the subject of a long conflict between India and Pakistan. However, in 2004 and 2005, both countries sought ways of easing the tension, including the opening up of cross-border transport services.

In February 2006 India and Pakistan reopened a second rail link connecting Munabao in Rajasthan with Khokrapar, a border town in Pakistan's Sindh province. Against this a wave of violence by Islamic militants occurred in Kashmir; the prime minister Manmohan Singh said that this would not halt peace efforts.

On July 11, 2006 more than 180 people died with over 700 injured in coordinated terrorist bomb attacks on moving trains and in stations in Mumbai.

ECONOMY

According to the World Bank, India is a "low-income" developing country. Despite initiatives, its socialist policies have failed to raise the living standards of the poor. In the 1990s, the government introduced private enterprise policies to stimulate growth.

Farming employs 64% of the workforce. The main crops are rice, wheat, millet, sorghum, peas, and beans. India has more cattle than any other country. Milk is produced but Hindus do not eat beef. India has reserves of coal, iron ore, and oil, and manufacturing has expanded greatly since 1947 to include high-tech goods, iron and steel, machinery, refined petroleum, textiles, jewelry, and transportation equipment. India has begun to capitalize on its large numbers of fluent English speakers, with many working in call centers for multinational businesses. Another important provider of income is the large cinema industry, the most famous of which is the Hindi Bollywood.

CHRISTMAS ISLAND

Area 52 sq mi [135 sq km]
Population 2,771
Capital (population) The Settlement (1,508)
Government Territory of Australia
Ethnic groups Chinese 70%, European 20%, Malay 10%
Languages English (official), Chinese, Malay
Religions Buddhist 36%, Muslim 25%, Christian 18%, others
Currency Australian dollar = 100 cents
Website www.christmas.net.au

Island in the east Indian Ocean 200 mi [320 km] south of Java. Named by Captain William Mynors when he landed on Christmas Day 1643. Once under British rule, it was annexed to Australia in 1958. It has important lime phosphate deposits. The Australian Government has agreed to support a commercial space-launching site to aid the economy. Two-thirds of the island is national park making it good for bird-watching.

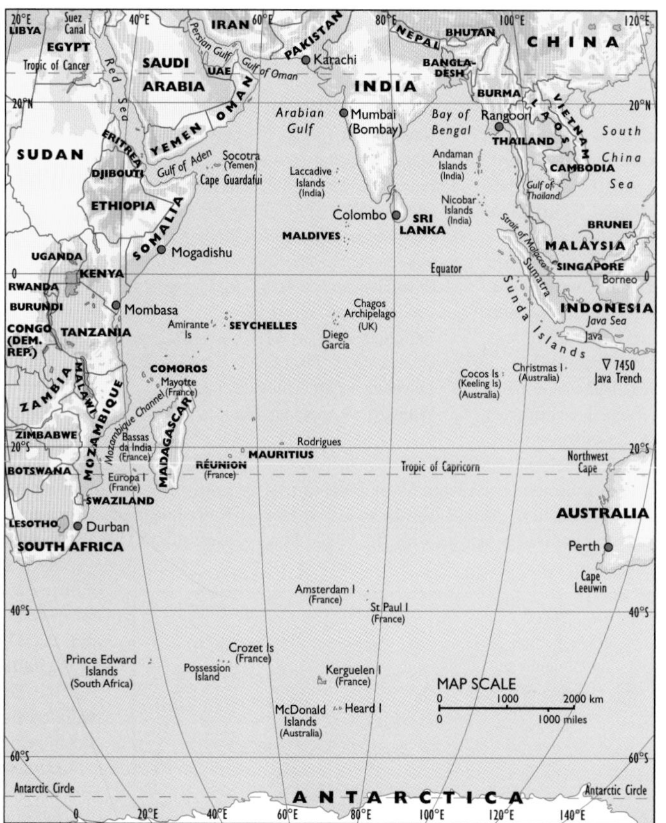

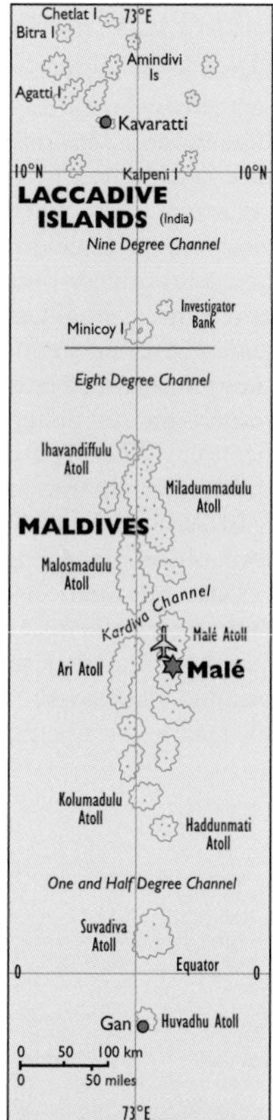

COCOS ISLANDS

Area 5.4 sq mi [14 sq km]
Population 628
Capital (population) West Island (120)
Government Territory of Australia
Ethnic groups Europeans, Cocos Malays
Languages Malay (Cocos dialect), English
Religions Sunni Muslim 80%, others
Currency Australian dollar = 100 cents
Website www.cocos-tourism.cc

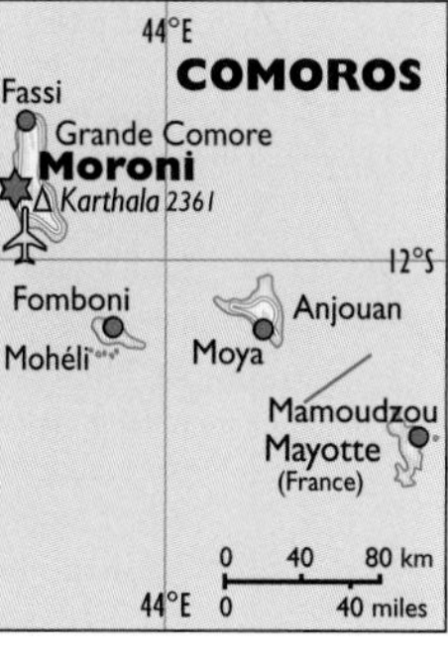

Cocos (Keeling) Islands is made up of 27 coral islands. The islands are located 1,700 mi (2,750 km) northwest of Perth. The climate is consistent with the temperature remaining at 84°F [29°C] all year round no matter what the season. The average annual rainfall is 74 in (2,000 mm). Discovered in 1609 by Captain William Keeling, but uninhabited until the 19th century, the islands were annexed by the UK in 1857 and transferred to the Australian Government in 1955. Only two of the islands are inhabited and their population is split along ethnic lines, with ethnic Europeans on West Island and ethnic Malays on Home Island. Most food and other necessities are imported from Australia. Coconuts are the sole cash crop and there is a small tourist industry.

COMOROS

The Union des Isles Comoros, consists of three large volcanic islands and some smaller ones, at the northern end of the Mozambique Channel. The three major islands are Grande Comore (site of the capital), Anjouan, and Mohéli. They are mountainous, with tropical climate and fertile soil.

Area 838 sq mi [2,170 sq km]
Population 652,000
Capital (population) Moroni (30,000)
Government Independent republic
Ethnic groups Antalote, Cafre, Makoa, Oimatsaha, Sakalava
Languages Arabic and French (both official), Shikomoro
Religions Sunni Muslim 98%, Roman Catholic 2%
Currency Comoran franc = 100 centimes
Website www.arab.net/comoros

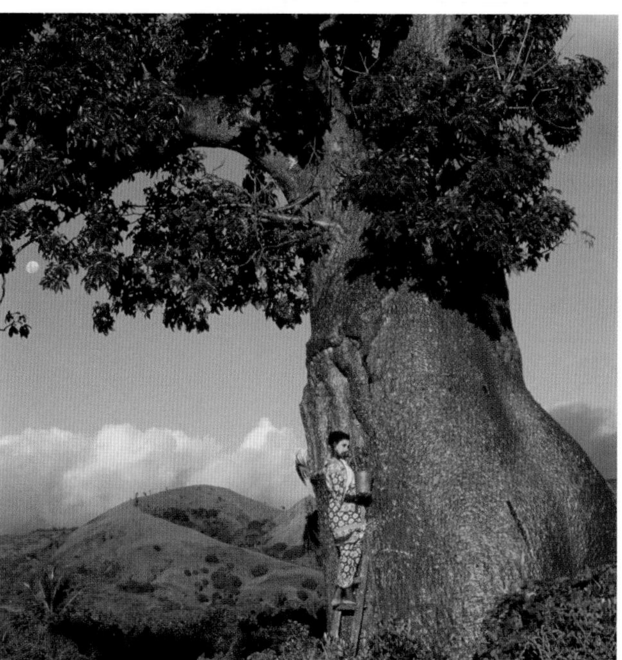

Grand Comore Island, Comoros; *a man taps water from a baobab tree, which acts as a natural water reservoir*

France took over one of the islands, Mayotte, in 1843 and, in 1886, the other islands came under French protection. The Comoros became independent in 1974, but the people of Mayotte opted to remain French. In the late 1990s, separatists on Anjouan and Mohéli islands sought to secede, but in 2004 each of the large islands was granted autonomy with its own president and legislature. The Comoros is a poor country. It exports cloves, perfume oils, coconuts, copra, and vanilla.

MALDIVES

The Republic of the Maldives, Asia's smallest independent country, comprises some 1,200 low-lying coral islands grouped into 26 atolls, 202 of the islands are inhabited. They are scattered along a broad north–south line in the Indian Ocean about 400 mi [640 km] south west of Sri Lanka.

Area 115 sq mi [298 sq km]
Population 339,000
Capital (population) Malé (74,000)
Government Republic
Ethnic groups South Indians, Sinhalese, Arabs
Languages Maldivian Dhivehi (dialect of Sinhala, script derived from Arabic), English
Religion Sunni Muslim
Currency Rufiyaa = 100 laari
Website www.maldivesinfo.gov.mv

HISTORY AND POLITICS The islands are prone to flooding. They have a tropical climate and the monsoon season is from April to October.

Sri Lanka settled the islands in about 500 BC. From the 14th century, the ad-Din dynasty ruled the Maldives. In 1518, the Portuguese claimed the islands. From 1665 to 1886, the Maldives were a dependency of Ceylon (Sri Lanka).

They became a British protectorate in 1887. In 1965 they achieved independence as a sultanate and then became a republic when the sultan was deposed in 1968. Maumoon Abdul Gayoom has served as president since 1978. In 1982, the Maldives joined the Commonwealth. In 1988, Indian troops helped suppress an attempted coup.

A tsunami struck the islands in December 2004 killing 82 people.

Political parties are banned, though political activity is permitted, at least nominally. The president is chosen in a yes-no referendum. The voters are presented with just one candidate, chosen on their behalf by parliament. President Gayoom came under increasing pressure from human rights groups to ease up on his autocratic style of governance. There was anti-government violence on the streets. As a result of this he announced in 2005 that he planned to introduce a multiparty democracy.

ECONOMY The chief crops are bananas, coconuts, copra, mangoes, sweet potatoes, and spices, but much food is imported. Fishing is important and the leading export is the bonito (Maldives tuna). Since 1972 the growth in tourism boosted foreign reserves, but the Maldives remain one of the world's poorest countries.

MAYOTTE

A French administered archipelago in the Indian Ocean to the east of the Comoros. The two major islands are Grande Terre and Petite Terre (Pamanzi). Grande Terre includes the new capital, Mamoudzou. Pamanzi is the site of the old capital, Dzaoudzi.

Mayotte has a tropical climate. It is generally hot and humid. The rainy season is from November to May, during northeastern monsoon. The dry season, from May to November, is cooler.

Area 144 sq mi [373 sq km]
Population 173,300
Capital (population) Mamoudzou (4,000)
Government Territorial collectivity of France
Ethnic groups Comorian (mixture of Bantu, Arab and Malagasy) 92%
Languages Mahorian (a Swahili dialect), French (official)
Religions Muslim 97%, Christian (mostly Roman Catholic)
Currency Euro = 100 cents
Website http://ctt.mayotte.free.fr/anglais/Eaccueil.htm

HISTORY AND POLITICS Mayotte was a French colony from 1843 to 1914 when it was attached to the Comoro group and collectively achieved administrative autonomy as a French Overseas Territory. In 1974, the rest of the Comoros became independent while Mayotte voted to remain a French dependency. In 1976 it became an overseas collectivity of France.

ECONOMY The economy is primarily agricultural, the chief products being bananas and mangoes.

RÉUNION

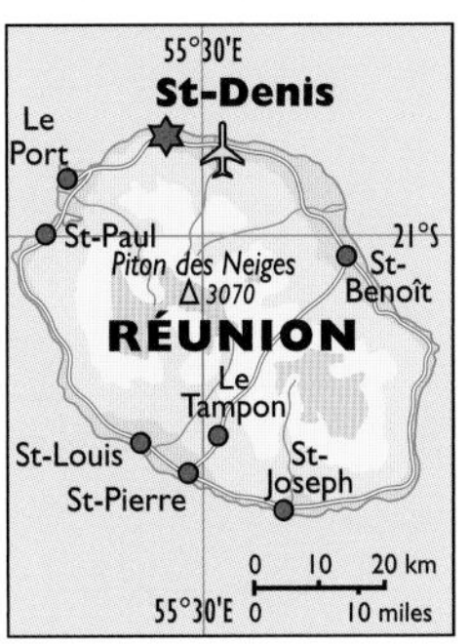

Area 969 sq mi [2,510 sq km]
Population 766,000
Capital (population) St-Denis (122,000)
Government Overseas department of France
Ethnic groups French, African, Malagasy, Chinese, Pakistani, Indian
Languages French (official), Creole
Religions Roman Catholic 86%, Hindu, Muslim, Buddhist
Currency Euro = 100 cents
Website www.la-reunion-tourisme.com/gb_entere.htm

The Department of Réunion is a volcanic island in the Mascarene group lying about 440 mi [700 km] east of Madagascar in the Indian Ocean. It has a mountainous, wooded center, surrounded by a fertile coastal plain. The climate is tropical, but the temperature moderates with elevation. It is cool and dry from May to November and hot and rainy from November to April.

HISTORY AND POLITICS Discovered in 1513 by the Portuguese, France claimed Réunion in 1638. It became a French department in 1946. The island became part of an administrative region in 1973. There is increasing pressure on France for independence.

ECONOMY Sugar cane dominates the economy, though vanilla, perfume oils and tea also produce revenue. Tourism is the big hope for the future, but unemployment is high and the island relies on French aid.

SEYCHELLES

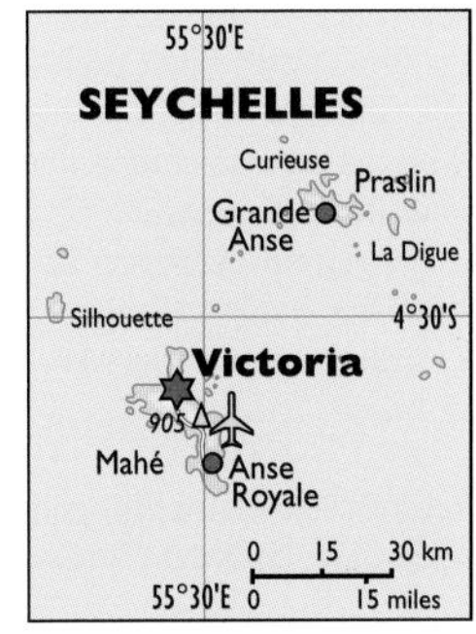

Area 176 sq mi [455 sq km]
Population 81,000
Capital (population) Victoria (24,000)
Government Republic
Ethnic groups French, African, Indian, Chinese, and Arab
Languages Creole 92%, English 5% (both official)
Religions Roman Catholic 82%, Anglican 6%, others
Currency Seychelles rupee = 100 cents
Website www.virtualseychelles.sc

The Republic of Seychelles includes a group of four large and 36 small granitic islands, plus a wide scattering of coralline islands, 14 of them inhabited, lying to the south and west. The islands experience a tropical oceanic climate.

Formerly part of the British Indian Ocean Territory (BIOT), Farquhar, Des Roches and Aldabra (famous for its unique wildlife) were returned to the Seychelles in 1976. The BIOT now consists only of the Chagos Archipelago, with Diego Garcia, the largest island, supporting a US Navy base.

HISTORY AND POLITICS French from 1756 and British from 1814, the islands gained their independence in 1976. A year later, a coup resulted in the setting up of a one-party socialist state that several attempts failed to remove. Multiparty elections were held in 1992 and France-Albert René, who had been elected president unopposed in 1979 and 1984, was reelected president under a new constitution adopted in 1993. René was again reelected president in 1998, but in 2004 he stepped down in favor of vice-president James Michel.

ECONOMY The Seychelles produces copra, cinnamon, and tea, although rice is imported. Fishing and luxury tourism are the two main industries, with much fish produced for export.

Indonesia

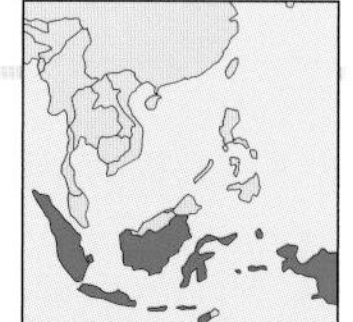

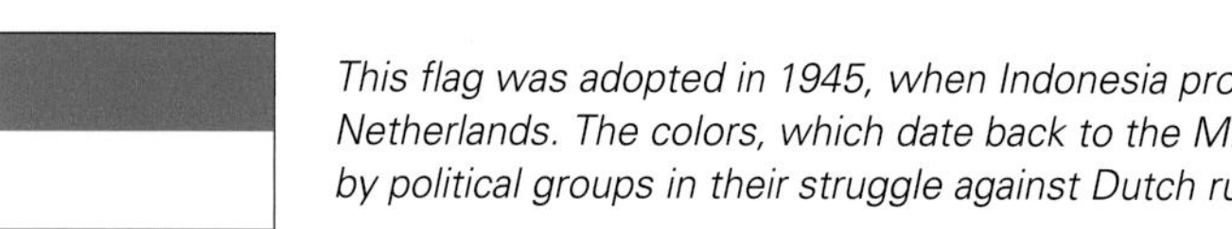

This flag was adopted in 1945, when Indonesia proclaimed itself independent from the Netherlands. The colors, which date back to the Middle Ages, were adopted in the 1920s by political groups in their struggle against Dutch rule.

The Republic of Indonesia, in Southeast Asia, consists of about 13,600 islands, less than 6,000 of which are inhabited. The island of Java covers only 7% of the country's area but it contains more than half of Indonesia's population. Three-quarters of the country is made up of five main areas: the islands of Sumatra, Java, and Sulawesi (Celebes), together with Kalimantan (southern Borneo and Papua (western New Guinea). The islands are mountainous and many have extensive coastal lowlands. Indonesia contains more than 200 volcanoes, but the highest peak is Puncak Jaya, which reaches 16,503 ft [5,029 m] above sea level, is in West Papua.

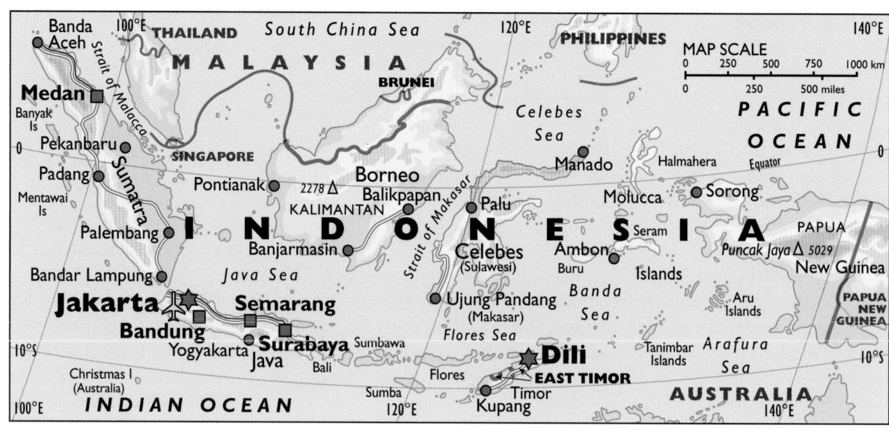

CLIMATE

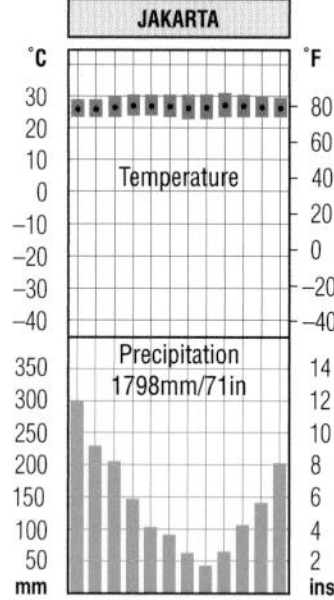

Indonesia has a hot and humid monsoon climate. Only Java and the Sunda Islands have a relatively dry season. From December to March, moist prevailing winds blow from mainland Asia. Between mid-June and October, dry prevailing winds blow from Australia.

HISTORY

From the 8th century, the empire of Sri Vijaya, which was centered on Palembang, held sway until it was replaced in the 14th century by the kingdom of Madjapahit, whose center was east-central Java. Indonesia is the world's most populous Muslim nation, though Islam was introduced as recently as the 15th century. The area came under the domination of the Dutch East India Company in the 17th century. The Dutch government took over the islands in 1799. Japan occupied the islands in World War II and Indonesia declared its independence in 1945. The Dutch finally recognized Indonesia's independence in 1949.

POLITICS

Indonesia's first president, the anti-Western Achmed Sukarno, plunged his country into chaos. In 1962, Indonesia invaded Dutch New Guinea (now West Papua), and between 1963 and 1966 Sukarno sought to destabilize the Federation of Malaysia through incursions into northern Borneo. In 1967, Sukarno was toppled by General Suharto, following Sukarno's suppression of an alleged Communist-inspired uprising that cost 80,000 lives. Suharto's military regime, with US help, achieved significant economic growth, though corruption was rife. In 1975, Indonesian troops invaded East Timor, opposed by the local people. Suharto was forced to stand down in 1998 and his deputy, Bacharuddin Jusuf Habibie, succeeded him. In June 1999, Habibie's ruling Golkar Party was defeated in elections and, in October, the parliament elected Abdurrahman Wahid as president. However, Wahid, charged with corruption and general incompetence, was dismissed in 2001 and succeeded by the vice-president, Megawati Sukarnoputri (daughter of President Sukarno).

In the early 21st century, Indonesia faced many problems. East Timor seceded in 2002, while secessionist groups in Aceh province, northern Sumatra, and the Free Papua Movement in West Papua also demanded independence. Muslim-Christian clashes broke out in the Moluccas at the end of 1999, while indigenous Dyaks in Kalimantan clashed with immigrants from Madura.

In December 2004, more than 120,000 people were killed in Indonesia by a tsunami. Worst hit was Aceh, though the tragedy was followed by peace talks in 2005, ending the separatist conflict.

Area 1,904,569 sq km [735,354 sq mi]
Population 238,453,000
Capital (population) Jakarta (9,374,000)
Government Multiparty republic
Ethnic groups Javanese 45%, Sundanese 14|%, Madurese 7%, coastal Malays 7%, approximately 300 others
Languages Bahasa Indonesian (official), many others
Religions Islam 88%, Roman Catholic 3%, Hinduism 2%, Buddhism 1%
Currency Indonesian rupiah = 100 sen
Website www.indonesiamission-ny.org

ECONOMY

The World Bank describes Indonesia as a "lower-middle-income" developing country. Agriculture employs more than 40% of the workforce and rice is the main food crop. Bananas, cassava, coconuts, groundnuts, corn, spices, and sweet potatoes are also grown. Major cash crops include coffee, palm oil, rubber, sugar cane, tea, and tobacco. Fishing and forestry are also important.

There are important mineral reserves, including oil and natural gas. Bauxite, coal, iron ore, nickel, and tin are also mined.

JAKARTA

Capital of Indonesia, on the northwest coast of Java. Founded in 1619 as Batavia by the Dutch as a fort and trading post, it became the headquarters of the Dutch East India Company. It became the capital after Indonesia gained its independence in 1949. Industries include ironworking, printing, and timber.

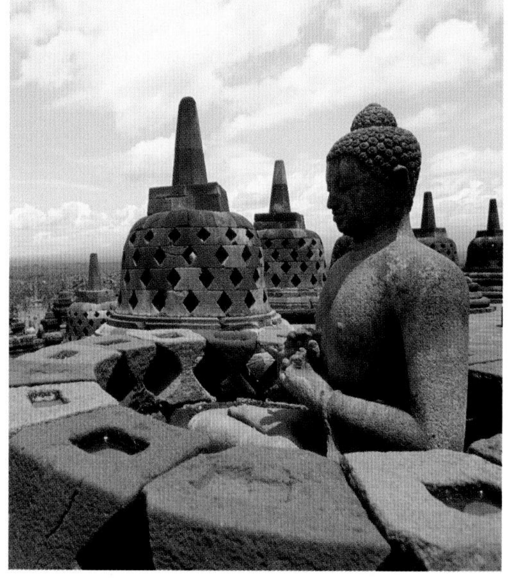

Borobudur Buddha; *the statue is part of the Borobudur Stupa on Java, the stupa represents the Buddhist cosmos*

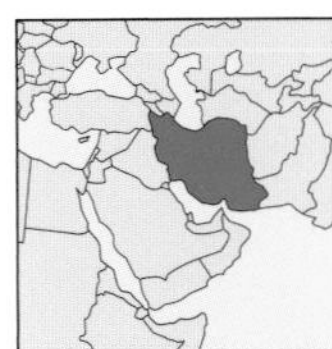

Iran's flag was adopted in 1980 by the country's Islamic government. The white stripe contains the national emblem, which is the word for Allah (God) in formal Arabic script. The words Allah Akbar (God is Great) is repeated 11 times on both the green and red stripes.

The Islamic Republic of Iran contains a barren central plateau which covers about half the country. It includes the Great Salt Desert (Dasht-e-Kavir) and the Great Sand Desert (Dasht-e-Lut). The Elburz Mountains (Alborz), which border the plateau to the north, contain Iran's highest peak, Damavand (18,386 ft [5,604 m]). North of the Elburz Mountains are the fertile, densely populated lowlands around the Caspian Sea, with a mild climate and abundant rainfall. Bordering the plateau to the west are the Zagros Mountains which separate the central plateau from the Khuzistan Plain, a region of sugar plantations and oil fields, which extends to the Iraqi border.

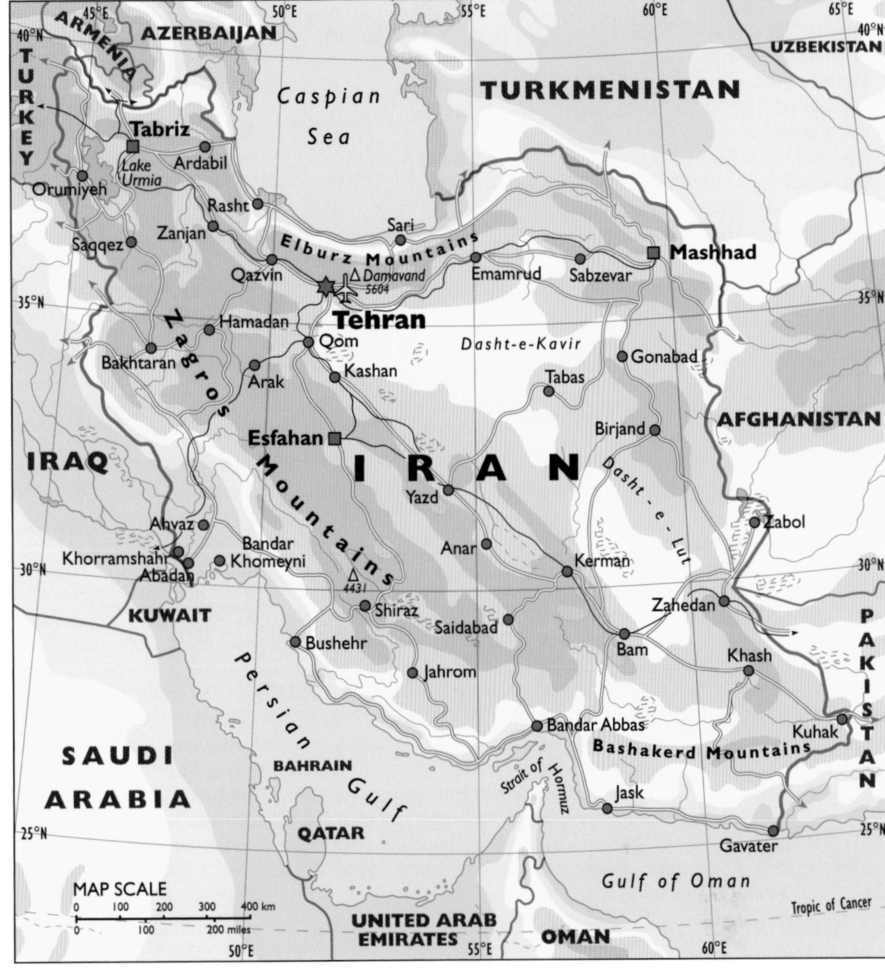

CLIMATE

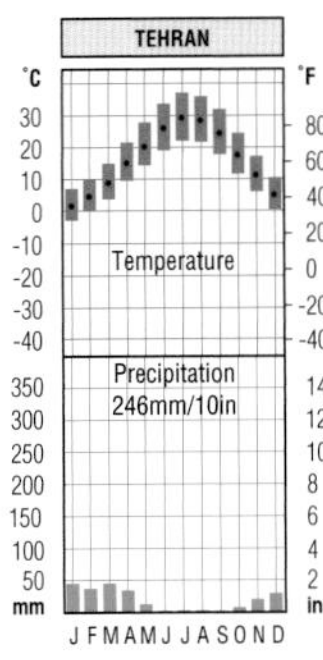

Much of Iran has a severe, dry climate, with hot summers and cold winters. Rain falls only about 30 days a year in Tehran and the annual temperature range is of more than 45°F [25°C]. The lowlands are generally milder.

HISTORY

Ancient Persia was a powerful empire. It flourished from 550 BC, when its king, Cyrus the Great, conquered the Medes, to 331 BC, when the empire was conquered by Alexander the Great. Arab armies introduced Islam in AD 641 and made Iran a great center of learning.

Britain and Russia competed for influence in the area in the 19th century, and in the early 20th century the British began to develop the country's oil resources. In 1925, the Pahlavi family took power. Reza Khan became shah (king) and worked to modernize the country. Persia was renamed Iran in 1935. The Pahlavi Dynasty ended in 1979 when religious leader, Ayatollah Ruhollah Khomeini, made Iran an Islamic republic.

POLITICS

Iran and Iraq fought over disputed borders from 1980–8, the war led to a great reduction in Iran's vital oil production, but output returned to its mid-1970s levels by 1994. Ayatollah Khomeini died in 1989 but his views and anti-Western attitudes continued to dominate. In 1997, the liberal Mohammad Khatami, was elected president, but conservative clerics made actual reform difficult with spiritual leader, Ayatollah Al Khameni, retaining much power. Khatami was reelected in 2001, but the clerical establishment and institutions such as the judiciary and the Expediency Council, still blocked most of his reformist plans and he was left isolated. Between 2003 and 2005 the United States accused Iran of developing nuclear weapons, a charge Iran denied.

In 2005 Mahmoud Ahmadinejad, former mayor of Tehran, was voted in as president. Upon election he promised a period of peace and moderation, however, his subsequent statements that Israel should be wiped off the map and that the Holocaust was but a myth did little to endear him with the West. His promise to proceed with a nuclear programme for Iran continued to cause concern and in 2006 he announced that Iran had successfully enriched uranium and should now be deemed a nuclear power.

ECONOMY

Iran's prosperity is based on its oil which accounts for 95% of the country's exports. Oil revenues have been used to develop a manufacturing sector, but agriculture still accounts for 25% of the gross domestic product, even though farms cover only a tenth of the land. The main crops are wheat and barley. Livestock farming and fishing are also important.

Area 636,368 sq mi [1,648,195 sq km]
Population 69,019,000
Capital (population) Tehran (7,723,000)
Government Islamic Republic
Ethnic groups Persian 51%, Azeri 24%, Gilaki and Mazandarani 8%, Kurd 7%, Arab 3%, Lur 2%, Baluchi 2%, Turkmen 2%
Languages Persian, Turkic 26%, Kurdish
Religions Islam (Shi'ite Muslim 89%)
Currency Iranian rial = 100 dinars
Website www.netiran.com

TEHRAN

Capital of Iran, 65 mi [105 km] south of the Caspian Sea. Strategically placed on the edge of the plains, in the foothills of the country's highest mountains. In 1788, it replaced Isfahan as the capital of Persia. In the early 20th century, the old fortifications were demolished and a planned city established by the Shah. Now Iran's industrial, commercial, administrative and cultural center.

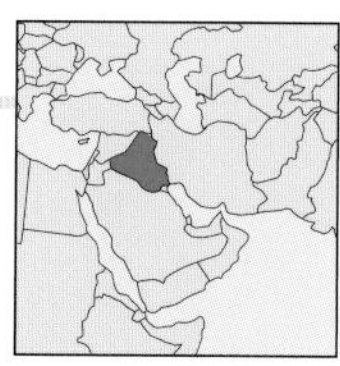

Iraq

Iraq's flag was adopted in 1963, when the country was planning to federate with Egypt and Syria. It uses the four Pan-Arab colors. The three green stars symbolize the three countries. Iraq retained these stars even though the union failed to come into being.

Area 169,234 sq mi [438,317 sq km]
Population 25,375,000
Capital (population) Baghdad (4,865,000)
Government Republic
Ethnic groups Arab 77%, Kurdish 19%, Assyrian and others
Languages Arabic (official), Kurdish (official in Kurdish areas), Assyrian, Armenian
Religions Islam 97%, Christianity and others
Currency New Iraqi dinar
Website www.un.int/iraq/homepage.htm

The Republic of Iraq is a southwest Asian country at the head of the Persian Gulf. Deserts cover western and southwestern Iraq, with part of the Zagros Mountains in the northeast, where farming can be practiced without irrigation. Western Iraq contains a large slice of the Hamad (or Syrian) Desert, but essentially comprises lower valleys of the rivers Euphrates (Nahr al Furat) and Tigris (Nahr Dijlah). The region is arid, but has fertile alluvial soils. The Euphrates and Tigris join south of Al Qurnah, to form the Shatt al Arab. The Shatt al Arab's delta is an area of irrigated farmland and marshes. This waterway is shared with Iran.

CLIMATE

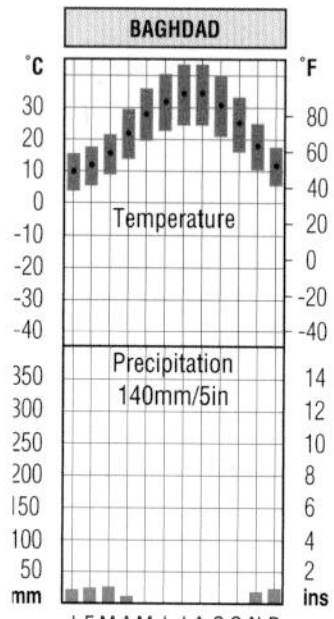

The climate of Iraq varies from temperate in the north to subtropical in the south and east. Baghdad, in central Iraq, has cool winters, with occasional frosts, and hot summers. Rainfall is generally low.

HISTORY

Mesopotamia was the home of several great civilizations, including Sumer, Babylon and Assyria. It later became part of the Persian Empire. Islam was introduced in AD 637 and Baghdad became the brilliant capital of the powerful Arab Empire. However, Mesopotamia declined after the Mongols invaded it in 1258. From 1534, Mesopotamia became part of the Turkish Ottoman Empire. Britain invaded the area in 1916. In 1921, Britain renamed the country Iraq and set up an Arab monarchy. Iraq finally became independent in 1932.

By the 1950s, oil dominated Iraq's economy. In 1952, Iraq agreed to take 50% of the profits of the foreign oil companies. This revenue enabled the government to pay for welfare services and development projects. But many Iraqis felt that they should benefit more from their oil.

Since 1958, when army officers killed the king and made Iraq a republic, the country has undergone turbulent times. In the 1960s, the Kurds, who live in northern Iraq, Iran, Turkey, Syria, and Armenia, asked for self-rule. The government rejected their demands and war broke out. A peace treaty was signed in 1975, but conflict continued.

POLITICS

In 1979, Saddam Hussein became Iraq's president. Under his leadership, Iraq invaded Iran in 1980, starting an eight-year war. During this war, Iraqi Kurds supported Iran and the Iraqi government attacked Kurdish villages with poison gas.

In 1990, Iraqi troops occupied Kuwait, but an international force drove them out in 1991. Since 1991, Iraqi troops have attacked Shi'ite Marsh Arabs and Kurds. In 1996, the government aided the forces of the Kurdish Democratic Party in an offensive against the Patriotic Union of Kurdistan, a rival Kurdish faction. In 1998, Iraq's failure to permit UNSCOM, the UN body charged with disposing of Iraq's deadliest weapons, access to all suspect sites led to Western bombardment of military sites. Periodic bombardment and economic sanctions continued, but Iraq was allowed to export a limited amount of oil in exchange for food and medicines.

The threat of war mounted after the terrorist attacks on the United States in 2001 and the rejection by Iraq in 2002 of the return of UN weapons inspectors. In 2002 and 2003, presure mounted on Iraq to dispose of its alleged weapons of mass destruction. Its failure to do so led to a coalition force, headed by the United States and the UK, to invade Iraq and overthrow the Saddam regime in March–April 2003. The coalition forces rapidly achieved their main objectives, but violence continued even after the capture of Saddam Hussein in December 2003.

Although largely boycotted by the Sunni Arabs, who make up a fifth of the population, elections took place in Iraq in 2005, but this still in an atmosphere of constant battle as civil order was still in disarray with daily attacks on civilians, Iraqi security forces and international agencies.

ECONOMY

Civil war and war damage in 1991 and 2003, UN sanctions, and economic mismanagement have all contributed to economic chaos. Oil remains Iraq's main resource, but a UN trade embargo in 1990 halted oil exports. Farmland covers around one-fifth of the land. Products include barley, cotton, dates, fruit, livestock, wheat, and wool. Iraq still has to import food. Industries include oil refining and the manufacture of petrochemicals and consumer goods.

***Visitors climb** the spiral stairway of the 9th-century mosque minaret at Samarra, Iraq*

BAGHDAD

Capital of Iraq, on the River Tigris. Established in 762 as capital of the Abbasid caliphate, it became a center of Islamic civilization and focus of caravan routes between Asia and Europe. It was almost destroyed by the Mongols in 1258. In 1921 Baghdad became the capital of newly independent Iraq. Notable sites include the 13th-century Abbasid Palace. In 1991 and 2003 Baghdad was badly damaged by bombing in the two Gulf Wars. Industries include building materials, textiles, tanning, bookbinding.

Ireland's flag was adopted in 1922 after the country had become independent from Britain, though nationalists had used it as early as 1848. Green represents Ireland's Roman Catholics, orange the Protestants, and the white a desire for peace between the two.

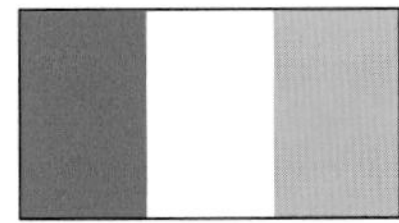

The Republic of Ireland consists of a large lowland region surrounded by a broken rim of low mountains. The lowlands include peat bogs. The uplands include the Mountains of Kerry with Carrauntoohill, Ireland's highest peak (3,415 ft [1,041 m]). The River Shannon is the longest in the Ireland, flowing through three large lakes, loughs Allen, Ree, and Derg. Forests cover approximately 5% of Ireland. Much of the land is under pasture and a very small percentage is set aside for crops.

Area 27,132 sq mi [70,273 sq km]
Population 3,970,000
Capital (population) Dublin (482,000)
Government Multiparty republic
Ethnic groups Irish 94%
Languages Irish (Gaelic) and English (both official)
Religions Roman Catholic 92%, Protestant 3%
Currency Euro = 100 cents
Website www.irlgov.ie

DUBLIN (BAILE ÁTHA CLIATH)

Capital of the Republic of Ireland, at the mouth of the River Liffey on Dublin Bay. In 1014, Brian Boru recaptured it from the Danish. In 1170, it was taken by the English and became the seat of colonial government. Dublin suffered much bloodshed in nationalist attempts to free Ireland from English rule. Strikes beginning in 1913 finally resulted in the Easter Rising (1916). Dublin was the center of the late 19th-century Irish literary renaissance. It is now the commercial and cultural center of the Republic. Notable sites include Christ Church Cathedral (1053), St. Patrick's Cathedral (1190), Trinity College (1591), and the Abbey Theatre (1904).

CLIMATE

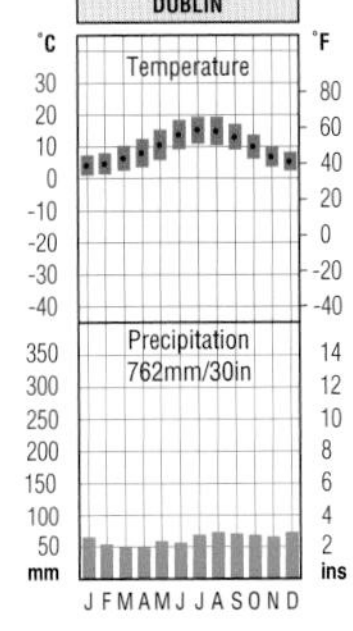

Ireland has a mild, damp climate influenced by the Gulf Stream current which warms the west coast, with Dublin in the east somewhat cooler. Rain occurs thoughout the year.

HISTORY

Celts settled in Ireland from about 400 BC. They were followed by the Vikings, Normans and the English. Vikings raided Ireland from the 790s, establishing settlements in the 9th century. But Norse domination was ended in 1014 when they were defeated by Ireland's king, Brian Boru. The Normans arrived in 1169 and, gradually, Ireland came under English influence.

In 1801, the Act of Union created the United Kingdom of Great Britain and Ireland. But Irish discontent intensified in the 1840s when a potato blight caused a famine in which a million people died and nearly a million emigrated. Britain was blamed for not having done enough to help. In 1905, Arthur Griffith founded Sinn Féin ("We Ourselves"), a movement advocating self-government for Ireland. Another secret organization, the Irish Republican Brotherhood, was also active in the early 20th century and its supporters became known as republicans. In 1916, republicans launched what was called the Easter Rebellion in Dublin, but the uprising was crushed. The republicans took over the Sinn Féin movement in 1918. They won a majority of Ireland's seats in the British parliament, but instead of going to London, they set up the Dáil Éireann (House of Representatives) in Dublin and declared Ireland an independent republic in January 1919.

In 1920, the British parliament passed the Government of Ireland Act, partitioning Ireland. The six Ulster counties accepted the Act, but fighting broke out in southern Ireland. In 1921, a treaty was agreed allowing southern Ireland to become a self-governing dominion, called the Irish Free State, within the British Commonwealth. With one Irish group accepting the treaty and another group, wanting complete independence civil war occurred between 1922 and 1923.

POLITICS

Ireland became a republic in 1949 and has subsequently played an independent role in Europe, joining the EEC in 1973 and, unlike the UK, adopting the euro as its currency in 2002. The government of Ireland has worked with British governments in attempts to solve the problems of Northern Ireland. In 1998, it supported the creation of a Northern Ireland Assembly, the setting up of north–south political structures, and the amendment of the 1937 constitution removing from it the republic's claim to Northern Ireland. A referendum showed strong support for the proposals and the amendments to the constitution. The 1998 Good Friday Agreement in Northern Ireland, aimed to end the long-standing conflict, it met with much support but ran into difficulties when the underground Irish Republican Army (IRA) refused to disarm. In July 2005 the IRA issued a statement of full disarmament.

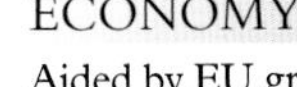

ECONOMY

Aided by EU grants, farming is now relatively prosperous and includes cattle and dairy, sheep, pigs, potatoes, and barley. Manufacturing is now the leading activity, with high-tech industries producing chemicals and pharmaceuticals, electronic equipment, machinery, paper, and textiles. Tourism and racehorses are important industries.

***Hore Abbey ruins** at Cashel, County Tipperary, founded in 1266 by Cistercians*

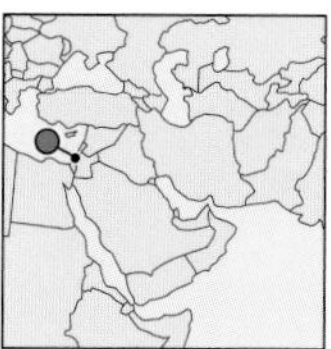

Israel

Israel's flag was adopted when the Jewish state declared itself independent in 1948. The blue and white stripes are based on the tallit, a Hebrew prayer shawl. The ancient, six-pointed Star of David is in the center. The flag was designed in America in 1891.

Area 7,954 sq mi [20,600 sq km]
Population 6,199,000
Capital (population) Jerusalem (685,000)
Government Multiparty republic
Ethnic groups Jewish 80%, Arab and others 20%
Languages Hebrew and Arabic (both official)
Religions Judaism 80%, Islam (mostly Sunni) 14%, Christianity 2%, Druze and others 2%
Currency New Israeli shekel = 100 agorat
Website www.mfa.gov.il/MFA

The State of Israel is a small country in the eastern Mediterranean. The fertile Mediterranean plains are the most densely populated region. Inland lie the Judaeo-Galilean highlands, a series of ranges that extend from northern Israel to the northern tip of the Negev Desert in the south. To the east lie part of the Great Rift Valley, River Jordan, Sea of Galilee and the Dead Sea, whose shoreline is 1,371 ft [418 m] below sea level, the world's lowest point on land.

CLIMATE

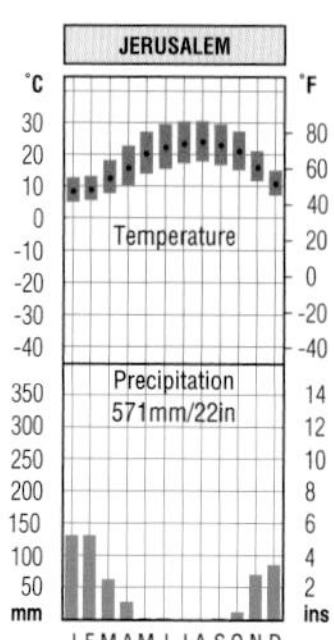

Northern Israel enjoys a typical Mediterranean climate, with hot, dry, summers and mild winters when heavy rains may occur, though generally on a small number of days. The average annual rainfall decreases west to east with only 2.5 in [70 mm] in the Dead Sea region. The driest region is the Negev Desert, where the average annual rainfall ranges from 8 in [200 mm] in the north to 2 in [50 mm] at the resort of Eilat on the Gulf of Aqaba. The most unpleasant conditions occur when hot dry khamsin winds blow from the Arabian peninsula, especially in early and late summer.

HISTORY

Israel is part of the ancient region of Palestine, which, because of its location at a crossroad of cultures, has long been a center of conflict. Between about 1800 and 1500 BC, a group of people called Hebrews or Israelites settled in what was then known as the Land of Canaan. Later, Hebrews settled in Egypt, but they returned to Canaan in the 13th century BC. The southern group of Hebrews established a state called Judah and they

MAP SCALE
0 25 50 75 km
0 25 50 miles
35°E
LEBANON
Mediterranean Sea
SYRIA
Golan Heights
Nahariyya
Mt Meron 1208
Acre
33°N
Haifa
Tiberias
Sea of Galilee -210
Nazareth
Yarmuk
ISRAEL
Netanya
Nabulus
Jordan
Tel Aviv-Jaffa
Petah Tiqwa
WEST BANK
Bat Yam
Ramat Gan
32°N
Rishon Le Ziyyon
Lod
Ram Allah
Ramla
Jericho
Ashdod
Rehovot
Jerusalem
Ashqelon
Bethlehem
Dead Sea
Gaza
GAZA STRIP
Hebron
-418
JORDAN
Beersheba
31°N
Negev Desert
EGYPT
30°N
Eilat
Aqaba
Gulf of Aqaba
SAUDI ARABIA

became known as Jews. Their capital was Jerusalem. The area later came under the Persians and, from 63 BC, the Romans. Following the suppression of Jewish revolts, the Romans drove the Jews out of Jerusalem and most Jews fled from Palestine. Muslim Arabs moved into the area in the AD 600s.

Most modern Israelis are descendants of Jewish immigrants who began to settle from the 1880s. Britain ruled Palestine from 1917. Large numbers of Jews escaping Nazi persecution arrived in the 1930s, provoking an Arab uprising against British rule. In 1947, the UN agreed to partition Palestine into an Arab and a Jewish state. Fighting broke out after Arabs rejected the plan.

The State of Israel came into being in May 1948, but fighting continued into 1949. Other Arab-Israeli wars were fought in 1956, 1967, and 1973. The Six Day War in 1967 led to the acquisition by Israel of the West Bank and East Jerusalem. Israel also occupied the Gaza Strip, the Sinai Peninsula (Egyptian), and the Golan Heights (Syrian). In 1982, Israel invaded Lebanon to destroy the stronghold of the PLO (Palestine Liberation Organization), but they left in 1985.

POLITICS

In 1978 Israel signed a treaty with Egypt leading to the return of the Sinai Peninsula to Egypt in 1979. Conflict continued between Israel and the PLO. In 1993, the PLO and Israel agreed to establish Palestinian self-rule in the Gaza Strip and in Jericho on the West Bank. The agreement was extended in 1995 to include more

Houses on the side of Mount of Olives, *Jerusalem; the mount is of historical importance to Jews and they have long sought to be buried there, as a result of this it is home to more than 150,000 graves, including the tomb of Zechariah the prophet*

JERUSALEM

Jerusalem is a sacred site for Christians, Jews, and Muslims. It is capital of Israel, though the UN does not recognize this status and East Jerusalem is also claimed as the intended capital of a future Palestinian state. Jerusalem has repeatedly been occupied and destroyed throughout history. Jews were expelled from Jerusalem by the Romans (AD 135). It was occupied by the Ottoman Turks from the Middle Ages until 1917, when it became the capital of the British-mandated territory of Palestine. In 1948, it was divided between Jordan (east) and Israel (west). In 1967, the Israeli army captured the Old City of East Jerusalem and the united city became the capital of Israel. The Old City was the political and religious center of the Jews in Biblical times and the Western (Wailing) Wall is the last remaining part of the holy Jewish Temple of Biblical times. Muslims believe that the Prophet Muhammad rose to Heaven from the site now occupied by the Dome of the Rock. For Christians, the principal site is the Church of the Sepulchre, which occupies the place believed to be Calvary (Golgotha), where Jesus was crucified. Jerusalem is located on a ridge which forms part of the watershed that divides the Mediterranean plains to the west from the Jordan River and the Dead Sea to the east. Government and service industries, including tourism, are the main employers. Other light industrial activities include diamond cutting, the manufacture of clothing and shoes, printing, and a variety of high-tech industries.

than 30% of the West Bank. Israel's prime minister, Yitzhak Rabin, who had been seeking a "land for peace" settlement, was assassinated in 1995 and in 1996 the right-wing hardliner Binyamin Netanyahu became prime minister.

In 1999 the left-wing Ehud Barak won elections, promising to resume the peace process. Many problems remained, particularly the extension of Jewish settlements in the occupied areas and attacks on Israel by the militant Islamic group, Hezbollah, based in southern Lebanon. In 2001, Ariel Sharon, former general and leader of the right-wing Likud, was elected prime minister adopting a hardline policy against the Palestinians. In 2003, Western powers pressed Israel to adopt a "road map" that would lead to the creation of two states, Israel and a democratic Palestine. In late 2004 the death of Palestinian leader Yasser Arafat held out hope that moderate policies might lead to the creation of a Palestinian state. Israel forcibly evicted Israeli settlers from Gaza and four settlements on the West Bank in August 2005. However, tension and conflict continued, making negotiations extremely difficult.

In late 2005, Sharon formed a new political party, Kadima. Its aim was to impose a peace settlement should negotiations with the Palestinian National Authority prove unsuccessful. However, before his party could be tested at the polls, he suffered a severe stroke. Ehud Olmert became the Kadima leader and, in elections in 2006, Kadima won most seats. Following lengthy talks with other parties, Olmert became prime minister heading a coalition government.

WEST BANK

Region west of River Jordan, northwest of the Dead Sea. Designated an Arab district in the 1947 UN plan for the partition of Palestine. Administered by Jordan after the first Arab-Israeli War (1948), but captured by Israel in the Six-Day War (1967). In 1988, Jordan passed its claim to the West Bank to the PLO. The 1994 Israeli-Palestinian Accord gave the Palestinian National Authority (PNA) limited autonomy in the West Bank. Difficulties resulting particularly from the growth of Israeli settlements and security disputes halted progress towards any Israeli withdrawal.

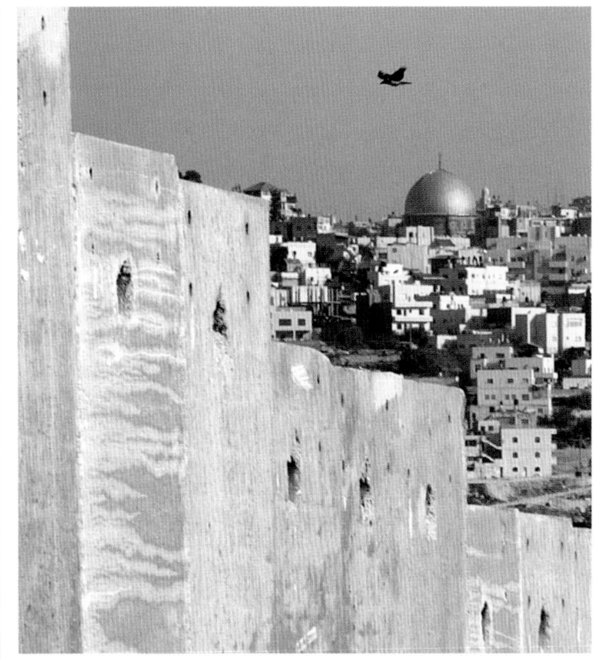

***The golden Dome of the Rock** mosque in Jerusalem's Old City is seen behind the controversial security barrier separating Jerusalem from the West Bank*

ECONOMY

The State of Israel has a high standard of living. Agriculture employs less than 3% of the population, but farming is highly efficient. Major products include beef, citrus fruits, cotton, dairy products, and poultry. However, manufacturing accounts for around 38% of the gross domestic product. Israel produces a wide range of manufactures, including many high-technology projects. Machinery and equipment, computer software, cut diamonds, agricultural products, chemicals, textiles, and clothing are exported. The United States is Israel's leading trading partner. Tourism is another major activity.

GAZA STRIP

Region bordering the Mediterranean Sea. From 1920, the region was part of the British Mandate of Palestine. It came under the control of Egypt, under the ceasefire arrangements following the Arab-Israeli War (1948). Israel seized the area during the Six-Day War (1967) when it became an Occupied Territory. But it came under the control of the Palestinian National Authority in 2005, when Israel withdrew all its settlers and armed forces. Palestinian Arabs make up the bulk of the population. Agriculture is important and exports include citrus fruits, flowers, and textiles.

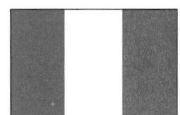

The Italian flag is based on the military standard carried by the French Republican National Guard when Napoleon invaded Italy in 1796, causing great changes in Italy's map. It was finally adopted as the national flag after Italy was unified in 1861.

Area 116,339 sq mi [301,318 sq km]
Population 58,057,000
Capital (population) Rome (2,460,000)
Government Multiparty republic
Ethnic groups Italian 94%, German, French, Albanian, Slovene, Greek
Languages Italian (official),German, French, Slovene
Religions Roman Catholic
Currency Euro = 100 cents
Website www.enit.it

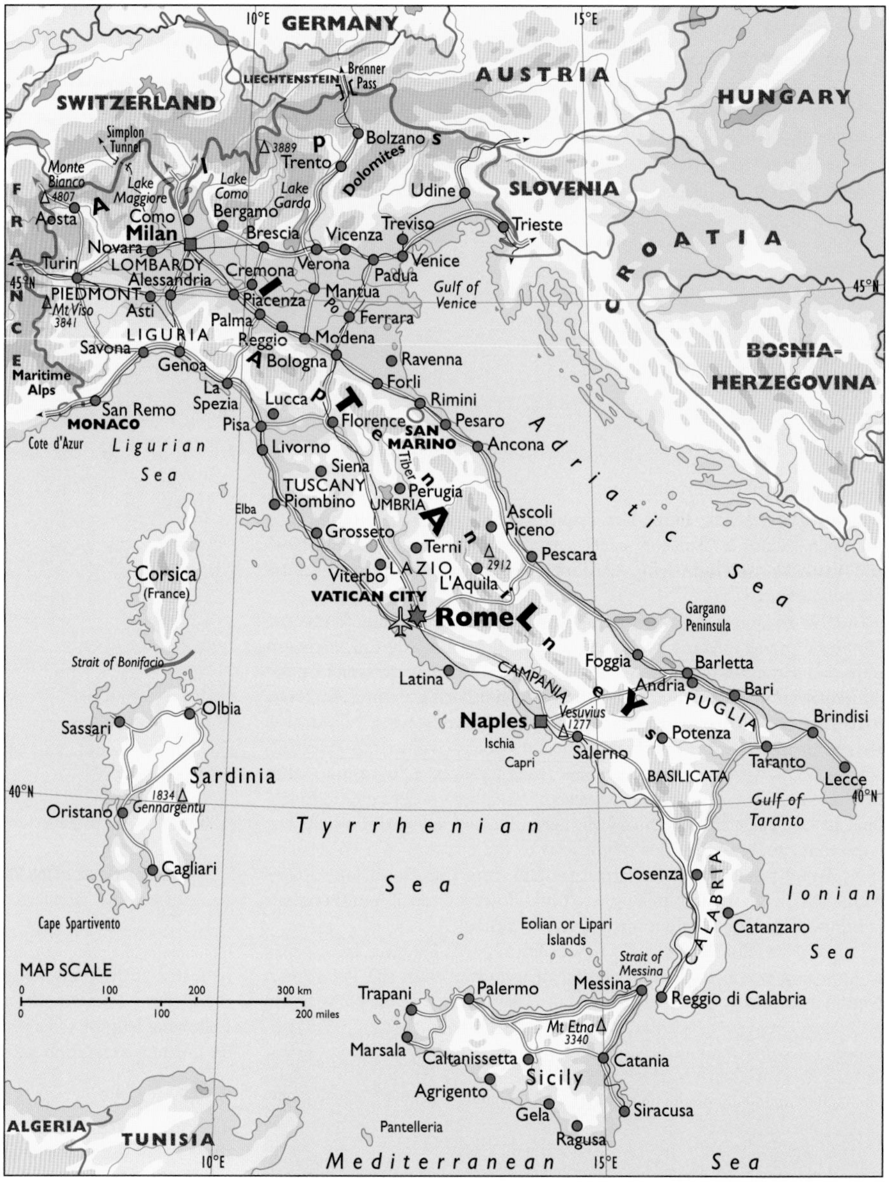

The Republic of Italy is bordered to the north by the Alps which overlook the northern plains, Italy's most fertile and densely populated region, drained by the River Po. The Apennines (Appennini), which form the backbone of southern Italy, reach their highest peaks (9,800 ft [3,000 m]), in the Gran Sasso Range overlooking the the central Adriatic Sea, near Pescara. Limestones are the most common rocks. Between the mountains are long, narrow basins, some with lakes.

Southern Italy contains a string of volcanoes, stretching from Vesuvius, near Naples (Nápoli), through the Lipari Islands, to Mount Etna on Sicily. Traces of volcanic activity are found throughout Italy. Ancient lava flows cover large areas and produce fertile soils. Italy is still subject to earthquakes and volcanic eruptions. Sicily is the largest island in the Mediterranean. Sardinia is more isolated from the mainland and its rugged, windswept terrain and lack of resources have set it apart.

CLIMATE

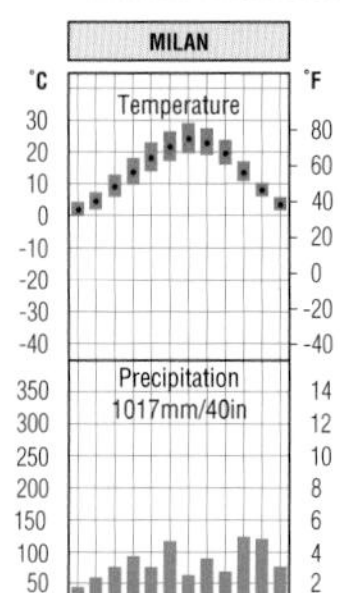

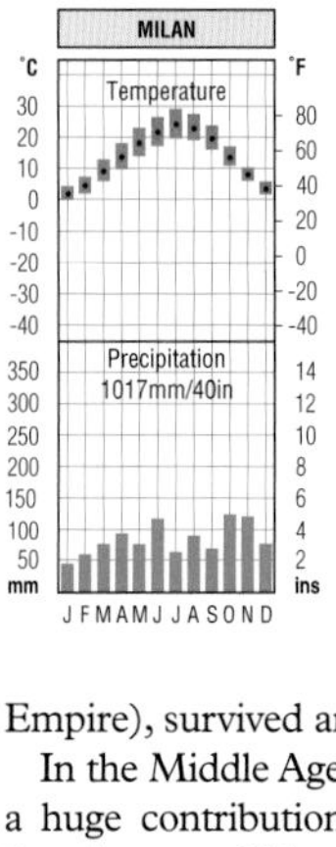

The north has cold, snowy winters, but warm and sunny summer months. Rainfall is plentiful, with brief but powerful thunderstorms in summer. Southern Italy has mild, moist winters and warm, dry summers.

HISTORY

Magnificent ruins throughout Italy testify to the glories of the ancient Roman Empire, which was founded in 753 BC. It reached its peak in the AD 100s and finally collapsed in the 400s, although the Eastern Roman Empire (the Byzantine Empire), survived another 1,000 years.

In the Middle Ages, Italy was split into many tiny states.and they made a huge contribution to the revival of art and learning, known as the Renaissance. Cities, such as Florence and Venice, testify to the artistic achievements of this period.

The struggle for unification (the Risorgimento) began early in the 19th century, but little progress was made until an alliance between France and Piedmont (then part of the Kingdom of Sardinia) drove Austria from Lombardy in 1859. Tuscany, Parma and Modena joined

Capalbio, *Tuscany; located on the coast in the province of Grosseto, the area that is now Capalbio was first settled in Etruscan times, around 900 BC*

ROME (ROMA)

Capital of Italy, on the River Tiber, west central Italy. Founded in the 8th century BC. The Roman Republic was founded around 500 BC. By the 3rd century BC, Rome ruled most of Italy and began to expand overseas. In the 1st century AD, the city was transformed as successive emperors built temples, palaces, public baths, arches, and columns. It remained the capital of the Roman Empire until AD 330. In the 5th century, Rome was sacked during the Barbarian invasions, and its population fell rapidly. In the Middle Ages, Rome became the seat of the papacy. In 1527, it was sacked by the army of Charles V. The city flourished once more in the 16th and 17th centuries. Italian troops occupied it in 1870, and in 1871 it became the capital of a unified Italy. The 1922 Fascist march on Rome brought Mussolini to power; he did much to turn Rome into a modern capital city.

Piedmont-Lombardy in 1860, and the Papal States, Sicily, Naples—including most of the southern peninsula—and Romagna were brought into the alliance. King Victor Emmanuel II was proclaimed ruler of a united Italy the following year. Venetia was acquired from Austria in 1866 and Rome was finally annexed in 1871. Since then, Italy has been a unified state, though the pope and his successors disputed the takeover of the Papal States. This dispute was resolved in 1929, when Vatican City was established as a fully independent state.

Since unification, the population has doubled, and though the rate of increase is notoriously slow today, the rapid growth of population, in a poor country attempting to develop its resources, forced millions of Italians to emigrate during the first quarter of the 20th century. Large numbers settled in the United States, South America, and Australia. More recently, large numbers of Italians have moved into northern Europe for similar reasons.

In 1915, Italy entered World War I alongside the Allies (Britain, France and Russia). After the war, Italy was given nearly 9,000 sq mi [23,000 sq km] of territory that had belonged to Austria-Hungary. Benito Mussolini (Il Duce) became prime minister of Italy in 1922 and, from 1925 ruled as a dictator. In 1936, Italian forces invaded Ethiopia, while military personnel were sent to support the rebellion of General Franco in Spain. Italy agreed to fight alongside Germany in the event of war, though did not enter World War II until June 1940. During the war, Italy lost much of its colonial empire to the Allies and, in late 1943, declared war on Germany. Mussolini was captured and shot by partisans in 1945, when he tried to escape to Switzerland.

Italy became a republic in 1946 following a referendum. Allied troops left in 1947. Italy was a founder member of NATO in 1949, and of the EEC, now the European Union, in 1957. After the establishment of the EEC, Italy's economy began to expand. Much of the economic development took place in the industrialized north. Central Italy is less developed and represents a transition zone between the developed north and the poor agrarian south known as the Mezzogiorno.

POLITICS

In 1992, the old political establishment was driven from office with several prominent leaders accused of links to organized crime and some imprisoned. In 1996, the left-wing Olive Tree alliance led by Romano Prodi took office, but Prodi was forced to resign in 1998 following his rejection of demands made by his Communist allies. He was replaced by Massimo D'Alemo, the first former Communist to become prime minister. His attempts to create a two-party system in Italy failed in 1999.

By the late 1990s, it had the world's sixth largest economy and, on 1 January 2002, the euro became its currency. In 2001, Italy moved towards the political right when a coalition of center-right parties won a substantial majority in parliament. Media tycoon Silvio Berlusconi, who had briefly served as prime minister in 1994 and who had spent several years fighting tax evasion charges, became prime minister.

ECONOMY

Fifty years ago, Italy was a mainly agricultural society. Today it is a major industrial power. It imports most of the raw materials used in industry. Industries include cars, chemicals, processed food, machinery, textiles. Major crops include grapes for wine-making, and olives, citrus fruits, sugar beet and vegetables. Cattle, pigs, poultry and sheep are raised.

VATICAN CITY

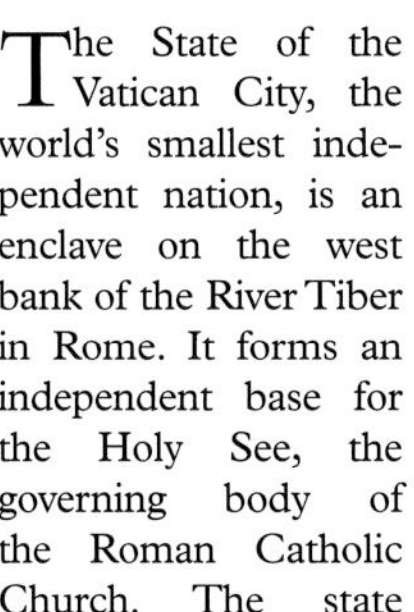

Area 0.17 sq mi [0.44 sq km]
Population 921
Capital (population) Vatican City (921)
Government Ecclesiastical
Ethnic groups Italian, Swiss, others
Languages Italian, Latin, French, others
Religions Roman Catholic
Currency Euro = 100 cents
Website www.vatican.va

The State of the Vatican City, the world's smallest independent nation, is an enclave on the west bank of the River Tiber in Rome. It forms an independent base for the Holy See, the governing body of the Roman Catholic Church. The state includes St Peter's Square, St Peter's Basilica, and Vatican Palace. The Vatican treasures include Michelangelo's frescoes in the Sistine Chapel and attract tourists from all over the world. The Vatican Library contains a priceless collection of both Christian and pre-Christian manuscripts. The popes have lived in the Vatican almost continuously since the 5th century. Sustained by investment income and voluntary contributions, the Vatican City is all that remains of the Papal States which, until 1870, occupied most of central Italy. In 1929, Mussolini recognized the Vatican's independence in return for papal recognition of the kingdom of Italy.

The population, including 100 Swiss Guards, the country's armed force, is entirely of unmarried males. The Commission appointed by the Pope to administer the affairs of the Vatican controls a radio station, the Pope's summer palace at Castel Gandolfo, and several churches in Rome. Vatican City has its own newspaper, police, and railway stations, and issues its own stamps and coins.

SAN MARINO

Area 24 sq mi [61 sq km]
Population 27,000
Capital (population) San Marino (2,395)
Government Republic
Ethnic groups Sanmarinese, Italian
Languages Italian (official)
Religions Roman Catholic
Currency Euro = 100 cents
Website www.visitsanmarino.com

The Republic of San Marino, the world's smallest republic lies 12 mi [20 km] southwest of the Adriatic port of Rimini and is wholly surrounded by Italy. It consists largely of the limestone mass of Monte Titano (2,382 ft [725 m]) around which cluster wooded mountains, pastures, fortresses, and medieval villages. San Marino has pleasant, mild summers and cool winters.

The republic was named after St Marinus, the stonemason saint who is said to have first established a community here in 301 AD. It has a friendship and cooperation treaty with Italy dating back to 1862 and uses Italian currency, but issues its own stamps, which are an important source of revenue. The state is governed by an elected council and has its own legal system. San Marino has no armed forces and its police are from the Italian constabulary. Most of the people live in the medieval city of San Marino, which receives more than 3 million tourists a year.

Chief occupations are tourism, limestone quarrying, ceramics, textiles, and wine-making. The customs union with Italy makes San Marino an easy conduit for the illegal export of currency and certain kinds of tax evasion for Italians.

Ivory Coast

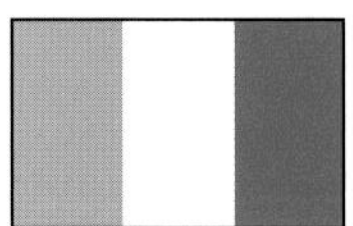

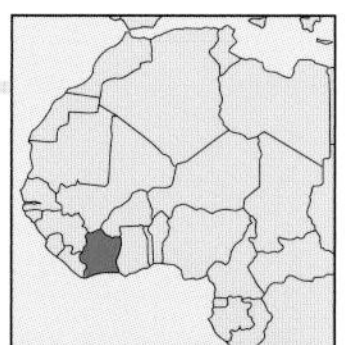

This flag was adopted in 1960 when the country became independent from France. It combines elements from the French tricolor and the Pan-African colors. Orange represents the northern savanna, white is for peace and unity, and green for the forests in the south.

Area 124,503 sq mi [322,463 sq km]
Population 17,328,000
Capital (population) Yamoussoukro (107,000)
Government Multiparty republic
Ethnic groups Akan 42%, Voltaiques 18%, Northern Mandes 16%, Krous 11%, Southern Mandes 10%
Languages French (official), many native dialects
Religions Islam 40%, Christianity 30%, traditional beliefs 30%
Currency CFA franc = 100 centimes
Website www.afrika.no/index/Countries/C_te_d_Ivoire/index.html

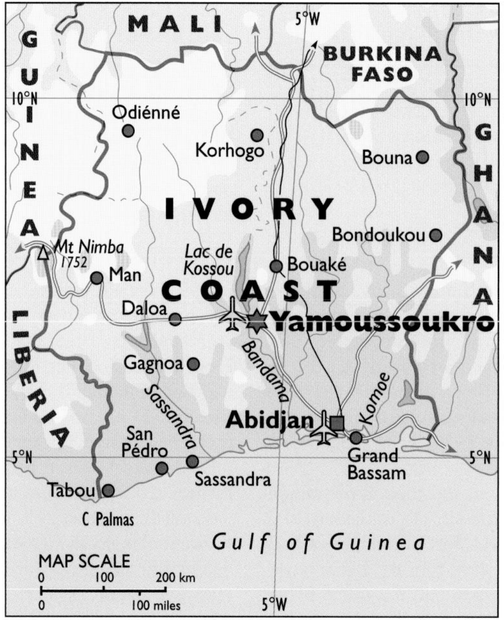

YAMOUSSOUKRO

Capital of Ivory Coast since 1983. Originally a small Baouké tribal village and birthplace of Ivory Coast's first president, Félix Houphouët-Boigny, it developed rapidly into the administrative and transport center of Ivory Coast. Yamoussoukro's Our Lady of Peace Cathedral (consecrated by Pope John Paul II in 1990) is the world's largest Christian church.

The Republic of the Ivory Coast, in West Africa, is officially known as Côte d'Ivoire. The southeast coast is bordered by sand bars that enclose lagoons, on one of which the former capital and chief port of Abidjan is situated. But the southwestern coast is lined by rocky cliffs. Behind the coast is a coastal plain, but the land rises inland to high plains. The highest land is an extension of the Guinea Highlands in the northwest, along the borders with Liberia and Guinea. Most of the country's rivers run north–south.

CLIMATE

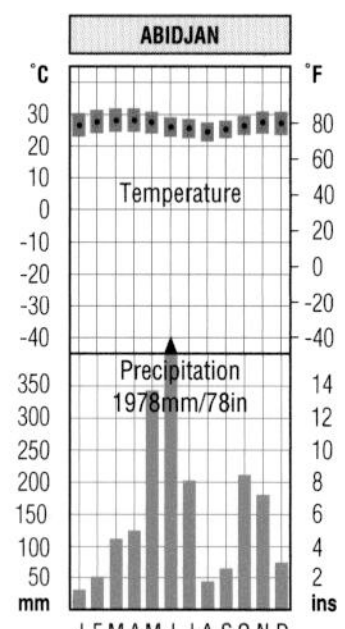

Ivory Coast has a hot and humid tropical climate, with high temperatures throughout the year. There are two distinct rainy seasons in the south of the country: between May and July, and from October to November. Inland, the rainfall decreases. Northern Ivory Coast has a dry season and only one rainy season. As a result, the forests in central Ivory Coast thin out to the north, giving way to savanna.

HISTORY

The region that is now Ivory Coast came under successive black African rulers until the late 15th century, when Europeans, attracted by the chance to trade in slaves and such local products as ivory, began to establish contacts along the coast. French missionaries reached the area in 1637 and, by the end of the 17th century, the French had set up trading posts on the coast. In 1842, France brought the Grand-Bassam area under its protection and Ivory Coast became a French colony in 1893. From 1895, it was ruled as part of French West Africa, a massive union which also included Benin, Burkina Faso, Guinea, Mali, Mauritania, Niger, and Senegal. In 1946, Ivory Coast became a territory in the French Union. The port of Abidjan was built in the early 1950s, but the country achieved autonomy in 1958.

POLITICS

Ivory Coast became fully independent in 1960. Its first president, Félix Houphouët-Boigny, became the longest serving head of state in Africa with an uninterrupted period in office that ended with his death in 1993. Houphouët-Boigny was a paternalistic, pro-Western leader, who made his country a one-party state. In 1983, the National Assembly agreed to move the capital from Abidjan to Yamoussoukro, Houphouët-Boigny's birthplace. Visitors to Abidjan, where most of the country's Europeans live, are usually impressed by the city's general air of prosperity, but the cost of living for local people is high and there are great social and regional inequalities. Despite its political stability since independence, the country faces such economic problems as variations in the price of its export commodities, unemployment, and high foreign debt.

Following the death of Houphouët-Boigny in 1993, the Speaker of the National Assembly, Henri Konan Bédié, proclaimed himself president. He was reelected president in 1995. However, in December 1999, Bédié was overthrown during an army mutiny and a new administration was set up by General Robert Guei. Presidential elections, held after a new constitution was adopted in 2000, resulted in defeat for Guei by a veteran politician, Laurent Gbago. However, conflict began in 2002. By 2004 the country was divided into the government-held south and the rebel-held, mainly Muslim, north.

ECONOMY

Ivory Coast is one of Africa's more prosperous countries. Its free-market economy has proved attractive to foreign investors, especially French firms, while France has given much aid. It has an agrarian economy, which employs about three-fifths of the workforce. The chief farm products are cocoa, coffee, and cotton and make up nearly half the value of the total exports. Food crops include cassava, corn, plantains, rice, vegetables, and yams. Manufactures include processed farm products, timber, and textiles.

Biankouma, Pays Yacouba; *this old village in the mountainous west of the country is noted for its impeccable round huts*

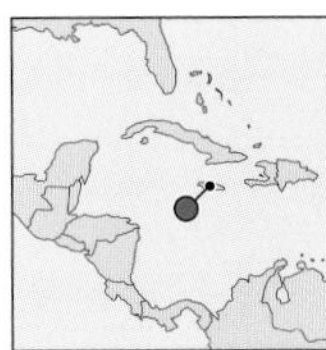

A committee of Jamaica's House of Representatives designed the national flag. the gold represents Jamaica's sunshine and natural resources; the green symbolizes agriculture and hope for the future; the black is for the hardships faced and overcome by its people.

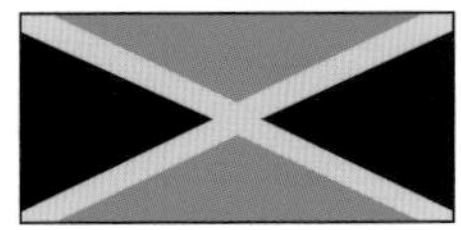

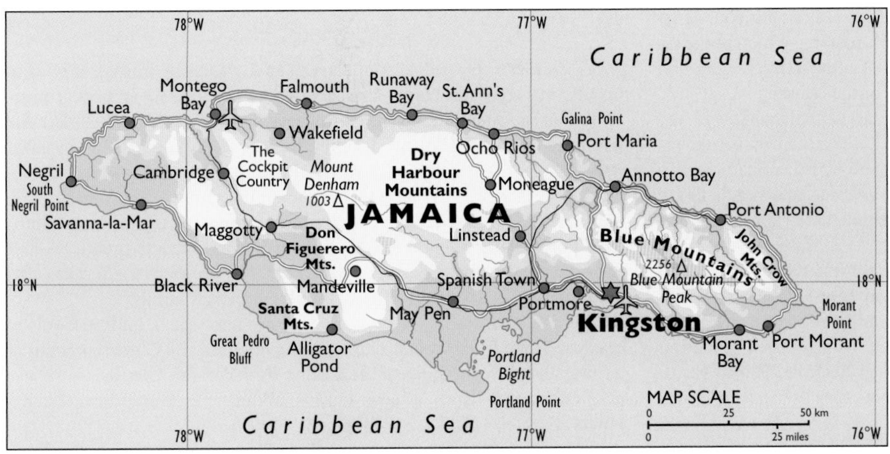

Area 4,244 sq mi [10,990 sq km]
Population 2,713,000
Capital (population) Kingston (104,000)
Government Constitutional monarchy
Ethnic groups Black 91%, Mixed 7%, East Indian
Languages English (official), patois English
Religions Protestant 61%, Roman Catholic 4%
Currency Jamaican dollar = 100 cents
Website www.jis.gov.jm

Jamaica is the third largest Caribbean island. It is a parliamentary democracy, with the monarch of the UK as its head of state. The coastal plain is narrow and discontinuous. Inland are hills, plateaus and mountains. The country's central range culminates in the Blue Mountain Peak (7,402 ft [2,256 m]). The Cockpit Country in the northwest of the island is an inaccessible limestone area, known for its many deep depressions, (cockpits). Jamaica is a lush, green island.

CLIMATE

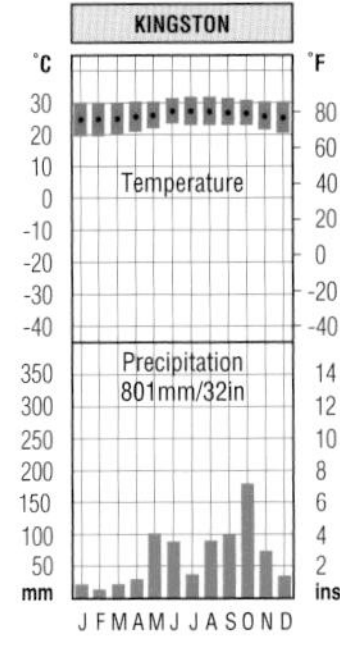

The climate is hot and humid. Temperatures range from 77°F [25°C] in January to 81°F [27°C] in July. Moist southeast trade winds bring rain to the more temperate highlands. Annual rainfall on the northern slopes may reach 200 in [5,000 mm]. But the sheltered south coast is much drier, about 30 in [750 mm] per year. The island is prone to periodic hurricanes.

HISTORY

In 1509, Spaniards occupied the island. Soon, the local Arawak Amerindian population had died out. The Spaniards imported African slaves to work the sugar plantations. The British took the island in 1655 and, with sugar as its staple product, it became a prized possession. The African slaves were the forefathers of much of the present population. But the plantations on which they worked disappeared when the sugar market collapsed in the 19th century.

In 1865, after 200 years of having their own elected body to help the British rule the island, Jamaica came under direct British rule as a crown colony, following the Moranty Bay rebellion. This peasant uprising, led by Baptist deacon Paul Bogle, was staged by freed slaves who were suffering acute hardship, but it was put down by British troops. In the 1930s, Jamaican leaders called for more power and riots took place in 1938, with people protesting against unemployment and Britain's racial policies. In that year, the People's National Party (PNP) was founded. In 1944, Britain granted Jamaica a new constitution, providing for an elected House of Representatives. In 1958, the island became a member of the British-sponsored Federation of the West Indies, but it withdrew in 1961.

POLITICS

Jamaica became an independent nation and a member of the British Commonwealth in 1962. It joined the Organization of American States in 1969. In the 1970s, economic problems developed. Michael Manley, leader of the PNP, became prime minister in 1972 and he pursued socialist policies, advocating a policy of non-alignment. The PNP won a second term in office in 1976. It nationalized businesses and sought closer ties with Cuba. In 1980, the Jamaica Labor Party (JLP), led by Edward Seaga defeated the PNP in elections. Seaga privatized much state-owned business and distanced Jamaica from Cuba. His moderate policies led to increased investment and better relations with Western countries. In 1989, the PNP defeated the JLP and Manley was returned to power as prime minister. However, Manley broadly followed Seaga's moderate policies. Manley retired on health grounds in 1992 and was succeeded by Percival J Patterson. The PNP was reelected in 1993, 1998 and 2002.

Jamaica faces many problems, including drug trafficking. It has become a major transshipment point for cocaine being transported from South America to North America and Europe. Cannabis is produced in Jamaica. Corruption and money-laundering are major concerns. Price and tax increases led to riots in 1999, while in 2001, gun battles occurred with 27 people killed when the police searched for drugs in a poor district of Kingston. The murder rate in 2004 was 1,145. This figure was attributed by the police to street-gang violence.

In 2004 Hurricane Ivan destroyed thousands of homes, described as the worst natural disaster in living memory.

ECONOMY

Jamaica is a developing country. Agriculture employs about 20% of the workforce. The chief crop is sugar cane, other products include allspice, bananas, citrus fruits, cocoa, coconuts, coffee, milk, poultry, vegetables, and yams. The country's chief resource is bauxite (aluminum ore) and Jamaica is one of the world's top producers. Cement, chemicals, cigars, clothing, and textiles, fertilizers, machinery, molasses and petroleum products are also produced. Service industries account for 60% of the gross domestic product. Tourism brings in vital revenue.

KINGSTON

Capital and largest city of Jamaica. It was founded in 1693. It rapidly developed into Jamaica's commercial center, based on the export of raw cane sugar, bananas and rum. In 1872 it became the island's capital. Kingston is the cultural heart of Jamaica, the home of calypso and reggae music.

Bog Walk Gorge, *St Catherine; the gorge is located between Spanish Town and Linstead and takes its name from the Spanish "Boca de Agua" meaning "water's mouth"*

Japan

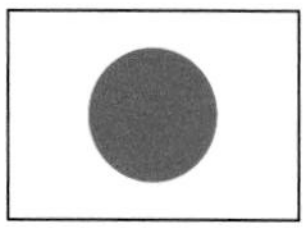

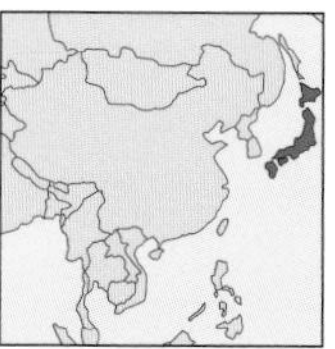

Japan's flag was officially adopted in 1870, although Japanese emperors had used this simple design for many centuries. The flag shows a red sun on a white background. The geographical position of Japan is expressed in its name "Nippon" or "Nihon," meaning "source of the Sun."

Japan is an island nation in northeastern Asia containing four large islands—Honshu, Hokkaido, Kyushu, and Shikoku—which make up more than 98% of the country. Thousands of small islands, including the Ryukyu island chain, make up the rest of the country.

The four main islands are mainly mountainous, while many of the small islands are the tips of volcanoes rising from the sea bed. Japan has more than 150 volcanoes, about 60 of which are active. Volcanic eruptions, earthquakes and tsunamis often occur, because the islands lie on an unstable part of Earth where the continental plates are constantly moving.

Throughout Japan, complex folding and faulting has produced an intricate mosaic of landforms. Mountains and forested hills alternate with small basins and coastal lowlands, covered by alluvium deposited there by the short rivers that rise in the uplands. Most of the population lives on the coastal plains, one being the stretch from the Kanto Plain, where Tokyo is situated, along the narrow plains that border the southern coasts of Honshu, to northern Kyushu.

The pattern of landforms is further complicated by the presence of volcanic cones and calderas. The highest mountain in Japan, Fuji-san (12,388 ft [3,776 m]), is a long dormant volcano which last erupted in 1707. It is considered sacred, and is visited by thousands of pilgrims every year.

CLIMATE

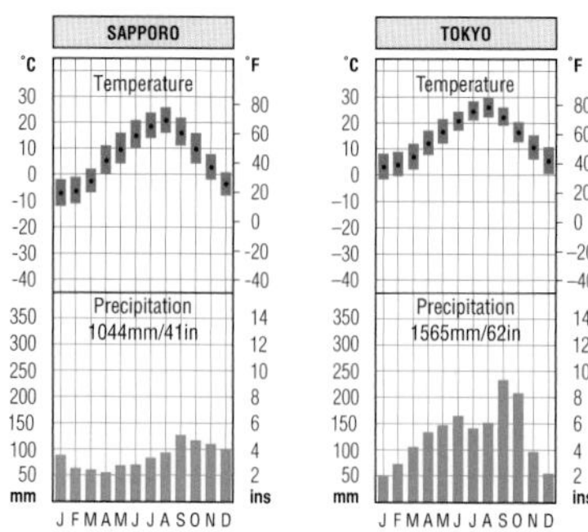

The climate of Japan varies greatly. Hokkaido in the north has cold, snowy winters. At Sapporo, temperatures below 4°F [–20°C] have been recorded between December and March. Summers are warm, with temperatures often exceeding 86°F [30°C]. Rain falls throughout the year. Tokyo has the higher rainfall and temperatures while the southern islands of Shikoku and Kyushu in the south have warm temperate climates with hot summers and cold winters.

Area 145,880 sq mi [377,829 sq km]
Population 127,333,000
Capital (population) Tokyo (8,130,000)
Government Constitutional monarchy
Ethnic groups Japanese 99%, Chinese, Korean, Brazilian and others
Languages Japanese (official)
Religions Shintoism and Buddhism 84% (most Japanese consider themselves to be both Shinto and Buddhist), others
Currency Yen = 100 sen
Website http://web-japan.org

HISTORY

Most modern Japanese are descendants of early immigrants who arrived in successive waves from the Korean Peninsula and other parts of the Asian mainland. The earliest zone of settlement included the northern part of Kyushu Island and the coastlands of Setonaikai (Inland Sea). By the 5th century AD, Japan was divided among numerous clans, of which the largest and most powerful was the Yamato. The Yamato ruled from the area which now contains the city of Nara. Shinto, a polytheistic religion based on nature worship, was practiced, and the Japanese imperial dynasty established. The chiefs of the Yamato clan are regarded as ancestors of the Japanese imperial family.

The 5th century AD was a time when new ideas and technology reached Japan from China. The Japanese adopted the Chinese system of writing and their methods of calculating the calendar. Confucianism was also introduced from China and, in about 552, Buddhism reached Japan.

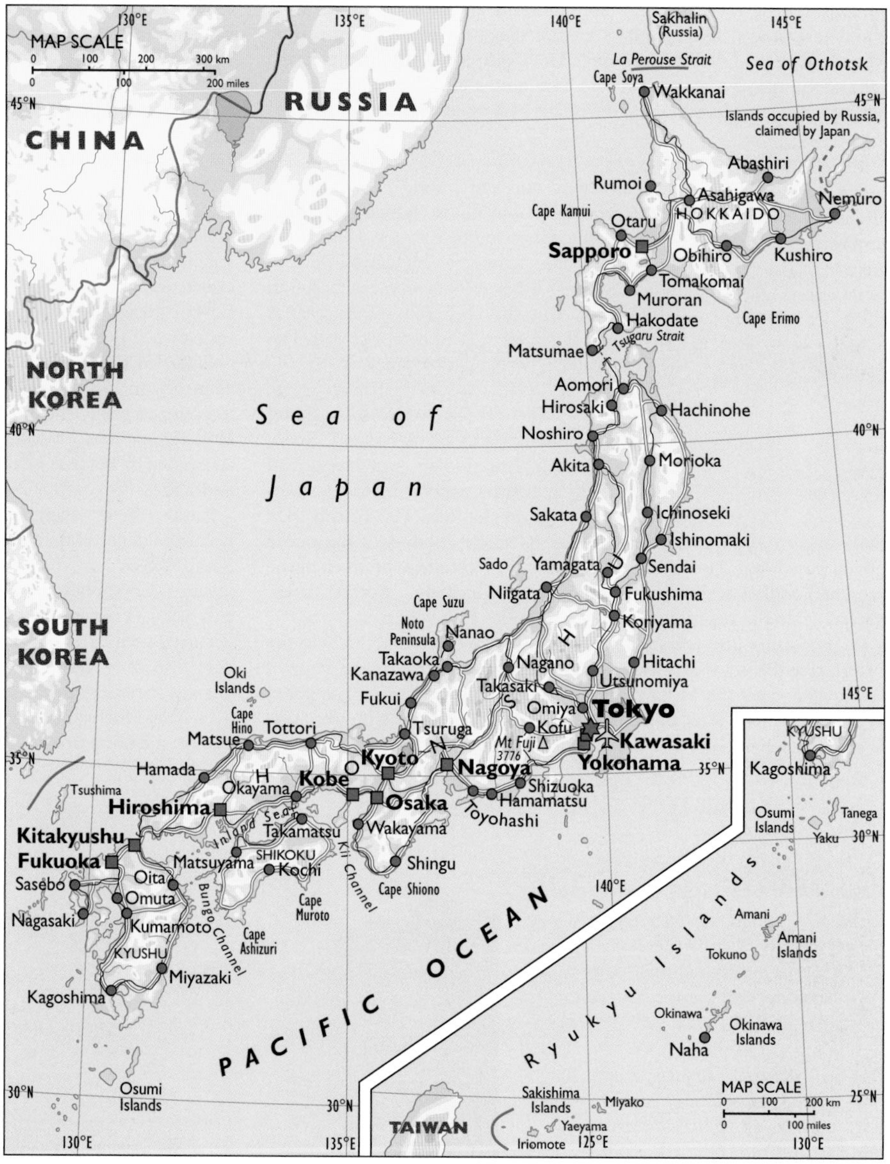

From the early 12th century, political power passed increasingly to military aristocrats. Government was conducted in the name of the emperor by warrior leaders called *shoguns*. Civil warfare between rival groups of feudal lords was endemic over long periods, but, under the rule of the Tokugawa *shoguns*, between 1603 and 1867, Japan enjoyed a great period of peace and prosperity. Military families (the feudal lords and their retainers, or *samurai*) formed a powerful elite. During the *shogun* era, a code of conduct called *bushido* ("the way of the warrior") was developed for the *samurai*, it stressed military skills and fearlessness, frugality, kindness, honesty and filial piety. The *samurai's* supreme obligation was, above all, to his feudal lord.

European contact began with the arrival of Portuguese sailors in 1543, then in 1549 a Spanish missionary came to convert the Japanese to Christianity. The Japanese put an end to missionary work in the 1630s when they ordered all Christian missionaries to leave the country, and forced Japanese converts to give up their faith. The only Europeans allowed to stay were Dutch traders, as they were not involved in missionary work. Japan only opened its ports to Western trade again in 1854 after American intervention.

The Meiji period from 1867 to 1912 was marked by the adoption of Western ideas and technology. An educational system and a telegraph network were set up, railways built, and modern systems of banking and taxation introduced. In addition the samurai was abolished and a modern army and navy established.

In 1889, Japan introduced its first constitution under which the emperor became head of state and supreme commander of the army and navy. The emperor appointed government ministers, responsible to him. The constitution also allowed for a parliament, called the Diet, with two houses.

From the 1890s, Japan began to build up an overseas empire. In 1894–5, Japan fought China over the control of Korea. Under the Treaty of Shimonoseki (1895), Japan took Taiwan. Korea was made an independent territory, leaving it open to Japanese influence. Rivalry with Russia led to the Russo-Japanese War (1904–5). Under the Treaty of Portsmouth, Japan gained the Liaodong peninsula, which Russia had leased from China, while Russia recognized the supremacy of Japan's interests in Korea. Thus Japan was established as a world power.

In World War I Japan supported the Allies. After the war Japan's foreign policy strongly supported the maintenance of world peace, becoming a founding member of the League of Nations in 1920. The army seized Manchuria in 1931 and made it a puppet state called Manchukuo, they then extended their influence into other parts of northern China. In 1933, after the League of Nations condemned its actions in Manchuria Japan was forced to rescind its membership

During the 1930s, and especially after the outbreak of war between Japan and China in 1937, militarist control of Japan's government grew steadily. By the end of 1938, when Japan controlled most of eastern China, there was talk of bringing all of eastern Asia under Japanese control. In September 1939, Japan occupied the northern part of French Indo-China and, later that month, signed an agreement with Italy and Germany, assuring their co-operation in building a "new world order," and acknowledging Japan's leadership in Asia.

In 1941 Japan launched a surprise attack on the American naval base of Pearl Harbor, in Hawaii, an action that drew the United States into World War II. On 6 August 1945, American bombers dropped the first atomic bomb on Hiroshima. The USSR declared war on Japan and invaded Manchuria and Korea. On August 9, the Americans dropped an atomic bomb on Nagasaki. World War II ended on September 2, 1945 when Japan officially surrendered.

TOKYO

Capital of Japan, on east-central Honshu, at the head of Tokyo Bay. The modern city divides into distinct districts: Kasumigaseki, Japan's administrative center; Marunouchi, its commercial center; Ginza, its shopping and cultural center; the west shore of Tokyo Bay, its industrial center. Modern Tokyo also serves as the country's educational center with more than 100 universities. Founded in the 12th century as Edo, it became capital of the Tokugawa shogunate in 1603. In 1868, the Japanese Reformation reestablished imperial power, and the last shogun surrendered Edo Castle. Emperor Meiji renamed the city Tokyo, and it replaced Kyoto as the capital of Japan. In 1923, an earthquake and subsequent fire claimed more than 150,000 lives and necessitated the city's reconstruction. In 1944–5, intensive US bombing destroyed more than half of Tokyo, and another modernization and restoration program began. Industries include electronics, cameras, automobile manufacture, metals, chemicals, textiles.

POLITICS

The Allies occupied Japan in August 1945. Under a new constitution, power was transferred from the emperor to the people. The army and navy were abolished and the country renounced war as a political weapon. The emperor became a constitutional monarch.

Japan signed a Treaty of Peace that took effect on 28 April 1952. The Allied occupation ended on that day. When, in 1956, the Soviet Union and Japan agreed to end the state of war between them, Japan became a member of the UN.

The conservative Liberal-Democratic Party was formed in 1955, made up of rival Japanese parties. The LDP controlled Japan's government until the 1990s, when a series of coalition governments were formed. A true opposition party emerged in the late 1990s, when the Democratic Party of Japan united with several small parties. The country underwent a serious economic crisis in 1997. In 2001, the LDP chose Junichiro Koizumi as prime minister. Koizumi promised drastic reforms to revive the economy. He won a landslide victory in September 2005 after calling a snap election when his plans to privatize Japan's postal system were defeated in the upper house. After this victory his government announced plans to continue his reform program and also to revise Japan's pacifist constitution.

ECONOMY

Japan has the world's second highest GDP after the United States. The most important sector of the economy is industry, though Japan has to import most of the raw materials and fuels it needs for its industries. Its success is based on the use of the latest technology, a skilled and hard-working labor force, vigorous export policies and a comparatively small spend on defense. Manufactures dominate its exports which include machinery, electrical and electronic equipment, vehicles and transport equipment, iron and steel, chemicals, textiles, and ships. Japan is one of the world's top fishing nations and fish is an important source of protein. Only 15% of the land can be farmed due to its rugged nature yet the country produces about 70% of the food it requires. Rice is the chief crop, taking up about half of the farmland. Other major products include fruits, sugar beets, tea, and vegetables.

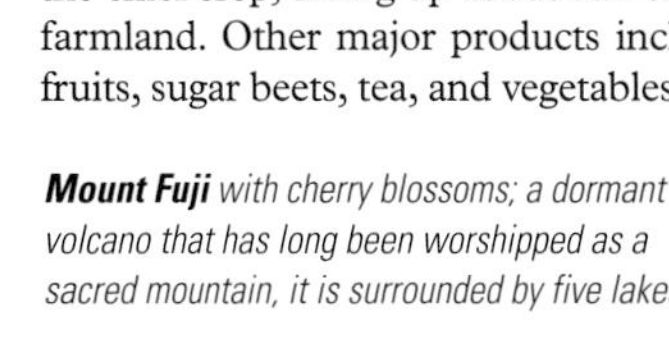

Mount Fuji *with cherry blossoms; a dormant volcano that has long been worshipped as a sacred mountain, it is surrounded by five lakes*

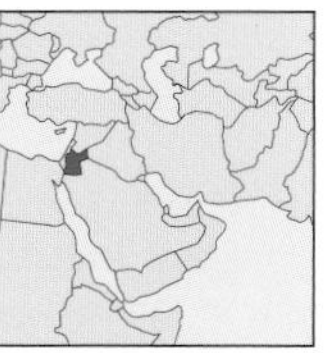

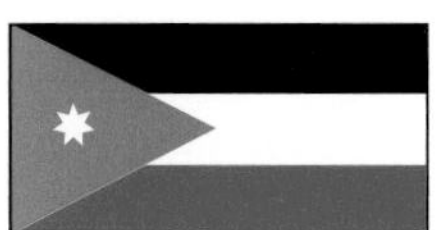

The green, white, and black on this flag are the colors of the three tribes who led the Arab Revolt against the Turks in 1917; red is the color of the Hussein Dynasty. The star was added in 1928. Its seven points represent the first seven verses of the Koran.

Area 34,495 sq mi [89,342 sq km]
Population 5,611,000
Capital (population) Amman (1,148,000)
Government Constitutional monarchy
Ethnic groups Arab 98% (Palestinians 50%)
Languages Arabic (official)
Religions Islam (mostly Sunni) 94%, Christianity (mostly Greek Orthodox) 6%
Currency Jordanian dinar = 1,000 fils
Website www.tourism.jo

The Hashemite Kingdom of Jordan is an Arab country in southwestern Asia. The Great Rift Valley in the west contains the River Jordan and the Dead Sea. East of the Rift Valley is the Transjordan Plateau, where most Jordanians live. To the east and south lie vast areas of desert. Jordan has a short coastline on an arm of the Red Sea, the Gulf of Aqaba. The country's highest peak is Jabal Ram (1,754 m [5,755 ft]).

CLIMATE

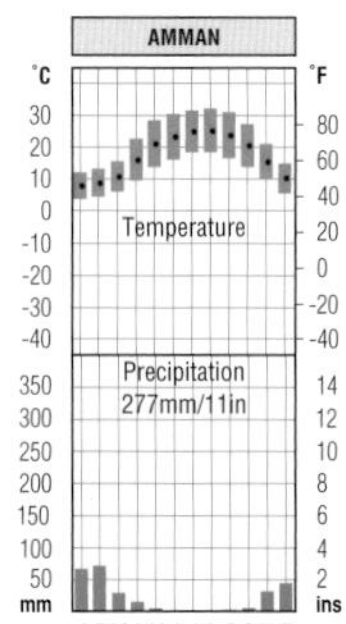

About 90% of Jordan has a desert climate, with an average annual rainfall of less than 8 in [200 mm]. Summers are hot, winters can be cold, with snow on higher areas. The northwest is the wettest area, with an average annual rainfall of 31 in [800 mm] in higher areas.

HISTORY

Jordan was first settled by Semitic peoples about 4,000 years ago, and later conquered by Egyptian, Assyrian, Chaldean, Persian and Roman forces. The area fell to Muslim Arabs in AD 636, the Arab culture they introduced survives to this day.

By the end of the 12th century, Christian crusaders controlled parts of western Jordan, but were driven out by the great Muslim warrior Saladin in 1187. The Egyptian Mamelukes overthrew Saladin's successors in 1250 and ruled until 1517, when the area was conquered by the Ottoman Turks. Jordan stagnated under their rule, but the opening of a railway in 1908 stimulated the economy. Arab and British forces defeated the Turks during World War I and after the war, the area east of the River Jordan was awarded to Britain by the League of Nations.

Britain created a territory called Transjordan, east of the River Jordan in 1921. It then became self-governing in 1923, but Britain retained control of its defenses, finances, and foreign affairs. This territory became fully independent as Jordan in 1946.

Since the creation of the State of Israel in 1948 Jordan has suffered from instability arising from Arab-Israeli conflict. After the first Arab-Israeli War (1948-9), Jordan acquired the West Bank, which was officially incorporated into the state in 1950. This crucial area, including East Jerusalem, was lost to Israel in the war of 1967, causing many Palestinians to seek refuge in Jordan. In the 1970s, Palestinian guerrillas using Jordan as a base became a challenge to the authority of King Hussein's government. After a short civil war, the Palestinian leadership fled.

POLITICS

In 1988 King Hussein suddenly renounced all responsibility for the West Bank, thereby recognizing that the Palestine Liberation Organization, not Jordan, was the legitimate representative of the Palestinian people. Palestinians were still in the majority and the refugees, numbering around 900,000, placed a huge burden on an already weak economy. Jordan was further undermined by the 1991 Gulf War when, despite its official neutrality, the pro-Iraq, anti-Western stance of the Palestinians in Jordan damaged prospects of trade and aid deals with Europe and the United States, Jordan's vital economic links with Israel having already been severed. A ban on political parties was removed in 1991, and martial law lifted after 21 years. Multiparty elections were held in 1993 and, in 1994, Jordan and Israel signed a peace treaty, ending a 40-year-long state of war. The treaty restored some land in the south to Jordan.

King Hussein, who had commanded great respect for his role in Middle Eastern affairs, died in 1999. He was succeeded by his eldest son who became King Abdullah II. Following the path of his father, Abdullah sought to further the Israeli-Palestinian peace process. He also worked to consolidate his country's relations with other nations in the region. Despite local opposition to the invasion of Iraq in 2003, he supported the US-led war on terrorism and worked to improve relations with Israel. However, in November 2005 suicide bombers killed 57 in Amman and terrorist group al-Qaida claimed responsibility.

ECONOMY

Classified as a "lower-middle-income" developing country, Jordan's economy depends substantially on aid. Less than 6% of the land is farmed. It has an oil refinery and manufactures include pharmaceuticals, cement, ceramics, fertilizers, shoes, and textiles. Service industries, including tourism, employ more than 70% of the workforce.

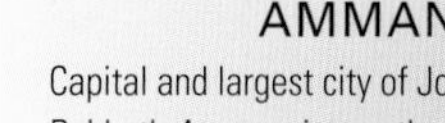

AMMAN

Capital and largest city of Jordan. Known as Rabbath-Ammon, it was the chief city of the Ammonites in biblical times. Ptolemy II Philadelphus renamed it Philadelphia. A new city was built on seven hills from 1875, and it became the capital of Trans-Jordan in 1921. From 1948 it grew rapidly, partly as a result of the influx of Palestinian refugees. Industries include cement, textiles, tobacco, and leather.

***The facade of the treasury** (El-Khazneh), Petra; an amazing rock-carved city created by the Nabateans over 2,000 years ago*

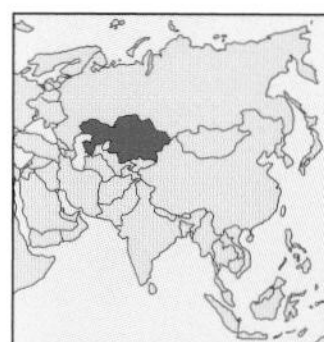

Kazakhstan's flag was adopted on June 4, 1992, about six months after it had become independent. The blue represents cloudless skies, while the golden sun and the soaring eagle represent love of freedom. A vertical strip of gold ornamentation is on the left.

Area 1,052,084 sq mi [2,724,900 sq km]
Population 15,144,000
Capital (population) Astana (322,000)
Government Multiparty republic
Ethnic groups Kazakh 53%, Russian 30%, Ukranian 4%, German 2%, Uzbek 2%
Languages Kazakh (official), Russian, the former official language, is widely spoken
Religions Islam 47%, Russian Orthodox 44%
Currency Tenge = 100 tiyn
Website www.kz

The Republic of Kazakhstan is a large country in west-central Asia. In the west, the Caspian Sea lowlands include the Karagiye Depression, which reaches 433 ft [132 m] below sea level. The lowlands extend eastward through the Aral Sea area. The north contains high plains, but the highest land is along the eastern and southern borders. These areas include parts of the Altai and Tian Shan mountain ranges.

Eastern Kazakhstan contains several freshwater lakes, the largest of which is Lake Balkhash (Balqash Köl). The water in the rivers has been used for irrigation, causing ecological problems. The Aral Sea, deprived of water, shrank from 25,830 sq mi [66,900 sq km] in 1960, to 12,989 sq mi [33,642 sq km] in 1993. Areas which once provided fish have dried up and are now barren desert.

Kazakhstan has very little woodland. Grassy steppe covers much of the north, while the south is desert or semidesert. Large, dry areas between the Aral Sea and Lake Balkhash have become irrigated farmland.

CLIMATE

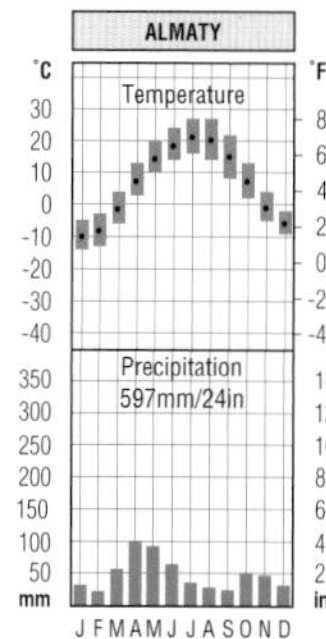

The extreme climate reflects position in the heart of Asia, far from the influence of the oceans. Winters are cold and snow covers the land for about 100 days, on average, at Almaty (Alma Ata). Rainfall is generally quite low.

HISTORY

From the late 15th century, the Kazakhs built up a large nomadic empire ruled by *khans*. But Kazakh power declined in the 17th century. In the early 18th century, Russia became influential in the area. In 1731, the Kazakhs in the west accepted Russian rule to gain protection from attack from neighboring peoples. By the mid-1740s, Russia ruled most of the region and, in the early 19th century, Russia abolished the *khanates*. They also encouraged Russians and Ukrainians to settle in Kazakhstan.

After the Russian Revolution of 1917, many Kazakhs wanted independence, but the Communists prevailed and in 1936 Kazakhstan became a republic of the Soviet Union, called the Kazakh Soviet Socialist Republic. During and after World War II, the Soviet government moved many people from the west into Kazakhstan. From the 1950s, people were encouraged to work on a "Virgin Lands" project, which involved bringing large areas of grassland under cultivation.

POLITICS

Reforms in the Soviet Union in the 1980s led to the breakup of the country in December 1991. Kazakhstan kept contacts with Russia and most of the former Soviet republics by joining the Commonwealth of Independent States (CIS), and in 1995 Kazakhstan announced that its army would unite with that of Russia. In December 1997, the government moved the capital from Alma Ata to Aqmola (later renamed Astana), a town in the Russian-dominated north. It was hoped that this move would bring some Kazakh identity to the area.

Under Soviet rule, Kazakhstan was a dumping ground and test bed. The rocket-launching site at Baykonur (Bayqongyr) suffered great environmental damage, including the shrinking of the Aral Sea by 70%. But Kazakhstan has emerged as a powerful entity, wealthier and more diversified than other Asian republics. It could provide the "new order" between East and West. It is the only former Soviet republic whose ethnic population is almost outnumbered by another group (the Russians), and its Muslim revival is relatively muted. Its first elected president, Nursultan Nazarbayev, a former Communist leader, introduced many reforms, including a multiparty system. However, he has been criticized for his authoritarian rule and the elections of 2004 and 2005, were widely considered to be flawed.

ECONOMY

The World Bank classifies Kazakhstan as a "lower-middle-income" developing country. Livestock farming, especially sheep and cattle, is an important activity, and major crops include barley, cotton, rice, and wheat.

The country is rich in mineral resources, including coal and oil reserves, together with bauxite, copper, lead, tungsten, and zinc. Manufactures include chemicals, food products, machinery, and textiles. The first major pipeline transporting oil direct from the Caspian opened in 2001 and runs through Russia. To reduce dependence on Russia, Kazakhstan signed an agreement in 1997 to build a new pipeline to China.

Produce market, *Almaty; a vast array of vibrantly colored fruit and vegetables being sold by the producers themselves in the town's central market*

ASTANA (formerly AQMOLA)

Capital of Kazakhstan, on the River Ishim in the steppes of north-central Kazakhstan. Under Soviet rule, Aqmola functioned as capital of the Virgin Lands. From 1961 to 1993 it was known as Tselinograd, and from 1993 to 1998 as Aqmola.

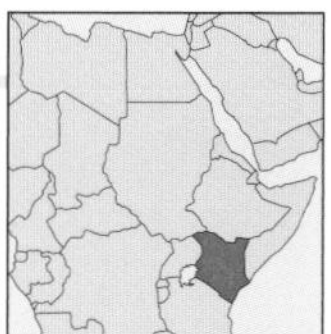

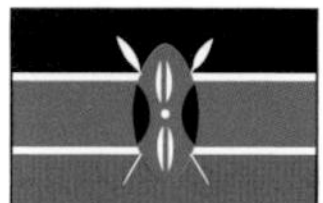

Kenya's flag dates from 1963, when the country became independent. It is based on the flag of KANU (Kenya African National Union), the political party which led the nationalist struggle. The Masai warrior's shield and crossed spears represent the defense of freedom.

Area 224,080 sq mi [580,367 sq km]
Population 32,022,000
Capital (population) Nairobi (2,143,000)
Government Multiparty republic
Ethnic groups Kikuyu 22%, Luhya 14%, Luo 13%, Kalenjin 12%, Kamba 11%, others
Languages Kiswahili and English (both official)
Religions Protestant 45%, Roman Catholic 33%, traditional beliefs 10%, Islam 10%
Currency Kenyan shilling = 100 cents
Website www.kenya.go.ke

The Republic of Kenya is located in East Africa straddling the Equator. Behind the narrow coastal plain on the Indian Ocean, the land rises to high plains and highlands, broken by volcanic mountains, including Mount Kenya, the highest peak at 17,057 ft [5,199 m].

Crossing the country is an arm of the Great Rift Valley with several lakes including Baringo, Magadi, Naivasha, Nakuru and, on the northern frontier, Lake Turkana (formerly Lake Rudolf).

CLIMATE

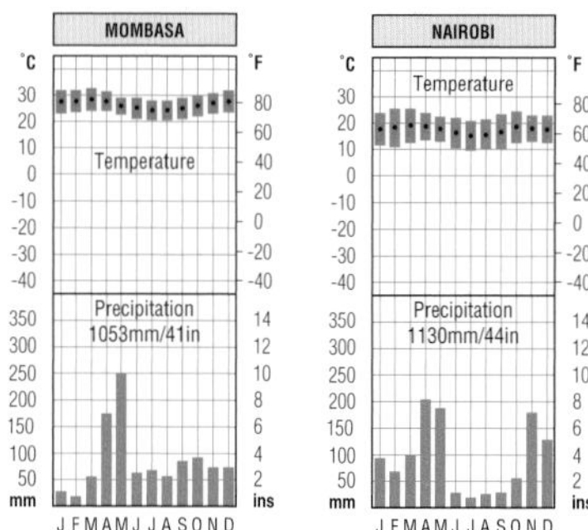

The coast is hot and humid, but inland the climate is moderated by the height of the land. The thickly populated southwestern highlands have summer temperatures 18°F [10°C] lower than the coast. Nights can be cool, but temperatures stay above zero. The main rainy season is from April to May. Only 15% of the country has a reliable rainfall of 31 in [800 mm].

HISTORY

The Kenyan coast has been an important trading center for more than 2,000 years. Early Arab traders carried goods from eastern Asia and exchanged them for items from the local people. Portuguese explorer Vasco da Gama reached the coast in 1498. Later, the Portuguese competed with the Arabs for control of the coast.

The British took control of the coast in 1895, soon extending their influence inland with many Britons setting up large farms. Opposition to British rule mounted in the 1940s, and, in 1953, a secret movement called Mau Mau launched an armed struggle. Mau Mau was eventually defeated, but Kenya finally gained independence in 1963. Kenya's first president was nationalist veteran Jomo Kanyatta.

***Bare tree** by Lake Turkana, Loyangalani; situated to the north of Kenya, crossing the border with Ethiopia at its northernmost tip; the lake measures 2,606 sq mi (6,750 sq km)*

POLITICS

Many Kenyan leaders felt that the division of the population into 40 ethnic groups might lead to instability. They argued that Kenya should have a strong central government and, as a result, Kenya has been a one-party state for much of the time since independence. Multiparty democracy was restored in the early 1990s with elections in 1992, 1997 and 2002.

In the 1960s, attempts by Kenya, Tanzania, and Uganda to collaborate collapsed due to the deep differences between the political and economic policies of the countries. Hopes were revived in 1999, when a new East African Community was created. Its aim was to establish a customs union, a common market, a monetary union, and, ultimately, a political union.

Jomo Kanyatta died in 1978 and was succeeded by the vice-president Daniel arap Moi, who stood down in 2002 after having been criticized for his autocratic rule, as well as corruption. The veteran Mwai Kibaki was elected president in 2002, promising to stamp out corruption. But by 2005 he was widely criticized for failing to fulfill his election pledge.

ECONOMY

According to the United Nations, Kenya is a "low-income" developing country. Agriculture employs about 80% of the people, but many Kenyans are subsistence farmers. The chief food crop is maize. Bananas, beans, cassava, and sweet potatoes are also grown. The main cash crops are coffee and tea. Manufactures include chemicals, leather, footwear, processed food, petroleum products, and textiles.

NAIROBI

Capital and largest city of Kenya, in the south central part of the country. Founded in 1899, Nairobi replaced Mombasa as the capital of the British East Africa Protectorate in 1905. Nairobi has a national park (1946), a university (1970,) and several institutions of higher education. It is an administrative and commercial center. Industries: cigarettes, textiles, chemicals, food processing, furniture, glass.

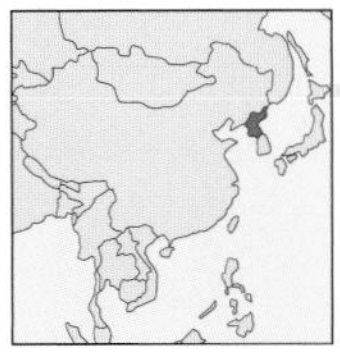

The flag of the Democratic People's Republic of Korea (North Korea) has been flown since Korea was split into two states in 1948. The colors are traditional ones in Korea. The design, with the red star, indicates that North Korea is a Communist country.

PYONGYANG

Capital of North Korea, in the west of the country, on the River Taedong. An ancient city, it was the capital of the Choson, Koguryo and Koryo kingdoms. In the 16th and 17th centuries, it came under both Japanese and Chinese rule. Pyongyang's industry developed during the Japanese occupation from 1910–45. It became the capital of North Korea in 1948. During the Korean War (1950–3), it suffered considerable damage.

Area 46,540 sq mi [120,538 sq km]
Population 22,698,000
Capital (population) Pyongyang (2,725,000)
Government Single-party people's republic
Ethnic groups Korean 99%
Languages Korean (official)
Religions Buddhism and Confucianism (religious freedom now an illusion created by government-sponsored religious groups)
Currency North Korean won = 100 chon
Website www.korea-dpr.com

The Democratic People's Republic of Korea occupies the northern part of the Korean Peninsula extending south from northeastern China. Mountains form the heart of the country. The highest peak, Paektu-san (9,003 ft [2,744 m]) is on the northern border. East of the mountains lie the eastern coastal plains, which are densely populated, as are the coastal plains to the west which contain the capital, Pyonyang. Another small highland region in the southeast borders South Korea.

The coastal plains are mostly farmed, but some patches of chestnut, elm, and oak woodland survive on the hilltops. The mountains contain forests of such trees cedar, fir, pine, and spruce.

CLIMATE

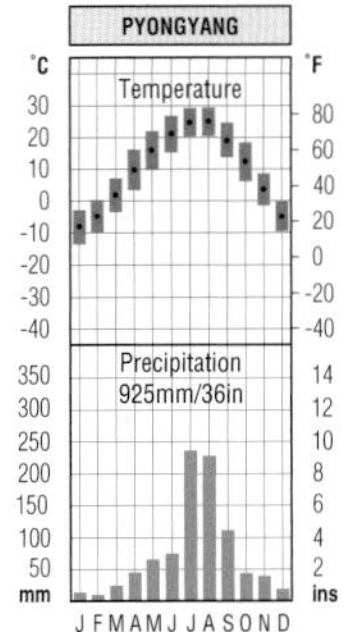

North Korea has a fairly severe climate, with bitterly cold winters when winds blow from across central Asia, bringing snow. Rivers freeze over and sea-ice may block harbors on the coast. In summer, moist winds from the oceans bring rain.

HISTORY

North Korea's history is described on page 120 [*see Korea, South*]. North Korea was created in 1945, when the peninsula, a Japanese colony since 1910, was divided in two. Soviet forces occupied the north, with US forces in the south. Soviet occupation led to a Communist government being established in 1948 under the leadership of Kim Il Sung.

The Korean War began in June 1950 when North Korean troops invaded the south. North Korea, aided by China and the Soviet Union, fought with South Korea, which was supported by troops from the United States and other UN members. The war ended in July 1953. An armistice was signed but no permanent peace treaty was agreed. The war caused great destruction and loss of life, with 1.6 million Communist troops killed, wounded, or reported missing.

POLITICS

Between 1948 and his death in 1994, Kim Il Sung was a virtual dictator, ruling along similar lines to Stalin in the Soviet Union. After the war, North Korea adopted a hostile policy towards South Korea in pursuit of its aim of reunification. The situation was at times so tense as to warrant international concern.

The end of the Cold War in the late 1980s eased relations between North and South and they both joined the UN in 1991. The two countries made several agreements, including one in which they agreed not to use force against each other. However, the collapse of Communism in the Soviet Union meant that North Korea remained isolated.

In 1993, North Korea triggered a new international crisis by announcing that it was withdrawing from the Nuclear Non-Proliferation Treaty, leading to suspicions that it, was developing its own nuclear weapons. Upon his death in 1994, Kim Il Sung was succeeded by his son, Kim Jong Il.

In the early 2000s, uncertainty surrounding North Korea's nuclear capabilities cast unease across the entire region.The United States accused North Korea of supporting international terrorism, while at the same time, talks between North and South Korea continued in an attempt to normalize relations between them. In 2003 North Korea's relations with the United States further deteriorated when the US accused the country of having a secret nuclear weapons program. North Korea withdrew from international talks in early 2005 stating that it had already produced nuclear weapons. However in September North Korea agreed to give up all its nuclear activities and rejoin the nuclear Non-Proliferation Treaty. Despite reports of malnutrition North Korea formally requested an end to food aid in September 2005. It was thought that the government might be worried that taking more food aid might be perceived as a sign of weakness.

ECONOMY

North Korea's considerable resources include coal, copper, iron ore, lead, tin, tungsten, and zinc. Under Communism, North Korea has concentrated on developing heavy, state-owned industries. Manufactures include chemicals, iron and steel, machinery, processed food, and textiles. Agriculture employs about a third of the population and rice is the leading crop. Economic decline and mismanagement, aggravated by three successive crop failures caused by floods in 1995 and 1996, and a drought in 1997, led to famine on a large scale.

***Music students** from the Children's Palace in Pyongyang performing*

Korea, South

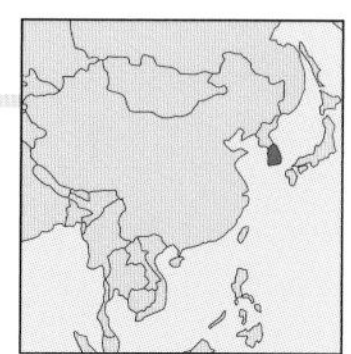

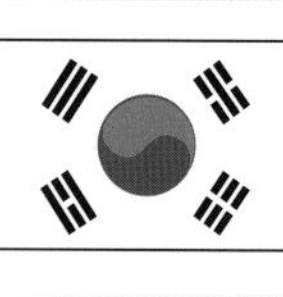

South Korea's flag, adopted in 1950, is white, the traditional symbol for peace. The central "yin-yang" symbol signifies the opposing forces of nature. The four black symbols stand for the four seasons, the points of the compass, and the Sun, Moon, Earth, and Heaven.

Area 38,327 sq mi [99,268 sq km]
Population 48,598,000
Capital (population) Seoul (9,888,000)
Government Multiparty republic
Ethnic groups Korean 99%
Languages Korean (official)
Religions No affiliation 46%, Christianity 26%, Buddhism 26%, Confucianism 1%
Currency South Korean won = 100 chon
Website www.kois.go.kr

The Republic of Korea, as South Korea is officially known, occupies the southern part of the Korean Peninsula. Mountains cover much of the country. The southern and western coasts are major farming regions. There are many islands along the west and south coasts, the largest of which is Cheju-do, with South Korea's highest peak, Halla-san (6,398 ft [1,950 m]).

CLIMATE

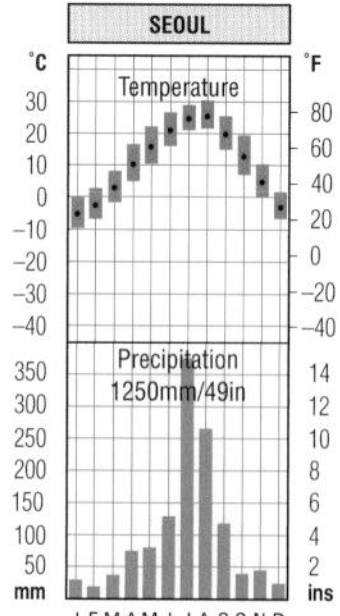

South Korea is chilled in winter by cold, dry winds blowing from central Asia. Snow often covers the mountains in the east. The summers are hot and wet, especially in July and August.

HISTORY

The Chinese conquered the north in 108 BC and ruled until they were thrown out in AD 313. Mongol armies attacked Korea in the 13th century, but in 1388, a general, Yi Songgye, founded a dynasty of rulers which lasted until 1910.

From the 17th century, Korea prevented foreigners from entering the country, earning it the name the "Hermit Kingdom" until 1876, when Japan forced it to open some of its ports. Soon, the United States, Russia and some European countries were trading with Korea. In 1910, Korea became a Japanese colony.

After Japan's defeat in World War II, North Korea was occupied by Soviet troops, while South Korea was occupied by United States forces. Attempts at reunification failed and, in 1948, a National Assembly was elected in South Korea. This Assembly created the Republic of Korea, with North Korea becoming a Communist state. North Korean troops invaded the South in June 1950, sparking off the Korean War (1950–3).

POLITICS

The story of South Korea after the civil war differs greatly from that of the North. Land reform based on smallholdings worked to produce some of the world's highest rice yields and self-sufficiency in food grains.

The real economic miracle came with industrial expansion started in the early 1960s. Initiated by a military government and based on limited natural resources, the country used its cheap, plentiful, well-educated labor force to transform the economy. The manufacturing base of textiles remained important, South Korea also became a world leader in footwear, shipbuilding, consumer electronics, toys and, vehicles.

In 1988, a new constitution came into force, enabling presidential elections to be held every five years. Evidence of the new spirit of democracy came in 1997 when, in presidential elections, Kim Dae-jung, leader of past pro-democracy campaigns, narrowly defeated Hoi-chang, the governing party's candidate. In foreign affairs, a major breakthrough had occurred in 1991 when both North and South Korea were admitted as full members of the United Nations. The two countries signed several agreements, including one in which they agreed not to use force against each other, but tensions between them continued. In 2000, South Korea's President Dae-jung met with North Korea's Kim Jong Il in talks aimed at establishing better relations between the countries. But the prospect of reunification seemed as distant as ever.

ECONOMY

The World Bank classifies South Korea as an "upper-middle-income" developing country. It is one of the world's fastest growing industrial economies. Resources include coal and tungsten. The main manufactures are processed food and textiles. The heavy industries are chemicals, fertilizers, iron, steel, and ships. Computers, automobiles and televisions are leading industrial products. Farming and fishing remain important activities. Rice is the chief food crop.

SEOUL (KYONGSONG)

Capital of South Korea, on the River Han. The political, commercial, industrial and cultural center of South Korea, it was founded in 1392 as the capital of the Yi dynasty. It developed rapidly under the Japanese (1910–45). Following the 1948 partition, it became capital of South Korea. Seoul's capture by North Korean troops precipitated the start of the Korean War (1950–3), and the following months witnessed the city's virtual destruction. In 1951, it became the headquarters of the UN command in Korea and a rebuilding program commenced. By the 1970s, it was the hub of one of the most successful economies of South east Asia. In 1996, there were violent student demonstrations for reunification with North Korea. Seoul hosted the Summer Olympics in 1988 and the semifinal of the 2002 Fifa World Cup.

***Ginseng is displayed** for sale in jars, at a stall in Namdaemun Market, Seoul; the largest market in the country it has over 1,000 vendors from tiny street stalls to more established shops; it takes its name from the nearby Great South Gate and is situated close to the center of the city*

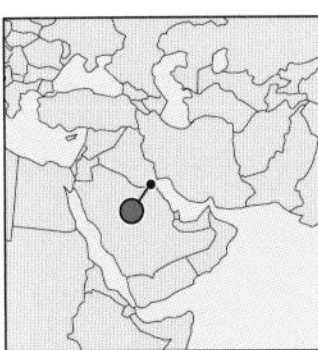

The colors of Kuwait's flag are pan-Arab. The green symbolizes Kuwaiti hospitality. The white represents the commitment to peace. The red symbolizes Kuwait's determination to resist aggression. The black signifies decisiveness.

The State of Kuwait is a small, oil-rich, Arab country at the head of the Persian Gulf. It consists of a mainland area and several offshore islands. The capital, Kuwait City, stands on a natural harbor called Kuwait Bay.

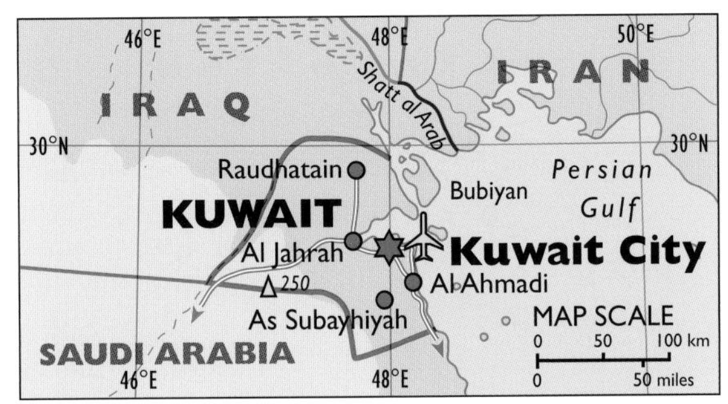

Area 6,880 sq mi [17,818 sq km]
Population 2,258,000
Capital (population) Kuwait City (29,000)
Government Constitutional monarchy
Ethnic groups Kuwaiti 45%, other Arab 35%, South Asian 9%, Iranian 4%, other 7%
Languages Arabic (official), English
Religions Islam 85%, Christianity, Hinduism
Currency Kuwaiti dinar = 1000 fils
Website www.kuwait-info.org

Most of the land is a flat or gently undulating plain. The highest point is about 820 ft [250 m]. There are no rivers or lakes and water supply is a problem. Water is imported, but drinking water is also produced by desalination plants. Desert scrub covers some areas, but much of Kuwait has no vegetation.

CLIMATE

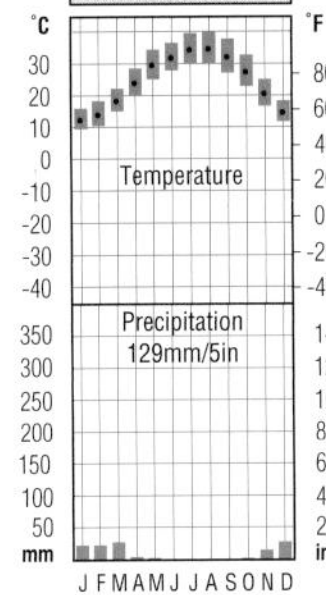

Kuwait has a hot desert climate. Annual rainfall is around 5 in [125 mm] and most rain occurs between November and March. Winters are mild and pleasant. But summers are hot, with average temperatures reaching 91 to 95°F [33°C–35°C] between June and September. August to September are the most uncomfortable months, because the humidity is then at its highest. Periodically, conditions become most unpleasant in the interior when hot sandstorms or duststorms blow from central Arabia.

HISTORY

In the 17th century, the northwestern part of the Arabian peninsula became part of the Turkish Ottoman empire. But the area was thinly populated until about 1710, when people from Arabia settled there and built the port that later became Kuwait City. They elected the head of the Al Sabah family as their ruler, and this family still rules Kuwait today.

British interest in the area began near the end of the 18th century when Kuwait's leader, Sheikh Mubarak, feared Turkish domination. In 1899, Britain became responsible for Kuwait's defense and, in 1914, the territory became a British protectorate. Britain provided naval protection, while taking control of Kuwait's external affairs.

Drilling for oil began in 1936 and large reserves were discovered by the US-British Kuwait Oil Company. Production was delayed by World War II (1939–45), but oil was produced commercially in 1946. Kuwait soon became a prosperous oil exporter. The country financed great improvements to the infrastructure, and Kuwaitis soon enjoyed a high standard of living.

KUWAIT CITY

Capital of Kuwait, it sits on the natural harbor Kuwait Bay in the Persian Gulf. It was first settled in the early 18th century and by the 19th century it was an important trading port. The city was invaded by Iraqi forces in the 1991 Gulf War and under Iraqi occupation renamed Saddam City, after Iraqi leader Saddam Hussein. It returned to its original name once Iraqi troops were expelled. Known as "The City" to the people of Kuwait it includes the Majlis Al-Umma (Kuwait's parliament), most governmental offices, and the headquarters of most Kuwaiti businesses.

POLITICS

Kuwait became an independent state on June 19, 1961, and the Sheikh, the head of state, became an Amir (Emir). Kuwait joined the Arab League and Iraq renewed its claim that Kuwait was legally part of its territory. But British military intervention forced Iraq to back down. In 1963, elections were held for the National Assembly under a new constitution. However, the Amir suspended the National Assembly in 1976 saying that it was not acting in the interests of the nation. The National Assembly was restored in 1981 but dissolved again in 1986.

In the Iran-Iraq War, which began in 1980, Kuwait supported Iraq. But in August 1990, Iraq invaded Kuwait, after accusing it of taking oil from an Iraqi oilfield near the border. The Amir and his cabinet fled to Saudi Arabia. When Iraq refused to withdraw, a United States-led and UN-supported international force began an aerial bombing campaign, called "Operation Desert Storm," in January 1991. They took Kuwait City in late February and expelled the Iraqis; however, prior to expulsion the Iraqis set fire to more than 500 oil wells, causing massive pollution, and destroying almost all the country's commercial and industrial installations. Kuwait's revenge was directed mainly at the huge contingent of Palestinian, Jordanian, and Yemeni immigrant workers, who were seen as pro-Iraq. In 1994, Iraq, under pressure from the UN, officially recognized Kuwait's independence and boundaries, although the countries still have no recognized maritime boundaries in the Persian Gulf.

In 1992, elections were held for a new National Assembly. In 1999, the Amir, Jabir al-Ahmad al-Jabir Al Sabah, suspended the Assembly, but liberals and Islamists predominated in the new Assembly. But the liberals did badly in elections in 2003, though Islamists again did well. In 1999, the Assembly had narrowly rejected a proposal to give women full political rights, but parliament approved these rights in May 2005. Kuwait's first woman cabinet minister was appointed in June. In 2006, women were given the opportunity to exercise their right to vote in national elections for the first time. The Amir died in 2006 and was succeeded by his cousin Sheikh Sabah al-Sabah.

A recent problem faced by Kuwait is violent activity by Islamist militants, some of whom are alleged to be linked to al-Qaida. These groups have been accused of conspiring to attack Western targets.

ECONOMY

The economy is based on oil, and this accounts for more than 90% of the exports. Kuwait has about 10% of the world's known reserves. Agriculture is practically non-existent, though the country has a small fishing fleet. Kuwait has to import most of its food. The shortage of water has inhibited the development of industries. However, industrial products include petrochemicals, cement, food products, and construction materials.

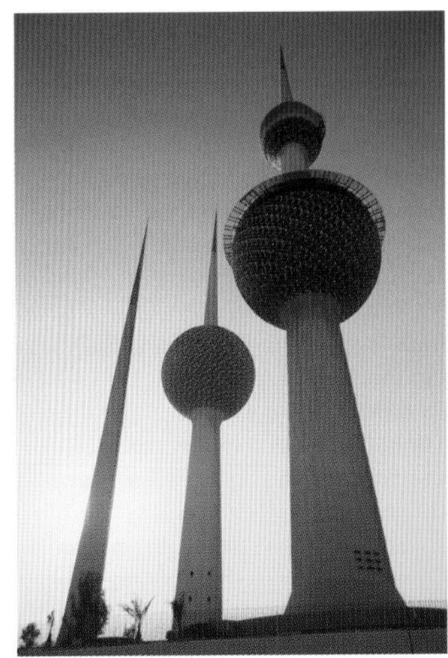

Opened in 1979, *Kuwait Towers in Kuwait City rise high above the city; a symbol of the city's vast oil wealth, two of the towers hold water, a less accessible, but equally vital commodity for the city*

Kyrgyzstan

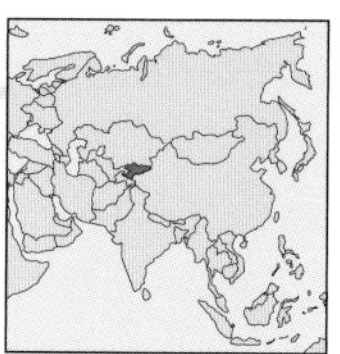

Kyrgyzstan's flag was adopted in March 1992. The flag depicts a bird's-eye view of a "yurt" (circular tent) within a radiant sun. The "yurt" recalls the traditional nomadic way of life. The 40 rays of the sun stand for the 40 traditional tribes.

Area 77,181 sq mi [199,900 sq km]
Population 5,081,000
Capital (population) Bishkek (824,000)
Government Multiparty republic
Ethnic groups Kyrgyz 65%, Russian 13%, Uzbek 13%, Ukranian 1%, others
Languages Kyrgyz and Russian (both official)
Religions Islam 75%, Russian Orthodox 20%
Currency Kyrgyzstani som = 100 tyiyn
Website www.gov.kg

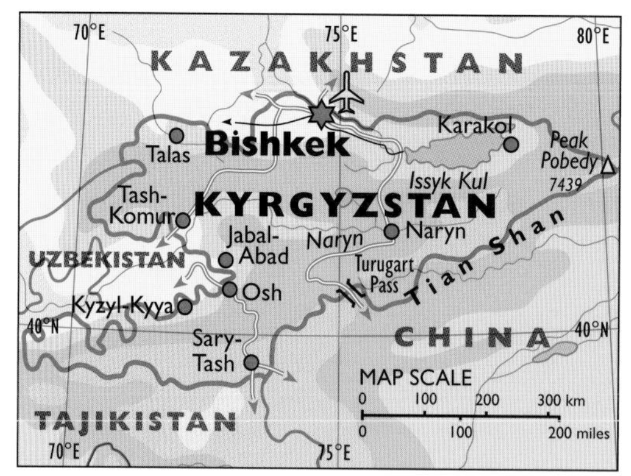

TIAN SHAN (TIEN SHAN)

Mountain range in central Asia, 1,500 mi [2,400 km] long, forming the border between Kyrgyzstan and Xinjiang, northwest China. At their western edge, the Tian Shan ("Celestial Mountains") divide the Tarim and Junggar Basins. The range rises to 24,406 ft [7,439 m] at Pik Pobedy, on the Chinese border with Kazakhstan and Kyrgyzstan. The Issyk Kul in Kyrgyzstan is one of the world's largest mountain lakes.

The Kyrgyz Republic, is a landlocked country between China, Tajikistan, Uzbekistan and Kazakhstan. The country is mountainous, with spectacular scenery. The highest mountain, Pik Pobedy (Peak of Victory) in the Tian Shan Range, reaches 24,406 ft [7,439 m] above sea level in the east. Less than a sixth of the country is below 2,950 ft [900 m].

The largest of the country's many lakes is Lake Issyk Kul (Ysyk-Köl) in the northeast which is 113 mi (182 km) long and up to 38 mi (61 km) wide.

CLIMATE

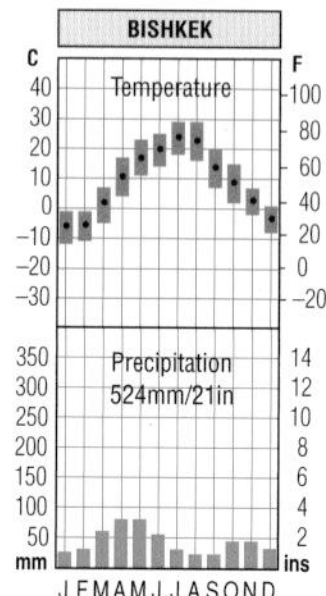

The lowlands of Kyrgyzstan have warm summers and cold winters. The altitude influences the climate in the mountains, where the January temperatures drop plummet to 18°F [–28°C]. Far from any sea, Kyrgyzstan has a low annual rainfall.

HISTORY

The area that is now Kyrgyzstan was populated in ancient times by nomadic herders. Mongol armies conquered the region in the early 13th century. They set up areas called *khanates*, ruled by chieftains, or *khans*. Islam was introduced in the 17th century.

China gained control of the area in the mid-18th century, but, in 1876, Kyrgyzstan became a province of Russia, and Russian settlement in the area began. In 1916, Russia crushed a rebellion among the Kyrgyz, and many subsequently fled to China.

In 1922, the area became an autonomous *oblast* (self-governing region) of the newly formed Soviet Union and, in 1936, it became one of the Soviet Socialist Republics. Under Communist rule, nomads were forced to work on government-run farms, while local customs and religious worship were suppressed. However, education and health services were greatly improved.

POLITICS

In 1991, Kyrgyzstan became an independent country following the breakup of the Soviet Union. The Communist Party was dissolved, but the country retained ties with Russia through the Commonwealth of Independent States. Kyrgyzstan adopted a new constitution in 1994 and elections were held in 1995.

In the late 1990s, Askar Akayev, president since 1990, introduced constitutional changes and other measures which gave him greater powers and limited press freedom. In 2000, Akayev was elected to a third five-year term as president. Alleged government interference in the parliamentary elections of March 2005 sparked massive popular protest, with the people demanding a rerun of the vote and the resignation of Askar Akayev. Official buildings in the capital were seized and, with virtually no resistance from the security forces, Akayev fled to Russia. Kurmanbek Bakiev was appointed acting president and prime minister and he subsequently won a landslide victory in a presidential election in July 2005. The election was deemed to have shown clear progress in democratic standards, according to independent foreign observers. However, one year on civil unrest remained a problem for the government.

Kyrgyzstan has the potential to be an ethnic tinderbox, with its large Russian minority (who held positions of power in Soviet days), disenchanted Uzbeks, and an influx of Chinese Muslim immigrants. In the early 2000s, many people were alarmed when Islamic guerrillas staged border raids on Kyrgyzstan as they sought to set up an Islamic state in the Fergana valley, where Kyrgyzstan borders Uzbekistan and Tajikistan.

ECONOMY

The chief economic activity is agriculture, especially livestock rearing. The main products include cotton, eggs, fruits, grain, tobacco, vegetables, and wool. Food is imported. Manufactures include machinery, processed food, metals, and textiles.

BISHKEK

Capital of Kyrgyzstan, central Asia, on the River Chu. Founded in 1862 as Pishpek, it was the birthplace of a Soviet general, Mikhail Frunze, after whom it was renamed in 1926 when it became administrative center of the Kyrghyz Soviet Republic. Its name changed to Bishkek in 1991, when Kyrgyzstan declared independence. The city has a university (1951). Industries include textiles, food processing, and agricultural machinery.

***Kyrgyz villagers** from Bash Chimghan return home after attending a Nazir, or funeral, ceremony in Tom Kurghan*

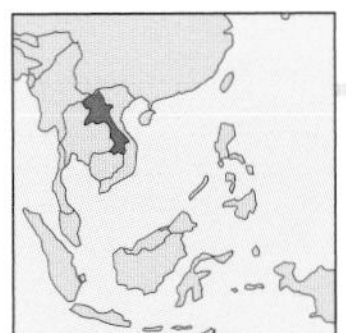

Since 1975, Laos has flown the flag of the Pathet Lao, the Communist movement which won control of the country after a long struggle. The blue stands for the River Mekong, the white disk for the Moon, and the red for the unity and purpose of the people.

The Lao People's Democratic Republic is a landlocked country in Southeast Asia. Mountains and plateaux cover much of the country. The highest point is Mount Bia in central Laos, which reaches 9,242 ft [2,817 m].

Most people live on the plains bordering the River Mekong and its tributaries. This river, one of Asia's longest, forms much of the country's northwestern and southwestern borders. A range of mountains called the Annam Cordillera (Chaîne Annamatique) runs along the eastern border with Vietnam.

Area 91,428 sq mi [236,800 sq km]
Population 6,068,000
Capital (population) Vientiane (528,000)
Government Single-party republic
Ethnic groups Lao Loum 68%, Lao Theung 22%, Lao Soung 9%
Languages Lao (official), French, English
Religions Buddhism 60%, traditional beliefs and others 40%
Currency Kip = 100 at
Website www.un.int/lao

CLIMATE

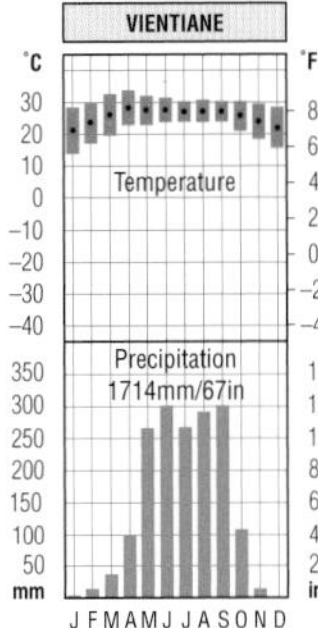

Laos has a tropical monsoon climate. Winters are dry and sunny, with winds blowing in from the northeast. The temperatures rise until April, when the wind directions are reversed and moist southwesterly winds reach Laos, heralding the start of the wet monsoon season.

HISTORY

From the 9th century AD, Lao and Tai peoples set up a number of small states ruled by princes. In 1353 the area that is now Laos was united in a kingdom called Lan Xang ("land of a million elephants"). Apart from a period of Burmese rule between 1574 and 1637, the Lan Xang ruled Laos until the early 18th century. The region was divided into three separate kingdoms, Champasak, Vientiane, and Louangphrabang, which became vassals of Siam (now Thailand).

In the 19th century, Chao Anou, the king of Vientiane, united his kingdom with Vietnam in an attempt to break Siamese domination, but he was defeated and Vientiane became a Siamese province. In the late 19th century, France gradually gained control of all Siamese territory east of the River Mekong and made it a protectorate, ruling it as part of French Indochina, a region which also included Cambodia and Vietnam. After France's surrender to Germany in 1945, Japanese forces moved into Indochina. They allowed the French to continue as puppet rulers until 1945, when they interned all French authorities and military units. A Free Laos movement set up a government, but it collapsed when the French returned in 1946.

POLITICS

Under a new constitution, Laos became a monarchy in 1947 and, in 1949, the country became a self-governing state within the French Union. After full independence in 1954, Laos suffered from instability caused by a power struggle between royalist government forces and a pro-Communist group called the Pathet Lao. The Pathet Lao took power in 1975 after two decades of chaotic civil war in which the royalist forces were supported by American bombing and Thai mercenaries, while the Pathet Lao was assisted by North Vietnam. The king, Savang Vatthana, abdicated in 1975, and the People's Democratic Republic of Laos was proclaimed. Over 300,000 Laotians, including technicians and other experts, as well as farmers, and members of ethnic minorities, fled the country. Many opponents of the government who remained were sent to reeducation camps.

Communist policies brought isolation and stagnation under the domination of the Vietnamese government in Hanoi, which had used Laos as a supply line in their war against the US. In 1986, the Laotian Politburo embarked upon its own *perestroika*, opening its doors to tourists and opening trade links with its neighbors, notably China and Japan. Laos became a member of the Association of Southeast Asian Nations (ASEAN) in 1997.

The economy deteriorated from the 1980s and latterly opposition has appeared with sporadic bombings occurring in Vientiane. These have been attributed to rebels in the minority Hmong tribe. Any dissent is dealt with harshly by the authorities.

ECONOMY

Laos is one of the world's poorest countries. Agriculture employs about 76% of the workforce even though only 5% of the land is suitable for such cultivation. 7% of the people work in industry and 17% in services. Rice is the main crop, and timber and coffee are both exported. The most valuable export is electricity, which is produced at hydroelectric power stations on the River Mekong and exported to Thailand.

Laos also produces opium and in the early 1990s was thought to be the world's third biggest source of this illegal drug. Most enterprises are now outside state control. The government is working to develop alternative crops to opium.

VIENTIANE (VIANGCHAN)

Capital and chief port of Laos, on the River Mekong, close to the Thai border, north central Laos. It was the capital of the Lao kingdom (1707–1828). It became part of French Indo-China in 1893, and in 1899 became the capital of the French Protectorate. It is a major source of opium for world markets. Industries include textiles, brewing, cigarettes, hides, wood products.

Reclining Buddha Statue *at Buddha Park in Vientiane*

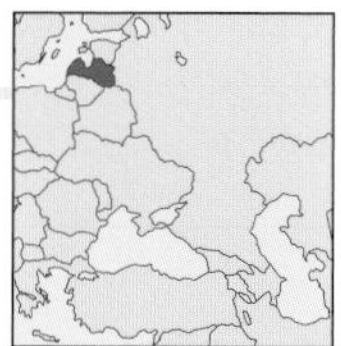

The burgundy and white Latvian flag, which dates back to at least 1280, was revived after Latvia achieved its independence in 1991. According to one legend, the flag was first made from a white sheet which had been stained with the blood of a Latvian hero.

Area 24,942 sq mi [64,600 sq km]
Population 2,306,000
Capital (population) Riga (793,000)
Government Multiparty republic
Ethnic groups Latvian 58%, Russian 30%, Belarusian, Ukranian, Polish, Lithuanian
Languages Latvian (official), Lithuanian, Russian
Religions Lutheran, Roman Catholic, Russian Orthodox
Currency Latvian lat = 100 santimi
Website www.lv

The Republic of Latvia is one of three states on the southeastern corner of the Baltic Sea, known as the Baltic States. Latvia consists mainly of flat plains separated by low hills, composed of moraine (ice-worn rocks) that was dumped there by ice sheets during the Ice Age. The country's highest point is only 1,020 ft [311 m] above sea level. Small lakes and peat bogs are common. The country's main river, the Daugava, is also known as the Western Dvina.

CLIMATE

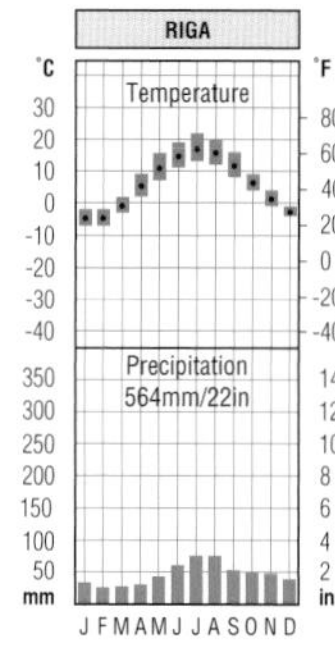

Air masses from the Atlantic influence the climate of Latvia, bringing warm and rainy conditions in summer. Winters are cold. The average temperature range is 61–64°F [16°C–18°C] in July, and 19-27°F [–7°C to –3°C] in January.

HISTORY

Between the 9th and 11th centuries, the region was attacked by Vikings from the west and Russians from the east. In the 13th century, German invaders took over, naming the country Livland.

In 1561, Latvia was partitioned and most of the land came under Polish or Lithuanian rule. A Germany duchy was also established there. In 1621, the Swedish king Gustavus II Adolphus took over Riga. In 1629, the greater part of the country north of the Daugava River was ceded to Sweden, with the southeast remaining under Lithuanian rule. But, in 1710, Peter the Great took control of Riga and, by the end of the 18th century, all of Latvia was under Russian control, although the German landowners and merchants continued to exercise considerable power. The 19th century saw the rise of Latvian nationalism and calls for independence became increasingly frequent.

After the Russian Revolution of March 1917, the Latvian National Political Conference demanded independence, but Germany occupied Riga in September. However, after the October Revolution, the Latvian National Political Conference proclaimed the country's independence in November 1918. Russia and Germany, finally recognized Latvia's independence in 1920. In 1922, Latvia adopted a democratic constitution and the elected government introduced land reforms. However, a coup in May 1934 ended this period of democratic rule. In 1939, Germany and the Soviet Union agreed to divide up much of eastern Europe. Soviet troops invaded Latvia in June 1940 and Latvia was made a part of the Soviet Union. But German forces invaded the area in 1941 and held it until 1944, when Soviet troops reoccupied the country. Many Latvians opposed to Russian rule were killed or deported.

POLITICS

Under Soviet rule, many Russians settled in Latvia leading Latvians to fear that the Russians would become the dominant ethnic group. From the mid-1980s, when Mikhail Gorbachev was introducing reforms in the Soviet Union, Latvian nationalists campaigned against Soviet rule. In the late 1980s, the Latvian government ended absolute Communist rule and voted to restore the banned national flag and anthem. It also proclaimed Latvian the official language.

In 1990, Latvia established a multiparty political system. In elections in March, candidates in favor of separation from the Soviet Union won two-thirds of parliamentary seats. The parliament declared Latvia independent on May 4, 1990, though the Soviet Union declared this act illegal. However, the Soviet government recognized Latvia's independence in September 1991, shortly before the Soviet Union itself was dissolved.

Latvia held its first free elections to its parliament (the Saeima) in 1993. Voting was limited only to those who were citizens on June 17, 1940 and their descendants. This meant that about 34% of Latvian residents were unable to vote. In 1994, Latvia restricted the naturalization of non-Latvians, denying them the vote and land ownership. In 1998, the government agreed that all children born since independence should have automatic citizenship, regardless of their parents' status. There are tests in place that ethnic Russians must take in order to gain citizenship, however many have not taken them and so remain stateless.

Latvia became a member of NATO and the EU in 2004.

ECONOMY

The World Bank classifies Latvia as a "lower-middle-income" country. The country's only natural resources are land and forests, so many raw materials have to be imported. Its industries include electronic goods, farm machinery, fertilizers, processed food, plastics, radios, washing machines, and vehicles. Farm products include barley, dairy, beef, oats, potatoes and rye. Latvia produces only about a tenth of its electricity needs. The rest has to be imported from Belarus, Russia, and Ukraine.

Statue of St. Roland *in Ratslaukums, Riga with the tower of St. Peter's Church in the background; St. Roland was said to represent freedom*

RIGA

Capital of Latvia, on the River Daugava, Gulf of Riga. Founded at the beginning of the 13th century, it joined the Hanseatic League in 1282, growing into a major Baltic port. Tsar Peter the Great took the city in 1710. In 1918, it became capital of independent Latvia. In 1940, when Latvia was incorporated into the Soviet Union, thousands of its citizens were deported or executed. Under German occupation from 1941, the city reverted to Soviet rule in 1944 and subsequently suffered further deportations and an influx of Russian immigrants. In 1991, it reassumed its status as capital of an independent Latvia.

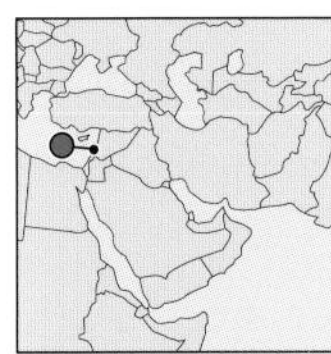

Lebanon's flag was adopted in 1943. It uses the colors of Lebanese nationalists in World War I (1914–18). The cedar tree on the white stripe has been a Lebanese symbol since Biblical times. Because of deforestation, only a few of Lebanon's giant cedars survive.

The Republic of Lebanon is a country on the eastern shores of the Mediterranean Sea. Behind the coastal plain are the rugged Lebanon Mountains (Jabal Lubnán), which rise to 10,131 ft [3,088 m]. Another range, the Anti-Lebanon Mountains (Al Jabal ash Sharqi), form the eastern border with Syria. Between the two ranges is the Bekaa (Beqaa) Valley, a fertile farming region.

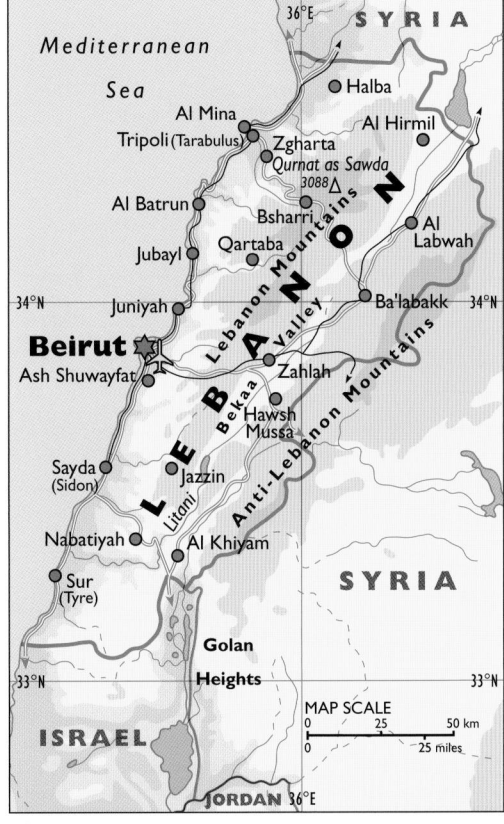

Area 4,015 sq mi [10,400 sq km]
Population 3,777,000
Capital (population) Beirut (1,148,000)
Government Multiparty republic
Ethnic groups Arab 95%, Armenian 4%, others
Languages Arabic (official),French, English
Religions Islam 70%, Christianity 30%
Currency Lebanese pound = 100 piastres
Website www.lebanon-tourism.gov.lb

CLIMATE

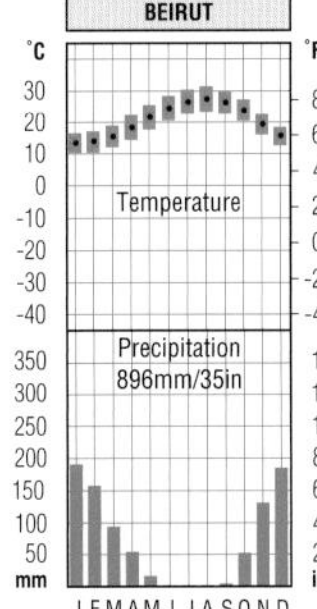

The Lebanese coast has hot, dry summers and mild, wet winters. Inland, onshore winds bring heavy rain to the western slopes of the mountains in the winter months, with snow on the western slopes of the mountains.

HISTORY

There were waves of invaders from 800 BC—Egyptians, Hittites, Assyrians, Babylonians and Persians. The armies of Alexander the Great seized the area in 332 BC and the Romans took control in 64 BC. Christianity was introduced in AD 325 and in 395, the area became part of the Byzantine Empire. Muslim Arabs occupied the area in the early 7th century, converting many people to Islam.

European Crusaders arrived in Lebanon in about 1100 and the area became a battlefield between Christian and Muslim armies. The Muslim Mamelukes of Egypt drove the last of the Crusaders out of the area around 1300. In 1516, Lebanon was taken over by the Turkish Ottoman Empire. Turkish rule continued until World War I, when British and French forces defeated the Ottoman Turks. France took over Lebanon's political affairs from 1923 until 1944 with Lebanon becoming independent in 1946.

POLITICS

The Muslims and Christians agreed to share power and Lebanon made rapid economic progress. But from the late 1950s, development was slowed by periodic conflict between Sunni and Shia Muslims, Druze, and Christians. The situation was further complicated by the presence of Palestinian refugees who used bases in Lebanon to attack Israel.

In March 1975, fierce civil war broke out between Christians, Muslims and Druzes. Lebanon sank into a state of chaos. Assassinations, bombings, and kidnappings became routine as numerous factions fought for control.

The situation was complicated by interventions by Palestinian refugees, the Syrian army, Western and then UN forces as the country became a patchwork of occupied zones and "no-go areas." The core religious confrontation has deep roots. In 1860, thousands of Maronites, who are aligned to the Roman Catholic Church, were murdered by Druzes, who are so tangential to other Islamic sects that they are not now regarded as Muslims.

Although not directly involved, Lebanon was destabilized by the Arab-Israel War of 1967 and by the exile of the PLO leadership to Beirut in 1970. By 1990, the Syrian army had crushed the two-year revolt of Christian rebels against the Lebanese government, peace proved fragile and a solution elusive. In 1996, Israeli forces launched a sustained attack on the pro-Iranian Hezbollah positions in southern Lebanon, with heavy civilian casualties. Sporadic fighting continued in southern Lebanon in 1997, flaring up again in early 2000. In 2005, former prime minister Rafik Hariri, a critic of Syria's military presence in Lebanon, was assassinated. Opposition groups accused Syria of involvement, a charge denied by the Damascus government. Following demonstrations, Syria withdrew its forces.

ECONOMY

Civil war almost destroyed valuable trade and financial services which, together with tourism, had been Lebanon's chief source of income. Manufactures also suffered: they now include chemicals, electrical goods, processed food, and textiles. Fruits, vegetables, and sugar beets are farmed.

The Church of Le Christ Roi *sits above a bay along the Mediterranean Sea near Beirut*

BEIRUT (BAYRUT)

Capital and chief port of Lebanon, on the Mediterranean. From AD 635 Beirut was under Arab rule. Christian crusaders made it part of the Latin Kingdom of Jerusalem from 1110–1291. In 1516, under Druze control, it became part of the Ottoman Empire and remained so until World War I. In 1920 it became capital of Lebanon under French mandate. With the creation of Israel, thousands of Arabs sought refuge there. The outbreak of civil war in 1976 saw Beirut rapidly fracture along religious lines. In 1982, Israel devastated West Beirut in the war against the PLO. Israel began a phased withdrawal in 1985. Syrian troops entered in 1987 as part of an Arab peace-keeping force and in 1990, they dismantled the "Green Line" separating Muslim West from Christian East Beirut. All militias withdrew by 1991and restoration began. The infrastructure, economy, and culture of Beirut suffered terribly during the civil war.

Lesotho

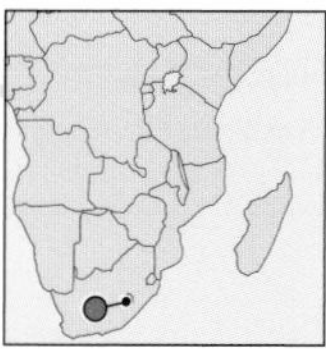

Based on the national motto: white for peace, blue for rain, and green for prosperity. The brown animal-skin shield is supported by an assegai (stabbing spear), a plumed spine, and a bludgeon, signifying the nation's traditional peace safeguards.

Area 11,720 sq mi [30,355 sq km]
Population 1,865,000
Capital (population) Maseru (109,000)
Government Constitutional monarchy
Ethnic groups Sotho 99%
Languages Sotho and English (both official)
Religions Christianity 80%, traditional beliefs 20%
Currency Loti = 100 lisente
Website www.lesotho.gov.ls

The Kingdom of Lesotho is a landlocked country, surrounded by South Africa on all sides. The scenic Drakensberg Range covers most of the country and forms Lesotho's north eastern border with KwaZulu Natal. It includes Lesotho's highest peak Thabana Ntlenyana, at 11,424 ft [3,482 m].

Most people live in the western lowlands, site of Maseru, or in the southern valley of the River Orange, which rises in northeast Lesotho and flows through South Africa to the Atlantic Ocean. Grassland covers much of Lesotho. The King holds all land in Lesotho, in trust for the Sotho nation.

CLIMATE

MASERU — Temperature (°C / °F); Precipitation 647mm/25in; J F M A M J J A S O N D

The climate is greatly affected by altitude, with 66% of the country lying above 4,921 ft [1,500 m]. Maseru has warm summers, but the temperatures fall below freezing in the winter and the mountains are colder. Rainfall varies, averaging around 28 in [700 mm].

HISTORY

The early 19th century tribal wars dispersed the Sotho. The Basotho nation was founded in the 1820s by King Moshoeshoe I, who united various groups fleeing from tribal wars in southern Africa. Moshoeshoe I was forced to yield to the British and Britain made the area a protectorate in 1868. In 1871, it became part of the British Cape Colony in South Africa. However, in 1884, Basutoland, as the area was called, was reconstituted as a British protectorate, where whites were not allowed to own land.

POLITICS

In 1966, Sotho opposition to incorporation into the Union of South Africa saw the creation of the independent Kingdom of Lesotho, with Moshoeshoe II, great-grandson of Moshoeshoe I, as its king.

In 1970, Leabua Jonathan suspended the constitution and banned opposition parties. Civil conflict between the government and Basuto Congress Party (BCP) forces characterized the next 16 years. In 1986, a military coup led to the reinstatement of Moshoeshoe II. In 1990, he was deposed and replaced by his son, Letsie III, as monarch. The BCP won the 1992 multiparty elections, and the military council dissolved. In 1994, Letsie III attempted to overthrow the government. In 1995, Moshoeshoe II returned to the throne. But after his death in a car crash in 1996, Letsie III again became king. In 1997, a majority of BCP politicians formed a new governing party, the Lesotho Congress for Democracy (LCD).

In 1998, an army revolt, following an election in which the ruling party won 79 out of the 80 seats, caused much damage to the economy, despite the intervention of a South African force intended to maintain order. In 2004, the government declared a state of emergency following three years of drought

ECONOMY

Lesotho is a "low-income" developing country. It lacks natural resources except diamonds. Agriculture employs two-thirds of the workforce, but most farmers live at subsistence level. Livestock farming is important. Major crops include corn and sorghum. Tourism is developing. Other sources of income include the products of light manufacturing and remittances sent home by Basotho working abroad, mainly in the mines of South Africa.

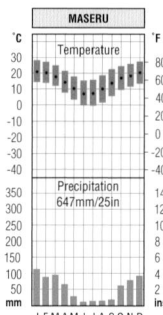

MASERU

Capital of Lesotho, located on the River Caledon, near the western border with South Africa. It is the only large city in the whole country. Originally a small trading town, it was capital of British Basutoland protectorate (1869–71, 1884–1966). It remained the capital when the Kingdom of Lesotho achieved independence in 1966. It is a commercial, transport, and administrative center. Places of interest include the Catholic Cathedral of Our Lady of Victories and Lancer's Gap which has great views of the city and the Caledon Valley. The National University of Lesotho is in the town of Roma, some 21 mi (35 km) away; and the country's main international airport is also adjacent.

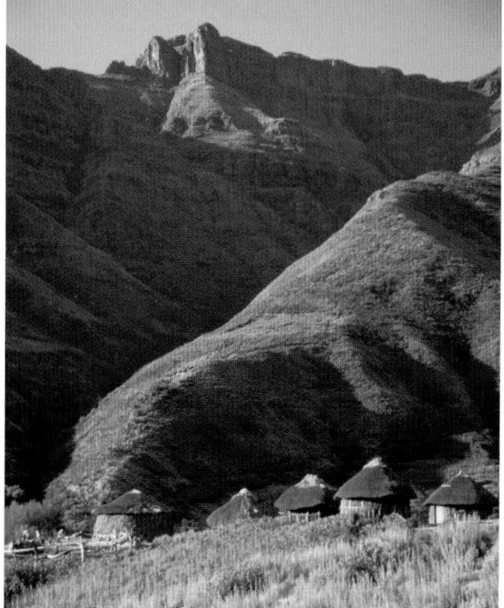

Round stone huts *in verdant mountains*

SOTHO

Major cultural and linguistic group of southern Africa. Includes the Northern Sotho of Transvaal, South Africa, the Western Sotho (better known as the Tswana) of Botswana, and the Southern Sotho (Basotho or Basuto) of Lesotho. Although dominating the rural territories they inhabit, the 4 million Sotho share the areas with people of other Bantu-speaking tribes. Many work and live in the urban areas and surrounding townships.

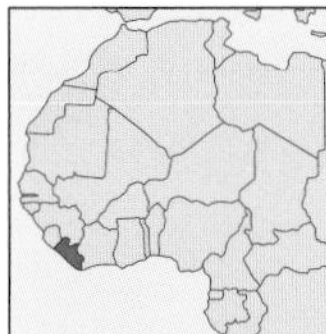

Liberia was founded in the early 19th century as an American colony for freed slaves who wanted to return to Africa. Its flag was adopted upon its independence in 1847. The 11 red and white stripes represent the 11 men who signed the Declaration of Independence.

The Republic of Liberia is located on the Atlantic coast of west Africa. Behind the coastline 311 mi [500 km] long, lies a narrow coastal plain. Beyond, the land rises to a plateau region, with the highest land along the border with Guinea. The most important rivers are the Cavally, which forms the border with Ivory Coast, and the St Paul.

Mangrove swamps and lagoons line the coast, while inland, forests cover nearly 40% of the land. Liberia also has areas of tropical savanna. Only 5% of the land is cultivated.

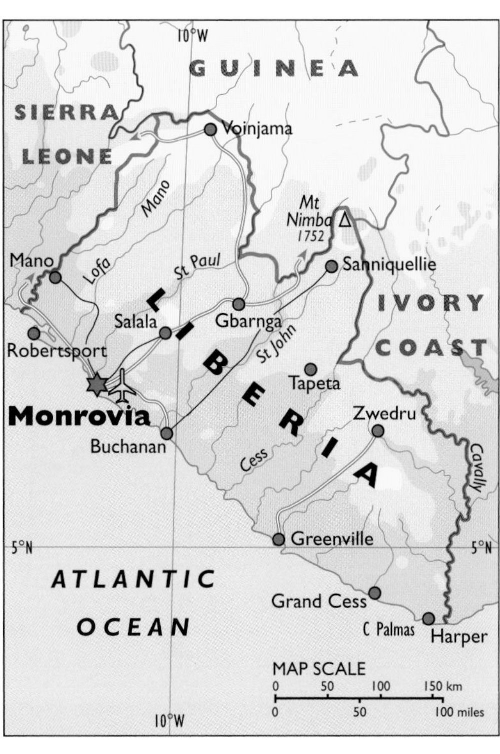

Area 43,000 sq mi [111,369 sq km]
Population 3,391,000
Capital (population) Monrovia (421,000)
Government Multiparty republic
Ethnic groups Indigenous African tribes 95% (including Kpelle, Bassa, Grebo, Gio, Kru, Mano)
Languages English (official), ethnic languages
Religions Christianity 40%, Islam 20%, traditional beliefs and others 40%
Currency Liberian dollar = 100 cents
Website www.un.org/Depts/dpko/missions/unmil/index.html

CLIMATE

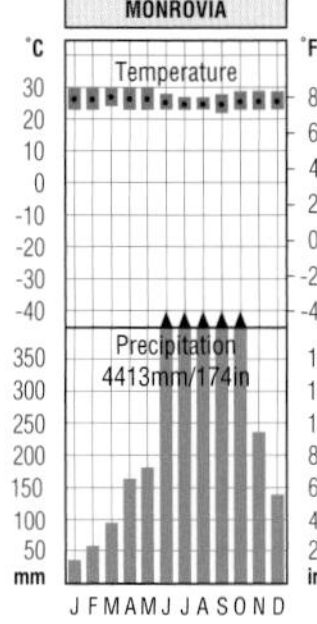

Liberia has a tropical climate. There are high temperatures and humidity throughout the year. Rainfall is abundant all year round, but there is a particularly wet period from June to November. The rainfall generally increases from east to west.

HISTORY

In the late 18th century, some white Americans in the United States wanted to help freed black slaves to return to Africa. They set up the American Colonization Society in 1816, which bought land in what is now Liberia.

In 1822, the Society landed former slaves at a settlement on the coast which they named Monrovia. In 1847, Liberia became a fully independent republic with a constitution much like that of the United States. For many years, the Americo-Liberians controlled the government. US influence remained strong and the American Firestone Company, which ran Liberia's rubber plantations covering more than 1 million acres [400,000 ha], was especially influential. Foreign countries were also involved in exploiting Liberia's mineral resources, including its huge iron-ore deposits.

POLITICS

Under the leadership (1944–71) of William Tubman, Liberia's economy grew and it adopted social reforms. In 1980, a military force composed of people from the local population killed the Americo-Liberian president William R. Tolbert, Tubman's successor. An army sergeant, Samuel K. Doe, became president. In 1985, Doe's brutal and corrupt regime won a fraudulent election.

Civil war broke out in 1989, and the Economic Community of West African States (ECOWAS) sent a five-nation peacekeeping force. Doe was assassinated and an interim government, led by Amos Sawyer, took office. Civil war raged on, claiming 150,000 lives and leaving hundreds of thousands of people homeless by 1994. In 1995, a ceasefire occurred and the former warring factions formed a council of state. Former warlord Charles Taylor of the National Patriotic Council secured a resounding victory in 1997 elections. In 2001, the UN imposed an arms embargo on Liberia for trading weapons for diamonds with rebels in Sierra Leone. In 2002, Taylor imposed a state of emergency as fighting intensified with rebels. In 2003, the fighting largely ended; Taylor went into exile. The UN helped to restore order and, in 2005, Ellen Johnson-Sirleaf was elected president. After a lengthy campaign Charles Taylor was extradited to the international court in The Hague to be tried for war crimes.

ECONOMY

Liberia's civil war devastated the economy. Agriculture employs 75% of the workforce, but many families live at subsistence level. Food crops include cassava, fruits, rice, and sugar cane. Rubber is grown on plantations and cash crops include cocoa and coffee. Liberia's natural resources include its forests and iron ore, while gold and diamonds are also mined. Liberia has an oil refinery, but manufacturing is small-scale. Exports include rubber, timber, diamonds, gold, and coffee. Revenue is also obtained from its "flag of convenience," which is used by about one-sixth of the world's commercial shipping, exploiting low taxes.

MONROVIA

Capital and chief port of Liberia, west Africa, on the estuary of the River St Paul. In 1822 freed US slaves settled Monrovia, on a site chosen by the American Colonization Society. The city is named after James Monroe, US president from 1817–25. Monrovia is Liberia's largest city and the administrative, commercial, and financial center of the country. It suffered extensive damage in the civil war with the city's infrastructure bearing the brunt. It exports latex and iron ore. Industries include bricks and cement.

***Mud bricks** set out to dry at the edge of a street in Monrovia*

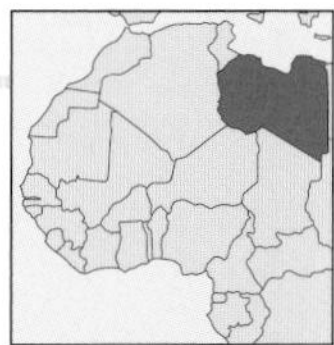

Libya's flag was adopted in 1977. It replaced the flag of the Federation of Arab Republics which Libya left in that year. Libya's flag is the simplest of all world flags. It represents the country's quest for a green revolution in agriculture.

Area 679,358 sq mi [1,759,540 sq km]
Population 5,632,000
Capital (population) Tripoli (1,500,000)
Government Single-party socialist state
Ethnic groups Libyan Arab and Berber 97%
Languages Arabic (official), Berber
Religions Islam (Sunni Muslim) 97%
Currency Libyan dinar = 1000 dirhams
Website www.libyana.org

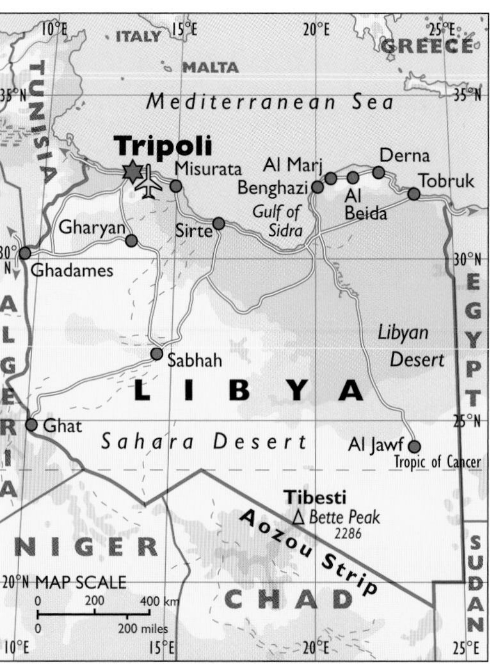

The Great Socialist People's Libyan Arab Jamahiriya (Libya's official name) is located in North Africa. The majority live on the Mediterranean coastal plains in the northeast and northwest. The Sahara, the world's largest desert, occupies 95% of Libya, reaching the Mediterranean coast along the Gulf of Sidra (Khalij Surt). The Sahara is virtually uninhabited except around scattered oases.

The land rises towards the south, reaching 7,500 ft [2,286 m] at Bette Peak (Bikku Bitti) on the border with Chad. Shrubs and grasses grow on northern coasts, with some trees in wetter areas. Few plants grow in the desert, except at oases where date palms provide protection from the hot sun.

CLIMATE

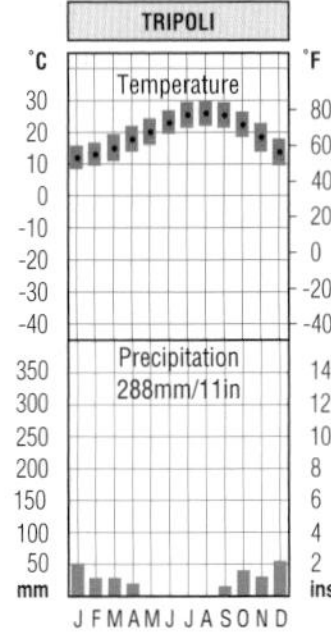

The coastal plains experience hot summers. Winters are mild with some rain. Inland, the average yearly rainfall drops to around 4 in [100 mm] or less. Daytime temperatures are high but nights are cool.

HISTORY

Libya's first known inhabitants were the Berbers. From the 7th century BC to the 5th century AD, Libya came under the Carthaginians, Greeks and Romans. The Romans left superb ruins, but the Arabs, who invaded the area in AD 642, imposed their culture, including their religion, Islam. From 1551, Libya was part of the Ottoman empire. Italy took control in 1911, but lost the territory in World War II. Britain and France then jointly ruled Libya until 1951, when it became an independent kingdom.

POLITICS

In 1969, a military group headed by Colonel Muammar Gaddafi deposed the king and set up a military government. Under Gaddafi, the government took control of the economy and used money from oil exports to finance welfare services and development projects. However, although Libya appears to be democratic, political parties are not permitted.

Gaddafi has attracted international criticism for his support for radical movements, such as the PLO (Palestine Liberation Organization) and various terrorist groups. In 1986, his policies led the United States to bomb installations in the capital and in Benghazi. In 1994, the International Court of Justice ruled against Libya's claim to an area in northern Chad.

In 1999, Gaddafi sought to restore good relations with the outside world by surrendering for trial two Libyans suspected of planting a bomb on a PanAm plane, which exploded over the Scottish town of Lockerbie in 1988. In addition Libya agreed to pay compensation to victims of the bombing. Gaddafi also accepted Libya's responsibility for the shooting of a British policewoman in London in 1984 and diplomatic relations with Britain were restored. In 2004 it was announced that Libya was abandoning programs to produce weapons of mass destruction, an initiative that was rewarded by visits to Libya by many Western leaders.

ECONOMY

Libya is Africa's richest country, per capita, but remains a developing country because of its dependence on oil, which accounts for nearly all of its export revenues.

Agriculture is important, although Libya still imports food. Crops include barley, citrus fruits, dates, olives, potatoes, and wheat. Cattle, sheep and poultry are raised. Libya has oil refineries and petrochemical plants. It also manufactures cement, processed food, and steel.

The "Great Man-Made River" is an ambitious project involving the tapping of subterranean water from rocks beneath the Sahara and piping it to the dry, populated areas in the north. But, the water in the aquifers is non-renewable and will eventually run dry.

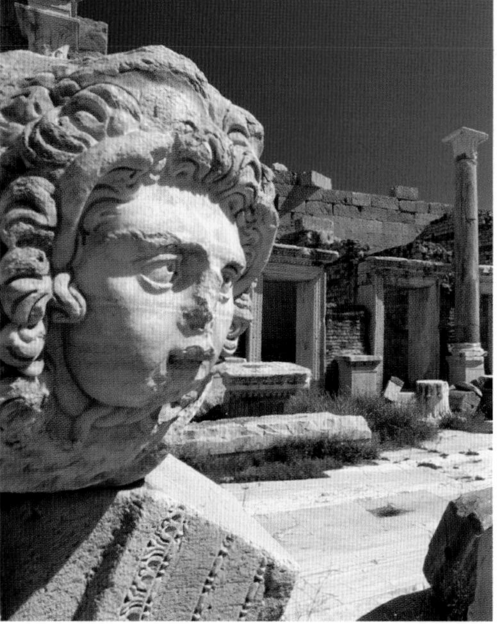

Leptis Magna, *on the Mediterranean coast; originally founded by the Phoenicians in the 10th century BC it flourished under the Romans; granted UNESCO World Heritage Site status in 1982*

TRIPOLI (TARABULUS)

Capital and chief port of Libya, on the Mediterranean Sea. Founded as Oea in the 7th century BC by the Phoenicians and developed by the Romans. From the 7th century AD, the Arabs developed Tripoli as a market center for the trans-Saharan caravans. In 1551, it was captured by the Ottoman Turks. It was made capital of the Italian colony of Libya in 1911, and was an important base for Axis forces during World War II. After intensive Allied bombing in 1941–2, Britain captured the city. In 1986, the US Air Force bombed Tripoli in retaliation for Libya's alleged support of worldwide terrorism. The city is the commercial, industrial, transport and communications center of Libya. Its oases are the most fertile agricultural area in northern Africa.

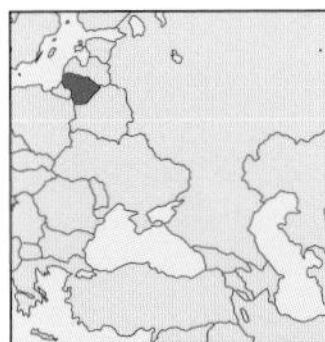

This flag was created in 1918 when Lithuania became an independent republic. After the Soviet Union annexed Lithuania in 1940, the flag was suppressed. It was revived in 1988 and again became the national flag when Lithuania became fully independent in 1991.

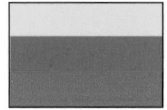

The Republic of Lithuania is the southernmost of the three Baltic states. The land is essentially flat with the highest point a hill, northeast of Vilnius (958 ft [292 m]). From the southeast, the land slopes down to the fertile central lowland. In the west is an area of forested sandy ridges, dotted with lakes. South of Klaipeda, sand dunes separate a large lagoon from the Baltic Sea.

Most of the land is covered by moraine deposited by ice sheets during the Ice Age. Hollows in the moraine contain about 3,000 lakes. The longest river is the Neman, which rises in Belarus and flows through Lithuania to the Baltic Sea.

Area 25,174 sq mi [65,200 sq km]
Population 3,608,000
Capital (population) Vilnius (578,000)
Government Multiparty republic
Ethnic groups Lithuanian 80%, Russian 9%, Polish 7%, Belarusian 2%
Languages Lithuanian (official), Russian, Polish
Religions Mainly Roman Catholic
Currency Litas
Website www.lietuva.lt

CLIMATE

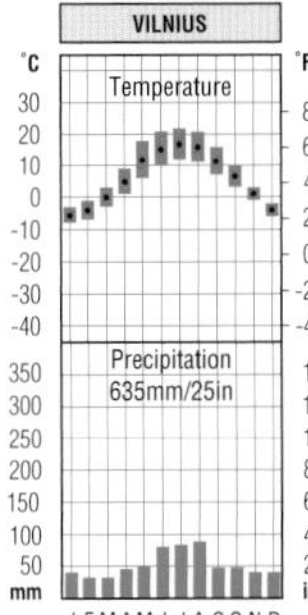

Winters are cold with temperatures averaging 27°F [–3°C] in January. But summers are warm, with average temperatures in July of 63°F [17°C]. The average rainfall in the west is 25 in [630 mm]. Inland areas are drier.

VILNIUS

Capital of Lithuania, on the River Nerisr. Founded in 1323 as the capital of the Grand Duchy of Lithuania, the city declined after the union of Lithuania-Poland. Vilnius was captured by Russia in 1795. After World War I, it was made capital of an independent Lithuania. In 1939, Soviet troops occupied the city and, in 1940, Lithuania became a Soviet republic. During World War II, the city was occupied by German troops, and its Jewish population was all but exterminated. In 1944, it reverted to its Soviet status. In 1990, Lithuania unilaterally declared independence, leading to clashes with Soviet troops and battles on the streets of Vilnius. In 1991, the Soviet Union recognized Lithuanian independence. The old city has many historic synagogues, churches, and civic buildings, and the ruins of a 14th-century castle.

HISTORY

The Lithuanian people were united into a single nation in the 12th century. The first great ruler was Mindaugas who became king in 1251. By the 14th century, Lithuania's territory extended nearly to Moscow in the east and the Black Sea in the south. Lithuania and Poland became a single state in 1569. This state collapsed in the 18th century and, by 1795, Lithuania was under Russian control. Despite rebellions, Lithuania failed to regain its independence.

In 1905, a conference of elected representatives called for self-government, Russia refused. German troops occupied Lithuania during World War I and, in February 1918, Lithuania declared its independence from Germany and Russia. Lithuania established a democratic form of government, and in 1920, Russia and Lithuania signed a peace treaty. Poland occupied Vilnius from 1920 until 1939, having incorporated it into Poland in 1923. In 1926, a coup overthrew Lithuania's democratic regime.

In 1939, Germany and the USSR agreed to divide up much of eastern Europe. Lithuania and Vilnius were ceded to the USSR in 1940 and a government was set up. German forces invaded in 1941 and held it until 1944, when Soviet troops reoccupied the country. Many Lithuanian guerrillas fought against Soviet rule between 1944 and 1952. Thousands of Lithuanians were killed and many sent to labor camps.

POLITICS

From 1988, Lithuania led the way among the Baltic states in the drive to shed Communism and regain nationhood. In 1989, the parliament in Lithuania declared Soviet laws invalid unless approved by the Lithuanian parliament and that Lithuanian should be the official language. Religious freedom and the freedom of the press were restored, abolishing the monopoly of power held by the Communist Party and establishing a multiparty system.

Following parliamentary elections in February 1990, in which pro-independence candidates won more than 90% of the seats, Lithuania declared itself independent in March 1990, a declaration that was rejected by the Soviet leaders. Most of the capital was then occupied by Soviet troops and a crippling economic blockade put in place. After negotiations to end the sanctions failed, Soviet troops moved into Lithuania and 14 people were killed when the troops fired on demonstrators. Finally, on September 6, 1991, the Soviet government recognized Lithuania's independence.

Parliamentary elections in 1992 were won by the Lithuanian Democratic Labor Party (former Communists). Russian troops withdrew from the country in 1993. In 1996, following new parliamentary elections, a coalition government was set up by the conservative Homeland Union and the Christian Democratic Party. In 1998, an independent, Valdas Adamkus, a Lithuanian-American who had fled in 1944, was elected president. Lithuania had better relations with Russia than the other two Baltic states, partly because ethnic Russians make up a lower proportion of the population than in Estonia and Latvia. Lithuania became a member of NATO and of the EU in 2004.

ECONOMY

The World Bank classifies Lithuania as a "lower-middle-income" developing country. Manufacturing is the most valuable activity. Products include chemicals, electronic goods, processed food, and machine tools. Dairy and meat farming are important, as also is fishing.

View of Vilnius, *from the Hill of Three Crosses*

Luxembourg

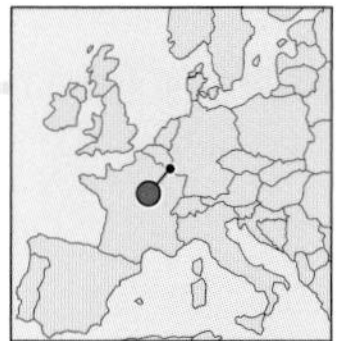

Luxembourg's tri-color flag derives from its coat of arms which shows a red lion on front of blue and white horizontal stripes. The first recorded use of the coat of arms is on the banner of Earl Heinrich VI in 1228.

Area 998 sq mi [2,586 sq km]
Population 463,000
Capital (population) Luxembourg (77,000)
Government Constitutional monarchy (Grand Duchy)
Ethnic groups Luxembourger 71%, Portuguese, Italian, French, Belgian, Slav
Languages Luxembourgish (official), French, German
Religions Roman Catholic 87%, others 13%
Currency Euro = 100 cents
Website www.luxembourg.lu

The Grand Duchy of Luxembourg is one of the smallest and oldest countries in Europe. The north belongs to an upland region which includes the wooded plateau of the Ardennes in Belgium and Luxembourg, and the Eiffel Highlands in Germany. This scenic region contains the country's highest point, Buurgplaatz, in the north which reaches 1,854 ft [565 m] above sea level.

The southern two-thirds of Belgium, which is geographically part of French Lorraine, is a hilly or rolling plateau called the Bon Pays or Gut Land ("Good Land"). This region contains rich farmland, especially in the fertile Alzette, Moselle and Sûre (or Sauer) river valleys in the south and east.

Forests cover about one-fifth of Luxembourg, mainly in the north, where deer and wild boar are found. Farms cover about 25% of the land and pasture another 20%.

CLIMATE

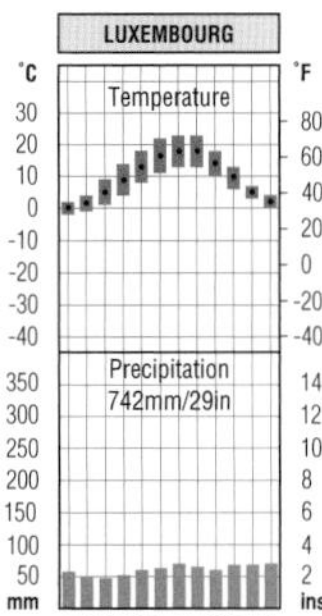

Luxembourg has a temperate climate. In the south of the country summers and falls are warm. This is when grapes ripen in the sheltered southeastern valleys. Winters are sometimes severe, particularly in the Ardennes region, where snow can cover the land for some weeks.

HISTORY

Luxembourg became an independent state in AD 963 and a duchy in 1354. In the 1440s, Luxembourg came under the House of Burgundy and, in the early 16th century, under the rule of the Habsburgs. From 1684, it came successively under France (between 1684 and 1697), Spain (from 1697 to 1714), and Austria until 1795, when it reverted to French rule. In 1815, following the defeat of France, Luxembourg became a Grand Duchy under the Netherlands. This was due to the Grand Duke also being the king of the Netherlands.

In 1890, when Wilhelmina became queen of the Netherlands, Luxembourg broke away as its laws did not permit a woman monarch. The Grand Duchy then passed to Adolphus, Duke of Nassau-Weilburg. But, in 1912, Luxembourg's laws were changed to allow Marie Adélaïde of Nassau to become the ruling grand duchess. Her sister Charlotte succeeded in 1919, but she abdicated in 1964 in favor of her son, Jean. In 2000, Grand Duke Jean handed over the role as head of state to his son, Prince Henri.

Germany occupied Luxembourg in both World Wars. In 1944–5, northern Luxembourg was the scene of the Battle of the Bulge. Following World War II, the economy recovered rapidly.

LUXEMBOURG

Capital of the Grand Duchy of Luxembourg, at the confluence of the Alzette and Pétrusse rivers. Luxembourg was a Roman stronghold. The walled town developed around a 10th-century fortress. The Treaty of London (1867) dismantled the fortress and demilitarized the city. It is the seat of the European Court of Justice, the Secretariat of the Parliament of the European Union, the European Monetary Fund, the European Investment Bank, and the European Coal and Steel Union. Industries include iron and steel, chemicals, textiles, and tourism.

POLITICS

In 1948, Luxembourg joined Belgium and the Netherlands in a union by the name of Benelux and, in the 1950s, was one of the six founders of what is now the European Union. The country's capital, a major financial center, contains the headquarters of several international agencies, including the European Coal and Steel Community and the European Court of Justice.

ECONOMY

Luxembourg has iron-ore reserves and is a major steel producer. It also has many high-technology industries, producing electronic goods and computers. Steel and other manufactures, including chemicals, glass, and rubber products, are exported.

Other activities include tourism and financial services. Half the land area is farmed, but agriculture employs only 3% of the workforce. Crops include barley, fruits, oats, potatoes, and wheat. Cattle, sheep, pigs, and poultry are reared.

***View over Luxembourg** with the Bisserbreck viaduct to the fore; constructed in 1861, the viaduct carries a railway line and crosses the river Pétrusse; it is 951 ft (290 m) in length and has 24 arches*

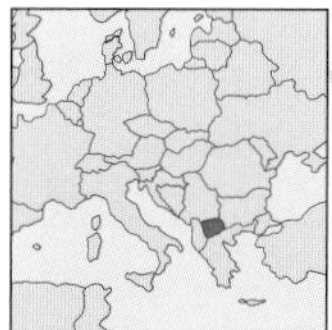

Macedonia's flag was introduced in August 1992. The emblem in the center of the flag was the device from the war-chest of Philip of Macedon; however, the Greeks claimed this symbol as their own. In 1995, Macedonia agreed to redesign their flag, as shown here.

The Republic of Macedonia is in southeastern Europe. This landlocked country is largely mountainous or hilly, the highest point being Mount Korab (9,068 ft [2,764 m]) on the border with Albania. Most of the country is drained by the River Vardar and its many tributaries. In the southwest, Macedonia shares two large lakes—Ohrid and Prespa—with Albania and Greece. Forests of beech, oak, and pine cover large areas, especially in the west.

Area 9,928 sq mi [25,713 sq km]
Population 2,071,000
Capital (population) Skopje (430,000)
Government Multiparty republic
Ethnic groups Macedonian 64%, Albanian 25%, Turkish 4%, Romanian 3%, Serb 2%
Languages Macedonian and Albanian (official)
Religions Macedonian Orthodox 70%, Islam 29%
Currency Macedonian denar = 100 paras
Website www.vlada.mk/english/index_en.htm

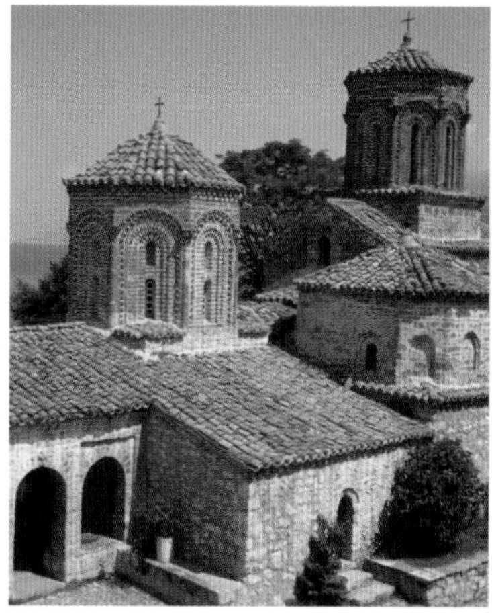

The small church of Sv. Jovan Kaneo *in the town of Orid, overlooking Lake Ohrid; built in the 13th century in the plan of a Greek cross, it is constructed in layers of brick and stone*

CLIMATE

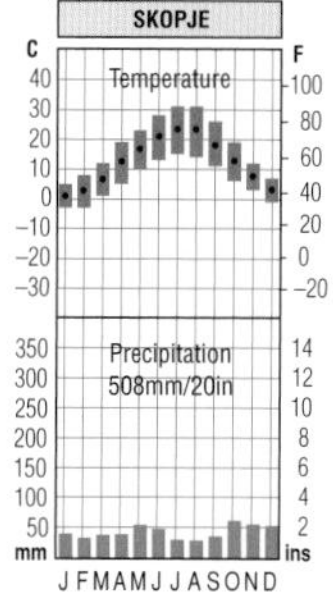

Summers are hot, though highland areas are cooler. Winters are cold and snowfall is often heavy. The climate is fairly continental with rainfall throughout the year. Average temperatures in Skopje range from 34°F [1°C] in January to 75°F [24°C] in July. The average annual rainfall in the city is 21 in [550 mm].

HISTORY

Until the 20th century, Macedonia's history was closely tied to that of a larger area, also called Macedonia, which covered of northern Greece and southwestern Bulgaria. This region reached its peak in power at the time of Philip II (382–336 BC) and his son Alexander the Great (336–323 BC), who conquered an empire that stretched from Greece to India. The area became a Roman province in the 140s BC and part of the Byzantine Empire from AD 395. In the 6th century, Slavs from eastern Europe attacked and settled in the area, followed by Bulgars from central Asia in the late 9th century. The Byzantine Empire regained control in 1018. Serbia took Macedonia in the early 14th century.

The area was conquered by the Ottoman Turks in 1371 and was under their rule for more than 500 years. The Ottoman Empire began to collapse in the late 19th century and in 1913, at the end of the Balkan Wars, the area was divided between Bulgaria, Greece, and Serbia.

POLITICS

As a result of the division of the area known as Macedonia, Serbia took the north and center of the region, Bulgaria took a small area in the southeast, and Greece gained the south. At the end of World War I, Serbian Macedonia became part of the Kingdom of the Serbs, Croats, and Slovenes, which was renamed Yugoslavia in 1929. Yugoslavia was conquered by Germany during World War II, but when the war ended in 1945 the Communist partisan leader Josip Broz Tito set up a Communist government. Tito maintained unity among the diverse peoples of Yugoslavia but, after his death in 1980, the ethnic and religious differences began to reassert themselves. Yugoslavia broke apart into five sovereign republics with Macedonia declaring its independence on September 18, 1991 thereby avoiding the civil war that shattered other parts of the former Yugoslavia.

However, Macedonia ran into problems concerning recognition. Greece, worried by the consequences for its own Macedonian region, vetoed any acknowledgement of an independent Macedonia on its borders. It considered Macedonia to be a Greek name. It also objected to a symbol on Macedonia's flag, which was associated with Philip of Macedon, and a reference in the country's constitution to the desire to reunite the three parts of the old Macedonia.

Macedonia adopted a new clause in its constitution rejecting all claims on Greek territory and, in 1993, joined the United Nations under the name of The Former Yugoslav Republic of Macedonia (FYROM). In late 1993, all EU countries, except Greece, established diplomatic relations with the FYROM. Greece barred Macedonian trade in 1994, but this ban was subsequently lifted in 1995. Macedonia's stability was threatened in 1999 when Albanian-speaking refugees flooded into Macedonia from Kosovo. In 2001, Albanian-speaking Macedonians in northern Macedonia launched an armed struggle. The uprising ended when the government introduced changes that gave Albanian-speakers increased rights, including the recognition of Albanian as an official language. In 2004, the USA recognized the name Republic of Macedonia instead of FYROM, with other countries expected to follow this lead, despite objections from Greece.

ECONOMY

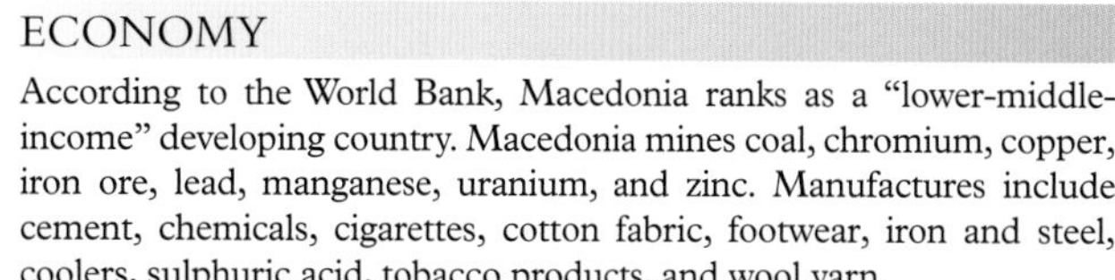

According to the World Bank, Macedonia ranks as a "lower-middle-income" developing country. Macedonia mines coal, chromium, copper, iron ore, lead, manganese, uranium, and zinc. Manufactures include cement, chemicals, cigarettes, cotton fabric, footwear, iron and steel, coolers, sulphuric acid, tobacco products, and wool yarn.

Agriculture employs 9% of the workforce, as compared with 23% in manufacturing and mining. About a quarter of the land is farmed and major crops include cotton, fruits, corn, potatoes, tobacco, vegetables, and wheat. Cattle, pigs, poultry, and sheep are also raised. Forestry is another important activity in some areas.

SKOPJE

Capital of Macedonia, on the River Vardar. Founded in Roman times, it became capital of the Serbian Empire in the 14th century, fell to the Ottoman Turks in 1392, and incorporated into Yugoslavia in 1918. In 1963 an earthquake destroyed most of the city. Industries include metals, textiles, chemicals, glassware.

Madagascar

The colors on this flag are those used on historic flags in Southeast Asia. It was from this region that the ancestors of many Madagascans came around 2,000 years ago. This flag was adopted in 1958, when Madagascar became a self-governing republic under French rule.

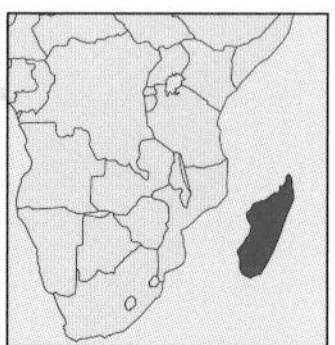

Area 226,657 sq mi [587,041 sq km]
Population 17,502,000
Capital (population) Antananarivo (1,250,000)
Government Republic
Ethnic groups Merina, Betsimisaraka, Betsileo, Tsimihety, Sakalava and others
Languages Malagasy and French (both official)
Religions Traditional beliefs 52%, Christianity 41%, Islam 7%
Currency Malagasy franc = 100 centimes
Website www.madagascar.gov.mg

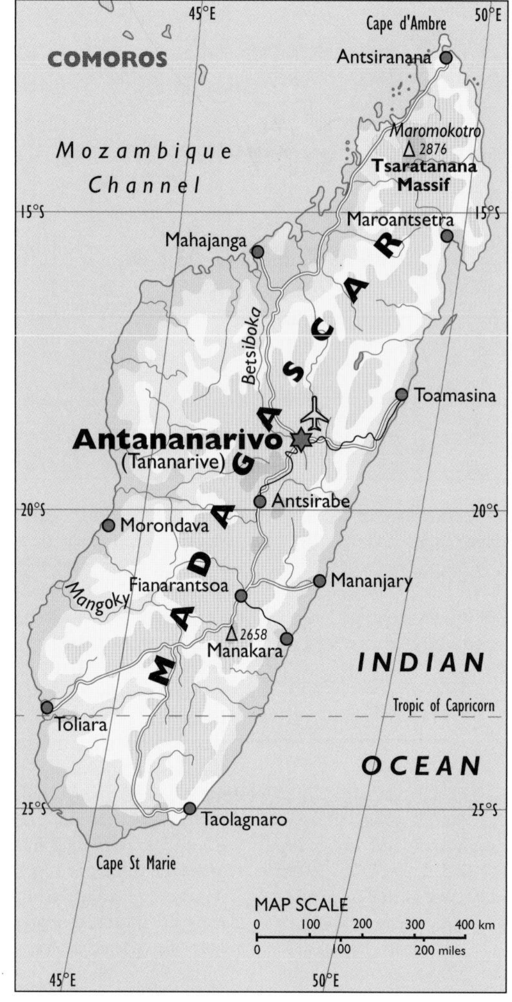

The Republic of Madagascar, lies 240 mi [390 km] off the southeast coast of Africa and is the world's fourth largest island. In the west, a wide coastal plain gives way to a central highland region, mostly between 2,000ft and 4,000ft [600 m to 1,220 m]. This is Madagascar's most densely populated region and home of the capital, Antananarivo. The land rises in the north to the volcanic peak of Tsaratanana, at 9,436 ft [2,876 m]. The land slopes off in the east to a narrow coastal strip.

Grass and scrub grow in the south. Forest and tropical savanna once covered much of Madagascar, but farming cleared large areas, destroying natural habitats and seriously threatening the island's unique and diverse wildlife.

CLIMATE

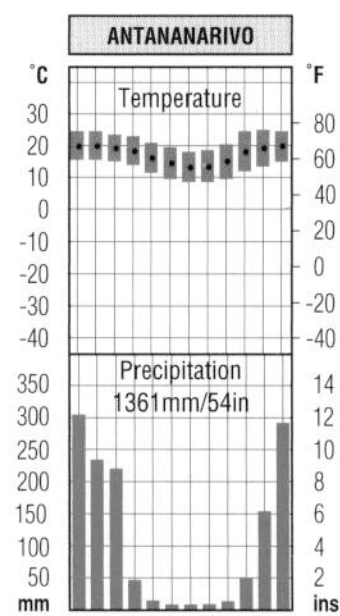

Altitude moderates temperatures in the highlands. Winters (April to September) are dry, but heavy rains occur in summer. Coastlands to the east are warm and humid. The west is drier, and the south and southwest are hot and dry.

HISTORY

People from Southeast Asia began to settle on Madagascar around 2,000 years ago. Subsequent influxes from Africa and Arabia added to the island's diverse heritage, culture and language. The Malagasy language is of Southeast Asian origin, though it included words from Arabic, Bantu languages, and European languages.

The first Europeans to reach Madagascar were Portuguese missionaries who in the early 17th century vainly sought to convert the native population. The 17th century saw the creation of small kingdoms and later the French established trading posts along the east coast. The island became a haven for pirates from the late 18th to early 19th century. A major part of the island was was under Merina rule from the late 18th century.

In 1817, the Merina ruler and the British governor of Mauritius agreed to the abolition of the slave trade. As a result of this, the island received British military and financial assistance. British influence remained strong for several decades. France made contacts with the island in the 1860s. Finally, French troops defeated a Malagasy army in 1895 and Madagascar became a French colony. In 1942, the British overthrew Vichy colonial rule and the Free French reasserted control. In 1946–8 France brutally crushed a rebellion against colonial rule, killing perhaps as many as 80,000 islanders.

POLITICS

In 1960, the country achieved full independence as the Malagasy Republic. In 1972, the military took control of government. Malagasy was renamed Madagascar in 1975, and Lieutenant Commander Didier Ratsiraka became president. He proclaimed martial law, banned opposition parties, and nationalized many industries.

In 1992 Ratsiraka bowed to political pressure and approved a new, democratic constitution. Multiparty elections in 1993 saw Albert Zafy become president. Zafy was impeached in 1996, and Ratsiraka regained the presidency in 1997 elections. In 2000, floods and tropical storms devastated Madagascar.

Madagascar came to the brink of civil war in 2002 when Ratsiraka and his opponent, Marc Ravalomanana, both claimed victory in presidential elections. Ravalomanana was eventually recognized as president and Ratsiraka went into exile.

ECONOMY

Madagascar is one of the world's poorest countries. The land has been eroded due to the cutting down of the forests and overgrazing of the grasslands. Farming, fishing, and forestry employ about 80% of the people.

The country's food crops include bananas, cassava, rice, and sweet potatoes. Coffee is the leading export. Other exports include cloves, sisal, sugar, and vanilla. There are few manufacturing industries.

***Seaweed farmers** harvest their crop*

ANTANANARIVO (TANANARIVE)

Capital and largest city of Madagascar. Founded around 1625, the city became the residence for Imerina rulers in 1794 and the capital of Madagascar. Antananarivo was taken by the French in 1895, and became part of a French protectorate. It is the seat of the University of Madagascar (1961). A trade center for a rice-producing region, it has textile, tobacco, and leather industries.

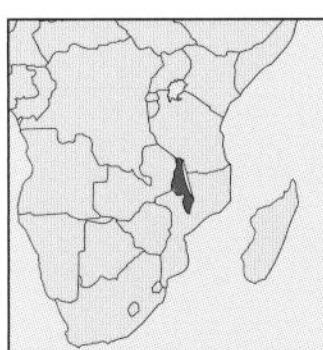

The colors in Malawi's flag come from the flag of the Malawi Congress Party, which was adopted in 1953. The symbol of the rising sun was added when Malawi became independent from Britain in 1964. It represents the beginning of a new era for Malawi and Africa.

The Republic of Malawi in southern Africa is a small, landlocked country, which is nowhere more than 100 mi [160 km] wide. Its dominant physical feature is Lake Malawi, which is drained in the south by the River Shire, a tributary of the Zambezi. The land is mostly mountainous, the highest point being Mulanje, in the southeast, which reaches 9,843 ft [3,000 m].

Area 45,747 sq mi [118,484 sq km]
Population 11,907,000
Capital (population) Lilongwe (440,000)
Government Multiparty republic
Ethnic groups Chewa, Nyanja, Tonga, Tumbuka, Lomwe, Yao, Ngoni and others
Languages Chichewa and English (both official)
Religions Protestant 55%, Roman Catholic 20%, Islam 20%
Currency Malawian kwacha = 100 tambala
Website www.malawi.gov.mw

CLIMATE

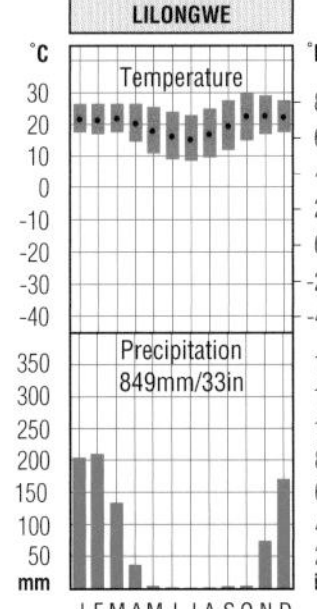

The low-lying regions of Malawi remain hot and humid all year long; the uplands have a pleasant climate. Lilongwe, at about 3,609 ft [1,100 m] above sea level, has a warm and sunny climate. Frosts can sometimes occur in July and August, the middle of the long dry season. The wet season extends from November to May.

Wooded savanna and tropical grasslands cover much of the country, with swampy vegetation in many river valleys.

LILONGWE

Capital of Malawi, southeast Africa, in the center of the country, 50 mi [80 km] west of Lake Malawi. It replaced Zomba as the capital in 1975, and rapidly became Malawi's second-largest city.

HISTORY

The Bantu-speaking ancestors of the people of Malawi first reached the area around 2,000 years ago, introducing an iron age culture and developing kingdoms in the region. In the first half of the 19th century, two other Bantu-speaking groups, the Ngoni (or Angoni) and the Yao invaded the area. The Yao took slaves and sold them to Arabs who traded along the coast. In 1859, the British missionary-explorer David Livingstone reached the area and was horrified by the cruelty of the slave trade. The Free Church of Scotland established a mission in 1875, while Scottish businessmen worked to found businesses to replace the slave trade. The British made treaties with local chiefs on the western banks of what was then called Lake Nyasa and, in 1891, the area was made the British Protectorate of Nyasaland.

The Federation of Rhodesia and Nyasaland was established by Britain in 1953. This included Northern Rhodesia (Zambia) and Southern Rhodesia (Zimbabwe). The people of Nyasaland opposed the creation of the federation, fearing domination by the white minority community in Southern Rhodesia. In 1958, Dr Hastings Banda took over leadership of the opposition to the federation and also to the continuance of British rule. Faced with mounting protests, Britain dissolved the federation in 1963. During 1964, Nyasaland became fully independent as Malawi. Banda became the country's first prime minister and, in 1966, after the adoption of a new constitution, making the country a single-party republic, Banda became the first president.

POLITICS

Banda declared himself president for life in 1971. His autocratic regime differed from most of black Africa in being conservative and pragmatic, hostile to its socialist neighbors, but friendly with South Africa. His austerity program and agricultural policies seemed to have wrought an economic miracle, but a swift decline in the 1980s, combined with the arrival of a million refugees from war-torn Mozambique, led to a return to poverty, despite massive aid packages. Another immediate and ongoing problem was the high incidence of AIDS putting pressure on the country's limited welfare services. Political dissent led to the restoration of a multiparty system in 1993. Banda and his party were defeated in the elections of 1994 with Bakili Muluzi becoming president. Banda was arrested and charged with murder, but he died in 1997.

ECONOMY

The overthrow of Banda led to a restoration of political freedoms. The abolition of school fees and school uniforms nearly doubled school enrolment. Malawi remains one of the world's poorest countries. Reforms in the 1990s included encouraging small farmers to diversify production, but free enterprise and privatization angered some farmers who have suffered from the ending of subsidies.

Although fertile farmland is limited, agriculture dominates the economy employing more than 80% of the workforce. Tobacco is the leading export, followed by tea, sugar, and cotton. The main food crops include cassava, groundnuts, corn, rice and sorghum. Many farmers raise cattle, goats, and other livestock.

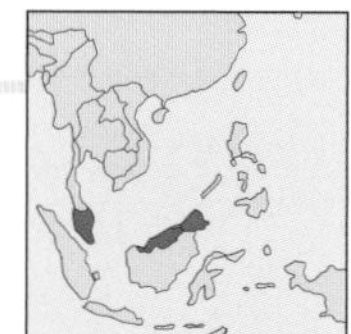

This flag was adopted when the Federation of Malaysia was set up in 1963. The red and white bands date back to a revolt in the 13th century. The star and crescent are symbols of Islam. The blue represents Malaysia's role in the Commonwealth.

Malaysia consists of two main parts, Peninsular Malaysia (the Malay peninsula) and northern Borneo. Peninsular Malaysia is made up of 11 states and two of the three components of the federal territory (Kuala Lumpur and Putrajaya). Northern Borneo comprises two states and one component of the federal territory (Labuan)

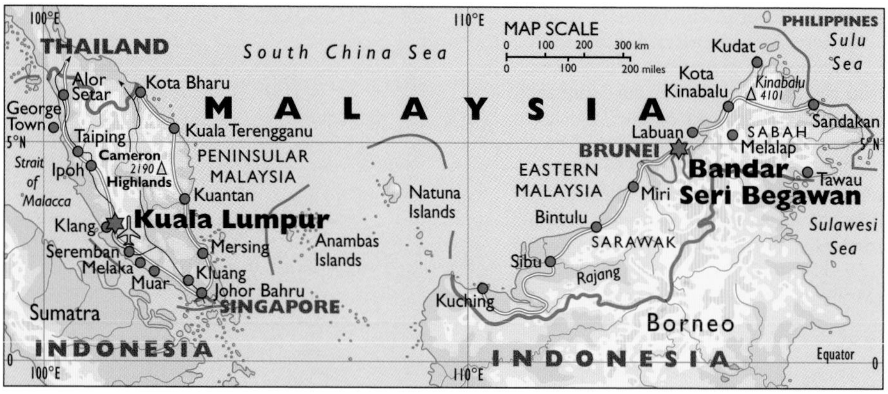

Peninsular Malaysia is dominated by fold mountains with a north–south axis. The most important is the Main Range, which runs from the Thai border to the southeast of Kuala Lumpur, reaching 7,159 ft [2,182 m] at its highest point, Gunong Kerbau. South of the Main Range lie the flat, poorly drained lowlands of Johor. The short rivers have built up a margin of lowlands around the coast.

Northern Borneo has a mangrove-fringed coastal plain, backed by hill country, with east–west fold mountains in the interior. The most striking mountain, and Malaysia's highest point, is the granite peak of Mount Kinabalu, in Sabah, at 13,455 ft [4,101 m].

CLIMATE

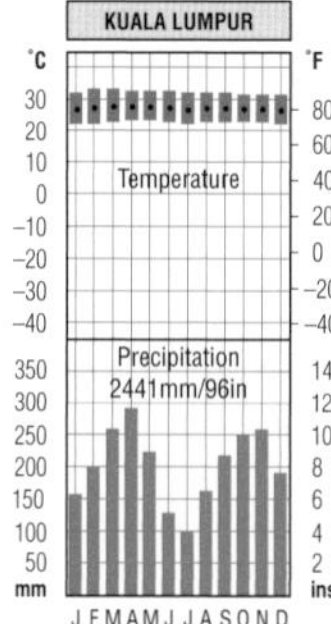

Malaysia has a hot equatorial climate. Temperatures are high all year, though the mountains are much cooler than lowland areas. Rainfall affects the whole country and is heavy throughout the year.

HISTORY

The Malay peninsula has long been a crossroads for sea traders from China and India. Hinduism and Buddhism were introduced from India in the 9th century AD. An early golden age of Malay political power came in the 15th century with the rise of the Kingdom of Malacca (now Melaka), on the southwestern coast of the Malay peninsula. Malacca controlled the important sea routes and attracted traders from all parts of Asia. Arab traders introduced Islam and, in 1414, Malacca's ruler became a Muslim. Many of the people on the peninsula soon embraced Islam, which remains the official religion of Malaysia today.

The first Europeans to reach the area were the Portuguese and Malacca became a Portuguese possession in 1511. The Dutch, who had been trading in the area during the early 17th century, took Malacca in 1641, and many people from the Dutch-controlled Sulawesi and Sumatra settled in the peninsula, adding to the region's complex ethnic mix. The British, who had been seeking a suitable trading post in Southeast Asia, took over Malacca in 1794 and though Malacca was returned to the Dutch in 1814, it reverted to British rule in 1824. Through the activities of Stamford Raffles, an agent for the British-owned East India Company, Singapore was occupied by the British in 1819 and made a British territory in 1824. The Straits Settlement, consisting of Penang (now Pinang), Malacca and Singapore, was founded by the British in 1826. In 1867, the Straits Settlement became a British colony. British rule was gradually extended, with Sabah and Sarawak becoming a British protectorate in 1888. In 1896, Negeri Sembilan, Penang, Perak, and Selangor became the Federated Malay States. Under British rule, the economy developed and thousands of Chinese and Indian workers came to work on the rubber plantations.

Japan occupied the area that is now Malaysia and Singapore during World War II, but British rule was restored in 1945 following Japan's defeat. In the late 1940s and 1950s, inspired by the Chinese revolution, Communists fought the British, but guerrilla warfare ended with the independence of the Federation of Malaya in 1957. In 1963, Malaya joined with Singapore, and what is now Sabah and Sarawak, to form the nation of Malaysia, with Tunku Abdul Rahman of the Alliance Party as prime minister. Brunei was invited to join, but no agreement was achieved on entry terms. Arguments between Singapore and the Malaysian government occurred from the outset, causing Singapore to withdraw in 1965, and become an independent sovereign state.

One of the problems faced by the nation has been its great ethnic and religious diversity, with Malays of both Chinese and Indian origin, many brought in by the British to work the tin mines and rubber plantations. There are also a number of Eurasians, Europeans, and aboriginal peo-

Area 127,320 sq mi [329,758 sq km]
Population 23,522,000
Capital (population) Kuala Lumpur (1,145,000), Putrajaya (administrative center)
Government Constitutional monarchy
Ethnic groups Malay and other indigenous groups 58%, Chinese 24%, Indian 8%, others
Languages Malay (official), Chinese, English
Religions Islam, Buddhism, Daoism, Hinduism, Christianity, Sikhism
Currency Ringgit = 100 cents
Website www.tourism.gov.my

KUALA LUMPUR (MALAY, "ESTUARY MUD")

Capital of Malaysia, southern Malay Peninsula. Founded in 1857, Kuala Lumpur became the capital of the Federated Malay States in 1895, capital of the Federation of Malaya in 1957, and capital of Malaysia in 1963. A commercial city, its striking modern architecture includes one of the world's tallest buildings, the twin Petronas Towers, at 452 m [1,483 ft]. Industries include tin and rubber.

***Dragon Sculpture** at Buddhist Temple, Penang Island*

ples, notably in Sabah and Sarawak. This patchwork has caused tensions, especially between the Muslim Malays and the politically dominant, mainly Buddhist, Chinese. But while riots did break out in 1969, there was never any escalation into serious armed conflict, nor was economic development effected.

Malaysia faced attacks by Indonesia, which objected to Sabah and Sarawak joining Malaysia. Indonesia's policy of "confrontation" forced Malaysia to increase its defense expenditure. Malaysia was also reluctant to have dealings with Communist countries, but at the same time was keen to remain independent of the Western bloc and aware of the need for Southeast Asian nations to work together. From 1967, it was playing a major part in regional affairs, especially through its membership of ASEAN (Association of Southeast Asian Nations), together with Indonesia, the Philippines, Singapore, and Thailand. (Later members of ASEAN include Brunei in 1984, Vietnam in 1995, Laos and Burma (Myanmar) in 1997, and Cambodia in 1999.)

POLITICS

From the 1970s, Malaysia achieved rapid economic progress, especially under the leadership of Dr Mahathir Mohamad, who became prime minister in 1981. Mahathir encouraged the development of industry in order to diversify the economy and reduce the country's reliance on agriculture and mining. The first Malaysian car, the Proton Saga, went into production in 1985 and by the early 1990s, manufacturing accounted for about 20% of the gross domestic product. and by 1996 its share of the GDP had risen to nearly 35%. However, as with many of the economic "tigers" in Asia's eastern rim, Malaysia was hit by a recession in 1997–8. In response to the crisis, the government ordered the repatriation of many temporary foreign workers and initiated a series of austerity measures aimed at restoring confidence and avoiding the chronic debt problems affecting some other Asian countries. In 1998, the economy shrank by about 5%.

During the economic crisis, differences developed between Mahathir Mohamad and his deputy prime minister and finance minister, Anwar Ibrahim. Anwar wanted Malaysia to work closely with the International Monetary Fund (IMF) to promote domestic reforms and strict monetary and fiscal policies. By the summer of 1998, he had gone further, attacking corruption and nepotism in government. Mahathir, who was suspicious of international "plots" to undermine Malaysia's economy, put much of the blame for the crisis on foreign speculators. He sacked Anwar from the government and also from the ruling United Malays National Organization (UMNO). Anwar was later convicted of conspiracy and charged with sexual misconduct. He was jailed for six years.

In late 1999, Mahathir called a snap election to consolidate his power and strengthen his mandate to deal with the economy. With the economy appearing to be rebounding from recession, Mahathir's coalition retained its two-thirds majority in parliament. But many Malays voted for the conservative Muslim Parti Islam. This meant that Mahathir had to rely more on the Chinese and Indian parties in his coalition. The opposition also gained strength by forming a united front at the 1999 elections. In 2003, Mahathir was succeeded by Abdullah Ahmad Badawi, who won a landslide victory in 2004.

ECONOMY

The World Bank classifies Malaysia as an "upper-middle-income" developing country. Manufacturing is the most important sector of the economy and accounts for a sizeable proportion of the exports. The manufacture of electronic equipment is now a major industry, and, by 1994, Malaysia ranked second in the world in producing radios and fifth in television receivers. Other electronic products include clocks, semiconductors for computers, stereo equipment, tape recorders, and telephones. Other major industrial products include chemicals, petroleum products, plastics, processed food, textiles and clothing, rubber, and wood products. Partly because of industrialization, Malaysia is becoming increasingly urbanized. By 2000, about 57% of the population lived in cities and towns.

Malaysia leads the world in the production of palm oil, and, in the mid-1990s, it ranked third in producing natural rubber. Malaysia also ranked fifth in the production of cocoa beans. Other important crops include apples, bananas, coconuts, pepper, pineapples and many other tropical fruits, rice (Malaysia's chief food crop), sugar cane, tea and tobacco. Some farmers raise livestock, including cattle, pigs, and poultry. The country's rainforests contain large reserves of timber, and wood and wood products, including plywood and furniture, play an important part in the economy.

The mining of tin is important with Malaysia the eighth largest producer of tin ore in the world. There is also bauxite, copper, gold, iron ore, and ilmenite (an ore from which titanium is obtained). Since the 1970s, the production of oil and natural gas has steadily increased.

By the mid-1990s, the country's leading exports were machinery and transport equipment, accounting for about 55% of the value of the exports. Other exports included manufactures, mineral fuels, animal and vegetable oils, inedible raw materials, and food.

BRUNEI

Negara Brunei Darussalam (as Brunei is offically known), is a sultanate located in north Borneo, southeast Asia.

Bounded in the northwest by the South China Sea, the country consists of humid plains with forested mountains that run along its southern border with Malaysia.

Area 2,226 sq mi [5,765 sq km]
Population 358,000
Capital (population) Banda Seri Begawan (55,000)
Government Constitutional sultanate
Ethnic groups Malay 67%, Chinese 15%, others
Languages Malay (official), Chinese, English
Religions Islam (official) 67%, Buddhist 13%, Christian 10%, indigenous beliefs and others
Currency Bruneian dollar = 100 cents
Website www.brunei.gov.bn/index.htm

CLIMATE Brunei has an equatorial climate. Temperatures range from 73-90°F [23-32°C]. There is high humidity. Rainfall varies from 98 in [2,500 mm] on the coast to 295 in [7,500 mm] inland, but there is no defined rainy season.

HISTORY AND POLITICS During the 16th century, Brunei ruled over the whole of Borneo and parts of the Philippines. Brunei gradually lost its influence in the region. This was caused by problems regarding royal succession combined with European colonialism. It became a British protectorate in 1888.

In 1970 the capital, Brunei Town, was renamed Banda Seri Begawan. Brunei achieved independence in 1983. It has been ruled by the same family for over six centuries. The Sultan has executive authority.

ECONOMY Oil and gas are the main source of income, accounting for 70% of GDP. Recently, attempts have been made to increase agricultural production.

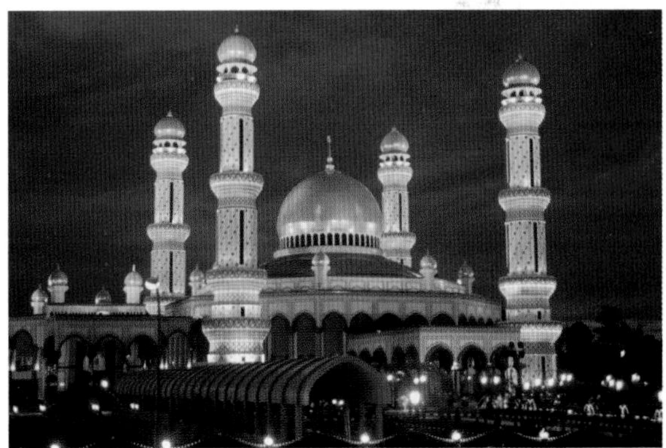

Lights illuminate *the Waqaf Mosque in Bandar Seri Begawan*

Mali

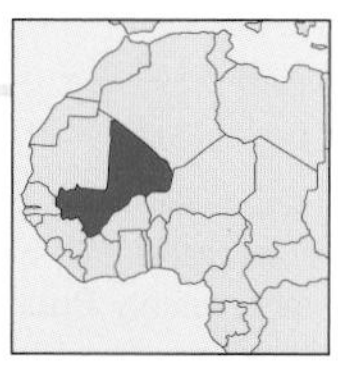

The colors on Mali's flag are those used on the flag of Ethiopia, Africa's oldest independent nation. They symbolize African unity. This flag was used by Mali's African Democratic Rally prior to the country becoming independent from France in 1960.

Area 478,838 sq mi [1,240,192 sq km]
Population 11,957,000
Capital (population) Bamako (1,016,000)
Government Multiparty republic
Ethnic groups Mande 50% (Bambara, Malinke, Soninke), Peul 17%, Voltaic 12%, Songhai 6%, Tuareg and Moor 10%, others
Languages French (official) and many African languages
Religions Islam 90%, Traditional beliefs 9%, Christianity 1%
Currency CFA franc = 100 centimes
Website www.officetourisme-mali.com

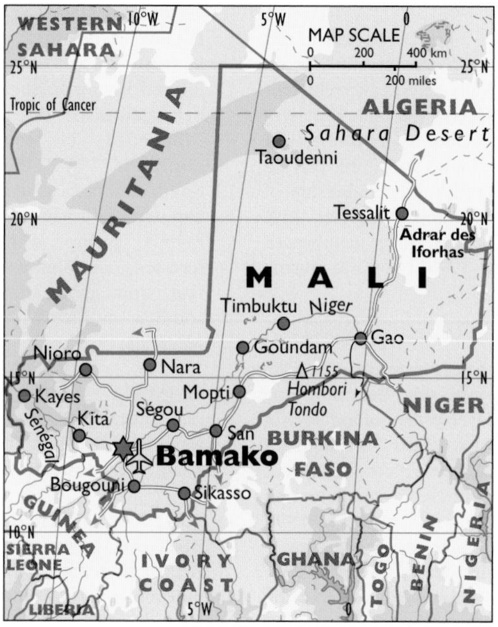

The Republic of Mali is the largest country in west Africa. It is mainly flat, with the highest land in the Adrar des Iforhas on the border with Algeria. Saharan Mali contains many wadis (dry river valleys). The old trading city of Timbuktu lies on the edge of the desert. The only permanent rivers are in the south, the main rivers being the Sénégal, which flows westwards to the Atlantic Ocean to the north of Kayes, and the Niger, which makes a large turn, called the Niger Bend, in south-central Mali.

More than 70% of Mali is desert or semidesert with sparse vegetation. Central and southeastern Mali is a dry grassland region known as the Sahel. In prolonged droughts, the northern Sahel dries up and becomes part of the Sahara. Fertile farmland and tropical savanna covers southern Mali, the most densely populated region.

CLIMATE

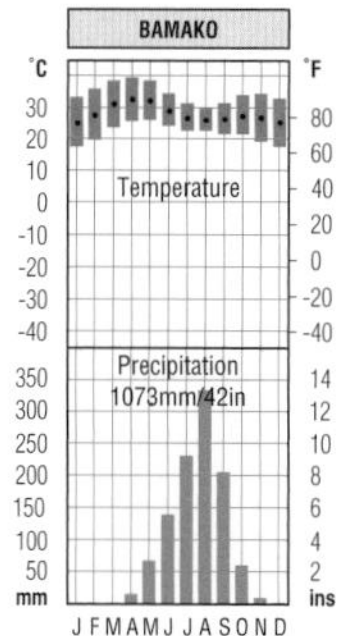

Northern Mali is part of the Sahara, with a hot, practically rainless climate. But the south has enough rain for farming. In the southwest of the country, unpleasant weather is experienced when dry and dusty harmattan winds blow from the Sahara Desert.

HISTORY

From the 4th to the 16th centuries, Mali was part of three major black African cultures—ancient Ghana, Mali, and Songhai. Reports on these empires were made by Arab scholars who crossed the Sahara to visit them. One major center was Timbuktu (Tombouctou), in central Mali. In the 14th century, this town was a great center of learning in history, law, and the Muslim religion. It was also a trading center and stopping point for Arabs and their camel caravans. At its height, the Mali Empire was West Africa's richest and most powerful state. However, following the defeat of the Songhai empire by Morocco in 1591, the area was divided into small kingdoms.

In 1893, the region became known as French Sudan, and was incorporated into the Federation of West Africa in 1898. Nationalist movements grew more vocal in their opposition to colonialism. In 1958, French Sudan voted to join the French Community as an autonomous republic. In 1959, it joined with Senegal to form the Federation of Mali.

BAMAKO

Capital of Mali, on the River Niger, 145 km [90 mi] northeast of the border with Guinea. Once a center of Muslim learning (11th–15th centuries), it was occupied by the French in 1883 and became capital of the French Sudan (1908). Industries include shipping, groundnuts, meat, and metal products.

POLITICS

Shortly after gaining independence, Senegal seceded and, in 1960, Mali became a one-party republic. Its first president, Modibo Keita, committed Mali to nationalization and pan-Africanism. Mali adopted its own currency in 1962 and in 1963, it joined the Organization of African States (OAS). Economic crisis forced Keita to revert to the franc zone, and permit France greater economic influence. Opposition led to Keita's overthrow in a military coup in 1968. The military formed a National Liberation Committee and appointed Moussa Traoré as prime minister. During the 1970s, the Sahel suffered a series of droughts that contributed to a devastating famine in which thousands of people died.

In 1979, Mali adopted a new constitution, and Traoré was elected president. In 1991, a military coup overthrew Traoré, and a new constitution (1992) saw the establishment of a multiparty democracy. Alpha Oumar Konaré, leader of the Alliance for Democracy in Mali (ADEMA), won the ensuing presidential election. A political settlement provided a special administration for Tuaregs in northern Mali. Konaré was reelected in 1997. In 1999, he commuted Traoré's death sentence for corruption to life imprisonment. General Amadou Toumani Toure succeeded Konaré as president in 2002 elections.

ECONOMY

Mali is one of the world's poorest countries and 70% of the land is desert or semidesert. Only about 2% of the land is used for growing crops, while 25% is used for grazing animals. Despite this, agriculture employs nearly 85% of the workforce, many of whom still subsist by nomadic livestock rearing. Farming is hampered by water shortages, and the severe droughts in the 1970s and 1980s led to a great loss of animals and much human suffering. The farmers in the south grow millet, rice, sorghum, and other food crops to feed their families.

The chief cash crops are cotton, groundnuts, and sugar cane. Many of these crops are grown on land which is irrigated with river water. Only a few small areas in the south are worked without irrigation, while the barren deserts in the north are populated only by a few poor nomads. Fishing is an important economic activity. Mali has vital mineral deposits of gold and salt.

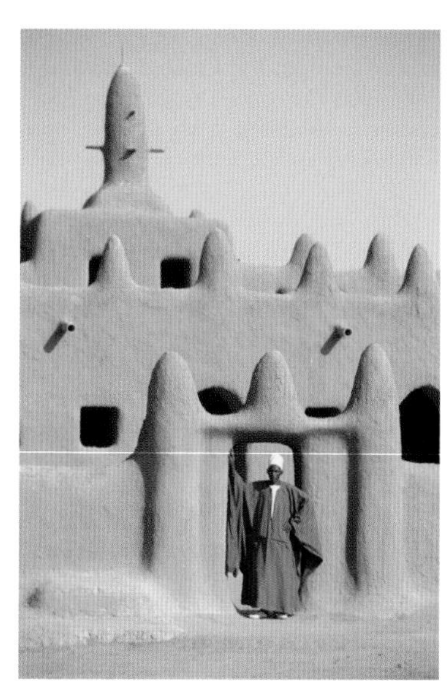

***A Peul man** stands outside the village mosque in Djenne*

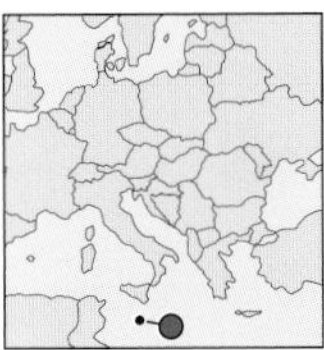

A red flag with a white cross was used by the Knights of Malta. In 1943 a George Cross was added after the award bestowed by King George VI of Britain. Upon independence, in 1964 a red edge was added to the cross.

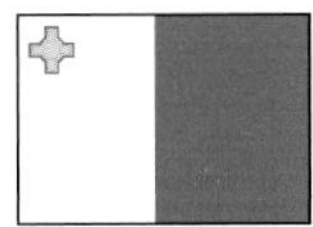

VALLETTA

Port and capital of Malta, on the northeast coast of the island. Founded in the 16th century, it was named after Jean Parisot de la Valette, Grand Master of the Order of the Knights of St John, who organized the reconstruction of the city after repelling the Turks' Great Siege of 1565. Notable sights include the Royal University of Malta (1592) and the Cathedral of San Giovanni (1576).

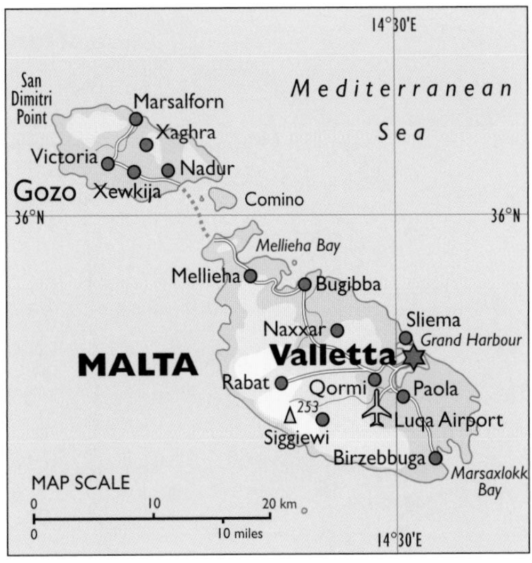

Area 122 sq mi [316 sq km]
Population 397,000
Capital (population) Valetta (9,000)
Government Multiparty republic
Ethnic groups Maltese 96%, British 2%
Languages Maltese and English (both official)
Religions Roman Catholic 98%
Currency Maltese lira = 100 cents
Website www.gov.mt

The Republic of Malta is an archipelago republic in the Mediterranean Sea, 60 mi [100 km] south of Sicily. Malta consists of two main islands, Malta (95 sq mi [246 sq km]) and Gozo (26 sq mi [67 sq km]), the small island of Comino, lies between the two large islands. There are also two tiny islets.

The islands are low-lying. Malta island is composed mostly of limestone. Gozo is largely covered by clay, and as a result its landscapes are less arid. Malta has no forests, and 38% of the land is arable.

CLIMATE

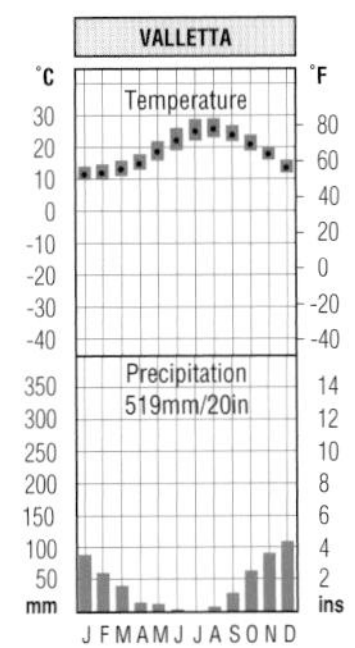

Malta is typically Mediterranean. Summers are hot and dry. Winters are mild and wet. The sirocco, a hot wind from North Africa, can raise temperatures considerably in the spring.

HISTORY

Malta has evidence of Stone Age settlement dating back 4,000 years. In 850 BC, the Phoenicians colonized Malta. The Carthaginians, Greeks, and Romans followed. In AD 395, Malta became part of the Eastern Roman (Byzantine) Empire. In 870, the Arab invasion brought Islam, but Roger I, Norman King of Sicily, restored Christian rule in 1091. In 1530, the Holy Roman Emperor gave Malta to the Knights Hospitallers. In 1565, the Knights, held Malta against a Turkish siege. In 1798, the French captured Malta but, with help from Britain, they were driven out in 1800. In 1814, Malta became a British colony and a strategic military base.

During World War I, Malta was an important naval base. In World War II, Italian and German aircraft bombed the islands. In recognition of the bravery of the Maltese resistance, the British King George VI awarded the George Cross to Malta in 1942. Malta became a base for NATO in 1953.

POLITICS

Malta became independent in 1964, and a republic in 1974. Britain's military agreement with Malta expired in 1979, with Malta then ceasing to be a military base. In the 1980s, the people declared Malta neutral. Malta applied to join the European Union in the 1990s, but the application was scrapped when the Labor Party won the elections in 1996. But, following its election defeat in 1998, the bid for EU membership was renewed and Malta finally became a member in 2004.

ECONOMY

The World Bank classifies Malta as an "upper-middle income" developing country, although it lacks natural resources. Most of the workforce is employed in commercial shipbuilding, manufacturing and the tourist industry. Machinery and transportation equipment account for more than 50% of exports. Manufacturing industries include chemicals, electronic equipment, and textiles. The rocky soil makes farming difficult, Malta produces only 20% of its food. It has a small fishing industry.

MALTESE (MALTI)

Maltese is a Semitic language, that is, one of a group of languages spoken by peoples native to North Africa and the Middle East and forming one of the five branches of the Afro-Asiatic language family. It is spoken by about 340,000 people in Malta and Gozo, and is the only Semitic tongue officially written in the Latin alphabet. The modern language is closely related to western Arabic dialects, but it also shows the strong influence of the Latin that was spoken in Malta. The language developed from the Arabic spoken by the Arabs who invaded Malta in 870. French-speaking Roger I, Norman King of Sicily, ruled from 1091. In 1530 the Knights Hospitallers, who spoke Italian and Latin, were given Malta by the Holy Roman Emperor and it remained under their rule until 1798. In 1814, Malta became a British colony and the British endeavoured to make English the local language. After independence in 1964 Maltese became the national language.

***Marsaxlokk Bay**, on the southeast coast*

Mauritania

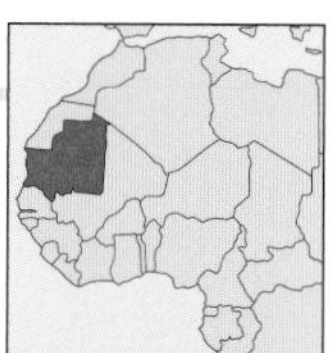

The Islamic Republic of Mauritania adopted its flag in 1959, the year before it became fully independent from France. It features a yellow star and crescent. These are traditional symbols of the national religion, Islam, as also is the color green.

Area 395,953 sq mi [1,025,520 sq km]
Population 2,999,000
Capital (population) Nouakchott (735,000)
Government Multiparty Islamic republic
Ethnic groups Mixed Moor/Black 40%, Moor 30%, Black 30%
Languages Arabic and Wolof (both official), French
Religions Islam
Currency Ouguiya = 100 5 khoums
Website www.mauritania.mr

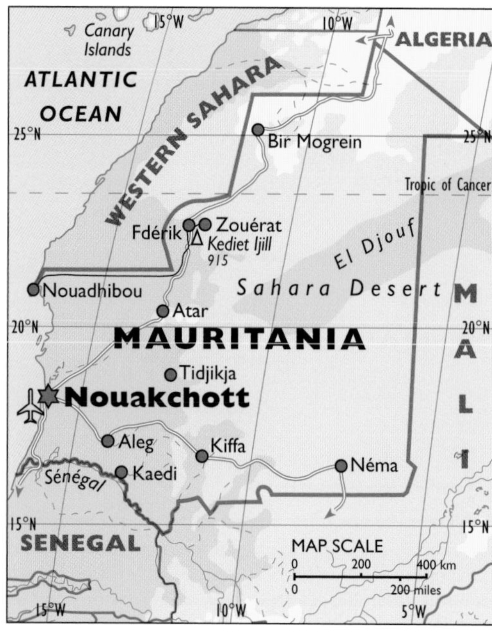

The Islamic Republic of Mauritania in northwestern Africa is nearly twice the size of France, though France's population is more than 28 times that of Mauritania. Over two-thirds of the land is barren, most of it being part of the Sahara. Apart from a small nomadic population, most Mauritanians live in the south, either on the plains bordering the Senegal River in the southwest or on the tropical savanna in the southeast. The highest point is Kediet Ijill (3,002 ft [915 m]). It is an area rich in haematite (high-quality iron ore).

CLIMATE

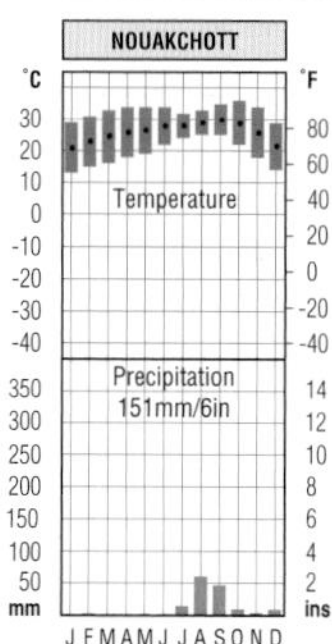

The amount of rain and the length of the rainy season increases north to south. The desert has dry northeast and easterly winds throughout the year. Southwesterly winds bring summer rain to the south.

HISTORY

From the 4th to the 16th centuries, parts of Mauritania belonged to two great African empires—ancient Ghana and Mali. Portuguese explorers arrived in the 1440s.

European contact did not begin in the area until the 17th century when trade in gum arabic, a substance obtained from an acacia tree, became important, with Britain, France, and the Netherlands to the fore. France set up a protectorate in Mauritania in 1903, attempting to exploit the trade in gum arabic. In 1920 the country became a French colony and a territory of French West Africa (an area that included present-day Benin, Burkina Faso, Guinea, Ivory Coast, Mali, Niger, and Senegal, as well as Mauritania). Mauritania became a self-governing territory in the French Union in 1958, achieving full independence in 1960.

BANC D'ARGUIN

Lying on the coast of Mauritania, the Banc d'Arguin is the most important area of intertidal flats on the coast of Africa. In winter it is home to over 2 million shorebirds, while some 40,000 waterbirds, including great white pelicans, greater flamingos, spoonbills, and several species of tern also breed here. The Banc d'Arguin is also an important fishing area and the Imraguen fishing community and their predecessors have lived from the local fishery for the past 500 years or more. The sight of their lanteen sailed boats working their way up the channels between the mudflats, backed by the dunes of the Sahara, is a unique spectacle in Africa.

Courtyard embellished *with a relief design of pigment-filled shapes, cut into a mud wall, Oualata in the southeast of the country*

POLITICS

In 1961, Mauritania's political parties were merged into one by the president, Mokhtar Ould Daddah, who made the country a one-party state. Upon the withdrawal by Spain from Spanish (now Western) Sahara, a territory bordering Mauritania to the north, in 1976,. Morocco occupied the northern two-thirds of the territory, while Mauritania took the rest. Saharan guerrillas belonging to POLISARIO (the Popular Front for the Liberation of Saharan Territories) then began an armed struggle for independence. In 1979, Mauritania withdrew from the southern part of Western Sahara, then occupied by Morocco.

From 1978, Mauritania was ruled by a series of military regimes. In 1991, the country adopted a new constitution when the people voted to create a multiparty democracy. In 1992, an army colonel, Maaouiya Ould Sidi Ahmed Taya, who had served as leader of a military administration since December 1984, was elected president. However, subsequent legislative elections in 1992 were boycotted by opposition parties. Taya was reelected in 1997 and 2003.

ECONOMY

The World Bank classifies Mauritania as a "low-income" developing country. Agriculture employs over half the workforce, with the majority living at subsistence level. Many are still cattle herders who drive their herds from the Senegal River through the Sahelian steppelands, coinciding with the seasonal rains. However, droughts in the 1980s greatly reduced the domestic animal populations, forcing many nomadic farmers to seek help in urban areas. Plagues of locusts in 2004 also caused severe damage. Farmers in the southeast grow such crops as beans, dates, millet, rice, and sorghum. Rich fishing grounds lie off the coast. The country's chief natural resource is iron ore and the vast reserves around Fderik provide a major source of revenue.

NOUAKCHOTT

Capital of Mauritania, north west Africa, in the southwestern part of the country, 5 mi [8 km] from the Atlantic Ocean. Originally a small fishing village, it was chosen as capital when Mauritania became independent in 1960. Nouakchott now has an international airport and is the site of modern storage facilities for petroleum. Light industries have been developed and handicrafts are important.

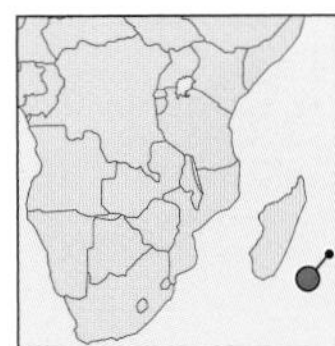

The flag is unique in having four equal horizontal bands. The colors derive from Mauritius' coat of arms. Red is for the blood shed in the liberation struggle, blue for the Indian Ocean, yellow for the bright future afforded by independence, and green for the islands' lush vegetation.

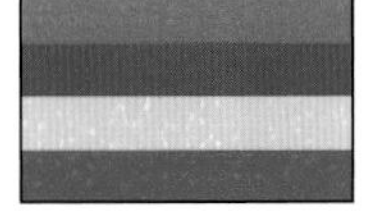

The Republic of Mauritius consists of the large island of Mauritius, which is situated 500 mi [800 km] east of Madagascar. This island makes up just over 90% of the country, which also includes the island of Rodrigues, about 348 mi [560 km] east of Mauritius, and several small islands. The main island is fringed by coral reefs, lagoons and sandy beaches. The land in the interior rises to a high lava plateau (2,717 ft [828 m]) enclosed by rocky peaks.

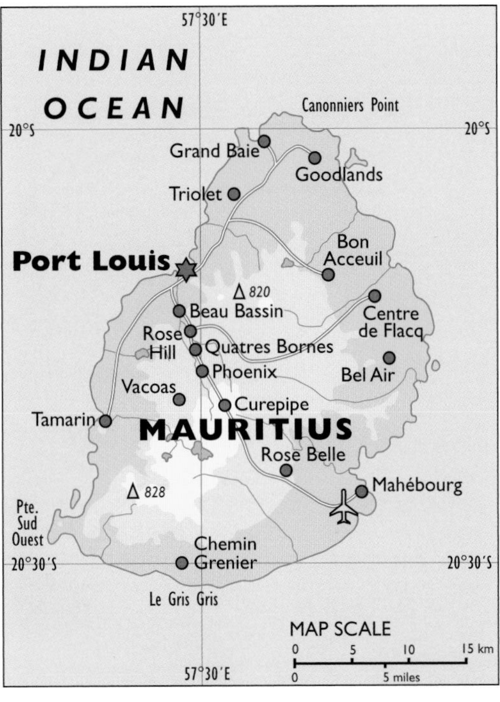

Area 788 sq mi [2,040 sq km]
Population 1,220,000
Capital (population) Port Louis (148,000)
Government Multiparty republic
Ethnic groups Indo-Mauritian 68%, Creole 27%, Sino-Mauritian 3%, Franco-Mauritian 2%
Languages English (official), Creole, French, Hindi, Urdu, Hakka, Bojpoori
Religions Hindu 50%, Roman Catholic 27%, Muslim (largely Sunni) 16%, Protestant 5%
Currency Mauritian rupee = 100 cents
Website www.gov.mu

CLIMATE

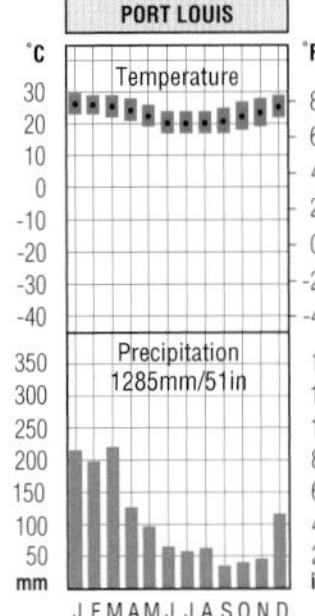

Mauritius has a tropical climate, with heavy rains in the winter. Southeast winds bring rain to the interior plateau of the main island, which is also occasionally hit by destructive tropical cyclones in summer. Average annual rainfall on the interior plateau may reach 200 in [5,100 mm]. The southwest is much drier, with about 35 in [890 mm]. Temperatures range from 72°F [22°C] in the winter (June to October) to 79°F [26°C] in the summer (November to April).

HISTORY

In 1498, Vasco da Gama's fleet accidentally saw the island and, in 1510, a Portuguese navigator, Pedro Mascarenhas, arrived and named it Cimé. Later Portuguese navigators used the island as a port of call, but no permanent settlement was established. In 1598, the Dutch became the first nation to claim the island and they renamed it after Maurice, Prince of Orange and Count of Nassau. However, an attempt at settlement failed in the 1650s. A second attempt was abandoned in 1710, by which time the famous dodo, which was unique to Mauritius, had become extinct. Following the Dutch withdrawal, the island became a haven for pirates.

The French East India Company claimed Mauritius for France in 1715 and named it the Isle de France. The French developed the economy and imported African slaves. In 1767, control of the island passed to the French government, although the settlers revolted in 1796 when the French government tried to abolish slavery.

British forces landed on Mauritius in 1810, starting a period of British rule. In 1834, Britain abolished slavery on the island which they renamed Mauritius. Most former slaves refused to work on the sugar plantations and so Britain introduced indentured laborers from India, recruiting around 450,000 workers between 1837 and 1910, when indentured labor was ended.

In 1926, the first Indo-Mauritians were elected to the government council while, in 1936, a Creole politician, Dr Maurice Cure, founded the Mauritian Labor Party (MLP). In 1942, representatives from all Mauritian communities were invited to serve on consultative committees and, in 1948, many Indian and Creole were given the vote in elections to a new, enlarged legislature. Internal self-government was introduced in 1957. Elections were held under universal adult suffrage following the introduction of a new constitution in 1958. The MLP, led by Dr Seewoosagur Ramgoolam, won a majority. However, ethnic riots between Indians and Creoles occurred in 1964.

PORT LOUIS

Capital of Mauritius, a seaport in the northwest of the island. It was founded by the French in 1735. Taken by the British during the Napoleonic Wars, it grew in importance as a trading port after the opening of the Suez Canal. Industries include sugar, electrical equipment, and textiles.

Women harvest peanuts *from the roots of a peanut plant*

POLITICS

Mauritius became independent in 1968. In 1969, Paul Berenger founded the socialist Mauritian Militant Movement (MMM). In 1971, the MMM supported strikers and organized opposition to the government. In response, the government declared a state of emergency which lasted until 1976. The MMM won the 1992 elections and Anerood Jugnauth became prime minister.

Mauritius became a republic in 1992 and Caseem Uteem of the MMM was elected president. In 1995, an alliance led by Navin Ramgoolam and Paul Berenger won the elections and Ramgoolam became prime minister. But Jugnauth was returned to power in 2000. He served as prime minister until 2003, when he handed over to Paul Berenger, who had been his deputy. Berenger was the first non-Hindu to become prime minister. Navin Ramgoolam again became prime minister after elections in July 2005.

Despite tensions between the Indian and Creole communities, Mauritius is a stable democracy with free elections and a good human rights record. As a result, it has attracted foreign investment.

ECONOMY

Mauritius has become one of Africa's success stories. It is now a middle-income country with a diversified economy. Arable land covers more than half of the country and sugar cane plantations cover about 90% of the cultivated land. Sugar remains a major export, tea and tobacco are also grown. Agriculture and fishing employ 14% of the workforce, compared with 36% in construction and industry. Textiles and clothing are the leading exports. Mauritius has growing industrial and financial sectors and is now a major tourist center.

Mexico

Mexico's flag dates from 1821. The stripes were inspired by the French tricolor. The emblem in the center contains an eagle, a snake, and a cactus. It is based on an ancient Aztec legend about the founding of their capital, Tenochtitlán (now Mexico City).

Area 756,061 sq mi [1,958,201 sq km]
Population 104,960,000
Capital (population) Mexico City (4,000)
Government Federal republic
Ethnic groups Mestizo 60%, Amerindian 30%, White 9%
Languages Spanish (official)
Religions Roman Catholic 90%, Protestant 6%
Currency Mexican peso = 100 centavos
Website www.presidencia.gob.mx

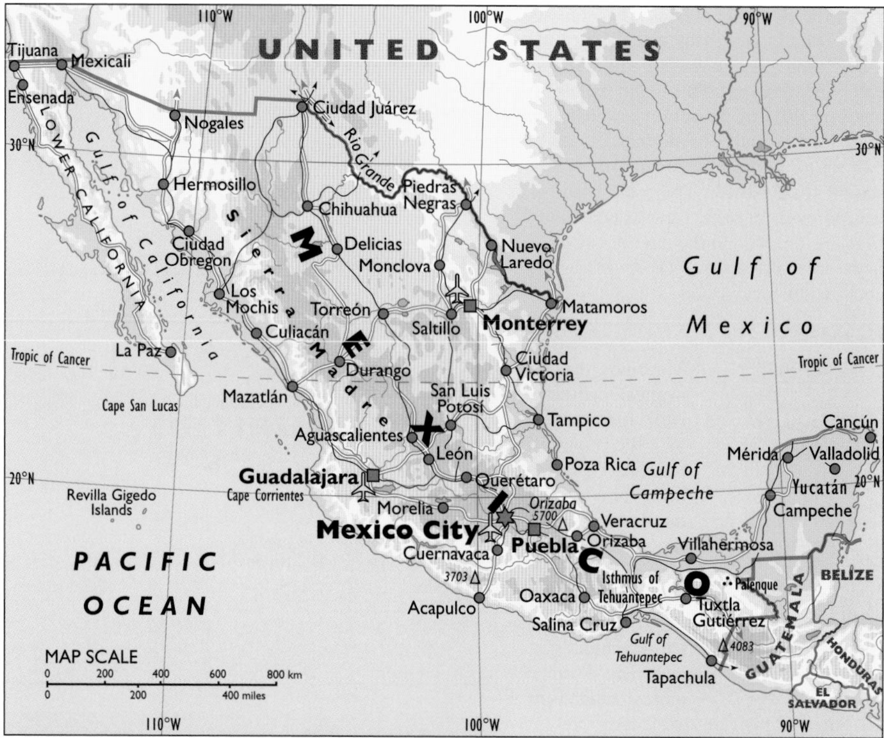

The United Mexican States is the world's largest Spanish-speaking country. It is largely mountainous. The Sierra Madre Occidental begins in the northwest state of Chihuahua, and runs parallel to Mexico's west coast and the Sierra Madre Oriental. Monterrey lies in the foothills of the latter. Between the two ranges lies the Mexican Plateau. The southern part of the plateau contains a series of extinct volcanoes, rising to Orizaba, at 18,701 ft [5,700 m]. The southern highlands of the Sierra Madre del Sur include the archaeological sites in Oaxaca. Mexico contains two large peninsulas: the Baja California in the northwest; and the Yucatán peninsula in the southeast.

CLIMATE

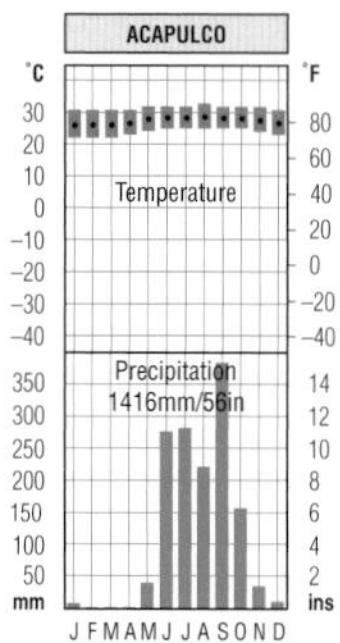

Mexico's climate is hugely varied according to altitude. Most rain occurs between June and September. More than 70% of Mexico experiences desert or semidesert conditions.

Pyramid of Kukulcan, *Chichen-Itza*

HISTORY

Many Native American civilizations flourished in Mexico. The Olmec (800–400 BC), the Maya (AD 300–900), and the Toltec Empire (900–1200). But it was the Aztec who dominated the central plateau from their capital at Tenochtitlán.

In 1519, Spanish conquistadors captured the capital and the Aztec emperor Montezuma. In 1535, the territory became the Viceroyalty of New Spain. Christianity was introduced. Spanish rule was harsh, divisive, and unpopular. Hidalgo y Costillo's revolt (1810) failed to win the support of creoles.

Mexico became independent in 1821 and a republic in 1824. War with Texas escalated into the Mexican War (1846–8) with the United States. Under the terms of the Treaty of Guadalupe-Hidalgo (1848), Mexico lost 50% of its territory. Liberal forces, led by Benito Juárez, triumphed in the War of Reform (1858–61), but conservatives with support from France installed Maximilian of Austria as Emperor in 1864. In 1867, republican rule was restored and Juárez became president. In 1876, an armed revolt gave Porfirio Díaz the presidency, his dictatorship lasted until 1910. Huerta's took power in 1913: his dictatorship prolonged the Mexican Revolution (1910–40) and led to US intervention. During the 1920s and 1930s, Mexico introduced land and social reforms. After World War II, Mexico's economy developed with the introduction of liberal reforms. Relations with the US improved but problems remain over Mexican economic migration and drug trafficking.

MEXICO CITY

Capital of Mexico, at 7,800 ft [2,380 m], in a volcanic basin in the center of the country. As the nation's political, economic and cultural center, it suffers from overcrowding and pollution. Hernán Cortés destroyed the former Aztec capital (Tenochtitlán) in 1521. A new city was built, acting as the capital of Spain's New World colonies for 300 years. US troops occupied it in 1847, during the Mexican War. In 1863, French troops took the city, establishing Maximilian as Emperor. Benito Juárez's forces recaptured it in 1867. From 1914–15, Emiliano Zapata and Francisco Villa's revolutionary forces captured and lost the city three times.

POLITICS

The Institutional Revolutionary Party (PRI) ruled Mexico continuously from 1929 to 2000. In 1994 the Zapatista National Liberation Army (ZNLA) staged an armed revolt in the southern state of Chiapas, calling for land reforms and recognition of Native American rights. Vicente Fox became the first non-PRI leader of Mexico in 2000. In 2001, after a nationwide march by the Zapatistas, the Mexican parliament passed a new rights' bill for indigenous peoples.

ECONOMY

The World Bank classifies Mexico as an "upper-middle-income" developing country. Agriculture is important. Oil and oil products are the chief exports, while manufacturing is the most valuable activity. Many factories near the northern border assemble goods such as automobile parts and electrical products, for US companies, known as *maquiladoras.*

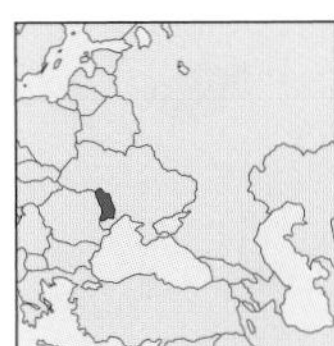

Adopted in 1990, using the same colors as the Romanian flag to emphasize their strong ties. Blue is for Transylvania, yellow for Wallachia, red for Moldavia. The eagle symbolizes the Byzantine Empire; the bison's head, star, rose, and crescent, the medieval principality.

Area 13,070 sq mi [33,851 sq km]
Population 4,446,000
Capital (population) Chisinau (658,000)
Government Multiparty republic
Ethnic groups Moldovan/Romanian 65%, Ukrainian 14%, Russian 13%, others
Languages Moldovan/Romanian, Russian (official)
Religions Eastern Orthodox 98%
Currency Moldovan leu = 100 bani
Website www.moldova.org/index/eng/

The Republic of Moldova is a small country sandwiched between Ukraine and Romania. It was formerly one of the 15 republics that made up the Soviet Union. Much of the land is hilly and the highest areas are near the center of the country. The main river is the Dniester, which flows through eastern Moldova.

Forests of hornbeam and oak grow in northern and central Moldova. In the drier south, most of the region is now used for farming, with rich pasture along the rivers.

CLIMATE

Moldova has a moderately continental climate, with warm summers and fairly cold winters when temperatures dip below freezing point. Most of the rain falls in the warmer months.

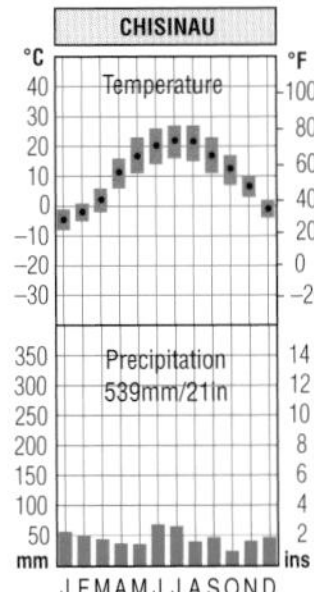

HISTORY

Moldavia was a historic Balkan region, between the Carpathian Mountains in Romania and the Dniester River.

Under Roman rule, it formed the major part of the province of Dacia, and today's population is Romanian-speaking. In the 14th century, it became an independent principality ruled by the Vlachs; its lands included Bessarabia and Bukovina. In 1504, the Turks conquered Moldavia, and it remained part of the Ottoman Empire until the 19th century.

In 1775, the Austrians gained Bukovina, and in 1815 Russia conquered Bessarabia. After the Russo-Turkish War (1828–9), Russia became the dominant power. In 1856, the twin principalities of Moldavia and Wallachia gained considerable autonomy. Three years later, they united under one crown to form Romania, but Russia reoccupied southern Bessarabia in 1878.

In 1920, Bessarabia and Bukovina were incorporated into the Romanian state. In 1924, the Soviet republic of Moldavia was formed, which in 1947 enlarged to include Bessarabia and northern Bukovina. In 1989, the Moldavians asserted their independence by making Romanian the official language, and in 1991, following the dissolution of the Soviet Union, Moldavia became the independent republic of Moldova.

POLITICS

Following independence in 1991, the majority Moldovan population wished to rejoin Romania, but this alienated the Ukrainian and Russian populations east of the Dniester, who declared their independence from Moldova as the Transdniester Republic. War raged between the two, with Transdniester supported by the Russian 14th Army. In August 1992, a ceasefire was declared.

The former Communists of the Agrarian Democratic Party won multiparty elections in 1994. A referendum rejected reunification with Romania. Parliament voted to join the Commonwealth of Independent States (CIS).

In 1994 a new constitution established a presidential parliamentary republic. In 1995, Transdniester voted in favor of independence in a referendum and in 1996, Russian troops began their withdrawal. On January 1, 1997, a former Communist, Petru Lucinschi, became president. In 1998 and 2001, the Party of the Moldovan Communists (PCRM) won the highest share of the votes. The constitution was changed in 2000, turning Moldova from a semipresidential republic to a parliamentary republic. In 2001, the Communist leader Vladimir Voronin was elected president. The Communist party was reelected in 2005, though it now advocates close ties with the West, a matter of some concern to Russia.

ECONOMY

According to the World Bank, Moldova is a lower-middle income developing country, and in terms of GNP per capita, Europe's poorest country. It is fertile and agriculture remains central to the economy. Major products include fruits, corn, tobacco, and grapes for wine-making. Farmers also raise livestock, including dairy cattle and pigs.

There are few natural resources within Moldova, which means that the government is obliged to import materials and fuels for its industries. Light industries, such as food processing and the manufacturing of household appliances, are expanding.

CHISINAU (KISHINEV)

Capital of Moldova, in the center of the country, on the River Byk. Founded in the early 15th century, it came under Turkish then Russian rule. Romania held the city from 1918 to 1940 when it was annexed by the Soviet Union. In 1991 it became capital of independent Moldova. It has a 19th-century cathedral and a university (1945). Industries include plastics, rubber, textiles, tobacco.

The Palace of Culture *in Chisinau*

Mongolia

ASIA

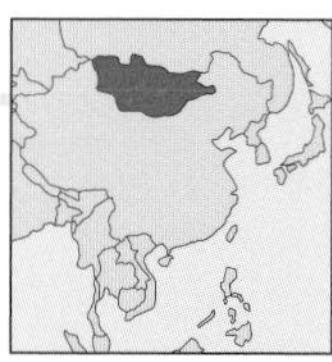

Mongolia's flag contains blue, the national color, together with red for Communism. The traditional Mongolian golden "soyonbo" symbol represents freedom. Within this, the flame is seen as a promise of prosperity and progress.

Area 604,826 sq mi [1,566,500 sq km]
Population 2,751,000
Capital (population) Ulan Bator (760,000)
Government Multiparty republic
Ethnic groups Khalkha Mongol 85%, Kazakh 6%
Languages Khalkha Mongolian (official), Turkic, Russian
Religions Tibetan Buddhist Lamaism 96%
Currency Tugrik = 100 möngös
Website www.mongoliatourism.gov.mn

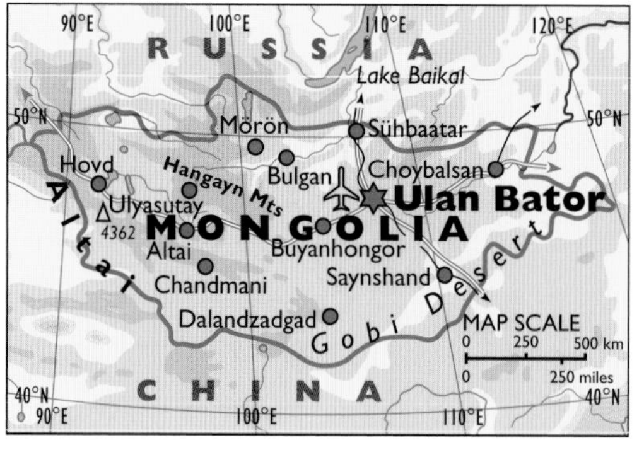

ULAN BATOR

Capital of Mongolia, on the River Tola. Ulan Bator dates back to the founding of the Lamaistic Temple of the Living Buddha in 1639. It grew as a stop for caravans between Russia and China and was later a focus for the Mongolian autonomy movement, becaming the capital in 1921. It is the political, cultural, and economic center of Mongolia. Industries include textiles, building materials, leather, paper, alcohol, and carpets.

Mongolia, which is sandwiched between China and Russia, is the world's largest landlocked country. It consists mainly of high plateaus, the highest of which are in the west, between the Altai Mountains (or Aerhtai Shan) and the Hangayn Mountains (or Hangayn Nuruu).

The Altai Mountains contain the country's highest peaks (14,311 ft [4,362 m]). The land descends towards the east and south, where part of the Gobi Desert is situated.

CLIMATE

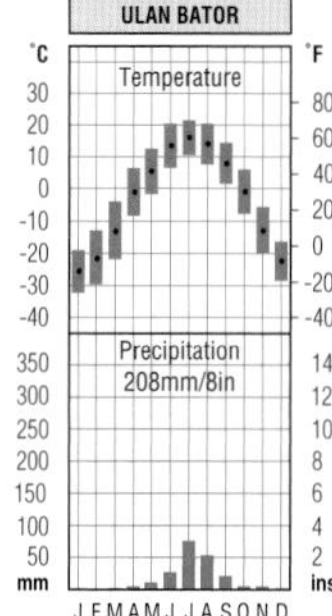

Due to its remote position, Mongolia has an extreme continental climate, with long, bitterly cold winters and short, warm summers. Annual rainfall ranges from no more than 20 in [500 mm] in the highlands to 5 in [125 mm] in the lowlands.

HISTORY

In the 13th century, the great Mongol conqueror Genghis Khan united the Mongol people, created a ruthless army, and founded the largest land empire in history. Under his grandson, Kublai Khan, the Mongol empire stretched from Korea and China, across Asia into what is now Iraq. In the northwest, Mongol rule extended beyond the Black Sea into eastern Europe. Learning flourished under Kublai Khan, but, after his death in 1294, the empire broke up into several parts. It was not until the late 16th century that Mongol princes reunited Mongolia. During their rule, they introduced Lamaism (a form of Buddhism).

In the early 17th century, the Manchu leaders of Manchuria took over Inner Mongolia. They conquered China in 1644 and Outer Mongolia some 40 years later. Present-day Mongolia then became a remote Chinese province scarcely in contact with the outside world.

Outer Mongolia broke away from China following the collapse of the Qing Dynasty in 1911, and the Mongols appointed a priest, the Living Buddha, as their king. Legally, Outer Mongolia remained Chinese territory, but China and Russia agreed to grant it control over its own affairs in 1913. Russian influence increased and, in 1921, Mongolian and Russian Communists took control of Outer Mongolia, proclaiming the Mongolian People's Republic in 1924.

POLITICS

Mongolia became an ally of the Soviet Union, its support being particularly significant from the 1950s, when the Soviet Union was in dispute with Mongolia's neighbor, China. The Soviet Union helped develop Mongolia's mineral reserves so by the late 1980s, minerals had overtaken agriculture as the country's main source of revenue.

In 1990, the people, influenced by reforms taking place in the Soviet Union, held demonstrations, demanding more freedom. Free elections in June 1990 resulted in victory for the Communist Mongolian People's Revolutionary Party (MPRP). The new government began to move away from Communist policies, launching into privatization and developing a free-market economy. The "People's Democracy" was abolished in 1992 and democratic institutions were introduced.

The MPRP was defeated in elections in 1996 by the opposition Mongolian Democratic Union coalition. The Democratic Union ran into economic problems and, in the presidential elections of 1997, the MPRP candidate, Natasagiyn Babagandi, defeated the Democratic Union nominee. This achievement was followed by the parliamentary elections in July 2000, which resulted in a landslide victory for the MPRP, who gained 72 out of the 76 available seats in the Great Hural (parliament). The MPRP chairman, Nambaryn Enhbayar, became prime minister. Following disputed elections in 2004 a coalition government was set up.

ECONOMY

The World Bank classifies Mongolia as a "lower-middle-income" developing country. Many Mongolians were once nomads, moving around with their livestock. Under Communist rule, most were moved into permanent homes on government-owned farms. Livestock and animal products remain important.

The Communists developed mining and manufacturing and by 1996, mineral products accounted for nearly 60% of the country's exports. Minerals produced in Mongolia include coal, copper, fluorspar, gold, molybdenum, tin, and tungsten. The leading manufactures are textiles and metal products.

Taking a break during eagle training; *it takes between four to six months to train an eagle for the hunt, after six or seven years, the eagle is released so it can breed in the wild and produce offspring for the next generation of Kazaks*

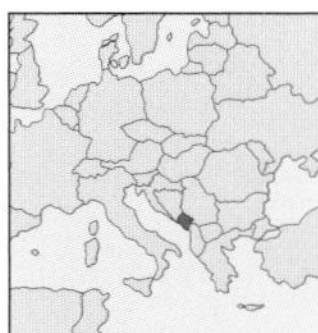

The flag of Montenegro has been in existence since 2004 when it was adopted by the Parliament of Montenegro. It is made up of a red background with the country's coat of arms which themselves derive from the coat of arms of King Nikola I who ruled 1910–1918.

The Republic of Montenegro, together with Serbia, was formerly part of Yugoslavia. In 2003, it became part of the Union of Serbia and Montenegro, but, in 2006, it became fully independent. Ethnic Montenegrins make up 62% of the population. There are Albanian, Croat, Muslim, and Serb minorities.

Area 5,415 sq mi [14,026 sq km]
Population 630,540
Capital (population) Podgorica (152,000)
Government Federal republic
Ethnic groups Montenegrin 43%, Serbian 32%, Bosniak 8%, Albanian 5%, others
Languages Serbian (Ijekavian dialect)
Religions Orthodox, Muslim, Roman Catholic
Currency Euro = 100 cents
Website www.montenegro.yu/english/naslovna

CLIMATE

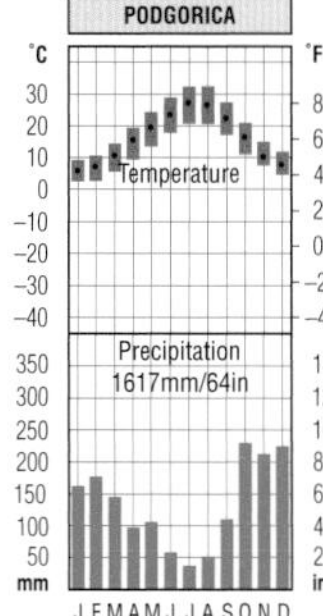

The coast has a Mediterranean climate, with hot, generally dry summers, with occasional thunderstorms, and mild, moist winters. Inland, the mountains have a more extreme climate, with heavy rainfall on the Dinaric Alps.

HISTORY

South Slavs began to move into the region around 1,500 years ago. Each group founded its own state. In the late 12th century, the province of Zeta (modern Montenegro) was incorporated into the Serbian empire. But it began to reassert its independence in the 14th century following the Turkish defeat of the Serbians in 1389. Between the 15th and 18th centuries, Serbia was part of the Turkish Ottoman Empire, while Montenegro was ruled by Christian dynasties headed by bishops who were elected by popular assemblies.

Montenegro's independence was recognized at the Congress of Berlin in 1878. Between 1860 and 1918, the country was ruled by Nicholas I, who declared himself king of Montenegro in 1910. In 1912-1913, Montenegro and Serbia joined in the fight against Turkey and, during World War I, Montenegro supported Serbia.

In 1918, Nicholas was dethroned and Montenegro was absorbed into Serbia. The South Slavs were united in the Kingdom of the Serbs, Croats and Slovenes. In 1929, King Alexander renamed the kingdom Yugoslavia. Italy occupied parts of Montenegro in 1941. But resistance continued until 1944, with Montenegrins prominent among the Communist-led partisans of Josip Broz Tito, who emerged victorious in 1945.

PODGORICA

Capital of Montenegro at the confluence of the Ribnica and Moraca rivers. Podgorica has the mountains close by to the north, and to the south, the Adriatic Sea. The name Podgorica was first documented in the early 14th century, formerly Ribnica, after the river. It came under Turkish occupation from the late 15th to the late 19th century. After freedom from Turkish rule the city developed quickly as a financial and commercial center. In 1946 it was renamed Titograd and became capital of Montenegro. The city flourished under Communist rule. The name Podgorica was reinstated in 1992.

POLITICS

The new Federal People's Republic of Yugoslavia adopted a constitution in 1946, which recognized Montenegro as one of the six autonomous federal units in the republic. The capital of Montenegro was moved to Podgorica, then called Titograd. After Tito's death in 1980, the country was divided. In 1991-2, Yugoslavia broke up. Bosnia-Herzegovina, Croatia, Macedonia, and Slovenia each proclaimed its independence, while the remaining republics of Serbia and Montenegro were jointly called Yugoslavia.

The breakup of the country was marked by ethnic conflict. In 1992, the United Nations withdrew recognition of Yugoslavia due to its failure to halt atrocities committed by Serbs living in Croatia and Bosnia-Herzegovina. However, in 1995, Yugoslavia took part in talks that led to the Dayton Peace Accord. In the 1990s, Yugoslavia was rocked by conflict in the autonomous province of Kosovo in southern Serbia. NATO forces intervened by launching attacks on administrative and industrial targets in Kosovo and Serbia.

Many people became increasingly opposed to Serbia's dominance in Yugoslavia and, in 2003, the country was reconstituted in a loose union called the Union of Serbia and Montenegro. Both republics became semi-independent, each with their own customs, currencies and laws. However, most ethnic Montenegrins and Albanians still favored full independence. In 2006, by a narrow majority, Montenegrins voted to withdraw from the Union. Montenegro then became a fully independent republic led by its pro-independence prime minister, Milo Djukanovic.

ECONOMY

From the 1990s, the economy has been increasingly privatized. Manufacturing is the most valuable activity and steel and aluminium are major products. Farmers produce meat, dairy products, and a variety of crops, including citrus fruits and olives. Forests cover about 54% of the country's surface area.

The Bay of Kotor, *on the Adriatic Sea in Montenegro is often regarded as one of the most beautiful in the world*

Morocco

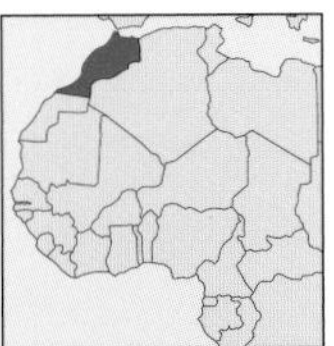

Morocco has flown a red flag since the 16th century. The green pentagram (five-pointed star), called the Seal of Solomon, was added in 1915. This design was retained when Morocco gained its independence from French and Spanish rule in 1956.

Area 172,413 sq mi [446,550 sq km]
Population 32,209,000
Capital (population) Rabat (1,220,000)
Government Constitutional monarchy
Ethnic groups Arab-Berber 99%
Languages Arabic (official), Berber dialects, French
Religions Islam 99%
Currency Moroccan dirham = 100 centimes
Website www.mincom.gov.ma

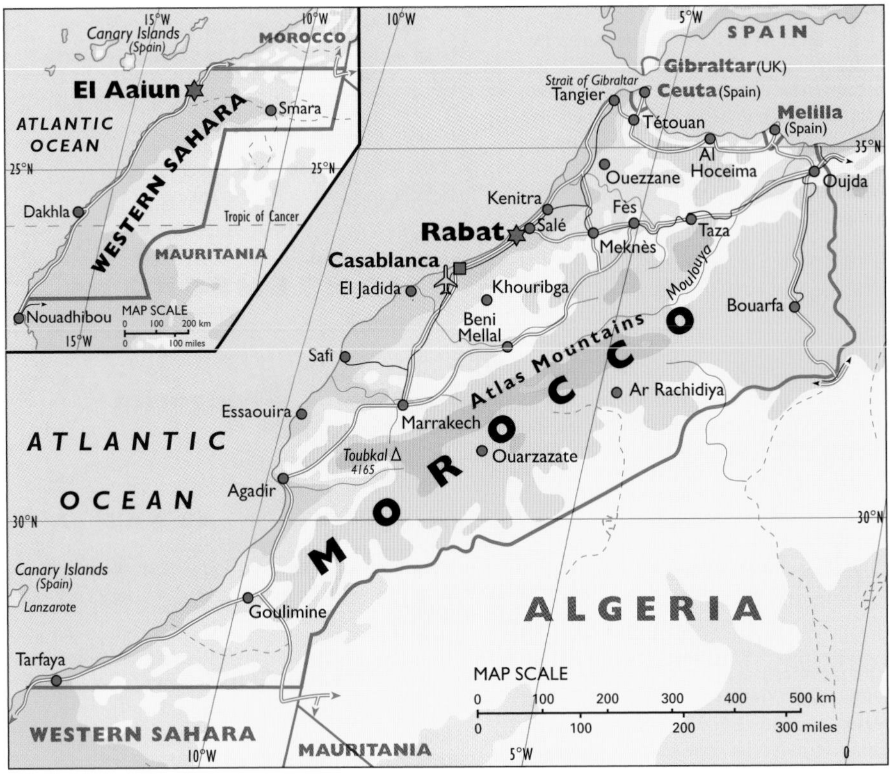

The Kingdom of Morocco lies in northwestern Africa. Its name comes from the Arabic Maghreb-el-Aksa (the farthest west). Behind the western coastal plain the land rises to a broad plateau and the Atlas Mountains. The High (Haut) Atlas contains the highest peak, Djebel Toubkal, at 13,665 ft [4,165 m]. Other ranges include the Anti Atlas, the Middle (Moyen) Atlas and the Rif Atlas (or Er Rif). East of the mountains the land lies the arid Sahara.

CLIMATE

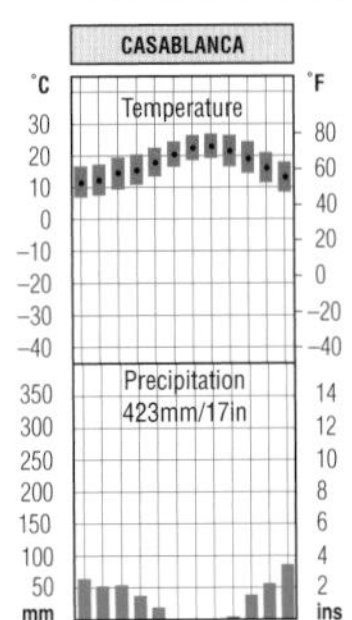

The Atlantic coast is cooled by the Canaries Current. Inland, summers are very hot and dry while winters are mild. From October to April southwesterly Atlantic winds bring rain; there is frequent snowfall in the High Atlas.

HISTORY

The original people of Morocco were the Berbers. In the 680s, Arab invaders introduced Islam and the Arabic language. By the early 20th century, France and Spain controlled Morocco. It finally became an independent kingdom in 1956, becoming an independent monarchy in 1957 when Sidi Muhammad changed his title to King Muhammad V. In 1961, his son succeeded as King Hassan II.

POLITICS

King Hassan II ruled the country in an authoritarian way until his death in 1999. His successor, King Mohamed VI, faced a number of problems, including finding a solution to the future of Western Sahara. Relations with Spain became strained in 2002 over the disputed island of Leila (Perejil in Spanish), in the Strait of Gibraltar. Diplomatic relations were restored in 2003. Another problem faced by Morocco is activity by Islamic extremists. Its opposition to extremism led the United States to designate Morocco as a major non-NATO ally in 2004.

ECONOMY

Morocco is classified as a "lower-middle-income" developing country. It is the world's third largest producer of phosphate rock. Farming employs 38% of Moroccans. Fishing and tourism are important.

RABAT

Capital of Morocco, on the Atlantic coast, northern Morocco. Rabat dates from Phoenician times, but the fortified city was founded in the 12th century by the Almohad ruler, Abd al-Mumin. Under French rule, it was made the capital of the protectorate of Morocco.

WESTERN SAHARA

Desert territory on the Atlantic coast of northwest Africa, covering 102,680 sq mi [266,769 sq km]; the capital is El Aaiun. It comprises two districts: Saguia el Hamra in the north, and Río de Oro in the south. The population consists of Arabs, Berbers, and pastoral nomads, most of whom are Sunni Muslims.

The first European discovery was in 1434, but it remained unexploited until Spain took control of the coastal area in the 19th century. In 1957, a nationalist movement temporarily overthrew the Spanish but they regained control of the region in 1958, and merged the two districts to form the province of Spanish Sahara. Large phosphate deposits were discovered in 1963.

The Polisario Front began a guerrilla war in 1973, eventually forcing a Spanish withdrawal in 1976. Within a month, Morocco and Mauritania partitioned the country. Polisario (backed by Algeria) continued to fight for independence, renaming the country the Saharawi Arab Democratic Republic. In 1979, Mauritania withdrew and Morocco assumed full control. In 1982, the Saharawi Republic became a member of the Organization of African Unity. By 1988 it controlled most of the desert up to the Moroccan defensive line. Fragile ceasefires were agreed in 1988 and 1991. About 200,000 Saharawis continue to live in refugee camps, mostly in Algeria. Talks between Morocco and Western Sahara began in 1997 and have been inconclusive.

Livestock-rearing dominates agriculture. The government hopes to diversify the economy and explore the prospects of offshore oil and gas fields. The islands benefit from a Danish subsidy which accounts for 15% of the GDP.

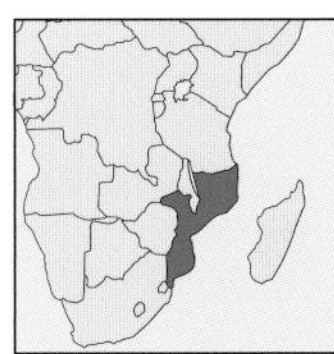

Mozambique

Mozambique's flag was adopted when the country became independent from Portugal in 1975. The green stripe represents fertile land, the black stands for Africa, and the yellow for mineral wealth. The badge on the red triangle contains a rifle, a hoe, a cogwheel and a book.

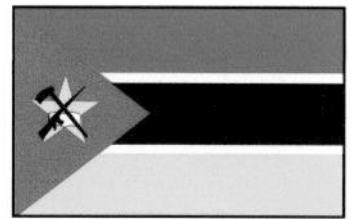

The Republic of Mozambique borders the Indian Ocean in southeastern Africa. The coastal plains are narrow in the north but broaden to the south making up nearly half of the country. Inland lie plateaus and hills, which make up another two-fifths of the country, with highlands along the borders with Zimbabwe, Zambia, Malawi, and Tanzania.

Area 309,494 sq mi [801,590 sq km]
Population 18,812,000
Capital (population) Maputo (1,015,000)
Government Multiparty republic
Ethnic groups Indigenous tribal groups (Shangaan, Chokwe, Manyika, Sena, Makua, others) 99%
Languages Portuguese (official), many others
Religions Traditional beliefs 50%, Christianity 30%, Islam 20%
Currency Metical = 100 centavos
Website www.mozambique.mz

CLIMATE

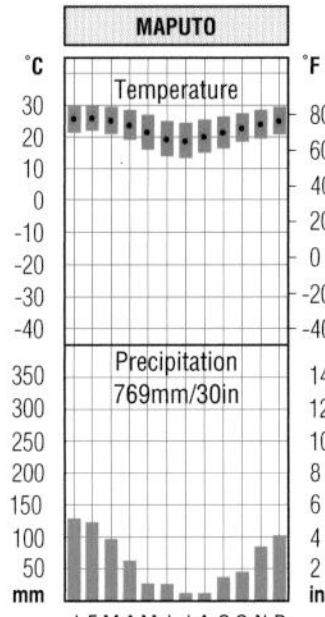

Most of Mozambique has a tropical maritime climate, with two main seasons. The hot, wet season runs from November to March, with a dry, milder season between April and October. Rainfall varies, being greatest on the northwestern highlands and lowest on the southeastern lowlands.

Temperatures in the lowlands vary from between 79 and 86°F [20°C–30°C] in January, and between 52–59°F [11°C–15°C] in July. The interior highlands are much cooler and generally less humid.

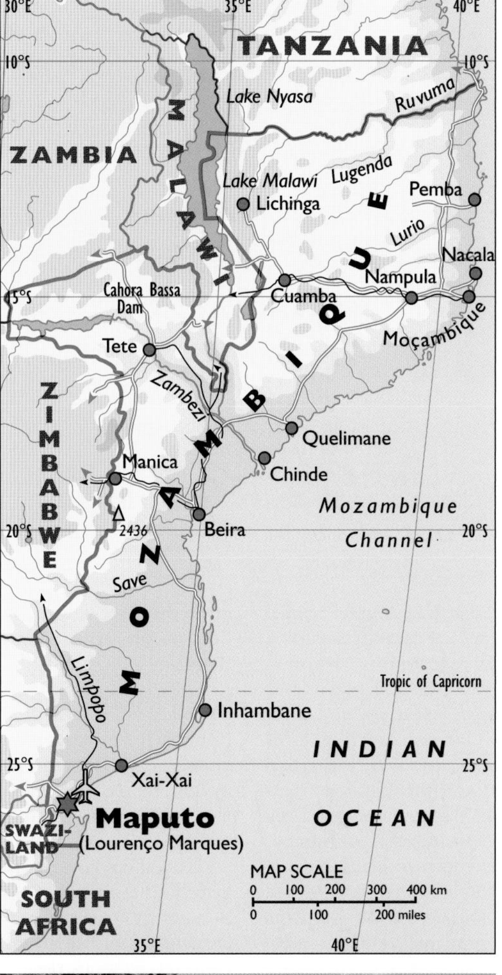

HISTORY

Arab traders began to operate in the area in the 9th century AD, with Portuguese explorers arriving in 1497. The Portuguese set up trading stations in the early 16th century and the area became a source of slaves. When the European powers divided Africa in 1885, Mozambique was recognized as a Portuguese colony. Black African opposition to European rule gradually increased and in 1961, the Front for the Liberation of Mozambique (FRELIMO) was founded to oppose Portuguese rule. FRELIMO launched a guerrilla war in 1964, which continued for ten years. Mozambique achieved independence in 1975, when the Marxist-Leninist FRELIMO, took over the government.

***Oxen pull a cart** filled with coconuts during the coconut harvest on a plantation, Quelimane*

POLITICS

After independence, Mozambique became a one-party state. Its government aided African nationalists in Rhodesia (now Zimbabwe) and South Africa. However, the white governments of these countries helped an opposition group, the Mozambique National Resistance Movement (RENAMO), to lead an armed struggle against Mozambique's government. This civil war, combined with severe droughts, caused much human suffering in the 1980s.

In 1989, FRELIMO declared that it had dropped its Communist policies and ended one-party rule. The war officially ended in 1992 and multiparty elections in 1994 were won by FRELIMO, whose leader, Joaquim A. Chissano, became president. RENAMO's leader, Afonso Dhlakama, accepted the election results and stated that the civil war would not be resumed. This led to a period of relative stability. In 1995, Mozambique became the 53rd member of the Commonwealth, joining its English-speaking allies in southern Africa.

MAPUTO (LOURENÇO MARQUES)

Capital and chief port of Mozambique, on Maputo Bay, southern Mozambique. It was visited by the Portuguese in 1502, and was made the capital of Portuguese East Africa in 1907, being known as Lourenço Marques until 1976. It is linked by rail to South Africa, Swaziland, and Zimbabwe, and is a popular resort area. Industries include footwear, textiles, rubber.

ECONOMY

By the early 1990s, Mozambique was one of the world's poorest countries. Battered by a civil war, which had killed around a million people and had driven 5 million from their homes, and combined with devastating droughts, and floods, the economy collapsed.

By the end of the twentieth century, economists were praising Mozambique for its economic recovery. Although 80% of the people are poor, support from the World Bank and other international institutions, privatization and rescheduling of the country's foreign debts, led to an expansion of the economy and the bringing down of inflation to less than 10% by 1999.

Massive floods at the start of 2000 affected about a quarter of the population making thousands homeless and devastating the economy for many years to come.

Agriculture is important. Crops include cassava, cotton, cashew nuts, fruits, corn, rice, sugar cane, and tea. Fishing is important and shrimps, cashew nuts, sugar, and copra are exported. Despite its large hydroelectric plant at the Cahora Bassa Dam on the River Zambezi, manufacturing is at a small-scale. Electricity is exported to South Africa.

Namibia

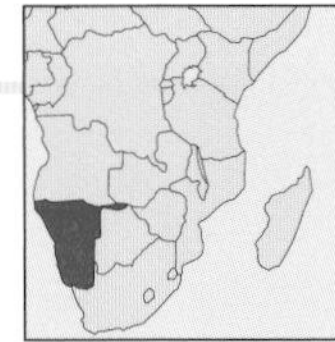

Namibia adopted this flag in 1990 when it gained its independence from South Africa. The red diagonal stripe and white borders are symbols of Namibia's human resources. The green and blue triangles and the gold sun represent the country's resources.

The Republic of Namibia lies on the Atlantic coast to the south of Angola and to the north of South Africa. The coastal region contains the arid Namib Desert, mostly between 900 m and 2,950–6,560 ft [2,000 m] above sea level, which is virtually uninhabited. Inland is a central plateau, bordered by a rugged spine of mountains stretching north–south.

Eastern Namibia contains part of the Kalahari, a semidesert area which extends into Botswana. The Orange River forms Namibia's southern border, while the Cunene and Cubango rivers form parts of the northern borders.

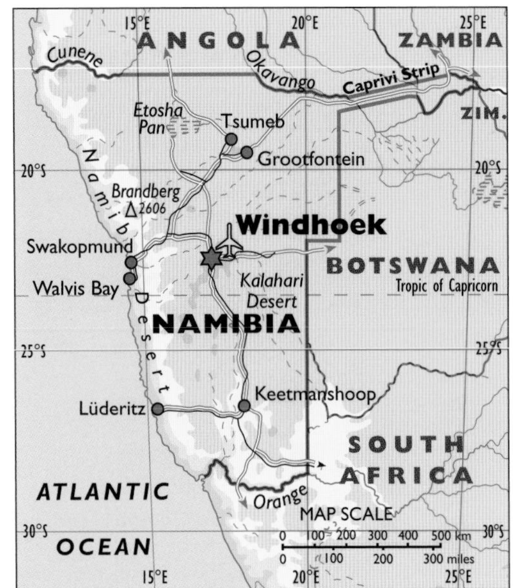

Area 318,259 sq mi [824,292 sq km]
Population 1,954,000
Capital (population) Windhoek (147,000)
Government Multiparty republic
Ethnic groups Ovambo 50%, Kavango 9%, Herero 7%, Damara 7%, White 6%, Nama 5%
Languages English (official), Afrikaans, German, indigenous dialects
Religions Christianity 90% (Lutheran 51%)
Currency Namibian dollar = 100 cents
Website www.grnnet.gov.na

CLIMATE

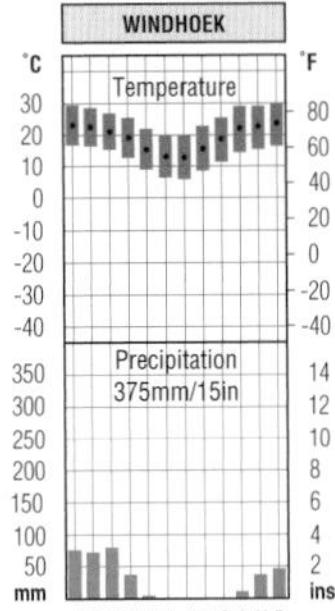

Namibia has a warm and largely arid climate. Daily temperatures range from about 75°F [24°C] in January to 68°F [20°C] in July. Annual rainfall ranges from about 20 in [500 mm] in northern areas to between 1 and 6 in [25 mm–150 mm] in the south. Most of the rain falls in summer.

HISTORY

The earliest people in Namibia were the San (also called Bushmen) and the Damara (Hottentots). Later arrivals were people who spoke Bantu languages. They migrated into Namibia from the north and included the Ovambo, Kavango and Herero. From 1868, Germans began to operate along the coast and, in 1884, Germany annexed the entire territory which they called German South West Africa. In the 1890s, the Germans forcibly removed the Damara and Herero from the Windhoek area. About 65,000 Herero were killed when they revolted against their eviction.

South African troops took over the territory in 1915 and five years later the League of Nations gave South Africa a mandate to govern the country, however, South Africa chose to rule it as though it were a South African province.

After World War II, many people challenged South Africa's right to govern the territory. A civil war began during the 1960s between African guerrillas and South African troops, with a ceasefire as finally being agreed in 1989. The country became independent in 1990.

Namibia's Caprivi Strip is a geographical oddity. The Strip was given to Germany by European powers in the late 19th century in order that Germany would have access to the River Zambezi. It became the scene of a rebellion in 1999 when a small band of rebels tried, unsuccessfully, to seize the regional capital, Kutima Mulilo, as part of an attempt to make the Caprivi Strip independent. The Strip is populated mainly by Lozi people, who resent SWAPO rule. Lozi separatists also live in Botswana and Zambia.

ECONOMY

Namibia has important mineral reserves, including diamonds, zinc, uranium, copper, lead, and tin. Mining is the most valuable economic activity and, by the mid-1990s, minerals accounted for as much as 90% of the exports, with diamonds making up over half the total revenue from minerals.

Farming employs around two out of every five Namibians, although many farmers live at subsistence level, contributing little to the economy. Because most of the land in Namibia has too little rainfall for arable farming, the principal agricultural activities are cattle and sheep raising. However, livestock raising has been hit in the last 20 years by extended droughts that have depleted the number of farm animals. The chief crops are corn, millet, and vegetables.

Fishing in the Atlantic Ocean is also important, though overfishing has reduced the yields of Namibia's fishing fleet. The country has few manufacturing industries apart from jewelry-making, some metal smelting, the processing of farm products, such as karakul pelts (sheepskins that are used to make fur coats), and textiles. Tourism is developing, especially in the Etosha National Park in northern Namibia, which is rich in wildlife.

POLITICS

After achieving independence, the government pursued a policy of "national reconciliation." An enclave on Namibia's coast, called Walvis Bay (Walvisbaai), remained part of South Africa until 1994, when South Africa transferred it to Namibia. In 2004, Sam Nujoma of the South West African People's Organization (SWAPO), who had been president since independence, retired. His successor was Hifikepunye Pohama.

Himba settlement, *girl standing beside herd; the Himba are a seminomadic pastoralist Herero people who live in Kaokoland to the northwest of Namibia; they herd sheep, goats and cattle*

WINDHOEK

Capital and largest city of Namibia, situated some 190 mi [300 km] inland from the Atlantic at a height of 5,410 ft [1,650 m]. Originally serving as the headquarters of a Nama chief, in 1892 it was made the capital of the new German colony of South West Africa. It was taken by South African troops in World War I. In 1990, it became capital of independent Namibia. An important world trade market for karakul sheepskins, its industries include diamonds, copper, and meat-packing. The German heritage is still very much in evidence with German restaurants selling traditional food and the German language still prevalent.

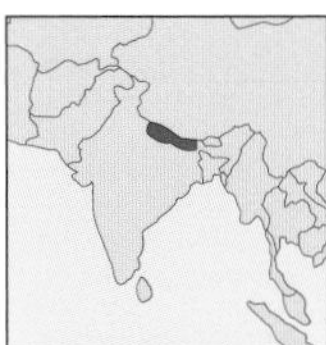

This Himalayan kingdom's uniquely shaped flag was adopted in 1962. It came about in the 19th century when two triangular pennants—the royal family's crescent moon symbol and the powerful Rana family's sun symbol—were joined together.

The Kingdom of Nepal in central Asia, lies between India to the south and China to the north. More than three-quarters of the country is in the Himalayan mountain heartland, culminating in the world's highest peak Mount Everest (or Chomolongma in Nepali), at 29,035 ft [8,850 m].

Nepal comprises three distinct regions. A southern lowland area (*terai*) of grassland and forests is the main location of Nepal's agriculture and timber industry. The central Siwalik mountains and valleys are divided between the basins of the Ghaghara, Gandak, and Kosi rivers. Between the Gandak and Kosi lies Katmandu valley, Nepal's most populous area. The last region is the main section of the Himalayas. Vegetation varies widely according to altitude.

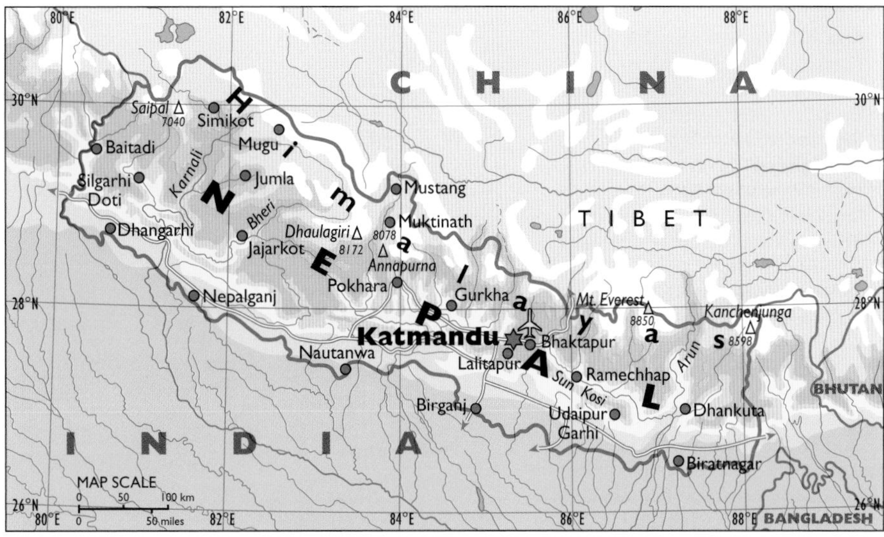

CLIMATE

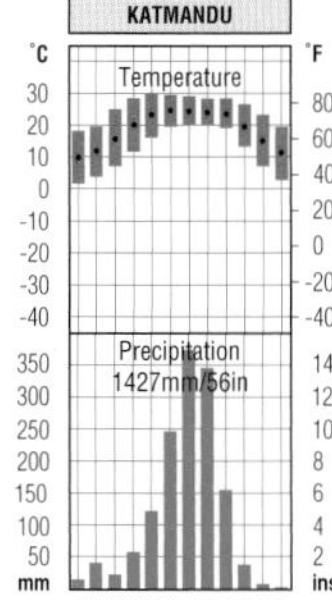

The huge differences in altitude give Nepal a wide variety of climatic regions.

HISTORY

In 1482 the kingdom of Nepal was divided into three, Bhadgaon, Kathmandu and Patan. It was nearly four hundred years later in 1768 when the three kingdoms finally resolved their differences and unified to form what is now known as Nepal. Between 1815 and 1816 the Anglo-Nepalese War took place as a result of rivalry between Nepal and the British East India Company over the annexation of minor states bordering Nepal. In exchange for autonomy the Nepalese signed The Treaty of Sugauli ceding parts of the Terrai and Sikkim to the British East India Company.

From 1846 to 1951, hereditary prime ministers from the Rana family ruled Nepal. In 1923, Britain recognized Nepal as a sovereign state. Gurkha soldiers fought in the British Army during both World Wars. In 1951, the Rana government was overthrown and the monarchy reestablished. The first national constitution was adopted in 1959, and free elections were held. In 1960, King Mahendra dissolved parliament and introduced a political system based on village councils (*panchayat*). In 1972, Birendra succeeded his father as king.

POLITICS

In 1990, after mass protests, a new constitution limited the power of the monarchy. In 1991 the Nepali Congress Party (NCP), led by G.P. Koirala, won multiparty elections. The NCP dominated the unstable politics of the 1990s, and Koirala led nine governments in ten years. Since the 1990s, a Maoist revolt has claimed more than 3,500 lives. A brief ceasefire was agreed in 2003, but fighting continued.

In 2001, King Birendra, his queen, and six other members of his family were shot dead by his heir, Crown Prince Dipendra, who then took his own life. Gyanendra, Birendra's brother, became king.

Increasing Maoist activity led the king to take direct control of the government and appoint a new cabinet early in 2005.

ECONOMY

Nepal is one of the world's poorest countries, with a per capita gross national product of US$220 in 1999. Agriculture employs over 80% of the workforce, accounting for two-fifths of the gross domestic product. Export crops include herbs, jute, rice, spices, and wheat. Tourism, which is centered around the high Himalayas, has grown in importance since 1951, when the country first opened to foreigners. The government is highly dependent on aid to develop the infrastructure. There are also plans to exploit the hydroelectric potential offered by the Himalayan rivers.

Area 56,827 sq miles [147,181 sq km]
Population 27,071,000
Capital (population) Katmandu (695,000)
Government Constitutional monarchy
Ethnic groups Brahman, Chetri, Newar, Gurung, Magar, Tamang, Sherpa and others
Languages Nepali (official), local languages
Religions Hinduism 86%, Buddhism 8%, Islam 4%
Currency Nepalese rupee = 100 paisa
Website www.welcomenepal.com

Tengboche Monastery, *in the Everest region*

KATMANDU (KATHMANDU)

Capital of Nepal, situated 4,500 ft [1,370 m] above sea level in a Himalayan valley. Founded in AD 723, it was independent from the 15th century to 1768, when Gurkhas captured it. Katmandu is Nepal's administrative, commercial, and religious center. Sights of interest include many beautiful temples including Kasthamandap from which the city derives its name, the Royal Palace (Narayanhity Durbar), and the neo-classical Singha Durbar, former private residence of Rana prime ministers.

HIMALAYAS

System of mountains in southern Asia, extending 1,500 mi [2,400 km] north–south in an arc between Tibet and India-Pakistan. The mountains are divided into three ranges: the Greater Himalayas (north), which include Mount Everest and K2; the Lesser Himalayas; and the Outer Himalayas (south)

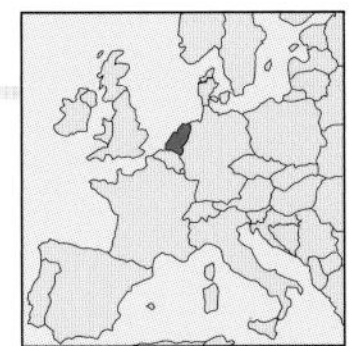

The flag of the Netherlands, one of Europe's oldest, dates from 1630, during the long struggle for independence from Spain which began in 1568. The tricolor became a symbol of liberty which inspired many other revolutionary flags around the world.

Area 16,033 sq mi [41,526 sq km]
Population 16,318,000
Capital (population) Amsterdam (729,000); The Hague (seat of government, 440,000)
Government Constitutional monarchy
Ethnic groups Dutch 83%, Indonesian, Turkish, Moroccan and others
Languages Dutch (official), Frisian
Religions Roman Catholic 31%, Protestant 21%, Islam 4%, others
Currency Euro = 100 cents
Website www.holland.com

The Kingdom of the Netherlands lies at the western end of the North European Plain, which extends to the Ural Mountains in Russia. The country is largely flat, about 40% being below sea level at high tide. To prevent flooding, dikes have been built to hold back the waves. There are large areas called polders made up of land reclaimed from the sea.

CLIMATE

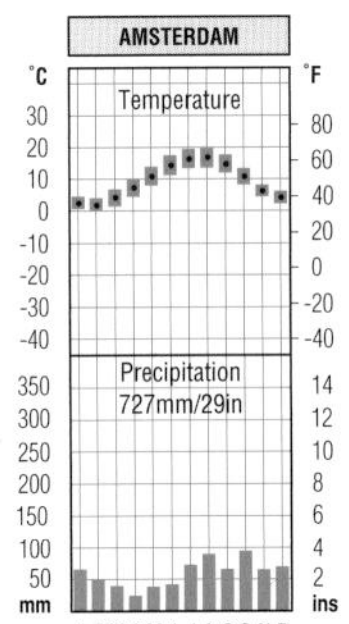

Because of its position on the North Sea, the Netherlands has a temperate climate. Winters are mild, with rain coming from the Atlantic depressions which pass over the country. North Sea storms often batter the coasts. Storm waves have periodically breached the dikes, causing flooding and sometimes loss of life.

HISTORY

Before the 16th century, the area that is now the Netherlands was under a succession of foreign rulers, including the Romans, the Germanic Franks, the French, and the Spanish. The Dutch declared their independence from Spain in 1581 this status finally being recognized by Spain in 1648. In the 17th century the Dutch built up a great overseas empire, especially in Southeast Asia.

France controlled the Netherlands from 1795 to 1813 and in 1815 the Netherlands, then containing both Belgium and Luxembourg, became an independent kingdom. Belgium broke away in 1830, Luxembourg followed in 1890.

The Netherlands was neutral in World War I, but occupied by German troops in World War II. Much of the Dutch fleet escaped and served with the Allies, but around three-quarters of the country's Jews were murdered, while many other people were forced to work in German factories. By the end of the war, about 270,000 Netherlanders had been killed or had died of starvation.

POLITICS

In 1948, the Netherlands formed an economic union called Benelux with Belgium and Luxembourg and, in 1949, it became a member of NATO. Economic recovery was rapid and in 1957 it became a founder member of the EEC.

In 1949, after much fighting, the Dutch recognized the independence of its largest overseas possession, Indonesia. In 1954, Suriname and the Netherlands Antilles were granted self-government. In 1962, the Dutch handed over Netherlands New Guinea to the United Nations, which handed it over, as Irian Jaya, to Indonesia in 1963. Suriname became fully independent in 1975.

In 1953, waves penetrated the coastal defenses in the southwestern delta region, flooding about 4.3% of the country, destroying or damaging more than 30,000 houses and killing 1,800 people. Within three weeks, a commission of enquiry had recommended the Delta Plan, a huge project to protect the delta region. Completed in 1986, it involved the construction of massive dams and floodgates, which are closed during severe storms.

The Maastricht Treaty, which transformed the EEC into the European Union, was signed in the Dutch city of Maastricht in 1991. Since January 1, 2002, the euro has been its sole currency.

ECONOMY

The Netherlands has the world's 14th largest economy, it is a highly industrialized country. Manufacturing and commerce are the most valuable activities. Mineral resources include china clay, natural gas, oil and salt. It imports many of the materials needed by its industries. The products are wide-ranging, including aircraft, chemical products, electronic equipment, machinery, textiles and vehicles. In the area south of Rotterdam, the Dutch have constructed a vast port and industrial area, Europoort. Together with Rotterdam's own facilities, the complex is the largest and busiest in the world.

Agriculture employs only 5% of the workforce, but, through the use of scientific techniques, yields are high. The Dutch cut and sell more than 3 billion flowers a year. Dairy farming is the leading farming activity. In the areas above sea level, farming includes both cattle and crops. Major food crops include barley, potatoes, sugar beets, and wheat.

***Keizersgracht,** Amsterdam; one of the canals that runs from the Amstel clockwise towards het IJ*

AMSTERDAM

Capital and largest city in the Netherlands, on the River Amstel, linked to the North Sea by the North Sea Canal. Amsterdam was chartered in 1300 and joined the Hanseatic League in 1369. The Dutch East India Company (1602) brought great prosperity to the city. It became a notable center of learning and book printing during the 17th century. It was captured by the French in 1795 and blockaded by the British during the Napoleonic Wars. Amsterdam was badly damaged during the German occupation during World War II. A major port and one of Europe's leading financial and cultural centers, it has an important stock exchange and diamond-cutting industry.

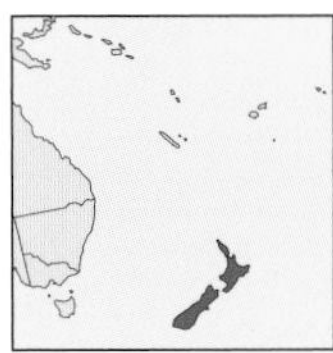

New Zealand's flag was designed in 1869 and adopted as the national flag in 1907 when New Zealand became an independent dominion. The flag includes the British Blue Ensign and four of the five stars in the Southern Cross constellation.

New Zealand lies about 994 mi [1,600 km] southeast of Australia. It consists of two main islands and several other small ones. New Zealand is mountainous and partly volcanic. The Southern Alps contain the country's highest peak, Aoraki Mount Cook, at 12,313 ft3,753 m []. Minor earthquakes are common and there are several areas of volcanic and geothermal activity, especially on North Island.

About 75% of New Zealand lies above the 650 ft [200 m] contour. In the south east, broad, fertile valleys have been cut by rivers between the low ranges. The only extensive lowland area of New Zealand is the Canterbury Plains. As a result of its isolation, almost 90% of the indigenous plants are unique to the country.

Much of the original vegetation has been destroyed and only small areas of the kauri forests have survived. Mixed evergreen forest grows on the western side of South Island. Beech forests grow in the highlands and large plantations are grown for timber.

Area 104,453 sq miles [270,534 sq km]
Population 3,994,000
Capital (population) Wellington (167,000)
Government Constitutional monarchy
Ethnic groups New Zealand European 74%, New Zealand Maori 10%, Polynesian 4%
Languages English and Maori (both official)
Religions Anglican 24%, Presbyterian 18%, Roman Catholic 15%, others
Currency New Zealand dollar = 100 cents
Website www.govt.nz

CLIMATE

Auckland in the north has a warm, humid climate throughout the year. Wellington has cooler summers, while in Dunedin, to the southeast, temperatures sometimes dip below freezing in winter. The rainfall is heaviest on the western highlands.

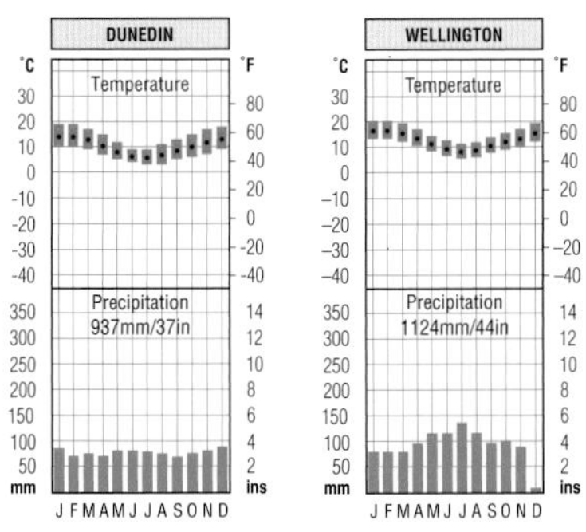

HISTORY

Early Maori settlers arrived in New Zealand more than 1,000 years ago. The Dutch navigator Abel Janszoon Tasman reached the area in 1642, but after several of his men were killed by Maoris, he made no further attempt to land. His discovery was not followed up until 1769, when the British Captain James Cook rediscovered the islands.

British settlers arrived in the early 19th century and in 1840, under the Treaty of Waitangi, Britain took possession of the islands. Clashes occurred with the Maoris in the 1860s, but from the 1870s the Maoris were gradually integrated into society. In 1893, New Zealand became the first country in the world to give women the vote and in 1907, it became a self-governing dominion in the British Empire.

New Zealanders fought alongside the Allies in both World Wars. In 1952, New Zealand signed the ANZUS treaty, a mutual defense pact with Australia and the United States. Troops from New Zealand served in the Korean War (1950–3) and a few units later served in the war in Vietnam.

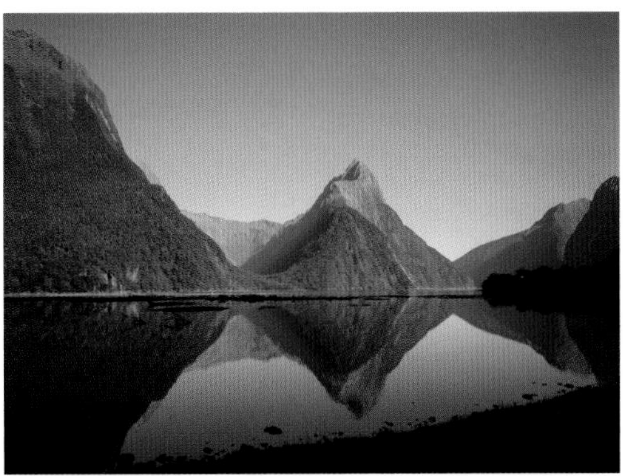

***The peaceful waters of Milford Sound** reflect surrounding wooded mountains, South Island*

POLITICS

After Britain joined the EEC (now the EU) in 1973, New Zealand's exports to Britain shrank from 70% to 10%. Along with its reevaluation of its defense position through ANZUS, it also had to reassess its economic strategy. This has involved seeking new markets in Asia, cutting subsidies to farmers, privatization, and cutting back on its extensive welfare programs in the 1990s. The rights of Maoris and the preservation of their culture are other major political issues in New Zealand. In 1998, New Zealand completed a NZ$170 million settlement with the Ngai Tahu group on South Island in compensation for forced land purchases in the 19th century. The government expressed its profound regret for past suffering and for injustices that had impaired the development of the Ngai Tahu. Ties with Britain have been gradually reduced and in 2005 the prime minister, Helen Clark, stated that the country would eventually abolish the monarchy and become a republic.

ECONOMY

Manufacturing now employs twice as many people as agriculture. Meat and dairy products are the most valuable agricultural products. The country has more than 45 million sheep, 4.3 million dairy cattle, and 4.6 million beef cattle. Major crops include barley, fruits, potatoes and other vegetables, and wheat. Fishing is also important. The chief manufactures are processed food products, including butter, cheese, frozen meat, and woollen products.

WELLINGTON

Capital and region of New Zealand, in the extreme south of North Island, on Port Nicholson, an inlet of Cook Strait. First visited by Europeans in 1826, it was founded in 1840. In 1865 it replaced Auckland as capital. Wellington's excellent harbor furthered its development as a transportation and trading center. It is the world's southernmost capital city.

Nicaragua

The colors of the flag are in homage to Argentina. Central America is represented by the white stripe; the Atlantic and Pacific Oceans are the blue stripes. The coat of arms features five volcanoes, a rainbow for hope and red Liberty cap for freedom.

Area 50,193 sq mi [130,000 sq km]
Population 5,360,000
Capital (population) Managua (1,109,000)
Government Multiparty republic
Ethnic groups Mestizo 69%, White 17%, Black 9%, Amerindian 5%
Languages Spanish (official)
Religions Roman Catholic 85%, Protestant
Currency Córdoba oro (gold córdoba) = 100 centavos
Website www.intur.gob.ni/index_eng.html

MANAGUA

Capital of Nicaragua, on the southern shore of Lake Managua, west-central Nicaragua. It became the capital in 1855. Managua suffered damage from earthquakes in 1931 and 1962. It is the economic, industrial, and commercial hub of Nicaragua. Industries include textiles, tobacco, and cement.

The Republic of Nicaragua is the largest country in Central America. The Central Highlands rise in the north west Cordillera Isabella to more than 6,000 ft [1,800 m] and are the source for many of the rivers that drain the eastern plain. The Caribbean coast forms part of the Mosquito Coast. Lakes Managua and Nicaragua lie on the edge of a narrow volcanic region, which contains Nicaragua's major urban areas, including the capital, Managua, and the second-largest city, León. This region is highly unstable, with many active volcanoes, and is prone to earthquakes.

Rainforests cover large areas in the east, with trees such as cedar, mahogany, and walnut. Tropical savanna is common in the drier west.

CLIMATE

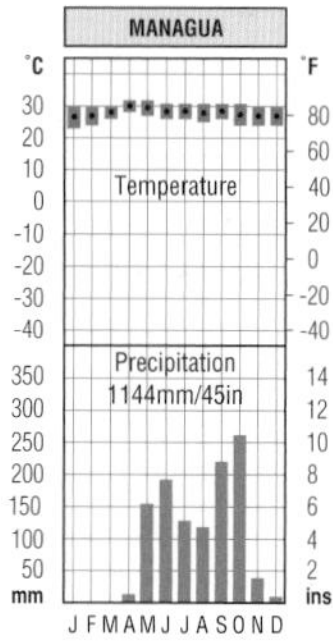

Nicaragua has a tropical climate, with a rainy season from June to October. Cooler weather is found in the Central Highlands. The wettest part is the Mosquito Coast, with 165 in [4,200 mm] of rain.

HISTORY

Spanish explorer Christopher Columbus reached Nicaragua in 1502, and claimed the land for Spain. Colonization claimed the lives of c. 100,000 Native Americans. By 1518 Nicaragua had become part of the Spanish Captaincy-General of Guatemala.

In 1821, Nicaragua gained independence, later forming part of the Central American Federation from 1825 to 1838. In the mid-19th century, civil war and US and British interference ravaged Nicaragua. The USA sought the construction of a trans-isthmian canal through Nicaragua. In 1855, William Walker invaded and briefly established himself as president. José Santos Zemalya's dictatorship from 1893 to 1909 gained control of Mosquito Coast and formed close links with the British. Following his downfall, civil war raged once more. In 1912, US marines landed to protect the pro-US regime, and in 1916 the USA gained exclusive rights to the canal. Opposition to US occupation resulted in guerrilla war, led by Augusto César Sandino. In 1933, the US marines withdrew but set up a National Guard to help defeat the rebels.

In 1934 Anastasio Somoza, director of the National Guard, assassinated Sandino. Somoza became president in 1937. His dictatorial regime led to political isolation. Somoza was succeeded by his sons Luis in 1956 and Anastasio in 1967. Anastasio's diversion of international relief aid following the devastating 1972 Managua earthquake cemented opposition.

POLITICS

In 1979, the Sandinista National Liberation Front (FSLN) overthrew the Somoza regime. The Sandinista government, led by Daniel Ortega, instigated wide-ranging socialist reforms. The USA, concerned about the Sandinistas' ties with communist regimes, sought to destabilize the government by supporting the Contra rebels. A ten-year civil war devastated the economy and led to political dissatisfaction. The conflict ended when the Sandinista agreed to free elections.

In the 1990 elections, the National Opposition Union coalition, led by Violeta Chamorro, defeated the Sandinistas. However, the Contra were disbanded and Chamorro's coalition partners and the Sandinista-controlled trade unions blocked many of her reforms. In 1996 elections, Liberal leader Arnoldo Aleman defeated Chamorro.

In 1998, Hurricane Mitch killed c.4,000 people and caused extensive damage. Enrique Bolanos became president at elections in 2001. In 2003, former president Arnoldo Aleman was sentenced to 20 years in prison for corruption.

ECONOMY

Nicaragua faces problems in rebuilding its economy and introducing free-market reforms. Agriculture is the main activity, employing 50% of the workforce and accounting for 70% of exports. Major cash crops include coffee, cotton, sugar, and bananas. Rice is the main food crop.

There is some copper, gold, and silver, but mining is underdeveloped. Most manufacturing is based around Managua.

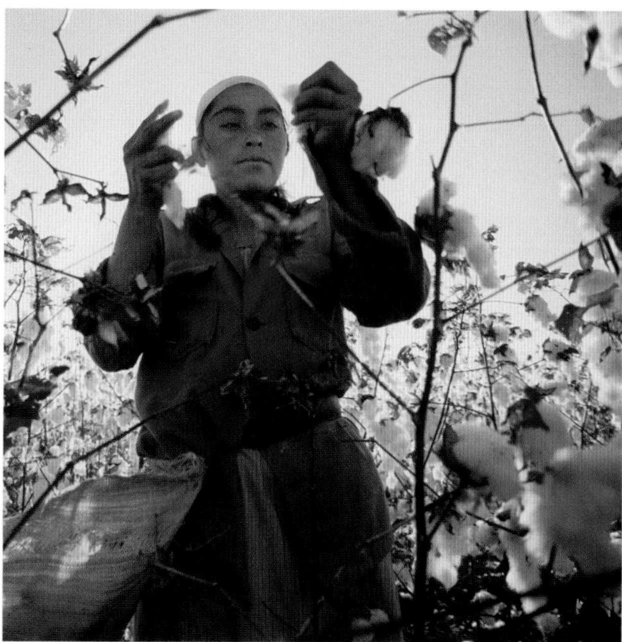

Cotton picking; *cotton is one of the key crops of Nicaragua*

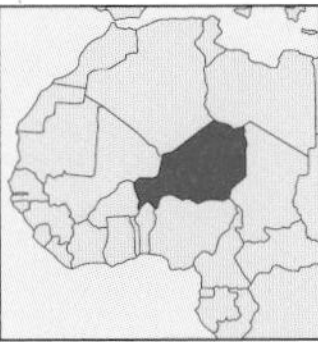

This flag was adopted shortly before Niger became independent from France in 1960. The orange stripe represents the Sahara in the north and the green represents the grasslands in the south. Between them, the white stripe represents the River Niger, with a circle for the sun.

The Republic of Niger is a landlocked nation in north-central Africa. The northern plateaus lie in the Sahara, while north-central Niger contains the rugged Aïr Mountains, which reach a height of 6,632 ft [2,022 m] above sea level near Agadez. The rainfall in the mountains—averaging around 7 in [175 mm] per year—is sufficient in places to permit the growth of thorny shrub. Severe droughts since the 1970s have crippled the traditional lifestyle of the nomads in northern and central Niger as the Sahara has slowly advanced south. The southern region has also been hit by droughts.

The south consists of broad plains. The Lake Chad Basin lies in southeastern Niger on the borders with Chad and Nigeria. The only permanent rivers are the Niger and its tributaries in the southwest. The narrow Niger Valley is the country's most fertile and densely populated region and includes the capital Niamey. Yet Niger, a title which comes from a Tuareg word meaning "flowing water," seems scarcely appropriate for a country which consists mainly of hot, arid, sandy, and stony basins.

Buffaloes, elephants, giraffes. and lions are found in the "W" National Park, which Niger shares with Benin and Burkina Faso. Most of southern Niger lies in the Sahel region of dry grassland. The Aïr Mountains support grass and scrub. The northern deserts are generally barren.

CLIMATE

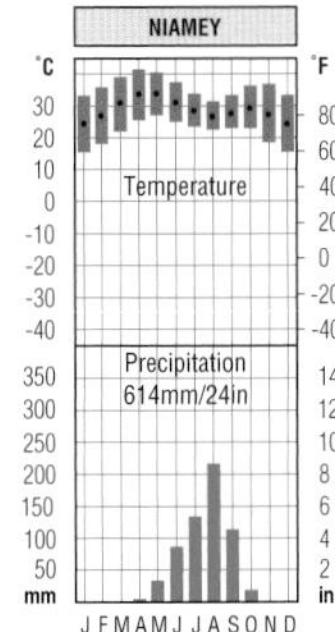

Niger is one of the world's hottest countries. The warmest months are March to May, when the harmattan wind blows from the Sahara. Niamey has a tropical climate, with a rainy season from June to September. Rainfall decreases from south to north. Northern Niger is practically rainless. The far south consists of tropical savanna.

HISTORY

Neolithic remains have been found in the northern desert. Nomadic Tuareg settled in the Aïr Mountains in the 11th century AD, and by the 13th century established a state centered around Agadez and the trans-Saharan trade. In the 14th century, the Hausa settled in southern Niger. In the early 16th century, the Songhai Empire controlled much of Niger, but the Moroccans supplanted the Songhai at the turn of the century.

NIAMEY

Capital of Niger, West Africa, in the southwestern part of the country, on the River Niger. It became capital of the French colony of Niger in 1926. It grew rapidly after World War II and is now the country's largest city and its commercial and administrative center. Manufactures include textiles, ceramics, plastics, and chemicals.

Grand Marché, Niamey; *the largest of Niamey's markets and one of the best in west Africa, selling everything from beads to mosquito nets*

Area 489,189 sq mi [1,267,000 sq km]
Population 11,361,000
Capital (population) Niamcy (732,000)
Government Multiparty republic
Ethnic groups Hausa 56%, Djerma 22%, Tuareg 8%, Fula 8%, others
Languages French (official), Hausa, Djerma
Religions Islam 80%, indigenous beliefs, Christianity
Currency CFA franc = 100 centimes
Website www.un.int/niger

Later on, the Hausa and then the Fulani set up kingdoms in the region. In the early 19th century, the Fulani gained control of much of southern Niger. The first French expedition arrived in 1891, but Tuareg resistance prevented full occupation until 1914.

POLITICS

In 1922, Niger became a colony within French West Africa. In 1958, Niger voted to remain an autonomous republic within the French Community. It gained full independence in 1960, and Hamani Diori became Niger's first president. He maintained close ties with France.

Drought in the Sahel began in 1968, and killed many livestock and destroyed crops. In 1974, a group of army officers, led by Lieutenant Colonel Seyni Kountché, overthrew Hamani Diori and suspended the constitution. Kountché died in 1987, and was succeeded by his cousin General Ali Saibou. In 1991, the Tuareg in northern Niger began an armed campaign for greater autonomy. A national conference removed Saibou and established a transitional government. In 1993 multiparty elections, Mahamane Ousmane of the Alliance of Forces for Change (AFC) coalition became president. The collapse of the coalition led to fresh elections in 1995, which were won by the National Movement for a Development Society (MNSD), but a military coup, led by Colonel Ibrahim Bare Mainassara, seized power. In 1995, the government and the Tuaregs signed a peace accord. Elections in 1996 confirmed Mainassara as president. In 1999, bodyguards assassinated Mainassara and he was replaced briefly by Major Daouda Malam Wanke. Parliamentary rule was restored and, later that year, Tandjou Mamadou was elected president. He was reelected in 2004.

ECONOMY

Droughts have caused great hardship and food shortages in Niger, and have destroyed much of the traditional nomadic lifestyle. Niger's chief resource is uranium, and it is the world's second-largest producer. Uranium accounts for more than 80% of exports, most of which goes to France. Some tin and tungsten are also mined. Other mineral resources are largely unexploited.

Niger is one of the world's poorest countries, despite its resources. Farming employs 85% of the workforce, although only 3% of the land is arable and 7% is used for grazing. Food crops include beans, cassava, millet, rice, and sorghum. Cotton and groundnuts are leading cash crops.

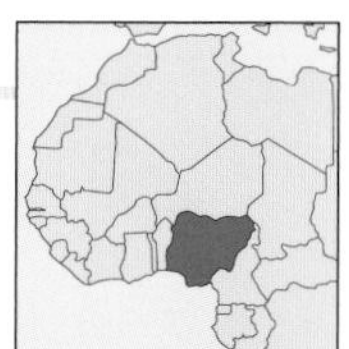

Nigeria's flag was adopted in 1960 when Nigeria became independent from Britain. It was selected after a competition to find a suitable design. The green represents Nigeria's forests. The white in the center stands for peace.

The Federal Republic of Nigeria is the most populous nation in Africa. The country's main rivers are the Niger and Benue, which meet in central Nigeria. North of the two river valleys are high plains and plateaus. The Lake Chad Basin is in the northeast, with the Sokoto plains in the northwest. Southern Nigeria contains hilly uplands and broad coastal plains, including the swampy Niger Delta. Highlands form the border with Cameroon. Mangrove swamps line the coast, behind which are rainforests. The north contains large areas of savanna with forests along the rivers. Open grassland and semidesert occur in drier areas.

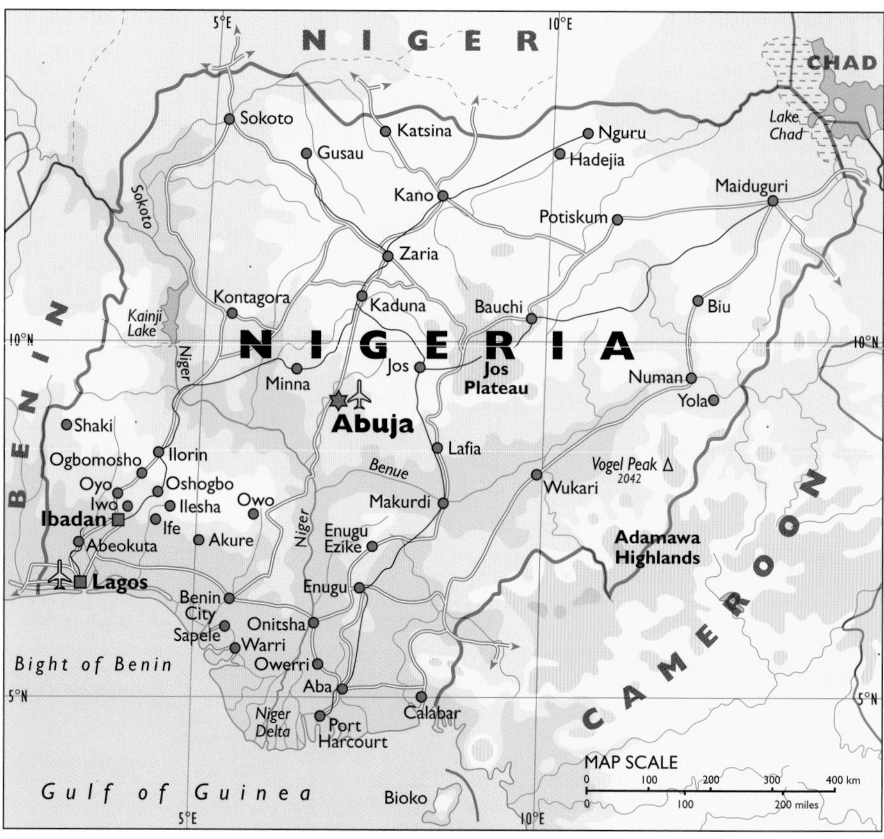

ABUJA

Nigeria's administrative capital since 1991. The new city was designed by the Japanese architect Kenzo Tange, and work began in 1976. The change was decided upon because it was thought that the capital city should be in the center of the country. The previous capital, Lagos, which lies on the coast close to the border of Benin is still the commercial capital. Although the government has moved to Abuja, much of the city remains under construction.

Area 356,667 sq mi [923,768 sq km]
Population 137,253,000
Capital (population) Abuja (339,000)
Government Federal multiparty republic
Ethnic groups Hausa and Fulani 29%, Yoruba 21%, Ibo (or Igbo) 18%, Ijaw 10%, Kanuri 4%
Languages English (official), Hausa, Yoruba, Ibo
Religions Islam 50%, Christianity 40%, traditional beliefs
Currency Naira = 100 kobo
Website www.nigeria.gov.ng

CLIMATE

The south of the country has high temperatures and rain all year. Parts of the coast have an average annual rainfall of 150 in [3,800 mm]. The north has a marked dry season and higher temperatures than the south.

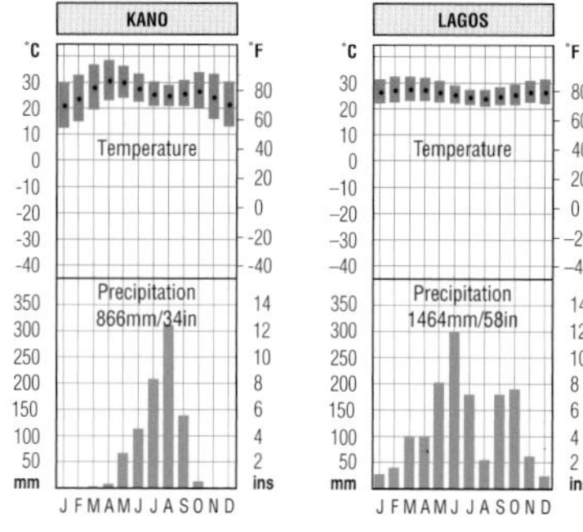

HISTORY

Nigeria has a long artistic tradition. Major cultures include the Nok (500 BC to AD 200), Ife, which developed about 1,000 years ago, and Benin, which flourished between the 15th and 17th centuries.

Britain outlawed slavery in 1807 and soon afterwards the British began to trade in agricultural products. In 1851, Britain made Lagos a base from which they could continue their efforts to stop the slave trade. During the second half of the 19th century, Britain gradually extended its influence over Nigeria. By 1914 it ruled the entire country.

POLITICS

Nigeria became independent in 1960 and a federal republic in 1963. A federal constitution dividing the country into regions was necessary because Nigeria contains more than 250 ethnic and linguistic groups, as well as several religious ones. Local rivalries have long been a threat to national unity. In 1967, in an attempt to meet the demands of more ethnic groups, the country's four regions were replaced by 12 states. The division of the Eastern Region provoked an uprising. In 1967, the governor of the Eastern Region, Colonel Odumegwu Ojukwu, proclaimed it an independent republic called Biafra. Civil war continued until Biafra's surrender in January 1970.

The country had only nine years of civilian government between independence in 1960 and 1998. In 1998-9 civilian rule was restored. A former military leader, Olusegun Obasanjo, was elected president and reelected in 2003. Ethnic and religious differences are a threat to national unity. In the late 1990s and early 2000s, ethnic riots broke out between Yorubas and Hausas in the southwest, while the introduction of *sharia* (Islamic law) in northern states has caused friction between Muslims and Christians. The government declared in 2004 that it had put down an uprising in the northeast aimed at creating a Muslim state, while ethnic and religious conflict continued in other parts of the country. In 2006 parliament blocked an attempt by Obasanjo's supporters to amend the charter to allow the president to stand for a third term.

ECONOMY

Despite its many natural resources, including oil reserves, metals, forests, and fertile farmland, Nigeria is a "low-income" developing economy. Agriculture employs 43% of the workforce and Nigeria is one of the world's leading producers of cocoa beans, groundnuts, palm oil and kernels, and natural rubber. Leading food crops include beans, cassava, corn, millet, plantains, rice, sorghum, and yams.

This flag became the national flag of Norway in 1898, although merchant ships had used it since 1821. The design is based on the Dannebrog, the flag of Denmark, the country which ruled Norway from the 14th century until the early 19th century.

The Kingdom of Norway forms the western part of the mountainous Scandinavian Peninsula. The landscape is dominated by rolling plateaux, the vidda, which are generally between 1,000–3,000 ft [300 m and 900 m] high, but some peaks rise from 5,000–8,000 ft [1,500 m to 2,400 m] in the area between Oslo, Bergen and Trondheim. The highest areas retain permanent icefields, as in the Jotunheimen Mountains above Sognefjord.

Norway's jagged coastline is the longest in Europe. The vidda are cut by long, narrow, steep-sided fjords on the west coast. The largest of the fjords, is Sognefjord, which is 127 mi [203 km] long and less than 3 mi [5 km] wide.

CLIMATE

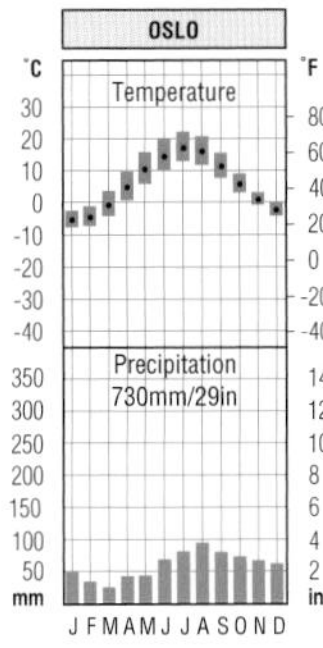

The warm North Atlantic Drift flows off the coast and moderates the country's climate, with milder winters and cooler summers. Most of Norway's ports remain ice-free all year. Inland, away from the moderating effects of the sea, the climate becomes more severe. Winters are bitterly cold with snow cover for at least three months of the year.

HISTORY

From about AD 800, Vikings from Norway roamed the northern seas, raiding and founding colonies around the coasts of Britain, Iceland and even North America. In about 900, Norway was united under Harold I, the country's first king. Viking power ended in the late 11th century. In 1380, Norway was united with Denmark and in 1397 Sweden joined the union. Sweden broke away in 1523 and, in 1526, Denmark, which had become increasingly powerful, made Norway a Danish province.

In 1814, Denmark ceded Norway to Sweden, but retained Norway's colonies of Greenland, Iceland, and the Faeroe Islands. Norway finally ended its union with Sweden in 1905. The Norwegians chose as their king a Danish prince, who took the title Haakon VII.

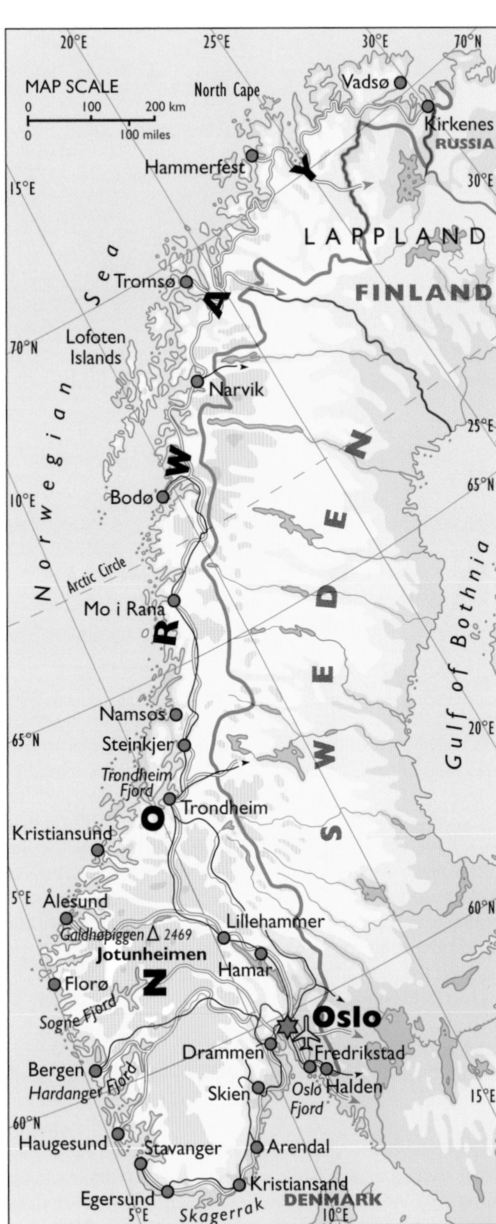

Area 125,049 sq mi [323,877 sq km]
Population 4,575,000
Capital (population) Oslo (513,000)
Government Constitutional monarchy
Ethnic groups Norwegian 97%
Languages Norwegian (official)
Religions Evangelical Lutheran 86%
Currency Norwegian krone = 100 øre
Website www.norge.no

Despite being neutral in World War I, and seeking to remain so in World War II, German troops invaded in 1940.

POLITICS

After World War II, Norwegians worked to rebuild their economy and their merchant fleet. The economy was boosted in the 1970s, when Norway began producing petroleum and natural gas from wells in the North Sea. Rapid economic growth has ensured that Norwegians are among the most prosperous in Europe.

In 1949, it became a member of NATO, though neither NATO bases nor nuclear weapons were permitted on its soil for fear of provoking its neighbor, the Soviet Union. In 1960, Norway and six other countries formed the European Free Trade Association while continuing to work with its Scandinavian neighbors through the Nordic Council. In 1994, Norwegians again voted against membership of the EU. The 1990s–2000s saw Norwegian diplomats seeking to broker peace deals in Sri Lanka and Palestine.

ECONOMY

Norway's chief resources and exports are oil and natural gas. Dairy farming and meat production are the chief farming activities, though Norway has to import food. Industries include petroleum products, chemicals, aluminum, wood products, machinery, and clothing.

OSLO

Capital of Norway, in the south of the country. The city is located at the head of Oslo Fjord and is surrounded by forest. Founded in the 11th century it was largely destroyed by fire in 1624. Christian IV rebuilt the city, naming it Christiania. In 1905, it became the capital of independent Norway. It acquired the name Oslo in 1925. Home to the Vigeland Sculpture Park, the Viking Ship Museum, and the Munch Museum, it is an important tourist center.

Farmer with a reindeer herd, *Arrisovarre, Norwegian Lappland*

Oman

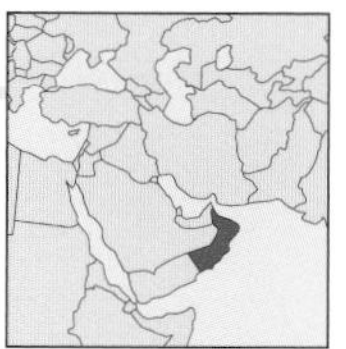

White symbolizes peace. Green is traditional Islamic color, also standing for the fertility of the land. Red represents the blood shed in the struggle for liberation. The Sultanate's white coat of arms consists of two crossed swords, a khnajar (dagger), and belt.

Area 119,498 sq mi [309,500 sq km]
Population 2,903,000
Capital (population) Muscat (41,000)
Government Monarchy with consultative council
Ethnic groups Arab, Baluchi, Indian, Pakistani
Languages Arabic (official), Baluchi, English
Religions Islam (mainly Ibadhi), Hinduism
Currency Omani rial = 100 baizas
Website www.omanet.om/english/home.asp

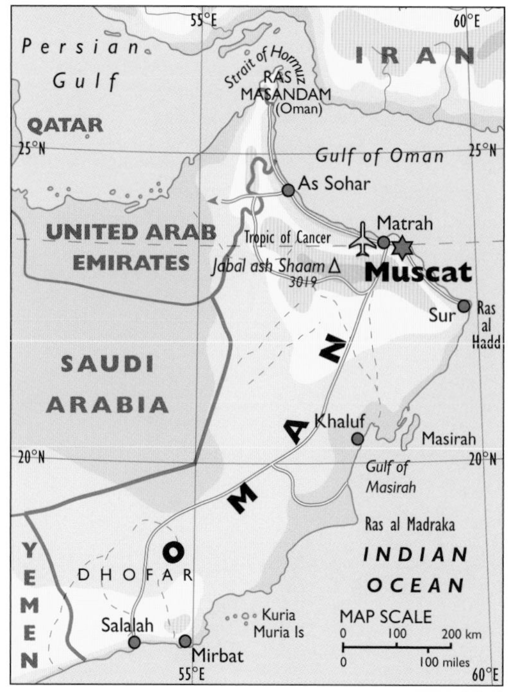

The Sultanate of Oman is the oldest independent nation in the Arab world. It occupies the southeastern corner of the Arabian peninsula and includes the tip of the Musandam Peninsula which is separated from the rest of Oman by UAE territory. This peninsula overlooks the strategic Strait of Hormuz.

The Al Halar al Gharbi range, rising to 9,904 ft [3,019 m] above sea level, borders the narrow coastal plain in the north. This fertile plain along the Gulf of Oman is called Al Battinah. Inland are deserts, including part of the Rub' al Khali (Empty Quarter). Much of the land along the Arabian Sea is barren, but the province of Zufar (or Dhofar) in the southeast is a hilly, fertile region.

CLIMATE

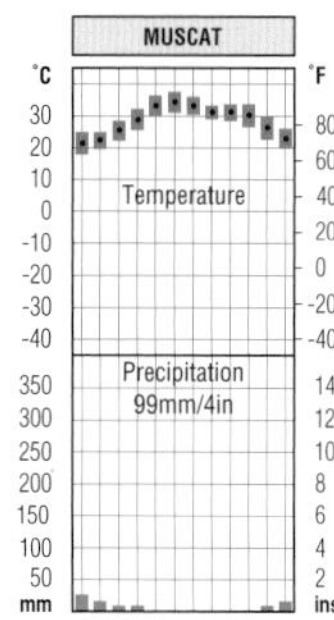

Temperatures in Oman can reach 129°F [54°C] in summer, but winters are mild to warm. Rainfall in the northern mountains can exceed 16 in [400 mm] per year, while in the southeast it can be up to 25 in [630 mm], but for most of Oman the desert climate means less than 6 in [150 mm] per year.

Sandstorms, duststorms, and droughts feature and occasionally, tropical cyclones bring stormy weather.

HISTORY

Oman first became a major trading region 5,000 years ago. Islam was introduced into the area in the 7th century and today, 75% of the population follow the strict Ibadi Islam sect.

The Portuguese conquered its ports in the early 16th century, but local Arabs forced them out in 1650. The Al Bu Said family came to power in the 1740s and has ruled the country ever since. British influence dates back to the end of the 18th century, when the two countries entered into the first of several treaties.

In 1920, Britain brokered an agreement whereby the interior was ruled by imams, with coastal areas under the control of the Sultan. Clashes between the two groups continued into the 1950s, but Sultan Said bin Taimur regained control of the whole country in 1959.

***New houses in Al Khuwair,** Muscat*

POLITICS

Under Sultan Said bin Taimur, Oman had been an isolated, feudal country. Its economy was backward compared to its oil-rich Gulf neighbors. However, after Sultan Said bin Taimur was deposed by his son, Sultan Qaboos ibn Said, in 1970, Oman made substantial strides. With the help of soldiers from Iran and Jordan, he saw an end to war against Yemen-backed separatist guerrillas in the province of Zufar (1965–1975). He also led the way in developing an expanding economy based on oil reserves far larger than expected when production began in 1967. Qaboos opened up Oman to the outside world, ending the isolation it had long endured. At home, he avoided the prestigious projects favored by Arab leaders to concentrate on social programs, including the education of girls. His leadership proved popular despite the lack of a democratic government.

In 1991, Oman took part in the military campaign to liberate Kuwait. In 1997, Oman held its first direct elections to a Consultative Council. Unusually for the Gulf region, two women were elected. In 1999, Oman and the United Arab Emirates signed an agreement, confirming most of the borders between them. In 2001, while a military campaign was being launched in Afghanistan, Britain held military exercises in the Omani desert. This was an example of the longstanding political and military relationship between the two countries. In 2003, elections were held to the Consultative Council. For the first time, all citizens over 21 were allowed to vote although no parties are allowed. In 2004, the Sultan appointed the first woman minister with portfolio. In 2005, nearly 100 suspected Islamists were arrested and 31 were convicted of trying to overthrow the government, but they were later pardoned.

ECONOMY

The World Bank classifies Oman as an "upper-middle-income" developing country. It has sizeable oil and natural gas deposits, a large trade surplus and low inflation. Oil accounts for more than 90% of Oman's export revenues. Huge natural gas deposits, equal to all the finds of the previous 20 years, were discovered in 1991. Although only about 0.3% of the land is cultivated, agriculture and fishing are the traditional economic activities. Major crops include alfalfa, bananas, coconuts, dates, tobacco, and wheat. Water supply is a major problem. Oman depends on water from underground aquifers, which will eventually run dry. and also from desalination plants. Industries include copper smelting, cement, and chemicals, as well as food processing and import substitution. Tourism is a growing activity.

MUSCAT (MASQAT, MASKAT)

Capital of Oman, on the Gulf of Oman, in the southeast Arabian Peninsula. The Portuguese held Muscat from 1508 to 1650, when it passed to Persia. After 1741 it became capital of Oman. In the 20th century, Muscat's rulers developed treaty relations with Britain.

AMERICAN SAMOA

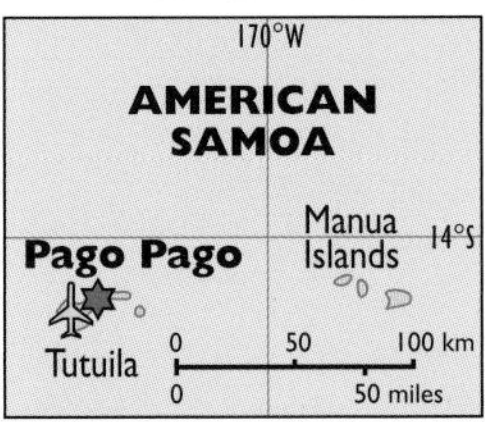

The Territory of American Samoa is an unincorporated territory of the United States and lies in the south-central Pacific Ocean. Two of its islands are coral islands, the other five are extinct volcanoes. The US took control of the islands between 1900 and 1904. The main industry is the canning of tuna; fish products dominate the economy.

Area 77 sq mi [199 sq km]
Population 58,000
Capital (population) Pago Pago (4,000)
Government Territory of the USA
Ethnic groups Native Pacific Islander 93%, Asian, White
Languages Samoan 91%, English 3%, Tongan 2%, other Pacific islander 2%
Religions Christian Congregationalist 50%, Protestant 30%, Roman Catholic 20%
Currency US dollar = 100 cents
Website www.asg-gov.net

COOK ISLANDS

A group of 15 islands in the south Pacific Ocean to the northeast of New Zealand consisting of the Northern (Manihiki) Cook Islands and the Southern (Lower) Cook Islands. A self-governing territory in free association with New Zealand. Discovered in 1773 by Captain James Cook, the islands became a British protectorate in 1888 and were annexed to New Zealand in 1901. They became self-governing in 1965. Products include copra and citrus fruits.

Area 113 sq mi [293 sq km]
Population 21,388
Capital (population) Avarua (12,188)
Government Self-governing parliamentary democracy
Ethnic groups Cook Island Maori (Polynesian) 88%
Languages English (official), Maori
Religions Cook Islands Christian Church 57%, Roman Catholic 17%, Seventh Day Saint 8%, Church of Latter Day Saints 4%, other Protestant 6%, others
Currency New Zealand dollar = 100 cents
Website www.ck

FRENCH POLYNESIA

French Polynesia consists of 130 islands, scattered over 1 million sq mi [2.5 million sq km] of the Pacific Ocean. The most densely populated island is Tahiti which is part of a group called the Society Islands. Tribal chiefs agreed to a French protectorate in 1843. They gained increased autonomy in 1984. Links with France ensure a high standard of living. Some favor independence. Following a struggle for power in 2004, the pro-independence Union for Democracy party, ousted the pro-French ruling party. The government is based in Papeete on Tahiti.

Area 1,544 sq mi [4,000 sq km]
Population 266,000
Capital (population) Papeete (24,000)
Government Overseas territory of France
Ethnic groups Polynesian 78%, Chinese 12%, local French 6%, metropolitan French 4%
Languages French 61%, Polynesian 31% (both official), Asian languages
Religions Protestant 54%, Roman Catholic 30%
Currency Comptoirs Francais du Pacifique franc = 100 centimes
Website www.presidence.pf

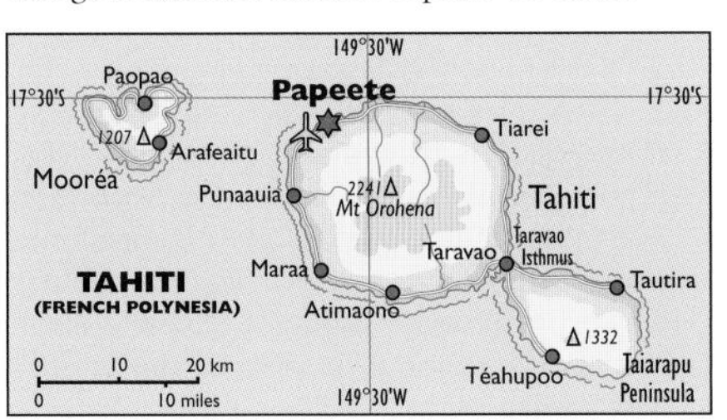

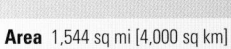

GUAM

The Territory of Guam is a strategically important "unincorporated territory" of the USA and the largest of the Mariana Islands in the Pacific Ocean. It is composed of a coralline limestone plateau. Guam was ruled by Spain from 1668 until it was ceded to the US in 1899 after the Spanish-American War in an agreement whereby the US paid $20 million for Guam and other Spanish-held territorie. Temperatures range from 75–86°F (26–30°C).

Area 212 sq mi [549 sq km]
Population 166,000
Capital (population) Hagatna (Agana) (1,000)
Government Territory of the USA
Ethnic groups Chamorro 37%, Filipino 26%, other Pacific islander 11%, white 7%, other Asian 6%
Languages English 38%, Chamorro 22%, Philippine languages 22%, other Pacific island languages 7%, Asian languages 7%, others
Religions Roman Catholic 85%, others 15%
Currency US dollar = 100 cents
Website www.visitguam.org

KIRIBATI

The Republic of Kiribati is an independent nation in the west Pacific Ocean. It comprises about 33 islands, including the Gilbert, Phoenix, and Line Islands, and straddles the Equator over an area of 2 million sq mi (5 million sq km). The islands are threatened by global warming and consequent rising sea levels. Rainfall is abundant.

British navigators first visited the Gilbert and Ellice Islands during the late 18th century. They became a British protectorate in 1892 and a colony in 1915. In 1975 the Ellice Islands, following a referendum, officially severed links with the Gilbert Islands and became a separate territory called Tuvalu in 1978. The Gilbert Islands became fully independent within the Commonwealth of Nations in 1979 as the Republic of Kiribati. Agriculture is now the major economic activity.

Area 280 sq mi [726 sq km]
Population 101,000
Capital (population) Bairiki (on Tarawa) (32,000)
Government Multiparty republic
Ethnic groups Micronesian 99%
Languages I-Kiribati and English (both official)
Religions Roman Catholic 52%, Protestant (Congregational) 40%, others
Currency Australian dollar = 100 cents
Website www.janeresture.com/kirihome/index.htm

MARSHALL ISLANDS

The Republic of the Marshall Islands consists of 31 coral atolls, five single islands, and more than 1,000 islets. It lies north of Kiribati in the region of Micronesia. The temperature averages 81°F [27°C]. The islands came under German rule in 1885 and became a Japanese mandate after World War I. US forces took the main islands in 1944 and they became a US Trust Territory in 1947. Independence was achieved in 1991, but the islands remain heavily dependent on US aid. The main activities are agriculture and tourism.

Area 70 sq mi [181 sq km]
Population 58,000
Capital (population) Majuro (20,000)
Government Constitutional government in free association with the US
Ethnic groups Micronesian
Languages Marshallese 98% and English (both official)
Religions Protestant 55%, Assembly of God 26%, Roman Catholic 9%, Bukot nan Jesus 3%, Mormon 2%
Currency US dollar = 100 cents
Website www.visitmarshallislands.com

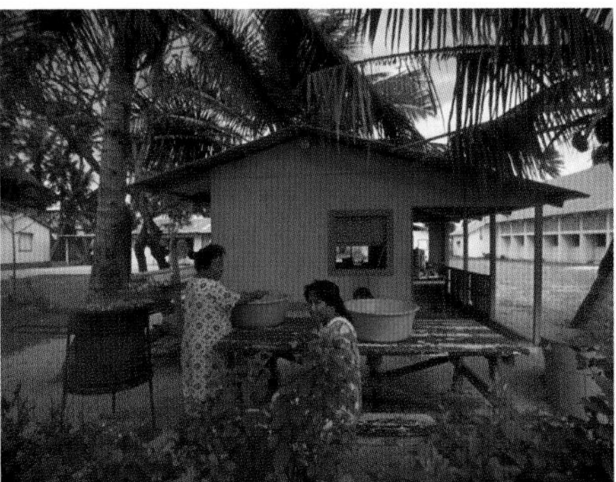

Woman cooking on outdoor grill, *Laura Island, Marshall Islands*

MICRONESIA

Area 271 sq mi [702 sq km]
Population 108,000
Capital (population) Palikir (on Pohnpei) (5,000)
Government Constitutional government in free association with the US
Ethnic groups Micronesian and Polynesian
Languages English (official), others
Religions Roman Catholic 50%, Protestant 47%
Currency US dollar = 100 at
Website www.visit-fsm.org

Federated States of Micronesia is a republic in the western Pacific Ocean, consisting of all the Caroline Islands except Belau. The 607 islands of the republic divide into four states: Chuuk, Pohnpei, Yap, and Kosrae. The government is based in Palikir on Pohnpei. The temperature remains around 80°F [27°C] all year.

After 1874 the islands were under a succession of rulers from Spain to Germany in 1899, to Japan in 1920. They came under US administration in 1947. In 1979, the Federated States of Micronesia came into being, with Belau remaining a US trust territory. In 1986, a compact of free association with the USA was signed. In 1991 Micronesia became a full member of the UN. The economy depends heavily on US aid. Land use is limited to subsistence agriculture.

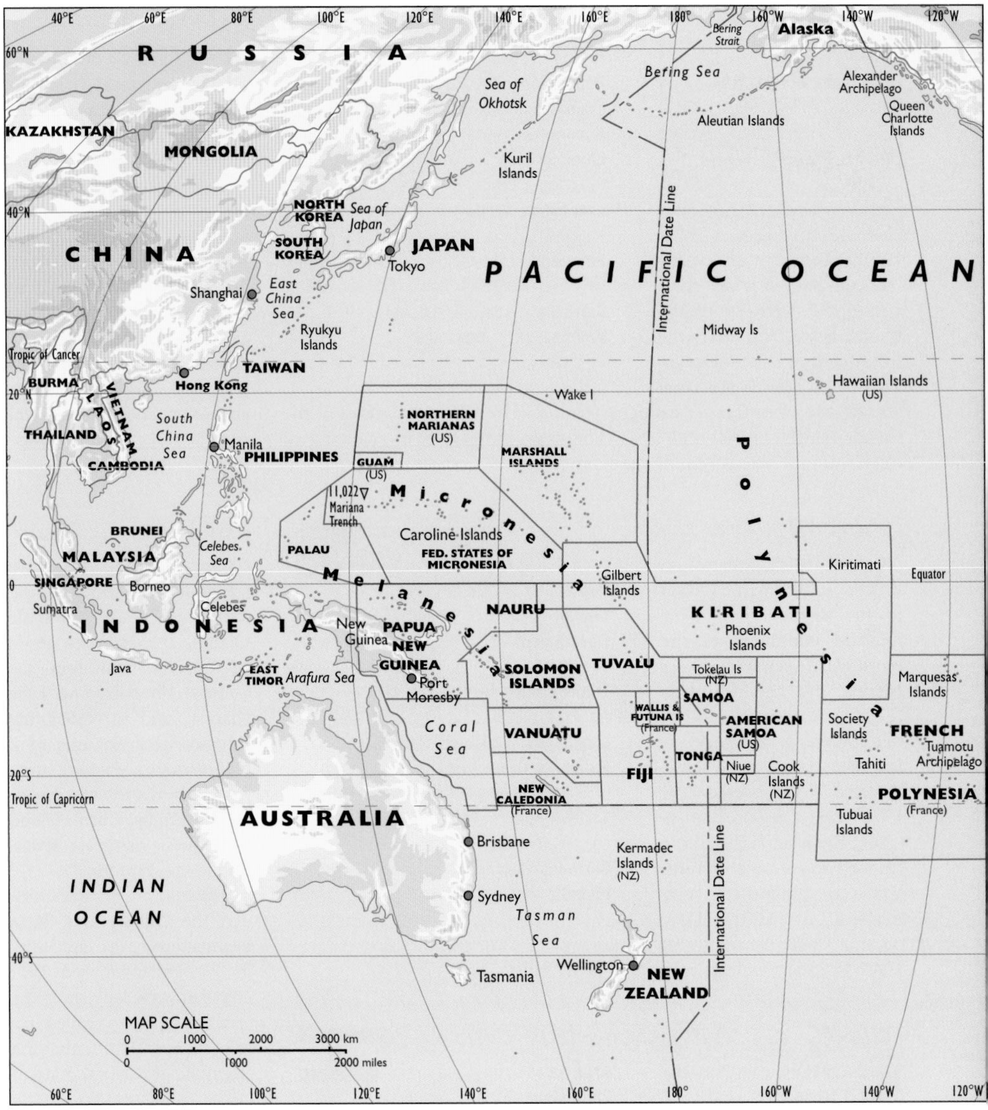

NAURU

Area 8 sq mi [21 sq km]
Population 13,000
Capital (population) Yaren (4,500)
Government Multiparty republic
Ethnic groups Nauruan 58%, other Pacific Islander 26%, Chinese 8%, European 8%
Languages Nauruan (official), English
Religions Protestant 66%, Roman Catholic 33%
Currency Australian dollar = 100 cents
Website www.un.int/nauru/

A former UN Trust Territory ruled by Australia, Nauru became independent in 1968. It has its government offices in the Yaren district though there is no official capital. Located in the western Pacific close to the Equator, it is the world's smallest republic. Nauru's prosperity is based on phosphate mining, but reserves are running out. It relies on Australia for support as well as for its day-to-day needs. Tourism and offshore banking are being developed to off-set the lack of income when the phosphate runs out.

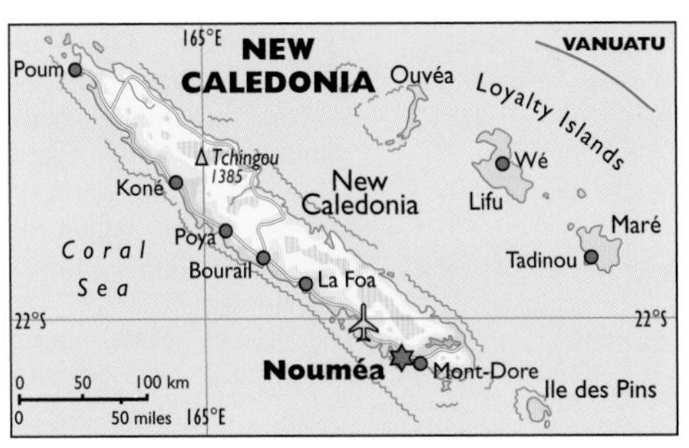

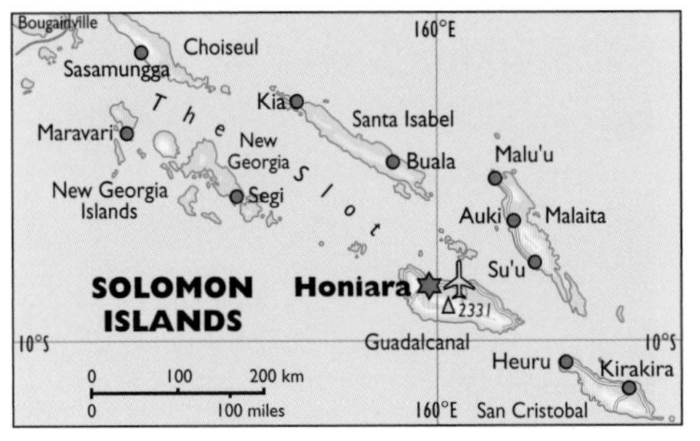

NEW CALEDONIA

Area 7,172 sq mi [18,575 sq km]
Population 214,000
Capital (population) Nouméa (76,000)
Government Overseas territory of France
Ethnic groups Melanesian 43%, European 37%, Wallisian 8%, Polynesian 4%, Indonesian 4%
Languages French (official), 33 Melanesian-Polynesian dialects
Religions Roman Catholic 60%, Protestant 30%
Currency Comptoirs Français du Pacifique franc = 100 centimes
Website www.newcaledoniatourism-south.com

New Caledonia is the most southerly of the Melanesian countries in the Pacific. A French possession since 1853 and an Overseas Territory since 1958. In 1998, France announced an agreement with local Melanesians that a vote on independence would be postponed until 2014. The country is rich in mineral resources. Experts claim that it has about a quarter of the world's nickel reserves.

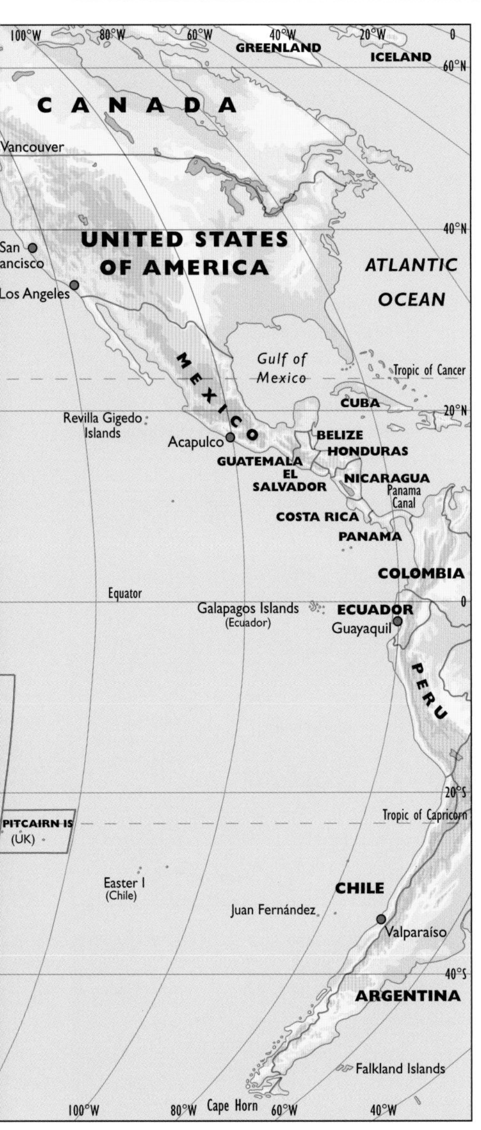

NIUE

Area 100 sq mi [260 sq km]
Population 2,000
Capital (population) Alofi (404)
Government Self-governing parliamentary democracy
Ethnic groups Niuen 78%, Pacific islander 10%, European 4%, others
Languages Niuean, English
Religions Ekalesia Niue 61%, Latter-Day Saints 9%, Roman Catholic 7%, others
Currency New Zealand dollar = 100 cents
Website www.niueisland.com

Niue is an island territory in the southern Pacific Ocean, 1,340 mi [2,160 km] northeast of New Zealand. It has an average temperature of 27°F [25°C]. The largest coral island in the world, Niue was first visited by Europeans in 1774. In 1901 it was annexed to New Zealand. In 1974 it achieved self-government in free association with New Zealand. Its economy is mainly agricultural; the major export is coconuts.

NORFOLK ISLAND

Area 13 sq mi [34 sq km]
Population 1,828
Capital (population) Kingston
Government Territory of Australia
Ethnic groups Descendants of the Bounty mutineers, Australian, New Zealander, Polynesians
Languages English, Norfolk
Religions Anglican 35%, Roman Catholic 12%, Uniting Church in Australia 11%, others
Currency Australian dollar = 100 cents
Website www.nf

The Territory of Norfolk Island lies in the southwest Pacific Ocean 900 mi [1,450 km] east of Australia. Visited in 1774 by Captain James Cook, it was a British penal colony. Many Pitcairn Islanders, decendents of the *Bounty* mutineers, resettled here in 1856. The chief economic activities are agriculture and tourism.

NORTHERN MARIANA ISLANDS

Area 179 sq mi [464 sq km]
Population 78,000
Capital (population) Saipan (39,000)
Government Commonwealth in political union with the US
Ethnic groups Asian 56%, Pacific islander 36%
Languages Philippine languages 24%, Chinese 23%, Chamorro 22%, English 10%, others
Religions Christianity
Currency US dollar = 100 cents
Website www.cnmi.net

The Commonwealth of the Northern Mariana Islands contains 16 mountainous islands north of Guam in the western Pacific Ocean. In a 1975 plebescite, the islanders voted for Commonwealth status in union with the USA and in 1986 they were granted US citizenship. The economy is reliant upon tourism and the export of clothing.

PALAU

Area 459 sq km [177 sq mi]
Population 20,000
Capital (population) Koror (11,000)
Government Multiparty republic
Ethnic groups Palauan 70%, Filipino 15%, Chinese 5%, others
Languages Palauan (official except – Sonsoral:Sonsoralese and English; Tobi: Tobi and English; Anguar: Anguar, Japanese and English), Filipino, English Chinese
Religions Roman Catholic 42%, Protestant 23%, Modekngei 9% (indigenous)
Currency US dollar = 100 cents
Website www.visit-palau.com

The Republic of Palau became fully independent in 1994 after the US refused to accede to a 1979 referendum that declared this island nation a nuclear-free zone. The economy relies on US aid, tourism, fishing, and subsistence agriculture. The main crops include cassava, coconuts, and copra.

PITCAIRN ISLAND

Area 21 sq mi [55 sq km]
Population 46
Capital (population) Adamstown
Government Overseas territory of the UK
Ethnic groups Descendants of the Bounty mutineers and their Tahitian wives
Languages English (official), Pitcairnese
Religions Seventh-Day Adventist
Currency New Zealand dollar = 100 cents
Website www.government.pn/homepage.htm

Pitcairn Island is a British overseas territory in the Pacific Ocean. Its inhabitants are descendents of the original settlers—nine mutineers from HMS *Bounty* and 18 Tahitians who arrived on this formerly uninhabited island in 1790.

SAMOA

Area 1,093 sq mi [2,831 sq km]
Population 178,000
Capital (population) Apia (32,000)
Government Parliamentary democracy and constitutional monarchy
Ethnic groups Samoan 93%, Euronesians
Languages Samoan, English
Religions Congregationalist 35%, Roman Catholic 20%, Methodist 15%, Latter-Day Saints 13%
Currency Tala = 100 sene
Website www.visitsamoa.ws

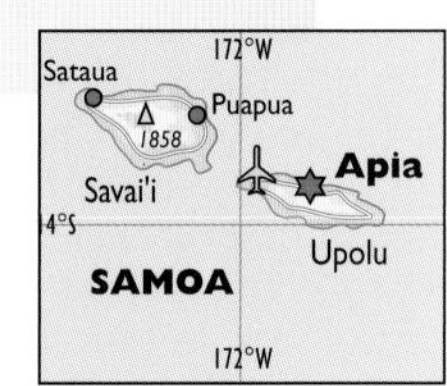

The Independent State of Samoa comprises two islands in the South Pacific Ocean. The ownership of these Polynesian islands was disputed by European powers, but Germany took control in 1900. Following Germany's defeat in World War I, New Zealand governed from 1920 until 1961. The country became independent in 1962. The economy is based on agriculture, plus coconut products, copra, and fishing.

SOLOMON ISLANDS

Area 11,157 sq mi [28,896 sq km]
Population 524,000
Capital (population) Honiara (49,000)
Government Parliamentary democracy
Ethnic groups Melanesian 95%, others
Languages Melanesian pidgin
Religions Church of Melanesia 33%, Roman Catholic 19%, South Seas Evangelical 17%, Seventh-Day Adventist 11%, United Church 10%
Currency Solomon Islands dollar = 100 cents
Website www.solomons.com

The Solomon Islands, a chain of mainly volcanic islands in the Pacific Ocean, extending 1,400 mi [2,250 km]. A British territory between 1893 and 1978. In 2003 an Australian peacekeeping force was sent in the belief that the islands were threatened with anarchy. Fish, coconuts, and cocoa are important.

see map pages 148–9

TOKELAU

Tokelau was originally settled by Polynesian emigrants from surrounding islands. It was made a British protectorate in 1889 and transferred to New Zealand administration in 1925. It is made up of three villages, there is little economic development and agriculture is at subsistence level. The people produce copra, postage stamps, souvenir coins, and handicrafts, but rely heavily on aid from New Zealand.

Area 3.86 sq mi [10 sq km]
Population 1,405
Government Self-administering territory of New Zealand
Ethnic groups Polynesian
Languages Tokelauan, English
Religions Congregational Christian Church 70%, Roman Catholic 28%
Currency New Zealand dollar = 100 cents
Website www.tokelau.org.nz

TONGA

Originally called the Friendly Islands, the Kingdom of Tonga is an island kingdom in the South Pacific, 1,370 mi [2,200 km] northeast of New Zealand. The archipelago consists of c.170 islands in five administrative groups. Only 36 of the islands are inhabited. They are mainly coral atolls, but the western group are volcanic, with some active craters. The largest island is Tongatapu, the seat of the capital, Nukualofa, and home to 66% of the population.

The northern islands were discovered by Europeans in 1616, and the rest by Abel Tasman in 1643. During the 19th century, British missionaries converted the indigenous population to Christianity. In 1900, Tonga became a British Protectorate.

In 1970, the country achieved independence. The economy is dominated by agriculture, the chief crops are yams, tapioca, and fish.

Area 251 sq mi [650 sq km]
Population 110,000
Capital (population) Nuku'alofa 22,000)
Government Constitutional monarchy
Ethnic groups Polynesian
Languages Tongan, English
Religions Christian (Free Wesleyan Church)
Currency Pa'anga = 100 seniti
Website http://pmo.gov.to

TUVALU

Tuvalu, formerly the Ellice Islands (see Kiribati), is an independent republic in western Pacific Ocean. None of the cluster of nine low-lying coral islands rises more than 15 ft [4.6 m] out of the Pacific, making them vulnerable to rising sea levels. There are no streams or rivers, so the collection of rainwater is vital.

The first European to discover the islands was the Spanish navigator Alvaro de Mendaña in 1568. Between 1850 and 1880, the population was reduced from around 20,000 to just 3,000 by Europeans abducting workers for other Pacific plantations. In 1892, the British assumed control, and Tuvalu was subsequently administered with the nearby Gilbert Islands (now Kiribati). In 1978, Tuvalu became a separate self-governing colony within the Commonwealth.

Poor soil restricts vegetation to coconut palms, breadfruit, and bush. The population survives by subsistence farming, raising pigs and poultry, and by fishing. Copra is the only significant export crop, but more foreign exchange is derived from the sale of elaborate postage stamps. In addition, it has sold its internet suffix—.tv—for several million dollars a year.

Area 10 sq mi [26 sq km]
Population 11,000
Capital (population) Fongafale (3,000)
Government Constitutional monarchy with a parliamentary democracy
Ethnic groups Polynesian 96%, Micronesian 4%
Languages Tuvaluan, English, Samoan, Kiribati
Religions Church of Tuvalu (Congregationalist) 97%, others
Currency Tuvaluan dollar and Australian dollar = 100 cents
Website www.tuvaluislands.com

VANUATU

The Republic of Vanuatu, formerly the Anglo-French Condominium of the New Hebrides, became independent in 1980. The word Vanuatu means "Our Land Forever." The republic consists of a chain of 80 islands in the South Pacific Ocean. Espiritu Santo is the largest island, though Efate is home to the government and the republic's capital, Port Vila.

The oldest archaeological evidence dates back to 2000 BC. Efate and Espiritu Santo were used as allied bases in World War II. The economy of Vanuatu is based on agriculture and it exports copra, beef and veal, timber, and cocoa. Fishing, offshore financial services, and tourism are also important. 113 languages are spoken across the islands.

Area 4,706 sq mi [12,189 sq km]
Population 203,000
Capital (population) Port Vila (19,000)
Government Multiparty republic
Ethnic groups Ni-Vanuatu 99%
Languages Local languages (more than 100) 73%, pidgin (known as Bislama or Bichelama) 23%, others
Religions Presbyterian 31%, Anglican 13%, Roman Catholic 13%, Seventh-Day Adventist 11%, indigenous beliefs 6% (including Jon Frum cargo cult), others
Currency Vatu
Website www.vanuatugovernment.gov.vu

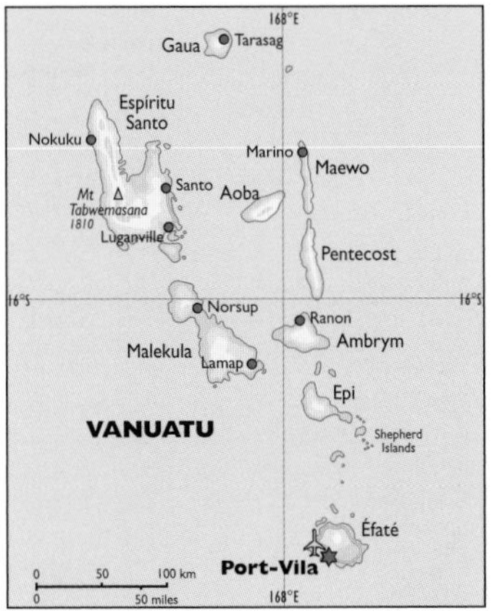

***Yassur volcano** throws smoke high into the air on Tanna Island, Vanuatu*

WALLIS & FUTUNA

The Territory of the Wallis and Futuna Islands in the South Pacific Ocean form the smallest and the poorest of France's overseas territories, although they were in fact discovered by the Dutch and the British in the 17th and 18th centuries.

In 1959, the inhabitants of the islands voted to become a French overseas territory. A French dependency since 1842, the territory comprises two groups of islands. The Isles de Hoorn, which includes Futuna is situated to the north east of the Fiji Islands. The other is the Wallis Archipelago.

The economy is based on subsistence agriculture, and 80% of the workforce makes their living from either coconuts and vegetables, livestock or fishing. Other revenue comes from the licensing of fishing rights to Japan and South Korea.

Area 77 sq mi [200 sq km]
Population 16,000
Capital (population) Mata-Utu (1,000)
Government Overseas territory of France
Ethnic groups Polynesian
Languages Wallisian 59%, Futunian 30%, French 11%
Religions Roman Catholic
Currency Comptoirs Français du Pacifique franc = 100 centimes
Website www.wallis.co.nc

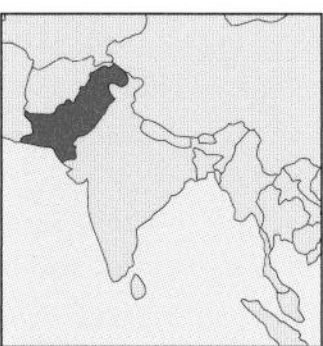

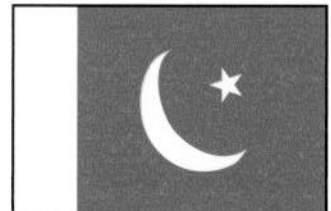

Pakistan's flag was adopted in 1947, when the country gained independence. The color green, the crescent Moon and the five-pointed star are all traditional symbols of Islam. The white stripe represents the other religions in Pakistan.

The Islamic Republic of Pakistan, a federal republic, contains high mountains, fertile plains and rocky deserts. The Karakoram range contains K2, the world's second highest peak at 28,251 ft [8,611 m] It lies in the northern part of Jammu and Kashmir.

The Punjab plains, which are drained by the Indus River and its tributaries, the Chenab, Jhelum, Ravi, and Sutlej, and the Sind plains to the south contain fertile agricultural land, irrigated by river water. East of the Sind plains lies the Thar (or Great Indian) Desert, while the arid Baluchistan Plateau covers the southwest, bordering Iran and Afghanistan.

CLIMATE

Most of Pakistan has hot summers and cool winters. The country is generally arid, though occasional storms cause floods. The eastern part of the Punjab plains has the highest average annual rainfall with around 20 in [500 mm]. Winters in the mountains are cold and snowy. The coastal region has a generally mild, humid climate.

HISTORY

Around 4,500 years ago, what is now the Indus Valley in Pakistan became the home of one of the world's great early civilizations. At its

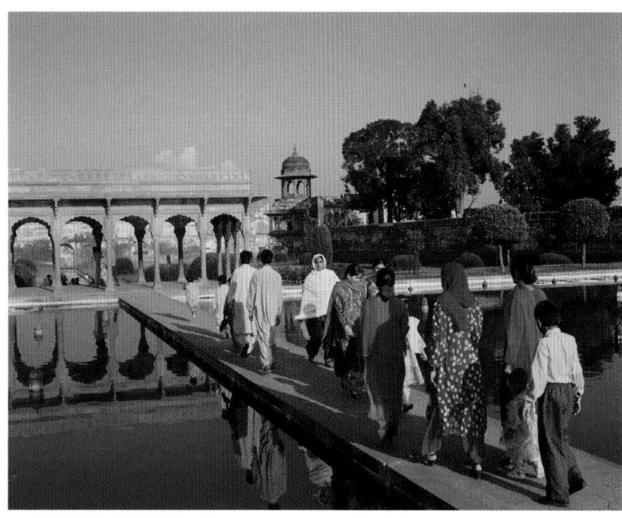

Shalimar Gardens, *Lahore; the gardens date from the mid-17th century and were built during the reign of the Emperor Shah Jahan; they were inscribed as a UNESCO World Heritage Site in 1981*

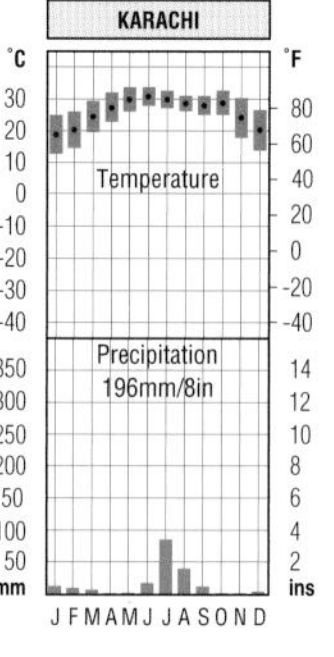

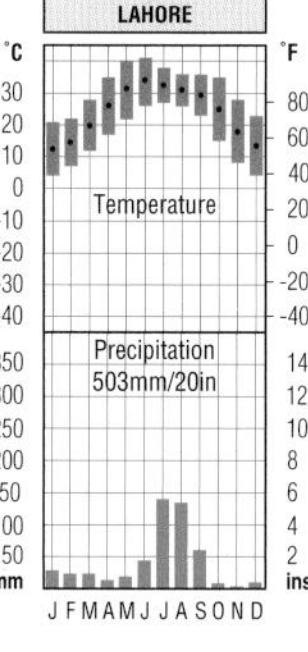

Area 307,372 sq mi [796,095 sq km]
Population 159,196,000
Capital (population) Islamabad (529,000)
Government Federal republic
Ethnic groups Punjabi, Sindhi, Pashtun (Pathan), Baluchi, Muhajir
Languages Urdu (official), many others
Religions Islam 97%, Christianity, Hinduism
Currency Pakistani rupee = 100 paisa
Website www.infopak.gov.pk

KASHMIR

In 1947, British India was partitioned into India and Pakistan. The region known as Kashmir (officially Jammu and Kashmir) was claimed by both India and Pakistan. Muslims formed the majority, but there were also large numbers of Hindus and people of other faiths. In 1947, the region was ruled by a maharaja, who was a Hindu, and he made Kashmir part of India. But Pakistani Muslims invaded in an attempt to make Kashmir part of Pakistan. War ensued until 1949, when a truce line was established, leaving the northwestern two-thirds of the territory under Pakistani control. This area was named Azad (or "Free") Kashmir. In 1957, under a new constitution, India declared Jammu and Kashmir to be part of India. China seized part of Kashmir in 1959 and 1962 and, in 1965, fighting again broke out between India and Pakistan. Finally, in 1972, a new truce line was established and this line remains the boundary on the ground. In the 21st century, India and Pakistan have sought to improve relations between them and, in 2005, bus services began to operate across the cease-fire line. But no solution has been found to the problem of Kashmir, the most explosive issue dividing them.

Prayer flags lead to Tsemo Gompa, *Ladakh, Jammu-Kashmir State*

height, the Indus Valley civilization included most of what is now Pakistan and parts of Afghanistan and India. Ruins have been excavated at Harrappa and Mohenjodaro, revealing that these ancient people developed planned cities and had their own systems of writing and weights and measures. The break-up of this civilization into smaller cultures in around 1700 BC may have been caused by changes in the courses of the rivers.

The region was later conquered by waves of invaders from central and south-western Asia, including the Persians and, briefly by Alexander the Great. Islam was introducedby Arab Muslims in AD 711. In 1526, what is now Pakistan became part of the Mogul Empire, under which Sikhism emerged, combining elements of Hinduism and Islam, and Urdu became a dominant language. The Mogul Empire, included most of what is now Pakistan, India, and Bangladesh, began to decline in the 18th century. In the 1840s, the British East India Company gained areas in Punjab and Sind. The British government took over this region, together with all of the company's other possessions. It became known as British India.

POLITICS

Independence movements began to develop in the early 20th century and, in 1947, British India was divided into Pakistan, led by Muhammed Ali Jinnah, who is regarded as "father of the nation," who died in 1948. Slaughter ensued as Hindus and Sikhs fled Pakistan and Muslims fled India. In 1947, Pakistan consisted of two areas: West and East Pakistan. Following a bitter civil war, East Pakistan broke away in 1971 to become Bangladesh. In 1948-9, 1965 and 1971, Pakistan and India clashed over the disputed territory of Kashmir—the present ceasefire line was agreed in 1972 under the Simla peace agreement.

Pakistan has been ruled by a succession of civilian and military regimes. Following a period of military rule, elections were held in 1988 and Benazir Bhutto, daughter of a previous prime minister, became prime minister. She was removed from office in 1990 but returned as prime minister from 1993 to 1996. In 1997 Narwaz Sharif was elected prime minister but a military coup brought General Pervez Musharraf to power.

In 2001 Pakistan supported the Western assault on Taliban forces in Afghanistan. In 2002, voters agreed to extend Musharraf's term in office by five years. He then changed the constitution to increase his own powers. Pakistan's declaration of support for the international coalition against terrorism provoked a backlash by Islamic fundamentalists. In 2004, Musharraf announced, despite much criticism, that he would remain army chief as well as head of state.

In 1998 Pakistan responded to a series of Indian nuclear weapon tests by conducting its own nuclear tests, provoking global controversy. In the 21st century, Pakistan and India sought to normalize relations through a series of peace moves, raising hopes of a settlement in Kashmir, though activity by Kashmiri militants continued.

In October 2005 nearly 75,000 people were killed and 3 million left homeless in an earthquake centered on Pakistan-administered Kashmir. Among the worst hit areas was the city of Muzaffarabad.

ISLAMABAD

Capital of Pakistan, Islamabad lies northeast of Rawalpindi, which became the interim capital following the decision in 1959 to build a new capital replacing Karachi. Islamabad became the official capital in 1967 and most government offices had been relocated in the city by the end of the 1960s. This new city has been carefully planned and contains a blend of modern and traditional Islamic architectural styles. The city stands on the Potwar Plateau, at the heart of an agricultural region. The city is divided into administrative, diplomatic, business, and residential zones. Most of the people work in administrative and governmental posts. Some people in nongovernment jobs have homes in nearby Rawalpindi. Islamabad lies in a region of seismic activity and suffered damage during the 2005 earthquake in northwestern Pakistan and Kashmir. The city has hot summers, with monsoon rains in July–August and mild winters.

ECONOMY

Pakistan is a "low-income" developing country, whose economy has been damaged by internal political disputes, the ongoing confrontation with India, and the low level of foreign investment. However, some economic progress has been made since 2001, especially because of generous foreign assistance, which has come partly because of the country's support for the war against international terrorism.

Agriculture employs 42% of the workforce, industry 20%, and services 38%. Major crops are cotton, fruits, rice, sugar cane, vegetables, and wheat. Livestock include goats and sheep. Manufactures include bicycles, car tires, cement, industrial chemicals, and jute. Textiles, including cotton fabric, knitwear, bedding, garments, and cotton yarn, are the leading exports. Other exports include rice, leather products, and petroleum products.

The blue quarter stands for the Conservative Party. The red quarter represents the Liberal Party. The white quarters symbolize peace between the parties The blue star stands for purity and honesty. The red star denotes government and law.

Area 29,157 sq mi [75,517 sq km]
Population 3,000,000
Capital (population) Panamá (484,000)
Government Multiparty republic
Ethnic groups Mestizo 70%, Black and Mulatto 14%, White 10%, Amerindian 6%
Languages Spanish (official), English
Religions Roman Catholic 85%, Protestant 15%
Currency US dollar; Balboa = 100 centésimos
Website www.visitpanama.com

The Republic of Panama forms an isthmus linking Central America to South America. The narrowest part of Panama is less than 37 mi [60 km] wide. The Panama Canal, which is 81.6 km [50.7 mi] long and cuts straight across the isthmus, has made the country a major transport center. and most Panamanians live within 20 km [12 mi] of it. Most of the land between the Pacific and Caribbean coastal plains is mountainous, rising to 3,475 m [11,400 ft] at the volcano Barú.

Tropical forests cover approximately 50% of Panama. Mangrove swamps line the coast, though in recent years more than 400 sq km [150 sq mi] have been lost to agriculture, ranching and shrimp mariculture. Subtropical woodland grows on the mountains, while tropical savanna occurs along the Pacific coast.

CLIMATE

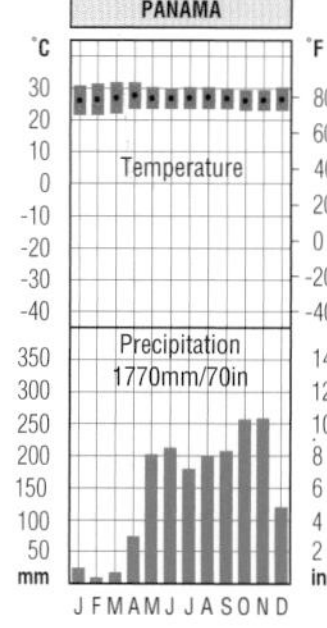

Panama has a tropical climate, though the mountains are much cooler than the coastal plains. The rainy season is between May and December. The Caribbean side of has about twice as much rain as the Pacific side.

HISTORY

Christopher Columbus landed in Panama in 1502. In 1510, Vasco Núñez de Balboa became the first European to cross Panama and see the Pacific Ocean. The indigenous population was soon wiped out and Spain established control. In 1821, Panama became a province of Colombia. The USA exerted great influence from the mid-19th century.

After a revolt in 1903, Panama declared independence from Colombia. In 1904, the USA began construction of the Panama Canal, and established the Panama Canal Zone. Since it opened in 1914, the status of the Canal has dominated Panamanian politics. The Panama Canal Zone, a strip of land along the canal, was then administered by the United States. US forces intervened in 1908, 1912, and 1918 to protect US interests.

POLITICS

Panama has been politically unstable throughout the 20th century, with a series of dictatorial regimes and military coups.

Civil strife during the 1950s and 1960s led to negotiations with the USA for the transfer of the Canal Zone. In 1977, a treaty confirmed Panama's sovereignty over the Canal, while providing for US bases in the Canal Zone. The USA agreed to hand over control of the Canal on December 31, 1999. In 1979, the Canal Zone disestablished.

In 1983, General Noriega took control of the National Guard and ruled Panama through a succession of puppet governments. In 1987, the USA withdrew its support for Noriega after he was accused of murder, electoral fraud, and aiding drug smuggling. In 1988, the USA imposed sanctions and in 1989, Noriega annulled elections, made himself president, and declared war on the USA. On December 20, 1989, 25,000 US troops invaded Panama. Noriega was quickly captured, and taken to the USA for trial.

Pérez Balladares became president in 1994 elections. In 1999, Mireya Moscoso, Panama's first woman president, succeeded Balladares. She was succeeded in 2004 by Martin Torrijos, son of a former military dictator.

Revenues from the Canal rose in the early 21st century, but, overall, the economy slowed, causing social discontent and problems for the government.

PANAMA CITY

Capital of Panama, on the shore of the Gulf of Panama, near the Pacific end of the Panama Canal. It was founded by Pedro Arias de Avila in 1519, and was destroyed and rebuilt in the 17th century. It includes an area known as Casco Antiguo (Colonial Panama), which was constructed inland after the destruction of the first city. Casco Antiguo has been declared "Patrimony of Humanity" by UNESCO. The city became the capital of Panama in 1903 and it developed rapidly after the construction of the Panama Canal in 1914. Industries include brewing, shoes, textiles, oil-refining,and plastics.

ECONOMY

The World Bank classifies Panama as a "lower-middle-income" developing country. The Panama Canal is a major source of revenue, generating jobs in commerce, trade, manufacturing, and transportation.

After the Canal, the main activity is agriculture, which employs 27% of the workforce. Rice is the main food crop. Bananas, shrimps, sugar, and coffee are exported. Tourism is also important. Many ships are registered under Panama's flag, due to its low taxes.

PANAMA CANAL

Waterway connecting the Atlantic and Pacific oceans across the Isthmus of Panama. A canal, begun in 1882 by Ferdinand de Lesseps, was subsequently abandoned because of bankruptcy. The US government decided to finance the project to provide a convenient route for its warships. The main construction took about ten years to complete, and the first ship passed through in 1914. The 51 mi [82 km] waterway reduces the sea voyage between San Francisco and New York by about 7,800 mi [12,500 km]. Control of the Canal passed from the USA to Panama at the end of 1999.

Papua New Guinea

MELANESIA

Papua New Guinea's flag was first adopted in 1971, four years before the country became independent from Australia. It includes a local bird of paradise, the "kumul," in flight, together with the stars of the Southern Cross. The colors are those often used by local artists.

Area 178,703 sq mi [462,840 sq km]
Population 5,420,000
Capital (population) Port Moresby (193,000)
Government Constitutional monarchy
Ethnic groups Papuan, Melanesian, Micronesian
Languages English (official), Melanesian Pidgin, more than 700 other indigenous languages
Religions Traditional beliefs 34%, Roman Catholic 22%, Lutheran 16%, others
Currency Kina = 100 toea
Website www.pngonline.gov.pg

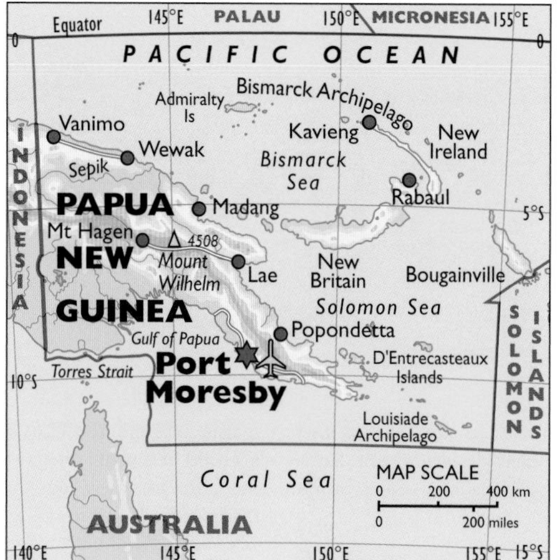

The Independent State of Papua New Guinea is part of a southwest Pacific island region called Melanesia 100 mi [160 km] northeast of Australia that includes the eastern part of New Guinea, Bismarck Archipelago, Solomon Islands, New Hebrides, the Trobriand, and D'Entercasteaux Islands, the Louisiade Archipelago, and the Tonga group.

The land is largely mountainous, rising to Mount Wilhelm, at 14,790 ft [4,508 m], eastern New Guinea. In 1995, two volcanoes erupted in Eastern New Britain. East New Guinea also has extensive coastal lowlands.

Forests cover more than 70% of the land. The dominant vegetation is rainforest. Mangrove swamps line the coast. "Cloud" forest and tussock grass are found on the higher peaks.

CLIMATE

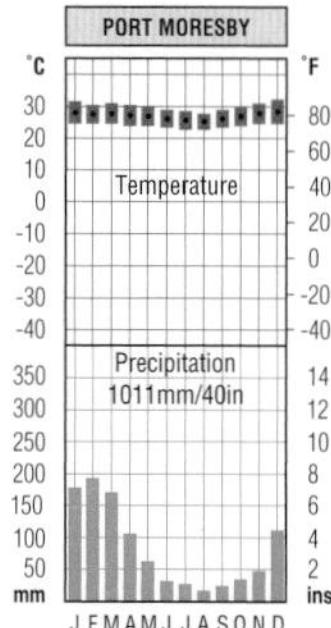

The climate is tropical. It is hot all year with most rain occurring during the monsoon from December to April, when winds blow from the northeast. Winds blow from the southwest during the dry season.

HISTORY

The Portuguese made the first European sighting of the island in 1526, although no settlements were established until the late 19th century. The Dutch took western New Guinea (now Papua part of Indonesia) in 1828, but it was not until 1884 that Germany took northeastern New Guinea as German New Guinea and Britain formed the protectorate of British New Guinea in southeast New Guinea. In 1906, Britain handed the southeast over to Australia. It then became known as the Territory of Papua. When World War I broke out in 1914, Australia took German New Guinea. In 1921, the League of Nations gave Australia a mandate to rule the area, which was named the Territory of New Guinea.

Japan invaded New Guinea in 1942, but the Allies reconquered in 1944. In 1949, Papua and New Guinea were combined into the Territory of Papua and New Guinea. In 1973, the Territory achieved self-government as a prelude to full independence as Papua New Guinea in 1975.

POLITICS

Since independence, the government has worked to develop mineral reserves. One of the most valuable reserves was a copper mine at Panguna on Bougainville. Conflict developed when the people of Bougainville demanded a larger share in mining profits.

Following an insurrection, the Bougainville Revolutionary Army proclaimed independence in 1990. Bougainville's secession was not recognized internationally. In 1992 and 1996, Papua New Guinea launched offensives against the rebels. The use of highly paid mercenaries created unrest in the army. In 1997, troops and civilians surrounded Parliament, forcing the resignation of Prime Minister Sir Julius Chan. He was succeeded by Bill Skate. In April 1998, a ceasefire was declared on Bougainville.

In July 1998, a tidal wave hit northern Papua New Guinea, killing more than 1,600 people. Local autonomy was granted to Bougainville in 2000. In 2004 Australia sent police to the country to help fight crime after a report had stated that the country was heading for social and economic collapse. In 2005 global warming lead to the proposed evacuation of all the residents of the Cartaret atolls due to rising sea levels.

ECONOMY

The World Bank classifies Papua New Guinea as a "lower-middle-income" developing country. Agriculture employs 75% of the workforce, many at subsistence level. Minerals, notably copper and gold, are the most valuable exports. Papua New Guinea is the world's ninth-largest producer of gold.

House and boat *along Sepik River; the river is fundamental to the lives of those who live by it, depending on it as they do for transport, food and water*

PORT MORESBY

Capital of Papua New Guinea, on the south east coast of New Guinea, built around Fairfax Harbor, the island's largest harbor. Settled by the British in the 1880s and named after British explorer John Moresby, its sheltered harbor was the site of an important Allied base in World War II. It developed rapidly in the post-war period. In recent years it has experienced problems with a growing disparity in income which has lead to an increase in crime. Exports include gold, copper, and rubber.

The front (obverse) side of Paraguay's tricolor flag, which evolved in the early 19th century, contains the state emblem, which displays the May Star, commemorating liberation from Spain in 1811. The reverse side shows the treasury seal—a lion and staff.

Area 157,047 sq mi [406,752 sq km]
Population 6,191,000
Capital (population) Asunción (547,000)
Government Multiparty republic
Ethnic groups Mestizo 95%
Languages Spanish and Guarani (both official)
Religions Roman Catholic 90%, Protestant
Currency Guarani = 100 céntimos
Website www.paraguay.com

The Republic of Paraguay is a landlocked country in South America. Rivers, form most of its borders. They include the Paraná in the south and the east, the Pilcomayo (Brazo Sur) in the southwest, and the Paraguay in the northeast. West of the River Paraguay is a region known as the Gran Chaco, which extends into Bolivia and Argentina. The Gran Chaco is mostly flat, but the land rises to the northwest. East of the Paraguay is a region of plains, hills, and, in the east, the Paraná Plateau region.

CLIMATE

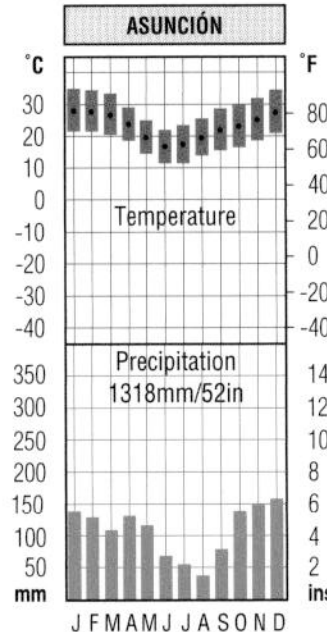

The northern half of Paraguay lies in the tropics, while the southern half is subtropical. Most of the country has a warm, humid climate. The Gran Chaco is the driest and hottest part of the country. Rainfall increases to the Paraná Plateau in the southeast.

HISTORY

The Guarani, an Amerindian people, were the indigenous people of what is now Paraguay. Spanish and Portuguese explorers reached the area in the early 16th century and, in 1537, a Spanish expedition built a fort at Asunción, which later became the capital of Spain's colonies in southeastern South America. The Spaniards were attracted by the potential labor supply of the Guarani and the chance to find a short cut to the silver mines of Peru. From the late 16th century, Jesuit missionaries arrived to convert the Guarani to Christianity and to protect them against those who wanted to exploit them as cheap labor. Complaints against the Jesuits' power led to their expulsion in 1767.

From 1776, Paraguay formed part of the Rio de la Plata Viceroyalty, with its capital at Buenos Aires. However, this proved unpopular and Paraguay broke free in 1811, achieving its independence from Buenos Aires in 1813.

Between 1865 and 1870, war against Brazil, Argentina and Uruguay cost the country more than half of its 600,000 population, and much of its territory. Some territory was regained after the Chaco Wars against Bolivia between 1920 and 1935, and, in 1947, a period of civil war was followed by a spell of political and economic stability. While most other South American countries were attracting European settlers and foreign capital, Paraguay remained isolated and forbidding.

ASUNCIÓN

Capital, chief port, and largest city of Paraguay, located on the e bank of the Paraguay River near its junction with the River Pilcomayo. Founded by the Spanish 1536 as a trading post, Asunción was the scene of the Communeros rebellion against Spanish rule in 1721 and was later occupied by Brazil (1868–76). City sites include the Pantéon Nacional, Encarnación Church, National University (1889) and the Catholic University (1960). It is an administrative, industrial and cultural center. Industries include vegetable oil and textiles.

Harvest of sugar cane *in San Pedro; the capital of the department also called San Pedro, it is located in the center of the country*

POLITICS

In 1954, General Alfredo Stroessner seized power and assumed the presidency. During his dictatorship, there was considerable economic growth, with an emphasis on developing hydroelectricity. By 1976, Paraguay was self-sufficient in electrical energy due to the completion of the Aracay complex. A second hydroelectric project, the world's largest, started production in 1984, at Itaipu. This was a joint US$20 billion venture with Brazil to harness the Paraná. Paraguay was then generating 99.9% of its electricity from water power. However, demand slackened and income declined, making it difficult for Paraguay to repay foreign debts incurred on the projects. High inflation and balance of payments problems followed.

Stroessner's regime was an unpleasant variety of nepotism. He ruled with an increasing disregard for human rights during nearly 35 years of fear and fraud until his supporters deposed him in 1989.

Three elections were held in the 1990s. The fragility of democracy was demonstrated in 1998, when the newly elected president, Raul Cubas Grau, was threatened with impeachment after issuing a decree freeing his former running mate, General Lino Oviedo, who had been imprisoned for attempting a coup against the previous president, Juan Carlos Wasmosy. In March 1999, Paraguay's vice-president, an opponent of Cubas, was assassinated and the Congress impeached Cubas, who resigned and fled to Argentina. In 2003, Nicanor Duarte Frutos was elected president.

ECONOMY

The World Bank classifies Paraguay as a "lower-middle-income" developing country. Agriculture and forestry are the leading activities, employing 48% of the workforce. The country has very large cattle ranches, while crops are grown in the fertile soils of eastern Paraguay. Major exports include cotton, soybeans, timber, vegetable oils, sugar cane, coffee, tannin, and meat products.

The country has abundant hydroelectricity and exports power to Argentina and Brazil. Its factories produce cement, processed food, leather goods, and textiles.

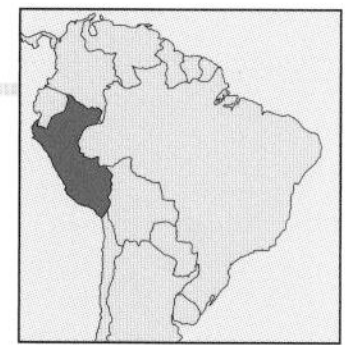

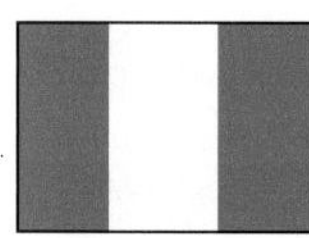

Peru's flag was adopted in 1825. The colors are said to have been inspired by a flock of red and white flamingos which the Argentine patriot General José de San Martín saw flying over his marching army when he arrived in 1820 to liberate Peru from Spain.

Area 496,222 sq mi [1,285,216 sq km]
Population 27,544,000
Capital (population) Lima (5,681,000)
Government Constitutional republic
Ethnic groups Mestizo (Spanish-Indian) 44%, Creole (mainly African American) 30%, Mayan Indian 11%, Garifuna (Black-Carib Indian) 7%, others 8%
Languages English (official), Creole, Spanish
Religions Roman Catholic 62%, Protestant 30%
Currency Belize dollar = 100 cents
Website www.peru.info/perueng.asp

The Republic of Peru lies in the tropics in western South America. A narrow coastal plain borders the Pacific Ocean in the west. Inland are ranges of the Andes Mountains, which rise to 22,205 ft [6,768 m] at Mount Huascarán, an extinct volcano. The Andes also contain active volcanoes, windswept plateaux, broad valleys and, in the far south, part of Lake Titicaca, the world's highest navigable lake. To the east the Andes descend to a hilly region and a huge plain. Eastern Peru is part of the Amazon basin.

CLIMATE

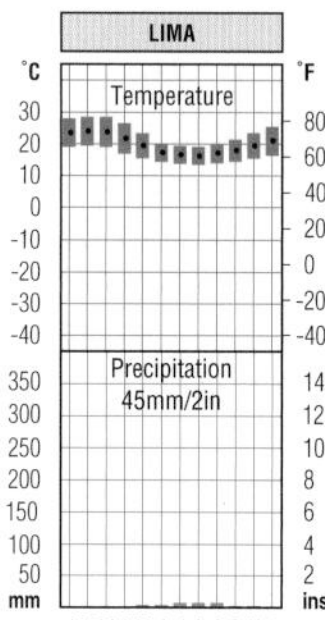

Lima, on the coastal plain has an arid climate. The coastal region is chilled by the cold offshore Humboldt Current. In the Andes, temperatures are moderated by the altitude and many mountains are snow-capped. The eastern lowlands are hot and humid.

HISTORY

Amerindian people reached the area about 12,000 years ago. Several civilizations developed in the Andes region. By about AD 1200, the Inca were established in southern Peru. In 1500, their empire extended from Ecuador to Chile. The Spanish adventurer Francisco Pizarro visited Peru in the 1520s. Hearing of Inca riches, he returned in 1532. By 1533, he had conquered most of Peru.

In 1820, the Argentinian José de San Martín led an army into Peru and declared the country to be independent. However, Spain still held large areas. In 1823, the Venezuelan Simón Bolívar led another army into Peru and, in 1824, one of his generals defeated the Spaniards at Ayacucho. The Spaniards surrendered in 1826. Peru suffered much instability throughout the 19th century.

POLITICS

Instability continued into the 20th century. When civilian rule was restored in 1980, a left-wing group called the Sendero Luminoso (Shining Path), began guerrilla warfare against the government. In 1990, Alberto Fujimori, son of Japanese immigrants, became president. In 1992, he suspended the constitution and dismissed the legislature. The guerrilla leader, Abimael Guzmán, was arrested in 1992, but instability continued.

A new constitution was introduced in 1993, giving increased power to President Albert Fujimori. In 1996, Tupac Amaru (MRTA) rebels seized the Japanese ambassador's residence, taking hostages and demanding the release of guerrilla prisoners. The stalemate ended in April 1997, when Peruvian troops attacked and freed the remaining 72 hostages.

Peru faced many problems in the 1990s, including a cholera outbreak, the worst El Niño in the 20th century, and a border dispute with Ecuador which was finally settled in 1998. Fujimori began his third term as president in 2000, but, in November, the Congress declared him "morally unfit" to govern. He resigned and sought sanctuary in Japan. In his absence he was banned from holding office until 2011. In 2005 the government began its attempt to extradite him and try him for financial corruption and sanctioning death squads. In 2001, Alejandro Toledo became the first Peruvian of Amerindian descent to hold the office of president. Toledo faced many problems including in 2003–4, a resurgence of activity by the "Shining Path" guerillas.

ECONOMY

The World Bank classifies Peru as a "lower-middle-income" developing country. Agriculture employs 35% of the workforce and major food crops include beans, corn, potatoes, and rice. Coffee, cotton, and sugar are the chief cash crops. Many farmers live at subsistence level. Other farms are cooperatives. Fishing is important.

Peru is one of the world's main producers of copper, silver, and zinc. Iron ore, lead, and oil are also produced, while gold is mined in the highlands. Most manufacturing is small-scale.

LIMA

Capital and largest city of Peru, on the River Rímac at the foot of the Cerro San Cristóbal. Founded in 1535, it was the capital of Spain's New World colonies until the 19th century. Chilean forces occupied Lima during the War of the Pacific (1881–3). It is the commercial and cultural center of Peru. With the oil-refining port of Callao, the Lima metropolitan area forms the third-largest city of South America, and handles more than 75% of all Peru's manufacturing. Lima has the oldest university (1551) in the Western Hemisphere.

Machu Picchu ruins; *created by the Inca empire and situated in the middle of tropical mountain forest the ruins are a World Heritage Site*

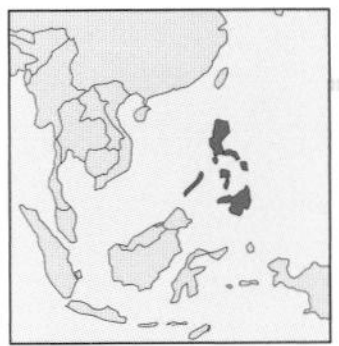

This flag was adopted in 1946, when the country won its independence from the United States. The eight rays of the large sun represent the eight provinces which led the revolt against Spanish rule in 1898. The three smaller stars stand for the three main island groups.

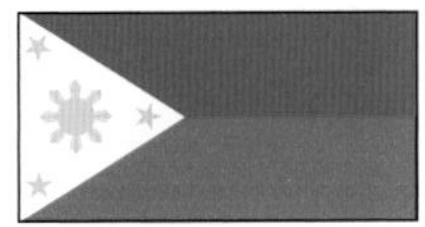

The Republic of the Philippines is an island country in southeastern Asia. It includes about 7,100 islands, of which 2,770 are named and about 1,000 are inhabited. Luzon and Mindanao, the two largest islands, make up more than two-thirds of the country.

The land is mainly mountainous, it is also unstable and prone to earthquakes. The islands also have several active volcanoes, one of which is the highest peak, Mount Apo, at 9,692 ft [2,954 m].

CLIMATE

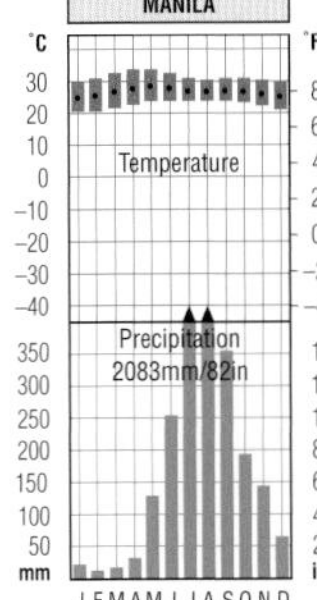

The climate is tropical with high temperatures all year. The dry season runs from December to April. The rest of the year is wet. Typhoons periodically strike the east coast bringing high rainfall.

HISTORY

The first European to reach the Philippines was Ferdinand Magellan in 1521. Spanish explorers claimed the region in 1565 when they established their first permanent settlement on Cebu. Manila was founded in 1571. The Spaniards regarded their new territory as a stepping stone to the Spice Islands to the south. But they also converted most people (except the Muslims on Mindanao and Sulu) to Roman Catholicism.

The economy grew from the late 18th century when the islands were opened up to foreign trade. In 1896 a secret revolutionary society called Katipunan launched a revolt against Spanish rule. The revolt was put down and the rebel leader Emilio Aguinaldo left the country. In 1898, the United States declared war on Spain and the first major engagement was the destruction of all the Spanish ships in Manila Bay. Aguinaldo returned to the Philippines and formed an army which fought alongside the Americans. He proclaimed the Philippines an independent nation and a peace treaty between Spain and the United States was signed with the US taking over the government of the Philippines. However, Aguinaldo still wanted independence and fighting continued between 1899 and 1901.

The Philippines became a self-governing US Commonwealth in 1935 and was guaranteed full independence after a ten-year transitional period. During World War II Japanese troops occupied the islands but the Philippines finally achieved independence on 4 July 1946.

POLITICS

From 1946 until 1971, the country was governed under a constitution similar to that of the United States. In 1971, constitutional changes were proposed, but before ratification, President Ferdinand Marcos declared martial law. In 1977, the main opposition leader, Benigno Aquino, Jr, was sentenced to death. He was allowed a stay of execution and went to the United States for medical treatment. Martial law was lifted in 1981, but Aquino was shot dead on his return to the Philippines in 1983.

Following presidential elections in 1986, Marcos was proclaimed president, but the elections proved to be fraudulent and his opponent, Corazon Aquino, the widow of Benigno Aquino, became president. In 2001 Gloria Macapagal-Arroyo, became president and set out to try to find peace in the southern Philippines. In 2003, the government put down military rebellion. Gloria Arroyo was reelected president in 2004 and a ceasefire was agreed in the south with the Moro Islamic Liberation Front. This ceasefire was broken in 2005.

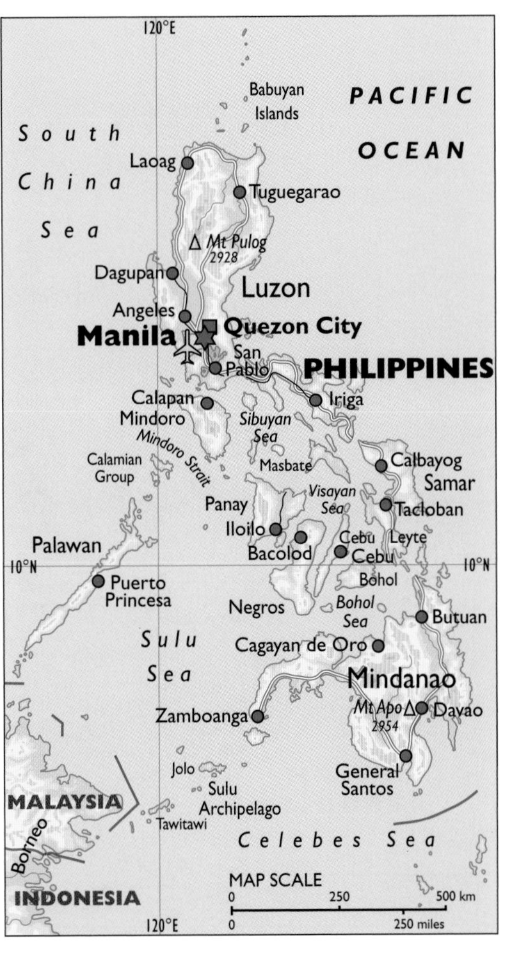

Area 115,830 sq mi [300,000 sq km]
Population 86,242,000
Capital (population) Manila (1,581,000)
Government Multiparty republic
Ethnic groups Christian Malay 92%, Muslim Malay 4%, Chinese and others
Languages Filipino (Tagalog) and English (both official), Spanish and many others
Religions Roman Catholic 83%, Protestant 9%, Islam 5%
Currency Philippine peso = 100 centavos
Website www.gov.ph

MANILA

Capital of the Philippines, on Manila Bay, southwest Luzon island. Industrial, commercial, and administrative heart of the Philippines. The River Pasig bisects the city. On the south bank is the old walled city (Intramuros), built by the Spanish in the 16th century on the site of a Muslim settlement. It became a trading center for the Pacific area. On the north bank lies Ermita, the administrative and tourist center. Japan occupied the city in 1942 and in 1945 a battle between Japanese and Allied forces destroyed the old city.

ECONOMY

The Philippines is a "lower-middle-income" developing country. Agriculture employs 40% of the workforce. Rice and corn are the main food crops, with bananas, cassava, coconuts, coffee, cocoa, fruits, sugar cane, sweet potatoes, and tobacco. Water buffalo, goats, and pigs are farmed. Forestry is valuable as nearly half the land is forested. Sea fishing is important, shellfish come from inshore waters.

__Vintas__, the traditional sailing outrigger of the Badjao, Zamboanga, Mindanao

Poland

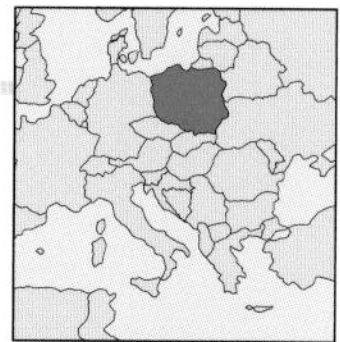

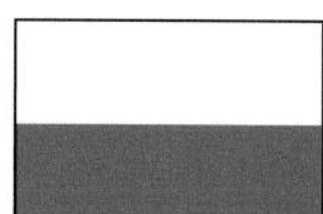

Poland's flag was adopted when the country became a republic in 1919. Its colors were taken from the 13th-century coat of arms of a white eagle on a red field. This coat of arms still appears on Poland's merchant flag.

The Republic of Poland faces the Baltic Sea in north-central Europe. Behind the lagoon-fringed coast is a broad plain.The land rises to a plateau region in the southeast of the country.The Sudeten Highlands straddle the border with the Czech Republic. Part of the Carpathian Range lies on the southeastern border with the Slovak Republic.

CLIMATE

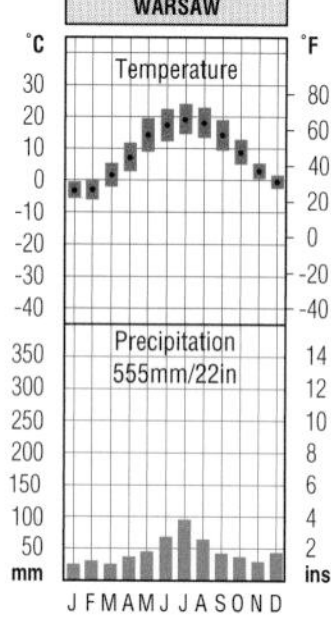

Poland's climate is influenced by its geographical position. Warm, moist air masses come from the west, while cold air masses come from the north and east. Summers are warm, winters cold and snowy.

HISTORY

Poland's boundaries have changed several times in the last 200 years. It disappeared from the map in the late 18th century, when a Polish state called the Grand Duchy ofWarsaw was set up. In 1815, the country was partitioned, between Austria, Prussia and Russia. Poland became independent in 1918, but in 1939 it was divided between Germany and the USSR.The country again became independent in 1945, when it lost land (poor agricultural land), and around 6 million people, to the Soviet Union. In compensation, it gained parts of Germany as far as the River Oder, an important industrial region in the west. Other gains were, in the southwest, Silesia and Breslau (now Wroclaw), in the northwest the Baltic port of Stettin (now Szczecin), and in the north the port of Danzig (now Gda´nsk). Acquisition of a length of Baltic coastline gave Poland an opportunity to develop maritime interests.

POLITICS

Communists took power in 1948. Opposition mounted and focused through an organization called Solidarity, led by trade unionist, Lech Walesa. A coalition government was formed between Solidarity and the Communists in 1989. In 1990, the Communist Party was dissolved and Walesa became president. He faced many problems in turning Poland towards a market economy. Solidarity divided in 1990 over personality and the speed of reform. The adoption of its reforms was interrupted in 1993, when the former Communists won the parliamentary elections. In 1995, the ex-Communist Aleksander Krasniewski defeated Walesa in presidential elections, but he continued to follow westward-looking policies. Poland became a member of NATO in 1999 and of the EU in 2004. Having lost elections in 1997, Krasniewski was reelected president in 2000. In 2005, Lech Kaczynski of the right-wing Law and Justice party became president.

Area 124,807 sq mi [323,250 sq km]
Population 38,626,000
Capital (population) Warsaw (1,615,000)
Government Multiparty republic
Ethnic groups Polish 97%, Belarusian, Ukranian, German
Languages Polish (official)
Religions Roman Catholic 95%, Eastern Orthodox
Currency Zloty = 100 groszy
Website www.poland.pl

ECONOMY

Poland has large reserves of coal and deposits of minerals which are used in its factories. Manufactures include chemicals, processed food, machinery, ships, steel, and textiles. Major crops include barley, potatoes, rye, sugar beets, and wheat.

WARSAW

Capital city of Poland, on the River Vistula. Dating from the 11th century it became Poland's capital in 1596. Controlled by Russia from 1813 to 1915, German troops occupied it during World War I. The 1939 German invasion and occupation of Warsaw marked the beginning of World War II. In 1940, the Germans isolated the Jewish ghetto. In January 1945, the Red Army liberated Warsaw and found only 200 surviving Jews. The old town was painstakingly reconstructed. Warsaw became a major transportation and industrial center.

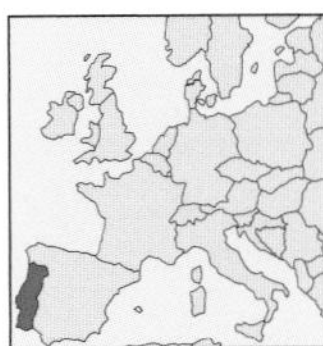

Portugal's colors, which were adopted in 1910 when the country became a republic, represent the soldiers who died in the war (red), and hope (green). The armillary sphere —an early navigational instrument—reflects Portugal's leading role in world exploration.

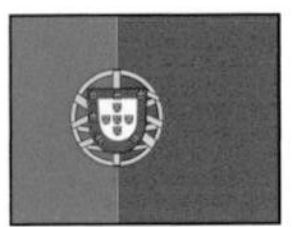

The Portuguese Republic shares the Iberian Peninsula with Spain. It is the most westerly of Europe's mainland countries. The land rises from the coastal plains on the Atlantic Ocean to the western edge of the huge plateau, or Meseta, which occupies most of the Iberian Peninsula. In central Portugal, the Sera da Estrela contains Portugal's highest point, at 6,537 ft1,993 m []. Portugal also contains two autonomous regions, the Azores and Madeira islands.

CLIMATE

Winds blowing in from the Atlantic Ocean moderate the climate. Portugal experiences cooler summers and milder winters than in other lands on the Mediterranean. In the south, temperatures range from 59–82°F [15–28°C], temperatures in the north are only a few degrees lower year round.

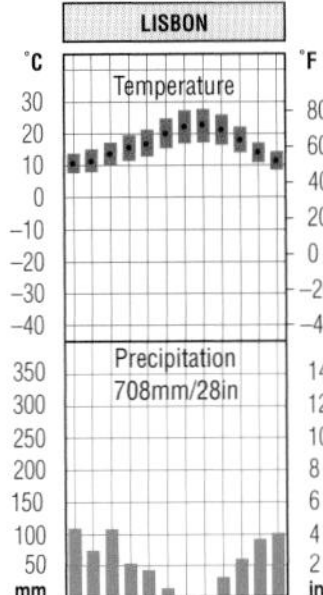

HISTORY

The Romans completed their conquest of the Iberian Peninsula around 2,000 years ago and Christianity was introduced in the 4th century AD. The Romans called Portugal Lusitania. Following the collapse of the Roman Empire in the 5th century, Portugal was conquered by the Christian Visigoths, but in the early 8th century, the Iberian Peninsula was conquered by Muslim Moors. The Christians strove to drive out the Muslims and, by the mid-13th century, they had retaken Portugal and most of Spain.

In 1143, Portugal became a separate country, independent from Spain. In the 15th century, the Portuguese, who were skilled navigators, led the "Age of Exploration," pioneering routes around Africa onwards to Asia.

Although Portugal set up colonies in Africa and Asia, the most valuable was Brazil. Portugal became wealthy through trade and the exploitation of its colonies. Its power began to decline in the 16th century, when it could no longer defend its far-flung empire. Spain ruled Portugal from 1580 until 1640, when Portugal's independence was restored by John, Duke of Braganza, who took the title of John IV. England supported Portuguese independence and several times defended it from invasion or threats by Spain and its allies. In 1822, Portugal lost Brazil.

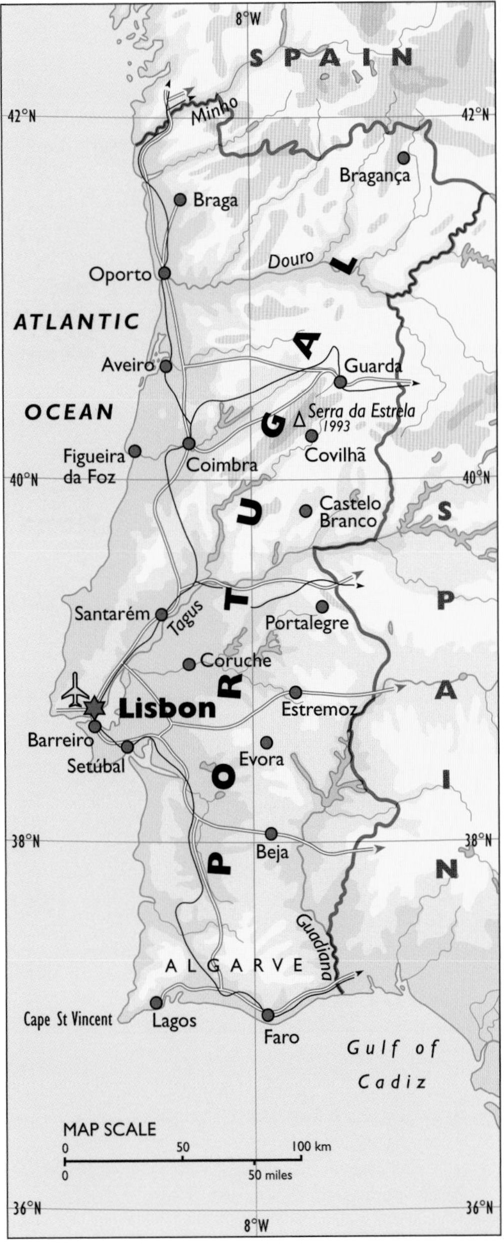

LISBON (LISBOA)

Capital, largest city and chief port of Portugal, at the mouth of the River Tagus, on the Atlantic Ocean. An ancient Phoenician settlement, the Romans conquered the city in 205 BC. After Teutonic invasions in the 5th century AD, it fell to the Moors in 716. In 1147, the Portuguese reclaimed Lisbon, and in 1260 it became the capital. It declined under Spanish occupation (1580–1640). In 1755, an earthquake devastated the city and Marques de Pombal oversaw its reconstruction. It is an international port and tourist center. Baixa is the neoclassical heart of Lisbon with the Praça do Comércio and Rosso squares. São Jorge castle is surrounded by the medieval quarters. The Monastery of Jerónimos is exceptional.

Area 34,285 sq mi [88,797 sq km]
Population 10,524,000
Capital (population) Lisbon (663,000)
Government Multiparty republic
Ethnic groups Portuguese 99%
Languages Portuguese (official)
Religions Roman Catholic 94%, Protestant
Currency Euro = 100 cents
Website www.portugal.org

POLITICS

Portugal became a republic in 1910, but its first attempts at democracy led to great instability. Portugal fought alongside the Allies in World War I. A coup in 1926 brought an army group to power. They abolished the parliament and set up a dictatorial regime. In 1928, they selected António de Oliviera Salazar, an economist, as minister of finance. He became prime minister in 1932 and ruled as a dictator from 1933. After World War II, when other European powers began to grant independence to their colonies, Salazar was determined to maintain his country's empire. Colonial wars flared up and weakened Portugal's economy. Salazar suffered a stroke in 1968 and died two years later. His successor, Marcello Caetano, was overthrown by another military coup in 1974 and the new military leaders set about granting independence to Portugal's colonies. Free elections were held in 1978 and full democracy was restored in 1982, when a new constitution abolished the military Council of the Revolution and reduced the powers of the president.

Portugal joined the European Community (now the EU) in 1986, and in 1999 became one of the 12 EU countries to adopt the euro, the single currency of the EU. In 2005 the Socialists led by a moderate, José Socrates, won a decisive victory in parliamentary elections.

ECONOMY

Although its economy was growing strongly in the late 1990s, Portugal remains one of the EU's poorer members. Agriculture and fishing were the mainstays of the economy until the mid-20th century. But manufacturing is now the most valuable sector. Textiles, processed food, paper products, and machinery are important manufactures. Major crops include grapes for winemaking, olives, potatoes, rice, corn, and wheat. Cattle and other livestock are raised and fishing catches include cod, sardines, and tuna.

Forest products including timber and cork are important, though forest fires often cause much damage.

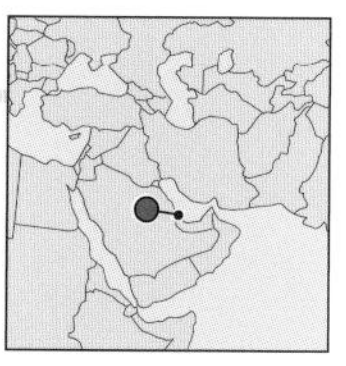

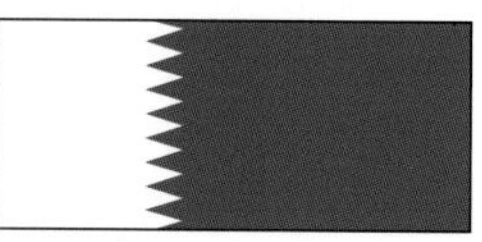

The white stripe, added at the request of the British, denotes friendly Arab states. The nine point serrated line indicates Qatar is the ninth member of the reconciled Emirates of the Arabian Gulf. The maroon area represents blood shed in the 19th-century wars.

Area 4,415 sq mi [11,437 sq km]
Population 522,000
Capital (population) Doha (264,000)
Government Absolute monarchy
Ethnic groups Arab 40%, Pakistani 18%, Indian 18%, Iranian 10%
Languages Arabic (official), English
Religions Islam 95% (all native Qataris are Wahhabi Sunni)
Currency Rial = 100 dirham
Website http://english.mofa.gov.qa

The State of Qatar occupies a long, narrow peninsula jutting into the Persian Gulf. The peninsula is about 124 mi [200 km] long, with a greatest width of 56 mi [90 km]. The land is mostly flat desert covered by gravel and loose, windblown sand. Sand dunes occur in the southeast. There are also some barren salt flats. The highest point, on a central limestone plateau, is only 321 ft [98 m] above sea level. Qatar also includes several offshore islands and coral reefs. Fresh water is scarce and much of the water supply comes from desalination plants.

CLIMATE

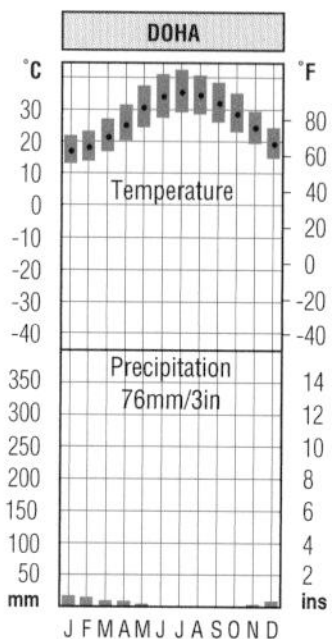

The weather from May to September is extremely hot and dry, with temperatures soaring to 120°F [49°C]. Sand and dust storms are common. Winters are mild to warm, with the weather generally sunny and pleasant. The total annual rainfall seldom exceeds 4 in [100 mm]. Most of the rain occurs in winter.

HISTORY

In the 18th century, migrants established trading settlements along the coast of the peninsula. Since the mid-19th century, members of the Al-Thani family have been the leaders of Qatar. Between 1871 and 1913, the Ottoman Turks, with Qatar's consent, occupied a garrison on the peninsula. In 1916, Qatar agreed that Britain would take responsibility for the country's foreign affairs. Oil was struck in 1939 but exploitation was delayed by World War II. Commercial exploitation began in 1949, leading to the rapid development and modernization of the country's infrastructure.

In 1968, Britain announced the withdrawal of its forces from the Gulf. Qatar negotiated with Bahrain and the United Arab Emirates concerning the formation of a federation, but this proposal was finally rejected.

DOHA

Capital of Qatar, on the east coast of the Qatar peninsula, in the Persian (Arabian) Gulf. Doha was a small fishing village until oil production began in 1949. It is now a modern city and trade center. Industries include oil refining, shipping, engineering.

POLITICS

Qatar became fully independent on September 3, 1971. In 1972, because of rivalries in the ruling family, the deputy ruler Khalifa bin Hamad Al Thani seized power, from his cousin, Emir Ahmad in Al-Thani, in a coup. In 1982, Qatar together with Bahrain, Kuwait, Oman, Saudi Arabia and the United Arab Emirates united to form the Gulf Cooperation Council, which is concerned with such matters as defence and economic development.

In 1990, following Iraq's invasion of Kuwait, Qatar agreed to allow foreign troops on its soil and, in 1991, Qatari troops were involved in the military campaign to free Kuwait. In 1995, Qatar signed a security pact with the United States. A bloodless coup occurred in 1995, when the heir apparent, Sheikh Hamad bin Khalifa Al-Thani, deposed his father, while Khalifa was abroad. An attempted countercoup failed in 1996.

In 1996, the Al-Jazeera satellite television was launched in Qatar. It soon won a worldwide reputation for tackling controversial issues, especially those connected with the Arab world. In 2001, it became famous when it became the first station to air recorded statements by the al Qaida leader Osama bin Laden and, from 2003, it covered the conflict in Iraq graphically. Qatar is an emirate, ruled by the Emir and his appointed Council of Ministers. Municipal elections in 1999 heralded moves towards democracy.

A new constitution introduced in 2004 provided for a 45-member Consultative Council. This Council consisted of 45 members, two-thirds of whom would be elected by the public and one-third appointed by the Emir. The new constitution came into force in 2005 with elections expected by 2007. In foreign affairs, Qatar resolved long-standing boundary disputes with Bahrain and Saudi Arabia in 2001. In 2003, the US Central Command forward base on Qatar became the main center for the US-led invasion of Iraq.

ECONOMY

The people of Qatar enjoy a high standard of living, which derives from oil revenues. The country has a comprehensive welfare system, and many of its services are free or highly subsidized. Oil production has given Qatar one of the world's highest per capita incomes and accounts for more than 80% of the country's export revenues. Qatar has about 5% of the world's proved oil reserves and more than 15% of the world's proven natural gas reserves.

Besides oil refining, they produce ammonia, cement, fertilizers, petrochemicals, and steel bars. Wells have been dug to develop agriculture and products include beef, dairy products, fruits, poultry, and vegetables.

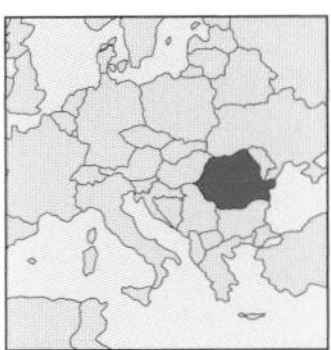

Romania's flag, adopted in 1948, uses colors from the arms of the provinces, which united in 1861to form Romania. A central coat of arms, added in 1965, was deleted in 1990 after the fall of the Communist regime under the dictator Nicolae Ceaucescu.

Romania is on the Black Sea in eastern Europe. Eastern and southern Romania form part of the Danube River Basin. The delta region where the river flows into the Black Sea, is one of Europe's finest wetlands. The southern part of the coast contains several resorts.

The country is dominated by the Carpathian mountains which curve around the plateaus of Transylvania in central Romania. The southern arm of the mountains, including Mount Moldoveanu (8,341 ft [2,543 m]), is known as the Transylvanian Alps. On the border with Serbia and Montenegro, the River Danube (Dunav/Dunǎrea) has cut a gorge, the Iron Gate (Portile de Fier) whose rapids have been tamed by a huge dam. Forests cover large areas in Transylvania and the Carpathians, while farmland dominates in the Danubian lowlands and the plateaus.

Area 92,043 sq mi [238,391 sq km]
Population 22,356,000
Capital (population) Bucharest (2,001,000)
Government Multiparty republic
Ethnic groups Romanian 89%, Hungarian 7%, Roma 2%, Ukranian
Languages Romanian (official), Hungarian, German
Religions Eastern Orthodox 87%, Protestant 7%, Roman Catholic 5%
Currency Leu = 100 bani
Website www.gov.ro/engleza/

CLIMATE

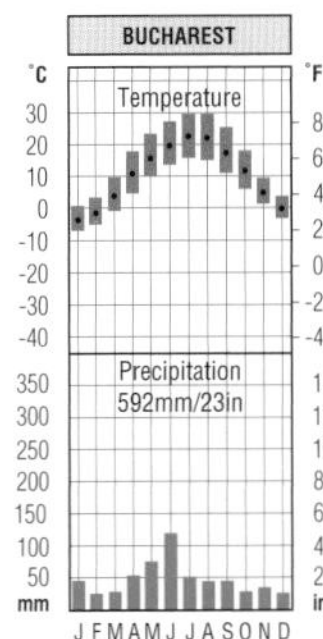

Romania has hot summers and cold winters. Rainfall is heaviest in spring and early summer, when thundery showers are common.

HISTORY

Around 2,300 years ago, Romania was called Dacia. After the Romans conquered the area in AD 106, the Dacians embraced Roman culture and language so completely that the region became known as Romania. The first step towards the creation of the modern state occurred in the 14th century when two principalities were formed: Walachia (or Valachi) in the south and Moldavia in the east. But they were conquered by the Ottoman Turks around 1500.

***Museum of Peles**, Sinaia, Transylvania*

BUCHAREST (BUCURESTI)

Capital and largest city of Romania, on the River Dimbovita, southern Romania. Founded in the 14th century on an important trade route, it became capital in 1862. Occupied by Germany in both World Wars. An industrial, commercial, and cultural center. The seat of the patriarch of the Romanian Orthodox Church, it has notable churches, museums and galleries. The infamous 1980s Civic Center is a symbol of dictatorial aggrandisement.

Walachia and Moldavia united in 1861 to form modern Romania. After World War I, Romania, which had fought with the Allies, gained much land, including Transylvania, almost doubling the country's size and population. In 1939 Romania lost territory to Bulgaria, Hungary, and the Soviet Union. Romania fought alongside Germany in World War II, and was occupied by Soviet in 1944. Hungary returned northern Transylvania to Romania in 1945, but Bulgaria and the Soviet Union kept former Romanian territory when King Michael was forcibly removed from the throne.

In the 1960s, Romania's Communist Party, led by Gheorghe Gheorghiu-Dej, began to oppose Soviet control, a policy continued by Nicolae Ceaucescu, who became Communist Party chief in 1965.

Under Ceaucescu Romania developed industries based on its oil and natural gas reserves. His rule was corrupt and self-seeking, but he won plaudits from the West for his independent stance against Soviet control, including a knighthood from Queen Elizabeth II. However, he pursued a strict Stalinist approach and the remorseless industrialization and urbanization programs of the 1970s caused severe debt. In the 1980s, he cut imports and diverted output to exports. Self-sufficiency turned to subsistence and shortages, with savage rationing of food and energy.

Ceaucescu's building schemes desecrated some of the country's finest architecture and demolished thousands of villages. In December 1989, mass anti-government demonstrations were held in Timisoara with protests across Romania. Security forces fired on crowds, causing many deaths. But after army units joined the protests, Nicolae Ceaucescu and his wife Elena fled from Bucharest on December 22. Both were executed on Christmas Day on charges of genocide and corruption. A provisional government of the National Salvation Front (NSF), took control, much of the old administrative apparatus was dismantled, and the Communist Party was dissolved.

POLITICS

In May 1990, under Ion Iliescu, the NSF won Romania's first free elections since World War II, a result judged to be flawed but not fraudulent.A new constitution enshrining pluralist democracy, human rights, and a market economy was passed by parliament in 1991. There were strikes and protests against the new authorities and also against the effects of the switch to a market economy, which caused food shortages, rampant inflation, and increased unemployment. Foreign investment was sluggish, deterred by the political instability. Presidential elections in 1996 led to defeat for Iliescu and victory for the center-right Emil Constantinescu. In 2000, Iliescu was reelected president, though the government continued its privatization policies. He stood down in 2004. Romania became a member of NATO in 2004 and is expected to join the EU in 2007.

ECONOMY

According to the World Bank, Romania is a "lower-middle-income" economy. Oil and natural gas are the chief mineral resources and the aluminum, copper, lead, and zinc industries use domestic supplies. Manufactures include cement, processed food, petroleum products, textiles, and wood. Agriculture employs nearly a third of the workforce. Crops include fruits, corn, potatoes, sugar beets, and wheat. Sheep are the chief livestock.

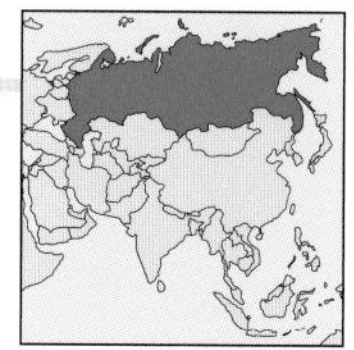

In August 1991, Russia's traditional flag, which had first been used in 1699, was restored as Russia's national flag. It uses colors from the flag of the Netherlands. This flag was suppressed when Russia was part of the Soviet Union.

The Russian Federation is the world's largest country. About 25% lies west of the Ural Mountains (Uralskie Gory) in European Russia, where 80% of the population lives. It is mostly flat or undulating, but the land rises to the Caucasus Mountains in the south, with Russia's highest peak, Elbrus (18,481 ft [5,633 m]). Siberia, contains vast plains and plateaus, with mountains in the east and south. The Kamchatka peninsula in the far east has many active volcanoes.

Russia contains many of the world's longest rivers, including Yenisey-Angara and the Ob-Irtysh. It also includes part of the world's largest inland body of water, the Caspian Sea, and Lake Baikal, the world's deepest lake.

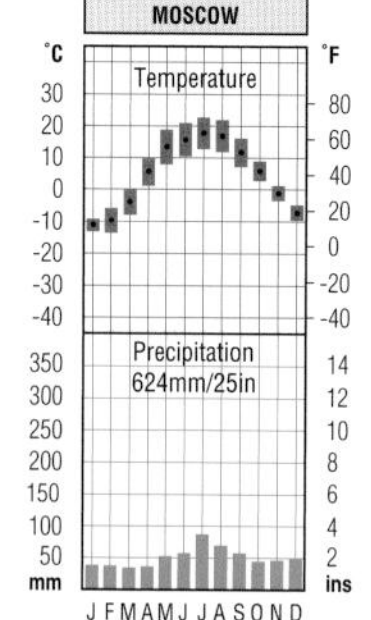

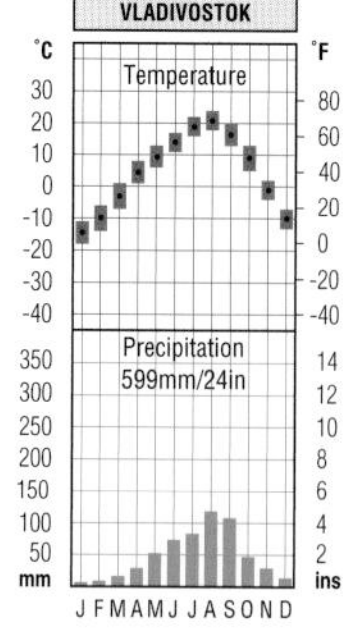

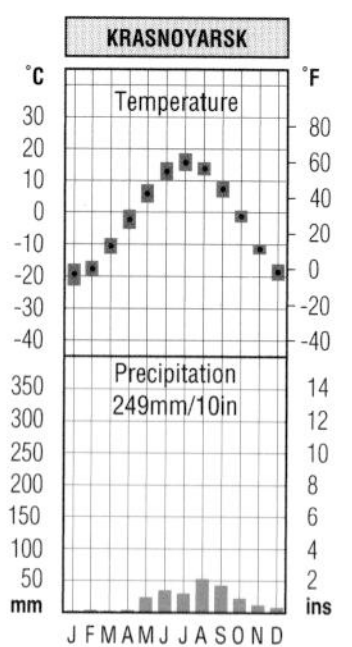

CLIMATE

The Moscow climate is continental with cold and snowy winters and warm summers. While Krasnoyarsk in south-central Siberia has a harsher, drier climate, but it is not as severe as parts of northern Siberia.

HISTORY

In the 9th century AD, a state called Kievan Rus was formed at the junction of the forest and the steppe in what is now Ukraine. Other states then formed further to the north and all were eventually united under the principality of Muscovy. In the 13th century, Mongol armies from the east penetrated the forests and held sway over the Slavic peoples there. It was only in the 16th century that the Mongol yoke was thrown off as the Slavs, under Ivan the Terrible (1530–84), began to advance across the steppes.

There began a period of expansion from the core area of Slavic settlement to the south, east, and west. Expansion across Siberia was rapid and the first Russian settlement on the Pacific, Okhotsk, was established in 1649. By 1696, Azov, the key to the Black Sea, was secured. A series of struggles in the 17th and 18th centuries against the Swedes and the Poles resulted in the addition of the Gulf of Finland, the Baltic coast, and part of Poland to the growing Russian Empire, while, in the 19th century, the Caucasus, Central Asia, and new territories in the Far East were added.

The Russian Revolution took place in 1917, Tsar Nicholas II was forced to abdicate and a Bolshevik (Communist) government was established under Vladimir Ilyich Lenin (1870–1924). The Union of Soviet Socialist Republics (the USSR or the Soviet Union) was established in 1922.

POLITICS

From 1924 Joseph Stalin introduced a socialist economic program, suppressing all opposition both within the Party and among the population. His authority was consolidated with the Great Purge, a period of widespread arrests and execu-

ST. PETERSBURG

Second-largest city in Russia, and a major Gulf of Finland seaport, on the delta of the River Neva. Founded in 1703 by Peter I (the Great), the city was the capital of Russia from 1712 to 1918. It was the scene of the Decembrist revolt (1825) and the Bloody Sunday incident in the Russian Revolution of 1905. Renamed Petrograd in 1914, it was a center of the political unrest that culminated in the Russian Revolution. Petrograd workers were the spearhead of the 1917 Revolution, and the city was renamed Leningrad in 1924. Damaged during World War II, it has since been rebuilt. Renamed St. Petersburg (1991), following the breakup of the Soviet Union, it has federal status within the Russian Republic.

Area 6,592,812 sq mi [17,075,400 sq km]
Population 143,782,000
Capital (population) Moscow (8,297,000)
Government Federal multiparty republic
Ethnic groups Russian 82%, Tatar 4%, Ukrainian 3%, Chuvash 1%, more than 100 others
Languages Russian (official), plus many others
Religions Russian Orthodox, Islam, Judaism
Currency Russian rouble = 100 kopeks
Website www.kremlin.ru/eng

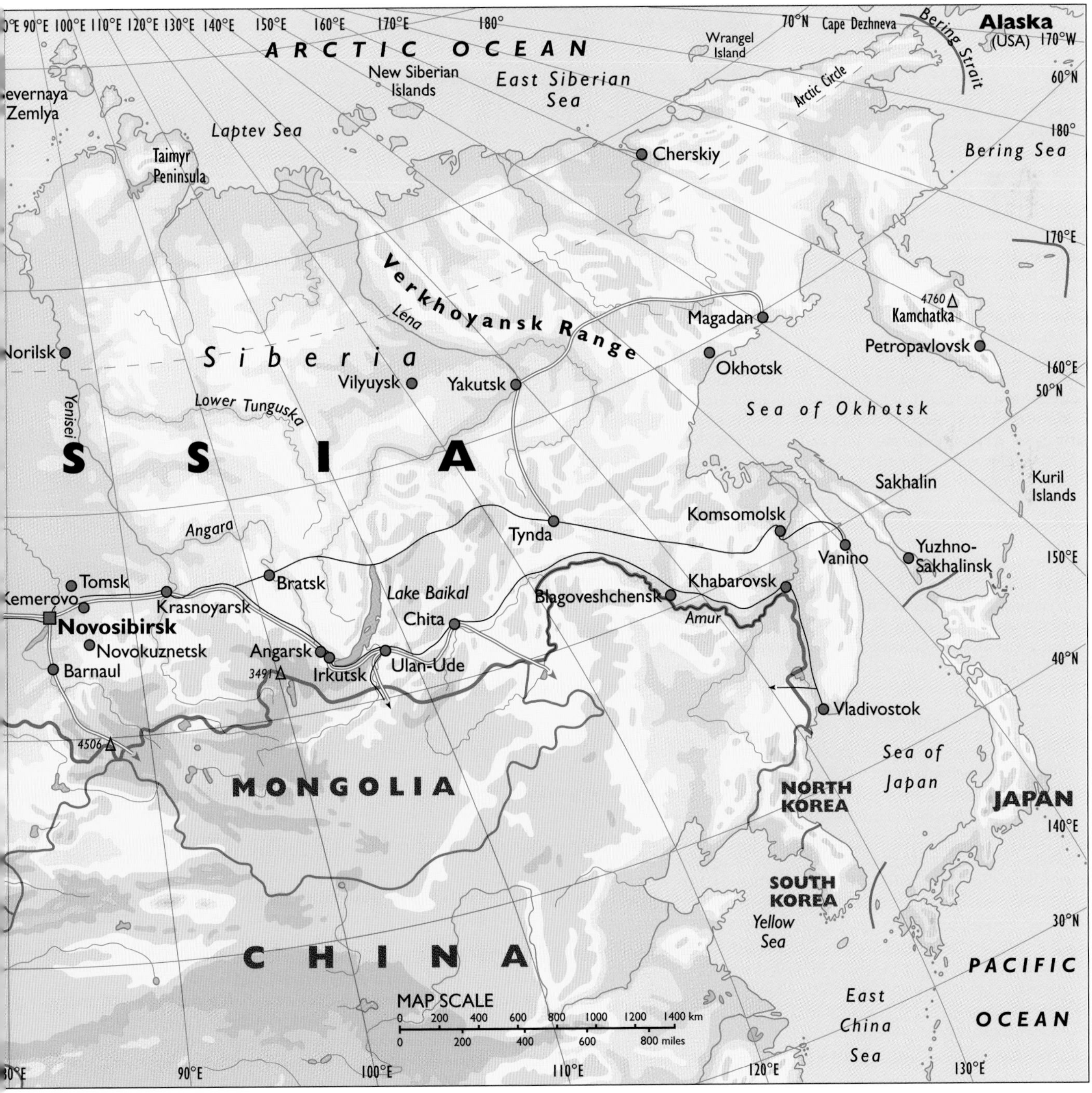

ARCTIC OCEAN
East Siberian Sea
Laptev Sea
New Siberian Islands
Wrangel Island
Cape Dezhneva
Bering Strait
Alaska (USA)
Arctic Circle
Bering Sea
Severnaya Zemlya
Taimyr Peninsula
Cherskiy
Verkhoyansk Range
Lena
Magadan
Kamchatka
4760
Petropavlovsk
Norilsk
Siberia
Vilyuysk
Yakutsk
Okhotsk
Sea of Okhotsk
Lower Tunguska
Yenisei
ASIA
Sakhalin
Kuril Islands
Komsomolsk
Tynda
Angara
Vanino
Yuzhno-Sakhalinsk
Tomsk
Kemerovo
Bratsk
Krasnoyarsk
Lake Baikal
Blagoveshchensk
Khabarovsk
Amur
Novosibirsk
Chita
Novokuznetsk
Angarsk
Barnaul
3491
Irkutsk
Ulan-Ude
Vladivostok
4506
Sea of Japan
MONGOLIA
NORTH KOREA
JAPAN
SOUTH KOREA
Yellow Sea
CHINA
PACIFIC OCEAN
East China Sea
MAP SCALE
0 200 400 600 800 1000 1200 1400 km
0 200 400 600 800 miles
90°E 100°E 110°E 120°E 130°E 140°E 150°E 160°E 170°E 180° 170°W
70°N 60°N 50°N 40°N 30°N

LAKE BAIKAL

World's deepest lake in southern Siberia, Russia; the largest freshwater feature in Asia. Fed by numerous small rivers, its outlet is the River Angara. Framed by mountains, Baikal has rich fish stocks and the world's only freshwater seal species. Its ecology is threatened by pollutants from lakeside factories. Government schemes have been introduced to protect the environment. Irkutsk is on the north shore and the Trans-Siberian Railway runs along the south shore. Area: 31,494 sq km (12,160 sq mi),.maximum depth: 1,743 m (5,714 ft).

Russian fishermen *net a catch of omul on Lake Baikal*

tions which reached its peak in 1937. His introduction of five-year plans and collective farming transformed the Soviet Union from a largely peasant society to a major world industrial power by the end of the 1930s. Collectivization was violently resisted by many peasants, resulting in millions of casualties from famine and mass repression of peasants (*kulaks*) by the authorities. After Stalin's death, the Soviet leaders modified some policies, but remained true to the principles of Communism until Mikhail Gorbachev changed the face of Russia in the 1980s.

The Soviet Union joined World War II (known in Russia as the Great Patriotic War) in June 1941. The armed forces of the Soviet Union inflicted about 80% of losses suffered by German land forces in World War II (about 3 million soldiers). The Soviet Union, suffered enormous losses with 25 million dead.

Under Soviet rule, changes took place in the distribution of the population so that the former pattern of a small highly populated core and "empty" periphery began to break down. As a result, a far higher proportion of the Russian population lives east of the Ural Mountains than before the Revolution. The redistribution was actively encouraged by a regime committed to developing the east. Migration to the towns and cities has also been marked and by 1997 73% of the population lived in cities and towns.

In the 1980s, Mikhail Gorbachev sought to introduce economic and political reforms necessitated by the failures of Communist economic policies. This was a time of *glasnost* (openness) and *perestroika* (restructuring). The Soviet Union broke up in December 1991. Russia maintained relations with 11 of the 15 former Soviet republics through a confederation called the Commonwealth of Independent States (CIS).

MOSCOW (MOSKVA)

Capital of Russia and largest city in Europe, on the River Moskva. The site has been inhabited since Neolithic times, but Russian records do not mention it until 1147. It had become a principality by the end of the 13th century, and in 1367 the first stone walls of the Kremlin were constructed. By the end of the 14th century, Moscow emerged as the focus of Russian opposition to the Mongols. Polish troops occupied the city in 1610, but were driven out two years later. Moscow was the capital of the Grand Duchy of Russia from 1547 to 1712, when the capital moved to St Petersburg. In 1812 Napoleon and his army occupied Moscow, but were forced to flee when the city burned to the ground. In 1918, following the Russian Revolution, it became the capital of the Soviet Union. The failure of the German army to seize the city in 1941 was the Nazis' first major setback in World War II. The Kremlin is the center of the city, and the administrative heart of the country. Adjoining it are Red Square, the Lenin Mausoleum, and the 16th-century cathedral of Basil the Beatified. Industries include metalworking, oil-refining, motor vehicles, film-making, precision instruments, chemicals, publishing, wood and paper products, and tourism.

Despite Gorbachev's brave efforts at reform, his successor Boris Yeltsin inherited an economy in crisis. The abolition of price controls sent the cost of basic commodities rocketing, there were food shortages and rising unemployment. Despite these difficulties, including rising corruption and crime, the government's program of reforms was supported in a 1993 referendum and Yeltsin returned as president in July 1996.

Yeltsin resigned on December 1999 31, due to poor health and appointed the prime minister Vladimir Putin as the acting president. Putin, was elected president by a landslide in March 2000.

Fighting began in the secessionist Chechnya during the 1990s and flared up into full-scale war in 1999. The conflict slowed in 2000, but Russia faced a new threat, namely bombings of its cities by Chechen terrorists. After the attacks on the United States on September 11, 2001, Putin and President George W. Bush found common cause in the campaign against international terrorism and the assault on the Taliban in Afghanistan, though relations soured when Russia opposed the attack on Iraq in 2003.

The conflict in Chechnya mounted and has lead to hundreds of deaths in Russia in a series of major terrorist attacks, such as the attack on a Moscow theater in 2002, the bombing of two passenger flights in 2004, and the occupation of a school by Muslim extremists in 2004 which led to more than 300 deaths, caused international outrage.

ECONOMY

Under Soviet rule, Russia transformed from an agrarian economy into the world's second greatest industrial power. By the 1970s, concentration on the military-industrial complex and a bloated bureaucracy caused the economy to stagnate. Gorbachev's policy of perestroika was an attempt to correct this weakness. Yeltsin sped up the pace of reform. In 1993, the command economy was abolished, private ownership was reintroduced, and mass privatization began. In 1997 Russia was admitted to the Council of Europe, the same year Russia attended the G7 summit, suggesting that it was now counted among the world's leading economies. Industry employs 46% of the workforce and contributes 48% of GDP. Mining is the most valuable activity. Russia is the world's leading producer of natural gas and nickel, and the world's third-largest producer of crude oil, lignite, and brown coal. It is the world's second-largest manufacturer of aluminum and phosphates. Light industries are growing in importance. Most farmland is still government-owned or run as collectives. Russia is the largest producer of barley, oats, rye, and potatoes. It is the world's second-largest producer of beef and veal.

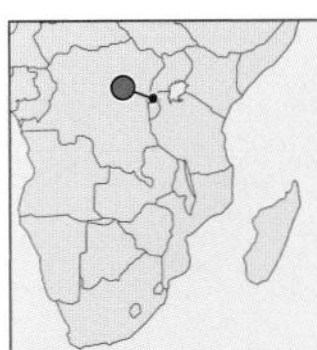

Rwanda's new flag was adopted in 2002. The blue is used to symbolize peace and tranquillity. Yellow represents wealth as the country works to achieve sustainable economic growth, while green denotes prosperity, work and productivity. The 24-ray golden sun symbolizes new hope.

Area 10,169 sq mi [26,338 sq km]
Population 7,954,000
Capital (population) Kigali (234,000)
Government Republic
Ethnic groups Hutu 84%, Tutsi 15%, Twa 1%
Languages French, English and Kinyarwanda (all official)
Religions Roman Catholic 57%, Protestant 26%, Adventist 11%, Islam 5%
Currency Rwandan franc = 100 centimes
Website www.gov.rw

The Republic of Rwanda is Africa's most densely populated country. It is a small state in the heart of Africa. The western border is formed by Lake Kivu and the River Ruzizi. Rwanda has a rugged landscape, dominated by high, volcanic mountains, rising to Mount Karisimbi, at 14,787 ft [4,507 m]. The capital, Kigali, stands on the central plateau. East Burundi consists of stepped plateaus, which descend to the lakes and marshland of the Kagera National Park on the Tanzania border.

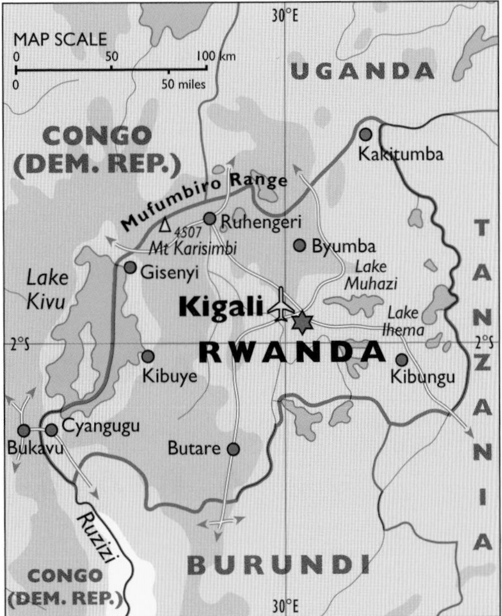

The lush rainforests in the west are one of the last refuges for the mountain gorilla. Many of Rwanda's forests have been cleared and 35% of the land is now arable. The steep mountain slopes are intensively cultivated. Despite contour ploughing, heavy rains cause severe soil erosion.

CLIMATE

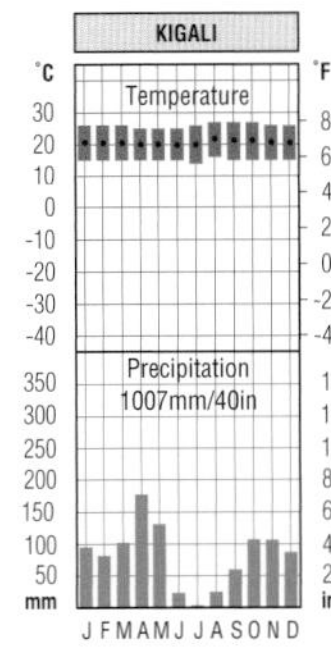

Temperatures in Kigali are moderated by the altitude. The rainfall is abundant, but much heavier rain falls on the western mountains. The dry season is June–August. The floor of the Great Rift Valley is warmer and drier than the rest of the country.

HISTORY

The Twa, a pygmy people, were the first known people to live in Rwanda. About 1,000 years ago, a farming people, the Hutu, settled in the area, gradually displacing the Twa.

From the 15th century, a cattle-owning people from the north, the Tutsi, began to dominate the Hutu, who had to serve the Tutsi overlords.

By the late 18th century, Rwanda and Burundi formed a single Tutsi-dominated state, ruled by a King (Mwami). In 1890, Germany conquered the area and subsumed it into German East Africa. During World War 1, Belgian forces occupied (1916) both Rwanda and Burundi. In 1919, it became part of the Belgian League of Nations mandate territory of Ruanda-Urundi (which in 1946 became a UN Trust Territory). The Hutu majority intensified their demands for political representation. In 1959, the Tutsi Mwami died. The ensuing civil war between Hutus and Tutsis claimed more than 150,000 lives. Hutu victory led to a mass exodus of Tutsis. The Hutu Emancipation Movement, led by Grégoire Kayibanda, won the 1960 elections. In 1961, Rwanda declared itself a republic. Belgium granted independence in 1962, and Kayibanda became president.

POLITICS

Rwanda was subject to continual Tutsi incursions from Burundi and Uganda. In 1973, Major General Habyarimana overthrew Kayibanda in a military coup. In 1978, Habyarimana became president. Drought devastated Rwanda in the 1980s. More than 50,000 refugees fled to Burundi. In 1990, the Tutsi-dominated Rwandan Patriotic Front (RPF) invaded Rwanda, forcing Habyarimana to adopt a multiparty constitution. In April 1994, Habyarimana and the president of Burundi died in a rocket attack. The Hutu army and militia launched an act of genocide against the Tutsi minority, massacring more than 800,000 Tutsis. In July 1994, an RPF offensive toppled the government, creating 2 million Hutu refugees. A government of national unity, comprising Tutsis and Hutus, emerged. More than 50,000 people died in refugee camps in eastern Zaïre (now DR Congo). Hutu militia controlled the camps, their leaders facing prosecution for genocide. The sheer number of refugees (1995, one million in Zaïre and 500,000 in Tanzania) destabilized the region. In 1997, Rwandan troops supported Laurent Kabila's successful overthrow of President Mobutu in Zaïre. Kabila failed to expel the Hutu militia from Congo, and Rwanda switched to supporting rebel forces. In 1998, the UN International Criminal Tribunal sentenced Rwanda's former prime minister Jean Kambanda to life imprisonment for genocide. Paul Kagame became president in 2000. He was reelected in 2003.

In the early 21st century, prosecutions began in both Belgium and Tanzania of people accused of genocide. Rwanda finally withdrew from DR Congo in late 2002 after signing a peace deal with Kinshasa.

KIGALI

Capital city lying in the center of Rwanda. It was a trade center during the period of German and Belgian colonial administration, becoming the capital when Rwanda achieved independence in 1962. Industries include tin mining, cotton, and coffee.

ECONOMY

According to the World Bank, Rwanda is a "low-income" developing country. Agriculture employs 90% of the workforce, but many farmers live at subsistence level. Chief food crops include bananas, beans, cassava, plantains, potatoes, sorghum, and sweet potatoes. Some farmers raise cattle and other livestock. The chief cash crop is coffee, also the leading export, followed by tea and hides and skins. Rwanda also produces pyrethrum, which is used to make insecticide. The country produces some cassiterite (tin ore) and wolframite (tungsten ore). Manufacturing is small-scale and include beverages, cement and sugar.

***Kinigi farmland** extending to Virunga National Park*

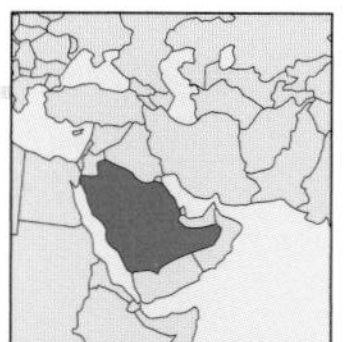

Saudi Arabia's flag was adopted in 1938. It is the only national flag with an inscription as its main feature. The Arabic inscription above the sword means "There is no God but Allah, and Muhammad is the Prophet of Allah."

Area 829,995 sq mi [2,149,690 sq km]
Population 25,796,000
Capital (population) Riyadh (3,000,000)
Government Absolute monarchy
Ethnic groups Arab 90%, Afro-Asian 10%
Languages Arabic (official)
Religions Islam 100%
Currency Saudi riyal = 100 halalas
Website www.saudinf.com

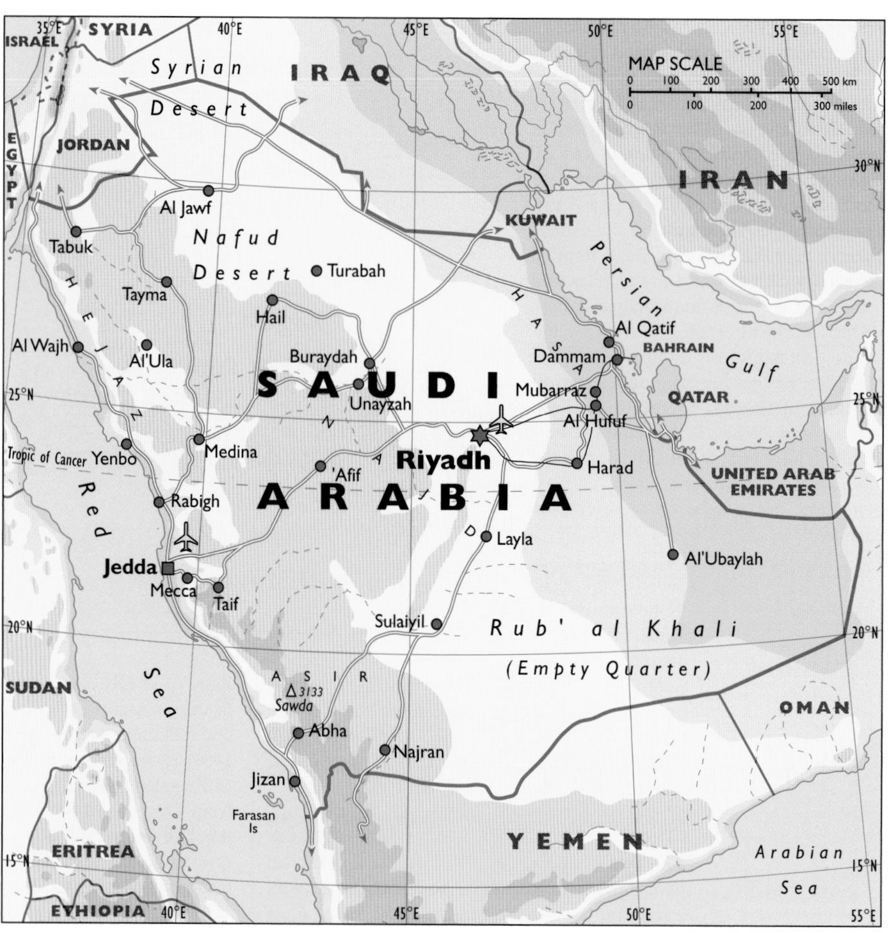

The Kingdom of Saudi Arabia occupies about three-quarters of the Arabian Peninsula in southwest Asia. The land is mostly desert and includes the largest expanse of sand in the world, the Rub' al Khali (Empty Quarter), covering an area of 250,000 sq mi [647,500 sq km]. Mountains to the west border the Red Sea plains.

CLIMATE

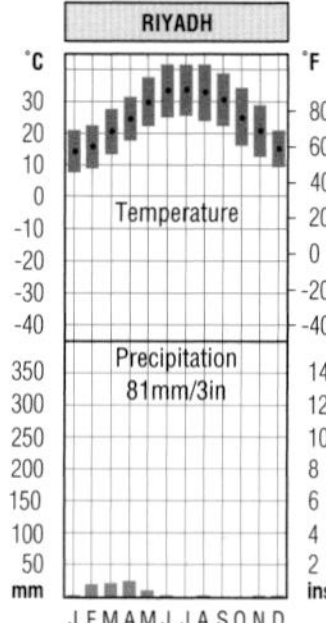

Saudi Arabia has a hot, dry climate. In the summer, the temperatures are extremely high and often exceed 104°F [40°C], though the nights are cool. Winter temperatures rarely go below 68°F [20°C].

HISTORY

Saudi Arabia contains the two holiest places in Islam—Mecca, the birthplace of the Prophet Muhammad in 570, and Medina where Muhammad and his followers went in 622.

In the mid-15th century, the Saud Dynasty established control over a small area near present-day Riyadh. In the mid-18th century an alliance was established with a religious leader, Muhammad Ibn Abd al-Wahhab, who wanted to restore strict observance of Islam. The Wahhabi movement swept across Arabia and the Saud family took over areas converted to the Wahhabi beliefs. By the early 19th century, they had taken Mecca and Medina. The Ottoman governor of Egypt attacked to halt their expansion and by the late 19th century, most of the Arabian Peninsula was under the rule of Ottoman Turks.

In 1902 Abd al-Aziz Ibn Saud, led a force from Kuwait, where he had been living in exile, and captured Riyadh. From 1906, the Saud family gradually won control over the territory held by their ancestors and extended their land following the defeat of the Ottoman Empire in World War I. After further conquests in the 1920s, Ibn Saud proclaimed the country the Kingdom of Saudi Arabia in 1932.

RIYADH

Capital of Saudi Arabia, in the east-central part of the country, 235 mi [380 km] inland from the Persian Gulf. In the early 19th century, it was the domain of the Saudi dynasty, becoming capital of Saudi Arabia in 1932. The chief industry is oil refining.

POLITICS

The first major oil discovery was made in 1938, and full-scale production began after World War II. Saudi Arabia eventually became the world's leading oil exporter and highly influential in the Arab world where it played a major role in supplying development aid.

Saudi Arabia supported Egypt, Jordan, and Syria in the Six-Day War against Israel, in 1967. It did not send troops, but gave aid to the Arab combatants.

King Fahd suffered a stroke in 1995 and appointed his half-brother, Crown Prince Abdullah Ibn Abdulaziz, to act on his behalf. Fahd died in 2005 and Abdullah succeeded him as king.

Although assisted by a Consultative Council, the monarch holds executive and legislative powers and is also the imam (supreme religious ruler). Saudi Arabia is an absolute monarchy with no formal constitution.

Despite its support of Iraq against Iran in the First Gulf War in the 1980s, Saudi Arabia asked for the protection of Western forces against possible Iraqi aggression following the invasion of Kuwait in 1990. In 1991, the country played a significant role in the quick victory over Iraq's Saddam Hussein.

Relations between Saudi Arabia and the United States became strained following the terrorist attacks on the US on September 11. 2001, in part because Osama bin Laden and many of his followers were Saudi-born. Saudi authorities denounced the attacks and severed relations with Afghanistan's Taliban regime. In 2003 and 2004, Saudi Arabia was hit by Islamic attacks. The government held nationwide municipal elections in 2005, its first exercise in democracy. However, political parties are banned and activists who publicly broach the subject of reform risk jail.

ECONOMY

Saudi Arabia has about 25% of the world's known oil reserves, and oil and oil products make up 85% of its exports.

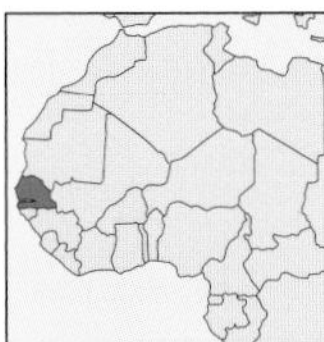

This flag was adopted in 1960 when Senegal became independent from France. It uses the three colors that symbolize African unity. It is identical to the flag of Mali, except for the five-pointed green star. This star symbolizes the Muslim faith of most of the people.

The Republic of Senegal is situated on the northwest coast of Africa. The volcanic Cape Verde (Cap Vert), on which Dakar stands, is the most westerly point in Africa. The country entirely surrounds Gambia. The Atlantic coastline from St. Louis to Dakar is sandy. Plains cover most of Senegal, though the land rises gently in the southeast. The north forms part of the Sahel. The main rivers are the Sénégal, which forms the north border, and the Casamance in the south. The River Gambia flows into the Gambia.

Desert and semidesert cover north east Senegal. In central Senegal, dry grasslands and scrub predominate. Mangrove swamps border parts of the south coast. The far south is a region of tropical savanna, though large areas have been cleared for farming. Senegal has several protected parks, the largest is the Niokolo-Kobo Wildlife Park.

Area 75,954 sq mi [196,722 sq km]
Population 10,852,000
Capital (population) Dakar (880,000)
Government Multiparty republic
Ethnic groups Wolof 44%, Pular 24%, Serer 15%
Languages French (official), tribal languages
Religions Islam 94%, Christianity (mainly Roman Catholic) 5%, traditional beliefs 1%
Currency CFA franc = 100 centimes
Website www.senegalembassy.co.uk

CLIMATE

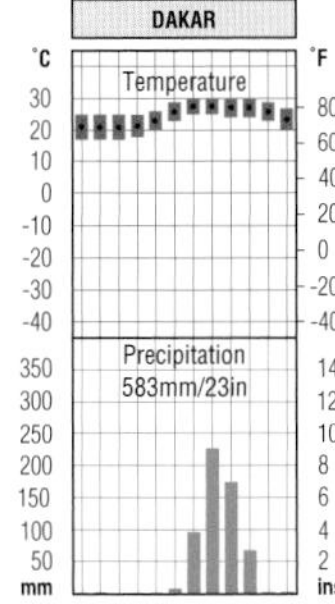

Dakar has a tropical climate, with a short rainy season between June and September when moist winds blow from the southwest. Temperatures are higher inland. Rainfall is greatest in the south.

HISTORY

From the 6th to the 10th century, Senegal formed part of the Empire of ancient Ghana. Between the 10th and 14th centuries, the Tukolor state of Tekrur dominated the Sénégal valley. The Almoravid dynasty of Zenega Berbers introduced Islam and it is from the Zenega that Senegal got its name. In the 14th century, the Wolof established the Jolof Empire. The Songhai Empire began to dominate the region.

In 1444, Portuguese sailors became the first Europeans to reach Cape Verde. Trading stations were rapidly established in the area. In the 17th century, France and the Netherlands replaced Portuguese influence. France gradually gained control of the valuable slave trade and founded St. Louis in 1658. By 1763 Britain expelled the French from Senegal and in 1765, set up Senegambia, the first British colony in Africa. In 1783 France regained control and in the mid 19th century, battled for control of the interior. The French founded Dakar in 1857. In 1895, Senegal became a French colony within the Federation of French West Africa. In 1902, the capital of this huge empire transferred from St. Louis to Dakar. Dakar became a major trading center. In 1946, Senegal joined the French Union.

POLITICS

In 1959, Senegal joined French Sudan (now Mali) to form the Federation of Mali. Senegal withdrew in 1960 to become the separate Republic of Senegal, within the French community. Its first post-colonial president, Léopold Sédar Senghor, was a noted African poet.

Following an unsuccessful coup in 1962, Senghor gradually assumed wider powers. During the 1960s Senegal's economy deteriorated and a succession of droughts caused starvation and widespread civil unrest.

During the 1970s southern Senegal was a base for guerrilla movements in Guinea and Portuguese Guinea (modern Guinea-Bissau). In 1974, Senegal was a founding member of the West African Economic Community.

Senghor continued in office until 1981, when he was succeeded by the prime minister, Abdou Diouf. In that same year, Senegalese troops suppressed a coup in the Gambia. In 1982 the two countries joined to form the Confederation of Senegambia, but the union collapsed in 1989. From 1989 to 1992, Senegal was at war with Mauritania.

In 2000, Diouf was surprisingly beaten in presidential elections by veteran opposition leader Abdoulaye Wade of the Senegalese Democratic Party, ending 40 years of Socialist Party rule. In 2001, the government signed a peace treaty with the separatist rebels in the southern Casamance province.

ECONOMY

According to the World Bank, Senegal is a "lower-middle-income" developing country. Agriculture still employs 65% of the population, though many farmers produce little more than they need to feed their families. Food crops include cassava, millet, and rice. Senegal is the world's sixth largest producer of groundnuts. Phosphates are the chief resource, and Senegal also refines oil imported from Gabon and Nigeria. Fishing is important.

***A group of fishermen** sit at the base of a large fig tree along the bank of the Casamance river in Kafountine, Senegal*

DAKAR

Capital and largest city of Senegal. Founded in 1857 as a French fort, the city grew rapidly with the arrival of a railroad (1885). A major Atlantic port, it later became capital of French West Africa. There is a Roman Catholic cathedral and a presidential palace. Dakar has excellent educational and medical facilities, including the Pasteur Institute. Industries include textiles, oil refining, brewing.

Serbia

The tricolor flag uses the Pan-Slavic colors of blue, white, and red. These colors derive from the 19th-century flag of Russia.

Area 34, 116 sq mi [88,361 sq km]
Population 9,396,411
Capital (population) Belgrade (1,594,000)
Government Federal republic
Ethnic groups Serb 66%, Albanian 17%, Hungarian 3.5%, others
Languages Serbian (official), Romanian, Hungarian, Slovak, and Croatian (all official in Vojvodina); Albanian (official in Kosovo)
Religions Orthodox 65%, Islam 19%, others
Currency New dinar = 100 paras
Website
www.srbija.sr.gov.yu/?change_lang=en

The Republic of Serbia, with Montenegro, was formerly part of Yugoslavia, in the central part of the Balkan peninsula. From 2003, it was part of the Union of Serbia and Montenegro, but, in 2006, after the Montenegrins had voted for full independence, Serbia became a separate republic. Serbia includes the semi-independent Kosovo in the south. Serbia is a landlocked country. The southeast is mountainous, while the Pannonian Plains, drained by the River Danube, lie in the north.

BELGRADE (BEOGRAD)

Capital of Serbia, at the confluence of the Sava and Danube rivers. Belgrade became capital of Serbia in the 12th century, but fell to the Ottoman Turks in 1521. Freed from Ottoman rule in 1867, it became capital of the newly created Yugoslavia in 1929. The city suffered much damage under German occupation in World War II. In 1999 it was further damaged by Allied air strikes after Milosevic sent federal troops into Kosovo. In October 2000, more than 300,000 people marched through the streets of Belgrade, forcing Milosevic to step down as president.

CLIMATE

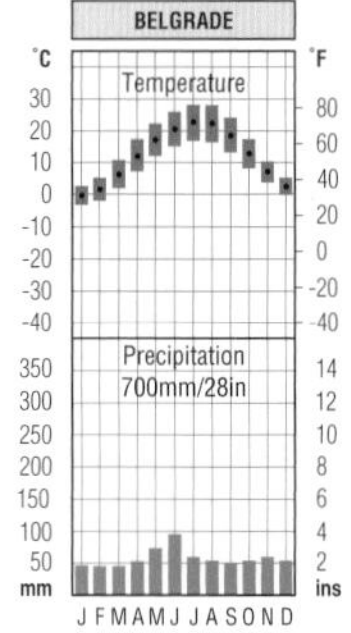

Central and northern Serbia has a continental climate, with hot, dry summers, with heavy rains in the spring and fall, while the southeast has a more Mediterranean climate.

HISTORY

South Slavs began to move into the region around 1,500 years ago. Each group founded its own state, but by the 15th century Serbia was under the Turkish Ottoman Empire. In 1914, Austria-Hungary declared war on Serbia, blaming it for the assassination of Archduke Franz Ferdinand of Austria-Hungary. This led to World War I and the defeat of Austria-Hungary. In 1918, the South Slavs united in the Kingdom of the Serbs, Croats, and Slovenes. In 1929, King Alexander abolished the constitution and renamed the country Yugoslavia. Ruling as a dictator, he sought to enforce the use of one language, Serbo-Croatian. His new political divisions failed to acknowledge the historic boundaries determined by the ethnic groups so the unity of the new state was under constant threat from nationalist and ethnic tensions. After the Germans invaded in 1941, Yugoslavs fought the Germans and themselves. The Communist-led partisans of Josip Broz Tito (a Croat) emerged victorious in 1945.

POLITICS

From 1945, the Communists ruled the country, then called the Federal People's Republic of Yugoslavia. But after Tito's death in 1980, the country was divided. In 1991-2, Yugoslavia split apart with Bosnia-Herzegovina, Croatia, Macedonia, and Slovenia each proclaiming their independence. The remaining two republics, Serbia and Montenegro, retained the name of Yugoslavia.

Fighting broke out in Croatia and Bosnia-Herzegovina as rival groups struggled for power. In 1992, the United Nations withdrew recognition of the rump Yugoslavia due to its failure to halt atrocities committed by Serbs living in Croatia and Bosnia-Herzegovina. However, in 1995, Yugoslavia took part in talks that led to the Dayton Peace Accord, but it had problems of its own as international sanctions struck the war-ravaged economy.

In 1998, the fragility of the region was again highlighted, in Kosovo, a former autonomous region in southern Serbia where most people are Albanian-speaking Muslims. Serbians forced Muslim Albanians to leave their homes, but they were opposed by the Kosovo Liberation Army (KLA). The Serbs hit back and thousands of civilians fled for their lives.

In March 1999, after attempts to find an agreement had failed, NATO forces intervened by launching aerial attacks on administrative and industrial targets in Kosovo and Serbia. Serbian forces stepped up attacks on Albanian- speaking villages, forcibly expelling the people, who fled into Albania and Macedonia. The NATO offensive ended when Serbian forces withdrew from Kosovo and the KLA was disbanded. In 2000, the Yugoslav leader Slobodan Milosevic was defeated in presidential elections and, in February 2002, he faced charges at the UN War Crimes Tribunal in The Hague. Milosevic died in 2006.

In 2003, Yugoslavia became the Union of Serbia and Montenegro, making both republics semi-independent. But, in 2006, the people of Montenegro voted by a narrow majority for independence, and Serbia and Montenegro became separate republics. The Albanian-speakers in Kosovo also continue to press for full independence from Serbia.

ECONOMY

Serbia's resources include bauxite, coal, copper, and other metals, together with oil and natural gas. Manufactures include aluminum, machinery, plastics, steel, textiles, and vehicles. Agriculture remains important.

***A quiet street** in the city of Novi Sad, situated on a bend of the Danube River, in the region of Vojvodina*

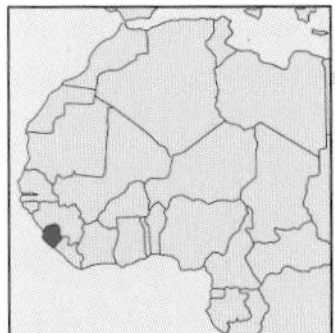

The green of the flag represents the nation's agriculture and its lush mountain slopes. Blue stands for the waters of the Atlantic that lap Sierra Leone's coast. White symbolizes the desire for peace, justice, and unity

The Republic of Sierra Leone on the west coast of Africa is about the same size as the Republic of Ireland. The coast contains several deep estuaries in the north, with lagoons in the south. The most prominent feature is the mountainous Freetown (or Sierra Leone) peninsula. North of the peninsula is the River Rokel estuary, west Africa's best natural harbor. Behind the coastal plain, the land rises to mountains, with the highest peak, Loma Mansa, reaching 6,391 ft [1,948 m].

Swamps cover large areas near the coast. Inland, much of the rainforest has been destroyed. The north is largely covered by tropical savanna.

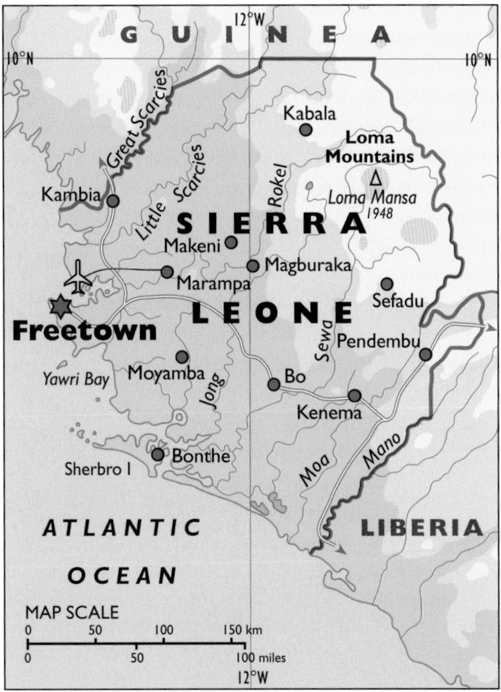

Area 27,699 sq mi [71,740 sq km]
Population 5,884,000
Capital (population) Freetown (470,000)
Government Single-party republic
Ethnic groups Native African tribes 90%
Languages English (official), Mende, Temne, Krio
Religions Islam 60%, traditional beliefs 30%, Christianity 10%
Currency Leone = 100 cents
Website www.visitsierraleone.org

CLIMATE

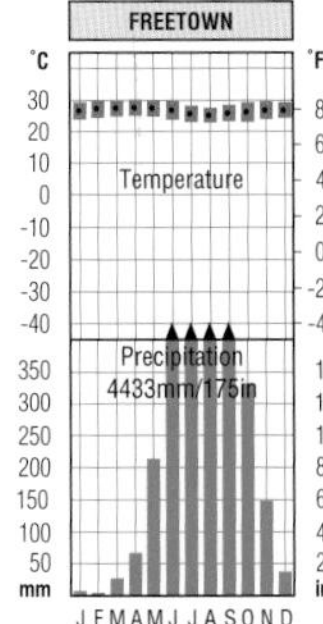

The climate is tropical, with heavy rainfall. In the north, it is dry between December and March. In the south, it is dry in January and February.

HISTORY

Portuguese sailors reached the coast in 1460. In the 16th century, the area became a source of slaves. Freetown was founded in 1787 as a home for freed slaves. In 1808, the settlement became a British Crown Colony. The interior was made a Protectorate in 1896 and in 1951, the Protectorate and Colony united.

Sierra Leone gained independence in 1961 and in 1971 became a republic.

POLITICS

A 1991 referendum voted for the restoration of multiparty democracy, but the military seized power in 1992. A civil war raged between government forces and the Revolutionary United Front (RUF). The RUF fought to end foreign interference and to nationalize the diamond mines. After 1996 elections, Ahmad Tejan Kabbah led a civilian government. In 1997, Major Johnny Paul Koroma seized power in a military coup. The Economic Community of West African States (ECOWAS) imposed sanctions, and Nigeria led an intervention force that restored Kabbah as president in 1998.

A 1999 peace treaty and the arrival of UN peacekeeping forces seemed to signal an end to the civil war, but in 2000 RUF rebels, led by Foday Sankoh and backed by Liberia, abducted UN troops and renewed the war. British soldiers arrived to bolster the UN peacekeeping effort. Disarmament continued throughout 2001 through a UN-brokered peace plan. Sankoh was captured and, in 2002, the war, which had left about 50,000 people dead, appeared to be over. Rebel raids from Liberia in 2003 failed to disturb the country's fragile peace. Stability was gradually restored and, in late 2005, the last contingent of UN soldiers left the country.

ECONOMY

The World Bank classifies Sierra Leone among the "low-income" economies. Agriculture provides a living for 70% of the workforce, though farming is mostly at subsistence level. Food crops include cassava, corn and rice, the staple food and export crops include cocoa and coffee. The most valuable exports include diamonds, bauxite, and rutile (titanium ore).

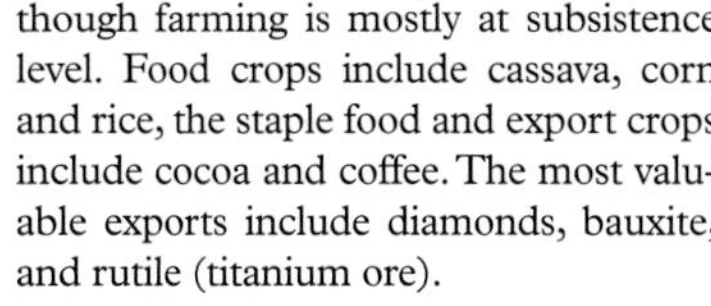

FREETOWN

Capital and chief port of Sierra Leone, west Africa. First explored by the Portuguese in the 15th century and visited by Sir John Hawkins in 1562. Freetown was founded by the British in 1787 as a settlement for freed slaves from England, Nova Scotia, and Jamaica. It was the capital of British West Africa (1808–74). West Africa's oldest university, Fourah Bay, was founded here in 1827. Freetown was made capital of independent Sierra Leone in 1961. Industries include platinum, gold, diamonds, oil refining, and palm oil.

DIAMOND

Crystalline form of carbon (C). The hardest natural substance known, it is found in kimberlite pipes and alluvial deposits. Appearance varies according to impurities. Bort, inferior in crystal and color, carborondo, an opaque gray to black variety, and other non-gem varieties are used in industry. Industrial diamonds are used as abrasives, bearings in precision instruments such as watches, and in the cutting heads of drills for mining. Synthetic diamonds, made by subjecting graphite, with a catalyst, to high pressure and temperatures of 5,400°F [3,000°C] are fit only for industry. Diamonds are weighed in carats (0.2gm) and points (1/100 carat).

***Sierra Leonian women** walking in village near Freetown*

Singapore

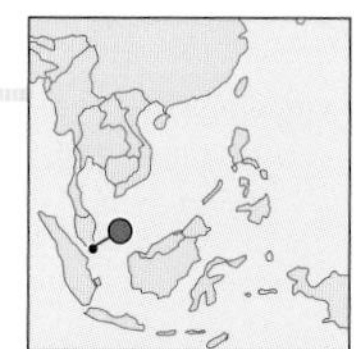

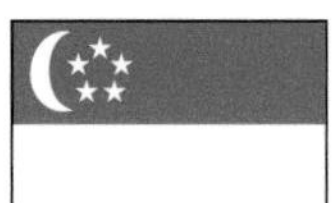

Singapore's flag was adopted in 1959 and it was retained when Singapore became part of the Federation of Malaysia in 1963. The crescent stands for the nation's ascent. The stars stand for Singapore's aims of democracy, peace, progress, justice and equality.

Area 264 sq mi [683 sq km]
Population 4,354,000
Capital (population) Singapore City (3,894,000)
Government Multiparty republic
Ethnic groups Chinese 77%, Malay 14%, Indian 8%
Languages Chinese, Malay, Tamil and English (all official)
Religions Buddhism, Islam, Hinduism, Christianity
Currency Singaporean dollar = 100 cents
Website www.gov.sg

103°40'E 104°E
MALAYSIA
Johore Strait
Kranji Sembawang Mandai Nee Soon Selator Punggol Ubin Tekong Changi
SINGAPORE
Jurong Bukit Timah 176 Bukit Timah Serangoon
1°20'N
Tuas Katong
Singapore City
Straits of Singapore
MAP SCALE 0 5 10 km 0 5 miles
INDONESIA

The Republic of Singapore is an island country at the southern tip of the Malay Peninsula. It consists of the large Singapore Island and 59 small islands, 20 of which are inhabited.

Singapore Island is 26 mi [42 km] wide and 14 mi [28 km] across. It is linked to the peninsula by a 3,465 ft [1,056 m] long causeway. The land is mostly low-lying; the highest point, Bukit Timah, is only 577 ft [176 m] above sea level. Its strategic position, at the convergence of some of the world's most vital shipping lanes, ensured its growth.

Rainforest once covered Singapore, but forests now grow on only 5% of the land. Today, about 50% of Singapore is built up. The distinction between island and city has all but disappeared. Most of the rest consists of open spaces, including parks, granite quarries, and inland waters. Farmland covers 4% of the land and plantations of permanent crops make up 7%.

SINGAPORE CITY

The capital of Singapore, on Singapore Island, the largest island in the Republic of Singapore, at the mouth of the Singapore River. The city is home to an ethnic mix of Chinese, Malaysians and Indians with English the main language. It has a very high standard of living due to its very healthy export-based economy. Tourism is one of the largest industries with attractions including the Singapore Zoological Gardens and the Jurong Bird Park, not to mention the Orchard Road area which is the shopping and entertainment center.

CLIMATE

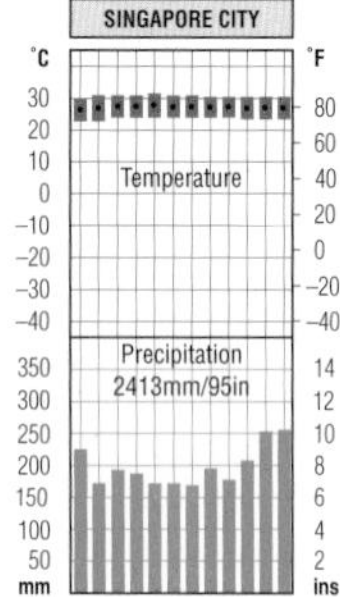

Singapore has a hot, humid equatorial climate, with temperatures averaging 86°F [30°C]. Total average annual rainfall is, 95 in [2,413 mm], with Rain occuring (on average) 180 days each year.

HISTORY

According to legend, Singapore was founded in 1299. It was first called Temasak ("sea town"), but was named Singapura ("city of the lion") when an Indian prince thought he saw a lion there. Singapore soon became a busy trading center within the Sumatran Srivijaya kingdom. Javanese raiders destroyed it in 1377. Subsumed into Johor, Singapore became part of the powerful Malacca sultanate.

In 1819, Sir Thomas Stamford Raffles, agent of the British East India Company, made a treaty with the Sultan of Johor which allowed the British to build a settlement on Singapore Island. In 1826, Singapore, Pinang, and Malacca formed the Straits Settlement. Singapore soon became the most important British trading center in Southeast Asia, and the Straits Settlement became a Crown Colony in 1867. Despite British defensive reinforcements in the early 20th century, Japanese forces seized the island in 1942.

POLITICS

British rule returned in 1945. In 1946, the Straits Settlement dissolved and Singapore became a separate colony. In 1959, Singapore achieved self-government. Following a referendum in 1963, Singapore merged with Malaya, Sarawak, and Sabah to form the Federation of Malaysia. In 1965, Singapore broke away from the Federation to become an independent republic within the Commonwealth of Nations.

The People's Action Party (PAP) has ruled Singapore since 1959. Its leader, Lee Kuan Yew, served as prime minister from 1959 until 1990, when he resigned and was succeeded by Goh Chok Tong. Under the PAP, the economy has expanded rapidly, although some people consider that the PAP's rule has been dictatorial and oversensitive to criticism. In 2004, Lee Hsien Loong, eldest son of Lee Kuan Yew, succeeded Goh Chok Tong as prime minister and called for a more open society. He also called for more people to marry and have babies, a reflection of the country's falling birth rate.

ECONOMY

The World Bank classifies Singapore as a "high-income" economy. It is one of the world's fastest growing (tiger) economies. Historically, Singapore's economy has been based on transshipment, and this remains a vital component. It is one of the world's busiest ports, annually handling more than 290 million tons of cargo. Post-1945 the economy diversified. Singapore has a highly skilled and productive workforce. The service sector employs 65% of the workforce; banking and insurance provide many jobs.

Manufacturing is the largest export sector. Industries include computers and electronics, telecommunications, chemicals, machinery, scientific instruments, ships, and textiles. It has a large oil refinery. Agriculture is relatively unimportant. Most farming is highly intensive, and farmers use the latest technology and scientific methods.

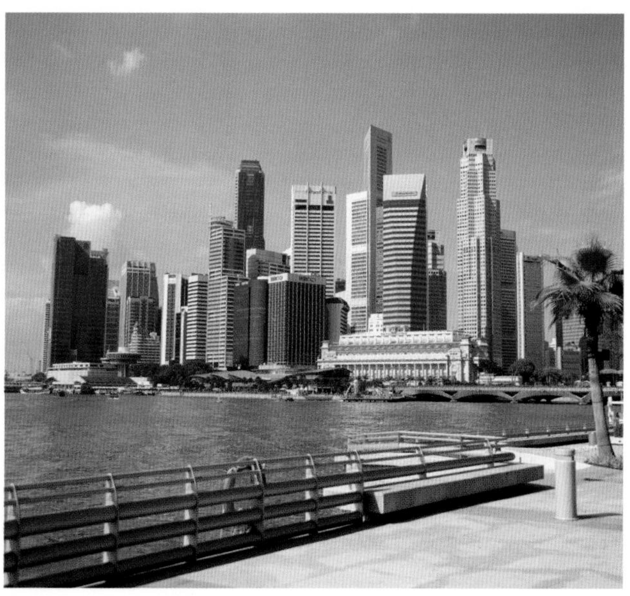

Skyline of Singapore City *from the water's edge*

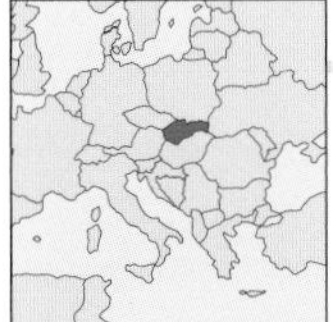

The flag uses the typical red, white, and blue Slavic colors. The coat of arms is taken from part of the Hungarian arms and shows a double cross set on three hills to commemorate the arrival of Christianity in the Carpathian region in the 9th century.

Slovak Republic

The Slovak Republic (Slovakia), is a predominantly mountainous country, part of the Carpathian system that divides the Slovak Republic from Poland is found in the north. The highest peak (Gerlachovka 8,711 ft [2,655 m]) is in the scenic Tatra (Tatry) Mountains on the Polish border.

Forests cover much of the mountain slopes and there is also extensive pasture. The southwestern Danubian lowlands form a fertile lowland region. The Danube forms part of the southern border with Hungary.

Area 18,924 sq mi [49,012 sq km]
Population 5,424,000
Capital (population) Bratislava (449,000)
Government Multiparty republic
Ethnic groups Slovak 86%, Hungarian 11%
Languages Slovak (official), Hungarian
Religions Roman Catholic 60%, Protestant 8%, Orthodox 4%, others
Currency Slovak koruna = 100 halierov
Website www.government.gov.sk/english

A fine example of *the traditional painted houses of the Slovak Republic*

CLIMATE

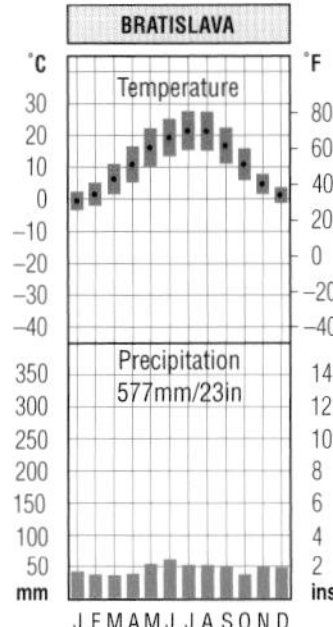

Slovakia has a transitional climate, in between the mild conditions of western Europe, and the continental conditions of Russia to the east. The conditions in Kosice, eastern Slovakia are fairly typical. Temperatures can range from 27°F [–3°C] in January to 68°F [20°C] in July. Kosice has an average annual rainfall of 24 in [600 mm]. The mountains have a more extreme climate, with snow or rain throughout the year.

HISTORY

Slav peoples settled in the region in the 5th century AD. In the 9th century, the region, together with Bohemia and Moravia in what is now the Czech Republic, became part of the Greater Moravian Empire. Hungarians conquered this empire in 907 and ruled for nearly a thousand years. Religious wars in the 15th century led many Czech nobles to settle in what is now the Slovak Republic. Hungary was defeated by the Turkish Ottomans in 1526 and, soon afterward, the Ottomans occupied much of eastern and central Hungary. As a result, the center of Hungarian power shifted into Slovakia.

Slovak nationalism developed from the late 18th century, but it was kept in check by the Hungarians who enforced "Magyarization." In 1867, Hungary and Austria were united to form the dual monarchy of Austria-Hungary. At the end of World War I, Austria-Hungary collapsed and the Czechs and Slovaks united to form a new nation called Czechoslovakia. In 1938, Hungary forced Czechoslovakia to give up several areas with large Hungarian populations. These areas included Kosice in the east.

In 1939, fearing that it might be divided up between Germany, Poland and Hungary, Slovakia declared itself independent, but the country was then conquered by Germany. At the end of World War II, Slovakia again became part of Czechoslovakia. Communists seized control in 1948. In the late 1960s, many Czechs and Slovaks, led by Alexander Dubcek, tried to reform the Communist system. This movement, known as "the Prague Spring," was put down in 1968 by Soviet troops. Demands for democracy reemerged in the 1980s, when Soviet leader Mikhail Gorbachev launched a series of reforms in the USSR.

BRATISLAVA

Capital of Slovakia, on the River Danube, western Slovakia. It became part of Hungary after the 13th century, and was the Hungarian capital from 1526–1784. Incorporated into Czechoslovakia in 1918, it became the capital of Slovakia in 1992. Industries include oil refining, textiles, chemicals, electrical goods.

POLITICS

At the end of November 1989, Czechoslovakia's parliament abolished the Communist Party's sole right to govern. In December, the head of the Communist Gustáv Hável, resigned. Non-Communists led by the playwright and dissident Václav Havel formed a new government, they then won a majority in the elections of June 1990.

In the elections of 1992, the Movement for Democratic Slovakia, led by Vladimir Meciar, campaigned for Slovak independence and won a majority in Slovakia's parliament. The Slovak National Council then approved a new constitution for the Slovak Republic, which came into existence on 1 January 1993.

The Slovak Republic became a member of the OECD in 1997 and maintained close contacts with its former partner. Slovak independence raised national aspirations among the Magyar-speaking community. Relations with Hungary were not helped in 1996, when the Slovak government initiated eight new administrative regions which the Hungarian minority claimed underrepresented them politically. The government also made Slovak the only official language. The government's autocratic rule, human rights record, and apparent tolerance of organized crime led to mounting international criticism. In 1998, Meciar's party was defeated in a general election by a four-party coalition and Mikulas Dzurinda, leader of the center-right Slovak Democratic Coalition, became prime minister. Dzurinda narrowly won the parliamentary elections of 2002 and his government continued its policy of strengthening ties with the West. Slovakia became a member of both NATO and the EU in 2004.

ECONOMY

Communist governments developed manufacturing industries, producing chemicals, machinery, steel, and weapons. Since the late 1980s, many state-run businesses have been handed over to private owners. Manufacturing employs around 33% of workers. Bratislava and Kosice are the chief industrial cities. Products include ceramics, machinery, and steel. The armaments industry is based at Martin, in the northwest. Farming employs about 12% of the workforce. Major crops include barley, grapes for wine-making, corn, sugar beets, and wheat.

Slovenia

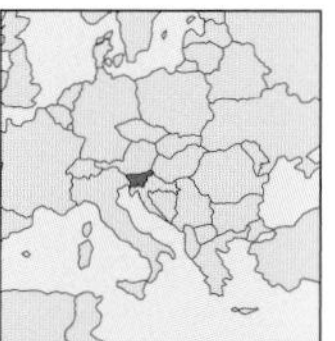

Slovenia's flag, based on the Russian flag, was originally adopted in 1848. A red star appeared at the center under Communist rule. This flag, which was adopted in 1991 when Slovenia proclaimed independence, has a new emblem, the national coat of arms.

Area 7,821 sq mi [20,256 sq km]
Population 2,011,000
Capital (population) Ljubljana (264,000)
Government Multiparty republic
Ethnic groups Slovene 92%, Croat 1%, Serb, Hungarian, Bosniak
Languages Slovenian (official), Serbo-Croatian
Religions Mainly Roman Catholic
Currency Tolar = 100 stotin
Website www.slovenia-tourism.si

The Republic of Slovenia was one of the six republics which made up Yugoslavia. Much of the land is mountainous and forested. The highest peak is Mount Triglav (9,393 ft [2,863 m]) in the Julian Alps (Julijske Alpe), an extension of the main Alpine ranges in the northwest. Much of central and eastern Slovenia is hilly. The River Sava which flows through central Slovenia is a tributary of the Danube, as is the Drava in the northeast.

Central Slovenia contains the limestone Karst region, with numerous underground streams and cave networks. The Postojna Caves, southwest of Ljubljana, are among the largest in Europe. The country has a short coastline on the Adriatic Sea.

Forests cover about half of Slovenia. Mountain pines grow on higher slopes, with beech, oak, and hornbeam at lower levels. The Karst region is largely bare of vegetation because of the lack of surface water. Farmland covers about one-third of Slovenia.

CLIMATE

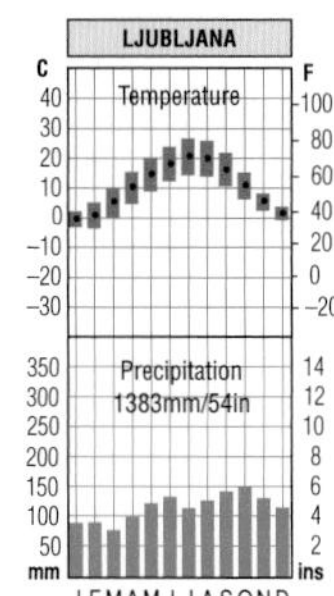

The Slovenian coast has a mild Mediterranean climate. The climate inland is more continental, with snow capping the mountains in winter. Eastern Slovenia has cold winters and hot summers. Rain occurs in every month in Ljubljana, late summer being the rainiest.

HISTORY

The ancestors of the Slovenes, the western branch of a group of people called the South Slavs, settled in the area around 1,400 years ago. An independent Slovene state was formed in AD 623, but the area came under Bavarian-Frankish rule in 748. Austrian royal family the Habsburgs took control of the region in 1278 and, apart from a short period of French rule between 1809 and 1815, it remained under Austrian control until 1918, when the dual monarchy of Austria-Hungary collapsed.

At the end of World War I, Slovenia became part of a new country called the Kingdom of the Serbs, Croats, and Slovenes, renamed Yugoslavia in 1929. Slovenia was invaded by Germany and Italy in 1941 and was partitioned between them and Hungary. At the end of the war, Slovenia again became one of the six republics of Yugoslavia.

In the late 1960s and early 1970s, some Slovenes called for the secession of their federal republic from Yugoslavia, but the dissidents were removed from the Communist Party by President Josip Broz Tito, whose strong rule maintained the unity of his country.

POLITICS

After Tito's death in 1980, the federal government in Belgrade found it increasingly difficult to maintain the unity of the disparate elements of the population. It was also weakened by the fact that Communism was increasingly seen to have failed in Eastern Europe and the Soviet Union. In 1990, Slovenia held multiparty elections and a non-Communist coalition was formed to rule the country.

Slovenia and neighboring Croatia proclaimed their independence in June 1991, but these acts were not accepted by the central government. After a few days of fighting between the Slovene militia and Yugoslav forces, Slovenia, the most ethnically homogenous of Yugoslavia's six component parts, found ready support from Italy and Austria (which had Slovene minorities of about 100,000 and 80,000, respectively), as well as Germany (an early supporter of Slovene independence). After a three-month moratorium, during which there was a negotiated, peaceful withdrawal, Slovenia became independent on October 8, 1991, thereby avoiding the conflict that was to plague other former Yugoslav states.

Slovenia's independence was recognized by the European Community in 1992. Multiparty elections were held and Milan Kucan (a former Communist) of the Party of Democratic Reform became president, while Janez Drnovsek, of the center-left Liberal Democratic Party, became prime minister, heading a coalition government. The Liberal Democrat coalition government was returned again in 1996 and 2000. Slovenia became a member of NATO and the EU in 2004 and later that year, the center-right Slovenian Democratic Party topped the polls in parliamentary elections and a center-right coalition was formed.

ECONOMY

The reform of the formerly state-run economy, and the fighting in areas to the south caused problems for Slovenia. It remains one of the fastest growing economies in Europe.

Manufacturing is the principal activity and manufactures include chemicals, machinery, and transportation equipment, metal goods and textiles. Slovenia mines some iron ore, lead, lignite, and mercury. The leading crops are corn, potatoes, and wheat.

Lake Bled *in the northwest of Slovenia; the lake formed after the recession of the Bohinj glacier*

LJUBLJANA

Capital and largest city of Slovenia, at the confluence of the rivers Sava and Ljubljanica. In 34 BC Roman Emperor Augustus founded Ljubljana as Emona. From 1244 it was the capital of Carniola, an Austrian province of the Habsburg Empire. During the 19th century, it was the center of the Slovene nationalist movement. The city remained under Austrian rule until 1918, when it became part of the Kingdom of Serbs, Croats, and Slovenes (later Yugoslavia). When Slovenia achieved independence in 1991, Ljubljana became the capital.

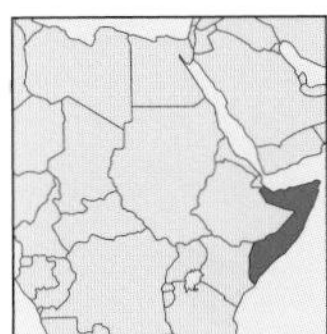

This flag was adopted in 1960, when Italian Somaliland in the south united with British Somaliland in the north to form Somalia. The colors are based on the United Nations flag and the points of the star represent the five regions of East Africa where Somalis live.

Area 246,199 sq mi [637,657 sq km]
Population 8,305,000
Capital (population) Mogadishu (900,000)
Government Transitional, parliamentary federal government
Ethnic groups Somali 85%, Bantu, Arab, others
Languages Somali (official), Arabic, English, Italian
Religions Islam (Sunni Muslim)
Currency CFA franc = 100 centimes
Website www.unsomalia.net

Somalia, is in a region known as the "Horn of Africa." A narrow, mostly barren, coastal plain borders the Indian Ocean and the Gulf of Aden. In the interior, the land rises to a plateau, of 3,300 ft [1,000 m]. In the north is a highland region. The south contains the only rivers, the Juba and the Scebeli.

Much of Somalia is dry grassland or semidesert. There are areas of wooded grassland, with trees such as acacia and baobab. Plants are most abundant in the the lower Juba valley.

CLIMATE

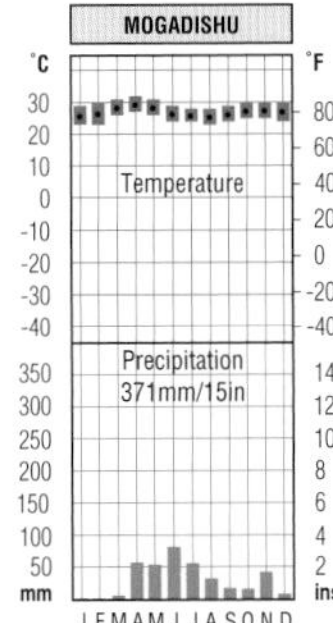

Rainfall is light throughout, the wettest regions being in the south and the northern mountains. The country is prone to droughts, with temperatures on the plateaux and the plains often reaching 90°F [32°C].

HISTORY

In the 7th century, Arab traders established coastal settlements and introduced Islam. Around 900, Mogadishu was founded as a trading center. The interest of European imperial powers increased after the opening of the Suez Canal in 1869. In 1887, Britain established a protectorate in what is now northern Somalia. In 1889, Italy formed a protectorate in the central region, and extended its power to the south by 1905. The new boundaries divided the Somalis into five areas: the two Somalilands, Djibouti (taken by France in 1896), Ethiopia, and Kenya. In 1936 Italian Somaliland united with the Somali regions of Ethiopia to form Italian East Africa. During World War II, Italy invaded British Somaliland, but, British forces conquered the region in 1941 and ruled both Somalilands until 1950, when Italian Somaliland returned to Italy as a UN Trust Territory. In 1960, both Somalilands gained independence and joined to form the United Republic of Somalia.

POLITICS

The new republic faced calls for the creation of a "Greater Somalia" to include the Somali-majority areas in Ethiopia, Kenya, and Djibouti. In 1969, the army, led by Siad Barre, seized power and formed a socialist, Islamic republic. During the 1970s, Somalia and Ethiopia fought for control of the Ogaden Desert, inhabited mainly by Somali nomads. In 1978 Ethiopia forced Somalia to withdraw, but resistance continued, forcing one million refugees to flee to Somalia. In 1991, Barre was overthrown and the United Somali Congress (USC), led by Ali Mahdi Muhammad, gained power. Somalia disintegrated into civil war between rival clans. The Ethiopian-backed Somali National Movement (SNM) gained control of northwest Somalia, and seceded as the Somaliland Republic in 1991. An attack from the Somali National Alliance (SNA), led by General Muhammad Aideed, shattered Mogadishu. War and drought resulted in a devastating famine. The UN was slow to provide relief and unable to secure distribution. US marines led a taskforce to aid food distribution, but became embroiled in conflict with Somali warlords.

In 1994, 30 US marines died in the fighting and US forces withdrew. Civil strife continued, and in 1996 Aideed was killed. The Cairo Declaration (1997), signed by 26 of the 28 warring factions, held out hope of an end to factional feuding. In 2000, clan leaders elected Abdulkassim Salat Hassan as president, but factional fighting continued. An interim parliament was set up in Kenya (for safety) in 2004, but attempts to move it to Somalia in 2005 saw limited success.

ECONOMY

Somalia is a developing country whose economy has been shattered by drought and war. Catastrophic flooding in late 1997 displaced tens of thousands of people, further damaging the country's infrastrucure, destroying hopes of economic recovery.

Many Somalis are nomads who raise livestock. Live animals, meat, and hides are major exports, plus bananas grown in the wetter south. Other crops include citrus fruits, cotton, corn, and sugar cane.

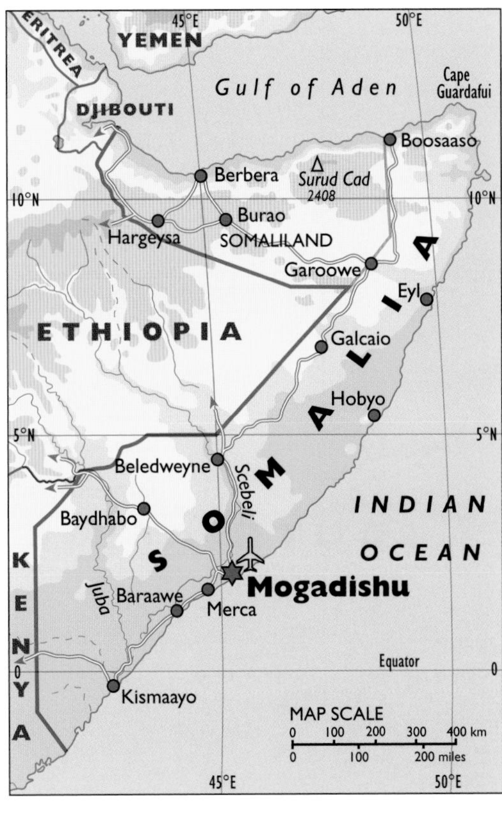

MOGADISHU

Capital and chief port of Somalia, on the Indian Ocean. It was founded by Arabs in the 10th century. In the 16th century, the Portuguese captured the city and it became a cornerstone of their trade with Africa. In 1871 the Sultan of Zanzibar took control. He first leased (1892) and then sold (1905) the port to the Italians. The city then became the capital of Italian Somaliland. It was occupied by the British during World War II. In 1960, Mogadishu became the capital of independent Somalia. The civil war of the 1980s/1990s devastated the city, its population swelled by refugees escaping famine and drought in the outlying regions. In 1992, UN troops flew in to control aid distribution but withdrew in 1995 after little success.

***A Somali herdsman** watches over his mixed herd of cattle and a few camels in a dry riverbed Lugh Ganane, west of Mogadishu*

South Africa

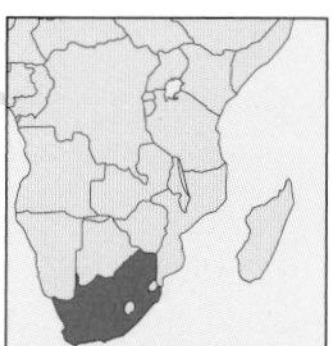

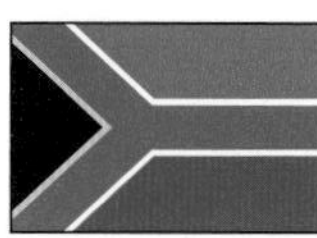

South Africa's flag was first flown in 1994 when the country adopted a new, non-racial constitution. It incorporates the red, white, and blue of former colonial powers, Britain and the Netherlands, together with the green, black, and gold of black organizations.

CAPE TOWN

City and seaport at the foot of Table Mountain, South Africa. It is South Africa's legislative capital and the capital of Western Cape province. Founded in 1652 by the Dutch East India Company, it came under British rule in 1795. Places of interest include the Union Parliament, a 17th-century castle, the National Historic Museum, and the University of Cape Town (founded 1829). It is an important industrial and commercial center. Industries include clothing, engineering equipment, motor vehicles, and wine.

The Republic of South Africa is geologically very ancient, with few deposits less than 600 million years old. The country can be divided into two main regions, the interior plateau, the southern part of the huge plateau that makes up most of southern Africa; and the coastal fringes.

The interior consists of two main parts. Most of Northern Cape Province and Free State are drained by the Orange River and its right-bank tributaries that flow over level plateaus, varying in height from 4,000–6,000 ft [1,200 m to 2,000 m]. The Northern Province is occupied by the Bushveld, an area of granites and igneous intrusions.

The Fringing Escarpment divides the interior from the coastal fringe. This escarpment makes communication within the country very difficult. In the east, the massive basalt-capped rock wall of the Drakensberg, at its most majestic near Mont-aux-Sources and rising to more than 10,000 ft [3,000 m], overlooks KwaZulu-Natal and Eastern Cape coastlands.

In the west there is a similar, though less well developed, divide between the interior plateau and the coastlands. The Fringing Escarpment also parallels the south coast, where it is fronted by a series of ranges, including the folded Cape Ranges.

CLIMATE

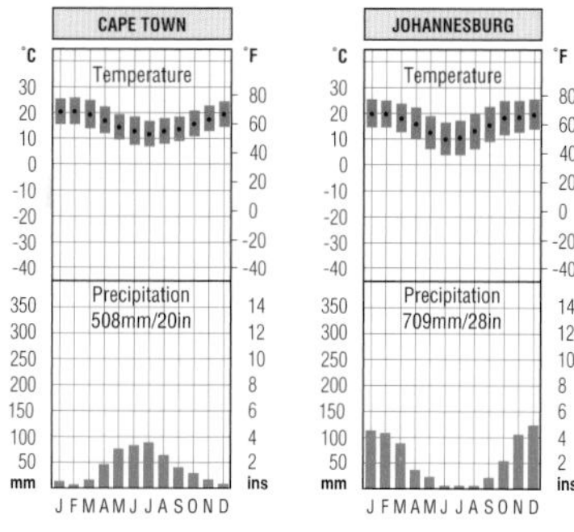

Most of South Africa is subtropical and has a mild, sunny climate. Much of the coastal strip, including the city of Cape Town, has warm, dry summers and mild, rainy winters, like the Mediterranean lands of northern Africa. Inland, large areas are arid and the Namib Desert is almost rainless.

Area 471,442 sq mi [1,221,037 sq km]
Population 42,719,000
Capital (population) Cape Town (legislative, 855,000); Tshwane/Pretoria (administrative, 2,200,000); Bloemfontein (judiciary, 350,000)
Government Multiparty republic
Ethnic groups Black 76%, White 13%, Colored 9%, Asian 2%
Languages Afrikaans, English, Ndebele, Pedi, Sotho, Swazi, Tsonga, Tswana, Venda, Xhosa and Zulu (all official)
Religions Christianity 68%, Islam 2%, Hlnduism 1%
Currency CFA franc = 100 centimes
Website www.gov.za

HISTORY

Early inhabitants were the Khoisan (also called Hottentots and Bushmen). However, the majority of the people today are Bantu-speakers from the north who entered the country, introducing a cattle-keeping, grain-growing culture. Arriving via the plateaus of the northeast, they continued southward into the well-watered zones below the Fringing Escarpment of KwaZulu-Natal and Eastern Cape. By the 18th century, these people had reached the southeast. They formed large groups, including the Zulu, Xhosa, Sotho and Tswana.

Also at this time, a group of Europeans was establishing a supply base for the Dutch East India Company on the site of present-day Cape Town. The first group was led by Jan van Riebeeck who founded the base in 1652. In 1657, some Company employees set up their own farms and were known as Boers (farmers). After Britain took over the Cape Town settlement in the early 19th century, many Boers, who resented British rule, began to move inland to develop their own Afrikaaner culture. Beginning in 1836, this migration was known as the Great Trek. Their advance was channeled in the south by parallel coastal ranges, and eventually black and white met near the Kei River. To the north, once the Fringing Escarpment had been overcome, the level plateau surfaces allowed a rapid spread northward, with the Boers founding the Transvaal in 1852 and Orange Free State in 1854.

In 1870, diamonds were found near the site where Kimberley now stands. Both the British and the Boers claimed the area, but Britain annexed it in 1871. In 1880, the Boers rebeled and defeated the British in the First Boer War. In 1886, gold was discovered in the Witwatersrand in what is now Gauteng. Many immigrants, called *uitlanders* (foreigners), flooded to the area. Most of them were British and, to maintain their control, the Boers restricted their freedom. Tension developed, culminating in the Second Boer War (1899–1902). The Boer republics of Orange Free State and Transvaal then surrendered and became British colonies. Meanwhile, British forces had overcome Zulu resistance to European settlement. By 1898, all opposition had been suppressed and the black people had lost their independence.

POLITICS

In 1906, Transvaal was granted self-rule, followed by Orange Free State in 1907. The other two parts of the country, Cape Colony and Natal, already had self-rule. In 1910, the entire country was united as the Union of South Africa, a self-governing country within the British Empire. During World War I, two Boer generals led South African forces against Germany. In German South West Africa (now Namibia), General Louis Botha conquered the Germans, while General Jan Christiaan Smuts led Allied forces in German East Africa (now Tanzania). In 1920, the League of Nations gave South Africa control over South West Africa, under a trusteeship agreement. In 1931, Britain granted South Africa full independence as a member of the Commonwealth of Nations.

The development of minerals and urban complexes in South Africa caused an even greater divergence between black and white. The African farmers gained little from the mineral boom. With taxes to pay, they had little alternative but to seek employment in the mines or on European-owned farms. Migrant labor became the normal way of life for many men, while agriculture in black areas stagnated. Groups of Africans took up urban life, living in communities set apart from the white settlements. These townships, with their rudimentary housing often supplemented by shanty dwellings and without any real services, mushroomed during World War II and left South Africa with a major housing problem in the late 1940s. Nowhere was this problem greater than in Johannesburg, where a vast complex of brick boxes called SOWETO (South Western Townships) was built. The contrast between the living standards of blacks and whites increased rapidly.

At the start of World War II, opinion was divided as to whether South Africa should remain neutral or support Britain. The pro-British General Smuts triumphed. He became prime minister and South African forces served in Ethiopia, northern Africa, and Europe. During the war, Daniel Malan, a supporter of Afrikaner nationalism, reorganized the National Party. The Nationalists came to power in 1948, with Malan as prime minister, and introduced the policy of apartheid. The African National Congress, which had been founded in 1912, became the leading black opposition group. Opposition to South Africa's segregationist policies mounted around the world. Stung by criticism from Britain and other Commonwealth members, South Africa became a republic and withdrew from the Commonwealth in 1961. In 1966, the United Nations voted to end South Africa's control over South West Africa, though it was not until 1990 that the territory finally became independent as Namibia.

In response to continuing opposition, South Africa repealed some apartheid laws and, in 1984, under a new constitution, a new three-house parliament was set up. The three houses were for whites, Coloreds, and Asians, but there was still no provision for the black majority. In 1986, the European Community (now the European Union), the Commonwealth, and the United States applied sanctions on South Africa, banning trade in certain areas. In 1989, F. W. de Klerk was elected president and in 1990 he released the banned ANC leader Nelson Mandela from prison.

In the early 1990s, more apartheid laws were repealed. The country began to prepare a new constitution giving all non-whites the right to vote, though progress toward majority rule was marred by fighting between the Zulu-dominated Inkatha Freedom Party and the ANC.

Elections held in 1994 resulted in victory for the ANC and Nelson Mandela became president. Mandela advocated reconciliation between whites and non-whites, and his government sought to alleviate the poverty of Africans in the townships. The slow rate of progress disappointed many as did other problems, including an increase in crime and the continuing massive gap in living standards between the whites and the blacks. However, in 1999, following the retirement of Nelson Mandela, his successor, Thabo Mbeki, led the African National Congress to an overwhelming electoral victory. Besides poverty, one of the biggest problems facing the country is the estimate given in a government study that one in five South Africans is infected with the HIV virus.

TSHWANE (PRETORIA)

Administrative capital of South Africa, Gauteng province. Founded in 1855 and named after Andries Pretorius, a hero for the Afrikaaners who set up apartheid. It became the capital of the Transvaal in 1860, and of the South African Republic in 1881. The Peace of Vereeniging, which ended the South African Wars, was signed here in 1902. In 1910, it became the capital of the Union of South Africa.Early African people named the area Tshwane which means "We are the same." The city was renamed in 2005, Pretoria is still the name of the city center.

ECONOMY

South Africa is Africa's most developed country. However, most of the black people—rural and urban—are poor with low standards of living. Natural resources include diamonds and gold, which formed the basis of its economy from the late 19th century. Today, South Africa ranks first in the world in gold production and fifth in diamond production. South Africa also produces coal, chromite, copper, iron ore, manganese, platinum, phosphate rock, silver, uranium, and vanadium. Mining and manufacturing are the most valuable economic activities and gold, metals and metal products, and gem diamonds are the chief exports.

Manufactures include chemicals, processed food, iron and steel, machinery, motor vehicles, and textiles. The main industrial areas lie in and around the cities of Cape Town, Durban, Johannesburg, Port Elizabeth, and Pretoria. Investment in South African mining and manufacturing declined in the 1980s, but foreign companies began to invest again following the abolition of apartheid.

Farmland is limited by the aridity of many areas, but the country produces most of the food it needs and food products make up around 7% of South Africa's exports. Major crops include apples, grapes (for wine-making), corn, oranges, pineapples, sugar cane, tobacco, and wheat. Sheep-rearing is important on land which is unfit for arable farming. Other livestock products include beef, dairy products, eggs, and milk.

The Outeniqua Choo-Tjoe steam train *crossing a bridge at Dolphin Point near Wilderness on the Garden Route.*

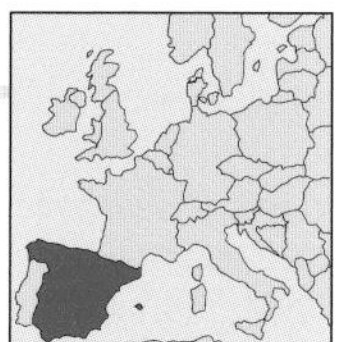

The colors on the Spanish flag date back to those used by the old kingdom of Aragon in the 12th century. The present design, in which the central yellow stripe is twice as wide as each of the red stripes, was adopted in 1938, during the Civil War.

The Kingdom of Spain is the second largest country in Western Europe after France. It shares the Iberian Peninsula with Portugal. A plateau, called the Meseta, covers most of Spain. Much of it is flat, but crossed by several mountain ranges (*sierras*).

The northern highlands include the Cantabrian Mountains (Cordillera Cantabrica) and the high Pyrenees, which form Spain's border with France. Mulhacén, the highest peak on the Spanish mainland, is in the Sierra Nevada in the southeast. Spain also contains fertile coastal plains. Other lowlands are the Ebro River Basin in the northeast and the Guadalquivir River Basin in the southwest.

Spain also includes the Balearic Islands (Islas Baleares) in the Mediterranean Sea and the Canary Islands off the northwest coast of Africa. Tenerife in the Canary Islands contains Pico de Teide, Spain's highest peak (12,918 ft [3,718 m]).

Forests lie to the rainier north and northwest, with beech and deciduous oak being common. Toward the drier south and east, Mediterranean pines and evergreen oaks take over, and the forests resemble open parkland. Large areas are matorral, a Mediterranean scrub. Where soils are thin and drought is prevalent, matorral gives way to steppe.

CLIMATE

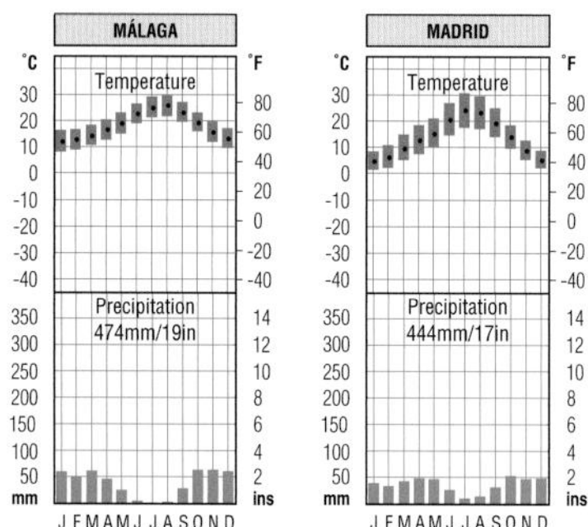

Spain has the widest range of climate in Western Europe. One of the most striking contrasts is between the humid north and northwest, where winds from the Atlantic bring mild, wet weather throughout the year, and the mainly arid remainder of the country. Droughts are common in much of Spain, though these are occasionally interrupted by thunderstorms.

The Meseta, removed from the influence of the sea, has a continental climate, with hot summers and cold winters, when frosts often occur and snow blankets the mountain ranges that rise above the plateau surface. By contrast, the Mediterranean coastlands and the Balearic Islands have mild, moist winters. Summers along the Mediterranean coast are hot and dry. The Canary Islands have mild to warm weather throughout the year.

Wave-like balconies *and roof on the colorful Casa Ballto, Barcelona designed by the Catalan architect of the Art Nouveau Movement Antonio Gaudi y Cornet*

Area 192,103 sq mi [497,548 sq km]
Population 40,281,000
Capital (population) Madrid (2,939,000)
Government Constitutional monarchy
Ethnic groups Mediterranean and Nordic types
Languages Castillian Spanish (official) 74%, Catalan 17%, Galician 7%, Basque 2%
Religions Roman Catholic 94%, others
Currency Euro = 100 cents
Website www.spain.info

HISTORY

5,000 years ago, Spain was inhabited by farming people called Iberians. Some historians believe the Basques in northern Spain may be descendants of these people. Around 3,000 years ago, Phoenicians from the eastern Mediterranean reached the Iberian Peninsula and began to establish trading colonies, some on the sites of modern cities, such as Cádiz and Málaga. Celtic peoples arrived later from the north, while Greeks reached the east coast of Spain around 600 BC.

In the 5th century BC, Carthaginians conquered much of Spain, but after the Second Punic War (218–201 BC), the Iberian Peninsula gradually came under Roman rule. The Romans made Iberia a Roman province called Hispania.

By 573, the Visigoths had conquered the entire peninsula, including what is now Portugal, and they ruled until the early 8th century when the Muslim Moors invaded from North Africa. They introduced their culture and scholarship, far ahead of that of Europe, building superb mosques and palaces, some of which still stand. In the 11th century, the country began to divide into many small Moorish kingdoms, leaving them open to attack by the Christian kingdoms in the north. Portugal broke away from Spain in the 11th–12th centuries. By the late 13th century, Muslim power was confined to the southern Kingdom of Granada.

The rest of Spain was ruled by the Christian kingdoms of Aragon, Navarre, and, the most powerful of all, Castile. In 1469, Prince Ferdinand of Aragon married Princess Isabella of Castile. Ferdinand and Isabella started the Spanish Inquisition which persecuted Jews, Muslims and other non-Roman Catholics. In 1492, Ferdinand's forces captured the last Muslim stronghold of Granada and, in 1512, the Kingdom of Navarre was taken by Ferdinand. This completed the union of Spain.

By the mid-16th century, Spain was a great world power controlling much of Central and South America, parts of Africa and the Philippines in Asia. A major disaster occurred in 1588, when King Philip II sent a fleet, the Armada, to conquer England, but the English navy and bad weather destroyed half of the Spanish ships. By the 20th century all that remained of Spain's empire were a few small African territories.

A military government was established in 1923 and King Alfonso III allowed General Miguel Primo de Rivera, the prime minister, to rule as a dictator. After Primo de Rivera was forced to resign in 1930, Alfonso called for city elections. Republican candidates scored such a major victory in these elections that he left the country, though he did not renounce his claim to the throne. The republicans took over the government.

In October 1936, rebel Nationalists chose General Francisco Franco (1892–1975) as their commander and, and in 1939 he became the dictator of Spain, though technically the country was a monarchy. During World War II, Spain was officially neutral.

POLITICS

The revival of Spain's shattered economy began in the 1950s through the growth of manufacturing industries and tourism. As standards of living rose, people began to demand more freedom. After Franco died in 1975, the monarchy was restored and Juan Carlos, grandson of Alfonso III, became king. The ban on political parties was lifted and, in 1977, elections were held. A new constitution making Spain a parliamentary democracy, with the king as head of state, came into effect in December 1978.

From the late 1970s, Spain began to tackle the problem of its regions. In 1980, a regional parliament was set up in the Basque Country (Euskadi in Basque and Pais Vasco in Spanish). Similar parliaments were initiated in Catalonia (Cataluña) in the northeast and Galicia in the northwest. While regional devolution was welcomed in Catalonia and Galicia, it did not end the terrorist campaign of the Basque separatist movement, Euskadi Ta Askatasuna (ETA). ETA announced an indefinite ceasefire in September 1998, but the truce was ended in December 1999 and the conflict continued. The Supreme Court voted in 2003, to ban Batasuna, the Basque separatist party deemed to be the political wing of ETA.

In March 2004 terrorist bombs exploded in Madrid killing 191 people. This was seem as the work of Al Qaeda, though the govenerment were keen to persuade the people that it was the work of ETA. The country went to the polls three days later and voted out the right-wing Aznar. This was largely seen as a reaction to his support of the US in Iraq and the sending of troops which was to blame for the bombing some three days earlier. The new prime minister Zapatero immediately withdrew all troops from Iraq.

MADRID

Capital and largest city of Spain, lying on a high plain in the center of Spain on the River Manzanares. It is Europe's highest capital city, at 2,149 ft [655 m]. Founded as a Moorish fortress in the 10th century, Alfonso VI of Castile captured Madrid in 1083. In 1561, Philip II moved the capital to Madrid. The French occupied the city during the Peninsular War (1808–14). Madrid expanded considerably in the 19th century. During the Spanish Civil War, it remained loyal to the Republican cause and was under siege for almost three years. Its capitulation in March 1939 brought the war to an end. Modern Madrid is a thriving center of commerce and industry.

ECONOMY

Spain has the fifth largest economy in the EU. By the early 2000s, agriculture employed only 6% of the workforce as compared with industry at 17% and services including tourism who employ 77%. Farmland makes up two-thirds of the land, and forest most of the rest. Major crops include barley, citrus fruits, grapes for wine-making, olives, potatoes, and wheat.

There is some high-grade iron ore in the north. Spain's many manufacturing industries include automobiles, chemicals, clothing, electronics, processed food, metal goods, steel, and textiles.

ANDORRA

Area 175 sq mi [453 sq km]
Population 68,000
Capital (population) Andorra La Vella (22,000)
Government Co-principality
Ethnic groups Spanish 43%, Andorran 33%, Portuguese 11%, French 7%
Languages Catalan (official)
Religions Mainly Roman Catholic
Currency Euro = 100 cents
Website www.turisme.ad

Andorra is a tiny state sandwiched between France and Spain. It lies in the Pyrenees Mountains. Most Andorrans live in the sheltered valleys.

The winters are cold and fairly dry. The summers are a little more wet, but pleasantly cool.

Tourism is Andorra's chief activity in both winter, for winter sports, and summer.

There is some farming in the valleys and tobacco is the main crop. Cattle and sheep are grazed on the mountain slopes.

GIBRALTAR

Area 2.5 sq mi [6.5 sq km]
Population 28,000
Capital (population) Gibraltar Town (28,000)
Government British dependency
Ethnic groups English, Spanish, Maltese, Italian, Portuguese
Languages English (official), Spanish, Italian, Portuguese
Religions Mainly Roman Catholic
Currency Gibraltar pound = 100 pence
Website www.gibraltar.gov.uk

Gibraltar is a tiny British dependency on the south coast of Spain, occupying a strategic position overlooking the narrow Strait of Gibraltar which links the Mediterranean Sea with the Atlantic Ocean. The majority of the population works for the government or in tourism.

Most of the land is a huge mass of limestone, known as the Rock of Gibraltar. Between AD 711 and 1309, and again between 1333 and 1462, Gibraltar was held by Moors from North Africa. Spaniards retook the area in 1462, but it became a British territory in 1713. Gibraltar became a vital British military base, but was still claimed by Spain.

In 1967 the Gibraltarians voted to remain British. Between 1969 and 1985 Spain closed its border with Gibraltar. Britain withdrew its military forces in 1991. In 2002, proposals that Gibraltar should come under joint Anglo-Spanish sovreignty were rejected by nearly all Gibraltarians.

Sri Lanka

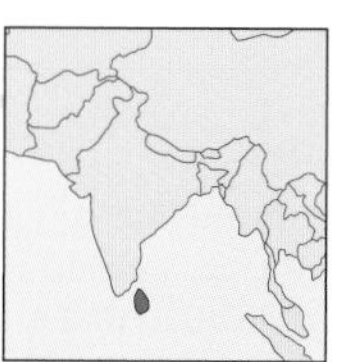

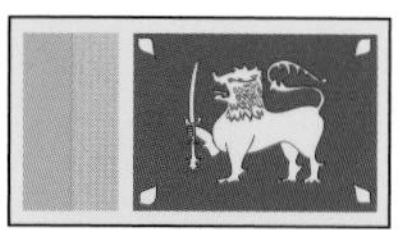

Sri Lanka's unusual flag was adopted in 1951, three years after the country, then called Ceylon, became independent from Britain. The lion banner represents the ancient Buddhist kingdom. The stripes symbolize the minorities—Muslims (green) and Hindus (orange).

Area 25,332 sq mi [65,610 sq km]
Population 19,905,000
Capital (population) Colombo (642,000)
Government Multiparty republic
Ethnic groups Sinhalese 74%, Tamil 18%, Moor 7%
Languages Sinhala and Tamil (both official)
Religions Buddhism 70%, Hinduism 15%, Christianity 8%, Islam 7%
Currency Sri Lankan rupee = 100 cents
Website www.gov.lk

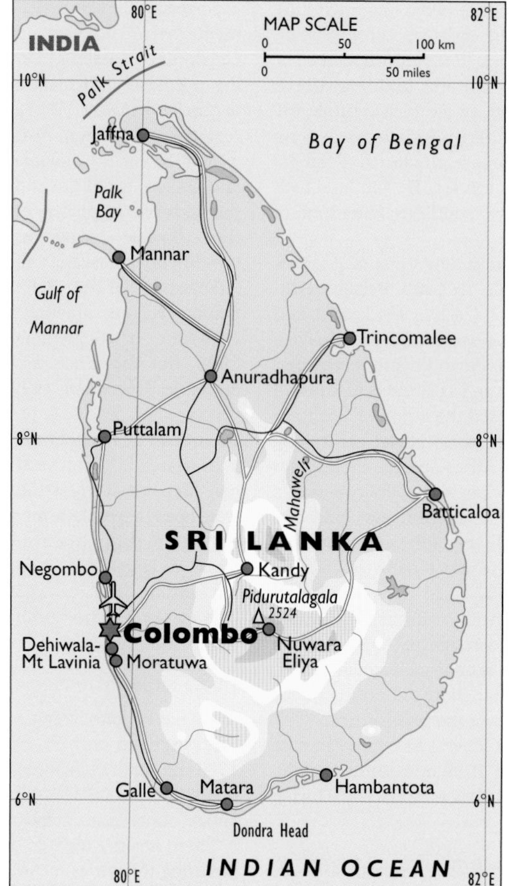

The Democratic Socialist Republic of Sri Lanka is an island nation, often called the "pearl of the Indian Ocean." It lies on the same continental shelf as India, separated by the shallow Palk Strait. Most of the land is low-lying but, in the south-central part of Sri Lanka, the land rises to a mountain massif. The nation's highest peak is Pidurutalagala (8,281 ft [2,524 m]). The nearby Adam's Peak, at 7,359 ft [2,243 m], is a place of pilgrimage. The southwest is also mountainous, with long ridges.

Around the south-central highlands are broad plains, while the Jaffna Peninsula in the far north is made of limestone. Cliffs overlook the sea in the southwest, while elsewhere lagoons line the coast. Forests cover nearly two-fifths of the land, with open grasslands in the eastern highlands. Farmland, including pasture, covers another two-fifths of the country.

CLIMATE

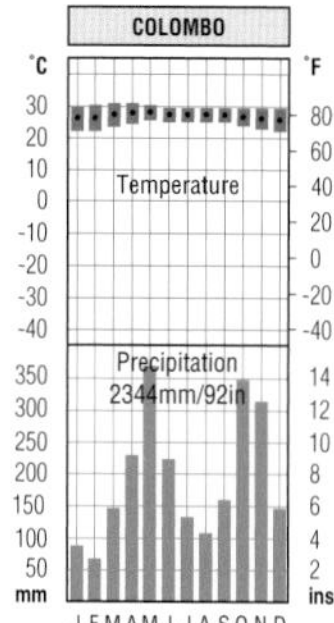

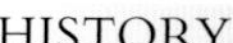

The western part of Sri Lanka has a wet equatorial climate. Temperatures are high and the rainfall is heavy. The wettest months are May and October as these months mark the advance and the retreat of the summer monsoon. Eastern Sri Lanka is drier.

HISTORY

The ancestors of the Sinhalese people settled on the island around 2,400 years ago pushing the Veddahs, descendants of the earliest inhabitants, into the interior. The Sinhalese founded the city of Anuradhapura, which was their center from the 3rd century BC to the 10th century AD. Tamils arrived around 2,100 years ago and the early history of Ceylon, as the island was known, was concerned with a struggle between the Sinhalese and the Tamils. Victory for the Tamils led the Sinhalese to move south. From the 16th century, Ceylon was ruled successively by the Portuguese, Dutch and British.

Tea leaf picking, *Nuwara Eliya;tea plantation built during the 19th century in an English style*

POLITICS

Independence was achieved in 1948 and the country was renamed Sri Lanka in 1972. After independence, rivalries between the two main ethnic groups, the Sinhalese and Tamils, marred progress. In the 1950s, the government made Sinhala the official language. Following protests, the prime minister made provisions for Tamil to be used in some areas. In 1959, the prime minister was assassinated by a Sinhalese extremist and he was succeeded by Sirimavo Bandanaraike, the world's first woman prime minister.

Conflict between Tamils and Sinhalese continued in the 1970s and 1980s. In 1987, India helped to engineer a ceasefire. Indian troops arrived to enforce the agreement. They withdrew in 1990 after failing to subdue the main guerrilla group, the Tamil Tigers, who wanted an independent Tamil homeland in northern Sri Lanka. In 1993, the country's president, Ranasinghe Premadasa, was assassinated by a suspected Tamil separatist. A ceasefire was signed in May 1993, but fighting soon broke out. In 1995, government forces captured Jaffna, the stronghold of the "Liberation Tigers of the Tamil Eelam" (LTTE). But the 1998 bombing of the Temple of the Tooth in Kandy created great outrage among the Sinhalese Buddhists, who believe that the temple's treasured tooth belonged to Buddha.

The bombing led to rioting and provoked President Chandrika Kumaratunga to ban the LTTE. These events led to some of the fiercest fighting in the civil war, including several suicide bombings. The government lost most of the gains it had made in the mid-1990s. A long-term ceasefire agreement was signed in 2002. In December 2004, Sri Lanka was hit by a tsunami, which killed more than 30,000 people. In 2005 Mahinda Rajapakse was elected president. At the time of election he was in fact prime minister and it was hoped that under his leadership a long-sought-after resolution would be found to the conflict in the north.

ECONOMY

The World Bank classifies Sri Lanka as a "low-income" developing country. Agriculture employs around a third of the workforce, coconuts, rubber, and tea are the cash crops. Rice is the chief food crop. Cattle, water buffalo, and goats are the chief farm animals, while fish provide another source of protein. Manufacturing is mainly the processing of agricultural products and textile production. The leading exports are clothing and accessories, gemstones, tea, and rubber.

COLOMBO

Capital and chief seaport of Sri Lanka, on the southwest coast. Settled in the 6th century BC, it was taken by Portugal in the 16th century and later by the Dutch. Captured by the British in 1796, it gained independence in 1948. The town hall is of great interest.

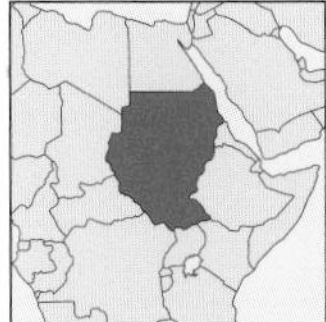

Adopted in 1969, Sudan's flag uses colors associated with the Pan-Arab movement. The Islamic green triangle symbolizes prosperity and spiritual wealth. The flag is based on the one used in the Arab revolt against Turkish rule in World War I (1914–18).

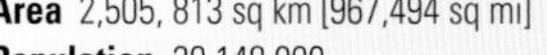

The Republic of the Sudan is the largest country in Africa. It extends from the arid Sahara in the north to an equatorial swamp region (the Sudd) in the south.

Much of the land is flat, but there are mountains in the north east and south-east; the highest point is Kinyeti, at 10,456 ft [3,187 m]. The River Nile (Bahr el Jebel) runs south to north, entering Sudan as the White Nile, converging with the Blue Nile at Khartoum, and flowing north to Egypt.

Khartoum is prone to summer dust storms (*haboobs*). From the bare deserts of the north, the land merges into dry grasslands and savanna. Dense rainforests grow in the south.

CLIMATE

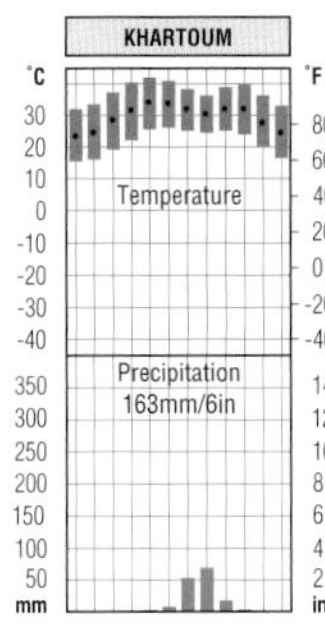

Northern Sudan is hot and arid. The center has an average annual rainfall of 4 to 32 in [100 to 510 mm], while the tropical south has between 32 and 55 in [810 and 1,400 mm] of rain per year.

HISTORY

One of the earliest civilizations in the Nile region of northern Sudan was Nubia, which came under Ancient Egypt around 4,000 years ago. Another Nubian civilization, called Kush, developed from about 1000 BC, finally collapsing in AD 350. Christianity was introduced to northern Sudan in the 6th century. From the 13th to 15th centuries, northern Sudan came under Muslim control, and Islam became the dominant religion.

In 1821 Muhammad Ali's forces occupied Sudan. Anglo-Egyptian forces, led by General Gordon, attempted to extend Egypt's influence into the south. Muhammad Ahmad led a Mahdi uprising, which briefly freed Sudan from Anglo-Egyptian influence. In 1898, General Kitchener's forces defeated the Mahdists, and in 1899 Sudan became Anglo-Egyptian Sudan, governed jointly by Britain and Egypt.

POLITICS

After Sudan's independence in 1952, the southern Sudanese, who are mostly Christian or of traditional beliefs, revolted against the dominance of the Muslim north, and civil war broke out. In 1958, the military seized power. Civilian rule was reestablished in 1964, but overthrown again in 1969, when Gaafar Muhammad Nimeri seized control. Southern Sudan received considerable autonomy in 1972, but unrest persisted.

In 1983, the imposition of strict Islamic law sparked off further conflict between the government and the Sudan People's Liberation Army (SPLA) in the south. In 1985, Nimeri was deposed and a civilian government installed. In 1989, the military, led by Omar Hassan Ahmed al-Bashir, established a Revolutionary Command Council. Civil war continued in the south. In 1996, Bashir was reelected, virtually unopposed. The National Islamic Front (NIF) dominated the government and was believed to have strong links with Iranian terrorist groups.

In 1996, the UN imposed sanctions on Sudan. A South African peace initiative in 1997 led to the formation of a Southern States' Coordination Council. The US imposed sanctions on Bashir's regime and American Secretary of State Madeleine Albright met rebel leaders. In 1998, the USA bombed a pharmaceuticals factory in Khartoum in the mistaken belief that it produced chemical weapons. In 2003, conflict broke out in the Darfur region in the west, primarily involving rebels and government-backed militias. A severe humanitarian crisis developed, and the militias were accused of ethnic cleansing. In the south, government and rebels signed a comprehensive peace deal in 2005. The humanitarian crisis continued to worsen in 2006.

ECONOMY

The World Bank classifies Sudan as a "low-income" economy. Food shortages and a refugee crisis worsened its economic plight. Agriculture employs 60% of the population. The chief crop is cotton. Other crops include groundnuts, gum arabic, millet, sesame, sorghum, and sugar cane, while many people raise livestock.

Minerals include chromium, gold, gypsum, and oil. Manufacturing industries process foods, and produce such things as cement, fertilizers, and textiles. The main exports are cotton, gum arabic and sesame seeds, but the most valuable exports are oil and oil products.

KHARTOUM

Capital of Sudan, at the junction of the Blue Nile and White Nile rivers. Khartoum was founded in the 1820s by Muhammad Ali and was besieged by the Mahdists in 1885, when General Gordon was killed. In 1898, it became the seat of government of the Anglo-Egyptian Sudan, and from 1956 the capital of independent Sudan. It was at the center of controversy in 1998 when the US bombed a pharmaceuticals plant thinking it was producing chemical weapons. Industries include cement, gum arabic, chemicals, glass, cotton, and textiles.

Area 2,505, 813 sq km [967,494 sq mi]
Population 39,148,000
Capital (population) Khartoum (947,000)
Government Military regime
Ethnic groups Black 52%, Arab 39%, Beja 6%, others
Languages Arabic (officia)l, Nubian, Ta Bedawie
Religions Islam 70%, traditional beliefs
Currency Sudanese dinar = 10 Sudanese pounds
Website www.sudan.net

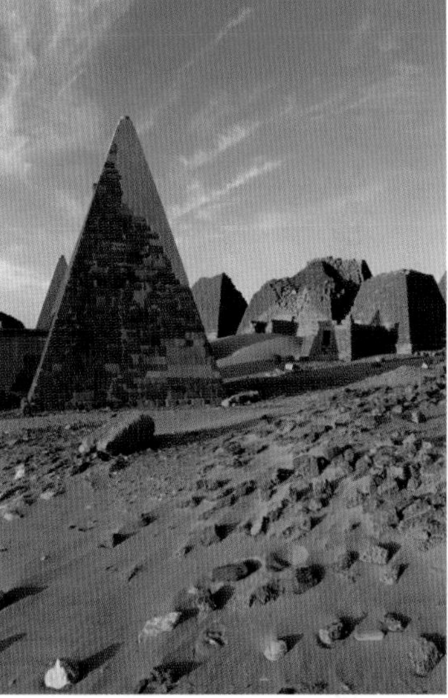

Burial pyramids *at the Royal Necropolis of the ancient Kingdom of Kush, dated between 300 BC and 300 AD, at Meroe near Bejwaria*

Suriname

The star symbolizes national unity—each point being one of Suriname's five main ethnic groups. Yellow is for Suriname's golden future. Red stands for progress and the struggle for a better life. Green signifies hope and fertility. White symbolizes freedom and justice.

Area 63,037 sq mi [163,265 sq km]
Population 437,000
Capital (population) Paramaribo (216,000)
Government Multiparty republic
Ethnic groups Hindustani/East Indian 37%, Creole (mixed White and Black) 31%, Javanese 15%, Black 10%, Amerindian 2%, Chinese 2%, others
Languages Dutch (official), Sranang Tonga
Religions Hinduism 27%, Protestant 25%, Roman Catholic 23%, Islam 20%
Currency Surinamese dollar = 100 cents
Website www.parbo.com/tourism/

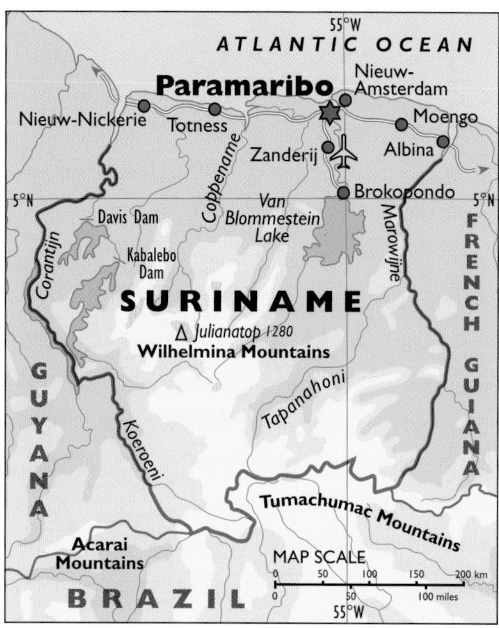

PARAMARIBO

Capital of Suriname, a port on the River Suriname. It was founded in the early 17th century by the French and became a British colony in 1651. It was held intermittently by the British and the Dutch until 1816, when the latter finally took control until independence. Paramaribo is the administrative and economic center. The name is derived from Paramurubo, meaning "city of parwa blossoms" after an old Arrawak village. Places of interest include Fort Zeelandia/ Suriname Museum, the Palm Gardens and the Presidential Palace. Industries include bauxite, timber, sugar cane, rice, rum,coffee and cacao.

The Republic of Suriname is on the Atlantic Ocean in northeastern South America bordered by Brazil to the south, French Guiana to the east, and Guyana to the west.

Suriname is made up of the Guiana Highlands plateau, a flat coastal plain, and a forested inland region. Its many rivers serve as a source of hydroelectric power. The narrow coastal plain was once swampy, but it has been drained and now consists mainly of farmland. Inland lie hills and low mountains which rise to 4,199 ft [1,280 m].

CLIMATE

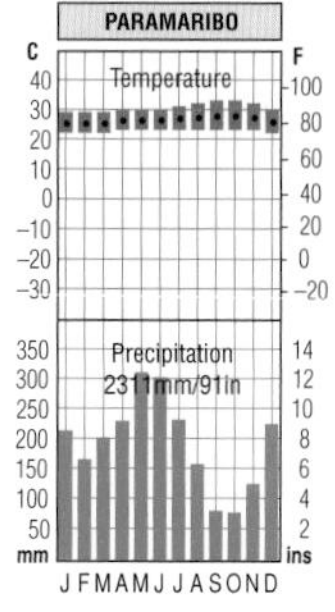

Suriname has a hot, wet and humid climate. Temperatures are high throughout the year.

HISTORY

Spanish explorer Alfonso de Ojeda discovered Suriname in 1499, but it was the British who founded the first colony in 1651. In 1667, Britain handed Suriname to the Dutch in return for New Amsterdam, an area that is now the state of New York. Slave revolts and Dutch neglect hampered development.

In the early 19th century Britain and the Netherlands disputed the ownership of the area. The British gave up their claims in 1813 and in 1815 the Congress of Vienna gave the Guyana region to Britain and reaffirmed Dutch control of "Dutch Guiana." Slavery was abolished in 1863 and soon afterward Indian and Indonesian laborers were introduced to work on plantations. It gained autonomy in 1954.

POLITICS

Suriname became fully independent from the Netherlands in 1975 and gained membership of the United Nations, but the economy was weakened when thousands of skilled people emigrated to the Netherlands.

Following a coup in 1980, Suriname was ruled by a military dictator, Dési Bouterse, who banned all political parties. Guerrilla warfare disrupted the economy. In 1987, a new constitution provided for a 51-member National Assembly, with powers to elect the president. Rameswak Shankar became president in 1988 elections, but he was overthrown by a military coup in 1990

In 1991, Ronald Venetiaan, leader of the New Front for Democracy and Development, became president. In 1992 the government negotiated a peace agreement with the *boschneger*, descendants of African slaves, who had launched a struggle against the government. That same year, the constitution was amended in order to limit the power of the military and a peace agreement was reached with the rebels. Elections were held in 1996 and again in 2000.

In 1999, Bouterse was convicted in absentia in the Netherlands of having led a cocaine-trafficking ring during and after his tenure in office. In 2004, the government announced that he and others would face trial over the killings of 15 people in 1982.

ECONOMY

The World Bank classifies Suriname as an "upper-middle-income" developing country. Its economy is based on mining and metal processing. Suriname is a leading producer of bauxite, from which the metal aluminum is made.

The chief agricultural products are rice, bananas, sugar cane, coffee, coconuts, timber, and citrus fruits.

***A woman trims a cassava cake** with a leaf, as it cooks upon a griddle in Bigi Poika, a Carib Indian village in north-central Suriname*

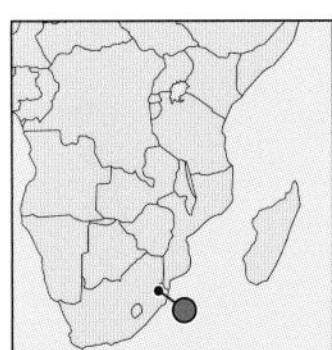

The oxhide shield with two spears and a fighting staff represent the defense of Swaziland, the tassels symbolize the Swazi monarchy. Black and white represent racial harmony, blue is for peace, yellow stands for the nation's mineral wealth; red signifies blood shed in past struggles.

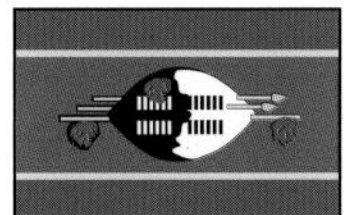

The Kingdom of Swaziland is a small, landlocked country in southern Africa bounded by South Africa to the north, west, and south and by Mozambique to the east. The country has four regions which run north–south.

In the west, the Highveld, with an average height of 3,937 ft [1,200 m], makes up 30% of Swaziland. The Middleveld, between 1,148 and 3,281 ft [350 m and 1,000 m], covers 28% of the country. The Lowveld, with an average height of 886 ft [270 m], covers another 33%. The Lebombo Mountains reach 2,600 ft [800 m] along the eastern border.

Meadows and pasture cover 65% of Swaziland. Arable land covers 8% of the land, and forests only 6%.

CLIMATE

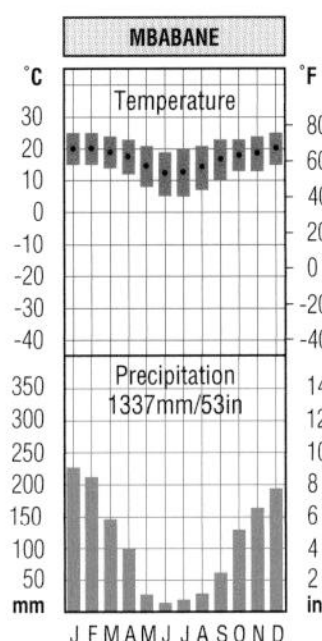

The Lowveld is almost tropical, with an average temperature of 72°F [22°C] and a low rainfall of 20 in [500 mm] a year. The altitude moderates the climate in the west of the country. Mbabane has a climate typical of the Highveld with warm summers and cool winters.

HISTORY

In the 18th century, according to tradition, a group of Bantu-speaking people, under the Swazi Chief Ngwane II, crossed the Lebombo range and united with local African groups to form the Swazi nation. In the 1840s, under attack from the Zulu, the Swazi sought British protection. Gold was discovered in the 1880s, and many Europeans sought land concessions from the King, who did not realize that in acceding to their demands he lost control of the land. In 1894, Britain and the Boers of South Africa agreed to put Swaziland under the control of the South African Republic (the Transvaal). Britain took control at the end of the second South African War (1899–1902).

MBABANE

Capital of Swaziland, in the northwest of the country, at the northern end of the Ezulwini Valley in the Dlangeni Hills, which are part of the Highveld region of southern Africa. It is both an administrative and commercial center, serving the surrounding agricultural region. Tin and iron ore are mined nearby.

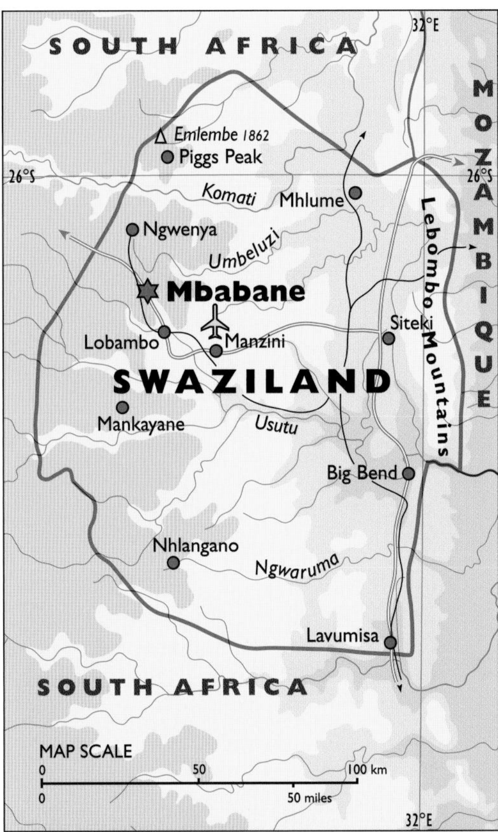

***Man carving** soapstone sculpture in Swaziland; soapstone is a soft stone that feels soapy to the touch,,hence its name. It is commonly used in African sculpture*

Area 6,704 sq mi [17,364 sq km]
Population 1,169,000
Capital (population) Mbabane (38,000)
Government Monarchy
Ethnic groups African 97%, European 3%
Languages Siswati and English (both official)
Religions Zionist (a mixture of Christianity and traditional beliefs) 40%, Roman Catholic 20%, Islam 10%
Currency Lilangeni = 100 cents
Website www.gov.sz

LOBAMBO

The traditional royal capital of Swaziland, lying in the Ezulwini Valley 10 mi [16 km] from Mbabane. It is the home of the Queen Mother. The National Assembly, National Museum, and parliament are all based here.

POLITICS

In 1968, when Swaziland became fully independent as a constitutional monarchy, the head of state was King Sobhuza II. In 1973, Sobhuza suspended the constitution and assumed supreme power. In 1978, he banned all political parties. Sobhuza died in 1982 after a reign of 82 years.

In 1983, his son, Prince Makhosetive, was chosen as his heir. In 1986, he became King Mswati III. Elections in 1993 and 1998, in which political parties were banned, failed to satisfy protesters who opposed the absolute monarchy.

Mswati continued to rule by decree and in 2004 he announced plans to build palaces for each of his 11 wives. At the same time the government appealed for aid in the face of a national disaster caused by the spread of HIV/AIDS and a severe drought.

ECONOMY

The World Bank classifies Swaziland as a "lower-middle-income" developing country. Agriculture employs 50% of the workforce, with many farmers living at subsistence level. Farm products and processed foods, including sugar, wood pulp, citrus fruits, and canned fruit, are the leading exports. Swaziland exhausted its high-grade iron ore reserves in 1978, while the world demand for its asbestos fell. Swaziland is heavily dependent on South Africa and the two countries are linked through a customs union.

Sweden's flag was adopted in 1906, though it had been in use since the reign of Gustavus Vasa (r. 1523–60), a king who won many victories for Sweden and laid the foundations of the modern nation. The colors on the flag come from a coat of arms dating from 1364.

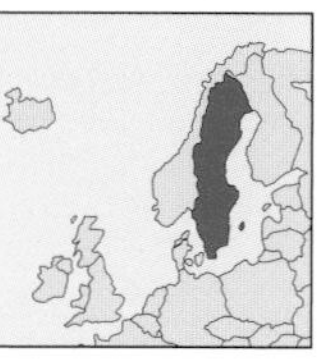

Area 173,731 sq mi [449,964 sq km]
Population 8,986,000
Capital (population) Stockholm (744,000)
Government Constitutional monarchy
Ethnic groups Swedish 91%, Finnish, Sami
Languages Swedish (official), Finnish, Sami
Religions Lutheran 87%, Roman Catholic, Orthodox
Currency Swedish krona = 100 öre
Website www.sweden.gov.se

The Kingdom of Sweden is the largest of the countries of Scandinavia both in terms of area and population. It shares the Scandinavian Peninsula with Norway. The western part of the country, along the border with Norway, is mountainous. The highest point is Kebnekaise, which reaches 6,946 ft [2,117 m] in the northwest. The southern lowlands contain two of Europe's largest lakes, Vänern and Vättern, and Sweden's largest cities: the capital, Stockholm, and Gothenburg.

CLIMATE

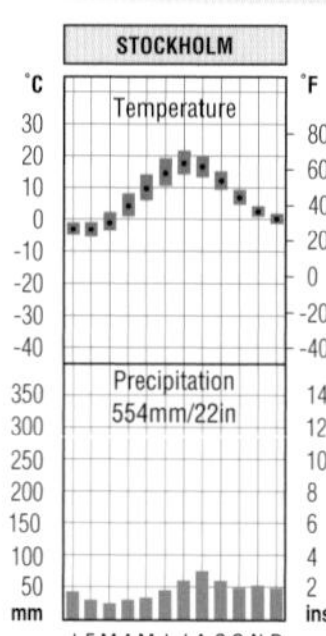

The northerly latitude and high mountains and plateaus of Norway cut Sweden off from the mild influences of the Atlantic in the west. The Gulf Stream warms the southern coastlands. The February temperature in the central lowlands is just below freezing, but in the north it is 5°F [–15°C].

Precipitation is low throughout Sweden, but lies as snow for more than six months in the north. In summer there is little difference between the north and south. Most areas have an average temperature range between 59 and 68°F [15°–20°C].

HISTORY

People began to settle in Sweden around 8,000 years ago. Accounts were recorded in about AD 100.

By the seventh century, Teutonic peoples had occupied much of central Sweden. Between the 9th and 11th centuries the Swedish Vikings sailed to the east, across Russia and down to the Black and Caspian seas.

In the 11th century, Sweden, Norway and Denmark were separate kingdoms. However, in 1388, Sweden, fearing the growing influence of Germany on Swe-

STOCKHOLM

Port and capital of Sweden, on Lake Mälaren's outlet to the Baltic Sea. Founded in the mid-13th century, it became a trade center dominated by the Hanseatic League. Gustavus I made it the center of his kingdom, and ended the privileges of Hanseatic merchants. Stockholm became the capital of Sweden in 1436, and developed as an intellectual center in the 17th century. Industrial development dates from the mid-19th century. Industries include textiles, clothing, paper and printing, rubber, chemicals, shipbuilding, beer, and electronics.

den's affairs, turned to Queen Margaret of Denmark, and Norway for help. The Germans were defeated in 1389 and, in 1397, Sweden, Denmark and Norway were united by a treaty called the Union of Kalmar. Sweden defeated the Danes in 1523 and under Gustavus Vasa, a Swedish noble, Sweden broke away from the union. Gustavus encouraged followers of Martin Luther to spread their ideas and by 1540, Lutheranism had become the official religion.

From the late 16th century, Sweden became involved in a series of wars, during which it gained territory around the Baltic Ocean. In 1658, Sweden forced Denmark to give up its provinces on the Swedish mainland. Following defeat at the hands of Tsar Peter the Great in 1709, a coalition of Russia, Poland and Denmark forced Sweden to give up most of its European possessions.

Sweden lost Finland to Russia in 1809, though it gained Norway from Denmark in 1814. By the late 19th century, Sweden was a major industrial nation. The Social Democratic Party was set up in 1889 to improve the conditions of workers. In 1905, Norway's parliament voted for independence from Sweden.

POLITICS

Sweden has a high standard of living, more than 70% of the national budget goes on one of the widest ranging welfare programs in the world. In turn, the tax burden is the world's highest.

The elections of September 1991 saw the end of the Social Democratic government, which had been in power since 1932, with voters swinging toward parties advocating lower taxes. But the Social Democrats returned to power in 1994, advocating economic stringency.

A founder member of EFTA (European Free Trade Association), Sweden joined the European Union in 1985 following a referendum. However, it did not adopt the euro in 2001. In 2003, the government launched a referendum on replacing the krona with the euro. During the campaign Sweden's foreign minister, Anna Lindh, was murdered. Shortly afterward Swedish voters rejected the adoption of the euro.

ECONOMY

Sweden is a highly developed industrial country. It has rich iron ore deposits, but imports other materials. Steel is a major product, and is used to manufacture aircraft, automobiles, machinery, and ships. Forestry and fishing are important. Farmland covers 10% of the land. Livestock and dairy farming are valuable; crops include barley and oats.

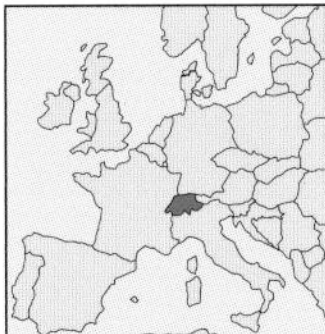

Switzerland has used this square flag since 1848, though the white cross on the red shield has been Switzerland's emblem since the 14th century. The flag of the International Red Cross, which is based in Geneva, was derived from this flag.

The Swiss Confederation is a landlocked country in Western Europe. Much of the land is mountainous. The Jura Mountains lie along Switzerland's western border with France, while the Swiss Alps make up about 60% of the country in the south and east. Four-fifths of the people of Switzerland live on the fertile Swiss Plateau, which contains most of Switzerland's large cities.

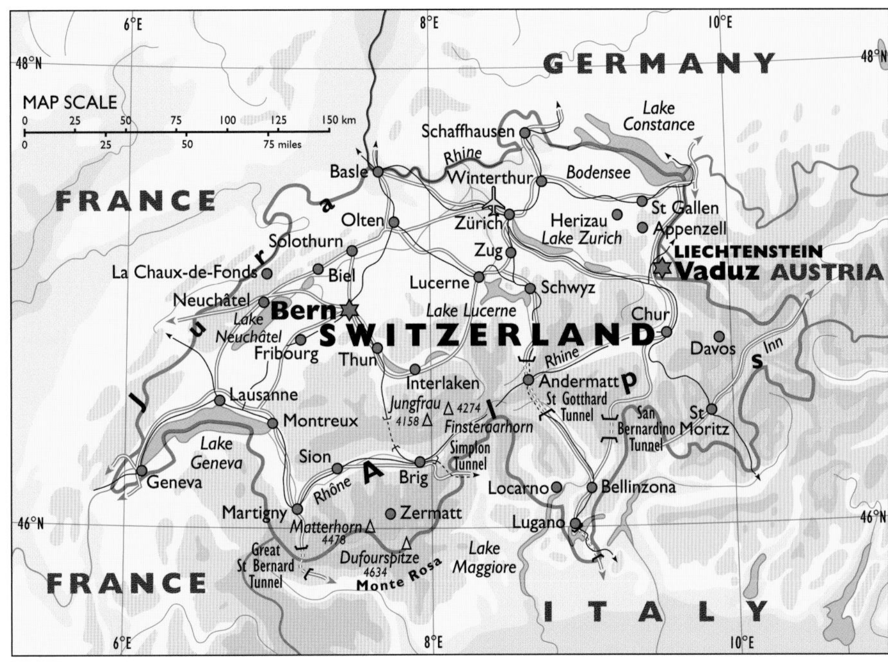

CLIMATE

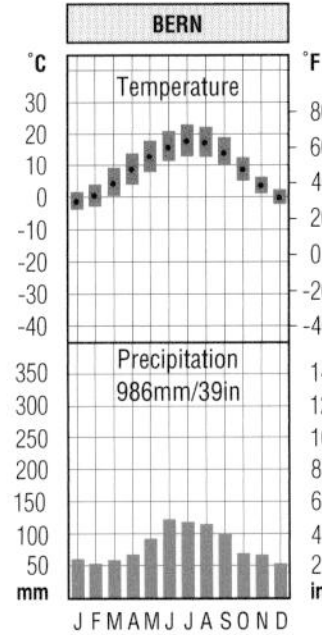

The climate varies greatly according to the height of the land. The plateau region has a central European climate with warm summers, but cold and snowy winters. Rain occurs throughout the year.

HISTORY

In 1291, three small cantons (states) united to defend their freedom against the Habsburg rulers of the Holy Roman Empire. They were Schwyz, Uri, and Unterwalden, and they called the confederation "Switzerland." In the 14th century, Switzerland defeated Austria in three wars of independence. But after a defeat by the French in 1515, the Swiss adopted a policy of neutrality, which they still follow.

In 1815, the Congress of Vienna expanded Switzerland to 22 cantons and guaranteed its neutrality. Switzerland's 23rd canton, Jura, was created in 1979 from part of the capital Bern (Berne).

POLITICS

A referendum in 1986 rejected Swiss membership of the UN to avoid compromising its neutrality. In 1993 the Swiss voted against joining the EU. In 1999, Ruth Dreifuss became Switzerland's first woman president. However, in 2002, the Swiss voted by a narrow majority to end its centuries-old political isolationism and join the United Nations.

Area 15,940 sq mi [41,284 sq km]
Population 7,451,000
Capital (population) Bern (124,000)
Government Federal republic
Ethnic groups German 65%, French 18%, Italian 10%, Romansch 1%, others
Languages French, German, Italian and Romansch (all official)
Religions Roman Catholic 46%, Protestant 40%
Currency Swiss franc = 100 centimes
Website www.vlada.hr/default.asp?ru=2

ECONOMY

Although lacking in natural resources, Switzerland is a wealthy, industrialized country with many highly skilled workers. Major products include chemicals, electrical equipment, machinery and machine tools, precision instruments, processed food, watches, and textiles. Farmers produce about three-fifths of the country's food—the rest is imported. Livestock raising, especially dairy farming, is the chief agricultural activity. Crops include fruits, potatoes, and wheat. Tourism and banking are important. Swiss banks attract investors from all over the world.

BERN (BERNE)

Capital of Switzerland, on the River Aare in Bern region. Founded in 1191 as a military post, it became part of the Swiss Confederation in 1353. Bern was occupied by France during the French Revolutionary Wars (1798). It has a Gothic cathedral, a 15th-century town hall, and is the headquarters of the Swiss National Library.

LIECHTENSTEIN

The Principality of Liechtenstein is sandwiched between Switzerland and Austria. The River Rhine flows along its western border, while Alpine peaks rise in the east and the south. The capital, Vaduz, is situated on the Oberland Plateau above the fields and meadows of the Rhine Valley. The climate is relatively mild and the average annual precipitation is about 35 in [890 mm].

Liechtenstein, whose people speak a German dialect, has been an independent principality since 1719. Switzerland has represented Liechtenstein abroad since 1918 and Swiss currency was adopted in 1921. It has been in customs union with Switzerland since 1924.

Liechtenstein is best known abroad for its postage stamps, but is a haven for international companies, attracted by the low taxation and the strictest banking codes in the world.

In 2003, the people voted to give the head of state, Prince Hans Adam III, sovereign powers. In 2004, he handed the running of the country to his son, Prince Alois, but remained titular head of state.

Area 62 sq mi [160 sq km]
Population 33,000
Capital (population) Vaduz (5,000)
Government Hereditary constitutional monarchy
Ethnic groups Alemannic 86%, Italian, Turkish
Languages German (official), Alemannic dialect
Religions Roman Catholic 76%, Protestant 7%
Currency Swiss franc = 100 centimes
Website www.liechtenstein.li

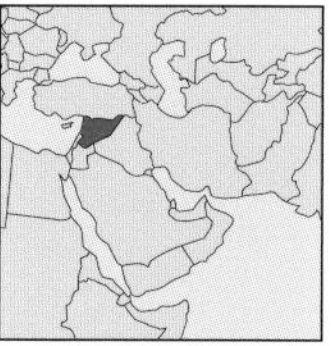

Syria has used this flag since 1980. The colors are those used by the Pan-Arab movement. This flag is the one that was used by the United Arab Republic between 1958 and 1961, when Syria was linked with Egypt and North Yemen.

Area 71,498 sq mi [185,180 sq km]
Population 18,017,000
Capital (population) Damascus (1,394,000)
Government Multiparty republic
Ethnic groups Arab 90%, Kurdish, Armenian, others
Languages Arabic (official), Kurdish, Armenian
Religions Sunni Muslim 74%, other Islam 16%
Currency Syrian pound = 100 piastres
Website www.syriatourism.org

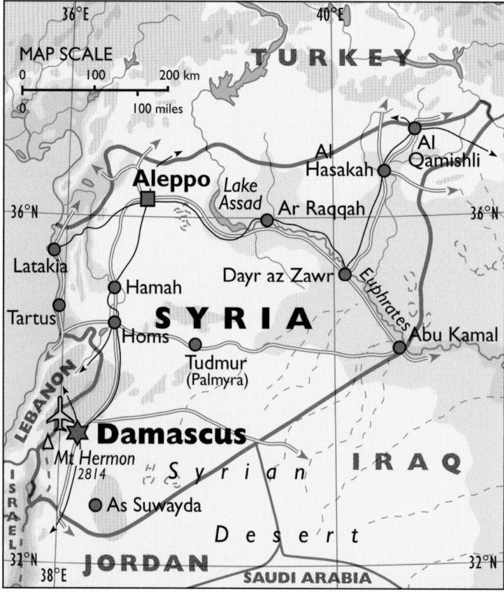

The Syrian Arab Republic is in southwestern Asia. The narrow coastal plain is overlooked by a low mountain range which runs north–south. Another range, the Jabal ash Sharqi, runs along the border with Lebanon. South of this range is a region called the Golan Heights. Israel has occupied this region since 1967. East of the mountains, the bulk of Syria consists of fertile valleys, grassy plains, and large sandy deserts. This region contains the valley of the River Euphrates (Nahr al Furat).

CLIMATE

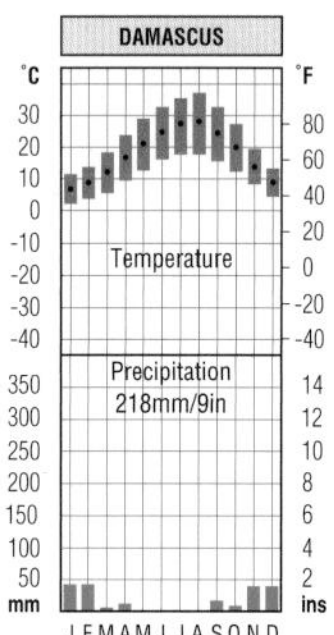

The coast has a Mediterranean climate, with dry, warm summers and wet, mild winters. The low mountains cut off Damascus from the sea. It has less rainfall than the coastal areas and becomes drier to the east.

The Central Bank of Syria *stands on the north side of Tajrida Al-Maghribiya Square in Damascus*

HISTORY

Syria is rich in historic sites from a wide range of periods. The earliest known settlers were Semites who arrived around 3,500 years ago. They set up city-states, such as Ebla, which existed between about 2700 and 2200 BC. The people of Ebla used clay tablets inscribed in cuneiform, an ancient system of writing developed by the Sumer people of Mesopotamia. Later conquerors of the area included the Akkadians, Canaanites, Phoenicians, Amorites, Aramaeans, and the Hebrews, who introduced monotheism. The Assyrians occupied the area from 732 BC until 612 BC, when the Babylonians took over. The ancient Persians conquered the Babylonians in 539 BC, but the armies of Alexander the Great swept into the region in 331 BC, introducing Greek culture in their wake. The Romans took over in 64 BC, and Syria remained under Roman law for nearly 700 years.

Christianity became the state religion of Syria in the 4th century AD, but, in 636, Muslims from Arabia invaded the region. Islam gradually replaced Christianity as the main religion, and Arabic became the chief language. From 661, Damascus became the capital of a vast Muslim empire which was ruled by the Ummayad Dynasty. But the Abbasid Dynasty took over in 750 and the center of power passed to Baghdad.

From the late 11th century, Crusaders sought to win the Holy Land from the Muslims. But the Crusaders were unsuccessful in their aim because Saladin, a Muslim ruler of Egypt, defeated the Crusaders and ruled most of the area by the end of the 12th century. The Mameluke Dynasty of Egypt ruled Syria from 1260–1516, when the region became part of the huge Turkish Ottoman Empire. During World War I, Syrians and other Arabs fought alongside British forces and overthrew the Turks.

POLITICS

After the collapse of the Turkish Ottoman empire in World War I, Syria was ruled by France. Syria became fully independent from France in 1946. The partition of Palestine and the creation of Israel in 1947 led to the first Arab-Israeli war, when Syria and other Arab nations failed to defeat Israeli forces. In 1949, a military coup established a military regime, starting a long period of revolts and changes of government. In 1967, in the third Arab-Israeli war (known as the Six-Day War), Syria lost the strategically important Golan Heights to Israel.

In 1970, Lieutenant-General Hafez al Assad led a military revolt, becoming Syria's president in 1971. His repressive but stable regime attracted much Western criticism and was heavily reliant on Arab aid. But Syria's anti-Iraq stance in the 1991 Gulf War, and the involvement of about 20,000 Syrian troops in the conflict, greatly improved its standing in the West. In the mid-1990s, Syria had talks with Israel over the future of the Golan Heights. Negotiations were suspended after the election of Binyamin Netanyahu's right-wing government in Israel in 1996. Assad died in 2000 and was succeeded by his son, Bashar al Assad, raising hopes of a more pliable policy on the Golan Heights.

Syria has been criticised for supporting Palestinian terrorist groups and keeping its troops in Lebanon. In 2005, following demonstrations against its continuing military presence in Lebanon, Syria announced the phased withdrawal of its troops.

ECONOMY

The World Bank classifies Syria as a "lower-middle-income" developing country. Its main resources are oil, hydroelectricity, and fertile land. Agriculture employs about 26% of the population. Oil is the chief mineral product, and phosphates are mined to make fertilizers.

DAMASCUS

Capital of Syria, on the River Barada, southwest Syria. Thought to be the oldest continuously occupied city in the world, in ancient times it belonged to the Egyptians, Persians, and Greeks, and under Roman rule was a prosperous commercial center. It was held by the Ottoman Turks for 400 years, and after World War I came under French administration. It became capital of an independent Syria in 1941. Sites include the Great Mosque and the Citadel. It is Syria's administrative and financial center. Industries include damask fabric, metalware, leather goods, and sugar.

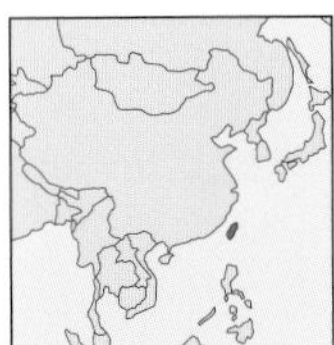

In 1928, the Chinese Nationalists adopted this design as China's national flag and used it in the long struggle against Mao Zedong's Communist army. When the nationalists were forced to retreat to Taiwan in 1949, their flag went with them.

Taiwan (formerly Formosa), is an island about 87 mi [140 km] off the south coast of mainland China. The country administers a number of islands close to the mainland. They include Quemoy (Jinmen) and Matsu (Mazu).

High mountain ranges, extending the length of the island, occupy the central and eastern regions, and only a quarter of the island's surface is used for agriculture. The highest peak is Yü Shan (Morrison Mountain), 12,966 ft [3,952 m] above sea level. Several peaks in the central ranges rise to more than 10,000 ft [3,000 m], and carry dense forests of broadleaved evergreen trees, such as camphor and Chinese cork oak. Above 5,000 ft [1,500 m], conifers, such as pine, larch and cedar, dominate. In the east, where the mountains often drop steeply down to the sea, the short rivers have cut deep gorges. The western slopes are more gentle.

CLIMATE

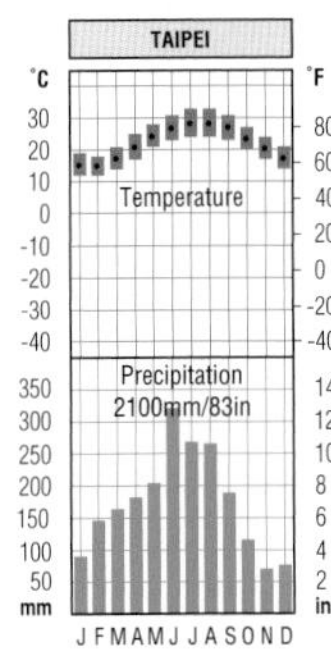

Taiwan has a tropical monsoon climate. The annual rainfall exceeds 79 in [2,000 mm] in almost all areas. From July to September, the island is often hit by typhoons. When humidity is high in the heat can be oppressive.

HISTORY

Chinese settlers arrived in Taiwan from the 7th century AD, displacing the Aboriginal people, but large settlements were not established until the 17th century. When the Portuguese first reached the island in 1590, they named the island Formosa (meaning "beautiful island"), but chose not to settle there. The Dutch occupied a trading port in 1624, but they were driven out in 1661 by refugees from the deposed Ming Dynasty on the mainland. A Ming official tried to use the island as a base for attacking the Manchu Dynasty, but without success as the Manchus took the island in 1683 and incorporated it into what is now Fujian province.

The Manchus settled the island in the late 18th century and, by the mid-19th century, the population had increased to about 2,500,000. The island was a major producer of sugar and rice, which were exported to the mainland. In 1886, the island became a Chinese province and Taipei became its capital in 1894. However, in 1895, Taiwan was ceded to Japan following the Chinese-Japanese War. Japan used the island as a source of food crops and, from the 1930s, they developed manufacturing industries based on hydroelectricity.

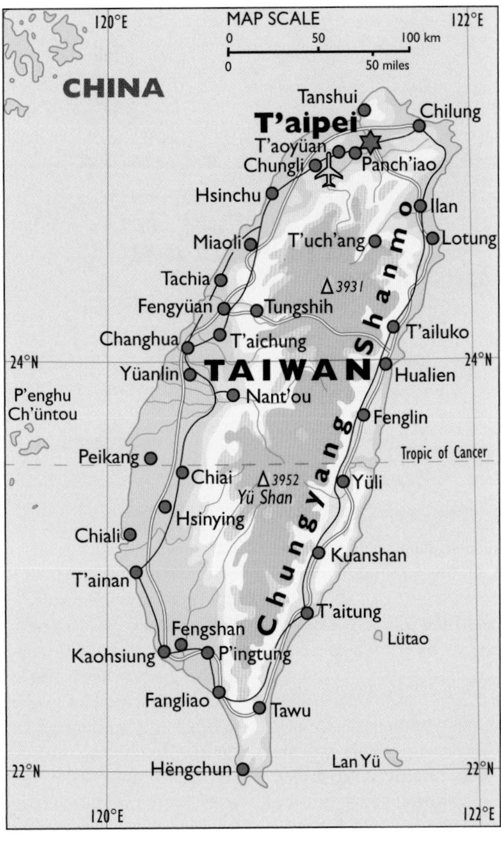

TAIPEI

Capital and largest city of Taiwan, at the northern end of the island. A major trade center for tea in the 19th century, the city enlarged under Japanese rule (1895–1945), and became the seat of the Chinese Nationalist government in 1949. Industries include textiles, chemicals, fertilizers, metals, machinery. The city expanded from 335,000 people in 1945 to 2,619,022 in 2005.

Area 36,000 sq mi [13,900 sq km]
Population 22,750,000
Capital (population) Taipei (2,619,022)
Government Unitary multiparty republic
Ethnic groups Taiwanese 84%, mainland Chinese 14%
Languages Mandarin Chinese (official), Min, Hakka
Religions Buddhism, Taoism, Confucianism
Currency New Taiwan dollar = 100 cents
Website www.roc-taiwan.org.uk

POLITICS

In 1945, the Japanese army surrendered Taiwan to General Chiang Kai-shek's Nationalist Chinese government. Following victories by Mao Zedong's Communists, about 2 million Nationalists, together with their leader, fled the mainland to Taiwan in the two years before 1949, when the People's Republic of China was proclaimed. The influx was met with hostility by the 8 million Taiwanese, and the new regime, the "Republic of China", was imposed with force. Boosted by help from the United States, Chiang's government set about ambitious programs for land reform and industrial expansion and, by 1980, Taiwan had become one of the top 20 industrial nations. Economic development was accompanied by a marked rise in living standards.

Nevertheless, Taiwan remained politically isolated and it lost its seat in the United Nations to Communist China in 1971. It was then abandoned diplomatically by the United States in 1979, when the US switched its recognition to mainland China. However, in 1987 with continuing progress in the economy, martial law was lifted by the authoritarian regime in Taiwan. In 1988, a native Taiwanese became president and in 1991 the country's first general election was held.

China continued to regard Taiwan as a Chinese province and, in 1999, tension developed when the Taiwanese President Lee Teng-hui stated that relations between China and Taiwan should be on a "special state-by-state" basis. This angered the Chinese President Jiang Zemin, whose "one-nation" policy was based on the concept that China and Taiwan should be regarded as one country with two equal governments. Tension mounted in 2000, when Taiwan's opposition leader, Chen Shui-bian, was elected president, because Chen had adopted a pro-independence stance. However, after the elections, Chen adopted a more conciliatory approach to mainland China.

ECONOMY

The economy depends on manufacturing and trade. Manufactures include electronic goods, footwear and clothing, ships and television sets. The western coastal plains produce large rice crops. Other products include bananas, pineapples, sugar cane, sweet potatoes, and tea.

Tajikistan

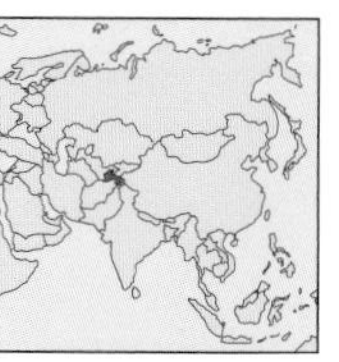

Tajikistan's flag was adopted in 1993. It replaced the flag used during the Communist period which showed a hammer and sickle. The new flag shows an unusual gold crown under an arc of seven stars on the central white band.

Area 55,521 sq mi [143,100 sq km]
Population 7,012,000
Capital (population) Dushanbe (529,000)
Government Republic
Ethnic groups Tajik 65%,Uzbek 25%, Russian
Languages Tajik (official), Russian
Religions Islam (Sunni Muslim 85%)
Currency Somoni = 100 dirams
Website www.tajiktour.taknet.com

The Republic of Tajikistan is one of the five central Asian republics that formed part of the former Soviet Union. Only 7% of the land is below 3,280 ft [1,000 m], while almost all of eastern Tajikistan is above 3,000 m [9,840 ft]. The highest point is Communism Peak (Pik Kommunizma), which reaches 24,590 ft [7,495 m]. The main ranges are the westward extension of the Tian Shan Range in the north and the snow-capped Pamirs (Pamir) in the southeast. Earthquakes are common throughout the country.

Vegetation varies greatly according to altitude. Much of Tajikistan consists of desert or rocky mountain landscapes capped by snow and ice.

CLIMATE

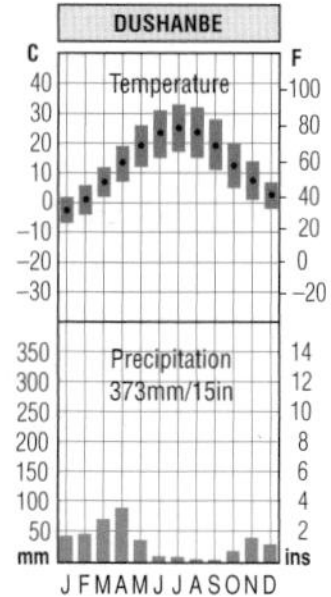

Tajikistan has an extreme continental climate. Summers are hot and dry in the lower valleys, and winters are long and bitterly cold in the mountains. Much of the country is arid, but the south east has heavy snowfalls.

HISTORY

Persians settled in the area about 2,500 years ago. The area was conquered many times with first the Persians in the 6th century BC, then the Macedonian Greeks led by Alexander the Great in 331 BC. From 323 BC, the area was split into several independent states. Arab armies conquered the area in the mid-7th century and introduced Islam, which remains the chief religion today. The region was later ruled by various Turkic tribes and later by the Mongols, led by Genghis Khan. Uzbeks, a Turkic people, ruled the area as the Khanate of Bukhara from the 16th to the 19th centuries.

The fragmentation of the region aided Russian conquest from 1868. Following the Russian Revolution (1917), Tajikistan rebelled against Russian rule. Although Soviet troops annexed northern Tajikistan into Turkistan in 1918, the Bukhara Emirate held out against the Red Army until 1921. In 1924 Tajikistan became an autonomous part of the Republic of Uzbekistan. In 1929 Tajikistan achieved full republic status, but Bukhara and Samarkand remained in the Republic of Uzbekistan. During the 1930s vast irrigation schemes greatly increased agricultural land. Many Russians and Uzbeks were settled in Tajikistan.

POLITICS

While the Soviet Union began to introduce reforms in the 1980s, many Tajiks demanded freedom. In 1989, the Tajik government made Tajik the official language in place of Russian and, in 1990, it stated that its local laws overruled Soviet laws. Tajikistan became fully independent in 1991, following the breakup of the Soviet Union. As the poorest of the ex-Soviet republics, Tajikistan faced many problems in trying to introduce a free-market system.

In 1992, civil war broke out between the government, which was run by former Communists, and an alliance of democrats and Islamic forces. The government maintained control, but it relied heavily on aid from the Commonwealth of Independent States, the organization through which most of the former Soviet republics kept in touch. Presidential elections in 1994 resulted in victory for Imomali Rakhmonov, though the Islamic opposition did not recognize the result.

A ceasefire was signed in December 1996. Further agreements in 1997 provided for the opposition to have 30% of the ministerial posts in the government. But many small groups excluded from the agreement continued to undermine the peace process through a series of killings and military actions. In 1999, Rakhmonov was reelected president. Changes to the constitution in 2003 enabled Rakhmonov to serve two more seven-year terms after the elections in 2006. His party won parliamentary elections in 2005, though independent Western observers said that the vote did not meet international standards.

ECONOMY

The World Bank classifies Tajikistan as a "low-income" developing country. Agriculture, mainly on irrigated land, is the main activity and cotton is the chief product. Other crops include fruits, grains and vegetables. The country has large hydroelectric power resources and it produces aluminum.

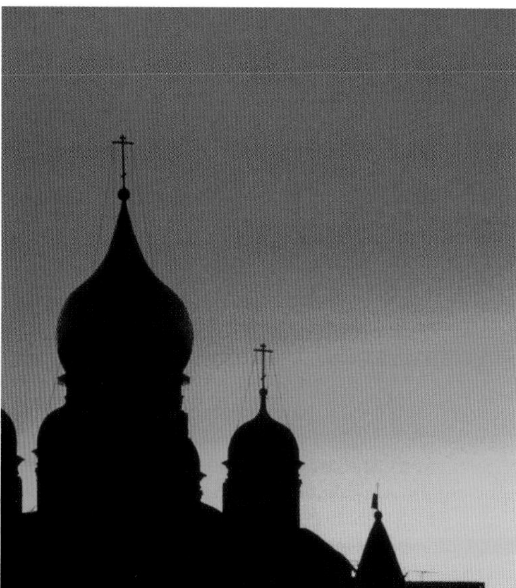

Cathedrals at sunset, *Dushanbe*

PAMIRS

A central Asian mountainous region, lying mostly in Tajikistan and partly in Pakistan, Afghanistan and China. The region forms a geological structural knot from which the Tian Shan, Karakoram, Kunlun, and Hindu Kush mountain ranges radiate. The terrain includes grasslands and sparse trees. The highest peak is Pik Imeni Ismail Samani (Pik Kommunizma) at 24,590 ft [7,495 m].

DUSHANBE

Capital of Tajikistan, at the foot of the Gissar Mountains, central Asia. Founded in the 1920s, it was known as Stalinabad from 1929–61. An industrial, trade and transportation center, it is the site of Tajik University and Academy of Sciences. Industries include cotton milling, engineering, leather goods, and food processing.

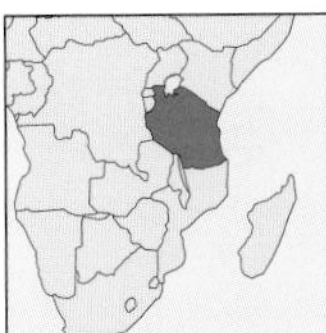

Tanzania's flag was adopted in 1964 when mainland Tanganyika joined with the island nation of Zanzibar to form the United Republic of Tanzania. The green represents agriculture and the yellow minerals. The black represents the people, while the blue symbolizes Zanzibar.

The United Republic of Tanzania consists of the former mainland country of Tanganyika and the island nation of Zanzibar, which also includes the island of Pemba.

Behind a narrow coastal plain, the majority of Tanzania is a plateau lying between 2,950 and 4,920 ft [900–1,500 m] above sea level. The plateau is broken by arms of the Great African Rift Valley. The western arm contains lakes Nyasa (also called Malawi) and Tanganyika, while the eastern arm contains the strongly alkaline Lake Natron, together with lakes Eyasi and Manyara. Lake Victoria occupies a shallow depression in the plateau and it is not situated within the Rift Valley.

Kilimanjaro, the highest peak, is an extinct volcano. At 19,340 ft [5,895 m], it is also Africa's highest mountain. Zanzibar and Pemba are coral islands.

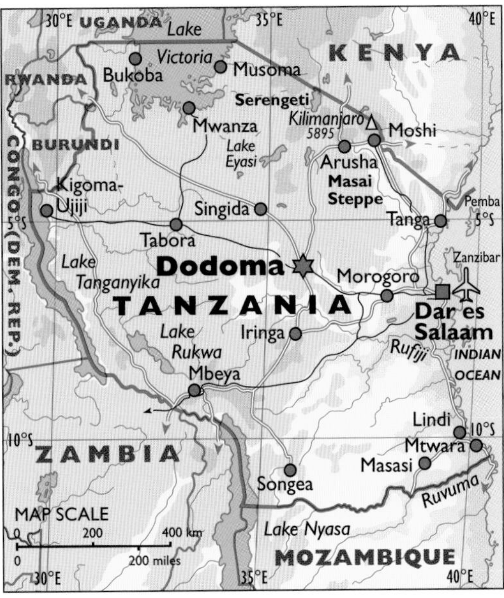

Area 364,899 sq mi [945,090 sq km]
Population 36,588,000
Capital (population) Dodoma (204,000)
Government Multiparty republic
Ethnic groups Native African 99% (Bantu 95%)
Languages Swahili (Kiswahili) and English (both official)
Religions Islam 35% (99% in Zanzibar), traditional beliefs 35%, Christianity 30%
Currency Tanzanian shilling = 100 cents
Website www.tanzania.go.tz/index2E.html

CLIMATE

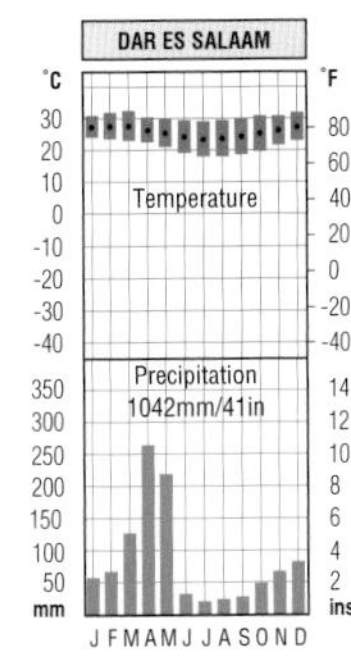

The coast has a hot, humid climate. The greatest rainfall is in April and May. Inland mountains and plateaux are cooler and less humid. The Rift Valley is hot. Mount Kilimanjaro is permanently snow and ice covered.

HISTORY

Around 2,000 years ago, Arabs, Persians and Chinese traded along the Tanzanian coast. The old cities and ruins testify to its importance. Arab traders often intermarried with local people and the Arab-African people produced the distinctive Arab-Swahili culture. The Portuguese took control of coastal trade in the early 16th century, but the Arabs regained control in the 17th century.

In 1698, Arabs from Oman took control of Zanzibar. From this base, they developed inland trade, bringing gold, ivory, and slaves from the interior. During the 19th century, European explorers and missionaries were active, mapping the country and striving to stop the slave trade.

POLITICS

Mainland Tanganyika became a German territory in the 1880s, while Zanzibar (including Pemba) became a British protectorate in 1890. The Germans introduced a system of forced labor to develop plantations. This led to a major rebellion in 1905, which was put down with great brutality.

Following Germany's defeat in World War I Britain gained control of Tanganyika and was granted a mandate to rule it by the League of Nations. Tanganyika remained a British territory until winning its independence in 1961, followed by Zanzibar in 1963. Tanganyika and Zanzibar united to form the United Republic of Tanzania in 1964.

The country's first president, Julius Nyerere, pursued socialist policies of self-help (called *ujamaa* in Swahili) and egalitarianism. While many of its social reforms were successful, the country failed to make economic progress.

DODOMA

Capital and third biggest city of Tanzania, it was chosen as the new capital due to its location in the center of the country and replaced Dar es Salaam in 1974. It is in an agricultural region, crops include grain, seeds, and nuts.

Nyerere resigned as president in 1985, though he remained influential until his death in 1999. His successors, Ali Hassan Mwinyi, who served from 1985 until 1995, and Benjamin Mkapa, who was reelected in 2000, pursued more liberal economic policies. In 2005, Mkapa was succeeded by Jakaya Kikwete, another CCM (Chama Cha Mapinduzi) candidate.

ECONOMY

Tanzania is one of the world's poorest countries. Although crops are grown on only 5% of the land, agriculture employs 85% of the people. Most farmers grow only enough to feed their families. Food crops include bananas, cassava, corn, millet, rice and vegetables. Export crops include coffee, cotton, cashew nuts, tea, and tobacco. Other crops grown for export include cloves, coconuts, and sisal. Some farmers raise animals, but sleeping sickness and drought restrict the areas for livestock farming.

Diamonds and other gems are mined, together with some coal and gold. Industry is mostly small-scale. Manufactures include processed food, fertilizers, petroleum products, and textiles.

Tourism is increasing. Tanzania has beautiful beaches, but its main attractions are its magnificent national parks and reserves, including the celebrated Serengeti and the Ngorongoro Crater. These are renowned for their wildlife and are among the world's finest.

Tanzania also contains a major archaeological site, Olduvai Gorge, west of the Serengeti. Here, in 1964, the British archaeologist and anthropologist, Louis Leakey, discovered the remains of ancient human-like creatures.

Dhow *Sailing into the harbor, Zanzibar*

Thailand

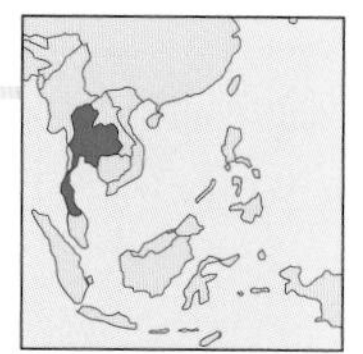

Thailand's flag was adopted in 1917. In the late 19th century, it featured a white elephant on a plain red flag. In 1916, white stripes were introduced above and below the elephant, but in 1917 the elephant was dropped and a central blue band was added.

Area 198,114 sq mi [513,115 sq km]
Population 64,866,000
Capital (population) Bangkok (6,320,000)
Government Constitutional monarchy
Ethnic groups Thai 75%, Chinese 14%, others
Languages Thai (official), English, ethnic and regional dialects
Religions Buddhism 95%, Islam, Christianity
Currency Baht = 100 satang
Website www.thaigov.go.th

The Kingdom of Thailand is one of ten nations in Southeast Asia. Central Thailand is a fertile plain drained mainly by the Chao Phraya. A densely populated region, it includes the capital, Bangkok. The highest land occurs in the north and includes the second largest city Chiang Mai and Doi Inthanon, the highest peak, which reaches 8,514 ft [2,595 m].

The Khorat Plateau, in the northeast, makes up about 30% of the country and extends to the River Mekong border with Laos. In the south, Thailand shares the finger-like Malay Peninsula with Burma and Malaysia.

The vegetation of Thailand includes many hardwood trees to the north. The south has rubber plantations. Grass, shrub and swamp make up 20% of land. 33% of the land is arable, mainly comprising rice fields.

CLIMATE

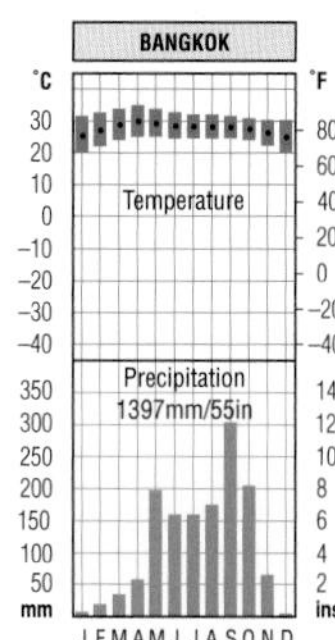

Thailand has a tropical climate. Monsoon winds from the southwest bring heavy rains May to October. Bangkok is drier than many parts of Southeast Asia because mountains shelter the central plains from the rain-bearing winds.

HISTORY

The Mongol capture in 1253 of a Thai kingdom in southwest China forced the Thai people to move south. A new kingdom was established around Sukothai. In the 14th century the kingdom expanded and the capital moved to Ayutthaya.

European contact began in the early 16th century. But, in the late 17th century, the Thais, fearing interference in their affairs, forced all Europeans to leave. This policy continued for 150 years. Thailand remained the only Southeast Asian nation to resist colonization.

In 1782, a Thai General, Chao Phraya Chakkri, became king, founding a dynasty which continues today. The country became known as Siam, and Bangkok became its capital. From the mid-19th century, contacts with the West were restored. In World War I, Siam supported the Allies against Germany and Austria-Hungary. In 1932, Thailand became a constitutional monarchy.

POLITICS

In 1938, Pibul Songkhram became premier and changed the country's name to Thailand. In 1941, Pibul, despite opposition, invited Japanese forces into Thailand. Pibul was overthrown in a military coup in 1957. The military governed Thailand until 1973.

Since 1967, when Thailand became a member of ASEAN (Association of Southeast Asian Nations), its economy has grown, especially its manufacturing and service industries. However, in 1997, it suffered recession along with other eastern Asian countries and this persisted into the 21st century.

A military group seized power in 1991, but elections were held in 1992, 1995, and 2001. Then in 2004 Thailand was rocked by sectarian violence in the south where the majority of the population is Muslim, many of whom claim that they suffer discrimination by the central government.

ECONOMY

Despite its rapid progress, the World Bank classifies the country as a "lower-middle-income" developing country. Manufactures, including commercial vehicles, food products, machinery, timber products, and textiles, are exported.

Agriculture still employs two-thirds of the workforce. Rice is the chief crop, while other major crops include cassava, cotton, corn, pineapples, rubber, sugar cane and tobacco. Thailand also mines tin and other minerals.

Tourism is a major source of income, though the December 2004 tsunami, which killed over 5,000 people, cast a shadow over its future growth.

Traffic in Bangkok's Chinatown *surrounded by colorful signage*

BANGKOK

Capital and chief port of Thailand, located on the east bank of the River Chao Phraya. Bangkok became the capital in 1782, when King Rama I built a royal palace here. It quickly became Thailand's largest city. The Grand Palace (including the sacred Emerald Buddha) and more than 400 Buddhist temples (wats) are notable examples of Thai culture. During World War II it was occupied by the Japanese. Bangkok is a busy market center, much of the city's commerce taking place on the numerous canals (klongs) on the Thonburi (original site of the capital) side of the river that connect the city with the suburbs.

The five stripes represent action and the five regions of Togo, the alternation of colors is for unity in diversity. Red represents the blood shed in the struggle for independence, the star is for life, liberty, and labor. Green is for hope and agriculture. Yellow is for Togo's mineral wealth.

The Republic of Togo is a long, narrow country in West Africa. From north to south, it extends about 311 mi [500 km]. Its coastline on the Gulf of Guinea is only 40 mi [64 km] long, and it is only 90 mi [145 km] at its widest point. The coastal plain is sandy. North of the coast is an area of fertile, clay soil. North again is the Mono Tableland which reaches an altitude of 1,500 ft [450 m], and is drained by the River Mono. The Atakora Mountains are the fourth region. The vegetation is mainly open grassland.

CLIMATE

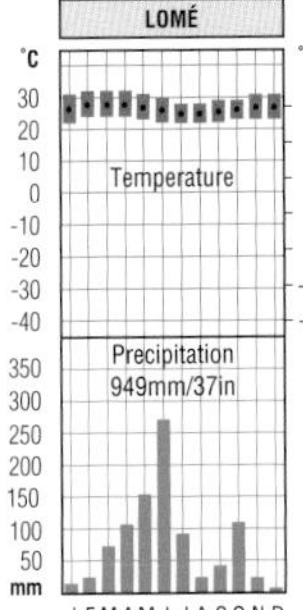

Togo has year-round high temperatures with a long dry season running from October to April. The main wet season runs from March to July, with a minor wet season in October and November. Rainfall is lower on the coast than even a short way inland.

HISTORY

The historic region of Togoland comprised what is now the Republic of Togo and West Ghana. From the 17th to the 19th century, the Ashanti raided Togoland and sold the indigenous inhabitants, the Ewe, to Europeans as slaves.

Togo became a German protectorate in 1884; it developed economically and Lomé was built. At the start of World War I, Britain and France captured Togoland from Germany. In 1922, it divided into two mandates, which in 1942 became UN Trust Territories. In 1956, the people of British Togoland voted to join Ghana, while French Togoland gained independent as the Republic of Togo in 1960.

In 1961 Sylvanus Olympio became Togo's first president. He was assassinated in 1963. Nicolas Grunitzky became president, but he was overthrown in the military coup of 1967, led by the head of the armed forces, General Gnassingbé Eyadéma who then became president. In 1969 a new constitution confirmed Togo as a single-party state, the sole legal party being the Rassemblement du Peuple Togolais (RPT).

Reelected in 1972 and 1986, Eyadéma was forced to resign in 1991 after pro-democracy riots. Kokou Koffigoh led an interim government. Unrest continued with troops loyal to Eyadéma attempting to overthrow Koffigoh.

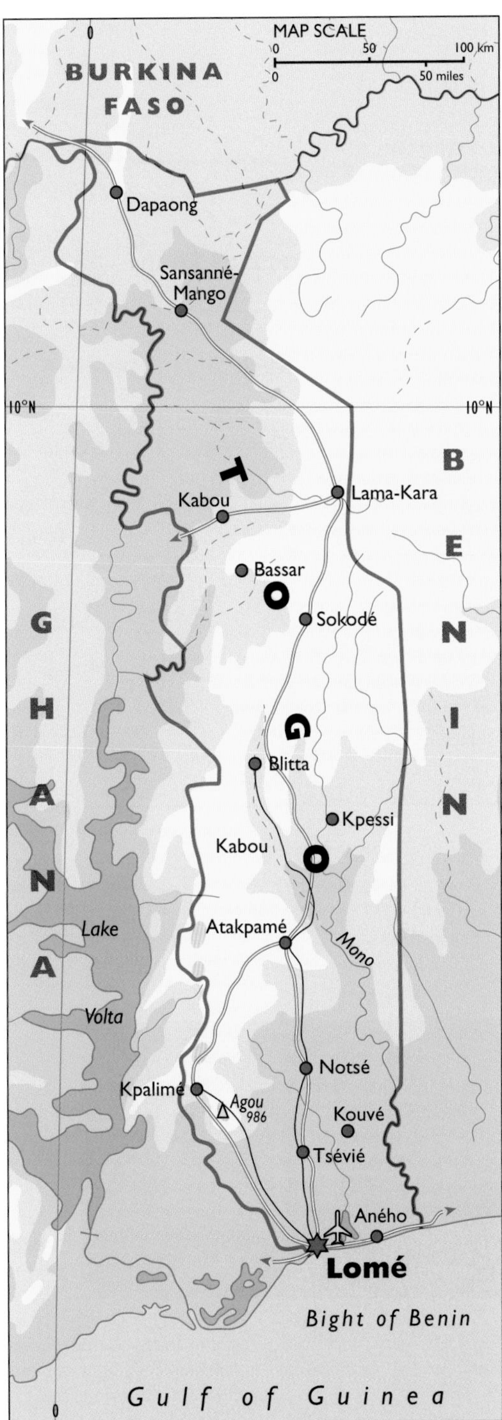

LOMÉ

Capital and largest city of Togo, on the Gulf of Guinea. Made capital of German Togoland in 1897, it later became an important commercial center. It was the site of two conferences (1975, 1979) that produced a trade agreement (known as the Lomé Convention) between Europe and 46 African, Caribbean and Pacific states. Its main exports are coffee, cocoa, palm nuts, copra and phosphates.

Area 21,925 sq mi [56,785 sq km]
Population 5,557,000
Capital (population) Lomé (658,000)
Government Multiparty republic
Ethnic groups Native African 99% (largest tribes are Ewe, Mina and Kabre)
Languages French (official), African languages
Religions Traditional beliefs 51%, Christianity 29%, Islam 20%
Currency CFA franc = 100 centimes
Website www.republicoftogo.com

POLITICS

A new constitution was adopted in 1992. In 1993 Eyadéma won rigged elections. Multiparty elections were held in 1994 and though these were won by an opposition alliance, Eyadéma formed a coalition government. In 1998, paramilitary police prevented the completion of the count in presidential elections when it became clear that Eyadéma had lost. Eyadéma continued in office and the main opposition parties boycotted the general elections in 1999. In late 2002 the constitution was changed to allow Eyadéma to stand for reelection. He won the subsequent 2003 elections.

Eyadéma died in 2005 and his son, Faure, became president. After international pressure he stepped down and called elections. Faure won these two months later amid claims by the opposition that the vote was rigged. In addition, the political violence surrounding the presidential poll was such that around 40,000 Togolese fled to neighboring countries. These events called into question Togo's commitment to democracy which had been declared in 2004 when trying to normalize ties with the EU. The EU had cut off aid to Togo in 1993 over the country's human rights record.

In 2006 Togo played in the FIFA World Cup Finals for the first time in the country's history.

ECONOMY

Togo is a poor developing country. Farming employs 65% of the people, but most farmers grow little more than they need to feed their families. Major food crops include cassava, corn, millet, and yams. The chief cash crops are cocoa, coffee and cotton. The leading exports are phosphate rock, which is used to make fertilizers, and palm oil.

Togo's small-scale manufacturing and mining industries employ about 6% of the people.

Trinidad and Tobago

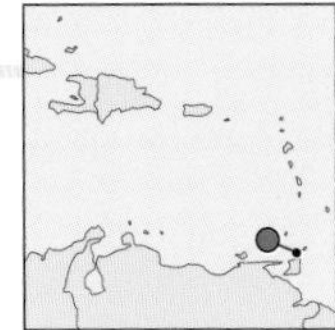

The colors represent earth, water, and fire. The black stripe stands for the country's abundant oil and gas resources and the unity and determination of the people. The white stripes are for the Caribbean Sea, as well as purity and equality. The red field represents the Caribbean sun.

The Republic of Trinidad and Tobago consists of two main islands and is the most southerly in the Lesser Antilles. The largest island, Trinidad, is just 10 mi [16 km] off Venezuela's Orinoco delta. Tobago, a detached extension of Trinidad's hilly Northern Range, lies 21 mi [34 km] to the north. The country's highest point is Mount Aripo (3,085 ft [940 m]) in Trinidad's rugged and forested Northern Range. Fertile plains cover much of the country.

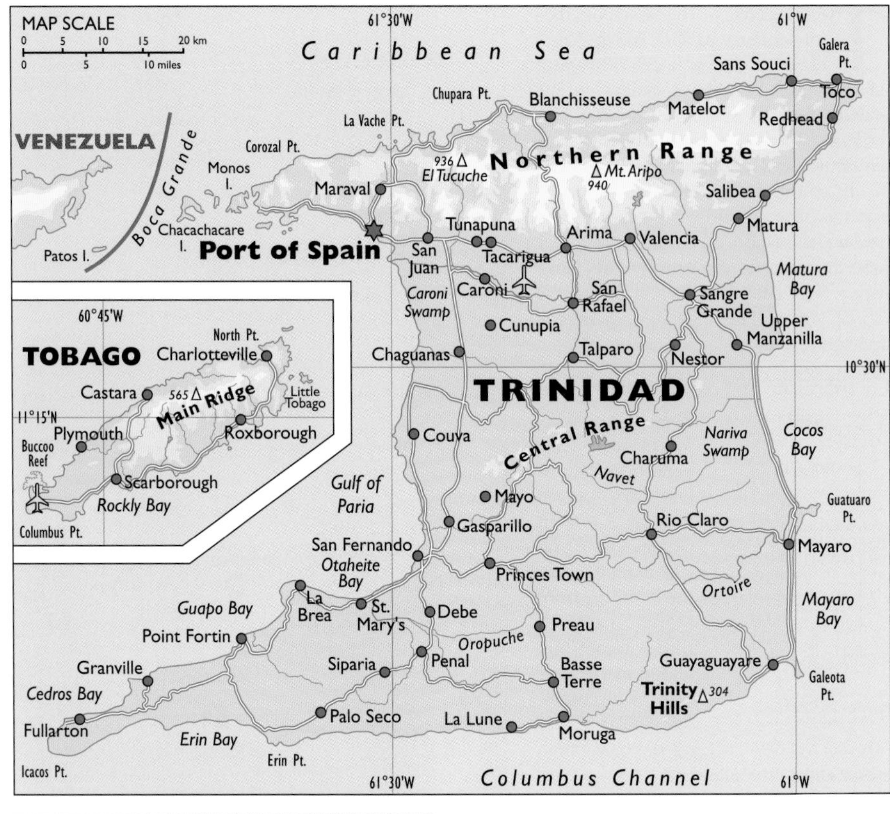

CLIMATE

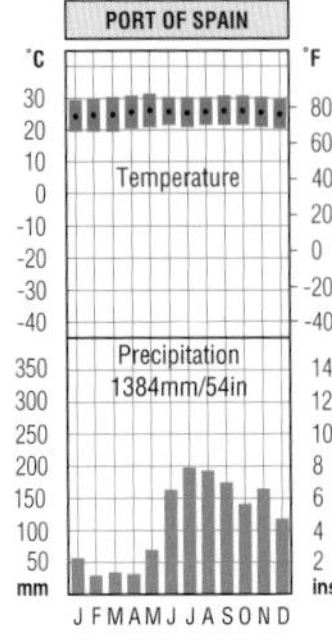

Temperatures are high throughout the year, ranging from 64°F to 92°F [18°C to 33°C]. Rainfall is heavy, with the wettest months from June to November. Annual rainfall ranges from 50 in [1,270 mm] on southwestern Trinidad to more than 100 in [2,540 mm] on the highlands of Tobago.

HISTORY

Christopher Columbus visited the islands, then populated by Arawak and Carib Amerindians in 1498. He named Trinidad after three peaks at its southern tip, and Tobago after a local tobacco pipe. Spain colonized Trinidad in 1532, while Dutch settlers planted sugar on plantations in Tobago in the 1630s. In 1781, France colonized Tobago and further developed its plantation economy. The British captured Trinidad from Spain in 1797 and, in 1802, Spain formally ceded the island to Britain. In 1814, France also ceded Tobago to Britain and, in 1869, the two islands were combined into one colony. Slaves worked on the plantations until slavery was abolished in 1834. To meet the problem of labor shortages, the British recruited Indian and Chinese indentured laborers. The presence of people of African, Asian, and European origin has resulted in a complex cultural mix in present-day Trinidad and Tobago.

PORT OF SPAIN

Capital of Trinidad and Tobago, on the northwest coast of Trinidad. Founded by the Spanish in the late 16th century, it was seized by Britain in 1797. From 1958 to 1962 it was the capital of the Federation of the West Indies. It is a major tourist and shipping center.

Area 1,981 sq mi [5,130 sq km]
Population 1,097,000
Capital (population) Port of Spain (51,000)
Government Multiparty republic
Ethnic groups Indian (South Asian) 40%, African 38%, mixed 21%, others
Languages English (official), Hindi, French, Spanish, Chinese
Religions Roman Catholic 26%, Hindu 23%, Anglican 8%, Baptist 7%, Pentecostal 7%, others
Currency Trinidad and Tobago dollar = 100 cents
Website www.visittnt.com

POLITICS

Independence was achieved in 1962. Eric Williams, moderate leader of the People's National Movement (PNP), which he had founded in 1956, became prime minister. In 1970, the government declared a state of emergency following violence by black power supporters, who called for an end to foreign influence and unemployment. The emergency was lifted in 1972, but strikes caused problems in 1975. Trinidad and Tobago became a republic in 1976, with Williams continuing as prime minister. In 1986, after 30 years in office, the PNP was defeated in elections. The National Alliance for Reconstruction (NAR) coalition took office under Arthur Robinson. In 1990, Islamists seized parliament and held Robinson and other officials hostage for several days. In 1991, Patrick Manning became prime minister following an election victory for the PNP, but, in 1994, Baseo Panday, leader of the Indian-based United National Congress (UNC), became prime minister, leading a coalition with the NAR. In the 2002 elections the PNP was victorious and Patrick Manning returned as prime minister.

Trinidad and Tobago is a major transshipment point for cocaine being moved from South America to North America and Europe. Cannabis is also produced in the country. The drug trade has fueled gang violence and corruption. The death penalty was reintroduced in 1999, despite strong international pressure. In 2005, a Caribbean Court of Justice was set up in Trinidad as a final court of appeal to replace the British Privy Council.

ECONOMY

Oil is vital to the economy. Chief exports include refined and crude petroleum, anhydrous ammonia, and iron and steel.

NORTH AFRICA

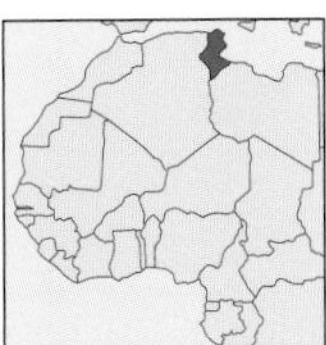

Tunisia's flag originated in about 1835 when the country was officially under Turkish rule. It became the national flag in 1956, when Tunisia became independent from France. The flag contains two traditional symbols of Islam, the crescent and the star.

The Republic of Tunisia is the smallest country in North Africa. The mountains in the north are an eastward and comparatively low extension of the Atlas Mountains.

To the north and east of the mountains lie fertile plains, especially between Sfax, Tunis, and Bizerte. South of the mountains lie broad plateaus which descend toward the south. This low-lying region contains a large salt pan, called the Chott Djerid, and part of the Sahara.

CLIMATE

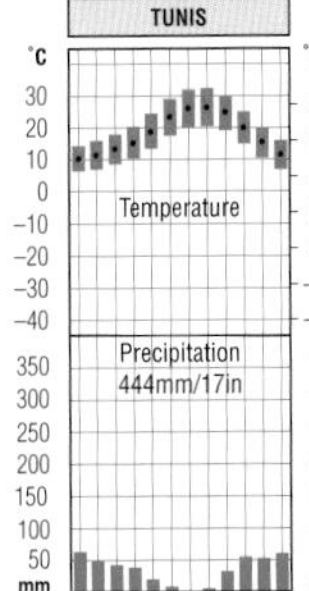

Northern Tunisia has a Mediterranean climate, with dry summers, and mild winters with a moderate rainfall. The average yearly rainfall decreases toward the south, which forms part of the Sahara.

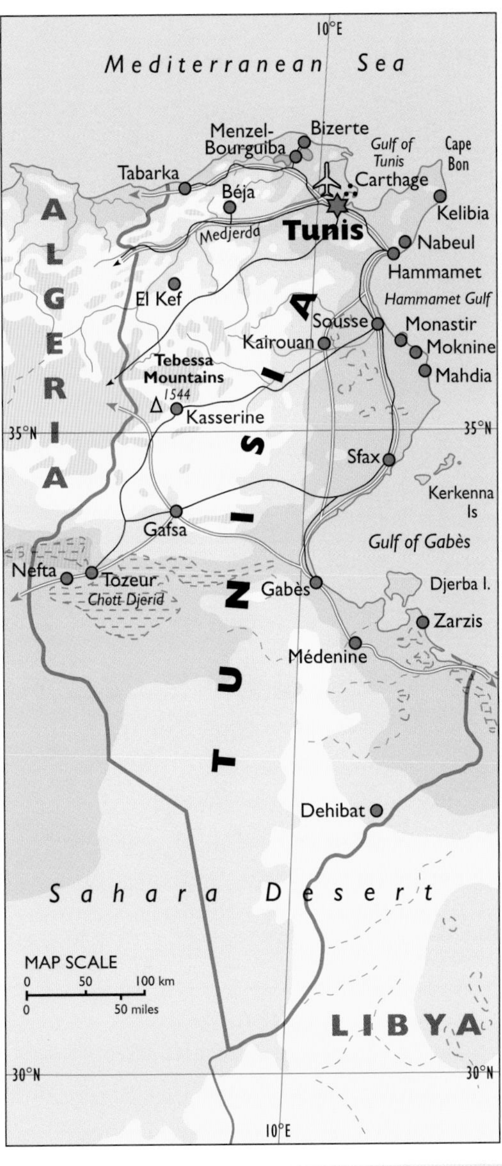

HISTORY

Tunisia has come under the influence of a succession of cultures, each of which has left its mark on the country, giving Tunisia a distinct identity and a long tradition of urban life.

The Phoenicians began the Carthaginian Empire in Tunisia around 1100 BC and, according to legend, the colony of Carthage was established in 814 BC on a site near present-day Tunis. At its peak, Carthage controlled large areas in the eastern Mediterranean but, following the three Punic Wars with Rome, Carthage was destroyed in 146 BC. The Romans ruled the area for 600 years until the Vandals defeated the Romans in AD 439. The Vandals were finally conquered by the Byzantines. Arabs reached the area in the mid-7th century, introducing Islam and the Arabic language. In 1547, Tunisia came under the rule of the Turkish Ottoman Empire.

In 1881, France established a protectorate over Tunisia and ruled the country until 1956. Tunisian aspirations for independence were felt before World War I, but it was not until 1934 that Habib Bourguiba founded the first effective opposition group, the Neo-Destour (New Constitution) Party, which was renamed the Socialist Destour Party in 1964, and is now known as the Constitutional Assembly.

Tunisia supported the Allies during World War II and it was the scene of much fierce fighting. Following independence, the new parliament abolished the monarchy and declared Tunisia to be a republic in 1957. The nationalist leader, Habib Bourguiba, became president.

Area 63,170 sq mi [163,610 sq km]
Population 9,975,000
Capital (population) Tunis (702,000)
Government Multiparty republic
Ethnic groups Arab 98%, European 1%
Languages Arabic (official), French
Religions Islam 98%, Christianity 1%, others
Currency Tunisian dinar = 100 1,000 millimes
Website www.tourismtunisia.com

POLITICS

In 1975, Bourguiba was elected president for life. His government introduced many reforms, including votes for women. But problems arose from the government's successes. For example, the establishment of a national school system led to a very rapid increase in the number of educated people who were unable to find jobs that measured up to their qualifications. The growth of tourism, which provided a valuable source of foreign currency, also led to fears that Western influences might undermine traditional Muslim values.

Finally, the prime minister, Zine el Abidine Ben Ali, removed Bourguiba from office in 1987 and succeeded him as president. He was elected president in 1989, 1994, 1999, and 2004 with his party dominating the Chamber of Deputies, though some seats were reserved for opposition parties whatever their proportion of the popular vote. But he faced opposition from Islamic fundamentalists. Occasional violence and suppression of human rights, including the banning of al-Nahda, the main Islamic party, marred his presidency. However, Islamic fundamentalism in Tunisia did not prove to be anything like as effective as in Algeria.

ECONOMY

The World Bank classifies Tunisia as a "middle-income" developing country. Its main natural resources are oil and phosphates. Agriculture employs 22% of the people. Chief crops are barley, citrus fruits, dates, grapes, olives, sugar beets, tomatoes, and wheat. Sheep are the most important livestock, but goats and cattle are also raised. Tourism has grown considerably. Since independence, new industries and tourism have transformed a number of coastal towns. Major manufactures include cement, flour, phosphoric acid, processed food, and steel. An important stimulus was the signing of a free-trade agreement with the EU in 1995. In doing so Tunisia became the first Arab country on the Mediterranean to sign such an agreement.

TUNIS

Capital and largest city of Tunisia it lies to the north of the country, adjacent to the Gulf of Tunis on the Mediterranean.

Tunis became the capital in the 13th century under the Hafsid dynasty. Seized by Barbarossa in 1534 and controlled by Turkey, it attained infamy as a haven for pirates. The French assumed control in 1881. During World War II it was held by the Axis forces from November 1942 to May 1943.

Tunis gained independence in 1956. The ruins of Carthage are nearby. The medina of Tunis is a UNESCO World Heritage Site and has been so since 1979 featuring as it does over 700 monuments, including fountains, palaces, mosques, mausoleums, and madrasas (schools). Products include olive oil, carpets, textiles, and handicrafts.

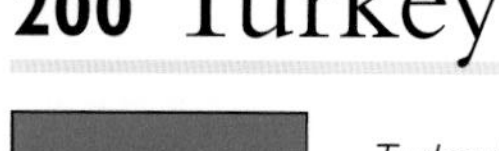

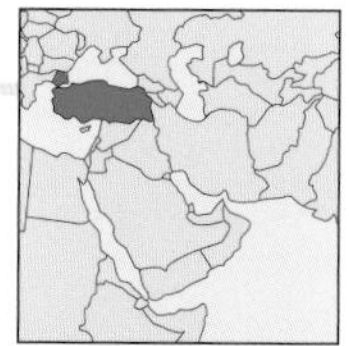

Turkey's flag was adopted when the Republic of Turkey was established in 1923. The crescent moon and the five-pointed star are traditional symbols of Islam. They were used on earlier Turkish flags used by the Turkish Ottoman Empire.

Area 299,156 sq mi [774,815 sq km]
Population 68,894,000
Capital (population) Ankara (2,984,000)
Government Multiparty republic
Ethnic groups Turkish 80%, Kurdish 20%
Languages Turkish (official), Kurdish, Arabic
Religions Islam (mainly Sunni Muslim) 99%
Currency New Turkish lira = 100 kurus
Website www.kultur.gov.tr/EN

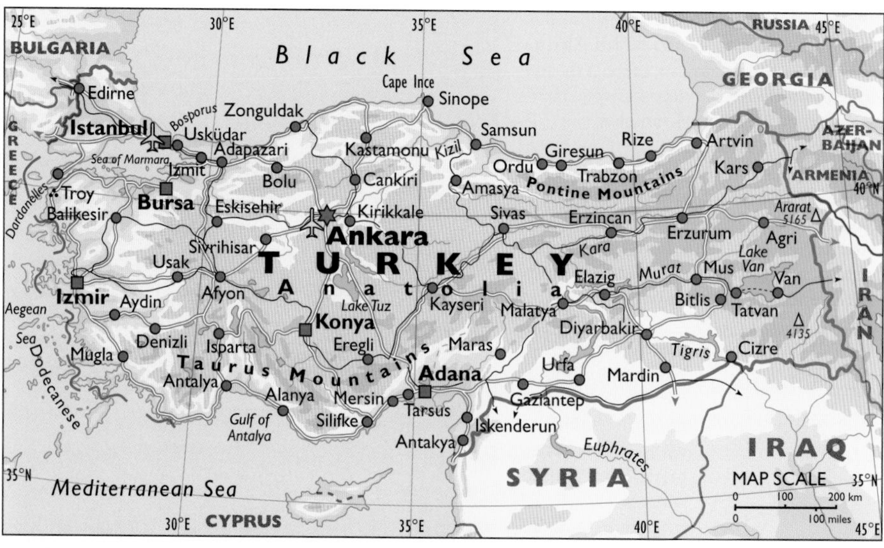

The Republic of Turkey lies in two continents. The European section (Thrace) lies west of a waterway between the Black and Mediterranean seas. This waterway consists of the Bosphorus, on which the city of Istanbul stands, the Sea of Marmara (Marmara Denizi) and a narrow strait called the Dardanelles.

Most of the Asian part of Turkey consists of plateaux and mountains, which rise to 16,945 ft [5,165 m] at Mount Ararat (Agri Dagi) near the border with Armenia. Earthquakes are common.

Deciduous forest grow inland with conifers on the mountains. The plateau is mainly dry steppe.

CLIMATE

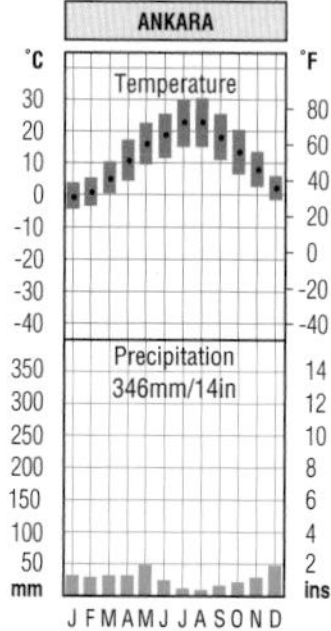

Central Turkey has a dry climate, with hot, sunny summers and cold winters. The driest part of the central plateau lies south of Ankara, around Lake Tuz. Western Turkey has a Mediterranean climate, while the Black Sea coast has cooler summers.

HISTORY

In AD 330, the Roman Empire moved its capital to Byzantium, renaming it Constantinople. Constantinople became the capital of the East Roman (or Byzantine) Empire in 395. Muslim Seljuk Turks from central Asia invaded Anatolia in the 11th century. In the 14th century, another group of Turks, the Ottomans, conquered the area. In 1453, the Ottoman Turks took Constantinople, which they called Istanbul. The Ottoman Turks built up a large empire which finally collapsed during World War I (1914–18). In 1923, Turkey became a republic. Its leader Mustafa Kemal, or Atatürk ("father of the Turks"), launched policies to modernize and secularize the country.

It joined NATO in 1951 and applied to join the European Economic Community in 1987. But Turkey's conflict with Greece, together with its invasion of northern Cyprus in 1974, have led many Europeans to treat Turkey's aspirations with caution. Political instability, military coups, conflict with Kurdish nationalists in eastern Turkey, and concern about the country's record on human rights are other problems.

Pamukkale (Cotton Palace); *this landscape of mineral forests and petrified waterfalls is a designated UNESCO World Heritage Site*

ANKARA

Capital of Turkey, at the confluence of the Cubuk and Ankara rivers. In ancient times it was known as Ancyra, and was an important commercial center as early as the 8th century BC. It flourished under Augustus as a Roman provincial capital. Tamerlane took the city in 1402. Kemal Atatürk set up a provisional government here in 1920. It replaced Istanbul as the capital in 1923, changing its name to Ankara in 1930. It is noted for its angora wool and mohair.

POLITICS

Turkey has enjoyed democracy since 1983, though, in 1998, the government banned the Islamist Welfare Party, accusing it of violating secular principles. In 1999, the largest numbers of parliamentary seats were won by the ruling Democratic Left Party and the far-right Nationalist Action Party. In 2001, the Turkish parliament adopted reforms to ease the country's entry into the European Union. One reform formally recognized men and women as equals—the former code designated the man as the head of the family.

In the elections of 2002 the moderate Islamic Justice and Development Party (AKP) won 362 of the 500 seats in parliament. None of the parties in the former ruling coalition won even 10%.

Turkey finally agreed to recognize Cyprus as an EU member and this led to EU membership talks being formally launched in October 2005 with negotiations expected to take about 10 years.

In the 1980s and 1990s civil war was a problem in the east and southeast of Turkey. Fighting took place between Turkish forces and those of the secessionist Kurdistan Workers' Party (PKK). Over 30,000 people died. The PKK seeks greater political and cultural rights for the Kurdish community. A five-year ceasefire was called off in 2004 by Kurdish secessionists after what they called annihilation operations against their fighters by the Turkish authorities. There have been subsequent clashes between Kurdish fighters and Turkish forces in the southeast causing many deaths.

ECONOMY

Turkey is a "lower-middle-income" developing country. Agriculture employs 40% of the people, and barley, cotton, fruits, corn, tobacco, and wheat are major crops. Livestock farming is important and wool is a leading product. Manufacturing is the chief activity, including processed farm products and textiles, automobiles, fertilizers, iron and steel, machinery, metal products, and paper products. Turkey receives more than 9 million tourists a year.

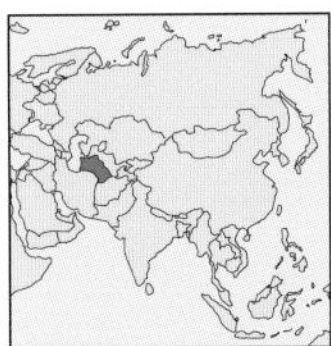

Turkmenistan's flag was adopted in 1992. It incorporates a typical Turkmen carpet design. The crescent is a symbol of Islam, while the five stars and the five elements in the carpet represent the traditional tribal groups of Turkmenistan.

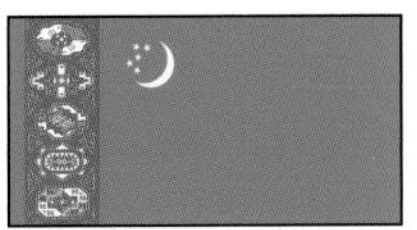

The Republic of Turkmenistan is one of five central Asian republics which once formed part of the Soviet Union. Most of the land is low-lying, with mountains on the southern and southwestern borders.

In the west lies the salty Caspian Sea. A depression called the Kara Bogaz Gol Bay contains the country's lowest point. Most of the country is arid and Asia's largest sand desert, the Garagum, covers 80% of the country, though parts of it are irrigated by the Garagum Canal.

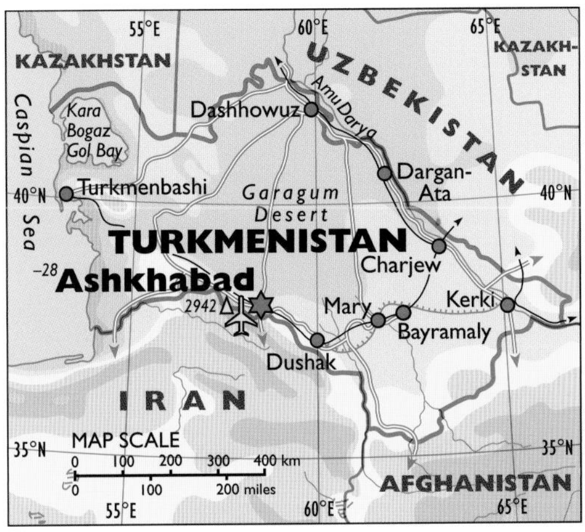

Area 188,455 sq mi [488,100 sq km]
Population 4,863,000
Capital (population) Ashkhabad (521,000)
Government Single-party republic
Ethnic groups Turkmen 85%, Uzbek 5%, Russian 4%, others
Languages Turkmen (official), Russian, Uzbek
Religions Islam 89%, Eastern Orthodox 9%
Currency Turkmen manat = 100 tenesi
Website www.turkmenistan.gov.tm/index_eng.html

CLIMATE

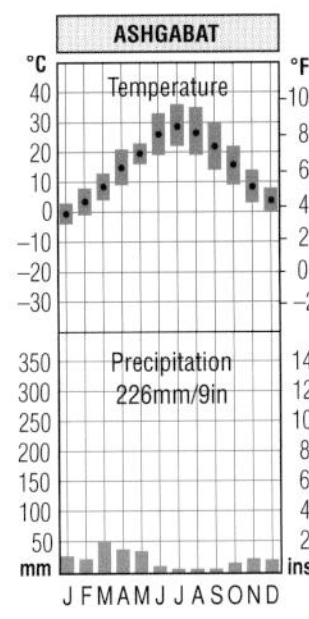

Turkmenistan has a continental climate, with average annual rainfall varying from 3 in [80 mm] in the desert to 12 in [300 mm] in the mountains. Summers are very hot, but temperatures during winter drop below freezing.

HISTORY

Just over 1,000 years ago, Turkic people settled in the lands east of the Caspian Sea and the name "Turkmen" comes from this time. Genghis Khan and his Mongol armies conquered the area in the 13th century and it subsequently became part of Tamerlane's vast empire. With the break up of the Timurid dynasty, Turkmenistan came under Uzbek control. Islam was introduced in the 14th century.

Russia took over the region during the 1870s and 1880s. In 1899, despite resistance, Turkmenistan became part of Russian Turkistan. After the Russian Revolution of 1917, the area came under Communist rule and, in 1924, as part of the Turkistan Autonomous Soviet Socialist Republic, it joined the Soviet Union. The Communists strictly controlled all aspects of life and, in particular, they discouraged religious worship. But they also improved such services as education, health, housing, and transport.

POLITICS

During the 1980s, the Soviet Union introduced reforms, and the Turkmen began to demand more freedom. In 1990, the Turkmen government stated that its laws overruled Soviet laws. In 1991, Turkmenistan became fully independent after the breakup of the Soviet Union, but kept ties with Russia through the Commonwealth of Independent States (CIS).

In 1992, Turkmenistan adopted a new constitution, allowing for political parties, providing that they were not ethnic or religious in character. But effectively Turkmenistan remained a one-party state and, in 1992, Saparmurad Niyazov, the former Communist and now Democratic leader, was the only candidate. In 1994 a referendum prolonged Niyazov's term of office to 2002, while in 1999 the parliament declared him president for life. In 2004, parliamentary elections were described as a "sham" because all the candidates supported the president. In 2005 he surprised observers by calling for contested presidential elections to take place in 2009.

Islamic buildings; with a strong Islamic heritage Turkmenistan is rich in monuments to its past in the form of mosques and palaces

Niyazov seeks to influence every aspect of his people's lives. Turkmens are expected to take spiritual guidance from his book, *Ruhnama*, a collection of thoughts on Turkmen culture, and history. After giving up smoking due to major heart surgery in 1997, he ordered all his ministers to give up and then banned smoking in public places. Subsequent bans include one on young men having beards and long hair, opera, ballet, and the playing of recorded music on television, at public events, and at weddings.

ECONOMY

Turkmenistan joined the Economic Cooperation Organization which was set up in 1985 by Iran, Pakistan, and Turkey. In 1996, the completion of a rail link from Turkmenistan to the Iranian coast was seen as an important step in the development of Central Asia. The World Bank classifies Turkmenistan as a "lower-middle-income" country. The chief resources are oil and natural gas, but agriculture is important. The chief crop, grown on irrigated land, is cotton. Grains and vegetables are also important. Manufactures include cement, glass, petrochemicals, and textiles. Turkmenistan has extensive hydrocarbon and natural gas reserves that could be of major economic assistance.

ASHGABAT (ASHKHABAD)

Capital of Turkmenistan, located 25 mi [40 km] from the Iranian border. Founded in 1881 as a Russian fortress between the Garagum Desert and the Kopet Dagh Mountains, it was largely rebuilt after a severe earthquake in 1948. The city was known as Poltaratsk from 1919 to 1927. Its present name was adopted after the republic attained independence from the former Soviet Union in 1991.

The flag used by the party that won the first national election was adopted as the national flag when Uganda became independent from Britain in 1962. The black represents the people, the yellow the sun, and the red brotherhood. The crested crane is the country's emblem.

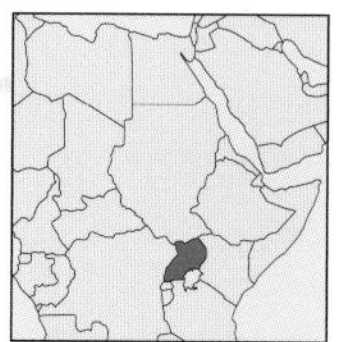

Area 93,065 sq mi [241,038 sq km]
Population 26,405,000
Capital (population) Kampala (774,000)
Government Republic
Ethnic groups Baganda 17%, Ankole 8%, Basogo 8%, Iteso 8%, Bakiga 7%, Langi 6%, Rwanda 6%, Bagisu 5%, Acholi 4%, Lugbara 4% and others
Languages English and Swahili (both official), Ganda
Religions Roman Catholic 33%, Protestant 33%, traditional beliefs 18%, Islam 16%
Currency Ugandan shilling = 100 cents
Website www.statehouse.go.ug

The Republic of Uganda is a landlocked country on the East African Plateau. It contains part of Lake Victoria, Africa's largest lake and a source of the River Nile, which occupies a shallow depression in the plateau.

The plateau varies in height from about 4,921 ft [1,500 m] in the south to 2,953 ft [900 m] in the north. The highest mountain is Margherita Peak, which reaches 16,762 ft [5,109 m] in the Ruwenzori Range in the southwest. Other mountains, including Mount Elgon at 14,177 ft [4,321 m], rise along Uganda's eastern border.

Part of the Great African Rift Valley, which contains lakes Edward and Albert, lies in western Uganda. The landscapes range from rainforests in the south, through savanna in the center, to semidesert in the north.

CLIMATE

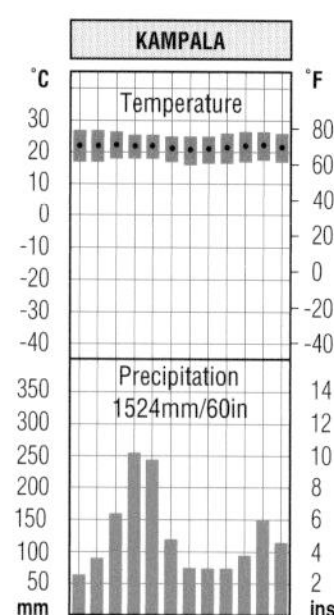

The Equator runs through Uganda and the country is warm throughout the year, though the high altitude moderates the temperature. The lands to the north of Lake Victoria, and the western mountains, especially the high Ruwenzori Range are the wettest regions. Much of Uganda has two rainy seasons from Apri to May and from October to December. In the center and the north, these merge into one, with a distinct dry season.

HISTORY

In around 1500, the Nilotic-speaking Lwo people formced various kingdoms in southwestern Uganda, including Buganda (kingdom of the Ganda) and Bunyoro. During the 18th century, the Buganda kingdom expanded and trade flourished. In 1862, a British explorer, John Speke, became the first European to reach Buganda. He was closely followed in 1875 by Sir Henry Stanley. The conversion activities of Christian missionaries led to conflict with Muslims. The Kabaka (king) came to depend on Christian support. In 1894, Uganda became a British Protectorate.

In 1962, Uganda gained independence with Buganda's Kabaka, Sir Edward Mutesa II, as president and Milton Obote as prime minister. In 1966, Mutesa II was forced into exile. Obote also abolished the traditional kingdoms, including Buganda. Obote was overthrown in 1971 in a military coup led by General Idi Amin Dada. Amin quickly established a personal dictatorship and launched a war against foreign interference that resulted in the mass expulsion of Asians. Amin's regime was responsible for the murder of more than 250,000 Ugandans. Obote loyalists resisted the regime from neighboring Tanzania. In 1976, Amin declared himself president for life and Israel launched a successful raid on Entebbe Airport to end the hijack of one of its passenger planes. In 1978 Uganda annexed the Kagera region of northwest Tanzania.

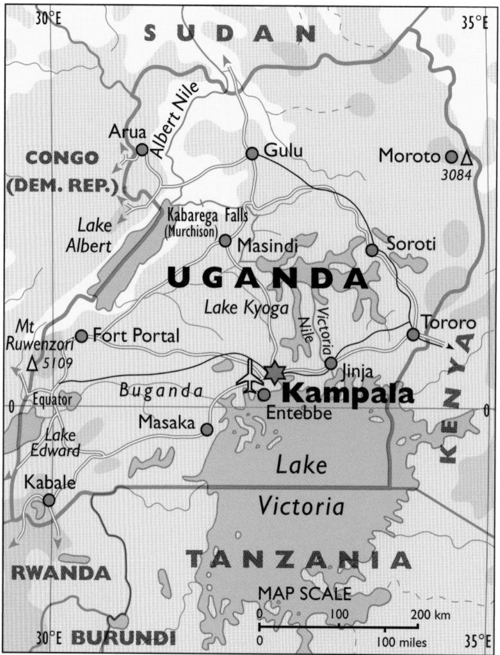

***Terraced fields** of crops, Kisoro*

POLITICS

In 1979 Tanzanian troops helped the Uganda National Liberation Front (UNLF) to overthrow Amin and capture Kampala. In 1980, Apollo Milton Obote led his party to victory in the national elections. But after charges of fraud, Obote's opponents the National Resistance Movement (NRA) began guerrilla warfare. More than 200,000 Ugandans sought refuge in Rwanda and Zaïre. A military group overthrew Obote in 1985 and he lived in exile in Zambia for the last 20 years of his life. Upon his death in 2005 he was granted a state funeral, much to the surprise of his opponents.

Strife continued until 1986, when the NRA captured Kampala and Yoweri Museveni became president. Musveni began to rebuild the domestic economy and improve foreign relations. In 1993 the Kabaka of Uganda returned as monarch. Museveni won Uganda's first direct presidential elections in 1996 and was reelected in 2001.

In 2005, the people voted in favor of restoring multiparty politics after years of non-party politics. Parliament also voted to remove presidential time limits, enabling Museveni to contest the elections in 2006 and beyond.

KAMPALA

Capital and largest city in Uganda, on the northern shore of Lake Victoria. Founded in the late 19th century on the remains of a royal palace of the Kings of Buganda, it replaced Entebbe as capital when Uganda attained independence in 1962. It is the trading center for the agricultural goods and livestock produced in Uganda. Industries include textiles, food processing, tea blending, coffee and brewing.

ECONOMY

Stability was restored to the economy under President Museveni and it finally expanded. Agriculture dominates, employing 80% of the people. Food crops include bananas, cassava, corn, millet, sorghum, and sweet potatoes, while the chief cash crops are coffee, cotton, sugar cane, and tea. The only important metal is copper. The Owen Falls Dam at Jinja, on the outlet of Lake Victoria, produces cheap electricity.

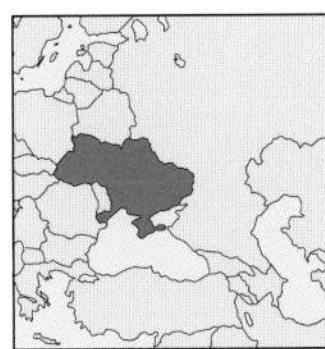

Ukraine's flag was first used between 1918 and 1922. It was readopted in September 1991. The colors were first used in 1848. They are heraldic in origin and were first used on the coat of arms of one of the Ukrainian kingdoms in the Middle Ages.

Ukraine is the second largest country in Europe after Russia. This mostly flat country faces the Black Sea in the south. The Crimean Peninsula includes a highland region overlooking Yalta. The highest point of the country is in the eastern Carpathian Mountains. The most extensive land region is the central plateau which descends in the north to the Dnipro-Pripet Lowlands. A low plateau occupies the northeast.

CLIMATE

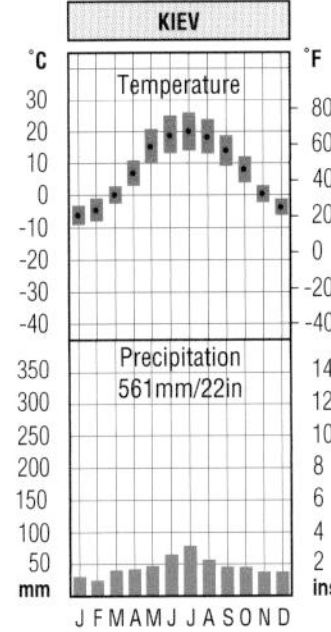

Ukraine has warm summers, but the winters are cold, becoming more severe from west to east. In the summer, the east of the country is often warmer than the west. The heaviest rainfall occurs in the summer.

HISTORY

In the 9th century AD, a civilization called Kievan Rus was founded, with its capital at Kiev. Russians took over the area in 980 and the region prospered. In the 13th century, Mongol armies ravaged the area. Later, the region was split into small kingdoms and large areas fell under foreign rule. In the 17th and 18th centuries, parts of Ukraine came under Polish and Russian rule. But Russia gained most of Ukraine in the late 18th century, although Austria held an area in the west, called Galicia. After the Bolshevik Revolution of 1917, the Ukrainians set up an independent, non-Communist republic. Austrian Ukraine declared itself a republic in 1918 and the two parts joined together, but in 1919, Ukrainian Communists set up a second government and proclaimed the country a Soviet Socialist Republic. The Communists ultimately triumphed and, during 1922, Ukraine became one of the four founding republics of the Soviet Union.

Millions of people died in the 1930s as the result of Soviet policies. Millions more died during the Nazi occupation between 1941 and 1944. In 1945, areas that were formerly in Czechoslovakia, Poland and Romania were added to Ukraine by the Soviet Union.

Area 233,089 sq mi [603,700 sq km]
Population 47,732,000
Capital (population) Kiev (2,590,000)
Government Multiparty republic
Ethnic groups Ukranian 78%, Russian 17%, Belarusian, Moldovan, Bulgarian, Hungarian, Polish
Languages Ukranian (official), Russian
Religions Mainly Ukranian Orthodox
Currency Hryvnia = 100 kopiykas
Website www.president.gov.ua/en

KIEV (KYYIV)

Capital of Ukraine and a seaport on the Dnieper River. Founded in the 6th century AD, Kiev was the capital of Kievan Russia. It later came under Lithuanian, then Polish rule before being absorbed into Russia. It became the capital of the Ukrainian Soviet Socialist Republic in 1934, and of an independent Ukraine in 1991.

***First day at elementary school** in Crimea*

Leonid Kuchma, who became president in 1994, came under fire in the early 2000s for maladministration and for his alleged involvement in the murder of a journalist. In 2004, the prime minister, a supporter of Kuchma, was declared the winner in presidential elections, but after massive demonstrations, the election was declared invalid. The opposition and pro-Western leader Victor Yuschenko was elected president. This led to tensions with Russia. Russia feared that Ukraine might become aligned with the West. A dispute with Russia over the price of the gas it supplies to Ukraine in 2005–6 was said to be politically motivated.

POLITICS

In the 1980s, the people demanded more say over their affairs. The country finally became independent when the Soviet Union broke up in 1991. Ukraine continued to work with Russia through the Commonwealth of Independent States. But Ukraine differed with Russia on some issues, including control over Crimea. In 1999, a treaty ratifying Ukraine's present boundaries failed to get the approval of Russia's upper house.

ECONOMY

The World Bank classifies Ukraine as a "lower-middle-income" economy. Agriculture is important, the major export crops are wheat and sugar beet. Livestock rearing and fishing are also important. Manufacturing is the chief economic activity and includes iron and steel, machinery, and vehicles. The country has large coalfields and hydroelectric and nuclear power stations, but it imports oil and natural gas. In 1986, an accident at the Chernobyl nuclear power plant caused widespread nuclear radiation. The plant was finally closed in 2000.

United Arab Emirates

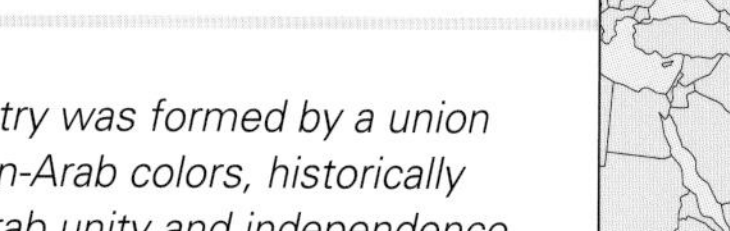

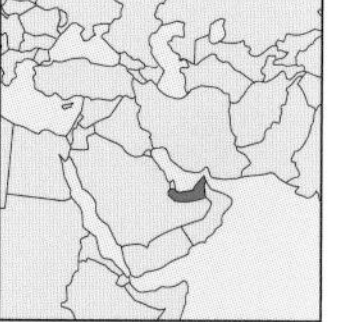

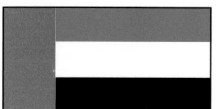

The flag was adopted on December 2, 1971, when the country was formed by a union of seven sheikdoms. Red, white, black and green are the Pan-Arab colors, historically linked to the Arab people and Islamic faith. They stand for Arab unity and independence.

Area 32,278 sq mi [83,600 sq km]
Population 2,524,000
Capital (population) Abu Dhabi (363,000)
Government Federation of Sheikdoms
Ethnic groups South Asian 50%, other Arab and Iranian 23%, Emirati 19%
Languages Arabic (official), Persian, English, Hindi, Urdu
Religions Muslim 96% (Shi'a 16%), others
Currency Emirati dirham = 100 fils
Website www.government.ae/gov/en/index.jsp

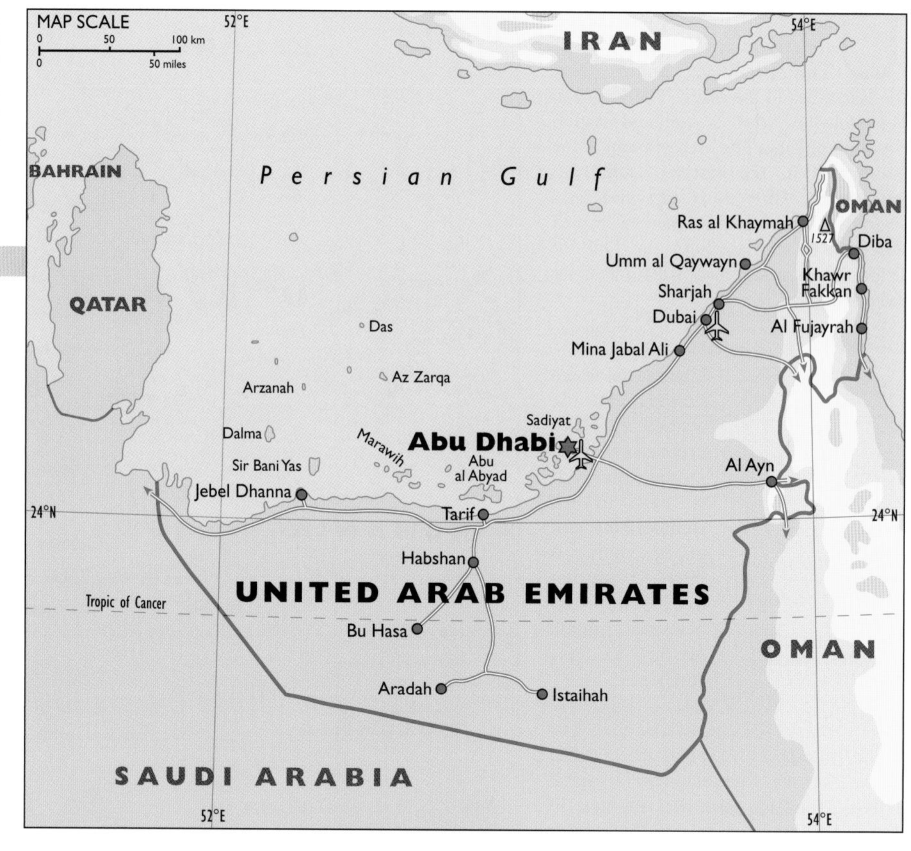

The United Arab Emirates (UAE) consists of a union of seven small Arab emirates (or sheikhdoms). Swamps and salt marshes border much of the coast in the north. The land is a flat, stony desert, with occasional oases. Sand dunes occur in the east. Highlands rise in the east, near the border with Oman. In the south, the land merges into the bleak Rub' al Khali (Empty Quarter) of Saudi Arabia.

CLIMATE

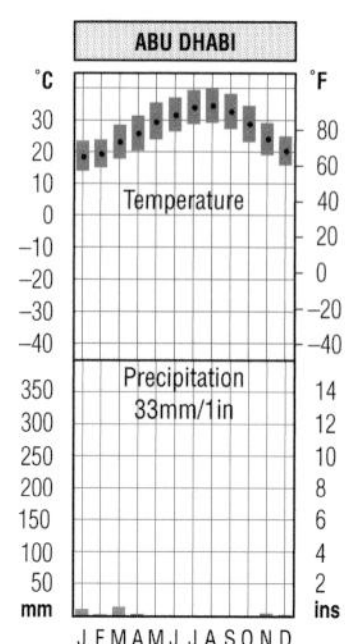

In most of the country, the average annual rainfall is less than 5 in [130 mm], most of it occurring between November and March. In summer (May to September), temperatures can soar to 120°F [49°C], with high humidity along the coast where conditions can become unpleasant. Winters are warm to mild. The eastern highlands are generally cooler and rainier than the rest of the country. Sandstorms and duststorms are common.

HISTORY

The area has its roots as a trading center between the Mesopotamian and Indus Valley civilizations, later coming under Persian control and, in the 7th century AD, embracing Islam. In the 16th century various European nations set up coastal trading posts. The emirates of today began to develop in the 18th century. Their economies were based on pearl fishing and trading. In 1820, conflict between local rulers and piracy along the coast led Britain to force the states to sign a series of truces. Britain took control of the foreign affairs of the states, while promising protection from attack by outsiders. The states retained control over internal affairs. Because of these truces, the region became known as the Trucial States. In 1952, the emirates set up a Trucial Council to increase cooperation between them. Oil was discovered in 1958 and first exported in 1962. In 1968, Britain announced the withdrawal of its forces.

ABU DHABI (ABU ZABY)

Largest and wealthiest of the United Arab Emirates, lying on the south coast of the Persian Gulf. Also the name of its capital city, the federal capital of the UAE. Ruled since the 18th century by the Al-bu-Falah clan of the Bani Yas tribe. There are long-standing frontier disputes with Saudi Arabia and Oman. Abu Dhabi's economy is based almost entirely on crude oil production.

POLITICS

The country became independent in 1971, when six of its seven states, Abu Zaby (Abu Dhabi), Ajman, Dubayy (Dubai), Al Fujayrah, Ash Shariqah (Sharjah), and Umm-al-Qaywayn, agreed to form a single country, the United Arab Emirates. A seventh state, Ras al Khaymah, joined in 1972. Each of the seven Emirates has its own Emir, who controls internal affairs. The federal government controls foreign affairs and defence and plays a leading role in the social and economic development of the country. The seven Emirs form a Federal Supreme Council, which elects the federation's president and vice-president who serve five-year terms. The president appoints the prime minister. The country also has a Federal National Council with 40 members appointed by the rulers of the states. There are no elections and the role of the National Council is to review legislation; it cannot change or veto it. The country is one of the most liberal and tolerant of the Persian Gulf countries, but it is the only one without elected bodies. The UAE joined the allied force against Iraq in 1991 following the invasion of Kuwait, and the United States stationed forces there during the 2003 invasion of Iraq.

ECONOMY

The economy is based on oil production and the country is the world's sixth largest oil exporter.

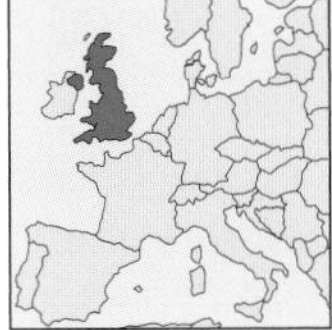

The flag of the United Kingdom was officially adopted in 1801. The first Union flag, combining the cross of St George (England) and St Andrew (Scotland), dates back from 1603. In 1801, the cross of St Patrick, Ireland's emblem, was added to form the present flag.

The United Kingdom of Great Britain and Northern Ireland is a union of four countries. Three of them—England, Scotland, and Wales—make up Great Britain. The Isle of Man and the Channel Islands, including Jersey and Guernsey, are not part of the UK, but are instead self-governing British dependencies.

Much of Scotland and Wales is mountainous, the highest peak is Scotland's Ben Nevis at 4,404 ft [1,342 m], with Snowdon in Wales reaching 3,560 ft [1,085 m]. England has some highland areas, including the Cumbrian Mountains (Lake District) and the Pennine range in the north. England also has large areas of fertile lowland. Northern Ireland is a mixture of lowlands and uplands and contains the United Kingdom's largest lake, Lough Neagh.

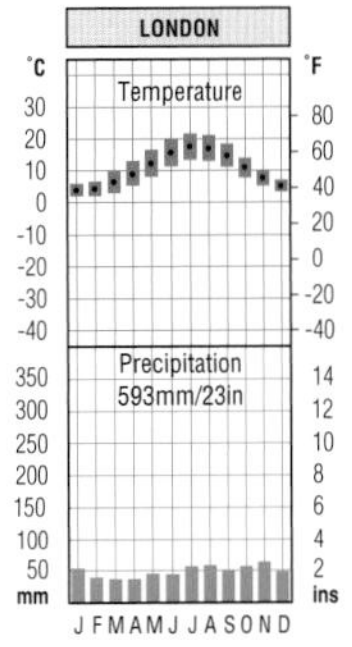

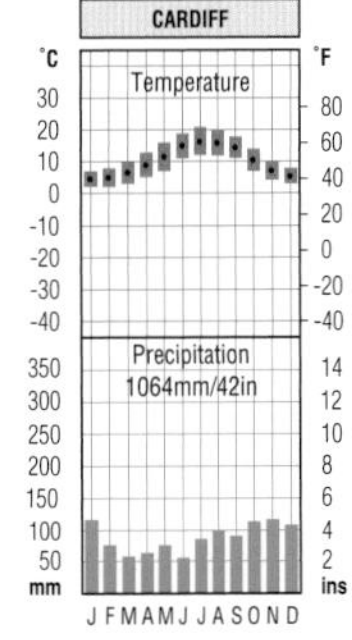

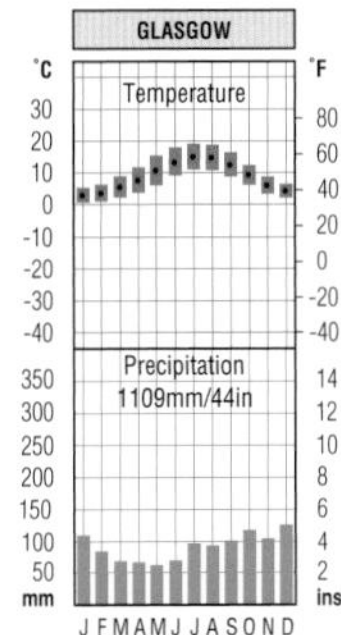

CLIMATE

The UK has a mild climate, influenced by the warm Gulf Stream flowing across the Atlantic from the Gulf of Mexico, then past the British Isles. Moist winds from the southwest bring rain, which diminishes west to east. Winds from the east and north bring cold conditions in winter. The weather is markedly changeable, because of the common occurrence of depressions with their associated fronts.

HISTORY

The isolation of the United Kingdom from mainland Europe has made a major impact on its history. Despite insularity, Britons are of mixed stock.

In ancient times, Britain was invaded by many peoples, including Iberians, celts, Romans, Angles, Saxons, Jutes, Norsemen, Danes, and Normans, who arrived in 1066 and were the last people to successfully invade Britain. The Normans finally overcame Welsh resistance in 1282, when King Edward I annexed Wales and united it with England. Union with Scotland was achieved by the Act of Union of 1707. This created a country known as the United Kingdom of Great Britain.

Ireland came under Norman rule in the 11th century, and much of its later history was concerned with a struggle against English domination. In 1801, Ireland became part of the United Kingdom of Great Britain and Ireland, but in 1921 southern Ireland broke away to become

Area 93,381 sq mi [241,857 sq km]
Population 60,271,000
Capital (population) London (8,089,000)
Government Constitutional monarchy
Ethnic groups English 82%, Scottish 10%, Irish 2%, Welsh 2%, Ulster 2%, West Indian, Indian, Pakistani, others
Languages English (official), Welsh, Gaelic
Religions Christianity, Islam, Sikhism, Hinduism, Judaism
Currency Pound sterling = 100 pence
Website www.pm.gov.uk

UNITED KINGDOM
SCOTLAND
WALES
ENGLAND
NORTHERN IRELAND
IRELAND
ATLANTIC OCEAN
North Sea
Irish Sea
English Channel
St George's Channel
North Channel
FRANCE
Orkney Islands
Shetland Islands
Mainland
Kirkwall
Lerwick
John o' Groats
Thurso
Wick
C. Wrath
Stornoway
Lewis
Outer Hebrides
St Kilda
Ullapool
North West Highlands
Moray Firth
Inner Hebrides
Skye
Loch Ness
Inverness
Spey
Grampians
Dee
Aberdeen
Fort William
1342 Ben Nevis
Mull
Oban
Dundee
Perth
Jura
Islay
Stirling
Dunfermline
Firth of Forth
Glasgow
Edinburgh
Berwick-upon-Tweed
Arran
Firth of Clyde
Ayr
Southern Uplands
Hawick
Malin Head
Londonderry
Coleraine
Larne
Ballymena
Neagh
Lurgan
Bangor
Belfast
Portadown
Enniskillen
Armagh
Newry
Stranraer
Dumfries
Newcastle-upon-Tyne
Sunderland
Carlisle
Solway Firth
Middlesbrough
LAKE DISTRICT
Sca Fell 978
Kendal
Pennines
Scarborough
Douglas
Isle of Man
Barrow-in-Furness
Lancaster
Bradford
York
Leeds
Hull
Blackpool
Preston
Huddersfield
Humber
Grimsby
Anglesey
Holyhead
Liverpool
Manchester
Chester
Doncaster
Sheffield
Trent
Lincoln
The Wash
Conwy
Snowdon 1085
Stoke-on-Trent
Derby
Nottingham
King's Lynn
Great Yarmouth
Stafford
Leicester
EAST ANGLIA
Norwich
Cardigan Bay
Telford
Birmingham
Coventry
Peterborough
Ouse
Lowestoft
Aberystwyth
Severn
Cambridge
Worcester
Northampton
Bedford
Ipswich
Fishguard
Carmarthen
Hereford
Cheltenham
Milton Keynes
Luton
Colchester
Gloucester
Cotswolds
Thames
Oxford
Chelmsford
Swansea
Newport
Slough
London
Southend
Swindon
Reading
Margate
Cardiff
Bristol
Bath
Canterbury
Bristol Channel
Guildford
Dover
Salisbury
Crawley
Folkestone
Taunton
EXMOOR
Winchester
Southampton
Hastings
Exeter
Bournemouth
Brighton
Eastbourne
Portsmouth
Poole
DARTMOOR
Weymouth
Isle of Wight
Torquay
Plymouth
Land's End
Penzance
Isles of Scilly
MAP SCALE
0 50 100 km
0 50 miles
8°W
6°W
4°W
2°W
0
2°E
60°N
58°N
56°N
54°N
52°N
50°N
Channel Is see page 118

Irish Free State. Most of the people in Irish Free State were Roman Catholics. In Northern Ireland, where the majority were Protestants, most wanted to remain citizens of the United Kingdom, as a result the country's official name changed to the United Kingdom of Great Britain and Northern Ireland.

The British empire began to develop in the 18th century, despite the loss in 1783 of its North American colonies. In the late 18th century the UK was the first country to industrialize its economy.

The British Empire broke up after World War II (1939–45), though the UK still administers many small, territories around the world. The empire was transformed into the Commonwealth of Nations, a free association of independent countries, numbering 53 in 2005.

CHANNEL ISLANDS

Group of islands at the south west end of the English Channel, 10 mi [16 km] off the west coast of France. The main islands are Jersey, Guernsey, Alderney, and Sark; the chief towns are St. Helier (Jersey) and St. Peter Port (Guernsey). A dependency of the British crown since the Norman Conquest, they were under German occupation during World War II. They are divided into the administrative bailiwicks of Guernsey and Jersey, each with its own legislative assembly. The islands have a warm, sunny climate and fertile soil. The major industries are tourism and agriculture. They cover an area of 75 sq mi (194 sq km).

POLITICS

A welfare state was set up in 1945, with a social security system that provided welfare for people "from the cradle to the grave." In 1960, the UK helped to set up the European Free Trade Association with six other nations. In 1963, Britain's request to join the EEC was rejected, the UK finally joined the EEC in 1973, though a strong body of opinion still feared that the development of a federal Europe would jeopardize British sovereignty. Membership was endorsed by a referendum in 1975, but, at the turn of the century, Britons were still debating whether it was advisable for Britain to adopt the euro, the single European currency adopted by 12 of the 15 European Union members in 1999.

Since the 1960s, Northern Ireland has been the scene of conflict between the Protestant majority, who favor continuing union with the UK, and the Roman Catholic minority, many of whom are republicans who would like to see Ireland reunified. British troops were sent to the province in 1969 to control violence between the communities and, at various times, Britain has imposed direct rule. In 1998, the "Good Friday" agreement held out hope for the future, when unionists and nationalists agreed that Northern Ireland would remain part of the United Kingdom, until a majority of its people voted in favor of a change. The agreement also allowed Ireland to play a part in the affairs of the north, while the republic amended its constitution to remove all claims to Northern Ireland. A Northern Ireland Assembly was set up to handle local affairs. In July 2005 the IRA issued a statement of full disarmament.

LONDON

Capital of the United Kingdom, second-largest city in Europe, after Moscow. Located on the River Thames, 40mi [65km] from its mouth in the North Sea. Greater London, comprises the City of London "square mile" plus 13 inner and 19 outer boroughs, covering a total of 610sq mi [1,580 sq km]. The Romans called it Londinium. In the 9th century, Alfred the Great made it the seat of government. Edward the Confessor built Westminster Abbey and made Westminster his capital in 1042. The Plague of 1665 killed 75,000 Londoners, and the following year the Fire of London destroyed many buildings. Sir Christopher Wren designed many churches, including St. Paul's. The 19th century saw the population reach 4 million. and London become the world's biggest city. Further growth between the World Wars was accompanied by extensions to the transport system. Much of London was rebuilt after bomb damage during World War II, and the docklands were regenerated in the late 1980s. London is one of the world's most important administrative, financial, and commercial cities.

ISLE OF MAN

Island off the northwest coast of England, in the Irish Sea; the capital is Douglas. In the Middle Ages, it was a Norwegian dependency, subsequently coming under Scottish then English rule. It has been a British crown possession since 1828, but has its own government (the Tynwald). The basis of the economy is tourism although agriculture is important, the chief products being oats, fruit and vegetables. It covers an area of 221 sq mi [572 sq km].

Before 1999, Scotland and Wales were directly ruled by the British parliament in London. In 1997, following the landslide victory of the Labour Party under Tony Blair, 74% of voters in Scotland and 50.3% of voters in Wales opted for the setting up local assemblies.

The Scottish parliament is responsible for local affairs with limited powers to raise or reduce taxes. The Welsh Assembly has no powers over taxation. Both met for the first time in 1999. Devolution has caused concern among those who fear that it might lead to the break-up of the UK, also focusing attention on the question of nationality.

The high cost of welfare services is a matter of political controversy. There is also concern about the changing economy, with a decline in traditional manufacturing and the growth of service industries, both of which affect employment. Another issue is immigration and the fear that economic migrants entering the UK will lessen the job opportunities of the indigenous workforce.

After the terrorist attacks on the United States on September 11, 2001, Britain was prominent in its support for the United States, helping to create the broad alliance that launched the attack on the Taliban government of Afghanistan. However, others are concerned at the cost and morality of British military operations especially the war with Iraq. In July 2005 four suicide bombers struck in central London, killing 52 and injuring hundreds.

ECONOMY

The UK is a major industrial and trading nation. Its natural resources are coal, iron ore, oil, and natural gas, but it has to import most of the materials it needs for industry. It also has to import food. Service and high-technology industries are vital, financial and insurance services bring in much-needed foreign exchange. Historic and cultural attractions make tourism a vital industry and a major earner.

Agriculture employs only 2% of the workforce. Production is high. Major crops include barley, potatoes, sugar beets, and wheat. Sheep are the leading livestock, beef and dairy cattle, pigs, and poultry are also important as are cheese, milk, and fishing.

Ullswater Lake *in the England's Lake District*

United States

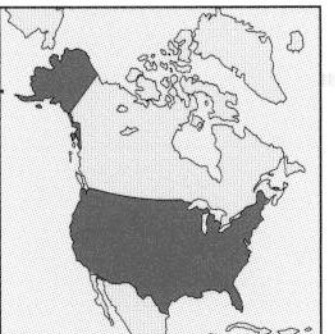

This flag, known as the "Stars and Stripes," has had the same basic design since 1777, during the War of Independence. The 13 stripes represent the 13 original colonies in the eastern United States. The 50 stars represent the 50 states of the Union.

The United States of America is the world's fourth largest country in area and the third largest in population. It contains 50 states, 48 of which lie between Canada and Mexico, plus Alaska in northwestern North America and Hawaii, a group of volcanic islands in the North Pacific Ocean.

Densely populated coastal plains lie toe the east and south of the Appalachian Mountains. The central lowlands drained by the Mississippi-Missouri rivers stretch from the Appalachians to the Rocky Mountains in the west. The Pacific region contains fertile valleys separated by mountain ranges.

CLIMATE

The climates of the United States vary greatly, ranging from the Arctic conditions in northern Alaska, where average temperatures plummet to 9°F [–13°C], to the intense heat of Death Valley. which holds the record for the highest shade temperature ever recorded in the United States—134°F [57°C].

The Midwest, New England and the Middle Atlantic States experience cold winters and warm summers. By contrast, the southern states have long, hot summers and mild, wet winters. In the central United States, a lack of topographical features bars the northward movement of hot, moist air from the Gulf of Mexico, and in winter the southward movement of dry, cold air from the Arctic. These air masses produce contrasts of climate, exacerbated by storms, blizzards, and tornadoes. Parts of California have a pleasant Mediterranean-type climate, but the mountains of the west are much cooler and wetter. The central plains are arid, while deserts occur in parts of the west and southwest.

HISTORY

The first people in North America, the ancestors of the Native Americans arrived around 40,000 years ago from Asia. AlthoughVikings probably reached North America 1,000 years ago, European exploration proper did not begin until the late 15th century.

The first Europeans to settle in large numbers were the British, who founded settlements on the eastern coast in the early 17th century. British rule ended with the War of Independence (1775–83). The country expanded in 1803 when a vast territory in the south and west was acquired through the Louisiana Purchase, while the border with Mexico was fixed in the mid-19th century. The Civil War (1861–5) ended slavery and the serious threat that the nation might split into two parts. In the late 19th century the West was opened up, while immigrants flooded in from Europe and elsewhere.

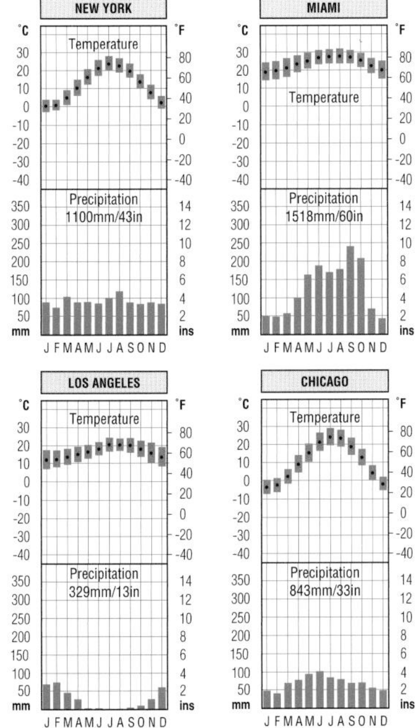

Area 3,717,792 sq mi [9,629,091 sq km]
Population 293,028,000
Capital (population) Washington, DC (572,000)
Government Federal republic
Ethnic groups White 77%, African American 13%, Asian 4%, Amerindian 2%, others
Languages English (official), Spanish, more than 30 others
Religions Protestant 56%, Roman Catholic 28%, Islam 2%, Judaism 2%
Currency US dollar = 100 cents
Website www.firstgov.gov

Manhattan, *New York, New York State; New York's population of over 8 million is the largest for a city in the USA*

POLITICS

The United States has long played a leading role in industrial, economic, social, and technological innovation. The majority of Americans continue to enjoy one of the world's highest material standards of living and the country continues to produce a highly skilled, literate, and imaginative population. Yet at the same time, the country faces many problems. One concerns the maintenance of social cohesion as the composition of American society changes. Another is the issue of poverty and the low standards of living of a sizeable underclass of poor and inadequately educated people, many of whom are members of ethnic minorities. Other associated problems include crime, drug addiction, and racial conflict.

Until about 1860, the population, with the exception of the Native Americans and the southern African Americans, was made up largely of immigrants of British and Irish origin, with small numbers of Spaniards and French. However, after the Civil War, increasing numbers of immigrants arrived from the countries of central and southeastern Europe, including Italy, the Balkans, Poland, Scandinavia, and Russia. This vast influx of Europeans, numbering about 30 million between 1860 and 1920, was vastly different in culture and language from the established population. More recently, the country has received lesser influxes of Japanese, Chinese, Filipinos, Cubans, Puerto Ricans, and large numbers of Mexicans, many of them illegal immigrants. Although strong influences and pressures toward Americanization still exist, members of these groups have tended to maintain their own culture, establishing social and cultural enclaves within American society. Although the nation has never adopted an official language, English was readily adopted by most immigrants in the late 19th and early 20th century, because they sought acceptance in the "melting pot" that makes up the United States. However, many of the recent Hispanic immigrants persist in speaking Spanish, which has become the country's second language. Many Americans are concerned about this trend toward "cultural pluralism" rather than integration through the "melting pot." They argue that Hispanics who do not speak English are at a disadvantage in American society and believe that everyone should speak English, either as a first or second language. According to some population forecasts, today's white majority will be outnumbered by other ethnic groups in 2050. With a total projected population of 380 million, Hispanics are expected to number around 80 million by 2050, while African Americans will account for another 62 million. Such a rapid growth of these communities is seen by some as a threat to the majority.

From the 1890s, the United States developed into a world power, and played a leading role in international affairs throughout the 20th century. It played a key role in World Wars I and II, after which it was one of the world's two superpowers the other being the Soviet Union. After World War II, it assumed the leadership of the West during the Cold War. Since the end of the Cold War, the United States has faced new threats from terrorists and rogue states. Its vulnerability was demonstrated by the terrorist attacks on New York City and Washington, DC, on September 11, 2001. The United States responded vigorously, creating an international alliance to combat terrorism and the nations which shelter or aid terrorists. In 2001 it led a coalition force against the Taliban regime in Afghanistan which was protecting al Qaida terrorists. Then in 2003 the US led another coalition force to over throw the repressive regime of Saddam Hussein in Iraq. However, despite early military successes, the conflict continued. George W. Bush was reelected in 2004.

WASHINGTON, DC

Capital of the USA, on the east bank of the Potomac River, covering the District of Columbia and extending into the neighboring states of Maryland and Virginia. The site was chosen as the seat of government in 1790, and French engineer Pierre Charles L'Enfant planned the city. Construction of the White House began in 1793, and the building of the Capitol the following year. In 1800, Congress moved from Philadelphia to Washington. During the War of 1812, the British occupied the city and many public buildings were burned, including the White House and the Capitol. Washington is the legislative, judicial, and administrative center of the USA. Despite its role, Washington has severe social problems; many of the large African-American population live in slum housing.

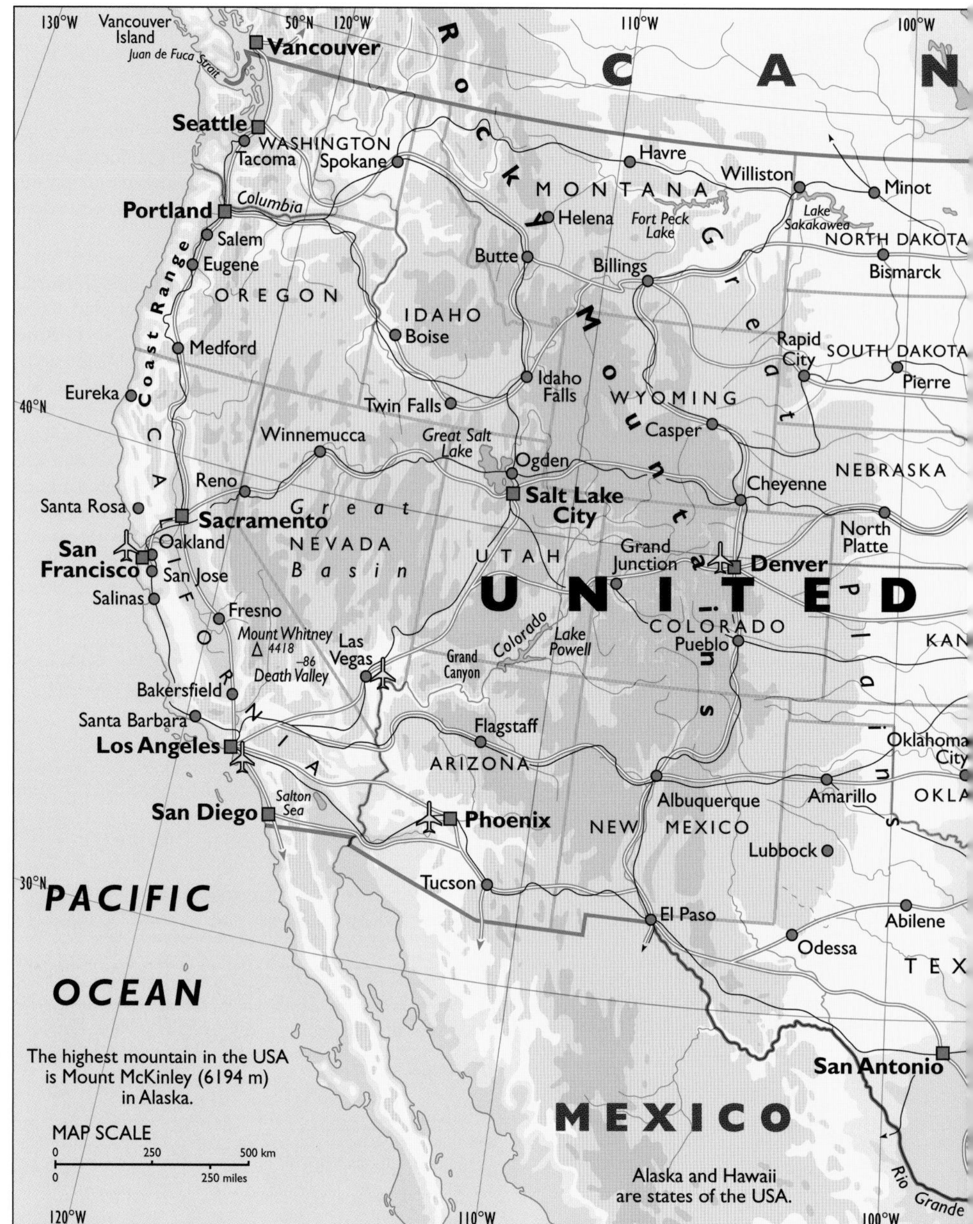

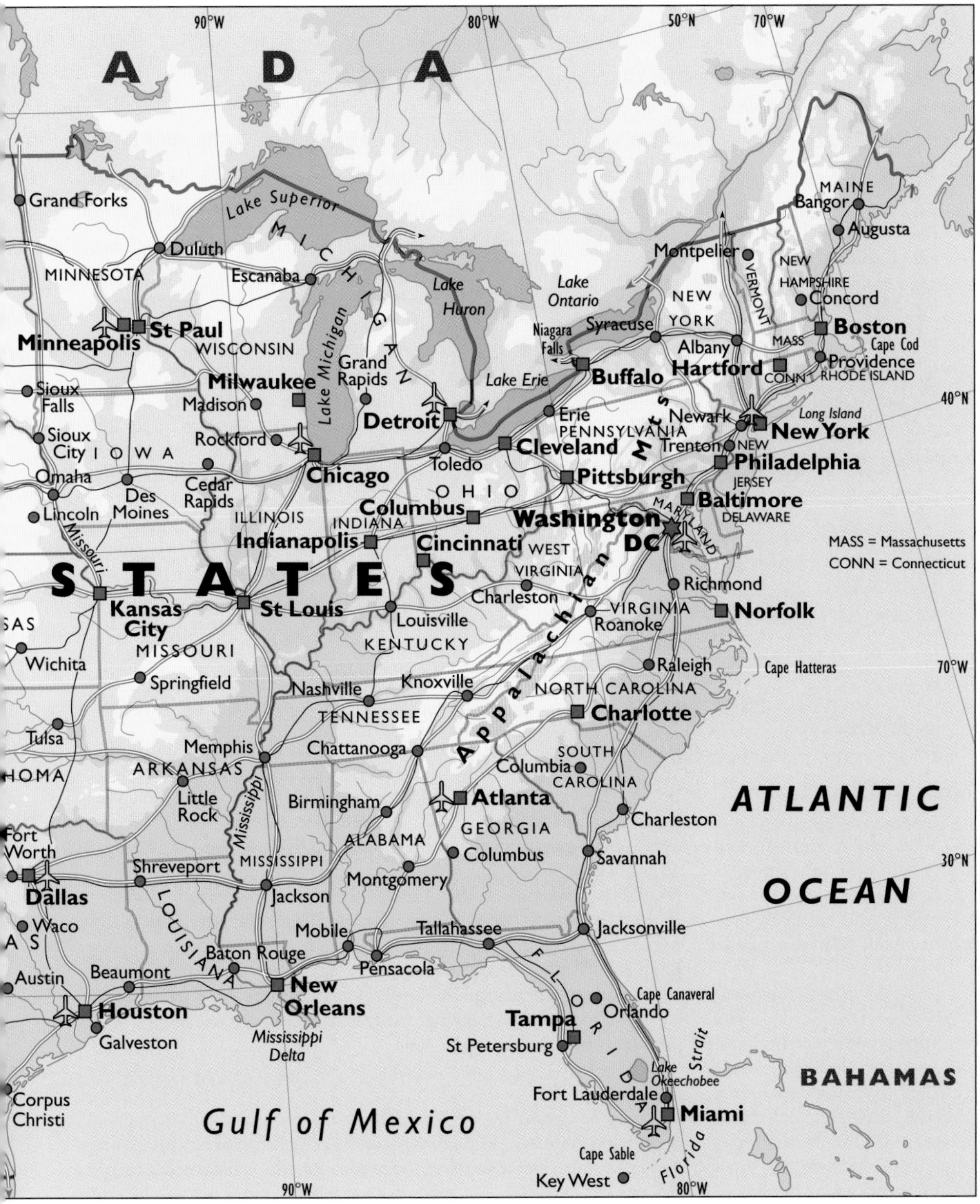

ECONOMY

Agriculture employs only 2.4% of the work force. The western plains are the main centers of production. Much of the land farmed by the Pilgrim Fathers and other settlers is now built over, or has reverted to forest. The US has become a leading producer of meat, dairy products, soybeans, corn, oats, wheat, barley, cotton, and sugar.

The spread of prosperity generated new consumer industries to satisfy the demands of a large middle class for ever-increasing standards of comfort. The US was a pioneer of large-scale industrial production. With almost every raw material available within its own boundaries, or readily gained through trading, its mining and extractive industries have been heavily exploited. Anthracite from eastern Pennsylvania, and good bituminous and coking coals from the Appalachians, Indiana, Illinois, Colorado, and Utah are still in demand, and vast reserves remain.

Oil, first drilled in Pennsylvania in 1859, was subsequently found in major fields underlying the Midwest, the eastern and central mountain states, the Gulf of Mexico, California and Alaska. Home consumption of petroleum products has grown steadily. Although the US is a major producer, it is also by far the world's greatest consumer and has long been a net importer of oil. In the Gulf Coast states, the exploitation of oil in Oklahoma, Texas and Louisiana has shifted the former dependence on agriculture to the refining and petrochemical industries. Dallas-Fort Worth has transformed into a major conurbation; Denver has changed from a small railhead town into a wealthy state capital. Natural gas is also found in abundance, usually associated with oil.

ALASKA

State in northwest North America, separated from the rest of continental USA by the province of British Columbia, Canada, and from Russia by the Bering Strait. The capital is Juneau. The largest city is Anchorage on the southern coast. The USA purchased Alaska for US$7.2 million from Russia in 1867. Fishing drew settlers and, after the gold rush of the 1890s, the population doubled within a decade. It became the 49th state of the Union in 1959. About 25% lies inside the Arctic Circle. The main Alaska Range includes Mount McKinley (Denali), the highest peak in North America. The chief river is the Yukon. The Alaskan economy is based on fish, natural gas, timber, quartz, and, primarily, oil. The national parks encourage tourism. Because of its strategic position and oil reserves, Alaska developed as a military area and is linked to the rest of the USA by the 1,500 mi (2,450 km) Alaska Highway. Although by far the largest US state, it has the third smallest population (after Wyoming and Vermont). Of the total state population, 98,043 are Native Americans (mainly Inuit-Aleut). It has an area of 591,004 sq mi (1,530,700 sq km) and a population of626,932.

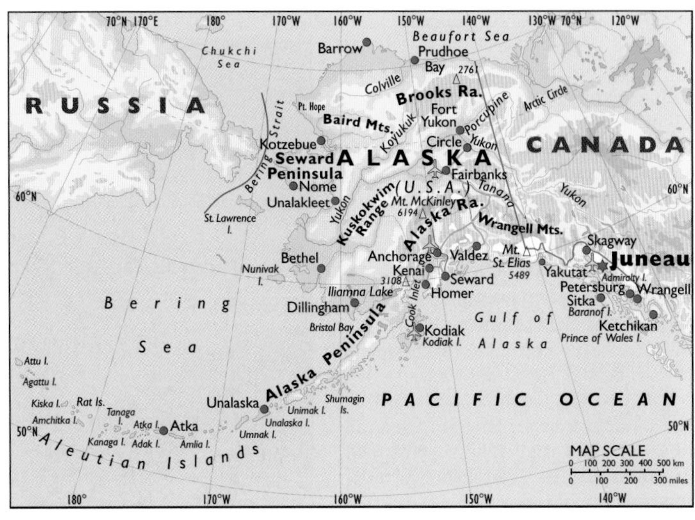

Uruguay has used this flag since 1830. The nine stripes represent the nine provinces which formed the country when it became an independent republic in 1828. The colors and the May Sun had originally been used by Argentina during its struggle against Spanish rule.

Area 67,574 sq mi [175,016 sq km]
Population 3,399,000
Capital (population) Montevideo (1,303,000)
Government Multiparty republic
Ethnic groups White 88%, Mestizo 8%, Mulatto or Black 4%
Languages Spanish (official)
Religions Roman Catholic 66%, Protestant 2%, Judaism 1%
Currency Uruguayan peso = 100 centésimos
Website www.turismo.gub.uy

The Oriental Republic of Uruguay, as Uruguay is officially known, is South America's second smallest independent nation after Suriname. The River Uruguay, which forms the country's western border, flows into the Río de la Plata (River Plate), a large estuary fringed with lagoons and sand dunes, which leads into the South Atlantic Ocean.

The land consists mainly of low-lying plains and hills. The highest point lies south of Minas and is only 501 m [1,644 ft] above sea level. The main river in the interior is the Rio Negro.

CLIMATE

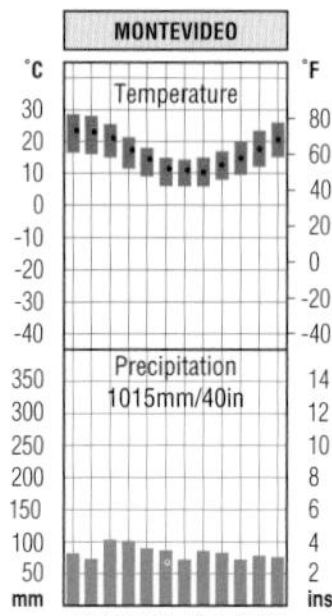

Uruguay has a mild climate, with rain throughout the year, though droughts sometimes occur. The summer is pleasantly warm, especially near the coast. The weather remains relatively mild in winter.

HISTORY

The first people of Uruguay were Amerindians. But the Amerindian population has largely disappeared. Many were killed by Europeans, some died of European diseases, while others fled into the interior. The majority of Uruguayans today are of European origin, though there are some mestizos (of mixed European and Amerindian descent). The first European to arrive in Uruguay was a Spanish navigator, Juan Diaz de Solis, in 1516. But he and part of his crew were killed by the local Charrúa Amerindians when they went ashore.

Few Europeans settled until the late 17th century. Spanish settlers founded Montevideo in order to prevent the Portuguese from gaining influence in the area. Uruguay was then little more than a buffer zone between the Portuguese territory to the north and Spanish territories to the west. By the late 18th century, Spaniards had settled in most of the country. Uruguay became part of a colony called the Viceroyalty of La Plata, which included Argentina, Paraguay, and parts of Bolivia, Brazil and Chile.

Uruguay was annexed by Brazil in 1820, bringing about an end to Spanish rule. In 1825, Uruguayans, supported by Argentina, began a struggle for independence.

POLITICS

Uruguay was recognized as an independent republic by Brazil and Argentina in 1828. Social and economic developments were slow in the 19th century, but, from 1903, governments made Uruguay a democratic and stable country. Since 1828, two political parties—the Colorados (Liberals) and the Blancos (Conservatives)—have dominated.

During World War II, Uruguay prospered because of its export trade, especially in meat and wool. However, from the 1950s, economic problems caused unrest. Terrorist groups, notably the Tupumaros (Marxist urban guerrillas), carried out murders and kidnappings in the 1960s and early 1970s. In 1972, President Juan Maria Bordaberry declared war on the Tupumaros and the army crushed them. In 1973, the military seized power, suspended the constitution and ruled with great severity, committing major human rights abuses.

Military rule continued until 1984, when elections were held. General Gregorio Alvarez, who had been president since 1981, resigned and Julio Maria Sanguinetti, leader of the Colorado Party, became president in February 1985, leading a government of National Unity. He ordered the release of all political prisoners. In the 1990s, Uruguay faced problems in trying to rebuild its weakened economy and shoring up its democratic traditions. In 1991, Uruguay joined with Argentina, Brazil, and Paraguay to form Mercosur, which aimed to create a common market. Mercosur's secretariat is in Montevideo. The early 21st century brought economic problems, many of which were the result of the economic crisis in Argentina, and its imposition of banking controls. Uruguay elected its first leftist president, Tabare Vasquez, in 2004.

ECONOMY

Uruguay is classed by the World Bank as an "upper-middle-income" developing country. Although 90% of the population live in urban areas and agriculture employs 3% of the population, the economy depends on the exports of hides and leather goods, beef, and wool. Main crops include corn, potatoes, rice, sugar beets, and wheat. Manufacturing concentrates on food processing and packing. The economy has diversified into cement, chemicals, leather goods, textiles, and steel. Uruguay depends largely on hydroelectric power for energy and exports electricity to Argentina.

MONTEVIDEO

Capital of Uruguay, located in the south, on the River Plate. Originally a Portuguese fort (1717), it was captured by the Spanish in 1726 and became the capital in 1828. One of South America's major ports, Montevideo is the base of a large fishing fleet and handles most of the country's exports. Products include textiles, dairy goods, wine, and packaged meat.

Punta del Este, *known as the St. Tropez of South America it lies on a peninsula that separates the Rio de la Plata and the Atlantic Ocean*

The white crescent moon is a traditional symbol of Islam and represents the rebirth of the nation. The white stars recall the 12 signs of the zodiac. Blue stands for water and the eternal sky. Red represents life. White symbolizes peace and green denotes nature.

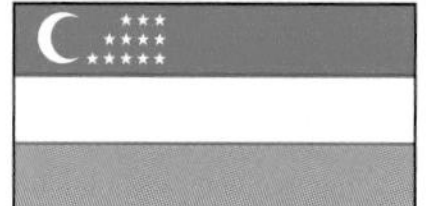

The Republic of Uzbekistan is one of five republics in Central Asia which were once part of the Soviet Union. Plains cover most of western Uzbekistan, with highlands in the east. The main rivers, the Amu (or Amu Darya) and Syr (or Syr Darya), drain into the Aral Sea. So much water has been taken from these rivers for irrigation that the Aral Sea is now only a quarter of its size in 1960. Much of the former sea is now desert.

Area 172,741sq mi [447,400 sq km]
Population 26,410,000
Capital (population) Tashkent (2,143,000)
Government Socialist republic
Ethnic groups Uzbek 80%, Russian 5%, Tajik 5%, Kazakh 3%, Tatar 2%, Kara-Kalpak 2%
Languages Uzbek (official), Russian
Religions Islam 88%, Eastern Orthodox 9%
Currency Uzbekistani sum = 100 tyiyn
Website www.gov.uz

CLIMATE

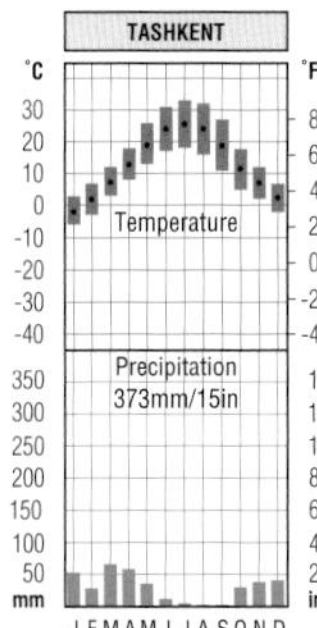

Uzbekistan has a continental climate. Winters are cold, but temperatures soar in the summer. In the west conditions are extremely arid with an average annual rainfall of about 8 in [200 mm].

TASHKENT

Largest city and capital of Uzbekistan, in the Tashkent oasis in the foothills of the Tian Shan (Celestial Range) mountains (a 1,500 mi [2,400 km] long mountain range). Tashkent is watered by the River Chirchik. It was ruled by the Arabs from the 8th until the 11th century. The city was captured by Tamerlane in 1361, and by the Russians in 1865. The modern city is the transport and economic center of the region. Industries include textiles, chemicals, food processing, mining machinery, paper, porcelain, clothing, leather, and furniture.

HISTORY

Uzbekistan lies on the ancient Silk Road between Europe and Asia. Great cities such as Samarkand and Bukhara, famed for their architectural opulence were important trade and cultural centers. Russia took the area in the 19th century. After the Russian Revolution of 1917, Communists took over, setting up the Uzbek Soviet Socialist Republic in 1924. Under Communism, all aspects of Uzbek life were controlled and religious worship was discouraged. The country did benefit though and health, housing, education, and transportation were all improved. In the late 1980s, people demanded more freedom and, in 1990, the government stated that its laws overruled those of the Soviet Union.

POLITICS

Uzbekistan became independent in 1991 with the breakup of the Soviet Union, but retained links with Russia through the Commonwealth of Independent States, but it subsequently pulled out due to the leader's opposition to closer integration on post-Soviet territory. Islam Karimov, leader of the People's Democratic Party (formerly the Communist Party), was elected president in December 1991. In 1992–3, many opposition leaders were arrested because the government said that they threatened national stability. In 1994-5, the PDP was victorious in national elections and in 1995 a referendum extended Karimov's term in office until 2000, when he was again reelected.

In 2001, Karimov declared Uzbekistan's support for the United States in its campaign against the terrorist al Qaida bases in Afghanistan and indeed allowed the US forces to have a base on Uzbek territory.

Due to the country's poor record on human rights the European Bank for Reconstruction and Development announced in 2004 that it would cut aid to Uzbekistan.

Recent years have seen bombings and shootings for which the authorities have blamed Islamic extremists. In 2005 protests against the jailing of several people charged with Islamic extremism in the city of Andijan turned to violence with troops opening fire. Several hundred civilians were killed, though the government claimed a toll of 180.

Karimov blamed fundamentalists out to destabilise the country, his opponents blamed the determination of those in power to crush all dissent and maintain a repressive state. There were calls for an international enquiry which the government rejected, as a result of which the US threatened to withold aid. Uzbekistan's reaction to this was to order US forces to leave their base.

ECONOMY

The World Bank classifies Uzbekistan as a "lower-middle-income" developing country. The government still controls most economic activity and economic reform has been very slow. Uzbekistan produces coal, copper, gold, oil, and natual gas, while manufacturing industries include agricultural machinery, chemicals and textiles. Agriculture is important with cotton the main crop. Other crops include fruits, rice, and vegetables; cattle, sheep, and goats are raised.

Nomad Camp *in Pamir Mountains; the main activity is sheep herding, though some coal is mined; the terrain is largely grasslands and sparse trees*

SAMARKAND

City in the fertile Zeravshan Valley, southeast Uzbekistan. One of the oldest cities in Asia, it was conquered by Alexander the Great in 329 BC. A vital trading center on the Silk Road, it flourished in the 8th century as part of the Umayyad Empire. Samarkand was destroyed in 1220 by Genghis Khan but became capital of the Mongol empire of Tamerlane in 1370. Ruled by the Uzbeks from the 16th century, it was captured by Russia in 1868, though it remained a center of Muslim culture. It is now a major scientific research center and has a population of 361,800.

Venezuela

Venezuela's flag, adopted in 1954, has the same basic tricolor as the flags of Colombia and Ecuador. The colors were used by the Venezuelan patriot Francisco de Miranda. The seven stars represent the provinces in the Venezuelan Federation in 1811.

Area 352,143 sq mi [912,050 sq km]
Population 25,017,000
Capital (population) Caracas (1,823,000)
Government Federal republic
Ethnic groups Spanish, Italian, Portuguese, Arab, German, African, indigenous people
Languages Spanish (official), indigenous dialects
Religions Roman Catholic 96%
Currency Bolívar = 100 céntimos
Website www.venezlon.co.uk

The Bolivarian Republic of Venezuela, in northern South America, contains the Maracaibo Lowlands in the west. The lowlands surround the oil-rich Lake Maracaibo (Lago de Maracaibo). Arms of the Andes Mountains enclose the lowlands and extend across most of northern Venezuela. Between the northern mountains and the scenic Guiana Highlands in the southeast, where the Angel Falls are found, lie the *llanos* (tropical grasslands), a low-lying region drained by the River Orinoco and its tributaries. The Orinoco is Venezuela's longest river.

CLIMATE

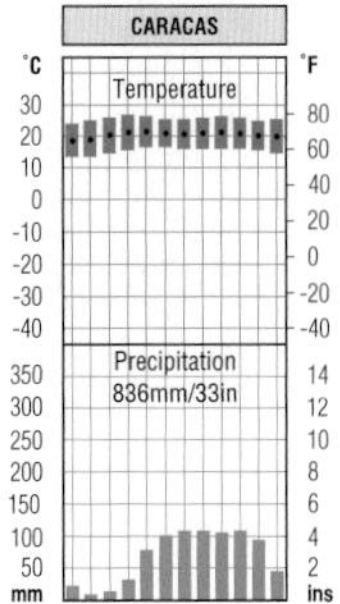

Venezuela has a tropical climate. Temperatures are high throughout the year on the lowlands, though far cooler in the mountains. There is a marked dry season in much of the country that falls between December and April. Most rainfall is in the mountains.

HISTORY

Arawak and Carib Amerindians were the main inhabitants of Venezuela before the arrival of Europeans. The first European to arrive was Christopher Columbus, who sighted the area in 1498. Spaniards began to settle in the early 16th century, but economic development was slow.

In the early 19th century, Spain's colonies in South America began their struggle for independence. The Venezuelan patriots Simón Bolívar and Francisco Miranda were prominent in the struggle. Venezuela was the first South American country to demand freedom and, in July 1811, it declared its independence, though Spaniards still held most of the country. In 1819, Venezuela became part of Gran Colombia, a republic led by Simón Bolívar that also included Colombia, Ecuador, and Panama.

The country became fully independent in 1821, after the Venezuelans had defeated the Spanish in a battle at Carabobo, near Valencia. Venezuela broke away from Gran Colombia in 1829 and in 1830 a new constitution was drafted. The country's first president was General José Antonio Páez, one of the leaders of Venezuela's independence movement.

POLITICS

The development of Venezuela in the 19th century and the first half of the 20th century was marred by instability, violence, and periods of harsh dictatorial rule. However, the country has had elected governments since 1958.

Venezuela has greatly benefited from its oil resources, which were first exploited in 1917. In 1960, Venezuela helped to form OPEC (the Organization of Petroleum Exporting Countries) and, in 1976, the government of Venezuela took control of the entire oil industry. Money from oil exports has helped Venezuela to raise living standards and diversify the economy.

Financial problems in the late 1990s led to the election of Hugo Chávez as president. Chávez, leader of the Patriotic Pole, a left-wing coalition, who had led an abortive military uprising in 1992, became president in February 1999. He announced that the country's official name would be changed to the Bolivarian Republic of Venezuela and held a referendum on a new constitution. This gave the president increased power over military and civilian institutions. Chávez argued that these powers were needed to counter corruption. In 2002, Chávez himself survived a coup and then in 2004 he won a majority in a referendum that had been intended by the opposition to remove him from office.

ECONOMY

The World Bank classifies Venezuela as an "upper-middle-income" developing country. Oil accounts for 80% of the exports. Other exports include bauxite and aluminum, iron ore, and farm products. Agriculture employs 9% of the people. Cattle ranching is important and dairy cattle and poultry are also raised. Major crops include bananas, cassava, citrus fruits, coffee, corn, plantains, rice, and sorghum. Most commercial crops are grown on large farms, but many people in remote areas farm small plots and produce barely enough to feed their families.

Manufacturing industries now employ 21% of the population. The leading industry is petroleum refining, centered on Maracaibo. Other manufactures include aluminum, cement, processed food, steel, and textiles.

CARACAS

Capital of Venezuela, on the River Guaire. Caracas was under Spanish rule until 1821. It was the birthplace of Venezuelan patriot Simón Bolívar. The city grew after 1930, encouraged by the exploitation of oil. It has the Central University of Venezuela (1725) and a cathedral (1614). Industries include motor vehicles, oil, brewing, chemicals, and rubber.

Angel Falls, *the world's highest uninterrupted falls, descend through the clouds, dropping 3,000 ft (980 m) from a high cliff in Venezuela's Canaima National Park*

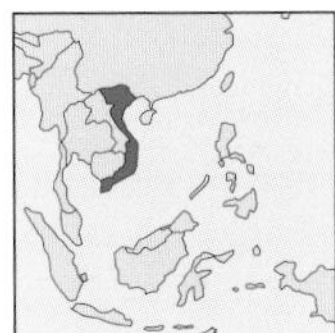

Vietnam's flag was first used by forces led by the Communist Ho Chi Minh during the liberation struggle against Japan in World War II (1939–45). It became the flag of North Vietnam in 1945 and it was retained when North and South Vietnam were reunited in 1975.

Area 128,065 sq mi [331,689 sq km]
Population 82,690,000
Capital (population) Hanoi (1,074,000)
Government Socialist republic
Ethnic groups Vietnamese 87%, Chinese, Hmong, Thai, Khmer, Cham, mountain groups
Languages Vietnamese (official), English, French, Chinese, Khmer, mountain languages
Religions Buddhism, Christianity, indigenous beliefs
Currency Dong = 10 hao - 100 xu
Website www.vietnamtourism.com

The Socialist Republic of Vietnam occupies an S-shaped strip of land facing the South China Sea in Southeast Asia. The coastal plains include two densely populated, fertile river delta areas. The Red (Hong) Delta faces the Gulf of Tonkin in the north, while the Mekong Delta is in the south.

Inland are thinly populated highland regions, including the Annam Cordillera (Chaîne Annamitique), which forms much of the boundary with Cambodia. The highlands in the northwest extend into Laos and China.

CLIMATE

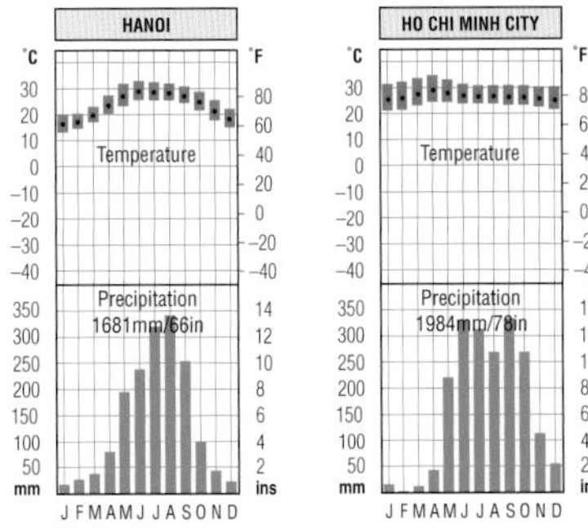

Vietnam has a tropical climate, though the drier months of January to March are cooler than the wet, hot summer months, when monsoon winds blow from the southwest. Typhoons sometimes hit the coast, causing much damage.

HISTORY

In 111 BC, China seized Vietnam, naming it Annam. In 939 AD, it became independent. In 1558, it split into two parts: Tonkin in the north, ruled from Hanoi; and Annam in the south, ruled from Hué. In 1802, with French support, Vietnam was united as the Empire of Vietnam, under Nguyen Anh. In 1859, the French seized Saigon, and by 1887 had formed Indo-China from the union of Tonkin, Annam, and Cochin China.

Japan conquered Vietnam during World War II, and established a Vietnamese state under Emperor Bao Dai. After the war, Bao Dai's government collapsed, and the nationalist Viet Minh, led by Ho Chi Minh, set up a Vietnamese republic. In 1946, the French tried to reassert control and war broke out. Despite aid from the USA, the Viet Minh defeated the French at Dien Bien Phu.

POLITICS

In 1954, Vietnam divided along the 17th Parallel—with North Vietnam under the communist government of Ho Chi Minh, and South Vietnam under the French-supported Bao Dai. In 1955, Bao Dai was deposed and Ngo Dinh Diem was elected president. Despite his authoritarian regime, many western countries recognized Diem as the legal ruler of Vietnam. North Vietnam, supported by China and the Soviet Union, extended its influence into South Vietnam, mainly through the Viet Cong. The USA became increasingly involved in what they perceived to be a fight against Communism. The conflict escalated into the Vietnam War (1954–75). In 1975, after the withdrawal of US troops, Ho Chi Minh's forces overran South Vietnam and it surrendered.

In 1976, the reunited Vietnam became a socialist republic. In 1979, Vietnam helped overthrow the Khmer Rouge government in Cambodia, only withdrawing in 1989. The United States opened an embassy in Hanoi in 1995 and in 2002 it implemented a trade agreement which normalized the trade status between the two countries.

The suppression of political dissent and religious belief has been noted along with the poor treatment of ethnic minorities.

ECONOMY

The World Bank classifies Vietnam as a "low-income" developing country. Agriculture employs 67% of the workforce. The main food crop is rice. Other products include corn and sweet potatoes; commercial crops include bananas, coffee, groundnuts, rubber, soybeans, and tea. Fishing is also important. Northern Vietnam has most of the country's natural resources, including coal. The country also produces chromium, oil, phosphates, and tin. Manufactures include cement, fertilizers, processed food, machinery, steel, and textiles.

HANOI

Capital of Vietnam and its second largest city, on the Red River. In the 7th century the Chinese ruled Vietnam from Hanoi; it later became capital of the Vietnamese empire. Taken by the French in 1883, the city became the capital of French Indo-China (1887–1945). In 1946–54, it was the scene of fierce fighting between the French and the Viet Minh. Hanoi was heavily bombed by the US during the Vietnam War.

***The harvesting of tea leaves** in a field near Bao Loc, to the south of the country*

Yemen

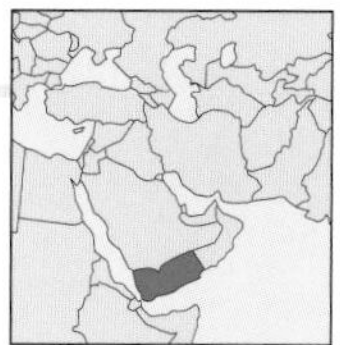

Yemen's flag was adopted in 1990 when the Yemen Arab Republic (or North Yemen) united with the People's Democratic Republic of Yemen (or South Yemen). This simple flag is a tricolor of red, white, and black—colors associated with the Pan-Arab movement.

Area 203,848 sq mi [527,968 sq km]
Population 20,025,000
Capital (population) Sana'a (954,000)
Government Multiparty republic
Ethnic groups Predominantly Arab
Languages Arabic (official)
Religions Islam
Currency Yemeni rial = 100 fils
Website www.yemeninfo.gov.ye/ENGLISH/home.htm

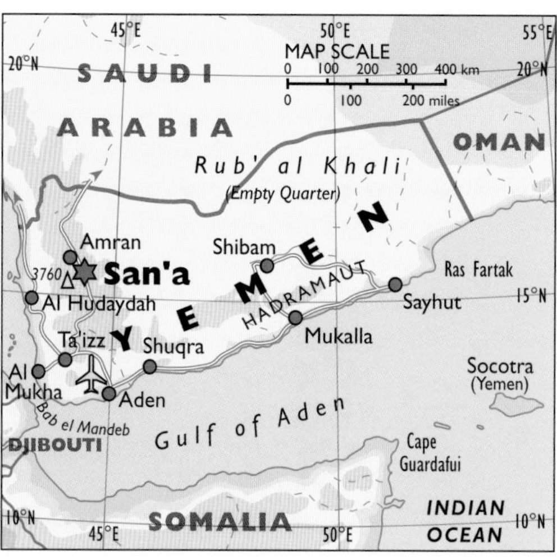

The Republic of Yemen faces the Red Sea and the Gulf of Aden in the southwestern corner of the Arabian Peninsula. Behind the narrow coastal plain along the Red Sea, the land rises to a mountain region called High Yemen. Beyond the mountains, the land slopes down toward the Rub' al Khali Desert. Other mountains rise behind the coastal plain along the Gulf of Aden. To the east lies a fertile valley called the Hadramaut and also the deserts of the Arabian Empty Quarter.

Palm trees grow along the coast. Plants such as acacia and eucalyptus flourish in the interior. Thorn shrubs and mountain pasture are found in the highlands.

SAN'A

Capital and largest city of Yemen, 65 km [40 mi] northeast of the Red Sea port of Hodeida. Situated on a high plateau at 2,286 m [7,500 ft], it claims to be the world's oldest city, founded by Shem, eldest son of Noah. During the 17th century and from 1872 to 1918, it was part of the Ottoman Empire. In 1918, it became capital of an independent Yemen Arab Republic, and in 1990 capital of the new, unified Yemen. It is noted for its handicrafts. Agriculture (grapes) and industry (iron) are also important.

CLIMATE

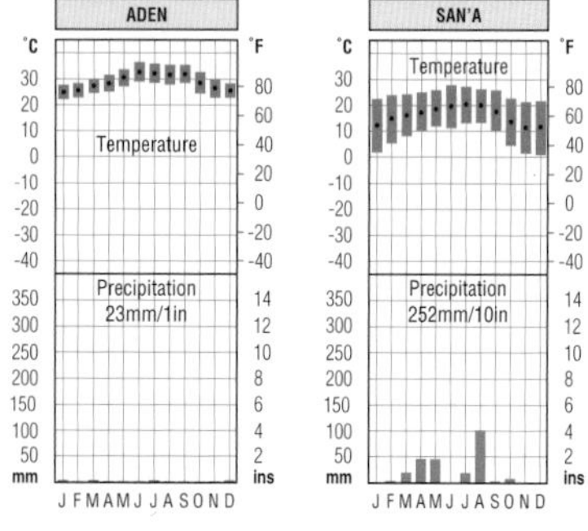

The climate in San'a is moderated by its altitude. Temperatures are much lower than in Aden (Al' Adan), which is at sea level. In summer, southwest monsoon winds bring thunderstorms. But most of Yemen is arid. The south coasts are particularly hot and humid, especially from June to September. There are two seasonal rainfalls, during March to May and from July to September. The average rainfall is about 2 in [50 mm] on most parts of the plateaus, but may rise to 40 in [1,000 mm] in the highlands, while the coastal lowlands may have no more than 0.5 in [12 mm].

HISTORY

From around 1400 BC, Yemen lay on an important trading route, with frankincense, pearls and spices being the major commodities. But its prosperity declined in the 4th century AD, when it became divided between warring groups.

Islam was introduced during the 7th century by the son-in-law of the Prophet Muhammad. From 897, the country was ruled by a Muslim leader. In 1517, the area was taken over by the Turkish Ottoman Empire and remained under Turkish rule for the next 400 years.

POLITICS

After World War I, northern Yemen, which had been ruled by Turkey, began to evolve into a separate state from the south, where Britain was in control. Britain withdrew in 1967 and a left-wing regime took power in the south. North Yemen became a republic in 1962 when the monarchy was abolished.

Clashes occurred between the traditionalist Yemen Arab Republic in the north and the formerly British Marxist People's Democratic Republic of Yemen. But, in 1990, the two Yemens merged to form one country. The marrying of the needs of the two parts of Yemen has proved difficult. In May 1994, civil war erupted, with President Saleh, a northerner, attempting to remove the vice-president (a southerner). The war ended in July 1994, following the capture of Aden by government forces. In 1995, Yemen resolved border disputes with Oman and Saudi Arabia, but clashed with Eritrea over uninhabited islands in the Red Sea. In 1998 and 1999, militants in the Aden-Abyan Islamic Army sought to destabilize the country. In 2000, a suicide bomb attack on the USS Cole in Aden killed 17 US personnel. In 2001, President Salih offered support to the USA in its "war on terrorism."

President Saleh has said that although the constitution entitles him to run for president again in 2006, he has chosen not to.

Dar al-Hajar *(The Palace of the Rock) stands in the fertile valley of Wadi Dahr*

ECONOMY

The World Bank classifies Yemen as a "low-income" developing country. Agriculture employs up to 63% of the people. Herders raise sheep and other animals, while farmers grow such crops as barley, fruits, wheat, and vegetables in highland valleys and around oases. Cash crops include coffee and cotton.

Imported oil is refined at Aden and petroleum extraction began in the northwest in the 1980s. Handicrafts, leather goods, and textiles are manufactured.

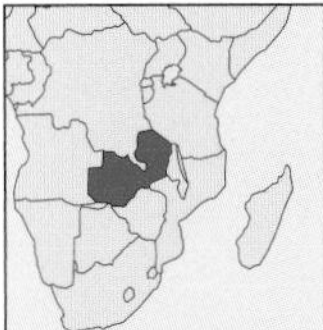

Zambia's flag was adopted when the country became independent from Britain in 1964. The colors are those of the United Nationalist Independence Party, which led the struggle against Britain and ruled until 1991. The flying eagle represents freedom.

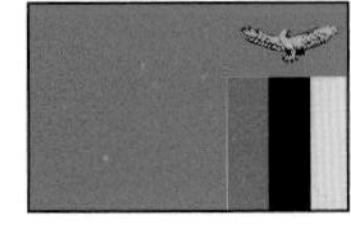

The Republic of Zambia is a landlocked country in southern Africa. The country lies on the plateau that makes up most of southern Africa. Much of the land is between 2,950 and 4,920 ft [900–1,500 m] above sea level. The Muchinga Mountains in the northeast rise above this flat land.

Lakes include Bangweulu, which is entirely within Zambia, together with parts of lakes Mweru and Tanganyika in the north. Most of the land is drained by the Zambezi (from which the country takes its name) and its two main tributaries, the Kafue and Luangwa. Occupying part of the Zambezi Vally and stretching along the southern border Lake Kariba, which was dammed in 1961 is the largest artificial lake in Africa and the second largest in the world (174 mi [280 km] long and 25 mi [40 km] across at its widest point). Zambia shares Lake Kariba and the Victoria Falls with Zimbabwe.

Grassland and wooded savanna cover much of Zambia. There are also swamps. Evergreen forests exist in the drier southwest.

CLIMATE

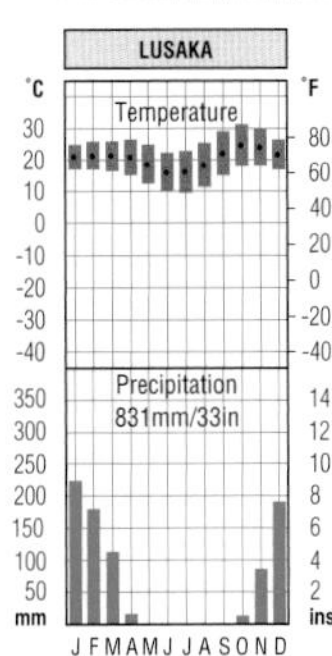

Zambia lies in the tropics, although temperatures are moderated by the altitude. The rainy season runs between November and March, when the rivers sometimes flood. Northern Zambia is the wettest region of the country. The average annual rainfall ranges from about 51 in [1,300 mm] in the north down to between 20 and30 in [510–760 mm] in the south.

HISTORY

European contact with Zambia began in the 19th century, when the explorer David Livingstone crossed the River Zambezi. In the 1890s, the British South Africa Company, set up by Cecil Rhodes (1853–1902), the British financier and statesman, made treaties with local chiefs and gradually took over the area. In 1911, the Company named the area Northern Rhodesia. In 1924, Britain took over the government of the country and the discovery of copper led to a large influx of Europeans in the late 1920s.

Following World War II, the majority of Europeans living in Zambia wanted greater control of their government and some favored a merger with their southern neighbor, Southern Rhodesia (now Zimbabwe). In 1953, Britain set up a federation of Northern Rhodesia, Southern Rhodesia and Nyasaland (now Malawi). Local Africans opposed the setting up of the federation arguing that it concentrated power in the hands of the white minority in Southern Rhodesia. Their opposition proved effective and the federation was dissolved in 1963. In 1964, Northern Rhodesia became an independent nation called Zambia.

LUSAKA

Capital and largest city of Zambia, in the south-central part of the country, at an altitude of 4,200 ft [1,280 m]. Founded by Europeans in 1905 to service the local lead-mining, it replaced Livingstone as the capital of Northern Rhodesia (later Zambia) in 1935. A vital road and rail junction, Lusaka is the center of a fertile agricultural region, and is a major financial and commercial city.

Area 290,586 sq mi [752,618 sq km]
Population 10,462,000
Capital (population) Lusaka (1,270,000)
Government Multiparty republic
Ethnic groups Native African (Bemba, Tonga, Maravi/Nyanja)
Languages English (official), Bemba, Kaonda
Religions Christianity 70%, Islam, IHinduism
Currency Zambian kwacha = 100 ngwee
Website www.zambiatourism.com

Greater Kudus *nuzzling in open area, Kafue National Park; the park is located in southern Zambia to the west of Lusaka and covers over 8,649 sq mi (22,400 sq km)*

POLITICS

The leading opponent of British rule, Kenneth Kaunda, became president in 1964. His government enjoyed reasonable income until copper prices crashed in the mid-1970s, but his collectivist policies failed to diversify the economy and neglected agriculture. In 1972, he declared the United Nationalist Independence Party (UNIP) the only legal party, and it was nearly 20 years before the country returned to democracy.

Under a new constitution, adopted in 1990, elections were held in 1991 in which Kaunda was trounced by Frederick Chiluba of the Movement for Multiparty Democracy (MMD)—Kaunda's first challenger in the post-colonial period. Chiluba was reelected in 1996, but he stood down in 2001 after an MMD proposal to amend the constitution to allow Chiluba to stand for a third term met with substantial popular and parliamentary opposition. In the 2001 elections, the MMD candidate, Levy Mwanawasa, was elected president. In 2005 the Supreme Court rejected a challenge to his election, but stated that the 2001 ballot had been flawed.

ECONOMY

Zambia holds 6% of the world's copper reserves and copper is the leading export, accounting for 49% of Zambia's total exports. Zambia also produces cobalt, lead, zinc, and various gemstones, but the country's dependence on minerals has created problems, especially when prices fluctuate. Agriculture employs 69% of the workforce, compared with 4% in mining and manufacturing. Major food crops include cassava, fruits and vegetables, corn, millet, and sorghum, while cash crops include coffee, sugar cane, and tobacco.

The Copperbelt, centered on Kitwe, is the main urban region, while Lusaka, provides the other major growth pole. Rural to urban migration has increased since 1964, but work is scarce. The production of copper products is the leading industrial activity. Other manufactures include beverages, processed food, iron and steel, textiles, and tobacco.

Zimbabwe

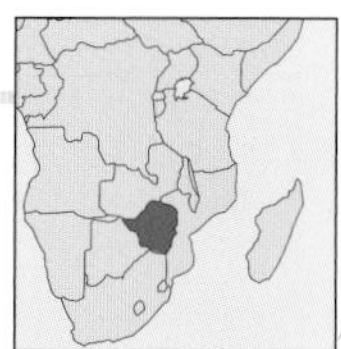

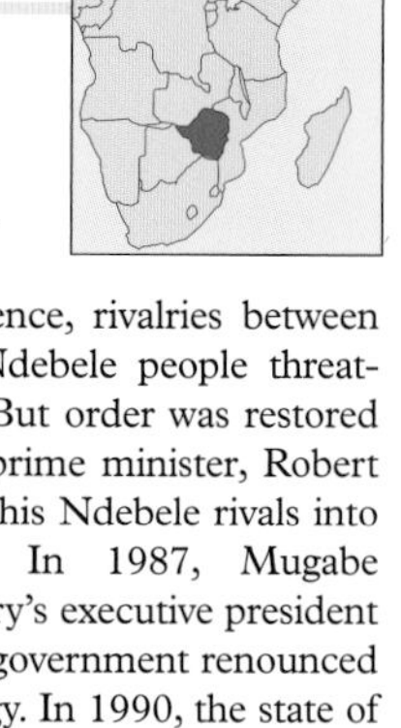

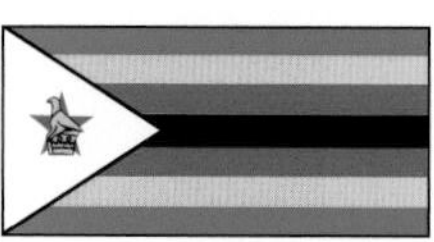

Zimbabwe's flag, adopted in 1980, is based on the colors used by the ruling Zimbabwe African National Union Patriotic Front. Within the white triangle is the Great Zimbabwe soapstone bird, the national emblem. The red star symbolizes the party's socialist policies.

Area 150,871 sq mi [390,757 sq km]
Population 12,672,000
Capital (population) Harare (1,189,000)
Government Multiparty republic
Ethnic groups Shona 82%, Ndebele 14%, other African groups 2%, mixed and Asian 1%
Languages English (official), Shona, Ndebele
Religions Christianity, traditional belief
Currency Zimbabwean dollar= 100 cents
Website www.zim.gov.zw

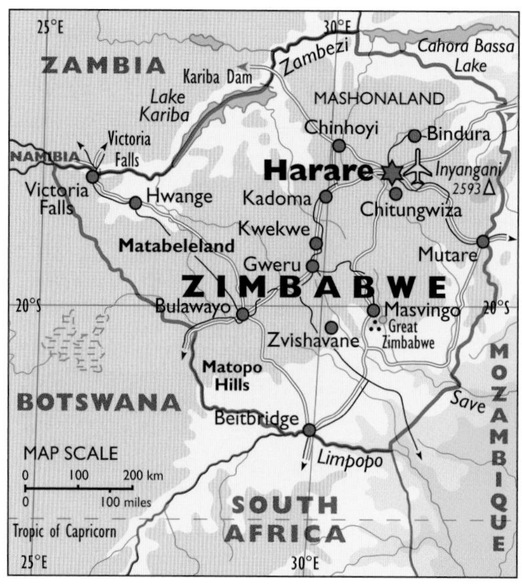

The Republic of Zimbabwe is a landlocked country in southern Africa. Most of the country lies on a high plateau between the Zambezi and Limpopo Rivers between 2,950 and 4,920 ft [900–1,500 m] above sea level.

The principal land feature is the High Veld, a ridge that crosses Zimbabwe from northeast to southwest. Harare lies on the northeast edge, Bulawayo on the southwest edge. Bordering the High Veld is the Middle Veld, the country's largest region and the site of many large ranches. Below 2,950 ft [900 m] is the Low Veld.

The country's highest point is Mount Inyangani, which reaches 8,507 ft [2,593 m] near the Mozambique border. Zimbabwe's best-known physical feature, Victoria Falls, is in the northeast. The Falls are shared with Zambia, as too is the artificial Lake Kariba which is also on the River Zambezi.

Wooded savanna covers much of Zimbabwe. The Eastern Highlands and river valleys are forested. There are many tobacco plantations.

CLIMATE

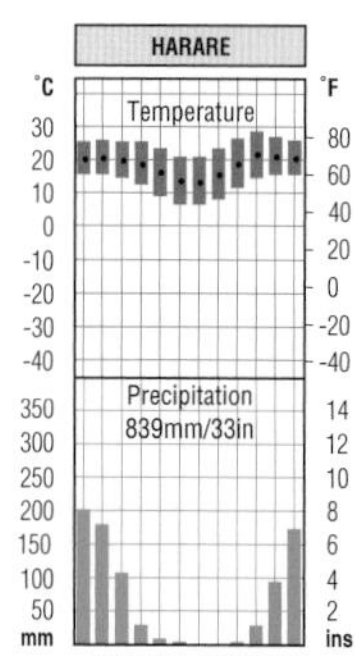

The subtropical climate varies greatly according to altitude. The Low Veld is much warmer and drier than the High Veld. November to March is mainly hot and wet. Winter in Harare is dry but cold. Frosts have been recorded between June and August.

HISTORY

The Shona people were dominant in the region about 1,000 years ago. They built the Great Zimbabwe, a city of stone buildings. Under the statesman Cecil Rhodes (1853–1902), the British South Africa Company occupied the area in the 1890s, after obtaining mineral rights from local chiefs. The area was named Rhodesia and later Southern Rhodesia. It became a self-governing British colony in 1923. Between 1953 and 1963, Southern and Northern Rhodesia (now Zambia) were joined to Nyasaland (Malawi) in the Central African Federation.

POLITICS

In 1965, the European government of Southern Rhodesia (then known as Rhodesia) declared their country independent. However, Britain refused to accept this declaration. Finally, after a civil war, the country became legally independent in 1980.

After independence, rivalries between the Shona and Ndebele people threatened its stability. But order was restored when the Shona prime minister, Robert Mugabe, brought his Ndebele rivals into his government. In 1987, Mugabe became the country's executive president and, in 1991, the government renounced its Marxist ideology. In 1990, the state of emergency that had lasted since 1965 was allowed to lapse—three months after Mugabe had secured a landslide election victory. Mugabe was reelected in 1996. In the late 1990s, Mugabe threatened to seize white-owned farms without paying compensation to owners. His announcement caused much disquiet among white farmers. The situation worsened in the early 2000s, when landless "war veterans" began to occupy white-owned farms, resulting in violence and deaths.

Food shortages have become a major problem with aid agencies blaming the land reform program while the government blames drought.

In 2002, amid accusations of electoral irregularities, Mugabe was reelected president. Mounting criticism of Mugabe led the Commonwealth to suspend Zimbabwe's membership. Later Zimbabwe confirmed that it had pulled out of the Commonwealth permanently. In 2004 the European Union renewed sanctions against the country. Zimbabwe was named by the United States, in 2005, as one of the world's six "outposts of tyranny," an accusation that was rejected by Zimbabwe.

ECONOMY

The World Bank classifies Zimbabwe as a "low-income" economy. Its economy has become significantly more diverse since the 1960s, having evolved to virtual self-sufficiency during the days of international sanctions between 1965 and 1980. After independence, the economy underwent a surge in most sectors, with successful agrarian policies and the exploitation of the country's mineral resources. However, a fast-growing population continues to exert pressure both on land and resources .

Agriculture employs approximately 30% of the people. Corn is the chief food crop, while cash crops include cotton, sugar, and tobacco. Cattle ranching is another important activity. Gold, asbestos, chromium, and nickel are mined and the country also has some coal and iron ore. Manufactures include beverages, chemicals, iron and steel, metal products, processed food, textiles, and tobacco. The principal exports include tobacco, gold, other metals, cotton, and asbestos.

HARARE

Capital of Zimbabwe, in the northeast of the country. Settled by Europeans in 1890 as Fort Salisbury, it became capital of Southern Rhodesia in 1902. The city served as capital of the Federation of Rhodesia and Nyasaland (1953–63) and of Rhodesia (1965–79). It has a university (1957) and two cathedrals. Industries include gold mining, textiles, steel, tobacco, chemicals, and furniture.

Lake Kariba, *hippopotamus and waterbuck; the lake was formed as a result of the damming of the Zambezi River floodplain in the early 1960s, a process that caused the displacement of the Batonga tribe*

A
Abdullah bin Abdulaziz, King 174
Abdullah II, King 116
Abu Dhabi 204
Abuja 152
Accra 90
Adamkus, Valdas 129
Adamstown 157
Addis Ababa 79
Aden, Gulf of 70
Afghanistan 17
Ahmadinejad, Mahmoud 105
Aideed, Gen Muhammad 181
Alaska 209
Albania 18
Albert, Prince 83
Aleman, Arnoldo 150
Alexandre, Boniface 96
Algeria 19
Algiers 19
Aliev, Heydar 29
Aliev, Ilham 29
al-Jabir, Jabir al-Ahmad 121
Al-Khalifa, Sheikh Hamad bin Isa 30
Allende Gossens, Salvador 56
Alofi 157
al-Saba, Sabah Sheikh 121
Al-Thani, Emir Ahmad 168
Al-Thani, Hamad bin Khalifa 168
Al-Thani, Kalifa bin Hamad 168
Alvarez, Gen Gregorio 210
American Samoa 155
Amin Dada, Gen Idi 202
Amman 116
Amsterdam 148
Andorra 185
Andorra La Vella 185
Angola 20
Anguilla 50
Ankara 200
Antananarivo (Tananarive) 132
Antarctic Circle 21
Antarctica 21
Antigua & Barbuda 50
Apia 157
Aptidon, Hassen Gouled 70
Aquino, Corazon 165
Argentina 22
Aristide, Jean-Bertrand 96
Armenia 23
Arroya, Gloria Macapagal 165
Aruba 50
Ashgabat 201
Asmara (Asmera) 77
Assad, Bashar al 192
Assad, Lt-Gen Hafez al 192
Astana 117
Asunción 163
Athens (Athínai) 91
Atlantic Islands 24
Aung San 44
Aung San Suu Kyi 44
Australia 26
Austria 28
Avarua 155
Aylwin, Patrico 56
Azerbaijan 29
Azores 24

B
Babagandi, Natasagiyn 142
Badawi, Abdulla Ahmad 135
Bagaza, Jean-Baptiste 45
Baghdad 106
Bahamas 150
Bahrain 30
Baikal, Lake 172
Bairiki 155
Bakiev, Kurmanbek 122
Baku 29
Balaguer, Joaqun 71
Balladares, Pérez 161
Bamako 136
Banda Seri Begawn 135
Banda, Dr Hastings 133
Bandanaraike, Sirimavo 186
Bangkok 196
Bangladesh 31
Bangui 54
Banjul 86
Barak, Ehud 109
Barbados 51
Barre, Siad 181
Barre, Siad 181
Bashir, Oman Hassan Ahmed al- 187
Basseterre 52
Basse-Terre 52
Batista, Fulgencio 65
Bavadra, Timoci 80
Bédié, Henri Konan 112
Beijing (Peking) 57
Beirut (Bayrut) 125
Belarus 32
Belgium 33
Belgrade 176
Belize 34
Belmopan 34
Ben Ali, Zine el Abidine 199
Benin 35
Berenger, Paul 139
Berlin 89
Berlusconi, Silvio 111
Bermuda 24
Bern 191
Bhutan 36
Bhutto, Benazir 160
Bihendra, King 147
Bijagos archipelago 94
Bishkek 122
Bissau 94
Biya, Paul 47
Blair, Tony 206
Bloemfontein 182
Bogotá 60
Bokassa I, Emperor 54
Bolanos, Enrique 150
Bolivia 37
Bongo, Bernard-Albert 85
Bordavetty, Juan Maria 210
Bosch, Juan 71
Bosnia-Herzegovina 38
Botswana 39
Bourguiba, Habib 199
Bouterse, Dési 188
Boutflika, Abdelaziz 19
Bozize, Gen. François 54
Brades Estate 52
Brasília 41
Bratislava 179
Brazil 40
Brazzaville 61
Bridgetown 51
British Virgin Islands 53
Brunei 135
Brussels (Bruxelles) 33
Bucharest 159
Budapest 98
Buenos Aires 22
Bujumbura 45
Bulgaria 42
Burkina Faso 43
Burma (Myanmar) 44
Burnham, Forbes 95
Burundi 45
Bush, George W. 208
Buyoya, Pierre 45

C
Caetano, Marcello 167
Cairo (Al-Qahirah) 74
Calderón Sol, Armando 75
Cambodia 46
Cameroon 47
Campaore, Blaise 43
Canada 48
Canary Islands 24
Canberra 27
Cape Town 182
Cape Verde 24
Caracas 212
Cardoso, Fernando Henrique 41
Caribbean Islands 50
Caribbean Sea 50
Castries 52
Castro, Fidel 65
Cayenne 84
Cayman Islands 51
Ceaucescu, Nicolae 169
Central African Republic 54
Chad (Tchad), Lake
Chad 55
Chamoro, Violetta 150
Chan, Sir Julius 162
Channel Islands 206
Charlotte Amalie 53
Chaudhry, Mahendra 80
Chávez, Hugo 212
Chen Shui-bian 193
Chiang Kai-shek 193
Chile 56
Chiluba, Frederick 215
China 57
Chirac, Jacques 83
Chisinau (Kishinev) 141
Chissano, Joaquim A 145
Christmas Island 102
Clark, Helen 149
Cockburn Town 53
Cocos Islands 102
Collor de Mello, Fernando 41
Colombia 60
Colombo 186
Comoros 102
Conakry 93
Congo (Democratic Republic of the) 62
Congo 61
Constantinescu, Emil 169
Conté, Col Lansana 93
Cook Islands 155
Copenhagen (København) 68
Costa Rica 63
Croatia 64
Cuba 65
Cure, Dr Maurice 139
Cyprus 66
Czech Republic 67

D
Dacko, David 54
Daddah, Mokhtar Ould 138
Dakar 175
D'Alemi, Massimo 111
Damascus 192
d'Arguin, Banc 138
da Silva, Luiz Inácio Lula 41
Déby, Idriss 55
Deng Xiaoping 58
Denmark 68
Desai, Morarji R 101
Devil's Island (Île du Diable) 84
Dhaka (Dacca) 31
Dhlakama, Afonso 145
Dili 72
Diori, Hamani 151
Diouf, Abdou 175
Djibouti (Jibuti) 70
Djibouti 70
Djukanovic, Milo 143
Dodoma 195
Doe, Samuel K 127
Doha 168
Dominica 51
Dominican Republic 71
Dos Santos, Jose Eduardo 20
Dreifuss, Ruth 191
Drnovsek, Janez 180
Duarte Frutos, Nicanor 163
Dublin (Baile átha Cliath) 107
Dushanbe 194
Duvalier, Baby Doc 96
Duvalier, Papa Doc 96
Dzurinda, Mikulas 179

E
East Timor 72
Ecuador 73
Edinburgh (Tristan da Cunha) 25
Egypt 74
El Aaiun 144
El Salvador 75
Elchibey, Abulfaz 29
Enhbayar, Nambaryn 142
Equatorial Guinea 76
Eritrea 77
Ershad, Gen Hossein Mohammad 31
Estonia 78
Ethiopia 79
Eyadéma, Gen Gnassinghé 197

F
Faeroe Islands 69
Fahd, King 174
Falkland Islands 24
Fernandez, Leionel 71
Ferrer, Jose Figueres 63
Fiji 80
Finland 81
Flores, Carlos 97

Flores, Francisco 75
Fongafale 158
Fort de France 52
France 82
Franco, Gen Francisco 185
Franco, Itamar 41
Freetown 177
French Guiana 84
French Polynesia 155
Fujimori, Alberto 164
Funchal 24

G
Gabon 85
Gaborone 39
Gaddafi, Col Muammar 128
Galtieri, Gen Leopoldo 22
Gambia, The 86
Gamsakhardia, Zviad 87
Gayoom, Maumoon Abdul 103
Gaza Strip 109
Gbago, Laurent 112
Gelleh, Ismael Omar 70
Georgetown (Cayman Islands) 51
Georgetown (Guyana) 95
Georgia 87
Germany 88
Ghana 90
Ghandi, Indira 101
Ghandi, Mohandas K 100-101
Ghandi, Rajiv 101
Gibraltar 185
Gibraltar Town 185
Gnassingbe, Faure 197
Goh Chok Tong 178
Gorbachev, Mikail 172
Grau, Raúl Cubas 163
Great Barrier Reef 27
Greece 91
Greenland 69
Grenada 52
Grunitzky, Nicolas 197
Guadeloupe 52
Guam 155
Guatemala 92
Guatemala City (Ciudad Guatemala) 92
Guei, General Robert 112
Guinea 93
Guinea-Bissau 94
Gusmao, Xanana 72
Guyana 95
Gyanendra, King 147

H
Haakon VII, King 153
Habibie, Bacharuddin Jusuf 104
Habré, Hissène 55
Habyarimana, Maj Gen Juvénal 173
Hagatna 155
Haider, Jörg 28
Haiti 96
Hamilton 24
Hanoi 213
Hans Adam III, Prince 191
Harare 216
Hariri, Rafik 123
Hassan II, King 144
Hassan, Abdulkassim Salat 181
Havana (La Habana) 65
Havel, Gustáv 179
Havel, Václav 67, 179
Hawke, Bob 26
Helsinki 81
Himalayas 147
Ho Chi Min 213
Honduras 97
Hong Kong 50
Honiara 157
Houphouët-Boigny, Félix 112
Howard, John, 26-27
Hoyte, Desmond 95
Hu Jintao 58
Hu Sen 46
Hungary 98
Hussein, King 116
Hussein, Saddam 106

I
Ialá, Kumba 94
Ibrahim, Anwar 135
Iceland 99
Iliescu, Ion 169
India 100
Indian Ocean Islands 102
Indonesia 104
Iran 105
Iraq 106
Ireland 107
Islamabad 160
Israel 108
Italy 110
Ivory Coast 112
Izetbegovic, Alija 38

J
Jagan, Cheddi 95
Jagan, Janet 95
Jagdeo, Bharrat 95
Jakarta 104
Jamaica 113
James, Michel 103
Jamestown 25
Jammeh, Yahye 86
Japan 104
Jawara, Dawda 86
Jerusalem 109
Jinnah, Muhammed Ali 160
Johnson-Sirleaf, Ellen 127
Jordan 116
Jospin, Lionel 83
Juan Carlos, King 185
Jugnauth, Anerood 139

K
Kabbah, Ahmad Tejan 177
Kabila, Joseph 62
Kabila, Laurent 62
Kabul 17
Kaczynski, Lech 166
Kádár, Janos 98
Kafuor, John Agyekum 90
Kagame, Paul 173
Kambanda, Jean 173
Kampala 202
Kanyatta, Jomo 118
Karimov, Islam 211
Karzai, Hamid 17
Kashmir 160
Katmandu (Kathmandu) 147
Kaunda, Kenneth 215
Kayibanda, Grégoir 173
Kazakhstan 117
Keating, Paul 26
Keita, Modibo 136
Kemal, Mustafa 200
Kenya 118
Kérékou, Lt-Col Matthieu 35
Khama, Sir Seretsc 39
Khan, Resa 105
Khartoum 187
Khatami, Mohammad 105
Khomeni, Ayatollah Ruholla 105
Kibaki, Mwai 118
Kiev 203
Kigali 173
Kikwete, Jakaya 195
Kim Dae-Jung 120
Kim il Sung 119
Kim John II 119
Kingston (Jamaica) 113
Kingston (Norfolk Island) 157
Kingstown 53
Kinshasa 62
Kiribati 155
Klerk, FW de 183
Kocharian, Robert 23
Koffigoh, Kokou 197
Kohl, Helmut 89
Koizumi, Junichero 115
Kolingba, André 54
Konaré, Alpha Oumar 136
Korea, North 119
Korea, South 120
Koroma, Maj Johnny Paul 177
Koror 157
Kountché, Lt-Col Sengi 151
Krasniewski, Aleksander 166
Kuala Lumpur 134
Kucan, Milan 180
Kuchma, Leonid 203
Kumaratunga, Chandrika 186
Kuwait 121
Kuwait City 121
Kyrgyzstan 122

L
La Paz 37
Lagos, Ricardo 56
Lamizana, Sangoule 43
Laos 123
Las Palmas (Gran Canaria) 24
Latottue, Gerald 96
Latvia 124
Lebanon 125
Lee Hsien Loong 178
Lee Kwan Yew 178
Lee Teng-hui 193
Lesotho 126
Letsie III, King 126
Liberia 127
Libreville 85
Libya 128
Liechtenstein 191
Lilongwe 133
Lima 164
Lisbon 167
Lissouba, Pascal 61
Lithuania 129
Ljubljana 180
Lobambo 189
Lomé 197
London 206
Luanda 20
Lucinschi, Petru 141
Lukashenko, Alexander 32
Lumumba, Patrice 62
Lusaka 215
Luxembourg (city) 130
Luxembourg 130

M
Macau 59
Macedonia 131
Madagascar 132
Madeira 24
Madrid 185
Maduro, Ricardo 97
Maga, Hubert 35
Magae, Festus 39
Mahaud, Jamil 73
Mahendra, King 147
Mainassara, Col Ibrahim Bare 151
Majuro 155
Makarios, Archbishop 66
Malabo 76
Malan, Daniel 183
Malawi 133
Malaysia 134
Maldives 103
Malé 103
Mali 136
Malta 137
Mamadou, Tandjou 151
Mamoudzou 103
Man, Isle of 206
Managua 150
Manama (Al-Manamah) 30
Mandela, Nelson 183
Manila 165
Manley, Michael 113
Manning, Patrick 198
Mao Zedong 58
Maputo (Lourenço Marques) 145
Mara, Ratu Sir 80 Kamisese
Marcos, Ferdinand 165
Marshall Islands 155
Martinez, Maximiliano Hernández 75
Martinique 52
Maseru 126
Masire, Sir Ketumile 39
Mata-Utu 158
Mauritania 138
Mauritius 139
Mayotte 103
Mba, Léon 85
Mbabane 189
Mbeki, Thabo 183
Meciar, Vladimir 179
Medgysy, Peter 98
Mengistu, Mariam 79
Merkel, Angela 89
Mesic, Stipe 64
Mexico 140
Mexico City (Ciudad de México) 140
Miccombero, Michel 45
Micronesia 156

Milosevic, Slobodan 176
Minsk 32
Mkapa, Benjamin 195
Mogadishu 181
Mohamad, Dr Mahathir 135
Mohammed VI, King 144
Moi, Daniel Arap 118
Moldova 141
Monaco 83
Mongolia 142
Monrovia 127
Montenegro 143
Montevideo 210
Montserrat 52
Morales, Evo 37
Morocco 144
Moroni 102
Moscoso, Mireya 161
Moscow (Moskva) 171, 172
Moshoeshoe I, King 126
Moshoshoe II, King 126
Motubu, Joseph 62
Mozambique 145
Mswati, King 189
Mubarek, Hosni 74
Mugabe, Robert 216
Muhammad V, King 144
Muhammad, Ali Mahdi 181
Muluzi, Bakili 133
Muscat (Masqat, Maskat) 154
Musharraf, Gen Pervez 159
Musveni, Yoweri 202
Mwambutsa IV, Mwami 45
Mwanawasa, Levy 215
Mwinyi, Ali Hassan 195

N

Naguib, Gen Muhammad 74
Nagy, Imry 98
Nairobi 118
Namibia 146
Nassau 50
Nasser, Col Gamal Abdel 74
Natare V, Mwami 45
Nauru 156
Nazarbayev, Nursultan 117
Ndadaye, Melchior 45
Ndayizeye, Domitien 45
Ndjamena 55
Ne Win 44
Nehru, Jawaharlat 101
Nepal 147
Netanyahu, Binyamin 109
Netherlands Antilles 52
Netherlands, The 148
New Caledonia 156
New Delhi 100
New Zealand 149
Ngo Dinh Diem 213
Ngouabi, Marien 61
Nguema, Francisco Macias 76
Niamey 151
Nicaragua 150
Nicosia (Levkosía) 66
Niger 151
Nigeria 152
Nimeri, Gaafar Muhammad 187
Niue 157
Niyasov, Saparmurad 201
Noeiega, Gen Manuel Antonio Morena 161
Norfolk Island 157
Northern Mariana Islands 157
Norway 153
Nouakchott 139
Nouméa 156
Ntaryamira, Cyprien 45
Nujoma, Sam 146
Nuku'Alofa 158
Nuuk (Godthåb) 69
Nyerere, Julius 195

O

Obasanjo, Olusegun 152
Obiang Neguma Mbasogo, Lt-Col Teodoro 76
Obote, Apollo Milton
Ojukwu, Col Odumegwu 152
Olmert, Ehud 109
Olympio, Sylvanus 197
Oman 154
Oranjestad 50
Orbán, Victor 98
Ortega, Daniel 150
Oslo 153
Ottawa 49
Ouagadougou 43
Oueddi, Goukouni 55
Ousmane, Mahamane 151
Oviedo, Gen Lino 163

P

Pacific Ocean 155
Páez, Gen. José Antonio 212
Pago Pago 155
Pakistan 159
Palau 157
Palikir 156
Palma, Tomás Estrada 65
Pamirs 194
Panama 161
Panama Canal 161
Panama City 161
Pancho, Abel 63
Panday, Baseo 198
Papeete 155
Papua New Guinea 162
Paraguay 263
Paramaribo 188
Paris 83
Pastrana Arango, Andrés 60
Patassé, Ange-Félix 54
Patterson, Percival J 113
Peru 164
Philippines 165
Phnom Penh (Phnum Pénh) 46
Pibul Songkhram 196
Pinochet Ugarte, Gen Augusto 56
Pitcairn Island 157
Podgorica 143
Pohama, Hifikepunye 146
Poland 166
Ponta Delgada 24
Port Louis 137
Port Moresby 162
Port of Spain 198
Port Vila 158
Port-au-Prince 96
Portillo, Alfonso 92
Porto-Novo 35
Portugal 167
Pot, Pol 46
Prague (Praha) 67
Praia 67
Premadasa, Ranansinghe 186
Préval, René 96
Prodi, Romano 111
Puerto Rico 52
Putin, Vladimir 172
Pyongyang 119

Q

Qaboos bin Said, Sultan 154
Qarase, Laisenia 80
Qatar 168
Quito 73

R

Rabat 144
Rabin, Yitzhak 109
Rabuka, Lt-Col Sitiveni 80
Raffarin, Jean-Pierre 83
Rahman, Gen Zia 31
Rahman, Sheikh Mujibur 31
Rainier, Prince 83
Rajapakse, Mahinda 186
Rakhmonov, Imomali 194
Rákosi, Mathias 98
Ramgoolam, Dr Seewoosagur 139
Ramiz, Alia 18
Rangoon (Yangon) 44
Rasmussen, Anders Fogh 68
Ratsiraka, Didier 132
Ravalomanana, Marc 132
Rawlings, Flt-Lt Jerry 90
Red Sea 70
René, France-Albert 103
Reunion 103
Reykjavík 99
Riga 124
Rivera, Julio Adalberto 75
Riyadh 171
Road Town 53
Robinson, Arthur 198
Romania 169
Rome (Roma) 111
Roseau 51
Russia 170
Rwanda 173

S

Saaskashvili, Michhail 87
Sadat, Anwar el- 74
Saibou, Gen Ali 151
Said bin Taimur, Sultan 154
St Denis 103
St Helena 25
St John's 50
St Kitts & Nevis 52
St Lucia 52
St Petersburg 171
St Pierre 25
St Pierre & Miquelon 25
St Vincent & Grenadines 52
Saipan 157
Salazar, António de Oliviera 167
Saleh, Ali Abdullah 214
Samarkand 211
Samoa 157
San José 63
San Juan 52
San Marino 111
San Salvador 75
San'a 214
Sanchez, Oscar Arias 63
Sanguinetti, Julio Maria 210
Sankara, Thomas 43
Santa Cruz (Tenerife) 24
Santiago 56
Santo Domingo 71
São Tomé & Príncipe 25
Sarajevo 38
Sassou-Nguesso, Col Denis 61
Saudi Arabia 174
Savimbi, Jonas 20
Saw Muang 44
Sawyer, Amos 127
Saxe-Coburg Gotha, Siméon 42
Schröder, Gerhard 89
Seaga, Edward 113
Sékou, Touré 93
Selassie, Haile 79
Senegal 175
Senghor, Léopold Sédar 175
Seoul (Kyongsong) 120
Serbia 176
Settlement, The 102
Seychelles 103
Shankar, Rameswak 188
Sharif, Narwaz 160
Sharon, Ariel 109
Shevardnadze, Eduard 87
Sierra Leone 177
Sihanouk, King Norodom 46
Sihanouk, King Norodom Ranariddh 46
Singapore 178
Singapore City 178
Skate, Bill 162
Skopje 131
Slovak Republic 179
Slovenia 180
Sobhuza, King 189
Sofia (Sofija) 42
Soglo, Nicéphore 35
Solomon Islands 157
Somalia 181
Somoza, Anastasio 150
South Africa 182
Spain 184
Sri Lanka 186
St George's 52
Stalin, Joseph 170
Stanley 24
Stockholm 190
Stroessner, Gen Alfredo 163
Suárez, Gen Hugo 37
Sudan 187
Suharto, Gen Raden 104
Sukarno, Achmed 104
Sukarnoputri, Megawati 104
Suriname 188
Suva 80
Swaziland 189
Sweden 190
Switzerland 191
Syria 192

T

Taipei 193
Taiwan 193

Tajikistan 194
Tallinn 78
Tanzania 195
Tashkent 211
Taya, Col Maaoyiya Ould Sidi Ahmed 138
Taylor, Charles 127
Tbilisi (Tiflis) 87
Tegucigalpa 97
Tehran 105
Thailand 196
Thimphu 36
Tian Shan (Tien Shan) 122
Tirana (Tiranë) 18
Tito, Josep Broz 38, 64, 131, 143, 176, 180
Togo 197
Tokelau 158
Tokyo 115
Tolbert, William R 127
Toledo, Alejandro 164
Tombalbaye, François 55
Tonga 158
Torijos, Martin 161
Tórshavn 69
Touré, Gen Amadou Toumani 136
Traoré, Moussa 136
Trinidad & Tobago 198
Tripoli (Tarabulus) 128
Tristan da Cunha 25
Tshwane (Pretoria) 183
Tubman, William 127
Tudjman, Franco 64
Tung Chee-hwa 59
Tunis 199
Tunisia 199
Turkey 200
Turkmenistan 201
Turks & Caicos 53
Tuvalu 158

U

U Nu 44
Ubangi 54
Uganda 202
Ukraine 203
Ulan Bator 142
United Arab Emirates 204
United Kingdom 205
United States of America 207
Uribe, Alvaro 60
Uruguay 210
US Virgin Islands 53
Utem, Caseem 139
Uzbekistan 211

V

Vaduz 191
Valletta 137
Valley, The 50
Vanuatu 158
Vargas, Getulio 41
Vatican City 111
Venetiaan, Ronald 188
Venezuela 212
Victoria 103
Vieira, Major João 94
Vienna (Wien) 28
Vientiane (Viangchan) 123
Vietnam 213
Vilnius 129
Voronin, Vladimir 141

W

Wade, Abdoulaye 175
Wahid, Abdurrahman 104
Wajed, Sheikh Hasina 31
Walesa, Lech 166
Wallis & Futuna 158
Wangchuk, King Jigme Dorji 36
Wangchuk, King Jigme Singye 36
Wanke, Maj Douda Malam 151
Warsaw 166
Washington, D.C. 208
Wellington 149
West Bank 109
West Island 102
Western Sahara 144
Whitlam, Gough 26
Willemstadt 52
Williams, Eric 198
Windhoek 146
Windward Islands 53

Y

Yamoussoukro 112
Yaoundé 47
Yaren 156
Yeltsin, Boris 172
Yemen 214
Yerevan 23
Yuschenko, Victor 203

Z

Zafy, Albert 132
Zagreb 64
Zambia 215
Zapatero, Jose Luis Rodriguez 185
Zenawi, Meles 79
Zhikov, Todor 42
Zia, Kaleda 31
Zimbabwe 216

PICTURE ACKNOWLEDGEMENTS

17 Robert Harding World Imagery/Corbis; 19 Frans Lemmens/zefa/Corbis; 20 Paul Velasco Gallo Images/Corbis; 21 Dave G. Houser/Post-Houserstock/Corbis; 23 Charles & Josette Lenars/Corbis; 27 Theo Allofs/zefa/Corbis; 28 W. Geiersperger/Corbis; 29 Remi Benali/Corbis; 31 Karen Kasmauski/Corbis; 32 Nik Wheeler/Corbis; 33 Fridmar Damm/zefa/Corbis; 34 Kevin Schafer/Corbis; 36 Keren Su/Corbis; 37 Anders Ryman/Corbis; 38 Fehim Demir/epa/Corbis; 39 Theo Allofs/zefa/Corbis; 40 Richard T. Nowitz/Corbis; 42 Ladislav Janicek/zefa/Corbis; 43 Nicolas Cotto/Corbis; 45 Tom Craig/Corbis; 46 Jeremy Horner/Corbis; 47 Michael & Patricia Fogden/Corbis; 49 Rudy Sulgan/Corbis; 50 Paul C. Pet/zefa/Corbis; 51 Tom Bean/Corbis; 53 Owen Franken/Corbis; 54 Martin Harvey/Corbis; 55 Patrick Robert/Corbis; 57 Vittoriano Rastelli/Corbis; 58 Free Agents Limited/Corbis; 59t Jose Fuste Raga/Corbis; 59b Royalty-Free/Corbis; 60 Enzo & Paolo Ragazzini/Corbis; 61 Karl Ammann/Corbis; 63 Jose Fuste Raga/Corbis; 64 Robert Harding World Imagery/Corbis; 65 James Sparshatt/Corbis; 66 Chris Lisle/Corbis; 67 Jose Fuste Raga/Corbis; 68 José Fuste Raga/zefa/Corbis; 70 1996-98 AccuSoft Inc. All right/Robert Harding World Imagery/Corbis; 71 Danny Lehman/Corbis; 72 Robert Garvey/Corbis; 73 Pablo Corral V/Corbis; 74 Free Agents Limited/Corbis; 75 Galen Rowell/Corbis; 76 Robert van der Hilst/Corbis; 77 Chris Hellier/Corbis; 78 Jon Hicks/Corbis; 79 Caroline Penn/Corbis; 80 Larry Dale Gordon/zefa/Corbis; 81 Hans Strand/Corbis; 82 Owen Franken/Corbis; 83 Sergio Pitamitz/Corbis; 84 Nogues Alain/Corbis Sygma; 85 Le Segretain Pascal/Corbis Sygma; 86 Christine Osborne/Corbis; 87 Brooks Kraft/Corbis; 89 Bob Krist/Corbis; 90 Margaret Courtney-Clarke/Corbis; 91 Jose Fuste Raga/Corbis; 92 Royalty-Free/Corbis; 93 Pierre Holtz/epa/Corbis; 94 Dave G. Houser/Post-Houserstock/Corbis; 95 Louie Psihoyos/Corbis; 96 Gideon Mendel/Corbis; 97 Macduff Everton/Corbis; 98 Sandro Vannini/Corbis; 99 Mike McQueen/Corbis; 100 Charles & Josette Lenars/Corbis; 102 Robert van der Hilst/Corbis; 104 Jan Butchofsky-Houser/Corbis; 106 Michael S. Yamashita/Corbis; 107 Bo Zaunders/Corbis; 108 Sandro Vannini/Corbis; 109 Reinhard Krause/Reuters/Corbis; 110 Sandro Vannini/Corbis; 112 Charles & Josette Lenars/Corbis; 113 Denis Anthony Valentine/Corbis; 115 Jose Fuste Raga/Corbis; 116 Richard T. Nowitz/Corbis; 117 Buddy Mays/Corbis; 118 Wendy Stone/Corbis; 119 Jeremy Horner/Corbis; 120 Neil Beer/Corbis; 121 Royalty-Free/Corbis; 122 Nevada Wier/Corbis; 123 Michael Freeman/Corbis; 124 Jon Hicks/Corbis; 125 Roger Wood/Corbis; 126 Earl & Nazima Kowall/Corbis; 127 Eldad Rafaeli/Corbis; 128 Sergio Pitamitz/zefa/Corbis; 129 Keren Su/Corbis; 130 Fridmar Damm/zefa/Corbis; 131 Otto Lang/Corbis; 132 Chris Hellier/Corbis; 134 Bob Krist/Corbis; 135 Michael S. Yamashita/Corbis; 136 Nik Wheeler/Corbis; 137 Jose Fuste Raga/Corbis; 138 Margaret Courtney-Clarke/Corbis; 139 Wolfgang Kaehler/Corbis; 140 Free Agents Limited/Corbis; 141 Nik Wheeler/Corbis; 142 Hamid Sardar/Corbis; 143 Philippe Giraud/Goodlook/Corbis; 145 Jon Spaull/Corbis; 146 Frans Lemmens/zefa/Corbis; 147 Craig Lovell/Corbis; 148 Free Agents Limited/Corbis; 149 Robert Dowling/Corbis; 150 Bill Gentile/Corbis; 151 Nik Wheeler/Corbis; 153 Farrell Grehan/Corbis; 154 Arthur Thévenart/Corbis; 155 Douglas Peebles/Corbis; 158 Matthew McKee/Eye Ubiquitous/Corbis; 159 Chris Lisle/Corbis; 160 David Samuel Robbins/Corbis; 161 Danny Lehman/Corbis; 162 Robert Harding World Imagery/Corbis; 163 Pablo Corral Vega/Corbis; 164 Galen Rowell/Corbis; 165 Otto Lang/Corbis; 166 Yiorgos Nikiteas/Eye Ubiquitous/Corbis; 168 Jon Hicks/Corbis; 169 José Fuste Raga/zefa/Corbis; 171 David Ball/Corbis; 172 Dean Conger/Corbis; 173 Michael S. Lewis/Corbis; 175 Robert van der Hilst/Corbis; 176 Adam Woolfitt/Corbis; 177 Bill Gentile/Corbis; 178 Jose Fuste Raga/Corbis; 179 David Ball/Corbis; 180 Jose Fuste Raga/Corbis; 181 Kevin Fleming/Corbis; 183 Jon Hicks/Corbis; 184 Patrick Ward/Corbis; 186 Dallas and John Heaton/Free Agents Limited/Corbis; 187 Michael Freeman/Corbis; 188 Nicole Duplaix/Corbis; 189 Nik Wheeler/Corbis; 192 Eye Ubiquitous/Corbis; 193 Jose Fuste Raga/Corbis; 194 Jim Richardson/Corbis; 195 Nik Wheeler/Corbis; 196 William Manning/Corbis; 198 Bob Krist/Corbis; 200 Lawrence Manning/Corbis; 201 Gérard Degeorge/Corbis; 202 Michael S. Lewis/Corbis; 203 Ed Kashi/Corbis; 204 Jon Hicks/Corbis; 206 Richard Klune/Corbis; 207 Royalty-Free/Corbis; 210 Dave G. Houser/Post-Houserstock/Corbis; 211 Ludovic Maisant/Corbis; 212 James Marshall/Corbis; 213 Wolfgang Kaehler/Corbis; 214 Sergio Pitamitz/Corbis; 215 Peter Johnson/Corbis; 216 Frans Lemmens/zefa/Corbis.

WORLD CITIES

Amsterdam 222
Athens 222
Atlanta 223
Baghdad 223
Bangkok 223
Barcelona 224
Beijing 224
Berlin 225
Boston 226
Brussels 226
Budapest 227
Buenos Aires 227
Cairo 227
Cape Town 228
Copenhagen 228
Chicago 229
Delhi 230
Dublin 230
Edinburgh 231
Guangzhou 231
Helsinki 231
Hong Kong 232
Istanbul 232
Jakarta 232
Jerusalem 233
Johannesburg 233
Karachi 233
Kolkata 234
Lagos 234
Las Vegas 234
Lima 234
London 235
Los Angeles 236
Lisbon 236
Madrid 237
Manila 237
Melbourne 238
Mexico City 238
Miami 238
Milan 239
Moscow 239
Montréal 240
Mumbai 240
Munich 241
New Orleans 241
New York 242
Orlando 243
Osaka 243
Oslo 243
Paris 244
Prague 245
Rio de Janeiro 245
Rome 246
San Francisco 246
St Petersburg 247
Santiago 247
São Paulo 247
Seoul 247
Shanghai 248
Singapore 248
Stockholm 249
Sydney 249
Tokyo 250
Tehran 251
Toronto 251
Vienna 252
Warsaw 252
Washington 253
Wellington 253

Index 254–263

WORLD CITIES SATELLITE IMAGES

Cape Town 264
Chicago 265
Karachi 266
London 267
New York 268
San Francisco 269
Santiago 270
Sydney 271
Tokyo 272

CITY MAPS

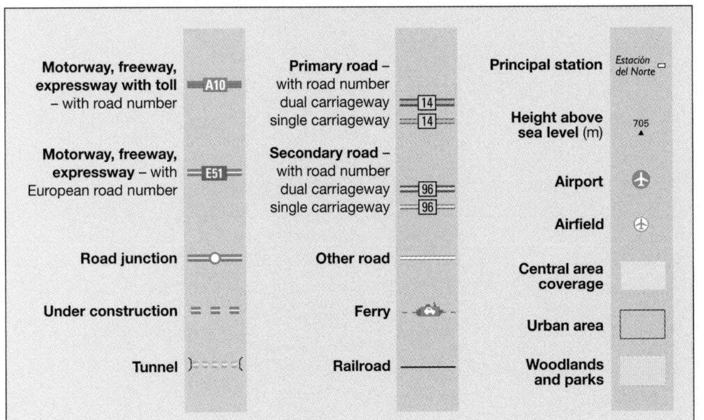

CENTRAL AREA MAPS

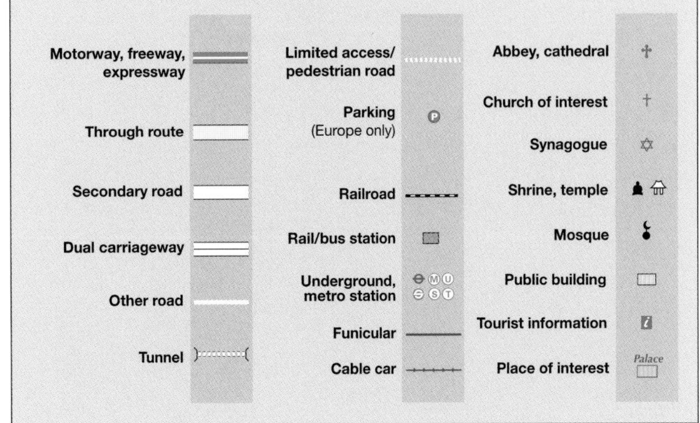

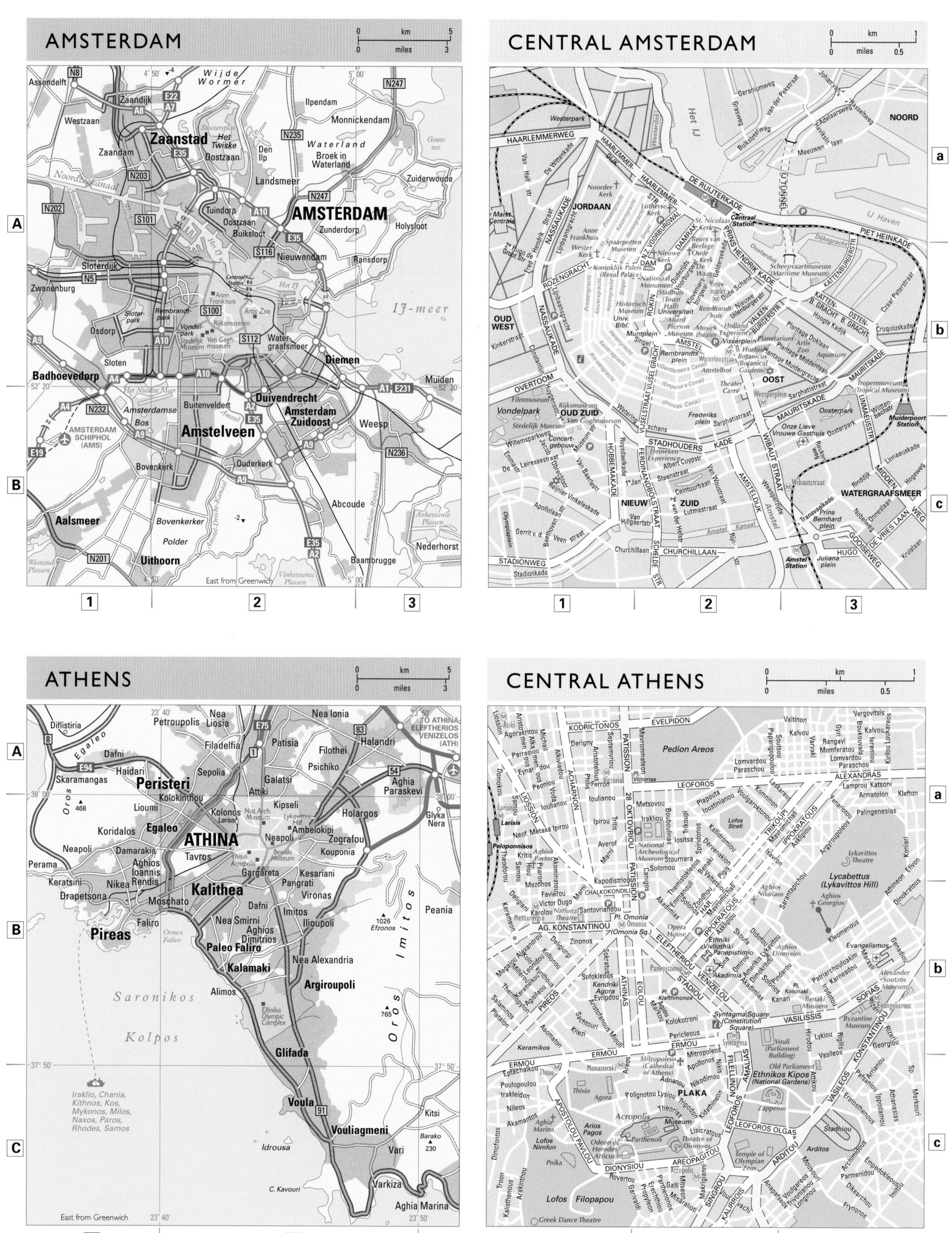
AMSTERDAM
0 km 5
0 miles 3
Assendelft
Wijde Wormer
Zaandijk
Westzaan
Zaanstad
Het Twiske
Oostzaan
Ilpendam
Monnickendam
Waterland
Broek in Waterland
Den Ilp
Landsmeer
Zuiderwoude
Zaandam
Noordzeekanaal
Tuindorp Oostzaan
Buiksloot
AMSTERDAM
Zunderdorp
Holysloot
Nieuwendam
Ransdorp
Sloterdijk
Zwanenburg
IJ-meer
Sloterpark
Rembrandtpark
Vondelpark
Osdorp
Artis Zoo
Rijksmuseum
Watergraafsmeer
Diemen
Sloten
Badhoevedorp
Het Nieuwe Meer
Muiden
Buitenveldert
Duivendrecht
Amsterdam Zuidoost
Amsterdamse Bos
AMSTERDAM SCHIPHOL (AMS)
Amstelveen
Weesp
Bovenkerk
Ouderkerk
Abcoude
Aalsmeer
Bovenkerker Polder
Nederhorst
Uithoorn
Baambrugge
East from Greenwich
CENTRAL AMSTERDAM
0 km 1
0 miles 0.5
Westerpark
Het IJ
NOORD
HAARLEMMERWEG
JORDAAN
DE RUIJTERKADE
Centraal Station
IJ Haven
PIET HEINKADE
Anne Frankhuis
Westerkerk
DAM
Koninklijk Paleis (Royal Palace)
Scheepvaartmuseum (Maritime Museum)
ROZENGRACHT
OUD WEST
Rembrandtsplein
AMSTEL
Hortus Botanicus (Botanical Gardens)
Artis Zoo
OOST
Tropenmuseum (Tropical Museum)
OVERTOOM
Vondelpark
OUD ZUID
Rijksmuseum
Van Goghmuseum
Stedelijk Museum
Concertgebouw
STADHOUDERSKADE
Heineken Experience
Muiderpoort Station
WATERGRAAFSMEER
NIEUW ZUID
Amstel Station
STADIONWEG
CHURCHILLAAN
ATHENS
0 km 5
0 miles 3
Diflistiria
Nea Liosia
Petroupolis
Nea Ionia
TO ATHINA-ELEFTHERIOS VENIZELOS (ATH)
Halandri
Dafni
Filadelfia
Patisia
Filothei
Psichiko
Skaramangas
Haidari
Peristeri
Sepolia
Galatsi
Aghia Paraskevi
Kolokinthou
Attiki
Holargos
Glyka Nera
Liomi
Kolonos
Kipseli
Koridalos
Egaleo
Ambelokipi
Zografou
Neapoli
ATHINA
Kouponia
Perama
Damarakia
Tavros
Aghios Ioannis Rendis
Kesariani
Keratsini
Nikea
Kalithea
Pangrati
Drapetsona
Moschato
Vironas
Faliro
Dafni
Imitos
Peania
Pireas
Nea Smirni
Ilioupoli
Aghios Dimitrios
Paleo Faliro
Nea Alexandria
Kalamaki
Argiroupoli
Alimos
Saronikos Kolpos
Ellinko Olympic Complex
Oros Imitos
Glifada
Voula
Kitsi
Vouliagmeni
Iraklio, Chania, Kithnos, Kos, Mykonos, Milos, Naxos, Paros, Rhodes, Samos
Idrousa
Vari
C. Kavouri
Varkiza
Aghia Marina
East from Greenwich
CENTRAL ATHENS
0 km 1
0 miles 0.5
Pedion Areos
LEOFOROS ALEXANDRAS
Larisis
Peloponnisos
National Archaeological Museum
Lofos Strefi
Lycabettus (Lykavittos Hill)
Pl. Omonia (Omonia Sq.)
PATISSION
Panepistimio
Akadimia
Ethniki Vivliothiki
Syntagma Square (Constitution Square)
VASILISSIS SOFIAS
Benaki Museum
Byzantine Museum
ERMOU
Mitropoleos (Cathedral of Athens)
Vouli (Parliament Building)
Ethnikos Kipos (National Gardens)
PLAKA
Zappeion
Acropolis
Parthenon
Theatre of Dionysos
Odeon of Herodes Atticus
Temple of Olympian Zeus
Agora
Thisio
DIONYSIOU AREOPAGITOU
LEOFOROS OLGAS
Stadhiou
Lofos Filopapou
Greek Dance Theatre

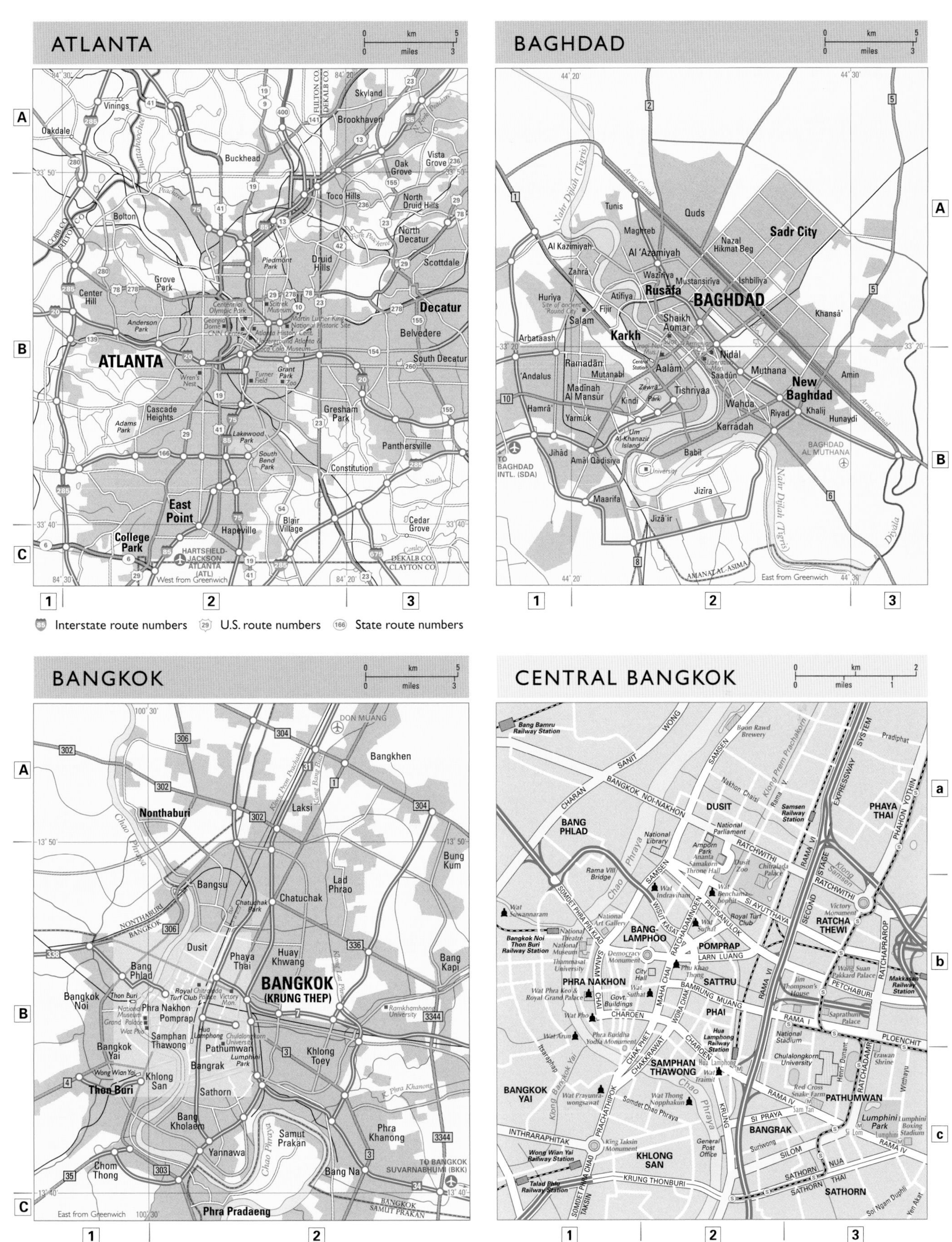
ATLANTA
BAGHDAD
BANGKOK
CENTRAL BANGKOK
Interstate route numbers
U.S. route numbers
State route numbers
Skytrain

BARCELONA

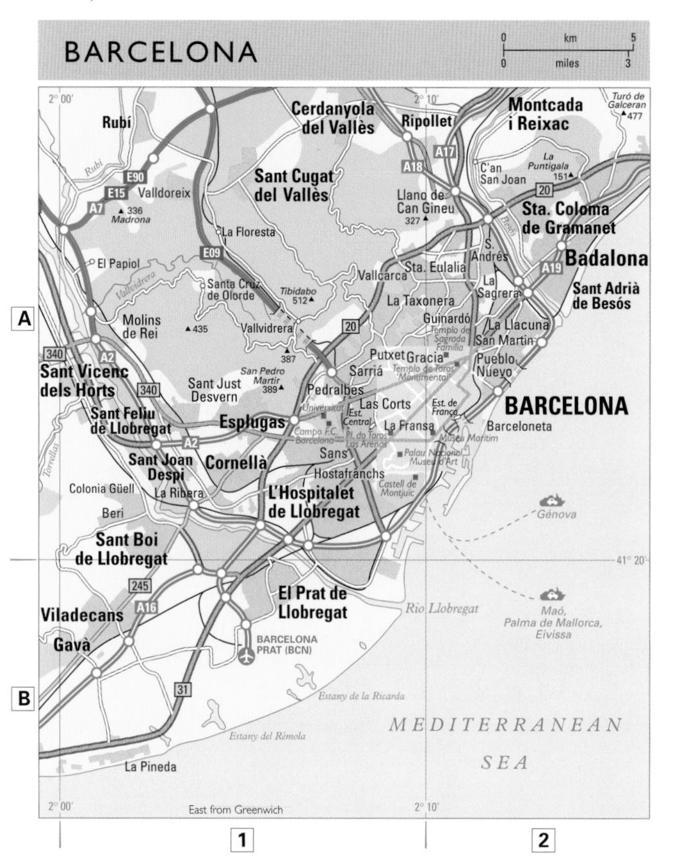

CENTRAL BARCELONA

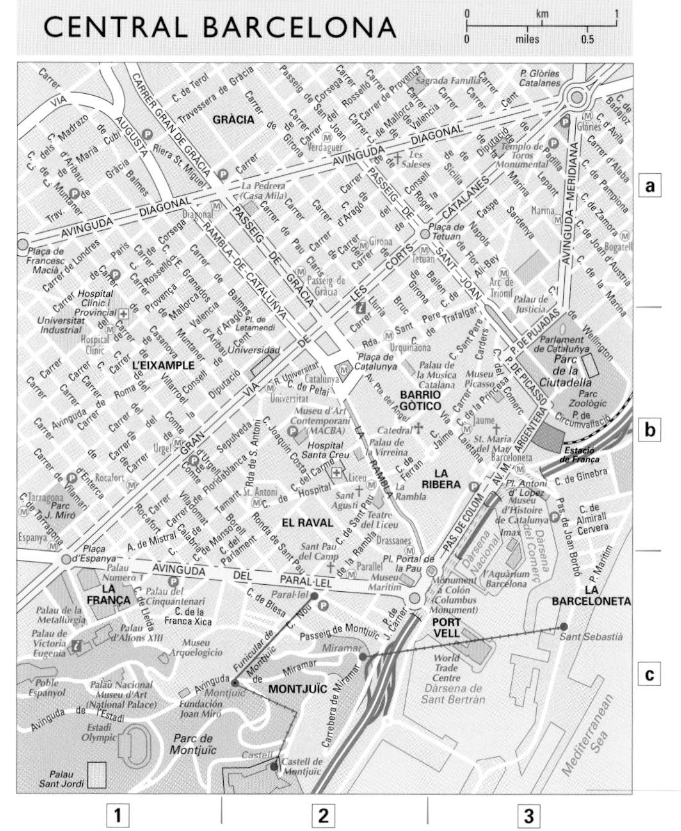

BEIJING

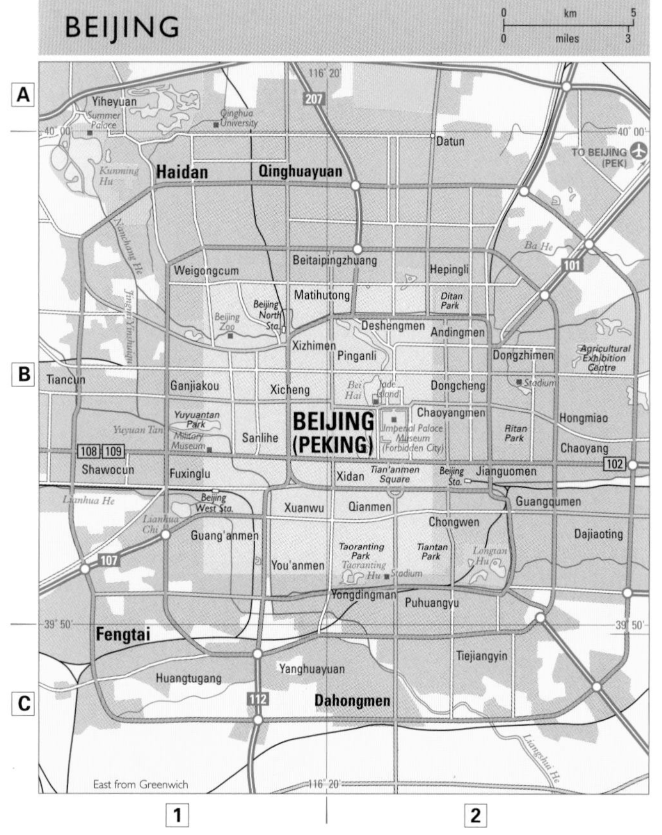

CENTRAL BEIJING

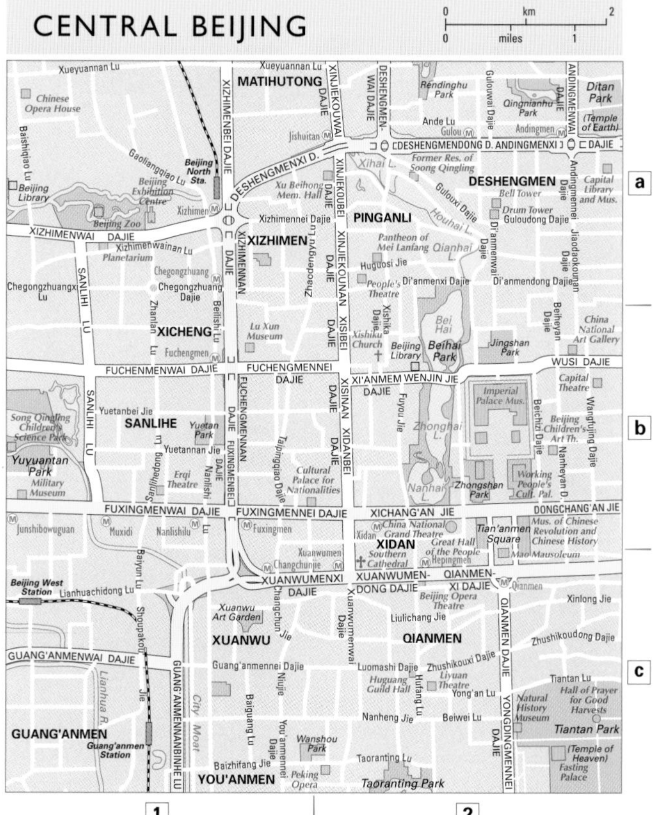

BERLIN

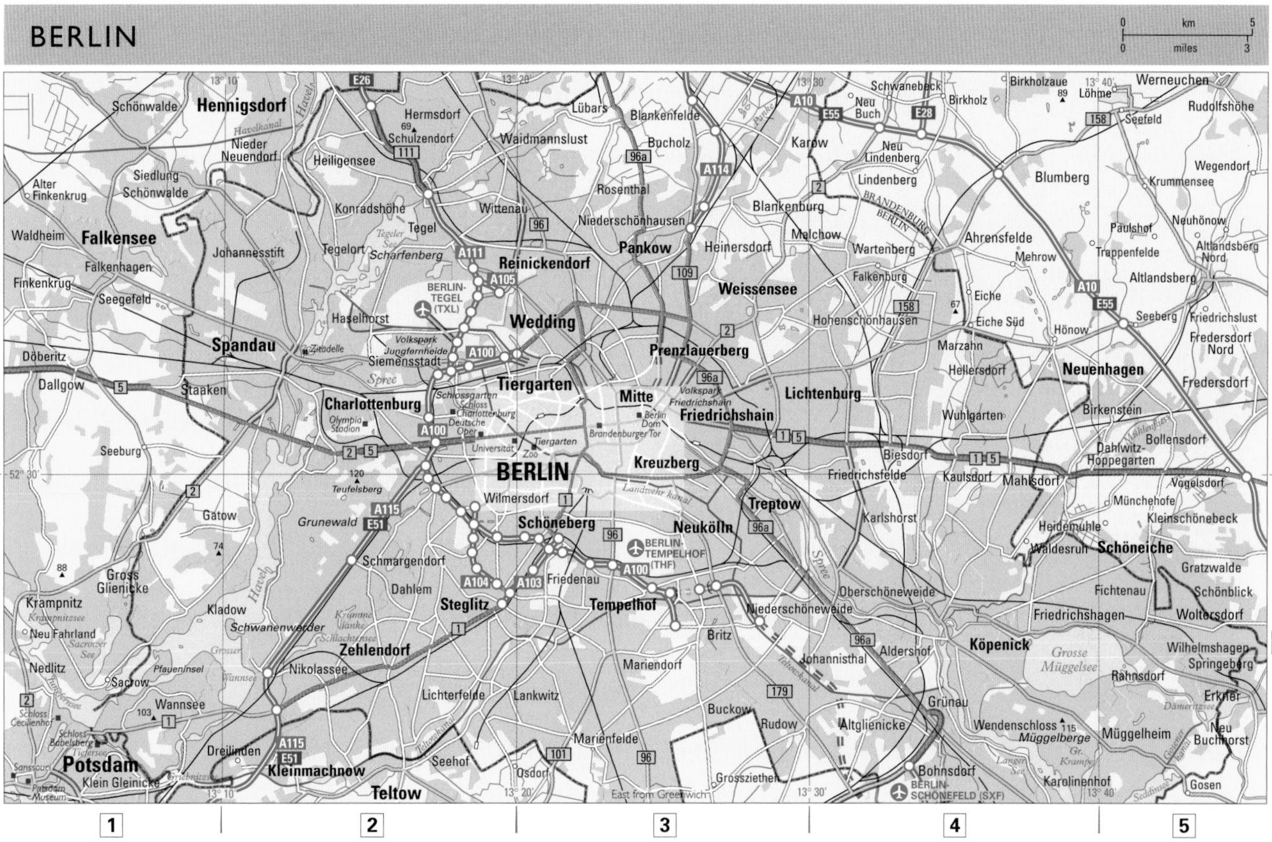

CENTRAL BERLIN

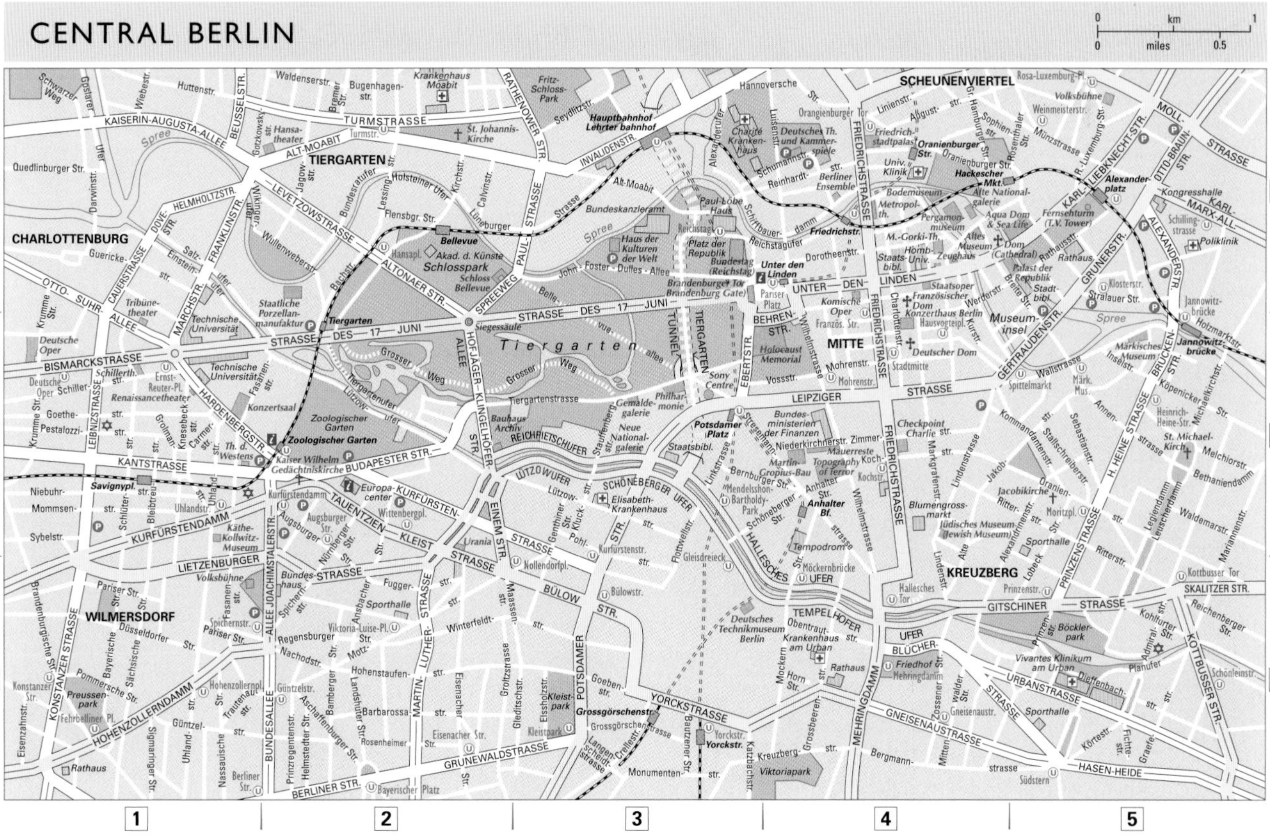

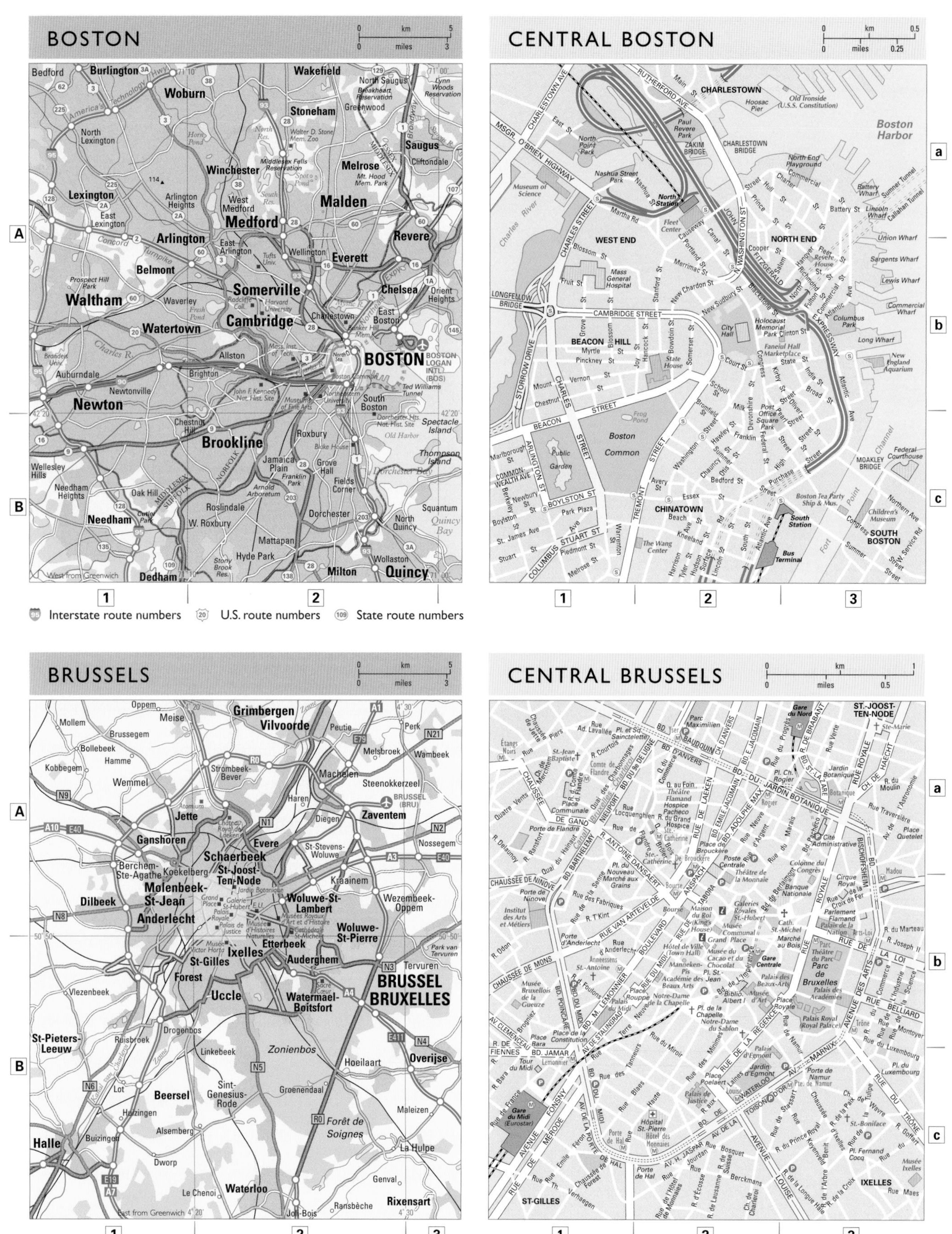
BOSTON
0 km 5
0 miles 3
Bedford
Burlington
Woburn
Wakefield
Stoneham
Lexington
Winchester
Melrose
Saugus
Malden
Medford
Revere
Arlington
Everett
Belmont
Chelsea
Waltham
Somerville
Cambridge
Watertown
East Boston
BOSTON
BOSTON LOGAN INTL (BOS)
Newton
South Boston
Brookline
Roxbury
Jamaica Plain
Dorchester
Needham
Roslindale
W. Roxbury
Mattapan
Hyde Park
Milton
Quincy
Dedham
Wellesley Hills
Needham Heights
North Quincy
Squantum
West from Greenwich
1
2
A
B
Interstate route numbers
U.S. route numbers
State route numbers
CENTRAL BOSTON
0 km 0.5
0 miles 0.25
CHARLESTOWN
Boston Harbor
WEST END
NORTH END
BEACON HILL
Boston Common
CHINATOWN
SOUTH BOSTON
North Station
South Station
Bus Terminal
Mass General Hospital
State House
Faneuil Hall Marketplace
City Hall
Public Garden
New England Aquarium
Children's Museum
Museum of Science
CAMBRIDGE STREET
STORROW DRIVE
CHARLES STREET
BEACON STREET
TREMONT STREET
BOYLSTON ST
a
b
c
1
2
3
BRUSSELS
0 km 5
0 miles 3
Grimbergen
Vilvoorde
Meise
Machelen
Zaventem
Jette
Ganshoren
Evere
Schaerbeek
Berchem-Ste-Agathe
Koekelberg
St-Joost-Ten-Node
Molenbeek-St-Jean
Dilbeek
Anderlecht
Woluwe-St-Lambert
Woluwe-St-Pierre
Etterbeek
Ixelles
St-Gilles
Forest
Auderghem
Uccle
Watermael-Boitsfort
BRUSSEL BRUXELLES
Tervuren
St-Pieters-Leeuw
Drogenbos
Linkebeek
Beersel
Sint-Genesius-Rode
Zonienbos
Hoeilaart
Overijse
Halle
Forêt de Soignes
Waterloo
Rixensart
La Hulpe
East from Greenwich
A
B
1
2
3
CENTRAL BRUSSELS
0 km 1
0 miles 0.5
ST.-JOOST-TEN-NODE
Gare du Nord
Gare Centrale
Gare du Midi (Eurostar)
Grand Place
Parc de Bruxelles
Palais Royal (Royal Palace)
Place Royale
Palais de Justice
Cath. St.-Michel
Place de la Chapelle
Place du Grand Sablon
Hôtel de Ville (Town Hall)
Manneken-Pis
Porte de Hal
IXELLES
ST-GILLES
a
b
c
1
2
3

BUDAPEST

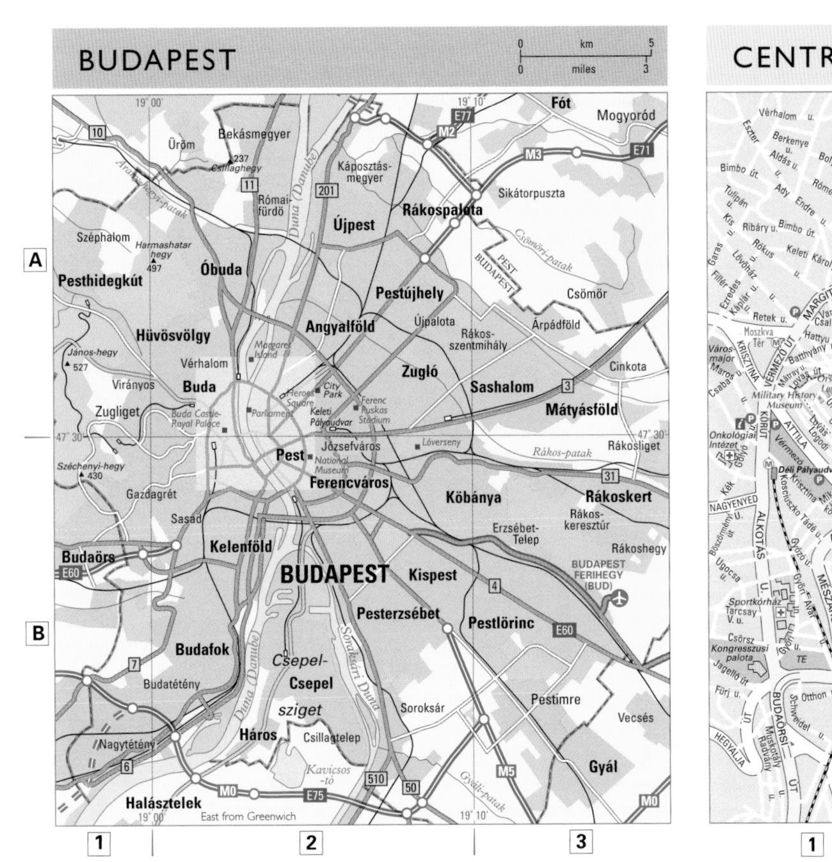

CENTRAL BUDAPEST

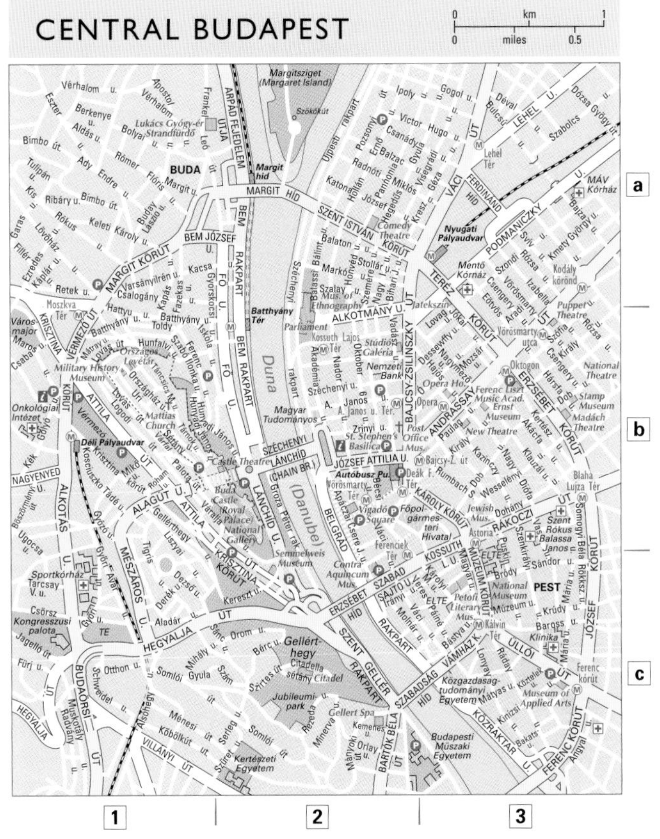

BUENOS AIRES

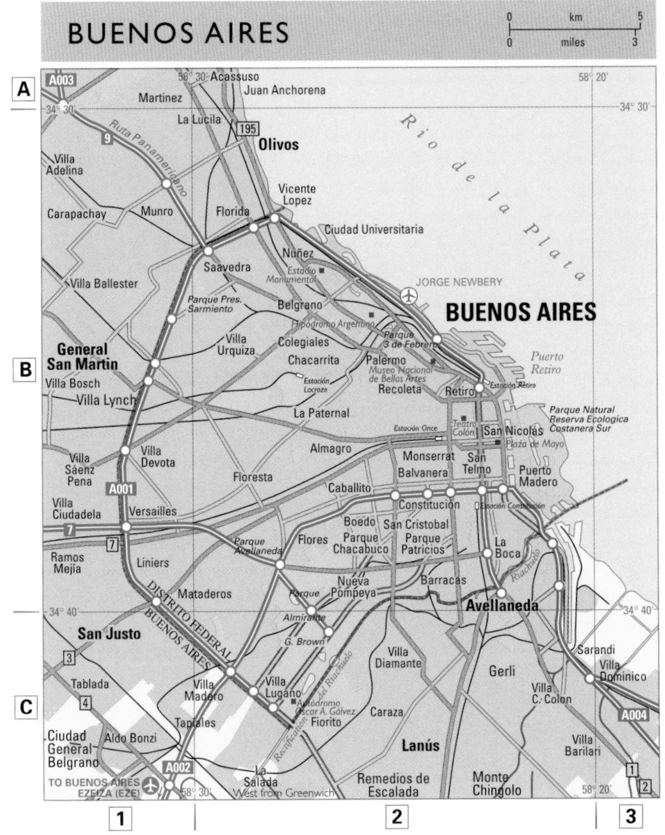

CAIRO

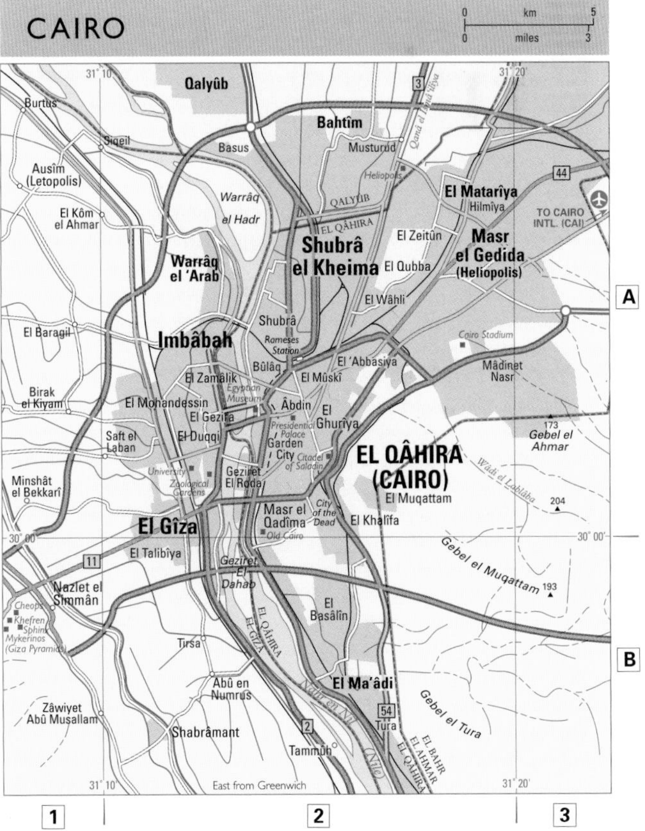

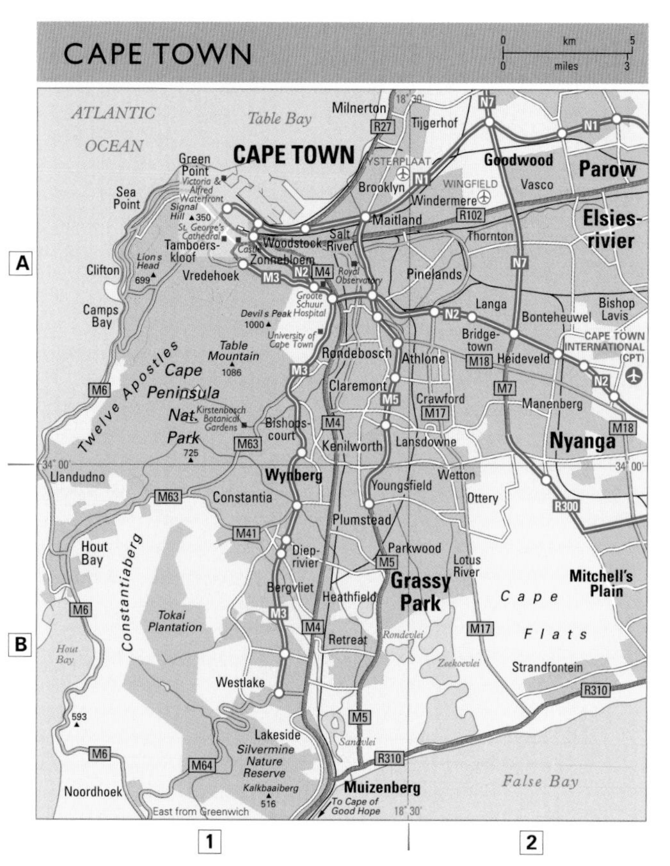
CAPE TOWN
ATLANTIC OCEAN
Table Bay
Milnerton
Tijgerhof
CAPE TOWN
Goodwood
Parow
Green Point
Sea Point
Brooklyn
Vasco
Windermere
Maitland
Elsies-rivier
Woodstock
Salt River
Thornton
Tamboers-kloof
Zonnebloem
Clifton
Vredehoek
Pinelands
Camps Bay
Langa
Bonteheuwel
Bishop Lavis
Rondebosch
Athlone
Bridge-town
Heideveld
CAPE TOWN INTERNATIONAL (CPT)
Table Mountain
Twelve Apostles
Cape Peninsula Nat. Park
Claremont
Crawford
Manenberg
Kenilworth
Lansdowne
Nyanga
Llandudno
Wynberg
Wetton
Constantia
Youngsfield
Ottery
Plumstead
Hout Bay
Parkwood
Lotus River
Grassy Park
Mitchell's Plain
Bergvliet
Heathfield
Cape Flats
Tokai Plantation
Retreat
Strandfontein
Westlake
Lakeside
Silvermine Nature Reserve
Muizenberg
Noordhoek
False Bay
East from Greenwich

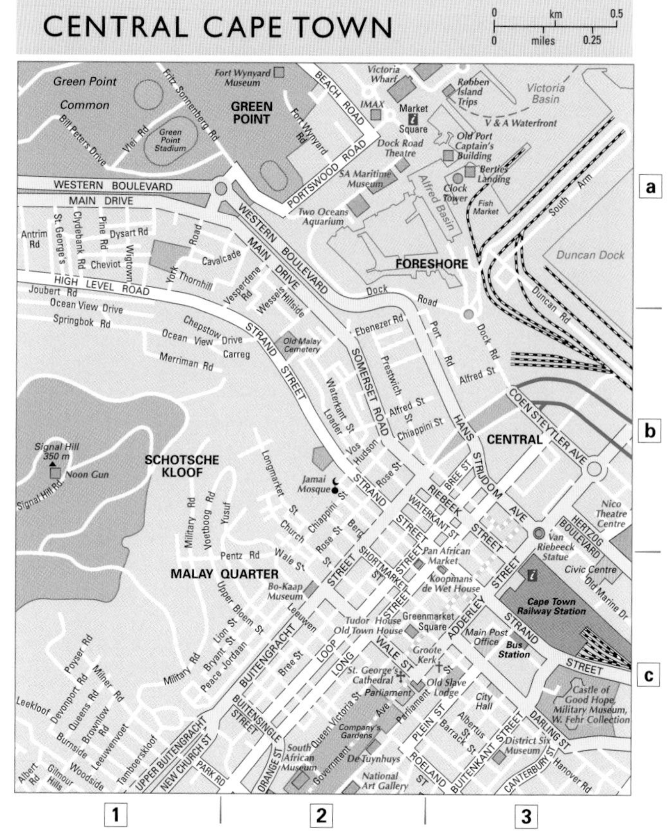
CENTRAL CAPE TOWN
Green Point Common
GREEN POINT
Fort Wynyard Museum
Victoria Wharf
Robben Island Trips
Victoria Basin
V & A Waterfront
Market Square
Dock Road Theatre
Old Port Captain's Building
SA Maritime Museum
Two Oceans Aquarium
Clock Tower
Fish Market
WESTERN BOULEVARD
MAIN DRIVE
HIGH LEVEL ROAD
FORESHORE
Duncan Dock
Signal Hill 350 m
Noon Gun
SCHOTSCHE KLOOF
CENTRAL
Jamai Mosque
Nico Theatre Centre
Van Riebeeck Statue
Civic Centre
MALAY QUARTER
Bo-Kaap Museum
Pan African Market
Koopmans de Wet House
Cape Town Railway Station
Tudor House
Old Town House
Greenmarket Square
Main Post Office
Bus Station
Groote Kerk
St. George's Cathedral
Parliament
Old Slave Lodge
City Hall
Castle of Good Hope Military Museum, W. Fehr Collection
Company's Gardens
South African Museum
De Tuynhuys
National Art Gallery
District Six Museum

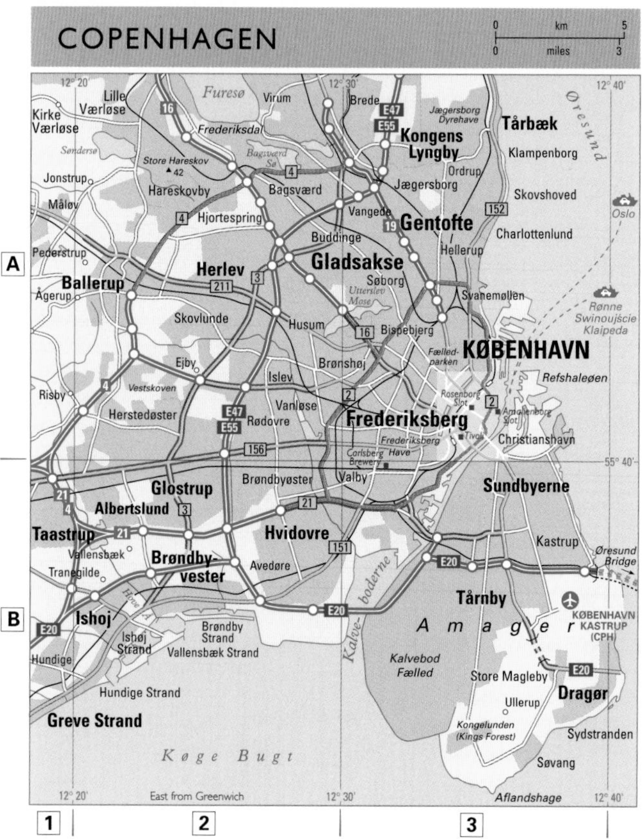
COPENHAGEN
Furesø
Virum
Brede
Lille Værløse
Kirke Værløse
Tårbæk
Kongens Lyngby
Klampenborg
Øresund
Store Hareskov
Jonstrup
Bagsværd
Jægersborg
Hareskovby
Ordrup
Skovshoved
Måløv
Hjortespring
Vangede
Gentofte
Charlottenlund
Buddinge
Pederstrup
Herlev
Gladsakse
Hellerup
Ballerup
Søborg
Svanemøllen
Skovlunde
Husum
Bispebjerg
KØBENHAVN
Brønshøj
Ejby
Islev
Refshaleøen
Risby
Vestskoven
Herstedøster
Vanløse
Rødovre
Frederiksberg
Christianshavn
Glostrup
Brøndbyøster
Valby
Sundbyerne
Albertslund
Taastrup
Hvidovre
Kastrup
Øresund Bridge
Vallensbæk
Brøndby-vester
Avedøre
Tranegilde
Tårnby
KØBENHAVN KASTRUP (CPH)
Ishøj
Ishøj Strand
Brøndby Strand
Vallensbæk Strand
Amager
Hundige
Kalvebod Fælled
Store Magleby
Dragør
Hundige Strand
Ullerup
Greve Strand
Kongelunden (Kings Forest)
Sydstranden
Køge Bugt
Søvang
Aflandshage
East from Greenwich

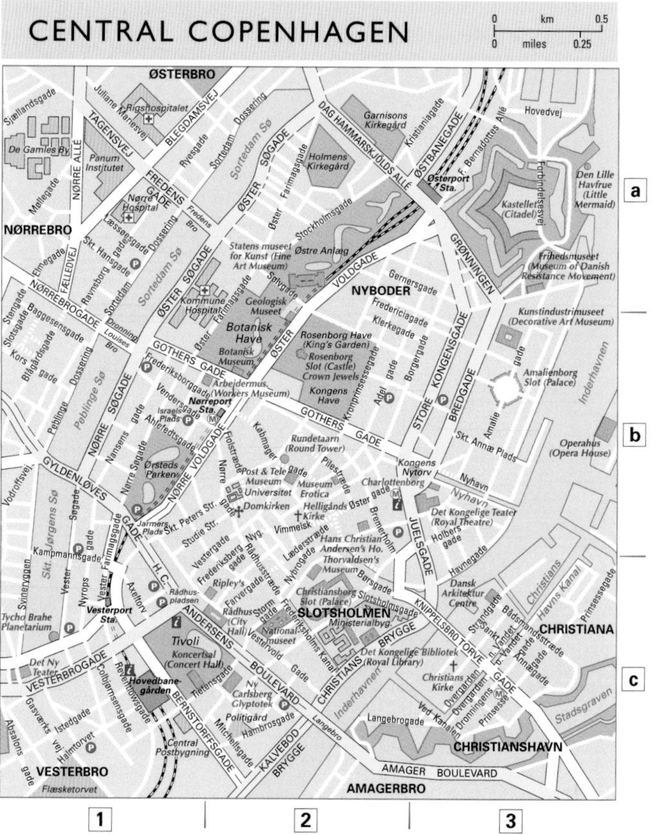
CENTRAL COPENHAGEN
ØSTERBRO
Rigshospitalet
Garnisons Kirkegård
Hovedvej
Panum Instituttet
Holmens Kirkegård
Østerport Sta.
Den Lille Havfrue (Little Mermaid)
Kastellet (Citadel)
NØRREBRO
Statens museum for Kunst (Fine Art Museum)
Østre Anlæg
Frihedsmuseet Museum of Danish Resistance Movement
NYBODER
Kommune Hospital
Geologisk Museet
Kunstindustrimuseet (Decorative Art Museum)
Botanisk Have
Rosenborg Have (King's Garden)
Rosenborg Slot (Castle) Crown Jewels
Amalienborg Slot (Palace)
Kongens Have
Nørreport Sta.
Rundetårn (Round Tower)
Operahus (Opera House)
Ørsteds Parken
Kongens Nytorv
Charlottenborg
Nyhavn
Det Kongelige Teater (Royal Theatre)
Thorvaldsens Museum
SLOTSHOLMEN
Christiansborg Slot (Palace)
Rådhus (City Hall)
Nationalmuseet
Tycho Brahe Planetarium
Vesterport Sta.
Tivoli
Koncertsal (Concert Hall)
Det Kongelige Bibliotek (Royal Library)
CHRISTIANIA
Hovedbanegården
Ny Carlsberg Glyptotek
Christians Kirke
CHRISTIANSHAVN
VESTERBRO
AMAGERBRO
AMAGER BOULEVARD

CHICAGO

0 km 5
0 miles 3

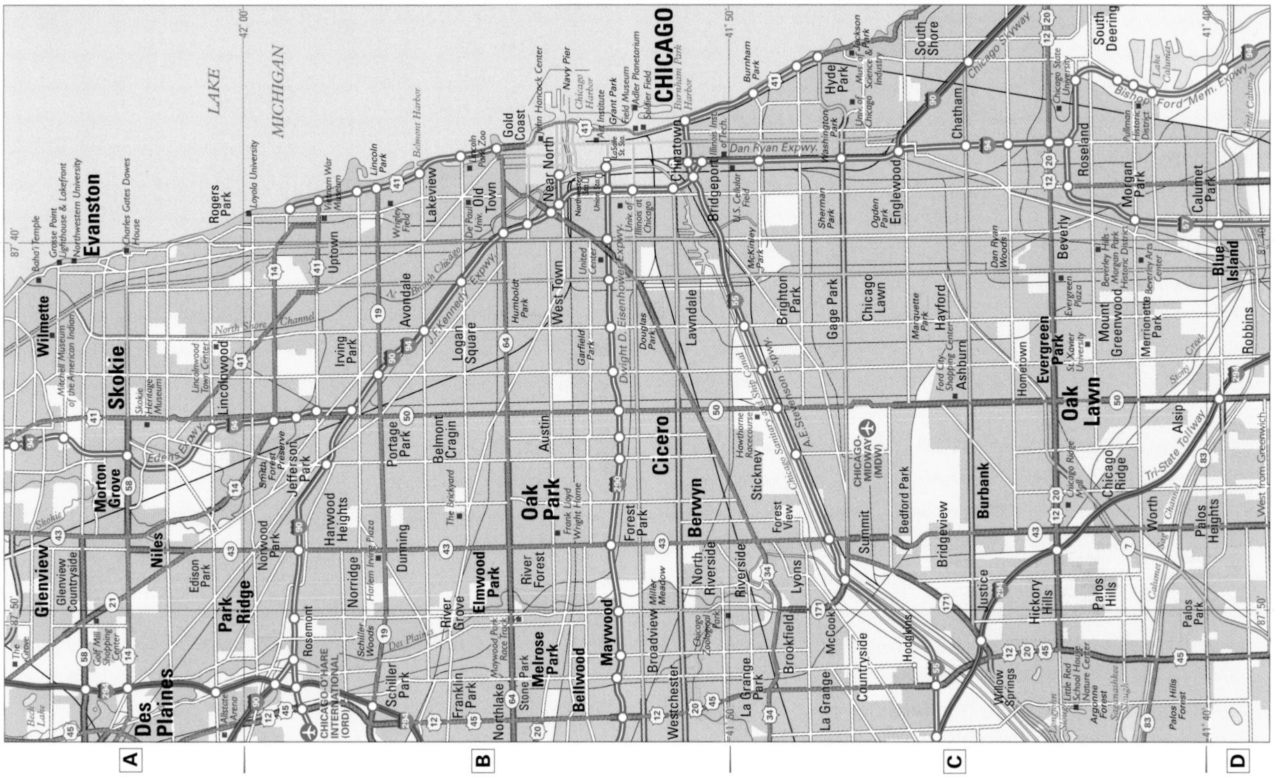

Interstate route numbers
U.S. route numbers
State route numbers

CENTRAL CHICAGO

0 km 1
0 miles 0.5

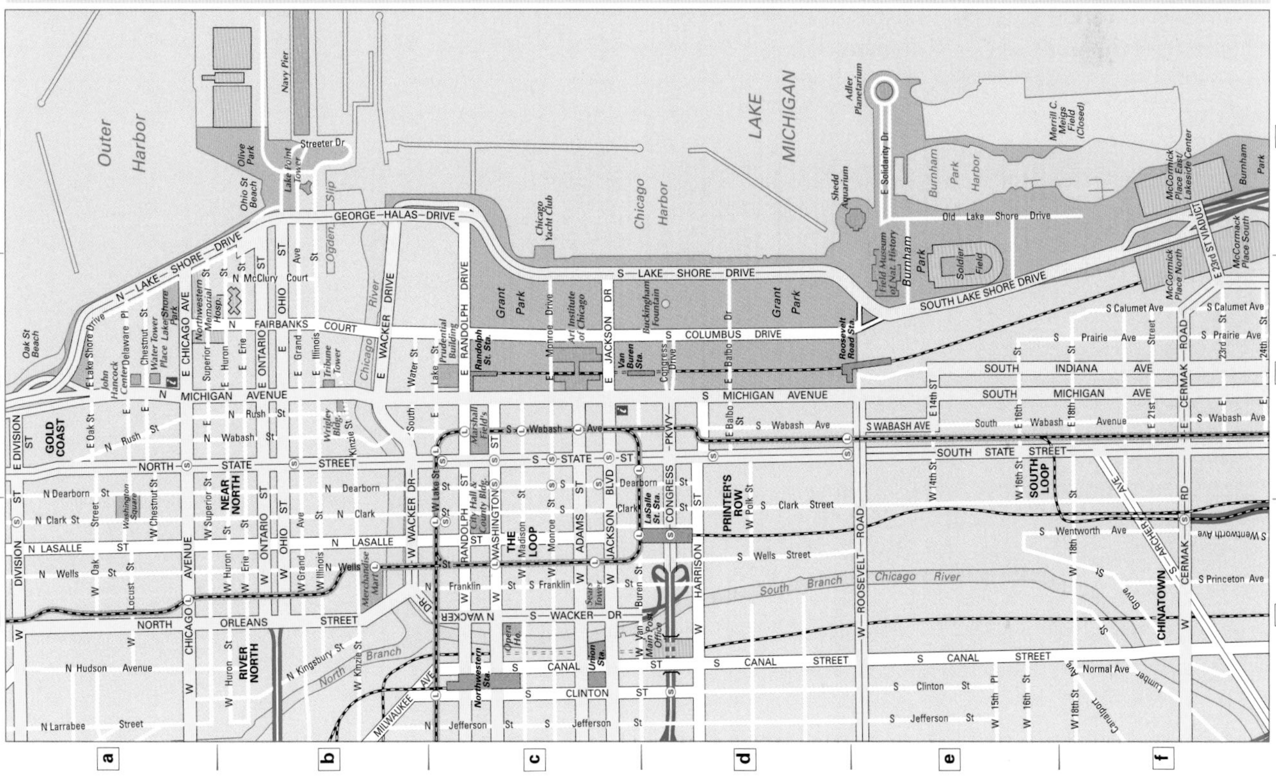

Elevated rail lines

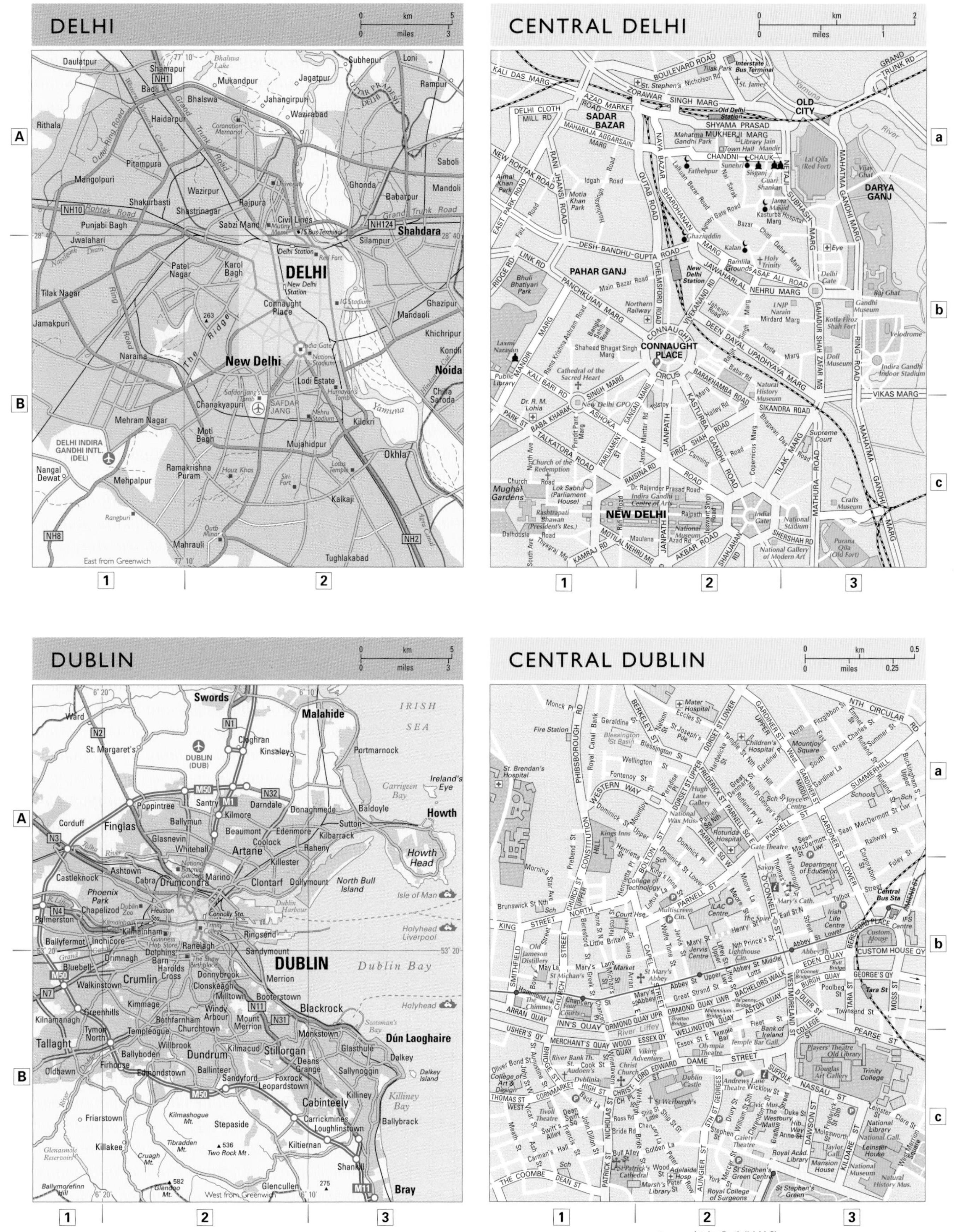

Light Rail (LUAS)

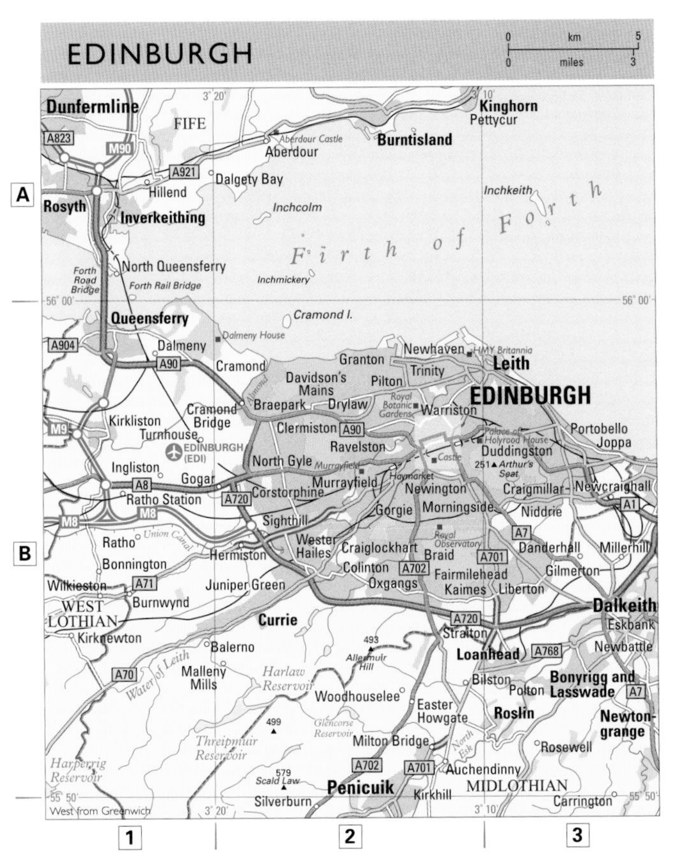
EDINBURGH
0 km 5
0 miles 3
Dunfermline
FIFE
Kinghorn
Pettycur
Aberdour Castle
Aberdour
Burntisland
Hillend
Dalgety Bay
Rosyth
Inverkeithing
Inchkeith
Inchcolm
Firth of Forth
North Queensferry
Forth Road Bridge
Forth Rail Bridge
Inchmickery
Queensferry
Cramond I.
Dalmeny
Dalmeny House
Cramond
Granton
Newhaven
HMY Britannia
Leith
Trinity
Davidson's Mains
Pilton
Royal Botanic Gardens
EDINBURGH
Braepark
Drylaw
Warriston
Kirkliston
Cramond Bridge
Turnhouse
Clermiston
Ravelston
Portobello
Joppa
EDINBURGH (EDI)
Duddingston
Ingliston
North Gyle
Murrayfield
Arthur's Seat
Gogar
Corstorphine
Ratho Station
Newington
Craigmillar
Newcraighall
Morningside
Niddrie
Sighthill
Gorgie
Ratho
Union Canal
Royal Observatory
Bonnington
Hermiston
Wester Hailes
Craiglockhart
Braid
Danderhall
Millerhill
Colinton
Fairmilehead
Gilmerton
Wilkieston
Juniper Green
Oxgangs
Kaimes
Liberton
WEST LOTHIAN
Burnwynd
Currie
Dalkeith
Eskbank
Kirknewton
Straiton
Newbattle
Balerno
Allermuir Hill
Loanhead
Malleny Mills
Water of Leith
Harlaw Reservoir
Bilston
Polton
Bonyrigg and Lasswade
Woodhouselee
Easter Howgate
Roslin
Newtongrange
Glencorse Reservoir
Milton Bridge
Threipmuir Reservoir
Rosewell
Harperrig Reservoir
Scald Law
Auchendinny
Penicuik
MIDLOTHIAN
Silverburn
Kirkhill
Carrington
West from Greenwich
A823 M90 A921 A904 A90 M9 A8 M8 A720 A71 A70 A702 A701 A1 A7 A768 A720 A702 A701
493 499 579 251
1 2 3
A B

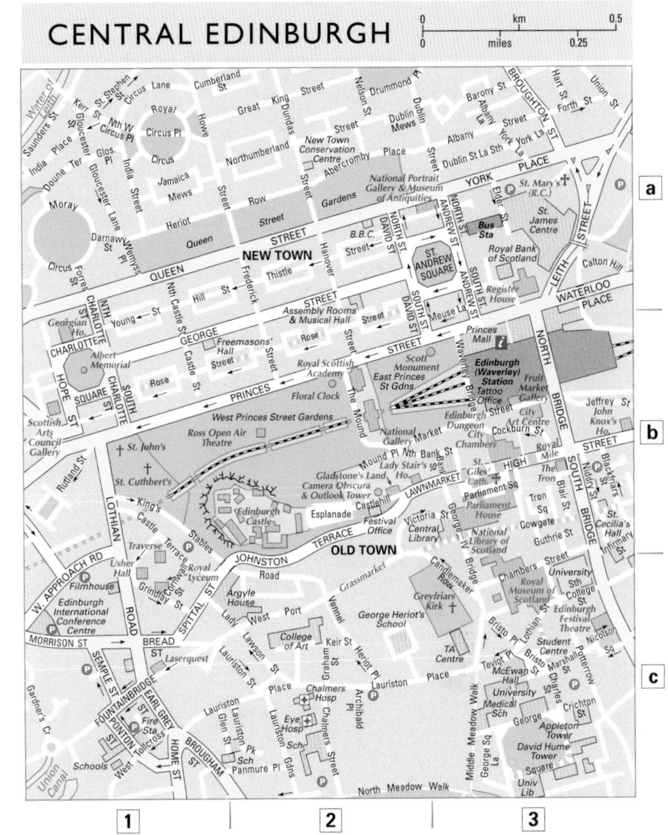
CENTRAL EDINBURGH
0 km 0.5
0 miles 0.25
Water of Leith
St. Stephen St.
Cumberland St.
Drummond Pl.
Broughton St.
Great King Street
Royal Circus
Dublin St.
Barony St.
Dublin Mews
Albany St.
New Town Conservation Centre
Abercromby Place
Dublin St. La Sth
York La.
Northumberland St.
Heriot Row
Queen Street
National Portrait Gallery & Museum of Antiquities
York Place
St. Mary's (R.C.)
Queen Street Gardens
B.B.C.
Bus Sta
St. James Centre
Royal Bank of Scotland
Leith Street
Calton Hill
NEW TOWN
St. Andrew Square
Register House
Waterloo Place
Queen Street
Thistle Street
George Street
Assembly Rooms & Musical Hall
Rose Street
Princes Mall
Freemasons' Hall
Georgian Ho.
Charlotte Square
Albert Memorial
Scott Monument
Royal Scottish Academy
East Princes St Gdns
Edinburgh (Waverley) Station
Fruit Market Gallery
Princes Street
Tattoo Office
Floral Clock
Hope Street
West Princes Street Gardens
Edinburgh Dungeon
City Art Centre
Jeffrey St
John Knox's Ho.
Scottish Arts Council Gallery
Ross Open Air Theatre
National Gallery
St. John's
St. Cuthbert's
The Mound
Market Street
Cockburn St
Mound Pl
Lady Stair's Ho.
Royal Mile
High Street
Gladstone's Land
Camera Obscura & Outlook Tower
Castlehill
Lawnmarket
St. Giles' Cath.
Tron
Parliament House
Parliament Sq
King's Stables
Castle Terrace
Edinburgh Castle
Esplanade
Festival Office
Victoria St
Central Library
National Library of Scotland
Cowgate
Guthrie St
Blackfriars St
St. Cecilia's Hall
Infirmary St
Traverse
Usher Hall
Royal Lyceum
Johnston Terrace
OLD TOWN
Filmhouse
Grindlay St
Argyle House
Grassmarket
Candlemaker Row
Chambers Street
Royal Museum of Scotland
University College
Edinburgh International Conference Centre
Spittal St
West Port
Greyfriars Kirk
George Heriot's School
Edinburgh Festival Theatre
Morrison St
Bread St
College of Art
Keir St
Student Centre
Nicolson Sq
Laserquest
Lauriston St
TA Centre
Bristo Pl
Teviot Pl
McEwan Hall
Lauriston Place
Chalmers Hosp
University Medical Sch
Crichton St
George Sq
Appleton Tower
Fountainbridge
Earl Grey St
Fire Sta
Eye Hosp
David Hume Tower
Lothian Road
Gardner's Cr
Lonsdale St
Panmure Pl
Home St
Brougham St
Schools
Union Canal
Middle Meadow Walk
North Meadow Walk
Univ Lib
1 2 3
a b c

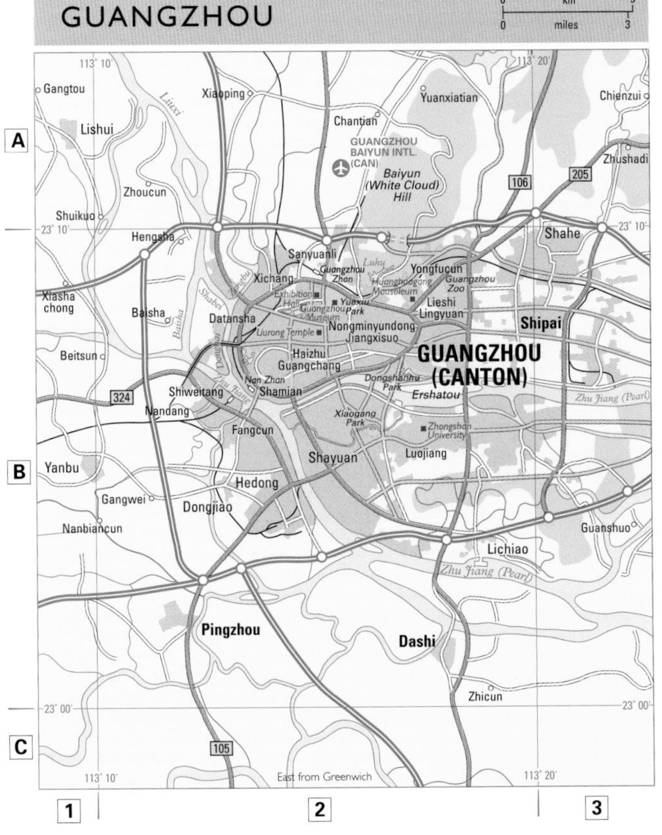
GUANGZHOU
0 km 5
0 miles 3
113° 10'
113° 20'
Gangtou
Xiaoping
Yuanxiatian
Chienzui
Lishui
Chantian
GUANGZHOU BAIYUN INTL. (CAN)
Zhushadi
Baiyun (White Cloud) Hill
Zhoucun
Shuikuo
Hengsha
Shahe
Sanyuanli
Yongfucun
Xichang
Guangzhou Zoo
Lieshi Lingyuan
Xiasha chong
Baisha
Datansha
Nongminyundong Jiangxisuo
Shipai
Beitsun
Haizhu Guangchang
GUANGZHOU (CANTON)
Nan Zhan
Dongshanhu Park
Shiweitang
Shamian
Ershatou
Zhu Jiang (Pearl)
Nandang
Fangcun
Xiaogang Park
Zhongshan University
Yanbu
Shayuan
Luojiang
Hedong
Gangwei
Dongjiao
Nanbiancun
Guanshuo
Lichiao
Pingzhou
Dashi
Zhicun
East from Greenwich
23° 10'
23° 00'
106 205 324 105
1 2 3
A B C

HELSINKI
0 km 5
0 miles 3
Kongo
Linna
Seutula
Mäkiniitty
Maantiekylä
Hanala
Rekola
Ketunkorpi
Vestra
Keimola
HELSINKI-VANTAA (HEL)
Kivistö
Koivupää
Lahnus
Harjusuo
Odilampi
Petas
Vantaanpuisto
Hiekkaharju
Röylä
Vantaankoski
Vantaa
Simonkylä
Ita Hakkila
Perusmaki
Askisto
Ylästö
Tikkurila
Gobbacka
Niiperi
Martinkylä
Hämeenkylä
Friherrs
Haltiala
Tapanila
Puistola
Hakunila
Haltiavuori
Kaivoksela
Paloheinä
Malmi
Rastaala
Laaksolahti
Pakila
Pukinmäki
Rajakylä
Mellunmäki
Konala
Lintuvaara
Pirkkola
Pihlajamäki
Mellunkylä
Oulunkylä
Myllypuro
Vartiokylä
Kauniainen
Haaga
Käpylä
Viikki
Kilo
Leppävaara
Puotila
Pasila
Herttoniemi
Rastila
Tuomarila
Henttaa
Nuijala
Munkkiniemi
HELSINKI
Roihuvuori
Mankkaa
Otaniemi
Olympic Stadium
Tammisalo
Vartiosaari
Olari
Tapiola
Lehtisaari
Kulosaari
Nöykkiö
Hietaniemi
Cathedral
Laajasalo
Jollas
Westend
Villinki
Lauttasaari
Suomenlinna
Nokkala
Santahamina
Miessaari
Pihlajasaari
Svinö
Melkki
Vallisaari
Stockholm, Lubeck, Travemund, Tallinn, Rostock
Harmaja
East from Greenwich
24° 50'
25° 00'
60° 20'
60° 10'
E12 E18 E75 130 120 110 101 170 50 45 51 3 4 1
1 2 3
A B C

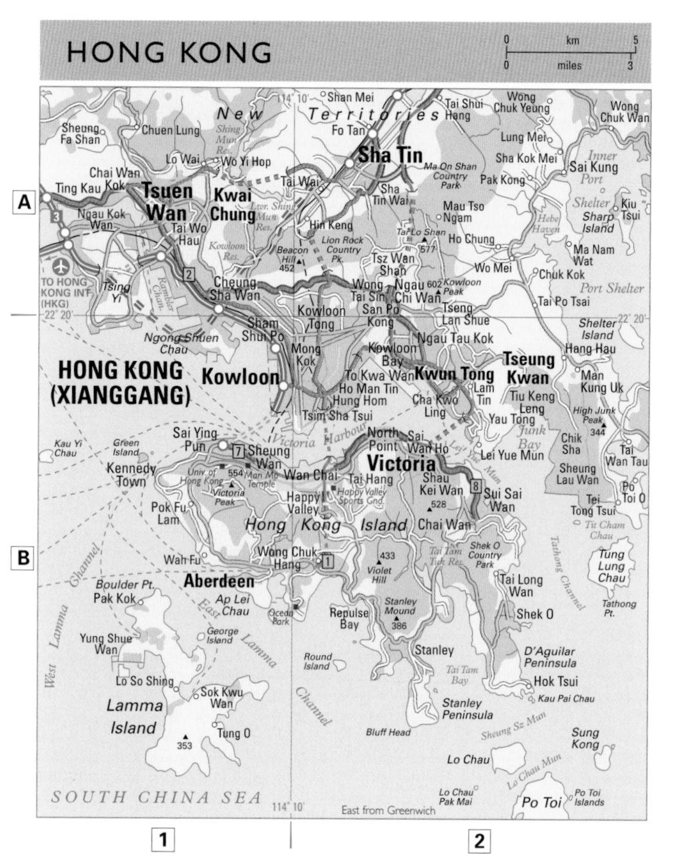
HONG KONG
km 0 5
miles 0 3
New Territories
Sheung Fa Shan
Chuen Lung
Shan Mei
Tai Shui Hang
Wong Chuk Yeung
Wong Chuk Wan
Fo Tan
Sha Tin
Lung Mei
Sha Kok Mei
Inner Port Shelter
Sai Kung
Lo Wai
Wo Yi Hop
Chai Wan Kok
Ting Kau
Tsuen Wan
Kwai Chung
Tai Wai
Ma On Shan Country Park
Pak Kong
Sha Tin Wai
Mau Tso Ngam
Shelter Island
Kiu Tsui
Sharp Island
Ngau Kok Wan
Tai Wo Hau
Hin Keng
Lion Rock Country Pk.
Ho Chung
Hebe Haven
Ma Nam Wat
Beacon Hill 452
Tsz Wan Shan
Wo Mei
Chuk Kok
TO HONG KONG INT. (HKG)
Tsing Yi
Cheung Sha Wan
Wong Tai Sin
Ngau Chi Wan
Kowloon Peak 602
Tai Po Tsai
Port Shelter
Kowloon Tong
San Po Kong
Tseng Lan Shue
Shelter Island
22° 20'
Sham Shui Po
Ngau Tau Kok
Hang Hau
Ngong Shuen Chau
Mong Kok
Kowloon Bay
Tseung Kwan
HONG KONG (XIANGGANG)
Kowloon
To Kwa Wan
Kwun Tong
Man Kung Uk
Ho Man Tin
Hung Hom
Lam Tin
Tiu Keng Leng
Tsim Sha Tsui
Cha Kwo Ling
Yau Tong
High Junk Peak 344
Sai Ying Pun
Victoria Harbour
Sheung Wan
North Point
Sai Wan Ho
Junk Bay
Chik Sha
Tai Wan Tau
Kau Yi Chau
Green Island
Kennedy Town
Victoria Peak 554
Man Mo Temple
Wan Chai
Victoria
Lei Yue Mun
Tai Hang
Shau Kei Wan
Sheung Lau Wan
Po Toi O
Pok Fu Lam
Happy Valley
Happy Valley Sports Gnd.
528
Sai Wan
Tei Tong Tsui
Hong Kong Island
Chai Wan
Tu Cham Chau
Wah Fu
Wong Chuk Hang
433
Tai Tam Country Park
Shek O Country Park
Tung Lung Chau
Aberdeen
Violet Hill
Tai Long Wan
Boulder Pt.
Pak Kok
Ap Lei Chau
Tathong Channel
Tathong Pt.
Ocean Park
Repulse Bay
Stanley Mound 386
Shek O
West Lamma Channel
Yung Shue Wan
George Island
Stanley
D'Aguilar Peninsula
East Lamma Channel
Round Island
Tai Tam Bay
Hok Tsui
Lo So Shing
Sok Kwu Wan
Kau Pai Chau
Lamma Island
Stanley Peninsula
353
Tung O
Bluff Head
Sheung Sz Mun
Sung Kong
Lo Chau
Lo Chau Mun
SOUTH CHINA SEA
114° 10'
East from Greenwich
Lo Chau Pak Mai
Po Toi
Po Toi Islands
A
B
1
2

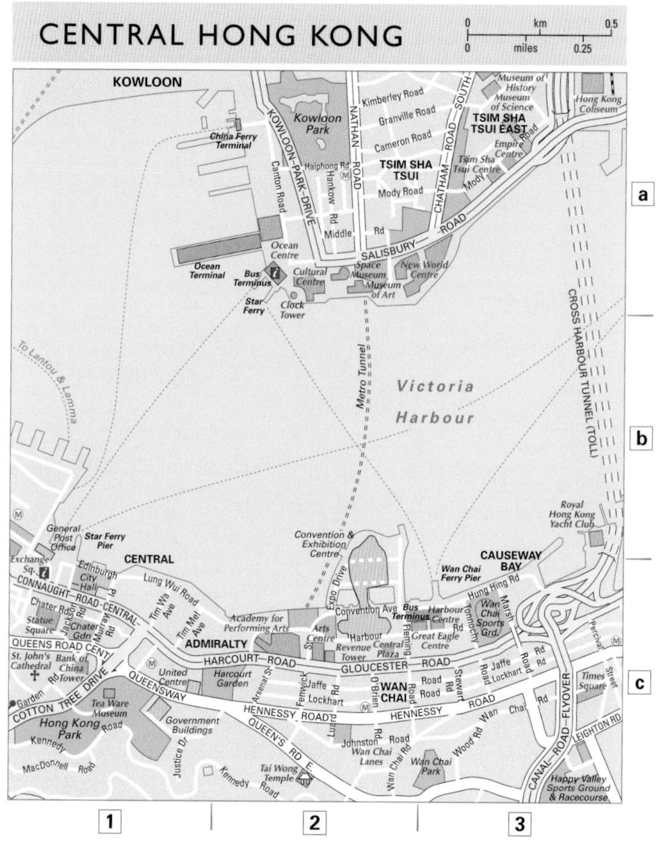
CENTRAL HONG KONG
km 0 0.5
miles 0 0.25
KOWLOON
Kowloon Park
Kimberley Road
Granville Road
Cameron Road
Museum of History
Museum of Science
Hong Kong Coliseum
TSIM SHA TSUI EAST
Empire Centre
TSIM SHA TSUI
Tsim Sha Tsui Centre
China Ferry Terminal
Haiphong Rd
Hankow Rd
Canton Road
KOWLOON PARK DRIVE
NATHAN ROAD
CHATHAM ROAD SOUTH
Mody Road
Middle Rd
SALISBURY ROAD
Ocean Centre
Ocean Terminal
Bus Terminus
Star Ferry
Clock Tower
Cultural Centre
Space Museum
Museum of Art
New World Centre
CROSS HARBOUR TUNNEL (TOLL)
To Lantau & Lamma
Metro Tunnel
Victoria Harbour
Royal Hong Kong Yacht Club
General Post Office
Star Ferry Pier
Exchange Sq.
CENTRAL
Convention & Exhibition Centre
Expo Drive
Wan Chai Ferry Pier
CAUSEWAY BAY
Edinburgh Pl
City Hall
Lung Wui Road
Hung Hing Rd
CONNAUGHT ROAD CENTRAL
Chater Road
Statue Square
Chater Gdn
Tim Wa Ave
Tim Mei Ave
Academy for Performing Arts
Convention Ave
Bus Terminus
Harbour Centre
Wan Chai Sports Grd
Arts Centre
Harbour Rd
Great Eagle Centre
QUEENS ROAD CENTRAL
ADMIRALTY
Revenue Tower
Central Plaza
St. John's Cathedral
Bank of China Tower
HARCOURT ROAD
GLOUCESTER ROAD
Garden Rd
COTTON TREE DRIVE
QUEENSWAY
United Centre
Harcourt Garden
Jaffe Rd
Lockhart Rd
WAN CHAI
Times Square
Tea Ware Museum
Hong Kong Park
HENNESSY ROAD
Government Buildings
QUEEN'S RD E.
Johnston Rd
Wan Chai Lanes
Wan Chai Park
Kennedy Road
MacDonnell Road
Justice Dr.
Tai Wong Temple
CANAL ROAD FLYOVER
LEIGHTON RD
Happy Valley Sports Ground & Racecourse
a
b
c
1
2
3

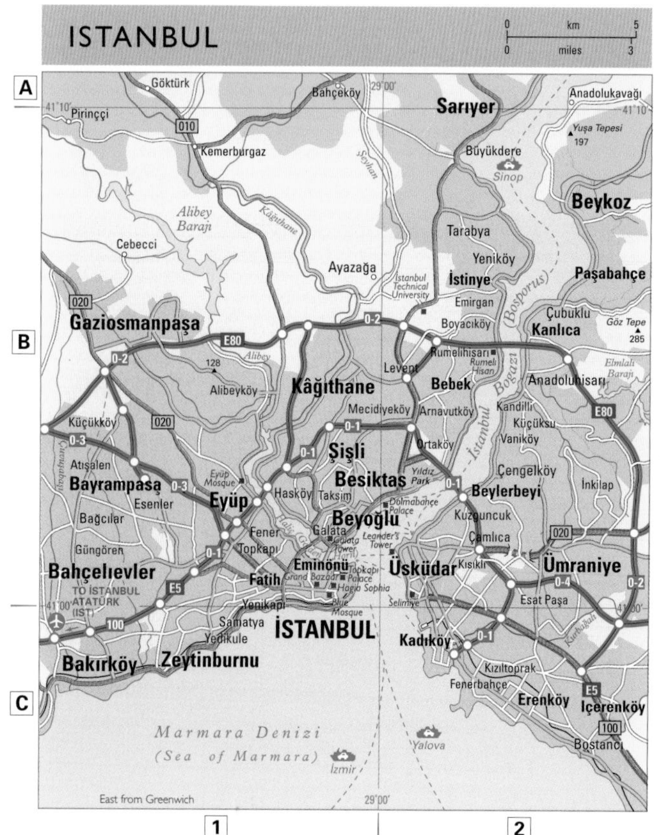
ISTANBUL
km 0 5
miles 0 3
Göktürk
Bahçeköy
29°00'
Sarıyer
Anadolukavağı
41°10'
Pirinççi
010
Yuşa Tepesi 197
Kemerburgaz
Büyükdere
Sinop
Alibey Barajı
Beykoz
Tarabya
Cebecci
Yeniköy
Ayazağa
İstanbul Technical University
İstinye
Paşabahçe
020
Emirgan
Gaziosmanpaşa
E80
Boyacıköy
Çubuklu
Kanlıca
Göz Tepe 285
Rumelihisarı
Bebek
Anadoluhisarı
128
Alibeyköy
Kâğıthane
Levent
Elmalı Barajı
Mecidiyeköy
Arnavutköy
Kandilli
Küçükköy
Şişli
Kuçüksu
Vaniköy
Ortaköy
Atışalen
Bayrampaşa
Beşiktaş
Yıldız Park
Çengelköy
Beylerbeyi
İnkılap
Esenler
Eyüp
Eyüp Mosque
Hasköy
Taksim
Dolmabahçe Palace
Bağcılar
Beyoğlu
Kuzguncuk
Galata
Leander's Tower
Çamlıca
Güngören
Fener
Topkapı
Bahçelıevler
Eminönü
Grand Bazaar
Topkapı Palace
Üsküdar
Ümraniye
Fatih
Hagia Sophia
Kısıklı
TO ISTANBUL ATATÜRK (IST)
Blue Mosque
Selimiye
Esat Paşa
41°00'
Yenikapı
100
Samatya
Yedikule
İSTANBUL
Kadıköy
Bakırköy
Zeytinburnu
Kızıltoprak
Fenerbahçe
Erenköy
İçerenköy
Marmara Denizi (Sea of Marmara)
Yalova
İzmir
Bostancı
East from Greenwich
29°00'
A
B
C
1
2

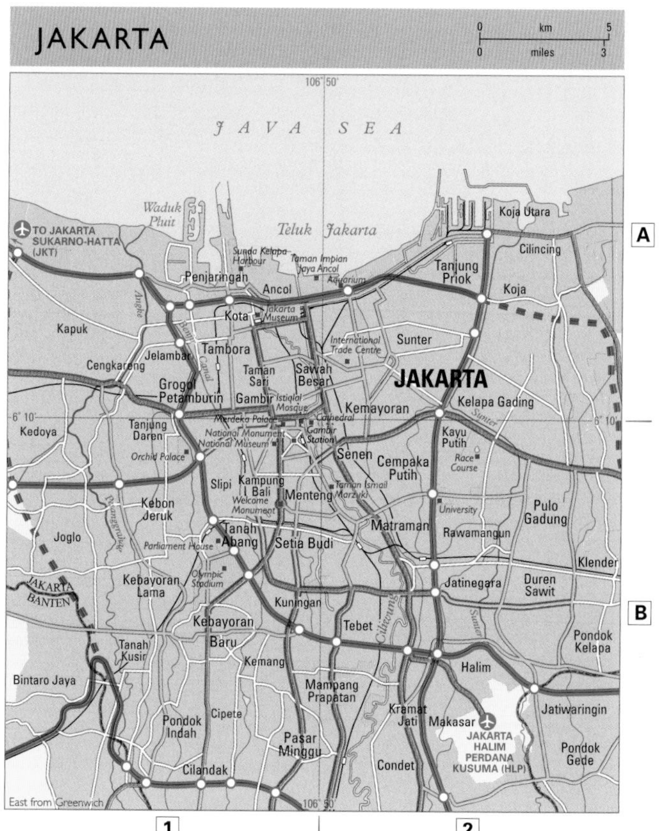
JAKARTA
km 0 5
miles 0 3
106°50'
JAVA SEA
Koja Utara
Waduk Pluit
Teluk Jakarta
TO JAKARTA SUKARNO-HATTA (JKT)
Cilincing
Sunda Kelapa Harbour
Taman Impian Jaya Ancol
Aquarium
Penjaringan
Tanjung Priok
Ancol
Koja
Kapuk
Kota
Jakarta Museum
International Trade Centre
Sunter
Jelambar
Tambora
Cengkareng
Taman Sari
Sawah Besar
JAKARTA
Grogol Petamburin
Gambir
Istiqlal Mosque
Kemayoran
Kelapa Gading
Merdeka Palace
Cathedral
6°10'
Kedoya
Tanjung Duren
National Monument
National Museum
Gambir Station
Kayu Putih
Orchid Palace
Senen
Cempaka Putih
Race Course
Slipi
Kampung Bali
Taman Ismail Marzuki
University
Pulo Gadung
Kebon Jeruk
Welcome Monument
Menteng
Matraman
Rawamangun
Joglo
Parliament House
Tanah Abang
Setia Budi
Klender
Kebayoran Lama
Olympic Stadium
Jatinegara
Duren Sawit
JAKARTA BANTEN
Kuningan
Kebayoran Baru
Tebet
Pondok Kelapa
Tanah Kusir
Kemang
Halim
Bintaro Jaya
Mampang Prapatan
Kramat Jati
Makasar
Jatiwaringin
Pondok Indah
Cipete
JAKARTA HALIM PERDANA KUSUMA (HLP)
Pasar Minggu
Condet
Pondok Gede
Cilandak
East from Greenwich
106°50'
A
B
1
2

JERUSALEM

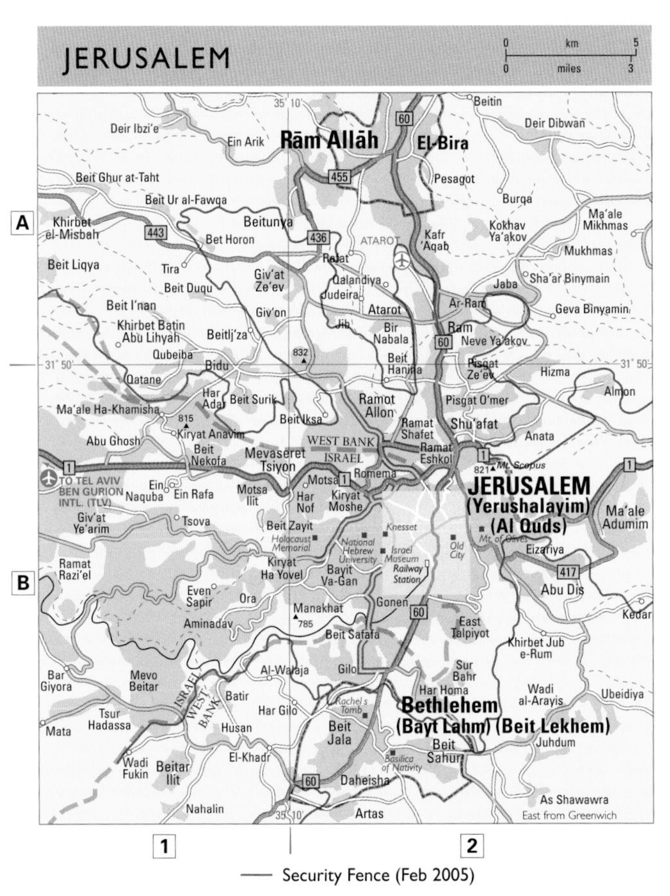

— Security Fence (Feb 2005)

CENTRAL JERUSALEM

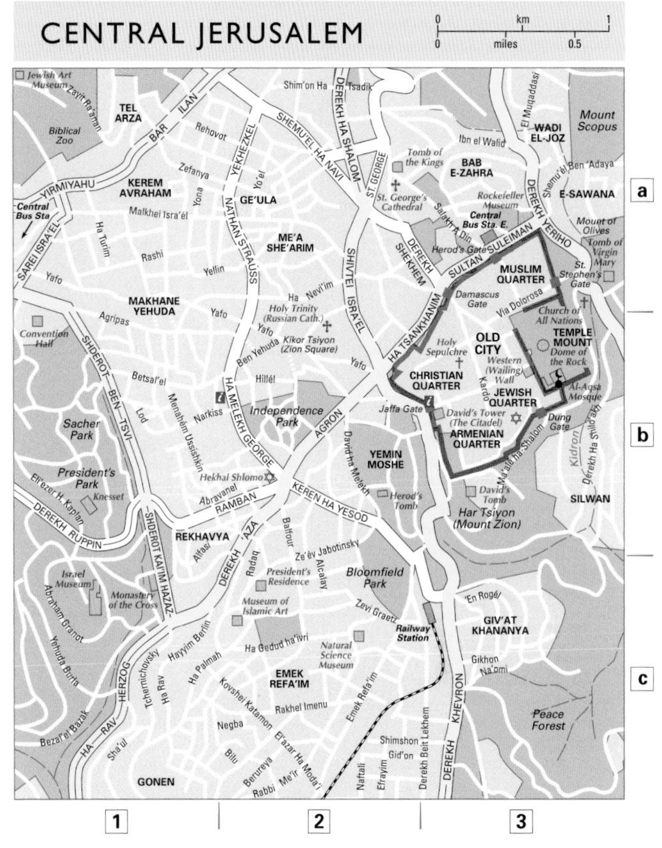

JOHANNESBURG

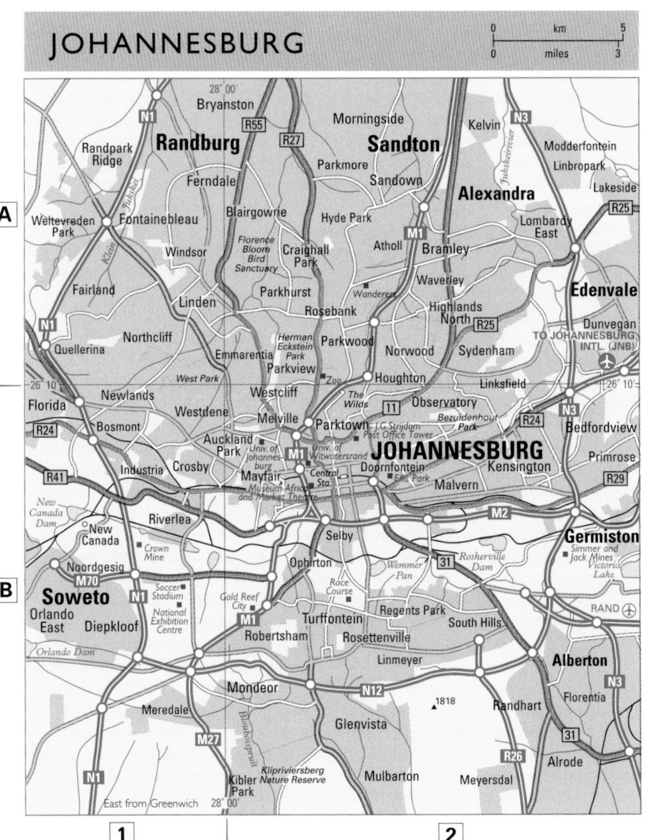

KARACHI

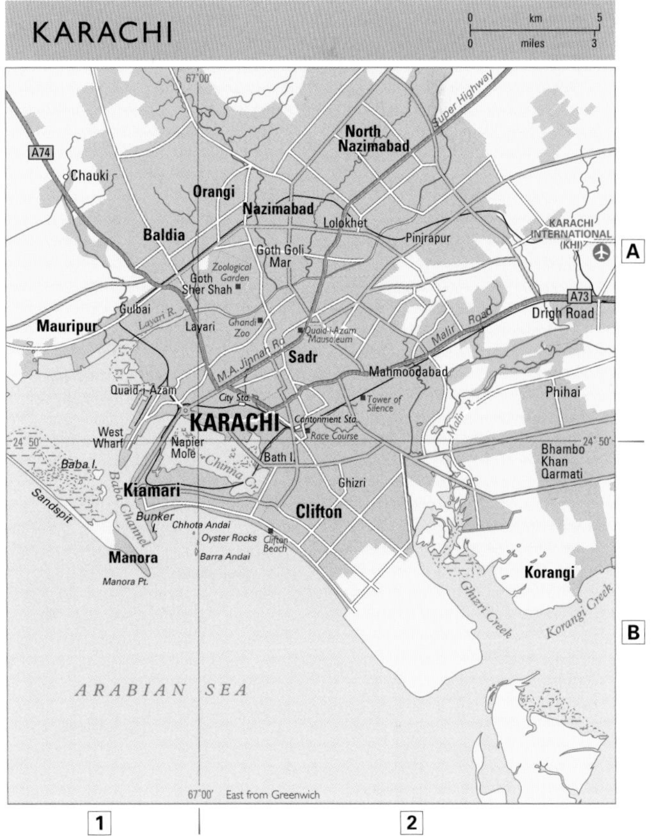

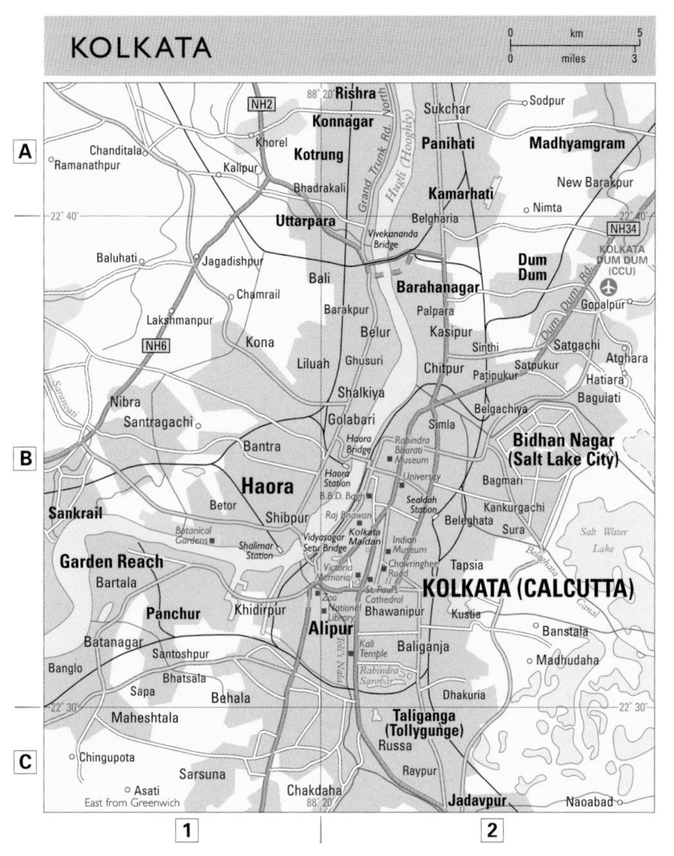

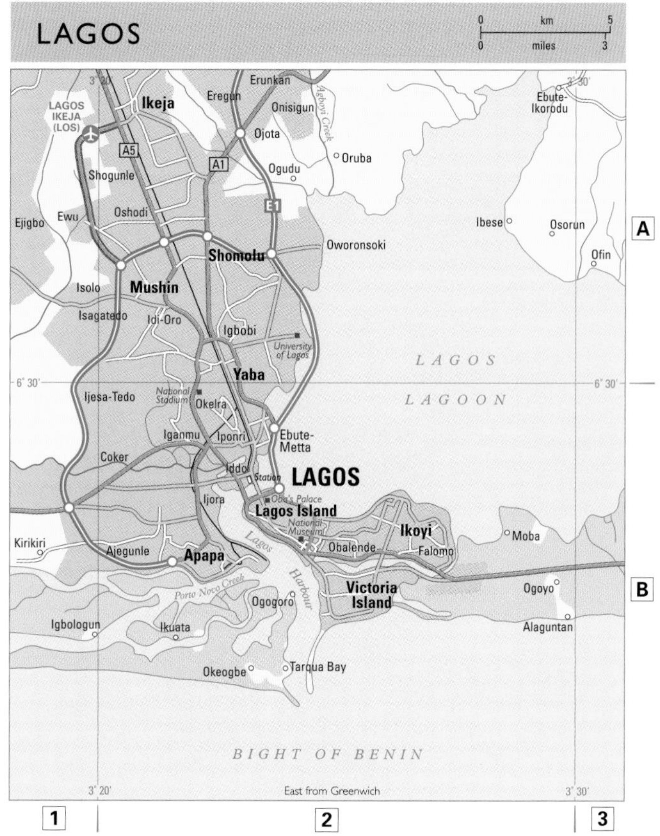

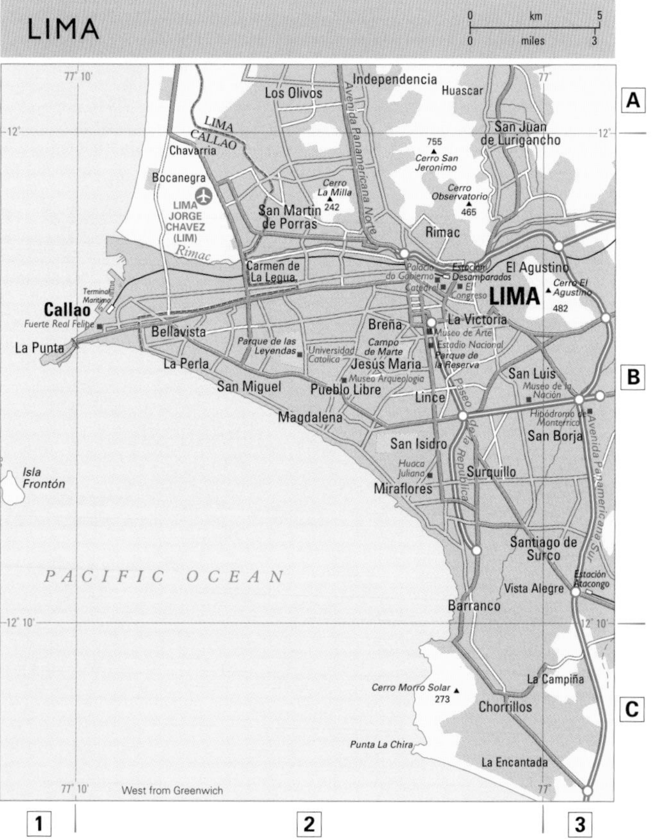

Interstate route numbers U.S. route numbers State route numbers

LONDON

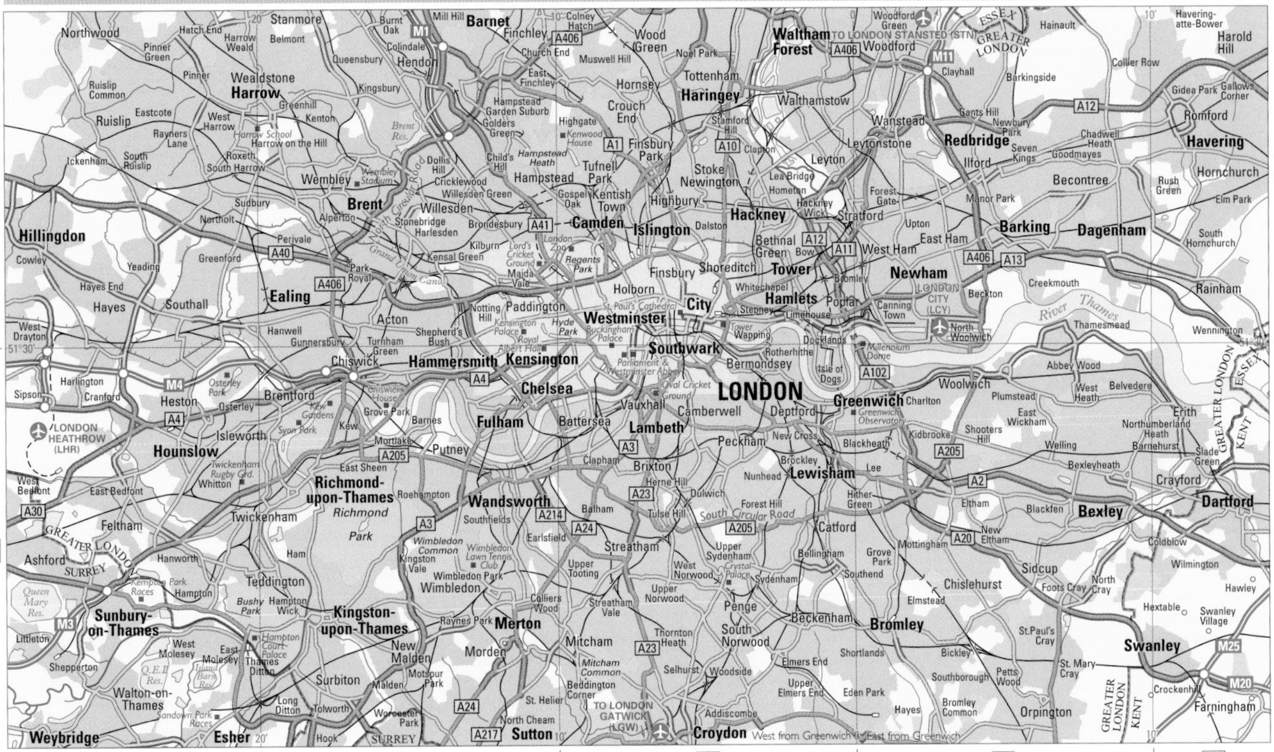

0 km 5
0 miles 3

CENTRAL LONDON

0 km 2
0 miles 1

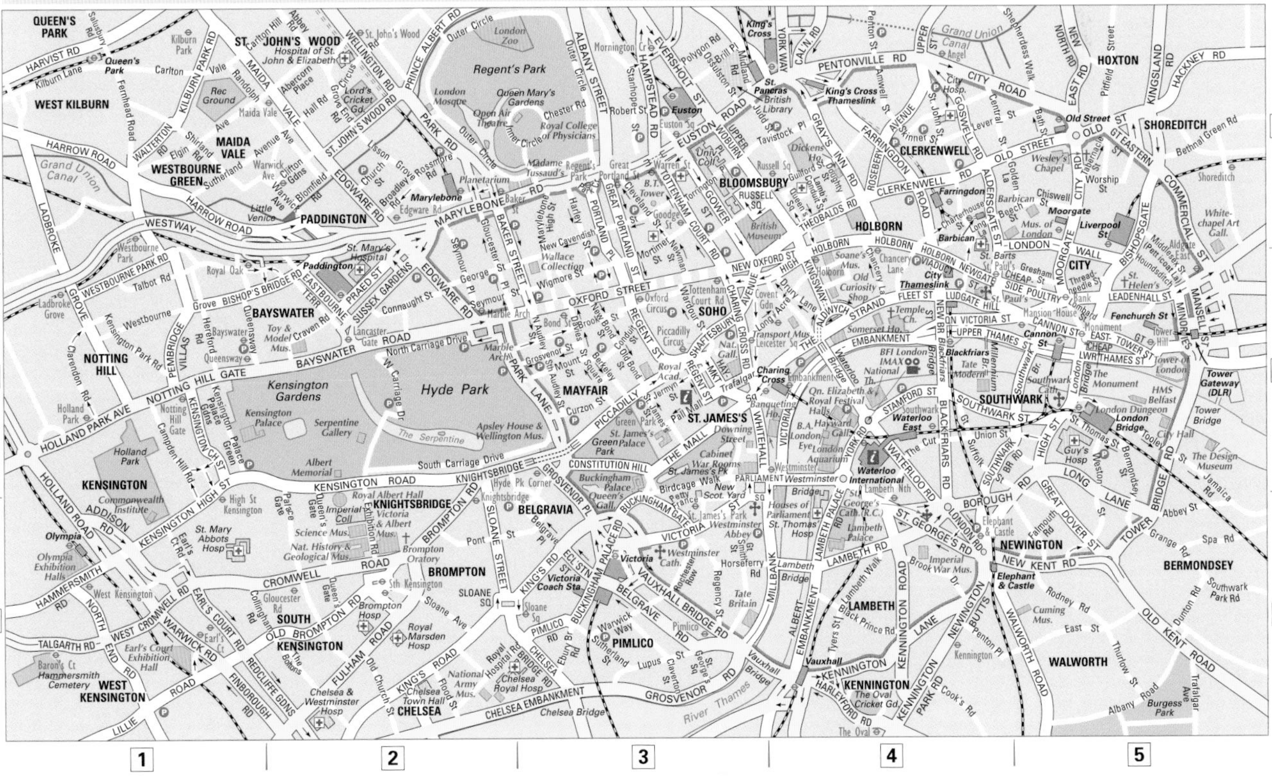

Congestion Charging Zone

LISBON

0 km 5
0 miles 3

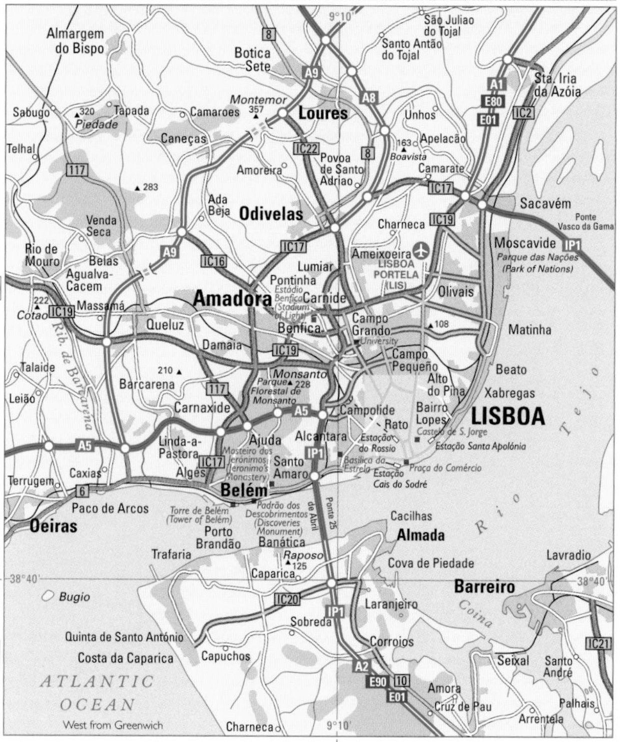

West from Greenwich

CENTRAL LISBON

0 km 1
0 miles 0.5

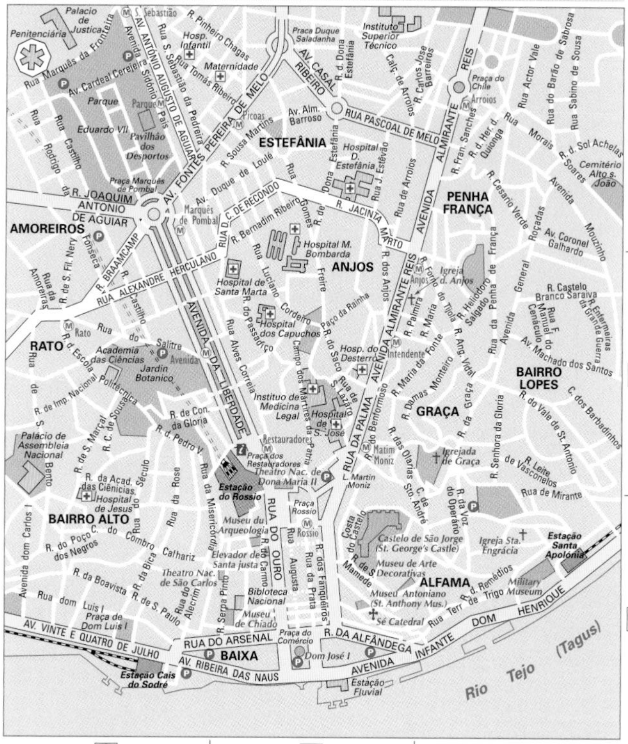

LOS ANGELES

0 km 5
0 miles 3

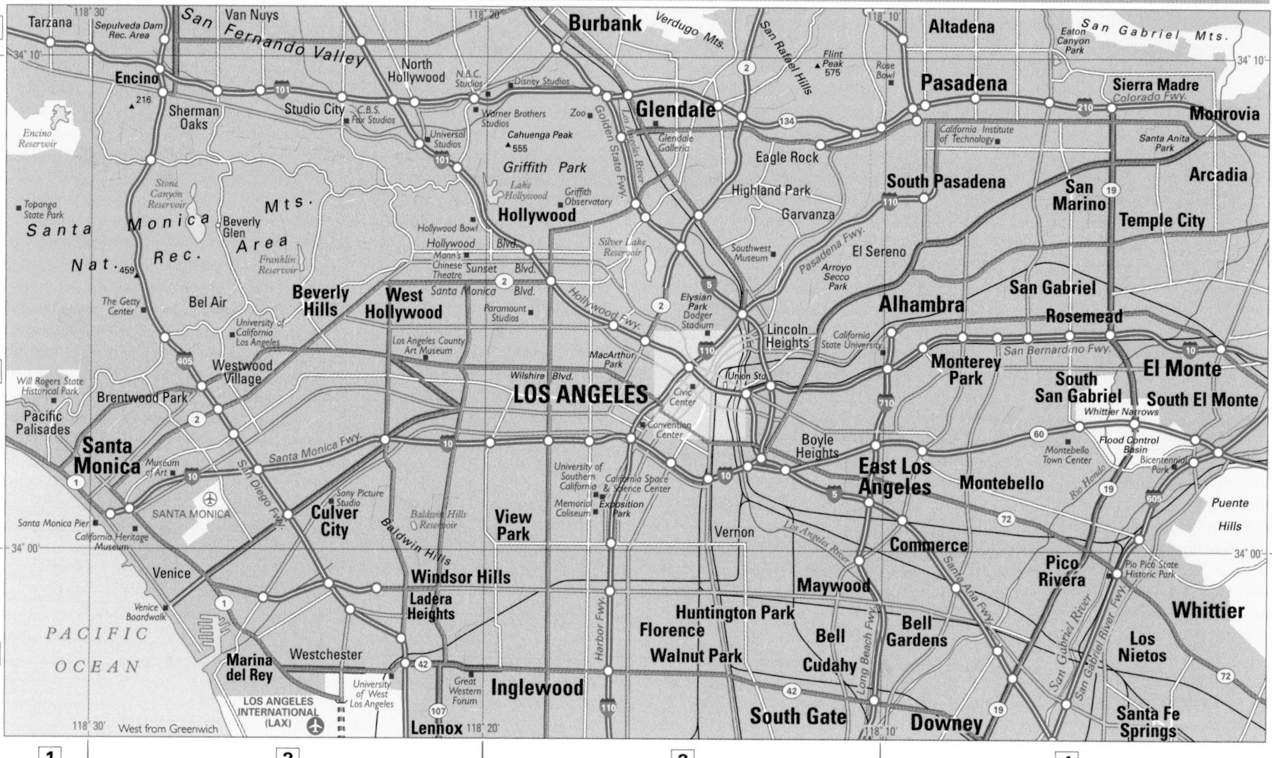

West from Greenwich

Interstate route numbers
State route numbers

MADRID

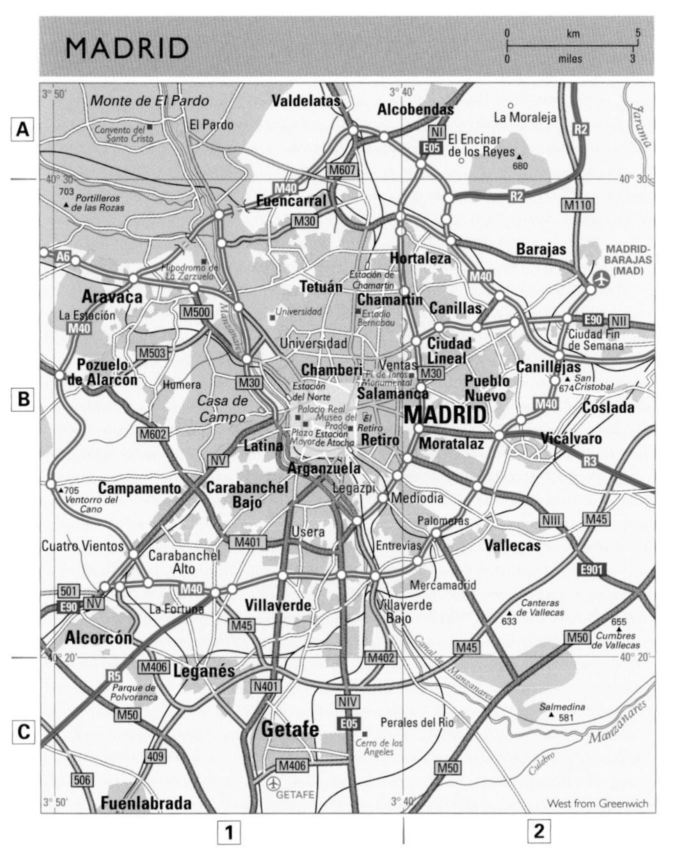

CENTRAL MADRID

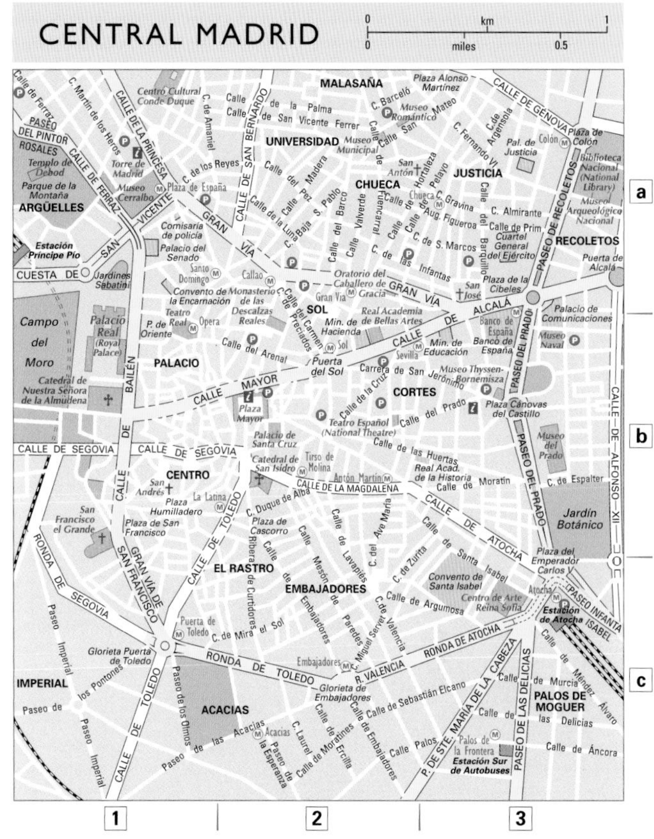

CENTRAL LOS ANGELES

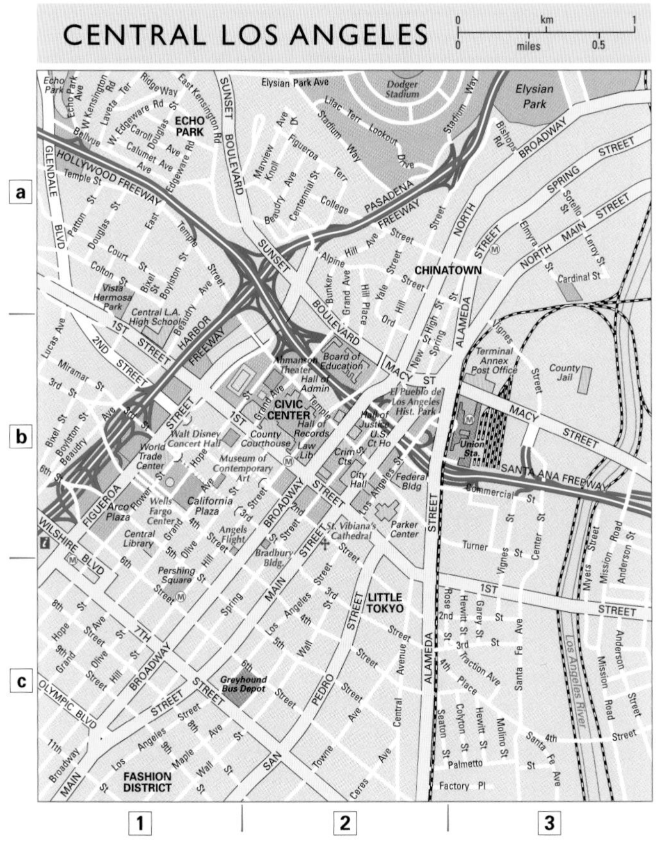

MANILA

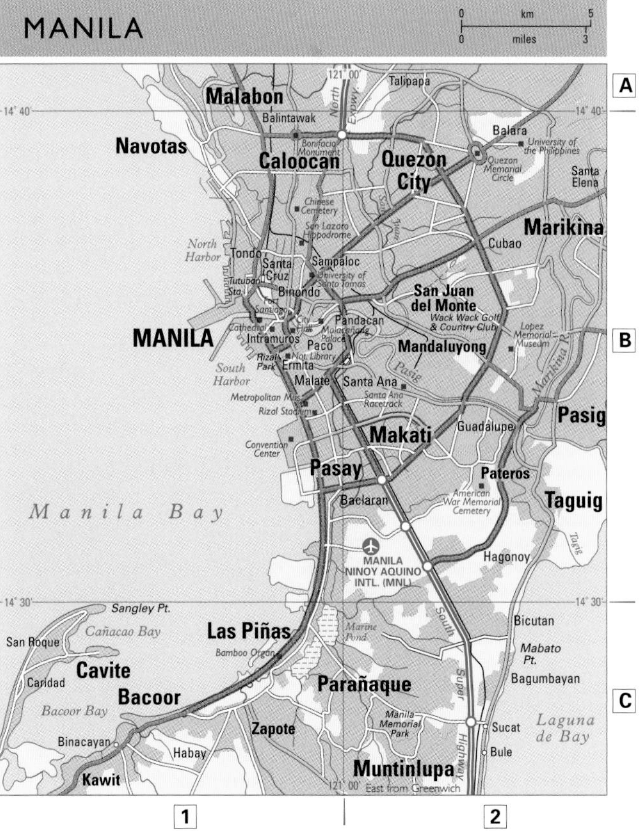

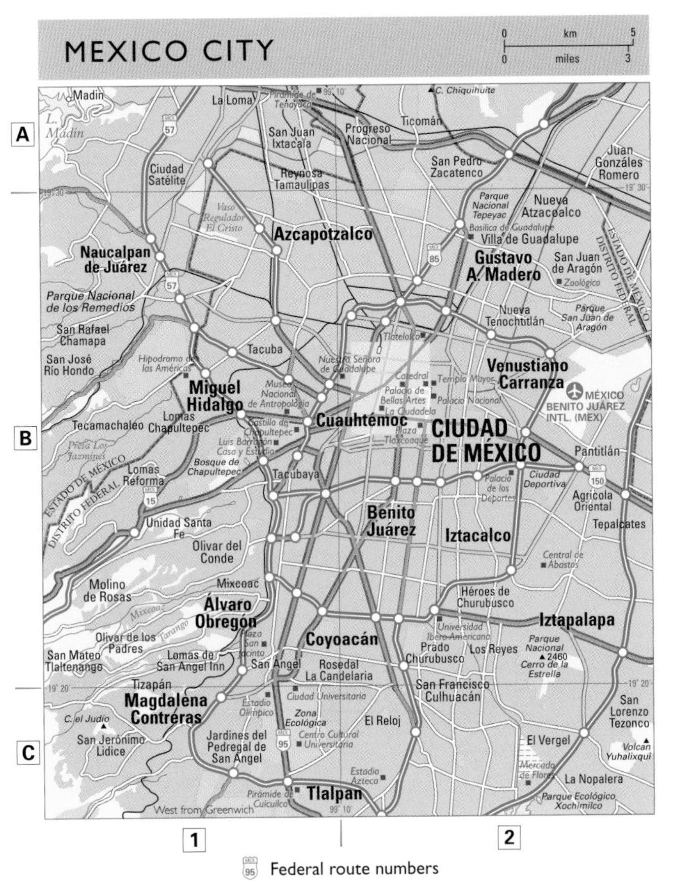
MEXICO CITY
km
miles
Madin
L. Madin
La Loma
Pirámide de Tenayuca
C. Chiquihuite
Ticomán
San Juan Ixtacala
Progreso Nacional
Juan Gonzáles Romero
Ciudad Satélite
Reynosa Tamaulipas
San Pedro Zacatenco
Vaso Regulador El Cristo
Azcapotzalco
Parque Nacional Tepeyac
Nueva Atzacoalco
Basilica de Guadalupe
Villa de Guadalupe
Naucalpan de Juárez
Gustavo A. Madero
San Juan de Aragón
Zoológico
ESTADO DE MÉXICO
DISTRITO FEDERAL
Parque Nacional de los Remedios
San Rafael Chamapa
Nueva Tenochtitlán
Parque San Juan de Aragón
Tlatelolco
San José Río Hondo
Tacuba
Hipodromo de las Américas
Nuestra Señora de Guadalupe
Venustiano Carranza
Miguel Hidalgo
Museo Nacional de Antropología
Catedral
Templo Mayor
Palacio de Bellas Artes
Palacio Nacional
MÉXICO BENITO JUÁREZ INTL. (MEX)
Tecamachalco
Lomas Chapultepec
Cuauhtémoc
La Ciudadela
Plaza Tlaxcoaque
CIUDAD DE MÉXICO
Castillo de Chapultepec
Presa Los Jazmines
Luis Barragán Casa y Estudio
Pantitlán
Bosque de Chapultepec
Lomas Reforma
Tacubaya
Palacio de los Deportes
Ciudad Deportiva
Agricola Oriental
Unidad Santa Fe
Benito Juárez
Iztacalco
Tepalcates
Olivar del Conde
Central de Abastos
Molino de Rosas
Mixcoac
Alvaro Obregón
Héroes de Churubusco
Iztapalapa
Olivar de los Padres
Coyoacán
Universidad Ibero-Americana
Parque Nacional Cerro de la Estrella
San Mateo Tlaltenango
Lomas de San Angel Inn
San Angel
Rosedal La Candelaria
Prado Churubusco
Los Reyes
Tizapán
San Francisco Culhuacán
Magdalena Contreras
Estadio Olímpico
Ciudad Universitaria
C. el Judío
Zona Ecológica
El Reloj
San Lorenzo Tezonco
San Jerónimo Lídice
Centro Cultural Universitario
Jardines del Pedregal de San Angel
El Vergel
Volcán Yuhalixqui
Estadio Azteca
Mercado de Flores
La Nopalera
Pirámide de Cuicuilco
Tlalpan
Parque Ecológico Xochimilco
West from Greenwich
A
B
C
1
2
Federal route numbers

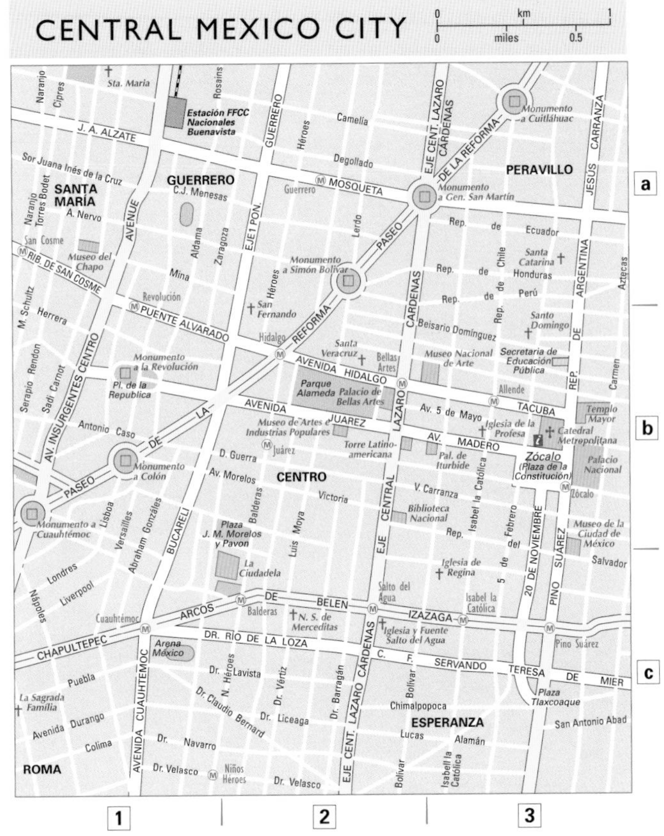
CENTRAL MEXICO CITY
km
miles
Sta. María
Estación FFCC Nacionales Buenavista
Monumento a Cuitláhuac
J. A. ALZATE
GUERRERO
Camelia
Degollado
PERAVILLO
Sor Juana Inés de la Cruz
SANTA MARÍA
GUERRERO
C.J. Menesas
MOSQUETA
Monumento a Gen. San Martín
Ecuador
Museo del Chopo
Monumento a Simón Bolívar
Santa Catarina
Honduras
RIB. DE SAN COSME
Perú
Revolución
PUENTE ALVARADO
San Fernando
REFORMA
Beisario Dominguez
Santo Domingo
Santa Veracruz
Bellas Artes
Museo Nacional de Arte
Secretaria de Educación Pública
Monumento a la Revolución
AVENIDA HIDALGO
Pl. de la República
Parque Alameda
Palacio de Bellas Artes
Allende
TACUBA
Templo Mayor
AVENIDA JUAREZ
Av. 5 de Mayo
Iglesia de la Profesa
Catedral Metropolitana
Museo de Artes e Industrias Populares
Torre Latino-americana
MADERO
Pal. de Iturbide
Zócalo (Plaza de la Constitución)
Palacio Nacional
Monumento a Colón
CENTRO
V. Carranza
Biblioteca Nacional
Monumento a Cuauhtémoc
Plaza J. M. Morelos y Pavon
La Ciudadela
Iglesia de Regina
Museo de la Ciudad de México
Salvador
Salto del Agua
Isabel la Católica
BELEN
IZAZAGA
ARCOS
N. S. de Mercedites
Iglesia y Fuente Salto del Agua
CHAPULTEPEC
DR. RIO DE LA LOZA
Arena México
Pino Suárez
SERVANDO
TERESA
DE MIER
La Sagrada Familia
Plaza Tlaxcoaque
Chimalpopoca
ESPERANZA
San Antonio Abad
ROMA
Niños Héroes
Dr. Velasco
a
b
c
1
2
3

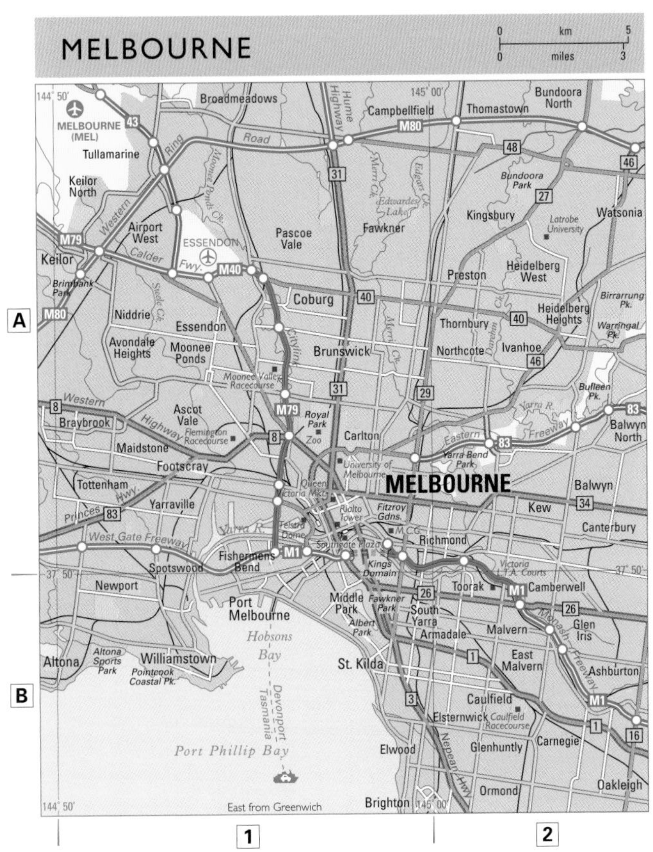
MELBOURNE
km
miles
Broadmeadows
Campbellfield
Thomastown
Bundoora North
MELBOURNE (MEL)
Tullamarine
Keilor North
Bundoora Park
Kingsbury
Watsonia
Latrobe University
Airport West
ESSENDON
Pascoe Vale
Fawkner
Keilor
Preston
Heidelberg West
Coburg
Heidelberg Heights
Niddrie
Essendon
Thornbury
Avondale Heights
Moonee Ponds
Brunswick
Northcote
Ivanhoe
Moonee Valley Racecourse
Braybrook
Ascot Vale
Royal Park
Flemington Racecourse
Zoo
Carlton
Balwyn North
Maidstone
Footscray
Yarra Bend Park
University of Melbourne
Tottenham
MELBOURNE
Balwyn
Yarraville
Fitzroy Gdns.
Kew
West Gate Freeway
Richmond
Canterbury
Spotswood
Fishermens Bend
Victoria Mkt.
Kings Domain
Toorak
Camberwell
Newport
Port Melbourne
Middle Park
Albert Park
South Yarra
Armadale
Malvern
Glen Iris
Hobsons Bay
East Malvern
Altona
Altona Sports Park
Williamstown
Pointcook Coastal Pk.
St. Kilda
Ashburton
Caulfield
Elsternwick
Caulfield Racecourse
Port Phillip Bay
Elwood
Glenhuntly
Carnegie
Ormond
Oakleigh
Brighton
East from Greenwich
A
B
1
2

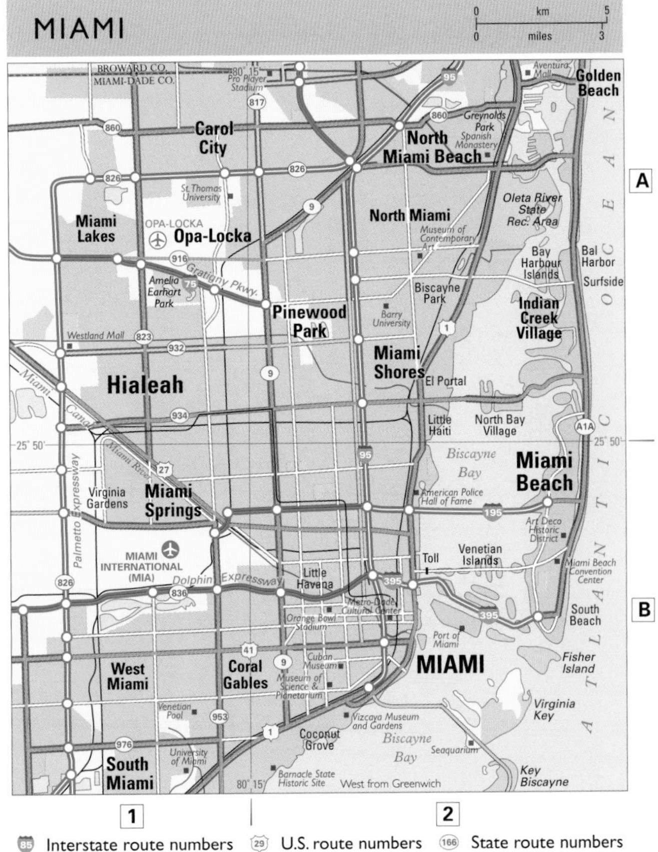
MIAMI
km
miles
BROWARD CO.
MIAMI-DADE CO.
Pro Player Stadium
Golden Beach
Carol City
Greynolds Park
Spanish Monastery
North Miami Beach
St. Thomas University
Oleta River State Rec. Area
Miami Lakes
OPA-LOCKA
Opa-Locka
North Miami
Museum of Contemporary Art
Bay Harbour Islands
Bal Harbour
Amelia Earhart Park
Surfside
Biscayne Park
Pinewood Park
Indian Creek Village
Barry University
Westland Mall
Miami Shores
Hialeah
El Portal
Little Haiti
North Bay Village
Biscayne Bay
Virginia Gardens
Miami Springs
Miami Beach
American Police Hall of Fame
Art Deco Historic District
MIAMI INTERNATIONAL (MIA)
Dolphin Expressway
Little Havana
Toll
Venetian Islands
Miami Beach Convention Center
Orange Bowl Stadium
Metro-Dade Cultural Center
South Beach
Port of Miami
West Miami
Coral Gables
Cuban Museum
Museum of Science & Planetarium
MIAMI
Fisher Island
Venetian Pool
Vizcaya Museum and Gardens
Virginia Key
University of Miami
Coconut Grove
Seaquarium
South Miami
Barnacle State Historic Site
West from Greenwich
Key Biscayne
ATLANTIC OCEAN
A
B
1
2
Interstate route numbers
U.S. route numbers
State route numbers

MILAN

0 km 5
0 miles 3

CENTRAL MOSCOW

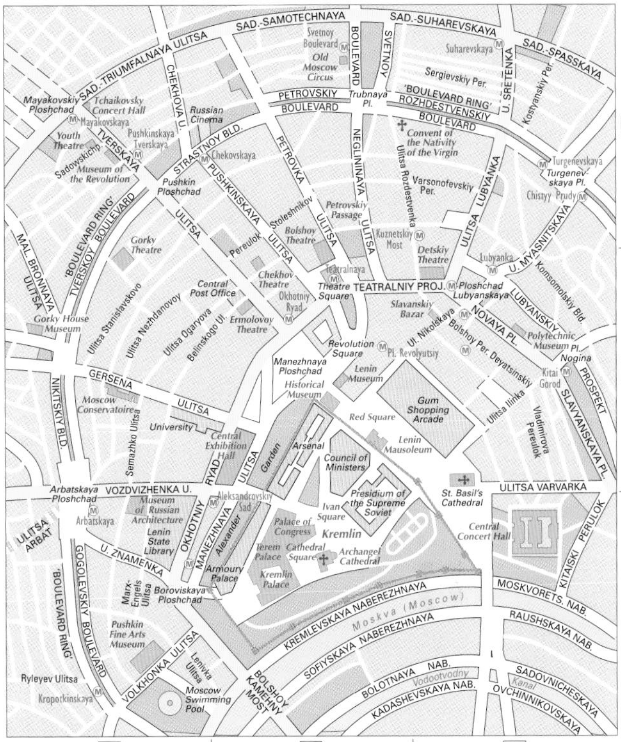

0 km 1
0 miles 0.5

MOSCOW

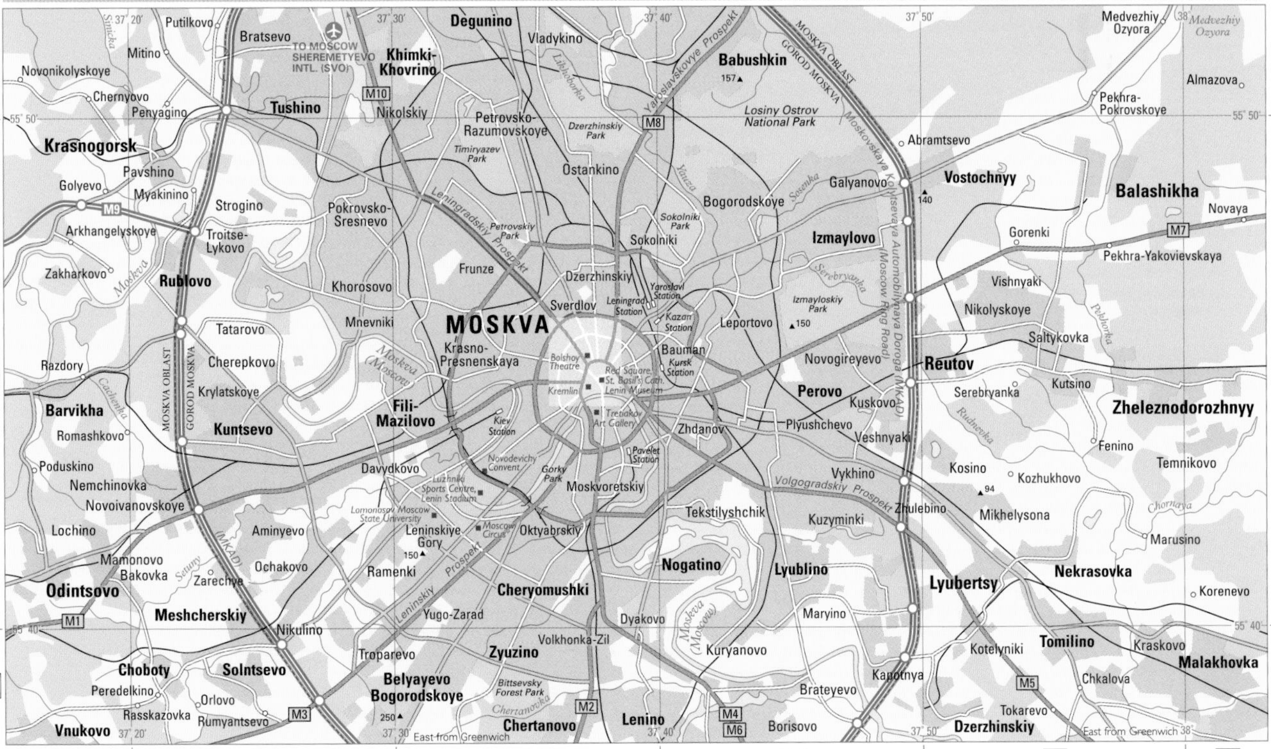

0 km 5
0 miles 3

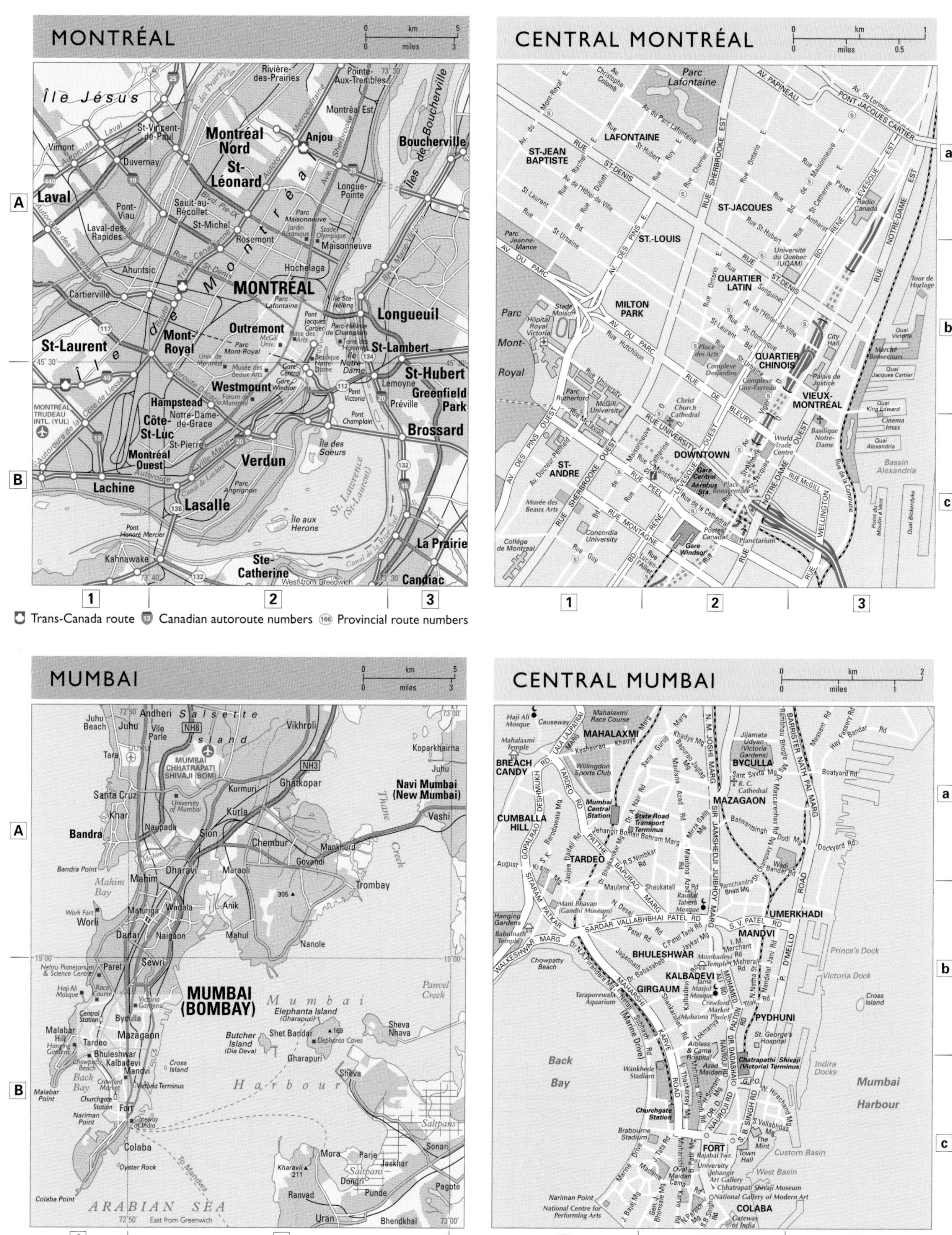
MONTRÉAL
CENTRAL MONTRÉAL
MUMBAI
CENTRAL MUMBAI
km
miles
Trans-Canada route
Canadian autoroute numbers
Provincial route numbers
Île Jésus
Laval
Vimont
Duvernay
Pont-Viau
Laval-des-Rapides
Montréal Nord
St-Léonard
Anjou
Montréal Est
Rivière-des-Prairies
Pointe-Aux-Trembles
Boucherville
Îles de Boucherville
Longue-Pointe
Sault-au-Récollet
St-Michel
Rosemont
Maisonneuve
Hochelaga
Ahuntsic
Cartierville
MONTRÉAL
Longueuil
St-Laurent
Mont-Royal
Outremont
St-Lambert
St-Hubert
Greenfield Park
Westmount
Hampstead
Côte-St-Luc
Lemoyne
Préville
Brossard
Montréal Ouest
Verdun
Île des Soeurs
Lachine
Lasalle
Île aux Herons
St. Lawrence (St-Laurent)
La Prairie
Kahnawake
Ste-Catherine
Candiac
MONTRÉAL TRUDEAU INTL. (YUL)
West from Greenwich
Parc Lafontaine
LAFONTAINE
ST-JEAN BAPTISTE
ST-JACQUES
ST.-LOUIS
QUARTIER LATIN
MILTON PARK
QUARTIER CHINOIS
VIEUX-MONTRÉAL
DOWNTOWN
ST-ANDRE
Parc Mont-Royal
McGill University
Christ Church Cathedral
Gare Central
Gare Windsor
Concordia University
City Hall
Bassin Alexandria
Salsette Island
Andheri
Juhu
Vile Parle
Vikhroli
Ghatkopar
Kurla
Santa Cruz
Khar
Bandra
Navi Mumbai (New Mumbai)
Vashi
Sion
Chembur
Mankhurd
Trombay
Mahim
Dharavi
Worli
Wadala
Dadar
Sewri
Parel
Thane Creek
MUMBAI (BOMBAY)
Mumbai Harbour
Elephanta Island
Sheva
Nhava
Byculla
Mazagaon
Tardeo
Bhuleshwar
Kalbadevi
Mandvi
Back Bay
Colaba
ARABIAN SEA
East from Greenwich
MUMBAI CHHATRAPATI SHIVAJI (BOM)
MAHALAXMI
BREACH CANDY
CUMBALLA HILL
TARDEO
BYCULLA
MAZAGAON
UMERKHADI
MANDVI
BHULESHWAR
KALBADEVI
GIRGAUM
PYDHUNI
FORT
COLABA
Back Bay
Mumbai Harbour
Chatrapathi Shivaji (Victoria) Terminus
Churchgate Station
Mumbai Central Station
Prince's Dock
Victoria Dock
Indira Docks
Gateway of India

MUNICH

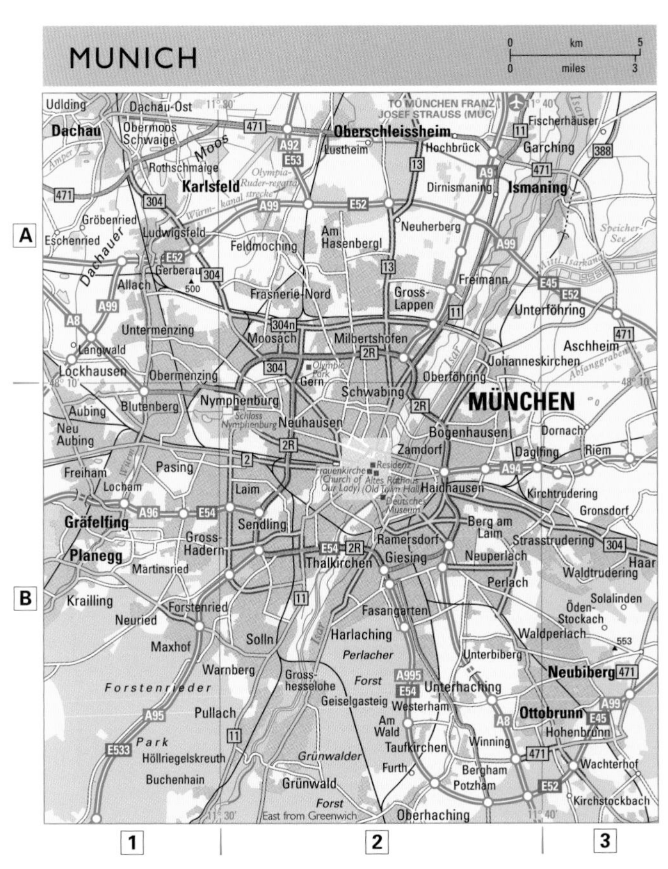

CENTRAL MUNICH

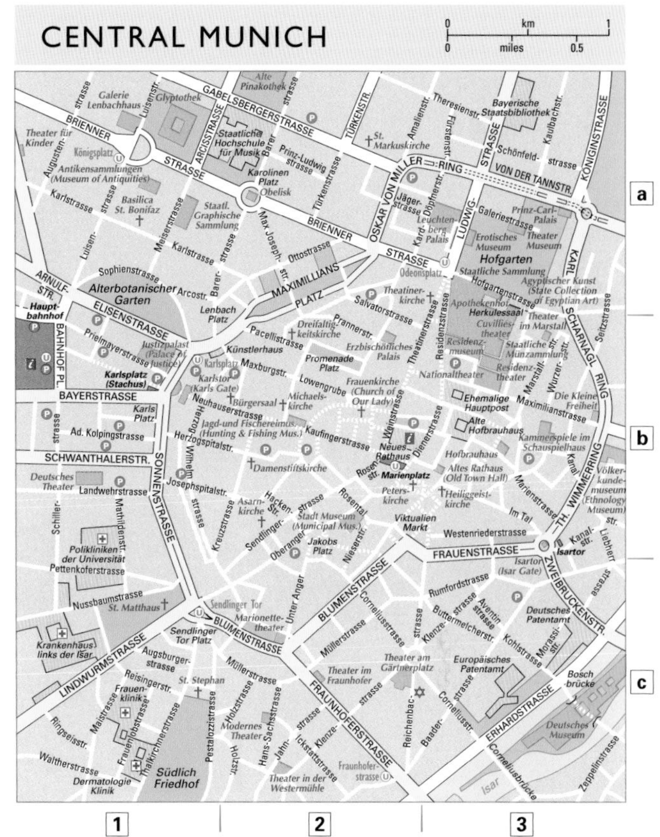

NEW ORLEANS

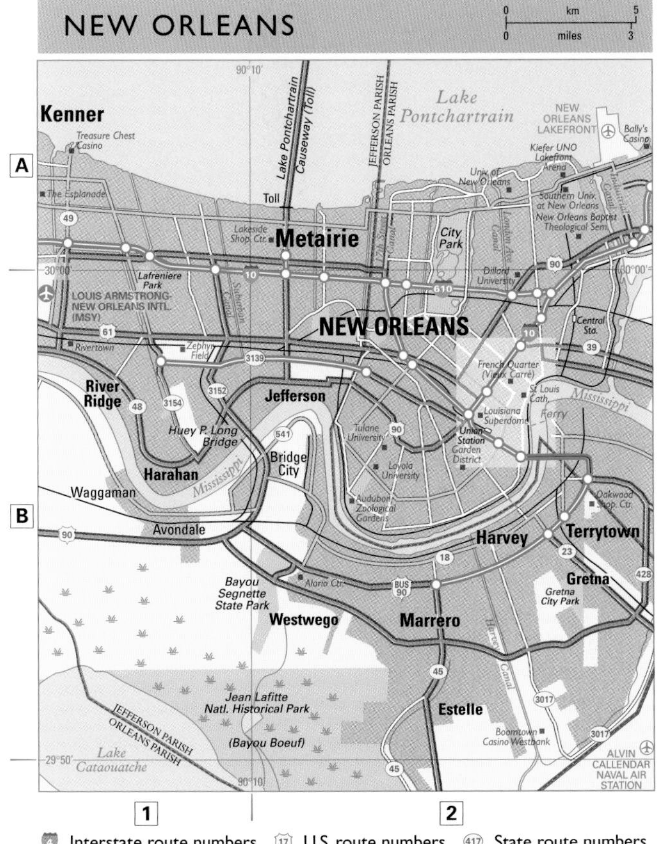

CENTRAL NEW ORLEANS

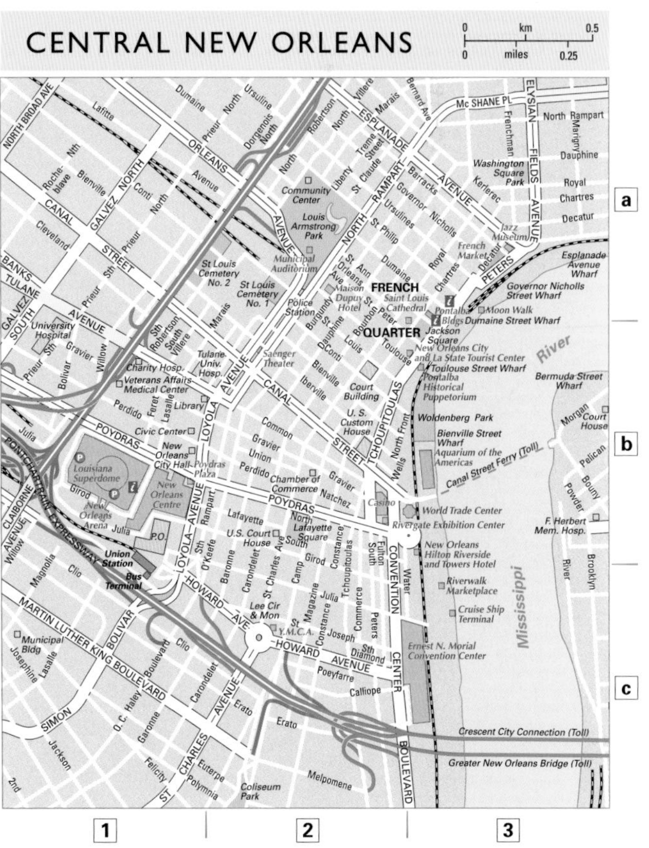

Interstate route numbers · U.S. route numbers · State route numbers

NEW YORK

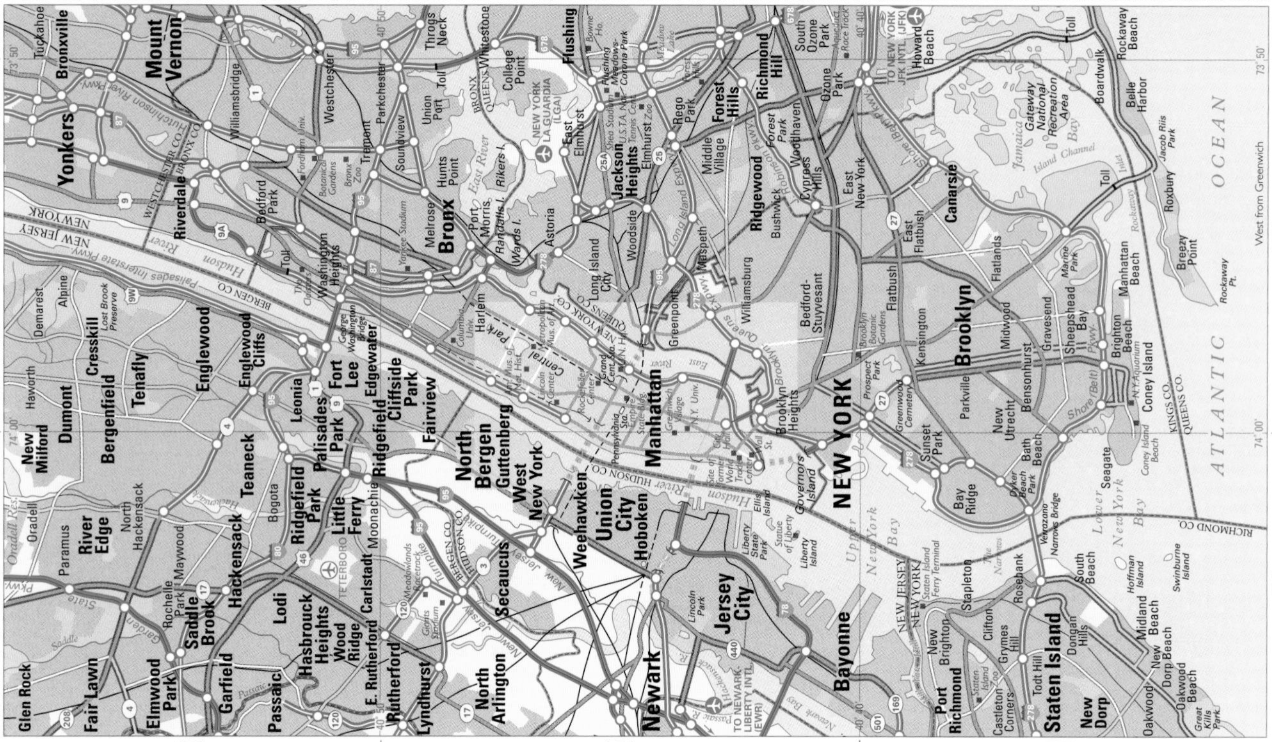

0 km 5
0 miles 3

Interstate route numbers
U.S. route numbers
State route numbers

CENTRAL NEW YORK

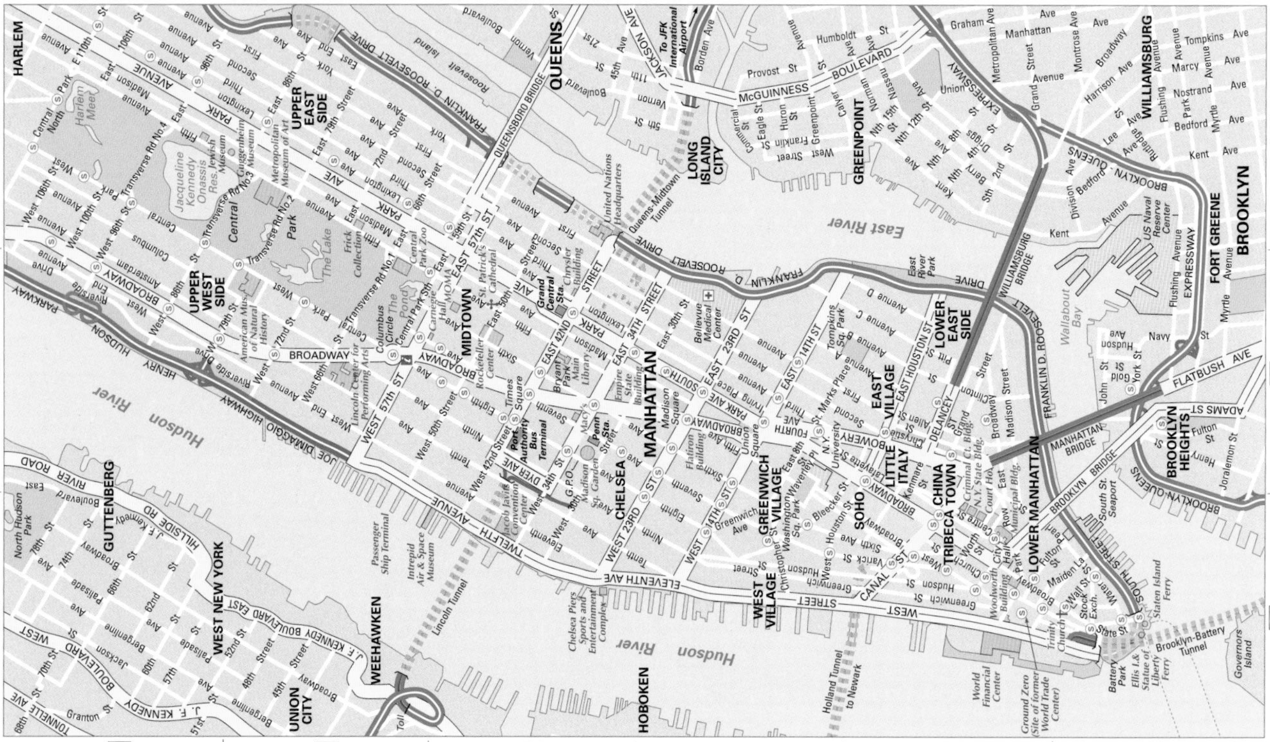

0 km 2
0 miles 1

ORLANDO

0 km 5
0 miles 3

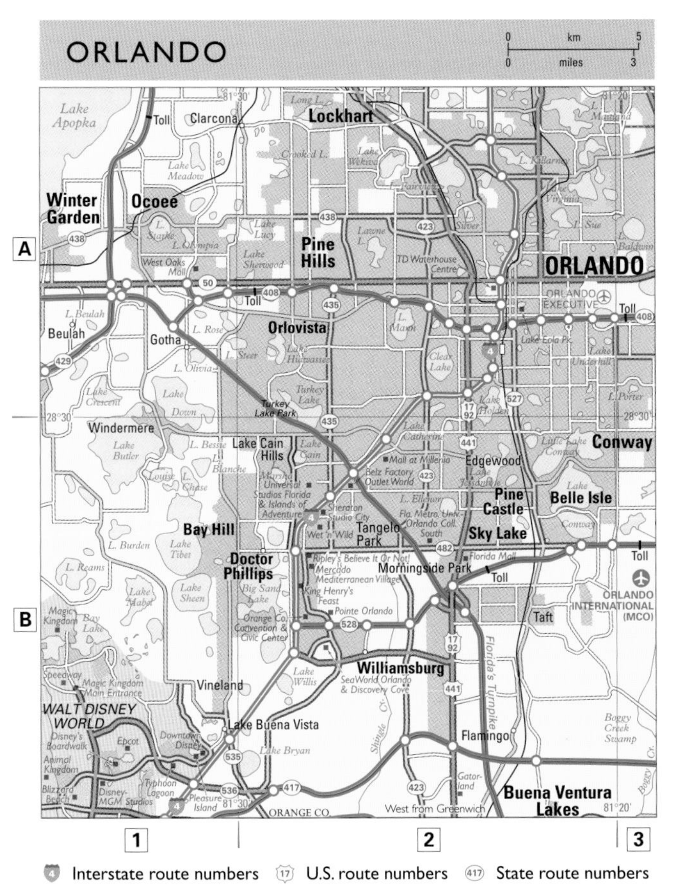

Interstate route numbers U.S. route numbers State route numbers

OSAKA

0 km 5
0 miles 3

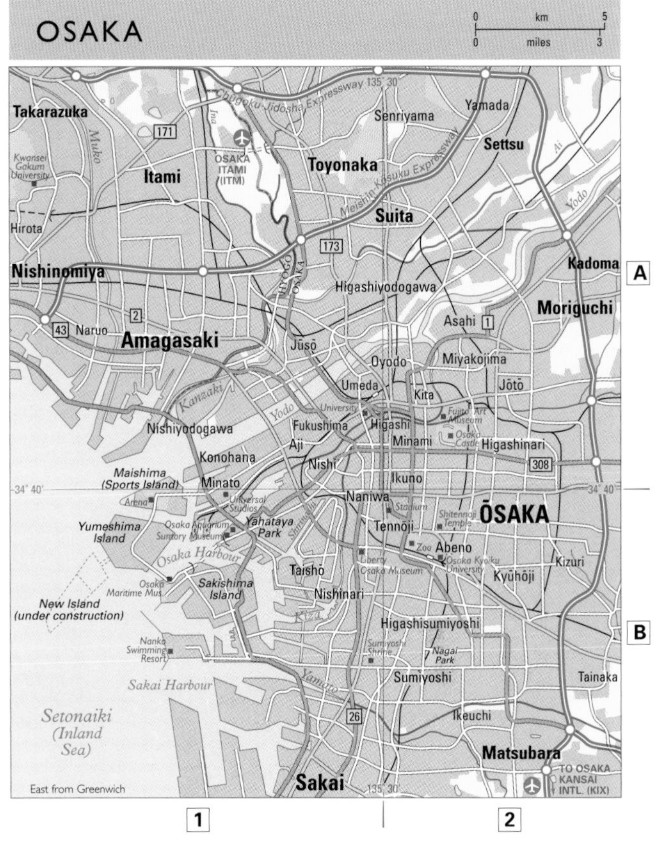

OSLO

0 km 5
0 miles 3

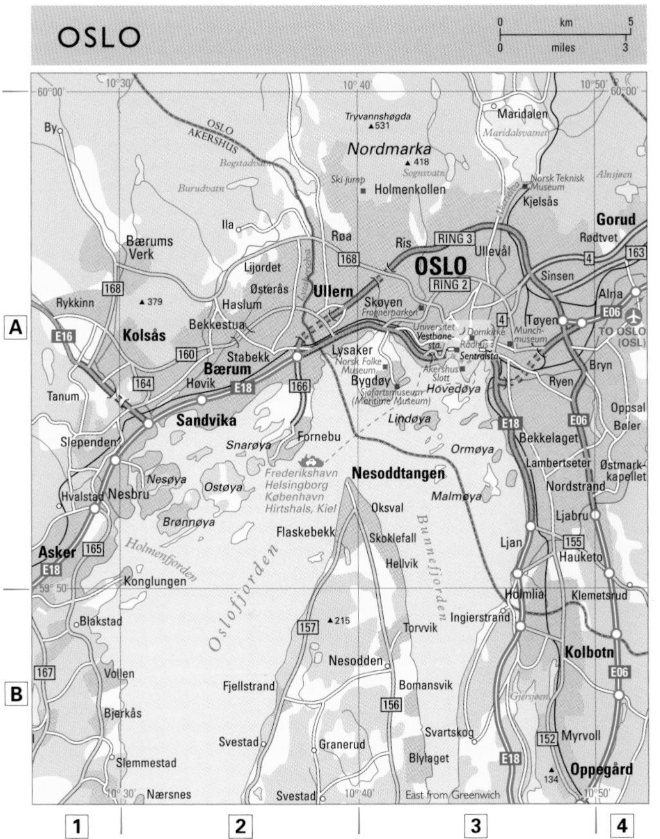

CENTRAL OSLO

0 km 0.5
0 miles 0.25

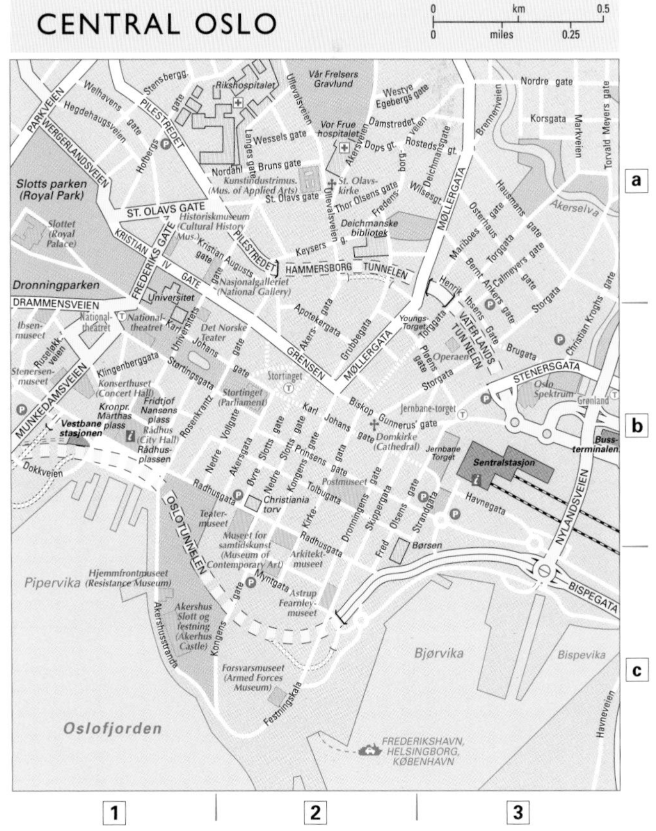

PARIS

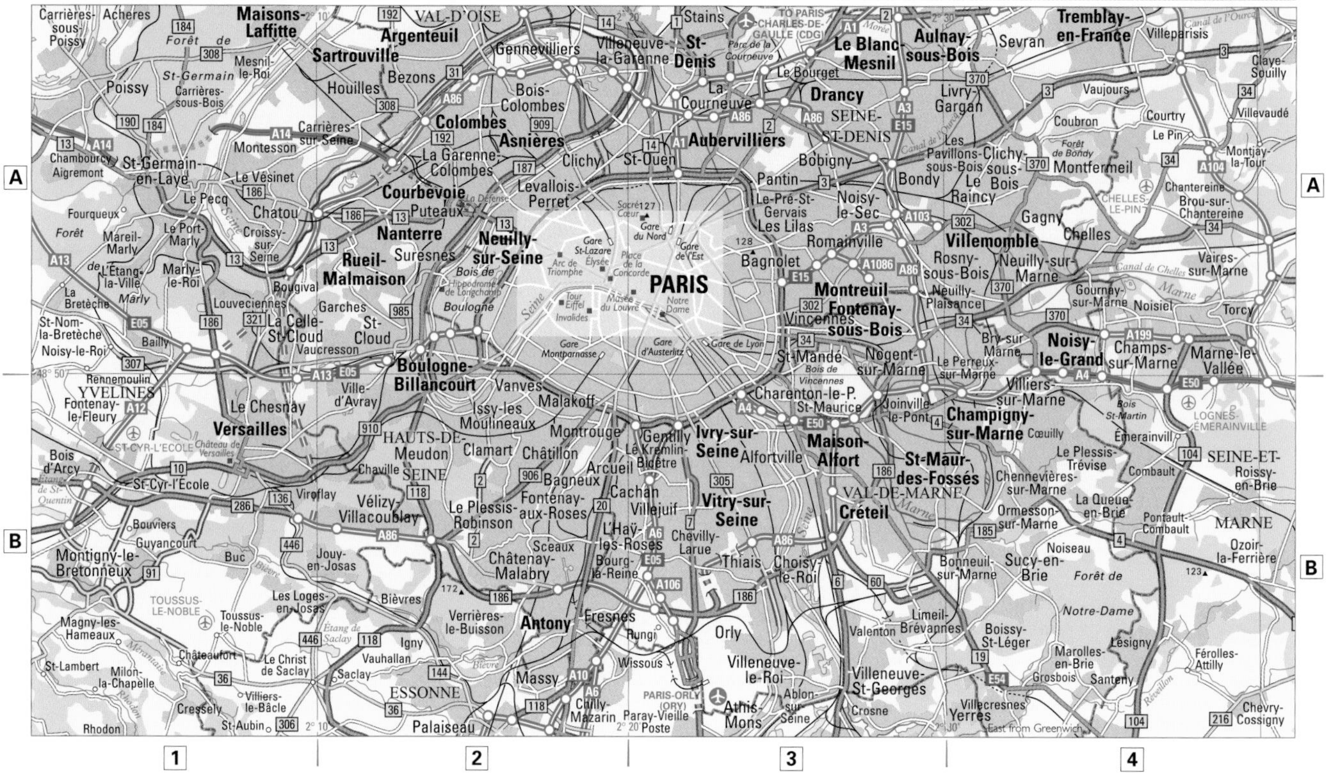

0 km 5
0 miles 3

CENTRAL PARIS

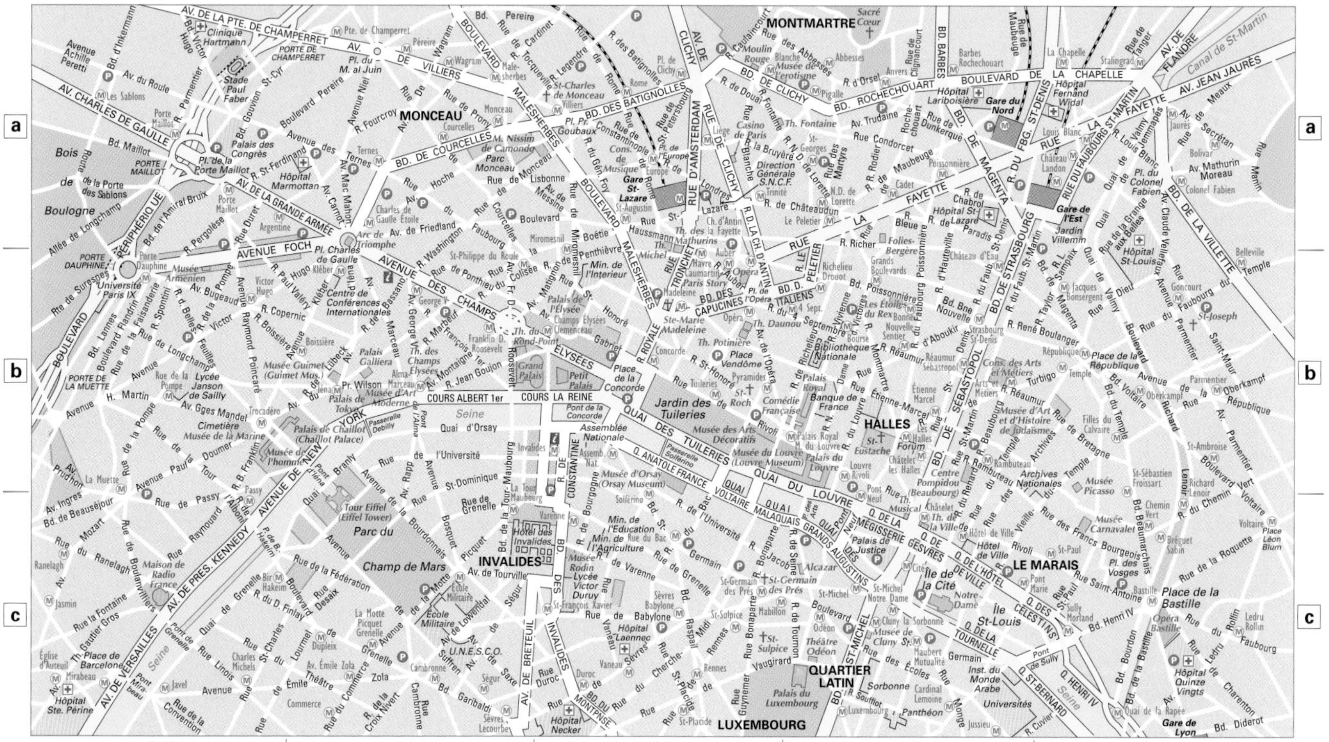

0 km 1
0 miles 0.5

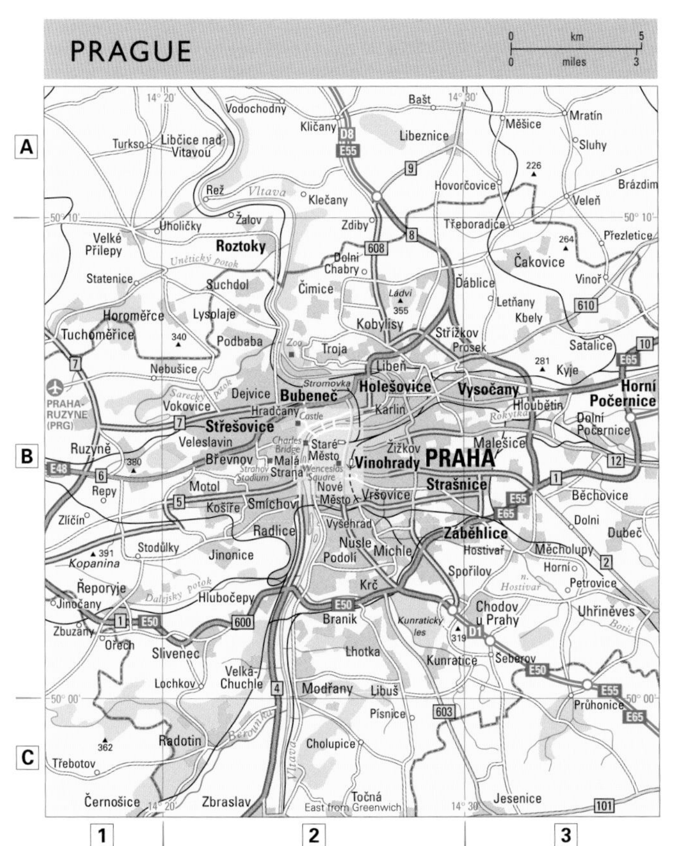
PRAGUE
0 km 5
0 miles 3
Vodochodný
Klíčany
Bašt
Měšice
Mratín
Turkso
Libčice nad Vltavou
Libeznice
Sluhy
Hovorčovice
Brázdim
Řež
Vltava
Klecany
Veleň
Úholičky
Žalov
Zdiby
Třeboradice
Přezletice
Velké Přílepy
Roztoky
Dolní Chabry
Čakovice
Statenice
Suchdol
Čimice
Ďáblice
Vinoř
Horoměřice
Lysolaje
Ládví
Letňany
Kbely
Tuchoměřice
Podbaba
Kobylisy
Střížkov
Satalice
Nebušice
Troja
Prosek
Libeň
Kyje
PRAHA-RUZYNĚ (PRG)
Vokovice
Dejvice
Bubeneč
Holešovice
Vysočany
Hloubětín
Horní Počernice
Hradčany
Střešovice
Karlín
Dolní Počernice
Ruzyně
Veleslavin
Břevnov
Malá Strana
Staré Město
Nové Město
Žižkov
Vinohrady
PRAHA
Malešice
Řepy
Motol
Košíře
Smíchov
Vršovice
Strašnice
Běchovice
Zličín
Radlice
Vyšehrad
Nusle
Michle
Záběhlice
Dolní
Dubeč
Kopanina
Stodůlky
Jinonice
Podolí
Hostivař
Měcholupy
Řeporyje
Jinočany
Hlubočepy
Krč
Spořilov
Horní
Petrovice
Zbuzany
Ořech
Braník
Chodov u Prahy
Uhříněves
Slivenec
Lhotka
Kunratice
Šeberov
Lochkov
Velká Chuchle
Modřany
Libuš
Průhonice
Písnice
Radotín
Třebotov
Cholupice
Černošice
Zbraslav
Točná
Jesenice
East from Greenwich
A
B
C
1
2
3

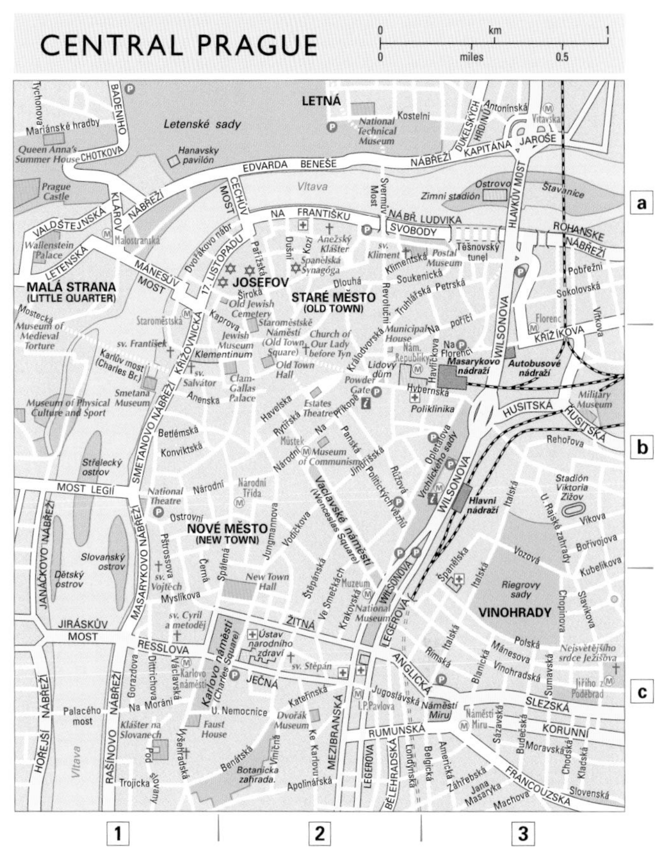
CENTRAL PRAGUE
0 km 1
0 miles 0.5
LETNÁ
Letenské sady
National Technical Museum
Hanavsky pavilon
Queen Anna's Summer House
Prague Castle
Vltava
Zimní stadión
MALÁ STRANA (LITTLE QUARTER)
JOSEFOV
STARÉ MĚSTO (OLD TOWN)
Old Jewish Cemetery
Jewish Museum
Klementinum
Clam-Gallas Palace
Karlův most (Charles Br.)
Old Town Hall
Powder Gate
Masarykovo nádraží
Autobusové nádraží
Museum of Physical Culture and Sport
Estates Theatre
National Theatre
NOVÉ MĚSTO (NEW TOWN)
Museum of Communism
Slovanský ostrov
Dětský ostrov
New Town Hall
Hlavní nádraží
VINOHRADY
Riegrovy sady
Dvořák Museum
Faust House
Botanická zahrada
WILSONOVA
a
b
c
1
2
3

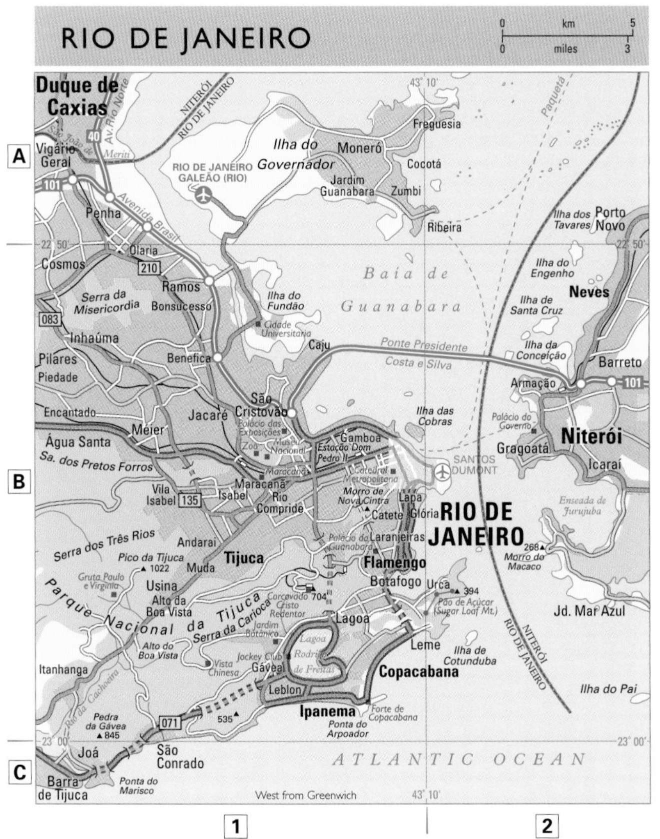
RIO DE JANEIRO
0 km 5
0 miles 3
Duque de Caxias
Vigário Geral
Penha
Olaria
Cosmos
Ramos
Serra da Misericordia
Bonsucesso
Inhaúma
Pilares
Piedade
Encantado
Méier
Água Santa
Sa. dos Pretos Forros
Ilha do Governador
RIO DE JANEIRO GALEÃO (RIO)
Moneró
Cocotá
Jardim Guanabara
Zumbi
Freguesia
Ribeira
Ilha do Fundão
Baía de Guanabara
Ilha do Engenho
Neves
Ilha de Santa Cruz
Ponte Presidente Costa e Silva
Caju
Benfica
Jacaré
São Cristovão
Barreto
Niterói
Gragoatá
Icaraí
SANTOS DUMONT
Vila Isabel
Maracanã
Rio Comprido
RIO DE JANEIRO
Flamengo
Botafogo
Urca
Pão de Açúcar (Sugar Loaf Mt.)
Morro do Macaco
Jd. Mar Azul
Serra dos Três Rios
Pico da Tijuca 1022
Andaraí
Tijuca
Muda
Usina
Parque Nacional da Tijuca
Lagoa
Leme
Copacabana
Gávea
Leblon
Ipanema
Itanhanga
Pedra da Gávea 845
Joá
São Conrado
Barra de Tijuca
ATLANTIC OCEAN
Ilha do Pai
West from Greenwich
A
B
C
1
2

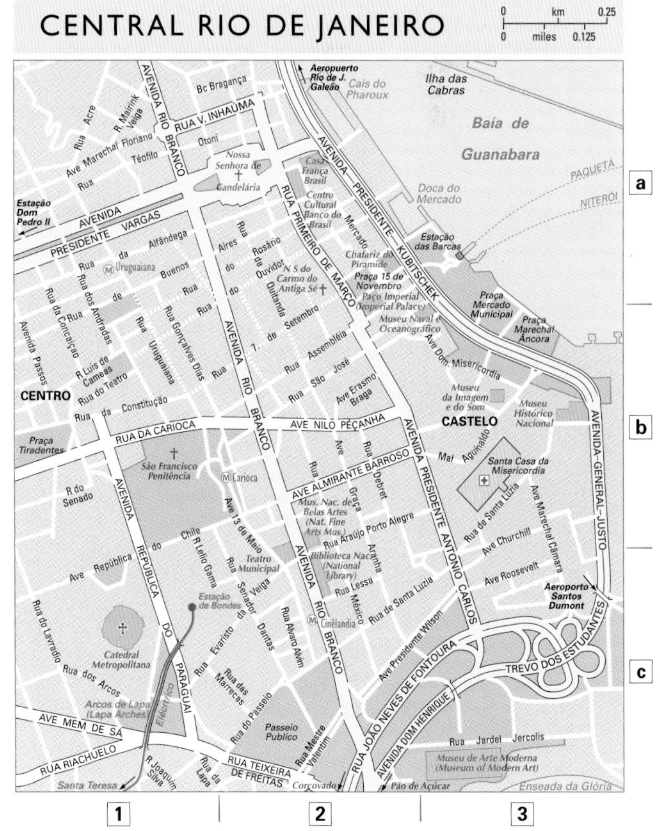
CENTRAL RIO DE JANEIRO
0 km 0.25
0 miles 0.125
Aeropuerto Rio de J. Galeão
Cais do Pharoux
Ilha das Cabras
Baía de Guanabara
Doca do Mercado
Estação Dom Pedro II
AVENIDA PRESIDENTE VARGAS
AVENIDA RIO BRANCO
Candelária
Casa França Brasil
Centro Cultural Banco do Brasil
Estação das Barcas
AVENIDA PRESIDENTE KUBITSCHEK
Praça 15 de Novembro
Paço Imperial (Imperial Palace)
Museu Naval e Oceanográfico
Praça Mercado Municipal
Praça Marechal Âncora
CENTRO
Museu da Imagem e do Som
CASTELO
Museu Histórico Nacional
Praça Tiradentes
RUA DA CARIOCA
AVE NILO PEÇANHA
São Francisco Penitência
AVE ALMIRANTE BARROSO
Santa Casa da Misericórdia
Mus. Nac. de Belas Artes (Nat. Fine Arts Mus.)
Teatro Municipal
Biblioteca Nacional (National Library)
Aeroporto Santos Dumont
Catedral Metropolitana
AVENIDA REPÚBLICA DO PARAGUAI
Estação de Bondes
Arcos de Lapa (Lapa Arches)
Passeio Publico
TREVO DOS ESTUDANTES
AVE MEM DE SÁ
RUA RIACHUELO
RUA TEIXEIRA DE FREITAS
Museu de Arte Moderna (Museum of Modern Art)
Pão de Açúcar
Enseada da Glória
Santa Teresa
a
b
c
1
2
3

ROME

0 km 5
0 miles 3

CENTRAL ROME

0 km 1
0 miles 0.5

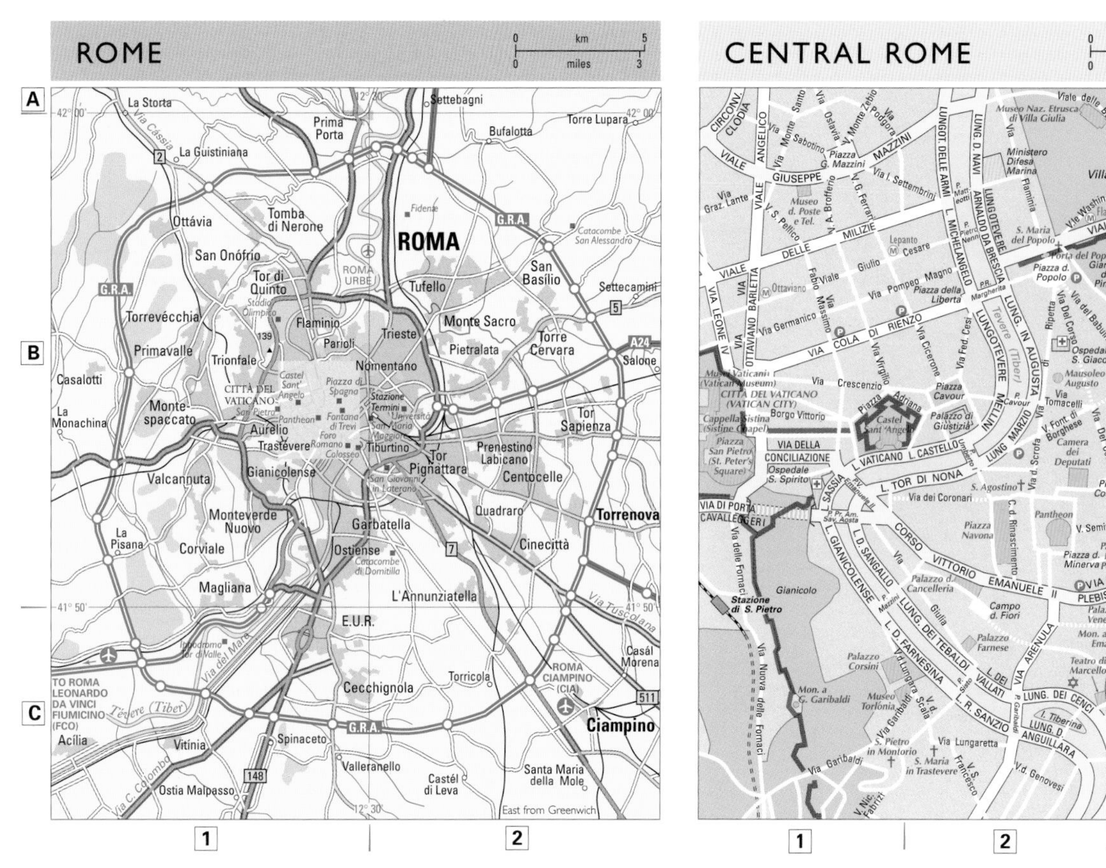

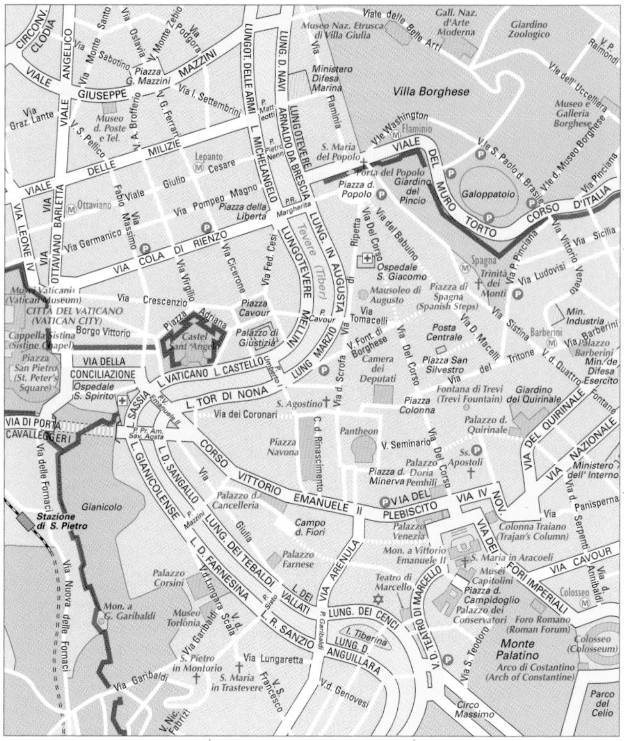

SAN FRANCISCO

0 km 5
0 miles 3

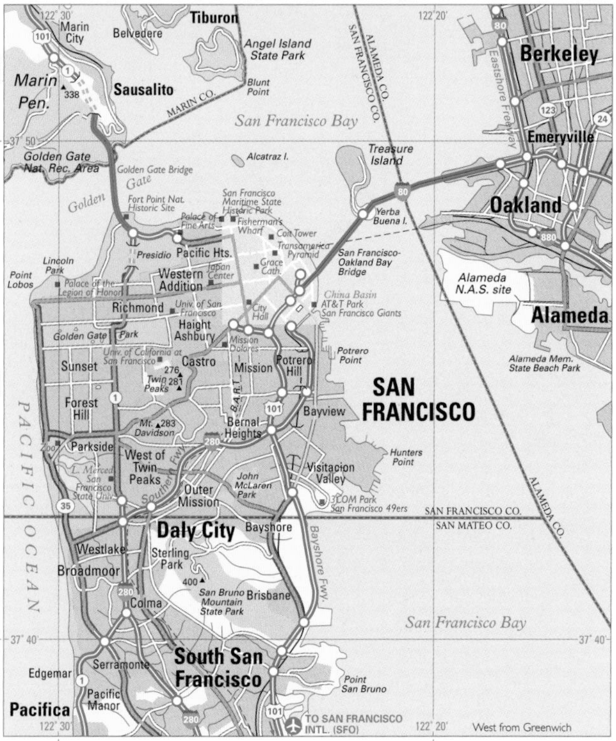

Tiburon, Marin City, Belvedere, Angel Island State Park, Sausalito, Marin Pen., San Francisco Bay, Golden Gate Nat. Rec. Area, Golden Gate Bridge, Alcatraz I., Treasure Island, Yerba Buena I., Berkeley, Emeryville, Oakland, Alameda, Alameda N.A.S. site, Presidio, Pacific Hts., Western Addition, Richmond, Haight Ashbury, Sunset, Castro, Mission, Potrero Hill, Twin Peaks, Forest Hill, Bayview, SAN FRANCISCO, Hunters Point, Parkside, West of Twin Peaks, Outer Mission, Visitacion Valley, Daly City, Bayshore, Westlake, Sterling Park, Broadmoor, Colma, Brisbane, San Bruno Mountain State Park, Edgemar, Serramonte, South San Francisco, Pacifica, Pacific Manor, Point San Bruno, TO SAN FRANCISCO INTL. (SFO), PACIFIC OCEAN, SAN FRANCISCO CO., SAN MATEO CO., West from Greenwich

CENTRAL SAN FRANCISCO

0 km 0.25
0 miles 0.125

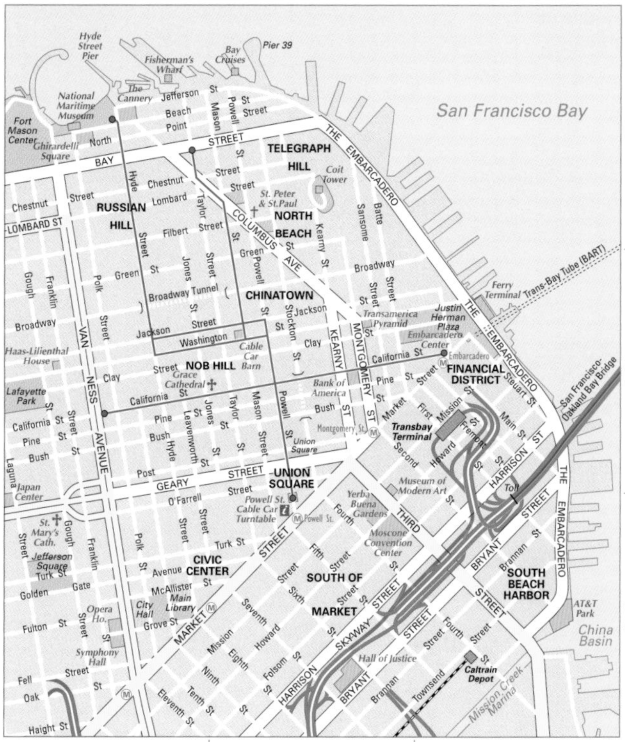

Hyde Street Pier, Fisherman's Wharf, Pier 39, San Francisco Bay, National Maritime Museum, Fort Mason Center, Ghirardelli Square, TELEGRAPH HILL, Coit Tower, RUSSIAN HILL, NORTH BEACH, CHINATOWN, Transamerica Pyramid, Justin Herman Plaza, FINANCIAL DISTRICT, NOB HILL, Grace Cathedral, Cable Car Barn, Transbay Terminal, UNION SQUARE, Museum of Modern Art, Yerba Buena Gardens, Moscone Convention Center, CIVIC CENTER, City Hall, SOUTH OF MARKET, SOUTH BEACH HARBOR, AT&T Park, China Basin, Caltrain Depot, Hall of Justice, Japan Center, Lafayette Park, Opera Ho., Symphony Hall

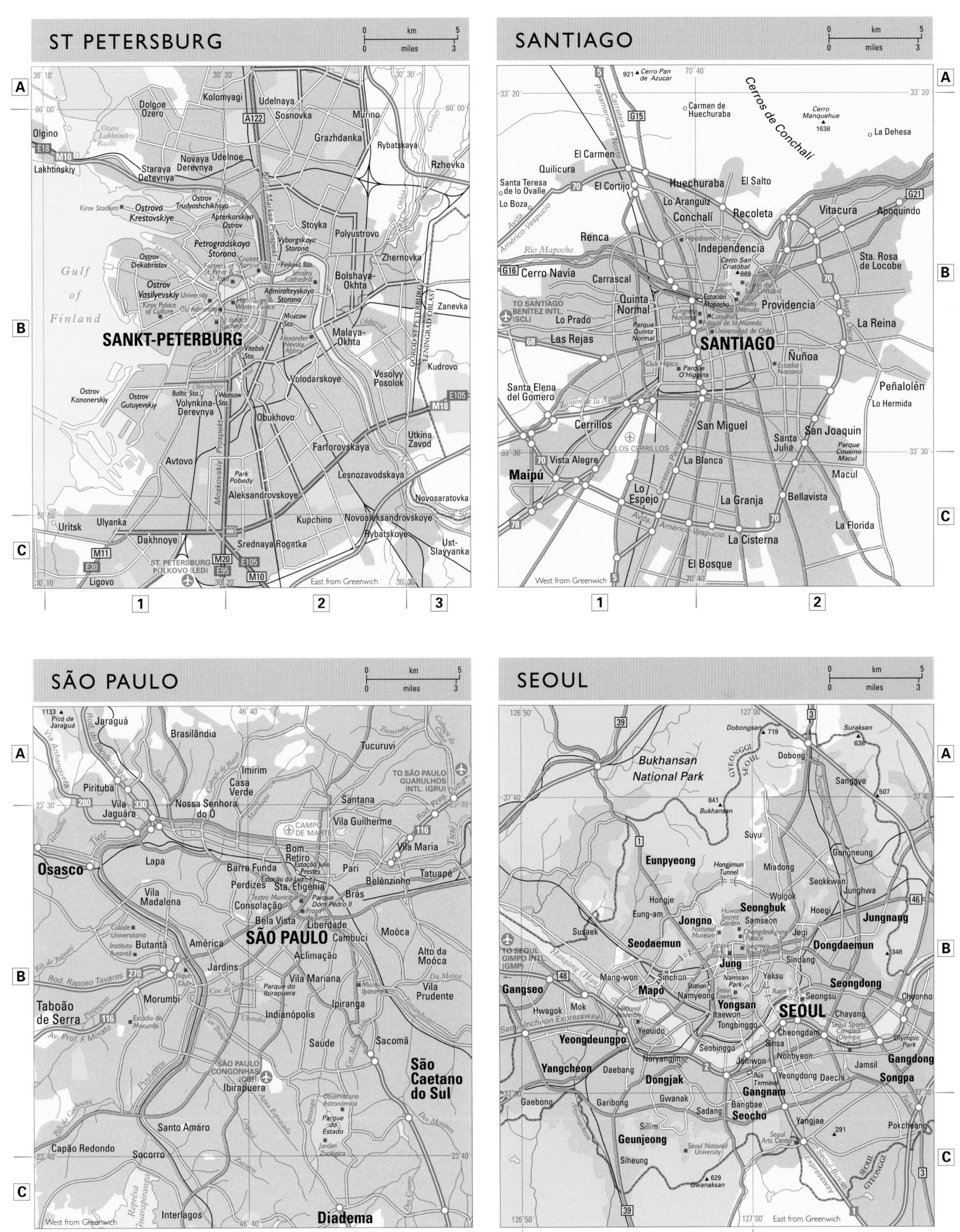
ST PETERSBURG
km
miles
Kolomyagi
Udelnaya
Dolgoe Ozero
Sosnovka
Murino
Olgino
Grazhdanka
Rybatskaya
Novaya Derevnya
Udelnoe
Lakhtinskiy
Staraya Derevnya
Rzhevka
Kirov Stadium
Ostrova Krestovskiye
Apterkarskiy Ostrov
Stoyka
Polyustrovo
Petrogradskaya Storona
Vyborgskaya Storona
Zhernovka
Ostrov Dekabristov
Finland Sta.
Smolny Cathedral
Bolshaya-Okhta
Gulf of Finland
Ostrov Vasilyevskiy
Admiralteyskaya Storona
Zanevka
Moscow Sta.
Malaya-Okhta
SANKT-PETERBURG
Vitebsk Sta.
Alexander Nevsky Abbey
Kudrovo
Volodarskoye
Vesolyy Posolok
Ostrov Kanonerskiy
Ostrov Gutuyevskiy
Baltic Sta.
Warsaw Sta.
Volynkina-Derevnya
Obukhovo
Utkina Zavod
Farforovskaya
Avtovo
Moskovskiy Prospekt
Park Pobedy
Lesnozavodskaya
Aleksandrovskoye
Novosaratovka
Uritsk
Ulyanka
Kupchino
Novoaleksandrovskoye
Dakhnoye
Srednaya Rogatka
Rybatskoye
Ust-Slavyanka
ST. PETERSBURG PULKOVO (LED)
Ligovo
East from Greenwich
SANTIAGO
Cerro Pan de Azucar
Carmen de Huechuraba
Cerros de Conchalí
Cerro Manquehue
La Dehesa
El Carmen
Quilicura
Santa Teresa de lo Ovalle
El Cortijo
Huechuraba
El Salto
Lo Boza
Lo Aranguiz
Conchalí
Recoleta
Vitacura
Apoquindo
Renca
Hipódromo Chile
Independencia
Río Mapocho
Cerro San Cristóbal
Sta. Rosa de Locobe
Cerro Navia
Carrascal
Quinta Normal
Providencia
TO SANTIAGO BENITEZ INTL. (SCL)
Lo Prado
La Reina
Las Rejas
SANTIAGO
Ñuñoa
Club Hípico
Parque O'Higgins
Estadio Nacional
Peñalolén
Santa Elena del Gomero
Lo Hermida
Cerrillos
San Miguel
San Joaquín
Santa Julia
LOS CERRILLOS
Vista Alegre
La Blanca
Maipú
Macul
Lo Espejo
La Granja
Bellavista
La Florida
La Cisterna
El Bosque
West from Greenwich
SÃO PAULO
Pico de Jaraguá
Jaraguá
Brasilândia
Tucuruvi
Imirim
Casa Verde
TO SÃO PAULO GUARULHOS INTL. (GRU)
Pirituba
Santana
Vila Jaguára
Nossa Senhora do Ó
CAMPO DE MARTE
Vila Guilherme
Vila Maria
Osasco
Lapa
Bom Retiro
Barra Funda
Pari
Tatuapé
Perdizes
Sta. Efigênia
Belènzinho
Vila Madalena
Brás
Consolação
Bela Vista
Liberdade
Moóca
Butantã
América
SÃO PAULO
Cambuci
Aclimação
Alto da Moóca
Jardins
Vila Mariana
Vila Prudente
Taboão de Serra
Morumbi
Ipiranga
Indianópolis
Saúde
Sacomã
SÃO PAULO CONGONHAS (CGH)
São Caetano do Sul
Ibirapuera
Santo Amaro
Capão Redondo
Socorro
Interlagos
Diadema
West from Greenwich
SEOUL
Dobongsan
Suraksan
Bukhansan National Park
Dobong
Sanggye
Bukhansan
Suyu
Gongneung
Eunpyeong
Miadong
Seokkwan
Junghwa
Hongje
Seongbuk
Hoegi
Jungnang
Eung-am
Jongno
Samseon
Susaek
Jegi
Seodaemun
Dongdaemun
TO SEOUL GIMPO INTL. (GMP)
Jung
Sindang
Mang-won
Sinchon
Yaksu
Seongdong
Gangseo
Mapo
Seongsu
Cheonho
Namyeong
Yongsan
Hwagok
Mok
Itaewon
SEOUL
Chayang
Tongbinggo
Yeongdeungpo
Yeouido
Cheongdam
Seobinggo
Sinsa
Noryangjin
Nonhyeon
Jamsil
Gangdong
Yangcheon
Daebang
Dongjak
Jamwon
Yeongdong
Daechi
Songpa
Gangnam
Gaebong
Garibong
Gwanak
Bangbae
Sadang
Seocho
Yangjae
Pokcheong
Sillim
Geunjeong
Seoul National University
Seoul Arts Center
Siheung
Gwanaksan
East from Greenwich

SHANGHAI

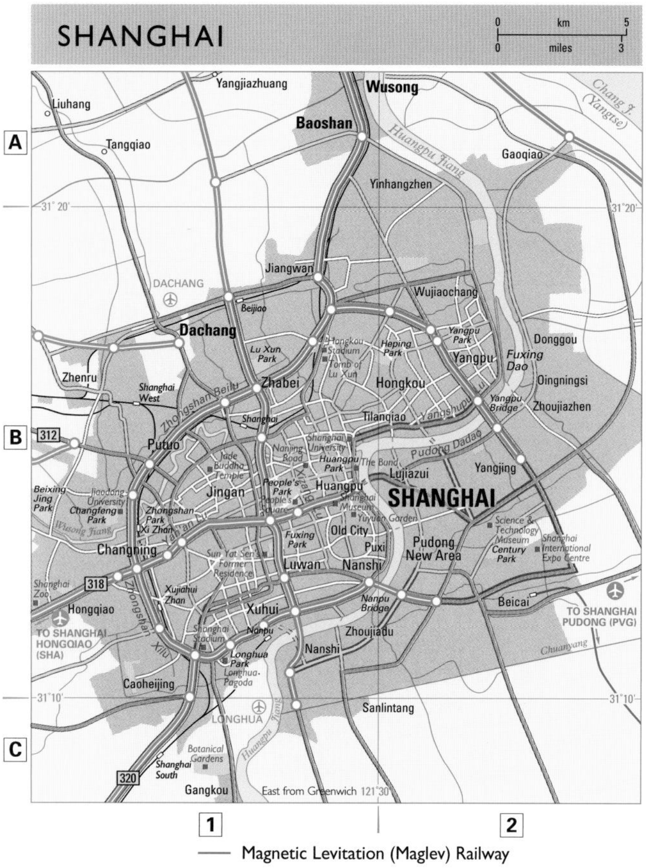

0 km 5
0 miles 3

— Magnetic Levitation (Maglev) Railway

CENTRAL SINGAPORE

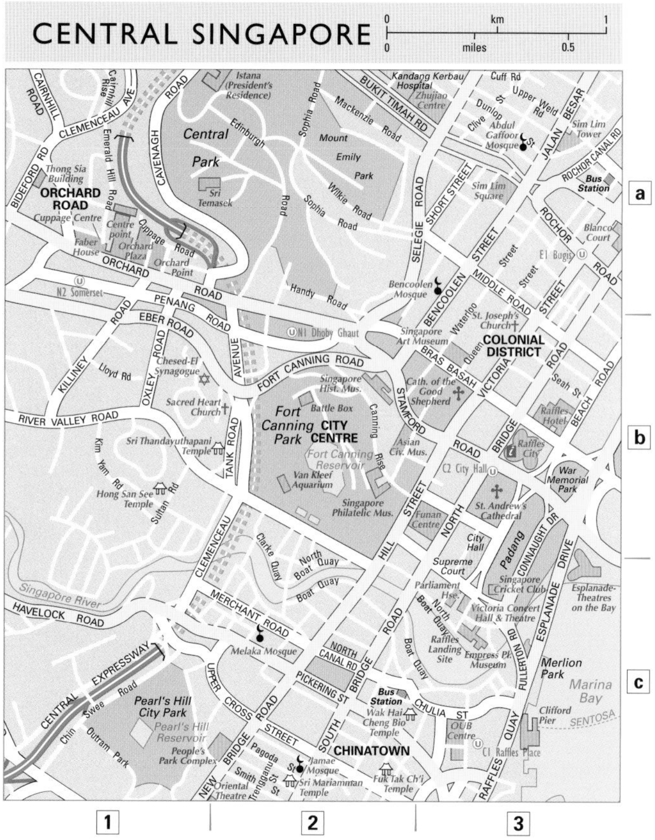

0 km 1
0 miles 0.5

SINGAPORE

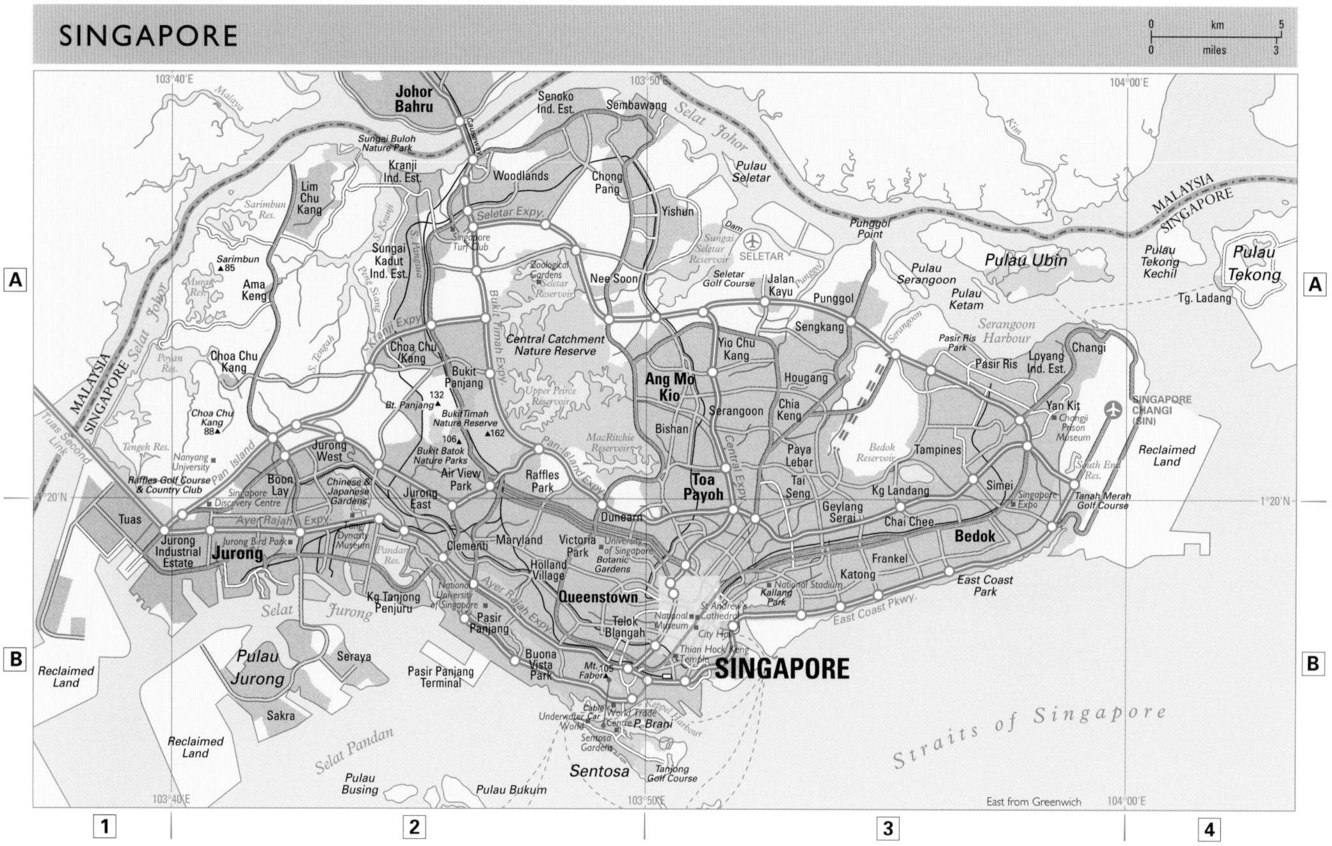

0 km 5
0 miles 3

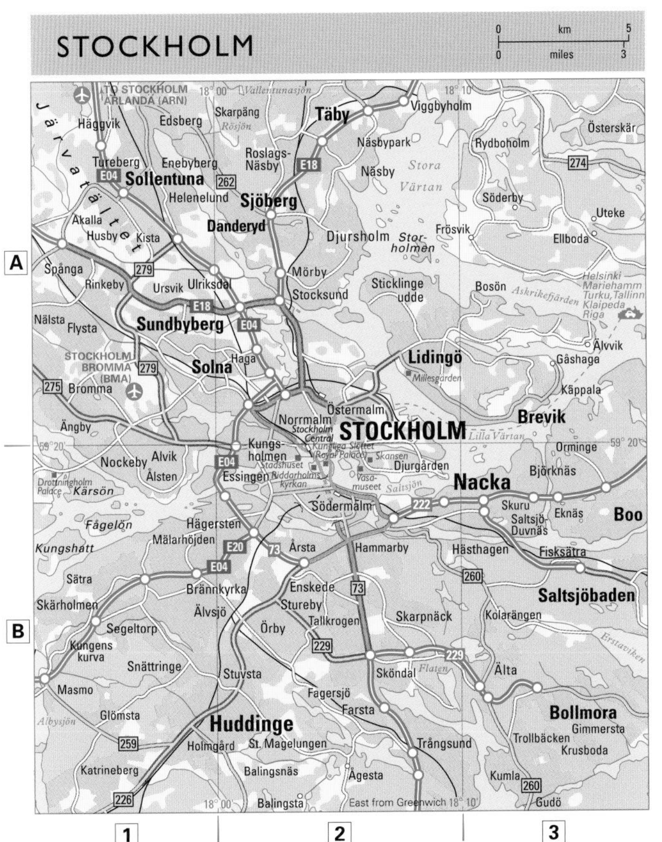
STOCKHOLM
0 km 5
0 miles 3
TO STOCKHOLM ARLANDA (ARN)
Järvafältet
Häggvik
Edsberg
Skarpäng
Täby
Viggbyholm
Österskär
Tureberg
Sollentuna
Enebyberg
Roslags-Näsby
Näsbypark
Rydboholm
Näsby
Stora Värtan
Helenelund
Sjöberg
Söderby
Uteke
Akalla
Husby
Kista
Danderyd
Djursholm
Stor-holmen
Frösvik
Ellboda
Spånga
Rinkeby
Ursvik
Ulriksdal
Mörby
Stocksund
Sticklinge udde
Bosön
Helsinki Mariehamn Turku, Tallinn Klaipeda Riga
Nälsta
Flysta
Sundbyberg
Älvvik
Lidingö
Gåshaga
STOCKHOLM BROMMA (BMA)
Solna
Haga
Millesgården
Bromma
Käppala
Östermalm
Brevik
Ängby
Norrmalm
STOCKHOLM
Lilla Värtan
Orminge
Nockeby
Alvik
Kungs-holmen
Skansen
Djurgården
Ålsten
Essingen
Nacka
Björknäs
Drottningholm Palace
Kärsön
Vasa-museet
Saltsjön
Södermalm
Skuru
Saltsjö-Duvnäs
Eknäs
Boo
Fågelön
Hägersten
Mälarhöjden
Årsta
Hammarby
Hästhagen
Fisksätra
Kungshatt
Sätra
Brännkyrka
Enskede
Stureby
Skärholmen
Älvsjö
Saltsjöbaden
Segeltorp
Örby
Tallkrogen
Skarpnäck
Kolarängen
Kungens kurva
Snättringe
Stuvsta
Sköndal
Flaten
Älta
Erstaviken
Masmo
Fagersjö
Farsta
Bollmora
Gimmersta
Albysjön
Glömsta
Huddinge
Trollbäcken
Krusboda
Holmgård
St. Magelungen
Trångsund
Katrineberg
Balingsnäs
Ågesta
Kumla
Balingsta
Gudö
East from Greenwich 18°10'
18°00'
59°20'
A
B
1
2
3

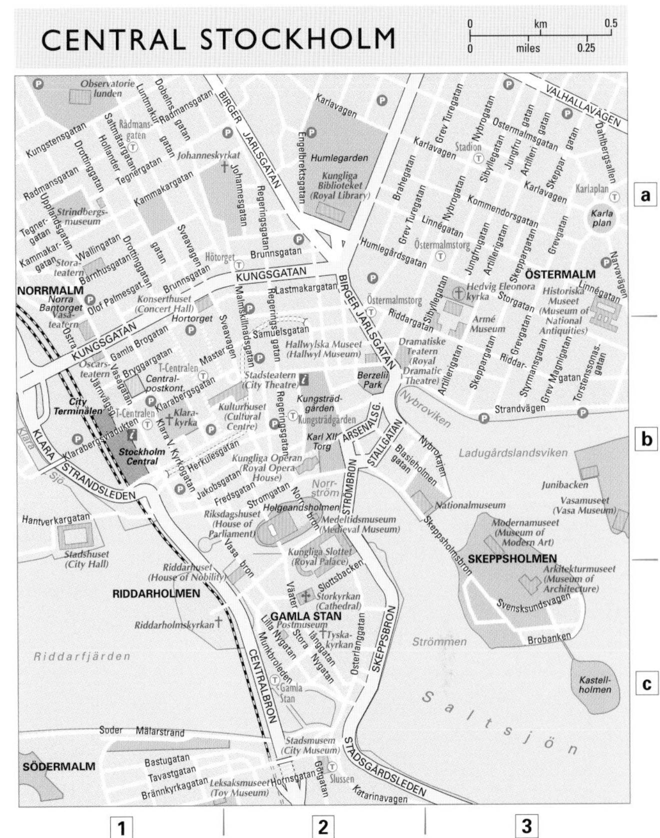
CENTRAL STOCKHOLM
0 km 0.5
0 miles 0.25
Observatorie lunden
VALHALLAVÄGEN
Karlavägen
Humlegarden
Kungliga Biblioteket (Royal Library)
Johanneskyrkat
BIRGER JARLSGATAN
Stadion
Karlaplan
Karla plan
Strindbergs-museum
Humlegårdsgatan
Östermalmstorg
ÖSTERMALM
Hötorget
Brunnsgatan
KUNGSGATAN
Lastmakargatan
Hedvig Eleonora kyrka
Historiska Museet (Museum of National Antiquities)
NORRMALM
Norra Bantorget
Konserthuset (Concert Hall)
Hortorget
Samuelsgatan
Hallwylska Museet (Hallwyl Museum)
Armé Museum
Dramatiske Teatern (Royal Dramatic Theatre)
KUNGSGATAN
Oscars-teatern
T-Centralen
Central-postkont.
Stadsteatern (City Theatre)
Berzelii Park
Kungstrad-garden
Nybroviken
Strandvägen
City Terminalen
Klara kyrka
Kulturhuset (Cultural Centre)
Karl XII Torg
ARSENALSG.
Stockholm Central
Kungliga Operan (Royal Opera House)
Ladugårdslandsviken
Junibacken
Vasamuseet (Vasa Museum)
KLARA STRANDSLEDEN
Norr-ström
Helgeandsholmen
Medeltidsmuseum (Medieval Museum)
Nationalmuseum
Moderna museet (Museum of Modern Art)
Hantverkargatan
Riksdagshuset (House of Parliament)
SKEPPSHOLMEN
Arkitekturmuseet (Museum of Architecture)
Stadshuset (City Hall)
Riddarhuset (House of Nobility)
Kungliga Slottet (Royal Palace)
Storkyrkan (Cathedral)
RIDDARHOLMEN
GAMLA STAN
Postmuseum
Tyska-kyrkan
Riddarholmskyrkan
Strömmen
Brobanken
Riddarfjärden
CENTRALBRON
SKEPPSBRON
Kastell-holmen
Gamla Stan
Saltsjön
Söder Mälarstrand
Bastugatan
Tavastgatan
Brännkyrkagatan
SÖDERMALM
Stadsmuseum (City Museum)
Leksaksmuseet (Toy Museum)
Hornsgatan
Götgatan
Slussen
Katarinavägen
STADSGÅRDSLEDEN
a
b
c
1
2
3

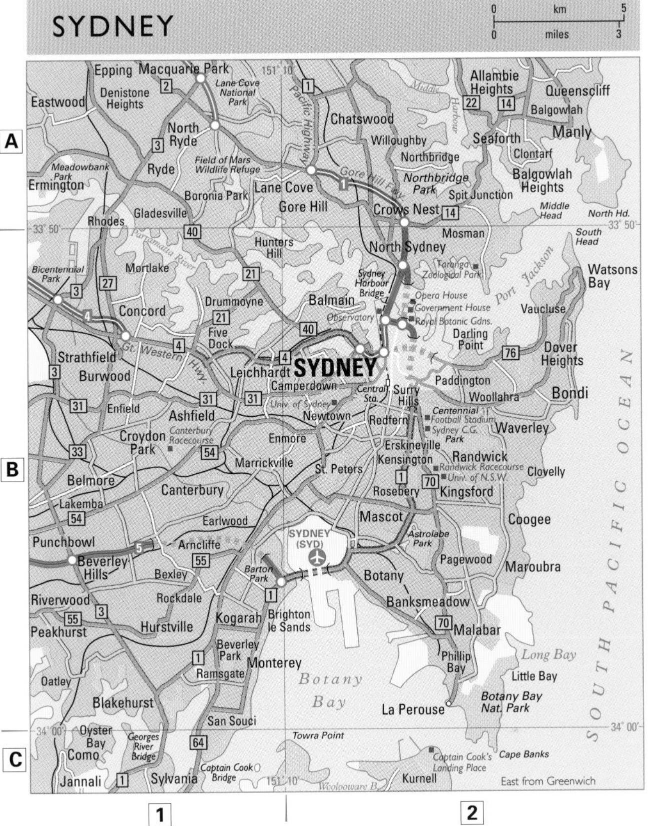
SYDNEY
0 km 5
0 miles 3
Epping
Macquarie Park
Lane Cove National Park
Allambie Heights
Queenscliff
Eastwood
Denistone Heights
Balgowlah
North Ryde
Chatswood
Manly
Seaforth
Willoughby
Clontarf
Meadowbank Park
Ryde
Field of Mars Wildlife Refuge
Northbridge
Ermington
Northbridge Park
Balgowlah Heights
Lane Cove
Spit Junction
Boronia Park
Middle Head
Gladesville
Gore Hill
Crows Nest
North Hd.
Rhodes
Mosman
South Head
Hunters Hill
North Sydney
Bicentennial Park
Mortlake
Taronga Zoological Park
Watsons Bay
Sydney Harbour Bridge
Port Jackson
Drummoyne
Balmain
Opera House
Government House
Vaucluse
Concord
Five Dock
Observatory
Royal Botanic Gdns.
Darling Point
Strathfield
Dover Heights
Burwood
Leichhardt
SYDNEY
Camperdown
Paddington
Bondi
Univ. of Sydney
Central Sta.
Surry Hills
Woollahra
Enfield
Ashfield
Newtown
Centennial Football Stadium
Sydney C.G. Park
Waverley
Croydon Park
Canterbury Racecourse
Redfern
Erskineville
Enmore
Randwick
Marrickville
Kensington
Randwick Racecourse
Univ. of N.S.W.
Clovelly
Belmore
St. Peters
Canterbury
Rosebery
Kingsford
Lakemba
Mascot
Coogee
Earlwood
Punchbowl
Arncliffe
SYDNEY (SYD)
Astrolabe Park
Beverley Hills
Pagewood
Maroubra
Bexley
Barton Park
Botany
Riverwood
Rockdale
Banksmeadow
Peakhurst
Hurstville
Kogarah
Brighton le Sands
Malabar
Beverley Park
Phillip Bay
Long Bay
Monterey
Little Bay
Oatley
Ramsgate
Botany Bay
Botany Bay Nat. Park
Blakehurst
La Perouse
San Souci
Oyster Bay
Georges River Bridge
Towra Point
Como
Captain Cook's Landing Place
Cape Banks
Captain Cook Bridge
Jannali
Sylvania
Woolooware B.
Kurnell
East from Greenwich
SOUTH PACIFIC OCEAN
151°10'
33°50'
34°00'
A
B
C
1
2

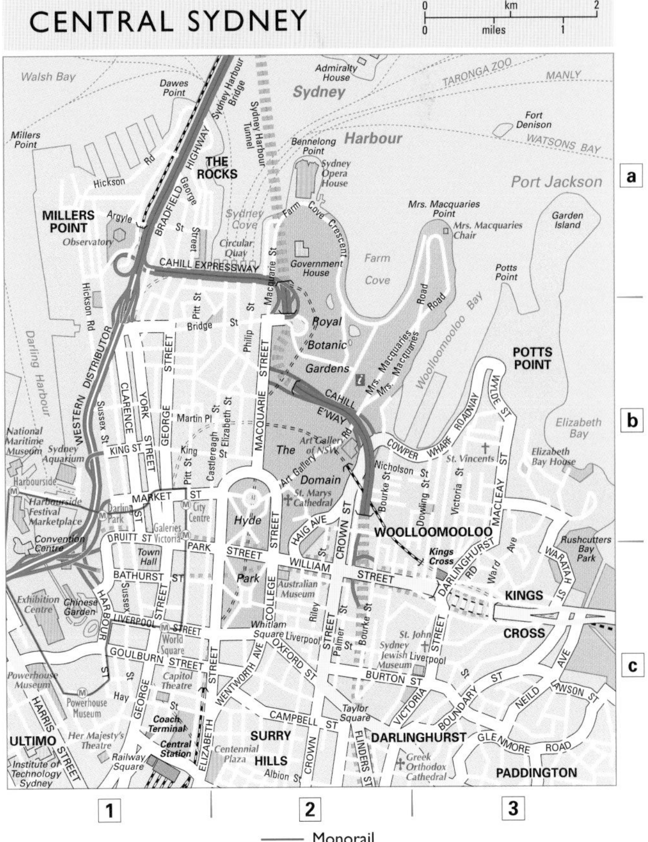
CENTRAL SYDNEY
0 km 2
0 miles 1
Walsh Bay
Dawes Point
Admiralty House
TARONGA ZOO
MANLY
Sydney
Fort Denison
Millers Point
Sydney Harbour Bridge
Sydney Harbour Tunnel
Harbour
WATSONS BAY
Bennelong Point
THE ROCKS
Sydney Opera House
Hickson Rd
Port Jackson
MILLERS POINT
Observatory
BRADFIELD HIGHWAY
Sydney Cove
Farm Cove
Mrs. Macquaries Point
Garden Island
Mrs. Macquaries Chair
Circular Quay
CAHILL EXPRESSWAY
Government House
Potts Point
Royal Botanic Gardens
Woolloomooloo Bay
POTTS POINT
Darling Harbour
WESTERN DISTRIBUTOR
CLARENCE ST
YORK ST
GEORGE ST
Pitt St
Macquarie St
CAHILL E'WAY
Martin Pl
Elizabeth St
Castlereagh St
The Art Gallery of NSW
The Domain
COWPER WHARF ROADWAY
Elizabeth Bay
National Maritime Museum
Sydney Aquarium
KING ST
St. Vincents
Elizabeth Bay House
Harbourside Festival Marketplace
MARKET ST
St. Marys Cathedral
Hyde Park
Convention Centre
DRUITT ST
Town Hall
PARK ST
WOOLLOOMOOLOO
Kings Cross
Rushcutters Bay Park
BATHURST ST
WILLIAM ST
KINGS CROSS
Exhibition Centre
Chinese Garden
Australian Museum
LIVERPOOL ST
Whitlam Square
Sydney Jewish Museum
GOULBURN ST
OXFORD ST
Powerhouse Museum
Capitol Theatre
BURTON ST
Coach Terminal
Central Station
Her Majesty's Theatre
Railway Square
Taylor Square
ULTIMO
SURRY HILLS
DARLINGHURST
Centennial Plaza
Institute of Technology Sydney
Greek Orthodox Cathedral
PADDINGTON
a
b
c
1
2
3

Monorail

CENTRAL TOKYO

0 km 5
0 miles 3

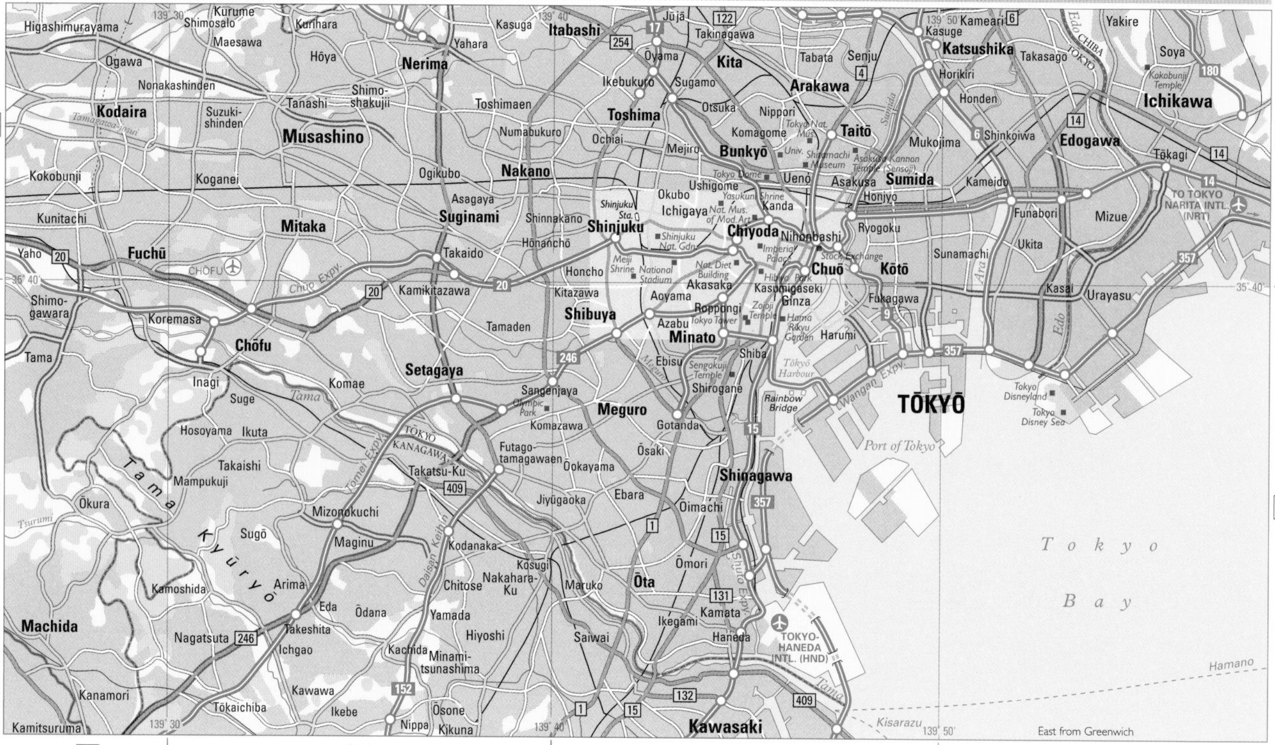

East from Greenwich

CENTRAL TOKYO

0 km 0.5
0 miles 0.25

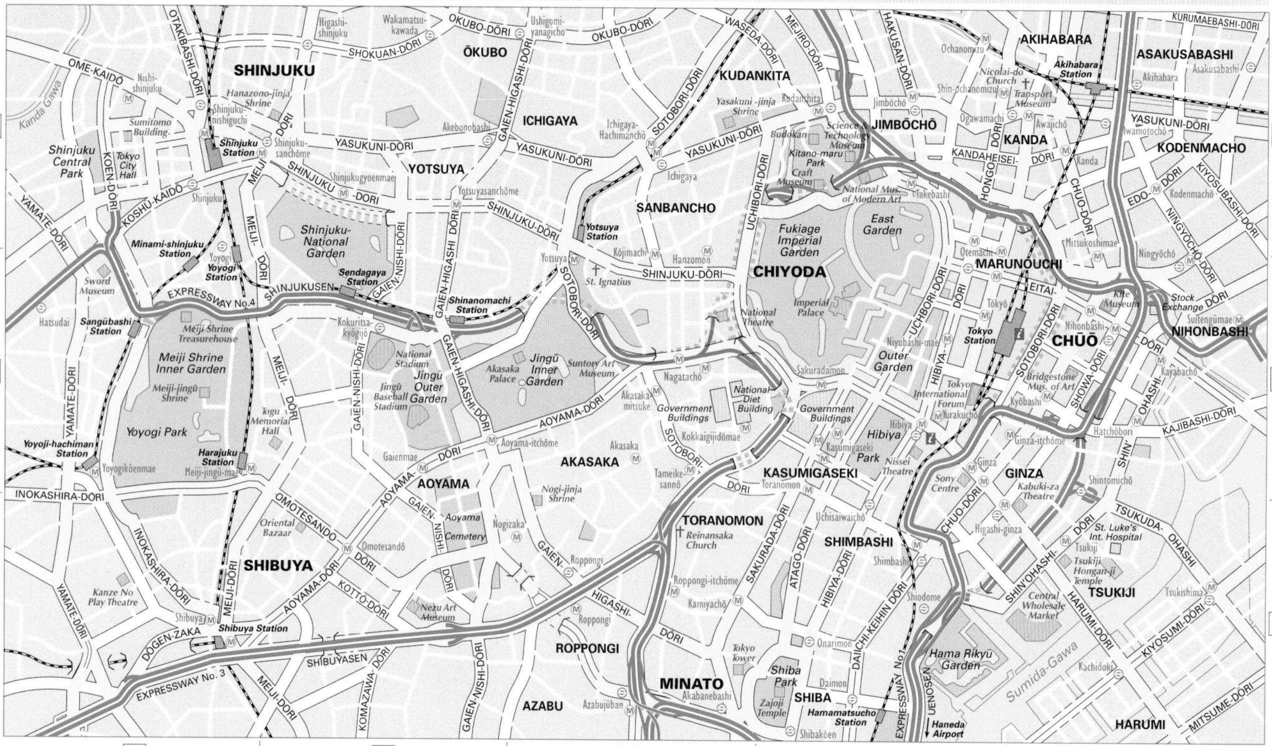

⊖ Toei Subway Ⓜ Tokyo Metro

TEHRAN

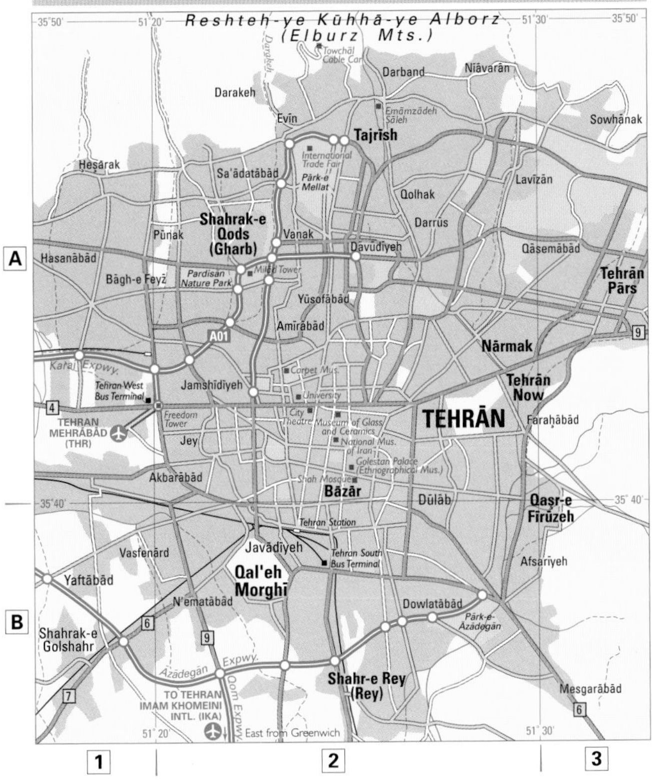

0 km 5
0 miles 3

Reshteh-ye Kūhhā-ye Alborz (Elburz Mts.)
35°50' 51°20' 51°30' 35°50'
Towchāl Cable Car
Darband
Niāvarān
Darakeh
Emāmzādeh Sāleh
Evīn
Tajrīsh
Sowhānak
Hesārak
International Trade Fair
Sa'ādatābād
Pārk-e Mellat
Lavīzān
Qolhak
Shahrak-e Qods (Gharb)
Darrūs
Pūnak
Vanak
Qāsemābād
Hasanābād
Davūdīyeh
Bāgh-e Feyz
Pardisan Nature Park
Milad Tower
Tehrān Pārs
Yūsofābād
Amīrābād
A01
Nārmak
Karaj Expwy.
Carpet Mus.
Tehran West Bus Terminal
Jamshīdīyeh
Tehrān Now
University
TEHRAN MEHRĀBĀD (THR)
Freedom Tower
City Theatre
Museum of Glass and Ceramics
National Mus. of Iran
TEHRĀN
Farahābād
Jey
Golestan Palace (Ethnographical Mus.)
Akbarābād
Shah Mosque
Bāzār
Dūlāb
Qasr-e Fīrūzeh
35°40'
Tehran Station
Javādīyeh
Vasfenārd
Tehran South Bus Terminal
Afsarīyeh
Yaftābād
Qal'eh Morghī
N'ematābād
Dowlatābād
Pārk-e Āzādegān
Shahrak-e Golshahr
Āzādegān Expwy.
Shahr-e Rey (Rey)
Mesgarābād
TO TEHRAN IMAM KHOMEINI INTL. (IKA)
Dom Expwy.
51°20'
East from Greenwich
51°30'
A B 1 2 3

CENTRAL TORONTO

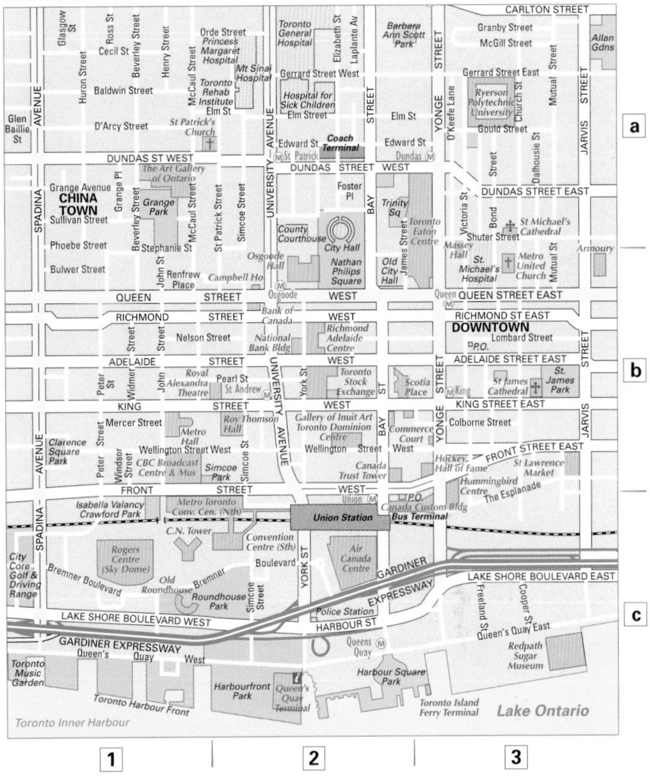

0 km 0.5
0 miles 0.25

CARLTON STREET
Glasgow St
Ross St
Beverley Street
Henry Street
Orde Street
Toronto General Hospital
Elizabeth St
Laplante Av
Barbara Ann Scott Park
Granby Street
McGill Street
Allan Gdns
Cecil St
Princess Margaret Hospital
Mt Sinai Hospital
Gerrard Street West
Gerrard Street East
Ryerson Polytechnic University
Baldwin Street
Huron Street
McCaul Street
Toronto Rehab Institute
Hospital for Sick Children
Elm Street
Elm St
Glen Baillie St
AVENUE
D'Arcy Street
St Patrick's Church
UNIVERSITY
Edward St
Coach Terminal
Edward St
Gould Street
JARVIS
DUNDAS ST WEST
St Patrick
DUNDAS STREET WEST
Dundas
Dalhousie St
The Art Gallery of Ontario
Foster Pl
DUNDAS STREET EAST
Grange Avenue
Grange Pl
CHINA TOWN
Grange Park
Trinity Sq
Toronto Eaton Centre
St Michael's Cathedral
SPADINA
Sullivan Street
County Courthouse
Shuter Street
Phoebe Street
Stephanie St
City Hall
Massey Hall
Armoury
Osgoode Hall
Nathan Philips Square
Old City Hall
St. Michael's Hospital
Metro United Church
Bulwer Street
Renfrew Place
Campbell Ho
James Street
Victoria St
Bond St
Mutual St
QUEEN STREET WEST
Osgoode
Queen
QUEEN STREET EAST
RICHMOND STREET WEST
Bank of Canada
RICHMOND ST EAST
Nelson Street
National Bank Bldg
Richmond Adelaide Centre
DOWNTOWN
Lombard Street
P.O.
ADELAIDE STREET WEST
ADELAIDE STREET EAST
Royal Alexandra Theatre
Pearl St
St Andrew
Toronto Stock Exchange
Scotia Plaza
St James Cathedral
St. James Park
Peter St
Widmer Street
John Street
York St
KING STREET WEST
King
KING STREET EAST
Mercer Street
Roy Thomson Hall
Gallery of Inuit Art
Toronto Dominion Centre
Commerce Court West
Colborne Street
Clarence Square Park
Metro Hall
Wellington Street West
Wellington Street
BAY
YONGE
Windsor Street
CBC Broadcast Centre & Mus
Simcoe Park
Canada Trust Tower
Hockey Hall of Fame
FRONT STREET EAST
St Lawrence Market
FRONT STREET WEST
Union
Hummingbird Centre
The Esplanade
Isabella Valancy Crawford Park
Metro Toronto Conv. Cen. (Nth)
P.O.
Union Station
Canada Custom Bldg
Bus Terminal
C.N. Tower
Convention Centre (Sth)
City Core Golf & Driving Range
Rogers Centre (Sky Dome)
Boulevard
Air Canada Centre
GARDINER EXPRESSWAY
Bremner Boulevard
Old Roundhouse
Roundhouse Park
Simcoe Street
LAKE SHORE BOULEVARD EAST
Freeland St
Cooper St
Police Station
LAKE SHORE BOULEVARD WEST
HARBOUR ST
Queen's Quay East
GARDINER EXPRESSWAY
Queen's Quay West
Queens Quay
Redpath Sugar Museum
Toronto Music Garden
Harbour Square Park
Harbourfront Park
Queen's Quay Terminal
Toronto Harbour Front
Toronto Island Ferry Terminal
Lake Ontario
Toronto Inner Harbour
a b c 1 2 3

TORONTO

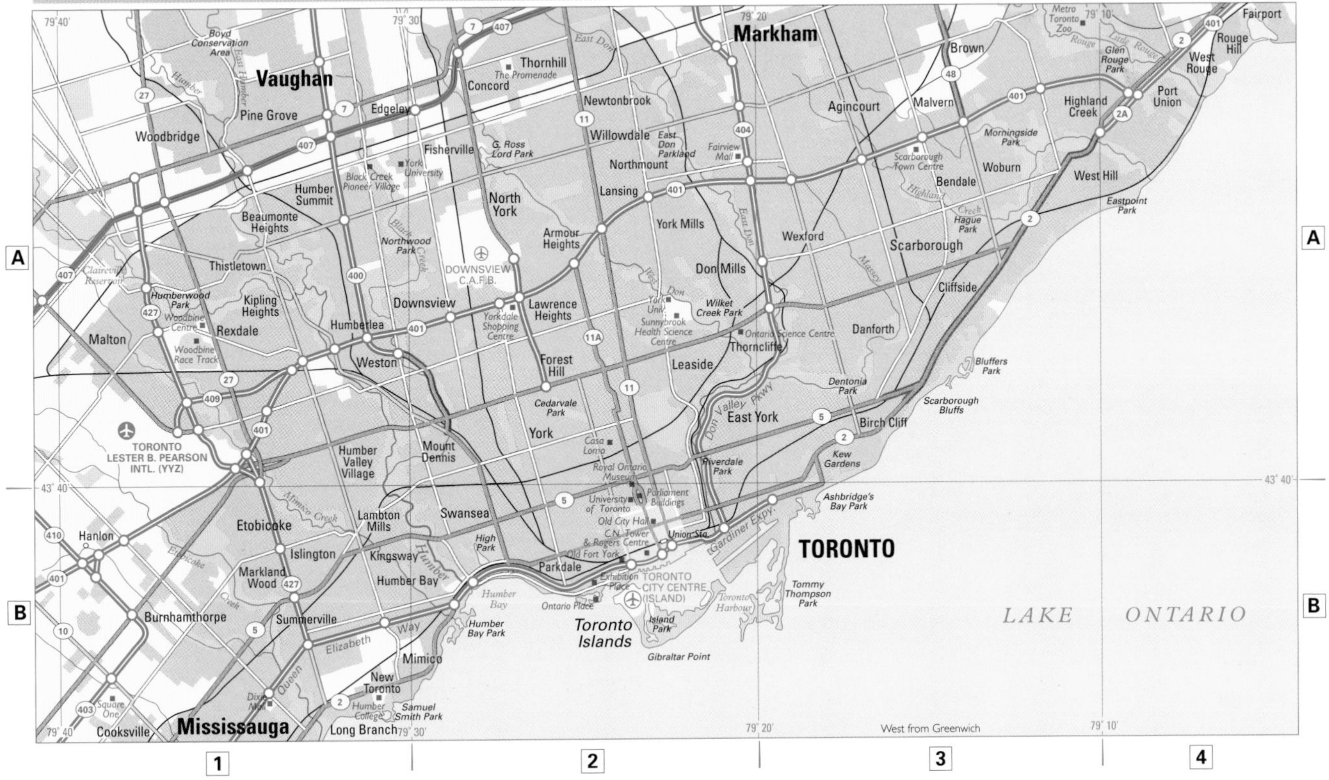

0 km 5
0 miles 3

79°40'
79°30'
79°20'
79°10'
Metro Toronto Zoo
Fairport
Boyd Conservation Area
Thornhill
The Promenade
Markham
Brown
Rouge Hill
Vaughan
Concord
Glen Rouge Park
West Rouge
Pine Grove
Edgeley
Newtonbrook
Agincourt
Malvern
Highland Creek
Port Union
Woodbridge
Willowdale
East Don Parkland
Fairview Mall
Morningside Park
Fisherville
G. Ross Lord Park
York University
Northmount
Scarborough Town Centre
Woburn
Black Creek Pioneer Village
Humber Summit
Lansing
Bendale
West Hill
North York
Eastpoint Park
Beaumonte Heights
York Mills
Hague Park
Armour Heights
Wexford
Scarborough
Northwood Park
Thistletown
DOWNSVIEW C.A.F.B.
Don Mills
Claireville Reservoir
Cliffside
Humberwood Park
Kipling Heights
Downsview
Lawrence Heights
York Univ.
Wilket Creek Park
Woodbine Centre
Yorkdale Shopping Centre
Sunnybrook Health Science Centre
Rexdale
Humberlea
Danforth
Malton
Woodbine Race Track
Ontario Science Centre
Thorncliffe
Weston
Forest Hill
Leaside
Bluffers Park
Dentonia Park
Cedarvale Park
Scarborough Bluffs
TORONTO LESTER B. PEARSON INTL. (YYZ)
York
Don Valley Pkwy
East York
Birch Cliff
Casa Loma
Kew Gardens
Humber Valley Village
Mount Dennis
Royal Ontario Museum
Riverdale Park
43°40'
Parliament Buildings
University of Toronto
Ashbridge's Bay Park
Lambton Mills
Swansea
Old City Hall
Etobicoke
Hanlon
C.N. Tower & Rogers Centre
Union Sta.
Gardiner Expy.
TORONTO
Islington
High Park
Old Fort York
Kingsway
Parkdale
Markland Wood
Humber Bay
Exhibition Place
TORONTO CITY CENTRE (ISLAND)
Tommy Thompson Park
Toronto Harbour
Burnhamthorpe
Ontario Place
LAKE ONTARIO
Summerville
Humber Bay Park
Toronto Islands
Island Park
Elizabeth Way
Gibraltar Point
Mimico
New Toronto
Dixie Mall
Square One
Humber College
Samuel Smith Park
Cooksville
Mississauga
Long Branch
West from Greenwich
A B 1 2 3 4

(427) Provincial route numbers

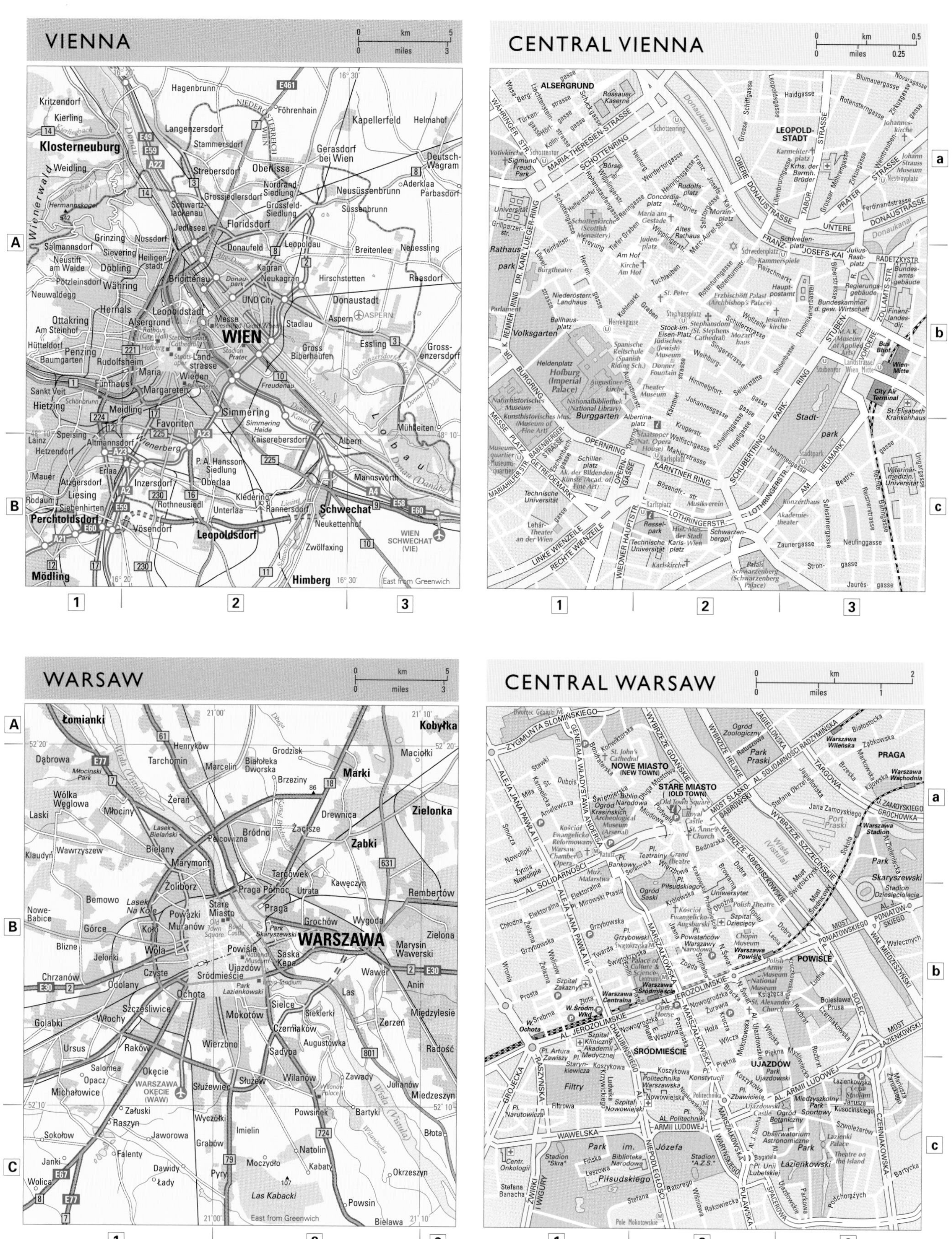
VIENNA
0 km 5
0 miles 3
Hagenbrunn
Föhrenhain
Kritzendorf
Kierling
Klosterneuburg
Langenzersdorf
Stammersdorf
Kapellerfeld
Helmahof
Gerasdorf bei Wien
Deutsch-Wagram
Weidling
Strebersdorf
Oberlisse
Nordrand-Siedlung
Aderklaa
Parbasdorf
Neusüssenbrunn
Grossjedlersdorf
Grossfeld-Siedlung
Süssenbrunn
Hermannskogel
542
Schwartz lackenau
Floridsdorf
Jedlesee
Grinzing
Nussdorf
Donaufeld
Leopoldau
Breitenlee
Neuessling
Salmannsdorf
Sievering
Heiligenstadt
Neustift am Walde
Döbling
Kagran
Pötzleinsdorf
Währing
Brigittenau
Neukagran
Hirschstetten
Raasdorf
Neuwaldegg
UNO City
Donaustadt
Hernals
Leopoldstadt
Ottakring
Alsergrund
Messe
Aspern
ASPERN
Am Steinhof
WIEN
Stadlau
Hütteldorf
Penzing
Landstrasse
Essling
Gross Biberhaufen
Gross-enzersdorf
Baumgarten
Rudolfsheim
Maria
Wieden
Sankt Veit
Fünfhaus
Margareten
Freudenau
Hietzing
Meidling
Simmering
Mühlleiten
Lainz
Speising
Favoriten
Simmeringer Heide
Hetzendorf
Altmannsdorf
Kaiserebersdorf
Albern
Wienerberg
Mauer
Atzgersdorf
P. A. Hansson Siedlung
Inzersdorf
Oberlaa
Mannswörth
Erlaa
Liesing
Rodaun
Siebenhirten
Rothneusiedl
Kledering
Unterlaa
Rannersdorf
Schwechat
Perchtoldsdorf
Vösendorf
Leopoldsdorf
Neukettenhof
WIEN SCHWECHAT (VIE)
Zwölfaxing
Mödling
Himberg
East from Greenwich
Wienerwald
Donau
Lobau
Donau (Danube)
NIEDERÖSTERREICH
WIEN
A
B
1
2
3

CENTRAL VIENNA
0 km 0.5
0 miles 0.25
ALSERGRUND
Rossauer Kaserne
Währinger Str.
Maria-Theresien-Strasse
Schottenring
Votivkirche
Sigmund Freud Park
LEOPOLDSTADT
Karmeliterplatz
Krhs. der Barmh. Brüder
Johann Strauss Museum
Obere Donaustrasse
Untere Donaustrasse
Universität
Schottenkirche (Scottish Monastery)
Freyung
Maria am Gestade
Altes Rathaus
Morzinplatz
Schwedenplatz
Franz-Josefs-Kai
Rathaus-park
Dr. Karl-Lueger-Ring
Burgtheater
Am Hof
Kirche Am Hof
Kammerspiele
Fleischmarkt
Hauptpostamt
Radetzkystr.
Bundesamtsgebäude
Regierungsgebäude
Niederösterr. Landhaus
St. Peter
Erzbischöfl Palast (Archbishop's Palace)
Bundeskammer d. gew. Wirtschaft
Finanzlandesdir.
Parlament
Volksgarten
Stephansplatz
Stephansdom (St. Stephens Cathedral)
Mozarthaus
Jesuitenkirche
M.A.K. Museum of Applied Arts
Stubenring
Bus Bhf.
Wien-Mitte
Heldenplatz
Hofburg (Imperial Palace)
Spanische Reitschule (Spanish Riding Sch.)
Jüdisches Museum (Jewish Museum)
Donner Fountain
Augustinerkirche
Theater Museum
Nationalbibliothek (National Library)
City Air Terminal
St. Elisabeth Krankenhaus
Naturhistorisches Museum
Kunsthistorisches Mus. (Museum of Fine Art)
Burggarten
Albertinaplatz
Stadtpark
Museumsquartier
Staatsoper (Nat. Opera House)
Karlsplatz
Schillerplatz
Ak. der Bildenden Künste (Acad. of Fine Art)
Opernring
Kärntner Ring
Schubertring
Parkring
Heumarkt
Veterinärmedizin. Universität
Technische Universität
Musikverein
Konzerthaus
Akademietheater
Lothringerstr.
Lehár-Theater an der Wien
Resselpark
Hist. Mus. der Stadt Wien
Schwarzenbergplatz
Technische Universität
Karlskirche
Palais Schwarzenberg (Schwarzenberg Palace)
Linke Wienzeile
Rechte Wienzeile
Wiedner Hauptstr.
a
b
c
1
2
3

WARSAW
0 km 5
0 miles 3
Łomianki
Kobyłka
Henryków
Grodzisk
Maciołki
Dąbrowa
Tarchomin
Marcelin
Białołęka Dworska
Brzeziny
Marki
Młocinski Park
Wólka Węglowa
Żerań
Drewnica
Zielonka
Laski
Młociny
Bródno
Zacisze
Kłudyń
Wawrzyszew
Bielany
Ząbki
Marymont
Targówek
Żoliborz
Praga Północ
Utrata
Kawęczyn
Rembertów
Bemowo
Lasek Na Kole
Stare Miasto
Praga
Nowe-Babice
Powązki
Grochów
Wygoda
Górce
Koło
Muranów
WARSZAWA
Marysin Wawerski
Blizne
Wola
Powiśle
Saska Kępa
Zielona
Jelonki
Czyste
Ujazdów
Wawer
Chrzanów
Odolany
Śródmieście
Anin
Ochota
Las
Szczęśliwice
Sielce
Siekierki
Międzylesie
Golabki
Włochy
Mokotów
Czerniaków
Zerzeń
Ursus
Raków
Wierzbno
Augustówka
Radość
Salomea
Opacz
Okęcie
Służewiec
Służew
Wilanów
Zawady
Julianów
Michałowice
WARSZAWA OKĘCIE (WAW)
Miedzeszyn
Załuski
Powsinek
Bartyki
Raszyn
Wyczółki
Jaworowa
Imielin
Błota
Sokołów
Grabów
Natolin
Falenty
Janki
Dawidy
Moczydło
Kabaty
Okrzeszyn
Łady
Pyry
107
Wolica
Las Kabacki
Powsin
Bielawa
East from Greenwich
Wisła (Vistula)
A
B
C
1
2
3

CENTRAL WARSAW
0 km 2
0 miles 1
Dworzec Gdański
Zygmunta Słomińskiego
Ogród Zoologiczny
Park Praski
Białostocka
Ząbkowska
PRAGA
Warszawa Wileńska
Warszawa Wschodnia
St. John's Cathedral
NOWE MIASTO (NEW TOWN)
STARE MIASTO (OLD TOWN)
Old Town Square
Royal Castle
St. Anne's Church
Most Śląsko-Dąbrowski
Wybrzeże Gdańskie
Wybrzeże Helskie
Al. Solidarności
Targowa
Jagiellońska
Jana Zamoyskiego
Grochowska
Warszawa Stadion
Al. Jana Pawła II
Biblio. Narodowa
Ogród Krasińskich
Archeological Museum (Arsenal)
Kościół Ewangelicko Reformowany
Warsaw Chamber Opera
Grand Theatre
Pl. Teatralny
Pl. Bankowy
Park Skaryszewski
Stadion Dziesięciolecia
Pl. Piłsudskiego
Uniwersytet
Ogród Saski
Kościół Ewangelicko Augsburski
Polish Theatre
Szpital Dziecięcy
Pl. Mirowski
Chopin Museum
Warszawa Powiśle
POWIŚLE
Most Poniatowskiego
Al. Poniatowskiego
Pl. Grzybowski
Pl. Powstańców Warszawy
Palace of Culture & Science
Warszawa Śródmieście
Polish Army Museum
National Museum
Warszawa Centralna
Szpital Zakaźny
W. Śródm. Wkd
W. Ochota
Al. Jerozolimskie
Pl. Artura Zawiszy
St. Alexander's Church
Bolesława Prusa
Szpital Kliniczny
Akademii Medycznej
ŚRÓDMIEŚCIE
Politechnika Warszawska
Pl. Konstytucji
UJAZDÓW
Park Ujazdowski
Filtry
Pl. Zbawiciela
Ujazdowski Castle
Międzyszkolny Park Sportowy
Pl. Narutowicza
Pl. Nowowiejski
Al. Politechniki
Al. Armii Ludowej
Ogród Botaniczny
Wawelska
Obserwatorium Astronomiczne
Łazienki Palace
Theatre on the Island
Park Łazienkowski
Park im. Józefa Piłsudskiego
Stadion "Skra"
Stadion "A.Z.S."
Biblioteka Narodowa
Centr. Onkologii
Pl. Unii Lubelskiej
Niepodległości
Marszałkowska
Puławska
Stefana Banacha
Batorego
Rakowiecka
Pole Mokotowskie
Podchorążych
Czerniakowska
Solec
Wisła (Vistula)
a
b
c
1
2
3

WASHINGTON

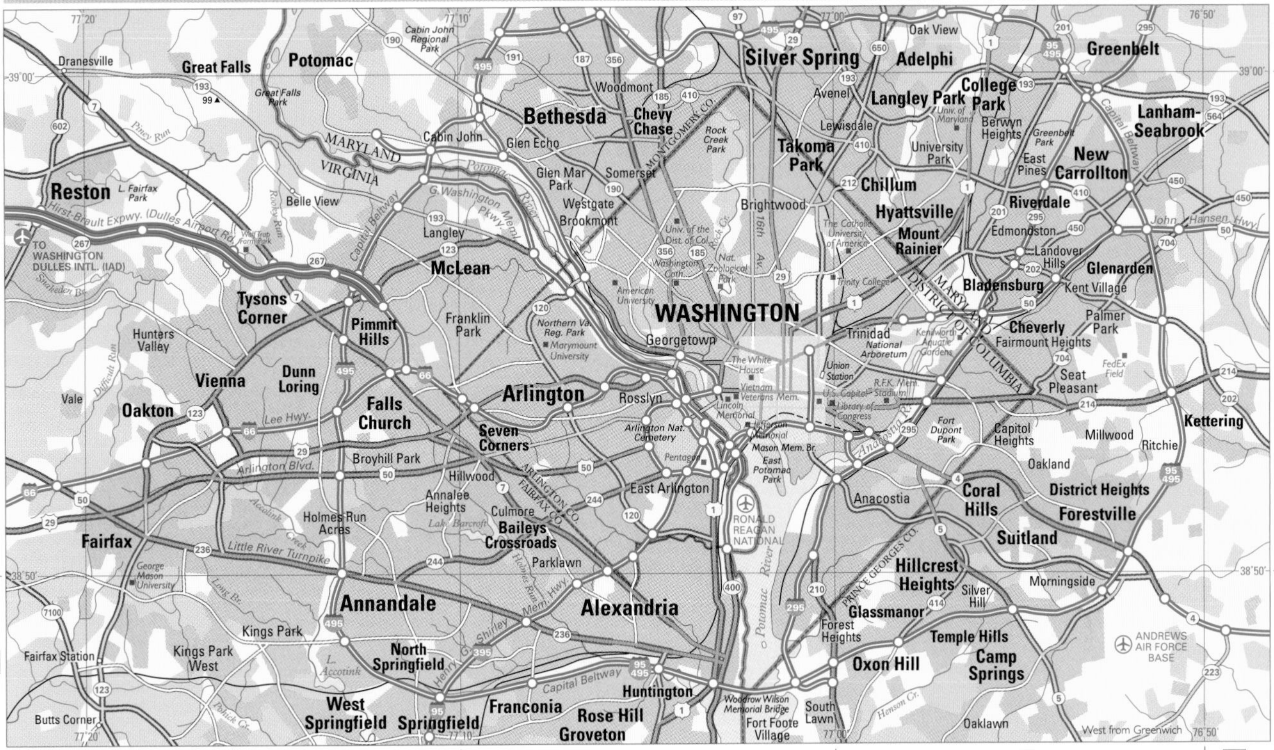

0 km 5
0 miles 3
Great Falls
Potomac
Dranesville
Great Falls Park
Cabin John Regional Park
Silver Spring
Adelphi
Oak View
Greenbelt
Woodmont
Bethesda
Chevy Chase
Takoma Park
Langley Park
College Park
Lanham-Seabrook
Avenel
Lewisdale
Univ. of Maryland
Berwyn Heights
Greenbelt Park
Rock Creek Park
MARYLAND
VIRGINIA
MONTGOMERY CO.
Cabin John
Glen Echo
University Park
East Pines
New Carrollton
Reston
L. Fairfax Park
Glen Mar Park
Somerset
Chillum
Riverdale
Belle View
Westgate
Brookmont
Brightwood
Hyattsville
Edmondston
Mount Rainier
Landover Hills
Glenarden
Hirst-Brault Expwy. (Dulles Airport Rd.)
TO WASHINGTON DULLES INTL. (IAD)
Langley
McLean
Univ. of the Dist. of Col.
Washington Cath.
Nat. Zoological Park
The Catholic University of America
Trinity College
DISTRICT OF COLUMBIA
Bladensburg
Kent Village
Tysons Corner
Pimmit Hills
Franklin Park
American University
WASHINGTON
Northern Va. Reg. Park
Marymount University
Georgetown
Trinidad
National Arboretum
Kenilworth Aquatic Gardens
Cheverly
Fairmount Heights
Palmer Park
Hunters Valley
Dunn Loring
Vienna
The White House
Union Station
FedEx Field
Arlington
Falls Church
Vale
Oakton
Lee Hwy.
Rosslyn
Lincoln Memorial
Vietnam Veterans Mem.
U.S. Capitol
R.F.K. Mem. Stadium
Library of Congress
Seat Pleasant
Kettering
Seven Corners
Arlington Nat. Cemetery
Jefferson Memorial
Mason Mem. Br.
Fort Dupont Park
Capitol Heights
Millwood
Ritchie
Arlington Blvd.
Broyhill Park
Pentagon
East Potomac Park
Oakland
Hillwood
ARLINGTON CO.
FAIRFAX CO.
East Arlington
Coral Hills
District Heights
Annalee Heights
Holmes Run Acres
Culmore
Lake Barcroft
Baileys Crossroads
RONALD REAGAN NATIONAL
Anacostia
Forestville
Fairfax
Little River Turnpike
Parklawn
Suitland
George Mason University
Hillcrest Heights
PRINCE GEORGES CO.
Morningside
Annandale
Alexandria
Potomac River
Silver Hill
Glassmanor
Kings Park
Shirley Mem. Hwy.
Forest Heights
Temple Hills
ANDREWS AIR FORCE BASE
Fairfax Station
Kings Park West
North Springfield
Oxon Hill
Camp Springs
Capital Beltway
Huntington
West Springfield
Springfield
Franconia
Rose Hill
Groveton
Woodrow Wilson Memorial Bridge
South Lawn
Fort Foote Village
Oaklawn
Butts Corner
West from Greenwich
77°20'
77°10'
77°00'
76°50'
39°00'
38°50'
A
B
C
1
2
3
4
5

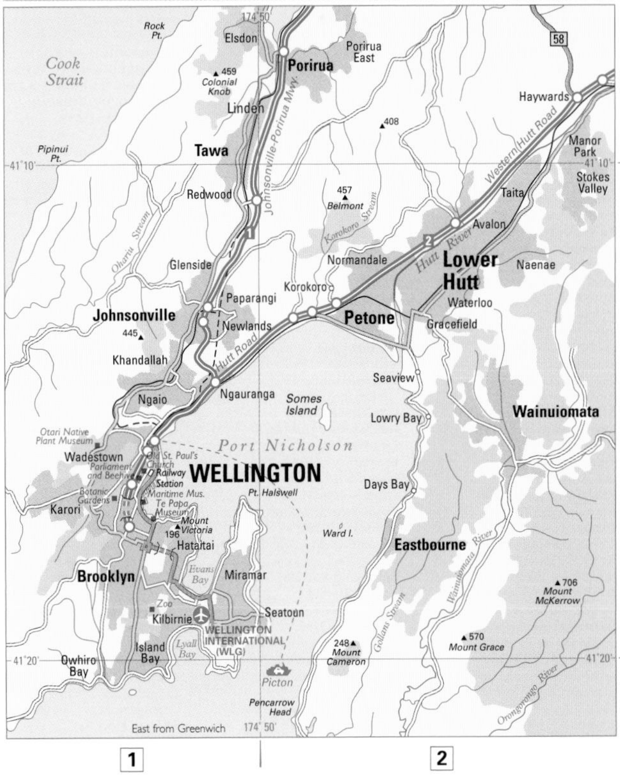

Interstate route numbers U.S. route numbers State route numbers

CENTRAL WASHINGTON

0 km 1
0 miles 0.5
P St.
Logan Circle
FLORIDA AVE.
N St.
Scott Circle
RHODE ISLAND AVE.
CONNECTICUT AVE.
NORTH WEST
NEW JERSEY AVE.
NEW YORK AVE.
NORTH CAPITOL ST.
M St.
Thomas Circle
MASSACHUSETTS AVE.
Mt. Vernon Sq.-UDC
Farragut North
L St.
VERMONT AVE.
K ST.
Mt. Vernon Square
Farragut West
McPherson Sq.
Franklin Square
Lafayette Square
Convention Center
Metro Center
Gallery Place
Union Station
PENNSYLVANIA AVE.
World Bank
The White House
National Place
Ford's Theater
Nat. Mus. of American Art
Judiciary Sq.
Columbus Circle
E ST.
Zero Milestone
Dept. of the Interior
The Ellipse
Federal Triangle
Nat. Museum of Natural History
Archives-Navy Memorial
LOUISIANA AVE.
Union Station Plaza
CONSTITUTION AVE.
Nat. Museum of American History
Supreme Court
Reflecting Pool
Washington Monument
Madison Dr.
National Gallery of Art
Grant Statue
U.S. Capitol
D. C. War Memorial (W.W. II Memorial)
The Mall
Jefferson Dr.
Smithsonian
Smithsonian Institution
National Air & Space Museum
Botanic Gardens
Library of Congress
INDEPENDENCE AVE.
Hirshhorn Museum
Kutz Bridge
US Holocaust Memorial Museum
MARYLAND AVE.
Federal Center SW
Tidal Basin
L'Enfant Plaza
Capitol South
Potomac Park
Jefferson Memorial
Outlet Bridge
14TH ST.
SOUTHWEST FREEWAY
Francis Case Meml. Bridge
MAINE AVE.
SOUTH WEST
SOUTH CAPITOL ST.
Potomac River
East Potomac Park
Washington Channel
Waterfront
M ST.
Navy Yard
a
b
c
1
2
3

WELLINGTON

0 km 5
0 miles 3
Rock Pt.
Elsdon
Porirua
Porirua East
Cook Strait
459 Colonial Knob
Linden
Haywards
Johnsonville-Porirua Mwy.
408
Pipinui Pt.
Tawa
Western Hutt Road
Manor Park
Stokes Valley
Taita
Redwood
457 Belmont
Avalon
Glenside
Normandale
Hutt River
Lower Hutt
Naenae
Korokoro
Paparangi
Johnsonville
Petone
Waterloo
Gracefield
Newlands
445
Khandallah
Hutt Road
Seaview
Ngaio
Ngauranga
Somes Island
Lowry Bay
Wainuiomata
Otari Native Plant Museum
Port Nicholson
Wadestown
Parliament and Beehive
Old St. Paul's Church
Railway Station
WELLINGTON
Botanic Gardens
Maritime Mus.
Te Papa Museum
Pt. Halswell
Days Bay
Karori
Mount Victoria
196
Ward I.
Hataitai
Eastbourne
Brooklyn
Evans Bay
Miramar
706 Mount McKerrow
Zoo
Kilbirnie
Seatoun
WELLINGTON INTERNATIONAL (WLG)
248 Mount Cameron
570 Mount Grace
Owhiro Bay
Island Bay
Lyall Bay
Picton
Pencarrow Head
East from Greenwich
174°50'
41°10'
41°20'
A
B
C
1
2

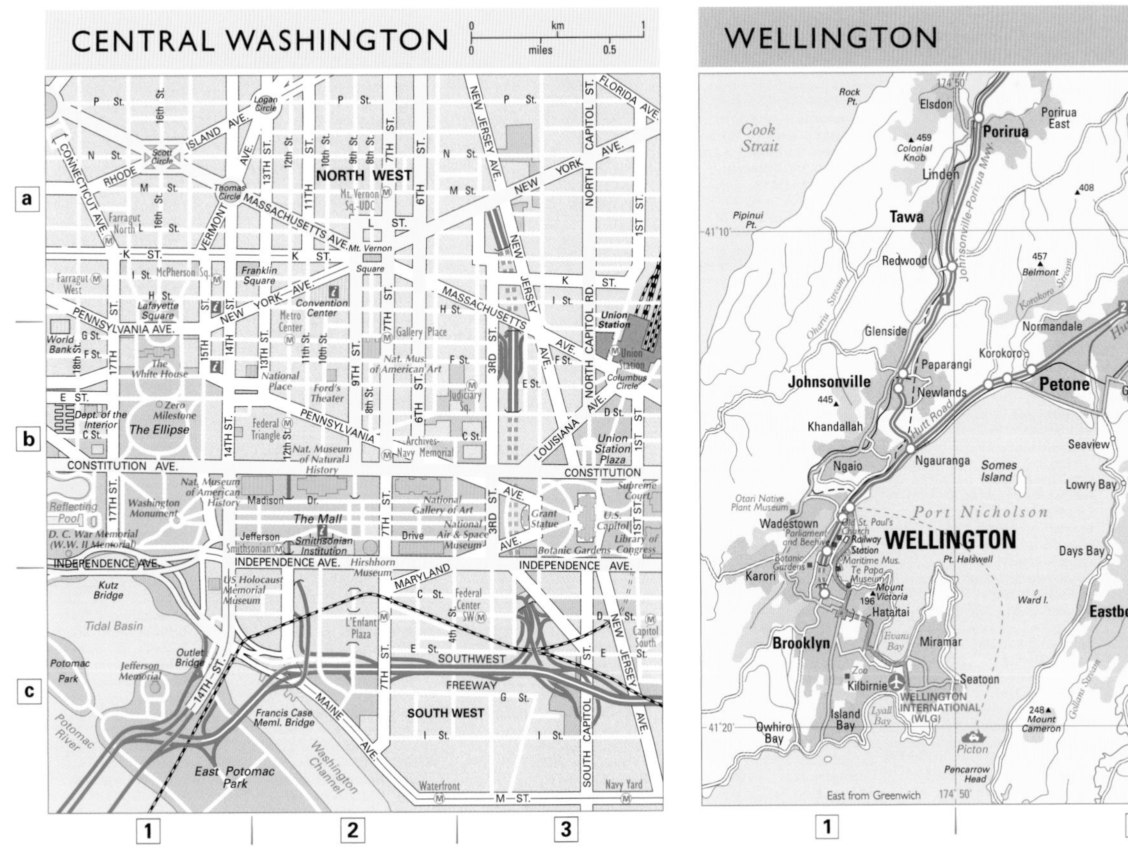

INDEX TO CITY MAPS

The index contains the names of all the principal places and features shown on the City Maps. Each name is followed by an additional entry in italics giving the name of the City Map within which it is located.

The number in bold type which follows each name refers to the number of the City Map page where that feature or place will be found.

The letter and figure which are immediately after the page number give the grid square on the map within which the feature or place is situated.

The letter represents the latitude and the figure the longitude. The full geographic reference is provided in the border of the City Maps.

The location given is the centre of the city, suburb or feature and is not necessarily the name. Rivers, canals and roads are indexed to their name. Rivers carry the symbol → after their name.

An explanation of the alphabetical order rules and a list of the abbreviations used are to be found at the beginning of the World Map Index.

A

Aalām *Baghdad* **223** B2
Abbey Wood *London* **235** B4
Abcoude *Amsterdam* **222** B2
Âbdin *Cairo* **227** A2
Abeno *Osaka* **243** B2
Aberdeen *Hong Kong* **232** B1
Aberdour *Edinburgh* **231** A2
Aberdour Castle *Edinburgh* **231** A2
Abfanggraben → *Munich* **241** A3
Ablon-sur-Seine *Paris* **244** B3
Abramtsevo *Moscow* **239** B3
Abu Dis *Jerusalem* **233** B2
Abû en Numrus *Cairo* **227** B2
Abu Ghosh *Jerusalem* **233** B1
Acassuso *Buenos Aires* **227** A1
Accotink, L. *Washington* **253** C2
Accotink Cr. → *Washington* **253** B2
Achères *Paris* **244** A1
Acília *Rome* **246** C1
Aclimação *São Paulo* **247** B2
Acropolis *Athens* **222** B2
Acton *London* **235** A2
Açúcar, Pão de *Rio de Janeiro* **245** B2
Ada Beja *Lisbon* **236** A1
Adams Park *Atlanta* **223** B2
Addiscombe *London* **235** B3
Adelphi *Washington* **253** A4
Aderklaa *Vienna* **252** A3
Adler Planetarium *Chicago* **229** B3
Admiralteyskaya Storona *St. Petersburg* **247** B2
Áffori *Milan* **239** A2
Aflandshage *Copenhagen* **228** B3
Afsarīyeh *Tehran* **251** B2
Agboyi Cr. → *Lagos* **234** A2
Ågerup *Copenhagen* **228** A1
Ågesta *Stockholm* **249** B2
Aghia Marina *Athens* **222** C3
Aghia Paraskevi *Athens* **222** A2
Aghios Dimitrios *Athens* **222** B2
Aghios Ioannis Rendis *Athens* **222** B1
Agincourt *Toronto* **251** A3
Agra Canal *Delhi* **230** B2
Agricola Oriental *Mexico City* **238** B2
Agua Espraiada → *São Paulo* **247** B2
Agualva-Cacem *Lisbon* **236** A1
Agustino, Cerro El *Lima* **234** B3
Ahrensfelde *Berlin* **225** A4
Ahuntsic *Montreal* **240** A1
Ai → *Osaka* **243** A2
Aigremont *Paris* **244** A1
Air View Park *Singapore* **248** A2
Airport West *Melbourne* **238** A1
Ajegunle *Lagos* **234** B2
Aji *Osaka* **243** A1
Ajuda *Lisbon* **236** A1
Akalla *Stockholm* **249** A1
Akasaka *Tokyo* **250** A3
Akbarābād *Tehran* **251** A2
Akershus Castle = Akershus Slott *Oslo* **243** A3
Akershus Slott *Oslo* **243** A3
Al 'Azamīyah *Baghdad* **223** A2
Al Quds = Jerusalem *Jerusalem* **233** B2
Al-Walaja *Jerusalem* **233** B1
Alaguntan *Lagos* **234** B2
Alameda *San Francisco* **246** B3
Alameda Memorial State Beach Park *San Francisco* **246** B3
Albern *Vienna* **252** B2
Albert Park *Melbourne* **238** B1
Alberton *Johannesburg* **233** B2
Albertslund *Copenhagen* **228** B2
Albysjön *Stockholm* **249** B1
Alcantara *Lisbon* **236** A1
Alcatraz I. *San Francisco* **246** B2
Alcobendas *Madrid* **237** A2
Alcorcón *Madrid* **237** B1
Aldershof *Berlin* **225** B4
Aldo Bonzi *Buenos Aires* **227** C1
Aleksandrovskoye *St. Petersburg* **247** B2
Alexander Nevsky Abbey *St. Petersburg* **247** B2
Alexandra *Johannesburg* **233** A2
Alexandra *Singapore* **248** B2
Alexandria *Washington* **253** C3
Alfortville *Paris* **244** B3
Algés *Lisbon* **236** A1
Alhambra *Los Angeles* **236** B4
Alibey → *Istanbul* **232** B1
Alibey Barajı *Istanbul* **232** B1
Alibeyköy *Istanbul* **232** B1
Alimos *Athens* **222** B2
Alipur *Kolkata* **234** B1
Allach *Munich* **241** A1
Allambie Heights *Sydney* **249** A2
Allermuir Hill *Edinburgh* **231** B2
Allstate Arena *Chicago* **229** A1
Allston *Boston* **226** A2
Almada *Lisbon* **236** A2
Almagro *Buenos Aires* **227** B2
Almargem do Bispo *Lisbon* **236** A1
Almirante G. Brown, Parque *Buenos Aires* **227** C2
Almon *Jerusalem* **233** B2
Almond → *Edinburgh* **231** B2
Alna *Oslo* **243** A4
Alnsjøen *Oslo* **243** A4
Alperton *London* **235** A2
Alpine *New York* **242** A2
Alrode *Johannesburg* **233** B2
Alsemberg *Brussels* **226** B1
Alsergrund *Vienna* **252** A2
Alsip *Chicago* **229** C2
Ålsten *Stockholm* **249** B1
Älta *Stockholm* **249** B3
Altadena *Los Angeles* **236** A4
Alte-Donau → *Vienna* **252** A2
Alter Finkenkrug *Berlin* **225** A1
Altes Rathaus *Munich* **241** B2
Altglienicke *Berlin* **225** B4
Altlandsberg *Berlin* **225** A5
Altlandsberg Nord *Berlin* **225** A5
Altmannsdorf *Vienna* **252** B1
Alto da Boa Vista *Rio de Janeiro* **245** B1
Alto da Moóca *São Paulo* **247** B2
Alto do Pina *Lisbon* **236** A2
Altona *Melbourne* **238** B1
Alvik *Stockholm* **249** B1
Älvsjo *Stockholm* **249** B2
Älvvik *Stockholm* **249** A3
Am Hasenbergl *Munich* **241** A2
Am Steinhof *Vienna* **252** A1
Am Wald *Munich* **241** B2
Ama Keng *Singapore* **248** A2
Amadora *Lisbon* **236** A1
Amagasaki *Osaka* **243** A1
Amager *Copenhagen* **228** B3
Amāl Qādisiya *Baghdad* **223** B2
Amalienborg Slot *Copenhagen* **228** A3
Amata *Milan* **239** A1
Ambelokipi *Athens* **222** B2
Ameixoeira *Lisbon* **236** A2
América *São Paulo* **247** B1
American Police Hall of Fame *Miami* **238** B2
American University *Washington* **253** B3
Amin *Baghdad* **223** B2
Aminadav *Jerusalem* **233** B1
Amīrābād *Tehran* **251** A2
Amora *Lisbon* **236** B2
Amoreira *Lisbon* **236** A1
Amper → *Munich* **241** A1
Amstel-Drecht-Kanaal *Amsterdam* **222** B2
Amstelveen *Amsterdam* **222** B2
Amsterdam *Amsterdam* **222** A2
Amsterdam ✕ (AMS) *Amsterdam* **222** B1
Amsterdam-Rijnkanaal *Amsterdam* **222** B3
Amsterdam Zuidoost *Amsterdam* **222** B2
Amsterdamse Bos *Amsterdam* **222** B1
Anacosta → *Washington* **253** B4
Anacostia *Washington* **253** B4
Anadoluhisarı *Istanbul* **232** B2
Anadolukavağı *Istanbul* **232** A2
Anata *Jerusalem* **233** B2
Ancol *Jakarta* **232** A1
'Andalus *Baghdad* **223** B1
Andaraí *Rio de Janeiro* **245** B1
Anderlecht *Brussels* **226** A1
Anderson Park *Atlanta* **223** B2
Andingmen *Beijing* **224** B2
Ang Mo Kio *Singapore* **248** A3
Ängby *Stockholm* **249** A1
Angel I. *San Francisco* **246** A2
Angel Island State Park ⌂ *San Francisco* **246** A2
Angke, Kali → *Jakarta* **232** A1
Angyalföld *Budapest* **227** A2
Anik *Mumbai* **240** A2
Anin *Warsaw* **252** B2
Anjou *Montreal* **240** A2
Annalee Heights *Washington* **253** B2
Annandale *Washington* **253** C2
Anne Frankhuis *Amsterdam* **222** A2
Antony *Paris* **244** B2
Aoyama *Tokyo* **250** B3
Ap Lei Chau *Hong Kong* **232** B1
Apapa *Lagos* **234** B2
Apelacão *Lisbon* **236** A2
Apopka, L. *Orlando* **243** A1
Apoquindo *Santiago* **247** B2
Apterkarskiy Ostrov *St. Petersburg* **247** B2
Ar Kazimiyah *Baghdad* **223** B1
Ar Ram *Jerusalem* **233** A2
Ara → *Tokyo* **250** A4
Arakawa *Tokyo* **250** A3
Arany-hegyi-patak → *Budapest* **227** A2
Aravaca *Madrid* **237** B1
Arbataash *Baghdad* **223** A1
Arc de Triomphe *Paris* **244** A2
Arcadia *Los Angeles* **236** B4
Arcueil *Paris* **244** B2
Arese *Milan* **239** A1
Arganzuela *Madrid* **237** B1
Argenteuil *Paris* **244** A2
Argiroupoli *Athens* **222** B2
Argonne Forest *Chicago* **229** C1
Arima *Tokyo* **250** B2
Arlanda ✕ (ARN) *Stockholm* **249** A1
Arlington *Boston* **226** A1
Arlington *Washington* **253** B3
Arlington Heights *Boston* **226** A1
Arlington Nat. Cemetery *Washington* **253** B3
Armação *Rio de Janeiro* **245** B2
Armadale *Melbourne* **238** B2
Armour Heights *Toronto* **251** A2
Arncliffe *Sydney* **249** B1
Arnold Arboretum *Boston* **226** B2
Árpádföld *Budapest* **227** A3
Arrentela *Lisbon* **236** B2
Arroyo Seco Park *Los Angeles* **236** B3
Årsta *Stockholm* **249** B2
Art Institute *Chicago* **229** B3
Artane *Dublin* **230** A2
Artas *Jerusalem* **233** B2
Arthur's Seat *Edinburgh* **231** B3
Arts, Place des *Montreal* **240** A2
As Shawawra *Jerusalem* **233** B2
Asagaya *Tokyo* **250** A2
Asahi *Osaka* **243** A2
Asakusa *Tokyo* **250** A3
Asati *Kolkata* **234** C1
Aschheim *Munich* **241** A3
Ascot Vale *Melbourne* **238** A1
Ashbridge's Bay Park *Toronto* **251** B3
Ashburn *Chicago* **229** C2
Ashburton *Melbourne* **238** B2
Ashfield *Sydney* **249** B1
Ashford *London* **235** B1
Ashtown *Dublin* **230** A2
Askisto *Helsinki* **231** B1
Askrikefjärden *Stockholm* **249** A3
Asnières *Paris* **244** A2
Aspern *Vienna* **252** A2
Aspern ✕ *Vienna* **252** A3
Assago *Milan* **239** B1
Assendelft *Amsterdam* **222** A1
Assiano *Milan* **239** B1
Astoria *New York* **242** B2
Astrolabe Park *Sydney* **249** B2
Atarot *Jerusalem* **233** A2
Atarot ✕ *Jerusalem* **233** A2
Atghara *Kolkata* **234** B2
Athens = Athina *Athens* **222** B2
Athina *Athens* **222** B2
Athina ✕ (ATH) *Athens* **222** A3
Athínai = Athina *Athens* **222** B2
Athis-Mons *Paris* **244** B3
Athlone *Cape Town* **228** A2
Atholl *Johannesburg* **233** A2
Atīfiya *Baghdad* **223** A2
Atişalen *Istanbul* **232** B1
Atlanta *Atlanta* **223** B2
Atlanta Hartsfield Int. ✕ (ATL) *Atlanta* **223** C2
Atlanta Zoo *Atlanta* **223** B2
Atomium *Brussels* **226** A2
Attiki *Athens* **222** A2
Atzgersdorf *Vienna* **252** B1
Aubervilliers *Paris* **244** A3
Aubing *Munich* **241** B1
Auburndale *Boston* **226** A1
Auchendinny *Edinburgh* **231** B2
Auckland Park *Johannesburg* **233** B2
Auderghem *Brussels* **226** B2
Augustówka *Warsaw* **252** B2
Aulnay-sous-Bois *Paris* **244** A3
Aurelio *Rome* **246** B1
Ausîm *Cairo* **227** A1
Austerlitz, Gare d' *Paris* **244** A3
Austin *Chicago* **229** B2
Avalon *Wellington* **253** B2
Avedøre *Copenhagen* **228** B2
Avellaneda *Buenos Aires* **227** C2
Avenel *Washington* **253** B4
Avondale *Chicago* **229** B2
Avondale Heights *Melbourne* **238** A1
Avtovo *St. Petersburg* **247** B1
Ayazağa *Istanbul* **232** B1
Ayer Chawan, Pulau *Singapore* **248** B2
Ayer Merbau, Pulau *Singapore* **248** B2
Azabu *Tokyo* **250** B3
Azcapotzalco *Mexico City* **238** B1
Azteca, Estadia *Mexico City* **238** C2
Azucar, Cerro Pan de *Santiago* **247** A1

B

Baambrugge *Amsterdam* **222** B2
Baba Ch. *Karachi* **233** B1
Baba I. *Karachi* **233** B1
Babarpur *Delhi* **230** A2
Babushkin *Moscow* **239** A3
Back B. *Mumbai* **240** B1
Baclaran *Manila* **237** B2
Bacoor *Manila* **237** C1
Bacoor B. *Manila* **237** C1
Badalona *Barcelona* **224** A2
Badhoevedorp *Amsterdam* **222** A1
Badli *Delhi* **230** A1
Bærum *Oslo* **243** A2
Bağcılar *Istanbul* **232** B1
Bággio *Milan* **239** B1
Bāgh-e-Feyz *Tehran* **251** A1
Baghdād *Baghdad* **223** A2
Baghdad al Muthana ✕ *Baghdad* **223** B2
Baghdad Int. ✕ (SDA) *Baghdad* **223** B1
Bagmari *Kolkata* **234** B2
Bagneux *Paris* **244** B2
Bagnolet *Paris* **244** A3
Bagsværd *Copenhagen* **228** A2
Bagsværd Sø *Copenhagen* **228** A2
Baguiati *Kolkata* **234** B2
Bagumbayan *Manila* **237** C2
Baha'i Temple *Chicago* **229** A2
Bahçeköy *Istanbul* **232** A1
Bahçelievler *Istanbul* **232** B1
Bahtîm *Cairo* **227** A2
Baile Atha Cliath = Dublin *Dublin* **230** A2
Baileys Crossroads *Washington* **253** B3
Bailly *Paris* **244** A1
Bairro Lopes *Lisbon* **236** A2
Baisha *Guangzhou* **231** B2
Baiyun Hill *Guangzhou* **231** B2
Baiyun Int. ✕ (CAN) *Guangzhou* **231** A2
Bakırköy *Istanbul* **232** C1
Bal Harbor *Miami* **238** A2
Balara *Manila* **237** B2
Baldia *Karachi* **233** A1
Baldoyle *Dublin* **230** A3
Baldwin, L. *Orlando* **243** A3
Baldwin Hills *Los Angeles* **236** B2
Baldwin Hills Res. *Los Angeles* **236** B2
Balgowlah *Sydney* **249** A2
Balgowlah Heights *Sydney* **249** A2
Balham *London* **235** B3
Bali *Kolkata* **234** B1
Baliganja *Kolkata* **234** B2
Balingsnäs *Stockholm* **249** B2
Balingsta *Stockholm* **249** B2
Balintawak *Manila* **237** B1
Ballerup *Copenhagen* **228** A2
Ballinteer *Dublin* **230** B2
Ballyboden *Dublin* **230** B2
Ballybrack *Dublin* **230** B3
Ballyfermot *Dublin* **230** A1
Ballymorefinn Hill *Dublin* **230** B1
Ballymun *Dublin* **230** A2
Balmain *Sydney* **249** B2
Baluhati *Kolkata* **234** B1
Balvanera *Buenos Aires* **227** B2
Balwyn *Melbourne* **238** A2
Balwyn North *Melbourne* **238** A2
Banática *Lisbon* **236** A1
Bandra *Mumbai* **240** A1
Bandra Pt. *Mumbai* **240** A1
Bang Kapi *Bangkok* **223** B2
Bang Na *Bangkok* **223** B2
Bangbae *Seoul* **247** C1
Bangkhen *Bangkok* **223** A2
Bangkok *Bangkok* **223** B2
Bangkok Noi *Bangkok* **223** B1
Bangkok Yai *Bangkok* **223** B1
Banglo *Kolkata* **234** B1
Bangrak *Bangkok* **223** B2
Bangsu *Bangkok* **223** B2
Banks, C. *Sydney* **249** C2
Banksmeadow *Sydney* **249** B2
Banstala *Kolkata* **234** B2
Bantra *Kolkata* **234** B1
Baoshan *Shanghai* **248** A1
Bar Giyora *Jerusalem* **233** B1
Barahanagar *Kolkata* **234** B2
Barajas *Madrid* **237** B2
Barajas, Madrid ✕ (MAD) *Madrid* **237** B2
Barakpur *Kolkata* **234** A2
Barcarena *Lisbon* **236** A1
Barcarena, Rib. de → *Lisbon* **236** A1
Barcelona *Barcelona* **224** A2
Barcelona-Prat ✕ (BCN) *Barcelona* **224** B1
Barceloneta *Barcelona* **224** A2
Barcroft, L. *Washington* **253** B3
Barking *London* **235** A4
Barkingside *London* **235** A4
Barnes *London* **235** B2
Barnet *London* **235** A2
Barra Andai *Karachi* **233** B2
Barra Funda *São Paulo* **247** B2
Barracas *Buenos Aires* **227** B2
Barrackpur = Barakpur *Kolkata* **234** A2
Barranco *Lima* **234** B2
Barreiro *Lisbon* **236** B2
Barreto *Rio de Janeiro* **245** B2
Bartala *Kolkata* **234** B1
Barton Park *Sydney* **249** B1
Bartyki *Warsaw* **252** C2
Basus *Cairo* **227** A2
Batanagar *Kolkata* **234** B1
Bath Beach *New York* **242** C1
Bath I. *Karachi* **233** B2
Batir *Jerusalem* **233** B1
Batok, Bukit *Singapore* **248** A2
Battersea *London* **235** B3
Bauman *Moscow* **239** B3
Baumgarten *Vienna* **252** A1
Bay, L. *Orlando* **243** A2
Bay Harbour Islands *Miami* **238** A2
Bay Hill *Orlando* **243** B1
Bay Ridge *New York* **242** C1
Bayit Va-Gan *Jerusalem* **233** B2
Bayonne *New York* **242** B1
Bayrampaşa *Istanbul* **232** B1
Bayshore *San Francisco* **246** B2
Bayt Lahm *Jerusalem* **233** B2
Bayview *San Francisco* **246** B2
Bāzār *Tehran* **251** A2
Beacon Hill *Hong Kong* **232** A2
Beato *Lisbon* **236** A2
Beaumont *Dublin* **230** A2
Beaumonte Heights *Toronto* **251** A1
Bebek *Istanbul* **232** B2
Běchovice *Prague* **245** B3
Beck L. *Chicago* **229** A1
Beckenham *London* **235** B3
Beckton *London* **235** A4
Becontree *London* **235** A4
Beddington Corner *London* **235** B3
Bedford *Boston* **226** A1
Bedford Park *Chicago* **229** C2
Bedford Park *New York* **242** A2
Bedford Stuyvesant *New York* **242** B2
Bedford View *Johannesburg* **233** B2
Bedok *Singapore* **248** B3
Bedok, Res. *Singapore* **248** A3
Beersel *Brussels* **226** B1
Behala *Kolkata* **234** B1
Bei Hai *Beijing* **224** B2
Beicai *Shanghai* **248** B2
Beijing *Beijing* **224** B1
Beit Duqu *Jerusalem* **233** A1
Beit Ghur at-Taht *Jerusalem* **233** A1
Beit Ghur el-Fawqa *Jerusalem* **233** A1
Beit Hanina *Jerusalem* **233** B2
Beit Ij'za *Jerusalem* **233** A1
Beit Iksa *Jerusalem* **233** B2
Beit I'nan *Jerusalem* **233** A1
Beit Jala *Jerusalem* **233** B2
Beit Lekhem = Bayt Lahm *Jerusalem* **233** B2
Beit Liqya *Jerusalem* **233** A1
Beit Nekofa *Jerusalem* **233** B1
Beit Sahur *Jerusalem* **233** B2
Beit Sofafa *Jerusalem* **233** B2
Beit Surik *Jerusalem* **233** B1
Beit Ur al-Fawqa *Jerusalem* **233** A1
Beit Zayit *Jerusalem* **233** B1
Beitaipingzhuan *Beijing* **224** B1
Beitar Ilit *Jerusalem* **233** B1
Beitin *Jerusalem* **233** A2
Beitsun *Guangzhou* **231** B2
Beitunya *Jerusalem* **233** A2
Beixing Jing Park *Shanghai* **248** B1
Békásmegyer *Budapest* **227** A2
Bekkelaget *Oslo* **243** A3
Bekkestua *Oslo* **243** A2
Bel Air *Los Angeles* **236** B2
Bela Vista *São Paulo* **247** B2
Bélanger *Montreal* **240** A1
Belas *Lisbon* **236** A1
Beleghata *Kolkata* **234** B2
Belém *Lisbon* **236** A1
Belém, Torre de *Lisbon* **236** A1
Belènzinho *São Paulo* **247** B2
Belgachiya *Kolkata* **234** B2
Belgharia *Kolkata* **234** B2
Belgrano *Buenos Aires* **227** B2
Bell *Los Angeles* **236** C3
Bell Gardens *Los Angeles* **236** C4
Bellavista *Lima* **234** B2
Bellavista *Santiago* **247** C2
Belle Harbor *New York* **242** C2
Belle Isle *Orlando* **243** B2
Belle View *Washington* **253** B2
Bellingham *London* **235** B3
Bellwood *Chicago* **229** B1
Belmont *Boston* **226** A1
Belmont *London* **235** A2
Belmont, Mt. *Wellington* **253** B2
Belmont Cragin *Chicago* **229** B2
Belmont Harbor *Chicago* **229** B3
Belmore *Sydney* **249** B1
Belur *Kolkata* **234** B2
Belvedere *Atlanta* **223** B3
Belvedere *London* **235** B4
Belvedere *San Francisco* **246** A2
Belyayevo Bogorodskoye *Moscow* **239** C2
Bemowo *Warsaw* **252** B1
Benaki Museum *Athens* **222** B2
Bendale *Toronto* **251** A3
Benefica *Rio de Janeiro* **245** B1
Benfica *Lisbon* **236** A1
Benito Juárez *Mexico City* **238** B2

Benito Juárez, Int. ✕ (MEX) Mexico City 238 B2
Bensonhurst New York 242 C2
Berchem-Ste-Agathe Brussels 226 A1
Berg am Laim Munich 241 B2
Bergenfield New York 242 A2
Bergham Munich 241 B2
Bergvliet Cape Town 228 B1
Beri Barcelona 224 A1
Berkeley San Francisco 246 A3
Berlin Berlin 225 A3
Berlin Dom Berlin 225 A3
Berlin Tegel ✕ (TXL) Berlin 225 A2
Berlin Tempelhof ✕ (THF) Berlin 225 B3
Bermondsey London 235 B3
Bernabeu, Estadio Madrid 237 B1
Bernal Heights San Francisco 246 B2
Berwyn Chicago 229 B2
Berwyn Heights Washington 253 B4
Besiktas Istanbul 232 B2
Besós → Barcelona 224 A2
Bessie, L. Orlando 243 B1
Bet Horon Jerusalem 233 A1
Bethesda Washington 253 B3
Bethlehem = Bayt Lahm Jerusalem 233 B2
Bethnal Green London 235 A3
Betor Kolkata 234 B1
Beulah Orlando 243 A1
Beulah, L. Orlando 243 A1
Beverley Hills Sydney 249 B1
Beverley Park Sydney 249 B1
Beverly Chicago 229 C3
Beverly Arts Center Chicago 229 C2
Beverly Glen Los Angeles 236 B2
Beverly Hills Los Angeles 236 B2
Beverly Hills -Morgan Park Historic District Chicago 229 C2
Bexley Sydney 249 B1
Bexley □ London 235 B4
Bexleyheath London 235 B4
Beykoz Istanbul 232 B2
Beylerbeyi Istanbul 232 B2
Beyoğlu Istanbul 232 B1
Bezons Paris 244 A2
Bezuidenhout Park Johannesburg 233 B2
Bhadrakali Kolkata 234 A2
Bhalswa Delhi 230 A2
Bhambo Khan Qarmati Karachi 233 B2
Bhatsala Kolkata 234 B1
Bhawanipur Kolkata 234 B2
Bhendkhal Mumbai 240 B2
Bhuleshwar Mumbai 240 B1
Białołeka Dworska Warsaw 252 B2
Bicentennial Park Los Angeles 236 B4
Bicentennial Park Sydney 249 B1
Bickley London 235 B4
Bicutan Manila 237 C2
Bidhan Nagar Kolkata 234 B2
Bidu Jerusalem 233 B1
Bielany Warsaw 252 B1
Bielawa Warsaw 252 C2
Biesdorf Berlin 225 A4
Bièvre → Paris 244 B1
Bièvres Paris 244 B2
Big Sand Lake Orlando 243 B2
Bilston Edinburgh 231 B2
Binacayan Manila 237 C1
Binondo Manila 237 B1
Bintaro Jaya Jakarta 232 B1
Bir Nabala Jerusalem 233 A2
Birak el Kiyam Cairo 227 A1
Birch Cliff Toronto 251 A3
Birkenstein Berlin 225 A5
Birkholz Berlin 225 A4
Birkholzaue Berlin 225 A4
Birrarrung Park Melbourne 238 A2
Biscayne Park Miami 238 A2
Bishop Lavis Cape Town 228 A2
Bishopscourt Cape Town 228 A1
Bispebjerg Copenhagen 228 A3
Bittsevsky Forest Park Moscow 239 C2
Björknäs Stockholm 249 B3
Black Cr. → Toronto 251 A2
Black Creek Pioneer Village Toronto 251 A1
Blackfen London 235 B4
Blackheath London 235 B4
Blackrock Dublin 230 B2
Bladensburg Washington 253 B4
Blair Village Atlanta 223 C2
Blairgowrie Johannesburg 233 A2
Blake House Boston 226 B2
Blakehurst Sydney 249 B1
Blakstad Oslo 243 B1
Blanche, L. Orlando 243 B1
Blankenburg Berlin 225 A3
Blankenfelde Berlin 225 A3
Blizne Warsaw 252 B1
Blota Warsaw 252 C3
Blue Island Chicago 229 D2
Blue Mosque = Sultanahme Camii Istanbul 232 B1
Bluebell Dublin 230 B1
Bluff Hd. Hong Kong 232 B2
Bluffers Park Toronto 251 A3
Blumberg Berlin 225 A4
Blunt Pt. San Francisco 246 A2
Blutenberg Munich 241 B1
Blylaget Oslo 243 B3
Boa Vista, Alto do Rio de Janeiro 245 B1
Boardwalk New York 242 C3
Boavista Lisbon 236 A2
Bobigny Paris 244 A3
Bocanegra Lima 234 B2
Boedo Buenos Aires 227 B2
Bogenhausen Munich 241 B2
Boggy Creek Swamp Orlando 243 B2
Bogorodskoye Moscow 239 B3
Bogota New York 242 A1
Bogstadvatnet Oslo 243 A2
Bohnsdorf Berlin 225 B4
Bois-Colombes Paris 244 A2
Bois-d'Arcy Paris 244 B1
Boissy-St-Léger Paris 244 B4
Boldinasco Milan 239 B1
Bøler Oslo 243 A4
Bollate Milan 239 A1
Bollebeek Brussels 226 A1
Bollensdorf Berlin 225 A5
Bollmora Stockholm 249 B3
Bolshaya Okhta St. Petersburg 247 B2
Bolton Atlanta 223 B2
Bom Retiro São Paulo 247 B2
Bombay = Mumbai Mumbai 240 B2
Bondi Sydney 249 B2
Bondy Paris 244 A3
Bondy, Forêt de Paris 244 A4
Bonifacio Monument Manila 237 B1
Bonneuil-sur-Marne Paris 244 B4
Bonnington Edinburgh 231 B1
Bonnyrigg and Lasswade Edinburgh 231 B3
Bonsucesso Rio de Janeiro 245 B1
Bonteheuwel Cape Town 228 A2
Boo Stockholm 249 A3
Booterstown Dublin 230 B2
Borisovo Moscow 239 C3
Borle Mumbai 240 A2
Boronia Park Sydney 249 A1
Bosmont Johannesburg 233 B1
Bosön Stockholm 249 A3
Bosporus = İstanbul Boğazı Istanbul 232 B2
Bostancı Istanbul 232 C2
Boston Boston 226 A2
Boston Common Boston 226 A2
Boston Logan Int. ✕ (BOS) Boston 226 A2
Botafogo Rio de Janeiro 245 B1
Botany Sydney 249 B2
Botany B. Sydney 249 B2
Botany Bay Nat. Park △ Sydney 249 B2
Botič → Prague 245 B3
Botica Sete Lisbon 236 A1
Boucherville Montreal 240 A3
Boucherville, Îs. de Montreal 240 A3
Bougival Paris 244 A1
Boulder Pt. Hong Kong 232 B1
Boulogne, Bois de Paris 244 A2
Boulogne-Billancourt Paris 244 A2
Bourg-la-Reine Paris 244 B2
Bouviers Paris 244 B1
Bovenkerk Amsterdam 222 B2
Bovenkerker Polder Amsterdam 222 B2
Bovisa Milan 239 A2
Bow London 235 A3
Boyacıköy Istanbul 232 B2
Boyd Conservation Area Toronto 251 A1
Boyle Heights Los Angeles 236 B3
Braepark Edinburgh 231 B2
Braid Edinburgh 231 B2
Bramley Johannesburg 233 A2
Brandeis University Boston 226 A1
Brandenburger Tor Berlin 225 A3
Brani, Pulau Singapore 248 B3
Branik Prague 245 B2
Brännkyrka Stockholm 249 B2
Brás São Paulo 247 B2
Brasilândia São Paulo 247 A1
Brateyevo Moscow 239 C3
Braybrook Melbourne 238 A1
Brázdim Prague 245 A3
Breakheart Reservation Boston 226 A2
Brede Copenhagen 228 A3
Breezy Point New York 242 C2
Breitenlee Vienna 252 A3
Breña Lima 234 B2
Brent □ London 235 A2
Brent Res. London 235 A2
Brentford London 235 B2
Brentwood Park Los Angeles 236 B2
Brera Milan 239 B2
Bresso Milan 239 A2
Brevik Stockholm 249 A3
Břevnov Prague 245 B2
Brickyard, The Chicago 229 B2
Bridgeport Chicago 229 B3
Bridgetown Cape Town 228 A2
Bridgeview Chicago 229 C2
Brighton Boston 226 A2
Brighton Melbourne 238 B1
Brighton Beach New York 242 C2
Brighton le Sands Sydney 249 B1
Brighton Park Chicago 229 C2
Brightwood Washington 253 B3
Brigittenau Vienna 252 A2
Brimbank Park Melbourne 238 A1
Brisbane San Francisco 246 B2
Britz Berlin 225 B3
Brixton London 235 B3
Broadmeadows Melbourne 238 A1
Broadmoor San Francisco 246 B2
Broadview Chicago 229 B1
Brockley London 235 B3
Bródno Warsaw 252 B2
Bródnowski, Kanal Warsaw 252 B2
Broek Amsterdam 222 A2
Bromley □ London 235 B4
Bromley Common London 235 B4
Bromma Stockholm 249 A1
Bromma ✕ Stockholm 249 A1
Brøndby Strand Copenhagen 228 B2
Brøndbyøster Copenhagen 228 B2
Brøndbyvester Copenhagen 228 B2
Brondesbury London 235 A2
Brønnøya Oslo 243 A2
Brønshøj Copenhagen 228 A2
Bronxville New York 242 A3
Brookfield Chicago 229 C1
Brookhaven Atlanta 223 A2
Brookline Boston 226 B2
Brooklyn Cape Town 228 A1
Brooklyn New York 242 C2
Brooklyn Wellington 253 B1
Brooklyn Heights New York 242 B2
Brookmont Washington 253 B3
Brossard Montreal 240 B3
Brou-sur-Chantereine Paris 244 A4
Brown Toronto 251 A3
Broyhill Park Washington 253 B2
Brughério Milan 239 A2
Brunswick Melbourne 238 A1
Brussegem Brussels 226 A1
Brussel Brussels 226 A2
Brussel ✕ (BRU) Brussels 226 A2
Brussels = Brussel Brussels 226 A2
Bruxelles = Brussel Brussels 226 A2
Bruzzano Milan 239 A2
Bry-sur-Marne Paris 244 A4
Bryan, L. Orlando 243 B2
Bryanston Johannesburg 233 A1
Bryn Oslo 243 A1
Brzeziny Warsaw 252 B2
Bubeneč Prague 245 B2
Buc Paris 244 B1
Buchenhain Munich 241 B1
Buchholz Berlin 225 A3
Buckhead Atlanta 223 A2
Buckingham Palace London 235 A3
Buckow Berlin 225 B3
Buda Budapest 227 A2
Buda Castle = Budavárípalota Budapest 227 A2
Budafok Budapest 227 B2
Budaörs Budapest 227 B1
Budapest Budapest 227 B2
Budapest ✕ (BUD) Budapest 227 B3
Budatétény Budapest 227 B2
Budavárípalota Budapest 227 A2
Buddinge Copenhagen 228 A3
Buena Ventura Lakes Orlando 243 B2
Buena Vista San Francisco 246 B2
Buenos Aires Buenos Aires 227 B2
Bufalotta Rome 246 B2
Bugio Lisbon 236 B1
Buiksloot Amsterdam 222 A2
Buitenveldert Amsterdam 222 B2
Buizingen Brussels 226 B1
Bukhansan Seoul 247 B1
Bukit Panjang Nature Reserve Singapore 248 A2
Bukit Timah Nature Reserve Singapore 248 A2
Bukum, Pulau Singapore 248 B2
Būlâq Cairo 227 A2
Bule Manila 237 C2
Bulim Singapore 248 A2
Bullen Park Melbourne 238 A2
Bund, The Shanghai 248 B1
Bundoora North Melbourne 238 A2
Bundoora Park Melbourne 238 A2
Bunker Hill Memorial Boston 226 A2
Bunker I. Karachi 233 B1
Bunkyō Tokyo 250 A3
Bunnefjorden Oslo 243 A3
Buona Vista Park Singapore 248 B2
Burbank Chicago 229 C2
Burbank Los Angeles 236 A3
Burden, L. Orlando 243 B1
Burlington Boston 226 A1
Burnham Park Chicago 229 C3
Burnham Park Harbor Chicago 229 B3
Burnhamthorpe Toronto 251 B1
Burnt Oak London 235 A2
Burntisland Edinburgh 231 A2
Burnwynd Edinburgh 231 B1
Burqa Jerusalem 233 A2
Burtus Cairo 227 A1
Burudvatn Oslo 243 A2
Burwood Sydney 249 B1
Bushwick New York 242 B2
Bushy Park London 235 B1
Butantã São Paulo 247 B1
Butcher I. Mumbai 240 B2
Butler, L. Orlando 243 B1
Butts Corner Washington 253 C2
Büyükdere Istanbul 232 B2
Byculla Mumbai 240 B2
Bygdøy Oslo 243 A3

C

C.B.S. Fox Studios Los Angeles 236 B2
C.N.N. Center Atlanta 223 B2
C.N. Tower Toronto 251 B2
Caballito Buenos Aires 227 B2
Cabin John Washington 253 B2
Cabin John Regional Park ⌂ Washington 253 A2
Cabinteely Dublin 230 B3
Cabra Dublin 230 A2
Cabuçú de Baixo → São Paulo 247 A1
Cabuçú de Cima → São Paulo 247 A2
Cachan Paris 244 B2
Cachoeira, Rib. da → São Paulo 247 B1
Cacilhas Lisbon 236 A2
Cahuenga Park Los Angeles 236 B3
Cain, L. Orlando 243 B2
Cairo = El Qâhira Cairo 227 A2
Cairo Int. ✕ (CAI) Cairo 227 A3
Caju Rio de Janeiro 245 B1
Čakovice Prague 245 B3
Calcutta = Kolkata Kolkata 234 B2
California Inst. of Tech. Los Angeles 236 B4
California Los Angeles, University of Los Angeles 236 B2
California State University Los Angeles 236 B3
Callao Lima 234 B2
Caloocan Manila 237 B1
Calumet L. Chicago 229 C3
Calumet Park Chicago 229 C3
Calumet Sag Channel → Chicago 229 C2
Calvairate Milan 239 B2
Camarate Lisbon 236 A2
Camaroes Lisbon 236 A1
Camberwell London 235 B3
Camberwell Melbourne 238 B2
Cambridge Boston 226 A2
Cambuci São Paulo 247 B2
Camden □ London 235 A3
Cameron, Mt. Wellington 253 B2
Çamlıca Istanbul 232 B2
Camp Springs Washington 253 C4
Campamento Madrid 237 B1
Campbellfield Melbourne 238 A1
Camperdown Sydney 249 B2
Campo, Casa de Madrid 237 B1
Campo F.C. Barcelona Barcelona 224 A1
Campo Grando Lisbon 236 A2
Campo Pequeño Lisbon 236 A2
Campolide Lisbon 236 A2
Camps Bay Cape Town 228 A1
C'an San Joan Barcelona 224 A2
Cañacao B. Manila 237 C1
Canarsie New York 242 C2
Candiac Montreal 240 B3
Caneças Lisbon 236 A1
Canillas Madrid 237 B2
Canillejas Madrid 237 B2
Canning Town London 235 A4
Canteras de Vallecas Madrid 237 B2
Canterbury Melbourne 238 A2
Canterbury Sydney 249 B1
Canton = Guangzhou Guangzhou 231 B2
Caoheijing Shanghai 248 B1
Capão Redondo São Paulo 247 B1
Caparica Lisbon 236 A2
Caparica, Costa da Lisbon 236 B1
Cape Flats Cape Town 228 B2
Cape Peninsula △ Cape Town 228 A1
Cape Town Cape Town 228 A1
Cape Town Int. ✕ (CPT) Cape Town 228 A2
Capitol Heights Washington 253 B4
Captain Cook Bridge Sydney 249 C1
Captain Cook Landing Place Park Sydney 249 C2
Capuchos Lisbon 236 B1
Carabanchel Alto Madrid 237 B1
Carabanchel Bajo Madrid 237 B1
Carapachay Buenos Aires 227 B1
Caraza Buenos Aires 227 C2
Caridad Manila 237 C1
Carioca, Sa. da Rio de Janeiro 245 B1
Carlstadt New York 242 A1
Carlton Melbourne 238 A1
Carmen de Huechuraba Santiago 247 B1
Carmen de la Legua Lima 234 B2
Carnaxide Lisbon 236 A1
Carnegie Melbourne 238 B2
Carnide Lisbon 236 A1
Carol City Miami 238 A1
Carrascal Santiago 247 B1
Carrickmines Dublin 230 B3
Carrières-sous-Bois Paris 244 A1
Carrières-sous-Poissy Paris 244 A1
Carrières-sur-Seine Paris 244 A2
Carrigeen B. Dublin 230 A3
Cartierville Montreal 240 A1
Casa Loma Toronto 251 A2
Casa Verde São Paulo 247 A1
Casál Morena Rome 246 C2
Casalotti Rome 246 B1
Cascade Heights Atlanta 223 B2
Castèl di Leva Rome 246 C2
Castèl Sant'Angelo Rome 246 B1
Castleknock Dublin 230 A1
Castleton Corners New York 242 C1
Catete Rio de Janeiro 245 B1
Catford London 235 B3
Catherine, L. Orlando 243 B2
Caulfield Melbourne 238 B2
Cavite Manila 237 C1
Caxias Lisbon 236 A1
Cebecci Istanbul 232 B1
Cecchignola Rome 246 C2
Cecilienhof, Schloss Berlin 225 B1
Cedar Grove Atlanta 223 C3
Cedarvale Park Toronto 251 A2
Cempaka Putih Jakarta 232 B2
Çengelköy Istanbul 232 B2
Cengkareng Jakarta 232 A1
Centennial Olympic Park Atlanta 223 B2
Centennial Park Sydney 249 B2
Center Hill Atlanta 223 B2
Centocelle Rome 246 B2
Central, Gare Montreal 240 B2
Central Park New York 242 B2
Cerdanyola del Vallès Barcelona 224 A1
Cerillos Santiago 247 B1
Cerro de la Estrella, Parque Nacional △ Mexico City 238 B2
Cerro de los Angeles Madrid 237 C1
Cerro Navia Santiago 247 B1
Cesano Boscone Milan 239 B1
Cesate Milan 239 A1
Cha Kwo Ling Hong Kong 232 B2
Chacarrita Buenos Aires 227 B2
Chadwell Heath London 235 A4
Chai Chee Singapore 248 B3
Chai Wan Hong Kong 232 B2
Chai Wan Kok Hong Kong 232 A1
Chakdaha Kolkata 234 C1
Chamartin Madrid 237 B1
Chamberi Madrid 237 B1
Chambourcy Paris 244 A1
Champigny-sur-Marne Paris 244 B4
Champlain, Pont Montreal 240 B2
Champs-sur-Marne Paris 244 A4
Chamrail Kolkata 234 B1
Chanakyapuri Delhi 230 B2
Chanditala Kolkata 234 A1
Changfeng Park Shanghai 248 B1
Changhai = Shanghai Shanghai 248 B2
Changi Singapore 248 A3
Changi, Singapore ✕ (SIN) Singapore 248 A3
Changning Shanghai 248 B1
Chantereine Paris 244 A4
Chantian Guangzhou 231 A2
Chaoyang Beijing 224 B2
Chaoyangmen Beijing 224 B2
Chapelizod Dublin 230 A1
Chapultepec, Bosque de Mexico City 238 B1
Chapultepec, Castillo de Mexico City 238 B1
Charenton-le-Pont Paris 244 B3
Charleroi, Kanal de → Brussels 226 B1
Charles Bridge = Karlův most Prague 245 B2
Charles Gates Dawes House Chicago 229 A2
Charlestown Boston 226 A2
Charlottenburg Berlin 225 A2
Charlottenburg, Schloss Berlin 225 A2
Charlottenlund Copenhagen 228 A3
Charlton London 235 B4
Charneca Lisbon 236 A2
Chase, L. Orlando 243 B1
Châteaufort Paris 244 B1
Châtenay-Malabry Paris 244 B2
Chatham Chicago 229 C3
Chatillon Paris 244 B2
Chatou Paris 244 A1
Chatpur Kolkata 234 B2
Chatswood Sydney 249 A2
Chatuchak Bangkok 223 B2
Chatuchak Park Bangkok 223 B2
Chauki Karachi 233 A1
Chavarria Lima 234 B2
Chaville Paris 244 B2
Chayang Seoul 247 B2
Chelles Paris 244 A4
Chelles, Canal de Paris 244 A4
Chells-le-Pin ✕ Paris 244 A4
Chelsea Boston 226 A2
Chelsea London 235 B2
Chembur Mumbai 240 A2
Chennevières-sur-Marne Paris 244 B4
Cheongdam Seoul 247 B2
Cheonho Seoul 247 B2
Cheops Cairo 227 B1
Chertanovka → Moscow 239 C2
Chertanovo Moscow 239 C2
Cheryomushki Moscow 239 B2
Chestnut Hill Boston 226 B1
Cheung Sha Wan Hong Kong 232 A1
Cheverly Washington 253 B4
Chevilly-Larue Paris 244 B3
Chevry-Cossigny Paris 244 B4
Chevy Chase Washington 253 B3
Chhatrapati Shivaji, Mumbai ✕ (BOM) Mumbai 240 A2
Chia Keng Singapore 248 A3
Chiaravalle Milanese Milan 239 B2
Chicago Chicago 229 B3
Chicago, University of Chicago 229 C3
Chicago Harbor Chicago 229 B3
Chicago Lawn Chicago 229 C2
Chicago-Midway ✕ (MDW) Chicago 229 C2
Chicago O'Hare Int. ✕ (ORD) Chicago 229 B1
Chicago Ridge Chicago 229 C2
Chicago River, North Branch → Chicago 229 B2
Chicago Sanitary and Ship Canal Chicago 229 C2
Chicago State University Chicago 229 C3
Chicago Zoo Chicago 229 B1
Chienzui Guangzhou 231 A3
Chik Sha Hong Kong 232 B2
Child's Hill London 235 A2
Chilla Saroda Delhi 230 B2
Chillum Washington 253 B4
Chilly-Mazarin Paris 244 B2
China Basin San Francisco 246 B2
Chingupota Kolkata 234 C1
Chinna Cr. → Karachi 233 B2
Chiquihuite, Cerro Mexico City 238 A2
Chislehurst London 235 B4
Chiswick London 235 B2
Chiswick House London 235 B2
Chitose Tokyo 250 B2
Chitralada Palace Bangkok 223 B2
Chiyoda Tokyo 250 A3
Choa Chu Kang Singapore 248 A2
Chodov u Prahy Prague 245 B3
Chōfu Tokyo 250 B2
Choisy-le-Roi Paris 244 B3
Cholupice Prague 245 C2
Chom Thong Bangkok 223 B1
Chong Pang Singapore 248 A2
Chongwen Beijing 224 B2
Chorrillos Lima 234 C2
Chowpatty Beach Mumbai 240 B1
Christianshavn Copenhagen 228 A3
Chrzanów Warsaw 252 B1
Chuen Lung Hong Kong 232 A1
Chuk Kok Hong Kong 232 A2
Chulalongkom Univ. Bangkok 223 B2
Chuō Tokyo 250 A3
Church End London 235 A2
Churchtown Dublin 230 B2
Ciampino Rome 246 C2
Ciampino ✕ Rome 246 C2
Cicero Chicago 229 B2
Cilandak Jakarta 232 B1
Cilincing Jakarta 232 A2
Ciliwung → Jakarta 232 B2
Čimice Prague 245 B2
Cinecittà Rome 246 B2
Cinisello Bálsamo Milan 239 A2
Cinkota Budapest 227 A3
Cipete Jakarta 232 B1
Citta degli Studi Milan 239 B2
Città del Vaticano = Vatican City ■ Rome 246 B1
City, The London 235 A3
City of the Dead Cairo 227 A2
Ciudad de México Mexico City 238 B2
Ciudad Deportiva Mexico City 238 B2
Ciudad Fin de Semana Madrid 237 B2
Ciudad General Belgrano Buenos Aires 227 C1
Ciudad Lineál Madrid 237 B2
Ciudad Satélite Mexico City 238 A1
Ciudad Universitaria Buenos Aires 227 B2
Ciudad Universitaria Mexico City 238 C1
Claireville Res. Toronto 251 A1
Clamart Paris 244 B2
Clapham London 235 B3
Clapton London 235 A3
Claremont Cape Town 228 A1
Clayhall London 235 A4
Clear, L. Orlando 243 A2
Clermiston Edinburgh 231 B2
Clichy Paris 244 A2
Clichy-sous-Bois Paris 244 A4
Cliffside Toronto 251 A3
Cliffside Park New York 242 B2
Clifton Cape Town 228 A1
Clifton Karachi 233 B2
Clifton New York 242 C1
Clifton Beach Karachi 233 B2
Cliftondale Boston 226 A2
Cloghran Dublin 230 A2
Clonskeagh Dublin 230 B2
Clontarf Dublin 230 A2
Clontarf Sydney 249 A2
Clovelly Sydney 249 B2
Cobras, I. das Rio de Janeiro 245 B2
Coburg Melbourne 238 A1
Cocotá Rio de Janeiro 245 A1
Cœuilly Paris 244 B4
Coina Lisbon 236 B2
Coker Lagos 234 B2
Colaba Mumbai 240 B1
Colaba Pt. Mumbai 240 B1

Colegiales Buenos Aires 227 B2
Colindale London 235 A2
Colinton Edinburgh 231 B2
College Park Atlanta 223 C2
College Park Washington 253 B4
College Point New York 242 B2
Collégien Paris 244 A4
Collier Row London 235 A4
Colliers Wood London 235 B2
Colma San Francisco 246 B2
Colney Hatch London 235 A3
Cologno Monzese Milan 239 A2
Colombes Paris 244 A2
Colonia Güell Barcelona 224 A1
Colonial Knob Wellington 253 A1
Colosseo Rome 246 B1
Colosseum = Colosseo Rome 246 B1
Combault Paris 244 B4
Comércio, Praça do Lisbon 236 A2
Commerce Los Angeles 236 B4
Como Sydney 249 C1
Conceição, I. da Rio de Janeiro 245 B2
Conchali Santiago 247 B2
Concord Sydney 249 B1
Concord Toronto 251 A2
Concorde, Place de la Paris 244 A2
Concorezzo Milan 239 A2
Condet Jakarta 232 A2
Coney Island New York 242 C2
Congonhas São Paulo ✈ (CGH) São Paulo 247 B2
Conley → Atlanta 223 C3
Connaught Place Delhi 230 B2
Consolação São Paulo 247 B2
Constantia Cape Town 228 B1
Constitución Buenos Aires 227 B2
Constitution Atlanta 223 B2
Convention Center Los Angeles 236 B3
Conway Orlando 243 B2
Conway, L. Orlando 243 B2
Coogee Sydney 249 B2
Cooksville Toronto 251 B1
Coolock Dublin 230 A2
Copacabana Rio de Janeiro 245 B1
Copenhagen = København Copenhagen 228 A2
Coral Gables Miami 238 B2
Coral Hills Washington 253 B4
Corcovado, Cristo Redentar Rio de Janeiro 245 B1
Corduff Dublin 230 A1
Cormano Milan 239 A2
Cornaredo Milan 239 A1
Córsico Milan 239 B1
Corstorphine Edinburgh 231 B2
Corviale Rome 246 B1
Coslada Madrid 237 B2
Cossigny Paris 244 B4
Cotao Lisbon 236 A1
Côte-St-Luc Montreal 240 B2
Cotunduba, I. de Rio de Janeiro 245 B2
Coubron Paris 244 A4
Countryside Chicago 229 C1
County Art Museum Los Angeles 236 B2
Courbevoie Paris 244 A2
Courtry Paris 244 A4
Cowley London 235 A1
Coyoacán Mexico City 238 B2
Craighall Park Johannesburg 233 A2
Craiglockhart Edinburgh 231 B2
Craigmillar Edinburgh 231 B3
Cramond Edinburgh 231 B2
Cramond Bridge Edinburgh 231 B1
Cramond I. Edinburgh 231 B2
Cranford London 235 B1
Crawford Cape Town 228 A2
Crayford London 235 B5
Creekmouth London 235 A4
Crescent, L. Orlando 243 A1
Crescenzago Milan 239 A2
Cressely Paris 244 B1
Cresskill New York 242 A2
Créteil Paris 244 B3
Cricklewood London 235 A2
Cristo Redentor, Estatua do Rio de Janeiro 245 B1
Crockenhill London 235 B4
Croissy-Beaubourg Paris 244 B4
Croissy-sur-Seine Paris 244 A1
Crosby Johannesburg 233 B1
Crosne Paris 244 B3
Cross I. Mumbai 240 B2
Crouch End London 235 A3
Crown Mine Johannesburg 233 B1
Crows Nest Sydney 249 A2
Croydon London 235 B3
Croydon Park Sydney 249 B1
Cruagh Mt. Dublin 230 B2
Crumlin Dublin 230 B2
Cruz de Pau Lisbon 236 B2
Crystal Palace London 235 B3
Csepel Budapest 227 B2
Csepelsziget Budapest 227 B2
Csillaghegy Budapest 227 A2
Csillagtelep Budapest 227 B2
Csömör Budapest 227 A3
Csömöri-patak → Budapest 227 A3
Cuatro Vientos Madrid 237 B1
Cuauhtémoc Mexico City 238 B2
Cuban Museum Miami 238 B2
Cubao Manila 237 B2
Çubuklu Istanbul 232 B2
Cudahy Los Angeles 236 C3
Cuicuilco, Pirámido de Mexico City 238 C1
Culmore Washington 253 B3
Culver City Los Angeles 236 B2
Cumbres de Vallecas Madrid 237 B2
Cupecé São Paulo 247 B1
Currie Edinburgh 231 B2
Cusago Milan 239 B1
Cusano Milanino Milan 239 A2
Cutler Park Boston 226 B1
Çuvuşabaşi → Istanbul 232 B1
Cypress Hills New York 242 B2
Czerniaków Warsaw 252 B2
Czyste Warsaw 252 B1

D

Da Moóca → São Paulo 247 B2
Ďablice Prague 245 B2
Dąbrowa Warsaw 252 B1
Dachang Shanghai 248 B1
Dachang ✈ Shanghai 248 B1
Dachau Munich 241 A1
Dachau-Ost Munich 241 A1
Dachauer Moos Munich 241 A1
Dadar Mumbai 240 A1
Daebang Seoul 247 B1
Daechi Seoul 247 B2
Dafni Athens 222 B2
Dagenham London 235 A4
Daglfing Munich 241 B2
Dahab, Gezîret el Cairo 227 B2
Daheisha Jerusalem 233 B2
Dahlem Berlin 225 B2
Dahlwitz-Hoppegarten Berlin 225 A5
Dahongmen Beijing 224 C2
Dajiaoting Beijing 224 B2
Dakhnoye St. Petersburg 247 C1
Dalejsky potok → Prague 245 B2
Dalgety Bay Edinburgh 231 A1
Dalkeith Edinburgh 231 B3
Dalkey Dublin 230 B3
Dalkey I. Dublin 230 B3
Dallgow Berlin 225 A1
Dalmeny Edinburgh 231 B1
Dalston London 235 A3
Daly City San Francisco 246 B2
Damaia Lisbon 236 A1
Damarakia Athens 222 B1
Dämeritzsee Berlin 225 B5
Dan Ryan Woods Chicago 229 C2
Danderhall Edinburgh 231 B3
Danderyd Stockholm 249 A2
Danforth Toronto 251 A3
Darakeh Tehran 251 A2
Darband Tehran 251 A2
Darling Point Sydney 249 B2
Darndale Dublin 230 A2
Darrūs Tehran 251 A2
Dartford London 235 B5
Dashi Guangzhou 231 B2
Datansha Guangzhou 231 B2
Datun Beijing 224 B2
Daulatpur Delhi 230 A1
Davidson, Mt. San Francisco 246 B2
Davidson's Mains Edinburgh 231 B2
Dāvūdiyeh Tehran 251 A2
Davydkovo Moscow 239 B1
Dawidy Warsaw 252 C1
Days Bay Wellington 253 B2
Decatur Atlanta 223 B3
Dedham Boston 226 B1
Degunino Moscow 239 A2
Deir Dibwan Jerusalem 233 A2
Deir Ibzi'e Jerusalem 233 A1
Dejvice Prague 245 B2
Dekabristov, Ostrov St. Petersburg 247 B1
Delhi Delhi 230 B2
Demarest New York 242 A2
Den Ilp Amsterdam 222 A2
Denistone Heights Sydney 249 A1
Dentonia Park Toronto 251 A3
DePaul University Chicago 229 B3
Deptford London 235 B3
Des Plaines Chicago 229 A1
Deshengmen Beijing 224 B2
Deutsch-Wagram Vienna 252 A3
Deutsche Oper Berlin 225 A2
Deutscher Museum Munich 241 B2
Devil's Peak Cape Town 228 A1
Dhakuria Kolkata 234 B2
Dharavi Mumbai 240 A2
Diadema São Paulo 247 C2
Diegen Brussels 226 A2
Diemen Amsterdam 222 A2
Diepkloof Johannesburg 233 B1
Dieprivier Cape Town 228 B1
Difficult Run → Washington 253 B2
Dilbeek Brussels 226 A1
Dilli = Delhi Delhi 230 B2
Dirnismaning Munich 241 A2
Disney-M.G.M. Studios Orlando 243 B1
Disney Studios Los Angeles 236 B3
District Heights Washington 253 B4
Djakarta = Jakarta Jakarta 232 A2
Djursholm Stockholm 249 A2
Döberitz Berlin 225 A1
Döbling Vienna 252 A2
Dobong Seoul 247 B2
Dobongsan Seoul 247 A2
Docklands London 235 A3
Doctor Phillips Orlando 243 B2
Dodder → Dublin 230 B1
Dodger Stadium Los Angeles 236 B3
Dogs, Isle of London 235 B3
Dolgoe Ozero St. Petersburg 247 A1
Dollis Hill London 235 A2
Dollymount Dublin 230 A2
Dolni Prague 245 B3
Dolni Chabry Prague 245 B2
Dolni Počernice Prague 245 B3
Dolphins Barn Dublin 230 B2
Dom Pedro II, Parque São Paulo 247 B2
Don Mills Toronto 251 A2
Don Muang Int. ✈ (BKK) Bangkok 223 A2
Donaghmede Dublin 230 A3
Donau-Oder Kanal Vienna 252 A3
Donaufeld Vienna 252 A2
Donaupark Vienna 252 A2
Donaustadt Vienna 252 A2
Dongan Hills New York 242 C1
Dongcheng Beijing 224 B2
Dongdaemung Seoul 247 B2
Donggou Shanghai 248 B2
Dongjak Seoul 247 B1
Dongjiao Guangzhou 231 B2
Dongri Mumbai 240 B2
Dongshanhu Park Guangzhou 231 B2
Dongzhimen Beijing 224 B2
Donnybrook Dublin 230 B2
Doornfontein Johannesburg 233 B2
Dorchester Boston 226 B2
Dorchester B. Boston 226 B2
Dorchester Heights Nat. Historical Site ⌂ Boston 226 B2
Dornach Munich 241 B3
Dorval Int., Montréal ✈ (YUL) Montreal 240 B1
Dos Couros → São Paulo 247 C2
Dos Moninos → São Paulo 247 C2
Douglas Park Chicago 229 B2
Dover Heights Sydney 249 B2
Dowlatābād Tehran 251 B2
Down, L. Orlando 243 A1
Downey Los Angeles 236 C4
Downsview Toronto 251 A1
Downsview C.A.F.B. ✈ Toronto 251 A2
Dragør Copenhagen 228 B3
Drancy Paris 244 A3
Dranesville Washington 253 A1
Drapetsona Athens 222 B1
Dreilinden Berlin 225 B2
Drewnica Warsaw 252 B2
Drigh Road Karachi 233 A2
Drimnagh Dublin 230 B2
Drogenbos Brussels 226 B1
Druid Hills Atlanta 223 B2
Drumcondra Dublin 230 A2
Drummoyne Sydney 249 B1
Drylaw Edinburgh 231 B2
Dubeč Prague 245 B3
Dublin Dublin 230 A2
Dublin ✈ (DUB) Dublin 230 A2
Dublin B. Dublin 230 B3
Dublin Harbour Dublin 230 A2
Duddingston Edinburgh 231 B3
Dugnano Milan 239 A2
Duivendrecht Amsterdam 222 B2
Dūlāb Tehran 251 B2
Dulwich London 235 B3
Dum Dum Kolkata 234 B2
Dum Dum Int. ✈ (CCU) Kolkata 234 B2
Dumont New York 242 A2
Dún Laoghaire Dublin 230 B3
Dundrum Dublin 230 B2
Dunearn Singapore 248 B2
Dúnleary = Dún Laoghaire Dublin 230 B3
Dunn Loring Washington 253 B2
Dunning Chicago 229 B2
Dunvegan Johannesburg 233 A2
Duomo Milan 239 B2
Duque de Caxias Rio de Janeiro 245 A1
Duren Sawit Jakarta 232 A2
Dusit Bangkok 223 B2
Dworp Brussels 226 B1
Dyakovo Moscow 239 B2
Dyker Beach Park New York 242 C1
Dzerzhinskiy Moscow 239 B2
Dzerzhinskiy Park Moscow 239 B2

E

E.U.R. = Esposizione Universale di Roma Rome 246 C1
Eagle Rock Los Angeles 236 B3
Ealing □ London 235 A2
Earlsfield London 235 B2
Earlwood Sydney 249 B1
East Arlington Boston 226 A2
East Arlington Washington 253 B3
East Bedfont London 235 B1
East Boston Boston 226 A2
East Don → Toronto 251 A2
East Don Parkland Toronto 251 A2
East Elmhurst New York 242 B2
East Finchley London 235 A2
East Flatbush New York 242 C2
East Ham London 235 A4
East Humber → Toronto 251 A1
East Lamma Channel Hong Kong 232 B1
East Lexington Boston 226 A1
East Los Angeles Los Angeles 236 B3
East Molesey London 235 B1
East New York New York 242 B2
East Pines Washington 253 B4
East Point Atlanta 223 B2
East Potomac Park Washington 253 B3
East River → New York 242 B2
East Rutherford New York 242 A1
East Sheen London 235 B2
East Talpiyot Jerusalem 233 B2
East Wickham London 235 B4
East York Toronto 251 A2
Eastbourne Wellington 253 B2
Eastcote London 235 A1
Easter Howgate Edinburgh 231 B2
Eastpoint Park Toronto 251 A4
Eastwood Sydney 249 A1
Eaton Canyon Park Los Angeles 236 A4
Ebara Tokyo 250 B3
Ebisu Tokyo 250 B3
Ebute-Ikorodu Lagos 234 A2
Ebute-Metta Lagos 234 B2
Eda Tokyo 250 B2
Edendale Johannesburg 233 A2
Edenmore Dublin 230 A2
Edgars Cr. → Melbourne 238 A1
Edgeley Toronto 251 A1
Edgemar San Francisco 246 C2
Edgewater New York 242 B2
Edgewood Orlando 243 B2
Edinburgh Edinburgh 231 B2
Edinburgh ✈ (EDI) Edinburgh 231 B1
Edinburgh Castle Edinburgh 231 B2
Edison Park Chicago 229 A2
Edmondston Washington 253 B4
Edmondstown Dublin 230 B2
Edo → Tokyo 250 B4
Edogawa Tokyo 250 A4
Edsberg Stockholm 249 A1
Edwards L. Melbourne 238 A1
Efzonos Athens 222 B2
Egaleo Athens 222 B2
Egaleo, Oros Athens 222 B1
Eiche Berlin 225 A4
Eiche Sud Berlin 225 A4
Eiffel, Tour Paris 244 A2
Ein Arik Jerusalem 233 A1
Ein Naquba Jerusalem 233 B1
Ein Rafa Jerusalem 233 B1
Eizariya Jerusalem 233 B2
Ejby Copenhagen 228 A2
Ejigbo Lagos 234 A1
Ekeberg Oslo 243 A3
Eknäs Stockholm 249 B3
El 'Abbasiya Cairo 227 A2
El Agustino Lima 234 B2
El Baragil Cairo 227 A1
El Basâtîn Cairo 227 B2
El Bira Jerusalem 233 A2
El Bosque Santiago 247 C2
El Carmen Santiago 247 B1
El Cortijo Santiago 247 B1
El Cristo, Vaso Regulador Mexico City 238 B1
El Duqqi Cairo 227 A2
El Encinar de los Reyes Madrid 237 A2
El Gezira Cairo 227 A2
El Ghurîya Cairo 227 A2
El Gîza Cairo 227 A2
El Khadr Jerusalem 233 B1
El Khalîfa Cairo 227 A2
El Kôm el Ahmar Cairo 227 A2
El Ma'âdi Cairo 227 B2
El Matarîya Cairo 227 A2
El Mohandessin Cairo 227 A2
El Monte Los Angeles 236 B4
El Muqattam Cairo 227 A2
El Mûskî Cairo 227 A2
El Pardo Madrid 237 A1
El Portal Miami 238 A2
El Prat de Llobregat Barcelona 224 B1
El Qâhira Cairo 227 A2
El Qubba Cairo 227 A2
El Reloj Mexico City 238 C2
El Retiro Madrid 237 B1
El Salto Santiago 247 B2
El Sereno Los Angeles 236 B3
El Talibîya Cairo 227 B2
El Vergel Mexico City 238 C2
El Wâhli Cairo 227 A2
El Zamâlik Cairo 227 A2
El Zeitûn Cairo 227 A2
Elephanta Caves Mumbai 240 B2
Elephanta I. Mumbai 240 B2
Ellboda Stockholm 249 A3
Ellenor, L. Orlando 243 B2
Elliniko Olympic Complex Athens 222 B2
Ellis I. New York 242 B1
Elm Park London 235 A5
Elmers End London 235 B3
Elmhurst New York 242 B2
Elmstead London 235 B4
Elmwood Park Chicago 229 B2
Elmwood Park New York 242 A1
Elsdon Wellington 253 A1
Elsiesrivier Cape Town 228 A2
Elsternwick Melbourne 238 B2
Eltham London 235 B4
Elwood Melbourne 238 B1
Élysée Paris 244 A2
Elysian Park Los Angeles 236 B3
Emāmzādeh Sāleh Tehran 251 A2
Émerainville Paris 244 B4
Emeryville San Francisco 246 A3
Eminönü Istanbul 232 B1
Emirgan Istanbul 232 B2
Emmarentia Johannesburg 233 A2
Empire State Building New York 242 B2
Encantado Rio de Janeiro 245 B1
Encino Los Angeles 236 B2
Encino Res. Los Angeles 236 B1
Enebyberg Stockholm 249 A1
Enfield Sydney 249 B1
Engenho, I. do Rio de Janeiro 245 B2
Englewood Chicago 229 C3
Englewood New York 242 A2
Englewood Cliffs New York 242 A2
Enmore Sydney 249 B2
Enskede Stockholm 249 B2
Entrevias Madrid 237 B1
Epcot Orlando 243 B1
Epping Sydney 249 A1
Eregun Lagos 234 A2
Erenköy Istanbul 232 C2
Erith London 235 B5
Erlaa Vienna 252 B1
Ermington Sydney 249 A1
Ermita Manila 237 B1
Ershatou Guangzhou 231 B2
Erskineville Sydney 249 B2
Erunkan Lagos 234 A2
Erzsébet-Telep Budapest 227 B3
Eschenried Munich 241 A1
Esenler Istanbul 232 B1
Esher London 235 B1
Eskbank Edinburgh 231 B3
Esplugas Barcelona 224 A1
Esposizione Universale di Roma Rome 246 C1
Essendon Melbourne 238 A1
Essendon ✈ (MEB) Melbourne 238 A1
Essingen Stockholm 249 B1
Essling Vienna 252 A3
Est, Gare de l' Paris 244 A3
Estado, Parque do São Paulo 247 B2
Estrela, Basilica da Lisbon 236 A2
Etobicoke Toronto 251 B1
Etobicoke Cr. → Toronto 251 B1
Etterbeek Brussels 226 B2
Eung-am Seoul 247 B1
Eunpyeong Seoul 247 B1
Evanston Chicago 229 A2
Even Sapir Jerusalem 233 B1
Evere Brussels 226 A2
Everett Boston 226 A2
Evergreen Park Chicago 229 C2
Evīn Tehran 251 A2
Ewu Lagos 234 A1
Exhibition Place Toronto 251 B2
Exposições, Palácio das Rio de Janeiro 245 B1
Eyüp Istanbul 232 B1
Ezeiza ✈ (EZE) Buenos Aires 227 B2

F

Fabour, Mt. Singapore 248 B2
Fælledparken Copenhagen 228 A3
Fågelön Stockholm 249 B1
Fagersjö Stockholm 249 B2
Fair Lawn New York 242 A1
Fairfax Washington 253 B2
Fairfax Station Washington 253 C2
Fairland Johannesburg 233 A1
Fairmilehead Edinburgh 231 B2
Fairmount Heights Washington 253 B4
Fairport Toronto 251 A4
Fairview New York 242 B2
Fairview, L. Orlando 243 A2
Falenty Warsaw 252 C1
Faliro Athens 222 B1
Faliro, Ormos Athens 222 B2
Falkenburg Berlin 225 A4
Falkenhagen Berlin 225 A1
Falkensee Berlin 225 A1
Falls Church Washington 253 B2
Falomo Lagos 234 B2
False Bay Cape Town 228 B2
Fangcun Guangzhou 231 B2
Faraḥābād Tehran 251 A2
Farforovskaya St. Petersburg 247 B2
Farningham London 235 B5
Farsta Stockholm 249 B2
Fasanerie-Nord Munich 241 A2
Fasangarten Munich 241 B2
Fatih Istanbul 232 B1
Favoriten Vienna 252 B2
Fawkner Melbourne 238 A1
Fawkner Park Melbourne 238 B1
FedEx Stadium Washington 253 B4
Feijó Lisbon 236 B2
Feldkirchen Munich 241 B3
Feldmoching Munich 241 A2
Feltham London 235 B1
Fener Istanbul 232 B1
Fenerbahçe Istanbul 232 C2
Fengtai Beijing 224 C1
Ferencváros Budapest 227 B2
Ferihegy, Budapest ✈ (BUD) Budapest 227 B3
Ferndale Johannesburg 233 A2
Férolles-Attilly Paris 244 B4
Fichtenau Berlin 225 B5
Field Museum of Natural History Chicago 229 B3
Fields Corner Boston 226 B2
Fiera Camp Milan 239 B1
Figino Milan 239 B1
Fijir Baghdad 223 A2
Filadelfia Athens 222 A2
Fili-Mazilovo Moscow 239 B1
Filothei Athens 222 A2
Finchley London 235 A2
Fine Arts, Museum of Boston 226 A2
Finglas Dublin 230 A2
Finsbury London 235 A3
Finsbury Park London 235 A3
Fiorito Buenos Aires 227 C2
Firhouse Dublin 230 B2
Fischerhäuser Munich 241 A3
Fisher Island Miami 238 B2
Fishermans Bend Melbourne 238 A1
Fisherville Toronto 251 A2
Fisksätra Stockholm 249 B3
Fitzroy Gardens Melbourne 238 A1
Five Dock Sydney 249 B1
Fjellstrand Oslo 243 B2
Flamengo Rio de Janeiro 245 B1
Flamingo Orlando 243 B2
Flaminio Rome 246 B1
Flaskebekk Oslo 243 A2
Flatbush New York 242 C2
Flaten Stockholm 249 B2
Flatlands New York 242 C2
Flemington Racecourse Melbourne 238 A1
Flint Pk. Los Angeles 236 B3
Florence Los Angeles 236 C3
Florence Bloom Bird Sanctuary ⌂ Johannesburg 233 A2
Florentia Johannesburg 233 B2
Flores Buenos Aires 227 B2
Flores, Mercado de Mexico City 238 C2
Floresta Buenos Aires 227 B2
Florida Buenos Aires 227 B2
Florida Johannesburg 233 B1
Floridsdorf Vienna 252 A2
Flushing New York 242 B3
Flushing Meadows Corona Park New York 242 B2
Flysta Stockholm 249 A1
Fo Tan Hong Kong 232 A2
Föhrenhain Vienna 252 A2
Fontainebleau Johannesburg 233 A1
Fontenay-aux-Roses Paris 244 B2
Fontenay-le-Fleury Paris 244 B1
Fontenay-sous-Bois Paris 244 A3
Foots Cray London 235 B4
Footscray Melbourne 238 A1
Forbidden City = Imperial Palace Museum Beijing 224 B2
Forest Brussels 226 B1
Forest Gate London 235 A4
Forest Heights Washington 253 C3
Forest Hill London 235 B3
Forest Hill Toronto 251 A2
Forest Hills New York 242 B2
Forest Park Chicago 229 B2
Forest Park New York 242 B2
Forest View Chicago 229 C2
Forestville Washington 253 B4
Fornebu Oslo 243 A2
Foro Romano Rome 246 B1
Forstenried Munich 241 B1
Forstenrieder Park Munich 241 B1
Fort Mumbai 240 B1
Fort Dupont Park Washington 253 B4
Fort Foote Village Washington 253 C3
Fort Lee New York 242 A2
Forth, Firth of Edinburgh 231 A2
Forth Rail Bridge Edinburgh 231 A1
Forth Road Bridge Edinburgh 231 A1
Fót Budapest 227 A3
Fourqueux Paris 244 A1
Foxrock Dublin 230 B2
Franconia Washington 253 C3
Frank Lloyd Wright Home Chicago 229 B2
Frankel Singapore 248 B3
Franklin Park Boston 226 B2
Franklin Park Chicago 229 B1
Franklin Park Washington 253 B3
Franklin Res. Los Angeles 236 B2
Frauenkirche Munich 241 B2
Frederiksberg Copenhagen 228 A3
Frederiksdal Copenhagen 228 A2
Fredersdorf Berlin 225 A5
Freguesia Rio de Janeiro 245 A1
Freidrichshain, Volkspark Berlin 225 A3
Freiham Munich 241 B1
Freimann Munich 241 A2
French Quarter New Orleans 241 B2
Fresh Pond Boston 226 A2
Fresnes Paris 244 B2
Freudenau Vienna 252 A2
Friarstown Dublin 230 B1
Friedenau Berlin 225 B3
Friedrichsfelde Berlin 225 B4
Friedrichshagen Berlin 225 B4

Friedrichshain *Berlin* 225 A3
Friedrichslust *Berlin* 225 A5
Friherrs *Helsinki* 231 B1
Frilufts Museum *Helsinki* 231 B2
Frontón, I. *Lima* 234 B1
Frunze *Moscow* 239 B2
Fūchū *Tokyo* 250 A1
Fuencarral *Madrid* 237 B1
Fuenlabrada *Madrid* 237 C1
Fukagawa *Tokyo* 250 B3
Fukushima *Osaka* 243 A1
Fulham *London* 235 B2
Funabori *Tokyo* 250 A4
Fundão, I. do *Rio de Janeiro* 245 B1
Fünfhaus *Vienna* 252 A2
Furesø *Copenhagen* 228 A2
Fürth *Munich* 241 B2
Futago-tamagawaen *Tokyo* 250 B2
Fuxing Dao *Shanghai* 248 B2
Fuxing Park *Shanghai* 248 B1
Fuxinglu *Beijing* 224 B1

G

G. Ross Lord Park *Toronto* 251 A2
Gaebong *Seoul* 247 C1
Gage Park *Chicago* 229 C2
Gagny *Paris* 244 A4
Galata *Istanbul* 232 B1
Galata Tower *Istanbul* 232 B1
Galatsi *Athens* 222 A2
Galeão, Int. de ✕ (GIG) *Rio de Janeiro* 245 A1
Galyanovo *Moscow* 239 B3
Gambir *Jakarta* 232 A1
Gamboa *Rio de Janeiro* 245 B1
Gambolóita *Milan* 239 B2
Gamlebyen *Oslo* 243 A3
Gangdong *Seoul* 247 B2
Gangnam *Seoul* 247 B1
Gangseo *Seoul* 247 B1
Gangtou *Guangzhou* 231 A1
Gangwei *Guangzhou* 231 B2
Ganjiakou *Beijing* 224 B1
Ganshoren *Brussels* 226 A1
Gants Hill *London* 235 A4
Gaoqiao *Shanghai* 248 A2
Garbagnate Milanese *Milan* 239 A1
Garbatella *Rome* 246 B2
Garches *Paris* 244 A2
Garching *Munich* 241 A3
Garden City *Cairo* 227 A2
Garden Reach *Kolkata* 234 B1
Garder *Oslo* 243 B2
Garfield *New York* 242 A1
Garfield Park *Chicago* 229 B2
Gargareta *Athens* 222 B2
Garibong *Seoul* 247 C1
Garvanza *Los Angeles* 236 B3
Gåshaga *Stockholm* 249 A3
Gateway ⌂ *New York* 242 C2
Gateway of India *Mumbai* 240 B2
Gatow *Berlin* 225 B1
Gavà *Barcelona* 224 B1
Gávea *Rio de Janeiro* 245 B1
Gávea, Pedra da *Rio de Janeiro* 245 B1
Gazdagrét *Budapest* 227 B1
Gaziosmanpaşa *Istanbul* 232 B1
Gebel el Ahmar *Cairo* 227 A3
Gebel el Muqattam *Cairo* 227 A2
Gebel el Tura *Cairo* 227 B2
Geiselgasteig *Munich* 241 B2
General San Martín *Buenos Aires* 227 B1
Gennevilliers *Paris* 244 A2
Gentilly *Paris* 244 B3
Gentofte *Copenhagen* 228 A3
Genval *Brussels* 226 B2
George I. *Hong Kong* 232 B1
Georges River Bridge *Sydney* 249 C1
Georgetown *Washington* 253 B3
Georgia Dome *Atlanta* 223 B2
Gerasdorf bei Wien *Vienna* 252 A2
Gerberau *Munich* 241 A1
Gerli *Buenos Aires* 227 C2
Germiston *Johannesburg* 233 B2
Gern *Munich* 241 B2
Getafe *Madrid* 237 C1
Getty Center, The *Los Angeles* 236 B2
Geunjeong *Seoul* 247 C1
Geva Binyamin *Jerusalem* 233 A2
Geylang Serai *Singapore* 248 B3
Gharapuri *Mumbai* 240 B2
Gharb = Shahrak-e Qods *Tehran* 251 A2
Ghatkopar *Mumbai* 240 A2
Ghazipur *Delhi* 230 B2
Ghizri *Karachi* 233 B2
Ghizri Cr. → *Karachi* 233 B2
Ghonda *Delhi* 230 A2
Ghusuri *Kolkata* 234 B2
Gianicolense *Rome* 246 B1
Giant Wheel = Riesenrad *Vienna* 252 A2
Gibraltar Pt. *Toronto* 251 B2
Gidea Park *London* 235 A5
Giesing *Munich* 241 B2
Gilmerton *Edinburgh* 231 B3
Gilo *Jerusalem* 233 B2
Gimmersta *Stockholm* 249 B3
Ginza *Tokyo* 250 B3
Giv'at Ram *Jerusalem* 233 B2
Giv'at Ye'arim *Jerusalem* 233 B1
Giv'at Ze'ev *Jerusalem* 233 A2
Giv'on *Jerusalem* 233 A1
Giza = El Gîza *Cairo* 227 A2
Giza Pyramids *Cairo* 227 B1
Gjersjøen *Oslo* 243 B3
Gladesville *Sydney* 249 B1
Gladsakse *Copenhagen* 228 A2
Glasnevin *Dublin* 230 A2
Glassmanor *Washington* 253 C4
Glasthule *Dublin* 230 B3
Glen Iris *Melbourne* 238 B2
Glen Mar Park *Washington* 253 B3
Glen Rock *New York* 242 A1
Glen Rouge Park *Toronto* 251 A4
Glenarden *Washington* 253 B4
Glenasmole Reservoirs *Dublin* 230 B1
Glencorse Res. *Edinburgh* 231 B2
Glencullen *Dublin* 230 B2
Glendale *Los Angeles* 236 B3
Glendoo Mt. *Dublin* 230 B2
Glenhuntly *Melbourne* 238 B2
Glenside *Wellington* 253 B1
Glenview *Chicago* 229 A2
Glenview Countryside *Chicago* 229 A2
Glenvista *Johannesburg* 233 B2
Glifada *Athens* 222 B2
Glömsta *Stockholm* 249 B1
Glostrup *Copenhagen* 228 B2
Gogar *Edinburgh* 231 B2
Göktürk *Istanbul* 232 A1
Golabari *Kolkata* 234 B2
Golabki *Warsaw* 252 B1
Gold Coast *Chicago* 229 B3
Golden Gate *San Francisco* 246 B2
Golden Gate ⌂ *San Francisco* 246 A2
Golden Gate Bridge *San Francisco* 246 B2
Golden Gate Park *San Francisco* 246 B2
Golden Horn = Haliç *Istanbul* 232 B1
Golders Green *London* 235 A2
Golestan Palace *Tehran* 251 A2
Gollans Stream → *Wellington* 253 B2
Gonen *Jerusalem* 233 B2
Gongneung *Seoul* 247 B2
Goodmayes *London* 235 A4
Goodwood *Cape Town* 228 A2
Gopalpur *Kolkata* 234 B2
Górce *Warsaw* 252 B1
Gore Hill *Sydney* 249 A2
Gorelyy → *St. Petersburg* 247 A3
Gorgie *Edinburgh* 231 B2
Gorky Park *Moscow* 239 B2
Gosen *Berlin* 225 B5
Gosener kanal *Berlin* 225 B5
Gospel Oak *London* 235 A3
Gotanda *Tokyo* 250 B3
Goth Goli Mar *Karachi* 233 A2
Goth Sher Shah *Karachi* 233 A1
Gotha *Orlando* 243 A1
Gournay-sur-Marne *Paris* 244 A4
Governador, I. do *Rio de Janeiro* 245 A1
Governors I. *New York* 242 B1
Grabów *Warsaw* 252 C1
Grace, Mt. *Wellington* 253 B2
Gracefield *Wellington* 253 B2
Gracia *Barcelona* 224 A2
Gräfelfing *Munich* 241 B1
Gragoatá *Rio de Janeiro* 245 B2
Grand Bazaar = Kapalı Carsı *Istanbul* 232 B1
Grand Central Station *New York* 242 B2
Grand Palace *Bangkok* 223 B1
Grande Place *Brussels* 226 A2
Grankulla = Kauniainen *Helsinki* 231 B1
Grant Park *Chicago* 229 B3
Granton *Edinburgh* 231 B2
Grassy Park *Cape Town* 228 B2
Gratosóglio *Milan* 239 B2
Gratzwalde *Berlin* 225 B5
Gravesend *New York* 242 C2
Grazhdanka *St. Petersburg* 247 B2
Great Falls *Washington* 253 B2
Great Falls Park *Washington* 253 B2
Great Western Forum *Los Angeles* 236 C2
Greco *Milan* 239 A2
Green I. *Hong Kong* 232 B1
Green Point *Cape Town* 228 A1
Greenbelt *Washington* 253 A4
Greenbelt Park *Washington* 253 B4
Greenfield Park *Montreal* 240 B3
Greenford *London* 235 A1
Greenhill *London* 235 A2
Greenhills *Dublin* 230 B1
Greenpoint *New York* 242 B2
Greenwich ☐ *London* 235 B3
Greenwich Observatory *London* 235 B3
Greenwich Village *New York* 242 B2
Greenwood *Boston* 226 A2
Grefsen *Oslo* 243 A3
Gresham Park *Atlanta* 223 B2
Greve Strand *Copenhagen* 228 B1
Griebnitzsee *Berlin* 225 B1
Griffith Park *Los Angeles* 236 B3
Grimbergen *Brussels* 226 A2
Grinzing *Vienna* 252 A2
Gröbenried *Munich* 241 A1
Grochów *Warsaw* 252 B2
Grodzisk *Warsaw* 252 B2
Groenendaal *Brussels* 226 B2
Grogol Petamburin *Jakarta* 232 A1
Gronsdorf *Munich* 241 B3
Grorud *Oslo* 243 A4
Gross-Glienicke *Berlin* 225 B1
Gross-Hadern *Munich* 241 B1
Gross-Lappen *Munich* 241 A2
Grosse Krampe *Berlin* 225 B5
Grosse Müggelsee *Berlin* 225 B4
Grosse Point Lighthouse *Chicago* 229 A2
Grossenzersdorf *Vienna* 252 A3
Grossenzersdorfer Arm → *Vienna* 252 A3
Grosser Biberhaufen *Vienna* 252 A2
Grosser Wannsee *Berlin* 225 B2
Grossfeld-Siedlung *Vienna* 252 A2
Grosshesselohe *Munich* 241 B2
Grossjedlersdorf *Vienna* 252 A2
Grossziethen *Berlin* 225 B3
Ground Zero *New York* 242 B1
Grove, The *Chicago* 229 A1
Grove Hall *Boston* 226 B2
Grove Park *Atlanta* 223 B2
Grove Park *Hounslow, London* 235 B2
Grove Park *Lewisham, London* 235 B4
Groveton *Washington* 253 C3
Grünau *Berlin* 225 B4
Grunewald *Berlin* 225 B2
Grünwald *Munich* 241 B2
Grünwalder Forst *Munich* 241 B2
Grymes Hill *New York* 242 C1
Guadalupe *Manila* 237 B2
Guadalupe, Basílica de *Mexico City* 238 B2
Guanabara, B. de *Rio de Janeiro* 245 B1
Guanabara, Jardim *Rio de Janeiro* 245 A1
Guanabara, Palácio da *Rio de Janeiro* 245 B1
Guang'anmen *Beijing* 224 B1
Guangqumen *Beijing* 224 B2
Guangzhou *Guangzhou* 231 B2
Guanshuo *Guangzhou* 231 B3
Gudö *Stockholm* 249 B3
Güell, Parque de *Barcelona* 224 A2
Guinardó *Barcelona* 224 A2
Gulbai *Karachi* 233 A1
Güngören *Istanbul* 232 B1
Gunnersbury *London* 235 B2
Gustavo A. Madero *Mexico City* 238 B2
Guttenberg *New York* 242 B1
Gutuyevskiy, Ostrov *St. Petersburg* 247 B1
Guyancourt *Paris* 244 B1
Gwanak *Seoul* 247 C1
Gwanaksan *Seoul* 247 C1
Gyál *Budapest* 227 B3
Gyáli-patak → *Budapest* 227 B2

H

Haaga *Helsinki* 231 B2
Haar *Munich* 241 B3
Habay *Manila* 237 C1
Hackbridge *London* 235 B3
Hackensack *New York* 242 A1
Hackensack → *New York* 242 B1
Hackney ☐ *London* 235 A3
Hackney Wick *London* 235 A3
Hadr, Warrâq el *Cairo* 227 A2
Haga *Stockholm* 249 A2
Hagenbrunn *Vienna* 252 A2
Hägersten *Stockholm* 249 B1
Häggvik *Stockholm* 249 A1
Hagonoy *Manila* 237 B2
Hague Park *Toronto* 251 A3
Haidan *Beijing* 224 B1
Haidari *Athens* 222 A1
Haidarpur *Delhi* 230 A1
Haidhausen *Munich* 241 B2
Haight-Ashbury *San Francisco* 246 B2
Hainault *London* 235 A4
Haizhu Guangchang *Guangzhou* 231 B2
Hakunila *Helsinki* 231 B3
Halandri *Athens* 222 A2
Halásztelek *Budapest* 227 B1
Haliç *Istanbul* 232 B1
Halim Perdana Kusuma Int. ✕ (HLP) *Jakarta* 232 B2
Halle *Brussels* 226 B1
Haltiala *Helsinki* 231 B2
Haltiavuori *Helsinki* 231 B2
Ham *London* 235 B2
Hämeenkylä *Helsinki* 231 B1
Hammarby *Stockholm* 249 B2
Hamme *Brussels* 226 A1
Hammersmith *London* 235 B2
Hampstead *London* 235 A2
Hampstead *Montreal* 240 B2
Hampstead Garden Suburb *London* 235 A2
Hampstead Heath *London* 235 A2
Hampton *London* 235 B1
Hampton Court Palace *London* 235 B1
Hampton Wick *London* 235 B2
Hamrā' *Baghdad* 223 B1
Hanala *Helsinki* 231 A3
Haneda *Tokyo* 250 B3
Haneda, Tōkyō ✕ (HND) *Tokyo* 250 B3
Hang Hau *Hong Kong* 232 B2
Hanging Gardens *Mumbai* 240 B1
Hanlon *Toronto* 251 B1
Hanwell *London* 235 A1
Hanworth *London* 235 B1
Haora *Kolkata* 234 B1
Hapeville *Atlanta* 223 C2
Happy Valley *Hong Kong* 232 B2
Har Adar *Jerusalem* 233 B1
Har Gilo *Jerusalem* 233 B2
Har Homa *Jerusalem* 233 B2
Har Nof *Jerusalem* 233 B2
Haren *Brussels* 226 A2
Hareskovby *Copenhagen* 228 A2
Haringey ☐ *London* 235 A3
Harjusuo *Helsinki* 231 B3
Harlaching *Munich* 241 B2
Harlaw Res. *Edinburgh* 231 B2
Harlem *New York* 242 B2
Harlesden *London* 235 A2
Harlington *London* 235 B1
Harmaja *Helsinki* 231 C2
Harmashatar hegy *Budapest* 227 A2
Harolds Cross *Dublin* 230 B2
Háros *Budapest* 227 B2
Harperrig Res. *Edinburgh* 231 B1
Harrow ☐ *London* 235 A1
Harrow on the Hill *London* 235 A1
Harrow School *London* 235 A1
Harrow Weald *London* 235 A1
Hartsfield-Atlanta Int. ✕ (ATL) *Atlanta* 223 C2
Harumi *Tokyo* 250 B3
Harvard University *Boston* 226 A2
Harwood Heights *Chicago* 229 B2
Ḥasanābād *Tehran* 251 A1
Hasbrouck Heights *New York* 242 A1
Haselhorst *Berlin* 225 A2
Hasköy *Istanbul* 232 B1
Hasle *Oslo* 243 B2
Haslum *Oslo* 243 A2
Hästhagen *Stockholm* 249 B2
Hataitai *Wellington* 253 B1
Hatch End *London* 235 A1
Hatiara *Kolkata* 234 B2
Hauketo *Oslo* 243 A3
Hauz Khas *Delhi* 230 B2
Havel → *Berlin* 225 A2
Havelkanal *Berlin* 225 A2
Havering ☐ *London* 235 A5
Havering-atte-Bower *London* 235 A5
Haworth *New York* 242 A2
Hawthorne Racecourse *Chicago* 229 C2
Hayes *Bromley, London* 235 B4
Hayes *Hillingdon, London* 235 A1
Hayes End *London* 235 A1
Hayford *Chicago* 229 C2
Haywards *Wellington* 253 A2
Heathfield *Cape Town* 228 B1
Heathrow, London ✕ (LHR) *London* 235 B1
Hebe Haven *Hong Kong* 232 A2
Hedong *Guangzhou* 231 B2
Heidelberg Heights *Melbourne* 238 A2
Heidelberg West *Melbourne* 238 A2
Heidemühle *Berlin* 225 B5
Heideveld *Cape Town* 228 A2
Heiligensee *Berlin* 225 A2
Heiligenstadt *Vienna* 252 A2
Heinersdorf *Berlin* 225 A3
Hélène de Champlain, Parc ⌂ *Montreal* 240 A2
Helenelund *Stockholm* 249 A1
Heliopolis = Masr el Gedida *Cairo* 227 A2
Hellersdorf *Berlin* 225 A4
Hellerup *Copenhagen* 228 A3
Hellmahof *Vienna* 252 A3
Helsingfors = Helsinki *Helsinki* 231 B2
Helsinki *Helsinki* 231 B2
Helsinki-Vantaa ✕ (HEL) *Helsinki* 231 B2
Hendon *London* 235 A2
Hengsha *Guangzhou* 231 B2
Henningsdorf *Berlin* 225 A2
Henryków *Warsaw* 252 B1
Henson Cr. → *Washington* 253 C4
Henttaa *Helsinki* 231 B1
Heping Park *Shanghai* 248 B2
Hepingli *Beijing* 224 B2
Herlev *Copenhagen* 228 A2
Herman Eckstein Park *Johannesburg* 233 A2
Hermannskogel *Vienna* 252 A1
Hermiston *Edinburgh* 231 B2
Hermitage and Winter Palace *St. Petersburg* 247 B1
Hermsdorf *Berlin* 225 A2
Hernals *Vienna* 252 A2
Herne Hill *London* 235 B3
Héroes de Churubusco *Mexico City* 238 B2
Herons, Î. aux *Montreal* 240 B2
Herstedøster *Copenhagen* 228 A2
Herttoniemi *Helsinki* 231 B3
Ḥeṣārak *Tehran* 251 A1
Heston *London* 235 B1
Hetzendorf *Vienna* 252 B1
Hextable *London* 235 B5
Hialeah *Miami* 238 A1
Hiawassa, L. *Orlando* 243 A2
Hickory Hills *Chicago* 229 C2
Hiekkaharju *Helsinki* 231 B3
Hietaniemi *Helsinki* 231 B2
Hietzing *Vienna* 252 A1
Higashi *Osaka* 243 A2
Higashimurayama *Tokyo* 250 A1
Higashinari *Osaka* 243 A2
Higashisumiyoshi *Osaka* 243 B2
Higashiyodogawa *Osaka* 243 A1
High Park *Toronto* 251 B2
Highbury *London* 235 A3
Highgate *London* 235 A3
Highland Cr. → *Toronto* 251 A3
Highland Creek *Toronto* 251 A3
Highland Park *Los Angeles* 236 B3
Highlands North *Johannesburg* 233 A2
Hillcrest Heights *Washington* 253 C4
Hillend *Edinburgh* 231 A1
Hillingdon ☐ *London* 235 A1
Hillwood *Washington* 253 B3
Hilmîya *Cairo* 227 A2
Hin Keng *Hong Kong* 232 A2
Hirota *Osaka* 243 A1
Hirschstetten *Vienna* 252 A2
History Center *Atlanta* 223 B2
Hither Green *London* 235 B3
Hiyoshi *Tokyo* 250 B2
Hizma *Jerusalem* 233 B2
Hjortekær *Copenhagen* 228 A3
Hjortespring *Copenhagen* 228 A2
Hlubočepy *Prague* 245 B2
Ho Chung *Hong Kong* 232 A2
Ho Man Tin *Hong Kong* 232 B2
Hoboken *New York* 242 B1
Hobsons B. *Melbourne* 238 B1
Hochbrück *Munich* 241 A2
Hochelaga *Montreal* 240 A2
Hodgkins *Chicago* 229 C1
Hoegi *Seoul* 247 B2
Hoeilaart *Brussels* 226 B2
Hofburg *Vienna* 252 A2
Hoffman I. *New York* 242 C1
Hohenbrunn *Munich* 241 B3
Hohenschönhausen *Berlin* 225 A4
Holargos *Athens* 222 B2
Holborn *London* 235 A3
Holden, L. *Orlando* 243 B2
Holešovice *Prague* 245 B2
Holland Village *Singapore* 248 B2
Höllriegelskreuth *Munich* 241 B1
Hollywood *Los Angeles* 236 B3
Hollywood Bowl *Los Angeles* 236 B2
Holmenkollen *Oslo* 243 A3
Holmes Run Acres *Washington* 253 B2
Holmgård *Stockholm* 249 B1
Holmlia *Oslo* 243 B3
Holocaust Memorial *Jerusalem* 233 B2
Holyrood House, Palace of *Edinburgh* 231 B3
Holysloot *Amsterdam* 222 A3
Homerton *London* 235 A3
Hometown *Chicago* 229 C2
Hōnanchō *Tokyo* 250 A2
Honcho *Tokyo* 250 A3
Honden *Tokyo* 250 A4
Hondo, Rio → *Los Angeles* 236 B4
Hong Kong *Hong Kong* 232 B1
Hong Kong, Univ. of *Hong Kong* 232 B1
Hong Kong I. *Hong Kong* 232 B2
Hongje *Seoul* 247 B1
Hongjimun Tunnel *Seoul* 247 B1
Hongkou *Shanghai* 248 B1
Hongmiao *Beijing* 224 B2
Hongqiao *Shanghai* 248 B1
Honjyo *Tokyo* 250 A3
Honoré Mercier, Pont *Montreal* 240 B1
Hönow *Berlin* 225 A4
Hook *London* 235 B2
Horikiri *Tokyo* 250 A4
Horn Pond *Boston* 226 A1
Hornchurch *London* 235 A5
Horní *Prague* 245 B3
Horní Počernice *Prague* 245 B3
Hornsey *London* 235 A3
Horoměřice *Prague* 245 B1
Hortaleza *Madrid* 237 B2
Hosoyama *Tokyo* 250 B2
Hostafranchs *Barcelona* 224 A1
Hostivař *Prague* 245 B3
Houbětin *Prague* 245 B3
Houghton *Johannesburg* 233 B2
Houilles *Paris* 244 A2
Hounslow ☐ *London* 235 B1
Hout Bay *Cape Town* 228 B1
Hove Å → *Copenhagen* 228 A1
Hovedøya *Oslo* 243 A3
Høvik *Oslo* 243 A2
Hovorčovice *Prague* 245 A3
Howard Beach *New York* 242 C2
Howrah = Haora *Kolkata* 234 B1
Howth *Dublin* 230 A3
Howth Hd. *Dublin* 230 A3
Hōya *Tokyo* 250 A2
Hradčany *Prague* 245 B2
Huanghuagang Mausoleum *Guangzhou* 231 B2
Huangpu *Shanghai* 248 B2
Huangpu Jiang → *Shanghai* 248 B1
Huangpu Park *Shanghai* 248 B1
Huangtugang *Beijing* 224 C1
Huascar *Lima* 234 A2
Huay Khwang *Bangkok* 223 B2
Huddinge *Stockholm* 249 B2
Huechuraba *Santiago* 247 B1
Huertas de San Beltran *Barcelona* 224 A1
Huizingen *Brussels* 226 B1
Humayun's Tomb *Delhi* 230 B2
Humber → *Toronto* 251 A1
Humber B. *Toronto* 251 B2
Humber Bay *Toronto* 251 B2
Humber Bay Park *Toronto* 251 B2
Humber College *Toronto* 251 B1
Humber Summit *Toronto* 251 A1
Humber Valley Village *Toronto* 251 A1
Humberlea *Toronto* 251 A1
Humberwood Park *Toronto* 251 A1
Humboldt Park *Chicago* 229 B2
Humera *Madrid* 237 B1
Hunaydī *Baghdad* 223 B2
Hundige *Copenhagen* 228 B1
Hundige Strand *Copenhagen* 228 B2
Hung Hom *Hong Kong* 232 B2
Hunters Hill *Sydney* 249 B1
Hunters Pt. *San Francisco* 246 B2
Hunters Valley *Washington* 253 B2
Huntington *Washington* 253 C3
Huntington Park *Los Angeles* 236 C3
Hurīya *Baghdad* 223 A1
Hurstville *Sydney* 249 B1
Husan *Jerusalem* 233 B1
Husby *Stockholm* 249 A1
Husum *Copenhagen* 228 A2
Hutt → *Wellington* 253 B2
Hütteldorf *Vienna* 252 A1
Hűvösvölgy *Budapest* 227 A2
Huwon Secret Garden *Seoul* 247 B1
Hvalstad *Oslo* 243 A1
Hvalstrand *Oslo* 243 A2
Hvidovre *Copenhagen* 228 B2
Hwagok *Seoul* 247 B1
Hyattsville *Washington* 253 B4
Hyde Park *Boston* 226 B2
Hyde Park *Chicago* 229 C3
Hyde Park *Johannesburg* 233 A2
Hyde Park *London* 235 A2
Hyde Park *Sydney* 249 B2

I

Ibese *Lagos* 234 A2
Ibirapuera *São Paulo* 247 B1
Ibirapuera, Parque do *São Paulo* 247 B2
Icarai *Rio de Janeiro* 245 B2
Içerenköy *Istanbul* 232 C2
Ichgao *Tokyo* 250 B2
Ichigaya *Tokyo* 250 A3
Ichikawa *Tokyo* 250 A4
Ickenham *London* 235 A1
Iddo *Lagos* 234 B2
Idi-Oro *Lagos* 234 A2
Iganmu *Lagos* 234 B2
Igbobi *Lagos* 234 A2
Igbologun *Lagos* 234 B1
Igny *Paris* 244 B2
IJ, Het → *Amsterdam* 222 A2
IJ-meer *Amsterdam* 222 A3
Ijesa-Tedo *Lagos* 234 B1
Ijora *Lagos* 234 B2
Ikebe *Tokyo* 250 B2
Ikebukuro *Tokyo* 250 A3
Ikegami *Tokyo* 250 B3
Ikeja *Lagos* 234 A2
Ikeuchi *Osaka* 243 B2
Ikoyi *Lagos* 234 B2
Ikuata *Lagos* 234 B2
Ikuno *Osaka* 243 A2
Ikuta *Tokyo* 250 B2
Ila *Oslo* 243 A2
Ilford *London* 235 A4
Ilioupoli *Athens* 222 B2
Illinois at Chicago, University of *Chicago* 229 B3
Illinois Institute of Technology *Chicago* 229 B3
Ilpendam *Amsterdam* 222 A2
Ilsos → *Athens* 222 B2
Imbâbah *Cairo* 227 A2
Imielin *Warsaw* 252 C2
Imirim *São Paulo* 247 A2
Imitos *Athens* 222 B2
Imitos, Oros *Athens* 222 B2
Imperial Palace Museum *Beijing* 224 B2
Inagi *Tokyo* 250 B2
Inchcolm *Edinburgh* 231 A2
Inchicore *Dublin* 230 A1
Inchkeith *Edinburgh* 231 A3
Inchmickery *Edinburgh* 231 A2
Incirano *Milan* 239 A1
Independencia *Lima* 234 A2
Independencia *Santiago* 247 B2
India Gate *Delhi* 230 B2
Indian Creek Village *Miami* 238 A2
Indianópolis *São Paulo* 247 B2
Indira Gandhi Int. ✕ (DEL) *Delhi* 230 B1
Industria *Johannesburg* 233 B1
Ingierstrand *Oslo* 243 B3
Inglewood *Los Angeles* 236 C3

Ingliston *Edinburgh* 231 B1
Inhaúma *Rio de Janeiro* 245 B1
Inner Port Shelter *Hong Kong* 232 A2
Interlagos *São Paulo* 247 C1
Intramuros *Manila* 237 B1
Invalides *Paris* 244 A2
Inverkeithing *Edinburgh* 231 A1
Inzersdorf *Vienna* 252 B2
Ipanema *Rio de Janeiro* 245 B1
Ipiranga *São Paulo* 247 B2
Ipiranga → *São Paulo* 247 B2
Iponri *Lagos* 234 B2
Ireland's Eye *Dublin* 230 A3
Irving Park *Chicago* 229 B2
Isabel *Rio de Janeiro* 245 B1
Isagatedo *Lagos* 234 A1
Isar → *Munich* 241 A3
Ishbīlīya *Baghdad* 223 A2
Ishøj Strand *Copenhagen* 228 B2
Island Bay *Wellington* 253 B1
Island Park *Toronto* 251 B2
Islev *Copenhagen* 228 A2
Isleworth *London* 235 B2
Islington *Toronto* 251 B1
Islington □ *London* 235 A3
Ismaning *Munich* 241 A3
Ismayloskiy Park *Moscow* 239 B3
Isolo *Lagos* 234 A1
Issy-les-Moulineaux *Paris* 244 B2
İstanbul *Istanbul* 232 C1
İstanbul Boğazı *Istanbul* 232 B2
Istinye *Istanbul* 232 B2
Itä Hakkila *Helsinki* 231 B3
Itaewon *Seoul* 247 B1
Itami *Osaka* 243 A1
Itanhanga *Rio de Janeiro* 245 B1
Ivanhoe *Melbourne* 238 A2
Ivry-sur-Seine *Paris* 244 B3
Ixelles *Brussels* 226 B2
Izmaylovo *Moscow* 239 B3
Iztacalco *Mexico City* 238 B2
Iztapalapa *Mexico City* 238 B2

J

Jaba *Jerusalem* 233 A2
Jacaré *Rio de Janeiro* 245 B1
Jackson Heights *New York* 242 B2
Jackson Park *Chicago* 229 C3
Jacques-Cartier *Montreal* 240 A3
Jacques-Cartier, Pont *Montreal* 240 A2
Jadavpur *Kolkata* 234 C2
Jade Buddha Temple *Shanghai* 248 B1
Jægersborg *Copenhagen* 228 A3
Jægersborg Dyrehave *Copenhagen* 228 A3
Jagadishpur *Kolkata* 234 B1
Jagatpur *Delhi* 230 A2
Jaguaré, Rib. do → *São Paulo* 247 B1
Jahangirpur *Delhi* 230 A2
Jakarta *Jakarta* 232 A2
Jakarta, Teluk *Jakarta* 232 A1
Jalan Kayu *Singapore* 248 A3
Jamaica B. *New York* 242 C3
Jamaica Plain *Boston* 226 B2
Jamakpuri *Delhi* 230 B1
Jamshīdīyeh *Tehran* 251 A2
Jamsil *Seoul* 247 B2
Jamwon *Seoul* 247 B2
Janki *Warsaw* 252 C1
Jannali *Sydney* 249 C1
Jaraguá *São Paulo* 247 A1
Jaraguá, Pico de *São Paulo* 247 A1
Jardim Paulista *São Paulo* 247 B1
Järvatältet *Stockholm* 249 A1
Jaskhar *Mumbai* 240 B2
Jatinegara *Jakarta* 232 B2
Javādīyeh *Tehran* 251 B2
Jaworowa *Warsaw* 252 C1
Jedlesee *Vienna* 252 A2
Jefferson Memorial *Washington* 253 B3
Jefferson Park *Chicago* 229 B2
Jegi *Seoul* 247 B2
Jelambar *Jakarta* 232 A1
Jelonki *Warsaw* 252 B1
Jerónimos, Mosteiro dos *Lisbon* 236 A1
Jersey City *New York* 242 B1
Jerusalem *Jerusalem* 233 B2
Jessamine, L. *Orlando* 243 B2
Jésus, Î. *Montreal* 240 A1
Jesús Maria *Lima* 234 B2
Jette *Brussels* 226 A1
Jey *Tehran* 251 B2
Jianguomen *Beijing* 224 B2
Jiangwan *Shanghai* 248 B1
Jib *Jerusalem* 233 A2
Jihād *Baghdad* 223 B1
Jingan *Shanghai* 248 B1
Jinočany *Prague* 245 B1
Jinonice *Prague* 245 B2
Jiulong = Kowloon *Hong Kong* 232 B1
Jiyūgaoka *Tokyo* 250 B3
Jizā'ir *Baghdad* 223 B2
Jizīra *Baghdad* 223 B2
Joglo *Jakarta* 232 B1
Johannesburg *Johannesburg* 233 B2
Johannesburg, Univ. of *Johannesburg* 233 B2
Johannesburg Int. ✈ (GCJ) *Johannesburg* 233 A2
Johanneskirchen *Munich* 241 A2
Johannesstift *Berlin* 225 A2
Johannisthal *Berlin* 225 B4
John F. Kennedy Nat. Historic Site ⌂ *Boston* 226 A2
John McLaren Park *San Francisco* 246 B2
Johnsonville *Wellington* 253 B1
Joinville-le-Pont *Paris* 244 B3
Joli-Bois *Brussels* 226 B2
Jollas *Helsinki* 231 B3
Jongmyo Royal Shrine *Seoul* 247 B1
Jongno *Seoul* 247 B1
Jonstrup *Copenhagen* 228 A2
Joppa *Edinburgh* 231 B3
Jorge Chavez, Int. ✈ (LIM) *Lima* 234 B2
Jorge Newbery ✈ *Buenos Aires* 227 B2
Jósefa Pilsudskiego Park *Warsaw* 252 B1
Jōtō *Osaka* 243 A2
Jouy-en-Josas *Paris* 244 B2
Juan Anchorena *Buenos Aires* 227 A2
Juan González Romero *Mexico City* 238 A2
Juárez Int. ✈ (MEX) *Mexico City* 238 B2
Judeira *Jerusalem* 233 A2
Juhdum *Jerusalem* 233 B2
Juhu *Mumbai* 240 A2
Jūjā *Tokyo* 250 A3
Jukskeirivier → *Johannesburg* 233 A2
Julianów *Warsaw* 252 B2
Jung *Seoul* 247 B1
Jungfernheide, Volkspark *Berlin* 225 A2
Jungfernsee *Berlin* 225 B1
Junghwa *Seoul* 247 B2
Jungnang *Seoul* 247 B2
Jungnangcheon → *Seoul* 247 B1
Juniper Green *Edinburgh* 231 B2
Junk B. *Hong Kong* 232 B2
Jurong *Singapore* 248 B2
Jurong, Selat *Singapore* 248 B2
Jurong Industrial Estate *Singapore* 248 B1
Jurujuba, Enseada de *Rio de Janeiro* 245 B2
Jūsō *Osaka* 243 A1
Justice *Chicago* 229 C2
Jwalahari *Delhi* 230 B1

K

Kaapstad = Cape Town *Cape Town* 228 A1
Kabaty *Warsaw* 252 C2
Kadıköy *Istanbul* 232 C2
Kadoma *Osaka* 243 A2
Kafr 'Aqab *Jerusalem* 233 A2
Kâğıthane *Istanbul* 232 B1
Kâğıthane → *Istanbul* 232 B1
Kagran *Vienna* 252 A2
Kahnawake *Montreal* 240 B1
Kaimes *Edinburgh* 231 B2
Kaiserebersdorf *Vienna* 252 B2
Kaivoksela *Helsinki* 231 B2
Kalamaki *Athens* 222 B2
Kalbadevi *Mumbai* 240 B1
Kalipur *Kolkata* 234 A1
Kalithea *Athens* 222 B2
Kalkaji *Delhi* 230 B2
Kalvebod Fælled *Copenhagen* 228 B3
Kalveboderne *Copenhagen* 228 B3
Kamarhati *Kolkata* 234 A2
Kamata *Tokyo* 250 B3
Kameari *Tokyo* 250 A4
Kameido *Tokyo* 250 A4
Kami-Itabashi *Tokyo* 250 A3
Kamikitazawa *Tokyo* 250 B2
Kamitsuruma *Tokyo* 250 B1
Kamoshida *Tokyo* 250 B2
Kampong Landang *Singapore* 248 A3
Kampong Tanjong Penjuru *Singapore* 248 B2
Kampung Bali *Jakarta* 232 B1
Kanamori *Tokyo* 250 B1
Kanda *Tokyo* 250 A3
Kandilli *Istanbul* 232 B2
Kankurgachi *Kolkata* 234 B2
Kanlıca *Istanbul* 232 B2
Kanonerskiy, Ostrov *St. Petersburg* 247 B1
Kanzaki → *Osaka* 243 A1
Kapali Carsi *Istanbul* 232 B1
Kapellerfeld *Vienna* 252 A2
Káposztásmegyer *Budapest* 227 A2
Kapotnya *Moscow* 239 C3
Käppala *Stockholm* 249 A3
Kapuk *Jakarta* 232 A1
Käpylä *Helsinki* 231 B2
Karachi *Karachi* 233 A2
Karachi Int. ✈ (KHI) *Karachi* 233 A2
Karkh *Baghdad* 223 A2
Karlin *Prague* 245 B2
Karlsfeld *Munich* 241 A1
Karlshorst *Berlin* 225 B4
Karlův most *Prague* 245 B2
Karol Bagh *Delhi* 230 B2
Karolinenhof *Berlin* 225 B4
Karori *Wellington* 253 B1
Karow *Berlin* 225 A3
Karrādah *Baghdad* 223 B2
Kärsön *Stockholm* 249 B1
Kasai *Tokyo* 250 B4
Kasipur *Kolkata* 234 B2
Kastrup *Copenhagen* 228 B3
Kastrup, København ✈ (CPH) *Copenhagen* 228 B3
Kasuga *Tokyo* 250 A2
Kasuge *Tokyo* 250 A3
Kasumigaseki *Tokyo* 250 B3
Katong *Singapore* 248 B3
Katrineberg *Stockholm* 249 B1
Katsushika *Tokyo* 250 A4
Kau Pai Chau *Hong Kong* 232 B2
Kau Yi Chau *Hong Kong* 232 B1
Kaulsdorf *Berlin* 225 B4
Kauniainen *Helsinki* 231 B1
Kawasaki *Tokyo* 250 B3
Kawawa *Tokyo* 250 B2
Kawęczyn *Warsaw* 252 B2
Kayu Putih *Jakarta* 232 B2
Kbely *Prague* 245 B3
Kebayoran Baru *Jakarta* 232 B1
Kebayoran Lama *Jakarta* 232 B1
Kebon Jeruk *Jakarta* 232 B1
Kedar *Jerusalem* 233 B2
Kedoya *Jakarta* 232 B1
Keilor *Melbourne* 238 A1
Keilor North *Melbourne* 238 A1
Keimola *Helsinki* 231 A1
Kelapa Gading *Jakarta* 232 A2
Kelenföld *Budapest* 227 B2
Kelvin *Johannesburg* 233 A2
Kemang *Jakarta* 232 B1
Kemayoran *Jakarta* 232 B2
Kemerburgaz *Istanbul* 232 B1
Kempton Park Races *London* 235 B1
Kenilworth *Cape Town* 228 A1
Kennedy Town *Hong Kong* 232 B1
Kensal Green *London* 235 A2
Kensington *Johannesburg* 233 B2
Kensington *London* 235 B2
Kensington *New York* 242 C2
Kensington *Sydney* 249 B2
Kensington Palace *London* 235 A2
Kent Village *Washington* 253 B4
Kentish Town *London* 235 A3
Kenton *London* 235 A2
Kenwood House *London* 235 A3
Kepa *Warsaw* 252 B2
Keppel Harbour *Singapore* 248 B2
Kesariani *Athens* 222 B2
Kettering *Washington* 253 B5
Kew *London* 235 B2
Kew *Melbourne* 238 A2
Kew Gardens *London* 235 B2
Kew Gardens *Toronto* 251 A3
Key Biscayne *Miami* 238 B2
Khalīj *Baghdad* 223 B2
Khandallah *Wellington* 253 B1
Khansā' *Baghdad* 223 A2
Kharavli *Mumbai* 240 B2
Khefren *Cairo* 227 B1
Khichripur *Delhi* 230 B2
Khidirpur *Kolkata* 234 B1
Khimki-Khovrino *Moscow* 239 A2
Khirbet Batin Abu Lihyah *Jerusalem* 233 A1
Khirbet el-Misbah *Jerusalem* 233 A1
Khirbet Jub e-Rum *Jerusalem* 233 B2
Khlong San *Bangkok* 223 B2
Khlong Toey *Bangkok* 223 B2
Khorel *Kolkata* 234 A1
Khorosovo *Moscow* 239 B1
Kiamari *Karachi* 233 B1
Kierling *Vienna* 252 A1
Kierlingbach → *Vienna* 252 A1
Kifisos → *Athens* 222 B2
Kikuna *Tokyo* 250 B2
Kilbarrack *Dublin* 230 A3
Kilbirnie *Wellington* 253 B1
Kilburn *London* 235 A2
Killakee *Dublin* 230 B2
Killester *Dublin* 230 A2
Killiney *Dublin* 230 B3
Killiney B. *Dublin* 230 B3
Kilmacud *Dublin* 230 B2
Kilmainham *Dublin* 230 A2
Kilmainham Gaol *Dublin* 230 A2
Kilmashogue Mt. *Dublin* 230 B2
Kilmore *Dublin* 230 A2
Kilnamanagh *Dublin* 230 B1
Kilo *Helsinki* 231 B1
Kilokri *Delhi* 230 B2
Kiltiernan *Dublin* 230 B2
Kimmage *Dublin* 230 B2
Kindi *Baghdad* 223 B2
Kinghorn *Edinburgh* 231 A2
Kings Domain *Melbourne* 238 A1
Kings Forest = Kongelunden *Copenhagen* 228 B3
Kings Park *Washington* 253 C2
Kings Park West *Washington* 253 C2
Kingsbury *London* 235 A2
Kingsbury *Melbourne* 238 A2
Kingsford *Sydney* 249 B2
Kingsford Smith, Sydney ✈ (SYD) *Sydney* 249 B2
Kingston-upon-Thames □ *London* 235 B2
Kingston Vale *London* 235 B2
Kingsway *Toronto* 251 B1
Kinsaley *Dublin* 230 A2
Kipling Heights *Toronto* 251 A1
Kipseli *Athens* 222 B2
Kirchstockbach *Munich* 241 B3
Kirchtrudering *Munich* 241 B3
Kirikiri *Lagos* 234 B1
Kirke Værløse *Copenhagen* 228 A1
Kirkhill *Edinburgh* 231 B2
Kirkliston *Edinburgh* 231 B1
Kirknewton *Edinburgh* 231 B1
Kirov Palace of Culture *St. Petersburg* 247 B1
Kiryat Anavim *Jerusalem* 233 B1
Kiryat Ha Yovel *Jerusalem* 233 B1
Kısıklı *Istanbul* 232 B2
Kispest *Budapest* 227 B2
Kista *Stockholm* 249 A1
Kita *Osaka* 243 A2
Kita *Tokyo* 250 A3
Kitazawa *Tokyo* 250 B3
Kiu Tsiu *Hong Kong* 232 A2
Kivistö *Helsinki* 231 B2
Kızıltoprak *Istanbul* 232 C2
Kizuri *Osaka* 243 B2
Kjelsås *Oslo* 243 A3
Kladow *Berlin* 225 B1
Klampenborg *Copenhagen* 228 A3
Klaudyń *Warsaw* 252 B1
Klečany *Prague* 245 A2
Kledering *Vienna* 252 B2
Klein Jukskei → *Johannesburg* 233 A1
Kleinmachnow *Berlin* 225 B2
Kleinschönebeck *Berlin* 225 B5
Klemetsrud *Oslo* 243 A4
Klender *Jakarta* 232 B2
Kličany *Prague* 245 A2
Klipriviersberg Nature Reserve *Johannesburg* 233 B2
Klosterneuburg *Vienna* 252 A1
Kőbánya *Budapest* 227 B2
Kobbegem *Brussels* 226 A1
København *Copenhagen* 228 A2
København ✈ (CPH) *Copenhagen* 228 B3
Kobylisy *Prague* 245 B2
Kobyłka *Warsaw* 252 A3
Kodaira *Tokyo* 250 A1
Kodanaka *Tokyo* 250 B2
Koekelberg *Brussels* 226 A1
Koganei *Tokyo* 250 A2
Kogarah *Sydney* 249 B1
Koivupää *Helsinki* 231 B2
Koja *Jakarta* 232 A2
Koja Utara *Jakarta* 232 A2
Kokhav Ya'akov *Jerusalem* 233 A2
Kokobunji *Tokyo* 250 A1
Kokobunji-Temple *Tokyo* 250 A4
Kolarängen *Stockholm* 249 B3
Kolbotn *Oslo* 243 B3
Kolkata *Kolkata* 234 B2
Kolkata Dum Dum Int. ✈ (CCU) *Kolkata* 234 B2
Kolkata Maidan *Kolkata* 234 B1
Koło *Warsaw* 252 B1
Kolokinthou *Athens* 222 B2
Kolomyagi *St. Petersburg* 247 A1
Kolonos *Athens* 222 B2
Kolsås *Oslo* 243 A2
Komae *Tokyo* 250 B2
Komagome *Tokyo* 250 A3
Komazawa *Tokyo* 250 B3
Kona *Kolkata* 234 B1
Konala *Helsinki* 231 B2
Kondli *Delhi* 230 B2
Kongelunden *Copenhagen* 228 B3
Kongens Lyngby *Copenhagen* 228 A3
Kongo *Helsinki* 231 A1
Konnagar *Kolkata* 234 A2
Konohana *Osaka* 243 A1
Konradshöhe *Berlin* 225 A2
Kopanina *Prague* 245 B1
Koparkhairna *Mumbai* 240 A2
Köpenick *Berlin* 225 B4
Korangi *Karachi* 233 B2
Koremasa *Tokyo* 250 B1
Koridalos *Athens* 222 B1
Korokoro *Wellington* 253 B2
Korokoro Stream → *Wellington* 253 B2
Kosino *Moscow* 239 B4
Kosugi *Tokyo* 250 B2
Kota *Jakarta* 232 A1
Kōtō *Tokyo* 250 A3
Kotrung *Kolkata* 234 A2
Kouponia *Athens* 222 B2
Kowloon *Hong Kong* 232 B1
Kowloon Peak *Hong Kong* 232 A2
Kowloon Res. *Hong Kong* 232 A1
Kowloon Tong *Hong Kong* 232 A2
Kraainem *Brussels* 226 A2
Krailling *Munich* 241 B1
Krampnitz *Berlin* 225 B1
Krampnitzsee *Berlin* 225 B1
Kranji, Sungei → *Singapore* 248 A2
Kranji Industrial Estate *Singapore* 248 A2
Krasno-Presnenskaya *Moscow* 239 B2
Krč *Prague* 245 B2
Kremlin *Moscow* 239 B2
Krestovskiye, Ostrov *St. Petersburg* 247 B1
Kreuzberg *Berlin* 225 A3
Kritzendorf *Vienna* 252 A1
Krumme Lanke *Berlin* 225 B2
Krummensee *Berlin* 225 A5
Krung Thep = Bangkok *Bangkok* 223 B2
Krusboda *Stockholm* 249 B3
Kuangchou = Guangzhou *Guangzhou* 231 B2
Küçükköy *Istanbul* 232 B1
Küçüksu *Istanbul* 232 B2
Kudrovo *St. Petersburg* 247 B3
Kulosaari *Helsinki* 231 B3
Kumla *Stockholm* 249 B3
Kungens kurva *Stockholm* 249 B1
Kungliga Slottet *Stockholm* 249 B2
Kungshatt *Stockholm* 249 B1
Kungsholmen *Stockholm* 249 A2
Kuningan *Jakarta* 232 B1
Kunitachi *Tokyo* 250 A1
Kunming Hu *Beijing* 224 B1
Kunratice *Prague* 245 B2
Kupchino *St. Petersburg* 247 B2
Kurbağalı → *Istanbul* 232 C2
Kurihara *Tokyo* 250 A2
Kurla *Mumbai* 240 A2
Kurmuri *Mumbai* 240 A2
Kurume *Tokyo* 250 A2
Kuryanovo *Moscow* 239 C3
Kuskovo *Moscow* 239 B3
Kustia *Kolkata* 234 B2
Kuzguncuk *Istanbul* 232 B2
Kuzyminki *Moscow* 239 B3
Kwai Chung *Hong Kong* 232 A1
Kwangchow = Guangzhou *Guangzhou* 231 B2
Kwun Tong *Hong Kong* 232 B2
Kyje *Prague* 245 B3
Kyūhōji *Osaka* 243 B2

L

La Blanca *Santiago* 247 C2
La Boca *Buenos Aires* 227 B2
La Bretèche *Paris* 244 A1
La Campiña *Lima* 234 C2
La Celle-St-Cloud *Paris* 244 A1
La Cisterna *Santiago* 247 C2
La Courneuve *Paris* 244 A3
La Dehesa *Santiago* 247 B2
La Encantada *Lima* 234 C2
La Estación *Madrid* 237 B1
La Floresta *Barcelona* 224 A1
La Florida *Santiago* 247 C2
La Fortuna *Madrid* 237 B1
La Fransa *Barcelona* 224 A1
La Garenne-Colombes *Paris* 244 A2
La Giustiniana *Rome* 246 B1
La Grange *Chicago* 229 C1
La Grange Park *Chicago* 229 C1
La Granja *Santiago* 247 C2
La Guardia, New York ✈ (LGA) *New York* 242 B2
La Hulpe *Brussels* 226 B2
La Llacuna *Barcelona* 224 A2
La Loma *Mexico City* 238 A1
La Lucila *Buenos Aires* 227 B2
La Maladrerie *Paris* 244 A1
La Milla, Cerro *Lima* 234 B2
La Monachina *Rome* 246 B1
La Moraleja *Madrid* 237 A2
La Nopalera *Mexico City* 238 C2
La Paternal *Buenos Aires* 227 B2
La Perla *Lima* 234 B2
La Perouse *Sydney* 249 B2
La Pineda *Barcelona* 224 B1
La Pisana *Rome* 246 B1
La Prairie *Montreal* 240 B3
La Punta *Lima* 234 B1
La Puntigala *Barcelona* 224 A2
La Queue-en-Brie *Paris* 244 B4
La Reina *Santiago* 247 B2
La Ribera *Barcelona* 224 A1
La Sagrera *Barcelona* 224 A2
La Salada *Buenos Aires* 227 C2
La Scala *Milan* 239 B2
La Storta *Rome* 246 A1
La Taxonera *Barcelona* 224 A2
La Victoria *Lima* 234 B2
Laajalahti *Helsinki* 231 B1
Laajasalo *Helsinki* 231 B3
Laaksolahti *Helsinki* 231 B1
Lablâba, W. el → *Cairo* 227 A2
Lachine *Montreal* 240 B1
Lachine, Canal de *Montreal* 240 B2
Lad Phrao *Bangkok* 223 B2
Ladera Heights *Los Angeles* 236 C2
Ládví *Prague* 245 B2
Lady *Warsaw* 252 C1
Lafontaine, Parc *Montreal* 240 A2
Lagoa *Rio de Janeiro* 245 B1
Lagos *Lagos* 234 B2
Lagos Harbour *Lagos* 234 B2
Lagos-Ikeja ✈ (LOS) *Lagos* 234 A1
Lagos Island *Lagos* 234 B2
Lagos Lagoon *Lagos* 234 B2
Laguna de B. *Manila* 237 C2
Laim *Munich* 241 B2
Lainate *Milan* 239 A1
Lainz *Vienna* 252 B1
Lake Buena Vista *Orlando* 243 B1
Lake Cain Hills *Orlando* 243 B2
Lake Fairfax Park *Washington* 253 B2
Lakemba *Sydney* 249 B1
Lakeside *Cape Town* 228 B1
Lakeside *Johannesburg* 233 A2
Lakeview *Chicago* 229 B3
Lakewood Park *Atlanta* 223 B2
Lakhtinskiy *St. Petersburg* 247 B1
Lakhtinskiy Razliv, Oz. *St. Petersburg* 247 B1
Lakshmanpur *Kolkata* 234 B1
Laksi *Bangkok* 223 A2
Lal Qila *Delhi* 230 B2
Lam Tin *Hong Kong* 232 B2
Lambert *Oslo* 243 A3
Lambeth □ *London* 235 B3
Lambrate *Milan* 239 B2
Lambro, Parco *Milan* 239 B2
Lambton Mills *Toronto* 251 B1
Lamma I. *Hong Kong* 232 B1
Landover Hills *Washington* 253 B4
Landsmeer *Amsterdam* 222 A2
Landstrasse *Vienna* 252 A2
Landwehr kanal *Berlin* 225 B3
Lane Cove *Sydney* 249 A1
Lane Cove National Park △ *Sydney* 249 A1
Langa *Cape Town* 228 A2
Langenzersdorf *Vienna* 252 A2
Langer See *Berlin* 225 B4
Langley *Washington* 253 B2
Langley Park *Washington* 253 B4
Langwald *Munich* 241 A1
Lanham *Washington* 253 B4
Lankwitz *Berlin* 225 B3
L'Annunziatella *Rome* 246 C2
Lansdowne *Cape Town* 228 A2
Lansing *Toronto* 251 A2
Lanus *Buenos Aires* 227 C2
Lapa *Rio de Janeiro* 245 B1
Laranjeiras *Rio de Janeiro* 245 B1
Las *Warsaw* 252 B2
Las Corts *Barcelona* 224 A1
Las Kabacki *Warsaw* 252 C2
Las Pinas *Manila* 237 C1
Las Rejas *Santiago* 247 B1
Lasalle *Montreal* 240 B2
LaSalle Street Station *Chicago* 229 B3
Lasek Bielański *Warsaw* 252 B1
Lasek Na Kole *Warsaw* 252 B1
Laski *Warsaw* 252 B1
Latina *Madrid* 237 B1
Lauttasaari *Helsinki* 231 C2
Laval-des-Rapides *Montreal* 240 A1
Lavīzān *Tehran* 251 A2
Lavradio *Lisbon* 236 A2
Lawndale *Chicago* 229 B2
Lawne L. *Orlando* 243 A1
Lawrence Heights *Toronto* 251 A2
Layari *Karachi* 233 A2
Layari → *Karachi* 233 A1
Łazienkowski Park *Warsaw* 252 B2
Le Blanc-Mesnil *Paris* 244 A3
Le Bourget *Paris* 244 A3
Le Chenoi *Brussels* 226 B2
Le Chesnay *Paris* 244 B1
Le Christ de Saclay *Paris* 244 B2
Le Kremlin-Bicêtre *Paris* 244 B3
Le Mesnil-le-Roi *Paris* 244 A1
Le Pecq *Paris* 244 A1
Le Perreux *Paris* 244 A3
Le Pin *Paris* 244 A4
Le Plessis-Robinson *Paris* 244 B2
Le Plessis-Trévise *Paris* 244 B4
Le Port-Marly *Paris* 244 A1
Le Pré-St-Gervais *Paris* 244 A3
Le Raincy *Paris* 244 A4
Le Vésinet *Paris* 244 A1
Lea Bridge *London* 235 A3
Leaside *Toronto* 251 A2
Leblon *Rio de Janeiro* 245 B1
Lee *London* 235 B4
Leganés *Madrid* 237 C1
Legazpi *Madrid* 237 B1
Lehtisaari *Helsinki* 231 B2
Lei Yue Mun *Hong Kong* 232 B2
Leião *Lisbon* 236 A1
Leichhardt *Sydney* 249 B1
Leith *Edinburgh* 231 B3
Leme *Rio de Janeiro* 245 B1
Lemoyne *Montreal* 240 B3
Lenin *Moscow* 239 B2
Lenino *Moscow* 239 C2
Leninskiye Gory *Moscow* 239 B2
Lennox *Los Angeles* 236 C2
Leonia *New York* 242 A2
Leopardstown *Dublin* 230 B2
Leopoldau *Vienna* 252 A2
Leopoldsdorf *Vienna* 252 B2
Leopoldstadt *Vienna* 252 A2
Leportovo *Moscow* 239 B3
Leppävaara *Helsinki* 231 B1
Les Lilas *Paris* 244 A3
Les Loges-en-Josas *Paris* 244 B1
Les Pavillons-sous-Bois *Paris* 244 A4
Lésigny *Paris* 244 B4
Lesnozavodskaya *St. Petersburg* 247 B2
Lester B. Pearson Int., Toronto ✈ (YYZ) *Toronto* 251 A1
L'Étang-la-Ville *Paris* 244 A1
Letňany *Prague* 245 B3
Letopolis = Ausîm *Cairo* 227 A1
Levallois-Perret *Paris* 244 A2
Levent *Istanbul* 232 B2
Lewisdale *Washington* 253 B4
Lewisham □ *London* 235 B3
Lexington *Boston* 226 A1
Leyton *London* 235 A3
Leytonstone *London* 235 A4
L'Haÿ-les-Roses *Paris* 244 B3

L'Hospitalet de Llobregat Barcelona 224 A1
Lhotka Prague 245 B2
Liangshui He → Beijing 224 C2
Lianhua Chi Beijing 224 B1
Lianhua He → Beijing 224 B1
Libčice nad Vitavou Prague 245 A2
Libeň Prague 245 B2
Liberdade São Paulo 247 B2
Liberton Edinburgh 231 B3
Liberty I. New York 242 B1
Liberty Osaka Museum Osaka 243 B1
Liberty State Park ⌂ New York 242 B1
Libeznice Prague 245 A2
Libuš Prague 245 B2
Lichiao Guangzhou 231 B2
Lichtenburg Berlin 225 A4
Lichterfelde Berlin 225 B2
Lidingö Stockholm 249 A2
Lieshi Lingyuan Guangzhou 231 B2
Liesing Vienna 252 B1
Liesing → Vienna 252 B2
Ligovo St. Petersburg 247 C1
Lijordet Oslo 243 A2
Likhoborka → Moscow 239 A2
Lilla Värtan Stockholm 249 A3
Lille Værløse Copenhagen 228 A2
Liluah Kolkata 234 B1
Lim Chu Kang Singapore 248 A2
Lima Lima 234 B2
Limbiate Milan 239 A1
Limehouse London 235 A3
Limeil-Brévannes Paris 244 B3
Linate, Milano ✈ (LIN) Milan 239 B2
Linbropark Johannesburg 233 A2
Lincoln Center for Performing Arts New York 242 B2
Lincoln Heights Los Angeles 236 B3
Lincoln Memorial Washington 253 B3
Lincoln Park Chicago 229 B3
Lincoln Park New York 242 B1
Lincoln Park San Francisco 246 B1
Lincoln Park Zoo Chicago 229 B3
Lincolnwood Chicago 229 A2
Linda-a-Pastora Lisbon 236 A1
Linden Johannesburg 233 A2
Linden Wellington 253 A1
Lindenberg Berlin 225 A4
Lindøya Oslo 243 A3
Liniers Buenos Aires 227 B1
Linkebeek Brussels 226 B2
Linksfield Johannesburg 233 A2
Linmeyer Johannesburg 233 B2
Linna Helsinki 231 A2
Lintuvaara Helsinki 231 B1
Lion Rock Country Park ⌂ Hong Kong 232 A2
Lion's Head Cape Town 228 A1
Lioumi Athens 222 B2
Lisboa Lisbon 236 A2
Lisboa ✈ (LIS) Lisbon 236 A2
Lisbon = Lisboa Lisbon 236 A2
Lishui Guangzhou 231 A1
Little B. Sydney 249 B2
Little Calumet → Chicago 229 D3
Little Ferry New York 242 A1
Little Lake Conway Orlando 243 B2
Little Red School House Nature Center Chicago 229 C1
Little Rouge → Toronto 251 A4
Liuhang Shanghai 248 A1
Liurong Temple Guangzhou 231 B2
Livry-Gargan Paris 244 A4
Ljan Oslo 243 A3
Llano de Can Gineu Barcelona 224 A2
Lo Aranguiz Santiago 247 B2
Lo Boza Santiago 247 B1
Lo Chau Hong Kong 232 B2
Lo Chau Pak Mai Hong Kong 232 B2
Lo Espejo Santiago 247 C1
Lo Hermida Santiago 247 B2
Lo Prado Santiago 247 B1
Lo So Shing Hong Kong 232 B1
Lo Wai Hong Kong 232 A1
Loanhead Edinburgh 231 B3
Lobau Vienna 252 A3
Lobos, Pt. San Francisco 246 B1
Locham Munich 241 B1
Lochkov Prague 245 B2
Lockhausen Munich 241 A1
Lodi New York 242 A1
Lodi Estate Delhi 230 B2
Logan Int., Boston ✈ (BOS) Boston 226 A2
Logan Square Chicago 229 B2
Lognes-Émerainville ✈ Paris 244 B4
Löhme Berlin 225 A5
Lolokhet Karachi 233 A2
Lomas Chapultepec Mexico City 238 B1
Lomas de San Angel Inn Mexico City 238 B1
Lombardy East Johannesburg 233 A2
Lomianki Warsaw 252 A1
Lomus Reforma Mexico City 238 B1
London London 235 B3
London City ✈ (LCY) London 235 A4
London Heathrow ✈ (LHR) London 235 B1
London Zoo London 235 A3
Long B. Sydney 249 B2
Long Branch Toronto 251 B1
Long Brook → Washington 253 C2
Long Ditton London 235 B2
Long Island City New York 242 B2
Longchamp, Hippodrome de Paris 244 A2
Longhua Pagoda Shanghai 248 B1
Longhua Park Shanghai 248 B1
Longjohn Slough Chicago 229 C1
Longtan Hu → Beijing 224 B2
Longue-Pointe Montreal 240 A2
Longueuil Montreal 240 A3
Longueuil-St-Hubert = St-Hubert Montreal 240 B3
Loni Delhi 230 A2
Loop, The Chicago 229 B3
Lord's Cricket Ground London 235 A2
Loreto Milan 239 B2
Los Angeles Los Angeles 236 B3
Los Angeles Int. ✈ (LAX) Los Angeles 236 C2
Los Cerrillos ✈ (ULC) Santiago 247 B1
Los Nietos Los Angeles 236 C4
Los Olivos Lima 234 A2
Los Reyes Mexico City 238 B2
Losiny Ostrov △ Moscow 239 A3
Lot Brussels 226 B1
Lotus River Cape Town 228 B2
Lotus Temple Delhi 230 B2
Loughlinstown Dublin 230 B3
Louise, L. Orlando 243 B1
Louisiana Superdome New Orleans 241 B2
Loures Lisbon 236 A1
Louveciennes Paris 244 A1
Louvre, Musée du Paris 244 A3
Lower B. New York 242 C1
Lower Hutt Wellington 253 B2
Lower New York B. = Lower B. New York 242 C1
Lower Shing Mun Res. Hong Kong 232 A1
Lowry Bay Wellington 253 B2
Loyola University Chicago 229 B3
Lu Xun, Tomb of Shanghai 248 B1
Lu Xun Park Shanghai 248 B1
Lübars Berlin 225 A3
Lucy, L. Orlando 243 A2
Ludwigsfeld Munich 241 A1
Luhu Guangzhou 231 B2
Lumiar Lisbon 236 A2
Lundtofte Copenhagen 228 A3
Lung Mei Hong Kong 232 A2
Luojiang Guangzhou 231 B2
Lustheim Munich 241 A2
Luwan Shanghai 248 B1
Luzhniki Sports Centre Moscow 239 B2
Lyndhurst New York 242 B1
Lynn Woods Res. Boston 226 A2
Lyon, Gare de Paris 244 A3
Lyons Chicago 229 C2
Lysaker Oslo 243 A2
Lysakerselva → Oslo 243 A2
Lysolaje Prague 245 B2
Lyublino Moscow 239 B3

M

Ma Nam Wat Hong Kong 232 A2
Ma On Shan Country Park ⌂ Hong Kong 232 A2
Ma'ale Adumim Jerusalem 233 B2
Ma'ale Ha Khamisha Jerusalem 233 B1
Ma'ale Mikhmas Jerusalem 233 A2
Maantiekylä Helsinki 231 A3
Maarifa Baghdad 223 B2
Mabato Pt. Manila 237 C2
Mabel, L. Orlando 243 B1
Macaco, Morro do Rio de Janeiro 245 B2
McCook Chicago 229 C2
McGill University Montreal 240 A2
Machelen Brussels 226 A2
Machida Tokyo 250 B1
Maciołki Warsaw 252 B2
McKerrow, Mt. Wellington 253 B2
McKinley Park Chicago 229 C2
McLean Washington 253 B2
Macopocho → Santiago 247 B1
MacRitchie Res. Singapore 248 A2
Macul Santiago 247 C2
Madhudaha Kolkata 234 B2
Madhyamgram Kolkata 234 A2
Madín Mexico City 238 A1
Madín, L. Mexico City 238 A1
Madīnah Al Mansūr Baghdad 223 B2
Mâdinet Nasr Cairo 227 A2
Madrid Madrid 237 B1
Madrid Barajas ✈ (MAD) Madrid 237 B2
Madrona Barcelona 224 A1
Maesawa Tokyo 250 A2
Magdalena Lima 234 B2
Magdalena Contreras Mexico City 238 C1
Maghreb Baghdad 223 A2
Maginu Tokyo 250 B2
Magliana Rome 246 B1
Magny-les-Hameaux Paris 244 B1
Maheshtala Kolkata 234 C1
Mahim Mumbai 240 A2
Mahim B. Mumbai 240 A1
Mahlsdorf Berlin 225 A4
Mahmoodabad Karachi 233 A2
Mahrauli Delhi 230 B2
Mahul Mumbai 240 A2
Maida Vale London 235 A2
Maidstone Melbourne 238 A1
Maipú Santiago 247 C1
Maisonneuve, Parc Montreal 240 A2
Maisons-Alfort Paris 244 B3
Maisons-Laffitte Paris 244 A1
Maissoneuve Montreal 240 A2
Maitland Cape Town 228 A1
Makasar Jakarta 232 A2
Makati Manila 237 B2
Mäkiniitty Helsinki 231 A2
Malá Strana Prague 245 B2
Malabar Sydney 249 B2
Malabar Hill Mumbai 240 B1
Malabar Pt. Mumbai 240 B1
Malabon Manila 237 B1
Malacañang Palace Manila 237 B1
Malahide Dublin 230 A3
Malakoff Paris 244 B2
Mälarhöjaen Stockholm 249 B1
Malate Manila 237 B1
Malaya Neva St. Petersburg 247 B1
Malaya Okhta St. Petersburg 247 B2
Malchow Berlin 225 A3
Malden Boston 226 A2
Malden London 235 B2
Maleizen Brussels 226 B3
Malešice Prague 245 B3
Malir → Karachi 233 B2
Malleny Mills Edinburgh 231 B2
Malmi Helsinki 231 B2
Malmøya Oslo 243 A3
Måløv Copenhagen 228 A2
Malton Toronto 251 A1
Malvern Johannesburg 233 B2
Malvern Melbourne 238 B2
Malvern Toronto 251 A3
Mampang Prapatan Jakarta 232 B1
Mampukuji Tokyo 250 B2
Man Budrukh Mumbai 240 A2
Man Khurd Mumbai 240 A2
Manakhat Jerusalem 233 B2
Mandaluyong Manila 237 B2
Mandaoli Delhi 230 B2
Mandaqui → São Paulo 247 A2
Mandoli Delhi 230 A2
Mandvi Mumbai 240 B2
Manenberg Cape Town 228 A2
Mang Kung Uk Hong Kong 232 B2
Mang-won Seoul 247 B1
Mangolpuri Delhi 230 A1
Manguinhos ✈ Rio de Janeiro 245 B1
Manhattan New York 242 B2
Manhattan Beach New York 242 C2
Manila Manila 237 B1
Manila Ninoy Aquino Int. ✈ (MNL) Manila 237 B2
Mankkaa Helsinki 231 B1
Manly Sydney 249 A2
Mann, L. Orlando 243 A2
Mann's Chinese Theatre Los Angeles 236 B2
Mannswörth Vienna 252 B3
Manor Park London 235 A4
Manor Park Wellington 253 A2
Manora Karachi 233 B1
Manora Pt. Karachi 233 B1
Manquehue, Cerro Santiago 247 B2
Manzanares, Canal de Madrid 237 C2
Mapo Seoul 247 B1
Maracanã Rio de Janeiro 245 B1
Maraoli Mumbai 240 A2
Marcelin Warsaw 252 B1
Mareil-Marly Paris 244 A1
Margareten Vienna 252 A2
Maria Vienna 252 A2
Maridalen Oslo 243 A3
Maridalsvatnet Oslo 243 A3
Mariendorf Berlin 225 B3
Marienfelde Berlin 225 B3
Marikina Manila 237 B2
Marikina → Manila 237 B2
Marin City San Francisco 246 A1
Marin Pen. San Francisco 246 A1
Marina del Rey Los Angeles 236 C2
Marino Dublin 230 A2
Marisco, Ponta do Rio de Janeiro 245 C1
Markham Toronto 251 A2
Marki Warsaw 252 B2
Markland Wood Toronto 251 B1
Marly, Forêt de Paris 244 A1
Marly-le-Roi Paris 244 A1
Marne-la-Vallée Paris 244 A4
Marolles-en-Brie Paris 244 B4
Maroubra Sydney 249 B2
Marquette Park Chicago 229 C2
Marrickville Sydney 249 B1
Marsfield Sydney 249 A1
Marsha, L. Orlando 243 B2
Marte, Campo de São Paulo 247 B2
Martesana, Navíglio della Milan 239 A2
Martin Luther King Nat. Historic Site ⌂ Atlanta 223 B2
Martinez Buenos Aires 227 A1
Martinkylä Helsinki 231 B2
Martinsried Munich 241 B1
Maruko Tokyo 250 B3
Maryino Moscow 239 B3
Maryland Singapore 248 B2
Marymont Warsaw 252 B1
Marysin Wawerski Warsaw 252 B2
Marzahn Berlin 225 A4
Mascot Sydney 249 B2
Masmo Stockholm 249 B1
Maspeth New York 242 B2
Masr el Gedida Cairo 227 A2
Masr el Qadîma Cairo 227 A2
Massachusetts Inst. of Tech. Boston 226 A2
Massamá Lisbon 236 A1
Massey → Toronto 251 A3
Massy Paris 244 B2
Mata Jerusalem 233 B1
Matihutong Beijing 224 B1
Matinha Lisbon 236 A2
Matramam Jakarta 232 B2
Matsubara Osaka 243 B2
Mattapan Boston 226 B2
Mátyásföld Budapest 227 A3
Mau Tso Ngam Hong Kong 232 A2
Mauer Vienna 252 B1
Mauripur Karachi 233 A1
Maxhof Munich 241 B1
Mayfair Johannesburg 233 B2
Mayor, Plaza Madrid 237 B1
Maywood Chicago 229 B1
Maywood Los Angeles 236 C3
Maywood New York 242 A1
Maywood Park Race Track Chicago 229 B1
Mazagaon Mumbai 240 B2
Meadowbank Park Sydney 249 A1
Měcholupy Prague 245 B3
Měčice Prague 245 A3
Mecidiyeköy Istanbul 232 B2
Medford Boston 226 A2
Mediodia Madrid 237 B2
Meguro Tokyo 250 B3
Meguro → Tokyo 250 B3
Mehpalpur Delhi 230 B1
Mehrābād ✈ (THR) Tehran 251 A1
Mehram Nagar Delhi 230 B1
Mehrow Berlin 225 A4
Meidling Vienna 252 A2
Méier Rio de Janeiro 245 B1
Meiji Shrine Tokyo 250 A3
Meise Brussels 226 A1
Mejiro Tokyo 250 A3
Melbourne Melbourne 238 A1
Melbourne ✈ (MEL) Melbourne 238 A1
Melkki Helsinki 231 C2
Mellunkylä Helsinki 231 B3
Mellunmäki Helsinki 231 B3
Melrose Boston 226 A2
Melrose New York 242 B2
Melrose Park Chicago 229 B1
Melsbroek Brussels 226 A2
Melville Johannesburg 233 B2
Menteng Jakarta 232 B1
Mérantaise → Paris 244 B1
Mercamadrid Madrid 237 B2
Merced, L. San Francisco 246 B2
Meredale Johannesburg 233 B1
Merlimau, Pulau Singapore 248 B2
Merri Cr. → Melbourne 238 A1
Merrion Dublin 230 B2
Merrionette Park Chicago 229 C2
Merton □ London 235 B2
Mesgarābād Tehran 251 B3
Messe Vienna 252 A2
Metanópoli Milan 239 B2
Metro-Dade Cultural Centre Miami 238 B2
Metro Toronto Zoo Toronto 251 A3
Metropolitan Museum of Art New York 242 B2
Meudon Paris 244 B2
Mevaseret Tsiyon Jerusalem 233 B1
Mevo Beitar Jerusalem 233 B1
México Mexico City 238 B2
México, Ciudad de Mexico City 238 B2
Mexico City Int. ✈ (MEX) Mexico City 238 B2
Meyersdal Johannesburg 233 B2
Mezzate Milan 239 B2
Miadong Seoul 247 B2
Miami Miami 238 B2
Miami Beach Miami 238 B2
Miami Canal Miami 238 A1
Miami Int. ✈ (MIA) Miami 238 B1
Miami Shores Miami 238 A2
Miami Springs Miami 238 B1
Miasto Warsaw 252 B2
Michalowice Warsaw 252 B1
Michle Prague 245 B2
Middle Harbour Sydney 249 A2
Middle Hd. Sydney 249 A2
Middle Park Melbourne 238 B1
Middle Village New York 242 B2
Middlesex Fells Reservation Boston 226 A2
Midland Beach New York 242 C1
Midwood New York 242 C2
Miedzeszyn Warsaw 252 B3
Międzylesie Warsaw 252 B3
Miessaari Helsinki 231 C1
Miguel Hidalgo Mexico City 238 B1
Milan = Milano Milan 239 B1
Milanese, Parco Regionale ⌂ Milan 239 A1
Milano Milan 239 B1
Milano Due Milan 239 B2
Milano Linate ✈ (LIN) Milan 239 B2
Milano San Felice Milan 239 B2
Milbertshofen Munich 241 A2
Mill Hill London 235 A2
Millennium Dome London 235 A4
Miller Meadow Chicago 229 B2
Millerhill Edinburgh 231 B3
Milltown Dublin 230 B2
Millwood Washington 253 B4
Milnerton Cape Town 228 A1
Milon-la-Chapelle Paris 244 B1
Milton Boston 226 B2
Milton Bridge Edinburgh 231 B2
Mimico Toronto 251 B2
Mimico Creek → Toronto 251 B1
Minami Osaka 243 A2
Minamitsunashima Tokyo 250 B2
Minato Osaka 243 B1
Minato Tokyo 250 B3
Minshât el Bekkarî Cairo 227 A1
Miraflores Lima 234 B2
Miramar Wellington 253 B1
Misericordia, Sa. da Rio de Janeiro 245 B1
Mission San Francisco 246 B2
Mississauga Toronto 251 B1
Mitaka Tokyo 250 A2
Mitcham London 235 B2
Mitcham Common London 235 B3
Mitchell Museum of the American Indian Chicago 229 A2
Mitchell's Plain Cape Town 228 B2
Mitte Berlin 225 A3
Mittel Isarkanal → Munich 241 A3
Mixcoac Mexico City 238 B1
Miyakojima Osaka 243 A2
Mizonokuchi Tokyo 250 B2
Mizue Tokyo 250 A4
Mlocinski Park Warsaw 252 B1
Mlociny Warsaw 252 B1
Mnevniki Moscow 239 B1
Moba Lagos 234 B2
Moczydło Warsaw 252 C2
Modderfontein Johannesburg 233 A2
Modřany Prague 245 B2
Mogyoród Budapest 227 A3
Moinho Velho, Cor. → São Paulo 247 B2
Mok Seoul 247 B1
Mokotów Warsaw 252 B2
Molenbeek-St-Jean Brussels 226 A1
Molino de Rosas Mexico City 238 B1
Mollem Brussels 226 A1
Mollins de Rey Barcelona 224 A1
Mondeor Johannesburg 233 B2
Moneda, Palacio de la Santiago 247 B2
Moneró Rio de Janeiro 245 A1
Mong Kok Hong Kong 232 B2
Monkstown Dublin 230 B3
Monnickendam Amsterdam 222 A3
Monrovia Los Angeles 236 B4
Monsanto Lisbon 236 A1
Monsanto, Parque Florestal de Lisbon 236 A1
Mont-Royal Montreal 240 A2
Mont-Royal, Parc Montreal 240 A2
Montana de Montjuich Barcelona 224 A1
Montcada i Reixac Barcelona 224 A2
Monte Chingolo Buenos Aires 227 C2
Montebello Los Angeles 236 B4
Montemor Lisbon 236 A1
Monterey Park Los Angeles 236 B4
Montespaccato Rome 246 B1
Montesson Paris 244 A1
Monteverde Nuovo Rome 246 B1
Montfermeil Paris 244 A4
Montigny-le-Bretonneux Paris 244 B1
Montjay-la-Tour Paris 244 A4
Montparnasse, Gare Paris 244 A2
Montréal Montreal 240 A2
Montréal, Î. de Montreal 240 A2
Montréal, Université de Montreal 240 B2
Montréal Est Montreal 240 A2
Montréal-Nord Montreal 240 A2
Montréal-Ouest Montreal 240 B1
Montréal Trudeau Int. ✈ (YUL) Montreal 240 B1
Montreuil Paris 244 A3
Montrouge Paris 244 B2
Montserrat Buenos Aires 227 B2
Monza Milan 239 A2
Monzoro Milan 239 B1
Moóca São Paulo 247 B2
Moonachie New York 242 B1
Moonee Ponds Melbourne 238 A1
Moonee Valley Racecourse Melbourne 238 A1
Moosach Munich 241 A2
Mora Mumbai 240 B2
Moratalaz Madrid 237 B2
Mörby Stockholm 249 A2
Morden London 235 B2
Morée → Paris 244 A3
Morgan Park Chicago 229 C3
Moriguchi Osaka 243 A2
Morivione Milan 239 B2
Morningside Edinburgh 231 B2
Morningside Johannesburg 233 A2
Morningside Washington 253 C4
Morningside Park Orlando 243 B2
Morningside Park Toronto 251 A3
Morro Solar, Cerro Lima 234 C2
Mortlake London 235 B2
Mortlake Sydney 249 B1
Morton Grove Chicago 229 A2
Morumbi São Paulo 247 B1
Moscavide Lisbon 236 A2
Moschato Athens 222 B2
Moscow = Moskva Moscow 239 B2
Moskva Moscow 239 B2
Moskvoretskiy Moscow 239 B2
Mosman Sydney 249 A2
Móstoles Madrid 237 C1
Moti Bagh Delhi 230 B2
Motol Prague 245 B1
Motsa Jerusalem 233 B2
Motsa Ilit Jerusalem 233 B1
Motspur Park London 235 B2
Mottingham London 235 B4
Mount Dennis Toronto 251 A2
Mount Greenwood Chicago 229 C2
Mount Hood Memorial Park ⌂ Boston 226 A2
Mount Merrion Dublin 230 B2
Mount Rainier Washington 253 B4
Mount Vernon New York 242 A3
Müggelberge Berlin 225 B4
Müggelheim Berlin 225 B5
Muggiò Milan 239 A2
Mühleiten Vienna 252 A3
Mühlenfliess → Berlin 225 A5
Muiden Amsterdam 222 A3
Muizenberg Cape Town 228 B1
Mujahidpur Delhi 230 B2
Mukandpur Delhi 230 A2
Mukhmas Jerusalem 233 A2
Muko → Osaka 243 A1
Mukojima Tokyo 250 A3
Mulbarton Johannesburg 233 B2
Mumbai Mumbai 240 B2
Mumbai Chhatrapati Shivaji Int. ✈ (BOM) Mumbai 240 A2
Mumbai Harbour Mumbai 240 B2
Munch Museum Oslo 243 A3
Münchehofe Berlin 225 B5
München Munich 241 B2
München Franz Josef Straus ✈ (MUC) Munich 241 A2
Munich = München Munich 241 B2
Munkkiniemi Helsinki 231 B2
Munro Buenos Aires 227 B1
Muntinlupa Manila 237 C2
Murai Res. Singapore 248 A2
Muranów Warsaw 252 B1
Murino St. Petersburg 247 B2
Murrayfield Edinburgh 231 B2
Musashino Tokyo 250 A2
Museu Nacional Rio de Janeiro 245 B1
Mushin Lagos 234 A2
Musocco Milan 239 B1
Mustansirīya Baghdad 223 A2
Musturud Cairo 227 A2
Muswell Hill London 235 A3
Mutanabi Baghdad 223 B2
Muthana Baghdad 223 B2
Mykerinos Cairo 227 B1
Myllypuro Helsinki 231 B3
Mystic → Boston 226 A2

N

Nacka Stockholm 249 B3
Naenae Wellington 253 B2
Nærsnes Oslo 243 B1
Nagatsuta Tokyo 250 B2
Nagytétény Budapest 227 B1
Nahalin Jerusalem 233 B1
Najafgarh Drain → Delhi 230 B1
Nakahara Tokyo 250 B2
Nakano Tokyo 250 A2
Namsan Park Seoul 247 B1
Namyeong Seoul 247 B1
Nanbiancun Guangzhou 231 B1
Nanchang He → Beijing 224 B1
Nandang Guangzhou 231 B2
Nangal Dewat Delhi 230 B1
Naniwa Osaka 243 B1
Nanole Mumbai 240 A2
Nanpu Bridge Shanghai 248 B2
Nanshi Shanghai 248 B1
Nanterre Paris 244 A2
Naoabad Kolkata 234 C2
Napier Mole Karachi 233 B1
Naraina Delhi 230 B1
Nariman Point Mumbai 240 B1
Nariman Pt. Mumbai 240 B1
Närmak Tehran 251 A2
Naruo Osaka 243 A1
Näsby Stockholm 249 A2
Näsbypark Stockholm 249 A2
National Arboretum Washington 253 B3
National Zoological Park Washington 253 B3
Nativity, Basilica of Jerusalem 233 B2
Natolin Warsaw 252 C2
Naucalpan de Juárez Mexico City 238 B1
Naupada Mumbai 240 A2

Navi Mumbai Mumbai 240 A2
Navíglio di Pavia Milan 239 B1
Navíglio Grande Milan 239 B1
Navotas Manila 237 B1
Navy Pier Chicago 229 B3
Nazal Hikmat Beg Baghdad 223 A2
Nazimabad Karachi 233 A2
Nazlet el Simmân Cairo 227 B1
Nea Alexandria Athens 222 B2
Nea Ionia Athens 222 A2
Nea Liosia Athens 222 A2
Nea Smirni Athens 222 B2
Neapoli Athens 222 B2
Near North Chicago 229 B3
Nebušice Prague 245 B1
Nederhorst Amsterdam 222 B3
Nedlitz Berlin 225 B1
Nee Soon Singapore 248 A2
Needham Boston 226 B1
Needham Heights Boston 226 B1
N'ematābād Tehran 251 B2
Nerima Tokyo 250 A3
Nesodden Oslo 243 B3
Nesoddtangen Oslo 243 A3
Nesøya Oslo 243 A2
Neu Aubing Munich 241 B1
Neu Buch Berlin 225 A4
Neu Buchhorst Berlin 225 B5
Neu Fahrland Berlin 225 B1
Neu Lindenberg Berlin 225 A4
Neubiberg Munich 241 B3
Neuenhagen Berlin 225 A4
Neuessling Vienna 252 A3
Neuhausen Munich 241 B2
Neuherberg Munich 241 A2
Neuhönow Berlin 225 A5
Neuilly-Plaisance Paris 244 A4
Neuilly-sur-Marne Paris 244 A4
Neuilly-sur-Seine Paris 244 A2
Neukagran Vienna 252 A2
Neukettenhof Vienna 252 B2
Neukölln Berlin 225 B3
Neuperlach Munich 241 B2
Neuried Munich 241 B1
Neustift am Walde Vienna 252 A1
Neusüssenbrunn Vienna 252 A2
Neuwaldegg Vienna 252 A1
Neve Ya'akov Jerusalem 233 A2
Neves Rio de Janeiro 245 B2
New Baghdād Baghdad 223 B2
New Barakpur Kolkata 234 A2
New Brighton New York 242 C1
New Canada Johannesburg 233 B1
New Canada Dam Johannesburg 233 B1
New Carrollton Washington 253 B4
New Cross London 235 B3
New Delhi Delhi 230 B2
New Dorp New York 242 C1
New Dorp Beach New York 242 C1
New Malden London 235 B2
New Milford New York 242 A1
New Mumbai = Navi Mumbai Mumbai 240 A2
New Territories Hong Kong 232 A1
New Toronto Toronto 251 B1
New Utrecht New York 242 C2
New York New York 242 B3
New York La Guardia ✈ (LGA) New York 242 B2
Newark B. New York 242 B1
Newbattle Edinburgh 231 B3
Newbury Park London 235 A4
Newcraighall Edinburgh 231 B3
Newham □ London 235 A4
Newhaven Edinburgh 231 B2
Newington Edinburgh 231 B2
Newlands Johannesburg 233 B1
Newlands Wellington 253 B1
Newport Melbourne 238 B1
Newton Boston 226 B1
Newtonbrook Toronto 251 A2
Newtongrange Edinburgh 231 B3
Newtonville Boston 226 A1
Newtown Sydney 249 B2
Ngaio Wellington 253 B1
Ngau Chi Wan Hong Kong 232 A2
Ngau Tau Kok Hong Kong 232 B2
Ngauranga Wellington 253 B1
Ngong Shuen Chau Hong Kong 232 B1
Ngua Kok Wan Hong Kong 232 A1
Niāvarān Tehran 251 A2
Nibra Kolkata 234 B1
Nidāl Baghdad 223 B2
Niddrie Edinburgh 231 B3
Niddrie Melbourne 238 A1
Nieder Neuendorf Berlin 225 A2
Niederschöneweide Berlin 225 B3
Niederschönhausen Berlin 225 A3
Niemeyer Rio de Janeiro 245 B1
Nieuwendam Amsterdam 222 A2
Nihonbashi Tokyo 250 A3
Niipperi Helsinki 231 B1
Nikea Athens 222 B1
Nikolassee Berlin 225 B2
Nikolskiy Moscow 239 B1
Niles Chicago 229 A2
Nimta Kolkata 234 A2
Ninoy Aquino Int. ✈ (MNL) Manila 237 B2
Nippa Tokyo 250 B2
Nippori Tokyo 250 A3
Nishi Osaka 243 A1
Nishinari Osaka 243 B1
Nishinomiya Osaka 243 A1
Nishiyodogawa Osaka 243 A1
Niterói Rio de Janeiro 245 B2
Nockeby Stockholm 249 B1
Noel Park London 235 A3
Nogatino Moscow 239 B3
Nogent-sur-Marne Paris 244 A3
Noida Delhi 230 B2
Noiseau Paris 244 B4
Noisiel Paris 244 A4
Noisy-le-Grand Paris 244 A4
Noisy-le-Roi Paris 244 A1
Noisy-le-Sec Paris 244 A3
Nokkala Helsinki 231 C1
Nomentano Rome 246 B2
Nonakashinden Tokyo 250 A2
Nongminyundong Jiangxisuo Guangzhou 231 B2
Nonhyeon Seoul 247 B2
Nonthaburi Bangkok 223 A1
Noordgesig Johannesburg 233 B1
Noordzeekanaal Amsterdam 222 A1
Nord, Gare du Paris 244 A3
Nordmarka Oslo 243 A3
Nordrand-Siedlung Vienna 252 A2
Nordstrand Oslo 243 A3
Normandale Wellington 253 B2
Norridge Chicago 229 B2
Norrmalm Stockholm 249 A2
North Arlington New York 242 B1
North Bay Village Miami 238 A2
North Bergen New York 242 B1
North Bull I. Dublin 230 A3
North Cheam London 235 B2
North Cray London 235 B4
North Decatur Atlanta 223 B3
North Druid Hills Atlanta 223 B3
North Esk → Edinburgh 231 B2
North Gyle Edinburgh 231 B2
North Hackensack New York 242 A1
North Harbor Manila 237 B1
North Hd. Sydney 249 A2
North Hollywood Los Angeles 236 B2
North Lexington Boston 226 A1
North Miami Miami 238 A2
North Miami Beach Miami 238 A2
North Nazimabad Karachi 233 A2
North Pt. Hong Kong 232 B2
North Queensferry Edinburgh 231 A1
North Quincy Boston 226 B2
North Res. Boston 226 A2
North Riverside Chicago 229 B2
North Saugus Boston 226 A2
North Shore Channel → Chicago 229 B2
North Springfield Washington 253 C2
North Station Boston 226 A2
North Sydney Sydney 249 B2
North Woolwich London 235 A4
North York Toronto 251 A2
Northbridge Sydney 249 A2
Northbridge Park Sydney 249 A2
Northcliff Johannesburg 233 A1
Northcote Melbourne 238 A2
Northeastern University Boston 226 A2
Northern Virginia Regional Park ⌂ Washington 253 B3
Northlake Chicago 229 B1
Northmount Toronto 251 A2
Northolt London 235 A1
Northumberland Heath London 235 B5
Northwestern Station Chicago 229 B3
Northwestern University Chicago 229 A2
Northwood London 235 A1
Northwood Park Toronto 251 A1
Norwood Johannesburg 233 A2
Norwood Park Chicago 229 B2
Noryangjin Seoul 247 B1
Nossa Senhora do Ó São Paulo 247 B1
Nossegem Brussels 226 A3
Notre-Dame Paris 244 A3
Notre-Dame, Basilique Montreal 240 B2
Notre-Dame, Bois Paris 244 B4
Notre-Dame-de-Grace Montreal 240 B2
Notting Hill London 235 A2
Nova Milanese Milan 239 A2
Novate Milanese Milan 239 A1
Novaya Derevnya St. Petersburg 247 A1
Nové Město Prague 245 B2
Novoaleksandrovskoye St. Petersburg 247 B2
Novodevichy Convent Moscow 239 B2
Novogireyevo Moscow 239 B3
Novosaratovka St. Petersburg 247 B3
Nowe-Babice Warsaw 252 B1
Nowe Miasto Warsaw 252 B2
Nöykkiö Helsinki 231 B1
Nueva Atzacoalco Mexico City 238 B2
Nueva Pompeya Buenos Aires 227 C2
Nueva Tenochtitlán Mexico City 238 B2
Nuijala Helsinki 231 B1
Numabukuro Tokyo 250 A2
Nuñez Buenos Aires 227 B2
Nunhead London 235 B3
Ñuñoa Santiago 247 B2
Nusle Prague 245 B2
Nussdorf Vienna 252 A2
Nyanga Cape Town 228 A2
Nymphenburg Munich 241 B2
Nymphenburg, Schloss Munich 241 B2

O

Oak Grove Atlanta 223 A3
Oak Hill Boston 226 B1
Oak Lawn Chicago 229 C2
Oak Park Chicago 229 B2
Oak View Washington 253 A4
Oakdale Atlanta 223 A2
Oakland San Francisco 246 B3
Oakland Washington 253 B4
Oaklawn Washington 253 C4
Oakleigh Melbourne 238 B2
Oakton Washington 253 B2
Oakwood Beach New York 242 C1
Oatley Sydney 249 B1
Obalende Lagos 234 B2
Oba's Palace Lagos 234 B2
Oberföhring Munich 241 B2
Oberhaching Munich 241 B2
Oberlaa Vienna 252 B2
Oberlisse Vienna 252 A2
Obermenzing Munich 241 A1
Obermoos Schwaige Munich 241 A1
Oberschleissheim Munich 241 A2
Oberschöneweide Berlin 225 B4
Observatory Johannesburg 233 B2
Óbuda Budapest 227 A2
Obukhovo St. Petersburg 247 B2
Obvodnyy Kanal St. Petersburg 247 B1
Ocean Park Hong Kong 232 B2
Ochota Warsaw 252 B1
Ocoee Orlando 243 A1
Ōdana Tokyo 250 B2
Öden-Stockach Munich 241 B3
Odilampi Helsinki 231 B1
Odivelas Lisbon 236 A1
Odolany Warsaw 252 B1
Oeiras Lisbon 236 A1
Ofin Lagos 234 A3
Ogawa Tokyo 250 A1
Ogden Park Chicago 229 C2
Ogikubo Tokyo 250 A2
Ogogoro Lagos 234 B2
Ogoyo Lagos 234 B2
Ogudu Lagos 234 A2
O'Hare Int., Chicago ✈ (ORD) Chicago 229 B1
Ohariu Stream → Wellington 253 B1
O'Higgins, Parque Santiago 247 B2
Ōimachi Tokyo 250 B3
Ojota Lagos 234 A2
Okęcie Warsaw 252 B1
Okęcie, Warszawa ✈ (WAW) Warsaw 252 B1
Okelra Lagos 234 B2
Okeogbe Lagos 234 B2
Okhla Delhi 230 B2
Okhta → St. Petersburg 247 B2
Okkervil → St. Petersburg 247 B2
Okrzeszyn Warsaw 252 C2
Oksval Oslo 243 A3
Oktyabrskiy Moscow 239 B2
Okubo Tokyo 250 A3
Ōkura Tokyo 250 B1
Olari Helsinki 231 B1
Olaria Rio de Janeiro 245 B1
Old Admiralty St. Petersburg 247 B1
Old City Jerusalem 233 B2
Old City Shanghai 248 B1
Old City Hall Toronto 251 B2
Old Fort York Toronto 251 B2
Old Harbor Boston 226 B2
Old Town Chicago 229 B3
Old Town Hall = Altes Rathaus Munich 241 B2
Oldbawn Dublin 230 B1
Olgino St. Petersburg 247 A1
Olimpico, Estadio Mexico City 238 C1
Olivais Lisbon 236 A2
Olivar de los Padres Mexico City 238 B1
Olivar del Conde Mexico City 238 B1
Olives, Mt. of Jerusalem 233 B2
Olivia, L. Orlando 243 A1
Olivos Buenos Aires 227 B2
Olona → Milan 239 B1
Olympia, L. Orlando 243 A1
Olympic Stadium = Turner Field Atlanta 223 B2
Olympic Stadium Helsinki 231 B2
Olympique, Stade Montreal 240 A2
Ōmori Tokyo 250 B3
Onisigun Lagos 234 B2
Ontario Science Centre Toronto 251 A2
Ōokayama Tokyo 250 B3
Oostzaan Amsterdam 222 A2
Opa-Locka Miami 238 A1
Opa-Locka ✈ (OPF) Miami 238 A1
Opacz Warsaw 252 B1
Ophirton Johannesburg 233 B2
Oppegård Oslo 243 B3
Oppem Brussels 226 A1
Oppsal Oslo 243 A4
Ora Jerusalem 233 B1
Oradell New York 242 A1
Oradell Res. New York 242 A1
Orange Bowl Stadium Miami 238 B2
Orangi Karachi 233 A2
Ordrup Copenhagen 228 A3
Orech Prague 245 B1
Orient Heights Boston 226 A3
Orlando Orlando 243 A2
Orlando Dam Johannesburg 233 B1
Orlando East Johannesburg 233 B1
Orlando Executive ✈ Orlando 243 A2
Orlando Int. ✈ (MCO) Orlando 243 B3
Orlovista Orlando 243 A2
Orly Paris 244 B3
Orly, Paris ✈ (ORY) Paris 244 B3
Ormesson-sur-Marne Paris 244 B4
Ormond Melbourne 238 B2
Ormøya Oslo 243 A3
Orpington London 235 B4
Ortaköy Istanbul 232 B2
Ortica Milan 239 B2
Oruba Lagos 234 A2
Ōsaka Osaka 243 B2
Ōsaka Castle Osaka 243 A2
Ōsaka Harbour Osaka 243 B1
Ōsaka Itami Int. ✈ (ITM) Osaka 243 A1
Ōsaka Kansai ✈ (KIX) Osaka 243 B2
Ōsaki Tokyo 250 B3
Osasco São Paulo 247 B1
Osdorf Berlin 225 B3
Osdorp Amsterdam 222 A1
Oshodi Lagos 234 A2
Oslo Oslo 243 A3
Oslo ✈ (OSL) Oslo 243 A4
Ōsone Tokyo 250 B2
Osorun Lagos 234 A2
Ospiate Milan 239 A1
Ostankino Moscow 239 B2
Osterley London 235 B1
Osterley Park London 235 B1
Östermalm Stockholm 249 A2
Österskär Stockholm 249 A3
Óstia Malpasso Rome 246 C1
Ostiense Rome 246 B1
Østmarkkapellet Oslo 243 A4
Ostøya Oslo 243 A2
Østre Aker Oslo 243 A3
Ōta Tokyo 250 B3
Otaniemi Helsinki 231 B1
Otari Open Air Museum Wellington 253 B1
Otsuka Tokyo 250 A3
Ottakring Vienna 252 A1
Ottávia Rome 246 B1
Ottery Cape Town 228 B2
Ottobrunn Munich 241 B3
Ouderkerk Amsterdam 222 B2
Oulunkylä Helsinki 231 B2
Ourcq, Canal de l' Paris 244 A3
Outer Mission San Francisco 246 B2
Outremont Montreal 240 A2
Overijse Brussels 226 B3
Owhiro Bay Wellington 253 C1
Oworonsoki Lagos 234 A2
Oxgangs Edinburgh 231 B2
Oxon Hill Washington 253 C4
Oyodo Osaka 243 A1
Oyster B. Sydney 249 C1
Oyster Rock Mumbai 240 B1
Oyster Rocks Karachi 233 B2
Ozoir-la-Ferrière Paris 244 B4
Ozone Park New York 242 B2

P

Pacific Heights San Francisco 246 B2
Pacific Manor San Francisco 246 C2
Pacific Palisades Los Angeles 236 B1
Pacifica San Francisco 246 C2
Paco Manila 237 B1
Paco de Arcos Lisbon 236 A1
Paddington London 235 A2
Paddington Sydney 249 B2
Paderno Milan 239 A1
Pagewood Sydney 249 B2
Pagote Mumbai 240 B2
Pai, I. do Rio de Janeiro 245 B2
Pak Kok Hong Kong 232 B1
Pak Kong Hong Kong 232 A2
Pakila Helsinki 231 B2
Palacio Real Madrid 237 B1
Palaiseau Paris 244 B2
Palazzolo Milan 239 A1
Paleo Faliro Athens 222 B2
Palermo Buenos Aires 227 B2
Palhais Lisbon 236 B2
Palisades Park New York 242 A1
Palmer Park Washington 253 B4
Palmerston Dublin 230 A1
Paloheinä Helsinki 231 B2
Palomeras Madrid 237 B2
Palos Heights Chicago 229 D2
Palos Hills Chicago 229 C2
Palos Hills Forest Chicago 229 C1
Palos Park Chicago 229 C1
Palpara Kolkata 234 B2
Panchur Kolkata 234 B1
Pandacan Manila 237 B2
Pandan, Selat Singapore 248 B2
Pandan Res. Singapore 248 B2
Pangrati Athens 222 B2
Pangsua, Sungei → Singapore 248 A2
Panihati Kolkata 234 A2
Panjang, Bukit Singapore 248 A2
Panke → Berlin 225 A3
Pankow Berlin 225 A3
Pantheon Rome 246 B1
Panthersville Atlanta 223 B3
Pantin Paris 244 A3
Pantitlán Mexico City 238 B2
Panvel Cr. → Mumbai 240 B2
Paparangi Wellington 253 B1
Papiol Barcelona 224 A1
Paramount Studios Los Angeles 236 B3
Paramus New York 242 A1
Paranaque Manila 237 B1
Paray-Vieille-Poste Paris 244 B3
Pardisān Nature Park Tehran 251 A2
Parel Mumbai 240 B1
Pari São Paulo 247 B2
Parioli Rome 246 B1
Paris Paris 244 A3
Paris Orly ✈ (ORY) Paris 244 B3
Parje Mumbai 240 B2
Pārk-e Āzādegān Tehran 251 B2
Pārk-e Mellat Tehran 251 A2
Park Ridge Chicago 229 A1
Park Royal London 235 A2
Parkchester New York 242 B2
Parkdale Toronto 251 B2
Parkhurst Johannesburg 233 A2
Parklawn Washington 253 B3
Parkmore Johannesburg 233 A2
Parkside San Francisco 246 B2
Parktown Johannesburg 233 B2
Parkview Johannesburg 233 A2
Parkville New York 242 C2
Parkwood Cape Town 228 B1
Parkwood Johannesburg 233 A2
Parow Cape Town 228 A2
Parque Chacabuco Buenos Aires 227 B2
Parque Patricios Buenos Aires 227 B2
Parramatta → Sydney 249 A1
Paşabahçe Istanbul 232 B2
Pasadena Los Angeles 236 B4
Pasar Minggu Jakarta 232 B1
Pasay Manila 237 B1
Pascoe Vale Melbourne 238 A1
Pasig Manila 237 B2
Pasig → Manila 237 B2
Pasila Helsinki 231 B2
Pasing Munich 241 B1
Pasir Panjang Singapore 248 B2
Pasir Ris Singapore 248 A3
Passaic New York 242 A1
Passaic → New York 242 B1
Passirana Milan 239 A1
Patel Nagar Delhi 230 B1
Pateros Manila 237 B2
Pathumwan Bangkok 223 B2
Patipukur Kolkata 234 B2
Patisia Athens 222 A2
Paulo E. Virginia, Gruta Rio de Janeiro 245 B1
Paulshof Berlin 225 A5
Paya Lebar Singapore 248 A3
Peakhurst Sydney 249 B1
Peania Athens 222 B3
Pearson Int. Toronto ✈ (YYZ) Toronto 251 A1
Peckham London 235 B3
Pederstrup Copenhagen 228 A2
Pedralbes Barcelona 224 A1
Pedregal de San Angel, Jardines del Mexico City 238 C1
Peip'ing = Beijing Beijing 224 B1
Peking = Beijing Beijing 224 B1
Pelcowizna Warsaw 252 B2
Peñalolén Santiago 247 B2
Pencarrow Hd. Wellington 253 C2
Peng Siang → Singapore 248 A2
Penge London 235 B3
Penha Rio de Janeiro 245 A1
Penicuik Edinburgh 231 B2
Penjaringan Jakarta 232 A1
Pentagon Washington 253 B3
Penzing Vienna 252 A1
People's Park Shanghai 248 B1
People's Square Shanghai 248 B1
Perales del Rio Madrid 237 C2
Perchtoldsdorf Vienna 252 B1
Perdizes São Paulo 247 B2
Peristeri Athens 222 A2
Perivale London 235 A2
Perk Brussels 226 A2
Perlach Munich 241 B2
Perlacher Forst Munich 241 B2
Pero Milan 239 A1
Peropok, Bukit Singapore 248 B2
Perovo Moscow 239 B3
Pertusella Milan 239 A1
Pesagot Jerusalem 233 A2
Pesanggrahag, Kali → Jakarta 232 B1
Peschiera Borromeo Milan 239 B2
Pesek, Pulau Singapore 248 B2
Pest Budapest 227 B2
Pesterzsébet Budapest 227 B2
Pesthidegkút Budapest 227 A1
Pestimre Budapest 227 B3
Pestlőrinc Budapest 227 B3
Pestújhely Budapest 227 A2
Petas Helsinki 231 B2
Petone Wellington 253 B2
Petrogradskaya Storona St. Petersburg 247 B2
Petroupoli Athens 222 A2
Petrovice Prague 245 B3
Petrovskiy Park Moscow 239 B2
Petrovsko-Razumovskoye Moscow 239 B2
Pettycur Edinburgh 231 A2
Peutie Brussels 226 A2
Pfaueninsel Berlin 225 B1
Phaya Thai Bangkok 223 B2
Phihai Karachi 233 A2
Phillip B. Sydney 249 B2
Phoenix Park Dublin 230 A2
Phra Khanong Bangkok 223 B2
Phra Nakhon Bangkok 223 B2
Phra Pradaeng Bangkok 223 C2
Phranakhon Bangkok 223 B1
Pico Rivera Los Angeles 236 C4
Piedade Lisbon 236 A1
Piedade Rio de Janeiro 245 B1
Piedade, Cova da Lisbon 236 A2
Piedmont Park Atlanta 223 B2
Pierre Elliott Trudeau ✈ (YUL) Montreal 240 B1
Pietralata Rome 246 B2
Pihlajamäki Helsinki 231 B2
Pihlajasaari Helsinki 231 C2
Pilares Rio de Janeiro 245 B1
Pilton Edinburgh 231 B2
Pimmit Hills Washington 253 B2
Pine Castle Orlando 243 B2
Pine Grove Toronto 251 A1
Pine Hills Orlando 243 A2
Pinewood Park Miami 238 A2
Piney Run → Washington 253 B2
Pinganli Beijing 224 B2
Pingzhou Guangzhou 231 B2
Pinheiros → São Paulo 247 B1
Pinjrapur Karachi 233 A2
Pinner London 235 A1
Pinner Green London 235 A1
Pioltello Milan 239 A2
Pipinui Pt. Wellington 253 A1
Piræus = Pireas Athens 222 B1
Piraiévs = Pireas Athens 222 B1
Pirajuçara → São Paulo 247 B1
Pireas Athens 222 B1
Pirinççi Istanbul 232 B1
Pirituba São Paulo 247 A1
Pirkkola Helsinki 231 B2
Pisgat O'mer Jerusalem 233 B2
Pisgat Ze'ev Jerusalem 233 B2
Písnice Prague 245 C2
Pitampura Delhi 230 A1
Pitkäjärvi Helsinki 231 B1
Planegg Munich 241 B1
Pleasure Island Orlando 243 B1
Plumstead Cape Town 228 B1
Plumstead London 235 B4
Plyushchevo Moscow 239 B3
Po Toi Hong Kong 232 B2
Po Toi O Hong Kong 232 B2
Poasco Milan 239 B2
Podbaba Prague 245 B2
Podoli Prague 245 B2
Pohick Creek → Washington 253 C2
Pointe-Aux-Trembles Montreal 240 A2
Poissy Paris 244 A1
Pok Fu Lam Hong Kong 232 B1
Pokcheong Seoul 247 C2
Pokrovsko-Sresnevo Moscow 239 B1
Polton Edinburgh 231 B3
Polvoranca, Parque de Madrid 237 C1
Polyustrovo St. Petersburg 247 B2
Pomprap Bangkok 223 B2
Pondok Gede Jakarta 232 A2
Pondok Indah Jakarta 232 B1
Pont-Viau Montreal 240 A1
Pontault-Combault Paris 244 B4
Pontinha Lisbon 236 A1
Poplar London 235 A3
Poppintree Dublin 230 A2
Porirua Wellington 253 A2
Porirua East Wellington 253 A2
Port Melbourne Melbourne 238 B1
Port Nicholson Wellington 253 B2
Port Richmond New York 242 C1
Port Shelter Hong Kong 232 A2
Port Union Toronto 251 A4
Portage Park Chicago 229 B2
Portela, Lisboa ✈ (LIS) Lisbon 236 A2
Porter, L. Orlando 243 A3
Portmarnock Dublin 230 A3
Porto Brandão Lisbon 236 A1
Pôrto Novo Rio de Janeiro 245 A2
Porto Novo Cr. → Lagos 234 B2
Portobello Edinburgh 231 B3
Portrero San Francisco 246 B3
Potomac Washington 253 A2
Potrero Pt. San Francisco 246 B2
Potsdam Berlin 225 B1
Potzham Munich 241 B2
Pötzleinsdorf Vienna 252 A1

Povoa de Santo Adriao Lisbon 236 A2
Powązki Warsaw 252 B1
Powiśle Warsaw 252 B2
Powsin Warsaw 252 C2
Powsinek Warsaw 252 C2
Poyan Res. Singapore 248 A2
Pozuelo de Alarcón Madrid 237 B1
Prado, Museo del Madrid 237 B1
Prado Churubusco Mexico City 238 B2
Praga Warsaw 252 B2
Prague = Praha Prague 245 B2
Praha Prague 245 B2
Praha ✈ (PRG) Prague 245 B1
Praires, R. des → Montreal 240 A2
Prater Vienna 252 A2
Precotto Milan 239 A2
Prenestino Labicano Rome 246 B2
Prenzlauerberg Berlin 225 A3
Preston Melbourne 238 A1
Pretos Forros, Sa. dos Rio de Janeiro 245 B1
Préville Montreal 240 B3
Přezletice Prague 245 B3
Prima Porta Rome 246 B1
Primavalle Rome 246 B1
Primrose Johannesburg 233 B2
Progreso Nacional Mexico City 238 A2
Prosek Prague 245 B3
Prospect Hill Park Boston 226 A1
Providencia Santiago 247 B2
Průhonice Prague 245 C3
Psichiko Athens 222 A2
Pudong New Area Shanghai 248 B2
Pueblo Libre Lima 234 B2
Pueblo Nuevo Barcelona 224 A2
Pueblo Nuevo Madrid 237 B2
Puerto Madero Buenos Aires 227 B2
Puhuangyu Beijing 224 B2
Puistola Helsinki 231 B3
Pukinmäki Helsinki 231 B2
Pulkovo Int. ✈ (LED) St. Petersburg 247 C1
Pullach Munich 241 B1
Pullman Historic District Chicago 229 C3
Pulo Gadung Jakarta 232 B2
Pūnak Tehran 251 A2
Punchbowl Sydney 249 B1
Punde Mumbai 240 B2
Punggol Singapore 248 A3
Punggol, Sungei → Singapore 248 A3
Punggol Pt. Singapore 248 A3
Punjabi Bagh Delhi 230 A1
Puotila Helsinki 231 B3
Puteaux Paris 244 A2
Putney London 235 B2
Putuo Shanghai 248 B1
Putxet Barcelona 224 A1
Puxi Shanghai 248 B1
Pyramids Cairo 227 B1
Pyry Warsaw 252 C1

Q

Qalandiya Jerusalem 233 A2
Qal'eh Morghī Tehran 251 B2
Qanâ el Ismâ'ilîya Cairo 227 A2
Qāsemābād Tehran 251 A3
Qasr-e Firūzeh Tehran 251 B3
Qatane Jerusalem 233 B1
Qianmen Beijing 224 B2
Qinghuayuan Beijing 224 B1
Qingningsi Shanghai 248 B2
Qolhak Tehran 251 A2
Quadraro Rome 246 B2
Quaid-i-Azam Karachi 233 A1
Quartiere Zingone Milan 239 B1
Qubeiba Jerusalem 233 A1
Quds Baghdad 223 A2
Queen Mary Res. London 235 B1
Queen Victoria Market Melbourne 238 A1
Queensbury London 235 A2
Queenscliffe Sydney 249 A2
Queensferry Edinburgh 231 B1
Queenstown Singapore 248 B2
Quellerina Johannesburg 233 A1
Queluz Lisbon 236 A1
Quezon City Manila 237 B2
Quilicura Santiago 247 B1
Quincy Boston 226 B2
Quincy B. Boston 226 B3
Quinta Normal Santiago 247 B1
Quinto de Stampi Milan 239 B2
Quinto Romano Milan 239 B1
Quirinale Rome 246 B1

R

R.F.K. Memorial Stadium Washington 253 B4
Raasdorf Vienna 252 A3
Radcliffe College Boston 226 A2
Rådhus Oslo 243 A3
Radlice Prague 245 B2
Radość Warsaw 252 B3
Radotin Prague 245 C2
Rafat Jerusalem 233 A2
Raffles Park Singapore 248 B2
Raheny Dublin 230 A3
Rahnsdorf Berlin 225 B5
Rainham London 235 A5
Rajakylä Helsinki 231 B3
Rajpura Delhi 230 A2
Rákos-patak → Budapest 227 B3
Rákoshegy Budapest 227 B3
Rákoskeresztúr Budapest 227 B3
Rákoskert Budapest 227 B3
Rákosliget Budapest 227 B3
Rákospalota Budapest 227 A2
Rákosszentmihály Budapest 227 A2
Raków Warsaw 252 B1
Ram Jerusalem 233 A2
Rām Allāh Jerusalem 233 A2
Ramadān Baghdad 223 B2
Ramakrishna Puram Delhi 230 B1
Rāmallāh = Rām Allāh Jerusalem 233 A2
Ramanathpur Kolkata 234 A1
Ramat Allon Jerusalem 233 B2
Ramat Eshkol Jerusalem 233 B2
Ramat Razi'el Jerusalem 233 B1
Ramat Shafet Jerusalem 233 B1
Rambler Channel Hong Kong 232 A1
Ramenki Moscow 239 B1
Ramersdorf Munich 241 B2
Rameses Station Cairo 227 A2
Ramos Rio de Janeiro 245 B1
Ramos Mejía Buenos Aires 227 B1
Ramot Jerusalem 233 B2
Rampur Delhi 230 A2
Ramsgate Sydney 249 B1
Rand ✈ (QRA) Johannesburg 233 B2
Randalls I. New York 242 B2
Randburg Johannesburg 233 A1
Randhart Johannesburg 233 B2
Randpark Ridge Johannesburg 233 A1
Randwick Sydney 249 B2
Ranelagh Dublin 230 A2
Rangpuri Delhi 230 B1
Rannersdorf Vienna 252 B2
Ransbèche Brussels 226 B2
Ransdorp Amsterdam 222 A2
Ranvad Mumbai 240 B2
Raposo Lisbon 236 A1
Rastaala Helsinki 231 B1
Rastila Helsinki 231 B3
Raszyn Warsaw 252 C1
Rathfarnham Dublin 230 B2
Ratho Edinburgh 231 B1
Ratho Station Edinburgh 231 B1
Rato Lisbon 236 A2
Ravelston Edinburgh 231 B2
Rawamangun Jakarta 232 B2
Rayners Lane London 235 A1
Raynes Park London 235 B2
Raypur Kolkata 234 C2
Real Felipe, Fuerte Lima 234 B2
Reams, L. Orlando 243 B1
Recoleta Buenos Aires 227 B2
Recoleta Santiago 247 B2
Red Fort = Lal Qila Delhi 230 B2
Red Square Moscow 239 B2
Redbridge □ London 235 A4
Redfern Sydney 249 B2
Redwood Wellington 253 B1
Refshaleøen Copenhagen 228 A3
Regents Park Johannesburg 233 B2
Regent's Park London 235 A3
Rego Park New York 242 B2
Reinickendorf Berlin 225 A3
Rekola Helsinki 231 B3
Rembertów Warsaw 252 B2
Rembrandtpark Amsterdam 222 A2
Remedios, Parque Nacional de los △ Mexico City 238 B1
Remedios de Escalada Buenos Aires 227 C2
Rémola, Estany del Barcelona 224 B1
Renca Santiago 247 B1
Rennemoulin Paris 244 A1
Řeporyje Prague 245 B1
Repulse Bay Hong Kong 232 B2
Repy Prague 245 B1
Residenz Munich 241 B2
Reston Washington 253 B2
Retiro Buenos Aires 227 B2
Retiro Madrid 237 B1
Retiro, Puerto Buenos Aires 227 B2
Retreat Cape Town 228 B1
Reutov Moscow 239 B4
Réveillon → Paris 244 B4
Revere Boston 226 A2
Rexdale Toronto 251 A1
Reynosa Tamaulipas Mexico City 238 A1
Rho Milan 239 A1
Rhodes Sydney 249 A1
Rhodon Paris 244 B1
Rhodon → Paris 244 B1
Rialto Towers Melbourne 238 A1
Ribeira Rio de Janeiro 245 A1
Ricarda, Estany de la Barcelona 224 B1
Richmond Melbourne 238 A2
Richmond San Francisco 246 B2
Richmond Hill New York 242 B2
Richmond Park London 235 B2
Richmond-upon-Thames □ London 235 B2
Ridge, The Delhi 230 B2
Ridgefield New York 242 B1
Ridgefield Park New York 242 A1
Ridgewood New York 242 B2
Riem Munich 241 B3
Riesenrad Vienna 252 A2
Rijksmuseum Amsterdam 222 A2
Rikers I. New York 242 B2
Rimac Lima 234 B2
Ringsend Dublin 230 A2
Rinkeby Stockholm 249 A1
Rio Comprido Rio de Janeiro 245 B1
Rio de Janeiro Rio de Janeiro 245 B1
Rio de Janeiro Galeão ✈ (GIG) Rio de Janeiro 245 A1
Rio de Mouro Lisbon 236 A1
Ripollet Barcelona 224 A1
Ris Oslo 243 A3
Risby Copenhagen 228 A1
Rishra Kolkata 234 A2
Ritchie Washington 253 B4
Rithala Delhi 230 A1
Rive Sud, Canal de la Montreal 240 B2
River Edge New York 242 A1
River Forest Chicago 229 B2
River Grove Chicago 229 B1
Riverdale New York 242 A2
Riverdale Washington 253 B4
Riverdale Park Toronto 251 A2
Riverlea Johannesburg 233 B1
Riverside Chicago 229 C2
Riverwood Sydney 249 B1
Rivière-des-Praires Montreal 240 A2
Rixensart Brussels 226 B3
Riyad Baghdad 223 B2
Rizal Park Manila 237 B1
Rizal Stadium Manila 237 B1
Røa Oslo 243 A2
Robbins Chicago 229 D2
Robertsham Johannesburg 233 B2
Rochelle Park New York 242 A1
Rock Cr. → Washington 253 B3
Rock Creek Park Washington 253 B3
Rock Pt. Wellington 253 A1
Rockaway Beach New York 242 C3
Rockaway Pt. New York 242 C2
Rockdale Sydney 249 B1
Rockefeller Center New York 242 B2
Rocky Run → Washington 253 B2
Roda, Gezîret el Cairo 227 A2
Roda I. = Roda, Gezîret el Cairo 227 A2
Rodaon Vienna 252 B1
Rødovre Copenhagen 228 A2
Rodrigo de Freitas, L. Rio de Janeiro 245 B1
Roehampton London 235 B2
Rogers Park Chicago 229 A3
Roihuvuori Helsinki 231 B3
Roissy-en-Brie Paris 244 B4
Rokytka → Prague 245 B3
Roma Rome 246 B1
Roma Urbe ✈ Rome 246 B2
Római-Fürdö Budapest 227 A2
Romainville Paris 244 A3
Roman Forum = Foro Romano Rome 246 B1
Romano Banco Milan 239 B1
Rome = Roma Rome 246 B1
Romema Jerusalem 233 B2
Romford London 235 A5
Ronald Reagan National, Washington ✈ (DCA) Washington 253 B3
Rondebosch Cape Town 228 A1
Roppongi Tokyo 250 B3
Rose, L. Orlando 243 A1
Rose Bowl Los Angeles 236 B4
Rose Hill Washington 253 C3
Rosebank Johannesburg 233 A2
Rosebank New York 242 C1
Rosebery Sydney 249 B2
Rosedal La Candelaria Mexico City 238 B2
Roseland Chicago 229 C3
Rosemead Los Angeles 236 B4
Rosemont Chicago 229 B1
Rosemont Montreal 240 A2
Rosenborg Slot Copenhagen 228 A3
Rosenthal Berlin 225 A3
Rosettenville Johannesburg 233 B2
Rosewell Edinburgh 231 B3
Rosherville Dam Johannesburg 233 B2
Rösjön Stockholm 249 A2
Roslags-Näsby Stockholm 249 A2
Roslin Edinburgh 231 B3
Roslindale Boston 226 B2
Rosny-sous-Bois Paris 244 A4
Rosslyn Washington 253 B3
Rosyth Edinburgh 231 A1
Rotherhithe London 235 B3
Rothneusiedl Vienna 252 B2
Rothschmaige Munich 241 A1
Rouge Hill Toronto 251 A4
Round I. Hong Kong 232 B2
Roxbury Boston 226 B2
Roxeth London 235 A1
Royal Botanic Gardens Edinburgh 231 B2
Royal Observatory Edinburgh 231 B2
Royal Palace = Kungliga Slottet Stockholm 249 B2
Royal Park Melbourne 238 A1
Röylä Helsinki 231 B1
Rozas, Portilleros de las Madrid 237 B1
Roztoky Prague 245 B2
Rozzano Milan 239 B1
Rubí → Barcelona 224 A1
Rudolfsheim Vienna 252 A2
Rudolfshöhe Berlin 225 A5
Rudow Berlin 225 B3
Rueil-Malmaison Paris 244 A2
Ruisbroek Brussels 226 B1
Ruislip London 235 A1
Rumelihisarı Istanbul 232 B2
Rungis Paris 244 B3
Rusāfa Baghdad 223 A2
Rush Green London 235 A5
Russa Kolkata 234 C2
Rutherford New York 242 B1
Ruzyně Prague 245 B1
Ruzyne, Praha ✈ (PRG) Prague 245 B1
Rybatskaya St. Petersburg 247 B2
Rydboholm Stockholm 249 A3
Ryde Sydney 249 A1
Ryogoku Tokyo 250 A3
Rzhevka St. Petersburg 247 B3

S

Sa'ādatābād Tehran 251 A2
Saadūn Baghdad 223 B2
Saavedra Buenos Aires 227 B2
Saboli Delhi 230 A2
Sabugo Lisbon 236 A1
Sabzi Mand Delhi 230 A2
Sacavém Lisbon 236 A2
Saclay Paris 244 B2
Saclay, Étang de Paris 244 B1
Sacomã São Paulo 247 B2
Sacré Cœur Paris 244 A3
Sacrow Berlin 225 B1
Sacrower See Berlin 225 B1
Sadang Seoul 247 C1
Saddle → New York 242 A1
Saddle Brook New York 242 A1
Sadr Karachi 233 A2
Sadr City Baghdad 223 A2
Sadyba Warsaw 252 B2
Safdar Jang's Tomb Delhi 230 B2
Saft el Laban Cairo 227 A2
Saganashkee Slough Chicago 229 C1
Sagene Oslo 243 A3
Sagrada Família, Templo de Barcelona 224 A2
Sahar, Mumbai ✈ (BOM) Mumbai 240 A2
Sai Kung Hong Kong 232 A2
Sai Wan Ho Hong Kong 232 B2
Sai Ying Pun Hong Kong 232 B1
St-Aubin Paris 244 B1
St-Cloud Paris 244 A2
St-Cyr-l'École Paris 244 B1
St-Cyr-l'École ✈ Paris 244 B1
St-Denis Paris 244 A3
St-Germain, Forêt de Paris 244 A1
St-Germain-en-Laye Paris 244 A1
St-Gilles Brussels 226 B2
St. Helier London 235 B2
St-Hubert Montreal 240 B3
St. Hubert, Galeries Royales Brussels 226 A2
St. Isaac's Cathedral St. Petersburg 247 B1
St-Jacques → Montreal 240 B3
St-Joost-Ten-Node Brussels 226 A2
St. Kilda Melbourne 238 B1
St-Lambert Montreal 240 A3
St-Lambert Paris 244 B1
St-Laurent Montreal 240 A1
St-Léonard Montreal 240 A2
St. Magelungen Stockholm 249 B2
St-Mandé Paris 244 A3
St. Margaret's Dublin 230 A2
St-Martin, Bois Paris 244 B4
St. Mary Cray London 235 B4
St-Maur-des-Fossés Paris 244 B3
St-Maurice Paris 244 B3
St-Michel Montreal 240 A2
St. Nikolaus-Kirken Prague 245 B2
St-Ouen Paris 244 A3
St. Paul's Cray London 235 B4
St. Peters Sydney 249 B2
St. Petersburg = Sankt-Peterburg St. Petersburg 247 B1
St-Pierre Montreal 240 B2
St-Pieters Leew Brussels 226 B1
St-Quentin, Étang de Paris 244 B1
St-Stevens-Woluwe Brussels 226 A2
St-Vincent-de-Paul Montreal 240 A2
St. Xavier University Chicago 229 C2
Ste-Catherine Montreal 240 B2
Ste-Hélène, Î. Montreal 240 A2
Saiwai Tokyo 250 B3
Sakai Osaka 243 B1
Sakai Harbour Osaka 243 B1
Sakra, Pulau Singapore 248 B2
Salam Baghdad 223 A2
Salamanca Madrid 237 B1
Sallynoggin Dublin 230 B3
Salmannsdorf Vienna 252 A1
Salmedina Madrid 237 C2
Salomea Warsaw 252 B1
Salsette I. Mumbai 240 A2
Salt Lake City = Bidhan Nagar Kolkata 234 B2
Salt River Cape Town 228 A1
Salt Water L. Kolkata 234 B2
Saltsjö-Duvnäs Stockholm 249 B3
Samatya Istanbul 232 C1
Sampaloc Manila 237 B1
Samphan Thawong Bangkok 223 B2
Samseon Seoul 247 B2
Samuel Smith Park Toronto 251 B1
Samut Prakan Bangkok 223 B2
San Andrés Barcelona 224 A2
San Angel Mexico City 238 B1
San Basilio Rome 246 B2
San Borja Lima 234 B3
San Bóvio Milan 239 B2
San Bruno, Pt. San Francisco 246 C2
San Bruno Mountain State Park ⌂ San Francisco 246 B2
San Cristobal Buenos Aires 227 B2
San Cristobal Madrid 237 B2
San Cristóbal, Cerro Santiago 247 B2
San Cristoforo Milan 239 B1
San Donato Milanese Milan 239 B2
San Francisco San Francisco 246 B2
San Francisco B. San Francisco 246 B3
San Francisco Culhuacán Mexico City 238 C2
San Fruttuoso Milan 239 A2
San Gabriel Los Angeles 236 B4
San Gabriel → Los Angeles 236 C4
San Giuliano Milanese Milan 239 B2
San Isidro Lima 234 B2
San Jerónimo Lidice Mexico City 238 C1
San Joaquin Santiago 247 B2
San José Río Hondo Mexico City 238 B1
San Juan → Manila 237 B2
San Juan de Aragón Mexico City 238 B2
San Juan de Aragón, Parque Mexico City 238 B2
San Juan de Lurigancho Lima 234 A2
San Juan del Monte Manila 237 B2
San Juan Ixtacala Mexico City 238 A1
San Just Desvern Barcelona 224 A1
San Justo Buenos Aires 227 C1
San Lorenzo Tezonco Mexico City 238 C2
San Luis Lima 234 B2
San Marino Los Angeles 236 B4
San Martin Barcelona 224 A2
San Martin de Porras Lima 234 B2
San Mateo Tlaltenango Mexico City 238 B1
San Miguel Lima 234 B2
San Miguel Santiago 247 B2
San Nicolás Buenos Aires 227 B2
San Onófrio Rome 246 B1
San Pedro Martir Barcelona 224 A1
San Pedro Zacatenco Mexico City 238 A2
San Pietro, Piazza Rome 246 B1
San Po Kong Hong Kong 232 A2
San Rafael Chamapa Mexico City 238 B1
San Rafael Hills Los Angeles 236 A3
San Roque Manila 237 B2
San Siro Milan 239 B1
San Souci Sydney 249 B1
San Telmo Buenos Aires 227 B2
San Vicenc dels Horts Barcelona 224 A1
Sandown Johannesburg 233 A2
Sandown Park Races London 235 B1
Sandton Johannesburg 233 A2
Sandvika Oslo 243 A2
Sandyford Dublin 230 B2
Sandymount Dublin 230 B2
Sangenjaya Tokyo 250 B2
Sanggye Seoul 247 B2
Sangley Pt. Manila 237 C1
Sankrail Kolkata 234 B1
Sankt-Peterburg St. Petersburg 247 B1
Sankt Veit Vienna 252 A1
Sanlihe Beijing 224 B1
Sanlintang Shanghai 248 C1
Sans Barcelona 224 A1
Sanssouci Berlin 225 B1
Sant Ambrogio, Basilica di Milan 239 B2
Sant Boi de Llobregat Barcelona 224 A1
Sant Cugat Barcelona 224 A1
Sant Feliu de Llobregat Barcelona 224 A1
Sant Joan Despi Barcelona 224 A1
Santa Ana Manila 237 B2
Santa Anita Park Los Angeles 236 B4
Santa Coloma de Gramenet Barcelona 224 A2
Santa Cruz Manila 237 B1
Santa Cruz Mumbai 240 A1
Santa Cruz, I. de Rio de Janeiro 245 B2
Santa Cruz de Olorde Barcelona 224 A1
Santa Efigénia São Paulo 247 B2
Santa Elena Manila 237 B2
Santa Elena del Gomero Santiago 247 B1
Santa Eulalia Barcelona 224 A2
Santa Fe Springs Los Angeles 236 C4
Santa Iria da Azóia Lisbon 236 A2
Santa Julia Santiago 247 C2
Santa Monica Los Angeles 236 B2
Santa Monica Mts. Los Angeles 236 B2
Santa Rosa de Locobe Santiago 247 B2
Santa Teresa de la Ovalle Santiago 247 B1
Santahamina Helsinki 231 C3
Santana São Paulo 247 A2
Santeny Paris 244 B4
Santiago Santiago 247 B2
Santiago Benítez ✈ (SCL) Santiago 247 B1
Santiago de Surco Lima 234 B2
Santo Amaro Lisbon 236 A1
Santo Amaro São Paulo 247 B1
Santo Andre Lisbon 236 B2
Santo Antão do Tojal Lisbon 236 A2
Santo António, Qta. de Lisbon 236 B1
Santo Tomas, Univ. of Manila 237 B1
Santos Dumont ✈ (SDU) Rio de Janeiro 245 B2
Santoshpur Kolkata 234 B1
Santragachi Kolkata 234 B1
Santry Dublin 230 A2
Sanyuanli Guangzhou 231 B2
São Caetano do Sul São Paulo 247 B2
São Conrado Rio de Janeiro 245 C1
São Cristóvão Rio de Janeiro 245 B1
São Jorge, Castelo de Lisbon 236 A2
São Juliao do Tojal Lisbon 236 A2
São Paulo São Paulo 247 B2
São Paulo Congonhas ✈ (CGH) São Paulo 247 B2
Sapa Kolkata 234 B1
Sapateiro, Cor. do → São Paulo 247 B1
Sarandi Buenos Aires 227 C2
Saraswati → Kolkata 234 A1
Sarecky potok → Prague 245 B2
Sarimbun Singapore 248 A2
Sarimbun Res. Singapore 248 A2
Sarıyer Istanbul 232 A2
Sarriá Barcelona 224 A1
Sarsuna Kolkata 234 C1
Sartrouville Paris 244 A2
Sasad Budapest 227 B2
Sashalom Budapest 227 A3
Saska Warsaw 252 B2
Satalice Prague 245 B3
Satgachi Kolkata 234 B2
Satpukur Kolkata 234 B2
Sätra Stockholm 249 B1
Saúde São Paulo 247 B2
Saugus Boston 226 A2
Saugus → Boston 226 A2
Sault-au-Récollet Montreal 240 A2
Sausalito San Francisco 246 A2
Sawah Besar Jakarta 232 A1
Scald Law Edinburgh 231 B2
Scarborough Toronto 251 A3
Scarborough Bluffs Toronto 251 A3
Sceaux Paris 244 B2
Schaerbeek Brussels 226 A2
Scharfenberg Berlin 225 A2
Schiller Park Chicago 229 B1
Schiller Woods Chicago 229 B1
Schiphol, Amsterdam ✈ (AMS) Amsterdam 222 B1
Schlachtensee Berlin 225 B2
Schlossgarten Berlin 225 A2
Schmargendorf Berlin 225 B2
Schönblick Berlin 225 B5
Schönbrunn Vienna 252 A1
Schöneberg Berlin 225 B3
Schönefeld Berlin 225 B4
Schöneiche Berlin 225 B5
Schönwalde Berlin 225 A1
Schulzendorf Berlin 225 A2
Schwabing Munich 241 B2
Schwanebeck Berlin 225 A4
Schwanenwerder Berlin 225 B2
Schwarzlackenau Vienna 252 A2
Schwechat Vienna 252 B2
Schwechat, Wien ✈ (VIE) Vienna 252 B3
Science and Industry, Museum of Chicago 229 C3
Scitrek Museum Atlanta 223 B2
Scopus, Mt. Jerusalem 233 B2
Scottdale Atlanta 223 B3
Scutari = Üsküdar Istanbul 232 B2
Sea Point Cape Town 228 A1
Seabrook Washington 253 B5
Seacliff San Francisco 246 B2
Seaforth Sydney 249 A2
Seagate New York 242 C1
Seat Pleasant Washington 253 B4
Seaview Wellington 253 B2
SeaWorld Orlando 243 B2
Šeberov Prague 245 B3
Secaucus New York 242 B1
Seddinsee Berlin 225 B5
Seeberg Berlin 225 A5
Seeburg Berlin 225 A1
Seefeld Berlin 225 A5
Seegefeld Berlin 225 A1
Seehof Berlin 225 B2
Segeltorp Stockholm 249 B1
Segrate Milan 239 B2
Seguro Milan 239 B1
Seixal Lisbon 236 B2
Selby Johannesburg 233 B2

Seletar, Pulau Singapore 248 A3
Seletar Hills Singapore 248 A3
Seletar Res. Singapore 248 A2
Selhurst London 235 B3
Sembawang Singapore 248 A2
Senago Milan 239 A1
Sendling Munich 241 B2
Senju Tokyo 250 A3
Senriyama Osaka 243 A2
Sentosa Singapore 248 B2
Seobinggo Seoul 247 B1
Seocho Seoul 247 C1
Seodaemun Seoul 247 B1
Seokkwan Seoul 247 B2
Seongbuk Seoul 247 B2
Seongdong Seoul 247 B2
Seongsu Seoul 247 B2
Seoul Seoul 247 B2
Seoul National University Seoul 247 C1
Seoul Tower Seoul 247 B1
Sepolia Athens 222 A2
Sepulveda Dam Rec. Area ⌂ Los Angeles 236 A2
Serangoon Singapore 248 A3
Serangoon, Pulau Singapore 248 A3
Serangoon, Sungei ➜ Singapore 248 A3
Serangoon Harbour Singapore 248 A3
Seraya, Pulau Singapore 248 B2
Serebryanka ➜ Moscow 239 B3
Serramonte San Francisco 246 C2
Sesto San Giovanni Milan 239 A2
Sesto Ulteriano Milan 239 B2
Setagaya Tokyo 250 B2
Seter Oslo 243 A3
Setia Budi Jakarta 232 B1
Settebagni Rome 246 A2
Settecamini Rome 246 B2
Séttimo Milanese Milan 239 B1
Settsu Osaka 243 A2
Seutula Helsinki 231 A2
Seven Corners Washington 253 B3
Seven Kings London 235 A4
Sévesco ➜ Milan 239 A1
Sevran Paris 244 A4
Sewri Mumbai 240 B2
Sforzesso, Castello Milan 239 B2
Sha Kok Mei Hong Kong 232 A2
Sha Tin Hong Kong 232 A2
Sha Tin Wai Hong Kong 232 A2
Sha'ar Binyamin Jerusalem 233 A2
Shabrâmant Cairo 227 B2
Shah Mosque Tehran 251 A2
Shahdara Delhi 230 A2
Shahe Guangzhou 231 B2
Shahr-e Rey Tehran 251 B2
Shahrak-e Golshahr Tehran 251 B1
Shahrak-e Qods Tehran 251 A2
Shaikh Aomar Baghdad 223 A2
Shakurbasti Delhi 230 A1
Shalkiya Kolkata 234 B2
Sham Shui Po Hong Kong 232 B1
Shamapur Delhi 230 A1
Shamian Guangzhou 231 B2
Shan Mei Hong Kong 232 A2
Shanghai Shanghai 248 B2
Shanghai Hongqiao ✈ (SHA) Shanghai 248 B1
Shanghai Pudong ✈ (PVG) Shanghai 248 B2
Shankill Dublin 230 B3
Sharp I. Hong Kong 232 A2
Shastrinagar Delhi 230 A2
Shau Kei Wan Hong Kong 232 B2
Shawocun Beijing 224 B1
Shayuan Guangzhou 231 B2
Sheen, L. Orlando 243 B1
Sheepshead Bay New York 242 C2
Shek O Hong Kong 232 B2
Shelter I. Hong Kong 232 B2
Shepherds Bush London 235 A2
Shepperton London 235 B1
Sheremetyevo ✈ (SVO) Moscow 239 A2
Sherman Oaks Los Angeles 236 B2
Sherman Park Chicago 229 C2
Sherwood, L. Orlando 243 A2
Shet Bandar Mumbai 240 B2
Sheung Fa Shan Hong Kong 232 A1
Sheung Lau Wan Hong Kong 232 B2
Sheung Wan Hong Kong 232 B1
Sheva Mumbai 240 B2
Sheva Nhava Mumbai 240 B2
Shiba Tokyo 250 B3
Shibpur Kolkata 234 B1
Shibuya Tokyo 250 B3
Shimogawara Tokyo 250 B1
Shimosalo Tokyo 250 A2
Shimoshakujii Tokyo 250 A2
Shinagawa Tokyo 250 B3
Shing Mun Res. Hong Kong 232 A1
Shinjuku Tokyo 250 A3
Shinjuku National Garden Tokyo 250 A3
Shinkoiwa Tokyo 250 A4
Shinnakano Tokyo 250 A3
Shipai Guangzhou 231 B3
Shirinashi ➜ Osaka 243 B1
Shirogane Tokyo 250 B3
Shitennoji Temple Osaka 243 B2
Shiweitang Guangzhou 231 B2
Shogunle Lagos 234 A2
Shomolu Lagos 234 A2
Shooters Hill London 235 B4
Shoreditch London 235 A3
Shortlands London 235 B4
Shu'afat Jerusalem 233 B2
Shubrâ Cairo 227 A2
Shubrâ el Kheima Cairo 227 A2
Shuikuo Guangzhou 231 A2
Sidcup London 235 B4
Siebenhirten Vienna 252 B1
Siedlung Berlin 225 A1
Siekierki Warsaw 252 B2
Sielce Warsaw 252 B2
Siemensstadt Berlin 225 A2
Sierra Madre Los Angeles 236 B4
Sievering Vienna 252 A2
Sighthill Edinburgh 231 B2
Signal Hill Cape Town 228 A1
Siheung Seoul 247 C1
Sikátorpuszta Budapest 227 A3
Silampur Delhi 230 B2
Sillim Seoul 247 C1
Silver, L. Orlando 243 A2
Silver Hill Washington 253 C4
Silver Spring Washington 253 A3
Silvermine Nature Reserve Cape Town 228 B1
Silvolantekojärvi Helsinki 231 B2
Simei Singapore 248 A3
Simla Kolkata 234 B2
Simmering Vienna 252 A2
Simmering Heide Vienna 252 A2
Simonkylä Helsinki 231 B3
Sinchon Seoul 247 B1
Sindang Seoul 247 B2
Singapore ■ Singapore 248 B3
Singapore, Univ. of Singapore 248 B2
Singapore Changi ✈ (SIN) Singapore 248 A3
Sinki, Selat Singapore 248 B2
Sinsa Seoul 247 B2
Sint-Genesius-Rode Brussels 226 B2
Sion Mumbai 240 A2
Sipson London 235 B1
Siqeil Cairo 227 A1
Şişli Istanbul 232 B1
Site of Former World Trade Center = Ground Zero New York 242 B1
Skansen Stockholm 249 B2
Skärholmen Stockholm 249 B1
Skarpäng Stockholm 249 A2
Skarpnäck Stockholm 249 B2
Skaryszewski, Park Warsaw 252 B2
Skokie Chicago 229 A2
Skokie ➜ Chicago 229 A2
Skokie Heritage Museum Chicago 229 A2
Skoklefall Oslo 243 A3
Sköndal Stockholm 249 B2
Skovlunde Copenhagen 228 A2
Skovshoved Copenhagen 228 A3
Skuru Stockholm 249 B3
Sky Lake Orlando 243 B2
Skyland Atlanta 223 A3
Slade Green London 235 B5
Slemmestad Oslo 243 B1
Slependen Oslo 243 A2
Slipi Jakarta 232 B1
Slivenec Prague 245 B2
Sloten Amsterdam 222 A1
Sloterdijk Amsterdam 222 A1
Sloterpark Amsterdam 222 A1
Sluhy Prague 245 A3
Służew Warsaw 252 B2
Służewiec Warsaw 252 B2
Smíchov Prague 245 B2
Smith Forest Preserve Chicago 229 B2
Smolny St. Petersburg 247 B2
Smolny Cathedral St. Petersburg 247 B2
Snake Creek Canal Miami 238 A2
Snakeden Branch ➜ Washington 253 B1
Snarøya Oslo 243 A2
Snättringe Stockholm 249 B1
Søborg Copenhagen 228 A2
Sobreda Lisbon 236 B1
Söderby Stockholm 249 A3
Södermalm Stockholm 249 B2
Sodpur Kolkata 234 A2
Soeurs, Î. des Montreal 240 B2
Sognsvatn Oslo 243 A3
Soignes, Forêt de Brussels 226 B2
Sok Kwu Wan Hong Kong 232 B1
Sokolniki Moscow 239 B3
Sokolniki Park Moscow 239 B3
Sokolów Warsaw 252 C1
Solalinden Munich 241 B3
Sollentuna Stockholm 249 A1
Solln Munich 241 B2
Solna Stockholm 249 A1
Somerset Washington 253 B3
Somerville Boston 226 A2
Somes I. Wellington 253 B2
Sonari Mumbai 240 B2
Sønderso Copenhagen 228 A2
Songpa Seoul 247 B2
Sony Picture Studio Los Angeles 236 B2
Soroksár Budapest 227 B2
Soroksari Duna ➜ Budapest 227 B2
Sosenka ➜ Moscow 239 B3
Sosnovka St. Petersburg 247 B2
Söul = Seoul Seoul 247 B2
Soundview New York 242 B2
South Beach New York 242 C1
South Bend Park Atlanta 223 B2
South Boston Boston 226 A2
South Decatur Atlanta 223 B3
South Deering Chicago 229 C3
South El Monte Los Angeles 236 B4
South Gate Los Angeles 236 C3
South Harbor Manila 237 B1
South Harrow London 235 A1
South Hd. Sydney 249 B2
South Hills Johannesburg 233 B2
South Hornchurch London 235 A5
South Lawn Washington 253 C3
South Miami Miami 238 B1
South Norwood London 235 B3
South of Market San Francisco 246 B2
South Ozone Park New York 242 B3
South Pasadena Los Angeles 236 B4
South Res. Boston 226 A2
South Ruislip London 235 A1
South San Francisco San Francisco 246 C2
South San Gabriel Los Angeles 236 B4
South Shore Chicago 229 C3
Southall London 235 A1
Southborough London 235 B4
Southend London 235 B3
Southern California, University of Los Angeles 236 B3
Southfields London 235 B2
Southwark □ London 235 B3
Southwest Museum Los Angeles 236 B3
Søvang Copenhagen 228 B3
Soweto Johannesburg 233 B1
Sowhānak Tehran 251 A3
Soya Tokyo 250 A4
Spandau Berlin 225 A1
Spånga Stockholm 249 A1
Spanish Monastery Miami 238 A2
Spectacle I. Boston 226 A3
Speicher-See Munich 241 A3
Speising Vienna 252 B1
Sphinx Cairo 227 B1
Spinaceto Rome 246 C1
Spit Junction Sydney 249 A2
Spořilov Prague 245 B3
Spot Pond Boston 226 A2
Spotswood Melbourne 238 B1
Springeberg Berlin 225 B5
Springfield Washington 253 C2
Squantum Boston 226 B2
Srednaya Rogatka St. Petersburg 247 C2
Śródmieście Warsaw 252 B2
Staaken Berlin 225 A1
Stabekk Oslo 243 A2
Stadlau Vienna 252 A2
Stadshuset Stockholm 249 B2
Stains Paris 244 A3
Stamford Hill London 235 A3
Stammersdorf Vienna 252 A2
Stanley Hong Kong 232 B2
Stanley Pen. Hong Kong 232 B2
Stanmore London 235 A2
Stapleton New York 242 C1
Staraya Derevnya St. Petersburg 247 B1
Staré Město Prague 245 B2
Stare Miasto Warsaw 252 B2
Starke, L. Orlando 243 A1
Staten Island Zoo New York 242 C1
Staten Islands Ferry Terminal New York 242 C1
Statenice Prague 245 B1
Stedelijk Museum Amsterdam 222 A2
Steele Creek Melbourne 238 A1
Steenokkerzeel Brussels 226 A2
Steer, L. Orlando 243 A2
Steglitz Berlin 225 B2
Stepaside Dublin 230 B2
Stephansdom Vienna 252 A2
Stepney London 235 A3
Sterling Park San Francisco 246 B2
Sticklinge udde Stockholm 249 A2
Stickney Chicago 229 C2
Stillorgan Dublin 230 B2
Stockholm Stockholm 249 B2
Stocksund Stockholm 249 A2
Stodůlky Prague 245 B1
Stoke Newington London 235 A3
Stokes Valley Wellington 253 B2
Stone Canyon Res. Los Angeles 236 B2
Stone Park Chicago 229 B1
Stonebridge London 235 A2
Stoneham Boston 226 A2
Stony Brook Res. Boston 226 B2
Stony Creek ➜ Chicago 229 C2
Stora Värtan Stockholm 249 A2
Store Hareskov Copenhagen 228 A2
Store Magleby Copenhagen 228 B3
Storholmen Stockholm 249 A2
Stoyka St. Petersburg 247 B2
Straiton Edinburgh 231 B3
Strandfontein Cape Town 228 B2
Strašnice Prague 245 B2
Strasstrudering Munich 241 B3
Stratford London 235 A4
Strathfield Sydney 249 B1
Streatham London 235 B3
Streatham Vale London 235 B3
Strebersdorf Vienna 252 A2
Střešovice Prague 245 B2
Střížkov Prague 245 B2
Strombeek-Bever Brussels 226 A2
Stromovka Prague 245 B2
Studio City Los Angeles 236 B2
Stureby Stockholm 249 B2
Stuvsta Stockholm 249 B2
Subhepur Delhi 230 A2
Sucat Manila 237 C2
Suchdol Prague 245 B2
Sucy-en-Brie Paris 244 B4
Sue, L. Orlando 243 A2
Sugamo Tokyo 250 A3
Sugar Loaf Mt. = Açúcar, Pão de Rio de Janeiro 245 B2
Suge Tokyo 250 B2
Suginami Tokyo 250 A2
Sugō Tokyo 250 B2
Sui Sai Wan Hong Kong 232 B1
Suita Osaka 243 A2
Suitland Washington 253 B4
Sukchar Kolkata 234 A2
Sultanahme Camil Istanbul 232 B1
Sumida Tokyo 250 A3
Sumida ➜ Tokyo 250 A3
Sumiyoshi Osaka 243 B2
Sumiyoshi Shrine Osaka 243 B1
Summerville Toronto 251 B1
Summit Chicago 229 C2
Sunamachi Tokyo 250 A4
Sunbury-on-Thames London 235 B1
Sundbyberg Stockholm 249 A1
Sundbyerne Copenhagen 228 B3
Sung Kong Hong Kong 232 B2
Sungei Kadut Industrial Estate Singapore 248 A2
Sungei Selatar Res. Singapore 248 A3
Sunset Park New York 242 C2
Sunter Jakarta 232 A2
Sunter, Kali ➜ Jakarta 232 B2
Suomenlinna Helsinki 231 C2
Sur Bahr Jerusalem 233 B2
Sura Kolkata 234 B2
Suraksan Seoul 247 A2
Surbiton London 235 B2
Suresnes Paris 244 A2
Surfside Miami 238 A2
Surquillo Lima 234 B2
Surrey Hills Sydney 249 B2
Susaek Seoul 247 B1
Süssenbrunn Vienna 252 A2
Sutton Dublin 230 A3
Sutton London 235 B2
Suyu Seoul 247 B2
Suzukishinden Tokyo 250 A2
Svanemøllen Copenhagen 228 A3
Sveaborg = Suomenlinna Helsinki 231 C2
Sverdlov Moscow 239 B2
Svestad Oslo 243 B2
Svinö Helsinki 231 C1
Swanley London 235 B4
Swansea Toronto 251 B2
Swinburne I. New York 242 C1
Swords Dublin 230 A2
Sydenham Johannesburg 233 A2
Sydney Sydney 249 B2
Sydney, Univ. of Sydney 249 B2
Sydney Harbour Bridge Sydney 249 B2
Sydney Kingsford Smith ✈ (SYD) Sydney 249 A1
Sydstranden Copenhagen 228 B3
Sylvania Sydney 249 C1
Syon Park London 235 B2
Szczęśliwice Warsaw 252 B1
Széchnenyi-hegy Budapest 227 B1
Széphalom Budapest 227 A1

T

Taastrup Copenhagen 228 B1
Tabata Tokyo 250 A3
Tablada Buenos Aires 227 C1
Table B. Cape Town 228 A1
Table Mt. Cape Town 228 A1
Taboão da Serra São Paulo 247 B1
Täby Stockholm 249 A2
Tacuba Mexico City 238 B1
Tacubaya Mexico City 238 B1
Tafelbaai = Table B. Cape Town 228 A1
Taft Orlando 243 B2
Tagig ➜ Manila 237 B2
Taguig Manila 237 B2
Tai Hang Hong Kong 232 B2
Tai Lo Shan Hong Kong 232 A2
Tai Po Tsai Hong Kong 232 A2
Tai Seng Singapore 248 A3
Tai Shui Hang Hong Kong 232 A2
Tai Tam B. Hong Kong 232 B2
Tai Tam Tuk Res. Hong Kong 232 B2
Tai Wai Hong Kong 232 A2
Tai Wan Tau Hong Kong 232 B2
Tai Wo Hau Hong Kong 232 A1
Tainaka Osaka 243 B2
Taishō Osaka 243 B1
Taita Wellington 253 B2
Tajrīsh Tehran 251 A2
Takaido Tokyo 250 B2
Takaishi Tokyo 250 B2
Takarazuka Osaka 243 A1
Takasago Tokyo 250 A4
Takatsu Tokyo 250 B2
Takeshita Tokyo 250 B2
Takinegawa Tokyo 250 A3
Takoma Park Washington 253 B3
Taksim Istanbul 232 B1
Talaide Lisbon 236 A1
Taliganga Kolkata 234 B2
Talipapa Manila 237 A2
Tallaght Dublin 230 B1
Tallkrogen Stockholm 249 B2
Tama Tokyo 250 B1
Tama ➜ Tokyo 250 B2
Tama Kyūryō Tokyo 250 B2
Tamaden Tokyo 250 B2
Tamagawa-josui ➜ Tokyo 250 A1
Taman Sari Jakarta 232 A1
Tamanduateí ➜ São Paulo 247 B2
Tamboerskloof Cape Town 228 A1
Tambora Jakarta 232 A1
Tammisalo Helsinki 231 B3
Tammûh Cairo 227 B2
Tampines Singapore 248 A3
Tanah Abang Jakarta 232 B1
Tanah Kusir Jakarta 232 B1
Tangelo Park Orlando 243 B2
Tanjung Duren Jakarta 232 B1
Tanjung Priok Jakarta 232 A2
Tanum Oslo 243 A1
Tapada Lisbon 236 A1
Tapanila Helsinki 231 B3
Tapiales Buenos Aires 227 C1
Tapiola Helsinki 231 B1
Tapsia Kolkata 234 B2
Tara Mumbai 240 A1
Tarabya Istanbul 232 B2
Tårbæk Copenhagen 228 A3
Tarchomin Warsaw 252 B1
Tardeo Mumbai 240 B1
Targówek Warsaw 252 B2
Tårnby Copenhagen 228 B3
Tarqua Bay Lagos 234 B2
Tathong Channel Hong Kong 232 B2
Tathong Pt. Hong Kong 232 B2
Tatuapé São Paulo 247 B2
Taufkirchen Munich 241 B2
Tavares, I. dos Rio de Janeiro 245 A2
Tavros Athens 222 B2
Tawa Wellington 253 A1
Te Papa Museum Wellington 253 B1
Teaneck New York 242 A1
Tebet Jakarta 232 B2
Tecamachalco Mexico City 238 B1
Ted Williams Tunnel Boston 226 A2
Teddington London 235 B1
Tegel Berlin 225 A2
Tegel, Berlin ✈ (TXL) Berlin 225 A2
Tegeler See Berlin 225 A2
Tegelort Berlin 225 A2
Teheran = Tehrān Tehran 251 A2
Tehrān Tehran 251 A2
Tehrān Pārs Tehran 251 A3
Tei Tong Tsui Hong Kong 232 B2
Tejo, Rio ➜ Lisbon 236 A2
Tekstilyshchik Moscow 239 B3
Telhal Lisbon 236 A1
Telok Blangah Singapore 248 B2
Teltow Berlin 225 B2
Teltow kanal Berlin 225 B3
Tempelhof Berlin 225 B3
Tempelhof, Berlin ✈ (THF) Berlin 225 B3
Temple City Los Angeles 236 B4
Temple Hills Washington 253 C4
Templeogue Dublin 230 B2
Temppeliaukio Church Helsinki 231 B2
Tenafly New York 242 A2
Tenayuca, Piramide de Mexico City 238 A1
Tengah ➜ Singapore 248 A2
Tennoji Osaka 243 B2
Tepalcates Mexico City 238 B2
Tepeyac, Parque Nacional △ Mexico City 238 B2
Terrazzano Milan 239 A1
Terre des Hommes Montreal 240 A2
Terrugem Lisbon 236 A1
Tervuren Brussels 226 B3
Tervuren, Park van Brussels 226 B3
Tetuán Madrid 237 B1
Teufelsberg Berlin 225 B2
Thalkirchen Munich 241 B2
Thames Ditton London 235 B1
Thamesmead London 235 A4
Thana Cr. ➜ Mumbai 240 A2
Thiais Paris 244 B3
Thisio Athens 222 B2
Thistletown Toronto 251 A1
Thomastown Melbourne 238 A2
Thompson I. Boston 226 B3
Thon Buri Bangkok 223 B1
Thornbury Melbourne 238 A2
Thorncliffe Toronto 251 A2
Thornhill Toronto 251 A2
Thornton Cape Town 228 A2
Thornton Heath London 235 B3
Threipmuir Res. Edinburgh 231 B2
Throgs Neck New York 242 B3
Tian'anmen Square Beijing 224 B2
Tiancun Beijing 224 B1
Tibet, L. Orlando 243 B1
Tibidabo Barcelona 224 A1
Tibradden Mt. Dublin 230 B2
Tiburon San Francisco 246 A2
Tiburtino Rome 246 B2
Ticomán Mexico City 238 A2
Tiefersee Berlin 225 B1
Tiejiangyin Beijing 224 C2
Tiergarten Berlin 225 A3
Tijgerhof Cape Town 228 A2
Tijuca Rio de Janeiro 245 B1
Tijuca, Pico da Rio de Janeiro 245 B1
Tijuca △ Rio de Janeiro 245 B1
Tikkurila Helsinki 231 B3
Tilak Nagar Delhi 230 B1
Tilanqiao Shanghai 248 B1
Timah, Bukit Singapore 248 A2
Timiryazev Park Moscow 239 B2
Ting Kau Hong Kong 232 A1
Tira Jerusalem 233 A1
Tirsa Cairo 227 B2
Tishrīyaa Baghdad 223 B2
Tiu Keng Leng Hong Kong 232 B2
Tizapán Mexico City 238 C1
Tlalnepantla ➜ Mexico City 238 A1
Tlalpan Mexico City 238 C2
To Kwai Wan Hong Kong 232 B2
Toa Payoh Singapore 248 A3
Točná Prague 245 C2
Toco Hills Atlanta 223 B2
Todt Hill New York 242 C1
Tōkagi Tokyo 250 A4
Tokai Plantation Cape Town 228 B1
Tōkaichiba Tokyo 250 B2
Tōkyō Tokyo 250 B3
Tōkyō B. = Tōkyō-Wan Tokyo 250 B4
Tōkyō Disneyland Tokyo 250 B4
Tōkyō Haneda ✈ (HND) Tokyo 250 B3
Tōkyō Harbour Tokyo 250 B3
Tōkyō-Wan Tokyo 250 B4
Tolka ➜ Dublin 230 A1
Tollygunge = Taliganga Kolkata 234 B2
Tolworth London 235 B2
Tomba di Nerone Rome 246 B1
Tommy Thompson Park Toronto 251 B3
Tondo Manila 237 B1
Tongbinggo Seoul 247 B1
Tongqiao Shanghai 248 A1
Toorak Melbourne 238 B2
Topanga State Park ⌂ Los Angeles 236 B1
Topkapı Istanbul 232 B1
Topkapı Palaca Istanbul 232 B1
Tor di Quinto Rome 246 B1
Tor Pignattara Rome 246 B2
Tor Sapienza Rome 246 B2
Torcy Paris 244 A4
Toronto Toronto 251 B2
Toronto, Univ. of Toronto 251 B2
Toronto City Centre ✈ (YTZ) Toronto 251 B2
Toronto Harbour Toronto 251 B2
Toronto I. Toronto 251 B2
Toronto Lester B. Pearson Int. ✈ (YYZ) Toronto 251 A1
Torre Lupara Rome 246 B2
Torre Nova Rome 246 B2
Torrellas ➜ Barcelona 224 A1
Torrevécchia Rome 246 B1
Toshima Tokyo 250 A3
Toshimaen Tokyo 250 A2
Tottenham London 235 A3
Tottenham Melbourne 238 A1
Toussus-le-Noble Paris 244 B1
Toussus-le-Noble ✈ Paris 244 B1
Towchāl Cable Car Tehran 251 A2
Tower Hamlets □ London 235 A3
Tower of London London 235 A3
Towra Pt. Sydney 249 C2
Tøyen Oslo 243 A3
Toyonaka Osaka 243 A1
Trafaria Lisbon 236 A1
Traição, Cor. ➜ São Paulo 247 B2
Tranegilde Copenhagen 228 B2
Trångsund Stockholm 249 B2
Trappenfelde Berlin 225 A4
Trastévere Rome 246 B1
Treasure I. San Francisco 246 B2
Třeboradice Prague 245 B3
Třebotov Prague 245 C1
Tremblay-en-France Paris 244 A4
Tremembe ➜ São Paulo 247 A2
Tremont New York 242 A2
Trenno Milan 239 B1
Treptow Berlin 225 B3
Três Rios, Sa. dos Rio de Janeiro 245 B1
Trevi, Fontana di Rome 246 B1
Trezzano sul Naviglio Milan 239 B1
Trieste Rome 246 B2
Trinidad Washington 253 B4
Trinity Edinburgh 231 B2
Trinity College Dublin 230 A2
Trionfale Rome 246 B1
Triulzo Milan 239 B2
Troja Prague 245 B2
Trollbäcken Stockholm 249 B3
Trombay Mumbai 240 A2
Troparevo Moscow 239 C1
Trudeau, Montréal ✈ (YUL) Montreal 240 B1
Trudyashchikhsya, Ostrov St. Petersburg 247 B1
Tryvasshøgda Oslo 243 A3
Tseng Lan Shue Hong Kong 232 A2
Tseung Kwan Hong Kong 232 B2

Tsim Sha Tsui Hong Kong 232 B2
Tsing Yi Hong Kong 232 A1
Tsova Jerusalem 233 B1
Tsuen Wan Hong Kong 232 A1
Tsur Hadassa Jerusalem 233 B1
Tsurumi → Tokyo 250 B3
Tsz Wan Shan Hong Kong 232 A2
Tuas Singapore 248 B1
Tuchoměřice Prague 245 B1
Tuckahoe New York 242 A3
Tucuruvi São Paulo 247 A2
Tufello Rome 246 B2
Tufnell Park London 235 A3
Tufts University Boston 226 A2
Tughlakabad Delhi 230 B2
Tuindorp Amsterdam 222 A2
Tullamarine Melbourne 238 A1
Tulse Hill London 235 B3
Tung Lung Chau Hong Kong 232 B2
Tung O Hong Kong 232 B1
Tunis Baghdad 223 A2
Tuomarila Helsinki 231 B1
Tureberg Stockholm 249 A1
Turffontein Johannesburg 233 B2
Turkey L. Orlando 243 A2
Turkey Lake Park Orlando 243 A2
Turner Field Atlanta 223 B2
Turnham Green London 235 B2
Turnhouse Edinburgh 231 B1
Tuscolana, Via Rome 246 B2
Twelve Apostles Cape Town 228 A1
Twickenham London 235 B1
Twickenham Rugby Ground London 235 B1
Twin Peaks San Francisco 246 B2
Two Rock Mt. Dublin 230 B2
Tymon North Dublin 230 B1
Tysons Corner Washington 253 B2

U

U.S. Capitol Washington 253 B3
U.S. Cellular Field Chicago 229 C3
Ubeidiya Jerusalem 233 B2
Uberaba → São Paulo 247 B2
Ubin, Pulau Singapore 248 A3
Uccle Brussels 226 B2
Udelnaya St. Petersburg 247 A2
Udelnoe St. Petersburg 247 B1
Udlding Munich 241 A1
Ueno Tokyo 250 A3
Úholičky Prague 245 B1
Uhříněves Prague 245 B3
Uithoorn Amsterdam 222 B1
Ujazdów Warsaw 252 B2
Újpalota Budapest 227 A2
Újpest Budapest 227 A2
Ukita Tokyo 250 A4
Ullerup Copenhagen 228 B3
Ullevål Oslo 243 A3
Ulriksdal Stockholm 249 A1
Ulyanka St. Petersburg 247 B1
Um Al-Khanazir Island Baghdad 223 B2
Umeda Osaka 243 A1
Ümraniye Istanbul 232 B2
Underground Atlanta Atlanta 223 B2
Underhill, L. Orlando 243 A3
Unětický potok → Prague 245 B2
Unhos Lisbon 236 A2
Unidad Santa Fe Mexico City 238 B1
Union City New York 242 B1
Union Port New York 242 B2
Union Station Toronto 251 B2
United Center Chicago 229 B2
United Nations Headquarters New York 242 B2
Universal Studios Los Angeles 236 B2
Universal Studios Orlando 243 B2
Universidad Madrid 237 B1
Universidad de Chile Santiago 247 B2
University Park Washington 253 B4
Unterbiberg Munich 241 B2
Unterföhring Munich 241 A3
Unterhaching Munich 241 B2
Unterlaa Vienna 252 B2
Untermenzing Munich 241 A1
Upper B. New York 242 C1
Upper Elmers End London 235 B3
Upper New York B. = Upper B. New York 242 C1
Upper Norwood London 235 B3
Upper Peirce Res. Singapore 248 A2
Upper Sydenham London 235 B3
Upper Tooting London 235 B3
Upton London 235 A4
Uptown Chicago 229 B2
Uran Mumbai 240 B2
Urayasu Tokyo 250 B4
Urbe ✈ Rome 246 B2
Urca Rio de Janeiro 245 B2
Uritsk St. Petersburg 247 C1
Üröm Budapest 227 A2
Ursus Warsaw 252 B1
Ursvik Stockholm 249 A1
Usera Madrid 237 B1
Ushigome Tokyo 250 A3
Usina Rio de Janeiro 245 B1
Üsküdar Istanbul 232 B2
Ust-Slavyanka St. Petersburg 247 C3
Uteke Stockholm 249 A3
Utrata Warsaw 252 B2
Uttarpara Kolkata 234 B1
Utterslev Mose Copenhagen 228 A2

V

Vaclavské náměstí Prague 245 B2
Vadaul Mumbai 240 A2
Vaires-sur-Marne Paris 244 A4
Valby Copenhagen 228 B2
Valcannuta Rome 246 B1
Valdelatas Madrid 237 A1
Vale Washington 253 B1
Valenton Paris 244 B3
Valera Milan 239 A1
Vallcarca Barcelona 224 A1
Valldoreix Barcelona 224 A1
Vallecas Madrid 237 B2
Vallensbæk Copenhagen 228 B2
Vallensbæk Strand Copenhagen 228 B2
Vallentunasjön Stockholm 249 A2
Valleranello Rome 246 C1
Vallisaari Helsinki 231 C3
Vallvidrera Barcelona 224 A1
Valvidrera → Barcelona 224 A1
Van Gogh-museum Amsterdam 222 A2
Vanak Tehran 251 A2
Vanda = Vantaa Helsinki 231 B2
Vangede Copenhagen 228 A3
Vaniköy Istanbul 232 B2
Vanløse Copenhagen 228 A2
Vantaa Helsinki 231 B2
Vantaankoski Helsinki 231 B2
Vantaanpuisto Helsinki 231 B2
Vanves Paris 244 B2
Varedo Milan 239 A1
Varkiza Athens 222 C2
Vartiokylä Helsinki 231 B3
Vartiosaari Helsinki 231 B3
Vasamuseet Stockholm 249 B2
Vasco Cape Town 228 A2
Vasfanärd Tehran 251 B2
Vashi Mumbai 240 A2
Vasilyevskiy, Ostrov St. Petersburg 247 B1
Vatican City ■ Rome 246 B1
Vaucluse Sydney 249 B2
Vaucresson Paris 244 A1
Vaughan Toronto 251 A1
Vauhallan Paris 244 B2
Vaujours Paris 244 A4
Vauxhall London 235 B3
Vecsés Budapest 227 B3
Veleň Prague 245 A3
Veleslavin Prague 245 B2
Vélizy-Villacoublay Paris 244 B2
Velka-Chuchle Prague 245 B2
Velké Přílepy Prague 245 B1
Venda Seca Lisbon 236 A1
Venetian Islands Miami 238 B2
Venice Los Angeles 236 C2
Ventas Madrid 237 B1
Ventorro del Cano Madrid 237 B1
Venustiano Carranza Mexico City 238 B2
Verde → São Paulo 247 A1
Verdi Athens 222 B2
Verdugo Mts. Los Angeles 236 A2
Verdun Montreal 240 B2
Vérhalom Budapest 227 A2
Vermelho → São Paulo 247 B1
Vernon Los Angeles 236 B3
Verrières-le-Buisson Paris 244 B2
Versailles Buenos Aires 227 B1
Versailles Paris 244 B1
Veshnyaki Moscow 239 B3
Vesolyy Posolok St. Petersburg 247 B2
Vestra Helsinki 231 B1
Vestskoven Copenhagen 228 A2
Vicálvaro Madrid 237 B2
Vicente Lopez Buenos Aires 227 B2
Victoria Hong Kong 232 B2
Victoria, Mt. Wellington 253 B1
Victoria, Pont Montreal 240 B2
Victoria and Alfred Waterfront Cape Town 228 A1
Victoria Gardens Mumbai 240 B2
Victoria Harbour Hong Kong 232 B1
Victoria Island Lagos 234 B2
Victoria L. Johannesburg 233 B2
Victoria Lawn Tennis Courts Melbourne 238 B2
Victoria Park Singapore 248 B2
Victoria Peak Hong Kong 232 B1
Vienna = Wien Vienna 252 A2
Vienna Washington 253 B2
Vietnam Veterans Memorial Washington 253 B3
Vietnam War Museum Chicago 229 B3
View Park Los Angeles 236 B3
Vigário Geral Rio de Janeiro 245 A1
Vigentino Milan 239 B2
Viggbyholm Stockholm 249 A2
Vighignolo Milan 239 B1
Viikki Helsinki 231 B3
Vikhroli Mumbai 240 A2
Vila Guilherme São Paulo 247 B2
Vila Isabel Rio de Janeiro 245 B1
Vila Jaguára São Paulo 247 B1
Vila Madalena São Paulo 247 B1
Vila Maria São Paulo 247 B2
Vila Mariana São Paulo 247 B2
Vila Prudente São Paulo 247 B2
Viladecans Barcelona 224 B1
Vile Parle Mumbai 240 A2
Villa Adelina Buenos Aires 227 B1
Villa Ballester Buenos Aires 227 B1
Villa Barilari Buenos Aires 227 C2
Villa Bosch Buenos Aires 227 B1
Villa C. Colon Buenos Aires 227 C2
Villa Ciudadela Buenos Aires 227 B1
Villa de Guadalupe Mexico City 238 B2
Villa Devoto Buenos Aires 227 B1
Villa Diamante Buenos Aires 227 C2
Villa Dominico Buenos Aires 227 C3
Villa Lugano Buenos Aires 227 C2
Villa Lynch Buenos Aires 227 B1
Villa Madero Buenos Aires 227 C1
Villa Sáenz Pena Buenos Aires 227 B1
Villa Urquiza Buenos Aires 227 B2
Villaverde Madrid 237 B1
Villaverde Bajo Madrid 237 B1
Ville-d'Avray Paris 244 B2
Villecresnes Paris 244 B4
Villejuif Paris 244 B3
Villemomble Paris 244 A4
Villeneuve-la-Garenne Paris 244 A2
Villeneuve-le-Roi Paris 244 B3
Villeneuve-St-Georges Paris 244 B3
Villeparisis Paris 244 A4
Villevaudé Paris 244 A4
Villiers-le-Bâcle Paris 244 B1
Villiers-sur-Marne Paris 244 B4
Villinki Helsinki 231 C3
Villoresi, Canale Milan 239 A1
Vilvoorde Brussels 226 A2
Vimodrone Milan 239 A2
Vimont Montreal 240 A1
Vincennes Paris 244 A3
Vincennes, Bois de Paris 244 B3
Vineland Orlando 243 B1
Vinings Atlanta 223 A2
Vinohrady Prague 245 B2
Vinoř Prague 245 B3
Violet Hill Hong Kong 232 B2
Virányos Budapest 227 A1
Virgen del San Cristóbal Santiago 247 B2
Virginia, L. Orlando 243 A2
Virginia Gardens Miami 238 B1
Virginia Key Miami 238 B2
Viroflay Paris 244 B2
Vironas Athens 222 B2
Virum Copenhagen 228 A2
Visitacion Valley San Francisco 246 B2
Vista Alegre Lima 234 B3
Vista Alegre Santiago 247 C1
Vista Grove Atlanta 223 A3
Vitacura Santiago 247 B2
Vitínia Rome 246 C1
Vitry-sur-Seine Paris 244 B3
Vizcaya Museum and Gardens Miami 238 B2
Vladykino Moscow 239 A2
Vlezenbeek Brussels 226 B1
Vokovice Prague 245 B2
Volgelsdorf Berlin 225 B5
Volkhonka-Zil Moscow 239 C2
Vollen Oslo 243 B1
Volodarskoye St. Petersburg 247 B2
Volynkina-Derevnya St. Petersburg 247 B1
Vondelpark Amsterdam 222 A2
Vösendorf Vienna 252 B2
Voula Athens 222 C2
Vouliagmeni Athens 222 C2
Vredehoek Cape Town 228 A1
Vršovice Prague 245 B2
Vyborgskaya Storona St. Petersburg 247 B2
Vykhino Moscow 239 B3
Vyšehrad Prague 245 B2

W

Wachterhof Munich 241 B3
Wadala Mumbai 240 A2
Wadestown Wellington 253 B1
Wadi al-Arayis Jerusalem 233 B2
Wadi Fukin Jerusalem 233 B1
Waduk Pluit Jakarta 232 A1
Wah Fu Hong Kong 232 B1
Wahda Baghdad 223 B2
Währing Vienna 252 A2
Waidmannslust Berlin 225 A3
Wainuiomata Wellington 253 B2
Wainuiomata → Wellington 253 B2
Wakefield Boston 226 A2
Waldesruh Berlin 225 B4
Waldperlach Munich 241 B3
Waldtrudering Munich 241 B3
Walkinstown Dublin 230 B1
Wall Street New York 242 B1
Walt Disney World Orlando 243 B1
Walter D. Stone Memorial Zoo Boston 226 A2
Waltham Boston 226 A1
Waltham Forest □ London 235 A3
Walthamstow London 235 A3
Walton-on-Thames London 235 B1
Wambeek Brussels 226 A3
Wan Chai Hong Kong 232 B2
Wandsworth □ London 235 B2
Wannsee Berlin 225 B1
Wansdorf Berlin 225 A1
Wanstead London 235 A4
Wapping London 235 A3
Ward Dublin 230 A1
Ward I. Wellington 253 B2
Wards I. New York 242 B2
Warnberg Munich 241 B2
Warner Brothers Studios Los Angeles 236 B2
Warrâq el 'Arab Cairo 227 A2
Warringal Park Melbourne 238 A2
Warriston Edinburgh 231 B2
Warsaw = Warszawa Warsaw 252 B2
Warszawa Warsaw 252 B2
Warszawa ✈ (WAW) Warsaw 252 B1
Wartenberg Berlin 225 A4
Washington Washington 253 B3
Washington Heights New York 242 A2
Washington Park Chicago 229 C3
Washington Ronald Reagan National ✈ (DCA) Washington 253 B3
Wat Pho Bangkok 223 B1
Water of Leith → Edinburgh 231 B1
Watergraafsmeer Amsterdam 222 A2
Waterland Amsterdam 222 A2
Waterloo Brussels 226 B2
Waterloo Wellington 253 B2
Watermeal-Boitsfort Brussels 226 B2
Watertown Boston 226 A1
Watsonia Melbourne 238 A2
Waverley Boston 226 A1
Waverley Johannesburg 233 A2
Waverley Sydney 249 B2
Wawer Warsaw 252 B2
Wawrzyszew Warsaw 252 B1
Wazirabad Delhi 230 A2
Wazīrīya Baghdad 223 A2
Wazirpur Delhi 230 A2
Wealdstone London 235 A1
Wedding Berlin 225 A3
Weehawken New York 242 B1
Weesp Amsterdam 222 B3
Weidling Vienna 252 A1
Weidlingbach Vienna 252 A1
Weigongcum Beijing 224 B1
Weissensee Berlin 225 A3
Wellesley Hills Boston 226 B1
Welling London 235 B4
Wellington Boston 226 A2
Wellington Wellington 253 B1
Wellington Int. ✈ (WLE) Wellington 253 B1
Weltevreden Park Johannesburg 233 A1
Wembley London 235 A2
Wemmel Brussels 226 A1
Wemmer Pan Johannesburg 233 B2
Wenceslas Square = Vaclavské náměstí Prague 245 B2
Wendenschloss Berlin 225 B4
Wennington London 235 A5
Werneuchen Berlin 225 A5
West Don → Toronto 251 A2
West Drayton London 235 A1
West Ham London 235 A4
West Harrow London 235 A1
West Heath London 235 B4
West Hill Toronto 251 A3
West Hollywood Los Angeles 236 B2
West Lamma Channel Hong Kong 232 B1
West Los Angeles, University of Los Angeles 236 C2
West Medford Boston 226 A2
West Miami Miami 238 B1
West Molesey London 235 B1
West New York New York 242 B1
West of Twin Peaks San Francisco 246 B2
West Park Johannesburg 233 A1
West Rouge Toronto 251 A4
West Roxbury Boston 226 B2
West Springfield Washington 253 C2
West Town Chicago 229 B2
West Wharf Karachi 233 B1
Westchester Chicago 229 B1
Westchester Los Angeles 236 C2
Westchester New York 242 A2
Westcliff Johannesburg 233 B2
Westdene Johannesburg 233 B1
Westend Helsinki 231 C1
Wester Hailes Edinburgh 231 B2
Westerham Munich 241 B2
Western Addition San Francisco 246 B2
Westgate Washington 253 B3
Westlake Cape Town 228 B1
Westlake San Francisco 246 B2
Westminster London 235 A3
Westmount Montreal 240 B2
Weston Toronto 251 A1
Westwood Village Los Angeles 236 B2
Westzaan Amsterdam 222 A1
Wetton Cape Town 228 B2
Wexford Toronto 251 A3
Weybridge London 235 B1
Wezembeek-Oppem Brussels 226 A2
White Cloud Hill = Baiyun Hill Guangzhou 231 B2
White House, The Washington 253 B3
Whitechapel London 235 A3
Whitehall Dublin 230 A2
Whittier Los Angeles 236 C4
Whitton London 235 B1
Wieden Vienna 252 A2
Wien Vienna 252 A2
Wien-Schwechat ✈ (VIE) Vienna 252 B3
Wienerberg Vienna 252 B2
Wierzbno Warsaw 252 B2
Wijde Wormer Amsterdam 222 A2
Wilanów Warsaw 252 B2
Wilanówka → Warsaw 252 C2
Wilds, The Johannesburg 233 B2
Wilhelmshagen Berlin 225 B5
Wilket Creek Park Toronto 251 A2
Wilkieston Edinburgh 231 B1
Will Rogers State Historical Park ⌂ Los Angeles 236 B1
Willbrook Dublin 230 B2
Willesden London 235 A2
Willesden Green London 235 A2
Williamsbridge New York 242 A2
Williamsburg New York 242 B2
Williamsburg Orlando 243 B2
Williamstown Melbourne 238 B1
Willis, L. Orlando 243 B2
Willoughby Sydney 249 A2
Willow Springs Chicago 229 C1
Willowdale Toronto 251 A2
Wilmersdorf Berlin 225 B2
Wilmette Chicago 229 A2
Wilmington London 235 B5
Wimbledon London 235 B2
Wimbledon Common London 235 B2
Wimbledon Park London 235 B2
Wimbledon Tennis Ground London 235 B2
Winchester Boston 226 A2
Windermere Cape Town 228 A2
Windermere Orlando 243 B1
Windsor Johannesburg 233 A1
Windsor, Gare Montreal 240 B2
Windsor Hills Los Angeles 236 C2
Windy Arbour Dublin 230 B2
Winning Munich 241 B2
Wissous Paris 244 B2
Wittenau Berlin 225 A2
Witwatersrand, Univ. of Johannesburg 233 B2
Wlochy Warsaw 252 B1
Wo Mei Hong Kong 232 A2
Wo Yi Hop Hong Kong 232 A1
Woburn Boston 226 A2
Woburn Toronto 251 A3
Wola Warsaw 252 B1
Wolf Trap Farm Park Washington 253 B2
Wolgok Seoul 247 B2
Wolica Warsaw 252 C1
Wólka Węglowa Warsaw 252 B1
Wollaston Boston 226 B2
Woltersdorf Berlin 225 B5
Woluwe-St-Lambert Brussels 226 A2
Woluwe-St-Pierre Brussels 226 A2
Wong Chuk Hang Hong Kong 232 B2
Wong Chuk Wan Hong Kong 232 A2
Wong Chuk Yeung Hong Kong 232 A2
Wong Tai Sin Hong Kong 232 A2
Wood Green London 235 A3
Wood Ridge New York 242 A1
Woodbine Race Track Toronto 251 A1
Woodbridge Toronto 251 A1
Woodford London 235 A4
Woodford Bridge London 235 A4
Woodford Green London 235 A4
Woodhaven New York 242 B2
Woodhouselee Edinburgh 231 B2
Woodlands Singapore 248 A2
Woodmont Washington 253 B3
Woodside London 235 B3
Woodside New York 242 B2
Woodstock Cape Town 228 A1
Woollahra Sydney 249 B2
Woolooware B. Sydney 249 C1
Woolwich London 235 B4
World Trade Center, site of former New York 242 B1
Worli Mumbai 240 A1
Worth Chicago 229 C2
Wren's Nest Atlanta 223 B2
Wrigley Field Chicago 229 B3
Wuhlgarten Berlin 225 A4
Wujiaochang Shanghai 248 B2
Würm → Munich 241 B1
Würm-kanal Munich 241 A1
Wusong Shanghai 248 A1
Wyczółki Warsaw 252 C1
Wygoda Warsaw 252 B2
Wynberg Cape Town 228 B1

X

Xabregas Lisbon 236 A2
Xianggang = Hong Kong Hong Kong 232 B1
Xiaogang Park Guangzhou 231 B2
Xiaoping Guangzhou 231 A2
Xiasha chong Guangzhou 231 B1
Xichang Guangzhou 231 B2
Xicheng Beijing 224 B1
Xidan Beijing 224 B2
Xizhimen Beijing 224 B1
Xochimilco, Parque Ecológico Mexico City 238 C2
Xuanwu Beijing 224 B1
Xuhui Shanghai 248 B1

Y

Yaba Lagos 234 A2
Yaftābād Tehran 251 B1
Yahara Tokyo 250 A2
Yaho Tokyo 250 A1
Yakire Tokyo 250 A4
Yaksu Seoul 247 B2
Yamada Osaka 243 A2
Yamada Tokyo 250 B2
Yamato → Osaka 243 B1
Yan Kit Singapore 248 A3
Yanbu Guangzhou 231 B1
Yangcheon Seoul 247 B1
Yanghuayuan Beijing 224 C1
Yangjae Seoul 247 C2
Yangjiazhuang Shanghai 248 A1
Yangjing Shanghai 248 B2
Yangpu Shanghai 248 B2
Yangpu Park Shanghai 248 B2
Yannawa Bangkok 223 B2
Yarmūk Baghdad 223 B1
Yarra Bend Park Melbourne 238 A2
Yarraville Melbourne 238 A1
Yau Tong Hong Kong 232 B2
Yauza → Moscow 239 A3
Yeading London 235 A1
Yedikule Istanbul 232 C1
Yenikapı Istanbul 232 B1
Yeniköy Istanbul 232 B2
Yeongdeungpo Seoul 247 B1
Yeongdong Seoul 247 B2
Yeouido Seoul 247 B1
Yerba Buena I. San Francisco 246 B2
Yerres Paris 244 B4
Yerushalayim = Jerusalem Jerusalem 233 B2
Yiheyuan Beijing 224 A1
Yıldız Park Istanbul 232 B2
Yinhangzhen Shanghai 248 A2
Yishun Singapore 248 A3
Ylästö Helsinki 231 B2
Yodo → Osaka 243 A2
Yongdingman Beijing 224 B2
Yongfucun Guangzhou 231 B2
Yongsan Seoul 247 B1
Yonkers New York 242 A2
York Toronto 251 A2
York Mills Toronto 251 A2
York University Toronto 251 A1
You'anmen Beijing 224 B1
Youngsfield Cape Town 228 B1
Yuanxiatian Guangzhou 231 A2
Yuexiu Park Guangzhou 231 B2
Yugo-Zarad Moscow 239 B2
Yuhalixqui, Volcan Mexico City 238 C2
Yung Shue Wan Hong Kong 232 B1
Yūsofābād Tehran 251 A2

Z

Zaandam Amsterdam 222 A1
Zaandijk Amsterdam 222 A1
Zaanstad Amsterdam 222 A1
Záběhlice Prague 245 B2
Ząbki Warsaw 252 B2
Żacisze Warsaw 252 B2
Zahrā Baghdad 223 A1
Žalov Prague 245 A2
Załuski Warsaw 252 C1
Zamdorf Munich 241 B2
Zanevka St. Petersburg 247 B3
Zapote Manila 237 C1
Zaventem Brussels 226 A2
Zawady Warsaw 252 B2
Zâwiyet Abû Musallam Cairo 227 B1
Zawrā' Park Baghdad 223 B2
Zbraslav Prague 245 C2
Zbuzany Prague 245 B1
Zdiby Prague 245 B2
Zeekoevlei Cape Town 228 B2
Zehlendorf Berlin 225 B2
Zenne → Brussels 226 B1
Żerań Warsaw 252 B1
Zerzeń Warsaw 252 B2
Zeytinburnu Istanbul 232 C1
Zhabei Shanghai 248 B1
Zhdanov Moscow 239 B3
Zhenru Shanghai 248 B1
Zhernovka St. Petersburg 247 B2
Zhicun Guangzhou 231 B2
Zhongshan Park Shanghai 248 B1
Zhoucun Guangzhou 231 A2
Zhoujiadu Shanghai 248 B1
Zhoujiazhen Shanghai 248 B2
Zhulebino Moscow 239 B4
Zhushadi Guangzhou 231 A3
Zielona Warsaw 252 B3
Zielonka Warsaw 252 B2
Žižkov Prague 245 B2
Zličín Prague 245 B1
Zografou Athens 222 B2
Żoliborz Warsaw 252 B1
Zonnebloem Cape Town 228 A1
Zugliget Budapest 227 B1
Zugló Budapest 227 A2
Zuiderwoude Amsterdam 222 A3
Zumbi Rio de Janeiro 245 A1
Zunderdorp Amsterdam 222 A2
Zuvuvu → São Paulo 247 C1
Zwanenburg Amsterdam 222 A1
Zwölfaxing Vienna 252 B2

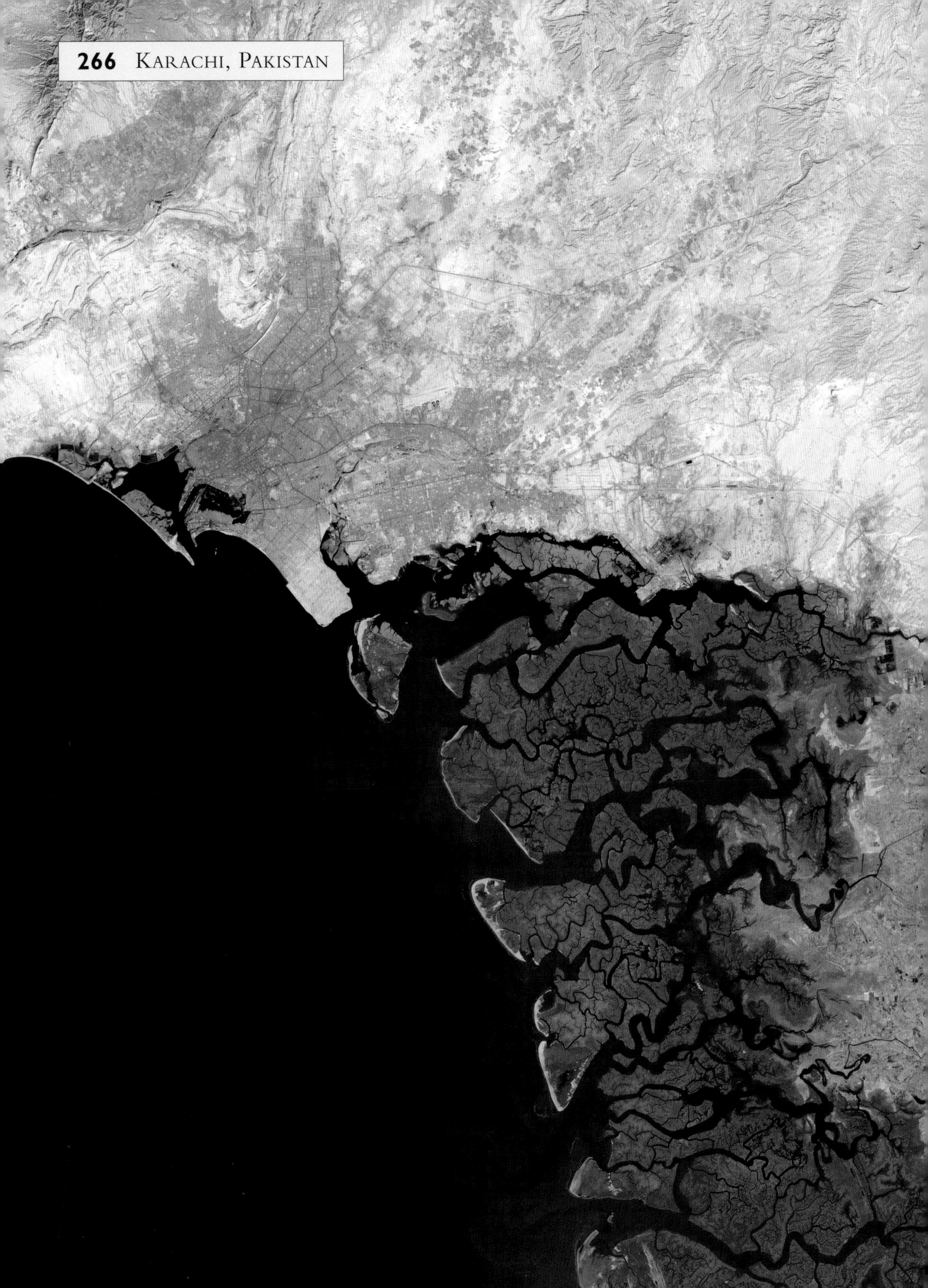
266 Karachi, Pakistan

268 NEW YORK, NY, USA

270 SANTIAGO, CHILE

272 TOKYO, JAPAN

WORLD MAPS

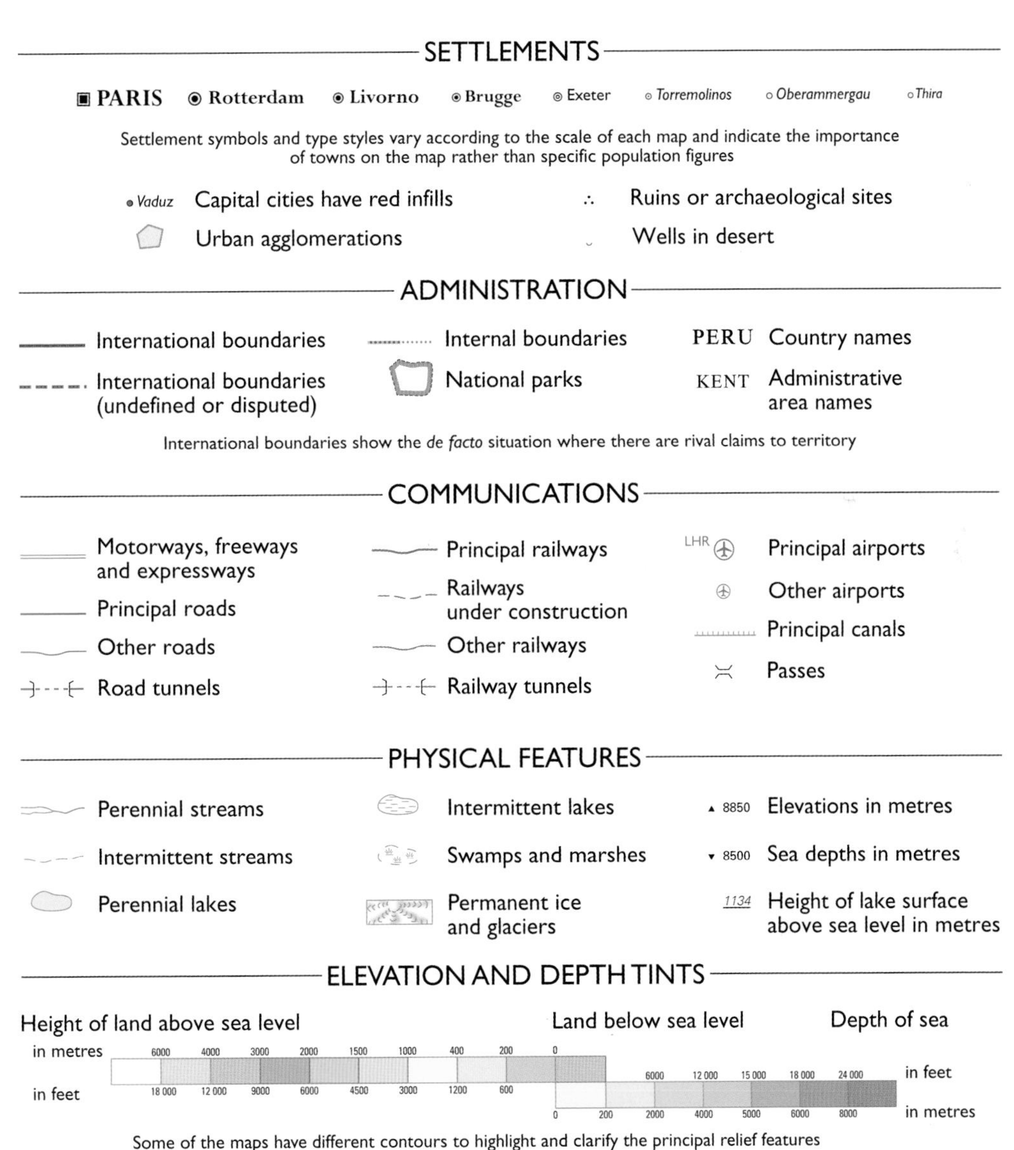
SETTLEMENTS
PARIS
Rotterdam
Livorno
Brugge
Exeter
Torremolinos
Oberammergau
Thira
Settlement symbols and type styles vary according to the scale of each map and indicate the importance of towns on the map rather than specific population figures
Vaduz
Capital cities have red infills
Ruins or archaeological sites
Urban agglomerations
Wells in desert
ADMINISTRATION
International boundaries
Internal boundaries
PERU
Country names
International boundaries (undefined or disputed)
National parks
KENT
Administrative area names
International boundaries show the de facto situation where there are rival claims to territory
COMMUNICATIONS
Motorways, freeways and expressways
Principal railways
LHR
Principal airports
Principal roads
Railways under construction
Other airports
Other roads
Other railways
Principal canals
Road tunnels
Railway tunnels
Passes
PHYSICAL FEATURES
Perennial streams
Intermittent lakes
8850
Elevations in metres
Intermittent streams
Swamps and marshes
8500
Sea depths in metres
Perennial lakes
Permanent ice and glaciers
1134
Height of lake surface above sea level in metres
ELEVATION AND DEPTH TINTS
Height of land above sea level
Land below sea level
Depth of sea
in metres
6000
4000
3000
2000
1500
1000
400
200
0
in feet
18 000
12 000
9000
6000
4500
3000
1200
600
6000
12 000
15 000
18 000
24 000
in feet
0
200
2000
4000
5000
6000
8000
in metres
Some of the maps have different contours to highlight and clarify the principal relief features

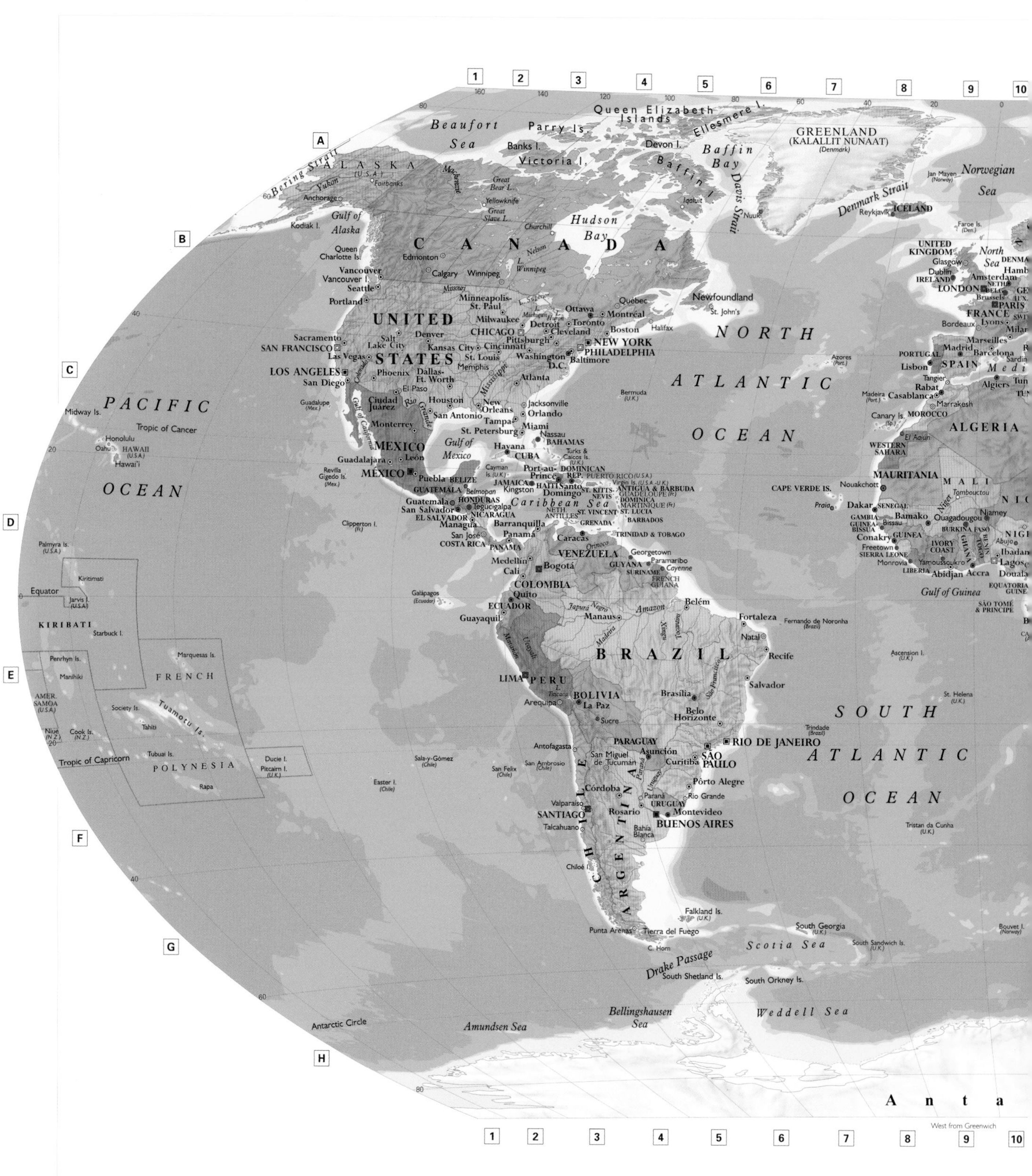

Projection: Winkel III

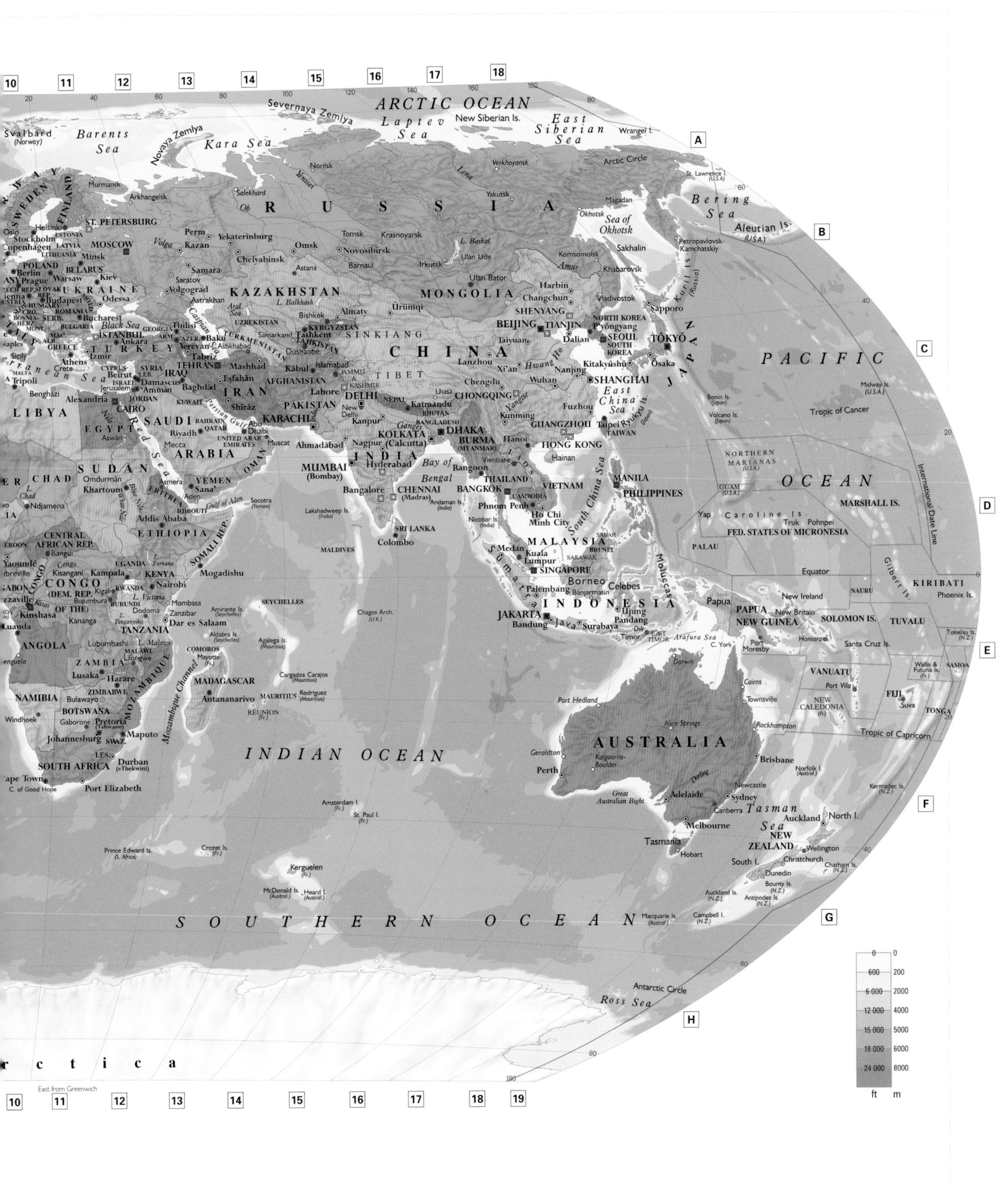
ARCTIC OCEAN
Barents Sea
Kara Sea
Laptev Sea
East Siberian Sea
R U S S I A
Bering Sea
Sea of Okhotsk
KAZAKHSTAN
MONGOLIA
C H I N A
TIBET
INDIA
IRAN
AFGHANISTAN
PAKISTAN
SAUDI ARABIA
TURKEY
EGYPT
LIBYA
SUDAN
CHAD
ETHIOPIA
CONGO (DEM. REP. OF THE)
TANZANIA
ANGOLA
ZAMBIA
NAMIBIA
BOTSWANA
SOUTH AFRICA
MADAGASCAR
PACIFIC OCEAN
INDIAN OCEAN
SOUTHERN OCEAN
AUSTRALIA
INDONESIA
PHILIPPINES
JAPAN
PAPUA NEW GUINEA
NEW ZEALAND
Tasman Sea
Antarctica
East from Greenwich
ft m

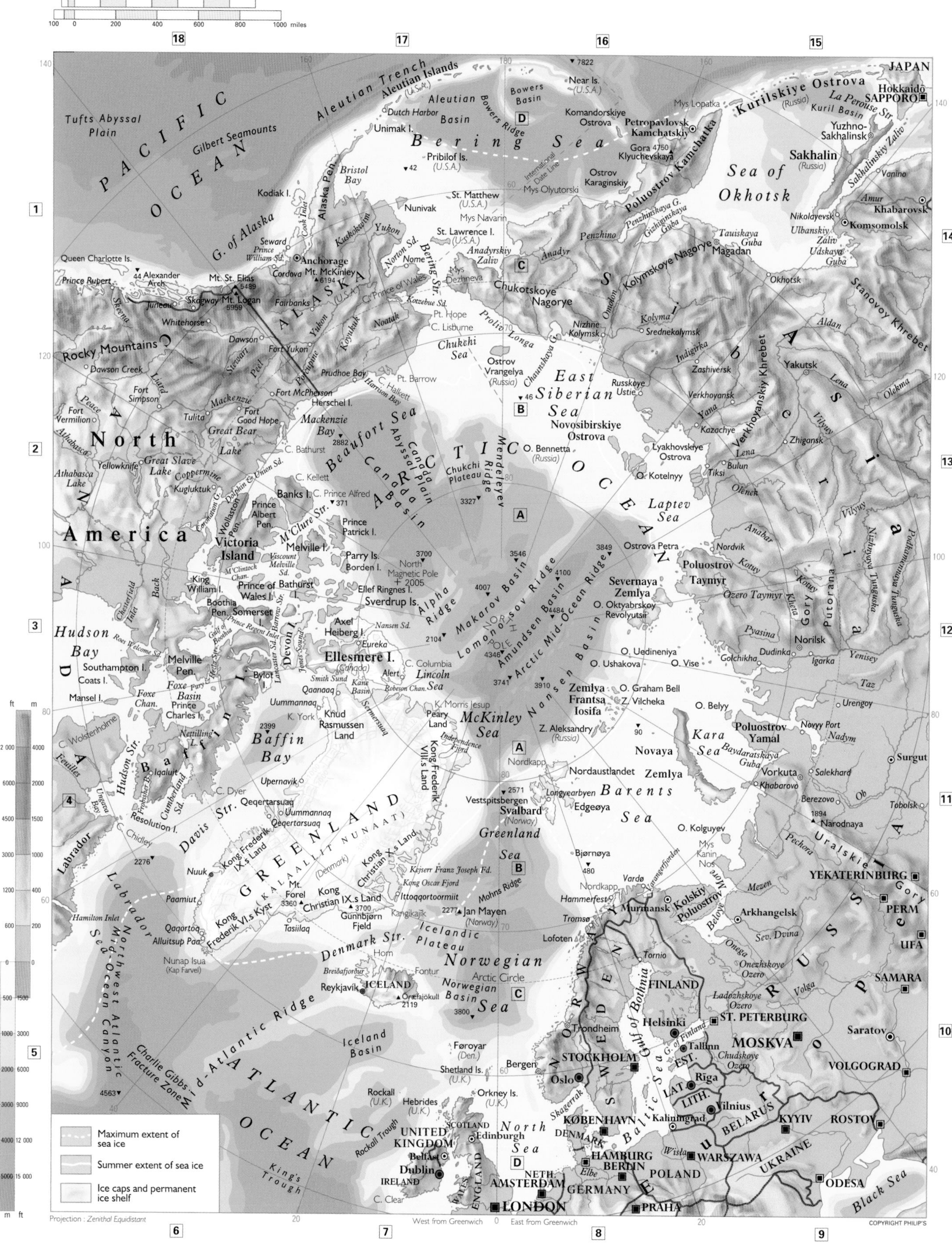

100 0 200 400 600 800 1000 1200 1400 km
100 0 200 400 600 800 1000 miles
PACIFIC OCEAN
Tufts Abyssal Plain
Gilbert Seamounts
Aleutian Trench
Aleutian Islands (U.S.A.)
Aleutian Basin
Bowers Basin
Bowers Ridge
Near Is. (U.S.A.)
Komandorskiye Ostrova
Dutch Harbor
Unimak I.
Bering Sea
Pribilof Is. (U.S.A.)
Bristol Bay
Kodiak I.
Alaska Pen.
G. of Alaska
Cook Inlet
Kuskokwim
Yukon
Nunivak
St. Matthew (U.S.A.)
Mys Navarin
St. Lawrence I. (U.S.A.)
Norton Sd.
Nome
Bering Str.
Seward
Prince William Sd.
Anchorage
Cordova
Mt. McKinley 6194
Queen Charlotte Is.
Prince Rupert
Alexander Arch.
Mt. St. Elias 5489
Mt. Logan 5959
Juneau
Skagway
Fairbanks
ALASKA (U.S.A.)
Whitehorse
Dawson
Fort Yukon
Kotzebue Sd.
Pt. Hope
C. Lisburne
Chukchi Sea
Prudhoe Bay
Pt. Barrow
Rocky Mountains
Dawson Creek
Fort Simpson
Fort McPherson
Herschel I.
Mackenzie Bay
Beaufort Sea
Fort Vermilion
Fort Good Hope
Tulita
Great Bear Lake
North
America
Athabasca Lake
Yellowknife
Great Slave Lake
Coppermine
Kugluktuk
C. Bathurst
C. Kellett
Banks I.
C. Prince Alfred
Prince Albert Pen.
M'Clure Str.
Prince Patrick I.
Victoria Island
Melville I.
Viscount Melville Sd.
Parry Is.
Borden I.
North Magnetic Pole 2005
King William I.
Prince of Wales I.
Bathurst I.
Ellef Ringnes I.
Sverdrup Is.
Boothia Pen.
Somerset I.
Axel Heiberg I.
Nansen Sd.
Eureka
Hudson Bay
Devon I.
Ellesmere I. (Canada)
C. Columbia
Lincoln Sea
Alert
Southampton I.
Coats I.
Melville Pen.
Bylot I.
Smith Sund
Qaanaaq
Kane Basin
Robeson Chan.
Mansel I.
Foxe Chan.
Foxe Basin
Prince Charles I.
Uummannaq
K. York
Knud Rasmussen Land
Peary Land
K. Morris Jesup
Baffin Bay
Baffin I.
Hudson Str.
Iqaluit
Cumberland Sd.
C. Dyer
Qeqertarsuaq
Upernavik
Davis Str.
Resolution I.
C. Chidley
Labrador
GREENLAND (KALAALLIT NUNAAT) (Denmark)
Nuuk
Paamiut
Qaqortoq
Alluitsup Paa
Nunap Isua (Kap Farvel)
Hamilton Inlet
Labrador Sea
Northwest Atlantic Mid-Ocean Canyon
Kong Frederik VIII.s Land
Independence Fjord
Kong Frederik IX.s Land
Kong Christian X.s Land
Kong Christian IX.s Land
Kong Frederik VI.s Kyst
Mt. Forel 3360
Gunnbjørn Fjeld 3700
Tasiilaq
Kangikajik
Ittoqqortoormiit
Kejserr Franz Joseph Fd.
Kong Oscar Fjord
Denmark Str.
Horn
Jan Mayen (Norway)
Mohns Ridge
Icelandic Plateau
Breiðafjörður
Fontur
Reykjavík
ICELAND
Öræfajökull 2119
Mid-Atlantic Ridge
Iceland Basin
Charlie Gibbs Fracture Zone
ATLANTIC OCEAN
Rockall (U.K.)
Rockall Trough
Hebrides (U.K.)
King's Trough
Føroyar (Den.)
Shetland Is. (U.K.)
Orkney Is. (U.K.)
UNITED KINGDOM
SCOTLAND
Edinburgh
Belfast
Dublin
IRELAND
C. Clear
WALES
ENGLAND
LONDON
North Sea
NETH.
AMSTERDAM
GERMANY
HAMBURG
BERLIN
Elbe
POLAND
Wisła
WARSZAWA
PRAHA
DENMARK
KØBENHAVN
Norwegian Sea
Norwegian Basin
Arctic Circle
Bergen
Oslo
Skagerrak
Trondheim
NORWAY
SWEDEN
STOCKHOLM
Lofoten
Tromsø
Hammerfest
Nordkapp
Vardø
Bjørnøya
Greenland Sea
Svalbard (Norway)
Vestspitsbergen
Longyearbyen
Edgeøya
Nordaustlandet
Nordkapp
Barents Sea
McKinley Sea
Z. Aleksandry (Russia)
Zemlya Frantsa Iosifa
Z. Vilcheka
O. Graham Bell
O. Belyy
Novaya Zemlya
Kara Sea
Baydaratskaya Guba
Poluostrov Yamal
O. Kolguyev
Mys Kanin Nos
Kolskiy Poluostrov
Murmansk
Belove More
Mezen
Arkhangelsk
Sev. Dvina
Onega
Onezhskoye Ozero
Ladozhskoye Ozero
FINLAND
Gulf of Bothnia
Tornio
Helsinki
G. of Finland
Tallinn
EST.
Riga
LAT.
LITH.
Vilnius
Kaliningrad
Baltic Sea
BELARUS
UKRAINE
KYYIV
ODESA
Black Sea
ROSTOV
VOLGOGRAD
Saratov
SAMARA
Volga
MOSKVA
ST. PETERBURG
Chudskoye Ozero
RUSSIA
Europe
UFA
PERM
YEKATERINBURG
Uralskie Gory
Pechora
Narodnaya 1894
Vorkuta
Khabarovo
Salekhard
Berezovo
Tobolsk
Ob
Nadym
Novyy Port
Surgut
Urengoy
Taz
Yenisey
Igarka
Dudinka
Norilsk
Golchikha
Pyasina
Putorana
Gory
Kotuy
Kheta
Ozero Taymyr
Poluostrov Taymyr
Nordvik
Anabar
Severnaya Zemlya
O. Oktyabrskoy Revolyutsii
O. Uedineniya
O. Ushakova
O. Vise
Ostrova Petra
Laptev Sea
Olenek
Tiksi
Bulun
Lena
Kotelnyy
Lyakhovskiye Ostrova
Novosibirskiye Ostrova
East Siberian Sea
Russkoye Ustie
O. Bennetta (Russia)
Zhigansk
Kazachye
Yana
Verkhoyansk
Verkhoyanskiy Khrebet
Indigirka
Zashiversk
Yakutsk
Aldan
Vilyuy
Olekma
Stanovoy Khrebet
Srednekolymsk
Kolyma
Nizhne Kolymsk
Chaunskaya G.
Ostrov Vrangelya (Russia)
Proliv Longa
Chukotskoye Nagorye
Mys Dezhneva
Anadyrskiy Zaliv
Anadyr
Penzhino
Mys Olyutorski
International Date Line
Ostrov Karaginskiy
Klyuchevskaya Gora 4750
Petropavlovsk Kamchatskiy
Poluostrov Kamchatka
Penzhinskaya G.
Gizhiginskaya Guba
Kolymskoye Nagorye
Omolon
Magadan
Tauiskaya Guba
Okhotsk
Sea of Okhotsk
Mys Lopatka
Kurilskiye Ostrova (Russia)
Kuril Basin
La Perouse Str.
Sakhalin (Russia)
Sakhalinskiy Zaliv
Yuzhno-Sakhalinsk
Hokkaido
SAPPORO
JAPAN
Vanino
Amur
Khabarovsk
Komsomolsk
Nikolayevsk
Ulbanskiy Zaliv
Udskaya Guba
Siberia
ARCTIC OCEAN
Canada Basin
Canada Abyssal Plain
Chukchi Plateau
Mendeleyev Ridge
Alpha Ridge
Makarov Basin
Lomonosov Ridge
NORTH POLE
Amundsen Basin
Arctic Mid-Ocean Ridge
Nansen Basin
CANADA
Maximum extent of sea ice
Summer extent of sea ice
Ice caps and permanent ice shelf
Projection : Zenithal Equidistant
West from Greenwich
East from Greenwich
COPYRIGHT PHILIP'S

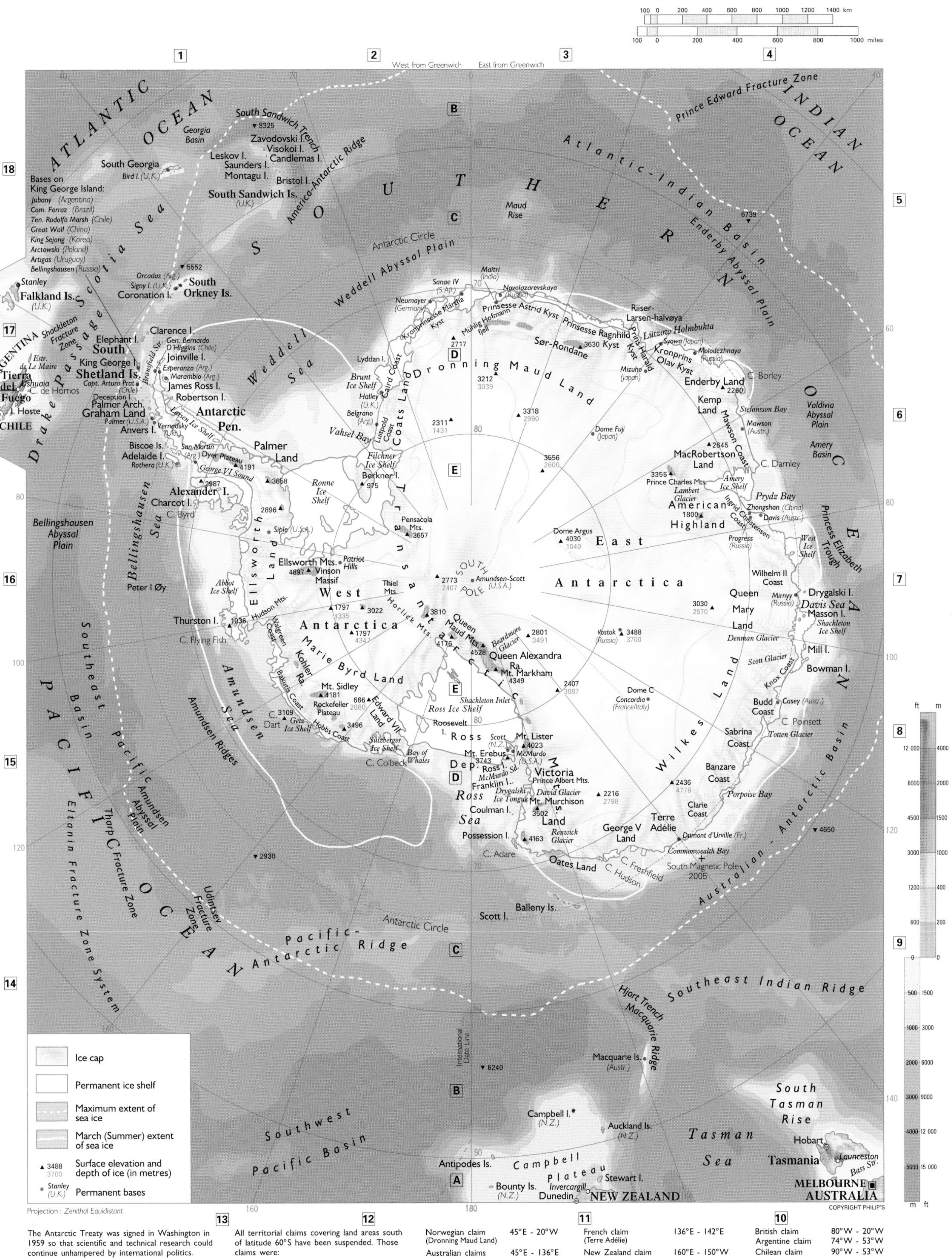

The Antarctic Treaty was signed in Washington in 1959 so that scientific and technical research could continue unhampered by international politics.

All territorial claims covering land areas south of latitude 60°S have been suspended. Those claims were:

Norwegian claim (Dronning Maud Land)	45°E - 20°W
Australian claims	45°E - 136°E 142°E - 160°E
French claim (Terre Adélie)	136°E - 142°E
New Zealand claim (Ross Dependency)	160°E - 150°W
British claim	80°W - 20°W
Argentine claim	74°W - 53°W
Chilean claim	90°W - 53°W

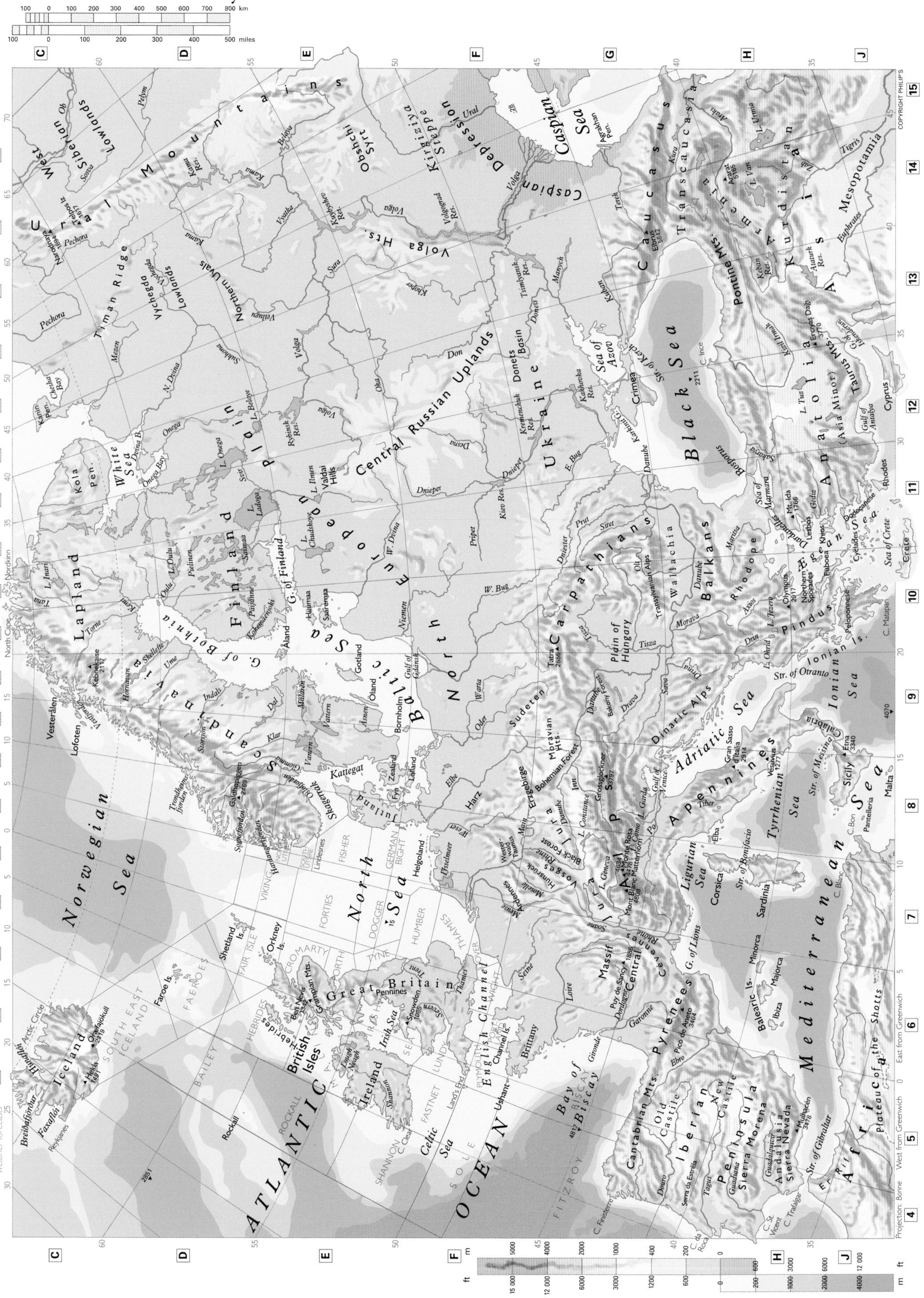

100 0 100 200 300 400 500 600 700 800 km

100 0 100 200 300 400 500 miles

m ft

5000 15 000

4000 12 000

2000 6000

1000 3000

400 1200

200 600

0

200 600

1000 3000

2000 6000

4000 12 000

m ft

Projection: Bonne

West from Greenwich | East from Greenwich

COPYRIGHT PHILIP'S

Sea areas named in weather forecasts

100 0 100 200 300 400 500 600 700 800 km

100 0 100 200 300 400 500 miles

■ LONDON Capital Cities

Projection: Bonne

West from Greenwich 0 East from Greenwich

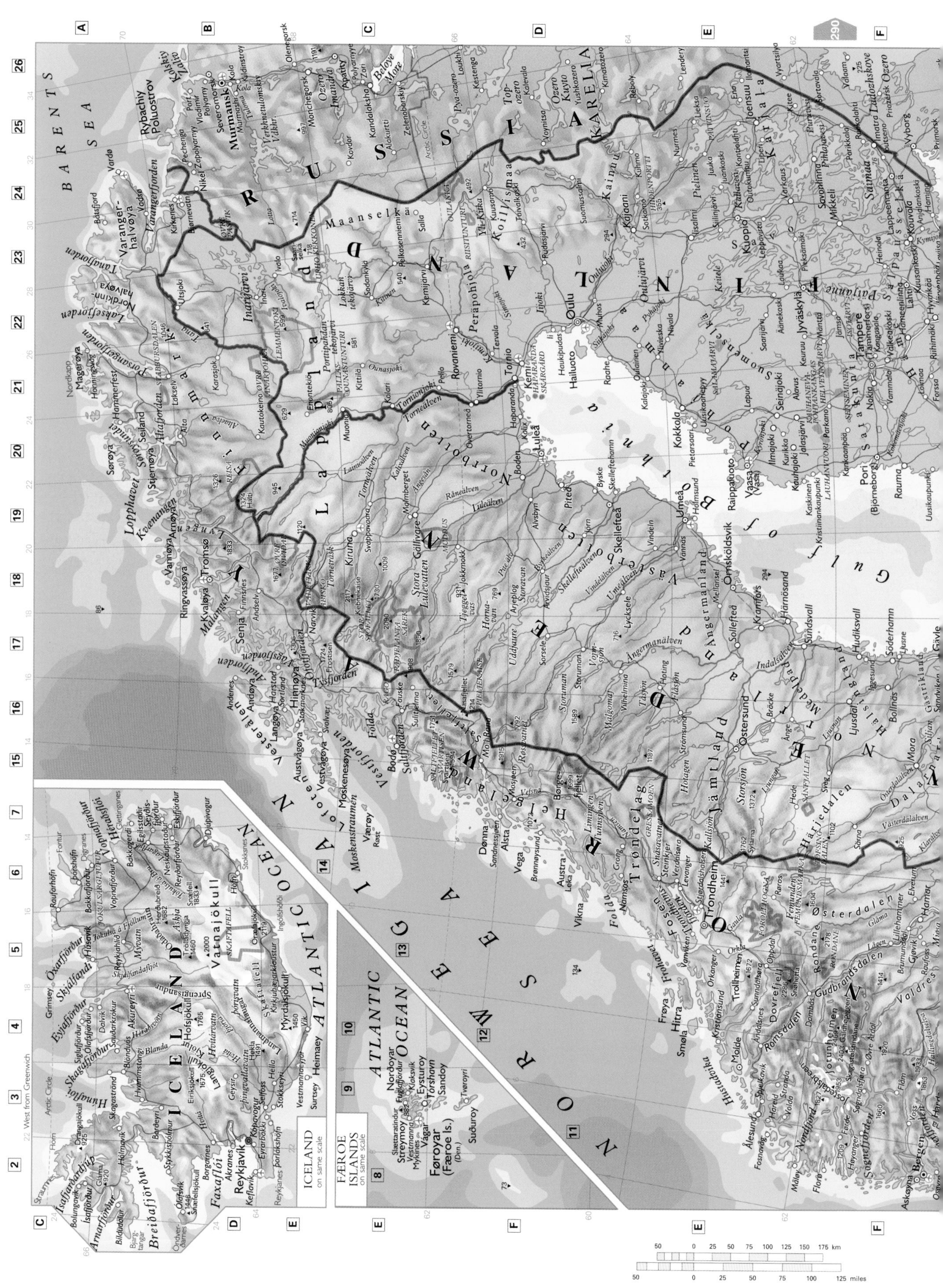
BARENTS SEA
NORWEGIAN SEA
ATLANTIC OCEAN
Gulf of Bothnia
RUSSIA
KARELIA
FINLAND
SWEDEN
NORWAY
Lappland
ICELAND
ICELAND on same scale
FÆROE ISLANDS on same scale
Føroyar (Færoe Is.) (Den.)
Lofoten
Vesterålen
Reykjavík
Tórshavn
Trondheim
Oulu
Murmansk
Tromsø
Bodø
Bergen
Ålesund
Tampere
Vaasa
Umeå
Luleå
Kiruna
Östersund
Sundsvall
Gävle
Arctic Circle
West from Greenwich
50 0 25 50 75 100 125 150 175 km
50 0 25 50 75 100 125 miles

NORTH SEA
BALTIC SEA
Gulf of Finland
Gulf of Riga
Skagerrak
Kattegat
Ålands hav
ESTONIA
LATVIA
LITHUANIA
BELARUS
POLAND
GERMANY
DENMARK
CZECH REP.
UKRAINE
KALININGRAD
STOCKHOLM
Oslo
KØBENHAVN (Copenhagen)
BERLIN
WARSZAWA (Warsaw)
PRAHA (Prague)
MINSK
Vilnius
Riga
Tallinn
Helsinki (Helsingfors)
PETERBURG (Leningrad)
HAMBURG
Göteborg (Gothenburg)
Gotland (Sweden)
Bornholm (Denmark)
Öland
Rügen
Gdańsk
Kraków
Łódź
Poznań
Wrocław
Hannover
Leipzig
Dresden
Frankfurt
Kaunas
Klaipėda
Kaliningrad (Russia)
Lviv (Lvov)
Brest
Hrodna
Pskov
Projection: Conical with two standard parallels
East from Greenwich
COPYRIGHT PHILIP'S
ft
m

National Parks

282 284

National Parks and Forest Parks in Scotland

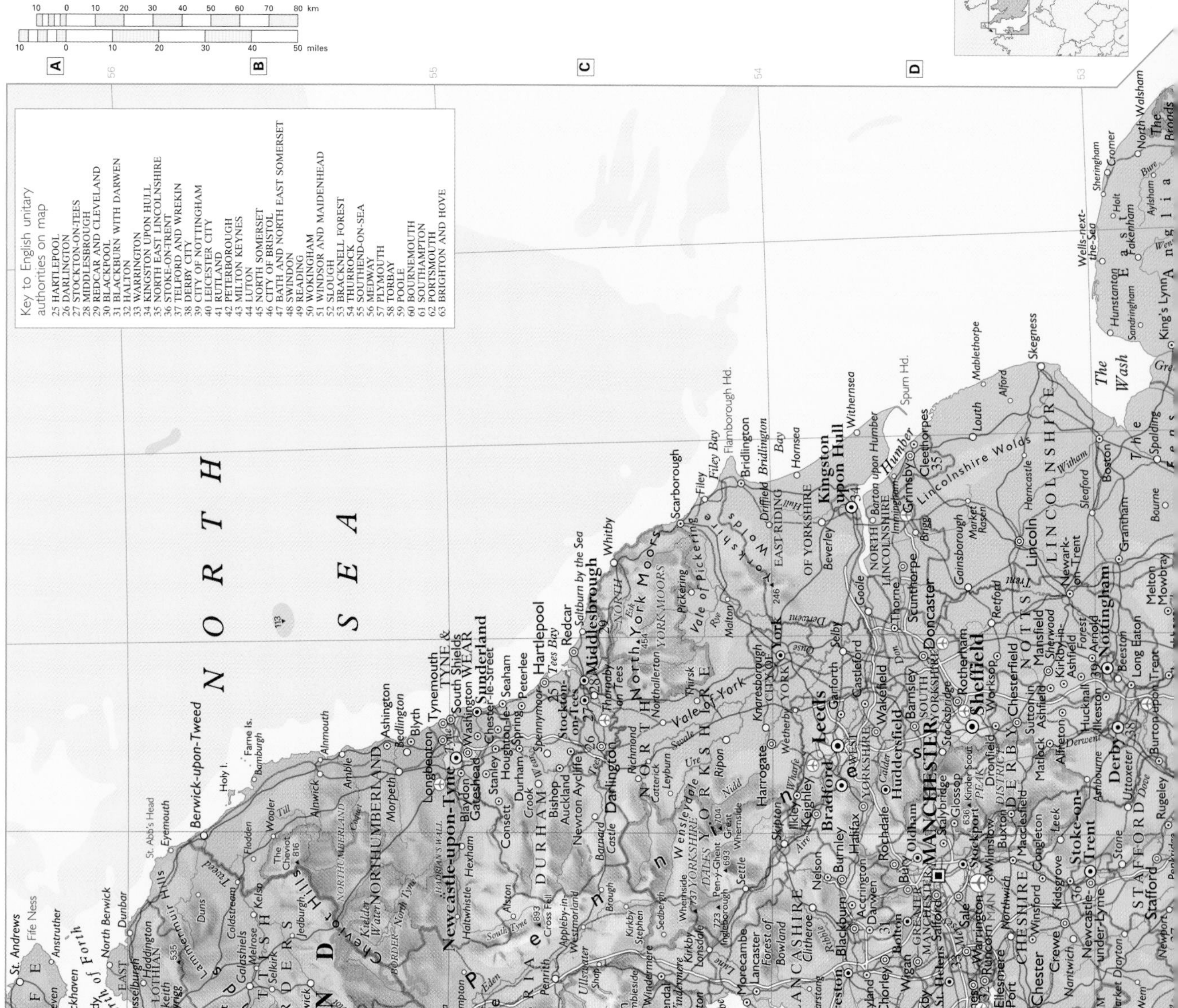

10 0 10 20 30 40 50 60 70 80 km
10 0 10 20 30 40 50 miles
Key to English unitary authorities on map
25 HARTLEPOOL
26 DARLINGTON
27 STOCKTON-ON-TEES
28 MIDDLESBROUGH
29 REDCAR AND CLEVELAND
30 BLACKPOOL
31 BLACKBURN WITH DARWEN
32 HALTON
33 WARRINGTON
34 KINGSTON UPON HULL
35 NORTH EAST LINCOLNSHIRE
36 STOKE-ON-TRENT
37 TELFORD AND WREKIN
38 DERBY CITY
39 CITY OF NOTTINGHAM
40 LEICESTER CITY
41 RUTLAND
42 PETERBOROUGH
43 MILTON KEYNES
44 LUTON
45 NORTH SOMERSET
46 CITY OF BRISTOL
47 BATH AND NORTH EAST SOMERSET
48 SWINDON
49 READING
50 WOKINGHAM
51 WINDSOR AND MAIDENHEAD
52 SLOUGH
53 BRACKNELL FOREST
54 THURROCK
55 SOUTHEND-ON-SEA
56 MEDWAY
57 PLYMOUTH
58 TORBAY
59 POOLE
60 BOURNEMOUTH
61 SOUTHAMPTON
62 PORTSMOUTH
63 BRIGHTON AND HOVE
Key to Welsh unitary authorities on map
15 SWANSEA
16 NEATH PORT TALBOT
17 BRIDGEND
18 RHONDDA CYNON TAFF
19 MERTHYR TYDFIL
20 CAERPHILLY
21 BLAENAU GWENT
22 TORFAEN
23 CARDIFF
24 NEWPORT
NORTH SEA
IRISH SEA
North Channel
SCOTLAND
NORTHERN IRELAND
ISLE OF MAN
283
282

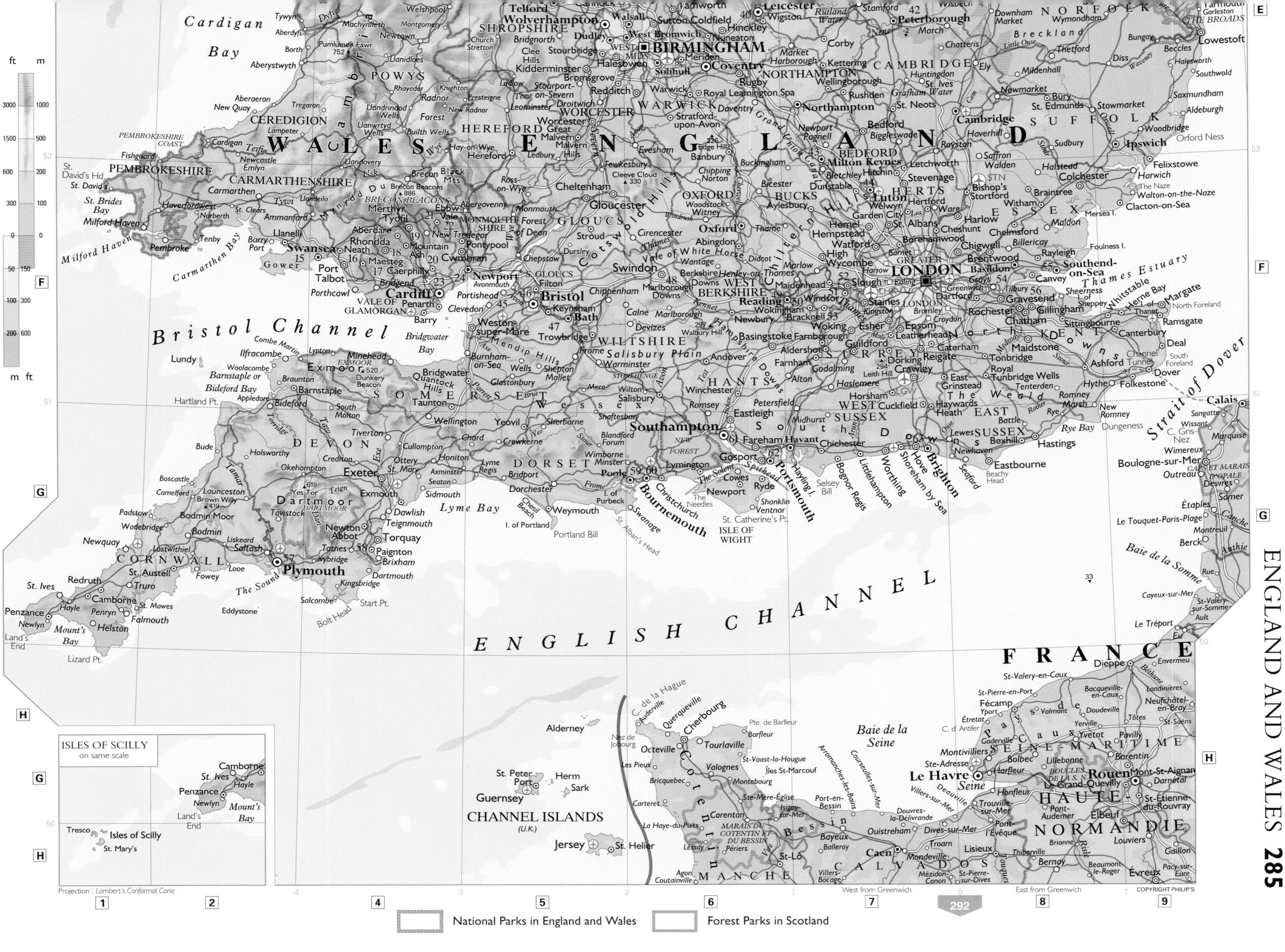
ENGLISH CHANNEL
FRANCE
ENGLAND
WALES
Bristol Channel
Cardigan Bay
Strait of Dover
Thames Estuary
Lyme Bay
Baie de la Seine
Baie de la Somme
CHANNEL ISLANDS (U.K.)
ISLE OF WIGHT
LONDON
BIRMINGHAM
Bristol
Cardiff
Southampton
Portsmouth
Plymouth
Brighton
Le Havre
Rouen
Cherbourg
ISLES OF SCILLY on same scale
National Parks in England and Wales
Forest Parks in Scotland
Projection : Lambert's Conformal Conic
COPYRIGHT PHILIP'S
West from Greenwich
East from Greenwich
292

ATLANTIC OCEAN
NORTH SEA
IRISH SEA
CELTIC SEA
English Channel
Bristol Channel
St. George's Channel
North Channel
North Minch
Sea of the Hebrides
Pentland Firth
Moray Firth
Firth of Clyde
Str. of Dover
The Wash
UNITED KINGDOM
SCOTLAND
ENGLAND
WALES
NORTHERN IRELAND
IRELAND
FRANCE
BELGIUM
NETHERLANDS
NORWAY
Shetland Is.
Orkney Is.
Outer Hebrides
Inner Hebrides
Channel Is. (U.K.)
Grampian Mts.
North West Highlands
Southern Uplands
Cheviot Hills
Pennines
Cambrian Mts.
Cotswold Hills
Cumbrian Mts.
London
Dublin
Edinburgh
Glasgow
Belfast
Cardiff
Manchester
Birmingham
Liverpool
Leeds
Sheffield
Newcastle-upon-Tyne
Aberdeen
Cork
Projection: Conical with two standard parallels
East from Greenwich
West from Greenwich

281 288 292

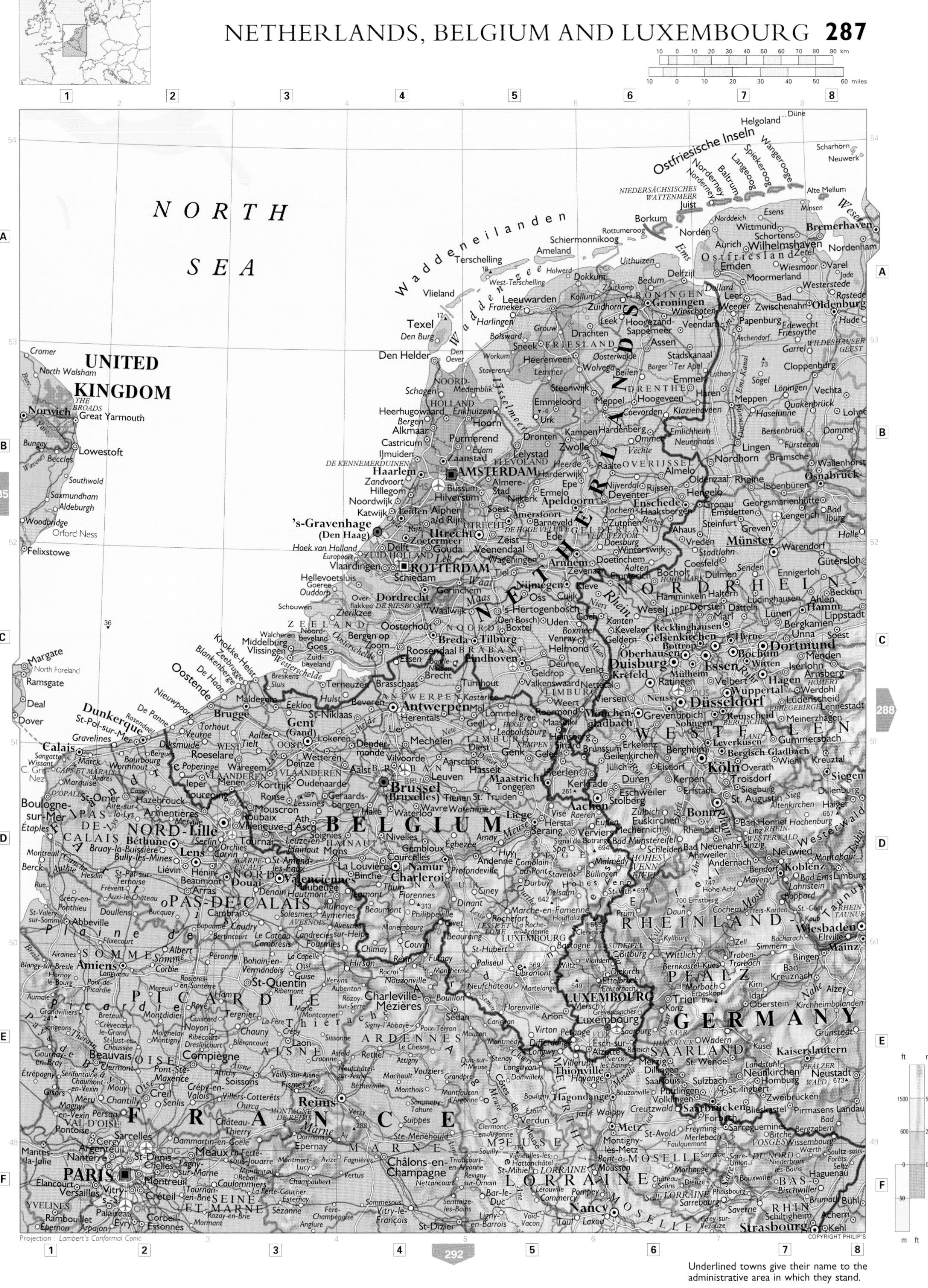

Underlined towns give their name to the administrative area in which they stand.

50 0 25 50 75 100 125 150 175 km

50 0 25 50 75 100 125 miles

Projection: Conical with two standard parallels

281
285
292
294

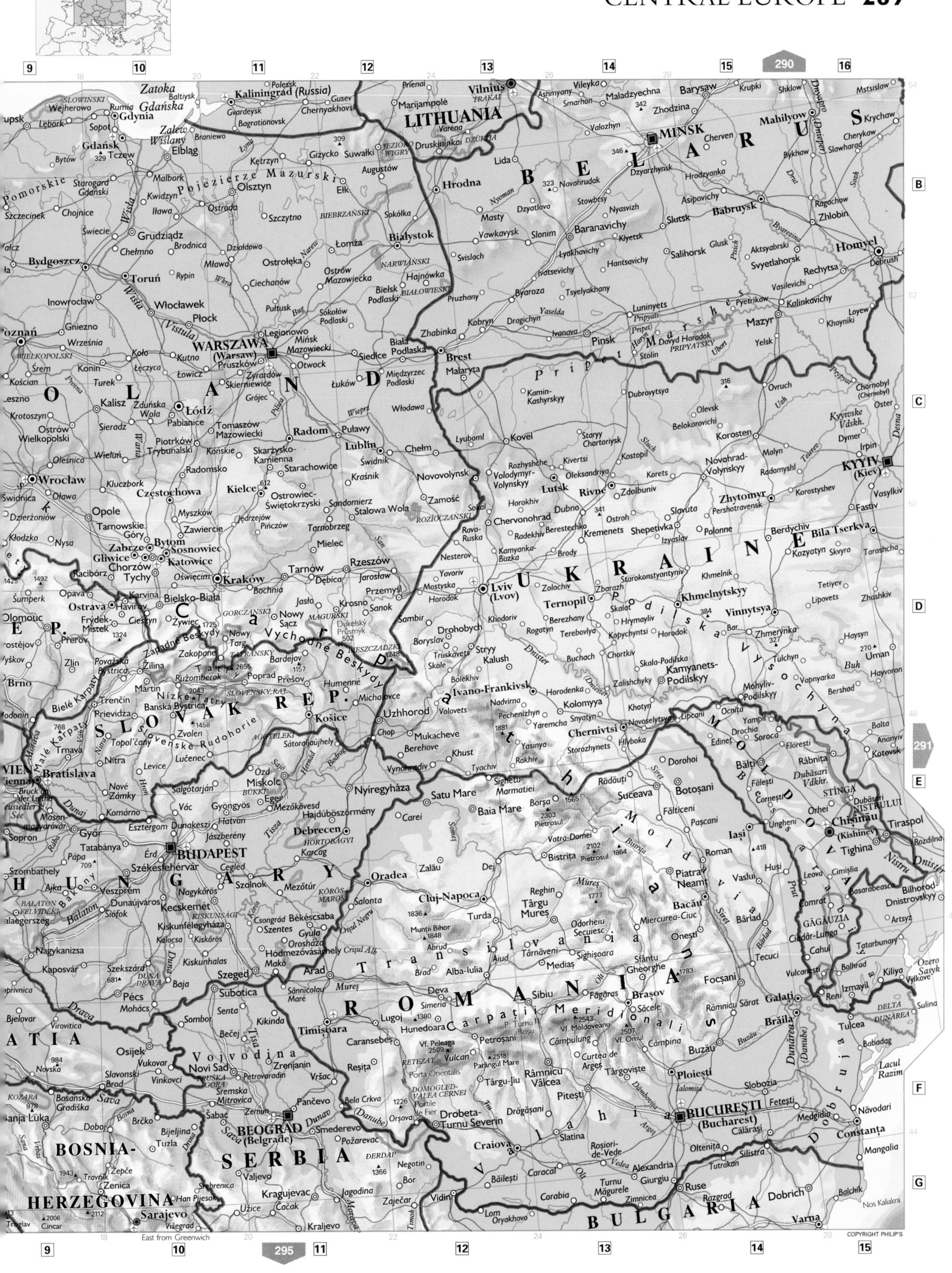
LITHUANIA
BELARUS
POLAND
UKRAINE
MOLDOVA
ROMANIA
SLOVAK REP.
HUNGARY
SERBIA
BOSNIA-HERZEGOVINA
CROATIA
BULGARIA
Vilnius
MINSK
WARSZAWA (Warsaw)
KYYIV (Kiev)
BUDAPEST
BUCUREȘTI (Bucharest)
BEOGRAD (Belgrade)
CHIȘINĂU (Kishinev)
Bratislava
Sarajevo
Kaliningrad (Russia)
Gdańsk
Gdynia
Zatoka Gdańska
Olsztyn
Białystok
Hrodna
Brest
Pinsk
Homyel
Mahilyow
Babruysk
Baranavichy
Mazyr
Łódź
Poznań
Wrocław
Kraków
Katowice
Lublin
Radom
Kielce
Częstochowa
Rzeszów
Lviv (Lvov)
Lutsk
Rivne
Zhytomyr
Vinnytsya
Khmelnytskyy
Ternopil
Ivano-Frankivsk
Chernivtsi
Uzhhorod
Košice
Žilina
Brno
Ostrava
Miskolc
Debrecen
Szeged
Győr
Pécs
Novi Sad
Timișoara
Arad
Oradea
Cluj-Napoca
Sibiu
Brașov
Iași
Bacău
Galați
Brăila
Constanța
Ploiești
Craiova
Varna
Ruse
Tiraspol
Bălți
Pripet Marshes
Transilvania
Carpații Meridionali
Moldavia
Podilska Vysochyna
Vojvodina
Wisła (Vistula)
Dnister
Dunărea (Danube)
Prut
Mureș
Tisza
Drava
Sava
Dunav
Pojezierze Mazurskie
Vychodné Beskydy
Tatry
Nízke Tatry
2655
2543
2509
2303
1881
Nos Kaliakra
East from Greenwich
COPYRIGHT PHILIP'S

290
291
295

50 0 100 200 300 400 km

50 0 50 100 150 200 250 miles

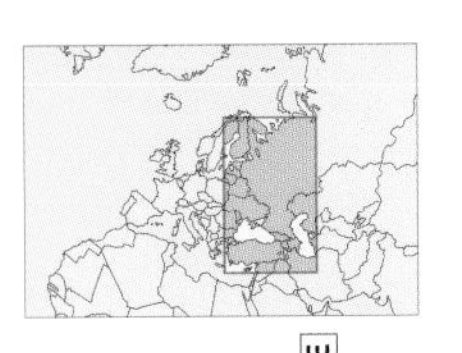

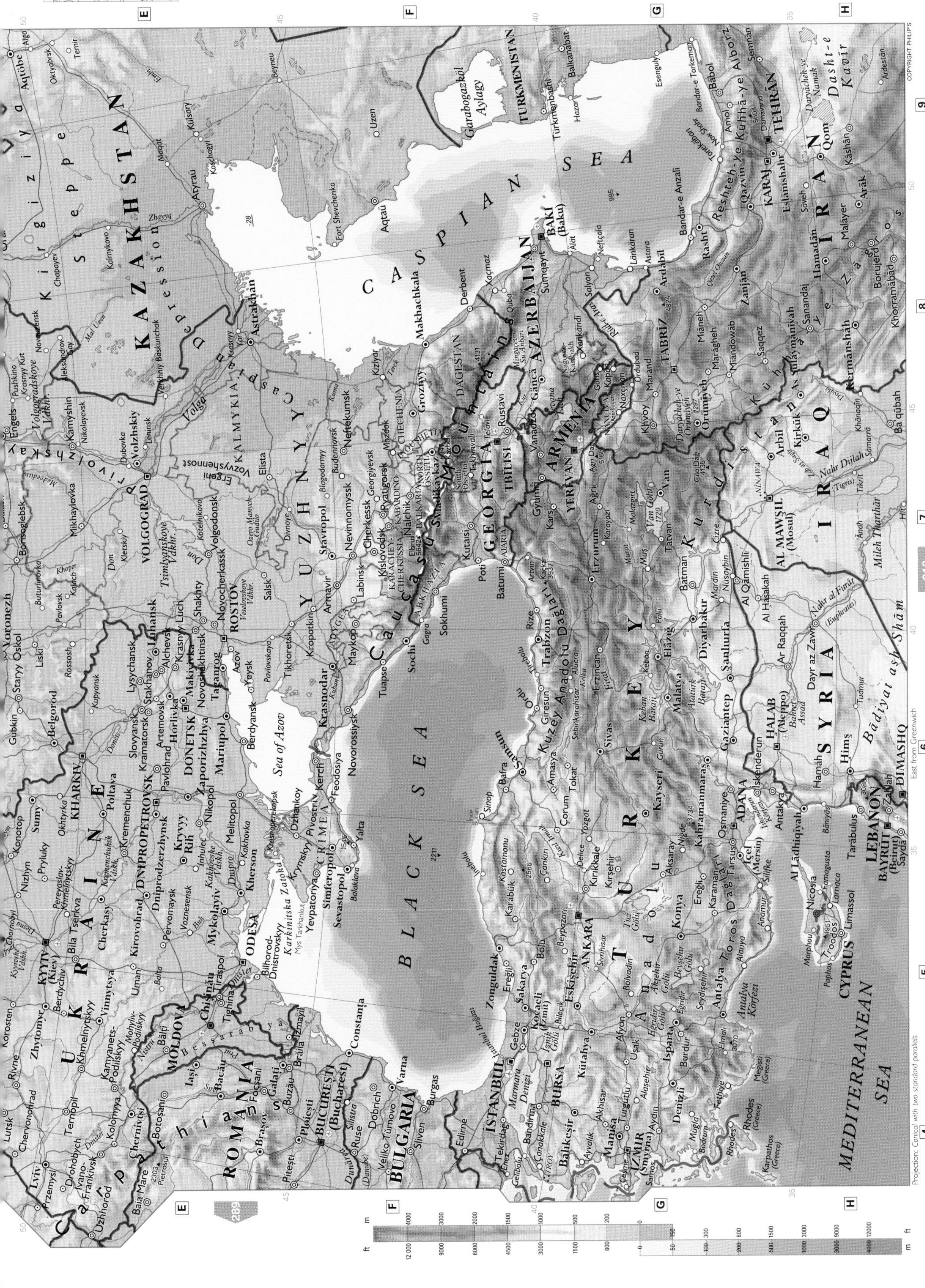

BLACK SEA
CASPIAN SEA
MEDITERRANEAN SEA
Sea of Azov
UKRAINE
KAZAKHSTAN
TURKMENISTAN
GEORGIA
ARMENIA
AZERBAIJAN
TURKEY
SYRIA
IRAQ
IRAN
LEBANON
CYPRUS
ROMANIA
MOLDOVA
BULGARIA
CRIMEA
KALMYKIA
DAGESTAN
ISTANBUL
ANKARA
TBILISI
YEREVAN
BAKI (Baku)
TEHRĀN
DIMASHQ
BAYRŪT (Beirut)
BUCUREȘTI (Bucharest)
KYIV (Kiev)
VOLGOGRAD
ROSTOV
ODESA
KHARKIV
DONETSK
DNIPROPETROVSK
Caucasus Mountains
Projection: Conical with two standard parallels
East from Greenwich
COPYRIGHT PHILIP'S

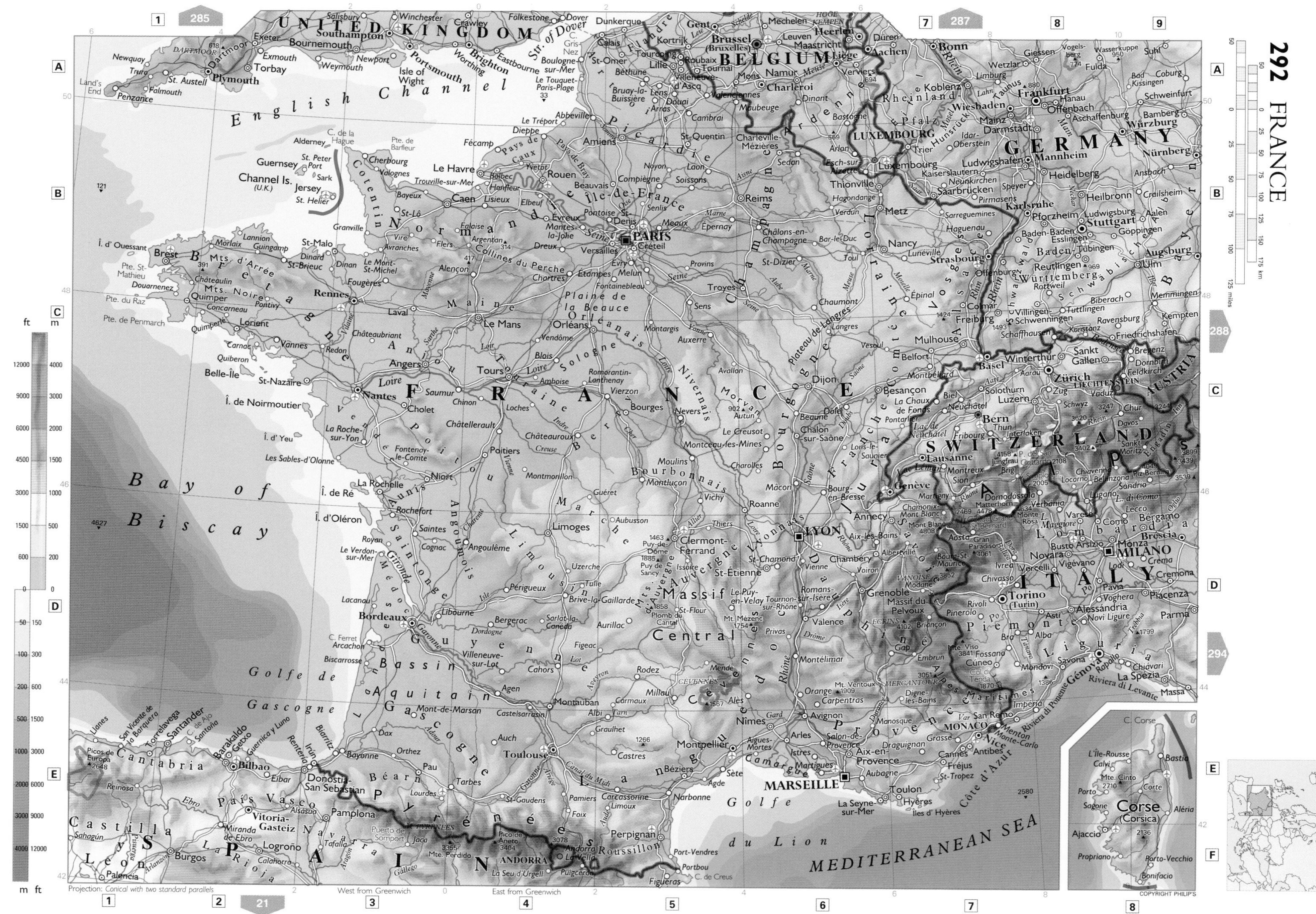
50 0 25 50 75 100 125 150 175 km
50 0 25 50 75 100 125 miles
FRANCE
PARIS
LYON
MARSEILLE
UNITED KINGDOM
BELGIUM
LUXEMBOURG
GERMANY
SWITZERLAND
LIECHTENSTEIN
AUSTRIA
ITALY
MILANO
MONACO
ANDORRA
SPAIN
English Channel
Bay of Biscay
Golfe de Gascogne
Golfe du Lion
MEDITERRANEAN SEA
Côte d'Azur
Corse (Corsica)
285
287
288
294
21
Projection: Conical with two standard parallels
West from Greenwich
East from Greenwich
COPYRIGHT PHILIP'S

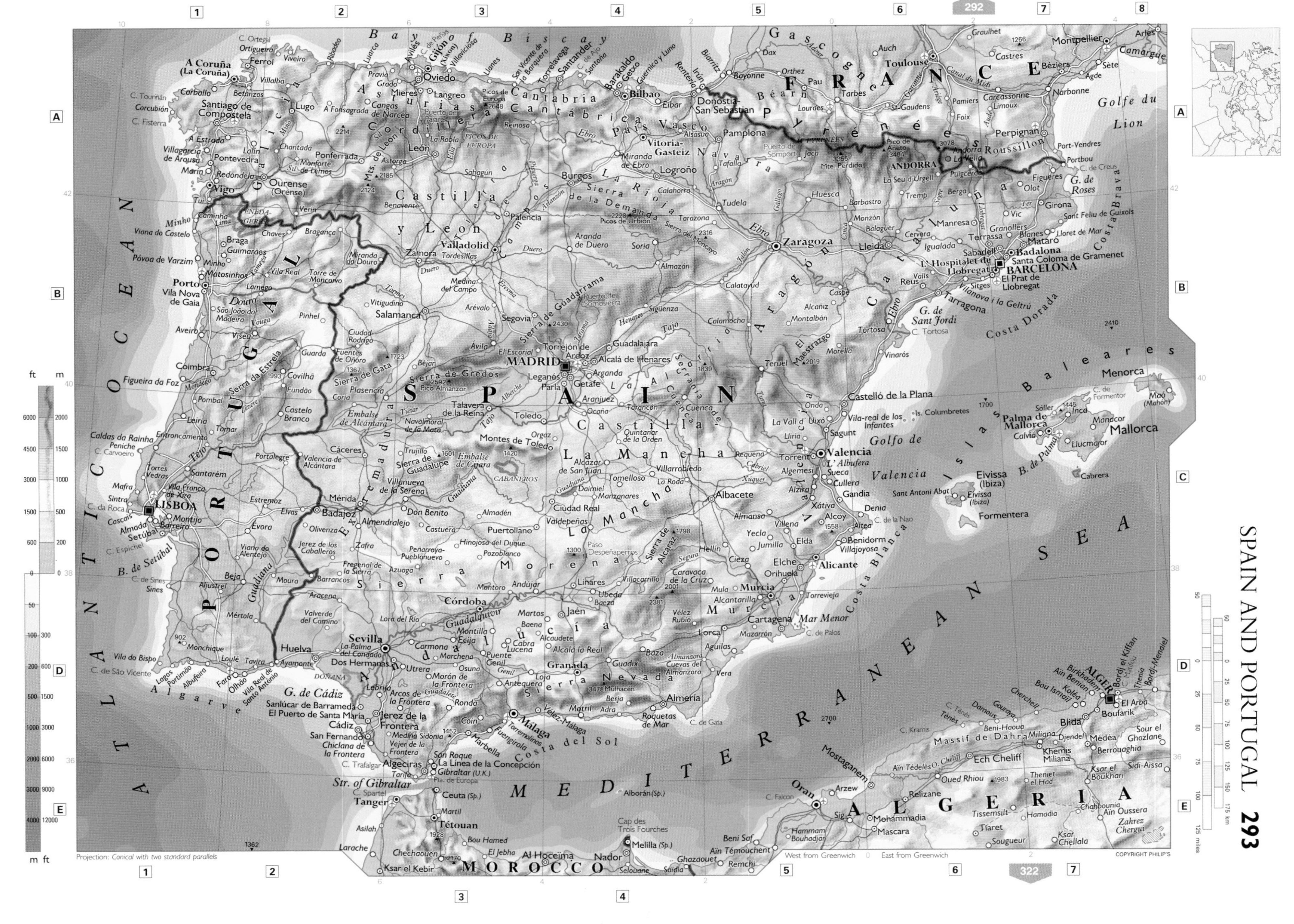
SPAIN
PORTUGAL
FRANCE
ANDORRA
MOROCCO
ALGERIA
Bay of Biscay
Golfe du Lion
Islas Baleares
Mallorca
Menorca
Eivissa (Ibiza)
Formentera
MEDITERRANEAN SEA
ATLANTIC OCEAN
Str. of Gibraltar
G. de Cádiz
Golfo de Valencia
MADRID
LISBOA
BARCELONA
ALGER
Pyrénées
Sierra Nevada
Sierra Morena
Castilla y León
Castilla-La Mancha
Andalucía
Costa del Sol
Costa Brava
Costa Dorada
Costa Blanca
Valencia
Zaragoza
Sevilla
Málaga
Bilbao
Porto
Granada
Córdoba
Murcia
Alicante
Valladolid
Toulouse
Oran
Projection: Conical with two standard parallels
West from Greenwich
East from Greenwich
COPYRIGHT PHILIP'S
292
322
50 0 25 50 75 100 125 150 175 km
50 0 25 50 75 100 125 miles
ft m
m ft

288
292
322
Projection: Conical with two standard parallels
SWITZERLAND
AUSTRIA
SLOVENIA
CROAT
FRANCE
ALGERIA
TUNISIA
MALTA
VATICAN CITY
SAN MARINO
MONACO
ADRIATIC SEA
LIGURIAN SEA
TYRRHENIAN SEA
MEDITER
Golfo di Génova
Golfo di Venézia
Str. of Sicily
Golfe de Tunis
Golfe de Hammamet
Bouches de Bonifacio
Golfo di Táranto
LYON
MARSEILLE
MILANO
Torino (Turin)
Génova
Venézia (Venice)
Firenze (Florence)
ROMA
Nápoli
Palermo
Cágliari
Bologna
Ljubljana
ZAGREB
TUNIS
Valletta
Sardegna (Sardinia)
Corse (Corsica)
Sicilia
Ísole Eólie
Ísole Égadi
Ísole Pelagie (Italy)
Lampedusa
Pantelleria (Italy)
Ústica (Italy)
Ísole Ponziane
Elba
Gozo
Messina
Catánia
Siracusa
Reggio di Calábria
Bari
Táranto
Ancona
Pescara
Perúgia
Trieste
Verona
Pádova
Parma
Módena
Pisa
Livorno
La Spézia
Bergamo
Brescia
Trento
Bolzano
Udine
Rijeka
Split
Zadar
Nice
Toulon
Grenoble
Constantine
Annaba
Bizerte
Sousse
Kairouan
Ajaccio
Bastia
Sássari
Olbia
Oristano
Foggia
Salerno
Cosenza
Catanzaro
Crotone
Agrigento
Trápani
Marsala

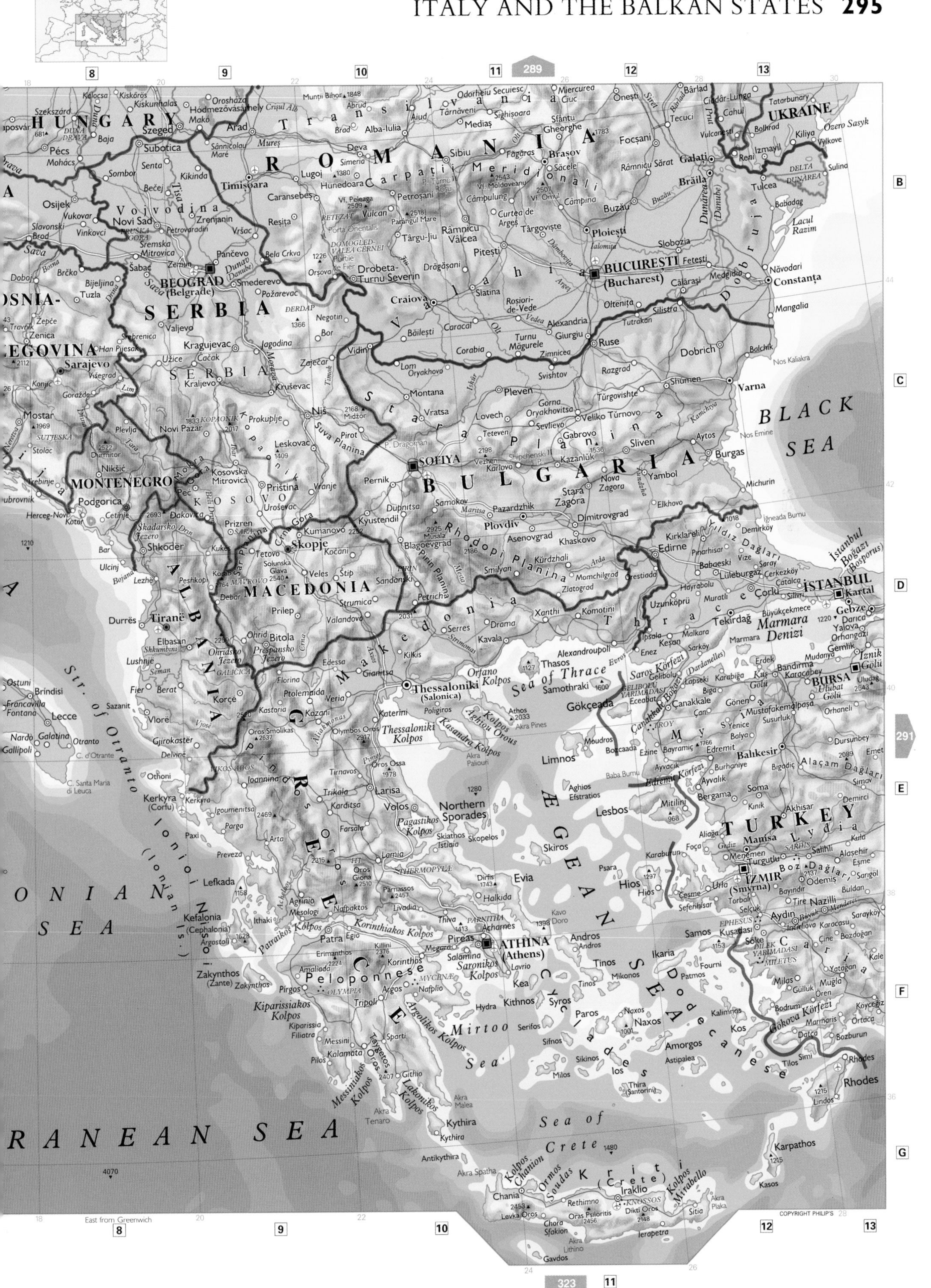
HUNGARY
ROMANIA
SERBIA
BOSNIA-
HERZEGOVINA
MONTENEGRO
KOSOVO
ALBANIA
MACEDONIA
BULGARIA
GREECE
TURKEY
UKRAINE
BLACK SEA
AEGEAN SEA
IONIAN SEA
MEDITERRANEAN SEA
Sea of Thrace
Sea of Crete
Mirtoo Sea
Marmara Denizi
BEOGRAD (Belgrade)
BUCUREŞTI (Bucharest)
SOFIYA
Skopje
Tiranë
Podgorica
Sarajevo
ATHINA (Athens)
İSTANBUL
BURSA
İZMIR (Smyrna)
Thessaloniki (Salonica)
Constanța
Varna
Burgas
Plovdiv
Craiova
Timişoara
Novi Sad
Niš
Priština
Edirne
Kriti (Crete)
Iraklio
Chania
Rhodes
Lesbos
Limnos
Evia
Kefalonia (Cephalonia)
Kerkyra (Corfu)
Zakynthos (Zante)
Peloponnese
Cyclades
Dodecanese
Northern Sporades
Str. of Otranto
Transilvania
Carpații Meridionali
Stara Planina
Rhodopi Planina
Makedonia
Thrace
Dobruja
Walachia
Pindos Oros
Kythira
Karpathos
Samos
Ikaria
Naxos
Paros
Milos
Thira (Santorini)
East from Greenwich
COPYRIGHT PHILIP'S
289
291
323

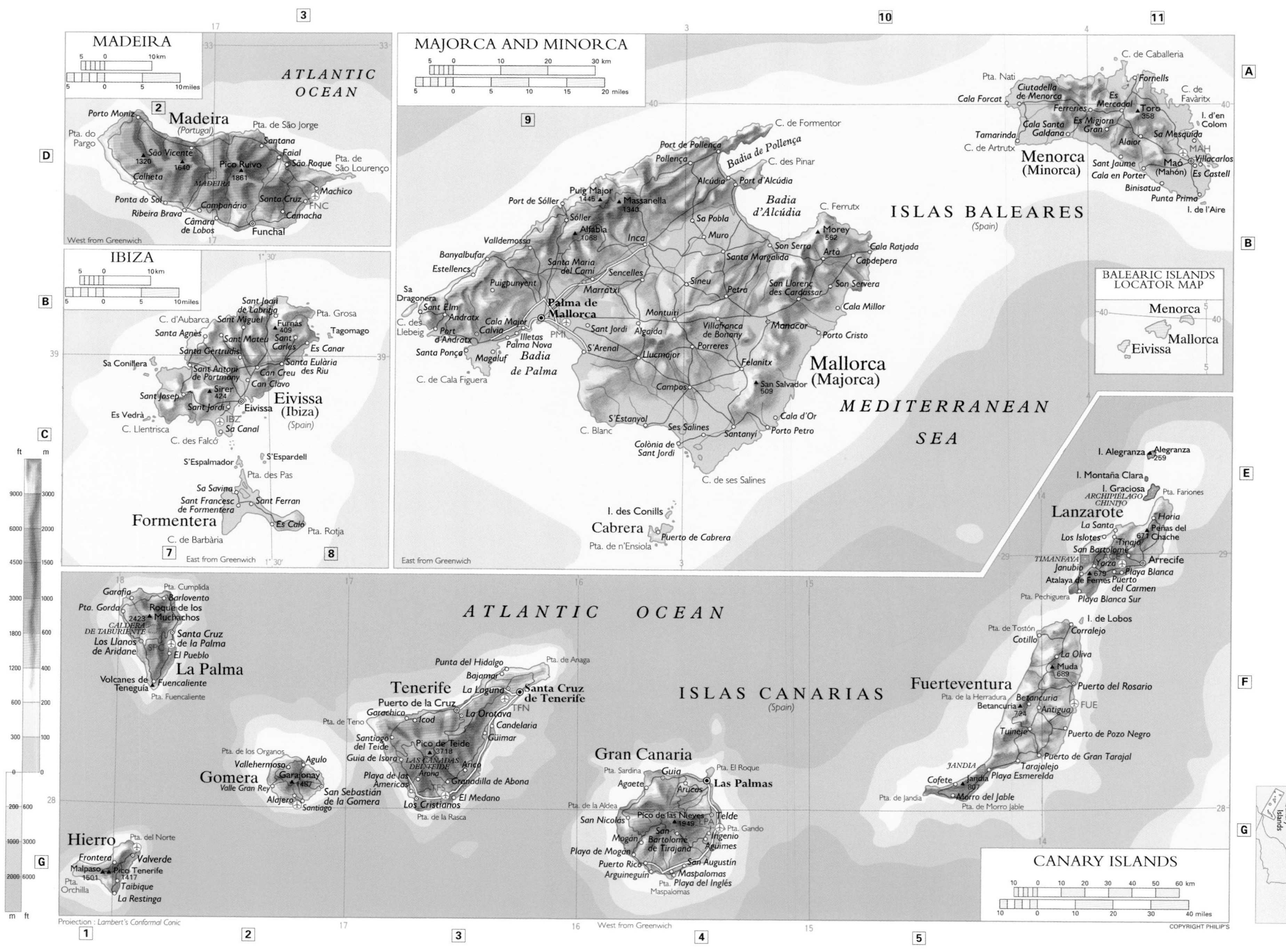

MADEIRA
ATLANTIC OCEAN
Madeira
(Portugal)
Funchal
IBIZA
Eivissa (Ibiza)
(Spain)
Formentera
MAJORCA AND MINORCA
ISLAS BALEARES
(Spain)
Menorca (Minorca)
Mallorca (Majorca)
Palma de Mallorca
Badia de Palma
Badia d'Alcúdia
Cabrera
MEDITERRANEAN SEA
BALEARIC ISLANDS LOCATOR MAP
Menorca
Mallorca
Eivissa
ATLANTIC OCEAN
ISLAS CANARIAS
(Spain)
La Palma
Hierro
Gomera
Tenerife
Santa Cruz de Tenerife
Gran Canaria
Las Palmas
Fuerteventura
Lanzarote
CANARY ISLANDS
Canary Islands
Madeira
Balearic Islands
East from Greenwich
West from Greenwich
Projection : Lambert's Conformal Conic
COPYRIGHT PHILIP'S

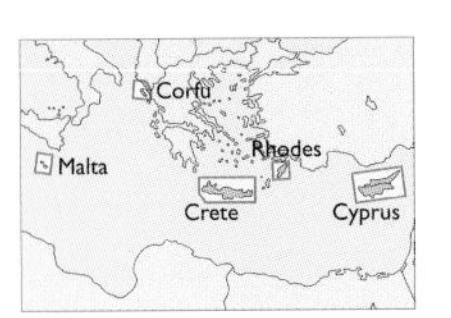

CRETE

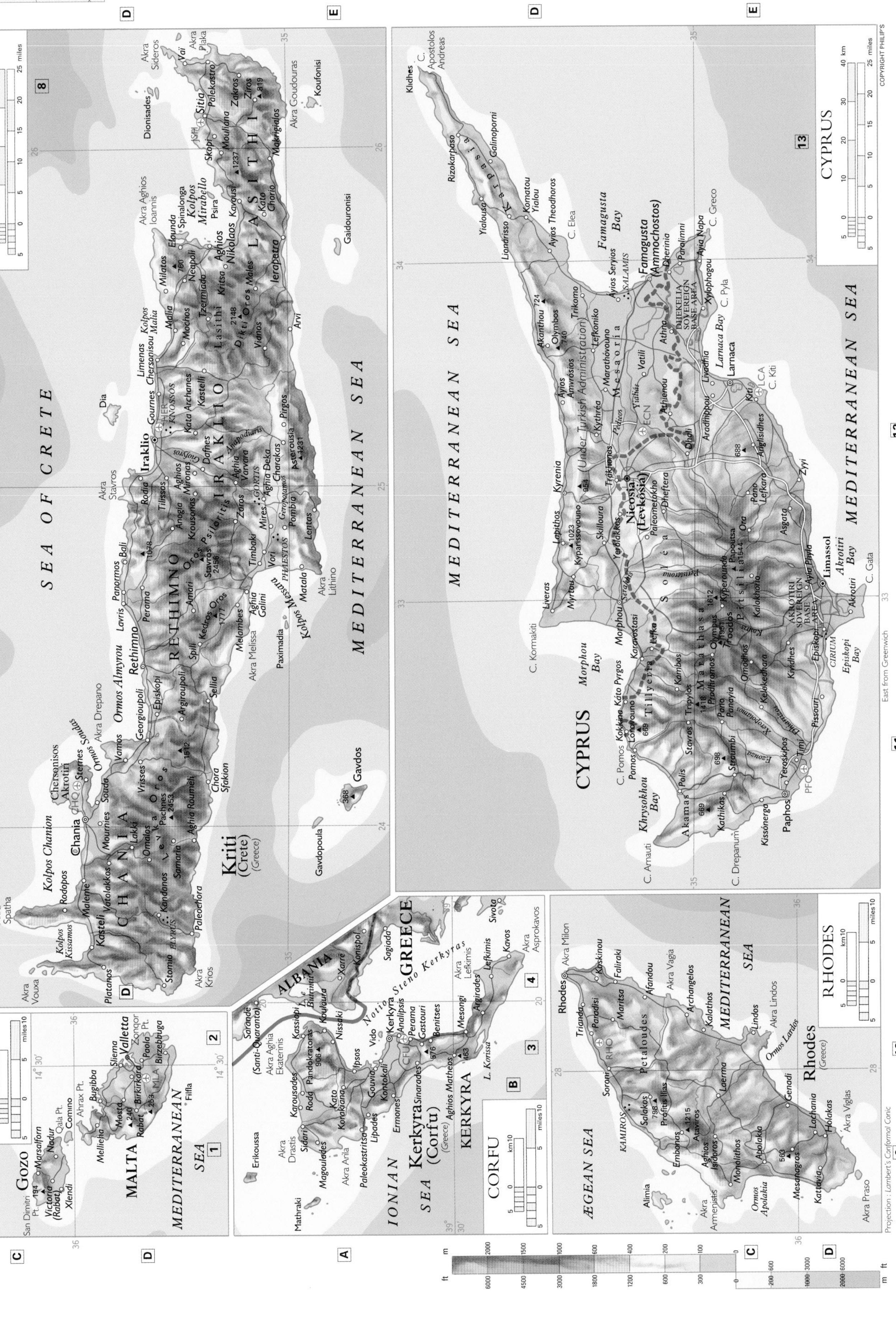

MALTA

CORFU

RHODES

CYPRUS

East from Greenwich

Projection : Lambert's Conformal Conic

ARCTIC OCEAN
PACIFIC OCEAN
INDIAN OCEAN
Norwegian Sea
Barents Sea
Kara Sea
Laptev Sea
East Siberian Sea
Bering Sea
Sea of Okhotsk
Sea of Japan (East Sea)
Yellow Sea
East China Sea
South China Sea
Philippine Sea
Celebes Sea
Sulu Sea
Banda Sea
Arafura Sea
Java Sea
Bay of Bengal
Arabian Sea
Persian Gulf
Gulf of Oman
G. of Aden
Red Sea
Caspian Sea
Black Sea
Mediterranean Sea
Aral Sea
Baltic Sea
North Sea
Adriatic Sea
Europe
Scandinavia
North European Plain
Central Russian Uplands
Ural Mts.
West Siberian Plain
Central Siberian Plateau
Siberia
Verkhoyansk Ra.
Cherski Ra.
Kolyma Ra.
Chukot Ra.
Kamchatka Pen.
Sredinny Ra.
Stanovoy Ra.
Yablonovyy Ra.
Sayan Mts.
Steppe
Altai
Gobi
Plateau of Mongolia
Great Khingan Mts.
Manchurian Plain
Korea
Japan
Honshū
Hokkaido
Kyūshū
Shikoku
Sakhalin
Kuril Is.
Aleutian Is.
Ryūkyū Is.
Taiwan
Philippines
Luzon
Mindanao
Borneo
Celebes
Sumatra
Java
East Indies
New Guinea
Australia
Timor
Indo-China
Malay Peninsula
Hainan
Great Plain of China
Far East
Kunlun Shan
Tien Shan
Takla Makan
Tarim Basin
Dzungarian Basin
Turfan Basin
Qaidam Basin
Qilian Shan
Plateau of Tibet
Himalaya
Mt. Everest 8850
Karakoram Ra.
K2 8611
Pamirs
Hindu Kush
India
Deccan
Thar Desert
Western Ghats
Eastern Ghats
Ceylon
Maldives
Chagos Arch.
Seychelles
Arabia
Rub' al Khālī (Empty Quarter)
Nafud Desert
Syrian Desert
Zagros Mts.
Elburz Mts.
Caucasus
Anatolia
Taurus Mts.
Mesopotamia
Middle East
Kara Kum
Kyzyl Kum
Ustyurt Plateau
Caspian Depression
Africa
Somali Peninsula
Ethiopian Highlands
Alps
Carpathians
Balkans
British Isles
Crete
Cyprus
East from Greenwich
Projection: Bonne
COPYRIGHT PHILIP'S

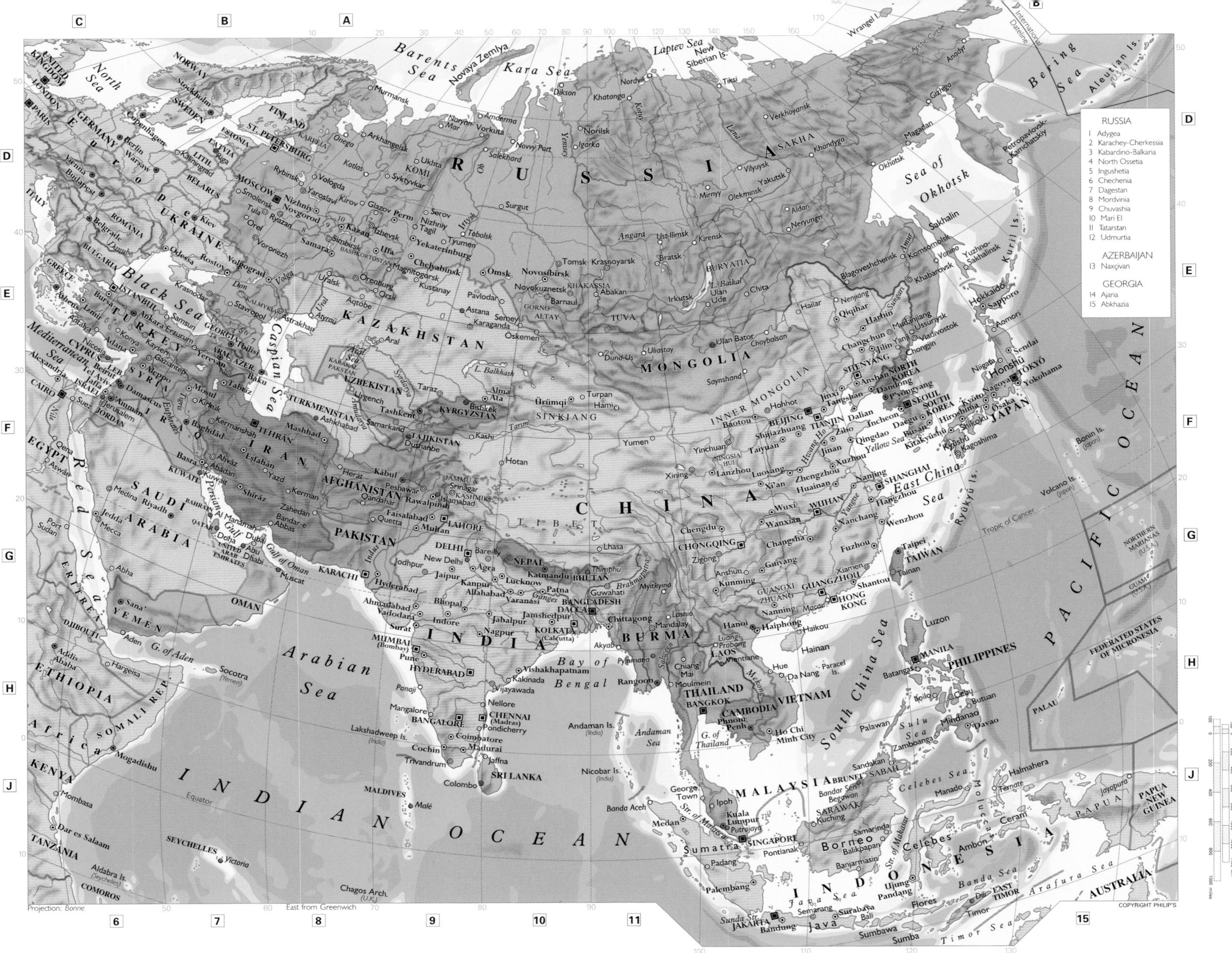
100 0 200 400 600 800 1000 1200 1400 km
100 0 200 400 600 800 1000 miles
RUSSIA
1 Adygea
2 Karachey-Cherkessia
3 Kabardino-Balkaria
4 North Ossetia
5 Ingushetia
6 Chechenia
7 Dagestan
8 Mordvinia
9 Chuvashia
10 Mari El
11 Tatarstan
12 Udmurtia
AZERBAIJAN
13 Naxçivan
GEORGIA
14 Ajaria
15 Abkhazia
RUSSIA
MONGOLIA
CHINA
KAZAKHSTAN
INDIA
PAKISTAN
IRAN
AFGHANISTAN
TURKEY
SAUDI ARABIA
JAPAN
PHILIPPINES
INDONESIA
MALAYSIA
THAILAND
VIETNAM
BURMA
NEPAL
SRI LANKA
YEMEN
OMAN
PACIFIC OCEAN
INDIAN OCEAN
Arabian Sea
Bay of Bengal
South China Sea
Caspian Sea
Black Sea
Red Sea
Mediterranean Sea
Sea of Okhotsk
Bering Sea
Kara Sea
Barents Sea
Laptev Sea
East China Sea
Yellow Sea
Andaman Sea
Java Sea
Banda Sea
Timor Sea
Arafura Sea
Celebes Sea
Sulu Sea
Persian Gulf
Gulf of Oman
G. of Aden
Tropic of Cancer
Equator
International Dateline
Projection: Bonne
East from Greenwich
COPYRIGHT PHILIP'S

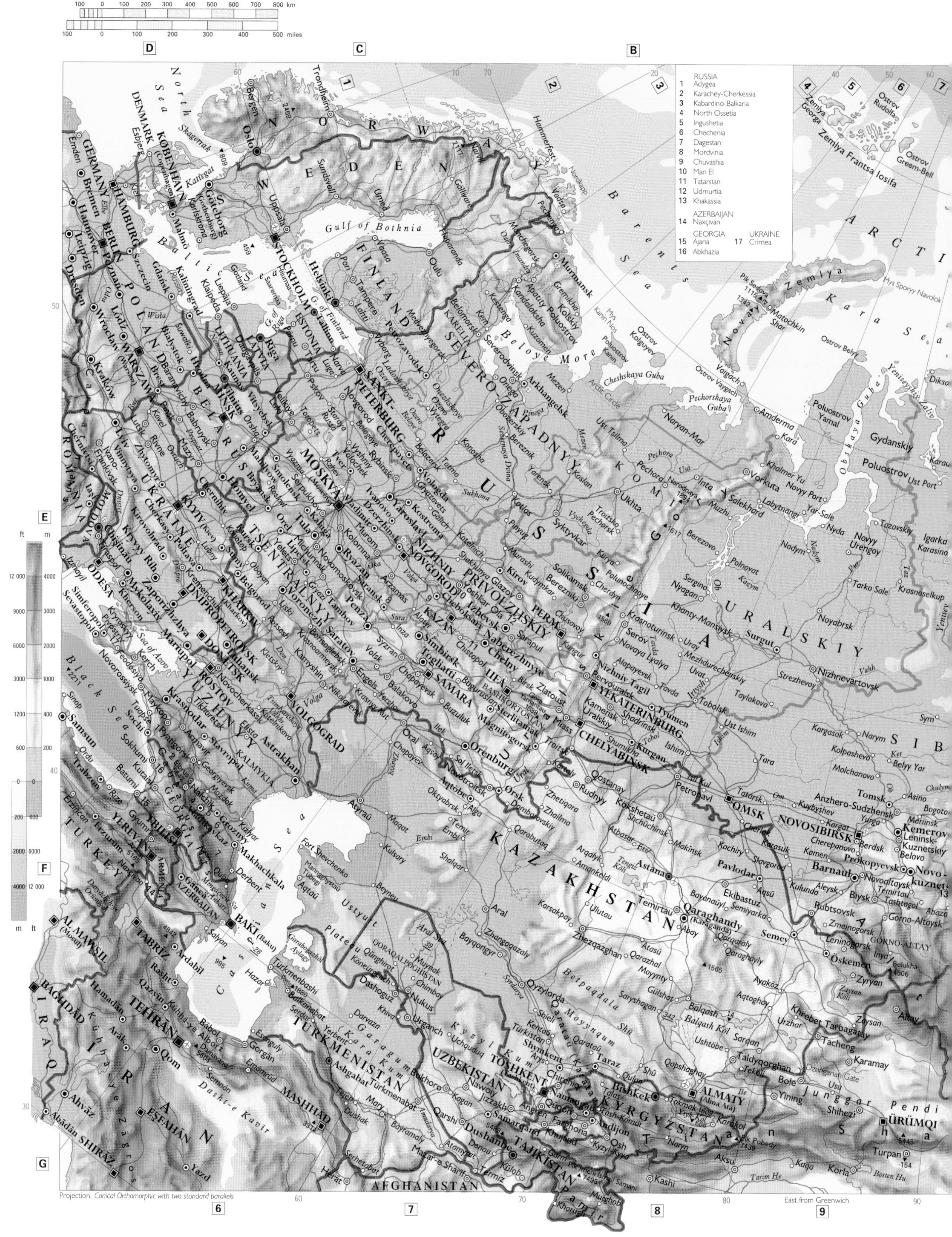
100 0 100 200 300 400 500 600 700 800 km
100 0 100 200 300 400 500 miles
RUSSIA
1 Adygea
2 Karachey-Cherkessia
3 Kabardino-Balkaria
4 North Ossetia
5 Ingushetia
6 Chechenia
7 Dagestan
8 Mordvinia
9 Chuvashia
10 Mari El
11 Tatarstan
12 Udmurtia
13 Khakassia
AZERBAIJAN
14 Naxçıvan
GEORGIA
15 Ajaria
16 Abkhazia
UKRAINE
17 Crimea
ft m
12 000 4000
9000 3000
6000 2000
3000 1000
1200 400
600 200
0 0
200 600
2000 6000
4000 12 000
m ft
NORWAY
SWEDEN
FINLAND
ESTONIA
LATVIA
LITHUANIA
POLAND
BELARUS
UKRAINE
MOLDOVA
ROMANIA
DENMARK
GERMANY
RUSSIA
KAZAKHSTAN
UZBEKISTAN
TURKMENISTAN
KYRGYZSTAN
TAJIKISTAN
AFGHANISTAN
IRAN
IRAQ
TURKEY
GEORGIA
ARMENIA
AZERBAIJAN
MOSKVA
SANKT-PETERBURG
KYYIV (Kiev)
MINSK
ASTANA
TOSHKENT
BISHKEK
ALMATY (Alma Ata)
DUSHANBE
ASHGABAT
BAKI (Baku)
TBILISI
YEREVAN
TEHRĀN
BAGHDĀD
HELSINKI
TALLINN
RIGA
VILNIUS
WARSZAWA (Warsaw)
STOCKHOLM
OSLO
KØBENHAVN (Copenhagen)
BERLIN
North Sea
Baltic Sea
Gulf of Bothnia
Barents Sea
Kara Sea
Beloye More
Black Sea
Sea of Azov
Caspian Sea
Aral Sea
Novaya Zemlya
Zemlya Frantsa Iosifa
Ural
Projection: Conical Orthomorphic with two standard parallels
East from Greenwich

SEA OF OKHOTSK
SEA OF JAPAN
(EAST SEA)
Sakhalin (Russia)
Ostrov Moneron (Russia)
La Perouse Strait
(Sōya-Kaikyō)
Hokkaidō
HOKKAIDŌ
SAPPORO
Otaru
Ebetsu
Tomakomai
Muroran
Hakodate
Asahikawa
Kitami
Obihiro
Kushiro
Wakkanai
Ishikari-Wan
(Otaru-Wan)
Uchiura-Wan
Okushiri-Tō
Tsugaru-Kaikyō
Honshū
TŌHOKU
Aomori
Hachinohe
Hirosaki
Akita
Morioka
Sakata
Yamagata
SENDAI
Sendai-Wan
Fukushima
Niigata
Sado
CHŪBU
RUSSIA
CHINA
HEILONG-JIANG
JILIN
NORTH KOREA
Ch'ŏngjin
Vladivostok
Nakhodka
Ussuriysk
Lake Khanka
Zaliv Petra Velikogo
Khrebet Sikhote-Alin
Yamato Rise
301
307

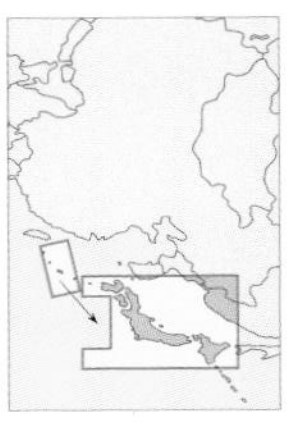

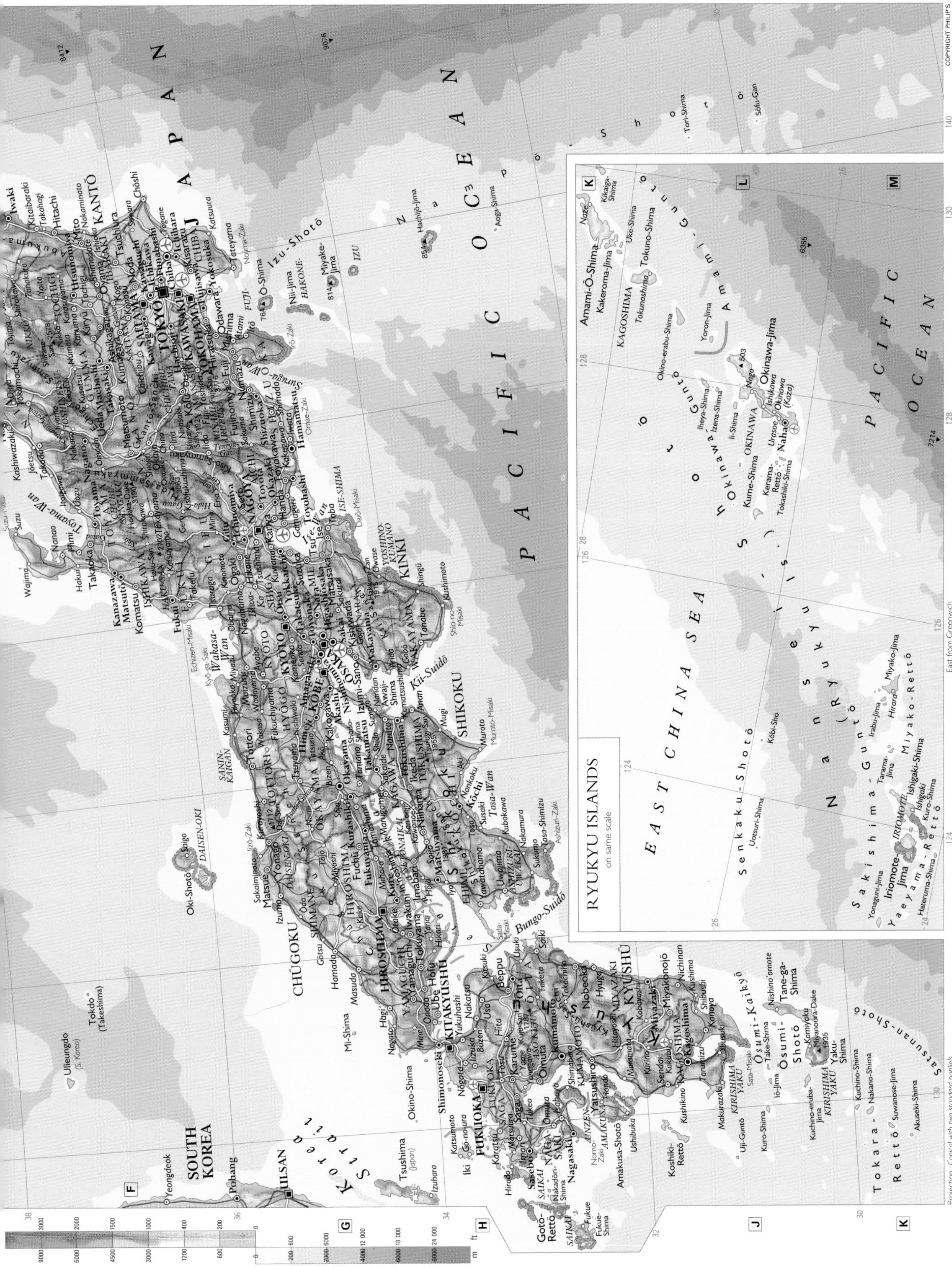

RYUKYU ISLANDS
on same scale

Projection: Conical with two standard parallels

East from Greenwich

100 0 100 200 300 400 500 600 km
100 0 100 200 300 400 miles
KAZAKHSTAN
RUSSIA
MONGOLIA
KYRGYZSTAN
Astana
Qaraghandy
Temirtau
Karsakpay
Zhezqazghan
Balqash
Balqash Köl
Betpaqdala
Moyynqum
Taldyqorghan
Bishkek
ALMATY
Ysyk-Köl
Semey
Rubtsovsk
Öskemen
Leninogorsk
Zaysan Köl
Gorno-Altaysk
Zapadnyy Sayan
Tannu Ola
Kyzyl
Irkutsk
Angarsk
Uvs Nuur
Ulaangom
Hövsgöl Nuur
Mörön
Ulaanbaatar
Hyargas Nuur
Har Us Nuur
Dund-Us (Hovd)
Uliastay
Hangayn Nuruu
Altay
Bayanhongor
Arvayheer
Mandalgovi
Dalandzadgad
Gurvan Sayhan Uul
Aerhtai Shan (Altai)
Khrebet Tarbagatay
Tacheng
Karamay
Gurbantünggüt Shamo
Junggar Pendi
Ala Tau
Bole
Yining
Borohoro Shan
Shihezi
ÜRÜMQI
Bogda Shan
Tian Shan
Turpan
Turpan Pendi
Hami
Barkol Kazak Zizhixian
Pik Khan-Tengri 6995
Pik Pobedy 7439
Aksu
Kuqa
Korla
Bosten Hu
Kuruktag
Kashi
XINJIANG UYGUR ZIZHIQU (SINKIANG)
Tarim Pendi
Taklamakan Shamo
Lop Nur
Dunhuang
Bei Shan
Badain Jaran Shamo
Yumen
Jiayuguan
Qilian Shan
Zhangye
Shache
Yecheng
Hotan
Qiemo
Ruoqiang
Kumtag Shamo
Altun Shan
Mangnai
Qaidam Pendi
Tengger Shamo
Wuwei
Yinchuan
NINGXIA HUIZU ZIZHIQU
Xining
LANZHOU
Qinghai Hu
Golmud
QINGHAI
Kunlun Shan
Hoh Xil Shan
Muz Tag 7723
Karakoram
K2 8611
JAMMU & KASHMIR
Aksai Chin
Srinagar
Leh
Zaskar Mts.
Hindu Kush
XIZANG ZIZHIQU (TIBET)
Tanggula (Dangla) Shan
Bayan Har Shan
Gangdisê Shan
Nyainqêntanglha Shan
Lhasa
Nagqu
Qamdo
Xigazê
Namcha Barwa 7756
NEPAL
KATMANDU
Mt. Everest 8850
Kanchenjunga
Himalaya
Annapurna
Dhaulagiri
BHUTAN
Thimphu
SIKKIM
ARUNACHAL PRADESH
ASSAM
Guwahati
BANGLADESH
DHAKA
KOLKATA (Calcutta)
Chittagong
INDIA
DELHI
New Delhi
MEERUT
AGRA
KANPUR
LUCKNOW
UTTAR PRADESH
ALLAHABAD
VARANASI
PATNA
BIHAR
JHARKHAND
Ranchi
JAMSHEDPUR
MADHYA PRADESH
JABALPUR
NAGPUR
CHHATTISGARH
ORISSA
Cuttack
VISHAKHAPATNAM
Tropic of Cancer
BAY OF BENGAL
BURMA (MYANMAR)
Mandalay
Arakan Yoma
Pegu Yoma
Sittwe (Akyab)
Kachin
THAILAND (SIAM)
LAOS
Luang Prabang
VIETNAM
HANOI
HAIPHONG
G. of Tonkin
Nanning
KUNMING
YUNNAN
Dali
Hengduan Shan
Shaluli Shan
Ningjing Shan
SICHUAN
CHENGDU
Leshan
ZIGONG
CHONGQING
GUIYANG
GUIZHOU
TIANSHUI
Baoji
Hanzhong
MIANYANG
NANCHONG
Xichang
Projection: Bonne
East from Greenwich

301
312
310

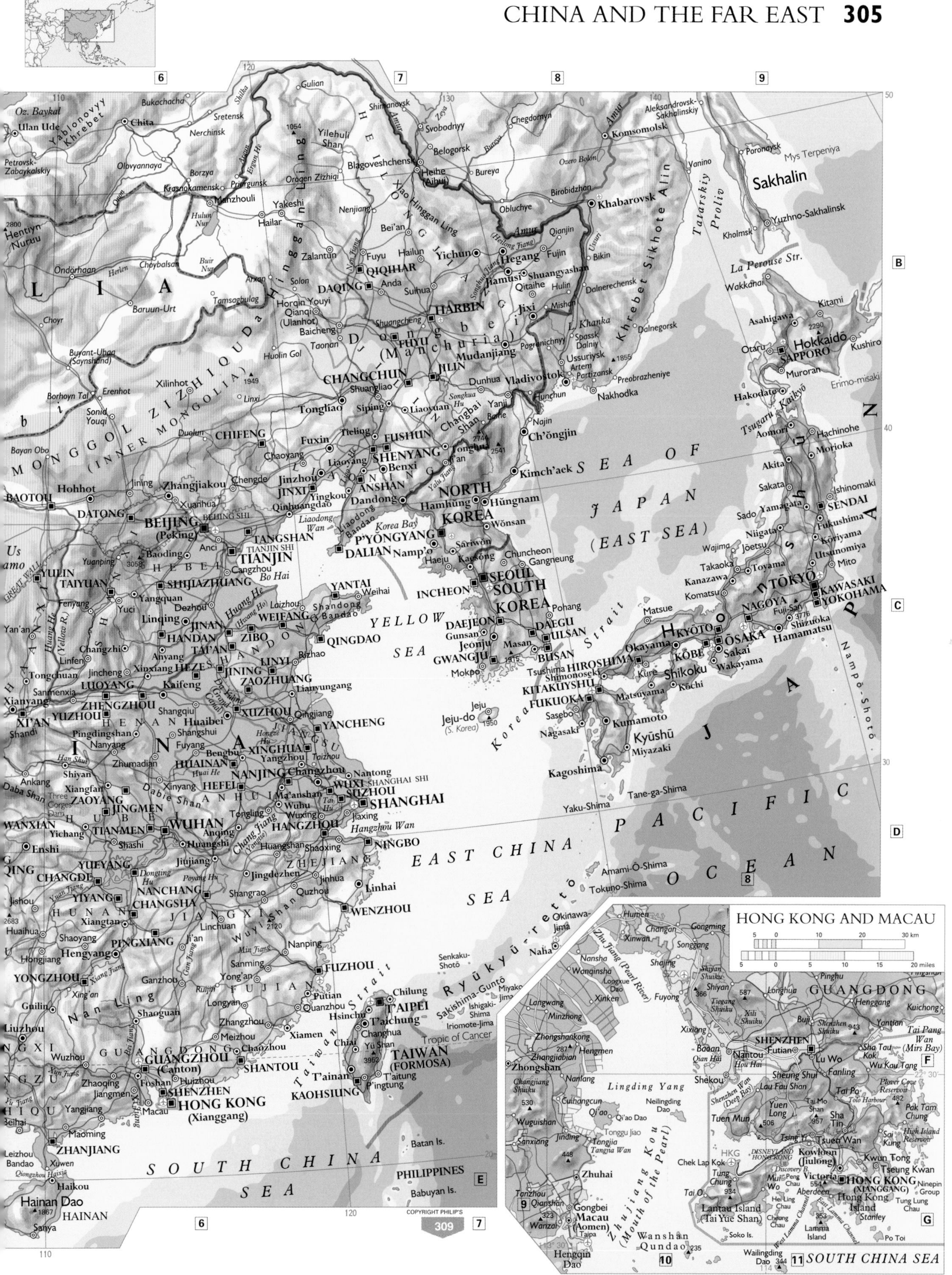
HONG KONG AND MACAU
COPYRIGHT PHILIP'S
309

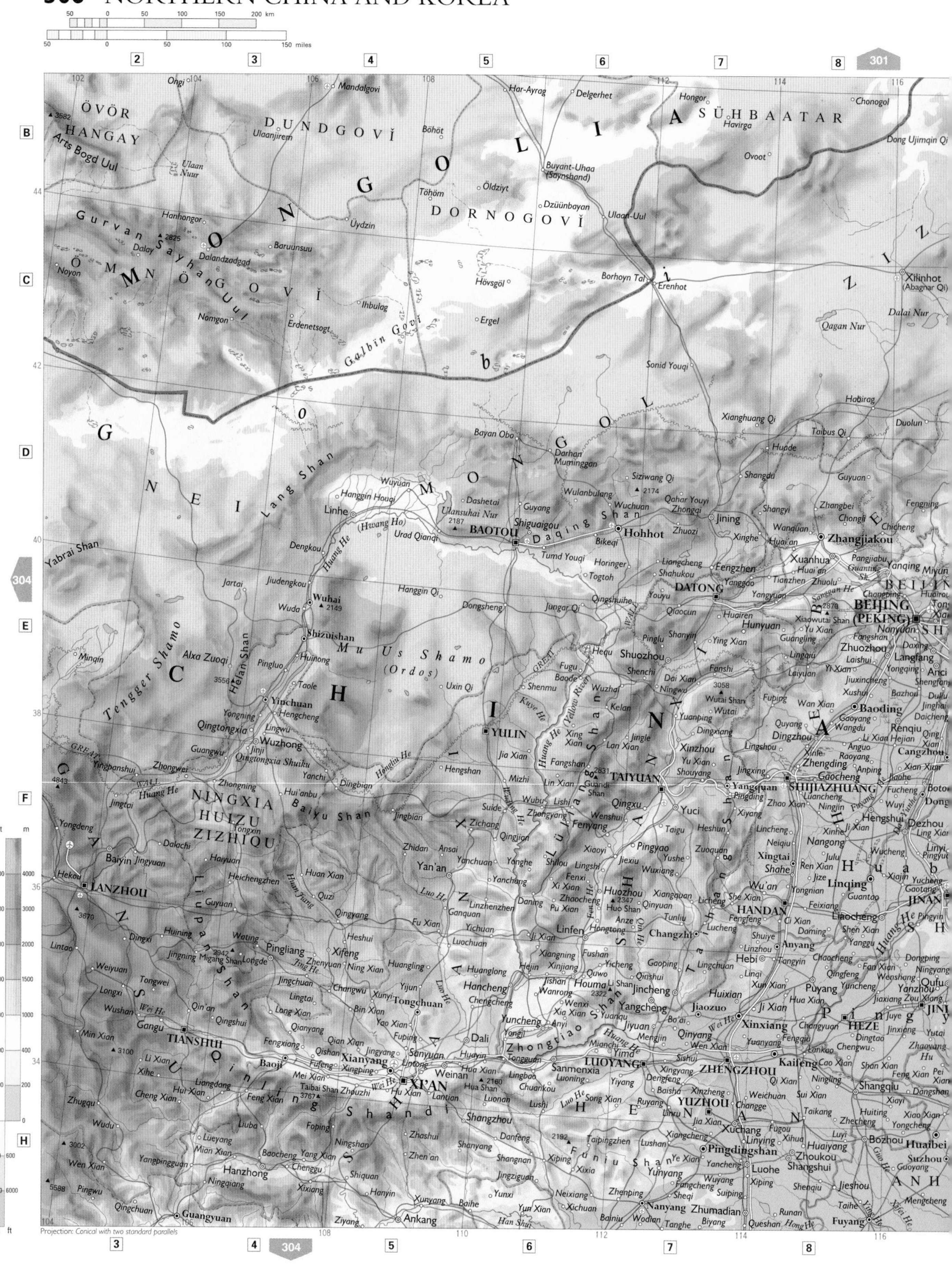
50 0 50 100 150 200 km
50 0 50 100 150 miles
2
3
4
5
6
7
8
301
304
B
C
D
E
F
H
ÖVÖR HANGAY
Arts Bogd Uul
Ongi
Mandalgovi
DUNDGOVĬ
Ulaanjirem
Böhöt
Har-Ayrag
Delgerhet
Hongor
SÜHBAATAR
Havirga
Chonogol
Dong Ujimqin Qi
Ovoot
Buyant-Uhaa (Saynshand)
Ulaan Nuur
MONGOLIA
Töhöm
Öldziyt
Dzüünbayan
DORNOGOVĬ
Ulaan-Uul
Hanhongor
Üydzin
Gurvan Sayhan Uul
Dalay
Dalandzadgad
Baruunsuu
ÖMNÖGOVĬ
Noyon
Hövsgöl
Borhoyn Tal
Erenhot
Xilinhot (Abagnar Qi)
Ihbulag
Nomgon
Erdenetsogt
Galbin Govi
Ergel
Dalai Nur
Qagan Nur
Sonid Youqi
Gobi
Habirag
Xianghuang Qi
Duolun
Taibus Qi
Bayan Obo
Darhan Muminggan
Huade
NEI MONGOL
Lang Shan
Siziwang Qi
Shangdu
Guyuan
Wuyuan
Hanggin Houqi
Dashetai
Guyang
Wulanbulang
Qahar Youyi Zhongqi
Wuchuan
Shangyi
Zhangbei
Fengning
Ulansuhai Nur
Linhe
2187
BAOTOU
Shiguaigou
Daqing Shan
Hohhot
Jining
Chongli
Chicheng
Urad Qianqi
Huang He (Hwang Ho)
Dengkou
Tumd Youqi
Bikeqi
Zhuozi
Xinghe
Wanquan
Huai'an
Zhangjiakou
Yabrai Shan
Horinger
Liangcheng
Shahukou
Fengzhen
Xuanhua
Togtoh
DATONG
Yanggao
Tianzhen
Yanqing
BEIJING (PEKING)
Jartai
Jiudengkou
Wuhai
2149
Wuda
Hanggin Qi
Dongsheng
Jungar Qi
Qingshuihe
Youyu
Huairen
Hunyuan
Qiaocun
Shizuishan
Huinong
Pingluo
Helan Shan
Mu Us Shamo (Ordos)
Tengger Shamo
Alxa Zuoqi
Minqin
CHINA
3556
Taole
Uxin Qi
Yinchuan
Hengcheng
Yongning
Qingtongxia
Lingwu
Wuzhong
Guangwu
Jinji
Qingtongxia Shuiku
Yingpanshui
Zhongwei
Zhongning
Yanchi
Dingbian
Hengshan
Jingtai
Huang He
NINGXIA HUIZU ZIZHIQU
Hui'anbu
Baiyu Shan
Jingbian
Tongxin
YULIN
Jia Xian
Mizhi
Suide
Zichang
Qingjian
Yongdeng
Dalachi
Baiyin
Jingyuan
Haiyuan
Heichengzhen
Hekou
LANZHOU
3670
Huan Xian
Quzi
Liupan Shan
Guyuan
Qingyang
Heshui
Zhidan
Ansai
Yan'an
Yanchuan
Yanhe
Yanchang
Huining
Dingxi
Lintao
Jingning
Migang Shan
2942
Longde
Pingliang
Xifeng
Jing He
Zhenyuan
Ning Xian
Huangling
Weiyuan
Tongwei
Longxi
Wei He
Wushan
Gangu
Qin'an
Qingshui
Jingchuan
Changwu
Lingtai
Long Xian
Xunyi
Yijun
Tongchuan
Bin Xian
Yao Xian
Fuping
Luo He
Huanglong
Hancheng
Chengcheng
TIANSHUI
Min Xian
3100
Li Xian
Xihe
Baoji
Fengxiang
Qishan
Fufeng
Qian Xian
Jingyang
Sanyuan
Xianyang
Xingping
Lintong
XI'AN
Weinan
Hua Xian
Huayin
Dali
Mei Xian
Zhouzhi
Taibai Shan
3767
Qinling Shandi
Hu Xian
Lantian
2160
Hua Shan
Luonan
Shangzhou
Liangdang
Hui Xian
Cheng Xian
Feng Xian
Zhugqu
Wudu
Liuba
Foping
Ningshan
Zhashui
Danfeng
Lüeyang
Mian Xian
Baocheng
Yang Xian
Chenggu
Hanzhong
Yangpingguan
Wen Xian
Ningqiang
Xixiang
Shiquan
Zhen'an
Shanyang
3002
5588
Pingwu
Qingchuan
Guangyuan
Hanyin
Xunyang
Baihe
Yunxi
Ziyang
Ankang
Han Shui
Yun Xian
Xichuan
Shangnan
Xixia
Jingziguan
Neixiang
Zhenping
Nanyang
Zhumadian
Funiu Shan
SHAANXI
Lüliang Shan
Taihang Shan
SHANXI
HEBEI
HENAN
Wutai Shan
3058
Wutai
Fugu
Baode
Shenmu
Kuye He
Huang He (Yellow River)
Wuzhai
Kelan
Xing Xian
Lan Xian
Jingle
Fangshan
2831
TAIYUAN
Lin Xian
Lishi
Zhongyang
Fenyang
Wenshui
Qingxu
Yuci
Pingyao
Jiexiu
Xiaoyi
Shilou
Lingshi
Fenxi
Xi Xian
Huozhou
2347
Huo Shan
Daning
Pu Xian
Zhaocheng
Linfen
Hongtong
Anze
Changzhi
Ji Xian
Xiangning
Fushan
Hejin
Xinjiang
Houma
Jishan
Wanrong
Wenxi
Yuncheng
Xia Xian
Yangcheng
Jincheng
Zhongtiao Shan
Sanmenxia
Lingbao
Luoning
LUOYANG
Yiyang
Dengfeng
ZHENGZHOU
Kaifeng
Xinzheng
YUZHOU
Pingdingshan
Ye Xian
Xuchang
Luohe
Zhoukou
Shangshui
Xiping
Jieshou
Fuyang
Huaibei
Bozhou
Suzhou
Shangqiu
Dangshan
Xuanwu
Heze
Puyang
Anyang
Hebi
Xinxiang
Jiaozuo
Ji Xian
HANDAN
Xingtai
Shahe
Nangong
Linqing
Guantao
Liaocheng
JINAN
Dezhou
Hengshui
Shijiazhuang
Xinji
Gaocheng
Yangquan
Pingding
Xinzhou
Dingxiang
Yuanping
Dai Xian
Ningwu
Shenchi
Shuozhou
Pinglu
Shanyin
Ying Xian
Hequ
Lingqiu
Laiyuan
Fanshi
Fuping
Wan Xian
Baoding
Quyang
Dingzhou
Anguo
Xian Xian
Cangzhou
Renqiu
Hejian
Zhuozhou
Laishui
Yi Xian
Langfang
Daxing
Fangshan
Guangling
Yu Xian
Xiaowutai Shan
2870
Zhangjiakou
Changping
Huairou
Miyun
Xushui
Gaoyang
Wangdu
Raoyang
Shenze
Wuji
Xinle
Zhengding
Jingxing
Shouyang
Heshun
Zuoquan
Xiyang
Taigu
Yushe
Wuxiang
Qinyuan
Xiangyuan
Licheng
She Xian
Wu'an
Cixian
Linzhou
Tangyin
Qingfeng
Fan Xian
Yuncheng
Juye
Jinxiang
Chengwu
Dingtao
Cao Xian
Shan Xian
Lankao
Yucheng
Sui Xian
Taikang
Luyi
Zhecheng
Huaiyang
Xiangcheng
Shenqiu
Yicheng
Xinyang
Huiting
Biyang
Tanghe
Queshan
Runan
Xiping
Wugang
Tongbai
Fangcheng
Sheqi
Yunyang
Lushan
Baofeng
Lushi
Luo He
Changge
Weichuan
Tongxu
Yuanyang
Wen Xian
Mengjin
Yima
Mianchi
Jiyuan
Qinyang
Wei He
Hua Xian
Changyuan
Song Xian
Ruyang
Ruzhou
Linru
Jia Xian
Yuzhou
Fugou
Xihua
Wuyang
Suiping
Wuhua
Projection: Conical with two standard parallels
ft m
12 000 4000
9000 3000
6000 2000
4500 1500
3000 1000
1200 400
600 200
0 0
200 600
2000 6000
m ft
102
104
106
108
110
112
114
116
44
42
40
38
36
34

HARBIN
CHANGCHUN
JILIN
SHENYANG
FUSHUN
ANSHAN
DALIAN
(Lüda)
TIANJIN
TIANJIN SHI
TANGSHAN
QINGDAO
YANTAI
WEIFANG
ZIBO
XUZHOU
HUAI'AN
YANCHENG
LINYI
ZAOZHUANG
XINTAI
CHIFENG
JINXI
FUYU
P'YŎNGYANG
SEOUL
SEONGNAM
INCHEON
SUWON
DAEJEON
DAEGU
BUSAN
ULSAN
GWANGJU
NORTH KOREA
SOUTH KOREA
RUSSIA
JAPAN
HEILONGJIANG
JILIN
LIAONING
SHANDONG
Vladivostok
Ussuriysk
Hunchun
Mudanjiang
Dandong
Sinŭiju
Hamhŭng
Ch'ŏngjin
Kaesŏng
Haeju
Nampo
Pohang
Gyeongju
Jeonju
Mokpo
Yeosu
Jeju
Jeju-do (S. Korea)
Tsushima (Japan)
Sasebo
Nagasaki
Qinhuangdao
Weihai
Rizhao
Lianyungang
Liaodong Wan
Liaodong Bandao
Shandong Bandao
Laizhou Wan
Bo Hai
Korea Bay
YELLOW SEA
(Huang Hai)
SEA OF JAPAN
(EAST SEA)
Tongjosŏn Man
Korea Strait
Changbai Shan
Paektu-san
Manchuria
Zhangguangcai Ling
Lake Khanka
Ulleungdo (S. Korea)
Baengnyeongdo (S. Korea)
Heuksando (S. Korea)
East from Greenwich

BURMA (MYANMAR)
RANGOON (Yangon)
THAILAND
BANGKOK
LAOS
VIETNAM
CAMBODIA
PHNOM PENH
THANH PHO HO CHI MINH
ANDAMAN SEA
SOUTH CHINA SEA
Gulf of Thailand
Malay Pen.
Straits of Malacca
MALAYSIA
PENINSULAR MALAYSIA
KUALA LUMPUR
SINGAPORE
BRUNEI
SARAWAK
SABAH
Kalimantan (Borneo)
INDONESIA
Sumatera
JAKARTA
Jawa (Java)
JAVA SEA
Greater Sunda Islands
INDIAN OCEAN
Java Trench
Spratly Is.
Paracel Is.
Projection: Mercator
East from Greenwich

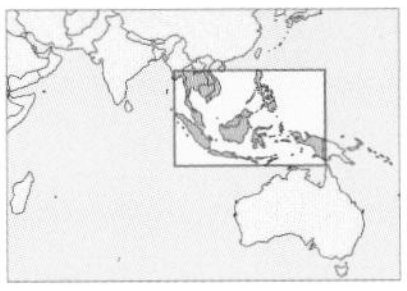

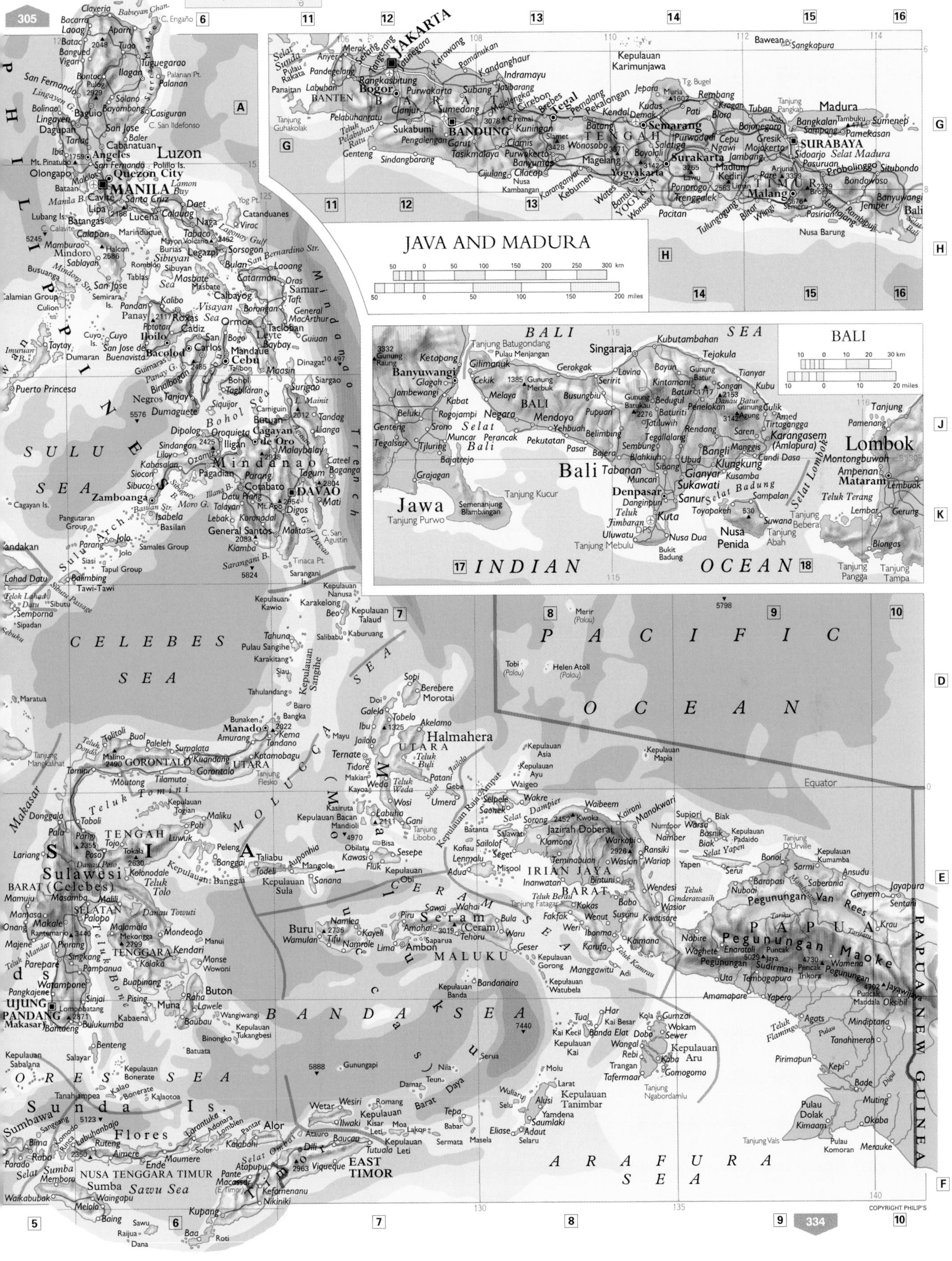

JAVA AND MADURA

BALI

305

334

BURMA
(MYANMAR)
THAILAND
LAOS
CAMBODIA
YUNNAN
GUANGXI ZHUANGZU ZIZHIQU
GUANGDONG
HAINAN
Hainan Dao
G. of Tonkin
G. of Martaban
ANDAMAN SEA
TENASSERIM
Dawna Range
Bilauk Taungdan
Tanen Tong Dan
Phnom Dangrek
Cao Nguyen Khorat
Chaine Annamitique
Mekong
Hanoi
Haiphong
Vientiane (Viangchan)
Bangkok
Rangoon (Yangon)
Mandalay
Luang Prabang
Chiang Mai
Nakhon Ratchasima
Da Nang
Hue
Nanning
Zhanjiang
Haikou
Moulmein
Pegu
Tavoy
Ubon Ratchathani
Battambang
Kompong Thom
304
313

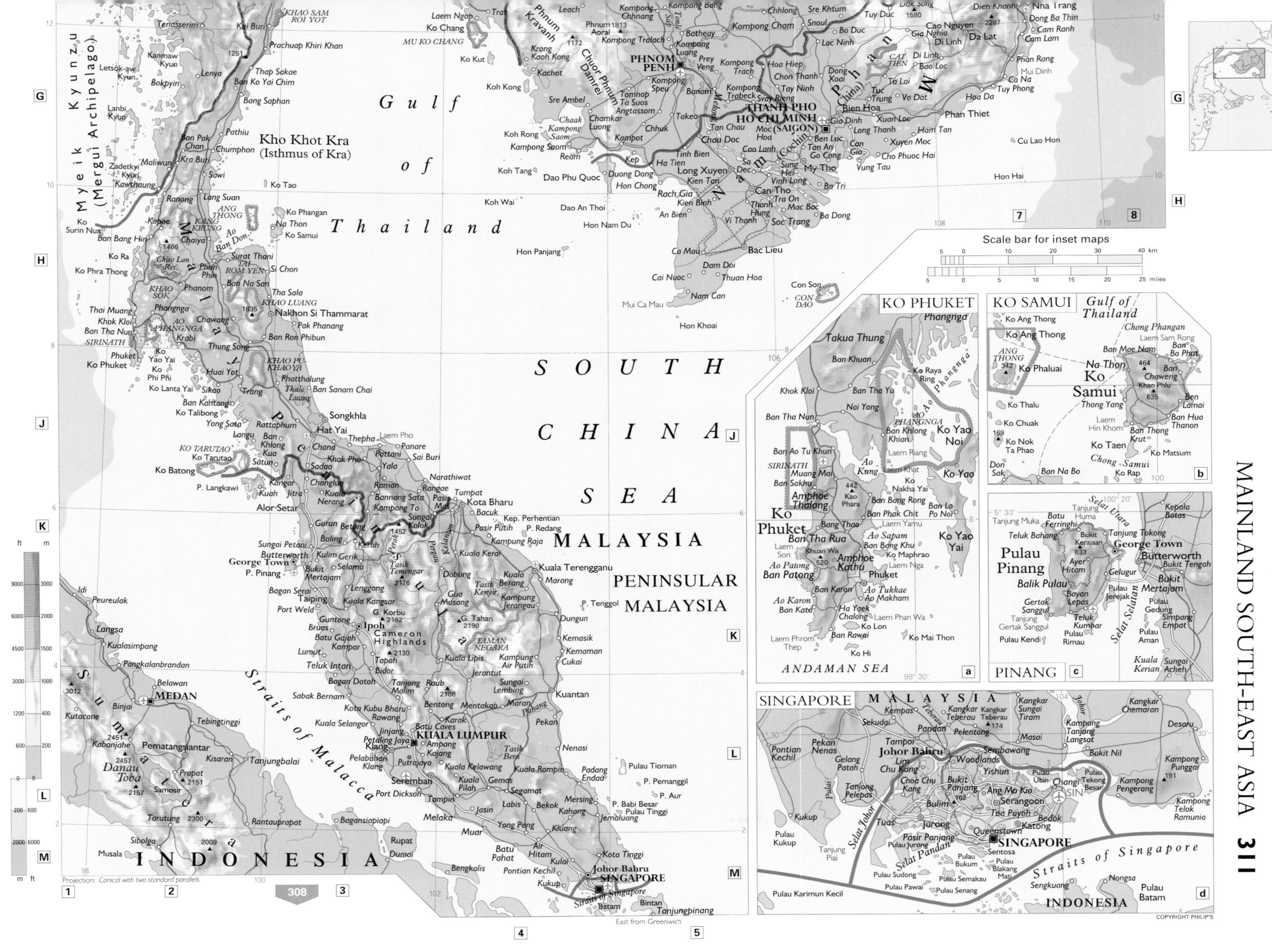

Gulf of Thailand
SOUTH CHINA SEA
MALAYSIA
PENINSULAR MALAYSIA
INDONESIA
Straits of Malacca
Myeik Kyunzu (Mergui Archipelago)
Kho Khot Kra (Isthmus of Kra)
PHNOM PENH
THANH PHO HO CHI MINH (SAIGON)
KUALA LUMPUR
SINGAPORE
MEDAN
Scale bar for inset maps
KO PHUKET
ANDAMAN SEA
KO SAMUI
Gulf of Thailand
PINANG
SINGAPORE
Straits of Singapore
Projection: Conical with two standard parallels
East from Greenwich
COPYRIGHT PHILIP'S
308

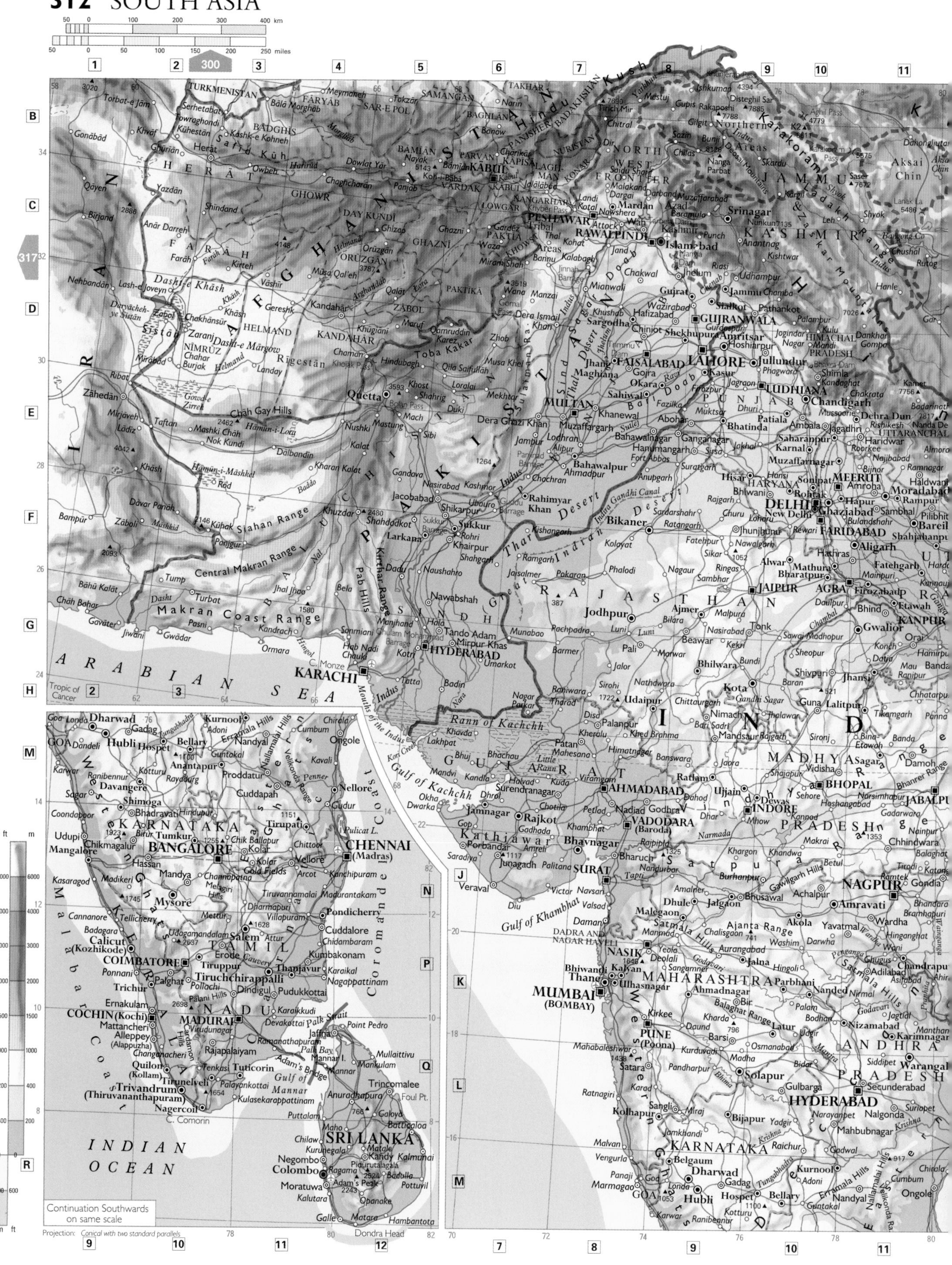

50 0 100 200 300 400 km
50 0 50 100 150 200 250 miles
300
317
TURKMENISTAN
IRAN
AFGHANISTAN
PAKISTAN
INDIA
SRI LANKA
ARABIAN SEA
INDIAN OCEAN
Gulf of Kachchh
Gulf of Khambhat
Gulf of Mannar
Palk Strait
Hindu Kush
Karakoram Range
Northern Areas
NORTH WEST FRONTIER
JAMMU & KASHMIR
Aksai Chin
PUNJAB
HARYANA
HIMACHAL PRADESH
UTTARANCHAL
RAJASTHAN
GUJARAT
MADHYA PRADESH
MAHARASHTRA
ANDHRA PRADESH
KARNATAKA
TAMIL NADU
KERALA
BALUCHISTAN
SINDH
Thar Desert
Great Indian Desert
Rann of Kachchh
Makran Coast Range
Central Makran Range
Siahan Range
Chagai Hills
Rigestan
Dasht-e Khash
Dasht-e Margow
Western Ghats
Eastern Ghats
Satpura Range
Coromandel Coast
Malabar Coast
Kathiawar
KABUL
Herat
Kandahar
Quetta
PESHAWAR
RAWALPINDI
Islamabad
FAISALABAD
LAHORE
MULTAN
HYDERABAD
KARACHI
Srinagar
Amritsar
LUDHIANA
Chandigarh
DELHI
New Delhi
MEERUT
FARIDABAD
JAIPUR
AGRA
KANPUR
Jodhpur
AHMADABAD
VADODARA (Baroda)
SURAT
Rajkot
INDORE
BHOPAL
JABALPUR
NAGPUR
NASIK
MUMBAI (BOMBAY)
PUNE (Poona)
HYDERABAD
BANGALORE
CHENNAI (Madras)
COIMBATORE
MADURAI
COCHIN (Kochi)
Trivandrum (Thiruvananthapuram)
Mysore
Pondicherry
Colombo
Jaffna
Trincomalee
Kandy
C. Comorin
Dondra Head
Tropic of Cancer
Continuation Southwards on same scale
Projection: Conical with two standard parallels
ft m
18 000 6000
12 000 4000
9000 3000
6000 2000
4500 1500
3000 1000
1200 400
600 200
0 0
200 600
m ft

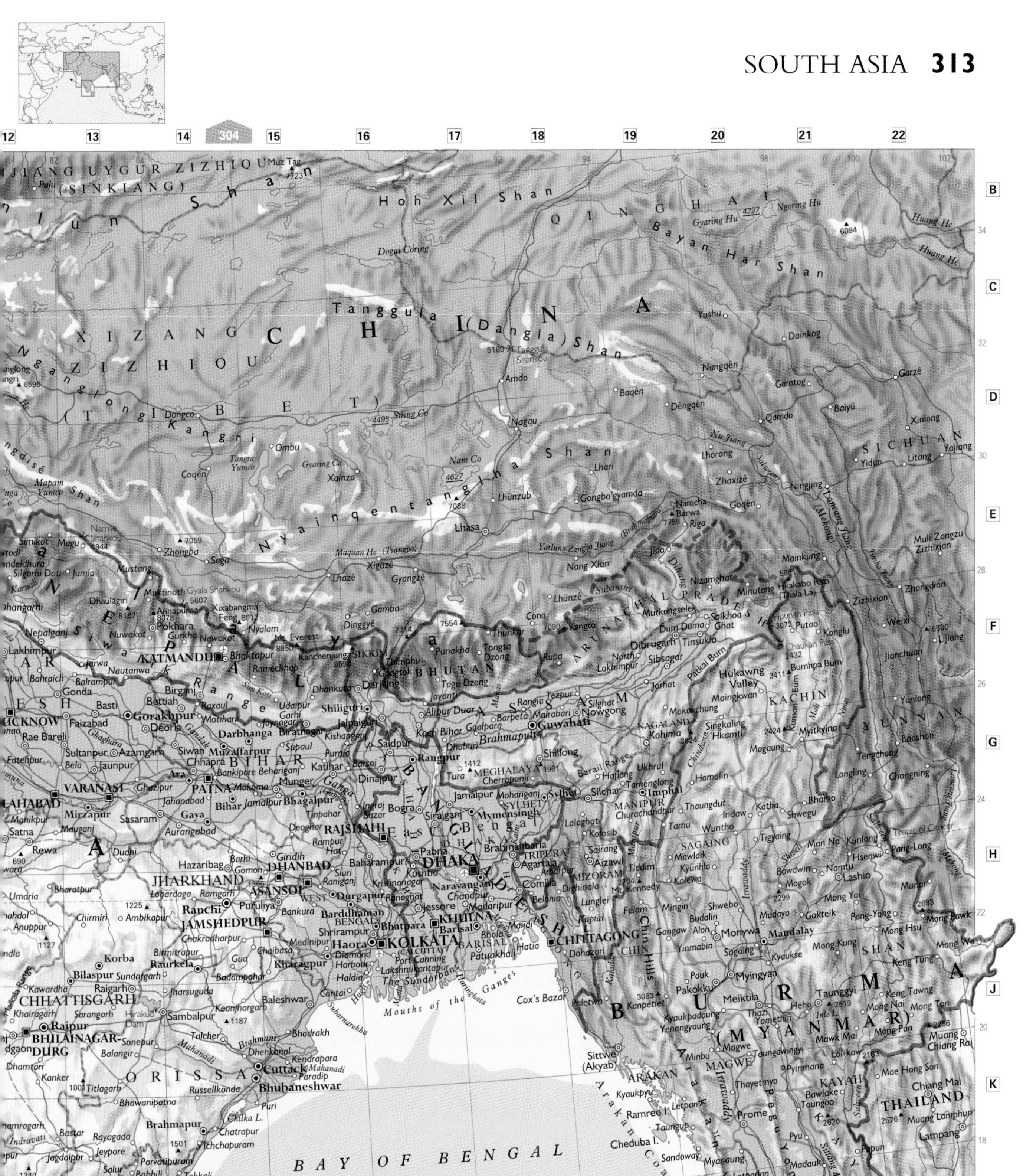
XIZANG ZIZHIQU (TIBET)
CHINA
QINGHAI
SICHUAN
YUNNAN
Hoh Xil Shan
Bayan Har Shan
Tanggula (Dangla) Shan
Nyainqentanglha Shan
Gangdisê Shan
Muz Tag 7723
Dogai Coring
Gyaring Hu
Ngoring Hu
Huang He
Yushu
Dainkog
Nangqên
Garzê
Amdo
Baqên
Dêngqên
Nagqu
Qamdo
Siling Co
Nam Co
Ombu
Xainza
Coqên
Lhünzub
Lhasa
Xigazê
Gyangzê
Lhazê
Saga
Zhongba
Gongbo'gyamda
Namcha Barwa 7756
Riga
Nu Jiang
Lhorong
Zhaxizê
Ningjing
Lancang Jiang (Mekong)
Jinsha Jiang
Yidun
Litang
Xinlong
Yajiang
Muli Zangzu Zizhixian
Zhongdian
Weixi
Lijiang
Jianchuan
Yarlung Zangbo Jiang (Tsangpo)
Maquan He (Tsangpo)
Nang Xian
Mainkung
Zayü
NEPAL
KATMANDU
Mt. Everest 8850
Kanchenjunga 8598
Annapurna 8078
Dhaulagiri 8167
Pokhara
Nepalganj
Bhaktapur
Siwalik Range
SIKKIM
Gangtok
BHUTAN
Thimphu
Punakha
Tongsa Dzong
Taga Dzong
ARUNACHAL PRADESH
Dibrugarh
Tinsukia
Sibsagar
North Lakhimpur
Jorhat
ASSAM
Tezpur
Guwahati
Nowgong
Shillong
MEGHALAYA
Cherrapunji
NAGALAND
Kohima
MANIPUR
Imphal
Silchar
Haflong
MIZORAM
Aizawl
TRIPURA
Agartala
BANGLADESH
DHAKA
Rangpur
Dinajpur
Bogra
RAJSHAHI
Pabna
Mymensingh
Sylhet
Comilla
Narayanganj
Chandpur
Jessore
KHULNA
Barisal
Bhola
Patuakhali
CHITTAGONG
Cox's Bazar
KOLKATA (CALCUTTA)
Haora
Bhatpara
Barddhaman
Asansol
Durgapur
Kharagpur
Haldia
The Sundarbans
Mouths of the Ganges
BIHAR
PATNA
Gaya
Bhagalpur
Munger
Darbhanga
Muzaffarpur
Chhapra
Purnia
Katihar
JHARKHAND
DHANBAD
Ranchi
Hazaribag
JAMSHEDPUR
Bokaro
ORISSA
Cuttack
Bhubaneshwar
Puri
Sambalpur
Raurkela
Baleshwar
Brahmapur
Chilka L.
CHHATTISGARH
Raipur
BHILAINAGAR-DURG
Bilaspur
Korba
UTTAR PRADESH
VARANASI
ALLAHABAD
LUCKNOW
Gorakhpur
Faizabad
Rae Bareli
Sultanpur
Azamgarh
Jaunpur
Mirzapur
Rewa
Satna
Northern Circars
Eastern Ghats
VISHAKHAPATNAM
Vizianagaram
Srikakulam
Kakinada
Vijayawada
Machilipatnam
Godavari Point
BAY OF BENGAL
INDIAN OCEAN
BURMA (MYANMAR)
KACHIN
Myitkyina
Bhamo
Putao
Hukawng Valley
SAGAING
Mandalay
Monywa
Shwebo
Sagaing
Myingyan
Meiktila
Pakokku
Magwe
MAGWE
Minbu
Taunggyi
SHAN
Lashio
Hsenwi
Kengtung
Chin Hills
Kalemyo
Mt. Kennedy
Sittwe (Akyab)
ARAKAN
Arakan Coast
Arakan Yoma
Pegu Yoma
Kyaukpyu
Ramree I.
Cheduba I.
Sandoway
Prome
Thayetmyo
Pyinmana
Toungoo
KAYAH
KAYIN
Irrawaddy
Sittang
Salween
Bassein
Henzada
RANGOON
PEGU
Pegu
IRRAWADDY
Myaungmya
Maubin
Pyapon
Mouths of the Irrawaddy
G. of Martaban
Martaban
Moulmein
MON
Thaton
Amherst
Ye
Tavoy
Dawna Range
Preparis North Channel
Preparis South Channel
Pariparit Kyun (Burma)
Koko Kyunzu (Burma)
Moscos Is.
THAILAND
Chiang Mai
Chiang Rai
Lampang
Tak
Tropic of Cancer
East from Greenwich
COPYRIGHT PHILIP'S

304
310
311

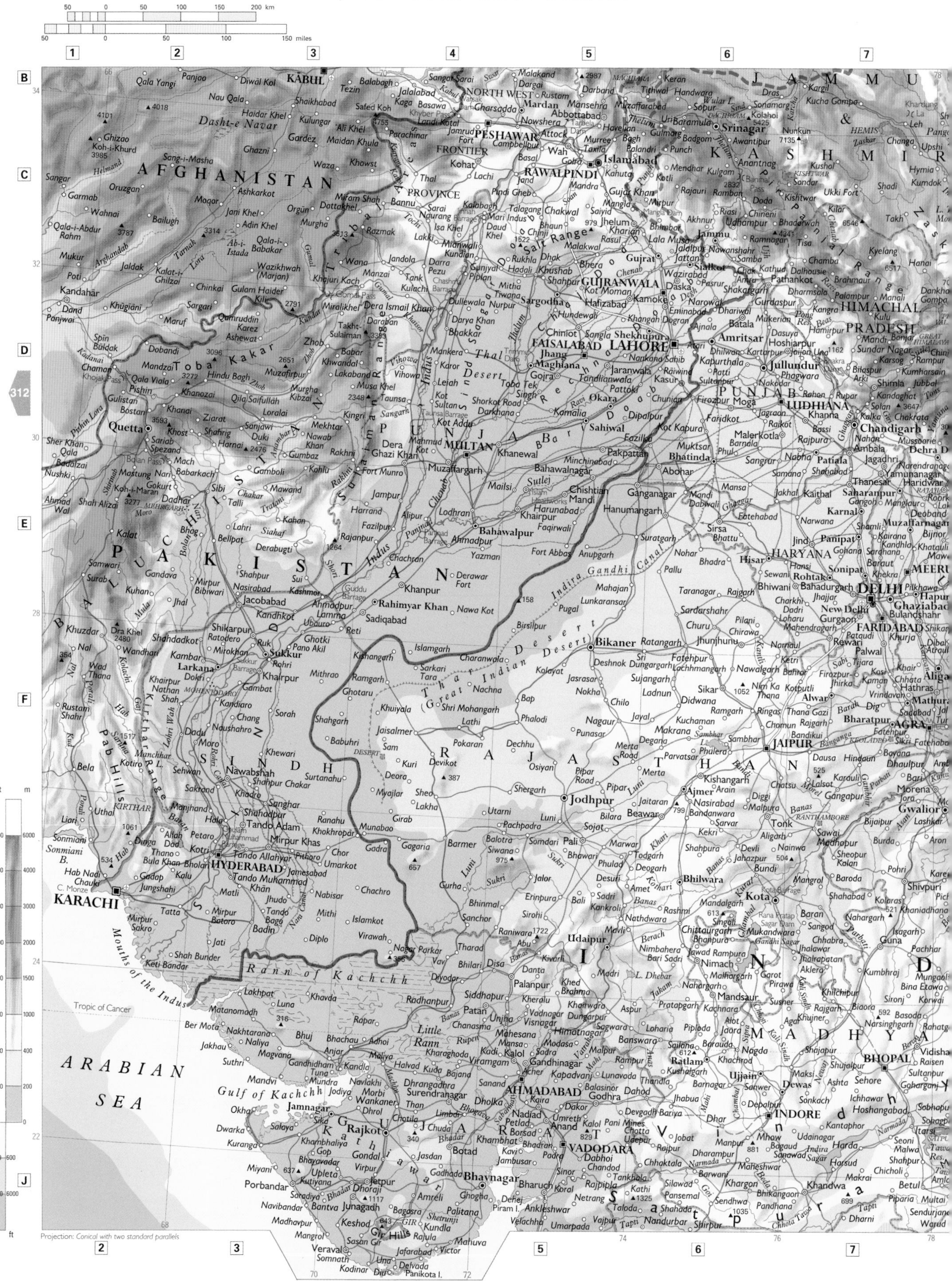
50 0 50 100 150 200 km
50 0 50 100 150 miles
AFGHANISTAN
PAKISTAN
BALUCHISTAN
NORTH WEST FRONTIER PROVINCE
PUNJAB
SINDH
JAMMU & KASHMIR
HIMACHAL PRADESH
HARYANA
RAJASTHAN
GUJARAT
MADHYA
INDIA
KABUL
PESHAWAR
Islamabad
RAWALPINDI
GUJRANWALA
FAISALABAD
LAHORE
Srinagar
Amritsar
Jullundur
LUDHIANA
Chandigarh
MULTAN
Quetta
Kandahār
Bahawalpur
Sukkur
HYDERABAD
KARACHI
Bikaner
Jodhpur
JAIPUR
DELHI
AGRA
Gwalior
Ajmer
Udaipur
AHMADABAD
VADODARA
INDORE
BHOPAL
Rajkot
Bhavnagar
Jamnagar
Thar Desert (Great Indian Desert)
Indira Gandhi Canal
Rann of Kachchh
Gulf of Kachchh
Mouths of the Indus
Tropic of Cancer
ARABIAN SEA
Salt Range
Toba Kakar
Kirthar Range
Sulaiman Range
Pab Hills
Dasht-e Navar
Thal Desert
Indus
Chenab
Jhelum
Sutlej
Ravi
Tropic of Cancer
312
Projection: Conical with two standard parallels

JAMMU AND KASHMIR
on same scale
AFGHANISTAN
CHINA
NORTH WEST FRONTIER
JAMMU AND KASHMIR
PUNJAB
HIMACHAL PRADESH
Islamabad
RAWALPINDI
Srinagar
Karakoram Range
Aksai Chin
Kunlun Shan
XIZANG ZIZHIQU (TIBET)
UTTARANCHAL
NEPAL
KATMANDU
Mt. Everest (Chomolungma or Sagarmatha) 8850
SIKKIM
BHUTAN
ASSAM
BANGLADESH
DHAKA
UTTAR PRADESH
LUCKNOW
KANPUR
ALLAHABAD
VARANASI
PATNA
BIHAR
JHARKHAND
WEST BENGAL
KOLKATA
CHHATTISGARH
MADHYA PRADESH
JABALPUR
Mouths of the Ganges
The Sandheads
East from Greenwich
COPYRIGHT PHILIP'S

304
313
312

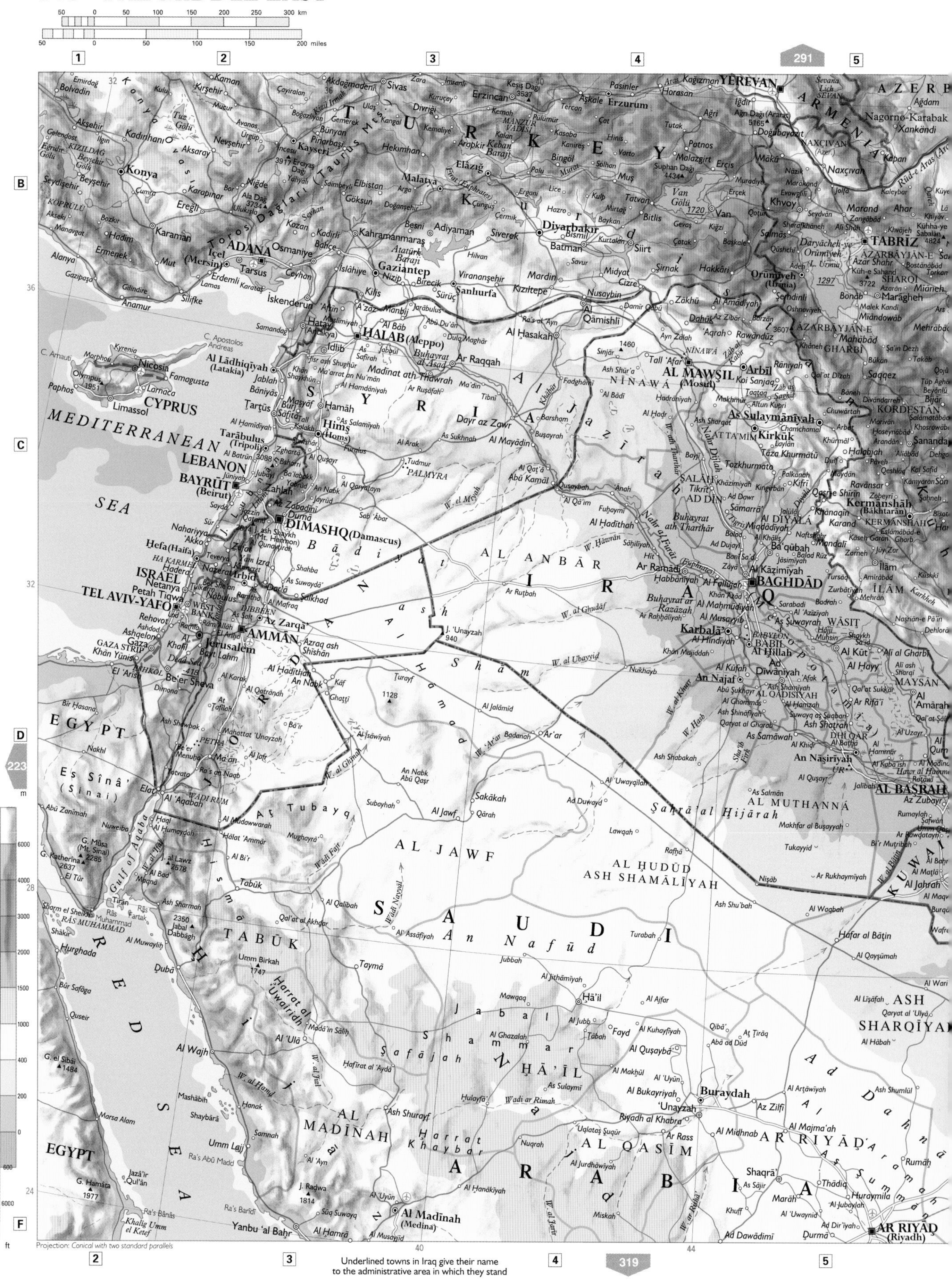

Underlined towns in Iraq give their name to the administrative area in which they stand

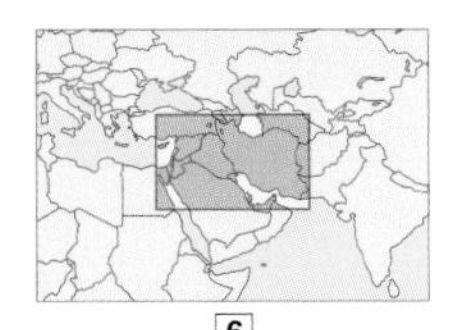

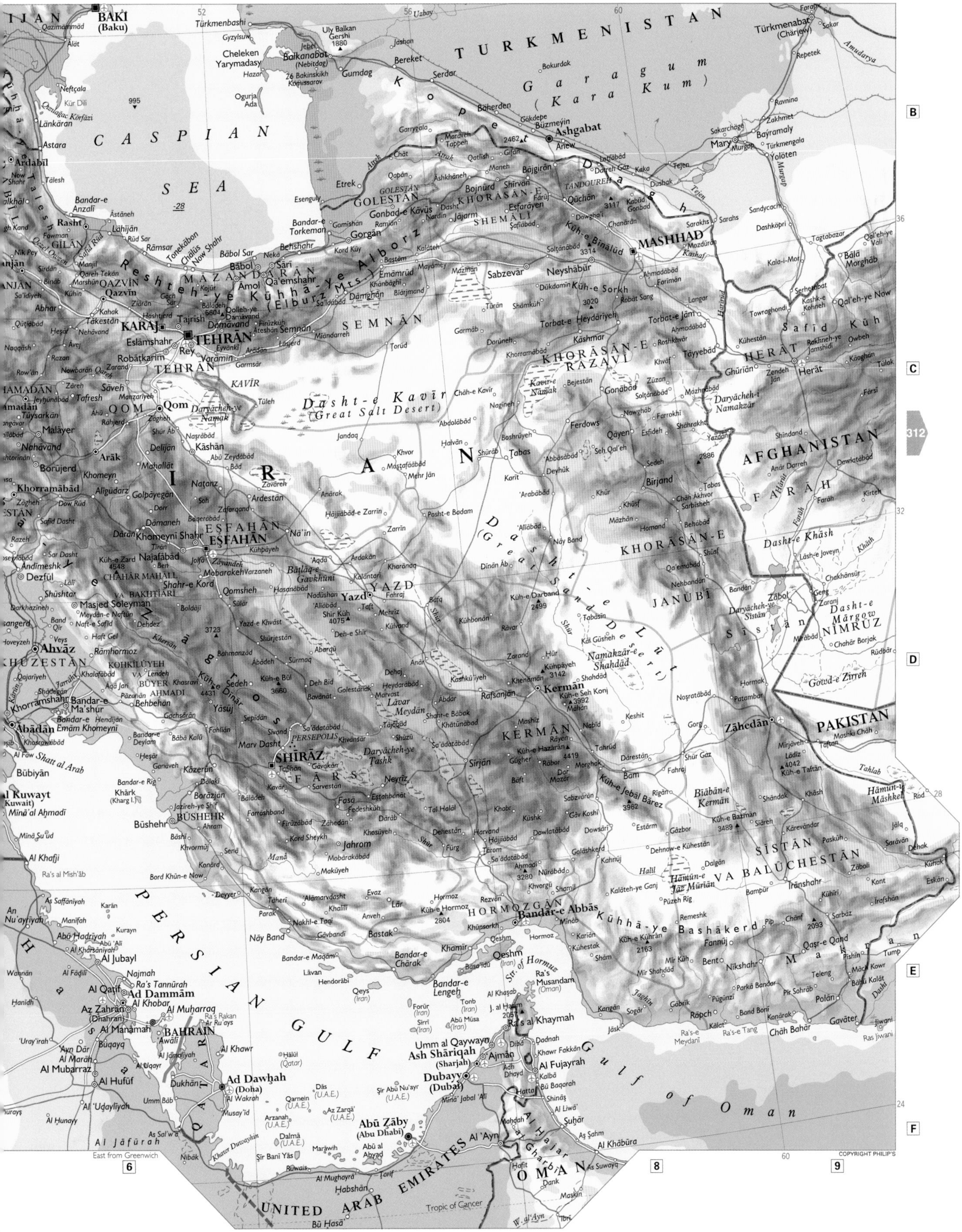

6 7 8 300 9 10

TURKMENISTAN
Garagum (Kara Kum)
Kopet Dagh
CASPIAN SEA
Baki (Baku)
Türkmenbashi
Balkanabat (Nebitdag)
Ashgabat
Mary
Türkmenabat (Chärjew)
Amudarya
IRAN
TEHRĀN
Karaj
Qom
Esfahān
Shīrāz
Yazd
Kermān
Mashhad
Tabrīz
Ahvāz
Abādān
Zāhedān
Bandar-e Abbās
Reshteh-ye Kūhhā-ye Alborz (Elburz Mts.)
Dasht-e Kavīr (Great Salt Desert)
Dasht-e Lūt (Great Sand Desert)
Zagros
AFGHANISTAN
Herāt
PAKISTAN
PERSIAN GULF
Gulf of Oman
Str. of Hormuz
Al Kuwayt (Kuwait)
BAHRAIN
Al Manāmah
QATAR
Ad Dawḩah (Doha)
Ad Dammām
UNITED ARAB EMIRATES
Abū Z̧aby (Abu Dhabi)
Dubayy (Dubai)
Ash Shāriqah (Sharjah)
OMAN
Tropic of Cancer

B C D E F

East from Greenwich

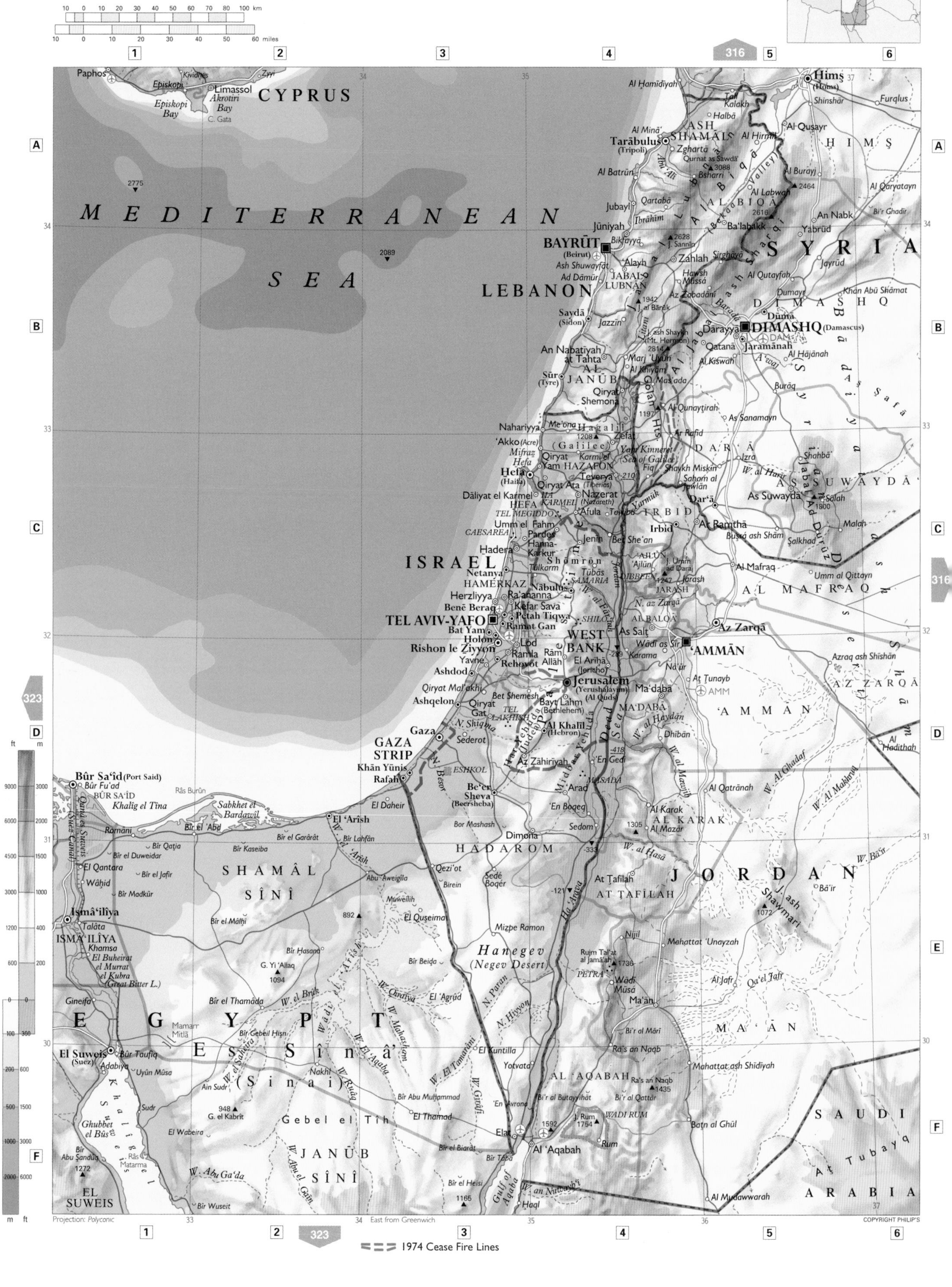

CYPRUS

MEDITERRANEAN SEA

LEBANON

SYRIA

ISRAEL

WEST BANK

GAZA STRIP

JORDAN

EGYPT

SAUDI ARABIA

Projection: Polyconic

East from Greenwich

1974 Cease Fire Lines

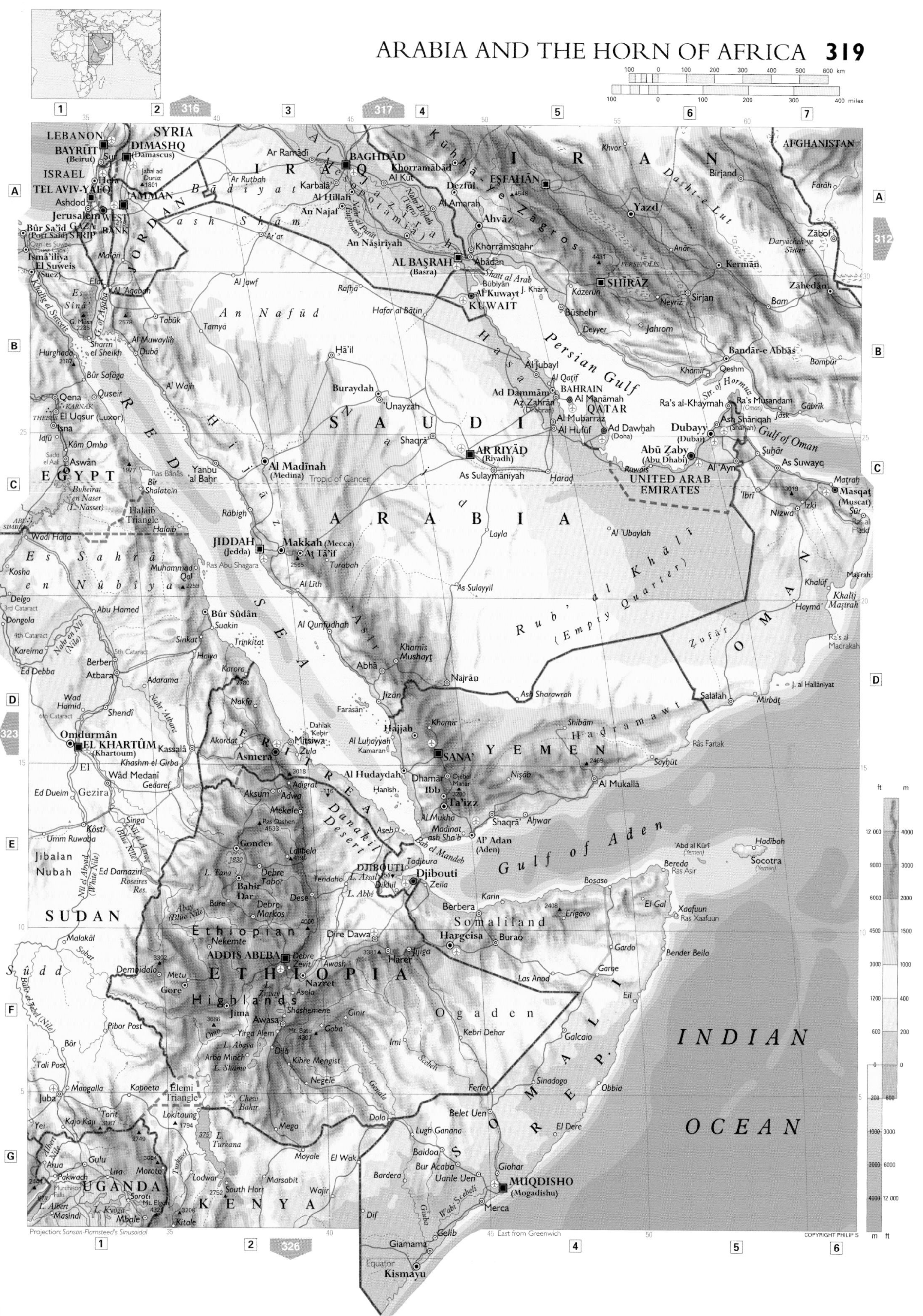

LEBANON
SYRIA
BAYRŪT (Beirut)
DIMASHQ (Damascus)
ISRAEL
TEL AVIV-YAFO
Ashdod
Jerusalem
WEST BANK
GAZA STRIP
'AMMĀN
JORDAN
Bûr Sa'îd (Port Said)
Ismâ'iliya
El Suweis (Suez)
Ar Ramādī
BAGHDĀD
I R A Q
Karbalā'
Al Ḩillah
An Najaf
Al Kūt
An Nāşirīyah
Ar Ruţbah
Bādiyat ash Shām
Ar'ar
AL BAŞRAH (Basra)
Al Kuwayt
KUWAIT
Khorramābād
Dezfūl
Ahvāz
Khorramshahr
Ābādān
EŞFAHĀN
I R A N
Yazd
Dasht-e Lut
Kūhhā-ye Zāgros
Kermān
SHĪRĀZ
Būshehr
Bandār-e Abbās
AFGHANISTAN
Birjand
Zābol
Zāhedān
Persian Gulf
Al Jubayl
Ad Dammām
BAHRAIN
Al Manāmah
QATAR
Ad Dawḩah (Doha)
Al Hufūf
Dubayy (Dubai)
Abū Ẓaby (Abu Dhabi)
UNITED ARAB EMIRATES
Str. of Hormuz
Gulf of Oman
Masqaţ (Muscat)
As Suwayq
S A U D I A R A B I A
AR RIYĀḐ (Riyadh)
An Nafūd
Ḩā'il
Buraydah
'Unayzah
Al Madīnah (Medina)
Tropic of Cancer
Yanbu 'al Baḩr
JIDDAH (Jedda)
Makkah (Mecca)
At Ţā'if
As Sulaymānīyah
Layla
As Sulayyil
Rub' al Khālī (Empty Quarter)
O M A N
Ẓufār
Şalālah
Najrān
Abhā
Jīzān
Y E M E N
SANA'
Ḩadramawt
Al Mukallā
Al Hudaydah
Ta'izz
Al 'Adan (Aden)
Gulf of Aden
Socotra
E G Y P T
Aswân
El Uqsur (Luxor)
Qena
Hurghada
Sharm el Sheikh
R E D S E A
Halaib Triangle
Wadi Halfa
Es Sahrâ en Nûbîya
Bûr Sûdân
Atbara
Omdurmân
EL KHARTÛM (Khartoum)
Kassalâ
Wad Medanî
Gezira
SUDAN
Malakâl
Sûdd
ERITREA
Asmera
Mitsiwa
Danakil Desert
DJIBOUTI
Djibouti
Bab el Mandeb
Gonder
L. Tana
Bahir Dar
Ethiopian Highlands
ADDIS ABEBA
ETHIOPIA
Dire Dawa
Harer
Hargeisa
Berbera
Somaliland
Ogaden
SOMALI REP.
MUQDISHO (Mogadishu)
Kismayu
Equator
INDIAN OCEAN
UGANDA
K E N Y A
L. Turkana
Elemi Triangle
Juba
Projection: Sanson-Flamsteed's Sinusoidal
East from Greenwich
COPYRIGHT PHILIP'S
316
317
312
323
326

Projection: Azimuthal Equidistant

West from Greenwich East from Greenwich

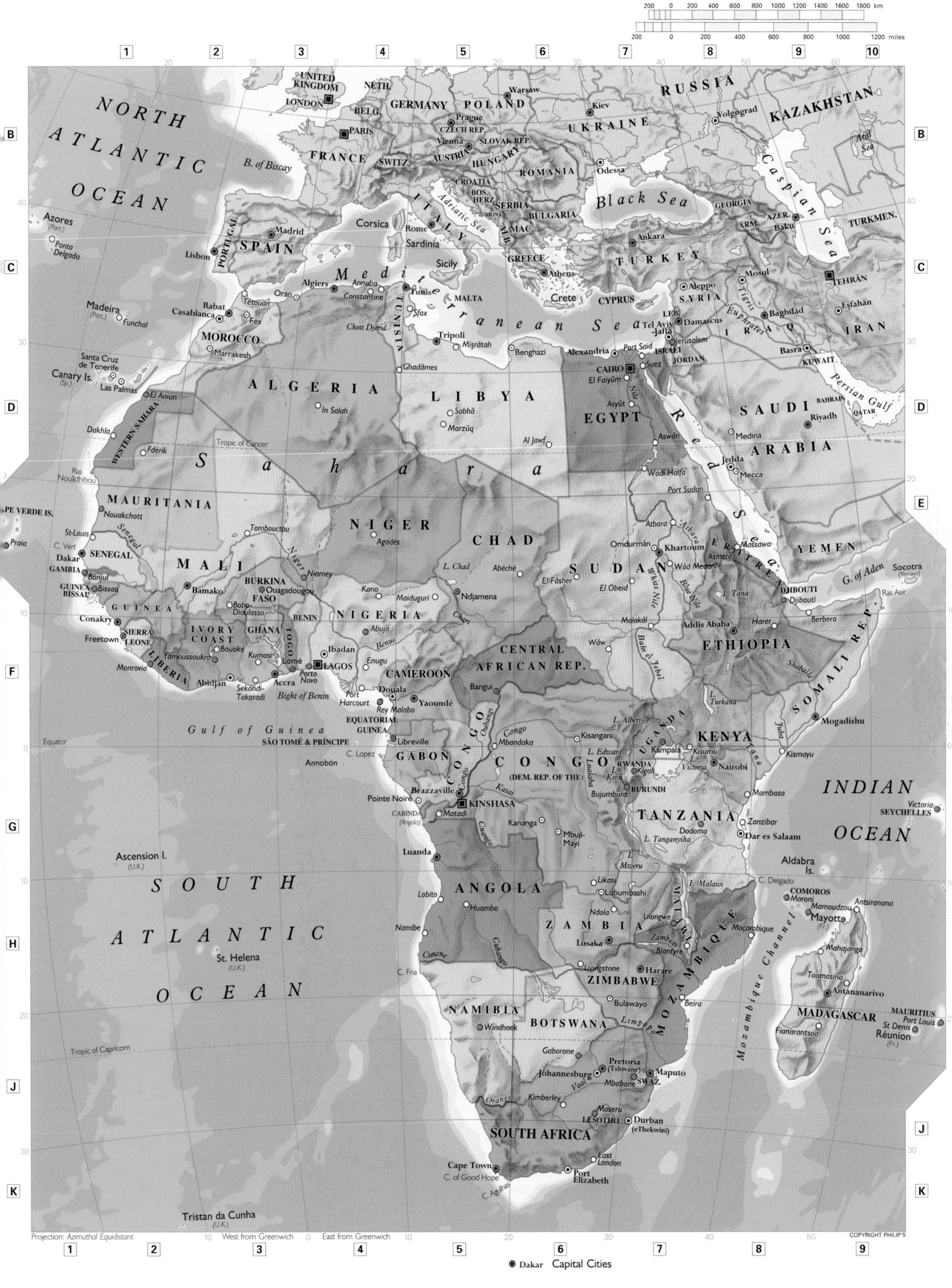

200 0 200 400 600 800 1000 1200 1400 1600 1800 km

200 0 200 400 600 800 1000 1200 miles

NORTH ATLANTIC OCEAN
Azores (Port.)
Ponta Delgada
Madeira (Port.)
Funchal
Santa Cruz de Tenerife
Canary Is. (Sp.)
Las Palmas
B. of Biscay
UNITED KINGDOM
LONDON
NETH.
BELG.
PARIS
FRANCE
GERMANY
POLAND
Warsaw
Prague
CZECH REP.
SLOVAK REP.
Vienna
AUSTRIA
SWITZ.
HUNGARY
ROMANIA
CROATIA
BOS.-HERZ.
SERBIA
MONT.
BULGARIA
ALB.
MAC.
GREECE
Athens
Crete
CYPRUS
ITALY
Rome
Corsica
Sardinia
Sicily
MALTA
Adriatic Sea
PORTUGAL
Lisbon
SPAIN
Madrid
RUSSIA
Kiev
UKRAINE
Odessa
Volgograd
KAZAKHSTAN
Aral Sea
Caspian Sea
Black Sea
GEORGIA
ARM.
AZER.
Baku
TURKMEN.
TURKEY
Ankara
SYRIA
Aleppo
Damascus
LEB.
Tel Aviv-Jaffa
Jerusalem
ISRAEL
JORDAN
IRAQ
Mosul
Baghdād
Tigris
Euphrates
Basra
KUWAIT
IRAN
TEHRĀN
Eşfahān
Persian Gulf
BAHRAIN
QATAR
SAUDI ARABIA
Riyadh
Medina
Jedda
Mecca
YEMEN
Socotra (Yemen)
G. of Aden
Mediterranean Sea
Algiers
Oran
Annaba
Constantine
Tunis
TUNISIA
Sfax
Chott Djerid
Tétouan
Rabat
Casablanca
Fès
MOROCCO
Marrakesh
El Aaiún
WESTERN SAHARA
Dakhla
Fdérik
ALGERIA
In Salah
Tropic of Cancer
Sahara
Tripoli
Mişrātah
Benghazi
Ghadāmes
LIBYA
Sabhā
Marzūq
Al Jawf
Alexandria
Port Said
CAIRO
Suez
El Faiyûm
Asyût
Nile
EGYPT
Aswân
Red Sea
Wadi Halfa
Port Sudan
Ras Nouâdhibou
MAURITANIA
Nouakchott
CAPE VERDE IS.
Praia
St-Louis
C. Vert
Dakar
SENEGAL
Senegal
GAMBIA
Banjul
GUINEA-BISSAU
Bissau
GUINEA
Conakry
Freetown
SIERRA LEONE
LIBERIA
Monrovia
MALI
Tombouctou
Bamako
Niger
BURKINA FASO
Ouagadougou
Bobo-Dioulasso
IVORY COAST
Yamoussoukro
Bouaké
Abidjan
GHANA
Kumasi
Accra
Sekondi-Takoradi
TOGO
Lomé
BENIN
Porto Novo
LAGOS
NIGER
Agadès
Niamey
NIGERIA
Kano
Maiduguri
Abuja
Ibadan
Enugu
Benue
Port Harcourt
Bight of Benin
CHAD
L. Chad
Abéché
Ndjamena
Chari
SUDAN
Atbara
Omdurmân
Khartoum
Wad Medani
El Fâsher
El Obeid
White Nile
Blue Nile
Atbara
Malakâl
Wâw
Bahr el Jebel
ERITREA
Asmera
Massawa
L. Tana
DJIBOUTI
Djibouti
Ras Asir
Berbera
Addis Ababa
Harer
ETHIOPIA
Shabeelle
SOMALI REP.
Mogadishu
Juba
Kismayu
CENTRAL AFRICAN REP.
Bangui
CAMEROON
Douala
Yaoundé
Rey Malabo
EQUATORIAL GUINEA
Gulf of Guinea
SÃO TOMÉ & PRÍNCIPE
Equator
Annobón
C. Lopez
Libreville
GABON
CONGO
Oubangi
Congo
Mbandaka
Brazzaville
Pointe Noire
CABINDA (Angola)
KINSHASA
Matadi
CONGO (DEM. REP. OF THE)
Kasai
Kisangani
Kananga
Mbuji-Mayi
Cuango
L. Albert
UGANDA
Kampala
L. Edward
Lualaba
RWANDA
Kigali
L. Kivu
Bujumbura
BURUNDI
L. Turkana
KENYA
Kisumu
L. Victoria
Nairobi
Tana
Mombasa
TANZANIA
Dodoma
Zanzibar
Dar es Salaam
L. Tanganyika
L. Mweru
Likasi
Lubumbashi
L. Malawi
MALAWI
Lilongwe
Blantyre
Ndola
Luanda
ANGOLA
Lobito
Huambo
Namibe
Cunene
Cubango
C. Fria
ZAMBIA
Lusaka
Zambezi
Livingstone
Harare
ZIMBABWE
Bulawayo
MOZAMBIQUE
Moçambique
Beira
Limpopo
Maputo
NAMIBIA
Windhoek
BOTSWANA
Gaborone
Pretoria (Tshwane)
Johannesburg
Mbabane
SWAZ.
Vaal
Orange
Kimberley
Maseru
LESOTHO
Durban (eThekwini)
SOUTH AFRICA
East London
Port Elizabeth
Cape Town
C. of Good Hope
C. Agulhas
Mozambique Channel
C. Delgado
COMOROS
Moroni
Mamoudzou
Mayotte (Fr.)
Antsiranana
Mahajanga
Toamasina
Antananarivo
MADAGASCAR
Fianarantsoa
MAURITIUS
Port Louis
St Denis
Réunion (Fr.)
Aldabra Is.
Victoria
SEYCHELLES
INDIAN OCEAN
Ascension I. (U.K.)
SOUTH ATLANTIC OCEAN
St. Helena (U.K.)
Tropic of Capricorn
Tristan da Cunha (U.K.)

Projection: Azimuthal Equidistant
West from Greenwich
East from Greenwich

● Dakar Capital Cities

AZORES
on same scale as main map

CAPE VERDE IS.

Projection : Sanson-Flamsteed's Sinusoidal

West from Greenwich 0 East from Greenwich

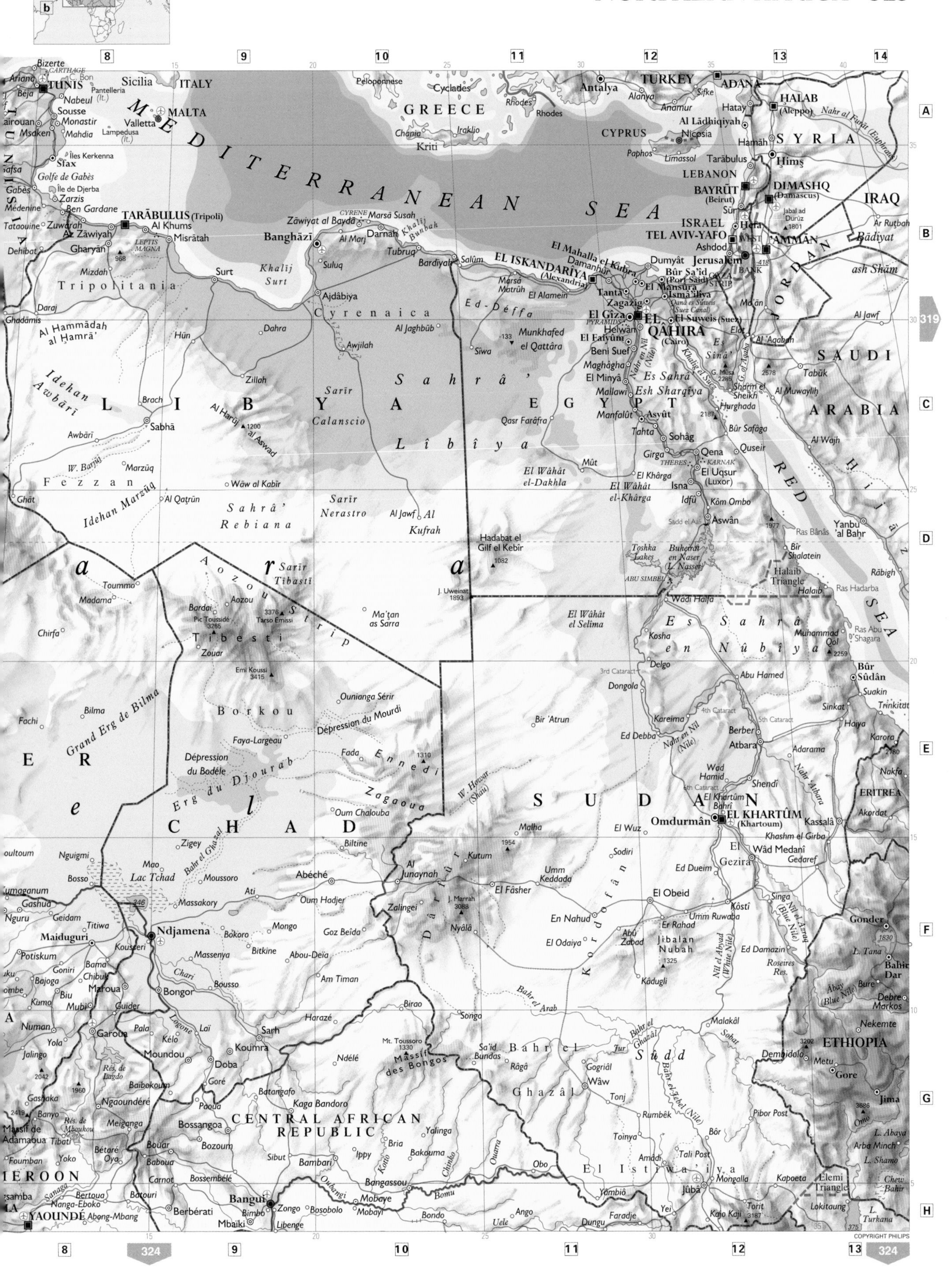
MEDITERRANEAN SEA
TUNIS
Sicilia
ITALY
MALTA
Valletta
GREECE
Kriti
Cyclades
Rhodes
TURKEY
Antalya
ADANA
HALAB (Aleppo)
CYPRUS
Nicosia
SYRIA
LEBANON
BAYRŪT (Beirut)
DIMASHQ (Damascus)
IRAQ
ISRAEL
TEL AVIV-YAFO
Jerusalem
'AMMĀN
JORDAN
TARĀBULUS (Tripoli)
Misrātah
Banghāzī
Tripolitania
Cyrenaica
EL ISKANDARĪYA (Alexandria)
EL QÂHIRA (Cairo)
El Gîza
Bûr Sa'îd (Port Said)
El Suweis (Suez)
LIBYA
EGYPT
Sahrâ' Lîbîya
Sabhā
Fezzan
Al Kufrah
Asyût
El Uqsur (Luxor)
Aswân
RED SEA
SAUDI ARABIA
Sinâ'
Aozou Strip
Tibesti
Borkou
Ennedi
CHAD
Ndjamena
Lac Tchad
SUDAN
Omdurmân
EL KHARTÛM (Khartoum)
Es Sahrâ en Nûbîya
Dongola
Atbara
Bûr Sûdân
Kassalâ
ERITREA
El Obeid
Kordofân
Darfûr
El Fâsher
Nyâlâ
Halaib Triangle
CENTRAL AFRICAN REPUBLIC
Bangui
Sudd
Bahr el Ghazâl
El Istiwa'iya
Jûba
ETHIOPIA
Gonder
Bahir Dar
L. Tana
Elemi Triangle
L. Turkana
Maiduguri
Garoua
Moundou
Ngaoundéré
YAOUNDÉ
CAMEROON
Berbérati
Niger
Grand Erg de Bilma
Erg du Djourab
Abéché
Sarh
Wadi Halfa
Kosti
Wâd Medanî
Malakâl
Wâw
COPYRIGHT PHILIPS

319
324
324

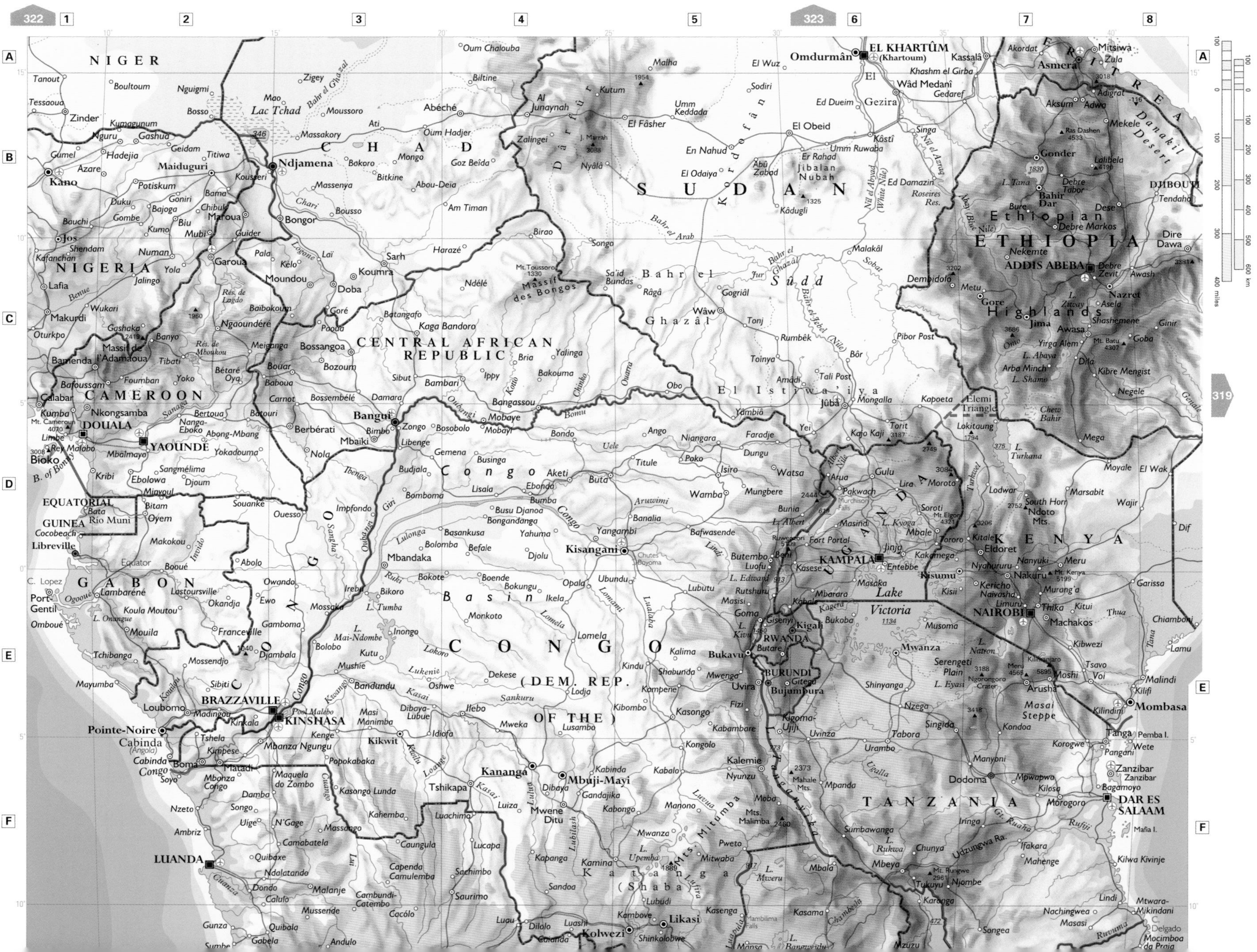

100 0 100 200 300 400 500 600 km
100 0 100 200 300 400 miles
322
323
319
NIGER
CHAD
SUDAN
ETHIOPIA
ERITREA
DJIBOUTI
KENYA
UGANDA
RWANDA
BURUNDI
TANZANIA
CENTRAL AFRICAN REPUBLIC
CAMEROON
NIGERIA
EQUATORIAL GUINEA
GABON
CONGO
CONGO (DEM. REP. OF THE)
EL KHARTÛM (Khartoum)
ADDIS ABEBA
NAIROBI
KAMPALA
DAR ES SALAAM
KINSHASA
BRAZZAVILLE
LUANDA
YAOUNDÉ
DOUALA
Ndjamena
Bangui
Libreville
Kigali
Bujumbura
Mombasa
Lake Victoria
Lac Tchad
Ethiopian Highlands
Congo Basin
Sudd
Bahr el Ghazâl
Danakil Desert
Serengeti Plain
Masai Steppe

ATLANTIC OCEAN
INDIAN OCEAN
ANGOLA
ZAMBIA
ZIMBABWE
MOZAMBIQUE
MALAWI
BOTSWANA
NAMIBIA
SOUTH AFRICA
LESOTHO
SWAZILAND
MADAGASCAR
COMOROS
SEYCHELLES
MAURITIUS
RÉUNION
LUSAKA
HARARE
MAPUTO
PRETORIA
JOHANNESBURG
CAPE TOWN
DURBAN
PORT ELIZABETH
ANTANANARIVO
Windhoek
Bulawayo
Lilongwe
Blantyre
Beira
Maseru
Bloemfontein
Kalahari
Namib Desert
Skeleton Coast
Tropic of Capricorn
Projection: Sanson-Flamsteed's Sinusoidal
COPYRIGHT PHILIPS

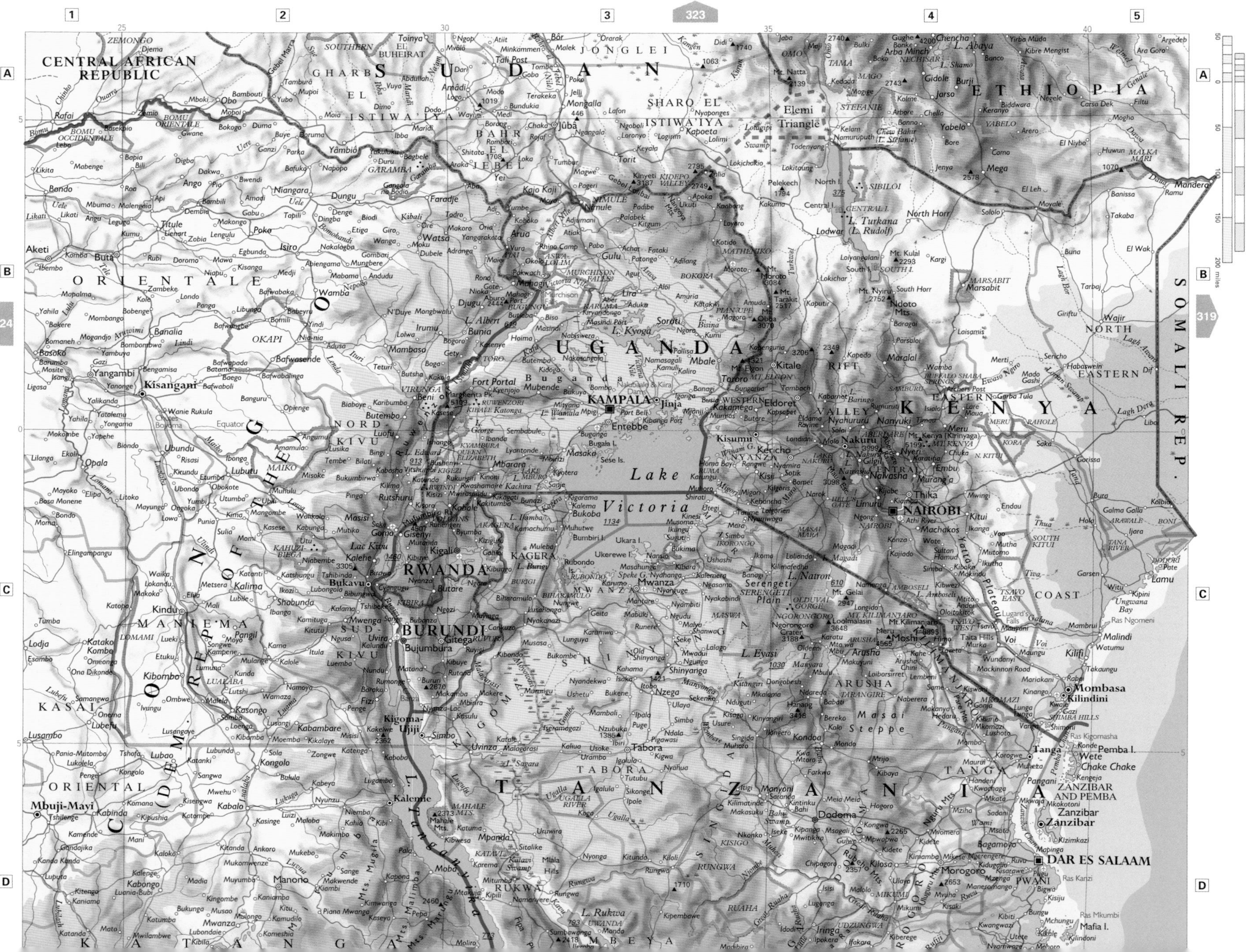
SOMALI REP.
ETHIOPIA
SUDAN
KENYA
UGANDA
TANZANIA
RWANDA
BURUNDI
CENTRAL AFRICAN REPUBLIC
NAIROBI
KAMPALA
DAR ES SALAAM
Mombasa
Zanzibar
Lake Victoria
L. Tanganyika
L. Turkana (L. Rudolf)
Kisangani
Bujumbura
Kigali
Elemi Triangle
319
323
324

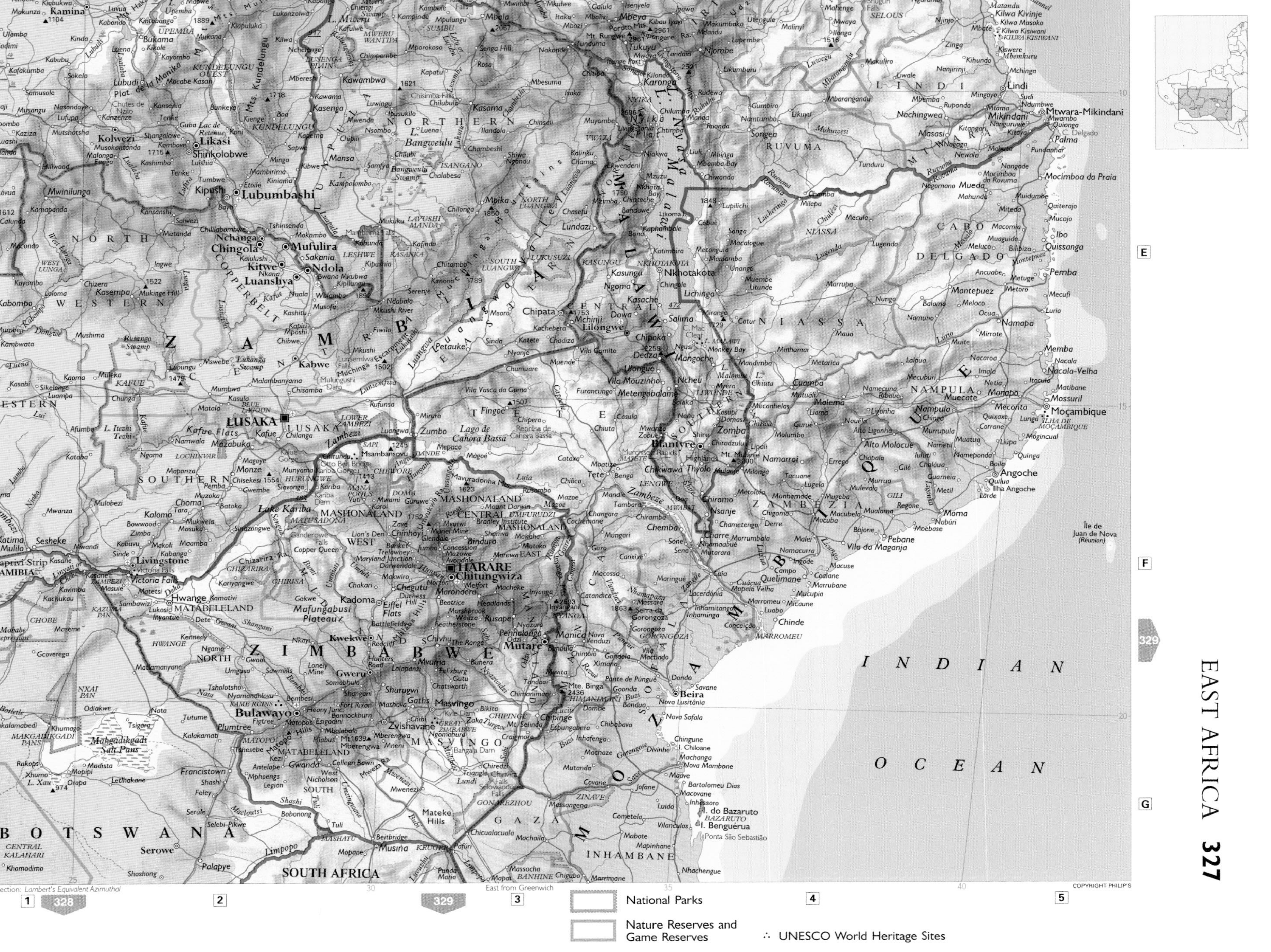
National Parks
Nature Reserves and
Game Reserves
∴ UNESCO World Heritage Sites
Projection: Lambert's Equivalent Azimuthal
East from Greenwich
COPYRIGHT PHILIP'S
INDIAN
OCEAN
ZAMBIA
MALAWI
ZIMBABWE
BOTSWANA
MOZAMBIQUE
SOUTH AFRICA
NAMIBIA
ANGOLA
LUSAKA
HARARE
Lilongwe
Blantyre
Bulawayo
Beira
Lubumbashi
Lake Kariba
L. Nyasa
Malawi
Zambezi
m
ft
328
329
325
E
F
G
1
2
3
4
5

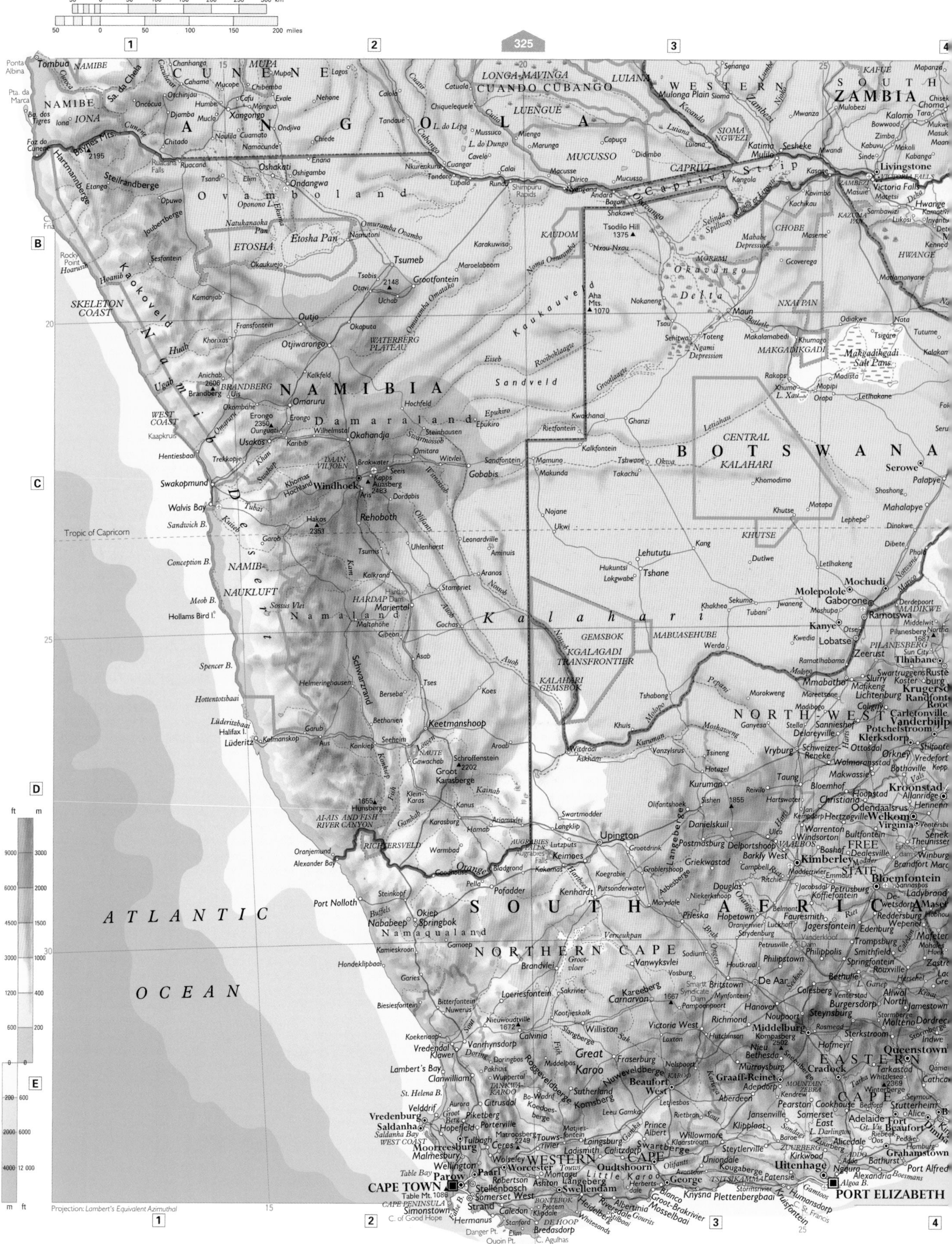

50 0 50 100 150 200 250 300 km
50 0 50 100 150 200 miles
325
ANGOLA
NAMIBIA
BOTSWANA
ZAMBIA
SOUTH AFRICA
NORTH-WEST
FREE STATE
NORTHERN CAPE
WESTERN CAPE
EASTERN CAPE
ATLANTIC OCEAN
Tropic of Capricorn
Namib Desert
Kalahari
Kaokoveld
Ovamboland
Damaraland
Namaland
Namaqualand
Sandveld
Great Karoo
Okavango Delta
Caprivi Strip
Etosha Pan
Makgadikgadi Salt Pans
SKELETON COAST
NAMIB-NAUKLUFT
CENTRAL KALAHARI
KGALAGADI TRANSFRONTIER
AI-AIS AND FISH RIVER CANYON
RICHTERSVELD
Windhoek
Swakopmund
Walvis Bay
Lüderitz
Keetmanshoop
Rehoboth
Tsumeb
Grootfontein
Otjiwarongo
Outjo
Okahandja
Gobabis
Oshakati
Ondangwa
Katima Mulilo
Maun
Ghanzi
Gaborone
Molepolole
Mochudi
Kanye
Lobatse
Serowe
Palapye
Mahalapye
Livingstone
Victoria Falls
Upington
Kimberley
Bloemfontein
Welkom
Kroonstad
Klerksdorp
Potchefstroom
Mafikeng
Mmabatho
Vryburg
Kuruman
De Aar
Beaufort West
Graaff-Reinet
Middelburg
Cradock
Queenstown
Grahamstown
Port Alfred
Uitenhage
PORT ELIZABETH
George
Oudtshoorn
Knysna
Plettenberg Baai
Mosselbaai
Swellendam
Worcester
Paarl
Stellenbosch
Somerset West
Wellington
Malmesbury
Moorreesburg
Saldanha
Vredenburg
CAPE TOWN
Table Mt. 1086
CAPE PENINSULA
Simonstown
C. of Good Hope
Hermanus
C. Agulhas
Springbok
Port Nolloth
Pofadder
Calvinia
Carnarvon
Victoria West
Hopetown
Prieska
Colesberg
Projection: Lambert's Equivalent Azimuthal
ft m
9000 3000
6000 2000
4500 1500
3000 1000
1200 400
600 200
0 0
200 600
2000 6000
4000 12 000
m ft

ZIMBABWE
MOZAMBIQUE
MOZAMBIQUE CHANNEL
MADAGASCAR
INDIAN OCEAN
HARARE
MAPUTO
ANTANANARIVO
PRETORIA (Tshwane)
JOHANNESBURG
DURBAN (eThekwini)
Bulawayo
Beira
Chitungwiza
Mutare
Masvingo
Gweru
Kadoma
Quelimane
Inhambane
Xai-Xai
Chinde
Mbabane
SWAZILAND
LESOTHO
LIMPOPO
MPUMALANGA
KWAZULU NATAL
EASTERN CAPE
Pietermaritzburg
East London
Umlazi
KwaMashu
Mahajanga
Toamasina (Tamatave)
Antsiranana (Diego Suarez)
Fianarantsoa
Toliara
Morondava
Taolanaro (Fort Dauphin)
Antsirabe
Maintirano
Tropic of Capricorn
Île de Juán de Nova (Fr.)
Îs. Glorieuses (Fr.)
I. do Bazaruto
I. Benguérua
Tete
Angoche
Moma
Pebane
Vila da Maganja
Nsanje
Musina
Zambeze
Limpopo
MADAGASCAR
on same scale
East from Greenwich
COPYRIGHT PHILIP'S
327
5
6
7
8
9
A
B
C
D
National Parks
Nature Reserves and Game Reserves
∴ UNESCO World Heritage Sites

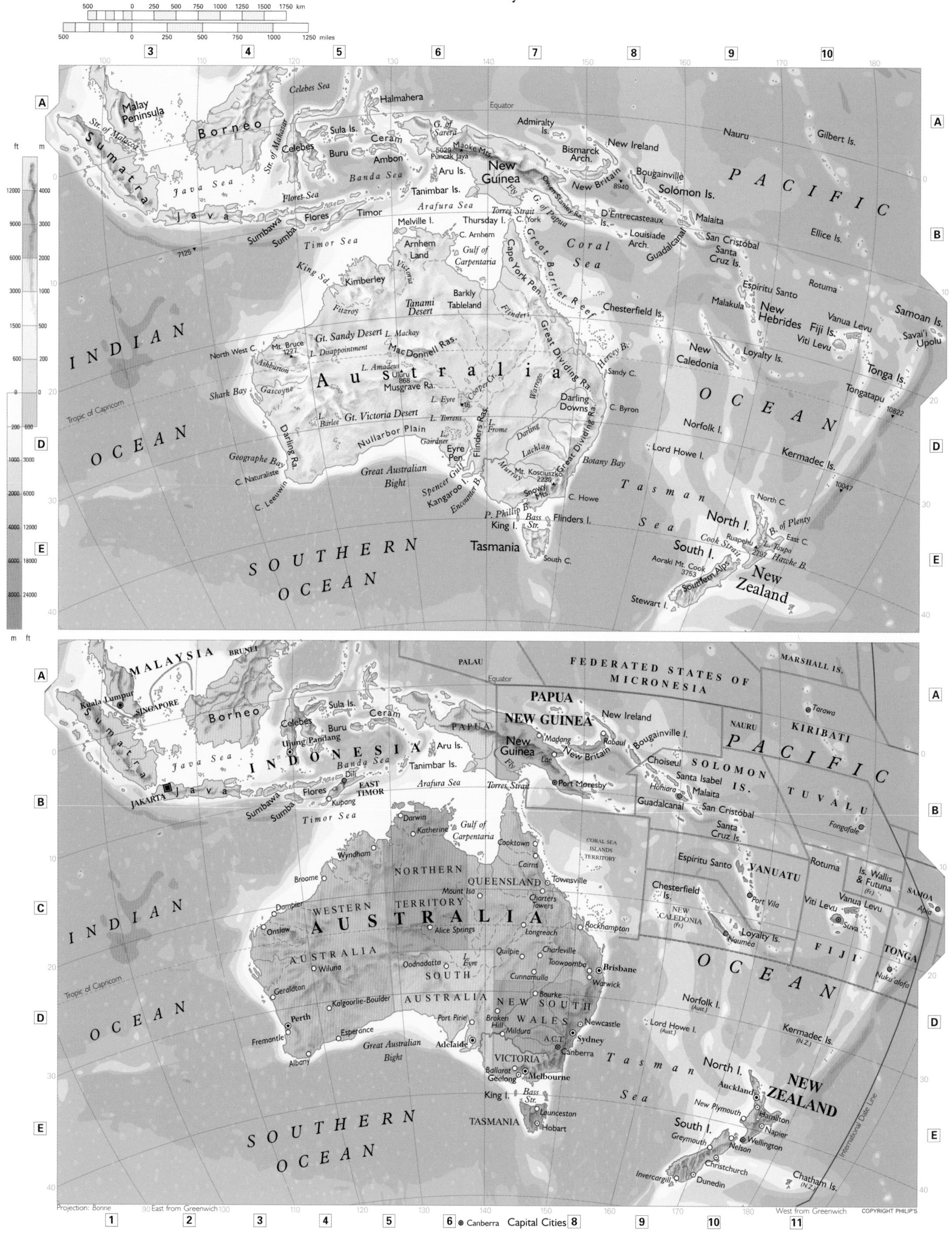

Malay Peninsula
Sumatra
Borneo
Celebes Sea
Halmahera
Celebes
Sula Is.
Ceram
Buru
Ambon
Banda Sea
Java Sea
Java
Flores Sea
Flores
Timor
Sumbawa
Sumba
Timor Sea
Arafura Sea
Aru Is.
Tanimbar Is.
New Guinea
Admiralty Is.
Bismarck Arch.
New Ireland
New Britain
Bougainville I.
Solomon Is.
Nauru
Gilbert Is.
PACIFIC OCEAN
INDIAN OCEAN
SOUTHERN OCEAN
Coral Sea
Great Barrier Reef
Gulf of Carpentaria
Cape York Pen.
Arnhem Land
Kimberley
Great Sandy Desert
MacDonnell Ras.
Australia
Gt. Victoria Desert
Nullarbor Plain
Great Australian Bight
Great Dividing Ra.
Tasman Sea
Tasmania
New Caledonia
New Hebrides
Fiji Is.
Tonga Is.
Samoan Is.
North I.
South I.
New Zealand
Equator
Tropic of Capricorn
MALAYSIA
BRUNEI
SINGAPORE
Kuala Lumpur
JAKARTA
INDONESIA
EAST TIMOR
Dili
PAPUA NEW GUINEA
Port Moresby
FEDERATED STATES OF MICRONESIA
PALAU
MARSHALL IS.
KIRIBATI
NAURU
TUVALU
SOLOMON IS.
VANUATU
FIJI
TONGA
SAMOA
WESTERN AUSTRALIA
NORTHERN TERRITORY
QUEENSLAND
SOUTH AUSTRALIA
NEW SOUTH WALES
VICTORIA
TASMANIA
A.C.T.
Canberra
Darwin
Perth
Adelaide
Melbourne
Sydney
Brisbane
Hobart
NEW ZEALAND
Auckland
Wellington
Christchurch
Projection: Bonne
East from Greenwich
West from Greenwich
Canberra Capital Cities
COPYRIGHT PHILIP'S

50 0 50 100 150 200 km
50 0 50 100 150 miles

336

FIJI a
on same scale

Great Sea Reef
Kia
Udu Pt.
Ringgold Is.
PACIFIC OCEAN
Yaqaga
Labasa
Vanua Levu
Natewa Bay
Rabi
Yasawa Group
Yasawa
Yadua
Bua
Savusavu
Buca
Somosomo
Qamea
Nacula
Savusavu Bay
Somosomo Str.
BOUMA
Taveuni
Nabouwalu
Kanacea
Naitaba
Viwa
Naviti
Bligh Water
Namenalala
Nanuku Passage
Kanacea
Vanua Balavu
Waya
Nasau
Koro
Vacata
Lomaloma
Lau
Rakiraki
Vatu Vara
Mago
Northern Lau Group
Vomo
Tavua
Makogai
Lautoka
Mba
Tomanivi 1323
Lawaki
Levuka
Wakaya
Cicia
Tuvuca
Malolo
Nadi
Navai
KOROYANITU
Ovalau
Mamanuca Group
Viti Levu
Korovou
KORO
Keiyasi
Batiki
Nairai
Nayau
Vunidawa
Sawaleke
Nausori
18 S
Sigatoka
Navua
Suva
Gau
SEA
Lakeba Passage
Group
Korolevu
Tubou
FIJI
Vanua Vatu
Lakeba
Yanuca
Beqa
Oneata
Vatulele
Moala
Southern Lau Group
Moce
Kadavu Passage
Namuka-i-Lau
Ono
Kadavu
Totoya
Kabara
Yagasa Cluster
Tavuki
Yuniseo
Matuku
Fulaga
Ogea Levu
Ogea Driki
178 E
East from Greenwich
180
West from Greenwich

SAMOA
Asau
Safune
Falelima
1858
Pu'apu'a
Savai'i
Salelologa
Satupa'itea
Apia
Taga
Mulifanua
Manono
Falefa
Faleolo
1113
Amaile
OLE PUPU PU'E
Safata Bay
'Upolu
14 S
172 W
SAMOAN ISLANDS b
on same scale

PACIFIC OCEAN
170 W
AMERICAN SAMOA
(U.S.A.)
AMERICAN SAMOA
Tutuila
Pago Pago
Leone
'Aunu'u
Vaitogi
Ofu
Olosega
Ta'u
Luma
AMERICAN SAMOA
Manu'a Is.
West from Greenwich

TONGA c
on same scale

174 W
18 S
Fonualei
Toku
PACIFIC OCEAN
Vava'u
Neiafu
Late
Vava'u Group
Home Reef
Disney Reef
Ofolanga
Ha'ano
Kao
Foa
Tofua
Lifuka
Ha'apai Group
Uiha
Kotu Group
20 S
Nomuka
Oto Tolu Group
Fonuafo'ou
Nomuka Group
Mango
Tonumea
Hunga Ha'apai
TONGA
Nuku'alofa
Tongatapu
Tongatapu Group
Eua
West from Greenwich

New Zealand

C. Reinga
C. Maria van Diemen
North C.
Rangaunu B.
Houhora Heads
Doubtless B.
Mangonui
Whangaroa Harb.
Ahipara B.
Kaitaia
Tauroa Pt.
B. of Islands
C. Brett
Okaihau
Waitangi
Opua
Rawene
Northland
Kaikohe
Hokianga Harbour
Hikurangi
Waipoua Forest
Whangarei
Whangarei Harb.
Bream Hd.
Bream B.
Dargaville
Waipu
Little Barrier I.
Great Barrier I.
Warkworth
C. Rodney
C. Colville
Kaipara Harbour
Cuvier I.
Hauraki Gulf
Helensville
Takapuna
Coromandel
Whitianga
AUCKLAND
Manukau
Papakura
Pukekohe
Thames
Waiuku
Waikato
Mercer
Whangamata
Mayor I.
North Island
Huntly
Paeroa
Waihi
Tauranga Harb.
Whakaari (White I.)
C. Runaway
Te Aroha
Mount Maunganui
Bay of Plenty
Morrinsville
Hamilton
Tauranga
Te Puke
East C.
Raglan
Cambridge
Whakatane
Opotiki
Raukumara Ra.
Hikurangi 1753
Kawhia Harbour
Te Awamutu
Putaruru
Kawerau
Te Teko
Otorohanga
Rotorua
Tarawera
Matata
Ruatoria
Waipiro
Waitomo Caves
Te Kuiti
Tokoroa
Murupara
Motu
Kinleith
UREWERA
Tolaga Bay
Mokau
Mokai
Wairakei
Taupo
Ormond
North Taranaki Bight
Ongarue
L. Taupo
Waitara
Taumarunui
Waikaremoana
Gisborne
Poverty Bay
New Plymouth
WHANGANUI
Turangi
Kaimanawa Mts.
Tarawera
Nuhaka
Waikokopu
Inglewood
Whangamomona
Ruapehu 2797
Wairoa
Mahia Pen.
Mt. Taranaki or Mt. Egmont 2518
EGMONT
Ohakune
TONGARIRO
C. Egmont
Stratford
Raetihi
Waiouru
Opunake
Eltham
Bay View
Hawke Bay
Kaponga
Hawera
Taihape
Napier
South Taranaki Bight
Patea
Waverley
Mangaweka
Ruahine Ra.
C. Kidnappers
Hastings
Wanganui
Hunterville
Waipawa
Marton
Bulls
Halcombe
Feilding
Waipukurau
Palmerston North
Dannevirke
Foxton
Woodville
Shannon
Pahiatua
Levin
C. Turnagain
Eketahuna
C. Farewell
Golden B.
D'Urville I.
Paraparaumu
Otaki
Tararua Ra.
Collingwood
ABEL TASMAN
Kapiti I.
KAHURANGI
Takaka
Tasman B.
Pelorus Sd.
Featherston
Masterton
Tasman Mts.
Motueka
Upper Hutt
Carterton
Karamea
Nelson
Havelock
Petone
Greytown
Karamea Bight
Lower Hutt
Martinborough
Tadmor
Richmond
Picton
Wellington
Eastbourne
L. Wairarapa
Seddonville
Wakefield
Blenheim
Cook Strait
Granity
Matiri Ra.
Wairau
Seddon
Westport
Murchison
Lyell
NELSON LAKES
Awatere
Ward
Inangahua
L. Rotoroa
Kaikoura Ra.
Tapuae-o-Uenuku 2885
Mt. Travers 2338
PAPAROA
Punakaiki
Reefton
Spenser Mts.
Clarence
Blackball
Grey
Lewis Pass
Kaikoura
Runanga
Stillwater
Hanmer Springs
Greymouth
Kumara
L. Brunner
Jacksons
Waiau
Hokitika
Waiau
Ross
ARTHUR'S PASS
Culverden
South Island
Hurunui
Abut Hd.
Arthur's Pass
Waikari
Waipara
Westland Bight
Amberley
Pegasus Bay
Oxford
Rangiora
Kaiapoi
Coleridge
Springfield
New Brighton
WESTLAND
Whitecliffs
Christchurch
Aoraki Mt. Cook 3753
Southern Alps (Tiritiri o te Moana)
Riccarton
Lyttelton
Methven
Lincoln
Banks Pen.
Mount Cook
MT. COOK
Staveley
Akaroa
Jackson B.
Okuru
Haast
Plains
Rakaia
Little River
Southbridge
L. Ellesmere
Tekapo
Ashburton
MOUNT ASPIRING
Fairlie
Canterbury
Temuka
Mt. Aspiring 3027
Pukaki
Canterbury Bight
Timaru
Ohau
Mt. Earnslaw 2818
Wanaka
Hawea
St. Andrews
Milford Sd.
Sutherland Falls
Waitaki
Bligh Sound
Milford Sound
Wanaka
Kurow
Waimate
George Sound
Dunstan Mts.
Tokarahi
Ngapara
Queenstown
Arrowtown
Cromwell
Secretary I.
Naseby
Kakanui Mts.
Oamaru
Doubtful Sd.
Wakatipu
Alexandra
Maheno
Clyde
Hampden
Te Anau
Kingston
Garvie Mts.
Otago
Dunback
Palmerston
Breaksea Sd.
FIORDLAND
Manapouri
Eyre Mts.
Umbrella Mts.
Taieri
Port Chalmers
Resolution I.
Manapouri
Mossburn
Roxburgh
Waikouaiti
Otago Harbour
Lumsden
L. Mahinerangi
Dusky Sd.
Southland
Edievale
C. Saunders
L. Poteriteri
Ohai
Nightcaps
Kelso
Tapanui
Mosgiel
Dunedin
Chalky Inlet
Clifden
Lawrence
Tuatapere
Winton
Clinton
Milton
Preservation Inlet
Te Waewae B.
Hedgehope
Gore
Balclutha
Orepuki
Mataura
Kaitangata
Riverton
Invercargill
Wyndham
Nugget Pt.
South Invercargill
Owaka
Foveaux Str.
Tokanui
Tahakopa
Solander I.
Bluff
Ruapuke I.
Halfmoon Bay
Stewart I. (Rakiura)
RAKIURA
Port Pegasus
South West C.
TASMAN SEA
PACIFIC OCEAN
34
36
38
40
42
44
46
166
168
170
172
174
176
178
East from Greenwich
Projection : Conical with two standard parallels

A
B
C
D
E
F
G
1
2
3
4
5
6
7

TAHITI & MOOREA d

10 0 10 km
10 0 10 miles

Pte. Aroa
Papetoai
Paopao
Mt. Tohiea 1207
Afareaitu
Haapiti
Pte. Nuupere
Moorea (France)
B. de Matavai
Pte. Vénus
Mahina
Papeete
Arue
Papenoo
Pirae
Tiarei
Faaa
Papenoo
Tahiti (France)
Hitiaa
Mt. Aorai 2060
Mt. Orohena 2241
Punaauia
Mt. Tetufera 1799
Lac Vaihiria
Faaone
Isthme de Taravao
PACIFIC OCEAN
Paea
Taravao
Afaahiti
Pte. Tatatua
Maraa
Papara
Pueu
Tautira
Atimaono
Mataiea
Vairao
Mt. Rooniu 1332
Teahupoo
Presqu'île de Taiarapu
17°30'S
17°45'S
149°45'W
149°30'W
149°15'W
West from Greenwich

ft m
9000 3000
6000 2000
3000 1000
1200 400
600 200
0 0
200 600
2000 6000
4000 12 000
6000 18 000
m ft

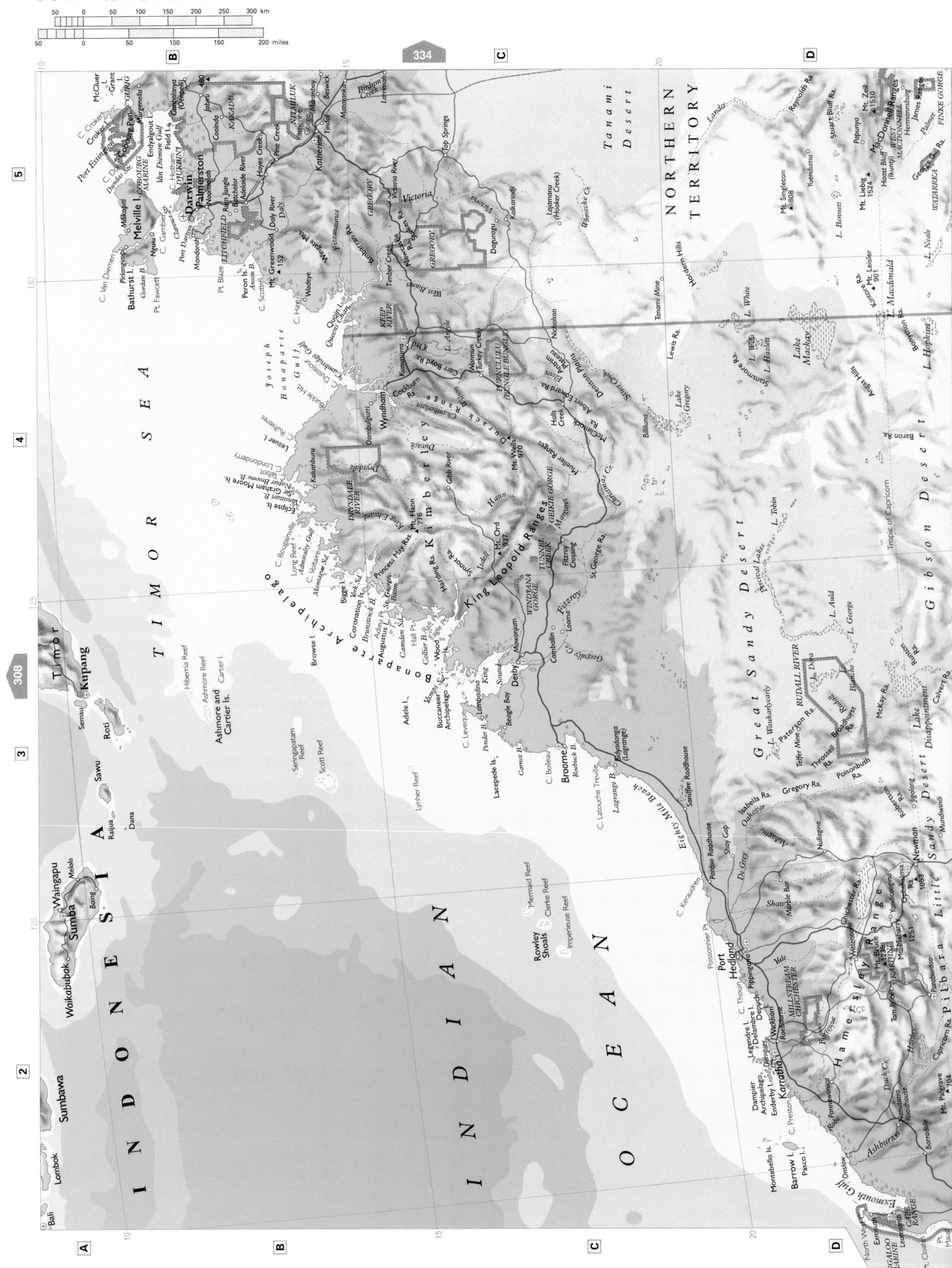

50 0 50 100 150 200 250 300 km
50 0 50 100 150 200 miles
334
308
INDONESIA
TIMOR SEA
INDIAN OCEAN
NORTHERN TERRITORY
Tanami Desert
Great Sandy Desert
Gibson Desert
Little Sandy Desert
Kimberley
King Leopold Ranges
Hamersley Range
Bonaparte Archipelago
Joseph Bonaparte Gulf
Eighty Mile Beach
Timor
Kupang
Sumba
Waingapu
Waikabubak
Sumbawa
Lombok
Bali
Sawu
Roti
Darwin
Palmerston
Melville I.
Bathurst I.
Katherine
Wyndham
Kununurra
Halls Creek
Fitzroy Crossing
Derby
Broome
Port Hedland
Karratha
Dampier
Roebourne
Onslow
Exmouth
Newman
Barrow I.
Montebello Is.
Rowley Shoals
Ashmore and Cartier Is.
Lake Mackay
Lake Disappointment
Lake Gregory
L. Hopkins
MacDonnell Ranges
Tropic of Capricorn

335

WESTERN AUSTRALIA

SOUTH AUSTRALIA

Great Victoria Desert

Nullarbor Plain

Hampton Tableland

Great Australian Bight

INDIAN OCEAN

SOUTHERN OCEAN

PERTH

Fremantle

Kwinana

Rockingham

Mandurah

Bunbury

Busselton

Albany

Geraldton

Carnarvon

Kalgoorlie-Boulder

Esperance

Norseman

Merredin

Northam

Katanning

Wiluna

Meekatharra

Eucla

Nullarbor

Ooldea

Cook

Maralinga

Uluru (Ayers Rock)

Kata Tjuta (The Olgas)

Petermann Ranges

Musgrave Ranges

Everard Ranges

Archipelago of the Recherche

Projection: Bonne

East from Greenwich

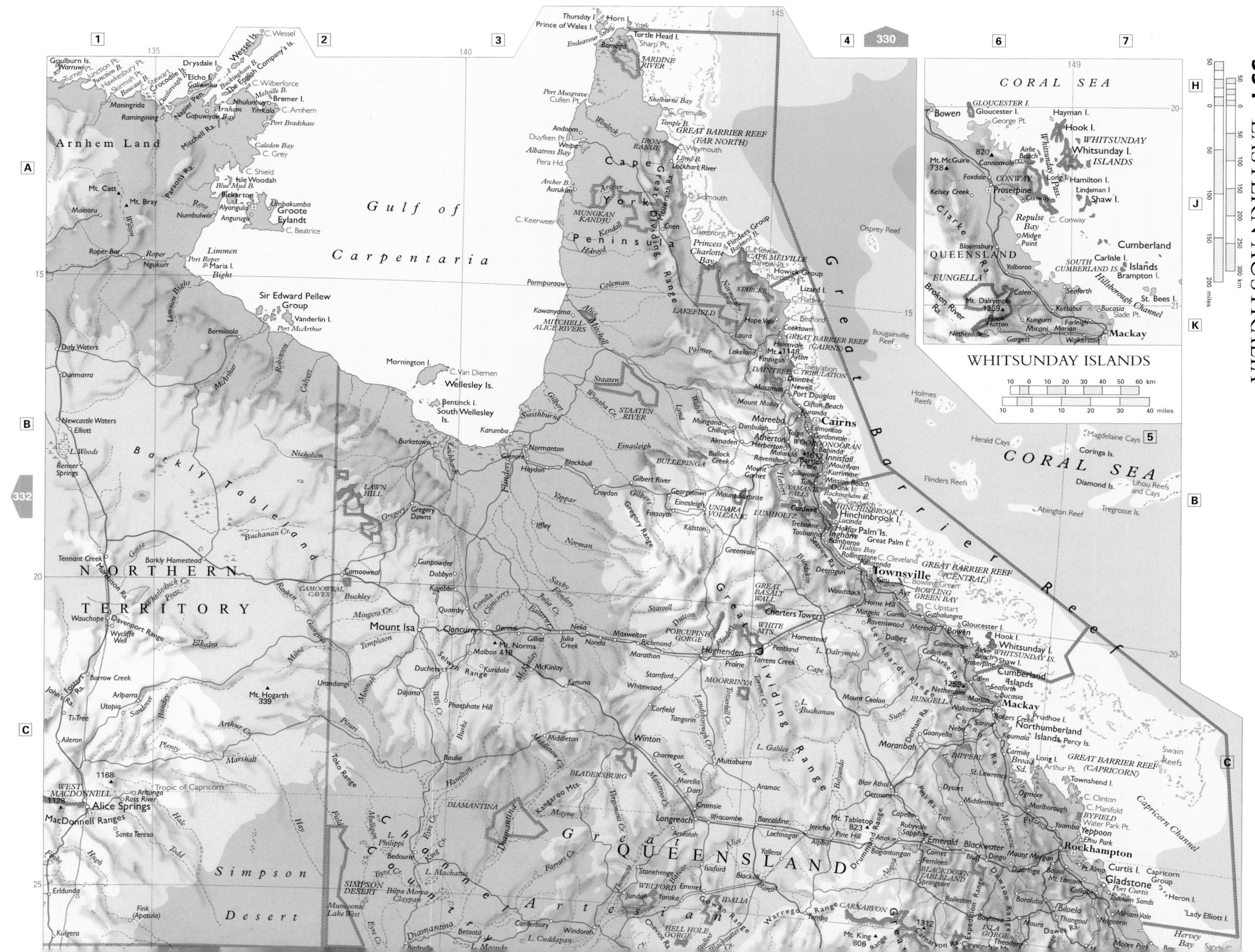

WHITSUNDAY ISLANDS
CORAL SEA
Whitsunday I.
Hook I.
Hayman I.
Cumberland Islands
Proserpine
Mackay
Bowen
QUEENSLAND
EUNGELLA
Great Barrier Reef
CORAL SEA
Gulf of Carpentaria
Cape York Peninsula
Great Dividing Range
Cairns
Townsville
Mackay
Rockhampton
Gladstone
Capricorn Channel
GREAT BARRIER REEF (FAR NORTH)
GREAT BARRIER REEF (CAIRNS)
GREAT BARRIER REEF (CENTRAL)
GREAT BARRIER REEF (CAPRICORN)
Charters Towers
Hughenden
Mount Isa
Cloncurry
Longreach
Winton
Emerald
Normanton
Karumba
Wellesley Is.
Mornington I.
Sir Edward Pellew Group
Groote Eylandt
Arnhem Land
Barkly Tableland
NORTHERN TERRITORY
QUEENSLAND
Simpson Desert
Channel Country
Great Artesian
Alice Springs
MacDonnell Ranges
Tennant Creek
Tropic of Capricorn
Prince of Wales I.
Thursday I.
Horn I.
Hinchinbrook I.

SOUTH AUSTRALIA
NEW SOUTH WALES
TASMANIA
TASMAN SEA
Bass Strait
BRISBANE
SYDNEY
MELBOURNE
ADELAIDE
Canberra
Hobart
Newcastle
Wollongong
Gold Coast
Sunshine Coast
Toowoomba
Broken Hill
Mildura
Wagga Wagga
Albury
Geelong
Ballarat
Bendigo
Launceston
Port Augusta
Port Lincoln
Mount Gambier
Kangaroo I.
King Island
Lake Eyre (North)
Lake Torrens
Strzelecki Desert
Sturt Stony Desert
East from Greenwich
Projection: Bonne
COPYRIGHT, GEORGE PHILIP LTD.

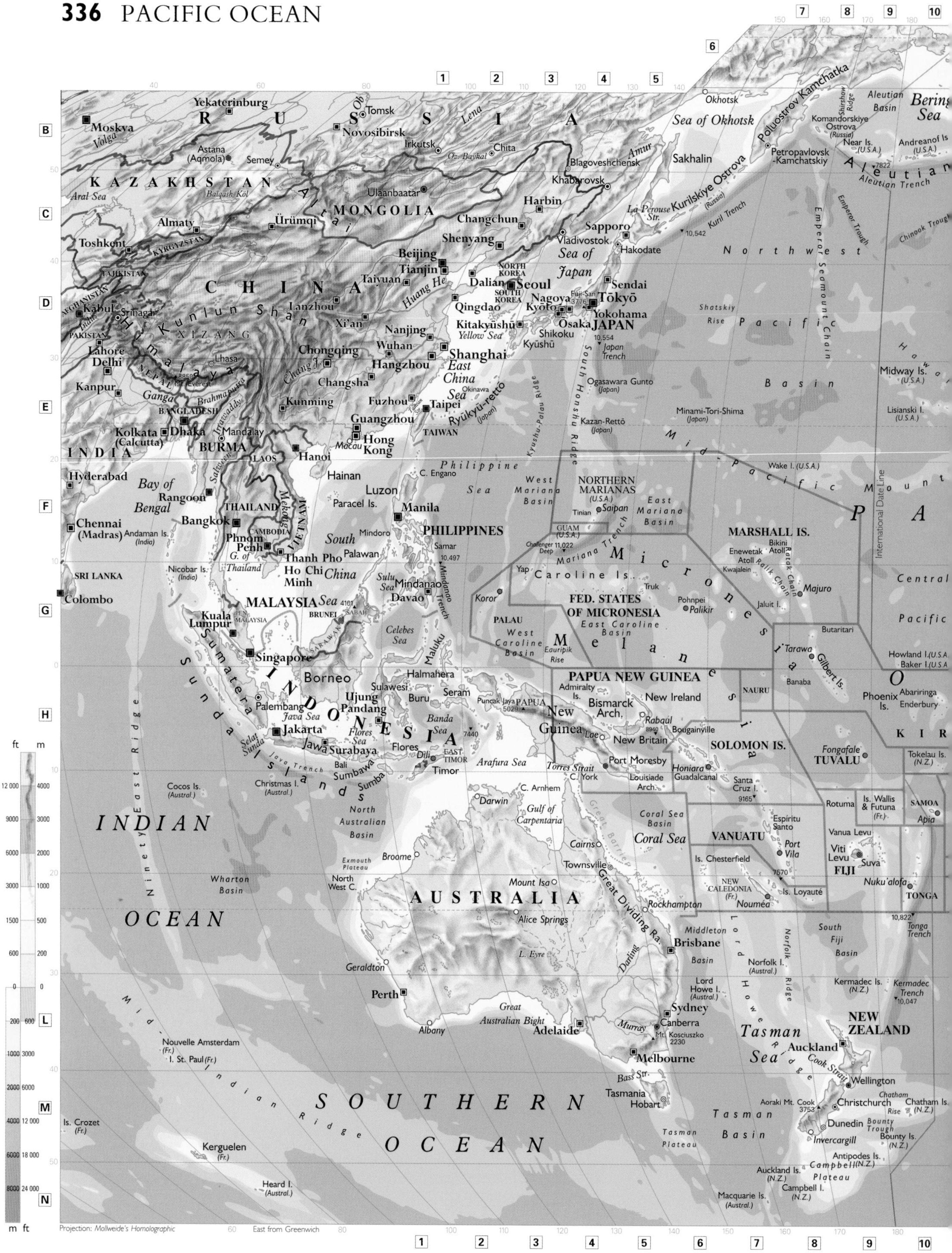

RUSSIA
Moskva
Yekaterinburg
Tomsk
Novosibirsk
Irkutsk
Chita
Astana (Aqmola)
Semey
KAZAKHSTAN
Aral Sea
MONGOLIA
Ulaanbaatar
Almaty
Ürümqi
Toshkent
KYRGYZSTAN
TAJIKISTAN
AFGHANISTAN
Kābul
Srīnagar
PAKISTAN
CHINA
Kunlun Shan
XIZANG
Lhasa
Himalaya
Mt Everest 8850
NEPAL
Lahore
Delhi
Kanpur
Ganga
Brahmaputra
BANGLADESH
Dhaka
Kolkata (Calcutta)
INDIA
Hyderabad
Bay of Bengal
Chennai (Madras)
SRI LANKA
Colombo
Andaman Is. (India)
Nicobar Is. (India)
Mandalay
BURMA
Rangoon
Irrawaddy
Salween
Bangkok
THAILAND
LAOS
Hanoi
CAMBODIA
Phnom Penh
VIETNAM
Mekong
Thanh Pho Ho Chi Minh
G. of Thailand
MALAYSIA
Kuala Lumpur
PEN. MALAYSIA
Singapore
Sumatera
Sunda Islands
Selat Sunda
Palembang
Jakarta
Java Sea
Jawa
Surabaya
Bali
Sumbawa
Sumba
Flores
Flores Sea
Dili
EAST TIMOR
Timor
INDONESIA
Borneo
SARAWAK
SABAH
BRUNEI
Sulawesi
Ujung Pandang
Halmahera
Buru
Seram
Banda Sea
7440
Maluku
Celebes Sea
Sulu Sea
Mindanao
Davao
Mindanao Trench
PHILIPPINES
Manila
Luzon
Mindoro
Palawan
Samar
10,497
South China Sea
Paracel Is.
Hainan
C. Engano
Lena
Oz. Baykal
Ob
Volga
Altai
Balqash Köl
Lanzhou
Xi'an
Taiyuan
Huang He
Beijing
Tianjin
Chongqing
Chang Jiang
Wuhan
Nanjing
Shanghai
Hangzhou
Changsha
Kunming
Fuzhou
Guangzhou
Hong Kong
Macau
Taipei
TAIWAN
East China Sea
Okinawa
Ryūkyū-rettō (Japan)
Qingdao
Dalian
Yellow Sea
NORTH KOREA
SOUTH KOREA
Seoul
Shenyang
Changchun
Harbin
Blagoveshchensk
Amur
Khabarovsk
Vladivostok
Sea of Japan
Sapporo
Hakodate
Sendai
Tōkyō
Yokohama
Fuji-San 3776
Nagoya
Kyōto
Ōsaka
JAPAN
Kitakyūshū
Shikoku
Kyūshū
10,554
Japan Trench
Okhotsk
Sea of Okhotsk
Sakhalin
La Perouse Str.
Kurilskiye Ostrova (Russia)
Kuril Trench
10,542
Poluostrov Kamchatka
Petropavlovsk-Kamchatskiy
Komandorskiye Ostrova (Russia)
Shirshov Ridge
Aleutian Basin
Bering Sea
Near Is. (U.S.A.)
Andreanof Is (U.S.A.)
Aleutian
7822
Aleutian Trench
Emperor Trough
Chinook Trough
Emperor Seamount Chain
Northwest Pacific Basin
Shatskiy Rise
Hawai
Midway Is. (U.S.A.)
Lisianski I. (U.S.A.)
Ogasawara Gunto (Japan)
Minami-Tori-Shima (Japan)
Kazan-Rettō (Japan)
South Honshu Ridge
Kyushu-Palau Ridge
Philippine Sea
West Mariana Basin
NORTHERN MARIANAS (U.S.A.)
Tinian
Saipan
East Mariana Basin
GUAM (U.S.A.)
Challenger Deep 11,022
Mariana Trench
Mid-Pacific Mountains
Wake I. (U.S.A.)
International Date Line
MARSHALL IS.
Bikini Atoll
Enewetak Atoll
Kwajalein
Ratak Chain
Ralik Chain
Majuro
Jaluit I.
Micronesia
Caroline Is.
Yap
Koror
PALAU
Truk
FED. STATES OF MICRONESIA
Pohnpei
Palikir
East Caroline Basin
West Caroline Basin
Eauripik Rise
Melanesia
Butaritari
Tarawa
Gilbert Is.
Banaba
NAURU
Central Pacific
Howland I. (U.S.A.)
Baker I. (U.S.A.)
Phoenix Is.
Abariringa
Enderbury
KIR
PA
O
PAPUA NEW GUINEA
Admiralty Is.
New Ireland
Bismarck Arch.
Rabaul
8940
Bougainville
New Britain
Puncak Jaya 5029
PAPUA
New Guinea
Lae
Port Moresby
SOLOMON IS.
Honiara
Guadalcanal
Santa Cruz I.
9165
Torres Strait
C. York
Louisiade Arch.
Arafura Sea
C. Arnhem
Darwin
Gulf of Carpentaria
North Australian Basin
Coral Sea Basin
Coral Sea
Great Barrier Reef
Cairns
Townsville
Broome
Exmouth Plateau
North West C.
Mount Isa
AUSTRALIA
Alice Springs
Great Dividing Ra.
Rockhampton
Brisbane
Darling
L. Eyre
Geraldton
Perth
Great Australian Bight
Albany
Adelaide
Murray
Sydney
Canberra
Mt. Kosciuszko 2230
Melbourne
Bass Str.
Tasmania
Hobart
VANUATU
Espiritu Santo
Port Vila
7570
Is. Chesterfield
NEW CALEDONIA (Fr.)
Nouméa
Is. Loyauté
Fongafale
TUVALU
Tokelau Is. (N.Z.)
Rotuma
Is. Wallis & Futuna (Fr.)
SAMOA
Apia
Vanua Levu
Viti Levu
Suva
FIJI
Nuku'alofa
TONGA
10,822
Tonga Trench
South Fiji Basin
Middleton Basin
Lord Howe Rise
Norfolk Ridge
Norfolk I. (Austral.)
Lord Howe I. (Austral.)
Kermadec Is. (N.Z.)
Kermadec Trench
10,047
NEW ZEALAND
Tasman Sea
Auckland
Cook Strait
Wellington
Aoraki Mt. Cook 3753
Christchurch
Chatham Rise
Chatham Is. (N.Z.)
Dunedin
Bounty Trough
Bounty Is. (N.Z.)
Invercargill
Antipodes Is. (N.Z.)
Campbell Plateau
Auckland Is. (N.Z.)
Campbell I. (N.Z.)
Macquarie Is. (Austral.)
Tasman Basin
Tasman Plateau
INDIAN OCEAN
Ninetyeast Ridge
Java Trench
Cocos Is. (Austral.)
Christmas I. (Austral.)
Wharton Basin
Mid-Indian Ridge
Nouvelle Amsterdam (Fr.)
I. St. Paul (Fr.)
SOUTHERN OCEAN
Is. Crozet (Fr.)
Kerguelen (Fr.)
Heard I. (Austral.)
ft m
12 000 4000
9000 3000
6000 2000
3000 1000
1500 500
600 200
0 0
200 600
1000 3000
2000 6000
4000 12 000
6000 18 000
8000 24 000
m ft
Projection: Mollweide's Homolographic
East from Greenwich

Arctic Circle
ALASKA (U.S.A.)
Anchorage
Bristol Bay
Gulf of Alaska
Juneau
Prince of Wales I. (U.S.A.)
Prince Rupert
Queen Charlotte Is. (Canada)
Rocky Mts.
CANADA
Edmonton
Calgary
Regina
Winnipeg
L. Winnipeg
Vancouver
Vancouver I.
Victoria
Seattle
Portland
Boise
Snake
Salt Lake City
Colorado
Denver
Minneapolis
Missouri
L. Superior
L. Michigan
L. Huron
L. Ontario
L. Erie
Chicago
Detroit
Toronto
Ottawa
Montréal
Québec
St. Lawrence
Newfoundland
St. John's
Buffalo
Boston
Pittsburgh
New York
Philadelphia
Baltimore
Washington D.C.
Cincinnati
St. Louis
Kansas City
UNITED STATES
Appalachian Mts.
Memphis
Oklahoma City
Atlanta
C. Hatteras
Mississippi
Dallas
Phoenix
Los Angeles
San Diego
Sacramento
San Francisco
C. Mendocino
Houston
San Antonio
New Orleans
Jacksonville
Tampa
Miami
Ciudad Juárez
Guadalupe (Mex.)
Baja California
Golfo de California
Monterrey
MEXICO
Gulf of Mexico
Florida Str.
BAHAMAS
C. San Lucas
Guadalajara
Mexico
Puebla
6610
Acapulco
La Habana
CUBA
Canal de Yucatán
Mérida
7680
JAMAICA
Kingston
HAITI
DOMINICAN REP.
9200
PUERTO RICO (U.S.A.)
Leeward Is.
BELIZE
GUATEMALA
HONDURAS
Guatemala
6662
Middle America Trench
San Salvador
EL SALVADOR
NICARAGUA
Managua
Guatemala Basin
Caribbean Sea
BARBADOS
Windward Is.
Barranquilla
Maracaibo
Caracas
Orinoco
VENEZUELA
San José
COSTA RICA
Colón
Panamá
PANAMA
Cocos Ridge
I. del Coco (Costa Rica)
Medellín
Bogotá
Cali
COLOMBIA
I. de Malpelo (Colombia)
Galápagos (Ecuador)
Carnegie Ridge
Quito
ECUADOR
Guayaquil
C. Paliñas
Iquitos
Amazonas
BRAZIL
Trujillo
6369
PERU
Lima
Cuzco
L. Titicaca
Arequipa
Nevada Ancohuma 6550
La Paz
BOLIVIA
6866
Peru-Chile Trench
8050
Arica
Iquique
Antofagasta
PARAGUAY
Asunción
San. Miguel de Tucumán
San Felix (Chile)
San Ambrosio (Chile)
Córdoba
Aconcagua 6962
Rosario
Porto Alegre
Valparaíso
Santiago
Buenos Aires
URUGUAY
Montevideo
Río de la Plata
Arch. de Juan Fernández (Chile)
Concepción
ARGENTINA
Andes
Patagonia
SOUTH ATLANTIC OCEAN
6212
Falkland Is. (U.K.)
South Georgia (U.K.)
Punta Arenas
Est. de Magallanes
Tierra del Fuego
C. de Hornos
Drake Passage
NORTH ATLANTIC OCEAN
Bermuda (U.K.)
Sargasso Sea
West Indies
Northeast Pacific Basin
Mendocino Fracture Zone
Murray Fracture Zone
6741
4418
Molokai Fracture Zone
Tropic of Cancer
Hawaiian Ridge
Honolulu
Kauai
Oahu
Maui
HAWAIIAN IS. (U.S.A.)
4205
Hilo
Hawaii
Johnston I. (U.S.A.)
Clarion Fracture Zone
Is. Revilla Gigedo (Mex.)
PACIFIC OCEAN
North West Christmas I. Ridge
I. Clipperton (Fr.)
Clipperton Fracture Zone
Palmyra Is. (U.S.A.)
Teraina
Tabuaeran
Kiritimati
Equator
Jarvis I. (U.S.A.)
Galápagos Fracture Zone
Line Islands
Malden I.
Starbuck I.
KIRIBATI
Penrhyn (Tongareva)
Manihiki
Pukapuka
Manihiki Plateau
Vostok I.
Caroline I. (Millennium I.)
Flint I.
Nuku Hiva
Is. Marquises
Hiva Oa
Marquesas Fracture Zone
East Pacific Ridge
Galápagos Rise
Peru Basin
Suwarrow Is.
Is. de la Société
Bora Bora
Huahine
Raiatea
Tahiti
Papeete
Rangiroa
Is. Tuamotu
Tuamotu Ridge
Niue (N.Z.)
Cook Is. (N.Z.)
Aitutaki
Atiu
Rarotonga
Mangaia
Austral Seamount Chain
FRENCH POLYNESIA
Gambier Is.
Mururoa
Is. Tubuai
Rapa
Oeno I.
Henderson I.
Pitcairn I. (U.K.)
Ducie I.
Tropic of Capricorn
Easter Fracture Zone
Sala y Gómez Ridge
Sala-y-Gómez (Chile)
I. de Pascua (Chile)
Nazca Ridge
Challenger Fracture Zone
Chile Rise
Southwest Pacific Basin
Menard Fracture Zone
Pacific-Antarctic Ridge
Southeast Pacific Basin
West from Greenwich

ARCTIC OCEAN
Beaufort Sea
Lincoln Sea
Greenland
Baffin Bay
Baffin Island
Hudson Bay
Labrador Sea
Canadian Shield
Rocky Mountains
Great Plains
Great Lakes
Great Basin
Mexican Plateau
Gulf of Mexico
NORTH ATLANTIC OCEAN
Sargasso Sea
PACIFIC OCEAN
Caribbean Sea
Central America
Alaska Range
Mackenzie Mts
Appalachian Mts
Western Sierra Madre
Eastern Sierra Madre
Gulf of Alaska
Bering Sea
Chukchi Sea
Asia
Iceland
Cuba
West Indies
Greater Antilles
Andes
Projection: Bonne
West from Greenwich

ARCTIC OCEAN
GREENLAND (Denmark)
ICELAND
Reykjavik
RUSSIA
Asia
Bering Sea
Bering Strait
Beaufort Sea
Queen Elizabeth Is.
Ellesmere I.
Victoria I.
Baffin Island
Baffin Bay
Davis Strait
Denmark Strait
Nuuk
ALASKA (U.S.A.)
Fairbanks
Anchorage
Gulf of Alaska
YUKON TERRITORY
Whitehorse
NORTHWEST TERRITORIES
Yellowknife
NUNAVUT
Iqaluit
Hudson Strait
Hudson Bay
CANADA
BRITISH COLUMBIA
ALBERTA
Edmonton
Calgary
SASKATCHEWAN
Regina
MANITOBA
Winnipeg
ONTARIO
QUÉBEC
NEWFOUNDLAND & LABRADOR
St. John's
PRINCE EDWARD I.
Charlottetown
NEW BRUNSWICK
Fredericton
NOVA SCOTIA
Halifax
St.-Pierre et Miquelon (Fr.)
Vancouver
Victoria
Québec
Montréal
Ottawa
Toronto
UNITED STATES
WASHINGTON
Seattle
Olympia
Portland
Salem
OREGON
IDAHO
Boise
MONTANA
Helena
WYOMING
NORTH DAKOTA
Bismarck
SOUTH DAKOTA
MINNESOTA
Minneapolis-St. Paul
WISCONSIN
Madison
Milwaukee
MICHIGAN
Lansing
Detroit
CHICAGO
IOWA
NEBRASKA
Lincoln
Sacramento
SAN FRANCISCO
San Jose
Carson City
NEVADA
UTAH
Salt Lake City
Denver
COLORADO
KANSAS
Topeka
Kansas City
MISSOURI
St. Louis
Springfield
ILLINOIS
INDIANA
Indianapolis
OHIO
Columbus
Cleveland
Cincinnati
Toledo
Buffalo
NEW YORK
PHILADELPHIA
Pittsburgh
Baltimore
Washington D.C.
Richmond
VIRGINIA
Raleigh
NORTH CAROLINA
Charlotte
Boston
Providence
Concord
Hartford
Augusta
MAINE
LOS ANGELES
CALIFORNIA
Las Vegas
San Diego
Tijuana
Mexicali
ARIZONA
Phoenix
Tucson
NEW MEXICO
Santa Fe
Albuquerque
OKLAHOMA
Oklahoma City
ARKANSAS
Little Rock
TENNESSEE
Nashville
Memphis
KENTUCKY
Atlanta
GEORGIA
SOUTH CAROLINA
Columbia
Charleston
ALABAMA
Birmingham
Montgomery
MISSISSIPPI
Jackson
El Paso
Ciudad Juárez
TEXAS
Dallas-Ft. Worth
Austin
Houston
San Antonio
LOUISIANA
Baton Rouge
New Orleans
FLORIDA
Tallahassee
Jacksonville
Orlando
Tampa-St. Petersburg
Miami
Bermuda (U.K.)
NORTH ATLANTIC OCEAN
PACIFIC OCEAN
Guadalupe (Mex.)
Hermosillo
MEXICO
Culiacán
Torreón
Monterrey
San Luis Potosí
León
Guadalajara
MÉXICO
Toluca
Puebla
Acapulco
Mérida
Revilla Gigedo Is. (Mex.)
Tropic of Cancer
Gulf of Mexico
BAHAMAS
Nassau
Turks & Caicos Is. (U.K.)
CUBA
Havana
Cayman Is. (U.K.)
JAMAICA
Kingston
HAITI
Port-au-Prince
DOMINICAN REP.
Santo Domingo
PUERTO RICO (U.S.A.)
San Juan
Caribbean Sea
BELIZE
Belmopan
GUATEMALA
Guatemala
HONDURAS
Tegucigalpa
San Salvador
EL SALVADOR
NICARAGUA
Managua
L. Nicaragua
COSTA RICA
San José
PANAMA
Panamá
COLOMBIA
Medellín
Barranquilla
Maracaibo
VENEZUELA
South America
International Date Line
Arctic Circle
Projection: Bonne
West from Greenwich
■ MÉXICO Capital Cities
COPYRIGHT PHILIP'S

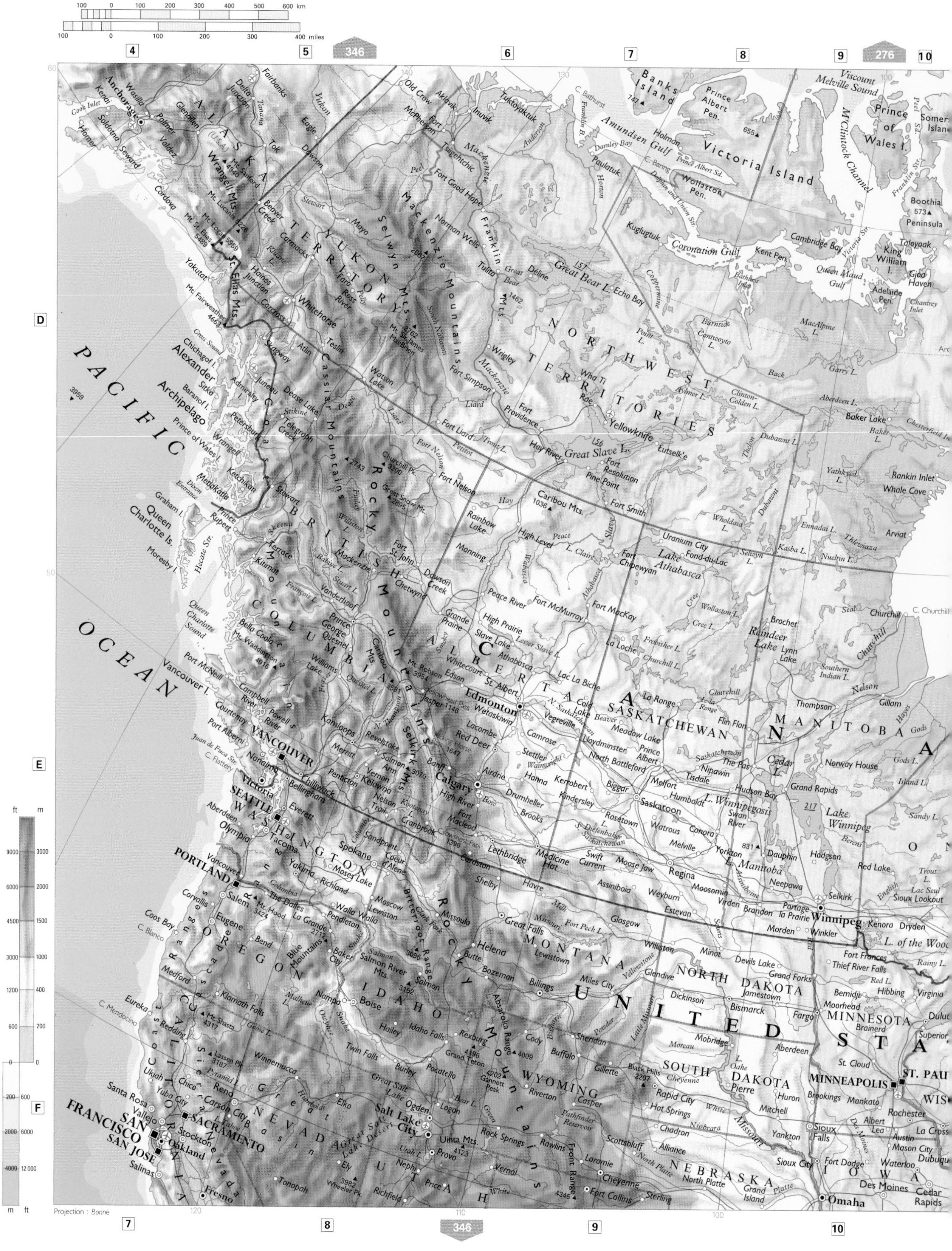

100 0 100 200 300 400 500 600 km
100 0 100 200 300 400 miles

4 5 346 6 7 8 9 276 10

PACIFIC OCEAN

ALASKA (U.S.A.)
YUKON TERRITORY
NORTHWEST TERRITORIES
BRITISH COLUMBIA
ALBERTA
SASKATCHEWAN
MANITOBA
WASHINGTON
OREGON
CALIFORNIA
NEVADA
IDAHO
MONTANA
WYOMING
UTAH
NORTH DAKOTA
SOUTH DAKOTA
NEBRASKA
MINNESOTA
IOWA
UNITED STATES

Anchorage, Fairbanks, Juneau, Whitehorse, Dawson, Inuvik, Tuktoyaktuk, Yellowknife, Norman Wells, Fort Simpson, Hay River, Fort Smith, Prince Rupert, Prince George, Kamloops, VANCOUVER, Victoria, Edmonton, Calgary, Red Deer, Lethbridge, Medicine Hat, Saskatoon, Regina, Prince Albert, Moose Jaw, Brandon, Winnipeg, Thompson, Flin Flon, Churchill, SEATTLE, Spokane, PORTLAND, Salem, Eugene, Boise, Helena, Great Falls, Billings, Salt Lake City, Reno, SACRAMENTO, SAN FRANCISCO, SAN JOSE, Fresno, Bismarck, Fargo, MINNEAPOLIS, ST. PAUL, Sioux Falls, Omaha, Cheyenne, Rapid City

Banks Island, Victoria Island, Prince of Wales I., King William I., Queen Charlotte Is., Vancouver I., Alexander Archipelago

Great Bear L., Great Slave L., Lake Athabasca, Reindeer Lake, Lake Winnipeg, L. Winnipegosis, L. Manitoba, L. of the Woods

Rocky Mountains, Mackenzie Mountains, Selwyn Mts., Cassiar Mountains, Coast Mountains, Columbia Mountains, Selkirk Mts., Cascade Range, Sierra Nevada, Great Basin, Wrangell Mts., St. Elias Mts.

Amundsen Gulf, Coronation Gulf, Queen Maud Gulf, Viscount Melville Sound, M'Clintock Channel

Projection : Bonne

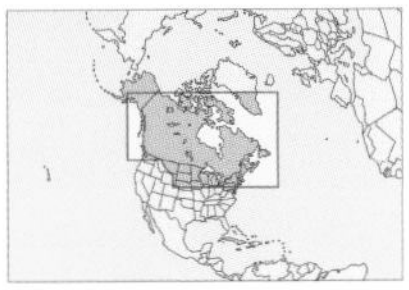

NORTHERN CANADA
continuation northwards on same scale as main map
ARCTIC OCEAN
Queen Elizabeth Is.
Sverdrup Islands
Parry Islands
Banks Island
Victoria Island
Melville I.
Devon Island
Ellesmere Island
Axel Heiberg I.
GREENLAND (Denmark)
NUNAVUT
NORTHWEST TERRITORIES
Prince of Wales Island
Somerset Island
Baffin Island
Baffin Bay
Baffin Island
Foxe Basin
Hudson Strait
Hudson Bay
James Bay
Ungava Bay
Labrador Sea
ATLANTIC OCEAN
Péninsule d'Ungava
NEWFOUNDLAND AND LABRADOR
Newfoundland
QUÉBEC
Gulf of St. Lawrence
NEW BRUNSWICK
NOVA SCOTIA
PR. EDWARD I.
ONTARIO
MAINE
VERMONT
NEW HAMPSHIRE
NEW YORK
MICHIGAN
Lake Superior
Lake Huron
L. Ontario
L. Erie
MONTRÉAL
OTTAWA
Québec
TORONTO
BOSTON
NEW YORK
CHICAGO
DETROIT
CLEVELAND
PROVIDENCE
MILWAUKEE
Halifax
St. John's
Iqaluit
West from Greenwich
COPYRIGHT PHILIP'S

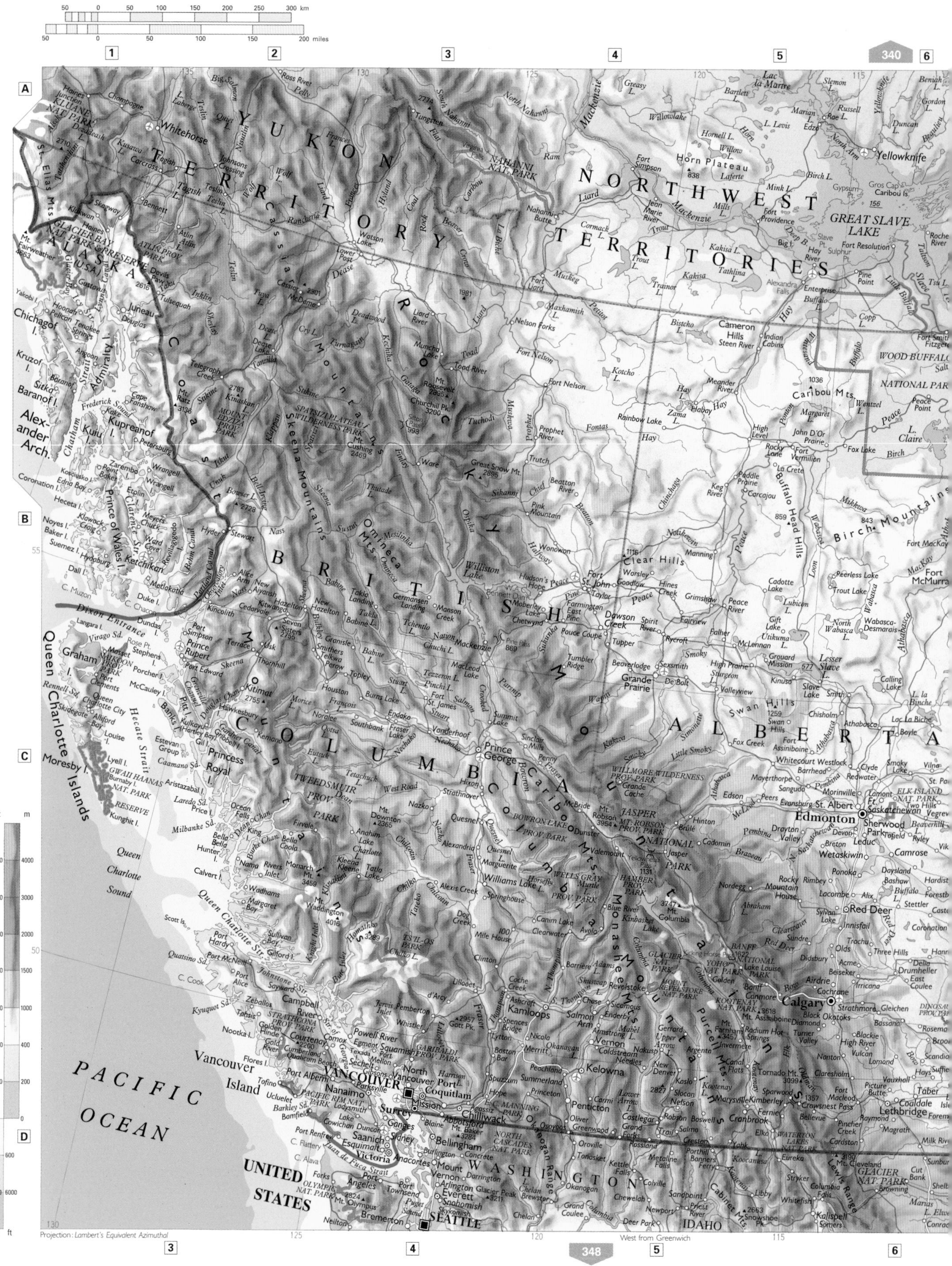

YUKON TERRITORY
NORTHWEST TERRITORIES
BRITISH COLUMBIA
ALBERTA
ALASKA
WASHINGTON
IDAHO
UNITED STATES
PACIFIC OCEAN
Queen Charlotte Islands
Vancouver Island
GREAT SLAVE LAKE
Whitehorse
Yellowknife
Edmonton
Calgary
Kamloops
Kelowna
Prince George
Prince Rupert
Fort St John
Dawson Creek
Grande Prairie
Red Deer
Lethbridge
Victoria
VANCOUVER
SEATTLE
Juneau
Ketchikan
Projection: Lambert's Equivalent Azimuthal
West from Greenwich

340
348

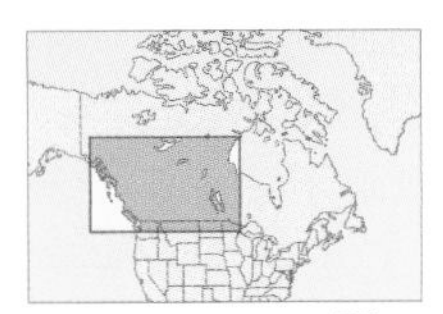

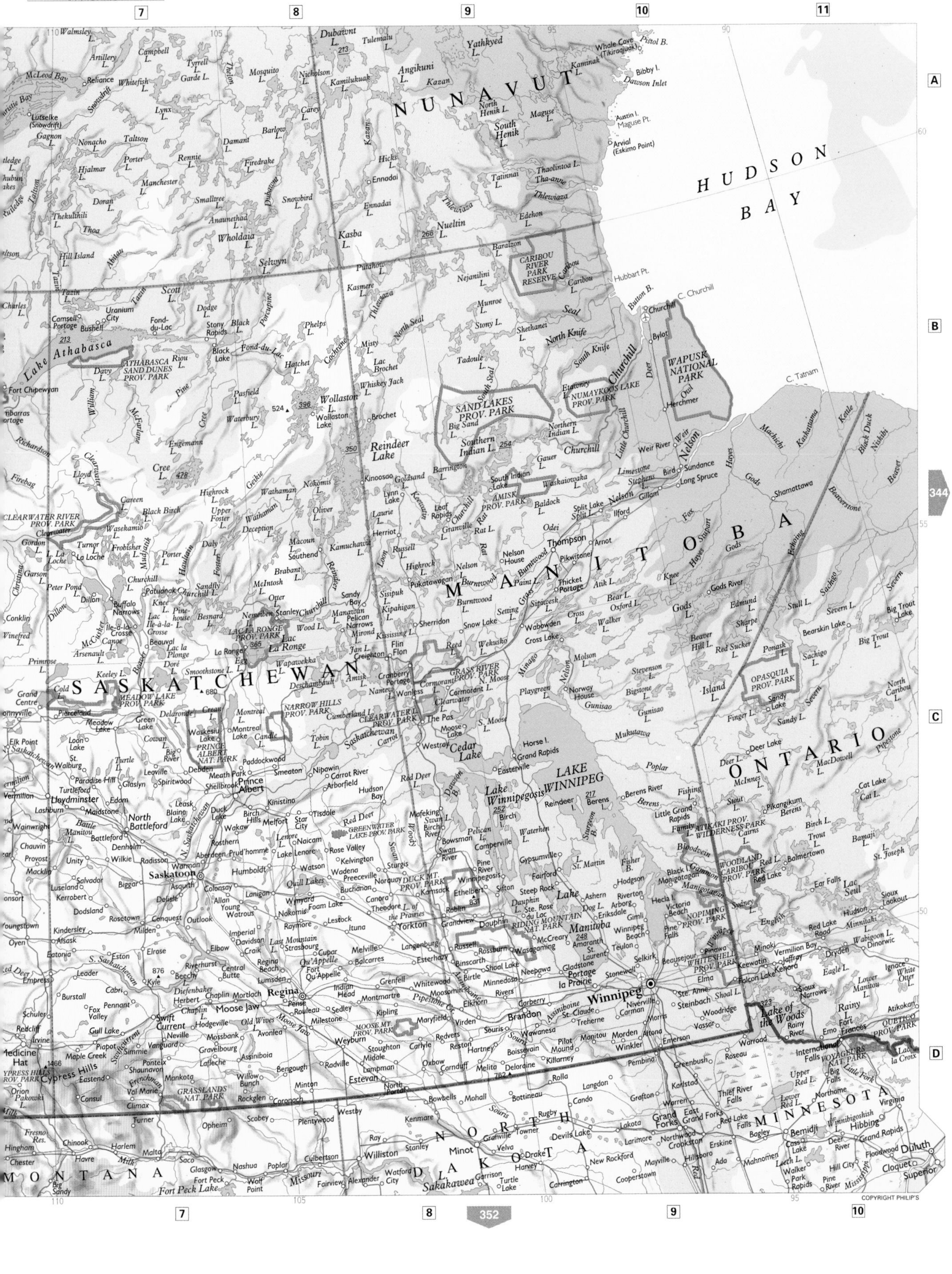

7
8
9
10
11
A
B
C
D
344
352
NUNAVUT
HUDSON
BAY
MANITOBA
SASKATCHEWAN
ONTARIO
MONTANA
NORTH DAKOTA
MINNESOTA
LAKE WINNIPEG
Lake Winnipegosis
Lake Manitoba
Cedar Lake
Lake of the Woods
Lake Athabasca
Reindeer Lake
Southern Indian L.
Wollaston L.
Nueltin L.
Dubawnt L.
Yathkyed L.
Kaminak L.
Whale Cove (Tikirarjuaq)
Pistol B.
Bibby I.
Dawson Inlet
Austin I.
Maguse Pt.
Arvial (Eskimo Point)
Hubbart Pt.
Button B.
C. Churchill
Churchill
C. Tatnam
WAPUSK NATIONAL PARK
CARIBOU RIVER PARK RESERVE
SAND LAKES PROV. PARK
NUMAYKOOS LAKE PROV. PARK
ATHABASCA SAND DUNES PROV. PARK
CLEARWATER RIVER PROV. PARK
LAC LA RONGE PROV. PARK
MEADOW LAKE PROV. PARK
NARROW HILLS PROV. PARK
PRINCE ALBERT NAT. PARK
GRASS RIVER PROV. PARK
CLEARWATER L. PROV. PARK
OPASQUIA PROV. PARK
ATIKAKI PROV. WILDERNESS PARK
WOODLAND CARIBOU PROV. PARK
NOPIMING PROV. PARK
WHITESHELL PROV. PARK
RIDING MOUNTAIN NAT. PARK
DUCK MT. PROV. PARK
MOOSE MT. PROV. PARK
GRASSLANDS NAT. PARK
CYPRESS HILLS INTER. PROV. PARK
GREENWATER LAKE PROV. PARK
QUETICO PROV. PARK
VOYAGEURS NAT. PARK
Uranium City
Fort Chipewyan
Thompson
Flin Flon
The Pas
Lynn Lake
La Ronge
Prince Albert
North Battleford
Lloydminster
Saskatoon
Yorkton
Dauphin
Brandon
Regina
Moose Jaw
Swift Current
Medicine Hat
Weyburn
Estevan
Portage la Prairie
Winnipeg
Steinbach
Selkirk
Kenora
Dryden
Fort Frances
International Falls
Grand Forks
Minot
Williston
Bemidji
Hibbing
Duluth
Superior
Sakakawea
Missouri
Fort Peck Lake
Cypress Hills
Churchill
Nelson
Hayes
Saskatchewan
S. Saskatchewan
N. Saskatchewan
Assiniboine
Souris
Red
Qu'Appelle
Winnipeg
COPYRIGHT PHILIP'S

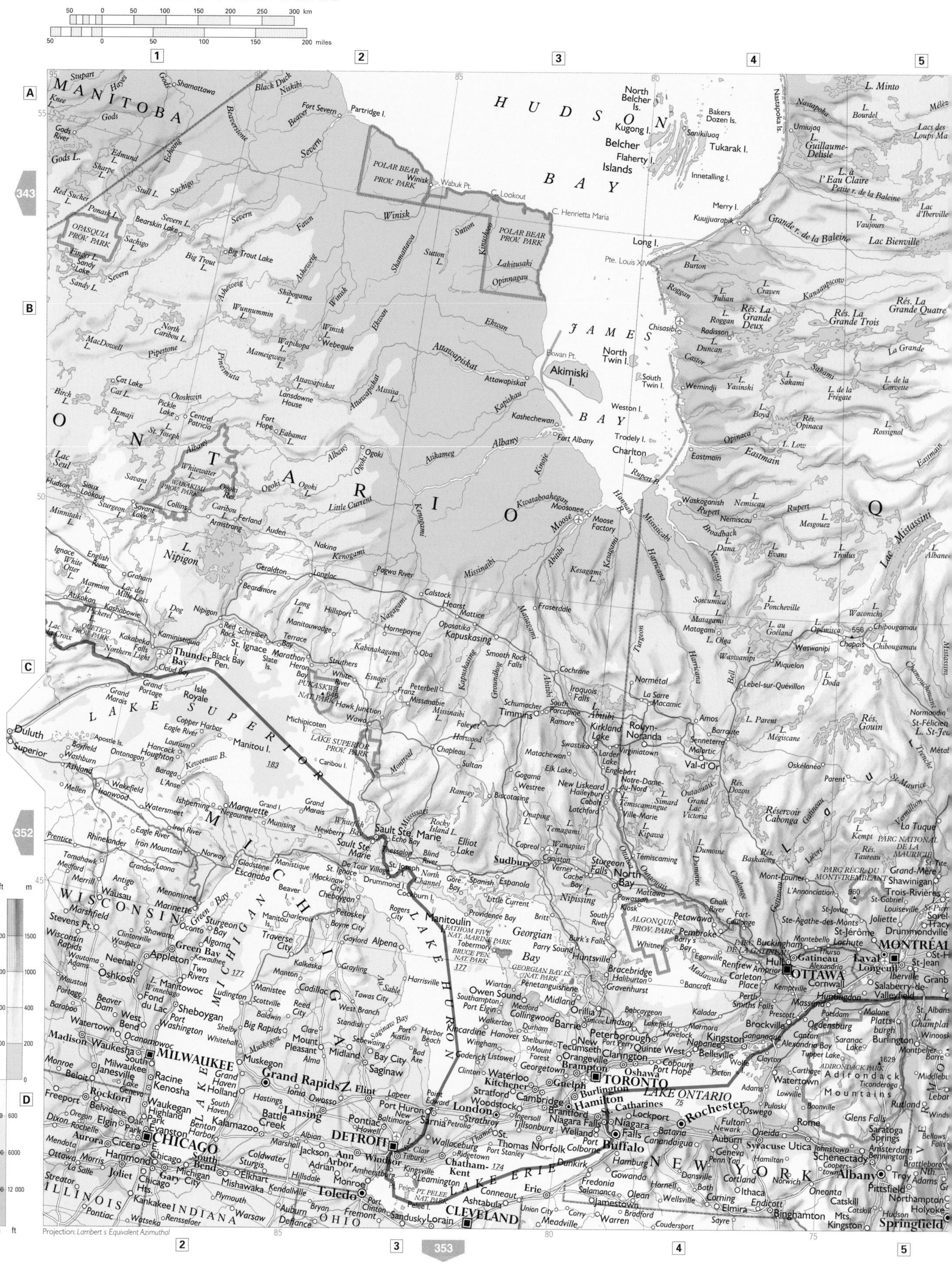
50 0 50 100 150 200 250 300 km
50 0 50 100 150 200 miles
1 2 3 4 5
A B C D
MANITOBA
ONTARIO
HUDSON BAY
JAMES BAY
POLAR BEAR PROV. PARK
OPASQUIA PROV. PARK
WABAKIMI PROV. PARK
QUETICO PROV. PARK
PUKASKWA NAT. PARK
LAKE SUPERIOR PROV. PARK
ALGONQUIN PROV. PARK
FATHOM FIVE NAT. MARINE PARK
BRUCE PEN. NAT. PARK
GEORGIAN BAY IS. NAT. PARK
PT. PELEE NAT. PARK
PARC NATIONAL DE LA MAURICIE
PARC RÉCR. DU MONT-TREMBLANT
ADIRONDACK PARK
Adirondack Mountains
LAKE SUPERIOR
LAKE MICHIGAN
LAKE HURON
LAKE ERIE
LAKE ONTARIO
Georgian Bay
L. Nipigon
L. Nipissing
L. Mistassini
Belcher Islands
Akimiski I.
MICHIGAN
WISCONSIN
ILLINOIS
INDIANA
OHIO
NEW YORK
Q
OTTAWA
MONTRÉAL
TORONTO
DETROIT
CHICAGO
MILWAUKEE
CLEVELAND
Buffalo
Rochester
Hamilton
London
Windsor
Sudbury
Thunder Bay
Sault Ste. Marie
Timmins
Duluth
Grand Rapids
Toledo
Albany
Kingston
Moosonee
Moose Factory
Fort Severn
Fort Albany
Attawapiskat
Chisasibi
Rouyn-Noranda
Val-d'Or
Projection: Lambert's Equivalent Azimuthal
ft m
4500 1500
3000 1000
1200 400
600 200
0 0
200 600
2000 6000
4000 12 000
m ft

343
352
353

100 0 100 200 300 400 500 km

100 0 50 100 150 200 250 300 350 miles

1 2 3 4 340 5 6 7

A B C D

CANADA
BRITISH COLUMBIA
ALBERTA
SASKATCHEWAN
MANITOBA
Calgary, Red Deer, High River, Lethbridge, Medicine Hat, Kindersley, Saskatoon, L. Diefenbaker, Swift Current, Moose Jaw, Regina, Assiniboia, Weyburn, Estevan, Moosomin, Yorkton, Dauphin, L. Winnipegosis, L. Manitoba, Neepawa, Brandon, Portage la Prairie, Morden
VANCOUVER, Vancouver I., Str. of Georgia, Str. of Juan de Fuca, Victoria, Chilliwack, Bellingham, Kelowna, Penticton, Nelson, Grand Forks, Trail, Cranbrook, Selkirk Mts., Mt. Assiniboine 3618

PACIFIC OCEAN

WASHINGTON
SEATTLE, Everett, Bremerton, Tacoma, Olympia, Aberdeen, Grays Harb., C. Disappointment, Centralia, Mt. Rainier 4392, Mt. St. Helens 2550, Longview, Yakima, Ellensburg, Wenatchee, Spokane, Moses Lake, Kennewick, Richland, Pullman, Walla Walla, Mt. Olympus 2428, Cascade Range

OREGON
PORTLAND, Vancouver, Astoria, McMinnville, Salem, Corvallis, Albany, Eugene, Springfield, Coos Bay, Roseburg, Grants Pass, Medford, Klamath Falls, Upper Klamath L., Bend, The Dalles, Pendleton, La Grande, Baker City, Burns, Ontario, Mt. Hood 3426, Blue Mountains, Columbia Plateau, Harney L., Malheur L., Summer L., C. Blanco

IDAHO
Sandpoint, Coeur d'Alene, Kellogg, Moscow, Lewiston, Grangeville, Boise, Caldwell, Nampa, Payette, Sun Valley, Hailey, Mountain Home, Twin Falls, Rupert, Burley, Pocatello, Idaho Falls, Rexburg, Salmon, Salmon River Mts., Hyndman Peak 3681, Snake, Bitterroot Range

MONTANA
Kalispell, Missoula, Helena, Butte, Anaconda, Bozeman, Great Falls, Havre, Shelby, Glasgow, Lewistown, Livingston, Billings, Miles City, Glendive, Big Belt Mts., Flathead Lake, Glacier Nat. Park, Fort Peck L., Missouri, Yellowstone, Milk

ROCKY MOUNTAINS

WYOMING
Cody, Sheridan, Buffalo, Gillette, Thermopolis, Riverton, Casper, Rawlins, Laramie, Cheyenne, Evanston, Rock Springs, Green River, Grand Teton 4196, Gannett Peak 4202, Yellowstone Nat. Park, Absaroka Range, Bighorn Mts., Wind River Range, Pathfinder Reservoir, Laramie Mts.

NORTH DAKOTA
Williston, Minot, Devils Lake, Dickinson, Mandan, Bismarck, Jamestown, Valley City, L. Sakakawea, Coteau du Missouri

SOUTH DAKOTA
Mobridge, Aberdeen, Pierre, Huron, Mitchell, Rapid City, Black Hills 2207, Badlands, Lake Oahe, Lake Francis Case

NEBRASKA
Chadron, Valentine, O'Neill, Scottsbluff, Alliance, Sidney, North Platte, Grand Island, Kearney, Hastings, McCook

CALIFORNIA
SACRAMENTO, SAN FRANCISCO, Oakland, Concord, Vallejo, Napa, Santa Rosa, Ukiah, Eureka, Redding, Red Bluff, Chico, Yuba City, Roseville, Stockton, Modesto, Merced, SAN JOSÉ, Santa Cruz, Salinas, Monterey, Fresno, Hanford, Visalia, Tulare, Bakersfield, Paso Robles, San Luis Obispo, Santa Maria, Santa Barbara, Oxnard, Santa Clarita, Glendale, Pasadena, LOS ANGELES, Long Beach, Anaheim, Santa Ana, Riverside, SAN BERNARDINO, Mission Viejo, Oceanside, SAN DIEGO, Palm Springs, El Centro, Barstow, Ridgecrest, Mt. Shasta 4317, Lassen Pk. 3187, Mt. Whitney 4418, Sierra Nevada, Coast Ranges, Yosemite Nat. Park, Sequoia Nat. Park, Death Valley -86, Mojave Desert, Salton Sea, Channel Islands, C. Mendocino, Pt. Conception

NEVADA
Reno, Sparks, Carson City, Winnemucca, Elko, Ely, Tonopah, Hawthorne, LAS VEGAS, Henderson, Great Basin, Walker Lake, Wheeler Pk. 3982, L. Tahoe, Lake Mead, Hoover Dam

UTAH
Salt Lake City, Ogden, Logan, Brigham City, Provo, Orem, Sandy, Nephi, Price, Richfield, Moab, Cedar City, St. George, Great Salt Lake, Great Salt Lake Desert, Uinta Mts., Wasatch Range, Kings Pk. 4123, Zion Nat. Park, L. Powell

COLORADO
Fort Collins, Greeley, Boulder, DENVER, Aurora, Vail, Aspen, Grand Junction, Montrose, Colorado Springs, Pueblo, Cañon City, Salida, Durango, Cortez, Alamosa, Trinidad, Walsenburg, La Junta, Lamar, Sterling, Fort Morgan, Craig, Mt. Elbert 4399, Pikes Pk. 4301, Blanca Peak 4372, Front Range, San Juan Mts., Sangre de Cristo Mts.

ARIZONA
Page, Kingman, Lake Havasu City, Bullhead City, Flagstaff, Prescott, Winslow, Payson, Glendale, PHOENIX, Mesa, Globe, Safford, Tucson, Casa Grande, Yuma, Sonoyta, Nogales, Grand Canyon, Grand Canyon Nat. Park, Humphreys Peak 3851, Colorado Plateau, Painted Desert, Sonoran Desert, Baldy Pk. 3476

NEW MEXICO
Farmington, Gallup, Los Alamos, Santa Fe, Taos, Raton, Las Vegas, Albuquerque, Mt. Taylor 3445, Tucumcari, Socorro, Silver City, Lordsburg, Deming, Las Cruces, Alamogordo, Roswell, Hobbs, Carlsbad, Sierra Blanca Peak 3659, Elephant Butte Res., Llano Estacado

TEXAS
Dalhart, Amarillo, Lubbock, Plainview, Childress, Midland, Odessa, Big Spring, San Angelo, Abilene, Sweetwater, Fort Worth, El Paso, Pecos, Fort Stockton, Alpine, Presidio, Del Rio, Uvalde, Eagle Pass, SAN ANTONIO, Austin, San Marcos, Laredo, Corpus Christi, Kingsville, McAllen, Harlingen, Edwards Plateau

OKLAHOMA, KANSAS
Clinton, El Reno, Norman, Lawton, Altus, Enid, Liberal, Dodge City, Garden City, Hays, Salina, Great Bend, McPherson, Hutchinson, Pratt, Concordia

MEXICO
Tijuana, Ensenada, Mexicali, San Felipe 3078, Nogales, Agua Prieta, Magdalena de Kino, SONORA, CIUDAD JUÁREZ, Villa Ahumada, CHIHUAHUA, Ojinaga, Ciudad Acuña, Piedras Negras, COAHUILA, Sabinas, Nuevo Laredo, Sabinas Hidalgo, MONTERREY, Matamoros, Falcon Res.

ALASKA a

100 0 100 200 300 400 500 600 km

100 0 100 200 300 400 miles

CHUKCHI SEA, Barrow, Prudhoe Bay, Point Hope, Brooks Range 2699, Kotzebue, Fort Yukon, Circle, Nome, Bering Strait, Seward Pen., Galena, Fairbanks, Dawson, Unalakleet, Norton Sound, Anderson, Mt. McKinley 6194, Alaska Range, Tok, St. Lawrence I., St. Matthew I., Nunivak I., Hooper Bay, Bethel, Anchorage, Valdez, Mt. Logan 5959, Whitehorse, Skagway, Juneau, Kenai, Seward, Homer, Dillingham, Bristol Bay, Iliamna Lake, Kodiak, Kodiak I., GULF OF ALASKA, Alexander Archipelago, Sitka, Petersburg, Ketchikan, Prince Rupert, Queen Charlotte Is., Trinity Is., Shumagin Is., Alaska Peninsula, Pribilof Is., Unimak I., Dutch Harbor, Unalaska I., Umnak I., Unalaska, Aleutian Is., Andreanof Is., Rat Is., Near Is., Attu I., Amchitka I., BERING SEA, RUSSIA, Koryakskoye Nagorye, Chukotskoye Nagorye, Uelen, Provideniya, Anadyrskiy Zaliv, Ugolnyi, Ossora, O. Karaginskiy, PACIFIC OCEAN

HAWAI'I b

50 0 100 km

50 0 50 100 miles

Kaua'i, Kapaa, Lihue, Ni'ihau, Kauai Channel, O'ahu, Wahiawa, Pearl City, Pearl Harbor, Kane'ohe, Honolulu, Moloka'i, Kaunakakai, Lāna'i, Wailuku, Kahului, Maui, Kaho'olawe, 'Alenuihāhā Channel, Waimea (Kamuela), Hilo, Hawai'i, Mauna Kea 4205, Mauna Loa 4169, Kailua, Kilauea, Mountain View, Pāhala, Hawaiian Islands, PACIFIC OCEAN

ft m: 12 000 4000, 9000 3000, 6000 2000, 4500 1500, 3000 1000, 1200 400, 600 200, 0 0, 200 600, 1000 3000, 2000 6000, 4000 12 000 m ft

Projection: Albers' Equal Area with two standard parallels

West from Greenwich

CANADA
Lake Winnipeg
Winnipeg
Lake of the Woods
Kenora
Dryden
Sioux Lookout
Nakina
Hearst
Cochrane
Moosonee
Lake Nipigon
Nipigon
Marathon
Greenstone
Timmins
Kirkland Lake
Rouyn-Noranda
Amos
Chibougamau
Roberval
Jonquière
Chicoutimi
Alma
La Tuque
Québec
Rimouski
Rivière-du-Loup
Edmundston
Fort Kent
Caribou
Presque Isle
Houlton
Millinocket
Saint John
Calais
Bangor
Augusta
Waterville
Belfast
Penobscot Bay
Lewiston
Brunswick
Portland
Gulf of Maine
Thunder Bay
I. Royale
Lake Superior
Wawa
Sault Ste. Marie
Sudbury
North Bay
Pembroke
Ottawa
Montréal
Sherbrooke
Drummondville
Trois-Rivières
Shawinigan
Joliette
Hull
Gatineau
Cornwall
Ogdensburg
Huntsville
Parry Sound
Manitoulin I.
Orillia
Peterborough
Kingston
Barrie
Oshawa
Toronto
Kitchener
London
Hamilton
Lake Ontario
Lake Huron
Lake Erie
Lake Michigan
Niagara Falls
Buffalo
Rochester
Syracuse
Utica
Schenectady
Albany
Troy
Burlington
Montpelier
Plattsburgh
Adirondack Mts.
White Mts.
Concord
Manchester
Nashua
Lowell
Boston
Worcester
Springfield
Providence
Hartford
New Haven
Bridgeport
Yonkers
New York
Jersey City
Newark
Paterson
Trenton
Philadelphia
Atlantic City
Allentown
Reading
Lancaster
Harrisburg
Scranton
Wilkes-Barre
Binghamton
Elmira
Ithaca
Jamestown
Erie
Pittsburgh
Johnstown
Altoona
Baltimore
Wilmington
Dover
Annapolis
Washington D.C.
Frederick
Harrisonburg
Charlottesville
Richmond
Newport News
Norfolk
Virginia Beach
Portsmouth
Petersburg
Lynchburg
Roanoke
Danville
Greensboro
Durham
Raleigh
Rocky Mount
Greenville
Fayetteville
Goldsboro
New Bern
Jacksonville
Wilmington
Charlotte
Winston-Salem
Hickory
Asheville
Spartanburg
Greenville
Rock Hill
Columbia
Florence
Myrtle Beach
Sumter
Charleston
Orangeburg
Hilton Head Island
Savannah
Statesboro
Brunswick
Augusta
Athens
Atlanta
Macon
Columbus
Dublin
Albany
Valdosta
Waycross
Tallahassee
Jacksonville
St. Augustine
Daytona Beach
Gainesville
Ocala
Deltona
Orlando
Lakeland
Tampa
Clearwater
St. Petersburg
Sarasota
Cape Coral
Fort Myers
Naples
Melbourne
Palm Bay
Fort Pierce
Port St. Lucie
West Palm Beach
Fort Lauderdale
Miami
Key West
Florida Keys
Straits of Florida
BAHAMAS
Grand Bahama I.
Freeport
Little Abaco I.
Abaco I.
Nassau
New Providence I.
Andros I.
Eleuthera I.
Cat I.
Great Exuma I.
Long I.
Duluth
Superior
Marquette
Ishpeming
Houghton
Escanaba
Green Bay
Appleton
Oshkosh
Sheboygan
Manitowoc
Wausau
Eau Claire
St. Paul
Minneapolis
Rochester
Mankato
Owatonna
Austin
La Crosse
Madison
Milwaukee
Racine
Kenosha
Janesville
Rockford
Chicago
Elgin
Aurora
Joliet
Gary
South Bend
Elkhart
Fort Wayne
Kalamazoo
Battle Creek
Grand Rapids
Muskegon
Lansing
Jackson
Ann Arbor
Detroit
Windsor
Flint
Saginaw
Midland
Bay City
Port Huron
Toledo
Sandusky
Findlay
Cleveland
Akron
Canton
Youngstown
Mansfield
Columbus
Dayton
Springfield
Cincinnati
Lima
Marion
Muncie
Kokomo
Lafayette
Indianapolis
Richmond
Terre Haute
Bloomington
Evansville
Louisville
Lexington
Frankfort
Owensboro
Henderson
Paducah
Bowling Green
Clarksville
Nashville
Murfreesboro
Knoxville
Chattanooga
Johnson City
Kingsport
Memphis
Jackson
Huntsville
Birmingham
Tuscaloosa
Montgomery
Dothan
Mobile
Pensacola
Panama City
Gulfport
Biloxi
Hattiesburg
Meridian
Jackson
Vicksburg
Greenville
Tupelo
New Orleans
Baton Rouge
Lafayette
Lake Charles
Alexandria
Shreveport
Monroe
Houston
Pasadena
Galveston
Beaumont
Port Arthur
Dallas
Arlington
Waco
Tyler
Longview
Texarkana
Little Rock
Pine Bluff
Hot Springs
Fort Smith
Fayetteville
Tulsa
Oklahoma City
Springfield
Joplin
Kansas City
St. Joseph
Topeka
Lawrence
Jefferson City
Columbia
St. Louis
East St. Louis
Peoria
Springfield
Decatur
Champaign
Quincy
Davenport
Cedar Rapids
Iowa City
Waterloo
Dubuque
Des Moines
Ames
Council Bluffs
Omaha
Lincoln
Sioux City
Sioux Falls
Fargo
Grand Forks
Wichita
Brownsville
Rio Grande
Laguna Madre
Padre I.
Matagorda I.
Aransas Pass
Victoria
Freeport
Port Lavaca
Mississippi River Delta
GULF OF MEXICO
ATLANTIC OCEAN
MINNESOTA
WISCONSIN
MICHIGAN
IOWA
ILLINOIS
INDIANA
OHIO
KENTUCKY
TENNESSEE
MISSOURI
ARKANSAS
MISSISSIPPI
ALABAMA
GEORGIA
LOUISIANA
FLORIDA
SOUTH CAROLINA
NORTH CAROLINA
VIRGINIA
WEST VIRGINIA
PENNSYLVANIA
NEW YORK
VERMONT
NEW HAMPSHIRE
MAINE
MASS.
NEW BRUNSWICK
New England
Midwest
Ozark Plateau
Appalachian Mts.
Cumberland Plateau
Allegheny Mts.
C. Cod
C. Hatteras
C. Fear
C. Canaveral
C. Sable
C. San Blas
Florida Bay
Charlotte Harbor
L. Okeechobee
Apalachee B.
Albemarle Sd.
Pamlico Sd.
Delaware B.
Chesapeake B.
Nantucket I.
Martha's Vineyard
Long I.
New Bedford
Fall River
Tallahassee ⊛ State capitals
COPYRIGHT PHILIP'S

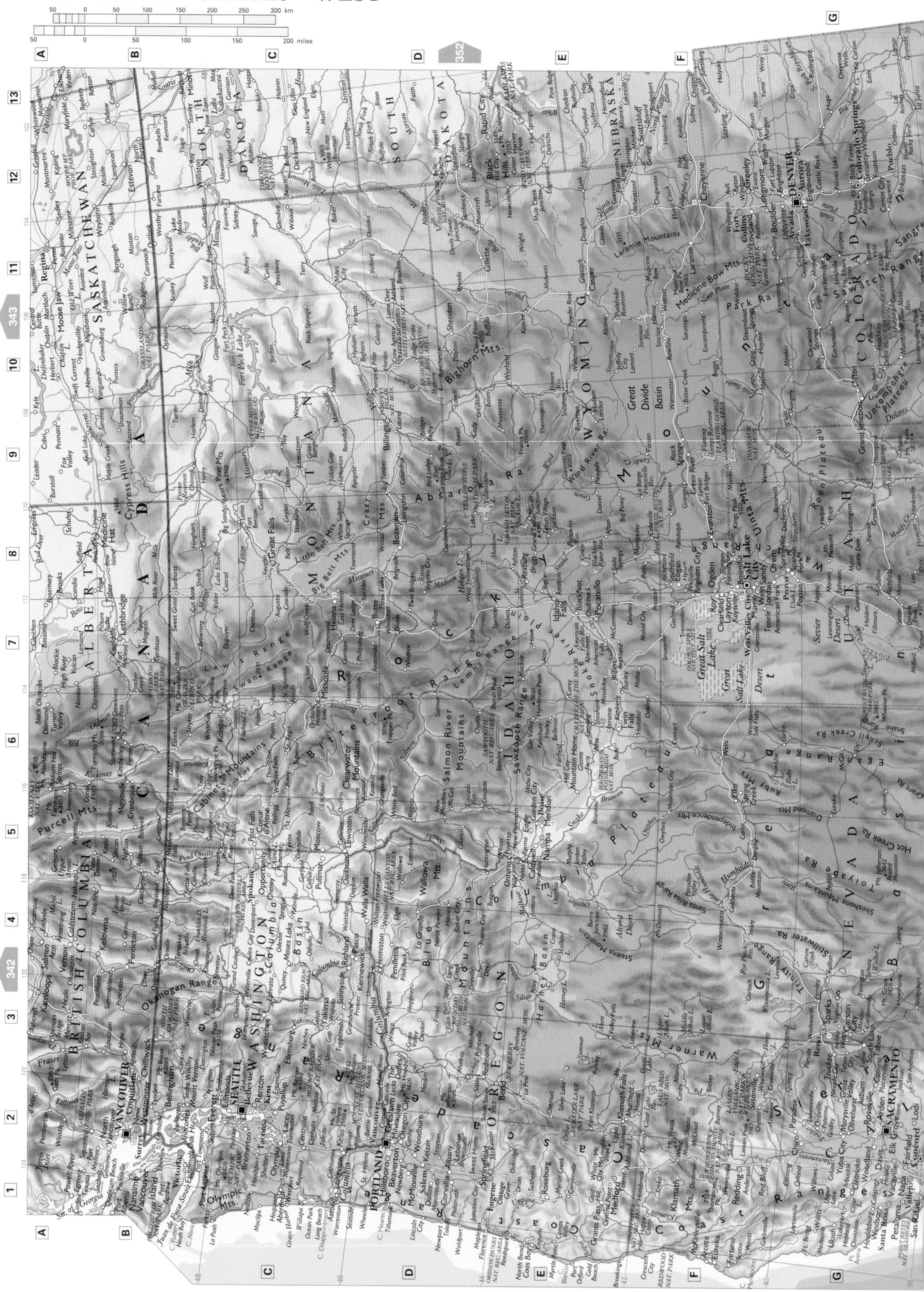
50 0 50 100 150 200 250 300 km
50 0 50 100 150 200 miles
352
343
342
BRITISH COLUMBIA
ALBERTA
SASKATCHEWAN
CANADA
WASHINGTON
OREGON
IDAHO
MONTANA
WYOMING
NORTH DAKOTA
SOUTH DAKOTA
NEBRASKA
COLORADO
UTAH
NEVADA
VANCOUVER
SEATTLE
PORTLAND
SACRAMENTO
Salt Lake City
DENVER
Boise
Helena
Cheyenne
Carson City
Salem
Olympia
Victoria
Regina
Spokane
Great Falls
Billings
Calgary
Lethbridge
Medicine Hat
Moose Jaw
Kamloops
Kelowna
Penticton
Pocatello
Idaho Falls
Twin Falls
Missoula
Butte
Bozeman
Casper
Rock Springs
Ogden
Provo
Reno
Elko
Eugene
Medford
Bend
Klamath Falls
Redding
Colorado Springs
Pueblo
Fort Collins
Grand Junction
Rapid City
Great Salt Lake
Great Basin
Snake River Plain
Columbia Basin
Cascade Range
Rocky Mountains
Bitterroot Range
Bighorn Mts.
Wind River Ra.
Laramie Mountains
Medicine Bow Mts.
Uinta Mts.
Sawatch Range
Blue Mountains
Salmon River Mountains
Sawtooth Range
Lemhi Range
Clearwater Mountains
Cabinet Mountains
Purcell Mts.
Okanogan Range
Olympic Mts.
Warner Mts.
Great Divide Basin
Roan Plateau
Uncompahgre Plateau
Great Salt Lake Desert
Cypress Hills
Fort Peck Lake
Yellowstone
Missouri
Columbia
Snake
Sierra Nevada

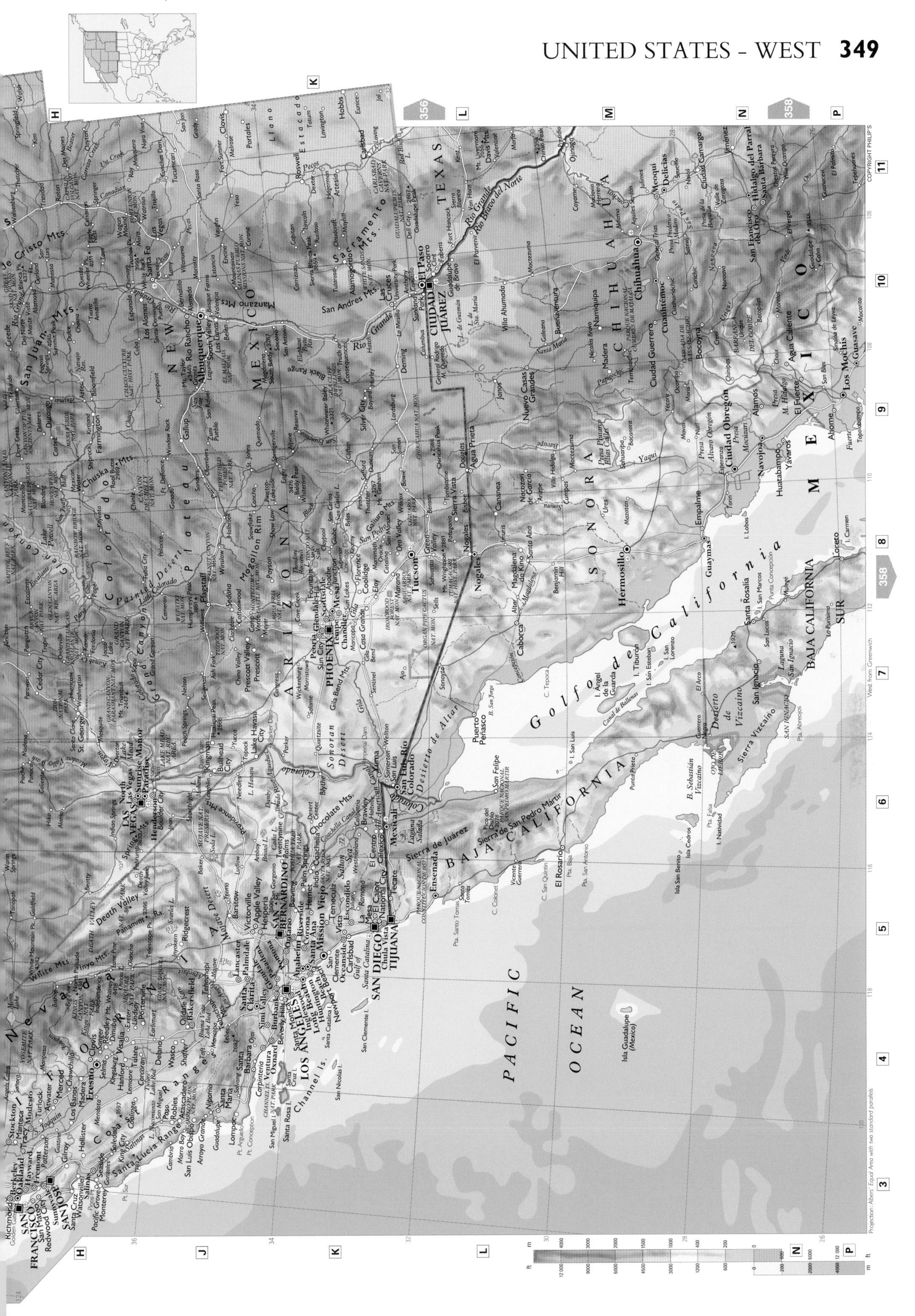
PACIFIC
OCEAN
Golfo de California
ARIZONA
NEW MEXICO
TEXAS
SONORA
CHIHUAHUA
BAJA CALIFORNIA
BAJA CALIFORNIA SUR
MEXICO
Colorado Plateau
Mojave Desert
Sonoran Desert
LOS ANGELES
SAN DIEGO
PHOENIX
Tucson
El Paso
CIUDAD JUÁREZ
Chihuahua
Hermosillo
Albuquerque
LAS VEGAS
Projection: Albers' Equal Area with two standard parallels
West from Greenwich
COPYRIGHT PHILIP'S

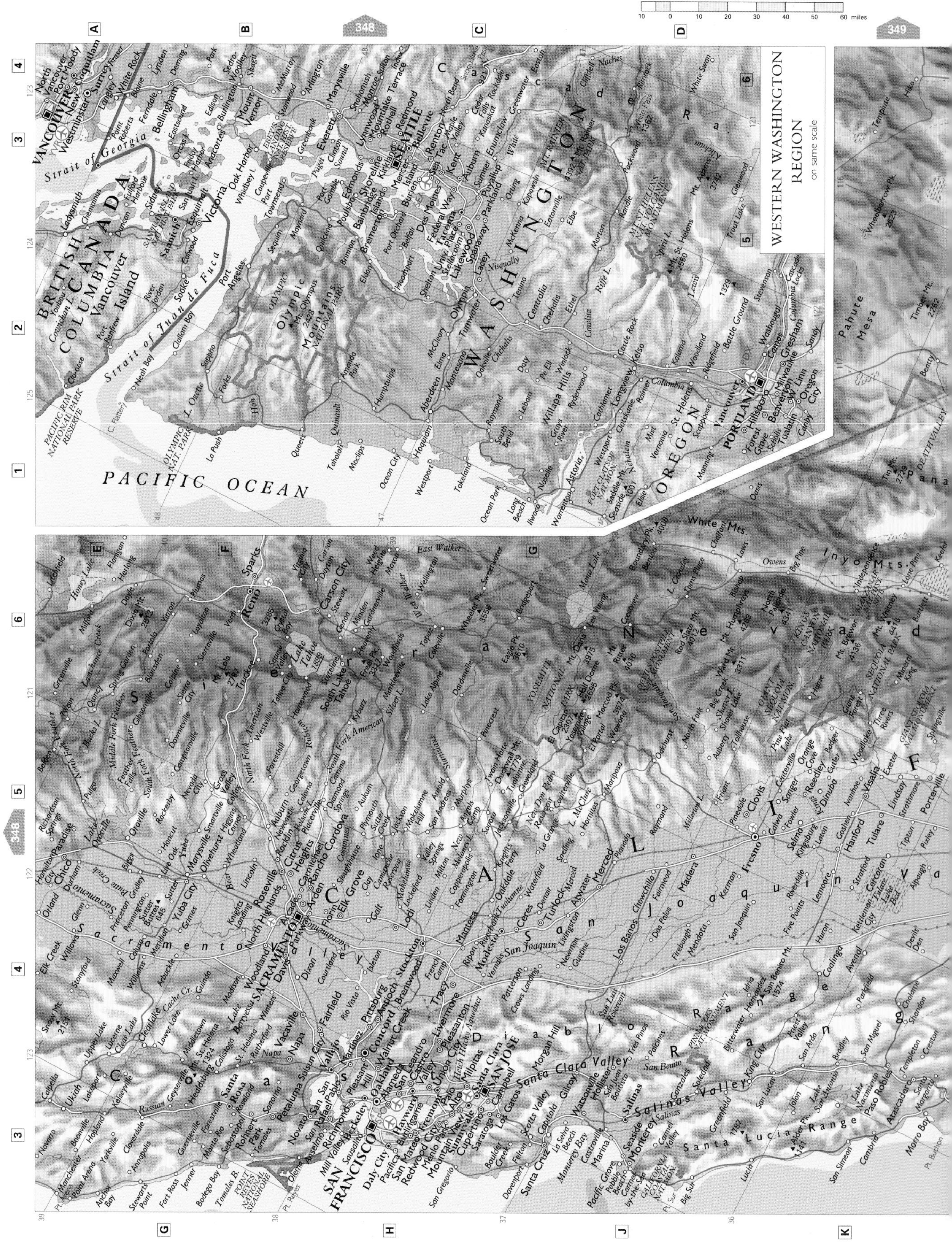

10 0 10 20 30 40 50 60 70 80 90 km
10 0 10 20 30 40 50 60 miles
348
349
A
B
C
D
E
F
G
H
J
K
1
2
3
4
5
6
WESTERN WASHINGTON REGION
on same scale
PACIFIC OCEAN
BRITISH COLUMBIA
CANADA
Vancouver Island
Strait of Georgia
Strait of Juan de Fuca
WASHINGTON
OREGON
Olympic Mountains
VANCOUVER
Victoria
SEATTLE
Tacoma
Olympia
PORTLAND
Vancouver
Mt. Rainier
Mt. St. Helens
Mt. Adams
SACRAMENTO
SAN FRANCISCO
SAN JOSE
Oakland
Stockton
Modesto
Fresno
Reno
Carson City
Lake Tahoe
White Mts.
Inyo Mts.
Pahute Mesa
Santa Lucia Range
Salinas Valley
Santa Clara Valley
Monterey
Santa Cruz
Sierra Nevada
San Joaquin Valley
Sacramento Valley
Coast Ranges

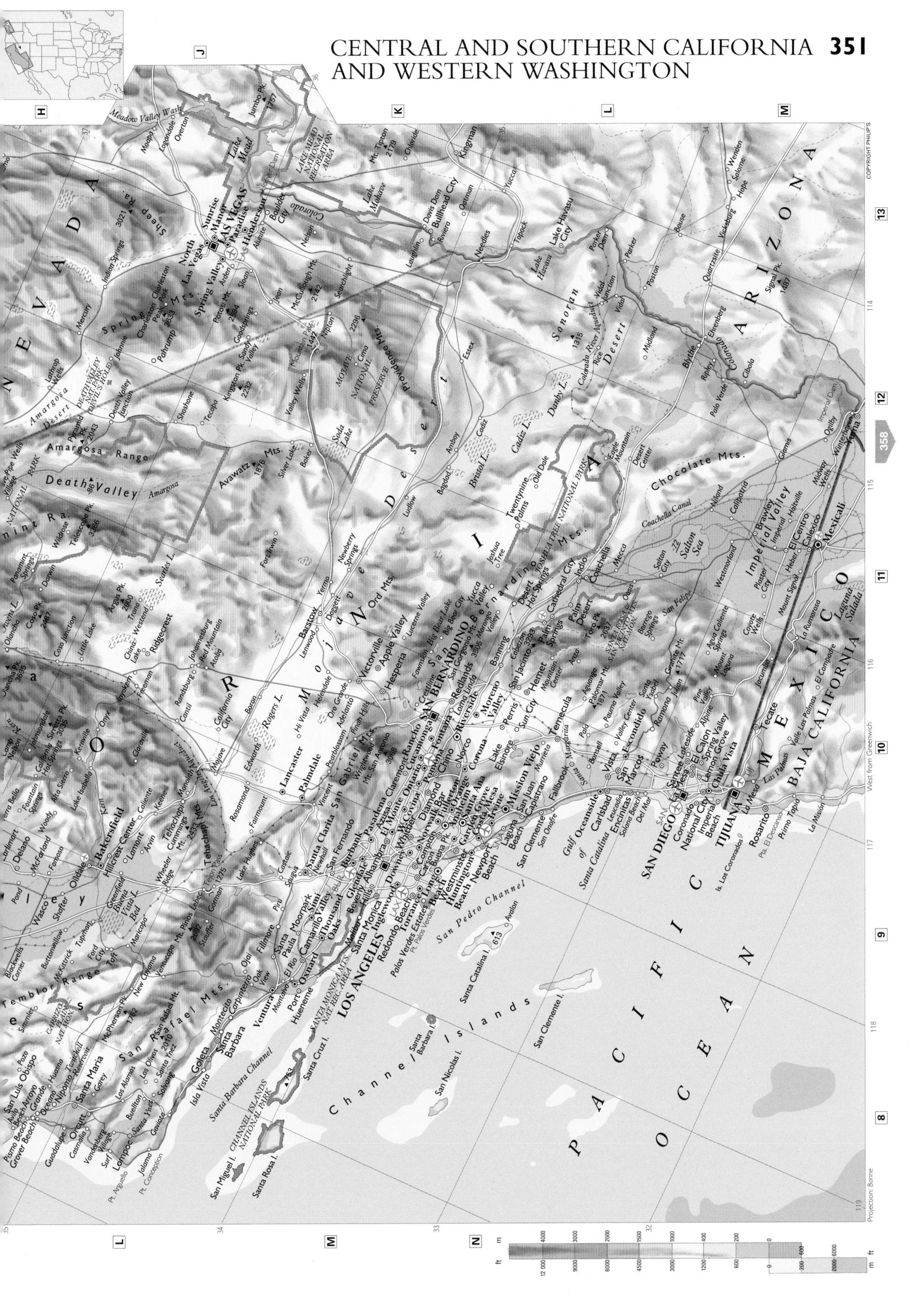
NEVADA
ARIZONA
CALIFORNIA
MEXICO
BAJA CALIFORNIA
PACIFIC OCEAN
Mojave Desert
Sonoran Desert
Las Vegas
North Las Vegas
Henderson
Boulder City
Lake Mead
Kingman
Bullhead City
Needles
Lake Havasu City
Parker
Blythe
Yuma
San Luis Obispo
Santa Maria
Lompoc
Santa Barbara
Goleta
Ventura
Oxnard
Port Hueneme
Bakersfield
Delano
Wasco
Tehachapi
Lancaster
Palmdale
Santa Clarita
Barstow
Victorville
Hesperia
Apple Valley
San Bernardino
Riverside
Moreno Valley
Ontario
Pomona
Pasadena
Glendale
Burbank
Los Angeles
Santa Monica
Inglewood
Torrance
Long Beach
Huntington Beach
Newport Beach
Santa Ana
Anaheim
Irvine
Mission Viejo
San Clemente
Oceanside
Carlsbad
Escondido
San Diego
Chula Vista
Tijuana
Mexicali
Calexico
El Centro
Brawley
Indio
Palm Springs
Twentynine Palms
Salton Sea
Death Valley
Amargosa Range
Spring Mts.
San Bernardino Mts.
San Gabriel Mts.
Santa Catalina I.
San Clemente I.
San Nicolas I.
Santa Cruz I.
Santa Rosa I.
San Miguel I.
Channel Islands
Santa Barbara Channel
San Pedro Channel
Gulf of Santa Catalina
Chocolate Mts.
Imperial Valley
JOSHUA TREE NATIONAL PARK
CHANNEL ISLANDS NATIONAL PARK
MOJAVE NATIONAL PRESERVE
LAKE MEAD NATIONAL RECREATION AREA
West from Greenwich
Projection: Bonne
COPYRIGHT PHILIP'S
358

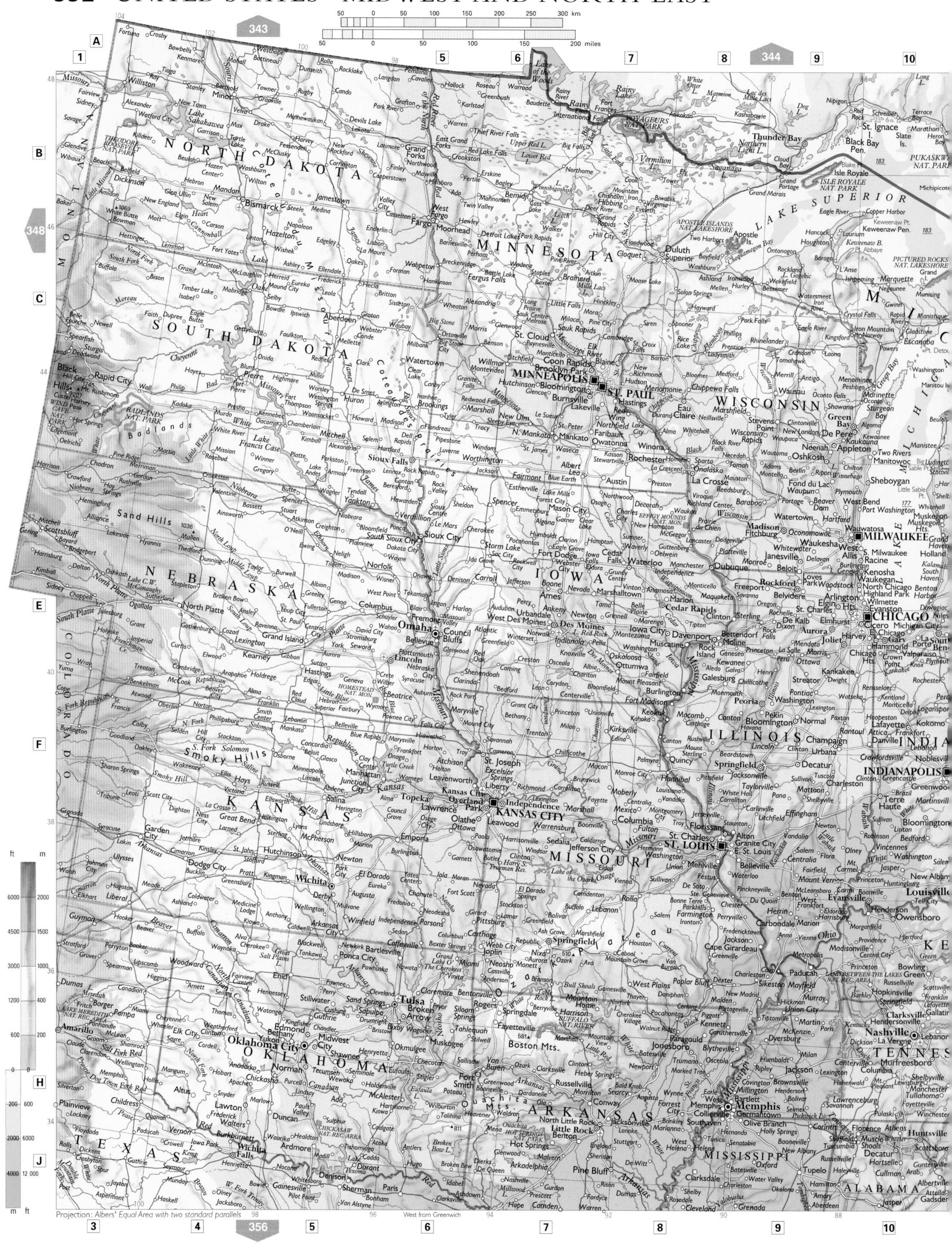
343
344
348
356
50 0 50 100 150 200 250 300 km
50 0 50 100 150 200 miles
NORTH DAKOTA
SOUTH DAKOTA
NEBRASKA
KANSAS
OKLAHOMA
TEXAS
MINNESOTA
IOWA
MISSOURI
ARKANSAS
WISCONSIN
ILLINOIS
MISSISSIPPI
LAKE SUPERIOR
Bismarck
Fargo
Pierre
Rapid City
Sioux Falls
Lincoln
Omaha
Topeka
Wichita
Kansas City
Oklahoma City
Tulsa
MINNEAPOLIS
ST. PAUL
Des Moines
MILWAUKEE
CHICAGO
ST. LOUIS
Memphis
Little Rock
Nashville
INDIANAPOLIS
Louisville
Duluth
Thunder Bay
Sand Hills
Smoky Hills
Badlands
Ozark Plateau
Boston Mts.
Ouachita Mts.
Projection: Albers' Equal Area with two standard parallels
West from Greenwich

344
345
357
ONTARIO
QUÉBEC
CANADA
NEW BRUNS.
MAINE
NEW HAMPSHIRE
VERMONT
NEW YORK
MA.
CT.
R.I.
PENNSYLVANIA
NEW JERSEY
DELAWARE
MARYLAND
OHIO
WEST VIRGINIA
VIRGINIA
NORTH CAROLINA
SOUTH CAROLINA
GEORGIA
KENTUCKY
LAKE HURON
LAKE ONTARIO
LAKE ERIE
Georgian Bay
Gulf of Maine
ATLANTIC OCEAN
Allegheny Plateau
Cumberland Plateau
Appalachian Mountains
Blue Ridge
Pamlico Sound
Chesapeake Bay
Delaware Bay
Long Island
Cape Cod
OTTAWA
MONTRÉAL
Québec
TORONTO
DETROIT
CLEVELAND
PITTSBURGH
PHILADELPHIA
BALTIMORE
WASHINGTON D.C.
NEW YORK
BOSTON
PROVIDENCE
COLUMBUS
CINCINNATI
NORFOLK
Richmond
Buffalo
Rochester
Hamilton
Albany
Hartford
Charlotte
Raleigh
Atlanta
COPYRIGHT PHILIP'S

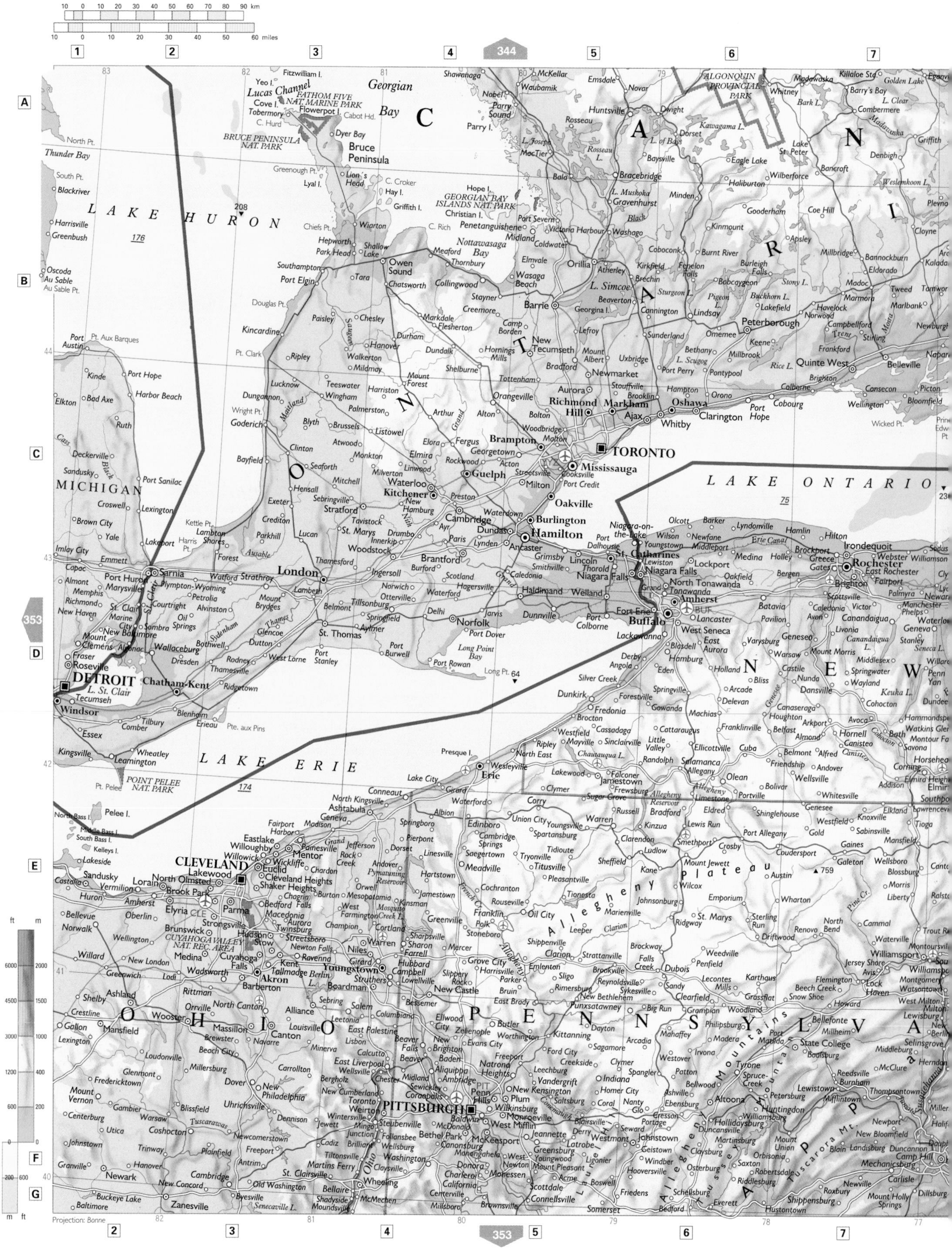
LAKE HURON
LAKE ONTARIO
LAKE ERIE
Georgian Bay
MICHIGAN
OHIO
ONTARIO
CANADA
NEW YORK
PENNSYLVANIA
TORONTO
DETROIT
CLEVELAND
PITTSBURGH
Hamilton
London
Buffalo
Rochester
Erie
Akron
Youngstown
Mississauga
Kitchener
Windsor
Allegheny Plateau
Projection: Bonne

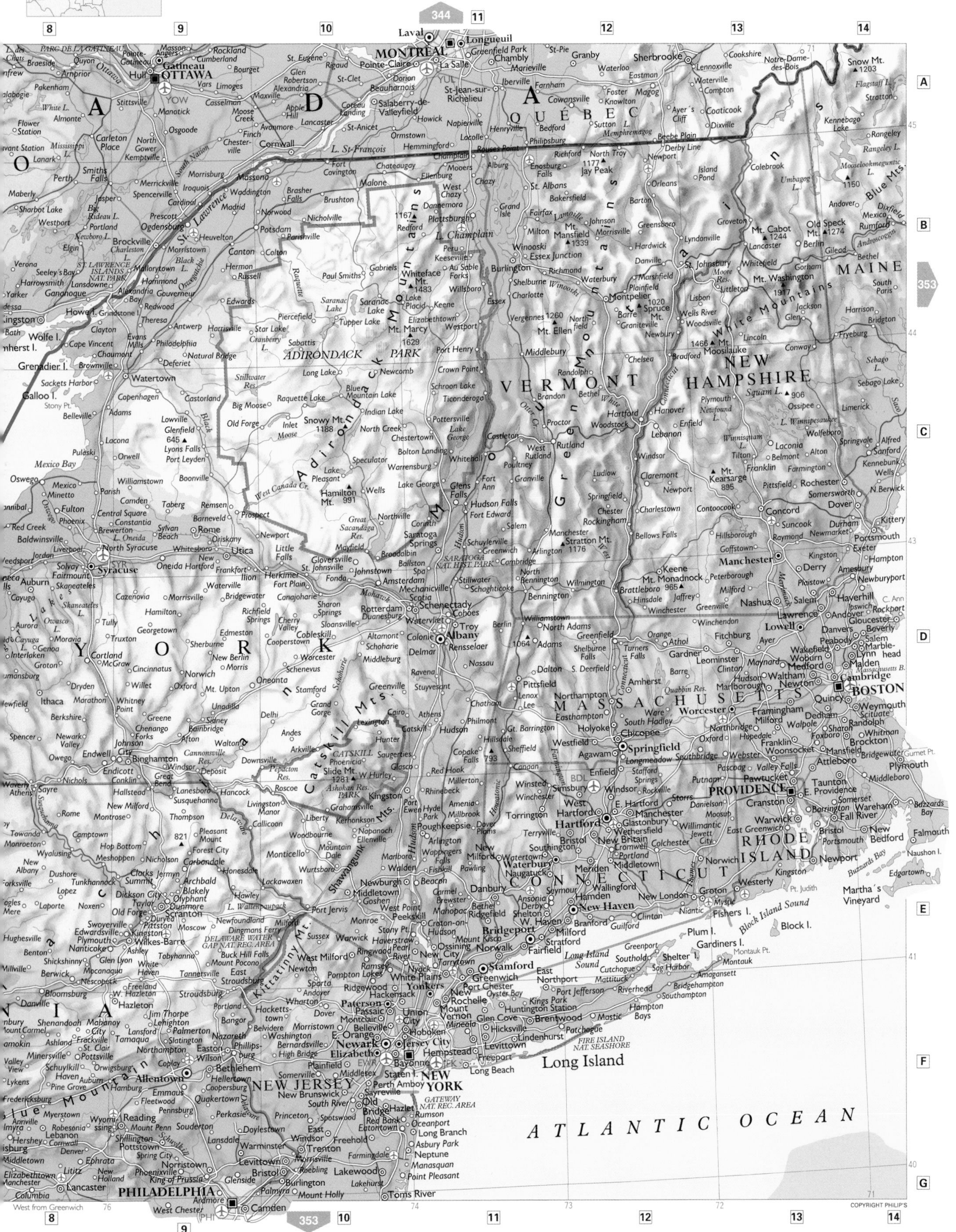

50 0 50 100 150 200 250 300 km
50 0 50 100 150 200 miles
1 2 3 4 5 6 7 8
352
349
NEBRASKA
IOWA
COLORADO
KANSAS
MISSOURI
OKLAHOMA
ARKANSAS
NEW MEXICO
TEXAS
LOUISIANA
MEXICO
COAHUILA
NUEVO LEÓN
CHIHUAHUA
GULF
Rocky Mts.
Sawatch Range
Sangre de Cristo Mts.
San Juan Mts.
Smoky Hills
Llano Estacado
Edwards Plateau
Stockton Plateau
Balcones Escarpment
Ouachita Mts.
Ozark Plateau
Boston Mts.
Bolsón de Mapimí
Sacramento Mts.
Rio Grande
Río Bravo del Norte
Arkansas
Canadian
Red
Pecos
Brazos
Colorado
Mississippi
DENVER
Colorado Springs
Pueblo
Santa Fe
Albuquerque
Amarillo
Lubbock
El Paso
Wichita
Topeka
KANSAS CITY
Oklahoma City
Tulsa
DALLAS
Fort Worth
Austin
SAN ANTONIO
HOUSTON
Corpus Christi
Galveston
Shreveport
Little Rock
Baton Rouge
MONTERREY
Saltillo
Torreón
Ciudad Acuña
Piedras Negras
Nuevo Laredo
Laredo
McAllen
Brownsville
Matamoros
Reynosa
Monclova
Lincoln
Springfield
Jefferson City
Columbia
Abilene
Midland
Odessa
San Angelo
Waco
Wichita Falls
Beaumont
Lake Charles
Tyler
Texarkana
Fort Smith
Padre I.
Matagorda I.
B
C
D
E
F
H
J
ft m
12 000 4000
9000 3000
6000 2000
4500 1500
3000 1000
1200 400
600 200
0 0
200 600
2000 6000
4000 12 000
m ft
Projection: Albers' Equal Area with two standard parallels
102 100 98 96 94 92
West from Greenwich
2 3 4 5 6 7 8 9
359

ILLINOIS
INDIANA
OHIO
PENNSYLVANIA
MARYLAND
DELAWARE
WEST VIRGINIA
VIRGINIA
KENTUCKY
TENNESSEE
NORTH CAROLINA
SOUTH CAROLINA
GEORGIA
ALABAMA
MISSISSIPPI
FLORIDA
BAHAMAS
ATLANTIC
OCEAN
OF MEXICO
PITTSBURGH
PHILADELPHIA
BALTIMORE
WASHINGTON D.C.
COLUMBUS
CINCINNATI
INDIANAPOLIS
ST. LOUIS
Louisville
Lexington
Nashville
Memphis
Knoxville
Chattanooga
Charlotte
Raleigh
Richmond
NORFOLK
ATLANTA
Birmingham
Montgomery
Jackson
NEW ORLEANS
Mobile
Tallahassee
Jacksonville
ORLANDO
TAMPA
St. Petersburg
MIAMI
Savannah
Charleston
Columbia
Greensboro
Appalachian Mts.
Cumberland Plateau
Blue Ridge
Mississippi River Delta
Florida Keys
Str. of Florida
Florida Bay
Key West
Dry Tortugas
Northwest Providence Channel
Nassau
Freeport

353
360

50 0 50 100 150 200 250 300 km

50 0 50 100 150 200 miles

349

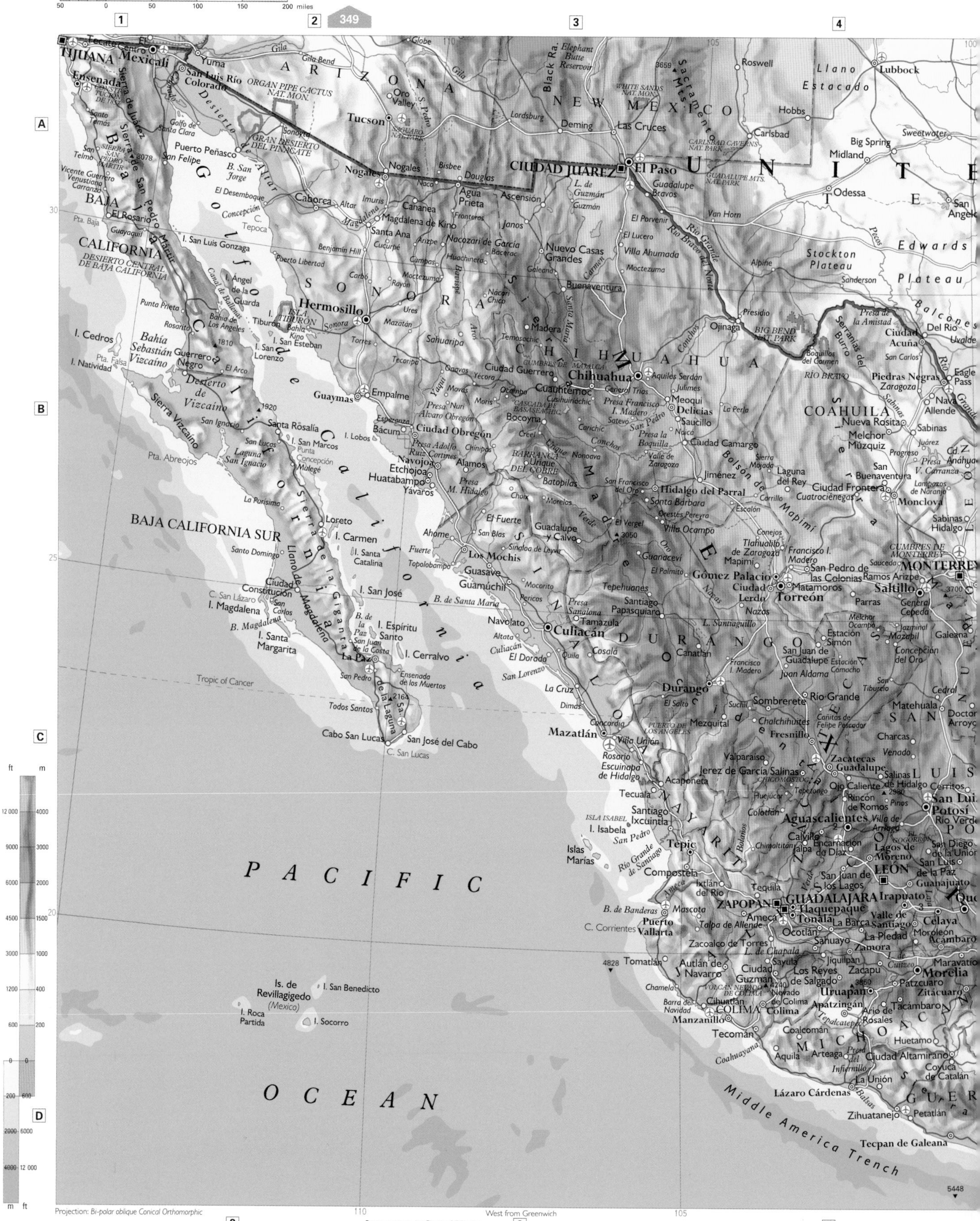

PACIFIC OCEAN

Projection: Bi-polar oblique Conical Orthomorphic

West from Greenwich

State names in Central Mexico

1	DISTRITO FEDERAL	5	MÉXICO
2	AGUASCALIENTES	6	MORELOS
3	GUANAJUATO	7	QUERÉTARO
4	HIDALGO	8	TLAXCALA

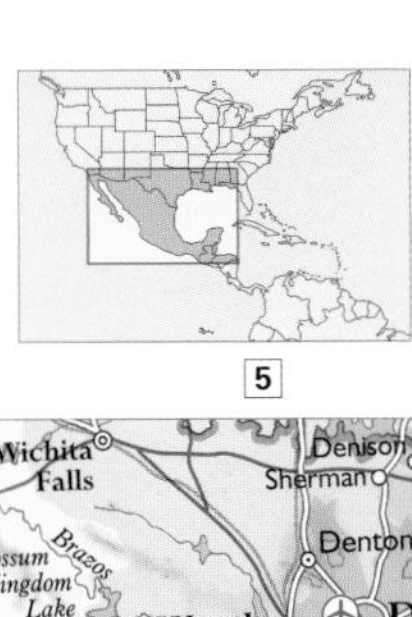

357

5 6 7 8

A B C D E

GULF OF MEXICO

Golfo de Campeche

Golfo de Tehuantepec

UNITED STATES

TEXAS

LOUISIANA

MISSISSIPPI

ALABAMA

GEORGIA

FLORIDA

ARKANSAS

TAMAULIPAS

VERACRUZ

PUEBLA

OAXACA

CHIAPAS

TABASCO

CAMPECHE

YUCATÁN

QUINTANA ROO

BELIZE

GUATEMALA

HONDURAS

CUBA

DALLAS

Fort Worth

HOUSTON

SAN ANTONIO

Austin

NEW ORLEANS

Baton Rouge

Shreveport

Jackson

Mobile

Pensacola

Tallahassee

Montgomery

Corpus Christi

Galveston

Laredo

Nuevo Laredo

McAllen

Reynosa

Brownsville

Matamoros

Tampico

Ciudad Victoria

Ciudad Madero

Tuxpan

Poza Rica

Xalapa

Veracruz

Puebla

MÉXICO

Toluca

Cuernavaca

Oaxaca

Acapulco

Chilpancingo

Salina Cruz

Tehuantepec

Coatzacoalcos

Minatitlán

Villahermosa

Ciudad del Carmen

Campeche

Champotón

Mérida

Progreso

Valladolid

Cancún

Isla Mujeres

Cozumel

Playa del Carmen

Chetumal

Belmopan

Belize City

Flores

Tuxtla Gutiérrez

San Cristóbal de las Casas

Tapachula

Huehuetenango

Cobán

GUATEMALA

Puerto Barrios

San Pedro Sula

La Ceiba

Tegucigalpa

Tropic of Cancer

Banco Campeche

Canal de Yucatán

Yucatan Basin

Mississippi River Delta

Laguna Madre

PADRE ISLAND NAT. SEASHORE

Istmo de Tehuantepec

Golfo de Honduras

Clearwater

360

Projection: Bi-polar oblique Conical Orthomorphic

PUERTO RICO d
VIRGIN ISLANDS e
ST. LUCIA f
BARBADOS g
ATLANTIC OCEAN
PUERTO RICO (U.S.A.)
SAN JUAN
Virgin Islands (U.K.)
Virgin Is. (U.S.A.)
ST. LUCIA
BARBADOS
Bridgetown
HAITI
DOMINICAN REP.
PORT-AU-PRINCE
SANTO DOMINGO
Hispaniola
Antilles
Puerto Rico Trench
Lesser Antilles
Leeward Islands
Windward Islands
GUADELOUPE
DOMINICA
MARTINIQUE
ST. VINCENT & THE GRENADINES
GRENADA
ANTIGUA & BARBUDA
ST. KITTS & NEVIS
Turks & Caicos (U.K.)
COLOMBIA
VENEZUELA
CARACAS
MARACAIBO
TRINIDAD & TOBAGO
NETH. ANTILLES
West from Greenwich
COPYRIGHT PHILIP'S

NORTH ATLANTIC OCEAN
SOUTH ATLANTIC OCEAN
PACIFIC OCEAN
Caribbean Sea
Greater Antilles
Lesser Antilles
West Indies
Cuba
Hispaniola
Puerto Rico
Jamaica
Bahamas
Turks & Caicos Is.
Gulf of Campeche
Yucatán Peninsula
Yucatan Channel
Isthmus of Tehuantepec
Central America
G. de Honduras
C. Gracias a Dios
Guatemala Trench
L. Nicaragua
Panama Canal
Isthmus of Panama
G. of Darién
Gulf of Panamá
I. del Coco
I. de Malpelo
B. de Buenaventura
C. de San Francisco
Galapagos Is.
G. of Guayaquil
Cotopaxi 5897
Chimborazo 6267
Pta. Pariñas
Pta. Negra
Des. de Sechura
Huascarán 6768
Nevado Coropuna 6425
Chincha Alta
Peru-Chile Trench
L. Titicaca 3812
Nevado Ancohuma 6550
Altiplano (Bolivian Plateau)
L. de Poopó
Salar de Uyuni
Pta. Tetas
8050
Atacama Desert
Cord. de Calalaste
Cerro Ojos del Salado 6863
Monte Pissis 6779
Cerro Bonete 6872
Salinas Grandes
Pta. Lengua da Vaca
Cerro Mercedario 6770
6960 Mt. Aconcagua
San Félix
San Ambrosio
Arch. de Juan Fernández
Pta. Lavapié
Chile Rise
Chiloé I.
Chonos Archipelago
Taitao Peninsula
G. de Penas
Wellington I.
Madre de Dios I.
Magellan's Str.
Riesco I.
Santa Inés I.
Canal Cockburn
Canal Beagle
Tierra del Fuego
Staten I.
C. Horn
Mte San Valentin 4058
L. Buenos Aires
L. Viedma
L. Argentino
C. Vírgenes
Patagonia
Andes
Pen. de la Guajira
G. de Venezuela
Curaçao
Pen. de Paraguana
L. Maracaibo
I. Margarita
Grenada
Tobago
Trinidad
C. de la Aguja
5800 Sierra Nevada de Santa Marta
Cordillera Occidental
Cordillera Central
Cordillera Oriental
Cord. de Mérida
Cauca
Magdalena
Leeward Islands
Guadeloupe
Dominica
Martinique
St. Lucia
St. Vincent
Barbados
9200
Llanos
Apure
Meta
Orinoco
Embalse de Guri
Cuyuni
Angel Falls
2772 Mt. Roraima
Guiana Highlands
Sierra Pacaraima
Casiquiare
Pico de Neblina 3014
Essequibo
Courantyne
Maroni
Oyapock
Serra Tumucumaque
Devil's I.
C. Orange
I. de Maracá
Guaviare
Vaupés
Caquetá
Putumayo
Japurá
Negro
Branco
Représa de Balbina
Amazon
Amazon Basin
Marajó I.
B. de Marajó
Equator
B. de São Marcos
Napo
Marañón
Montaña
Selvas
Ucayali
Juruá
Purus
Madeira
Tapajós
Xingu
Tocantins
Itapicuru
Parnaíba
C. de São Roque
Caatinga
Plat. of Borborema
Représa de Sobradinho
Sertão
Aripuanã
Roosevelt
Teles Pires
Araguaia
Arinos
Madre de Dios
Beni
Mamoré
Itonamas
Yungas
Sa. dos Parecis
Guaporé
Plateau of Mato Grosso
Brazilian Highlands
São Francisco
Serra do Espinhaço
Sa. Geral
B. de Todos os Santos
Abrolhos Bank
Doce
Pantanal
Paraguay
Paranaíba
Grande
Paraná
Tietê
Serra da Mantiqueira
2890 Pico da Bandeira
C. de São Tomé
C. Frio
I. de São Sebastião
Chaco Boreal
Gran Chaco
Chaco Austral
Pilcomayo
Bermejo
Rep. de Itaipú
Iguaçu Falls
Iguaçu
Campos
Serra do Mar
C. Santa Marta Grande
Dulce
Salado
Sa. de Córdoba
L. Mar Chiquita
Entre Ríos
Uruguay
Negro
L. dos Patos
L. Mirim
Paraná
Río de la Plata
B. Samborombón
C. San Antonio
Pampas
Colorado
Bahía Blanca
Limay
Negro
G. San Matías
Valdés Peninsula
40
Chubut
Chico
Golfo San Jorge
C. Tres Puntas
Argentine Abyssal Plain
6212
Falkland Is.
West Falkland
East Falkland
South Georgia
Tropic of Cancer
Tropic of Capricorn
Equator
West from Greenwich
Projection: Lambert's Azimuthal Equal Area
100 0 200 400 600 800 1000 1200 1400 km
100 0 200 400 600 800 1000 miles
ft m
12000 4000
9000 3000
6000 2000
3000 1000
1500 500
600 200
0 0
200 600
1000 3000
2000 6000
4000 12000
6000 18000
8000 24000
m ft
COPYRIGHT PHILIP'S

NORTH ATLANTIC OCEAN
Caribbean Sea
PACIFIC OCEAN
SOUTH ATLANTIC OCEAN
MEXICO
BELIZE
GUATEMALA
HONDURAS
EL SALVADOR
NICARAGUA
COSTA RICA
PANAMA
CUBA
JAMAICA
HAITI
DOMINICAN REP.
VENEZUELA
COLOMBIA
GUYANA
SURINAME
FRENCH GUIANA
ECUADOR
PERU
BRAZIL
BOLIVIA
PARAGUAY
CHILE
ARGENTINA
URUGUAY
BOGOTÁ
LIMA
SANTIAGO
BUENOS AIRES
SÃO PAULO
RIO DE JANEIRO
Galapagos Is. (Ecuador)
FALKLAND IS. (U.K.)
South Georgia (U.K.)
Tierra del Fuego
C. Horn
Projection: Lambert's Azimuthal Equal Area
West from Greenwich
COPYRIGHT PHILIP'S
LIMA Capital Cities

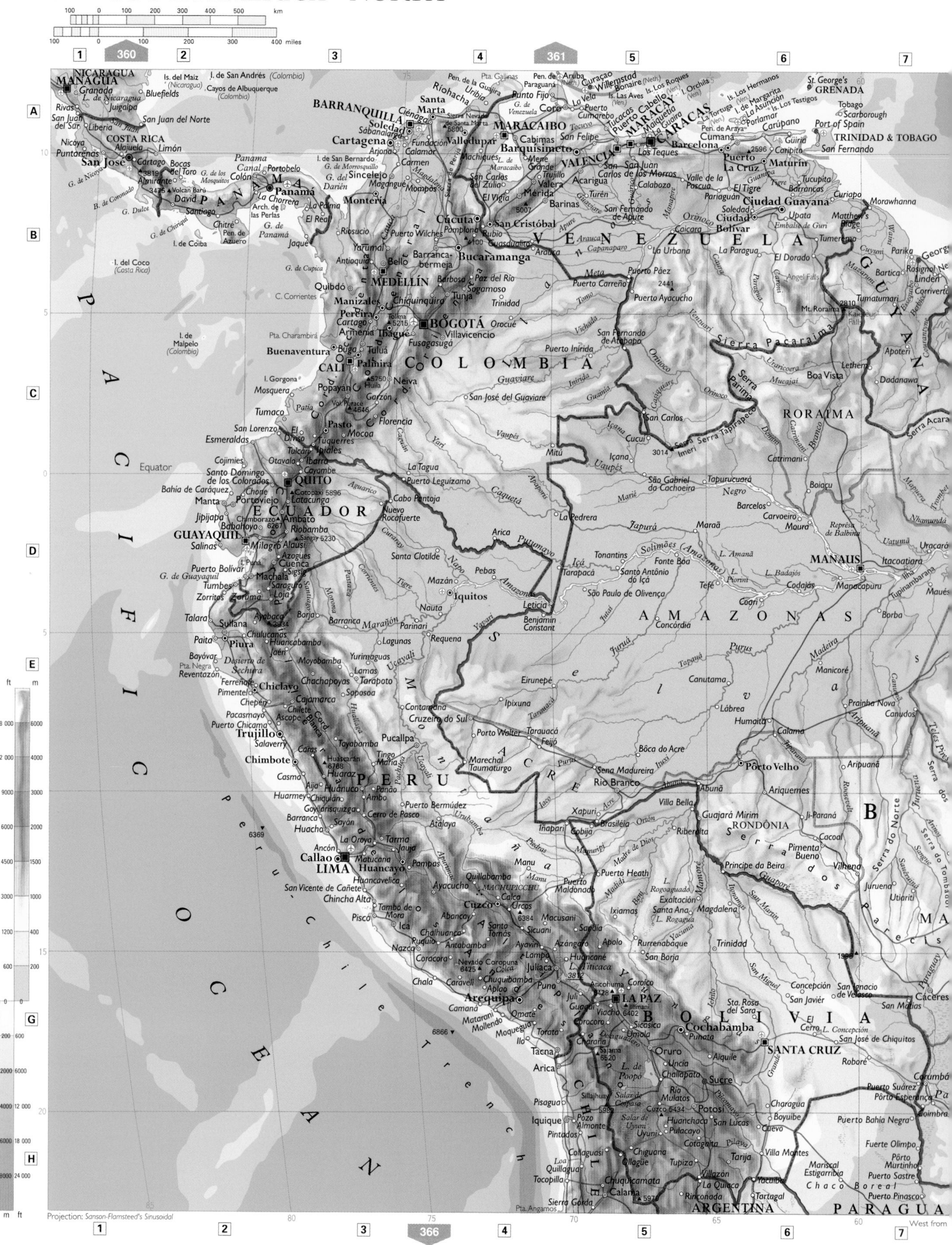

PACIFIC OCEAN
Peru-Chile Trench
Equator
NICARAGUA
MANAGUA
COSTA RICA
San José
PANAMA
Panamá
COLOMBIA
BOGOTÁ
MEDELLÍN
CALI
BARRANQUILLA
Cartagena
VENEZUELA
CARACAS
MARACAIBO
VALENCIA
MARACAY
Barquisimeto
Ciudad Guayana
TRINIDAD & TOBAGO
Port of Spain
GRENADA
GUYANA
ECUADOR
QUITO
GUAYAQUIL
PERU
LIMA
Callao
Trujillo
Arequipa
Cuzco
BOLIVIA
LA PAZ
Cochabamba
SANTA CRUZ
Sucre
CHILE
ARGENTINA
PARAGUAY
AMAZONAS
RORAIMA
RONDÔNIA
ACRE
MANAUS
Pôrto Velho
Rio Branco
Boa Vista
Iquitos
Amazonas
Orinoco
Sierra Pacaraima
L. Titicaca
Projection: Sanson-Flamsteed's Sinusoidal

TRINIDAD AND TOBAGO
10 0 10 20 30 40 50 km
10 0 10 20 30 miles
Tobago
Charlotteville
North Pt.
Little Tobago
Castara
Main Ridge
565
Roxborough
Plymouth
Buccoo Reef
Crown Pt.
Scarborough
Rocky Bay
VENEZUELA
Pen. de Paria
Macuro
Güiria
Dragon's Mouths
Corozal Pt.
Monos I.
Chupara Pt.
La Vache Pt.
Maracas Bay Village
Blanchisseuse
Maraval
Matelot
Sans Souci
Toco
Galera Pt.
Redhead
Northern Range
936
940 Mt. Aripo
Salybia
Port of Spain
Tunapuna
Valencia
Matura Bay
San Juan
Caroni
Arima
Guaico
Sangre Grande
Talparo
Upper Manzanilla
Chaguanas
Nariva Swamp
Cocos Bay
Golfo de Paria
Couva
ATLANTIC OCEAN
Trinidad
Point Lisas
Otaheite Bay
Gasparillo
Rio Claro
Guatuaro Pt.
San Fernando
Brighton
La Brea
Pierreville
Guapo Bay
Pitch Lake
Princes Town
Mayaro Bay
Point Fortin
Penal
Basse Terre
Guayaguayare
Cedros Bay
304
Trinity Hills
Galeota Pt.
Bonasse
Palo Seco
Siparia
Icacos Pt.
Erin Pt.
La Lune
Moruga
Serpent's Mouth
Pta. Bombedor
VENEZUELA
West from Greenwich
ATLANTIC
OCEAN
Equator
SURINAME
Paramaribo
Nieuw Amsterdam
Nieuw Nickerie
Totness
Moengo
Albina
Kwakoegron
St.-Laurent
Iracoubo
Sinnamary
Kourou
Cayenne
FRENCH GUIANA
Kaw
C. Orange
St. Georges
Oiapoque
Camopi
Amapá
I. de Maracá
Serra Tumucumaque
AMAPÁ
Araguari
Meriruma
Serra do Navio
Macapá
I. Caviana
I. Mexiana
C. Maguarinho
Mazagão
Afuá
Chaves
I. de Soure
Curuçá
Salinópolis
I. Grande de Gurupá
Marajó
BELÉM
Vigia
Bragança
Almeirim
Gurupá
Breves
Castanhal
Viseu
Gurupi
Óbidos
Monte Alegre
Prainha
Pôrto de Moz
Curralinho
Cametá
Abaetetuba
Turiaçu
Alenquer
Amazonas (Amazon)
Xingu
Alcântara
B. de São Marcos
São Luís
Barreirinhas
Tutóia
Luís Correia
Camocim
Juruti
Santarém
Belterra
Parintins
Altamira
Baião
Pinheiro
Rosário
Itapecuru-Mirim
Viana
Parnaíba
Granja
Itapipoca
Caucaia
FORTALEZA
Aveiro
Brasília Legal
P A R Á
Tucuruí
Santa Inês
Brejo
Piracuruca
Sobral
Maranguape
Cascavel
Bacabal
Coroatá
Codó
Piripiri
Baturité
Aracati
Itaituba
Iriri
Represa de Tucuruí
Açailândia
Pedreiras
Caxias
Campo Maior
Ipu
Quixadá
Russas
Areia Branca
Macau
Ceará Mirim
Marabá
MARANHÃO
Imperatriz
Teresina
Crateús
CEARÁ
Mossoró
RIO GRANDE DO NORTE
Natal
C. de São Roque
São João do Araguaia
Carajás
Barra do Corda
Senador Pompeu
Caraúbas
Currais Novos
Tocantinópolis
Pôrto Franco
Colinas
Amarante
Valença do Piauí
Iguatu
Caicó
Canguaretama
Mamanguape
Estreito
Floriano
Oeiras
Picos
Cajàzeiras
Sousa
Patos
Alagoa Grande
Cabedelo
Carolina
Loreto
Nova Iorque
Crato
Juàzeiro do Norte
PARAÍBA
Campina Grande
João Pessoa
Olinda
Araguaína
Riachão
Uruçuí
PIAUÍ
Ouricuri
Salgueiro
Caruaru
RECIFE
Jaboatão
Paulistana
PERNAMBUCO
Pesqueira
Conceição do Araguaia
São João do Piauí
Garanhuns
Palmares
Vitória de Santo Antão
Araguacema
Pedro Afonso
Santa Filomena
Petrolina
Petrolândia
Caracol
Novo Remanso
Nova Casa Nova
Juàzeiro
Paulo Afonso
Palmeira dos Índios
Rio Largo
Maceió
Arapiraca
Represa de Sobradinho
ALAGOAS
Palmas
Parnaguá
Senhor-do-Bonfim
Propriá
Penedo
SERGIPE
Capela
Aracaju
São Cristóvão
Estância
B R A Z I L
Pôrto Nacional
TOCANTINS
Barra
Xique-Xique
Jacobina
Queimadas
Serrinha
Alagoinhas
Feira de Santana
Mundo Novo
Santa Isabel do Morro
I. do Bananal
Gurupi
Peixe
Taguatinga
Barreiras
Ibotirama
Itaberaba
Cachoeira
Santo Amaro
SALVADOR
BAHIA
Paranã
Bom Jesus da Lapa
Castro Alves
Nazaré
Campos Belos
São Domingos
Santa Maria da Vitória
Valença
Jequié
Serra do Roncador
Serra Formosa
MATO GROSSO
Planalto do Mato Grosso
Diamantino
Barragem de Serra da Mesa
Niquelândia
Posse
Carinhanha
Caetité
Brumado
Ubaitaba
Itabuna
Ilhéus
Vitória da Conquista
Uruaçu
1678
Aruanã
Condeúba
Canavieiras
Cuiabá
Santo Antônio
Barra do Garças
DIST. FED.
Formosa
Taguatinga
BRASÍLIA
Januária
Monte Azul
São Francisco
Pedra Azul
Belmonte
Rondonópolis
Goiás
Anápolis
Luziânia
Janaúba
Montes Claros
Salinas
Jequitinhonha
Pôrto Seguro
GOIÂNIA
GOIÁS
Vianópolis
Araçuaí
Itamaraju
Alto Araguaia
Morrinhos
Paracatu
Pirapora
Teófilo Otoni
Prado
Nanuque
Caravelas
Jataí
Rio Verde
Ipameri
Patos de Minas
Diamantina
Governador Valadares
Mucuri
Banco
Coxim
Quirinópolis
Itumbiara
Catalão
Araguari
Corinto
1340
Conceição da Barra
São Mateus
MINAS GERAIS
Uberlândia
Patrocínio
Curvelo
Ipatinga
Nova Venécia
DO SUL
Ituiutaba
Prata
Araxá
Ibiá
Sête Lagoas
Itabira
Colatina
Linhares
Abrolhos
Paranaíba
Uberaba
Campo Grande
Miranda
Santa Fé do Sul
Frutal
BELO HORIZONTE
Sabará
Caratinga
Cariacica
Vitória
Vila Velha
Aquidauana
Água Clara
São José do Rio Prêto
Divinópolis
Nova Lima
Ponte Nova
ESPÍRITO SANTO
Ribas do Rio Pardo
Três Lagoas
Rio Prêto
Franca
Passos
Conselheiro Lafaiete
Ouro Prêto
2890
Cachoeiro de Itapemirim
Andradina
Araçatuba
Ribeirão Prêto
Guaxupé
São João del Rei
Ubá
Barbacena
Itaperuna
Panorama
Catanduva
Lins
Araraquara
Poços de Caldas
Juiz de Fora
Bela Vista
Dourados
Presidente Epitácio
Penápolis
SÃO PAULO
São Carlos
Três Rios
Campos
Presidente Prudente
Marília
Mogi-Mirim
São Lourenço
Nova Friburgo
Ponta Porã
Bauru
Jaú
Limeira
RIO DE JANEIRO
Petrópolis
Pedro Juan Caballero
Assis
Piracicaba
Volta Redonda
Botucatu
CAMPINAS
Niterói
Cabo Frio
RIO DE JANEIRO
Rocas
Fernando de Noronha (Braz.)
São Pedro & São Paulo (Braz.)
6059
27
Trindade (Braz.)
Greenwich
8 9 10 11 12 13 14 15 16
D E F G H J K L

367

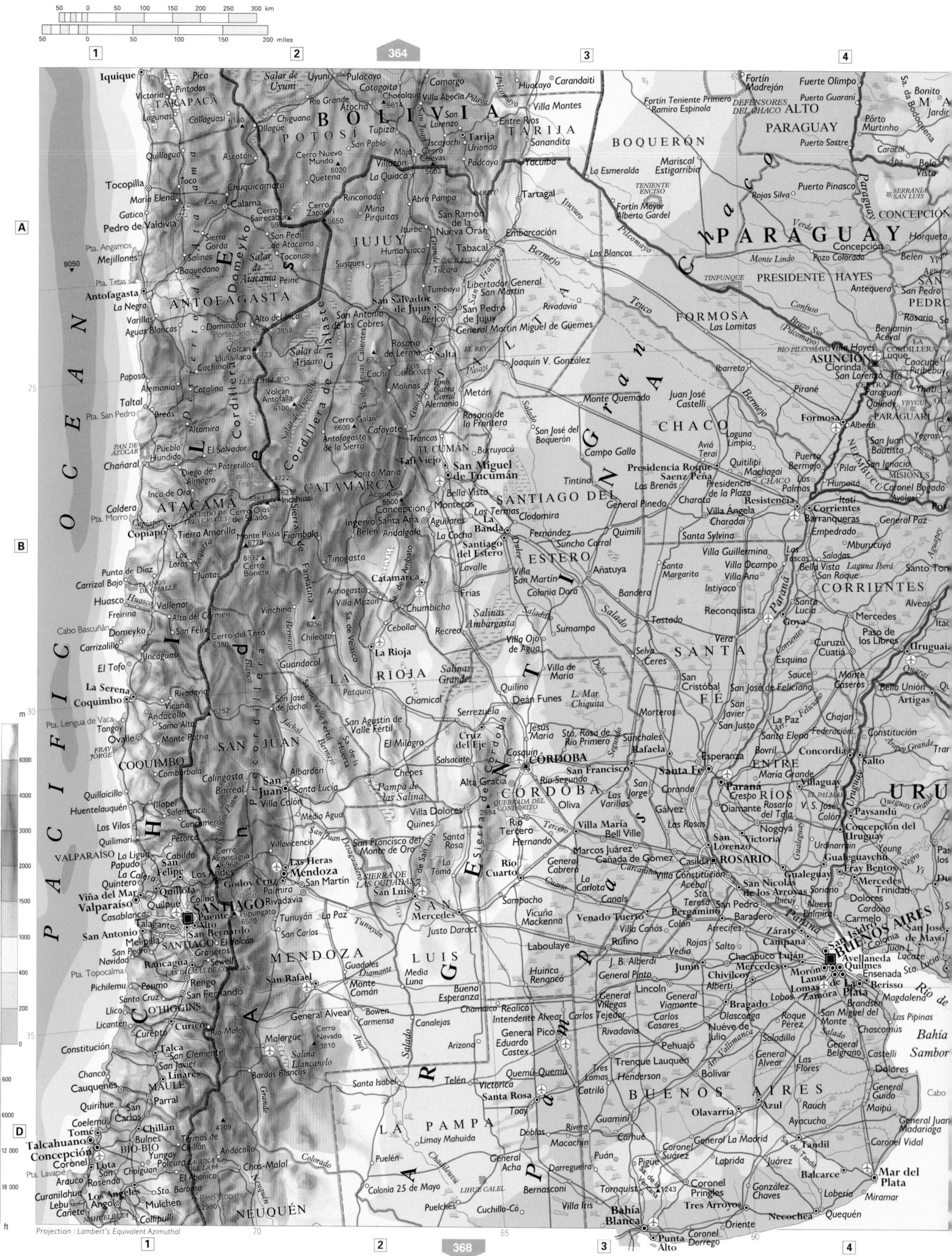
50 0 50 100 150 200 250 300 km
50 0 50 100 150 200 miles
364
368
Projection : Lambert's Equivalent Azimuthal
PACIFIC OCEAN
BOLIVIA
PARAGUAY
URU
CHILE
ARGENTINA
Gran Chaco
Chaco
Cordillera Domeyko
Cordillera de Calalaste
Cordillera de Famatina
Andes
Pampa
TARAPACÁ
ANTOFAGASTA
ATACAMA
COQUIMBO
VALPARAÍSO
SANTIAGO
O'HIGGINS
MAULE
BIO-BIO
POTOSÍ
TARIJA
BOQUERÓN
ALTO PARAGUAY
PRESIDENTE HAYES
CONCEPCIÓN
JUJUY
SALTA
FORMOSA
CHACO
TUCUMÁN
CATAMARCA
SANTIAGO DEL ESTERO
LA RIOJA
SAN JUAN
CÓRDOBA
SANTA FÉ
CORRIENTES
ENTRE RÍOS
MISIONES
MENDOZA
SAN LUIS
LA PAMPA
NEUQUÉN
BUENOS AIRES
Iquique
Pica
Pintados
Victoria
Lagunas
Collaguasi
Quillagua
Tocopilla
María Elena
Gatico
Pedro de Valdivia
Calama
Chuquicamata
Pta. Angamos
Mejillones
Baquedano
Pta. Tetas
Antofagasta
La Negra
Varillas
Aguas Blancas
Paposo
Taltal
Pta. San Pedro
Chañaral
Diego de Almagro
Inca de Oro
Caldera
Pta. Morro
Copiapó
Tierra Amarilla
Carrizal Bajo
Huasco
Vallenar
Freirina
Cabo Bascuñán
Domeyko
Carrizalillo
El Tofo
La Serena
Coquimbo
Vicuña
Andacollo
Pta. Lengua de Vaca
Tongoy
Ovalle
Combarbalá
Quilaicillo
Huentelauquén
Illapel
Salamanca
Los Vilos
Quilimarí
La Ligua
Cabildo
Papudo
La Calera
Quintero
Viña del Mar
Valparaíso
Quillota
Los Andes
San Felipe
Casablanca
Talagante
Puente Alto
San Bernardo
San Antonio
Melipilla
Rancagua
Sewell
Navidad
Pta. Topocalma
Pichilemu
Rengo
San Fernando
Santa Cruz
Licantén
Curicó
Curepto
Constitución
Talca
San Clemente
San Javier
Linares
Chanco
Cauquenes
Parral
Quirihue
San Carlos
Coelemu
Tomé
Chillán
Talcahuano
Concepción
Coronel
Lota
Pta. Lavapié
Arauco
Curanilahue
Lebu
Cañete
Los Angeles
Angol
Mulchen
Collipulli
Chos-Malal
Uyuni
Salar de Uyuni
Pulacayo
Cotagaita
Camargo
Atocha
Tupiza
San Pablo
Villazón
La Quiaca
Tarija
Uriondo
Padcaya
Villa Montes
Entre Ríos
Sanandita
Yacuiba
Carandaiti
Huacaya
Fortín Teniente Primero Ramiro Espínola
Fortín Madrejón
Fuerte Olimpo
Puerto Guaraní
Puerto Sastre
Bahía Negra
La Esmeralda
Mariscal Estigarribia
Fortín Mayor Alberto Gardel
Rojas Silva
Puerto Pinasco
Concepción
Horqueta
Belén
Pozo Colorado
Monte Lindo
Antequera
San Pedro
Rosario
Benjamin Aceval
Villa Hayes
ASUNCIÓN
Luque
Caacupé
Clorinda
San Lorenzo
Paraguarí
Quiindy
Pirané
Formosa
Alberdi
Las Lomitas
Ibarreta
Juan José Castelli
Pilar
Humaitá
Corrientes
Resistencia
Barranqueras
Empedrado
Mburucuyá
Saladas
Bella Vista
San Roque
Santo Tomé
Mercedes
Goya
Curuzú Cuatiá
Esquina
Sauce
Monte Caseros
Bella Unión
Artigas
Chajarí
Federación
Constitución
Salto
Concordia
Paysandú
Colón
Concepción del Uruguay
Gualeguaychú
Fray Bentos
Gualeguay
Mercedes
Dolores
Carmelo
Colonia
Tartagal
Embarcación
Orán
Tabacal
Libertador General San Martín
San Pedro de Jujuy
San Salvador de Jujuy
Humahuaca
Tilcara
Rivadavia
General Martín Miguel de Güemes
Salta
Rosario de Lerma
Joaquín V. González
Metán
Cafayate
Cachi
Molinos
Rosario de la Frontera
Monte Quemado
Campo Gallo
Presidencia Roque Sáenz Peña
Charata
Villa Ángela
Tintina
San Miguel de Tucumán
Tafí Viejo
Concepción
Aguilares
Santa María
Andalgalá
Belén
Fiambalá
Tinogasta
Catamarca
Santiago del Estero
La Banda
Fernández
Añatuya
Frías
Recreo
Chilecito
La Rioja
Chamical
Quilino
Deán Funes
Jesús María
Cosquín
CÓRDOBA
Alta Gracia
Villa Dolores
San Francisco
Rafaela
Sunchales
Ceres
Reconquista
Vera
San Javier
San Justo
Esperanza
Santa Fé
Paraná
Diamante
Victoria
Villa María
Bell Ville
Río Tercero
Río Cuarto
Marcos Juárez
Cañada de Gómez
ROSARIO
Casilda
Villa Constitución
San Nicolás de los Arroyos
San Pedro
Pergamino
Baradero
Zárate
Campana
Venado Tuerto
Rufino
Laboulaye
Huinca Renancó
Junín
Mercedes
Luján
Chivilcoy
BUENOS AIRES
Avellaneda
Quilmes
Lanús
La Plata
Ensenada
Berisso
Magdalena
Lobos
Bragado
Nueve de Julio
Pehuajó
Trenque Lauquen
Bolívar
Azul
Olavarría
Tandil
Ayacucho
Balcarce
Mar del Plata
Miramar
Necochea
Tres Arroyos
Coronel Pringles
Coronel Suárez
Tornquist
Bahía Blanca
Punta Alto
Chascomús
Dolores
Maipú
General Madariaga
Bahía Samborombón
San Juan
Jáchal
Calingasta
Barreal
Albardón
Villa Colón
Mendoza
Las Heras
Godoy Cruz
San Martín
Rivadavia
Tunuyán
San Carlos
San Rafael
General Alvear
Malargüe
San Luis
Villa Mercedes
Justo Daract
Buena Esperanza
General Pico
Eduardo Castex
Santa Rosa
Victorica
General Acha
Puelches
Cuchillo-Có
Colonia 25 de Mayo
Realicó
Intendente Alvear
Aconcagua 6962
Ojos del Salado
Llullaillaco 6723
Salar de Atacama
Salar de Arizaro
Salinas Grandes
Salinas Ambargasta
Laguna Mar Chiquita
Salado
Bermejo
Pilcomayo
Paraná
Uruguay
Río de la Plata
Colorado
Neuquén
Atuel

365
5
6
7
A
B
C
D
BELO HORIZONTE
Nova Lima
Itabirito
Congonhas
Conselheiro Lafaiete
Ouro Prêto
Ponte Nova
Vitória
Vila Velha
Guarapari
Castelo
Cachoeiro de Itapemirim
Itaperuna
Guarus
Campos
Cabo de São Tomé
Três Lagoas
Andradina
Mirassol
São José do Rio Prêto
Olímpia
Batatais
Passos
Oliveira
Barbacena
Cataguases
Juiz de Fora
Leopoldina
Três Rios
Além Paraíba
RIO DE JANEIRO
Nova Friburgo
Petrópolis
Macaé
Duque de Caxias
São Gonçalo
Niterói
Cabo Frio
Nova Iguaçu
Volta Redonda
Barra do Piraí
Barra Mansa
Angra dos Reis
Ilha Grande
Tropic of Capricorn
Araçatuba
Birigui
Catanduva
Bebedouro
Ribeirão Prêto
Jaboticabal
Araraquara
São Carlos
Rio Claro
Limeira
Piracicaba
CAMPINAS
Americana
Jundiaí
Sorocaba
Guarulhos
SÃO PAULO
Santo André
Mogi das Cruzes
São Bernardo do Campo
São Vicente
SANTOS
Guarujá
Ilha de São Sebastião
Pta. de Boi
Itanhaém
Taubaté
São José dos Campos
Guaratinguetá
Pouso Alegre
Poços de Caldas
Varginha
Três Corações
Lavras
São João del Rei
Santos Dumont
Presidente Prudente
Presidente Epitácio
Adamantina
Marília
Bauru
Jaú
Assis
Ourinhos
Avaré
Botucatu
Tatuí
Itapetininga
Itapeva
Registro
Iguape
Ilha Comprida
Ilha do Cardoso
Dourados
Ponta Porã
Pedro Juan Caballero
Amambai
Umuarama
Maringá
Londrina
Arapongas
Apucarana
Cornélio Procópio
Paranavaí
Campo Mourão
Goio-Erê
Toledo
Cascavel
Foz do Iguaçu
Ciudad del Este
Guarapuava
Ponta Grossa
Castro
Tibagi
Prudentópolis
Irati
CURITIBA
Paranaguá
Antonina
Matinhos
Guaratuba
Joinville
São Francisco do Sul
Rio Negro
Mafra
União da Vitória
Pato Branco
Francisco Beltrão
Pôrto União
Caçador
Blumenau
Itajaí
Brusque
Chapecó
Joaçaba
Xanxerê
SANTA CATARINA
Curitibanos
Campos Novos
Lajes
São José
Ilha de Santa Catarina
Florianópolis
Laguna
Cabo Santa Marta Grande
Tubarão
Criciúma
Araranguá
Torres
Erechim
Passo Fundo
Carazinho
Santo Angelo
Santa Rosa
Vacaria
Bento Gonçalves
Caxias do Sul
Nôvo Hamburgo
São Leopoldo
Taquara
Canoas
Osorio
PORTO ALEGRE
Viamão
Santa Maria
Santa Cruz do Sul
Cachoeira do Sul
Rio Pardo
RIO GRANDE DO SUL
Alegrete
Rosário do Sul
Santiago
São Borja
Cruz Alta
Santana do Livramento
Rivera
São Gabriel
Dom Pedrito
Bagé
Camaquã
Mostardas
LAGOA DE PEIXE
Lagoa dos Patos
Pelotas
São José do Norte
Rio Grande
Jaguarão
Lagoa Mirim
Lagoa Mangueira
Santa Vitória do Palmar
Chuy
Castillos
Rocha
Minas
San Carlos
Maldonado
MONTEVIDEO
Melo
Tacuarembó
Treinta y Tres
Posadas
Encarnación
Oberá
Apóstoles
MISIONES
ITAPUÁ
BRAZIL
PARANÁ
SÃO PAULO
ATLANTIC
OCEAN
5304
West from Greenwich
55
50
45
40
25
30
35
COPYRIGHT PHILIP'S

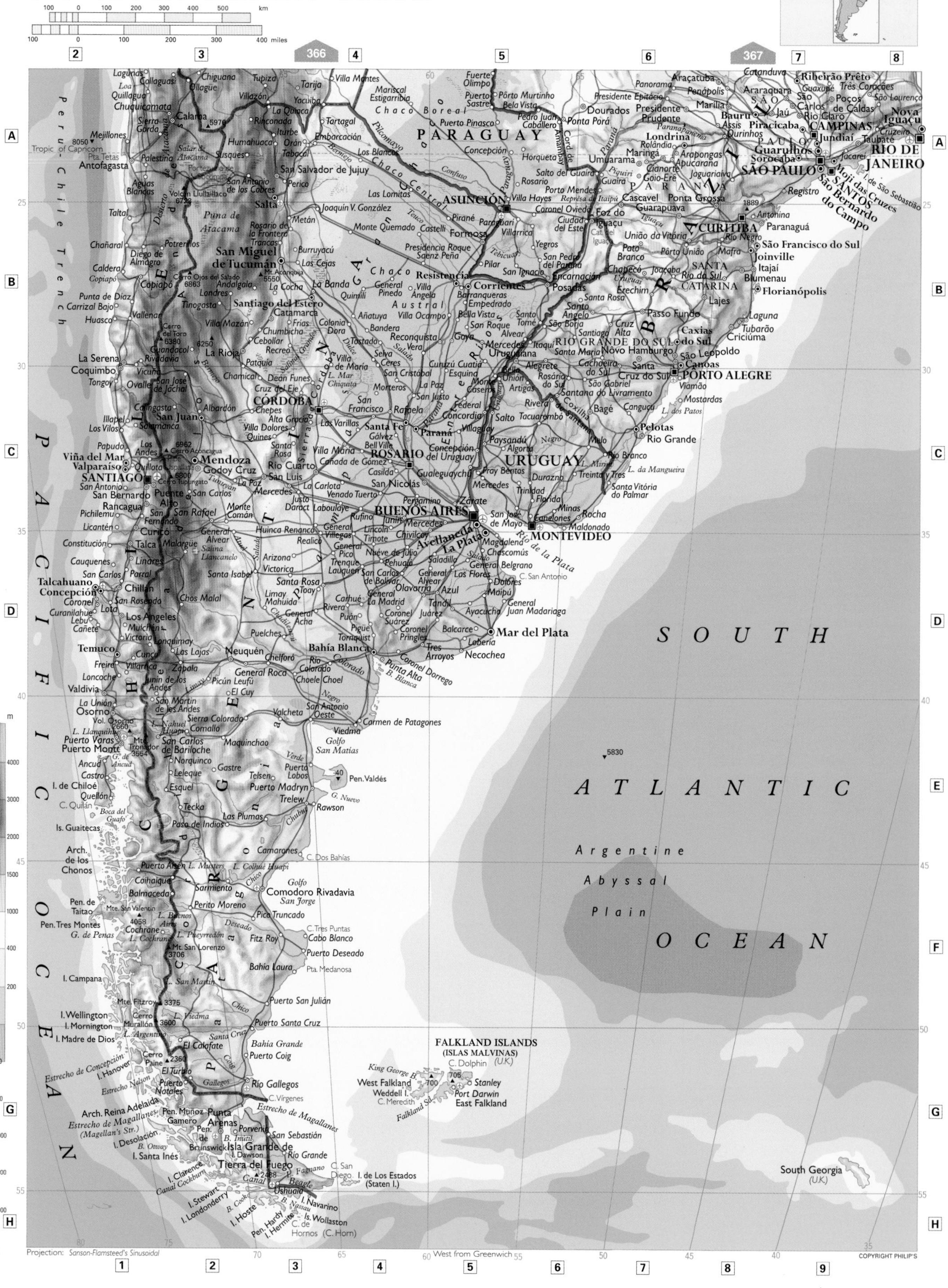

SOUTH AMERICA - SOUTH

INDEX TO WORLD MAPS

The index contains the names of all the principal places and features shown on the World Maps. Each name is followed by an additional entry in italics giving the country or region within which it is located. The alphabetical order of names composed of two or more words is governed primarily by the first word, then by the second, and then by the country or region name that follows. This is an example of the rule:

Mīr Kūh *Iran*	26°22N 58°55E	**317** E8
Mīr Shahdād *Iran*	26°15N 58°29E	**317** E8
Mira *Italy*	45°26N 12°8E	**294** B5
Mira por vos Cay *Bahamas*	22°9N 74°30W	**361** B5

Physical features composed of a proper name (Erie) and a description (Lake) are positioned alphabetically by the proper name. The description is positioned after the proper name and is usually abbreviated:

Erie, L. *N. Amer.*	42°15N 81°0W	**354** D4

Where a description forms part of a settlement or administrative name, however, it is always written in full and put in its true alphabetical position:

Mount Morris *U.S.A.*	42°44N 77°52W	**354** D7

Names beginning with M' and Mc are indexed as if they were spelled Mac. Names beginning St. are alphabetized under Saint, but Sankt, Sint, Sant', Santa and San are all spelt in full and are alphabetized accordingly. If the same place name occurs two or more times in the index and all are in the same country, each is followed by the name of the administrative subdivision in which it is located.

The geographical co-ordinates which follow each name in the index give the latitude and longitude of each place. The first co-ordinate indicates latitude – the distance north or south of the Equator. The second co-ordinate indicates longitude – the distance east or west of the Greenwich Meridian. Both latitude and longitude are measured in degrees and minutes (there are 60 minutes in a degree).

The latitude is followed by N(orth) or S(outh) and the longitude by E(ast) or W(est).

The number in bold type which follows the geographical co-ordinates refers to the number of the map page where that feature or place will be found. This is usually the largest scale at which the place or feature appears.

The letter and figure that are immediately after the page number give the grid square on the map page, within which the feature is situated. The letter represents the latitude and the figure the longitude. A lower-case letter immediately after the page number refers to an inset map on that page.

In some cases the feature itself may fall within the specified square, while the name is outside. This is usually the case only with features that are larger than a grid square.

Rivers are indexed to their mouths or confluences, and carry the symbol → after their names. The following symbols are also used in the index: ■ country, ☒ overseas territory or dependency, □ first-order administrative area, △ national park, ⌂ other park (provincial park, nature reserve or game reserve), ✈ (LHR) principal airport (and location identifier).

Abbreviations used in the index

A.C.T. – Australian Capital Territory
A.R. – Autonomous Region
Afghan. – Afghanistan
Afr. – Africa
Ala. – Alabama
Alta. – Alberta
Amer. – America(n)
Ant. – Antilles
Arch. – Archipelago
Ariz. – Arizona
Ark. – Arkansas
Atl. Oc. – Atlantic Ocean
B. – Baie, Bahía, Bay, Bucht, Bugt
B.C. – British Columbia
Bangla. – Bangladesh
Barr. – Barrage
Bos.-H. – Bosnia-Herzegovina
C. – Cabo, Cap, Cape, Coast
C.A.R. – Central African Republic
C. Prov. – Cape Province
Calif. – California
Cat. – Catarata
Cent. – Central
Chan. – Channel
Colo. – Colorado
Conn. – Connecticut
Cord. – Cordillera
Cr. – Creek
Czech. – Czech Republic
D.C. – District of Columbia
Del. – Delaware
Dem. – Democratic
Dep. – Dependency
Des. – Desert
Dét. – Détroit
Dist. – District
Dj. – Djebel
Dom. Rep. – Dominican Republic
E. – East
El Salv. – El Salvador
Eq. Guin. – Equatorial Guinea
Est. – Estrecho
Falk. Is. – Falkland Is.
Fd. – Fjord
Fla. – Florida
Fr. – French
G. – Golfe, Golfo, Gulf, Guba, Gebel
Ga. – Georgia
Gt. – Great, Greater
Guinea-Biss. – Guinea-Bissau
H.K. – Hong Kong
H.P. – Himachal Pradesh
Hants. – Hampshire
Harb. – Harbor, Harbour
Hd. – Head
Hts. – Heights
I.(s). – Île, Ilha, Insel, Isla, Island, Isle
Ill. – Illinois
Ind. – Indiana
Ind. Oc. – Indian Ocean
Ivory C. – Ivory Coast
J. – Jabal, Jebel
Jaz. – Jazīrah
Junc. – Junction
K. – Kap, Kapp
Kans. – Kansas
Kep. – Kepulauan
Ky. – Kentucky
L. – Lac, Lacul, Lago, Lagoa, Lake, Limni, Loch, Lough
La. – Louisiana
Ld. – Land
Liech. – Liechtenstein
Lux. – Luxembourg
Mad. P. – Madhya Pradesh
Madag. – Madagascar
Man. – Manitoba
Mass. – Massachusetts
Md. – Maryland
Me. – Maine
Medit. S. – Mediterranean Sea
Mich. – Michigan
Minn. – Minnesota
Miss. – Mississippi
Mo. – Missouri
Mont. – Montana
Mozam. – Mozambique
Mt.(s) – Mont, Montaña, Mountain
Mte. – Monte
Mti. – Monti
N. – Nord, Norte, North, Northern, Nouveau, Nahal, Nahr
N.B. – New Brunswick
N.C. – North Carolina
N. Cal. – New Caledonia
N. Dak. – North Dakota
N.H. – New Hampshire
N.I. – North Island
N.J. – New Jersey
N. Mex. – New Mexico
N.S. – Nova Scotia
N.S.W. – New South Wales
N.W.T. – North West Territory
N.Y. – New York
N.Z. – New Zealand
Nac. – Nacional
Nat. – National
Nebr. – Nebraska
Neths. – Netherlands
Nev. – Nevada
Nfld & L. – Newfoundland and Labrador
Nic. – Nicaragua
O. – Oued, Ouadi
Occ. – Occidentale
Okla. – Oklahoma
Ont. – Ontario
Or. – Orientale
Oreg. – Oregon
Os. – Ostrov
Oz. – Ozero
P. – Pass, Passo, Pasul, Pulau
P.E.I. – Prince Edward Island
Pa. – Pennsylvania
Pac. Oc. – Pacific Ocean
Papua N.G. – Papua New Guinea
Pass. – Passage
Peg. – Pegunungan
Pen. – Peninsula, Péninsule
Phil. – Philippines
Pk. – Peak
Plat. – Plateau
Prov. – Province, Provincial
Pt. – Point
Pta. – Ponta, Punta
Pte. – Pointe
Qué. – Québec
Queens. – Queensland
R. – Rio, River
R.I. – Rhode Island
Ra. – Range
Raj. – Rajasthan
Recr. – Recreational, Récréatif
Reg. – Region
Rep. – Republic
Res. – Reserve, Reservoir
Rhld-Pfz. – Rheinland-Pfalz
S. – South, Southern, Sur
Si. Arabia – Saudi Arabia
S.C. – South Carolina
S. Dak. – South Dakota
S.I. – South Island
S. Leone – Sierra Leone
Sa. – Serra, Sierra
Sask. – Saskatchewan
Scot. – Scotland
Sd. – Sound
Sev. – Severnaya
Sib. – Siberia
Sprs. – Springs
St. – Saint
Sta. – Santa
Ste. – Sainte
Sto. – Santo
Str. – Strait, Stretto
Switz. – Switzerland
Tas. – Tasmania
Tenn. – Tennessee
Terr. – Territory, Territoire
Tex. – Texas
Tg. – Tanjung
Trin. & Tob. – Trinidad & Tobago
U.A.E. – United Arab Emirates
U.K. – United Kingdom
U.S.A. – United States of America
Ut. P. – Uttar Pradesh
Va. – Virginia
Vdkhr. – Vodokhranilishche
Vdskh. – Vodoskhovyshche
Vf. – Vîrful
Vic. – Victoria
Vol. – Volcano
Vt. – Vermont
W. – Wadi, West
W. Va. – West Virginia
Wall. & F. Is. – Wallis and Futuna Is.
Wash. – Washington
Wis. – Wisconsin
Wlkp. – Wielkopolski
Wyo. – Wyoming
Yorks. – Yorkshire

A

A Coruña Spain 43°20N 8°25W 293 A1
A Estrada Spain 42°43N 8°27W 293 A1
A Fonsagrada Spain 43°8N 7°4W 293 A2
Aabenraa Denmark 55°3N 9°25E 281 J13
Aachen Germany 50°45N 6°6E 288 C4
Aalborg Denmark 57°2N 9°54E 281 H13
Aalen Germany 48°51N 10°6E 288 D6
Aalst Belgium 50°56N 4°2E 287 D4
Aalten Neths. 51°56N 6°35E 287 C6
Aalter Belgium 51°5N 3°28E 287 C3
Äänekoski Finland 62°36N 25°44E 280 E21
Aarau Switz. 47°23N 8°4E 292 C8
Aare → Switz. 47°33N 8°14E 292 C8
Aarhus = Århus Denmark 56°8N 10°11E 281 H14
Aarschot Belgium 50°59N 4°49E 287 D4
Aba Dem. Rep. of the Congo 3°58N 30°17E 326 B3
Aba Nigeria 5°10N 7°19E 322 G7
Abaco I. Bahamas 26°25N 77°10W 360 A4
Ābādān Iran 30°22N 48°20E 317 D6
Ābādeh Iran 31°8N 52°40E 317 D7
Abadla Algeria 31°2N 2°45W 322 B5
Abaetetuba Brazil 1°40S 48°50W 365 D9
Abagnar Qi China 43°52N 116°2E 306 C9
Abah, Tanjung Indonesia 8°46S 115°38E 309 K18
Abai Paraguay 25°58S 55°54W 367 B4
Abakan Russia 53°40N 91°10E 301 D10
Abancay Peru 13°35S 72°55W 364 F4
Abariringa Kiribati 2°50S 171°40W 336 H10
Abarqū Iran 31°10N 53°20E 317 D7
Abashiri Japan 44°0N 144°15E 302 B12
Abashiri-Wan Japan 44°0N 144°30E 302 C12
Ābay = Nîl el Azraq → Sudan 15°38N 32°31E 323 E12
Abay Kazakhstan 49°38N 72°53E 300 E8
Abaya, L. Ethiopia 6°30N 37°50E 319 F2
Abaza Russia 52°39N 90°6E 300 D9
'Abbāsābād Iran 33°34N 58°23E 317 C8
Abbay = Nîl el Azraq → Sudan 15°38N 32°31E 323 E12
Abbaye, Pt. U.S.A. 46°58N 88°8W 352 B9
Abbé, L. Ethiopia 11°8N 41°47E 319 E3
Abbeville France 50°6N 1°49E 292 A4
Abbeville Ala., U.S.A. 31°34N 85°15W 357 F12
Abbeville La., U.S.A. 29°58N 92°8W 356 G8
Abbeville S.C., U.S.A. 34°11N 82°23W 357 D13
Abbeyfeale Ireland 52°23N 9°18W 282 D2
Abbot Ice Shelf Antarctica 73°0S 92°0W 277 D16
Abbotsford Canada 49°5N 122°20W 342 D4
Abbottabad Pakistan 34°10N 73°15E 314 B5
ABC Islands = Netherlands Antilles ☒ W. Indies 12°15N 69°0W 364 A5
Abd al Kūrī Yemen 12°5N 52°20E 319 E5
Ābdar Iran 30°16N 55°19E 317 D7
'Abdolābād Iran 34°12N 56°30E 317 C8
Abdulpur Bangla. 24°15N 88°59E 315 G13
Abéché Chad 13°50N 20°35E 323 F10
Abel Tasman △ N.Z. 40°59S 173°3E 331 D4
Abengourou Ivory C. 6°42N 3°27W 322 G5
Åbenrå = Aabenraa Denmark 55°3N 9°25E 281 J13
Abeokuta Nigeria 7°3N 3°19E 322 G6
Aber Uganda 2°12N 32°25E 326 B3
Aberaeron U.K. 52°15N 4°15W 285 E3
Aberayron = Aberaeron U.K. 52°15N 4°15W 285 E3
Aberchirder U.K. 57°34N 2°37W 283 D6
Abercorn Australia 25°12S 151°5E 335 D5
Aberdare U.K. 51°43N 3°27W 285 F4
Aberdare △ Kenya 0°22S 36°44E 326 C4
Aberdare Ra. Kenya 0°15S 36°50E 326 C4
Aberdeen Australia 32°9S 150°56E 335 E5
Aberdeen Canada 52°20N 106°8W 343 C7
Aberdeen China 22°14N 114°8E 305 G11
Aberdeen S. Africa 32°28S 24°2E 328 E3
Aberdeen U.K. 57°9N 2°5W 283 D6
Aberdeen Ala., U.S.A. 33°49N 88°33W 357 E10
Aberdeen Idaho, U.S.A. 42°57N 112°50W 348 E7
Aberdeen Md., U.S.A. 39°31N 76°10W 353 F15
Aberdeen S. Dak., U.S.A. 45°28N 98°29W 352 C4
Aberdeen Wash., U.S.A. 46°59N 123°50W 350 D3
Aberdeen, City of □ U.K. 57°10N 2°10W 283 D6
Aberdeenshire □ U.K. 57°17N 2°36W 283 D6
Aberdovey = Aberdyfi U.K. 52°33N 4°3W 285 E3
Aberdyfi U.K. 52°33N 4°3W 285 E3
Aberfeldy U.K. 56°37N 3°51W 283 E5
Aberfoyle U.K. 56°11N 4°23W 283 E4
Abergavenny U.K. 51°49N 3°1W 285 F4
Abergele U.K. 53°17N 3°35W 284 D4
Abernathy U.S.A. 33°50N 101°51W 356 E4
Abert, L. U.S.A. 42°38N 120°14W 348 E3
Aberystwyth U.K. 52°25N 4°5W 285 E3
Abhā Si. Arabia 18°0N 42°34E 319 D3
Abhar Iran 36°9N 49°13E 317 B6
Abhayapuri India 26°24N 90°38E 315 F14
Abidjan Ivory C. 5°26N 3°58W 322 G5
Abilene Kans., U.S.A. 38°55N 97°13W 352 F5
Abilene Tex., U.S.A. 32°28N 99°43W 356 E5
Abingdon U.K. 51°40N 1°17W 285 F6
Abingdon U.S.A. 36°43N 81°59W 353 G13
Abington Reef Australia 18°0S 149°35E 334 B4
Abitau → Canada 59°53N 109°3W 343 B7
Abitibi → Canada 51°3N 80°55W 344 B3
Abitibi, L. Canada 48°40N 79°40W 344 C4
Abkhaz Republic = Abkhazia □ Georgia 43°12N 41°5E 291 F7
Abkhazia □ Georgia 43°12N 41°5E 291 F7
Abminga Australia 26°8S 134°51E 335 D1
Åbo = Turku Finland 60°30N 22°19E 281 F20
Abohar India 30°10N 74°10E 314 D6
Abomey Benin 7°10N 2°5E 322 G6
Abong-Mbang Cameroon 4°0N 13°8E 324 D2
Abou-Deïa Chad 11°20N 19°20E 323 F9
Aboyne U.K. 57°4N 2°47W 283 D6
Abra Pampa Argentina 22°43S 65°42W 366 A2
Abraham L. Canada 52°15N 116°35W 342 C5
Abreojos, Pta. Mexico 26°50N 113°40W 358 B2
Abrolhos, Banco Brazil 18°0S 38°0W 365 F11
Abrud Romania 46°19N 23°5E 289 E12
Absaroka Range U.S.A. 44°45N 109°50W 348 D9
Abu India 24°41N 72°50E 314 G5
Abū al Abyad U.A.E. 24°11N 53°50E 317 E7
Abū al Khaşīb Iraq 30°25N 48°0E 317 D6
Abū 'Alī Si. Arabia 27°20N 49°27E 317 E6
Abū 'Alī → Lebanon 34°25N 35°50E 318 A4
Abu Dhabi = Abū Ẓāby U.A.E. 24°28N 54°22E 317 E7
Abū Du'ān Syria 36°25N 38°15E 316 B3
Abu el Gaīn, W. → Egypt 29°35N 33°30E 318 F2
Abu Ga'da, W. → Egypt 29°15N 32°53E 318 F1
Abū Ḥadrīyah Si. Arabia 27°20N 48°58E 317 E6
Abu Hamed Sudan 19°32N 33°13E 323 E12
Abū Kamāl Syria 34°30N 41°0E 316 C4
Abū Madd, Ra's Si. Arabia 24°50N 37°7E 316 E3
Abū Mūsā U.A.E. 25°52N 55°3E 317 E7
Abū Qaşr Si. Arabia 30°21N 38°34E 316 D3
Abu Shagara, Ras Sudan 21°4N 37°19E 323 D13
Abu Simbel Egypt 22°18N 31°40E 323 D12
Abū Şukhayr Iraq 31°54N 44°30E 316 D5
Abu Zabad Sudan 12°25N 29°10E 323 F11
Abū Ẓāby U.A.E. 24°28N 54°22E 317 E7
Abū Zeydābād Iran 33°54N 51°45E 317 C6
Abuja Nigeria 9°5N 7°32E 322 G7
Abukuma-Gawa → Japan 38°6N 140°52E 302 E10
Abukuma-Sammyaku Japan 37°30N 140°45E 302 F10
Abunã Brazil 9°40S 65°20W 364 E5
Abunã → Brazil 9°41S 65°20W 364 E5
Aburo Dem. Rep. of the Congo 2°4N 30°53E 326 B3
Abut Hd. N.Z. 43°7S 170°15E 331 E3
Acadia △ U.S.A. 44°20N 68°13W 353 C19
Açailândia Brazil 4°57S 47°0W 365 D9
Acajutla El Salv. 13°36N 89°50W 360 D2
Acámbaro Mexico 20°2N 100°44W 358 D4
Acaponeta Mexico 22°30N 105°22W 358 C3
Acapulco Mexico 16°51N 99°55W 359 D5
Acarai, Serra Brazil 1°50N 57°50W 364 C7
Acarigua Venezuela 9°33N 69°12W 364 B5
Acatlán Mexico 18°12N 98°3W 359 D5
Acayucán Mexico 17°57N 94°55W 359 D6
Accomac U.S.A. 37°43N 75°40W 353 G16
Accra Ghana 5°35N 0°6W 322 G5
Accrington U.K. 53°45N 2°22W 284 D5
Acebal Argentina 33°20S 60°50W 366 C3
Aceh □ Indonesia 4°15N 97°30E 308 D1
Achalpur India 21°22N 77°32E 312 J10
Acharnes Greece 38°5N 23°44E 295 E10
Acheloos → Greece 38°19N 21°7E 295 E9
Acheng China 45°30N 126°58E 307 B14
Acher India 23°10N 72°32E 314 H5
Achill Hd. Ireland 53°58N 10°15W 282 C1
Achill I. Ireland 53°58N 10°1W 282 C1
Achinsk Russia 56°20N 90°20E 301 D10
Acireale Italy 37°37N 15°10E 294 F6
Ackerman U.S.A. 33°19N 89°11W 357 E10
Acklins I. Bahamas 22°30N 74°0W 361 B5
Acme Canada 51°33N 113°30W 342 C6
Acme U.S.A. 40°8N 79°26W 354 F5
Aconcagua, Cerro Argentina 32°39S 70°0W 366 C2
Aconquija, Mt. Argentina 27°0S 66°0W 366 B2
Açores, Is. dos Atl. Oc. 38°0N 27°0W 322 a
Acornhoek S. Africa 24°37S 31°2E 329 C5
Acraman, L. Australia 32°2S 135°23E 335 E2
Acre = 'Akko Israel 32°55N 35°4E 318 C4
Acre □ Brazil 9°1S 71°0W 364 E4
Acre → Brazil 8°45S 67°22W 364 E5
Acton Canada 43°38N 80°3W 354 C4
Ad Dammām Si. Arabia 26°20N 50°5E 317 E6
Ad Dāmūr Lebanon 33°43N 35°27E 318 B4
Ad Dawādimī Si. Arabia 24°35N 44°15E 316 E5
Ad Dawḥah Qatar 25°15N 51°35E 317 E6
Ad Dawr Iraq 34°27N 43°47E 316 C4
Ad Dir'īyah Si. Arabia 24°44N 46°35E 316 E5
Ad Dīwānīyah Iraq 32°0N 45°0E 316 D5
Ad Dujayl Iraq 33°51N 44°14E 316 C5
Ad Duwayd Si. Arabia 30°15N 42°17E 316 D4
Ada Minn., U.S.A. 47°18N 96°31W 352 B5
Ada Okla., U.S.A. 34°46N 96°41W 356 D6
Adabiya Egypt 29°53N 32°28E 318 F1
Adair, C. Canada 71°30N 71°34W 341 B12
Adaja → Spain 41°32N 4°52W 293 B3
Adak I. U.S.A. 51°45N 176°45W 346 a
Adamaoua, Massif de l' Cameroon 7°20N 12°20E 323 G8
Adamawa Highlands = Adamaoua, Massif de l' Cameroon 7°20N 12°20E 323 G8
Adamello, Mte. Italy 46°9N 10°30E 292 C9
Adaminaby Australia 36°0S 148°45E 335 F4
Adams Mass., U.S.A. 42°38N 73°7W 355 D11
Adams N.Y., U.S.A. 43°49N 76°1W 355 C8
Adams Wis., U.S.A. 43°57N 89°49W 352 D9
Adams, Mt. U.S.A. 46°12N 121°30W 350 D5
Adam's Bridge Sri Lanka 9°15N 79°40E 312 Q11
Adams L. Canada 51°10N 119°40W 342 C5
Adam's Peak Sri Lanka 6°48N 80°30E 312 R12
Adana Turkey 37°0N 35°16E 316 B2
Adapazarı = Sakarya Turkey 40°48N 30°25E 291 F5
Adarama Sudan 17°10N 34°52E 323 E12
Adare, C. Antarctica 71°0S 171°0E 277 D11
Adaut Indonesia 8°8S 131°7E 309 F8
Adavale Australia 25°52S 144°32E 335 D3
Adda → Italy 45°8N 9°53E 292 D8
Addis Ababa = Addis Abeba Ethiopia 9°2N 38°42E 319 F2
Addis Abeba Ethiopia 9°2N 38°42E 319 F2
Addison U.S.A. 42°1N 77°14W 354 D7
Addo S. Africa 33°32S 25°45E 328 E4
Addo △ S. Africa 33°30S 25°50E 328 E4
Ādeh Iran 37°42N 45°11E 316 B5
Adel U.S.A. 31°8N 83°25W 357 F13
Adelaide Australia 34°52S 138°30E 335 E2
Adelaide S. Africa 32°42S 26°20E 328 E4
Adelaide I. Antarctica 67°15S 68°30W 277 C17
Adelaide Pen. Canada 68°15N 97°30W 340 C10
Adelaide River Australia 13°15S 131°7E 332 B5
Adelaide Village Bahamas 25°0N 77°31W 360 A4
Adelanto U.S.A. 34°35N 117°22W 351 L9
Adele I. Australia 15°32S 123°9E 332 C3
Adélie, Terre Antarctica 68°0S 140°0E 277 C10
Adelie Land = Adélie, Terre Antarctica 68°0S 140°0E 277 C10
Aden = Al 'Adan Yemen 12°45N 45°0E 319 E4
Aden, G. of Asia 12°30N 47°30E 319 E4
Adendorp S. Africa 32°15S 24°30E 328 E3
Adh Dhayd U.A.E. 25°17N 55°53E 317 E7
Adhoi India 23°26N 70°32E 314 H4
Adi Indonesia 4°15S 133°30E 309 E8
Adieu, C. Australia 32°0S 132°10E 333 F5
Adieu Pt. Australia 15°14S 124°35E 332 C3
Adige → Italy 45°9N 12°20E 294 B5
Adigrat Ethiopia 14°20N 39°26E 319 E2
Adilabad India 19°33N 78°20E 312 K11
Adirondack ⌂ U.S.A. 44°0N 74°20W 355 C10
Adirondack Mts. U.S.A. 44°0N 74°0W 355 C10
Adis Abeba = Addis Abeba Ethiopia 9°2N 38°42E 319 F2
Adjumani Uganda 3°20N 31°50E 326 B3
Adjuntas Puerto Rico 18°10N 66°43W 361 d
Adlavik Is. Canada 55°0N 58°40W 345 B8
Admiralty G. Australia 14°20S 125°55E 332 B4
Admiralty I. U.S.A. 57°30N 134°30W 342 B2
Admiralty Is. Papua N. G. 2°0S 147°0E 330 B7
Adolfo Ruiz Cortines, Presa Mexico 27°15N 109°6W 358 B3
Adonara Indonesia 8°15S 123°5E 309 F6
Adoni India 15°33N 77°18E 312 M10
Adour → France 43°32N 1°32W 292 E3
Adra India 23°30N 86°42E 315 H12
Adra Spain 36°43N 3°3W 293 D4
Adrano Italy 37°40N 14°50E 294 F6
Adrar Algeria 27°51N 0°11E 322 C6
Adrar Mauritania 20°30N 7°30W 322 D3
Adrar des Iforas Africa 19°40N 1°40E 322 E6
Adrian Mich., U.S.A. 41°54N 84°2W 353 E11
Adrian Tex., U.S.A. 35°16N 102°40W 356 D3
Adriatic Sea Medit. S. 43°0N 16°0E 294 C6
Adua Indonesia 1°45S 129°50E 309 E7
Adwa Ethiopia 14°15N 38°52E 319 E2
Adygea □ Russia 45°0N 40°0E 291 F7
Adzhar Republic = Ajaria □ Georgia 41°30N 42°0E 291 F7
Adzopé Ivory C. 6°7N 3°49W 322 G5
Ægean Sea Medit. S. 38°30N 25°0E 295 E11
Aerhtai Shan Mongolia 46°40N 92°45E 304 B4
Afaahiti Tahiti 17°45S 149°17W 331 d
'Afak Iraq 32°4N 45°15E 316 C5
Afandou Greece 36°18N 28°12E 297 C10
Afareaitu Moorea 17°33S 149°47W 331 d
Afghanistan ■ Asia 33°0N 65°0E 312 C4
Aflou Algeria 34°7N 2°3E 322 B6
Africa 10°0N 20°0E 320 E6
'Afrīn Syria 36°32N 36°50E 316 B3
Afton N.Y., U.S.A. 42°14N 75°32W 355 D9
Afton Wyo., U.S.A. 42°44N 110°56W 348 E8
Afuá Brazil 0°15S 50°20W 365 D8
'Afula Israel 32°37N 35°17E 318 C4
Afyon Turkey 38°45N 30°33E 291 G5
Afyonkarahisar = Afyon Turkey 38°45N 30°33E 291 G5
Agadès = Agadez Niger 16°58N 7°59E 322 E7
Agadez Niger 16°58N 7°59E 322 E7
Agadir Morocco 30°28N 9°55W 322 B4
Agaete Canary Is. 28°6N 15°43W 296 F4
Agalega Is. Mauritius 11°0S 57°0E 275 E12
Agar India 23°40N 76°2E 314 H7
Agartala India 23°50N 91°23E 313 H17
Agassiz Canada 49°14N 121°46W 342 D4
Agats Indonesia 5°33S 138°0E 309 F9
Agawam U.S.A. 42°5N 72°37W 355 D12
Agboville Ivory C. 5°55N 4°15W 322 G5
Ağdam Azerbaijan 40°0N 46°58E 316 B5
Agde France 43°19N 3°28E 292 E5
Agen France 44°12N 0°38E 292 D4
Āgh Kand Iran 37°15N 48°4E 317 B6
Aghia Deka Greece 35°3N 24°58E 297 D6
Aghia Ekaterinis, Akra Greece 39°50N 19°50E 297 A3
Aghia Galini Greece 35°6N 24°41E 297 D6
Aghia Varvara Greece 35°8N 25°1E 297 D7
Aghios Efstratios Greece 39°34N 24°58E 295 E11
Aghios Ioannis, Akra Greece 35°20N 25°40E 297 D7
Aghios Isidoros Greece 36°9N 27°51E 297 C9
Aghios Matheos Greece 39°30N 19°47E 297 B3
Aghios Nikolaos Greece 35°11N 25°41E 297 D7
Aghiou Orous, Kolpos Greece 40°6N 24°0E 295 D11
Aginskoye Russia 51°6N 114°32E 301 D12
Agnew Australia 28°1S 120°31E 333 E3
Agori India 24°33N 82°57E 315 G10
Agra India 27°17N 77°58E 314 F7
Ağri Turkey 39°44N 43°3E 291 G7
Agri → Italy 40°13N 16°44E 294 D7
Ağrı Dağı Turkey 39°50N 44°15E 316 B5
Ağri Karakose = Ağri Turkey 39°44N 43°3E 291 G7
Agrigento Italy 37°19N 13°34E 294 F5
Agrinio Greece 38°37N 21°27E 295 E9
Agua Caliente Mexico 32°29N 116°59W 351 N10
Agua Caliente Springs U.S.A. 32°56N 116°19W 351 N10
Água Clara Brazil 20°25S 52°45W 365 H8
Agua Fria ⌂ U.S.A. 34°14N 112°0W 349 J8
Agua Hechicera Mexico 32°28N 116°15W 351 N10
Agua Prieta Mexico 31°18N 109°34W 358 A3
Aguadilla Puerto Rico 18°26N 67°10W 361 d
Aguadulce Panama 8°15N 80°32W 360 E3
Aguanga U.S.A. 33°27N 116°51W 351 M10
Aguanish Canada 50°14N 62°2W 345 B7
Aguanus → Canada 50°13N 62°5W 345 B7
Aguapey → Argentina 29°7S 56°36W 366 B4
Aguaray Guazú → Paraguay 24°47S 57°19W 366 A4
Aguarico → Ecuador 0°59S 75°11W 364 D3
Aguaro-Guariquito △ Venezuela 8°20N 66°35W 361 E6
Aguas Blancas Chile 24°15S 69°55W 366 A2
Aguas Calientes, Sierra de Argentina 25°26S 66°40W 366 B2
Aguascalientes Mexico 21°53N 102°18W 358 C4
Aguascalientes □ Mexico 22°0N 102°20W 358 C4
Aguila, Punta Puerto Rico 17°57N 67°13W 361 d
Aguilares Argentina 27°26S 65°35W 366 B2
Aguilas Spain 37°23N 1°35W 293 D5
Agüimes Canary Is. 27°58N 15°27W 296 G4
Aguja, C. de la Colombia 11°18N 74°12W 362 B3
Agujereada, Pta. Puerto Rico 18°30N 67°8W 361 d
Agulhas, C. S. Africa 34°52S 20°0E 328 E3
Agulo Canary Is. 28°11N 17°12W 296 F2
Agung, Gunung Indonesia 8°20S 115°28E 308 F5
Agur Uganda 2°28N 32°55E 326 B3
Agusan → Phil. 9°0N 125°30E 309 C7
Aha Mts. Botswana 19°45S 21°0E 328 B3
Ahaggar Algeria 23°0N 6°30E 322 D7
Ahar Iran 38°35N 47°0E 316 B5
Ahipara B. N.Z. 35°5S 173°5E 331 A4
Ahiri India 19°30N 80°0E 312 K12
Ahmad Wal Pakistan 29°18N 65°58E 314 E1
Ahmadabad India 23°0N 72°40E 314 H5
Aḩmadābād Khorāsān, Iran 35°3N 60°50E 317 C9
Aḩmadābād Khorāsān, Iran 35°49N 59°42E 317 C8
Aḩmadī Iran 27°56N 56°42E 317 E8
Ahmadnagar India 19°7N 74°46E 312 K9
Ahmadpur Pakistan 29°12N 71°10E 314 E4
Ahmadpur Lamma Pakistan 28°19N 70°3E 314 E4
Ahmedabad = Ahmadabad India 23°0N 72°40E 314 H5
Ahmednagar = Ahmadnagar India 19°7N 74°46E 312 K9
Ahome Mexico 25°55N 109°11W 358 B3
Ahoskie U.S.A. 36°17N 76°59W 357 C16
Ahram Iran 28°52N 51°16E 317 D6
Ahrax Pt. Malta 36°0N 14°22E 297 D1
Āhū Iran 34°33N 50°2E 317 C6
Ahuachapán El Salv. 13°54N 89°52W 360 D2
Ahvāz Iran 31°20N 48°40E 317 D6
Ahvenanmaa = Åland Finland 60°15N 20°0E 281 F19
Aḩwar Yemen 13°30N 46°40E 319 E4
Ai → India 26°26N 90°44E 315 F14
Ai-Ais Namibia 27°54S 17°59E 328 D2
Ai-Ais and Fish River Canyon △ Namibia 24°45S 17°15E 328 C2
Aichi □ Japan 35°0N 137°15E 303 G8
Aigrettes, Pte. des Réunion 21°3S 55°13E 325 c
Aigua Uruguay 34°13S 54°46W 367 C5
Aigues-Mortes France 43°35N 4°12E 292 E6
Aihui China 50°10N 127°30E 305 A7
Aija Peru 9°50S 77°45W 364 E3
Aikawa Japan 38°2N 138°15E 302 E9
Aiken U.S.A. 33°34N 81°43W 357 E14
Aileron Australia 22°39S 133°20E 334 C1
Aillik Canada 55°11N 59°18W 345 A8
Ailsa Craig U.K. 55°15N 5°6W 283 F3
Aim Russia 59°0N 133°55E 301 D14
Aimere Indonesia 8°45S 121°3E 309 F6
Aimogasta Argentina 28°33S 66°50W 366 B2
Aïn Ben Tili Mauritania 25°59N 9°27W 322 C4
Aïn Sefra Algeria 32°47N 0°37W 322 B5
Ain Sudr Egypt 29°50N 33°6E 318 F2
Aïn Témouchent Algeria 35°16N 1°8W 322 A5
Ainaži Latvia 57°50N 24°24E 281 H21
Ainsworth U.S.A. 42°33N 99°52W 352 D4
Aiquile Bolivia 18°10S 65°10W 364 G5
Aïr Niger 18°30N 8°0E 322 E7
Air Force I. Canada 67°58N 74°5W 341 C12
Air Hitam Malaysia 1°55N 103°11E 311 M4
Airdrie Canada 51°18N 114°2W 342 C6
Airdrie U.K. 55°52N 3°57W 283 F5
Aire → U.K. 53°43N 0°55W 284 D7
Aire, I. de l' Spain 39°48N 4°16E 296 B11
Airlie Beach Australia 20°16S 148°43E 334 J6
Aisne → France 49°26N 2°50E 292 B5
Ait India 25°54N 79°14E 315 G8
Aitkin U.S.A. 46°32N 93°42W 352 B7
Aitutaki Cook Is. 18°52S 159°45W 337 J12
Aiud Romania 46°19N 23°44E 289 E12
Aix-en-Provence France 43°32N 5°27E 292 E6
Aix-la-Chapelle = Aachen Germany 50°45N 6°6E 288 C4
Aix-les-Bains France 45°41N 5°53E 292 D6
Aizawl India 23°40N 92°44E 313 H18
Aizkraukle Latvia 56°36N 25°11E 281 H21
Aizpute Latvia 56°43N 21°40E 281 H19
Aizuwakamatsu Japan 37°30N 139°56E 302 F9
Ajaccio France 41°55N 8°40E 292 F8
Ajai ⌂ Uganda 2°52N 31°16E 326 B3
Ajaigarh India 24°52N 80°16E 315 G9
Ajalpan Mexico 18°22N 97°15W 359 D5
Ajanta Ra. India 20°28N 75°50E 312 J9
Ajari Rep. = Ajaria □ Georgia 41°30N 42°0E 291 F7
Ajaria □ Georgia 41°30N 42°0E 291 F7
Ajax Canada 43°50N 79°1W 354 C5
Ajdābiyā Libya 30°54N 20°4E 323 B10
Ajka Hungary 47°4N 17°31E 289 E9
'Ajlūn Jordan 32°18N 35°47E 318 C4
'Ajlūn □ Jordan 32°18N 35°47E 318 C4
'Ajmān U.A.E. 25°25N 55°30E 317 E7
Ajmer India 26°28N 74°37E 314 F6
Ajnala India 31°50N 74°48E 314 D6
Ajo U.S.A. 32°22N 112°52W 349 K7
Ajo, C. de Spain 43°31N 3°35W 293 A4
Akabira Japan 43°33N 142°5E 302 C11
Akagera △ Rwanda 1°31S 30°33E 326 C3
Akamas Cyprus 35°3N 32°18E 297 D11
Akan △ Japan 43°20N 144°20E 302 C12
Akanthou Cyprus 35°22N 33°45E 297 D12
Akaroa N.Z. 43°49S 172°59E 331 E4
Akashi Japan 34°45N 134°58E 303 G7
Akbarpur Bihar, India 24°39N 83°58E 315 G10
Akbarpur Ut. P., India 26°25N 82°32E 315 F10
Akelamo Indonesia 1°35N 129°40E 309 D7
Aketi Dem. Rep. of the Congo 2°38N 23°47E 324 D4
Akhisar Turkey 38°56N 27°48E 295 E12
Akhnur India 32°52N 74°45E 315 C6
Akhtyrka = Okhtyrka Ukraine 50°25N 35°0E 291 D5
Aki Japan 33°30N 133°54E 303 H6
Akimiski I. Canada 52°50N 81°30W 344 B3
Akita Japan 39°45N 140°7E 302 E10
Akita □ Japan 39°40N 140°30E 302 E10
Akjoujt Mauritania 19°45N 14°15W 322 E3
Akkeshi Japan 43°2N 144°51E 302 C12
'Akko Israel 32°55N 35°4E 318 C4
Aklavik Canada 68°12N 135°0W 340 C6
Aklera India 24°26N 76°32E 314 G7
Akō Japan 34°45N 134°24E 303 G7
Akola India 20°42N 77°2E 312 J10
Akordat Eritrea 15°30N 37°40E 319 D2
Akpatok I. Canada 60°25N 68°8W 341 C13
Åkrahamn Norway 59°15N 5°10E 281 G11
Akranes Iceland 64°19N 22°5W 280 D2
Akron Colo., U.S.A. 40°10N 103°13W 348 F12
Akron Ohio, U.S.A. 41°5N 81°31W 354 E3
Akrotiri Cyprus 34°36N 32°57E 297 E11
Akrotiri Bay Cyprus 34°35N 33°10E 297 E12
Aksai Chin China 35°15N 79°55E 315 B8
Aksaray Turkey 38°25N 34°2E 316 B2
Aksay = Aqsay Kazakhstan 51°11N 53°0E 291 D9
Akşehir Turkey 38°18N 31°30E 316 B1
Akşehir Gölü Turkey 38°30N 31°25E 291 G5
Aksu China 41°5N 80°10E 304 B3
Aksum Ethiopia 14°5N 38°40E 319 E2
Aktsyabrski Belarus 52°38N 28°53E 289 B15
Aktyubinsk = Aqtöbe Kazakhstan 50°17N 57°10E 291 D10
Akure Nigeria 7°15N 5°5E 322 G7
Akureyri Iceland 65°40N 18°6W 280 D4
Akuseki-Shima Japan 29°27N 129°37E 303 K4
Akyab = Sittwe Burma 20°18N 92°45E 313 J18
Al 'Adan Yemen 12°45N 45°0E 319 E4
Al Aḩsā' = Hasa Si. Arabia 25°50N 49°0E 317 E6
Al Ajfar Si. Arabia 27°26N 43°0E 316 E4
Al Amādīyah Iraq 37°5N 43°30E 316 B4
Al 'Amārah Iraq 31°55N 47°15E 316 D5
Al Anbār □ Iraq 33°25N 42°0E 316 C4
Al 'Aqabah Jordan 29°31N 35°0E 318 F4
Al 'Aqabah □ Jordan 29°30N 35°0E 318 F4
Al Arak Syria 34°38N 38°35E 316 C3
Al 'Aramah Si. Arabia 25°30N 46°0E 316 E5
Al 'Arṭāwīyah Si. Arabia 26°31N 45°20E 316 E5
Al 'Āṣimah = 'Ammān □ Jordan 31°40N 36°30E 318 D5
Al 'Assāfīyah Si. Arabia 28°17N 38°59E 316 D3
Al 'Ayn Si. Arabia 25°4N 38°6E 316 E3
Al 'Ayn U.A.E. 24°15N 55°45E 317 E7
Al 'Azīzīyah Iraq 32°54N 45°4E 316 C5
Al Bāb Syria 36°23N 37°29E 316 B3
Al Bad' Si. Arabia 28°28N 35°1E 316 D2
Al Bādī Iraq 35°56N 41°32E 316 C4
Al Baḩrah Kuwait 29°40N 47°52E 316 D5
Al Baḩral Mayyit = Dead Sea Asia 31°30N 35°30E 318 D4
Al Balqā' □ Jordan 32°5N 35°45E 318 C4
Al Bārūk, J. Lebanon 33°39N 35°40E 318 B4
Al Başrah Iraq 30°30N 47°50E 316 D5
Al Baṭḩā Iraq 31°6N 45°53E 316 D5
Al Batrūn Lebanon 34°15N 35°40E 318 A4
Al Bayḑā Libya 32°50N 21°44E 323 B10
Al Biqā Lebanon 34°10N 36°10E 318 A5
Al Bi'r Si. Arabia 28°51N 36°16E 316 D3
Al Bukayrīyah Si. Arabia 26°9N 43°40E 316 E4
Al Burayj Syria 34°15N 36°46E 318 A5
Al Faḑilī Si. Arabia 26°58N 49°10E 317 E6
Al Fallūjah Iraq 33°20N 43°55E 316 C4
Al Fāw Iraq 30°0N 48°30E 317 D6
Al Fujayrah U.A.E. 25°7N 56°18E 317 E8
Al Ghadaf, W. → Jordan 31°26N 36°43E 318 D5
Al Ghammās Iraq 31°45N 44°37E 316 D5
Al Ghazālah Si. Arabia 26°48N 41°19E 316 E4
Al Ḩadīthah Iraq 34°0N 41°13E 316 C4
Al Ḩadīthah Si. Arabia 31°28N 37°8E 318 D6
Al Ḩaḑr Iraq 35°35N 42°44E 316 C4

Al Ḩājānah *Syria* 33°20N 36°33E **318** B5
Al Ḩajar al Gharbī *Oman* 24°10N 56°15E **317** E8
Al Hāmad *Si. Arabia* 31°30N 39°30E **316** D3
Al Ḩamdānīyah *Syria* 35°25N 36°50E **316** C3
Al Ḩamīdīyah *Syria* 34°42N 35°57E **318** A4
Al Ḩammār *Iraq* 30°57N 46°51E **316** D5
Al Ḩamrā' *Si. Arabia* 24°2N 38°55E **316** E3
Al Ḩamzah *Iraq* 31°43N 44°58E **316** D5
Al Ḩanākīyah *Si. Arabia* 24°51N 40°31E **316** E4
Al Harūj al Aswad *Libya* 27°0N 17°10E **323** C9
Al Ḩasakah *Syria* 36°35N 40°45E **316** B4
Al Ḩayy *Iraq* 32°5N 46°5E **316** C5
Al Ḩijarah *Asia* 30°0N 44°0E **316** D4
Al Ḩillah *Iraq* 32°30N 44°25E **316** C5
Al Ḩillah *Si. Arabia* 23°35N 46°50E **319** B4
Al Hindīyah *Iraq* 32°30N 44°10E **316** C5
Al Hirmil *Lebanon* 34°26N 36°24E **318** A5
Al Hoceïma *Morocco* 35°8N 3°58W **322** A5
Al Ḩudaydah *Yemen* 14°50N 43°0E **319** E3
Al Ḩudūd ash Shamālīyah ☐ *Si. Arabia* 29°10N 42°30E **316** D4
Al Hufūf *Si. Arabia* 25°25N 49°45E **317** E6
Al Ḩumaydah *Si. Arabia* 29°14N 34°56E **316** D2
Al Ḩunayy *Si. Arabia* 25°58N 48°45E **317** E6
Al Īsāwīyah *Si. Arabia* 30°43N 37°59E **316** D3
Al Jafr *Jordan* 30°18N 36°14E **318** E5
Al Jāfūrah *Si. Arabia* 25°0N 50°15E **317** E7
Al Jaghbūb *Libya* 29°42N 24°38E **323** C10
Al Jahrah *Kuwait* 29°25N 47°40E **316** D5
Al Jalāmīd *Si. Arabia* 31°20N 40°6E **316** D3
Al Jamalīyah *Qatar* 25°37N 51°5E **317** E6
Al Janūb ☐ *Lebanon* 33°20N 35°20E **318** B4
Al Jawf *Libya* 24°10N 23°24E **323** D10
Al Jawf *Si. Arabia* 29°55N 39°40E **316** D3
Al Jawf ☐ *Si. Arabia* 29°30N 39°30E **316** D3
Al Jazair = Algeria ■ *Africa* 28°30N 2°0E **322** C6
Al Jazirah *Iraq* 33°30N 44°0E **316** C5
Al Jithāmīyah *Si. Arabia* 27°41N 41°43E **316** E4
Al Jubayl *Si. Arabia* 27°0N 49°50E **317** E6
Al Jubaylah *Si. Arabia* 24°55N 46°25E **316** E5
Al Jubb *Si. Arabia* 27°11N 42°17E **316** E4
Al Junaynah *Sudan* 13°27N 22°45E **323** F10
Al Kabā'ish *Iraq* 30°58N 47°0E **316** D5
Al Karak *Jordan* 31°11N 35°42E **318** D4
Al Karak ☐ *Jordan* 31°0N 36°0E **318** E5
Al Kāẓimīyah *Iraq* 33°22N 44°18E **316** C5
Al Khābūra *Oman* 23°57N 57°5E **317** F8
Al Khafjī *Si. Arabia* 28°24N 48°29E **317** E6
Al Khalīl *West Bank* 31°32N 35°6E **318** D4
Al Khāliş *Iraq* 33°49N 44°32E **316** C5
Al Kharsānīyah *Si. Arabia* 27°13N 49°18E **317** E6
Al Khaşab *Oman* 26°14N 56°15E **317** E8
Al Khawr *Qatar* 25°41N 51°30E **317** E6
Al Khiḑr *Iraq* 31°12N 45°33E **316** D5
Al Khiyām *Lebanon* 33°20N 35°36E **318** B4
Al Khobar *Si. Arabia* 26°17N 50°12E **317** E6
Al Khums *Libya* 32°40N 14°17E **323** B8
Al Kiswah *Syria* 33°23N 36°14E **318** B5
Al Kūfah *Iraq* 32°2N 44°24E **316** C5
Al Kufrah *Libya* 24°17N 23°15E **323** D10
Al Kuhayfīyah *Si. Arabia* 27°12N 43°3E **316** E4
Al Kūt *Iraq* 32°30N 46°0E **316** C5
Al Kuwayt *Kuwait* 29°30N 48°0E **316** D5
Al Labwah *Lebanon* 34°11N 36°20E **318** A5
Al Lādhiqīyah *Syria* 35°30N 35°45E **316** C2
Al Līth *Si. Arabia* 20°9N 40°15E **319** C3
Al Liwā' *Oman* 24°31N 56°36E **317** E8
Al Luḩayyah *Yemen* 15°45N 42°40E **319** D3
Al Madīnah *Iraq* 30°57N 47°16E **316** D5
Al Madīnah *Si. Arabia* 24°35N 39°52E **316** E3
Al Mafraq *Jordan* 32°17N 36°14E **318** C5
Al Mafraq ☐ *Jordan* 32°17N 36°15E **318** C5
Al Maghreb = Morocco ■ *N. Afr.* 32°0N 5°50W **322** B4
Al Maḩmūdīyah *Iraq* 33°3N 44°21E **316** C5
Al Majma'ah *Si. Arabia* 25°57N 45°22E **316** E5
Al Makhruq, W. → *Jordan* 31°28N 37°0E **318** D6
Al Makḩūl *Si. Arabia* 26°37N 42°39E **316** E4
Al Manāmah *Bahrain* 26°10N 50°30E **317** E6
Al Maqwa' *Kuwait* 29°10N 47°59E **316** D5
Al Marāḩ *Si. Arabia* 25°35N 49°35E **317** E6
Al Marj *Libya* 32°25N 20°30E **323** B10
Al Maţlā *Kuwait* 29°24N 47°40E **316** D5
Al Mawşil *Iraq* 36°15N 43°5E **316** B4
Al Mayādin *Syria* 35°1N 40°27E **316** C4
Al Mazār *Jordan* 31°4N 35°41E **318** D4
Al Midhnab *Si. Arabia* 25°50N 44°18E **316** E5
Al Minā' *Lebanon* 34°24N 35°49E **318** A4
Al Miqdādīyah *Iraq* 34°0N 45°0E **316** C5
Al Mubarraz *Si. Arabia* 25°30N 49°40E **317** E6
Al Mudawwarah *Jordan* 29°19N 36°0E **318** F5
Al Mughayrā' *U.A.E.* 24°5N 53°32E **317** E7
Al Muḩarraq *Bahrain* 26°15N 50°40E **317** E6
Al Mukallā *Yemen* 14°33N 49°2E **319** E4
Al Mukhā *Yemen* 13°18N 43°15E **319** E3
Al Musayjīd *Si. Arabia* 24°5N 39°5E **316** E3
Al Musayyib *Iraq* 32°49N 44°20E **316** C5
Al Muthanná ☐ *Iraq* 30°30N 45°15E **316** D5
Al Muwayliḩ *Si. Arabia* 27°40N 35°30E **316** E2
Al Qādisīyah ☐ *Iraq* 32°0N 45°0E **316** D5
Al Qā'im *Iraq* 34°21N 41°7E **316** C4
Al Qalībah *Si. Arabia* 28°24N 37°42E **316** D3
Al Qāmishlī *Syria* 37°2N 41°14E **316** B4
Al Qaryatayn *Syria* 34°12N 37°13E **318** A6
Al Qaşīm ☐ *Si. Arabia* 26°0N 43°0E **316** E4
Al Qaţ'ā *Syria* 34°40N 40°48E **316** C4
Al Qaţīf *Si. Arabia* 26°35N 50°0E **317** E6
Al Qaţrānah *Jordan* 31°12N 36°6E **318** D5
Al Qaţrūn *Libya* 24°56N 15°3E **323** D9
Al Qayşūmah *Si. Arabia* 28°20N 46°7E **316** D5
Al Quds = Jerusalem *Israel/West Bank* 31°47N 35°10E **318** D4
Al Qunayţirah *Syria* 32°55N 35°45E **318** C4
Al Qunfudhah *Si. Arabia* 19°3N 41°4E **319** D3
Al Qurnah *Iraq* 31°1N 47°25E **316** D5
Al Quşayr *Iraq* 30°39N 45°50E **316** D5
Al Quşayr *Syria* 34°31N 36°34E **318** A5
Al Qutayfah *Syria* 33°44N 36°36E **318** B5
Al 'Ubaylah *Si. Arabia* 21°59N 50°57E **319** C5
Al 'Uḑaylīyah *Si. Arabia* 25°8N 49°18E **317** E6
Al 'Ulā *Si. Arabia* 26°35N 38°0E **316** E3
Al 'Uqayr *Si. Arabia* 25°40N 50°15E **317** E6
Al 'Uwaynid *Si. Arabia* 24°50N 46°0E **316** E5
Al 'Uwayqīlah *Si. Arabia* 30°30N 42°10E **316** D4
Al 'Uyūn *Ḩijāz, Si. Arabia* 24°33N 39°35E **316** E3
Al 'Uyūn *Najd, Si. Arabia* 26°30N 43°50E **316** E4
Al 'Uzayr *Iraq* 31°19N 47°25E **316** D5
Al Wajh *Si. Arabia* 26°10N 36°30E **316** E3
Al Wakrah *Qatar* 25°10N 51°40E **317** E6
Al Waqbah *Si. Arabia* 28°48N 45°33E **316** D5
Al Wari'āh *Si. Arabia* 27°51N 47°25E **316** E5
Al Yaman = Yemen ■ *Asia* 15°0N 44°0E **319** E3
Ala Dağ *Turkey* 37°44N 35°9E **316** B2
Ala Tau Shankou = Dzungarian Gate *Asia* 45°10N 82°0E **304** B3
Alabama ☐ *U.S.A.* 33°0N 87°0W **357** E11
Alabama → *U.S.A.* 31°8N 87°57W **357** F11
Alabaster *U.S.A.* 33°15N 86°49W **357** E11
Alaçam Dağları *Turkey* 39°18N 28°49E **295** E13
Alacant = Alicante *Spain* 38°23N 0°30W **293** C5
Alachua *U.S.A.* 29°47N 82°30W **357** G13
Alagoa Grande *Brazil* 7°3S 35°35W **365** E11
Alagoas ☐ *Brazil* 9°0S 36°0W **365** E11
Alagoinhas *Brazil* 12°7S 38°20W **365** F11
Alaior *Spain* 39°57N 4°8E **296** B11
Alajero *Canary Is.* 28°3N 17°13W **296** F2
Alajuela *Costa Rica* 10°2N 84°8W **360** D3
Alakamisy *Madag.* 21°19S 47°14E **329** C8
Alaknanda → *India* 30°8N 78°36E **315** D8
Alakurtti *Russia* 66°58N 30°25E **280** C24
Alamarvdasht *Iran* 27°37N 52°59E **317** E7
Alameda *Calif., U.S.A.* 37°46N 122°15W **350** H4
Alameda *N. Mex., U.S.A.* 35°11N 106°37W **349** J10
Alamo *U.S.A.* 37°22N 115°10W **351** H11
Alamogordo *U.S.A.* 32°54N 105°57W **349** K11
Alamos *Mexico* 27°1N 108°56W **358** B3
Alamosa *U.S.A.* 37°28N 105°52W **349** H11
Åland *Finland* 60°15N 20°0E **281** F19
Ålands hav *Europe* 60°0N 19°30E **281** G18
Alania = North Ossetia ☐ *Russia* 43°30N 44°30E **291** F7
Alanya *Turkey* 36°38N 32°0E **316** B1
Alaotra, Farihin' *Madag.* 17°30S 48°30E **329** B8
Alapayevsk *Russia* 57°52N 61°42E **300** D7
Alappuzha = Alleppey *India* 9°30N 76°28E **312** Q10
Alarobia-Vohiposa *Madag.* 20°59S 47°9E **329** C8
Alaşehir *Turkey* 38°23N 28°30E **295** E13
Alaska ☐ *U.S.A.* 64°0N 154°0W **346** a
Alaska, G. of *Pac. Oc.* 58°0N 145°0W **346** a
Alaska Peninsula *U.S.A.* 56°0N 159°0W **346** a
Alaska Range *U.S.A.* 62°50N 151°0W **346** a
Älät *Azerbaijan* 39°58N 49°25E **317** B6
Alatyr *Russia* 54°55N 46°35E **290** D8
Alausi *Ecuador* 2°0S 78°50W **364** D3
Alava, C. *U.S.A.* 48°10N 124°44W **348** B1
Alavo = Alavus *Finland* 62°35N 23°36E **280** E20
Alavus *Finland* 62°35N 23°36E **280** E20
Alawoona *Australia* 34°45S 140°30E **335** E3
'Alayh *Lebanon* 33°46N 35°33E **318** B4
Alba *Italy* 44°42N 8°2E **292** D8
Alba-Iulia *Romania* 46°8N 23°39E **289** E12
Albacete *Spain* 39°0N 1°50W **293** C5
Albacutya, L. *Australia* 35°45S 141°58E **335** F3
Albanel, L. *Canada* 50°55N 73°12W **344** B5
Albania ■ *Europe* 41°0N 20°0E **295** D9
Albany *Australia* 35°1S 117°58E **333** G2
Albany *Ga., U.S.A.* 31°35N 84°10W **357** F12
Albany *N.Y., U.S.A.* 42°39N 73°45W **355** D11
Albany *Oreg., U.S.A.* 44°38N 123°6W **348** D2
Albany *Tex., U.S.A.* 32°44N 99°18W **356** E5
Albany → *Canada* 52°17N 81°31W **344** B3
Albardón *Argentina* 31°20S 68°30W **366** C2
Albatross B. *Australia* 12°45S 141°30E **334** A3
Albemarle *U.S.A.* 35°21N 80°12W **357** D14
Albemarle Sd. *U.S.A.* 36°5N 76°0W **357** C16
Alberche → *Spain* 39°58N 4°46W **293** C3
Alberdi *Paraguay* 26°14S 58°20W **366** B4
Alberga → *Australia* 27°6S 135°33E **335** D2
Albert, L. *Africa* 1°30N 31°0E **326** B3
Albert, L. *Australia* 35°30S 139°10E **335** F2
Albert Edward Ra. *Australia* 18°17S 127°57E **332** C4
Albert Lea *U.S.A.* 43°39N 93°22W **352** D7
Albert Nile → *Uganda* 3°36N 32°2E **326** B3
Albert Town *Bahamas* 22°37N 74°33W **361** B5
Alberta ☐ *Canada* 54°40N 115°0W **342** C6
Alberti *Argentina* 35°1S 60°16W **366** D3
Albertinia *S. Africa* 34°11S 21°34E **328** E3
Alberton *Canada* 46°50N 64°0W **345** C7
Albertville *France* 45°40N 6°22E **292** D7
Albertville *U.S.A.* 34°16N 86°13W **357** D11
Albi *France* 43°56N 2°9E **292** E5
Albia *U.S.A.* 41°2N 92°48W **352** E7
Albina *Suriname* 5°37N 54°15W **365** B8
Albina, Ponta *Angola* 15°52S 11°44E **328** B1
Albion *Mich., U.S.A.* 42°15N 84°45W **353** D11
Albion *Nebr., U.S.A.* 41°42N 98°0W **352** E4
Albion *Pa., U.S.A.* 41°53N 80°22W **354** E4
Alborán *Medit. S.* 35°57N 3°0W **293** E4
Ålborg = Aalborg *Denmark* 57°2N 9°54E **281** H13
Alborz, Reshteh-ye Kūhhā-ye *Iran* 36°0N 52°0E **317** C7
Albufeira *Portugal* 37°5N 8°15W **293** D1
Albuquerque *U.S.A.* 35°5N 106°39W **349** J10
Albuquerque, Cayos de *Caribbean* 12°10N 81°50W **360** D3
Alburg *U.S.A.* 44°59N 73°18W **355** B11
Albury *Australia* 36°3S 146°56E **335** F4
Alcalá de Henares *Spain* 40°28N 3°22W **293** B4
Alcalá la Real *Spain* 37°27N 3°57W **293** D4
Álcamo *Italy* 37°59N 12°55E **294** F5
Alcaníz *Spain* 41°2N 0°8W **293** B5
Alcântara *Brazil* 2°20S 44°30W **365** D10
Alcántara, Embalse de *Spain* 39°44N 6°50W **293** C2
Alcantarilla *Spain* 37°59N 1°12W **293** D5
Alcaraz, Sierra de *Spain* 38°40N 2°20W **293** C4
Alcaudete *Spain* 37°35N 4°5W **293** D3
Alcázar de San Juan *Spain* 39°24N 3°12W **293** C4
Alchevsk *Ukraine* 48°30N 38°45E **291** E6
Alcira = Alzira *Spain* 39°9N 0°30W **293** C5
Alcova *U.S.A.* 42°34N 106°43W **348** E10
Alcoy *Spain* 38°43N 0°30W **293** C5
Alcúdia *Spain* 39°51N 3°7E **296** B10
Alcúdia, B. d' *Spain* 39°47N 3°15E **296** B10
Aldabra Is. *Seychelles* 9°22S 46°28E **321** G8
Aldama *Mexico* 22°55N 98°4W **359** C5
Aldan *Russia* 58°40N 125°30E **301** D13
Aldan → *Russia* 63°28N 129°35E **301** C13
Aldea, Pta. de la *Canary Is.* 28°0N 15°50W **296** G4
Aldeburgh *U.K.* 52°10N 1°37E **285** E9
Alder Pk. *U.S.A.* 35°53N 121°22W **350** K5
Alderney *U.K.* 49°42N 2°11W **285** H5
Aldershot *U.K.* 51°15N 0°44W **285** F7
Aledo *U.S.A.* 41°12N 90°45W **352** E8
Aleg *Mauritania* 17°3N 13°55W **322** E3
Alegranza *Canary Is.* 29°23N 13°32W **296** E6
Alegranza, I. *Canary Is.* 29°23N 13°32W **296** E6
Alegre *Brazil* 20°50S 41°30W **367** A7
Alegrete *Brazil* 29°40S 56°0W **367** B4
Aleksandriya = Oleksandriya *Ukraine* 50°37N 26°19E **289** C14
Aleksandrov Gay *Russia* 50°9N 48°34E **291** D8
Aleksandrovsk-Sakhalinskiy *Russia* 50°50N 142°20E **301** D15
Aleksandry, Zemlya *Russia* 80°25N 48°0E **276** A10
Além Paraíba *Brazil* 21°52S 42°41W **367** A7
Alemania *Argentina* 25°40S 65°30W **366** B2
Alemania *Chile* 25°10S 69°55W **366** B2
Alençon *France* 48°27N 0°4E **292** B4
Alenquer *Brazil* 1°56S 54°46W **365** D8
'Alenuihähä Channel *U.S.A.* 20°30N 156°0W **346** b
Aleppo = Ḩalab *Syria* 36°10N 37°15E **316** B3
Aléria *France* 42°5N 9°26E **292** E9
Alert *Canada* 83°2N 60°0W **341** A13
Alès *France* 44°9N 4°5E **292** D6
Alessándria *Italy* 44°54N 8°37E **292** D8
Ålesund *Norway* 62°28N 6°12E **280** E12
Aleutian Basin *Pac. Oc.* 57°0N 177°0E **336** B9
Aleutian Is. *Pac. Oc.* 52°0N 175°0W **346** a
Aleutian Trench *Pac. Oc.* 48°0N 180°0E **276** D17
Alexander *U.S.A.* 47°51N 103°39W **352** B2
Alexander, Mt. *Australia* 28°58S 120°16E **333** E3
Alexander Arch. *U.S.A.* 56°0N 136°0W **346** a
Alexander Bay *S. Africa* 28°40S 16°30E **328** D2
Alexander City *U.S.A.* 32°56N 85°58W **357** E12
Alexander I. *Antarctica* 69°0S 70°0W **277** C17
Alexandra *Australia* 37°8S 145°40E **335** F4
Alexandra *N.Z.* 45°14S 169°25E **331** F2
Alexandra Falls *Canada* 60°29N 116°18W **342** A5
Alexandria = El Iskandarîya *Egypt* 31°13N 29°58E **323** B11
Alexandria *B.C., Canada* 52°35N 122°27W **342** C4
Alexandria *Ont., Canada* 45°19N 74°38W **355** A10
Alexandria *Romania* 43°57N 25°24E **289** G13
Alexandria *S. Africa* 33°38S 26°28E **328** E4
Alexandria *U.K.* 55°59N 4°35W **283** F4
Alexandria *La., U.S.A.* 31°18N 92°27W **356** F8
Alexandria *Minn., U.S.A.* 45°53N 95°22W **352** C6
Alexandria *S. Dak., U.S.A.* 43°39N 97°47W **352** D5
Alexandria *Va., U.S.A.* 38°49N 77°5W **353** F15
Alexandria Bay *U.S.A.* 44°20N 75°55W **355** B9
Alexandrina, L. *Australia* 35°25S 139°10E **335** F2
Alexandroupoli *Greece* 40°50N 25°54E **295** D11
Alexis → *Canada* 52°33N 56°8W **345** B8
Alexis Creek *Canada* 52°10N 123°20W **342** C4
Aleysk *Russia* 52°40N 83°0E **300** D9
Alfabia *Spain* 39°44N 2°44E **296** B9
Alfenas *Brazil* 21°20S 46°10W **367** A6
Alford *Aberds., U.K.* 57°14N 2°41W **283** D6
Alford *Lincs., U.K.* 53°15N 0°10E **284** D8
Alfred *Maine, U.S.A.* 43°29N 70°43W **355** C14
Alfred *N.Y., U.S.A.* 42°16N 77°48W **354** D7
Alfreton *U.K.* 53°6N 1°24W **284** D6
Alga *Kazakhstan* 49°53N 57°20E **291** E10
Algaida *Spain* 39°33N 2°53E **296** B9
Ålgård *Norway* 58°46N 5°53E **281** G11
Algarve *Portugal* 36°58N 8°20W **293** D1
Algeciras *Spain* 36°9N 5°28W **293** D3
Algemesí *Spain* 39°11N 0°27W **293** C5
Alger *Algeria* 36°42N 3°8E **322** A6
Algeria ■ *Africa* 28°30N 2°0E **322** C6
Alghero *Italy* 40°33N 8°19E **294** D3
Algiers = Alger *Algeria* 36°42N 3°8E **322** A6
Algoa B. *S. Africa* 33°50S 25°45E **328** E4
Algoma *U.S.A.* 44°36N 87°26W **352** C10
Algona *U.S.A.* 43°4N 94°14W **352** D6
Algonac *U.S.A.* 42°37N 82°32W **354** D2
Algonquin ⌂ *Canada* 45°50N 78°30W **344** C4
Algorta *Uruguay* 32°25S 57°23W **368** C5
Alhambra *U.S.A.* 34°5N 118°7W **351** L8
Alhucemas = Al Hoceïma *Morocco* 35°8N 3°58W **322** A5
'Alī al Gharbī *Iraq* 32°30N 46°45E **316** C5
'Alī ash Sharqī *Iraq* 32°7N 46°44E **316** C5
'Alī Khēl *Afghan.* 33°57N 69°43E **314** C3
Alī Shāh *Iran* 38°9N 45°50E **316** B5
'Alīābād *Khorāsān, Iran* 32°30N 57°30E **317** C8
'Alīābād *Kordestān, Iran* 35°4N 46°58E **316** C5
'Alīābād *Yazd, Iran* 31°41N 53°49E **317** D7
Aliağa *Turkey* 38°47N 26°59E **295** E12
Aliakmonas → *Greece* 40°30N 22°36E **295** D10
Alicante *Spain* 38°23N 0°30W **293** C5
Alice *S. Africa* 32°48S 26°55E **328** E4
Alice *U.S.A.* 27°45N 98°5W **356** H5
Alice → *Queens., Australia* 24°2S 144°50E **334** C3
Alice → *Queens., Australia* 15°35S 142°20E **334** B3
Alice Arm *Canada* 55°29N 129°31W **342** B3
Alice Springs *Australia* 23°40S 133°50E **334** C1
Alicedale *S. Africa* 33°15S 26°4E **328** E4
Aliceville *U.S.A.* 33°8N 88°9W **357** E10
Aliganj *India* 27°30N 79°10E **315** F8
Aligarh *Raj., India* 25°55N 76°15E **314** G7
Aligarh *Ut. P., India* 27°55N 78°10E **314** F8
Alīgūdarz *Iran* 33°25N 49°45E **317** C6
Alimia *Greece* 36°16N 27°43E **297** C9
Alingsås *Sweden* 57°56N 12°31E **281** H15
Alipur *Pakistan* 29°25N 70°55E **314** E4
Alipur Duar *India* 26°30N 89°35E **313** F16
Aliquippa *U.S.A.* 40°37N 80°15W **354** F4
Alitus = Alytus *Lithuania* 54°24N 24°3E **281** J21
Aliwal North *S. Africa* 30°45S 26°45E **328** E4
Alix *Canada* 52°24N 113°11W **342** C6
Aljustrel *Portugal* 37°55N 8°10W **293** D1
Alkmaar *Neths.* 52°37N 4°45E **287** B4
All American Canal *U.S.A.* 32°45N 115°15W **349** K6
Allagash → *U.S.A.* 47°5N 69°3W **353** B19
Allah Dad *Pakistan* 25°38N 67°34E **314** G2
Allahabad *India* 25°25N 81°58E **315** G9
Allan *Canada* 51°53N 106°4W **343** C7
Allanridge *S. Africa* 27°45S 26°40E **328** D4
Allegany *U.S.A.* 42°6N 78°30W **354** D6
Allegheny → *U.S.A.* 40°27N 80°1W **354** F5
Allegheny Mts. *U.S.A.* 38°15N 80°10W **353** F13
Allegheny Plateau *U.S.A.* 41°30N 78°30W **353** E14
Allegheny Res. *U.S.A.* 41°50N 79°0W **354** E6
Allègre, Pte. *Guadeloupe* 16°22N 61°46W **360** b
Allen, Bog of *Ireland* 53°15N 7°0W **282** C5
Allen, L. *Ireland* 54°8N 8°4W **282** B3
Allendale *U.S.A.* 33°1N 81°18W **357** E14
Allende *Mexico* 28°20N 100°51W **358** B4
Allentown *U.S.A.* 40°37N 75°29W **355** F9
Alleppey *India* 9°30N 76°28E **312** Q10
Aller → *Germany* 52°56N 9°12E **288** B5
Alleynes B. *Barbados* 13°13N 59°39W **361** g
Alliance *Nebr., U.S.A.* 42°6N 102°52W **352** D2
Alliance *Ohio, U.S.A.* 40°55N 81°6W **354** F3
Allier → *France* 46°57N 3°4E **292** C5
Alliford Bay *Canada* 53°12N 131°58W **342** C2
Alligator Pond *Jamaica* 17°52N 77°34W **360** a
Alliston = New Tecumseth *Canada* 44°9N 79°52W **354** B5
Alloa *U.K.* 56°7N 3°47W **283** E5
Allora *Australia* 28°2S 152°0E **335** D5
Alluitsup Paa *Greenland* 60°30N 45°35W **276** C5
Alma *Canada* 48°35N 71°40W **345** C5
Alma *Ga., U.S.A.* 31°33N 82°28W **357** F13
Alma *Kans., U.S.A.* 39°1N 96°17W **352** F5
Alma *Mich., U.S.A.* 43°23N 84°39W **353** D11
Alma *Nebr., U.S.A.* 40°6N 99°22W **352** E4
Alma *Wis., U.S.A.* 44°20N 91°55W **352** C8
Alma Ata = Almaty *Kazakhstan* 43°15N 76°57E **300** E8
Almada *Portugal* 38°41N 9°8W **293** C1
Almaden *Australia* 17°22S 144°40E **334** B3
Almadén *Spain* 38°49N 4°52W **293** C3
Almanor, L. *U.S.A.* 40°14N 121°9W **348** F3
Almansa *Spain* 38°51N 1°5W **293** C5
Almanzor, Pico *Spain* 40°15N 5°18W **293** B3
Almanzora → *Spain* 37°14N 1°46W **293** D5
Almaty *Kazakhstan* 43°15N 76°57E **300** E8
Almazán *Spain* 41°30N 2°30W **293** B4
Almeirim *Brazil* 1°30S 52°34W **365** D8
Almelo *Neths.* 52°22N 6°42E **287** B6
Almendralejo *Spain* 38°41N 6°26W **293** C2
Almere-Stad *Neths.* 52°20N 5°15E **287** B5
Almería *Spain* 36°52N 2°27W **293** D4
Almirante *Panama* 9°10N 82°30W **360** E3
Almond *U.S.A.* 42°19N 77°44W **354** D7
Almont *U.S.A.* 42°55N 83°3W **354** D1
Almonte *Canada* 45°14N 76°12W **355** A8
Almora *India* 29°38N 79°40E **315** E8
Almyrou, Ormos *Greece* 35°23N 24°20E **297** D6
Alness *U.K.* 57°41N 4°16W **283** D4
Alnmouth *U.K.* 55°24N 1°37W **284** B6
Alnwick *U.K.* 55°24N 1°42W **284** B6
Aloi *Uganda* 2°16N 33°10E **326** B3
Alon *Burma* 22°12N 95°5E **313** H19
Alor *Indonesia* 8°15S 124°30E **309** F6
Alor Setar *Malaysia* 6°7N 100°22E **311** J3
Alot *India* 23°56N 75°40E **314** H6
Aloysius, Mt. *Australia* 26°0S 128°38E **333** E4
Alpaugh *U.S.A.* 35°53N 119°29W **350** K7
Alpena *U.S.A.* 45°4N 83°27W **353** C12
Alpha *Australia* 23°39S 146°37E **334** C4
Alpha Ridge *Arctic* 84°0N 118°0W **276** A2
Alphen aan den Rijn *Neths.* 52°7N 4°40E **287** B4
Alpine *Ariz., U.S.A.* 33°51N 109°9W **349** K9
Alpine *Calif., U.S.A.* 32°50N 116°46W **351** N10
Alpine *Tex., U.S.A.* 30°22N 103°40W **356** F3
Alps *Europe* 46°30N 9°30E **292** C8
Alsace ☐ *France* 48°15N 7°25E **292** B7
Alsask *Canada* 51°21N 109°59W **343** C7
Alsasua *Spain* 42°54N 2°10W **293** A4
Alsek → *U.S.A.* 59°10N 138°12W **342** B1
Alsta *Norway* 65°58N 12°40E **280** D15
Alston *U.K.* 54°49N 2°25W **284** C5
Alta *Norway* 69°57N 23°10E **280** B20
Alta Gracia *Argentina* 31°40S 64°30W **366** C3
Alta Sierra *U.S.A.* 35°42N 118°33W **351** K8
Altaelva → *Norway* 69°54N 23°17E **280** B20
Altafjorden *Norway* 70°5N 23°5E **280** A20
Altai = Aerhtai Shan *Mongolia* 46°40N 92°45E **304** B4
Altai = Gorno-Altay ☐ *Russia* 51°0N 86°0E **300** D9
Altamaha → *U.S.A.* 31°20N 81°20W **357** F14
Altamira *Brazil* 3°12S 52°10W **365** D8
Altamira *Chile* 25°47S 69°51W **366** B2
Altamira *Mexico* 22°24N 97°55W **359** C5
Altamont *U.S.A.* 42°42N 74°2W **355** D10
Altamura *Italy* 40°49N 16°33E **294** D7
Altanbulag *Mongolia* 50°16N 106°30E **304** A5
Altar *Mexico* 30°43N 111°44W **358** A2
Altar, Gran Desierto de *Mexico* 31°50N 114°10W **358** B2
Altata *Mexico* 24°40N 107°55W **358** C3
Altavista *U.S.A.* 37°6N 79°17W **353** G14
Altay *China* 47°48N 88°10E **304** B3
Altea *Spain* 38°38N 0°2W **293** C5
Altiplano *Bolivia* 17°0S 68°0W **364** G5
Alto Araguaia *Brazil* 17°15S 53°20W **365** G8
Alto Cuchumatanes = Cuchumatanes, Sierra de los *Guatemala* 15°35N 91°25W **360** C1
Alto del Carmen *Chile* 28°46S 70°30W **366** B1
Alto del Inca *Chile* 24°10S 68°10W **366** A2
Alto Ligonha *Mozam.* 15°30S 38°11E **327** F4
Alto Molocue *Mozam.* 15°50S 37°35E **327** F4
Alto Paraguay ☐ *Paraguay* 21°0S 58°30W **366** A4
Alto Paraná ☐ *Paraguay* 25°30S 54°50W **367** B5
Alton *Canada* 43°54N 80°5W **354** C4
Alton *U.K.* 51°9N 0°59W **285** F7
Alton *Ill., U.S.A.* 38°53N 90°11W **352** F8
Alton *N.H., U.S.A.* 43°27N 71°13W **355** C13
Altona *Canada* 49°6N 97°33W **343** D9
Altoona *U.S.A.* 40°31N 78°24W **354** F6
Altun Kupri *Iraq* 35°45N 44°9E **316** C5
Altun Shan *China* 38°30N 88°0E **304** C3
Alturas *U.S.A.* 41°29N 120°32W **348** F3
Altus *U.S.A.* 34°38N 99°20W **356** D5
Alucra *Turkey* 40°22N 38°47E **291** F6
Alūksne *Latvia* 57°24N 27°3E **281** H22
Alunite *U.S.A.* 35°59N 114°55W **351** K12
Alusi *Indonesia* 7°35S 131°40E **309** F8
Alva *U.S.A.* 36°48N 98°40W **356** C5
Alvarado *Mexico* 18°46N 95°46W **359** D5
Alvarado *U.S.A.* 32°24N 97°13W **356** E6
Alvaro Obregón, Presa *Mexico* 27°52N 109°52W **358** B3
Alvear *Argentina* 29°5S 56°30W **366** B4
Alvesta *Sweden* 56°54N 14°35E **281** H16
Alvin *U.S.A.* 29°26N 95°15W **356** G7
Alvinston *Canada* 42°49N 81°52W **354** D3
Älvkarleby *Sweden* 60°34N 17°26E **281** F17
Alvord Desert *U.S.A.* 42°30N 118°25W **348** E4
Älvsbyn *Sweden* 65°40N 21°0E **280** D19
Alwar *India* 27°38N 76°34E **314** F7
Alxa Zuoqi *China* 38°50N 105°40E **306** E3
Alyangula *Australia* 13°55S 136°30E **334** A2
Alyata = Älät *Azerbaijan* 39°58N 49°25E **317** B6
Alyth *U.K.* 56°38N 3°13W **283** E5
Alytus *Lithuania* 54°24N 24°3E **281** J21
Alzada *U.S.A.* 45°2N 104°25W **348** D11
Alzira *Spain* 39°9N 0°30W **293** C5
Am Timan *Chad* 11°0N 20°10E **323** F10
Amadeus, L. *Australia* 24°54S 131°0E **333** D5
Amadi *Dem. Rep. of the Congo* 3°40N 26°40E **326** B2
Amâdi *Sudan* 5°29N 30°25E **323** G12
Amadjuak L. *Canada* 65°0N 71°8W **341** C12
Amagansett *U.S.A.* 40°59N 72°9W **355** F12
Amagasaki *Japan* 34°42N 135°23E **303** G7
Amahai *Indonesia* 3°20S 128°55E **309** E7
Amaile *Samoa* 13°59S 171°22W **331** b
Amakusa-Shotō *Japan* 32°15N 130°10E **303** H5
Åmål *Sweden* 59°3N 12°42E **281** G15
Amaliada *Greece* 37°47N 21°22E **295** F9
Amalner *India* 21°5N 75°5E **312** J9
Amamapare *Indonesia* 4°53S 136°38E **309** E9
Amambaí *Brazil* 23°5S 55°13W **367** A4
Amambaí → *Brazil* 23°22S 53°56W **367** A5
Amambay ☐ *Paraguay* 23°0S 56°0W **367** A4
Amambay, Cordillera de *S. Amer.* 23°0S 55°45W **367** A4
Amami-Guntō *Japan* 27°16N 129°21E **303** L4
Amami-Ō-Shima *Japan* 28°0N 129°0E **303** L4
Aman, Pulau *Malaysia* 5°16N 100°24E **311** c
Amaná, L. *Brazil* 2°35S 64°40W **364** D6
Amanat → *India* 24°7N 84°4E **315** G11
Amanda Park *U.S.A.* 47°28N 123°55W **350** C3
Amankeldi *Kazakhstan* 50°10N 65°10E **300** D7
Amapá *Brazil* 2°5N 50°50W **365** C8
Amapá ☐ *Brazil* 1°40N 52°0W **365** C8
Amarante *Brazil* 6°14S 42°50W **365** E10
Amaranth *Canada* 50°36N 98°43W **343** C9
Amargosa → *U.S.A.* 36°14N 116°51W **351** J10
Amargosa Desert *U.S.A.* 36°40N 116°30W **351** J10
Amargosa Range *U.S.A.* 36°20N 116°45W **351** J10
Amari *Greece* 35°13N 24°40E **297** D6
Amarillo *U.S.A.* 35°13N 101°50W **356** D4

Amarkantak *India* 22°40N 81°45E **315** H9
Amaro, Mte. *Italy* 42°5N 14°5E **294** C6
Amarpur *India* 25°5N 87°0E **315** G12
Amarwara *India* 22°18N 79°10E **315** H8
Amasya *Turkey* 40°40N 35°50E **291** F6
Amata *Australia* 26°9S 131°9E **333** E5
Amatikulu *S. Africa* 29°3S 31°33E **329** D5
Amatitlán *Guatemala* 14°29N 90°38W **360** D1
Amay *Belgium* 50°33N 5°19E **287** D5
Amazon = Amazonas ➝ *S. Amer.* 0°5S 50°0W **365** D8
Amazonas ☐ *Brazil* 5°0S 65°0W **364** E6
Amazonas ➝ *S. Amer.* 0°5S 50°0W **365** D8
Ambah *India* 26°43N 78°13E **314** F8
Ambahakily *Madag.* 21°36S 43°41E **329** C7
Ambahita *Madag.* 24°1S 45°16E **329** C8
Ambala *India* 30°23N 76°56E **314** D7
Ambalavao *Madag.* 21°50S 46°56E **329** C8
Ambanja *Madag.* 13°40S 48°27E **329** A8
Ambarata *Madag.* 15°3S 48°33E **329** B8
Ambarchik *Russia* 69°40N 162°20E **301** C17
Ambarijeby *Madag.* 14°56S 47°41E **329** A8
Ambaro, Helodranon' *Madag.* 13°23S 48°38E **329** A8
Ambato *Ecuador* 1°5S 78°42W **364** D3
Ambato *Madag.* 13°24S 48°29E **329** A8
Ambato, Sierra de *Argentina* 28°25S 66°10W **366** B2
Ambato Boeny *Madag.* 16°28S 46°43E **329** B8
Ambatofinandrahana *Madag.* 20°33S 46°48E **329** C8
Ambatolampy *Madag.* 19°20S 47°35E **329** B8
Ambatomainty *Madag.* 17°41S 45°40E **329** B8
Ambatomanoina *Madag.* 18°18S 47°37E **329** B8
Ambatondrazaka *Madag.* 17°55S 48°28E **329** B8
Ambatosoratra *Madag.* 17°37S 48°31E **329** B8
Ambenja *Madag.* 15°17S 46°58E **329** B8
Amberg *Germany* 49°26N 11°52E **288** D6
Ambergris Cay *Belize* 18°0N 87°55W **359** D7
Amberley *N.Z.* 43°9S 172°44E **331** E4
Ambikapur *India* 23°15N 83°15E **315** H10
Ambilobé *Madag.* 13°10S 49°3E **329** A8
Ambinanindrano *Madag.* 20°5S 48°23E **329** C8
Ambinanitelo *Madag.* 15°21S 49°35E **329** B8
Ambinda *Madag.* 16°25S 45°52E **329** B8
Amble *U.K.* 55°20N 1°36W **284** B6
Ambleside *U.K.* 54°26N 2°58W **284** C5
Ambo *Peru* 10°5S 76°10W **364** F3
Amboahangy *Madag.* 24°15S 46°22E **329** C8
Ambodifototra *Madag.* 16°59S 49°52E **329** B8
Ambodilazana *Madag.* 18°6S 49°10E **329** B8
Ambodiriana *Madag.* 17°55S 49°18E **329** B8
Ambohidratrimo *Madag.* 18°50S 47°26E **329** B8
Ambohidray *Madag.* 18°36S 48°18E **329** B8
Ambohimahamasina *Madag.* 21°56S 47°11E **329** C8
Ambohimahasoa *Madag.* 21°7S 47°13E **329** C8
Ambohimanga *Madag.* 20°52S 47°36E **329** C8
Ambohimitombo *Madag.* 20°43S 47°26E **329** C8
Ambohitra *Madag.* 12°30S 49°10E **329** A8
Amboise *France* 47°24N 1°2E **292** C4
Ambon *Indonesia* 3°43S 128°12E **309** E7
Ambondro *Madag.* 25°13S 45°44E **329** D8
Amboseli, L. *Kenya* 2°40S 37°10E **326** C4
Amboseli △ *Kenya* 2°37S 37°13E **326** C4
Ambositra *Madag.* 20°31S 47°25E **329** C8
Ambovombe *Madag.* 25°11S 46°5E **329** D8
Amboy *U.S.A.* 34°33N 115°45W **351** L11
Amboyna Cay *S. China Sea* 7°50N 112°50E **308** C4
Ambridge *U.S.A.* 40°36N 80°14W **354** F4
Ambriz *Angola* 7°48S 13°8E **324** F2
Amchitka I. *U.S.A.* 51°32N 179°0E **346** a
Amderma *Russia* 69°45N 61°30E **300** C7
Amdhi *India* 23°51N 81°27E **315** H9
Amdo *China* 32°20N 91°40E **313** C17
Ameca *Mexico* 20°33N 104°2W **358** C4
Ameca ➝ *Mexico* 20°41N 105°18W **358** C3
Amecameca de Juárez *Mexico* 19°8N 98°46W **359** D5
Ameland *Neths.* 53°27N 5°45E **287** A5
Amenia *U.S.A.* 41°51N 73°33W **355** E11
America-Antarctica Ridge *S. Ocean* 59°0S 16°0W **277** B2
American Falls *U.S.A.* 42°47N 112°51W **348** E7
American Falls Res. *U.S.A.* 42°47N 112°52W **348** E7
American Fork *U.S.A.* 40°23N 111°48W **348** F8
American Highland *Antarctica* 73°0S 75°0E **277** D6
American Samoa ☒ *Pac. Oc.* 14°20S 170°0W **331** b
American Samoa △ *Amer. Samoa* 14°15S 170°28W **331** b
Americana *Brazil* 22°45S 47°20W **367** A6
Americus *U.S.A.* 32°4N 84°14W **357** E12
Amersfoort *Neths.* 52°9N 5°23E **287** B5
Amersfoort *S. Africa* 26°59S 29°53E **329** D4
Amery Basin *S. Ocean* 68°15S 74°30E **277** C6
Amery Ice Shelf *Antarctica* 69°30S 72°0E **277** C6
Ames *U.S.A.* 42°2N 93°37W **352** D7
Amesbury *U.S.A.* 42°51N 70°56W **355** D14
Amet *India* 25°18N 73°56E **314** G5
Amga *Russia* 60°50N 132°0E **301** C14
Amga ➝ *Russia* 62°38N 134°32E **301** C14
Amgu *Russia* 45°45N 137°15E **302** B8
Amgun ➝ *Russia* 52°56N 139°38E **301** D14
Amherst *Canada* 45°48N 64°8W **345** C7
Amherst *Mass., U.S.A.* 42°23N 72°31W **355** D12
Amherst *N.Y., U.S.A.* 42°59N 78°48W **354** D6
Amherst *Ohio, U.S.A.* 41°24N 82°14W **354** E2
Amherst I. *Canada* 44°8N 76°43W **355** B8
Amherstburg *Canada* 42°6N 83°6W **344** D3
Amiata, Mte. *Italy* 42°53N 11°37E **294** C4
Amidon *U.S.A.* 46°29N 103°19W **352** B2
Amiens *France* 49°54N 2°16E **292** B5
Aminuis *Namibia* 23°43S 19°21E **328** C2
Amīrābād *Iran* 33°20N 46°16E **316** C5
Amirante Is. *Seychelles* 6°0S 53°0E **298** J7
Amisk ⌓ *Canada* 56°43N 98°0W **343** B9
Amisk L. *Canada* 54°35N 102°15W **343** C8
Amistad, Presa de la *Mexico* 29°26N 101°3W **358** B4
Amistad ⌓ *U.S.A.* 29°32N 101°12W **356** G4
Amite *U.S.A.* 30°44N 90°30W **357** F9
Amla *India* 21°56N 78°7E **314** J8
Amlapura = Karangasem *Indonesia* 8°27S 115°37E **309** J18
Amlia I. *U.S.A.* 52°4N 173°30W **346** a
Amlwch *U.K.* 53°24N 4°20W **284** D3
'Ammān *Jordan* 31°57N 35°52E **318** D4
'Ammān ☐ *Jordan* 31°40N 36°30E **318** D5
'Ammān ✈ **(AMM)** *Jordan* 31°45N 36°2E **318** D5
Ammanford *U.K.* 51°48N 3°59W **285** F4
Ammassalik = Tasiilaq *Greenland* 65°40N 37°20W **276** C6
Ammochostos = Famagusta *Cyprus* 35°8N 33°55E **297** D12
Ammon *U.S.A.* 43°28N 111°58W **348** E8
Amnat Charoen *Thailand* 15°51N 104°38E **310** E5
Amnura *Bangla.* 24°37N 88°25E **315** G13
Āmol *Iran* 36°23N 52°20E **317** B7
Amorgos *Greece* 36°50N 25°57E **295** F11
Amory *U.S.A.* 33°59N 88°29W **357** E10
Amos *Canada* 48°35N 78°5W **344** C4
Åmot *Norway* 59°57N 9°54E **281** G13
Amoy = Xiamen *China* 24°25N 118°4E **305** D6
Ampanavoana *Madag.* 15°41S 50°22E **329** B9
Ampang *Malaysia* 3°8N 101°45E **311** L3
Ampangalana, Lakandranon' *Madag.* 22°48S 47°50E **329** C8
Ampanihy *Madag.* 24°40S 44°45E **329** C7
Amparafaravola *Madag.* 17°35S 48°13E **329** B8
Ampasinambo *Madag.* 20°31S 48°0E **329** C8
Ampasindava, Helodranon' *Madag.* 13°40S 48°15E **329** A8
Ampasindava, Saikanosy *Madag.* 13°42S 47°55E **329** A8
Ampenan *Indonesia* 8°34S 116°4E **308** F5
Amper ➝ *Germany* 48°29N 11°55E **288** D6
Amphoe Kathu *Thailand* 7°55N 98°21E **311** a
Amphoe Thalang *Thailand* 8°1N 98°20E **311** a
Ampitsikinana *Madag.* 12°57S 49°49E **329** A8
Ampombiantambo *Madag.* 12°42S 48°57E **329** A8
Ampotaka *Madag.* 25°3S 44°41E **329** D7
Ampoza *Madag.* 22°20S 44°44E **329** C7
Amqui *Canada* 48°28N 67°27W **345** C6
Amravati *India* 20°55N 77°45E **312** J10
Amreli *India* 21°35N 71°17E **314** J4
Amritsar *India* 31°35N 74°57E **314** D6
Amroha *India* 28°53N 78°30E **315** E8
Amsterdam *Neths.* 52°23N 4°54E **287** B4
Amsterdam *U.S.A.* 42°56N 74°11W **355** D10
Amsterdam ✈ **(AMS)** *Neths.* 52°18N 4°45E **287** B4
Amsterdam, I. = Nouvelle Amsterdam, Î. *Ind. Oc.* 38°30S 77°30E **275** F13
Amstetten *Austria* 48°7N 14°51E **288** D8
Amudarya ➝ *Uzbekistan* 43°58N 59°34E **300** E6
Amund Ringnes I. *Canada* 78°20N 96°25W **341** B10
Amundsen Abyssal Plain *S. Ocean* 65°0S 125°0W **277** C14
Amundsen Basin *Arctic* 87°30N 80°0E **276** A
Amundsen Gulf *Canada* 71°0N 124°0W **340** B7
Amundsen Ridges *S. Ocean* 69°15S 123°0W **277** C14
Amundsen-Scott *Antarctica* 90°0S 166°0E **277** E
Amundsen Sea *Antarctica* 72°0S 115°0W **277** D15
Amuntai *Indonesia* 2°28S 115°25E **308** E5
Amur ➝ *Russia* 52°56N 141°10E **301** D15
Amurang *Indonesia* 1°5N 124°40E **309** D6
Amursk *Russia* 50°14N 136°54E **301** D14
Amyderya = Amudarya ➝ *Uzbekistan* 43°58N 59°34E **300** E6
An Bien *Vietnam* 9°45N 105°0E **311** H5
An Hoa *Vietnam* 15°40N 108°5E **310** E7
An Nabatīyah at Tahta *Lebanon* 33°23N 35°27E **318** B4
An Nabk *Si. Arabia* 31°20N 37°20E **316** D3
An Nabk *Syria* 34°2N 36°44E **318** A5
An Nafūd *Si. Arabia* 28°15N 41°0E **316** D4
An Najaf *Iraq* 32°3N 44°15E **316** C5
An Nāşirīyah *Iraq* 31°0N 46°15E **316** D5
An Nhon *Vietnam* 13°55N 109°7E **310** F7
An Nu'ayrīyah *Si. Arabia* 27°30N 48°30E **317** E6
An Thoi, Dao *Vietnam* 9°58N 104°0E **311** H4
An Uaimh *Ireland* 53°39N 6°41W **282** C5
Anabar ➝ *Russia* 73°8N 113°36E **301** B12
'Anabtā *West Bank* 32°19N 35°7E **318** C4
Anaconda *U.S.A.* 46°8N 112°57W **348** C7
Anacortes *U.S.A.* 48°30N 122°37W **350** B4
Anadarko *U.S.A.* 35°4N 98°15W **356** D5
Anadolu *Turkey* 39°0N 30°0E **291** G5
Anadyr *Russia* 64°35N 177°20E **301** C18
Anadyr ➝ *Russia* 64°55N 176°5E **301** C18
Anadyrskiy Zaliv *Russia* 64°0N 180°0E **301** C19
Anaga, Pta. de *Canary Is.* 28°34N 16°9W **296** F3
'Ānah *Iraq* 34°25N 42°0E **316** C4
Anaheim *U.S.A.* 33°50N 117°55W **351** M9
Anahim Lake *Canada* 52°28N 125°18W **342** C3
Anakapalle *India* 17°42N 83°6E **313** L13
Anakie *Australia* 23°32S 147°45E **334** C4
Analalava *Madag.* 14°35S 48°0E **329** A8
Analavoka *Madag.* 22°23S 46°30E **329** C8
Analipsis *Greece* 39°36N 19°55E **297** A3
Anambar ➝ *Pakistan* 30°15N 68°50E **314** D3
Anambas, Kepulauan *Indonesia* 3°20N 106°30E **308** D3
Anambas Is. = Anambas, Kepulauan *Indonesia* 3°20N 106°30E **308** D3
Anamosa *U.S.A.* 42°7N 91°17W **352** D8
Anamur *Turkey* 36°8N 32°58E **316** B2
Anan *Japan* 33°54N 134°40E **303** H7
Anand *India* 22°32N 72°59E **314** H5
Anantapur *India* 14°39N 77°42E **312** M10
Anantnag *India* 33°45N 75°10E **315** C6
Ananyiv *Ukraine* 47°44N 29°58E **289** E15
Anapodiaris ➝ *Greece* 34°59N 25°20E **297** E7
Anápolis *Brazil* 16°15S 48°50W **365** G9
Anapu ➝ *Brazil* 1°53S 50°53W **365** D8
Anār *Iran* 30°55N 55°13E **317** D7
Anārak *Iran* 33°25N 53°40E **317** C7
Anas ➝ *India* 23°26N 74°0E **314** H5
Anatolia = Anadolu *Turkey* 39°0N 30°0E **291** G5
Anatsogno *Madag.* 23°33S 43°46E **329** C7
Añatuya *Argentina* 28°20S 62°50W **366** B3
Anaunethad L. *Canada* 60°55N 104°25W **343** A8
Anbyŏn *N. Korea* 39°1N 127°35E **307** E14
Ancaster *Canada* 43°13N 79°59W **354** C5
Anchor Bay *U.S.A.* 38°48N 123°34W **350** G3
Anchorage *U.S.A.* 61°13N 149°54W **346** a
Anci *China* 39°20N 116°40E **306** E9
Ancohuma, Nevado *Bolivia* 16°0S 68°50W **364** G5
Ancón *Peru* 11°50S 77°10W **364** F3
Ancona *Italy* 43°38N 13°30E **294** C5
Ancud *Chile* 42°0S 73°50W **368** E2
Ancud, G. de *Chile* 42°0S 73°0W **368** E2
Anda *China* 46°24N 125°19E **305** B7
Andacollo *Argentina* 37°10S 70°42W **366** D1
Andacollo *Chile* 30°14S 71°6W **366** C1
Andaingo *Madag.* 18°12S 48°17E **329** B8
Andalgalá *Argentina* 27°40S 66°30W **366** B2
Åndalsnes *Norway* 62°35N 7°43E **280** E12
Andalucía ☐ *Spain* 37°35N 5°0W **293** D3
Andalusia = Andalucía ☐ *Spain* 37°35N 5°0W **293** D3
Andalusia *U.S.A.* 31°18N 86°29W **357** F11
Andaman Is. *Ind. Oc.* 12°30N 92°45E **275** D14
Andaman Sea *Ind. Oc.* 13°0N 96°0E **308** B1
Andamooka *Australia* 30°27S 137°9E **335** E2
Andapa *Madag.* 14°39S 49°39E **329** A8
Andara *Namibia* 18°2S 21°9E **328** B3
Andenes *Norway* 69°19N 16°18E **280** B17
Andenne *Belgium* 50°28N 5°5E **287** D5
Anderson *Alaska, U.S.A.* 64°25N 149°15W **346** a
Anderson *Calif., U.S.A.* 40°27N 122°18W **348** F2
Anderson *Ind., U.S.A.* 40°10N 85°41W **353** E11
Anderson *Mo., U.S.A.* 36°39N 94°27W **352** G6
Anderson *S.C., U.S.A.* 34°31N 82°39W **357** D13
Anderson ➝ *Canada* 69°42N 129°0W **340** C7
Andes *U.S.A.* 42°12N 74°47W **355** D10
Andes, Cord. de los *S. Amer.* 20°0S 68°0W **364** H5
Andfjorden *Norway* 69°10N 16°20E **280** B17
Andhra Pradesh ☐ *India* 18°0N 79°0E **312** L11
Andijon *Uzbekistan* 41°10N 72°15E **300** E8
Andikíthira = Antikythira *Greece* 35°52N 23°15E **295** G10
Andilamena *Madag.* 17°1S 48°35E **329** B8
Andīmeshk *Iran* 32°27N 48°21E **317** C6
Andizhan = Andijon *Uzbekistan* 41°10N 72°15E **300** E8
Andoany *Madag.* 13°25S 48°16E **329** A8
Andohahela ⌓ *Madag.* 24°4S 46°44E **329** C8
Andong *S. Korea* 36°40N 128°43E **307** F15
Andongwei *China* 35°6N 119°20E **307** G10
Andoom *Australia* 12°25S 141°53E **334** A3
Andorra ■ *Europe* 42°30N 1°30E **292** E4
Andorra La Vella *Andorra* 42°31N 1°32E **292** E4
Andover *U.K.* 51°12N 1°29W **285** F6
Andover *Maine, U.S.A.* 44°38N 70°45W **355** B14
Andover *Mass., U.S.A.* 42°40N 71°8W **355** D13
Andover *N.J., U.S.A.* 40°59N 74°45W **355** F10
Andover *N.Y., U.S.A.* 42°10N 77°48W **354** D7
Andover *Ohio, U.S.A.* 41°36N 80°34W **354** E4
Andøya *Norway* 69°10N 15°50E **280** B16
Andradina *Brazil* 20°54S 51°23W **365** H8
Andrahary *Madag.* 13°37S 49°17E **329** A8
Andramasina *Madag.* 19°11S 47°35E **329** B8
Andranopasy *Madag.* 21°17S 43°44E **329** C7
Andranovory *Madag.* 23°8S 44°10E **329** C7
Andratx *Spain* 39°39N 2°25E **296** B9
Andreanof Is. *U.S.A.* 51°30N 176°0W **346** a
Andrews *S.C., U.S.A.* 33°27N 79°34W **357** E15
Andrews *Tex., U.S.A.* 32°19N 102°33W **356** E3
Ándria *Italy* 41°13N 16°17E **294** D7
Andriamena *Madag.* 17°26S 47°30E **329** B8
Andriandampy *Madag.* 22°45S 45°41E **329** C8
Andriba *Madag.* 17°30S 46°58E **329** B8
Andringitra ⌓ *Madag.* 22°13S 46°52E **329** C8
Androka *Madag.* 24°58S 44°2E **329** C7
Andros *Greece* 37°50N 24°57E **295** F11
Andros I. *Bahamas* 24°30N 78°0W **360** B4
Andros Town *Bahamas* 24°43N 77°47W **360** B4
Androscoggin ➝ *U.S.A.* 43°58N 69°52W **355** C14
Andselv *Norway* 69°4N 18°34E **280** B18
Andújar *Spain* 38°3N 4°5W **293** C3
Andulo *Angola* 11°25S 16°45E **324** G3
Anegada *Br. Virgin Is.* 18°45N 64°20W **361** e
Anegada Passage *W. Indies* 18°15N 63°45W **361** C7
Aneto, Pico de *Spain* 42°37N 0°40E **293** A6
Ang Mo Kio *Singapore* 1°23N 103°50E **311** d
Ang Thong *Thailand* 14°35N 100°31E **310** E3
Ang Thong, Ko *Thailand* 9°37N 99°41E **311** b
Ang Thong △ *Thailand* 9°40N 99°43E **311** H2
Angamos, Punta *Chile* 23°1S 70°32W **366** A1
Angara ➝ *Russia* 58°5N 94°20E **301** D10
Angarsk *Russia* 52°30N 104°0E **301** D11
Angas Hills *Australia* 23°0S 127°50E **332** D4
Angaston *Australia* 34°30S 139°8E **335** E2
Ånge *Sweden* 62°31N 15°35E **280** E16
Ángel, Salto = Angel Falls *Venezuela* 5°57N 62°30W **364** B6
Ángel de la Guarda, I. *Mexico* 29°20N 113°25W **358** B2
Angel Falls *Venezuela* 5°57N 62°30W **364** B6
Angeles *Phil.* 15°9N 120°33E **309** A6
Ängelholm *Sweden* 56°15N 12°58E **281** H15
Angels Camp *U.S.A.* 38°4N 120°32W **350** G6
Ångermanälven ➝ *Sweden* 64°0N 17°20E **280** E17
Ångermanland *Sweden* 63°36N 17°45E **280** E17
Angers *Canada* 45°31N 75°29W **355** A9
Angers *France* 47°30N 0°35W **292** C3
Ängesån ➝ *Sweden* 66°16N 22°47E **280** C20
Angikuni L. *Canada* 62°12N 99°59W **343** A9
Angkor *Cambodia* 13°22N 103°50E **310** F4
Anglesey *U.K.* 53°17N 4°20W **284** D3
Anglesey, Isle of ☐ *U.K.* 53°16N 4°18W **284** D3
Angleton *U.S.A.* 29°10N 95°26W **356** G7
Anglisidhes *Cyprus* 34°51N 33°27E **297** E12
Angmagssalik = Tasiilaq *Greenland* 65°40N 37°20W **276** C6
Ango *Dem. Rep. of the Congo* 4°10N 26°5E **326** B2
Angoche *Mozam.* 16°8S 39°55E **327** F4
Angoche, I. *Mozam.* 16°20S 39°50E **327** F4
Angol *Chile* 37°56S 72°45W **366** D1
Angola *Ind., U.S.A.* 41°38N 85°0W **353** E11
Angola *N.Y., U.S.A.* 42°38N 79°2W **354** D5
Angola ■ *Africa* 12°0S 18°0E **325** G3
Angoulême *France* 45°39N 0°10E **292** D4
Angoumois *France* 45°50N 0°25E **292** D3
Angra do Heroismo *Azores* 38°39N 27°13W **322** a
Angra dos Reis *Brazil* 23°0S 44°10W **367** A7
Angren *Uzbekistan* 41°1N 70°12E **300** E8
Angtassom *Cambodia* 11°1N 104°41E **311** G5
Angu *Dem. Rep. of the Congo* 3°23N 24°30E **326** B1
Anguang *China* 45°15N 123°45E **307** B12
Anguilla ☒ *W. Indies* 18°14N 63°5W **361** C7
Anguo *China* 38°28N 115°15E **306** E8
Angurugu *Australia* 14°0S 136°25E **334** A2
Angus ☐ *U.K.* 56°46N 2°56W **283** E6
Angwa ➝ *Zimbabwe* 16°0S 30°23E **329** B5
Anhanduí ➝ *Brazil* 21°46S 52°9W **367** A5
Anholt *Denmark* 56°42N 11°33E **281** H14
Anhui ☐ *China* 32°0N 117°0E **305** C6
Anhwei = Anhui ☐ *China* 32°0N 117°0E **305** C6
Anichab *Namibia* 21°0S 14°46E **328** C1
Animas ➝ *U.S.A.* 36°43N 108°13W **349** H9
Anivorano *Madag.* 18°44S 48°58E **329** B8
Anjalankoski *Finland* 60°45N 26°51E **280** F22
Anjar *India* 23°6N 70°10E **314** H4
Anjou *France* 47°20N 0°15W **292** C3
Anjouan *Comoros Is.* 12°15S 44°20E **325** a
Anjozorobe *Madag.* 18°22S 47°52E **329** B8
Anju *N. Korea* 39°36N 125°40E **307** E13
Ankaboa, Tanjona *Madag.* 21°58S 43°20E **329** C7
Ankang *China* 32°40N 109°1E **306** H5
Ankara *Turkey* 39°57N 32°54E **291** G5
Ankarafantsika ⌓ *Madag.* 16°8S 47°5E **329** B8
Ankaramena *Madag.* 21°57S 46°39E **329** C8
Ankaratra *Madag.* 19°25S 47°12E **325** H9
Ankasakasa *Madag.* 16°21S 44°52E **329** B7
Ankavandra *Madag.* 18°46S 45°18E **329** B8
Ankazoabo *Madag.* 22°18S 44°31E **329** C7
Ankazobe *Madag.* 18°20S 47°10E **329** B8
Ankeny *U.S.A.* 41°44N 93°36W **352** E7
Ankilimalinika *Madag.* 22°58S 43°45E **329** C7
Ankilizato *Madag.* 20°25S 45°1E **329** C8
Ankisabe *Madag.* 19°17S 46°29E **329** B8
Ankoro *Dem. Rep. of the Congo* 6°45S 26°55E **326** D2
Ankororoka *Madag.* 25°30S 45°11E **329** D8
Anmyeondo *S. Korea* 36°25N 126°25E **307** F14
Ann, C. *U.S.A.* 42°38N 70°35W **355** D14
Ann Arbor *U.S.A.* 42°17N 83°45W **353** D12
Anna *U.S.A.* 37°28N 89°15W **352** G9
Annaba *Algeria* 36°50N 7°46E **322** A7
Annalee ➝ *Ireland* 54°2N 7°24W **282** B4
Annam *Vietnam* 16°0N 108°0E **310** E7
Annamitique, Chaîne *Asia* 17°0N 106°0E **310** D6
Annan *U.K.* 54°59N 3°16W **283** G5
Annan ➝ *U.K.* 54°58N 3°16W **283** G5
Annapolis *U.S.A.* 38°59N 76°30W **353** F15
Annapolis Royal *Canada* 44°44N 65°32W **345** D6
Annapurna *Nepal* 28°34N 83°50E **315** E10
Annean, L. *Australia* 26°54S 118°14E **333** E2
Annecy *France* 45°55N 6°8E **292** D7
Anning *China* 24°55N 102°26E **304** D5
Anniston *U.S.A.* 33°39N 85°50W **357** E12
Annobón *Atl. Oc.* 1°25S 5°36E **321** G4
Annotto B. *Jamaica* 18°17N 76°45W **360** a
Annville *U.S.A.* 40°20N 76°31W **355** F8
Anogia *Greece* 35°16N 24°52E **297** D6
Anorotsangana *Madag.* 13°56S 47°55E **329** A8
Anosibe *Madag.* 19°26S 48°13E **329** B8
Anping *Hebei, China* 38°15N 115°30E **306** E8
Anping *Liaoning, China* 41°5N 123°30E **307** D12
Anqing *China* 30°30N 117°3E **305** C6
Anqiu *China* 36°25N 119°10E **307** F10
Ansai *China* 36°50N 109°20E **306** F5
Ansan *S. Korea* 37°21N 126°52E **307** F14
Ansbach *Germany* 49°28N 10°34E **288** D6
Anse Boileau *Seychelles* 4°43S 55°29E **325** b
Anse Royale *Seychelles* 4°44S 55°31E **325** b
Anshan *China* 41°5N 122°58E **307** D12
Anshun *China* 26°18N 105°57E **304** D5
Ansley *U.S.A.* 41°18N 99°23W **352** E4
Anson *U.S.A.* 32°45N 99°54W **356** E5
Anson B. *Australia* 13°20S 130°6E **332** B5
Ansongo *Mali* 15°25N 0°35E **322** E6
Ansonia *U.S.A.* 41°21N 73°5W **355** E11
Anstruther *U.K.* 56°14N 2°41W **283** E6
Ansudu *Indonesia* 2°11S 139°22E **309** E9
Antabamba *Peru* 14°40S 73°0W **364** F4
Antakya = Hatay *Turkey* 36°14N 36°10E **316** B3
Antalaha *Madag.* 14°57S 50°20E **329** A9
Antalya *Turkey* 36°52N 30°45E **291** G5
Antalya Körfezi *Turkey* 36°15N 31°30E **291** G5
Antambohobe *Madag.* 22°20S 46°47E **329** C8
Antanambao-Manampotsy *Madag.* 19°29S 48°34E **329** B8
Antanambe *Madag.* 16°26S 49°52E **329** B8
Antananarivo *Madag.* 18°55S 47°31E **329** B8
Antananarivo ☐ *Madag.* 19°0S 47°0E **329** B8
Antanifotsy *Madag.* 19°39S 47°19E **329** B8
Antanimbaribe *Madag.* 21°30S 44°48E **329** C7
Antanimora *Madag.* 24°49S 45°40E **329** C8
Antarctic Pen. *Antarctica* 67°0S 60°0W **277** C18
Antarctica 90°0S 0°0 **277** E3
Antelope *Zimbabwe* 21°2S 28°31E **327** G2
Antequera *Paraguay* 24°8S 57°7W **366** A4
Antequera *Spain* 37°5N 4°33W **293** D3
Antero, Mt. *U.S.A.* 38°41N 106°15W **348** G10
Antevamena *Madag.* 21°2S 44°8E **329** C7
Anthony *Kans., U.S.A.* 37°9N 98°2W **352** G4
Anthony *N. Mex., U.S.A.* 32°0N 106°36W **349** K10
Anti Atlas *Morocco* 30°0N 8°30W **322** C4
Anti-Lebanon = Sharqi, Al Jabal ash *Lebanon* 33°40N 36°10E **318** B5
Antibes *France* 43°34N 7°6E **292** E7
Anticosti, Î. d' *Canada* 49°30N 63°0W **345** C7
Antigo *U.S.A.* 45°9N 89°9W **352** C9
Antigonish *Canada* 45°38N 61°58W **345** C7
Antigua *Canary Is.* 28°24N 14°1W **296** F5
Antigua *Guatemala* 14°34N 90°41W **360** D1
Antigua *W. Indies* 17°0N 61°50W **361** C7
Antigua & Barbuda ■ *W. Indies* 17°20N 61°48W **361** C7
Antikythira *Greece* 35°52N 23°15E **295** G10
Antilla *Cuba* 20°40N 75°50W **360** B4
Antilles = West Indies *Cent. Amer.* 15°0N 65°0W **361** D7
Antioch *U.S.A.* 38°1N 121°48W **350** G5
Antioquia *Colombia* 6°40N 75°55W **364** B3
Antipodes Is. *Pac. Oc.* 49°45S 178°40E **336** M9
Antlers *U.S.A.* 34°14N 95°37W **356** D7
Antoetra *Madag.* 20°46S 47°20E **329** C8
Antofagasta *Chile* 23°50S 70°30W **366** A1
Antofagasta ☐ *Chile* 24°0S 69°0W **366** A2
Antofagasta de la Sierra *Argentina* 26°5S 67°20W **366** B2
Antofalla *Argentina* 25°30S 68°5W **366** B2
Antofalla, Salar de *Argentina* 25°40S 67°45W **366** B2
Anton *U.S.A.* 33°49N 102°10W **356** E3
Antongila, Helodrano *Madag.* 15°30S 49°50E **329** B8
Antonibé *Madag.* 15°7S 47°24E **329** B8
Antonibé, Presqu'île d' *Madag.* 14°55S 47°20E **329** A8
Antonina *Brazil* 25°26S 48°42W **367** B6
Antrim *U.K.* 54°43N 6°14W **282** B5
Antrim *U.S.A.* 40°7N 81°21W **354** F3
Antrim ☐ *U.K.* 54°56N 6°25W **282** B5
Antrim, Mts. of *U.K.* 55°3N 6°14W **282** A5
Antrim Plateau *Australia* 18°8S 128°20E **332** C4
Antsakabary *Madag.* 15°3S 48°56E **329** B8
Antsalova *Madag.* 18°40S 44°37E **329** B7
Antsenavolo *Madag.* 21°24S 48°3E **329** C8
Antsiafabositra *Madag.* 17°18S 46°57E **329** B8
Antsirabe *Antananarivo, Madag.* 19°55S 47°2E **329** B8
Antsirabe *Antsiranana, Madag.* 14°0S 49°59E **329** A8
Antsirabe *Mahajanga, Madag.* 15°57S 48°58E **329** B8
Antsiranana *Madag.* 12°25S 49°20E **329** A8
Antsiranana ☐ *Madag.* 12°16S 49°17E **329** A8
Antsohihy *Madag.* 14°50S 47°59E **329** A8
Antsohimbondrona Seranana *Madag.* 13°7S 48°48E **329** A8
Antu *China* 42°30N 128°20E **307** C15
Antwerp = Antwerpen *Belgium* 51°13N 4°25E **287** C4
Antwerp *U.S.A.* 44°12N 75°37W **355** B9
Antwerpen *Belgium* 51°13N 4°25E **287** C4
Antwerpen ☐ *Belgium* 51°15N 4°40E **287** C4
Anupgarh *India* 29°10N 73°10E **314** E5
Anuppur *India* 23°6N 81°41E **315** H9
Anuradhapura *Sri Lanka* 8°22N 80°28E **312** Q12
Anveh *Iran* 27°23N 54°11E **317** E7
Anvers = Antwerpen *Belgium* 51°13N 4°25E **287** C4
Anvers I. *Antarctica* 64°30S 63°40W **277** C17
Anxi *China* 40°30N 95°43E **304** B4
Anxious B. *Australia* 33°24S 134°45E **335** E1
Anyang *China* 36°5N 114°21E **306** F8
Anyang *S. Korea* 37°23N 126°55E **307** F14
Anyer *Indonesia* 6°4S 105°53E **309** G11
Anyi *China* 35°2N 111°2E **306** G6
Anza *U.S.A.* 33°35N 116°39W **351** M10
Anze *China* 36°10N 112°12E **306** F7
Anzhero-Sudzhensk *Russia* 56°10N 86°0E **300** D9
Ánzio *Italy* 41°27N 12°37E **294** D5

Ao Makham Thailand 7°50N 98°24E 311 a
Ao Phangnga △ Thailand 8°10N 98°32E 311 a
Aoga-Shima Japan 32°28N 139°46E 303 H9
Aoji N. Korea 42°31N 130°23E 307 C16
Aomen = Macau China 22°12N 113°33E 305 G10
Aomori Japan 40°45N 140°45E 302 D10
Aomori □ Japan 40°45N 140°40E 302 D10
Aonla India 28°16N 79°11E 315 E8
Aorai, Mt. Tahiti 17°34S 149°30W 331 d
Aoraki Mount Cook N.Z. 43°36S 170°9E 331 E3
Aoral, Phnum Cambodia 12°0N 104°15E 311 G5
Aosta Italy 45°45N 7°20E 292 D7
Aotearoa = New Zealand ■ Oceania 40°0S 176°0E 331 D6
Aoukâr Mauritania 17°40N 10°0W 322 E4
Aozou Strip Chad 22°0N 19°0E 323 D9
Apa → S. Amer. 22°6S 58°2W 366 A4
Apache U.S.A. 34°54N 98°22W 356 D5
Apache Junction U.S.A. 33°25N 111°33W 349 K8
Apalachee B. U.S.A. 30°0N 84°0W 357 G13
Apalachicola U.S.A. 29°43N 84°59W 357 G12
Apalachicola → U.S.A. 29°43N 84°58W 357 G12
Apaporis → Colombia 1°23S 69°25W 364 D5
Aparados da Serra △ Brazil 29°10S 50°8W 367 B5
Aparri Phil. 18°22N 121°38E 309 A6
Apatity Russia 67°34N 33°22E 280 C25
Apatula = Finke Australia 25°34S 134°35E 334 D1
Apatzingán Mexico 19°5N 102°21W 358 D4
Apeldoorn Neths. 52°13N 5°57E 287 B5
Apennines = Appennini Italy 44°30N 10°0E 294 B4
Apia Samoa 13°50S 171°50W 331 b
Apiacás, Serra dos Brazil 9°50S 57°0W 364 E7
Apies → S. Africa 25°15S 28°8E 329 D4
Apizaco Mexico 19°25N 98°8W 359 D5
Aplao Peru 16°0S 72°40W 364 G4
Apo, Mt. Phil. 6°53N 125°14E 309 C7
Apolakia Greece 36°5N 27°48E 297 C9
Apolakia, Ormos Greece 36°5N 27°45E 297 C9
Apollonia = Marsá Susah Libya 32°52N 21°59E 323 B10
Apolo Bolivia 14°30S 68°30W 364 F5
Aporé → Brazil 19°27S 50°57W 365 G8
Apostle Is. U.S.A. 47°0N 90°40W 352 B8
Apostle Islands ⌂ U.S.A. 46°55N 91°0W 352 B8
Apóstoles Argentina 28°0S 56°0W 367 B4
Apostolos Andreas, C. Cyprus 35°42N 34°35E 297 D13
Apoteri Guyana 4°2N 58°32W 364 C7
Appalachian Mts. U.S.A. 38°0N 80°0W 353 G14
Appennini Italy 44°30N 10°0E 294 B4
Apple Hill Canada 45°13N 74°46W 355 A10
Apple Valley U.S.A. 34°32N 117°14W 351 L9
Appleby-in-Westmorland U.K. 54°35N 2°29W 284 C5
Appledore U.K. 51°3N 4°13W 285 F3
Appleton U.S.A. 44°16N 88°25W 352 C9
Approuague → Fr. Guiana 4°30N 51°57W 365 C8
Aprilia Italy 41°36N 12°39E 294 D5
Apsley Canada 44°45N 78°6W 354 B6
Apucarana Brazil 23°55S 51°33W 367 A5
Apure → Venezuela 7°37N 66°25W 364 B5
Apurímac → Peru 12°17S 73°56W 364 F4
Āqā Jarī Iran 30°42N 49°50E 317 D6
Aqaba = Al 'Aqabah Jordan 29°31N 35°0E 318 F4
Aqaba, G. of Red Sea 29°0N 34°40E 316 D2
'Aqabah, Khalīj al = Aqaba, G. of Red Sea 29°0N 34°40E 316 D2
'Aqdā Iran 32°26N 53°37E 317 C7
'Aqrah Iraq 36°46N 43°45E 316 B4
Aqsay Kazakhstan 51°11N 53°0E 291 D9
Aqtaū Kazakhstan 43°39N 51°12E 291 F9
Aqtöbe Kazakhstan 50°17N 57°10E 291 D10
Aqtoghay Kazakhstan 46°57N 79°40E 300 E8
Aquidauana Brazil 20°30S 55°50W 365 H7
Aquila Mexico 18°36N 103°30W 358 D4
Aquiles Serdán Mexico 28°36N 105°53W 358 B3
Aquin Haiti 18°16N 73°24W 361 C5
Aquitain, Bassin France 44°0N 0°30W 292 D3
Ar Rachidiya = Er Rachidia Morocco 31°58N 4°20W 322 B5
Ar Rafid Syria 32°57N 35°52E 318 C4
Ar Raḥḥālīyah Iraq 32°44N 43°23E 316 C4
Ar Ramādī Iraq 33°25N 43°20E 316 C4
Ar Ramthā Jordan 32°34N 36°0E 318 C5
Ar Raqqah Syria 35°59N 39°8E 316 C3
Ar Rass Si. Arabia 25°50N 43°40E 316 E4
Ar Rifā'ī Iraq 31°50N 46°10E 316 D5
Ar Riyāḍ Si. Arabia 24°41N 46°42E 316 E5
Ar Ru'ays Qatar 26°8N 51°12E 317 E6
Ar Rukhaymīyah Iraq 29°22N 45°38E 316 D5
Ar Ruṣāfah Syria 35°45N 38°49E 316 C3
Ar Ruṭbah Iraq 33°0N 40°15E 316 C4
Ara India 25°35N 84°32E 315 G11
Arab U.S.A. 34°19N 86°30W 357 D11
'Arab, Bahr el → Sudan 9°0N 29°30E 323 G11
Arab, Shatt al → Asia 29°57N 48°34E 317 D6
'Arabābād Iran 33°2N 57°41E 317 C8
Arabia Asia 25°0N 45°0E 298 F6
Arabian Desert = Es Sahrâ' Esh Sharqîya Egypt 27°30N 32°30E 323 C12
Arabian Gulf = Persian Gulf Asia 27°0N 50°0E 317 E6
Arabian Sea Ind. Oc. 16°0N 65°0E 298 G8
Aracaju Brazil 10°55S 37°4W 365 F11
Aracati Brazil 4°30S 37°44W 365 D11
Araçatuba Brazil 21°10S 50°30W 367 A5
Aracena Spain 37°53N 6°38W 293 D2
Araçuaí Brazil 16°52S 42°4W 365 G10
'Arad Israel 31°15N 35°12E 318 D4
Arad Romania 46°10N 21°20E 289 E11
Arādān Iran 35°21N 52°30E 317 C7
Aradhippou Cyprus 34°57N 33°36E 297 E12
Arafura Sea E. Indies 9°0S 135°0E 330 B6
Aragón □ Spain 41°25N 0°40W 293 B5
Aragón → Spain 42°13N 1°44W 293 A5
Araguacema Brazil 8°50S 49°20W 365 E9
Araguaia → Brazil 5°21S 48°41W 365 E9
Araguaína Brazil 7°12S 48°12W 365 E9
Araguari Brazil 18°38S 48°11W 365 G9
Araguari → Brazil 1°15N 49°55W 365 C9
Arain India 26°27N 75°2E 314 F6
Arak Algeria 25°20N 3°45E 322 C6
Arāk Iran 34°0N 49°40E 317 C6
Arakan Coast Burma 19°0N 94°0E 313 K19
Arakan Yoma Burma 20°0N 94°40E 313 K19
Araks = Aras, Rūd-e → Asia 40°5N 48°29E 316 B5
Aral Kazakhstan 46°41N 61°45E 300 E7
Aral Sea Asia 44°30N 60°0E 300 E7
Aral Tengizi = Aral Sea Asia 44°30N 60°0E 300 E7
Aralsk = Aral Kazakhstan 46°41N 61°45E 300 E7
Aralskoye More = Aral Sea Asia 44°30N 60°0E 300 E7
Aramac Australia 22°58S 145°14E 334 C4
Aran I. Ireland 55°0N 8°30W 282 A3
Aran Is. Ireland 53°6N 9°38W 282 C2
Aranda de Duero Spain 41°39N 3°42W 293 B4
Arandān Iran 35°23N 46°55E 316 C5
Aranjuez Spain 40°1N 3°40W 293 B4
Aranos Namibia 24°9S 19°7E 328 C2
Aransas Pass U.S.A. 27°55N 97°9W 356 H6
Aranyaprathet Thailand 13°41N 102°30E 310 F4
Arapahoe U.S.A. 40°18N 99°54W 352 E4
Arapey Grande → Uruguay 30°55S 57°49W 366 C4
Arapgir Turkey 39°5N 38°30E 316 B3
Arapiraca Brazil 9°45S 36°39W 365 E11
Arapongas Brazil 23°29S 51°28W 367 A5
Ar'ar Si. Arabia 30°59N 41°2E 316 D4
Araranguá Brazil 29°0S 49°30W 367 B6
Araraquara Brazil 21°50S 48°0W 365 H9
Ararás, Serra das Brazil 25°0S 53°10W 367 B5
Ararat Australia 37°16S 142°58E 335 F3
Ararat, Mt. = Ağrı Dağı Turkey 39°50N 44°15E 316 B5
Araria India 26°9N 87°33E 315 F12
Araripe, Chapada do Brazil 7°20S 40°0W 365 E11
Araruama, L. de Brazil 22°53S 42°12W 367 A7
Aras, Rūd-e → Asia 40°5N 48°29E 316 B5
Arauca Colombia 7°0N 70°40W 364 B4
Arauca → Venezuela 7°24N 66°35W 364 B5
Arauco Chile 37°16S 73°25W 366 D1
Arawale ⌂ Kenya 1°24S 40°9E 326 C5
Araxá Brazil 19°35S 46°55W 365 G9
Araya, Pen. de Venezuela 10°40N 64°0W 364 A6
Arba Minch Ethiopia 6°0N 37°30E 319 F2
Arbat Iraq 35°25N 45°35E 316 C5
Árbatax Italy 39°56N 9°42E 294 E3
Arbīl Iraq 36°15N 44°5E 316 B5
Arborfield Canada 53°6N 103°39W 343 C8
Arborg Canada 50°54N 97°13W 343 C9
Arbroath U.K. 56°34N 2°35W 283 E6
Arbuckle U.S.A. 39°1N 122°3W 350 F4
Arcachon France 44°40N 1°10W 292 D3
Arcade U.S.A. 42°32N 78°25W 354 D6
Arcadia Fla., U.S.A. 27°13N 81°52W 357 H14
Arcadia La., U.S.A. 32°33N 92°55W 356 E8
Arcadia Pa., U.S.A. 40°47N 78°51W 354 F6
Arcata U.S.A. 40°52N 124°5W 348 F1
Archangel = Arkhangelsk Russia 64°38N 40°36E 290 B7
Archangelos Greece 36°13N 28°7E 297 C10
Archbald U.S.A. 41°30N 75°32W 355 E9
Archer → Australia 13°28S 141°41E 334 A3
Archer B. Australia 13°20S 141°30E 334 A3
Archer Bend = Mungkan Kandju △ Australia 13°35S 142°52E 334 A3
Archers Post Kenya 0°35N 37°35E 326 B4
Arches △ U.S.A. 38°45N 109°25W 348 G9
Archipel-de-Mingan △ Canada 50°13N 63°10W 345 B7
Archipiélago Chinijo △ Canary Is. 29°20N 13°30W 296 E6
Archipiélago Los Roques △ Venezuela 11°50N 66°44W 361 D6
Arckaringa Cr. → Australia 28°10S 135°22E 335 D2
Arco U.S.A. 43°38N 113°18W 348 E7
Arcos de la Frontera Spain 36°45N 5°49W 293 D3
Arcot India 12°53N 79°20E 312 N11
Arctic Bay Canada 73°1N 85°7W 341 B11
Arctic Mid-Ocean Ridge Arctic 87°0N 90°0E 276 A
Arctic Ocean Arctic 78°0N 160°0W 276 B18
Arctic Red River = Tsiigehtchic Canada 67°15N 134°0W 340 C6
Arctowski Antarctica 62°30S 58°0W 277 C18
Arda → Bulgaria 41°40N 26°30E 295 D12
Ardabīl Iran 38°15N 48°18E 317 B6
Ardabīl □ Iran 38°15N 48°20E 317 B6
Ardakān = Sepīdān Iran 30°20N 52°5E 317 D7
Ardakān Iran 32°19N 53°59E 317 C7
Ardara Ireland 54°46N 8°25W 282 B3
Ardee Ireland 53°52N 6°33W 282 C5
Arden Canada 44°43N 76°56W 354 B8
Arden Calif., U.S.A. 38°36N 121°33W 350 G5
Arden Nev., U.S.A. 36°1N 115°14W 351 J11
Ardenne Belgium 49°50N 5°5E 287 E5
Ardennes = Ardenne Belgium 49°50N 5°5E 287 E5
Arderin Ireland 53°2N 7°39W 282 C4
Ardestān Iran 33°20N 52°25E 317 C7
Ardfert Ireland 52°20N 9°47W 282 D2
Ardglass U.K. 54°17N 5°36W 282 B6
Ardivachar Pt. U.K. 57°23N 7°26W 283 D1
Ardlethan Australia 34°22S 146°53E 335 E4
Ardmore Okla., U.S.A. 34°10N 97°8W 356 D6
Ardmore Pa., U.S.A. 40°2N 75°17W 355 F9
Ardnamurchan, Pt. of U.K. 56°43N 6°14W 283 E2
Ardnave Pt. U.K. 55°53N 6°20W 283 F2
Ardrossan Australia 34°26S 137°53E 335 E2
Ardrossan U.K. 55°39N 4°49W 283 F4
Ards Pen. U.K. 54°33N 5°34W 282 B6
Arecibo Puerto Rico 18°29N 66°43W 361 d
Areia Branca Brazil 5°0S 37°0W 365 E11
Arena, Pt. U.S.A. 38°57N 123°44W 350 G3
Arenal Honduras 15°21N 86°50W 360 C2
Arendal Norway 58°28N 8°46E 281 G13
Arequipa Peru 16°20S 71°30W 364 G4
Arévalo Spain 41°3N 4°43W 293 B3
Arezzo Italy 43°25N 11°53E 294 C4
Arga Turkey 38°21N 37°59E 316 B3
Arganda Spain 40°19N 3°26W 293 B4
Argenta Canada 50°11N 116°56W 342 C5
Argentan France 48°45N 0°1W 292 B3
Argentário, Mte. Italy 42°24N 11°9E 294 C4
Argentia Canada 47°18N 53°58W 345 C9
Argentina ■ S. Amer. 35°0S 66°0W 368 D3
Argentine Basin Atl. Oc. 45°0S 45°0W 368 F6
Argentino, L. Argentina 50°10S 73°0W 368 G2
Argeş → Romania 44°5N 26°38E 289 F14
Arghandab → Afghan. 31°30N 64°15E 314 D1
Argirades Greece 39°27N 19°58E 297 B3
Argiroupoli Greece 35°17N 24°20E 297 D6
Argolikos Kolpos Greece 37°20N 22°52E 295 F10
Argos Greece 37°40N 22°43E 295 F10
Argostoli Greece 38°11N 20°29E 295 E9
Arguello, Pt. U.S.A. 34°35N 120°39W 351 L6
Arguineguín Canary Is. 27°46N 15°41W 296 G4
Argun → Russia 53°20N 121°28E 301 D13
Argungu Nigeria 12°40N 4°31E 322 F6
Argus Pk. U.S.A. 35°52N 117°26W 351 K9
Argyle, L. Australia 16°20S 128°40E 332 C4
Argyll ⌂ U.K. 56°6N 5°0W 283 E4
Argyll & Bute □ U.K. 56°13N 5°28W 283 E3
Århus Denmark 56°8N 10°11E 281 H14
Ariadnoye Russia 45°8N 134°25E 302 B7
Ariamsvlei Namibia 28°9S 19°51E 328 D2
Ariana Tunisia 36°52N 10°12E 323 A8
Arica Chile 18°32S 70°20W 364 G4
Arica Colombia 2°0S 71°50W 364 D4
Arico Canary Is. 28°9N 16°29W 296 F3
Arid, C. Australia 34°1S 123°10E 333 F3
Arida Japan 34°5N 135°8E 303 G7
Aride Seychelles 4°13S 55°40E 325 b
Ariège → France 43°30N 1°25E 292 E4
Arila, Akra Greece 39°43N 19°39E 297 A3
Arima Trin. & Tob. 10°38N 61°17W 361 D7
Arinos → Brazil 10°25S 58°20W 364 F7
Ario de Rosales Mexico 19°12N 101°43W 358 D4
Aripo, Mt. Trin. & Tob. 10°45N 61°15W 365 K15
Aripuanã Brazil 9°25S 60°30W 364 E6
Aripuanã → Brazil 5°7S 60°25W 364 E6
Ariquemes Brazil 9°55S 63°6W 364 E6
Arisaig U.K. 56°55N 5°51W 283 E3
Aristazabal I. Canada 52°40N 129°10W 342 C3
Arivonimamo Madag. 19°1S 47°11E 329 B8
Arizaro, Salar de Argentina 24°40S 67°50W 366 A2
Arizona Argentina 35°45S 65°25W 366 D2
Arizona □ U.S.A. 34°0N 112°0W 349 J8
Arizpe Mexico 30°20N 110°10W 358 A2
Arjeplog Sweden 66°3N 17°54E 280 C17
Arjepluovve = Arjeplog Sweden 66°3N 17°54E 280 C17
Arjona Colombia 10°14N 75°22W 364 A3
Arjuna Indonesia 7°49S 112°34E 309 G15
Arka Russia 60°15N 142°0E 301 C15
Arkadelphia U.S.A. 34°7N 93°4W 356 D8
Arkaig, L. U.K. 56°59N 5°10W 283 E3
Arkalyk = Arqalyk Kazakhstan 50°13N 66°50E 300 D7
Arkansas □ U.S.A. 35°0N 92°30W 356 D8
Arkansas → U.S.A. 33°47N 91°4W 356 E9
Arkansas City U.S.A. 37°4N 97°2W 352 G5
Arkaroola Australia 30°20S 139°22E 335 E2
Arkhangelsk Russia 64°38N 40°36E 290 B7
Arki India 31°9N 76°58E 314 D7
Arklow Ireland 52°48N 6°10W 282 D5
Arkport U.S.A. 42°24N 77°42W 354 D7
Arkticheskiy, Mys Russia 81°10N 95°0E 301 A10
Arkville U.S.A. 42°9N 74°37W 355 D10
Arlanzón → Spain 42°3N 4°17W 293 A3
Arlbergpass Austria 47°9N 10°12E 288 E6
Arles France 43°41N 4°40E 292 E6
Arlington S. Africa 28°1S 27°53E 329 D4
Arlington N.Y., U.S.A. 41°42N 73°54W 355 E11
Arlington Oreg., U.S.A. 45°43N 120°12W 348 D3
Arlington S. Dak., U.S.A. 44°22N 97°8W 352 C5
Arlington Tex., U.S.A. 32°44N 97°6W 356 E6
Arlington Va., U.S.A. 38°53N 77°7W 353 F15
Arlington Vt., U.S.A. 43°5N 73°9W 355 C11
Arlington Wash., U.S.A. 48°12N 122°8W 350 B4
Arlington Heights U.S.A. 42°5N 87°59W 352 D10
Arlit Niger 19°0N 7°38E 322 E7
Arlon Belgium 49°42N 5°49E 287 E5
Arlparra Australia 22°11S 134°30E 334 C1
Arltunga Australia 23°26S 134°41E 334 C1
Armagh U.K. 54°21N 6°39W 282 B5
Armagh □ U.K. 54°18N 6°37W 282 B5
Armando Bermudez △ Dom. Rep. 19°3N 71°0W 361 C5
Armavir Russia 45°2N 41°7E 291 E7
Armenia Colombia 4°35N 75°45W 364 C3
Armenia ■ Asia 40°20N 45°0E 291 F7
Armenistis, Akra Greece 36°8N 27°42E 297 C9
Armidale Australia 30°30S 151°40E 335 E5
Armour U.S.A. 43°19N 98°21W 352 D4
Armstrong B.C., Canada 50°25N 119°10W 342 C5
Armstrong Ont., Canada 50°18N 89°4W 344 B2
Arnarfjörður Iceland 65°48N 23°40W 280 D2
Arnaud → Canada 59°59N 69°46W 341 D13
Arnauti, C. Cyprus 35°6N 32°17E 297 D11
Arnett U.S.A. 36°8N 99°46W 356 C5
Arnhem Neths. 51°58N 5°55E 287 C5
Arnhem, C. Australia 12°20S 137°30E 334 A2
Arnhem B. Australia 12°20S 136°10E 334 A2
Arnhem Land Australia 13°10S 134°30E 334 A1
Arno → Italy 43°41N 10°17E 294 C4
Arno Bay Australia 33°54S 136°34E 335 E2
Arnold U.K. 53°1N 1°7W 284 D6
Arnold U.S.A. 38°15N 120°21W 350 G6
Arnot Canada 55°56N 96°41W 343 B9
Arnøya Norway 70°9N 20°40E 280 A19
Arnprior Canada 45°26N 76°21W 355 A8
Arnsberg Germany 51°24N 8°5E 288 C5
Aroa, Pte. Moorea 17°28S 149°46W 331 d
Aroab Namibia 26°41S 19°39E 328 D2
Aron India 25°57N 77°56E 314 G6
Arona Canary Is. 28°6N 16°40W 296 F3
Aros → Mexico 29°9N 107°57W 358 B3
Arqalyk Kazakhstan 50°13N 66°50E 300 D7
Arrah = Ara India 25°35N 84°32E 315 G11
Arrah Ivory C. 6°40N 3°58W 322 G5
Arran U.K. 55°34N 5°12W 283 F3
Arras France 50°17N 2°46E 292 A5
Arrecife Canary Is. 28°57N 13°37W 296 F6
Arrecifes Argentina 34°6S 60°9W 366 C3
Arrée, Mts. d' France 48°26N 3°55W 292 B2
Arriaga Mexico 16°14N 93°54W 359 D6
Arrilalah Australia 23°43S 143°54E 334 C3
Arrino Australia 29°30S 115°40E 333 E2
Arrow, L. Ireland 54°3N 8°19W 282 B3
Arrowtown N.Z. 44°57S 168°50E 331 F2
Arroyo Grande U.S.A. 35°7N 120°35W 351 K6
Ars Iran 37°9N 47°46E 316 B5
Arsenault L. Canada 55°6N 108°32W 343 B7
Arsenev Russia 44°10N 133°15E 302 B6
Arta Greece 39°8N 21°2E 295 E9
Artà Spain 39°41N 3°21E 296 B10
Arteaga Mexico 18°28N 102°25W 358 D4
Artem Russia 43°22N 132°13E 302 C6
Artemovsk Russia 54°45N 93°35E 301 D10
Artemovsk Ukraine 48°35N 38°0E 291 E6
Artesia = Mosomane Botswana 24°2S 26°19E 328 C4
Artesia U.S.A. 32°51N 104°24W 349 K11
Arthur Canada 43°50N 80°32W 354 C4
Arthur → Australia 41°2S 144°40E 335 G3
Arthur Cr. → Australia 22°30S 136°25E 334 C2
Arthur Pt. Australia 22°7S 150°3E 334 C5
Arthur River Australia 33°20S 117°2E 333 F2
Arthur's Pass N.Z. 42°54S 171°35E 331 E3
Arthur's Pass △ N.Z. 42°53S 171°42E 331 E3
Arthur's Town Bahamas 24°38N 75°42W 361 B4
Artigas Antarctica 62°30S 58°0W 277 C18
Artigas Uruguay 30°20S 56°30W 366 C4
Artillery L. Canada 63°9N 107°52W 343 A7
Artois France 50°20N 2°30E 292 A5
Artrutx, C. de Spain 39°55N 3°49E 296 B10
Artsyz Ukraine 46°4N 29°26E 289 E15
Artux China 39°40N 76°10E 304 C2
Artvin Turkey 41°14N 41°44E 291 F7
Aru, Kepulauan Indonesia 6°0S 134°30E 309 F8
Aru Is. = Aru, Kepulauan Indonesia 6°0S 134°30E 309 F8
Arua Uganda 3°1N 30°58E 326 B3
Aruanã Brazil 14°54S 51°10W 365 F8
Aruba ☒ W. Indies 12°30N 70°0W 361 D6
Arucas Canary Is. 28°7N 15°32W 296 F4
Arué Tahiti 17°31S 149°30W 331 d
Arun → Nepal 26°55N 87°10E 315 F12
Arun → U.K. 50°49N 0°33W 285 G7
Arunachal Pradesh □ India 28°0N 95°0E 313 F19
Arusha Tanzania 3°20S 36°40E 326 C4
Arusha □ Tanzania 4°0S 36°30E 326 C4
Arusha △ Tanzania 3°16S 36°47E 326 C4
Arusha Chini Tanzania 3°32S 37°20E 326 C4
Aruwimi → Dem. Rep. of the Congo 1°13N 23°36E 326 B1
Arvada Colo., U.S.A. 39°48N 105°5W 348 G11
Arvada Wyo., U.S.A. 44°39N 106°8W 348 D10
Arvayheer Mongolia 46°15N 102°48E 304 B5
Arvi Greece 34°59N 25°28E 297 E7
Arviat Canada 61°6N 93°59W 343 A10
Arvidsjaur Sweden 65°35N 19°10E 280 D18
Arvika Sweden 59°40N 12°36E 281 G15
Arvin U.S.A. 35°12N 118°50W 351 K8
Arwal India 25°15N 84°41E 315 G11
Arxan China 47°11N 119°57E 305 B6
Arys Kazakhstan 42°26N 68°48E 300 E7
Arzamas Russia 55°27N 43°55E 290 C7
Arzanah U.A.E. 24°47N 52°34E 317 E7
Aş Şafā Syria 33°10N 37°0E 318 B6
As Saffānīyah Si. Arabia 27°55N 48°50E 317 E6
As Safīrah Syria 36°5N 37°21E 316 B3
Aş Şahm Oman 24°10N 56°53E 317 E8
As Sājir Si. Arabia 25°11N 44°36E 316 E5
As Salamīyah Syria 35°1N 37°2E 316 C3
As Salmān Iraq 30°30N 44°32E 316 D5
As Salṭ Jordan 32°2N 35°43E 318 C4
As Sal'w'a Qatar 24°23N 50°50E 317 E6
As Samāwah Iraq 31°15N 45°15E 316 D5
As Sanamayn Syria 33°3N 36°10E 318 B5
As Sohar = Şuḥār Oman 24°20N 56°40E 317 E8
As Sukhnah Syria 34°52N 38°52E 316 C3
As Sulaymānīyah Iraq 35°35N 45°29E 316 C5
As Sulaymī Si. Arabia 26°17N 41°21E 316 E4
As Sulayyil Si. Arabia 20°27N 45°34E 319 C4
As Summān Si. Arabia 25°0N 47°0E 316 E5
As Suwaydā' Syria 32°40N 36°30E 318 C5
As Suwaydā' □ Syria 32°45N 36°45E 318 C5
As Suwayq Oman 23°51N 57°26E 317 F8
Aş Şuwayrah Iraq 32°55N 45°0E 316 C5
Asab Namibia 25°30S 18°0E 328 D2
Asad, Buḥayrat al Syria 36°0N 38°15E 316 C3
Asahi-Gawa → Japan 34°36N 133°58E 303 G6
Asahigawa Japan 43°46N 142°22E 302 C11
Asamankese Ghana 5°50N 0°40W 322 G5
Asan → India 26°37N 78°24E 315 F8
Asansol India 23°40N 87°1E 315 H12
Asau Samoa 13°27S 172°33W 331 b
Asbesberge S. Africa 29°0S 23°0E 328 D3
Asbestos Canada 45°47N 71°58W 345 C5
Asbury Park U.S.A. 40°13N 74°1W 355 F10
Ascensión Mexico 31°6N 107°59W 358 A3
Ascensión, B. de la Mexico 19°40N 87°30W 359 D7
Ascension I. Atl. Oc. 7°57S 14°23W 321 G2
Aschaffenburg Germany 49°58N 9°6E 288 D5
Aschersleben Germany 51°45N 11°29E 288 C6
Áscoli Piceno Italy 42°51N 13°34E 294 C5
Ascope Peru 7°46S 79°8W 364 E3
Ascotán Chile 21°45S 68°17W 366 A2
Aseb Eritrea 13°0N 42°40E 319 E3
Asela Ethiopia 8°0N 39°0E 319 F2
Asenovgrad Bulgaria 42°1N 24°51E 295 C11
Aşgabat = Ashgabat Turkmenistan 38°0N 57°50E 317 B8
Asgata Cyprus 34°46N 33°15E 297 E12
Ash Fork U.S.A. 35°13N 112°29W 349 J7
Ash Grove U.S.A. 37°19N 93°35W 352 G7
Ash Shabakah Iraq 30°49N 43°39E 316 D4
Ash Shamāl □ Lebanon 34°25N 36°0E 318 A5
Ash Shāmīyah Iraq 31°55N 44°35E 316 D5
Ash Shāriqah U.A.E. 25°23N 55°26E 317 E7
Ash Sharmah Si. Arabia 28°1N 35°16E 316 D2
Ash Sharqāt Iraq 35°27N 43°16E 316 C4
Ash Shaṭrah Iraq 31°30N 46°10E 316 D5
Ash Shawbak Jordan 30°32N 35°34E 316 D2
Ash Shināfīyah Iraq 31°35N 44°39E 316 D5
Ash Shu'bah Si. Arabia 28°54N 44°44E 316 D5
Ash Shumlūl Si. Arabia 26°31N 47°20E 316 E5
Ash Shūr'a Iraq 35°58N 43°13E 316 C4
Ash Shurayf Si. Arabia 25°43N 39°14E 316 E3
Ash Shuwayfāt Lebanon 33°45N 35°30E 318 B4
Asha Russia 55°0N 57°16E 290 D10
Ashau Vietnam 16°6N 107°22E 310 D6
Ashbourne U.K. 53°2N 1°43W 284 D6
Ashburn U.S.A. 31°43N 83°39W 357 F13
Ashburton N.Z. 43°53S 171°48E 331 E3
Ashburton → Australia 21°40S 114°56E 332 D1
Ashcroft Canada 50°40N 121°20W 342 C4
Ashdod Israel 31°49N 34°35E 318 D3
Ashdown U.S.A. 33°40N 94°8W 356 E7
Asheboro U.S.A. 35°43N 79°49W 357 D15
Ashern Canada 51°11N 98°21W 343 C9
Asherton U.S.A. 28°27N 99°46W 356 G5
Asheville U.S.A. 35°36N 82°33W 357 D13
Ashewat Pakistan 31°22N 68°32E 314 D3
Asheweig → Canada 54°17N 87°12W 344 B2
Ashford Australia 29°15S 151°3E 335 D5
Ashford U.K. 51°8N 0°53E 285 F8
Ashgabat Turkmenistan 38°0N 57°50E 317 B8
Ashibetsu Japan 43°31N 142°11E 302 C11
Ashikaga Japan 36°28N 139°29E 303 F9
Ashington U.K. 55°11N 1°33W 284 B6
Ashizuri-Uwakai △ Japan 32°56N 132°32E 303 H6
Ashizuri-Zaki Japan 32°44N 133°0E 303 H6
Ashkarkot Afghan. 33°3N 67°58E 314 C2
Ashkhabad = Ashgabat Turkmenistan 38°0N 57°50E 317 B8
Āshkhāneh Iran 37°26N 56°55E 317 B8
Ashland Kans., U.S.A. 37°11N 99°46W 352 G4
Ashland Ky., U.S.A. 38°28N 82°38W 353 F12
Ashland Maine, U.S.A. 46°38N 68°24W 353 B19
Ashland Mont., U.S.A. 45°36N 106°16W 348 D10
Ashland Ohio, U.S.A. 40°52N 82°19W 354 F2
Ashland Oreg., U.S.A. 42°12N 122°43W 348 E2
Ashland Pa., U.S.A. 40°45N 76°22W 355 F8
Ashland Va., U.S.A. 37°46N 77°29W 353 G15
Ashland Wis., U.S.A. 46°35N 90°53W 352 B8
Ashley N. Dak., U.S.A. 46°2N 99°22W 352 B4
Ashley Pa., U.S.A. 41°12N 75°55W 355 E9
Ashmore and Cartier Is. Ind. Oc. 12°15S 123°0E 332 B3
Ashmore Reef Australia 12°14S 123°5E 332 B3
Ashmyany Belarus 54°26N 25°52E 289 A13
Ashokan Res. U.S.A. 41°56N 74°13W 355 E10
Ashqelon Israel 31°42N 34°35E 318 D3
Ashta India 23°1N 76°43E 314 H7
Ashtabula U.S.A. 41°52N 80°47W 354 E4
Ashton S. Africa 33°50S 20°5E 328 E3
Ashton U.S.A. 44°4N 111°27W 348 D8
Ashuanipi, L. Canada 52°45N 66°15W 345 B6
Ashuapmushuan → Canada 48°37N 72°20W 344 C5
Ashville U.S.A. 40°34N 78°33W 354 F6
Asia 45°0N 75°0E 298 E9
Asia, Kepulauan Indonesia 1°0N 131°13E 309 D8
Asifabad India 19°20N 79°24E 312 K11
Asinara Italy 41°4N 8°16E 294 D3
Asinara, G. dell' Italy 41°0N 8°30E 294 D3
Asino Russia 57°0N 86°0E 300 D9
Asipovichy Belarus 53°19N 28°33E 289 B15
'Asīr Si. Arabia 18°40N 42°30E 319 D3
Asir, Ras Somali Rep. 11°55N 51°10E 319 E5
Askham S. Africa 26°59S 20°47E 328 D3

Askim Norway 59°35N 11°10E 281 G14
Askja Iceland 65°3N 16°48W 280 D5
Askøyna Norway 60°29N 5°10E 280 F11
Asmara = Asmera Eritrea 15°19N 38°55E 319 D2
Asmera Eritrea 15°19N 38°55E 319 D2
Åsnen Sweden 56°37N 14°45E 281 H16
Aso Kuju △ Japan 32°53N 131°6E 303 H5
Aspatria U.K. 54°47N 3°19W 284 C4
Aspen U.S.A. 39°11N 106°49W 348 G10
Aspermont U.S.A. 33°8N 100°14W 356 E4
Aspiring, Mt. N.Z. 44°23S 168°46E 331 F2
Asprokavos, Akra Greece 39°21N 20°6E 297 B4
Aspur India 23°58N 74°7E 314 H6
Asquith Canada 52°8N 107°13W 343 C7
Assab = Aseb Eritrea 13°0N 42°40E 319 E3
Assal, L. Djibouti 11°40N 42°26E 319 E3
Assam □ India 26°0N 93°0E 313 G18
Assateague Island ⌓ U.S.A. 38°15N 75°10W 353 F16
Asse Belgium 50°24N 4°10E 287 D4
Assen Neths. 53°0N 6°35E 287 A6
Assiniboia Canada 49°40N 105°59W 343 D7
Assiniboine → Canada 49°53N 97°8W 343 D9
Assiniboine, Mt. Canada 50°52N 115°39W 342 C5
Assis Brazil 22°40S 50°20W 367 A5
Assisi Italy 43°4N 12°37E 294 C5
Assynt, L. U.K. 58°10N 5°3W 283 C3
Astana Kazakhstan 51°10N 71°30E 300 D8
Āstāneh Iran 37°17N 49°59E 317 B6
Astara Azerbaijan 38°30N 48°50E 317 B6
Asterousia Greece 34°59N 25°3E 297 E7
Asti Italy 44°54N 8°12E 292 D8
Astipalea Greece 36°32N 26°22E 295 F12
Astorga Spain 42°29N 6°8W 293 A2
Astoria U.S.A. 46°11N 123°50W 350 D3
Astrakhan Russia 46°25N 48°5E 291 E8
Asturias □ Spain 43°15N 6°0W 293 A3
Asunción Paraguay 25°10S 57°30W 366 B4
Asunción Nochixtlán Mexico 17°28N 97°14W 359 D5
Aswa → Uganda 3°43N 31°55E 326 B3
Aswa-Lolim ⌓ Uganda 2°43N 31°35E 326 B3
Aswân Egypt 24°4N 32°57E 323 D12
Aswan Dam = Sadd el Aali Egypt 23°54N 32°54E 323 D12
Asyût Egypt 27°11N 31°4E 323 C12
At Ţafīlah Jordan 30°45N 35°30E 318 E4
At Ţafīlah □ Jordan 30°45N 35°30E 318 E4
Aţ Ţā'if Si. Arabia 21°5N 40°27E 319 C3
At Ta'mīm □ Iraq 35°30N 44°20E 316 C5
Aţ Ţirāq Si. Arabia 27°19N 44°33E 316 E5
Aţ Ţubayq Si. Arabia 29°30N 37°0E 316 D3
Aţ Ţunayb Jordan 31°48N 35°57E 318 D4
Atacama □ Chile 27°30S 70°0W 366 B2
Atacama, Desierto de Chile 24°0S 69°20W 366 A2
Atacama, Salar de Chile 23°30S 68°20W 366 A2
Atakpamé Togo 7°31N 1°13E 322 G6
Atalaya Peru 10°45S 73°50W 364 F4
Atalaya de Femes Canary Is. 28°56N 13°47W 296 F6
Atami Japan 35°5N 139°4E 303 G9
Atamyrat Turkmenistan 37°50N 65°12E 300 F7
Atapupu Indonesia 9°0S 124°51E 309 F6
Atâr Mauritania 20°30N 13°5W 322 D3
Atari Pakistan 30°56N 74°2E 314 D6
Atascadero U.S.A. 35°29N 120°40W 350 K6
Atasū Kazakhstan 48°30N 71°0E 300 E8
Atatürk Barajı Turkey 37°28N 38°30E 291 G6
Atauro E. Timor 8°10S 125°30E 309 F7
Ataviros Greece 36°12N 27°50E 297 C9
Atbara Sudan 17°42N 33°59E 323 E12
'Atbara, Nahr → Sudan 17°40N 33°56E 323 E12
Atbasar Kazakhstan 51°48N 68°20E 300 D7
Atchafalaya B. U.S.A. 29°25N 91°25W 356 G9
Atchison U.S.A. 39°34N 95°7W 352 F6
Āteshān Iran 35°35N 52°37E 317 C7
Ath Belgium 50°38N 3°47E 287 D3
Athabasca Canada 54°45N 113°20W 342 C6
Athabasca → Canada 58°40N 110°50W 343 B6
Athabasca, L. Canada 59°15N 109°15W 343 B7
Athabasca Sand Dunes ⌓ Canada 59°4N 108°43W 343 B7
Athboy Ireland 53°37N 6°56W 282 C5
Athenry Ireland 53°18N 8°44W 282 C3
Athens = Athina Greece 37°58N 23°43E 295 F10
Athens Ala., U.S.A. 34°48N 86°58W 357 D11
Athens Ga., U.S.A. 33°57N 83°23W 357 E13
Athens N.Y., U.S.A. 42°16N 73°49W 355 D11
Athens Ohio, U.S.A. 39°20N 82°6W 353 F12
Athens Pa., U.S.A. 41°57N 76°31W 355 E8
Athens Tenn., U.S.A. 35°27N 84°36W 357 D12
Athens Tex., U.S.A. 32°12N 95°51W 356 E7
Atherley Canada 44°37N 79°20W 354 B5
Atherton Australia 17°17S 145°30E 334 B4
Athi River Kenya 1°28S 36°58E 326 C4
Athienou Cyprus 35°3N 33°32E 297 D12
Athina Greece 37°58N 23°43E 295 F10
Athínai = Athina Greece 37°58N 23°43E 295 F10
Athlone Ireland 53°25N 7°56W 282 C4
Athna Cyprus 35°3N 33°47E 297 D12
Athol U.S.A. 42°36N 72°14W 355 D12
Atholl, Forest of U.K. 56°51N 3°50W 283 E5
Atholville Canada 47°59N 66°43W 345 C6
Athos Greece 40°9N 24°22E 295 D11
Athy Ireland 53°0N 7°0W 282 C5
Ati Chad 13°13N 18°20E 323 F9
Atiak Uganda 3°12N 32°2E 326 B3
Atik L. Canada 55°15N 96°0W 343 B9
Atikaki ⌓ Canada 51°30N 95°31W 343 C9
Atikameg → Canada 52°30N 82°46W 344 B3
Atikokan Canada 48°45N 91°37W 344 C1
Atikonak L. Canada 52°40N 64°32W 345 B7
Atimaono Tahiti 17°46S 149°28W 331 d
Atitlán △ Cent. Amer. 14°38N 91°10W 359 E6
Atiu Cook Is. 20°0S 158°10W 337 J12
Atka Russia 60°50N 151°48E 301 C16
Atka I. U.S.A. 52°7N 174°30W 346 a
Atkinson U.S.A. 42°32N 98°59W 352 D4
Atlanta Ga., U.S.A. 33°45N 84°23W 357 E12
Atlanta Tex., U.S.A. 33°7N 94°10W 356 E7
Atlantic U.S.A. 41°24N 95°1W 352 E6
Atlantic City U.S.A. 39°21N 74°27W 353 F16
Atlantic-Indian Basin Antarctica 60°0S 30°0E 277 B4
Atlantic Ocean 0°0 20°0W 274 D8
Atlas Mts. = Haut Atlas Morocco 32°30N 5°0W 322 B4
Atlin Canada 59°31N 133°41W 342 B2
Atlin, L. Canada 59°26N 133°45W 342 B2
Atlin ⌓ Canada 59°10N 134°30W 342 B2
Atmore U.S.A. 31°2N 87°29W 357 F11
Atoka U.S.A. 34°23N 96°8W 356 D6
Atolia U.S.A. 35°19N 117°37W 351 K9
Atrai → Bangla. 24°7N 89°22E 315 G13
Atrak = Atrek → Turkmenistan 37°35N 53°58E 317 B8
Atrauli India 28°2N 78°20E 314 E8
Atrek → Turkmenistan 37°35N 53°58E 317 B8
Atsuta Japan 43°24N 141°26E 302 C10
Attalla U.S.A. 34°1N 86°6W 357 D11
Attapu Laos 14°48N 106°50E 310 E6
Attawapiskat Canada 52°56N 82°24W 344 B3
Attawapiskat → Canada 52°57N 82°18W 344 B3
Attawapiskat L. Canada 52°18N 87°54W 344 B2
Attica Ind., U.S.A. 40°18N 87°15W 352 E10
Attica Ohio, U.S.A. 41°4N 82°53W 354 E2
Attikamagen L. Canada 55°0N 66°30W 345 B6
Attleboro U.S.A. 41°57N 71°17W 355 E13
Attock Pakistan 33°52N 72°20E 314 C5
Attopeu = Attapu Laos 14°48N 106°50E 310 E6
Attu I. U.S.A. 52°55N 172°55E 346 a
Attur India 11°35N 78°30E 312 P11
Atuel → Argentina 36°17S 66°50W 366 D2
Åtvidaberg Sweden 58°12N 16°0E 281 G17
Atwater U.S.A. 37°21N 120°37W 350 H6
Atwood Canada 43°40N 81°1W 354 C3
Atwood U.S.A. 39°48N 101°3W 352 F3
Atyraū Kazakhstan 47°5N 52°0E 291 E9
Au Sable U.S.A. 44°25N 83°20W 354 B1
Au Sable → U.S.A. 44°25N 83°20W 353 C12
Au Sable Forks U.S.A. 44°27N 73°41W 355 B11
Au Sable Pt. U.S.A. 44°20N 83°20W 354 B1
Auasberg Namibia 22°37S 17°13E 328 C2
Aubagne France 43°17N 5°37E 292 E6
Aubarca, C. d' Spain 39°4N 1°22E 296 B7
Aube → France 48°34N 3°43E 292 B5
Auberry U.S.A. 37°7N 119°29W 350 H7
Auburn Ala., U.S.A. 32°36N 85°29W 357 E12
Auburn Calif., U.S.A. 38°54N 121°4W 350 G5
Auburn Ind., U.S.A. 41°22N 85°4W 353 E11
Auburn Maine, U.S.A. 44°6N 70°14W 353 C18
Auburn N.Y., U.S.A. 42°56N 76°34W 355 D8
Auburn Nebr., U.S.A. 40°23N 95°51W 352 E6
Auburn Pa., U.S.A. 40°36N 76°6W 355 F8
Auburn Wash., U.S.A. 47°18N 122°14W 350 C4
Auburn Ra. Australia 25°15S 150°30E 335 D5
Auburndale U.S.A. 28°4N 81°48W 357 G14
Aubusson France 45°57N 2°11E 292 D5
Auch France 43°39N 0°36E 292 E4
Auchterarder U.K. 56°18N 3°41W 283 E5
Auchtermuchty U.K. 56°18N 3°13W 283 E5
Auckland N.Z. 36°52S 174°46E 331 B5
Auckland Is. Pac. Oc. 50°40S 166°5E 336 N8
Aude → France 43°13N 3°14E 292 E5
Auden Canada 50°14N 87°53W 344 B2
Audubon U.S.A. 41°43N 94°56W 352 E6
Augathella Australia 25°48S 146°35E 335 D4
Aughnacloy U.K. 54°25N 6°59W 282 B5
Aughrim Ireland 53°18N 8°19W 282 C3
Augrabies Falls S. Africa 28°35S 20°20E 328 D3
Augrabies Falls △ S. Africa 28°40S 20°22E 328 D3
Augsburg Germany 48°25N 10°52E 288 D6
Augusta Australia 34°19S 115°9E 333 F2
Augusta Italy 37°13N 15°13E 294 F6
Augusta Ark., U.S.A. 35°17N 91°22W 356 D9
Augusta Ga., U.S.A. 33°28N 81°58W 357 E14
Augusta Kans., U.S.A. 37°41N 96°59W 352 G5
Augusta Maine, U.S.A. 44°19N 69°47W 353 C19
Augusta Mont., U.S.A. 47°30N 112°24W 348 C7
Augustów Poland 53°51N 23°0E 289 B12
Augustus, Mt. Australia 24°20S 116°50E 333 D2
Augustus I. Australia 15°20S 124°30E 332 C3
Aujuittuq = Grise Fiord Canada 76°25N 82°57W 341 B11
Aukštaitija △ Lithuania 55°15N 26°0E 281 J22
Aukum U.S.A. 38°34N 120°43W 350 G6
Auld, L. Australia 22°25S 123°50E 332 D3
Ault U.S.A. 40°35N 104°44W 348 F11
Aunis France 46°5N 0°50W 292 C3
Aunu'u Amer. Samoa 14°20S 170°31W 331 b
Auponhia Indonesia 1°58S 125°27E 309 E7
Aur, Pulau Malaysia 2°35N 104°10E 311 L5
Auraiya India 26°28N 79°33E 315 F8
Aurangabad Bihar, India 24°45N 84°18E 315 G11
Aurangabad Maharashtra, India 19°50N 75°23E 312 K9
Aurich Germany 53°28N 7°28E 288 B4
Aurillac France 44°55N 2°26E 292 D5
Aurora Canada 44°0N 79°28W 354 C5
Aurora S. Africa 32°40S 18°29E 328 E2
Aurora Colo., U.S.A. 39°43N 104°49W 348 G11
Aurora Ill., U.S.A. 41°45N 88°19W 352 E9
Aurora Mo., U.S.A. 36°58N 93°43W 352 G7
Aurora N.Y., U.S.A. 42°45N 76°42W 355 D8
Aurora Nebr., U.S.A. 40°52N 98°0W 352 E5
Aurora Ohio, U.S.A. 41°21N 81°20W 354 E3
Aurukun Australia 13°20S 141°45E 334 A3
Aus Namibia 26°35S 16°12E 328 D2
Ausable → Canada 43°19N 81°46W 354 C3
Auschwitz = Oświęcim Poland 50°2N 19°11E 289 C10
Austin Minn., U.S.A. 43°40N 92°58W 352 D7
Austin Nev., U.S.A. 39°30N 117°4W 348 G5
Austin Pa., U.S.A. 41°38N 78°6W 354 E6
Austin Tex., U.S.A. 30°17N 97°45W 356 F6
Austin, L. Australia 27°40S 118°0E 333 E2
Austin I. Canada 61°10N 94°0W 343 A10
Austra Norway 65°8N 11°55E 280 D14
Austral Is. = Tubuaï, Îs. French Polynesia 25°0S 150°0W 337 K13
Austral Seamount Chain Pac. Oc. 24°0S 150°0W 337 K13
Australia ■ Oceania 23°0S 135°0E 330 D6
Australian-Antarctic Basin S. Ocean 60°0S 120°0E 277 C9
Australian Capital Territory □ Australia 35°30S 149°0E 335 F4
Australind Australia 33°17S 115°42E 333 F2
Austria ■ Europe 47°0N 14°0E 288 E8
Austvågøya Norway 68°20N 14°40E 280 B16
Autlán de Navarro Mexico 19°46N 104°22W 358 D4
Autun France 46°58N 4°17E 292 C6
Auvergne □ France 45°20N 3°15E 292 D5
Auvergne, Mts. d' France 45°20N 2°55E 292 D5
Auxerre France 47°48N 3°32E 292 C5
Ava U.S.A. 36°57N 92°40W 352 G7
Avallon France 47°30N 3°53E 292 C5
Avalon U.S.A. 33°21N 118°20W 351 M8
Avalon Pen. Canada 47°30N 53°20W 345 C9
Avanos Turkey 38°43N 34°51E 316 B2
Avaré Brazil 23°4S 48°58W 367 A6
Avawatz Mts. U.S.A. 35°40N 116°30W 351 K10
Aveiro Brazil 3°10S 55°5W 365 D7
Aveiro Portugal 40°37N 8°38W 293 B1
Āvej Iran 35°40N 49°15E 317 C6
Avellaneda Argentina 34°40S 58°22W 366 C4
Avellino Italy 40°54N 14°47E 294 D6
Avenal U.S.A. 36°0N 120°8W 350 K6
Aversa Italy 40°58N 14°12E 294 D6
Avery U.S.A. 47°15N 115°49W 348 C6
Aves, I. de W. Indies 15°45N 63°55W 361 C7
Aves, Is. las Venezuela 12°0N 67°30W 361 D6
Avesta Sweden 60°9N 16°10E 281 F17
Aveyron → France 44°5N 1°16E 292 D4
Avezzano Italy 42°2N 13°25E 294 C5
Aviá Terai Argentina 26°45S 60°50W 366 B3
Aviemore U.K. 57°12N 3°50W 283 D5
Avignon France 43°57N 4°50E 292 E6
Ávila Spain 40°39N 4°43W 293 B3
Avila Beach U.S.A. 35°11N 120°44W 351 K6
Avilés Spain 43°35N 5°57W 293 A3
Avis U.S.A. 41°11N 77°19W 354 E7
Avoca U.S.A. 42°25N 77°25W 354 D7
Avoca → Australia 35°40S 143°43E 335 F3
Avoca → Ireland 52°48N 6°10W 282 D5
Avola Canada 51°45N 119°19W 342 C5
Avola Italy 36°56N 15°7E 294 F6
Avon U.S.A. 42°55N 77°45W 354 D7
Avon → Australia 31°40S 116°7E 333 F2
Avon → Bristol, U.K. 51°29N 2°41W 285 F5
Avon → Dorset, U.K. 50°44N 1°46W 285 G6
Avon → Warks., U.K. 52°0N 2°8W 285 E5
Avon Park U.S.A. 27°36N 81°31W 357 H14
Avondale Zimbabwe 17°43S 30°58E 327 F3
Avonlea Canada 50°0N 105°0W 343 D8
Avonmore Canada 45°10N 74°58W 355 A10
Avonmouth U.K. 51°30N 2°42W 285 F5
Avranches France 48°40N 1°20W 292 B3
Awa-Shima Japan 38°27N 139°14E 302 E9
A'waj → Syria 33°23N 36°20E 318 B5
Awaji-Shima Japan 34°30N 134°50E 303 G7
'Awālī Bahrain 26°0N 50°30E 317 E6
Awantipur India 33°55N 75°3E 315 C6
Awasa Ethiopia 7°2N 38°28E 319 F2
Awash Ethiopia 9°1N 40°10E 319 F3
Awatere → N.Z. 41°37S 174°10E 331 D5
Awbārī Libya 26°46N 12°57E 323 C8
Awbārī, Idehan Libya 27°10N 11°30E 323 C8
Awe, L. U.K. 56°17N 5°16W 283 E3
Awjilah Libya 29°8N 21°7E 323 C10
Axe → U.K. 50°42N 3°4W 285 F5
Axel Heiberg I. Canada 80°0N 90°0W 341 B11
Axim Ghana 4°51N 2°15W 322 H5
Axios → Greece 40°57N 22°35E 295 D10
Axminster U.K. 50°46N 3°0W 285 G4
Ayabaca Peru 4°40S 79°53W 364 D3
Ayabe Japan 35°20N 135°20E 303 G7
Ayacucho Argentina 37°5S 58°20W 366 D4
Ayacucho Peru 13°0S 74°0W 364 F4
Ayaguz = Ayaköz Kazakhstan 48°10N 80°10E 300 E9
Ayaköz Kazakhstan 48°10N 80°10E 300 E9
Ayamonte Spain 37°12N 7°24W 293 D2
Ayan Russia 56°30N 138°16E 301 D14
Ayaviri Peru 14°50S 70°35W 364 F4
Aydın Turkey 37°51N 27°51E 295 F12
Aydingkol Hu China 42°40N 89°15E 304 B3
Ayer U.S.A. 42°34N 71°35W 355 D13
Ayer Hitam Malaysia 5°24N 100°16E 311 c
Ayer's Cliff Canada 45°10N 72°3W 355 A12
Ayers Rock = Uluru Australia 25°23S 131°5E 333 E5
Áyia Napa Cyprus 34°59N 34°0E 297 E13
Áyia Phyla Cyprus 34°43N 33°1E 297 E12
Áyios Amvrósios Cyprus 35°20N 33°35E 297 D12
Áyios Seryios Cyprus 35°12N 33°53E 297 D12
Áyios Theodhoros Cyprus 35°22N 34°1E 297 D13
Aykino Russia 62°15N 49°56E 290 B8
Aylesbury U.K. 51°49N 0°49W 285 F7
Aylmer Canada 42°46N 80°59W 354 D4
Aylmer, L. Canada 64°5N 108°30W 340 C9
'Ayn, Wādī al Oman 22°15N 55°28E 317 F7
Ayn Dār Si. Arabia 25°55N 49°10E 317 E7
Ayn Zālah Iraq 36°45N 42°35E 316 B4
Ayolas Paraguay 27°10S 56°59W 366 B4
Ayon, Ostrov Russia 69°50N 169°0E 301 C17
'Ayoûn el 'Atroûs Mauritania 16°38N 9°37W 322 E4
Ayr Australia 19°35S 147°25E 334 B4
Ayr Canada 43°17N 80°27W 354 C4
Ayr U.K. 55°28N 4°38W 283 F4
Ayr → U.K. 55°28N 4°38W 283 F4
Ayre, Pt. of I. of Man 54°25N 4°21W 284 C3
Ayton Australia 15°56S 145°22E 334 B4
Aytos Bulgaria 42°42N 27°16E 295 C12
Ayu, Kepulauan Indonesia 0°35N 131°5E 309 D8
Ayutla Guatemala 14°40N 92°10W 360 D1
Ayutla de los Libres Mexico 16°54N 99°13W 359 D5
Ayvacık Turkey 39°36N 26°24E 295 E12
Ayvalık Turkey 39°20N 26°46E 295 E12
Az Zabadānī Syria 33°43N 36°5E 318 B5
Az Ẓāhirīyah West Bank 31°25N 34°58E 318 D3
Az Ẓahrān Si. Arabia 26°10N 50°7E 317 E6
Az Zarqā Jordan 32°5N 36°4E 318 C5
Az Zarqā' U.A.E. 24°53N 53°4E 317 E7
Az Zarqā □ Jordan 32°5N 36°4E 318 C5
Az Zāwiyah Libya 32°52N 12°56E 323 B8
Az Zībār Iraq 36°52N 44°4E 316 B5
Az Zilfī Si. Arabia 26°12N 44°52E 316 E5
Az Zubayr Iraq 30°26N 47°40E 316 D5
Azad Kashmir □ Pakistan 33°50N 73°50E 315 C5
Azamgarh India 26°5N 83°13E 315 F10
Azangaro Peru 14°55S 70°13W 364 F4
Azaouad Mali 19°0N 3°0W 322 E5
Āzār Shahr Iran 37°45N 45°59E 316 B5
Azarān Iran 37°25N 47°16E 316 B5
Azärbayjan = Azerbaijan ■ Asia 40°20N 48°0E 291 F8
Āzarbāyjān-e Gharbī □ Iran 37°0N 44°30E 316 B5
Āzarbāyjān-e Sharqī □ Iran 37°20N 47°0E 316 B5
Azare Nigeria 11°55N 10°10E 322 F8
A'zāz Syria 36°36N 37°4E 316 B3
Azbine = Aïr Niger 18°30N 8°0E 322 E7
Azerbaijan ■ Asia 40°20N 48°0E 291 F8
Azerbaijchan = Azerbaijan ■ Asia 40°20N 48°0E 291 F8
Azimganj India 24°14N 88°16E 315 G13
Azogues Ecuador 2°35S 78°0W 364 D3
Azores = Açores, Is. dos Atl. Oc. 38°0N 27°0W 322 a
Azov Russia 47°3N 39°25E 291 E6
Azov, Sea of Europe 46°0N 36°30E 291 E6
Azovskoye More = Azov, Sea of Europe 46°0N 36°30E 291 E6
Azraq ash Shīshān Jordan 31°50N 36°49E 318 D5
Aztec U.S.A. 36°49N 107°59W 349 H10
Azúa de Compostela Dom. Rep. 18°25N 70°44W 361 C5
Azuaga Spain 38°16N 5°39W 293 C3
Azuero, Pen. de Panama 7°30N 80°30W 360 E3
Azul Argentina 36°42S 59°43W 366 D4
Azusa U.S.A. 34°8N 117°52W 351 L9
Azzel Matti, Sebkra Algeria 26°10N 0°43E 322 C6

B

Ba Be △ Vietnam 22°25N 105°37E 310 A5
Ba Don Vietnam 17°45N 106°26E 310 D6
Ba Dong Vietnam 9°40N 106°33E 311 H6
Ba Ngoi = Cam Lam Vietnam 11°54N 109°10E 311 G7
Ba Tri Vietnam 10°2N 106°36E 311 G6
Ba Vi △ Vietnam 21°1N 105°22E 310 B5
Ba Xian = Bazhou China 39°8N 116°22E 306 E9
Baa Indonesia 10°50S 123°0E 309 F6
Baardeere = Bardera Somali Rep. 2°20N 42°27E 319 G3
Baarle-Nassau Belgium 51°27N 4°56E 287 C4
Bab el Mandeb Red Sea 12°35N 43°25E 319 E3
Bābā, Koh-i- Afghan. 34°30N 67°0E 312 B5
Baba Burnu Turkey 39°29N 26°2E 295 E12
Bābā Kalū Iran 30°7N 50°49E 317 D6
Babadag Romania 44°53N 28°44E 289 F15
Babaeski Turkey 41°26N 27°6E 295 D12
Babahoyo Ecuador 1°40S 79°30W 364 D3
Babai = Sarju → India 27°21N 81°23E 315 F9
Babar Indonesia 8°0S 129°30E 309 F7
Babar Pakistan 31°7N 69°32E 314 D3
Babarkach Pakistan 29°45N 68°0E 314 E3
Babb U.S.A. 48°51N 113°27W 348 B7
Baberu India 25°33N 80°43E 315 G9
Babi Besar, Pulau Malaysia 2°25N 103°59E 311 L4
Bābil □ Iraq 32°30N 44°30E 316 C5
Babinda Australia 17°20S 145°56E 334 B4
Babine Canada 55°22N 126°37W 342 B3
Babine → Canada 55°45N 127°44W 342 B3
Babine L. Canada 54°48N 126°0W 342 C3
Babo Indonesia 2°30S 133°30E 309 E8
Bābol Iran 36°40N 52°50E 317 B7
Bābol Sar Iran 36°45N 52°45E 317 B7
Baboua C.A.R. 5°49N 14°58E 324 C2
Babruysk Belarus 53°10N 29°15E 289 B15
Babuhri India 26°49N 69°43E 314 F3
Babusar Pass Pakistan 35°12N 73°59E 315 B5
Babuyan Chan. Phil. 18°40N 121°30E 309 A6
Babylon Iraq 32°34N 44°22E 316 C5
Bac Can Vietnam 22°8N 105°49E 310 A5
Bac Giang Vietnam 21°16N 106°11E 310 B6
Bac Lieu Vietnam 9°17N 105°43E 311 H5
Bac Ninh Vietnam 21°13N 106°4E 310 B6
Bac Phan Vietnam 22°0N 105°0E 310 B5
Bac Quang Vietnam 22°30N 104°48E 310 A5
Bacabal Brazil 4°15S 44°45W 365 D10
Bacalar Mexico 18°43N 88°27W 359 D7
Bacan, Kepulauan Indonesia 0°35S 127°30E 309 E7
Bacarra Phil. 18°15N 120°37E 309 A6
Bacău Romania 46°35N 26°55E 289 E14
Bacerac Mexico 30°18N 108°50W 358 A3
Bach Long Vi, Dao Vietnam 20°10N 107°40E 310 B6
Bach Ma △ Vietnam 16°11N 107°49E 310 D6
Bachhwara India 25°35N 85°54E 315 G11
Back → Canada 65°10N 104°0W 340 C9
Bacolod Phil. 10°40N 122°57E 309 B6
Bacuk Malaysia 6°4N 102°25E 311 J4
Bácum Mexico 27°33N 110°5W 358 B2
Bād Iran 33°41N 52°1E 317 C7
Bad → U.S.A. 44°21N 100°22W 352 C3
Bad Axe U.S.A. 43°48N 83°0W 354 C2
Bad Ischl Austria 47°44N 13°38E 288 E7
Bad Kissingen Germany 50°11N 10°4E 288 C6
Bada Barabil India 22°7N 85°24E 315 H11
Badagara India 11°35N 75°40E 312 P9
Badajós, L. Brazil 3°15S 62°50W 364 D6
Badajoz Spain 38°50N 6°59W 293 C2
Badakhshān □ Afghan. 36°30N 71°0E 312 A7
Badalona Spain 41°26N 2°15E 293 B7
Badalzai Afghan. 29°50N 65°35E 314 E1
Badampahar India 22°10N 86°10E 313 H15
Badanah Si. Arabia 30°58N 41°30E 316 D4
Badarinath India 30°45N 79°30E 315 D8
Badas, Kepulauan Indonesia 0°45N 107°5E 308 D3
Baddo → Pakistan 28°0N 64°20E 312 F4
Bade Indonesia 7°10S 139°35E 309 F9
Baden Austria 48°1N 16°13E 288 D9
Baden U.S.A. 40°38N 80°14W 354 F4
Baden-Baden Germany 48°44N 8°13E 288 D5
Baden-Württemberg □ Germany 48°20N 8°40E 288 D5
Badgastein Austria 47°7N 13°9E 288 E7
Badger Canada 49°0N 56°4W 345 C8
Badger U.S.A. 36°38N 119°1W 350 J7
Bādghīs □ Afghan. 35°0N 63°0E 312 B3
Badgingarra △ Australia 30°23S 115°22E 333 F2
Badgom India 34°1N 74°45E 315 B6
Badin Pakistan 24°38N 68°54E 314 G3
Badlands U.S.A. 43°55N 102°30W 352 D2
Badlands △ U.S.A. 43°38N 102°56W 352 D2
Badrah Iraq 33°6N 45°58E 316 C5
Badrinath India 30°44N 79°29E 315 D8
Badulla Sri Lanka 7°1N 81°7E 312 R12
Badung, Selat Indonesia 8°40S 115°22E 309 K18
Baena Spain 37°37N 4°20W 293 D3
Baengnyeongdo S. Korea 37°57N 124°40E 307 F13
Baeza Spain 37°57N 3°25W 293 D4
Bafatá Guinea-Biss. 12°8N 14°40W 322 F3
Baffin B. N. Amer. 72°0N 64°0W 341 B13
Baffin I. Canada 68°0N 75°0W 341 C12
Bafing → Mali 13°49N 10°50W 322 F3
Bafliyūn Syria 36°37N 36°59E 316 B3
Bafoulabé Mali 13°50N 10°55W 322 F3
Bafoussam Cameroon 5°28N 10°25E 324 C2
Bāfq Iran 31°40N 55°25E 317 D7
Bafra Turkey 41°34N 35°54E 291 F6
Bāft Iran 29°15N 56°38E 317 D8
Bafwasende Dem. Rep. of the Congo 1°3N 27°5E 326 B2
Bagamoyo Tanzania 6°28S 38°55E 326 D4
Bagan Datoh Malaysia 3°59N 100°47E 311 L3
Bagan Serai Malaysia 5°1N 100°32E 311 K3
Baganga Phil. 7°34N 126°33E 309 C7
Bagani Namibia 18°7S 21°41E 328 B3
Bagansiapiapi Indonesia 2°12N 100°50E 308 D2
Bagasra India 21°30N 71°0E 314 J4
Bagaud India 22°19N 75°53E 314 H6
Bagdad U.S.A. 34°35N 115°53W 351 L11
Bagdarin Russia 54°26N 113°36E 301 D12
Bagé Brazil 31°20S 54°15W 367 C5
Bagenalstown = Muine Bheag Ireland 52°42N 6°58W 282 D5
Baggs U.S.A. 41°2N 107°39W 348 F10
Bagh Pakistan 33°59N 73°45E 315 C5
Baghain → India 25°32N 81°1E 315 G9
Baghdād Iraq 33°20N 44°23E 316 C5
Bagheria Italy 38°5N 13°30E 294 E5
Baghlān Afghan. 32°12N 68°46E 312 A6
Baghlān □ Afghan. 36°0N 68°30E 312 B6
Bagley U.S.A. 47°32N 95°24W 352 B6
Bago = Pegu Burma 17°20N 96°29E 313 L20
Bagodar India 24°5N 85°52E 315 G11
Bagrationovsk Russia 54°23N 20°39E 281 J19
Baguio Phil. 16°26N 120°34E 309 A6
Bah India 26°53N 78°36E 315 F8
Bahadurganj India 26°16N 87°49E 315 F12
Bahadurgarh India 28°40N 76°57E 314 E7
Bahama, Canal Viejo de W. Indies 22°10N 77°30W 360 B4
Bahamas ■ N. Amer. 24°0N 75°0W 361 B5
Baharampur India 24°2N 88°27E 315 G13
Baharu Pandan = Pandan Malaysia 1°32N 103°46E 311 d
Bahawalnagar Pakistan 30°0N 73°15E 314 E5
Bahawalpur Pakistan 29°24N 71°40E 314 E4
Bäherden Turkmenistan 38°25N 57°26E 317 B8
Baheri India 28°45N 79°34E 315 E8
Bahgul → India 27°45N 79°36E 315 F8
Bahi Tanzania 5°58S 35°21E 326 D4
Bahi Swamp Tanzania 6°10S 35°0E 326 D4
Bahía = Salvador Brazil 13°0S 38°30W 365 F11

Bahía □ Brazil 12°0S 42°0W 365 F10
Bahía, Is. de la Honduras 16°45N 86°15W 360 C2
Bahía Blanca Argentina 38°35S 62°13W 366 D3
Bahía de Caráquez Ecuador 0°40S 80°27W 364 D2
Bahía Kino Mexico 28°47N 111°58W 358 B2
Bahía Laura Argentina 48°10S 66°30W 368 F3
Bahía Negra Paraguay 20°5S 58°5W 364 H7
Bahir Dar Ethiopia 11°37N 37°10E 319 E2
Bahmanzād Iran 31°15N 51°47E 317 D6
Bahraich India 27°38N 81°37E 315 F9
Bahrain ■ Asia 26°0N 50°35E 317 E6
Bahror India 27°51N 76°20E 314 F7
Bāhū Kalāt Iran 25°43N 61°25E 317 E9
Bai Bung, Mui = Ca Mau, Mui Vietnam 8°38N 104°44E 311 H5
Bai Duc Vietnam 18°3N 105°49E 310 C5
Bai Thuong Vietnam 19°54N 105°23E 310 C5
Baia Mare Romania 47°40N 23°35E 289 E12
Baião Brazil 2°40S 49°40W 365 D9
Baïbokoum Chad 7°46N 15°43E 323 G9
Baicheng China 45°38N 122°42E 307 B12
Baidoa Somali Rep. 3°8N 43°30E 319 G3
Baie-Comeau Canada 49°12N 68°10W 345 C6
Baie-St-Paul Canada 47°28N 70°32W 345 C5
Baie Ste-Anne Seychelles 4°18S 55°45E 325 b
Baie-Trinité Canada 49°25N 67°20W 345 C6
Baie Verte Canada 49°55N 56°12W 345 C8
Baihar India 22°6N 80°33E 315 H9
Baihe China 32°50N 110°5E 306 H6
Ba'ījī Iraq 35°0N 43°30E 316 C4
Baijnath India 29°55N 79°37E 315 E8
Baikal, L. = Baykal, Oz. Russia 53°0N 108°0E 301 D11
Baikonur = Bayqongyr Kazakhstan 45°40N 63°20E 300 E7
Baikunthpur India 23°15N 82°33E 315 H10
Baile Atha Cliath = Dublin Ireland 53°21N 6°15W 282 C5
Băileşti Romania 44°1N 23°20E 289 F12
Bainbridge Ga., U.S.A. 30°55N 84°35W 357 F12
Bainbridge N.Y., U.S.A. 42°18N 75°29W 355 D9
Bainbridge Island U.S.A. 47°38N 122°32W 350 C4
Baing Indonesia 10°14S 120°34E 309 F6
Bainiu China 32°50N 112°15E 306 H7
Bā'ir Jordan 30°45N 36°55E 318 E5
Bairiki = Tarawa Kiribati 1°30N 173°0E 336 G9
Bairin Youqi China 43°30N 118°35E 307 C10
Bairin Zuoqi China 43°58N 119°15E 307 C10
Bairnsdale Australia 37°48S 147°36E 335 F4
Baisha China 34°20N 112°32E 306 G7
Baitadi Nepal 29°35N 80°25E 315 E9
Baiyin China 36°45N 104°14E 306 F3
Baiyu Shan China 37°15N 107°30E 306 F4
Baj Baj India 22°30N 88°5E 315 H13
Baja Hungary 46°12N 18°59E 289 E10
Baja, Pta. Mexico 29°58N 115°49W 358 B1
Baja California Mexico 31°10N 115°12W 358 A1
Baja California □ Mexico 30°0N 115°0W 358 B2
Baja California Sur □ Mexico 25°50N 111°50W 358 B2
Bajag India 22°40N 81°21E 315 H9
Bajamar Canary Is. 28°33N 16°20W 296 F3
Bajana India 23°7N 71°49E 314 H4
Bajatrejo Indonesia 8°29S 114°19E 309 J17
Bajera Indonesia 8°31S 115°2E 309 J18
Bājgīrān Iran 37°36N 58°24E 317 B8
Bajimba, Mt. Australia 29°17S 152°6E 335 D5
Bajo Nuevo Caribbean 15°40N 78°50W 360 C4
Bajoga Nigeria 10°57N 11°20E 323 F8
Bajool Australia 23°40S 150°35E 334 C5
Bakel Senegal 14°56N 12°20W 322 F3
Baker Calif., U.S.A. 35°16N 116°4W 351 K10
Baker Mont., U.S.A. 46°22N 104°17W 348 C11
Baker, L. Canada 64°0N 96°0W 340 C10
Baker, Mt. U.S.A. 48°50N 121°49W 348 B3
Baker City U.S.A. 44°47N 117°50W 348 D5
Baker I. Pac. Oc. 0°10N 176°35W 336 G10
Baker I. U.S.A. 55°20N 133°40W 342 B2
Baker L. Australia 26°54S 126°5E 333 E4
Baker Lake Canada 64°20N 96°3W 340 C10
Bakers Creek Australia 21°13S 149°7E 334 C4
Bakers Dozen Is. Canada 56°45N 78°45W 344 A4
Bakersfield Calif., U.S.A. 35°23N 119°1W 351 K8
Bakersfield Vt., U.S.A. 44°45N 72°48W 355 B12
Bakharden = Bäherden Turkmenistan 38°25N 57°26E 317 B8
Bākhtarān = Kermānshāh Iran 34°23N 47°0E 316 C5
Bākhtarān = Kermānshāh □ Iran 34°0N 46°30E 316 C5
Bakı Azerbaijan 40°29N 49°56E 317 A6
Bakkafjörður Iceland 66°2N 14°48W 280 C6
Bakouma C.A.R. 5°40N 22°56E 324 C4
Bakswaho India 24°15N 79°18E 315 G8
Baku = Bakı Azerbaijan 40°29N 49°56E 317 A6
Bakutis Coast Antarctica 74°0S 120°0W 277 D15
Baky = Bakı Azerbaijan 40°29N 49°56E 317 A6
Bala Canada 45°1N 79°37W 354 A5
Bala U.K. 52°54N 3°36W 284 E4
Bala, L. U.K. 52°53N 3°37W 284 E4
Balabac I. Phil. 8°0N 117°0E 308 C5
Balabac Str. E. Indies 7°53N 117°5E 308 C5
Balabagh Afghan. 34°25N 70°12E 314 B4
Ba'labakk Lebanon 34°0N 36°10E 318 B5
Balabalangan, Kepulauan Indonesia 2°20S 117°30E 308 E5
Balad Iraq 34°0N 44°9E 316 C5
Balad Rūz Iraq 33°42N 45°5E 316 C5
Bālādeh Fārs, Iran 29°17N 51°56E 317 D6
Bālādeh Māzandaran, Iran 36°12N 51°48E 317 B6
Balaghat India 21°49N 80°12E 312 J12
Balaghat Ra. India 18°50N 76°30E 312 K10
Balaguer Spain 41°50N 0°50E 293 B6
Balaklava Ukraine 44°30N 33°30E 291 F5
Balakovo Russia 52°4N 47°55E 290 D8
Balamau India 27°10N 80°21E 315 F9
Balancán Mexico 17°48N 91°32W 359 D6
Balashov Russia 51°30N 43°10E 291 D7
Balasinor India 22°57N 73°23E 314 H5
Balasore = Baleshwar India 21°35N 87°3E 313 J15
Balaton Hungary 46°50N 17°40E 289 E9
Balbina, Reprêsa de Brazil 2°0S 59°30W 364 D7
Balboa Panama 8°57N 79°34W 360 E4
Balbriggan Ireland 53°37N 6°11W 282 C5
Balcarce Argentina 38°0S 58°10W 366 D4
Balcarres Canada 50°50N 103°35W 343 C8
Balchik Bulgaria 43°28N 28°11E 295 C13
Balclutha N.Z. 46°15S 169°45E 331 G2
Balcones Escarpment U.S.A. 29°30N 99°15W 356 G5
Bald Hd. Australia 35°6S 118°1E 333 G2
Bald I. Australia 34°57S 118°27E 333 F2
Bald Knob U.S.A. 35°19N 91°34W 356 D9
Baldock L. Canada 56°33N 97°57W 343 B9
Baldwin Mich., U.S.A. 43°54N 85°51W 353 D11
Baldwin Pa., U.S.A. 40°21N 79°58W 354 F5
Baldwinsville U.S.A. 43°10N 76°20W 355 C8
Baldy Peak U.S.A. 33°54N 109°34W 349 K9
Baleares, Is. Spain 39°30N 3°0E 296 B10
Balearic Is. = Baleares, Is. Spain 39°30N 3°0E 296 B10
Baleine = Whale → Canada 58°15N 67°40W 345 A6
Baleine, Petite R. de la → Canada 56°0N 76°45W 344 A4
Baler Phil. 15°46N 121°34E 309 A6
Baleshare U.K. 57°31N 7°22W 283 D1
Baleshwar India 21°35N 87°3E 313 J15
Balfate Honduras 15°48N 86°25W 360 C2
Bali Greece 35°25N 24°47E 297 D6
Bali India 25°11N 73°17E 314 G5
Bali Indonesia 8°20S 115°0E 308 F4
Bali □ Indonesia 8°20S 115°0E 308 F5
Bali, Selat Indonesia 8°18S 114°25E 309 J17
Bali Sea Indonesia 8°0S 115°0E 309 J17
Baliapal India 21°40N 87°17E 315 J12
Balik Pulau Malaysia 5°21N 100°14E 311 c
Balıkeşir Turkey 39°39N 27°53E 295 E12
Balikpapan Indonesia 1°10S 116°55E 308 E5
Balimbing Phil. 5°5N 119°58E 309 C5
Baling Malaysia 5°41N 100°55E 311 K3
Balkan Mts. = Stara Planina Bulgaria 43°15N 23°0E 295 C10
Balkanabat Turkmenistan 39°30N 54°22E 317 B7
Balkhash = Balqash Kazakhstan 46°50N 74°50E 300 E8
Balkhash, Ozero = Balqash Köl Kazakhstan 46°0N 74°50E 300 E8
Ballachulish U.K. 56°41N 5°8W 283 E3
Balladonia Australia 32°27S 123°51E 333 F3
Ballaghaderreen Ireland 53°55N 8°34W 282 C3
Ballarat Australia 37°33S 143°50E 335 F3
Ballard, L. Australia 29°20S 120°40E 333 E3
Ballater U.K. 57°3N 3°3W 283 D5
Ballenas, Canal de Mexico 29°10N 113°29W 358 B2
Balleny Is. Antarctica 66°30S 163°0E 277 C11
Ballia India 25°46N 84°12E 315 G11
Ballina Australia 28°50S 153°31E 335 D5
Ballina Ireland 54°7N 9°9W 282 B2
Ballinasloe Ireland 53°20N 8°13W 282 C3
Ballinger U.S.A. 31°45N 99°57W 356 F5
Ballinrobe Ireland 53°38N 9°13W 282 C2
Ballinskelligs B. Ireland 51°48N 10°13W 282 E1
Ballston Spa U.S.A. 43°0N 73°51W 355 D11
Ballyboghil Ireland 53°32N 6°16W 282 C5
Ballybunion Ireland 52°31N 9°40W 282 D2
Ballycanew Ireland 52°37N 6°19W 282 D5
Ballycastle U.K. 55°12N 6°15W 282 A5
Ballyclare U.K. 54°46N 6°0W 282 B5
Ballydehob Ireland 51°34N 9°28W 282 E2
Ballygawley U.K. 54°27N 7°2W 282 B4
Ballyhaunis Ireland 53°46N 8°46W 282 C3
Ballyheige Ireland 52°23N 9°49W 282 D2
Ballymena U.K. 54°52N 6°17W 282 B5
Ballymoney U.K. 55°5N 6°31W 282 A5
Ballymote Ireland 54°5N 8°31W 282 B3
Ballynahinch U.K. 54°24N 5°54W 282 B6
Ballyquintin Pt. U.K. 54°20N 5°30W 282 B6
Ballyshannon Ireland 54°30N 8°11W 282 B3
Balmaceda Chile 46°0S 71°50W 368 F2
Balmertown Canada 51°4N 93°41W 343 C10
Balmoral Australia 37°15S 141°48E 335 F3
Balmorhea U.S.A. 30°59N 103°45W 356 F3
Balochistan = Baluchistan □ Pakistan 27°30N 65°0E 312 F4
Balonne → Australia 28°47S 147°56E 335 D4
Balotra India 25°50N 72°14E 314 G5
Balqash Kazakhstan 46°50N 74°50E 300 E8
Balqash Köl Kazakhstan 46°0N 74°50E 300 E8
Balrampur India 27°30N 82°20E 315 F10
Balranald Australia 34°38S 143°33E 335 E3
Balsas → Brazil 7°15S 44°35W 365 E9
Balsas → Mexico 17°55N 102°10W 358 D4
Balsas del Norte Mexico 18°0N 99°46W 359 D5
Balta Ukraine 48°2N 29°45E 289 D15
Bălţi Moldova 47°48N 27°58E 289 E14
Baltic Sea Europe 57°0N 19°0E 281 H18
Baltimore Ireland 51°29N 9°22W 282 E2
Baltimore Md., U.S.A. 39°17N 76°36W 353 F15
Baltimore Ohio, U.S.A. 39°51N 82°36W 354 G2
Baltinglass Ireland 52°56N 6°43W 282 D5
Baltit Pakistan 36°15N 74°40E 315 A6
Baltiysk Russia 54°41N 19°58E 281 J18
Baluchistan □ Pakistan 27°30N 65°0E 312 F4
Balurghat India 25°15N 88°44E 315 G13
Balvi Latvia 57°8N 27°15E 281 H22
Balya Turkey 39°44N 27°35E 295 E12
Bam Iran 29°7N 58°14E 317 D8
Bama Nigeria 11°33N 13°41E 323 F8
Bamaga Australia 10°50S 142°25E 334 A3
Bamaji L. Canada 51°9N 91°25W 344 B1
Bamako Mali 12°34N 7°55W 322 F4
Bambari C.A.R. 5°40N 20°35E 324 C4
Bambaroo Australia 18°50S 146°10E 334 B4
Bamberg Germany 49°54N 10°54E 288 D6
Bamberg U.S.A. 33°18N 81°2W 357 E14
Bambili Dem. Rep. of the Congo 3°40N 26°0E 326 B2
Bamburgh U.K. 55°37N 1°43W 284 B6
Bamenda Cameroon 5°57N 10°11E 324 C2
Bamfield Canada 48°45N 125°10W 342 D3
Bāmīān □ Afghan. 35°0N 67°0E 312 B5
Bamiancheng China 43°15N 124°2E 307 C13
Bampūr Iran 27°15N 60°21E 317 E9
Ban Ao Tu Khun Thailand 8°9N 98°20E 311 a
Ban Ban Laos 19°31N 103°30E 310 C4
Ban Bang Hin Thailand 9°32N 98°35E 311 H2
Ban Bang Khu Thailand 7°57N 98°23E 311 a
Ban Bang Rong Thailand 8°3N 98°25E 311 a
Ban Bo Phut Thailand 9°33N 100°2E 311 b
Ban Chaweng Thailand 9°32N 100°3E 311 b
Ban Chiang Klang Thailand 19°25N 100°55E 310 C3
Ban Chik Laos 17°15N 102°22E 310 D4
Ban Choho Thailand 15°2N 102°9E 310 E4
Ban Dan Lan Hoi Thailand 17°0N 99°35E 310 D2
Ban Don = Surat Thani Thailand 9°6N 99°20E 311 H2
Ban Don Vietnam 12°53N 107°48E 310 F6
Ban Don, Ao → Thailand 9°20N 99°25E 311 H2
Ban Dong Thailand 19°30N 100°59E 310 C3
Ban Hong Thailand 18°18N 98°50E 310 C2
Ban Hua Thanon Thailand 9°26N 100°1E 311 b
Ban Kaeng Thailand 17°29N 100°7E 310 D3
Ban Kantang Thailand 7°25N 99°31E 311 J2
Ban Karon Thailand 7°51N 98°18E 311 a
Ban Kata Thailand 7°50N 98°18E 311 a
Ban Keun Laos 18°22N 102°35E 310 C4
Ban Khai Thailand 12°46N 101°18E 310 F3
Ban Kheun Laos 20°13N 101°7E 310 B3
Ban Khlong Khian Thailand 8°10N 98°26E 311 a
Ban Khlong Kua Thailand 6°57N 100°8E 311 J3
Ban Khuan Thailand 8°20N 98°25E 311 a
Ban Khuan Mao Thailand 7°50N 99°37E 311 J2
Ban Ko Yai Chim Thailand 11°17N 99°26E 311 G2
Ban Kok Thailand 16°40N 103°40E 310 D4
Ban Laem Thailand 13°13N 99°59E 310 F2
Ban Lamai Thailand 9°28N 100°3E 311 b
Ban Lao Ngam Laos 15°28N 106°10E 310 E6
Ban Le Kathe Thailand 15°49N 98°53E 310 E2
Ban Lo Po Noi Thailand 8°1N 98°34E 311 a
Ban Mae Chedi Thailand 19°11N 99°31E 310 C2
Ban Mae Laeng Thailand 20°1N 99°17E 310 B2
Ban Mae Nam Thailand 9°34N 100°0E 311 b
Ban Mae Sariang Thailand 18°10N 97°56E 310 C1
Ban Mê Thuôt = Buon Ma Thuot Vietnam 12°40N 108°3E 310 F7
Ban Mi Thailand 15°3N 100°32E 310 E3
Ban Muong Mo Laos 19°4N 103°58E 310 C4
Ban Na Bo Thailand 9°19N 99°41E 311 b
Ban Na Mo Laos 17°7N 105°40E 310 D5
Ban Na San Thailand 8°53N 99°52E 311 H2
Ban Na Tong Laos 20°56N 101°47E 310 B3
Ban Nam Bac Laos 20°38N 102°20E 310 B4
Ban Nam Ma Laos 22°2N 101°37E 310 A3
Ban Ngang Laos 15°59N 106°11E 310 E6
Ban Nong Bok Laos 17°5N 104°48E 310 D5
Ban Nong Boua Laos 15°40N 106°33E 310 E6
Ban Nong Pling Thailand 15°40N 100°10E 310 E3
Ban Pak Chan Thailand 10°32N 98°51E 311 G2
Ban Patong Thailand 7°54N 98°18E 311 a
Ban Phai Thailand 16°4N 102°44E 310 D4
Ban Phak Chit Thailand 8°0N 98°24E 311 a
Ban Pong Thailand 13°50N 99°55E 310 F2
Ban Rawai Thailand 7°47N 98°20E 311 a
Ban Ron Phibun Thailand 8°9N 99°51E 311 H2
Ban Sakhu Thailand 8°4N 98°18E 311 a
Ban Sanam Chai Thailand 7°33N 100°25E 311 J3
Ban Sangkha Thailand 14°37N 103°52E 310 E4
Ban Tak Thailand 17°2N 99°4E 310 D2
Ban Tako Thailand 14°5N 102°40E 310 E4
Ban Tha Dua Thailand 17°59N 98°39E 310 D2
Ban Tha Li Thailand 17°37N 101°25E 310 D3
Ban Tha Nun Thailand 8°12N 98°18E 311 a
Ban Tha Rua Thailand 7°59N 98°22E 311 a
Ban Tha Yu Thailand 8°17N 98°22E 311 a
Ban Thahine Laos 14°12N 105°33E 310 E5
Ban Thong Krut Thailand 9°25N 99°57E 311 b
Ban Xien Kok Laos 20°54N 100°39E 310 B3
Ban Yen Nhan Vietnam 20°57N 106°2E 310 B6
Banaba Kiribati 0°45S 169°50E 336 H8
Banalia Dem. Rep. of the Congo 1°32N 25°5E 326 B2
Banam Cambodia 11°20N 105°17E 311 G5
Bananal, I. do Brazil 11°30S 50°30W 365 F8
Banaras = Varanasi India 25°22N 83°0E 315 G10
Banas → Gujarat, India 23°45N 71°25E 314 H4
Banas → Mad. P., India 24°15N 81°30E 315 G9
Bânâs, Ras Egypt 23°57N 35°59E 323 D13
Banbridge U.K. 54°22N 6°16W 282 B5
Banbury U.K. 52°4N 1°20W 285 E6
Banchory U.K. 57°3N 2°29W 283 D6
Bancroft Canada 45°3N 77°51W 354 A7
Band Bonī Iran 25°30N 59°33E 317 E8
Band Qīr Iran 31°39N 48°53E 317 D6
Banda Mad. P., India 24°3N 78°57E 315 G8
Banda Ut. P., India 25°30N 80°26E 315 G9
Banda, Kepulauan Indonesia 4°37S 129°50E 309 E7
Banda Aceh Indonesia 5°35N 95°20E 308 C1
Banda Banda, Mt. Australia 31°10S 152°28E 335 E5
Banda Elat Indonesia 5°40S 133°5E 309 F8
Banda Is. = Banda, Kepulauan Indonesia 4°37S 129°50E 309 E7
Banda Sea Indonesia 6°0S 130°0E 309 F7
Bandai-Asahi △ Japan 37°38N 140°5E 302 F10
Bandai-San Japan 37°36N 140°4E 302 F10
Bandān Iran 31°23N 60°44E 317 D9
Bandanaira Indonesia 4°32S 129°54E 309 E7
Bandanwara India 26°9N 74°38E 314 F6
Bandar = Machilipatnam India 16°12N 81°8E 313 L12
Bandar-e Abbās Iran 27°15N 56°15E 317 E8
Bandar-e Anzalī Iran 37°30N 49°30E 317 B6
Bandar-e Bushehr = Būshehr Iran 28°55N 50°55E 317 D6
Bandar-e Chārak Iran 26°45N 54°20E 317 E7
Bandar-e Deylam Iran 30°5N 50°10E 317 D6
Bandar-e Emām Khomeynı Iran 30°30N 49°5E 317 D6
Bandar-e Lengeh Iran 26°35N 54°58E 317 E7
Bandar-e Maqām Iran 26°56N 53°29E 317 E7
Bandar-e Ma'shur Iran 30°35N 49°10E 317 D6
Bandar-e Rīg Iran 29°29N 50°38E 317 D6
Bandar-e Torkeman Iran 37°0N 54°10E 317 B7
Bandar Lampung = Tanjungkarang Telukbetung Indonesia 5°20S 105°10E 308 F3
Bandar Maharani = Muar Malaysia 2°3N 102°34E 311 L4
Bandar Penggaram = Batu Pahat Malaysia 1°50N 102°56E 311 M4
Bandar Seri Begawan Brunei 4°52N 115°0E 308 C4
Bandar Sri Aman = Sri Aman Malaysia 1°15N 111°32E 308 D4
Bandawe Malawi 11°58S 34°5E 327 E3
Bandeira, Pico da Brazil 20°26S 41°47W 367 A7
Bandera Argentina 28°55S 62°20W 366 B3
Banderas, B. de Mexico 20°40N 105°25W 358 C3
Bandhavgarh India 23°40N 81°2E 315 H9
Bandi → India 26°12N 75°47E 314 F6
Bandikui India 27°3N 76°34E 314 F7
Bandırma Turkey 40°20N 28°0E 295 D13
Bandjarmasin = Banjarmasin Indonesia 3°20S 114°35E 308 E4
Bandon Ireland 51°44N 8°44W 282 E3
Bandon → Ireland 51°43N 8°37W 282 E3
Bandula Mozam. 19°0S 33°7E 327 F3
Bandundu Dem. Rep. of the Congo 3°15S 17°22E 324 E3
Bandung Indonesia 6°54S 107°36E 308 F3
Bāneh Iran 35°59N 45°53E 316 C5
Banes Cuba 21°0N 75°42W 361 B4
Banff Canada 51°10N 115°34W 342 C5
Banff U.K. 57°40N 2°33W 283 D6
Banff △ Canada 51°30N 116°15W 342 C5
Bang Fai → Laos 16°57N 104°45E 310 D5
Bang Hieng → Laos 16°10N 105°10E 310 D5
Bang Krathum Thailand 16°34N 100°18E 310 D3
Bang Lamung Thailand 13°3N 100°56E 310 F3
Bang Mun Nak Thailand 16°2N 100°23E 310 D3
Bang Pa In Thailand 14°14N 100°35E 310 E3
Bang Rakam Thailand 16°45N 100°7E 310 D3
Bang Saphan Thailand 11°14N 99°28E 311 G2
Bang Thao Thailand 7°59N 98°18E 311 a
Bangaduni I. India 21°34N 88°52E 315 J13
Bangala Dam Zimbabwe 21°7S 31°25E 327 G3
Bangalore India 12°59N 77°40E 312 N10
Banganga → India 27°6N 77°25E 314 F6
Bangaon India 23°0N 88°47E 315 H13
Bangassou C.A.R. 4°55N 23°7E 324 D4
Banggai Indonesia 1°34S 123°30E 309 E6
Banggai, Kepulauan Indonesia 1°40S 123°30E 309 E6
Banggai Arch. = Banggai, Kepulauan Indonesia 1°40S 123°30E 309 E6
Banggi, Pulau Malaysia 7°17N 117°12E 308 C5
Banghāzī Libya 32°11N 20°3E 323 B10
Bangka Sulawesi, Indonesia 1°50N 125°5E 309 D7
Bangka Sumatera, Indonesia 2°0S 105°50E 308 E3
Bangka, Selat Indonesia 2°30S 105°30E 308 E3
Bangka-Belitung □ Indonesia 2°30S 107°0E 308 E3
Bangkalan Indonesia 7°2S 112°46E 309 G15
Bangkinang Indonesia 0°18N 101°5E 308 D2
Bangko Indonesia 2°5S 102°9E 308 E2
Bangkok Thailand 13°45N 100°35E 310 F3
Bangladesh ■ Asia 24°0N 90°0E 313 H17
Bangli Indonesia 8°27S 115°21E 309 J18
Bangong Co China 33°45N 78°43E 315 B8
Bangor Down, U.K. 54°40N 5°40W 282 B6
Bangor Gwynedd, U.K. 53°14N 4°8W 284 D3
Bangor Maine, U.S.A. 44°48N 68°46W 353 C19
Bangor Pa., U.S.A. 40°52N 75°13W 355 F9
Bangued Phil. 17°40N 120°37E 309 A6
Bangui C.A.R. 4°23N 18°35E 324 D3
Banguru Dem. Rep. of the Congo 0°30N 27°10E 326 B2
Bangweulu, L. Zambia 11°0S 30°0E 327 E3
Bangweulu Swamp Zambia 11°20S 30°15E 327 E3
Banhine △ Mozam. 22°49S 32°55E 329 C5
Baní Dom. Rep. 18°16N 70°22W 361 C5
Banī Sa'd Iraq 33°34N 44°32E 316 C5
Banihal Pass India 33°30N 75°12E 315 C6
Banissa Kenya 3°55N 40°19E 326 B4
Bāniyās Syria 35°10N 36°0E 316 C3
Banja Luka Bos.-H. 44°49N 17°11E 294 B7
Banjar India 31°38N 77°21E 314 D7
Banjar → India 22°36N 80°22E 315 H9
Banjarmasin Indonesia 3°20S 114°35E 308 E4
Banjul Gambia 13°28N 16°40W 322 F2
Banka India 24°53N 86°55E 315 G12
Banket Zimbabwe 17°27S 30°19E 327 F3
Bankipore India 25°35N 85°10E 313 G14
Banks I. B.C., Canada 53°20N 130°0W 342 C3
Banks I. N.W.T., Canada 73°15N 121°30W 340 B7
Banks Pen. N.Z. 43°45S 173°15E 331 E4
Banks Str. Australia 40°40S 148°10E 335 G4
Bankura India 23°11N 87°18E 315 H12
Banmankhi India 25°53N 87°11E 315 G12
Bann → Armagh, U.K. 54°30N 6°31W 282 B5
Bann → L'derry., U.K. 55°8N 6°41W 282 A5
Bannang Sata Thailand 6°16N 101°16E 311 J3
Banning U.S.A. 33°56N 116°53W 351 M10
Bannockburn Canada 44°39N 77°33W 354 B7
Bannockburn U.K. 56°5N 3°55W 283 E5
Bannockburn Zimbabwe 20°17S 29°48E 327 G2
Bannu Pakistan 33°0N 70°18E 312 C7
Bano India 22°40N 84°55E 315 H11
Bansgaon India 26°33N 83°21E 315 F10
Banská Bystrica Slovak Rep. 48°46N 19°14E 289 D10
Banswara India 23°32N 74°24E 314 H6
Bantaeng Indonesia 5°32S 119°56E 309 F5
Banten □ Indonesia 6°30S 106°0E 309 G11
Bantry Ireland 51°41N 9°27W 282 E2
Bantry B. Ireland 51°37N 9°44W 282 E2
Bantul Indonesia 7°55S 110°19E 309 G14
Bantva India 21°29N 70°12E 314 J4
Banyak, Kepulauan Indonesia 2°10N 97°10E 308 D1
Banyalbufar Spain 39°42N 2°31E 296 B9
Banyo Cameroon 6°52N 11°45E 324 C2
Banyumas Indonesia 7°32S 109°18E 309 G13
Banyuwangi Indonesia 8°13S 114°21E 309 J17
Banzare Coast Antarctica 68°0S 125°0E 277 C9
Bao Ha Vietnam 22°11N 104°21E 310 A5
Bao Lac Vietnam 22°57N 105°40E 310 A5
Bao Loc Vietnam 11°32N 107°48E 311 G6
Bao'an = Shenzhen China 22°32N 114°5E 305 F10
Baocheng China 33°12N 106°56E 306 H4
Baode China 39°1N 111°5E 306 E6
Baodi China 39°38N 117°20E 307 E9
Baoding China 38°50N 115°28E 306 E8
Baoji China 34°20N 107°5E 306 G4
Baoshan China 25°10N 99°5E 304 D4
Baotou China 40°32N 110°2E 306 D6
Baoying China 33°17N 119°20E 307 H10
Baoyou = Ledong China 18°41N 109°5E 310 C7
Bap India 27°23N 72°18E 314 F5
Bapatla India 15°55N 80°30E 313 M12
Bāqerābād Iran 33°2N 51°58E 317 C6
Ba'qūbah Iraq 33°45N 44°50E 316 C5
Baquedano Chile 23°20S 69°52W 366 A2
Bar Montenegro 42°8N 19°6E 295 C8
Bar Ukraine 49°4N 27°40E 289 D14
Bar Bigha India 25°21N 85°47E 315 G11
Bar Harbor U.S.A. 44°23N 68°13W 353 C19
Bar-le-Duc France 48°47N 5°10E 292 B6
Bara India 25°16N 81°43E 315 G9
Bara Banki India 26°55N 81°12E 315 F9
Barabai Indonesia 2°32S 115°34E 308 E5
Baraboo U.S.A. 43°28N 89°45W 352 D9
Baracoa Cuba 20°20N 74°30W 361 B5
Baradā → Syria 33°33N 36°34E 318 B5
Baradero Argentina 33°52S 59°29W 366 C4
Baraga U.S.A. 46°47N 88°30W 352 B9
Baragoi Kenya 1°47N 36°47E 326 B4
Barah → India 27°42N 77°5E 314 F6
Barahona Dom. Rep. 18°13N 71°7W 361 C5
Barail Range India 25°15N 93°20E 313 G18
Barakaldo Spain 43°18N 2°59W 293 A4
Barakar → India 24°7N 86°14E 315 G12
Barakot India 21°33N 84°59E 315 J11
Barakpur India 22°47N 88°21E 315 H13
Baralaba Australia 24°13S 149°50E 334 C4
Baralzon L. Canada 60°0N 98°3W 343 B9
Baramula India 34°15N 74°20E 315 B6
Baran India 25°9N 76°40E 314 G7
Baran → Pakistan 25°13N 68°17E 314 G3
Baranavichy Belarus 53°10N 26°0E 289 B14
Baranof U.S.A. 57°5N 134°50W 342 B2
Baranof I. U.S.A. 57°0N 135°0W 340 D6
Barapasi Indonesia 2°15S 137°5E 309 E9
Barasat India 22°46N 88°31E 315 H13
Barat Daya, Kepulauan Indonesia 7°30S 128°0E 309 F7
Barataria B. U.S.A. 29°20N 89°55W 357 G10
Barauda India 23°33N 75°15E 314 H6
Baraut India 29°13N 77°7E 314 E7
Barbacena Brazil 21°15S 43°56W 367 A7
Barbados ■ W. Indies 13°10N 59°30W 361 g
Barbària, C. de Spain 38°39N 1°24E 296 C7
Barbas, C. W. Sahara 22°20N 16°42W 322 D2
Barbastro Spain 42°2N 0°5E 293 A6
Barberton S. Africa 25°42S 31°2E 329 D5
Barberton U.S.A. 41°1N 81°39W 354 E3
Barbosa Colombia 5°57N 73°37W 364 B4
Barbourville U.S.A. 36°52N 83°53W 353 G12
Barbuda W. Indies 17°30N 61°40W 361 C7
Barcaldine Australia 23°43S 145°6E 334 C4
Barcellona Pozzo di Gotto Italy 38°9N 15°13E 294 E6
Barcelona Spain 41°22N 2°10E 293 B7
Barcelona Venezuela 10°10N 64°40W 364 A6
Barceloneta Puerto Rico 18°27N 66°32W 361 d

Barcelos Brazil 1°0S 63°0W 364 D6
Barcoo → Australia 25°30S 142°50E 334 D3
Bardaï Chad 21°25N 17°0E 323 D9
Bardas Blancas Argentina 35°49S 69°45W 366 D2
Bardawîl, Sabkhet el Egypt 31°10N 33°15E 318 D2
Barddhaman India 23°14N 87°39E 315 H12
Bardejov Slovak Rep. 49°18N 21°15E 289 D11
Bardera Somali Rep. 2°20N 42°27E 319 G3
Bardīyah Libya 31°45N 25°5E 323 B10
Bardsey I. U.K. 52°45N 4°47W 284 E3
Bardstown U.S.A. 37°49N 85°28W 353 G11
Bareilly India 28°22N 79°27E 315 E8
Barela India 23°6N 80°3E 315 H9
Barents Sea Arctic 73°0N 39°0E 276 B9
Barfleur, Pte. de France 49°42N 1°16W 292 B3
Bargara Australia 24°50S 152°25E 334 C5
Barguzin Russia 53°37N 109°37E 301 D11
Barh India 25°29N 85°46E 315 G11
Barhaj India 26°18N 83°44E 315 F10
Barharwa India 24°52N 87°47E 315 G12
Barhi India 24°15N 85°25E 315 G11
Bari India 26°39N 77°39E 314 F7
Bari Italy 41°8N 16°51E 294 D7
Bari Doab Pakistan 30°20N 73°0E 314 D5
Bari Sadri India 24°28N 74°30E 314 G6
Barīdī, Ra's Si. Arabia 24°17N 37°31E 316 E3
Barīm Yemen 12°39N 43°25E 320 E8
Barinas Venezuela 8°36N 70°15W 364 B4
Baring, C. Canada 70°0N 117°30W 340 C8
Baringo, L. Kenya 0°47N 36°16E 326 B4
Barisal Bangla. 22°45N 90°20E 313 H17
Barisal □ Bangla. 22°45N 90°20E 313 H17
Barisan, Pegunungan Indonesia 3°30S 102°15E 308 E2
Barito → Indonesia 4°0S 114°50E 308 E4
Baritú △ Argentina 23°43S 64°40W 366 A3
Barjūj, Wadi → Libya 25°26N 12°12E 323 C8
Bark L. Canada 45°27N 77°51W 354 A7
Barkakana India 23°37N 85°29E 315 H11
Barker U.S.A. 43°20N 78°33W 354 C6
Barkley, L. U.S.A. 37°1N 88°14W 357 C10
Barkley Sound Canada 48°50N 125°10W 342 D3
Barkly East S. Africa 30°58S 27°33E 328 E4
Barkly Homestead Australia 19°52S 135°50E 334 B2
Barkly Tableland Australia 17°50S 136°40E 334 B2
Barkly West S. Africa 28°5S 24°31E 328 D3
Barkol Kazak Zizhixian China 43°37N 93°2E 304 B4
Bârlad Romania 46°15N 27°38E 289 E14
Bârlad → Romania 45°38N 27°32E 289 F14
Barlee, L. Australia 29°15S 119°30E 333 E2
Barlee, Mt. Australia 24°38S 128°13E 333 D4
Barletta Italy 41°19N 16°17E 294 D7
Barlovento Canary Is. 28°48N 17°48W 296 F2
Barlovento C. Verde Is. 17°0N 25°0W 322 b
Barlow L. Canada 62°0N 103°0W 343 A8
Barmedman Australia 34°9S 147°21E 335 E4
Barmer India 25°45N 71°20E 314 G4
Barmera Australia 34°15S 140°28E 335 E3
Barmouth U.K. 52°44N 4°4W 284 E3
Barna → India 25°21N 83°3E 315 G10
Barnagar India 23°7N 75°19E 314 H6
Barnala India 30°23N 75°33E 314 D6
Barnard Castle U.K. 54°33N 1°55W 284 C6
Barnaul Russia 53°20N 83°40E 300 D9
Barnesville Ga., U.S.A. 33°3N 84°9W 357 E12
Barnesville Minn., U.S.A. 46°43N 96°28W 352 B5
Barnet □ U.K. 51°38N 0°9W 285 F7
Barneveld Neths. 52°7N 5°36E 287 B5
Barneveld U.S.A. 43°16N 75°14W 355 C9
Barnhart U.S.A. 31°8N 101°10W 356 F4
Barnsley U.K. 53°34N 1°27W 284 D6
Barnstaple U.K. 51°5N 4°4W 285 F3
Barnstaple Bay = Bideford Bay U.K. 51°5N 4°20W 285 F3
Barnwell U.S.A. 33°15N 81°23W 357 E14
Baro Nigeria 8°35N 6°18E 322 G7
Baroda = Vadodara India 22°20N 73°10E 314 H5
Baroda India 25°29N 76°35E 314 G7
Baroe S. Africa 33°13S 24°33E 328 E3
Baron Ra. Australia 23°30S 127°45E 332 D4
Barotseland Zambia 15°0S 24°0E 325 H4
Barpeta India 26°20N 91°10E 313 F17
Barques, Pt. Aux U.S.A. 44°4N 82°58W 354 B2
Barquísimeto Venezuela 10°4N 69°19W 364 A5
Barr Smith Range Australia 27°4S 120°20E 333 E3
Barra Brazil 11°5S 43°10W 365 F10
Barra U.K. 57°0N 7°29W 283 E1
Barra, Sd. of U.K. 57°4N 7°25W 283 D1
Barra de Navidad Mexico 19°12N 104°41W 358 D4
Barra do Corda Brazil 5°30S 45°10W 365 E9
Barra do Piraí Brazil 22°30S 43°50W 367 A7
Barra Falsa, Pta. da Mozam. 22°58S 35°37E 329 C6
Barra Hd. U.K. 56°47N 7°40W 283 E1
Barra Mansa Brazil 22°35S 44°12W 367 A7
Barraba Australia 30°21S 150°35E 335 E5
Barrackpur = Barakpur India 22°47N 88°21E 315 H13
Barradale Australia 22°42S 114°58E 332 D1
Barraigh = Barra U.K. 57°0N 7°29W 283 E1
Barranca Lima, Peru 10°45S 77°50W 364 F3
Barranca Loreto, Peru 4°50S 76°50W 364 D3
Barranca del Cobre ⌂ Mexico 27°18N 107°40W 358 B3
Barrancabermeja Colombia 7°0N 73°50W 364 B4
Barrancas Venezuela 8°55N 62°5W 364 B6
Barrancos Portugal 38°10N 6°58W 293 C2
Barranqueras Argentina 27°30S 59°0W 366 B4
Barranquilla Colombia 11°0N 74°50W 364 A4
Barraute Canada 48°26N 77°38W 344 C4
Barre Mass., U.S.A. 42°25N 72°6W 355 D12
Barre Vt., U.S.A. 44°12N 72°30W 355 B12
Barreal Argentina 31°33S 69°28W 366 C2
Barreiras Brazil 12°8S 45°0W 365 F10
Barreirinhas Brazil 2°30S 42°50W 365 D10
Barreiro Portugal 38°39N 9°5W 293 C1
Barren, Nosy Madag. 18°25S 43°40E 329 B7
Barretos Brazil 20°30S 48°35W 365 H9
Barrhead Canada 54°10N 114°24W 342 C6
Barrie Canada 44°24N 79°40W 354 B5
Barrier Ra. Australia 31°0S 141°30E 335 E3
Barrier Reef Belize 17°9N 88°3W 359 D7
Barrière Canada 51°12N 120°7W 342 C4
Barrington U.S.A. 41°44N 71°18W 355 E13
Barrington L. Canada 56°55N 100°15W 343 B8
Barrington Tops Australia 32°6S 151°28E 335 E5
Barringun Australia 29°1S 145°41E 335 D4
Barro do Garças Brazil 15°54S 52°16W 365 G8
Barron U.S.A. 45°24N 91°51W 352 C8
Barrow U.S.A. 71°18N 156°47W 346 a
Barrow → Ireland 52°25N 6°58W 282 D5
Barrow, Pt. U.S.A. 71°23N 156°29W 338 B4
Barrow Creek Australia 21°30S 133°55E 334 C1
Barrow I. Australia 20°45S 115°20E 332 D2
Barrow-in-Furness U.K. 54°7N 3°14W 284 C4
Barrow Pt. Australia 14°20S 144°40E 334 A3
Barrow Ra. Australia 26°0S 127°40E 333 E4
Barrow Str. Canada 74°20N 95°0W 276 B3
Barry U.K. 51°24N 3°16W 285 F4
Barry's Bay Canada 45°29N 77°41W 354 A7
Barsat Pakistan 36°10N 72°45E 315 A5
Barsham Syria 35°21N 40°33E 316 C4
Barsi India 18°10N 75°50E 312 K9
Barsoi India 25°48N 87°57E 313 G15
Barstow U.S.A. 34°54N 117°1W 351 L9
Barthélemy, Col Vietnam 19°26N 104°6E 310 C5
Bartica Guyana 6°25N 58°40W 364 B7
Bartle Frere Australia 17°27S 145°50E 334 B4
Bartlesville U.S.A. 36°45N 95°59W 356 C7
Bartlett Calif., U.S.A. 36°29N 118°2W 350 J8
Bartlett Tenn., U.S.A. 35°12N 89°52W 357 D10
Bartlett, L. Canada 63°5N 118°20W 342 A5
Bartolomeu Dias Mozam. 21°10S 35°8E 327 G4
Barton U.S.A. 44°45N 72°11W 355 B12
Barton upon Humber U.K. 53°41N 0°25W 284 D7
Bartow U.S.A. 27°54N 81°50W 357 H14
Barú, Volcan Panama 8°55N 82°35W 360 E3
Barumba Dem. Rep. of the Congo 1°3N 23°37E 326 B1
Baruunsuu Mongolia 43°43N 105°35E 306 C3
Barwani India 22°2N 74°57E 314 H6
Barysaw Belarus 54°17N 28°28E 289 A15
Barzān Iraq 36°55N 44°3E 316 B5
Bāsa'idū Iran 26°35N 55°20E 317 E7
Basal Pakistan 33°33N 72°13E 314 C5
Basankusa Dem. Rep. of the Congo 1°5N 19°50E 324 D3
Basarabeasca Moldova 46°21N 28°58E 289 E15
Basarabia = Bessarabiya Moldova 47°0N 28°10E 289 E15
Basawa Afghan. 34°15N 70°50E 314 B4
Bascuñán, C. Chile 28°52S 71°35W 366 B1
Basel Switz. 47°35N 7°35E 292 C7
Bashākerd, Kūhhā-ye Iran 26°42N 58°35E 317 E8
Bashaw Canada 52°35N 112°58W 342 C6
Bāshī Iran 28°41N 51°4E 317 D6
Bashkir Republic = Bashkortostan □ Russia 54°0N 57°0E 290 D10
Bashkortostan □ Russia 54°0N 57°0E 290 D10
Basibasy Madag. 22°10S 43°40E 329 C7
Basilan Phil. 6°35N 122°0E 309 C6
Basilan Str. Phil. 6°50N 122°0E 309 C6
Basildon U.K. 51°34N 0°28E 285 F8
Basim = Washim India 20°3N 77°0E 312 J10
Basin U.S.A. 44°23N 108°2W 348 D9
Basingstoke U.K. 51°15N 1°5W 285 F6
Baskatong, Rés. Canada 46°46N 75°50W 344 C4
Basle = Basel Switz. 47°35N 7°35E 292 C7
Basoda India 23°52N 77°54E 314 H7
Basoko Dem. Rep. of the Congo 1°16N 23°40E 326 B1
Basque Provinces = País Vasco □ Spain 42°50N 2°45W 293 A4
Basra = Al Başrah Iraq 30°30N 47°50E 316 D5
Bass Str. Australia 39°15S 146°30E 335 F4
Bassano Canada 50°48N 112°20W 342 C6
Bassano del Grappa Italy 45°46N 11°44E 294 B4
Bassas da India Ind. Oc. 22°0S 39°0E 325 J7
Basse-Pointe Martinique 14°52N 61°8W 360 c
Basse-Terre Guadeloupe 16°0N 61°44W 360 b
Basse Terre Trin. & Tob. 10°7N 61°19W 365 K15
Bassein Burma 16°45N 94°30E 313 L19
Basses, Pte. des Guadeloupe 15°52N 61°17W 360 b
Basseterre St. Kitts & Nevis 17°17N 62°43W 361 C7
Bassett U.S.A. 42°35N 99°32W 352 D4
Bassi India 30°44N 76°21E 314 D7
Bastak Iran 27°15N 54°25E 317 E7
Baştām Iran 36°29N 55°4E 317 B7
Bastar India 19°15N 81°40E 313 K12
Basti India 26°52N 82°55E 315 F10
Bastia France 42°40N 9°30E 292 E8
Bastogne Belgium 50°1N 5°43E 287 D5
Bastrop La., U.S.A. 32°47N 91°55W 356 E9
Bastrop Tex., U.S.A. 30°7N 97°19W 356 F6
Basuo = Dongfang China 18°50N 108°33E 310 C7
Bat Yam Israel 32°2N 34°44E 318 C3
Bata Eq. Guin. 1°57N 9°50E 324 D1
Bataan □ Phil. 14°40N 120°25E 309 B6
Batabanó Cuba 22°41N 82°18W 360 B3
Batabanó, G. de Cuba 22°30N 82°30W 360 B3
Batac Phil. 18°3N 120°34E 309 A6
Batagai Russia 67°38N 134°38E 301 C14
Batala India 31°48N 75°12E 314 D6
Batama Dem. Rep. of the Congo 0°58N 26°33E 326 B2
Batamay Russia 63°30N 129°15E 301 C13
Batang Indonesia 6°55S 109°45E 309 G13
Batangafo C.A.R. 7°25N 18°20E 324 C3
Batangas Phil. 13°35N 121°10E 309 B6
Batanta Indonesia 0°55S 130°40E 309 E8
Batatais Brazil 20°54S 47°37W 367 A6
Batavia U.S.A. 43°0N 78°11W 354 D6
Batchelor Australia 13°4S 131°1E 332 B5
Batdambang Cambodia 13°7N 103°12E 310 F4
Batemans B. Australia 35°40S 150°12E 335 F5
Batemans Bay Australia 35°44S 150°11E 335 F5
Bates Ra. Australia 27°27S 121°5E 333 E3
Batesburg-Leesville U.S.A. 33°54N 81°33W 357 E14
Batesville Ark., U.S.A. 35°46N 91°39W 356 D9
Batesville Miss., U.S.A. 34°19N 89°57W 357 D10
Batesville Tex., U.S.A. 28°58N 99°37W 356 G5
Bath Canada 44°11N 76°47W 355 B8
Bath U.K. 51°23N 2°22W 285 F5
Bath Maine, U.S.A. 43°55N 69°49W 353 D19
Bath N.Y., U.S.A. 42°20N 77°19W 354 D7
Bath & North East Somerset □ U.K. 51°21N 2°27W 285 F5
Batheay Cambodia 11°59N 104°57E 311 G5
Bathsheba Barbados 13°13N 59°32W 361 g
Bathurst Australia 33°25S 149°31E 335 E4
Bathurst Canada 47°37N 65°43W 345 C6
Bathurst S. Africa 33°30S 26°50E 328 E4
Bathurst, C. Canada 70°34N 128°0W 340 B7
Bathurst B. Australia 14°16S 144°25E 334 A3
Bathurst Harb. Australia 43°15S 146°10E 335 G4
Bathurst I. Australia 11°30S 130°10E 332 B5
Bathurst I. Canada 76°0N 100°30W 341 B11
Bathurst Inlet Canada 66°50N 108°1W 340 C9
Batiki Fiji 17°48S 179°10E 331 a
Batlow Australia 35°31S 148°9E 335 F4
Batman Turkey 37°55N 41°5E 316 B4
Baṭn al Ghūl Jordan 29°36N 35°56E 318 F4
Batna Algeria 35°34N 6°15E 322 A7
Batoka Zambia 16°45S 27°15E 327 F2
Baton Rouge U.S.A. 30°27N 91°11W 356 F9
Batong, Ko Thailand 6°32N 99°12E 311 J2
Batopilas Mexico 27°1N 107°44W 358 B3
Batouri Cameroon 4°30N 14°25E 324 D2
Båtsfjord Norway 70°38N 29°39E 280 A23
Battambang = Batdambang Cambodia 13°7N 103°12E 310 F4
Batticaloa Sri Lanka 7°43N 81°45E 312 R12
Battipáglia Italy 40°37N 14°58E 294 D6
Battle U.K. 50°55N 0°30E 285 G8
Battle → Canada 52°43N 108°15W 343 C7
Battle Creek U.S.A. 42°19N 85°11W 353 D11
Battle Ground U.S.A. 45°47N 122°32W 350 E4
Battle Harbour Canada 52°16N 55°35W 345 B8
Battle Lake U.S.A. 46°17N 95°43W 352 B6
Battle Mountain U.S.A. 40°38N 116°56W 348 F5
Battlefields Zimbabwe 18°37S 29°47E 327 F2
Battleford Canada 52°45N 108°15W 343 C7
Batu Ethiopia 6°55N 39°45E 319 F2
Batu, Kepulauan Indonesia 0°30S 98°25E 308 E1
Batu Caves Malaysia 3°15N 101°40E 311 L3
Batu Ferringhi Malaysia 5°28N 100°15E 311 c
Batu Gajah Malaysia 4°28N 101°3E 311 K3
Batu Is. = Batu, Kepulauan Indonesia 0°30S 98°25E 308 E1
Batu Pahat Malaysia 1°50N 102°56E 311 M4
Batuata Indonesia 6°12S 122°42E 309 F6
Batugondang, Tanjung Indonesia 8°6S 114°29E 309 J17
Batukau, Gunung Indonesia 8°20S 115°5E 309 J18
Batumi Georgia 41°39N 41°44E 291 F7
Batur Indonesia 8°15S 115°20E 309 J18
Batur, Danau Indonesia 8°15S 115°24E 309 J18
Batur, Gunung Indonesia 8°14S 115°23E 309 J18
Baturaja Indonesia 4°11S 104°15E 308 E2
Baturité Brazil 4°28S 38°45W 365 D11
Baturiti Indonesia 8°19S 115°11E 309 J18
Bau Malaysia 1°25N 110°9E 308 D4
Baubau Indonesia 5°25S 122°38E 309 F6
Baucau E. Timor 8°27S 126°27E 309 F7
Bauchi Nigeria 10°22N 9°48E 322 F7
Baudette U.S.A. 48°43N 94°36W 352 A6
Bauer, C. Australia 32°44S 134°4E 335 E1
Bauhinia Australia 24°35S 149°18E 334 C4
Baukau = Baucau E. Timor 8°27S 126°27E 309 F7
Bauld, C. Canada 51°38N 55°26W 341 D14
Bauru Brazil 22°10S 49°0W 367 A6
Bausi India 24°48N 87°1E 315 G12
Bauska Latvia 56°24N 24°15E 281 H21
Bautzen Germany 51°10N 14°26E 288 C8
Bavānāt Iran 30°28N 53°27E 317 D7
Bavaria = Bayern □ Germany 48°50N 12°0E 288 D6
Bavispe → Mexico 29°15N 109°11W 358 B3
Bawdwin Burma 23°5N 97°20E 313 H20
Bawean Indonesia 5°46S 112°35E 308 F4
Bawku Ghana 11°3N 0°19W 322 F5
Bawlake Burma 19°11N 97°21E 313 K20
Baxley U.S.A. 31°47N 82°21W 357 F13
Baxter U.S.A. 46°21N 94°17W 352 B6
Baxter Springs U.S.A. 37°2N 94°44W 352 G6
Baxter State ⌂ U.S.A. 46°5N 68°57W 353 B19
Bay City Mich., U.S.A. 43°36N 83°54W 353 D12
Bay City Tex., U.S.A. 28°59N 95°58W 356 G7
Bay Minette U.S.A. 30°53N 87°46W 357 F11
Bay Roberts Canada 47°36N 53°16W 345 C9
Bay St. Louis U.S.A. 30°19N 89°20W 357 F10
Bay Springs U.S.A. 31°59N 89°17W 357 F10
Bay View N.Z. 39°25S 176°50E 331 C6
Baya Dem. Rep. of the Congo 11°53S 27°25E 327 E2
Bayamo Cuba 20°20N 76°40W 360 B4
Bayamón Puerto Rico 18°24N 66°9W 361 d
Bayan Har Shan China 34°0N 98°0E 304 C4
Bayan Hot = Alxa Zuoqi China 38°50N 105°40E 306 E3
Bayan Lepas Malaysia 5°17N 100°16E 311 c
Bayan Obo China 41°52N 109°59E 306 D5
Bayan-Ovoo = Erdenetsogt Mongolia 42°55N 106°5E 306 C4
Bayana India 26°55N 77°18E 314 F7
Bayanaūyl Kazakhstan 50°45N 75°45E 300 D8
Bayandalay Mongolia 43°30N 103°29E 306 C2
Bayanhongor Mongolia 46°8N 102°43E 304 B5
Bayard N. Mex., U.S.A. 32°46N 108°8W 349 K9
Bayard Nebr., U.S.A. 41°45N 103°20W 352 E2
Baybay Phil. 10°40N 124°55E 309 B6
Baydhabo = Baidoa Somali Rep. 3°8N 43°30E 319 G3
Bayern □ Germany 48°50N 12°0E 288 D6
Bayeux France 49°17N 0°42W 292 B3
Bayfield Canada 43°34N 81°42W 354 C3
Bayfield U.S.A. 46°49N 90°49W 352 B8
Bayındır Turkey 38°13N 27°39E 295 E12
Baykal, Oz. Russia 53°0N 108°0E 301 D11
Baykan Turkey 38°7N 41°44E 316 B4
Baymak Russia 52°36N 58°19E 290 D10
Baynes Mts. Namibia 17°15S 13°0E 328 B1
Bayombong Phil. 16°30N 121°10E 309 A6
Bayonne France 43°30N 1°28W 292 E3
Bayonne U.S.A. 40°40N 74°6W 355 F10
Bayovar Peru 5°50S 81°0W 364 E2
Bayqongyr Kazakhstan 45°40N 63°20E 300 E7
Bayram-Ali = Baýramaly Turkmenistan 37°37N 62°10E 317 B9
Baýramaly Turkmenistan 37°37N 62°10E 317 B9
Bayramiç Turkey 39°48N 26°36E 295 E12
Bayreuth Germany 49°56N 11°35E 288 D6
Bayrūt Lebanon 33°53N 35°31E 318 B4
Bays, L. of Canada 45°15N 79°4W 354 A5
Baysville Canada 45°9N 79°7W 354 A5
Bayt Lahm West Bank 31°43N 35°12E 318 D4
Baytown U.S.A. 29°43N 94°59W 356 G7
Bayun Indonesia 8°11S 115°16E 309 J18
Baza Spain 37°30N 2°47W 293 D4
Bazaruto, I. do Mozam. 21°40S 35°28E 329 C6
Bazaruto △ Mozam. 21°42S 35°26E 329 C6
Bazhou China 39°8N 116°22E 306 E9
Bazmān, Kūh-e Iran 28°4N 60°1E 317 D9
Beach U.S.A. 46°58N 104°0W 352 B2
Beach City U.S.A. 40°39N 81°35W 354 F3
Beachport Australia 37°29S 140°0E 335 F3
Beachy Hd. U.K. 50°44N 0°15E 285 G8
Beacon Australia 30°26S 117°52E 333 F2
Beacon U.S.A. 41°30N 73°58W 355 E11
Beaconsfield Australia 41°11S 146°48E 335 G4
Beagle, Canal S. Amer. 55°0S 68°30W 368 H3
Beagle Bay Australia 16°58S 122°40E 332 C3
Bealanana Madag. 14°33S 48°44E 329 A8
Beals Cr. → U.S.A. 32°10N 100°51W 356 E4
Beamsville = Lincoln Canada 43°12N 79°28W 354 C5
Bear → Calif., U.S.A. 38°56N 121°36W 350 G5
Bear → Utah, U.S.A. 41°30N 112°8W 346 B4
Bear I. Ireland 51°38N 9°50W 282 E2
Bear L. Canada 55°8N 96°0W 343 B9
Bear L. U.S.A. 41°59N 111°21W 348 F8
Beardmore Canada 49°36N 87°57W 344 C2
Beardmore Glacier Antarctica 84°30S 170°0E 277 E11
Beardstown U.S.A. 40°1N 90°26W 352 E8
Bearma → India 24°20N 79°51E 315 G8
Béarn France 43°20N 0°30W 292 E3
Bearpaw Mts. U.S.A. 48°12N 109°30W 348 B9
Bearskin Lake Canada 53°58N 91°2W 344 B1
Beas → India 31°10N 74°59E 314 D6
Beata, C. Dom. Rep. 17°40N 71°30W 361 C5
Beata, I. Dom. Rep. 17°34N 71°31W 361 C5
Beatrice U.S.A. 40°16N 96°45W 352 E5
Beatrice Zimbabwe 18°15S 30°55E 327 F3
Beatrice, C. Australia 14°20S 136°55E 334 A2
Beatton → Canada 56°15N 120°45W 342 B4
Beatton River Canada 57°26N 121°20W 342 B4
Beatty U.S.A. 36°54N 116°46W 350 J10
Beau Bassin Mauritius 20°13S 57°27E 325 d
Beauce, Plaine de la France 48°10N 1°45E 292 B4
Beauceville Canada 46°13N 70°46W 345 C5
Beaudesert Australia 27°59S 153°0E 335 D5
Beaufort Malaysia 5°30N 115°40E 308 C5
Beaufort N.C., U.S.A. 34°43N 76°40W 357 D16
Beaufort S.C., U.S.A. 32°26N 80°40W 357 E14
Beaufort Sea Arctic 72°0N 140°0W 338 B5
Beaufort West S. Africa 32°18S 22°36E 328 E3
Beauharnois Canada 45°20N 73°52W 355 A11
Beaulieu → Canada 62°3N 113°11W 342 A6
Beauly U.K. 57°30N 4°28W 283 D4
Beauly → U.K. 57°29N 4°27W 283 D4
Beaumaris U.K. 53°16N 4°6W 284 D3
Beaumont Belgium 50°15N 4°14E 287 D4
Beaumont U.S.A. 30°5N 94°6W 356 F7
Beaune France 47°2N 4°50E 292 C6
Beaupré Canada 47°3N 70°54W 345 C5
Beauraing Belgium 50°7N 4°57E 287 D4
Beausejour Canada 50°5N 96°35W 343 C9
Beauvais France 49°25N 2°8E 292 B5
Beauval Canada 55°9N 107°37W 343 B7
Beaver Okla., U.S.A. 36°49N 100°31W 356 C4
Beaver Pa., U.S.A. 40°42N 80°19W 354 F4
Beaver Utah, U.S.A. 38°17N 112°38W 348 G7
Beaver → B.C., Canada 59°52N 124°20W 342 B4
Beaver → Ont., Canada 55°55N 87°48W 344 A2
Beaver → Sask., Canada 55°26N 107°45W 343 B7
Beaver → U.S.A. 36°35N 99°30W 356 C5
Beaver City U.S.A. 40°8N 99°50W 352 E4
Beaver Creek Canada 63°0N 141°0W 340 C5
Beaver Dam U.S.A. 43°28N 88°50W 352 D9
Beaver Falls U.S.A. 40°46N 80°20W 354 F4
Beaver Hill L. Canada 54°5N 94°50W 343 C10
Beaver I. U.S.A. 45°40N 85°33W 353 C11
Beavercreek U.S.A. 39°43N 84°11W 353 F11
Beaverhill L. Canada 53°27N 112°32W 342 C6
Beaverlodge Canada 55°11N 119°29W 342 B5
Beaverstone → Canada 54°59N 89°25W 344 B2
Beaverton Canada 44°26N 79°9W 354 B5
Beaverton U.S.A. 45°29N 122°48W 350 E4
Beawar India 26°3N 74°18E 314 F6
Bebedouro Brazil 21°0S 48°25W 367 A6
Bebera, Tanjung Indonesia 8°44S 115°51E 309 K18
Beboa Madag. 17°22S 44°33E 329 B7
Becán Mexico 18°34N 89°31W 359 D7
Bécancour Canada 46°20N 72°26W 353 B17
Beccles U.K. 52°27N 1°35E 285 E9
Bečej Serbia 45°36N 20°3E 295 B9
Béchar Algeria 31°38N 2°18W 322 B5
Beckley U.S.A. 37°47N 81°11W 353 G13
Beddouza, Ras Morocco 32°33N 9°9W 322 B4
Bedford Canada 45°7N 72°59W 355 A12
Bedford S. Africa 32°40S 26°10E 328 E4
Bedford U.K. 52°8N 0°28W 285 E7
Bedford Ind., U.S.A. 38°52N 86°29W 352 F10
Bedford Iowa, U.S.A. 40°40N 94°44W 352 E6
Bedford Ohio, U.S.A. 41°23N 81°32W 354 E3
Bedford Pa., U.S.A. 40°1N 78°30W 354 F6
Bedford Va., U.S.A. 37°20N 79°31W 353 G14
Bedford, C. Australia 15°14S 145°21E 334 B4
Bedfordshire □ U.K. 52°4N 0°28W 285 E7
Bedok Singapore 1°19N 103°56E 311 d
Bedourie Australia 24°30S 139°30E 334 C2
Bedum Neths. 53°18N 6°36E 287 A6
Beebe Plain Canada 45°1N 72°9W 355 A12
Beech Creek U.S.A. 41°5N 77°36W 354 E7
Beechy Canada 50°53N 107°24W 343 C7
Beef I. Br. Virgin Is. 18°26N 64°30W 361 e
Beenleigh Australia 27°43S 153°10E 335 D5
Be'er Menuḥa Israel 30°19N 35°8E 316 D2
Be'er Sheva Israel 31°15N 34°48E 318 D3
Beersheba = Be'er Sheva Israel 31°15N 34°48E 318 D3
Beestekraal S. Africa 25°23S 27°38E 329 D4
Beeston U.K. 52°56N 1°14W 284 E6
Beeville U.S.A. 28°24N 97°45W 356 G6
Befale Dem. Rep. of the Congo 0°25N 20°45E 324 D4
Befandriana Mahajanga, Madag. 15°16S 48°32E 329 B8
Befandriana Toliara, Madag. 21°55S 44°0E 329 C7
Befasy Madag. 20°33S 44°23E 329 C7
Befotaka Antsiranana, Madag. 13°15S 48°16E 329 A8
Befotaka Fianarantsoa, Madag. 23°49S 47°0E 329 C8
Bega Australia 36°41S 149°51E 335 F4
Begusarai India 25°24N 86°9E 315 G12
Behābād Iran 32°24N 59°47E 317 C8
Behala India 22°30N 88°18E 315 H13
Behara Madag. 24°55S 46°20E 329 C8
Behbehān Iran 30°30N 50°15E 317 D6
Behm Canal U.S.A. 55°10N 131°0W 342 B2
Behshahr Iran 36°45N 53°35E 317 B7
Bei Jiang → China 23°2N 112°58E 305 D6
Bei'an China 48°10N 126°20E 305 B7
Beihai China 21°28N 109°6E 305 D5
Beijing China 39°53N 116°21E 306 E9
Beijing □ China 39°55N 116°20E 306 E9
Beilen Neths. 52°52N 6°27E 287 B6
Beilpajah Australia 32°54S 143°52E 335 E3
Beinn na Faoghla = Benbecula U.K. 57°26N 7°21W 283 D1
Beipiao China 41°52N 120°32E 307 D11
Beira Mozam. 19°50S 34°52E 327 F3
Beirut = Bayrūt Lebanon 33°53N 35°31E 318 B4
Beiseker Canada 51°23N 113°32W 342 C6
Beit Lekhem = Bayt Lahm West Bank 31°43N 35°12E 318 D4
Beitaolaizhao China 44°58N 125°58E 307 B13
Beitbridge Zimbabwe 22°12S 30°0E 327 G3
Beizhen = Binzhou China 37°20N 118°2E 307 F10
Beizhen China 41°38N 121°54E 307 D11
Beizhengzhen China 44°31N 123°30E 307 B12
Beja Portugal 38°2N 7°53W 293 C2
Béja Tunisia 36°43N 9°12E 323 A7
Bejaïa Algeria 36°42N 5°2E 322 A7
Béjar Spain 40°23N 5°46W 293 B3
Bejestān Iran 34°30N 58°5E 317 C8
Bekaa Valley = Al Biqā Lebanon 34°10N 36°10E 318 A5
Békéscsaba Hungary 46°40N 21°5E 289 E11
Bekily Madag. 24°13S 45°19E 329 C8
Bekisopa Madag. 21°40S 45°54E 329 C8
Bekitro Madag. 24°33S 45°18E 329 C8
Bekodoka Madag. 16°58S 45°7E 329 B8
Bekok Malaysia 2°20N 103°7E 311 L4
Bekopaka Madag. 19°9S 44°48E 329 B7
Bekuli Indonesia 8°22S 114°13E 309 J17
Bela India 25°50N 82°0E 315 G10
Bela Pakistan 26°12N 66°20E 314 F2
Bela Bela S. Africa 24°51S 28°19E 329 C4
Bela Crkva Serbia 44°55N 21°27E 295 B9
Bela Vista Brazil 22°12S 56°20W 366 A4
Bela Vista Mozam. 26°10S 32°44E 329 D5

Belan → *India* 24°2N 81°45E **315** G9
Belarus ■ *Europe* 53°30N 27°0E **289** B14
Belau = Palau ■ *Palau* 7°30N 134°30E **330** A6
Belavenona *Madag.* 24°50S 47°4E **329** C8
Belawan *Indonesia* 3°33N 98°32E **308** D1
Belaya → *Russia* 54°40N 56°0E **290** C9
Belaya Tserkov = Bila Tserkva *Ukraine* 49°45N 30°10E **289** D16
Belcher Chan. *Canada* 77°15N 95°0W **341** B10
Belcher Is. *Canada* 56°15N 78°45W **344** A3
Belden *U.S.A.* 40°2N 121°17W **350** E5
Belebey *Russia* 54°7N 54°7E **290** D9
Beled Weyne = Belet Uen *Somali Rep.* 4°30N 45°5E **319** G4
Belém *Brazil* 1°20S 48°30W **365** D9
Belén *Argentina* 27°40S 67°5W **366** B2
Belén *Paraguay* 23°30S 57°6W **366** A4
Belen *U.S.A.* 34°40N 106°46W **349** J10
Belet Uen *Somali Rep.* 4°30N 45°5E **319** G4
Belev *Russia* 53°50N 36°5E **290** D6
Belfair *U.S.A.* 47°27N 122°50W **350** C4
Belfast *S. Africa* 25°42S 30°2E **329** D5
Belfast *U.K.* 54°37N 5°56W **282** B6
Belfast *Maine, U.S.A.* 44°26N 69°1W **353** C19
Belfast *N.Y., U.S.A.* 42°21N 78°7W **354** D6
Belfast L. *U.K.* 54°40N 5°50W **282** B6
Belfield *U.S.A.* 46°53N 103°12W **352** B2
Belfort *France* 47°38N 6°50E **292** C7
Belfry *U.S.A.* 45°9N 109°1W **348** D9
Belgaum *India* 15°55N 74°35E **312** M9
Belgium ■ *Europe* 50°30N 5°0E **287** D4
Belgorod *Russia* 50°35N 36°35E **291** D6
Belgorod-Dnestrovskiy = Bilhorod-Dnistrovskyy *Ukraine* 46°11N 30°23E **291** E5
Belgrade = Beograd *Serbia* 44°50N 20°37E **295** B9
Belgrade *U.S.A.* 45°47N 111°11W **348** D8
Belgrano *Antarctica* 77°52S 34°37W **277** D1
Belhaven *U.S.A.* 35°33N 76°37W **357** D16
Beli Drim → *Europe* 42°6N 20°25E **295** C9
Belimbing *Indonesia* 8°24S 115°2E **309** J18
Belinyu *Indonesia* 1°35S 105°50E **308** E3
Beliton Is. = Belitung *Indonesia* 3°10S 107°50E **308** E3
Belitung *Indonesia* 3°10S 107°50E **308** E3
Belize ■ *Cent. Amer.* 17°0N 88°30W **359** D7
Belize City *Belize* 17°25N 88°10W **359** D7
Belkovskiy, Ostrov *Russia* 75°32N 135°44E **301** B14
Bell → *Canada* 49°48N 77°38W **344** C4
Bell I. *Canada* 50°46N 55°35W **345** B8
Bell-Irving → *Canada* 56°12N 129°5W **342** B3
Bell Peninsula *Canada* 63°50N 82°0W **341** C11
Bell Ville *Argentina* 32°40S 62°40W **366** C3
Bella Bella *Canada* 52°10N 128°10W **342** C3
Bella Coola *Canada* 52°25N 126°40W **342** C3
Bella Unión *Uruguay* 30°15S 57°40W **366** C4
Bella Vista *Corrientes, Argentina* 28°33S 59°0W **366** B4
Bella Vista *Tucuman, Argentina* 27°10S 65°25W **366** B2
Bellaire *U.S.A.* 40°1N 80°45W **354** F4
Bellary *India* 15°10N 76°56E **312** M10
Bellata *Australia* 29°53S 149°46E **335** D4
Belle Fourche *U.S.A.* 44°40N 103°51W **352** C2
Belle Fourche → *U.S.A.* 44°26N 102°18W **346** B6
Belle Glade *U.S.A.* 26°41N 80°40W **357** H14
Belle-Île *France* 47°20N 3°10W **292** C2
Belle Isle *Canada* 51°57N 55°25W **345** B8
Belle Isle, Str. of *Canada* 51°30N 56°30W **345** B8
Belle Plaine *U.S.A.* 41°54N 92°17W **352** E7
Bellefontaine *U.S.A.* 40°22N 83°46W **353** E12
Bellefonte *U.S.A.* 40°55N 77°47W **354** F7
Belleoram *Canada* 47°31N 55°25W **345** C8
Belleplaine *Barbados* 13°15N 59°34W **361** g
Belleville *Canada* 44°10N 77°23W **354** B7
Belleville *Ill., U.S.A.* 38°31N 89°59W **352** F9
Belleville *Kans., U.S.A.* 39°50N 97°38W **352** F5
Belleville *N.J., U.S.A.* 40°47N 74°9W **355** F10
Belleville *N.Y., U.S.A.* 43°46N 76°10W **355** C8
Bellevue *Canada* 49°35N 114°22W **342** D6
Bellevue *Idaho, U.S.A.* 43°28N 114°16W **348** E6
Bellevue *Nebr., U.S.A.* 41°9N 95°54W **352** E6
Bellevue *Ohio, U.S.A.* 41°17N 82°51W **354** E2
Bellevue *Wash., U.S.A.* 47°37N 122°12W **350** C4
Bellin = Kangirsuk *Canada* 60°0N 70°0W **341** D13
Bellingen *Australia* 30°25S 152°50E **335** E5
Bellingham *U.S.A.* 48°46N 122°29W **350** B4
Bellingshausen Abyssal Plain *S. Ocean* 64°0S 90°0W **277** C16
Bellingshausen Sea *Antarctica* 66°0S 80°0W **277** C17
Bellinzona *Switz.* 46°11N 9°1E **292** C8
Bello *Colombia* 6°20N 75°33W **364** B3
Bellows Falls *U.S.A.* 43°8N 72°27W **355** C12
Bellpat *Pakistan* 29°0N 68°5E **314** E3
Belluno *Italy* 46°9N 12°13E **294** A5
Bellwood *U.S.A.* 40°36N 78°20W **354** F6
Belmont *Canada* 42°53N 81°5W **354** D3
Belmont *S. Africa* 29°28S 24°22E **328** D3
Belmont *U.S.A.* 42°14N 78°2W **354** D6
Belmonte *Brazil* 16°0S 39°0W **365** G11
Belmopan *Belize* 17°18N 88°30W **359** D7
Belmullet *Ireland* 54°14N 9°58W **282** B2
Belo Horizonte *Brazil* 19°55S 43°56W **365** G10
Belo-sur-Mer *Madag.* 20°42S 44°0E **329** C7
Belo-Tsiribihina *Madag.* 19°40S 44°30E **329** B7
Belogorsk *Russia* 51°0N 128°20E **301** D13
Beloha *Madag.* 25°10S 45°3E **329** D8
Beloit *Kans., U.S.A.* 39°28N 98°6W **352** F4
Beloit *Wis., U.S.A.* 42°31N 89°2W **352** D9
Belokorovichi *Ukraine* 51°7N 28°2E **289** C15
Belomorsk *Russia* 64°35N 34°54E **290** B5
Belonia *India* 23°15N 91°30E **313** H17
Beloretsk *Russia* 53°58N 58°24E **290** D10
Belorussia = Belarus ■ *Europe* 53°30N 27°0E **289** B14
Belovo *Russia* 54°30N 86°0E **300** D9
Beloye, Ozero *Russia* 60°10N 37°35E **290** B6
Beloye More *Russia* 66°30N 38°0E **280** C25
Belozersk *Russia* 60°1N 37°45E **290** B6
Belpre *U.S.A.* 39°17N 81°34W **353** F13
Belrain *India* 28°23N 80°55E **315** E9
Belt *U.S.A.* 47°23N 110°55W **348** C8
Beltana *Australia* 30°48S 138°25E **335** E2
Belterra *Brazil* 2°45S 55°0W **365** D8
Belton *U.S.A.* 31°3N 97°28W **356** F6
Belton L. *U.S.A.* 31°6N 97°28W **356** F6
Beltsy = Bălţi *Moldova* 47°48N 27°58E **289** E14
Belturbet *Ireland* 54°6N 7°26W **282** B4
Belukha *Russia* 49°50N 86°50E **300** E9
Beluran *Malaysia* 5°48N 117°35E **308** C5
Belvidere *Ill., U.S.A.* 42°15N 88°50W **352** D9
Belvidere *N.J., U.S.A.* 40°50N 75°5W **355** F9
Belyando → *Australia* 21°38S 146°50E **334** C4
Belyy, Ostrov *Russia* 73°30N 71°0E **300** B8
Belyy Yar *Russia* 58°26N 84°39E **300** D9
Belzoni *U.S.A.* 33°11N 90°29W **357** E9
Bemaraha, Lembalemban' i *Madag.* 18°40S 44°45E **329** B7
Bemarivo *Madag.* 21°45S 44°45E **329** C7
Bemarivo → *Antsiranana, Madag.* 14°9S 50°9E **329** A9
Bemarivo → *Mahajanga, Madag.* 15°27S 47°40E **329** B8
Bemavo *Madag.* 21°33S 45°25E **329** C8
Bembéréke *Benin* 10°11N 2°43E **322** F6
Bembesi *Zimbabwe* 20°0S 28°58E **327** G2
Bembesi → *Zimbabwe* 18°57S 27°47E **327** F2
Bemetara *India* 21°42N 81°32E **315** J9
Bemidji *U.S.A.* 47°28N 94°53W **352** B6
Bemolanga *Madag.* 17°44S 45°6E **329** B8
Ben *Iran* 32°32N 50°45E **317** C6
Ben Cruachan *U.K.* 56°26N 5°8W **283** E3
Ben Dearg *U.K.* 57°47N 4°56W **283** D4
Ben En △ *Vietnam* 19°37N 105°30E **310** C5
Ben Gardane *Tunisia* 33°11N 11°11E **323** B8
Ben Hope *U.K.* 58°25N 4°36W **283** C4
Ben Lawers *U.K.* 56°32N 4°14W **283** E4
Ben Lomond *N.S.W., Australia* 30°1S 151°43E **335** E5
Ben Lomond *Tas., Australia* 41°38S 147°42E **335** G4
Ben Lomond *U.K.* 56°11N 4°38W **283** E4
Ben Lomond △ *Australia* 41°33S 147°39E **335** G4
Ben Luc *Vietnam* 10°39N 106°29E **311** G6
Ben Macdhui *U.K.* 57°4N 3°40W **283** D5
Ben Mhor *U.K.* 57°15N 7°18W **283** D1
Ben More *Argyll & Bute, U.K.* 56°26N 6°1W **283** E2
Ben More *Stirling, U.K.* 56°23N 4°32W **283** E4
Ben More Assynt *U.K.* 58°8N 4°52W **283** C4
Ben Nevis *U.K.* 56°48N 5°1W **283** E3
Ben Quang *Vietnam* 17°3N 106°55E **310** D6
Ben Vorlich *U.K.* 56°21N 4°14W **283** E4
Ben Wyvis *U.K.* 57°40N 4°35W **283** D4
Bena *Nigeria* 11°20N 5°50E **322** F7
Benalla *Australia* 36°30S 146°0E **335** F4
Benares = Varanasi *India* 25°22N 83°0E **315** G10
Benavente *Spain* 42°2N 5°43W **293** A3
Benavides *U.S.A.* 27°36N 98°25W **356** H5
Benbecula *U.K.* 57°26N 7°21W **283** D1
Benbonyathe Hill *Australia* 30°25S 139°11E **335** E2
Bend *U.S.A.* 44°4N 121°19W **348** D3
Bender Beila *Somali Rep.* 9°30N 50°48E **319** F5
Bendery = Tighina *Moldova* 46°50N 29°30E **289** E15
Bendigo *Australia* 36°40S 144°15E **335** F3
Benē Beraq *Israel* 32°6N 34°51E **318** C3
Benenitra *Madag.* 23°27S 45°5E **329** C8
Benevento *Italy* 41°8N 14°45E **294** D6
Benga *Mozam.* 16°11S 33°40E **327** F3
Bengal, Bay of *Ind. Oc.* 15°0N 90°0E **313** M17
Bengalûru = Bangalore *India* 12°59N 77°40E **312** N10
Bengbu *China* 32°58N 117°20E **307** H9
Benghazi = Banghāzī *Libya* 32°11N 20°3E **323** B10
Bengkalis *Indonesia* 1°30N 102°10E **308** D2
Bengkulu *Indonesia* 3°50S 102°12E **308** E2
Bengkulu □ *Indonesia* 3°48S 102°16E **308** E2
Bengough *Canada* 49°25N 105°10W **343** D7
Benguela *Angola* 12°37S 13°25E **325** G2
Benguérua, I. *Mozam.* 21°58S 35°28E **329** C6
Beni *Dem. Rep. of the Congo* 0°30N 29°27E **326** B2
Beni → *Bolivia* 10°23S 65°24W **364** F5
Beni Mellal *Morocco* 32°21N 6°21W **322** B4
Beni Suef *Egypt* 29°5N 31°6E **323** C12
Beniah L. *Canada* 63°23N 112°17W **342** A6
Benidorm *Spain* 38°33N 0°9W **293** C5
Benin ■ *Africa* 10°0N 2°0E **322** G6
Benin, Bight of *W. Afr.* 5°0N 3°0E **322** H6
Benin City *Nigeria* 6°20N 5°31E **322** G7
Benitses *Greece* 39°32N 19°55E **297** A3
Benjamin Aceval *Paraguay* 24°58S 57°34W **366** A4
Benjamin Constant *Brazil* 4°40S 70°15W **364** D4
Benjamín Hill *Mexico* 30°9N 111°7W **358** A2
Benkelman *U.S.A.* 40°3N 101°32W **352** E3
Bennett *Canada* 59°51N 135°0W **342** B2
Bennett, L. *Australia* 22°50S 131°2E **332** D5
Bennetta, Ostrov *Russia* 76°21N 148°56E **301** B15
Bennettsville *U.S.A.* 34°37N 79°41W **357** D15
Bennington *N.H., U.S.A.* 43°0N 71°55W **355** D11
Bennington *Vt., U.S.A.* 42°53N 73°12W **355** D11
Benoni *S. Africa* 26°11S 28°18E **329** D4
Benque Viejo *Belize* 17°5N 89°8W **359** D7
Benson *Ariz., U.S.A.* 31°58N 110°18W **349** L8
Benson *Minn., U.S.A.* 45°19N 95°36W **352** C6
Bent *Iran* 26°20N 59°31E **317** E8
Benteng *Indonesia* 6°10S 120°30E **309** F6
Bentinck I. *Australia* 17°3S 139°35E **334** B2
Bento Gonçalves *Brazil* 29°10S 51°31W **367** B5
Benton *Ark., U.S.A.* 34°34N 92°35W **356** D8
Benton *Calif., U.S.A.* 37°48N 118°32W **350** H8
Benton *Ill., U.S.A.* 38°0N 88°55W **352** F9
Benton *Pa., U.S.A.* 41°12N 76°23W **355** E8
Benton Harbor *U.S.A.* 42°6N 86°27W **352** D10
Bentong *Malaysia* 3°31N 101°55E **311** L3
Bentonville *U.S.A.* 36°22N 94°13W **356** C7
Benue → *Nigeria* 7°48N 6°46E **322** G7
Benxi *China* 41°20N 123°48E **307** D12
Beo *Indonesia* 4°25N 126°50E **309** D7
Beograd *Serbia* 44°50N 20°37E **295** B9
Beolgyo *S. Korea* 34°51N 127°21E **307** G14
Beppu *Japan* 33°15N 131°30E **303** H5
Beqa *Fiji* 18°23S 178°8E **331** a
Beqaa Valley = Al Biqā *Lebanon* 34°10N 36°10E **318** A5
Ber Mota *India* 23°27N 68°34E **314** H3
Berach → *India* 25°15N 75°2E **314** G6
Beraketa *Madag.* 23°7S 44°25E **329** C7
Berat *Albania* 40°43N 19°59E **295** D8
Berau, Teluk *Indonesia* 2°30S 132°30E **309** E8
Beravina *Madag.* 18°10S 45°14E **329** B8
Berber *Sudan* 18°0N 34°0E **323** E12
Berbera *Somali Rep.* 10°30N 45°2E **319** E4
Berbérati *C.A.R.* 4°15N 15°40E **324** D3
Berbice → *Guyana* 6°20N 57°32W **364** B7
Berdichev = Berdychiv *Ukraine* 49°57N 28°30E **289** D15
Berdsk *Russia* 54°47N 83°2E **300** D9
Berdyansk *Ukraine* 46°45N 36°50E **291** E6
Berdychiv *Ukraine* 49°57N 28°30E **289** D15
Berea *U.S.A.* 37°34N 84°17W **353** G11
Berebere *Indonesia* 2°25N 128°45E **309** D7
Bereda *Somali Rep.* 11°45N 51°0E **319** E5
Berehove *Ukraine* 48°15N 22°35E **289** D12
Bereket *Turkmenistan* 39°16N 55°32E **317** B7
Berekum *Ghana* 7°29N 2°34W **322** G5
Berens → *Canada* 52°25N 97°2W **343** C9
Berens I. *Canada* 52°18N 97°18W **343** C9
Berens River *Canada* 52°25N 97°0W **343** C9
Beresford *U.S.A.* 43°5N 96°47W **352** D5
Berestechko *Ukraine* 50°22N 25°5E **289** C13
Berevo *Mahajanga, Madag.* 17°14S 44°17E **329** B7
Berevo *Toliara, Madag.* 19°44S 44°58E **329** B7
Berezhany *Ukraine* 49°26N 24°58E **289** D13
Berezina = Byarezina → *Belarus* 52°33N 30°14E **289** B16
Bereznik *Russia* 62°51N 42°40E **290** B7
Berezniki *Russia* 59°24N 56°46E **290** C10
Berezovo *Russia* 64°0N 65°0E **300** C7
Berga *Spain* 42°6N 1°48E **293** A6
Bergama *Turkey* 39°8N 27°11E **295** E12
Bérgamo *Italy* 45°41N 9°43E **292** D8
Bergen *Neths.* 52°40N 4°43E **287** B4
Bergen *Norway* 60°20N 5°20E **280** F11
Bergen *U.S.A.* 43°5N 77°57W **354** C7
Bergen op Zoom *Neths.* 51°28N 4°18E **287** C4
Bergerac *France* 44°51N 0°30E **292** D4
Bergholz *U.S.A.* 40°31N 80°53W **354** F4
Bergisch Gladbach *Germany* 50°59N 7°8E **287** D7
Bergville *S. Africa* 28°52S 29°18E **329** D4
Berhala, Selat *Indonesia* 1°0S 104°15E **308** E2
Berhampore = Baharampur *India* 24°2N 88°27E **315** G13
Berhampur = Brahmapur *India* 19°15N 84°54E **313** K14
Bering Sea *Pac. Oc.* 58°0N 171°0W **346** a
Bering Strait *Pac. Oc.* 65°30N 169°0W **346** a
Beringovskiy *Russia* 63°3N 179°19E **301** C18
Berisso *Argentina* 34°56S 57°50W **366** C4
Berja *Spain* 36°50N 2°56W **293** D4
Berkeley *U.S.A.* 37°51N 122°16W **350** H4
Berkner I. *Antarctica* 79°30S 50°0W **277** D18
Berkshire *U.S.A.* 42°19N 76°11W **355** D8
Berkshire Downs *U.K.* 51°33N 1°29W **285** F6
Berlin *Germany* 52°31N 13°23E **288** B7
Berlin *Md., U.S.A.* 38°20N 75°13W **353** F16
Berlin *N.H., U.S.A.* 44°28N 71°11W **355** B13
Berlin *N.Y., U.S.A.* 42°42N 73°23W **355** D11
Berlin *Wis., U.S.A.* 43°58N 88°57W **352** D9
Berlin L. *U.S.A.* 41°3N 81°0W **354** E4
Bermejo → *Formosa, Argentina* 26°51S 58°23W **366** B4
Bermejo → *San Juan, Argentina* 32°30S 67°30W **366** C2
Bermen, L. *Canada* 53°35N 68°55W **345** B6
Bermuda ☑ *Atl. Oc.* 32°45N 65°0W **339** F13
Bern *Switz.* 46°57N 7°28E **292** C7
Bernalillo *U.S.A.* 35°18N 106°33W **349** J10
Bernardo de Irigoyen *Argentina* 26°15S 53°40W **367** B5
Bernardo O'Higgins □ *Chile* 34°15S 70°45W **366** C1
Bernardsville *U.S.A.* 40°43N 74°34W **355** F10
Bernasconi *Argentina* 37°55S 63°44W **366** D3
Bernburg *Germany* 51°47N 11°44E **288** C6
Berne = Bern *Switz.* 46°57N 7°28E **292** C7
Berneray *U.K.* 57°43N 7°11W **283** D1
Bernier I. *Australia* 24°50S 113°12E **333** D1
Bernina, Piz *Switz.* 46°20N 9°54E **292** C8
Beroroha *Madag.* 21°40S 45°10E **329** C8
Beroun *Czech Rep.* 49°57N 14°5E **288** D8
Berri *Australia* 34°14S 140°35E **335** E3
Berriane *Algeria* 32°50N 3°46E **322** B6
Berry *Australia* 34°46S 150°43E **335** E5
Berry *France* 46°50N 2°0E **292** C5
Berry Is. *Bahamas* 25°40N 77°50W **360** A4
Berryessa, L. *U.S.A.* 38°31N 122°6W **350** G4
Berryville *U.S.A.* 36°22N 93°34W **356** C8
Berseba *Namibia* 26°0S 17°46E **328** D2
Bershad *Ukraine* 48°22N 29°31E **289** D15
Berthold *U.S.A.* 48°19N 101°44W **352** A3
Berthoud *U.S.A.* 40°19N 105°5W **348** F11
Bertoua *Cameroon* 4°30N 13°45E **324** D2
Bertraghboy B. *Ireland* 53°22N 9°54W **282** C2
Berwick *U.S.A.* 41°3N 76°14W **355** E8
Berwick-upon-Tweed *U.K.* 55°46N 2°0W **284** B6
Berwyn Mts. *U.K.* 52°54N 3°26W **284** E4
Besal *Pakistan* 35°4N 73°56E **315** B5
Besalampy *Madag.* 16°43S 44°29E **329** B7
Besançon *France* 47°15N 6°2E **292** C7
Besar *Indonesia* 2°40S 116°0E **308** E5
Besnard L. *Canada* 55°25N 106°0W **343** B7
Besni *Turkey* 37°41N 37°52E **316** B3
Besor, N. → *Egypt* 31°28N 34°22E **318** D3
Bessarabiya *Moldova* 47°0N 28°10E **289** E15
Bessarabka = Basarabeasca *Moldova* 46°21N 28°58E **289** E15
Bessemer *Ala., U.S.A.* 33°24N 86°58W **357** E11
Bessemer *Mich., U.S.A.* 46°29N 90°3W **352** B8
Bessemer *Pa., U.S.A.* 40°59N 80°30W **354** F4
Beswick *Australia* 14°34S 132°53E **332** B5
Bet She'an *Israel* 32°30N 35°30E **318** C4
Bet Shemesh *Israel* 31°44N 35°0E **318** D4
Betafo *Madag.* 19°50S 46°51E **329** B8
Betancuria *Canary Is.* 28°25N 14°3W **296** F5
Betanzos *Spain* 43°15N 8°12W **293** A1
Bétaré Oya *Cameroon* 5°40N 14°5E **324** C2
Betatao *Madag.* 18°11S 47°52E **329** B8
Bethal *S. Africa* 26°27S 29°28E **329** D4
Bethanien *Namibia* 26°31S 17°8E **328** D2
Bethany *Canada* 44°11N 78°34W **354** B6
Bethany *Mo., U.S.A.* 40°16N 94°2W **352** E6
Bethany *Okla., U.S.A.* 35°31N 97°38W **356** D6
Bethel *Alaska, U.S.A.* 60°48N 161°45W **346** a
Bethel *Conn., U.S.A.* 41°22N 73°25W **355** E11
Bethel *Maine, U.S.A.* 44°25N 70°47W **355** B14
Bethel *Vt., U.S.A.* 43°50N 72°38W **355** C12
Bethel Park *U.S.A.* 40°19N 80°2W **354** F4
Bethlehem = Bayt Lahm *West Bank* 31°43N 35°12E **318** D4
Bethlehem *S. Africa* 28°14S 28°18E **329** D4
Bethlehem *U.S.A.* 40°37N 75°23W **355** F9
Bethulie *S. Africa* 30°30S 25°59E **328** E4
Béthune *France* 50°30N 2°38E **292** A5
Betioky *Madag.* 23°48S 44°20E **329** C7
Betong *Malaysia* 1°24N 111°31E **308** D4
Betong *Thailand* 5°45N 101°5E **311** K3
Betoota *Australia* 25°45S 140°42E **334** D3
Betpaqdala *Kazakhstan* 45°45N 70°30E **300** E8
Betroka *Madag.* 23°16S 46°0E **329** C8
Betsiamites *Canada* 48°56N 68°40W **345** C6
Betsiamites → *Canada* 48°56N 68°38W **345** C6
Betsiboka → *Madag.* 16°3S 46°36E **329** B8
Bettendorf *U.S.A.* 41°32N 90°30W **352** E8
Bettiah *India* 26°48N 84°33E **315** F11
Betul *India* 21°58N 77°59E **312** J10
Betws-y-Coed *U.K.* 53°5N 3°48W **284** D4
Beulah *Mich., U.S.A.* 44°38N 86°6W **352** C10
Beulah *N. Dak., U.S.A.* 47°16N 101°47W **352** B3
Beveren *Belgium* 51°12N 4°16E **287** C4
Beverley *Australia* 32°9S 116°56E **333** F2
Beverley *U.K.* 53°51N 0°26W **284** D7
Beverly *U.S.A.* 42°33N 70°53W **355** D14
Beverly Hills *Calif., U.S.A.* 34°5N 118°24W **351** L8
Beverly Hills *Fla., U.S.A.* 28°55N 82°28W **357** G13
Bevoalavo *Madag.* 25°13S 45°26E **329** D7
Bewas → *India* 23°59N 79°21E **315** H8
Bexhill *U.K.* 50°51N 0°29E **285** G8
Beyānlū *Iran* 36°0N 47°51E **316** C5
Beyneu *Kazakhstan* 45°18N 55°9E **291** E10
Beypazarı *Turkey* 40°10N 31°56E **291** F5
Beyşehir Gölü *Turkey* 37°41N 31°33E **316** B1
Béziers *France* 43°20N 3°12E **292** E5
Bezwada = Vijayawada *India* 16°31N 80°39E **313** L12
Bhabua *India* 25°3N 83°37E **315** G10
Bhachau *India* 23°20N 70°16E **312** H7
Bhadar → *Gujarat, India* 22°17N 72°20E **314** H5
Bhadar → *Gujarat, India* 21°27N 69°47E **314** J3
Bhadarwah *India* 32°58N 75°46E **315** C6
Bhadgaon = Bhaktapur *Nepal* 27°38N 85°24E **315** F11
Bhadohi *India* 25°25N 82°34E **315** G10
Bhadra *India* 29°8N 75°14E **314** E6
Bhadrakh *India* 21°10N 86°30E **313** J15
Bhadran *India* 22°19N 72°6E **314** H5
Bhadravati *India* 13°49N 75°40E **312** N9
Bhag *Pakistan* 29°2N 67°49E **314** E2
Bhagalpur *India* 25°10N 87°0E **315** G12
Bhagirathi → *Uttaranchal, India* 30°8N 78°35E **315** D8
Bhagirathi → *W. Bengal, India* 23°25N 88°23E **315** H13
Bhakkar *Pakistan* 31°40N 71°5E **314** D4
Bhakra Dam *India* 31°30N 76°45E **314** D7
Bhaktapur *Nepal* 27°38N 85°24E **315** F11
Bhamo *Burma* 24°15N 97°15E **313** G20
Bhandara *India* 21°5N 79°42E **312** J11
Bhanpura *India* 24°31N 75°44E **314** G6
Bhanrer Ra. *India* 23°40N 79°45E **315** H8
Bhaptiahi *India* 26°19N 86°44E **315** F12
Bharat = India ■ *Asia* 20°0N 78°0E **312** K11
Bharatpur *Chhattisgarh, India* 23°44N 81°46E **315** H9
Bharatpur *Raj., India* 27°15N 77°30E **314** F7
Bharno *India* 23°14N 84°53E **315** H11
Bharuch *India* 21°47N 73°0E **312** J8
Bhatinda *India* 30°15N 74°57E **314** D6
Bhatpara *India* 22°50N 88°25E **315** H13
Bhattu *India* 29°36N 75°19E **314** E6
Bhaun *Pakistan* 32°55N 72°40E **314** C5
Bhaunagar = Bhavnagar *India* 21°45N 72°10E **312** J8
Bhavnagar *India* 21°45N 72°10E **312** J8
Bhawari *India* 25°42N 73°4E **314** G5
Bhayavadar *India* 21°51N 70°15E **314** J4
Bhera *Pakistan* 32°29N 72°57E **314** C5
Bhikangaon *India* 21°52N 75°57E **314** J6
Bhilai = Bhilainagar-Durg *India* 21°13N 81°26E **313** J12
Bhilainagar-Durg *India* 21°13N 81°26E **313** J12
Bhilsa = Vidisha *India* 23°28N 77°53E **314** H7
Bhilwara *India* 25°25N 74°38E **314** G6
Bhima → *India* 16°25N 77°17E **312** L10
Bhimbar *Pakistan* 32°59N 74°3E **315** C6
Bhind *India* 26°30N 78°46E **315** F8
Bhinga *India* 27°43N 81°56E **315** F9
Bhinmal *India* 25°0N 72°15E **314** G5
Bhiwandi *India* 19°20N 73°0E **312** K8
Bhiwani *India* 28°50N 76°9E **314** E7
Bhogava → *India* 22°26N 72°20E **314** H5
Bhola *Bangla.* 22°45N 90°35E **313** H17
Bholari *Pakistan* 25°19N 68°13E **314** G3
Bhopal *India* 23°20N 77°30E **314** H7
Bhubaneshwar *India* 20°15N 85°50E **313** J14
Bhuj *India* 23°15N 69°49E **314** H3
Bhumiphol Res. *Thailand* 17°20N 98°40E **310** D2
Bhusawal *India* 21°3N 75°46E **312** J9
Bhutan ■ *Asia* 27°25N 90°30E **313** F17
Biafra, B. of = Bonny, Bight of *Africa* 3°30N 9°20E **324** D1
Biak *Indonesia* 1°10S 136°6E **309** E9
Biała Podlaska *Poland* 52°4N 23°6E **289** B12
Białogard *Poland* 54°2N 15°58E **288** A8
Białystok *Poland* 53°10N 23°10E **289** B12
Biaora *India* 23°56N 76°56E **314** H7
Bīārjmand *Iran* 36°6N 55°53E **317** B7
Biaro *Indonesia* 2°5N 125°26E **309** D7
Biarritz *France* 43°29N 1°33W **292** E3
Bias *Indonesia* 8°24S 115°36E **309** J18
Bibai *Japan* 43°19N 141°52E **302** C10
Bibby I. *Canada* 61°55N 93°0W **343** A10
Biberach *Germany* 48°5N 9°47E **288** D5
Bibungwa *Dem. Rep. of the Congo* 2°40S 28°15E **326** C2
Bicester *U.K.* 51°54N 1°9W **285** F6
Bicheno *Australia* 41°52S 148°18E **335** G4
Bichia *India* 22°27N 80°42E **315** H9
Bickerton I. *Australia* 13°45S 136°10E **334** A2
Bida *Nigeria* 9°3N 5°58E **322** G7
Bidar *India* 17°55N 77°35E **312** L10
Biddeford *U.S.A.* 43°30N 70°28W **353** D18
Bideford *U.K.* 51°1N 4°13W **285** F3
Bideford Bay *U.K.* 51°5N 4°20W **285** F3
Bidhuna *India* 26°49N 79°31E **315** F8
Bidor *Malaysia* 4°6N 101°15E **311** K3
Bidyadanga *Australia* 18°45S 121°43E **332** C3
Bié, Planalto de *Angola* 12°0S 16°0E **325** G3
Bieber *U.S.A.* 41°7N 121°8W **348** F3
Biel *Switz.* 47°8N 7°14E **292** C7
Bielefeld *Germany* 52°1N 8°33E **288** B5
Biella *Italy* 45°34N 8°3E **292** D8
Bielsk Podlaski *Poland* 52°47N 23°12E **289** B12
Bielsko-Biała *Poland* 49°50N 19°2E **289** D10
Bien Hoa *Vietnam* 10°57N 106°49E **311** G6
Bienne = Biel *Switz.* 47°8N 7°14E **292** C7
Bienville, L. *Canada* 55°5N 72°40W **344** A5
Biesiesfontein *S. Africa* 30°57S 17°58E **328** E2
Big → *Canada* 54°50N 58°55W **345** B8
Big B. *Canada* 55°43N 60°35W **345** A7
Big Bear City *U.S.A.* 34°16N 116°51W **351** L10
Big Bear Lake *U.S.A.* 34°15N 116°56W **351** L10
Big Belt Mts. *U.S.A.* 46°30N 111°25W **348** C8
Big Bend *Swaziland* 26°50S 31°58E **329** D5
Big Bend △ *U.S.A.* 29°20N 103°5W **356** G3
Big Blue → *U.S.A.* 39°35N 96°34W **352** F5
Big Creek *U.S.A.* 37°11N 119°14W **350** H7
Big Cypress ⌂ *U.S.A.* 26°0N 81°10W **357** H14
Big Desert *Australia* 35°45S 141°10E **335** F3
Big Falls *U.S.A.* 48°12N 93°48W **352** A7
Big Fork → *U.S.A.* 48°31N 93°43W **352** A7
Big Horn Mts. = Bighorn Mts. *U.S.A.* 44°25N 107°0W **348** D10
Big I. *Canada* 61°7N 116°45W **342** A5
Big Lake *U.S.A.* 31°12N 101°28W **356** F4
Big Moose *U.S.A.* 43°49N 74°58W **355** C10
Big Muddy Cr. → *U.S.A.* 48°8N 104°36W **348** B11
Big Pine *U.S.A.* 37°10N 118°17W **350** H8
Big Piney *U.S.A.* 42°32N 110°7W **348** E8
Big Rapids *U.S.A.* 43°42N 85°29W **353** D11
Big Rideau L. *Canada* 44°40N 76°15W **355** B8
Big River *Canada* 53°50N 107°0W **343** C7
Big Run *U.S.A.* 40°57N 78°55W **354** F6
Big Sable Pt. *U.S.A.* 44°3N 86°1W **352** C10
Big Salmon → *Canada* 61°52N 134°55W **342** A2
Big Sand L. *Canada* 57°45N 99°45W **343** B9
Big Sandy *U.S.A.* 48°11N 110°7W **348** B8
Big Sandy → *U.S.A.* 38°25N 82°36W **353** F12
Big Sandy Cr. = Sandy Cr. → *U.S.A.* 41°51N 109°47W **348** F9
Big Sandy Cr. → *U.S.A.* 38°7N 102°29W **348** G12
Big Sioux → *U.S.A.* 42°29N 96°27W **352** D5
Big South Fork ⌂ *U.S.A.* 36°27N 84°47W **357** C12
Big Spring *U.S.A.* 32°15N 101°28W **356** E4
Big Stone City *U.S.A.* 45°18N 96°28W **352** C5
Big Stone Gap *U.S.A.* 36°52N 82°47W **353** G12
Big Stone L. *U.S.A.* 45°18N 96°27W **352** C5
Big Sur *U.S.A.* 36°15N 121°48W **350** J5
Big Timber *U.S.A.* 45°50N 109°57W **348** D9
Big Trout L. *Canada* 53°40N 90°0W **344** B2
Big Trout Lake *Canada* 53°45N 90°0W **344** B2
Biğa *Turkey* 40°13N 27°14E **295** D12

Bigadiç Turkey 39°22N 28°7E 295 E13
Biggar Canada 52°4N 108°0W 343 C7
Biggar U.K. 55°38N 3°32W 283 F5
Bigge I. Australia 14°35S 125°10E 332 B4
Biggenden Australia 25°31S 152°4E 335 D5
Biggleswade U.K. 52°5N 0°14W 285 E7
Biggs U.S.A. 39°25N 121°43W 350 F5
Bighorn U.S.A. 46°10N 107°27W 348 C10
Bighorn → U.S.A. 46°10N 107°28W 348 C10
Bighorn Canyon ⌂ U.S.A. 45°10N 108°0W 348 D10
Bighorn L. U.S.A. 44°55N 108°15W 348 D9
Bighorn Mts. U.S.A. 44°25N 107°0W 348 D10
Bight, The Bahamas 24°19N 75°24W 361 B4
Bigstone L. Canada 53°42N 95°44W 343 C9
Bigwa Tanzania 7°10S 39°10E 326 D4
Bihać Bos.-H. 44°49N 15°57E 288 F8
Bihar India 25°5N 85°40E 315 G11
Bihar □ India 25°0N 86°0E 315 G12
Biharamulo Tanzania 2°25S 31°25E 326 C3
Biharamulo ⌂ Tanzania 2°24S 31°26E 326 C3
Bihariganj India 25°44N 86°59E 315 G12
Bihor, Munţii Romania 46°29N 22°47E 289 E12
Bijagós, Arquipélago dos Guinea-Biss. 11°15N 16°10W 322 F2
Bijaipur India 26°2N 77°20E 314 F7
Bijapur Chhattisgarh, India 18°50N 80°50E 313 K12
Bijapur Karnataka, India 16°50N 75°55E 312 L9
Bījār Iran 35°52N 47°35E 316 C5
Bijawar India 24°38N 79°30E 315 G8
Bijeljina Bos.-H. 44°46N 19°14E 295 B8
Bijnor India 29°27N 78°11E 314 E8
Bikaner India 28°2N 73°18E 314 E5
Bikapur India 26°30N 82°7E 315 F10
Bikeqi China 40°43N 111°20E 306 D6
Bikfayyā Lebanon 33°55N 35°41E 318 B4
Bikin Russia 46°50N 134°20E 302 A7
Bikin → Russia 46°51N 134°2E 302 A7
Bikini Atoll Marshall Is. 12°0N 167°30E 336 F8
Bikita Zimbabwe 20°6S 31°41E 329 C5
Bila Tserkva Ukraine 49°45N 30°10E 289 D16
Bilara India 26°14N 73°53E 314 F5
Bilaspur Chhattisgarh, India 22°2N 82°15E 315 H10
Bilaspur Punjab, India 31°19N 76°50E 314 D7
Bilauk Taungdan Thailand 13°0N 99°0E 310 F2
Bilbao Spain 43°16N 2°56W 293 A4
Bilbo = Bilbao Spain 43°16N 2°56W 293 A4
Bíldudalur Iceland 65°41N 23°36W 280 D2
Bílé Karpaty Europe 49°5N 18°0E 289 D9
Bilecik Turkey 40°5N 30°5E 291 F5
Bilgram India 27°11N 80°2E 315 F9
Bilhaur India 26°51N 80°5E 315 F9
Bilhorod-Dnistrovskyy Ukraine 46°11N 30°23E 291 E5
Bilibino Russia 68°3N 166°20E 301 C17
Bilibiza Mozam. 12°30S 40°20E 327 E5
Billiluna Australia 19°37S 127°41E 332 C4
Billings U.S.A. 45°47N 108°30W 348 D9
Billiton Is. = Belitung Indonesia 3°10S 107°50E 308 E3
Bilma Niger 18°50N 13°30E 323 E8
Biloela Australia 24°24S 150°31E 334 C5
Biloxi U.S.A. 30°24N 88°53W 357 F10
Bilpa Morea Claypan Australia 25°0S 140°0E 334 D3
Biltine Chad 14°40N 20°50E 323 F10
Bima Indonesia 8°22S 118°49E 309 F5
Bimbo C.A.R. 4°15N 18°33E 324 D3
Bimini Is. Bahamas 25°42N 79°25W 360 A4
Bin Xian Heilongjiang, China 45°42N 127°32E 307 B14
Bin Xian Shaanxi, China 35°2N 108°4E 306 G5
Bina-Etawah India 24°13N 78°14E 314 G8
Bināb Iran 36°35N 48°41E 317 B6
Binalbagan Phil. 10°12N 122°50E 309 B6
Binalong Australia 34°40S 148°39E 335 E4
Bīnālūd, Kūh-e Iran 36°30N 58°30E 317 B8
Binatang = Bintangau Malaysia 2°10N 111°40E 308 D4
Binche Belgium 50°26N 4°10E 287 D4
Bindki India 26°2N 80°36E 315 F9
Bindura Zimbabwe 17°18S 31°18E 327 F3
Bingara Australia 29°52S 150°36E 335 D5
Bingham U.S.A. 45°3N 69°53W 353 C19
Binghamton U.S.A. 42°6N 75°55W 355 D9
Bingöl Turkey 38°53N 40°29E 316 B4
Binh Dinh = An Nhon Vietnam 13°55N 109°7E 310 F7
Binh Khe Vietnam 13°57N 108°51E 310 F7
Binh Son Vietnam 15°20N 108°40E 310 E7
Binhai China 34°2N 119°49E 307 G10
Binisatua Spain 39°50N 4°11E 296 B11
Binjai Indonesia 3°20N 98°30E 308 D3
Binnaway Australia 31°28S 149°24E 335 E4
Binongko Indonesia 5°57S 124°2E 309 F6
Binscarth Canada 50°37N 101°17W 343 C8
Bintan Indonesia 1°0N 104°0E 308 D2
Bintangau Malaysia 2°10N 111°40E 308 D4
Bintulu Malaysia 3°10N 113°0E 308 D4
Bintuni Indonesia 2°7S 133°32E 309 E8
Binzert = Bizerte Tunisia 37°15N 9°50E 323 A7
Binzhou China 37°20N 118°2E 307 F10
Bío Bío □ Chile 37°35S 72°0W 366 D1
Bioko Eq. Guin. 3°30N 8°40E 324 D1
Bir India 19°4N 75°46E 312 K9
Bîr Abu Muḥammad Egypt 29°44N 34°14E 318 F3
Bi'r ad Dabbāghāt Jordan 30°26N 35°32E 318 E4
Bi'r al Butayyihāt Jordan 29°47N 35°20E 318 F4
Bi'r al Mārī Jordan 30°4N 35°33E 318 E4
Bi'r al Qattār Jordan 29°47N 35°32E 318 F4
Bir Atrun Sudan 18°15N 26°40E 323 E11
Bîr Beiḍa Egypt 30°25N 34°29E 318 E3
Bîr el 'Abd Egypt 31°2N 33°0E 318 D2
Bîr el Biarât Egypt 29°30N 34°43E 318 F3
Bîr el Duweidar Egypt 30°56N 32°32E 318 E1
Bîr el Garârât Egypt 31°3N 33°34E 318 D2
Bîr el Heisi Egypt 29°22N 34°36E 318 F3
Bîr el Jafir Egypt 30°50N 32°41E 318 E1
Bîr el Mâlḥi Egypt 30°38N 33°19E 318 E2
Bîr el Thamâda Egypt 30°12N 33°27E 318 E2
Bîr Gebeil Ḥiṣn Egypt 30°2N 33°18E 318 E2
Bi'r Ghadīr Syria 34°6N 37°3E 318 A6
Bîr Ḥasana Egypt 30°29N 33°46E 318 E2
Bîr Kaseiba Egypt 31°0N 33°17E 318 E2
Bîr Lahfân Egypt 31°0N 33°51E 318 E2
Bîr Madkûr Egypt 30°44N 32°33E 318 E1
Bîr Mogreïn Mauritania 25°10N 11°25W 322 C3
Bi'r Muṭribah Kuwait 29°54N 47°17E 316 D5
Bîr Qaṭia Egypt 30°58N 32°45E 318 E1
Bîr Shalatein Egypt 23°5N 35°25E 323 D13
Biratnagar Nepal 26°27N 87°17E 315 F12
Birawa Dem. Rep. of the Congo 2°20S 28°48E 326 C2
Birch → Canada 58°28N 112°17W 342 B6
Birch Hills Canada 52°59N 105°25W 343 C7
Birch I. Canada 52°26N 99°54W 343 C9
Birch L. N.W.T., Canada 62°4N 116°33W 342 A5
Birch L. Ont., Canada 51°23N 92°18W 344 B1
Birch Mts. Canada 57°30N 113°10W 342 B6
Birch River Canada 52°24N 101°6W 343 C8
Birchip Australia 35°56S 142°55E 335 F3
Bird Canada 56°30N 94°13W 343 B10
Bird I. = Aves, I. de W. Indies 15°45N 63°55W 361 C7
Bird I. Antarctica 54°0S 38°0W 277 B1
Birdsville Australia 25°51S 139°20E 334 D2
Birdum Cr. → Australia 15°14S 133°0E 332 C5
Birecik Turkey 37°2N 38°0E 316 B3
Bireim Israel 30°50N 34°28E 318 E3
Bireuen Indonesia 5°14N 96°39E 308 C1
Birigui Brazil 21°18S 50°16W 367 A5
Birjand Iran 32°53N 59°13E 317 C8
Birkenhead U.K. 53°23N 3°2W 284 D4
Bîrlad = Bârlad Romania 46°15N 27°38E 289 E14
Birmingham U.K. 52°29N 1°52W 285 E6
Birmingham U.S.A. 33°31N 86°48W 357 E11
Birmingham Int. ✕ (BHX) U.K. 52°26N 1°45W 285 E6
Birmitrapur India 22°24N 84°46E 313 H14
Birni Nkonni Niger 13°55N 5°15E 322 F7
Birnin Kebbi Nigeria 12°32N 4°12E 322 F6
Birobidzhan Russia 48°50N 132°50E 301 E14
Birr Ireland 53°6N 7°54W 282 C4
Birrie → Australia 29°43S 146°37E 335 D4
Birsilpur India 28°11N 72°15E 314 E5
Birsk Russia 55°25N 55°30E 290 C10
Birtle Canada 50°30N 101°5W 343 C8
Birur India 13°30N 75°55E 312 N9
Biržai Lithuania 56°11N 24°45E 281 H21
Birżebbugga Malta 35°50N 14°32E 297 D2
Bisa Indonesia 1°15S 127°28E 309 E7
Bisalpur India 28°14N 79°48E 315 E8
Bisbee U.S.A. 31°27N 109°55W 349 L9
Biscarrosse France 44°22N 1°20W 292 D3
Biscay, B. of Atl. Oc. 45°0N 2°0W 292 D1
Biscayne B. U.S.A. 25°40N 80°12W 357 J14
Biscoe Is. Antarctica 66°0S 67°0W 277 C17
Biscotasing Canada 47°18N 82°9W 344 C3
Bishkek Kyrgyzstan 42°54N 74°46E 300 E8
Bishnupur India 23°8N 87°20E 315 H12
Bisho S. Africa 32°50S 27°23E 329 E4
Bishop Calif., U.S.A. 37°22N 118°24W 350 H8
Bishop Tex., U.S.A. 27°35N 97°48W 356 H6
Bishop Auckland U.K. 54°39N 1°40W 284 C6
Bishop's Falls Canada 49°2N 55°30W 345 C8
Bishop's Stortford U.K. 51°52N 0°10E 285 F8
Bisina, L. Uganda 1°38N 33°56E 326 B3
Biskra Algeria 34°50N 5°44E 322 B7
Bismarck U.S.A. 46°48N 100°47W 352 B3
Bismarck Arch. Papua N. G. 2°30S 150°0E 330 B7
Biso Uganda 1°44N 31°26E 326 B3
Bison U.S.A. 45°31N 102°28W 352 C2
Bīsotūn Iran 34°23N 47°26E 316 C5
Bissagos = Bijagós, Arquipélago dos Guinea-Biss. 11°15N 16°10W 322 F2
Bissau Guinea-Biss. 11°45N 15°45W 322 F2
Bistcho L. Canada 59°45N 118°50W 342 B5
Bistrița Romania 47°9N 24°35E 289 E13
Bistrița → Romania 46°30N 26°57E 289 E14
Biswan India 27°29N 81°2E 315 F9
Bitam Gabon 2°5N 11°25E 324 D2
Bitkine Chad 11°59N 18°13E 323 F9
Bitlis Turkey 38°20N 42°3E 316 B4
Bitola Macedonia 41°1N 21°20E 295 D9
Bitolj = Bitola Macedonia 41°1N 21°20E 295 D9
Bitter Creek U.S.A. 41°33N 108°33W 348 F9
Bitterfontein S. Africa 31°1S 18°32E 328 E2
Bitterroot → U.S.A. 46°52N 114°7W 348 C6
Bitterroot Range U.S.A. 46°0N 114°20W 348 C6
Bitterwater U.S.A. 36°23N 121°0W 350 J6
Biu Nigeria 10°40N 12°3E 323 F8
Biwa-Ko Japan 35°15N 136°10E 303 G8
Biwabik U.S.A. 47°32N 92°21W 352 B7
Bixby U.S.A. 35°57N 95°53W 356 D7
Biyang China 32°38N 113°21E 306 H7
Biysk Russia 52°40N 85°0E 300 D9
Bizana S. Africa 30°50S 29°52E 329 E4
Bizen Japan 34°43N 134°8E 303 G7
Bizerte Tunisia 37°15N 9°50E 323 A7
Bjargtangar Iceland 65°30N 24°30W 280 D1
Bjelovar Croatia 45°56N 16°49E 294 B7
Björneborg = Pori Finland 61°29N 21°48E 280 F19
Bjørnevatn Norway 69°40N 30°0E 280 B24
Bjørnøya Arctic 74°30N 19°0E 276 B8
Black = Da → Vietnam 21°15N 105°20E 310 B5
Black → Canada 44°42N 79°19W 354 B5
Black → Ariz., U.S.A. 33°44N 110°13W 349 K8
Black → Ark., U.S.A. 35°38N 91°20W 356 D9
Black → La., U.S.A. 31°16N 91°50W 356 F9
Black → Mich., U.S.A. 42°59N 82°27W 354 D2
Black → N.Y., U.S.A. 43°59N 76°4W 355 C8
Black → Wis., U.S.A. 43°57N 91°22W 352 D8
Black Bay Pen. Canada 48°38N 88°21W 344 C2
Black Birch L. Canada 56°53N 107°45W 343 B7
Black Canyon of the Gunnison ⌂ U.S.A. 38°40N 107°35W 348 G10
Black Diamond Canada 50°45N 114°14W 342 C6
Black Duck → Canada 56°51N 89°2W 344 A2
Black Forest = Schwarzwald Germany 48°30N 8°20E 288 D5
Black Forest U.S.A. 39°0N 104°43W 348 G11
Black Hd. Ireland 53°9N 9°16W 282 C2
Black Hills U.S.A. 44°0N 103°45W 352 D2
Black I. Canada 51°12N 96°30W 343 C9
Black L. Canada 59°12N 105°15W 343 B7
Black L. Mich., U.S.A. 45°28N 84°16W 353 C11
Black L. N.Y., U.S.A. 44°31N 75°36W 355 B9
Black Lake Canada 59°11N 105°20W 343 B7
Black Mesa U.S.A. 36°58N 102°58W 356 C3
Black Mt. = Mynydd Du U.K. 51°52N 3°50W 285 F4
Black Mts. U.K. 51°55N 3°7W 285 F4
Black Range U.S.A. 33°15N 107°50W 349 K10
Black River Jamaica 18°0N 77°50W 360 a
Black River Falls U.S.A. 44°18N 90°51W 352 C8
Black Rock Barbados 13°7N 59°37W 361 g
Black Sea Eurasia 43°30N 35°0E 291 F6
Black Tickle Canada 53°28N 55°45W 345 B8
Black Volta → Africa 8°41N 1°33W 322 G5
Black Warrior → U.S.A. 32°32N 87°51W 357 E11
Blackall Australia 24°25S 145°45E 334 C4
Blackball N.Z. 42°22S 171°26E 331 E3
Blackbull Australia 17°55S 141°45E 334 B3
Blackburn U.K. 53°45N 2°29W 284 D5
Blackburn with Darwen □ U.K. 53°45N 2°29W 284 D5
Blackdown Tableland △ Australia 23°52S 149°8E 334 C4
Blackfoot U.S.A. 43°11N 112°21W 348 E7
Blackfoot → U.S.A. 46°52N 113°53W 348 C7
Blackfoot Res. U.S.A. 42°55N 111°39W 348 E8
Blackpool U.K. 53°49N 3°3W 284 D4
Blackpool □ U.K. 53°49N 3°3W 284 D4
Blackriver U.S.A. 44°46N 83°17W 354 B1
Blacks Harbour Canada 45°3N 66°49W 345 C6
Blacksburg U.S.A. 37°14N 80°25W 353 G13
Blacksod B. Ireland 54°6N 10°0W 282 B1
Blackstairs Mt. Ireland 52°33N 6°48W 282 D5
Blackstone U.S.A. 37°5N 78°0W 353 G14
Blackstone Ra. Australia 26°0S 128°30E 333 E4
Blacktown Australia 33°48S 150°55E 335 E5
Blackwater = West Road → Canada 53°18N 122°53W 342 C4
Blackwater Australia 23°35S 148°53E 334 C4
Blackwater → Meath, Ireland 53°39N 6°41W 282 C4
Blackwater → Waterford, Ireland 52°4N 7°52W 282 D4
Blackwater → U.K. 54°31N 6°35W 282 B5
Blackwell U.S.A. 36°48N 97°17W 356 C6
Blackwells Corner U.S.A. 35°37N 119°47W 351 K7
Bladensburg △ Australia 22°30S 142°59E 334 C3
Blaenau Ffestiniog U.K. 53°0N 3°56W 284 E4
Blaenau Gwent □ U.K. 51°48N 3°12W 285 F4
Blagodarnoye = Blagodarnyy Russia 45°7N 43°37E 291 E7
Blagodarnyy Russia 45°7N 43°37E 291 E7
Blagoevgrad Bulgaria 42°2N 23°5E 295 C10
Blagoveshchensk Russia 50°20N 127°30E 301 D13
Blahkiuh Indonesia 8°31S 115°12E 309 J18
Blain U.S.A. 40°20N 77°31W 354 F7
Blaine Minn., U.S.A. 45°10N 93°13W 352 C7
Blaine Wash., U.S.A. 48°59N 122°45W 350 B4
Blaine Lake Canada 52°51N 106°52W 343 C7
Blair U.S.A. 41°33N 96°8W 352 E5
Blair Athol Australia 22°42S 147°31E 334 C4
Blair Atholl U.K. 56°46N 3°50W 283 E5
Blairgowrie U.K. 56°35N 3°21W 283 E5
Blairsden U.S.A. 39°47N 120°37W 350 F6
Blairsville U.S.A. 40°26N 79°16W 354 F5
Blakang Mati, Pulau Singapore 1°15N 103°50E 311 d
Blake Pt. U.S.A. 48°11N 88°25W 352 A9
Blakely Ga., U.S.A. 31°23N 84°56W 357 F12
Blakely Pa., U.S.A. 41°28N 75°37W 355 E9
Blanc, C. Spain 39°21N 2°51E 296 B9
Blanc, Mont Europe 45°48N 6°50E 292 D7
Blanca, B. Argentina 39°10S 61°30W 368 D4
Blanca, Cord. Peru 9°10S 77°35W 364 E3
Blanca Peak U.S.A. 37°35N 105°29W 349 H11
Blanche, C. Australia 33°1S 134°9E 335 E1
Blanche, L. S. Austral., Australia 29°15S 139°40E 335 D2
Blanche, L. W. Austral., Australia 22°25S 123°17E 332 D3
Blanchisseuse Trin. & Tob. 10°48N 61°18W 365 K15
Blanco S. Africa 33°55S 22°23E 328 E3
Blanco U.S.A. 30°6N 98°25W 356 F5
Blanco → Argentina 30°20S 68°42W 366 C2
Blanco, C. Costa Rica 9°34N 85°8W 360 E2
Blanco, C. U.S.A. 42°51N 124°34W 348 E1
Blanda → Iceland 65°37N 20°9W 280 D3
Blandford Forum U.K. 50°51N 2°9W 285 G5
Blanding U.S.A. 37°37N 109°29W 349 H9
Blanes Spain 41°40N 2°48E 293 B7
Blankenberge Belgium 51°20N 3°9E 287 C3
Blanquilla Venezuela 11°51N 64°37W 361 D7
Blanquillo Uruguay 32°53S 55°37W 367 C4
Blantyre Malawi 15°45S 35°0E 327 F4
Blarney Ireland 51°56N 8°33W 282 E3
Blasdell U.S.A. 42°48N 78°50W 354 D6
Blåvands Huk Denmark 55°33N 8°4E 281 J13
Blaydon U.K. 54°58N 1°42W 284 C6
Blayney Australia 33°32S 149°14E 335 E4
Blaze, Pt. Australia 12°56S 130°11E 332 B5
Blekinge Sweden 56°25N 15°20E 281 H16
Blenheim Canada 42°20N 82°0W 354 D3
Blenheim N.Z. 41°38S 173°57E 331 D4
Bletchley U.K. 51°59N 0°44W 285 F7
Blida Algeria 36°30N 2°49E 322 A6
Bligh Sound N.Z. 44°47S 167°32E 331 F1
Bligh Water Fiji 17°0S 178°0E 331 a
Blind River Canada 46°10N 82°58W 344 C3
Bliss Idaho, U.S.A. 42°56N 114°57W 348 E6
Bliss N.Y., U.S.A. 42°34N 78°15W 354 D6
Blissfield U.S.A. 40°24N 81°58W 354 F3
Blitar Indonesia 8°5S 112°11E 309 H15
Block I. U.S.A. 41°11N 71°35W 355 E13
Block Island Sd. U.S.A. 41°15N 71°40W 355 E13
Bloemfontein S. Africa 29°6S 26°7E 328 D4
Bloemhof S. Africa 27°38S 25°32E 328 D4
Blois France 47°35N 1°20E 292 C4
Blönduós Iceland 65°40N 20°12W 280 D3
Blongas Indonesia 8°53S 116°2E 309 K19
Bloodvein → Canada 51°47N 96°43W 343 C9
Bloody Foreland Ireland 55°10N 8°17W 282 A3
Bloomer U.S.A. 45°6N 91°29W 352 C8
Bloomfield Canada 43°59N 77°14W 354 C7
Bloomfield Iowa, U.S.A. 40°45N 92°25W 352 E7
Bloomfield N. Mex., U.S.A. 36°43N 107°59W 349 H10
Bloomfield Nebr., U.S.A. 42°36N 97°39W 352 D5
Bloomington Ill., U.S.A. 40°28N 89°0W 352 E9
Bloomington Ind., U.S.A. 39°10N 86°32W 352 F10
Bloomington Minn., U.S.A. 44°50N 93°17W 352 C7
Bloomsburg U.S.A. 41°0N 76°27W 355 F8
Bloomsbury Australia 20°48S 148°38E 334 J6
Blora Indonesia 6°57S 111°25E 309 G14
Blossburg U.S.A. 41°41N 77°4W 354 E7
Blouberg S. Africa 23°8S 28°59E 329 C4
Blountstown U.S.A. 30°27N 85°3W 357 F12
Blue Earth U.S.A. 43°38N 94°6W 352 D6
Blue Hole △ Belize 17°24N 88°30W 360 C2
Blue Lagoon △ Zambia 15°28S 27°26E 327 F2
Blue Mesa Res. U.S.A. 38°28N 107°20W 348 G10
Blue Mountain Lake U.S.A. 43°51N 74°27W 355 C10
Blue Mountain Pk. Jamaica 18°3N 76°36W 360 a
Blue Mt. U.S.A. 40°30N 76°30W 355 F8
Blue Mts. Jamaica 18°3N 76°36W 360 a
Blue Mts. Maine, U.S.A. 44°50N 70°35W 355 B14
Blue Mts. Oreg., U.S.A. 45°0N 118°20W 348 D4
Blue Mud B. Australia 13°30S 136°0E 334 A2
Blue Nile = Nîl el Azraq → Sudan 15°38N 32°31E 323 E12
Blue Rapids U.S.A. 39°41N 96°39W 352 F5
Blue Ridge U.S.A. 36°40N 80°50W 353 G13
Blue River Canada 52°6N 119°18W 342 C5
Bluefield U.S.A. 37°15N 81°17W 353 G13
Bluefields Nic. 12°20N 83°50W 360 D3
Bluff Australia 23°35S 149°4E 334 C4
Bluff N.Z. 46°37S 168°20E 331 G2
Bluff U.S.A. 37°17N 109°33W 349 H9
Bluff Knoll Australia 34°24S 118°15E 333 F2
Bluff Pt. Australia 27°50S 114°5E 333 E1
Bluffton U.S.A. 40°44N 85°11W 353 E11
Blumenau Brazil 27°0S 49°0W 367 B6
Blunt U.S.A. 44°31N 99°59W 352 C4
Bly U.S.A. 42°24N 121°3W 348 E3
Blyde River Canyon ⌂ S. Africa 24°37S 31°2E 329 C5
Blyth Canada 43°44N 81°26W 354 C3
Blyth U.K. 55°8N 1°31W 284 B6
Blythe U.S.A. 33°37N 114°36W 351 M12
Blytheville U.S.A. 35°56N 89°55W 357 D10
Bo S. Leone 7°55N 11°50W 322 G3
Bo Duc Vietnam 11°58N 106°50E 311 G6
Bo Hai China 39°0N 119°0E 307 E10
Bo Xian = Bozhou China 33°55N 115°41E 306 H8
Boa Vista Brazil 2°48N 60°30W 364 C6
Boa Vista C. Verde Is. 16°0N 22°49W 322 b
Boaco Nic. 12°29N 85°35W 360 D2
Bo'ai China 35°10N 113°3E 306 G7
Boalsburg U.S.A. 40°47N 77°49W 354 F7
Boane Mozam. 26°6S 32°19E 329 D5
Boardman U.S.A. 41°2N 80°40W 354 E4
Bobadah Australia 32°19S 146°41E 335 E4
Bobbili India 18°35N 83°30E 313 K13
Bobcaygeon Canada 44°33N 78°33W 354 B6
Bobo-Dioulasso Burkina Faso 11°8N 4°13W 322 F5
Bóbr → Poland 52°4N 15°4E 288 B8
Bobraomby, Tanjon' i Madag. 12°40S 49°10E 329 A8
Bobruysk = Babruysk Belarus 53°10N 29°15E 289 B15
Boby, Pic Madag. 22°12S 46°55E 325 J9
Boca de Drago Venezuela 11°0N 61°50W 365 K15
Boca del Río Mexico 19°5N 96°4W 359 D5
Bôca do Acre Brazil 8°50S 67°27W 364 E5
Boca Raton U.S.A. 26°21N 80°5W 357 H14
Bocas del Toro Panama 9°15N 82°20W 360 E3
Bochnia Poland 49°58N 20°27E 289 D11
Bochum Germany 51°28N 7°13E 288 C4
Bocoyna Mexico 27°52N 107°35W 358 B3
Bodaybo Russia 57°50N 114°0E 301 D12
Boddam U.K. 59°56N 1°17W 283 B7
Boddington Australia 32°50S 116°30E 333 F2
Bodega Bay U.S.A. 38°20N 123°3W 350 G3
Boden Sweden 65°50N 21°42E 280 D19
Bodensee Europe 47°35N 9°25E 292 C8
Bodhan India 18°40N 77°44E 312 K10
Bodmin U.K. 50°28N 4°43W 285 G3
Bodmin Moor U.K. 50°33N 4°36W 285 G3
Bodø Norway 67°17N 14°24E 280 C16
Bodrog → Hungary 48°11N 21°22E 289 D11
Bodrum Turkey 37°3N 27°30E 295 F12
Boende Dem. Rep. of the Congo 0°24S 21°12E 324 E4
Boerne U.S.A. 29°47N 98°44W 356 G5
Boesmans → S. Africa 33°42S 26°39E 328 E4
Bogalusa U.S.A. 30°47N 89°52W 357 F10
Bogan → Australia 30°20S 146°55E 335 D4
Bogan Gate Australia 33°7S 147°49E 335 E4
Bogantungan Australia 23°41S 147°17E 334 C4
Bogata U.S.A. 33°28N 95°13W 356 E7
Bogda Shan China 43°35N 89°40E 304 B3
Boggabilla Australia 28°36S 150°24E 335 D5
Boggabri Australia 30°45S 150°5E 335 E5
Boggeragh Mts. Ireland 52°2N 8°55W 282 D3
Boglan = Solhan Turkey 38°57N 41°3E 316 B4
Bognor Regis U.K. 50°47N 0°40W 285 G7
Bogo Phil. 11°3N 124°0E 309 B6
Bogong, Mt. Australia 36°47S 147°17E 335 F4
Bogor Indonesia 6°36S 106°48E 308 F3
Bogotá Colombia 4°34N 74°0W 364 C4
Bogotol Russia 56°15N 89°50E 300 D9
Bogra Bangla. 24°51N 89°22E 313 G16
Boguchany Russia 58°40N 97°30E 301 D10
Bogué Mauritania 16°45N 14°10W 322 E3
Bohemian Forest = Böhmerwald Germany 49°8N 13°14E 288 D7
Böhmerwald Germany 49°8N 13°14E 288 D7
Bohol □ Phil. 9°50N 124°10E 309 C6
Bohol Sea Phil. 9°0N 124°0E 309 C6
Bohuslän Sweden 58°25N 12°0E 281 G15
Boi, Pta. de Brazil 23°55S 45°15W 367 A6
Boiaçu Brazil 0°27S 61°46W 364 D6
Boileau, C. Australia 17°40S 122°7E 332 C3
Boise U.S.A. 43°37N 116°13W 348 E5
Boise City U.S.A. 36°44N 102°31W 356 C3
Boissevain Canada 49°15N 100°5W 343 D8
Bojador, C. W. Sahara 26°0N 14°30W 322 C3
Bojana → Albania 41°52N 19°22E 295 D8
Bojnūrd Iran 37°30N 57°20E 317 B8
Bojonegoro Indonesia 7°11S 111°54E 309 G14
Bokaro India 23°46N 85°55E 315 H11
Boké Guinea 10°56N 14°17W 322 F3
Bokhara → Australia 29°55S 146°42E 335 D4
Boknafjorden Norway 59°14N 5°40E 281 G11
Bokora ⌂ Uganda 2°12N 31°32E 326 B3
Bokoro Chad 12°25N 17°14E 323 F9
Bokpyin Burma 11°18N 98°42E 311 G2
Bokungu Dem. Rep. of the Congo 0°35S 22°50E 324 E4
Bolan → Pakistan 28°38N 67°42E 314 E2
Bolan Pass Pakistan 29°50N 67°20E 312 E5
Bolaños → Mexico 21°12N 104°5W 358 C4
Bolbec France 49°30N 0°30E 292 B4
Boldājī Iran 31°56N 51°3E 317 D6
Bole China 45°11N 81°37E 304 B3
Bolekhiv Ukraine 49°0N 23°57E 289 D12
Bolesławiec Poland 51°17N 15°37E 288 C8
Bolgatanga Ghana 10°44N 0°53W 322 F5
Bolgrad = Bolhrad Ukraine 45°40N 28°32E 289 F15
Bolhrad Ukraine 45°40N 28°32E 289 F15
Bolívar Argentina 36°15S 60°53W 366 D3
Bolivar Mo., U.S.A. 37°37N 93°25W 352 G7
Bolivar N.Y., U.S.A. 42°4N 78°10W 354 D6
Bolivar Tenn., U.S.A. 35°12N 89°0W 357 D10
Bolivia ■ S. Amer. 17°6S 64°0W 364 G6
Bolivian Plateau = Altiplano Bolivia 17°0S 68°0W 364 G5
Bollnäs Sweden 61°21N 16°24E 280 F17
Bollon Australia 28°2S 147°29E 335 D4
Bolmen Sweden 56°55N 13°40E 281 H15
Bolobo Dem. Rep. of the Congo 2°6S 16°20E 324 E3
Bologna Italy 44°29N 11°20E 294 B4
Bologoye Russia 57°55N 34°5E 290 C5
Bolomba Dem. Rep. of the Congo 0°35N 19°0E 324 D3
Bolonchén Mexico 20°1N 89°45W 359 D7
Boloven, Cao Nguyen Laos 15°10N 106°30E 310 E6
Bolpur India 23°40N 87°45E 315 H12
Bolsena, L. di Italy 42°36N 11°56E 294 C4
Bolshevik, Ostrov Russia 78°30N 102°0E 301 B11
Bolshoy Anyuy → Russia 68°30N 160°49E 301 C17
Bolshoy Begichev, Ostrov Russia 74°20N 112°30E 301 B12
Bolshoy Kavkas = Caucasus Mountains Eurasia 42°50N 44°0E 291 F7
Bolshoy Lyakhovskiy, Ostrov Russia 73°35N 142°0E 301 B15
Bolshoy Tyuters, Ostrov Russia 59°51N 27°13E 281 G22
Bolsward Neths. 53°3N 5°32E 287 A5
Bolt Head U.K. 50°12N 3°48W 285 G4
Bolton Canada 43°54N 79°45W 354 C5
Bolton U.K. 53°35N 2°26W 284 D5
Bolton Landing U.S.A. 43°32N 73°35W 355 C11
Bolu Turkey 40°45N 31°35E 291 F5
Bolungavík Iceland 66°9N 23°15W 280 C2
Bolvadin Turkey 38°45N 31°4E 316 B1
Bolzano Italy 46°31N 11°22E 294 A4
Bom Jesus da Lapa Brazil 13°15S 43°25W 365 F10
Boma Dem. Rep. of the Congo 5°50S 13°4E 324 F2

Bombala *Australia* 36°56S 149°15E **335** F4
Bombay = Mumbai *India* 18°56N 72°50E **312** K8
Bombedor, Pta. *Venezuela* 9°53N 61°37W **365** L15
Bomboma *Dem. Rep. of the Congo* 2°25N 18°55E **324** D3
Bombombwa *Dem. Rep. of the Congo* 1°40N 25°40E **326** B2
Bomili *Dem. Rep. of the Congo* 1°45N 27°5E **326** B2
Bømlo *Norway* 59°37N 5°13E **281** G11
Bomokandi → *Dem. Rep. of the Congo* 3°39N 26°8E **326** B2
Bomu → *C.A.R.* 4°40N 22°30E **324** D4
Bon, C. *Tunisia* 37°1N 11°2E **294** F4
Bon Acceuil *Mauritius* 20°10S 57°39E **325** d
Bon Sar Pa *Vietnam* 12°24N 107°35E **310** F6
Bonaigarh *India* 21°50N 84°57E **315** J11
Bonaire *Neth. Ant.* 12°10N 68°15W **361** D6
Bonampak *Mexico* 16°44N 91°5W **359** D6
Bonang *Australia* 37°11S 148°41E **335** F4
Bonanza *Nic.* 13°54N 84°35W **360** D3
Bonaparte Arch. *Australia* 14°0S 124°30E **332** B3
Bonar Bridge *U.K.* 57°54N 4°20W **283** D4
Bonasse *Trin. & Tob.* 10°5N 61°54W **365** K15
Bonaventure *Canada* 48°5N 65°32W **345** C6
Bonavista *Canada* 48°40N 53°5W **345** C9
Bonavista, C. *Canada* 48°42N 53°5W **345** C9
Bonavista B. *Canada* 48°45N 53°25W **345** C9
Bondo *Dem. Rep. of the Congo* 3°55N 23°53E **326** B1
Bondoukou *Ivory C.* 8°2N 2°47W **322** G5
Bondowoso *Indonesia* 7°55S 113°49E **309** G15
Bone, Teluk *Indonesia* 4°10S 120°50E **309** E6
Bonerate *Indonesia* 7°25S 121°5E **309** F6
Bonerate, Kepulauan *Indonesia* 6°30S 121°10E **309** F6
Bo'ness *U.K.* 56°1N 3°37W **283** E5
Bonete, Cerro *Argentina* 27°55S 68°40W **366** B2
Bong Son = Hoai Nhon *Vietnam* 14°28N 109°1E **310** E7
Bongandanga *Dem. Rep. of the Congo* 1°24N 21°3E **324** D4
Bongor *Chad* 10°35N 15°20E **323** F9
Bongos, Massif des *C.A.R.* 8°40N 22°25E **324** C4
Bonham *U.S.A.* 33°35N 96°11W **356** E6
Boni ⌂ *Kenya* 1°35S 41°18E **326** C5
Bonifacio *France* 41°24N 9°10E **292** F8
Bonifacio, Bouches de *Medit. S.* 41°12N 9°15E **294** D3
Bonin Is. = Ogasawara Gunto *Pac. Oc.* 27°0N 142°0E **336** E6
Bonn *Germany* 50°46N 7°6E **288** C4
Bonne Terre *U.S.A.* 37°55N 90°33W **352** G8
Bonners Ferry *U.S.A.* 48°42N 116°19W **348** B5
Bonney, L. *Australia* 37°50S 140°20E **335** F3
Bonnie Rock *Australia* 30°29S 118°22E **333** F2
Bonny, Bight of *Africa* 3°30N 9°20E **324** D1
Bonnyrigg *U.K.* 55°53N 3°6W **283** F5
Bonnyville *Canada* 54°20N 110°45W **343** C6
Bonoi *Indonesia* 1°45S 137°41E **309** E9
Bonsall *U.S.A.* 33°16N 117°14W **351** M9
Bontang *Indonesia* 0°10N 117°30E **308** D5
Bontebok ⌂ *S. Africa* 34°5S 20°28E **328** E3
Bonthe *S. Leone* 7°30N 12°33W **322** G3
Bontoc *Phil.* 17°7N 120°58E **309** A6
Bonython Ra. *Australia* 23°40S 128°45E **332** D4
Bookabie *Australia* 31°50S 132°41E **333** F5
Booker *U.S.A.* 36°27N 100°32W **356** C4
Booligal *Australia* 33°58S 144°53E **335** E3
Boonah *Australia* 27°58S 152°41E **335** D5
Boone *Iowa, U.S.A.* 42°4N 93°53W **352** D7
Boone *N.C., U.S.A.* 36°13N 81°41W **357** C14
Booneville *Ark., U.S.A.* 35°8N 93°55W **356** D8
Booneville *Miss., U.S.A.* 34°39N 88°34W **357** D10
Boonville *Calif., U.S.A.* 39°1N 123°22W **350** F3
Boonville *Ind., U.S.A.* 38°3N 87°16W **352** F10
Boonville *Mo., U.S.A.* 38°58N 92°44W **352** F7
Boonville *N.Y., U.S.A.* 43°29N 75°20W **355** C9
Boorabbin ⌂ *Australia* 31°30S 120°10E **333** F3
Boorindal *Australia* 30°22S 146°11E **335** E4
Boorowa *Australia* 34°28S 148°44E **335** E4
Boosaaso = Bosaso *Somali Rep.* 11°12N 49°18E **319** E4
Boothia, Gulf of *Canada* 71°0N 90°0W **341** B11
Boothia Pen. *Canada* 71°0N 94°0W **340** B10
Bootle *U.K.* 53°28N 3°1W **284** D4
Booué *Gabon* 0°5S 11°55E **324** E2
Boquete *Panama* 8°46N 82°27W **360** E3
Boquilla, Presa de la *Mexico* 27°31N 105°30W **358** B3
Boquillas del Carmen *Mexico* 29°11N 102°58W **358** B4
Bor *Serbia* 44°5N 22°7E **295** B10
Bôr *Sudan* 6°10N 31°40E **323** G12
Bor Mashash *Israel* 31°7N 34°50E **318** D3
Bora Bora *French Polynesia* 16°30S 151°45W **337** J12
Borah Peak *U.S.A.* 44°8N 113°47W **348** D7
Borås *Sweden* 57°43N 12°56E **281** H15
Borāzjān *Iran* 29°22N 51°10E **317** D6
Borba *Brazil* 4°12S 59°34W **364** D7
Borborema, Planalto da *Brazil* 7°0S 37°0W **362** D7
Bord Khūn-e Now *Iran* 28°3N 51°28E **317** D6
Borda, C. *Australia* 35°45S 136°34E **335** F2
Bordeaux *France* 44°50N 0°36W **292** D3
Borden *Australia* 34°3S 118°12E **333** F2
Borden-Carleton *Canada* 46°18N 63°47W **345** C7
Borden I. *Canada* 78°30N 111°30W **341** B8
Borden Pen. *Canada* 73°0N 83°0W **341** B11
Border Ranges ⌂ *Australia* 28°24S 152°56E **335** D5
Borders = Scottish Borders □ *U.K.* 55°35N 2°50W **283** F6
Bordertown *Australia* 36°19S 140°45E **335** F3
Borðeyri *Iceland* 65°12N 21°6W **280** D3
Bordj Fly Ste. Marie *Algeria* 27°19N 2°32W **322** C5
Bordj-in-Eker *Algeria* 24°9N 5°3E **322** D7
Bordj Omar Driss *Algeria* 28°10N 6°40E **322** C7
Borehamwood *U.K.* 51°40N 0°15W **285** F7
Borgarfjörður *Iceland* 65°33N 13°47W **280** D7
Borgarnes *Iceland* 64°32N 21°55W **280** D3
Børgefjellet *Norway* 65°20N 13°45E **280** D15
Borger *Neths.* 52°54N 6°44E **287** B6
Borger *U.S.A.* 35°39N 101°24W **356** D4
Borgholm *Sweden* 56°52N 16°39E **281** H17
Borhoyn Tal *Mongolia* 43°50N 111°58E **306** C6
Borikhane *Laos* 18°33N 103°43E **310** C4
Borisoglebsk *Russia* 51°27N 42°5E **291** D7
Borisov = Barysaw *Belarus* 54°17N 28°28E **289** A15
Borja *Peru* 4°20S 77°40W **364** D3
Borkou *Chad* 18°15N 18°50E **323** E9
Borkum *Germany* 53°34N 6°40E **288** B4
Borlänge *Sweden* 60°29N 15°26E **281** F16
Borley, C. *Antarctica* 66°15S 52°30E **277** C5
Borneo *E. Indies* 1°0N 115°0E **308** D5
Bornholm *Denmark* 55°10N 15°0E **281** J16
Borogontsy *Russia* 62°42N 131°8E **301** C14
Borohoro Shan *China* 44°6N 83°10E **304** B3
Boron *U.S.A.* 35°0N 117°39W **351** L9
Borongan *Phil.* 11°37N 125°26E **309** B7
Borovichi *Russia* 58°25N 33°55E **290** C5
Borrego Springs *U.S.A.* 33°15N 116°23W **351** M10
Borrisokane *Ireland* 53°0N 8°7W **282** D3
Borroloola *Australia* 16°4S 136°17E **334** B2
Borşa *Romania* 47°41N 24°50E **289** E13
Borsad *India* 22°25N 72°54E **314** H5
Borth *U.K.* 52°29N 4°2W **285** E3
Borūjerd *Iran* 33°55N 48°50E **317** C6
Boryeong *S. Korea* 36°21N 126°36E **307** F14
Boryslav *Ukraine* 49°18N 23°28E **289** D12
Borzya *Russia* 50°24N 116°31E **301** D12
Bosa *Italy* 40°18N 8°30E **294** D3
Bosanska Gradiška *Bos.-H.* 45°10N 17°15E **294** B7
Bosaso *Somali Rep.* 11°12N 49°18E **319** E4
Boscastle *U.K.* 50°41N 4°42W **285** G3
Boscobelle *Barbados* 13°17N 59°35W **361** g
Bose *China* 23°53N 106°35E **304** D5
Boseong *S. Korea* 34°46N 127°5E **307** G14
Boshan *China* 36°28N 117°49E **307** F9
Boshof *S. Africa* 28°31S 25°13E **328** D4
Boshrūyeh *Iran* 33°50N 57°30E **317** C8
Bosna → *Bos.-H.* 45°4N 18°29E **295** B8
Bosna i Hercegovina = Bosnia-Herzegovina ■ *Europe* 44°0N 18°0E **294** B7
Bosnia-Herzegovina ■ *Europe* 44°0N 18°0E **294** B7
Bosnik *Indonesia* 1°5S 136°10E **309** E9
Bosobolo *Dem. Rep. of the Congo* 4°15N 19°50E **324** D3
Bosporus = İstanbul Boğazı *Turkey* 41°5N 29°3E **295** D13
Bosque Farms *U.S.A.* 35°51N 106°42W **349** J10
Bossangoa *C.A.R.* 6°35N 17°30E **324** C3
Bossier City *U.S.A.* 32°31N 93°44W **356** E8
Bosso *Niger* 13°43N 13°19E **323** F8
Bostan *Pakistan* 30°26N 67°2E **314** D2
Bostānābād *Iran* 37°50N 46°50E **316** B5
Bosten Hu *China* 41°55N 87°40E **304** B3
Boston *U.K.* 52°59N 0°2W **284** E7
Boston *U.S.A.* 42°22N 71°3W **355** D13
Boston Bar *Canada* 49°52N 121°30W **342** D4
Boston Mts. *U.S.A.* 35°42N 93°15W **356** D8
Boswell *Canada* 49°28N 116°45W **342** D5
Boswell *U.S.A.* 40°10N 79°2W **354** F5
Botad *India* 22°15N 71°40E **314** H4
Botany B. *Australia* 33°58S 151°11E **330** E8
Botene *Laos* 17°35N 101°12E **310** D3
Bothaville *S. Africa* 27°23S 26°34E **328** D4
Bothnia, G. of *Europe* 62°0N 20°0E **280** F19
Bothwell *Australia* 42°20S 147°1E **335** G4
Bothwell *Canada* 42°38N 81°52W **354** D3
Botletle → *Botswana* 20°10S 23°15E **328** C3
Botoşani *Romania* 47°42N 26°41E **289** E14
Botou *Burkina Faso* 12°42N 1°59E **322** F6
Botshabelo *S. Africa* 29°14S 26°44E **325** K5
Botswana ■ *Africa* 22°0S 24°0E **328** C3
Bottineau *U.S.A.* 48°50N 100°27W **352** A3
Bottrop *Germany* 51°31N 6°58E **287** C6
Botucatu *Brazil* 22°55S 48°30W **367** A6
Botwood *Canada* 49°6N 55°23W **345** C8
Bou Saâda *Algeria* 35°11N 4°9E **322** A6
Bouaflé *Ivory C.* 7°1N 5°47W **322** G4
Bouaké *Ivory C.* 7°40N 5°2W **322** G4
Bouar *C.A.R.* 6°0N 15°40E **324** C3
Bouârfa *Morocco* 32°32N 1°58W **322** B5
Boucaut B. *Australia* 12°0S 134°25E **334** A1
Bouctouche *Canada* 46°30N 64°45W **345** C7
Bougainville, C. *Australia* 13°57S 126°4E **332** B4
Bougainville I. *Papua N. G.* 6°0S 155°0E **330** B8
Bougainville Reef *Australia* 15°30S 147°5E **334** B4
Bougie = Bejaïa *Algeria* 36°42N 5°2E **322** A7
Bougouni *Mali* 11°30N 7°20W **322** F4
Bouillon *Belgium* 49°44N 5°3E **287** E5
Boulder *Colo., U.S.A.* 40°1N 105°17W **348** F11
Boulder *Mont., U.S.A.* 46°14N 112°7W **348** C7
Boulder City *U.S.A.* 35°58N 114°49W **351** K12
Boulder Creek *U.S.A.* 37°7N 122°7W **350** H4
Boulder Dam = Hoover Dam *U.S.A.* 36°1N 114°44W **351** K12
Boulia *Australia* 22°52S 139°51E **334** C2
Boulogne-sur-Mer *France* 50°42N 1°36E **292** A4
Boulsa *Burkina Faso* 12°39N 0°34W **322** F5
Boultoum *Niger* 14°45N 10°25E **323** F8
Bouma ⌂ *Fiji* 16°50S 179°52E **331** a
Boun Neua *Laos* 21°38N 101°54E **310** B3
Boun Tai *Laos* 21°23N 101°58E **310** B3
Bouna *Ivory C.* 9°10N 3°0W **322** G5
Boundary Peak *U.S.A.* 37°51N 118°21W **350** H8
Boundiali *Ivory C.* 9°30N 6°20W **322** G4
Bountiful *U.S.A.* 40°53N 111°52W **348** F8
Bounty Is. *Pac. Oc.* 48°0S 178°30E **336** M9
Bounty Trough *Pac. Oc.* 46°0S 178°0E **336** M9
Bourbonnais *France* 46°28N 3°0E **292** C5
Bourdel L. *Canada* 56°43N 74°10W **344** A5
Bourem *Mali* 17°0N 0°24W **322** E5
Bourg-en-Bresse *France* 46°13N 5°12E **292** C6
Bourg-St-Maurice *France* 45°35N 6°46E **292** D7
Bourgas = Burgas *Bulgaria* 42°33N 27°29E **295** C12
Bourges *France* 47°9N 2°25E **292** C5
Bourget *Canada* 45°26N 75°9W **355** A9
Bourgogne □ *France* 47°0N 4°50E **292** C6
Bourke *Australia* 30°8S 145°55E **335** E4
Bourne *U.K.* 52°47N 0°22W **284** E7
Bournemouth *U.K.* 50°43N 1°52W **285** G6
Bournemouth □ *U.K.* 50°43N 1°52W **285** G6
Bouse *U.S.A.* 33°56N 114°0W **351** M13
Bousso *Chad* 10°34N 16°52E **323** F9
Bouvet I. = Bouvetøya *Antarctica* 54°26S 3°24E **274** G10
Bouvetøya *Antarctica* 54°26S 3°24E **274** G10
Bovill *U.S.A.* 46°51N 116°24W **348** C5
Bovril *Argentina* 31°21S 59°26W **366** C4
Bow → *Canada* 49°57N 111°41W **342** C6
Bow Island *Canada* 49°50N 111°23W **348** B8
Bowbells *U.S.A.* 48°48N 102°15W **352** A2
Bowdle *U.S.A.* 45°27N 99°39W **352** C4
Bowelling *Australia* 33°25S 116°30E **333** F2
Bowen *Argentina* 35°0S 67°31W **366** D2
Bowen *Australia* 20°0S 148°16E **334** J6
Bowen Mts. *Australia* 37°0S 147°50E **335** F4
Bowers Basin *Pac. Oc.* 53°45N 176°0E **276** D16
Bowers Ridge *Pac. Oc.* 54°0N 180°0E **276** D17
Bowie *Ariz., U.S.A.* 32°19N 109°29W **349** K9
Bowie *Tex., U.S.A.* 33°34N 97°51W **356** E6
Bowland, Forest of *U.K.* 54°0N 2°30W **284** D5
Bowling Green *Ky., U.S.A.* 36°59N 86°27W **352** G10
Bowling Green *Ohio, U.S.A.* 41°23N 83°39W **353** E12
Bowling Green, C. *Australia* 19°19S 147°25E **334** B4
Bowling Green Bay ⌂ *Australia* 19°26S 146°57E **334** B4
Bowman *U.S.A.* 46°11N 103°24W **352** B2
Bowman I. *Antarctica* 65°0S 104°0E **277** C8
Bowmanville = Clarington *Canada* 43°55N 78°41W **354** C6
Bowmore *U.K.* 55°45N 6°17W **283** F2
Bowral *Australia* 34°26S 150°27E **335** E5
Bowraville *Australia* 30°37S 152°52E **335** E5
Bowron → *Canada* 54°3N 121°50W **342** C4
Bowron Lake ⌂ *Canada* 53°10N 121°5W **342** C4
Bowser L. *Canada* 56°30N 129°30W **342** B3
Bowsman *Canada* 52°14N 101°12W **343** C8
Bowwood *Zambia* 17°5S 26°20E **327** F2
Box Cr. → *Australia* 34°10S 143°50E **335** E3
Boxmeer *Neths.* 51°38N 5°56E **287** C5
Boxtel *Neths.* 51°36N 5°20E **287** C5
Boyce *U.S.A.* 31°23N 92°40W **356** F8
Boyd L. *Canada* 52°46N 76°42W **344** B4
Boyle *Canada* 54°35N 112°49W **342** C6
Boyle *Ireland* 53°59N 8°18W **282** C3
Boyne → *Ireland* 53°43N 6°15W **282** C5
Boyne City *U.S.A.* 45°13N 85°1W **353** C11
Boynton Beach *U.S.A.* 26°32N 80°4W **357** H14
Boyolali *Indonesia* 7°32S 110°35E **309** G14
Boyoma, Chutes *Dem. Rep. of the Congo* 0°35N 25°23E **326** B2
Boysen Res. *U.S.A.* 43°25N 108°11W **348** E9
Boyuibe *Bolivia* 20°25S 63°17W **364** G6
Boyup Brook *Australia* 33°50S 116°23E **333** F2
Boz Dağları *Turkey* 38°20N 28°0E **295** E13
Bozburun *Turkey* 36°43N 28°4E **295** F13
Bozcaada *Turkey* 39°49N 26°3E **295** E12
Bozdoğan *Turkey* 37°40N 28°17E **295** F13
Bozeman *U.S.A.* 45°41N 111°2W **348** D8
Bozen = Bolzano *Italy* 46°31N 11°22E **294** A4
Bozhou *China* 33°55N 115°41E **306** H8
Bozoum *C.A.R.* 6°25N 16°35E **324** C3
Bra *Italy* 44°42N 7°51E **292** D7
Brabant □ *Belgium* 50°46N 4°30E **287** D4
Brabant L. *Canada* 55°58N 103°43W **343** B8
Brač *Croatia* 43°20N 16°40E **294** C7
Bracadale, L. *U.K.* 57°20N 6°30W **283** D2
Bracciano, L. di *Italy* 42°7N 12°14E **294** C5
Bracebridge *Canada* 45°2N 79°19W **354** A5
Brach *Libya* 27°31N 14°20E **323** C8
Bräcke *Sweden* 62°45N 15°26E **280** E16
Brackettville *U.S.A.* 29°19N 100°25W **356** G4
Bracknell *U.K.* 51°25N 0°43W **285** F7
Bracknell Forest □ *U.K.* 51°25N 0°44W **285** F7
Brad *Romania* 46°10N 22°50E **289** E12
Bradenton *U.S.A.* 27°30N 82°34W **357** H13
Bradford *Canada* 44°7N 79°34W **354** B5
Bradford *U.K.* 53°47N 1°45W **284** D6
Bradford *Pa., U.S.A.* 41°58N 78°38W **354** E6
Bradford *Vt., U.S.A.* 43°59N 72°9W **355** C12
Bradley *Ark., U.S.A.* 33°6N 93°39W **356** E8
Bradley *Calif., U.S.A.* 35°52N 120°48W **350** K6
Bradley Institute *Zimbabwe* 17°7S 31°25E **327** F3
Brady *U.S.A.* 31°9N 99°20W **356** F5
Braeside *Canada* 45°28N 76°24W **355** A8
Braga *Portugal* 41°35N 8°25W **293** B1
Bragado *Argentina* 35°2S 60°27W **366** D3
Bragança *Brazil* 1°0S 47°2W **365** D9
Bragança *Portugal* 41°48N 6°50W **293** B2
Bragança Paulista *Brazil* 22°55S 46°32W **367** A6
Brahestad = Raahe *Finland* 64°40N 24°28E **280** D21
Brahmanbaria *Bangla.* 23°58N 91°15E **313** H17
Brahmani → *India* 20°39N 86°46E **313** J15
Brahmapur *India* 19°15N 84°54E **313** K14
Brahmaputra → *Asia* 23°40N 90°35E **315** H13
Braich-y-pwll *U.K.* 52°47N 4°46W **284** E3
Braidwood *Australia* 35°27S 149°49E **335** F4
Brăila *Romania* 45°19N 27°59E **289** F14
Brainerd *U.S.A.* 46°22N 94°12W **352** B6
Braintree *U.K.* 51°53N 0°34E **285** F8
Braintree *U.S.A.* 42°13N 71°0W **355** D14
Brak → *S. Africa* 29°35S 22°55E **328** D3
Brakwater *Namibia* 22°28S 17°3E **328** C2
Brampton *Canada* 43°45N 79°45W **354** C5
Brampton *U.K.* 54°57N 2°44W **284** C5
Bramton I. *Australia* 20°50S 149°17E **334** J7
Branco → *Brazil* 1°20S 61°50W **364** D6
Brandberg *Namibia* 21°10S 14°33E **328** C1
Brandberg ⌂ *Namibia* 21°10S 14°30E **328** C1
Brandenburg = Neubrandenburg *Germany* 53°33N 13°15E **288** B7
Brandenburg *Germany* 52°25N 12°33E **288** B7
Brandenburg □ *Germany* 52°50N 13°0E **288** B6
Brandfort *S. Africa* 28°40S 26°30E **328** D4
Brandon *Canada* 49°50N 99°57W **343** D9
Brandon *U.S.A.* 43°48N 73°6W **355** C11
Brandon B. *Ireland* 52°17N 10°8W **282** D1
Brandon Mt. *Ireland* 52°15N 10°15W **282** D1
Brandsen *Argentina* 35°10S 58°15W **366** D4
Brandvlei *S. Africa* 30°25S 20°30E **328** E3
Branford *U.S.A.* 41°17N 72°49W **355** E12
Braniewo *Poland* 54°25N 19°50E **289** A10
Bransfield Str. *Antarctica* 63°0S 59°0W **277** C18
Branson *U.S.A.* 36°39N 93°13W **352** G7
Brantford *Canada* 43°10N 80°15W **354** C4
Bras d'Or L. *Canada* 45°50N 60°50W **345** C7
Brasher Falls *U.S.A.* 44°49N 74°47W **355** B10
Brasil = Brazil ■ *S. Amer.* 12°0S 50°0W **365** F9
Brasil, Planalto *Brazil* 18°0S 46°30W **362** E6
Brasiléia *Brazil* 11°0S 68°45W **364** F5
Brasília *Brazil* 15°47S 47°55W **365** G9
Brasília Legal *Brazil* 3°49S 55°36W **365** D7
Braslaw *Belarus* 55°38N 27°0E **281** J22
Braşov *Romania* 45°38N 25°35E **289** F13
Brasschaat *Belgium* 51°19N 4°27E **287** C4
Brassey, Banjaran *Malaysia* 5°0N 117°15E **308** D5
Brassey Ra. *Australia* 25°8S 122°15E **333** E3
Brasstown Bald *U.S.A.* 34°53N 83°49W **357** D13
Brastad *Sweden* 58°23N 11°30E **281** G14
Bratislava *Slovak Rep.* 48°10N 17°7E **289** D9
Bratsk *Russia* 56°10N 101°30E **301** D11
Brattleboro *U.S.A.* 42°51N 72°34W **355** D12
Braunau *Austria* 48°15N 13°3E **288** D7
Braunschweig *Germany* 52°15N 10°31E **288** B6
Braunton *U.K.* 51°7N 4°10W **285** F3
Brava *C. Verde Is.* 15°0N 24°40W **322** b
Bravo del Norte, Rio = Grande, Rio → *N. Amer.* 25°58N 97°9W **356** J6
Brawley *U.S.A.* 32°59N 115°31W **351** N11
Bray *Ireland* 53°13N 6°7W **282** C5
Bray, Mt. *Australia* 14°0S 134°30E **334** A1
Bray, Pays de *France* 49°46N 1°26E **292** B4
Brazeau → *Canada* 52°55N 115°14W **342** C5
Brazil *U.S.A.* 39°32N 87°8W **352** F10
Brazil ■ *S. Amer.* 12°0S 50°0W **365** F9
Brazilian Highlands = Brasil, Planalto *Brazil* 18°0S 46°30W **362** E6
Brazo Sur → *S. Amer.* 25°21S 57°42W **366** B4
Brazos → *U.S.A.* 28°53N 95°23W **356** G7
Brazzaville *Congo* 4°9S 15°12E **324** E3
Brčko *Bos.-H.* 44°54N 18°46E **295** B8
Breaden, L. *Australia* 25°51S 125°28E **333** E4
Breaksea Sd. *N.Z.* 45°35S 166°35E **331** F1
Bream B. *N.Z.* 35°56S 174°28E **331** A5
Bream Hd. *N.Z.* 35°51S 174°36E **331** A5
Breas *Chile* 25°29S 70°24W **366** B1
Brebes *Indonesia* 6°52S 109°3E **309** G13
Brechin *Canada* 44°32N 79°10W **354** B5
Brechin *U.K.* 56°44N 2°39W **283** E6
Brecht *Belgium* 51°21N 4°38E **287** C4
Breckenridge *Colo., U.S.A.* 39°29N 106°3W **348** G10
Breckenridge *Minn., U.S.A.* 46°16N 96°35W **352** B5
Breckenridge *Tex., U.S.A.* 32°45N 98°54W **356** E5
Breckland *U.K.* 52°30N 0°40E **285** E8
Brecon *U.K.* 51°57N 3°23W **285** F4
Brecon Beacons *U.K.* 51°53N 3°26W **285** F4
Brecon Beacons ⌂ *U.K.* 51°50N 3°30W **285** F4
Breda *Neths.* 51°35N 4°45E **287** C4
Bredasdorp *S. Africa* 34°33S 20°2E **328** E3
Bree *Belgium* 51°8N 5°35E **287** C5
Bregenz *Austria* 47°30N 9°45E **288** E5
Breiðafjörður *Iceland* 65°15N 23°15W **280** D2
Brejo *Brazil* 3°41S 42°47W **365** D10
Bremen *Germany* 53°4N 8°47E **288** B5
Bremer Bay *Australia* 34°21S 119°20E **333** F2
Bremer I. *Australia* 12°5S 136°45E **334** A2
Bremerhaven *Germany* 53°33N 8°36E **288** B5
Bremerton *U.S.A.* 47°34N 122°37W **350** C4
Brenham *U.S.A.* 30°10N 96°24W **356** F6
Brennerpass *Austria* 47°2N 11°30E **288** E6
Brent *U.S.A.* 32°56N 87°10W **357** E11
Brentwood *U.K.* 51°37N 0°19E **285** F8
Brentwood *Calif., U.S.A.* 37°56N 121°42W **350** H5
Brentwood *N.Y., U.S.A.* 40°47N 73°15W **355** F11
Bréscia *Italy* 45°33N 10°15E **292** D9
Breskens *Neths.* 51°23N 3°33E **287** C3
Breslau = Wrocław *Poland* 51°5N 17°5E **289** C9
Bressanone *Italy* 46°43N 11°39E **294** A4
Bressay *U.K.* 60°9N 1°6W **283** A7
Brest *Belarus* 52°10N 23°40E **289** B12
Brest *France* 48°24N 4°31W **292** B1
Brest-Litovsk = Brest *Belarus* 52°10N 23°40E **289** B12
Bretagne □ *France* 48°10N 3°0W **292** B2
Breton *Canada* 53°7N 114°28W **342** C6
Breton Sd. *U.S.A.* 29°35N 89°15W **357** G10
Brett, C. *N.Z.* 35°10S 174°20E **331** A5
Brevard *U.S.A.* 35°14N 82°44W **357** D13
Breves *Brazil* 1°40S 50°29W **365** D8
Brewarrina *Australia* 30°0S 146°51E **335** E4
Brewer *U.S.A.* 44°48N 68°46W **353** C19
Brewer, Mt. *U.S.A.* 36°44N 118°28W **350** J8
Brewster *N.Y., U.S.A.* 41°24N 73°36W **355** E11
Brewster *Ohio, U.S.A.* 40°43N 81°36W **354** F3
Brewster *Wash., U.S.A.* 48°6N 119°47W **348** B4
Brewster, Kap = Kangikajik *Greenland* 70°7N 22°0W **276** B6
Brewton *U.S.A.* 31°7N 87°4W **357** F11
Breyten *S. Africa* 26°16S 30°0E **329** D5
Bria *C.A.R.* 6°30N 21°58E **324** C4
Briançon *France* 44°54N 6°39E **292** D7
Bribie I. *Australia* 27°0S 153°10E **335** D5
Bribri *Costa Rica* 9°38N 82°50W **360** E3
Bridgefield *Barbados* 13°9N 59°36W **361** g
Bridgehampton *U.S.A.* 40°56N 72°19W **355** F12
Bridgend *U.K.* 51°30N 3°34W **285** F4
Bridgend □ *U.K.* 51°36N 3°36W **285** F4
Bridgeport *Calif., U.S.A.* 38°15N 119°14W **350** G7
Bridgeport *Conn., U.S.A.* 41°11N 73°12W **355** E11
Bridgeport *Nebr., U.S.A.* 41°40N 103°6W **352** E2
Bridgeport *Tex., U.S.A.* 33°13N 97°45W **356** E6
Bridger *U.S.A.* 45°18N 108°55W **348** D9
Bridgeton *U.S.A.* 39°26N 75°14W **353** F16
Bridgetown *Australia* 33°58S 116°7E **333** F2
Bridgetown *Barbados* 13°6N 59°37W **361** g
Bridgetown *Canada* 44°55N 65°18W **345** D6
Bridgewater *Australia* 42°44S 147°14E **335** G4
Bridgewater *Canada* 44°25N 64°31W **345** D7
Bridgewater *Mass., U.S.A.* 41°59N 70°58W **355** E14
Bridgewater *N.Y., U.S.A.* 42°53N 75°15W **355** D9
Bridgewater, C. *Australia* 38°23S 141°23E **335** F3
Bridgnorth *U.K.* 52°32N 2°25W **285** E5
Bridgton *U.S.A.* 44°3N 70°42W **355** B14
Bridgwater *U.K.* 51°8N 2°59W **285** F5
Bridgwater B. *U.K.* 51°15N 3°15W **285** F4
Bridlington *U.K.* 54°5N 0°12W **284** C7
Bridlington B. *U.K.* 54°4N 0°10W **284** C7
Bridport *Australia* 40°59S 147°23E **335** G4
Bridport *U.K.* 50°44N 2°45W **285** G5
Brig *Switz.* 46°18N 7°59E **292** C7
Brigg *U.K.* 53°34N 0°28W **284** D7
Brigham City *U.S.A.* 41°31N 112°1W **348** F7
Bright *Australia* 36°42S 146°56E **335** F4
Brighton *Australia* 35°5S 138°30E **335** F2
Brighton *Canada* 44°2N 77°44W **354** B7
Brighton *Trin. & Tob.* 10°13N 61°39W **365** K15
Brighton *U.K.* 50°49N 0°7W **285** G7
Brighton *U.S.A.* 43°8N 77°34W **354** C7
Brilliant *U.S.A.* 40°15N 80°39W **354** F4
Bríndisi *Italy* 40°39N 17°55E **295** D7
Brinkley *U.S.A.* 34°53N 91°12W **356** D9
Brinnon *U.S.A.* 47°41N 122°54W **350** C4
Brion, Î. *Canada* 47°46N 61°26W **345** C7
Brisbane *Australia* 27°25S 153°2E **335** D5
Brisbane → *Australia* 27°24S 153°9E **335** D5
Bristol *U.K.* 51°26N 2°35W **285** F5
Bristol *Conn., U.S.A.* 41°40N 72°57W **355** E12
Bristol *Pa., U.S.A.* 40°6N 74°51W **355** F10
Bristol *R.I., U.S.A.* 41°40N 71°16W **355** E13
Bristol *Tenn., U.S.A.* 36°36N 82°11W **357** C13
Bristol, City of □ *U.K.* 51°27N 2°36W **285** F5
Bristol B. *U.S.A.* 58°0N 160°0W **346** a
Bristol Channel *U.K.* 51°18N 4°30W **285** F3
Bristol I. *Antarctica* 58°45S 28°0W **277** B1
Bristol L. *U.S.A.* 34°28N 115°41W **349** J6
Bristow *U.S.A.* 35°50N 96°23W **356** D6
Britain = Great Britain *Europe* 54°0N 2°15W **278** E5
British Columbia □ *Canada* 55°0N 125°15W **342** C3
British Indian Ocean Terr. = Chagos Arch. ⊠ *Ind. Oc.* 6°0S 72°0E **298** J9
British Isles *Europe* 54°0N 4°0W **286** D5
British Virgin Is. ⊠ *W. Indies* 18°30N 64°30W **361** e
Brits *S. Africa* 25°37S 27°48E **329** D4
Britstown *S. Africa* 30°37S 23°30E **328** E3
Britt *Canada* 45°46N 80°34W **344** C3
Brittany = Bretagne □ *France* 48°10N 3°0W **292** B2
Britton *U.S.A.* 45°48N 97°45W **352** C5
Brive-la-Gaillarde *France* 45°10N 1°32E **292** D4
Brixen = Bressanone *Italy* 46°43N 11°39E **294** A4
Brixham *U.K.* 50°23N 3°31W **285** G4
Brno *Czech Rep.* 49°10N 16°35E **289** D9
Broach = Bharuch *India* 21°47N 73°0E **312** J8
Broad → *U.S.A.* 34°1N 81°4W **357** D14
Broad Arrow *Australia* 30°23S 121°15E **333** F3
Broad B. *U.K.* 58°14N 6°18W **283** C2
Broad Haven *Ireland* 54°20N 9°55W **282** B2
Broad Law *U.K.* 55°30N 3°21W **283** F5
Broad Sd. *Australia* 22°0S 149°45E **334** C4
Broadalbin *U.S.A.* 43°4N 74°12W **355** C10
Broadback → *Canada* 51°21N 78°52W **344** B4
Broadhurst Ra. *Australia* 22°30S 122°30E **332** D3

Broads, The U.K. 52°45N 1°30E 284 E9
Broadus U.S.A. 45°27N 105°25W 348 D11
Brochet Canada 57°53N 101°40W 343 B8
Brochet, L. Canada 58°36N 101°35W 343 B8
Brock I. Canada 77°52N 114°19W 341 B8
Brocken Germany 51°47N 10°37E 288 C6
Brockport U.S.A. 43°13N 77°56W 354 C7
Brockton U.S.A. 42°5N 71°1W 355 D13
Brockville Canada 44°35N 75°41W 355 B9
Brockway Mont., U.S.A. 47°18N 105°45W 348 C11
Brockway Pa., U.S.A. 41°15N 78°47W 354 E6
Brocton U.S.A. 42°23N 79°26W 354 D5
Brodeur Pen. Canada 72°30N 88°10W 341 B11
Brodick U.K. 55°35N 5°9W 283 F3
Brodnica Poland 53°15N 19°25E 289 B10
Brody Ukraine 50°5N 25°10E 289 C13
Brogan U.S.A. 44°15N 117°31W 348 D5
Broken Arrow U.S.A. 36°3N 95°48W 356 C7
Broken Bow Nebr., U.S.A. 41°24N 99°38W 352 E4
Broken Bow Okla., U.S.A. 34°2N 94°44W 356 D7
Broken Bow Lake U.S.A. 34°9N 94°40W 356 D7
Broken Hill Australia 31°58S 141°29E 335 E3
Broken Ridge Ind. Oc. 30°0S 94°0E 336 L1
Broken River Ra. Australia 21°0S 148°22E 334 K6
Bromley □ U.K. 51°24N 0°2E 285 F8
Bromo Indonesia 7°55S 112°55E 309 G15
Bromsgrove U.K. 52°21N 2°2W 285 E5
Brønderslev Denmark 57°16N 9°57E 281 H13
Bronkhorstspruit S. Africa 25°46S 28°45E 329 D4
Brønnøysund Norway 65°28N 12°14E 280 D15
Brook Park U.S.A. 41°23N 81°48W 354 E4
Brookhaven U.S.A. 31°35N 90°26W 357 F9
Brookings Oreg., U.S.A. 42°3N 124°17W 348 E1
Brookings S. Dak., U.S.A. 44°19N 96°48W 352 C5
Brooklin Canada 43°55N 78°55W 354 C6
Brooklyn Park U.S.A. 45°6N 93°23W 352 C7
Brooks Canada 50°35N 111°55W 342 C6
Brooks Range U.S.A. 68°0N 152°0W 346 a
Brooksville U.S.A. 28°33N 82°23W 357 G13
Brookton Australia 32°22S 117°0E 333 F2
Brookville U.S.A. 41°10N 79°5W 354 E5
Broom, L. U.K. 57°55N 5°15W 283 D3
Broome Australia 18°0S 122°15E 332 C3
Brora U.K. 58°0N 3°52W 283 C5
Brora → U.K. 58°0N 3°51W 283 C5
Brosna → Ireland 53°14N 7°58W 282 C4
Brothers U.S.A. 43°49N 120°36W 348 E3
Brough U.K. 54°32N 2°18W 284 C5
Brough Hd. U.K. 59°8N 3°20W 283 B5
Broughton Island = Qikiqtarjuaq Canada 67°33N 63°0W 341 C13
Brown, L. Australia 31°5S 118°15E 333 F2
Brown, Pt. Australia 32°32S 133°50E 335 E1
Brown City U.S.A. 43°13N 82°59W 354 C2
Brown Willy U.K. 50°35N 4°37W 285 G3
Brownfield U.S.A. 33°11N 102°17W 356 E3
Browning U.S.A. 48°34N 113°1W 348 B7
Brownsville Oreg., U.S.A. 44°24N 122°59W 348 D2
Brownsville Pa., U.S.A. 40°1N 79°53W 354 F5
Brownsville Tenn., U.S.A. 35°36N 89°16W 357 D10
Brownsville Tex., U.S.A. 25°54N 97°30W 356 J6
Brownville U.S.A. 44°0N 75°59W 355 C9
Brownwood U.S.A. 31°43N 98°59W 356 F5
Browse I. Australia 14°7S 123°33E 332 B3
Bruas Malaysia 4°30N 100°47E 311 K3
Bruay-la-Buissière France 50°29N 2°33E 292 A5
Bruce, Mt. Australia 22°37S 118°8E 332 D2
Bruce Pen. Canada 45°0N 81°30W 354 B3
Bruce Peninsula △ Canada 45°14N 81°36W 354 A3
Bruce Rock Australia 31°52S 118°8E 333 F2
Bruck an der Leitha Austria 48°1N 16°47E 289 D9
Bruck an der Mur Austria 47°24N 15°16E 288 E8
Brue → U.K. 51°13N 2°59W 285 F5
Bruges = Brugge Belgium 51°13N 3°13E 287 C3
Brugge Belgium 51°13N 3°13E 287 C3
Bruin U.S.A. 41°3N 79°43W 354 E5
Brûk, W. el → Egypt 30°15N 33°50E 318 E2
Brûlé Canada 53°15N 117°58W 342 C5
Brumado Brazil 14°14S 41°40W 365 F10
Brumunddal Norway 60°53N 10°56E 280 F14
Bruneau U.S.A. 42°53N 115°48W 348 E6
Bruneau → U.S.A. 42°56N 115°57W 348 E6
Brunei = Bandar Seri Begawan Brunei 4°52N 115°0E 308 C4
Brunei ■ Asia 4°50N 115°0E 308 D4
Brunner, L. N.Z. 42°37S 171°27E 331 E3
Brunssum Neths. 50°57N 5°59E 287 D5
Brunswick = Braunschweig Germany 52°15N 10°31E 288 B6
Brunswick Ga., U.S.A. 31°10N 81°30W 357 F14
Brunswick Maine, U.S.A. 43°55N 69°58W 353 D19
Brunswick Md., U.S.A. 39°19N 77°38W 353 F15
Brunswick Mo., U.S.A. 39°26N 93°8W 352 F7
Brunswick Ohio, U.S.A. 41°14N 81°51W 354 E3
Brunswick, Pen. de Chile 53°30S 71°30W 368 G2
Brunswick B. Australia 15°15S 124°50E 332 C3
Brunswick Junction Australia 33°15S 115°50E 333 F2
Brunt Ice Shelf Antarctica 75°30S 25°0W 277 D2
Brus Laguna Honduras 15°47N 84°35W 360 C3
Brush U.S.A. 40°15N 103°37W 348 F12
Brushton U.S.A. 44°50N 74°31W 355 B10
Brusque Brazil 27°5S 49°0W 367 B6
Brussel Belgium 50°51N 4°21E 287 D4
Brussel ✕ (BRU) Belgium 50°54N 4°29E 287 D5
Brussels = Brussel Belgium 50°51N 4°21E 287 D4
Brussels Canada 43°44N 81°15W 354 C3
Bruthen Australia 37°42S 147°50E 335 F4
Bruxelles = Brussel Belgium 50°51N 4°21E 287 D4
Bryan Ohio, U.S.A. 41°28N 84°33W 353 E11
Bryan Tex., U.S.A. 30°40N 96°22W 356 F6
Bryan, Mt. Australia 33°30S 139°5E 335 E2
Bryansk Russia 53°13N 34°25E 290 D4
Bryce Canyon △ U.S.A. 37°30N 112°10W 349 H7
Bryne Norway 58°44N 5°38E 281 G11
Bryson City U.S.A. 35°26N 83°27W 357 D13
Bsharri Lebanon 34°15N 36°0E 318 A5
Bū Baqarah U.A.E. 25°35N 56°25E 317 E8
Bu Craa W. Sahara 26°45N 12°50W 322 C3
Bū Ḥasā U.A.E. 23°30N 53°20E 317 F7
Bua Fiji 16°48S 178°37E 331 a
Bua Yai Thailand 15°33N 102°26E 310 E4
Buan S. Korea 35°44N 126°44E 307 G14
Buapinang Indonesia 4°40S 121°30E 309 E6
Bubanza Burundi 3°6S 29°23E 326 C2
Bubi → Zimbabwe 22°20S 31°7E 327 G3
Būbiyān Kuwait 29°45N 48°15E 317 D6
Buca Fiji 16°38S 179°52E 331 a
Bucaramanga Colombia 7°0N 73°0W 364 B4
Bucasia Australia 21°2S 149°10E 334 K7
Buccaneer Arch. Australia 16°7S 123°20E 332 C3
Buccoo Reef Trin. & Tob. 11°10N 60°51W 365 J16
Buchach Ukraine 49°5N 25°25E 289 D13
Buchan U.K. 57°32N 2°21W 283 D6
Buchan Ness U.K. 57°29N 1°46W 283 D7
Buchanan Canada 51°40N 102°45W 343 C8
Buchanan Liberia 5°57N 10°2W 322 G3
Buchanan, L. Queens., Australia 21°35S 145°52E 334 C4
Buchanan, L. W. Austral., Australia 25°33S 123°2E 333 E3
Buchanan, L. U.S.A. 30°45N 98°25W 356 F5
Buchanan Cr. → Australia 19°13S 136°33E 334 B2
Buchans Canada 48°50N 56°52W 345 C8
Bucharest = București Romania 44°27N 26°10E 289 F14
Bucheon S. Korea 37°28N 126°45E 307 F14
Buchon, Pt. U.S.A. 35°15N 120°54W 350 K6
Buck Hill Falls U.S.A. 41°11N 75°16W 355 E9
Buckeye Lake U.S.A. 39°55N 82°29W 354 G2
Buckhannon U.S.A. 39°0N 80°8W 353 F13
Buckhaven U.K. 56°11N 3°3W 283 E5
Buckhorn L. Canada 44°29N 78°23W 354 B6
Buckie U.K. 57°41N 2°58W 283 D6
Buckingham Canada 45°37N 75°24W 344 C4
Buckingham U.K. 51°59N 0°57W 285 F7
Buckingham B. Australia 12°10S 135°40E 334 A2
Buckinghamshire □ U.K. 51°53N 0°55W 285 F7
Buckle Hd. Australia 14°26S 127°52E 332 B4
Buckleboo Australia 32°54S 136°12E 335 E2
Buckley U.K. 53°10N 3°5W 284 D4
Buckley → Australia 20°10S 138°49E 334 C2
Bucklin U.S.A. 37°33N 99°38W 352 G4
Bucks L. U.S.A. 39°54N 121°12W 350 F5
București Romania 44°27N 26°10E 289 F14
Bucyrus U.S.A. 40°48N 82°59W 353 E12
Budalin Burma 22°20N 95°10E 313 H19
Budapest Hungary 47°29N 19°3E 289 E10
Budaun India 28°5N 79°10E 315 E8
Budd Coast Antarctica 68°0S 112°0E 277 C8
Bude U.K. 50°49N 4°34W 285 G3
Budennovsk Russia 44°50N 44°10E 291 F7
Budge Budge = Baj Baj India 22°30N 88°5E 315 H13
Budgewoi Australia 33°13S 151°34E 335 E5
Budjala Dem. Rep. of the Congo 2°50N 19°40E 324 D3
Buellton U.S.A. 34°37N 120°12W 351 L6
Buena Esperanza Argentina 34°45S 65°15W 366 C2
Buena Park U.S.A. 33°52N 117°59W 351 M9
Buena Vista Colo., U.S.A. 38°51N 106°8W 348 G10
Buena Vista Va., U.S.A. 37°44N 79°21W 353 G14
Buena Vista Lake Bed U.S.A. 35°12N 119°18W 351 K7
Buenaventura Colombia 3°53N 77°4W 364 C3
Buenaventura Mexico 29°51N 107°29W 358 B3
Buenos Aires Argentina 34°36S 58°22W 366 C4
Buenos Aires Costa Rica 9°10N 83°20W 360 E3
Buenos Aires □ Argentina 36°30S 60°0W 366 D4
Buenos Aires, L. Argentina 46°35S 72°30W 368 F2
Buffalo Mo., U.S.A. 37°39N 93°6W 352 G7
Buffalo N.Y., U.S.A. 42°53N 78°53W 354 D6
Buffalo Okla., U.S.A. 36°50N 99°38W 356 C5
Buffalo S. Dak., U.S.A. 45°35N 103°33W 352 C2
Buffalo Wyo., U.S.A. 44°21N 106°42W 348 D10
Buffalo → Canada 60°5N 115°5W 342 A5
Buffalo → S. Africa 28°43S 30°37E 329 D5
Buffalo ⌂ U.S.A. 36°14N 92°36W 356 C8
Buffalo Head Hills Canada 57°25N 115°55W 342 B5
Buffalo L. Alta., Canada 52°27N 112°54W 342 C6
Buffalo L. N.W.T., Canada 60°12N 115°25W 342 A5
Buffalo Narrows Canada 55°51N 108°29W 343 B7
Buffalo Springs ⌂ Kenya 0°32N 37°35E 326 B4
Buffels → S. Africa 29°36S 17°3E 328 D2
Buford U.S.A. 34°10N 84°0W 357 D12
Bug = Buh → Ukraine 46°59N 31°58E 291 E5
Bug → Poland 52°31N 21°5E 289 B11
Buga Colombia 4°0N 76°15W 364 C3
Bugala I. Uganda 0°40S 32°20E 326 C3
Buganda Uganda 0°0 31°30E 326 C3
Buganga Uganda 0°3S 32°0E 326 C3
Bugel, Tanjung Indonesia 6°26S 111°3E 309 G14
Bugibba Malta 35°57N 14°25E 297 D1
Bugsuk I. Phil. 8°12N 117°18E 308 C5
Bugulma Russia 54°33N 52°48E 290 D9
Bugun Shara Mongolia 49°0N 104°0E 304 B5
Bugungu ⌂ Uganda 2°17N 31°50E 326 B3
Buguruslan Russia 53°39N 52°26E 290 D9
Buh → Ukraine 46°59N 31°58E 291 E5
Buhera Zimbabwe 19°18S 31°29E 329 B5
Buhl U.S.A. 42°36N 114°46W 348 E6
Builth Wells U.K. 52°9N 3°25W 285 E4
Buir Nur Mongolia 47°50N 117°42E 305 B6
Buji China 22°37N 114°5E 305 F11
Bujumbura Burundi 3°16S 29°18E 326 C2
Bukachacha Russia 52°55N 116°50E 301 D12
Bukama Dem. Rep. of the Congo 9°10S 25°50E 327 D2
Būkān Iran 36°31N 46°12E 316 B5
Bukavu Dem. Rep. of the Congo 2°20S 28°52E 326 C2
Bukene Tanzania 4°15S 32°48E 326 C3
Bukhara = Bukhoro Uzbekistan 39°48N 64°25E 300 F7
Bukhoro Uzbekistan 39°48N 64°25E 300 F7
Bukima Tanzania 1°50S 33°25E 326 C3
Bukit Badung Indonesia 8°49S 115°10E 309 K18
Bukit Kerajaan Malaysia 5°25N 100°15E 311 c
Bukit Mertajam Malaysia 5°22N 100°28E 311 c
Bukit Ni Malaysia 1°22N 104°12E 311 d
Bukit Panjang Singapore 1°23N 103°46E 311 d
Bukit Tengah Malaysia 5°22N 100°25E 311 c
Bukittinggi Indonesia 0°20S 100°20E 308 E2
Bukoba Tanzania 1°20S 31°49E 326 C3
Bukum, Pulau Singapore 1°14N 103°46E 311 d
Bukuya Uganda 0°40N 31°52E 326 B3
Būl, Kuh-e Iran 30°48N 52°45E 317 D7
Bula Indonesia 3°6S 130°30E 309 E8
Bulahdelah Australia 32°23S 152°13E 335 E5
Bulan Phil. 12°40N 123°52E 309 B6
Bulandshahr India 28°28N 77°51E 314 E7
Bulawayo Zimbabwe 20°7S 28°32E 327 G2
Buldan Turkey 38°2N 28°50E 295 E13
Bulgan Mongolia 48°45N 103°34E 304 B5
Bulgar Russia 54°57N 49°4E 290 D8
Bulgaria ■ Europe 42°35N 25°30E 295 C11
Buli, Teluk Indonesia 0°48N 128°25E 309 D7
Buliluyan, C. Phil. 8°20N 117°15E 308 C5
Bulim Singapore 1°22N 103°43E 311 d
Bulkley → Canada 55°15N 127°40W 342 B3
Bull Shoals L. U.S.A. 36°22N 92°35W 356 C8
Bulleringa △ Australia 17°39S 143°56E 334 B3
Bullhead City U.S.A. 35°8N 114°32W 351 K12
Büllingen Belgium 50°25N 6°16E 287 D6
Bullock Creek Australia 17°43S 144°31E 334 B3
Bulloo → Australia 28°43S 142°30E 335 D3
Bulloo L. Australia 28°43S 142°25E 335 D3
Bulls N.Z. 40°10S 175°24E 331 D5
Bulnes Chile 36°42S 72°19W 366 D1
Bulsar = Valsad India 20°40N 72°58E 312 J8
Bultfontein S. Africa 28°18S 26°10E 328 D4
Bulukumba Indonesia 5°33S 120°11E 309 F6
Bulun Russia 70°37N 127°30E 301 B13
Bumba Dem. Rep. of the Congo 2°13N 22°30E 324 D4
Bumbiri I. Tanzania 1°40S 31°55E 326 C3
Bumhpa Bum Burma 26°51N 97°14E 313 F20
Bumi → Zimbabwe 17°0S 28°20E 327 F2
Buna Kenya 2°58N 39°30E 326 B4
Bunaken Indonesia 1°37N 124°46E 309 D6
Bunazi Tanzania 1°3S 31°23E 326 C3
Bunbah, Khalīj Libya 32°20N 23°15E 323 B10
Bunbury Australia 33°20S 115°35E 333 F2
Bunclody Ireland 52°39N 6°40W 282 D5
Buncrana Ireland 55°8N 7°27W 282 A4
Bundaberg Australia 24°54S 152°22E 335 C5
Bundey → Australia 21°46S 135°37E 334 C2
Bundi India 25°30N 75°35E 314 G6
Bundjalung △ Australia 29°16S 153°21E 335 D5
Bundoran Ireland 54°28N 8°16W 282 B3
Bung Kan Thailand 18°23N 103°37E 310 C4
Bungay U.K. 52°27N 1°28E 285 E9
Bungil Cr. → Australia 27°5S 149°5E 335 D4
Bungle Bungle = Purnululu △ Australia 17°20S 128°20E 332 C4
Bungo-Suidō Japan 33°0N 132°15E 303 H6
Bungoma Kenya 0°34N 34°34E 326 B3
Bungotakada Japan 33°35N 131°25E 303 H5
Bungu Tanzania 7°35S 39°0E 326 D4
Bunia Dem. Rep. of the Congo 1°35N 30°20E 326 B3
Bunji Pakistan 35°45N 74°40E 315 B6
Bunkie U.S.A. 30°57N 92°11W 356 F8
Bunnell U.S.A. 29°28N 81°16W 357 G14
Buntok Indonesia 1°40S 114°58E 308 E4
Bunya Mts. △ Australia 26°51S 151°34E 335 D5
Bunyu Indonesia 3°35N 117°50E 308 D5
Buol Indonesia 1°15N 121°32E 309 D6
Buon Brieng Vietnam 13°9N 108°12E 310 F7
Buon Ma Thuot Vietnam 12°40N 108°3E 310 F7
Buong Long Cambodia 13°44N 106°59E 310 F6
Buorkhaya, Mys Russia 71°50N 132°40E 301 B14
Buqayq Si. Arabia 26°0N 49°45E 317 E6
Bur Acaba Somali Rep. 3°12N 44°20E 319 G3
Bûr Safâga Egypt 26°43N 33°57E 316 E2
Bûr Sa'îd Egypt 31°16N 32°18E 323 B12
Bûr Sûdân Sudan 19°32N 37°9E 323 E13
Bura Kenya 1°4S 39°58E 326 C4
Burakin Australia 30°31S 117°10E 333 F2
Burao Somali Rep. 9°32N 45°32E 319 F4
Burāq Syria 33°11N 36°29E 318 B5
Buraydah Si. Arabia 26°20N 43°59E 316 E4
Burbank U.S.A. 34°12N 118°18W 351 L8
Burda India 25°50N 77°35E 314 G6
Burdekin → Australia 19°38S 147°25E 334 B4
Burdur Turkey 37°45N 30°17E 291 G5
Burdwan = Barddhaman India 23°14N 87°39E 315 H12
Bure Ethiopia 10°40N 37°4E 319 E2
Bure → U.K. 52°38N 1°43E 284 E9
Bureya → Russia 49°27N 129°30E 301 E13
Burford Canada 43°7N 80°27W 354 C4
Burgas Bulgaria 42°33N 27°29E 295 C12
Burgeo Canada 47°37N 57°38W 345 C8
Burgersdorp S. Africa 31°0S 26°20E 328 E4
Burges, Mt. Australia 30°50S 121°5E 333 F3
Burghead U.K. 57°43N 3°30W 283 D5
Burgos Spain 42°21N 3°41W 293 A4
Burgsvik Sweden 57°3N 18°19E 281 H18
Burgundy = Bourgogne □ France 47°0N 4°50E 292 C6
Burhaniye Turkey 39°30N 26°58E 295 E12
Burhanpur India 21°18N 76°14E 312 J10
Burhi Gandak → India 25°20N 86°37E 315 G12
Burhner → India 22°43N 80°31E 315 H9
Burias I. Phil. 12°55N 123°5E 309 B6
Burica, Pta. Costa Rica 8°3N 82°51W 360 E3
Burien U.S.A. 47°28N 122°20W 350 C4
Burigi, L. Tanzania 2°2S 31°22E 326 C3
Burigi ⌂ Tanzania 2°20S 31°6E 326 C3
Burin Canada 47°1N 55°14W 345 C8
Buriram Thailand 15°0N 103°0E 310 E4
Burkburnett U.S.A. 34°6N 98°34W 356 D5
Burke → Australia 23°12S 139°33E 334 C2
Burke Chan. Canada 52°10N 127°30W 342 C3
Burketown Australia 17°45S 139°33E 334 B2
Burkina Faso ■ Africa 12°0N 1°0W 322 F5
Burk's Falls Canada 45°37N 79°24W 344 C4
Burleigh Falls Canada 44°33N 78°12W 354 B6
Burley U.S.A. 42°32N 113°48W 348 E7
Burlingame U.S.A. 37°35N 122°21W 350 H4
Burlington Canada 43°18N 79°45W 354 C5
Burlington Colo., U.S.A. 39°18N 102°16W 348 G12
Burlington Iowa, U.S.A. 40°49N 91°14W 352 E8
Burlington Kans., U.S.A. 38°12N 95°45W 352 F6
Burlington N.C., U.S.A. 36°6N 79°26W 357 C15
Burlington N.J., U.S.A. 40°4N 74°51W 355 F10
Burlington Vt., U.S.A. 44°29N 73°12W 355 B11
Burlington Wash., U.S.A. 48°28N 122°20W 350 B4
Burlington Wis., U.S.A. 42°41N 88°17W 352 D9
Burma ■ Asia 21°0N 96°30E 313 J20
Burnaby I. Canada 52°25N 131°19W 342 C2
Burnet U.S.A. 30°45N 98°14W 356 F5
Burney U.S.A. 40°53N 121°40W 348 F3
Burnham U.S.A. 40°38N 77°34W 354 F7
Burnham-on-Sea U.K. 51°14N 3°0W 285 F5
Burnie Australia 41°4S 145°56E 335 G4
Burnley U.K. 53°47N 2°14W 284 D5
Burns U.S.A. 43°35N 119°3W 348 E4
Burns Junction U.S.A. 42°47N 117°51W 348 E5
Burns Lake Canada 54°14N 125°45W 342 C3
Burnside → Canada 66°51N 108°4W 340 C9
Burnside, L. Australia 25°22S 123°0E 333 E3
Burnsville U.S.A. 44°47N 93°17W 352 C7
Burnt, L. Canada 53°35N 64°4W 345 B7
Burnt River Canada 44°41N 78°42W 354 B6
Burntwood → Canada 56°8N 96°34W 343 B9
Burntwood L. Canada 55°22N 100°26W 343 B8
Burqān Kuwait 29°0N 47°57E 316 D5
Burqin China 47°43N 87°0E 304 B3
Burra Australia 33°40S 138°55E 335 E2
Burray U.K. 58°51N 2°54W 283 C6
Burren Ireland 53°9N 9°5W 282 C2
Burren △ Ireland 53°1N 8°58W 282 C3
Burren Junction Australia 30°7S 148°58E 335 E4
Burrinjuck Res. Australia 35°0S 148°36E 335 F4
Burro, Serranías del Mexico 28°56N 102°5W 358 B4
Burrow Hd. U.K. 54°41N 4°24W 283 G4
Burrum Coast △ Australia 25°13S 152°36E 335 D5
Burruyacú Argentina 26°30S 64°40W 366 B3
Burry Port U.K. 51°41N 4°15W 285 F3
Bursa Turkey 40°15N 29°5E 295 D13
Burstall Canada 50°39N 109°54W 343 C7
Burton Ohio, U.S.A. 41°28N 81°8W 354 E3
Burton S.C., U.S.A. 32°26N 80°43W 357 E14
Burton, L. Canada 54°45N 78°20W 344 B4
Burton upon Trent U.K. 52°48N 1°38W 284 E6
Buru Indonesia 3°30S 126°30E 309 E7
Burûn, Râs Egypt 31°14N 33°7E 318 D2
Burundi ■ Africa 3°15S 30°0E 326 C3
Bururi Burundi 3°57S 29°37E 326 C2
Burutu Nigeria 5°20N 5°29E 322 G7
Burwell U.S.A. 41°47N 99°8W 352 E4
Burwick U.K. 58°45N 2°58W 283 C5
Bury U.K. 53°35N 2°17W 284 D5
Bury St. Edmunds U.K. 52°15N 0°43E 285 E8
Buryatia □ Russia 53°0N 110°0E 301 D11
Busan S. Korea 35°5N 129°0E 307 G15
Busango Swamp Zambia 14°15S 25°45E 327 E2
Buşayrah Syria 35°9N 40°26E 316 C4
Būshehr Iran 28°55N 50°55E 317 D6
Būshehr □ Iran 28°20N 51°45E 317 D6
Bushell Canada 59°31N 108°45W 343 B7
Bushenyi Uganda 0°35S 30°10E 326 C3
Bushire = Būshehr Iran 28°55N 50°55E 317 D6
Businga Dem. Rep. of the Congo 3°16N 20°59E 324 D4
Buşra ash Shām Syria 32°30N 36°25E 318 C5
Busselton Australia 33°42S 115°15E 333 F2
Bussum Neths. 52°16N 5°10E 287 B5
Busto Arsízio Italy 45°37N 8°51E 292 D8
Busu Djanoa Dem. Rep. of the Congo 1°43N 21°23E 324 D4
Busuanga I. Phil. 12°10N 120°0E 309 B5
Busungbiu Indonesia 8°16S 114°58E 309 J17
Buta Dem. Rep. of the Congo 2°50N 24°53E 326 B1
Butare Rwanda 2°31S 29°52E 326 C2
Butaritari Kiribati 3°30N 174°0E 336 G9
Bute U.K. 55°48N 5°2W 283 F3
Bute Inlet Canada 50°40N 124°53W 342 C4
Butemba Uganda 1°9N 31°37E 326 B3
Butembo Dem. Rep. of the Congo 0°9N 29°18E 326 B2
Butere Kenya 0°13N 34°30E 326 B3
Butha Qi China 48°0N 122°32E 305 B7
Butiaba Uganda 1°50N 31°20E 326 B3
Butler Mo., U.S.A. 38°16N 94°20W 352 F6
Butler Pa., U.S.A. 40°52N 79°54W 354 F5
Buton Indonesia 5°0S 122°45E 309 E6
Butte Mont., U.S.A. 46°0N 112°32W 348 C7
Butte Nebr., U.S.A. 42°58N 98°51W 352 D4
Butte Creek → U.S.A. 39°12N 121°56W 350 F5
Butterworth = Gcuwa S. Africa 32°20S 28°11E 329 E4
Butterworth Malaysia 5°24N 100°23E 311 c
Buttevant Ireland 52°14N 8°40W 282 D3
Buttfield, Mt. Australia 24°45S 128°9E 333 D4
Button B. Canada 58°45N 94°23W 343 B10
Buttonwillow U.S.A. 35°24N 119°28W 351 K7
Butty Hd. Australia 33°54S 121°39E 333 F3
Butuan Phil. 8°57N 125°33E 309 C7
Butung = Buton Indonesia 5°0S 122°45E 309 E6
Buturlinovka Russia 50°50N 40°35E 291 D7
Buur Hakaba = Bur Acaba Somali Rep. 3°12N 44°20E 319 G3
Buxa Duar India 27°45N 89°35E 315 F13
Buxar India 25°34N 83°58E 315 G10
Buxoro = Bukhoro Uzbekistan 39°48N 64°25E 300 F7
Buxtehude Germany 53°28N 9°39E 288 B5
Buxton U.K. 53°16N 1°54W 284 D6
Buy Russia 58°28N 41°28E 290 C7
Buyant-Uhaa Mongolia 44°55N 110°11E 305 B6
Buyo, L. de Ivory C. 6°16N 7°10W 322 G4
Büyük Menderes → Turkey 37°28N 27°11E 295 F12
Büyükçekmece Turkey 41°2N 28°35E 295 D13
Buzău Romania 45°10N 26°50E 289 F14
Buzău → Romania 45°26N 27°44E 289 F14
Buzen Japan 33°35N 131°5E 303 H5
Buzi → Mozam. 19°50S 34°43E 327 F3
Büzmeýin Turkmenistan 38°3N 58°12E 317 B8
Buzuluk Russia 52°48N 52°12E 290 D9
Buzzards Bay U.S.A. 41°45N 70°37W 355 E14
Bwana Mkubwe Dem. Rep. of the Congo 13°8S 28°38E 327 E2
Bwindi △ Uganda 1°2S 29°42E 326 C2
Byarezina → Belarus 52°33N 30°14E 289 B16
Bydgoszcz Poland 53°10N 18°0E 289 B9
Byelarus = Belarus ■ Europe 53°30N 27°0E 289 B14
Byelorussia = Belarus ■ Europe 53°30N 27°0E 289 B14
Byers U.S.A. 39°43N 104°14W 348 G11
Byesville U.S.A. 39°58N 81°32W 354 G3
Byfield △ Australia 22°52S 150°45E 334 C5
Byford Australia 32°15S 116°0E 333 F2
Bykhaw Belarus 53°31N 30°14E 289 B16
Bykhov = Bykhaw Belarus 53°31N 30°14E 289 B16
Bylas U.S.A. 33°8N 110°7W 349 K8
Bylot Canada 58°25N 94°8W 343 B10
Bylot I. Canada 73°13N 78°34W 341 B12
Byrd, C. Antarctica 69°38S 76°7W 277 C17
Byrock Australia 30°40S 146°27E 335 E4
Byron, C. Australia 28°43S 153°38E 335 D5
Byron Bay Australia 28°43S 153°37E 335 D5
Byrranga, Gory Russia 75°0N 100°0E 301 B11
Byrranga Mts. = Byrranga, Gory Russia 75°0N 100°0E 301 B11
Byske Sweden 64°57N 21°11E 280 D19
Byskeälven → Sweden 64°57N 21°13E 280 D19
Bytom Poland 50°25N 18°54E 289 C10
Bytów Poland 54°10N 17°30E 289 A9
Byumba Rwanda 1°35S 30°4E 326 C3

C

C.W. McConaughy, L. U.S.A. 41°14N 101°40W 352 E3
Ca → Vietnam 18°45N 105°45E 310 C5
Ca Mau Vietnam 9°7N 105°8E 311 H5
Ca Mau, Mui Vietnam 8°38N 104°44E 311 H5
Ca Na Vietnam 11°20N 108°54E 311 G7
Caacupé Paraguay 25°23S 57°5W 366 B4
Caaguazú △ Paraguay 26°5S 55°31W 367 B4
Caála Angola 12°46S 15°30E 325 G3
Caamaño Sd. Canada 52°55N 129°25W 342 C3
Caazapá Paraguay 26°8S 56°19W 366 B4
Caazapá □ Paraguay 26°10S 56°0W 367 B4
Caballeria, C. de Spain 40°5N 4°5E 296 A11
Cabanatuan Phil. 15°30N 120°58E 309 A6
Cabano Canada 47°40N 68°56W 345 C6
Cabazon U.S.A. 33°55N 116°47W 351 M10
Cabedelo Brazil 7°0S 34°50W 365 E12
Cabildo Chile 32°30S 71°5W 366 C1
Cabimas Venezuela 10°23N 71°25W 364 A4
Cabinda Angola 5°33S 12°11E 324 F2

Cabinda □ *Angola* 5°0S 12°30E **324** F2
Cabinet Mts. *U.S.A.* 48°10N 115°50W **348** B6
Cabo Blanco *Argentina* 47°15S 65°47W **368** F3
Cabo Frio *Brazil* 22°51S 42°3W **367** A7
Cabo Pantoja *Peru* 1°0S 75°10W **364** D3
Cabo San Lucas *Mexico* 22°53N 109°54W **358** C3
Cabo Verde = Cape Verde Is. ■ *Atl. Oc.* 16°0N 24°0W **322** b
Cabonga, Réservoir *Canada* 47°20N 76°40W **344** C4
Cabool *U.S.A.* 37°7N 92°6W **352** G7
Caboolture *Australia* 27°5S 152°58E **335** D5
Cabora Bassa Dam = Cahora Bassa, Reprêsa de *Mozam.* 15°20S 32°50E **327** F3
Caborca *Mexico* 30°37N 112°6W **358** A2
Cabot, Mt. *U.S.A.* 44°30N 71°25W **355** B13
Cabot Hd. *Canada* 45°14N 81°17W **354** A3
Cabot Str. *Canada* 47°15N 59°40W **345** C8
Cabra *Spain* 37°30N 4°28W **293** D3
Cabrera *Spain* 39°8N 2°57E **296** B9
Cabri *Canada* 50°35N 108°25W **343** C7
Cabriel → *Spain* 39°14N 1°3W **293** C5
Caçador *Brazil* 26°47S 51°0W **367** B5
Čačak *Serbia* 43°54N 20°20E **295** C9
Caçapava do Sul *Brazil* 30°30S 53°30W **367** C5
Cáceres *Brazil* 16°5S 57°40W **364** G7
Cáceres *Spain* 39°26N 6°23W **293** C2
Cache Bay *Canada* 46°22N 80°0W **344** C4
Cache Cr. → *U.S.A.* 38°42N 121°42W **350** G5
Cache Creek *Canada* 50°48N 121°19W **342** C4
Cachi *Argentina* 25°5S 66°10W **366** B2
Cachimbo, Serra do *Brazil* 9°30S 55°30W **365** E7
Cachinal de la Sierra *Chile* 24°58S 69°32W **366** A2
Cachoeira *Brazil* 12°30S 39°0W **365** F11
Cachoeira do Sul *Brazil* 30°3S 52°53W **367** C5
Cachoeiro de Itapemirim *Brazil* 20°51S 41°7W **367** A7
Cacoal *Brazil* 11°32S 61°18W **364** F6
Cacólo *Angola* 10°9S 19°21E **324** G3
Caconda *Angola* 13°48S 15°8E **325** G3
Caddo *U.S.A.* 34°7N 96°16W **356** D6
Cader Idris *U.K.* 52°42N 3°53W **285** E4
Cadereyta de Jiménez *Mexico* 25°36N 100°0W **358** B5
Cadibarrawirracanna, L. *Australia* 28°52S 135°27E **335** D2
Cadillac *U.S.A.* 44°15N 85°24W **353** C11
Cadiz *Phil.* 10°57N 123°15E **309** B6
Cádiz *Spain* 36°30N 6°20W **293** D2
Cadiz *Calif., U.S.A.* 34°30N 115°28W **351** L11
Cadiz *Ohio, U.S.A.* 40°22N 81°0W **354** F4
Cádiz, G. de *Spain* 36°40N 7°0W **293** D2
Cadiz L. *U.S.A.* 34°18N 115°24W **349** J6
Cadney Park *Australia* 27°55S 134°3E **335** D1
Cadomin *Canada* 53°2N 117°20W **342** C5
Cadotte Lake *Canada* 56°26N 116°23W **342** B5
Cadoux *Australia* 30°46S 117°7E **333** F2
Caen *France* 49°10N 0°22W **292** B3
Caernarfon *U.K.* 53°8N 4°16W **284** D3
Caernarfon B. *U.K.* 53°4N 4°40W **284** D3
Caernarvon = Caernarfon *U.K.* 53°8N 4°16W **284** D3
Caerphilly *U.K.* 51°35N 3°13W **285** F4
Caerphilly □ *U.K.* 51°37N 3°12W **285** F4
Caesarea *Israel* 32°30N 34°53E **318** C3
Caetité *Brazil* 13°50S 42°32W **365** F10
Cafayate *Argentina* 26°2S 66°0W **366** B2
Cafu *Angola* 16°30S 15°8E **328** B2
Cagayan de Oro *Phil.* 8°30N 124°40E **309** C6
Cagayan Is. *Phil.* 9°40N 121°16E **309** C5
Cágliari *Italy* 39°13N 9°7E **294** E3
Cágliari, G. di *Italy* 39°8N 9°11E **294** E3
Caguán → *Colombia* 0°8S 74°18W **364** D4
Caguas *Puerto Rico* 18°14N 66°2W **361** d
Caha Mts. *Ireland* 51°45N 9°40W **282** E2
Cahama *Angola* 16°17S 14°19E **328** B1
Caher *Ireland* 52°22N 7°56W **282** D4
Cahersiveen *Ireland* 51°56N 10°14W **282** E1
Cahora Bassa, L. de *Mozam.* 15°35S 32°0E **327** F3
Cahora Bassa, Reprêsa de *Mozam.* 15°20S 32°50E **327** F3
Cahore Pt. *Ireland* 52°33N 6°12W **282** D5
Cahors *France* 44°27N 1°27E **292** D4
Cahul *Moldova* 45°50N 28°15E **289** F15
Cai Bau, Dao *Vietnam* 21°10N 107°27E **310** B6
Cai Nuoc *Vietnam* 8°56N 105°1E **311** H5
Caia *Mozam.* 17°51S 35°24E **327** F4
Caianda *Angola* 11°2S 23°31E **327** E1
Caibarién *Cuba* 22°30N 79°30W **360** B4
Caicara *Venezuela* 7°38N 66°10W **364** B5
Caicó *Brazil* 6°20S 37°0W **365** E11
Caicos Is. *Turks & Caicos* 21°40N 71°40W **361** B5
Caicos Passage *W. Indies* 22°45N 72°45W **361** B5
Caird Coast *Antarctica* 75°0S 25°0W **277** D1
Cairn Gorm *U.K.* 57°7N 3°39W **283** D5
Cairngorm Mts. *U.K.* 57°6N 3°42W **283** D5
Cairngorms △ *U.K.* 57°10N 3°50W **283** D5
Cairnryan *U.K.* 54°59N 5°1W **283** G3
Cairns *Australia* 16°57S 145°45E **334** B4
Cairns L. *Canada* 51°42N 94°30W **343** C10
Cairo = El Qâhira *Egypt* 30°2N 31°13E **323** B12
Cairo *Ga., U.S.A.* 30°52N 84°13W **357** F12
Cairo *Ill., U.S.A.* 37°0N 89°11W **352** G9
Cairo *N.Y., U.S.A.* 42°18N 74°0W **355** D10
Caithness *U.K.* 58°25N 3°35W **283** C5
Caithness, Ord of *U.K.* 58°8N 3°36W **283** C5
Caja de Muertos, I. *Puerto Rico* 17°54N 66°32W **361** d
Cajamarca *Peru* 7°5S 78°28W **364** E3
Cajàzeiras *Brazil* 6°52S 38°30W **365** E11
Cala d'Or *Spain* 39°23N 3°14E **296** B10
Cala en Porter *Spain* 39°52N 4°8E **296** B11
Cala Figuera, C. de *Spain* 39°27N 2°31E **296** B9
Cala Forcat *Spain* 40°0N 3°47E **296** B10
Cala Major *Spain* 39°33N 2°37E **296** B9
Cala Mezquida = Sa Mesquida *Spain* 39°55N 4°16E **296** B11
Cala Millor *Spain* 39°35N 3°22E **296** B10
Cala Ratjada *Spain* 39°43N 3°27E **296** B10
Cala Santa Galdana *Spain* 39°56N 3°58E **296** B10
Calabar *Nigeria* 4°57N 8°20E **322** H7
Calabogie *Canada* 45°18N 76°43W **355** A8
Calabozo *Venezuela* 9°0N 67°28W **364** B5
Calábria □ *Italy* 39°0N 16°30E **294** E7
Calafate *Argentina* 50°19S 72°15W **368** G2
Calahorra *Spain* 42°18N 1°59W **293** A5
Calais *France* 50°57N 1°56E **292** A4
Calais *U.S.A.* 45°11N 67°17W **353** C20
Calakmul ⌂ *Mexico* 18°14N 89°48W **359** D7
Calalaste, Cord. de *Argentina* 25°0S 67°0W **366** B2
Calama *Brazil* 8°0S 62°50W **364** E6
Calama *Chile* 22°30S 68°55W **366** A2
Calamar *Colombia* 10°15N 74°55W **364** A4
Calamian Group *Phil.* 11°50N 119°55E **309** B5
Calamocha *Spain* 40°50N 1°17W **293** B5
Calang *Indonesia* 4°37N 95°37E **308** D1
Calanscio, Sarīr *Libya* 27°30N 21°30E **323** C10
Calapan *Phil.* 13°25N 121°7E **309** B6
Călăraşi *Romania* 44°12N 27°20E **289** F14
Calatayud *Spain* 41°20N 1°40W **293** B5
Calauag *Phil.* 13°55N 122°15E **309** B6
Calavite, C. *Phil.* 13°26N 120°20E **309** B6
Calbayog *Phil.* 12°4N 124°38E **309** B6
Calca *Peru* 13°22S 72°0W **364** F4
Calcasieu L. *U.S.A.* 29°55N 93°18W **356** G8
Calcutta = Kolkata *India* 22°34N 88°21E **315** H13
Calcutta *U.S.A.* 40°40N 80°34W **354** F4
Caldas da Rainha *Portugal* 39°24N 9°8W **293** C1
Calder → *U.K.* 53°44N 1°22W **284** D6
Caldera *Chile* 27°5S 70°55W **366** B1
Caldera de Taburiente △ *Canary Is.* 28°43N 17°52W **296** F2
Caldwell *Idaho, U.S.A.* 43°40N 116°41W **348** E5
Caldwell *Kans., U.S.A.* 37°2N 97°37W **352** G5
Caldwell *Tex., U.S.A.* 30°32N 96°42W **356** F6
Caledon *S. Africa* 34°14S 19°26E **328** E2
Caledon → *S. Africa* 30°31S 26°5E **328** E4
Caledon B. *Australia* 12°45S 137°0E **334** A2
Caledonia *Canada* 43°7N 79°58W **354** C5
Caledonia *U.S.A.* 42°58N 77°51W **354** D7
Calemba *Angola* 16°0S 15°44E **328** B2
Calen *Australia* 20°56S 148°48E **334** J6
Caletones *Chile* 34°6S 70°27W **366** C1
Calexico *U.S.A.* 32°40N 115°30W **351** N11
Calf of Man *I. of Man* 54°3N 4°48W **284** C3
Calgary *Canada* 51°0N 114°10W **342** C6
Calheta *Madeira* 32°44N 17°11W **296** D2
Calhoun *U.S.A.* 34°30N 84°57W **357** D12
Cali *Colombia* 3°25N 76°35W **364** C3
Calicut *India* 11°15N 75°43E **312** P9
Caliente *U.S.A.* 37°37N 114°31W **349** H6
California *Mo., U.S.A.* 38°38N 92°34W **352** F7
California *Pa., U.S.A.* 40°4N 79°54W **354** F5
California □ *U.S.A.* 37°30N 119°30W **350** H7
California, Baja, T.N. = Baja California □ *Mexico* 30°0N 115°0W **358** B2
California, Baja, T.S. = Baja California Sur □ *Mexico* 25°50N 111°50W **358** B2
California, G. de *Mexico* 27°0N 111°0W **358** B2
California City *U.S.A.* 35°10N 117°55W **351** K9
California Hot Springs *U.S.A.* 35°51N 118°41W **351** K8
Calilegua △ *Argentina* 25°36S 64°50W **366** B3
Calingasta *Argentina* 31°15S 69°30W **366** C2
Calipatria *U.S.A.* 33°8N 115°31W **351** M11
Calistoga *U.S.A.* 38°35N 122°35W **350** G4
Calitzdorp *S. Africa* 33°33S 21°42E **328** E3
Callabonna, L. *Australia* 29°40S 140°5E **335** D3
Callan *Ireland* 52°32N 7°24W **282** D4
Callander *U.K.* 56°15N 4°13W **283** E4
Callao *Peru* 12°3S 77°8W **364** F3
Callicoon *U.S.A.* 41°46N 75°3W **355** E9
Calling Lake *Canada* 55°15N 113°12W **342** B6
Calliope *Australia* 24°0S 151°16E **334** C5
Calne *U.K.* 51°26N 2°0W **285** F6
Calola *Angola* 16°25S 17°48E **328** B2
Caloundra *Australia* 26°45S 153°10E **335** D5
Calpella *U.S.A.* 39°14N 123°12W **350** F3
Calpine *U.S.A.* 39°40N 120°27W **350** F6
Calstock *Canada* 49°47N 84°9W **344** C3
Caltagirone *Italy* 37°14N 14°31E **294** F6
Caltanissetta *Italy* 37°29N 14°4E **294** F6
Calulo *Angola* 10°1S 14°56E **324** G2
Calvert → *Australia* 16°17S 137°44E **334** B2
Calvert I. *Canada* 51°30N 128°0W **342** C3
Calvert Ra. *Australia* 24°0S 122°30E **332** D3
Calvi *France* 42°34N 8°45E **292** E8
Calviá *Spain* 39°34N 2°31E **293** C7
Calvillo *Mexico* 21°51N 102°43W **358** C4
Calvinia *S. Africa* 31°28S 19°45E **328** E2
Calwa *U.S.A.* 36°42N 119°46W **350** J7
Cam → *U.K.* 52°21N 0°16E **285** E8
Cam Lam *Vietnam* 11°54N 109°10E **311** G7
Cam Pha *Vietnam* 21°7N 107°18E **310** B6
Cam Ranh *Vietnam* 11°54N 109°12E **311** G7
Cam Xuyen *Vietnam* 18°15N 106°0E **310** C6
Camabatela *Angola* 8°20S 15°26E **324** F3
Camacha *Madeira* 32°41N 16°49W **296** D3
Camacupa *Angola* 11°58S 17°22E **325** G3
Camagüey *Cuba* 21°20N 77°55W **360** B4
Camaná *Peru* 16°30S 72°50W **364** G4
Camanche Res. *U.S.A.* 38°14N 121°1W **350** G6
Camaquã *Brazil* 30°51S 51°49W **367** C5
Camaquã → *Brazil* 31°17S 51°47W **367** C5
Câmara de Lobos *Madeira* 32°39N 16°59W **296** D3
Camargo *Mexico* 26°19N 98°50W **359** B5
Camarillo *U.S.A.* 34°13N 119°2W **351** L7
Camarón, C. *Honduras* 16°0N 85°5W **360** C2
Camarones *Argentina* 44°50S 65°40W **368** E3
Camas *U.S.A.* 45°35N 122°24W **350** E4
Camas Valley *U.S.A.* 43°2N 123°40W **348** E2
Camballin *Australia* 17°59S 124°12E **332** C3
Cambará *Brazil* 23°2S 50°5W **367** A5
Cambay = Khambhat *India* 22°23N 72°33E **314** H5
Cambay, G. of = Khambhat, G. of *India* 20°45N 72°30E **312** J8
Cambodia ■ *Asia* 12°15N 105°0E **310** F5
Camborne *U.K.* 50°12N 5°19W **285** G2
Cambrai *France* 50°11N 3°14E **292** A5
Cambria *U.S.A.* 35°34N 121°5W **350** K5
Cambrian Mts. *U.K.* 52°3N 3°57W **285** E4
Cambridge *Canada* 43°23N 80°15W **354** C4
Cambridge *Jamaica* 18°18N 77°54W **360** a
Cambridge *N.Z.* 37°54S 175°29E **331** B5
Cambridge *U.K.* 52°12N 0°8E **285** E8
Cambridge *Mass., U.S.A.* 42°23N 71°7W **355** D13
Cambridge *Minn., U.S.A.* 45°34N 93°13W **352** C7
Cambridge *N.Y., U.S.A.* 43°2N 73°22W **355** C11
Cambridge *Nebr., U.S.A.* 40°17N 100°10W **352** E3
Cambridge *Ohio, U.S.A.* 40°2N 81°35W **354** F3
Cambridge Bay = Ikaluktutiak *Canada* 69°10N 105°0W **340** C9
Cambridge G. *Australia* 14°55S 128°15E **332** B4
Cambridge Springs *U.S.A.* 41°48N 80°4W **354** E4
Cambridgeshire □ *U.K.* 52°25N 0°7W **285** E7
Cambuci *Brazil* 21°35S 41°55W **367** A7
Cambundi-Catembo *Angola* 10°10S 17°35E **324** G3
Camden *Ala., U.S.A.* 31°59N 87°17W **357** F11
Camden *Ark., U.S.A.* 33°35N 92°50W **356** E8
Camden *Maine, U.S.A.* 44°13N 69°4W **353** C19
Camden *N.J., U.S.A.* 39°55N 75°7W **355** G9
Camden *N.Y., U.S.A.* 43°20N 75°45W **355** C9
Camden *S.C., U.S.A.* 34°16N 80°36W **357** D14
Camden Sd. *Australia* 15°27S 124°25E **332** C3
Camdenton *U.S.A.* 38°1N 92°45W **352** F7
Camelford *U.K.* 50°37N 4°42W **285** G3
Cameron *Ariz., U.S.A.* 35°53N 111°25W **349** J8
Cameron *La., U.S.A.* 29°48N 93°20W **356** G8
Cameron *Mo., U.S.A.* 39°44N 94°14W **352** F6
Cameron *Tex., U.S.A.* 30°51N 96°59W **356** F6
Cameron Highlands *Malaysia* 4°27N 101°22E **311** K3
Cameron Hills *Canada* 59°48N 118°0W **342** B5
Cameroon ■ *Africa* 6°0N 12°30E **323** G7
Cameroun, Mt. *Cameroon* 4°13N 9°10E **324** D1
Cametá *Brazil* 2°12S 49°30W **365** D9
Camiguin I. *Phil.* 18°56N 121°55E **309** C6
Camilla *U.S.A.* 31°14N 84°12W **357** F12
Caminha *Portugal* 41°50N 8°50W **293** B1
Camino *U.S.A.* 38°44N 120°41W **350** G6
Camira Creek *Australia* 29°15S 152°58E **335** D5
Cammal *U.S.A.* 41°24N 77°28W **354** E7
Camocim *Brazil* 2°55S 40°50W **365** D10
Camooweal *Australia* 19°56S 138°7E **334** B2
Camooweal Caves △ *Australia* 20°1S 138°11E **334** C2
Camopi *Fr. Guiana* 3°12N 52°17W **365** C8
Camp Borden *Canada* 44°18N 79°56W **354** B5
Camp Hill *U.S.A.* 40°14N 76°55W **354** F8
Camp Nelson *U.S.A.* 36°8N 118°39W **351** J8
Camp Pendleton *U.S.A.* 33°13N 117°24W **351** M9
Camp Verde *U.S.A.* 34°34N 111°51W **349** J8
Camp Wood *U.S.A.* 29°40N 100°1W **356** G4
Campana *Argentina* 34°10S 58°55W **366** C4
Campana, I. *Chile* 48°20S 75°20W **368** F1
Campanário *Madeira* 32°39N 17°2W **296** D2
Campánia □ *Italy* 41°0N 14°30E **294** D6
Campbell *S. Africa* 28°48S 23°44E **328** D3
Campbell *Calif., U.S.A.* 37°17N 121°57W **350** H5
Campbell *Ohio, U.S.A.* 41°5N 80°37W **354** E4
Campbell I. *Pac. Oc.* 52°30S 169°0E **336** N8
Campbell L. *Canada* 63°14N 106°55W **343** A7
Campbell Plateau *S. Ocean* 50°0S 170°0E **277** A11
Campbell River *Canada* 50°5N 125°20W **342** C3
Campbell Town *Australia* 41°52S 147°30E **335** G4
Campbellford *Canada* 44°18N 77°48W **354** B7
Campbellpur *Pakistan* 33°46N 72°26E **314** C5
Campbellsville *U.S.A.* 37°21N 85°20W **353** G11
Campbellton *Canada* 47°57N 66°43W **345** C6
Campbelltown *Australia* 34°4S 150°49E **335** E5
Campbeltown *U.K.* 55°26N 5°36W **283** F3
Campeche *Mexico* 19°51N 90°32W **359** D6
Campeche □ *Mexico* 19°0N 90°30W **359** D6
Campeche, Golfo de *Mexico* 19°30N 93°0W **359** D6
Camperdown *Australia* 38°14S 143°9E **335** F3
Camperville *Canada* 51°59N 100°9W **343** C8
Câmpina *Romania* 45°10N 25°45E **289** F13
Campina Grande *Brazil* 7°20S 35°47W **365** E11
Campinas *Brazil* 22°50S 47°0W **367** A6
Campo Grande *Brazil* 20°25S 54°40W **365** H8
Campo Maior *Brazil* 4°50S 42°12W **365** D10
Campo Mourão *Brazil* 24°3S 52°22W **367** A5
Campobasso *Italy* 41°34N 14°39E **294** D6
Campos *Brazil* 21°50S 41°20W **367** A7
Campos *Spain* 39°26N 3°1E **296** B10
Campos Belos *Brazil* 13°10S 47°3W **365** F9
Campos Novos *Brazil* 27°21S 51°50W **367** B5
Camptonville *U.S.A.* 39°27N 121°3W **350** F5
Camptown *U.S.A.* 41°44N 76°14W **355** E8
Câmpulung *Romania* 45°17N 25°3E **289** F13
Camrose *Canada* 53°0N 112°50W **342** C6
Camsell Portage *Canada* 59°37N 109°15W **343** B7
Çan *Turkey* 40°2N 27°3E **295** D12
Can Clavo *Spain* 38°57N 1°27E **296** C7
Can Creu *Spain* 38°58N 1°28E **296** C7
Can Gio *Vietnam* 10°25N 106°58E **311** G6
Can Tho *Vietnam* 10°2N 105°46E **311** G5
Canaan *U.S.A.* 42°2N 73°20W **355** D11
Canada ■ *N. Amer.* 60°0N 100°0W **340** D10
Canada Abyssal Plain *Arctic* 80°0N 140°0W **276** B18
Canada Basin *Arctic* 80°0N 145°0W **276** B18
Cañada de Gómez *Argentina* 32°40S 61°30W **366** C3
Canadian *U.S.A.* 35°55N 100°23W **356** D4
Canadian → *U.S.A.* 35°28N 95°3W **356** D7
Canadian Shield *Canada* 53°0N 75°0W **338** D12
Canajoharie *U.S.A.* 42°54N 74°35W **355** D10
Çanakkale *Turkey* 40°8N 26°24E **295** D12
Çanakkale Boğazı *Turkey* 40°17N 26°32E **295** D12
Canal Flats *Canada* 50°10N 115°48W **342** C5
Canalejas *Argentina* 35°15S 66°34W **366** D2
Canals *Argentina* 33°35S 62°53W **366** C3
Canandaigua *U.S.A.* 42°54N 77°17W **354** D7
Canandaigua L. *U.S.A.* 42°47N 77°19W **354** D7
Cananea *Mexico* 31°0N 110°18W **358** A2
Canarias, Is. *Atl. Oc.* 28°30N 16°0W **296** F4
Canaries *St. Lucia* 13°55N 61°4W **361** f
Canarreos, Arch. de los *Cuba* 21°35N 81°40W **360** B3
Canary Is. = Canarias, Is. *Atl. Oc.* 28°30N 16°0W **296** F4
Canaseraga *U.S.A.* 42°27N 77°45W **354** D7
Canatlán *Mexico* 24°31N 104°47W **358** C4
Canaveral, C. *U.S.A.* 28°27N 80°32W **357** G14
Canaveral ⌂ *U.S.A.* 28°28N 80°34W **357** G14
Canavieiras *Brazil* 15°39S 39°0W **365** G11
Canberra *Australia* 35°15S 149°8E **335** F4
Canby *Calif., U.S.A.* 41°27N 120°52W **348** F3
Canby *Minn., U.S.A.* 44°43N 96°16W **352** C5
Canby *Oreg., U.S.A.* 45°16N 122°42W **350** E4
Cancún *Mexico* 21°8N 86°44W **359** C7
Candelaria *Argentina* 27°29S 55°44W **367** B4
Candelaria *Canary Is.* 28°22N 16°22W **296** F3
Candelo *Australia* 36°47S 149°43E **335** F4
Candi Dasa *Indonesia* 8°30S 115°34E **309** J18
Candia = Iraklio *Greece* 35°20N 25°12E **297** D7
Candle L. *Canada* 53°50N 105°18W **343** C7
Candlemas I. *Antarctica* 57°3S 26°40W **277** B1
Cando *U.S.A.* 48°32N 99°12W **352** A4
Canea = Chania *Greece* 35°30N 24°4E **297** D6
Canelones *Uruguay* 34°32S 56°17W **367** C4
Cañete *Chile* 37°50S 73°30W **366** D1
Cañete *Peru* 13°8S 76°30W **364** F3
Cangas de Narcea *Spain* 43°10N 6°32W **293** A2
Canguaretama *Brazil* 6°20S 35°5W **365** E11
Canguçu *Brazil* 31°22S 52°43W **367** C5
Canguçu, Serra do *Brazil* 31°20S 52°40W **367** C5
Cangzhou *China* 38°19N 116°52E **306** E9
Caniapiscau → *Canada* 56°40N 69°30W **345** A6
Caniapiscau, L. *Canada* 54°10N 69°55W **345** B6
Canicattì *Italy* 37°21N 13°51E **294** F5
Canim Lake *Canada* 51°47N 120°54W **342** C4
Canindeyu □ *Paraguay* 24°10S 55°0W **367** A5
Canisteo *U.S.A.* 42°16N 77°36W **354** D7
Canisteo → *U.S.A.* 42°7N 77°8W **354** D7
Cañitas de Felipe Pescador *Mexico* 23°36N 102°43W **358** C4
Çankırı *Turkey* 40°40N 33°37E **291** F5
Cankuzo *Burundi* 3°10S 30°31E **326** C3
Canmore *Canada* 51°7N 115°18W **342** C5
Cann River *Australia* 37°35S 149°7E **335** F4
Canna *U.K.* 57°3N 6°33W **283** D2
Cannanore *India* 11°53N 75°27E **312** P9
Cannes *France* 43°32N 7°1E **292** E7
Canning Town = Port Canning *India* 22°23N 88°40E **315** H13
Cannington *Canada* 44°20N 79°2W **354** B5
Cannock *U.K.* 52°41N 2°1W **285** E5
Cannonball → *U.S.A.* 46°26N 100°35W **352** B3
Cannondale Mt. *Australia* 25°13S 148°57E **334** D4
Cannonsville Res. *U.S.A.* 42°4N 75°22W **355** D9
Cannonvale *Australia* 20°17S 148°43E **334** J6
Canoas *Brazil* 29°56S 51°11W **367** B5
Canoe L. *Canada* 55°10N 108°15W **343** B7
Cañon City *U.S.A.* 38°27N 105°14W **348** G11
Cañón de Río Blanco △ *Mexico* 18°43N 97°15W **359** D5
Cañón del Sumidero △ *Mexico* 19°22N 96°24W **359** D5
Canonniers Pt. *Mauritius* 20°2S 57°32E **325** d
Canora *Canada* 51°40N 102°30W **343** C8
Canowindra *Australia* 33°35S 148°38E **335** E4
Canso *Canada* 45°20N 61°0W **345** C7
Cantabria □ *Spain* 43°10N 4°0W **293** A4
Cantabrian Mts. = Cantábrica, Cordillera *Spain* 43°0N 5°10W **293** A3
Cantábrica, Cordillera *Spain* 43°0N 5°10W **293** A3
Cantal, Plomb du *France* 45°3N 2°45E **292** D5
Canterbury *Australia* 25°23S 141°53E **334** D3
Canterbury *U.K.* 51°16N 1°6E **285** F9
Canterbury Bight *N.Z.* 44°16S 171°55E **331** F3
Canterbury Plains *N.Z.* 43°55S 171°22E **331** E3
Cantil *U.S.A.* 35°18N 117°58W **351** K9
Canton = Guangzhou *China* 23°6N 113°13E **305** D6
Canton *Ga., U.S.A.* 34°14N 84°29W **357** D12
Canton *Ill., U.S.A.* 40°33N 90°2W **352** E8
Canton *Miss., U.S.A.* 32°37N 90°2W **357** E9
Canton *Mo., U.S.A.* 40°8N 91°32W **352** E8
Canton *N.Y., U.S.A.* 44°36N 75°10W **355** B9
Canton *Ohio, U.S.A.* 40°48N 81°23W **354** F3
Canton *Pa., U.S.A.* 41°39N 76°51W **354** E8
Canton *S. Dak., U.S.A.* 43°18N 96°35W **352** D5
Canton L. *U.S.A.* 36°6N 98°35W **356** C5
Canudos *Brazil* 7°13S 58°5W **364** E7
Canumã → *Brazil* 3°55S 59°10W **364** D7
Canutama *Brazil* 6°30S 64°20W **364** E6
Canutillo *U.S.A.* 31°55N 106°36W **356** F1
Canvey *U.K.* 51°31N 0°37E **285** F8
Canyon *U.S.A.* 34°59N 101°55W **356** D4
Canyon De Chelly ⌂ *U.S.A.* 36°10N 109°20W **349** H9
Canyonlands △ *U.S.A.* 38°15N 110°0W **349** G9
Canyons of the Ancients ⌂ *U.S.A.* 37°30N 108°55W **349** H9
Canyonville *U.S.A.* 42°56N 123°17W **348** E2
Cao Bang *Vietnam* 22°40N 106°15E **310** A6
Cao He → *China* 40°10N 124°32E **307** D13
Cao Lanh *Vietnam* 10°27N 105°38E **311** G5
Cao Xian *China* 34°50N 115°35E **306** G8
Cap-aux-Meules *Canada* 47°23N 61°52W **345** C7
Cap-Chat *Canada* 49°6N 66°40W **345** C6
Cap-de-la-Madeleine *Canada* 46°22N 72°31W **344** C5
Cap-Haïtien *Haiti* 19°40N 72°20W **361** C5
Cap Pt. *St. Lucia* 14°7N 60°57W **361** f
Capac *U.S.A.* 43°1N 82°56W **354** C2
Capanaparo → *Venezuela* 7°1N 67°7W **364** B5
Cape → *Australia* 20°59S 146°51E **334** C4
Cape Arid △ *Australia* 33°58S 123°13E **333** F3
Cape Barren I. *Australia* 40°25S 148°15E **335** G4
Cape Breton Highlands △ *Canada* 46°50N 60°40W **345** C7
Cape Breton I. *Canada* 46°0N 60°30W **345** C7
Cape Charles *U.S.A.* 37°16N 76°1W **353** G15
Cape Coast *Ghana* 5°5N 1°15W **322** G5
Cape Cod ⌂ *U.S.A.* 41°56N 70°6W **353** E18
Cape Coral *U.S.A.* 26°33N 81°57W **357** H14
Cape Dorset *Canada* 64°14N 76°32W **341** C12
Cape Fear → *U.S.A.* 33°53N 78°1W **357** E15
Cape Girardeau *U.S.A.* 37°19N 89°32W **352** G9
Cape Hatteras ⌂ *U.S.A.* 35°30N 75°28W **357** D17
Cape Le Grand △ *Australia* 33°54S 122°26E **333** F3
Cape Lookout ⌂ *U.S.A.* 35°45N 76°25W **357** D16
Cape May *U.S.A.* 38°56N 74°56W **353** F16
Cape May Point *U.S.A.* 38°56N 74°58W **353** F16
Cape Melville △ *Australia* 14°26S 144°28E **334** A3
Cape Peninsula △ *S. Africa* 34°20S 18°28E **328** E2
Cape Range △ *Australia* 22°3S 114°0E **332** D1
Cape Tormentine *Canada* 46°8N 63°47W **345** C7
Cape Town *S. Africa* 33°55S 18°22E **328** E2
Cape Tribulation △ *Australia* 16°5S 145°25E **334** B4
Cape Verde Is. ■ *Atl. Oc.* 16°0N 24°0W **322** b
Cape Vincent *U.S.A.* 44°8N 76°20W **355** B8
Cape York Peninsula *Australia* 12°0S 142°30E **334** A3
Capela *Brazil* 10°30S 37°0W **365** F11
Capella *Australia* 23°2S 148°1E **334** C4
Capesterre-Belle-Eau *Guadeloupe* 16°4N 61°36W **360** b
Capesterre-de-Marie-Galante *Guadeloupe* 15°53N 61°14W **360** b
Capim → *Brazil* 1°40S 47°47W **365** D9
Capitan *U.S.A.* 33°35N 105°35W **349** K11
Capitán Arturo Prat *Antarctica* 63°0S 61°0W **277** C17
Capitol Reef △ *U.S.A.* 38°15N 111°10W **349** G8
Capitola *U.S.A.* 36°59N 121°57W **350** J5
Capoche → *Mozam.* 15°35S 33°0E **327** F3
Capraia *Italy* 43°2N 9°50E **292** E8
Capreol *Canada* 46°43N 80°56W **344** C3
Capri *Italy* 40°33N 14°14E **294** D6
Capricorn Group *Australia* 23°30S 151°55E **334** C5
Capricorn Ra. *Australia* 23°20S 116°50E **332** D2
Caprivi Game ⌂ *Namibia* 17°55S 22°37E **328** B3
Caprivi Strip *Namibia* 18°0S 23°0E **328** B3
Captain's Flat *Australia* 35°35S 149°27E **335** F4
Capulin Volcano ⌂ *U.S.A.* 36°47N 103°58W **356** C3
Caquetá → *Colombia* 1°15S 69°15W **364** D5
Caracal *Romania* 44°8N 24°22E **289** F13
Caracas *Venezuela* 10°30N 66°55W **364** A5
Caracol *Belize* 16°45N 89°6E **360** C2
Caracol *Mato Grosso do Sul, Brazil* 22°18S 57°1W **366** A4
Caracol *Piauí, Brazil* 9°15S 43°22W **365** E10
Carajas *Brazil* 6°5S 50°23W **365** E8
Carajás, Serra dos *Brazil* 6°0S 51°30W **365** E8
Carangola *Brazil* 20°44S 42°5W **367** A7
Caransebeş *Romania* 45°28N 22°18E **289** F12
Caraquet *Canada* 47°48N 64°57W **345** C6
Caras *Peru* 9°3S 77°47W **364** E3
Caratasca, L. *Honduras* 15°20N 83°40W **360** C3
Caratinga *Brazil* 19°50S 42°10W **365** G10
Caraúbas *Brazil* 5°43S 37°33W **365** E11
Caravaca de la Cruz *Spain* 38°8N 1°52W **293** C5
Caravelas *Brazil* 17°45S 39°15W **365** G11
Caraveli *Peru* 15°45S 73°25W **364** G4
Caravelle, Presqu'île de la *Martinique* 14°46N 60°48W **360** c
Carazinho *Brazil* 28°16S 52°46W **367** B5
Carballo *Spain* 43°13N 8°41W **293** A1
Carberry *Canada* 49°50N 99°25W **343** D9

Carbó *Mexico* 29°42N 110°58W **358** B2
Carbonara, C. *Italy* 39°6N 9°31E **294** E3
Carbondale *Colo., U.S.A.* 39°24N 107°13W **348** G10
Carbondale *Ill., U.S.A.* 37°44N 89°13W **352** G9
Carbondale *Pa., U.S.A.* 41°35N 75°30W **355** E9
Carbonear *Canada* 47°42N 53°13W **345** C9
Carbónia *Italy* 39°10N 8°30E **294** E3
Carcajou *Canada* 57°47N 117°6W **342** B5
Carcarana → *Argentina* 32°27S 60°48W **366** C3
Carcasse, C. *Haiti* 18°30N 74°28W **361** C5
Carcassonne *France* 43°13N 2°20E **292** E5
Carcross *Canada* 60°13N 134°45W **342** A2
Cardamon Hills *India* 9°30N 77°15E **312** Q10
Cárdenas *Cuba* 23°0N 81°30W **360** B3
Cárdenas *San Luis Potosí, Mexico* 22°0N 99°38W **359** C5
Cárdenas *Tabasco, Mexico* 17°59N 93°22W **359** D6
Cardiff *U.K.* 51°29N 3°10W **285** F4
Cardiff ☐ *U.K.* 51°31N 3°12W **285** F4
Cardiff-by-the-Sea *U.S.A.* 33°1N 117°17W **351** M9
Cardigan *U.K.* 52°5N 4°40W **285** E3
Cardigan B. *U.K.* 52°30N 4°30W **285** E3
Cardinal *Canada* 44°47N 75°23W **355** B9
Cardona *Uruguay* 33°53S 57°18W **366** C4
Cardoso, Ilha do *Brazil* 25°8S 47°58W **367** B5
Cardston *Canada* 49°15N 113°20W **342** D6
Cardwell *Australia* 18°14S 146°2E **334** B4
Careen L. *Canada* 57°0N 108°11W **343** B7
Carei *Romania* 47°40N 22°29E **289** E12
Careme = Ciremay *Indonesia* 6°55S 108°27E **309** G13
Carey *U.S.A.* 43°19N 113°57W **348** E7
Carey, L. *Australia* 29°0S 122°15E **333** E3
Carey L. *Canada* 62°12N 102°55W **343** A8
Carhué *Argentina* 37°10S 62°50W **366** D3
Caria *Turkey* 37°20N 28°10E **295** F13
Cariacica *Brazil* 20°16S 40°25W **365** H10
Caribbean Sea *W. Indies* 15°0N 75°0W **361** D5
Cariboo Mts. *Canada* 53°0N 121°0W **342** C4
Caribou *U.S.A.* 46°52N 68°1W **353** B19
Caribou → *Man., Canada* 59°20N 94°44W **343** B10
Caribou → *N.W.T., Canada* 61°27N 125°45W **342** A3
Caribou I. *Canada* 47°22N 85°49W **344** C2
Caribou Is. *Canada* 61°55N 113°15W **342** A6
Caribou L. *Man., Canada* 59°21N 96°10W **343** B9
Caribou L. *Ont., Canada* 50°25N 89°5W **344** B2
Caribou Mts. *Canada* 59°12N 115°40W **342** B5
Caribou River ⌓ *Canada* 59°35N 96°35W **343** B9
Carichic *Mexico* 27°56N 107°3W **358** B3
Carinda *Australia* 30°28S 147°41E **335** E4
Carinhanha *Brazil* 14°15S 44°46W **365** F10
Carinhanha → *Brazil* 14°20S 43°47W **365** F10
Carinthia = Kärnten ☐ *Austria* 46°52N 13°30E **288** E8
Caripito *Venezuela* 10°8N 63°6W **364** A6
Carleton, Mt. *Canada* 47°23N 66°53W **345** C6
Carleton Place *Canada* 45°8N 76°9W **355** A8
Carletonville *S. Africa* 26°23S 27°22E **328** D4
Carlin *U.S.A.* 40°43N 116°7W **348** F5
Carlingford L. *U.K.* 54°3N 6°9W **282** B5
Carlinville *U.S.A.* 39°17N 89°53W **352** F9
Carlisle *U.K.* 54°54N 2°56W **284** C5
Carlisle *U.S.A.* 40°12N 77°12W **354** F7
Carlisle B. *Barbados* 13°5N 59°37W **361** g
Carlisle I. *Australia* 20°49S 149°18E **334** J7
Carlos Casares *Argentina* 35°32S 61°20W **366** D3
Carlos Tejedor *Argentina* 35°25S 62°25W **366** D3
Carlow *Ireland* 52°50N 6°56W **282** D5
Carlow ☐ *Ireland* 52°43N 6°50W **282** D5
Carlsbad *Calif., U.S.A.* 33°10N 117°21W **351** M9
Carlsbad *N. Mex., U.S.A.* 32°25N 104°14W **349** K11
Carlsbad Caverns △ *U.S.A.* 32°10N 104°35W **349** K11
Carluke *U.K.* 55°45N 3°50W **283** F5
Carlyle *Canada* 49°40N 102°20W **343** D8
Carmacks *Canada* 62°5N 136°16W **340** C6
Carman *Canada* 49°30N 98°0W **343** D9
Carmarthen *U.K.* 51°52N 4°19W **285** F3
Carmarthen B. *U.K.* 51°40N 4°30W **285** F3
Carmarthenshire ☐ *U.K.* 51°55N 4°13W **285** F3
Carmaux *France* 44°3N 2°10E **292** D5
Carmel *U.S.A.* 41°26N 73°41W **355** E11
Carmel-by-the-Sea *U.S.A.* 36°33N 121°55W **350** J5
Carmel Valley *U.S.A.* 36°29N 121°43W **350** J5
Carmelo *Uruguay* 34°0S 58°20W **366** C4
Carmen *Colombia* 9°43N 75°8W **364** B3
Carmen *Paraguay* 27°13S 56°12W **367** B4
Carmen → *Mexico* 30°42N 106°29W **358** A3
Carmen, I. *Mexico* 25°57N 111°12W **358** B2
Carmen de Patagones *Argentina* 40°50S 63°0W **368** E4
Carmensa *Argentina* 35°15S 67°40W **366** D2
Carmi *Canada* 49°36N 119°8W **342** D5
Carmi *U.S.A.* 38°5N 88°10W **352** F9
Carmichael *U.S.A.* 38°38N 121°19W **350** G5
Carmila *Australia* 21°55S 149°24E **334** C4
Carmona *Costa Rica* 10°0N 85°15W **360** E2
Carmona *Spain* 37°28N 5°42W **293** D3
Carn Ban *U.K.* 57°7N 4°15W **283** D4
Carn Eige *U.K.* 57°17N 5°8W **283** D3
Carnamah *Australia* 29°41S 115°53E **333** E2
Carnarvon *Australia* 24°51S 113°42E **333** D1
Carnarvon *S. Africa* 30°56S 22°8E **328** E3
Carnarvon △ *Australia* 24°54S 148°2E **334** C4
Carnarvon Ra. *Queens., Australia* 25°15S 148°30E **334** D4
Carnarvon Ra. *W. Austral., Australia* 25°20S 120°45E **333** E3
Carnation *U.S.A.* 47°39N 121°55W **350** C5
Carncastle *U.K.* 54°54N 5°53W **282** B6
Carndonagh *Ireland* 55°16N 7°15W **282** A4
Carnduff *Canada* 49°10N 101°50W **343** D8
Carnegie *U.S.A.* 40°24N 80°5W **354** F4
Carnegie, L. *Australia* 26°5S 122°30E **333** E3
Carnegie Ridge *Pac. Oc.* 1°0S 87°0W **337** H19
Carnic Alps = Karnische Alpen *Europe* 46°36N 13°0E **288** E7
Carniche Alpi = Karnische Alpen *Europe* 46°36N 13°0E **288** E7
Carnot *C.A.R.* 4°59N 15°56E **324** D3
Carnot, C. *Australia* 34°57S 135°38E **335** E2
Carnot B. *Australia* 17°20S 122°15E **332** C3
Carnoustie *U.K.* 56°30N 2°42W **283** E6
Carnsore Pt. *Ireland* 52°10N 6°22W **282** D5
Caro *U.S.A.* 43°29N 83°24W **353** D12
Carol City *U.S.A.* 25°56N 80°14W **357** J14
Carolina *Brazil* 7°10S 47°30W **365** E9
Carolina *Puerto Rico* 18°23N 65°58W **361** d
Carolina *S. Africa* 26°5S 30°6E **329** D5
Caroline I. *Kiribati* 9°58S 150°13W **337** H12
Caroline Is. *Micronesia* 8°0N 150°0E **336** G6
Caroni *Trin. & Tob.* 10°34N 61°23W **365** K15
Caroni → *Venezuela* 8°21N 62°43W **364** B6
Caronie = Nébrodi, Monti *Italy* 37°54N 14°35E **294** F6
Caroona *Australia* 31°24S 150°26E **335** E5
Carpathians *Europe* 49°30N 21°0E **289** D11
Carpații Meridionali *Romania* 45°30N 25°0E **289** F13
Carpentaria, G. of *Australia* 14°0S 139°0E **334** A2
Carpentras *France* 44°3N 5°2E **292** D6
Carpi *Italy* 44°47N 10°53E **294** B4
Carpinteria *U.S.A.* 34°24N 119°31W **351** L7
Carr Boyd Ra. *Australia* 16°15S 128°35E **332** C4
Carra, L. *Ireland* 53°41N 9°14W **282** C2
Carrabelle *U.S.A.* 29°51N 84°40W **357** G12
Carranza, Presa V. *Mexico* 27°20N 100°50W **358** B4
Carrara *Italy* 44°5N 10°6E **292** D9
Carrauntoohill *Ireland* 52°0N 9°45W **282** D2
Carrick-on-Shannon *Ireland* 53°57N 8°5W **282** C3
Carrick-on-Suir *Ireland* 52°21N 7°24W **282** D4
Carrickfergus *U.K.* 54°43N 5°49W **282** B6
Carrickmacross *Ireland* 53°59N 6°43W **282** C5
Carrieton *Australia* 32°25S 138°31E **335** E2
Carrillo *Mexico* 26°54N 103°55W **358** B4
Carrington *U.S.A.* 47°27N 99°8W **352** B4
Carrizal Bajo *Chile* 28°5S 71°20W **366** B1
Carrizalillo *Chile* 29°5S 71°30W **366** B1
Carrizo Cr. → *U.S.A.* 36°55N 103°55W **349** H12
Carrizo Plain ⌓ *U.S.A.* 35°11N 119°47W **350** K7
Carrizo Springs *U.S.A.* 28°31N 99°52W **356** G5
Carrizozo *U.S.A.* 33°38N 105°53W **349** K11
Carroll *U.S.A.* 42°4N 94°52W **352** D6
Carrollton *Ga., U.S.A.* 33°35N 85°5W **357** E12
Carrollton *Ill., U.S.A.* 39°18N 90°24W **352** F8
Carrollton *Ky., U.S.A.* 38°41N 85°11W **353** F11
Carrollton *Mo., U.S.A.* 39°22N 93°30W **352** F7
Carrollton *Ohio, U.S.A.* 40°34N 81°5W **354** F3
Carron → *U.K.* 57°53N 4°22W **283** D4
Carron, L. *U.K.* 57°22N 5°35W **283** D3
Carrot → *Canada* 53°50N 101°17W **343** C8
Carrot River *Canada* 53°17N 103°35W **343** C8
Carruthers *Canada* 52°52N 109°16W **343** C7
Carson *Calif., U.S.A.* 33°49N 118°16W **351** M8
Carson *N. Dak., U.S.A.* 46°25N 101°34W **352** B3
Carson → *U.S.A.* 39°45N 118°40W **350** F8
Carson City *U.S.A.* 39°10N 119°46W **350** F7
Carson Sink *U.S.A.* 39°50N 118°25W **348** G4
Cartagena *Colombia* 10°25N 75°33W **364** A3
Cartagena *Spain* 37°38N 0°59W **293** D5
Cartago *Colombia* 4°45N 75°55W **364** C3
Cartago *Costa Rica* 9°50N 83°55W **360** E3
Cartersville *U.S.A.* 34°10N 84°48W **357** D12
Carterton *N.Z.* 41°2S 175°31E **331** D5
Carthage *Tunisia* 36°52N 10°20E **294** F4
Carthage *Ill., U.S.A.* 40°25N 91°8W **352** E8
Carthage *Mo., U.S.A.* 37°11N 94°19W **352** G6
Carthage *N.Y., U.S.A.* 43°59N 75°37W **353** D16
Carthage *Tex., U.S.A.* 32°9N 94°20W **356** E7
Cartier I. *Australia* 12°31S 123°29E **332** B3
Cartwright *Canada* 53°41N 56°58W **345** B8
Caruaru *Brazil* 8°15S 35°55W **365** E11
Carúpano *Venezuela* 10°39N 63°15W **364** A6
Caruthersville *U.S.A.* 36°11N 89°39W **352** G9
Carvoeiro *Brazil* 1°30S 61°59W **364** D6
Carvoeiro, C. *Portugal* 39°21N 9°24W **293** C1
Cary *U.S.A.* 35°47N 78°46W **357** D15
Casa Grande *U.S.A.* 32°53N 111°45W **349** K8
Casablanca *Chile* 33°20S 71°25W **366** C1
Casablanca *Morocco* 33°36N 7°36W **322** B4
Cascada de Basaseachic △ *Mexico* 28°9N 108°15W **358** B3
Cascade *Seychelles* 4°39S 55°29E **325** b
Cascade *Idaho, U.S.A.* 44°31N 116°2W **348** D5
Cascade *Mont., U.S.A.* 47°16N 111°42W **348** C8
Cascade Locks *U.S.A.* 45°40N 121°54W **350** E5
Cascade Ra. *U.S.A.* 47°0N 121°30W **350** D5
Cascade Res. *U.S.A.* 44°32N 116°3W **348** D5
Cascades, Pte. des *Réunion* 21°9S 55°51E **325** c
Cascais *Portugal* 38°41N 9°25W **293** C1
Cascavel *Brazil* 24°57S 53°28W **367** A5
Cáscina *Italy* 43°41N 10°33E **294** C4
Casco B. *U.S.A.* 43°45N 70°0W **353** D19
Caserta *Italy* 41°4N 14°20E **294** D6
Casey *Antarctica* 66°0S 76°0E **277** C8
Caseyr, Raas = Asir, Ras *Somali Rep.* 11°55N 51°10E **319** E5
Cashel *Ireland* 52°30N 7°53W **282** D4
Casiguran *Phil.* 16°22N 122°7E **309** A6
Casilda *Argentina* 33°10S 61°10W **366** C3
Casino *Australia* 28°52S 153°3E **335** D5
Casiquiare → *Venezuela* 2°1N 67°7W **364** C5
Casma *Peru* 9°30S 78°20W **364** E3
Casmalia *U.S.A.* 34°50N 120°32W **351** L6
Caspe *Spain* 41°14N 0°1W **293** B5
Casper *U.S.A.* 42°51N 106°19W **348** E10
Caspian Depression *Eurasia* 47°0N 48°0E **291** E8
Caspian Sea *Eurasia* 43°0N 50°0E **291** F9
Cass Lake *U.S.A.* 47°23N 94°37W **352** B6
Cassadaga *U.S.A.* 42°20N 79°19W **354** D5
Casselman *Canada* 45°19N 75°5W **355** A9
Casselton *U.S.A.* 46°54N 97°13W **352** B5
Cassiar *Canada* 59°16N 129°40W **342** B3
Cassiar Mts. *Canada* 59°30N 130°30W **342** B2
Cassino *Italy* 41°30N 13°49E **294** D5
Cassville *U.S.A.* 36°41N 93°52W **352** G7
Castaic *U.S.A.* 34°30N 118°38W **351** L8
Castalia *U.S.A.* 41°24N 82°49W **354** E2
Castanhal *Brazil* 1°18S 47°55W **365** D9
Castara *Trin. & Tob.* 11°17N 60°42W **365** J16
Castellammare di Stábia *Italy* 40°42N 14°29E **294** D6
Castelli *Argentina* 36°7S 57°47W **366** D4
Castelló de la Plana *Spain* 39°58N 0°3W **293** C5
Castelo *Brazil* 20°33S 41°14W **367** A7
Castelo Branco *Portugal* 39°50N 7°31W **293** C2
Castelsarrasin *France* 44°2N 1°7E **292** E4
Castelvetrano *Italy* 37°41N 12°47E **294** F5
Casterton *Australia* 37°30S 141°30E **335** F3
Castile *U.S.A.* 42°38N 78°3W **354** D6
Castilla-La Mancha ☐ *Spain* 39°30N 3°30W **293** C4
Castilla y Leon ☐ *Spain* 42°0N 5°0W **293** B3
Castillos *Uruguay* 34°12S 53°52W **367** C5
Castle Dale *U.S.A.* 39°13N 111°1W **348** G8
Castle Douglas *U.K.* 54°56N 3°56W **283** G5
Castle Rock *Colo., U.S.A.* 39°22N 104°51W **348** G11
Castle Rock *Wash., U.S.A.* 46°17N 122°54W **350** D4
Castlebar *Ireland* 53°52N 9°18W **282** C2
Castlebay *U.K.* 56°57N 7°31W **283** E1
Castleblaney *Ireland* 54°7N 6°44W **282** B5
Castlederg *U.K.* 54°42N 7°35W **282** B4
Castleford *U.K.* 53°43N 1°21W **284** D6
Castlegar *Canada* 49°20N 117°40W **342** D5
Castlemaine *Australia* 37°2S 144°12E **335** F3
Castlemaine *Ireland* 52°10N 9°42W **282** D2
Castlepollard *Ireland* 53°41N 7°19W **282** C4
Castlerea *Ireland* 53°46N 8°29W **282** C3
Castlereagh → *Australia* 30°12S 147°32E **335** E4
Castlereagh B. *Australia* 12°10S 135°10E **334** A2
Castleton *U.S.A.* 43°37N 73°11W **355** C11
Castletown *I. of Man* 54°5N 4°38W **284** C3
Castletown Bearhaven *Ireland* 51°39N 9°55W **282** E2
Castor *Canada* 52°15N 111°50W **342** C6
Castor → *Canada* 53°24N 78°58W **344** B4
Castorland *U.S.A.* 43°53N 75°31W **355** C9
Castres *France* 43°37N 2°13E **292** E5
Castricum *Neths.* 52°33N 4°40E **287** B4
Castries *St. Lucia* 14°2N 60°58W **361** f
Castro *Brazil* 24°45S 50°0W **367** A6
Castro *Chile* 42°30S 73°50W **368** E2
Castro Alves *Brazil* 12°46S 39°33W **365** F11
Castro Valley *U.S.A.* 37°41N 122°5W **350** H4
Castroville *U.S.A.* 36°46N 121°45W **350** J5
Castuera *Spain* 38°43N 5°37W **293** C3
Cat Ba, Dao *Vietnam* 20°50N 107°0E **310** B6
Cat Ba △ *Vietnam* 20°47N 107°3E **310** B6
Cat I. *Bahamas* 24°30N 75°30W **361** B4
Cat L. *Canada* 51°40N 91°50W **344** B1
Cat Lake *Canada* 51°40N 91°50W **344** B1
Cat Tien △ *Vietnam* 11°25N 107°17E **311** G6
Catacamas *Honduras* 14°54N 85°56W **360** D2
Cataguases *Brazil* 21°23S 42°39W **367** A7
Catalão *Brazil* 18°10S 47°57W **365** G9
Çatalca *Turkey* 41°8N 28°27E **295** D13
Catalina *Canada* 48°31N 53°4W **345** C9
Catalina *Chile* 25°13S 69°43W **366** B2
Catalina *U.S.A.* 32°30N 110°50W **349** K8
Catalonia = Cataluña ☐ *Spain* 41°40N 1°15E **293** B6
Cataluña ☐ *Spain* 41°40N 1°15E **293** B6
Catamarca *Argentina* 28°30S 65°50W **366** B2
Catamarca ☐ *Argentina* 27°0S 65°50W **366** B2
Catanduanes ☐ *Phil.* 13°50N 124°20E **309** B6
Catanduva *Brazil* 21°5S 48°58W **367** A6
Catánia *Italy* 37°30N 15°6E **294** F6
Catanzaro *Italy* 38°54N 16°35E **294** E7
Catarman *Phil.* 12°28N 124°35E **309** B6
Catatumbo-Bari △ *Colombia* 9°3N 73°12W **361** E5
Cateel *Phil.* 7°47N 126°24E **309** C7
Catembe *Mozam.* 26°0S 32°33E **329** D5
Caterham *U.K.* 51°15N 0°4W **285** F7
Cathcart *S. Africa* 32°18S 27°10E **328** E4
Cathedral City *U.S.A.* 33°47N 116°28W **351** M10
Cathlamet *U.S.A.* 46°12N 123°23W **350** D3
Catlettsburg *U.S.A.* 38°25N 82°36W **353** F12
Catoche, C. *Mexico* 21°35N 87°5W **359** C7
Catriló *Argentina* 36°26S 63°24W **366** D3
Catrimani *Brazil* 0°27N 61°41W **364** C6
Catrimani → *Brazil* 0°28N 61°44W **364** C6
Catskill *U.S.A.* 42°14N 73°52W **355** D11
Catskill ⌓ *U.S.A.* 42°8N 74°39W **355** D10
Catskill Mts. *U.S.A.* 42°10N 74°25W **355** D10
Catt, Mt. *Australia* 13°49S 134°23E **334** A1
Cattaraugus *U.S.A.* 42°20N 78°52W **354** D6
Catterick *U.K.* 54°23N 1°37W **284** C6
Catuala *Angola* 16°25S 19°2E **328** B2
Catuane *Mozam.* 26°48S 32°18E **329** D5
Catur *Mozam.* 13°45S 35°30E **327** E4
Cauca → *Colombia* 8°54N 74°28W **364** B4
Caucaia *Brazil* 3°40S 38°35W **365** D11
Caucasus Mountains *Eurasia* 42°50N 44°0E **291** F7
Caungula *Angola* 8°26S 18°38E **324** F3
Cauquenes *Chile* 36°0S 72°22W **366** D1
Caura → *Venezuela* 7°38N 64°53W **364** B6
Cauresi → *Mozam.* 17°8S 33°0E **327** F3
Causapscal *Canada* 48°19N 67°12W **345** C6
Cauvery → *India* 11°9N 78°52E **312** P11
Caux, Pays de *France* 49°38N 0°35E **292** B4
Cavalier *U.S.A.* 48°48N 97°37W **352** A5
Cavan *Ireland* 54°0N 7°22W **282** B4
Cavan ☐ *Ireland* 54°1N 7°16W **282** C4
Cave Creek *U.S.A.* 33°50N 111°57W **349** K8
Cavenagh Ra. *Australia* 26°12S 127°55E **333** E4
Cavendish *Australia* 37°31S 142°2E **335** F3
Caviana, I. *Brazil* 0°10N 50°10W **365** C8
Cavite *Phil.* 14°29N 120°54E **309** B6
Cawndilla L. *Australia* 32°30S 142°15E **335** E3
Cawnpore = Kanpur *India* 26°28N 80°20E **315** F9
Caxias *Brazil* 4°55S 43°20W **365** D10
Caxias do Sul *Brazil* 29°10S 51°10W **367** B5
Cay Sal Bank *Bahamas* 23°45N 80°0W **360** B4
Cayambe *Ecuador* 0°3N 78°8W **364** C3
Cayenne *Fr. Guiana* 5°5N 52°18W **365** B8
Cayey *Puerto Rico* 18°7N 66°10W **361** d
Cayman Brac *Cayman Is.* 19°43N 79°49W **360** C4
Cayman Is. ⊠ *W. Indies* 19°40N 80°30W **360** C3
Cayman Trough *Caribbean* 19°0N 81°0W **338** H11
Cayuga *U.S.A.* 42°54N 76°44W **355** D8
Cayuga L. *U.S.A.* 42°41N 76°41W **355** D8
Cazenovia *U.S.A.* 42°56N 75°51W **355** D9
Cazombo *Angola* 11°54S 22°56E **325** G4
Ceanannus Mor *Ireland* 53°44N 6°53W **282** C5
Ceará = Fortaleza *Brazil* 3°45S 38°35W **365** D11
Ceará ☐ *Brazil* 5°0S 40°0W **365** E11
Ceará Mirim *Brazil* 5°38S 35°25W **365** E11
Cebaco, I. de *Panama* 7°33N 81°9W **360** E3
Cebollar *Argentina* 29°10S 66°35W **366** B2
Cebu *Phil.* 10°18N 123°54E **309** B6
Cecil Plains *Australia* 27°30S 151°11E **335** D5
Cedar → *U.S.A.* 41°17N 91°21W **352** E8
Cedar City *U.S.A.* 37°41N 113°4W **349** H7
Cedar Creek Res. *U.S.A.* 32°11N 96°4W **356** E6
Cedar Falls *Iowa, U.S.A.* 42°32N 92°27W **352** D7
Cedar Falls *Wash., U.S.A.* 47°25N 121°45W **350** C5
Cedar Key *U.S.A.* 29°8N 83°2W **357** G13
Cedar L. *Canada* 53°10N 100°0W **343** C9
Cedar Park *U.S.A.* 30°30N 97°49W **356** F6
Cedar Rapids *U.S.A.* 41°59N 91°40W **352** E8
Cedartown *U.S.A.* 34°1N 85°15W **357** D12
Cedarvale *Canada* 55°1N 128°22W **342** B3
Cedarville *S. Africa* 30°23S 29°3E **329** E4
Cedral *Mexico* 23°50N 100°45W **358** C4
Cedro *Brazil* 6°34S 39°3W **365** E11
Cedros, I. *Mexico* 28°12N 115°15W **358** B1
Cedros B. *Trin. & Tob.* 10°16N 61°54W **365** K15
Ceduna *Australia* 32°7S 133°46E **335** E1
Ceerigaabo = Erigavo *Somali Rep.* 10°35N 47°20E **319** E4
Cefalù *Italy* 38°2N 14°1E **294** E6
Cegléd *Hungary* 47°11N 19°47E **289** E10
Cekik *Indonesia* 8°12S 114°27E **309** J17
Celaque △ *Honduras* 14°30N 88°43W **360** D2
Celaya *Mexico* 20°31N 100°37W **358** C4
Celebes Sea *Indonesia* 3°0N 123°0E **309** D6
Celina *U.S.A.* 40°33N 84°35W **353** E11
Celje *Slovenia* 46°16N 15°18E **288** E8
Celle *Germany* 52°37N 10°4E **288** B6
Celtic Sea *Atl. Oc.* 50°9N 9°34W **286** F2
Cenderwasih, Teluk *Indonesia* 3°0S 135°20E **309** E9
Center *N. Dak., U.S.A.* 47°7N 101°18W **352** B3
Center *Tex., U.S.A.* 31°48N 94°11W **356** F7
Centerburg *U.S.A.* 40°18N 82°42W **354** F2
Centerville *Calif., U.S.A.* 36°44N 119°30W **350** J7
Centerville *Iowa, U.S.A.* 40°44N 92°52W **352** E7
Centerville *Pa., U.S.A.* 40°3N 79°59W **354** F5
Centerville *Tenn., U.S.A.* 35°47N 87°28W **357** D11
Centerville *Tex., U.S.A.* 31°16N 95°59W **356** F7
Central = Tsentralnyy ☐ *Russia* 52°0N 40°0E **300** D4
Central ☐ *Kenya* 0°30S 37°30E **326** C4
Central ☐ *Malawi* 13°30S 33°30E **327** E3
Central ☐ *Zambia* 14°25S 28°50E **327** E2
Central, Cordillera *Colombia* 5°0N 75°0W **364** C4
Central, Cordillera *Costa Rica* 10°10N 84°5W **360** D3
Central, Cordillera *Dom. Rep.* 19°15N 71°0W **361** C5
Central, Cordillera *Puerto Rico* 18°8N 66°35W **361** d
Central African Rep. ■ *Africa* 7°0N 20°0E **323** G9
Central America *America* 12°0N 85°0W **338** H11
Central Butte *Canada* 50°48N 106°31W **343** C7
Central City *Colo., U.S.A.* 39°48N 105°31W **348** G11
Central City *Ky., U.S.A.* 37°18N 87°7W **352** G10
Central City *Nebr., U.S.A.* 41°7N 98°0W **352** E4
Central I. *Kenya* 3°30N 36°0E **326** B4
Central Island △ *Kenya* 2°33N 36°1E **326** B4
Central Kalahari ⌓ *Botswana* 22°36S 23°58E **328** C3
Central Makran Range *Pakistan* 26°30N 64°15E **312** F4
Central Pacific Basin *Pac. Oc.* 8°0N 175°0W **336** G10
Central Patricia *Canada* 51°30N 90°9W **344** B1
Central Point *U.S.A.* 42°23N 122°55W **348** E2
Central Russian Uplands *Europe* 54°0N 36°0E **278** E13
Central Siberian Plateau *Russia* 65°0N 105°0E **298** B12
Central Square *U.S.A.* 43°17N 76°9W **355** C8
Centralia *Ill., U.S.A.* 38°32N 89°8W **352** F9
Centralia *Mo., U.S.A.* 39°13N 92°8W **352** F7
Centralia *Wash., U.S.A.* 46°43N 122°58W **350** D4
Centre de Flacq *Mauritius* 20°12S 57°43E **325** d
Cephalonia = Kefalonia *Greece* 38°15N 20°30E **295** E9
Cepu *Indonesia* 7°9S 111°35E **309** G14
Ceram = Seram *Indonesia* 3°10S 129°0E **309** E7
Ceram Sea = Seram Sea *Indonesia* 2°30S 128°30E **309** E7
Ceredigion ☐ *U.K.* 52°16N 4°15W **285** E3
Ceres *Argentina* 29°55S 61°55W **366** B3
Ceres *S. Africa* 33°21S 19°18E **328** E2
Ceres *U.S.A.* 37°35N 120°57W **350** H6
Cerf *Seychelles* 4°38S 55°40E **325** b
Cerignola *Italy* 41°17N 15°53E **294** D6
Cerigo = Kythira *Greece* 36°8N 23°0E **295** F10
Çerkezköy *Turkey* 41°17N 28°0E **295** D12
Cerralvo, I. *Mexico* 24°15N 109°55W **358** C3
Cerritos *Mexico* 22°25N 100°16W **358** C4
Cerro Chato *Uruguay* 33°6S 55°8W **367** C4
Cerro Cofre de Perote △ *Mexico* 19°29N 97°8W **359** D5
Cerro Corá △ *Paraguay* 22°35S 56°2W **367** A4
Cerro el Copey △ *Venezuela* 10°59N 63°53W **361** D7
Cerro Hoya △ *Panama* 7°17N 80°45W **360** E3
Cerro Saroche △ *Venezuela* 10°8N 69°38W **361** D6
Cerventes *Australia* 30°31S 115°3E **333** F2
Cervera *Spain* 41°40N 1°16E **293** B6
Cesena *Italy* 44°8N 12°15E **294** B5
Cēsis *Latvia* 57°18N 25°15E **281** H21
Ceská Rep. = Czech Rep. ■ *Europe* 50°0N 15°0E **288** D8
České Budějovice *Czech Rep.* 48°55N 14°25E **288** D8
Českomoravská Vrchovina *Czech Rep.* 49°30N 15°40E **288** D8
Çeşme *Turkey* 38°20N 26°23E **295** E12
Cessnock *Australia* 32°50S 151°21E **335** E5
Cetinje *Montenegro* 42°23N 18°59E **295** C8
Cetraro *Italy* 39°31N 15°55E **294** E6
Ceuta *N. Afr.* 35°52N 5°18W **293** E3
Cévennes *France* 44°10N 3°50E **292** D5
Ceyhan *Turkey* 37°4N 35°47E **316** B2
Ceylon = Sri Lanka ■ *Asia* 7°30N 80°50E **312** R12
Cha-am *Thailand* 12°48N 99°58E **310** F2
Cha Pa *Vietnam* 22°20N 103°47E **310** A4
Chacabuco *Argentina* 34°40S 60°27W **366** C3
Chachapoyas *Peru* 6°15S 77°50W **364** E3
Chachoengsao *Thailand* 13°42N 101°5E **310** F3
Chachran *Pakistan* 28°55N 70°30E **314** E4
Chachro *Pakistan* 25°5N 70°15E **314** G4
Chaco ☐ *Argentina* 26°30S 61°0W **366** B3
Chaco ☐ *Paraguay* 26°0S 60°0W **366** B4
Chaco → *U.S.A.* 36°46N 108°39W **349** H9
Chaco △ *Argentina* 27°0S 59°30W **366** B4
Chaco Austral *S. Amer.* 27°0S 61°30W **368** B4
Chaco Boreal *S. Amer.* 22°0S 60°0W **364** H6
Chaco Central *S. Amer.* 24°0S 61°0W **368** A4
Chaco Culture ⌓ *U.S.A.* 36°3N 107°58W **349** H10
Chacon, C. *U.S.A.* 54°42N 132°0W **342** C2
Chad ■ *Africa* 15°0N 17°15E **323** F8
Chad, L. = Tchad, L. *Chad* 13°30N 14°30E **323** F8
Chadan *Russia* 51°17N 91°35E **301** D10
Chadileuvú → *Argentina* 37°46S 66°0W **366** D2
Chadiza *Zambia* 14°45S 32°27E **327** E3
Chadron *U.S.A.* 42°50N 103°0W **352** D2
Chadyr-Lunga = Ciadâr-Lunga *Moldova* 46°3N 28°51E **289** E15
Chae Hom *Thailand* 18°43N 99°35E **310** C2
Chae Son △ *Thailand* 18°42N 99°20E **310** C2
Chaem → *Thailand* 18°11N 98°38E **310** C2
Chaeryŏng *N. Korea* 38°24N 125°36E **307** E13
Chagai Hills = Chāh Gay Hills *Afghan.* 29°30N 64°0E **312** E3
Chagda *Russia* 58°45N 130°38E **301** D14
Chaghcharān *Afghan.* 34°31N 65°15E **312** B4
Chagos Arch. ⊠ *Ind. Oc.* 6°0S 72°0E **298** J9
Chagres △ *Panama* 9°33N 79°37W **360** E4
Chagrin Falls *U.S.A.* 41°26N 81°24W **354** E3
Chaguanas *Trin. & Tob.* 10°30N 61°26W **365** K15
Chāh Ākhvor *Iran* 32°41N 59°40E **317** C8
Chāh Bahar *Iran* 25°20N 60°40E **317** E9
Chāh-e Kavīr *Iran* 34°29N 56°52E **317** C8
Chāh Gay Hills *Afghan.* 29°30N 64°0E **312** E3
Chahār Borjak *Afghan.* 30°17N 62°3E **312** D3
Chahār Mahāll va Bakhtīarī ☐ *Iran* 32°0N 49°0E **317** C6
Chai Wan *China* 22°16N 114°14E **305** G11
Chaibasa *India* 22°42N 85°49E **315** H11
Chainat *Thailand* 15°11N 100°8E **310** E3
Chaiya *Thailand* 9°23N 99°14E **311** H2
Chaiyaphum *Thailand* 15°48N 102°2E **310** E4
Chaj Doab *Pakistan* 32°15N 73°0E **314** C5
Chajari *Argentina* 30°42S 58°0W **366** C4
Chak Amru *Pakistan* 32°22N 75°11E **314** C6
Chakar → *Pakistan* 29°29N 68°2E **314** E3
Chakari *Zimbabwe* 18°5S 29°51E **329** B4
Chake Chake *Tanzania* 5°15S 39°45E **326** D4
Chakhānsūr *Afghan.* 31°10N 62°0E **312** D3
Chakonipau, L. *Canada* 56°18N 68°30W **345** A6
Chakradharpur *India* 22°45N 85°40E **315** H11
Chakrata *India* 30°42N 77°51E **314** D7

Chakwal Pakistan 32°56N 72°53E 314 C5
Chala Peru 15°48S 74°20W 364 G4
Chalchihuites Mexico 23°29N 103°53W 358 C4
Chalcis = Halkida
Greece 38°27N 23°42E 295 E10
Chaleur B. Canada 47°55N 65°30W 345 C6
Chalfant U.S.A. 37°32N 118°21W 350 H8
Chalhuanca Peru 14°15S 73°15W 364 F4
Chalisgaon India 20°30N 75°10E 312 J9
Chalk River Canada 46°1N 77°27W 344 C4
Chalky Inlet N.Z. 46°3S 166°31E 331 G1
Challapata Bolivia 18°53S 66°50W 364 G5
Challenger Deep
Pac. Oc. 11°30N 142°0E 336 F6
Challenger Fracture Zone
Pac. Oc. 35°0S 105°0W 337 L17
Challis U.S.A. 44°30N 114°14W 348 D6
Chalmette U.S.A. 29°56N 89°57W 357 G10
Chalon-sur-Saône France 46°48N 4°50E 292 C6
Châlons-en-Champagne
France 48°58N 4°20E 292 B6
Chālūs Iran 36°38N 51°26E 317 B6
Cham, Cu Lao Vietnam 15°57N 108°30E 310 E7
Chama U.S.A. 36°54N 106°35W 349 H10
Chamaicó Argentina 35°3S 64°58W 366 D3
Chaman Pakistan 30°58N 66°25E 312 D5
Chamba India 32°35N 76°10E 314 C7
Chamba Tanzania 11°37S 37°0E 327 E4
Chambal → India 26°29N 79°15E 315 F8
Chamberlain U.S.A. 43°49N 99°20W 352 D4
Chamberlain →
Australia 15°30S 127°54E 332 C4
Chamberlain L. U.S.A. 46°14N 69°19W 353 B19
Chambers U.S.A. 35°11N 109°26W 349 J9
Chambersburg U.S.A. 39°56N 77°40W 353 F15
Chambéry France 45°34N 5°55E 292 D6
Chambeshi → Zambia 11°53S 29°48E 324 G6
Chambly Canada 45°27N 73°17W 355 A11
Chambord Canada 48°25N 72°6W 345 C5
Chamchamal Iraq 35°32N 44°50E 316 C5
Chamela Mexico 19°32N 105°5W 358 D3
Chamical Argentina 30°22S 66°27W 366 C2
Chamkar Luong
Cambodia 11°0N 103°45E 311 G4
Chamoli India 30°24N 79°21E 315 D8
Chamonix-Mont Blanc
France 45°55N 6°51E 292 D7
Champa India 22°2N 82°43E 315 H10
Champagne Canada 60°49N 136°30W 342 A1
Champagne France 48°40N 4°20E 292 B6
Champaign U.S.A. 40°7N 88°15W 352 E9
Champassak Laos 14°53N 105°52E 310 E5
Champawat India 29°20N 80°6E 315 E9
Champdoré, L. Canada 55°55N 65°49W 345 A6
Champion U.S.A. 41°19N 80°51W 354 E4
Champlain U.S.A. 44°59N 73°27W 355 B11
Champlain, L. U.S.A. 44°40N 73°20W 355 B11
Champotón Mexico 19°21N 90°43W 359 D6
Champua India 22°5N 85°40E 315 H11
Chana Thailand 6°55N 100°44E 311 J3
Chañaral Chile 26°23S 70°40W 366 B1
Chanārān Iran 36°39N 59°6E 317 B8
Chanasma India 23°44N 72°5E 314 H5
Chancery Lane Barbados 13°3N 59°30W 361 g
Chanco Chile 35°44S 72°32W 366 D1
Chand India 21°57N 79°7E 315 J8
Chandan India 24°38N 86°40E 315 G12
Chandan Chauki India 28°33N 80°47E 315 E9
Chandannagar India 22°52N 88°24E 315 H13
Chandausi India 28°27N 78°49E 315 E8
Chandeleur Is. U.S.A. 29°55N 88°57W 357 G10
Chandeleur Sd. U.S.A. 29°55N 89°0W 357 G10
Chandigarh India 30°43N 76°47E 314 D7
Chandil India 22°58N 86°3E 315 H12
Chandler Australia 27°0S 133°19E 335 D1
Chandler Canada 48°18N 64°46W 345 C7
Chandler Ariz., U.S.A. 33°18N 111°50W 349 K8
Chandler Okla., U.S.A. 35°42N 96°53W 356 D6
Chandod India 21°59N 73°28E 314 J5
Chandpur Bangla. 23°8N 90°45E 313 H17
Chandrapur India 19°57N 79°25E 312 K11
Chānf Iran 26°38N 60°29E 317 E9
Chang Pakistan 26°59N 68°30E 314 F3
Chang, Ko Thailand 12°0N 102°23E 311 F4
Ch'ang Chiang = Chang Jiang →
China 31°48N 121°10E 305 C7
Chang Jiang → China 31°48N 121°10E 305 C7
Chang-won S. Korea 35°16N 128°37E 307 G15
Changa India 33°53N 77°35E 315 C7
Changan China 22°48N 113°48E 305 F10
Changanacheri India 9°25N 76°31E 312 Q10
Changane → Mozam. 24°30S 33°30E 329 C5
Changbai China 41°25N 128°5E 307 D15
Changbai Shan China 42°20N 129°0E 307 C15
Changchiak'ou = Zhangjiakou
China 40°48N 114°55E 306 D8
Ch'angchou = Changzhou
China 31°47N 119°58E 305 C6
Changchun China 43°57N 125°17E 307 C13
Changchunling China 45°18N 125°27E 307 B13
Changde China 29°4N 111°35E 305 D6
Changdo-ri N. Korea 38°30N 127°40E 307 E14
Changhai = Shanghai
China 31°15N 121°26E 305 C7
Changhua Taiwan 24°2N 120°30E 305 D7
Changhŭngni
N. Korea 40°24N 128°19E 307 D15
Changi Singapore 1°23N 103°59E 311 d
Changi, Singapore ✈ (SIN)
Singapore 1°23N 103°59E 311 M4
Changji China 44°1N 87°19E 304 B3
Changjiang China 19°20N 108°55E 310 C7
Changjiang Shuiku
China 22°29N 113°27E 305 G10
Changjin N. Korea 40°23N 127°15E 307 D14
Changjin-ho N. Korea 40°30N 127°15E 307 D14
Changli China 39°40N 119°13E 307 E10
Changling China 44°20N 123°58E 307 B12
Changlun Malaysia 6°25N 100°26E 311 J3
Changping China 40°14N 116°12E 306 D9
Changsha China 28°12N 113°0E 305 D6
Changshan Qundao
China 39°11N 122°32E 307 E12
Changwu China 35°10N 107°45E 306 G4
Changyi China 36°40N 119°30E 307 F10
Changyŏn N. Korea 38°15N 125°6E 307 E13
Changyuan China 35°15N 114°42E 306 G8
Changzhi China 36°10N 113°6E 306 F7
Changzhou China 31°47N 119°58E 305 C6
Chanhanga Angola 16°0S 14°8E 328 B1
Chania Greece 35°30N 24°4E 297 D6
Chania □ Greece 35°30N 24°0E 297 D6
Chanion, Kolpos Greece 35°33N 23°55E 297 D5
Channapatna India 12°40N 77°15E 312 N10
Channel Is. U.K. 49°19N 2°24W 285 H5
Channel Is. U.S.A. 33°40N 119°15W 351 M7
Channel Islands △
U.S.A. 34°0N 119°24W 351 L7
Channel-Port aux Basques
Canada 47°30N 59°9W 345 C8
Channel Tunnel Europe 51°0N 1°30E 285 F9
Channing U.S.A. 35°41N 102°20W 356 D3
Chantada Spain 42°36N 7°46W 293 A2
Chanthaburi Thailand 12°38N 102°12E 310 F4
Chantrey Inlet Canada 67°48N 96°20W 340 C10
Chanute U.S.A. 37°41N 95°27W 352 G6
Chao Phraya →
Thailand 13°40N 100°31E 310 F3
Chao Phraya Lowlands
Thailand 15°30N 100°0E 310 E3
Chaocheng China 36°4N 115°37E 306 F8
Chaoyang China 41°35N 120°22E 307 D11
Chaozhou China 23°42N 116°32E 305 D6
Chapais Canada 49°47N 74°51W 344 C5
Chapala Mozam. 15°50S 37°35E 327 F4
Chapala, L. de Mexico 20°15N 103°0W 358 C4
Chapayev Kazakhstan 50°25N 51°10E 291 D9
Chapayevsk Russia 53°0N 49°40E 290 D8
Chapecó Brazil 27°14S 52°41W 367 B5
Chapel Hill U.S.A. 35°55N 79°4W 357 D15
Chapleau Canada 47°50N 83°24W 344 C3
Chaplin Canada 50°28N 106°40W 343 C7
Chaplin L. Canada 50°22N 106°36W 343 C7
Chappell U.S.A. 41°6N 102°28W 352 E2
Chapra = Chhapra
India 25°48N 84°44E 315 G11
Chara Russia 56°54N 118°20E 301 D12
Charadai Argentina 27°35S 59°55W 366 B4
Charagua Bolivia 19°45S 63°10W 364 G6
Charakas Greece 35°1N 25°7E 297 D7
Charambirá, Punta
Colombia 4°16N 77°32W 364 C3
Charaña Bolivia 17°30S 69°25W 364 G5
Charanwala India 27°51N 72°10E 314 F5
Charata Argentina 27°13S 61°14W 366 B3
Charcas Mexico 23°8N 101°7W 358 C4
Charcot I. Antarctica 70°0S 70°0W 277 C17
Chard U.K. 50°52N 2°58W 285 G5
Chardon U.S.A. 41°35N 81°12W 354 E3
Chardzhou = Türkmenabat
Turkmenistan 39°6N 63°34E 317 B9
Charente → France 45°57N 1°5W 292 D3
Chari → Chad 12°58N 14°31E 323 F8
Chārīkār Afghan. 35°0N 69°10E 312 B6
Chariton U.S.A. 41°1N 93°19W 352 E7
Chariton → U.S.A. 39°19N 92°58W 352 F7
Chärjew = Türkmenabat
Turkmenistan 39°6N 63°34E 317 B9
Charkhari India 25°24N 79°45E 315 G8
Charkhi Dadri India 28°37N 76°17E 314 E7
Charleroi Belgium 50°24N 4°27E 287 D4
Charleroi U.S.A. 40°9N 79°57W 354 F5
Charles, C. U.S.A. 37°7N 75°58W 353 G16
Charles, Peak Australia 32°52S 121°11E 333 F3
Charles City U.S.A. 43°4N 92°41W 352 D7
Charles L. Canada 59°50N 110°33W 343 B6
Charles Town U.S.A. 39°17N 77°52W 353 F15
Charlesbourg Canada 46°51N 71°16W 353 B18
Charleston Ill., U.S.A. 39°30N 88°10W 352 F9
Charleston Miss., U.S.A. 34°1N 90°4W 357 D9
Charleston Mo., U.S.A. 36°55N 89°21W 352 G9
Charleston S.C., U.S.A. 32°46N 79°56W 357 E15
Charleston W. Va.,
U.S.A. 38°21N 81°38W 353 F13
Charleston L. Canada 44°32N 76°0W 355 B9
Charleston Peak
U.S.A. 36°16N 115°42W 351 J11
Charlestown Ireland 53°58N 8°48W 282 C3
Charlestown S. Africa 27°26S 29°53E 329 D4
Charlestown Ind.,
U.S.A. 38°27N 85°40W 353 F11
Charlestown N.H.,
U.S.A. 43°14N 72°25W 355 C12
Charlestown of Aberlour
U.K. 57°28N 3°14W 283 D5
Charleville = Rath Luirc
Ireland 52°21N 8°40W 282 D3
Charleville Australia 26°24S 146°15E 335 D4
Charleville-Mézières
France 49°44N 4°40E 292 B6
Charlevoix U.S.A. 45°19N 85°16W 353 C11
Charlotte Mich., U.S.A. 42°34N 84°50W 353 D11
Charlotte N.C., U.S.A. 35°13N 80°50W 357 D14
Charlotte Vt., U.S.A. 44°19N 73°16W 355 B11
Charlotte Amalie
U.S. Virgin Is. 18°21N 64°56W 361 e
Charlotte Harbor
U.S.A. 26°57N 82°4W 357 H13
Charlotte L. Canada 52°12N 125°19W 342 C3
Charlottesville U.S.A. 38°2N 78°30W 353 F14
Charlottetown Nfld. & L.,
Canada 52°46N 56°7W 345 B8
Charlottetown P.E.I.,
Canada 46°14N 63°8W 345 C7
Charlotteville
Trin. & Tob. 11°20N 60°33W 365 J16
Charlton Australia 36°16S 143°24E 335 F3
Charlton I. Canada 52°0N 79°20W 344 B4
Charny Canada 46°43N 71°15W 345 C5
Charolles France 46°27N 4°16E 292 C6
Charre Mozam. 17°13S 35°10E 327 F4
Charsadda Pakistan 34°7N 71°45E 314 B4
Charters Towers
Australia 20°5S 146°13E 334 C4
Chartres France 48°29N 1°30E 292 B4
Chascomús Argentina 35°30S 58°0W 366 D4
Chase Canada 50°50N 119°41W 342 C5
Chasefu Zambia 11°55S 33°8E 327 E3
Chashma Barrage
Pakistan 32°27N 71°20E 314 C4
Chāt Iran 37°59N 55°16E 317 B7
Châteaubriant France 47°43N 1°23W 292 C3
Chateaugay U.S.A. 44°56N 74°5W 355 B10
Châteauguay, L. Canada 56°26N 70°3W 345 A5
Châteaulin France 48°11N 4°8W 292 B1
Châteauroux France 46°50N 1°40E 292 C4
Châteaux, Pte. des
Guadeloupe 16°15N 61°10W 360 b
Châtellerault France 46°50N 0°30E 292 C4
Chatham = Chatham-Kent
Canada 42°24N 82°11W 354 D2
Chatham = Miramichi
Canada 47°2N 65°28W 345 C6
Chatham U.K. 51°22N 0°32E 285 F8
Chatham U.S.A. 42°21N 73°36W 355 D11
Chatham Is. Pac. Oc. 44°0S 176°40W 336 M10
Chatham-Kent Canada 42°24N 82°11W 354 D2
Chatham Rise Pac. Oc. 43°30S 180°0E 336 M10
Chatmohar Bangla. 24°15N 89°15E 315 G13
Chatra India 24°12N 84°56E 315 G11
Chatrapur India 19°22N 85°2E 313 K14
Chats, L. des Canada 45°30N 76°20W 355 A8
Chatsu India 26°36N 75°57E 314 F6
Chatsworth Canada 44°27N 80°54W 354 B4
Chatsworth Zimbabwe 19°38S 31°13E 327 F3
Châttagâm = Chittagong
Bangla. 22°19N 91°48E 313 H17
Chattahoochee U.S.A. 30°42N 84°51W 357 F12
Chattahoochee →
U.S.A. 30°54N 84°57W 357 F12
Chattanooga U.S.A. 35°3N 85°19W 357 D12
Chatteris U.K. 52°28N 0°2E 285 E8
Chaturat Thailand 15°40N 101°51E 310 E3
Chau Doc Vietnam 10°42N 105°7E 311 G5
Chaukan Pass Burma 27°8N 97°10E 313 F20
Chaumont France 48°7N 5°8E 292 B6
Chaumont U.S.A. 44°4N 76°8W 355 B8
Chaunskaya G. Russia 69°0N 169°0E 276 C16
Chautauqua L. U.S.A. 42°10N 79°24W 354 D5
Chauvin Canada 52°45N 110°10W 343 C6
Chaves Brazil 0°15S 49°55W 365 D9
Chaves Portugal 41°45N 7°32W 293 B2
Chawang Thailand 8°25N 99°30E 311 H2
Chaykovskiy Russia 56°47N 54°9E 290 C9
Chazy U.S.A. 44°53N 73°26W 355 B11
Cheb Czech Rep. 50°9N 12°28E 288 C7
Cheboksary Russia 56°8N 47°12E 290 C8
Cheboygan U.S.A. 45°39N 84°29W 353 C11
Chech, Erg Africa 25°0N 2°15W 322 D5
Chechenia □ Russia 43°30N 45°29E 291 F8
Checheno-Ingush Republic =
Chechenia □ Russia 43°30N 45°29E 291 F8
Chechnya = Chechenia □
Russia 43°30N 45°29E 291 F8
Checotah U.S.A. 35°28N 95°31W 356 D7
Chedabucto B. Canada 45°25N 61°8W 345 C7
Cheduba I. Burma 18°45N 93°40E 313 K18
Cheepie Australia 26°33S 145°1E 335 D4
Chegdomyn Russia 51°7N 133°1E 301 D14
Chegga Mauritania 25°27N 5°40W 322 C4
Chegutu Zimbabwe 18°10S 30°14E 327 F3
Chehalis U.S.A. 46°40N 122°58W 350 D4
Chehalis → U.S.A. 46°57N 123°50W 350 D3
Cheju = Jeju S. Korea 33°31N 126°32E 307 H14
Cheju-do = Jeju-do
S. Korea 33°29N 126°34E 307 H14
Chekiang = Zhejiang □
China 29°0N 120°0E 305 D7
Chela, Sa. da Angola 16°20S 13°20E 328 B1
Chelan U.S.A. 47°51N 120°1W 348 C3
Chelan, L. U.S.A. 48°11N 120°30W 348 B3
Cheleken = Hazar
Turkmenistan 39°34N 53°16E 291 G9
Cheleken Yarymadasy
Turkmenistan 39°30N 53°15E 317 B7
Chelforó Argentina 39°0S 66°33W 368 D3
Chelkar = Shalqar
Kazakhstan 47°48N 59°39E 300 E6
Chelm Poland 51°8N 23°30E 289 C12
Chelmno Poland 53°20N 18°30E 289 B10
Chelmsford U.K. 51°44N 0°29E 285 F8
Chelsea Australia 38°5S 145°8E 335 F4
Chelsea U.S.A. 43°59N 72°27W 355 C12
Cheltenham U.K. 51°54N 2°4W 285 F5
Chelyabinsk Russia 55°10N 61°24E 279 D18
Chelyuskin, C. = Chelyuskin, Mys
Russia 77°30N 103°0E 301 B11
Chelyuskin, Mys
Russia 77°30N 103°0E 301 B11
Chemainus Canada 48°55N 123°42W 350 B3
Chemba Mozam. 17°9S 34°53E 325 H6
Chemin Grenier
Mauritius 20°29S 57°28E 325 d
Chemnitz Germany 50°51N 12°54E 288 C7
Chemult U.S.A. 43°14N 121°47W 348 E3
Chen, Gora Russia 65°16N 141°50E 301 C15
Chenab → Pakistan 30°23N 71°2E 314 D4
Chenango Forks U.S.A. 42°15N 75°51W 355 D9
Cheney U.S.A. 47°30N 117°35W 348 C5
Cheng Xian China 33°43N 105°42E 306 H3
Chengcheng China 35°8N 109°56E 306 G5
Chengchou = Zhengzhou
China 34°45N 113°34E 306 G7
Chengde China 40°59N 117°58E 307 D9
Chengdu China 30°38N 104°2E 304 C5
Chenggu China 33°10N 107°21E 306 H4
Chengjiang China 24°39N 103°0E 304 D5
Chengmai China 19°50N 109°58E 310 C7
Ch'engtu = Chengdu
China 30°38N 104°2E 304 C5
Chengwu China 34°58N 115°50E 306 G8
Chengyang China 36°18N 120°21E 307 F11
Chenjiagang China 34°23N 119°47E 307 G10
Chennai India 13°8N 80°19E 312 N12
Cheom Ksan Cambodia 14°13N 104°56E 310 E5
Cheonan S. Korea 36°48N 127°9E 307 F14
Cheongdo S. Korea 35°38N 128°42E 307 G15
Cheongju S. Korea 36°39N 127°27E 307 F14
Cheorwon S. Korea 38°15N 127°10E 307 E14
Chepén Peru 7°15S 79°23W 364 E3
Chepes Argentina 31°20S 66°35W 366 C2
Chepo Panama 9°10N 79°6W 360 E4
Chepstow U.K. 51°38N 2°41W 285 F5
Chequamegon B.
U.S.A. 46°39N 90°51W 352 B8
Cher → France 47°21N 0°29E 292 C4
Cheraw U.S.A. 34°42N 79°53W 357 D15
Cherbourg France 49°39N 1°40W 292 B3
Cherdyn Russia 60°24N 56°29E 290 B10
Cheremkhovo Russia 53°8N 103°1E 301 D11
Cherepanovo Russia 54°15N 83°30E 300 D9
Cherepovets Russia 59°5N 37°55E 290 C6
Chergui, Chott ech
Algeria 34°21N 0°25E 322 B6
Cherikov = Cherykaw
Belarus 53°32N 31°20E 289 B16
Cherkasy Ukraine 49°27N 32°4E 291 E5
Cherkessk Russia 44°15N 42°5E 291 F7
Cherlak Russia 54°15N 74°55E 300 D8
Chernaya Russia 70°30N 89°10E 301 B9
Chernigov = Chernihiv
Ukraine 51°28N 31°20E 290 D5
Chernihiv Ukraine 51°28N 31°20E 290 D5
Chernivtsi Ukraine 48°15N 25°52E 289 D13
Chernobyl = Chornobyl
Ukraine 51°20N 30°15E 289 C16
Chernogorsk Russia 53°49N 91°18E 301 D10
Chernovtsy = Chernivtsi
Ukraine 48°15N 25°52E 289 D13
Chernyakhovsk Russia 54°36N 21°48E 281 J19
Chernysheyskiy Russia 63°0N 112°30E 301 C12
Cherokee Iowa, U.S.A. 42°45N 95°33W 352 D6
Cherokee Okla., U.S.A. 36°45N 98°21W 356 C5
Cherokee Village
U.S.A. 36°18N 91°31W 356 C9
Cherokees, Grand Lake O' The
U.S.A. 36°28N 94°55W 356 C7
Cherrapunji India 25°17N 91°47E 313 G17
Cherry Valley U.S.A. 42°48N 74°45W 355 D10
Cherskiy Russia 68°45N 161°18E 301 C17
Cherskogo Khrebet
Russia 65°0N 143°0E 301 C15
Chersonisos Greece 35°18N 25°22E 297 D7
Chersonisos Akrotiri
Greece 35°30N 24°10E 297 D6
Cherven Belarus 53°45N 28°28E 289 B15
Chervonohrad Ukraine 50°25N 24°10E 289 C13
Cherwell → U.K. 51°44N 1°14W 285 F6
Cherykaw Belarus 53°32N 31°20E 289 B16
Chesapeake U.S.A. 36°49N 76°16W 353 G15
Chesapeake B. U.S.A. 38°0N 76°10W 353 F14
Cheshire □ U.K. 53°14N 2°30W 284 D5
Cheshskaya Guba Russia 67°20N 47°0E 290 A8
Cheshunt U.K. 51°43N 0°1W 285 F7
Chesil Beach U.K. 50°37N 2°33W 285 G5
Chesley Canada 44°17N 81°5W 354 B3
Chester U.K. 53°12N 2°53W 284 D5
Chester Calif., U.S.A. 40°19N 121°14W 348 F3
Chester Ill., U.S.A. 37°55N 89°49W 352 G9
Chester Mont., U.S.A. 48°31N 110°58W 348 B8
Chester Pa., U.S.A. 39°51N 75°22W 353 F16
Chester S.C., U.S.A. 34°43N 81°12W 357 D14
Chester Vt., U.S.A. 43°16N 72°36W 355 C12
Chester W. Va., U.S.A. 40°37N 80°34W 354 F4
Chester-le-Street U.K. 54°51N 1°34W 284 C6
Chesterfield U.K. 53°15N 1°25W 284 D6
Chesterfield, Îs. N. Cal. 19°52S 158°15E 330 C8
Chesterfield Inlet
Canada 63°30N 90°45W 340 C10
Chesterton Ra.
Australia 25°30S 147°27E 335 D4
Chesterton Range △
Australia 26°16S 147°22E 335 D4
Chestertown U.S.A. 43°40N 73°48W 355 C11
Chesterville Canada 45°6N 75°14W 355 A9
Chesuncook L. U.S.A. 46°0N 69°21W 353 C19
Chéticamp Canada 46°37N 60°59W 345 C7
Chetumal Mexico 18°30N 88°20W 359 D7
Chetumal, B. de
Cent. Amer. 18°40N 88°10W 359 D7
Chetwynd Canada 55°45N 121°36W 342 B4
Cheviot, The U.K. 55°29N 2°9W 284 B5
Cheviot Hills U.K. 55°20N 2°30W 284 B5
Cheviot Ra. Australia 25°20S 143°45E 334 D3
Chew Bahir Ethiopia 4°40N 36°50E 319 G2
Chewelah U.S.A. 48°17N 117°43W 348 B5
Chewore ⌂ Zimbabwe 16°0S 29°52E 327 F2
Cheyenne Okla., U.S.A. 35°37N 99°40W 356 D5
Cheyenne Wyo., U.S.A. 41°8N 104°49W 348 F11
Cheyenne → U.S.A. 44°41N 101°18W 352 C3
Cheyenne Wells
U.S.A. 38°49N 102°21W 348 G12
Cheyne B. Australia 34°35S 118°50E 333 F2
Chhabra India 24°40N 76°54E 314 G7
Chhaktala India 22°6N 74°11E 314 H6
Chhapra India 25°48N 84°44E 315 G11
Chhata India 27°42N 77°30E 314 F7
Chhatarpur Jharkhand,
India 24°23N 84°11E 315 G11
Chhatarpur Mad. P.,
India 24°55N 79°35E 315 G8
Chhattisgarh □ India 22°0N 82°0E 315 J10
Chhep Cambodia 13°45N 105°24E 310 F5
Chhindwara Mad. P.,
India 23°3N 79°29E 315 H8
Chhindwara Mad. P.,
India 22°2N 78°59E 315 H8
Chhlong Cambodia 12°15N 105°58E 311 F5
Chhota Tawa → India 22°14N 76°36E 314 H7
Chhoti Kali Sindh →
India 24°2N 75°31E 314 G6
Chhuikhadan India 21°32N 80°59E 315 J9
Chhuk Cambodia 10°46N 104°28E 311 G5
Chi → Thailand 15°11N 104°43E 310 E5
Chiai Taiwan 23°29N 120°25E 305 D7
Chiamboni Somali Rep. 1°39S 41°35E 324 E8
Chiang Dao Thailand 19°22N 98°58E 310 C2
Chiang Kham Thailand 19°32N 100°18E 310 C3
Chiang Khan Thailand 17°52N 101°36E 310 D3
Chiang Khong
Thailand 20°17N 100°24E 310 B3
Chiang Mai Thailand 18°47N 98°59E 310 C2
Chiang Rai Thailand 19°52N 99°50E 310 C2
Chiang Saen Thailand 20°16N 100°5E 310 B3
Chiapa → Mexico 16°42N 93°0W 359 D6
Chiapa de Corzo Mexico 16°42N 93°0W 359 D6
Chiapas □ Mexico 16°30N 92°30W 359 D6
Chiapas, Sa. Madre de
Mexico 15°40N 93°0W 359 D6
Chiautla de Tapia
Mexico 18°18N 98°36W 359 D5
Chiávari Italy 44°19N 9°19E 292 D8
Chiavenna Italy 46°19N 9°24E 292 C8
Chiba Japan 35°30N 140°7E 303 G10
Chiba □ Japan 35°30N 140°20E 303 G10
Chibabava Mozam. 20°17S 33°35E 329 C5
Chibemba Cunene, Angola 15°48S 14°8E 325 H2
Chibemba Huila, Angola 16°20S 15°20E 328 B2
Chibi Zimbabwe 20°18S 30°25E 329 C5
Chibia Angola 15°10S 13°42E 325 H2
Chibougamau Canada 49°56N 74°24W 344 C5
Chibougamau, L.
Canada 49°50N 74°20W 344 C5
Chibuk Nigeria 10°52N 12°50E 323 F8
Chibuto Mozam. 24°40S 33°33E 329 C5
Chic-Chocs, Mts. Canada 48°55N 66°0W 345 C6
Chicacole = Srikakulam
India 18°14N 83°58E 313 K13
Chicago U.S.A. 41°52N 87°38W 352 E10
Chicago Heights
U.S.A. 41°30N 87°38W 352 E10
Chichagof I. U.S.A. 57°30N 135°30W 340 D6
Chichaoua Morocco 31°32N 8°44W 322 B4
Chichén-Itzá Mexico 20°37N 88°35W 359 C7
Chicheng China 40°55N 115°55E 306 D8
Chichester U.K. 50°50N 0°47W 285 G7
Chichester Ra.
Australia 22°12S 119°15E 332 D2
Chichibu Japan 35°59N 139°10E 303 F9
Chichibu-Tama △
Japan 35°52N 138°42E 303 G9
Ch'ich'ihaerh = Qiqihar
China 47°26N 124°0E 305 B7
Chicholi India 22°1N 77°40E 314 H8
Chickasaw ⌂ U.S.A. 34°26N 97°0W 356 D6
Chickasha U.S.A. 35°3N 97°58W 356 D6
Chiclana de la Frontera
Spain 36°26N 6°9W 293 D2
Chiclayo Peru 6°42S 79°50W 364 E3
Chico U.S.A. 39°44N 121°50W 350 F5
Chico → Chubut,
Argentina 44°0S 67°0W 368 E3
Chico → Santa Cruz,
Argentina 50°0S 68°30W 368 G3
Chicomo Mozam. 24°31S 34°6E 329 C5
Chicomostoc Mexico 22°28N 102°46W 358 C4
Chicontepec Mexico 20°58N 98°10W 359 C5
Chicopee U.S.A. 42°9N 72°37W 355 D12
Chicoutimi Canada 48°28N 71°5W 345 C5
Chicualacuala Mozam. 22°6S 31°42E 329 C5
Chidambaram India 11°20N 79°45E 312 P11
Chidenguele Mozam. 24°55S 34°11E 329 C5
Chidley, C. Canada 60°23N 64°26W 341 C13
Chiducuane Mozam. 24°35S 34°25E 329 C5
Chiede Angola 17°15S 16°22E 328 B2
Chiefs Pt. Canada 44°41N 81°18W 354 B3
Chiem Hoa Vietnam 22°12N 105°17E 310 A5
Chiemsee Germany 47°53N 12°28E 288 E7
Chiengi Zambia 8°45S 29°10E 327 D2
Chiengmai = Chiang Mai
Thailand 18°47N 98°59E 310 C2
Chiese → Italy 45°8N 10°25E 292 D9
Chieti Italy 42°21N 14°10E 294 C6
Chifeng China 42°18N 118°58E 307 C10
Chignecto B. Canada 45°30N 64°40W 345 C7
Chiguana Bolivia 21°0S 67°58W 366 A2
Chigwell U.K. 51°37N 0°6E 285 F8
Chihli, G. of = Bo Hai
China 39°0N 119°0E 307 E10
Chihuahua Mexico 28°38N 106°5W 358 B3
Chihuahua □ Mexico 28°30N 106°0W 358 B3
Chiili = Shīeli
Kazakhstan 44°20N 66°15E 300 E7
Chik Bollapur India 13°25N 77°45E 312 N10
Chikmagalur India 13°15N 75°45E 312 N9
Chikwawa Malawi 16°2S 34°50E 327 F3
Chilam Chavki Pakistan 35°5N 75°5E 315 B6
Chilanga Zambia 15°33S 28°16E 327 F2
Chilapa Mexico 17°36N 99°10W 359 D5
Chilas Pakistan 35°25N 74°5E 315 B6
Chilaw Sri Lanka 7°30N 79°50E 312 R11
Chilcotin → Canada 51°44N 122°23W 342 C4
Childers Australia 25°15S 152°17E 335 D5
Childress U.S.A. 34°25N 100°13W 356 D4
Chile ■ S. Amer. 35°0S 72°0W 368 D2
Chile Rise Pac. Oc. 38°0S 92°0W 337 L18

Chilecito Argentina 29°10S 67°30W 366 B2
Chilete Peru 7°10S 78°50W 364 E3
Chililabombwe Zambia 12°18S 27°43E 327 E2
Chilin = Jilin China 43°44N 126°30E 307 C14
Chilka L. India 19°40N 85°25E 313 K14
Chilko → Canada 52°0N 123°40W 342 C4
Chilko L. Canada 51°20N 124°10W 342 C4
Chillagoe Australia 17°7S 144°33E 334 B3
Chillán Chile 36°40S 72°10W 366 D1
Chillicothe Ill., U.S.A. 40°55N 89°29W 352 E9
Chillicothe Mo., U.S.A. 39°48N 93°33W 352 F7
Chillicothe Ohio, U.S.A. 39°20N 82°59W 353 F12
Chilliwack Canada 49°10N 121°54W 342 D4
Chilo India 27°25N 73°32E 314 F5
Chiloane, I. Mozam. 20°40S 34°55E 329 C5
Chiloé, I. de Chile 42°30S 73°50W 368 E2
Chilpancingo Mexico 17°33N 99°30W 359 D5
Chiltern Hills U.K. 51°40N 0°53W 285 F7
Chilton U.S.A. 44°2N 88°10W 352 C9
Chilubi Zambia 11°5S 29°58E 327 E2
Chilubula Zambia 10°14S 30°51E 327 E3
Chilumba Malawi 10°28S 34°12E 327 E3
Chilung Taiwan 25°3N 121°45E 305 D7
Chilwa, L. Malawi 15°15S 35°40E 327 F4
Chimaltitán Mexico 21°35N 103°50W 358 C4
Chimán Panama 8°45N 78°40W 360 E4
Chimanimani Zimbabwe 19°48S 32°52E 329 B5
Chimay Belgium 50°3N 4°20E 287 D4
Chimayo U.S.A. 36°0N 105°56W 349 J11
Chimbay Uzbekistan 42°57N 59°47E 300 E6
Chimborazo Ecuador 1°29S 78°55W 364 D3
Chimbote Peru 9°0S 78°35W 364 E3
Chimkent = Shymkent Kazakhstan 42°18N 69°36E 300 E7
Chimoio Mozam. 19°4S 33°30E 327 F3
Chimpembe Zambia 9°31S 29°33E 327 D2
Chin □ Burma 22°0N 93°0E 313 J18
Chin Hills Burma 22°30N 93°30E 313 H18
Chin Ling Shan = Qinling Shandi China 33°50N 108°10E 306 H5
China Mexico 25°42N 99°14W 359 B5
China ■ Asia 30°0N 110°0E 305 C6
China, Great Plain of Asia 35°0N 115°0E 298 E13
China Lake U.S.A. 35°44N 117°37W 351 K9
Chinan = Jinan China 36°38N 117°1E 306 F9
Chinandega Nic. 12°35N 87°12W 360 D2
Chinati Peak U.S.A. 29°57N 104°29W 356 G2
Chincha Alta Peru 13°25S 76°7W 364 F3
Chinchaga → Canada 58°53N 118°20W 342 B5
Chinchilla Australia 26°45S 150°38E 335 D5
Chinchorro, Banco Mexico 18°35N 87°22W 359 D7
Chinchou = Jinzhou China 41°5N 121°3E 307 D11
Chincoteague U.S.A. 37°56N 75°23W 353 G16
Chinde Mozam. 18°35S 36°30E 327 F4
Chindwin → Burma 21°26N 95°15E 313 J19
Chineni India 33°2N 75°15E 315 C6
Chinga Mozam. 15°13S 38°35E 327 F4
Chingola Zambia 12°31S 27°53E 327 E2
Chingole Malawi 13°4S 34°17E 327 E3
Ch'ingtao = Qingdao China 36°5N 120°20E 307 F11
Chinguetti Mauritania 20°25N 12°24W 322 D3
Chingune Mozam. 20°33S 34°58E 329 C5
Chinhanguanine Mozam. 25°21S 32°30E 329 D5
Chinhoyi Zimbabwe 17°20S 30°8E 327 F3
Chini India 31°32N 78°15E 314 D8
Chiniot Pakistan 31°45N 73°0E 314 D5
Chínipas Mexico 27°23N 108°32W 358 B3
Chinji Pakistan 32°42N 72°22E 314 C5
Chinju = Jinju S. Korea 35°12N 128°2E 307 G15
Chinko → C.A.R. 4°50N 23°53E 324 D4
Chinle U.S.A. 36°9N 109°33W 349 H9
Chinnampo = Namp'o N. Korea 38°52N 125°10E 307 E13
Chino Japan 35°59N 138°9E 303 G9
Chino U.S.A. 34°1N 117°41W 351 L9
Chino Valley U.S.A. 34°45N 112°27W 349 J7
Chinon France 47°10N 0°15E 292 C4
Chinook U.S.A. 48°35N 109°14W 348 B9
Chinook Trough Pac. Oc. 44°0N 175°0W 336 C10
Chinsali Zambia 10°30S 32°2E 327 E3
Chióggia Italy 45°13N 12°17E 294 B5
Chíos = Hios Greece 38°27N 26°9E 295 E12
Chipata Zambia 13°38S 32°28E 327 E3
Chipindo Angola 13°49S 15°48E 325 G3
Chipinge Zimbabwe 20°13S 32°28E 327 G3
Chipinge ⌂ Zimbabwe 20°14S 33°0E 327 G3
Chipley U.S.A. 30°47N 85°32W 357 F12
Chipman Canada 46°6N 65°53W 345 C6
Chipoka Malawi 13°57S 34°28E 327 E3
Chippenham U.K. 51°27N 2°6W 285 F5
Chippewa → U.S.A. 44°25N 92°5W 352 C7
Chippewa Falls U.S.A. 44°56N 91°24W 352 C8
Chipping Norton U.K. 51°56N 1°32W 285 F6
Chiputneticook Lakes N. Amer. 45°35N 67°35W 353 C20
Chiquián Peru 10°10S 77°0W 364 F3
Chiquibul △ Belize 16°49N 88°52W 360 C2
Chiquimula Guatemala 14°51N 89°37W 360 D2
Chiquinquira Colombia 5°37N 73°50W 364 B4
Chirala India 15°50N 80°26E 312 M12
Chiramba Mozam. 16°55S 34°39E 327 F3
Chirawa India 28°14N 75°42E 314 E6
Chirchiq Uzbekistan 41°29N 69°35E 300 E7
Chiredzi Zimbabwe 21°0S 31°38E 329 C5
Chiricahua ⌂ U.S.A. 32°0N 109°20W 349 K9
Chiricahua Peak U.S.A. 31°51N 109°18W 349 L9
Chiriquí, G. de Panama 8°0N 82°10W 360 E3
Chiriquí, L. de Panama 9°10N 82°0W 360 E3
Chirisa ⌂ Zimbabwe 17°53S 28°15E 327 F2
Chirivira Falls Zimbabwe 21°10S 32°12E 327 G3
Chirmiri India 23°15N 82°20E 315 H10
Chirripó Grande, Cerro Costa Rica 9°29N 83°29W 360 E3
Chirundu Zimbabwe 16°3S 28°50E 329 B4
Chisamba Zambia 14°55S 28°20E 327 E2
Chisapani Nepal 28°37N 81°16E 315 E9
Chisasibi Canada 53°50N 79°0W 344 B4
Chisholm Canada 54°55N 114°10W 342 C6
Chisholm U.S.A. 47°29N 92°53W 352 B7
Chishtian Mandi Pakistan 29°50N 72°55E 314 E5
Chisimaio Somali Rep. 0°22S 42°32E 319 H3
Chisimba Falls Zambia 10°12S 30°56E 327 E3
Chişinău Moldova 47°2N 28°50E 289 E15
Chisos Mts. U.S.A. 29°5N 103°15W 356 G3
Chistopol Russia 55°25N 50°38E 290 C9
Chita Russia 52°0N 113°35E 301 D12
Chitipa Malawi 9°41S 33°19E 327 D3
Chitose Japan 42°49N 141°39E 302 C10
Chitral Pakistan 35°50N 71°56E 312 B7
Chitré Panama 7°59N 80°27W 360 E3
Chittagong Bangla. 22°19N 91°48E 313 H17
Chittagong □ Bangla. 24°5N 91°0E 313 G17
Chittaurgarh India 24°52N 74°38E 314 G6
Chittoor India 13°15N 79°5E 312 N11
Chitungwiza Zimbabwe 18°0S 31°6E 327 F3
Chiusi Italy 43°1N 11°57E 294 C4
Chivasso Italy 45°11N 7°53E 292 D7
Chivhu Zimbabwe 19°2S 30°52E 327 F3
Chivilcoy Argentina 34°55S 60°0W 366 C4
Chiwanda Tanzania 11°23S 34°55E 327 E3
Chizarira Zimbabwe 17°36S 27°45E 327 F2
Chizarira △ Zimbabwe 17°44S 27°52E 327 F2
Chizela Zambia 13°8S 25°0E 327 E2
Chkalov = Orenburg Russia 51°45N 55°6E 290 D10
Chloride U.S.A. 35°25N 114°12W 351 K12
Cho Bo Vietnam 20°46N 105°10E 310 B5
Cho-do N. Korea 38°30N 124°40E 307 E13
Cho Phuoc Hai Vietnam 10°26N 107°18E 311 G6
Choa Chu Kang Singapore 1°22N 103°41E 311 d
Choba Kenya 2°30N 38°5E 326 B4
Chobe △ Botswana 18°37S 24°23E 328 B4
Chocolate Mts. U.S.A. 33°15N 115°15W 351 M11
Choctawhatchee → U.S.A. 30°25N 86°8W 357 F11
Choele Choel Argentina 39°11S 65°40W 368 D3
Choiseul St. Lucia 13°47N 61°3W 361 f
Choiseul Solomon Is. 7°0S 156°40E 330 B8
Choix Mexico 26°43N 108°17W 358 B3
Chojnice Poland 53°42N 17°32E 289 B9
Chōkai-San Japan 39°6N 140°3E 302 E10
Choke Canyon Res. U.S.A. 28°30N 98°20W 356 G5
Chokurdakh Russia 70°38N 147°55E 301 B15
Cholame U.S.A. 35°44N 120°18W 350 K6
Cholet France 47°4N 0°52W 292 C3
Cholguan Chile 37°10S 72°3W 366 D1
Choluteca Honduras 13°20N 87°14W 360 D2
Choluteca → Honduras 13°0N 87°20W 360 D2
Chom Bung Thailand 13°37N 99°36E 310 F2
Chom Thong Thailand 18°25N 98°41E 310 C2
Choma Zambia 16°48S 26°59E 327 F2
Chomolungma = Everest, Mt. Nepal 28°5N 86°58E 315 E12
Chomun India 27°15N 75°40E 314 F6
Chomutov Czech Rep. 50°28N 13°23E 288 C7
Chon Buri Thailand 13°21N 101°1E 310 F3
Chon Thanh Vietnam 11°24N 106°36E 311 G6
Chone Ecuador 0°40S 80°0W 364 D3
Chong Kai Cambodia 13°57N 103°35E 310 F4
Chong Mek Thailand 15°10N 105°27E 310 E5
Chong Phangan Thailand 9°39N 100°0E 311 b
Chong Samui Thailand 9°21N 99°50E 311 b
Ch'ŏngjin N. Korea 41°47N 129°50E 307 D15
Chŏngju N. Korea 39°40N 125°5E 307 E13
Chongli China 40°58N 115°15E 306 D8
Chongqing China 29°35N 106°25E 304 D5
Chongqing Shi □ China 30°0N 108°0E 304 C5
Chonguene Mozam. 25°3S 33°49E 329 C5
Chonos, Arch. de los Chile 45°0S 75°0W 368 F2
Chop Ukraine 48°26N 22°12E 289 D12
Chopim → Brazil 25°35S 53°5W 367 B5
Chor Pakistan 25°31N 69°46E 314 G3
Chora Sfakion Greece 35°15N 24°9E 297 D6
Chorbat La India 34°42N 76°37E 315 B7
Chorley U.K. 53°39N 2°38W 284 D5
Chornobyl Ukraine 51°20N 30°15E 289 C16
Chorolque, Cerro Bolivia 20°59S 66°5W 366 A2
Chorregon Australia 22°40S 143°32E 334 C3
Chorro el Indio △ Venezuela 7°43N 72°9W 361 E5
Chortkiv Ukraine 49°2N 25°46E 289 D13
Chorzów Poland 50°18N 18°57E 289 C10
Chos-Malal Argentina 37°20S 70°15W 366 D1
Ch'osan N. Korea 40°50N 125°47E 307 D13
Choszczno Poland 53°7N 15°25E 288 B8
Choteau U.S.A. 47°49N 112°11W 348 C7
Chotila India 22°23N 71°15E 314 H4
Chotta Udepur India 22°19N 74°1E 314 H6
Chowchilla U.S.A. 37°7N 120°16W 350 H6
Choybalsan Mongolia 48°4N 114°30E 305 B6
Christchurch N.Z. 43°33S 172°47E 331 E4
Christchurch U.K. 50°44N 1°47W 285 G6
Christian I. Canada 44°50N 80°12W 354 B4
Christiana S. Africa 27°52S 25°8E 328 D4
Christiansted U.S. Virgin Is. 17°45N 64°42W 361 C7
Christie B. Canada 62°32N 111°10W 343 A6
Christina → Canada 56°40N 111°3W 343 B6
Christmas Cr. → Australia 18°29S 125°23E 332 C4
Christmas I. = Kiritimati Kiribati 1°58N 157°27W 337 G12
Christmas I. Ind. Oc. 10°30S 105°40E 336 J2
Christopher, L. Australia 24°49S 127°42E 333 D4
Chtimba Malawi 10°35S 34°13E 327 E3
Chū = Shū Kazakhstan 43°36N 73°42E 300 E8
Chu → Vietnam 19°53N 105°45E 310 C5
Chu Lai Vietnam 15°28N 108°45E 310 E7
Chuak, Ko Thailand 9°28N 99°41E 311 b
Ch'uanchou = Quanzhou China 24°55N 118°34E 305 D6
Chuankou China 34°20N 110°59E 306 G6
Chubbuck U.S.A. 42°55N 112°28W 348 E7
Chūbu □ Japan 36°45N 137°30E 303 F8
Chubu-Sangaku △ Japan 36°30N 137°40E 303 F8
Chubut → Argentina 43°20S 65°5W 368 E3
Chuchi L. Canada 55°12N 124°30W 342 B4
Chuda India 22°29N 71°41E 314 H4
Chudskoye, Ozero Russia 58°13N 27°30E 281 G22
Chūgoku □ Japan 35°0N 133°0E 303 G6
Chūgoku-Sanchi Japan 35°0N 133°0E 303 G6
Chugwater U.S.A. 41°46N 104°50W 348 F11
Chuka Kenya 0°20S 37°39E 326 C4
Chukchi Plateau Arctic 78°0N 165°0W 276 B17
Chukchi Sea Russia 68°0N 175°0W 301 C19
Chukotskoye Nagorye Russia 68°0N 175°0E 301 C18
Chula Vista U.S.A. 32°38N 117°5W 351 N9
Chulucanas Peru 5°8S 80°10W 364 E2
Chulym → Russia 57°43N 83°51E 300 D9
Chum Phae Thailand 16°40N 102°6E 310 D4
Chum Saeng Thailand 15°55N 100°15E 310 E3
Chumar India 32°40N 78°35E 315 C8
Chumbicha Argentina 29°0S 66°10W 366 B2
Chumikan Russia 54°40N 135°10E 301 D14
Chumphon Thailand 10°35N 99°14E 311 G2
Chumuare Mozam. 14°31S 31°50E 327 E3
Chuna → Russia 57°47N 94°37E 301 D10
Chuncheon S. Korea 37°58N 127°44E 307 F14
Chunchura India 22°53N 88°27E 315 H13
Chunga Zambia 15°0S 26°2E 327 F2
Chunggang-ŭp N. Korea 41°48N 126°48E 307 D14
Chunghwa N. Korea 38°52N 125°47E 307 E13
Chungju S. Korea 36°58N 127°58E 307 F14
Chungking = Chongqing China 29°35N 106°25E 304 D5
Chungt'iaoshan = Zhongtiao Shan China 35°0N 111°10E 306 G6
Chunian Pakistan 30°57N 74°0E 314 D6
Chunya Tanzania 8°30S 33°27E 327 D3
Chunyang China 43°38N 129°23E 307 C15
Chupara Pt. Trin. & Tob. 10°49N 61°22W 365 K15
Chuquibamba Peru 15°47S 72°44W 364 G4
Chuquicamata Chile 22°15S 69°0W 366 A2
Chur Switz. 46°52N 9°32E 292 C8
Churachandpur India 24°20N 93°40E 313 G18
Church Stretton U.K. 52°32N 2°48W 285 E5
Churchill Canada 58°47N 94°11W 343 B10
Churchill → Man., Canada 58°47N 94°12W 343 B10
Churchill → Nfld. & L., Canada 53°19N 60°10W 345 B7
Churchill, C. Canada 58°46N 93°12W 343 B10
Churchill Falls Canada 53°36N 64°19W 345 B7
Churchill L. Canada 55°55N 108°20W 343 B7
Churchill Pk. Canada 58°10N 125°10W 342 B3
Churki India 23°50N 83°12E 315 H10
Churu India 28°20N 74°50E 314 E6
Churún Merú = Angel Falls Venezuela 5°57N 62°30W 364 B6
Chushal India 33°40N 78°40E 315 C8
Chuska Mts. U.S.A. 36°15N 108°50W 349 H9
Chusovoy Russia 58°22N 57°50E 290 C10
Chute-aux-Outardes Canada 49°7N 68°24W 345 C6
Chuuk = Truk Micronesia 7°25N 151°46E 336 G7
Chuvash Republic = Chuvashia □ Russia 55°30N 47°0E 290 C8
Chuvashia □ Russia 55°30N 47°0E 290 C8
Chuwārtah Iraq 35°43N 45°34E 316 C5
Chuy Uruguay 33°41S 53°27W 367 C5
Ci Xian China 36°20N 114°25E 306 F8
Ciadăr-Lunga Moldova 46°3N 28°51E 289 E15
Ciamis Indonesia 7°20S 108°21E 309 G13
Cianjur Indonesia 6°49S 107°8E 309 G12
Cianorte Brazil 23°37S 52°37W 367 A5
Cibola U.S.A. 33°17N 114°42W 351 M12
Cicero U.S.A. 41°51N 87°44W 352 E10
Cicia Fiji 17°45S 179°18W 331 a
Ciéagas del Cataumbo △ Venezuela 9°25N 71°54W 361 E5
Ciechanów Poland 52°52N 20°38E 289 B11
Ciego de Ávila Cuba 21°50N 78°50W 360 B4
Ciénaga Colombia 11°1N 74°15W 364 A4
Cienfuegos Cuba 22°10N 80°30W 360 B3
Cieszyn Poland 49°45N 18°35E 289 D10
Cieza Spain 38°17N 1°23W 293 C5
Cihuatlán Mexico 19°14N 104°35W 358 D4
Cijara, Embalse de Spain 39°18N 4°52W 293 C3
Cijulang Indonesia 7°42S 108°27E 309 G13
Cilacap Indonesia 7°43S 109°0E 309 G13
Cill Chainnigh = Kilkenny Ireland 52°39N 7°15W 282 D4
Cilo Dağı Turkey 37°28N 43°55E 291 G7
Cima U.S.A. 35°14N 115°30W 351 K11
Cimarron Kans., U.S.A. 37°48N 100°21W 352 G3
Cimarron N. Mex., U.S.A. 36°31N 104°55W 349 H11
Cimarron → U.S.A. 36°10N 96°16W 356 C6
Cimişlia Moldova 46°34N 28°44E 289 E15
Cimone, Mte. Italy 44°12N 10°42E 294 B4
Cinca → Spain 41°26N 0°21E 293 B6
Cincar Bos.-H. 43°55N 17°5E 294 C7
Cincinnati U.S.A. 39°9N 84°27W 353 F11
Cincinnatus U.S.A. 42°33N 75°54W 355 D9
Çine Turkey 37°37N 28°2E 295 F13
Ciney Belgium 50°18N 5°5E 287 D5
Cinto, Mte. France 42°24N 8°54E 292 E8
Circle Alaska, U.S.A. 65°50N 144°4W 346 a
Circle Mont., U.S.A. 47°25N 105°35W 348 C11
Circleville U.S.A. 39°36N 82°57W 353 F12
Cirebon Indonesia 6°45S 108°32E 308 F3
Ciremay Indonesia 6°55S 108°27E 309 G13
Cirencester U.K. 51°43N 1°57W 285 F6
Cirium Cyprus 34°40N 32°53E 297 E11
Cisco U.S.A. 32°23N 98°59W 356 E5
Citlaltépetl = Orizaba, Pico de Mexico 18°58N 97°15W 359 D5
Citrus Heights U.S.A. 38°42N 121°17W 350 G5
Citrusdal S. Africa 32°35S 19°0E 328 E2
Città del Vaticano = Vatican City ■ Europe 41°54N 12°27E 294 D5
Città di Castello Italy 43°27N 12°14E 294 C5
Ciudad Acuña Mexico 29°18N 100°55W 358 B4
Ciudad Altamirano Mexico 18°20N 100°40W 358 D4
Ciudad Anáhuac Mexico 27°14N 100°7W 358 B4
Ciudad Bolívar Venezuela 8°5N 63°36W 364 B6
Ciudad Camargo Mexico 27°40N 105°10W 358 B3
Ciudad de México Mexico 19°24N 99°9W 359 D5
Ciudad de Valles Mexico 22°0N 99°0W 359 C5
Ciudad del Carmen Mexico 18°38N 91°50W 359 D6
Ciudad del Este Paraguay 25°30S 54°50W 367 B5
Ciudad Delicias = Delicias Mexico 28°13N 105°28W 358 B3
Ciudad Frontera Mexico 26°56N 101°27W 358 B4
Ciudad Guayana Venezuela 8°0N 62°30W 364 B6
Ciudad Guerrero Mexico 28°33N 107°30W 358 B3
Ciudad Guzmán Mexico 19°41N 103°29W 358 D4
Ciudad Juárez Mexico 31°44N 106°29W 358 A3
Ciudad Lerdo Mexico 25°32N 103°32W 358 B4
Ciudad Madero Mexico 22°19N 97°50W 359 C5
Ciudad Mante Mexico 22°44N 98°59W 359 C5
Ciudad Obregón Mexico 27°29N 109°56W 358 B3
Ciudad Real Spain 38°59N 3°55W 293 C4
Ciudad Rodrigo Spain 40°35N 6°32W 293 B2
Ciudad Victoria Mexico 23°44N 99°8W 359 C5
Ciudadela Spain 40°0N 3°50E 296 B10
Civitanova Marche Italy 43°18N 13°44E 294 C5
Civitavécchia Italy 42°6N 11°48E 294 C4
Cizre Turkey 37°19N 42°10E 316 B4
Clackmannanshire □ U.K. 56°10N 3°43W 283 E5
Clacton-on-Sea U.K. 51°47N 1°11E 285 F9
Claire, L. Canada 58°35N 112°5W 342 B6
Clairton U.S.A. 40°18N 79°53W 354 F5
Clallam Bay U.S.A. 48°15N 124°16W 350 B2
Clanton U.S.A. 32°51N 86°38W 357 E11
Clanwilliam S. Africa 32°11S 18°52E 328 E2
Clara Ireland 53°21N 7°37W 282 C4
Claraville U.S.A. 35°24N 118°20W 351 K8
Clare Australia 33°50S 138°37E 335 E2
Clare U.S.A. 43°49N 84°46W 353 D11
Clare □ Ireland 52°45N 9°0W 282 D3
Clare → Ireland 53°20N 9°2W 282 C2
Clare I. Ireland 53°49N 10°0W 282 C1
Claremont Calif., U.S.A. 34°6N 117°43W 351 L9
Claremont N.H., U.S.A. 43°23N 72°20W 355 C12
Claremont Pt. Australia 14°1S 143°41E 334 A3
Claremore U.S.A. 36°19N 95°36W 356 C7
Claremorris Ireland 53°45N 9°0W 282 C3
Clarence → Australia 29°25S 153°22E 335 D5
Clarence → N.Z. 42°10S 173°56E 331 E4
Clarence, I. Chile 54°0S 72°0W 368 G2
Clarence I. Antarctica 61°10S 54°0W 277 C18
Clarence Str. Australia 12°0S 131°0E 332 B5
Clarence Town Bahamas 23°6N 74°59W 361 B5
Clarendon Pa., U.S.A. 41°47N 79°6W 354 E5
Clarendon Tex., U.S.A. 34°56N 100°53W 356 D4
Clarenville-Shoal Harbour Canada 48°10N 54°1W 345 C9
Claresholm Canada 50°2N 113°33W 342 D6
Clarie Coast Antarctica 68°0S 135°0E 277 C9
Clarinda U.S.A. 40°44N 95°2W 352 E6
Clarington Canada 43°55N 78°41W 354 C6
Clarion Iowa, U.S.A. 42°44N 93°44W 352 D7
Clarion Pa., U.S.A. 41°13N 79°23W 354 E5
Clarion → U.S.A. 41°7N 79°41W 354 E5
Clarion Fracture Zone Pac. Oc. 20°0N 120°0W 338 H7
Clark U.S.A. 44°53N 97°44W 352 C5
Clark, Pt. Canada 44°4N 81°45W 354 B3
Clark Fork U.S.A. 48°9N 116°11W 348 B5
Clark Fork → U.S.A. 48°9N 116°15W 348 B5
Clarkdale U.S.A. 34°46N 112°3W 349 J7
Clarke City Canada 50°12N 66°38W 345 B6
Clarke I. Australia 40°32S 148°10E 335 G4
Clarke Ra. Australia 20°40S 148°30E 334 J6
Clarks Fork Yellowstone → U.S.A. 45°32N 108°50W 348 D9
Clark's Harbour Canada 43°25N 65°38W 345 D6
Clarks Hill L. = J. Strom Thurmond L. U.S.A. 33°40N 82°12W 357 E13
Clarks Summit U.S.A. 41°30N 75°42W 355 E9
Clarksburg U.S.A. 39°17N 80°30W 353 F13
Clarksdale U.S.A. 34°12N 90°35W 357 D9
Clarkston U.S.A. 46°25N 117°3W 348 C5
Clarksville Ark., U.S.A. 35°28N 93°28W 356 D8
Clarksville Tenn., U.S.A. 36°32N 87°21W 357 C11
Clarksville Tex., U.S.A. 33°37N 95°3W 356 E7
Clatskanie U.S.A. 46°6N 123°12W 350 D3
Claude U.S.A. 35°7N 101°22W 356 D4
Claveria Phil. 18°37N 121°4E 309 A6
Clay U.S.A. 38°17N 121°10W 350 G5
Clay Center U.S.A. 39°23N 97°8W 352 F5
Claypool U.S.A. 33°25N 110°51W 349 K8
Claysburg U.S.A. 40°17N 78°27W 354 F6
Claysville U.S.A. 40°7N 80°25W 354 F4
Clayton N. Mex., U.S.A. 36°27N 103°11W 349 H12
Clayton N.Y., U.S.A. 44°14N 76°5W 355 B8
Clear, C. Ireland 51°25N 9°32W 282 E2
Clear, L. Canada 45°26N 77°12W 354 A7
Clear Hills Canada 56°40N 119°30W 342 B5
Clear I. Ireland 51°26N 9°30W 282 E2
Clear L. U.S.A. 39°2N 122°47W 350 F4
Clear Lake Iowa, U.S.A. 43°8N 93°23W 352 D7
Clear Lake S. Dak., U.S.A. 44°45N 96°41W 352 C5
Clear Lake Res. U.S.A. 41°56N 121°5W 348 F3
Clearfield Pa., U.S.A. 41°2N 78°27W 354 E6
Clearfield Utah, U.S.A. 41°7N 112°2W 348 F7
Clearlake U.S.A. 38°57N 122°38W 350 G4
Clearwater Canada 51°38N 120°2W 342 C4
Clearwater U.S.A. 27°59N 82°48W 357 H13
Clearwater → Alta., Canada 52°22N 114°57W 342 C6
Clearwater → Alta., Canada 56°44N 111°23W 343 B6
Clearwater L. Canada 53°34N 99°49W 343 C9
Clearwater Lake ⌂ Canada 54°0N 101°0W 343 C8
Clearwater Mts. U.S.A. 46°5N 115°20W 348 C6
Clearwater River ⌂ Canada 56°55N 109°10W 343 B7
Cleburne U.S.A. 32°21N 97°23W 356 E6
Clee Hills U.K. 52°26N 2°35W 285 E5
Cleethorpes U.K. 53°33N 0°3W 284 D7
Cleeve Cloud U.K. 51°56N 2°0W 285 F6
Clemson U.S.A. 34°41N 82°50W 357 D13
Clerke Reef Australia 17°22S 119°20E 332 C2
Clermont Australia 22°49S 147°39E 334 C4
Clermont U.S.A. 28°33N 81°46W 357 G14
Clermont-Ferrand France 45°46N 3°4E 292 D5
Clervaux Lux. 50°4N 6°2E 287 D6
Clevedon U.K. 51°26N 2°52W 285 F5
Cleveland Miss., U.S.A. 33°45N 90°43W 357 E9
Cleveland Ohio, U.S.A. 41°29N 81°41W 354 E3
Cleveland Okla., U.S.A. 36°19N 96°28W 356 C6
Cleveland Tenn., U.S.A. 35°10N 84°53W 357 D12
Cleveland Tex., U.S.A. 30°21N 95°5W 356 F7
Cleveland, C. Australia 19°11S 147°1E 334 B4
Cleveland, Mt. U.S.A. 48°56N 113°51W 348 B7
Cleveland Heights U.S.A. 41°31N 81°33W 354 E3
Clevelândia Brazil 26°24S 52°23W 367 B5
Clew B. Ireland 53°50N 9°49W 282 C2
Clewiston U.S.A. 26°45N 80°56W 357 H14
Clifden Ireland 53°29N 10°1W 282 C1
Clifden N.Z. 46°1S 167°42E 331 G1
Cliffdell U.S.A. 46°56N 121°5W 350 D5
Cliffy Hd. Australia 35°1S 116°29E 333 G2
Clifton Australia 27°59S 151°53E 335 D5
Clifton Ariz., U.S.A. 33°3N 109°18W 349 K9
Clifton Colo., U.S.A. 39°7N 108°25W 348 G9
Clifton Tex., U.S.A. 31°47N 97°35W 356 F6
Clifton Beach Australia 16°46S 145°39E 334 B4
Climax Canada 49°10N 108°20W 343 D7
Clinch → U.S.A. 35°53N 84°29W 357 D12
Clingmans Dome U.S.A. 35°34N 83°30W 357 D13
Clint U.S.A. 31°35N 106°14W 356 F1
Clinton B.C., Canada 51°6N 121°35W 342 C4
Clinton Ont., Canada 43°37N 81°32W 354 C3
Clinton N.Z. 46°12S 169°23E 331 G2
Clinton Ark., U.S.A. 35°36N 92°28W 356 D8
Clinton Conn., U.S.A. 41°17N 72°32W 355 E12
Clinton Ill., U.S.A. 40°9N 88°57W 352 E9
Clinton Ind., U.S.A. 39°40N 87°24W 352 F10
Clinton Iowa, U.S.A. 41°51N 90°12W 352 E8
Clinton Mass., U.S.A. 42°25N 71°41W 355 D13
Clinton Miss., U.S.A. 32°20N 90°20W 357 E9
Clinton Mo., U.S.A. 38°22N 93°46W 352 F7
Clinton N.C., U.S.A. 35°0N 78°22W 357 D15
Clinton Okla., U.S.A. 35°31N 98°58W 356 D5
Clinton S.C., U.S.A. 34°29N 81°53W 357 D14
Clinton Tenn., U.S.A. 36°6N 84°8W 357 C12
Clinton Wash., U.S.A. 47°59N 122°21W 350 C4
Clinton, C. Australia 22°30S 150°45E 334 C5
Clinton Colden L. Canada 63°58N 107°27W 340 C9
Clintonville U.S.A. 44°37N 88°46W 352 C9
Clipperton, I. Pac. Oc. 10°18N 109°13W 337 F17
Clipperton Fracture Zone Pac. Oc. 19°0N 122°0W 337 G16
Clisham U.K. 57°58N 6°49W 283 D2
Clitheroe U.K. 53°53N 2°22W 284 D5
Clo-oose Canada 48°39N 124°49W 350 B2
Cloates, Pt. Australia 22°43S 113°40E 332 D1
Clocolan S. Africa 28°55S 27°34E 329 D4
Clodomira Argentina 27°35S 64°14W 366 B3
Clogher Hd. Ireland 53°48N 6°14W 282 C5
Clonakilty Ireland 51°37N 8°53W 282 E3
Clonakilty B. Ireland 51°35N 8°51W 282 E3
Cloncurry Australia 20°40S 140°28E 334 C3
Cloncurry Ireland 53°25N 6°48W 282 C5
Cloncurry → Australia 18°37S 140°40E 334 B3
Clondalkin Ireland 53°19N 6°25W 282 C5
Clones Ireland 54°11N 7°15W 282 B4
Clonmel Ireland 52°21N 7°42W 282 D4
Cloquet U.S.A. 46°43N 92°28W 352 B7

Clorinda Argentina 25°16S 57°45W 366 B4
Cloud Bay Canada 48°5N 89°26W 344 C2
Cloud Peak U.S.A. 44°23N 107°11W 348 D10
Cloudcroft U.S.A. 32°58N 105°45W 349 K11
Cloverdale U.S.A. 38°48N 123°1W 350 G4
Clovis Calif., U.S.A. 36°49N 119°42W 350 J7
Clovis N. Mex., U.S.A. 34°24N 103°12W 349 J12
Cloyne Canada 44°49N 77°11W 354 B7
Cluj-Napoca Romania 46°47N 23°38E 289 E12
Clunes Australia 37°20S 143°45E 335 F3
Clutha → N.Z. 46°20S 169°49E 331 G2
Clwyd → U.K. 53°19N 3°31W 284 D4
Clyde Canada 54°9N 113°39W 342 C6
Clyde N.Z. 45°12S 169°20E 331 F2
Clyde U.S.A. 43°5N 76°52W 354 C8
Clyde → U.K. 55°55N 4°30W 283 F4
Clyde, Firth of U.K. 55°22N 5°1W 283 F3
Clyde Muirshiel ⌂ U.K. 55°50N 4°40W 283 F4
Clyde River Canada 70°30N 68°30W 341 B13
Clydebank U.K. 55°54N 4°23W 283 F4
Clymer N.Y., U.S.A. 42°1N 79°37W 354 D5
Clymer Pa., U.S.A. 40°40N 79°1W 354 D5
Coachella U.S.A. 33°41N 116°10W 351 M10
Coachella Canal U.S.A. 32°43N 114°57W 351 N12
Coahoma U.S.A. 32°18N 101°18W 356 E4
Coahuayana → Mexico 18°41N 103°45W 358 D4
Coahuila □ Mexico 27°20N 102°0W 358 B4
Coal → Canada 59°39N 126°57W 342 B3
Coalane Mozam. 17°48S 37°2E 327 F4
Coalcomán Mexico 18°47N 103°9W 358 D4
Coaldale Canada 49°45N 112°35W 342 D6
Coalgate U.S.A. 34°32N 96°13W 356 D6
Coalinga U.S.A. 36°9N 120°21W 350 J6
Coalisland U.K. 54°33N 6°42W 282 B5
Coalville U.K. 52°44N 1°23W 284 E6
Coalville U.S.A. 40°55N 111°24W 348 F8
Coamo Puerto Rico 18°5N 66°22W 361 d
Coari Brazil 4°8S 63°7W 364 D6
Coast □ Kenya 2°40S 39°45E 326 C4
Coast Mts. Canada 55°0N 129°20W 342 C3
Coast Ranges U.S.A. 39°0N 123°0W 350 G4
Coatbridge U.K. 55°52N 4°6W 283 F4
Coatepec Mexico 19°27N 96°58W 359 D5
Coatepeque Guatemala 14°46N 91°55W 360 D1
Coatesville U.S.A. 39°59N 75°50W 353 F16
Coaticook Canada 45°10N 71°46W 355 A13
Coats I. Canada 62°30N 83°0W 341 C11
Coats Land Antarctica 77°0S 25°0W 277 D1
Coatzacoalcos Mexico 18°7N 94°25W 359 D6
Cobá Mexico 20°31N 87°45W 359 C7
Cobalt Canada 47°25N 79°42W 344 C4
Cobán Guatemala 15°30N 90°21W 360 C1
Cobar Australia 31°27S 145°48E 335 E4
Cóbh Ireland 51°51N 8°17W 282 E3
Cobija Bolivia 11°0S 68°50W 364 F5
Cobleskill U.S.A. 42°41N 74°29W 355 D10
Coboconk Canada 44°39N 78°48W 354 B6
Cobourg Canada 43°58N 78°10W 354 C6
Cobourg ⌂ Australia 11°26S 131°58E 332 B5
Cobourg Pen. Australia 11°20S 132°15E 332 B5
Cobram Australia 35°54S 145°40E 335 F4
Cóbué Mozam. 12°0S 34°58E 327 E3
Coburg Germany 50°15N 10°58E 288 C6
Cocanada = Kakinada India 16°57N 82°11E 313 L13
Cochabamba Bolivia 17°26S 66°10W 364 G5
Cochemane Mozam. 17°0S 32°54E 327 F3
Cochin India 9°58N 76°20E 312 Q10
Cochin China = Nam-Phan Vietnam 10°30N 106°0E 311 G6
Cochran U.S.A. 32°23N 83°21W 357 E13
Cochrane Alta., Canada 51°11N 114°30W 342 C6
Cochrane Ont., Canada 49°0N 81°0W 344 C3
Cochrane Chile 47°15S 72°33W 368 F2
Cochrane → Canada 59°0N 103°40W 343 B8
Cochrane, L. Chile 47°10S 72°0W 368 F2
Cochranton U.S.A. 41°31N 80°3W 354 E4
Cockburn Australia 32°5S 141°0E 335 E3
Cockburn, Canal Chile 54°30S 72°0W 368 G2
Cockburn I. Canada 45°55N 83°22W 344 C3
Cockburn Ra. Australia 15°46S 128°0E 332 C4
Cockermouth U.K. 54°40N 3°22W 284 C4
Cocklebiddy Australia 32°0S 126°3E 333 F4
Cockpit Country, The Jamaica 18°15N 77°45W 360 a
Coco → Cent. Amer. 15°0N 83°8W 360 D3
Coco, I. del Pac. Oc. 5°25N 87°55W 337 G19
Cocoa U.S.A. 28°21N 80°44W 357 G14
Cocobeach Gabon 0°59N 9°34E 324 D1
Cocos B. Trin. & Tob. 10°25N 61°2W 365 K15
Cocos Is. Ind. Oc. 12°10S 96°55E 336 J1
Cocos Ridge Pac. Oc. 4°0N 88°0W 337 G19
Cod, C. U.S.A. 42°5N 70°10W 353 D18
Codajás Brazil 3°55S 62°0W 364 D6
Codó Brazil 4°30S 43°55W 365 D10
Cody U.S.A. 44°32N 109°3W 348 D9
Coe Hill Canada 44°52N 77°50W 354 B7
Coelemu Chile 36°30S 72°48W 366 D1
Coen Australia 13°52S 143°12E 334 A3
Coeur d'Alene U.S.A. 47°41N 116°46W 348 C5
Coeur d'Alene L. U.S.A. 47°32N 116°49W 348 C5
Coevorden Neths. 52°40N 6°44E 287 B6
Cofete Canary Is. 28°6N 14°23W 296 F5
Coffeyville U.S.A. 37°2N 95°37W 352 G6
Coffin B. Australia 34°38S 135°28E 335 E2
Coffin Bay Australia 34°37S 135°29E 335 E2
Coffin Bay △ Australia 34°34S 135°19E 335 E2
Coffin Bay Peninsula Australia 34°32S 135°15E 335 E2
Coffs Harbour Australia 30°16S 153°5E 335 E5
Cognac France 45°41N 0°20W 292 D3
Cohocton U.S.A. 42°30N 77°30W 354 D7
Cohocton → U.S.A. 42°9N 77°6W 354 D7
Cohoes U.S.A. 42°46N 73°42W 355 D11
Cohuna Australia 35°45S 144°15E 335 F3
Coiba, I. de Panama 7°30N 81°40W 360 E3
Coig → Argentina 51°0S 69°10W 368 G3
Coigeach, Rubha U.K. 58°6N 5°26W 283 C3
Coihaique Chile 45°30S 71°45W 368 F2
Coimbatore India 11°2N 76°59E 312 P10
Coimbra Brazil 19°55S 57°48W 364 G7
Coimbra Portugal 40°15N 8°27W 293 B1
Coín Spain 36°40N 4°48W 293 D3
Coipasa, Salar de Bolivia 19°26S 68°9W 364 G5
Cojimies Ecuador 0°20N 80°0W 364 C3
Cojutepequé El Salv. 13°41N 88°54W 360 D2
Cokeville U.S.A. 42°5N 110°57W 348 E8
Colac Australia 38°21S 143°35E 335 F3
Colatina Brazil 19°32S 40°37W 365 G10
Colbeck, C. Antarctica 77°6S 157°48W 277 D13
Colborne Canada 44°0N 77°53W 354 C7
Colby U.S.A. 39°24N 101°3W 352 F3
Colca → Peru 15°55S 72°43W 364 G4
Colchester U.K. 51°54N 0°55E 285 F8
Colchester U.S.A. 41°35N 72°20W 355 E12
Cold L. Canada 54°33N 110°5W 343 C7
Coldstream Canada 50°13N 119°11W 342 C5
Coldstream U.K. 55°39N 2°15W 283 F6
Coldwater Canada 44°42N 79°40W 354 B5
Coldwater Kans., U.S.A. 37°16N 99°20W 352 G4
Coldwater Mich., U.S.A. 41°57N 85°0W 353 E11
Colebrook U.S.A. 44°54N 71°30W 355 B13
Coleman U.S.A. 31°50N 99°26W 356 F5
Coleman → Australia 15°6S 141°38E 334 B3
Colenso S. Africa 28°44S 29°50E 329 D4
Coleraine Australia 37°36S 141°40E 335 F3
Coleraine U.K. 55°8N 6°41W 282 A5
Coleridge, L. N.Z. 43°17S 171°30E 331 E3
Colesberg S. Africa 30°45S 25°5E 328 E4
Coleville U.S.A. 38°34N 119°30W 350 G7
Colfax Calif., U.S.A. 39°6N 120°57W 350 F6
Colfax La., U.S.A. 31°31N 92°42W 356 F8
Colfax Wash., U.S.A. 46°53N 117°22W 348 C5
Colhué Huapi, L. Argentina 45°30S 69°0W 368 F3
Coligny S. Africa 26°17S 26°15E 329 D4
Colima Mexico 19°14N 103°43W 358 D4
Colima □ Mexico 19°10N 104°0W 358 D4
Colima, Nevado de Mexico 19°33N 103°38W 358 D4
Colina Chile 33°13S 70°45W 366 C1
Colinas Brazil 6°0S 44°10W 365 E10
Coll U.K. 56°39N 6°34W 283 E2
Collaguasi Chile 21°5S 68°45W 366 A2
Collarenebri Australia 29°33S 148°34E 335 D4
Colleen Bawn Zimbabwe 21°0S 29°12E 327 G2
College Park U.S.A. 33°39N 84°27W 357 E12
College Station U.S.A. 30°37N 96°21W 356 F6
Collie Australia 33°22S 116°8E 333 F2
Collier B. Australia 16°10S 124°15E 332 C3
Collier Ra. Australia 24°45S 119°10E 333 D2
Collier Range △ Australia 24°39S 119°7E 333 D2
Collierville U.S.A. 35°3N 89°40W 357 D10
Collina, Passo di Italy 44°2N 10°56E 294 B4
Collingwood Canada 44°29N 80°13W 354 B4
Collingwood N.Z. 40°41S 172°40E 331 D4
Collins Canada 50°17N 89°27W 344 B2
Collinsville Australia 20°30S 147°56E 334 C4
Collipulli Chile 37°55S 72°30W 366 D1
Collooney Ireland 54°11N 8°29W 282 B3
Colmar France 48°5N 7°20E 292 B7
Colo → Australia 33°25S 150°52E 335 E5
Cologne = Köln Germany 50°56N 6°57E 288 C4
Colom, I. d'en Spain 39°58N 4°16E 296 B11
Coloma U.S.A. 38°48N 120°53W 350 G6
Colomb-Béchar = Béchar Algeria 31°38N 2°18W 322 B5
Colombia ■ S. Amer. 3°45N 73°0W 364 C4
Colombian Basin S. Amer. 14°0N 76°0W 338 H12
Colombo Sri Lanka 6°56N 79°58E 312 R11
Colón B. Aires, Argentina 33°53S 61°7W 366 C3
Colón Entre Ríos, Argentina 32°12S 58°10W 366 C4
Colón Cuba 22°42N 80°54W 360 B3
Colón Panama 9°20N 79°54W 360 E4
Colón, Arch. de Ecuador 0°0 91°0W 362 D1
Colònia de Sant Jordi Spain 39°19N 2°59E 296 B9
Colonia del Sacramento Uruguay 34°25S 57°50W 366 C4
Colonia Dora Argentina 28°34S 62°59W 366 B3
Colonial Beach U.S.A. 38°15N 76°58W 353 F15
Colonie U.S.A. 42°43N 73°50W 355 D11
Colonsay Canada 51°59N 105°52W 343 C7
Colonsay U.K. 56°5N 6°12W 283 E2
Colorado □ U.S.A. 39°30N 105°30W 348 G11
Colorado → Argentina 39°50S 62°8W 368 D4
Colorado → N. Amer. 31°45N 114°40W 349 L6
Colorado → U.S.A. 28°36N 95°59W 356 G7
Colorado City U.S.A. 32°24N 100°52W 356 E4
Colorado Plateau U.S.A. 37°0N 111°0W 349 H8
Colorado River Aqueduct U.S.A. 33°50N 117°23W 351 L12
Colorado Springs U.S.A. 38°50N 104°49W 348 G11
Colotlán Mexico 22°6N 103°16W 358 C4
Colstrip U.S.A. 45°53N 106°38W 348 D10
Colton U.S.A. 44°33N 74°56W 355 B10
Columbia Ky., U.S.A. 37°6N 85°18W 353 G11
Columbia La., U.S.A. 32°6N 92°5W 356 E8
Columbia Miss., U.S.A. 31°15N 89°50W 357 F10
Columbia Mo., U.S.A. 38°57N 92°20W 352 F7
Columbia Pa., U.S.A. 40°2N 76°30W 355 F8
Columbia S.C., U.S.A. 34°0N 81°2W 357 D14
Columbia Tenn., U.S.A. 35°37N 87°2W 357 D11
Columbia → N. Amer. 46°15N 124°5W 350 D2
Columbia, C. Canada 83°6N 69°57W 341 A11
Columbia, District of □ U.S.A. 38°55N 77°0W 353 F15
Columbia, Mt. Canada 52°8N 117°20W 342 C5
Columbia Basin U.S.A. 46°45N 119°5W 348 C4
Columbia Falls U.S.A. 48°23N 114°11W 348 B6
Columbia Mts. Canada 52°0N 119°0W 342 C5
Columbia Plateau U.S.A. 44°0N 117°30W 348 E5
Columbiana U.S.A. 40°53N 80°42W 354 F4
Columbretes, Is. Spain 39°50N 0°50E 293 C6
Columbus Ga., U.S.A. 32°28N 84°59W 357 E12
Columbus Ind., U.S.A. 39°13N 85°55W 353 F11
Columbus Kans., U.S.A. 37°10N 94°50W 352 G6
Columbus Miss., U.S.A. 33°30N 88°25W 357 E10
Columbus Mont., U.S.A. 45°38N 109°15W 348 D9
Columbus N. Mex., U.S.A. 31°50N 107°38W 349 L10
Columbus Nebr., U.S.A. 41°26N 97°22W 352 E5
Columbus Ohio, U.S.A. 39°58N 83°0W 353 F12
Columbus Tex., U.S.A. 29°42N 96°33W 356 G6
Colusa U.S.A. 39°13N 122°1W 350 F4
Colville U.S.A. 48°33N 117°54W 348 B5
Colville → U.S.A. 70°25N 150°30W 346 a
Colville, C. N.Z. 36°29S 175°21E 331 B5
Colwood Canada 48°26N 123°29W 350 B3
Colwyn Bay U.K. 53°18N 3°44W 284 D4
Comácchio Italy 44°42N 12°11E 294 B5
Comalcalco Mexico 18°16N 93°13W 359 D6
Comallo Argentina 41°0S 70°5W 368 E2
Comanche U.S.A. 31°54N 98°36W 356 F5
Comandante Ferraz Antarctica 62°30S 58°0W 277 C18
Comayagua Honduras 14°25N 87°37W 360 D2
Combahee → U.S.A. 32°31N 80°31W 357 E14
Combarbalá Chile 31°11S 71°2W 366 C1
Combe Martin U.K. 51°12N 4°3W 285 F3
Comber Canada 42°14N 82°33W 354 D2
Comber U.K. 54°33N 5°45W 282 B6
Combermere Canada 45°22N 77°37W 354 A7
Comblain-au-Pont Belgium 50°29N 5°35E 287 D5
Comeragh Mts. Ireland 52°18N 7°34W 282 D4
Comet Australia 23°36S 148°38E 334 C4
Comilla Bangla. 23°28N 91°10E 313 H17
Comino Malta 36°1N 14°20E 297 C1
Comino, C. Italy 40°32N 9°49E 294 D3
Comitán de Domínguez Mexico 16°15N 92°8W 359 D6
Commerce Ga., U.S.A. 34°12N 83°28W 357 D13
Commerce Tex., U.S.A. 33°15N 95°54W 356 E7
Committee B. Canada 68°30N 86°30W 341 C11
Commonwealth B. Antarctica 67°0S 144°0E 277 C10
Commoron Cr. → Australia 28°22S 150°8E 335 D5
Communism Pk. = imeni Ismail Samani, Pik Tajikistan 39°0N 72°2E 300 F8
Como Italy 45°47N 9°5E 292 D8
Como, Lago di Italy 46°0N 9°11E 292 D8
Comodoro Rivadavia Argentina 45°50S 67°40W 368 F3
Comorin, C. India 8°3N 77°40E 312 Q10
Comoros ■ Ind. Oc. 12°10S 44°15E 325 a
Comox Canada 49°42N 124°55W 342 D4
Compiègne France 49°24N 2°50E 292 B5
Compostela Mexico 21°14N 104°55W 358 C4
Comprida, I. Brazil 24°50S 47°42W 367 A6
Compton Canada 45°14N 71°49W 355 A13
Compton U.S.A. 33°53N 118°13W 351 M8
Comrat Moldova 46°18N 28°40E 289 E15
Con Cuong Vietnam 19°2N 104°54E 310 C5
Con Dao △ Vietnam 8°42N 106°35E 311 H6
Con Son Vietnam 8°41N 106°37E 311 H6
Conakry Guinea 9°29N 13°49W 322 G3
Conara Australia 41°50S 147°26E 335 G4
Concarneau France 47°52N 3°56W 292 C2
Conceição Mozam. 18°47S 36°7E 327 F4
Conceição da Barra Brazil 18°35S 39°45W 365 G11
Conceição do Araguaia Brazil 8°0S 49°2W 365 E9
Concepción Argentina 27°20S 65°35W 366 B2
Concepción Bolivia 16°15S 62°8W 364 G6
Concepción Chile 36°50S 73°0W 366 D1
Concepción Mexico 18°15N 90°5W 359 D6
Concepción Paraguay 23°22S 57°26W 366 A4
Concepción □ Chile 37°0S 72°30W 366 D1
Concepción → Mexico 30°32N 113°2W 358 A2
Concepción, Est. de Chile 50°30S 74°55W 368 G2
Concepción, L. Bolivia 17°20S 61°20W 364 G6
Concepción, Pta. Mexico 26°53N 111°50W 358 B2
Concepción del Oro Mexico 24°38N 101°25W 358 C4
Concepción del Uruguay Argentina 32°35S 58°20W 366 C4
Conception, Pt. U.S.A. 34°27N 120°28W 351 L6
Conception B. Canada 47°45N 53°0W 345 C9
Conception B. Namibia 23°55S 14°22E 328 C1
Conception I. Bahamas 23°52N 75°9W 361 B4
Concession Zimbabwe 17°27S 30°56E 327 F3
Conchas Dam U.S.A. 35°22N 104°11W 349 J11
Concho U.S.A. 34°28N 109°36W 349 J9
Concho → U.S.A. 31°34N 99°43W 356 F5
Conchos → Chihuahua, Mexico 29°35N 104°25W 358 B4
Conchos → Chihuahua, Mexico 27°29N 106°45W 358 B3
Conchos → Tamaulipas, Mexico 24°55N 97°38W 359 B5
Concord Calif., U.S.A. 37°59N 122°2W 350 H4
Concord N.C., U.S.A. 35°25N 80°35W 357 D14
Concord N.H., U.S.A. 43°12N 71°32W 355 C13
Concordia Antarctica 75°6S 123°23E 277 D17
Concordia Argentina 31°20S 58°2W 366 C4
Concórdia Brazil 4°36S 66°36W 364 D5
Concordia Mexico 23°17N 106°4W 358 C3
Concordia U.S.A. 39°34N 97°40W 352 F5
Concrete U.S.A. 48°32N 121°45W 348 B3
Condamine Australia 26°56S 150°9E 335 D5
Conde U.S.A. 45°9N 98°6W 352 C4
Condeúba Brazil 14°52S 42°0W 365 F10
Condobolin Australia 33°4S 147°6E 335 E4
Condon U.S.A. 45°14N 120°11W 348 D3
Conegliano Italy 45°53N 12°18E 294 B5
Conejera, I. = Conills, I. des Spain 39°11N 2°58E 296 B9
Conejos Mexico 26°14N 103°53W 358 B4
Conemaugh → U.S.A. 40°28N 79°19W 354 F5
Confuso → Paraguay 25°9S 57°34W 366 B4
Congleton U.K. 53°10N 2°13W 284 D5
Congo (Brazzaville) = Congo ■ Africa 1°0S 16°0E 324 E3
Congo (Kinshasa) = Congo, Dem. Rep. of the ■ Africa 3°0S 23°0E 324 E4
Congo ■ Africa 1°0S 16°0E 324 E3
Congo → Africa 6°4S 12°24E 324 F2
Congo, Dem. Rep. of the ■ Africa 3°0S 23°0E 324 E4
Congo Basin Africa 0°10S 24°30E 324 E4
Congonhas Brazil 20°30S 43°52W 367 A7
Congress U.S.A. 34°9N 112°51W 349 J7
Conills, I. des Spain 39°11N 2°58E 296 B9
Coniston Canada 46°29N 80°51W 344 C3
Conjeeveram = Kanchipuram India 12°52N 79°45E 312 N11
Conklin Canada 55°38N 111°5W 343 B6
Conklin U.S.A. 42°2N 75°49W 355 D9
Conn, L. Ireland 54°3N 9°15W 282 B2
Connacht □ Ireland 53°43N 9°12W 282 C2
Conneaut U.S.A. 41°57N 80°34W 354 E4
Connecticut □ U.S.A. 41°30N 72°45W 355 E12
Connecticut → U.S.A. 41°16N 72°20W 355 E12
Connell U.S.A. 46°40N 118°52W 348 C4
Connellsville U.S.A. 40°1N 79°35W 354 F5
Connemara Ireland 53°29N 9°45W 282 C2
Connemara △ Ireland 53°32N 9°52W 282 C2
Connersville U.S.A. 39°39N 85°8W 353 F11
Connors Ra. Australia 21°40S 149°10E 334 C4
Conquest Canada 51°32N 107°14W 343 C7
Conrad U.S.A. 48°10N 111°57W 348 B8
Conran, C. Australia 37°49S 148°44E 335 F4
Conroe U.S.A. 30°19N 95°27W 356 F7
Consecon Canada 44°0N 77°31W 354 C7
Conselheiro Lafaiete Brazil 20°40S 43°48W 367 A7
Consett U.K. 54°51N 1°50W 284 C6
Consort Canada 52°1N 110°46W 343 C6
Constance = Konstanz Germany 47°40N 9°10E 288 E5
Constance, L. = Bodensee Europe 47°35N 9°25E 292 C8
Constanţa Romania 44°14N 28°38E 289 F15
Constantia U.S.A. 43°15N 76°1W 355 C8
Constantine Algeria 36°25N 6°42E 322 A7
Constitución Chile 35°20S 72°30W 366 D1
Constitución Uruguay 31°0S 57°50W 366 C4
Constitución de 1857 △ Mexico 32°4N 115°55W 358 A1
Consul Canada 49°20N 109°30W 343 D7
Contact U.S.A. 41°46N 114°45W 348 F6
Contai India 21°54N 87°46E 315 J12
Contamana Peru 7°19S 74°55W 364 E4
Contas → Brazil 14°17S 39°1W 365 F11
Contoocook U.S.A. 43°13N 71°45W 355 C13
Contra Costa Mozam. 25°9S 33°30E 329 D5
Contwoyto L. Canada 65°42N 110°50W 340 C8
Conway = Conwy U.K. 53°17N 3°50W 284 D4
Conway = Conwy → U.K. 53°17N 3°50W 284 D4
Conway Australia 20°24S 148°41E 334 J6
Conway Ark., U.S.A. 35°5N 92°26W 356 D8
Conway N.H., U.S.A. 43°59N 71°7W 355 C13
Conway S.C., U.S.A. 33°51N 79°3W 357 E15
Conway, C. Australia 20°34S 148°46E 334 J6
Conway, L. Australia 28°17S 135°35E 335 D2
Conwy U.K. 53°17N 3°50W 284 D4
Conwy □ U.K. 53°10N 3°44W 284 D4
Conwy → U.K. 53°17N 3°50W 284 D4
Coober Pedy Australia 29°1S 134°43E 335 D1
Cooch Behar = Koch Bihar India 26°22N 89°29E 313 F16
Cooinda Australia 13°15S 130°5E 332 B5
Cook Australia 30°37S 130°25E 333 F5
Cook U.S.A. 47°51N 92°41W 352 B7
Cook, B. Chile 55°10S 70°0W 368 H3
Cook, C. Canada 50°8N 127°55W 342 C3
Cook, Mt. = Aoraki Mount Cook N.Z. 43°36S 170°9E 331 E3
Cook Inlet U.S.A. 60°0N 152°0W 340 D4
Cook Is. Pac. Oc. 17°0S 160°0W 337 J12
Cook Strait N.Z. 41°15S 174°29E 331 D5
Cookeville U.S.A. 36°10N 85°30W 357 C12
Cookhouse S. Africa 32°44S 25°47E 328 E4
Cookshire Canada 45°25N 71°38W 355 A13
Cookstown U.K. 54°39N 6°45W 282 B5
Cooksville Canada 43°35N 79°38W 354 C5
Cooktown Australia 15°30S 145°16E 334 B4
Coolabah Australia 31°1S 146°43E 335 E4
Cooladdi Australia 26°37S 145°23E 335 D4
Coolah Australia 31°48S 149°41E 335 E4
Coolamon Australia 34°46S 147°8E 335 E4
Coolgardie Australia 30°55S 121°8E 333 F3
Coolidge U.S.A. 32°59N 111°31W 349 K8
Coolidge Dam U.S.A. 33°10N 110°32W 349 K8
Cooma Australia 36°12S 149°8E 335 F4
Coon Rapids U.S.A. 45°9N 93°19W 352 C7
Coonabarabran Australia 31°14S 149°18E 335 E4
Coonamble Australia 30°56S 148°27E 335 E4
Coonana Australia 31°0S 123°0E 333 F3
Coondapoor India 13°42N 74°40E 312 N9
Cooninnie, L. Australia 26°4S 139°59E 335 D2
Cooper U.S.A. 33°23N 96°42W 356 E7
Cooper Cr. → Australia 28°29S 137°46E 335 D2
Cooper Ridge Pac. Oc. 10°15N 150°30W 337 F12
Cooperstown N. Dak., U.S.A. 47°27N 98°8W 352 B4
Cooperstown N.Y., U.S.A. 42°42N 74°56W 355 D10
Coorabie Australia 31°54S 132°18E 333 F5
Coorong, The Australia 35°50S 139°20E 335 F2
Coorow Australia 29°53S 116°2E 333 E2
Cooroy Australia 26°22S 152°54E 335 D5
Coos Bay U.S.A. 43°22N 124°13W 348 E1
Coosa → U.S.A. 32°30N 86°16W 357 E11
Cootamundra Australia 34°36S 148°1E 335 E4
Cootehill Ireland 54°4N 7°5W 282 B4
Copahue Paso Argentina 37°49S 71°8W 366 D1
Copainalá Mexico 17°4N 93°18W 359 D6
Copake U.S.A. 42°7N 73°31W 355 D11
Copán Honduras 14°50N 89°9W 360 D2
Cope U.S.A. 39°40N 102°51W 348 G12
Copenhagen = København Denmark 55°40N 12°26E 281 J15
Copenhagen U.S.A. 43°54N 75°41W 355 C9
Copiapó Chile 27°30S 70°20W 366 B1
Copiapó → Chile 27°19S 70°56W 366 B1
Coplay U.S.A. 40°44N 75°29W 355 F9
Copp L. Canada 60°14N 114°40W 342 A6
Coppename → Suriname 5°48N 55°55W 365 B7
Copper Canyon = Barranca del Cobre ⌂ Mexico 27°18N 107°40W 358 B3
Copper Harbor U.S.A. 47°28N 87°53W 352 B10
Copper Queen Zimbabwe 17°29S 29°18E 327 F2
Copperas Cove U.S.A. 31°8N 97°54W 356 F6
Copperbelt □ Zambia 13°15S 27°30E 327 E2
Coppermine = Kugluktuk Canada 67°50N 115°5W 340 C8
Coppermine → Canada 67°49N 116°4W 340 C8
Copperopolis U.S.A. 37°58N 120°38W 350 H6
Coquet → U.K. 55°20N 1°32W 284 B6
Coquille U.S.A. 43°11N 124°11W 348 E1
Coquimbo Chile 30°0S 71°20W 366 C1
Coquimbo □ Chile 31°0S 71°0W 366 C1
Corabia Romania 43°48N 24°30E 289 G13
Coracora Peru 15°5S 73°45W 364 G4
Coraki Australia 28°59S 153°17E 335 D5
Coral U.S.A. 40°29N 79°10W 354 F5
Coral Gables U.S.A. 25°43N 80°16W 357 J14
Coral Harbour Canada 64°8N 83°10W 341 C11
Coral Sea Pac. Oc. 15°0S 150°0E 330 C8
Coral Sea Basin Pac. Oc. 14°0S 152°0E 336 J7
Coral Sea Islands Terr. □ Australia 20°0S 155°0E 330 C8
Coral Springs U.S.A. 26°16N 80°16W 357 H14
Coraopolis U.S.A. 40°31N 80°10W 354 F4
Corato Italy 41°9N 16°25E 294 D7
Corbett △ India 29°20N 79°0E 315 E8
Corbin U.S.A. 36°57N 84°6W 353 G11
Corby U.K. 52°30N 0°41W 285 E7
Corcaigh = Cork Ireland 51°54N 8°29W 282 E3
Corcoran U.S.A. 36°6N 119°33W 350 J7
Corcovado △ Costa Rica 8°33N 83°35W 360 E3
Corcubión Spain 42°56N 9°12W 293 A1
Cordele U.S.A. 31°58N 83°47W 357 F13
Cordell U.S.A. 35°17N 98°59W 356 D5
Córdoba Argentina 31°20S 64°10W 366 C3
Córdoba Mexico 18°53N 96°56W 359 D5
Córdoba Spain 37°50N 4°50W 293 D3
Córdoba □ Argentina 31°22S 64°15W 366 C3
Córdoba, Sierra de Argentina 31°10S 64°25W 366 C3
Cordova U.S.A. 60°33N 145°45W 340 C5
Corella → Australia 19°34S 140°47E 334 B3
Corfield Australia 21°40S 143°21E 334 C3
Corfu = Kerkyra Greece 39°38N 19°50E 297 A3
Corfu, Str. of = Kerkyras, Notio Steno Greece 39°34N 20°0E 297 A4
Coria Spain 39°58N 6°33W 293 C2
Corigliano Cálabro Italy 39°36N 16°31E 294 E7
Coringa Is. Australia 16°58S 149°58E 334 B4
Corinth = Korinthos Greece 37°56N 22°55E 295 F10
Corinth Miss., U.S.A. 34°56N 88°31W 357 D10
Corinth N.Y., U.S.A. 43°15N 73°49W 355 C11
Corinth, G. of = Korinthiakos Kolpos Greece 38°16N 22°30E 295 E10
Corinto Brazil 18°20S 44°30W 365 G10
Corinto Nic. 12°30N 87°10W 360 D2
Cork Ireland 51°54N 8°29W 282 E3
Cork □ Ireland 51°57N 8°40W 282 E3
Cork Harbour Ireland 51°47N 8°16W 282 E3
Çorlu Turkey 41°11N 27°49E 295 D12
Cormack L. Canada 60°56N 121°37W 342 A4
Cormorant Canada 54°14N 100°35W 343 C8
Cormorant L. Canada 54°15N 100°50W 343 C8
Corn Is. = Maíz, Is. del Nic. 12°15N 83°4W 360 D3
Cornélio Procópio Brazil 23°7S 50°40W 367 A5
Corner Brook Canada 48°57N 57°58W 345 C8
Corneşti Moldova 47°21N 28°1E 289 E15
Corning Ark., U.S.A. 36°25N 90°35W 357 C9
Corning Calif., U.S.A. 39°56N 122°11W 348 G2
Corning Iowa, U.S.A. 40°59N 94°44W 352 E6
Corning N.Y., U.S.A. 42°9N 77°3W 354 D7
Cornwall Canada 45°2N 74°44W 355 A10
Cornwall U.S.A. 40°17N 76°25W 355 F8
Cornwall □ U.K. 50°26N 4°40W 285 G3
Cornwall I. Canada 77°37N 94°38W 341 B10
Cornwallis I. Canada 75°8N 95°0W 341 B10
Corny Pt. Australia 34°55S 137°0E 335 E2
Coro Venezuela 11°25N 69°41W 364 A5
Coroatá Brazil 4°8S 44°0W 365 D10
Corocoro Bolivia 17°15S 68°28W 364 G5
Coroico Bolivia 16°0S 67°50W 364 G5
Coromandel N.Z. 36°45S 175°31E 331 B5
Coromandel Coast India 12°30N 81°0E 312 N12
Corona Calif., U.S.A. 33°53N 117°34W 351 M9
Corona N. Mex., U.S.A. 34°15N 105°36W 349 J11

Coronach Canada 49°7N 105°31W 343 D7
Coronado U.S.A. 32°41N 117°10W 351 N9
Coronado, B. de Costa Rica 9°0N 83°40W 360 E3
Coronados, Is. Los Mexico 32°26N 117°19W 351 N9
Coronation Canada 52°5N 111°27W 342 C6
Coronation Gulf Canada 68°25N 110°0W 340 C9
Coronation I. Antarctica 60°45S 46°0W 277 C18
Coronation Is. Australia 14°57S 124°55E 332 B3
Coronda Argentina 31°58S 60°56W 366 C3
Coronel Chile 37°0S 73°10W 366 D1
Coronel Bogado Paraguay 27°11S 56°18W 366 B4
Coronel Dorrego Argentina 38°40S 61°10W 366 D3
Coronel Oviedo Paraguay 25°24S 56°30W 366 B4
Coronel Pringles Argentina 38°0S 61°30W 366 D3
Coronel Suárez Argentina 37°30S 61°52W 366 D3
Coronel Vidal Argentina 37°28S 57°45W 366 D4
Coropuna, Nevado Peru 15°30S 72°41W 364 G4
Corowa Australia 35°58S 146°21E 335 F4
Corozal □ Belize 18°23N 88°23W 359 D7
Corozal Pt. Trin. & Tob. 10°45N 61°37W 365 K15
Corpus Argentina 27°10S 55°30W 367 B4
Corpus Christi U.S.A. 27°47N 97°24W 356 H6
Corpus Christi, L. U.S.A. 28°2N 97°52W 356 G6
Corralejo Canary Is. 28°43N 13°53W 296 F6
Corraun Pen. Ireland 53°54N 9°54W 282 C2
Correntes, C. das Mozam. 24°6S 35°34E 329 C6
Corrib, L. Ireland 53°27N 9°16W 282 C2
Corrientes Argentina 27°30S 58°45W 366 B4
Corrientes □ Argentina 28°0S 57°0W 366 B4
Corrientes → Argentina 30°42S 59°38W 366 C4
Corrientes → Peru 3°43S 74°35W 364 D4
Corrientes, C. Colombia 5°30N 77°34W 364 B3
Corrientes, C. Cuba 21°43N 84°30W 360 B3
Corrientes, C. Mexico 20°25N 105°42W 358 C3
Corrigan U.S.A. 31°0N 94°52W 356 F7
Corrigin Australia 32°20S 117°53E 333 F2
Corriverton Guyana 5°55N 57°20W 364 B7
Corry U.S.A. 41°55N 79°39W 354 E5
Corse □ France 42°0N 9°0E 292 F8
Corse, C. France 43°1N 9°25E 292 E8
Corsica = Corse □ France 42°0N 9°0E 292 F8
Corsicana U.S.A. 32°6N 96°28W 356 E6
Corte France 42°19N 9°11E 292 E8
Cortés, Mar de = California, G. de Mexico 27°0N 111°0W 358 B2
Cortez U.S.A. 37°21N 108°35W 349 H9
Cortland N.Y., U.S.A. 42°36N 76°11W 355 D8
Cortland Ohio, U.S.A. 41°20N 80°44W 354 E4
Çorum Turkey 40°30N 34°57E 291 F5
Corumbá Brazil 19°0S 57°30W 364 G7
Corunna = A Coruña Spain 43°20N 8°25W 293 A1
Corvallis U.S.A. 44°34N 123°16W 348 D2
Corvette, L. de la Canada 53°25N 74°3W 344 B5
Corvo Azores 39°43N 31°8W 322 a
Corydon U.S.A. 40°46N 93°19W 352 E7
Cosalá Mexico 24°23N 106°41W 358 C3
Cosamaloapan de Carpio Mexico 18°22N 95°48W 359 D5
Cosenza Italy 39°18N 16°15E 294 E7
Coshocton U.S.A. 40°16N 81°51W 354 F3
Cosmo Newberry Australia 28°0S 122°54E 333 E3
Coso Junction U.S.A. 36°3N 117°57W 351 J9
Coso Pk. U.S.A. 36°13N 117°44W 351 J9
Cosquín Argentina 31°15S 64°30W 366 C3
Costa Blanca Spain 38°25N 0°10W 293 C5
Costa Brava Spain 41°30N 3°0E 293 B7
Costa del Sol Spain 36°30N 4°30W 293 D3
Costa Dorada Spain 41°12N 1°15E 293 B6
Costa Mesa U.S.A. 33°38N 117°55W 351 M9
Costa Rica ■ Cent. Amer. 10°0N 84°0W 360 E3
Costa Smeralda Italy 41°5N 9°35E 294 D3
Cosumnes → U.S.A. 38°16N 121°26W 350 G5
Cotabato Phil. 7°14N 124°15E 309 C6
Cotagaita Bolivia 20°45S 65°40W 366 A2
Côte d'Azur France 43°25N 7°10E 292 E7
Côte-d'Ivoire = Ivory Coast ■ Africa 7°30N 5°0W 322 G4
Coteau des Prairies U.S.A. 45°20N 97°50W 352 C5
Coteau du Missouri U.S.A. 47°0N 100°0W 352 B4
Cotentin France 49°15N 1°30W 292 B3
Cotillo Canary Is. 28°41N 14°1W 296 F5
Cotonou Benin 6°20N 2°25E 322 G6
Cotopaxi Ecuador 0°40S 78°30W 364 D3
Cotswold Hills U.K. 51°42N 2°10W 285 F5
Cottage Grove U.S.A. 43°48N 123°3W 348 E2
Cottbus Germany 51°45N 14°20E 288 C8
Cottonwood U.S.A. 34°45N 112°1W 349 J7
Cotulla U.S.A. 28°26N 99°14W 356 G5
Coudersport U.S.A. 41°46N 78°1W 354 E6
Couedic, C. du Australia 36°5S 136°40E 335 F2
Coulee City U.S.A. 47°37N 119°17W 348 C4
Coulee Dam Nat. Recr. Area = Lake Roosevelt ⌂ U.S.A. 48°5N 118°14W 348 B4
Coulman I. Antarctica 73°35S 170°0E 277 D11
Coulonge → Canada 45°52N 76°46W 344 C4
Coulterville U.S.A. 37°43N 120°12W 350 H6
Council U.S.A. 44°44N 116°26W 348 D5
Council Bluffs U.S.A. 41°16N 95°52W 352 E6
Council Grove U.S.A. 38°40N 96°29W 352 F5
Coupeville U.S.A. 48°13N 122°41W 350 B4
Courantyne → S. Amer. 5°55N 57°5W 364 B7
Courcelles Belgium 50°28N 4°22E 287 D4
Courtenay Canada 49°45N 125°0W 342 D4
Courtland U.S.A. 38°20N 121°34W 350 G5
Courtrai = Kortrijk Belgium 50°50N 3°17E 287 D3
Courtright Canada 42°49N 82°28W 354 D2
Coushatta U.S.A. 32°1N 93°21W 356 E8
Coutts Crossing Australia 29°49S 152°55E 335 D5
Couva Trin. & Tob. 10°25N 61°27W 365 K15
Couvin Belgium 50°3N 4°29E 287 D4
Cove I. Canada 45°17N 81°44W 354 A3
Coventry U.K. 52°25N 1°28W 285 E6
Covilhã Portugal 40°17N 7°31W 293 B2
Covington Ga., U.S.A. 33°36N 83°51W 357 E13
Covington Ky., U.S.A. 39°5N 84°30W 353 F11
Covington Tenn., U.S.A. 35°34N 89°39W 357 D10
Covington Va., U.S.A. 37°47N 79°59W 353 G14
Cowal, L. Australia 33°40S 147°25E 335 E4
Cowan, L. Australia 31°45S 121°45E 333 F3
Cowan L. Canada 54°0N 107°15W 343 C7
Cowangie Australia 35°12S 141°26E 335 F3
Cowansville Canada 45°14N 72°46W 355 A12
Coward Springs Australia 29°24S 136°49E 335 D2
Cowcowing Lakes Australia 30°55S 117°20E 333 F2
Cowdenbeath U.K. 56°7N 3°21W 283 E5
Cowell Australia 33°39S 136°56E 335 E2
Cowes U.K. 50°45N 1°18W 285 G6
Cowichan L. Canada 48°53N 124°17W 350 B2
Cowlitz → U.S.A. 46°6N 122°55W 350 D4
Cowra Australia 33°49S 148°42E 335 E4
Coxilha Grande Brazil 28°18S 51°30W 367 B5
Coxim Brazil 18°30S 54°55W 365 G8
Cox's Bazar Bangla. 21°26N 91°59E 313 J17
Coyote Wells U.S.A. 32°44N 115°58W 351 N11
Coyuca de Benitez Mexico 17°2N 100°4W 359 D4
Coyuca de Catalán Mexico 18°20N 100°39W 358 D4
Cozad U.S.A. 40°52N 99°59W 352 E4
Cozumel Mexico 20°31N 86°55W 359 C7
Cozumel, Isla Mexico 20°30N 86°40W 359 C7
Crab Hill Barbados 13°19N 59°38W 361 g
Cracow = Kraków Poland 50°4N 19°57E 289 C10
Cracow Australia 25°17S 150°17E 335 D5
Cradle Mt.-Lake St. Clair △ Australia 41°49S 147°56E 335 G4
Cradock Australia 32°6S 138°31E 335 E2
Cradock S. Africa 32°8S 25°36E 328 E4
Craig U.S.A. 40°31N 107°33W 348 F10
Craigavon U.K. 54°27N 6°23W 282 B5
Craigmore Zimbabwe 20°28S 32°50E 327 G3
Craik Canada 51°3N 105°49W 343 C7
Crailsheim Germany 49°8N 10°5E 288 D6
Craiova Romania 44°21N 23°48E 289 F12
Cramsie Australia 23°20S 144°15E 334 C3
Cranberry L. U.S.A. 44°11N 74°50W 355 B10
Cranberry Portage Canada 54°35N 101°23W 343 C8
Cranbrook Australia 34°18S 117°33E 333 F2
Cranbrook Canada 49°30N 115°46W 342 D5
Crandon U.S.A. 45°34N 88°54W 352 C9
Crane Oreg., U.S.A. 43°25N 118°35W 348 E4
Crane Tex., U.S.A. 31°24N 102°21W 356 F3
Crane, The Barbados 13°6N 59°27W 361 g
Cranston U.S.A. 41°47N 71°26W 355 E13
Crater L. U.S.A. 42°56N 122°6W 348 E2
Crater Lake △ U.S.A. 42°55N 122°10W 348 E2
Craters of the Moon ⌂ U.S.A. 43°25N 113°30W 348 E7
Crateús Brazil 5°10S 40°39W 365 E10
Crato Brazil 7°10S 39°25W 365 E11
Craven, L. Canada 54°20N 76°56W 344 B4
Crawford U.S.A. 42°41N 103°25W 352 D2
Crawfordsville U.S.A. 40°2N 86°54W 352 E10
Crawley U.K. 51°7N 0°11W 285 F7
Crazy Mts. U.S.A. 46°12N 110°20W 348 C8
Crean L. Canada 54°5N 106°9W 343 C7
Crediton Canada 43°17N 81°33W 354 C3
Crediton U.K. 50°47N 3°40W 285 G4
Cree → Canada 58°57N 105°47W 343 B7
Cree → U.K. 54°55N 4°25W 283 G4
Cree L. Canada 57°30N 106°30W 343 B7
Creede U.S.A. 37°51N 106°56W 349 H10
Creekside U.S.A. 40°40N 79°11W 354 F5
Creel Mexico 27°45N 107°38W 358 B3
Creemore Canada 44°19N 80°6W 354 B4
Creighton Canada 54°45N 101°54W 343 C8
Creighton U.S.A. 42°28N 97°54W 352 D5
Crema Italy 45°22N 9°41E 292 D8
Cremona Italy 45°7N 10°2E 292 D9
Cres Croatia 44°58N 14°25E 288 F8
Crescent City U.S.A. 41°45N 124°12W 348 F1
Crespo Argentina 32°2S 60°19W 366 C3
Cresson U.S.A. 40°28N 78°36W 354 F6
Crestline Calif., U.S.A. 34°14N 117°18W 351 L9
Crestline Ohio, U.S.A. 40°47N 82°44W 354 F2
Creston Canada 49°10N 116°31W 342 D5
Creston Calif., U.S.A. 35°32N 120°33W 350 K6
Creston Iowa, U.S.A. 41°4N 94°22W 352 E6
Crestview Calif., U.S.A. 37°46N 118°58W 350 H8
Crestview Fla., U.S.A. 30°46N 86°34W 357 F11
Crete = Kriti Greece 35°15N 25°0E 297 D7
Crete U.S.A. 40°38N 96°58W 352 E5
Créteil France 48°47N 2°27E 292 B5
Creus, C. de Spain 42°20N 3°19E 293 A7
Creuse → France 47°0N 0°34E 292 C4
Crewe U.K. 53°6N 2°26W 284 D5
Crewkerne U.K. 50°53N 2°48W 285 G5
Crianlarich U.K. 56°24N 4°37W 283 E4
Criciúma Brazil 28°40S 49°23W 367 B6
Crieff U.K. 56°22N 3°50W 283 E5
Crimea □ Ukraine 45°30N 33°10E 291 E5
Crimean Pen. = Krymskyy Pivostriv Ukraine 45°0N 34°0E 291 F5
Crişul Alb → Romania 46°42N 21°17E 289 E11
Crişul Negru → Romania 46°42N 21°16E 289 E11
Crna → Macedonia 41°33N 21°59E 295 D9
Crna Gora = Montenegro ■ Europe 42°40N 19°20E 295 C8
Crna Gora Macedonia 42°10N 21°30E 295 C9
Crna Reka = Crna → Macedonia 41°33N 21°59E 295 D9
Croagh Patrick Ireland 53°46N 9°40W 282 C2
Croatia ■ Europe 45°20N 16°0E 288 F9
Crocker, Banjaran Malaysia 5°40N 116°30E 308 C5
Crockett U.S.A. 31°19N 95°27W 356 F7
Crocodile = Krokodil → Mozam. 25°14S 32°18E 329 D5
Crocodile Is. Australia 12°3S 134°58E 334 A1
Crohy Hd. Ireland 54°55N 8°26W 282 B3
Croix, L. la Canada 48°20N 92°15W 344 C1
Croker, C. Australia 10°58S 132°35E 332 B5
Croker, C. Canada 44°58N 80°59W 354 B4
Croker I. Australia 11°12S 132°32E 332 B5
Cromarty U.K. 57°40N 4°2W 283 D4
Cromer U.K. 52°56N 1°17E 284 E9
Cromwell N.Z. 45°3S 169°14E 331 F2
Cromwell U.S.A. 41°36N 72°39W 355 E12
Crook U.K. 54°43N 1°45W 284 C6
Crooked → Canada 54°50N 122°54W 342 C4
Crooked → U.S.A. 44°32N 121°16W 348 D3
Crooked I. Bahamas 22°50N 74°10W 361 B5
Crooked Island Passage Bahamas 22°55N 74°35W 361 B5
Crookston Minn., U.S.A. 47°47N 96°37W 352 B5
Crookston Nebr., U.S.A. 42°56N 100°45W 352 D3
Crookwell Australia 34°28S 149°24E 335 E4
Crosby U.K. 53°30N 3°3W 284 D4
Crosby N. Dak., U.S.A. 48°55N 103°18W 352 A2
Crosby Pa., U.S.A. 41°45N 78°23W 354 E6
Crosbyton U.S.A. 33°40N 101°14W 356 E4
Cross City U.S.A. 29°38N 83°7W 357 G13
Cross Fell U.K. 54°43N 2°28W 284 C5
Cross L. Canada 54°45N 97°30W 343 C9
Cross Lake Canada 54°37N 97°47W 343 C9
Cross Sound U.S.A. 58°0N 135°0W 340 D6
Crossett U.S.A. 33°8N 91°58W 356 E9
Crosshaven Ireland 51°47N 8°17W 282 E3
Crossmaglen U.K. 54°5N 6°36W 282 B5
Crossmolina Ireland 54°6N 9°20W 282 B2
Crossville U.S.A. 35°57N 85°2W 357 D12
Croswell U.S.A. 43°16N 82°37W 354 C2
Croton-on-Hudson U.S.A. 41°12N 73°55W 355 E11
Crotone Italy 39°5N 17°8E 294 E7
Crow → Canada 59°41N 124°20W 342 B4
Crow Agency U.S.A. 45°36N 107°28W 348 D10
Crow Hd. Ireland 51°35N 10°9W 282 E1
Crowell U.S.A. 33°59N 99°43W 356 E5
Crowley U.S.A. 30°13N 92°22W 356 F8
Crowley, L. U.S.A. 37°35N 118°42W 350 H8
Crown Point Ind., U.S.A. 41°25N 87°22W 352 E10
Crown Point N.Y., U.S.A. 43°57N 73°26W 355 C11
Crown Pt. Trin. & Tob. 11°18N 60°51W 365 J16
Crownpoint U.S.A. 35°41N 108°9W 349 J9
Crows Landing U.S.A. 37°23N 121°6W 350 H5
Crows Nest Australia 27°16S 152°4E 335 D5
Crowsnest Pass Canada 49°40N 114°40W 342 D6
Croydon Australia 18°13S 142°14E 334 B3
Croydon □ U.K. 51°22N 0°5W 285 F7
Crozet, Is. Ind. Oc. 46°27S 52°0E 275 G12
Crusheen Ireland 52°57N 8°53W 282 D3
Cruz, C. Cuba 19°50N 77°50W 360 C4
Cruz Alta Brazil 28°45S 53°40W 367 B5
Cruz Bay U.S. Virgin Is. 18°20N 64°48W 361 e
Cruz del Eje Argentina 30°45S 64°50W 366 C3
Cruzeiro Brazil 22°33S 45°0W 367 A7
Cruzeiro do Oeste Brazil 23°46S 53°4W 367 A5
Cruzeiro do Sul Brazil 7°35S 72°35W 364 E4
Cry L. Canada 58°45N 129°0W 342 B3
Crystal Bay U.S.A. 39°15N 120°0W 350 F7
Crystal Brook Australia 33°21S 138°12E 335 E2
Crystal City U.S.A. 28°41N 99°50W 356 G5
Crystal Falls U.S.A. 46°5N 88°20W 352 B9
Crystal River U.S.A. 28°54N 82°35W 357 G13
Crystal Springs U.S.A. 31°59N 90°21W 357 F9
Csongrád Hungary 46°43N 20°12E 289 E11
Cu Lao Hon Vietnam 10°54N 108°18E 311 G7
Cua Rao Vietnam 19°16N 104°27E 310 C5
Cuácua → Mozam. 17°54S 37°0E 327 F4
Cuamato Angola 17°2S 15°7E 328 B2
Cuamba Mozam. 14°45S 36°22E 327 E4
Cuando → Angola 17°30S 23°15E 325 H4
Cuando Cubango □ Angola 16°25S 20°0E 328 B3
Cuangar Angola 17°36S 18°39E 328 B2
Cuango = Kwango → Dem. Rep. of the Congo 3°14S 17°22E 324 E3
Cuanza → Angola 9°21S 13°9E 324 F2
Cuarto → Argentina 33°25S 63°2W 366 C3
Cuatrociénegas Mexico 26°59N 102°5W 358 B4
Cuauhtémoc Mexico 28°25N 106°52W 358 B3
Cuba N. Mex., U.S.A. 36°1N 107°4W 349 H10
Cuba N.Y., U.S.A. 42°13N 78°17W 354 D6
Cuba ■ W. Indies 22°0N 79°0W 360 B4
Cubango → Africa 18°50S 22°25E 328 B3
Cuc Phuong △ Vietnam 20°17N 105°38E 310 B5
Cuchumatanes, Sierra de los Guatemala 15°35N 91°25W 360 C1
Cuckfield U.K. 51°1N 0°8W 285 F7
Cucuí Brazil 1°12N 66°50W 364 C5
Cucurpé Mexico 30°20N 110°43W 358 A2
Cúcuta Colombia 7°54N 72°31W 364 B4
Cuddalore India 11°46N 79°45E 312 P11
Cuddapah India 14°30N 78°47E 312 M11
Cuddapan, L. Australia 25°45S 141°26E 334 D3
Cue Australia 27°25S 117°54E 333 E2
Cuenca Ecuador 2°50S 79°9W 364 D3
Cuenca Spain 40°5N 2°10W 293 B4
Cuenca, Serranía de Spain 39°55N 1°50W 293 C5
Cuernavaca Mexico 18°55N 99°15W 359 D5
Cuero U.S.A. 29°6N 97°17W 356 G6
Cueva de la Quebrada del Toro △ Venezuela 10°46N 69°3W 361 D6
Cuevas del Almanzora Spain 37°18N 1°58W 293 D5
Cuevo Bolivia 20°15S 63°30W 364 H6
Cuiabá Brazil 15°30S 56°0W 365 G7
Cuiabá → Brazil 17°5S 56°36W 365 G7
Cuihangcun China 22°27N 113°32E 305 G10
Cuijk Neths. 51°44N 5°50E 287 C5
Cuilco Guatemala 15°24N 91°58W 360 C1
Cuillin Hills U.K. 57°13N 6°15W 283 D2
Cuillin Sd. U.K. 57°4N 6°20W 283 D2
Cuilo = Kwilu → Dem. Rep. of the Congo 3°22S 17°22E 324 E3
Cuito → Angola 18°1S 20°48E 328 B3
Cuitzeo, L. de Mexico 19°55N 101°5W 358 D4
Cukai Malaysia 4°13N 103°25E 311 K4
Culbertson U.S.A. 48°9N 104°31W 348 B11
Culcairn Australia 35°41S 147°3E 335 F4
Culebra Puerto Rico 18°19N 65°18W 361 d
Culgoa → Australia 29°56S 146°20E 335 D4
Culgoa Flood Plain △ Australia 28°58S 147°5E 335 D4
Culiacán Mexico 24°50N 107°23W 358 C3
Culiacán → Mexico 24°30N 107°42W 358 C3
Culik Indonesia 8°21S 115°37E 309 J18
Culion Phil. 11°54N 119°58E 309 B6
Cullarin Ra. Australia 34°30S 149°30E 335 E4
Cullen U.K. 57°42N 2°49W 283 D6
Cullen Pt. Australia 11°57S 141°54E 334 A3
Cullera Spain 39°9N 0°17W 293 C5
Cullman U.S.A. 34°11N 86°51W 357 D11
Cullompton U.K. 50°51N 3°24W 285 G4
Culpeper U.S.A. 38°30N 78°0W 353 F14
Culuene → Brazil 12°56S 52°51W 365 F8
Culver, Pt. Australia 32°54S 124°43E 333 F3
Culverden N.Z. 42°47S 172°49E 331 E4
Cumaná Venezuela 10°30N 64°5W 364 A6
Cumberland B.C., Canada 49°40N 125°0W 342 D4
Cumberland Ont., Canada 45°29N 75°24W 355 A9
Cumberland U.S.A. 39°39N 78°46W 353 F14
Cumberland → U.S.A. 37°9N 88°25W 352 G9
Cumberland, L. U.S.A. 36°52N 85°9W 353 G11
Cumberland Gap ⌂ U.S.A. 36°36N 83°40W 353 G12
Cumberland I. U.S.A. 30°50N 81°25W 357 F14
Cumberland Is. Australia 20°35S 149°10E 334 J7
Cumberland Island ⌂ U.S.A. 30°12N 81°24W 357 F14
Cumberland L. Canada 54°3N 102°18W 343 C8
Cumberland Pen. Canada 67°0N 64°0W 341 C13
Cumberland Plateau U.S.A. 36°0N 85°0W 357 D12
Cumberland Sd. Canada 65°30N 66°0W 341 C13
Cumbernauld U.K. 55°57N 3°58W 283 F5
Cumborah Australia 29°40S 147°45E 335 D4
Cumbres de Majalca △ Mexico 28°48N 106°30W 358 B3
Cumbres de Monterrey △ Mexico 25°26N 100°25W 358 B4
Cumbria □ U.K. 54°42N 2°52W 284 C5
Cumbrian Mts. U.K. 54°30N 3°0W 284 C5
Cumbum India 15°40N 79°10E 312 M11
Cuminá → Brazil 1°30S 56°0W 365 D7
Cummings Mt. U.S.A. 35°2N 118°34W 351 K8
Cummins Australia 34°16S 135°43E 335 E2
Cumnock Australia 32°59S 148°46E 335 E4
Cumnock U.K. 55°28N 4°17W 283 F4
Cumpas Mexico 30°2N 109°48W 358 B3
Cumplida, Pta. Canary Is. 28°50N 17°48W 296 F2
Cunco Chile 38°55S 72°2W 368 D2
Cuncumén Chile 31°53S 70°38W 366 C1
Cunderdin Australia 31°37S 117°12E 333 F2
Cunene → Angola 17°20S 11°50E 328 B1
Cúneo Italy 44°23N 7°32E 292 D7
Çüngüş Turkey 38°13N 39°17E 316 B3
Cunillera, I. = Sa Conillera Spain 38°59N 1°13E 296 C7
Cunnamulla Australia 28°2S 145°38E 335 D4
Cupar Canada 50°57N 104°10W 343 C8
Cupar U.K. 56°19N 3°1W 283 E5
Cupertino U.S.A. 37°19N 122°2W 350 H4
Cupica, G. de Colombia 6°25N 77°30W 364 B3
Curaçao Neth. Ant. 12°10N 69°0W 361 D6
Curanilahue Chile 37°29S 73°28W 366 D1
Curaray → Peru 2°20S 74°5W 364 D4
Curepipe Mauritius 20°19S 57°31E 325 d
Curepto Chile 35°8S 72°1W 366 D1
Curiapo Venezuela 8°33N 61°5W 364 B6
Curicó Chile 34°55S 71°20W 366 C1
Curieuse Seychelles 4°15S 55°44E 325 b
Curitiba Brazil 25°20S 49°10W 367 B6
Curitibanos Brazil 27°18S 50°36W 367 B5
Currabubula Australia 31°16S 150°44E 335 E5
Currais Novos Brazil 6°13S 36°30W 365 E11
Curral Velho C. Verde Is. 16°8N 22°48W 322 b
Curralinho Brazil 1°45S 49°46W 365 D9
Currane, L. Ireland 51°49N 10°4W 282 E1
Currant U.S.A. 38°44N 115°28W 348 G6
Currawinya △ Australia 28°55S 144°27E 335 D3
Current → U.S.A. 36°15N 90°55W 356 C9
Currie Australia 39°56S 143°53E 335 F3
Currie U.S.A. 40°16N 114°45W 348 F6
Curtea de Argeş Romania 45°12N 24°42E 289 F13
Curtis U.S.A. 40°38N 100°31W 352 E3
Curtis Group Australia 39°30S 146°37E 335 F4
Curtis I. Australia 23°35S 151°10E 334 C5
Curuápanema → Brazil 2°25S 55°2W 365 D7
Curuçá Brazil 0°43S 47°50W 365 D9
Curuguaty Paraguay 24°31S 55°42W 367 A4
Curup Indonesia 4°26S 102°13E 308 E2
Cururupu Brazil 1°50S 44°50W 365 D10
Curuzú Cuatiá Argentina 29°50S 58°5W 366 B4
Curvelo Brazil 18°45S 44°27W 365 G10
Cusco = Cuzco Peru 13°32S 72°0W 364 F4
Cushendall U.K. 55°5N 6°4W 282 A5
Cushing U.S.A. 35°59N 96°46W 356 D6
Cushing, Mt. Canada 57°35N 126°57W 342 B3
Cusihuiriáchic Mexico 28°14N 106°50W 358 B3
Custer U.S.A. 43°46N 103°36W 352 D2
Cut Bank U.S.A. 48°38N 112°20W 348 B7
Cutchogue U.S.A. 41°1N 72°30W 355 E12
Cuthbert U.S.A. 31°46N 84°48W 357 F12
Cutler U.S.A. 36°31N 119°17W 350 J7
Cuttaburra → Australia 29°43S 144°22E 335 D3
Cuttack India 20°25N 85°57E 313 J14
Cuvier, C. Australia 23°14S 113°22E 333 D1
Cuvier I. N.Z. 36°27S 175°50E 331 B5
Cuxhaven Germany 53°51N 8°41E 288 B5
Cuyahoga Falls U.S.A. 41°8N 81°29W 354 E3
Cuyahoga Valley △ U.S.A. 41°14N 81°33W 354 E3
Cuyo Phil. 10°51N 121°2E 309 B6
Cuyuni → Guyana 6°23N 58°41W 364 B7
Cuzco Bolivia 20°0S 66°50W 364 H5
Cuzco Peru 13°32S 72°0W 364 F4
Cwmbran U.K. 51°39N 3°2W 285 F4
Cyangugu Rwanda 2°29S 28°54E 326 C2
Cyclades Greece 37°0N 24°30E 295 F11
Cygnet Australia 43°8S 147°1E 335 G4
Cynthiana U.S.A. 38°23N 84°18W 353 F11
Cypress Hills Canada 49°40N 109°30W 343 D7
Cypress Hills ⌂ Canada 49°40N 109°30W 343 D7
Cyprus ■ Asia 35°0N 33°0E 297 E12
Cyrenaica Libya 27°0N 23°0E 323 C10
Cyrene Libya 32°53N 21°52E 323 B10
Czar Canada 52°27N 110°50W 343 C6
Czech Rep. ■ Europe 50°0N 15°0E 288 D8
Częstochowa Poland 50°49N 19°7E 289 C10

D

Da → Vietnam 21°15N 105°20E 310 B5
Da Hinggan Ling China 48°0N 121°0E 305 B7
Da Lat Vietnam 11°56N 108°25E 311 G7
Da Nang Vietnam 16°4N 108°13E 310 D7
Da Qaidam China 37°50N 95°15E 304 C4
Da Yunhe → Hopei, China 39°10N 117°10E 307 E9
Da Yunhe → Jiangsu, China 34°25N 120°5E 307 G11
Da'an China 45°30N 124°7E 307 B13
Daan Viljoen ⌂ Namibia 22°2S 16°45E 328 C2
Daba Shan China 32°0N 109°0E 305 C5
Dabbagh, Jabal Si. Arabia 27°52N 35°45E 316 E2
Dabhoi India 22°10N 73°20E 314 H5
Dabo = Pasirkuning Indonesia 0°30S 104°33E 308 E2
Dabola Guinea 10°50N 11°5W 322 F3
Dabung Malaysia 5°23N 102°1E 311 K4
Dacca = Dhaka Bangla. 23°43N 90°26E 315 H14
Dacca = Dhaka □ Bangla. 24°25N 90°25E 315 G14
Dachau Germany 48°15N 11°26E 288 D6
Dachigam △ India 34°10N 75°0E 314 B6
Dadanawa Guyana 2°50N 59°30W 364 C7
Dade City U.S.A. 28°22N 82°11W 357 G13
Dadhar Pakistan 29°28N 67°39E 314 E2
Ḍadnah U.A.E. 25°32N 56°22E 317 E8
Dadra & Nagar Haveli □ India 20°5N 73°0E 312 J8
Dadri = Charkhi Dadri India 28°37N 76°17E 314 E7
Dadu Pakistan 26°45N 67°45E 314 F2
Daegu S. Korea 35°50N 128°37E 307 G15
Daejeon S. Korea 36°20N 127°28E 307 F14
Daejeong S. Korea 33°8N 126°17E 307 H14
Daet Phil. 14°2N 122°55E 309 B6
Dafnes Greece 35°13N 25°3E 297 D7
Dagana Senegal 16°30N 15°35W 322 E2
Dagestan □ Russia 42°30N 47°0E 291 F8
Daggett U.S.A. 34°52N 116°52W 351 L10
Daghestan Republic = Dagestan □ Russia 42°30N 47°0E 291 F8
Dağlıq Qarabağ = Nagorno-Karabakh □ Azerbaijan 39°55N 46°45E 316 B5
Dagö = Hiiumaa Estonia 58°50N 22°45E 281 G20
Dagu China 38°59N 117°40E 307 E9
Dagupan Phil. 16°3N 120°20E 309 A6
Daguragu Australia 17°33S 130°30E 332 C5
Dahlak Kebir Eritrea 15°50N 40°10E 319 D3
Dahlonega U.S.A. 34°32N 83°59W 357 D13
Dahod India 22°50N 74°15E 314 H6
Dahongliutan China 35°45N 79°20E 315 B8
Dahra Libya 29°30N 17°50E 323 C9
Dahūk Iraq 36°50N 43°1E 316 B3
Dai Hao Vietnam 18°1N 106°25E 310 C6
Dai-Sen Japan 35°22N 133°32E 303 G6
Dai Xian China 39°4N 112°58E 306 E7
Daicheng China 38°42N 116°38E 306 E9
Daikondi = Day Kundī □ Afghan. 34°0N 66°0E 312 C5

Daingean *Ireland* 53°18N 7°17W **282** C4
Daintree *Australia* 16°20S 145°20E **334** B4
Daintree △ *Australia* 16°8S 145°2E **334** B4
Daiō-Misaki *Japan* 34°15N 136°45E **303** G8
Daisen-Oki △ *Japan* 35°23N 133°34E **303** G6
Daisetsu-Zan *Japan* 43°30N 142°57E **302** C11
Daisetsu-Zan △ *Japan* 43°30N 142°55E **302** C11
Dajarra *Australia* 21°42S 139°30E **334** C2
Dajiawa *China* 37°9N 119°0E **307** F10
Dak Dam *Cambodia* 12°20N 107°21E **310** F6
Dak Nhe *Vietnam* 15°28N 107°48E **310** E6
Dak Pek *Vietnam* 15°4N 107°44E **310** E6
Dak Song *Vietnam* 12°19N 107°35E **311** F6
Dak Sui *Vietnam* 14°55N 107°43E **310** E6
Dakar *Senegal* 14°34N 17°29W **322** F2
Dakhla *W. Sahara* 23°50N 15°53W **322** D2
Dakhla, El Wâhât el-
Egypt 25°30N 28°50E **323** C11
Dakor *India* 22°45N 73°11E **314** H5
Dakota City *U.S.A.* 42°25N 96°25W **352** D5
Đakovica *Serbia* 42°22N 20°26E **295** C9
Dalachi *China* 36°48N 105°0E **306** F3
Dalai Nur *China* 43°20N 116°45E **306** C9
Dālakī *Iran* 29°26N 51°17E **317** D6
Dalälven → *Sweden* 60°12N 16°43E **281** F17
Dalaman → *Turkey* 36°41N 28°43E **295** F13
Dalandzadgad
Mongolia 43°27N 104°30E **306** C3
Dalap-Uliga-Darrit = Majuro
Marshall Is. 7°9N 171°12E **336** G9
Dalarna *Sweden* 61°0N 14°0E **280** F16
Dālbandīn *Pakistan* 29°0N 64°23E **312** E4
Dalbeattie *U.K.* 54°56N 3°50W **283** G5
Dalbeg *Australia* 20°16S 147°18E **334** C4
Dalby *Australia* 27°10S 151°17E **335** D5
Dale City *U.S.A.* 38°38N 77°19W **353** F15
Dale Hollow L. *U.S.A.* 36°32N 85°27W **357** C12
Dalgān *Iran* 27°31N 59°19E **317** E8
Dalhart *U.S.A.* 36°4N 102°31W **356** C3
Dalhousie *Canada* 48°5N 66°26W **345** C6
Dalhousie *India* 32°38N 75°58E **314** C6
Dali *Shaanxi, China* 34°48N 109°58E **306** G5
Dali *Yunnan, China* 25°40N 100°10E **304** D5
Dalian *China* 38°50N 121°40E **307** E11
Daliang Shan *China* 28°0N 102°45E **304** D5
Daling He → *China* 40°55N 121°40E **307** D11
Dāliyat el Karmel *Israel* 32°43N 35°2E **318** C4
Dalkeith *U.K.* 55°54N 3°4W **283** F5
Dallas *Oreg., U.S.A.* 44°55N 123°19W **348** D2
Dallas *Tex., U.S.A.* 32°47N 96°48W **356** E6
Dalles, The *U.S.A.* 45°36N 121°10W **348** D3
Dalmā *U.A.E.* 24°30N 52°20E **317** E7
Dalmacija *Croatia* 43°20N 17°0E **294** C7
Dalmas, L. *Canada* 53°30N 71°50W **345** B5
Dalmatia = Dalmacija
Croatia 43°20N 17°0E **294** C7
Dalmau *India* 26°4N 81°2E **315** F9
Dalmellington *U.K.* 55°19N 4°23W **283** F4
Dalnegorsk *Russia* 44°32N 135°33E **302** B7
Dalnerechensk *Russia* 45°50N 133°40E **302** B6
Dalnevostochnyy □
Russia 67°0N 140°0E **301** C14
Daloa *Ivory C.* 7°0N 6°30W **322** G4
Dalry *U.K.* 55°42N 4°43W **283** F4
Dalrymple, L. *Australia* 20°40S 147°0E **334** C4
Dalrymple, Mt.
Australia 21°1S 148°39E **334** K6
Dalsland *Sweden* 58°50N 12°15E **281** G15
Daltenganj *India* 24°0N 84°4E **315** H11
Dalton *Ga., U.S.A.* 34°46N 84°58W **357** D12
Dalton *Mass., U.S.A.* 42°28N 73°11W **355** D11
Dalton *Nebr., U.S.A.* 41°25N 102°58W **352** E2
Dalton-in-Furness *U.K.* 54°10N 3°11W **284** C4
Dalvík *Iceland* 65°58N 18°32W **280** D4
Dálvvadis = Jokkmokk
Sweden 66°35N 19°50E **280** C18
Dalwallinu *Australia* 30°17S 116°40E **333** F2
Daly → *Australia* 13°35S 130°19E **332** B5
Daly City *U.S.A.* 37°42N 122°27W **350** H4
Daly L. *Canada* 56°32N 105°39W **343** B7
Daly River *Australia* 13°46S 130°42E **332** B5
Daly Waters *Australia* 16°15S 133°24E **334** B1
Dam Doi *Vietnam* 8°50N 105°12E **311** H5
Dam Ha *Vietnam* 21°21N 107°36E **310** B6
Daman *India* 20°25N 72°57E **312** J8
Dāmaneh *Iran* 33°1N 50°29E **317** C6
Damanhûr *Egypt* 31°0N 30°30E **323** B12
Damant L. *Canada* 61°45N 105°5W **343** A7
Damanzhuang *China* 38°5N 116°35E **306** E9
Damar *Indonesia* 7°7S 128°40E **309** F7
Damara *C.A.R.* 4°58N 18°42E **324** D3
Damaraland *Namibia* 20°0S 15°0E **328** C2
Damascus = Dimashq
Syria 33°30N 36°18E **318** B5
Damāvand *Iran* 35°47N 52°0E **317** C7
Damāvand, Qolleh-ye
Iran 35°56N 52°10E **317** C7
Damba *Angola* 6°44S 15°20E **324** F3
Dâmboviţa →
Romania 44°12N 26°26E **289** F14
Dame Marie *Haiti* 18°36N 74°26W **361** C5
Dāmghān *Iran* 36°10N 54°17E **317** B7
Damiel *Spain* 39°4N 3°37W **293** C4
Damietta = Dumyât
Egypt 31°24N 31°48E **323** B12
Daming *China* 36°15N 115°6E **306** F8
Damīr Qābū *Syria* 36°58N 41°51E **316** B4
Dammam = Ad Dammām
Si. Arabia 26°20N 50°5E **317** E6
Damodar → *India* 23°17N 87°35E **315** H12
Damoh *India* 23°50N 79°28E **315** H8
Dampier *Australia* 20°41S 116°42E **332** D2
Dampier, Selat *Indonesia* 0°40S 131°0E **309** E8
Dampier Arch.
Australia 20°38S 116°32E **332** D2
Damrei, Chuor Phnum
Cambodia 11°30N 103°0E **311** G4
Damyang *S. Korea* 35°19N 126°59E **307** G14
Dana *Indonesia* 11°0S 122°52E **309** F6
Dana, L. *Canada* 50°53N 77°20W **344** B4
Dana, Mt. *U.S.A.* 37°54N 119°12W **350** H7
Danakil Desert *Ethiopia* 12°45N 41°0E **319** E3
Danané *Ivory C.* 7°16N 8°9W **322** G4
Danau Poso *Indonesia* 1°52S 120°35E **309** E6
Danbury *U.S.A.* 41°24N 73°28W **355** E11
Danby L. *U.S.A.* 34°13N 115°5W **349** J6
Dand *Afghan.* 31°28N 65°32E **314** D1
Dande ⌓ *Zimbabwe* 15°56S 30°16E **327** F3
Dandeldhura *Nepal* 29°20N 80°35E **315** E9
Dandeli *India* 15°5N 74°30E **312** M9
Dandenong *Australia* 38°0S 145°15E **335** F4
Dandong *China* 40°10N 124°20E **307** D13
Danfeng *China* 33°45N 110°25E **306** H6
Danger Is. = Pukapuka
Cook Is. 10°53S 165°49W **337** J11
Danger Pt. *S. Africa* 34°40S 19°17E **328** E2
Danginpuri *Indonesia* 8°40S 115°13E **309** K18
Dangla Shan = Tanggula Shan
China 32°40N 92°10E **304** C4
Dangrek, Phnom
Thailand 14°15N 105°0E **310** E5
Dangriga *Belize* 17°0N 88°13W **359** D7
Dangshan *China* 34°27N 116°22E **306** G9
Daniel *U.S.A.* 42°52N 110°4W **348** E8
Daniel's Harbour
Canada 50°13N 57°35W **345** B8
Danielskuil *S. Africa* 28°11S 23°33E **328** D3
Danielson *U.S.A.* 41°48N 71°53W **355** E13
Danilov *Russia* 58°16N 40°13E **290** C7
Daning *China* 36°28N 110°45E **306** F6
Ḑank *Oman* 23°33N 56°16E **317** F8
Dankhar Gompa *India* 32°10N 78°10E **314** C8
Danlí *Honduras* 14°4N 86°35W **360** D2
Danmark = Denmark ■
Europe 55°45N 10°0E **281** J14
Dannemora *U.S.A.* 44°43N 73°44W **355** B11
Dannevirke *N.Z.* 40°12S 176°8E **331** D6
Dannhauser *S. Africa* 28°0S 30°3E **329** D5
Dansville *U.S.A.* 42°34N 77°42W **354** D7
Danta *India* 24°11N 72°46E **314** G5
Dantan *India* 21°57N 87°20E **315** J12
Danube = Dunărea →
Europe 45°20N 29°40E **289** F15
Danvers *U.S.A.* 42°34N 70°56W **355** D14
Danville *Ill., U.S.A.* 40°8N 87°37W **352** E10
Danville *Ky., U.S.A.* 37°39N 84°46W **353** G11
Danville *Pa., U.S.A.* 40°58N 76°37W **355** F8
Danville *Va., U.S.A.* 36°36N 79°23W **353** G14
Danville *Vt., U.S.A.* 44°25N 72°9W **355** B12
Danzhou *China* 19°31N 109°33E **310** C7
Danzig = Gdańsk
Poland 54°22N 18°40E **289** A10
Dapaong *Togo* 10°55N 0°16E **322** F6
Daqing Shan *China* 40°40N 111°0E **306** D6
Dar Banda *Africa* 8°0N 23°0E **320** F6
Dar el Beida = Casablanca
Morocco 33°36N 7°36W **322** B4
Dar es Salaam *Tanzania* 6°50S 39°12E **326** D4
Dar Mazār *Iran* 29°14N 57°20E **317** D8
Dar'ā *Syria* 32°36N 36°7E **318** C5
Dar'ā □ *Syria* 32°55N 36°10E **318** C5
Dārāb *Iran* 28°50N 54°30E **317** D7
Daraban *Pakistan* 31°44N 70°20E **314** D4
Daraina *Madag.* 13°12S 49°40E **329** A8
Daraj *Libya* 30°10N 10°28E **323** B8
Dārān *Iran* 32°59N 50°24E **317** C6
Dārayyā *Syria* 33°28N 36°15E **318** B5
Darband *Pakistan* 34°20N 72°50E **314** B5
Darband, Kūh-e *Iran* 31°34N 57°8E **317** D8
Darbhanga *India* 26°15N 85°55E **315** F11
D'Arcy *Canada* 50°33N 122°29W **342** C4
Dardanelle *Ark., U.S.A.* 35°13N 93°9W **356** D8
Dardanelle *Calif.,*
U.S.A. 38°20N 119°50W **350** G7
Dardanelles = Çanakkale Boğazı
Turkey 40°17N 26°32E **295** D12
Dārestān *Iran* 29°9N 58°42E **317** D8
Dârfûr *Sudan* 13°40N 24°0E **323** F10
Dargai *Pakistan* 34°25N 71°55E **314** B4
Dargaville *N.Z.* 35°57S 173°52E **331** A4
Darhan *Mongolia* 49°37N 106°21E **304** B5
Darhan Muminggan Lianheqi
China 41°40N 110°28E **306** D6
Darıca *Turkey* 40°45N 29°23E **295** D13
Darién, G. del *Colombia* 9°0N 77°0W **364** B3
Darién △ *Panama* 7°36N 77°57W **360** E4
Dariganga = Ovoot
Mongolia 45°21N 113°45E **306** B7
Darjeeling = Darjiling
India 27°3N 88°18E **315** F13
Darjiling *India* 27°3N 88°18E **315** F13
Darkan *Australia* 33°20S 116°43E **333** F2
Darkhana *Pakistan* 30°39N 72°11E **314** D5
Darkhazīneh *Iran* 31°54N 48°39E **317** D6
Darkot Pass *Pakistan* 36°45N 73°26E **315** A5
Darling → *Australia* 34°4S 141°54E **335** E3
Darling Downs
Australia 27°30S 150°30E **335** D5
Darling Ra. *Australia* 32°30S 116°20E **333** F2
Darlington *U.K.* 54°32N 1°33W **284** C6
Darlington *U.S.A.* 34°18N 79°52W **357** D15
Darlington □ *U.K.* 54°32N 1°33W **284** C6
Darlington, L. *S. Africa* 33°10S 25°9E **328** E4
Darlot, L. *Australia* 27°48S 121°35E **333** E3
Darlowo *Poland* 54°25N 16°25E **288** A9
Darmstadt *Germany* 49°51N 8°39E **288** D5
Darnah *Libya* 32°45N 22°45E **323** B10
Darnall *S. Africa* 29°23S 31°18E **329** D5
Darnley, C. *Antarctica* 68°0S 69°0E **277** C6
Darnley B. *Canada* 69°30N 123°30W **340** C7
Darr → *Australia* 23°39S 143°50E **334** C3
Darra Pezu *Pakistan* 32°19N 70°44E **314** C4
Darrequeira *Argentina* 37°42S 63°10W **366** D3
Darrington *U.S.A.* 48°15N 121°36W **348** B3
Dart → *U.K.* 50°24N 3°39W **285** G4
Dart, C. *Antarctica* 73°6S 126°20W **277** D14
Dartford *U.K.* 51°26N 0°13E **285** F8
Dartmoor *U.K.* 50°38N 3°57W **285** G4
Dartmoor △ *U.K.* 50°37N 3°59W **285** G4
Dartmouth *Canada* 44°40N 63°30W **345** D7
Dartmouth *U.K.* 50°21N 3°36W **285** G4
Dartmouth Res.
Australia 26°4S 145°18E **335** D4
Dartuch, C. = Artrutx, C. de
Spain 39°55N 3°49E **296** B10
Darvaza *Turkmenistan* 40°11N 58°24E **300** E6
Darvel, Teluk = Lahad Datu,
Telok *Malaysia* 4°50N 118°20E **309** D5
Darwen *U.K.* 53°42N 2°29W **284** D5
Darwendale *Zimbabwe* 17°41S 30°33E **329** B5
Darwha *India* 20°15N 77°45E **312** J10
Darwin *Australia* 12°25S 130°51E **332** B5
Darwin *U.S.A.* 36°15N 117°35W **351** J9
Darya Khan *Pakistan* 31°48N 71°6E **314** D4
Daryoi Amu = Amudarya →
Uzbekistan 43°58N 59°34E **300** E6
Dās *U.A.E.* 25°20N 53°30E **317** E7
Dashen, Ras *Ethiopia* 13°8N 38°26E **319** E2
Dashetai *China* 41°0N 109°5E **306** D5
Dashköpri *Turkmenistan* 36°16N 62°8E **317** B9
Dashoguz *Turkmenistan* 41°49N 59°58E **300** E6
Dasht *Iran* 37°17N 56°7E **317** B8
Dasht → *Pakistan* 25°10N 61°40E **312** G2
Daska *Pakistan* 32°20N 74°20E **314** C6
Dasuya *India* 31°49N 75°38E **314** D6
Datça *Turkey* 36°46N 27°40E **295** F12
Datia *India* 25°39N 78°27E **315** G8
Datong *China* 40°6N 113°18E **306** D7
Dattakhel *Pakistan* 32°54N 69°46E **314** C3
Datu, Tanjung *Indonesia* 2°5N 109°39E **308** D3
Datu Piang *Phil.* 7°2N 124°30E **309** C6
Datuk, Tanjong = Datu, Tanjung
Indonesia 2°5N 109°39E **308** D3
Daud Khel *Pakistan* 32°53N 71°34E **314** C4
Daudnagar *India* 25°2N 84°24E **315** G11
Daugava → *Latvia* 57°4N 24°3E **281** H21
Daugavpils *Latvia* 55°53N 26°32E **281** J22
Daulpur *India* 26°45N 77°59E **314** F7
Dauphin *Canada* 51°9N 100°5W **343** C8
Dauphin *U.S.A.* 40°22N 76°56W **354** F8
Dauphin L. *Canada* 51°20N 99°45W **343** C9
Dauphiné *France* 45°15N 5°25E **292** D6
Dausa *India* 26°52N 76°20E **314** F7
Davangere *India* 14°25N 75°55E **312** M9
Davao *Phil.* 7°0N 125°40E **309** C7
Davao G. *Phil.* 6°30N 125°48E **309** C7
Dāvar Panāh = Sarāvān
Iran 27°25N 62°15E **317** E9
Davenport *Calif., U.S.A.* 37°1N 122°12W **350** H4
Davenport *Iowa, U.S.A.* 41°32N 90°35W **352** E8
Davenport *Wash.,*
U.S.A. 47°39N 118°9W **348** C4
Davenport Ra. *Australia* 20°28S 134°0E **334** C1
Daventry *U.K.* 52°16N 1°10W **285** E6
David *Panama* 8°30N 82°30W **360** E3
David City *U.S.A.* 41°15N 97°8W **352** E5
David Glacier
Antarctica 75°20S 162°0E **277** D21
David Gorodok = Davyd Haradok
Belarus 52°4N 27°8E **289** B14
Davidson *Canada* 51°16N 105°59W **343** C7
Davis *Antarctica* 68°34S 77°55E **277** C6
Davis *U.S.A.* 38°33N 121°44W **350** G5
Davis Dam *U.S.A.* 35°12N 114°34W **351** K12
Davis Inlet *Canada* 55°50N 60°59W **345** A7
Davis Mts. *U.S.A.* 30°50N 103°55W **356** F3
Davis Sea *Antarctica* 66°0S 92°0E **277** C7
Davis Str. *N. Amer.* 65°0N 58°0W **338** C14
Davos *Switz.* 46°48N 9°49E **292** C8
Davy L. *Canada* 58°53N 108°18W **343** B7
Davyd Haradok *Belarus* 52°4N 27°8E **289** B14
Dawei = Tavoy *Burma* 14°2N 98°12E **310** E2
Dawes Ra. *Australia* 24°40S 150°40E **334** C5
Dawlish *U.K.* 50°35N 3°28W **285** G4
Dawna Ra. *Burma* 16°30N 98°30E **310** D2
Dawros Hd. *Ireland* 54°50N 8°33W **282** B3
Dawson *Canada* 64°10N 139°30W **340** C6
Dawson *U.S.A.* 31°46N 84°27W **357** F12
Dawson, I. *Chile* 53°50S 70°50W **368** G2
Dawson B. *Canada* 52°53N 100°49W **343** C8
Dawson Creek *Canada* 55°45N 120°15W **342** B4
Dawson Inlet *Canada* 61°50N 93°25W **343** A10
Dawson Ra. *Australia* 24°30S 149°48E **334** C4
Dax *France* 43°44N 1°3W **292** E3
Daxian *China* 31°15N 107°23E **304** C5
Daxindian *China* 37°30N 120°50E **307** F11
Daxinggou *China* 43°25N 129°40E **307** C15
Daxue Shan *China* 30°30N 101°30E **304** C5
Day Kundī □ *Afghan.* 34°0N 66°0E **312** C5
Daylesford *Australia* 37°21S 144°9E **335** F3
Dayr az Zawr *Syria* 35°20N 40°5E **316** C4
Daysland *Canada* 52°50N 112°20W **342** C6
Dayton *Nev., U.S.A.* 39°14N 119°36W **350** F7
Dayton *Ohio, U.S.A.* 39°45N 84°12W **353** F11
Dayton *Pa., U.S.A.* 40°53N 79°15W **354** F5
Dayton *Tenn., U.S.A.* 35°30N 85°1W **357** D12
Dayton *Wash., U.S.A.* 46°19N 117°59W **348** C5
Dayton *Wyo., U.S.A.* 44°53N 107°16W **348** D10
Daytona Beach *U.S.A.* 29°13N 81°1W **357** G14
Dayville *U.S.A.* 44°28N 119°32W **348** D4
De Aar *S. Africa* 30°39S 24°0E **328** E3
De Biesbosch △ *Neths.* 51°45N 4°48E **287** C4
De Funiak Springs
U.S.A. 30°43N 86°7W **357** F11
De Grey → *Australia* 20°12S 119°13E **332** D2
De Haan *Belgium* 51°16N 3°2E **287** C3
De Hoge Veluwe △ *Neths.* 52°5N 5°46E **287** B5
De Hoop ⌓ *S. Africa* 34°30S 20°28E **328** E3
De Kennemerduinen △
Neths. 52°27N 4°33E **287** B4
De Land *U.S.A.* 29°2N 81°18W **357** G14
De Leon *U.S.A.* 32°7N 98°32W **356** E5
De Panne *Belgium* 51°6N 2°34E **287** C2
De Pere *U.S.A.* 44°27N 88°4W **352** C9
De Queen *U.S.A.* 34°2N 94°21W **356** D7
De Quincy *U.S.A.* 30°27N 93°26W **356** F8
De Smet *U.S.A.* 44°23N 97°33W **352** C5
De Soto *U.S.A.* 38°8N 90°34W **352** F8
De Tour Village *U.S.A.* 46°0N 83°56W **353** B12
De Witt *U.S.A.* 34°18N 91°20W **356** D9
Dead Sea *Asia* 31°30N 35°30E **318** D4
Deadwood *U.S.A.* 44°23N 103°44W **352** C2
Deadwood L. *Canada* 59°10N 128°30W **342** B3
Deal *U.K.* 51°13N 1°25E **285** F9
Deal I. *Australia* 39°30S 147°20E **335** F4
Dealesville *S. Africa* 28°41S 25°44E **328** D4
Dean → *Canada* 52°49N 126°58W **342** C3
Dean, Forest of *U.K.* 51°45N 2°33W **285** F5
Dean Chan. *Canada* 52°30N 127°15W **342** C3
Deán Funes *Argentina* 30°20S 64°20W **366** C3
Dease → *Canada* 59°56N 128°32W **342** B3
Dease L. *Canada* 58°40N 130°5W **342** B2
Dease Lake *Canada* 58°25N 130°6W **342** B2
Death Valley *U.S.A.* 36°15N 116°50W **351** J10
Death Valley △ *U.S.A.* 36°29N 117°6W **351** J9
Death Valley Junction
U.S.A. 36°20N 116°25W **351** J10
Debar *Macedonia* 41°31N 20°30E **295** D9
Debden *Canada* 53°30N 106°50W **343** C7
Dębica *Poland* 50°2N 21°25E **289** C11
DeBolt *Canada* 55°12N 118°1W **342** B5
Deborah East, L.
Australia 30°45S 119°30E **333** F2
Deborah West, L.
Australia 30°45S 119°5E **333** F2
Debre Markos *Ethiopia* 10°20N 37°40E **319** E2
Debre Tabor *Ethiopia* 11°50N 38°26E **319** E2
Debre Zebit *Ethiopia* 11°48N 38°30E **319** F2
Debrecen *Hungary* 47°33N 21°42E **289** E11
Decatur *Ala., U.S.A.* 34°36N 86°59W **357** D11
Decatur *Ga., U.S.A.* 33°46N 84°16W **357** E12
Decatur *Ill., U.S.A.* 39°51N 88°57W **352** F9
Decatur *Ind., U.S.A.* 40°50N 84°56W **353** E11
Decatur *Tex., U.S.A.* 33°14N 97°35W **356** E6
Deccan *India* 18°0N 79°0E **312** L11
Deception Bay *Australia* 27°10S 153°5E **335** D5
Deception I. *Antarctica* 63°0S 60°15W **277** C17
Deception L. *Canada* 56°33N 104°13W **343** B8
Dechhu *India* 26°46N 72°20E **314** F5
Děčín *Czech Rep.* 50°47N 14°12E **288** C8
Deckerville *U.S.A.* 43°32N 82°44W **354** C2
Decorah *U.S.A.* 43°18N 91°48W **352** D8
Dedéagach = Alexandroupoli
Greece 40°50N 25°54E **295** D11
Dedham *U.S.A.* 42°15N 71°10W **355** D13
Dedza *Malawi* 14°20S 34°20E **327** E3
Dee → *Aberds., U.K.* 57°9N 2°5W **283** D6
Dee → *Dumf. & Gall., U.K.* 54°51N 4°3W **283** G4
Dee → *Wales, U.K.* 53°22N 3°17W **284** D4
Deep B. *Canada* 61°15N 116°35W **342** A5
Deep Bay = Shenzhen Wan
China 22°27N 113°55E **305** G10
Deepwater *Australia* 29°25S 151°51E **335** D5
Deer → *Canada* 58°23N 94°13W **343** B10
Deer L. *Canada* 52°40N 94°20W **343** C10
Deer Lake *Nfld. & L.,*
Canada 49°11N 57°27W **345** C8
Deer Lake *Ont., Canada* 52°36N 94°20W **343** C10
Deer Lodge *U.S.A.* 46°24N 112°44W **348** C7
Deer Park *U.S.A.* 47°57N 117°28W **348** C5
Deer River *U.S.A.* 47°20N 93°48W **352** B7
Deeragun *Australia* 19°16S 146°33E **334** B4
Deerdepoort *S. Africa* 24°37S 26°27E **328** C4
Deferiet *U.S.A.* 44°2N 75°41W **355** B9
Defiance *U.S.A.* 41°17N 84°22W **353** E11
Degana *India* 26°50N 74°20E **314** F6
Dégelis *Canada* 47°30N 68°35W **345** C6
Deggendorf *Germany* 48°50N 12°57E **288** D7
Degh → *Pakistan* 31°3N 73°21E **314** D5
Deh Bīd *Iran* 30°39N 53°11E **317** D7
Deh-e Shīr *Iran* 31°29N 53°45E **317** D7
Dehaj *Iran* 30°42N 54°53E **317** D7
Dehak *Iran* 27°11N 62°37E **317** E9
Dehdez *Iran* 31°43N 50°17E **317** D6
Dehej *India* 21°44N 72°40E **314** J5
Dehestān *Iran* 28°30N 55°35E **317** D7
Dehgolān *Iran* 35°17N 47°25E **316** C5
Dehibat *Tunisia* 32°0N 10°47E **323** B8
Dehlorān *Iran* 32°41N 47°16E **316** C5
Dehnow-e Kūhestān
Iran 27°58N 58°32E **317** E8
Dehra Dun *India* 30°20N 78°4E **314** D8
Dehri *India* 24°50N 84°15E **315** G11
Dehui *China* 44°30N 125°40E **307** B13
Deinze *Belgium* 50°59N 3°32E **287** D3
Dej *Romania* 47°10N 23°52E **289** E12
Deka → *Zimbabwe* 18°4S 26°42E **328** B4
DeKalb *U.S.A.* 41°56N 88°46W **352** E9
Dekese
Dem. Rep. of the Congo 3°24S 21°24E **324** E4
Del Mar *U.S.A.* 32°58N 117°16W **351** N9
Del Norte *U.S.A.* 37°41N 106°21W **349** H10
Del Rio *U.S.A.* 29°22N 100°54W **356** G4
Delambre I. *Australia* 20°26S 117°5E **332** D2
Delano *U.S.A.* 35°46N 119°15W **351** K7
Delano Peak *U.S.A.* 38°22N 112°22W **348** G7
Delareyville *S. Africa* 26°41S 25°26E **328** D4
Delaronde L. *Canada* 54°3N 107°3W **343** C7
Delavan *U.S.A.* 42°38N 88°39W **352** D9
Delaware *U.S.A.* 40°18N 83°4W **353** E12
Delaware □ *U.S.A.* 39°0N 75°20W **353** F16
Delaware → *U.S.A.* 39°15N 75°20W **355** G9
Delaware B. *U.S.A.* 39°0N 75°10W **353** F16
Delaware Water Gap ⌓
U.S.A. 41°10N 74°55W **355** E10
Delay → *Canada* 56°56N 71°28W **345** A5
Delegate *Australia* 37°4S 148°56E **335** F4
Delevan *U.S.A.* 42°29N 78°29W **354** D6
Delft *Neths.* 52°1N 4°22E **287** B4
Delfzijl *Neths.* 53°20N 6°55E **287** A6
Delgado, C. *Mozam.* 10°45S 40°40E **327** E5
Delgerhet *Mongolia* 45°50N 110°30E **306** B6
Delgo *Sudan* 20°6N 30°40E **323** D12
Delhi *Canada* 42°51N 80°30W **354** D4
Delhi *India* 28°39N 77°13E **314** E7
Delhi *La., U.S.A.* 32°28N 91°30W **356** E9
Delhi *N.Y., U.S.A.* 42°17N 74°55W **355** D10
Delia *Canada* 51°38N 112°23W **342** C6
Delice *Turkey* 39°54N 34°2E **291** G5
Delicias *Mexico* 28°13N 105°28W **358** B3
Delījān *Iran* 33°59N 50°40E **317** C6
Déline *Canada* 65°11N 123°25W **340** C7
Delisle *Canada* 51°55N 107°8W **343** C7
Dell City *U.S.A.* 31°56N 105°12W **356** F2
Dell Rapids *U.S.A.* 43°50N 96°43W **352** D5
Delmar *U.S.A.* 42°37N 73°47W **355** D11
Delmenhorst *Germany* 53°3N 8°37E **288** B5
Delonga, Ostrova
Russia 76°40N 149°20E **301** B15
Deloraine *Australia* 41°30S 146°40E **335** G4
Deloraine *Canada* 49°15N 100°29W **343** D8
Delphi *U.S.A.* 40°36N 86°41W **352** E10
Delphos *U.S.A.* 40°51N 84°21W **353** E11
Delportshoop *S. Africa* 28°22S 24°20E **328** D3
Delray Beach *U.S.A.* 26°28N 80°4W **357** H14
Delta *Colo., U.S.A.* 38°44N 108°4W **348** G9
Delta *Utah, U.S.A.* 39°21N 112°35W **348** G7
Delta Dunărea ⌓
Romania 45°15N 29°25E **289** F15
Delta Junction *U.S.A.* 64°2N 145°44W **340** C5
Deltona *U.S.A.* 28°54N 81°16W **357** G14
Delungra *Australia* 29°39S 150°51E **335** D5
Delvada *India* 20°46N 71°2E **314** J4
Delvinë *Albania* 39°59N 20°6E **295** E9
Demak *Indonesia* 6°53S 110°38E **309** G14
Demanda, Sierra de la
Spain 42°15N 3°0W **293** A4
Demavend = Damāvand,
Qolleh-ye *Iran* 35°56N 52°10E **317** C7
Dembia
Dem. Rep. of the Congo 3°33N 25°48E **326** B2
Dembidolo *Ethiopia* 8°34N 34°50E **319** F1
Demchok *India* 32°42N 79°29E **315** C8
Demer → *Belgium* 50°57N 4°42E **287** D4
Deming *N. Mex.,*
U.S.A. 32°16N 107°46W **349** K10
Deming *Wash., U.S.A.* 48°50N 122°13W **350** B4
Demini → *Brazil* 0°46S 62°56W **364** D6
Demirci *Turkey* 39°2N 28°38E **295** E13
Demirköy *Turkey* 41°49N 27°45E **295** D12
Demopolis *U.S.A.* 32°31N 87°50W **357** E11
Dempo *Indonesia* 4°2S 103°15E **308** E2
Den Bosch = 's-Hertogenbosch
Neths. 51°42N 5°17E **287** C5
Den Burg *Neths.* 53°3N 4°47E **287** A4
Den Chai *Thailand* 17°59N 100°4E **310** D3
Den Haag = 's-Gravenhage
Neths. 52°7N 4°17E **287** B4
Den Helder *Neths.* 52°57N 4°45E **287** B4
Den Oever *Neths.* 52°56N 5°2E **287** B5
Denair *U.S.A.* 37°32N 120°48W **350** H6
Denali = McKinley, Mt.
U.S.A. 63°4N 151°0W **346** a
Denau *Uzbekistan* 38°16N 67°54E **300** F7
Denbigh *Canada* 45°8N 77°15W **354** A7
Denbigh *U.K.* 53°12N 3°25W **284** D4
Denbighshire □ *U.K.* 53°8N 3°22W **284** D4
Dendang *Indonesia* 3°7S 107°56E **308** E3
Dendermonde *Belgium* 51°2N 4°5E **287** C4
Dengfeng *China* 34°25N 113°2E **306** G7
Dengkou *China* 40°18N 106°55E **306** D4
Denham *Australia* 25°56S 113°31E **333** E1
Denham, Mt. *Jamaica* 18°13N 77°32W **360** a
Denham Ra. *Australia* 21°55S 147°46E **334** C4
Denham Sd. *Australia* 25°45S 113°15E **333** E1
Denholm *Canada* 52°39N 108°1W **343** C7
Denia *Spain* 38°49N 0°8E **293** C6
Denial B. *Australia* 32°14S 133°32E **335** E1
Deniliquin *Australia* 35°30S 144°58E **335** F3
Denison *Iowa, U.S.A.* 42°1N 95°21W **352** D6
Denison *Tex., U.S.A.* 33°45N 96°33W **356** E6
Denison Plains *Australia* 18°35S 128°0E **332** C4
Denizli *Turkey* 37°42N 29°2E **291** G4
Denman Glacier
Antarctica 66°45S 99°25E **277** C7
Denmark *Australia* 34°59S 117°25E **333** F2
Denmark ■ *Europe* 55°45N 10°0E **281** J14
Denmark Str. *Atl. Oc.* 66°0N 30°0W **338** C17
Dennery *St. Lucia* 13°55N 60°54W **361** f
Dennison *U.S.A.* 40°24N 81°19W **354** F3
Denny *U.K.* 56°1N 3°55W **283** E5
Denpasar *Indonesia* 8°39S 115°13E **308** F5
Denpasar ✕ (DPS)
Indonesia 8°44S 115°10E **309** K18
Denton *Mont., U.S.A.* 47°19N 109°57W **348** C9
Denton *Tex., U.S.A.* 33°13N 97°8W **356** E6
D'Entrecasteaux, Pt.
Australia 34°50S 115°57E **333** F2
D'Entrecasteaux △
Australia 34°20S 115°33E **333** F2
D'Entrecasteaux Is.
Papua N. G. 9°0S 151°0E **330** B8
Denver *Colo., U.S.A.* 39°42N 104°59W **348** G11
Denver *Pa., U.S.A.* 40°14N 76°8W **355** F8
Denver City *U.S.A.* 32°58N 102°50W **356** E3
Deoband *India* 29°42N 77°43E **314** E7
Deogarh *India* 25°32N 73°54E **314** G5
Deoghar *India* 24°30N 86°42E **315** G12
Deolali *India* 19°58N 73°50E **312** K8
Deoli = Devli *India* 25°50N 75°20E **314** G6
Deora *India* 26°22N 70°55E **314** F4
Deori *India* 23°24N 79°1E **315** H8
Deoria *India* 26°31N 83°48E **315** F10
Deosai Mts. *Pakistan* 35°40N 75°0E **315** B6
Deosri *India* 26°46N 90°29E **315** F14

Depalpur India 22°51N 75°33E 314 H6
Deping China 37°25N 116°58E 307 F9
Deposit U.S.A. 42°4N 75°25W 355 D9
Depuch I. Australia 20°37S 117°44E 332 D2
Deputatskiy Russia 69°18N 139°54E 301 C14
Dera Ghazi Khan Pakistan 30°5N 70°43E 314 D4
Dera Ismail Khan Pakistan 31°50N 70°50E 314 D4
Derabugti Pakistan 29°2N 69°9E 314 E3
Derawar Fort Pakistan 28°46N 71°20E 314 E4
Derbent Russia 42°5N 48°15E 291 F8
Derby Australia 17°18S 123°38E 332 C3
Derby U.K. 52°56N 1°28W 284 E6
Derby Conn., U.S.A. 41°19N 73°5W 355 E11
Derby Kans., U.S.A. 37°33N 97°16W 352 G5
Derby N.Y., U.S.A. 42°41N 78°58W 354 D6
Derby City □ U.K. 52°56N 1°28W 284 E6
Derby Line U.S.A. 45°0N 72°6W 355 B12
Derbyshire □ U.K. 53°11N 1°38W 284 D6
Derdepoort S. Africa 24°38S 26°24E 328 C4
Dereham U.K. 52°41N 0°57E 285 E8
Derg → U.K. 54°44N 7°26W 282 B4
Derg, L. Ireland 53°0N 8°20W 282 D3
Deridder U.S.A. 30°51N 93°17W 356 F8
Dermott U.S.A. 33°32N 91°26W 356 E9
Derry = Londonderry U.K. 55°0N 7°20W 282 B4
Derry = Londonderry □ U.K. 55°0N 7°20W 282 B4
Derry N.H., U.S.A. 42°53N 71°19W 355 D13
Derry Pa., U.S.A. 40°20N 79°18W 354 F5
Derryveagh Mts. Ireland 54°56N 8°11W 282 B3
Derwent → Cumb., U.K. 54°39N 3°33W 284 C4
Derwent → Derby, U.K. 52°57N 1°28W 284 E6
Derwent → N. Yorks., U.K. 53°45N 0°58W 284 D7
Derwent Water U.K. 54°35N 3°9W 284 C4
Des Moines Iowa, U.S.A. 41°35N 93°37W 352 E7
Des Moines N. Mex., U.S.A. 36°46N 103°50W 349 H12
Des Moines Wash., U.S.A. 47°24N 122°19W 350 C4
Des Moines → U.S.A. 40°23N 91°25W 352 E8
Desaguadero → Argentina 34°30S 66°46W 366 C2
Desaguadero → Bolivia 16°35S 69°5W 364 G5
Desar Malaysia 1°31N 104°17E 311 d
Descanso, Pta. Mexico 32°21N 117°3W 351 N9
Deschaillons-sur-St-Laurent Canada 46°32N 72°7W 345 C5
Deschambault L. Canada 54°50N 103°30W 343 C8
Deschutes → U.S.A. 45°38N 120°55W 348 D3
Dese Ethiopia 11°5N 39°40E 319 E2
Deseado → Argentina 47°45S 65°54W 368 F3
Desert Center U.S.A. 33°43N 115°24W 351 M11
Desert Hot Springs U.S.A. 33°58N 116°30W 351 M10
Deshnok India 27°48N 73°21E 314 F5
Desierto Central de Baja California ⌂ Mexico 29°40N 114°50W 358 B2
Desna → Ukraine 50°33N 30°32E 289 C16
Desolación, I. Chile 53°0S 74°0W 368 G2
Despeñaperros, Paso Spain 38°24N 3°30W 293 C4
Dessau Germany 51°51N 12°14E 288 C7
Dessye = Dese Ethiopia 11°5N 39°40E 319 E2
D'Estrees B. Australia 35°55S 137°45E 335 F2
Desuri India 25°18N 73°35E 314 G5
Det Udom Thailand 14°54N 105°5E 310 E5
Dete Zimbabwe 18°38S 26°50E 328 B4
Detmold Germany 51°56N 8°52E 288 C5
Detour, Pt. U.S.A. 45°40N 86°40W 352 C10
Detroit U.S.A. 42°19N 83°12W 354 D1
Detroit Lakes U.S.A. 46°49N 95°51W 352 B6
Deua △ Australia 35°32S 149°46E 335 F4
Deurne Neths. 51°27N 5°49E 287 C5
Deutsche Bucht Germany 54°15N 8°0E 288 A5
Deutschland = Germany ■ Europe 51°0N 10°0E 288 C6
Deva Romania 45°53N 22°55E 289 F12
Devakottai India 9°55N 78°45E 312 Q11
Devaprayag India 30°13N 78°35E 315 D8
Deventer Neths. 52°15N 6°10E 287 B6
Deveron → U.K. 57°41N 2°32W 283 D6
Devgadh Bariya India 22°40N 73°55E 314 H5
Devikot India 26°42N 71°12E 314 F4
Devils Den U.S.A. 35°46N 119°58W 350 K7
Devils Hole = Death Valley △ U.S.A. 36°29N 117°6W 351 J9
Devils Lake U.S.A. 48°7N 98°52W 352 A4
Devils Paw Canada 58°47N 134°0W 342 B2
Devils Postpile ⌂ U.S.A. 37°37N 119°5W 350 H7
Devils Tower U.S.A. 44°35N 104°42W 348 D11
Devils Tower △ U.S.A. 44°48N 104°55W 348 D11
Devine U.S.A. 29°8N 98°54W 356 G5
Devizes U.K. 51°22N 1°58W 285 F6
Devli India 25°50N 75°20E 314 G6
Devon Canada 53°24N 113°44W 342 C6
Devon □ U.K. 50°50N 3°40W 285 G4
Devon I. Canada 75°10N 85°0W 341 B11
Devonport Australia 41°10S 146°22E 335 G4
Devonport N.Z. 36°49S 174°49E 331 B5
Dewas India 22°59N 76°3E 314 H7
Dewetsdorp S. Africa 29°33S 26°39E 328 D4
Dewey Puerto Rico 18°18N 65°18W 361 d
Dexter Maine, U.S.A. 45°1N 69°18W 353 C19
Dexter Mo., U.S.A. 36°48N 89°57W 352 G9
Dexter N. Mex., U.S.A. 33°12N 104°22W 349 K11
Dey-Dey, L. Australia 29°12S 131°4E 333 E5
Deyang China 31°3N 104°27E 304 C5
Deyhūk Iran 33°15N 57°30E 317 C8
Deyyer Iran 27°55N 51°55E 317 E6
Dezadeash L. Canada 60°28N 136°58W 342 A1
Dezfūl Iran 32°20N 48°30E 317 C6
Dezhneva, Mys Russia 66°5N 169°40W 301 C19
Dezhou China 37°26N 116°18E 306 F9
Dhadhar → India 24°56N 85°24E 315 G11
Dhahiriya = Aẓ Ẓāhirīyah West Bank 31°25N 34°58E 318 D3
Dhahran = Aẓ Ẓahrān Si. Arabia 26°10N 50°7E 317 E6
Dhak Pakistan 32°25N 72°33E 314 C5
Dhaka Bangla. 23°43N 90°26E 315 H14
Dhaka □ Bangla. 24°25N 90°25E 315 G14
Dhali Cyprus 35°1N 33°25E 297 D12
Dhamār Yemen 14°30N 44°20E 319 E3
Dhampur India 29°19N 78°33E 315 E8
Dhamtari India 20°42N 81°35E 313 J12
Dhanbad India 23°50N 86°30E 315 H12
Dhangarhi Nepal 28°55N 80°40E 315 E9
Dhankuta Nepal 26°55N 87°40E 315 F12
Dhar India 22°35N 75°26E 314 H6
Dharampur India 22°13N 75°18E 314 H6
Dharamsala = Dharmsala India 32°16N 76°23E 314 C7
Dhariwal India 31°57N 75°19E 314 D6
Dharla → Bangla. 25°46N 89°42E 315 G13
Dharmapuri India 12°10N 78°10E 312 N11
Dharmjaygarh India 22°28N 83°13E 315 H10
Dharmsala India 32°16N 76°23E 314 C7
Dharni India 21°33N 76°53E 314 J7
Dharwad India 15°30N 75°4E 312 M9
Dhasan → India 25°48N 79°24E 315 G8
Dhaulagiri Nepal 28°39N 83°28E 315 E10
Dhebar, L. India 24°10N 74°0E 314 G6
Dheftera Cyprus 35°5N 33°16E 297 D12
Dhenkanal India 20°45N 85°35E 313 J14
Dherinia Cyprus 35°3N 33°57E 297 D12
Dhī Qār □ Iraq 31°0N 46°15E 316 D5
Dhiarrizos → Cyprus 34°41N 32°34E 297 E11
Dhībān Jordan 31°30N 35°46E 318 D4
Dhilwan India 31°31N 75°21E 314 D6
Dhimarkhera India 23°28N 80°22E 315 H9
Dhodhekánisos = Dodecanese Greece 36°35N 27°0E 295 F12
Dholka India 22°44N 72°29E 314 H5
Dhoraji India 21°45N 70°37E 314 J4
Dhrangadhra India 22°59N 71°31E 314 H4
Dhrol India 22°33N 70°25E 314 H4
Dhuburi India 26°2N 89°59E 313 F16
Dhule India 20°58N 74°50E 312 J9
Di Linh Vietnam 11°35N 108°4E 311 G7
Di Linh, Cao Nguyen Vietnam 11°30N 108°0E 311 G7
Dia Greece 35°28N 25°14E 297 D7
Diablo Range U.S.A. 37°20N 121°25W 350 J5
Diafarabé Mali 14°9N 4°57W 322 F5
Diamante Argentina 32°5S 60°40W 366 C3
Diamante → Argentina 34°30S 66°46W 366 C2
Diamantina Brazil 18°17S 43°40W 365 G10
Diamantina → Australia 26°45S 139°10E 335 D2
Diamantina △ Australia 23°33S 141°23E 334 C3
Diamantino Brazil 14°30S 56°30W 365 F7
Diamond Bar U.S.A. 34°1N 117°48W 351 L9
Diamond Harbour India 22°11N 88°14E 315 H13
Diamond Is. Australia 17°25S 151°5E 334 B5
Diamond Mts. U.S.A. 39°40N 115°50W 348 G6
Diamond Springs U.S.A. 38°42N 120°49W 350 G6
Diaoyu Tai = Senkaku-Shotō E. China Sea 25°45N 123°30E 303 M1
Dībā U.A.E. 25°45N 56°16E 317 E8
Dibai India 28°13N 78°15E 314 E8
Dibaya Dem. Rep. of the Congo 6°30S 22°57E 324 F4
Dibaya-Lubue Dem. Rep. of the Congo 4°12S 19°54E 324 E3
Dibbeen △ Jordan 32°20N 35°45E 318 C4
Dibete Botswana 23°45S 26°32E 328 C4
Dibrugarh India 27°29N 94°55E 313 F19
Dickens U.S.A. 33°37N 100°50W 356 E4
Dickinson U.S.A. 46°53N 102°47W 352 B2
Dickson U.S.A. 36°5N 87°23W 357 C11
Dickson City U.S.A. 41°28N 75°36W 355 E9
Didiéni Mali 13°53N 8°6W 322 F4
Didsbury Canada 51°35N 114°10W 342 C6
Didwana India 27°23N 74°36E 314 F6
Diefenbaker, L. Canada 51°0N 106°55W 343 C7
Diego de Almagro Chile 26°22S 70°3W 366 B1
Diego Suarez = Antsiranana Madag. 12°25S 49°20E 329 A8
Diekirch Lux. 49°52N 6°10E 287 E6
Dien Ban Vietnam 15°53N 108°16E 310 E7
Dien Bien Vietnam 21°20N 103°0E 310 B4
Dien Khanh Vietnam 12°15N 109°6E 311 F7
Dieppe France 49°54N 1°4E 292 B4
Dierks U.S.A. 34°7N 94°1W 356 D7
Diest Belgium 50°58N 5°4E 287 D5
Dif Somali Rep. 0°59N 40°58E 319 G3
Differdange Lux. 49°31N 5°54E 287 E5
Dig India 27°28N 77°20E 314 F7
Digba Dem. Rep. of the Congo 4°25N 25°48E 326 B2
Digby Canada 44°38N 65°50W 345 D6
Diggi India 26°22N 75°26E 314 F6
Dighinala Bangla. 23°15N 92°5E 313 H18
Dighton U.S.A. 38°29N 100°28W 352 F3
Digne-les-Bains France 44°5N 6°12E 292 D7
Digos Phil. 6°45N 125°20E 309 C7
Digranes Iceland 66°4N 14°44W 280 C6
Digul → Indonesia 7°7S 138°42E 309 F9
Dihang = Brahmaputra → Asia 23°40N 90°35E 315 H13
Dijlah, Nahr → Asia 31°0N 47°25E 316 D5
Dijon France 47°20N 5°3E 292 C6
Dikhil Djibouti 11°8N 42°20E 319 E3
Dikkil = Dikhil Djibouti 11°8N 42°20E 319 E3
Diksmuide Belgium 51°2N 2°52E 287 C2
Dikson Russia 73°40N 80°5E 300 B9
Dikti Oros Greece 35°8N 25°30E 297 D7
Dila Ethiopia 6°21N 38°22E 319 F2
Dili E. Timor 8°39S 125°34E 309 F7
Dilley U.S.A. 28°40N 99°10W 356 G5
Dilli = Delhi India 28°39N 77°13E 314 E7
Dillingham U.S.A. 59°3N 158°28W 346 a
Dillon Canada 55°56N 108°35W 343 B7
Dillon Mont., U.S.A. 45°13N 112°38W 348 D7
Dillon S.C., U.S.A. 34°25N 79°22W 357 D15
Dillon → Canada 55°56N 108°56W 343 B7
Dillsburg U.S.A. 40°7N 77°2W 354 F7
Dilolo Dem. Rep. of the Congo 10°28S 22°18E 324 G4
Dimas Mexico 23°43N 106°47W 358 C3
Dimashq Syria 33°30N 36°18E 318 B5
Dimashq □ Syria 33°30N 36°30E 318 B5
Dimbaza S. Africa 32°50S 27°14E 329 E4
Dimboola Australia 36°28S 142°7E 335 F3
Dîmboviţa = Dâmboviţa → Romania 44°12N 26°26E 289 F14
Dimbulah Australia 17°8S 145°4E 334 B4
Dimitrovgrad Bulgaria 42°5N 25°35E 295 C11
Dimitrovgrad Russia 54°14N 49°39E 290 D8
Dimitrovo = Pernik Bulgaria 42°35N 23°2E 295 C10
Dimmitt U.S.A. 34°33N 102°19W 356 D3
Dimona Israel 31°2N 35°1E 318 D4
Dinagat Phil. 10°10N 125°40E 309 B7
Dinajpur Bangla. 25°33N 88°43E 313 G16
Dinan France 48°28N 2°2W 292 B2
Dīnān Āb Iran 32°4N 56°49E 317 C8
Dinant Belgium 50°16N 4°55E 287 D4
Dinapur India 25°38N 85°5E 315 G11
Dīnār, Kūh-e Iran 30°42N 51°46E 317 D6
Dinara Planina Croatia 44°0N 16°30E 294 C7
Dinard France 48°38N 2°6W 292 B2
Dinaric Alps = Dinara Planina Croatia 44°0N 16°30E 294 C7
Dindigul India 10°25N 78°0E 312 P11
Dindori India 22°57N 81°5E 315 H9
Ding Xian = Dingzhou China 38°30N 114°59E 306 E8
Dinga Pakistan 25°26N 67°10E 314 G2
Ding'an China 19°42N 110°19E 310 C8
Dingbian China 37°35N 107°32E 306 F4
Dingle Ireland 52°9N 10°17W 282 D1
Dingle B. Ireland 52°3N 10°20W 282 D1
Dingmans Ferry U.S.A. 41°13N 74°55W 355 E10
Dingo Australia 23°38S 149°19E 334 C4
Dingtao China 35°5N 115°35E 306 G8
Dingwall U.K. 57°36N 4°26W 283 D4
Dingxi China 35°30N 104°33E 306 G3
Dingxiang China 38°30N 112°58E 306 E7
Dingzhou China 38°30N 114°59E 306 E8
Dinh, Mui Vietnam 11°22N 109°1E 311 G7
Dinh Lap Vietnam 21°33N 107°6E 310 B6
Dinin → Ireland 52°43N 7°18W 282 D4
Dinira △ Venezuela 9°57N 70°6W 361 E6
Dinokwe Botswana 23°29S 26°37E 328 C4
Dinorwic Canada 49°41N 92°30W 343 D10
Dinosaur ⌂ Canada 50°47N 111°30W 342 C6
Dinosaur ⌂ U.S.A. 40°30N 108°45W 348 F9
Dinuba U.S.A. 36°32N 119°23W 350 J7
Dionisades Greece 35°20N 26°10E 297 D8
Diourbel Senegal 14°39N 16°12W 322 F2
Dipalpur Pakistan 30°40N 73°39E 314 D5
Diplo Pakistan 24°35N 69°35E 314 G3
Dipolog Phil. 8°36N 123°20E 309 C6
Dipperu △ Australia 21°56S 148°42E 334 C4
Dir Pakistan 35°8N 71°59E 312 B7
Dire Dawa Ethiopia 9°35N 41°45E 319 F3
Dirfis Oros Greece 38°40N 23°54E 295 E10
Diriamba Nic. 11°51N 86°19W 360 D2
Dirk Hartog I. Australia 25°50S 113°5E 333 E1
Dirranbandi Australia 28°33S 148°17E 335 D4
Disa India 24°18N 72°10E 314 G5
Disappointment, C. U.S.A. 46°18N 124°5W 348 C1
Disappointment, L. Australia 23°20S 122°40E 332 D3
Disaster B. Australia 37°15S 149°58E 335 F4
Discovery B. Australia 38°10S 140°40E 335 F3
Discovery B. China 22°18N 114°1E 305 G11
Disko = Qeqertarsuaq Greenland 69°45N 53°30W 338 C14
Disney Reef Tonga 19°17S 174°7W 331 c
Diss U.K. 52°23N 1°7E 285 E9
Disteghil Sar Pakistan 36°20N 75°12E 315 A6
District of Columbia □ U.S.A. 38°55N 77°0W 353 F15
Distrito Federal □ Brazil 15°45S 47°45W 365 G9
Distrito Federal □ Mexico 19°15N 99°10W 359 D5
Diu India 20°45N 70°58E 314 J4
Dīvāndarreh Iran 35°55N 47°2E 316 C5
Divide U.S.A. 45°45N 112°45W 348 D7
Dividing Ra. Australia 27°45S 116°0E 333 E2
Divinópolis Brazil 20°10S 44°54W 365 H10
Divnoye Russia 45°55N 43°21E 291 E7
Divo Ivory C. 5°48N 5°15W 322 G4
Dīwāl Kol Afghan. 34°23N 67°52E 314 B2
Dixie Mt. U.S.A. 39°55N 120°16W 350 F6
Dixon Calif., U.S.A. 38°27N 121°49W 350 G5
Dixon Ill., U.S.A. 41°50N 89°29W 352 E9
Dixon Entrance U.S.A. 54°30N 132°0W 340 D6
Dixville Canada 45°4N 71°46W 355 A13
Diyālā □ Iraq 33°45N 44°50E 316 C5
Diyālā → Iraq 33°13N 44°30E 316 C5
Diyarbakır Turkey 37°55N 40°18E 316 B4
Diyodar India 24°8N 71°50E 314 G4
Djakarta = Jakarta Indonesia 6°9S 106°52E 308 F3
Djamba Angola 16°45S 13°58E 328 B1
Djambala Congo 2°32S 14°30E 324 E2
Djanet Algeria 24°35N 9°32E 322 D7
Djawa = Jawa Indonesia 7°0S 110°0E 308 F3
Djelfa Algeria 34°40N 3°15E 322 B6
Djema C.A.R. 6°3N 25°15E 326 A2
Djerba, Î. de Tunisia 33°50N 10°48E 323 B8
Djerid, Chott Tunisia 33°42N 8°30E 322 B7
Djibouti Djibouti 11°30N 43°5E 319 E3
Djibouti ■ Africa 12°0N 43°0E 319 E3
Djolu Dem. Rep. of the Congo 0°35N 22°5E 324 D4
Djougou Benin 9°40N 1°45E 322 G6
Djoum Cameroon 2°41N 12°35E 324 D2
Djourab, Erg du Chad 16°40N 18°50E 323 E9
Djugu Dem. Rep. of the Congo 1°55N 30°35E 326 B3
Djukbinj △ Australia 12°11S 131°2E 332 B5
Djúpivogur Iceland 64°39N 14°17W 280 D6
Dmitriya Lapteva, Proliv Russia 73°0N 140°0E 301 B15
Dnepr = Dnipro → Ukraine 46°30N 32°18E 291 E5
Dneprodzerzhinsk = Dniprodzerzhynsk Ukraine 48°32N 34°37E 291 E5
Dnepropetrovsk = Dnipropetrovsk Ukraine 48°30N 35°0E 291 E6
Dnestr = Dnister → Europe 46°18N 30°17E 289 E16
Dnieper = Dnipro → Ukraine 46°30N 32°18E 291 E5
Dniester = Dnister → Europe 46°18N 30°17E 289 E16
Dnipro → Ukraine 46°30N 32°18E 291 E5
Dniprodzerzhynsk Ukraine 48°32N 34°37E 291 E5
Dnipropetrovsk Ukraine 48°30N 35°0E 291 E6
Dnister → Europe 46°18N 30°17E 289 E16
Dno Russia 57°50N 29°58E 281 H23
Dnyapro = Dnipro → Ukraine 46°30N 32°18E 291 E5
Doaktown Canada 46°33N 66°8W 345 C6
Doan Hung Vietnam 21°30N 105°10E 310 B5
Doany Madag. 14°21S 49°30E 329 A8
Doba Chad 8°40N 16°50E 323 G9
Dobandi Pakistan 31°13N 66°50E 314 D2
Dobbyn Australia 19°44S 140°2E 334 B3
Dobele Latvia 56°37N 23°16E 281 H20
Doberai, Jazirah Indonesia 1°25S 133°0E 309 E8
Doblas Argentina 37°5S 64°0W 366 D3
Dobo Indonesia 5°45S 134°15E 309 F8
Doboj Bos.-H. 44°46N 18°4E 295 B8
Dobrich Bulgaria 43°37N 27°49E 295 C12
Dobruja Europe 44°30N 28°15E 289 F15
Dobrush Belarus 52°25N 31°22E 289 B16
Doc, Mui Vietnam 17°58N 106°30E 310 D6
Docker River = Kaltukatjara Australia 24°52S 129°5E 333 D4
Doctor Arroyo Mexico 23°40N 100°11W 358 C4
Doda India 33°10N 75°34E 315 C6
Doda, L. Canada 49°25N 75°13W 344 C4
Dodecanese Greece 36°35N 27°0E 295 F12
Dodekanisa = Dodecanese Greece 36°35N 27°0E 295 F12
Dodge City U.S.A. 37°45N 100°1W 352 G3
Dodge L. Canada 59°50N 105°36W 343 B7
Dodgeville U.S.A. 42°58N 90°8W 352 D8
Dodoma Tanzania 6°8S 35°45E 326 D4
Dodoma □ Tanzania 6°0S 36°0E 326 D4
Dodori ⌂ Kenya 1°55S 41°7E 326 C5
Dodsland Canada 51°50N 108°45W 343 C7
Dodson U.S.A. 48°24N 108°15W 348 B9
Doesburg Neths. 52°1N 6°9E 287 B6
Doetinchem Neths. 51°59N 6°18E 287 C6
Dog Creek Canada 51°35N 122°14W 342 C4
Dog L. Man., Canada 51°2N 98°31W 343 C9
Dog L. Ont., Canada 48°48N 89°30W 344 C2
Dogran Pakistan 31°48N 73°35E 314 D5
Doğubayazıt Turkey 39°31N 44°5E 316 B5
Doha = Ad Dawḥah Qatar 25°15N 51°35E 317 E6
Dohazari Bangla. 22°10N 92°5E 313 H18
Dohrighat India 26°16N 83°31E 315 F10
Doi Indonesia 2°14N 127°49E 309 D7
Doi Inthanon △ Thailand 18°33N 98°34E 310 C2
Doi Khuntan △ Thailand 18°33N 99°14E 310 C2
Doi Luang Thailand 18°30N 101°0E 310 C3
Doi Luang △ Thailand 19°22N 99°35E 310 C2
Doi Saket Thailand 18°52N 99°9E 310 C2
Doi Suthep △ Thailand 18°49N 98°53E 310 C2
Dois Irmãos, Sa. Brazil 9°0S 42°30W 365 E10
Dokkum Neths. 53°20N 5°59E 287 A5
Dokri Pakistan 27°25N 68°7E 314 F3
Dolak, Pulau Indonesia 8°0S 138°30E 309 F9
Dolbeau-Mistassini Canada 48°53N 72°14W 345 C5
Dole France 47°7N 5°31E 292 C6
Dolgellau U.K. 52°45N 3°53W 284 E4
Dolgelley = Dolgellau U.K. 52°45N 3°53W 284 E4
Dollard Neths. 53°20N 7°10E 287 A7
Dolo Ethiopia 4°11N 42°3E 319 G3
Dolomites = Dolomiti Italy 46°23N 11°51E 294 A4
Dolomiti Italy 46°23N 11°51E 294 A4
Dolores Argentina 36°20S 57°40W 366 D4
Dolores Uruguay 33°34S 58°15W 366 C4
Dolores U.S.A. 37°28N 108°30W 349 H9
Dolores → U.S.A. 38°49N 109°17W 348 G9
Dolphin, C. Falk. Is. 51°10S 59°0W 368 G5
Dolphin and Union Str. Canada 69°5N 114°45W 340 C8
Dom Pedrito Brazil 31°0S 54°40W 367 C5
Doma ⌂ Zimbabwe 16°28S 30°12E 327 F3
Domariaganj → India 26°17N 83°44E 315 F10
Domasi Malawi 15°15S 35°22E 327 F4
Dombarovskiy Russia 50°46N 59°32E 300 D6
Dombås Norway 62°4N 9°8E 280 E13
Dome Argus Antarctica 80°50S 76°30E 277 E12
Dome C. Antarctica 75°12S 123°37E 277 D17
Dome Fuji Antarctica 77°20S 39°45E 277 D5
Domel I. = Letsôk-aw Kyun Burma 11°30N 98°25E 311 G2
Domeyko Chile 29°0S 71°0W 366 B1
Domeyko, Cordillera Chile 24°30S 69°0W 366 A2
Dominador Chile 24°21S 69°20W 366 A2
Dominica ■ W. Indies 15°20N 61°20W 361 C7
Dominica Passage W. Indies 15°10N 61°20W 361 C7
Dominican Rep. ■ W. Indies 19°0N 70°30W 361 C5
Domodóssola Italy 46°7N 8°17E 292 C8
Domville, Mt. Australia 28°1S 151°15E 335 D5
Don → Russia 47°4N 39°18E 291 E6
Don → Aberds., U.K. 57°11N 2°5W 283 D6
Don → S. Yorks., U.K. 53°41N 0°52W 284 D7
Don, C. Australia 11°18S 131°46E 332 B5
Don Benito Spain 38°53N 5°51W 293 C3
Don Figuerero Mts. Jamaica 18°5N 77°36W 360 a
Don Sak Thailand 9°18N 99°41E 311 b
Dona Ana = Nhamaabué Mozam. 17°25S 35°5E 327 F4
Donaghadee U.K. 54°39N 5°33W 282 B6
Donaghmore Ireland 52°52N 7°36W 282 D4
Donald Australia 36°23S 143°0E 335 F3
Donaldsonville U.S.A. 30°6N 90°59W 356 F9
Donalsonville U.S.A. 31°3N 84°53W 357 F12
Donau = Dunărea → Europe 45°20N 29°40E 289 F15
Donauwörth Germany 48°43N 10°47E 288 D6
Doncaster U.K. 53°32N 1°6W 284 D6
Dondo Angola 9°45S 14°25E 324 F2
Dondo Mozam. 19°33S 34°46E 327 F3
Dondo, Teluk Indonesia 0°50N 120°30E 309 D6
Dondra Head Sri Lanka 5°55N 80°40E 312 S12
Donegal Ireland 54°39N 8°5W 282 B3
Donegal □ Ireland 54°53N 8°0W 282 B4
Donegal B. Ireland 54°31N 8°49W 282 B3
Donets → Russia 47°33N 40°55E 291 E7
Donets Basin Ukraine 49°0N 38°0E 278 F13
Donetsk Ukraine 48°0N 37°45E 291 E6
Dong Ba Thin Vietnam 12°8N 109°13E 311 F7
Dong Dang Vietnam 21°54N 106°42E 310 B6
Dong Giam Vietnam 19°25N 105°31E 310 C5
Dong Ha Vietnam 16°55N 107°8E 310 D6
Dong Hene Laos 16°40N 105°18E 310 D5
Dong Hoi Vietnam 17°29N 106°36E 310 D6
Dong Khe Vietnam 22°26N 106°27E 310 A6
Dong Ujimqin Qi China 45°32N 116°55E 306 B9
Dong Van Vietnam 23°16N 105°22E 310 A5
Dong Xoai Vietnam 11°32N 106°55E 311 G6
Dongara Australia 29°14S 114°57E 333 E1
Dongbei China 45°0N 125°0E 307 D13
Dongchuan China 26°8N 103°1E 304 D5
Dongco China 32°8N 84°50E 313 C14
Dongfang China 18°50N 108°33E 310 C7
Dongfeng China 42°40N 125°34E 307 C13
Donggala Indonesia 0°30S 119°40E 309 E5
Donggang China 39°52N 124°10E 307 E13
Dongguang China 37°50N 116°30E 306 F9
Donghae S. Korea 37°29N 129°7E 307 F15
Dongjingcheng China 44°5N 129°10E 307 B15
Dongnae S. Korea 35°12N 129°5E 307 G15
Dongning China 44°2N 131°5E 307 B16
Dongola Sudan 19°9N 30°22E 323 E12
Dongping China 35°55N 116°20E 306 G9
Dongsheng China 39°50N 110°0E 306 E6
Dongtai China 32°51N 120°21E 307 H11
Dongting Hu China 29°18N 112°45E 305 D6
Donington, C. Australia 34°45S 136°0E 335 E2
Doniphan U.S.A. 36°37N 90°50W 352 G8
Dønna Norway 66°6N 12°30E 280 C15
Donna U.S.A. 26°9N 98°4W 356 H5
Donnacona Canada 46°41N 71°41W 345 C5
Donnelly's Crossing N.Z. 35°42S 173°38E 331 A4
Donnybrook Australia 33°34S 115°48E 333 F2
Donnybrook S. Africa 29°59S 29°48E 329 D4
Donora U.S.A. 40°11N 79°52W 354 F5
Donostia = Donostia-San Sebastián Spain 43°17N 1°58W 293 A5
Donostia-San Sebastián Spain 43°17N 1°58W 293 A5
Doon → U.K. 55°27N 4°39W 283 F4
Dora, L. Australia 22°0S 123°0E 332 D3
Dora Báltea → Italy 45°11N 8°3E 292 D8
Doran L. Canada 61°13N 108°6W 343 A7
Dorchester U.K. 50°42N 2°27W 285 G5
Dorchester, C. Canada 65°27N 77°27W 341 C12
Dordabis Namibia 22°52S 17°38E 328 C2
Dordogne → France 45°2N 0°36W 292 D3
Dordrecht Neths. 51°48N 4°39E 287 C4
Dordrecht S. Africa 31°20S 27°3E 328 E4
Doré L. Canada 54°46N 107°17W 343 C7
Dori Burkina Faso 14°3N 0°2W 322 F5
Doring → S. Africa 31°54S 18°39E 328 E2
Doringbos S. Africa 31°59S 19°16E 328 E2
Dorking U.K. 51°14N 0°19W 285 F7
Dornbirn Austria 47°25N 9°45E 288 E5
Dornie U.K. 57°17N 5°31W 283 D3
Dornoch U.K. 57°53N 4°2W 283 D4
Dornoch Firth U.K. 57°51N 4°4W 283 D4
Dornogovĭ □ Mongolia 44°0N 110°0E 306 C6
Doro, Kavo Greece 38°9N 24°38E 295 E11
Dorohoi Romania 47°56N 26°23E 289 E14
Döröö Nuur Mongolia 48°0N 93°0E 304 B4
Dorr Iran 33°17N 50°38E 317 C6
Dorre I. Australia 25°13S 113°12E 333 E1
Dorrigo Australia 30°20S 152°44E 335 E5

Dorris U.S.A. 41°58N 121°55W 348 F3
Dorset Canada 45°14N 78°54W 354 A6
Dorset U.S.A. 41°40N 80°40W 354 E4
Dorset □ U.K. 50°45N 2°26W 285 G5
Dortmund Germany 51°30N 7°28E 288 C4
Doruma Dem. Rep. of the Congo 4°42N 27°33E 326 B2
Dorūneh Iran 35°10N 57°18E 317 C8
Dos Bahías, C. Argentina 44°58S 65°32W 368 E3
Dos Hermanas Spain 37°16N 5°55W 293 D3
Dos Palos U.S.A. 36°59N 120°37W 350 J6
Dosso Niger 13°0N 3°13E 322 F6
Dothan U.S.A. 31°13N 85°24W 357 F12
Doty U.S.A. 46°38N 123°17W 350 D3
Douai France 50°21N 3°4E 292 A5
Douala Cameroon 4°0N 9°45E 324 D1
Douarnenez France 48°6N 4°21W 292 B1
Double Island Pt. Australia 25°56S 153°11E 335 D5
Double Mountain Fork → U.S.A. 33°16N 100°0W 356 E4
Doubs → France 46°53N 5°1E 292 C6
Doubtful Sd. N.Z. 45°20S 166°49E 331 F1
Doubtless B. N.Z. 34°55S 173°26E 331 A4
Douglas I. of Man 54°10N 4°28W 284 C3
Douglas S. Africa 29°4S 23°46E 328 D3
Douglas Ariz., U.S.A. 31°21N 109°33W 349 L9
Douglas Ga., U.S.A. 31°31N 82°51W 357 F13
Douglas Wyo., U.S.A. 42°45N 105°24W 348 E11
Douglas Apsley △ Australia 41°45S 148°11E 335 G4
Douglas Chan. Canada 53°40N 129°20W 342 C3
Douglas Pt. Canada 44°19N 81°37W 354 B3
Douglasville U.S.A. 33°45N 84°45W 357 E12
Dounreay U.K. 58°35N 3°44W 283 C5
Dourada, Serra Brazil 13°10S 48°45W 365 F9
Dourados Brazil 22°9S 54°50W 367 A5
Dourados → Brazil 21°58S 54°18W 367 A5
Dourados, Serra dos Brazil 23°30S 53°30W 367 A5
Douro → Europe 41°8N 8°40W 293 B1
Dove → U.K. 52°51N 1°36W 284 E6
Dove Creek U.S.A. 37°46N 108°54W 349 H9
Dover Australia 43°18S 147°2E 335 G4
Dover U.K. 51°7N 1°19E 285 F9
Dover Del., U.S.A. 39°10N 75°32W 353 F16
Dover N.H., U.S.A. 43°12N 70°56W 355 C14
Dover N.J., U.S.A. 40°53N 74°34W 355 F10
Dover Ohio, U.S.A. 40°32N 81°29W 354 F3
Dover, Pt. Australia 32°32S 125°32E 333 F4
Dover, Str. of Europe 51°0N 1°30E 285 G9
Dover-Foxcroft U.S.A. 45°11N 69°13W 353 C19
Dover Plains U.S.A. 41°43N 73°35W 355 E11
Dovey = Dyfi → U.K. 52°32N 4°3W 285 E3
Dovrefjell Norway 62°15N 9°33E 280 E13
Dow Rūd Iran 33°28N 49°4E 317 C6
Dowa Malawi 13°38S 33°58E 327 E3
Dowagiac U.S.A. 41°59N 86°6W 352 E10
Dowerin Australia 31°12S 117°2E 333 F2
Dowgha'i Iran 36°54N 58°32E 317 B8
Dowlatābād Iran 28°20N 56°40E 317 D8
Down □ U.K. 54°23N 6°2W 282 B5
Downey Calif., U.S.A. 33°56N 118°9W 351 M8
Downey Idaho, U.S.A. 42°26N 112°7W 348 E7
Downham Market U.K. 52°37N 0°23E 285 E8
Downieville U.S.A. 39°34N 120°50W 350 F6
Downpatrick U.K. 54°20N 5°43W 282 B6
Downpatrick Hd. Ireland 54°20N 9°21W 282 B2
Downsville U.S.A. 42°5N 75°0W 355 D10
Downton, Mt. Canada 52°42N 124°52W 342 C4
Dowsārī Iran 28°25N 57°59E 317 D8
Doyle U.S.A. 40°2N 120°6W 350 E6
Doylestown U.S.A. 40°21N 75°10W 355 F9
Dozois, Rés. Canada 47°30N 77°5W 344 C4
Dra Khel Pakistan 27°58N 66°45E 314 F2
Drâa, C. Morocco 28°47N 11°0W 322 C3
Drâa, Oued → Morocco 28°40N 11°10W 322 C3
Drachten Neths. 53°7N 6°5E 287 A6
Drăgăşani Romania 44°39N 24°17E 289 F13
Dragichyn Belarus 52°15N 25°8E 289 B13
Dragoman, Prokhod Bulgaria 42°58N 22°53E 295 C10
Dragon's Mouths = Boca de Dragon Venezuela 11°0N 61°50W 365 K15
Draguignan France 43°32N 6°27E 292 E7
Drain U.S.A. 43°40N 123°19W 348 E2
Drake U.S.A. 47°55N 100°23W 352 B3
Drake Passage S. Ocean 58°0S 68°0W 277 B17
Drakensberg S. Africa 31°0S 28°0E 329 D4
Drama Greece 41°9N 24°10E 295 D11
Drammen Norway 59°42N 10°12E 281 G14
Drangajökull Iceland 66°9N 22°15W 280 C2
Dras India 34°25N 75°48E 315 B6
Drastis, Akra Greece 39°48N 19°40E 297 A3
Drau = Drava → Croatia 45°33N 18°55E 295 B8
Drava → Croatia 45°33N 18°55E 295 B8
Drayton Valley Canada 53°12N 114°58W 342 C6
Drenthe □ Neths. 52°52N 6°40E 287 B6
Drepano, Akra Greece 35°28N 24°14E 297 D6
Drepanum, C. Cyprus 34°54N 32°19E 297 E11
Dresden Canada 42°35N 82°11W 354 D2
Dresden Germany 51°3N 13°44E 288 C7
Dreux France 48°44N 1°23E 292 B4
Driffield U.K. 54°0N 0°26W 284 C7
Driftwood U.S.A. 41°20N 78°8W 354 E6
Driggs U.S.A. 43°44N 111°6W 348 E8
Drin → Albania 42°1N 19°38E 295 C8
Drina → Bos.-H. 44°53N 19°21E 295 B8
Drøbak Norway 59°39N 10°39E 281 G14
Drobeta-Turnu Severin Romania 44°39N 22°41E 289 F12
Drochia Moldova 48°2N 27°48E 289 D14
Drogheda Ireland 53°43N 6°22W 282 C5
Drogichin = Dragichyn Belarus 52°15N 25°8E 289 B13
Drogobych = Drohobych Ukraine 49°20N 23°30E 289 D12
Drohobych Ukraine 49°20N 23°30E 289 D12
Droichead Atha = Drogheda Ireland 53°43N 6°22W 282 C5
Droichead Nua Ireland 53°11N 6°48W 282 C5
Droitwich U.K. 52°16N 2°8W 285 E5
Drôme → France 44°46N 4°46E 292 D6
Dromedary, C. Australia 36°17S 150°10E 335 F5
Dromore U.K. 54°31N 7°28W 282 B4
Dromore West Ireland 54°15N 8°52W 282 B3
Dronfield U.K. 53°19N 1°27W 284 D6
Dronning Maud Land Antarctica 72°30S 12°0E 277 D3
Dronten Neths. 52°32N 5°43E 287 B5
Druk Yul = Bhutan ■ Asia 27°25N 90°30E 313 F17
Drumbo Canada 43°16N 80°35W 354 C4
Drumcliff Ireland 54°20N 8°29W 282 B3
Drumheller Canada 51°25N 112°40W 342 C6
Drummond U.S.A. 46°40N 113°9W 348 C7
Drummond I. U.S.A. 46°1N 83°39W 353 B12
Drummond Pt. Australia 34°9S 135°16E 335 E2
Drummond Ra. Australia 23°45S 147°10E 334 C4
Drummondville Canada 45°55N 72°25W 344 C5
Drumright U.S.A. 35°59N 96°36W 356 D6
Druskininkai Lithuania 54°3N 23°58E 281 J20
Drut → Belarus 53°8N 30°5E 289 B16
Druzhina Russia 68°14N 145°18E 301 C15
Dry Harbour Mts. Jamaica 18°19N 77°24W 360 a
Dry Tortugas U.S.A. 24°38N 82°55W 357 F13
Dryden Canada 49°47N 92°50W 343 D10
Dryden U.S.A. 42°30N 76°18W 355 D8
Drygalski I. Antarctica 66°0S 92°0E 277 C7
Drygalski Ice Tongue Antarctica 75°24S 163°30E 277 D21
Drysdale → Australia 13°59S 126°51E 332 B4
Drysdale I. Australia 11°41S 136°0E 334 A2
Drysdale River △ Australia 14°56S 127°2E 332 B4
Du Gué → Canada 57°21N 70°45W 344 A5
Du Quoin U.S.A. 38°1N 89°14W 352 F9
Duanesburg U.S.A. 42°45N 74°11W 355 D10
Duaringa Australia 23°42S 149°42E 334 C4
Duarte, Pico Dom. Rep. 19°2N 70°59W 361 D5
Ḍubā Si. Arabia 27°10N 35°40E 316 E2
Dubai = Dubayy U.A.E. 25°18N 55°20E 317 E7
Dubăsari Moldova 47°15N 29°10E 289 E15
Dubăsari Vdkhr. Moldova 47°30N 29°0E 289 E15
Dubawnt → Canada 64°33N 100°6W 343 A8
Dubawnt L. Canada 63°8N 101°28W 343 A8
Dubayy U.A.E. 25°18N 55°20E 317 E7
Dubbo Australia 32°11S 148°35E 335 E4
Dubele Dem. Rep. of the Congo 2°56N 29°35E 326 B2
Dublin Ireland 53°21N 6°15W 282 C5
Dublin Ga., U.S.A. 32°32N 82°54W 357 E13
Dublin Tex., U.S.A. 32°5N 98°21W 356 E5
Dublin □ Ireland 53°24N 6°20W 282 C5
Dublin ✕ (DUB) Ireland 53°26N 6°15W 282 C5
Dubno Ukraine 50°25N 25°45E 289 C13
Dubois Idaho, U.S.A. 44°10N 112°14W 348 D7
Dubois Pa., U.S.A. 41°7N 78°46W 354 E6
Dubossary = Dubăsari Moldova 47°15N 29°10E 289 E15
Dubossary Vdkhr. = Dubăsari Vdkhr. Moldova 47°30N 29°0E 289 E15
Dubovka Russia 49°5N 44°50E 291 E7
Dubrajpur India 23°48N 87°25E 315 H12
Dubréka Guinea 9°46N 13°31W 322 G3
Dubrovitsa = Dubrovytsya Ukraine 51°31N 26°35E 289 C14
Dubrovnik Croatia 42°39N 18°6E 295 C8
Dubrovytsya Ukraine 51°31N 26°35E 289 C14
Dubuque U.S.A. 42°30N 90°41W 352 D8
Duchesne U.S.A. 40°10N 110°24W 348 F8
Duchess Australia 21°20S 139°50E 334 C2
Ducie I. Pac. Oc. 24°40S 124°48W 337 K15
Duck → U.S.A. 36°2N 87°52W 357 C11
Duck Cr. → Australia 22°37S 116°53E 332 D2
Duck Lake Canada 52°50N 106°16W 343 C7
Duck Mountain ⌂ Canada 51°45N 101°0W 343 C8
Duckwall, Mt. U.S.A. 37°58N 120°7W 350 H6
Dudhi India 24°15N 83°10E 315 G10
Dudinka Russia 69°30N 86°13E 301 C9
Dudley U.K. 52°31N 2°5W 285 E5
Dudwa India 28°30N 80°41E 315 E9
Dudwa △ India 28°30N 80°40E 315 E9
Duero = Douro → Europe 41°8N 8°40W 293 B1
Dufftown U.K. 57°27N 3°8W 283 D5
Dugi Otok Croatia 44°0N 15°3E 288 G8
Duisburg Germany 51°26N 6°45E 288 C4
Duiwelskloof = Modjadjiskloof S. Africa 23°42S 30°10E 329 C5
Dūkdamīn Iran 35°59N 57°43E 317 C8
Dukelský Průsmyk Slovak Rep. 49°25N 21°42E 289 D11
Dukhān Qatar 25°25N 50°50E 317 E6
Duki Pakistan 30°14N 68°25E 312 D6
Duku Nigeria 10°43N 10°43E 323 F8
Dulce U.S.A. 36°56N 107°0W 349 H10
Dulce → Argentina 30°32S 62°33W 366 C3
Dulce, G. Costa Rica 8°40N 83°20W 360 E3
Dulf Iraq 35°7N 45°51E 316 C5
Duliu China 39°2N 116°55E 306 E9
Dullewala Pakistan 31°50N 71°25E 314 D4
Dullstroom S. Africa 25°27S 30°7E 329 D5
Dulq Maghār Syria 36°22N 38°39E 316 B3
Duluth U.S.A. 46°47N 92°6W 352 B7
Dum Dum India 22°39N 88°33E 315 H13
Dum Duma India 27°40N 95°40E 313 F19
Dūmā Syria 33°34N 36°24E 318 B5
Dumaguete Phil. 9°17N 123°15E 309 C6
Dumai Indonesia 1°35N 101°28E 308 D2
Dumaran Phil. 10°33N 119°50E 309 B5
Dumas Ark., U.S.A. 33°53N 91°29W 356 E9
Dumas Tex., U.S.A. 35°52N 101°58W 356 D4
Ḍumayr Syria 33°39N 36°42E 318 B5
Dumbarton U.K. 55°57N 4°33W 283 F4
Dumbleyung Australia 33°17S 117°42E 333 F2
Dumfries U.K. 55°4N 3°37W 283 F5
Dumfries & Galloway □ U.K. 55°9N 3°58W 283 F5
Dumka India 24°12N 87°15E 315 G12
Dumoine → Canada 46°13N 77°51W 344 C4
Dumoine, L. Canada 46°55N 77°55W 344 C4
Dumont d'Urville Antarctica 67°0S 110°0E 277 C10
Dumraon India 25°33N 84°8E 315 G11
Dumyât Egypt 31°24N 31°48E 323 B12
Dún Dealgan = Dundalk Ireland 54°1N 6°24W 282 B5
Dún Laoghaire Ireland 53°17N 6°8W 282 C5
Duna = Dunărea → Europe 45°20N 29°40E 289 F15
Dunagiri India 30°31N 79°52E 315 D8
Dunaj = Dunărea → Europe 45°20N 29°40E 289 F15
Dunakeszi Hungary 47°37N 19°8E 289 E10
Dunărea → Europe 45°20N 29°40E 289 F15
Dunaújváros Hungary 46°58N 18°57E 289 E10
Dunav = Dunărea → Europe 45°20N 29°40E 289 F15
Dunay Russia 42°52N 132°22E 302 C6
Dunback N.Z. 45°23S 170°36E 331 F3
Dunbar U.K. 56°0N 2°31W 283 E6
Dunblane U.K. 56°11N 3°58W 283 E5
Duncan Canada 48°45N 123°40W 350 B3
Duncan Ariz., U.S.A. 32°43N 109°6W 349 K9
Duncan Okla., U.S.A. 34°30N 97°57W 356 D6
Duncan, L. Canada 53°29N 77°58W 344 B4
Duncan L. Canada 62°51N 113°58W 342 A6
Duncan Town Bahamas 22°15N 75°45W 360 B4
Duncannon U.S.A. 40°23N 77°2W 354 F7
Duncansby Head U.K. 58°38N 3°1W 283 C5
Duncansville U.S.A. 40°25N 78°26W 354 F6
Dundalk Canada 44°10N 80°24W 354 B4
Dundalk Ireland 54°1N 6°24W 282 B5
Dundalk U.S.A. 39°15N 76°31W 353 F15
Dundalk Bay Ireland 53°55N 6°15W 282 C5
Dundas = Uummannaq Greenland 77°28N 69°13W 276 B4
Dundas Canada 43°17N 79°59W 354 C5
Dundas, L. Australia 32°35S 121°50E 333 F3
Dundas I. Canada 54°30N 130°50W 342 C2
Dundas Str. Australia 11°15S 131°35E 332 B5
Dundee S. Africa 28°11S 30°15E 329 D5
Dundee U.K. 56°28N 2°59W 283 E6
Dundee U.S.A. 42°32N 76°59W 354 D8
Dundee City □ U.K. 56°30N 2°58W 283 E6
Dundgovĭ □ Mongolia 45°10N 106°0E 306 B4
Dundrum U.K. 54°16N 5°52W 282 B6
Dundrum B. U.K. 54°13N 5°47W 282 B6
Dunedin N.Z. 45°50S 170°33E 331 F3
Dunedin U.S.A. 28°1N 82°46W 357 G13
Dunfanaghy Ireland 55°11N 7°58W 282 A4
Dunfermline U.K. 56°5N 3°27W 283 E5
Dungannon Canada 43°51N 81°36W 354 C3
Dungannon U.K. 54°31N 6°46W 282 B5
Dungarpur India 23°52N 73°45E 314 H5
Dungarvan Ireland 52°5N 7°37W 282 D4
Dungarvan Harbour Ireland 52°4N 7°35W 282 D4
Dungeness U.K. 50°54N 0°59E 285 G8
Dunglow Ireland 54°57N 8°21W 282 B3
Dungo, L. do Angola 17°15S 19°0E 328 B2
Dungog Australia 32°22S 151°46E 335 E5
Dungu Dem. Rep. of the Congo 3°40N 28°32E 326 B2
Dungun Malaysia 4°45N 103°25E 311 K4
Dunhua China 43°20N 128°14E 307 C15
Dunhuang China 40°8N 94°36E 304 B4
Dunk I. Australia 17°59S 146°29E 334 B4
Dunkeld Australia 33°25S 149°29E 335 E4
Dunkeld U.K. 56°34N 3°35W 283 E5
Dunkerque France 51°2N 2°20E 292 A5
Dunkery Beacon U.K. 51°9N 3°36W 285 F4
Dunkirk = Dunkerque France 51°2N 2°20E 292 A5
Dunkirk U.S.A. 42°29N 79°20W 354 D5
Dúnleary = Dún Laoghaire Ireland 53°17N 6°8W 282 C5
Dunleer Ireland 53°50N 6°24W 282 C5
Dunmanus B. Ireland 51°31N 9°50W 282 E2
Dunmanway Ireland 51°43N 9°6W 282 E2
Dunmarra Australia 16°42S 133°25E 334 B1
Dunmore U.S.A. 41°25N 75°38W 355 E9
Dunmore East Ireland 52°9N 7°0W 282 D5
Dunmore Hd. Ireland 52°10N 10°35W 282 D1
Dunmore Town Bahamas 25°30N 76°39W 360 A4
Dunn U.S.A. 35°19N 78°37W 357 D15
Dunnellon U.S.A. 29°3N 82°28W 357 G13
Dunnet Hd. U.K. 58°40N 3°21W 283 C5
Dunning U.S.A. 41°50N 100°6W 352 E3
Dunnville Canada 42°54N 79°36W 354 D5
Dunolly Australia 36°51S 143°44E 335 F3
Dunoon U.K. 55°57N 4°56W 283 F4
Duns U.K. 55°47N 2°20W 283 F6
Dunseith U.S.A. 48°50N 100°3W 352 A3
Dunshaughlin Ireland 53°31N 6°33W 282 C5
Dunsmuir U.S.A. 41°13N 122°16W 348 F2
Dunstable U.K. 51°53N 0°32W 285 F7
Dunstan Mts. N.Z. 44°53S 169°35E 331 F2
Dunster Canada 53°8N 119°50W 342 C5
Dunvegan U.K. 57°27N 6°35W 283 D2
Dunvegan L. Canada 60°8N 107°10W 343 A7
Duolun China 42°12N 116°28E 306 C9
Duong Dong Vietnam 10°13N 103°58E 311 G4
Dupree U.S.A. 45°4N 101°35W 352 C3
Dupuyer U.S.A. 48°13N 112°30W 348 B7
Duque de Caxias Brazil 22°46S 43°18W 367 A7
Durack → Australia 15°33S 127°52E 332 C4
Durack Ra. Australia 16°50S 127°40E 332 C4
Durance → France 43°55N 4°45E 292 E6
Durand U.S.A. 44°38N 91°58W 352 C8
Durango Mexico 24°3N 104°39W 358 C4
Durango U.S.A. 37°16N 107°53W 349 H10
Durango □ Mexico 24°50N 105°20W 358 C4
Durant Miss., U.S.A. 33°4N 89°51W 357 E10
Durant Okla., U.S.A. 33°59N 96°25W 356 E6
Durazno Uruguay 33°25S 56°31W 366 C4
Durazzo = Durrës Albania 41°19N 19°28E 295 D8
Durban S. Africa 29°49S 31°1E 329 D5
Durbuy Belgium 50°21N 5°28E 287 D5
Düren Germany 50°48N 6°29E 288 C4
Durg = Bhilainagar-Durg India 21°13N 81°26E 313 J12
Durgapur India 23°30N 87°20E 315 H12
Durham Canada 44°10N 80°49W 354 B4
Durham U.K. 54°47N 1°34W 284 C6
Durham Calif., U.S.A. 39°39N 121°48W 350 F5
Durham N.C., U.S.A. 35°59N 78°54W 357 D15
Durham N.H., U.S.A. 43°8N 70°56W 355 C14
Durham □ U.K. 54°42N 1°45W 284 C6
Ḍurmā Si. Arabia 24°37N 46°8E 316 E5
Durmitor Montenegro 43°10N 19°0E 295 C8
Durness U.K. 58°34N 4°45W 283 C4
Durrës Albania 41°19N 19°28E 295 D8
Durrow Ireland 52°51N 7°24W 282 D4
Dursey I. Ireland 51°36N 10°12W 282 E1
Dursley U.K. 51°40N 2°21W 285 F5
Dursunbey Turkey 39°35N 28°37E 295 E13
Duru Dem. Rep. of the Congo 4°14N 28°50E 326 B2
Durūz, Jabal ad Jordan 32°35N 36°40E 318 C5
D'Urville, Tanjung Indonesia 1°28S 137°54E 309 E9
D'Urville I. N.Z. 40°50S 173°55E 331 D4
Duryea U.S.A. 41°20N 75°45W 355 E9
Dushak Turkmenistan 37°13N 60°1E 317 B9
Dushanbe Tajikistan 38°33N 68°48E 300 F7
Dushore U.S.A. 41°31N 76°24W 355 E8
Dusky Sd. N.Z. 45°47S 166°30E 331 F1
Dussejour, C. Australia 14°45S 128°13E 332 B4
Düsseldorf Germany 51°14N 6°47E 288 C4
Dutch Harbor U.S.A. 53°53N 166°32W 346 a
Dutlwe Botswana 23°58S 23°46E 328 C3
Dutton Canada 42°39N 81°30W 354 D3
Dutton → Australia 20°44S 143°10E 334 C3
Dutywa S. Africa 32°8S 28°18E 329 E4
Duwayhin, Khawr U.A.E. 24°20N 51°25E 317 E6
Duyfken Pt. Australia 12°33S 141°38E 334 A3
Duyun China 26°18N 107°29E 304 D5
Dvina, Severnaya → Russia 64°32N 40°30E 290 B7
Dvinsk = Daugavpils Latvia 55°53N 26°32E 281 J22
Dvinskaya Guba Russia 65°0N 39°0E 290 B6
Dwarka India 22°18N 69°8E 314 H3
Dwellingup Australia 32°43S 116°4E 333 F2
Dwight Canada 45°20N 79°1W 354 A5
Dwight U.S.A. 41°5N 88°26W 352 E9
Dyatlovo = Dzyatlava Belarus 53°28N 25°28E 289 B13
Dyce U.K. 57°13N 2°12W 283 D6
Dyer, C. Canada 66°37N 61°16W 341 C13
Dyer Bay Canada 45°10N 81°20W 354 A3
Dyer Plateau Antarctica 70°45S 65°30W 277 D17
Dyersburg U.S.A. 36°3N 89°23W 357 C10
Dyfi → U.K. 52°32N 4°3W 285 E3
Dymer Ukraine 50°47N 30°18E 289 C16
Dysart Australia 22°32S 148°23E 334 C4
Dzaoudzi Mayotte 12°47S 45°16E 325 a
Dzerzhinsk Russia 56°14N 43°30E 290 C7
Dzhalinda Russia 53°26N 124°0E 301 D13
Dzhambul = Taraz Kazakhstan 42°54N 71°22E 300 E8
Dzhankoy Ukraine 45°40N 34°20E 291 E5
Dzhezkazgan = Zhezqazghan Kazakhstan 47°44N 67°40E 300 E7
Dzhizak = Jizzakh Uzbekistan 40°6N 67°50E 300 E7
Dzhugdzur, Khrebet Russia 57°30N 138°0E 301 D14
Dzhungarskiye Vorota = Dzungarian Gate Asia 45°10N 82°0E 304 B3
Działdowo Poland 53°15N 20°15E 289 B11
Dzibilchaltún Mexico 21°10N 89°35W 359 C7
Dzierżoniów Poland 50°45N 16°39E 289 C9
Dzilam de Bravo Mexico 21°24N 88°53W 359 C7
Dzūkija △ Lithuania 54°10N 24°30E 281 J21
Dzungaria = Junggar Pendi China 44°30N 86°0E 304 B3
Dzungarian Basin = Junggar Pendi China 44°30N 86°0E 304 B3
Dzungarian Gate Asia 45°10N 82°0E 304 B3
Dzüünmod Mongolia 47°45N 106°58E 306 B4
Dzyarzhynsk Belarus 53°40N 27°1E 289 B14
Dzyatlava Belarus 53°28N 25°28E 289 B13

E

E.C. Manning ⌂ Canada 49°5N 120°45W 342 D4
Eabamet L. Canada 51°30N 87°46W 344 B2
Eads U.S.A. 38°29N 102°47W 348 G12
Eagar U.S.A. 34°6N 109°17W 349 J9
Eagle Alaska, U.S.A. 64°47N 141°12W 340 C5
Eagle Colo., U.S.A. 39°39N 106°50W 348 G10
Eagle → Canada 53°36N 57°26W 345 B8
Eagle Butte U.S.A. 45°0N 101°10W 352 C3
Eagle Grove U.S.A. 42°40N 93°54W 352 D7
Eagle L. Canada 49°42N 93°13W 343 D10
Eagle L. Calif., U.S.A. 40°39N 120°45W 348 F3
Eagle L. Maine, U.S.A. 46°20N 69°22W 353 B19
Eagle Lake Canada 45°8N 78°29W 354 A6
Eagle Lake Maine, U.S.A. 47°3N 68°36W 353 B19
Eagle Lake Tex., U.S.A. 29°35N 96°20W 356 G6
Eagle Mountain U.S.A. 33°49N 115°27W 351 M11
Eagle Nest U.S.A. 36°33N 105°16W 349 H11
Eagle Pass U.S.A. 28°43N 100°30W 356 G4
Eagle Pk. U.S.A. 38°10N 119°25W 350 G7
Eagle Pt. Australia 16°11S 124°23E 332 C3
Eagle River Mich., U.S.A. 47°25N 88°18W 352 B9
Eagle River Wis., U.S.A. 45°55N 89°15W 352 C9
Eaglehawk Australia 36°44S 144°15E 335 F3
Eagles Mere U.S.A. 41°25N 76°33W 355 E8
Ealing □ U.K. 51°31N 0°20W 285 F7
Ear Falls Canada 50°38N 93°13W 343 C10
Earle U.S.A. 35°16N 90°28W 357 D9
Earlimart U.S.A. 35°53N 119°16W 351 K7
Earn → U.K. 56°21N 3°18W 283 E5
Earn, L. U.K. 56°23N 4°13W 283 E4
Earnslaw, Mt. N.Z. 44°32S 168°27E 331 F2
Earth U.S.A. 34°14N 102°24W 356 D3
Easley U.S.A. 34°50N 82°36W 357 D13
East Anglia U.K. 52°30N 1°0E 284 E9
East Angus Canada 45°30N 71°40W 345 C5
East Antarctica Antarctica 80°0S 90°0E 277 D7
East Aurora U.S.A. 42°46N 78°37W 354 D6
East Ayrshire □ U.K. 55°26N 4°11W 283 F4
East Bengal Bangla. 24°0N 90°0E 313 G17
East Beskids = Vychodné Beskydy Europe 49°20N 22°0E 289 D11
East Brady U.S.A. 40°59N 79°37W 354 F5
East C. = Dezhneva, Mys Russia 66°5N 169°40W 301 C19
East C. N.Z. 37°42S 178°35E 331 B7
East Caroline Basin Pac. Oc. 4°0N 146°45E 336 G6
East Chicago U.S.A. 41°38N 87°27W 352 E10
East China Sea Asia 30°0N 126°0E 305 D7
East Coulee Canada 51°23N 112°27W 342 C6
East Dereham = Dereham U.K. 52°41N 0°57E 285 E8
East Dunbartonshire □ U.K. 55°57N 4°13W 283 F4
East Falkland Falk. Is. 51°30S 58°30W 368 G5
East Grand Forks U.S.A. 47°56N 97°1W 352 B5
East Greenwich U.S.A. 41°40N 71°27W 355 E13
East Grinstead U.K. 51°7N 0°0 285 F8
East Hartford U.S.A. 41°46N 72°39W 355 E12
East Helena U.S.A. 46°35N 111°56W 348 C8
East Indies Asia 0°0 120°0E 298 J14
East Kilbride U.K. 55°47N 4°11W 283 F4
East Lamma Channel China 22°14N 114°9E 305 G11
East Lansing U.S.A. 42°44N 84°29W 353 D11
East Liverpool U.S.A. 40°37N 80°35W 354 F4
East London S. Africa 33°0S 27°55E 329 E4
East Lothian □ U.K. 55°58N 2°44W 283 F6
East Main = Eastmain Canada 52°10N 78°30W 344 B4
East Mariana Basin Pac. Oc. 12°0N 153°0E 336 F7
East Northport U.S.A. 40°53N 73°20W 355 F11
East Orange U.S.A. 40°46N 74°12W 355 F10
East Pacific Rise Pac. Oc. 15°0S 110°0W 337 J17
East Palestine U.S.A. 40°50N 80°33W 354 F4
East Pine Canada 55°48N 120°12W 342 B4
East Point U.S.A. 33°41N 84°25W 357 E12
East Providence U.S.A. 41°49N 71°23W 355 E13
East Pt. Br. Virgin Is. 18°40N 64°18W 361 e
East Pt. Canada 46°27N 61°58W 345 C7
East Renfrewshire □ U.K. 55°46N 4°21W 283 F4
East Retford = Retford U.K. 53°19N 0°56W 284 D7
East Riding of Yorkshire □ U.K. 53°55N 0°30W 284 D7
East Rochester U.S.A. 43°7N 77°29W 354 C7
East St. Louis U.S.A. 38°37N 90°9W 352 F8
East Schelde = Oosterschelde → Neths. 51°33N 4°0E 287 C4
East Sea = Japan, Sea of Asia 40°0N 135°0E 302 E7
East Siberian Sea Russia 73°0N 160°0E 301 B17
East Stroudsburg U.S.A. 41°1N 75°11W 355 E9
East Sussex □ U.K. 50°56N 0°19E 285 G8
East Tasman Plateau Pac. Oc. 43°30S 152°0E 336 M7
East Tawas U.S.A. 44°17N 83°29W 353 C12
East Timor ■ Asia 8°50S 126°0E 309 F7
East Toorale Australia 30°27S 145°28E 335 E4
East Walker → U.S.A. 38°52N 119°10W 350 G7
East Windsor U.S.A. 40°17N 74°34W 355 F10
Eastbourne N.Z. 41°19S 174°55E 331 D5
Eastbourne U.K. 50°46N 0°18E 285 G8
Eastend Canada 49°32N 108°50W 343 D7
Easter Fracture Zone Pac. Oc. 25°0S 115°0W 337 K16
Easter I. = Pascua, I. de Chile 27°7S 109°23W 337 K17
Eastern □ Kenya 0°0 38°30E 326 C4
Eastern Cape □ S. Africa 32°0S 26°0E 328 E4
Eastern Cr. → Australia 20°40S 141°35E 334 C3
Eastern Ghats India 14°0N 78°50E 312 N11
Eastern Group = Lau Group Fiji 17°0S 178°30W 331 a
Eastern Group Australia 33°30S 124°30E 333 F3

Eastern Transvaal = Mpumalanga □ S. Africa 26°0S 30°0E 329 D5
Easterville Canada 53°8N 99°49W 343 C9
Easthampton U.S.A. 42°16N 72°40W 355 D12
Eastlake U.S.A. 41°40N 81°26W 354 E3
Eastland U.S.A. 32°24N 98°49W 356 E5
Eastleigh U.K. 50°58N 1°21W 285 G6
Eastmain Canada 52°10N 78°30W 344 B4
Eastmain → Canada 52°27N 78°26W 344 B4
Eastman Canada 45°18N 72°19W 355 A12
Eastman U.S.A. 32°12N 83°11W 357 E13
Easton Md., U.S.A. 38°47N 76°5W 353 F15
Easton Pa., U.S.A. 40°41N 75°13W 355 F9
Easton Wash., U.S.A. 47°14N 121°11W 350 C5
Eastport U.S.A. 44°56N 67°0W 353 C20
Eastsound U.S.A. 48°42N 122°55W 350 B4
Eaton U.S.A. 40°32N 104°42W 348 F11
Eatonia Canada 51°13N 109°25W 343 C7
Eatonton U.S.A. 33°20N 83°23W 357 E13
Eatontown U.S.A. 40°19N 74°4W 355 F10
Eatonville U.S.A. 46°52N 122°16W 350 D4
Eau Claire U.S.A. 44°49N 91°30W 352 C8
Eau Claire, L. à l' Canada 56°10N 74°25W 344 A5
Eauripik Rise Pac. Oc. 2°0N 142°0E 336 G6
Ebano Mexico 22°13N 98°24W 359 C5
Ebbw Vale U.K. 51°46N 3°12W 285 F4
Ebeltoft Denmark 56°12N 10°41E 281 H14
Ebensburg U.S.A. 40°29N 78°44W 354 F6
Eberswalde-Finow Germany 52°50N 13°49E 288 B7
Ebetsu Japan 43°7N 141°34E 302 C10
Ebey's Landing ⌂ U.S.A. 48°12N 122°41W 350 B4
Ebinur Hu China 44°55N 82°55E 304 B3
Ebolowa Cameroon 2°55N 11°10E 324 D2
Ebonda Dem. Rep. of the Congo 2°12N 22°21E 324 D4
Ebro → Spain 40°43N 0°54E 293 B6
Ecatepec de Morelos Mexico 19°36N 99°3W 359 D5
Eceabat Turkey 40°11N 26°21E 295 D12
Ech Chéliff Algeria 36°10N 1°20E 322 A6
Echigo-Sammyaku Japan 36°50N 139°50E 303 F9
Echizen-Misaki Japan 35°59N 135°57E 303 G7
Echo Bay N.W.T., Canada 66°5N 117°55W 340 C8
Echo Bay Ont., Canada 46°29N 84°4W 344 C3
Echoing → Canada 55°51N 92°5W 344 B1
Echternach Lux. 49°49N 6°25E 287 E6
Echuca Australia 36°10S 144°45E 335 F3
Ecija Spain 37°30N 5°10W 293 D3
Eclipse I. Australia 35°5S 117°58E 333 G2
Eclipse Is. Australia 13°54S 126°19E 332 B4
Eclipse Sd. Canada 72°38N 79°0W 341 B12
Ecuador ■ S. Amer. 2°0S 78°0W 364 D3
Ed Damazin Sudan 11°46N 34°21E 323 F12
Ed Dar el Beida = Casablanca Morocco 33°36N 7°36W 322 B4
Ed Debba Sudan 18°0N 30°51E 323 E12
Ed Déffa Egypt 30°40N 26°30E 323 B11
Ed Dueim Sudan 14°0N 32°10E 323 F12
Edam Canada 53°11N 108°46W 343 C7
Edam Neths. 52°31N 5°3E 287 B5
Eday U.K. 59°11N 2°47W 283 B6
Eddrachillis B. U.K. 58°17N 5°14W 283 C3
Eddystone U.K. 50°11N 4°16W 285 G3
Eddystone Pt. Australia 40°59S 148°20E 335 G4
Ede Neths. 52°4N 5°40E 287 B5
Edehon L. Canada 60°25N 97°15W 343 A9
Edekel, Adrar Algeria 23°56N 6°47E 322 D7
Eden Australia 37°3S 149°55E 335 F4
Eden N.C., U.S.A. 36°29N 79°53W 357 C15
Eden N.Y., U.S.A. 42°39N 78°55W 354 D6
Eden Tex., U.S.A. 31°13N 99°51W 356 F5
Eden → U.K. 54°57N 3°1W 284 C4
Edenburg S. Africa 29°43S 25°58E 328 D4
Edendale S. Africa 29°39S 30°18E 329 D5
Edenderry Ireland 53°21N 7°4W 282 C4
Edenton U.S.A. 36°4N 76°39W 357 C16
Edenville S. Africa 27°37S 27°34E 329 D4
Eder → Germany 51°12N 9°28E 288 C5
Edessa Greece 40°48N 22°5E 295 D10
Edgar U.S.A. 40°22N 97°58W 352 E5
Edgartown U.S.A. 41°23N 70°31W 355 E14
Edge Hill U.K. 52°8N 1°26W 285 E6
Edgefield U.S.A. 33°47N 81°56W 357 E14
Edgeley U.S.A. 46°22N 98°43W 352 B4
Edgemont U.S.A. 43°18N 103°50W 352 D2
Edgeøya Svalbard 77°45N 22°30E 276 B9
Édhessa = Edessa Greece 40°48N 22°5E 295 D10
Edievale N.Z. 45°49S 169°22E 331 F2
Edina U.S.A. 40°10N 92°11W 352 E7
Edinboro U.S.A. 41°52N 80°8W 354 E4
Edinburg U.S.A. 26°18N 98°10W 356 H5
Edinburgh U.K. 55°57N 3°13W 283 F5
Edinburgh ✕ (EDI) U.K. 55°54N 3°22W 283 F5
Edinburgh, City of □ U.K. 55°57N 3°17W 283 F5
Edineţ Moldova 48°9N 27°18E 289 D14
Edirne Turkey 41°40N 26°34E 295 D12
Edison U.S.A. 48°33N 122°27W 350 B4
Edithburgh Australia 35°5S 137°43E 335 F2
Edmeston U.S.A. 42°42N 75°15W 355 D9
Edmond U.S.A. 35°39N 97°29W 356 D6
Edmonds U.S.A. 47°48N 122°22W 350 C4
Edmonton Australia 17°2S 145°46E 334 B4
Edmonton Canada 53°30N 113°30W 342 C6
Edmund L. Canada 54°45N 93°17W 344 B1
Edmundston Canada 47°23N 68°20W 345 C6
Edna U.S.A. 28°59N 96°39W 356 G6
Edremit Turkey 39°34N 27°0E 295 E12
Edremit Körfezi Turkey 39°30N 26°45E 295 E12
Edson Canada 53°35N 116°28W 342 C5
Eduardo Castex Argentina 35°50S 64°18W 366 D3
Edward → Australia 35°5S 143°30E 335 F3
Edward, L. Africa 0°25S 29°40E 326 C2
Edward VII Land Antarctica 80°0S 150°0W 277 E13
Edwards Calif., U.S.A. 34°50N 117°40W 351 L9
Edwards N.Y., U.S.A. 44°20N 75°15W 355 B9
Edwards Plateau U.S.A. 30°45N 101°20W 356 F4
Edwardsville U.S.A. 41°15N 75°56W 355 E9
Edzná Mexico 19°39N 90°19W 359 D6
Edzo Canada 62°49N 116°4W 342 A5
Eeklo Belgium 51°11N 3°33E 287 C3
Eesti = Estonia ■ Europe 58°30N 25°30E 281 G21
Effigy Mounds ⌂ U.S.A. 43°5N 91°11W 352 D8
Effingham U.S.A. 39°7N 88°33W 352 F9
Égadi, Ísole Italy 37°55N 12°16E 294 F5
Egan Range U.S.A. 39°35N 114°55W 348 G6
Eganville Canada 45°32N 77°5W 354 A7
Eger = Cheb Czech Rep. 50°9N 12°28E 288 C7
Eger Hungary 47°53N 20°27E 289 E11
Egersund Norway 58°26N 6°1E 281 G12
Egg L. Canada 55°5N 105°30W 343 B7
Éghezée Belgium 50°35N 4°55E 287 D4
Egio Greece 38°15N 22°5E 295 E10
Eglinton I. Canada 75°48N 118°30W 341 B8
Egmont Canada 49°45N 123°56W 342 D4
Egmont, C. N.Z. 39°16S 173°45E 331 C4
Egmont, Mt. = Taranaki, Mt. N.Z. 39°17S 174°5E 331 C5
Egmont △ N.Z. 39°17S 174°4E 331 C5
Egra India 21°54N 87°32E 315 J12
Eğridir Turkey 37°52N 30°51E 291 G5
Eğridir Gölü Turkey 37°53N 30°50E 316 B1
Egvekinot Russia 66°19N 179°50W 301 C19
Egypt ■ Africa 28°0N 31°0E 323 C12
Ehime □ Japan 33°30N 132°40E 303 H6
Ehrenberg U.S.A. 33°36N 114°31W 351 M12
Eibar Spain 43°11N 2°28W 293 A4
Eidsvold Australia 25°25S 151°12E 335 D5
Eidsvoll Norway 60°19N 11°14E 281 F14
Eifel Germany 50°15N 6°50E 288 C4
Eiffel Flats Zimbabwe 18°20S 30°0E 327 F3
Eigg U.K. 56°54N 6°10W 283 E2
Eighty Mile Beach Australia 19°30S 120°40E 332 C3
Eil Somali Rep. 8°0N 49°50E 319 F4
Eil, L. U.K. 56°51N 5°16W 283 E3
Eildon, L. Australia 37°10S 146°0E 335 F4
Eilean Sar = Western Isles □ U.K. 57°30N 7°10W 283 D1
Einasleigh Australia 18°32S 144°5E 334 B3
Einasleigh → Australia 17°30S 142°17E 334 B3
Eindhoven Neths. 51°26N 5°28E 287 C5
Eire = Ireland ■ Europe 53°50N 7°52W 282 C4
Eiríksjökull Iceland 64°46N 20°24W 280 D3
Eirunepé Brazil 6°35S 69°53W 364 E5
Eiseb → Namibia 20°33S 20°59E 328 C2
Eisenach Germany 50°58N 10°19E 288 C6
Eisenerz Austria 47°32N 14°54E 288 E8
Eivissa Spain 38°54N 1°26E 296 C7
Ejeda Madag. 24°20S 44°31E 329 C7
Ejutla Mexico 16°34N 96°44W 359 D5
Ekalaka U.S.A. 45°53N 104°33W 348 D11
Ekenäs = Tammisaari Finland 60°0N 23°26E 281 G20
Eketahuna N.Z. 40°38S 175°43E 331 D5
Ekibastuz Kazakhstan 51°50N 75°10E 300 D8
Ekoli Dem. Rep. of the Congo 0°23S 24°13E 326 C1
Eksjö Sweden 57°40N 14°58E 281 H16
Ekuma → Namibia 18°40S 16°2E 328 B2
Ekwan → Canada 53°12N 82°15W 344 B3
Ekwan Pt. Canada 53°16N 82°7W 344 B3
El Aaiún W. Sahara 27°9N 13°12W 322 C3
El Abanico Chile 37°20S 71°31W 366 D1
El 'Agrûd Egypt 30°14N 34°24E 318 E3
El 'Alamein Egypt 30°48N 28°58E 323 B11
El 'Aqaba, W. → Egypt 30°7N 33°54E 318 E2
El Arīḥā West Bank 31°52N 35°27E 318 D4
El 'Arîsh Egypt 31°8N 33°50E 318 D2
El 'Arîsh, W. → Egypt 31°8N 33°47E 318 D2
El Asnam = Ech Chéliff Algeria 36°10N 1°20E 322 A6
El Bayadh Algeria 33°40N 1°1E 322 B6
El Bluff Nic. 11°59N 83°40W 360 D3
El Cajon U.S.A. 32°48N 116°58W 351 N10
El Campo U.S.A. 29°12N 96°16W 356 G6
El Capitan U.S.A. 37°44N 119°38E 350 H7
El Centro U.S.A. 32°48N 115°34W 351 N11
El Cerro Bolivia 17°30S 61°40W 364 G6
El Compadre Mexico 32°20N 116°14W 351 N10
El Cuy Argentina 39°55S 68°25W 368 D3
El Cuyo Mexico 21°31N 87°41W 359 C7
El Daheir Egypt 31°13N 34°10E 318 D3
El Dere Somali Rep. 3°50N 47°8E 319 G4
El Descanso Mexico 32°12N 116°58W 351 N10
El Desemboque Mexico 30°33N 113°1W 358 A2
El Diviso Colombia 1°22N 78°14W 364 C3
El Djouf Mauritania 20°0N 9°0W 322 D4
El Dorado Mexico 24°17N 107°21W 358 C3
El Dorado Ark., U.S.A. 33°12N 92°40W 356 E8
El Dorado Kans., U.S.A. 37°49N 96°52W 352 G5
El Dorado Venezuela 6°55N 61°37W 364 B6
El Dorado Springs U.S.A. 37°52N 94°1W 352 G6
El Escorial Spain 40°35N 4°7W 293 B3
El Faiyûm Egypt 29°19N 30°50E 323 C12
El Fâsher Sudan 13°33N 25°26E 323 F11
El Ferrol = Ferrol Spain 43°29N 8°15W 293 A1
El Fuerte Mexico 26°25N 108°39W 358 B3
El Gal Somali Rep. 10°58N 50°20E 319 E5
El Geneina = Al Junaynah Sudan 13°27N 22°45E 323 F10
El Gezira □ Sudan 15°0N 33°0E 323 F12
El Gîza Egypt 30°0N 31°12E 323 C12
El Gogorrón △ Mexico 21°49N 100°57W 358 C4
El Goléa Algeria 30°30N 2°50E 322 B6
El Golfo de Santa Clara Mexico 31°42N 114°30W 358 A2
El Guácharo △ Venezuela 10°8N 63°21W 361 D7
El Guache △ Venezuela 9°45N 69°30W 361 E6
El Iskandariya Egypt 31°13N 29°58E 323 B11
El Istiwa'iya Sudan 5°0N 28°0E 323 G11
El Jadida Morocco 33°11N 8°17W 322 B4
El Jardal Honduras 14°54N 88°50W 360 D2
El Kef □ Tunisia 36°0N 9°0E 323 A7
El Khârga Egypt 25°30N 30°33E 323 C12
El Khartûm Sudan 15°31N 32°35E 323 E12
El Khartûm Bahrî Sudan 15°40N 32°31E 323 E12
El Kuntilla Egypt 30°1N 34°45E 318 E3
El Lucero Mexico 30°37N 106°31W 358 A3
El Maestrazgo Spain 40°30N 0°25W 293 B5
El Mahalla el Kubra Egypt 31°0N 31°0E 323 B12
El Malpais ⌂ U.S.A. 34°53N 108°0W 349 J10
El Mansûra Egypt 31°0N 31°19E 323 B12
El Medano Canary Is. 28°3N 16°32W 296 F3
El Milagro Argentina 30°59S 65°59W 366 C2
El Minyâ Egypt 28°7N 30°33E 323 C12
El Monte U.S.A. 34°4N 118°1W 351 L8
El Obeid Sudan 13°8N 30°10E 323 F12
El Odaiya Sudan 12°8N 28°12E 323 F11
El Oro Mexico 19°51N 100°7W 359 D4
El Oued Algeria 33°20N 6°58E 322 B7
El Palmar △ Argentina 32°10S 58°31W 366 C4
El Palmito, Presa Mexico 25°40N 105°30W 358 B3
El Paso U.S.A. 31°45N 106°29W 356 F1
El Pinacate y Gran Desierto de Altar = Gran Desierto del Pinacate ⌂ Mexico 31°51N 113°32W 358 A2
El Portal U.S.A. 37°41N 119°47W 350 H7
El Porvenir Mexico 31°15N 105°51W 358 A3
El Prat de Llobregat Spain 41°19N 2°5E 293 B7
El Progreso Honduras 15°26N 87°51W 360 C2
El Pueblito Mexico 29°6N 105°7W 358 B3
El Pueblo Canary Is. 28°36N 17°47W 296 F2
El Puerto de Santa María Spain 36°36N 6°13W 293 D2
El Qâhira Egypt 30°2N 31°13E 323 B12
El Qantara Egypt 30°51N 32°20E 318 E1
El Quseima Egypt 30°40N 34°15E 318 E3
El Real Panama 8°0N 77°40W 364 B3
El Reno U.S.A. 35°32N 97°57W 346 C7
El Rey △ Argentina 24°40S 64°34W 366 A3
El Rio U.S.A. 34°14N 119°10W 351 L7
El Roque, Pta. Canary Is. 28°10N 15°25W 296 F4
El Rosarito Mexico 28°38N 114°4W 358 B2
El Salto Mexico 23°47N 105°22W 358 C3
El Salvador ■ Cent. Amer. 13°50N 89°0W 360 D2
El Sauce Nic. 13°0N 86°40W 360 D2
El Sueco Mexico 29°54N 106°24W 358 B3
El Suweis Egypt 29°58N 32°31E 323 C12
El Tamarâni, W. → Egypt 30°7N 34°43E 318 E3
El Thamad Egypt 29°40N 34°28E 318 F3
El Tigre Venezuela 8°44N 64°15W 364 B6
El Tîh, Gebel Egypt 29°40N 33°50E 318 F2
El Tofo Chile 29°22S 71°18W 366 B1
El Tránsito Chile 28°52S 70°17W 366 B1
El Tûr Egypt 28°14N 33°36E 316 D2
El Turbio Argentina 51°45S 72°5W 368 G2
El Uqsur Egypt 25°41N 32°38E 323 C12
El Vergel Mexico 26°28N 106°22W 358 B3
El Vigía Venezuela 8°38N 71°39W 364 B4
El Wabeira Egypt 29°34N 33°6E 318 F2
El Wak Kenya 2°49N 40°56E 326 B5
El Wuz Sudan 15°5N 30°7E 323 E12
Elat Israel 29°30N 34°56E 318 F3
Elâzığ Turkey 38°37N 39°14E 316 B3
Elba Italy 42°46N 10°17E 294 C4
Elba U.S.A. 31°25N 86°4W 357 F11
Elbasan Albania 41°9N 20°9E 295 D9
Elbe U.S.A. 46°45N 122°10W 350 D4
Elbe → Europe 53°50N 9°0E 288 B5
Elbert, Mt. U.S.A. 39°7N 106°27W 348 G10
Elberton U.S.A. 34°7N 82°52W 357 D13
Elbeuf France 49°17N 1°2E 292 B4
Elbing = Elbląg Poland 54°10N 19°25E 289 A10
Elbistan Turkey 38°13N 37°15E 316 B3
Elbląg Poland 54°10N 19°25E 289 A10
Elbow Canada 51°7N 106°35W 343 C7
Elbrus Asia 43°21N 42°30E 291 F7
Elburz Mts. = Alborz, Reshteh-ye Kūhhā-ye Iran 36°0N 52°0E 317 C7
Elche Spain 38°15N 0°42W 293 C5
Elcho I. Australia 11°55S 135°45E 334 A2
Elda Spain 38°29N 0°47W 293 C5
Eldama Ravine Kenya 0°3N 35°43E 326 B4
Elde → Germany 53°7N 11°15E 288 B6
Eldon Mo., U.S.A. 38°21N 92°35W 352 F7
Eldon Wash., U.S.A. 47°33N 123°3W 350 C3
Eldora U.S.A. 42°22N 93°5W 352 D7
Eldorado Argentina 26°28S 54°43W 367 B5
Eldorado Canada 44°35N 77°31W 354 B7
Eldorado Ill., U.S.A. 37°49N 88°26W 352 G9
Eldorado Tex., U.S.A. 30°52N 100°36W 356 F4
Eldoret Kenya 0°30N 35°17E 326 B4
Eldred U.S.A. 41°58N 78°23W 354 E6
Elea, C. Cyprus 35°19N 34°4E 297 D13
Eleanora, Pk. Australia 32°57S 121°9E 333 F3
Elefantes → Africa 24°10S 32°40E 329 C5
Elektrostal Russia 55°41N 38°32E 290 C6
Elemi Triangle Africa 5°0N 35°20E 326 B4
Elephant Butte Res. U.S.A. 33°9N 107°11W 349 K10
Elephant I. Antarctica 61°0S 55°0W 277 C18
Eleuthera Bahamas 25°0N 76°20W 360 B4
Elgin Canada 44°36N 76°13W 355 B8
Elgin U.K. 57°39N 3°19W 283 D5
Elgin Ill., U.S.A. 42°2N 88°17W 352 D9
Elgin N. Dak., U.S.A. 46°24N 101°51W 352 B3
Elgin Oreg., U.S.A. 45°34N 117°55W 348 D5
Elgin Tex., U.S.A. 30°21N 97°22W 356 F6
Elgon, Mt. Africa 1°10N 34°30E 326 B3
Eliase Indonesia 8°21S 130°48E 309 F8
Elim Namibia 17°48S 15°31E 328 B2
Elim S. Africa 34°35S 19°45E 328 E2
Elista Russia 46°16N 44°14E 291 E7
Elizabeth Australia 34°42S 138°41E 335 E2
Elizabeth U.S.A. 40°39N 74°12W 355 F10
Elizabeth City U.S.A. 36°18N 76°14W 357 C16
Elizabethton U.S.A. 36°21N 82°13W 357 C13
Elizabethtown Ky., U.S.A. 37°42N 85°52W 353 G11
Elizabethtown N.Y., U.S.A. 44°13N 73°36W 355 B11
Elizabethtown Pa., U.S.A. 40°9N 76°36W 355 F8
Ełk Poland 53°50N 22°21E 289 B12
Elk → Canada 49°11N 115°14W 342 C5
Elk → U.S.A. 34°46N 87°16W 357 D11
Elk City U.S.A. 35°25N 99°25W 356 D5
Elk Creek U.S.A. 39°36N 122°32W 350 F4
Elk Grove U.S.A. 38°25N 121°22W 350 G5
Elk Island △ Canada 53°35N 112°59W 342 C6
Elk Lake Canada 47°40N 80°25W 344 C3
Elk Point Canada 53°54N 110°55W 343 C6
Elk River Idaho, U.S.A. 46°47N 116°11W 348 C5
Elk River Minn., U.S.A. 45°18N 93°35W 352 C7
Elkedra → Australia 21°8S 136°22E 334 C2
Elkhart Ind., U.S.A. 41°41N 85°58W 353 E11
Elkhart Kans., U.S.A. 37°0N 101°54W 352 G3
Elkhorn Canada 49°59N 101°14W 343 D8
Elkhorn → U.S.A. 41°8N 96°19W 352 E5
Elkhovo Bulgaria 42°10N 26°35E 295 C12
Elkin U.S.A. 36°15N 80°51W 357 C14
Elkins U.S.A. 38°55N 79°51W 353 F14
Elkland U.S.A. 41°59N 77°19W 354 E7
Elko Canada 49°20N 115°10W 342 D5
Elko U.S.A. 40°50N 115°46W 348 F6
Elkton U.S.A. 43°49N 83°11W 354 C1
Ellas = Greece ■ Europe 40°0N 23°0E 295 E9
Ellef Ringnes I. Canada 78°30N 102°2W 341 B9
Ellen, Mt. U.S.A. 44°9N 72°56W 355 B12
Ellenburg U.S.A. 44°54N 73°48W 355 B11
Ellendale U.S.A. 46°0N 98°32W 352 B4
Ellensburg U.S.A. 46°59N 120°34W 348 C3
Ellenville U.S.A. 41°43N 74°24W 355 E10
Ellerton Barbados 13°7N 59°33W 361 g
Ellery, Mt. Australia 37°28S 148°47E 335 F4
Ellesmere, L. N.Z. 43°47S 172°28E 331 G4
Ellesmere I. Canada 79°30N 80°0W 341 B12
Ellesmere Port U.K. 53°17N 2°54W 284 D5
Ellice Is. = Tuvalu ■ Pac. Oc. 8°0S 178°0E 330 B10
Ellicottville U.S.A. 42°17N 78°40W 354 D6
Elliot Australia 17°33S 133°32E 334 B1
Elliot S. Africa 31°22S 27°48E 329 E4
Elliot Lake Canada 46°25N 82°35W 344 C3
Elliotdale = Xhora S. Africa 31°55S 28°38E 329 E4
Ellis U.S.A. 38°56N 99°34W 352 F4
Elliston Australia 33°39S 134°53E 335 E1
Ellisville U.S.A. 31°36N 89°12W 357 F10
Ellon U.K. 57°22N 2°4W 283 D6
Ellore = Eluru India 16°48N 81°8E 313 L12
Ellsworth Kans., U.S.A. 38°44N 98°14W 352 F4
Ellsworth Maine, U.S.A. 44°33N 68°25W 353 C19
Ellsworth Land Antarctica 76°0S 89°0W 277 D16
Ellsworth Mts. Antarctica 78°30S 85°0W 277 D16
Ellwood City U.S.A. 40°52N 80°17W 354 F4
Elma Canada 49°52N 95°55W 343 D9
Elma U.S.A. 47°0N 123°25W 350 D3
Elmalı Turkey 36°44N 29°56E 291 G4
Elmhurst U.S.A. 41°53N 87°56W 352 E10
Elmira Canada 43°36N 80°33W 354 C4
Elmira U.S.A. 42°6N 76°48W 354 D8
Elmira Heights U.S.A. 42°8N 76°50W 354 D8
Elmore Australia 36°30S 144°37E 335 F3
Elmshorn Germany 53°43N 9°40E 288 B5
Elmvale Canada 44°35N 79°52W 354 B5
Elora Canada 43°41N 80°26W 354 C4
Elounda Greece 35°16N 25°42E 297 D7
Eloy U.S.A. 32°45N 111°33W 349 K8
Elrose Canada 51°12N 108°0W 343 C7
Elsie U.S.A. 45°52N 123°36W 350 E3
Elsinore = Helsingør Denmark 56°2N 12°35E 281 H15
Eltanin Fracture Zone System S. Ocean 54°0S 130°0W 277 B14
Eltham N.Z. 39°26S 174°19E 331 C5
Eluru India 16°48N 81°8E 313 L12
Elvas Portugal 38°50N 7°10W 293 C2
Elverum Norway 60°53N 11°34E 280 F14
Elvire → Australia 17°51S 128°11E 332 C4
Elvire, Mt. Australia 29°22S 119°36E 333 E2
Elwell, L. = Tiber Res. U.S.A. 48°19N 111°6W 348 B8
Elwood Ind., U.S.A. 40°17N 85°50W 353 E11
Elwood Nebr., U.S.A. 40°36N 99°52W 352 E4
Elx = Elche Spain 38°15N 0°42W 293 C5
Ely U.K. 52°24N 0°16E 285 E8
Ely Minn., U.S.A. 47°55N 91°51W 352 B8
Ely Nev., U.S.A. 39°15N 114°54W 348 G6
Elyria U.S.A. 41°22N 82°7W 354 E2
Emāmrūd Iran 36°30N 55°0E 317 B7
Embarcación Argentina 23°10S 64°0W 366 A3
Embarras Portage Canada 58°27N 111°28W 343 B6
Embetsu Japan 44°44N 141°47E 302 B10
Embi Kazakhstan 48°50N 58°8E 300 E6
Embi → Kazakhstan 46°55N 53°28E 291 E9
Embonas Greece 36°13N 27°51E 297 C9
Embrun France 44°34N 6°30E 292 D7
Embu Kenya 0°32S 37°38E 326 C4
Emden Germany 53°21N 7°12E 288 B4
Emerald Australia 23°32S 148°10E 334 C4
Emerson Canada 49°0N 97°10W 343 D9
Emet Turkey 39°20N 29°15E 295 E13
Emi Koussi Chad 19°45N 18°55E 323 E9
Eminabad Pakistan 32°2N 74°8E 314 C6
Emine, Nos Bulgaria 42°40N 27°56E 295 C12
Emissi, Tarso Chad 21°27N 18°36E 323 D9
Emlenton U.S.A. 41°11N 79°43W 354 E5
Emmaus S. Africa 29°2S 25°15E 328 D4
Emmaus U.S.A. 40°32N 75°30W 355 F9
Emmeloord Neths. 52°44N 5°46E 287 B5
Emmen Neths. 52°48N 6°57E 287 B6
Emmet Australia 24°45S 144°30E 334 C3
Emmetsburg U.S.A. 43°7N 94°41W 352 D6
Emmett Idaho, U.S.A. 43°52N 116°30W 348 E5
Emmett Mich., U.S.A. 42°59N 82°46W 354 D2
Emmonak U.S.A. 62°47N 164°31W 346 a
Emo Canada 48°38N 93°50W 343 D10
Empalme Mexico 27°58N 110°51W 358 B2
Empangeni S. Africa 28°50S 31°52E 329 D5
Empedrado Argentina 28°0S 58°46W 366 B4
Emperor Seamount Chain Pac. Oc. 40°0N 170°0E 336 D9
Emperor Trough Pac. Oc. 43°0N 175°30E 336 C9
Emporia Kans., U.S.A. 38°25N 96°11W 352 F5
Emporia Va., U.S.A. 36°42N 77°32W 353 G15
Emporium U.S.A. 41°31N 78°14W 354 E6
Empress Canada 50°57N 110°0W 343 C7
Empty Quarter = Rub' al Khālī Si. Arabia 19°0N 48°0E 319 D4
Ems → Germany 53°20N 7°12E 288 B4
Emsdale Canada 45°32N 79°19W 354 A5
Emu China 43°40N 128°6E 307 C15
Emu Park Australia 23°13S 150°50E 334 C5
'En 'Avrona Israel 29°43N 35°0E 318 F4
'En Boqeq Israel 31°12N 35°21E 317 D4
'En Gedi Israel 31°28N 35°25E 317 D4
En Nahud Sudan 12°45N 28°25E 323 F11
Ena Japan 35°25N 137°25E 303 G8
Enana Namibia 17°30S 16°23E 328 B2
Enard B. U.K. 58°5N 5°20W 283 C3
Enare = Inarijärvi Finland 69°0N 28°0E 280 B23
Enarotali Indonesia 3°55S 136°21E 309 E9
Encampment U.S.A. 41°12N 106°47W 348 F10
Encantadas, Serra Brazil 30°40S 53°0W 367 C5
Encarnación Paraguay 27°15S 55°50W 367 B4
Encarnación de Díaz Mexico 21°31N 102°14W 358 C4
Encinitas U.S.A. 33°3N 117°17W 351 M9
Encino U.S.A. 34°39N 105°28W 349 J11
Encounter B. Australia 35°45S 138°45E 335 F2
Endako Canada 54°6N 125°2W 342 C3
Endau Kenya 1°18S 38°31E 326 C4
Ende Indonesia 8°45S 121°40E 309 F6
Endeavour Str. Australia 10°45S 142°0E 334 A3
Enderbury I. Kiribati 3°8S 171°5W 336 H10
Enderby Canada 50°35N 119°10W 342 C5
Enderby Abyssal Plain S. Ocean 60°0S 40°0E 277 C5
Enderby I. Australia 20°35S 116°30E 332 D2
Enderby Land Antarctica 66°0S 53°0E 277 C5
Enderlin U.S.A. 46°38N 97°36W 352 B5
Endicott U.S.A. 42°6N 76°4W 355 D8
Endwell U.S.A. 42°6N 76°2W 355 D8
Endyalgout I. Australia 11°40S 132°35E 332 B5
Eneabba Australia 29°49S 115°16E 333 E2
Enewetak Atoll Marshall Is. 11°30N 162°15E 336 F8
Enez Turkey 40°45N 26°5E 295 D12
Enfer, Pte. d' Martinique 14°22N 60°54W 360 c
Enfield Canada 44°56N 63°32W 345 D7
Enfield Conn., U.S.A. 41°58N 72°36W 355 E12
Enfield N.C., U.S.A. 36°11N 77°41W 357 C16
Enfield N.H., U.S.A. 43°39N 72°9W 355 C12
Engadin Switz. 46°45N 10°10E 292 C9
Engaño, C. Dom. Rep. 18°30N 68°20W 361 C6
Engaño, C. Phil. 18°35N 122°23E 309 A6
Engaru Japan 44°3N 143°31E 302 B11
Engcobo = Ngcobo S. Africa 31°37S 28°0E 329 E4
Engels Russia 51°28N 46°6E 291 D8
Engemann L. Canada 58°0N 106°55W 343 B7
Enggano Indonesia 5°20S 102°40E 308 F2
England U.S.A. 34°33N 91°58W 356 D9
England □ U.K. 53°0N 2°0W 285 E5
Englee Canada 50°45N 56°5W 345 B8
Englehart Canada 47°49N 79°52W 344 C4
Englewood U.S.A. 39°38N 104°59W 348 G11
English → Canada 49°12N 91°5W 343 C10
English Bazar = Ingraj Bazar India 24°58N 88°10E 315 G13
English Channel Europe 50°0N 2°0W 285 G6
English Company's Is., The Australia 11°50S 136°32E 334 A2
English River Canada 49°14N 91°0W 344 C1
Enid U.S.A. 36°24N 97°53W 356 C6
Enkhuizen Neths. 52°42N 5°17E 287 B5
Enna Italy 37°34N 14°16E 294 F6
Ennadai Canada 61°8N 100°53W 343 A8
Ennadai L. Canada 60°58N 101°20W 343 A8
Ennedi Chad 17°15N 22°0E 323 E10
Enngonia Australia 29°21S 145°50E 335 D4
Ennis Ireland 52°51N 8°59W 282 D3
Ennis Mont., U.S.A. 45°21N 111°44W 348 D8
Ennis Tex., U.S.A. 32°20N 96°38W 356 E6
Enniscorthy Ireland 52°30N 6°34W 282 D5
Enniskillen U.K. 54°21N 7°39W 282 B4
Ennistimon Ireland 52°57N 9°17W 282 D2
Enns → Austria 48°14N 14°32E 288 D8
Eno Finland 62°47N 30°10E 280 E24
Enontekiö Finland 68°23N 23°37E 280 B20
Enosburg Falls U.S.A. 44°55N 72°48W 355 B12

Enriquillo, L. *Dom. Rep.* 18°20N 72°5W **361** C5
Enschede *Neths.* 52°13N 6°53E **287** B6
Ensenada *Argentina* 34°55S 57°55W **366** C4
Ensenada *Mexico* 31°52N 116°37W **358** A1
Ensenada de los Muertos *Mexico* 23°59N 109°51W **358** C2
Ensiola, Pta. de n' *Spain* 39°7N 2°55E **296** B9
Entebbe *Uganda* 0°4N 32°28E **326** B3
Enterprise *Canada* 60°47N 115°45W **342** A5
Enterprise *Ala., U.S.A.* 31°19N 85°51W **357** F12
Enterprise *Oreg., U.S.A.* 45°25N 117°17W **348** D5
Entre Ríos *Bolivia* 21°30S 64°25W **366** A3
Entre Ríos □ *Argentina* 30°30S 58°30W **366** C4
Entroncamento *Portugal* 39°28N 8°28W **293** C1
Enugu *Nigeria* 6°30N 7°30E **322** G7
Enumclaw *U.S.A.* 47°12N 121°59W **350** C5
Eólie, Ís. *Italy* 38°30N 14°57E **294** E6
Epe *Neths.* 52°21N 5°59E **287** B5
Épernay *France* 49°3N 3°56E **292** B5
Ephesus *Turkey* 37°55N 27°22E **295** F12
Ephraim *U.S.A.* 39°22N 111°35W **348** G8
Ephrata *Pa., U.S.A.* 40°11N 76°11W **355** F8
Ephrata *Wash., U.S.A.* 47°19N 119°33W **348** C4
Épinal *France* 48°10N 6°27E **292** B7
Episkopi *Cyprus* 34°40N 32°54E **297** E11
Episkopi *Greece* 35°20N 24°20E **297** D6
Episkopi Bay *Cyprus* 34°35N 32°50E **297** E11
Epsom *U.K.* 51°19N 0°16W **285** F7
Epukiro *Namibia* 21°40S 19°9E **328** C2
Equatoria = El Istiwa'iya *Sudan* 5°0N 28°0E **323** G11
Equatorial Guinea ■ *Africa* 2°0N 8°0E **324** D1
Er Rachidia *Morocco* 31°58N 4°20W **322** B5
Er Rahad *Sudan* 12°45N 30°32E **323** F12
Er Rif *Morocco* 35°1N 4°1W **322** A5
Erāwadī Myit = Irrawaddy → *Burma* 15°50N 95°6E **313** M19
Erāwadī Myitwanya = Irrawaddy, Mouths of the *Burma* 15°30N 95°0E **313** M19
Erbil = Arbīl *Iraq* 36°15N 44°5E **316** B5
Erçek *Turkey* 38°39N 43°36E **316** B4
Erciyaş Dağı *Turkey* 38°30N 35°30E **316** B2
Érd *Hungary* 47°22N 18°56E **289** E10
Erdao Jiang → *China* 42°37N 128°0E **307** C14
Erdek *Turkey* 40°23N 27°47E **295** D12
Erdene = Ulaan-Uul *Mongolia* 44°13N 111°10E **306** B6
Erdenet *Mongolia* 49°2N 104°5E **304** B5
Erdenetsogt *Mongolia* 42°55N 106°5E **306** C4
Erebus, Mt. *Antarctica* 77°35S 167°0E **277** D11
Erechim *Brazil* 27°35S 52°15W **367** B5
Ereğli *Konya, Turkey* 37°31N 34°4E **316** B2
Ereğli *Zonguldak, Turkey* 41°15N 31°24E **291** F5
Erenhot *China* 43°48N 112°2E **306** C7
Eresma → *Spain* 41°26N 4°45W **293** B3
Erfenisdam *S. Africa* 28°30S 26°50E **328** D4
Erfurt *Germany* 50°58N 11°2E **288** C6
Ergani *Turkey* 38°17N 39°49E **316** B3
Ergel *Mongolia* 43°8N 109°5E **306** C5
Ergeni Vozvyshennost *Russia* 47°0N 44°0E **291** E7
Ērgli *Latvia* 56°54N 25°38E **281** H21
Eriboll, L. *U.K.* 58°30N 4°42W **283** C4
Érice *Italy* 38°2N 12°35E **294** E5
Erie *U.S.A.* 42°8N 80°5W **354** D4
Erie, L. *N. Amer.* 42°15N 81°0W **354** D4
Erie Canal *U.S.A.* 43°5N 78°43W **354** C7
Erieau *Canada* 42°16N 81°57W **354** D3
Erigavo *Somali Rep.* 10°35N 47°20E **319** E4
Erikoussa *Greece* 39°53N 19°34E **297** A3
Eriksdale *Canada* 50°52N 98°7W **343** C9
Erimanthos *Greece* 37°57N 21°50E **295** F9
Erimo-misaki *Japan* 41°50N 143°15E **302** D11
Erin Pt. *Trin. & Tob.* 10°3N 61°39W **365** K15
Erinpura *India* 25°9N 73°3E **314** G5
Eriskay *U.K.* 57°4N 7°18W **283** D1
Eritrea ■ *Africa* 14°0N 38°30E **319** D2
Erlangen *Germany* 49°36N 11°0E **288** D6
Erldunda *Australia* 25°14S 133°12E **334** D1
Ermelo *Neths.* 52°18N 5°35E **287** B5
Ermelo *S. Africa* 26°31S 29°59E **329** D4
Ermenek *Turkey* 36°38N 33°0E **316** B2
Ermones *Greece* 39°37N 19°46E **297** A3
Ernakulam *India* 9°59N 76°22E **312** Q10
Erne → *Ireland* 54°30N 8°16W **282** B3
Erne, Lower L. *U.K.* 54°28N 7°47W **282** B4
Erne, Upper L. *U.K.* 54°14N 7°32W **282** B4
Ernest Giles Ra. *Australia* 27°0S 123°45E **333** E3
Erode *India* 11°24N 77°45E **312** P10
Eromanga *Australia* 26°40S 143°11E **335** D3
Erongo *Namibia* 21°39S 15°58E **328** C2
Erramala Hills *India* 15°30N 78°15E **312** M11
Erri-Nundra △ *Australia* 37°28S 148°5E **335** F4
Errigal *Ireland* 55°2N 8°6W **282** A3
Erris Hd. *Ireland* 54°19N 10°0W **282** B1
Erskine *U.S.A.* 47°40N 96°0W **352** B6
Ertis = Irtysh → *Russia* 61°4N 68°52E **300** C7
Erwin *U.S.A.* 36°9N 82°25W **357** C13
Erzgebirge *Germany* 50°27N 12°55E **288** C7
Erzin *Russia* 50°15N 95°10E **301** D10
Erzincan *Turkey* 39°46N 39°30E **316** B3
Erzurum *Turkey* 39°57N 41°15E **316** B4
Es Caló *Spain* 38°40N 1°30E **296** C8
Es Canar *Spain* 39°2N 1°36E **296** B8
Es Mercadal *Spain* 39°59N 4°5E **296** B11
Es Migjorn Gran *Spain* 39°57N 4°3E **296** B11
Es Sahrā' Esh Sharqîya *Egypt* 27°30N 32°30E **323** C12
Es Sînâ' *Egypt* 29°0N 34°0E **318** F3
Es Vedrà *Spain* 38°52N 1°12E **296** C7
Esambo *Dem. Rep. of the Congo* 3°48S 23°30E **326** C1
Esan-Misaki *Japan* 41°40N 141°10E **302** D10
Esashi *Hokkaidō, Japan* 44°56N 142°35E **302** B11
Esashi *Hokkaidō, Japan* 41°52N 140°7E **302** D10
Esbjerg *Denmark* 55°29N 8°29E **281** J13
Esbo = Espoo *Finland* 60°12N 24°40E **281** F21
Escalante *U.S.A.* 37°47N 111°36W **349** H8
Escalante → *U.S.A.* 37°24N 110°57W **349** H8
Escalón *Mexico* 26°45N 104°20W **358** B4
Escambia → *U.S.A.* 30°32N 87°11W **357** F11
Escanaba *U.S.A.* 45°45N 87°4W **352** C10
Esch-sur-Alzette *Lux.* 49°32N 6°0E **287** E6
Escondido *U.S.A.* 33°7N 117°5W **351** M9
Escuinapa de Hidalgo *Mexico* 22°50N 105°50W **358** C3
Escuintla *Guatemala* 14°20N 90°48W **360** D1
Esenguly *Turkmenistan* 37°37N 53°59E **300** F6
Eşfahān *Iran* 32°39N 51°43E **317** C6
Eşfahān □ *Iran* 32°50N 51°50E **317** C6
Esfarāyen *Iran* 37°4N 57°30E **317** B8
Esfideh *Iran* 33°39N 59°46E **317** C8
Esh Sham = Dimashq *Syria* 33°30N 36°18E **318** B5
Esha Ness *U.K.* 60°29N 1°38W **283** A7
Esher *U.K.* 51°21N 0°20W **285** F7
Eshkol △ *Israel* 31°20N 34°30E **318** D3
Eshowe *S. Africa* 28°50S 31°30E **329** D5
Esigodini *Zimbabwe* 20°18S 28°56E **329** C4
Esil = Ishim → *Russia* 57°45N 71°10E **300** D8
Esira *Madag.* 24°20S 46°42E **329** C8
Esk → *Dumf. & Gall., U.K.* 54°58N 3°2W **283** G5
Esk → *N. Yorks., U.K.* 54°30N 0°37W **284** C7
Eskān *Iran* 26°48N 63°9E **317** E9
Esker *Canada* 53°53N 66°25W **345** B6
Eskifjörður *Iceland* 65°3N 13°55W **280** D7
Eskilstuna *Sweden* 59°22N 16°32E **281** G17
Eskimo Point = Arviat *Canada* 61°6N 93°59W **343** A10
Eskişehir *Turkey* 39°50N 30°30E **291** G5
Esla → *Spain* 41°29N 6°3W **293** B2
Eslāmābād-e Gharb *Iran* 34°10N 46°30E **316** C5
Eslāmshahr *Iran* 35°40N 51°10E **317** C6
Eşme *Turkey* 38°23N 28°58E **295** E13
Esmeraldas *Ecuador* 1°0N 79°40W **364** C3
Esnagi L. *Canada* 48°36N 84°33W **344** C3
España = Spain ■ *Europe* 39°0N 4°0W **293** B4
Espanola *Canada* 46°15N 81°46W **344** C3
Espanola *U.S.A.* 35°59N 106°5W **349** J10
Esparta *Costa Rica* 9°59N 84°40W **360** E3
Esperance *Australia* 33°45S 121°55E **333** F3
Esperance B. *Australia* 33°48S 121°55E **333** F3
Esperance Harbour *St. Lucia* 14°4N 60°55W **361** f
Esperanza *Antarctica* 65°0S 55°0W **277** C18
Esperanza *Argentina* 31°29S 61°3W **366** C3
Esperanza *Puerto Rico* 18°6N 65°28W **361** d
Espichel, C. *Portugal* 38°22N 9°16W **293** C1
Espigão, Serra do *Brazil* 26°35S 50°30W **367** B5
Espinazo, Sierra del = Espinhaço, Serra do *Brazil* 17°30S 43°30W **365** G10
Espinhaço, Serra do *Brazil* 17°30S 43°30W **365** G10
Espinilho, Serra do *Brazil* 28°30S 55°0W **367** B5
Espírito Santo □ *Brazil* 20°0S 40°45W **365** H10
Espíritu Santo *Vanuatu* 15°15S 166°50E **330** C9
Espíritu Santo, B. del *Mexico* 19°20N 87°35W **359** D7
Espíritu Santo, I. *Mexico* 24°30N 110°22W **358** C2
Espita *Mexico* 21°1N 88°19W **359** C7
Espoo *Finland* 60°12N 24°40E **281** F21
Espungabera *Mozam.* 20°29S 32°45E **329** C5
Esquel *Argentina* 42°55S 71°20W **368** E2
Esquimalt *Canada* 48°26N 123°25W **350** B3
Esquina *Argentina* 30°0S 59°30W **366** C4
Essaouira *Morocco* 31°32N 9°42W **322** B4
Essebie *Dem. Rep. of the Congo* 2°58N 30°40E **326** B3
Essen *Belgium* 51°28N 4°28E **287** C4
Essen *Germany* 51°28N 7°2E **288** C4
Essendon, Mt. *Australia* 25°0S 120°29E **333** E3
Essequibo → *Guyana* 6°50N 58°30W **364** B7
Essex *Canada* 42°10N 82°49W **354** D2
Essex *Calif., U.S.A.* 34°44N 115°15W **351** L11
Essex *N.Y., U.S.A.* 44°19N 73°21W **355** B11
Essex □ *U.K.* 51°54N 0°27E **285** F8
Essex Junction *U.S.A.* 44°29N 73°7W **355** B11
Esslingen *Germany* 48°44N 9°18E **288** D5
Estación Camacho *Mexico* 24°25N 102°18W **358** C4
Estación Simón *Mexico* 24°42N 102°35W **358** C4
Estados, I. de Los *Argentina* 54°40S 64°30W **368** G4
Eşţahbānāt *Iran* 29°8N 54°4E **317** D7
Estância *Brazil* 11°16S 37°26W **365** F11
Estancia *U.S.A.* 34°46N 106°4W **349** J10
Estārm *Iran* 28°21N 58°21E **317** D8
Estcourt *S. Africa* 29°0S 29°53E **329** D4
Este △ *Dom. Rep.* 18°14N 68°42W **361** C6
Estelí *Nic.* 13°9N 86°22W **360** D2
Estellencs *Spain* 39°39N 2°29E **296** B9
Esterhazy *Canada* 50°37N 102°5W **343** C8
Estevan *Canada* 49°10N 102°59W **343** D8
Estevan Group *Canada* 53°3N 129°38W **342** C3
Estherville *U.S.A.* 43°24N 94°50W **352** D6
Eston *Canada* 51°8N 108°40W **343** C7
Estonia ■ *Europe* 58°30N 25°30E **281** G21
Estreito *Brazil* 6°32S 47°25W **365** E9
Estrela, Serra da *Portugal* 40°10N 7°45W **293** B2
Estremoz *Portugal* 38°51N 7°39W **293** C2
Estrondo, Serra do *Brazil* 7°20S 48°0W **365** E9
Esztergom *Hungary* 47°47N 18°44E **289** E10
Etah *India* 27°35N 78°40E **315** F8
Étampes *France* 48°26N 2°10E **292** B5
Etanga *Namibia* 17°55S 13°0E **328** B1
Etawah *India* 26°48N 79°6E **315** F8
Etawney L. *Canada* 57°50N 96°50W **343** B9
Etchojoa *Mexico* 26°55N 109°38W **358** B3
eThekwini = Durban *S. Africa* 29°49S 31°1E **329** D5
Ethel *U.S.A.* 46°32N 122°46W **350** D4
Ethelbert *Canada* 51°32N 100°25W **343** C8
Ethiopia ■ *Africa* 8°0N 40°0E **319** F3
Ethiopian Highlands *Ethiopia* 10°0N 37°0E **319** F2
Etive, L. *U.K.* 56°29N 5°10W **283** E3
Etna *Italy* 37°50N 14°55E **294** F6
Etoile *Dem. Rep. of the Congo* 11°33S 27°30E **327** E2
Etosha △ *Namibia* 19°0S 16°0E **328** B2
Etosha Pan *Namibia* 18°40S 16°30E **328** B2
Etowah *U.S.A.* 35°20N 84°32W **357** D12
Etrek *Turkmenistan* 37°36N 54°46E **317** B7
Ettelbruck *Lux.* 49°51N 6°5E **287** E6
Ettrick Water → *U.K.* 55°31N 2°55W **283** F6
Etuku *Dem. Rep. of the Congo* 3°42S 25°45E **326** C2
Etzná-Tixmucuy = Edzná *Mexico* 19°39N 90°19W **359** D6
Eua *Tonga* 21°22S 174°56W **331** c
Euboea = Evia *Greece* 38°30N 24°0E **295** E11
Eucla *Australia* 31°41S 128°52E **333** F4
Euclid *U.S.A.* 41°34N 81°32W **354** E3
Eucumbene, L. *Australia* 36°2S 148°40E **335** F4
Eudora *U.S.A.* 33°7N 91°16W **356** E9
Eufaula *Ala., U.S.A.* 31°54N 85°9W **357** F12
Eufaula *Okla., U.S.A.* 35°17N 95°35W **356** D7
Eufaula L. *U.S.A.* 35°18N 95°21W **356** D7
Eugene *U.S.A.* 44°5N 123°4W **348** D2
Eugowra *Australia* 33°22S 148°24E **335** E4
Eulo *Australia* 28°10S 145°3E **335** D4
Eungella △ *Australia* 20°57S 148°40E **334** C4
Eunice *La., U.S.A.* 30°30N 92°25W **356** F8
Eunice *N. Mex., U.S.A.* 32°26N 103°10W **349** K12
Eupen *Belgium* 50°37N 6°3E **287** D6
Euphrates = Furāt, Nahr al → *Asia* 31°0N 47°25E **316** D5
Eureka *Canada* 80°0N 85°56W **341** B11
Eureka *Calif., U.S.A.* 40°47N 124°9W **348** F1
Eureka *Kans., U.S.A.* 37°49N 96°17W **352** G5
Eureka *Mont., U.S.A.* 48°53N 115°3W **348** B6
Eureka *Nev., U.S.A.* 39°31N 115°58W **348** G6
Eureka *S. Dak., U.S.A.* 45°46N 99°38W **352** C4
Eureka, Mt. *Australia* 26°35S 121°35E **333** E3
Euroa *Australia* 36°44S 145°35E **335** F4
Europa, Île *Ind. Oc.* 22°20S 40°22E **325** J8
Europa, Picos de *Spain* 43°10N 4°49W **293** A3
Europa, Pta. de *Gib.* 36°3N 5°21W **293** D3
Europe 50°0N 20°0E **278** E10
Europoort *Neths.* 51°57N 4°10E **287** C4
Eustis *U.S.A.* 28°51N 81°41W **357** G14
Eutsuk L. *Canada* 53°20N 126°45W **342** C3
Evale *Angola* 16°33S 15°44E **328** B2
Evans *U.S.A.* 40°23N 104°41W **348** F11
Evans, L. *Canada* 50°50N 77°0W **344** B4
Evans City *U.S.A.* 40°46N 80°4W **354** F4
Evans Head *Australia* 29°7S 153°27E **335** D5
Evans Mills *U.S.A.* 44°6N 75°48W **355** B9
Evansburg *Canada* 53°36N 114°59W **342** C5
Evanston *Ill., U.S.A.* 42°3N 87°40W **352** D10
Evanston *Wyo., U.S.A.* 41°16N 110°58W **348** F8
Evansville *U.S.A.* 37°58N 87°35W **352** G10
Evaz *Iran* 27°46N 53°59E **317** E7
Eveleth *U.S.A.* 47°28N 92°32W **352** B7
Evensk *Russia* 62°12N 159°30E **301** C16
Everard, L. *Australia* 31°30S 135°0E **335** E2
Everard Ranges *Australia* 27°5S 132°28E **333** E5
Everest, Mt. *Nepal* 28°5N 86°58E **315** E12
Everett *Pa., U.S.A.* 40°1N 78°23W **354** F6
Everett *Wash., U.S.A.* 47°59N 122°12W **350** C4
Everglades, The *U.S.A.* 25°50N 81°0W **357** J14
Everglades △ *U.S.A.* 25°30N 81°0W **357** J14
Everglades City *U.S.A.* 25°52N 81°23W **357** J14
Evergreen *Ala., U.S.A.* 31°26N 86°57W **357** F11
Evergreen *Mont., U.S.A.* 48°14N 114°17W **348** B6
Evesham *U.K.* 52°6N 1°56W **285** E6
Evia *Greece* 38°30N 24°0E **295** E11
Evje *Norway* 58°36N 7°51E **281** G12
Évora *Portugal* 38°33N 7°57W **293** C2
Evowghlī *Iran* 38°43N 45°13E **316** B5
Évreux *France* 49°3N 1°8E **292** B4
Evros → *Greece* 41°40N 26°34E **295** D12
Évry *France* 48°38N 2°27E **292** B5
Évvoia = Evia *Greece* 38°30N 24°0E **295** E11
Ewe, L. *U.K.* 57°49N 5°38W **283** D3
Ewing *U.S.A.* 42°16N 98°21W **352** D4
Ewo *Congo* 0°48S 14°45E **324** E2
Exaltación *Bolivia* 13°10S 65°20W **364** F5
Excelsior Springs *U.S.A.* 39°20N 94°13W **352** F6
Exe → *U.K.* 50°41N 3°29W **285** G4
Exeter *Canada* 43°21N 81°29W **354** C3
Exeter *U.K.* 50°43N 3°31W **285** G4
Exeter *Calif., U.S.A.* 36°18N 119°9W **350** J7
Exeter *N.H., U.S.A.* 42°59N 70°57W **355** D14
Exmoor *U.K.* 51°12N 3°45W **285** F4
Exmoor △ *U.K.* 51°8N 3°42W **285** F4
Exmouth *Australia* 21°54S 114°10E **332** D1
Exmouth *U.K.* 50°37N 3°25W **285** G4
Exmouth G. *Australia* 22°15S 114°15E **332** D1
Exmouth Plateau *Ind. Oc.* 19°0S 114°0E **336** J3
Expedition △ *Australia* 25°41S 149°7E **335** D4
Expedition Ra. *Australia* 24°30S 149°12E **334** C4
Extremadura □ *Spain* 39°30N 6°5W **293** C2
Exuma Sound *Bahamas* 24°30N 76°20W **360** B4
Eyasi, L. *Tanzania* 3°30S 35°0E **326** C4
Eye Pen. *U.K.* 58°13N 6°10W **283** C2
Eyemouth *U.K.* 55°52N 2°5W **283** F6
Eyjafjörður *Iceland* 66°15N 18°30W **280** C4
Eyre (North), L. *Australia* 28°30S 137°20E **335** D2
Eyre (South), L. *Australia* 29°18S 137°25E **335** D2
Eyre, L. *Australia* 29°30S 137°26E **330** D6
Eyre Mts. *N.Z.* 45°25S 168°25E **331** F2
Eyre Pen. *Australia* 33°30S 136°17E **335** E2
Eysturoy *Færoe Is.* 62°13N 6°54W **280** E9
Eyvānkī *Iran* 35°24N 51°56E **317** C6
Ezine *Turkey* 39°48N 26°20E **295** E12
Ezouza → *Cyprus* 34°44N 32°27E **297** E11

F

F.Y.R.O.M. = Macedonia ■ *Europe* 41°53N 21°40E **295** D9
Faaa *Tahiti* 17°34S 149°35W **331** d
Faaone *Tahiti* 17°40S 149°21W **331** d
Fabala *Guinea* 9°44N 9°5W **322** G4
Fabens *U.S.A.* 31°30N 106°10W **356** F1
Fabriano *Italy* 43°20N 12°54E **294** C5
Fachi *Niger* 18°6N 11°34E **323** E8
Fada *Chad* 17°13N 21°34E **323** E10
Fada-n-Gourma *Burkina Faso* 12°10N 0°30E **322** F6
Faddeyevskiy, Ostrov *Russia* 76°0N 144°0E **301** B15
Fadghāmī *Syria* 35°53N 40°52E **316** C4
Faenza *Italy* 44°17N 11°53E **294** B4
Færoe Is. = Føroyar ☒ *Atl. Oc.* 62°0N 7°0W **280** F9
Făgăras *Romania* 45°48N 24°58E **289** F13
Fagersta *Sweden* 60°1N 15°46E **281** F16
Fagnano, L. *Argentina* 54°30S 68°0W **368** G3
Fahliān *Iran* 30°11N 51°28E **317** D6
Fahraj *Kermān, Iran* 29°0N 59°0E **317** D8
Fahraj *Yazd, Iran* 31°46N 54°36E **317** D7
Faial *Azores* 38°34N 28°42W **322** a
Faial *Madeira* 32°47N 16°53W **296** D3
Fair Haven *U.S.A.* 43°36N 73°16W **353** D17
Fair Hd. *U.K.* 55°14N 6°9W **282** A5
Fair Isle *U.K.* 59°32N 1°38W **286** B6
Fair Oaks *U.S.A.* 38°39N 121°16W **350** G5
Fairbanks *U.S.A.* 64°51N 147°43W **346** a
Fairbury *U.S.A.* 40°8N 97°11W **352** E5
Fairfax *U.S.A.* 44°40N 73°1W **355** B11
Fairfield *Ala., U.S.A.* 33°29N 86°55W **357** E11
Fairfield *Calif., U.S.A.* 38°15N 122°3W **350** G4
Fairfield *Conn., U.S.A.* 41°9N 73°16W **355** E11
Fairfield *Idaho, U.S.A.* 43°21N 114°44W **348** E6
Fairfield *Ill., U.S.A.* 38°23N 88°22W **352** F9
Fairfield *Iowa, U.S.A.* 40°56N 91°57W **352** E8
Fairfield *Tex., U.S.A.* 31°44N 96°10W **356** F6
Fairford *Canada* 51°37N 98°38W **343** C9
Fairhope *U.S.A.* 30°31N 87°54W **357** F11
Fairlie *N.Z.* 44°5S 170°49E **331** F3
Fairmead *U.S.A.* 37°5N 120°10W **350** H6
Fairmont *Minn., U.S.A.* 43°39N 94°28W **352** D6
Fairmont *W. Va., U.S.A.* 39°29N 80°9W **353** F13
Fairmount *Calif., U.S.A.* 34°45N 118°26W **351** L8
Fairmount *N.Y., U.S.A.* 43°5N 76°12W **355** C8
Fairplay *U.S.A.* 39°15N 106°2W **348** G10
Fairport *U.S.A.* 43°6N 77°27W **354** C7
Fairport Harbor *U.S.A.* 41°45N 81°17W **354** E3
Fairview *Canada* 56°5N 118°25W **342** B5
Fairview *Mont., U.S.A.* 47°51N 104°3W **348** C11
Fairview *Okla., U.S.A.* 36°16N 98°29W **356** C5
Fairweather, Mt. *U.S.A.* 58°55N 137°32W **342** B1
Faisalabad *Pakistan* 31°30N 73°5E **314** D5
Faith *U.S.A.* 45°2N 102°2W **352** C2
Faizabad *India* 26°45N 82°10E **315** F10
Fajardo *Puerto Rico* 18°20N 65°39W **361** d
Fajr, W. → *Si. Arabia* 29°10N 38°10E **316** D3
Fakenham *U.K.* 52°51N 0°51E **284** E8
Fakfak *Indonesia* 2°55S 132°18E **309** E8
Faku *China* 42°32N 123°21E **307** C12
Falaise *France* 48°54N 0°12W **292** B3
Falaise, Mui *Vietnam* 19°6N 105°45E **310** C5
Falam *Burma* 23°0N 93°45E **313** H18
Falcó, C. des *Spain* 38°50N 1°23E **296** C7
Falcón, Presa *Mexico* 26°35N 99°10W **359** B5
Falcon Lake *Canada* 49°42N 95°15W **343** D9
Falcon Res. *U.S.A.* 26°34N 99°10W **356** H5
Falconara Marittima *Italy* 43°37N 13°24E **294** C5
Falcone, C. del *Italy* 40°58N 8°12E **294** D3
Falconer *U.S.A.* 42°7N 79°12W **354** D5
Falefa *Samoa* 13°54S 171°31W **331** b
Falelatai *Samoa* 13°55S 171°59W **331** b
Falelima *Samoa* 13°32S 172°41W **331** b
Faleshty = Făleşti *Moldova* 47°32N 27°44E **289** E14
Făleşti *Moldova* 47°32N 27°44E **289** E14
Falfurrias *U.S.A.* 27°14N 98°9W **356** H5
Falher *Canada* 55°44N 117°15W **342** B5
Faliraki *Greece* 36°22N 28°12E **297** C10
Falkenberg *Sweden* 56°54N 12°30E **281** H15
Falkirk *U.K.* 56°0N 3°47W **283** F5
Falkirk □ *U.K.* 55°58N 3°49W **283** F5
Falkland *U.K.* 56°16N 3°12W **283** E5
Falkland Is. ☒ *Atl. Oc.* 51°30S 59°0W **368** G5
Falkland Sd. *Falk. Is.* 52°0S 60°0W **368** G5
Fall River *U.S.A.* 41°43N 71°10W **355** E13
Fallbrook *U.S.A.* 33°23N 117°15W **351** M9
Fallon *U.S.A.* 39°28N 118°47W **348** G4
Falls City *U.S.A.* 40°3N 95°36W **352** E6
Falls Creek *U.S.A.* 41°9N 78°48W **354** E6
Falmouth *Jamaica* 18°30N 77°40W **360** a
Falmouth *U.K.* 50°9N 5°5W **285** G2
Falmouth *U.S.A.* 41°33N 70°37W **355** E14
Falsa, Pta. *Mexico* 27°51N 115°3W **358** B1
False B. *S. Africa* 34°15S 18°40E **328** E2
Falso, C. *Honduras* 15°12N 83°21W **360** C3
Falster *Denmark* 54°45N 11°55E **281** J14
Falsterbo *Sweden* 55°23N 12°50E **281** J15
Fălticeni *Romania* 47°21N 26°20E **289** E14
Falun *Sweden* 60°37N 15°37E **280** F16
Famagusta *Cyprus* 35°8N 33°55E **297** D12
Famagusta Bay *Cyprus* 35°15N 34°0E **297** D13
Famalé *Niger* 14°33N 1°5E **322** F6
Famatina, Sierra de *Argentina* 27°30S 68°0W **366** B2
Family L. *Canada* 51°54N 95°27W **343** C9
Famoso *U.S.A.* 35°37N 119°12W **351** K7
Fan Xian *China* 35°55N 115°38E **306** G8
Fanad Hd. *Ireland* 55°17N 7°38W **282** A4
Fandriana *Madag.* 20°14S 47°21E **329** C8
Fang *Thailand* 19°55N 99°13E **310** C2
Fangcheng *China* 33°18N 112°59E **306** H7
Fangshan *China* 38°3N 111°25E **306** E6
Fangzi *China* 36°33N 119°10E **307** F10
Fanjakana *Madag.* 21°10S 46°53E **329** C8
Fanjiatun *China* 43°40N 125°15E **307** C13
Fanling *China* 22°30N 114°8E **305** F11
Fannich, L. *U.K.* 57°38N 4°59W **283** D4
Fannūj *Iran* 26°35N 59°38E **317** E8
Fanø *Denmark* 55°25N 8°25E **281** J13
Fano *Italy* 43°50N 13°1E **294** C5
Fanshi *China* 39°12N 113°20E **306** E7
Fao = Al Fāw *Iraq* 30°0N 48°30E **317** D6
Faqirwali *Pakistan* 29°27N 73°0E **314** E5
Far East = Dalnevostochnyy □ *Russia* 67°0N 140°0E **301** C14
Far East *Asia* 40°0N 130°0E **298** E14
Faradje *Dem. Rep. of the Congo* 3°50N 29°45E **326** B2
Farafangana *Madag.* 22°49S 47°50E **329** C8
Farāh *Afghan.* 32°20N 62°7E **312** C3
Farāh □ *Afghan.* 32°25N 62°10E **312** C3
Farahalana *Madag.* 14°26S 50°10E **329** A9
Faranah *Guinea* 10°3N 10°45W **322** F3
Farasān, Jazā'ir *Si. Arabia* 16°45N 41°55E **319** D3
Farasan Is. = Farasān, Jazā'ir *Si. Arabia* 16°45N 41°55E **319** D3
Faratsiho *Madag.* 19°24S 46°57E **329** B8
Fareham *U.K.* 50°51N 1°11W **285** G6
Farewell, C. *N.Z.* 40°29S 172°43E **331** D4
Farewell C. = Nunap Isua *Greenland* 59°48N 43°55W **338** D15
Farghona *Uzbekistan* 40°23N 71°19E **300** E8
Fargo *U.S.A.* 46°53N 96°48W **352** B5
Fār'iah, W. al → *West Bank* 32°12N 35°27E **318** C4
Faribault *U.S.A.* 44°18N 93°16W **352** C7
Faridabad *India* 28°26N 77°19E **314** E6
Faridkot *India* 30°44N 74°45E **314** D6
Faridpur *Bangla.* 23°15N 89°55E **315** H13
Faridpur *India* 28°13N 79°33E **315** E8
Farīmān *Iran* 35°40N 59°49E **317** C8
Farina *Australia* 30°3S 138°15E **335** E2
Fariones, Pta. *Canary Is.* 29°13N 13°28W **296** E6
Farleigh *Australia* 21°4S 149°8E **334** K7
Farmerville *U.S.A.* 32°47N 92°24W **356** E8
Farmingdale *U.S.A.* 40°12N 74°10W **355** F10
Farmington *Canada* 55°54N 120°30W **342** B4
Farmington *Calif., U.S.A.* 37°55N 120°59W **350** H6
Farmington *Maine, U.S.A.* 44°40N 70°9W **353** C18
Farmington *Mo., U.S.A.* 37°47N 90°25W **352** G8
Farmington *N.H., U.S.A.* 43°24N 71°4W **355** C13
Farmington *N. Mex., U.S.A.* 36°44N 108°12W **349** H9
Farmington *Utah, U.S.A.* 40°59N 111°53W **348** F8
Farmington → *U.S.A.* 41°51N 72°38W **355** E12
Farmville *U.S.A.* 37°18N 78°24W **353** G14
Farne Is. *U.K.* 55°38N 1°37W **284** B6
Farnham *Canada* 45°17N 72°59W **355** A12
Farnham, Mt. *Canada* 50°29N 116°30W **342** C5
Faro *Brazil* 2°10S 56°39W **365** D7
Faro *Canada* 62°11N 133°22W **340** C6
Faro *Portugal* 37°2N 7°55W **293** D2
Fårö *Sweden* 57°55N 19°5E **281** H18
Farquhar, C. *Australia* 23°50S 113°36E **333** D1
Farrars Cr. → *Australia* 25°35S 140°43E **334** D3
Farrāshband *Iran* 28°57N 52°5E **317** D7
Farrell *U.S.A.* 41°13N 80°30W **354** E4
Farrokhī *Iran* 33°50N 59°31E **317** C8
Farruch, C. = Ferrutx, C. *Spain* 39°47N 3°21E **296** B10
Fārs □ *Iran* 29°30N 55°0E **317** D7
Farsala *Greece* 39°17N 22°23E **295** E10
Farson *U.S.A.* 42°47N 109°26W **348** E9
Farsund *Norway* 58°5N 6°55E **281** G12
Fartak, Râs *Si. Arabia* 28°5N 34°34E **316** D2
Fartak, Ra's *Yemen* 15°38N 52°15E **319** D5
Fartura, Serra da *Brazil* 26°21S 52°52W **367** B5
Fārūj *Iran* 37°14N 58°14E **317** B8
Farvel, Kap = Nunap Isua *Greenland* 59°48N 43°55W **338** D15
Farwell *U.S.A.* 34°23N 103°2W **356** D3
Fāryāb □ *Afghan.* 36°0N 65°0E **312** B4
Fasā *Iran* 29°0N 53°39E **317** D7
Fasano *Italy* 40°50N 17°22E **294** D7
Fastiv *Ukraine* 50°7N 29°57E **289** C15
Fastnet Rock *Ireland* 51°22N 9°37W **282** E2
Fastov = Fastiv *Ukraine* 50°7N 29°57E **289** C15
Fatagar, Tanjung *Indonesia* 2°46S 131°57E **309** E8
Fatehabad *Haryana, India* 29°31N 75°27E **314** E6
Fatehabad *Ut. P., India* 27°1N 78°19E **314** F8
Fatehgarh *India* 27°25N 79°35E **315** F8
Fatehpur *Bihar, India* 24°38N 85°14E **315** G11
Fatehpur *Raj., India* 28°0N 74°40E **314** F6
Fatehpur *Ut. P., India* 25°56N 81°13E **315** G9
Fatehpur *Ut. P., India* 27°10N 81°13E **315** F9
Fatehpur Sikri *India* 27°6N 77°40E **314** F6
Fathom Five ⌂ *Canada* 45°17N 81°40W **354** A3
Fatima *Canada* 47°24N 61°53W **345** C7

Faulkton U.S.A. 45°2N 99°8W 352 C4
Faure I. Australia 25°52S 113°50E 333 E1
Fauresmith S. Africa 29°44S 25°17E 328 D4
Fauske Norway 67°17N 15°25E 280 C16
Favara Italy 37°19N 13°39E 294 F5
Favàritx, C. de Spain 40°0N 4°15E 296 B11
Favignana Italy 37°56N 12°20E 294 F5
Fawcett, Pt. Australia 11°46S 130°2E 332 B5
Fawn → Canada 55°20N 87°35W 344 A2
Fawnskin U.S.A. 34°16N 116°56W 351 L10
Faxaflói Iceland 64°29N 23°0W 280 D2
Faya-Largeau Chad 17°58N 19°6E 323 E9
Fayd Si. Arabia 27°1N 42°52E 316 E4
Fayette Ala., U.S.A. 33°41N 87°50W 357 E11
Fayette Mo., U.S.A. 39°9N 92°41W 352 F7
Fayetteville Ark., U.S.A. 36°4N 94°10W 356 C7
Fayetteville N.C., U.S.A. 35°3N 78°53W 357 D15
Fayetteville Tenn., U.S.A. 35°9N 86°34W 357 D11
Fazilka India 30°27N 74°2E 314 D6
Fazilpur Pakistan 29°18N 70°29E 314 E4
Fdérik Mauritania 22°40N 12°45W 322 D3
Feakle Ireland 52°56N 8°40W 282 D3
Feale → Ireland 52°27N 9°37W 282 D2
Fear, C. U.S.A. 33°50N 77°58W 357 E16
Feather → U.S.A. 38°47N 121°36W 348 G3
Feather Falls U.S.A. 39°36N 121°16W 350 F5
Featherston N.Z. 41°6S 175°20E 331 D5
Featherstone Zimbabwe 18°42S 30°55E 327 F3
Fécamp France 49°45N 0°22E 292 B4
Fedala = Mohammedia Morocco 33°44N 7°21W 322 B4
Federación Argentina 31°0S 57°55W 366 C4
Féderal Argentina 30°57S 58°48W 368 C5
Federal Way U.S.A. 47°18N 122°19W 350 C4
Fedeshkūh Iran 28°49N 53°50E 317 D7
Fehmarn Germany 54°27N 11°7E 288 A6
Fehmarn Bælt Europe 54°35N 11°20E 281 J14
Fehmarn Belt = Fehmarn Bælt Europe 54°35N 11°20E 281 J14
Fei Xian China 35°18N 117°59E 307 G9
Feijó Brazil 8°9S 70°21W 364 E4
Feilding N.Z. 40°13S 175°35E 331 D5
Feira de Santana Brazil 12°15S 38°57W 365 F11
Feixiang China 36°30N 114°45E 306 F8
Felanitx Spain 39°28N 3°9E 296 B10
Feldkirch Austria 47°15N 9°37E 288 E5
Félicité Seychelles 4°19S 55°52E 325 b
Felipe Carrillo Puerto Mexico 19°38N 88°3W 359 D7
Felixburg Zimbabwe 19°29S 30°51E 329 B5
Felixstowe U.K. 51°58N 1°23E 285 F9
Felton U.S.A. 37°3N 122°4W 350 H4
Femer Bælt = Fehmarn Bælt Europe 54°35N 11°20E 281 J14
Femunden Norway 62°10N 11°53E 280 E14
Fen He → China 35°36N 110°42E 306 G6
Fenelon Falls Canada 44°32N 78°45W 354 B6
Feng Xian Jiangsu, China 34°43N 116°35E 306 G9
Feng Xian Shaanxi, China 33°54N 106°40E 306 H4
Fengcheng China 40°28N 124°5E 307 D13
Fengfeng China 36°28N 114°8E 306 F8
Fengning China 41°10N 116°33E 306 D9
Fengqiu China 35°2N 114°25E 306 G8
Fengrun China 39°48N 118°8E 307 E10
Fengtai China 39°49N 116°14E 306 E9
Fengxiang China 34°29N 107°25E 306 G4
Fengyang China 32°51N 117°29E 307 H9
Fengzhen China 40°25N 113°2E 306 D7
Fenoarivo Fianarantsoa, Madag. 21°43S 46°24E 329 C8
Fenoarivo Fianarantsoa, Madag. 20°52S 46°53E 329 C8
Fenoarivo Afovoany Madag. 18°26S 46°34E 329 B8
Fenoarivo Atsinanana Madag. 17°22S 49°25E 329 B8
Fens, The U.K. 52°38N 0°2W 284 E7
Fenton U.S.A. 42°48N 83°42W 353 D12
Fenxi China 36°40N 111°31E 306 F6
Fenyang China 37°18N 111°48E 306 F6
Feodosiya Ukraine 45°2N 35°16E 291 E6
Ferbane Ireland 53°16N 7°50W 282 C4
Ferdows Iran 33°58N 58°2E 317 C8
Ferfer Somali Rep. 5°4N 45°9E 319 F4
Fergana = Farghona Uzbekistan 40°23N 71°19E 300 E8
Fergus Canada 43°43N 80°24W 354 C4
Fergus Falls U.S.A. 46°17N 96°4W 352 B5
Ferkéssédougou Ivory C. 9°35N 5°6W 322 G4
Ferland Canada 50°19N 88°27W 344 B2
Ferlo, Vallée du Senegal 15°15N 14°15W 322 E3
Fermanagh □ U.K. 54°21N 7°40W 282 B4
Fermo Italy 43°9N 13°43E 294 C5
Fermont Canada 52°47N 67°5W 345 B6
Fermoy Ireland 52°9N 8°16W 282 D3
Fernández Argentina 27°55S 63°50W 366 B3
Fernandina Beach U.S.A. 30°40N 81°27W 357 F14
Fernando de Noronha Brazil 4°0S 33°10W 365 D12
Fernando Póo = Bioko Eq. Guin. 3°30N 8°40E 324 D1
Ferndale U.S.A. 48°51N 122°36W 350 B4
Fernie Canada 49°30N 115°5W 342 D5
Fernlees Australia 23°51S 148°7E 334 C4
Fernley U.S.A. 39°36N 119°15W 348 G4
Ferozepore = Firozpur India 30°55N 74°40E 314 D6
Ferrara Italy 44°50N 11°35E 294 B4
Ferreñafe Peru 6°42S 79°50W 364 E3
Ferrerías Spain 39°59N 4°1E 296 B11
Ferret, C. France 44°38N 1°15W 292 D3
Ferriday U.S.A. 31°38N 91°33W 356 F9
Ferrol Spain 43°29N 8°15W 293 A1
Ferron U.S.A. 39°5N 111°8W 348 G8
Ferrutx, C. Spain 39°47N 3°21E 296 B10
Ferryland Canada 47°2N 52°53W 345 C9
Fertile U.S.A. 47°32N 96°17W 352 B5
Fès Morocco 34°0N 5°0W 322 B5
Fessenden U.S.A. 47°39N 99°38W 352 B4
Festus U.S.A. 38°13N 90°24W 352 F8
Feteşti Romania 44°22N 27°51E 289 F14
Fethiye Turkey 36°36N 29°6E 291 G4
Fetlar U.K. 60°36N 0°52W 283 A8
Feuilles → Canada 58°47N 70°4W 341 D12
Fez = Fès Morocco 34°0N 5°0W 322 B5
Fezzan Libya 27°0N 13°0E 323 C8
Fiambalá Argentina 27°45S 67°37W 366 B2
Fianarantsoa Madag. 21°26S 47°5E 329 C8
Fianarantsoa □ Madag. 19°30S 47°0E 329 B8
Ficksburg S. Africa 28°51S 27°53E 329 D4
Field → Australia 23°48S 138°0E 334 C2
Field I. Australia 12°5S 132°23E 332 B5
Fier Albania 40°43N 19°33E 295 D8
Fife □ U.K. 56°16N 3°1W 283 E5
Fife ⌂ U.K. 56°15N 3°15W 283 E5
Fife Ness U.K. 56°17N 2°35W 283 E6
Fifth Cataract Sudan 18°22N 33°50E 323 E12
Figeac France 44°37N 2°2E 292 D5
Figtree Zimbabwe 20°22S 28°20E 327 G2
Figueira da Foz Portugal 40°7N 8°54W 293 B1
Figueres Spain 42°18N 2°58E 293 A7
Figuig Morocco 32°5N 1°11W 322 B5
Fihaonana Madag. 18°36S 47°12E 329 B8
Fiherenana Madag. 18°29S 48°24E 329 B8
Fiherenana → Madag. 23°19S 43°37E 329 C7
Fiji ■ Pac. Oc. 17°20S 179°0E 331 a
Filabusi Zimbabwe 20°34S 29°20E 329 C4
Filchner Ice Shelf Antarctica 79°0S 40°0W 277 D1
Filey U.K. 54°12N 0°18W 284 C7
Filey B. U.K. 54°12N 0°15W 284 C7
Filfla Malta 35°47N 14°24E 297 D1
Filiatra Greece 37°9N 21°35E 295 F9
Filingué Niger 14°21N 3°22E 322 F6
Filipstad Sweden 59°43N 14°9E 281 G16
Fillmore Calif., U.S.A. 34°24N 118°55W 351 L8
Fillmore Utah, U.S.A. 38°58N 112°20W 348 G7
Finch Canada 45°11N 75°7W 355 A9
Finch Hatton Australia 20°25S 148°39E 334 K6
Findhorn → U.K. 57°38N 3°38W 283 D5
Findlay U.S.A. 41°2N 83°39W 353 E12
Finger L. Canada 53°33N 93°30W 344 B1
Finger Lakes U.S.A. 42°40N 76°30W 355 D8
Fingoè Mozam. 14°55S 31°50E 327 E3
Finisterre, C. = Fisterra, C. Spain 42°50N 9°19W 293 A1
Finke Australia 25°34S 134°35E 334 D1
Finke Gorge △ Australia 24°8S 132°49E 332 D5
Finland ■ Europe 63°0N 27°0E 280 E22
Finland, G. of Europe 60°0N 26°0E 281 G22
Finlay → Canada 57°0N 125°10W 342 B3
Finley Australia 35°38S 145°35E 335 F4
Finley U.S.A. 47°31N 97°50W 352 B5
Finn → Ireland 54°51N 7°28W 282 B4
Finnigan, Mt. Australia 15°49S 145°17E 334 B4
Finniss, C. Australia 33°8S 134°51E 335 E1
Finnmark Norway 69°37N 23°57E 280 B20
Finnsnes Norway 69°14N 18°0E 280 B18
Finspång Sweden 58°43N 15°47E 281 G16
Fiora → Italy 42°20N 11°34E 294 C4
Fiordland △ N.Z. 45°46S 167°0E 331 F1
Fīq Syria 32°46N 35°41E 318 C4
Firat = Furāt, Nahr al → Asia 31°0N 47°25E 316 D5
Fire Island ⌂ U.S.A. 40°38N 73°8W 355 F11
Firebag → Canada 57°45N 111°21W 343 B6
Firebaugh U.S.A. 36°52N 120°27W 350 J6
Firedrake L. Canada 61°25N 104°30W 343 A8
Firenze Italy 43°46N 11°15E 294 C4
Firk, Sha'ib → Iraq 30°59N 44°34E 316 D5
Firozabad India 27°10N 78°25E 315 F8
Firozpur India 30°55N 74°40E 314 D6
Firozpur-Jhirka India 27°48N 76°57E 314 F7
Fīrūzābād Iran 28°52N 52°35E 317 D7
Fīrūzkūh Iran 35°50N 52°50E 317 C7
Firvale Canada 52°27N 126°13W 342 C3
Fish → Namibia 28°7S 17°10E 328 D2
Fish → S. Africa 31°30S 20°16E 328 E3
Fish River Canyon Namibia 27°40S 17°35E 328 D2
Fisher B. Canada 51°35N 97°13W 343 C9
Fishers I. U.S.A. 41°15N 72°0W 355 E13
Fishguard U.K. 52°0N 4°58W 285 E3
Fishing L. Canada 52°10N 95°24W 343 C9
Fishkill U.S.A. 41°32N 73°54W 355 E11
Fisterra, C. Spain 42°50N 9°19W 293 A1
Fitchburg Mass., U.S.A. 42°35N 71°48W 355 D13
Fitchburg Wis., U.S.A. 42°58N 89°28W 352 D9
Fitz Roy Argentina 47°0S 67°0W 368 F3
Fitzgerald Canada 59°51N 111°36W 342 B6
Fitzgerald U.S.A. 31°43N 83°15W 357 F13
Fitzgerald River △ Australia 33°53S 119°55E 333 F3
Fitzmaurice → Australia 14°45S 130°5E 332 B5
Fitzroy → Queens., Australia 23°32S 150°52E 334 C5
Fitzroy → W. Austral., Australia 17°31S 123°35E 332 C3
Fitzroy, Mte. Argentina 49°17S 73°5W 368 F2
Fitzroy Crossing Australia 18°9S 125°38E 332 C4
Fitzwilliam I. Canada 45°30N 81°45W 354 A3
Fiume = Rijeka Croatia 45°20N 14°21E 288 F8
Five Points U.S.A. 36°26N 120°6W 350 J6
Fizi Dem. Rep. of the Congo 4°17S 28°55E 326 C2
Flagstaff U.S.A. 35°12N 111°39W 349 J8
Flagstaff L. U.S.A. 45°12N 70°18W 355 A14
Flaherty I. Canada 56°15N 79°15W 344 A4
Flåm Norway 60°50N 7°7E 280 F12
Flambeau → U.S.A. 45°18N 91°14W 352 C8
Flamborough Hd. U.K. 54°7N 0°5W 284 C7
Flaming Gorge ⌂ U.S.A. 41°10N 109°25W 348 F9
Flaming Gorge Res. U.S.A. 41°10N 109°25W 348 F9
Flamingo, Teluk Indonesia 5°30S 138°0E 309 F9
Flanders = Flandre Europe 50°50N 2°30E 287 B9
Flandre Europe 50°50N 2°30E 287 B9
Flandre-Occidentale = West-Vlaanderen □ Belgium 51°0N 3°0E 287 D2
Flandre-Orientale = Oost-Vlaanderen □ Belgium 51°5N 3°50E 287 C3
Flandreau U.S.A. 44°3N 96°36W 352 C5
Flanigan U.S.A. 40°10N 119°53W 350 E7
Flannan Is. U.K. 58°9N 7°52W 283 C1
Flåsjön Sweden 64°5N 15°40E 280 D16
Flat → Canada 61°33N 125°18W 342 A3
Flat I. Mauritius 19°53S 57°35E 325 d
Flathead L. U.S.A. 47°51N 114°8W 348 C6
Flattery, C. Australia 14°58S 145°21E 334 A4
Flattery, C. U.S.A. 48°23N 124°29W 350 B2
Flatwoods U.S.A. 38°31N 82°43W 353 F12
Fleetwood U.K. 53°55N 3°1W 284 D4
Fleetwood U.S.A. 40°27N 75°49W 355 F9
Flekkefjord Norway 58°18N 6°39E 281 G12
Flemington U.S.A. 41°7N 77°28W 354 E7
Flensburg Germany 54°47N 9°27E 288 A5
Flers France 48°47N 0°33W 292 B3
Flesherton Canada 44°16N 80°33W 354 B4
Flesko, Tanjung Indonesia 0°29N 124°30E 309 D6
Fleurieu Pen. Australia 35°40S 138°5E 335 F2
Flevoland □ Neths. 52°30N 5°30E 287 B5
Flin Flon Canada 54°46N 101°53W 343 C8
Flinders → Australia 17°36S 140°36E 334 B3
Flinders B. Australia 34°19S 115°19E 333 F2
Flinders Group Australia 14°11S 144°15E 334 A3
Flinders I. S. Austral., Australia 33°44S 134°41E 335 E1
Flinders I. Tas., Australia 40°0S 148°0E 335 G4
Flinders Ranges Australia 31°30S 138°30E 335 E2
Flinders Reefs Australia 17°37S 148°31E 334 B4
Flint U.K. 53°15N 3°8W 284 D4
Flint U.S.A. 43°1N 83°41W 353 D12
Flint → U.S.A. 30°57N 84°34W 357 F12
Flint I. Kiribati 11°26S 151°48W 337 J12
Flintshire □ U.K. 53°17N 3°17W 284 D4
Flodden U.K. 55°37N 2°8W 284 B5
Floodwood U.S.A. 46°56N 92°55W 352 B7
Flora U.S.A. 38°40N 88°29W 352 F9
Florala U.S.A. 31°0N 86°20W 357 F11
Florence = Firenze Italy 43°46N 11°15E 294 C4
Florence Ala., U.S.A. 34°48N 87°41W 357 D11
Florence Ariz., U.S.A. 33°2N 111°23W 349 K8
Florence Colo., U.S.A. 38°23N 105°8W 348 G11
Florence Oreg., U.S.A. 43°58N 124°7W 348 D1
Florence S.C., U.S.A. 34°12N 79°46W 357 D15
Florence, L. Australia 28°53S 138°9E 335 D2
Florencia Colombia 1°36N 75°36W 364 C3
Florennes Belgium 50°15N 4°35E 287 D4
Florenville Belgium 49°40N 5°19E 287 E5
Flores Azores 39°26N 31°13W 322 a
Flores Guatemala 16°59N 89°50W 360 C2
Flores Indonesia 8°35S 121°0E 309 F6
Flores I. Canada 49°20N 126°10W 342 D3
Flores Sea Indonesia 6°30S 120°0E 309 F6
Floreşti Moldova 47°53N 28°17E 289 E15
Floresville U.S.A. 29°8N 98°10W 356 G5
Floriano Brazil 6°50S 43°0W 365 E10
Florianópolis Brazil 27°30S 48°30W 367 B6
Florida Cuba 21°32N 78°14W 360 B4
Florida Uruguay 34°7S 56°10W 367 C4
Florida □ U.S.A. 28°0N 82°0W 357 G14
Florida, Straits of U.S.A. 25°0N 80°0W 360 B4
Florida B. U.S.A. 25°0N 80°45W 360 B3
Florida Keys U.S.A. 24°40N 81°0W 357 J14
Florin U.S.A. 38°30N 121°24W 350 G5
Florina Greece 40°48N 21°26E 295 D9
Florissant U.S.A. 38°47N 90°19W 352 F8
Florø Norway 61°35N 5°1E 280 F11
Flower Station Canada 45°10N 76°41W 355 A8
Flowerpot I. Canada 45°18N 81°38W 354 A3
Floydada U.S.A. 33°59N 101°20W 356 E4
Fluk Indonesia 1°42S 127°44E 309 E7
Flushing = Vlissingen Neths. 51°26N 3°34E 287 C3
Fly → Papua N. G. 8°25S 143°0E 330 B7
Flying Fish, C. Antarctica 72°6S 102°29W 277 D15
Foa Tonga 19°45S 174°18W 331 c
Foam Lake Canada 51°40N 103°32W 343 C8
Foça Turkey 38°39N 26°46E 295 E12
Fochabers U.K. 57°37N 3°6W 283 D5
Focşani Romania 45°41N 27°15E 289 F14
Fóggia Italy 41°27N 15°34E 294 D6
Fogo Canada 49°43N 54°17W 345 C9
Fogo C. Verde Is. 15°5N 24°20W 322 b
Fogo I. Canada 49°40N 54°5W 345 C9
Föhr Germany 54°43N 8°30E 288 A5
Foix France 42°58N 1°38E 292 E4
Folda Nord-Trøndelag, Norway 64°32N 10°30E 280 D14
Folda Nordland, Norway 67°38N 14°50E 280 C16
Foley Botswana 21°34S 27°21E 328 C4
Foley U.S.A. 30°24N 87°41W 357 F11
Foleyet Canada 48°15N 82°25W 344 C3
Folgefonna Norway 60°3N 6°23E 281 F12
Foligno Italy 42°57N 12°42E 294 C5
Folkestone U.K. 51°5N 1°12E 285 F9
Folkston U.S.A. 30°50N 82°0W 357 F13
Follansbee U.S.A. 40°19N 80°35W 354 F4
Folsom L. U.S.A. 38°42N 121°9W 350 G5
Fomboni Comoros Is. 12°18S 43°46E 325 a
Fond-du-Lac Canada 59°19N 107°12W 343 B7
Fond du Lac U.S.A. 43°47N 88°27W 352 D9
Fond-du-Lac → Canada 59°17N 106°0W 343 B7
Fonda U.S.A. 42°57N 74°22W 355 D10
Fondi Italy 41°21N 13°25E 294 D5
Fongafale Tuvalu 8°31S 179°13E 330 B10
Fonsagrada = A Fonsagrada Spain 43°8N 7°4W 293 A2
Fonseca, G. de Cent. Amer. 13°10N 87°40W 360 D2
Fontainebleau France 48°24N 2°40E 292 B5
Fontana U.S.A. 34°6N 117°26W 351 L9
Fontas → Canada 58°14N 121°48W 342 B4
Fonte Boa Brazil 2°33S 66°0W 364 D5
Fontenay-le-Comte France 46°28N 0°48W 292 C3
Fontenelle Res. U.S.A. 42°1N 110°3W 348 E8
Fontur Iceland 66°23N 14°32W 280 C6
Fonuafo'ou Tonga 20°19S 175°25W 331 c
Fonualei Tonga 18°1S 174°19W 331 c
Foochow = Fuzhou China 26°5N 119°16E 305 D6
Foping China 33°41N 108°0E 306 H5
Forbes Australia 33°22S 148°5E 335 E4
Forbesganj India 26°17N 87°18E 315 F12
Ford City Calif., U.S.A. 35°9N 119°27W 351 K7
Ford City Pa., U.S.A. 40°46N 79°32W 354 F5
Førde Norway 61°27N 5°53E 280 F11
Fords Bridge Australia 29°41S 145°29E 335 D4
Fordyce U.S.A. 33°49N 92°25W 356 E8
Forel, Mt. Greenland 66°52N 36°55W 338 C16
Foremost Canada 49°26N 111°34W 342 D6
Forest Canada 43°6N 82°0W 354 C3
Forest U.S.A. 32°22N 89°29W 357 E10
Forest City Iowa, U.S.A. 43°16N 93°39W 352 D7
Forest City N.C., U.S.A. 35°20N 81°52W 357 D14
Forest City Pa., U.S.A. 41°39N 75°28W 355 E9
Forest Grove U.S.A. 45°31N 123°7W 350 E3
Forestburg Canada 52°35N 112°1W 342 C6
Foresthill U.S.A. 39°1N 120°49W 350 F6
Forestier Pen. Australia 43°0S 148°0E 335 G4
Forestville Canada 48°48N 69°2W 345 C6
Forestville Calif., U.S.A. 38°28N 122°54W 350 G4
Forestville N.Y., U.S.A. 42°28N 79°10W 354 D5
Forfar U.K. 56°39N 2°53W 283 E6
Forillon △ Canada 48°46N 64°12W 345 C7
Forks U.S.A. 47°57N 124°23W 350 C2
Forksville U.S.A. 41°29N 76°35W 355 E8
Forlì Italy 44°13N 12°3E 294 B5
Forman U.S.A. 46°7N 97°38W 352 B5
Formby Pt. U.K. 53°33N 3°6W 284 D4
Formentera Spain 38°43N 1°27E 296 C7
Formentor, C. de Spain 39°58N 3°13E 296 B10
Former Yugoslav ■ Republic of Macedonia = Macedonia Europe 41°53N 21°40E 295 D9
Fórmia Italy 41°15N 13°37E 294 D5
Formosa = Taiwan ■ Asia 23°30N 121°0E 305 D7
Formosa Argentina 26°15S 58°10W 366 B4
Formosa Brazil 15°32S 47°20W 365 G9
Formosa □ Argentina 25°0S 60°0W 366 B4
Formosa, Serra Brazil 12°0S 55°0W 365 F8
Formosa B. = Ungwana B. Kenya 2°45S 40°20E 326 C5
Fornells Spain 40°3N 4°7E 296 A11
Føroyar ☒ Atl. Oc. 62°0N 7°0W 280 F9
Forres U.K. 57°37N 3°37W 283 D5
Forrest Australia 30°51S 128°6E 333 F4
Forrest, Mt. Australia 24°48S 127°45E 333 D4
Forsayth Australia 18°33S 143°34E 334 B3
Forssa Finland 60°49N 23°38E 280 F20
Forst Germany 51°45N 14°37E 288 C8
Forster Australia 32°12S 152°31E 335 E5
Forsyth U.S.A. 46°16N 106°41W 348 C10
Fort Abbas Pakistan 29°12N 72°52E 314 E5
Fort Albany Canada 52°15N 81°35W 344 B3
Fort Ann U.S.A. 43°25N 73°29W 355 C11
Fort Assiniboine Canada 54°20N 114°45W 342 C6
Fort Augustus U.K. 57°9N 4°42W 283 D4
Fort Beaufort S. Africa 32°46S 26°40E 328 E4
Fort Benton U.S.A. 47°49N 110°40W 348 C8
Fort Bragg U.S.A. 39°26N 123°48W 348 G2
Fort Bridger U.S.A. 41°19N 110°23W 348 F8
Fort Chipewyan Canada 58°42N 111°8W 343 B6
Fort Clatsop ⌂ U.S.A. 46°8N 123°53W 350 D3
Fort Collins U.S.A. 40°35N 105°5W 348 F11
Fort-Coulonge Canada 45°50N 76°45W 344 C4
Fort Covington U.S.A. 44°59N 74°29W 355 B10
Fort Dauphin = Taolanaro Madag. 25°2S 47°0E 329 D8
Fort Davis U.S.A. 30°35N 103°54W 356 F3
Fort-de-France Martinique 14°36N 61°2W 360 c
Fort Defiance U.S.A. 35°45N 109°5W 349 J9
Fort Dodge U.S.A. 42°30N 94°11W 352 D6
Fort Edward U.S.A. 43°16N 73°35W 355 C11
Fort Erie Canada 42°54N 78°56W 354 D6
Fort Fairfield U.S.A. 46°46N 67°50W 353 B20
Fort Frances Canada 48°36N 93°24W 343 D10
Fort Franklin = Déline Canada 65°11N 123°25W 340 C7
Fort Garland U.S.A. 37°26N 105°26W 349 H11
Fort George = Chisasibi Canada 53°50N 79°0W 344 B4
Fort Good Hope Canada 66°14N 128°40W 340 C7
Fort Hancock U.S.A. 31°18N 105°51W 356 F2
Fort Hope Canada 51°30N 88°0W 344 B2
Fort Irwin U.S.A. 35°16N 116°41W 351 K10
Fort Kent U.S.A. 47°15N 68°36W 353 B19
Fort Klamath U.S.A. 42°42N 122°0W 348 D3
Fort Laramie U.S.A. 42°13N 104°31W 348 E11
Fort Lauderdale U.S.A. 26°7N 80°8W 357 H14
Fort Liard Canada 60°14N 123°30W 342 A4
Fort Liberté Haiti 19°42N 71°51W 361 C5
Fort Lupton U.S.A. 40°5N 104°49W 348 F11
Fort MacKay Canada 57°12N 111°41W 342 B6
Fort Macleod Canada 49°45N 113°30W 342 D6
Fort McMurray Canada 56°44N 111°7W 342 B6
Fort McPherson Canada 67°30N 134°55W 340 C6
Fort Madison U.S.A. 40°38N 91°27W 352 E8
Fort Meade U.S.A. 27°45N 81°48W 357 H14
Fort Morgan U.S.A. 40°15N 103°48W 348 F12
Fort Myers U.S.A. 26°39N 81°52W 357 H14
Fort Nelson Canada 58°50N 122°44W 342 B4
Fort Nelson → Canada 59°32N 124°0W 342 B4
Fort Norman = Tulita Canada 64°57N 125°30W 340 C7
Fort Payne U.S.A. 34°26N 85°43W 357 D12
Fort Peck U.S.A. 48°1N 106°27W 348 B10
Fort Peck Dam U.S.A. 48°0N 106°26W 348 C10
Fort Peck L. U.S.A. 48°0N 106°26W 348 C10
Fort Pierce U.S.A. 27°27N 80°20W 357 H14
Fort Pierre U.S.A. 44°21N 100°22W 352 C3
Fort Plain U.S.A. 42°56N 74°37W 355 D10
Fort Portal Uganda 0°40N 30°20E 326 B3
Fort Providence Canada 61°3N 117°40W 342 A5
Fort Qu'Appelle Canada 50°45N 103°50W 343 C8
Fort Resolution Canada 61°10N 113°40W 342 A6
Fort Rixon Zimbabwe 20°2S 29°17E 327 G2
Fort Ross U.S.A. 38°32N 123°13W 350 G3
Fort Rupert = Waskaganish Canada 51°30N 78°40W 344 B4
Fort St. James Canada 54°30N 124°10W 342 C4
Fort St. John Canada 56°15N 120°50W 342 B4
Fort Saskatchewan Canada 53°40N 113°15W 342 C6
Fort Scott U.S.A. 37°50N 94°42W 352 G6
Fort Severn Canada 56°0N 87°40W 344 A2
Fort Shevchenko Kazakhstan 44°35N 50°23E 291 F9
Fort Simpson Canada 61°45N 121°15W 342 A4
Fort Smith Canada 60°0N 111°51W 342 B6
Fort Smith U.S.A. 35°23N 94°25W 356 D7
Fort Stockton U.S.A. 30°53N 102°53W 356 F3
Fort Sumner U.S.A. 34°28N 104°15W 349 J11
Fort Thompson U.S.A. 44°3N 99°26W 352 C4
Fort Union ⌂ U.S.A. 35°54N 105°1W 349 J11
Fort Valley U.S.A. 32°33N 83°53W 357 E13
Fort Vermilion Canada 58°24N 116°0W 342 B5
Fort Walton Beach U.S.A. 30°25N 86°36W 357 F11
Fort Wayne U.S.A. 41°4N 85°9W 353 E11
Fort William U.K. 56°49N 5°7W 283 E3
Fort Worth U.S.A. 32°43N 97°19W 356 E6
Fort Yates U.S.A. 46°5N 100°38W 352 B3
Fort Yukon U.S.A. 66°34N 145°16W 346 a
Fortaleza Brazil 3°45S 38°35W 365 D11
Forteau Canada 51°28N 56°58W 345 B8
Fortescue → Australia 21°0S 116°4E 332 D2
Forth → U.K. 56°9N 3°50W 283 E5
Forth, Firth of U.K. 56°5N 2°55W 283 E6
Fortrose U.K. 57°35N 4°9W 283 D4
Fortuna Calif., U.S.A. 40°36N 124°9W 348 F1
Fortuna N. Dak., U.S.A. 48°55N 103°47W 352 A2
Fortune Canada 47°4N 55°50W 345 C8
Fortune B. Canada 47°30N 55°22W 345 C8
Forūr Iran 26°17N 54°32E 317 E7
Fosen Norway 63°50N 10°20E 280 E14
Foshan China 23°4N 113°5E 305 D6
Fosnavåg Norway 62°22N 5°38E 280 E11
Fossano Italy 44°33N 7°43E 292 D7
Fossil U.S.A. 45°0N 120°9W 348 D3
Fossil Butte ⌂ U.S.A. 41°50N 110°27W 348 F8
Foster Canada 45°17N 72°30W 355 A12
Foster → Canada 55°47N 105°49W 343 B7
Fosters Ra. Australia 21°35S 133°48E 334 C1
Fostoria U.S.A. 41°10N 83°25W 353 E12
Fotadrevo Madag. 24°3S 45°1E 329 C8
Fougères France 48°21N 1°14W 292 B3
Foul Pt. Sri Lanka 8°35N 81°18E 312 Q12
Foula U.K. 60°10N 2°5W 283 A6
Foulness I. U.K. 51°36N 0°55E 285 F8
Foulpointe Madag. 17°41S 49°31E 329 B8
Foumban Cameroon 5°45N 10°50E 324 C2
Foumbouni Comoros Is. 11°51S 43°29E 325 a
Fountain U.S.A. 38°41N 104°42W 348 G11
Fountain Hills U.S.A. 33°37N 111°43W 349 K8
Fountain Springs U.S.A. 35°54N 118°51W 351 K8
Fouriesburg S. Africa 28°38S 28°14E 328 D4
Fourni Greece 37°36N 26°32E 295 F12
Fourth Cataract Sudan 18°47N 32°3E 323 E12
Fouta Djallon Guinea 11°20N 12°10W 322 F3
Foux, Cap-à- Haiti 19°43N 73°27W 361 C5
Foveaux Str. N.Z. 46°42S 168°10E 331 G2
Fowey U.K. 50°20N 4°39W 285 G3
Fowler Calif., U.S.A. 36°38N 119°41W 350 J7
Fowler Colo., U.S.A. 38°8N 104°2W 348 G11
Fowler, Pt. Australia 32°2S 132°3E 333 F5
Fowlers B. Australia 31°59S 132°34E 333 F5
Fowman Iran 37°13N 49°19E 317 B6
Fox → Canada 56°3N 93°18W 343 B10
Fox Creek Canada 54°24N 116°48W 342 C5
Fox Lake Canada 58°28N 114°31W 342 B6
Fox Valley Canada 50°30N 109°25W 343 C7
Foxboro U.S.A. 42°4N 71°16W 355 D13
Foxdale Australia 20°22S 148°35E 334 J6
Foxe Basin Canada 66°0N 77°0W 341 C12
Foxe Chan. Canada 65°0N 80°0W 341 C12
Foxe Pen. Canada 65°0N 76°0W 341 C12
Foxford Ireland 53°59N 9°7W 282 C2
Foxton N.Z. 40°29S 175°18E 331 D5
Foyle, Lough U.K. 55°7N 7°4W 282 A4
Foynes Ireland 52°37N 9°7W 282 D2

Foz do Cunene Angola 17°15S 11°48E 328 B1
Foz do Iguaçu Brazil 25°30S 54°30W 367 B5
Frackville U.S.A. 40°47N 76°14W 355 F8
Fraile Muerto Uruguay 32°31S 54°32W 367 C5
Framingham U.S.A. 42°18N 71°24W 355 D13
Franca Brazil 20°33S 47°30W 365 H9
Francavilla Fontana Italy 40°32N 17°35E 295 D7
France ■ Europe 47°0N 3°0E 292 C5
Frances Australia 36°41S 140°55E 334 D3
Frances → Canada 60°16N 129°10W 342 A3
Frances L. Canada 61°23N 129°30W 342 A3
Franceville Gabon 1°40S 13°32E 324 E2
Franche-Comté □ France 46°50N 5°55E 292 C6
Francis Case, L. U.S.A. 43°4N 98°34W 352 D4
Francisco Beltrão Brazil 26°5S 53°4W 367 B5
Francisco Ignacio Madero Coahuila, Mexico 25°48N 103°18W 358 B4
Francisco Ignacio Madero Durango, Mexico 24°26N 104°18W 358 C4
Francisco Ignacio Madero, Presa Mexico 28°10N 105°37W 358 B3
Francistown Botswana 21°7S 27°33E 329 C4
François Canada 47°35N 56°45W 345 C8
François L. Canada 54°0N 125°30W 342 C3
Francois Peron △ Australia 25°42S 113°33E 333 E1
Francs Pk. U.S.A. 43°58N 109°20W 348 E9
Franeker Neths. 53°12N 5°33E 287 A5
Frank Hann △ Australia 32°52S 120°19E 333 F3
Frankford Canada 44°12N 77°36W 354 B7
Frankfort S. Africa 27°17S 28°30E 329 D4
Frankfort Ind., U.S.A. 40°17N 86°31W 352 E10
Frankfort Kans., U.S.A. 39°42N 96°25W 352 F5
Frankfort Ky., U.S.A. 38°12N 84°52W 353 F11
Frankfort N.Y., U.S.A. 43°2N 75°4W 355 C9
Frankfurt Brandenburg, Germany 52°20N 14°32E 288 B8
Frankfurt Hessen, Germany 50°7N 8°41E 288 C5
Fränkische Alb Germany 49°10N 11°23E 288 D6
Frankland → Australia 35°0S 116°48E 333 G2
Franklin Ky., U.S.A. 36°43N 86°35W 352 G10
Franklin La., U.S.A. 29°48N 91°30W 356 G9
Franklin Mass., U.S.A. 42°5N 71°24W 355 D13
Franklin N.H., U.S.A. 43°27N 71°39W 355 C13
Franklin Nebr., U.S.A. 40°6N 98°57W 352 E4
Franklin Pa., U.S.A. 41°24N 79°50W 354 E5
Franklin Va., U.S.A. 36°41N 76°56W 353 G15
Franklin W. Va., U.S.A. 38°39N 79°20W 353 F14
Franklin B. Canada 69°45N 126°0W 340 C7
Franklin D. Roosevelt L. U.S.A. 48°18N 118°9W 348 B4
Franklin-Gordon Wild Rivers △ Australia 42°19S 145°51E 335 G4
Franklin I. Antarctica 76°10S 168°30E 277 D11
Franklin L. U.S.A. 40°25N 115°22W 348 F6
Franklin Mts. Canada 65°0N 125°0W 340 C7
Franklin Str. Canada 72°0N 96°0W 340 B10
Franklinton U.S.A. 30°51N 90°9W 357 F9
Franklinville U.S.A. 42°20N 78°27W 354 D6
Frankston Australia 38°8S 145°8E 335 F4
Fransfontein Namibia 20°12S 15°1E 328 C2
Frantsa Iosifa, Zemlya Russia 82°0N 55°0E 300 A6
Franz Canada 48°25N 84°30W 344 C3
Franz Josef Land = Frantsa Iosifa, Zemlya Russia 82°0N 55°0E 300 A6
Fraser U.S.A. 42°32N 82°57W 354 D2
Fraser → B.C., Canada 49°7N 123°11W 350 A3
Fraser → Nfld. & L., Canada 56°39N 62°10W 345 A7
Fraser, Mt. Australia 25°35S 118°20E 333 E2
Fraser I. Australia 25°15S 153°10E 335 D5
Fraser Lake Canada 54°0N 124°50W 342 C4
Fraserburg S. Africa 31°55S 21°30E 328 E3
Fraserburgh U.K. 57°42N 2°1W 283 D6
Fraserdale Canada 49°55N 81°37W 344 C3
Fray Bentos Uruguay 33°10S 58°15W 366 C4
Fray Jorge △ Chile 30°42S 71°40W 366 C1
Fredericia Denmark 55°34N 9°45E 281 J13
Frederick Md., U.S.A. 39°25N 77°25W 353 F15
Frederick Okla., U.S.A. 34°23N 99°1W 356 D5
Frederick S. Dak., U.S.A. 45°50N 98°31W 352 C4
Fredericksburg Pa., U.S.A. 40°27N 76°26W 355 F8
Fredericksburg Tex., U.S.A. 30°16N 98°52W 356 F5
Fredericksburg Va., U.S.A. 38°18N 77°28W 353 F15
Fredericktown Mo., U.S.A. 37°34N 90°18W 352 G8
Fredericktown Ohio, U.S.A. 40°29N 82°33W 354 F2
Frederico Westphalen Brazil 27°22S 53°24W 367 B5
Fredericton Canada 45°57N 66°40W 345 C6
Fredericton Junction Canada 45°41N 66°40W 345 C6
Frederikshåb = Paamiut Greenland 62°0N 49°43W 276 C5
Frederikshamn = Hamina Finland 60°34N 27°12E 280 F22
Frederikshavn Denmark 57°28N 10°31E 281 H14
Frederiksted U.S. Virgin Is. 17°43N 64°53W 361 C7
Fredonia Ariz., U.S.A. 36°57N 112°32W 349 H7
Fredonia Kans., U.S.A. 37°32N 95°49W 352 G6
Fredonia N.Y., U.S.A. 42°26N 79°20W 354 D5
Fredrikstad Norway 59°13N 10°57E 281 G14
Free State □ S. Africa 28°30S 27°0E 328 D4
Freehold U.S.A. 40°16N 74°17W 355 F10
Freeland U.S.A. 41°1N 75°54W 355 E9
Freels, C. Canada 49°15N 53°30W 345 C9
Freeman Calif., U.S.A. 35°35N 117°53W 351 K9
Freeman S. Dak., U.S.A. 43°21N 97°26W 352 D5
Freeport Bahamas 26°30N 78°47W 360 A4
Freeport Ill., U.S.A. 42°17N 89°36W 352 D9
Freeport N.Y., U.S.A. 40°39N 73°35W 355 F11
Freeport Ohio, U.S.A. 40°12N 81°15W 354 F3
Freeport Pa., U.S.A. 40°41N 79°41W 354 F5
Freeport Tex., U.S.A. 28°57N 95°21W 356 G7
Freetown S. Leone 8°30N 13°17W 322 G3
Frégate, L. de la Canada 53°15N 74°45W 344 B5
Fregenal de la Sierra Spain 38°10N 6°39W 293 C2
Freibourg = Fribourg Switz. 46°49N 7°9E 292 C7
Freiburg Germany 47°59N 7°51E 288 E4
Freire Chile 38°54S 72°38W 368 D2
Freirina Chile 28°30S 71°10W 366 B1
Freising Germany 48°24N 11°45E 288 D6
Freistadt Austria 48°30N 14°30E 288 D8
Fréjus France 43°25N 6°44E 292 E7
Fremantle Australia 32°7S 115°47E 333 F2
Fremont Calif., U.S.A. 37°32N 121°57W 350 H4
Fremont Mich., U.S.A. 43°28N 85°57W 353 D11
Fremont Nebr., U.S.A. 41°26N 96°30W 352 E5
Fremont Ohio, U.S.A. 41°21N 83°7W 353 E12
Fremont → U.S.A. 38°24N 110°42W 348 G8
French Camp U.S.A. 37°53N 121°16W 350 H5
French Cays = Plana Cays Bahamas 22°38N 73°30W 361 B5
French Creek → U.S.A. 41°24N 79°50W 354 E5
French Guiana ⊡ S. Amer. 4°0N 53°0W 365 C8
French Polynesia ⊡ Pac. Oc. 20°0S 145°0W 337 J13
Frenchman → N. Amer. 48°31N 107°10W 348 B10
Frenchman Cr. → U.S.A. 40°14N 100°50W 352 E3
Fresco → Brazil 7°15S 51°30W 365 E8
Freshfield, C. Antarctica 68°25S 151°10E 277 C10
Fresnillo Mexico 23°10N 102°53W 358 C4
Fresno U.S.A. 36°44N 119°47W 350 J7
Fresno Res. U.S.A. 48°36N 109°57W 348 B9
Frew → Australia 20°0S 135°38E 334 C2
Frewsburg U.S.A. 42°3N 79°10W 354 D5
Freycinet △ Australia 42°11S 148°19E 335 G4
Freycinet Pen. Australia 42°10S 148°25E 335 G4
Fria Guinea 10°27N 13°38W 322 F3
Fria, C. Namibia 18°0S 12°0E 328 B1
Friant U.S.A. 36°59N 119°43W 350 J7
Frías Argentina 28°40S 65°5W 366 B2
Fribourg Switz. 46°49N 7°9E 292 C7
Friday Harbor U.S.A. 48°32N 123°1W 350 B3
Friedens U.S.A. 40°3N 78°59W 354 F6
Friedrichshafen Germany 47°39N 9°30E 288 E5
Friendship U.S.A. 42°12N 78°8W 354 D6
Friesland □ Neths. 53°5N 5°50E 287 A5
Frigate Seychelles 4°35S 55°56E 325 b
Frio → U.S.A. 28°26N 98°11W 356 G5
Frio, C. Brazil 22°50S 41°50W 362 F6
Friona U.S.A. 34°38N 102°43W 356 D3
Fritch U.S.A. 35°38N 101°36W 356 D4
Frobisher B. Canada 62°30N 66°0W 341 C13
Frobisher Bay = Iqaluit Canada 63°44N 68°31W 341 C13
Frobisher L. Canada 56°20N 108°15W 343 B7
Frohavet Norway 64°0N 9°30E 280 E13
Frome U.K. 51°14N 2°19W 285 F5
Frome → U.K. 50°41N 2°6W 285 G5
Frome, L. Australia 30°45S 139°45E 335 E2
Front Range U.S.A. 40°25N 105°45W 346 C5
Front Royal U.S.A. 38°55N 78°12W 353 F14
Frontera Canary Is. 27°47N 17°59W 296 G2
Frontera Mexico 18°32N 92°38W 359 D6
Fronteras Mexico 30°56N 109°31W 358 A3
Frosinone Italy 41°38N 13°19E 294 D5
Frostburg U.S.A. 39°39N 78°56W 353 F14
Frostisen Norway 68°14N 17°10E 280 B17
Frøya Norway 63°43N 8°40E 280 E13
Frunze = Bishkek Kyrgyzstan 42°54N 74°46E 300 E8
Frutal Brazil 20°0S 49°0W 365 H9
Frýdek-Místek Czech Rep. 49°40N 18°20E 289 D10
Fryeburg U.S.A. 44°1N 70°59W 355 B14
Fu Xian = Wafangdian China 39°38N 121°58E 307 E11
Fu Xian China 36°0N 109°20E 306 G5
Fucheng China 37°50N 116°10E 306 F9
Fuchou = Fuzhou China 26°5N 119°16E 305 D6
Fuchū Japan 34°34N 133°14E 303 G6
Fuencaliente Canary Is. 28°28N 17°50W 296 F2
Fuencaliente, Pta. Canary Is. 28°27N 17°51W 296 F2
Fuengirola Spain 36°32N 4°41W 293 D3
Fuentes de Oñoro Spain 40°33N 6°52W 293 B2
Fuerte → Mexico 25°54N 109°22W 358 B3
Fuerte Olimpo Paraguay 21°0S 57°51W 366 A4
Fuerteventura Canary Is. 28°30N 14°0W 296 F6
Fuerteventura ✕ (FUE) Canary Is. 28°24N 13°52W 296 F6
Fufeng China 34°22N 108°0E 306 G5
Fugou China 34°3N 114°25E 306 G8
Fugu China 39°2N 111°3E 306 E6
Fuhai China 47°2N 87°25E 304 B3
Fuḥaymī Iraq 34°16N 42°10E 316 C4
Fuji Japan 35°9N 138°39E 303 G9
Fuji-Hakone-Izu △ Japan 35°15N 138°45E 303 G9
Fuji-San Japan 35°22N 138°44E 303 G9
Fuji-Yoshida Japan 35°30N 138°46E 303 G9
Fujian □ China 26°0N 118°0E 305 D6
Fujinomiya Japan 35°10N 138°40E 303 G9
Fujisawa Japan 35°22N 139°29E 303 G9
Fujiyama, Mt. = Fuji-San Japan 35°22N 138°44E 303 G9
Fukagawa Japan 43°43N 142°2E 302 C11
Fukien = Fujian □ China 26°0N 118°0E 305 D6
Fukuchiyama Japan 35°19N 135°9E 303 G7
Fukue-Shima Japan 32°40N 128°45E 303 H4
Fukui Japan 36°5N 136°10E 303 F8
Fukui □ Japan 36°0N 136°12E 303 G8
Fukuoka Japan 33°39N 130°21E 303 H5
Fukuoka □ Japan 33°30N 131°0E 303 H5
Fukushima Japan 37°44N 140°28E 302 F10
Fukushima □ Japan 37°30N 140°15E 302 F10
Fukuyama Japan 34°35N 133°20E 303 G6
Fulaga Fiji 19°8S 178°33W 331 a
Fulda Germany 50°32N 9°40E 288 C5
Fulda → Germany 51°25N 9°39E 288 C5
Fulford Harbour Canada 48°47N 123°27W 350 B3
Fullerton Calif., U.S.A. 33°53N 117°56W 351 M9
Fullerton Nebr., U.S.A. 41°22N 97°58W 352 E5
Fulongquan China 44°20N 124°42E 307 B13
Fulton Mo., U.S.A. 38°52N 91°57W 352 F8
Fulton N.Y., U.S.A. 43°19N 76°25W 355 C8
Funabashi Japan 35°45N 140°0E 303 G10
Funafuti = Fongafale Tuvalu 8°31S 179°13E 330 B10
Funchal Madeira 32°38N 16°54W 296 D3
Funchal ✕ (FNC) Madeira 32°42N 16°45W 296 D3
Fundación Colombia 10°31N 74°11W 364 A4
Fundão Portugal 40°8N 7°30W 293 B2
Fundy, B. of Canada 45°0N 66°0W 345 D6
Fundy △ Canada 45°35N 65°10W 345 C6
Funhalouro Mozam. 23°3S 34°25E 329 C5
Funing Hebei, China 39°53N 119°12E 307 E10
Funing Jiangsu, China 33°45N 119°50E 307 H10
Funiu Shan China 33°30N 112°20E 306 H7
Funtua Nigeria 11°30N 7°18E 322 F7
Fuping Hebei, China 38°48N 114°12E 306 E8
Fuping Shaanxi, China 34°42N 109°10E 306 G5
Furano Japan 43°21N 142°23E 302 C11
Furat, Nahr al → Asia 31°0N 47°25E 316 D5
Fūrg Iran 28°18N 55°13E 317 D7
Furnás Spain 39°3N 1°32E 296 B8
Furnas, Représa de Brazil 20°50S 45°30W 367 A6
Furneaux Group Australia 40°10S 147°50E 335 G4
Furqlus Syria 34°36N 37°8E 318 A6
Fürstenwalde Germany 52°22N 14°3E 288 B8
Fürth Germany 49°28N 10°59E 288 D6
Furukawa Japan 38°34N 140°58E 302 E10
Fury and Hecla Str. Canada 69°56N 84°0W 341 C11
Fusagasuga Colombia 4°21N 74°22W 364 C4
Fushan Shandong, China 37°30N 121°15E 307 F11
Fushan Shanxi, China 35°58N 111°51E 306 G6
Fushun China 41°50N 123°56E 307 D12
Fusong China 42°20N 127°15E 307 C14
Fustic Barbados 13°16N 59°38W 361 g
Futian China 22°32N 114°4E 305 F11
Fuxin China 42°5N 121°48E 307 C11
Fuyang China 33°0N 115°48E 306 H8
Fuyang He → China 38°12N 117°0E 306 E9
Fuyong China 22°40N 113°49E 305 F10
Fuyu Heilongjiang, China 47°49N 124°27E 305 B7
Fuyu Jilin, China 45°12N 124°43E 307 B13
Fuyun China 47°0N 89°28E 304 B3
Fuzhou China 26°5N 119°16E 305 D6
Fyn Denmark 55°20N 10°30E 281 J14
Fyne, L. U.K. 55°59N 5°23W 283 F3

G

Gabela Angola 11°0S 14°24E 324 G2
Gabès Tunisia 33°53N 10°2E 323 B8
Gabès, G. de Tunisia 34°0N 10°30E 323 B8
Gabon ■ Africa 0°10S 10°0E 324 E2
Gaborone Botswana 24°45S 25°57E 328 C4
Gabriels U.S.A. 44°26N 74°12W 355 B10
Gābrīk Iran 25°44N 58°28E 317 E8
Gabrovo Bulgaria 42°52N 25°19E 295 C11
Gāch Sār Iran 36°7N 51°19E 317 B6
Gachsārān Iran 30°15N 50°45E 317 D6
Gadag India 15°30N 75°45E 312 M9
Gadap Pakistan 25°5N 67°28E 314 G2
Gadarwara India 22°50N 78°50E 315 H8
Gadhada India 22°0N 71°35E 314 J4
Gadra Pakistan 25°40N 70°38E 314 G4
Gadsden U.S.A. 34°1N 86°1W 357 D11
Gadwal India 16°10N 77°50E 312 L10
Gaffney U.S.A. 35°5N 81°39W 357 D14
Gafsa Tunisia 34°24N 8°43E 322 B7
Gagaria India 25°43N 70°46E 314 G4
Găgăuzia □ Moldova 46°10N 28°40E 289 E15
Gagnoa Ivory C. 6°56N 5°16W 322 G4
Gagnon Canada 51°50N 68°5W 345 B6
Gagnon, L. Canada 62°3N 110°27W 343 A6
Gahini Rwanda 1°50S 30°30E 326 C3
Gahmar India 25°27N 83°49E 315 G10
Gai Xian = Gaizhou China 40°22N 122°20E 307 D12
Gaidouronisi Greece 34°53N 25°41E 297 E7
Gail U.S.A. 32°46N 101°27W 356 E4
Gaillimh = Galway Ireland 53°17N 9°3W 282 C2
Gaines U.S.A. 41°46N 77°35W 354 E7
Gainesville Fla., U.S.A. 29°40N 82°20W 357 G13
Gainesville Ga., U.S.A. 34°18N 83°50W 357 D13
Gainesville Mo., U.S.A. 36°36N 92°26W 352 G7
Gainesville Tex., U.S.A. 33°38N 97°8W 356 E6
Gainsborough U.K. 53°24N 0°46W 284 D7
Gairdner, L. Australia 31°30S 136°0E 335 E2
Gairloch U.K. 57°43N 5°41W 283 D3
Gairloch, L. U.K. 57°43N 5°45W 283 D3
Gaizhou China 40°22N 122°20E 307 D12
Gaj → Pakistan 26°26N 67°21E 314 F2
Gakuch Pakistan 36°7N 73°45E 315 A5
Galán, Cerro Argentina 25°55S 66°52W 366 B2
Galana → Kenya 3°9S 40°8E 326 C5
Galápagos = Colón, Arch. de Ecuador 0°0 91°0W 362 D1
Galapagos Fracture Zone Pac. Oc. 3°0N 110°0W 337 G17
Galapagos Rise Pac. Oc. 15°0S 95°0W 337 J18
Galashiels U.K. 55°37N 2°49W 283 F6
Galați Romania 45°27N 28°2E 289 F15
Galatina Italy 40°10N 18°10E 295 D8
Galax U.S.A. 36°40N 80°56W 353 G13
Galcaio Somali Rep. 6°30N 47°30E 319 F4
Galdhøpiggen Norway 61°38N 8°18E 280 F13
Galeana Chihuahua, Mexico 30°7N 107°38W 358 A3
Galeana Nuevo León, Mexico 24°50N 100°4W 358 A3
Galela Indonesia 1°50N 127°49E 309 D7
Galena U.S.A. 64°44N 156°56W 346 a
Galeota Pt. Trin. & Tob. 10°8N 60°59W 365 K16
Galera Pt. Trin. & Tob. 10°49N 60°54W 361 D7
Galesburg U.S.A. 40°57N 90°22W 352 E8
Galestan △ Iran 37°30N 56°0E 317 B8
Galeton U.S.A. 41°44N 77°39W 354 E7
Galich Russia 58°22N 42°24E 290 C7
Galicia □ Spain 42°43N 7°45W 293 A2
Galilee = Hagalil Israel 32°53N 35°18E 318 C4
Galilee, L. Australia 22°20S 145°50E 334 C4
Galilee, Sea of = Yam Kinneret Israel 32°45N 35°35E 318 C4
Galina Pt. Jamaica 18°24N 76°58W 360 a
Galinoporni Cyprus 35°31N 34°18E 297 D13
Galion U.S.A. 40°44N 82°47W 354 F2
Galiuro Mts. U.S.A. 32°30N 110°20W 349 K8
Galiwinku Australia 12°2S 135°34E 334 A2
Gallan Hd. U.K. 58°15N 7°2W 283 C1
Gallatin U.S.A. 36°24N 86°27W 357 C11
Galle Sri Lanka 6°5N 80°10E 312 R12
Gállego → Spain 41°39N 0°51W 293 B5
Gallegos → Argentina 51°35S 69°0W 368 G3
Galley Hd. Ireland 51°32N 8°55W 282 E3
Gallinas, Pta. Colombia 12°28N 71°40W 364 A4
Gallipoli = Gelibolu Turkey 40°28N 26°43E 295 D12
Gallípoli Italy 40°3N 17°58E 295 D8
Gallipolis U.S.A. 38°49N 82°12W 353 F12
Gällivare Sweden 67°9N 20°40E 280 C19
Galloo I. U.S.A. 43°55N 76°25W 355 C8
Galloway U.K. 55°1N 4°29W 283 F4
Galloway, Mull of U.K. 54°39N 4°52W 283 G4
Galloway ⌂ U.K. 55°3N 4°20W 283 F4
Gallup U.S.A. 35°32N 108°45W 349 J9
Galoya Sri Lanka 8°10N 80°55E 312 Q12
Galt U.S.A. 38°15N 121°18W 350 G5
Galty Mts. Ireland 52°22N 8°10W 282 D3
Galtymore Ireland 52°21N 8°11W 282 D3
Galva U.S.A. 41°10N 90°3W 352 E8
Galveston U.S.A. 29°18N 94°48W 356 G7
Galveston B. U.S.A. 29°36N 94°50W 356 G7
Gálvez Argentina 32°0S 61°14W 366 C3
Galway Ireland 53°17N 9°3W 282 C2
Galway □ Ireland 53°22N 9°1W 282 C2
Galway B. Ireland 53°13N 9°10W 282 C2
Gam → Vietnam 21°55N 105°12E 310 B5
Gamagōri Japan 34°50N 137°14E 303 G8
Gambat Pakistan 27°17N 68°26E 314 F3
Gambhir → India 26°58N 77°27E 314 F6
Gambia ■ W. Afr. 13°25N 16°0W 322 F2
Gambia → W. Afr. 13°28N 16°34W 322 F2
Gambier U.S.A. 40°22N 82°23W 354 F2
Gambier, C. Australia 11°56S 130°57E 332 B5
Gambier, Îs. French Polynesia 23°8S 134°58W 337 K14
Gambier Is. Australia 35°3S 136°30E 335 F2
Gambo Canada 48°47N 54°13W 345 C9
Gamboli Pakistan 29°53N 68°24E 314 E3
Gamboma Congo 1°55S 15°52E 324 E3
Gamka → S. Africa 33°18S 21°39E 328 E3
Gamkab → Namibia 28°4S 17°54E 328 D2
Gamlakarleby = Kokkola Finland 63°50N 23°8E 280 E20
Gammon → Canada 51°24N 95°44W 343 C9
Gammon Ranges △ Australia 30°38S 139°8E 335 E2
Gamtoos → S. Africa 33°58S 25°1E 328 E4
Gan Jiang → China 29°15N 116°0E 305 D6
Ganado U.S.A. 35°43N 109°33W 349 J9
Gananoque Canada 44°20N 76°10W 355 B8
Ganāveh Iran 29°35N 50°35E 317 D6
Gäncä Azerbaijan 40°45N 46°20E 291 F8
Gancheng China 18°51N 108°37E 310 C7
Gand = Gent Belgium 51°2N 3°42E 287 C3
Ganda Angola 13°3S 14°35E 325 G2
Gandajika Dem. Rep. of the Congo 6°46S 23°58E 324 F4
Gandak → India 25°39N 85°13E 315 G11
Gandava Pakistan 28°32N 67°32E 314 E2
Gander Canada 48°58N 54°35W 345 C9
Gander L. Canada 48°58N 54°35W 345 C9
Ganderowe Falls Zimbabwe 17°20S 29°10E 327 F2
Gandhi Sagar India 24°40N 75°40E 314 G6
Gandhinagar India 23°15N 72°45E 314 H5
Gandia Spain 38°58N 0°9W 293 C5
Gando, Pta. Canary Is. 27°55N 15°22W 296 G4
Ganedidalem = Gani Indonesia 0°48S 128°14E 309 E7
Ganga → India 23°20N 90°30E 315 H14
Ganga Sagar India 21°38N 88°5E 315 J13
Gangan → India 28°38N 78°58E 315 E8
Ganganagar India 29°56N 73°56E 314 E5
Gangapur India 26°32N 76°49E 314 F7
Gangaw Burma 22°5N 94°5E 313 H19
Gangdisê Shan China 31°20N 81°0E 315 D9
Ganges = Ganga → India 23°20N 90°30E 315 H14
Ganges Canada 48°51N 123°31W 342 D4
Ganges, Mouths of the India 21°30N 90°0E 315 J14
Ganggyeong S. Korea 36°10N 127°0E 307 F14
Ganghwa S. Korea 37°45N 126°30E 307 F14
Gangneung S. Korea 37°45N 128°54E 307 F15
Gangoh India 29°46N 77°18E 314 E7
Gangotri India 30°50N 79°10E 315 D8
Gangotri △ India 30°50N 79°10E 315 D8
Gangseong S. Korea 38°24N 128°30E 307 E15
Gangtok India 27°20N 88°37E 313 F16
Gangu China 34°40N 105°15E 306 G3
Gangyao China 44°12N 126°37E 307 B14
Gani Indonesia 0°48S 128°14E 309 E7
Ganj India 27°45N 78°57E 315 F8
Gannett Peak U.S.A. 43°11N 109°39W 348 E9
Ganquan China 36°20N 109°20E 306 F5
Gansu □ China 36°0N 104°0E 306 G3
Ganta Liberia 7°15N 8°59W 322 G4
Gantheaume, C. Australia 36°4S 137°32E 335 F2
Gantheaume B. Australia 27°40S 114°10E 333 E1
Gantsevichi = Hantsavichy Belarus 52°49N 26°30E 289 B14
Ganyem = Genyem Indonesia 2°46S 140°12E 309 E10
Ganyu China 34°50N 119°8E 307 G10
Ganzhou China 25°51N 114°56E 305 D6
Gao Mali 16°15N 0°5W 322 E5
Gaomi China 36°20N 119°42E 307 F10
Gaoping China 35°45N 112°55E 306 G7
Gaotang China 36°50N 116°15E 306 F9
Gaoua Burkina Faso 10°20N 3°8W 322 F5
Gaoual Guinea 11°45N 13°25W 322 F3
Gaoxiong = Kaohsiung Taiwan 22°35N 120°16E 305 D7
Gaoyang China 38°40N 115°45E 306 E8
Gaoyou Hu China 32°45N 119°20E 307 H10
Gaoyuan China 37°8N 117°58E 307 F9
Gap France 44°33N 6°5E 292 D7
Gapat → India 24°30N 82°28E 315 G10
Gapuwiyak Australia 12°25S 135°43E 334 A2
Gar China 32°10N 79°58E 304 C2
Gara, L. Ireland 53°57N 8°26W 282 C3
Garabogazköl Aylagy Turkmenistan 41°0N 53°30E 291 F9
Garachico Canary Is. 28°22N 16°46W 296 F3
Garachiné Panama 8°0N 78°12W 360 E4
Garafia Canary Is. 28°48N 17°57W 296 F2
Garagum Turkmenistan 39°30N 60°0E 317 B8
Garah Australia 29°5S 149°38E 335 D4
Garajonay Canary Is. 28°7N 17°14W 296 F2
Garamba △ Dem. Rep. of the Congo 4°10N 29°40E 326 B2
Garanhuns Brazil 8°50S 36°30W 365 E11
Garautha India 25°34N 79°18E 315 G8
Garba Tula Kenya 0°30N 38°32E 326 B4
Garberville U.S.A. 40°6N 123°48W 348 F2
Garbiyang India 30°8N 80°54E 315 D9
Gard → France 43°51N 4°37E 292 E6
Garda, L. di Italy 45°40N 10°41E 294 B4
Garde L. Canada 62°50N 106°13W 343 A7
Garden City Ga., U.S.A. 32°6N 81°9W 357 E14
Garden City Kans., U.S.A. 37°58N 100°53W 352 G3
Garden City Tex., U.S.A. 31°52N 101°29W 356 F4
Garden Grove U.S.A. 33°47N 117°55W 351 M9
Gardēz Afghan. 33°37N 69°9E 314 C3
Gardiner Maine, U.S.A. 44°14N 69°47W 353 C19
Gardiner Mont., U.S.A. 45°2N 110°22W 348 D8
Gardiners I. U.S.A. 41°6N 72°6W 355 E12
Gardner U.S.A. 42°34N 71°59W 355 D13
Gardner Canal Canada 53°27N 128°8W 342 C3
Gardnerville U.S.A. 38°56N 119°45W 350 G7
Gardo Somali Rep. 9°30N 49°6E 319 F4
Garey U.S.A. 34°53N 120°19W 351 L6
Garfield U.S.A. 47°1N 117°9W 348 C5
Garforth U.K. 53°47N 1°24W 284 D6
Gargantua, C. Canada 47°36N 85°2W 353 B11
Gargett Australia 21°9S 148°46E 334 K6
Garibaldi ⌂ Canada 49°50N 122°40W 342 D4
Gariep, L. S. Africa 30°40S 25°40E 328 E4
Garies S. Africa 30°32S 17°59E 328 E2
Garigliano → Italy 41°13N 13°45E 294 D5
Garissa Kenya 0°25S 39°40E 326 C4
Garland Tex., U.S.A. 32°54N 96°38W 356 E6
Garland Utah, U.S.A. 41°45N 112°10W 348 F7
Garm Tajikistan 39°0N 70°20E 300 F8
Garmāb Iran 35°25N 56°45E 317 C8
Garmisch-Partenkirchen Germany 47°30N 11°6E 288 E6
Garmsār Iran 35°20N 52°25E 317 C7
Garner U.S.A. 43°6N 93°36W 352 D7
Garnett U.S.A. 38°17N 95°14W 352 F6
Garo Hills India 25°30N 90°30E 315 G14
Garoe Somali Rep. 8°25N 48°33E 319 F4
Garonne → France 45°2N 0°36W 292 D3
Garoowe = Garoe Somali Rep. 8°25N 48°33E 319 F4
Garot India 24°19N 75°41E 314 G6
Garoua Cameroon 9°19N 13°21E 323 G8
Garrauli India 25°5N 79°22E 315 G8
Garrison Mont., U.S.A. 46°31N 112°49W 348 C7
Garrison N. Dak., U.S.A. 47°40N 101°25W 352 B3
Garrison Res. = Sakakawea, L. U.S.A. 47°30N 101°25W 352 B3
Garron Pt. U.K. 55°3N 5°59W 282 A6
Garry → U.K. 56°44N 3°47W 283 E5
Garry, L. Canada 65°58N 100°18W 340 C9
Garrygala Turkmenistan 38°31N 56°29E 317 B8
Garsen Kenya 2°20S 40°5E 326 C5
Garson L. Canada 56°19N 110°2W 343 B6
Garstang U.K. 53°55N 2°46W 284 D5
Garu India 23°40N 84°14E 315 H11
Garub Namibia 26°37S 16°0E 328 D2

Garut Indonesia 7°14S 107°53E 309 G12
Garvie Mts. N.Z. 45°30S 168°50E 331 F2
Garwa = Garoua Cameroon 9°19N 13°21E 323 G8
Garwa India 24°11N 83°47E 315 G10
Gary U.S.A. 41°36N 87°20W 352 E10
Garzê China 31°38N 100°1E 304 C5
Garzón Colombia 2°10N 75°40W 364 C3
Gas-San Japan 38°32N 140°1E 302 E10
Gasan Kuli = Esenguly Turkmenistan 37°37N 53°59E 300 F6
Gascogne France 43°45N 0°20E 292 E4
Gascogne, G. de Europe 44°0N 2°0W 292 D2
Gascony = Gascogne France 43°45N 0°20E 292 E4
Gascoyne → Australia 24°52S 113°37E 333 D1
Gascoyne Junction Australia 25°2S 115°17E 333 E2
Gashaka Nigeria 7°20N 11°29E 323 G8
Gasherbrum Pakistan 35°40N 76°40E 315 B7
Gashua Nigeria 12°54N 11°0E 323 F8
Gasparillo Trin. & Tob. 10°18N 61°26W 365 K15
Gaspé Canada 48°52N 64°30W 345 C7
Gaspé, C. Canada 48°48N 64°7W 345 C7
Gaspé Pen. = Gaspésie, Pén. de la Canada 48°45N 65°40W 345 C6
Gaspésie, Pén. de la Canada 48°45N 65°40W 345 C6
Gaspésie ⌓ Canada 48°55N 66°10W 345 C6
Gasteiz = Vitoria-Gasteiz Spain 42°50N 2°41W 293 A4
Gastonia U.S.A. 35°16N 81°11W 357 D14
Gastre Argentina 42°20S 69°15W 368 E3
Gata, C. Cyprus 34°34N 33°2E 297 E12
Gata, C. de Spain 36°41N 2°13W 293 D4
Gata, Sierra de Spain 40°20N 6°45W 293 B2
Gataga → Canada 58°35N 126°59W 342 B3
Gatchina Russia 59°35N 30°9E 281 G24
Gatehouse of Fleet U.K. 54°53N 4°12W 283 G4
Gates U.S.A. 43°9N 77°42W 354 C7
Gateshead U.K. 54°57N 1°35W 284 C6
Gatesville U.S.A. 31°26N 97°45W 356 F6
Gateway ⌓ U.S.A. 40°38N 73°51W 355 F11
Gaths Zimbabwe 20°2S 30°32E 327 G3
Gatico Chile 22°29S 70°20W 366 A1
Gatineau Canada 45°29N 75°39W 355 A9
Gatineau → Canada 45°27N 75°42W 344 C4
Gatineau △ Canada 45°40N 76°0W 344 C4
Gatton Australia 27°32S 152°17E 335 D5
Gatun, L. Panama 9°7N 79°56W 360 E4
Gatwick, London ✈ (LGW) U.K. 51°10N 0°11W 285 F7
Gatyana S. Africa 32°16S 28°31E 329 E4
Gau Fiji 18°2S 179°18E 331 a
Gauer L. Canada 57°0N 97°50W 343 B9
Gauhati = Guwahati India 26°10N 91°45E 313 F17
Gauja → Latvia 57°10N 24°16E 281 H21
Gaujas △ Latvia 57°10N 24°50E 281 H21
Gaula → Norway 63°21N 10°14E 280 E14
Gauri Phanta India 28°41N 80°36E 315 E9
Gaustatoppen Norway 59°48N 8°40E 281 G13
Gauteng □ S. Africa 26°0S 28°0E 329 D4
Gāv Koshī Iran 28°38N 57°12E 317 D8
Gāvakān Iran 29°37N 53°10E 317 D7
Gavāter Iran 25°10N 61°31E 317 E9
Gāvbandī Iran 27°12N 53°4E 317 E7
Gavdopoula Greece 34°56N 24°0E 297 E6
Gavdos Greece 34°50N 24°5E 297 E6
Gaviota U.S.A. 34°29N 120°13W 351 L6
Gāvkhūnī, Bāṭlāq-e Iran 32°6N 52°52E 317 C7
Gävle Sweden 60°40N 17°9E 280 F17
Gawachab Namibia 27°4S 17°55E 328 D2
Gawilgarh Hills India 21°15N 76°45E 312 J10
Gawler Australia 34°30S 138°42E 335 E2
Gawler Ranges Australia 32°30S 135°45E 335 E2
Gaxun Nur China 42°22N 100°30E 304 B5
Gay Russia 51°27N 58°27E 290 D10
Gaya India 24°47N 85°4E 315 G11
Gaya Niger 11°52N 3°28E 322 F6
Gaylord U.S.A. 45°2N 84°41W 353 C11
Gayndah Australia 25°35S 151°32E 335 D5
Gaysin = Haysyn Ukraine 48°57N 29°25E 289 D15
Gayvoron = Hayvoron Ukraine 48°22N 29°52E 289 D15
Gaza Gaza Strip 31°30N 34°28E 318 D3
Gaza □ Mozam. 23°10S 32°45E 329 C5
Gaza Strip ■ Asia 31°29N 34°25E 318 D3
Gazanjyk = Bereket Turkmenistan 39°16N 55°32E 317 B7
Gāzbor Iran 28°5N 58°51E 317 D8
Gazi Dem. Rep. of the Congo 1°3N 24°30E 326 B1
Gaziantep Turkey 37°6N 37°23E 316 B3
Gazimağusa = Famagusta Cyprus 35°8N 33°55E 297 D12
Gcoverega Botswana 19°8S 24°18E 328 B3
Gcuwa S. Africa 32°20S 28°11E 329 E4
Gdańsk Poland 54°22N 18°40E 289 A10
Gdańska, Zatoka Poland 54°30N 19°20E 289 A10
Gdov Russia 58°48N 27°55E 281 G22
Gdynia Poland 54°35N 18°33E 289 A10
Gebe Indonesia 0°5N 129°25E 309 D7
Gebze Turkey 40°47N 29°25E 295 D13
Gedaref Sudan 14°2N 35°28E 323 F13
Gediz → Turkey 38°35N 26°48E 295 E12
Gedser Denmark 54°35N 11°55E 281 J14
Gedung, Pulau Malaysia 5°17N 100°23E 311 c
Geegully Cr. → Australia 18°32S 123°41E 332 C3
Geel Belgium 51°10N 4°59E 287 C4
Geelong Australia 38°10S 144°22E 335 F3
Geelvink B. = Cenderwasih, Teluk Indonesia 3°0S 135°20E 309 E9
Geelvink Chan. Australia 28°30S 114°0E 333 E1
Geesthacht Germany 53°26N 10°22E 288 B6
Geidam Nigeria 12°57N 11°57E 323 F8
Geikie → Canada 57°45N 103°52W 343 B8
Geikie Gorge △ Australia 18°3S 125°41E 332 C4
Geistown U.S.A. 40°18N 78°52W 354 F6
Geita Tanzania 2°48S 32°12E 326 C3
Gejiu China 23°20N 103°10E 304 D5
Gel, Meydān-e Iran 29°4N 54°50E 317 D7
Gela Italy 37°4N 14°15E 294 F6
Gelang Patah Malaysia 1°27N 103°35E 311 d
Gelderland □ Neths. 52°5N 6°10E 287 B6
Geldrop Neths. 51°25N 5°32E 287 C5
Geleen Neths. 50°57N 5°49E 287 D5
Gelib Somali Rep. 0°29N 42°46E 319 G3
Gelibolu Turkey 40°28N 26°43E 295 D12
Gelsenkirchen Germany 51°32N 7°6E 288 C4
Gelugur Malaysia 5°22N 100°18E 311 c
Gemas Malaysia 2°37N 102°36E 311 L4
Gembloux Belgium 50°34N 4°43E 287 D4
Gemena Dem. Rep. of the Congo 3°13N 19°48E 324 D3
Gemerek Turkey 39°15N 36°10E 316 B3
Gemlik Turkey 40°26N 29°9E 295 D13
Gemsbok △ Botswana 25°5S 21°1E 328 D3
Genadi Greece 36°2N 27°56E 297 C9
Genale → Ethiopia 6°2N 39°1E 319 F2
General Acha Argentina 37°20S 64°38W 366 D3
General Alvear B. Aires, Argentina 36°0S 60°0W 366 D4
General Alvear Mendoza, Argentina 35°0S 67°40W 366 D2
General Artigas Paraguay 26°52S 56°16W 366 B4
General Belgrano Argentina 36°35S 58°47W 366 D4
General Bernardo O'Higgins Antarctica 63°0S 58°3W 277 C18
General Cabrera Argentina 32°53S 63°52W 366 C3
General Cepeda Mexico 25°21N 101°22W 358 B4
General Guido Argentina 36°40S 57°50W 366 D4
General Juan Madariaga Argentina 37°0S 57°0W 366 D4
General La Madrid Argentina 37°17S 61°20W 366 D3
General MacArthur Phil. 11°18N 125°28E 309 B7
General Martin Miguel de Güemes Argentina 24°50S 65°0W 366 A3
General Paz Argentina 27°45S 57°36W 366 B4
General Pico Argentina 35°45S 63°50W 366 D3
General Pinedo Argentina 27°15S 61°20W 366 B3
General Pinto Argentina 34°45S 61°50W 366 C3
General Roca Argentina 39°2S 67°35W 368 D3
General Santos Phil. 6°5N 125°14E 309 C7
General Treviño Mexico 26°14N 99°29W 359 B5
General Trías Mexico 28°21N 106°22W 358 B3
General Viamonte Argentina 35°1S 61°3W 366 D3
General Villegas Argentina 35°5S 63°0W 366 D3
Genesee Idaho, U.S.A. 46°33N 116°56W 348 C5
Genesee Pa., U.S.A. 41°59N 77°54W 354 E7
Genesee → U.S.A. 43°16N 77°36W 354 C7
Geneseo Ill., U.S.A. 41°27N 90°9W 352 E8
Geneseo N.Y., U.S.A. 42°48N 77°49W 354 D7
Geneva = Genève Switz. 46°12N 6°9E 292 C7
Geneva Ala., U.S.A. 31°2N 85°52W 357 F12
Geneva N.Y., U.S.A. 42°52N 76°59W 354 D8
Geneva Nebr., U.S.A. 40°32N 97°36W 352 E5
Geneva Ohio, U.S.A. 41°48N 80°57W 354 E4
Geneva, L. = Léman, L. Europe 46°26N 6°30E 292 C7
Genève Switz. 46°12N 6°9E 292 C7
Genil → Spain 37°42N 5°19W 293 D3
Genk Belgium 50°58N 5°32E 287 D5
Gennargentu, Mti. del Italy 40°1N 9°19E 294 D3
Genoa = Génova Italy 44°25N 8°57E 292 D8
Genoa Australia 37°29S 149°35E 335 F4
Genoa N.Y., U.S.A. 42°40N 76°32W 355 D8
Genoa Nebr., U.S.A. 41°27N 97°44W 352 E5
Genoa Nev., U.S.A. 39°2N 119°50W 350 F7
Génova Italy 44°25N 8°57E 292 D8
Génova, G. di Italy 44°0N 9°0E 294 C3
Genriyetty, Ostrov Russia 77°6N 156°30E 301 B16
Gent Belgium 51°2N 3°42E 287 C3
Genteng Bali, Indonesia 8°22S 114°9E 309 J17
Genteng Jawa Barat, Indonesia 7°22S 106°24E 309 G12
Genyem Indonesia 2°46S 140°12E 309 E10
Geochang S. Korea 35°41N 127°55E 307 G14
Geographe B. Australia 33°30S 115°15E 333 F2
Geographe Chan. Australia 24°30S 113°0E 333 D1
Georga, Zemlya Russia 80°30N 49°0E 300 A5
George S. Africa 33°58S 22°29E 328 E3
George → Canada 58°49N 66°10W 345 A6
George, L. N.S.W., Australia 35°10S 149°25E 335 F4
George, L. S. Austral., Australia 37°25S 140°0E 335 F3
George, L. W. Austral., Australia 22°45S 123°40E 332 D3
George, L. Uganda 0°5N 30°10E 326 B3
George, L. Fla., U.S.A. 29°17N 81°36W 357 G14
George, L. N.Y., U.S.A. 43°37N 73°33W 355 C11
George Gill Ra. Australia 24°22S 131°45E 332 D5
George Pt. Australia 20°6S 148°36E 334 J6
George River = Kangiqsualujjuaq Canada 58°30N 65°59W 341 D13
George Sound N.Z. 44°52S 167°25E 331 F1
George Town Australia 41°6S 146°49E 335 G4
George Town Bahamas 23°33N 75°47W 360 B4
George Town Cayman Is. 19°20N 81°24W 360 C3
George Town Malaysia 5°25N 100°20E 311 c
George V Land Antarctica 69°0S 148°0E 277 C10
George VI Sound Antarctica 71°0S 68°0W 277 D17
George West U.S.A. 28°20N 98°7W 356 G5
Georgetown = Janjanbureh Gambia 13°30N 14°47W 322 F3
Georgetown Australia 18°17S 143°33E 334 B3
Georgetown Ont., Canada 43°40N 79°56W 354 C5
Georgetown P.E.I., Canada 46°13N 62°24W 345 C7
Georgetown Guyana 6°50N 58°12W 364 B7
Georgetown Calif., U.S.A. 38°54N 120°50W 350 G6
Georgetown Colo., U.S.A. 39°42N 105°42W 348 G11
Georgetown Ky., U.S.A. 38°13N 84°33W 353 F11
Georgetown N.Y., U.S.A. 42°46N 75°44W 355 D9
Georgetown Ohio, U.S.A. 38°52N 83°54W 353 F12
Georgetown S.C., U.S.A. 33°23N 79°17W 357 E15
Georgetown Tex., U.S.A. 30°38N 97°41W 356 F6
Georgia □ U.S.A. 32°50N 83°15W 357 E13
Georgia ■ Asia 42°0N 43°0E 291 F7
Georgia, Str. of N. Amer. 49°25N 124°0W 350 A3
Georgia Basin S. Ocean 50°45S 35°30W 277 B1
Georgian B. Canada 45°15N 81°0W 354 A4
Georgian Bay Islands △ Canada 44°53N 79°52W 354 B5
Georgina → Australia 23°30S 139°47E 334 C2
Georgina I. Canada 44°22N 79°17W 354 B5
Georgioupoli Greece 35°20N 24°15E 297 D6
Georgiyevsk Russia 44°12N 43°28E 291 F7
Gera Germany 50°53N 12°4E 288 C7
Geraardsbergen Belgium 50°45N 3°53E 287 D3
Geral, Serra Brazil 26°25S 50°0W 367 B6
Geral de Goiás, Serra Brazil 12°0S 46°0W 365 F9
Geraldine U.S.A. 47°36N 110°16W 348 C8
Geraldton Australia 28°48S 114°32E 333 E1
Geraldton Canada 49°44N 86°59W 344 C2
Gereshk Afghan. 31°47N 64°35E 312 D4
Gerik Malaysia 5°50N 101°15E 311 K3
Gering U.S.A. 41°50N 103°40W 352 E2
Gerlach U.S.A. 40°39N 119°21W 348 F4
Germansen Landing Canada 55°43N 124°40W 342 B4
Germantown U.S.A. 35°5N 89°49W 357 D10
Germany ■ Europe 51°0N 10°0E 288 C6
Germī Iran 39°1N 48°3E 317 B6
Germiston S. Africa 26°13S 28°10E 329 D4
Gernika-Lumo Spain 43°19N 2°40W 293 A4
Gero Japan 35°48N 137°14E 303 G8
Gerokgak Indonesia 8°11S 114°27E 309 J17
Gerona = Girona Spain 41°58N 2°46E 293 B7
Geropotamos → Greece 35°3N 24°50E 297 D6
Gerrard Canada 50°30N 117°17W 342 C5
Gertak Sanggul Malaysia 5°17N 100°12E 311 c
Gertak Sanggul, Tanjung Malaysia 5°16N 100°11E 311 c
Gerung Indonesia 8°43S 116°7E 309 K19
Geser Indonesia 3°50S 130°54E 309 E8
Getafe Spain 40°18N 3°43W 293 B4
Gettysburg Pa., U.S.A. 39°50N 77°14W 353 F15
Gettysburg S. Dak., U.S.A. 45°1N 99°57W 352 C4
Getxo Spain 43°21N 2°59W 293 A4
Getz Ice Shelf Antarctica 75°0S 130°0W 277 D14
Geyser U.S.A. 47°16N 110°30W 348 C8
Geyserville U.S.A. 38°42N 122°54W 350 G4
Ghadāmis Libya 30°11N 9°29E 323 B8
Ghaggar → India 29°30N 74°53E 314 E6
Ghaghara → India 25°45N 84°40E 315 G11
Ghaghat → Bangla. 25°19N 89°38E 315 G13
Ghagra India 23°17N 84°33E 315 H11
Ghagra → India 27°29N 81°9E 315 F9
Ghallamane Mauritania 23°15N 10°0W 322 D4
Ghana ■ W. Afr. 8°0N 1°0W 322 G5
Ghansor India 22°39N 80°1E 315 H9
Ghanzi Botswana 21°50S 21°34E 328 C3
Ghardaïa Algeria 32°20N 3°37E 322 B6
Gharyān Libya 32°10N 13°0E 323 B8
Ghat Libya 24°59N 10°11E 323 D8
Ghatal India 22°40N 87°46E 315 H12
Ghatampur India 26°8N 80°13E 315 F9
Ghats, Eastern India 14°0N 78°50E 312 N11
Ghats, Western India 14°0N 75°0E 312 N9
Ghatsila India 22°36N 86°29E 315 H12
Ghaṭṭī Si. Arabia 31°16N 37°31E 316 D3
Ghawdex = Gozo Malta 36°3N 14°15E 297 C1
Ghazal, Bahr el → Chad 13°0N 15°47E 323 F9
Ghazâl, Bahr el → Sudan 9°31N 30°25E 323 G12
Ghaziabad India 28°42N 77°26E 314 E7
Ghazipur India 25°38N 83°35E 315 G10
Ghaznī Afghan. 33°30N 68°28E 314 C3
Ghaznī □ Afghan. 32°10N 68°20E 312 C6
Ghent = Gent Belgium 51°2N 3°42E 287 C3
Gheorghe Gheorghiu-Dej = Oneşti Romania 46°17N 26°47E 289 E14
Ghīnah, Wādī al → Si. Arabia 30°27N 38°14E 316 D3
Ghizar → Pakistan 36°15N 73°43E 315 A5
Ghotaru India 27°20N 70°1E 314 F4
Ghotki Pakistan 28°5N 69°21E 314 E3
Ghowr □ Afghan. 34°0N 64°20E 312 C4
Ghudāf, W. al → Iraq 32°56N 43°30E 316 C4
Ghughri India 22°39N 80°41E 315 H9
Ghugus India 19°58N 79°12E 312 K11
Ghulam Mohammad Barrage Pakistan 25°30N 68°20E 314 G3
Ghūrīān Afghan. 34°17N 61°25E 312 B2
Gia Dinh Vietnam 10°49N 106°42E 311 G6
Gia Lai = Plei Ku Vietnam 13°57N 108°0E 310 F7
Gia Nghia Vietnam 11°58N 107°42E 311 G6
Gia Ngoc Vietnam 14°50N 108°58E 310 E7
Gia Vuc Vietnam 14°42N 108°34E 310 E7
Giamama Somali Rep. 0°4N 42°44E 319 G3
Giannitsa Greece 40°46N 22°24E 295 D10
Giant Forest U.S.A. 36°36N 118°43W 350 J8
Giant Sequoia ⌓ U.S.A. 36°10N 118°35W 350 K8
Giants Causeway U.K. 55°16N 6°29W 282 A5
Gianyar Indonesia 8°32S 115°20E 309 K18
Giarabub = Al Jaghbūb Libya 29°42N 24°38E 323 C10
Giarre Italy 37°43N 15°11E 294 F6
Gibara Cuba 21°9N 76°11W 360 B4
Gibb River Australia 16°26S 126°26E 332 C4
Gibbon U.S.A. 40°45N 98°51W 352 E4
Gibeon Namibia 25°9S 17°43E 328 D2
Gibraltar ☒ Europe 36°7N 5°22W 293 D3
Gibraltar, Str. of Medit. S. 35°55N 5°40W 293 E3
Gibraltar Range △ Australia 29°31S 152°19E 335 D5
Gibson Desert Australia 24°0S 126°0E 332 D4
Gibsons Canada 49°24N 123°32W 342 D4
Gibsonville U.S.A. 39°46N 120°54W 350 F6
Giddings U.S.A. 30°11N 96°56W 356 F6
Giebnegáisi = Kebnekaise Sweden 67°53N 18°33E 280 C18
Giessen Germany 50°34N 8°41E 288 C5
Gīfān Iran 37°54N 57°28E 317 B8
Gift Lake Canada 55°53N 115°49W 342 B5
Gifu Japan 35°30N 136°45E 303 G8
Gifu □ Japan 35°40N 137°0E 303 G8
Giganta, Sa. de la Mexico 26°0N 111°39W 358 B2
Gigha U.K. 55°42N 5°44W 283 F3
Giglio Italy 42°20N 10°52E 294 C4
Gijón Spain 43°32N 5°42W 293 A3
Gil I. Canada 53°12N 129°15W 342 C3
Gila → U.S.A. 32°43N 114°33W 349 K6
Gila Bend U.S.A. 32°57N 112°43W 349 K7
Gila Bend Mts. U.S.A. 33°10N 113°0W 349 K7
Gila Cliff Dwellings ⌓ U.S.A. 33°12N 108°16W 349 K9
Gīlān □ Iran 37°0N 50°0E 317 B6
Gilbert → Australia 16°35S 141°15E 334 B3
Gilbert Is. Kiribati 1°0N 172°0E 330 A10
Gilbert River Australia 18°9S 142°52E 334 B3
Gilbert Seamounts Pac. Oc. 52°50N 150°10W 276 D18
Gilead U.S.A. 44°24N 70°59W 355 B14
Gilf el Kebîr, Hadabat el Egypt 23°50N 25°50E 323 D11
Gilford I. Canada 50°40N 126°30W 342 C3
Gilgandra Australia 31°43S 148°39E 335 E4
Gilgil Kenya 0°30S 36°20E 326 C4
Gilgit India 35°50N 74°15E 315 B6
Gilgit → Pakistan 35°44N 74°37E 315 B6
Gili ⌓ Mozam. 16°39S 38°27E 327 F4
Gilimanuk Indonesia 8°10S 114°26E 309 J17
Gillam Canada 56°20N 94°40W 343 B10
Gillen, L. Australia 26°11S 124°38E 333 E3
Gilles, L. Australia 32°50S 136°45E 335 E2
Gillette U.S.A. 44°18N 105°30W 348 D11
Gilliat Australia 20°40S 141°28E 334 C3
Gillingham U.K. 51°23N 0°33E 285 F8
Gilmer U.S.A. 32°44N 94°57W 356 E7
Gilmore, L. Australia 32°29S 121°37E 333 F3
Gilroy U.S.A. 37°1N 121°34W 350 H5
Gimcheon S. Korea 36°11N 128°4E 307 F15
Gimhae S. Korea 35°14N 128°53E 307 G15
Gimhwa S. Korea 38°17N 127°28E 307 E14
Gimie, Mt St. Lucia 13°54N 61°0W 361 f
Gimje S. Korea 35°48N 126°45E 307 G14
Gimli Canada 50°40N 97°0W 343 C9
Gin Gin Australia 25°0S 151°58E 335 D5
Gingin Australia 31°22S 115°54E 333 F2
Gingindlovu S. Africa 29°2S 31°30E 329 D5
Ginir Ethiopia 7°6N 40°40E 319 F3
Giofyros → Greece 35°20N 25°6E 297 D7
Giohar Somali Rep. 2°48N 45°30E 319 G4
Giona, Oros Greece 38°38N 22°14E 295 E10
Gir △ India 21°0N 71°0E 314 J4
Gir Hills India 21°0N 71°0E 314 J4
Girab India 26°2N 70°38E 314 F4
Girâfi, W. → Egypt 29°58N 34°39E 318 F3
Girard Kans., U.S.A. 37°31N 94°51W 352 G6
Girard Ohio, U.S.A. 41°9N 80°42W 354 E4
Girard Pa., U.S.A. 42°0N 80°19W 354 E4
Girdle Ness U.K. 57°9N 2°3W 283 D6
Giresun Turkey 40°55N 38°30E 291 F6
Girga Egypt 26°17N 31°55E 323 C12
Giri → India 30°28N 77°41E 314 D7
Giridih India 24°10N 86°21E 315 G12
Giriftu Kenya 1°59N 39°46E 326 B4
Girne = Kyrenia Cyprus 35°20N 33°20E 297 D12
Giron = Kiruna Sweden 67°52N 20°15E 280 C19
Girona Spain 41°58N 2°46E 293 B7
Gironde → France 45°32N 1°7W 292 D3
Girraween △ Australia 28°46S 151°54E 335 D5
Giru Australia 19°30S 147°5E 334 B4
Girvan U.K. 55°14N 4°51W 283 F4
Gisborne N.Z. 38°39S 178°5E 331 C7
Gisenyi Rwanda 1°41S 29°15E 326 C2
Gislaved Sweden 57°19N 13°32E 281 H15
Gitega Burundi 3°26S 29°56E 326 C2
Githio Greece 36°46N 22°34E 295 F10
Giuba → Somali Rep. 1°30N 42°35E 319 G3
Giurgiu Romania 43°52N 25°57E 289 G13
Giza = El Gîza Egypt 30°0N 31°12E 323 C12
Giza Pyramids Egypt 29°58N 31°9E 323 C12
Gizab Afghan. 33°22N 66°17E 314 C1
Gizhiga Russia 62°3N 160°30E 301 C17
Gizhiginskaya Guba Russia 61°0N 158°0E 301 C16
Giżycko Poland 54°2N 21°48E 289 A11
Gjirokastër Albania 40°7N 20°10E 295 D9
Gjoa Haven Canada 68°38N 95°53W 340 C10
Gjøvik Norway 60°47N 10°43E 280 F14
Glace Bay Canada 46°11N 59°58W 345 C8
Glacier △ Canada 51°15N 117°30W 342 C5
Glacier △ U.S.A. 48°42N 113°48W 348 B7
Glacier Bay ⌓ U.S.A. 58°45N 136°30W 342 B1
Glacier Peak U.S.A. 48°7N 121°7W 348 B3
Gladewater U.S.A. 32°33N 94°56W 356 E7
Gladstone Queens., Australia 23°52S 151°16E 334 C5
Gladstone S. Austral., Australia 33°15S 138°22E 335 E2
Gladstone Canada 50°13N 98°57W 343 C9
Gladstone U.S.A. 45°51N 87°1W 352 C10
Gladwin U.S.A. 43°59N 84°29W 353 D11
Glagah Indonesia 8°13S 114°18E 309 J17
Glåma = Glomma → Norway 59°12N 10°57E 281 G14
Gláma Iceland 65°48N 23°0W 280 D2
Glamis U.S.A. 32°55N 115°5W 351 N11
Glamorgan, Vale of □ U.K. 51°28N 3°25W 285 F4
Glasco Kans., U.S.A. 39°22N 97°50W 352 F5
Glasco N.Y., U.S.A. 42°3N 73°57W 355 D11
Glasgow U.K. 55°51N 4°15W 283 F4
Glasgow Ky., U.S.A. 37°0N 85°55W 353 G11
Glasgow Mont., U.S.A. 48°12N 106°38W 348 B10
Glasgow, City of □ U.K. 55°51N 4°12W 283 F4
Glasgow Int. ✈ (GLA) U.K. 55°51N 4°21W 283 F4
Glaslyn Canada 53°22N 108°21W 343 C7
Glastonbury U.K. 51°9N 2°43W 285 F5
Glastonbury U.S.A. 41°43N 72°37W 355 E12
Glazov Russia 58°9N 52°40E 290 C9
Gleichen Canada 50°52N 113°3W 342 C6
Gleiwitz = Gliwice Poland 50°22N 18°41E 289 C10
Glen U.S.A. 44°7N 71°11W 355 B13
Glen Affric U.K. 57°17N 5°1W 283 D3
Glen Canyon U.S.A. 37°30N 110°40W 349 H8
Glen Canyon ⌓ U.S.A. 37°15N 111°0W 349 H8
Glen Canyon Dam U.S.A. 36°57N 111°29W 349 H8
Glen Coe U.K. 56°40N 5°0W 283 E3
Glen Cove U.S.A. 40°51N 73°38W 355 F11
Glen Garry U.K. 57°3N 5°7W 283 D3
Glen Innes Australia 29°44S 151°44E 335 D5
Glen Lyon U.S.A. 41°10N 76°5W 355 E8
Glen Mor U.K. 57°9N 4°37W 283 D4
Glen More ⌓ U.K. 57°8N 3°40W 283 D5
Glen Moriston U.K. 57°11N 4°52W 283 D4
Glen Robertson Canada 45°22N 74°30W 355 A10
Glen Spean U.K. 56°53N 4°40W 283 E4
Glen Ullin U.S.A. 46°49N 101°50W 352 B3
Glenallen U.S.A. 62°7N 145°33W 340 C5
Glenariff △ Ireland 55°2N 6°10W 282 A5
Glenbeigh Ireland 52°3N 9°58W 282 D2
Glencoe Canada 42°45N 81°43W 354 D3
Glencoe S. Africa 28°11S 30°11E 329 D5
Glencoe U.S.A. 44°46N 94°9W 352 C6
Glencolumbkille Ireland 54°43N 8°42W 282 B3
Glendale Ariz., U.S.A. 33°32N 112°11W 349 K7
Glendale Calif., U.S.A. 34°9N 118°15W 351 L8
Glendale Zimbabwe 17°22S 31°5E 327 F3
Glendive U.S.A. 47°7N 104°43W 348 C11
Glendo U.S.A. 42°30N 105°2W 348 E11
Glenelg → Australia 38°4S 140°59E 335 F3
Glenfield U.S.A. 43°43N 75°24W 355 C9
Glengad Hd. Ireland 55°20N 7°10W 282 A4
Glengarriff Ireland 51°45N 9°34W 282 E2
Glenmont U.S.A. 40°31N 82°6W 354 F2
Glenmorgan Australia 27°14S 149°42E 335 D4
Glenn U.S.A. 39°31N 122°1W 350 F4
Glennamaddy Ireland 53°37N 8°33W 282 C3
Glenns Ferry U.S.A. 42°57N 115°18W 348 E6
Glenorchy Australia 42°49S 147°18E 335 G4
Glenore Australia 17°50S 141°12E 334 B3
Glenreagh Australia 30°2S 153°1E 335 E5
Glenrock U.S.A. 42°52N 105°52W 348 E11
Glenrothes U.K. 56°12N 3°10W 283 E5
Glens Falls U.S.A. 43°19N 73°39W 355 C11
Glenside U.S.A. 40°6N 75°9W 355 F9
Glenties Ireland 54°49N 8°16W 282 B3
Glenveagh △ Ireland 55°3N 8°1W 282 A3
Glenville U.S.A. 38°56N 80°50W 353 F13
Glenwood Canada 49°0N 54°58W 345 C9
Glenwood Ark., U.S.A. 34°20N 93°33W 356 D8
Glenwood Iowa, U.S.A. 41°3N 95°45W 352 E6
Glenwood Minn., U.S.A. 45°39N 95°23W 352 C6
Glenwood Wash., U.S.A. 46°1N 121°17W 350 D5
Glenwood Springs U.S.A. 39°33N 107°19W 348 G10
Glettinganes Iceland 65°30N 13°37W 280 D7
Glin Ireland 52°34N 9°17W 282 D2
Gliwice Poland 50°22N 18°41E 289 C10
Globe U.S.A. 33°24N 110°47W 349 K8
Głogów Poland 51°37N 16°5E 288 C9
Glomma → Norway 59°12N 10°57E 281 G14
Glorieuses, Îs. Ind. Oc. 11°30S 47°20E 329 A8
Glossop U.K. 53°27N 1°56W 284 D6
Gloucester Australia 32°0S 151°59E 335 E5
Gloucester U.K. 51°53N 2°15W 285 F5
Gloucester U.S.A. 42°37N 70°40W 355 D14

Gloucester I. Australia 20°0S 148°30E 334 J6
Gloucester Island △ Australia 20°2S 148°30E 334 J6
Gloucester Point U.S.A. 37°15N 76°30W 353 G15
Gloucestershire □ U.K. 51°46N 2°15W 285 F5
Gloversville U.S.A. 43°3N 74°21W 355 C10
Glovertown Canada 48°40N 54°3W 345 C9
Glusk Belarus 52°53N 28°41E 289 B15
Gmünd Austria 48°45N 15°0E 288 D8
Gmunden Austria 47°55N 13°48E 288 E7
Gniezno Poland 52°30N 17°35E 289 B9
Gnowangerup Australia 33°58S 117°59E 333 F2
Go Cong Vietnam 10°22N 106°40E 311 G6
Gō-no-ura Japan 33°44N 129°40E 303 H4
Goa India 15°33N 73°59E 312 M8
Goa □ India 15°33N 73°59E 312 M8
Goalen Hd. Australia 36°33S 150°4E 335 F5
Goalpara India 26°10N 90°40E 313 F17
Goaltor India 22°43N 87°10E 315 H12
Goalundo Ghat Bangla. 23°50N 89°47E 315 H13
Goat Fell U.K. 55°38N 5°11W 283 F3
Goba Ethiopia 7°1N 39°59E 319 F2
Goba Mozam. 26°15S 32°13E 329 D5
Gobabis Namibia 22°30S 19°0E 328 C2
Gobi Asia 44°0N 110°0E 306 C6
Gobō Japan 33°53N 135°10E 303 H7
Gochas Namibia 24°59S 18°55E 328 C2
Godalming U.K. 51°11N 0°36W 285 F7
Godavari → India 16°25N 82°18E 313 L13
Godavari Pt. India 17°0N 82°20E 313 L13
Godbout Canada 49°20N 67°38W 345 C6
Godda India 24°50N 87°13E 315 G12
Goderich Canada 43°45N 81°41W 354 C3
Godfrey Ra. Australia 24°0S 117°0E 333 D2
Godhavn = Qeqertarsuaq Greenland 69°15N 53°38W 276 C5
Godhra India 22°49N 73°40E 314 H5
Godoy Cruz Argentina 32°56S 68°52W 366 C2
Gods → Canada 56°22N 92°51W 344 A1
Gods L. Canada 54°40N 94°15W 344 B1
Gods River Canada 54°50N 94°5W 343 C10
Godthåb = Nuuk Greenland 64°10N 51°35W 339 C14
Goeie Hoop, Kaap die = Good Hope, C. of S. Africa 34°24S 18°30E 328 E2
Goéland, L. au Canada 49°50N 76°48W 344 C4
Goélands, L. aux Canada 55°27N 64°17W 345 A7
Goeree Neths. 51°50N 4°0E 287 C3
Goes Neths. 51°30N 3°55E 287 C3
Goffstown U.S.A. 43°1N 71°36W 355 C13
Gogama Canada 47°35N 81°43W 344 C3
Gogebic, L. U.S.A. 46°30N 89°35W 352 B9
Gogra = Ghaghara → India 25°45N 84°40E 315 G11
Gogriâl Sudan 8°30N 28°8E 323 G11
Gohana India 29°8N 76°42E 314 E7
Goharganj India 23°1N 77°41E 314 H7
Goi → India 22°4N 74°46E 314 H6
Goiânia Brazil 16°43S 49°20W 365 G9
Goiás Brazil 15°55S 50°10W 365 G8
Goiás □ Brazil 12°10S 48°0W 365 F9
Goio-Erê Brazil 24°12S 53°1W 367 A5
Gojō Japan 34°21N 135°42E 303 G7
Gojra Pakistan 31°10N 72°40E 314 D5
Gökçeada Turkey 40°10N 25°50E 295 D11
Gökova Körfezi Turkey 36°55N 27°50E 295 F12
Gokteik Burma 22°26N 97°0E 313 H20
Gokurt Pakistan 29°40N 67°26E 314 E2
Gokwe Zimbabwe 18°7S 28°58E 329 B4
Gola India 28°3N 80°32E 315 E9
Golakganj India 26°8N 89°52E 315 F13
Golan Heights = Hagolan Syria 33°0N 35°45E 318 C4
Golāshkerd Iran 27°59N 57°16E 317 E8
Golchikha Russia 71°45N 83°30E 276 B12
Golconda U.S.A. 40°58N 117°30W 348 F5
Gold U.S.A. 41°52N 77°50W 354 E7
Gold Beach U.S.A. 42°25N 124°25W 348 E1
Gold Coast W. Afr. 4°0N 1°40W 322 H5
Gold Hill U.S.A. 42°26N 123°3W 348 E2
Gold River Canada 49°46N 126°3W 342 D3
Golden Canada 51°20N 116°59W 342 C5
Golden B. N.Z. 40°40S 172°50E 331 D4
Golden Gate U.S.A. 37°48N 122°29W 349 H2
Golden Gate Highlands △ S. Africa 28°40S 28°40E 329 D4
Golden Hinde Canada 49°40N 125°44W 342 D3
Golden Lake Canada 45°34N 77°21W 354 A7
Golden Spike △ U.S.A. 41°37N 112°33W 348 F7
Golden Vale Ireland 52°33N 8°17W 282 D3
Goldendale U.S.A. 45°49N 120°50W 348 D3
Goldfield U.S.A. 37°42N 117°14W 349 H5
Goldsand L. Canada 57°2N 101°8W 343 B8
Goldsboro U.S.A. 35°23N 77°59W 357 D16
Goldsmith U.S.A. 31°59N 102°37W 356 F3
Goldthwaite U.S.A. 31°27N 98°34W 356 F5
Goleniów Poland 53°35N 14°50E 288 B8
Golestān □ Iran 37°20N 55°25E 317 B7
Golestānak Iran 30°36N 54°14E 317 D7
Goleta U.S.A. 34°27N 119°50W 351 L7
Golfito Costa Rica 8°41N 83°5W 360 E3
Golfo Aranci Italy 40°59N 9°38E 294 D3
Goliad U.S.A. 28°40N 97°23W 356 G6
Golpāyegān Iran 33°27N 50°18E 317 C6
Golra Pakistan 33°37N 72°56E 314 C5
Golspie U.K. 57°58N 3°59W 283 D5
Goma Dem. Rep. of the Congo 1°37S 29°10E 326 C2
Gomal Pass Pakistan 31°56N 69°20E 314 D3
Gomati → India 25°32N 83°11E 315 G10
Gombari Dem. Rep. of the Congo 2°45N 29°3E 326 B2
Gombe Nigeria 10°19N 11°2E 323 F8
Gombe → Tanzania 4°38S 31°40E 326 C3
Gomel = Homyel Belarus 52°28N 31°0E 289 B16
Gomera Canary Is. 28°7N 17°14W 296 F2
Gómez Palacio Mexico 25°34N 103°30W 358 B4
Gomīshān Iran 37°4N 54°6E 317 B7
Gomogomo Indonesia 6°39S 134°43E 309 F8
Gomoh India 23°52N 86°10E 315 H12
Gompa = Ganta Liberia 7°15N 8°59W 322 G4
Gonābād Iran 34°15N 58°45E 317 C8
Gonaïves Haiti 19°20N 72°42W 361 C5
Gonarezhou △ Zimbabwe 21°32S 31°55E 327 G3
Gonâve, G. de la Haiti 19°29N 72°42W 361 C5
Gonâve, Île de la Haiti 18°51N 73°3W 361 C5
Gonbad-e Kāvūs Iran 37°20N 55°25E 317 B7
Gonda India 27°9N 81°58E 315 F9
Gondal India 21°58N 70°52E 314 J4
Gonder Ethiopia 12°39N 37°30E 319 E2
Gondia India 21°23N 80°10E 312 J12
Gondola Mozam. 19°10S 33°37E 327 F3
Gönen Turkey 40°6N 27°39E 295 D12
Gongbei China 22°12N 113°32E 305 G10
Gonghe China 36°18N 100°32E 304 C5
Gongju S. Korea 36°27N 127°7E 307 F14
Gongming China 22°47N 113°53E 305 F10
Gongolgon Australia 30°21S 146°54E 335 E4
Gongzhuling China 43°30N 124°40E 307 C13
Goniri Nigeria 11°30N 12°15E 323 F8
Gonzales Calif., U.S.A. 36°30N 121°26W 350 J5
Gonzales Tex., U.S.A. 29°30N 97°27W 356 G6
González Mexico 22°48N 98°25W 359 C5
González Chaves Argentina 38°2S 60°5W 366 D3
Good Hope, C. of S. Africa 34°24S 18°30E 328 E2
Gooderham Canada 44°54N 78°21W 354 B6
Goodhouse S. Africa 28°57S 18°13E 328 D2
Gooding U.S.A. 42°56N 114°43W 348 E6
Goodland U.S.A. 39°21N 101°43W 352 F3
Goodlands Mauritius 20°2S 57°39E 325 d
Goodlow Canada 56°20N 120°8W 342 B4
Goodooga Australia 29°3S 147°28E 335 D4
Goodsprings U.S.A. 35°49N 115°27W 351 K11
Goole U.K. 53°42N 0°53W 284 D7
Goolgowi Australia 33°58S 145°41E 335 E4
Goomalling Australia 31°15S 116°49E 333 F2
Goomeri Australia 26°12S 152°6E 335 D5
Goonda Mozam. 19°48S 33°57E 327 F3
Goondiwindi Australia 28°30S 150°21E 335 D5
Goongarrie, L. Australia 30°3S 121°9E 333 F3
Goongarrie △ Australia 30°7S 121°30E 333 F3
Goonyella Australia 21°47S 147°58E 334 C4
Goose → Canada 53°20N 60°35W 345 B7
Goose Creek U.S.A. 32°59N 80°2W 357 E14
Goose L. U.S.A. 41°56N 120°26W 348 F3
Gop India 22°5N 69°50E 314 H3
Gopalganj India 26°28N 84°30E 315 F11
Göppingen Germany 48°42N 9°39E 288 D5
Gorakhpur India 26°47N 83°23E 315 F10
Goražde Bos.-H. 43°38N 18°58E 295 C8
Gorda, Pta. Canary Is. 28°45N 18°0W 296 F2
Gorda, Pta. Nic. 14°20N 83°10W 360 D3
Gordan B. Australia 11°35S 130°10E 332 B5
Gordon U.S.A. 42°48N 102°12W 352 D2
Gordon → Australia 42°27S 145°30E 335 G4
Gordon L. Alta., Canada 56°30N 110°25W 343 B6
Gordon L. N.W.T., Canada 63°5N 113°11W 342 A6
Gordonvale Australia 17°5S 145°50E 334 B4
Goré Chad 7°59N 16°31E 323 G9
Gore Ethiopia 8°12N 35°32E 319 F2
Gore N.Z. 46°5S 168°58E 331 G2
Gore Bay Canada 45°57N 82°28W 344 C3
Gorey Ireland 52°41N 6°18W 282 D5
Gorg Iran 29°29N 59°43E 317 D8
Gorgān Iran 36°55N 54°30E 317 B7
Gorgona, I. Colombia 3°0N 78°10W 364 C3
Gorham U.S.A. 44°23N 71°10W 355 B13
Goriganga → India 29°45N 80°23E 315 E9
Gorinchem Neths. 51°50N 4°59E 287 C4
Goris Armenia 39°31N 46°22E 291 G8
Gorízia Italy 45°56N 13°37E 294 B5
Gorkiy = Nizhniy Novgorod Russia 56°20N 44°0E 290 C7
Gorkovskoye Vdkhr. Russia 57°2N 43°4E 290 C7
Gorleston U.K. 52°35N 1°44E 285 E9
Görlitz Germany 51°9N 14°58E 288 C8
Gorlovka = Horlivka Ukraine 48°19N 38°5E 291 E6
Gorman U.S.A. 34°47N 118°51W 351 L8
Gorna Dzhumayo = Blagoevgrad Bulgaria 42°2N 23°5E 295 C10
Gorna Oryakhovitsa Bulgaria 43°7N 25°40E 295 C11
Gorno-Altay □ Russia 51°0N 86°0E 300 D9
Gorno-Altaysk Russia 51°50N 86°5E 300 D9
Gornyatski Russia 67°32N 64°3E 290 A11
Gornyy Russia 44°57N 133°59E 302 B6
Gorodenka = Horodenka Ukraine 48°41N 25°29E 289 D13
Gorodok = Horodok Ukraine 49°46N 23°32E 289 D12
Gorokhov = Horokhiv Ukraine 50°30N 24°45E 289 C13
Goromonzi Zimbabwe 17°52S 31°22E 327 F3
Gorong, Kepulauan Indonesia 3°59S 131°25E 309 E8
Gorongosa △ Mozam. 18°50S 34°29E 329 B5
Gorongose → Mozam. 20°30S 34°40E 329 C5
Gorongoza Mozam. 18°44S 34°2E 327 F3
Gorongoza, Sa. da Mozam. 18°27S 34°2E 327 F3
Gorontalo Indonesia 0°35N 123°5E 309 D6
Gorontalo □ Indonesia 0°50N 122°20E 309 D6
Gort Ireland 53°3N 8°49W 282 C3
Gortis Greece 35°4N 24°58E 297 D6
Goryeong S. Korea 35°44N 128°15E 307 G15
Gorzów Wielkopolski Poland 52°43N 15°15E 288 B8
Gosford Australia 33°23S 151°18E 335 E5
Goshen Calif., U.S.A. 36°21N 119°25W 350 J7
Goshen Ind., U.S.A. 41°35N 85°50W 353 E11
Goshen N.Y., U.S.A. 41°24N 74°20W 355 E10
Goshogawara Japan 40°48N 140°27E 302 D10
Goslar Germany 51°54N 10°25E 288 C6
Gospič Croatia 44°35N 15°23E 288 F8
Gosport U.K. 50°48N 1°9W 285 G6
Gosse → Australia 19°32S 134°37E 334 B1
Göta älv → Sweden 57°42N 11°54E 281 H14
Göta kanal Sweden 58°30N 15°58E 281 G16
Götaland Sweden 57°30N 14°30E 281 H16
Göteborg Sweden 57°43N 11°59E 281 H14
Gotha Germany 50°56N 10°42E 288 C6
Gothenburg = Göteborg Sweden 57°43N 11°59E 281 H14
Gothenburg U.S.A. 40°56N 100°10W 352 E3
Gotland Sweden 57°30N 18°33E 281 H18
Gotō-Rettō Japan 32°55N 129°5E 303 H4
Gotska Sandön Sweden 58°24N 19°15E 281 G18
Gōtsu Japan 35°0N 132°14E 303 G6
Gott Pk. Canada 50°18N 122°16W 342 C4
Göttingen Germany 51°31N 9°55E 288 C5
Gottwaldov = Zlín Czech Rep. 49°14N 17°40E 289 D9
Goubangzi China 41°20N 121°52E 307 D11
Gouda Neths. 52°1N 4°42E 287 B4
Goudouras, Akra Greece 34°59N 26°6E 297 E8
Gouin, Rés. Canada 48°35N 74°40W 344 C5
Goulburn Australia 34°44S 149°44E 335 E4
Goulburn Is. Australia 11°40S 133°20E 334 A1
Goulimine Morocco 28°56N 10°0W 322 C3
Goundam Mali 16°27N 3°40W 322 E5
Gourits → S. Africa 34°21S 21°52E 328 E3
Gournes Greece 35°19N 25°16E 297 D7
Gourock U.K. 55°57N 4°49W 283 F4
Gouverneur U.S.A. 44°20N 75°28W 355 B9
Gouvia Greece 39°39N 19°50E 297 A3
Governador Valadares Brazil 18°15S 41°57W 365 G10
Governor's Harbour Bahamas 25°10N 76°14W 360 A4
Govindgarh India 24°23N 81°18E 315 G9
Gowan Ra. Australia 25°0S 145°0E 334 D4
Gowanda U.S.A. 42°28N 78°56W 354 D6
Gower U.K. 51°35N 4°10W 285 F3
Gowna, L. Ireland 53°51N 7°34W 282 C4
Goya Argentina 29°10S 59°10W 366 B4
Goyder Lagoon Australia 27°3S 138°58E 335 D2
Goyllarisquisga Peru 10°31S 76°24W 364 F3
Goz Beïda Chad 12°10N 21°20E 323 F10
Gozo Malta 36°3N 14°15E 297 C1
Graaff-Reinet S. Africa 32°13S 24°32E 328 E3
Gračac Croatia 44°18N 15°57E 288 F8
Gracias a Dios, C. Honduras 15°0N 83°10W 360 D3
Graciosa Azores 39°4N 28°0W 322 a
Graciosa, I. Canary Is. 29°15N 13°32W 296 E6
Grado Spain 43°23N 6°4W 293 A2
Grady U.S.A. 34°49N 103°19W 349 J12
Grafham Water U.K. 52°19N 0°18W 285 E7
Grafton Australia 29°38S 152°58E 335 D5
Grafton N. Dak., U.S.A. 48°25N 97°25W 352 A5
Grafton W. Va., U.S.A. 39°21N 80°2W 353 F13
Graham Canada 49°20N 90°30W 344 C1
Graham U.S.A. 33°6N 98°35W 356 E5
Graham, Mt. U.S.A. 32°42N 109°52W 349 K9
Graham Bell, Ostrov = Greem-Bell, Ostrov Russia 81°0N 62°0E 300 A7
Graham I. Canada 53°40N 132°30W 342 C2
Graham Land Antarctica 65°0S 64°0W 277 C17
Grahamstown S. Africa 33°19S 26°31E 328 E4
Grahamsville U.S.A. 41°51N 74°33W 355 E10
Grain Coast W. Afr. 4°20N 10°0W 322 H3
Grajagan Indonesia 8°35S 114°13E 309 K17
Grajagan, Teluk Indonesia 8°40S 114°18E 309 K17
Grajaú Brazil 5°50S 46°4W 365 E9
Grajaú → Brazil 3°41S 44°48W 365 D10
Grampian U.S.A. 40°58N 78°37W 354 F6
Grampian Highlands = Grampian Mts. U.K. 56°50N 4°0W 283 E5
Grampian Mts. U.K. 56°50N 4°0W 283 E5
Grampians, The Australia 37°15S 142°20E 335 F3
Gran Canaria Canary Is. 27°55N 15°35W 296 G4
Gran Chaco S. Amer. 25°0S 61°0W 366 B3
Gran Desierto del Pinacate ⌂ Mexico 31°51N 113°32W 358 A2
Gran Paradiso Italy 45°33N 7°17E 292 D7
Gran Sasso d'Itália Italy 42°27N 13°42E 294 C5
Granada Nic. 11°58N 86°0W 360 D2
Granada Spain 37°10N 3°35W 293 D4
Granada U.S.A. 38°4N 102°19W 348 G12
Granadilla de Abona Canary Is. 28°7N 16°33W 296 F3
Granard Ireland 53°47N 7°30W 282 C4
Granbury U.S.A. 32°27N 97°47W 356 E6
Granby Canada 45°25N 72°45W 355 A12
Granby U.S.A. 40°5N 105°56W 348 F11
Grand → Canada 42°51N 79°34W 354 D5
Grand → Mo., U.S.A. 39°23N 93°7W 352 F7
Grand → S. Dak., U.S.A. 45°40N 100°45W 352 C3
Grand Bahama I. Bahamas 26°40N 78°30W 360 A4
Grand Baie Mauritius 20°0S 57°35E 325 d
Grand Bank Canada 47°6N 55°48W 345 C8
Grand Bassam Ivory C. 5°10N 3°49W 322 G5
Grand-Bourg Guadeloupe 15°53N 61°19W 360 b
Grand Canal = Da Yunhe → China 39°10N 117°10E 307 E9
Grand Canyon U.S.A. 36°3N 112°9W 349 H7
Grand Canyon △ U.S.A. 36°15N 112°30W 349 H7
Grand Canyon-Parashant ⌂ U.S.A. 36°30N 113°45W 349 H7
Grand Cayman Cayman Is. 19°20N 81°20W 360 C3
Grand Centre Canada 54°25N 110°13W 343 C6
Grand Coulee U.S.A. 47°57N 119°0W 348 C4
Grand Coulee Dam U.S.A. 47°57N 118°59W 348 C4
Grand Erg de Bilma Niger 18°30N 14°0E 323 E8
Grand Falls Canada 47°3N 67°44W 345 C6
Grand Falls-Windsor Canada 48°56N 55°40W 345 C8
Grand Forks Canada 49°0N 118°30W 342 D5
Grand Forks U.S.A. 47°55N 97°3W 352 B5
Grand Gorge U.S.A. 42°21N 74°29W 355 D10
Grand Haven U.S.A. 43°4N 86°13W 352 D10
Grand I. Mich., U.S.A. 46°31N 86°40W 352 B10
Grand I. N.Y., U.S.A. 43°0N 78°58W 354 D6
Grand Island U.S.A. 40°55N 98°21W 352 E4
Grand Isle La., U.S.A. 29°14N 90°0W 357 G9
Grand Isle Vt., U.S.A. 44°43N 73°18W 355 B11
Grand Junction U.S.A. 39°4N 108°33W 348 G9
Grand L. N.B., Canada 45°57N 66°7W 345 C6
Grand L. Nfld. & L., Canada 49°0N 57°30W 345 C8
Grand L. Nfld. & L., Canada 53°40N 60°30W 345 B7
Grand L. U.S.A. 29°55N 92°47W 356 G8
Grand Lake U.S.A. 40°15N 105°49W 348 F11
Grand Manan I. Canada 44°45N 66°52W 345 D6
Grand Marais Mich., U.S.A. 46°40N 85°59W 353 B11
Grand Marais Minn., U.S.A. 47°45N 90°25W 344 C1
Grand-Mère Canada 46°36N 72°40W 344 C5
Grand Portage U.S.A. 47°58N 89°41W 352 B9
Grand Prairie U.S.A. 32°44N 96°59W 356 E6
Grand Rapids Canada 53°12N 99°19W 343 C9
Grand Rapids Mich., U.S.A. 42°58N 85°40W 353 D11
Grand Rapids Minn., U.S.A. 47°14N 93°31W 352 B7
Grand St-Bernard, Col du Europe 45°50N 7°10E 292 D7
Grand Staircase-Escalante ⌂ U.S.A. 37°25N 111°33W 349 H8
Grand Teton U.S.A. 43°54N 110°50W 348 E8
Grand Teton △ U.S.A. 43°50N 110°50W 348 E8
Grand Union Canal U.K. 52°7N 0°53W 285 E7
Grande → Jujuy, Argentina 24°20S 65°2W 366 A2
Grande → Mendoza, Argentina 36°52S 69°45W 366 D2
Grande → Bolivia 15°51S 64°39W 364 G6
Grande → Bahia, Brazil 11°30S 44°30W 365 F10
Grande → Minas Gerais, Brazil 20°6S 51°4W 365 H8
Grande, B. Argentina 50°30S 68°20W 368 G3
Grande, Rio → N. Amer. 25°58N 97°9W 356 J6
Grande Anse Seychelles 4°18S 55°45E 325 b
Grande Baleine, R. de la → Canada 55°16N 77°47W 344 A4
Grande Cache Canada 53°53N 119°8W 342 C5
Grande Comore Comoros Is. 11°35S 43°20E 325 a
Grande-Entrée Canada 47°30N 61°40W 345 C7
Grande Prairie Canada 55°10N 118°50W 342 B5
Grande-Rivière Canada 48°26N 64°30W 345 C7
Grande-Terre Guadeloupe 16°20N 61°25W 360 b
Grande-Vallée Canada 49°14N 65°8W 345 C6
Grande Vigie, Pte. de la Guadeloupe 16°32N 61°27W 360 b
Grandfalls U.S.A. 31°20N 102°51W 356 F3
Grands-Jardins ⌂ Canada 47°41N 70°51W 345 C5
Grandview Canada 51°10N 100°42W 343 C8
Grandview U.S.A. 46°15N 119°54W 348 C4
Graneros Chile 34°5S 70°45W 366 C1
Grangemouth U.K. 56°1N 3°42W 283 E5
Granger U.S.A. 41°35N 109°58W 348 F9
Grangeville U.S.A. 45°56N 116°7W 348 D5
Granisle Canada 54°53N 126°13W 342 C3
Granite City U.S.A. 38°42N 90°8W 352 F8
Granite Falls U.S.A. 44°49N 95°33W 352 C6
Granite L. Canada 48°8N 57°5W 345 C8
Granite Mt. U.S.A. 33°5N 116°28W 351 M10
Granite Pk. U.S.A. 45°10N 109°48W 348 D9
Graniteville U.S.A. 44°8N 72°29W 355 B12
Granity N.Z. 41°39S 171°51E 331 D3
Granja Brazil 3°7S 40°50W 365 D10
Granollers Spain 41°39N 2°18E 293 B7
Grant U.S.A. 40°50N 101°43W 352 E3
Grant, Mt. U.S.A. 38°34N 118°48W 348 G4
Grant City U.S.A. 40°29N 94°25W 352 E6
Grant I. Australia 11°10S 132°52E 332 B5
Grant Range U.S.A. 38°30N 115°25W 348 G6
Grantham U.K. 52°55N 0°38W 284 E7
Grantown-on-Spey U.K. 57°20N 3°36W 283 D5
Grants U.S.A. 35°9N 107°52W 349 J10
Grants Pass U.S.A. 42°26N 123°19W 348 E2
Grantsville U.S.A. 40°36N 112°28W 348 F7
Granville France 48°50N 1°35W 292 B3
Granville N. Dak., U.S.A. 48°16N 100°47W 352 A3
Granville N.Y., U.S.A. 43°24N 73°16W 355 C11
Granville Ohio, U.S.A. 40°4N 82°31W 354 F2
Granville L. Canada 56°18N 100°30W 343 B8
Graskop S. Africa 24°56S 30°49E 329 C5
Grass → Canada 56°3N 96°33W 343 B9
Grass Range U.S.A. 47°2N 108°48W 348 C9
Grass River ⌂ Canada 54°40N 100°50W 343 C8
Grass Valley Calif., U.S.A. 39°13N 121°4W 350 F6
Grass Valley Oreg., U.S.A. 45°22N 120°47W 348 D3
Grasse France 43°38N 6°56E 292 E7
Grassflat U.S.A. 41°0N 78°6W 354 E6
Grasslands △ Canada 49°11N 107°38W 343 D7
Grassy Australia 40°3S 144°5E 335 G3
Graulhet France 43°45N 1°59E 292 E4
Gravelbourg Canada 49°50N 106°35W 343 D7
's-Gravenhage Neths. 52°7N 4°17E 287 B4
Gravenhurst Canada 44°52N 79°20W 354 B5
Gravesend Australia 29°35S 150°20E 335 D5
Gravesend U.K. 51°26N 0°22E 285 F8
Gravois, Pointe-à- Haiti 18°15N 73°56W 361 C5
Grayling U.S.A. 44°40N 84°43W 353 C11
Grays U.K. 51°28N 0°21E 285 F8
Grays Harbor U.S.A. 46°59N 124°1W 348 C1
Grays L. U.S.A. 43°4N 111°26W 348 E8
Grays River U.S.A. 46°21N 123°37W 350 D3
Graz Austria 47°4N 15°27E 288 E8
Greasy L. Canada 62°55N 122°12W 342 A4
Great Abaco I. = Abaco I. Bahamas 26°25N 77°10W 360 A4
Great Artesian Basin Australia 23°0S 144°0E 334 C3
Great Australian Bight Australia 33°30S 130°0E 333 F5
Great Bahama Bank Bahamas 23°15N 78°0W 360 B4
Great Barrier I. N.Z. 36°11S 175°25E 331 B5
Great Barrier Reef Australia 18°0S 146°50E 334 B4
Great Barrier Reef ⌂ Australia 20°0S 150°0E 334 B4
Great Barrington U.S.A. 42°12N 73°22W 355 D11
Great Basalt Wall △ Australia 19°52S 145°43E 334 B4
Great Basin U.S.A. 40°0N 117°0W 348 G5
Great Basin △ U.S.A. 38°56N 114°15W 348 G6
Great Bear → Canada 65°0N 124°0W 340 C7
Great Bear L. Canada 65°30N 120°0W 340 C8
Great Belt = Store Bælt Denmark 55°20N 11°0E 281 J14
Great Bend Kans., U.S.A. 38°22N 98°46W 352 F4
Great Bend Pa., U.S.A. 41°58N 75°45W 355 E9
Great Blasket I. Ireland 52°6N 10°32W 282 D1
Great Britain Europe 54°0N 2°15W 278 E5
Great Camanoe Br. Virgin Is. 18°30N 64°35W 361 e
Great Codroy Canada 47°51N 59°16W 345 C8
Great Divide, The = Great Dividing Ra. Australia 23°0S 146°0E 334 C4
Great Divide Basin U.S.A. 42°0N 108°0W 348 E9
Great Dividing Ra. Australia 23°0S 146°0E 334 C4
Great Driffield = Driffield U.K. 54°0N 0°26W 284 C7
Great Exuma I. Bahamas 23°30N 75°50W 360 B4
Great Falls U.S.A. 47°30N 111°17W 348 C8
Great Fish = Groot-Vis → S. Africa 33°28S 27°5E 328 E4
Great Guana Cay Bahamas 24°0N 76°20W 360 B4
Great Harbour Deep Canada 50°25N 56°32W 345 B8
Great Himalayan △ India 31°30N 77°30E 314 D7
Great Inagua I. Bahamas 21°0N 73°20W 361 B5
Great Indian Desert = Thar Desert India 28°0N 72°0E 314 F5
Great Karoo S. Africa 31°55S 21°0E 328 E3
Great Khingan Mts. = Da Hinggan Ling China 48°0N 121°0E 305 B7
Great Lake Australia 41°50S 146°40E 335 G4
Great Lakes N. Amer. 46°0N 84°0W 347 A10
Great Malvern U.K. 52°7N 2°18W 285 E5
Great Miami → U.S.A. 39°7N 84°49W 353 F11
Great Ormes Head U.K. 53°20N 3°52W 284 D4
Great Ouse → U.K. 52°48N 0°21E 284 E8
Great Palm I. Australia 18°45S 146°40E 334 B4
Great Pedro Bluff Jamaica 17°51N 77°44W 360 a
Great Pee Dee → U.S.A. 33°21N 79°10W 357 E15
Great Plains N. Amer. 47°0N 105°0W 346 A6
Great Ruaha → Tanzania 7°56S 37°52E 326 D4
Great Sacandaga L. U.S.A. 43°6N 74°16W 355 C10
Great Saint Bernard Pass = Grand St-Bernard, Col du Europe 45°50N 7°10E 292 D7
Great Salt Desert = Kavīr, Dasht-e Iran 34°30N 55°0E 317 C7
Great Salt L. U.S.A. 41°15N 112°40W 348 F7
Great Salt Lake Desert U.S.A. 40°50N 113°30W 348 F7
Great Salt Plains L. U.S.A. 36°45N 98°8W 356 C5
Great Sand Dunes ⌂ U.S.A. 37°48N 105°45W 349 H11
Great Sandy △ Australia 26°13S 153°2E 335 D5
Great Sandy Desert Australia 21°0S 124°0E 332 D3
Great Sandy Desert U.S.A. 43°35N 120°15W 346 B2
Great Sangi = Sangihe, Pulau Indonesia 3°35N 125°30E 309 D7
Great Sea Reef Fiji 16°15S 179°0E 331 a
Great Skellig Ireland 51°47N 10°33W 282 E1
Great Slave L. Canada 61°23N 115°38W 342 A5
Great Smoky Mts. △ U.S.A. 35°40N 83°40W 357 D13
Great Snow Mt. Canada 57°26N 124°0W 342 B4

Great Stour = Stour → *U.K.* 51°18N 1°22E **285** F9
Great Victoria Desert *Australia* 29°30S 126°30E **333** E4
Great Wall *Antarctica* 62°30S 58°0W **277** C18
Great Wall *China* 38°30N 109°30E **306** E5
Great Whernside *U.K.* 54°10N 1°58W **284** C6
Great Yarmouth *U.K.* 52°37N 1°44E **285** E9
Great Zab = Zāb al Kabīr → *Iraq* 36°1N 43°24E **316** C4
Great Zimbabwe *Zimbabwe* 20°16S 30°54E **327** G3
Greater Antilles *W. Indies* 17°40N 74°0W **361** C5
Greater London □ *U.K.* 51°31N 0°6W **285** F7
Greater Manchester □ *U.K.* 53°30N 2°15W **284** D5
Greater St. Lucia Wetlands ⌓ *S. Africa* 28°6S 32°27E **329** D5
Greater Sudbury = Sudbury *Canada* 46°30N 81°0W **344** C3
Greater Sunda Is. *Indonesia* 7°0S 112°0E **308** F4
Greco, C. *Cyprus* 34°57N 34°5E **297** E13
Gredos, Sierra de *Spain* 40°20N 5°0W **293** B3
Greece *U.S.A.* 43°13N 77°41W **354** C7
Greece ■ *Europe* 40°0N 23°0E **295** E9
Greeley *Colo., U.S.A.* 40°25N 104°42W **348** F11
Greeley *Nebr., U.S.A.* 41°33N 98°32W **352** E4
Greely Fd. *Canada* 80°30N 85°0W **341** A11
Greem-Bell, Ostrov *Russia* 81°0N 62°0E **300** A7
Green → *Ky., U.S.A.* 37°54N 87°30W **352** G10
Green → *Utah, U.S.A.* 38°11N 109°53W **348** G9
Green B. *U.S.A.* 45°0N 87°30W **352** C10
Green Bay *U.S.A.* 44°31N 88°0W **352** C9
Green C. *Australia* 37°13S 150°1E **335** F5
Green Cove Springs *U.S.A.* 29°59N 81°42W **357** G14
Green Lake *Canada* 54°17N 107°47W **343** C7
Green Mts. *U.S.A.* 43°45N 72°45W **355** C12
Green River *Utah, U.S.A.* 38°59N 110°10W **348** G8
Green River *Wyo., U.S.A.* 41°32N 109°28W **348** F9
Green Valley *U.S.A.* 31°52N 110°56W **349** L8
Greenbank *U.S.A.* 48°6N 122°34W **350** B4
Greenbush *Mich., U.S.A.* 44°35N 83°19W **354** B1
Greenbush *Minn., U.S.A.* 48°42N 96°11W **352** A5
Greencastle *U.S.A.* 39°38N 86°52W **352** F10
Greene *U.S.A.* 42°20N 75°46W **355** D9
Greeneville *U.S.A.* 36°10N 82°50W **357** C13
Greenfield *Calif., U.S.A.* 36°19N 121°15W **350** J5
Greenfield *Calif., U.S.A.* 35°15N 119°0W **351** K8
Greenfield *Ind., U.S.A.* 39°47N 85°46W **353** F11
Greenfield *Iowa, U.S.A.* 41°18N 94°28W **352** E6
Greenfield *Mass., U.S.A.* 42°35N 72°36W **355** D12
Greenfield *Mo., U.S.A.* 37°25N 93°51W **352** G7
Greenfield Park *Canada* 45°29N 73°28W **355** A11
Greenland ⧄ *N. Amer.* 66°0N 45°0W **339** C15
Greenland Sea *Arctic* 73°0N 10°0W **276** B7
Greenock *U.K.* 55°57N 4°46W **283** F4
Greenore *Ireland* 54°2N 6°8W **282** B5
Greenore Pt. *Ireland* 52°14N 6°19W **282** D5
Greenough *Australia* 28°58S 114°43E **333** E1
Greenough → *Australia* 28°51S 114°38E **333** E1
Greenough Pt. *Canada* 44°58N 81°26W **354** B3
Greenport *U.S.A.* 41°6N 72°22W **355** E12
Greensboro *Ga., U.S.A.* 33°35N 83°11W **357** E13
Greensboro *N.C., U.S.A.* 36°4N 79°48W **357** C15
Greensboro *Vt., U.S.A.* 44°36N 72°18W **355** B12
Greensburg *Ind., U.S.A.* 39°20N 85°29W **353** F11
Greensburg *Kans., U.S.A.* 37°36N 99°18W **352** G4
Greensburg *Pa., U.S.A.* 40°18N 79°33W **354** F5
Greenstone Pt. *U.K.* 57°55N 5°37W **283** D3
Greenvale *Australia* 18°59S 145°7E **334** B4
Greenville *Liberia* 5°1N 9°6W **322** G4
Greenville *Ala., U.S.A.* 31°50N 86°38W **357** F11
Greenville *Calif., U.S.A.* 40°8N 120°57W **350** E6
Greenville *Maine, U.S.A.* 45°28N 69°35W **353** C19
Greenville *Mich., U.S.A.* 43°11N 85°15W **353** D11
Greenville *Mo., U.S.A.* 37°8N 90°27W **352** G8
Greenville *N.C., U.S.A.* 35°37N 77°23W **357** D16
Greenville *N.H., U.S.A.* 42°46N 71°49W **355** D13
Greenville *N.Y., U.S.A.* 42°25N 74°1W **355** D10
Greenville *Ohio, U.S.A.* 40°6N 84°38W **353** E11
Greenville *Pa., U.S.A.* 41°24N 80°23W **354** E4
Greenville *S.C., U.S.A.* 34°51N 82°24W **357** D13
Greenville *Tex., U.S.A.* 33°8N 96°7W **356** E6
Greenwater Lake ⌓ *Canada* 52°32N 103°30W **343** C8
Greenwich *Conn., U.S.A.* 41°2N 73°38W **355** E11
Greenwich *N.Y., U.S.A.* 43°5N 73°30W **355** C11
Greenwich *Ohio, U.S.A.* 41°2N 82°31W **354** E2
Greenwich □ *U.K.* 51°29N 0°1E **285** F8
Greenwood *Canada* 49°10N 118°40W **342** D5
Greenwood *Ark., U.S.A.* 35°13N 94°16W **356** D7
Greenwood *Ind., U.S.A.* 39°37N 86°7W **352** F10
Greenwood *Miss., U.S.A.* 33°31N 90°11W **357** E9
Greenwood *S.C., U.S.A.* 34°12N 82°10W **357** D13
Greenwood, Mt. *Australia* 13°48S 130°4E **332** B5
Gregory *U.S.A.* 43°14N 99°26W **352** D4
Gregory → *Australia* 17°53S 139°17E **334** B2
Gregory, L. *S. Austral., Australia* 28°55S 139°0E **335** D2
Gregory, L. *W. Austral., Australia* 20°0S 127°40E **332** D4
Gregory, L. *W. Austral., Australia* 25°38S 119°58E **333** E2
Gregory △ *Australia* 15°38S 131°15E **332** C5
Gregory Downs *Australia* 18°35S 138°45E **334** B2
Gregory Ra. *Queens., Australia* 19°30S 143°40E **334** B3
Gregory Ra. *W. Austral., Australia* 21°20S 121°12E **332** D3
Greifswald *Germany* 54°5N 13°23E **288** A7
Greiz *Germany* 50°39N 12°10E **288** C7
Gremikha *Russia* 67°59N 39°47E **290** A6
Grenaa *Denmark* 56°25N 10°53E **281** H14
Grenada *U.S.A.* 33°47N 89°49W **357** E10
Grenada ■ *W. Indies* 12°10N 61°40W **361** D7
Grenadier I. *U.S.A.* 44°3N 76°22W **355** B8
Grenadines, The *St. Vincent* 12°40N 61°20W **361** D7
Grenen *Denmark* 57°44N 10°40E **281** H14
Grenfell *Australia* 33°52S 148°8E **335** E4
Grenfell *Canada* 50°30N 102°56W **343** C8
Grenoble *France* 45°12N 5°42E **292** D6
Grenville, C. *Australia* 12°0S 143°13E **334** A3
Grenville Chan. *Canada* 53°40N 129°46W **342** C3
Gresham *U.S.A.* 45°29N 122°25W **350** E4
Gresik *Indonesia* 7°13S 112°38E **309** G15
Gretna *U.K.* 55°0N 3°3W **283** F5
Gretna *U.S.A.* 29°54N 90°3W **357** G9
Grevenmacher *Lux.* 49°41N 6°26E **287** E6
Grey → *Canada* 47°34N 57°6W **345** C8
Grey → *N.Z.* 42°27S 171°12E **331** E3
Grey, C. *Australia* 13°0S 136°35E **334** A2
Grey Ra. *Australia* 27°0S 143°30E **335** D3
Greybull *U.S.A.* 44°30N 108°3W **348** D9
Greymouth *N.Z.* 42°29S 171°13E **331** E3
Greystones *Ireland* 53°9N 6°5W **282** C5
Greytown *N.Z.* 41°5S 175°29E **331** D5
Greytown *S. Africa* 29°1S 30°36E **329** D5
Gribbell I. *Canada* 53°23N 129°0W **342** C3
Gridley *U.S.A.* 39°22N 121°42W **350** F5
Griekwastad *S. Africa* 28°49S 23°15E **328** D3
Griffin *U.S.A.* 33°15N 84°16W **357** E12
Griffith *Australia* 34°18S 146°2E **335** E4
Griffith *Canada* 45°15N 77°10W **354** A7
Griffith I. *Canada* 44°50N 80°55W **354** B4
Grimaylov = Hrymayliv *Ukraine* 49°20N 26°5E **289** D14
Grimes *U.S.A.* 39°4N 121°54W **350** F5
Grimsay *U.K.* 57°29N 7°14W **283** D1
Grimsby *Canada* 43°12N 79°34W **354** C5
Grimsby *U.K.* 53°34N 0°5W **284** D7
Grímsey *Iceland* 66°33N 17°58W **280** C5
Grimshaw *Canada* 56°10N 117°40W **342** B5
Grimstad *Norway* 58°20N 8°35E **281** G13
Grindstone I. *Canada* 44°43N 76°14W **355** B8
Grinnell *U.S.A.* 41°45N 92°43W **352** E7
Gris-Nez, C. *France* 50°52N 1°35E **292** A4
Grise Fiord *Canada* 76°25N 82°57W **341** B11
Groais I. *Canada* 50°55N 55°35W **345** B8
Groblersdal *S. Africa* 25°15S 29°25E **329** D4
Grodno = Hrodna *Belarus* 53°42N 23°52E **289** B12
Grodzyanka = Hrodzyanka *Belarus* 53°31N 28°42E **289** B15
Groesbeck *U.S.A.* 31°31N 96°32W **356** F6
Grójec *Poland* 51°50N 20°58E **289** C11
Grong *Norway* 64°25N 12°8E **280** D15
Groningen *Neths.* 53°15N 6°35E **287** A6
Groningen □ *Neths.* 53°16N 6°40E **287** A6
Groom *U.S.A.* 35°12N 101°6W **356** D4
Groot → *S. Africa* 33°45S 24°36E **328** E3
Groot-Berg → *S. Africa* 32°47S 18°8E **328** E2
Groot-Brakrivier *S. Africa* 34°2S 22°18E **328** E3
Groot Karasberge *Namibia* 27°20S 18°40E **328** D2
Groot-Kei → *S. Africa* 32°41S 28°22E **329** E4
Groot-Vis → *S. Africa* 33°28S 27°5E **328** E4
Grootdrink *S. Africa* 28°33S 21°42E **328** D3
Groote Eylandt *Australia* 14°0S 136°40E **334** A2
Grootfontein *Namibia* 19°31S 18°6E **328** B2
Grootlaagte → *Africa* 20°55S 21°27E **328** C3
Grootvloer → *S. Africa* 30°0S 20°40E **328** E3
Gros C. *Canada* 61°59N 113°32W **342** A6
Gros Islet *St. Lucia* 14°5N 60°58W **361** f
Gros Morne △ *Canada* 49°40N 57°50W **345** C8
Gros Piton *St. Lucia* 13°49N 61°5W **361** f
Gros Piton Pt. *St. Lucia* 13°49N 61°5W **361** f
Grossa, Pta. *Spain* 39°6N 1°36E **296** B8
Grosser Arber *Germany* 49°6N 13°8E **288** D7
Grosseto *Italy* 42°46N 11°8E **294** C4
Grossglockner *Austria* 47°5N 12°40E **288** E7
Groswater B. *Canada* 54°20N 57°40W **345** B8
Groton *Conn., U.S.A.* 41°21N 72°5W **355** E12
Groton *N.Y., U.S.A.* 42°36N 76°22W **355** D8
Groton *S. Dak., U.S.A.* 45°27N 98°6W **352** C4
Grouard Mission *Canada* 55°33N 116°9W **342** B5
Groundhog → *Canada* 48°45N 82°58W **344** C3
Grouw *Neths.* 53°5N 5°51E **287** A5
Grove City *U.S.A.* 41°10N 80°5W **354** E4
Grove Hill *U.S.A.* 31°42N 87°47W **357** F11
Groveland *U.S.A.* 37°50N 120°14W **350** H6
Grover Beach *U.S.A.* 35°7N 120°37W **351** K6
Groves *U.S.A.* 29°57N 93°54W **356** G8
Groveton *U.S.A.* 44°36N 71°31W **355** B13
Groznyy *Russia* 43°20N 45°45E **291** F8
Grudziądz *Poland* 53°30N 18°47E **289** B10
Gruinard B. *U.K.* 57°56N 5°35W **283** D3
Grundy Center *U.S.A.* 42°22N 92°47W **352** D7
Gruver *U.S.A.* 36°16N 101°24W **356** C4
Gryazi *Russia* 52°30N 39°58E **290** D6
Gryazovets *Russia* 58°50N 40°10E **290** C7
Gua *India* 22°18N 85°20E **315** H11
Gua Musang *Malaysia* 4°53N 101°58E **311** K3
Guacanayabo, G. de *Cuba* 20°40N 77°20W **360** B4
Guachípas → *Argentina* 25°40S 65°30W **366** B2
Guadalajara *Mexico* 20°40N 103°20W **358** C4
Guadalajara *Spain* 40°37N 3°12W **293** B4
Guadalcanal *Solomon Is.* 9°32S 160°12E **330** B9
Guadales *Argentina* 34°30S 67°55W **366** C2
Guadalete → *Spain* 36°35N 6°13W **293** D2
Guadalquivir → *Spain* 36°47N 6°22W **293** D2
Guadalupe = Guadeloupe ⧄ *W. Indies* 16°20N 61°40W **360** b
Guadalupe *Mexico* 32°4N 116°32W **351** N10
Guadalupe *Zacatecas, Mexico* 22°45N 102°31W **358** C4
Guadalupe *U.S.A.* 34°58N 120°34W **351** L6
Guadalupe → *Mexico* 32°6N 116°51W **351** N10
Guadalupe → *U.S.A.* 28°27N 96°47W **356** G6
Guadalupe, Sierra de *Spain* 39°28N 5°30W **293** C3
Guadalupe Bravos *Mexico* 31°20N 106°10W **358** A3
Guadalupe I. *Pac. Oc.* 29°0N 118°50W **338** G8
Guadalupe Mts. △ *U.S.A.* 31°40N 104°30W **356** F2
Guadalupe Peak *U.S.A.* 31°50N 104°52W **356** F2
Guadalupe y Calvo *Mexico* 26°6N 106°58W **358** B3
Guadarrama, Sierra de *Spain* 41°0N 4°0W **293** B4
Guadeloupe ⧄ *W. Indies* 16°20N 61°40W **360** b
Guadeloupe △ *Guadeloupe* 16°10N 61°40W **360** b
Guadeloupe Passage *W. Indies* 16°50N 62°15W **361** C7
Guadiana → *Portugal* 37°14N 7°22W **293** D2
Guadix *Spain* 37°18N 3°11W **293** D4
Guafo, Boca del *Chile* 43°35S 74°0W **368** E2
Guaico *Trin. & Tob.* 10°35N 61°9W **365** K15
Guainía → *Colombia* 2°1N 67°7W **364** C5
Guaíra *Brazil* 24°5S 54°10W **367** A5
Guaíra □ *Paraguay* 25°45S 56°30W **366** B4
Guaitecas, Is. *Chile* 44°0S 74°30W **368** E2
Guajará-Mirim *Brazil* 10°50S 65°20W **364** F5
Guajira, Pen. de la *Colombia* 12°0N 72°0W **364** A4
Gualán *Guatemala* 15°8N 89°22W **360** C2
Gualeguay *Argentina* 33°10S 59°14W **366** C4
Gualeguaychú *Argentina* 33°3S 59°31W **366** C4
Gualequay → *Argentina* 33°19S 59°39W **366** C4
Guam ⧄ *Pac. Oc.* 13°27N 144°45E **336** F6
Guaminí *Argentina* 37°1S 62°28W **366** D3
Guamúchil *Mexico* 25°28N 108°6W **358** B3
Guana I. *Br. Virgin Is.* 18°30N 64°30W **361** e
Guanabacoa *Cuba* 23°8N 82°18W **360** B3
Guanacaste, Cordillera del *Costa Rica* 10°40N 85°4W **360** D2
Guanacaste △ *Costa Rica* 10°57N 85°30W **360** D2
Guanaceví *Mexico* 25°56N 105°57W **358** B3
Guanahani = San Salvador I. *Bahamas* 24°0N 74°40W **361** B5
Guanajay *Cuba* 22°56N 82°42W **360** B3
Guanajuato *Mexico* 21°1N 101°15W **358** C4
Guanajuato □ *Mexico* 21°0N 101°0W **358** C4
Guandacol *Argentina* 29°30S 68°40W **366** B2
Guane *Cuba* 22°10N 84°7W **360** B3
Guangdong □ *China* 23°0N 113°0E **305** D6
Guangling *China* 39°47N 114°22E **306** E8
Guangrao *China* 37°5N 118°25E **307** F10
Guangwu *China* 37°48N 105°57E **306** F3
Guangxi Zhuangzu Zizhiqu □ *China* 24°0N 109°0E **305** D5
Guangzhou *China* 23°6N 113°13E **305** D6
Guanica *Puerto Rico* 17°58N 66°55W **361** d
Guanipa → *Venezuela* 9°56N 62°26W **364** B6
Guannan *China* 34°8N 119°21E **307** G10
Guantánamo *Cuba* 20°10N 75°14W **361** B4
Guantánamo B. *Cuba* 19°59N 75°10W **361** C4
Guantao *China* 36°42N 115°25E **306** F8
Guanyun *China* 34°20N 119°18E **307** G10
Guápiles *Costa Rica* 10°10N 83°46W **360** D3
Guapo B. *Trin. & Tob.* 10°12N 61°41W **365** K15
Guaporé *Brazil* 28°51S 51°54W **367** B5
Guaporé → *Brazil* 11°55S 65°4W **364** F5
Guaqui *Bolivia* 16°41S 68°54W **364** G5
Guaramacal △ *Venezuela* 9°13N 70°12W **361** E5
Guarapari *Brazil* 20°40S 40°30W **367** A7
Guarapuava *Brazil* 25°20S 51°30W **367** B5
Guaratinguetá *Brazil* 22°49S 45°9W **367** A6
Guaratuba *Brazil* 25°53S 48°38W **367** B6
Guarda *Portugal* 40°32N 7°20W **293** B2
Guardafui, C. = Asir, Ras *Somali Rep.* 11°55N 51°10E **319** E5
Guárico □ *Venezuela* 8°40N 66°35W **364** B5
Guarujá *Brazil* 24°2S 46°25W **367** A6
Guarulhos *Brazil* 23°29S 46°33W **367** A6
Guarus *Brazil* 21°44S 41°20W **367** A7
Guasave *Mexico* 25°34N 108°27W **358** B3
Guasdualito *Venezuela* 7°15N 70°44W **364** B4
Guatemala *Guatemala* 14°40N 90°22W **360** D1
Guatemala ■ *Cent. Amer.* 15°40N 90°30W **360** C1
Guatemala Basin *Pac. Oc.* 11°0N 95°0W **337** F18
Guatemala Trench *Pac. Oc.* 14°0N 95°0W **338** H10
Guatopo △ *Venezuela* 10°5N 66°30W **361** D6
Guatuaro Pt. *Trin. & Tob.* 10°19N 60°59W **365** K16
Guaviare → *Colombia* 4°3N 67°44W **364** C5
Guaxupé *Brazil* 21°10S 47°5W **367** A6
Guayaguayare *Trin. & Tob.* 10°8N 61°2W **365** K15
Guayama *Puerto Rico* 17°59N 66°7W **361** d
Guayaquil *Ecuador* 2°15S 79°52W **364** D3
Guayaquil *Mexico* 29°59N 115°4W **358** B1
Guayaquil, G. de *Ecuador* 3°10S 81°0W **364** D2
Guaymas *Mexico* 27°56N 110°54W **358** B2
Guba *Dem. Rep. of the Congo* 10°38S 26°27E **327** E2
Gubkin *Russia* 51°17N 37°32E **291** D6
Gudbrandsdalen *Norway* 61°33N 10°10E **280** F14
Guddu Barrage *Pakistan* 28°30N 69°50E **314** E3
Gudur *India* 14°12N 79°55E **312** M11
Guecho = Getxo *Spain* 43°21N 2°59W **293** A4
Guékédou *Guinea* 8°40N 10°5W **322** G3
Guelmine = Goulimine *Morocco* 28°56N 10°0W **322** C3
Guelph *Canada* 43°35N 80°20W **354** C4
Guéret *France* 46°11N 1°51E **292** C4
Guerneville *U.S.A.* 38°30N 123°0W **350** G4
Guernica = Gernika-Lumo *Spain* 43°19N 2°40W **293** A4
Guernsey *U.K.* 49°26N 2°35W **285** H5
Guernsey *U.S.A.* 42°16N 104°45W **348** E11
Guerrero □ *Mexico* 17°40N 100°0W **359** D5
Gūgher *Iran* 29°28N 56°27E **317** D8
Guhakolak, Tanjung *Indonesia* 6°50S 105°14E **309** G11
Guia *Canary Is.* 28°8N 15°38W **296** F4
Guia de Isora *Canary Is.* 28°12N 16°46W **296** F3
Guia Lopes da Laguna *Brazil* 21°26S 56°7W **367** A4
Guiana Highlands *S. Amer.* 5°10N 60°40W **362** C4
Guidónia-Montecélio *Italy* 42°1N 12°45E **294** C5
Guijá *Mozam.* 24°27S 33°0E **329** C5
Guildford *U.K.* 51°14N 0°34W **285** F7
Guilford *U.S.A.* 41°17N 72°41W **355** E12
Guilin *China* 25°18N 110°15E **305** D6
Guillaume-Delisle, L. *Canada* 56°15N 76°17W **344** A4
Güímar *Canary Is.* 28°18N 16°24W **296** F3
Guimarães *Portugal* 41°28N 8°24W **293** B1
Guimaras □ *Phil.* 10°35N 122°37E **309** B6
Guinda *U.S.A.* 38°50N 122°12W **350** G4
Guinea *Africa* 8°0N 8°0E **320** F4
Guinea ■ *W. Afr.* 10°20N 11°30W **322** F3
Guinea, Gulf of *Atl. Oc.* 3°0N 2°30E **321** F4
Guinea-Bissau ■ *Africa* 12°0N 15°0W **322** F3
Güines *Cuba* 22°50N 82°0W **360** B3
Guingamp *France* 48°34N 3°10W **292** B2
Güiria *Venezuela* 10°32N 62°18W **364** A6
Guiuan *Phil.* 11°5N 125°55E **309** B7
Guiyang *China* 26°32N 106°40E **304** D5
Guizhou □ *China* 27°0N 107°0E **304** D5
Gujar Khan *Pakistan* 33°16N 73°19E **314** C5
Gujarat □ *India* 23°20N 71°0E **314** H4
Gujranwala *Pakistan* 32°10N 74°12E **314** C6
Gujrat *Pakistan* 32°40N 74°2E **314** C6
Gulbarga *India* 17°20N 76°50E **312** L10
Gulbene *Latvia* 57°8N 26°52E **281** H22
Gulf, The = Persian Gulf *Asia* 27°0N 50°0E **317** E6
Gulf Islands ⌓ *U.S.A.* 30°10N 87°10W **357** F11
Gulfport *U.S.A.* 30°22N 89°6W **357** F10
Gulgong *Australia* 32°20S 149°49E **335** E4
Gulistan *Pakistan* 30°30N 66°35E **314** D2
Gull Lake *Canada* 50°10N 108°29W **343** C7
Güllük *Turkey* 37°14N 27°35E **295** F12
Gulmarg *India* 34°3N 74°25E **315** B6
Gülshat *Kazakhstan* 46°38N 74°21E **300** C8
Gulu *Uganda* 2°48N 32°17E **326** B3
Gulwe *Tanzania* 6°30S 36°25E **326** D4
Gumal → *Pakistan* 31°40N 71°50E **314** D4
Gumbaz *Pakistan* 30°2N 69°0E **314** D3
Gumel *Nigeria* 12°39N 9°22E **322** F7
Gumi *S. Korea* 36°10N 128°12E **307** F15
Gumla *India* 23°3N 84°33E **315** H11
Gumlu *Australia* 19°53S 147°41E **334** B4
Gumma □ *Japan* 36°30N 138°20E **303** F9
Gumzai *Indonesia* 5°28S 134°42E **309** F8
Guna *India* 24°40N 77°19E **314** G7
Gunbalanya *Australia* 12°20S 133°4E **332** B5
Gundabooka △ *Australia* 30°30S 145°20E **335** E4
Gunisao → *Canada* 53°56N 97°53W **343** C9
Gunisao L. *Canada* 53°33N 96°15W **343** C9
Gunjyal *Pakistan* 32°20N 71°55E **314** C4
Gunnbjørn Fjeld *Greenland* 68°55N 29°47W **276** C6
Gunnedah *Australia* 30°59S 150°15E **335** E5
Gunnewin *Australia* 25°59S 148°33E **335** D4
Gunningbar Cr. → *Australia* 31°14S 147°6E **335** E4
Gunnison *Colo., U.S.A.* 38°33N 106°56W **348** G10
Gunnison *Utah, U.S.A.* 39°9N 111°49W **348** G8
Gunnison → *U.S.A.* 39°4N 108°35W **348** G9
Gunpowder *Australia* 19°42S 139°22E **334** B2
Gunsan *S. Korea* 35°59N 126°45E **307** G14
Guntakal *India* 15°11N 77°27E **312** M10
Guntersville *U.S.A.* 34°21N 86°18W **357** D11
Guntong *Malaysia* 4°36N 101°3E **311** K3
Guntur *India* 16°23N 80°30E **313** L12
Gunungapi *Indonesia* 6°45S 126°30E **309** F7
Gunungsitoli *Indonesia* 1°15N 97°30E **308** D1
Gunza *Angola* 10°50S 13°50E **324** G2
Guo He → *China* 32°59N 117°10E **307** H9
Guoyang *China* 33°32N 116°12E **306** H9
Gupis *Pakistan* 36°15N 73°20E **315** A5
Gurdaspur *India* 32°5N 75°31E **314** C6
Gurdon *U.S.A.* 33°55N 93°9W **356** E8
Gurgaon *India* 28°27N 77°1E **314** E7
Gurgueia → *Brazil* 6°50S 43°24W **365** E10
Gurha *India* 25°12N 71°39E **314** G4
Guri, Embalse de *Venezuela* 7°50N 62°52W **364** B6
Gurig △ *Australia* 11°36S 132°7E **332** B5
Gurkha *Nepal* 28°5N 84°40E **315** E11
Gurley *Australia* 29°45S 149°48E **335** D4
Gurnet Point *U.S.A.* 42°1N 70°34W **355** D14
Guro *Mozam.* 17°26S 32°30E **327** F3
Guruè *Mozam.* 15°25S 36°58E **327** F4
Gurun *Malaysia* 5°49N 100°27E **311** K3
Gürün *Turkey* 38°43N 37°15E **291** G6
Gurupá *Brazil* 1°25S 51°35W **365** D8
Gurupá, I. Grande de *Brazil* 1°25S 51°45W **365** D8
Gurupi *Brazil* 11°43S 49°4W **365** F9
Gurupi → *Brazil* 1°13S 46°6W **365** D9
Guruwe *Zimbabwe* 16°40S 30°42E **329** B5
Gurvan Sayhan Uul *Mongolia* 43°50N 104°0E **304** B5
Guryev = Atyraū *Kazakhstan* 47°5N 52°0E **291** E9
Gusau *Nigeria* 12°12N 6°40E **322** F7
Gushan *China* 39°50N 123°35E **307** E12
Gushgy = Serhetabat *Turkmenistan* 35°20N 62°18E **317** C9
Gusinoozersk *Russia* 51°16N 106°27E **301** D11
Gustavus *U.S.A.* 58°25N 135°44W **342** B1
Gustine *U.S.A.* 37°16N 121°0W **350** H6
Güstrow *Germany* 53°47N 12°10E **288** B7
Gütersloh *Germany* 51°54N 8°24E **288** C5
Gutha *Australia* 28°58S 115°55E **333** E2
Guthalungra *Australia* 19°52S 147°50E **334** B4
Guthrie *Okla., U.S.A.* 35°53N 97°25W **356** D6
Guthrie *Tex., U.S.A.* 33°37N 100°19W **356** E4
Guttenberg *U.S.A.* 42°47N 91°6W **352** D8
Gutu *Zimbabwe* 19°41S 31°9E **329** B5
Guwahati *India* 26°10N 91°45E **313** F17
Guy Fawkes River △ *Australia* 30°0S 152°20E **335** D5
Guyana ■ *S. Amer.* 5°0N 59°0W **364** C7
Guyane française = French Guiana ⧄ *S. Amer.* 4°0N 53°0W **365** C8
Guyang *China* 41°0N 110°5E **306** D6
Guyenne *France* 44°30N 0°40E **292** D4
Guymon *U.S.A.* 36°41N 101°29W **356** C4
Guyra *Australia* 30°15S 151°40E **335** E5
Guyuan *Hebei, China* 41°37N 115°40E **306** D8
Guyuan *Ningxia Huizu, China* 36°0N 106°20E **306** G4
Güzelyurt = Morphou *Cyprus* 35°12N 32°59E **297** D11
Guzhen *China* 33°22N 117°18E **307** H9
Guzmán, L. de *Mexico* 31°20N 107°30W **358** A3
Gwa *Burma* 17°36N 94°34E **313** L19
Gwaai *Zimbabwe* 19°15S 27°45E **327** F2
Gwaai → *Zimbabwe* 17°59S 26°52E **327** F2
Gwabegar *Australia* 30°37S 148°59E **335** E4
Gwādar *Pakistan* 25°10N 62°18E **312** G3
Gwaii Haanas △ *Canada* 52°21N 131°26W **342** C2
Gwalior *India* 26°12N 78°10E **314** F8
Gwanda *Zimbabwe* 20°55S 29°0E **327** G2
Gwane *Dem. Rep. of the Congo* 4°45N 25°48E **326** B2
Gwangju *S. Korea* 35°9N 126°54E **307** G14
Gwanju = Gwangju *S. Korea* 35°9N 126°54E **307** G14
Gweebarra B. *Ireland* 54°51N 8°23W **282** B3
Gweedore *Ireland* 55°3N 8°13W **282** A3
Gweru *Zimbabwe* 19°28S 29°45E **327** F2
Gwinn *U.S.A.* 46°19N 87°27W **352** B10
Gwydir → *Australia* 29°27S 149°48E **335** D4
Gwynedd □ *U.K.* 52°52N 4°10W **284** E3
Gyandzha = Gäncä *Azerbaijan* 40°45N 46°20E **291** F8
Gyaring Hu *China* 34°50N 97°40E **304** C4
Gydanskiy Poluostrov *Russia* 70°0N 78°0E **300** C8
Gyeongju *S. Korea* 35°51N 129°14E **307** G15
Gympie *Australia* 26°11S 152°38E **335** D5
Gyöngyös *Hungary* 47°48N 19°56E **289** E10
Győr *Hungary* 47°41N 17°40E **289** E9
Gypsum Pt. *Canada* 61°53N 114°35W **342** A6
Gypsumville *Canada* 51°45N 98°40W **343** C9
Gyula *Hungary* 46°38N 21°17E **289** E11
Gyumri *Armenia* 40°47N 43°50E **291** F7
Gyzylarbat = Serdar *Turkmenistan* 39°4N 56°23E **317** B8
Gyzyletrek = Etrek *Turkmenistan* 37°36N 54°46E **317** B7

H

Ha 'Arava → *Israel* 30°50N 35°20E **318** E4
Ha Coi *Vietnam* 21°26N 107°46E **310** B6
Ha Dong *Vietnam* 20°58N 105°46E **310** B5
Ha Giang *Vietnam* 22°50N 104°59E **310** A5
Ha Karmel △ *Israel* 32°45N 35°5E **318** C4
Ha Long, Vinh *Vietnam* 20°56N 107°3E **310** B6
Ha Tien *Vietnam* 10°23N 104°29E **311** G5
Ha Tinh *Vietnam* 18°20N 105°54E **310** C5
Ha Trung *Vietnam* 19°58N 105°50E **310** C5
Ha Yaek Chalong *Thailand* 7°50N 98°22E **311** a
Haaksbergen *Neths.* 52°9N 6°45E **287** B6
Ha'ano *Tonga* 19°41S 174°18W **331** c
Ha'apai Group *Tonga* 19°47S 174°27W **331** c
Haapiti *Moorea* 17°34S 149°52W **331** d
Haapsalu *Estonia* 58°56N 23°30E **281** G20
Haarlem *Neths.* 52°23N 4°39E **287** B4
Haast → *N.Z.* 43°50S 169°2E **331** E2
Haast Bluff *Australia* 23°22S 132°0E **332** D5
Hab → *Pakistan* 24°53N 66°41E **314** G3
Hab Nadi Chauki *Pakistan* 25°0N 66°50E **314** G2
Habahe *China* 48°3N 86°23E **304** B3
Habaswein *Kenya* 1°2N 39°30E **326** B4
Habay *Canada* 58°50N 118°44W **342** B5
Ḩabbānīyah *Iraq* 33°17N 43°29E **316** C4
Haboro *Japan* 44°22N 141°42E **302** B10
Ḩabshān *U.A.E.* 23°50N 53°37E **317** F7
Hachijō-Jima *Japan* 33°5N 139°45E **303** H9
Hachinohe *Japan* 40°30N 141°29E **302** D10

Hachiōji Japan 35°40N 139°20E 303 G9
Hackensack U.S.A. 40°52N 74°4W 355 F10
Hackettstown U.S.A. 40°51N 74°50W 355 F10
Hadali Pakistan 32°16N 72°11E 314 C5
Hadarba, Ras Sudan 22°4N 36°51E 323 D13
Hadarom □ Israel 31°0N 35°0E 318 E4
Ḥadd, Ra's al Oman 22°35N 59°50E 319 C6
Haddington U.K. 55°57N 2°47W 283 F6
Hadejia Nigeria 12°30N 10°5E 322 F7
Ḥadera Israel 32°27N 34°55E 318 C3
Ḥadera, N. → Israel 32°28N 34°52E 318 C3
Haderslev Denmark 55°15N 9°30E 281 J13
Hadhramaut = Ḥaḍramawt Yemen 15°30N 49°30E 319 D4
Hadībоh Yemen 12°39N 54°2E 319 E5
Hadong S. Korea 35°5N 127°44E 307 G14
Ḥaḍramawt Yemen 15°30N 49°30E 319 D4
Ḥadrānīyah Iraq 35°38N 43°14E 316 C4
Hadrian's Wall U.K. 55°0N 2°30W 284 B5
Haeju N. Korea 38°3N 125°45E 307 E13
Haenam S. Korea 34°34N 126°35E 307 G14
Haenertsburg S. Africa 24°0S 29°50E 329 C4
Haerhpin = Harbin China 45°48N 126°40E 307 B14
Hafar al Bāṭin Si. Arabia 28°32N 45°52E 316 D5
Ḥafīrat al 'Aydā Si. Arabia 26°26N 39°12E 316 E3
Ḥafit Oman 23°59N 55°49E 317 F7
Hafizabad Pakistan 32°5N 73°40E 314 C5
Haflong India 25°10N 93°5E 313 G18
Haft Gel Iran 31°30N 49°32E 317 D6
Hagalil Israel 32°53N 35°18E 318 C4
Hagen Germany 51°21N 7°27E 288 C4
Hagerman U.S.A. 33°7N 104°20W 349 K11
Hagerman Fossil Beds ⌂ U.S.A. 42°48N 114°57W 348 E6
Hagerstown U.S.A. 39°39N 77°43W 353 F15
Hagersville Canada 42°58N 80°3W 354 D4
Hagfors Sweden 60°3N 13°45E 281 F15
Hagi Japan 34°30N 131°22E 303 G5
Hagolan Syria 33°0N 35°45E 318 C4
Hagondange France 49°16N 6°11E 292 B7
Hags Hd. Ireland 52°57N 9°28W 282 D2
Hague, C. de la France 49°44N 1°56W 292 B3
Hague, The = 's-Gravenhage Neths. 52°7N 4°17E 287 B4
Haguenau France 48°49N 7°47E 292 B7
Hai Duong Vietnam 20°56N 106°19E 310 B6
Haicheng China 40°50N 122°45E 307 D12
Haidar Khel Afghan. 33°58N 68°38E 314 C3
Haidarâbâd = Hyderabad India 17°22N 78°29E 312 L11
Haidargarh India 26°37N 81°22E 315 F9
Haifa = Ḥefa Israel 32°46N 35°0E 318 C4
Haikou China 20°1N 110°16E 310 B8
Ḥā'il Si. Arabia 27°28N 41°45E 316 E4
Ḥā'il □ Si. Arabia 26°40N 41°40E 316 E4
Hailar China 49°10N 119°38E 305 B6
Hailey U.S.A. 43°31N 114°19W 348 E6
Haileybury Canada 47°30N 79°38W 344 C4
Hailin China 44°37N 129°30E 307 B15
Hailuoto Finland 65°3N 24°45E 280 D21
Hainan □ China 19°0N 109°30E 310 C7
Hainan Dao China 19°0N 109°30E 310 C7
Hainan Str. = Qiongzhou Haixia China 20°10N 110°15E 310 B8
Hainaut □ Belgium 50°30N 4°0E 287 D4
Haines Alaska, U.S.A. 59°14N 135°26W 342 B1
Haines Oreg., U.S.A. 44°55N 117°56W 348 D5
Haines City U.S.A. 28°7N 81°38W 357 G14
Haines Junction Canada 60°45N 137°30W 342 A1
Haiphong Vietnam 20°47N 106°41E 310 B6
Haiti ■ W. Indies 19°0N 72°30W 361 C5
Haiya Sudan 18°20N 36°21E 323 E13
Haiyang China 36°47N 121°9E 307 F11
Haiyuan China 36°35N 105°52E 306 F3
Haizhou China 34°37N 119°7E 307 G10
Haizhou Wan China 34°50N 119°20E 307 G10
Hajdúböszörmény Hungary 47°40N 21°30E 289 E11
Hajipur India 25°45N 85°13E 315 G11
Ḥajjah Yemen 15°42N 43°36E 319 D3
Ḥājjī Muḥsin Iraq 32°35N 45°29E 316 C5
Ḥājjīābād Iran 28°19N 55°55E 317 D7
Ḥājjīābād-e Zarrīn Iran 33°9N 54°51E 317 C7
Hajnówka Poland 52°47N 23°35E 289 B12
Hakansson, Mts. Dem. Rep. of the Congo 8°40S 25°45E 327 D2
Hakkâri Turkey 37°34N 43°44E 316 B4
Hakken-Zan Japan 34°10N 135°54E 303 G7
Hakodate Japan 41°45N 140°44E 302 D10
Hakos Namibia 23°13S 16°21E 328 C2
Haku-San Japan 36°9N 136°46E 303 F8
Haku-San △ Japan 36°15N 136°45E 303 F8
Hakui Japan 36°53N 136°47E 303 F8
Hala Pakistan 25°43N 68°20E 312 G6
Ḥalab Syria 36°10N 37°15E 316 B3
Ḥalabjah Iraq 35°10N 45°58E 316 C5
Halaib Sudan 22°12N 36°30E 323 D13
Halaib Triangle Africa 22°30N 35°20E 323 D13
Hālat 'Ammār Si. Arabia 29°10N 36°4E 316 D3
Halbā Lebanon 34°34N 36°6E 318 A5
Halberstadt Germany 51°54N 11°3E 288 C6
Halcombe N.Z. 40°8S 175°30E 331 D5
Halcon Phil. 13°0N 121°30E 309 B6
Halde Fjäll = Haltiatunturi Finland 69°17N 21°18E 280 B19
Halden Norway 59°9N 11°23E 281 G14
Haldimand Canada 42°59N 79°52W 354 D5
Haldwani India 29°31N 79°30E 315 E8
Hale → Australia 24°56S 135°53E 334 C2
Halesowen U.K. 52°27N 2°3W 285 E5
Halesworth U.K. 52°20N 1°31E 285 E9
Haleyville U.S.A. 34°14N 87°37W 357 D11
Half Dome U.S.A. 37°44N 119°32E 350 H7
Halfmoon Bay N.Z. 46°50S 168°5E 331 G2
Halfway → Canada 56°12N 121°32W 342 B4
Halia India 24°50N 82°19E 315 G10
Haliburton Canada 45°3N 78°30W 354 A6
Halifax Australia 18°32S 146°22E 334 B4
Halifax Canada 44°38N 63°35W 345 D7
Halifax U.K. 53°43N 1°52W 284 D6
Halifax U.S.A. 40°25N 76°55W 354 F8
Halifax B. Australia 18°50S 147°0E 334 B4
Halifax I. Namibia 26°38S 15°4E 328 D2
Halīl → Iran 27°40N 58°30E 317 E8
Halkida Greece 38°27N 23°42E 295 E10
Halkirk U.K. 58°30N 3°29W 283 C5
Hall Beach = Sanirajak Canada 68°46N 81°12W 341 C11
Hall Pen. Canada 63°30N 66°0W 341 C13
Hall Pt. Australia 15°40S 124°23E 332 C3
Halland Sweden 57°8N 12°47E 281 H15
Hallāniyat, Jazā'ir al Oman 17°30N 55°58E 319 D6
Hallasan S. Korea 33°22N 126°32E 307 H14
Halle Belgium 50°44N 4°13E 287 D4
Halle Germany 51°30N 11°56E 288 C6
Hällefors Sweden 59°47N 14°31E 281 G16
Hallett Australia 33°25S 138°55E 335 E2
Hallettsville U.S.A. 29°27N 96°57W 356 G6
Hallim S. Korea 33°24N 126°15E 307 H14
Hallingdalselva → Norway 60°23N 9°35E 280 F13
Hallock U.S.A. 48°47N 96°57W 352 A5
Halls Creek Australia 18°16S 127°38E 332 C4
Halls Gap Australia 37°8S 142°34E 335 F3
Hallsberg Sweden 59°5N 15°7E 281 G16
Hallstead U.S.A. 41°58N 75°45W 355 E9
Halmahera Indonesia 0°40N 128°0E 309 D7
Halmstad Sweden 56°41N 12°52E 281 H15
Hälsingborg = Helsingborg Sweden 56°3N 12°42E 281 H15
Hälsingland Sweden 61°40N 16°5E 280 F17
Halstead U.K. 51°57N 0°40E 285 F8
Haltiatunturi Finland 69°17N 21°18E 280 B19
Halton □ U.K. 53°22N 2°45W 284 D5
Haltwhistle U.K. 54°58N 2°26W 284 C5
Ḥālūl Qatar 25°40N 52°40E 317 E7
Halvad India 23°1N 71°11E 314 H4
Ḥalvān Iran 33°57N 56°15E 317 C8
Ham Tan Vietnam 10°40N 107°45E 311 G6
Ham Yen Vietnam 22°4N 105°3E 310 A5
Hamab Namibia 28°7S 19°16E 328 D2
Hamada Japan 34°56N 132°4E 303 G6
Hamadān Iran 34°52N 48°32E 317 C6
Hamadān □ Iran 35°0N 49°0E 317 C6
Ḥamāh Syria 35°5N 36°40E 316 C3
Hamamatsu Japan 34°45N 137°45E 303 G8
Hamar Norway 60°48N 11°7E 280 F14
Hamâta, Gebel Egypt 24°17N 35°0E 316 E2
Hambantota Sri Lanka 6°10N 81°10E 312 R12
Hamber ⌂ Canada 52°20N 118°0W 342 C5
Hamburg Germany 53°33N 9°59E 288 B5
Hamburg Ark., U.S.A. 33°14N 91°48W 356 E9
Hamburg N.Y., U.S.A. 42°43N 78°50W 354 D6
Hamburg Pa., U.S.A. 40°33N 75°59W 355 F9
Ḥamḍ, W. al → Si. Arabia 24°55N 36°20E 316 E3
Hamden U.S.A. 41°23N 72°54W 355 E12
Häme Finland 61°38N 25°10E 280 F21
Hämeenlinna Finland 61°0N 24°28E 280 F21
Hamelin Pool Australia 26°22S 114°20E 333 E1
Hameln Germany 52°6N 9°21E 288 B5
Hamerkaz □ Israel 32°15N 34°55E 318 C3
Hamersley Ra. Australia 22°0S 117°45E 332 D2
Hamhŭng N. Korea 39°54N 127°30E 307 E14
Hami China 42°55N 93°25E 304 B4
Hamilton Australia 37°45S 142°2E 335 F3
Hamilton Canada 43°15N 79°50W 354 C5
Hamilton N.Z. 37°47S 175°19E 331 B5
Hamilton U.K. 55°46N 4°2W 283 F4
Hamilton Ala., U.S.A. 34°9N 87°59W 357 D11
Hamilton Mont., U.S.A. 46°15N 114°10W 348 C6
Hamilton N.Y., U.S.A. 42°50N 75°33W 355 D9
Hamilton Ohio, U.S.A. 39°24N 84°34W 353 F11
Hamilton Tex., U.S.A. 31°42N 98°7W 356 F5
Hamilton → Queens., Australia 23°30S 139°47E 334 C2
Hamilton → S. Austral., Australia 26°40S 135°19E 335 D2
Hamilton City U.S.A. 39°45N 122°1W 350 F4
Hamilton I. Australia 20°21S 148°56E 334 J6
Hamilton Inlet Canada 54°0N 57°30W 345 B8
Hamilton Mt. U.S.A. 43°25N 74°22W 355 C10
Hamina Finland 60°34N 27°12E 280 F22
Hamirpur H.P., India 31°41N 76°31E 314 D7
Hamirpur Ut. P., India 25°57N 80°9E 315 G9
Hamju N. Korea 39°51N 127°26E 307 E14
Hamlet U.S.A. 34°53N 79°42W 357 D15
Hamley Bridge Australia 34°17S 138°35E 335 E2
Hamlin = Hameln Germany 52°6N 9°21E 288 B5
Hamlin N.Y., U.S.A. 43°17N 77°55W 354 C7
Hamlin Tex., U.S.A. 32°53N 100°8W 356 E4
Hamm Germany 51°40N 7°50E 288 C4
Ḥammār, Hawr al Iraq 30°50N 47°10E 316 D5
Hammerfest Norway 70°39N 23°41E 280 A20
Hammond Ind., U.S.A. 41°38N 87°30W 352 E10
Hammond La., U.S.A. 30°30N 90°28W 357 F9
Hammond N.Y., U.S.A. 44°27N 75°42W 355 B9
Hammondsport U.S.A. 42°25N 77°13W 354 D7
Hammonton U.S.A. 39°39N 74°48W 353 F16
Hampden N.Z. 45°18S 170°50E 331 F3
Hampshire □ U.K. 51°7N 1°23W 285 F6
Hampshire Downs U.K. 51°15N 1°10W 285 F6
Hampton N.B., Canada 45°32N 65°51W 345 C6
Hampton Ont., Canada 43°58N 78°45W 354 C6
Hampton Ark., U.S.A. 33°32N 92°28W 356 E8
Hampton Iowa, U.S.A. 42°45N 93°13W 352 D7
Hampton N.H., U.S.A. 42°57N 70°50W 355 D14
Hampton S.C., U.S.A. 32°52N 81°7W 357 E14
Hampton Va., U.S.A. 37°2N 76°21W 353 G15
Hampton Bays U.S.A. 40°53N 72°30W 355 F12
Hampton Tableland Australia 32°0S 127°0E 333 F4
Hamyang S. Korea 35°32N 127°42E 307 G14
Han Pijesak Bos.-H. 44°5N 18°57E 295 B8
Hanak Si. Arabia 25°32N 37°0E 316 E3
Hanamaki Japan 39°23N 141°7E 302 E10
Hanang Tanzania 4°30S 35°25E 326 C4
Hanau Germany 50°7N 8°56E 288 C5
Hanbogd = Ihbulag Mongolia 43°11N 107°10E 306 C4
Hancheng China 35°31N 110°25E 306 G6
Hancock Mich., U.S.A. 47°8N 88°35W 352 B9
Hancock N.Y., U.S.A. 41°57N 75°17W 355 E9
Handa Japan 34°53N 136°55E 303 G8
Handa I. U.K. 58°23N 5°11W 283 C3
Handan China 36°35N 114°28E 306 F8
Handeni Tanzania 5°25S 38°2E 326 D4
Handwara India 34°21N 74°20E 315 B6
Hanegev Israel 30°50N 35°0E 318 E4
Hanford U.S.A. 36°20N 119°39W 350 J7
Hanford Reach ⌂ U.S.A. 46°40N 119°30W 348 C4
Hang Chat Thailand 18°20N 99°21E 310 C2
Hang Dong Thailand 18°41N 98°55E 310 C2
Hangang → S. Korea 37°50N 126°30E 307 F14
Hangayn Nuruu Mongolia 47°30N 99°0E 304 B4
Hangchou = Hangzhou China 30°18N 120°11E 305 C7
Hanggin Houqi China 40°58N 107°4E 306 D4
Hanggin Qi China 39°52N 108°50E 306 E5
Hangu China 39°18N 117°53E 307 E9
Hangzhou China 30°18N 120°11E 305 C7
Hangzhou Wan China 30°15N 120°45E 305 C7
Hanhongor Mongolia 43°55N 104°28E 306 C3
Hania = Chania Greece 35°30N 24°4E 297 D6
Ḥanīdh Si. Arabia 26°35N 48°38E 317 E6
Ḥanīsh Yemen 13°45N 42°46E 319 E3
Hankinson U.S.A. 46°4N 96°54W 352 B5
Hankö Finland 59°50N 22°57E 281 G20
Hanksville U.S.A. 38°22N 110°43W 348 G8
Hanle India 32°42N 79°4E 315 C8
Hanmer Springs N.Z. 42°32S 172°50E 331 E4
Hann → Australia 17°26S 126°17E 332 C4
Hann, Mt. Australia 15°45S 126°0E 332 C4
Hanna Canada 51°40N 111°54W 342 C6
Hanna U.S.A. 41°52N 106°34W 348 F10
Hannah B. Canada 51°40N 80°0W 344 B4
Hannibal Mo., U.S.A. 39°42N 91°22W 352 F8
Hannibal N.Y., U.S.A. 43°19N 76°35W 355 C8
Hannover Germany 52°22N 9°46E 288 B5
Hanoi Vietnam 21°5N 105°55E 310 B5
Hanover = Hannover Germany 52°22N 9°46E 288 B5
Hanover Canada 44°9N 81°2W 354 B3
Hanover S. Africa 31°4S 24°29E 328 E3
Hanover N.H., U.S.A. 43°42N 72°17W 355 C12
Hanover Ohio, U.S.A. 40°4N 82°16W 354 F2
Hanover Pa., U.S.A. 39°48N 76°59W 353 F15
Hanover, I. Chile 51°0S 74°50W 368 G2
Hans Lollik I. U.S. Virgin Is. 18°24N 64°53W 361 e
Hansdiha India 24°36N 87°5E 315 G12
Hansi India 29°10N 75°57E 314 E6
Hanson, L. Australia 31°0S 136°15E 335 E2
Hantsavichy Belarus 52°49N 26°30E 289 B14
Hanumangarh India 29°35N 74°19E 314 E6
Hanzhong China 33°10N 107°1E 306 H4
Hanzhuang China 34°33N 117°23E 307 G9
Haora India 22°34N 88°18E 315 H13
Haparanda Sweden 65°52N 24°8E 280 D21
Happy U.S.A. 34°45N 101°52W 356 D4
Happy Camp U.S.A. 41°48N 123°23W 348 F2
Happy Valley-Goose Bay Canada 53°15N 60°20W 345 B7
Hapsu N. Korea 41°13N 128°51E 307 D15
Hapur India 28°45N 77°45E 314 E7
Ḥaql Si. Arabia 29°10N 34°58E 318 F3
Har Indonesia 5°16S 133°14E 309 F8
Har-Ayrag Mongolia 45°47N 109°16E 306 B5
Har Hu China 38°20N 97°38E 304 C4
Har Us Nuur Mongolia 48°0N 92°0E 304 B4
Har Yehuda Israel 31°35N 34°57E 318 D3
Ḥaraḍ Si. Arabia 24°22N 49°0E 319 C4
Haranomachi Japan 37°38N 140°58E 302 F10
Harare Zimbabwe 17°43S 31°2E 327 F3
Harazé Chad 9°57N 20°48E 323 G10
Harbin China 45°48N 126°40E 307 B14
Harbor Beach U.S.A. 43°51N 82°39W 354 C2
Harbour Breton Canada 47°29N 55°50W 345 C8
Harda India 22°27N 77°5E 314 H7
Hardangerfjorden Norway 60°5N 6°0E 281 F12
Hardangervidda Norway 60°7N 7°20E 280 F12
Hardap ⌂ Namibia 24°29S 17°45E 328 C2
Hardap Dam Namibia 24°32S 17°50E 328 C2
Hardenberg Neths. 52°34N 6°37E 287 B6
Harderwijk Neths. 52°21N 5°38E 287 B5
Hardey → Australia 22°45S 116°8E 332 D2
Hardin U.S.A. 45°44N 107°37W 348 D10
Harding S. Africa 30°35S 29°55E 329 E4
Harding Ra. Australia 16°17S 124°55E 332 C3
Hardisty Canada 52°40N 111°18W 342 C6
Hardoi India 27°26N 80°6E 315 F9
Hardwar = Haridwar India 29°58N 78°9E 314 E8
Hardwick U.S.A. 44°30N 72°22W 355 B12
Hardy, Pen. Chile 55°30S 68°20W 368 H3
Hardy, Pte. St. Lucia 14°6N 60°56W 361 f
Hare B. Canada 51°15N 55°45W 345 B8
Hareid Norway 62°22N 6°1E 280 E12
Harer Ethiopia 9°20N 42°8E 319 F3
Hargeisa Somali Rep. 9°30N 44°2E 319 F3
Hari → Indonesia 1°16S 104°5E 308 E2
Haria Canary Is. 29°8N 13°32W 296 E6
Haridwar India 29°58N 78°9E 314 E8
Harim, Jabal al Oman 25°58N 56°14E 317 E8
Haringhata → Bangla. 22°0N 89°58E 313 J16
Harīr, W. al → Syria 32°44N 35°59E 318 C4
Harīrūd → Asia 37°24N 60°38E 317 B9
Härjedalen Sweden 62°22N 13°5E 280 E15
Harlan Iowa, U.S.A. 41°39N 95°19W 352 E6
Harlan Ky., U.S.A. 36°51N 83°19W 353 G12
Harlech U.K. 52°52N 4°6W 284 E3
Harlem U.S.A. 48°32N 108°47W 348 B9
Harlingen Neths. 53°11N 5°25E 287 A5
Harlingen U.S.A. 26°12N 97°42W 356 H6
Harlow U.K. 51°46N 0°8E 285 F8
Harlowton U.S.A. 46°26N 109°50W 348 C9
Harnai Pakistan 30°6N 67°56E 314 D2
Harney Basin U.S.A. 43°0N 119°30W 348 E4
Harney L. U.S.A. 43°14N 119°8W 348 E4
Harney Peak U.S.A. 43°52N 103°32W 352 D2
Härnösand Sweden 62°38N 17°55E 280 E17
Haroldswick U.K. 60°48N 0°50W 283 A8
Harp L. Canada 55°5N 61°50W 345 A7
Harper Liberia 4°25N 7°43W 322 H4
Harrai India 22°37N 79°13E 315 H8
Harrand Pakistan 29°28N 70°3E 314 E4
Harricana → Canada 50°56N 79°32W 344 B4
Harriman U.S.A. 35°56N 84°33W 357 D12
Harrington Harbour Canada 50°31N 59°30W 345 B8
Harris U.K. 57°50N 6°55W 283 D2
Harris, L. Australia 31°10S 135°10E 335 E2
Harris, Sd. of U.K. 57°44N 7°6W 283 D1
Harris Pt. Canada 43°6N 82°9W 354 C2
Harrisburg Ill., U.S.A. 37°44N 88°32W 352 G9
Harrisburg Nebr., U.S.A. 41°33N 103°44W 352 E2
Harrisburg Pa., U.S.A. 40°16N 76°53W 354 F8
Harrismith S. Africa 28°15S 29°8E 329 D4
Harrison Ark., U.S.A. 36°14N 93°7W 356 C8
Harrison Maine, U.S.A. 44°7N 70°39W 355 B14
Harrison Nebr., U.S.A. 42°41N 103°53W 352 D2
Harrison, C. Canada 54°55N 57°55W 345 B8
Harrison L. Canada 49°33N 121°50W 342 D4
Harrisonburg U.S.A. 38°27N 78°52W 353 F14
Harrisonville U.S.A. 38°39N 94°21W 352 F6
Harriston Canada 43°57N 80°53W 354 C4
Harrisville Mich., U.S.A. 44°39N 83°17W 354 B1
Harrisville N.Y., U.S.A. 44°9N 75°19W 355 B9
Harrisville Pa., U.S.A. 41°8N 80°0W 354 E5
Harrodsburg U.S.A. 37°46N 84°51W 353 G11
Harrogate U.K. 54°0N 1°33W 284 C6
Harrow □ U.K. 51°35N 0°21W 285 F7
Harrowsmith Canada 44°24N 76°40W 355 B8
Harry S. Truman Res. U.S.A. 38°16N 93°24W 352 F7
Harsīn Iran 34°18N 47°33E 316 C5
Harstad Norway 68°48N 16°30E 280 B17
Harsud India 22°6N 76°44E 314 H7
Hart U.S.A. 43°42N 86°22W 352 D10
Hart, L. Australia 31°10S 136°25E 335 E2
Hartbees → S. Africa 28°45S 20°32E 328 D3
Hartford Conn., U.S.A. 41°46N 72°41W 355 E12
Hartford Ky., U.S.A. 37°27N 86°55W 352 G10
Hartford S. Dak., U.S.A. 43°38N 96°57W 352 D5
Hartford Vt., U.S.A. 43°40N 72°20W 355 C12
Hartford Wis., U.S.A. 43°19N 88°22W 352 D9
Hartford City U.S.A. 40°27N 85°22W 353 E11
Hartland Canada 46°20N 67°32W 345 C6
Hartland Pt. U.K. 51°1N 4°32W 285 F3
Hartlepool U.K. 54°42N 1°13W 284 C6
Hartlepool □ U.K. 54°42N 1°17W 284 C6
Hartley Bay Canada 53°25N 129°15W 342 C3
Hartmannberge Namibia 17°0S 13°0E 328 B1
Hartney Canada 49°30N 100°35W 343 D8
Harts → S. Africa 28°24S 24°17E 328 D3
Hartselle U.S.A. 34°27N 86°56W 357 D11
Hartshorne U.S.A. 34°51N 95°34W 356 D7
Hartstown U.S.A. 41°33N 80°23W 354 E4
Hartsville U.S.A. 34°23N 80°4W 357 D14
Hartswater S. Africa 27°34S 24°43E 328 D3
Hartwell U.S.A. 34°21N 82°56W 357 D13
Harunabad Pakistan 29°35N 73°8E 314 E5
Harvand Iran 28°25N 55°43E 317 D7
Harvey Australia 33°5S 115°54E 333 F2
Harvey Ill., U.S.A. 41°36N 87°50W 352 E10
Harvey N. Dak., U.S.A. 47°47N 99°56W 352 B4
Harwich U.K. 51°56N 1°17E 285 F9
Haryana □ India 29°0N 76°10E 314 E7
Haryn → Belarus 52°7N 27°17E 289 B14
Harz Germany 51°38N 10°44E 288 C6
Hasa Si. Arabia 25°50N 49°0E 317 E6
Ḥasā, W. al → Jordan 31°4N 35°29E 318 D4
Ḥasanābād Iran 32°8N 52°44E 317 C7
Ḥasb, W. → Iraq 31°45N 44°17E 316 D5
Hasdo → India 21°44N 82°44E 315 J10
Hashimoto Japan 34°19N 135°37E 303 G7
Hashtjerd Iran 35°52N 50°40E 317 C6
Haskell U.S.A. 33°10N 99°44W 356 E5
Haskovo = Khaskovo Bulgaria 41°56N 25°30E 295 D11
Haslemere U.K. 51°5N 0°43W 285 F7
Hasselt Belgium 50°56N 5°21E 287 D5
Hassi Messaoud Algeria 31°51N 6°1E 322 B7
Hässleholm Sweden 56°10N 13°46E 281 H15
Hastings N.Z. 39°39S 176°52E 331 C6
Hastings U.K. 50°51N 0°35E 285 G8
Hastings Mich., U.S.A. 42°39N 85°17W 353 D11
Hastings Minn., U.S.A. 44°44N 92°51W 352 C7
Hastings Nebr., U.S.A. 40°35N 98°23W 352 E4
Hastings Ra. Australia 31°15S 152°14E 335 E5
Hat Yai Thailand 7°1N 100°27E 311 J3
Hatanbulag = Ergel Mongolia 43°8N 109°5E 306 C5
Hatay Turkey 36°14N 36°10E 316 B3
Hatch U.S.A. 32°40N 107°9W 349 K10
Hatchet L. Canada 58°36N 103°40W 343 B8
Hateruma-Shima Japan 24°3N 123°47E 303 M1
Hatfield P.O. Australia 33°54S 143°49E 335 E3
Hatgal Mongolia 50°26N 100°9E 304 A5
Hathras India 27°36N 78°6E 314 F8
Hatia Bangla. 22°30N 91°5E 313 H17
Hato Mayor Dom. Rep. 18°46N 69°15W 361 C6
Hatta India 24°7N 79°36E 315 G8
Hatta U.A.E. 24°45N 56°4E 317 E8
Hattah Australia 34°48S 142°17E 335 E3
Hattah-Kulkyne △ Australia 34°16S 142°33E 335 E3
Hatteras, C. U.S.A. 35°14N 75°32W 357 D17
Hattiesburg U.S.A. 31°20N 89°17W 357 F10
Hatvan Hungary 47°40N 19°45E 289 E10
Hau Duc Vietnam 15°20N 108°13E 310 E7
Haugesund Norway 59°23N 5°13E 281 G11
Haukipudas Finland 65°12N 25°20E 280 D21
Haultain → Canada 55°51N 106°46W 343 B7
Hauraki G. N.Z. 36°35S 175°5E 331 B5
Haut Atlas Morocco 32°30N 5°0W 322 B4
Hautes Fagnes = Hohes Venn Belgium 50°30N 6°5E 287 D6
Hauts Plateaux Algeria 35°0N 1°0E 322 B6
Havana = La Habana Cuba 23°8N 82°22W 360 B3
Havana U.S.A. 40°18N 90°4W 352 E8
Havant U.K. 50°51N 0°58W 285 G7
Havasor = Kığzı Turkey 38°18N 43°25E 316 B4
Havasu, L. U.S.A. 34°18N 114°28W 351 L12
Havel → Germany 52°50N 12°3E 288 B7
Havelian Pakistan 34°2N 73°10E 314 B5
Havelock Canada 44°26N 77°53W 354 B7
Havelock N.Z. 41°17S 173°48E 331 D4
Havelock U.S.A. 34°53N 76°54W 357 D16
Haverfordwest U.K. 51°48N 4°58W 285 F3
Haverhill U.K. 52°5N 0°28E 285 E8
Haverhill U.S.A. 42°47N 71°5W 355 D13
Haverstraw U.S.A. 41°12N 73°58W 355 E11
Havirga Mongolia 45°41N 113°5E 306 B7
Havířov Czech Rep. 49°46N 18°20E 289 D10
Havlíčkův Brod Czech Rep. 49°36N 15°33E 288 D8
Havre U.S.A. 48°33N 109°41W 348 B9
Havre-Aubert Canada 47°12N 61°56W 345 C7
Havre-St.-Pierre Canada 50°18N 63°33W 345 B7
Haw → U.S.A. 35°36N 79°3W 357 D15
Hawai'i U.S.A. 19°30N 155°30W 346 b
Hawai'i □ U.S.A. 19°30N 156°30W 346 b
Hawaiian Is. Pac. Oc. 20°30N 156°0W 346 b
Hawaiian Ridge Pac. Oc. 24°0N 165°0W 337 E11
Hawarden U.S.A. 43°0N 96°29W 352 D5
Hawea, L. N.Z. 44°28S 169°19E 331 F2
Hawera N.Z. 39°35S 174°19E 331 C5
Hawick U.K. 55°26N 2°47W 283 F6
Hawk Junction Canada 48°5N 84°38W 344 C3
Hawke B. N.Z. 39°25S 177°20E 331 C6
Hawker Australia 31°59S 138°22E 335 E2
Hawke's Bay Canada 50°36N 57°10W 345 B8
Hawkesbury Canada 45°37N 74°37W 344 C5
Hawkesbury I. Canada 53°37N 129°3W 342 C3
Hawkesbury Pt. Australia 11°55S 134°5E 334 A1
Hawkinsville U.S.A. 32°17N 83°28W 357 E13
Hawley Minn., U.S.A. 46°53N 96°19W 352 B5
Hawley Pa., U.S.A. 41°28N 75°11W 355 E9
Ḥawrān, W. → Iraq 33°58N 42°34E 316 C4
Hawsh Mūssá Lebanon 33°45N 35°55E 318 B4
Hawthorne U.S.A. 38°32N 118°38W 348 G4
Hay Australia 34°30S 144°51E 335 E3
Hay → Australia 24°50S 138°0E 334 C2
Hay → Canada 60°50N 116°26W 342 A5
Hay, C. Australia 14°5S 129°29E 332 B4
Hay I. Canada 44°53N 80°58W 354 B4
Hay L. Canada 58°50N 118°50W 342 B5
Hay-on-Wye U.K. 52°5N 3°8W 285 E4
Hay River Canada 60°51N 115°44W 342 A5
Hay Springs U.S.A. 42°41N 102°41W 352 D2
Haya = Tehoru Indonesia 3°23S 129°30E 309 E7
Hayachine-San Japan 39°34N 141°29E 302 E10
Hayastan = Armenia ■ Asia 40°20N 45°0E 291 F7
Haydān, W. al → Jordan 31°29N 35°34E 318 D4
Hayden U.S.A. 40°30N 107°16W 348 F10
Haydon Australia 18°0S 141°30E 334 B3
Hayes U.S.A. 44°23N 101°1W 352 C3
Hayes → Canada 57°3N 92°12W 344 A1
Hayes Creek Australia 13°43S 131°22E 332 B5
Hayle U.K. 50°11N 5°26W 285 G2
Hayling I. U.K. 50°48N 0°59W 285 G7
Haymen I. Australia 20°3S 148°52E 334 J6
Hayrabolu Turkey 41°12N 27°5E 295 D12
Hays Canada 50°6N 111°48W 342 C6
Hays U.S.A. 38°53N 99°20W 352 F4
Haysyn Ukraine 48°57N 29°25E 289 D15
Hayvoron Ukraine 48°22N 29°52E 289 D15
Hayward Calif., U.S.A. 37°40N 122°4W 350 H4
Hayward Wis., U.S.A. 46°1N 91°29W 352 B8
Haywards Heath U.K. 51°0N 0°5W 285 G7
Hazafon □ Israel 32°40N 35°20E 318 C4
Hazar Turkmenistan 39°34N 53°16E 291 G9
Hazārān, Kūh-e Iran 29°35N 57°20E 317 D8
Hazard U.S.A. 37°15N 83°12W 353 G12
Hazaribag India 23°58N 85°26E 315 H11
Hazaribag Road India 24°12N 85°57E 315 G11
Hazelton Canada 55°20N 127°42W 342 B3
Hazelton U.S.A. 46°29N 100°17W 352 B3
Hazen U.S.A. 47°18N 101°38W 352 B3
Hazlehurst Ga., U.S.A. 31°52N 82°36W 357 F13
Hazlehurst Miss., U.S.A. 31°52N 90°24W 357 F9
Hazlet U.S.A. 40°25N 74°12W 355 F10
Hazleton U.S.A. 40°57N 75°59W 355 F9
Hazlett, L. Australia 21°30S 128°48E 332 D4
Hazro Turkey 38°15N 40°47E 316 B4
Head of Bight Australia 31°30S 131°25E 333 F5
Headlands Zimbabwe 18°15S 32°2E 327 F3

Healdsburg *U.S.A.* 38°37N 122°52W **350** G4
Healdton *U.S.A.* 34°14N 97°29W **356** D6
Healesville *Australia* 37°35S 145°30E **335** F4
Heany Junction *Zimbabwe* 20°6S 28°54E **329** C4
Heard I. *Ind. Oc.* 53°0S 74°0E **275** G13
Hearne *U.S.A.* 30°53N 96°36W **356** F6
Hearst *Canada* 49°40N 83°41W **344** C3
Heart → *U.S.A.* 46°46N 100°50W **352** B3
Heart's Content *Canada* 47°54N 53°27W **345** C9
Heath, Pte. *Canada* 49°8N 61°40W **345** C7
Heathrow, London ✕ **(LHR)** *U.K.* 51°28N 0°27W **285** F7
Heavener *U.S.A.* 34°53N 94°36W **356** D7
Hebbronville *U.S.A.* 27°18N 98°41W **356** H5
Hebei □ *China* 39°0N 116°0E **306** E9
Hebel *Australia* 28°58S 147°47E **335** D4
Heber *U.S.A.* 32°44N 115°32W **351** N11
Heber Springs *U.S.A.* 35°30N 92°2W **356** D8
Hebgen L. *U.S.A.* 44°52N 111°20W **348** D8
Hebi *China* 35°57N 114°7E **306** G8
Hebrides *U.K.* 57°30N 7°0W **278** D4
Hebrides, Sea of the *U.K.* 57°5N 7°0W **283** D2
Hebron = Al Khalīl *West Bank* 31°32N 35°6E **318** D4
Hebron *Canada* 58°5N 62°30W **341** D13
Hebron *N. Dak., U.S.A.* 46°54N 102°3W **352** B2
Hebron *Nebr., U.S.A.* 40°10N 97°35W **352** E5
Hecate Str. *Canada* 53°10N 130°30W **342** C2
Heceta I. *U.S.A.* 55°46N 133°40W **342** B2
Hechi *China* 24°40N 108°2E **304** D5
Hechuan *China* 30°2N 106°12E **304** C5
Hecla *U.S.A.* 45°53N 98°9W **352** C4
Hecla I. *Canada* 51°10N 96°43W **343** C9
Hede *Sweden* 62°23N 13°30E **280** E15
Hedemora *Sweden* 60°18N 15°58E **281** F16
Heerde *Neths.* 52°24N 6°2E **287** B6
Heerenveen *Neths.* 52°57N 5°55E **287** B5
Heerhugowaard *Neths.* 52°40N 4°51E **287** B4
Heerlen *Neths.* 50°55N 5°58E **287** D5
Ḥefa *Israel* 32°46N 35°0E **318** C4
Ḥefa □ *Israel* 32°40N 35°0E **318** C4
Hefei *China* 31°52N 117°18E **305** C6
Hegang *China* 47°20N 130°19E **305** B8
Hei Ling Chau *China* 22°15N 114°2E **305** G11
Heichengzhen *China* 36°24N 106°3E **306** F4
Heidelberg *Germany* 49°24N 8°42E **288** D5
Heidelberg *S. Africa* 34°6S 20°59E **328** E3
Heilbron *S. Africa* 27°16S 27°59E **329** D4
Heilbronn *Germany* 49°9N 9°13E **288** D5
Heilongjiang □ *China* 48°0N 126°0E **305** B7
Heilunkiang = Heilongjiang □ *China* 48°0N 126°0E **305** B7
Heimaey *Iceland* 63°26N 20°17W **280** E3
Heinola *Finland* 61°13N 26°2E **280** F22
Heinze Kyun *Burma* 14°25N 97°45E **310** E1
Heishan *China* 41°40N 122°5E **307** D12
Heishui *China* 42°8N 119°30E **307** C10
Hejaz = Ḥijāz *Si. Arabia* 24°0N 40°0E **316** E3
Hejian *China* 38°25N 116°5E **306** E9
Hejin *China* 35°35N 110°42E **306** G6
Hekımhan *Turkey* 38°50N 37°55E **316** B3
Hekla *Iceland* 63°56N 19°35W **280** E4
Hekou *China* 22°30N 103°59E **304** D5
Helan Shan *China* 38°30N 105°55E **306** E3
Helen Atoll *Pac. Oc.* 2°40N 132°0E **309** D8
Helena *Ark., U.S.A.* 34°32N 90°36W **357** D9
Helena *Mont., U.S.A.* 46°36N 112°2W **348** C7
Helendale *U.S.A.* 34°44N 117°19W **351** L9
Helensburgh *U.K.* 56°1N 4°43W **283** E4
Helensville *N.Z.* 36°41S 174°29E **331** B5
Helenvale *Australia* 15°43S 145°14E **334** B4
Helgeland *Norway* 66°7N 13°29E **280** C15
Helgoland *Germany* 54°10N 7°53E **288** A4
Heligoland = Helgoland *Germany* 54°10N 7°53E **288** A4
Heligoland B. = Deutsche Bucht *Germany* 54°15N 8°0E **288** A5
Hell Hole Gorge △ *Australia* 25°31S 144°12E **334** D3
Hella *Iceland* 63°50N 20°24W **280** E3
Hellas = Greece ■ *Europe* 40°0N 23°0E **295** E9
Hellertown *U.S.A.* 40°35N 75°21W **355** F9
Hellespont = Çanakkale Boğazı *Turkey* 40°17N 26°32E **295** D12
Hellevoetsluis *Neths.* 51°50N 4°8E **287** C4
Hellín *Spain* 38°31N 1°40W **293** C5
Hells Canyon ⌂ *U.S.A.* 45°30N 117°45W **348** D5
Hell's Gate △ *Kenya* 0°54S 36°19E **326** C4
Helmand □ *Afghan.* 31°20N 64°0E **312** D4
Helmand → *Afghan.* 31°12N 61°34E **312** D2
Helmeringhausen *Namibia* 25°54S 16°57E **328** D2
Helmond *Neths.* 51°29N 5°41E **287** C5
Helmsdale *U.K.* 58°7N 3°39W **283** C5
Helmsdale → *U.K.* 58°8N 3°43W **283** C5
Helong *China* 42°40N 129°0E **307** C15
Helper *U.S.A.* 39°41N 110°51W **348** G8
Helsingborg *Sweden* 56°3N 12°42E **281** H15
Helsingfors = Helsinki *Finland* 60°10N 24°55E **281** F21
Helsingør *Denmark* 56°2N 12°35E **281** H15
Helsinki *Finland* 60°10N 24°55E **281** F21
Helston *U.K.* 50°6N 5°17W **285** G2
Helvellyn *U.K.* 54°32N 3°1W **284** C4
Helwân *Egypt* 29°50N 31°20E **323** C12
Hemel Hempstead *U.K.* 51°44N 0°28W **285** F7
Hemet *U.S.A.* 33°45N 116°58W **351** M10
Hemingford *U.S.A.* 42°19N 103°4W **352** D2
Hemis △ *India* 34°10N 77°15E **314** B7
Hemmingford *Canada* 45°3N 73°35W **355** A11
Hempstead *N.Y., U.S.A.* 40°42N 73°37W **355** F11
Hempstead *Tex., U.S.A.* 30°6N 96°5W **356** F6
Hemse *Sweden* 57°15N 18°22E **281** H18
Henan □ *China* 34°0N 114°0E **306** H8
Henares → *Spain* 40°24N 3°30W **293** B4
Henashi-Misaki *Japan* 40°37N 139°51E **302** D9
Henderson *Argentina* 36°18S 61°43W **366** D3
Henderson *Ky., U.S.A.* 37°50N 87°35W **352** G10
Henderson *N.C., U.S.A.* 36°20N 78°25W **357** C15
Henderson *Nev., U.S.A.* 36°2N 114°58W **351** J12
Henderson *Tenn., U.S.A.* 35°26N 88°38W **357** D10
Henderson *Tex., U.S.A.* 32°9N 94°48W **356** E7
Henderson I. *Pac. Oc.* 24°22S 128°19W **337** K15
Hendersonville *N.C., U.S.A.* 35°19N 82°28W **357** D13
Hendersonville *Tenn., U.S.A.* 36°18N 86°37W **357** C11
Hendījān *Iran* 30°14N 49°43E **317** D6
Hendorābī *Iran* 26°40N 53°37E **317** E7
Hengcheng *China* 38°18N 106°28E **306** E4
Hengdaohezi *China* 44°52N 129°0E **307** B15
Hengelo *Neths.* 52°16N 6°48E **287** B6
Henggang *China* 22°39N 114°12E **305** F11
Hengmen *China* 22°33N 113°35E **305** F10
Hengqin Dao *China* 22°7N 113°34E **305** G10
Hengshan *China* 37°58N 109°5E **306** F5
Hengshui *China* 37°41N 115°40E **306** F8
Hengyang *China* 26°59N 112°22E **305** D6
Henley-on-Thames *U.K.* 51°32N 0°54W **285** F7
Henlopen, C. *U.S.A.* 38°48N 75°6W **353** F16
Hennenman *S. Africa* 27°59S 27°1E **328** D4
Hennessey *U.S.A.* 36°6N 97°54W **356** C6
Henri Pittier △ *Venezuela* 10°26N 67°37W **361** D6
Henrietta *U.S.A.* 33°49N 98°12W **356** E5
Henrietta, Ostrov = Genriyetty, Ostrov *Russia* 77°6N 156°30E **301** B16
Henrietta Maria, C. *Canada* 55°9N 82°20W **344** A3
Henry *U.S.A.* 41°7N 89°22W **352** E9
Henryetta *U.S.A.* 35°27N 95°59W **356** D7
Henryville *Canada* 45°8N 73°11W **355** A11
Hensall *Canada* 43°26N 81°30W **354** C3
Hentiesbaai *Namibia* 22°8S 14°18E **328** C1
Hentiyn Nuruu *Mongolia* 48°30N 108°30E **305** B5
Henty *Australia* 35°30S 147°3E **335** F4
Henzada *Burma* 17°38N 95°26E **313** L19
Heppner *U.S.A.* 45°21N 119°33W **348** D4
Hepworth *Canada* 44°37N 81°9W **354** B3
Hequ *China* 39°20N 111°15E **306** E6
Héraðsflói *Iceland* 65°42N 14°12W **280** D6
Héraðsvötn → *Iceland* 65°45N 19°25W **280** D4
Heraklion = Iraklio *Greece* 35°20N 25°12E **297** D7
Herald Cays *Australia* 16°58S 149°9E **334** B4
Herāt *Afghan.* 34°20N 62°7E **312** B3
Herāt □ *Afghan.* 35°0N 62°0E **312** B3
Herbert *Canada* 50°30N 107°10W **343** C7
Herbert → *Australia* 18°31S 146°17E **334** B4
Herberton *Australia* 17°20S 145°25E **334** B4
Herbertsdale *S. Africa* 34°1S 21°46E **328** E3
Herceg-Novi *Montenegro* 42°30N 18°33E **295** C8
Herchmer *Canada* 57°22N 94°10W **343** B10
Herðubreið *Iceland* 65°11N 16°21W **280** D5
Hereford *U.K.* 52°4N 2°43W **285** E5
Hereford *U.S.A.* 34°49N 102°24W **356** D3
Herefordshire □ *U.K.* 52°8N 2°40W **285** E5
Herentals *Belgium* 51°12N 4°51E **287** C4
Herford *Germany* 52°7N 8°39E **288** B5
Herington *U.S.A.* 38°40N 96°57W **352** F5
Herkimer *U.S.A.* 43°2N 74°59W **355** D10
Herlong *U.S.A.* 40°8N 120°8W **350** E6
Herm *U.K.* 49°30N 2°28W **285** H5
Hermann *U.S.A.* 38°42N 91°27W **352** F8
Hermannsburg *Australia* 23°57S 132°45E **332** D5
Hermanus *S. Africa* 34°27S 19°12E **328** E2
Hermidale *Australia* 31°30S 146°42E **335** E4
Hermiston *U.S.A.* 45°51N 119°17W **348** D4
Hermite, I. *Chile* 55°50S 68°0W **368** H3
Hermon *U.S.A.* 44°28N 75°14W **355** B9
Hermon, Mt. = Shaykh, J. ash *Lebanon* 33°25N 35°50E **318** B4
Hermosillo *Mexico* 29°10N 111°0W **358** B2
Hernád → *Hungary* 47°56N 21°8E **289** D11
Hernandarias *Paraguay* 25°20S 54°40W **367** B5
Hernandez *U.S.A.* 36°24N 120°46W **350** J6
Hernando *Argentina* 32°28S 63°40W **366** C3
Hernando *U.S.A.* 34°50N 90°0W **357** D10
Herndon *U.S.A.* 40°43N 76°51W **354** F8
Herne *Germany* 51°32N 7°14E **287** C7
Herne Bay *U.K.* 51°21N 1°8E **285** F9
Herning *Denmark* 56°8N 8°58E **281** H13
Heroica Caborca = Caborca *Mexico* 30°37N 112°6W **358** A2
Heroica Nogales = Nogales *Mexico* 31°19N 110°56W **358** A2
Heron Bay *Canada* 48°40N 86°25W **344** C2
Heron I. *Australia* 23°27S 151°55E **334** C5
Herradura, Pta. de la *Canary Is.* 28°26N 14°8W **296** F5
Herreid *U.S.A.* 45°50N 100°4W **352** C3
Herrin *U.S.A.* 37°48N 89°2W **352** G9
Herriot *Canada* 56°22N 101°16W **343** B8
Herschel I. *Canada* 69°35N 139°5W **276** C1
Hershey *U.S.A.* 40°17N 76°39W **355** F8
Herstal *Belgium* 50°40N 5°38E **287** D5
Hertford *U.K.* 51°48N 0°4W **285** F7
Hertfordshire □ *U.K.* 51°51N 0°5W **285** F7
's-Hertogenbosch *Neths.* 51°42N 5°17E **287** C5
Hertzogville *S. Africa* 28°9S 25°30E **328** D4
Hervey B. *Australia* 25°0S 152°52E **334** C5
Herzliyya *Israel* 32°10N 34°50E **318** C3
Ḥeṣār *Fārs, Iran* 29°52N 50°16E **317** D6
Ḥeṣār *Markazī, Iran* 35°50N 49°12E **317** C6
Heshui *China* 35°48N 108°0E **306** G5
Heshun *China* 37°22N 113°32E **306** F7
Hesperia *U.S.A.* 34°25N 117°18W **351** L9
Hesse = Hessen □ *Germany* 50°30N 9°0E **288** C5
Hessen □ *Germany* 50°30N 9°0E **288** C5
Hetch Hetchy Aqueduct *U.S.A.* 37°29N 122°19W **350** H5
Hettinger *U.S.A.* 46°0N 102°42W **352** B2
Heuksando *S. Korea* 34°40N 125°30E **307** G13
Heunghae *S. Korea* 36°12N 129°21E **307** F15
Heuvelton *U.S.A.* 44°37N 75°25W **355** B9
Hewitt *U.S.A.* 31°28N 97°12W **356** F6
Hexham *U.K.* 54°58N 2°4W **284** C5
Hexigten Qi *China* 43°18N 117°30E **307** C9
Ḥeydarābād *Iran* 30°33N 55°38E **317** D7
Heysham *U.K.* 54°3N 2°53W **284** C5
Heywood *Australia* 38°8S 141°37E **335** F3
Heze *China* 35°14N 115°20E **306** G8
Hi, Ko *Thailand* 7°44N 98°22E **311** a
Hi Vista *U.S.A.* 34°45N 117°46W **351** L9
Hialeah *U.S.A.* 25°51N 80°16W **357** J14
Hiawatha *U.S.A.* 39°51N 95°32W **352** F6
Hibbing *U.S.A.* 47°25N 92°56W **352** B7
Hibbs B. *Australia* 42°35S 145°15E **335** G4
Hibernia Reef *Australia* 12°0S 123°23E **332** B3
Hickman *U.S.A.* 36°34N 89°11W **352** G9
Hickory *U.S.A.* 35°44N 81°21W **357** D14
Hicks, Pt. *Australia* 37°49S 149°17E **335** F4
Hicks L. *Canada* 61°25N 100°0W **343** A9
Hicksville *U.S.A.* 40°46N 73°32W **355** F11
Hida-Gawa → *Japan* 35°26N 137°3E **303** G8
Hida-Sammyaku *Japan* 36°30N 137°40E **303** F8
Hidaka-Sammyaku *Japan* 42°35N 142°45E **302** C11
Hidalgo □ *Mexico* 20°30N 99°0W **359** C5
Hidalgo, Presa M. *Mexico* 26°30N 108°35W **358** B3
Hidalgo del Parral *Mexico* 26°56N 105°40W **358** B3
Hierro *Canary Is.* 27°44N 18°0W **296** G1
Higashiajima-San *Japan* 37°40N 140°10E **302** F10
Higashiōsaka *Japan* 34°39N 135°37E **303** G7
Higgins *U.S.A.* 36°7N 100°2W **356** C4
Higgins Corner *U.S.A.* 39°2N 121°5W **350** F5
High Bridge *U.S.A.* 40°40N 74°54W **355** F10
High Island Res. *China* 22°22N 114°21E **305** G11
High Level *Canada* 58°31N 117°8W **342** B5
High Point *U.S.A.* 35°57N 80°0W **357** D15
High Prairie *Canada* 55°30N 116°30W **342** B5
High River *Canada* 50°30N 113°50W **342** C6
High Tatra = Tatry *Slovak Rep.* 49°20N 20°0E **289** D11
High Veld *Africa* 27°0S 27°0E **320** J6
High Wycombe *U.K.* 51°37N 0°45W **285** F7
Highland □ *U.K.* 57°17N 4°21W **283** D4
Highland Park *U.S.A.* 42°11N 87°48W **352** D10
Highmore *U.S.A.* 44°31N 99°27W **352** C4
Highrock L. *Man., Canada* 55°45N 100°30W **343** B8
Highrock L. *Sask., Canada* 57°5N 105°32W **343** B7
Higüey *Dom. Rep.* 18°37N 68°42W **361** C6
Hiiumaa *Estonia* 58°50N 22°45E **281** G20
Ḥijāz *Si. Arabia* 24°0N 40°0E **316** E3
Hijo = Tagum *Phil.* 7°33N 125°53E **309** C7
Hikari *Japan* 33°58N 131°58E **303** H5
Hiko *U.S.A.* 37°32N 115°14W **350** H11
Hikone *Japan* 35°15N 136°10E **303** G8
Hikurangi *Gisborne, N.Z.* 37°55S 178°4E **331** C6
Hikurangi *Northland, N.Z.* 35°36S 174°17E **331** A5
Hildesheim *Germany* 52°9N 9°56E **288** B5
Hill → *Australia* 30°23S 115°3E **333** F2
Hill City *Idaho, U.S.A.* 43°18N 115°3W **348** E6
Hill City *Kans., U.S.A.* 39°22N 99°51W **352** F4
Hill City *Minn., U.S.A.* 46°59N 93°36W **352** B7
Hill City *S. Dak., U.S.A.* 43°56N 103°35W **352** D2
Hill Island L. *Canada* 60°30N 109°50W **343** A7
Hillaby, Mt. *Barbados* 13°12N 59°35W **361** g
Hillcrest *Barbados* 13°13N 59°31W **361** g
Hillcrest Center *U.S.A.* 35°23N 118°57W **351** K8
Hillegom *Neths.* 52°18N 4°35E **287** B4
Hillsboro *Kans., U.S.A.* 38°21N 97°12W **352** F5
Hillsboro *N. Dak., U.S.A.* 47°26N 97°3W **352** B5
Hillsboro *Ohio, U.S.A.* 39°12N 83°37W **353** F12
Hillsboro *Oreg., U.S.A.* 45°31N 122°59W **350** E4
Hillsboro *Tex., U.S.A.* 32°1N 97°8W **356** E6
Hillsborough *Grenada* 12°28N 61°28W **361** D7
Hillsborough *U.S.A.* 43°7N 71°54W **355** C13
Hillsborough Channel *Australia* 20°56S 149°15E **334** J7
Hillsdale *Mich., U.S.A.* 41°56N 84°38W **353** E11
Hillsdale *N.Y., U.S.A.* 42°11N 73°32W **355** D11
Hillsport *Canada* 49°27N 85°34W **344** C2
Hillston *Australia* 33°30S 145°31E **335** E4
Hilo *U.S.A.* 19°44N 155°5W **346** b
Hilton *U.S.A.* 43°17N 77°48W **354** C7
Hilton Head Island *U.S.A.* 32°13N 80°45W **357** E14
Hilversum *Neths.* 52°14N 5°10E **287** B5
Himachal Pradesh □ *India* 31°30N 77°0E **314** D7
Himalaya *Asia* 29°0N 84°0E **315** E11
Himatnagar *India* 23°37N 72°57E **314** H5
Himeji *Japan* 34°50N 134°40E **303** G7
Himi *Japan* 36°50N 136°55E **303** F8
Ḥimṣ *Syria* 34°40N 36°45E **318** A5
Ḥimṣ □ *Syria* 34°30N 37°0E **318** A6
Hinche *Haiti* 19°9N 72°1W **361** C5
Hinchinbrook I. *Australia* 18°20S 146°15E **334** B4
Hinchinbrook Island △ *Australia* 18°14S 146°6E **334** B4
Hinckley *U.K.* 52°33N 1°22W **285** E6
Hinckley *U.S.A.* 46°1N 92°56W **352** B7
Hindaun *India* 26°44N 77°5E **314** F7
Hindmarsh, L. *Australia* 36°5S 141°55E **335** F3
Hindu Bagh *Pakistan* 30°56N 67°50E **314** D2
Hindu Kush *Asia* 36°0N 71°0E **312** B7
Hindupur *India* 13°49N 77°32E **312** N10
Hines Creek *Canada* 56°20N 118°40W **342** B5
Hinesville *U.S.A.* 31°51N 81°36W **357** F14
Hinganghat *India* 20°30N 78°52E **312** J11
Hingham *U.S.A.* 48°33N 110°25W **348** B8
Hingir *India* 21°57N 83°41E **315** J10
Hingoli *India* 19°41N 77°15E **312** K10
Hinna = Imi *Ethiopia* 6°28N 42°10E **319** F3
Hinnøya *Norway* 68°35N 15°50E **280** B16
Hinojosa del Duque *Spain* 38°30N 5°9W **293** C3
Hinsdale *U.S.A.* 42°47N 72°29W **355** D12
Hinthada = Henzada *Burma* 17°38N 95°26E **313** L19
Hinton *Canada* 53°26N 117°34W **342** C5
Hinton *U.S.A.* 37°40N 80°54W **353** G13
Hios *Greece* 38°27N 26°9E **295** E12
Hirado *Japan* 33°22N 129°33E **303** H4
Hirakud Dam *India* 21°32N 83°45E **313** J13
Hiran → *India* 23°6N 79°21E **315** H8
Hirapur *India* 24°22N 79°13E **315** G8
Hirara *Japan* 24°48N 125°17E **303** M2
Hiratsuka *Japan* 35°19N 139°21E **303** G9
Hiroo *Japan* 42°17N 143°19E **302** C11
Hirosaki *Japan* 40°34N 140°28E **302** D10
Hiroshima *Japan* 34°24N 132°30E **303** G6
Hiroshima □ *Japan* 34°50N 133°0E **303** G6
Hisar *India* 29°12N 75°45E **314** E6
Hisb, Sha'ib = Ḥasb, W. → *Iraq* 31°45N 44°17E **316** D5
Ḥismá *Si. Arabia* 28°30N 36°0E **316** D3
Hispaniola *W. Indies* 19°0N 71°0W **361** C5
Hīt *Iraq* 33°38N 42°49E **316** C4
Hita *Japan* 33°20N 130°58E **303** H5
Hitachi *Japan* 36°36N 140°39E **303** F10
Hitchin *U.K.* 51°58N 0°16W **285** F7
Hitiaa *Tahiti* 17°36S 149°18W **331** d
Hitoyoshi *Japan* 32°13N 130°45E **303** H5
Hitra *Norway* 63°30N 8°45E **280** E13
Hiva Oa *French Polynesia* 9°45S 139°0W **337** H14
Hixon *Canada* 53°25N 122°35W **342** C4
Ḥiyyon, N. → *Israel* 30°25N 35°10E **318** E4
Hjalmar L. *Canada* 61°33N 109°25W **343** A7
Hjälmaren *Sweden* 59°18N 15°40E **281** G16
Hjørring *Denmark* 57°29N 9°59E **281** H13
Hjort Trench *S. Ocean* 58°0S 157°30E **277** B10
Hkakabo Razi *Burma* 28°25N 97°23E **313** E20
Hlobane *S. Africa* 27°42S 31°0E **329** D5
Hluhluwe *S. Africa* 28°1S 32°15E **329** D5
Hluhluwe ⌂ *S. Africa* 22°10S 32°5E **329** C5
Hlyboka *Ukraine* 48°5N 25°56E **289** D13
Ho *Ghana* 6°37N 0°27E **322** G6
Ho Chi Minh City = Thanh Pho Ho Chi Minh *Vietnam* 10°58N 106°40E **311** G6
Ho Thuong *Vietnam* 19°32N 105°48E **310** C5
Hoa Binh *Vietnam* 20°50N 105°20E **310** B5
Hoa Da *Vietnam* 11°16N 108°40E **311** G7
Hoa Hiep *Vietnam* 11°34N 105°51E **311** G5
Hoai Nhon *Vietnam* 14°28N 109°1E **310** E7
Hoang Lien Son *Vietnam* 22°0N 104°0E **310** A4
Hoanib → *Namibia* 19°27S 12°46E **328** B2
Hoare B. *Canada* 65°17N 62°30W **341** C13
Hoarusib → *Namibia* 19°3S 12°36E **328** B2
Hobart *Australia* 42°50S 147°21E **335** G4
Hobart *U.S.A.* 35°1N 99°6W **356** D5
Hobbs *U.S.A.* 32°42N 103°8W **349** K12
Hobbs Coast *Antarctica* 74°50S 131°0W **277** D14
Hobe Sound *U.S.A.* 27°4N 80°8W **357** H14
Hoboken *U.S.A.* 40°44N 74°3W **355** F10
Hobro *Denmark* 56°39N 9°46E **281** H13
Hoburgen *Sweden* 56°55N 18°7E **281** H18
Hochfeld *Namibia* 21°28S 17°58E **328** C2
Hodaka-Dake *Japan* 36°17N 137°39E **303** F8
Hodeida = Al Ḥudaydah *Yemen* 14°50N 43°0E **319** E3
Hodgeville *Canada* 50°7N 106°58W **343** C7
Hodgson *Canada* 51°13N 97°36W **343** C9
Hódmezővásárhely *Hungary* 46°28N 20°22E **289** E11
Hodna, Chott el *Algeria* 35°26N 4°43E **322** A6
Hodonín *Czech Rep.* 48°50N 17°10E **289** D9
Hoek van Holland *Neths.* 52°0N 4°7E **287** C4
Hoengseong *S. Korea* 37°29N 127°59E **307** F14
Hoeryong *N. Korea* 42°30N 129°45E **307** C15
Hoeyang *N. Korea* 38°43N 127°36E **307** E14
Hof *Germany* 50°19N 11°55E **288** C6
Hofmeyr *S. Africa* 31°39S 25°50E **328** E4
Höfn *Iceland* 64°15N 15°13W **280** D6
Hofors *Sweden* 60°31N 16°15E **281** F17
Hofsjökull *Iceland* 64°49N 18°48W **280** D4
Hōfu *Japan* 34°3N 131°34E **303** G5
Hogan Group *Australia* 39°13S 147°1E **335** F4
Hogarth, Mt. *Australia* 21°48S 136°58E **334** C2
Hoge Kempen △ *Belgium* 51°6N 5°35E **287** C5
Hoggar = Ahaggar *Algeria* 23°0N 6°30E **322** D7
Hogsty Reef *Bahamas* 21°41N 73°48W **361** B5
Hoh → *U.S.A.* 47°45N 124°29W **350** C2
Hoh Xil Shan *China* 35°0N 89°0E **304** C3
Hohenwald *U.S.A.* 35°33N 87°33W **357** D11
Hoher Rhön = Rhön *Germany* 50°24N 9°58E **288** C5
Hohes Venn *Belgium* 50°30N 6°5E **287** D6
Hohhot *China* 40°52N 111°40E **306** D6
Hoi An *Vietnam* 15°30N 108°19E **310** E7
Hoi Xuan *Vietnam* 20°25N 105°9E **310** B5
Hoisington *U.S.A.* 38°31N 98°47W **352** F4
Hōjō *Japan* 33°58N 132°46E **303** H6
Hokianga Harbour *N.Z.* 35°31S 173°22E **331** A4
Hokitika *N.Z.* 42°42S 171°0E **331** E3
Hokkaidō □ *Japan* 43°30N 143°0E **302** C11
Hola *Kenya* 1°29S 40°2E **326** B4
Holakas *Greece* 35°57N 27°53E **297** D9
Holbrook *Australia* 35°42S 147°18E **335** F4
Holbrook *U.S.A.* 34°54N 110°10W **349** J8
Holden *U.S.A.* 39°6N 112°16W **348** G7
Holdenville *U.S.A.* 35°5N 96°24W **356** D6
Holdrege *U.S.A.* 40°26N 99°23W **352** E4
Holetown *Barbados* 13°11N 59°38W **361** g
Holguín *Cuba* 20°50N 76°20W **360** B4
Hollams Bird I. *Namibia* 24°40S 14°30E **328** C1
Holland *Mich., U.S.A.* 42°47N 86°7W **352** D10
Holland *N.Y., U.S.A.* 42°38N 78°32W **354** D6
Holley *U.S.A.* 43°14N 78°2W **354** C6
Hollidaysburg *U.S.A.* 40°26N 78°24W **354** F6
Hollis *U.S.A.* 34°41N 99°55W **356** D5
Hollister *Calif., U.S.A.* 36°51N 121°24W **350** J5
Hollister *Idaho, U.S.A.* 42°21N 114°35W **348** E6
Holly Hill *U.S.A.* 29°16N 81°3W **357** G14
Holly Springs *U.S.A.* 34°46N 89°27W **357** D10
Hollywood *U.S.A.* 26°0N 80°8W **357** J14
Holman *Canada* 70°44N 117°44W **340** B8
Hólmavík *Iceland* 65°42N 21°40W **280** D3
Holmen *U.S.A.* 43°58N 91°15W **352** D8
Holmes Reefs *Australia* 16°27S 148°0E **334** B4
Holmsund *Sweden* 63°41N 20°20E **280** E19
Holroyd → *Australia* 14°10S 141°36E **334** A3
Holstebro *Denmark* 56°22N 8°37E **281** H13
Holsworthy *U.K.* 50°48N 4°22W **285** G3
Holton *Canada* 54°31N 57°12W **345** B8
Holton *U.S.A.* 39°28N 95°44W **352** F6
Holtville *U.S.A.* 32°49N 115°23W **351** N11
Holwerd *Neths.* 53°22N 5°54E **287** A5
Holy I. *Anglesey, U.K.* 53°17N 4°37W **284** D3
Holy I. *Northumberland, U.K.* 55°40N 1°47W **284** B6
Holyhead *U.K.* 53°18N 4°38W **284** D3
Holyoke *Colo., U.S.A.* 40°35N 102°18W **348** F12
Holyoke *Mass., U.S.A.* 42°12N 72°37W **355** D12
Holyrood *Canada* 47°27N 53°8W **345** C9
Homa Bay *Kenya* 0°36S 34°30E **326** C3
Homalin *Burma* 24°55N 95°0E **313** G19
Homand *Iran* 32°28N 59°37E **317** C8
Homathko → *Canada* 51°0N 124°56W **342** C4
Hombori *Mali* 15°20N 1°38W **322** E5
Home B. *Canada* 68°40N 67°10W **341** C13
Home Hill *Australia* 19°43S 147°25E **334** B4
Home Reef *Tonga* 18°59S 174°47W **331** c
Homedale *U.S.A.* 43°37N 116°56W **348** E5
Homer *Alaska, U.S.A.* 59°39N 151°33W **346** a
Homer *La., U.S.A.* 32°48N 93°4W **356** E8
Homer City *U.S.A.* 40°32N 79°10W **354** F5
Homestead *Australia* 20°20S 145°40E **334** C4
Homestead *U.S.A.* 25°28N 80°29W **357** J14
Homestead ⌂ *U.S.A.* 40°17N 96°50W **352** E5
Homoine *Mozam.* 23°55S 35°8E **329** C6
Homs = Ḥimṣ *Syria* 34°40N 36°45E **318** A5
Homyel *Belarus* 52°28N 31°0E **289** B16
Hon Chong *Vietnam* 10°25N 104°30E **311** G5
Hon Hai *Vietnam* 10°0N 109°0E **311** G7
Hon Me *Vietnam* 19°23N 105°56E **310** C5
Honan = Henan □ *China* 34°0N 114°0E **306** H8
Honbetsu *Japan* 43°7N 143°37E **302** C11
Honcut *U.S.A.* 39°20N 121°32W **350** F5
Honda, Bahía *Cuba* 22°54N 83°10W **360** B3
Hondeklipbaai *S. Africa* 30°19S 17°17E **328** E2
Hondo *Japan* 32°27N 130°12E **303** H5
Hondo *U.S.A.* 29°21N 99°9W **356** G5
Hondo, Río → *Belize* 18°25N 88°21W **359** D7
Honduras ■ *Cent. Amer.* 14°40N 86°30W **360** D2
Honduras, G. de *Caribbean* 16°50N 87°0W **360** C2
Hønefoss *Norway* 60°10N 10°18E **281** F14
Honesdale *U.S.A.* 41°34N 75°16W **355** E9
Honey L. *U.S.A.* 40°15N 120°19W **350** E6
Honfleur *France* 49°25N 0°13E **292** B4
Hong → *Vietnam* 22°0N 104°0E **304** D5
Hong Gai *Vietnam* 20°57N 107°5E **310** B6
Hong He → *China* 32°25N 115°35E **306** H8
Hong Kong □ *China* 22°11N 114°14E **305** G11
Hong Kong I. *China* 22°16N 114°12E **305** G11
Hong Kong Int. ✕ **(HKG)** *China* 22°19N 113°57E **305** G10
Hongcheon *S. Korea* 37°44N 127°53E **307** F14
Hongjiang *China* 27°7N 109°59E **305** D5
Hongliu He → *China* 38°0N 109°50E **306** F5
Hongor *Mongolia* 45°45N 112°50E **306** B7
Hongsa *Laos* 19°43N 101°20E **310** C3
Hongseong *S. Korea* 36°37N 126°38E **307** F14
Hongshui He → *China* 23°48N 109°30E **305** D5
Hongtong *China* 36°16N 111°40E **306** F6
Honguedo, Détroit d' *Canada* 49°15N 64°0W **345** C7
Hongwon *N. Korea* 40°0N 127°56E **307** E14
Hongze Hu *China* 33°15N 118°35E **307** H10
Honiara *Solomon Is.* 9°27S 159°57E **330** B8
Honiton *U.K.* 50°47N 3°11W **285** G4
Honjō *Japan* 39°23N 140°3E **302** E10
Honningsvåg *Norway* 70°59N 25°59E **280** A21
Honolulu *U.S.A.* 21°19N 157°52W **346** b
Honshū *Japan* 36°0N 138°0E **305** C8
Hood, Mt. *U.S.A.* 45°23N 121°42W **348** D3
Hood, Pt. *Australia* 34°23S 119°34E **333** F2
Hood River *U.S.A.* 45°43N 121°31W **348** D3
Hoodsport *U.S.A.* 47°24N 123°9W **350** C3
Hoogeveen *Neths.* 52°44N 6°28E **287** B6
Hoogezand-Sappemeer *Neths.* 53°9N 6°45E **287** A6
Hooghly = Hugli → *India* 21°56N 88°4E **315** J13
Hooghly-Chinsura = Chunchura *India* 22°53N 88°27E **315** H13
Hook Hd. *Ireland* 52°7N 6°56W **282** D5
Hook I. *Australia* 20°4S 149°0E **334** J6
Hook of Holland = Hoek van Holland *Neths.* 52°0N 4°7E **287** C4
Hooker *U.S.A.* 36°52N 101°13W **356** C4
Hooker Creek = Lajamanu *Australia* 18°23S 130°38E **332** C5

Hoonah U.S.A. 58°7N 135°27W 342 B1
Hooper Bay U.S.A. 61°32N 166°6W 346 a
Hoopeston U.S.A. 40°28N 87°40W 352 E10
Hoopstad S. Africa 27°50S 25°55E 328 D4
Hoorn Neths. 52°38N 5°4E 287 B5
Hoover U.S.A. 33°24N 86°49W 357 E11
Hoover Dam U.S.A. 36°1N 114°44W 351 K12
Hooversville U.S.A. 40°9N 78°55W 354 F6
Hop Bottom U.S.A. 41°42N 75°46W 355 E9
Hope Canada 49°25N 121°25W 342 D4
Hope Ariz., U.S.A. 33°43N 113°42W 351 M13
Hope Ark., U.S.A. 33°40N 93°36W 356 E8
Hope, L. S. Austral., Australia 28°24S 139°18E 335 D2
Hope, L. W. Austral., Australia 32°35S 120°15E 333 F3
Hope, Pt. U.S.A. 68°21N 166°47W 338 C3
Hope I. Canada 44°55N 80°11W 354 B4
Hope Town Bahamas 26°35N 76°57W 360 A4
Hope Vale Australia 15°16S 145°20E 334 B4
Hopedale Canada 55°28N 60°13W 345 A7
Hopedale U.S.A. 42°8N 71°33W 355 D13
Hopefield S. Africa 33°3S 18°22E 328 E2
Hopei = Hebei □ China 39°0N 116°0E 305 E9
Hopelchén Mexico 19°46N 89°51W 359 D7
Hopetoun Vic., Australia 35°42S 142°22E 335 F3
Hopetoun W. Austral., Australia 33°57S 120°7E 333 F3
Hopetown S. Africa 29°34S 24°3E 328 D3
Hopewell U.S.A. 37°18N 77°17W 353 G15
Hopkins, L. Australia 24°15S 128°35E 332 D4
Hopkinsville U.S.A. 36°52N 87°29W 352 G10
Hopland U.S.A. 38°58N 123°7W 350 G3
Hoquiam U.S.A. 46°59N 123°53W 350 D3
Hordern Hills Australia 20°15S 130°0E 332 D5
Horinger China 40°28N 111°48E 306 D6
Horlick Mts. Antarctica 84°0S 102°0W 277 E15
Horlivka Ukraine 48°19N 38°5E 291 E6
Hormak Iran 29°58N 60°51E 317 D9
Hormoz Iran 27°35N 55°0E 317 E7
Hormoz, Jaz.-ye Iran 27°8N 56°28E 317 E8
Hormozgān □ Iran 27°30N 56°0E 317 E8
Hormuz, Kūh-e Iran 27°27N 55°10E 317 E7
Hormuz, Str. of The Gulf 26°30N 56°30E 317 E8
Horn Austria 48°39N 15°40E 288 D8
Horn → Canada 61°30N 118°1W 342 A5
Horn, Cape = Hornos, C. de Chile 55°50S 67°30W 368 H3
Horn Head Ireland 55°14N 8°0W 282 A3
Horn I. Australia 10°37S 142°17E 334 A3
Horn Plateau Canada 62°15N 119°15W 342 A5
Hornavan Sweden 66°15N 17°30E 280 C17
Hornbeck U.S.A. 31°20N 93°24W 356 F8
Hornbrook U.S.A. 41°55N 122°33W 348 F2
Horncastle U.K. 53°13N 0°7W 284 D7
Hornell U.S.A. 42°20N 77°40W 354 D7
Hornell L. Canada 62°20N 119°25W 342 A5
Hornepayne Canada 49°14N 84°48W 344 C3
Hornings Mills Canada 44°9N 80°12W 354 B4
Hornitos U.S.A. 37°30N 120°14W 350 H6
Hornos, C. de Chile 55°50S 67°30W 368 H3
Hornsea U.K. 53°55N 0°11W 284 D7
Horobetsu = Noboribetsu Japan 42°24N 141°6E 302 C10
Horodenka Ukraine 48°41N 25°29E 289 D13
Horodok Khmelnytskyy, Ukraine 49°10N 26°34E 289 D14
Horodok Lviv, Ukraine 49°46N 23°32E 289 D12
Horokhiv Ukraine 50°30N 24°45E 289 C13
Horqin Youyi Qianqi China 46°5N 122°3E 307 A12
Horqueta Paraguay 23°15S 56°55W 366 A4
Horse Cr. → U.S.A. 41°57N 103°58W 348 F12
Horse I. Canada 53°20N 99°6W 343 C9
Horse Is. Canada 50°15N 55°50W 345 B8
Horsefly L. Canada 52°25N 121°0W 342 C4
Horseheads U.S.A. 42°10N 76°49W 354 D8
Horsens Denmark 55°52N 9°51E 281 J13
Horsham Australia 36°44S 142°13E 335 F3
Horsham U.K. 51°4N 0°20W 285 F7
Horta Azores 38°32N 28°38W 322 a
Horten Norway 59°25N 10°32E 281 G14
Horton U.S.A. 39°40N 95°32W 352 F6
Horton → Canada 69°56N 126°52W 340 C7
Horwood L. Canada 48°5N 82°20W 344 C3
Hoseynābād Khuzestān, Iran 32°45N 48°20E 317 C6
Hoseynābād Kordestān, Iran 35°33N 47°8E 316 C5
Hoshangabad India 22°45N 77°45E 314 H7
Hoshiarpur India 31°30N 75°58E 314 D6
Hospet India 15°15N 76°20E 312 M10
Hoste, I. Chile 55°0S 69°0W 368 H3
Hot Thailand 18°8N 98°29E 310 C2
Hot Creek Range U.S.A. 38°40N 116°20W 348 G5
Hot Springs Ark., U.S.A. 34°31N 93°3W 356 D8
Hot Springs S. Dak., U.S.A. 43°26N 103°29W 352 D2
Hot Springs △ U.S.A. 34°31N 93°3W 356 D8
Hotagen Sweden 63°59N 14°12E 280 E16
Hotan China 37°25N 79°55E 304 C2
Hotazel S. Africa 27°17S 22°58E 328 D3
Hotchkiss U.S.A. 38°48N 107°43W 348 G10
Hotham, C. Australia 12°2S 131°18E 332 B5
Hoting Sweden 64°8N 16°15E 280 D17
Hotte, Massif de la Haiti 18°30N 73°45W 361 C5
Hottentotsbaai Namibia 26°8S 14°59E 328 D1
Hou Hai China 22°32N 113°56E 305 F10
Houei Sai Laos 20°18N 100°26E 310 B3
Houffalize Belgium 50°8N 5°48E 287 D5
Houghton Mich., U.S.A. 47°7N 88°34W 352 B9
Houghton N.Y., U.S.A. 42°25N 78°10W 354 D6
Houghton L. U.S.A. 44°21N 84°44W 353 C11
Houghton-le-Spring U.K. 54°51N 1°28W 284 C6
Houhora Heads N.Z. 34°49S 173°9E 331 A4
Houlton U.S.A. 46°8N 67°51W 353 B20
Houma U.S.A. 29°36N 90°43W 357 G9
Housatonic → U.S.A. 41°10N 73°7W 355 E11
Houston Canada 54°25N 126°39W 342 C3
Houston Mo., U.S.A. 37°22N 91°58W 352 G8
Houston Tex., U.S.A. 29°45N 95°21W 356 G7
Hout → S. Africa 23°4S 29°36E 329 C4
Houtkraal S. Africa 30°23S 24°5E 328 E3
Houtman Abrolhos Australia 28°43S 113°48E 333 E1
Hovd □ Mongolia 48°2N 91°37E 304 B4
Hove U.K. 50°50N 0°10W 285 G7
Hovenweep △ U.S.A. 37°20N 109°0W 349 H9
Hoveyzeh Iran 31°27N 48°4E 317 D6
Hövsgöl Mongolia 43°37N 109°39E 306 C5
Hövsgöl Nuur Mongolia 51°0N 100°30E 304 A5
Howar, Wadi → Sudan 17°30N 27°8E 323 E11
Howard Australia 25°16S 152°32E 335 D5
Howard Pa., U.S.A. 41°1N 77°40W 354 F7
Howard S. Dak., U.S.A. 44°1N 97°32W 352 C5
Howe U.S.A. 43°48N 113°0W 348 E7
Howe, C. Australia 37°30S 150°0E 335 F5
Howe, West Cape Australia 35°8S 117°36E 333 G2
Howe I. Canada 44°16N 76°17W 355 B8
Howell U.S.A. 42°36N 83°56W 353 D12
Howick Canada 45°11N 73°51W 355 A11
Howick S. Africa 29°28S 30°14E 329 D5
Howick Group Australia 14°20S 145°30E 334 A4
Howitt, L. Australia 27°40S 138°40E 335 D2
Howland I. Pac. Oc. 0°48N 176°38W 336 G10
Howrah = Haora India 22°34N 88°18E 315 H13
Howth Ireland 53°23N 6°6W 282 C5
Howth Hd. Ireland 53°22N 6°4W 282 C5
Höxter Germany 51°46N 9°22E 288 C5
Hoy U.K. 58°50N 3°15W 283 C5
Høyanger Norway 61°13N 6°4E 280 F12
Hoyerswerda Germany 51°26N 14°14E 288 C8
Hoylake U.K. 53°24N 3°10W 284 D4
Hpa-an = Pa-an Burma 16°51N 97°40E 313 L20
Hpunan Pass Burma 27°30N 96°55E 313 F20
Hradec Králové Czech Rep. 50°15N 15°50E 288 C8
Hrodna Belarus 53°42N 23°52E 289 B12
Hrodzyanka Belarus 53°31N 28°42E 289 B15
Hron → Slovak Rep. 47°49N 18°45E 289 E10
Hrvatska = Croatia ■ Europe 45°20N 16°0E 288 F9
Hrymayliv Ukraine 49°20N 26°5E 289 D14
Hsenwi Burma 23°22N 97°55E 313 H20
Hsiamen = Xiamen China 24°25N 118°4E 305 D6
Hsian = Xi'an China 34°15N 109°0E 306 G5
Hsinchu Taiwan 24°48N 120°58E 305 D7
Hsinhailien = Lianyungang China 34°40N 119°11E 307 G10
Hsüchou = Xuzhou China 34°18N 117°10E 307 G9
Hu Xian China 34°8N 108°42E 306 G5
Hua Hin Thailand 12°34N 99°58E 310 F2
Hua Xian Henan, China 35°30N 114°30E 306 G8
Hua Xian Shaanxi, China 34°30N 109°48E 306 G5
Huab → Namibia 20°52S 13°25E 328 B2
Huachinera Mexico 30°9N 108°55W 358 A3
Huacho Peru 11°10S 77°35W 364 F3
Huade China 41°55N 113°59E 306 D7
Huadian China 43°0N 126°40E 307 C14
Huahine, Î. French Polynesia 16°46S 150°58W 337 J12
Huai Had △ Thailand 16°52N 104°17E 310 D5
Huai He → China 33°0N 118°30E 305 C6
Huai Nam Dang △ Thailand 19°30N 98°30E 310 C2
Huai Yot Thailand 7°45N 99°37E 311 J2
Huai'an Hebei, China 40°30N 114°20E 306 D8
Huai'an Jiangsu, China 33°30N 119°10E 307 H10
Huaibei China 34°0N 116°48E 306 G9
Huaide = Gongzhuling China 43°30N 124°40E 307 C13
Huaidezhen China 43°48N 124°50E 307 C13
Huainan China 32°38N 116°58E 305 C6
Huairen China 39°48N 113°20E 306 E7
Huairou China 40°20N 116°35E 306 D9
Huaiyang China 33°40N 114°52E 306 H8
Huaiyin China 33°30N 119°2E 307 H10
Huaiyuan China 32°55N 117°10E 307 H9
Huajuapán de León Mexico 17°48N 97°46W 359 D5
Hualapai Peak U.S.A. 35°5N 113°54W 349 J7
Huallaga → Peru 5°15S 75°30W 364 E3
Huambo Angola 12°42S 15°54E 325 G3
Huan Jiang → China 34°28N 109°0E 306 G5
Huan Xian China 36°33N 107°7E 306 F4
Huancabamba Peru 5°10S 79°15W 364 E3
Huancane Peru 15°10S 69°44W 364 G5
Huancavelica Peru 12°50S 75°5W 364 F3
Huancayo Peru 12°5S 75°12W 364 F3
Huanchaca Bolivia 20°15S 66°40W 364 H5
Huang Hai = Yellow Sea China 35°0N 123°0E 307 G12
Huang He → China 37°55N 118°50E 307 F10
Huang Xian China 37°38N 120°30E 307 F11
Huangling China 35°34N 109°15E 306 G5
Huanglong China 35°30N 109°59E 306 G5
Huangshan China 29°42N 118°25E 305 D6
Huangshi China 30°10N 115°3E 305 C6
Huangsongdian China 43°45N 127°25E 307 C14
Huanren China 41°23N 125°20E 307 D13
Huantai China 36°58N 117°56E 307 F9
Huánuco Peru 9°55S 76°15W 364 E3
Huaraz Peru 9°30S 77°32W 364 E3
Huarmey Peru 10°5S 78°5W 364 F3
Huascarán, Nevado Peru 9°7S 77°37W 364 E3
Huasco Chile 28°30S 71°15W 366 B1
Huasco → Chile 28°27S 71°13W 366 B1
Huasna U.S.A. 35°6N 120°24W 351 K6
Huatabampo Mexico 26°50N 109°38W 358 B3
Huauchinango Mexico 20°12N 98°3W 359 C5
Huautla de Jiménez Mexico 18°8N 96°51W 359 D5
Huayin China 34°35N 110°5E 306 G6
Hubbard Ohio, U.S.A. 41°9N 80°34W 354 E4
Hubbard Tex., U.S.A. 31°51N 96°48W 356 F6
Hubbart Pt. Canada 59°21N 94°41W 343 B10
Hubei □ China 31°0N 112°0E 305 C6
Hubli India 15°22N 75°15E 312 M9
Huch'ang N. Korea 41°25N 127°2E 307 D14
Hucknall U.K. 53°3N 1°13W 284 D6
Huddersfield U.K. 53°39N 1°47W 284 D6
Hudiksvall Sweden 61°43N 17°10E 280 F17
Hudson Canada 50°6N 92°9W 344 B1
Hudson Mass., U.S.A. 42°23N 71°34W 355 D13
Hudson N.Y., U.S.A. 42°15N 73°46W 355 D11
Hudson Wis., U.S.A. 44°58N 92°45W 352 C7
Hudson Wyo., U.S.A. 42°54N 108°35W 348 E9
Hudson → U.S.A. 40°42N 74°2W 355 F10
Hudson, C. Antarctica 68°21S 153°45E 277 C20
Hudson Bay Nunavut, Canada 60°0N 86°0W 341 D11
Hudson Bay Sask., Canada 52°51N 102°23W 343 C8
Hudson Falls U.S.A. 43°18N 73°35W 355 C11
Hudson Mts. Antarctica 74°32S 99°20W 277 D16
Hudson Str. Canada 62°0N 70°0W 341 C13
Hudson's Hope Canada 56°0N 121°54W 342 B4
Hue Vietnam 16°30N 107°35E 310 D6
Huehuetenango Guatemala 15°20N 91°28W 360 C1
Huejúcar Mexico 22°21N 103°13W 358 C4
Huelva Spain 37°18N 6°57W 293 D2
Huentelauquén Chile 31°38S 71°33W 366 C1
Huerta, Sa. de la Argentina 31°10S 67°30W 366 C2
Huesca Spain 42°8N 0°25W 293 A5
Huetamo Mexico 18°35N 100°53W 358 D4
Hugh → Australia 25°1S 134°1E 334 D1
Hughenden Australia 20°52S 144°10E 334 C3
Hughesville U.S.A. 41°14N 76°44W 355 E8
Hugli → India 21°56N 88°4E 315 J13
Hugo Colo., U.S.A. 39°8N 103°28W 348 G12
Hugo Okla., U.S.A. 34°1N 95°31W 356 D7
Hugoton U.S.A. 37°11N 101°21W 352 G3
Hui Xian = Huixian China 35°27N 113°12E 306 G7
Hui Xian China 33°50N 106°4E 306 H4
Hui'anbu China 37°28N 106°38E 306 F4
Huichapan Mexico 20°23N 99°39W 359 C5
Huichon N. Korea 40°10N 126°16E 307 D14
Huifa He → China 43°0N 127°50E 307 C14
Huila, Nevado del Colombia 3°0N 76°0W 364 C3
Huimin China 37°27N 117°28E 307 F9
Huinan China 42°40N 126°2E 307 C14
Huinca Renancó Argentina 34°51S 64°22W 366 C3
Huining China 35°38N 105°0E 306 G3
Huinong China 39°5N 106°35E 306 E4
Huiting China 34°5N 116°5E 306 G9
Huixian China 35°27N 113°12E 306 G7
Huixtla Mexico 15°9N 92°28W 359 D6
Huize China 26°24N 103°15E 304 D5
Hukawng Valley Burma 26°30N 96°30E 313 F20
Hukuntsi Botswana 23°58S 21°45E 328 C3
Ḥulayfā' Si. Arabia 25°58N 40°45E 316 E4
Hulin He → China 45°0N 122°10E 307 B12
Hull = Kingston upon Hull U.K. 53°45N 0°21W 284 D7
Hull Canada 45°26N 75°43W 355 A9
Hull → U.K. 53°44N 0°20W 284 D7
Hulst Neths. 51°17N 4°2E 287 C4
Hulun Nur China 49°0N 117°30E 305 B6
Huma, Tanjung Malaysia 5°29N 100°16E 311 c
Humacao Puerto Rico 18°9N 65°50W 361 d
Humahuaca Argentina 23°10S 65°25W 366 A2
Humaitá Brazil 7°35S 63°1W 364 E6
Humaitá Paraguay 27°2S 58°31W 366 B4
Humansdorp S. Africa 34°2S 24°46E 328 E3
Humbe Angola 16°40S 14°55E 328 B1
Humber → U.K. 53°42N 0°27W 284 D7
Humboldt Canada 52°15N 105°9W 343 C7
Humboldt Iowa, U.S.A. 42°44N 94°13W 352 D6
Humboldt Tenn., U.S.A. 35°50N 88°55W 357 D10
Humboldt → U.S.A. 39°59N 118°36W 348 G4
Humboldt Gletscher = Sermersuaq Greenland 79°30N 62°0W 276 B4
Hume U.S.A. 36°48N 118°54W 350 J8
Hume, L. Australia 36°0S 147°5E 335 F4
Humen China 22°50N 113°40E 305 F10
Humenné Slovak Rep. 48°55N 21°50E 289 D11
Humphreys, Mt. U.S.A. 37°17N 118°40W 350 H8
Humphreys Peak U.S.A. 35°21N 111°41W 349 J8
Humptulips U.S.A. 47°14N 123°57W 350 C3
Hūn Libya 29°2N 16°0E 323 C9
Hun Jiang → China 40°50N 125°38E 307 D13
Húnaflói Iceland 65°50N 20°50W 280 D3
Hunan □ China 27°30N 112°0E 305 D6
Hunchun China 42°52N 130°28E 307 C16
Hundewali Pakistan 31°55N 72°38E 314 D5
Hundred Mile House Canada 51°38N 121°18W 342 C4
Hunedoara Romania 45°40N 22°50E 289 F12
Hung Yen Vietnam 20°39N 106°4E 310 B6
Hunga Ha'apai Tonga 20°41S 175°7W 331 c
Hungary ■ Europe 47°20N 19°20E 289 E10
Hungary, Plain of Europe 47°0N 20°0E 278 F10
Hungerford Australia 28°58S 144°24E 335 D3
Hŭngnam N. Korea 39°49N 127°45E 307 E14
Hunjiang China 41°54N 126°26E 307 D14
Hunsberge Namibia 27°45S 17°12E 328 D2
Hunsrück Germany 49°56N 7°27E 288 D4
Hunstanton U.K. 52°56N 0°29E 284 E8
Hunter U.S.A. 42°13N 74°13W 355 D10
Hunter I. Australia 40°30S 144°45E 335 G3
Hunter I. Canada 51°55N 128°0W 342 C3
Hunter Ra. Australia 32°45S 150°15E 335 E5
Hunters Road Zimbabwe 19°9S 29°49E 327 F2
Hunterville N.Z. 39°56S 175°35E 331 C5
Huntingburg U.S.A. 38°18N 86°57W 352 F10
Huntingdon Canada 45°6N 74°10W 344 C5
Huntingdon U.K. 52°20N 0°11W 285 E7
Huntingdon U.S.A. 40°30N 78°1W 354 F6
Huntington Ind., U.S.A. 40°53N 85°30W 353 E11
Huntington N.Y., U.S.A. 40°52N 73°26W 355 F11
Huntington Oreg., U.S.A. 44°21N 117°16W 348 D5
Huntington Utah, U.S.A. 39°20N 110°58W 348 G8
Huntington W. Va., U.S.A. 38°25N 82°27W 353 F12
Huntington Beach U.S.A. 33°40N 118°5W 351 M9
Huntly N.Z. 37°34S 175°11E 331 B5
Huntly U.K. 57°27N 2°47W 283 D6
Huntsville Canada 45°20N 79°14W 354 A5
Huntsville Ala., U.S.A. 34°44N 86°35W 357 D11
Huntsville Tex., U.S.A. 30°43N 95°33W 356 F7
Hunyani → Zimbabwe 15°57S 30°39E 327 F3
Hunyuan China 39°42N 113°42E 306 E7
Hunza → India 35°54N 74°20E 315 B6
Huo Xian = Huozhou China 36°36N 111°42E 306 F6
Huong Khe Vietnam 18°13N 105°41E 310 C5
Huonville Australia 43°0S 147°5E 335 G4
Huozhou China 36°36N 111°42E 306 F6
Hupeh = Hubei □ China 31°0N 112°0E 305 C6
Ḩūr Iran 30°50N 57°7E 317 D8
Ḩuraymīla Si. Arabia 25°8N 46°8E 316 E5
Hurd, C. Canada 45°13N 81°44W 354 A3
Hure Qi China 42°45N 121°45E 307 C11
Hurghada Egypt 27°15N 33°50E 323 C12
Hurley N. Mex., U.S.A. 32°42N 108°8W 349 K9
Hurley Wis., U.S.A. 46°27N 90°11W 352 B8
Huron Calif., U.S.A. 36°12N 120°6W 350 J6
Huron Ohio, U.S.A. 41°24N 82°33W 354 E2
Huron S. Dak., U.S.A. 44°22N 98°13W 352 C4
Huron, L. U.S.A. 44°30N 82°40W 354 B2
Huron East Canada 43°37N 81°18W 354 C3
Hurricane U.S.A. 37°11N 113°17W 349 H7
Hurungwe △ Zimbabwe 16°7S 29°5E 327 F2
Hurunui → N.Z. 42°54S 173°18E 331 E4
Húsavík Iceland 66°3N 17°21W 280 C5
Huşi Romania 46°41N 28°7E 289 E15
Hustadvika Norway 63°0N 7°0E 280 E12
Hustontown U.S.A. 40°3N 78°2W 354 F6
Hutchinson Kans., U.S.A. 38°5N 97°56W 352 F5
Hutchinson Minn., U.S.A. 44°54N 94°22W 352 C6
Hutte Sauvage, L. de la Canada 56°15N 64°45W 345 A7
Hutton, Mt. Australia 25°51S 148°20E 335 D4
Huy Belgium 50°31N 5°15E 287 D5
Huzhou China 30°51N 120°8E 305 C7
Hvammstangi Iceland 65°24N 20°57W 280 D3
Hvar Croatia 43°11N 16°28E 294 C7
Hvítá → Iceland 64°30N 21°58W 280 D3
Hwacheon-Cheosuji S. Korea 38°5N 127°50E 307 E14
Hwang Ho = Huang He → China 37°55N 118°50E 307 F10
Hwange Zimbabwe 18°18S 26°30E 327 F2
Hwange △ Zimbabwe 19°0S 26°30E 328 B4
Hyannis Mass., U.S.A. 41°39N 70°17W 353 E18
Hyannis Nebr., U.S.A. 42°0N 101°46W 352 E3
Hyargas Nuur Mongolia 49°0N 93°0E 304 B4
Hydaburg U.S.A. 55°15N 132°50W 342 B2
Hyde Park U.S.A. 41°47N 73°56W 355 E11
Hyden Australia 32°24S 118°53E 333 F2
Hyder U.S.A. 55°55N 130°5W 342 B2
Hyderabad India 17°22N 78°29E 312 L11
Hyderabad Pakistan 25°23N 68°24E 314 G3
Hydra Greece 37°20N 23°28E 295 F10
Hyères France 43°8N 6°9E 292 E7
Hyères, Îs. d' France 43°0N 6°20E 292 E7
Hyesan N. Korea 41°20N 128°10E 307 D15
Hyland → Canada 59°52N 128°12W 342 B3
Hymia India 33°40N 78°2E 315 C8
Hyndman Peak U.S.A. 43°45N 114°8W 348 E6
Hyōgo □ Japan 35°15N 134°50E 303 G7
Hyrum U.S.A. 41°38N 111°51W 348 F8
Hysham U.S.A. 46°18N 107°14W 348 C10
Hythe U.K. 51°4N 1°5E 285 F9
Hyūga Japan 32°25N 131°35E 303 H5
Hyvinge = Hyvinkää Finland 60°38N 24°50E 280 F21
Hyvinkää Finland 60°38N 24°50E 280 F21

I

I-n-Gall Niger 16°51N 7°1E 322 E7
Iaco → Brazil 9°3S 68°34W 364 E5
Iakora Madag. 23°6S 46°40E 329 C8
Ialomiţa → Romania 44°42N 27°51E 289 F14
Iaşi Romania 47°10N 27°40E 289 E14
Ib → India 21°34N 83°48E 315 J10
Iba Phil. 15°22N 120°0E 309 A6
Ibadan Nigeria 7°22N 3°58E 322 G6
Ibagué Colombia 4°20N 75°20W 364 C3
Ibar → Serbia 43°43N 20°45E 295 C9
Ibaraki □ Japan 36°10N 140°10E 303 F10
Ibarra Ecuador 0°21N 78°7W 364 C3
Ibb Yemen 14°2N 44°10E 319 E3
Ibembo Dem. Rep. of the Congo 2°35N 23°35E 326 B1
Ibenga → Congo 2°19N 18°9E 324 D3
Ibera, L. Argentina 28°30S 57°9W 366 B4
Iberian Peninsula Europe 40°0N 5°0W 278 H5
Iberville Canada 45°19N 73°17W 355 A11
Iberville, Lac d' Canada 55°55N 73°15W 344 A5
Ibiá Brazil 19°30S 46°30W 365 G9
Ibiapaba, Sa. da Brazil 4°0S 41°30W 365 D10
Ibicui → Brazil 29°25S 56°47W 367 B4
Ibicuy Argentina 33°55S 59°10W 366 C4
Ibiza = Eivissa Spain 38°54N 1°26E 296 C7
Ibo Mozam. 12°22S 40°40E 327 E5
Ibonma Indonesia 3°29S 133°31E 309 E8
Ibotirama Brazil 12°13S 43°12W 365 F10
Ibrāhīm → Lebanon 34°4N 35°38E 318 A4
'Ibrī Oman 23°14N 56°30E 317 F8
Ibu Indonesia 1°35N 127°33E 309 D7
Ibusuki Japan 31°12N 130°40E 303 J5
Ica Peru 14°0S 75°48W 364 F3
Iça → Brazil 2°55S 67°58W 364 D5
Icacos Pt. Trin. & Tob. 10°3N 61°57W 365 K15
Içana Brazil 0°21N 67°19W 364 C5
Içana → Brazil 0°26N 67°19W 364 C5
İçel Turkey 36°51N 34°36E 316 B2
Iceland ■ Europe 64°45N 19°0W 280 D4
Iceland Basin Atl. Oc. 61°0N 19°0W 276 C7
Icelandic Plateau Arctic 64°0N 10°0W 276 C7
Ich'ang = Yichang China 30°40N 111°20E 305 C6
Ichchapuram India 19°10N 84°40E 313 K14
Icheon S. Korea 37°17N 127°27E 307 F14
Ichhawar India 23°1N 77°1E 314 H7
Ichihara Japan 35°28N 140°5E 303 G10
Ichikawa Japan 35°43N 139°54E 303 G9
Ichilo → Bolivia 15°57S 64°50W 364 G6
Ichinohe Japan 40°13N 141°17E 302 D10
Ichinomiya Japan 35°18N 136°48E 303 G8
Ichinoseki Japan 38°55N 141°8E 302 E10
Icod Canary Is. 28°22N 16°43W 296 F3
Icy C. U.S.A. 70°20N 161°52W 338 B3
Ida Grove U.S.A. 42°21N 95°28W 352 D6
Idabel U.S.A. 33°54N 94°50W 356 E7
Idaho □ U.S.A. 45°0N 115°0W 348 D6
Idaho City U.S.A. 43°50N 115°50W 348 E6
Idaho Falls U.S.A. 43°30N 112°2W 348 E7
Idalia △ Australia 24°49S 144°36E 334 C3
Idar-Oberstein Germany 49°43N 7°16E 288 D4
Idensalmi = Iisalmi Finland 63°32N 27°10E 280 E22
Idfû Egypt 24°55N 32°49E 323 D12
Ídhra = Hydra Greece 37°20N 23°28E 295 F10
Idi Indonesia 5°2N 97°37E 308 C1
Idi, Oros = Psiloritis, Oros Greece 35°15N 24°45E 297 D6
Idiofa Dem. Rep. of the Congo 4°55S 19°42E 324 E3
Idlib Syria 35°55N 36°36E 316 C3
Idria U.S.A. 36°25N 120°41W 350 J6
Idutywa = Dutywa S. Africa 32°8S 28°18E 329 E4
Ieper Belgium 50°51N 2°53E 287 D2
Ierapetra Greece 35°1N 25°44E 297 E7
Iesi Italy 43°31N 13°14E 294 C5
Ifakara Tanzania 8°8S 36°41E 324 F7
'Ifāl, W. al → Si. Arabia 28°7N 35°3E 316 D2
Ifanadiana Madag. 21°19S 47°39E 329 C8
Ife Nigeria 7°30N 4°31E 322 G6
Iffley Australia 18°53S 141°12E 334 B3
Iforas, Adrar des Africa 19°40N 1°40E 322 E6
Ifould, L. Australia 30°52S 132°6E 333 F5
Iganga Uganda 0°37N 33°28E 326 B3
Igarapava Brazil 20°3S 47°47W 365 H9
Igarka Russia 67°30N 86°33E 300 C9
Igatimi Paraguay 24°5S 55°40W 367 A4
Iggesund Sweden 61°39N 17°10E 280 F17
Iglésias Italy 39°19N 8°32E 294 E3
Igloolik Canada 69°20N 81°49W 341 C11
Igluligaarjuk = Chesterfield Inlet Canada 63°30N 90°45W 340 C10
Iglulik = Igloolik Canada 69°20N 81°49W 341 C11
Ignace Canada 49°30N 91°40W 344 C1
İğneada Burnu Turkey 41°53N 28°2E 295 D13
Igoumenitsa Greece 39°32N 20°18E 295 E9
Iguaçu → Brazil 25°36S 54°36W 367 B5
Iguaçu, Cat. del Brazil 25°41S 54°26W 367 B5
Iguaçu △ Brazil 25°30S 54°0W 367 B5
Iguaçu Falls = Iguaçu, Cat. del Brazil 25°41S 54°26W 367 B5
Iguala Mexico 18°21N 99°32W 359 D5
Igualada Spain 41°37N 1°37E 293 B6
Iguassu = Iguaçu → Brazil 25°36S 54°36W 367 B5
Iguatu Brazil 6°20S 39°18W 365 E11
Iguazú △ Argentina 25°42S 54°22W 367 B5
Iguidi, Erg Africa 27°0N 7°0W 322 C4
Iharana Madag. 13°25S 50°0E 329 A9
Ihbulag Mongolia 43°11N 107°10E 306 C4
Iheya-Shima Japan 27°4N 127°58E 303 L3
Ihosy Madag. 22°24S 46°8E 329 C8
Ihotry, Farihy Madag. 21°56S 43°41E 329 C7
Ii Finland 65°19N 25°22E 280 D21
Ii-Shima Japan 26°43N 127°47E 303 L3
Iida Japan 35°35N 137°50E 303 G8
Iijoki → Finland 65°20N 25°20E 280 D21
Iisalmi Finland 63°32N 27°10E 280 E22
Iiyama Japan 36°51N 138°22E 303 F9
Iizuka Japan 33°38N 130°42E 303 H5
Ijâfene Mauritania 20°40N 8°0W 322 D4
Ijebu-Ode Nigeria 6°47N 3°58E 322 G6
IJmuiden Neths. 52°28N 4°35E 287 B4
Ijo älv = Iijoki → Finland 65°20N 25°20E 280 D21
IJssel → Neths. 52°35N 5°50E 287 B5
IJsselmeer Neths. 52°45N 5°20E 287 B5

Ijuí Brazil 28°23S 53°55W 367 B5
Ijuí → Brazil 27°58S 55°20W 367 B4
Ikalamavony Madag. 21°9S 46°35E 329 C8
Ikaluktutiak Canada 69°10N 105°0W 340 C9
Ikanga Kenya 1°42S 38°4E 326 C4
Ikare Nigeria 7°32N 5°40E 322 G7
Ikaria Greece 37°35N 26°10E 295 F12
Ikeda Japan 34°1N 133°48E 303 G6
Ikela Dem. Rep. of the Congo 1°6S 23°6E 324 E4
Iki Japan 33°45N 129°42E 303 H4
Ikimba L. Tanzania 1°30S 31°20E 326 C3
Ikongo Madag. 21°52S 47°27E 329 C8
Ikopa → Madag. 16°45S 46°40E 329 B8
Ikorongo ⌂ Tanzania 1°50S 34°53E 326 C3
Ikparjuk = Arctic Bay Canada 73°1N 85°7W 341 B11
Iksan S. Korea 35°59N 127°0E 307 G14
Ikungu Tanzania 1°33S 33°42E 326 C3
Ikuntji = Haast Bluff Australia 23°22S 132°0E 332 D5
Ilagan Phil. 17°7N 121°53E 309 A6
Ilaka Madag. 19°33S 48°52E 329 B8
Īlām Iran 33°36N 46°36E 316 C5
Ilam Nepal 26°58N 87°58E 315 F12
Īlām □ Iran 33°0N 47°0E 316 C5
Ilanskiy Russia 56°14N 96°3E 301 D10
Iława Poland 53°36N 19°34E 289 B10
Ile → Kazakhstan 45°53N 77°10E 300 E8
Île-à-la-Crosse Canada 55°27N 107°53W 343 B7
Île-à-la-Crosse, Lac Canada 55°40N 107°45W 343 B7
Île-de-France □ France 49°0N 2°20E 292 B5
Ilebo Dem. Rep. of the Congo 4°17S 20°55E 324 E4
Ilek Russia 51°32N 53°21E 300 D6
Ilek → Russia 51°30N 53°22E 290 D9
Ilesha Nigeria 7°37N 4°40E 322 G6
Ilford Canada 56°4N 95°35W 343 B9
Ilfracombe Australia 23°30S 144°30E 334 C3
Ilfracombe U.K. 51°12N 4°8W 285 F3
Ilha de Moçambique Mozam. 15°4S 40°52E 327 F5
Ilhéus Brazil 14°49S 39°2W 365 F11
Ili = Ile → Kazakhstan 45°53N 77°10E 300 E8
Iliamna L. U.S.A. 59°30N 155°0W 346 a
Ilias, Profitis Greece 36°17N 27°56E 297 C9
Iligan Phil. 8°12N 124°13E 309 C6
Ilion U.S.A. 43°1N 75°2W 355 D9
Ilkeston U.K. 52°58N 1°19W 284 E6
Ilkley U.K. 53°56N 1°48W 284 D6
Illampu = Ancohuma, Nevado Bolivia 16°0S 68°50W 364 G5
Illana B. Phil. 7°35N 123°45E 309 C6
Illapel Chile 32°0S 71°10W 366 C1
Iller → Germany 48°23N 9°58E 288 D6
Illetas Spain 39°32N 2°35E 296 B9
Illimani, Nevado Bolivia 16°30S 67°50W 364 G5
Illinois □ U.S.A. 40°15N 89°30W 352 E9
Illinois → U.S.A. 38°58N 90°28W 352 F8
Illizi Algeria 26°31N 8°32E 322 C7
Ilma, L. Australia 29°13S 127°46E 333 E4
Ilmajoki Finland 62°44N 22°34E 280 E20
Ilmen, Ozero Russia 58°15N 31°10E 290 C5
Ilo Peru 17°40S 71°20W 364 G4
Iloilo Phil. 10°45N 122°33E 309 B6
Ilomantsi Finland 62°38N 30°57E 280 E24
Ilorin Nigeria 8°30N 4°35E 322 G6
Ilwaco U.S.A. 46°19N 124°3W 350 D2
Ilwaki Indonesia 7°55S 126°30E 309 F7
Imabari Japan 34°4N 133°0E 303 G6
Imaloto → Madag. 23°27S 45°13E 329 C8
Imandra, Ozero Russia 67°30N 33°0E 280 C25
Imanombo Madag. 24°26S 45°49E 329 C8
Imari Japan 33°15N 129°52E 303 H4
Imatra Finland 61°12N 28°48E 280 F23
imeni 26 Bakinskikh Komissarov = Neftçala Azerbaijan 39°19N 49°12E 317 B6
imeni 26 Bakinskikh Komissarov Turkmenistan 39°22N 54°10E 317 B7
imeni Ismail Samani, Pik Tajikistan 39°0N 72°2E 300 F8
Imeri, Serra Brazil 0°50N 65°25W 364 C5
Imerimandroso Madag. 17°26S 48°35E 329 B8
Imfolozi ⌂ S. Africa 28°18S 31°50E 329 D5
Imi Ethiopia 6°28N 42°10E 319 F3
Imlay U.S.A. 40°40N 118°9W 348 F4
Imlay City U.S.A. 43°2N 83°5W 354 D1
Immingham U.K. 53°37N 0°13W 284 D7
Immokalee U.S.A. 26°25N 81°25W 357 H14
Ímola Italy 44°20N 11°42E 294 B4
Imperatriz Brazil 5°30S 47°29W 365 E9
Impéria Italy 43°53N 8°3E 292 E8
Imperial Canada 51°21N 105°28W 343 C7
Imperial Calif., U.S.A. 32°51N 115°34W 351 N11
Imperial Nebr., U.S.A. 40°31N 101°39W 352 E3
Imperial Beach U.S.A. 32°35N 117°6W 351 N9
Imperial Dam U.S.A. 32°55N 114°25W 351 N12
Imperial Res. U.S.A. 32°53N 114°28W 351 N12
Imperial Valley U.S.A. 33°0N 115°30W 351 N11
Imperieuse Reef Australia 17°36S 118°50E 332 C2
Impfondo Congo 1°40N 18°0E 324 D3
Imphal India 24°48N 93°56E 313 G18
İmroz = Gökçeada Turkey 40°10N 25°50E 295 D11
Imuris Mexico 30°47N 110°52W 358 A2
Imuruan B. Phil. 10°40N 119°10E 309 B5
In Salah Algeria 27°10N 2°32E 322 C6
Ina Japan 35°50N 137°55E 303 G8
Inagua △ Bahamas 21°5N 73°24W 361 B5
Inangahua N.Z. 41°52S 171°59E 331 D3
Inanwatan Indonesia 2°8S 132°10E 309 E8
Iñapari Peru 11°0S 69°40W 364 F5
Inari Finland 68°54N 27°1E 280 B22
Inarijärvi Finland 69°0N 28°0E 280 B23
Inawashiro-Ko Japan 37°29N 140°6E 302 F10
Inca Spain 39°43N 2°54E 296 B9
Inca de Oro Chile 26°45S 69°54W 366 B2
Incaguasi Chile 29°12S 71°5W 366 B1
Incahuasi Argentina 27°2S 68°18W 366 B2
İnce Burun Turkey 42°7N 34°56E 291 F5
İncesu Turkey 38°38N 35°11E 316 B2
Incheon S. Korea 37°27N 126°40E 307 F14
İncirliova Turkey 37°50N 27°41E 295 F12
Incline Village U.S.A. 39°10N 119°58W 348 G4
Incomáti → Mozam. 25°46S 32°43E 329 D5
Indalsälven → Sweden 62°36N 17°30E 280 E17
Indaw Burma 24°15N 96°5E 313 G20
Independence Calif., U.S.A. 36°48N 118°12W 350 J8
Independence Iowa, U.S.A. 42°28N 91°54W 352 D8
Independence Kans., U.S.A. 37°14N 95°42W 352 G6
Independence Ky., U.S.A. 38°57N 84°33W 353 F11
Independence Mo., U.S.A. 39°6N 94°25W 352 F6
Independence Fjord Greenland 82°10N 29°0W 276 A6
Independence Mts. U.S.A. 41°20N 116°0W 348 F5
Index U.S.A. 47°50N 121°33W 350 C5
India ■ Asia 20°0N 78°0E 312 K11
Indian → U.S.A. 27°59N 80°34W 357 H14
Indian Cabins Canada 59°52N 117°40W 342 B5
Indian Harbour Canada 54°27N 57°13W 345 B8
Indian Head Canada 50°30N 103°41W 343 C8
Indian Lake U.S.A. 43°47N 74°16W 355 C10
Indian Springs U.S.A. 36°35N 115°40W 351 J11
Indiana U.S.A. 40°37N 79°9W 354 F5
Indiana □ U.S.A. 40°0N 86°0W 353 F11
Indianapolis U.S.A. 39°46N 86°9W 352 F10
Indianola Iowa, U.S.A. 41°22N 93°34W 352 E7
Indianola Miss., U.S.A. 33°27N 90°39W 357 E9
Indiga Russia 67°38N 49°9E 290 A8
Indigirka → Russia 70°48N 148°54E 301 B15
Indio U.S.A. 33°43N 116°13W 351 M10
Indira Gandhi Canal India 28°0N 72°0E 314 F5
Indira Sagar India 22°15N 76°40E 314 H7
Indo-China Asia 15°0N 102°0E 298 G12
Indonesia ■ Asia 5°0S 115°0E 308 F5
Indore India 22°42N 75°53E 314 H6
Indramayu Indonesia 6°20S 108°19E 309 G13
Indravati → India 19°20N 80°20E 313 K12
Indre → France 47°16N 0°11E 292 C4
Indulkana Australia 26°58S 133°5E 335 D1
Indus → Pakistan 24°20N 67°47E 314 G2
Indus, Mouths of the Pakistan 24°0N 68°0E 314 H3
İnebolu Turkey 41°55N 33°40E 291 F5
Infiernillo, Presa del Mexico 18°35N 101°50W 358 D4
Ingenio Canary Is. 27°55N 15°26W 296 G4
Ingenio Santa Ana Argentina 27°25S 65°40W 366 B2
Ingersoll Canada 43°4N 80°55W 354 C4
Ingham Australia 18°43S 146°10E 334 B4
Ingleborough U.K. 54°10N 2°22W 284 C5
Inglewood Queens., Australia 28°25S 151°2E 335 D5
Inglewood Vic., Australia 36°29S 143°53E 335 F3
Inglewood N.Z. 39°9S 174°14E 331 C5
Inglewood U.S.A. 33°58N 118°21W 351 M8
Ingólfshöfði Iceland 63°48N 16°39W 280 E5
Ingolstadt Germany 48°46N 11°26E 288 D6
Ingomar U.S.A. 46°35N 107°23W 348 C10
Ingonish Canada 46°42N 60°18W 345 C7
Ingraj Bazar India 24°58N 88°10E 315 G13
Ingrid Christensen Coast Antarctica 69°30S 76°0E 277 C6
Ingulec = Inhulec Ukraine 47°42N 33°14E 291 E5
Ingushetia □ Russia 43°20N 44°50E 291 F8
Ingwavuma S. Africa 27°9S 31°59E 329 D5
Inhaca Mozam. 26°1S 32°57E 329 D5
Inhafenga Mozam. 20°36S 33°53E 329 C5
Inhambane Mozam. 23°54S 35°30E 329 C6
Inhambane □ Mozam. 22°30S 34°20E 329 C5
Inhaminga Mozam. 18°26S 35°0E 327 F4
Inharrime Mozam. 24°30S 35°0E 329 C6
Inharrime → Mozam. 24°30S 35°0E 329 C6
Inhulec Ukraine 47°42N 33°14E 291 E5
Ining = Yining China 43°58N 81°10E 304 B3
Inírida → Colombia 3°55N 67°52W 364 C5
Inishbofin Ireland 53°37N 10°13W 282 C1
Inisheer Ireland 53°3N 9°32W 282 C2
Inishfree B. Ireland 55°4N 8°23W 282 A3
Inishkea North Ireland 54°9N 10°11W 282 B1
Inishkea South Ireland 54°7N 10°12W 282 B1
Inishmaan Ireland 53°5N 9°35W 282 C2
Inishmore Ireland 53°8N 9°45W 282 C2
Inishmurray I. Ireland 54°26N 8°39W 282 B3
Inishowen Pen. Ireland 55°14N 7°15W 282 A4
Inishshark Ireland 53°37N 10°16W 282 C1
Inishturk Ireland 53°42N 10°7W 282 C1
Inishvickillane Ireland 52°3N 10°37W 282 D1
Injune Australia 25°53S 148°32E 335 D4
Inklin → N. Amer. 58°50N 133°10W 342 B2
Inland Kaikoura Ra. N.Z. 41°59S 173°41E 331 D4
Inland Sea = Setonaikai Japan 34°20N 133°30E 303 G6
Inle L. Burma 20°30N 96°58E 313 J20
Inlet U.S.A. 43°45N 74°48W 355 C10
Inn → Austria 48°35N 13°28E 288 D7
Innamincka Australia 27°44S 140°46E 335 D3
Inner Hebrides U.K. 57°0N 6°30W 283 E2
Inner Mongolia = Nei Monggol Zizhiqu □ China 42°0N 112°0E 306 D7
Inner Sound U.K. 57°30N 5°55W 283 D3
Innerkip Canada 43°13N 80°42W 354 C4
Innetalling I. Canada 56°0N 79°0W 344 A4
Innisfail Australia 17°33S 146°5E 334 B4
Innisfail Canada 52°2N 113°57W 342 C6
In'noshima Japan 34°19N 133°10E 303 G6
Innsbruck Austria 47°16N 11°23E 288 E6
Inny → Ireland 53°30N 7°50W 282 C4
Inongo Dem. Rep. of the Congo 1°55S 18°30E 324 E3
Inoucdjouac = Inukjuak Canada 58°25N 78°15W 341 D12
Inowrocław Poland 52°50N 18°12E 289 B10
Inscription, C. Australia 25°29S 112°59E 333 E1
Insein Burma 16°50N 96°5E 313 L20
Inta Russia 66°5N 60°8E 290 A11
Intendente Alvear Argentina 35°12S 63°32W 366 D3
Interlaken Switz. 46°41N 7°50E 292 C7
Interlaken U.S.A. 42°37N 76°44W 355 D8
International Falls U.S.A. 48°36N 93°25W 352 A7
Intiyaco Argentina 28°43S 60°5W 366 B3
Inukjuak Canada 58°25N 78°15W 341 D12
Inútil, B. Chile 53°30S 70°15W 368 G2
Inuvik Canada 68°16N 133°40W 340 C6
Inveraray U.K. 56°14N 5°5W 283 E3
Inverbervie U.K. 56°51N 2°17W 283 E6
Invercargill N.Z. 46°24S 168°24E 331 G2
Inverclyde □ U.K. 55°55N 4°49W 283 F4
Inverell Australia 29°45S 151°8E 335 D5
Invergordon U.K. 57°41N 4°10W 283 D4
Inverloch Australia 38°38S 145°45E 335 F4
Invermere Canada 50°30N 116°2W 342 C5
Inverness Canada 46°15N 61°19W 345 C7
Inverness U.K. 57°29N 4°13W 283 D4
Inverness U.S.A. 28°50N 82°20W 357 G13
Inverurie U.K. 57°17N 2°23W 283 D6
Investigator Group Australia 34°45S 134°20E 335 E1
Investigator Str. Australia 35°30S 137°0E 335 F2
Inya Russia 50°28N 86°37E 300 D9
Inyanga Zimbabwe 18°12S 32°40E 327 F3
Inyangani Zimbabwe 18°5S 32°50E 327 F3
Inyantue Zimbabwe 18°33S 26°39E 328 B4
Inyo Mts. U.S.A. 36°40N 118°0W 350 J9
Inyokern U.S.A. 35°39N 117°49W 351 K9
Inza Russia 53°55N 46°25E 290 D8
Iō-Jima Japan 30°48N 130°18E 303 J5
Ioannina Greece 39°42N 20°47E 295 E9
Iola U.S.A. 37°55N 95°24W 352 G6
Iona U.K. 56°20N 6°25W 283 E2
Ione U.S.A. 38°21N 120°56W 350 G6
Ionia U.S.A. 42°59N 85°4W 353 D11
Ionian Is. = Ionioi Nisoi Greece 38°40N 20°0E 295 E9
Ionian Sea Medit. S. 37°30N 17°30E 295 E7
Ionioi Nisoi Greece 38°40N 20°0E 295 E9
Ios Greece 36°41N 25°20E 295 F11
Iowa □ U.S.A. 42°18N 93°30W 352 D7
Iowa → U.S.A. 41°10N 91°1W 352 E8
Iowa City U.S.A. 41°40N 91°32W 352 E8
Iowa Falls U.S.A. 42°31N 93°16W 352 D7
Iowa Park U.S.A. 33°57N 98°40W 356 E5
Ipala Tanzania 4°30S 32°52E 326 C3
Ipameri Brazil 17°44S 48°9W 365 G9
Ipatinga Brazil 19°32S 42°30W 365 G10
Ipiales Colombia 0°50N 77°37W 364 C3
Ipin = Yibin China 28°45N 104°32E 304 D5
Ipixuna Brazil 7°0S 71°40W 364 E4
Ipoh Malaysia 4°35N 101°5E 311 K3
Ippy C.A.R. 6°5N 21°7E 324 C4
İpsala Turkey 40°55N 26°23E 295 D12
Ipswich Australia 27°35S 152°40E 335 D5
Ipswich U.K. 52°4N 1°10E 285 E9
Ipswich Mass., U.S.A. 42°41N 70°50W 355 D14
Ipswich S. Dak., U.S.A. 45°27N 99°2W 352 C4
Ipu Brazil 4°23S 40°44W 365 D10
Iqaluit Canada 63°44N 68°31W 341 C13
Iquique Chile 20°19S 70°5W 364 H4
Iquitos Peru 3°45S 73°10W 364 D4
Irabu-Jima Japan 24°50N 125°10E 303 M2
Iracoubo Fr. Guiana 5°30N 53°10W 365 B8
Īrafshān Iran 26°42N 61°56E 317 E9
Iraklio Greece 35°20N 25°12E 297 D7
Iraklio □ Greece 35°10N 25°10E 297 D7
Iráklion = Iraklio Greece 35°20N 25°12E 297 D7
Irala Paraguay 25°55S 54°35W 367 B5
Iran ■ Asia 33°0N 53°0E 317 C7
Iran, Pegunungan Malaysia 2°20N 114°50E 308 D4
Iran Ra. = Iran, Pegunungan Malaysia 2°20N 114°50E 308 D4
Īrānshahr Iran 27°15N 60°40E 317 E9
Irapuato Mexico 20°41N 101°28W 358 C4
Iraq ■ Asia 33°0N 44°0E 316 C5
Irati Brazil 25°25S 50°38W 367 B5
Irbid Jordan 32°35N 35°48E 318 C4
Irbid □ Jordan 32°30N 35°50E 318 C5
Irebu Dem. Rep. of the Congo 0°40S 17°46E 324 E3
Ireland ■ Europe 53°50N 7°52W 282 C4
Iri = Iksan S. Korea 35°59N 127°0E 307 G14
Irian Jaya = Papua □ Indonesia 4°0S 137°0E 309 E9
Irian Jaya Barat □ Indonesia 2°5S 132°50E 309 E8
Iringa Tanzania 7°48S 35°43E 326 D4
Iringa □ Tanzania 7°48S 35°43E 326 D4
Iriomote △ Japan 24°29N 123°53E 303 M1
Iriomote-Jima Japan 24°19N 123°48E 303 M1
Iriona Honduras 15°57N 85°11W 360 C2
Iriri → Brazil 3°52S 52°37W 365 D8
Irish Republic ■ Europe 53°50N 7°52W 282 C4
Irish Sea Europe 53°38N 4°48W 284 D3
Irkutsk Russia 52°18N 104°20E 301 D11
Irma Canada 52°55N 111°14W 343 C6
Irō-Zaki Japan 34°36N 138°51E 303 G9
Iron Baron Australia 32°58S 137°11E 335 E2
Iron Gate = Portile de Fier Europe 44°44N 22°30E 289 F12
Iron Knob Australia 32°46S 137°8E 335 E2
Iron Mountain U.S.A. 45°49N 88°4W 352 C9
Iron Range △ Australia 12°34S 143°18E 334 A3
Iron River U.S.A. 46°6N 88°39W 352 B9
Irondequoit U.S.A. 43°13N 77°35W 354 C7
Ironton Mo., U.S.A. 37°36N 90°38W 352 G8
Ironton Ohio, U.S.A. 38°32N 82°41W 353 F12
Ironwood U.S.A. 46°27N 90°9W 352 B8
Ironwood Forest ⌂ U.S.A. 32°32N 111°28W 349 K8
Iroquois Canada 44°51N 75°19W 355 B9
Iroquois Falls Canada 48°46N 80°41W 344 C3
Irpin Ukraine 50°30N 30°15E 289 C16
Irrara Cr. → Australia 29°35S 145°31E 335 D4
Irrawaddy □ Burma 17°0N 95°0E 313 L19
Irrawaddy → Burma 15°50N 95°6E 313 M19
Irrawaddy, Mouths of the Burma 15°30N 95°0E 313 M19
Irricana Canada 51°19N 113°37W 342 C6
Irtysh → Russia 61°4N 68°52E 300 C7
Irumu Dem. Rep. of the Congo 1°32N 29°53E 326 B2
Irún Spain 43°20N 1°52W 293 A5
Iruñea = Pamplona Spain 42°48N 1°38W 293 A5
Irvine Canada 49°57N 110°16W 343 D6
Irvine U.K. 55°37N 4°41W 283 F4
Irvine Calif., U.S.A. 33°41N 117°46W 351 M9
Irvine Ky., U.S.A. 37°42N 83°58W 353 G12
Irvinestown U.K. 54°28N 7°39W 282 B4
Irving U.S.A. 32°48N 96°56W 356 E6
Irvona U.S.A. 40°46N 78°33W 354 F6
Irwin → Australia 29°15S 114°54E 333 E1
Irymple Australia 34°14S 142°8E 335 E3
Isa Khel Pakistan 32°41N 71°17E 314 C4
Isaac → Australia 22°55S 149°20E 334 C4
Isabel U.S.A. 45°24N 101°26W 352 C3
Isabel, I. Mexico 21°51N 105°55W 358 C3
Isabela Phil. 6°40N 121°59E 309 C6
Isabela Puerto Rico 18°30N 67°2W 361 d
Isabella, Cord. Nic. 13°30N 85°25W 360 D2
Isabella Ra. Australia 21°0S 121°4E 332 D3
Ísafjarðardjúp Iceland 66°10N 23°0W 280 C2
Ísafjörður Iceland 66°5N 23°9W 280 C2
Isagarh India 24°48N 77°51E 314 G7
Isahaya Japan 32°52N 130°2E 303 H5
Isaka Tanzania 3°56S 32°59E 326 C3
Isalo △ Madag. 22°23S 45°16E 329 C8
Isan → India 26°51N 80°7E 315 F9
Isana = Içana → Brazil 0°26N 67°19W 364 C5
Isangano △ Zambia 11°8S 30°35E 327 E3
Isar → Germany 48°48N 12°57E 288 D7
Íschia Italy 40°44N 13°57E 294 D5
Isdell → Australia 16°27S 124°51E 332 C3
Ise Japan 34°25N 136°45E 303 G8
Ise-Shima △ Japan 34°25N 136°48E 303 G8
Ise-Wan Japan 34°43N 136°43E 303 G8
Iseramagazi Tanzania 4°37S 32°10E 326 C3
Isère → France 44°59N 4°51E 292 D6
Isérnia Italy 41°36N 14°14E 294 D6
Isfahan = Eşfahān Iran 32°39N 51°43E 317 C6
Ishigaki Japan 24°26N 124°10E 303 M2
Ishigaki-Shima Japan 24°20N 124°10E 303 M2
Ishikari-Gawa → Japan 43°15N 141°23E 302 C10
Ishikari-Sammyaku Japan 43°30N 143°0E 302 C11
Ishikari-Wan Japan 43°25N 141°1E 302 C10
Ishikawa Japan 26°25N 127°49E 303 L3
Ishikawa □ Japan 36°30N 136°30E 303 F8
Ishim Russia 56°10N 69°30E 300 D7
Ishim → Russia 57°45N 71°10E 300 D8
Ishinomaki Japan 38°32N 141°20E 302 E10
Ishioka Japan 36°11N 140°16E 303 F10
Ishkuman Pakistan 36°30N 73°50E 315 A5
Ishpeming U.S.A. 46°29N 87°40W 352 B10
Isil Kul Russia 54°55N 71°16E 300 D8
Isiolo Kenya 0°24N 37°33E 326 B4
Isiro Dem. Rep. of the Congo 2°53N 27°40E 326 B2
Isisford Australia 24°15S 144°21E 334 C3
İskenderun Turkey 36°32N 36°10E 316 B3
İskenderun Körfezi Turkey 36°40N 35°50E 291 G6
Iskŭr → Bulgaria 43°45N 24°25E 295 C11
Iskut → Canada 56°45N 131°49W 342 B2
Isla → U.K. 56°32N 3°20W 283 E5
Isla Coiba △ Panama 7°33N 81°36W 360 E3
Isla de Salamanca △ Colombia 10°59N 74°40W 361 D5
Isla Gorge △ Australia 25°10S 149°57E 334 D4
Isla Isabel, Parque Nacional △ Mexico 21°54N 105°58W 358 C3
Isla Tiburón y San Esteban ⌂ Mexico 29°0N 112°27W 358 B2
Isla Vista U.S.A. 34°25N 119°53W 351 L7
Islam Headworks Pakistan 29°49N 72°33E 314 E5
Islamabad Pakistan 33°40N 73°10E 314 C5
Islamgarh Pakistan 27°51N 70°48E 314 F4
Islamkot Pakistan 24°42N 70°13E 314 G4
Islampur India 25°9N 85°12E 315 G11
Island = Iceland ■ Europe 64°45N 19°0W 280 D4
Island L. Canada 53°47N 94°25W 343 C10
Island Lagoon Australia 31°30S 136°40E 335 E2
Island Pond U.S.A. 44°49N 71°53W 355 B13
Islands, B. of Canada 49°11N 58°15W 345 C8
Islands, B. of N.Z. 35°15S 174°6E 331 A5
Islay U.K. 55°46N 6°10W 283 F2
Isle → France 44°55N 0°15W 292 D3
Isle aux Morts Canada 47°35N 59°0W 345 C8
Isle of Wight □ U.K. 50°41N 1°17W 285 G6
Isle Royale △ U.S.A. 48°0N 88°55W 352 B9
Isleton U.S.A. 38°10N 121°37W 350 G5
Ismail = Izmayil Ukraine 45°22N 28°46E 289 F15
Ismâ'ilîya Egypt 30°37N 32°18E 323 B12
Isna Egypt 25°17N 32°30E 323 C12
Isoanala Madag. 23°50S 45°44E 329 C8
Isogstalo India 34°15N 78°46E 315 B8
Isparta Turkey 37°47N 30°30E 291 G5
Íspica Italy 36°47N 14°55E 294 F6
Israel ■ Asia 32°0N 34°50E 318 D3
Issoire France 45°32N 3°15E 292 D5
Issyk-Kul, Ozero = Ysyk-Köl Kyrgyzstan 42°25N 77°15E 300 E8
İstanbul Turkey 41°0N 28°58E 295 D13
İstanbul Boğazı Turkey 41°5N 29°3E 295 D13
Istiea Greece 38°57N 23°9E 295 E10
Istokpoga, L. U.S.A. 27°23N 81°17W 357 H14
Istra Croatia 45°10N 14°0E 288 F7
Istres France 43°31N 4°59E 292 E6
Istria = Istra Croatia 45°10N 14°0E 288 F7
Itá Paraguay 25°29S 57°21W 366 B4
Itaberaba Brazil 12°32S 40°18W 365 F10
Itabira Brazil 19°37S 43°13W 365 G10
Itabirito Brazil 20°15S 43°48W 367 A7
Itabuna Brazil 14°48S 39°16W 365 F11
Itacaunas → Brazil 5°21S 49°8W 365 E9
Itacoatiara Brazil 3°8S 58°25W 364 D7
Itaipú, Représa de Brazil 25°30S 54°30W 367 B5
Itaituba Brazil 4°10S 55°50W 365 D7
Itajaí Brazil 27°50S 48°39W 367 B6
Itajubá Brazil 22°24S 45°30W 367 A6
Itaka Tanzania 8°50S 32°49E 327 D3
Itala ⌂ S. Africa 27°30S 31°7E 329 D5
Italy ■ Europe 42°0N 13°0E 294 C5
Itamaraju Brazil 17°4S 39°32W 365 G11
Itampolo Madag. 24°41S 43°57E 329 C7
Itandrano Madag. 21°47S 45°17E 329 C8
Itapecuru-Mirim Brazil 3°24S 44°20W 365 D10
Itaperuna Brazil 21°10S 41°54W 367 A7
Itapetininga Brazil 23°36S 48°7W 367 A6
Itapeva Brazil 23°59S 48°59W 367 A6
Itapicuru → Bahia, Brazil 11°47S 37°32W 365 F11
Itapicuru → Maranhão, Brazil 2°52S 44°12W 365 D10
Itapipoca Brazil 3°30S 39°35W 365 D11
Itapuá □ Paraguay 26°40S 55°40W 367 B4
Itaquari Brazil 20°20S 40°25W 367 A7
Itaquí Brazil 29°8S 56°30W 366 B4
Itararé Brazil 24°6S 49°23W 367 A6
Itarsi India 22°36N 77°51E 314 H7
Itatí Argentina 27°16S 58°15W 366 B4
Itatiaia △ Brazil 22°22S 44°38W 367 A7
Itchen → U.K. 50°55N 1°22W 285 G6
Itezhi Tezhi, L. Zambia 15°30S 25°30E 327 F2
Ithaca = Ithaki Greece 38°25N 20°40E 295 E9
Ithaca U.S.A. 42°27N 76°30W 355 D8
Ithaki Greece 38°25N 20°40E 295 E9
Itiquira → Brazil 17°18S 56°44W 365 G7
Itō Japan 34°58N 139°5E 303 G9
Itoigawa Japan 37°2N 137°51E 303 F8
Itonamas → Bolivia 12°28S 64°24W 364 F6
Ittoqqortoormiit Greenland 70°20N 23°0W 276 B6
Itu Brazil 23°17S 47°15W 367 A6
Itu Aba I. S. China Sea 10°23N 114°21E 308 B4
Ituiutaba Brazil 19°0S 49°25W 365 G9
Itumbiara Brazil 18°20S 49°10W 365 G9
Ituna Canada 51°10N 103°24W 343 C8
Itunge Port Tanzania 9°40S 33°55E 327 D3
Iturbe Argentina 23°0S 65°25W 366 A2
Ituri → Dem. Rep. of the Congo 1°40N 27°1E 326 B2
Iturup, Ostrov Russia 45°0N 148°0E 301 E15
Ituxi → Brazil 7°18S 64°51W 364 E6
Ituyuro → Argentina 22°40S 63°50W 366 A3
Itzehoe Germany 53°55N 9°31E 288 B5
Ivahona Madag. 23°27S 46°10E 329 C8
Ivaí → Brazil 23°18S 53°42W 367 A5
Ivalo Finland 68°38N 27°35E 280 B22
Ivalojoki → Finland 68°40N 27°40E 280 B22
Ivanava Belarus 52°7N 25°29E 289 B13
Ivanhoe Australia 32°56S 144°20E 335 E3
Ivanhoe Calif., U.S.A. 36°23N 119°13W 350 J7
Ivanhoe Minn., U.S.A. 44°28N 96°15W 352 C5
Ivano-Frankivsk Ukraine 48°40N 24°40E 289 D13
Ivanovo = Ivanava Belarus 52°7N 25°29E 289 B13
Ivanovo Russia 57°5N 41°0E 290 C7
Ivato Madag. 20°37S 47°10E 329 C8
Ivatsevichy Belarus 52°43N 25°21E 289 B13
Ivdel Russia 60°42N 60°24E 290 B11
Ivinheima → Brazil 23°14S 53°42W 367 A5
Ivinhema Brazil 22°10S 53°37W 367 A5
Ivohibe Madag. 22°31S 46°57E 329 C8
Ivory Coast W. Afr. 4°20N 5°0W 322 H4
Ivory Coast ■ Africa 7°30N 5°0W 322 G4
Ivrea Italy 45°28N 7°52E 292 D7
Ivujivik Canada 62°24N 77°55W 341 C12
Ivybridge U.K. 50°23N 3°56W 285 G4
Iwaizumi Japan 39°50N 141°45E 302 E10
Iwaki Japan 37°3N 140°55E 303 F10
Iwakuni Japan 34°15N 132°8E 303 G6
Iwamizawa Japan 43°12N 141°46E 302 C10
Iwanai Japan 42°58N 140°30E 302 C10
Iwata Japan 34°42N 137°51E 303 G8
Iwate □ Japan 39°30N 141°30E 302 E10
Iwate-San Japan 39°51N 141°0E 302 E10
Iwo Nigeria 7°39N 4°9E 322 G6
Iwŏn N. Korea 40°19N 128°39E 307 D15
Ixiamas Bolivia 13°50S 68°5W 364 F5
Ixopo S. Africa 30°11S 30°5E 329 E5
Ixtepec Mexico 16°34N 95°6W 359 D5
Ixtlán del Río Mexico 21°2N 104°22W 358 C4
Iyo Japan 33°45N 132°45E 303 H6
Izabal, L. de Guatemala 15°30N 89°10W 360 C2

Izamal *Mexico* 20°56N 89°1W 359 C7
Izena-Shima *Japan* 26°56N 127°56E 303 L3
Izhevsk *Russia* 56°51N 53°14E 290 C9
Izhma → *Russia* 65°19N 52°54E 290 A9
Izmayil *Ukraine* 45°22N 28°46E 289 F15
İzmir *Turkey* 38°25N 27°8E 295 E12
İzmit = Kocaeli *Turkey* 40°45N 29°50E 291 F4
İznik Gölü *Turkey* 40°27N 29°30E 295 D13
Izra *Syria* 32°51N 36°15E 318 C5
Izu-Shotō *Japan* 34°30N 140°0E 303 G10
Izúcar de Matamoros *Mexico* 18°36N 98°28W 359 D5
Izumi-Sano *Japan* 34°23N 135°18E 303 G7
Izumo *Japan* 35°20N 132°46E 303 G6
Izyaslav *Ukraine* 50°5N 26°50E 289 C14

J

J.F.K. Int. ✕ (JFK) *U.S.A.* 40°38N 73°47W 355 F11
J. Strom Thurmond L. *U.S.A.* 33°40N 82°12W 357 E13
Jabalpur *India* 23°9N 79°58E 315 H8
Jabbūl *Syria* 36°4N 37°30E 316 B3
Jabiru *Australia* 12°40S 132°53E 332 B5
Jablah *Syria* 35°20N 36°0E 316 C3
Jablonec nad Nisou *Czech Rep.* 50°43N 15°10E 288 C8
Jaboatão *Brazil* 8°7S 35°1W 365 E11
Jaboticabal *Brazil* 21°15S 48°17W 367 A6
Jaca *Spain* 42°35N 0°33W 293 A5
Jacareí *Brazil* 23°20S 46°0W 367 A6
Jacarèzinho *Brazil* 23°5S 49°58W 367 A6
Jackman *U.S.A.* 45°37N 70°15W 353 C18
Jacksboro *U.S.A.* 33°13N 98°10W 356 E5
Jackson *Barbados* 13°7N 59°36W 361 g
Jackson *Ala., U.S.A.* 31°31N 87°53W 357 F11
Jackson *Calif., U.S.A.* 38°21N 120°46W 350 G6
Jackson *Ky., U.S.A.* 37°33N 83°23W 353 G12
Jackson *Mich., U.S.A.* 42°15N 84°24W 353 D11
Jackson *Minn., U.S.A.* 43°37N 95°1W 352 D6
Jackson *Miss., U.S.A.* 32°18N 90°12W 357 E9
Jackson *Mo., U.S.A.* 37°23N 89°40W 352 G9
Jackson *N.H., U.S.A.* 44°10N 71°11W 355 B13
Jackson *Ohio, U.S.A.* 39°3N 82°39W 353 F12
Jackson *Tenn., U.S.A.* 35°37N 88°49W 357 D10
Jackson *Wyo., U.S.A.* 43°29N 110°46W 348 E8
Jackson B. *N.Z.* 43°58S 168°42E 331 E2
Jackson L. *U.S.A.* 43°52N 110°36W 348 E8
Jacksons *N.Z.* 42°46S 171°32E 331 E3
Jackson's Arm *Canada* 49°52N 56°47W 345 C8
Jacksonville *Ala., U.S.A.* 33°49N 85°46W 357 E12
Jacksonville *Ark., U.S.A.* 34°52N 92°7W 356 D8
Jacksonville *Calif., U.S.A.* 37°52N 120°24W 350 H6
Jacksonville *Fla., U.S.A.* 30°20N 81°39W 357 F14
Jacksonville *Ill., U.S.A.* 39°44N 90°14W 352 F8
Jacksonville *N.C., U.S.A.* 34°45N 77°26W 357 D16
Jacksonville *Tex., U.S.A.* 31°58N 95°17W 356 F7
Jacksonville Beach *U.S.A.* 30°17N 81°24W 357 F14
Jacmel *Haiti* 18°14N 72°32W 361 C5
Jacob Lake *U.S.A.* 36°43N 112°13W 349 H7
Jacobabad *Pakistan* 28°20N 68°29E 314 E3
Jacobina *Brazil* 11°11S 40°30W 365 F10
Jacques-Cartier, Dét. de *Canada* 50°0N 63°30W 345 C7
Jacques-Cartier, Mt. *Canada* 48°57N 66°0W 345 C6
Jacques-Cartier ⌂ *Canada* 47°15N 71°33W 345 C5
Jacuí → *Brazil* 30°2S 51°15W 367 C5
Jacumba *U.S.A.* 32°37N 116°11W 351 N10
Jacundá → *Brazil* 1°57S 50°26W 365 D8
Jaén *Peru* 5°25S 78°40W 364 E3
Jaén *Spain* 37°44N 3°43W 293 D4
Jafarabad *India* 20°52N 71°22E 314 J4
Jaffa = Tel Aviv-Yafo *Israel* 32°4N 34°48E 318 C3
Jaffa, C. *Australia* 36°58S 139°40E 335 F2
Jaffna *Sri Lanka* 9°45N 80°2E 312 Q12
Jaffray *Canada* 49°47N 94°26W 343 D10
Jaffrey *U.S.A.* 42°49N 72°2W 355 D12
Jagadhri *India* 30°10N 77°20E 314 D7
Jagadishpur *India* 25°30N 84°21E 315 G11
Jagdalpur *India* 19°3N 82°0E 313 K13
Jagersfontein *S. Africa* 29°44S 25°27E 328 D4
Jaghīn → *Iran* 27°17N 57°13E 317 E8
Jagodina *Serbia* 44°5N 21°15E 295 C9
Jagraon *India* 30°50N 75°25E 314 D6
Jagtial *India* 18°50N 79°0E 312 K11
Jaguariaíva *Brazil* 24°10S 49°50W 367 A6
Jaguaribe → *Brazil* 4°25S 37°45W 365 D11
Jagüey Grande *Cuba* 22°35N 81°7W 360 B3
Jahanabad *India* 25°13N 84°59E 315 G11
Jahazpur *India* 25°37N 75°17E 314 G6
Jahrom *Iran* 28°30N 53°31E 317 D7
Jaijon *India* 31°21N 76°9E 314 D7
Jailolo *Indonesia* 1°5N 127°30E 309 D7
Jailolo, Selat *Indonesia* 0°5N 129°5E 309 D7
Jaipur *India* 27°0N 75°50E 314 F6
Jais *India* 26°15N 81°32E 315 F9
Jaisalmer *India* 26°55N 70°54E 314 F4
Jaisinghnagar *India* 23°38N 78°34E 315 H8
Jaitaran *India* 26°12N 73°56E 314 F5
Jaithari *India* 23°14N 78°37E 315 H8
Jājarm *Iran* 36°58N 56°27E 317 B8
Jakam → *India* 23°54N 74°13E 314 H6
Jakarta *Indonesia* 6°9S 106°52E 308 F3
Jakhal *India* 29°48N 75°50E 314 E6
Jakhau *India* 23°13N 68°43E 314 H3
Jakobstad = Pietarsaari *Finland* 63°40N 22°43E 280 E20
Jal *U.S.A.* 32°7N 103°12W 349 K12
Jalālābād *Afghan.* 34°30N 70°29E 314 B4
Jalalabad *India* 27°41N 79°42E 315 F8
Jalalpur Jattan *Pakistan* 32°38N 74°11E 314 C6
Jalama *U.S.A.* 34°29N 120°29W 351 L6
Jalapa *Guatemala* 14°39N 89°59W 360 D2
Jalapa Enríquez = Xalapa *Mexico* 19°32N 96°55W 359 D5
Jalasjärvi *Finland* 62°29N 22°47E 280 E20
Jalaun *India* 26°8N 79°25E 315 F8
Jaldhaka → *Bangla.* 26°16N 89°16E 315 F13
Jalesar *India* 27°29N 78°19E 314 F8
Jaleswar *Nepal* 26°38N 85°48E 315 F11
Jalgaon *India* 21°0N 75°42E 312 J9
Jalībah *Iraq* 30°35N 46°32E 316 D5
Jalingo *Nigeria* 8°55N 11°25E 323 G8
Jalisco □ *Mexico* 20°20N 103°40W 358 D4
Jalkot *Pakistan* 35°14N 73°24E 315 B5
Jalna *India* 19°48N 75°38E 312 K9
Jalón → *Spain* 41°47N 1°4W 293 B5
Jalor *India* 25°21N 72°37E 314 G5
Jalpa *Mexico* 21°38N 102°58W 358 C4
Jalpaiguri *India* 26°32N 88°46E 313 F16
Jalpan *Mexico* 21°14N 99°29W 359 C5
Jaluit I. *Marshall Is.* 6°0N 169°30E 336 G8
Jalūlā *Iraq* 34°16N 45°10E 316 C5
Jamaame = Giamama *Somali Rep.* 0°4N 42°44E 319 G3
Jamaica ■ *W. Indies* 18°10N 77°30W 360 a
Jamalpur *Bangla.* 24°52N 89°56E 313 G16
Jamalpur *India* 25°18N 86°28E 315 G12
Jamalpurganj *India* 23°2N 87°59E 315 H13
Jamanxim → *Brazil* 4°43S 56°18W 365 D7
Jambewangi *Indonesia* 8°17S 114°7E 309 J17
Jambi *Indonesia* 1°38S 103°30E 308 E2
Jambi □ *Indonesia* 1°30S 102°30E 308 E2
Jambongan, Pulau *Malaysia* 6°45N 117°20E 308 C5
Jambusar *India* 22°3N 72°51E 314 H5
James → *S. Dak., U.S.A.* 42°52N 97°18W 352 D5
James → *Va., U.S.A.* 36°56N 76°27W 353 G15
James B. *Canada* 54°0N 80°0W 344 B3
James Ranges *Australia* 24°10S 132°30E 332 D5
James Ross I. *Antarctica* 63°58S 57°50W 277 C18
Jamesabad *Pakistan* 25°17N 69°15E 314 G3
Jamestown *Australia* 33°10S 138°32E 335 E2
Jamestown *S. Africa* 31°6S 26°45E 328 E4
Jamestown *N. Dak., U.S.A.* 46°54N 98°42W 352 B4
Jamestown *N.Y., U.S.A.* 42°6N 79°14W 354 D5
Jamestown *Pa., U.S.A.* 41°29N 80°27W 354 E4
Jamīlābād *Iran* 34°24N 48°28E 317 C6
Jamira → *India* 21°35N 88°28E 315 J13
Jamkhandi *India* 16°30N 75°15E 312 L9
Jammu *India* 32°43N 74°54E 314 C6
Jammu & Kashmir □ *India* 34°25N 77°0E 315 B7
Jamnagar *India* 22°30N 70°6E 314 H4
Jamni → *India* 25°13N 78°35E 315 G8
Jampur *Pakistan* 29°39N 70°40E 314 E4
Jamrud *Pakistan* 33°59N 71°24E 314 C4
Jämsä *Finland* 61°53N 25°10E 280 F21
Jamshedpur *India* 22°44N 86°12E 315 H12
Jamtara *India* 23°59N 86°49E 315 H12
Jämtland *Sweden* 63°31N 14°0E 280 E16
Jan L. *Canada* 54°56N 102°55W 343 C8
Jan Mayen *Arctic* 71°0N 9°0W 276 B7
Janaúba *Brazil* 15°48S 43°19W 365 G10
Jand *Pakistan* 33°30N 72°6E 314 C5
Jandaq *Iran* 34°3N 54°22E 317 C7
Jandía *Canary Is.* 28°6N 14°21W 296 F5
Jandía, Pta. de *Canary Is.* 28°3N 14°31W 296 F5
Jandía △ *Canary Is.* 28°4N 14°19W 296 F5
Jandola *Pakistan* 32°20N 70°9E 314 C4
Jandowae *Australia* 26°45S 151°7E 335 D5
Janesville *U.S.A.* 42°41N 89°1W 352 D9
Jangamo *Mozam.* 24°6S 35°21E 329 C6
Janghai *India* 25°33N 82°19E 315 G10
Jangheung *S. Korea* 34°41N 126°52E 307 G14
Janjanbureh *Gambia* 13°30N 14°47W 322 F3
Janjgir *India* 22°1N 82°34E 315 J10
Janjina *Madag.* 20°30S 45°50E 329 C8
Janos *Mexico* 30°54N 108°10W 358 A3
Januária *Brazil* 15°25S 44°25W 365 G10
Janûb Sînî □ *Egypt* 29°30N 33°50E 318 F2
Janubio *Canary Is.* 28°56N 13°50W 296 F6
Jaora *India* 23°40N 75°10E 314 H6
Japan ■ *Asia* 36°0N 136°0E 303 G8
Japan, Sea of *Asia* 40°0N 135°0E 302 E7
Japan Trench *Pac. Oc.* 32°0N 142°0E 336 D6
Japen = Yapen *Indonesia* 1°50S 136°0E 309 E9
Japla *India* 24°33N 84°1E 315 G11
Japurá → *Brazil* 3°8S 65°46W 364 D5
Jaquarão *Brazil* 32°34S 53°23W 367 C5
Jaqué *Panama* 7°27N 78°8W 360 E4
Jarābulus *Syria* 36°49N 38°1E 316 B3
Jarama → *Spain* 40°24N 3°32W 293 B4
Jaranwala *Pakistan* 31°15N 73°26E 314 D5
Jarash *Jordan* 32°17N 35°54E 318 C4
Jarash □ *Jordan* 32°17N 35°54E 318 C4
Jardim *Brazil* 21°28S 56°2W 366 A4
Jardine River △ *Australia* 11°9S 142°21E 334 A3
Jardines de la Reina, Arch. de los *Cuba* 20°50N 78°50W 360 B4
Jargalang *China* 43°5N 122°55E 307 C12
Jari → *Brazil* 1°9S 51°54W 365 D8
Jarīr, W. al → *Si. Arabia* 25°38N 42°30E 316 E4
Jarosław *Poland* 50°2N 22°42E 289 C12
Jarrahdale *Australia* 32°24S 116°5E 333 F2
Jarrahi → *Iran* 30°49N 48°48E 317 D6
Jarres, Plaine des *Laos* 19°27N 103°10E 310 C4
Jartai *China* 39°45N 105°48E 306 E3
Jarud Qi *China* 44°28N 120°50E 307 B11
Järvenpää *Finland* 60°29N 25°5E 280 F21
Jarvis *Canada* 42°53N 80°6W 354 D4
Jarvis I. *Pac. Oc.* 0°15S 160°5W 337 H12
Jarwa *India* 27°38N 82°30E 315 F10
Jasdan *India* 22°2N 71°12E 314 H4
Jashpurnagar *India* 22°54N 84°9E 315 H11
Jasidih *India* 24°31N 86°39E 315 G12
Jāsimīyah *Iraq* 33°45N 44°41E 316 C5
Jasin *Malaysia* 2°20N 102°26E 311 L4
Jāsk *Iran* 25°38N 57°45E 317 E8
Jasło *Poland* 49°45N 21°30E 289 D11
Jaso *India* 24°30N 80°29E 315 G9
Jasper *Alta., Canada* 52°55N 118°5W 342 C5
Jasper *Ont., Canada* 44°52N 75°57W 355 B9
Jasper *Ala., U.S.A.* 33°50N 87°17W 357 E11
Jasper *Fla., U.S.A.* 30°31N 82°57W 357 F13
Jasper *Ind., U.S.A.* 38°24N 86°56W 352 F10
Jasper *Tex., U.S.A.* 30°56N 94°1W 356 F7
Jasper △ *Canada* 52°50N 118°8W 342 C5
Jasrasar *India* 27°43N 73°49E 314 F5
Jászberény *Hungary* 47°30N 19°55E 289 E10
Jataí *Brazil* 17°58S 51°48W 365 G8
Jati *Pakistan* 24°20N 68°19E 314 G3
Jatibarang *Indonesia* 6°28S 108°18E 309 G13
Jatiluwih *Indonesia* 8°23S 115°8E 309 J18
Jatinegara *Indonesia* 6°13S 106°52E 309 G12
Játiva = Xátiva *Spain* 38°59N 0°32W 293 C5
Jaú *Brazil* 22°10S 48°30W 367 A6
Jauja *Peru* 11°45S 75°15W 364 F3
Jaunpur *India* 25°46N 82°44E 315 G10
Java = Jawa *Indonesia* 7°0S 110°0E 308 F3
Java Sea *Indonesia* 4°35S 107°15E 308 E3
Java Trench *Ind. Oc.* 9°0S 105°0E 308 F3
Jawa *Indonesia* 7°0S 110°0E 308 F3
Jawa Barat □ *Indonesia* 7°0S 107°0E 309 G12
Jawa Tengah □ *Indonesia* 7°0S 110°0E 309 G14
Jawa Timur □ *Indonesia* 8°0S 113°0E 309 G15
Jawad *India* 24°36N 74°51E 314 G6
Jay Peak *U.S.A.* 44°55N 72°32W 355 B12
Jaya, Puncak *Indonesia* 3°57S 137°17E 309 E9
Jayanti *India* 26°45N 89°40E 313 F16
Jayapura *Indonesia* 2°28S 140°38E 309 E10
Jayawijaya, Pegunungan *Indonesia* 5°0S 139°0E 309 E9
Jaynagar *India* 26°43N 86°9E 315 F12
Jayrūd *Syria* 33°49N 36°44E 316 C3
Jayton *U.S.A.* 33°15N 100°34W 356 E4
Jāz Mūrīān, Hāmūn-e *Iran* 27°20N 58°55E 317 E8
Jazīreh-ye Shīf *Iran* 29°4N 50°54E 317 D6
Jazminal *Mexico* 24°52N 101°24W 358 C4
Jazzīn *Lebanon* 33°31N 35°35E 318 B4
Jean *U.S.A.* 35°47N 115°20W 351 K11
Jean Marie River *Canada* 61°32N 120°38W 342 A4
Jean-Rabel *Haiti* 19°50N 73°5W 361 C5
Jeanerette *U.S.A.* 29°55N 91°40W 356 G9
Jeanette, Ostrov = Zhannetty, Ostrov *Russia* 76°43N 158°0E 301 B16
Jeannette *U.S.A.* 40°20N 79°36W 354 F5
Jebāl Bārez, Kūh-e *Iran* 28°30N 58°20E 317 D8
Jebel, Bahr el → *Sudan* 9°30N 30°25E 323 G12
Jecheon *S. Korea* 37°8N 128°12E 307 F15
Jedburgh *U.K.* 55°29N 2°33W 283 F6
Jedda = Jiddah *Si. Arabia* 21°29N 39°10E 319 C2
Jeddore L. *Canada* 48°3N 55°55W 345 C8
Jędrzejów *Poland* 50°35N 20°15E 289 C11
Jefferson *Iowa, U.S.A.* 42°1N 94°23W 352 D6
Jefferson *Ohio, U.S.A.* 41°44N 80°46W 354 E4
Jefferson *Tex., U.S.A.* 32°46N 94°21W 356 E7
Jefferson, Mt. *Nev., U.S.A.* 38°47N 116°56W 348 G5
Jefferson, Mt. *Oreg., U.S.A.* 44°41N 121°48W 348 D3
Jefferson City *Mo., U.S.A.* 38°34N 92°10W 352 F7
Jefferson City *Tenn., U.S.A.* 36°7N 83°30W 357 C13
Jeffersontown *U.S.A.* 38°12N 85°35W 353 F11
Jeffersonville *U.S.A.* 38°17N 85°44W 353 F11
Jeffrey City *U.S.A.* 42°30N 107°49W 348 E10
Jega *Nigeria* 12°15N 4°23E 322 F6
Jeju *S. Korea* 33°31N 126°32E 307 H14
Jeju-do *S. Korea* 33°29N 126°34E 307 H14
Jēkabpils *Latvia* 56°29N 25°57E 281 H21
Jekyll I. *U.S.A.* 31°4N 81°25W 357 F14
Jelenia Góra *Poland* 50°50N 15°45E 288 C8
Jelgava *Latvia* 56°41N 23°49E 281 H20
Jemaja *Indonesia* 3°5N 105°45E 311 L5
Jemaluang *Malaysia* 2°16N 103°52E 311 L4
Jember *Indonesia* 8°11S 113°41E 309 H15
Jena *Germany* 50°54N 11°35E 288 C6
Jena *U.S.A.* 31°41N 92°8W 356 F8
Jenīn *West Bank* 32°28N 35°18E 318 C4
Jenkins *U.S.A.* 37°10N 82°38W 353 G12
Jenner *U.S.A.* 38°27N 123°7W 350 G3
Jennings *U.S.A.* 30°13N 92°40W 356 F8
Jeong-eup *S. Korea* 35°35N 126°50E 307 G14
Jeonju *S. Korea* 35°50N 127°4E 307 G14
Jepara *Indonesia* 7°40S 109°14E 309 G14
Jeparit *Australia* 36°8S 142°1E 335 F3
Jequié *Brazil* 13°51S 40°5W 365 F10
Jequitinhonha *Brazil* 16°30S 41°0W 365 G10
Jequitinhonha → *Brazil* 15°51S 38°53W 365 G11
Jerada *Morocco* 34°17N 2°10W 322 B5
Jerantut *Malaysia* 3°56N 102°22E 311 L4
Jerejak, Pulau *Malaysia* 5°19N 100°19E 311 c
Jérémie *Haiti* 18°40N 74°10W 361 C5
Jerez, Pta. *Mexico* 22°58N 97°40W 359 C5
Jerez de García Salinas *Mexico* 22°39N 103°0W 358 C4
Jerez de la Frontera *Spain* 36°41N 6°7W 293 D2
Jerez de los Caballeros *Spain* 38°20N 6°45W 293 C2
Jericho = El Arīḥā *West Bank* 31°52N 35°27E 318 D4
Jericho *Australia* 23°38S 146°6E 334 C4
Jerid, Chott el = Djerid, Chott *Tunisia* 33°42N 8°30E 322 B7
Jerilderie *Australia* 35°20S 145°41E 335 F4
Jermyn *U.S.A.* 41°31N 75°33W 355 E9
Jerome *U.S.A.* 42°44N 114°31W 348 E6
Jerramungup *Australia* 33°55S 118°55E 333 F2
Jersey *U.K.* 49°11N 2°7W 285 H5
Jersey City *U.S.A.* 40°42N 74°4W 355 F10
Jersey Shore *U.S.A.* 41°12N 77°15W 354 E7
Jerseyville *U.S.A.* 39°7N 90°20W 352 F8
Jerusalem *Israel/West Bank* 31°47N 35°10E 318 D4
Jervis B. *Australia* 35°8S 150°46E 335 F5
Jervis Inlet *Canada* 50°0N 123°57W 342 C4
Jesi = Iesi *Italy* 43°31N 13°14E 294 C5
Jessore *Bangla.* 23°10N 89°10E 313 H16
Jesup *U.S.A.* 31°36N 81°53W 357 F14
Jesús Carranza *Mexico* 17°26N 95°2W 359 D5
Jesús María *Argentina* 30°59S 64°5W 366 C3
Jetmore *U.S.A.* 38°4N 99°54W 352 F4
Jetpur *India* 21°45N 70°10E 314 J4
Jevnaker *Norway* 60°15N 10°26E 281 F14
Jewett *U.S.A.* 40°22N 81°2W 354 F3
Jewett City *U.S.A.* 41°36N 71°59W 355 E13
Jeyḥūnābād *Iran* 34°58N 48°59E 317 C6
Jeypore *India* 18°50N 82°38E 313 K13
Jha Jha *India* 24°46N 86°22E 315 G12
Jhaarkand = Jharkhand □ *India* 24°0N 85°50E 315 H11
Jhabua *India* 22°46N 74°36E 314 H6
Jhajjar *India* 28°37N 76°42E 314 E7
Jhal *Pakistan* 28°17N 67°27E 314 E2
Jhal Jhao *Pakistan* 26°20N 65°35E 312 F4
Jhalawar *India* 24°40N 76°10E 314 G7
Jhalida *India* 23°22N 85°58E 315 H11
Jhalrapatan *India* 24°33N 76°10E 314 G7
Jhang Maghiana *Pakistan* 31°15N 72°22E 314 D5
Jhansi *India* 25°30N 78°36E 315 G8
Jhargram *India* 22°27N 86°59E 315 H12
Jharia *India* 23°45N 86°26E 315 H12
Jharkhand □ *India* 24°0N 85°50E 315 H11
Jharsuguda *India* 21°56N 84°5E 313 J14
Jhelum *Pakistan* 33°0N 73°45E 314 C5
Jhelum → *Pakistan* 31°20N 72°10E 314 D5
Jhilmilli *India* 23°24N 82°51E 315 H10
Jhudo *Pakistan* 24°58N 69°18E 314 G3
Jhunjhunu *India* 28°10N 75°30E 314 E6
Ji-Paraná *Brazil* 10°52S 62°57W 364 F6
Ji Xian *Hebei, China* 37°35N 115°30E 306 F8
Ji Xian *Henan, China* 35°22N 114°5E 306 G8
Ji Xian *Shanxi, China* 36°7N 110°40E 306 F6
Jia Xian *Henan, China* 33°59N 113°12E 306 H7
Jia Xian *Shaanxi, China* 38°12N 110°28E 306 E6
Jiaji = Qionghai *China* 19°15N 110°26E 310 C8
Jiamusi *China* 46°40N 130°26E 305 B8
Ji'an *Jiangxi, China* 27°6N 114°59E 305 D6
Ji'an *Jilin, China* 41°5N 126°10E 307 D14
Jianchang *China* 40°55N 120°35E 307 D11
Jianchangying *China* 40°10N 118°50E 307 D10
Jiangcheng *China* 22°36N 101°52E 304 D5
Jiangmen *China* 22°32N 113°0E 305 D6
Jiangsu □ *China* 33°0N 120°0E 307 H11
Jiangxi □ *China* 27°30N 116°0E 305 D6
Jiao Xian = Jiaozhou *China* 36°18N 120°1E 307 F11
Jiaohe *Hebei, China* 38°2N 116°20E 306 E9
Jiaohe *Jilin, China* 43°40N 127°22E 307 C14
Jiaozhou *China* 36°18N 120°1E 307 F11
Jiaozhou Wan *China* 36°5N 120°10E 307 F11
Jiaozuo *China* 35°16N 113°12E 306 G7
Jiawang *China* 34°28N 117°26E 307 G9
Jiaxiang *China* 35°25N 116°20E 306 G9
Jiaxing *China* 30°49N 120°45E 305 C7
Jiayi = Chiai *Taiwan* 23°29N 120°25E 305 D7
Jibuti = Djibouti ■ *Africa* 12°0N 43°0E 319 E3
Jicarón, I. *Panama* 7°10N 81°50W 360 E3
Jiddah *Si. Arabia* 21°29N 39°10E 319 C2
Jido *India* 29°2N 94°58E 313 E19
Jieshou *China* 33°18N 115°22E 306 H8
Jiexiu *China* 37°2N 111°55E 306 F6
Jigalong *Australia* 23°21S 120°47E 332 D3
Jigni *India* 25°45N 79°25E 315 G8
Jihlava *Czech Rep.* 49°28N 15°35E 288 D8
Jihlava → *Czech Rep.* 48°55N 16°36E 289 D9
Jijiga *Ethiopia* 9°20N 42°50E 319 F3
Jilib = Gelib *Somali Rep.* 0°29N 42°46E 319 G3
Jilin *China* 43°44N 126°30E 307 C14
Jilin □ *China* 44°0N 127°0E 307 C14
Jilong = Chilung *Taiwan* 25°3N 121°45E 305 D7
Jim Thorpe *U.S.A.* 40°52N 75°44W 355 F9
Jima *Ethiopia* 7°40N 36°47E 319 F2
Jimbaran, Teluk *Indonesia* 8°46S 115°9E 309 K18
Jiménez *Mexico* 27°8N 104°54W 358 B4
Jimo *China* 36°23N 120°30E 307 F11
Jin Xian = Jinzhou *Hebei, China* 38°2N 115°2E 306 E8
Jin Xian = Jinzhou *Liaoning, China* 38°55N 121°42E 307 E11
Jinan *China* 36°38N 117°1E 306 F9
Jinchang *China* 38°30N 102°10E 304 C5
Jincheng *China* 35°29N 112°50E 306 G7
Jind *India* 29°19N 76°22E 314 E7
Jindabyne *Australia* 36°25S 148°35E 335 F4
Jinding *China* 22°22N 113°33E 305 G10
Jindo *S. Korea* 34°28N 126°15E 307 G14
Jindřichův Hradec *Czech Rep.* 49°10N 15°2E 288 D8
Jing He → *China* 34°27N 109°4E 306 G5
Jingbian *China* 37°20N 108°30E 306 F5
Jingchuan *China* 35°20N 107°20E 306 G4
Jingdezhen *China* 29°20N 117°11E 305 D6
Jinggu *China* 23°35N 100°41E 304 D5
Jinghai *China* 38°55N 116°55E 306 E9
Jingle *China* 38°20N 111°55E 306 E6
Jingning *China* 35°30N 105°43E 306 G3
Jingpo Hu *China* 43°55N 128°55E 307 C15
Jingtai *China* 37°10N 104°6E 306 F3
Jingxing *China* 38°2N 114°8E 306 E8
Jingyang *China* 34°30N 108°50E 306 G5
Jingyu *China* 42°25N 126°45E 307 C14
Jingyuan *China* 36°30N 104°40E 306 F3
Jingziguan *China* 33°15N 111°0E 306 H6
Jinhua *China* 29°8N 119°38E 305 D6
Jining *Nei Monggol Zizhiqu, China* 41°5N 113°0E 306 D7
Jining *Shandong, China* 35°22N 116°34E 306 G9
Jinja *Uganda* 0°25N 33°12E 326 B3
Jinjang *Malaysia* 3°13N 101°39E 311 L3
Jinji *China* 37°58N 106°8E 306 F4
Jinju *S. Korea* 35°12N 128°2E 307 G15
Jinnah Barrage *Pakistan* 32°58N 71°33E 314 C4
Jinotega *Nic.* 13°6N 85°59W 360 D2
Jinotepe *Nic.* 11°50N 86°10W 360 D2
Jinsha Jiang → *China* 28°50N 104°36E 304 D5
Jinxi *China* 40°52N 120°50E 307 D11
Jinxiang *China* 35°5N 116°22E 306 G9
Jinzhou *Hebei, China* 38°2N 115°2E 306 E8
Jinzhou *Liaoning, China* 38°55N 121°42E 307 E11
Jinzhou *Liaoning, China* 41°5N 121°3E 307 D11
Jiparaná → *Brazil* 8°3S 62°52W 364 E6
Jipijapa *Ecuador* 1°0S 80°40W 364 D2
Jiquilpan *Mexico* 19°59N 102°43W 358 D4
Jirisan *S. Korea* 35°20N 127°44E 307 G14
Jishan *China* 35°34N 110°58E 306 G6
Jisr ash Shughūr *Syria* 35°49N 36°18E 316 C3
Jitarning *Australia* 32°48S 117°57E 333 F2
Jitra *Malaysia* 6°16N 100°25E 311 J3
Jiu → *Romania* 43°47N 23°48E 289 F12
Jiudengkou *China* 39°56N 106°40E 306 E4
Jiujiang *China* 29°42N 115°58E 305 D6
Jiulong = Kowloon *China* 22°19N 114°11E 305 G11
Jiutai *China* 44°10N 125°50E 307 B13
Jiuxincheng *China* 39°17N 115°59E 306 E8
Jiwani *Pakistan* 25°1N 61°44E 312 G2
Jixi *China* 45°20N 130°50E 307 B16
Jiyang *China* 37°0N 117°12E 307 F9
Jiyuan *China* 35°7N 112°57E 306 G7
Jīzān *Si. Arabia* 17°0N 42°20E 319 D3
Jize *China* 36°54N 114°56E 306 F8
Jizl, Wādī al → *Si. Arabia* 25°39N 38°25E 316 E3
Jizō-Zaki *Japan* 35°34N 133°20E 303 G6
Jizzakh *Uzbekistan* 40°6N 67°50E 300 E7
Joaçaba *Brazil* 27°5S 51°31W 367 B5
João Pessoa *Brazil* 7°10S 34°52W 365 E12
Joaquín V. González *Argentina* 25°10S 64°0W 366 B3
Jobat *India* 22°25N 74°34E 314 H6
Jodhpur *India* 26°23N 73°8E 314 F5
Jodiya *India* 22°42N 70°18E 314 H4
Joensuu *Finland* 62°37N 29°49E 280 E23
Jōetsu *Japan* 37°12N 138°10E 303 F9
Jofane *Mozam.* 21°15S 34°18E 329 C5
Jogbani *India* 26°25N 87°15E 315 F12
Jõgeva *Estonia* 58°45N 26°24E 281 G22
Jogjakarta = Yogyakarta *Indonesia* 7°49S 110°22E 308 F4
Johannesburg *S. Africa* 26°11S 28°2E 329 D4
Johannesburg *U.S.A.* 35°22N 117°38W 351 K9
Johilla → *India* 23°37N 81°14E 315 H9
John Crow Mts. *Jamaica* 18°5N 76°25W 360 a
John Day *U.S.A.* 44°25N 118°57W 348 D4
John Day → *U.S.A.* 45°44N 120°39W 348 D3
John Day Fossil Beds ⌂ *U.S.A.* 44°33N 119°38W 348 D4
John D'Or Prairie *Canada* 58°30N 115°8W 342 B5
John H. Kerr Res. *U.S.A.* 36°36N 78°18W 357 C15
John o' Groats *U.K.* 58°38N 3°4W 283 C5
Johnnie *U.S.A.* 36°25N 116°5W 351 J10
John's Ra. *Australia* 21°55S 133°23E 334 C1
Johnson *U.S.A.* 44°38N 72°41W 355 B12
Johnson City *Kans., U.S.A.* 37°34N 101°45W 352 G3
Johnson City *N.Y., U.S.A.* 42°7N 75°58W 355 D9
Johnson City *Tenn., U.S.A.* 36°19N 82°21W 357 C13
Johnson City *Tex., U.S.A.* 30°17N 98°25W 356 F5
Johnsonburg *U.S.A.* 41°29N 78°41W 354 E6
Johnsondale *U.S.A.* 35°58N 118°32W 351 K8
Johnsons Crossing *Canada* 60°29N 133°18W 342 A2
Johnston, L. *Australia* 32°25S 120°30E 333 F3
Johnston Falls = Mambilima Falls *Zambia* 10°31S 28°45E 327 E2
Johnston I. *Pac. Oc.* 17°10N 169°8W 337 F11
Johnstone Str. *Canada* 50°28N 126°0W 342 C3
Johnstown *Ireland* 52°45N 7°33W 282 D4
Johnstown *N.Y., U.S.A.* 43°0N 74°22W 355 C10
Johnstown *Ohio, U.S.A.* 40°9N 82°41W 354 F2
Johnstown *Pa., U.S.A.* 40°20N 78°55W 354 F6
Johor, Selat *Asia* 1°28N 103°47E 311 d
Johor Bahru *Malaysia* 1°28N 103°46E 311 d
Jõhvi *Estonia* 59°22N 27°27E 281 G22
Joinville *Brazil* 26°15S 48°55W 367 B6
Joinville I. *Antarctica* 65°0S 55°30W 277 C18
Jojutla *Mexico* 18°37N 99°11W 359 D5
Jokkmokk *Sweden* 66°35N 19°50E 280 C18
Jökulsá á Bru → *Iceland* 65°40N 14°16W 280 D6
Jökulsá á Fjöllum → *Iceland* 66°10N 16°30W 280 C5
Jolfā *Āzarbājān-e Sharqī, Iran* 38°57N 45°38E 316 B5
Jolfā *Eşfahan, Iran* 32°58N 51°37E 317 C6
Joliet *U.S.A.* 41°32N 88°5W 352 E9
Joliette *Canada* 46°3N 73°24W 344 C5
Jolo *Phil.* 6°0N 121°0E 309 C6
Jolon *U.S.A.* 35°58N 121°9W 350 K5
Jombang *Indonesia* 7°33S 112°14E 309 G15

Jonava Lithuania 55°8N 24°12E 281 J21
Jones Sound Canada 76°0N 85°0W 341 B11
Jonesboro Ark., U.S.A. 35°50N 90°42W 357 D9
Jonesboro La., U.S.A. 32°15N 92°43W 356 E8
Joniškis Lithuania 56°13N 23°35E 281 H20
Jönköping Sweden 57°45N 14°8E 281 H16
Jonquière Canada 48°27N 71°14W 345 C5
Joplin U.S.A. 37°6N 94°31W 352 G6
Jora India 26°20N 77°49E 314 F6
Jordan Mont., U.S.A. 47°19N 106°55W 348 C10
Jordan N.Y., U.S.A. 43°4N 76°29W 355 C8
Jordan ■ Asia 31°0N 36°0E 318 E5
Jordan → Asia 31°48N 35°32E 318 D4
Jordan Valley U.S.A. 42°59N 117°3W 348 E5
Jorhat India 26°45N 94°12E 313 F19
Jörn Sweden 65°4N 20°1E 280 D19
Jorong Indonesia 3°58S 114°56E 308 E4
Jørpeland Norway 59°3N 6°1E 281 G12
Jorquera → Chile 28°3S 69°58W 366 B2
Jos Nigeria 9°53N 8°51E 322 G7
José Batlle y Ordóñez Uruguay 33°20S 55°10W 367 C4
Joseph, L. Nfld. & L., Canada 52°45N 65°18W 345 B6
Joseph, L. Ont., Canada 45°10N 79°44W 354 A5
Joseph Bonaparte G. Australia 14°35S 128°50E 332 B4
Joshinath India 30°34N 79°34E 315 D8
Joshinetsu-Kōgen △ Japan 36°42N 138°32E 303 F9
Joshua Tree U.S.A. 34°8N 116°19W 351 L10
Joshua Tree △ U.S.A. 33°55N 116°0W 351 M10
Jost Van Dyke I. Br. Virgin Is. 18°29N 64°47W 361 e
Jostedalsbreen Norway 61°40N 6°59E 280 F12
Jotunheimen Norway 61°35N 8°25E 280 F13
Joubertberge Namibia 18°30S 14°0E 328 B1
Jourdanton U.S.A. 28°55N 98°33W 356 G5
Jovellanos Cuba 22°40N 81°10W 360 B3
Jowhar = Giohar Somali Rep. 2°48N 45°30E 319 G4
Ju Xian China 36°35N 118°20E 307 F10
Juan Aldama Mexico 24°19N 103°21W 358 C4
Juan Bautista Alberdi Argentina 34°26S 61°48W 366 C3
Juan de Fuca, Str of. N. Amer. 48°15N 124°0W 350 B3
Juán de Nova Ind. Oc. 17°3S 43°45E 329 B7
Juan Fernández, Arch. de Pac. Oc. 33°50S 80°0W 362 G2
Juan José Castelli Argentina 25°27S 60°57W 366 B3
Juan L. Lacaze Uruguay 34°26S 57°25W 366 C4
Juankoski Finland 63°3N 28°19E 280 E23
Juárez Argentina 37°40S 59°43W 366 D4
Juárez Mexico 32°20N 115°57W 351 N11
Juárez Coahuila, Mexico 27°37N 100°44W 358 B4
Juárez, Sierra de Mexico 32°0N 116°0W 358 A1
Juàzeiro Brazil 9°30S 40°30W 365 E10
Juàzeiro do Norte Brazil 7°10S 39°18W 365 E11
Juba = Giuba → Somali Rep. 1°30N 42°35E 319 G3
Jûbâ Sudan 4°50N 31°35E 323 H12
Jubany Antarctica 62°30S 58°0W 277 C18
Jubayl Lebanon 34°5N 35°39E 318 A4
Jubbah Si. Arabia 28°2N 40°56E 316 D4
Jubbal India 31°5N 77°40E 314 D7
Jubbulpore = Jabalpur India 23°9N 79°58E 315 H8
Jubilee L. Australia 29°0S 126°50E 333 E4
Juby, C. Morocco 28°0N 12°59W 322 C3
Júcar = Xúquer → Spain 39°5N 0°10W 293 C5
Júcaro Cuba 21°37N 78°51W 360 B4
Juchitán de Zaragoza Mexico 16°26N 95°1W 359 D5
Judea = Har Yehuda Israel 31°35N 34°57E 318 D3
Judith → U.S.A. 47°44N 109°39W 348 C9
Judith, Pt. U.S.A. 41°22N 71°29W 355 E13
Judith Gap U.S.A. 46°41N 109°45W 348 C9
Jugoslavia = Serbia ■ Europe 43°20N 20°0E 295 B9
Juigalpa Nic. 12°6N 85°26W 360 D2
Juiz de Fora Brazil 21°43S 43°19W 367 A7
Jujuy □ Argentina 23°20S 65°40W 366 A2
Julesburg U.S.A. 40°59N 102°16W 348 F12
Juli Peru 16°10S 69°25W 364 G5
Julia Cr. → Australia 20°0S 141°11E 334 C3
Julia Creek Australia 20°39S 141°44E 334 C3
Juliaca Peru 15°25S 70°10W 364 G4
Julian U.S.A. 33°4N 116°38W 351 M10
Julian, L. Canada 54°25N 77°57W 344 B4
Julianatop Suriname 3°40N 56°30W 365 C7
Julianehåb = Qaqortoq Greenland 60°43N 46°0W 276 C5
Julimes Mexico 28°25N 105°27W 358 B3
Jullundur India 31°20N 75°40E 314 D6
Julu China 37°15N 115°2E 306 F8
Jumbo Zimbabwe 17°30S 30°58E 327 F3
Jumbo Pk. U.S.A. 36°12N 114°11W 351 J12
Jumentos Cays Bahamas 23°0N 75°40W 360 B4
Jumilla Spain 38°28N 1°19W 293 C5
Jumla Nepal 29°15N 82°13E 315 E10
Jumna = Yamuna → India 25°30N 81°53E 315 G9
Jumunjin S. Korea 37°55N 128°54E 307 F15
Junagadh India 21°30N 70°30E 314 J4
Junction Tex., U.S.A. 30°29N 99°46W 356 F5
Junction Utah, U.S.A. 38°14N 112°13W 349 G7
Junction B. Australia 11°52S 133°55E 334 A1
Junction City Kans., U.S.A. 39°2N 96°50W 352 F5
Junction City Oreg., U.S.A. 44°13N 123°12W 348 D2
Junction Pt. Australia 11°45S 133°50E 334 A1
Jundah Australia 24°46S 143°2E 334 C3
Jundiaí Brazil 24°30S 47°0W 367 A6
Juneau U.S.A. 58°18N 134°25W 342 B2
Junee Australia 34°53S 147°35E 335 E4
Jungfrau Switz. 46°32N 7°58E 292 C7
Junggar Pendi China 44°30N 86°0E 304 B3
Jungshahi Pakistan 24°52N 67°44E 314 G2
Juniata → U.S.A. 40°24N 77°1W 354 F7
Junín Argentina 34°33S 60°57W 366 C3
Junín de los Andes Argentina 39°45S 71°0W 368 D2
Jūniyah Lebanon 33°59N 35°38E 318 B4
Juntas Chile 28°24S 69°58W 366 B2
Juntura U.S.A. 43°45N 118°5W 348 E4
Jur, Nahr el → Sudan 8°45N 29°15E 323 G11
Jura = Jura, Mts. du Europe 46°40N 6°5E 292 C7
Jura = Schwäbische Alb Germany 48°20N 9°30E 288 D5
Jura U.K. 56°0N 5°50W 283 F3
Jura, Mts. du Europe 46°40N 6°5E 292 C7
Jura, Sd. of U.K. 55°57N 5°45W 283 F3
Jurbarkas Lithuania 55°4N 22°46E 281 J20
Jurien Australia 30°18S 115°2E 333 F2
Jūrmala Latvia 56°58N 23°34E 281 H20
Jurong Singapore 1°19N 103°42E 311 d
Juruá → Brazil 2°37S 65°44W 364 D5
Juruena Brazil 13°0S 58°10W 364 F7
Juruena → Brazil 7°20S 58°3W 364 E7
Juruti Brazil 2°9S 56°4W 365 D7
Justo Daract Argentina 33°52S 65°12W 366 C2
Jutaí → Brazil 2°43S 66°57W 364 D5
Juticalpa Honduras 14°40N 86°12W 360 D2
Jutland = Jylland Denmark 56°25N 9°30E 281 H13
Juuka Finland 63°13N 29°17E 280 E23
Juventud, I. de la Cuba 21°40N 82°40W 360 B3
Jūy Zar Iran 33°50N 46°18E 316 C5
Juye China 35°22N 116°5E 306 G9
Jwaneng Botswana 24°45S 24°50E 325 J4
Jylland Denmark 56°25N 9°30E 281 H13
Jyväskylä Finland 62°14N 25°50E 280 E21

K

K2 Pakistan 35°58N 76°32E 315 B7
Kaakha = Kaka Turkmenistan 37°21N 59°36E 317 B8
Kaap Plateau S. Africa 28°30S 24°0E 328 D3
Kaapkruis Namibia 21°55S 13°57E 328 C1
Kaapstad = Cape Town S. Africa 33°55S 18°22E 328 E2
Kabaena Indonesia 5°15S 122°0E 309 F6
Kabala S. Leone 9°38N 11°37W 322 G3
Kabale Uganda 1°15S 30°0E 326 C3
Kabalo Dem. Rep. of the Congo 6°0S 27°0E 326 D2
Kabambare Dem. Rep. of the Congo 4°41S 27°39E 326 C2
Kabango Dem. Rep. of the Congo 8°35S 28°30E 327 D2
Kabanjahe Indonesia 3°6N 98°30E 308 D1
Kabara Fiji 18°59S 178°56W 331 a
Kabardino-Balkar Republic = Kabardino-Balkaria □ Russia 43°30N 43°30E 291 F7
Kabardino-Balkaria □ Russia 43°30N 43°30E 291 F7
Kabarega Falls = Murchison Falls Uganda 2°15N 31°30E 326 B3
Kabarnet Kenya 0°30N 35°45E 326 B4
Kabasalan Phil. 7°47N 122°44E 309 C6
Kabat Indonesia 8°16S 114°19E 309 J17
Kabin Buri Thailand 13°57N 101°43E 310 F3
Kabinakagami L. Canada 48°54N 84°25W 344 C3
Kabinda Dem. Rep. of the Congo 6°19S 24°20E 324 F4
Kabompo Zambia 13°36S 24°14E 327 E1
Kabompo → Zambia 14°11S 23°11E 325 G4
Kabondo Dem. Rep. of the Congo 8°58S 25°40E 327 D2
Kabongo Dem. Rep. of the Congo 7°22S 25°33E 326 D2
Kabrīt, G. el Egypt 29°42N 33°16E 318 F2
Kabūd Gonbad Iran 37°5N 59°45E 317 B8
Kābul Afghan. 34°28N 69°11E 314 B3
Kābul □ Afghan. 34°30N 69°0E 312 B6
Kābul → Pakistan 33°55N 72°14E 314 C5
Kabunga Dem. Rep. of the Congo 1°38S 28°3E 326 C2
Kaburuang Indonesia 3°50N 126°30E 309 D7
Kabwe Zambia 14°30S 28°29E 327 E2
Kachchh, Gulf of India 22°50N 69°15E 314 H3
Kachchh, Rann of India 24°0N 70°0E 314 H4
Kachchhidhana India 21°44N 78°46E 315 J8
Kachebera Zambia 13°50S 32°50E 327 E3
Kachikau Botswana 18°8S 24°26E 328 B3
Kachin □ Burma 26°0N 97°30E 313 G20
Kachira, L. Uganda 0°40S 31°7E 326 C3
Kachiry Kazakhstan 53°10N 75°50E 300 D8
Kachnara India 23°50N 75°6E 314 H6
Kachot Cambodia 11°30N 103°3E 311 G4
Kaçkar Turkey 40°45N 41°10E 291 F7
Kadan Kyun Burma 12°30N 98°20E 310 F2
Kadanai → Afghan. 31°22N 65°45E 314 D1
Kadavu Fiji 19°0S 178°15E 331 a
Kadavu Passage Fiji 18°45S 178°0E 331 a
Kade Ghana 6°7N 0°56W 322 G5
Kadhimain = Al Kāzimīyah Iraq 33°22N 44°18E 316 C5
Kadi India 23°18N 72°23E 314 H5
Kadina Australia 33°55S 137°43E 335 E2
Kadipur India 26°10N 82°23E 315 F10
Kadirli Turkey 37°23N 36°5E 316 B3
Kadiyevka = Stakhanov Ukraine 48°35N 38°40E 291 E6
Kadoka U.S.A. 43°50N 101°31W 352 D3
Kadoma Zimbabwe 18°20S 29°52E 327 F2
Kâdugli Sudan 11°0N 29°45E 323 F11
Kaduna Nigeria 10°30N 7°21E 322 F7
Kaédi Mauritania 16°9N 13°28W 322 E3
Kaeng Khoï Thailand 14°35N 101°0E 310 E3
Kaeng Kra Chan △ Thailand 12°57N 99°23E 310 F2
Kaeng Tana △ Thailand 15°25N 105°32E 310 E5
Kaesŏng N. Korea 37°58N 126°35E 307 F14
Kāf Si. Arabia 31°25N 37°29E 316 D3
Kafan = Kapan Armenia 39°18N 46°27E 316 B5
Kafanchan Nigeria 9°40N 8°20E 322 G7
Kafinda Zambia 12°32S 30°20E 327 E3
Kafue Zambia 15°46S 28°9E 327 F2
Kafue → Zambia 15°30S 29°0E 325 H5
Kafue △ Zambia 15°12S 25°38E 327 F2
Kafue Flats Zambia 15°40S 27°25E 327 F2
Kafulwe Zambia 9°0S 29°1E 327 D2
Kaga Afghan. 34°14N 70°10E 314 B4
Kaga Bandoro C.A.R. 7°0N 19°10E 324 C3
Kagan Uzbekistan 39°43N 64°33E 300 F7
Kagawa □ Japan 34°15N 134°0E 303 G7
Kagera □ Tanzania 2°0S 31°30E 326 C3
Kagera → Uganda 0°57S 31°47E 326 C3
Kağızman Turkey 40°5N 43°10E 316 B4
Kagoshima Japan 31°35N 130°33E 303 J5
Kagoshima □ Japan 31°30N 130°30E 303 J5
Kagul = Cahul Moldova 45°50N 28°15E 289 F15
Kahak Iran 36°6N 49°46E 317 B6
Kahama Tanzania 4°8S 32°30E 326 C3
Kahan Pakistan 29°18N 68°54E 314 E3
Kahang Malaysia 2°12N 103°32E 311 L4
Kahayan → Indonesia 3°40S 114°0E 308 E4
Kahe Tanzania 3°30S 37°25E 326 C4
Kahemba Dem. Rep. of the Congo 7°18S 18°55E 324 F3
Kahnūj Iran 27°55N 57°40E 317 E8
Kahoka U.S.A. 40°25N 91°44W 352 E8
Kaho'olawe U.S.A. 20°33N 156°37W 346 b
Kahramanmaraş Turkey 37°37N 36°53E 316 B3
Kahului U.S.A. 20°54N 156°28W 346 b
Kahurangi △ N.Z. 41°10S 172°32E 331 D4
Kahuta Pakistan 33°35N 73°24E 314 C5
Kahuzi-Biega △ Dem. Rep. of the Congo 1°50S 27°55E 326 C2
Kai, Kepulauan Indonesia 5°55S 132°45E 309 F8
Kai Besar Indonesia 5°35S 133°0E 309 F8
Kai Is. = Kai, Kepulauan Indonesia 5°55S 132°45E 309 F8
Kai Kecil Indonesia 5°45S 132°40E 309 F8
Kaiapoi N.Z. 43°24S 172°40E 331 E4
Kaieteur Falls Guyana 5°1N 59°10W 364 B7
Kaifeng China 34°48N 114°21E 306 G8
Kaikohe N.Z. 35°25S 173°49E 331 A4
Kaikoura N.Z. 42°25S 173°43E 331 E4
Kailash = Kangrinboqe Feng China 31°0N 81°25E 315 D9
Kailu China 43°38N 121°18E 307 C11
Kailua U.S.A. 19°39N 155°59W 346 b
Kaimana Indonesia 3°39S 133°45E 309 E8
Kaimanawa Mts. N.Z. 39°15S 175°56E 331 C5
Kaimganj India 27°33N 79°24E 315 F8
Kaimur Hills India 24°30N 82°0E 315 G10
Kainab → Namibia 28°32S 19°34E 328 D2
Kainji Res. Nigeria 10°1N 4°40E 322 F6
Kainuu Finland 64°30N 29°7E 280 D23
Kaipara Harbour N.Z. 36°25S 174°14E 331 B5
Kaipokok B. Canada 54°54N 59°47W 345 B8
Kaira India 22°45N 72°50E 314 H5
Kairana India 29°24N 77°15E 314 E7
Kaironi Indonesia 0°47S 133°40E 309 E8
Kairouan Tunisia 35°45N 10°5E 323 A8
Kaiserslautern Germany 49°26N 7°45E 288 D4
Kaitaia N.Z. 35°8S 173°17E 331 A4
Kaitangata N.Z. 46°17S 169°51E 331 G2
Kaithal India 29°48N 76°26E 314 E7
Kaitu → Pakistan 33°10N 70°30E 314 C4
Kaiyuan Liaoning, China 42°28N 124°1E 307 C13
Kaiyuan Yunnan, China 23°40N 103°12E 304 D5
Kajaani Finland 64°17N 27°46E 280 D22
Kajabbi Australia 20°0S 140°1E 334 C3
Kajana = Kajaani Finland 64°17N 27°46E 280 D22
Kajang Malaysia 2°59N 101°48E 311 L3
Kajiado Kenya 1°53S 36°48E 326 C4
Kajo Kaji Sudan 3°58N 31°40E 323 H12
Kaka Turkmenistan 37°21N 59°36E 317 B8
Kakabeka Falls Canada 48°24N 89°37W 344 C2
Kakadu △ Australia 12°0S 132°3E 332 B5
Kakamas S. Africa 28°45S 20°33E 328 D3
Kakamega Kenya 0°20N 34°46E 326 B3
Kakanui Mts. N.Z. 45°10S 170°30E 331 F3
Kakdwip India 21°53N 88°11E 315 J13
Kake Japan 34°36N 132°19E 303 G6
Kake U.S.A. 56°59N 133°57W 342 B2
Kakegawa Japan 34°45N 138°1E 303 G9
Kakeroma-Jima Japan 28°8N 129°14E 303 K4
Kakhovka Ukraine 46°45N 33°30E 291 E5
Kakhovske Vdskh. Ukraine 47°5N 34°0E 291 E5
Kakinada India 16°57N 82°11E 313 L13
Kakisa → Canada 61°3N 118°10W 342 A5
Kakisa L. Canada 60°56N 117°43W 342 A5
Kakogawa Japan 34°46N 134°51E 303 G7
Kakuma Kenya 3°43N 34°52E 326 B3
Kakwa → Canada 54°37N 118°28W 342 C5
Kāl Gūsheh Iran 30°59N 58°12E 317 D8
Kal Safīd Iran 34°52N 47°23E 316 C5
Kalaallit Nunaat = Greenland ☒ N. Amer. 66°0N 45°0W 339 C15
Kalabagh Pakistan 33°0N 71°28E 314 C4
Kalabahi Indonesia 8°13S 124°31E 309 F6
Kalach Russia 50°22N 41°0E 291 D7
Kaladan → Burma 20°20N 93°5E 313 J18
Kaladar Canada 44°37N 77°5W 354 B7
Kalahari Africa 24°0S 21°30E 328 C3
Kalahari Gemsbok △ S. Africa 25°30S 20°30E 328 D3
Kalajoki Finland 64°12N 24°10E 280 D21
Kalakamati Botswana 20°40S 27°25E 329 C4
Kalakan Russia 55°15N 116°45E 301 D12
K'alak'unlun Shank'ou = Karakoram Pass Asia 35°33N 77°50E 315 B7
Kalam Pakistan 35°34N 72°30E 315 B5
Kalama Dem. Rep. of the Congo 2°52S 28°35E 326 C2
Kalama U.S.A. 46°1N 122°51W 350 E4
Kalamata Greece 37°3N 22°10E 295 F10
Kalamazoo U.S.A. 42°17N 85°35W 353 D11
Kalamazoo → U.S.A. 42°40N 86°10W 352 D10
Kalambo Falls Tanzania 8°37S 31°35E 327 D3
Kalan Turkey 39°7N 39°32E 316 B3
Kalannie Australia 30°22S 117°5E 333 F2
Kalāntarī Iran 32°10N 54°8E 317 C7
Kalao Indonesia 7°21S 121°0E 309 F6
Kalaotoa Indonesia 7°20S 121°50E 309 F6
Kalasin Thailand 16°26N 103°30E 310 D4
Kālat Iran 25°29N 59°22E 317 E8
Kalat Pakistan 29°8N 66°31E 312 E5
Kalāteh Iran 36°33N 55°41E 317 B7
Kalāteh-ye Ganj Iran 27°31N 57°55E 317 E8
Kalbā U.A.E. 25°5N 56°22E 317 E8
Kalbarri Australia 27°40S 114°10E 333 E1
Kalbarri △ Australia 27°51S 114°30E 333 E1
Kalce Slovenia 45°54N 14°13E 288 F8
Kale Turkey 37°27N 28°49E 295 F13
Kalegauk Kyun Burma 15°33N 97°35E 310 E1
Kalehe Dem. Rep. of the Congo 2°6S 28°50E 326 C2
Kalema Tanzania 1°12S 31°55E 326 C3
Kalemie Dem. Rep. of the Congo 5°55S 29°9E 326 D2
Kalewa Burma 23°10N 94°15E 313 H19
Kaleybar Iran 38°47N 47°2E 316 B5
Kalgoorlie-Boulder Australia 30°40S 121°22E 333 F3
Kali → India 27°6N 79°55E 315 F8
Kali Sindh → India 25°32N 76°17E 314 G6
Kaliakra, Nos Bulgaria 43°21N 28°30E 295 C13
Kalianda Indonesia 5°50S 105°45E 308 F3
Kalibo Phil. 11°43N 122°22E 309 B6
Kalima Dem. Rep. of the Congo 2°33S 26°32E 326 C2
Kalimantan Indonesia 0°0 114°0E 308 E4
Kalimantan Barat □ Indonesia 0°0 110°30E 308 E4
Kalimantan Selatan □ Indonesia 2°30S 115°30E 308 E5
Kalimantan Tengah □ Indonesia 2°0S 113°30E 308 E4
Kalimantan Timur □ Indonesia 1°30N 116°30E 308 D5
Kálimnos Greece 37°0N 27°0E 295 F12
Kalimpong India 27°4N 88°35E 315 F13
Kaliningrad Russia 54°42N 20°32E 281 J19
Kalinkavichy Belarus 52°12N 29°20E 289 B15
Kalinkovichi = Kalinkavichy Belarus 52°12N 29°20E 289 B15
Kaliro Uganda 0°56N 33°30E 326 B3
Kalispell U.S.A. 48°12N 114°19W 348 B6
Kalisz Poland 51°45N 18°8E 289 C10
Kaliua Tanzania 5°5S 31°48E 326 D3
Kalix = Kalixälven → Sweden 65°50N 23°11E 280 D20
Kalix Sweden 65°53N 23°12E 280 D20
Kalixälven → Sweden 65°50N 23°11E 280 D20
Kalka India 30°46N 76°57E 314 D7
Kalkarindji Australia 17°30S 130°47E 332 C5
Kalkaska U.S.A. 44°44N 85°11W 353 C11
Kalkfeld Namibia 20°57S 16°14E 328 C2
Kalkfontein Botswana 22°4S 20°57E 328 C3
Kalkrand Namibia 24°1S 17°35E 328 C2
Kallavesi Finland 62°58N 27°30E 280 E22
Kallsjön Sweden 63°38N 13°0E 280 E15
Kalmar Sweden 56°40N 16°20E 281 H17
Kalmyk Republic = Kalmykia □ Russia 46°5N 46°1E 291 E8
Kalmykia □ Russia 46°5N 46°1E 291 E8
Kalmykovo Kazakhstan 49°0N 51°47E 291 E9
Kalna India 23°13N 88°25E 315 H13
Kalnai India 22°46N 83°30E 315 H10
Kalocsa Hungary 46°32N 19°0E 289 E10
Kalokhorio Cyprus 34°51N 33°2E 297 E12
Kaloko Dem. Rep. of the Congo 6°47S 25°48E 326 D2
Kalol Gujarat, India 22°37N 73°31E 314 H5
Kalol Gujarat, India 23°15N 72°33E 314 H5
Kalomo Zambia 17°0S 26°30E 327 F2
Kalpi India 26°8N 79°47E 315 F8
Kaltukatjara Australia 24°52S 129°5E 333 D4
Kalu Pakistan 25°5N 67°39E 314 G2
Kaluga Russia 54°35N 36°10E 290 D6
Kalulushi Zambia 12°50S 28°3E 327 E2
Kalumburu Australia 13°55S 126°35E 332 B4
Kalush Ukraine 49°3N 24°23E 289 D13
Kalutara Sri Lanka 6°35N 80°0E 312 R12
Kalya Russia 60°15N 59°59E 290 B10
Kalyan India 19°15N 73°9E 312 K8
Kama Dem. Rep. of the Congo 3°30S 27°5E 326 C2
Kama → Russia 55°45N 52°0E 290 C9
Kamachumu Tanzania 1°37S 31°37E 326 C3
Kamaishi Japan 39°16N 141°53E 302 E10
Kamalia Pakistan 30°44N 72°42E 314 D5
Kaman India 27°39N 77°16E 314 F6
Kamanjab Namibia 19°35S 14°51E 328 B2
Kamapanda Zambia 12°5S 24°0E 327 E1
Kamarān Yemen 15°21N 42°35E 319 D3
Kamativi Zimbabwe 18°20S 27°6E 328 B4
Kambalda West Australia 31°10S 121°37E 333 F3
Kambar Pakistan 27°37N 68°1E 314 F3
Kambarka Russia 56°15N 54°11E 290 C9
Kambolé Zambia 8°47S 30°48E 327 D3
Kambos Cyprus 35°2N 32°44E 297 D11
Kambove Dem. Rep. of the Congo 10°51S 26°33E 327 E2
Kamchatka, Poluostrov Russia 57°0N 160°0E 301 D16
Kamchatka Pen. = Kamchatka, Poluostrov Russia 57°0N 160°0E 301 D16
Kamchiya → Bulgaria 43°4N 27°44E 295 C12
Kame Ruins Zimbabwe 20°7S 28°25E 327 G2
Kamen Russia 53°50N 81°30E 300 D9
Kamen-Rybolov Russia 44°46N 132°2E 302 B6
Kamenjak, Rt Croatia 44°47N 13°55E 288 F7
Kamenka Russia 65°58N 44°0E 290 A7
Kamenka Bugskaya = Kamyanka-Buzka Ukraine 50°8N 24°16E 289 C13
Kamensk Uralskiy Russia 56°25N 62°2E 300 D7
Kamenskoye Russia 62°45N 165°30E 301 C17
Kameoka Japan 35°0N 135°35E 303 G7
Kamet India 30°55N 79°35E 315 D8
Kamiah U.S.A. 46°14N 116°2W 348 C5
Kamieskroon S. Africa 30°9S 17°56E 328 E2
Kamilukuak L. Canada 62°22N 101°40W 343 A8
Kamin-Kashyrskyy Ukraine 51°39N 24°56E 289 C13
Kamina Dem. Rep. of the Congo 8°45S 25°0E 327 D2
Kaminak L. Canada 62°10N 95°0W 343 A10
Kaministiquia Canada 48°32N 89°35W 344 C1
Kaminoyama Japan 38°9N 140°17E 302 E10
Kamiros Greece 36°20N 27°56E 297 C9
Kamituga Dem. Rep. of the Congo 3°2S 28°10E 326 C2
Kamla → India 25°35N 86°36E 315 G12
Kamloops Canada 50°40N 120°20W 342 C4
Kamo Japan 37°39N 139°3E 302 F9
Kamoke Pakistan 32°4N 74°4E 314 C6
Kampala Uganda 0°20N 32°30E 326 B3
Kampar Malaysia 4°18N 101°9E 311 K3
Kampar → Indonesia 0°30N 103°8E 308 D2
Kampen Neths. 52°33N 5°53E 287 B5
Kampene Dem. Rep. of the Congo 3°36S 26°40E 324 E5
Kamphaeng Phet Thailand 16°28N 99°30E 310 D2
Kampolombo, L. Zambia 11°37S 29°42E 327 E2
Kampong Chhnang Cambodia 12°20N 104°35E 311 F5
Kampong Pengerang Malaysia 1°22N 104°7E 311 d
Kampong Punggai Malaysia 1°27N 104°18E 311 d
Kampong Saom Cambodia 10°38N 103°30E 311 G4
Kampong Saom, Chaak Cambodia 10°50N 103°32E 311 G4
Kampong Tanjong Langsat Malaysia 1°28N 104°1E 311 d
Kampong Telok Ramunia Malaysia 1°22N 104°15E 311 d
Kampong To Thailand 6°3N 101°13E 311 J3
Kampot Cambodia 10°36N 104°10E 311 G5
Kampuchea = Cambodia ■ Asia 12°15N 105°0E 310 F5
Kampung Air Putih Malaysia 4°15N 103°10E 311 K4
Kampung Jerangau Malaysia 4°50N 103°10E 311 K4
Kampung Raja Malaysia 5°45N 102°35E 311 K4
Kampungbaru = Tolitoli Indonesia 1°5N 120°50E 309 D6
Kamrau, Teluk Indonesia 3°30S 133°36E 309 E8
Kamsack Canada 51°34N 101°54W 343 C8
Kamskoye Vdkhr. Russia 58°41N 56°7E 290 C10
Kamuchawie L. Canada 56°18N 101°59W 343 B8
Kamuela U.S.A. 20°1N 155°41W 346 b
Kamui-Misaki Japan 43°20N 140°21E 302 C10
Kamyanets-Podilskyy Ukraine 48°45N 26°40E 289 D14
Kamyanka-Buzka Ukraine 50°8N 24°16E 289 C13
Kāmyārān Iran 34°47N 46°56E 316 C5
Kamyshin Russia 50°10N 45°24E 291 D8
Kanaaupscow Canada 53°39N 77°9W 341 D12
Kanaaupscow → Canada 54°2N 76°30W 344 B4
Kanab U.S.A. 37°3N 112°32W 349 H7
Kanab Cr. → U.S.A. 36°24N 112°38W 349 H7
Kanacea Lau Group, Fiji 17°15S 179°6W 331 a
Kanacea Taveuni, Fiji 16°59S 179°56E 331 a
Kanagi Japan 40°54N 140°27E 302 D10
Kanairiktok → Canada 55°2N 60°18W 345 A7
Kananga Dem. Rep. of the Congo 5°55S 22°18E 324 F4
Kanash Russia 55°30N 47°32E 290 C8
Kanaskat U.S.A. 47°19N 121°54W 350 C5
Kanastraíon, Ákra = Paliouri, Akra Greece 39°57N 23°45E 295 E10
Kanawha → U.S.A. 38°50N 82°9W 353 F12
Kanazawa Japan 36°30N 136°38E 303 F8
Kanchanaburi Thailand 14°2N 99°31E 310 E2
Kanchenjunga Nepal 27°50N 88°10E 315 F13
Kanchipuram India 12°52N 79°45E 312 N11
Kandaghat India 30°59N 77°7E 314 D7
Kandahār Afghan. 31°32N 65°43E 312 D4
Kandahār □ Afghan. 31°0N 65°0E 312 D4
Kandalaksha Russia 67°9N 32°30E 280 C25
Kandalakshskiy Zaliv Russia 66°0N 35°0E 290 A6

Kandangan Indonesia 2°50S 115°20E 308 E5
Kandanghaur Indonesia 6°21S 108°6E 309 G13
Kandanos Greece 35°19N 23°44E 297 D5
Kandavu = Kadavu Fiji 19°0S 178°15E 331 a
Kandavu Passage = Kadavu Passage Fiji 18°45S 178°0E 331 a
Kandhkot Pakistan 28°16N 69°8E 314 E3
Kandhla India 29°18N 77°19E 314 E7
Kandi Benin 11°7N 2°55E 322 F6
Kandi India 23°58N 88°5E 315 H13
Kandiaro Pakistan 27°4N 68°13E 314 F3
Kandla India 23°0N 70°10E 314 H4
Kandos Australia 32°45S 149°58E 335 E4
Kandreho Madag. 17°29S 46°6E 329 B8
Kandy Sri Lanka 7°18N 80°43E 312 R12
Kane U.S.A. 41°40N 78°49W 354 E6
Kane Basin Greenland 79°1N 70°0W 338 B12
Kāne'ohe U.S.A. 21°25N 157°48W 346 b
Kang Botswana 23°41S 22°50E 328 C3
Kang Krung △ Thailand 9°30N 98°50E 311 H2
Kangān Fārs, Iran 27°50N 52°3E 317 E7
Kangān Hormozgān, Iran 25°48N 57°28E 317 E8
Kangar Malaysia 6°27N 100°12E 311 J3
Kangaroo I. Australia 35°45S 137°0E 335 F2
Kangaroo Mts. Australia 23°29S 141°51E 334 C3
Kangasala Finland 61°28N 24°4E 280 F21
Kangāvar Iran 34°40N 48°0E 317 C6
Kangdong N. Korea 39°9N 126°5E 307 E14
Kangean, Kepulauan Indonesia 6°55S 115°23E 308 F5
Kangean Is. = Kangean, Kepulauan Indonesia 6°55S 115°23E 308 F5
Kanggye N. Korea 41°0N 126°35E 307 D14
Kangikajik Greenland 70°7N 22°0W 276 B6
Kangiqliniq = Rankin Inlet Canada 62°30N 93°0W 340 C10
Kangiqsualujjuaq Canada 58°30N 65°59W 341 D13
Kangiqsujuaq Canada 61°30N 72°0W 341 C12
Kangiqtugaapik = Clyde River Canada 70°30N 68°30W 341 B13
Kangirsuk Canada 60°0N 70°0W 341 D13
Kangkar Chemaran Malaysia 1°34N 104°12E 311 d
Kangkar Sungai Tiram Malaysia 1°35N 103°55E 311 d
Kangkar Teberau Malaysia 1°32N 103°51E 311 d
Kangping China 42°43N 123°18E 307 C12
Kangra India 32°6N 76°16E 314 C7
Kangrinboqe Feng China 31°0N 81°25E 315 D9
Kangto China 27°50N 92°35E 313 F18
Kanha △ India 22°15N 80°40E 315 H9
Kanhar → India 24°28N 83°8E 315 G10
Kaniama Dem. Rep. of the Congo 7°30S 24°12E 326 D1
Kaniapiskau = Caniapiscau → Canada 56°40N 69°30W 345 A6
Kaniapiskau, L. = Caniapiscau, L. Canada 54°10N 69°55W 345 B6
Kanin, Poluostrov Russia 68°0N 45°0E 290 A8
Kanin Nos, Mys Russia 68°39N 43°32E 290 A7
Kanin Pen. = Kanin, Poluostrov Russia 68°0N 45°0E 290 A8
Kaniva Australia 36°22S 141°18E 335 F3
Kanjut Sar Pakistan 36°7N 75°25E 315 A6
Kankaanpää Finland 61°44N 22°50E 280 F20
Kankakee U.S.A. 41°7N 87°52W 352 E10
Kankakee → U.S.A. 41°23N 88°15W 352 E9
Kankan Guinea 10°23N 9°15W 322 F4
Kankendy = Xankändi Azerbaijan 39°52N 46°49E 316 B5
Kanker India 20°10N 81°40E 313 J12
Kankroli India 25°4N 73°53E 314 G5
Kannapolis U.S.A. 35°30N 80°37W 357 D14
Kannauj India 27°3N 79°56E 315 F8
Kannod India 22°45N 76°40E 312 H10
Kano Nigeria 12°2N 8°30E 322 F7
Kan'onji Japan 34°7N 133°39E 303 G6
Kanowit Malaysia 2°14N 112°20E 308 D4
Kanoya Japan 31°25N 130°50E 303 J5
Kanpetlet Burma 21°10N 93°59E 313 J18
Kanpur India 26°28N 80°20E 315 F9
Kansas □ U.S.A. 38°30N 99°0W 352 F4
Kansas → U.S.A. 39°7N 94°37W 352 F6
Kansas City Kans., U.S.A. 39°7N 94°38W 352 F6
Kansas City Mo., U.S.A. 39°6N 94°35W 352 F6
Kansenia Dem. Rep. of the Congo 10°20S 26°0E 327 E2
Kansk Russia 56°20N 95°37E 301 D10
Kansu = Gansu □ China 36°0N 104°0E 306 G3
Kantaphor India 22°35N 76°34E 314 H7
Kantharalak Thailand 14°39N 104°39E 310 E5
Kantli → India 28°20N 75°30E 314 E6
Kantō □ Japan 36°15N 139°30E 303 F9
Kantō-Sanchi Japan 35°59N 138°50E 303 G9
Kanturk Ireland 52°11N 8°54W 282 D3
Kanuma Japan 36°34N 139°42E 303 F9
Kanus Namibia 27°50S 18°39E 328 D2
Kanye Botswana 24°55S 25°28E 328 C4
Kanzenze Dem. Rep. of the Congo 10°30S 25°12E 327 E2
Kanzi, Ras Tanzania 7°1S 39°33E 326 D4
Kao Tonga 19°40S 175°1W 331 c
Kao Phara Thailand 8°3N 98°22E 311 a
Kaohsiung Taiwan 22°35N 120°16E 305 D7
Kaokoveld Namibia 19°15S 14°30E 328 B1
Kaolack Senegal 14°5N 16°8W 322 F2
Kaoshan China 44°38N 124°50E 307 B13
Kapaa U.S.A. 22°5N 159°19W 346 b
Kapadvanj India 23°5N 73°0E 314 H5
Kapan Armenia 39°18N 46°27E 316 B5
Kapanga Dem. Rep. of the Congo 8°30S 22°40E 324 F4
Kapchagai = Qapshaghay Kazakhstan 43°51N 77°14E 300 E8
Kapedo Kenya 1°10N 36°6E 326 B4
Kapela = Velika Kapela Croatia 45°10N 15°5E 288 F8
Kapema Dem. Rep. of the Congo 10°45S 28°22E 327 E2
Kapenguria Kenya 1°14N 35°7E 326 B4
Kapfenberg Austria 47°26N 15°18E 288 E8
Kapiri Mposhi Zambia 13°59S 28°43E 327 E2
Kāpīsā □ Afghan. 35°0N 69°20E 312 B6
Kapiskau → Canada 52°47N 81°55W 344 B3
Kapit Malaysia 2°0N 112°55E 308 D4
Kapiti I. N.Z. 40°50S 174°56E 331 D5
Kaplan U.S.A. 30°0N 92°17W 356 F8
Kapoe Thailand 9°34N 98°32E 311 H2
Kapoeta Sudan 4°50N 33°35E 323 H12
Kaposvár Hungary 46°25N 17°47E 289 E9
Kapowsin U.S.A. 46°59N 122°13W 350 D4
Kapps Namibia 22°32S 17°18E 328 C2
Kapsabet Kenya 0°12N 35°6E 326 B4
Kapsan N. Korea 41°4N 128°19E 307 D15
Kapsukas = Marijampolė Lithuania 54°33N 23°19E 281 J20
Kaptai L. Bangla. 22°40N 92°20E 313 H18
Kapuas → Indonesia 0°25S 109°20E 308 E3
Kapuas Hulu, Pegunungan Malaysia 1°30N 113°30E 308 D4
Kapuas Hulu Ra. = Kapuas Hulu, Pegunungan Malaysia 1°30N 113°30E 308 D4
Kapulo Dem. Rep. of the Congo 8°18S 29°15E 327 D2
Kapunda Australia 34°20S 138°56E 335 E2
Kapuni N.Z. 39°29S 174°8E 331 C5
Kapurthala India 31°23N 75°25E 314 D6
Kapuskasing Canada 49°25N 82°30W 344 C3
Kapuskasing → Canada 49°49N 82°0W 344 C3
Kaputar, Mt. Australia 30°15S 150°10E 335 E5
Kaputir Kenya 2°5N 35°28E 326 B4
Kara Russia 69°10N 65°0E 300 C7
Kara Bogaz Gol, Zaliv = Garabogazköl Aylagy Turkmenistan 41°0N 53°30E 291 F9
Kara-Kala = Garrygala Turkmenistan 38°31N 56°29E 317 B8
Kara Kalpak Republic = Qoraqalpoghistan □ Uzbekistan 43°0N 58°0E 300 E6
Kara Kum = Garagum Turkmenistan 39°30N 60°0E 317 B8
Kara Sea Russia 75°0N 70°0E 300 B7
Karabiğa Turkey 40°23N 27°17E 295 D12
Karabük Turkey 41°12N 32°37E 291 F5
Karaburun Turkey 38°41N 26°28E 295 E12
Karabutak = Qarabutaq Kazakhstan 49°59N 60°14E 300 E7
Karacabey Turkey 40°12N 28°21E 295 D13
Karacasu Turkey 37°43N 28°35E 295 F13
Karachey-Cherkessia □ Russia 43°40N 41°30E 291 F7
Karachi Pakistan 24°50N 67°0E 314 G2
Karad India 17°15N 74°10E 312 L9
Karaganda = Qaraghandy Kazakhstan 49°50N 73°10E 300 E8
Karagayly = Qaraghayly Kazakhstan 49°26N 76°0E 300 E8
Karaginskiy, Ostrov Russia 58°45N 164°0E 301 D17
Karagiye, Vpadina Kazakhstan 43°27N 51°45E 291 F9
Karagiye Depression = Karagiye, Vpadina Kazakhstan 43°27N 51°45E 291 F9
Karagola Road India 25°29N 87°23E 315 G12
Karaikal India 10°59N 79°50E 312 P11
Karaikkudi India 10°5N 78°45E 312 P11
Karaj Iran 35°48N 51°0E 317 C6
Karak Malaysia 3°25N 102°2E 311 L4
Karakalpakstan = Qoraqalpoghistan □ Uzbekistan 43°0N 58°0E 300 E6
Karakelong Indonesia 4°35N 126°50E 309 D7
Karakitang Indonesia 3°14N 125°28E 309 D7
Karakol Kyrgyzstan 42°30N 78°20E 300 E8
Karakoram Pass Asia 35°33N 77°50E 315 B7
Karakoram Ra. Pakistan 35°30N 77°0E 315 B7
Karakuwisa Namibia 18°56S 19°40E 328 B2
Karalon Russia 57°5N 115°50E 301 D12
Karama Jordan 31°57N 35°35E 318 D4
Karaman Turkey 37°14N 33°13E 316 B2
Karamay China 45°30N 84°58E 304 B3
Karambu Indonesia 3°53S 116°6E 308 E5
Karamea Bight N.Z. 41°22S 171°40E 331 D3
Karamnasa → India 25°31N 83°52E 315 G10
Karān Si. Arabia 27°43N 49°49E 317 E6
Karand Iran 34°16N 46°15E 316 C5
Karanganyar Indonesia 7°38S 109°37E 309 G13
Karangasem Indonesia 8°27S 115°37E 309 J18
Karanjia India 21°47N 85°58E 315 J11
Karasburg Namibia 28°0S 18°44E 328 D2
Karasino Russia 66°50N 86°50E 300 C9
Karasjok Norway 69°27N 25°30E 280 B21
Karasuk Russia 53°44N 78°2E 300 D8
Karasuyama Japan 36°39N 140°9E 303 F10
Karatau, Khrebet = Qarataū Kazakhstan 43°30N 69°30E 300 E7
Karatax Shan China 35°57N 81°0E 304 C3
Karatsu Japan 33°26N 129°58E 303 H5
Karaul Russia 70°6N 82°15E 300 B9
Karauli India 26°30N 77°4E 314 F7
Karavostasi Cyprus 35°8N 32°50E 297 D11
Karawang Indonesia 6°30S 107°15E 309 G12
Karawanken Europe 46°30N 14°40E 288 E8
Karayazı Turkey 39°41N 42°9E 291 G7
Karazhal = Qarazhal Kazakhstan 48°2N 70°49E 300 E8
Karbalā' Iraq 32°36N 44°3E 316 C5
Karcag Hungary 47°19N 20°57E 289 E11
Karcha → Pakistan 34°45N 76°10E 315 B7
Karchana India 25°17N 81°56E 315 G9
Karditsa Greece 39°23N 21°54E 295 E9
Kärdla Estonia 59°0N 22°45E 281 G20
Kareeberge S. Africa 30°59S 21°50E 328 E3
Kareha → India 25°44N 86°21E 315 G12
Kareima Sudan 18°30N 31°49E 323 E12
Karelia □ Russia 65°30N 32°30E 280 D25
Karelian Republic = Karelia □ Russia 65°30N 32°30E 280 D25
Karera India 25°32N 78°9E 314 G8
Karevāndar Iran 27°53N 60°44E 317 E9
Kargasok Russia 59°3N 80°53E 300 D9
Kargat Russia 55°10N 80°15E 300 D9
Kargi Kenya 2°31N 37°34E 326 B4
Kargil India 34°32N 76°12E 315 B7
Kargopol Russia 61°30N 38°58E 290 B6
Karhal India 27°1N 78°57E 315 F8
Karīān Iran 26°57N 57°14E 317 E8
Karianga Madag. 22°25S 47°22E 329 C8
Kariba Zimbabwe 16°28S 28°50E 327 F2
Kariba, L. Zimbabwe 16°40S 28°25E 327 F2
Kariba Dam Zimbabwe 16°30S 28°35E 327 F2
Kariba Gorge Zambia 16°30S 28°50E 327 F2
Karibib Namibia 22°0S 15°56E 328 C2
Karijini △ Australia 23°8S 118°15E 332 D2
Karimata, Kepulauan Indonesia 1°25S 109°0E 308 E3
Karimata, Selat Indonesia 2°0S 108°40E 308 E3
Karimata Is. = Karimata, Kepulauan Indonesia 1°25S 109°0E 308 E3
Karimnagar India 18°26N 79°10E 312 K11
Karimun Kecil, Pulau Indonesia 1°8N 103°22E 311 d
Karimunjawa, Kepulauan Indonesia 5°50S 110°30E 308 F4
Karin Somali Rep. 10°50N 45°52E 319 E4
Karīt Iran 33°29N 56°55E 317 C8
Kariya Japan 34°58N 137°1E 303 G8
Kariyangwe Zimbabwe 18°0S 27°38E 329 B4
Karjala Finland 62°0N 30°25E 280 F24
Karkaralinsk = Qarqaraly Kazakhstan 49°26N 75°30E 300 E8
Karkheh → Iran 31°2N 47°29E 316 D5
Karkinitska Zatoka Ukraine 45°56N 33°0E 291 E5
Karkinitskiy Zaliv = Karkinitska Zatoka Ukraine 45°56N 33°0E 291 E5
Karkuk = Kirkūk Iraq 35°30N 44°21E 316 C5
Karleby = Kokkola Finland 63°50N 23°8E 280 E20
Karlovac Croatia 45°31N 15°36E 288 F8
Karlovo Bulgaria 42°38N 24°47E 295 C11
Karlovy Vary Czech Rep. 50°13N 12°51E 288 C7
Karlsbad = Karlovy Vary Czech Rep. 50°13N 12°51E 288 C7
Karlshamn Sweden 56°10N 14°51E 281 H16
Karlskoga Sweden 59°28N 14°33E 281 G16
Karlskrona Sweden 56°10N 15°35E 281 H16
Karlsruhe Germany 49°0N 8°23E 288 D5
Karlstad Sweden 59°23N 13°30E 281 G15
Karlstad U.S.A. 48°35N 96°31W 352 A5
Karmi'el Israel 32°55N 35°18E 318 C4
Karnak Egypt 25°43N 32°39E 323 C12
Karnal India 29°42N 77°2E 314 E7
Karnali → Nepal 28°45N 81°16E 315 E9
Karnaphuli Res. = Kaptai L. Bangla. 22°40N 92°20E 313 H18
Karnaprayag India 30°16N 79°15E 315 D8
Karnataka □ India 13°15N 77°0E 312 N10
Karnes City U.S.A. 28°53N 97°54W 356 G6
Karnische Alpen Europe 46°36N 13°0E 288 E7
Kärnten □ Austria 46°52N 13°30E 288 E8
Karoi Zimbabwe 16°48S 29°45E 327 F2
Karon, Ao Thailand 7°51N 98°17E 311 a
Karonga Malawi 9°57S 33°55E 327 D3
Karoo △ S. Africa 32°18S 22°27E 328 E3
Karoonda Australia 35°1S 139°59E 335 F2
Karor Pakistan 31°15N 70°59E 314 D4
Karora Sudan 17°44N 38°15E 323 E13
Karpasia Cyprus 35°32N 34°15E 297 D13
Karpathos Greece 35°37N 27°10E 295 G12
Karpinsk Russia 59°45N 60°1E 290 C11
Karpogory Russia 64°0N 44°27E 290 B7
Karpuz Burnu = Apostolos Andreas, C. Cyprus 35°42N 34°35E 297 D13
Karratha Australia 20°53S 116°40E 332 D2
Kars Turkey 40°40N 43°5E 291 F7
Karsakpay Kazakhstan 47°55N 66°40E 300 E7
Karshi = Qarshi Uzbekistan 38°53N 65°48E 300 F7
Karsiyang India 26°56N 88°18E 315 F13
Karsog India 31°23N 77°12E 314 D7
Kartala Comoros Is. 11°45S 43°21E 325 a
Kartaly Russia 53°3N 60°40E 300 D7
Kartapur India 31°27N 75°32E 314 D6
Karthaus U.S.A. 41°8N 78°9W 354 E6
Karufa Indonesia 3°50S 133°20E 309 E8
Karuma ⌂ Uganda 2°5N 32°15E 326 B3
Karumba Australia 17°31S 140°50E 334 B3
Karumo Tanzania 2°25S 32°50E 326 C3
Karumwa Tanzania 3°12S 32°38E 326 C3
Kārūn → Iran 30°26N 48°10E 317 D6
Karungu Kenya 0°50S 34°10E 326 C3
Karviná Czech Rep. 49°53N 18°31E 289 D10
Karwan → India 27°26N 78°4E 314 F8
Karwar India 14°55N 74°13E 312 M9
Karwi India 25°12N 80°57E 315 G9
Kasache Malawi 13°25S 34°20E 327 E3
Kasai → Dem. Rep. of the Congo 3°30S 16°10E 324 E3
Kasai-Oriental □ Dem. Rep. of the Congo 5°0S 24°30E 326 D1
Kasaji Dem. Rep. of the Congo 10°25S 23°27E 327 E1
Kasama Zambia 10°16S 31°9E 327 E3
Kasan N. Korea 41°18N 126°55E 307 D14
Kasandra Kolpos Greece 40°5N 23°30E 295 D10
Kasane Namibia 17°34S 24°50E 328 B3
Kasanga Tanzania 8°30S 31°10E 327 D3
Kasanka △ Zambia 11°34S 30°15E 327 E3
Kasaragod India 12°30N 74°58E 312 N9
Kasba L. Canada 60°20N 102°10W 343 A8
Kāseh Garān Iran 34°5N 46°2E 316 C5
Kasempa Zambia 13°30S 25°44E 327 E2
Kasenga Dem. Rep. of the Congo 10°20S 28°45E 327 E2
Kasese Uganda 0°13N 30°3E 326 B3
Kasewa Zambia 14°28S 28°53E 327 E2
Kasganj India 27°48N 78°42E 315 F8
Kashabowie Canada 48°40N 90°26W 344 C1
Kashaf Iran 35°58N 61°7E 317 C9
Kāshān Iran 34°5N 51°30E 317 C6
Kashechewan Canada 52°18N 81°37W 344 B3
Kashgar = Kashi China 39°30N 76°2E 304 C2
Kashi China 39°30N 76°2E 304 C2
Kashimbo Dem. Rep. of the Congo 11°12S 26°19E 327 E2
Kashipur India 29°15N 79°0E 315 E8
Kashiwazaki Japan 37°22N 138°33E 303 F9
Kashk-e Kohneh Afghan. 34°55N 62°30E 312 B3
Kashkū'īyeh Iran 30°31N 55°40E 317 D7
Kāshmar Iran 35°16N 58°26E 317 C8
Kashmir Asia 34°0N 76°0E 315 C7
Kashmor Pakistan 28°28N 69°32E 314 E3
Kashun Noerh = Gaxun Nur China 42°22N 100°30E 304 B5
Kasiari India 22°8N 87°14E 315 H12
Kasimov Russia 54°55N 41°20E 290 D7
Kasinge Dem. Rep. of the Congo 6°15S 26°58E 326 D2
Kasiruta Indonesia 0°25S 127°12E 309 E7
Kaskaskia → U.S.A. 37°58N 89°57W 352 G9
Kaskattama → Canada 57°3N 90°4W 343 B10
Kaskinen Finland 62°22N 21°15E 280 E19
Kaskö = Kaskinen Finland 62°22N 21°15E 280 E19
Kaslo Canada 49°55N 116°55W 342 D5
Kasmere L. Canada 59°34N 101°10W 343 B8
Kasongo Dem. Rep. of the Congo 4°30S 26°33E 326 C2
Kasongo Lunda Dem. Rep. of the Congo 6°35S 16°49E 324 F3
Kasos Greece 35°20N 26°55E 295 G12
Kassalâ Sudan 15°30N 36°0E 323 E13
Kassel Germany 51°18N 9°26E 288 C5
Kassiopi Greece 39°48N 19°53E 297 A3
Kasson U.S.A. 44°2N 92°45W 352 C7
Kastamonu Turkey 41°25N 33°43E 291 F5
Kasteli Greece 35°29N 23°38E 297 D5
Kastelli Greece 35°12N 25°20E 297 D7
Kasterlee Belgium 51°15N 4°59E 287 C4
Kastoria Greece 40°30N 21°19E 295 D9
Kasulu Tanzania 4°37S 30°5E 326 C3
Kasumi Japan 35°38N 134°38E 303 G7
Kasungu Malawi 13°0S 33°29E 327 E3
Kasungu △ Malawi 12°53S 33°9E 327 E3
Kasur Pakistan 31°5N 74°25E 314 D6
Kata Archanes Greece 35°15N 25°10E 297 D7
Kata Tjuta Australia 25°20S 130°50E 333 E5
Kataba Zambia 16°5S 25°10E 327 F2
Katahdin, Mt. U.S.A. 45°54N 68°56W 353 C19
Katako Kombe Dem. Rep. of the Congo 3°25S 24°20E 326 C1
Katale Tanzania 4°52S 31°7E 326 C3
Katanda Katanga, Dem. Rep. of the Congo 7°52S 24°13E 326 D1
Katanda Nord-Kivu, Dem. Rep. of the Congo 0°55S 29°21E 326 C2
Katanga □ Dem. Rep. of the Congo 8°0S 25°0E 326 D2
Katangi India 21°56N 79°50E 312 J11
Katanning Australia 33°40S 117°33E 333 F2
Katavi △ Tanzania 6°51S 31°3E 326 D3
Katavi Swamp Tanzania 6°50S 31°10E 326 D3
Katerini Greece 40°18N 22°37E 295 D10
Katghora India 22°30N 82°33E 315 H10
Katha Burma 24°10N 96°30E 313 G20
Katherîna, Gebel Egypt 28°30N 33°57E 316 D2
Katherine Australia 14°27S 132°20E 332 B5
Katherine Gorge Australia 14°18S 132°28E 332 B5
Kathi India 21°47N 74°3E 314 J6
Kathiawar India 22°20N 71°0E 314 H4
Kathikas Cyprus 34°55N 32°25E 297 E11
Kathmandu = Katmandu Nepal 27°45N 85°20E 315 F11
Kathua India 32°23N 75°34E 314 C6
Katihar India 25°34N 87°36E 315 G12
Katima Mulilo Zambia 17°28S 24°13E 328 B3
Katimbira Malawi 12°40S 34°0E 327 E3
Katingan = Mendawai → Indonesia 3°30S 113°0E 308 E4
Katiola Ivory C. 8°10N 5°10W 322 G4
Katmandu Nepal 27°45N 85°20E 315 F11
Katni India 23°51N 80°24E 315 H9
Kato Chorio Greece 35°3N 25°47E 297 D7
Kato Korakiana Greece 39°42N 19°45E 297 A3
Káto Pyrgos Cyprus 35°11N 32°41E 297 D11
Katompe Dem. Rep. of the Congo 6°2S 26°23E 326 D2
Katong Singapore 1°18N 103°53E 311 d
Katonga → Uganda 0°34N 31°50E 326 B3
Katoomba Australia 33°41S 150°19E 335 E5
Katowice Poland 50°17N 19°5E 289 C10
Katrine, L. U.K. 56°15N 4°30W 283 E4
Katrineholm Sweden 59°9N 16°12E 281 G17
Katsepe Madag. 15°45S 46°15E 329 B8
Katsina Nigeria 13°0N 7°32E 322 F7
Katsumoto Japan 33°51N 129°42E 303 H4
Katsuura Japan 35°10N 140°20E 303 G10
Katsuyama Japan 36°3N 136°30E 303 F8
Kattavia Greece 35°57N 27°46E 297 D9
Kattegat Denmark 56°40N 11°20E 281 H14
Katumba Dem. Rep. of the Congo 7°40S 25°17E 326 D2
Katwa India 23°30N 88°5E 315 H13
Katwijk Neths. 52°12N 4°24E 287 B4
Kaua'i U.S.A. 22°3N 159°30W 346 b
Kauai Channel U.S.A. 21°45N 158°50W 346 b
Kaudom ⌂ Namibia 18°45S 20°51E 328 B3
Kaufman U.S.A. 32°35N 96°19W 356 E6
Kauhajoki Finland 62°25N 22°10E 280 E20
Kaukauna U.S.A. 44°17N 88°17W 352 C9
Kaukauveld Namibia 20°0S 20°15E 328 C3
Kaunakakai U.S.A. 21°6N 157°1W 346 b
Kaunas Lithuania 54°54N 23°54E 281 J20
Kaunia Bangla. 25°46N 89°26E 315 G13
Kautokeino Norway 69°0N 23°4E 280 B20
Kauwapur India 27°31N 82°18E 315 F10
Kavacha Russia 60°16N 169°51E 301 C17
Kavala Greece 40°57N 24°28E 295 D11
Kavalerovo Russia 44°15N 135°4E 302 B7
Kavali India 14°55N 80°1E 312 M12
Kavār Iran 29°11N 52°44E 317 D7
Kavi India 22°12N 72°38E 314 H5
Kavimba Botswana 18°2S 24°38E 328 B3
Kavīr, Dasht-e Iran 34°30N 55°0E 317 C7
Kavīr △ Iran 34°40N 52°0E 317 C7
Kavos Greece 39°23N 20°3E 297 B4
Kaw Fr. Guiana 4°30N 52°15W 365 C8
Kawagama L. Canada 45°18N 78°45W 354 A6
Kawagoe Japan 35°55N 139°29E 303 G9
Kawaguchi Japan 35°52N 139°45E 303 G9
Kawambwa Zambia 9°48S 29°3E 327 D2
Kawanoe Japan 34°1N 133°34E 303 G6
Kawardha India 22°0N 81°17E 315 J9
Kawasaki Japan 35°31N 139°43E 303 G9
Kawasi Indonesia 1°38S 127°28E 309 E7
Kawawachikamach Canada 54°48N 66°50W 345 B6
Kawerau N.Z. 38°7S 176°42E 331 C6
Kawhia N.Z. 38°4S 174°49E 331 C5
Kawhia Harbour N.Z. 38°5S 174°51E 331 C5
Kawio, Kepulauan Indonesia 4°30N 125°30E 309 D7
Kawthaung Burma 10°5N 98°36E 311 H2
Kawthoolei = Kayin □ Burma 18°0N 97°30E 313 L20
Kawthule = Kayin □ Burma 18°0N 97°30E 313 L20
Kaya Burkina Faso 13°4N 1°10W 322 F5
Kayah □ Burma 19°15N 97°15E 313 K20
Kayan → Indonesia 2°55N 117°35E 308 D5
Kaycee U.S.A. 43°43N 106°38W 348 E10
Kayeli Indonesia 3°20S 127°10E 309 E7
Kayenta U.S.A. 36°44N 110°15W 349 H8
Kayes Mali 14°25N 11°30W 322 F3
Kayin □ Burma 18°0N 97°30E 313 L20
Kayoa Indonesia 0°1N 127°28E 309 D7
Kayomba Zambia 13°11S 24°2E 327 E1
Kayseri Turkey 38°45N 35°30E 316 B2
Kaysville U.S.A. 41°2N 111°56W 348 F8
Kazachye Russia 70°52N 135°58E 301 B14
Kazakhstan ■ Asia 50°0N 70°0E 300 E7
Kazan Russia 55°50N 49°10E 290 C8
Kazan → Canada 64°2N 95°29W 343 A9
Kazan-Rettō Pac. Oc. 25°0N 141°0E 336 E6
Kazanlŭk Bulgaria 42°38N 25°20E 295 C11
Kazatin = Kozyatyn Ukraine 49°45N 28°50E 289 D15
Kāzerūn Iran 29°38N 51°40E 317 D6
Kazi Magomed = Qazimämmäd Azerbaijan 40°3N 49°0E 317 A6
Kazuma Pan △ Zimbabwe 18°20S 25°48E 327 F2
Kazuno Japan 40°10N 140°45E 302 D10
Kazym → Russia 63°54N 65°50E 300 C7
Kea Greece 37°35N 24°22E 295 F11
Keady U.K. 54°15N 6°42W 282 B5
Kearney U.S.A. 40°42N 99°5W 352 E4
Kearny U.S.A. 33°3N 110°55W 349 K8
Kearsarge, Mt. U.S.A. 43°22N 71°50W 355 C13
Keban Turkey 38°50N 38°50E 291 G6
Keban Barajı Turkey 38°41N 38°33E 316 B3
Kebnekaise Sweden 67°53N 18°33E 280 C18
Kebri Dehar Ethiopia 6°45N 44°17E 319 F3
Kebumen Indonesia 7°42S 109°40E 309 G13
Kechika → Canada 59°41N 127°12W 342 B3
Kecskemét Hungary 46°57N 19°42E 289 E10
Kėdainiai Lithuania 55°15N 24°2E 281 J21
Kedarnath India 30°44N 79°4E 315 D8
Kedgwick Canada 47°40N 67°20W 345 C6
Kediri Indonesia 7°51S 112°1E 308 F4
Kedros Oros Greece 35°11N 24°37E 297 D6
Keeler U.S.A. 36°29N 117°52W 350 J9
Keeley L. Canada 54°54N 108°8W 343 C7
Keeling Is. = Cocos Is. Ind. Oc. 12°10S 96°55E 336 J1
Keelung = Chilung Taiwan 25°3N 121°45E 305 D7
Keene Canada 44°15N 78°10W 354 B6
Keene Calif., U.S.A. 35°13N 118°33W 351 K8
Keene N.H., U.S.A. 42°56N 72°17W 355 D12
Keene N.Y., U.S.A. 44°16N 73°46W 355 B11
Keep River △ Australia 15°49S 129°8E 332 C4
Keeper Hill Ireland 52°45N 8°16W 282 D3
Keerweer, C. Australia 14°0S 141°32E 334 A3
Keeseville U.S.A. 44°29N 73°30W 355 B11
Keetmanshoop Namibia 26°35S 18°8E 328 D2
Keewatin Canada 49°46N 94°34W 343 D10
Keewatin → Canada 56°29N 100°46W 343 B8
Kefalonia Greece 38°15N 20°30E 295 E9
Kefamenanu Indonesia 9°28S 124°29E 309 F6
Kefar Sava Israel 32°11N 34°54E 318 C3
Keffi Nigeria 8°55N 7°43E 322 G7
Keflavík Iceland 64°2N 22°35W 280 D2
Keg River Canada 57°54N 117°55W 342 B5
Kegaska Canada 50°9N 61°18W 345 B7
Kehancha Kenya 1°11S 34°37E 326 C3
Keighley U.K. 53°52N 1°54W 284 D6
Keila Estonia 59°18N 24°25E 281 G21
Keimoes S. Africa 28°41S 20°59E 328 D3
Keitele Finland 63°10N 26°20E 280 E22
Keith Australia 36°6S 140°20E 335 F3
Keith U.K. 57°32N 2°57W 283 D6

Keiyasi *Fiji* 17°53S 177°46E **331** a
Keizer *U.S.A.* 44°57N 123°1W **348** D2
Kejimkujik △ *Canada* 44°25N 65°25W **345** D6
Kejserr Franz Joseph Fd.
Greenland 73°30N 24°30W **276** B6
Kekri *India* 26°0N 75°10E **314** G6
Kelan *China* 38°43N 111°31E **306** E6
Kelang = Klang *Malaysia* 3°2N 101°26E **311** L3
Kelantan → *Malaysia* 6°13N 102°14E **311** J4
Kelkit → *Turkey* 40°45N 36°32E **291** F6
Kellerberrin *Australia* 31°36S 117°38E **333** F2
Kellett, C. *Canada* 72°0N 126°0W **341** B7
Kelleys I. *U.S.A.* 41°36N 82°42W **354** E2
Kellogg *U.S.A.* 47°32N 116°7W **348** C5
Kells = Ceanannus Mor
Ireland 53°44N 6°53W **282** C5
Kélo *Chad* 9°10N 15°45E **323** G9
Kelokedhara *Cyprus* 34°48N 32°39E **297** E11
Kelowna *Canada* 49°50N 119°25W **342** D5
Kelsey Creek *Australia* 20°26S 148°31E **334** J6
Kelseyville *U.S.A.* 38°59N 122°50W **350** G4
Kelso *N.Z.* 45°54S 169°15E **331** F2
Kelso *U.K.* 55°36N 2°26W **283** F6
Kelso *U.S.A.* 46°9N 122°54W **350** D4
Keluang = Kluang
Malaysia 2°3N 103°18E **311** L4
Kelvington *Canada* 52°10N 103°30W **343** C8
Kem *Russia* 65°0N 34°38E **290** B5
Kem → *Russia* 64°57N 34°41E **290** B5
Kema *Indonesia* 1°22N 125°8E **309** D7
Kemah *Turkey* 39°32N 39°5E **316** B3
Kemaman *Malaysia* 4°12N 103°18E **311** K4
Kemano *Canada* 53°35N 128°0W **342** C3
Kemasik *Malaysia* 4°25N 103°27E **311** K4
Kemerovo *Russia* 55°20N 86°5E **300** D9
Kemi *Finland* 65°44N 24°34E **280** D21
Kemi älv = Kemijoki →
Finland 65°47N 24°32E **280** D21
Kemi träsk = Kemijärvi
Finland 66°43N 27°22E **280** C22
Kemijärvi *Finland* 66°43N 27°22E **280** C22
Kemijoki → *Finland* 65°47N 24°32E **280** D21
Kemmerer *U.S.A.* 41°48N 110°32W **348** F8
Kemmuna = Comino
Malta 36°1N 14°20E **297** C1
Kemp, L. *U.S.A.* 33°46N 99°9W **356** E5
Kemp Land *Antarctica* 69°0S 55°0E **277** C5
Kempas *Malaysia* 1°33N 103°42E **311** d
Kempsey *Australia* 31°1S 152°50E **335** E5
Kempt, L. *Canada* 47°25N 74°22W **344** C5
Kempten *Germany* 47°45N 10°17E **288** E6
Kempton *Australia* 42°31S 147°12E **335** G4
Kemptville *Canada* 45°0N 75°38W **355** B9
Ken → *India* 25°13N 80°27E **315** G9
Kenai *U.S.A.* 60°33N 151°16W **346** a
Kendai *India* 22°45N 82°37E **315** H10
Kendal *Indonesia* 6°56S 110°14E **309** G14
Kendal *U.K.* 54°20N 2°44W **284** C5
Kendall *Australia* 31°35S 152°44E **335** E5
Kendall *U.S.A.* 25°40N 80°19W **357** J14
Kendall → *Australia* 14°4S 141°35E **334** A3
Kendallville *U.S.A.* 41°27N 85°16W **353** E11
Kendari *Indonesia* 3°50S 122°30E **309** E6
Kendawangan *Indonesia* 2°32S 110°17E **308** E4
Kendi, Pulau *Malaysia* 5°13N 100°11E **311** c
Kendrapara *India* 20°35N 86°30E **313** J15
Kendrew *S. Africa* 32°32S 24°30E **328** E3
Kene Thao *Laos* 17°44N 101°10E **310** D3
Kenedy *U.S.A.* 28°49N 97°51W **356** G6
Kenema *S. Leone* 7°50N 11°14W **322** G3
Keng Kok *Laos* 16°26N 105°12E **310** D5
Keng Tawng *Burma* 20°45N 98°18E **313** J21
Keng Tung *Burma* 21°0N 99°30E **313** J21
Kengeja *Tanzania* 5°26S 39°45E **326** D4
Kenhardt *S. Africa* 29°19S 21°12E **328** D3
Kenitra *Morocco* 34°15N 6°40W **322** B4
Kenli *China* 37°30N 118°20E **307** F10
Kenmare *Ireland* 51°53N 9°36W **282** E2
Kenmare *U.S.A.* 48°41N 102°5W **352** A2
Kenmare River *Ireland* 51°48N 9°51W **282** E2
Kennebago Lake
U.S.A. 45°4N 70°40W **355** A14
Kennebec *U.S.A.* 43°54N 99°52W **352** D4
Kennebec → *U.S.A.* 43°45N 69°46W **353** D19
Kennebunk *U.S.A.* 43°23N 70°33W **355** C14
Kennedy *Zimbabwe* 18°52S 27°10E **328** B4
Kennedy Ra. *Australia* 24°45S 115°10E **333** D2
Kennedy Range △
Australia 24°34S 115°2E **333** D2
Kenner *U.S.A.* 29°59N 90°14W **357** G9
Kennet → *U.K.* 51°27N 0°57W **285** F7
Kenneth Ra. *Australia* 23°50S 117°8E **333** D2
Kennett *U.S.A.* 36°14N 90°3W **352** G8
Kennewick *U.S.A.* 46°12N 119°7W **348** C4
Kenogami → *Canada* 51°6N 84°28W **344** B3
Kenora *Canada* 49°47N 94°29W **343** D10
Kenosha *U.S.A.* 42°35N 87°49W **352** D10
Kensington *Canada* 46°28N 63°34W **345** C7
Kent *Ohio, U.S.A.* 41°9N 81°22W **354** E3
Kent *Tex., U.S.A.* 31°4N 104°13W **356** F2
Kent *Wash., U.S.A.* 47°22N 122°14W **350** C4
Kent □ *U.K.* 51°12N 0°40E **285** F8
Kent Group *Australia* 39°30S 147°20E **335** F4
Kent Pen. *Canada* 68°30N 107°0W **340** C9
Kentaū *Kazakhstan* 43°32N 68°36E **300** E7
Kentland *U.S.A.* 40°46N 87°27W **352** E10
Kenton *U.S.A.* 40°39N 83°37W **353** E12
Kentucky □ *U.S.A.* 37°0N 84°0W **353** G11
Kentucky → *U.S.A.* 38°41N 85°11W **353** F11
Kentucky L. *U.S.A.* 37°1N 88°16W **352** G9
Kentville *Canada* 45°6N 64°29W **345** C7
Kentwood *U.S.A.* 30°56N 90°31W **357** F9
Kenya ■ *Africa* 1°0N 38°0E **326** B4
Kenya, Mt. *Kenya* 0°10S 37°18E **326** C4
Keo Neua, Deo
Vietnam 18°23N 105°10E **310** C5
Keokuk *U.S.A.* 40°24N 91°24W **352** E8
Keoladeo △ *India* 27°0N 77°20E **314** F7
Keonjhargarh *India* 21°28N 85°35E **315** J11
Kep *Cambodia* 10°29N 104°19E **311** G5
Kep *Vietnam* 21°24N 106°16E **310** B6
Kepala Batas *Malaysia* 5°31N 100°26E **311** c
Kepi *Indonesia* 6°32S 139°19E **309** F9
Kerala □ *India* 11°0N 76°15E **312** P10
Kerama-Rettō *Japan* 26°5N 127°15E **303** L3
Keran *Pakistan* 34°35N 73°59E **315** B5
Kerang *Australia* 35°40S 143°55E **335** F3
Keraudren, C. *Australia* 19°58S 119°45E **332** C2
Kerch *Ukraine* 45°20N 36°20E **291** E6
Kerguelen *Ind. Oc.* 49°15S 69°10E **275** G13
Kericho *Kenya* 0°22S 35°15E **326** C4
Kerinci *Indonesia* 1°40S 101°15E **308** E2
Kerki = Atamyrat
Turkmenistan 37°50N 65°12E **300** F7
Kerkrade *Neths.* 50°53N 6°4E **287** D6
Kerkyra *Greece* 39°38N 19°50E **297** A3
Kerkyras, Notio Steno
Greece 39°34N 20°0E **297** A4
Kermadec Is. *Pac. Oc.* 30°0S 178°15W **330** E11
Kermadec Trench
Pac. Oc. 30°30S 176°0W **336** L10
Kermān *Iran* 30°15N 57°1E **317** D8
Kerman *U.S.A.* 36°43N 120°4W **350** J6
Kermān □ *Iran* 30°0N 57°0E **317** D8
Kermān, Bīābān-e *Iran* 28°45N 59°45E **317** D8
Kermānshāh *Iran* 34°23N 47°0E **316** C5
Kermānshāh □ *Iran* 34°0N 46°30E **316** C5
Kermit *U.S.A.* 31°52N 103°6W **356** F3
Kern → *U.S.A.* 35°16N 119°18W **351** K7
Kernow = Cornwall □
U.K. 50°26N 4°40W **285** G3
Kernville *U.S.A.* 35°45N 118°26W **351** K8
Keroh *Malaysia* 5°43N 101°1E **311** K3
Kerrera *U.K.* 56°24N 5°33W **283** E3
Kerrobert *Canada* 51°56N 109°8W **343** C7
Kerrville *U.S.A.* 30°3N 99°8W **356** F5
Kerry □ *Ireland* 52°7N 9°35W **282** D2
Kerry Hd. *Ireland* 52°25N 9°56W **282** D2
Kerulen → *Asia* 48°48N 117°0E **305** B6
Kerzaz *Algeria* 29°29N 1°37W **322** C5
Kesagami → *Canada* 51°40N 79°45W **344** B4
Kesagami L. *Canada* 50°23N 80°15W **344** B3
Keşan *Turkey* 40°49N 26°38E **295** D12
Kesennuma *Japan* 38°54N 141°35E **302** E10
Keshit *Iran* 29°43N 58°17E **317** D8
Kestell *S. Africa* 28°17S 28°42E **329** D4
Kestenga *Russia* 65°50N 31°45E **280** D24
Keswick *U.K.* 54°36N 3°8W **284** C4
Ket → *Russia* 58°55N 81°32E **300** D9
Ketapang *Bali, Indonesia* 8°9S 114°23E **309** J17
Ketapang *Kalimantan, Indonesia* 1°55S 110°0E **308** E4
Ketchikan *U.S.A.* 55°21N 131°39W **342** B2
Ketchum *U.S.A.* 43°41N 114°22W **348** E6
Ketef, Khalîg Umm el
Egypt 23°40N 35°35E **316** F2
Keti Bandar *Pakistan* 24°8N 67°27E **314** G2
Ketri *India* 28°1N 75°50E **314** E6
Kętrzyn *Poland* 54°7N 21°22E **289** A11
Kettering *U.K.* 52°24N 0°43W **285** E7
Kettering *U.S.A.* 39°41N 84°10W **353** F11
Kettle → *Canada* 56°40N 89°34W **343** B11
Kettle Falls *U.S.A.* 48°37N 118°3W **348** B4
Kettle Pt. *Canada* 43°13N 82°1W **354** C2
Kettleman City *U.S.A.* 36°1N 119°58W **350** J7
Keuka L. *U.S.A.* 42°30N 77°9W **354** D7
Keuruu *Finland* 62°16N 24°41E **280** E21
Kewanee *U.S.A.* 41°14N 89°56W **352** E9
Kewaunee *U.S.A.* 44°27N 87°31W **352** C10
Keweenaw B. *U.S.A.* 47°0N 88°15W **352** B9
Keweenaw Pen. *U.S.A.* 47°15N 88°15W **352** B9
Keweenaw Pt. *U.S.A.* 47°25N 87°43W **352** B10
Key, L. *Ireland* 54°0N 8°15W **282** C3
Key Largo *U.S.A.* 25°5N 80°27W **357** J14
Key West *U.S.A.* 24°33N 81°48W **360** B3
Keynsham *U.K.* 51°24N 2°29W **285** F5
Keyser *U.S.A.* 39°26N 78°59W **353** F14
Kezhma *Russia* 58°59N 101°9E **301** D11
Kezi *Zimbabwe* 20°58S 28°32E **329** C4
Kgalagadi Transfrontier ⌓
Africa 25°10S 21°0E **328** D3
Khabarovsk *Russia* 48°30N 135°5E **301** E14
Khabr *Iran* 28°51N 56°22E **317** D8
Khābūr → *Syria* 35°17N 40°35E **316** C4
Khachmas = Xaçmaz
Azerbaijan 41°31N 48°42E **291** F8
Khachrod *India* 23°25N 75°20E **314** H6
Khadro *Pakistan* 26°11N 68°50E **314** F3
Khadzhilyangar = Dahongliutan
China 35°45N 79°20E **315** B8
Khaga *India* 25°47N 81°7E **315** G9
Khagaria *India* 25°30N 86°32E **315** G12
Khaipur *Pakistan* 29°34N 72°17E **314** E5
Khair *India* 27°57N 77°46E **314** F7
Khairabad *India* 27°33N 80°47E **315** F9
Khairagarh *India* 21°27N 81°2E **315** J9
Khairpur *Pakistan* 27°32N 68°49E **314** F3
Khairpur Nathan Shah
Pakistan 27°6N 67°44E **314** F2
Khairwara *India* 23°58N 73°38E **314** H5
Khaisor → *Pakistan* 31°17N 68°59E **314** D3
Khajuri Kach *Pakistan* 32°4N 69°51E **314** C3
Khakassia □ *Russia* 53°0N 90°0E **300** D9
Khakhea *Botswana* 24°48S 23°22E **328** C3
Khalafābād *Iran* 30°54N 49°24E **317** D6
Khalilabad *India* 26°48N 83°5E **315** F10
Khalīlī *Iran* 27°38N 53°17E **317** E7
Khalkhāl *Iran* 37°37N 48°32E **317** B6
Khalkís = Halkida
Greece 38°27N 23°42E **295** E10
Khalmer Yu *Russia* 67°58N 65°1E **300** C7
Khalturin *Russia* 58°40N 48°50E **290** C8
Khalūf *Oman* 20°30N 58°13E **319** C6
Kham Keut *Laos* 18°15N 104°43E **310** C5
Khamaria *India* 23°5N 80°48E **315** H9
Khambhaliya *India* 22°14N 69°41E **314** H3
Khambhat *India* 22°23N 72°33E **314** H5
Khambhat, G. of *India* 20°45N 72°30E **312** J8
Khamīr *Iran* 26°57N 55°36E **317** E7
Khamir *Yemen* 16°2N 44°0E **319** D3
Khamīs Mushayṭ
Si. Arabia 18°18N 42°44E **319** D3
Khamsa *Egypt* 30°27N 32°23E **318** E1
Khan → *Namibia* 22°37S 14°56E **328** C2
Khān Abū Shāmat
Syria 33°39N 36°53E **318** B5
Khān Azād *Iraq* 33°7N 44°22E **316** C5
Khān Mujiddah *Iraq* 32°21N 43°48E **316** C4
Khān Shaykhūn *Syria* 35°26N 36°38E **316** C3
Khān Yūnis *Gaza Strip* 31°21N 34°18E **318** D3
Khanai *Pakistan* 30°30N 67°8E **314** D2
Khānaqīn *Iraq* 34°23N 45°25E **316** C5
Khānbāghī *Iran* 36°10N 55°25E **317** B7
Khandwa *India* 21°49N 76°22E **312** J10
Khandyga *Russia* 62°42N 135°35E **301** C14
Khāneh *Iran* 36°41N 45°8E **316** B5
Khanewal *Pakistan* 30°20N 71°55E **314** D4
Khangah Dogran
Pakistan 31°50N 73°37E **314** D5
Khanh Duong *Vietnam* 12°44N 108°44E **310** F7
Khaniá = Chania *Greece* 35°30N 24°4E **297** D6
Khaniadhana *India* 25°1N 78°8E **314** G8
Khanka, L. *Asia* 45°0N 132°24E **302** B6
Khankendy = Xankändi
Azerbaijan 39°52N 46°49E **316** B5
Khanna *India* 30°42N 76°16E **314** D7
Khanozai *Pakistan* 30°37N 67°19E **314** D2
Khanpur *Pakistan* 28°42N 70°35E **314** E4
Khanty-Mansiysk *Russia* 61°0N 69°0E **300** C7
Khao Laem △ *Thailand* 14°56N 98°31E **310** E2
Khao Laem Res.
Thailand 14°50N 98°30E **310** E2
Khao Luang △ *Thailand* 8°34N 99°42E **311** H2
Khao Phlu *Thailand* 9°29N 99°59E **311** b
Khao Pu-Khao Ya △
Thailand 7°26N 99°57E **311** J2
Khao Sam Roi Yot △
Thailand 12°13N 99°57E **311** F2
Khao Sok △ *Thailand* 8°55N 98°38E **311** H2
Khao Yai △ *Thailand* 14°21N 101°29E **310** E3
Khaoen Si Nakarin △
Thailand 14°47N 99°0E **310** E2
Khapalu *Pakistan* 35°10N 76°20E **315** B7
Khapcheranga *Russia* 49°42N 112°24E **301** E12
Khaptao △ *Nepal* 29°20N 81°10E **315** E9
Kharaghoda *India* 23°11N 71°46E **314** H4
Kharagpur *India* 22°20N 87°25E **315** H12
Kharan Kalat *Pakistan* 28°34N 65°21E **312** E4
Kharānaq *Iran* 32°20N 54°45E **317** C7
Kharda *India* 18°40N 75°34E **312** K9
Khardung La *India* 34°20N 77°43E **315** B7
Kharg = Khārk, Jazīreh-ye
Iran 29°15N 50°28E **317** D6
Khârga, El Wâhât-el
Egypt 25°10N 30°35E **323** C12
Khargon *India* 21°45N 75°40E **312** J9
Khari → *India* 25°54N 74°31E **314** G6
Kharian *Pakistan* 32°49N 73°52E **314** C5
Khārk, Jazīreh-ye *Iran* 29°15N 50°28E **317** D6
Kharkiv *Ukraine* 49°58N 36°20E **291** E6
Kharkov = Kharkiv
Ukraine 49°58N 36°20E **291** E6
Kharovsk *Russia* 59°56N 40°13E **290** C7
Kharsawangarh *India* 22°48N 85°50E **315** H11
Kharta *Turkey* 40°55N 29°7E **295** D13
Khartoum = El Khartûm
Sudan 15°31N 32°35E **323** E12
Khasan *Russia* 42°25N 130°40E **302** C5
Khāsh *Iran* 28°15N 61°15E **317** D9
Khashm el Girba
Sudan 14°59N 35°58E **323** F13
Khaskovo *Bulgaria* 41°56N 25°30E **295** D11
Khatanga *Russia* 72°0N 102°20E **301** B11
Khatanga → *Russia* 72°55N 106°0E **301** B11
Khatauli *India* 29°17N 77°43E **314** E7
Khatra *India* 22°59N 86°51E **315** H12
Khātūnābād *Iran* 30°1N 55°25E **317** D7
Khatyrka *Russia* 62°3N 175°15E **301** C18
Khavda *India* 23°51N 69°43E **314** H3
Khawr Fakkān *U.A.E.* 25°21N 56°22E **317** E8
Khaybar, Ḥarrat
Si. Arabia 25°45N 40°0E **316** E4
Khāzimiyah *Iraq* 34°46N 43°37E **316** C4
Khe Bo *Vietnam* 19°8N 104°41E **310** C5
Khe Long *Vietnam* 21°29N 104°46E **310** B5
Khe Sanh *Vietnam* 16°37N 106°45E **310** D6
Khed Brahma *India* 24°7N 73°5E **314** G5
Khekra *India* 28°52N 77°20E **314** E7
Khemarak Phouminville = Krong Kaoh Kong
Cambodia 11°37N 102°59E **311** G4
Khemisset *Morocco* 33°50N 6°1W **322** B4
Khemmarat *Thailand* 16°10N 105°15E **310** D5
Khenāmān *Iran* 30°27N 56°29E **317** D8
Khenchela *Algeria* 35°28N 7°11E **322** A7
Khersān → *Iran* 31°33N 50°22E **317** D6
Kherson *Ukraine* 46°35N 32°35E **291** E5
Kheta → *Russia* 71°54N 102°6E **301** B11
Khewari *Pakistan* 26°36N 68°52E **314** F3
Khilchipur *India* 24°2N 76°34E **314** G7
Khilok *Russia* 51°30N 110°45E **301** D12
Khíos = Hios *Greece* 38°27N 26°9E **295** E12
Khirsadoh *India* 22°11N 78°47E **315** H8
Khiuma = Hiiumaa
Estonia 58°50N 22°45E **281** G20
Khiva *Uzbekistan* 41°30N 60°18E **300** E7
Khīyāv *Iran* 38°30N 47°45E **316** B5
Khlong Khlung
Thailand 16°12N 99°43E **310** D2
Khmelnik *Ukraine* 49°33N 27°58E **289** D14
Khmelnitskiy = Khmelnytskyy
Ukraine 49°23N 27°0E **289** D14
Khmelnytskyy *Ukraine* 49°23N 27°0E **289** D14
Khmer Rep. = Cambodia ■
Asia 12°15N 105°0E **310** F5
Khoai, Hon *Vietnam* 8°26N 104°50E **311** H5
Khodoriv *Ukraine* 49°24N 24°19E **289** D13
Khodzent = Khŭjand
Tajikistan 40°17N 69°37E **300** E7
Khojak Pass *Afghan.* 30°51N 66°34E **314** D2
Khok Kloi *Thailand* 8°17N 98°19E **311** a
Khok Pho *Thailand* 6°43N 101°6E **311** J3
Kholm *Russia* 57°10N 31°15E **290** C5
Kholmsk *Russia* 47°40N 142°5E **301** E15
Khomas Hochland
Namibia 22°40S 16°0E **328** C2
Khomeyn *Iran* 33°40N 50°7E **317** C6
Khomeynī Shahr *Iran* 32°41N 51°31E **317** C6
Khomodino *Botswana* 22°46S 23°52E **328** C3
Khon Kaen *Thailand* 16°30N 102°47E **310** D4
Khong → *Cambodia* 13°32N 105°58E **310** F5
Khong Sedone *Laos* 15°34N 105°49E **310** E5
Khonuu *Russia* 66°30N 143°12E **301** C15
Khoper → *Russia* 49°30N 42°20E **291** D6
Khorāsān □ *Iran* 34°0N 58°0E **317** C8
Khorat = Nakhon Ratchasima
Thailand 14°59N 102°12E **310** E4
Khorat, Cao Nguyen
Thailand 15°30N 102°50E **310** E4
Khorixas *Namibia* 20°16S 14°59E **328** C1
Khorramābād *Khorāsān, Iran* 35°6N 57°57E **317** C8
Khorramābād *Lorestān, Iran* 33°30N 48°25E **317** C6
Khorrāmshahr *Iran* 30°29N 48°15E **317** D6
Khorugh *Tajikistan* 37°30N 71°36E **300** F8
Khosravī *Iran* 30°48N 51°28E **317** D6
Khosrowābād *Khuzestān, Iran* 30°10N 48°25E **317** D6
Khosrowābād *Kordestān, Iran* 35°31N 47°38E **316** C5
Khost *Pakistan* 30°13N 67°35E **314** D2
Khosūyeh *Iran* 28°32N 54°26E **317** D7
Khotyn *Ukraine* 48°31N 26°27E **289** D14
Khouribga *Morocco* 32°58N 6°57W **322** B4
Khowst *Afghan.* 33°22N 69°58E **314** C3
Khowst □ *Afghan.* 33°20N 70°0E **312** C6
Khoyniki *Belarus* 51°54N 29°55E **289** C15
Khrysokhou B. *Cyprus* 35°6N 32°25E **297** D11
Khu Khan *Thailand* 14°42N 104°12E **310** E5
Khuan Wa *Thailand* 7°53N 98°17E **311** a
Khudzhand = Khŭjand
Tajikistan 40°17N 69°37E **300** E7
Khuff *Si. Arabia* 24°55N 44°53E **316** E5
Khūgīānī *Afghan.* 31°34N 66°32E **314** D2
Khuis *Botswana* 26°40S 21°49E **328** D3
Khuiyala *India* 27°9N 70°25E **314** F4
Khŭjand *Tajikistan* 40°17N 69°37E **300** E7
Khujner *India* 23°47N 76°36E **314** H7
Khulna *Bangla.* 22°45N 89°34E **313** H16
Khulna □ *Bangla.* 22°25N 89°35E **313** H16
Khumago *Botswana* 20°26S 24°32E **328** C3
Khunjerab △ *Pakistan* 36°40N 75°30E **315** A6
Khunjerab Pass = Kinjirap Daban
Asia 36°40N 75°25E **312** A9
Khūnsorkh *Iran* 27°9N 56°7E **317** E8
Khunti *India* 23°5N 85°17E **315** H11
Khūr *Iran* 32°55N 58°18E **317** C8
Khurai *India* 24°3N 78°23E **314** G8
Khurayṣ *Si. Arabia* 25°6N 48°2E **317** E6
Khurja *India* 28°15N 77°58E **314** E7
Khūrmāl *Iraq* 35°18N 46°2E **316** C5
Khurr, Wādī al *Iraq* 32°3N 43°52E **316** C4
Khūsf *Iran* 32°46N 58°53E **317** C8
Khushab *Pakistan* 32°20N 72°20E **314** C5
Khust *Ukraine* 48°10N 23°18E **289** D12
Khutse ⌓ *Botswana* 23°31S 24°12E **328** C3
Khuzdar *Pakistan* 27°52N 66°30E **314** F2
Khūzestān □ *Iran* 31°0N 49°0E **317** D6
Khvāf *Iran* 34°33N 60°8E **317** C9
Khvājeh *Iran* 38°9N 46°35E **316** B5
Khvānsār *Iran* 29°56N 54°8E **317** D7
Khvor *Iran* 33°45N 55°0E **317** C7
Khvorgū *Iran* 27°34N 56°27E **317** E8
Khvormūj *Iran* 28°40N 51°30E **317** D6
Khvoy *Iran* 38°35N 45°0E **316** B5
Khyber Pass *Afghan.* 34°10N 71°8E **314** B4
Kia *Fiji* 16°16S 179°8E **331** a
Kiabukwa
Dem. Rep. of the Congo 8°40S 24°48E **327** D1
Kiama *Australia* 34°40S 150°50E **335** E5
Kiamba *Phil.* 6°2N 124°46E **309** C6
Kiambi
Dem. Rep. of the Congo 7°15S 28°0E **326** D2
Kiambu *Kenya* 1°8S 36°50E **326** C4
Kiangara *Madag.* 17°58S 47°2E **329** B8
Kiangsi = Jiangxi □
China 27°30N 116°0E **305** D6
Kiangsu = Jiangsu □
China 33°0N 120°0E **307** H11
Kibale △ *Uganda* 0°16N 30°18E **326** B3
Kibanga Port *Uganda* 0°10N 32°58E **326** B3
Kibara *Tanzania* 2°8S 33°30E **326** C3
Kibare, Mts.
Dem. Rep. of the Congo 8°25S 27°10E **326** D2
Kibira △ *Burundi* 3°6S 30°24E **326** C3
Kibombo
Dem. Rep. of the Congo 3°57S 25°53E **326** C2
Kibondo *Tanzania* 3°35S 30°45E **326** C3
Kibre Mengist *Ethiopia* 5°54N 38°59E **319** F2
Kıbrıs = Cyprus ■ *Asia* 35°0N 33°0E **297** E12
Kibumbu *Burundi* 3°32S 29°45E **326** C2
Kibungo *Rwanda* 2°10S 30°32E **326** C3
Kibuye *Burundi* 3°39S 29°59E **326** C2
Kibuye *Rwanda* 2°3S 29°21E **326** C2
Kibwesa *Tanzania* 6°30S 29°58E **326** D2
Kibwezi *Kenya* 2°27S 37°57E **326** C4
Kichha *India* 28°53N 79°30E **315** E8
Kichha → *India* 28°41N 79°18E **315** E8
Kichmengskiy Gorodok
Russia 59°59N 45°48E **290** B8
Kicking Horse Pass
Canada 51°28N 116°16W **342** C5
Kidal *Mali* 18°26N 1°22E **322** E6
Kidderminster *U.K.* 52°24N 2°15W **285** E5
Kidepo Valley △ *Uganda* 3°52N 33°50E **326** B3
Kidete *Tanzania* 6°25S 37°17E **326** D4
Kidnappers, C. *N.Z.* 39°38S 177°5E **331** C6
Kidsgrove *U.K.* 53°5N 2°14W **284** D5
Kidston *Australia* 18°52S 144°8E **334** B3
Kidugallo *Tanzania* 6°49S 38°15E **326** D4
Kiel *Germany* 54°19N 10°8E **288** A6
Kiel Canal = Nord-Ostsee-Kanal
Germany 54°12N 9°32E **288** A5
Kielce *Poland* 50°52N 20°42E **289** C11
Kielder Water *U.K.* 55°11N 2°31W **284** B5
Kieler Bucht *Germany* 54°35N 10°25E **288** A6
Kien Binh *Vietnam* 9°55N 105°19E **311** H5
Kien Tan *Vietnam* 10°7N 105°17E **311** G5
Kienge
Dem. Rep. of the Congo 10°30S 27°30E **327** E2
Kiev = Kyyiv *Ukraine* 50°30N 30°28E **289** C16
Kiffa *Mauritania* 16°37N 11°24W **322** E3
Kifrī *Iraq* 34°45N 45°0E **316** C5
Kigali *Rwanda* 1°59S 30°4E **326** C3
Kigarama *Tanzania* 1°1S 31°50E **326** C3
Kigezi ⌓ *Uganda* 0°34S 29°55E **326** C2
Kigoma □ *Tanzania* 5°0S 30°0E **326** D3
Kigoma-Ujiji *Tanzania* 4°55S 29°36E **326** C2
Kigomasha, Ras *Tanzania* 4°58S 38°58E **326** C4
Kığzı *Turkey* 38°18N 43°25E **316** B4
Kihnu *Estonia* 58°9N 24°1E **281** G21
Kii-Sanchi *Japan* 34°20N 136°0E **303** G8
Kii-Suidō *Japan* 33°40N 134°45E **303** H7
Kiira Dam *Uganda* 0°25N 33°0E **326** B3
Kikaiga-Shima *Japan* 28°19N 129°59E **303** K4
Kikinda *Serbia* 45°50N 20°30E **295** B9
Kikládhes = Cyclades
Greece 37°0N 24°30E **295** F11
Kikwit
Dem. Rep. of the Congo 5°0S 18°45E **324** E3
Kilar *India* 33°6N 76°25E **314** C7
Kīlauea Caldera *U.S.A.* 19°25N 155°17W **346** b
Kilbeggan *Ireland* 53°22N 7°30W **282** C4
Kilbrannan Sd. *U.K.* 55°37N 5°26W **283** F3
Kilchu *N. Korea* 40°57N 129°25E **307** D15
Kilcoy *Australia* 26°59S 152°30E **335** D5
Kildare *Ireland* 53°9N 6°55W **282** C5
Kildare □ *Ireland* 53°10N 6°50W **282** C5
Kildinstroy *Russia* 68°48N 33°6E **280** B25
Kilfinnane *Ireland* 52°21N 8°28W **282** D3
Kilgarvan *Ireland* 51°54N 9°27W **282** E2
Kilgore *U.S.A.* 32°23N 94°53W **356** E7
Kilgoris *Kenya* 1°0S 34°53E **326** C3
Kilifi *Kenya* 3°40S 39°48E **326** C4
Kilimanjaro *Tanzania* 3°7S 37°20E **326** C4
Kilimanjaro □ *Tanzania* 4°0S 38°0E **326** C4
Kilindini *Kenya* 4°4S 39°40E **326** C4
Kilis *Turkey* 36°42N 37°6E **316** B3
Kiliya *Ukraine* 45°28N 29°16E **289** F15
Kilkee *Ireland* 52°41N 9°39W **282** D2
Kilkeel *U.K.* 54°4N 6°0W **282** B5
Kilkenny *Ireland* 52°39N 7°15W **282** D4
Kilkenny □ *Ireland* 52°35N 7°15W **282** D4
Kilkieran B. *Ireland* 53°20N 9°41W **282** C2
Kilkis *Greece* 40°58N 22°57E **295** D10
Killala *Ireland* 54°13N 9°12W **282** B2
Killala B. *Ireland* 54°16N 9°8W **282** B2
Killaloe *Canada* 45°33N 77°25W **354** A7
Killaloe *Ireland* 52°48N 8°28W **282** D3
Killarney *Australia* 28°20S 152°18E **335** D5
Killarney *Canada* 49°10N 99°40W **343** D9
Killarney *Ireland* 52°4N 9°30W **282** D2
Killarney △ *Ireland* 52°0N 9°33W **282** D2
Killary Harbour *Ireland* 53°38N 9°52W **282** C2
Killdeer *U.S.A.* 47°22N 102°45W **352** B2
Killeen *U.S.A.* 31°7N 97°44W **356** F6
Killin *U.K.* 56°28N 4°19W **283** E4
Killiney *Ireland* 53°15N 6°7W **282** C5
Killini *Greece* 37°54N 22°25E **295** F10
Killorglin *Ireland* 52°6N 9°47W **282** D2
Killybegs *Ireland* 54°38N 8°26W **282** B3
Kilmarnock *U.K.* 55°37N 4°29W **283** F4
Kilmore *Australia* 37°25S 144°53E **335** F3
Kilmore Quay *Ireland* 52°10N 6°36W **282** D5
Kilondo *Tanzania* 9°45S 34°20E **327** D3
Kilosa *Tanzania* 6°48S 37°0E **326** D4
Kilrush *Ireland* 52°38N 9°29W **282** D2
Kilwa Kisiwani *Tanzania* 8°58S 39°32E **327** D4
Kilwa Kivinje *Tanzania* 8°45S 39°25E **327** D4
Kilwa Masoko *Tanzania* 8°55S 39°30E **327** D4
Kilwinning *U.K.* 55°39N 4°43W **283** F4
Kim *U.S.A.* 37°15N 103°21W **349** H12
Kimaam *Indonesia* 7°58S 138°53E **309** F9
Kimamba *Tanzania* 6°45S 37°10E **326** D4
Kimba *Australia* 33°8S 136°23E **335** E2
Kimball *Nebr., U.S.A.* 41°14N 103°40W **352** E2
Kimball *S. Dak., U.S.A.* 43°45N 98°57W **352** D4
Kimberley *Australia* 16°20S 127°0E **332** C4
Kimberley *Canada* 49°40N 115°59W **342** D5
Kimberley *S. Africa* 28°43S 24°46E **328** D3
Kimberly *U.S.A.* 42°32N 114°22W **348** E6
Kimch'aek *N. Korea* 40°40N 129°10E **307** D15
Kimhae = Gimhae
S. Korea 35°14N 128°53E **307** G15
Kimmirut *Canada* 62°50N 69°50W **341** C13
Kimpese
Dem. Rep. of the Congo 5°35S 14°26E **324** F2
Kimry *Russia* 56°55N 37°15E **290** C6
Kinabalu, Gunung
Malaysia 6°3N 116°14E **308** C5
Kinango *Kenya* 4°8S 39°19E **326** C4
Kinaskan L. *Canada* 57°38N 130°8W **342** B2
Kinbasket L. *Canada* 52°0N 118°10W **342** C5
Kincardine *Canada* 44°10N 81°40W **354** B3
Kincolith *Canada* 55°0N 129°57W **342** C3
Kinda
Dem. Rep. of the Congo 9°18S 25°4E **327** D2
Kinde *U.S.A.* 43°56N 83°0W **354** C2

Kinder Scout U.K. 53°24N 1°52W 284 D6
Kindersley Canada 51°30N 109°10W 343 C7
Kindia Guinea 10°0N 12°52W 322 F3
Kindu Dem. Rep. of the Congo 2°55S 25°50E 326 C2
Kineshma Russia 57°30N 42°5E 290 C7
Kinesi Tanzania 1°25S 33°50E 326 C3
King, L. Australia 33°10S 119°35E 333 F2
King, Mt. Australia 25°10S 147°30E 334 D4
King City U.S.A. 36°13N 121°8W 350 J5
King Cr. → Australia 24°35S 139°30E 334 C2
King Edward → Australia 14°14S 126°35E 332 B4
King Frederick VI Land = Kong Frederik VI Kyst Greenland 63°0N 43°0W 276 C5
King George B. Falk. Is. 51°30S 60°30W 368 G4
King George I. Antarctica 60°0S 60°0W 277 C18
King George Is. Canada 57°20N 80°30W 341 D11
King I. = Kadan Kyun Burma 12°30N 98°20E 310 F2
King I. Australia 39°50S 144°0E 335 F3
King I. Canada 52°10N 127°40W 342 C3
King Leopold Ranges Australia 17°30S 125°45E 332 C4
King of Prussia U.S.A. 40°5N 75°23W 355 F9
King Sd. Australia 16°50S 123°20E 332 C3
King Sejong Antarctica 62°30S 58°0W 277 C18
King William I. Canada 69°10N 97°25W 340 C10
King William's Town S. Africa 32°51S 27°22E 328 E4
Kingait = Cape Dorset Canada 64°14N 76°32W 341 C12
Kingaok = Bathurst Inlet Canada 66°50N 108°1W 340 C9
Kingaroy Australia 26°32S 151°51E 335 D5
Kingfisher U.S.A. 35°52N 97°56W 356 D6
Kingirbān Iraq 34°40N 44°54E 316 C5
Kingisepp = Kuressaare Estonia 58°15N 22°30E 281 G20
Kingisepp Russia 59°25N 28°40E 281 G23
Kingman Ariz., U.S.A. 35°12N 114°4W 351 K12
Kingman Kans., U.S.A. 37°39N 98°7W 352 G4
Kingoonya Australia 30°55S 135°19E 335 E2
Kingri Pakistan 30°27N 69°49E 314 D3
Kings → U.S.A. 36°3N 119°50W 350 J7
Kings Canyon △ U.S.A. 36°50N 118°40W 350 J8
King's Lynn U.K. 52°45N 0°24E 284 E8
Kings Park U.S.A. 40°53N 73°16W 355 F11
Kings Peak U.S.A. 40°46N 110°23W 348 F8
Kingsbridge U.K. 50°17N 3°47W 285 G4
Kingsburg U.S.A. 36°31N 119°33W 350 J7
Kingscote Australia 35°40S 137°38E 335 F2
Kingscourt Ireland 53°55N 6°48W 282 C5
Kingsford U.S.A. 45°48N 88°4W 352 C9
Kingsland U.S.A. 30°48N 81°41W 357 F14
Kingsport U.S.A. 36°33N 82°33W 357 C13
Kingston Canada 44°14N 76°30W 355 B8
Kingston Jamaica 18°0N 76°50W 360 a
Kingston N.Z. 45°20S 168°43E 331 F2
Kingston N.H., U.S.A. 42°56N 71°3W 355 D13
Kingston N.Y., U.S.A. 41°56N 73°59W 355 E11
Kingston Pa., U.S.A. 41°16N 75°54W 355 E9
Kingston R.I., U.S.A. 41°29N 71°30W 355 E13
Kingston Pk. U.S.A. 35°44N 115°55W 351 K11
Kingston South East Australia 36°51S 139°55E 335 F2
Kingston upon Hull U.K. 53°45N 0°21W 284 D7
Kingston upon Hull □ U.K. 53°45N 0°21W 284 D7
Kingston-upon-Thames □ U.K. 51°24N 0°17W 285 F7
Kingstown St. Vincent 13°10N 61°10W 361 D7
Kingstree U.S.A. 33°40N 79°50W 357 E15
Kingsville Canada 42°2N 82°45W 354 D2
Kingsville U.S.A. 27°31N 97°52W 356 H6
Kingussie U.K. 57°6N 4°2W 283 D4
Kingwood U.S.A. 30°2N 95°16W 356 F7
Kınık Turkey 39°6N 27°24E 295 E12
Kinistino Canada 52°57N 105°2W 343 C7
Kinjirap Daban Asia 36°40N 75°25E 312 A9
Kinkala Congo 4°18S 14°49E 324 E2
Kinki □ Japan 33°45N 136°0E 303 H8
Kinleith N.Z. 38°20S 175°56E 331 C5
Kinlochleven U.K. 56°43N 5°0W 283 E4
Kinmount Canada 44°48N 78°45W 354 B6
Kinna Sweden 57°32N 12°42E 281 H15
Kinnairds Hd. U.K. 57°43N 2°1W 283 D6
Kino Nuevo Mexico 28°52N 112°3W 358 B2
Kinoje → Canada 52°8N 81°25W 344 B3
Kinomoto Japan 35°30N 136°13E 303 G8
Kinoni Uganda 0°41S 30°28E 326 C3
Kinoosao Canada 57°5N 102°1W 343 B8
Kinross U.K. 56°13N 3°25W 283 E5
Kinsale Ireland 51°42N 8°31W 282 E3
Kinsale, Old Hd. of Ireland 51°37N 8°33W 282 E3
Kinsha = Chang Jiang → China 31°48N 121°10E 305 C7
Kinshasa Dem. Rep. of the Congo 4°20S 15°15E 324 E3
Kinsley U.S.A. 37°55N 99°25W 352 G4
Kinsman U.S.A. 41°26N 80°35W 354 E4
Kinston U.S.A. 35°16N 77°35W 357 D16
Kintamani Indonesia 8°14S 115°19E 309 J18
Kintore U.K. 57°14N 2°20W 283 D6
Kintore Ra. Australia 23°15S 128°47E 332 D4
Kintyre U.K. 55°30N 5°35W 283 F3
Kintyre, Mull of U.K. 55°17N 5°47W 283 F3
Kinushseo → Canada 55°15N 83°45W 344 A3
Kinuso Canada 55°20N 115°25W 342 B5
Kinvarra Ireland 53°8N 8°56W 282 C3
Kinyangiri Tanzania 4°25S 34°37E 326 C3
Kinyeti Sudan 3°57N 32°54E 326 B3
Kinzua U.S.A. 41°52N 78°58W 354 E6
Kiosk Canada 46°6N 78°53W 344 C4
Kiowa Kans., U.S.A. 37°1N 98°29W 352 G4
Kiowa Okla., U.S.A. 34°43N 95°54W 356 D7
Kipahigan L. Canada 55°20N 101°55W 343 B8
Kipanga Tanzania 6°15S 35°20E 326 D4
Kiparissia Greece 37°15N 21°40E 295 F9
Kiparissiakos Kolpos Greece 37°25N 21°25E 295 F9
Kipawa, L. Canada 46°50N 79°0W 344 C4
Kipembawe Tanzania 7°38S 33°27E 326 D3
Kipengere Ra. Tanzania 9°12S 34°15E 327 D3
Kipili Tanzania 7°28S 30°32E 326 D3
Kipini Kenya 2°30S 40°32E 326 C5
Kipling Canada 50°6N 102°38W 343 C8
Kippure Ireland 53°11N 6°21W 282 C5
Kipushi Dem. Rep. of the Congo 11°48S 27°12E 327 E2
Kiranomena Madag. 18°17S 46°2E 329 B8
Kirensk Russia 57°50N 107°55E 301 D11
Kirghizia = Kyrgyzstan ■ Asia 42°0N 75°0E 300 E8
Kirghizstan = Kyrgyzstan ■ Asia 42°0N 75°0E 300 E8
Kirgiziya Steppe Eurasia 50°0N 55°0E 291 E10
Kiribati ■ Pac. Oc. 3°0S 180°0E 330 B10
Kırıkkale Turkey 39°51N 33°32E 291 G5
Kirillov Russia 59°49N 38°24E 290 C6
Kirin = Jilin China 43°44N 126°30E 307 C14
Kirinyaga = Kenya, Mt. Kenya 0°10S 37°18E 326 C4
Kirishima Yaku △ Japan 31°24N 130°50E 303 J5
Kiritimati Kiribati 1°58N 157°27W 337 G12
Kirkby U.K. 53°30N 2°54W 284 D5
Kirkby-in-Ashfield U.K. 53°6N 1°14W 284 D6
Kirkby Lonsdale U.K. 54°12N 2°36W 284 C5
Kirkby Stephen U.K. 54°29N 2°21W 284 C5
Kirkcaldy U.K. 56°7N 3°9W 283 E5
Kirkcudbright U.K. 54°50N 4°2W 283 G4
Kirkee India 18°34N 73°56E 312 K8
Kirkenes Norway 69°40N 30°5E 280 B24
Kirkfield Canada 44°34N 78°59W 354 B6
Kirkintilloch U.K. 55°56N 4°8W 283 F4
Kirkjubæjarklaustur Iceland 63°47N 18°4W 280 E4
Kirkkonummi Finland 60°8N 24°26E 281 F21
Kirkland U.S.A. 47°40N 122°12W 350 C4
Kirkland Lake Canada 48°9N 80°2W 344 C3
Kırklareli Turkey 41°44N 27°15E 295 D12
Kirksville U.S.A. 40°12N 92°35W 352 E7
Kirkūk Iraq 35°30N 44°21E 316 C5
Kirkwall U.K. 58°59N 2°58W 283 C6
Kirkwood S. Africa 33°22S 25°15E 328 E4
Kirov Russia 58°35N 49°40E 290 C8
Kirovabad = Gäncä Azerbaijan 40°45N 46°20E 291 F8
Kirovograd = Kirovohrad Ukraine 48°35N 32°20E 291 E5
Kirovohrad Ukraine 48°35N 32°20E 291 E5
Kirovsk Russia 67°32N 33°41E 290 A5
Kirovskiy Kamchatka, Russia 54°27N 155°42E 301 D16
Kirovskiy Primorsk, Russia 45°7N 133°30E 302 B6
Kirriemuir U.K. 56°41N 3°1W 283 E5
Kirsanov Russia 52°35N 42°40E 290 D7
Kırşehir Turkey 39°14N 34°5E 316 B2
Kirthar △ Pakistan 25°45N 67°30E 314 F2
Kirthar Range Pakistan 27°0N 67°0E 314 F2
Kirtland U.S.A. 36°44N 108°21W 349 H9
Kiruna Sweden 67°52N 20°15E 280 C19
Kirundu Dem. Rep. of the Congo 0°50S 25°35E 326 C2
Kiryū Japan 36°24N 139°20E 303 F9
Kisaga Tanzania 4°30S 34°23E 326 C3
Kisalaya Nic. 14°40N 84°3W 360 D3
Kisanga Dem. Rep. of the Congo 2°30N 26°35E 326 B2
Kisangani Dem. Rep. of the Congo 0°35N 25°15E 326 B2
Kisar Indonesia 8°5S 127°10E 309 F7
Kisarawe Tanzania 6°53S 39°0E 326 D4
Kisarazu Japan 35°23N 139°55E 303 G9
Kishanganga → Pakistan 34°18N 73°28E 315 B5
Kishanganj India 26°3N 88°14E 315 F13
Kishangarh Raj., India 26°34N 74°52E 314 F6
Kishangarh Raj., India 27°50N 70°30E 314 F4
Kishinev = Chişinău Moldova 47°2N 28°50E 289 E15
Kishiwada Japan 34°28N 135°22E 303 G7
Kishtwar India 33°20N 75°48E 314 C6
Kisigo ⌂ Tanzania 6°27S 34°17E 326 D3
Kisii Kenya 0°40S 34°45E 326 C3
Kisiju Tanzania 7°23S 39°19E 326 D4
Kisizi Uganda 1°0S 29°58E 326 C2
Kiskőrös Hungary 46°37N 19°20E 289 E10
Kiskunfélegyháza Hungary 46°42N 19°53E 289 E10
Kiskunhalas Hungary 46°28N 19°37E 289 E10
Kislovodsk Russia 43°50N 42°45E 291 F7
Kismayu = Chisimaio Somali Rep. 0°22S 42°32E 319 H3
Kiso-Gawa → Japan 35°20N 136°45E 303 G8
Kiso-Sammyaku Japan 35°45N 137°45E 303 G8
Kisofukushima Japan 35°52N 137°43E 303 G8
Kisoro Uganda 1°17S 29°48E 326 C2
Kissamos = Kasteli Greece 35°29N 23°38E 297 D5
Kissamos, Kolpos Greece 35°30N 23°38E 297 D5
Kissidougou Guinea 9°5N 10°5W 322 G3
Kissimmee U.S.A. 28°18N 81°24W 357 G14
Kissimmee → U.S.A. 27°9N 80°52W 357 H14
Kississing L. Canada 55°10N 101°20W 343 B8
Kissónerga Cyprus 34°49N 32°24E 297 E11
Kisumu Kenya 0°3S 34°45E 326 C3
Kiswani Tanzania 4°5S 37°57E 326 C4
Kiswere Tanzania 9°27S 39°30E 327 D4
Kit Carson U.S.A. 38°46N 102°48W 348 G12
Kita Mali 13°5N 9°25W 322 F4
Kitaibaraki Japan 36°50N 140°45E 303 F10
Kitakami Japan 39°20N 141°10E 302 E10
Kitakami-Gawa → Japan 38°25N 141°19E 302 E10
Kitakami-Sammyaku Japan 39°30N 141°30E 302 E10
Kitakata Japan 37°39N 139°52E 302 F9
Kitakyūshū Japan 33°50N 130°50E 303 H5
Kitale Kenya 1°0N 35°0E 326 B4
Kitami Japan 43°48N 143°54E 302 C11
Kitami-Sammyaku Japan 44°22N 142°43E 302 B11
Kitangiri, L. Tanzania 4°5S 34°20E 326 C3
Kitaya Tanzania 10°38S 40°8E 327 E5
Kitchener Canada 43°27N 80°29W 354 C4
Kitee Finland 62°5N 30°8E 280 E24
Kitega = Gitega Burundi 3°26S 29°56E 326 C2
Kitengo Dem. Rep. of the Congo 7°26S 24°8E 326 D1
Kitgum Uganda 3°17N 32°52E 326 B3
Kíthira = Kythira Greece 36°8N 23°0E 295 F10
Kíthnos Greece 37°26N 24°27E 295 F11
Kiti Cyprus 34°50N 33°34E 297 E12
Kiti, C. Cyprus 34°48N 33°36E 297 E12
Kitimat Canada 54°3N 128°38W 342 C3
Kitinen → Finland 67°14N 27°27E 280 C22
Kitsuki Japan 33°25N 131°37E 303 H5
Kittakittaooloo, L. Australia 28°3S 138°14E 335 D2
Kittanning U.S.A. 40°49N 79°31W 354 F5
Kittatinny Mt. U.S.A. 41°19N 74°39W 355 F10
Kittery U.S.A. 43°5N 70°45W 355 C14
Kittilä Finland 67°40N 24°51E 280 C21
Kitui Kenya 1°17S 38°0E 326 C4
Kitwanga Canada 55°6N 128°4W 342 B3
Kitwe Zambia 12°54S 28°13E 327 E2
Kivarli India 24°33N 72°46E 314 G5
Kivertsi Ukraine 50°50N 25°28E 289 C13
Kividhes Cyprus 34°46N 32°51E 297 E11
Kivu, L. Dem. Rep. of the Congo 1°48S 29°0E 326 C2
Kiyev = Kyyiv Ukraine 50°30N 30°28E 289 C16
Kiyevskoye Vdkhr. = Kyyivske Vdskh. Ukraine 51°0N 30°25E 289 C16
Kizel Russia 59°3N 57°40E 290 C10
Kiziguru Rwanda 1°46S 30°23E 326 C3
Kızıl Irmak → Turkey 41°44N 35°58E 291 F6
Kizil Jilga China 35°26N 78°50E 315 B8
Kızıldağ △ Turkey 38°5N 31°20E 316 B1
Kızıltepe Turkey 37°12N 40°35E 316 B4
Kizimkazi Tanzania 6°28S 39°30E 326 D4
Kizlyar Russia 43°51N 46°40E 291 F8
Kizyl-Arvat = Serdar Turkmenistan 39°4N 56°23E 317 B8
Kjölur Iceland 64°50N 19°25W 280 D4
Kladno Czech Rep. 50°10N 14°7E 288 C8
Klaeng Thailand 12°47N 101°39E 310 F3
Klagenfurt Austria 46°38N 14°20E 288 E8
Klaipėda Lithuania 55°43N 21°10E 281 J19
Klaksvík Færoe Is. 62°14N 6°35W 280 E9
Klamath → U.S.A. 41°33N 124°5W 348 F1
Klamath Falls U.S.A. 42°13N 121°46W 348 E3
Klamath Mts. U.S.A. 41°50N 123°20W 348 F2
Klamono Indonesia 1°8S 131°30E 309 E8
Klang Malaysia 3°2N 101°26E 311 L3
Klappan → Canada 58°0N 129°43W 342 B3
Klarälven → Sweden 59°23N 13°32E 281 G15
Klatovy Czech Rep. 49°23N 13°18E 288 D7
Klawer S. Africa 31°44S 18°36E 328 E2
Klazienaveen Neths. 52°44N 7°0E 287 B6
Kleena Kleene Canada 52°0N 124°59W 342 C4
Klein-Karas Namibia 27°33S 18°7E 328 D2
Klerksdorp S. Africa 26°53S 26°38E 328 D4
Kletsk = Klyetsk Belarus 53°5N 26°45E 289 B14
Kletskiy Russia 49°16N 43°11E 291 E7
Klickitat U.S.A. 45°49N 121°9W 348 D3
Klickitat → U.S.A. 45°42N 121°17W 350 E5
Klidhes Cyprus 35°42N 34°36E 297 D13
Klinaklini → Canada 51°21N 125°40W 342 C3
Klip → S. Africa 27°3S 29°3E 329 D4
Klipdale S. Africa 34°19S 19°57E 328 E2
Klipplaat S. Africa 33°1S 24°22E 328 E3
Kłodzko Poland 50°28N 16°38E 289 C9
Klong Wang Chao △ Thailand 16°20N 99°9E 310 D2
Klouto Togo 6°57N 0°44E 322 G6
Kluane △ Canada 60°45N 139°30W 342 A1
Kluane L. Canada 61°15N 138°40W 340 C6
Kluang Malaysia 2°3N 103°18E 311 L4
Kluczbork Poland 50°58N 18°12E 289 C10
Klukwan U.S.A. 59°24N 135°54W 342 B1
Klungkung Indonesia 8°32S 115°24E 309 K18
Klyetsk Belarus 53°5N 26°45E 289 B14
Klyuchevskaya, Gora Russia 55°50N 160°30E 301 D17
Knaresborough U.K. 54°1N 1°28W 284 C6
Knee L. Man., Canada 55°3N 94°45W 344 A1
Knee L. Sask., Canada 55°51N 107°0W 343 B7
Knight Inlet Canada 50°45N 125°40W 342 C3
Knighton U.K. 52°21N 3°3W 285 E4
Knights Ferry U.S.A. 37°50N 120°40W 350 H6
Knights Landing U.S.A. 38°48N 121°43W 350 G5
Knob, C. Australia 34°32S 119°16E 333 F2
Knock Ireland 53°48N 8°55W 282 C3
Knockmealdown Mts. Ireland 52°14N 7°56W 282 D4
Knokke-Heist Belgium 51°21N 3°17E 287 C3
Knossos Greece 35°16N 25°10E 297 D7
Knowlton Canada 45°13N 72°31W 355 A12
Knox U.S.A. 41°18N 86°37W 352 E10
Knox Coast Antarctica 66°30S 108°0E 277 C8
Knoxville Iowa, U.S.A. 41°19N 93°6W 352 E7
Knoxville Pa., U.S.A. 41°57N 77°27W 354 E7
Knoxville Tenn., U.S.A. 35°58N 83°55W 357 D13
Knud Rasmussen Land Greenland 78°0N 60°0W 276 A5
Knysna S. Africa 34°2S 23°2E 328 E3
Ko Kha Thailand 18°11N 99°24E 310 C2
Ko Tarutao △ Thailand 6°31N 99°26E 311 J2
Ko Yao Thailand 8°7N 98°35E 311 a
Koartac = Quaqtaq Canada 60°55N 69°40W 341 C13
Koba Indonesia 6°37S 134°37E 309 F8
Kobarid Slovenia 46°15N 13°30E 288 E7
Kobayashi Japan 31°56N 130°59E 303 J5
Kōbe Japan 34°41N 135°13E 303 G7
København Denmark 55°40N 12°26E 281 J15
Kōbi-Sho Japan 25°56N 123°41E 303 M1
Koblenz Germany 50°21N 7°36E 288 C4
Kobryn Belarus 52°15N 24°22E 289 B13
Kocaeli Turkey 40°45N 29°50E 291 F4
Kočani Macedonia 41°55N 22°25E 295 D10
Koch Bihar India 26°22N 89°29E 313 F16
Kochas India 25°15N 83°56E 315 G10
Kochi = Cochin India 9°58N 76°20E 312 Q10
Kōchi Japan 33°30N 133°35E 303 H6
Kōchi □ Japan 33°40N 133°30E 303 H6
Kochiu = Gejiu China 23°20N 103°10E 304 D5
Kodarma India 24°28N 85°36E 315 G11
Kodiak U.S.A. 57°47N 152°24W 346 a
Kodiak I. U.S.A. 57°30N 152°45W 346 a
Kodinar India 20°46N 70°46E 314 J4
Koedoesberge S. Africa 32°40S 20°11E 328 E3
Koes Namibia 26°0S 19°15E 328 D2
Koffiefontein S. Africa 29°30S 25°0E 328 D4
Kofiau Indonesia 1°11S 129°50E 309 E7
Koforidua Ghana 6°3N 0°17W 322 G5
Kōfu Japan 35°40N 138°30E 303 G9
Koga Japan 36°11N 139°43E 303 F9
Kogaluc → Canada 56°12N 61°44W 345 A7
Køge Denmark 55°27N 12°11E 281 J15
Koh-i-Khurd Afghan. 33°30N 65°59E 314 C1
Koh-i-Maran Pakistan 29°18N 66°50E 314 E2
Kohat Pakistan 33°40N 71°29E 314 C4
Kohima India 25°35N 94°10E 313 G19
Kohkīlūyeh va Būyer Aḥmadi □ Iran 31°30N 50°30E 317 D6
Kohler Ra. Antarctica 77°0S 110°0W 277 D15
Kohlu Pakistan 29°54N 69°15E 314 E3
Kohtla-Järve Estonia 59°20N 27°20E 281 G22
Koi Sanjaq Iraq 36°5N 44°38E 316 B5
Koillismaa Finland 65°44N 28°36E 280 D23
Koin N. Korea 40°28N 126°18E 307 D14
Kojŏ N. Korea 38°58N 127°58E 307 E14
Kojonup Australia 33°48S 117°10E 333 F2
Kojūr Iran 36°23N 51°43E 317 B6
Kokand = Qŭqon Uzbekistan 40°31N 70°56E 300 E8
Kokas Indonesia 2°42S 132°26E 309 E8
Kokchetav = Kökshetaū Kazakhstan 53°20N 69°25E 300 D7
Kokemäenjoki → Finland 61°32N 21°44E 280 F19
Kokkola Finland 63°50N 23°8E 280 E20
Koko Kyunzu Burma 14°10N 93°25E 313 M18
Kokomo U.S.A. 40°29N 86°8W 352 E10
Koksan N. Korea 38°46N 126°40E 307 E14
Kökshetaū Kazakhstan 53°20N 69°25E 300 D7
Koksoak → Canada 58°30N 68°10W 341 D13
Kokstad S. Africa 30°32S 29°29E 329 E4
Kokubu Japan 31°44N 130°46E 303 J5
Kola Indonesia 5°35S 134°30E 309 F8
Kola Russia 68°45N 33°8E 280 B25
Kola Pen. = Kolskiy Poluostrov Russia 67°30N 38°0E 290 A6
Kolachi → Pakistan 27°8N 67°2E 314 F2
Kolahoi India 34°12N 75°22E 315 B6
Kolaka Indonesia 4°3S 121°46E 309 E6
Kolar India 13°12N 78°15E 312 N11
Kolar Gold Fields India 12°58N 78°16E 312 N11
Kolaras India 25°14N 77°36E 314 G6
Kolari Finland 67°20N 23°48E 280 C20
Kolayat India 27°50N 72°50E 314 F5
Kolda Senegal 12°55N 14°57W 322 F3
Kolding Denmark 55°30N 9°29E 281 J13
Kolepom = Dolak, Pulau Indonesia 8°0S 138°30E 309 F9
Kolguyev, Ostrov Russia 69°20N 48°30E 290 A8
Kolhapur India 16°43N 74°15E 312 L9
Kolín Czech Rep. 50°2N 15°9E 288 C8
Kolkas rags Latvia 57°46N 22°37E 281 H20
Kolkata India 22°34N 88°21E 315 H13
Kollam = Quilon India 8°50N 76°38E 312 Q10
Kollum Neths. 53°17N 6°10E 287 A6
Kolmanskop Namibia 26°45S 15°14E 328 D2
Köln Germany 50°56N 6°57E 288 C4
Koło Poland 52°14N 18°40E 289 B10
Kołobrzeg Poland 54°10N 15°35E 288 A8
Kolomna Russia 55°8N 38°45E 290 C6
Kolomyya Ukraine 48°31N 25°2E 289 D13
Kolonodale Indonesia 2°0S 121°19E 309 E6
Kolosib India 24°15N 92°45E 313 G18
Kolpashevo Russia 58°20N 83°5E 300 D9
Kolpino Russia 59°44N 30°39E 290 C5
Kolskiy Poluostrov Russia 67°30N 38°0E 290 A6
Kolskiy Zaliv Russia 69°23N 34°0E 280 B26
Kolwezi Dem. Rep. of the Congo 10°40S 25°25E 327 E2
Kolyma → Russia 69°30N 161°0E 301 C17
Kolymskoye Nagorye Russia 63°0N 157°0E 301 C16
Kôm Ombo Egypt 24°25N 32°52E 323 D12
Komandorskiye Is. = Komandorskiye Ostrova Russia 55°0N 167°0E 301 D17
Komandorskiye Ostrova Russia 55°0N 167°0E 301 D17
Komárno Slovak Rep. 47°49N 18°5E 289 E10
Komatipoort S. Africa 25°25S 31°55E 329 D5
Komatou Yialou Cyprus 35°25N 34°8E 297 D13
Komatsu Japan 36°25N 136°30E 303 F8
Komatsushima Japan 34°0N 134°35E 303 H7
Komi □ Russia 64°0N 55°0E 290 B10
Kommunarsk = Alchevsk Ukraine 48°30N 38°45E 291 E6
Kommunizma, Pik = imeni Ismail Samani, Pik Tajikistan 39°0N 72°2E 300 F8
Komodo Indonesia 8°37S 119°20E 309 F5
Komoran, Pulau Indonesia 8°18S 138°45E 309 F9
Komoro Japan 36°19N 138°26E 303 F9
Komotini Greece 41°9N 25°26E 295 D11
Kompasberg S. Africa 31°45S 24°32E 328 E3
Kompong Bang Cambodia 12°24N 104°40E 311 F5
Kompong Cham Cambodia 12°0N 105°30E 311 F5
Kompong Chhnang = Kampong Chhnang Cambodia 12°20N 104°35E 311 F5
Kompong Chikreng Cambodia 13°5N 104°18E 310 F5
Kompong Kleang Cambodia 13°6N 104°8E 310 F5
Kompong Luong Cambodia 11°49N 104°48E 311 G5
Kompong Pranak Cambodia 13°35N 104°55E 310 F5
Kompong Som = Kampong Saom Cambodia 10°38N 103°30E 311 G4
Kompong Som, Chhung = Kampong Saom, Chaak Cambodia 10°50N 103°32E 311 G4
Kompong Speu Cambodia 11°26N 104°32E 311 G5
Kompong Sralau Cambodia 14°5N 105°46E 310 E5
Kompong Thom Cambodia 12°35N 104°51E 310 F5
Kompong Trabeck Cambodia 13°6N 105°14E 310 F5
Kompong Trabeck Cambodia 11°9N 105°28E 311 G5
Kompong Trach Cambodia 11°25N 105°48E 311 G5
Kompong Tralach Cambodia 11°54N 104°47E 311 G5
Komrat = Comrat Moldova 46°18N 28°40E 289 E15
Komsberg S. Africa 32°40S 20°45E 328 E3
Komsomolets, Ostrov Russia 80°30N 95°0E 301 A10
Komsomolsk Russia 50°30N 137°0E 301 D14
Kon Tum Vietnam 14°24N 108°0E 310 E7
Kon Tum, Plateau du Vietnam 14°30N 108°30E 310 E7
Konar □ Afghan. 34°30N 71°3E 312 B7
Konārī Iran 28°13N 51°36E 317 D6
Konch India 26°0N 79°10E 315 G8
Konde Tanzania 4°57S 39°45E 326 C4
Kondinin Australia 32°34S 118°8E 333 F2
Kondoa Tanzania 4°55S 35°50E 326 C4
Kondopaga Russia 62°12N 34°17E 290 B5
Kondratyevo Russia 57°22N 98°15E 301 D10
Köneürgench Turkmenistan 42°19N 59°10E 300 E6
Konevo Russia 62°8N 39°20E 290 B6
Kong = Khong → Cambodia 13°32N 105°58E 310 F5
Kong Ivory C. 8°54N 4°36W 322 G5
Kong, Koh Cambodia 11°20N 103°0E 311 G4
Kong Christian IX Land Greenland 68°0N 36°0W 276 C6
Kong Christian X Land Greenland 74°0N 29°0W 276 B6
Kong Frederik IX Land Greenland 67°0N 52°0W 276 C5
Kong Frederik VI Kyst Greenland 63°0N 43°0W 276 C5
Kong Frederik VIII Land Greenland 78°30N 26°0W 276 B6
Kong Oscar Fjord Greenland 72°20N 24°0W 276 B6
Konglu Burma 27°13N 97°57E 313 F20
Kongola Namibia 17°45S 23°20E 328 B3
Kongolo Kasai-Or., Dem. Rep. of the Congo 5°26S 24°49E 326 D1
Kongolo Katanga, Dem. Rep. of the Congo 5°22S 27°0E 326 D2
Kongsberg Norway 59°39N 9°39E 281 G13
Kongsvinger Norway 60°12N 12°2E 281 F15
Kongur Shan China 38°34N 75°18E 304 C2
Kongwa Tanzania 6°11S 36°26E 326 D4
Koni Dem. Rep. of the Congo 10°40S 27°11E 327 E2
Koni, Mts. Dem. Rep. of the Congo 10°36S 27°10E 327 E2
Konin Poland 52°12N 18°15E 289 B10
Konjic Bos.-H. 43°42N 17°58E 295 C7
Konkiep Namibia 26°49S 17°15E 328 D2
Konosha Russia 61°0N 40°5E 290 B7
Kōnosu Japan 36°3N 139°31E 303 F9
Konotop Ukraine 51°12N 33°7E 291 D5
Konqi He → China 41°0N 86°0E 304 B3
Końskie Poland 51°15N 20°23E 289 C11
Konstanz Germany 47°40N 9°10E 288 E5
Kont Iran 26°55N 61°50E 317 E9
Kontagora Nigeria 10°23N 5°27E 322 F7
Kontiolahti Finland 62°46N 29°50E 280 E23
Kontokali Greece 39°38N 19°51E 297 A3
Konya Turkey 37°52N 32°35E 316 B2
Konza Kenya 1°45S 37°7E 326 C4
Koocanusa, L. Canada 49°20N 115°15W 348 B6
Kookynie Australia 29°17S 121°22E 333 E3
Koolyanobbing Australia 30°48S 119°36E 333 F2
Koonibba Australia 31°54S 133°25E 335 E1

Koorawatha *Australia* 34°2S 148°33E **335** E4
Koorda *Australia* 30°48S 117°35E **333** F2
Kooskia *U.S.A.* 46°9N 115°59W **348** C6
Kootenay → *U.S.A.* 49°19N 117°39W **342** D5
Kootenay △ *Canada* 51°0N 116°0W **342** C5
Kootenay L. *Canada* 49°45N 116°50W **348** B5
Kootjieskolk *S. Africa* 31°15S 20°21E **328** E3
Kopaonik *Serbia* 43°10N 20°50E **295** C9
Kópavogur *Iceland* 64°6N 21°55W **280** D3
Koper *Slovenia* 45°31N 13°44E **288** F7
Kopervik *Norway* 59°17N 5°17E **281** G11
Kopet Dagh *Asia* 38°0N 58°0E **317** B8
Kopi *Australia* 33°24S 135°40E **335** E2
Köping *Sweden* 59°31N 16°3E **281** G17
Koppeh Dāgh = Kopet Dagh
Asia 38°0N 58°0E **317** B8
Koppies *S. Africa* 27°20S 27°30E **329** D4
Koprivnica *Croatia* 46°12N 16°45E **294** A7
Köprülü △ *Turkey* 37°20N 31°5E **316** B1
Kopychyntsi *Ukraine* 49°7N 25°58E **289** D13
Kora △ *Kenya* 0°14S 38°44E **326** C4
Korab *Macedonia* 41°44N 20°40E **295** D9
Koral *India* 21°50N 73°12E **314** J5
Korba *India* 22°20N 82°45E **315** H10
Korbu, G. *Malaysia* 4°41N 101°18E **311** K3
Korçë *Albania* 40°37N 20°50E **295** D9
Korčula *Croatia* 42°56N 16°57E **294** C7
Kord Kūy *Iran* 36°48N 54°7E **317** B7
Kord Sheykh *Iran* 28°31N 52°53E **317** D7
Kordestān □ *Iran* 36°0N 47°0E **316** C5
Kordofân *Sudan* 13°0N 29°0E **323** F11
Korea, North ■ *Asia* 40°0N 127°0E **307** E14
Korea, South ■ *Asia* 36°0N 128°0E **307** G15
Korea Bay *Korea* 39°0N 124°0E **307** E13
Korea Strait *Asia* 34°0N 129°30E **307** H15
Korets *Ukraine* 50°40N 27°5E **289** C14
Korhogo *Ivory C.* 9°29N 5°28W **322** G4
Korinthiakos Kolpos
Greece 38°16N 22°30E **295** E10
Korinthos *Greece* 37°56N 22°55E **295** F10
Korissa, L. *Greece* 39°27N 19°53E **297** B3
Kōriyama *Japan* 37°24N 140°23E **302** F10
Korla *China* 41°45N 86°4E **304** B3
Kormakiti, C. *Cyprus* 35°23N 32°56E **297** D11
Korneshty = Corneşti
Moldova 47°21N 28°1E **289** E15
Koro *Fiji* 17°19S 179°23E **331** a
Koro *Ivory C.* 8°32N 7°30W **322** G4
Koro Sea *Fiji* 17°30S 179°45W **331** a
Korogwe *Tanzania* 5°5S 38°25E **326** D4
Korolevu *Fiji* 18°12S 177°46E **331** a
Koronadal *Phil.* 6°12N 125°1E **309** C6
Koror *Palau* 7°20N 134°28E **336** G5
Körös → *Hungary* 46°43N 20°12E **289** E11
Korosten *Ukraine* 50°54N 28°36E **289** C15
Korostyshev *Ukraine* 50°19N 29°4E **289** C15
Korovou *Fiji* 17°47S 178°32E **331** a
Koroyanitu △ *Fiji* 17°40S 177°35E **331** a
Korraraika, Helodranon' i
Madag. 17°45S 43°57E **329** B7
Korsakov *Russia* 46°36N 142°42E **301** E15
Korshunovo *Russia* 58°37N 110°10E **301** D12
Korsør *Denmark* 55°20N 11°9E **281** J14
Kortrijk *Belgium* 50°50N 3°17E **287** D3
Korwai *India* 24°7N 78°5E **314** G8
Koryakskoye Nagorye
Russia 61°0N 171°0E **301** C18
Kos *Greece* 36°50N 27°15E **295** F12
Kosan *N. Korea* 38°52N 127°25E **307** E14
Koschagyl *Kazakhstan* 46°40N 54°0E **291** E9
Kościan *Poland* 52°5N 16°40E **288** B9
Kosciusko *U.S.A.* 33°4N 89°35W **357** E10
Kosciuszko, Mt.
Australia 36°27S 148°16E **335** F4
Kosha *Sudan* 20°50N 30°30E **323** D12
K'oshih = Kashi *China* 39°30N 76°2E **304** C2
Koshiki-Rettō *Japan* 31°45N 129°49E **303** J4
Kosi *India* 27°48N 77°29E **314** F7
Kosi → *India* 28°41N 78°57E **315** E8
Košice *Slovak Rep.* 48°42N 21°15E **289** D11
Koskinou *Greece* 36°23N 28°13E **297** C10
Koslan *Russia* 63°34N 49°14E **290** B8
Kosŏng *N. Korea* 38°40N 128°22E **307** E15
Kosovo □ *Serbia* 42°30N 21°0E **295** C9
Kosovska Mitrovica
Serbia 42°54N 20°52E **295** C9
Kossou, L. de *Ivory C.* 6°59N 5°31W **322** G4
Koster *S. Africa* 25°52S 26°54E **328** D4
Kôstî *Sudan* 13°8N 32°43E **323** F12
Kostopil *Ukraine* 50°51N 26°22E **289** C14
Kostroma *Russia* 57°50N 40°58E **290** C7
Kostrzyn *Poland* 52°35N 14°39E **288** B8
Koszalin *Poland* 54°11N 16°8E **288** A9
Kot Addu *Pakistan* 30°30N 71°0E **314** D4
Kot Kapura *India* 30°35N 74°50E **314** D6
Kot Moman *Pakistan* 32°13N 73°0E **314** C5
Kot Sultan *Pakistan* 30°46N 70°56E **314** D4
Kota *India* 25°14N 75°49E **314** G6
Kota Barrage *India* 25°6N 75°51E **314** G6
Kota Belud *Malaysia* 6°21N 116°26E **308** C5
Kota Bharu *Malaysia* 6°7N 102°14E **311** J4
Kota Kinabalu *Malaysia* 6°0N 116°4E **308** C5
Kota Kubu Bharu
Malaysia 3°34N 101°39E **311** L3
Kota Tinggi *Malaysia* 1°44N 103°53E **311** M4
Kotaagung *Indonesia* 5°38S 104°29E **308** F2
Kotabaru *Indonesia* 3°20S 116°20E **308** E5
Kotabumi *Indonesia* 4°49S 104°54E **308** E2
Kotamobagu *Indonesia* 0°57N 124°31E **309** D6
Kotcho L. *Canada* 59°7N 121°12W **342** B4
Kotdwara *India* 29°45N 78°32E **315** E8
Kotelnich *Russia* 58°22N 48°24E **290** C8
Kotelnikovo *Russia* 47°38N 43°8E **291** E7
Kotelnyy, Ostrov
Russia 75°10N 139°0E **301** B14
Kothari → *India* 25°20N 75°4E **314** G6
Kothi *Chhattisgarh, India* 23°21N 82°3E **315** H10
Kothi *Mad. P., India* 24°45N 80°40E **315** G9
Kotiro *Pakistan* 26°17N 67°13E **314** F2
Kotka *Finland* 60°28N 26°58E **280** F22
Kotlas *Russia* 61°17N 46°43E **290** B8
Kotli *Pakistan* 33°30N 73°55E **314** C5
Kotma *India* 23°12N 81°58E **315** H9
Kotmul *Pakistan* 35°32N 75°10E **315** B6
Kotor *Montenegro* 42°25N 18°47E **295** C8
Kotovsk *Ukraine* 47°45N 29°35E **289** E15
Kotputli *India* 27°43N 76°12E **314** F7
Kotri *Pakistan* 25°22N 68°22E **314** G3
Kotto → *C.A.R.* 4°14N 22°2E **324** D4
Kotturu *India* 14°45N 76°10E **312** M10
Kotu Group *Tonga* 20°0S 174°45W **331** c
Kotuy → *Russia* 71°54N 102°6E **301** B11
Kotzebue *U.S.A.* 66°53N 162°39W **346** a
Kotzebue Sound *U.S.A.* 66°20N 163°0W **338** C3
Kouchibouguac △
Canada 46°50N 65°0W **345** C6
Koudougou *Burkina Faso* 12°10N 2°20W **322** F5
Koufonisi *Greece* 34°56N 26°8E **297** E8
Kougaberge *S. Africa* 33°48S 23°50E **328** E3
Kouilou → *Congo* 4°10S 12°5E **324** E2
Koula Moutou *Gabon* 1°15S 12°25E **324** E2
Koulen = Kulen
Cambodia 13°50N 104°40E **310** F5
Kouloura *Greece* 39°42N 19°54E **297** A3
Koumala *Australia* 21°38S 149°15E **334** C4
Koumra *Chad* 8°50N 17°35E **323** G9
Kountze *U.S.A.* 30°22N 94°19W **356** F7
Kouris → *Cyprus* 34°38N 32°54E **297** E11
Kourou *Fr. Guiana* 5°9N 52°39W **365** B8
Kouroussa *Guinea* 10°45N 9°45W **322** F4
Koussseri *Cameroon* 12°0N 14°55E **323** F8
Koutiala *Mali* 12°25N 5°23W **322** F4
Kouvola *Finland* 60°52N 26°43E **280** F22
Kovdor *Russia* 67°34N 30°24E **280** C24
Kovel *Ukraine* 51°11N 24°38E **289** C13
Kovrov *Russia* 56°25N 41°25E **290** C7
Kowanyama *Australia* 15°29S 141°44E **334** B3
Kowloon *China* 22°19N 114°11E **305** G11
Kowŏn *N. Korea* 39°26N 127°14E **307** E14
Koyampattur = Coimbatore
India 11°2N 76°59E **312** P10
Köyceğiz *Turkey* 36°57N 28°40E **295** F13
Koyukuk → *U.S.A.* 64°55N 157°32W **338** C4
Koza = Okinawa *Japan* 26°19N 127°46E **303** L3
Kozan *Turkey* 37°26N 35°50E **316** B2
Kozani *Greece* 40°19N 21°47E **295** D9
Kozhikode = Calicut
India 11°15N 75°43E **312** P9
Kozhva *Russia* 65°10N 57°0E **290** A10
Kozyatyn *Ukraine* 49°45N 28°50E **289** D15
Kpalimé *Togo* 6°57N 0°44E **322** G6
Kra, Isthmus of = Kra, Kho Khot
Thailand 10°15N 99°30E **311** G2
Kra, Kho Khot *Thailand* 10°15N 99°30E **311** G2
Kra Buri *Thailand* 10°22N 98°46E **311** G2
Kraai → *S. Africa* 30°40S 26°45E **328** E4
Krabi *Thailand* 8°4N 98°55E **311** H2
Kracheh *Cambodia* 12°32N 106°10E **310** F6
Kragan *Indonesia* 6°43S 111°38E **309** G14
Kragerø *Norway* 58°52N 9°25E **281** G13
Kragujevac *Serbia* 44°2N 20°56E **295** B9
Krakatau = Rakata, Pulau
Indonesia 6°10S 105°20E **308** F3
Krakatoa = Rakata, Pulau
Indonesia 6°10S 105°20E **308** F3
Krakor *Cambodia* 12°32N 104°12E **310** F5
Kraków *Poland* 50°4N 19°57E **289** C10
Kralanh *Cambodia* 13°35N 103°25E **310** F4
Kraljevo *Serbia* 43°44N 20°41E **295** C9
Kramatorsk *Ukraine* 48°50N 37°30E **291** E6
Kramfors *Sweden* 62°55N 17°48E **280** E17
Kranj *Slovenia* 46°16N 14°22E **288** E8
Kranskop *S. Africa* 28°0S 30°47E **329** D5
Krasavino *Russia* 60°58N 46°29E **290** B8
Kraskino *Russia* 42°44N 130°48E **302** C5
Kraśnik *Poland* 50°55N 22°15E **289** C12
Krasnoarmeysk *Russia* 51°0N 45°42E **300** D5
Krasnodar *Russia* 45°5N 39°0E **291** E6
Krasnokamsk *Russia* 58°4N 55°48E **290** C10
Krasnoperekopsk
Ukraine 46°0N 33°54E **291** E5
Krasnorechenskiy
Russia 44°41N 135°14E **302** B7
Krasnoselkup *Russia* 65°20N 82°10E **300** C9
Krasnoturinsk *Russia* 59°46N 60°12E **290** C11
Krasnoufimsk *Russia* 56°36N 57°38E **290** C10
Krasnouralsk *Russia* 58°21N 60°3E **290** C11
Krasnovishersk *Russia* 60°23N 57°3E **290** B10
Krasnoyarsk *Russia* 56°8N 93°0E **301** D10
Krasnyy Kut *Russia* 50°50N 47°0E **291** D8
Krasnyy Luch *Ukraine* 48°13N 39°0E **291** E6
Krasnyy Yar *Russia* 46°43N 48°23E **291** E8
Kratie = Kracheh
Cambodia 12°32N 106°10E **310** F6
Krau *Indonesia* 3°19S 140°5E **309** E10
Kravanh, Chuor Phnum
Cambodia 12°0N 103°32E **311** G4
Krefeld *Germany* 51°20N 6°33E **288** C4
Kremen *Croatia* 44°28N 15°53E **288** F8
Kremenchuk *Ukraine* 49°5N 33°25E **291** E5
Kremenchuksk Vdskh.
Ukraine 49°20N 32°30E **291** E5
Kremenets *Ukraine* 50°8N 25°43E **289** C13
Kremmling *U.S.A.* 40°4N 106°24W **348** F10
Krems *Austria* 48°25N 15°36E **288** D8
Kretinga *Lithuania* 55°53N 21°15E **281** J19
Kribi *Cameroon* 2°57N 9°56E **324** D1
Krichev = Krychaw
Belarus 53°40N 31°41E **289** B16
Krios, Akra *Greece* 35°13N 23°34E **297** D5
Krishna → *India* 15°57N 80°59E **313** M12
Krishnanagar *India* 23°24N 88°33E **315** H13
Kristiansand *Norway* 58°8N 8°1E **281** G13
Kristianstad *Sweden* 56°2N 14°9E **281** H16
Kristiansund *Norway* 63°7N 7°45E **280** E12
Kristiinankaupunki
Finland 62°16N 21°21E **280** E19
Kristinehamn *Sweden* 59°18N 14°7E **281** G16
Kristinestad =
Kristiinankaupunki
Finland 62°16N 21°21E **280** E19
Kriti *Greece* 35°15N 25°0E **297** D7
Kritsa *Greece* 35°10N 25°41E **297** D7
Krivoy Rog = Kryvyy Rih
Ukraine 47°51N 33°20E **291** E5
Krk *Croatia* 45°8N 14°40E **288** F8
Krokodil → *Mozam.* 25°14S 32°18E **329** D5
Krong Kaoh Kong
Cambodia 11°37N 102°59E **311** G4
Kronprins Olav Kyst
Antarctica 69°0S 42°0E **277** C5
Kronprinsesse Märtha Kyst
Antarctica 73°30S 10°0W **277** D2
Kronshtadt *Russia* 59°57N 29°51E **290** B4
Kroonstad *S. Africa* 27°43S 27°19E **328** D4
Kropotkin *Russia* 45°28N 40°28E **291** E7
Krosno *Poland* 49°42N 21°46E **289** D11
Krotoszyn *Poland* 51°42N 17°23E **289** C9
Krousonas *Greece* 35°13N 24°59E **297** D6
Kruger △ *S. Africa* 24°50S 26°10E **329** C5
Krugersdorp *S. Africa* 26°5S 27°46E **329** D4
Kruisfontein *S. Africa* 33°59S 24°43E **328** E3
Krung Thep = Bangkok
Thailand 13°45N 100°35E **310** F3
Krupki *Belarus* 54°19N 29°8E **289** A15
Kruševac *Serbia* 43°35N 21°28E **295** C9
Krychaw *Belarus* 53°40N 31°41E **289** B16
Krymskiy Poluostrov = Krymskyy
Pivostriv *Ukraine* 45°0N 34°0E **291** F5
Krymskyy Pivostriv
Ukraine 45°0N 34°0E **291** F5
Kryvyy Rih *Ukraine* 47°51N 33°20E **291** E5
Ksar el Kebir *Morocco* 35°0N 6°0W **322** B4
Ksar es Souk = Er Rachidia
Morocco 31°58N 4°20W **322** B5
Kuah *Malaysia* 6°19N 99°51E **311** J2
Kuala Belait *Malaysia* 4°35N 114°11E **308** D4
Kuala Berang *Malaysia* 5°5N 103°1E **311** K4
Kuala Dungun = Dungun
Malaysia 4°45N 103°25E **311** K4
Kuala Kangsar
Malaysia 4°46N 100°56E **311** K3
Kuala Kelawang
Malaysia 2°56N 102°5E **311** L4
Kuala Kerai *Malaysia* 5°30N 102°12E **311** K4
Kuala Kerian *Malaysia* 5°10N 100°25E **311** c
Kuala Lipis *Malaysia* 4°10N 102°3E **311** K4
Kuala Lumpur *Malaysia* 3°9N 101°41E **311** L3
Kuala Nerang *Malaysia* 6°16N 100°37E **311** J3
Kuala Pilah *Malaysia* 2°45N 102°15E **311** L4
Kuala Rompin *Malaysia* 2°49N 103°29E **311** L4
Kuala Selangor
Malaysia 3°20N 101°15E **311** L3
Kuala Sepetang
Malaysia 4°49N 100°28E **311** K3
Kuala Terengganu
Malaysia 5°20N 103°8E **311** K4
Kualajelai *Indonesia* 2°58S 110°46E **308** E4
Kualakapuas *Indonesia* 2°55S 114°20E **308** E4
Kualakurun *Indonesia* 1°10S 113°50E **308** E4
Kualapembuang
Indonesia 3°14S 112°38E **308** E4
Kualasimpang *Indonesia* 4°17N 98°3E **308** D1
Kuancheng *China* 40°37N 118°30E **307** D10
Kuandang *Indonesia* 0°56N 123°1E **309** D6
Kuandian *China* 40°45N 124°45E **307** D13
Kuangchou = Guangzhou
China 23°6N 113°13E **305** D6
Kuantan *Malaysia* 3°49N 103°20E **311** L4
Kuba = Quba *Azerbaijan* 41°21N 48°32E **291** F8
Kuban → *Russia* 45°20N 37°30E **291** E6
Kubokawa *Japan* 33°12N 133°8E **303** H6
Kubu *Indonesia* 8°16S 115°35E **309** J18
Kubutambahan
Indonesia 8°5S 115°10E **309** J18
Kucar, Tanjung
Indonesia 8°39S 114°34E **309** K18
Kucha Gompa *India* 34°25N 76°56E **315** B7
Kuchaman *India* 27°13N 74°47E **314** F6
Kuchinda *India* 21°44N 84°21E **315** J11
Kuching *Malaysia* 1°33N 110°25E **308** D4
Kuchino-eruba-Jima
Japan 30°28N 130°12E **303** J5
Kuchino-Shima *Japan* 29°57N 129°55E **303** K4
Kuchinotsu *Japan* 32°36N 130°11E **303** H5
Kucing = Kuching
Malaysia 1°33N 110°25E **308** D4
Kud → *Pakistan* 26°5N 66°20E **314** F2
Kuda *India* 23°10N 71°15E **314** H4
Kudat *Malaysia* 6°55N 116°55E **308** C5
Kudus *Indonesia* 6°48S 110°51E **309** G14
Kudymkar *Russia* 59°1N 54°39E **290** C9
Kueiyang = Guiyang
China 26°32N 106°40E **304** D5
Kufra Oasis = Al Kufrah
Libya 24°17N 23°15E **323** D10
Kufstein *Austria* 47°35N 12°11E **288** E7
Kugaaruk = Pelly Bay
Canada 68°38N 89°50W **341** C11
Kugluktuk *Canada* 67°50N 115°5W **340** C8
Kugong I. *Canada* 56°18N 79°50W **344** A4
Kūh-e-Jebāl Bārez *Iran* 29°0N 58°0E **317** D8
Kūhak *Iran* 27°12N 63°10E **317** E9
Kuhan *Pakistan* 28°19N 67°14E **314** E2
Kūhbonān *Iran* 31°23N 56°19E **317** D8
Kūhestak *Iran* 26°47N 57°2E **317** E8
Kuhin *Iran* 36°22N 49°40E **317** B6
Kūhīrī *Iran* 26°55N 61°2E **317** E9
Kuhmo *Finland* 64°7N 29°31E **280** D23
Kūhpāyeh *Esfahan, Iran* 32°44N 52°20E **317** C7
Kūhpāyeh *Kermān, Iran* 30°35N 57°15E **317** D8
Kūhrān, Kūh-e *Iran* 26°46N 58°12E **317** E8
Kui Buri *Thailand* 12°3N 99°52E **311** F2
Kuichong *China* 22°38N 114°25E **305** F11
Kuiseb → *Namibia* 22°59S 14°31E **328** C1
Kuito *Angola* 12°22S 16°55E **325** G3
Kuiu I. *U.S.A.* 57°45N 134°10W **342** B2
Kujang *N. Korea* 39°57N 126°1E **307** E14
Kuji *Japan* 40°11N 141°46E **302** D10
Kujū-San *Japan* 33°5N 131°15E **303** H5
Kukës *Albania* 42°5N 20°27E **295** C9
Kukup *Malaysia* 1°20N 103°27E **311** d
Kukup, Pulau *Malaysia* 1°18N 103°25E **311** d
Kula *Turkey* 38°32N 28°40E **295** E13
Kulachi *Pakistan* 31°56N 70°27E **314** D4
Kulai *Malaysia* 1°44N 103°35E **311** M4
Kulasekarappattinam
India 8°20N 78°5E **312** Q11
Kuldīga *Latvia* 56°58N 21°59E **281** H19
Kulen *Cambodia* 13°50N 104°40E **310** F5
Kulgam *India* 33°36N 75°2E **315** C6
Kulgera *Australia* 25°50S 133°18E **334** D1
Kulim *Malaysia* 5°22N 100°34E **311** K3
Kulin *Australia* 32°40S 118°2E **333** F2
Kulkayu = Hartley Bay
Canada 53°25N 129°15W **342** C3
Kŭlob *Tajikistan* 37°55N 69°50E **300** F7
Kulsary *Kazakhstan* 46°59N 54°1E **291** E9
Kulti *India* 23°43N 86°50E **315** H12
Kulu *India* 31°58N 77°6E **314** D7
Kulunda *Russia* 52°35N 78°57E **300** D8
Kulungar *Afghan.* 34°0N 69°2E **314** C3
Kŭlvand *Iran* 31°21N 54°35E **317** D7
Kulwin *Australia* 35°2S 142°42E **335** F3
Kulyab = Kŭlob
Tajikistan 37°55N 69°50E **300** F7
Kuma → *Russia* 44°55N 47°0E **291** F8
Kumaganum *Nigeria* 13°8N 10°38E **323** F8
Kumagaya *Japan* 36°9N 139°22E **303** F9
Kumai *Indonesia* 2°44S 111°43E **308** E4
Kumamba, Kepulauan
Indonesia 1°36S 138°45E **309** E9
Kumamoto *Japan* 32°45N 130°45E **303** H5
Kumamoto □ *Japan* 32°55N 130°55E **303** H5
Kumanovo *Macedonia* 42°9N 21°42E **295** C9
Kumara *N.Z.* 42°37S 171°12E **331** E3
Kumarina Roadhouse
Australia 24°41S 119°32E **333** D2
Kumasi *Ghana* 6°41N 1°38W **322** G5
Kumba *Cameroon* 4°36N 9°24E **324** D1
Kumbakonam *India* 10°58N 79°25E **312** P11
Kumbarilla *Australia* 27°15S 150°55E **335** D5
Kumbhraj *India* 24°22N 77°3E **314** G7
Kumbia *Australia* 26°41S 151°39E **335** D5
Kŭmch'ŏn *N. Korea* 38°10N 126°29E **307** E14
Kumdok *India* 33°32N 78°10E **315** C8
Kume-Shima *Japan* 26°20N 126°47E **303** L3
Kumertau *Russia* 52°45N 55°57E **290** D10
Kumharsain *India* 31°19N 77°27E **314** D7
Kumi *Uganda* 1°30N 33°58E **326** B3
Kumo *Nigeria* 10°1N 11°12E **323** F8
Kumo älv = Kokemäenjoki →
Finland 61°32N 21°44E **280** F19
Kumon Bum *Burma* 26°30N 97°15E **313** F20
Kumtag Shamo *China* 39°40N 92°0E **304** C4
Kunashir, Ostrov
Russia 44°0N 146°0E **301** E15
Kunda *Estonia* 59°30N 26°34E **281** G22
Kunda *India* 25°43N 81°31E **315** G9
Kundar → *Pakistan* 31°56N 69°19E **314** D3
Kundelungu △
Dem. Rep. of the Congo 10°30S 27°40E **327** E2
Kundelungu Ouest △
Dem. Rep. of the Congo 9°55S 27°17E **327** D2
Kundian *Pakistan* 32°27N 71°28E **314** C4
Kundla *India* 21°21N 71°25E **314** J4
Kung, Ao *Thailand* 8°5N 98°24E **311** a
Kunga → *Bangla.* 21°46N 89°30E **315** J13
Kunghit I. *Canada* 52°6N 131°3W **342** C2
Kungrad = Qŭnghirot
Uzbekistan 43°2N 58°50E **300** E6
Kungsbacka *Sweden* 57°30N 12°5E **281** H15
Kungur *Russia* 57°25N 56°57E **290** C10
Kungurri *Australia* 21°4S 148°45E **334** C4
Kunhar → *Pakistan* 34°20N 73°30E **315** B5
Kuningan *Indonesia* 6°59S 108°29E **309** G13
Kunlong *Burma* 23°20N 98°50E **313** H21
Kunlun Shan *Asia* 36°0N 86°30E **304** C3
Kunming *China* 25°1N 102°41E **304** D5
Kununurra *Australia* 15°40S 128°50E **332** C4
Kunwari → *India* 26°26N 79°11E **315** F8
Kunya-Urgench = Köneürgench
Turkmenistan 42°19N 59°10E **300** E6
Kuopio *Finland* 62°53N 27°35E **280** E22
Kupa → *Croatia* 45°28N 16°24E **288** F9
Kupang *Indonesia* 10°19S 123°39E **309** F6
Kupreanof I. *U.S.A.* 56°50N 133°30W **342** B2
Kupyansk-Uzlovoi
Ukraine 49°40N 37°43E **291** E6
Kuqa *China* 41°35N 82°30E **304** B3
Kür → *Azerbaijan* 39°29N 49°15E **291** G8
Kür Dili *Azerbaijan* 39°3N 49°13E **317** B6
Kura = Kür →
Azerbaijan 39°29N 49°15E **291** G8
Kuranda *Australia* 16°48S 145°35E **334** B4
Kuranga *India* 22°4N 69°10E **314** H3
Kurashiki *Japan* 34°40N 133°50E **303** G6
Kurayn *Si. Arabia* 27°39N 49°50E **317** E6
Kurayoshi *Japan* 35°26N 133°50E **303** G6
Kŭrdzhali *Bulgaria* 41°38N 25°21E **295** D11
Kure *Japan* 34°14N 132°32E **303** G6
Kuressaare *Estonia* 58°15N 22°30E **281** G20
Kurgan *Russia* 55°26N 65°18E **300** D7
Kuri *India* 26°37N 70°43E **314** F4
Kuria Maria Is. = Ḥallāniyat,
Jazā'ir al *Oman* 17°30N 55°58E **319** D6
Kuridala *Australia* 21°16S 140°29E **334** C3
Kurigram *Bangla.* 25°49N 89°39E **313** G16
Kurikka *Finland* 62°36N 22°24E **280** E20
Kuril Basin *Pac. Oc.* 47°0N 150°0E **276** E15
Kuril Is. = Kurilskiye Ostrova
Russia 45°0N 150°0E **301** E15
Kuril-Kamchatka Trench
Pac. Oc. 44°0N 153°0E **336** C7
Kurilsk *Russia* 45°14N 147°53E **301** E15
Kurilskiye Ostrova
Russia 45°0N 150°0E **301** E15
Kurino *Japan* 31°57N 130°43E **303** J5
Kurinskaya Kosa = Kür Dili
Azerbaijan 39°3N 49°13E **317** B6
Kurnool *India* 15°45N 78°0E **312** M11
Kuro-Shima *Kagoshima,*
Japan 30°50N 129°57E **303** J4
Kuro-Shima *Okinawa,*
Japan 24°14N 124°1E **303** M2
Kurow *N.Z.* 44°44S 170°29E **331** F3
Kurram → *Pakistan* 32°36N 71°20E **314** C4
Kurri Kurri *Australia* 32°50S 151°28E **335** E5
Kurrimine *Australia* 17°47S 146°6E **334** B4
Kurshskiy Zaliv *Russia* 55°9N 21°6E **281** J19
Kursk *Russia* 51°42N 36°11E **290** D6
Kuruçay *Turkey* 39°39N 38°29E **316** B3
Kuruktag *China* 41°0N 89°0E **304** B3
Kuruman *S. Africa* 27°28S 23°28E **328** D3
Kuruman → *S. Africa* 26°56S 20°39E **328** D3
Kurume *Japan* 33°15N 130°30E **303** H5
Kurunegala *Sri Lanka* 7°30N 80°23E **312** R12
Kurya *Russia* 61°42N 57°9E **290** B10
Kus Gölü *Turkey* 40°10N 27°55E **295** D12
Kuşadası *Turkey* 37°52N 27°15E **295** F12
Kusamba *Indonesia* 8°34S 115°27E **309** K18
Kusatsu *Japan* 36°37N 138°36E **303** F9
Kusawa L. *Canada* 60°20N 136°13W **342** A1
Kushalgarh *India* 23°10N 74°27E **314** H6
Kushikino *Japan* 31°44N 130°16E **303** J5
Kushima *Japan* 31°29N 131°14E **303** J5
Kushimoto *Japan* 33°28N 135°47E **303** H7
Kushiro *Japan* 43°0N 144°25E **302** C12
Kushiro-Gawa →
Japan 42°59N 144°23E **302** C12
Kushiro Shitsugen △
Japan 43°9N 144°26E **302** C12
Kūshk *Iran* 28°46N 56°51E **317** D8
Kushka = Serhetabat
Turkmenistan 35°20N 62°18E **317** C9
Kūshkī *Iran* 33°31N 47°13E **316** C5
Kushol *India* 33°40N 76°36E **315** C7
Kushtia *Bangla.* 23°55N 89°5E **313** H16
Kushva *Russia* 58°18N 59°45E **290** C10
Kuskokwim → *U.S.A.* 60°5N 162°25W **338** C3
Kuskokwim B. *U.S.A.* 59°45N 162°25W **346** a
Kusmi *India* 23°17N 83°55E **315** H10
Kusŏng *N. Korea* 39°59N 125°15E **307** E13
Kussharo-Ko *Japan* 43°38N 144°21E **302** C12
Kustanay = Qostanay
Kazakhstan 53°10N 63°35E **300** D7
Kut, Ko *Thailand* 11°40N 102°35E **311** G4
Kuta *Indonesia* 8°43S 115°11E **309** K18
Kütahya *Turkey* 39°30N 30°2E **291** G5
Kutaisi *Georgia* 42°19N 42°40E **291** F7
Kutaraja = Banda Aceh
Indonesia 5°35N 95°20E **308** C1
Kutch, Gulf of = Kachchh, Gulf of
India 22°50N 69°15E **314** H3
Kutch, Rann of = Kachchh, Rann
of *India* 24°0N 70°0E **314** H4
Kutiyana *India* 21°36N 70°2E **314** J4
Kutno *Poland* 52°15N 19°23E **289** B10
Kutse *Botswana* 21°7S 22°16E **328** C3
Kuttabul *Australia* 21°1S 148°54E **334** K6
Kutu
Dem. Rep. of the Congo 2°40S 18°11E **324** E3
Kutum *Sudan* 14°10N 24°40E **323** F10
Kuujjuaq *Canada* 58°6N 68°15W **341** D13
Kuujjuarapik *Canada* 55°20N 77°35W **344** A4
Kuusamo *Finland* 65°57N 29°8E **280** D23
Kuusankoski *Finland* 60°55N 26°38E **280** F22
Kuwait = Al Kuwayt
Kuwait 29°30N 48°0E **316** D5
Kuwait ■ *Asia* 29°30N 47°30E **316** D5
Kuwana *Japan* 35°5N 136°43E **303** G8
Kuwana → *India* 26°25N 83°15E **315** F10
Kuybyshev = Samara
Russia 53°8N 50°6E **290** D9
Kuybyshev *Russia* 55°27N 78°19E **300** D8
Kuybyshevskoye Vdkhr.
Russia 55°2N 49°30E **290** C8
Kuye He → *China* 38°23N 110°46E **306** E6
Kūyeh *Iran* 38°45N 47°57E **316** B5
Kuyto, Ozero *Russia* 65°6N 31°20E **280** D24
Kuyumba *Russia* 60°58N 96°59E **301** C10
Kuzey Anadolu Dağları
Turkey 41°0N 36°45E **291** F6
Kuznetsk *Russia* 53°12N 46°40E **290** D8
Kuzomen *Russia* 66°22N 36°50E **290** A6
Kvænangen *Norway* 70°5N 21°15E **280** A19
Kvaløya *Norway* 69°40N 18°30E **280** B18
Kvarner *Croatia* 44°50N 14°10E **288** F8
Kvarnerič *Croatia* 44°43N 14°37E **288** F8
Kwabhaca *S. Africa* 30°51S 29°0E **329** E4
Kwajalein *Marshall Is.* 9°5N 167°20E **336** G8
Kwakhanai *Botswana* 21°39S 21°16E **328** C3
Kwakoegron *Suriname* 5°12N 55°25W **365** B7
Kwale *Kenya* 4°15S 39°31E **326** C4
KwaMashu *S. Africa* 29°45S 30°58E **329** D5
Kwando → *Africa* 18°27S 23°32E **328** B3
Kwangchow = Guangzhou
China 23°6N 113°13E **305** D6
Kwango →
Dem. Rep. of the Congo 3°14S 17°22E **324** E3
Kwangsi-Chuang = Guangxi
Zhuangzu Zizhiqu □
China 24°0N 109°0E **305** D5
Kwangtung = Guangdong □
China 23°0N 113°0E **305** D6
Kwataboahegan →
Canada 51°9N 80°50W **344** B3
Kwatisore *Indonesia* 3°18S 134°50E **309** E8

KwaZulu Natal □ S. Africa 29°0S 30°0E 329 D5
Kweichow = Guizhou □ China 27°0N 107°0E 304 D5
Kwekwe Zimbabwe 18°58S 29°48E 327 F2
Kwidzyn Poland 53°44N 18°55E 289 B10
Kwilu → Dem. Rep. of the Congo 3°22S 17°22E 324 E3
Kwinana Australia 32°15S 115°47E 333 F2
Kwoka Indonesia 0°31S 132°27E 309 E8
Kwun Tong China 22°19N 114°13E 305 G11
Kyabra Cr. → Australia 25°36S 142°55E 335 D3
Kyabram Australia 36°19S 145°4E 335 F4
Kyaikto Burma 17°20N 97°3E 310 D1
Kyakhta Russia 50°30N 106°25E 301 D11
Kyambura ⌓ Uganda 0°7S 30°9E 326 C3
Kyancutta Australia 33°8S 135°33E 335 E2
Kyaukpadaung Burma 20°52N 95°8E 313 J19
Kyaukpyu Burma 19°28N 93°30E 313 K18
Kyaukse Burma 21°36N 96°10E 313 J20
Kyburz U.S.A. 38°47N 120°18W 350 G6
Kyelang India 32°35N 77°2E 314 C7
Kyenjojo Uganda 0°40N 30°37E 326 B3
Kyle Canada 50°50N 108°2W 343 C7
Kyle Dam Zimbabwe 20°15S 31°0E 327 G3
Kyle of Lochalsh U.K. 57°17N 5°44W 283 D3
Kymijoki → Finland 60°30N 26°55E 280 F22
Kymmene älv = Kymijoki → Finland 60°30N 26°55E 280 F22
Kyneton Australia 37°10S 144°29E 335 F3
Kynuna Australia 21°37S 141°55E 334 C3
Kyō-ga-Saki Japan 35°45N 135°15E 303 G7
Kyoga, L. Uganda 1°35N 33°0E 326 B3
Kyogle Australia 28°40S 153°0E 335 D5
Kyŏngju = Gyeongju S. Korea 35°51N 129°14E 307 G15
Kyŏngsŏng N. Korea 41°35N 129°36E 307 D15
Kyonpyaw Burma 17°12N 95°10E 313 L19
Kyōto Japan 35°0N 135°45E 303 G7
Kyōto □ Japan 35°15N 135°45E 303 G7
Kyparissovouno Cyprus 35°19N 33°10E 297 D12
Kyperounda Cyprus 34°56N 32°58E 297 E11
Kypros = Cyprus ■ Asia 35°0N 33°0E 297 E12
Kyrenia Cyprus 35°20N 33°20E 297 D12
Kyrgyzstan ■ Asia 42°0N 75°0E 300 E8
Kyro älv = Kyrönjoki → Finland 63°14N 21°45E 280 E19
Kyrönjoki → Finland 63°14N 21°45E 280 E19
Kystatyam Russia 67°20N 123°10E 301 C13
Kythira Greece 36°8N 23°0E 295 F10
Kythréa Cyprus 35°15N 33°29E 297 D12
Kyunhla Burma 23°25N 95°15E 313 H19
Kyuquot Sound Canada 50°2N 127°22W 342 D3
Kyūshū Japan 33°0N 131°0E 303 H5
Kyūshū □ Japan 33°0N 131°0E 303 H5
Kyushu-Palau Ridge Pac. Oc. 20°0N 136°0E 336 E5
Kyūshū-Sanchi Japan 32°35N 131°17E 303 H5
Kyustendil Bulgaria 42°16N 22°41E 295 C10
Kyusyur Russia 70°19N 127°30E 301 B13
Kyyiv Ukraine 50°30N 30°28E 289 C16
Kyyivske Vdskh. Ukraine 51°0N 30°25E 289 C16
Kyzyl Russia 51°50N 94°30E 301 D10
Kyzyl Kum Uzbekistan 42°30N 65°0E 300 E7
Kyzyl-Kyya Kyrgyzstan 40°16N 72°8E 300 E8
Kyzyl-Orda = Qyzylorda Kazakhstan 44°48N 65°28E 300 E7

L

La Alcarria Spain 40°31N 2°45W 293 B4
La Amistad △ Cent. Amer. 9°28N 83°18W 360 E3
La Asunción Venezuela 11°2N 63°53W 364 A6
La Baie Canada 48°19N 70°53W 345 C5
La Banda Argentina 27°45S 64°10W 366 B3
La Barca Mexico 20°17N 102°34W 358 C4
La Barge U.S.A. 42°16N 110°12W 348 E8
La Belle U.S.A. 26°46N 81°26W 357 H14
La Biche → Canada 59°57N 123°50W 342 B4
La Biche, L. Canada 54°50N 112°3W 342 C6
La Brea Trin. & Tob. 10°15N 61°37W 365 K15
La Calera Chile 32°50S 71°10W 366 C1
La Campana △ Chile 32°58S 71°14W 366 C1
La Canal = Sa Canal Spain 38°51N 1°23E 296 C7
La Carlota Argentina 33°30S 63°20W 366 C3
La Ceiba Honduras 15°40N 86°50W 360 C2
La Chaux-de-Fonds Switz. 47°7N 6°50E 292 C7
La Chorrera Panama 8°53N 79°47W 360 E4
La Cocha Argentina 27°50S 65°40W 366 B2
La Concepción Panama 8°31N 82°37W 360 E3
La Concordia Mexico 16°5N 92°38W 359 D6
La Coruña = A Coruña Spain 43°20N 8°25W 293 A1
La Crescent U.S.A. 43°50N 91°18W 352 D8
La Crete Canada 58°11N 116°24W 342 B5
La Crosse Kans., U.S.A. 38°32N 99°18W 352 F4
La Crosse Wis., U.S.A. 43°48N 91°15W 352 D8
La Cruz Costa Rica 11°4N 85°39W 360 D2
La Cruz Mexico 23°55N 106°54W 358 C3
La Désirade Guadeloupe 16°18N 61°3W 360 b
La Digue Seychelles 4°20S 55°51E 325 b
La Esmeralda Paraguay 22°16S 62°33W 366 A3
La Esperanza Cuba 22°46N 83°44W 360 B3
La Esperanza Honduras 14°15N 88°10W 360 D2
La Estrada = A Estrada Spain 42°43N 8°27W 293 A1
La Fayette U.S.A. 34°42N 85°17W 357 D12
La Fé Cuba 22°2N 84°15W 360 B3
La Follette U.S.A. 36°23N 84°7W 357 C12
La Grande U.S.A. 45°20N 118°5W 348 D4
La Grande → Canada 53°50N 79°0W 344 B5
La Grande Deux, Rés. Canada 53°40N 76°55W 344 B4
La Grande Quatre, Rés. Canada 54°0N 73°15W 344 B5
La Grande Trois, Rés. Canada 53°40N 75°10W 344 B4
La Grange Calif., U.S.A. 37°42N 120°27W 350 H6
La Grange Ga., U.S.A. 33°2N 85°2W 357 E12
La Grange Ky., U.S.A. 38°24N 85°22W 353 F11
La Grange Tex., U.S.A. 29°54N 96°52W 356 G6
La Guaira Venezuela 10°36N 66°56W 364 A5
La Habana Cuba 23°8N 82°22W 360 B3
La Independencia Mexico 16°15N 92°1W 359 D6
La Isabela Dom. Rep. 19°58N 71°2W 361 C5
La Junta U.S.A. 37°59N 103°33W 348 H12
La Laguna Canary Is. 28°28N 16°18W 296 F3
La Libertad = Puerto Libertad Mexico 29°55N 112°43W 358 B2
La Libertad Guatemala 16°47N 90°7W 360 C1
La Ligua Chile 32°30S 71°16W 366 C1
La Línea de la Concepción Spain 36°15N 5°23W 293 D3
La Loche Canada 56°29N 109°26W 343 B7
La Louvière Belgium 50°27N 4°10E 287 D4
La Lune Trin. & Tob. 10°3N 61°22W 365 K15
La Malbaie Canada 47°40N 70°10W 345 C5
La Malinche △ Mexico 19°15N 98°3W 359 D5
La Mancha Spain 39°10N 2°54W 293 C4
La Martre, L. Canada 63°15N 117°55W 342 A5
La Mesa Mexico 32°30N 116°57W 351 N10
La Mesa U.S.A. 32°46N 117°1W 351 N9
La Mesilla U.S.A. 32°16N 106°48W 349 K10
La Misión Mexico 32°6N 116°53W 358 A1
La Moure U.S.A. 46°21N 98°18W 352 B4
La Negra Chile 23°46S 70°18W 366 A1
La Oliva Canary Is. 28°36N 13°57W 296 F6
La Orotava Canary Is. 28°22N 16°31W 296 F3
La Oroya Peru 11°32S 75°54W 364 F3
La Palma Canary Is. 28°40N 17°50W 296 F2
La Palma Panama 8°15N 78°0W 360 E4
La Palma del Condado Spain 37°21N 6°38W 293 D2
La Paloma Chile 30°35S 71°0W 366 C1
La Pampa □ Argentina 36°50S 66°0W 366 D2
La Paragua Venezuela 6°50N 63°20W 364 B6
La Paz Entre Ríos, Argentina 30°50S 59°45W 366 C4
La Paz San Luis, Argentina 33°30S 67°20W 366 C2
La Paz Bolivia 16°20S 68°10W 364 G5
La Paz Honduras 14°20N 87°47W 360 D2
La Paz Mexico 24°10N 110°18W 358 C2
La Paz Centro Nic. 12°20N 86°41W 360 D2
La Pedrera Colombia 1°18S 69°43W 364 D5
La Pérade Canada 46°35N 72°12W 345 C5
La Perla Mexico 28°18N 104°32W 358 B4
La Perouse Str. Asia 45°40N 142°0E 302 B11
La Pesca Mexico 23°46N 97°47W 359 C5
La Piedad Mexico 20°21N 102°0W 358 C4
La Pine U.S.A. 43°40N 121°30W 348 E3
La Plata Argentina 35°0S 57°55W 366 D4
La Pocatière Canada 47°22N 70°2W 345 C5
La Porte U.S.A. 29°40N 95°1W 356 G7
La Purísima Mexico 26°10N 112°4W 358 B2
La Push U.S.A. 47°55N 124°38W 350 C2
La Quiaca Argentina 22°5S 65°35W 366 A2
La Restinga Canary Is. 27°38N 17°59W 296 G2
La Rioja Argentina 29°20S 67°0W 366 B2
La Rioja □ Argentina 29°30S 67°0W 366 B2
La Rioja □ Spain 42°20N 2°20W 293 A4
La Robla Spain 42°50N 5°41W 293 A3
La Roche-en-Ardenne Belgium 50°11N 5°35E 287 D5
La Roche-sur-Yon France 46°40N 1°25W 292 C3
La Rochelle France 46°10N 1°9W 292 C3
La Roda Spain 39°13N 2°15W 293 C4
La Romaine Canada 50°13N 60°40W 345 B7
La Romana Dom. Rep. 18°27N 68°57W 361 C6
La Ronge Canada 55°5N 105°20W 343 B7
La Rumorosa Mexico 32°34N 116°6W 351 N10
La Sabina = Sa Savina Spain 38°44N 1°25E 296 C7
La Salle U.S.A. 41°20N 89°6W 352 E9
La Santa Canary Is. 29°5N 13°40W 296 E6
La Sarre Canada 48°45N 79°15W 344 C4
La Scie Canada 49°57N 55°36W 345 C8
La Selva Beach U.S.A. 36°56N 121°51W 350 J5
La Serena Chile 29°55S 71°10W 366 B1
La Seu d'Urgell Spain 42°22N 1°23E 293 A6
La Seyne-sur-Mer France 43°7N 5°52E 292 E6
La Soufrière St. Vincent 13°20N 61°11W 361 D7
La Spézia Italy 44°7N 9°50E 292 D8
La Tagua Colombia 0°3N 74°40W 364 C4
La Tortuga Venezuela 11°0N 65°22W 361 D6
La Trinité Martinique 14°43N 60°58W 360 c
La Tuque Canada 47°30N 72°50W 344 C5
La Unión Chile 40°10S 73°0W 368 E2
La Unión El Salv. 13°20N 87°50W 360 D2
La Unión Mexico 17°58N 101°49W 358 D4
La Urbana Venezuela 7°8N 66°56W 364 B5
La Vache Pt. Trin. & Tob. 10°47N 61°28W 365 K15
La Vall d'Uixó Spain 39°49N 0°15W 293 C5
La Vega Dom. Rep. 19°20N 70°30W 361 C5
La Vela de Coro Venezuela 11°27N 69°34W 364 A5
La Venta Mexico 18°5N 94°3W 359 D6
La Vergne U.S.A. 36°1N 86°35W 357 C11
Laas Caanood = Las Anod Somali Rep. 8°26N 47°19E 319 F4
Labasa Fiji 16°30S 179°27E 331 a
Labdah = Leptis Magna Libya 32°40N 14°12E 323 B8
Labe = Elbe → Europe 53°50N 9°0E 288 B5
Labé Guinea 11°24N 12°16W 322 F3
Laberge, L. Canada 61°11N 135°12W 342 A1
Labinsk Russia 44°40N 40°48E 291 F7
Labis Malaysia 2°22N 103°2E 311 L4
Laborie St. Lucia 13°45N 61°2W 361 f
Laboulaye Argentina 34°10S 63°30W 366 C3
Labrador Canada 53°20N 61°0W 345 B7
Labrador City Canada 52°57N 66°55W 345 B6
Labrador Sea Atl. Oc. 57°0N 54°0W 341 D14
Lábrea Brazil 7°15S 64°51W 364 E6
Labuan Malaysia 5°20N 115°14E 308 C5
Labuan, Pulau Malaysia 5°21N 115°13E 308 C5
Labuha Indonesia 0°30S 127°30E 309 E7
Labuhan Indonesia 6°22S 105°50E 309 G11
Labuhanbajo Indonesia 8°28S 119°54E 309 F6
Labuk, Telok Malaysia 6°10N 117°50E 308 C5
Labyrinth, L. Australia 30°40S 135°11E 335 E2
Labytnangi Russia 66°39N 66°21E 300 C7
Lac-Bouchette Canada 48°16N 72°11W 345 C5
Lac Édouard Canada 47°40N 72°16W 344 C5
Lac La Biche Canada 54°45N 111°58W 342 C6
Lac la Martre = Wha Ti Canada 63°8N 117°16W 340 C8
Lac La Ronge ⌓ Canada 55°9N 104°41W 343 B7
Lac-Mégantic Canada 45°35N 70°53W 345 C5
Lac Thien Vietnam 12°25N 108°11E 310 F7
Lacanau France 44°58N 1°5W 292 D3
Lacantún → Mexico 16°36N 90°39W 359 D6
Laccadive Is. = Lakshadweep Is. India 10°0N 72°30E 275 D13
Lacepede B. Australia 36°40S 139°40E 335 F2
Lacepede Is. Australia 16°55S 122°0E 332 C3
Lacerdónia Mozam. 18°3S 35°35E 327 F4
Lacey U.S.A. 47°7N 122°49W 350 C4
Lachania Greece 35°58N 27°54E 297 D9
Lachhmangarh India 27°50N 75°4E 314 F6
Lachi Pakistan 33°25N 71°20E 314 C4
Lachine Canada 45°26N 73°42W 344 C5
Lachlan → Australia 34°22S 143°55E 335 E3
Lachute Canada 45°39N 74°21W 344 C5
Lackagh Hills Ireland 54°16N 8°10W 282 B3
Lackawanna U.S.A. 42°50N 78°50W 354 D6
Lackawaxen U.S.A. 41°29N 74°59W 355 E10
Lacolle Canada 45°5N 73°22W 355 A11
Lacombe Canada 52°30N 113°44W 342 C6
Lacona U.S.A. 43°39N 76°10W 355 C8
Laconia U.S.A. 43°32N 71°28W 355 C13
Ladakh Ra. India 34°0N 78°0E 315 C8
Ladismith S. Africa 33°28S 21°15E 328 E3
Lādīz Iran 28°55N 61°15E 317 D9
Ladnun India 27°38N 74°25E 314 F6
Ladoga, L. = Ladozhskoye Ozero Russia 61°15N 30°30E 280 F24
Ladozhskoye Ozero Russia 61°15N 30°30E 280 F24
Lady Elliott I. Australia 24°7S 152°42E 334 C5
Lady Grey S. Africa 30°43S 27°13E 328 E4
Ladybrand S. Africa 29°9S 27°29E 328 D4
Ladysmith Canada 49°0N 123°49W 350 B3
Ladysmith S. Africa 28°32S 29°46E 329 D4
Ladysmith U.S.A. 45°28N 91°12W 352 C8
Lae Papua N. G. 6°40S 147°2E 330 B7
Laem Hin Khom Thailand 9°25N 99°56E 311 b
Laem Khat Thailand 8°6N 98°26E 311 a
Laem Nga Thailand 7°55N 98°27E 311 a
Laem Ngop Thailand 12°10N 102°26E 311 F4
Laem Phan Wa Thailand 7°47N 98°25E 311 a
Laem Pho Thailand 6°55N 101°19E 311 J3
Laem Phrom Thep Thailand 7°45N 98°19E 311 a
Laem Riang Thailand 8°7N 98°27E 311 a
Laem Sam Rong Thailand 9°35N 100°4E 311 b
Laem Son Thailand 7°59N 98°16E 311 a
Laem Yamu Thailand 7°59N 98°26E 311 a
Laerma Greece 36°9N 27°57E 297 C9
Læsø Denmark 57°15N 11°5E 281 H14
Lafayette Ind., U.S.A. 40°25N 86°54W 352 E10
Lafayette La., U.S.A. 30°14N 92°1W 356 F8
LaFayette Tenn., U.S.A. 36°31N 86°2W 357 C11
Laferte → Canada 61°53N 117°44W 342 A5
Lafia Nigeria 8°30N 8°34E 322 G7
Lafleche Canada 49°45N 106°40W 343 D7
Lagan → U.K. 54°36N 5°55W 282 B6
Lagarfljót → Iceland 65°40N 14°18W 280 D6
Lagdo, Rés. de Cameroon 8°40N 14°0E 323 G8
Lågen → Oppland, Norway 61°8N 10°25E 280 F14
Lågen → Vestfold, Norway 59°3N 10°3E 281 G14
Laghouat Algeria 33°50N 2°59E 322 B6
Lagoa do Peixe △ Brazil 31°12S 50°55W 367 C5
Lagoa Vermelha Brazil 28°13S 51°32W 367 B5
Lagonoy G. Phil. 13°35N 123°50E 309 B6
Lagos Nigeria 6°25N 3°27E 322 G6
Lagos Portugal 37°5N 8°41W 293 D1
Lagos de Moreno Mexico 21°21N 101°55W 358 C4
Lagrange = Bidyadanga Australia 18°45S 121°43E 332 C3
Lagrange B. Australia 18°38S 121°42E 332 C3
Laguna Brazil 28°30S 48°50W 367 B6
Laguna U.S.A. 35°2N 107°25W 349 J10
Laguna, Sa. de la Mexico 23°35N 109°55W 358 C3
Laguna Beach U.S.A. 33°33N 117°47W 351 M9
Laguna de la Restinga △ Venezuela 10°58N 64°0W 361 D6
Laguna del Laja △ Chile 37°27S 71°20W 366 D1
Laguna del Tigre △ Guatemala 17°32N 90°56W 360 C1
Laguna Limpia Argentina 26°32S 59°45W 366 B4
Lagunas Chile 21°0S 69°45W 366 A2
Lagunas Peru 5°10S 75°35W 364 E3
Lagunas de Chacahua △ Mexico 16°0N 97°43W 359 D5
Lagunas de Montebello △ Mexico 16°4N 91°42W 359 D6
Lahad Datu Malaysia 5°0N 118°20E 309 C5
Lahad Datu, Telok Malaysia 4°50N 118°20E 309 D5
Lahan Sai Thailand 14°25N 102°52E 310 E4
Lahanam Laos 16°16N 105°16E 310 D5
Lahar India 26°12N 78°57E 315 F8
Laharpur India 27°43N 80°56E 315 F9
Lahat Indonesia 3°45S 103°30E 308 E2
Lahewa Indonesia 1°22N 97°12E 308 D1
Lāhījān Iran 37°10N 50°6E 317 B6
Lahn → Germany 50°19N 7°37E 288 C4
Laholm Sweden 56°30N 13°2E 281 H15
Lahore Pakistan 31°32N 74°22E 314 D6
Lahri Pakistan 29°11N 68°13E 314 E3
Lahti Finland 60°58N 25°40E 280 F21
Lahtis = Lahti Finland 60°58N 25°40E 280 F21
Laï Chad 9°25N 16°18E 323 G9
Lai Chau Vietnam 22°5N 103°3E 310 A4
Laila = Layla Si. Arabia 22°10N 46°40E 319 C4
Laingsburg S. Africa 33°9S 20°52E 328 E3
Lainioälven → Sweden 67°35N 22°40E 280 C20
Lairg U.K. 58°2N 4°24W 283 C4
Laisamis Kenya 1°36N 37°48E 326 B4
Laishui China 39°23N 115°45E 306 E8
Laiwu China 36°15N 117°40E 307 F9
Laixi China 36°50N 120°31E 307 F11
Laiyang China 36°59N 120°45E 307 F11
Laiyuan China 39°20N 114°40E 306 E8
Laizhou China 37°8N 119°57E 307 F10
Laizhou Wan China 37°30N 119°30E 307 F10
Laja → Mexico 20°55N 100°46W 358 C4
Lajamanu Australia 18°23S 130°38E 332 C5
Lajes Brazil 27°48S 50°20W 367 B5
Lak Sao Laos 18°11N 104°59E 310 C5
Lakaband Pakistan 31°2N 69°15E 314 D3
Lake U.S.A. 44°33N 110°24W 348 D8
Lake Alpine U.S.A. 38°29N 120°0W 350 G7
Lake Andes U.S.A. 43°9N 98°32W 352 D4
Lake Arthur U.S.A. 30°5N 92°41W 356 F8
Lake Bindegolly △ Australia 28°0S 144°12E 335 D3
Lake Cargelligo Australia 33°15S 146°22E 335 E4
Lake Charles U.S.A. 30°14N 93°13W 356 F8
Lake City Colo., U.S.A. 38°2N 107°19W 348 G10
Lake City Fla., U.S.A. 30°11N 82°38W 357 F13
Lake City Mich., U.S.A. 44°20N 85°13W 353 C11
Lake City Minn., U.S.A. 44°27N 92°16W 352 C7
Lake City Pa., U.S.A. 42°1N 80°21W 354 D4
Lake City S.C., U.S.A. 33°52N 79°45W 357 E15
Lake Cowichan Canada 48°49N 124°3W 342 D4
Lake District △ U.K. 54°30N 3°21W 284 C4
Lake Elsinore U.S.A. 33°38N 117°20W 351 M9
Lake Eyre △ Australia 28°40S 137°31E 335 D2
Lake Gairdner △ Australia 31°41S 135°51E 335 E2
Lake George U.S.A. 43°26N 73°43W 355 C11
Lake Grace Australia 33°7S 118°28E 333 F2
Lake Harbour = Kimmirut Canada 62°50N 69°50W 341 C13
Lake Havasu City U.S.A. 34°27N 114°22W 351 L12
Lake Hughes U.S.A. 34°41N 118°26W 351 L8
Lake Isabella U.S.A. 35°38N 118°28W 351 K8
Lake Jackson U.S.A. 29°3N 95°27W 356 G7
Lake King Australia 33°5S 119°45E 333 F2
Lake Lenore Canada 52°24N 104°59W 343 C8
Lake Louise Canada 51°30N 116°10W 342 C5
Lake Malawi △ Malawi 14°2S 34°53E 327 E3
Lake Mburo △ Uganda 0°33S 30°56E 326 C3
Lake Mead ⌓ U.S.A. 36°30N 114°22W 351 K12
Lake Meredith ⌓ U.S.A. 35°50N 101°50W 356 D4
Lake Mills U.S.A. 43°25N 93°32W 352 D7
Lake Nakura △ Kenya 0°21S 36°8E 326 C4
Lake Placid U.S.A. 44°17N 73°59W 355 B11
Lake Pleasant U.S.A. 43°28N 74°25W 355 C10
Lake Providence U.S.A. 32°48N 91°10W 356 E9
Lake Roosevelt ⌓ U.S.A. 48°5N 118°14W 348 B4
Lake St. Peter Canada 45°18N 78°2W 354 A6
Lake Superior ⌓ Canada 47°45N 84°45W 344 C3
Lake Torrens △ Australia 30°55S 137°40E 335 E2
Lake Village U.S.A. 33°20N 91°17W 356 E9
Lake Wales U.S.A. 27°54N 81°35W 357 H14
Lake Worth U.S.A. 26°37N 80°3W 357 H14
Lakeba Fiji 18°13S 178°47W 331 a
Lakeba Passage Fiji 18°0S 178°45W 331 a
Lakefield Canada 44°25N 78°16W 354 B6
Lakefield △ Australia 15°24S 144°26E 334 B3
Lakehurst U.S.A. 40°1N 74°19W 355 F10
Lakeland Australia 15°49S 144°57E 334 B3
Lakeland U.S.A. 28°3N 81°57W 357 G14
Lakemba = Lakeba Fiji 18°13S 178°47W 331 a
Lakeport Calif., U.S.A. 39°3N 122°55W 350 F4
Lakeport Mich., U.S.A. 43°7N 82°30W 354 C2
Lakes Entrance Australia 37°50S 148°0E 335 F4
Lakeside Calif., U.S.A. 32°52N 116°55W 351 N10
Lakeside Nebr., U.S.A. 42°3N 102°26W 352 D2
Lakeside Ohio, U.S.A. 41°32N 82°46W 354 E2
Lakeview U.S.A. 42°11N 120°21W 348 E3
Lakeville U.S.A. 44°39N 93°14W 352 C7
Lakewood Colo., U.S.A. 39°42N 105°4W 348 G11
Lakewood N.J., U.S.A. 40°6N 74°13W 355 F10
Lakewood N.Y., U.S.A. 42°6N 79°19W 354 D5
Lakewood Ohio, U.S.A. 41°28N 81°47W 354 E3
Lakewood Wash., U.S.A. 47°11N 122°32W 350 C4
Lakha India 26°9N 70°54E 314 F4
Lakhimpur India 27°57N 80°46E 315 F9
Lakhnadon India 22°36N 79°36E 315 H8
Lakhnau = Lucknow India 26°50N 81°0E 315 F9
Lakhonpheng Laos 15°54N 105°34E 310 E5
Lakhpat India 23°48N 68°47E 314 H3
Lakin U.S.A. 37°57N 101°15W 352 G3
Lakitusaki → Canada 54°21N 82°25W 344 B3
Lakki Greece 35°24N 23°57E 297 D5
Lakki Pakistan 32°36N 70°55E 314 C4
Lakonikos Kolpos Greece 36°40N 22°40E 295 F10
Lakor Indonesia 8°15S 128°17E 309 F7
Lakota Ivory C. 5°50N 5°30W 322 G4
Lakota U.S.A. 48°2N 98°21W 352 A4
Laksar India 29°46N 78°3E 314 E8
Laksefjorden Norway 70°45N 26°50E 280 A22
Lakselv Norway 70°2N 25°0E 280 A21
Lakshadweep Is. India 10°0N 72°30E 275 D13
Lakshmanpur India 22°58N 83°3E 315 H10
Lakshmikantapur India 22°5N 88°20E 315 H13
Lala Musa Pakistan 32°40N 73°57E 314 C5
Lalaghat India 24°30N 92°40E 313 G18
Lalago Tanzania 3°28S 33°58E 326 C3
Lalapanzi Zimbabwe 19°20S 30°15E 327 F3
L'Albufera Spain 39°20N 0°27W 293 C5
Lalganj India 25°52N 85°13E 315 G11
Lalgola India 24°25N 88°15E 315 G13
Lālī Iran 32°21N 49°6E 317 C6
Lalibela Ethiopia 12°3N 39°0E 319 E2
Lalin China 45°12N 127°0E 307 B14
Lalín Spain 42°40N 8°5W 293 A1
Lalin He → China 45°32N 125°40E 307 B13
Lalitapur Nepal 27°40N 85°20E 315 F11
Lalitpur India 24°42N 78°28E 315 G8
Lalkua India 29°5N 79°31E 315 E8
Lalsot India 26°34N 76°20E 314 F7
Lam Vietnam 21°21N 106°31E 310 B6
Lam Pao Res. Thailand 16°50N 103°15E 310 D4
Lamaing Burma 15°25N 97°53E 310 E1
Lamar Colo., U.S.A. 38°5N 102°37W 348 G12
Lamar Mo., U.S.A. 37°30N 94°16W 352 G6
Lamas Peru 6°28S 76°31W 364 E3
Lambaréné Gabon 0°41S 10°12E 324 E2
Lambasa = Labasa Fiji 16°30S 179°27E 331 a
Lambay I. Ireland 53°29N 6°1W 282 C5
Lambert's Bay S. Africa 32°5S 18°17E 328 E2
Lambeth Canada 42°54N 81°18W 354 D3
Lambomakondro Madag. 22°41S 44°44E 329 C7
Lambton Shores Canada 43°10N 81°56W 354 C3
Lame Deer U.S.A. 45°37N 106°40W 348 D10
Lamego Portugal 41°5N 7°52W 293 B2
Lamèque Canada 47°45N 64°38W 345 C7
Lameroo Australia 35°19S 140°33E 335 F3
Lamesa U.S.A. 32°44N 101°58W 356 E4
Lamia Greece 38°55N 22°26E 295 E10
Lamington △ Australia 28°13S 153°12E 335 D5
Lamma I. China 22°12N 114°7E 305 G11
Lammermuir Hills U.K. 55°50N 2°40W 283 F6
Lamoille → U.S.A. 44°38N 73°13W 355 B11
Lamon B. Phil. 14°30N 122°20E 309 B6
Lamont Canada 53°46N 112°50W 342 C6
Lamont Calif., U.S.A. 35°15N 118°55W 351 K8
Lamont Wyo., U.S.A. 42°13N 107°29W 348 E10
Lampa Peru 15°22S 70°22W 364 G4
Lampang Thailand 18°16N 99°32E 310 C2
Lampasas U.S.A. 31°4N 98°11W 356 F5
Lampazos de Naranjo Mexico 27°1N 100°31W 358 B4
Lampedusa Medit. S. 35°36N 12°40E 294 G5
Lampeter U.K. 52°7N 4°4W 285 E3
Lampione Medit. S. 35°33N 12°20E 294 G5
Lampman Canada 49°25N 102°50W 343 D8
Lampung □ Indonesia 5°30S 104°30E 308 F2
Lamta India 22°8N 80°7E 315 H9
Lamu Kenya 2°16S 40°55E 326 C5
Lamy U.S.A. 35°29N 105°53W 349 J11
Lan Xian China 38°15N 111°35E 306 E6
Lāna'i U.S.A. 20°50N 156°55W 346 b
Lanak La China 34°27N 79°32E 315 B8
Lanak'o Shank'ou = Lanak La China 34°27N 79°32E 315 B8
Lanark Canada 45°1N 76°22W 355 A8
Lanark U.K. 55°40N 3°47W 283 F5
Lanbi Kyun Burma 10°50N 98°20E 311 G2
Lancang Jiang → China 21°40N 101°10E 304 D5
Lancashire □ U.K. 53°50N 2°48W 284 D5
Lancaster Canada 45°10N 74°30W 355 A10
Lancaster U.K. 54°3N 2°48W 284 C5
Lancaster Calif., U.S.A. 34°42N 118°8W 351 L8
Lancaster Ky., U.S.A. 37°37N 84°35W 353 G11
Lancaster N.H., U.S.A. 44°29N 71°34W 355 B13
Lancaster N.Y., U.S.A. 42°54N 78°40W 354 D6
Lancaster Ohio, U.S.A. 39°43N 82°36W 353 F12
Lancaster Pa., U.S.A. 40°2N 76°19W 355 F8
Lancaster S.C., U.S.A. 34°43N 80°46W 357 D14
Lancaster Wis., U.S.A. 42°51N 90°43W 352 D8
Lancaster Sd. Canada 74°13N 84°0W 341 B11
Lancelin Australia 31°0S 115°18E 333 F2
Lanchow = Lanzhou China 36°1N 103°52E 306 F2
Lanciano Italy 42°14N 14°23E 294 C6
Lancun China 36°25N 120°10E 307 F11
Land Between the Lakes ⌓ U.S.A. 36°25N 88°0W 357 C11
Landeck Austria 47°9N 10°34E 288 E6
Lander U.S.A. 42°50N 108°44W 348 E9
Lander → Australia 22°0S 132°0E 332 D5
Landes France 44°0N 1°0W 292 D3
Landi Kotal Pakistan 34°7N 71°6E 314 B4
Landisburg U.S.A. 40°21N 77°19W 354 F7
Landmannalaugar Iceland 63°59N 19°4W 280 E4
Land's End U.K. 50°4N 5°44W 285 G2
Landsborough Cr. → Australia 22°28S 144°35E 334 C3
Landshut Germany 48°34N 12°8E 288 D7
Lanesboro U.S.A. 41°57N 75°34W 355 E9
Lanett U.S.A. 32°52N 85°12W 357 E12
Lang Qua Vietnam 22°16N 104°27E 310 A5
Lang Shan China 41°0N 106°30E 306 D4

Lang Son Vietnam 21°52N 106°42E 310 B6
Lang Suan Thailand 9°57N 99°4E 311 H2
La'nga Co China 30°45N 81°15E 315 D9
Langar Iran 35°23N 60°25E 317 C9
Langara I. Canada 54°14N 133°1W 342 C2
Langdon U.S.A. 48°45N 98°22W 352 A4
Langeberg S. Africa 33°55S 21°0E 328 E3
Langeberge S. Africa 28°15S 22°33E 328 D3
Langeland Denmark 54°56N 10°48E 281 J14
Langenburg Canada 50°51N 101°43W 343 C8
Langholm U.K. 55°9N 3°0W 283 F5
Langjökull Iceland 64°39N 20°12W 280 D3
Langkawi, Pulau Malaysia 6°25N 99°45E 311 J2
Langklip S. Africa 28°12S 20°20E 328 D3
Langkon Malaysia 6°30N 116°40E 308 C5
Langlade St-P. & M. 46°50N 56°20W 345 C8
Langley Canada 49°7N 122°39W 350 A4
Langøya Norway 68°45N 14°50E 280 B16
Langreo Spain 43°18N 5°40W 293 A3
Langres France 47°52N 5°20E 292 C6
Langres, Plateau de France 47°45N 5°3E 292 C6
Langsa Indonesia 4°30N 97°57E 308 D1
Langtang △ Nepal 28°10N 85°30E 315 E11
Langtry U.S.A. 29°49N 101°34W 356 G4
Langu Thailand 6°53N 99°47E 311 J2
Languedoc France 43°58N 3°55E 292 E5
Langwang China 22°38N 113°27E 305 F9
Langxiangzhen China 39°43N 116°8E 306 E9
Lanigan Canada 51°51N 105°2W 343 C7
Lankao China 34°48N 114°50E 306 G8
Länkäran Azerbaijan 38°48N 48°52E 317 B6
Lannion France 48°46N 3°29W 292 B2
L'Annonciation Canada 46°25N 74°55W 344 C5
Lansdale U.S.A. 40°14N 75°17W 355 F9
Lansdowne Australia 31°48S 152°30E 335 E5
Lansdowne Canada 44°24N 76°1W 355 B8
Lansdowne India 29°50N 78°41E 315 E8
Lansdowne House Canada 52°14N 87°53W 344 B2
L'Anse U.S.A. 46°45N 88°27W 352 B9
L'Anse au Loup Canada 51°32N 56°50W 345 B8
L'Anse aux Meadows Canada 51°36N 55°32W 345 B8
L'Anse la Raye St. Lucia 13°55N 61°3W 361 f
Lansford U.S.A. 40°50N 75°53W 355 F9
Lansing U.S.A. 42°44N 84°33W 353 D11
Lanta Yai, Ko Thailand 7°35N 99°3E 311 J2
Lantau I. China 22°15N 113°56E 305 G10
Lantian China 34°11N 109°20E 306 G5
Lanus Argentina 34°42S 58°23W 366 C4
Lanusei Italy 39°52N 9°34E 294 E3
Lanzarote Canary Is. 29°0N 13°40W 296 F6
Lanzarote ✈ (ACE) Canary Is. 28°57N 13°40W 296 F6
Lanzhou China 36°1N 103°52E 306 F2
Lao Bao Laos 16°35N 106°30E 310 D6
Lao Cai Vietnam 22°30N 103°57E 310 A4
Laoag Phil. 18°7N 120°34E 309 A6
Laoang Phil. 12°32N 125°8E 309 B7
Laoha He → China 43°25N 120°35E 307 C11
Laois □ Ireland 52°57N 7°36W 282 D4
Laon France 49°33N 3°35E 292 B5
Laona U.S.A. 45°34N 88°40W 352 C9
Laos ■ Asia 17°45N 105°0E 310 D5
Lapa Brazil 25°46S 49°44W 367 B6
Lapeer U.S.A. 43°3N 83°19W 353 D12
Lapithos Cyprus 35°21N 33°11E 297 D12
Lapland = Lappland Europe 68°7N 24°0E 280 B21
LaPorte Ind., U.S.A. 41°36N 86°43W 352 E10
Laporte Pa., U.S.A. 41°25N 76°30W 355 E8
Lappeenranta Finland 61°3N 28°12E 280 F23
Lappland Europe 68°7N 24°0E 280 B21
Lappo = Lapua Finland 62°58N 23°0E 280 E20
Laprida Argentina 37°34S 60°45W 366 D3
Lapseki Turkey 40°20N 26°41E 295 D12
Laptev Sea Russia 76°0N 125°0E 301 B13
Lapua Finland 62°58N 23°0E 280 E20
L'Áquila Italy 42°22N 13°22E 294 C5
Lār Āzarbājān-e Sharqī, Iran 38°30N 47°52E 316 B5
Lār Fārs, Iran 27°40N 54°14E 317 E7
Laramie U.S.A. 41°19N 105°35W 348 F11
Laramie Mts. U.S.A. 42°0N 105°30W 348 F11
Laranjeiras do Sul Brazil 25°23S 52°23W 367 B5
Larantuka Indonesia 8°21S 122°55E 309 F6
Larat Indonesia 7°0S 132°0E 309 F8
Larde Mozam. 16°28S 39°43E 327 F4
Larder Lake Canada 48°5N 79°40W 344 C4
Lardos, Akra = Lindos, Akra Greece 36°4N 28°10E 297 C10
Lardos, Ormos Greece 36°4N 28°2E 297 C10
Lare Kenya 0°20N 37°56E 326 C4
Laredo U.S.A. 27°30N 99°30W 356 H5
Laredo Sd. Canada 52°30N 128°53W 342 C3
Largo U.S.A. 27°54N 82°47W 357 H13
Largs U.K. 55°47N 4°52W 283 F4
Lariang Indonesia 1°26S 119°17E 309 E5
Larimore U.S.A. 47°54N 97°38W 352 B5
Larisa Greece 39°36N 22°27E 295 E10
Larkana Pakistan 27°32N 68°18E 314 F3
Larnaca Cyprus 34°55N 33°38E 297 E12
Larnaca Bay Cyprus 34°53N 33°45E 297 E12
Larne U.K. 54°51N 5°51W 282 B6
Larned U.S.A. 38°11N 99°6W 352 F4
Larose U.S.A. 29°34N 90°23W 357 G9
Larrimah Australia 15°35S 133°12E 332 C5
Larsen Ice Shelf Antarctica 67°0S 62°0W 277 C17
Larvik Norway 59°4N 10°2E 281 G14
Las Animas U.S.A. 38°4N 103°13W 348 G12
Las Anod Somali Rep. 8°26N 47°19E 319 F4
Las Brenãs Argentina 27°5S 61°7W 366 B3
Las Cañadas del Teide △ Canary Is. 28°15N 16°37W 296 F3
Las Cejas Argentina 26°53S 64°44W 368 B4
Las Chimeneas Mexico 32°8N 116°5W 351 N10
Las Cruces U.S.A. 32°19N 106°47W 349 K10
Las Flores Argentina 36°10S 59°7W 366 D4
Las Heras Argentina 32°51S 68°49W 366 C2
Las Lajas Argentina 38°30S 70°25W 368 D2
Las Lomitas Argentina 24°43S 60°35W 366 A3
Las Palmas Argentina 27°8S 58°45W 366 B4
Las Palmas Canary Is. 28°7N 15°26W 296 F4
Las Palmas → Mexico 32°31N 116°58W 351 N10
Las Palmas ✈ (LPA) Canary Is. 27°55N 15°25W 296 G4
Las Palmas de Cocalán △ Chile 34°18S 71°4W 366 C1
Las Piedras Uruguay 34°44S 56°14W 367 C4
Las Pipinas Argentina 35°30S 57°19W 366 D4
Las Plumas Argentina 43°40S 67°15W 368 E3
Las Rosas Argentina 32°30S 61°35W 366 C3
Las Tablas Panama 7°49N 80°14W 360 E3
Las Termas Argentina 27°29S 64°52W 366 B3
Las Toscas Argentina 28°21S 59°18W 366 B4
Las Truchas Mexico 17°57N 102°13W 358 D4
Las Tunas Cuba 20°58N 76°59W 360 B4
Las Varillas Argentina 31°50S 62°50W 366 C3
Las Vegas N. Mex., U.S.A. 35°36N 105°13W 349 J11
Las Vegas Nev., U.S.A. 36°10N 115°8W 351 J11
Las Vegas McCarran Int. ✈ (LAS) U.S.A. 36°5N 115°9W 351 J11
Lascano Uruguay 33°35S 54°12W 367 C5
Lash-e Joveyn Afghan. 31°45N 61°30E 312 D2
Lashburn Canada 53°10N 109°40W 343 C7
Lashio Burma 22°56N 97°45E 313 H20
Lashkar India 26°10N 78°10E 314 F8
Lasithi Greece 35°11N 25°31E 297 D7
Lasithi □ Greece 35°5N 25°50E 297 D7
Lāsjerd Iran 35°24N 53°4E 317 C7
Lassen Pk. U.S.A. 40°29N 121°30W 348 F3
Lassen Volcanic △ U.S.A. 40°30N 121°20W 348 F3
Last Mountain L. Canada 51°5N 105°14W 343 C7
Lastchance Cr. → U.S.A. 40°2N 121°15W 350 E5
Lastoursville Gabon 0°55S 12°38E 324 E2
Lastovo Croatia 42°46N 16°55E 294 C7
Lat Yao Thailand 15°45N 99°48E 310 E2
Latacunga Ecuador 0°50S 78°35W 364 D3
Latakia = Al Lādhiqīyah Syria 35°30N 35°45E 316 C2
Latchford Canada 47°20N 79°50W 344 C4
Late Tonga 18°48S 174°39W 331 c
Latehar India 23°45N 84°30E 315 H11
Latham Australia 29°44S 116°20E 333 E2
Lathi India 27°43N 71°23E 314 F4
Lathrop Wells U.S.A. 36°39N 116°24W 351 J10
Latina Italy 41°28N 12°52E 294 D5
Latium = Lazio □ Italy 42°10N 12°30E 294 C5
Laton U.S.A. 36°26N 119°41W 350 J7
Latouche Treville, C. Australia 18°27S 121°49E 332 C3
Latrobe Australia 41°14S 146°30E 335 G4
Latrobe U.S.A. 40°19N 79°23W 354 F5
Latvia ■ Europe 56°50N 24°0E 281 H21
Lau Fau Shan China 22°28N 113°59E 305 G10
Lau Group Fiji 17°0S 178°30W 331 a
Lauchhammer Germany 51°29N 13°47E 288 C7
Laughlin U.S.A. 35°10N 114°34W 349 J6
Laukaa Finland 62°24N 25°56E 280 E21
Launceston Australia 41°24S 147°8E 335 G4
Launceston U.K. 50°38N 4°22W 285 G3
Laune → Ireland 52°7N 9°47W 282 D2
Launglon Bok Burma 13°50N 97°54E 310 F1
Laura Australia 15°32S 144°32E 334 B3
Laurel Miss., U.S.A. 31°41N 89°8W 357 F10
Laurel Mont., U.S.A. 45°40N 108°46W 348 D9
Laurel Hill U.S.A. 40°14N 79°6W 354 F5
Laurencekirk U.K. 56°50N 2°28W 283 E6
Laurens U.S.A. 34°30N 82°1W 357 D13
Laurentian Plateau Canada 52°0N 70°0W 345 B6
Lauria Italy 40°2N 15°50E 294 E6
Laurie L. Canada 56°35N 101°57W 343 B8
Laurinburg U.S.A. 34°47N 79°28W 357 D15
Laurium U.S.A. 47°14N 88°27W 352 B9
Lausanne Switz. 46°32N 6°38E 292 C7
Laut Indonesia 4°45N 108°0E 308 D3
Laut, Pulau Indonesia 3°40S 116°10E 308 E5
Laut Kecil, Kepulauan Indonesia 4°45S 115°40E 308 E5
Lautoka Fiji 17°37S 177°27E 331 a
Lava Beds ⌂ U.S.A. 41°40N 121°30W 348 F3
Lavagh More Ireland 54°46N 8°6W 282 B3
Laval France 48°4N 0°48W 292 B3
Laval-des-Rapides Canada 45°33N 73°42W 344 C5
Lavalle Argentina 28°15S 65°15W 366 B2
Lavant Station Canada 45°3N 76°42W 355 A8
Lāvar Meydān Iran 30°20N 54°30E 317 D7
Laverton Australia 28°44S 122°29E 333 E3
Lavras Brazil 21°20S 45°0W 367 A7
Lavrio Greece 37°40N 24°4E 295 F11
Lavris Greece 35°25N 24°40E 297 D6
Lavumisa Swaziland 27°20S 31°55E 329 D5
Lavushi Manda △ Zambia 12°46S 31°0E 327 E3
Lawaki Fiji 17°40S 178°35E 331 a
Lawas Malaysia 4°55N 115°25E 308 D5
Lawele Indonesia 5°13S 122°57E 309 F6
Lawn Hill △ Australia 18°15S 138°6E 334 B2
Lawqah Si. Arabia 29°49N 42°45E 316 D4
Lawrence N.Z. 45°55S 169°41E 331 F2
Lawrence Ind., U.S.A. 39°50N 86°2W 352 F10
Lawrence Kans., U.S.A. 38°58N 95°14W 352 F6
Lawrence Mass., U.S.A. 42°43N 71°10W 355 D13
Lawrenceburg Ind., U.S.A. 39°6N 84°52W 353 F11
Lawrenceburg Tenn., U.S.A. 35°14N 87°20W 357 D11
Lawrenceville Ga., U.S.A. 33°57N 83°59W 357 E13
Lawrenceville Pa., U.S.A. 41°59N 77°8W 354 E7
Laws U.S.A. 37°24N 118°20W 350 H8
Lawton U.S.A. 34°37N 98°25W 356 D5
Lawu Indonesia 7°40S 111°13E 309 G14
Laxford, L. U.K. 58°24N 5°6W 283 C3
Layla Si. Arabia 22°10N 46°40E 319 C4
Laylān Iraq 35°18N 44°31E 316 C5
Layton U.S.A. 41°4N 111°58W 348 F8
Laytonville U.S.A. 39°41N 123°29W 348 G2
Lazarivo Madag. 23°54S 44°59E 329 C8
Lázaro Cárdenas Mexico 17°55N 102°11W 358 D4
Lazio □ Italy 42°10N 12°30E 294 C5
Lazo Russia 43°25N 133°55E 302 C6
Le Bic Canada 48°20N 68°41W 345 C6
Le Creusot France 46°48N 4°24E 292 C6
Le François Martinique 14°38N 60°57W 360 c
Le Gosier Guadeloupe 16°14N 61°29W 360 b
Le Gris Gris Mauritius 20°31S 57°32E 325 d
Le Havre France 49°30N 0°5E 292 B4
Le Lamentin Martinique 14°35N 61°2W 360 c
Le Mans France 48°0N 0°10E 292 C4
Le Marin Martinique 14°27N 60°55W 360 c
Le Mars U.S.A. 42°47N 96°10W 352 D5
Le Mont-St-Michel France 48°40N 1°30W 292 B3
Le Moule Guadeloupe 16°20N 61°22W 360 b
Le Port Réunion 20°56S 55°18E 325 c
Le Prêcheur Martinique 14°50N 61°12W 360 c
Le Puy-en-Velay France 45°3N 3°52E 292 D5
Le Robert Martinique 14°40N 60°56W 360 c
Le St-Esprit Martinique 14°34N 60°56W 360 c
Le Sueur U.S.A. 44°28N 93°55W 352 C7
Le Tampon Réunion 21°16S 55°32E 325 c
Le Thuy Vietnam 17°14N 106°49E 310 D6
Le Touquet-Paris-Plage France 50°30N 1°36E 292 A4
Le Tréport France 50°3N 1°20E 292 A4
Le Verdon-sur-Mer France 45°33N 1°4W 292 D3
Lea → U.K. 51°31N 0°1E 285 F8
Leach Cambodia 12°21N 103°46E 311 F4
Lead U.S.A. 44°21N 103°46W 352 C2
Leader Canada 50°50N 109°30W 343 C7
Leadville U.S.A. 39°15N 106°18W 348 G10
Leaf → U.S.A. 30°59N 88°44W 357 F10
Leaf Rapids Canada 56°30N 99°59W 343 B9
Leamington Canada 42°3N 82°36W 354 D2
Leamington U.S.A. 39°32N 112°17W 348 G7
Leamington Spa = Royal Leamington Spa U.K. 52°18N 1°31W 285 E6
Leandro Norte Alem Argentina 27°34S 55°15W 367 B4
Leane, L. Ireland 52°2N 9°32W 282 D2
Learmonth Australia 22°13S 114°10E 332 D1
Leask Canada 53°5N 106°45W 343 C7
Leatherhead U.K. 51°18N 0°20W 285 F7
Leavenworth Kans., U.S.A. 39°19N 94°55W 352 F6
Leavenworth Wash., U.S.A. 47°36N 120°40W 348 C3
Leawood U.S.A. 38°58N 94°37W 352 F6
Lebak Phil. 6°32N 124°5E 309 C6
Lebam U.S.A. 46°34N 123°33W 350 D3
Lebanon Ind., U.S.A. 40°3N 86°28W 352 E10
Lebanon Kans., U.S.A. 39°49N 98°33W 352 F4
Lebanon Ky., U.S.A. 37°34N 85°15W 353 G11
Lebanon Mo., U.S.A. 37°41N 92°40W 352 G7
Lebanon N.H., U.S.A. 43°39N 72°15W 355 C12
Lebanon Oreg., U.S.A. 44°32N 122°55W 348 D2
Lebanon Pa., U.S.A. 40°20N 76°26W 355 F8
Lebanon Tenn., U.S.A. 36°12N 86°18W 357 C11
Lebanon ■ Asia 34°0N 36°0E 318 B5
Lebec U.S.A. 34°51N 118°52W 351 L8
Lebel-sur-Quévillon Canada 49°3N 76°59W 344 C4
Lebomboberge S. Africa 24°30S 32°0E 329 C5
Lębork Poland 54°33N 17°46E 289 A9
Lebrija Spain 36°53N 6°5W 293 D2
Lebu Chile 37°40S 73°47W 366 D1
Lecce Italy 40°23N 18°11E 295 D8
Lecco Italy 45°51N 9°23E 292 D8
Lech → Germany 48°43N 10°56E 288 D6
Lecontes Mills U.S.A. 41°5N 78°17W 354 E6
Łęczyca Poland 52°5N 19°15E 289 B10
Ledong China 18°41N 109°5E 310 C7
Leduc Canada 53°15N 113°30W 342 C6
Lee U.S.A. 42°19N 73°15W 355 D11
Lee → Ireland 51°53N 8°56W 282 E3
Lee Vining U.S.A. 37°58N 119°7W 350 H7
Leech L. U.S.A. 47°10N 94°24W 352 B6
Leechburg U.S.A. 40°37N 79°36W 354 F5
Leeds U.K. 53°48N 1°33W 284 D6
Leeds U.S.A. 33°33N 86°33W 357 E11
Leek Neths. 53°10N 6°24E 287 A6
Leek U.K. 53°7N 2°1W 284 D5
Leeman Australia 29°57S 114°58E 333 E1
Leeper U.S.A. 41°22N 79°18W 354 E5
Leer Germany 53°13N 7°26E 288 B4
Leesburg U.S.A. 28°49N 81°53W 357 G14
Leesville U.S.A. 31°8N 93°16W 356 F8
Leeton Australia 34°33S 146°23E 335 E4
Leetonia U.S.A. 40°53N 80°45W 354 F4
Leeu Gamka S. Africa 32°47S 21°59E 328 E3
Leeuwarden Neths. 53°15N 5°48E 287 A5
Leeuwin, C. Australia 34°20S 115°9E 333 F2
Leeuwin Naturaliste △ Australia 34°6S 115°3E 333 F2
Leeward Is. Atl. Oc. 16°30N 63°30W 361 C7
Lefka Cyprus 35°6N 32°51E 297 D11
Lefkada Greece 38°40N 20°43E 295 E9
Lefkimis Greece 39°25N 20°3E 297 B4
Lefkimis, Akra Greece 39°29N 20°4E 297 B4
Lefkímmi = Lefkimis Greece 39°25N 20°3E 297 B4
Lefkoniko Cyprus 35°18N 33°44E 297 D12
Lefroy Canada 44°16N 79°34W 354 B5
Lefroy, L. Australia 31°21S 121°40E 333 F3
Leganés Spain 40°19N 3°45W 293 B4
Legazpi Phil. 13°10N 123°45E 309 B6
Legendre I. Australia 20°22S 116°55E 332 D2
Leghorn = Livorno Italy 43°33N 10°19E 294 C4
Legionowo Poland 52°25N 20°50E 289 B11
Legnago Italy 45°11N 11°18E 294 B4
Legnica Poland 51°12N 16°10E 288 C9
Leh India 34°9N 77°35E 315 B7
Lehigh Acres U.S.A. 26°36N 81°39W 357 H14
Lehighton U.S.A. 40°50N 75°43W 355 F9
Lehututu Botswana 23°54S 21°55E 328 C3
Leiah Pakistan 30°58N 70°58E 314 D4
Leicester U.K. 52°38N 1°8W 285 E6
Leicester City □ U.K. 52°38N 1°8W 285 E6
Leicestershire □ U.K. 52°41N 1°17W 285 E6
Leichhardt → Australia 17°35S 139°48E 334 B2
Leichhardt Ra. Australia 20°46S 147°40E 334 C4
Leiden Neths. 52°9N 4°30E 287 B4
Leie → Belgium 51°2N 3°45E 287 C3
Leine → Germany 52°43N 9°36E 288 B5
Leinster Australia 27°51S 120°36E 333 E3
Leinster □ Ireland 53°3N 7°8W 282 C4
Leinster, Mt. Ireland 52°37N 6°46W 282 D5
Leipzig Germany 51°18N 12°22E 288 C7
Leiria Portugal 39°46N 8°53W 293 C1
Leirvik Norway 59°47N 5°28E 281 G11
Leisler, Mt. Australia 23°23S 129°20E 332 D4
Leith U.K. 55°59N 3°11W 283 F5
Leith Hill U.K. 51°11N 0°22W 285 F7
Leitrim Ireland 54°0N 8°5W 282 B3
Leitrim □ Ireland 54°8N 8°0W 282 B4
Leizhou Bandao China 21°0N 110°0E 305 D6
Lek → Neths. 51°54N 4°35E 287 C4
Leka Norway 65°5N 11°35E 280 D14
Lekva Oros Greece 35°18N 24°3E 297 D6
Leland U.S.A. 45°1N 85°45W 353 C11
Leleque Argentina 42°28S 71°0W 368 E2
Lelystad Neths. 52°30N 5°25E 287 B5
Léman, L. Europe 46°26N 6°30E 292 C7
Lembar Indonesia 8°45S 116°4E 309 K19
Lembuak Indonesia 8°36S 116°11E 309 K19
Lemera Dem. Rep. of the Congo 3°0S 28°55E 326 C2
Lemhi Ra. U.S.A. 44°0N 113°0W 348 D7
Lemmer Neths. 52°51N 5°43E 287 B5
Lemmon U.S.A. 45°57N 102°10W 352 C2
Lemon Grove U.S.A. 32°44N 117°1W 351 N9
Lemoore U.S.A. 36°18N 119°46W 350 J7
Lemvig Denmark 56°33N 8°20E 281 H13
Lena → Russia 72°52N 126°40E 301 B13
Lenadoon Pt. Ireland 54°18N 9°3W 282 B2
Lendeh Iran 30°58N 50°25E 317 D6
Lenggong Malaysia 5°6N 100°58E 311 K3
Lengua de Vaca, Pta. Chile 30°14S 71°38W 366 C1
Lengwe △ Malawi 16°14S 34°45E 327 F3
Leninogorsk Kazakhstan 50°20N 83°30E 300 D9
Leninsk Russia 48°40N 45°15E 291 E8
Leninsk-Kuznetskiy Russia 54°44N 86°10E 300 D9
Lenkoran = Länkäran Azerbaijan 38°48N 48°52E 317 B6
Lenmalu Indonesia 1°45S 130°15E 309 E8
Lennox U.S.A. 43°21N 96°53W 352 D5
Lennoxville Canada 45°22N 71°51W 355 A13
Lenoir U.S.A. 35°55N 81°32W 357 D14
Lenoir City U.S.A. 35°48N 84°16W 357 D12
Lenore L. Canada 52°30N 104°59W 343 C8
Lenox U.S.A. 42°22N 73°17W 355 D11
Lens France 50°26N 2°50E 292 A5
Lensk Russia 60°48N 114°55E 301 C12
Lentas Greece 34°56N 24°56E 297 E6
Lentini Italy 37°17N 15°0E 294 F6
Lenwood U.S.A. 34°53N 117°7W 351 L9
Lenya Burma 11°33N 98°57E 311 G2
Leoben Austria 47°22N 15°5E 288 E8
Leodhas = Lewis U.K. 58°9N 6°40W 283 C2
Leola U.S.A. 45°43N 98°56W 352 C4
Leominster U.K. 52°14N 2°43W 285 E5
Leominster U.S.A. 42°32N 71°46W 355 D13
León Mexico 21°6N 101°41W 358 C4
León Nic. 12°20N 86°51W 360 D2
León Spain 42°38N 5°34W 293 A3
Leon U.S.A. 40°44N 93°45W 352 E7
Leon → U.S.A. 31°14N 97°28W 356 F6
León, Montes de Spain 42°30N 6°18W 293 A2
Leonardtown U.S.A. 38°17N 76°38W 353 F15
Leonardville Namibia 23°29S 18°49E 328 C2
Leone Amer. Samoa 14°23S 170°48W 331 b
Leongatha Australia 38°30S 145°58E 335 F4
Leonora Australia 28°49S 121°19E 333 E3
Leopoldina Brazil 21°28S 42°40W 367 A7
Leopoldsburg Belgium 51°7N 5°13E 287 C5
Leoti U.S.A. 38°29N 101°21W 352 F3
Leova Moldova 46°28N 28°15E 289 E15
Leoville Canada 53°39N 107°33W 343 C7
Lepel = Lyepyel Belarus 54°50N 28°40E 281 J23
Lépo, L. do Angola 17°0S 19°0E 328 B2
Leppävirta Finland 62°29N 27°46E 280 E22
Leptis Magna Libya 32°40N 14°12E 323 B8
Leribe Lesotho 28°51S 28°3E 329 D4
Lérida = Lleida Spain 41°37N 0°39E 293 B6
Lerwick U.K. 60°9N 1°9W 283 A7
Les Cayes Haiti 18°15N 73°46W 361 C5
Les Coteaux Canada 45°15N 74°13W 355 A10
Les Escoumins Canada 48°21N 69°24W 345 C6
Les Sables-d'Olonne France 46°30N 1°45W 292 C3
Lesbos Greece 39°10N 26°20E 295 E12
Leshan China 29°33N 103°41E 304 D5
Leshukonskoye Russia 64°54N 45°46E 290 B8
Leshwe ⌂ Dem. Rep. of the Congo 12°45S 29°30E 327 E2
Leskov I. Antarctica 56°0S 28°0W 277 B1
Leskovac Serbia 43°0N 21°58E 295 C9
Lesopilnoye Russia 46°44N 134°20E 302 A7
Lesotho ■ Africa 29°40S 28°0E 329 D4
Lesozavodsk Russia 45°30N 133°29E 302 B6
Lesse → Belgium 50°15N 4°54E 287 D4
Lesse et Lomme ⌂ Belgium 50°8N 5°9E 287 D5
Lesser Antilles W. Indies 15°0N 61°0W 361 D7
Lesser Slave L. Canada 55°30N 115°25W 342 B5
Lesser Sunda Is. Indonesia 8°0S 120°0E 309 F6
Lessines Belgium 50°42N 3°50E 287 D3
Lester B. Pearson Int., Toronto ✈ (YYZ) Canada 43°46N 79°35W 354 C5
Lestock Canada 51°19N 103°59W 343 C8
Lesuer I. Australia 13°50S 127°17E 332 B4
Lesueur △ Australia 30°11S 115°10E 333 F2
Lésvos = Lesbos Greece 39°10N 26°20E 295 E12
Leszno Poland 51°50N 16°30E 289 C9
Letaba S. Africa 23°59S 31°50E 329 C5
Letchworth U.K. 51°59N 0°13W 285 F7
Lethbridge Canada 49°45N 112°45W 342 D6
Lethem Guyana 3°20N 59°50W 364 C7
Leti, Kepulauan Indonesia 8°10S 128°0E 309 F7
Leti Is. = Leti, Kepulauan Indonesia 8°10S 128°0E 309 F7
Letiahau → Botswana 21°16S 24°0E 328 C3
Leticia Colombia 4°9S 70°0W 364 D5
Leting China 39°23N 118°55E 307 E10
Letjiesbos S. Africa 32°34S 22°16E 328 E3
Letlhakane Botswana 21°27S 25°30E 328 C4
Letlhakeng Botswana 24°0S 24°59E 328 C3
Letpadan Burma 17°45N 95°45E 313 L19
Letpan Burma 19°28N 94°10E 313 K19
Letsôk-aw Kyun Burma 11°30N 98°25E 311 G2
Letterkenny Ireland 54°57N 7°45W 282 B4
Leucadia U.S.A. 33°4N 117°18W 351 M9
Leuchars U.K. 56°24N 2°53W 283 E6
Leuser, G. Indonesia 3°46N 97°12E 308 D1
Leuven Belgium 50°52N 4°42E 287 D4
Leuze-en-Hainaut Belgium 50°36N 3°37E 287 D3
Levanger Norway 63°45N 11°19E 280 E14
Levelland U.S.A. 33°35N 102°23W 356 E3
Leven U.K. 56°12N 3°0W 283 E6
Leven, L. U.K. 56°12N 3°22W 283 E5
Leven, Toraka Madag. 12°30S 47°45E 329 A8
Leveque C. Australia 16°20S 123°0E 332 C3
Levice Slovak Rep. 48°13N 18°35E 289 D10
Levin N.Z. 40°37S 175°18E 331 D5
Lévis Canada 46°48N 71°9W 345 C5
Levis, L. Canada 62°37N 117°58W 342 A5
Levittown N.Y., U.S.A. 40°44N 73°31W 355 F11
Levittown Pa., U.S.A. 40°9N 74°51W 355 F10
Levkás = Lefkada Greece 38°40N 20°43E 295 E9
Levkôsia = Nicosia Cyprus 35°10N 33°25E 297 D12
Levskigrad = Karlovo Bulgaria 42°38N 24°47E 295 C11
Levuka Fiji 17°34S 179°0E 331 a
Lewes U.K. 50°52N 0°1E 285 G8
Lewes U.S.A. 38°46N 75°9W 353 F16
Lewis U.K. 58°9N 6°40W 283 C2
Lewis → U.S.A. 45°51N 122°48W 350 E4
Lewis, Butt of U.K. 58°31N 6°16W 283 C2
Lewis Ra. Australia 20°3S 128°50E 332 D4
Lewis Range U.S.A. 48°5N 113°5W 348 B7
Lewis Run U.S.A. 41°52N 78°40W 354 E6
Lewisburg Pa., U.S.A. 40°58N 76°54W 354 F8
Lewisburg Tenn., U.S.A. 35°27N 86°48W 357 D11
Lewisburg W. Va., U.S.A. 37°48N 80°27W 353 G13
Lewisporte Canada 49°15N 55°3W 345 C8
Lewiston Idaho, U.S.A. 46°25N 117°1W 348 C5
Lewiston Maine, U.S.A. 44°6N 70°13W 353 C18
Lewiston N.Y., U.S.A. 43°11N 79°3W 354 C5
Lewistown Mont., U.S.A. 47°4N 109°26W 348 C9
Lewistown Pa., U.S.A. 40°36N 77°34W 354 F7
Lexington Ill., U.S.A. 40°39N 88°47W 352 E9
Lexington Ky., U.S.A. 38°3N 84°30W 353 F11
Lexington Mich., U.S.A. 43°16N 82°32W 354 C2
Lexington Mo., U.S.A. 39°11N 93°52W 352 F7
Lexington N.C., U.S.A. 35°49N 80°15W 357 D14
Lexington N.Y., U.S.A. 42°15N 74°22W 355 D10
Lexington Nebr., U.S.A. 40°47N 99°45W 352 E4
Lexington Ohio, U.S.A. 40°41N 82°35W 354 F2
Lexington Tenn., U.S.A. 35°39N 88°24W 357 D10
Lexington Va., U.S.A. 37°47N 79°27W 353 G14
Lexington Park U.S.A. 38°16N 76°27W 353 F15
Leyburn U.K. 54°19N 1°48W 284 C6
Leyland U.K. 53°42N 2°43W 284 D5
Leyte □ Phil. 11°0N 125°0E 309 B6
Lezhë Albania 41°47N 19°39E 295 D8
Lhasa China 29°25N 90°58E 304 D4
Lhazê China 29°5N 87°38E 304 D3
Lhokkruet Indonesia 4°55N 95°24E 308 D1
Lhokseumawe Indonesia 5°10N 97°10E 308 C1
L'Hospitalet de Llobregat Spain 41°21N 2°6E 293 B7
Li Thailand 17°48N 98°57E 310 D2
Li Xian Gansu, China 34°10N 105°5E 306 G3
Li Xian Hebei, China 38°30N 115°35E 306 E8
Liancourt Rocks = Tok-do Asia 37°15N 131°52E 303 F5
Lianga Phil. 8°38N 126°6E 309 C7
Liangcheng Nei Monggol Zizhiqu, China 40°28N 112°25E 306 D7
Liangcheng Shandong, China 35°32N 119°37E 307 G10
Liangdang China 33°56N 106°18E 306 H4
Liangpran Indonesia 1°4N 114°23E 308 D4

Lianshanguan China 40°53N 123°43E 307 D12
Lianshui China 33°42N 119°20E 307 H10
Lianyungang China 34°40N 119°11E 307 G10
Liao He → China 41°0N 121°50E 307 D11
Liaocheng China 36°28N 115°58E 306 F8
Liaodong Bandao China 40°0N 122°30E 307 E12
Liaodong Wan China 40°20N 121°10E 307 D11
Liaoning □ China 41°40N 122°30E 307 D12
Liaotung, G. of = Liaodong Wan China 40°20N 121°10E 307 D11
Liaoyang China 41°15N 122°58E 307 D12
Liaoyuan China 42°58N 125°2E 307 C13
Liaozhong China 41°23N 122°50E 307 D12
Liard → Canada 61°51N 121°18W 342 A4
Liard River Canada 59°25N 126°5W 342 B3
Liari Pakistan 25°37N 66°30E 314 G2
Libau = Liepāja Latvia 56°30N 21°0E 281 H19
Libby U.S.A. 48°23N 115°33W 348 B6
Libenge Dem. Rep. of the Congo 3°40N 18°55E 324 D3
Liberal U.S.A. 37°3N 100°55W 352 G3
Liberec Czech Rep. 50°47N 15°7E 288 C8
Liberia Costa Rica 10°40N 85°30W 360 D2
Liberia ■ W. Afr. 6°30N 9°30W 322 G4
Liberty Mo., U.S.A. 39°15N 94°25W 352 F6
Liberty N.Y., U.S.A. 41°48N 74°45W 355 E10
Liberty Pa., U.S.A. 41°34N 77°6W 354 E7
Liberty Tex., U.S.A. 30°3N 94°48W 356 F7
Liberty-Newark Int. ✕ (EWR) U.S.A. 40°42N 74°10W 355 F10
Lîbîya, Sahrâ' Africa 25°0N 25°0E 323 C10
Libobo, Tanjung Indonesia 0°54S 128°28E 309 E7
Libode S. Africa 31°33S 29°2E 329 E4
Libourne France 44°55N 0°14W 292 D3
Libramont Belgium 49°55N 5°23E 287 E5
Libreville Gabon 0°25N 9°26E 324 D1
Libya ■ N. Afr. 27°0N 17°0E 323 C9
Libyan Desert = Lîbîya, Sahrâ' Africa 25°0N 25°0E 323 C10
Libyan Plateau = Ed Déffa Egypt 30°40N 26°30E 323 B11
Licantén Chile 35°55S 72°0W 366 D1
Licata Italy 37°6N 13°56E 294 F5
Licheng China 36°28N 113°20E 306 F7
Lichfield U.K. 52°41N 1°49W 285 E6
Lichinga Mozam. 13°13S 35°11E 327 E4
Lichtenburg S. Africa 26°8S 26°8E 328 D4
Licking → U.S.A. 39°6N 84°30W 353 F11
Licungo → Mozam. 17°40S 37°15E 327 F4
Lida Belarus 53°53N 25°15E 289 B13
Lidköping Sweden 58°31N 13°7E 281 G15
Liebig, Mt. Australia 23°18S 131°22E 332 D5
Liechtenstein ■ Europe 47°8N 9°35E 292 C8
Liège Belgium 50°38N 5°35E 287 D5
Liège □ Belgium 50°32N 5°35E 287 D5
Liegnitz = Legnica Poland 51°12N 16°10E 288 C9
Lieksa Finland 63°18N 30°2E 280 E24
Lienart Dem. Rep. of the Congo 3°3N 25°31E 326 B2
Lienyünchiangshih = Lianyungang China 34°40N 119°11E 307 G10
Lienz Austria 46°50N 12°46E 288 E7
Liepāja Latvia 56°30N 21°0E 281 H19
Lier Belgium 51°7N 4°34E 287 C4
Lietuva = Lithuania ■ Europe 55°30N 24°0E 281 J21
Lièvre → Canada 45°31N 75°26W 344 C4
Liffey → Ireland 53°21N 6°13W 282 C5
Lifford Ireland 54°51N 7°29W 282 B4
Lifudzin Russia 44°21N 134°58E 302 B7
Lightning Ridge Australia 29°22S 148°0E 335 D4
Ligonha → Mozam. 16°54S 39°9E 327 F4
Ligonier U.S.A. 40°15N 79°14W 354 F5
Liguria □ Italy 44°30N 8°50E 292 D8
Ligurian Sea Medit. S. 43°20N 9°0E 294 C3
Lihou Reefs and Cays Australia 17°25S 151°40E 334 B5
Lihue U.S.A. 21°59N 159°23W 346 b
Lihué Calel △ Argentina 38°0S 65°10W 366 D2
Lijiang China 26°55N 100°20E 304 D5
Likasi Dem. Rep. of the Congo 10°55S 26°48E 327 E2
Likoma I. Malawi 12°3S 34°45E 327 E3
Likumburu Tanzania 9°43S 35°8E 327 D4
L'Île-Rousse France 42°38N 8°57E 292 E8
Lille France 50°38N 3°3E 292 A5
Lille Bælt Denmark 55°20N 9°45E 281 J13
Lillehammer Norway 61°8N 10°30E 280 F14
Lillesand Norway 58°15N 8°23E 281 G13
Lillian Pt. Australia 27°40S 126°6E 333 E4
Lillooet Canada 50°44N 121°57W 342 C4
Lillooet → Canada 49°15N 121°57W 342 D4
Lilongwe Malawi 14°0S 33°48E 327 E3
Liloy Phil. 8°4N 122°39E 309 C6
Lim → Europe 43°45N 19°15E 295 C8
Lim Chu Kang Singapore 1°26N 103°43E 311 d
Lima Indonesia 3°39S 127°58E 309 E7
Lima Peru 12°3S 77°2W 364 F3
Lima Mont., U.S.A. 44°38N 112°36W 348 D7
Lima Ohio, U.S.A. 40°44N 84°6W 353 E11
Lima → Portugal 41°41N 8°50W 293 B1
Liman Indonesia 7°48S 111°45E 309 G14
Limassol Cyprus 34°42N 33°1E 297 E12
Limavady U.K. 55°3N 6°56W 282 A5
Limay → Argentina 39°0S 68°0W 368 D3
Limay Mahuida Argentina 37°10S 66°45W 366 D2
Limbang Brunei 4°42N 115°6E 308 D5
Limbaži Latvia 57°31N 24°42E 281 H21
Limbdi India 22°34N 71°51E 314 H4
Limbe Cameroon 4°1N 9°10E 324 D1
Limburg Germany 50°22N 8°4E 288 C5
Limburg □ Belgium 51°2N 5°25E 287 C5
Limburg □ Neths. 51°20N 5°55E 287 C5
Limeira Brazil 22°35S 47°28W 367 A6
Limerick Ireland 52°40N 8°37W 282 D3
Limerick U.S.A. 43°41N 70°48W 355 C14
Limerick □ Ireland 52°30N 8°50W 282 D3
Limestone U.S.A. 42°2N 78°38W 354 D6
Limestone → Canada 56°31N 94°7W 343 B10
Limfjorden Denmark 56°55N 9°0E 281 H13
Limia = Lima → Portugal 41°41N 8°50W 293 B1
Limingen Norway 64°48N 13°35E 280 D15
Limmen Bight Australia 14°40S 135°35E 334 A2
Limmen Bight → Australia 15°7S 135°44E 334 B2
Limnos Greece 39°50N 25°5E 295 E11
Limoges Canada 45°20N 75°16W 355 A9
Limoges France 45°50N 1°15E 292 D4
Limón Costa Rica 10°0N 83°2W 360 E3
Limon U.S.A. 39°16N 103°41W 348 G12
Limousin □ France 45°30N 1°30E 292 D4
Limoux France 43°4N 2°12E 292 E5
Limpopo □ S. Africa 24°5S 29°0E 329 C4
Limpopo → Africa 25°5S 33°30E 329 D5
Limuru Kenya 1°2S 36°35E 326 C4
Lin Xian China 37°57N 110°58E 306 F6
Linares Chile 35°50S 71°40W 366 D1
Linares Mexico 24°52N 99°34W 359 C5
Linares Spain 38°10N 3°40W 293 C4
Lincheng China 37°25N 114°30E 306 F8
Lincoln Argentina 34°55S 61°30W 366 C3
Lincoln Canada 43°12N 79°28W 354 C5
Lincoln N.Z. 43°38S 172°30E 331 E4
Lincoln U.K. 53°14N 0°32W 284 D7
Lincoln Calif., U.S.A. 38°54N 121°17W 350 G5
Lincoln Ill., U.S.A. 40°9N 89°22W 352 E9
Lincoln Kans., U.S.A. 39°3N 98°9W 352 F4
Lincoln Maine, U.S.A. 45°22N 68°30W 353 C19
Lincoln N.H., U.S.A. 44°3N 71°40W 355 B13
Lincoln N. Mex., U.S.A. 33°30N 105°23W 349 K11
Lincoln Nebr., U.S.A. 40°49N 96°41W 352 E5
Lincoln City U.S.A. 44°57N 124°1W 348 D1
Lincoln Hav = Lincoln Sea Arctic 84°0N 55°0W 338 A14
Lincoln Sea Arctic 84°0N 55°0W 338 A14
Lincolnshire □ U.K. 53°14N 0°32W 284 D7
Lincolnshire Wolds U.K. 53°26N 0°13W 284 D7
Lincolnton U.S.A. 35°29N 81°16W 357 D14
Lind U.S.A. 46°58N 118°37W 348 C4
Linda U.S.A. 39°8N 121°34W 350 F5
Lindeman I. Australia 20°27S 149°3E 334 J7
Linden Guyana 6°0N 58°10W 364 B7
Linden Ala., U.S.A. 32°18N 87°48W 357 E11
Linden Calif., U.S.A. 38°1N 121°5W 350 G5
Linden Tex., U.S.A. 33°1N 94°22W 356 E7
Lindenhurst U.S.A. 40°41N 73°23W 355 F11
Lindesnes Norway 57°58N 7°3E 281 H12
Lindi Tanzania 9°58S 39°38E 327 D4
Lindi □ Tanzania 9°40S 38°30E 327 D4
Lindi → Dem. Rep. of the Congo 0°33N 25°5E 326 B2
Lindos Greece 36°6N 28°4E 297 C10
Lindos, Akra Greece 36°4N 28°10E 297 C10
Lindsay Canada 44°22N 78°43W 354 B6
Lindsay Calif., U.S.A. 36°12N 119°5W 350 J7
Lindsay Okla., U.S.A. 34°50N 97°38W 356 D6
Lindsborg U.S.A. 38°35N 97°40W 352 F5
Line Islands Pac. Oc. 7°0N 160°0W 337 H12
Linesville U.S.A. 41°39N 80°26W 354 E4
Linfen China 36°3N 111°30E 306 F6
Ling Xian China 37°22N 116°30E 306 F9
Lingao China 19°56N 109°42E 310 C7
Lingayen Phil. 16°1N 120°14E 309 A6
Lingayen G. Phil. 16°10N 120°15E 309 A6
Lingbi China 33°33N 117°33E 307 H9
Lingchuan China 35°45N 113°12E 306 G7
Lingding Yang China 22°25N 113°44E 305 G10
Lingen Germany 52°31N 7°19E 288 B4
Lingga Indonesia 0°12S 104°37E 308 E2
Lingga, Kepulauan Indonesia 0°10S 104°30E 308 E2
Lingga Arch. = Lingga, Kepulauan Indonesia 0°10S 104°30E 308 E2
Lingle U.S.A. 42°8N 104°21W 348 E11
Lingqiu China 39°28N 114°22E 306 E8
Lingshi China 36°48N 111°48E 306 F6
Lingshou China 38°20N 114°20E 306 E8
Lingshui China 18°27N 110°0E 310 C8
Lingtai China 35°0N 107°40E 306 G4
Linguère Senegal 15°25N 15°5W 322 E2
Lingwu China 38°6N 106°20E 306 E4
Lingyuan China 41°10N 119°15E 307 D10
Linhai China 28°50N 121°8E 305 D7
Linhares Brazil 19°25S 40°4W 365 G10
Linhe China 40°48N 107°20E 306 D4
Linjiang China 41°50N 127°0E 307 D14
Linköping Sweden 58°28N 15°36E 281 G16
Linkou China 45°15N 130°18E 307 B16
Linnhe, L. U.K. 56°36N 5°25W 283 E3
Linosa Medit. S. 35°51N 12°50E 294 G5
Linqi China 35°45N 113°52E 306 G7
Linqing China 36°50N 115°42E 306 F8
Linqu China 36°25N 118°30E 307 F10
Linru China 34°11N 112°52E 306 G7
Lins Brazil 21°40S 49°44W 367 A6
Linstead Jamaica 18°8N 77°2W 360 a
Linta → Madag. 25°2S 44°5E 329 D7
Linton Ind., U.S.A. 39°2N 87°10W 352 F10
Linton N. Dak., U.S.A. 46°16N 100°14W 352 B3
Lintong China 34°20N 109°10E 306 G5
Linwood Canada 43°35N 80°43W 354 C4
Linxi China 43°36N 118°2E 307 C10
Linxia China 35°36N 103°10E 304 C5
Linyanti → Africa 17°50S 25°5E 328 B4
Linyi China 35°5N 118°21E 307 G10
Linz Austria 48°18N 14°18E 288 D8
Linzhenzhen China 36°30N 109°59E 306 F5
Linzi China 36°50N 118°20E 307 F10
Lion, G. du France 43°10N 4°0E 292 E6
Lionárisso Cyprus 35°28N 34°8E 297 D13
Lions, G. of = Lion, G. du France 43°10N 4°0E 292 E6
Lion's Den Zimbabwe 17°15S 30°5E 327 F3
Lion's Head Canada 44°58N 81°15W 354 B3
Lipa Phil. 13°57N 121°10E 309 B6
Lipali Mozam. 15°50S 35°50E 327 F4
Lípari Italy 38°26N 14°58E 294 E6
Lípari, Is. = Eólie, Ís. Italy 38°30N 14°57E 294 E6
Lipcani Moldova 48°14N 26°48E 289 D14
Liperi Finland 62°31N 29°24E 280 E23
Lipetsk Russia 52°37N 39°35E 290 D6
Lipkany = Lipcani Moldova 48°14N 26°48E 289 D14
Lipovets Ukraine 49°12N 29°1E 289 D15
Lippe → Germany 51°39N 6°36E 288 C4
Lipscomb U.S.A. 36°14N 100°16W 356 C4
Liptrap, C. Australia 38°50S 145°55E 335 F4
Liquillo, Sierra de Puerto Rico 18°20N 65°47W 361 d
Lira Uganda 2°17N 32°57E 326 B3
Liria = Lliria Spain 39°37N 0°35W 293 C5
Lisala Dem. Rep. of the Congo 2°12N 21°38E 324 D4
Lisboa Portugal 38°42N 9°8W 293 C1
Lisbon = Lisboa Portugal 38°42N 9°8W 293 C1
Lisbon N. Dak., U.S.A. 46°27N 97°41W 352 B5
Lisbon N.H., U.S.A. 44°13N 71°55W 355 B13
Lisbon Ohio, U.S.A. 40°46N 80°46W 354 F4
Lisbon Falls U.S.A. 44°0N 70°4W 353 D18
Lisburn U.K. 54°31N 6°3W 282 B5
Lisburne, C. U.S.A. 68°53N 166°13W 276 C17
Liscannor B. Ireland 52°55N 9°24W 282 D2
Lisdoonvarna Ireland 53°2N 9°18W 282 C2
Lishi China 37°31N 111°8E 306 F6
Lishu China 43°20N 124°18E 307 C13
Lisianski I. U.S.A. 26°2N 174°0W 336 E10
Lisichansk = Lysychansk Ukraine 48°55N 38°30E 291 E6
Lisieux France 49°10N 0°12E 292 B4
Liski Russia 51°3N 39°30E 291 D6
Lismore Australia 28°44S 153°21E 335 D5
Lismore Ireland 52°8N 7°55W 282 D4
Lista Norway 58°7N 6°39E 281 G12
Lister, Mt. Antarctica 78°0S 162°0E 277 D11
Liston Australia 28°39S 152°6E 335 D5
Listowel Canada 43°44N 80°58W 354 C4
Listowel Ireland 52°27N 9°29W 282 D2
Litani → Lebanon 33°20N 35°15E 318 B4
Litchfield Calif., U.S.A. 40°24N 120°23W 350 E6
Litchfield Conn., U.S.A. 41°45N 73°11W 355 E11
Litchfield Ill., U.S.A. 39°11N 89°39W 352 F9
Litchfield Minn., U.S.A. 45°8N 94°32W 352 C6
Litchfield △ Australia 13°14S 131°1E 332 B5
Lithgow Australia 33°25S 150°8E 335 E5
Lithino, Akra Greece 34°55N 24°44E 297 E6
Lithuania ■ Europe 55°30N 24°0E 281 J21
Lititz U.S.A. 40°9N 76°18W 355 F8
Litoměřice Czech Rep. 50°33N 14°10E 288 C8
Little Abaco Bahamas 26°50N 77°30W 360 A4
Little Barrier I. N.Z. 36°12S 175°8E 331 B5
Little Belt Mts. U.S.A. 46°40N 110°45W 348 C8
Little Bighorn Battlefield △ U.S.A. 45°34N 107°25W 348 D10
Little Blue → U.S.A. 39°42N 96°41W 352 F5
Little Buffalo → Canada 61°0N 113°46W 342 A6
Little Cayman Cayman Is. 19°41N 80°3W 360 C3
Little Churchill → Canada 57°30N 95°22W 343 B9
Little Colorado → U.S.A. 36°12N 111°48W 349 H8
Little Current Canada 45°55N 82°0W 344 C3
Little Current → Canada 50°57N 84°36W 344 B3
Little Falls Minn., U.S.A. 45°59N 94°22W 352 C6
Little Falls N.Y., U.S.A. 43°3N 74°51W 355 C10
Little Fork → U.S.A. 48°31N 93°35W 352 A7
Little Grand Rapids Canada 52°0N 95°29W 343 C9
Little Humboldt → U.S.A. 41°1N 117°43W 348 F5
Little Inagua I. Bahamas 21°40N 73°50W 361 B5
Little Karoo S. Africa 33°45S 21°0E 328 E3
Little Khingan Mts. = Xiao Hinggan Ling China 49°0N 127°0E 305 B7
Little Lake U.S.A. 35°56N 117°55W 351 K9
Little Laut Is. = Laut Kecil, Kepulauan Indonesia 4°45S 115°40E 308 E5
Little Mecatina = Petit-Mécatina → Canada 50°40N 59°30W 345 B8
Little Minch U.K. 57°35N 6°45W 283 D2
Little Missouri → U.S.A. 47°36N 102°25W 352 B2
Little Ouse → U.K. 52°22N 1°12E 285 E9
Little Rann India 23°25N 71°25E 314 H4
Little Red → U.S.A. 35°11N 91°27W 356 D9
Little River N.Z. 43°45S 172°49E 331 E4
Little Rock U.S.A. 34°45N 92°17W 356 D8
Little Ruaha → Tanzania 7°57S 37°53E 326 D4
Little Sable Pt. U.S.A. 43°38N 86°33W 352 D10
Little Sioux → U.S.A. 41°48N 96°4W 352 E5
Little Smoky → Canada 54°44N 117°11W 342 C5
Little Snake → U.S.A. 40°27N 108°26W 348 F9
Little Tobago Trin. & Tob. 11°18N 60°30W 365 J16
Little Valley U.S.A. 42°15N 78°48W 354 D6
Little Wabash → U.S.A. 37°55N 88°5W 352 G9
Little White → U.S.A. 43°40N 100°40W 352 D3
Little Zab = Zāb aş Şaghīr → Iraq 35°17N 43°29E 316 C4
Littlefield U.S.A. 33°55N 102°20W 356 E3
Littlehampton U.K. 50°49N 0°32W 285 G7
Littleton U.S.A. 44°18N 71°46W 355 B13
Liu He → China 40°55N 118°15E 307 D11
Liuba China 33°38N 106°55E 306 H4
Liugou China 40°57N 118°15E 307 D10
Liuhe China 42°17N 125°43E 307 C13
Liukang Tenggaja = Sabalana, Kepulauan Indonesia 6°45S 118°50E 309 F5
Liuli Tanzania 11°3S 34°38E 327 E3
Liupanshui China 26°38N 104°48E 304 D5
Liuwa Plain Zambia 14°20S 22°30E 325 G4
Liuzhou China 24°22N 109°22E 305 D5
Liuzhuang China 33°12N 120°18E 307 H11
Livadhia Cyprus 34°57N 33°38E 297 E12
Livadia Greece 38°27N 22°54E 295 E10
Live Oak Calif., U.S.A. 39°17N 121°40W 350 F5
Live Oak Fla., U.S.A. 30°18N 82°59W 357 F13
Lively Canada 46°26N 81°9W 353 B13
Liveras Cyprus 35°23N 32°57E 297 D11
Livermore U.S.A. 37°41N 121°47W 350 H5
Livermore, Mt. U.S.A. 30°38N 104°11W 356 F2
Livermore Falls U.S.A. 44°29N 70°11W 353 C18
Liverpool Canada 44°5N 64°41W 345 D7
Liverpool U.K. 53°25N 3°0W 284 D4
Liverpool U.S.A. 43°6N 76°13W 355 C8
Liverpool Bay U.K. 53°30N 3°20W 284 D4
Liverpool Ra. Australia 31°50S 150°30E 335 E5
Livingston Guatemala 15°50N 88°50W 360 C2
Livingston U.K. 55°54N 3°30W 283 F5
Livingston Ala., U.S.A. 32°35N 88°11W 357 E10
Livingston Calif., U.S.A. 37°23N 120°43W 350 H6
Livingston Mont., U.S.A. 45°40N 110°34W 348 D8
Livingston S.C., U.S.A. 33°38N 81°7W 357 E14
Livingston Tenn., U.S.A. 36°23N 85°19W 357 C12
Livingston Tex., U.S.A. 30°43N 94°56W 356 F7
Livingston, L. U.S.A. 30°50N 95°10W 356 F7
Livingston Manor U.S.A. 41°54N 74°50W 355 E10
Livingstone Zambia 17°46S 25°52E 327 F2
Livingstone Mts. Tanzania 9°40S 34°20E 327 D3
Livingstonia Malawi 10°38S 34°5E 327 E3
Livny Russia 52°30N 37°30E 290 D6
Livonia Mich., U.S.A. 42°23N 83°23W 353 D12
Livonia N.Y., U.S.A. 42°49N 77°40W 354 D7
Livorno Italy 43°33N 10°19E 294 C4
Livramento Brazil 30°55S 55°30W 367 C4
Liwale Tanzania 9°48S 37°58E 327 D4
Liwonde △ Malawi 14°48S 35°20E 327 E4
Lizard I. Australia 14°42S 145°30E 334 A4
Lizard Pt. U.K. 49°57N 5°13W 285 H2
Ljubljana Slovenia 46°4N 14°33E 288 E8
Ljungan → Sweden 62°18N 17°23E 280 E17
Ljungby Sweden 56°49N 13°55E 281 H15
Ljusdal Sweden 61°46N 16°3E 280 F17
Ljusnan → Sweden 61°12N 17°8E 280 F17
Ljusne Sweden 61°13N 17°7E 280 F17
Llancanelo, Salina Argentina 35°40S 69°8W 366 D2
Llandeilo U.K. 51°53N 3°59W 285 F4
Llandovery U.K. 51°59N 3°48W 285 F4
Llandrindod Wells U.K. 52°14N 3°22W 285 E4
Llandudno U.K. 53°19N 3°50W 284 D4
Llanelli U.K. 51°41N 4°10W 285 F3
Llanes Spain 43°25N 4°50W 293 A3
Llangollen U.K. 52°58N 3°11W 284 E4
Llanidloes U.K. 52°27N 3°31W 285 E4
Llano U.S.A. 30°45N 98°41W 356 F5
Llano → U.S.A. 30°39N 98°26W 356 F5
Llano Estacado U.S.A. 33°30N 103°0W 356 E3
Llanos S. Amer. 5°0N 71°35W 364 C4
Llanos de Challe △ Chile 28°8S 71°1W 366 B1
Llanquihue, L. Chile 41°10S 72°50W 368 E1
Llanwrtyd Wells U.K. 52°7N 3°38W 285 E4
Llebeig, C. des Spain 39°33N 2°18E 296 B9
Lleida Spain 41°37N 0°39E 293 B6
Llentrisca, C. Spain 38°52N 1°15E 296 C7
Llera de Canales Mexico 23°19N 99°1W 359 C5
Lleyn Peninsula U.K. 52°51N 4°36W 284 E3
Llico Chile 34°46S 72°5W 366 C1
Lliria Spain 39°37N 0°35W 293 C5
Llobregat → Spain 41°19N 2°5E 293 B7
Lloret de Mar Spain 41°41N 2°53E 293 B7
Lloyd B. Australia 12°45S 143°27E 334 A3
Lloyd L. Canada 57°22N 108°57W 343 B7
Lloydminster Canada 53°17N 110°0W 343 C7
Llucmajor Spain 39°29N 2°53E 296 B9
Llullaillaco, Volcán S. Amer. 24°43S 68°30W 366 A2
Llullaillaco △ Chile 24°50S 68°51W 366 A2
Lo → Vietnam 21°18N 105°25E 310 B5
Loa U.S.A. 38°24N 111°39W 348 G8
Loa → Chile 21°26S 70°41W 366 A1
Loaita I. S. China Sea 10°41N 114°25E 308 B4
Loange → Dem. Rep. of the Congo 4°17S 20°2E 324 E4
Lobatse Botswana 25°12S 25°40E 328 D4
Lobería Argentina 38°10S 58°40W 366 D4
Lobito Angola 12°18S 13°35E 325 G2
Lobos Argentina 35°10S 59°0W 366 D4
Lobos, I. Mexico 27°20N 110°36W 358 B2
Lobos, I. de Canary Is. 28°45N 13°50W 296 F6
Loc Binh Vietnam 21°46N 106°54E 310 B6
Loc Ninh Vietnam 11°50N 106°34E 311 G6
Locarno Switz. 46°10N 8°47E 292 C8
Loch Baghasdail = Lochboisdale U.K. 57°9N 7°20W 283 D1
Loch Garman = Wexford Ireland 52°20N 6°28W 282 D5
Loch Lomond and the Trossachs △ U.K. 56°10N 4°40W 283 E4
Loch Nam Madadh = Lochmaddy U.K. 57°36N 7°10W 283 D1
Lochaber U.K. 56°59N 5°1W 283 E3
Locharbriggs U.K. 55°7N 3°35W 283 F5
Lochboisdale U.K. 57°9N 7°20W 283 D1
Loche, L. La Canada 56°30N 109°30W 343 B7
Lochem Neths. 52°9N 6°26E 287 B6
Loches France 47°7N 1°0E 292 C4
Lochgilphead U.K. 56°2N 5°26W 283 E3
Lochinvar △ Zambia 15°55S 27°15E 327 F2
Lochinver U.K. 58°9N 5°14W 283 C3
Lochmaddy U.K. 57°36N 7°10W 283 D1
Lochnagar Australia 23°33S 145°38E 334 C4
Lochnagar U.K. 56°57N 3°15W 283 E5
Lochy, L. U.K. 57°0N 4°53W 283 E4
Lock Australia 33°34S 135°46E 335 E2
Lock Haven U.S.A. 41°8N 77°28W 354 E7
Lockeford U.S.A. 38°10N 121°9W 350 G5
Lockeport Canada 43°47N 65°4W 345 D6
Lockerbie U.K. 55°7N 3°21W 283 F5
Lockhart U.S.A. 29°53N 97°40W 356 G6
Lockhart, L. Australia 33°15S 119°3E 333 F2
Lockhart River Australia 12°58S 143°30E 334 A3
Lockney U.S.A. 34°7N 101°27W 356 D4
Lockport U.S.A. 43°10N 78°42W 354 C6
Lod Israel 31°57N 34°54E 318 D3
Lodeinoye Pole Russia 60°44N 33°33E 290 B5
Lodge Bay Canada 52°14N 55°51W 345 B8
Lodge Grass U.S.A. 45°19N 107°22W 348 D10
Lodhran Pakistan 29°32N 71°30E 314 E4
Lodi Italy 45°19N 9°30E 292 D8
Lodi Calif., U.S.A. 38°8N 121°16W 350 G5
Lodi Ohio, U.S.A. 41°2N 82°1W 354 E3
Lodja Dem. Rep. of the Congo 3°30S 23°23E 326 C1
Lodwar Kenya 3°7N 35°36E 326 B4
Łódź Poland 51°45N 19°27E 289 C10
Loei Thailand 17°29N 101°35E 310 D3
Loengo Dem. Rep. of the Congo 4°48S 26°30E 326 C2
Loeriesfontein S. Africa 31°0S 19°26E 328 E2
Lofoten Norway 68°30N 14°0E 280 B16
Logan Iowa, U.S.A. 41°39N 95°47W 352 E6
Logan Ohio, U.S.A. 39°32N 82°25W 353 F12
Logan Utah, U.S.A. 41°44N 111°50W 348 F8
Logan W. Va., U.S.A. 37°51N 81°59W 353 G13
Logan, Mt. Canada 60°34N 140°23W 340 C5
Logandale U.S.A. 36°36N 114°29W 351 J12
Logansport Ind., U.S.A. 40°45N 86°22W 352 E10
Logansport La., U.S.A. 31°58N 94°0W 356 F8
Logone → Chad 12°6N 15°2E 323 F9
Logroño Spain 42°28N 2°27W 293 A4
Lohardaga India 23°27N 84°45E 315 H11
Loharia India 23°45N 74°14E 314 H6
Loharu India 28°27N 75°49E 314 E6
Lohri Wah → Pakistan 27°27N 67°37E 314 F2
Loi-kaw Burma 19°40N 97°17E 313 K20
Loimaa Finland 60°50N 23°5E 280 F20
Loir → France 47°33N 0°32W 292 C3
Loire → France 47°16N 2°10W 292 C2
Loja Ecuador 3°59S 79°16W 364 D3
Loja Spain 37°10N 4°10W 293 D3
Loji = Kawasi Indonesia 1°38S 127°28E 309 E7
Lokandu Dem. Rep. of the Congo 2°30S 25°45E 326 C2
Lokeren Belgium 51°6N 3°59E 287 C3
Lokgwabe Botswana 24°10S 21°50E 328 C3
Lokichar Kenya 2°23N 35°39E 326 B4
Lokichokio Kenya 4°19N 34°13E 326 B3
Lokitaung Kenya 4°12N 35°48E 326 B4
Lokkan tekojärvi Finland 67°55N 27°35E 280 C22
Lokoja Nigeria 7°47N 6°45E 322 G7
Lokolo → Dem. Rep. of the Congo 1°43S 18°23E 324 E3
Lola, Mt. U.S.A. 39°26N 120°22W 350 F6
Lolgorien Kenya 1°14S 34°48E 326 C3
Loliondo Tanzania 2°2S 35°39E 326 C4
Lolland Denmark 54°45N 11°30E 281 J14
Lolo U.S.A. 46°45N 114°5W 348 C6
Lom Bulgaria 43°48N 23°12E 295 C10
Lom Kao Thailand 16°53N 101°14E 310 D3
Lom Sak Thailand 16°47N 101°15E 310 D3
Loma U.S.A. 47°56N 110°30W 348 C8
Loma Linda U.S.A. 34°3N 117°16W 351 L9
Lomaloma Fiji 17°17S 178°59W 331 a
Lomami → Dem. Rep. of the Congo 0°46N 24°16E 326 B1
Lomas de Zamóra Argentina 34°45S 58°24W 366 C4
Lombadina Australia 16°31S 122°54E 332 C3
Lombárdia □ Italy 45°40N 9°30E 292 D8
Lombardy = Lombárdia □ Italy 45°40N 9°30E 292 D8
Lomblen Indonesia 8°30S 123°32E 309 F6
Lombok Indonesia 8°45S 116°30E 308 F5
Lombok, Selat Indonesia 8°30S 115°50E 309 K18
Lomé Togo 6°9N 1°20E 322 G6
Lomela Dem. Rep. of the Congo 2°19S 23°15E 324 E4
Lomela → Dem. Rep. of the Congo 0°15S 20°40E 324 E4
Lommel Belgium 51°14N 5°19E 287 C5
Lomond Canada 50°24N 112°36W 342 C6
Lomond, L. U.K. 56°8N 4°38W 283 E4
Lomonosov Ridge Arctic 88°0N 140°0E 276 A
Lomphat Cambodia 13°30N 106°59E 310 F6
Lompobatang Indonesia 5°24S 119°56E 309 F5
Lompoc U.S.A. 34°38N 120°28W 351 L6
Łomża Poland 53°10N 22°2E 289 B12
Lon, Ko Thailand 7°47N 98°23E 311 a
Loncoche Chile 39°20S 72°50W 368 D2
Londa India 15°30N 74°30E 312 M9
Londiani Kenya 0°10S 35°33E 326 C4
London Canada 42°59N 81°15W 354 D3
London U.K. 51°30N 0°3W 285 F7
London Ky., U.S.A. 37°8N 84°5W 353 G11
London Ohio, U.S.A. 39°53N 83°27W 353 F12
London, Greater □ U.K. 51°36N 0°5W 285 F7
London Gatwick ✕ (LGW) U.K. 51°10N 0°11W 285 F7

London Heathrow ✕ (LHR) U.K. 51°28N 0°27W 285 F7
London Stansted ✕ (STN) U.K. 51°54N 0°14E 285 F8
Londonderry U.K. 55°0N 7°20W 282 B4
Londonderry □ U.K. 55°0N 7°20W 282 B4
Londonderry, C. Australia 13°45S 126°55E 332 B4
Londonderry, I. Chile 55°0S 71°0W 368 H2
Londres Argentina 27°43S 67°7W 368 B3
Londrina Brazil 23°18S 51°10W 367 A5
Lone Pine U.S.A. 36°36N 118°4W 350 J8
Lonely Mine Zimbabwe 19°30S 28°49E 329 B4
Long B. U.S.A. 33°35N 78°45W 357 E15
Long Beach Calif., U.S.A. 33°46N 118°11W 351 M8
Long Beach N.Y., U.S.A. 40°35N 73°39W 355 F11
Long Beach Wash., U.S.A. 46°21N 124°3W 350 D2
Long Branch U.S.A. 40°18N 74°0W 355 F11
Long Creek U.S.A. 44°43N 119°6W 348 D4
Long Eaton U.K. 52°53N 1°15W 284 E6
Long I. Australia 20°22S 148°51E 334 J6
Long I. Bahamas 23°20N 75°10W 361 B4
Long I. Canada 54°50N 79°20W 344 B4
Long I. Ireland 51°30N 9°34W 282 E2
Long I. U.S.A. 40°45N 73°30W 355 F11
Long Island Sd. U.S.A. 41°10N 73°0W 355 E12
Long L. Canada 49°30N 86°50W 344 C2
Long Lake U.S.A. 43°58N 74°25W 355 C10
Long Point B. Canada 42°40N 80°10W 354 D4
Long Prairie U.S.A. 45°59N 94°52W 352 C6
Long Prairie → U.S.A. 46°20N 94°36W 352 B6
Long Pt. Canada 42°35N 80°2W 354 D4
Long Range Mts. Canada 49°30N 57°30W 345 C8
Long Reef Australia 14°1S 125°48E 332 B4
Long Spruce Canada 56°24N 94°21W 343 B10
Long Str. = Longa, Proliv Russia 70°0N 175°0E 276 C16
Long Thanh Vietnam 10°47N 106°57E 311 G6
Long Xian China 34°55N 106°55E 306 G4
Long Xuyen Vietnam 10°19N 105°28E 311 G5
Longa, Proliv Russia 70°0N 175°0E 276 C16
Longbenton U.K. 55°1N 1°31W 284 B6
Longboat Key U.S.A. 27°23N 82°39W 357 H13
Longde China 35°30N 106°20E 306 G4
Longford Australia 41°32S 147°3E 335 G4
Longford Ireland 53°43N 7°49W 282 C4
Longford □ Ireland 53°42N 7°45W 282 C4
Longhua Guangdong, China 22°39N 114°0E 305 F11
Longhua Hebei, China 41°18N 117°45E 307 D9
Longido Tanzania 2°43S 36°42E 326 C4
Longiram Indonesia 0°5S 115°45E 308 E5
Longkou China 37°40N 120°18E 307 F11
Longlac Canada 49°45N 86°25W 344 C2
Longmeadow U.S.A. 42°3N 72°34W 355 D12
Longmont U.S.A. 40°10N 105°6W 348 F11
Longnawan Indonesia 1°51N 114°55E 308 D4
Longreach Australia 23°28S 144°14E 334 C3
Longueuil Canada 45°31N 73°29W 355 A11
Longview Tex., U.S.A. 32°30N 94°44W 356 E7
Longview Wash., U.S.A. 46°8N 122°57W 350 D4
Longxi China 34°53N 104°40E 306 G3
Longxue Dao China 22°41N 113°38E 305 F10
Longyearbyen Svalbard 78°13N 15°40E 276 B8
Lonoke U.S.A. 34°47N 91°54W 356 D9
Lonquimay Chile 38°26S 71°14W 368 D2
Lons-le-Saunier France 46°40N 5°31E 292 C6
Looe U.K. 50°22N 4°28W 285 G3
Lookout, C. Canada 55°18N 83°56W 344 A3
Lookout, C. U.S.A. 34°35N 76°32W 357 D16
Loolmalasin Tanzania 3°0S 35°53E 326 C4
Loon → Alta., Canada 57°8N 115°3W 342 B5
Loon → Man., Canada 55°53N 101°59W 343 B8
Loon Lake Canada 54°2N 109°10W 343 C7
Loongana Australia 30°52S 127°5E 333 F4
Loop Hd. Ireland 52°34N 9°56W 282 D2
Lop China 37°3N 80°11E 304 C3
Lop Buri Thailand 14°48N 100°37E 310 E3
Lop Nor = Lop Nur China 40°20N 90°10E 304 B4
Lop Nur China 40°20N 90°10E 304 B4
Lopatina, Gora Russia 50°47N 143°10E 301 D15
Lopez U.S.A. 41°27N 76°20W 355 E8
Lopez, C. Gabon 0°47S 8°40E 324 E1
Lopphavet Norway 70°27N 21°15E 280 A19
Lora → Afghan. 31°35N 66°32E 312 D4
Lora, Hāmūn-i- Pakistan 29°38N 64°58E 312 E4
Lora Cr. → Australia 28°10S 135°22E 335 D2
Lora del Río Spain 37°39N 5°33W 293 D3
Lorain U.S.A. 41°28N 82°11W 354 E2
Loralai Pakistan 30°20N 68°41E 314 D3
Lorca Spain 37°41N 1°42W 293 D5
Lord Howe I. Pac. Oc. 31°33S 159°6E 330 E8
Lord Howe Rise Pac. Oc. 30°0S 162°30E 336 L8
Lordsburg U.S.A. 32°21N 108°43W 349 K9
Lorestān □ Iran 33°30N 48°40E 317 C6
Loreto Brazil 7°5S 45°10W 365 E9
Loreto Mexico 26°0N 111°21W 358 B2
Lorient France 47°45N 3°23W 292 C2
Lormi India 22°17N 81°41E 315 H9
Lorn U.K. 56°26N 5°10W 283 E3
Lorn, Firth of U.K. 56°20N 5°40W 283 E3
Lorne Australia 38°33S 143°59E 335 F3
Lorovouno Cyprus 35°8N 32°36E 297 D11
Lorraine □ France 48°53N 6°0E 292 B7
Los Alamos Calif., U.S.A. 34°44N 120°17W 351 L6
Los Alamos N. Mex., U.S.A. 35°53N 106°19W 349 J10
Los Altos U.S.A. 37°23N 122°7W 350 H4
Los Andes Chile 32°50S 70°40W 366 C1
Los Angeles Chile 37°28S 72°23W 366 D1
Los Angeles U.S.A. 34°4N 118°15W 351 M8
Los Angeles, Bahia de Mexico 28°56N 113°34W 358 B2
Los Angeles Aqueduct U.S.A. 35°22N 118°5W 351 K9
Los Angeles Int. ✕ (LAX) U.S.A. 33°57N 118°25W 351 M8
Los Banos U.S.A. 37°4N 120°51W 350 H6
Los Blancos Argentina 23°40S 62°30W 366 A3
Los Cardones △ Argentina 25°8S 65°55W 366 B2
Los Chiles Costa Rica 11°2N 84°43W 360 D3
Los Cristianos Canary Is. 28°3N 16°42W 296 F3
Los Gatos U.S.A. 37°14N 121°59W 350 H5
Los Haïtises △ Dom. Rep. 19°4N 69°36W 361 C6
Los Hermanos Is. Venezuela 11°45N 64°25W 361 D7
Los Islotes Canary Is. 29°4N 13°44W 296 E6
Los Llanos de Aridane Canary Is. 28°38N 17°54W 296 F2
Los Loros Chile 27°50S 70°6W 366 B1
Los Lunas U.S.A. 34°48N 106°44W 349 J10
Los Mochis Mexico 25°45N 108°57W 358 B3
Los Olivos U.S.A. 34°40N 120°7W 351 L6
Los Palacios Cuba 22°35N 83°15W 360 B3
Los Reyes de Salgado Mexico 19°35N 102°29W 358 D4
Los Roques Is. Venezuela 11°50N 66°45W 361 D6
Los Teques Venezuela 10°21N 67°2W 364 A5
Los Testigos, Is. Venezuela 11°23N 63°6W 364 A6
Los Vilos Chile 32°10S 71°30W 366 C1
Lošinj Croatia 44°30N 14°30E 288 F8
Loskop Dam S. Africa 25°23S 29°20E 329 D4
Lossiemouth U.K. 57°42N 3°17W 283 D5
Lostwithiel U.K. 50°24N 4°41W 285 G3
Lot → France 44°18N 0°20E 292 D4
Lota Chile 37°5S 73°10W 366 D1
Loṭfābād Iran 37°32N 59°20E 317 B8
Lothair S. Africa 26°22S 30°27E 329 D5
Lotta → Europe 68°42N 31°6E 280 B24
Loubomo Congo 4°9S 12°47E 324 E2
Loudonville U.S.A. 40°38N 82°14W 354 F2
Louga Senegal 15°45N 16°5W 322 E2
Loughborough U.K. 52°47N 1°11W 284 E6
Lougheed I. Canada 77°26N 105°6W 341 B9
Loughrea Ireland 53°12N 8°33W 282 C3
Loughros More B. Ireland 54°48N 8°32W 282 B3
Louis Trichardt S. Africa 23°1S 29°43E 329 C4
Louis XIV, Pte. Canada 54°37N 79°45W 344 B4
Louisa U.S.A. 38°7N 82°36W 353 F12
Louisbourg Canada 45°55N 60°0W 345 C8
Louisburgh Ireland 53°46N 9°49W 282 C2
Louise I. Canada 52°55N 131°50W 342 C2
Louiseville Canada 46°20N 72°56W 344 C5
Louisiade Arch. Papua N. G. 11°10S 153°0E 330 C8
Louisiana U.S.A. 39°27N 91°3W 352 F8
Louisiana □ U.S.A. 30°50N 92°0W 356 F9
Louisville Ky., U.S.A. 38°15N 85°46W 353 F11
Louisville Miss., U.S.A. 33°7N 89°3W 357 E10
Louisville Ohio, U.S.A. 40°50N 81°16W 354 F3
Louisville Ridge Pac. Oc. 31°0S 172°30W 336 L10
Loulé Portugal 37°9N 8°0W 293 D1
Loup City U.S.A. 41°17N 98°58W 352 E4
Loups Marins, Lacs des Canada 56°30N 73°45W 344 A5
Lourdes France 43°6N 0°3W 292 E3
Lourdes-de-Blanc-Sablon Canada 51°24N 57°12W 345 B8
Louth Australia 30°30S 145°8E 335 E4
Louth Ireland 53°58N 6°32W 282 C5
Louth U.K. 53°22N 0°1W 284 D7
Louth □ Ireland 53°56N 6°34W 282 C5
Louvain = Leuven Belgium 50°52N 4°42E 287 D4
Louwsburg S. Africa 27°37S 31°7E 329 D5
Lovech Bulgaria 43°8N 24°42E 295 C11
Loveland U.S.A. 40°24N 105°5W 348 F11
Lovell U.S.A. 44°50N 108°24W 348 D9
Lovelock U.S.A. 40°11N 118°28W 348 F4
Loviisa Finland 60°28N 26°12E 280 F22
Loving U.S.A. 32°17N 104°6W 349 K11
Lovington U.S.A. 32°57N 103°21W 349 K12
Lovisa = Loviisa Finland 60°28N 26°12E 280 F22
Low, L. Canada 52°29N 76°17W 344 B4
Low Pt. Australia 32°25S 127°25E 333 F4
Low Tatra = Nízké Tatry Slovak Rep. 48°55N 19°30E 289 D10
Lowa Dem. Rep. of the Congo 1°25S 25°47E 326 C2
Lowa → Dem. Rep. of the Congo 1°24S 25°51E 326 C2
Lowell U.S.A. 42°38N 71°19W 355 D13
Lowellville U.S.A. 41°2N 80°32W 354 E4
Löwen → Namibia 26°51S 18°17E 328 D2
Lower Alkali L. U.S.A. 41°16N 120°2W 348 F3
Lower Arrow L. Canada 49°40N 118°5W 342 D5
Lower California = Baja California Mexico 31°10N 115°12W 358 A1
Lower Hutt N.Z. 41°10S 174°55E 331 D5
Lower Lake U.S.A. 38°55N 122°37W 350 G4
Lower Manitou L. Canada 49°15N 93°0W 343 D10
Lower Post Canada 59°58N 128°30W 342 B3
Lower Red L. U.S.A. 47°58N 95°0W 352 B6
Lower Saxony = Niedersachsen □ Germany 52°50N 9°0E 288 B5
Lower Tunguska = Tunguska, Nizhnyaya → Russia 65°48N 88°4E 301 C9
Lower Zambezi △ Zambia 15°25S 29°40E 327 F2
Lowestoft U.K. 52°29N 1°45E 285 E9
Lowgar □ Afghan. 34°0N 69°0E 312 B6
Łowicz Poland 52°6N 19°55E 289 B10
Lowville U.S.A. 43°47N 75°29W 355 C9
Loxton Australia 34°28S 140°31E 335 E3
Loxton S. Africa 31°30S 22°22E 328 E3
Loyalton U.S.A. 39°41N 120°14W 350 F6
Loyalty Is. = Loyauté, Îs. N. Cal. 20°50S 166°30E 330 D9
Loyang = Luoyang China 34°40N 112°26E 306 G7
Loyauté, Îs. N. Cal. 20°50S 166°30E 330 D9
Loyev = Loyew Belarus 51°56N 30°46E 289 C16
Loyew Belarus 51°56N 30°46E 289 C16
Loyoro Uganda 3°22N 34°14E 326 B3
Lu Wo China 22°33N 114°6E 305 F11
Luachimo Angola 7°23S 20°48E 324 F4
Luajan → India 24°44N 85°1E 315 G11
Lualaba → Dem. Rep. of the Congo 0°26N 25°20E 326 B2
Luampa Zambia 15°4S 24°20E 327 F1
Luan Chau Vietnam 21°38N 103°24E 310 B4
Luan He → China 39°20N 119°5E 307 E10
Luan Xian China 39°40N 118°40E 307 E10
Luancheng China 37°53N 114°40E 306 F8
Luanda Angola 8°50S 13°15E 324 F2
Luang, Thale Thailand 7°30N 100°15E 311 J3
Luang Prabang Laos 19°52N 102°10E 310 C4
Luangwa Zambia 15°35S 30°16E 327 F3
Luangwa → Zambia 14°25S 30°25E 327 E3
Luangwa Valley Zambia 13°30S 31°30E 327 E3
Luanne China 40°55N 117°40E 307 D9
Luanping China 40°53N 117°23E 307 D9
Luanshya Zambia 13°3S 28°28E 327 E2
Luapula □ Zambia 11°0S 29°0E 327 E2
Luapula → Africa 9°26S 28°33E 327 D2
Luarca Spain 43°32N 6°32W 293 A2
Luashi Dem. Rep. of the Congo 10°50S 23°36E 327 E1
Luau Angola 10°40S 22°10E 324 G4
Lubana, Ozero = Lubānas Ezers Latvia 56°45N 27°0E 281 H22
Lubānas Ezers Latvia 56°45N 27°0E 281 H22
Lubang Is. Phil. 13°50N 120°12E 309 B6
Lubango Angola 14°55S 13°30E 325 G2
Lubao Dem. Rep. of the Congo 5°17S 25°42E 326 D2
Lubbock U.S.A. 33°35N 101°51W 356 E4
Lübeck Germany 53°52N 10°40E 288 B6
Lubefu Dem. Rep. of the Congo 4°47S 24°27E 326 C1
Lubefu → Dem. Rep. of the Congo 4°10S 23°0E 326 C1
Lubero = Luofu Dem. Rep. of the Congo 0°10S 29°15E 326 C2
Lubicon L. Canada 56°23N 115°56W 342 B5
Lubilash → Dem. Rep. of the Congo 6°2S 23°45E 324 F4
Lubin Poland 51°24N 16°11E 288 C9
Lublin Poland 51°12N 22°38E 289 C12
Lubnān = Lebanon ■ Asia 34°0N 36°0E 318 B5
Lubnān, Jabal Lebanon 33°45N 35°40E 318 B4
Lubny Ukraine 50°3N 32°58E 300 D4
Lubongola Dem. Rep. of the Congo 2°35S 27°50E 326 C2
Lubudi Dem. Rep. of the Congo 9°57S 25°58E 324 F5
Lubudi → Dem. Rep. of the Congo 9°0S 25°35E 327 D2
Lubuklinggau Indonesia 3°15S 102°55E 308 E2
Lubuksikaping Indonesia 0°10N 100°15E 308 D2
Lubumbashi Dem. Rep. of the Congo 11°40S 27°28E 327 E2
Lubunda Dem. Rep. of the Congo 5°12S 26°41E 326 D2
Lubungu Zambia 14°35S 26°24E 327 E2
Lubutu Dem. Rep. of the Congo 0°45S 26°30E 326 C2
Luc An Chau Vietnam 22°6N 104°43E 310 A5
Lucan Canada 43°11N 81°24W 354 C3
Lucania, Mt. Canada 61°1N 140°27W 340 C5
Lucas Channel Canada 45°21N 81°45W 354 A3
Lucca Italy 43°50N 10°29E 294 C4
Luce Bay U.K. 54°45N 4°48W 283 G4
Lucea Jamaica 18°27N 78°10W 360 a
Lucedale U.S.A. 30°56N 88°35W 357 F10
Lucena Phil. 13°56N 121°37E 309 B6
Lucena Spain 37°27N 4°31W 293 D3
Lučenec Slovak Rep. 48°18N 19°42E 289 D10
Lucerne = Luzern Switz. 47°3N 8°18E 292 C8
Lucerne U.S.A. 39°6N 122°48W 350 F4
Lucerne Valley U.S.A. 34°27N 116°57W 351 L10
Lucero Mexico 30°49N 106°30W 358 A3
Lucheng China 36°20N 113°11E 306 F7
Lucheringo → Mozam. 11°43S 36°17E 327 E4
Lucia U.S.A. 36°2N 121°33W 350 J5
Lucinda Australia 18°32S 146°20E 334 B4
Luckenwalde Germany 52°5N 13°10E 288 B7
Luckhoff S. Africa 29°44S 24°43E 328 D3
Lucknow Canada 43°57N 81°31W 354 C3
Lucknow India 26°50N 81°0E 315 F9
Lüda = Dalian China 38°50N 121°40E 307 E11
Lüderitz Namibia 26°41S 15°8E 328 D2
Lüderitzbaai Namibia 26°36S 15°8E 328 D2
Ludhiana India 30°57N 75°56E 314 D6
Ludington U.S.A. 43°57N 86°27W 352 D10
Ludlow U.K. 52°22N 2°42W 285 E5
Ludlow Calif., U.S.A. 34°43N 116°10W 351 L10
Ludlow Pa., U.S.A. 41°43N 78°56W 354 E6
Ludlow Vt., U.S.A. 43°24N 72°42W 355 C12
Ludvika Sweden 60°8N 15°14E 281 F16
Ludwigsburg Germany 48°53N 9°11E 288 D5
Ludwigshafen Germany 49°29N 8°26E 288 D5
Lueki Dem. Rep. of the Congo 3°20S 25°48E 326 C2
Luena Dem. Rep. of the Congo 9°28S 25°43E 327 D2
Luena Zambia 10°40S 30°25E 327 E3
Luena Flats Zambia 14°47S 23°17E 325 G4
Luenha = Ruenya → Africa 16°24S 33°48E 327 F3
Lüeyang China 33°22N 106°10E 306 H4
Lufira → Dem. Rep. of the Congo 9°30S 27°0E 327 D2
Lufkin U.S.A. 31°21N 94°44W 356 F7
Lufupa Dem. Rep. of the Congo 10°37S 24°56E 327 E1
Luga Russia 58°40N 29°55E 281 G23
Lugano Switz. 46°1N 8°57E 292 C8
Lugansk = Luhansk Ukraine 48°38N 39°15E 291 E6
Lugard's Falls Kenya 3°6S 38°41E 326 C4
Lugela Mozam. 16°25S 36°43E 327 F4
Lugenda → Mozam. 11°25S 38°33E 327 E4
Lugh Ganana Somali Rep. 3°48N 42°34E 319 G3
Lugnaquillia Ireland 52°58N 6°28W 282 D5
Lugo Italy 44°25N 11°54E 294 B4
Lugo Spain 43°2N 7°35W 293 A2
Lugoj Romania 45°42N 21°57E 289 F11
Lugovoy = Qulan Kazakhstan 42°55N 72°43E 300 E8
Luhansk Ukraine 48°38N 39°15E 291 E6
Lui → Angola 8°21S 17°33E 324 F3
Luiana Angola 17°25S 22°59E 328 B3
Luiana → Angola 17°24S 23°3E 325 H4
Luichow Pen. = Leizhou Bandao China 21°0N 110°0E 305 D6
Luimneach = Limerick Ireland 52°40N 8°37W 282 D3
Luing U.K. 56°14N 5°39W 283 E3
Luís Correia Brazil 3°0S 41°35W 365 D10
Luitpold Coast Antarctica 78°30S 32°0W 277 D1
Luiza Dem. Rep. of the Congo 7°40S 22°30E 324 F4
Luizi Dem. Rep. of the Congo 6°0S 27°25E 326 D2
Luján Argentina 34°45S 59°5W 366 C4
Lukanga Swamp Zambia 14°30S 27°40E 327 E2
Lukenie → Dem. Rep. of the Congo 3°0S 18°50E 324 E3
Lukhisaral India 25°11N 86°5E 315 G12
Lukolela Dem. Rep. of the Congo 5°23S 24°32E 326 D1
Lukosi Zimbabwe 18°30S 26°30E 327 F2
Łuków Poland 51°55N 22°23E 289 C12
Lukusuzi △ Zambia 12°43S 32°36E 327 E3
Luleå Sweden 65°35N 22°10E 280 D20
Luleälven → Sweden 65°35N 22°10E 280 D20
Lüleburgaz Turkey 41°23N 27°22E 295 D12
Luling U.S.A. 29°41N 97°39W 356 G6
Lulong China 39°53N 118°51E 307 E10
Lulonga → Dem. Rep. of the Congo 1°0N 18°10E 324 D3
Lulua → Dem. Rep. of the Congo 4°30S 20°30E 324 E4
Luma Amer. Samoa 14°16S 169°33W 331 b
Lumajang Indonesia 8°8S 113°13E 309 H15
Lumbala N'guimbo Angola 14°18S 21°18E 325 G4
Lumberton U.S.A. 34°37N 79°0W 357 D15
Lumholtz △ Australia 18°15S 145°32E 334 B4
Lumsden Canada 50°39N 104°52W 343 C8
Lumsden N.Z. 45°44S 168°27E 331 F2
Lumut Malaysia 4°13N 100°37E 311 K3
Lumut, Tanjung Indonesia 3°50S 105°58E 308 E3
Luna India 23°43N 69°16E 314 H3
Lunavada India 23°8N 73°37E 314 H5
Lund Sweden 55°44N 13°12E 281 J15
Lundazi Zambia 12°20S 33°7E 327 E3
Lundi → Zimbabwe 21°43S 32°34E 327 G3
Lundu Malaysia 1°40N 109°50E 308 D3
Lundy U.K. 51°10N 4°41W 285 F3
Lune → U.K. 54°0N 2°51W 284 C5
Lüneburg Germany 53°15N 10°24E 288 B6
Lüneburg Heath = Lüneburger Heide Germany 53°10N 10°12E 288 B6
Lüneburger Heide Germany 53°10N 10°12E 288 B6
Lunenburg Canada 44°22N 64°18W 345 D7
Lunéville France 48°36N 6°30E 292 B7
Lunga → Zambia 14°34S 26°25E 327 E2
Lunga Lunga Kenya 4°33S 39°7E 326 C4
Lunglei India 22°55N 92°45E 313 H18
Luni India 26°0N 73°6E 314 G5
Luni → India 24°41N 71°14E 314 G4
Luninets = Luninyets Belarus 52°15N 26°50E 289 B14
Luning U.S.A. 38°30N 118°11W 348 G4
Luninyets Belarus 52°15N 26°50E 289 B14
Lunkaransar India 28°29N 73°44E 314 E5
Lunsemfwa → Zambia 14°54S 30°12E 327 E3
Lunsemfwa Falls Zambia 14°30S 29°6E 327 E2
Luo He → China 34°35N 110°20E 306 G6
Luochuan China 35°45N 109°26E 306 G5
Luofu Dem. Rep. of the Congo 0°10S 29°15E 326 C2
Luohe China 33°32N 114°2E 306 H8
Luonan China 34°5N 110°10E 306 G6
Luoning China 34°35N 111°40E 306 G6
Luoyang China 34°40N 112°26E 306 G7
Luozigou China 43°42N 130°18E 307 C16
Lupilichi Mozam. 11°47S 35°13E 327 E4
Luque Paraguay 25°19S 57°25W 366 B4
Luray U.S.A. 38°40N 78°28W 353 F14
Lurgan U.K. 54°28N 6°19W 282 B5
Lusaka Zambia 15°28S 28°16E 327 F2
Lusaka □ Zambia 15°30S 29°0E 327 F2
Lusambo Dem. Rep. of the Congo 4°58S 23°28E 326 C1
Lusangaye Dem. Rep. of the Congo 4°54S 26°0E 326 C2
Luseland Canada 52°5N 109°24W 343 C7
Lusenga Plain △ Zambia 9°22S 29°14E 327 D2
Lushan China 33°45N 112°55E 306 H7
Lushi China 34°3N 111°3E 306 G6
Lushnjë Albania 40°55N 19°41E 295 D8
Lushoto Tanzania 4°47S 38°20E 326 C4
Lüshun China 38°45N 121°15E 307 E11
Lusk U.S.A. 42°46N 104°27W 348 E11
Lūt, Dasht-e Iran 31°30N 58°0E 317 D8
Luta = Dalian China 38°50N 121°40E 307 E11
Lutherstadt Wittenberg Germany 51°53N 12°39E 288 C7
Luton U.K. 51°53N 0°24W 285 F7
Luton □ U.K. 51°53N 0°24W 285 F7
Łutselk'e Canada 62°24N 110°44W 343 A6
Lutsk Ukraine 50°50N 25°15E 289 C13
Lutto = Lotta → Europe 68°42N 31°6E 280 B24
Lützow Holmbukta Antarctica 69°10S 37°30E 277 C4
Lutzputs S. Africa 28°3S 20°40E 328 D3
Luuq = Lugh Ganana Somali Rep. 3°48N 42°34E 319 G3
Luverne Ala., U.S.A. 31°43N 86°16W 357 F11
Luverne Minn., U.S.A. 43°39N 96°13W 352 D5
Luvua Dem. Rep. of the Congo 8°48S 25°17E 327 D2
Luvua → Dem. Rep. of the Congo 6°50S 27°30E 326 D2
Luvuvhu → S. Africa 22°25S 31°18E 329 C5
Luwegu → Tanzania 8°31S 37°23E 327 D4
Luwuk Indonesia 0°56S 122°47E 309 E6
Luxembourg Lux. 49°37N 6°9E 287 E6
Luxembourg □ Belgium 49°58N 5°30E 287 E5
Luxembourg ■ Europe 49°45N 6°0E 287 E5
Luxembourg ✕ (LUX) Lux. 49°37N 6°10E 287 E6
Luxi China 24°27N 98°36E 304 D4
Luxor = El Uqsur Egypt 25°41N 32°38E 323 C12
Luyi China 33°50N 115°35E 306 H8
Luza Russia 60°39N 47°10E 290 B8
Luzern Switz. 47°3N 8°18E 292 C8
Luzhou China 28°52N 105°20E 304 D5
Luziânia Brazil 16°20S 48°0W 365 G9
Luzon Phil. 16°0N 121°0E 309 A6
Lviv Ukraine 49°50N 24°0E 289 D13
Lvov = Lviv Ukraine 49°50N 24°0E 289 D13
Lyakhavichy Belarus 53°2N 26°32E 289 B14
Lyakhovskiye, Ostrova Russia 73°40N 141°0E 301 B15
Lyal I. Canada 44°57N 81°24W 354 B3
Lybster U.K. 58°18N 3°15W 283 C5
Lycksele Sweden 64°38N 18°40E 280 D18
Lydda = Lod Israel 31°57N 34°54E 318 D3
Lyddan I. Antarctica 74°0S 21°0W 277 D2
Lydenburg S. Africa 25°10S 30°29E 329 D5
Lydia Turkey 38°48N 28°19E 295 E13
Lyell N.Z. 41°48S 172°4E 331 D4
Lyell I. Canada 52°40N 131°35W 342 C2
Lyepyel Belarus 54°50N 28°40E 281 J23
Lykens U.S.A. 40°34N 76°42W 355 F8
Lyman U.S.A. 41°20N 110°18W 348 F8
Lyme B. U.K. 50°42N 2°53W 285 G4
Lyme Regis U.K. 50°43N 2°57W 285 G5
Lymington U.K. 50°45N 1°32W 285 G6
Łyna → Poland 54°37N 21°14E 289 A11
Lynchburg U.S.A. 37°25N 79°9W 353 G14
Lynd → Australia 16°28S 143°18E 334 B3
Lynd Ra. Australia 25°30S 149°20E 335 D4
Lynden Canada 43°14N 80°9W 354 C4
Lynden U.S.A. 48°57N 122°27W 350 B4
Lyndhurst Australia 30°15S 138°18E 335 E2
Lyndon → Australia 23°29S 114°6E 333 D1
Lyndonville N.Y., U.S.A. 43°20N 78°23W 354 C6
Lyndonville Vt., U.S.A. 44°31N 72°1W 355 B12
Lyngen Norway 69°45N 20°30E 280 B19
Lynher Reef Australia 15°27S 121°55E 332 C3
Lynn U.S.A. 42°28N 70°57W 355 D14
Lynn Haven U.S.A. 30°15N 85°39W 357 F12
Lynn Lake Canada 56°51N 101°3W 343 B8
Lynnwood U.S.A. 47°49N 122°18W 350 C4
Lynton U.K. 51°13N 3°50W 285 F4
Lyntupy Belarus 55°4N 26°23E 281 J22
Lynx L. Canada 62°25N 106°15W 343 A7
Lyon France 45°46N 4°50E 292 D6
Lyonnais France 45°45N 4°15E 292 D6
Lyons = Lyon France 45°46N 4°50E 292 D6
Lyons Ga., U.S.A. 32°12N 82°19W 357 E13
Lyons Kans., U.S.A. 38°21N 98°12W 352 F4
Lyons N.Y., U.S.A. 43°5N 77°0W 354 C8
Lyons → Australia 25°2S 115°9E 333 E2
Lyons Falls U.S.A. 43°37N 75°22W 355 C9
Lys = Leie → Belgium 51°2N 3°45E 287 C3
Lysva Russia 58°7N 57°49E 290 C10
Lysychansk Ukraine 48°55N 38°30E 291 E6
Lytham St. Anne's U.K. 53°45N 3°0W 284 D4
Lyttelton N.Z. 43°35S 172°44E 331 E4
Lytton Canada 50°13N 121°31W 342 C4
Lyubertsy Russia 55°40N 37°51E 290 C6
Lyuboml Ukraine 51°11N 24°4E 289 C13

M

Ma → Vietnam 19°47N 105°56E 310 C5
Ma'adaba Jordan 30°43N 35°47E 318 E4
Maamba Zambia 17°17S 26°28E 328 B4
Ma'ān Jordan 30°12N 35°44E 318 E4
Ma'ān □ Jordan 30°0N 36°0E 318 F5
Maanselkä Finland 63°52N 28°32E 280 E23
Ma'anshan China 31°44N 118°29E 305 C6
Maarianhamina = Mariehamn Finland 60°5N 19°55E 281 F18
Ma'arrat an Nu'mān Syria 35°43N 36°43E 316 C3
Maas → Neths. 51°45N 4°32E 287 C4
Maaseik Belgium 51°6N 5°45E 287 C5
Maasin Phil. 10°8N 124°50E 309 B6
Maastricht Neths. 50°50N 5°40E 287 D5
Maave Mozam. 21°4S 34°47E 329 C5
Mababe Depression Botswana 18°50S 24°15E 328 B3

Mabalane *Mozam.* 23°37S 32°31E **329** C5
Mabel L. *Canada* 50°35N 118°43W **342** C5
Mabenge *Dem. Rep. of the Congo* 4°15N 24°12E **326** B1
Maberly *Canada* 44°50N 76°32W **355** B8
Mablethorpe *U.K.* 53°20N 0°15E **284** D8
Maboma *Dem. Rep. of the Congo* 2°30N 28°10E **326** B2
Mabuasehube ⌓ *Botswana* 25°5S 21°10E **328** D3
Mac Bac *Vietnam* 9°46N 106°7E **311** H6
Macachín *Argentina* 37°10S 63°43W **366** D3
Macaé *Brazil* 22°20S 41°43W **367** A7
McAlester *U.S.A.* 34°56N 95°46W **356** D7
McAllen *U.S.A.* 26°12N 98°14W **356** H5
MacAlpine L. *Canada* 66°32N 102°45W **340** C9
Macamic *Canada* 48°45N 79°0W **344** C4
Macao = Macau *China* 22°12N 113°33E **305** G10
Macapá *Brazil* 0°5N 51°4W **365** C8
Macarao △ *Venezuela* 10°22N 67°7W **361** D6
McArthur → *Australia* 15°54S 136°40E **334** B2
McArthur, Port *Australia* 16°4S 136°23E **334** B2
Macau *Brazil* 5°15S 36°40W **365** E11
Macau *China* 22°12N 113°33E **305** G10
McBride *Canada* 53°20N 120°19W **342** C4
McCall *U.S.A.* 44°55N 116°6W **348** D5
McCamey *U.S.A.* 31°8N 102°14W **356** F3
McCammon *U.S.A.* 42°39N 112°12W **348** E7
McCarran Int., Las Vegas ✕ (LAS) *U.S.A.* 36°5N 115°9W **351** J11
McCauley I. *Canada* 53°40N 130°15W **342** C2
McCleary *U.S.A.* 47°3N 123°16W **350** C3
Macclenny *U.S.A.* 30°17N 82°7W **357** F13
Macclesfield *U.K.* 53°15N 2°8W **284** D5
M'Clintock Chan. *Canada* 72°0N 102°0W **340** B9
McClintock Ra. *Australia* 18°44S 127°38E **332** C4
McCloud *U.S.A.* 41°15N 122°8W **348** F2
McCluer I. *Australia* 11°5S 133°0E **332** B5
McClure *U.S.A.* 40°42N 77°19W **354** F7
McClure, L. *U.S.A.* 37°35N 120°16W **350** H6
M'Clure Str. *Canada* 75°0N 119°0W **341** B8
McClusky *U.S.A.* 47°29N 100°27W **352** B3
McComb *U.S.A.* 31°15N 90°27W **357** F9
McCook *U.S.A.* 40°12N 100°38W **352** E3
McCreary *Canada* 50°47N 99°29W **343** C9
McCullough Mt. *U.S.A.* 35°35N 115°13W **351** K11
McCusker → *Canada* 55°32N 108°39W **343** B7
McDame *Canada* 59°44N 128°59W **342** B3
McDermitt *U.S.A.* 41°59N 117°43W **348** F5
McDonald *U.S.A.* 40°22N 80°14W **354** F4
Macdonald, L. *Australia* 23°30S 129°0E **332** D4
McDonald Is. *Ind. Oc.* 53°0S 73°0E **275** G13
MacDonnell Ranges *Australia* 23°40S 133°0E **332** D5
MacDowell L. *Canada* 52°15N 92°45W **344** B1
Macduff *U.K.* 57°40N 2°31W **283** D6
Macedonia *U.S.A.* 41°19N 81°31W **354** E3
Macedonia □ *Greece* 40°39N 22°0E **295** D10
Macedonia ■ *Europe* 41°53N 21°40E **295** D9
Maceió *Brazil* 9°40S 35°41W **365** E11
Macerata *Italy* 43°18N 13°27E **294** C5
McFarland *U.S.A.* 35°41N 119°14W **351** K7
McFarlane → *Canada* 59°12N 107°58W **343** B7
Macfarlane, L. *Australia* 32°0S 136°40E **335** E2
McGehee *U.S.A.* 33°38N 91°24W **356** E9
McGill *U.S.A.* 39°23N 114°47W **348** G6
Macgillycuddy's Reeks *Ireland* 51°58N 9°45W **282** E2
McGraw *U.S.A.* 42°36N 76°8W **355** D8
McGregor *U.S.A.* 43°1N 91°11W **352** D8
McGregor Ra. *Australia* 27°0S 142°45E **335** D3
McGuire, Mt. *Australia* 20°18S 148°23E **334** J6
Mach *Pakistan* 29°50N 67°20E **314** E2
Māch Kowr *Iran* 25°48N 61°28E **317** E9
Machado = Jiparaná → *Brazil* 8°3S 62°52W **364** E6
Machagai *Argentina* 26°56S 60°2W **366** B3
Machakos *Kenya* 1°30S 37°15E **326** C4
Machala *Ecuador* 3°20S 79°57W **364** D3
Machanga *Mozam.* 20°59S 35°0E **329** C6
Machattie, L. *Australia* 24°50S 139°48E **334** C2
Machava *Mozam.* 25°54S 32°28E **329** D5
Machece *Mozam.* 19°15S 35°32E **327** F4
Macheke *Zimbabwe* 18°5S 31°51E **329** B5
Machhu → *India* 23°6N 70°46E **314** H4
Machiara △ *Pakistan* 34°40N 73°30E **314** B5
Machias *Maine, U.S.A.* 44°43N 67°28W **353** C20
Machias *N.Y., U.S.A.* 42°25N 78°29W **354** D6
Machichi → *Canada* 57°3N 92°6W **343** B10
Machico *Madeira* 32°43N 16°44W **296** D3
Machilipatnam *India* 16°12N 81°8E **313** L12
Machiques *Venezuela* 10°4N 72°34W **364** A4
Machupicchu *Peru* 13°8S 72°30W **364** F4
Machynlleth *U.K.* 52°35N 3°50W **285** E4
Macia *Mozam.* 25°2S 33°8E **329** D5
McIlwraith Ra. *Australia* 13°50S 143°20E **334** A3
McInnes L. *Canada* 52°13N 93°45W **343** C10
McIntosh *U.S.A.* 45°55N 101°21W **352** C3
McIntosh L. *Canada* 55°45N 105°0W **343** B8
Macintosh Ra. *Australia* 27°39S 125°32E **333** E4
Macintyre → *Australia* 28°37S 150°47E **335** D5
Mackay *Australia* 21°8S 149°11E **334** K7
Mackay *U.S.A.* 43°55N 113°37W **348** E7
MacKay → *Canada* 57°10N 111°38W **342** B6
Mackay, L. *Australia* 22°30S 129°0E **332** D4
McKay Ra. *Australia* 23°0S 122°30E **332** D3
McKeesport *U.S.A.* 40°20N 79°51W **354** F5
McKellar *Canada* 45°30N 79°55W **354** A5
McKenna *U.S.A.* 46°56N 122°33W **350** D4
Mackenzie *Canada* 55°20N 123°5W **342** B4
McKenzie *U.S.A.* 36°8N 88°31W **357** C10
Mackenzie → *Australia* 23°38S 149°46E **334** C4
Mackenzie → *Canada* 69°10N 134°20W **340** C6
McKenzie → *U.S.A.* 44°7N 123°6W **348** D2
Mackenzie Bay *Canada* 69°0N 137°30W **338** C6
Mackenzie City = Linden *Guyana* 6°0N 58°10W **364** B7
Mackenzie King I. *Canada* 77°45N 111°0W **341** B8
Mackenzie Mts. *Canada* 64°0N 130°0W **340** C7
Mackinaw City *U.S.A.* 45°47N 84°44W **353** C11
McKinlay *Australia* 21°16S 141°18E **334** C3
McKinlay → *Australia* 20°50S 141°28E **334** C3
McKinley, Mt. *U.S.A.* 63°4N 151°0W **346** a
McKinley Sea *Arctic* 82°0N 0°0 **276** A7
McKinney *U.S.A.* 33°12N 96°37W **356** E6
Mackinnon Road *Kenya* 3°40S 39°1E **326** C4
McKittrick *U.S.A.* 35°18N 119°37W **351** K7
Macklin *Canada* 52°20N 109°56W **343** C7
Macksville *Australia* 30°40S 152°56E **335** E5
McLaughlin *U.S.A.* 45°49N 100°49W **352** C3
Maclean *Australia* 29°26S 153°16E **335** D5
McLean *U.S.A.* 35°14N 100°36W **356** D4
McLeansboro *U.S.A.* 38°6N 88°32W **352** F9
Maclear *S. Africa* 31°2S 28°23E **329** E4
Maclear, C. *Malawi* 13°58S 34°49E **327** E3
Macleay → *Australia* 30°56S 153°0E **335** E5
McLennan *Canada* 55°42N 116°50W **342** B5
McLeod → *Canada* 54°9N 115°44W **342** C5
McLeod, L. *Australia* 24°9S 113°47E **333** D1
MacLeod B. *Canada* 62°53N 110°0W **343** A7
MacLeod Lake *Canada* 54°58N 123°0W **342** C4
McLoughlin, Mt. *U.S.A.* 42°27N 122°19W **348** E2
McMechen *U.S.A.* 39°57N 80°44W **354** G4
McMinnville *Oreg., U.S.A.* 45°13N 123°12W **348** D2
McMinnville *Tenn., U.S.A.* 35°41N 85°46W **357** D12
McMurdo *Antarctica* 77°0S 140°0E **277** D11
McMurdo Sd. *Antarctica* 77°0S 170°0E **277** D11
McMurray = Fort McMurray *Canada* 56°44N 111°7W **342** B6
McMurray *U.S.A.* 48°19N 122°14W **350** B4
Macodoene *Mozam.* 23°32S 35°5E **329** C6
Macomb *U.S.A.* 40°27N 90°40W **352** E8
Mâcon *France* 46°19N 4°50E **292** C6
Macon *Ga., U.S.A.* 32°51N 83°38W **357** E13
Macon *Miss., U.S.A.* 33°7N 88°34W **357** E10
Macon *Mo., U.S.A.* 39°44N 92°28W **352** F7
Macossa *Mozam.* 17°55S 33°56E **327** F3
Macoun L. *Canada* 56°32N 103°40W **343** B8
Macovane *Mozam.* 21°30S 35°2E **329** C6
McPherson *U.S.A.* 38°22N 97°40W **352** F5
McPherson Pk. *U.S.A.* 34°53N 119°53W **351** L7
McPherson Ra. *Australia* 28°15S 153°15E **335** D5
Macquarie → *Australia* 30°7S 147°24E **335** E4
Macquarie Harbour *Australia* 42°15S 145°23E **335** G4
Macquarie Is. *Pac. Oc.* 54°36S 158°55E **336** N7
Macquarie Ridge *S. Ocean* 57°0S 159°0E **277** B10
MacRobertson Land *Antarctica* 71°0S 64°0E **277** D6
Macroom *Ireland* 51°54N 8°57W **282** E3
MacTier *Canada* 45°8N 79°47W **354** A5
Macubela *Mozam.* 16°53S 37°49E **327** F4
Macuira △ *Colombia* 12°9N 71°21W **361** D5
Macuiza *Mozam.* 18°7S 34°29E **327** F3
Macumba → *Australia* 27°52S 137°12E **335** D2
Macuro *Venezuela* 10°42N 61°55W **365** K15
Macusani *Peru* 14°4S 70°29W **364** F4
Macuse *Mozam.* 17°45S 37°10E **327** F4
Macuspana *Mexico* 17°46N 92°36W **359** D6
Macusse *Angola* 17°48S 20°23E **328** B3
Ma'dabā □ *Jordan* 31°43N 35°47E **318** D4
Madadeni *S. Africa* 27°43S 30°3E **329** D5
Madagascar ■ *Africa* 20°0S 47°0E **329** C8
Madā'in Sālih *Si. Arabia* 26°46N 37°57E **316** E3
Madama *Niger* 22°0N 13°40E **323** D8
Madame, I. *Canada* 45°30N 60°58W **345** C7
Madang *Papua N. G.* 5°12S 145°49E **330** B7
Madaripur *Bangla.* 23°19N 90°15E **313** H17
Madauk *Burma* 17°56N 96°52E **313** L20
Madawaska *Canada* 45°30N 78°0W **354** A7
Madawaska → *Canada* 45°27N 76°21W **354** A7
Madaya *Burma* 22°12N 96°10E **313** H20
Maddalena *Italy* 41°16N 9°23E **294** D3
Madeira *Atl. Oc.* 32°50N 17°0W **296** D3
Madeira → *Brazil* 3°22S 58°45W **364** D7
Madeleine, Îs. de la *Canada* 47°30N 61°40W **345** C7
Madera *Mexico* 29°12N 108°7W **358** B3
Madera *Calif., U.S.A.* 36°57N 120°3W **350** J6
Madera *Pa., U.S.A.* 40°49N 78°26W **354** F6
Madha *India* 18°0N 75°30E **312** L9
Madhavpur *India* 21°15N 69°58E **314** J3
Madhepura *India* 26°11N 86°23E **315** F12
Madhubani *India* 26°21N 86°7E **315** F12
Madhupur *India* 24°16N 86°39E **315** G12
Madhya Pradesh □ *India* 22°50N 78°0E **314** J8
Madidi → *Bolivia* 12°32S 66°52W **364** F5
Madikeri *India* 12°30N 75°45E **312** N9
Madikwe ⌓ *S. Africa* 27°38S 32°15E **329** D5
Madill *U.S.A.* 34°6N 96°46W **356** D6
Madimba *Dem. Rep. of the Congo* 4°58S 15°5E **324** E3
Ma'din *Syria* 35°45N 39°36E **316** C3
Madingou *Congo* 4°10S 13°33E **324** E2
Madirovalo *Madag.* 16°26S 46°32E **329** B8
Madison *Calif., U.S.A.* 38°41N 121°59W **350** G5
Madison *Fla., U.S.A.* 30°28N 83°25W **357** F13
Madison *Ind., U.S.A.* 38°44N 85°23W **353** F11
Madison *Nebr., U.S.A.* 41°50N 97°27W **352** E5
Madison *Ohio, U.S.A.* 41°46N 81°3W **354** E3
Madison *S. Dak., U.S.A.* 44°0N 97°7W **352** C5
Madison *Wis., U.S.A.* 43°4N 89°24W **352** D9
Madison → *U.S.A.* 45°56N 111°31W **348** D8
Madison Heights *U.S.A.* 37°25N 79°8W **353** G14
Madisonville *Ky., U.S.A.* 37°20N 87°30W **352** G10
Madisonville *Tex., U.S.A.* 30°57N 95°55W **356** F7
Madista *Botswana* 21°15S 25°6E **328** C4
Madiun *Indonesia* 7°38S 111°32E **308** F4
Mado Gashi *Kenya* 0°44N 39°10E **326** B4
Madoc *Canada* 44°30N 77°28W **354** B7
Madona *Latvia* 56°53N 26°5E **281** H22
Madrakah, Ra's al *Oman* 19°0N 57°50E **319** D6
Madras = Chennai *India* 13°8N 80°19E **312** N12
Madras = Tamil Nadu □ *India* 11°0N 77°0E **312** P10
Madras *U.S.A.* 44°38N 121°8W **348** D3
Madre, L. *U.S.A.* 25°15N 97°30W **356** J6
Madre, Sierra *Phil.* 17°0N 122°0E **309** A6
Madre de Dios → *Bolivia* 10°59S 66°8W **364** F5
Madre de Dios, I. *Chile* 50°20S 75°10W **368** G1
Madre del Sur, Sierra *Mexico* 17°30N 100°0W **359** D5
Madre Occidental, Sierra *Mexico* 27°0N 107°0W **358** B3
Madre Oriental, Sierra *Mexico* 25°0N 100°0W **358** C5
Madri *India* 24°16N 73°32E **314** G5
Madrid *Spain* 40°24N 3°42W **293** B4
Madrid *U.S.A.* 44°45N 75°8W **355** B9
Madura *Australia* 31°55S 127°0E **333** F4
Madura *Indonesia* 7°30S 114°0E **309** G15
Madura, Selat *Indonesia* 7°30S 113°20E **309** G15
Madurai *India* 9°55N 78°10E **312** Q11
Madurantakam *India* 12°30N 79°50E **312** N11
Mae Chan *Thailand* 20°9N 99°52E **310** B2
Mae Hong Son *Thailand* 19°16N 97°56E **310** C2
Mae Khlong → *Thailand* 13°24N 100°0E **310** F3
Mae Phrik *Thailand* 17°27N 99°7E **310** D2
Mae Ping △ *Thailand* 17°37N 98°51E **310** D2
Mae Ramat *Thailand* 16°58N 98°31E **310** D2
Mae Rim *Thailand* 18°54N 98°57E **310** C2
Mae Sot *Thailand* 16°43N 98°34E **310** D2
Mae Suai *Thailand* 19°39N 99°33E **310** C2
Mae Tha *Thailand* 18°28N 99°8E **310** C2
Mae Wong △ *Thailand* 15°54N 99°12E **310** E2
Mae Yom △ *Thailand* 18°43N 100°15E **310** C3
Maebashi *Japan* 36°24N 139°4E **303** F9
Maesteg *U.K.* 51°36N 3°40W **285** F4
Maestra, Sierra *Cuba* 20°15N 77°0W **360** B4
Maevatanana *Madag.* 16°56S 46°49E **329** B8
Mafeking = Mafikeng *S. Africa* 25°50S 25°38E **328** D4
Mafeking *Canada* 52°40N 101°10W **343** C8
Mafeteng *Lesotho* 29°51S 27°15E **328** D4
Maffra *Australia* 37°53S 146°58E **335** F4
Mafia I. *Tanzania* 7°45S 39°50E **326** D4
Mafikeng *S. Africa* 25°50S 25°38E **328** D4
Mafra *Brazil* 26°10S 49°55W **367** B6
Mafra *Portugal* 38°55N 9°20W **293** C1
Mafungabusi Plateau *Zimbabwe* 18°30S 29°8E **327** F2
Magadan *Russia* 59°38N 150°50E **301** D16
Magadi *Kenya* 1°54S 36°19E **326** C4
Magadi, L. *Kenya* 1°54S 36°19E **326** C4
Magaliesburg *S. Africa* 26°0S 27°32E **329** D4
Magallanes, Estrecho de *Chile* 52°30S 75°0W **368** G2
Magangué *Colombia* 9°14N 74°45W **364** B4
Magdalen Is. = Madeleine, Îs. de la *Canada* 47°30N 61°40W **345** C7
Magdalena *Argentina* 35°5S 57°30W **366** D4
Magdalena *Bolivia* 13°13S 63°57W **364** F6
Magdalena *U.S.A.* 34°7N 107°15W **349** J10
Magdalena → *Colombia* 11°6N 74°51W **364** A4
Magdalena → *Mexico* 30°40N 112°25W **358** A2
Magdalena, B. *Mexico* 24°35N 112°0W **358** C2
Magdalena, I. *Mexico* 24°40N 112°15W **358** C2
Magdalena, Llano de *Mexico* 25°0N 111°25W **358** C2
Magdalena de Kino *Mexico* 30°38N 110°57W **358** A2
Magdeburg *Germany* 52°7N 11°38E **288** B6
Magdelaine Cays *Australia* 16°33S 150°18E **334** B5
Magee *U.S.A.* 31°52N 89°44W **357** F10
Magelang *Indonesia* 7°29S 110°13E **308** F4
Magellan's Str. = Magallanes, Estrecho de *Chile* 52°30S 75°0W **368** G2
Magenta, L. *Australia* 33°30S 119°2E **333** F2
Magerøya *Norway* 71°3N 25°40E **280** A21
Maggiore, Lago *Italy* 45°57N 8°39E **292** D8
Maggotty *Jamaica* 18°9N 77°46W **360** a
Maghâgha *Egypt* 28°38N 30°50E **323** C12
Magherafelt *U.K.* 54°45N 6°37W **282** B5
Maghreb *N. Afr.* 32°0N 4°0W **322** B5
Magistralnyy *Russia* 56°16N 107°36E **301** D11
Magnetic Pole (North) *Canada* 82°42N 114°24W **341** B9
Magnetic Pole (South) *Antarctica* 64°8S 138°8E **277** C9
Magnitogorsk *Russia* 53°27N 59°4E **290** D10
Magnolia *Ark., U.S.A.* 33°16N 93°14W **356** E8
Magnolia *Miss., U.S.A.* 31°9N 90°28W **357** F9
Mago *Fiji* 17°26S 179°8W **331** a
Magog *Canada* 45°18N 72°9W **355** A12
Magoro *Uganda* 1°45N 34°12E **326** B3
Magoša = Famagusta *Cyprus* 35°8N 33°55E **297** D12
Magoulades *Greece* 39°45N 19°42E **297** A3
Magoye *Zambia* 16°1S 27°30E **327** F2
Magpie, L. *Canada* 51°0N 64°41W **345** B7
Magrath *Canada* 49°25N 112°50W **342** D6
Maguarinho, C. *Brazil* 0°15S 48°30W **365** D9
Magude *Mozam.* 25°2S 32°40E **329** D5
Mağusa = Famagusta *Cyprus* 35°8N 33°55E **297** D12
Maguse L. *Canada* 61°37N 95°10W **343** A9
Maguse Pt. *Canada* 61°20N 93°50W **343** A10
Magvana *India* 23°13N 69°22E **314** H3
Magwe *Burma* 20°10N 95°0E **313** J19
Magyarorszag = Hungary ■ *Europe* 47°20N 19°20E **289** E10
Maha Sarakham *Thailand* 16°12N 103°16E **310** D4
Mahābād *Iran* 36°50N 45°45E **316** B5
Mahabharat Lekh *Nepal* 28°30N 82°0E **315** E10
Mahabo *Madag.* 20°23S 44°40E **329** C7
Mahadeo Hills *India* 22°20N 78°30E **315** H8
Mahaffey *U.S.A.* 40°53N 78°44W **354** F6
Mahagi *Dem. Rep. of the Congo* 2°20N 31°0E **326** B3
Mahajamba → *Madag.* 15°33S 47°8E **329** B8
Mahajamba, Helodranon' i *Madag.* 15°24S 47°5E **329** B8
Mahajan *India* 28°48N 73°56E **314** E5
Mahajanga *Madag.* 15°40S 46°25E **329** B8
Mahajanga □ *Madag.* 17°0S 47°0E **329** B8
Mahajilo → *Madag.* 19°42S 45°22E **329** B8
Mahakam → *Indonesia* 0°35S 117°17E **308** E5
Mahalapye *Botswana* 23°1S 26°51E **328** C4
Mahale Mts. *Tanzania* 6°20S 30°0E **326** D3
Mahale Mts. △ *Tanzania* 6°10S 29°50E **326** D2
Maḥallāt *Iran* 33°55N 50°30E **317** C6
Māhān *Iran* 30°5N 57°18E **317** D8
Mahan → *India* 23°30N 82°50E **315** H10
Mahanadi → *India* 20°20N 86°25E **313** J15
Mahananda → *India* 25°12N 87°52E **315** G12
Mahanoro *Madag.* 19°54S 48°48E **329** B8
Mahanoy City *U.S.A.* 40°49N 76°9W **355** F8
Maharashtra □ *India* 20°30N 75°30E **312** J9
Mahasham, W. → *Egypt* 30°15N 34°10E **318** E3
Mahasoa *Madag.* 22°12S 46°6E **329** C8
Mahasolo *Madag.* 19°7S 46°22E **329** B8
Mahattat ash Shīdīyah *Jordan* 29°55N 35°55E **318** F4
Mahattat 'Unayzah *Jordan* 30°30N 35°47E **318** E4
Mahavavy → *Madag.* 15°57S 45°54E **329** B8
Mahaxay *Laos* 17°22N 105°12E **310** D5
Mahbubnagar *India* 16°45N 77°59E **312** L10
Maḥḍah *Oman* 24°24N 55°59E **317** E7
Mahdia *Tunisia* 35°28N 11°0E **323** A8
Mahe *India* 33°10N 78°32E **315** C8
Mahé *Seychelles* 5°0S 55°30E **325** b
Mahé ✕ (SEZ) *Seychelles* 4°40S 55°31E **325** b
Mahébourg *Mauritius* 20°24S 57°42E **325** d
Mahendragarh *India* 28°17N 76°14E **314** E7
Mahendranagar *Nepal* 28°55N 80°20E **315** E9
Mahenge *Tanzania* 8°45S 36°41E **327** D4
Maheno *N.Z.* 45°10S 170°50E **331** F3
Mahesana *India* 23°39N 72°26E **314** H5
Maheshwar *India* 22°11N 75°35E **314** H6
Mahgawan *India* 26°29N 78°37E **315** F8
Mahi → *India* 22°15N 72°55E **314** H5
Mahia Pen. *N.Z.* 39°9S 177°55E **331** C6
Mahilyow *Belarus* 53°55N 30°18E **289** B16
Mahina *Tahiti* 17°30S 149°27W **331** d
Mahinerangi, L. *N.Z.* 45°50S 169°56E **331** F2
Mahmud Kot *Pakistan* 30°16N 71°0E **314** D4
Mahnomen *U.S.A.* 47°19N 95°58W **352** B6
Mahoba *India* 25°15N 79°55E **315** G8
Mahón = Maó *Spain* 39°53N 4°16E **296** B11
Mahone Bay *Canada* 44°27N 64°23W **345** D7
Mahopac *U.S.A.* 41°22N 73°45W **355** E11
Mahuva *India* 21°5N 71°48E **314** J4
Mai-Ndombe, L. *Dem. Rep. of the Congo* 2°0S 18°20E **324** E3
Mai-Sai *Thailand* 20°20N 99°55E **310** B2
Mai Thon, Ko *Thailand* 7°40N 98°28E **311** a
Maicurú → *Brazil* 2°14S 54°17W **365** D8
Maidan Khula *Afghan.* 33°36N 69°50E **314** C3
Maidenhead *U.K.* 51°31N 0°42W **285** F7
Maidstone *Canada* 53°5N 109°20W **343** C7
Maidstone *U.K.* 51°16N 0°32E **285** F8
Maiduguri *Nigeria* 12°0N 13°20E **323** F8
Maihar *India* 24°16N 80°45E **315** G9
Maijdi *Bangla.* 22°48N 91°10E **313** H17
Maikala Ra. *India* 22°0N 81°0E **313** J12
Maiko △ *Dem. Rep. of the Congo* 0°30S 27°50E **326** C2
Mailani *India* 28°17N 80°21E **315** E9
Mailsi *Pakistan* 29°48N 72°15E **314** E5
Main → *Germany* 50°0N 8°18E **288** C5
Main → *U.K.* 54°48N 6°18W **282** B5
Main Range △ *Australia* 28°11S 152°27E **335** D5
Main Ridge *Trin. & Tob.* 11°16N 60°40W **365** J16
Maine *France* 48°20N 0°15W **292** C3
Maine □ *U.S.A.* 45°20N 69°0W **353** C19
Maine → *Ireland* 52°9N 9°45W **282** D2
Maine, G. of *U.S.A.* 43°0N 68°30W **353** D19
Maingkwan *Burma* 26°15N 96°37E **313** F20
Mainit, L. *Phil.* 9°31N 125°30E **309** C7
Mainland *Orkney, U.K.* 58°59N 3°8W **283** C5
Mainland *Shet., U.K.* 60°15N 1°22W **283** A7
Mainoru *Australia* 14°0S 134°6E **334** A1
Mainpuri *India* 27°18N 79°4E **315** F8
Maintirano *Madag.* 18°3S 44°1E **329** B7
Mainz *Germany* 50°1N 8°14E **288** C5
Maio *C. Verde Is.* 15°10N 23°10W **322** b
Maipú *Argentina* 36°52S 57°50W **366** D4
Maiquetía *Venezuela* 10°36N 66°57W **364** A5
Mairabari *India* 26°30N 92°22E **313** F18
Maisí *Cuba* 20°17N 74°9W **361** B5
Maisí, Pta. de *Cuba* 20°10N 74°10W **361** B5
Maitland *N.S.W., Australia* 32°33S 151°36E **335** E5
Maitland *S. Austral., Australia* 34°23S 137°40E **335** E2
Maitland → *Canada* 43°45N 81°43W **354** C3
Maitri *Antarctica* 70°0S 3°0W **277** D3
Maiz, Is. del *Nic.* 12°15N 83°4W **360** D3
Maizuru *Japan* 35°25N 135°22E **303** G7
Majalengka *Indonesia* 6°50S 108°13E **309** G13
Majene *Indonesia* 3°38S 118°57E **309** E5
Majete ⌓ *Malawi* 15°54S 34°34E **327** F3
Majorca = Mallorca *Spain* 39°30N 3°0E **296** B10
Majuro *Marshall Is.* 7°9N 171°12E **336** G9
Maka *Senegal* 13°40N 14°10W **322** F3
Makaha *Zimbabwe* 17°20S 32°39E **329** B5
Makalamabedi *Botswana* 20°19S 23°51E **328** C3
Makale *Indonesia* 3°6S 119°51E **309** E5
Makalu-Barun △ *Nepal* 27°45N 87°10E **315** F12
Makamba *Burundi* 4°8S 29°49E **326** C2
Makarikari = Makgadikgadi Salt Pans *Botswana* 20°40S 25°45E **328** C4
Makarov Basin *Arctic* 87°0N 150°0W **276** A
Makarovo *Russia* 57°40N 107°45E **301** D11
Makasar = Ujung Pandang *Indonesia* 5°10S 119°20E **309** F5
Makasar, Selat *Indonesia* 1°0S 118°20E **309** E5
Makasar, Str. of = Makasar, Selat *Indonesia* 1°0S 118°20E **309** E5
Makat = Maqat *Kazakhstan* 47°39N 53°19E **291** E9
Makedonija = Macedonia ■ *Europe* 41°53N 21°40E **295** D9
Makeni *S. Leone* 8°55N 12°5W **322** G3
Makeyevka = Makiyivka *Ukraine* 48°0N 38°0E **291** E6
Makgadikgadi △ *Botswana* 20°27S 24°47E **328** C3
Makgadikgadi Salt Pans *Botswana* 20°40S 25°45E **328** C4
Makhachkala *Russia* 43°0N 47°30E **291** F8
Makhado = Louis Trichardt *S. Africa* 23°1S 29°43E **329** C4
Makhfar al Buşayyah *Iraq* 30°0N 46°10E **316** D5
Makhmūr *Iraq* 35°46N 43°35E **316** C4
Makian *Indonesia* 0°20N 127°20E **309** D7
Makindu *Kenya* 2°18S 37°50E **326** C4
Makīnsk *Kazakhstan* 52°37N 70°26E **300** D8
Makira = San Cristóbal *Solomon Is.* 10°30S 161°0E **330** C9
Makiyivka *Ukraine* 48°0N 38°0E **291** E6
Makkah *Si. Arabia* 21°30N 39°54E **319** C2
Makkovik *Canada* 55°10N 59°10W **345** A8
Makó *Hungary* 46°14N 20°33E **289** E11
Makogai *Fiji* 17°28S 179°0E **331** a
Makokou *Gabon* 0°40N 12°50E **324** D2
Makongo *Dem. Rep. of the Congo* 3°25N 26°17E **326** B2
Makoro *Dem. Rep. of the Congo* 3°10N 29°59E **326** B2
Makrai *India* 22°2N 77°0E **314** H7
Makran Coast Range *Pakistan* 25°40N 64°0E **312** G4
Makrana *India* 27°2N 74°46E **314** F6
Makrigialos *Greece* 35°2N 25°59E **297** D7
Mākū *Iran* 39°15N 44°31E **316** B5
Makunda *Botswana* 22°30S 20°7E **328** C3
Makurazaki *Japan* 31°15N 130°20E **303** J5
Makurdi *Nigeria* 7°43N 8°35E **322** G7
Makūyeh *Iran* 28°7N 53°9E **317** D7
Makwassie *S. Africa* 27°17S 26°0E **328** D4
Makwiro *Zimbabwe* 17°58S 30°25E **329** B5
Mal B. *Ireland* 52°50N 9°30W **282** D2
Mala, Pta. *Panama* 7°28N 80°2W **360** E3
Malabar Coast *India* 11°0N 75°0E **312** P9
Malacca, Straits of *Indonesia* 3°0N 101°0E **311** L3
Malad City *U.S.A.* 42°12N 112°15W **348** E7
Maladzyechna *Belarus* 54°20N 26°50E **289** A14
Málaga *Spain* 36°43N 4°23W **293** D3
Malagarasi *Tanzania* 5°5S 30°50E **326** D3
Malagarasi → *Tanzania* 5°12S 29°47E **326** D2
Malagasy Rep. = Madagascar ■ *Africa* 20°0S 47°0E **329** C8
Malahide *Ireland* 53°26N 6°9W **282** C5
Malaimbandy *Madag.* 20°20S 45°36E **329** C8
Malaita *Solomon Is.* 9°0S 161°0E **330** B9
Malakâl *Sudan* 9°33N 31°40E **323** G12
Malakand *Pakistan* 34°40N 71°55E **314** B4
Malakula *Vanuatu* 16°15S 167°30E **330** C9
Malakwal *Pakistan* 32°34N 73°13E **314** C5
Malamala *Indonesia* 3°21S 120°55E **309** E6
Malanda *Australia* 17°22S 145°35E **334** B4
Malang *Indonesia* 7°59S 112°45E **308** F4
Malangen *Norway* 69°24N 18°37E **280** B18
Malanje *Angola* 9°36S 16°17E **324** F3
Mälaren *Sweden* 59°30N 17°10E **281** G17
Malargüe *Argentina* 35°32S 69°30W **366** D2
Malartic *Canada* 48°9N 78°9W **344** C4
Malaryta *Belarus* 51°50N 24°3E **289** C13
Malatya *Turkey* 38°25N 38°20E **316** B3
Malawi ■ *Africa* 11°55S 34°0E **327** E3
Malawi, L. *Africa* 12°30S 34°30E **327** E3
Malay Pen. *Asia* 7°25N 100°0E **311** J3
Malaya Vishera *Russia* 58°55N 32°25E **290** C5
Malaybalay *Phil.* 8°5N 125°7E **309** C7
Malāyer *Iran* 34°19N 48°51E **317** C6
Malaysia ■ *Asia* 5°0N 110°0E **311** K4
Malazgirt *Turkey* 39°10N 42°33E **316** B4
Malbon *Australia* 21°5S 140°17E **334** C3
Malbooma *Australia* 30°41S 134°11E **335** E1
Malbork *Poland* 54°3N 19°1E **289** B10
Malcolm *Australia* 28°51S 121°25E **333** E3
Malcolm, Pt. *Australia* 33°48S 123°45E **333** F3
Maldah *India* 25°2N 88°9E **315** G13
Maldegem *Belgium* 51°14N 3°26E **287** C3
Malden *Mass., U.S.A.* 42°26N 71°3W **355** D13

Malden *Mo., U.S.A.* 36°34N 89°57W **352** G9
Malden I. *Kiribati* 4°3S 155°1W **337** H12
Maldives ■ *Ind. Oc.* 5°0N 73°0E **298** H9
Maldon *U.K.* 51°44N 0°42E **285** F8
Maldonado *Uruguay* 34°59S 55°0W **367** C5
Maldonado, Pta. *Mexico* 16°20N 98°33W **359** D5
Malé Karpaty *Slovak Rep.* 48°30N 17°20E **289** D9
Maleas, Akra *Greece* 36°28N 23°7E **295** F10
Malebo, Pool *Africa* 4°17S 15°20E **324** E3
Malegaon *India* 20°30N 74°38E **312** J9
Malei *Mozam.* 17°12S 36°58E **327** F4
Malek Kandī *Iran* 37°9N 46°6E **316** B5
Malela *Dem. Rep. of the Congo* 4°22S 26°8E **326** C2
Malema *Mozam.* 14°57S 37°20E **327** E4
Maleme *Greece* 35°31N 23°49E **297** D5
Malerkotla *India* 30°32N 75°58E **314** D6
Males *Greece* 35°6N 25°35E **297** D7
Malgomaj *Sweden* 64°40N 16°30E **280** D17
Malha *Sudan* 15°8N 25°10E **323** E11
Malhargarh *India* 24°17N 74°59E **314** G6
Malheur → *U.S.A.* 44°4N 116°59W **348** D5
Malheur L. *U.S.A.* 43°20N 118°48W **348** E4
Mali ■ *Africa* 17°0N 3°0W **322** E5
Mali → *Burma* 25°42N 97°30E **313** G20
Mali Kyun *Burma* 13°0N 98°20E **310** F2
Malia *Greece* 35°17N 25°32E **297** D7
Malia, Kolpos *Greece* 35°19N 25°27E **297** D7
Malibu *U.S.A.* 34°2N 118°41W **351** L8
Maliku *Indonesia* 0°39S 123°16E **309** E6
Malili *Indonesia* 2°42S 121°6E **309** E6
Malimba, Mts. *Dem. Rep. of the Congo* 7°30S 29°30E **326** D2
Malin Hd. *Ireland* 55°23N 7°23W **282** A4
Malin Pen. *Ireland* 55°20N 7°17W **282** A4
Malindi *Kenya* 3°12S 40°5E **326** C5
Malines = Mechelen *Belgium* 51°2N 4°29E **287** C4
Malino *Indonesia* 1°0N 121°0E **309** D6
Malinyi *Tanzania* 8°56S 36°0E **327** D4
Malita *Phil.* 6°19N 125°39E **309** C7
Maliwun *Burma* 10°17N 98°40E **311** G2
Maliya *India* 23°5N 70°46E **314** H4
Malka Mari △ *Kenya* 4°11N 40°46E **326** B5
Malkara *Turkey* 40°53N 26°53E **295** D12
Mallacoota Inlet *Australia* 37°34S 149°40E **335** F4
Mallaig *U.K.* 57°0N 5°50W **283** D3
Mallawan *India* 27°4N 80°12E **315** F9
Mallawi *Egypt* 27°44N 30°44E **323** C12
Mallicolo = Malakula *Vanuatu* 16°15S 167°30E **330** C9
Mallorca *Spain* 39°30N 3°0E **296** B10
Mallorytown *Canada* 44°29N 75°53W **355** B9
Mallow *Ireland* 52°8N 8°39W **282** D3
Malmberget *Sweden* 67°11N 20°40E **280** C19
Malmédy *Belgium* 50°25N 6°2E **287** D6
Malmesbury *S. Africa* 33°28S 18°41E **328** E2
Malmivaara = Malmberget *Sweden* 67°11N 20°40E **280** C19
Malmö *Sweden* 55°36N 12°59E **281** J15
Malolo *Fiji* 17°45S 177°11E **331** a
Malolos *Phil.* 14°50N 120°49E **309** B6
Malolotja ⌓ *Swaziland* 26°4S 31°6E **329** D5
Malombe L. *Malawi* 14°40S 35°15E **327** E4
Malone *U.S.A.* 44°51N 74°18W **355** B10
Måløy *Norway* 61°57N 5°6E **280** F11
Malpaso *Canary Is.* 27°43N 18°3W **296** G1
Malpaso, Presa = Netzahualcóyotl, Presa *Mexico* 17°8N 93°35W **359** D6
Malpelo, I. de *Colombia* 4°3N 81°35W **364** C2
Malpur *India* 23°21N 73°27E **314** H5
Malpura *India* 26°17N 75°23E **314** F6
Malta *Idaho, U.S.A.* 42°18N 113°22W **348** E7
Malta *Mont., U.S.A.* 48°21N 107°52W **348** B10
Malta ■ *Europe* 35°55N 14°26E **297** D2
Maltahöhe *Namibia* 24°55S 17°0E **328** C2
Malton *Canada* 43°42N 79°38W **354** C5
Malton *U.K.* 54°8N 0°49W **284** C7
Maluku *Indonesia* 1°0S 127°0E **309** E7
Maluku □ *Indonesia* 3°0S 128°0E **309** E7
Maluku Sea = Molucca Sea *Indonesia* 0°0 125°0E **309** E6
Malvan *India* 16°2N 73°30E **312** L8
Malvern *U.S.A.* 34°22N 92°49W **356** D8
Malvern Hills *U.K.* 52°0N 2°19W **285** E5
Malvinas, Is. = Falkland Is. ☑ *Atl. Oc.* 51°30S 59°0W **368** G5
Malya *Tanzania* 3°5S 33°38E **326** C3
Malyn *Ukraine* 50°46N 29°3E **289** C15
Malyy Lyakhovskiy, Ostrov *Russia* 74°7N 140°36E **301** B15
Mama *Russia* 58°18N 112°54E **301** D12
Mamanguape *Brazil* 6°50S 35°4W **365** E11
Mamanuca Group *Fiji* 17°35S 177°5E **331** a
Mamarr Mitlā *Egypt* 30°2N 32°54E **318** E1
Mamasa *Indonesia* 2°55S 119°20E **309** E5
Mambasa *Dem. Rep. of the Congo* 1°22N 29°3E **326** B2
Mamberamo → *Indonesia* 2°0S 137°50E **309** E9
Mambilima Falls *Zambia* 10°31S 28°45E **327** E2
Mambirima *Dem. Rep. of the Congo* 11°25S 27°33E **327** E2
Mambo *Tanzania* 4°52S 38°22E **326** C4
Mambrui *Kenya* 3°5S 40°5E **326** C5
Mamburao *Phil.* 13°13N 120°39E **309** B6
Mameigwess L. *Canada* 52°35N 87°50W **344** B2
Mammoth *U.S.A.* 32°43N 110°39W **349** K8
Mammoth Cave △ *U.S.A.* 37°8N 86°13W **352** G10
Mamoré → *Bolivia* 10°23S 65°53W **364** F5
Mamou *Guinea* 10°15N 12°0W **322** F3
Mamoudzou *Mayotte* 12°48S 45°14E **325** a
Mampikony *Madag.* 16°6S 47°38E **329** B8
Mamuju *Indonesia* 2°41S 118°50E **309** E5
Mamuno *Botswana* 22°16S 20°1E **328** C3
Man *Ivory C.* 7°30N 7°40W **322** G4
Man, I. of *U.K.* 54°15N 4°30W **284** C3
Man-Bazar *India* 23°4N 86°39E **315** H12
Man Na *Burma* 23°27N 97°19E **313** H20
Mana → *Fr. Guiana* 5°45N 53°55W **365** B8
Mana Pools △ *Zimbabwe* 15°56S 29°25E **327** F2
Manaar, G. of = Mannar, G. of *Asia* 8°30N 79°0E **312** Q11
Manacapuru *Brazil* 3°16S 60°37W **364** D6
Manacor *Spain* 39°34N 3°13E **296** B10
Manado *Indonesia* 1°29N 124°51E **309** D6
Managua *Nic.* 12°6N 86°20W **360** D2
Managua, L. de *Nic.* 12°20N 86°30W **360** D2
Manakara *Madag.* 22°8S 48°1E **329** C8
Manali *India* 32°16N 77°10E **314** C7
Manama = Al Manāmah *Bahrain* 26°10N 50°30E **317** E6
Manambao → *Madag.* 17°35S 44°0E **329** B7
Manambato *Madag.* 13°43S 49°7E **329** A8
Manambolo → *Madag.* 19°18S 44°22E **329** B7
Manambolosy *Madag.* 16°2S 49°40E **329** B8
Mananara *Madag.* 16°10S 49°46E **329** B8
Mananara → *Madag.* 23°21S 47°42E **329** C8
Mananara ⌓ *Madag.* 16°14S 49°45E **329** B8
Mananjary *Madag.* 21°13S 48°20E **329** C8
Manantenina *Madag.* 24°17S 47°19E **329** C8
Manaos = Manaus *Brazil* 3°0S 60°0W **364** D7
Manapire → *Venezuela* 7°42N 66°7W **364** B5
Manapouri *N.Z.* 45°34S 167°39E **331** F1
Manapouri, L. *N.Z.* 45°32S 167°32E **331** F1
Manār, Jabal *Yemen* 14°2N 44°17E **319** E3
Manaravolo *Madag.* 23°59S 45°39E **329** C8
Manas *China* 44°17N 85°56E **304** B3
Manas → *India* 26°12N 90°40E **313** F17
Manaslu *Nepal* 28°33N 84°33E **315** E11
Manasquan *U.S.A.* 40°8N 74°3W **355** F10
Manassa *U.S.A.* 37°11N 105°56W **349** H11
Manatí *Puerto Rico* 18°26N 66°29W **361** d
Manaung *Burma* 18°45N 93°40E **313** K18
Manaus *Brazil* 3°0S 60°0W **364** D7
Manawan L. *Canada* 55°24N 103°14W **343** B8
Manbij *Syria* 36°31N 37°57E **316** B3
Manchegorsk *Russia* 67°54N 32°58E **300** C4
Manchester *U.K.* 53°29N 2°12W **284** D5
Manchester *Calif., U.S.A.* 38°58N 123°41W **350** G3
Manchester *Conn., U.S.A.* 41°47N 72°31W **355** E12
Manchester *Ga., U.S.A.* 32°51N 84°37W **357** E12
Manchester *Iowa, U.S.A.* 42°29N 91°27W **352** D8
Manchester *Ky., U.S.A.* 37°9N 83°46W **353** G12
Manchester *N.H., U.S.A.* 42°59N 71°28W **355** D13
Manchester *N.Y., U.S.A.* 42°56N 77°16W **354** D7
Manchester *Pa., U.S.A.* 40°4N 76°43W **355** F8
Manchester *Tenn., U.S.A.* 35°29N 86°5W **357** D11
Manchester *Vt., U.S.A.* 43°10N 73°5W **355** C11
Manchester Int. ✕ **(MAN)** *U.K.* 53°21N 2°17W **284** D5
Manchester L. *Canada* 61°28N 107°29W **343** A7
Manchhar L. *Pakistan* 26°25N 67°39E **314** F2
Manchuria = Dongbei *China* 45°0N 125°0E **307** D13
Manchurian Plain *China* 47°0N 124°0E **298** D14
Mand → *India* 21°42N 83°15E **315** J10
Mand → *Iran* 28°20N 52°30E **317** D7
Manda *Ludewe, Tanzania* 10°30S 34°40E **327** E3
Manda *Mbeya, Tanzania* 7°58S 32°29E **326** D3
Manda *Mbeya, Tanzania* 8°30S 32°49E **327** D3
Mandabé *Madag.* 21°0S 44°55E **329** C7
Mandaguari *Brazil* 23°32S 51°42W **367** A5
Mandah = Töhöm *Mongolia* 44°27N 108°2E **306** B5
Mandal *Norway* 58°2N 7°25E **281** G12
Mandala, Puncak *Indonesia* 4°44S 140°20E **309** E10
Mandalay *Burma* 22°0N 96°4E **313** J20
Mandale = Mandalay *Burma* 22°0N 96°4E **313** J20
Mandalgarh *India* 25°12N 75°6E **314** G6
Mandalgovĭ *Mongolia* 45°45N 106°10E **306** B4
Mandalī *Iraq* 33°43N 45°28E **316** C5
Mandan *U.S.A.* 46°50N 100°54W **352** B3
Mandar, Teluk *Indonesia* 3°35S 119°15E **309** E5
Mandaue *Phil.* 10°20N 123°56E **309** B6
Mandera *Kenya* 3°55N 41°53E **326** B5
Mandeville *Jamaica* 18°2N 77°31W **360** a
Mandi *India* 31°39N 76°58E **314** D7
Mandi Dabwali *India* 29°58N 74°42E **314** E6
Mandimba *Mozam.* 14°20S 35°40E **327** E4
Mandioli *Indonesia* 0°40S 127°20E **309** E7
Mandla *India* 22°39N 80°30E **315** H9
Mandorah *Australia* 12°32S 130°42E **332** B5
Mandoto *Madag.* 19°34S 46°17E **329** B8
Mandra *Pakistan* 33°23N 73°12E **314** C5
Mandrare → *Madag.* 25°10S 46°30E **329** D8
Mandritsara *Madag.* 15°50S 48°49E **329** B8
Mandronarivo *Madag.* 21°7S 45°38E **329** C8
Mandsaur *India* 24°3N 75°8E **314** G6
Mandurah *Australia* 32°36S 115°48E **333** F2
Mandvi *India* 22°51N 69°22E **314** H3
Mandya *India* 12°30N 77°0E **312** N10
Mandzai *Pakistan* 30°55N 67°6E **314** D2
Maneh *Iran* 37°39N 57°7E **317** B8
Manera *Madag.* 22°55S 44°20E **329** C7
Maneroo Cr. → *Australia* 23°21S 143°53E **334** C3
Manfalût *Egypt* 27°20N 30°52E **323** C12
Manfredónia *Italy* 41°38N 15°55E **294** D6
Mangabeiras, Chapada das *Brazil* 10°0S 46°30W **365** F9
Mangaia *Cook Is.* 21°55S 157°55W **337** K12
Mangalia *Romania* 43°50N 28°35E **289** G15
Mangalore *India* 12°55N 74°47E **312** N9
Mangan *India* 27°31N 88°32E **315** F13
Mangawan *India* 24°41N 81°33E **315** G9
Mangaweka *N.Z.* 39°48S 175°47E **331** C5
Manggar *Indonesia* 2°50S 108°10E **308** E3
Manggawitu *Indonesia* 4°8S 133°32E **309** E8
Mangghystaū Tübegi *Kazakhstan* 44°30N 52°30E **300** E6
Manggis *Indonesia* 8°29S 115°31E **309** J18
Mangindrano *Madag.* 14°17S 48°58E **329** A8
Mangkalihat, Tanjung *Indonesia* 1°2N 118°59E **309** D5
Mangla *Pakistan* 33°7N 73°39E **314** C5
Mangla Dam *Pakistan* 33°9N 73°44E **315** C5
Manglaur *India* 29°44N 77°49E **314** E7
Mangnai *China* 37°52N 91°43E **304** C4
Mango *Togo* 10°20N 0°30E **322** F6
Mango *Tonga* 20°17S 174°29W **331** c
Mangoche *Malawi* 14°25S 35°16E **327** E4
Mangoky → *Madag.* 21°29S 43°41E **329** C7
Mangole *Indonesia* 1°50S 125°55E **309** E6
Mangombe *Dem. Rep. of the Congo* 1°20S 26°48E **326** C2
Mangonui *N.Z.* 35°1S 173°32E **331** A4
Mangoro → *Madag.* 20°0S 48°45E **329** B8
Mangrol *Mad. P., India* 21°7N 70°7E **314** J4
Mangrol *Raj., India* 25°20N 76°31E **314** G6
Mangueira, L. da *Brazil* 33°0S 52°50W **367** C5
Mangum *U.S.A.* 34°53N 99°30W **356** D5
Mangyshlak, Poluostrov = Mangghystaū Tübegi *Kazakhstan* 44°30N 52°30E **300** E6
Manhattan *U.S.A.* 39°11N 96°35W **352** F5
Manhiça *Mozam.* 25°23S 32°49E **329** D5
Mania → *Madag.* 19°42S 45°22E **329** B8
Manica *Mozam.* 18°58S 32°59E **329** B5
Manica □ *Mozam.* 19°10S 33°45E **329** B5
Manicaland □ *Zimbabwe* 19°0S 32°30E **327** F3
Manicoré *Brazil* 5°48S 61°16W **364** E6
Manicouagan → *Canada* 49°30N 68°30W **345** C6
Manicouagan, Rés. *Canada* 51°5N 68°40W **345** B6
Maniema □ *Dem. Rep. of the Congo* 3°0S 26°0E **326** C2
Manīfah *Si. Arabia* 27°44N 49°0E **317** E6
Manifold, C. *Australia* 22°41S 150°50E **334** C5
Manigotagan *Canada* 51°6N 96°18W **343** C9
Manigotagan → *Canada* 51°7N 96°20W **343** C9
Manihari *India* 25°21N 87°38E **315** G12
Manihiki *Cook Is.* 10°24S 161°1W **337** J11
Manihiki Plateau *Pac. Oc.* 11°0S 164°0W **337** J11
Manika, Plateau de la *Dem. Rep. of the Congo* 10°0S 25°5E **327** E2
Manikpur *India* 25°4N 81°7E **315** G9
Manila *Phil.* 14°35N 120°58E **309** B6
Manila *U.S.A.* 40°59N 109°43W **348** F9
Manila B. *Phil.* 14°40N 120°35E **309** B6
Manilla *Australia* 30°45S 150°43E **335** E5
Maningrida *Australia* 12°3S 134°13E **334** A1
Manipur □ *India* 25°0N 94°0E **313** G19
Manipur → *Burma* 23°45N 94°20E **313** H19
Manisa *Turkey* 38°38N 27°30E **295** E12
Manistee *U.S.A.* 44°15N 86°19W **352** C10
Manistee → *U.S.A.* 44°15N 86°21W **352** C10
Manistique *U.S.A.* 45°57N 86°15W **352** C10
Manitoba □ *Canada* 53°30N 97°0W **343** B9
Manitoba, L. *Canada* 51°0N 98°45W **343** C9
Manitou *Canada* 49°15N 98°32W **343** D9
Manitou, L. *Canada* 50°55N 65°17W **345** B6
Manitou Is. *U.S.A.* 45°8N 86°0W **353** C10
Manitou L. *Canada* 52°43N 109°43W **343** C7
Manitou Springs *U.S.A.* 38°52N 104°55W **348** G11
Manitoulin I. *Canada* 45°40N 82°30W **344** C3
Manitouwadge *Canada* 49°8N 85°48W **344** C2
Manitowoc *U.S.A.* 44°5N 87°40W **352** C10
Manizales *Colombia* 5°5N 75°32W **364** B3
Manja *Madag.* 21°26S 44°20E **329** C7
Manjacaze *Mozam.* 24°45S 34°0E **329** C5
Manjakandriana *Madag.* 18°55S 47°47E **329** B8
Manjhand *Pakistan* 25°50N 68°10E **314** G3
Manjil *Iran* 36°46N 49°30E **317** B6
Manjimup *Australia* 34°15S 116°6E **333** F2
Manjra → *India* 18°49N 77°52E **312** K10
Mankato *Kans., U.S.A.* 39°47N 98°13W **352** F4
Mankato *Minn., U.S.A.* 44°10N 94°0W **352** C6
Mankayane *Swaziland* 26°40S 31°4E **329** D5
Mankera *Pakistan* 31°23N 71°26E **314** D4
Mankota *Canada* 49°25N 107°5W **343** D7
Manlay = Üydzin *Mongolia* 44°9N 107°0E **306** B4
Manmad *India* 20°18N 74°28E **312** J9
Mann Ranges *Australia* 26°6S 130°5E **333** E5
Manna *Indonesia* 4°25S 102°55E **308** E2
Mannahill *Australia* 32°25S 140°0E **335** E3
Mannar *Sri Lanka* 9°1N 79°54E **312** Q11
Mannar, G. of *Asia* 8°30N 79°0E **312** Q11
Mannar I. *Sri Lanka* 9°5N 79°45E **312** Q11
Mannheim *Germany* 49°29N 8°29E **288** D5
Manning *Canada* 56°53N 117°39W **342** B5
Manning *Oreg., U.S.A.* 45°45N 123°13W **350** E3
Manning *S.C., U.S.A.* 33°42N 80°13W **357** E14
Mannum *Australia* 34°50S 139°20E **335** E2
Manoharpur *India* 22°23N 85°12E **315** H11
Manokwari *Indonesia* 0°54S 134°0E **309** E8
Manombo *Madag.* 22°57S 43°28E **329** C7
Manono *Dem. Rep. of the Congo* 7°15S 27°25E **326** D2
Manono *Samoa* 13°50S 172°5W **331** b
Manorhamilton *Ireland* 54°18N 8°9W **282** B3
Manosque *France* 43°49N 5°47E **292** E6
Manotick *Canada* 45°13N 75°41W **355** A9
Manouane → *Canada* 49°30N 71°10W **345** C5
Manouane, L. *Canada* 50°45N 70°45W **345** B5
Manp'o *N. Korea* 41°6N 126°24E **307** D14
Manpojin = Manp'o *N. Korea* 41°6N 126°24E **307** D14
Manpur *Chhattisgarh, India* 23°17N 83°35E **315** H10
Manpur *Mad. P., India* 22°26N 75°37E **314** H6
Manresa *Spain* 41°48N 1°50E **293** B6
Mansa *Gujarat, India* 23°27N 72°45E **314** H5
Mansa *Punjab, India* 30°0N 75°27E **314** E6
Mansa *Zambia* 11°13S 28°55E **327** E2
Mansehra *Pakistan* 34°20N 73°15E **314** B5
Mansel I. *Canada* 62°0N 80°0W **341** C12
Mansfield *Australia* 37°4S 146°6E **335** F4
Mansfield *U.K.* 53°9N 1°11W **284** D6
Mansfield *La., U.S.A.* 32°2N 93°43W **356** E8
Mansfield *Mass., U.S.A.* 42°2N 71°13W **355** D13
Mansfield *Ohio, U.S.A.* 40°45N 82°31W **354** F2
Mansfield *Pa., U.S.A.* 41°48N 77°5W **354** E7
Mansfield *Tex., U.S.A.* 32°33N 97°8W **356** E6
Mansfield, Mt. *U.S.A.* 44°33N 72°49W **355** B12
Manson Creek *Canada* 55°37N 124°32W **342** B4
Manta *Ecuador* 1°0S 80°40W **364** D2
Mantadia △ *Madag.* 18°54S 48°21E **329** B8
Mantalingajan, Mt. *Phil.* 8°55N 117°45E **308** C5
Mantare *Tanzania* 2°42S 33°13E **326** C3
Manteca *U.S.A.* 37°48N 121°13W **350** H5
Manteo *U.S.A.* 35°55N 75°40W **357** D17
Mantes-la-Jolie *France* 48°58N 1°41E **292** B4
Manthani *India* 18°40N 79°35E **312** K11
Manti *U.S.A.* 39°16N 111°38W **348** G8
Mantiqueira, Serra da *Brazil* 22°0S 44°0W **367** A7
Manton *U.S.A.* 44°25N 85°24W **353** C11
Mántova *Italy* 45°9N 10°48E **294** B4
Mänttä *Finland* 62°3N 24°40E **280** E21
Mantua = Mántova *Italy* 45°9N 10°48E **294** B4
Manu *Peru* 12°10S 70°51W **364** F4
Manu → *Peru* 12°16S 70°55W **364** F4
Manu'a Is. *Amer. Samoa* 14°13S 169°35W **331** b
Manuel Alves → *Brazil* 11°19S 48°28W **365** F9
Manui *Indonesia* 3°35S 123°5E **309** E6
Manukau *N.Z.* 37°0S 174°52E **331** B5
Manuripi → *Bolivia* 11°6S 67°36W **364** F5
Many *U.S.A.* 31°34N 93°29W **356** F8
Manyani *Kenya* 3°5S 38°30E **326** C4
Manyara, L. *Tanzania* 3°40S 35°50E **326** C4
Manych-Gudilo, Ozero *Russia* 46°24N 42°38E **291** E7
Manyonga → *Tanzania* 4°10S 34°15E **326** C3
Manyoni *Tanzania* 5°45S 34°55E **326** D3
Manzai *Pakistan* 32°12N 70°15E **314** C4
Manzanar ⌓ *U.S.A.* 36°44N 118°9W **350** J7
Manzanares *Spain* 39°2N 3°22W **293** C4
Manzanillo *Cuba* 20°20N 77°31W **360** B4
Manzanillo *Mexico* 19°3N 104°20W **358** D4
Manzanillo, Pta. *Panama* 9°30N 79°40W **360** E4
Manzano Mts. *U.S.A.* 34°40N 106°20W **349** J10
Manzarīyeh *Iran* 34°53N 50°50E **317** C6
Manzhouli *China* 49°35N 117°25E **305** B6
Manzini *Swaziland* 26°30S 31°25E **329** D5
Manzur Vadisi △ *Turkey* 39°10N 39°30E **316** B3
Mao *Chad* 14°4N 15°19E **323** F9
Maó *Spain* 39°53N 4°16E **296** B11
Maoke, Pegunungan *Indonesia* 3°40S 137°30E **309** E9
Maolin *China* 43°58N 123°30E **307** C12
Maoming *China* 21°50N 110°54E **305** D6
Maoxing *China* 45°28N 124°40E **307** B13
Mapam Yumco *China* 30°45N 81°28E **315** D9
Mapastepec *Mexico* 15°26N 92°54W **359** D6
Maphrao, Ko *Thailand* 7°56N 98°26E **311** a
Mapia, Kepulauan *Indonesia* 0°50N 134°20E **309** D8
Mapimí *Mexico* 25°49N 103°51W **358** B4
Mapimí, Bolsón de *Mexico* 27°0N 104°15W **358** B4
Mapinga *Tanzania* 6°40S 39°12E **326** D4
Mapinhane *Mozam.* 22°20S 35°0E **329** C6
Maple Creek *Canada* 49°55N 109°29W **343** D7
Maple Valley *U.S.A.* 47°25N 122°3W **350** C4
Mapleton *U.S.A.* 44°2N 123°52W **348** D2
Mapuera → *Brazil* 1°5S 57°2W **364** D7
Mapulanguene *Mozam.* 24°29S 32°6E **329** C5
Maputo *Mozam.* 25°58S 32°32E **329** D5
Maputo □ *Mozam.* 26°0S 32°25E **329** D5
Maputo, B. de *Mozam.* 25°50S 32°45E **329** D5
Maputo ⌓ *Mozam.* 26°23S 32°48E **329** D5
Maqat *Kazakhstan* 47°39N 53°19E **291** E9
Maqiaohe *China* 44°40N 130°30E **307** B16
Maqnā *Si. Arabia* 28°25N 34°50E **316** D2
Maquan He = Brahmaputra → *Asia* 23°40N 90°35E **315** H13
Maquela do Zombo *Angola* 6°0S 15°15E **324** F3
Maquinchao *Argentina* 41°15S 68°50W **368** E3
Maquoketa *U.S.A.* 42°4N 90°40W **352** D8
Mar, Serra do *Brazil* 25°30S 49°0W **367** B6
Mar Chiquita, L. *Argentina* 30°40S 62°50W **366** C3
Mar del Plata *Argentina* 38°0S 57°30W **366** D4
Mar Menor *Spain* 37°40N 0°45W **293** D5
Mara *Tanzania* 1°30S 34°32E **326** C3
Mara □ *Tanzania* 1°45S 34°20E **326** C3
Maraã *Brazil* 1°52S 65°25W **364** D5
Maraa *Tahiti* 17°46S 149°34W **331** d
Marabá *Brazil* 5°20S 49°5W **365** E9
Maracá, I. de *Brazil* 2°10N 50°30W **365** C8
Maracaibo *Venezuela* 10°40N 71°37W **364** A4
Maracaibo, L. de *Venezuela* 9°40N 71°30W **364** B4
Maracaju *Brazil* 21°38S 55°9W **367** A4
Maracas Bay Village *Trin. & Tob.* 10°46N 61°28W **365** K15
Maracay *Venezuela* 10°15N 67°28W **364** A5
Maradi *Niger* 13°29N 7°20E **322** F7
Marāgheh *Iran* 37°30N 46°12E **316** B5
Marāh *Si. Arabia* 25°0N 45°35E **316** E5
Marajó, I. de *Brazil* 1°0S 49°30W **365** D9
Marākand *Iran* 38°51N 45°16E **316** B5
Marakele △ *S. Africa* 32°14S 25°27E **329** E4
Maralal *Kenya* 1°0N 36°38E **326** B4
Maralinga *Australia* 30°13S 131°32E **333** F5
Marambio *Antarctica* 64°0S 56°0W **277** C18
Maran *Malaysia* 3°35N 102°45E **311** L4
Marana *U.S.A.* 32°27N 111°13W **349** K8
Maranboy *Australia* 14°40S 132°39E **332** B5
Marand *Iran* 38°30N 45°45E **316** B5
Marang *Malaysia* 5°12N 103°13E **311** K4
Maranguape *Brazil* 3°55S 38°50W **365** D11
Maranhão = São Luís *Brazil* 2°39S 44°15W **365** D10
Maranhão □ *Brazil* 5°0S 46°0W **365** E9
Maranoa → *Australia* 27°50S 148°37E **335** D4
Marañón → *Peru* 4°30S 73°35W **364** D4
Marão *Mozam.* 24°18S 34°2E **329** C5
Maraş = Kahramanmaraş *Turkey* 37°37N 36°53E **316** B3
Marathasa *Cyprus* 34°59N 32°51E **297** E11
Marathon *Australia* 20°51S 143°32E **334** C3
Marathon *Canada* 48°44N 86°23W **344** C2
Marathon *N.Y., U.S.A.* 42°27N 76°2W **355** D8
Marathon *Tex., U.S.A.* 30°12N 103°15W **356** F3
Marathóvouno *Cyprus* 35°13N 33°37E **297** D12
Maratua *Indonesia* 2°10N 118°35E **309** D5
Maraval *Trin. & Tob.* 10°42N 61°31W **365** K15
Maravatío *Mexico* 19°54N 100°27W **358** D4
Marāwih *U.A.E.* 24°18N 53°18E **317** E7
Marbella *Spain* 36°30N 4°57W **293** D3
Marble Bar *Australia* 21°9S 119°44E **332** D2
Marble Falls *U.S.A.* 30°35N 98°16W **356** F5
Marblehead *U.S.A.* 42°29N 70°51W **355** D14
Marburg *Germany* 50°47N 8°46E **288** C5
Marca, Pta. Da *Angola* 16°31S 11°43E **325** H2
March *U.K.* 52°33N 0°5E **285** E8
Marche *France* 46°5N 1°20E **292** C4
Marche-en-Famenne *Belgium* 50°14N 5°19E **287** D5
Marchena *Spain* 37°18N 5°23W **293** D3
Marco Island *U.S.A.* 25°58N 81°44W **357** J14
Marcos Juárez *Argentina* 32°42S 62°5W **366** C3
Marcus I. = Minami-Tori-Shima *Pac. Oc.* 24°20N 153°58E **336** E7
Marcy, Mt. *U.S.A.* 44°7N 73°56W **355** B11
Mardan *Pakistan* 34°20N 72°0E **314** B5
Mardin *Turkey* 37°20N 40°43E **316** B4
Maree, L. *U.K.* 57°40N 5°26W **283** D3
Mareeba *Australia* 16°59S 145°28E **334** B4
Mareetsane *S. Africa* 26°9S 25°25E **328** D4
Marek = Stanke Dimitrov *Bulgaria* 42°17N 23°9E **295** C10
Marengo *U.S.A.* 41°48N 92°4W **352** E7
Marerano *Madag.* 21°23S 44°52E **329** C7
Marfa *U.S.A.* 30°19N 104°1W **356** F2
Marfa Pt. *Malta* 35°59N 14°19E **297** D1
Margaret → *Australia* 18°9S 125°41E **332** C4
Margaret Bay *Canada* 51°20N 127°35W **342** C3
Margaret L. *Canada* 58°56N 115°25W **342** B5
Margaret River *Australia* 33°57S 115°4E **333** F2
Margarita, I. de *Venezuela* 11°0N 64°0W **364** A6
Margaritovo *Russia* 43°25N 134°45E **302** C7
Margate *S. Africa* 30°50S 30°20E **329** E5
Margate *U.K.* 51°23N 1°23E **285** F9
Margherita Pk. *Uganda* 0°22N 29°51E **326** B3
Mārgow, Dasht-e *Afghan.* 30°40N 62°30E **312** D3
Marguerite *Canada* 52°30N 122°25W **342** C4
Mari El □ *Russia* 56°30N 48°0E **290** C8
Mari Indus *Pakistan* 32°57N 71°34E **314** C4
Mari Republic = Mari El □ *Russia* 56°30N 48°0E **290** C8
María Elena *Chile* 22°18S 69°40W **366** A2
María Grande *Argentina* 31°45S 59°55W **366** C4
Maria I. *N. Terr., Australia* 14°52S 135°45E **334** A2
Maria I. *Tas., Australia* 42°35S 148°0E **335** G4
Maria Island △ *Australia* 42°38S 148°5E **335** G4
Maria van Diemen, C. *N.Z.* 34°29S 172°40E **331** A4
Mariakani *Kenya* 3°50S 39°27E **326** C4
Mariala △ *Australia* 25°57S 145°2E **335** D4
Marian *Australia* 21°9S 148°57E **334** K6
Marian L. *Canada* 63°0N 116°15W **342** A5
Mariana Trench *Pac. Oc.* 13°0N 145°0E **336** F6
Marianna *U.S.A.* 30°46N 85°14W **357** F12
Marias → *U.S.A.* 47°56N 110°30W **348** C8
Marías, Islas *Mexico* 21°25N 106°28W **358** C3
Mariato, Punta *Panama* 7°12N 80°52W **360** E3
Maribor *Slovenia* 46°36N 15°40E **288** E8
Marico → *Africa* 23°35S 26°57E **328** C4
Maricopa *Ariz., U.S.A.* 33°4N 112°3W **349** K7
Maricopa *Calif., U.S.A.* 35°4N 119°24W **351** K7
Marié → *Brazil* 0°27S 66°26W **364** D5
Marie Byrd Land *Antarctica* 79°30S 125°0W **277** D14
Marie-Galante *Guadeloupe* 15°56N 61°16W **360** b
Mariecourt = Kangiqsujuaq *Canada* 61°30N 72°0W **341** C12
Mariehamn *Finland* 60°5N 19°55E **281** F18
Mariembourg *Belgium* 50°6N 4°31E **287** D4
Mariental *Namibia* 24°36S 18°0E **328** C2
Marienville *U.S.A.* 41°28N 79°8W **354** E5
Mariestad *Sweden* 58°43N 13°50E **281** G15
Marietta *Ga., U.S.A.* 33°57N 84°33W **357** E12
Marietta *Ohio, U.S.A.* 39°25N 81°27W **353** F13
Marieville *Canada* 45°26N 73°10W **355** A11
Mariinsk *Russia* 56°10N 87°20E **300** D9
Marijampolė *Lithuania* 54°33N 23°19E **281** J20
Marília *Brazil* 22°13S 50°0W **367** A6
Marín *Spain* 42°23N 8°42W **293** A1
Marina *U.S.A.* 36°41N 121°48W **350** J5

Marinduque *Phil.* 13°25N 122°0E 309 B6
Marine City *U.S.A.* 42°43N 82°30W 354 D2
Marinette *U.S.A.* 45°6N 87°38W 352 C10
Maringá *Brazil* 23°26S 52°2W 367 A5
Marion *Ala., U.S.A.* 32°38N 87°19W 357 E11
Marion *Ill., U.S.A.* 37°44N 88°56W 352 G9
Marion *Ind., U.S.A.* 40°32N 85°40W 353 E11
Marion *Iowa, U.S.A.* 42°2N 91°36W 352 D8
Marion *Kans., U.S.A.* 38°21N 97°1W 352 F5
Marion *N.C., U.S.A.* 35°41N 82°1W 357 D13
Marion *Ohio, U.S.A.* 40°35N 83°8W 353 E12
Marion *S.C., U.S.A.* 34°11N 79°24W 357 D15
Marion *Va., U.S.A.* 36°50N 81°31W 353 G13
Marion, L. *U.S.A.* 33°28N 80°10W 357 E14
Mariposa *U.S.A.* 37°29N 119°58W 350 H7
Mariscal Estigarribia *Paraguay* 22°3S 60°40W 366 A3
Maritime Alps = Maritimes, Alpes *Europe* 44°10N 7°10E 292 D7
Maritimes, Alpes *Europe* 44°10N 7°10E 292 D7
Maritsa = Evros → *Greece* 41°40N 26°34E 295 D12
Maritsa *Greece* 36°22N 28°8E 297 C10
Mariupol *Ukraine* 47°5N 37°31E 291 E6
Mariusa △ *Venezuela* 9°24N 61°27W 361 E7
Marīvān *Iran* 35°30N 46°25E 316 C5
Marj 'Uyūn *Lebanon* 33°21N 35°34E 318 B4
Marka = Merca *Somali Rep.* 1°48N 44°50E 319 G3
Markam *China* 29°42N 98°38E 304 D4
Markdale *Canada* 44°19N 80°39W 354 B4
Marked Tree *U.S.A.* 35°32N 90°25W 357 D9
Market Drayton *U.K.* 52°54N 2°29W 284 E5
Market Harborough *U.K.* 52°29N 0°55W 285 E7
Market Rasen *U.K.* 53°24N 0°20W 284 D7
Markham *Canada* 43°52N 79°16W 354 C5
Markham, Mt. *Antarctica* 83°0S 164°0E 277 E11
Markleeville *U.S.A.* 38°42N 119°47W 350 G7
Markovo *Russia* 64°40N 170°24E 301 C17
Marks *Russia* 51°45N 46°50E 290 D8
Marksville *U.S.A.* 31°8N 92°4W 356 F8
Marla *Australia* 27°19S 133°33E 335 D1
Marlbank *Canada* 44°26N 77°6W 354 B7
Marlboro *U.S.A.* 41°36N 73°59W 355 E11
Marlborough *Australia* 22°46S 149°52E 334 C4
Marlborough *U.K.* 51°25N 1°43W 285 F6
Marlborough *U.S.A.* 42°21N 71°33W 355 D13
Marlborough Downs *U.K.* 51°27N 1°53W 285 F6
Marlin *U.S.A.* 31°18N 96°54W 356 F6
Marlow *U.K.* 51°34N 0°46W 285 F7
Marlow *U.S.A.* 34°39N 97°58W 356 D6
Marmagao *India* 15°25N 73°56E 312 M8
Marmara *Turkey* 40°35N 27°34E 295 D12
Marmara, Sea of = Marmara Denizi *Turkey* 40°45N 28°15E 295 D13
Marmara Denizi *Turkey* 40°45N 28°15E 295 D13
Marmaris *Turkey* 36°50N 28°14E 295 F13
Marmion, Mt. *Australia* 29°16S 119°50E 333 E2
Marmion L. *Canada* 48°55N 91°20W 344 C1
Marmolada, Mte. *Italy* 46°26N 11°51E 294 A4
Marmora *Canada* 44°28N 77°41W 354 B7
Marne → *France* 48°47N 2°29E 292 B5
Maroala *Madag.* 15°23S 47°59E 329 B8
Maroantsetra *Madag.* 15°26S 49°44E 329 B8
Maroelaboom *Namibia* 19°15S 18°53E 328 B2
Marofandilia *Madag.* 20°7S 44°34E 329 C7
Marojejy ⌓ *Madag.* 14°26S 49°21E 329 A8
Marolambo *Madag.* 20°2S 48°7E 329 C8
Maromandia *Madag.* 14°13S 48°5E 329 A8
Maromokotro *Madag.* 14°0S 49°0E 329 A8
Marondera *Zimbabwe* 18°5S 31°42E 327 F3
Maroni → *Fr. Guiana* 5°30N 54°0W 365 B8
Maroochydore *Australia* 26°29S 153°5E 335 D5
Maroona *Australia* 37°27S 142°54E 335 F3
Marosakoa *Madag.* 15°26S 46°38E 329 B8
Maroseranana *Madag.* 18°32S 48°51E 329 B8
Marotandrano *Madag.* 16°10S 48°50E 329 B8
Marotaolano *Madag.* 12°47S 49°15E 329 A8
Maroua *Cameroon* 10°40N 14°20E 323 F8
Marovato *Madag.* 15°48S 48°5E 329 B8
Marovoay *Madag.* 16°6S 46°39E 329 B8
Marquard *S. Africa* 28°40S 27°28E 328 D4
Marquesas Fracture Zone *Pac. Oc.* 9°0S 125°0W 337 H15
Marquesas Is. = Marquises, Îs. *French Polynesia* 9°30S 140°0W 337 H14
Marquette *U.S.A.* 46°33N 87°24W 352 B10
Marquis *St. Lucia* 14°2N 60°54W 361 f
Marquises, Îs. *French Polynesia* 9°30S 140°0W 337 H14
Marra, Djebel *Sudan* 13°10N 24°22E 323 F10
Marracuene *Mozam.* 25°45S 32°35E 329 D5
Marrakech *Morocco* 31°9N 8°0W 322 B4
Marrawah *Australia* 40°55S 144°42E 335 G3
Marree *Australia* 29°39S 138°1E 335 D2
Marrero *U.S.A.* 29°53N 90°6W 357 G9
Marrimane *Mozam.* 22°58S 33°34E 329 C5
Marromeu *Mozam.* 18°15S 36°25E 329 B6
Marromeu ⌓ *Mozam.* 19°0S 36°0E 329 B6
Marrowie Cr. → *Australia* 33°23S 145°40E 335 E4
Marrubane *Mozam.* 18°0S 37°0E 327 F4
Marrupa *Mozam.* 13°8S 37°30E 327 E4
Mars Hill *U.S.A.* 46°31N 67°52W 353 B20
Marsá Matrûh *Egypt* 31°19N 27°9E 323 B11
Marsá Susah *Libya* 32°52N 21°59E 323 B10
Marsabit *Kenya* 2°18N 38°0E 326 B4
Marsabit △ *Kenya* 2°23N 37°56E 326 B4
Marsala *Italy* 37°48N 12°26E 294 F5
Marsalforn *Malta* 36°4N 14°16E 297 C1
Marsden *Australia* 33°47S 147°32E 335 E4
Marseille *France* 43°18N 5°23E 292 E6
Marseilles = Marseille *France* 43°18N 5°23E 292 E6
Marsh I. *U.S.A.* 29°34N 91°53W 356 G9
Marshall *Ark., U.S.A.* 35°55N 92°38W 356 D8
Marshall *Mich., U.S.A.* 42°16N 84°58W 353 D11
Marshall *Minn., U.S.A.* 44°27N 95°47W 352 C6
Marshall *Mo., U.S.A.* 39°7N 93°12W 352 F7
Marshall *Tex., U.S.A.* 32°33N 94°23W 356 E7
Marshall → *Australia* 22°59S 136°59E 334 C2
Marshall Is. ■ *Pac. Oc.* 9°0N 171°0E 330 A10
Marshalltown *U.S.A.* 42°3N 92°55W 352 D7
Marshbrook *Zimbabwe* 18°33S 31°9E 329 B5
Marshfield *Mo., U.S.A.* 37°15N 92°54W 352 G7
Marshfield *Vt., U.S.A.* 44°20N 72°20W 355 B12
Marshfield *Wis., U.S.A.* 44°40N 90°10W 352 C8
Marshūn *Iran* 36°19N 49°23E 317 B6
Märsta *Sweden* 59°37N 17°52E 281 G17
Mart *U.S.A.* 31°33N 96°50W 356 F6
Martaban *Burma* 16°30N 97°35E 313 L20
Martaban, G. of *Burma* 16°5N 96°30E 313 L20
Martapura *Kalimantan, Indonesia* 3°22S 114°47E 308 E4
Martapura *Sumatera, Indonesia* 4°19S 104°22E 308 E2
Marte R. Gómez, Presa *Mexico* 26°10N 99°0W 359 B5
Martelange *Belgium* 49°49N 5°43E 287 E5
Martha's Vineyard *U.S.A.* 41°25N 70°38W 355 E14
Martigny *Switz.* 46°6N 7°3E 292 C7
Martigues *France* 43°24N 5°4E 292 E6
Martin *Slovak Rep.* 49°6N 18°58E 289 D10
Martin *S. Dak., U.S.A.* 43°11N 101°44W 352 D3
Martin *Tenn., U.S.A.* 36°21N 88°51W 357 C10
Martin L. *U.S.A.* 32°41N 85°55W 357 E12
Martina Franca *Italy* 40°42N 17°20E 294 D7
Martinborough *N.Z.* 41°14S 175°29E 331 D5
Martinez *Calif., U.S.A.* 38°1N 122°8W 350 G4
Martinez *Ga., U.S.A.* 33°31N 82°5W 357 E13
Martinique ☒ *W. Indies* 14°40N 61°0W 360 c
Martinique Passage *W. Indies* 15°15N 61°0W 361 C7
Martinópolis *Brazil* 22°11S 51°12W 367 A5
Martin's Bay *Barbados* 13°12N 59°29W 361 g
Martins Ferry *U.S.A.* 40°6N 80°44W 354 F4
Martinsburg *Pa., U.S.A.* 40°19N 78°20W 354 F6
Martinsburg *W. Va., U.S.A.* 39°27N 77°58W 353 F15
Martinsville *Ind., U.S.A.* 39°26N 86°25W 352 F10
Martinsville *Va., U.S.A.* 36°41N 79°52W 353 G14
Marton *N.Z.* 40°4S 175°23E 331 D5
Martos *Spain* 37°44N 3°58W 293 D4
Marudi *Malaysia* 4°11N 114°19E 308 D4
Maruf *Afghan.* 31°30N 67°6E 312 D5
Marugame *Japan* 34°15N 133°40E 303 G6
Marunga *Angola* 17°28S 20°2E 328 B3
Marungu, Mts. *Dem. Rep. of the Congo* 7°30S 30°0E 326 D3
Marv Dasht *Iran* 29°50N 52°40E 317 D7
Marvast *Iran* 30°30N 54°15E 317 D7
Marvel Loch *Australia* 31°28S 119°29E 333 F2
Marwar *India* 25°43N 73°45E 314 G5
Mary *Turkmenistan* 37°40N 61°50E 317 B9
Maryborough = Port Laoise *Ireland* 53°2N 7°18W 282 C4
Maryborough *Queens., Australia* 25°31S 152°37E 335 D5
Maryborough *Vic., Australia* 37°3S 143°44E 335 F3
Maryfield *Canada* 49°50N 101°35W 343 D8
Maryland □ *U.S.A.* 39°0N 76°30W 353 F15
Maryland Junction *Zimbabwe* 17°45S 30°31E 327 F3
Maryport *U.K.* 54°44N 3°28W 284 C4
Mary's Harbour *Canada* 52°18N 55°51W 345 B8
Marystown *Canada* 47°10N 55°10W 345 C8
Marysville *Canada* 49°35N 116°0W 342 D5
Marysville *Calif., U.S.A.* 39°9N 121°35W 350 F5
Marysville *Kans., U.S.A.* 39°51N 96°39W 352 F5
Marysville *Mich., U.S.A.* 42°54N 82°29W 354 D2
Marysville *Ohio, U.S.A.* 40°14N 83°22W 353 E12
Marysville *Wash., U.S.A.* 48°3N 122°11W 350 B4
Maryville *Mo., U.S.A.* 40°21N 94°52W 352 E6
Maryville *Tenn., U.S.A.* 35°46N 83°58W 357 D13
Marzūq *Libya* 25°53N 13°57E 323 C8
Marzūq, Idehān *Libya* 24°50N 13°51E 323 D8
Masada *Israel* 31°15N 35°20E 318 D4
Masahunga *Tanzania* 2°6S 33°18E 326 C3
Masai *Malaysia* 1°29N 103°55E 311 d
Masai Mara △ *Kenya* 1°25S 35°5E 326 C4
Masai Steppe *Tanzania* 4°30S 36°30E 326 C4
Masaka *Uganda* 0°21S 31°45E 326 C3
Masalembo, Kepulauan *Indonesia* 5°35S 114°30E 308 F4
Masalima, Kepulauan *Indonesia* 5°4S 117°5E 308 F5
Masamba *Indonesia* 2°30S 120°15E 309 E6
Masan *S. Korea* 35°11N 128°32E 307 G15
Masandam, Ra's *Oman* 26°30N 56°30E 317 E8
Masasi *Tanzania* 10°45S 38°52E 327 E4
Masaya *Nic.* 12°0N 86°7W 360 D2
Masbate *Phil.* 12°21N 123°36E 309 B6
Mascara *Algeria* 35°26N 0°6E 322 A6
Mascota *Mexico* 20°32N 104°49W 358 C4
Masela *Indonesia* 8°9S 129°51E 309 F7
Maseru *Lesotho* 29°18S 27°30E 328 D4
Mashaba *Zimbabwe* 20°2S 30°29E 327 G3
Mashābih *Si. Arabia* 25°35N 36°30E 316 E3
Mashatu ⌓ *Botswana* 22°5S 29°5E 329 C4
Masherbrum *Pakistan* 35°38N 76°18E 315 B7
Mashhad *Iran* 36°20N 59°35E 317 B8
Mashīz *Iran* 29°56N 56°37E 317 D8
Māshkel, Hāmūn-i- *Pakistan* 28°20N 62°56E 317 D9
Mashki Chāh *Pakistan* 29°5N 62°30E 312 E3
Mashonaland *Zimbabwe* 16°30S 31°0E 325 H6
Mashonaland Central □ *Zimbabwe* 17°30S 31°0E 329 B5
Mashonaland East □ *Zimbabwe* 18°0S 32°0E 329 B5
Mashonaland West □ *Zimbabwe* 17°30S 29°30E 329 B4
Mashrakh *India* 26°7N 84°48E 315 F11
Masi Manimba *Dem. Rep. of the Congo* 4°40S 17°54E 324 E3
Masindi *Uganda* 1°40N 31°43E 326 B3
Masindi Port *Uganda* 1°43N 32°2E 326 B3
Maşīrah *Oman* 21°0N 58°50E 319 C6
Maşīrah, Khalīj *Oman* 20°10N 58°10E 319 C6
Masisi *Dem. Rep. of the Congo* 1°23S 28°49E 326 C2
Masjed Soleyman *Iran* 31°55N 49°18E 317 D6
Mask, L. *Ireland* 53°36N 9°22W 282 C2
Maskin *Oman* 23°44N 56°52E 317 F8
Masoala, Tanjon' i *Madag.* 15°59S 50°13E 329 B9
Masoala △ *Madag.* 15°30S 50°12E 329 B9
Masoarivo *Madag.* 19°3S 44°19E 329 B7
Masohi = Amahai *Indonesia* 3°20S 128°55E 309 E7
Masomeloka *Madag.* 20°17S 48°37E 329 C8
Mason *Nev., U.S.A.* 38°56N 119°8W 350 G7
Mason *Tex., U.S.A.* 30°45N 99°14W 356 F5
Mason City *U.S.A.* 43°9N 93°12W 352 D7
Maspalomas *Canary Is.* 27°46N 15°35W 296 G4
Maspalomas, Pta. *Canary Is.* 27°43N 15°36W 296 G4
Masqat *Oman* 23°37N 58°36E 319 C6
Massa *Italy* 44°1N 10°9E 292 D9
Massachusetts □ *U.S.A.* 42°30N 72°0W 355 D13
Massachusetts B. *U.S.A.* 42°25N 70°50W 355 D14
Massakory *Chad* 13°0N 15°49E 323 F9
Massanella *Spain* 39°48N 2°51E 296 B9
Massangena *Mozam.* 21°34S 33°0E 329 C5
Massango *Angola* 8°2S 16°21E 324 F3
Massawa = Mitsiwa *Eritrea* 15°35N 39°25E 319 D2
Massena *U.S.A.* 44°56N 74°54W 355 B10
Massénya *Chad* 11°21N 16°9E 323 F9
Masset *Canada* 54°2N 132°10W 342 C2
Massiah Street *Barbados* 13°9N 59°29W 361 g
Massif Central *France* 44°55N 3°0E 292 D5
Massillon *U.S.A.* 40°48N 81°32W 354 F3
Massinga *Mozam.* 23°15S 35°22E 329 C6
Massingir *Mozam.* 23°51S 32°4E 329 C5
Masson-Angers *Canada* 45°32N 75°25W 355 A9
Masson I. *Antarctica* 66°10S 93°20E 277 C7
Mastanli = Momchilgrad *Bulgaria* 41°33N 25°23E 295 D11
Masterton *N.Z.* 40°56S 175°39E 331 D5
Mastic *U.S.A.* 40°47N 72°54W 355 F12
Mastuj *Pakistan* 36°20N 72°36E 315 A5
Mastung *Pakistan* 29°50N 66°56E 312 E5
Masty *Belarus* 53°27N 24°38E 289 B13
Masuda *Japan* 34°40N 131°51E 303 G5
Masvingo *Zimbabwe* 20°8S 30°49E 327 G3
Masvingo □ *Zimbabwe* 21°0S 31°30E 327 G3
Maswa ⌓ *Tanzania* 2°58S 34°19E 326 C3
Maşyāf *Syria* 35°4N 36°20E 316 C3
Mata-au = Clutha → *N.Z.* 46°20S 169°49E 331 G2
Matabeleland *Zimbabwe* 18°0S 27°0E 325 H5
Matabeleland North □ *Zimbabwe* 19°0S 28°0E 327 F2
Matabeleland South □ *Zimbabwe* 21°0S 29°0E 327 G2
Matachewan *Canada* 47°56N 80°39W 344 C3
Matadi *Dem. Rep. of the Congo* 5°52S 13°31E 324 F2
Matagalpa *Nic.* 13°0N 85°58W 360 D2
Matagami *Canada* 49°45N 77°34W 344 C4
Matagami, L. *Canada* 49°50N 77°40W 344 C4
Matagorda B. *U.S.A.* 28°40N 96°12W 356 G6
Matagorda I. *U.S.A.* 28°15N 96°30W 356 G6
Mataiea *Tahiti* 17°46S 149°25W 331 d
Matak *Indonesia* 3°18N 106°16E 308 D3
Matala *Greece* 34°59N 24°45E 297 E6
Matam *Senegal* 15°34N 13°17W 322 E3
Matamoros *Campeche, Mexico* 18°50N 90°50W 359 D6
Matamoros *Coahuila, Mexico* 25°32N 103°15W 358 B4
Matamoros *Tamaulipas, Mexico* 25°53N 97°30W 359 B5
Ma'ţan as Sarra *Libya* 21°45N 22°0E 323 D10
Matandu → *Tanzania* 8°45S 34°19E 327 D3
Matane *Canada* 48°50N 67°33W 345 C6
Matanomadh *India* 23°33N 68°57E 314 H3
Matanzas *Cuba* 23°0N 81°40W 360 B3
Matapa *Botswana* 23°11S 24°39E 328 C3
Matapan, C. = Tenaro, Akra *Greece* 36°22N 22°27E 295 F10
Matapédia *Canada* 48°0N 66°59W 345 C6
Matapo △ *Zimbabwe* 20°30S 29°40E 327 G2
Matara *Sri Lanka* 5°58N 80°30E 312 S12
Mataram *Indonesia* 8°35S 116°7E 308 F5
Matarani *Peru* 17°0S 72°10W 364 G4
Mataranka *Australia* 14°55S 133°4E 332 B5
Matarma, Râs *Egypt* 30°27N 32°44E 318 E1
Mataró *Spain* 41°32N 2°29E 293 B7
Matatiele *S. Africa* 30°20S 28°49E 329 E4
Mataura *N.Z.* 46°11S 168°51E 331 G2
Matavai, B. de *Tahiti* 17°30S 149°23W 331 d
Matehuala *Mexico* 23°39N 100°39W 358 C4
Mateke Hills *Zimbabwe* 21°48S 31°0E 327 G3
Matelot *Trin. & Tob.* 10°50N 61°7W 365 K15
Matera *Italy* 40°40N 16°36E 294 D7
Matetsi *Zimbabwe* 18°12S 26°0E 327 F2
Matheniko ⌓ *Uganda* 2°49N 34°27E 326 B3
Mathis *U.S.A.* 28°6N 97°50W 356 G6
Mathraki *Greece* 39°48N 19°31E 297 A3
Mathura *India* 27°30N 77°40E 314 F7
Mati *Phil.* 6°55N 126°15E 309 C7
Matiali *India* 26°56N 88°49E 315 F13
Matías Romero *Mexico* 16°53N 95°2W 359 D5
Matibane *Mozam.* 14°49S 40°45E 327 E5
Matiri Ra. *N.Z.* 41°38S 172°20E 331 D4
Matjiesfontein *S. Africa* 33°14S 20°35E 328 E3
Matla → *India* 21°40N 88°40E 315 J13
Matlamanyane *Botswana* 19°33S 25°57E 328 B4
Matli *Pakistan* 25°2N 68°39E 314 G3
Matlock *U.K.* 53°9N 1°33W 284 D6
Mato Grosso □ *Brazil* 14°0S 55°0W 365 F8
Mato Grosso, Planalto do *Brazil* 15°0S 55°0W 365 G8
Mato Grosso do Sul □ *Brazil* 18°0S 55°0W 365 G8
Matobo = Matapo △ *Zimbabwe* 20°30S 29°40E 327 G2
Matochkin Shar *Russia* 73°10N 56°40E 300 B6
Matopo Hills *Zimbabwe* 20°36S 28°20E 327 G2
Matopos *Zimbabwe* 20°20S 28°29E 327 G2
Matosinhos *Portugal* 41°11N 8°42W 293 B1
Matroosberg *S. Africa* 33°23S 19°40E 328 E2
Maţruḩ *Oman* 23°37N 58°30E 319 C6
Matsue *Japan* 35°25N 133°10E 303 G6
Matsum, Ko *Thailand* 9°22N 99°59E 311 b
Matsumae *Japan* 41°26N 140°7E 302 D10
Matsumoto *Japan* 36°15N 138°0E 303 F9
Matsusaka *Japan* 34°34N 136°32E 303 G8
Matsuura *Japan* 33°20N 129°49E 303 H4
Matsuyama *Japan* 33°45N 132°45E 303 H6
Mattagami → *Canada* 50°43N 81°29W 344 B3
Mattancheri *India* 9°50N 76°15E 312 Q10
Mattawa *Canada* 46°20N 78°45W 344 C4
Matterhorn *Switz.* 45°58N 7°39E 292 D7
Matthew Town *Bahamas* 20°57N 73°40W 361 B5
Matthews Ridge *Guyana* 7°37N 60°10W 364 B6
Mattice *Canada* 49°40N 83°20W 344 C3
Mattituck *U.S.A.* 40°59N 72°32W 355 F12
Mattō *Japan* 36°31N 136°34E 303 F8
Mattoon *U.S.A.* 39°29N 88°23W 352 F9
Matuba *Mozam.* 24°28S 32°49E 329 C5
Matucana *Peru* 11°55S 76°25W 364 F3
Matuku *Fiji* 19°10S 179°44E 331 a
Matūn = Khowst *Afghan.* 33°22N 69°58E 314 C3
Matura B. *Trin. & Tob.* 10°39N 61°1W 365 K15
Maturín *Venezuela* 9°45N 63°11W 364 B6
Matusadona △ *Zimbabwe* 16°58S 28°42E 327 F2
Mau *Mad. P., India* 26°17N 78°41E 315 F8
Mau *Ut. P., India* 25°56N 83°33E 315 G10
Mau *Ut. P., India* 25°17N 81°23E 315 G9
Mau Escarpment *Kenya* 0°40S 36°0E 326 C4
Mau Ranipur *India* 25°16N 79°8E 315 G8
Maua *Kenya* 0°14N 37°56E 326 C4
Maubeuge *France* 50°17N 3°57E 292 A6
Maubin *Burma* 16°44N 95°39E 313 L19
Maud, Pt. *Australia* 23°6S 113°45E 332 D1
Maud Rise *S. Ocean* 66°0S 3°0E 277 C3
Maude *Australia* 34°29S 144°18E 335 E3
Maudin Sun *Burma* 16°0N 94°30E 313 M19
Maués *Brazil* 3°20S 57°45W 364 D7
Mauganj *India* 24°50N 81°55E 315 G9
Maughold Hd. *I. of Man* 54°18N 4°18W 284 C3
Maui *U.S.A.* 20°48N 156°20W 346 b
Maulamyaing = Moulmein *Burma* 16°30N 97°40E 313 L20
Maule □ *Chile* 36°5S 72°30W 366 D1
Maumee *U.S.A.* 41°34N 83°39W 353 E12
Maumee → *U.S.A.* 41°42N 83°28W 353 E12
Maumere *Indonesia* 8°38S 122°13E 309 F6
Maun *Botswana* 20°0S 23°26E 328 C3
Mauna Kea *U.S.A.* 19°50N 155°28W 346 b
Mauna Loa *U.S.A.* 19°30N 155°35W 346 b
Maungmagan Kyunzu *Burma* 14°0N 97°48E 310 E1
Maungu *Kenya* 3°33S 38°45E 326 C4
Maupin *U.S.A.* 45°11N 121°5W 348 D3
Maurepas, L. *U.S.A.* 30°15N 90°30W 357 F9
Maurice, L. *Australia* 29°30S 131°0E 333 E5
Mauricie △ *Canada* 46°45N 73°0W 344 C5
Mauritania ■ *Africa* 20°50N 10°0W 322 E3
Mauritius ■ *Ind. Oc.* 20°0S 57°0E 325 d
Mauston *U.S.A.* 43°48N 90°5W 352 D8
Mavli *India* 24°45N 73°55E 314 G5
Mavuradonha Mts. *Zimbabwe* 16°30S 31°30E 327 F3
Mawa *Dem. Rep. of the Congo* 2°45N 26°40E 326 B2
Mawai *India* 22°30N 81°4E 315 H9
Mawana *India* 29°6N 77°58E 314 E7
Mawand *Pakistan* 29°33N 68°38E 314 E3
Mawjib, W. al → *Jordan* 31°28N 35°36E 318 D4
Mawk Mai *Burma* 20°14N 97°37E 313 J20
Mawlaik *Burma* 23°40N 94°26E 313 H19
Mawlamyine = Moulmein *Burma* 16°30N 97°40E 313 L20
Mawqaq *Si. Arabia* 27°25N 41°8E 316 E4
Mawson Base *Antarctica* 67°30S 62°53E 277 C6
Mawson Coast *Antarctica* 68°30S 63°0E 277 C6
Max *U.S.A.* 47°49N 101°18W 352 B3
Maxcanú *Mexico* 20°35N 90°0W 359 C6
Maxesibeni *S. Africa* 30°49S 29°23E 329 E4
Maxhamish L. *Canada* 59°50N 123°17W 342 B4
Maxixe *Mozam.* 23°54S 35°17E 329 C6
Maxville *Canada* 45°17N 74°51W 355 A10
Maxwell *U.S.A.* 39°17N 122°11W 350 F4
Maxwelton *Australia* 20°43S 142°41E 334 C3
May, C. *U.S.A.* 38°56N 74°58W 353 F16
May Pen *Jamaica* 17°58N 77°15W 360 a
Maya → *Russia* 60°28N 134°28E 301 D14
Maya Mts. *Belize* 16°30N 89°0W 359 D7
Mayaguana *Bahamas* 22°30N 72°44W 361 B5
Mayagüez *Puerto Rico* 18°12N 67°9W 361 d
Mayāmey *Iran* 36°24N 55°42E 317 B7
Mayanup *Australia* 33°57S 116°27E 333 F2
Mayapán *Mexico* 20°29N 89°11W 359 C7
Mayarí *Cuba* 20°40N 75°41W 361 B4
Mayaro B. *Trin. & Tob.* 10°14N 60°59W 365 K16
Maybell *U.S.A.* 40°31N 108°5W 348 F9
Maybole *U.K.* 55°21N 4°42W 283 F4
Maydān *Iraq* 34°55N 45°37E 316 C5
Maydena *Australia* 42°45S 146°30E 335 G4
Mayenne → *France* 47°30N 0°32W 292 C3
Mayer *U.S.A.* 34°24N 112°14W 349 J7
Mayerthorpe *Canada* 53°57N 115°8W 342 C5
Mayfield *Ky., U.S.A.* 36°44N 88°38W 352 G9
Mayfield *N.Y., U.S.A.* 43°6N 74°16W 355 C10
Mayhill *U.S.A.* 32°53N 105°29W 349 K11
Maykop *Russia* 44°35N 40°10E 291 F7
Maymyo *Burma* 22°2N 96°28E 310 A1
Maynard *Mass., U.S.A.* 42°26N 71°27W 355 D13
Maynard *Wash., U.S.A.* 47°59N 122°55W 350 C4
Maynard Hills *Australia* 28°28S 119°49E 333 E2
Mayne → *Australia* 23°40S 141°55E 334 C3
Maynooth *Ireland* 53°23N 6°34W 282 C5
Mayo *Canada* 63°38N 135°57W 340 C6
Mayo □ *Ireland* 53°53N 9°3W 282 C2
Mayon Volcano *Phil.* 13°15N 123°41E 309 B6
Mayor I. *N.Z.* 37°16S 176°17E 331 B6
Mayotte ☒ *Ind. Oc.* 12°50S 45°10E 325 a
Maysān □ *Iraq* 31°55N 47°15E 316 D5
Maysville *U.S.A.* 38°39N 83°46W 353 F12
Mayu *Indonesia* 1°30N 126°30E 309 D7
Mayville *N. Dak., U.S.A.* 47°30N 97°20W 352 B5
Mayville *N.Y., U.S.A.* 42°15N 79°30W 354 D5
Mayya *Russia* 61°44N 130°18E 301 C14
Mazabuka *Zambia* 15°52S 27°44E 327 F2
Mazagán = El Jadida *Morocco* 33°11N 8°17W 322 B4
Mazagão *Brazil* 0°7S 51°16W 365 D8
Mazán *Peru* 3°30S 73°0W 364 D4
Māzandarān □ *Iran* 36°30N 52°0E 317 B7
Mazapil *Mexico* 24°39N 101°34W 358 C4
Mazar *China* 36°32N 77°1E 304 C2
Mazara del Vallo *Italy* 37°39N 12°35E 294 F5
Mazarrón *Spain* 37°38N 1°19W 293 D5
Mazaruni → *Guyana* 6°25N 58°35W 364 B7
Mazatán *Mexico* 29°0N 110°8W 358 B2
Mazatenango *Guatemala* 14°35N 91°30W 360 D1
Mazatlán *Mexico* 23°13N 106°25W 358 C3
Mažeikiai *Lithuania* 56°20N 22°20E 281 H20
Māzhān *Iran* 32°30N 59°0E 317 C8
Mazīnān *Iran* 36°19N 56°56E 317 B8
Mazoe *Mozam.* 16°42S 33°7E 327 F3
Mazoe → *Mozam.* 16°20S 33°30E 327 F3
Mazowe *Zimbabwe* 17°28S 30°58E 327 F3
Mazurian Lakes = Mazurski, Pojezierze *Poland* 53°50N 21°0E 289 B11
Mazurski, Pojezierze *Poland* 53°50N 21°0E 289 B11
Mazyr *Belarus* 51°59N 29°15E 289 B15
Mba *Fiji* 17°33S 177°41E 331 a
Mbabane *Swaziland* 26°18S 31°6E 329 D5
Mbaïki *C.A.R.* 3°53N 18°1E 324 D3
Mbala *Zambia* 8°46S 31°24E 327 D3
Mbalabala *Zimbabwe* 20°27S 29°3E 329 C4
Mbale *Uganda* 1°8N 34°12E 326 B3
Mbalmayo *Cameroon* 3°33N 11°33E 324 D2
Mbamba Bay *Tanzania* 11°13S 34°49E 327 E3
Mbandaka *Dem. Rep. of the Congo* 0°1N 18°18E 324 D3
Mbanza Congo *Angola* 6°18S 14°16E 324 F2
Mbanza Ngungu *Dem. Rep. of the Congo* 5°12S 14°53E 324 F2
Mbarangandu *Tanzania* 10°11S 36°48E 327 D4
Mbarara *Uganda* 0°35S 30°40E 326 C3
Mbengga = Beqa *Fiji* 18°23S 178°8E 331 a
Mbenkuru → *Tanzania* 9°25S 39°50E 327 D4
Mberengwa *Zimbabwe* 20°29S 29°57E 327 G2
Mberengwa, Mt. *Zimbabwe* 20°37S 29°55E 327 G2
Mbesuma *Zambia* 10°0S 32°2E 327 E3
Mbeya *Tanzania* 8°54S 33°29E 327 D3
Mbeya □ *Tanzania* 8°15S 33°30E 326 D3
Mbhashe → *S. Africa* 32°15S 28°54E 329 E4
Mbinga *Tanzania* 10°50S 35°0E 327 E4
Mbini = Río Muni □ *Eq. Guin.* 1°30N 10°0E 324 D2
Mbour *Senegal* 14°22N 16°54W 322 F2
Mbuji-Mayi *Dem. Rep. of the Congo* 6°9S 23°40E 326 D1
Mbulu *Tanzania* 3°45S 35°30E 326 C4
Mburucuyá *Argentina* 28°1S 58°14W 366 B4
Mchinja *Tanzania* 9°44S 39°45E 327 D4
Mchinji *Malawi* 13°47S 32°58E 327 E3
Mdantsane *S. Africa* 32°56S 27°46E 325 L5
Mead, L. *U.S.A.* 36°0N 114°44W 351 J12
Meade *U.S.A.* 37°17N 100°20W 352 G3
Meadow Lake *Canada* 54°10N 108°26W 343 C7
Meadow Lake ⌓ *Canada* 54°27N 109°0W 343 C7
Meadow Valley Wash → *U.S.A.* 36°40N 114°34W 351 J12
Meadville *U.S.A.* 41°39N 80°9W 354 E4
Meaford *Canada* 44°36N 80°35W 354 B4
Mealy Mts. *Canada* 53°10N 58°0W 345 B8
Meander River *Canada* 59°2N 117°42W 342 B5
Meares, C. *U.S.A.* 45°37N 124°0W 348 D1
Mearim → *Brazil* 3°4S 44°35W 365 D10
Meath □ *Ireland* 53°40N 6°57W 282 C5
Meath Park *Canada* 53°27N 105°22W 343 C7
Meaux *France* 48°58N 2°50E 292 B5
Mebechi-Gawa → *Japan* 40°31N 141°31E 302 D10
Mebulu, Tanjung *Indonesia* 8°50S 115°5E 309 K18
Mecanhelas *Mozam.* 15°12S 35°54E 327 F4
Mecca = Makkah *Si. Arabia* 21°30N 39°54E 319 C2

Mecca U.S.A. 33°34N 116°5W 351 M10
Mechanicsburg U.S.A. 40°13N 77°1W 354 F8
Mechanicville U.S.A. 42°54N 73°41W 355 D11
Mechelen Belgium 51°2N 4°29E 287 C4
Mecheria Algeria 33°35N 0°18W 322 B5
Mecklenburg Germany 53°33N 11°40E 288 B7
Mecklenburger Bucht Germany 54°20N 11°40E 288 A6
Meconta Mozam. 14°59S 39°50E 327 E4
Medan Indonesia 3°40N 98°38E 308 D1
Médanos de Coro △ Venezuela 11°35N 69°44W 361 D6
Medanosa, Pta. Argentina 48°8S 66°0W 368 F3
Médéa Algeria 36°12N 2°50E 322 A6
Medellín Colombia 6°15N 75°35W 364 B3
Medelpad Sweden 62°33N 16°30E 280 E17
Medemblik Neths. 52°46N 5°8E 287 B5
Medford Mass., U.S.A. 42°25N 71°7W 355 D13
Medford Oreg., U.S.A. 42°19N 122°52W 348 E2
Medford Wis., U.S.A. 45°9N 90°20W 352 C8
Medgidia Romania 44°15N 28°19E 289 F15
Media Agua Argentina 31°58S 68°25W 366 C2
Media Luna Argentina 34°45S 66°44W 366 C2
Medianeira Brazil 25°17S 54°5W 367 B5
Mediaş Romania 46°9N 24°22E 289 E13
Medicine Bow U.S.A. 41°54N 106°12W 348 F10
Medicine Bow Mts. U.S.A. 40°40N 106°0W 348 F10
Medicine Bow Pk. U.S.A. 41°21N 106°19W 348 F10
Medicine Hat Canada 50°0N 110°45W 343 D6
Medicine Lake U.S.A. 48°30N 104°30W 348 B11
Medicine Lodge U.S.A. 37°17N 98°35W 352 G4
Medina = Al Madīnah Si. Arabia 24°35N 39°52E 316 E3
Medina N. Dak., U.S.A. 46°54N 99°18W 352 B4
Medina N.Y., U.S.A. 43°13N 78°23W 354 C6
Medina Ohio, U.S.A. 41°8N 81°52W 354 E3
Medina → U.S.A. 29°16N 98°29W 356 G5
Medina del Campo Spain 41°18N 4°55W 293 B3
Medina L. U.S.A. 29°32N 98°56W 356 G5
Medina Sidonia Spain 36°28N 5°57W 293 D3
Medinipur India 22°25N 87°21E 315 H12
Mediterranean Sea Europe 35°0N 15°0E 278 H7
Médoc France 45°10N 0°50W 292 D3
Medveditsa → Russia 49°35N 42°41E 291 E7
Medvezhi, Ostrava Russia 71°0N 161°0E 301 B17
Medvezhyegorsk Russia 63°0N 34°25E 290 B5
Medway □ U.K. 51°25N 0°32E 285 F8
Medway → U.K. 51°27N 0°46E 285 F8
Meekatharra Australia 26°32S 118°29E 333 E2
Meeker U.S.A. 40°2N 107°55W 348 F10
Meelpaeg L. Canada 48°20N 56°30W 345 C8
Meerut India 29°1N 77°42E 314 E7
Meeteetse U.S.A. 44°9N 108°52W 348 D9
Mega Ethiopia 3°57N 38°19E 319 G2
Megara Greece 37°58N 23°22E 295 F10
Megasini India 21°38N 86°21E 315 J12
Meghalaya □ India 25°50N 91°0E 313 G17
Meghna → Bangla. 22°50N 90°50E 313 H17
Mégiscane, L. Canada 48°35N 75°55W 344 C4
Meharry, Mt. Australia 22°59S 118°35E 332 D2
Mehlville U.S.A. 38°31N 90°19W 352 F8
Mehndawal India 26°58N 83°5E 315 F10
Mehr Jān Iran 33°50N 55°6E 317 C7
Mehrābād Iran 36°53N 47°55E 316 B5
Mehrān Iran 33°7N 46°10E 316 C5
Mehrgarh Pakistan 29°30N 67°30E 314 E2
Mehrīz Iran 31°35N 54°28E 317 D7
Mei Xian China 34°18N 107°55E 306 G4
Meighen I. Canada 80°0N 99°30W 341 B10
Meihekou China 42°32N 125°40E 307 C13
Meiktila Burma 20°53N 95°54E 313 J19
Meissen Germany 51°9N 13°29E 288 C7
Meizhou China 24°16N 116°6E 305 D6
Meja India 25°9N 82°7E 315 G10
Mejillones Chile 23°10S 70°30W 366 A1
Mekele Ethiopia 13°33N 39°30E 319 E2
Mekerghene, Sebkra Algeria 26°21N 1°30E 322 C6
Mekhtar Pakistan 30°30N 69°15E 312 D6
Meknès Morocco 33°57N 5°33W 322 B4
Mekong → Asia 9°30N 106°15E 311 H6
Mekongga Indonesia 3°39S 121°15E 309 E6
Mekvari = Kür → Azerbaijan 39°29N 49°15E 291 G8
Melagiri Hills India 12°20N 77°30E 312 N10
Melaka Malaysia 2°15N 102°15E 311 L4
Melalap Malaysia 5°10N 116°5E 308 C5
Melambes Greece 35°8N 24°40E 297 D6
Melanesia Pac. Oc. 4°0S 155°0E 336 H7
Melanesian Basin Pac. Oc. 0°5N 160°35E 336 G8
Melaya Indonesia 8°17S 114°30E 309 J17
Melbourne Australia 37°48S 144°58E 335 F4
Melbourne U.S.A. 28°5N 80°37W 357 G14
Melchor Múzquiz Mexico 27°53N 101°31W 358 B4
Melchor Ocampo Mexico 24°51N 101°39W 358 C4
Mélèzes → Canada 57°40N 69°29W 344 A5
Melfort Canada 52°50N 104°37W 343 C8
Melfort Zimbabwe 18°0S 31°25E 327 F3
Melhus Norway 63°17N 10°18E 280 E14
Melilla N. Afr. 35°21N 2°57W 293 E4
Melipilla Chile 33°42S 71°15W 366 C1
Melissa, Akra Greece 35°6N 24°33E 297 D6
Melita Canada 49°15N 101°0W 343 D8
Melitopol Ukraine 46°50N 35°22E 291 E6
Melk Austria 48°13N 15°20E 288 D8
Mellansel Sweden 63°26N 18°19E 280 E18
Mellen U.S.A. 46°20N 90°40W 352 B8
Mellerud Sweden 58°41N 12°28E 281 G15
Mellette U.S.A. 45°9N 98°30W 352 C4
Mellieha Malta 35°57N 14°22E 297 D1
Melo Uruguay 32°20S 54°10W 367 C5
Melolo Indonesia 9°53S 120°40E 309 F6
Melouprey Cambodia 13°48N 105°16E 310 F5
Melrhir, Chott Algeria 34°13N 6°30E 322 B7
Melrose Australia 32°42S 146°57E 335 E4
Melrose U.K. 55°36N 2°43W 283 F6
Melrose Minn., U.S.A. 45°40N 94°49W 352 C6
Melrose N. Mex., U.S.A. 34°26N 103°38W 349 J12
Melstone U.S.A. 46°36N 107°52W 348 C10
Melton Mowbray U.K. 52°47N 0°54W 284 E7
Melun France 48°32N 2°39E 292 B5
Melville Canada 50°55N 102°50W 343 C8
Melville, C. Australia 14°11S 144°30E 334 A3
Melville, L. Canada 53°30N 60°0W 345 B8
Melville B. Australia 12°0S 136°45E 334 A2
Melville I. Australia 11°30S 131°0E 332 B5
Melville I. Canada 75°30N 112°0W 341 B8
Melville Pen. Canada 68°0N 84°0W 341 C11
Melvin, Lough Ireland 54°26N 8°10W 282 B3
Memba Mozam. 14°11S 40°30E 327 E5
Memboro Indonesia 9°30S 119°30E 309 F5
Memel = Klaipėda Lithuania 55°43N 21°10E 281 J19
Memel S. Africa 27°38S 29°36E 329 D4
Memmingen Germany 47°58N 10°10E 288 E6
Mempawah Indonesia 0°30N 109°5E 308 D3
Memphis Mich., U.S.A. 42°54N 82°46W 354 D2
Memphis Tenn., U.S.A. 35°8N 90°2W 357 D9
Memphis Tex., U.S.A. 34°44N 100°33W 356 D4
Memphrémagog, L. N. Amer. 45°8N 72°17W 355 B12
Mena U.S.A. 34°35N 94°15W 356 D7
Menai Strait U.K. 53°11N 4°13W 284 D3
Ménaka Mali 15°59N 2°18E 322 E6
Menan = Chao Phraya → Thailand 13°40N 100°31E 310 F3
Menarandra → Madag. 25°17S 44°30E 329 D7
Menard U.S.A. 30°55N 99°47W 356 F5
Menard Fracture Zone Pac. Oc. 43°0S 97°0W 337 M18
Mendaña Fracture Zone Pac. Oc. 16°0S 91°0W 337 J18
Mendawai → Indonesia 3°30S 113°0E 308 E4
Mende France 44°31N 3°30E 292 D5
Mendeleyev Ridge Arctic 80°0N 178°0W 276 B17
Mendhar India 33°35N 74°10E 315 C6
Mendip Hills U.K. 51°17N 2°40W 285 F5
Mendocino U.S.A. 39°19N 123°48W 348 G2
Mendocino, C. U.S.A. 40°26N 124°25W 348 F1
Mendocino Fracture Zone Pac. Oc. 40°0N 142°0W 337 D13
Mendota Calif., U.S.A. 36°45N 120°23W 350 J6
Mendota Ill., U.S.A. 41°33N 89°7W 352 E9
Mendoyo Indonesia 8°23S 114°42E 309 J17
Mendoza Argentina 32°50S 68°52W 366 C2
Mendoza □ Argentina 33°0S 69°0W 366 C2
Mene Grande Venezuela 9°49N 70°56W 364 B4
Menemen Turkey 38°34N 27°3E 295 E12
Menen Belgium 50°47N 3°7E 287 D3
Menggala Indonesia 4°30S 105°15E 308 E3
Mengjin China 34°55N 112°45E 306 G7
Mengyin China 35°40N 117°58E 307 G9
Mengzi China 23°20N 103°22E 304 D5
Menihek Canada 54°28N 56°36W 345 B6
Menihek L. Canada 54°0N 67°0W 345 B6
Menin = Menen Belgium 50°47N 3°7E 287 D3
Menindee Australia 32°20S 142°25E 335 E3
Menindee L. Australia 32°20S 142°25E 335 E3
Meningie Australia 35°50S 139°18E 335 F2
Menjangan, Pulau Indonesia 8°7S 114°31E 309 J17
Menlo Park U.S.A. 37°27N 122°12W 350 H4
Menominee U.S.A. 45°6N 87°37W 352 C10
Menominee → U.S.A. 45°6N 87°35W 352 C10
Menomonie U.S.A. 44°53N 91°55W 352 C8
Menongue Angola 14°48S 17°52E 325 G3
Menorca Spain 40°0N 4°0E 296 B11
Mentakab Malaysia 3°29N 102°21E 311 L4
Mentawai, Kepulauan Indonesia 2°0S 99°0E 308 E1
Menton France 43°50N 7°29E 292 E7
Mentor U.S.A. 41°40N 81°21W 354 E3
Menzelinsk Russia 55°47N 53°11E 290 C9
Menzies Australia 29°40S 121°2E 333 E3
Meob B. Namibia 24°25S 14°34E 328 C1
Me'ona Israel 33°1N 35°15E 318 B4
Meoqui Mexico 28°17N 105°29W 358 B3
Mepaco Mozam. 15°57S 30°48E 327 F3
Meppel Neths. 52°42N 6°12E 287 B6
Merak Indonesia 6°10N 106°26E 309 F12
Meramangye, L. Australia 28°25S 132°13E 333 E5
Meran = Merano Italy 46°40N 11°9E 294 A4
Merano Italy 46°40N 11°9E 294 A4
Merauke Indonesia 8°29S 140°24E 309 F10
Merbein Australia 34°10S 142°2E 335 E3
Merbuk, Gunung Indonesia 8°13S 114°39E 309 J17
Merca Somali Rep. 1°48N 44°50E 319 G3
Merced U.S.A. 37°18N 120°29W 350 H6
Merced → U.S.A. 37°21N 120°59W 350 H6
Merced Pk. U.S.A. 37°36N 119°24W 350 H7
Mercedes B. Aires, Argentina 34°40S 59°30W 366 C4
Mercedes Corrientes, Argentina 29°10S 58°5W 366 B4
Mercedes San Luis, Argentina 33°40S 65°21W 366 C2
Mercedes Uruguay 33°12S 58°0W 366 C4
Merceditas Chile 28°20S 70°35W 366 B1
Mercer N.Z. 37°16S 175°5E 331 B5
Mercer U.S.A. 41°14N 80°15W 354 E4
Mercer Island U.S.A. 47°34N 122°13W 350 C4
Mercury U.S.A. 36°40N 115°59W 351 J11
Mercy, C. Canada 65°0N 63°30W 341 C13
Mere U.K. 51°6N 2°16W 285 F5
Meredith, C. Falk. Is. 52°15S 60°40W 368 G4
Meredith, L. U.S.A. 35°43N 101°33W 356 D4
Mergui Burma 12°26N 98°34E 310 F2
Mergui Arch. = Myeik Kyunzu Burma 11°30N 97°30E 311 G1
Mérida Mexico 20°58N 89°37W 359 C7
Mérida Spain 38°55N 6°25W 293 C2
Mérida Venezuela 8°24N 71°8W 364 B4
Mérida, Cord. de Venezuela 9°0N 71°0W 364 B4
Meriden U.K. 52°26N 1°38W 285 E6
Meriden U.S.A. 41°32N 72°48W 355 E12
Meridian Calif., U.S.A. 39°9N 121°55W 350 F5
Meridian Idaho, U.S.A. 43°37N 116°24W 348 E5
Meridian Miss., U.S.A. 32°22N 88°42W 357 E10
Merinda Australia 20°2S 148°11E 334 C4
Merir Pac. Oc. 4°10N 132°30E 309 D8
Merirumã Brazil 1°15N 54°50W 365 C8
Merkel U.S.A. 32°28N 100°1W 356 E4
Mermaid Reef Australia 17°6S 119°36E 332 C2
Merredin Australia 31°28S 118°18E 333 F2
Merrick U.K. 55°8N 4°28W 283 F4
Merrickville Canada 44°55N 75°50W 355 B9
Merrill Oreg., U.S.A. 42°1N 121°36W 348 E3
Merrill Wis., U.S.A. 45°11N 89°41W 352 C9
Merrimack → U.S.A. 42°49N 70°49W 355 D14
Merriman U.S.A. 42°55N 101°42W 352 D3
Merritt Canada 50°10N 120°45W 342 C4
Merritt Island U.S.A. 28°21N 80°42W 357 G14
Merriwa Australia 32°6S 150°22E 335 E5
Merry I. Canada 55°29N 77°31W 344 A4
Merryville U.S.A. 30°45N 93°33W 356 F8
Mersch Lux. 49°44N 6°7E 287 E6
Mersea I. U.K. 51°47N 0°58E 285 F8
Merseburg Germany 51°22N 11°59E 288 C6
Mersey → U.K. 53°25N 3°1W 284 D4
Merseyside □ U.K. 53°31N 3°2W 284 D4
Mersin = İçel Turkey 36°51N 34°36E 316 B2
Mersing Malaysia 2°25N 103°50E 311 L4
Merta India 26°39N 74°4E 314 F6
Merta Road India 26°43N 73°55E 314 F5
Merthyr Tydfil U.K. 51°45N 3°22W 285 F4
Merthyr Tydfil □ U.K. 51°46N 3°21W 285 F4
Merti Kenya 1°4N 38°40E 326 B4
Mértola Portugal 37°40N 7°40W 293 D2
Mertzon U.S.A. 31°16N 100°49W 356 F4
Meru Kenya 0°3N 37°40E 326 B4
Meru Tanzania 3°15S 36°46E 326 C4
Meru △ Kenya 0°5N 38°10E 326 B4
Mesa U.S.A. 33°25N 111°50W 349 K8
Mesa Verde △ U.S.A. 37°11N 108°29W 349 H9
Mesanagros Greece 36°1N 27°49E 297 C9
Mesaoría Cyprus 35°12N 33°14E 297 D12
Mesgouez, L. Canada 51°20N 75°0W 344 B5
Meshed = Mashhad Iran 36°20N 59°35E 317 B8
Meshoppen U.S.A. 41°36N 76°3W 355 E8
Mesilinka → Canada 56°6N 124°30W 342 B4
Mesologi Greece 38°21N 21°28E 295 E9
Mesongi Greece 39°29N 19°56E 297 B3
Mesopotamia = Al Jazirah Iraq 33°30N 44°0E 316 C5
Mesopotamia U.S.A. 41°27N 80°57W 354 E4
Mesquite U.S.A. 36°48N 114°4W 349 H6
Messaad Algeria 34°8N 3°30E 322 B6
Messalo → Mozam. 12°25S 39°15E 327 E4
Messara, Kolpos Greece 35°6N 24°47E 297 D6
Messina = Musina S. Africa 22°20S 30°5E 329 C5
Messina Italy 38°11N 15°34E 294 E6
Messina, Str. di Italy 38°15N 15°35E 294 F6
Messini Greece 37°4N 22°1E 295 F10
Messiniakos Kolpos Greece 36°45N 22°5E 295 F10
Mesta → Bulgaria 40°54N 24°49E 295 D11
Meta → S. Amer. 6°12N 67°28W 364 B5
Meta Incognita Pen. Canada 62°45N 68°30W 341 C13
Metabetchouan Canada 48°26N 71°52W 345 C5
Metairie U.S.A. 29°59N 90°9W 357 G9
Metaline Falls U.S.A. 48°52N 117°22W 348 B5
Metán Argentina 25°30S 65°0W 366 B3
Metangula Mozam. 12°40S 34°50E 327 E3
Metengobalame Mozam. 14°49S 34°30E 327 E3
Methven N.Z. 43°38S 171°40E 331 E3
Metil Mozam. 16°24S 39°0E 327 F4
Metlakatla U.S.A. 55°8N 131°35W 340 D6
Metropolis U.S.A. 37°9N 88°44W 352 G9
Metu Ethiopia 8°18N 35°35E 319 F2
Metz France 49°8N 6°10E 292 B7
Meulaboh Indonesia 4°11N 96°3E 308 D1
Meureudu Indonesia 5°19N 96°10E 308 C1
Meuse → Europe 50°45N 5°41E 287 D5
Mexia U.S.A. 31°41N 96°29W 356 F6
Mexiana, I. Brazil 0°0 49°30W 365 D9
Mexicali Mexico 32°40N 115°30W 351 N11
Mexican Plateau Mexico 25°0N 104°0W 338 G9
Mexican Water U.S.A. 36°57N 109°32W 349 H9
México Mexico 19°24N 99°9W 359 D5
Mexico Maine, U.S.A. 44°34N 70°33W 355 B14
Mexico Mo., U.S.A. 39°10N 91°53W 352 F8
Mexico N.Y., U.S.A. 43°28N 76°14W 355 C8
México □ Mexico 19°20N 99°30W 359 D5
Mexico ■ Cent. Amer. 25°0N 105°0W 358 C4
México, Ciudad de Mexico 19°24N 99°9W 359 D5
Mexico, G. of Cent. Amer. 25°0N 90°0W 359 C7
Mexico B. U.S.A. 43°35N 76°20W 355 C8
Meydān-e Naftūn Iran 31°56N 49°18E 317 D6
Meydani, Ra's-e Iran 25°24N 59°6E 317 E8
Meyers Chuck U.S.A. 55°45N 132°15W 342 B2
Meymaneh Afghan. 35°53N 64°38E 312 B4
Mezen Russia 65°50N 44°20E 290 A7
Mezen → Russia 65°44N 44°22E 290 A7
Mézenc, Mt. France 44°54N 4°11E 292 D6
Mezhdurechenskiy Russia 59°36N 65°56E 300 D7
Mezőkövesd Hungary 47°49N 20°35E 289 E11
Mezőtúr Hungary 47°1N 20°41E 289 E11
Mezquital Mexico 23°29N 104°23W 358 C4
Mfolozi → S. Africa 28°25S 32°26E 329 D5
Mgeta Tanzania 8°22S 36°6E 327 D4
Mhlaba Hills Zimbabwe 18°30S 30°30E 327 F3
Mhow India 22°33N 75°50E 314 H6
Miahuatlán Mexico 16°20N 96°36W 359 D5
Miami Fla., U.S.A. 25°46N 80°11W 357 J14
Miami Okla., U.S.A. 36°53N 94°53W 356 C7
Miami Tex., U.S.A. 35°42N 100°38W 356 D4
Miami Beach U.S.A. 25°47N 80°7W 357 J14
Mian Xian China 33°10N 106°32E 306 H4
Mianchi China 34°48N 111°48E 306 G6
Miāndarreh Iran 35°37N 53°39E 317 C7
Miāndowāb Iran 37°0N 46°5E 316 B5
Miandrivazo Madag. 19°31S 45°29E 329 B8
Miāneh Iran 37°30N 47°40E 316 B5
Mianwali Pakistan 32°38N 71°28E 314 C4
Mianyang China 31°22N 104°47E 304 C5
Miarinarivo Antananarivo, Madag. 18°57S 46°55E 329 B8
Miarinarivo Toamasina, Madag. 16°38S 48°15E 329 B8
Miariravaratra Madag. 20°13S 47°31E 329 C8
Miass Russia 54°59N 60°6E 290 D11
Mica S. Africa 24°10S 30°48E 329 C5
Michalovce Slovak Rep. 48°47N 21°58E 289 D11
Michigan □ U.S.A. 44°0N 85°0W 353 C11
Michigan, L. U.S.A. 44°0N 87°0W 352 D10
Michigan City U.S.A. 41°43N 86°54W 352 E10
Michipicoten I. Canada 47°40N 85°40W 344 C2
Michoacán □ Mexico 19°10N 101°50W 358 D4
Michurin Bulgaria 42°9N 27°51E 295 C12
Michurinsk Russia 52°58N 40°27E 290 D7
Mico, Pta. Nic. 12°0N 83°30W 360 D3
Micoud St. Lucia 13°49N 60°54W 361 f
Micronesia Pac. Oc. 11°0N 160°0E 336 G7
Micronesia, Federated States of ■ Pac. Oc. 9°0N 150°0E 330 A8
Mid-Pacific Seamounts Pac. Oc. 18°0N 177°0W 336 F10
Midai Indonesia 3°0N 107°47E 308 D3
Midale Canada 49°25N 103°20W 343 D8
Middelburg Neths. 51°30N 3°36E 287 C3
Middelburg Eastern Cape, S. Africa 31°30S 25°0E 328 E4
Middelburg Mpumalanga, S. Africa 25°49S 29°28E 329 D4
Middelpos S. Africa 31°55S 20°13E 328 E3
Middelwit S. Africa 24°51S 27°3E 328 C4
Middle Alkali L. U.S.A. 41°27N 120°5W 348 F3
Middle America Trench = Guatemala Trench Pac. Oc. 14°0N 95°0W 338 H10
Middle Bass I. U.S.A. 41°41N 82°48W 354 E2
Middle East Asia 35°0N 40°0E 298 E5
Middle Fork Feather → U.S.A. 38°33N 121°30W 350 F5
Middle I. Australia 34°6S 123°11E 333 F3
Middle Loup → U.S.A. 41°17N 98°24W 352 E4
Middle Sackville Canada 44°47N 63°42W 345 D7
Middleboro U.S.A. 41°54N 70°55W 355 E14
Middleburg Fla., U.S.A. 30°4N 81°52W 357 F14
Middleburg Pa., U.S.A. 40°47N 77°3W 354 F7
Middleburgh U.S.A. 42°36N 74°20W 355 D10
Middlebury U.S.A. 44°1N 73°10W 355 B11
Middlemount Australia 22°50S 148°40E 334 C4
Middleport N.Y., U.S.A. 43°13N 78°29W 354 C6
Middleport Ohio, U.S.A. 39°0N 82°3W 353 F12
Middlesboro U.S.A. 36°36N 83°43W 353 G12
Middlesbrough U.K. 54°35N 1°13W 284 C6
Middlesbrough □ U.K. 54°28N 1°13W 284 C6
Middlesex Belize 17°2N 88°31W 360 C2
Middlesex N.J., U.S.A. 40°36N 74°30W 355 F10
Middlesex N.Y., U.S.A. 42°42N 77°16W 354 D7
Middleton Australia 22°22S 141°32E 334 C3
Middleton Canada 44°57N 65°4W 345 D6
Middleton Cr. → Australia 22°35S 141°51E 334 C3
Middletown U.K. 54°17N 6°51W 282 B5
Middletown Calif., U.S.A. 38°45N 122°37W 350 G4
Middletown Conn., U.S.A. 41°34N 72°39W 355 E12
Middletown N.Y., U.S.A. 41°27N 74°25W 355 E10
Middletown Ohio, U.S.A. 39°31N 84°24W 353 F11
Middletown Pa., U.S.A. 40°12N 76°44W 355 F8
Midge Point Australia 20°39S 148°43E 334 J6
Midhurst U.K. 50°59N 0°44W 285 G7
Midi, Canal du → France 43°45N 1°21E 292 E4
Midland Australia 31°54S 116°1E 333 F2
Midland Canada 44°45N 79°50W 354 B5
Midland Calif., U.S.A. 33°52N 114°48W 351 M12
Midland Mich., U.S.A. 43°37N 84°14W 353 D11
Midland Pa., U.S.A. 40°39N 80°27W 354 F4
Midland Tex., U.S.A. 32°0N 102°3W 356 F3
Midlands □ Zimbabwe 19°40S 29°0E 327 F2
Midleton Ireland 51°55N 8°10W 282 E3
Midlothian □ U.K. 55°51N 3°5W 283 F5
Midongy, Tangorombohitr' i Madag. 23°30S 47°0E 329 C8
Midongy Atsimo Madag. 23°35S 47°1E 329 C8
Midway Is. Pac. Oc. 28°13N 177°22W 336 E10
Midway Wells U.S.A. 32°41N 115°7W 351 N11
Midwest U.S.A. 42°0N 90°0W 347 B9
Midwest Wyo., U.S.A. 43°25N 106°16W 348 E10
Midwest City U.S.A. 35°27N 97°24W 356 D6
Midyat Turkey 37°25N 41°23E 316 B4
Midžor Bulgaria 43°24N 22°40E 295 C10
Mie □ Japan 34°30N 136°10E 303 G8
Międzychód Poland 52°35N 15°53E 288 B8
Międzyrzec Podlaski Poland 51°58N 22°45E 289 C12
Mielec Poland 50°15N 21°25E 289 C11
Mienga Angola 17°12S 19°48E 328 B2
Miercurea-Ciuc Romania 46°21N 25°48E 289 E13
Mieres Spain 43°18N 5°48W 293 A3
Mifflintown U.S.A. 40°34N 77°24W 354 F7
Mifraz Ḥefa Israel 32°52N 35°0E 318 C4
Migori Kenya 1°4S 34°28E 326 C3
Miguel Alemán, Presa Mexico 18°15N 96°32W 359 D5
Mihara Japan 34°24N 133°5E 303 G6
Mikese Tanzania 6°48S 37°55E 326 D4
Mikhaylovgrad = Montana Bulgaria 43°27N 23°16E 295 C10
Mikhaylovka Russia 50°3N 43°5E 291 D7
Mikines Greece 37°43N 22°46E 295 F10
Mikkeli Finland 61°43N 27°15E 280 F22
Mikkwa → Canada 58°25N 114°46W 342 B6
Míkonos = Mykonos Greece 37°30N 25°25E 295 F11
Mikumi Tanzania 7°26S 37°0E 326 D4
Mikumi △ Tanzania 7°35S 37°15E 326 D4
Mikun Russia 62°20N 50°0E 290 B9
Milaca U.S.A. 45°45N 93°39W 352 C7
Milagro Ecuador 2°11S 79°36W 364 D3
Milan = Milano Italy 45°28N 9°10E 292 D8
Milan Mo., U.S.A. 40°12N 93°7W 352 E7
Milan Tenn., U.S.A. 35°55N 88°46W 357 D10
Milange Mozam. 16°3S 35°45E 327 F4
Milano Italy 45°28N 9°10E 292 D8
Milanoa Madag. 13°35S 49°47E 329 A8
Milâs Turkey 37°20N 27°50E 295 F12
Milatos Greece 35°18N 25°34E 297 D7
Milazzo Italy 38°13N 15°15E 294 E6
Milbank U.S.A. 45°13N 96°38W 352 C5
Milbanke Sd. Canada 52°19N 128°33W 342 C3
Milden Canada 51°29N 107°32W 343 C7
Mildenhall U.K. 52°21N 0°32E 285 E8
Mildmay Canada 44°3N 81°7W 354 B3
Mildura Australia 34°13S 142°9E 335 E3
Miles Australia 26°40S 150°9E 335 D5
Miles City U.S.A. 46°25N 105°51W 348 C11
Milestone Canada 49°59N 104°31W 343 D8
Miletus Turkey 37°30N 27°18E 295 F12
Milford Calif., U.S.A. 40°10N 120°22W 350 E6
Milford Conn., U.S.A. 41°14N 73°3W 355 E11
Milford Del., U.S.A. 38°55N 75°26W 353 F16
Milford Mass., U.S.A. 42°8N 71°31W 355 D13
Milford N.H., U.S.A. 42°50N 71°39W 355 D13
Milford Pa., U.S.A. 41°19N 74°48W 355 E10
Milford Utah, U.S.A. 38°24N 113°1W 348 G7
Milford Haven U.K. 51°42N 5°7W 285 F2
Milford Sd. N.Z. 44°41S 167°47E 331 F1
Milford Sound N.Z. 44°41S 167°55E 331 F1
Milḩ, Baḩr al = Razāzah, Buḩayrat ar Iraq 32°40N 43°35E 316 C4
Milikapiti Australia 11°26S 130°40E 332 B5
Miling Australia 30°30S 116°17E 333 F2
Milk River Canada 49°10N 112°5W 342 D6
Mill I. Antarctica 66°0S 101°30E 277 C8
Mill Valley U.S.A. 37°54N 122°32W 350 H4
Millau France 44°8N 3°4E 292 D5
Millbridge Canada 44°41N 77°36W 354 B7
Millbrook Canada 44°10N 78°29W 354 B6
Millbrook Ala., U.S.A. 32°29N 86°22W 357 E11
Millbrook N.Y., U.S.A. 41°47N 73°42W 355 E11
Mille Lacs, L. des Canada 48°45N 90°35W 344 C1
Mille Lacs L. U.S.A. 46°15N 93°39W 352 B7
Milledgeville U.S.A. 33°5N 83°14W 357 E13
Millen U.S.A. 32°48N 81°57W 357 E14
Millennium I. = Caroline I. Kiribati 9°58S 150°13W 337 H12
Miller U.S.A. 44°31N 98°59W 352 C4
Millersburg Ohio, U.S.A. 40°33N 81°55W 354 F3
Millersburg Pa., U.S.A. 40°32N 76°58W 354 F8
Millerton U.S.A. 41°57N 73°31W 355 E11
Millerton L. U.S.A. 37°1N 119°41W 350 J7
Millet St. Lucia 13°55N 60°59W 361 f
Millheim U.S.A. 40°54N 77°29W 354 F7
Millicent Australia 37°34S 140°21E 335 F3
Millington U.S.A. 35°20N 89°53W 357 D10
Millinocket U.S.A. 45°39N 68°43W 353 C19
Millmerran Australia 27°53S 151°16E 335 D5
Millom U.K. 54°13N 3°16W 284 C4
Mills L. Canada 61°30N 118°20W 342 A5
Millsboro U.S.A. 40°0N 80°0W 354 G5
Millstream Chichester △ Australia 21°35S 117°6E 332 D2
Millstreet Ireland 52°4N 9°4W 282 D2
Milltown Malbay Ireland 52°52N 9°24W 282 D2
Millville N.J., U.S.A. 39°24N 75°2W 353 F16
Millville Pa., U.S.A. 41°7N 76°32W 355 E8
Millwood L. U.S.A. 33°42N 93°58W 356 E8
Milne → Australia 21°10S 137°33E 334 C2
Milo U.S.A. 45°15N 68°59W 353 C19
Milon, Akra Greece 36°15N 28°11E 297 C10
Milos Greece 36°44N 24°25E 295 F11
Milparinka Australia 29°46S 141°57E 335 D3
Milpitas U.S.A. 37°26N 121°55W 350 H5
Milton N.S., Canada 44°4N 64°45W 345 D7
Milton Ont., Canada 43°31N 79°53W 354 C5
Milton N.Z. 46°7S 169°59E 331 G2
Milton Calif., U.S.A. 38°3N 120°51W 350 G6
Milton Fla., U.S.A. 30°38N 87°3W 357 F11
Milton Pa., U.S.A. 41°1N 76°51W 354 F8
Milton Vt., U.S.A. 44°38N 73°7W 355 B11
Milton-Freewater U.S.A. 45°56N 118°23W 348 D4
Milton Keynes U.K. 52°1N 0°44W 285 E7
Milton Keynes □ U.K. 52°1N 0°44W 285 E7
Milverton Canada 43°34N 80°55W 354 C4
Milwaukee U.S.A. 43°2N 87°54W 352 D10
Milwaukee Deep Atl. Oc. 19°50N 68°0W 361 C6
Milwaukie U.S.A. 45°26N 122°38W 350 E4
Min Jiang → Fujian, China 26°0N 119°35E 305 D6

Min Jiang → Sichuan, China 28°45N 104°40E 304 D5
Min Xian China 34°25N 104°5E 306 G3
Minā' Jabal 'Alī U.A.E. 25°2N 55°8E 317 E7
Mina Pirquitas Argentina 22°40S 66°30W 366 A2
Mīnā Su'ud Si. Arabia 28°45N 48°28E 317 D6
Mīnā'al Aḥmadī Kuwait 29°5N 48°10E 317 D6
Minago → Canada 54°33N 98°59W 343 C9
Minaki Canada 49°59N 94°40W 343 D10
Minamata Japan 32°10N 130°30E 303 H5
Minami-Arapusa △ Japan 35°30N 138°9E 303 G9
Minami-Tori-Shima Pac. Oc. 24°20N 153°58E 336 E7
Minas Uruguay 34°20S 55°10W 367 C4
Minas, Sierra de las Guatemala 15°9N 89°31W 360 C2
Minas Basin Canada 45°20N 64°12W 345 C7
Minas Gerais ☐ Brazil 18°50S 46°0W 365 G9
Minatitlán Mexico 17°59N 94°31W 359 D6
Minbu Burma 20°10N 94°52E 313 J19
Minchinabad Pakistan 30°10N 73°34E 314 D5
Mindanao Phil. 8°0N 125°0E 309 C6
Mindanao Sea = Bohol Sea Phil. 9°0N 124°0E 309 C6
Mindanao Trench Pac. Oc. 12°0N 126°6E 309 B7
Mindelo C. Verde Is. 16°24N 25°0W 322 b
Minden Canada 44°55N 78°43W 354 B6
Minden Germany 52°17N 8°55E 288 B5
Minden La., U.S.A. 32°37N 93°17W 356 E8
Minden Nev., U.S.A. 38°57N 119°46W 350 G7
Mindiptana Indonesia 5°55S 140°22E 309 F10
Mindoro Phil. 13°0N 121°0E 309 B6
Mindoro Str. Phil. 12°30N 120°30E 309 B6
Mine Japan 34°12N 131°7E 303 G5
Minehead U.K. 51°12N 3°29W 285 F4
Mineola N.Y., U.S.A. 40°44N 73°38W 355 F11
Mineola Tex., U.S.A. 32°40N 95°29W 356 E7
Mineral King U.S.A. 36°27N 118°36W 350 J8
Mineral Wells U.S.A. 32°48N 98°7W 356 E5
Minersville U.S.A. 40°41N 76°16W 355 F8
Minerva U.S.A. 40°44N 81°6W 354 F3
Minetto U.S.A. 43°24N 76°28W 355 C8
Minfeng China 37°4N 82°46E 304 C3
Mingäçevir Su Anbarı Azerbaijan 40°57N 46°50E 291 F8
Mingan Canada 50°20N 64°0W 345 B7
Mingechaurskoye Vdkhr. = Mingäçevir Su Anbarı Azerbaijan 40°57N 46°50E 291 F8
Mingela Australia 19°52S 146°38E 334 B4
Mingenew Australia 29°12S 115°21E 333 E2
Mingera Cr. → Australia 20°38S 137°45E 334 C2
Mingin Burma 22°50N 94°30E 313 H19
Mingo Junction U.S.A. 40°19N 80°37W 354 F4
Mingora Pakistan 34°48N 72°22E 315 B5
Mingteke Daban = Mintaka Pass Pakistan 37°0N 74°58E 315 A6
Mingyuegue China 43°2N 128°50E 307 C15
Minho = Miño → Spain 41°52N 8°40W 293 A2
Minho Portugal 41°25N 8°20W 293 B1
Minidoka U.S.A. 42°45N 113°29W 348 E7
Minigwal, L. Australia 29°31S 123°14E 333 E3
Minilya → Australia 23°45S 114°0E 333 D1
Minilya Roadhouse Australia 23°55S 114°0E 333 D1
Minipi L. Canada 52°25N 60°45W 345 B7
Mink L. Canada 61°54N 117°40W 342 A5
Minna Nigeria 9°37N 6°30E 322 G7
Minneapolis Kans., U.S.A. 39°8N 97°42W 352 F5
Minneapolis Minn., U.S.A. 44°57N 93°16W 352 C7
Minnedosa Canada 50°14N 99°50W 343 C9
Minnesota ☐ U.S.A. 46°0N 94°15W 352 B6
Minnesota → U.S.A. 44°54N 93°9W 352 C7
Minnewaukan U.S.A. 48°4N 99°15W 352 A4
Minnipa Australia 32°51S 135°9E 335 E2
Minnitaki L. Canada 49°57N 92°10W 344 C1
Mino Japan 35°32N 136°55E 303 G8
Miño → Spain 41°52N 8°40W 293 A2
Minorca = Menorca Spain 40°0N 4°0E 296 B11
Minot U.S.A. 48°14N 101°18W 352 A3
Minqin China 38°38N 103°20E 306 E2
Minsk Belarus 53°52N 27°30E 289 B14
Mińsk Mazowiecki Poland 52°10N 21°33E 289 B11
Mintabie Australia 27°15S 133°7E 335 D1
Mintaka Pass Pakistan 37°0N 74°58E 315 A6
Minto Canada 46°5N 66°5W 345 C6
Minto, L. Canada 57°13N 75°0W 344 A5
Minton Canada 49°10N 104°35W 343 D8
Minturn U.S.A. 39°35N 106°26W 348 G10
Minusinsk Russia 53°43N 91°20E 301 D10
Minutang India 28°15N 96°30E 313 E20
Minvoul Gabon 2°9N 12°8E 324 D2
Minzhong China 22°37N 113°30E 305 F10
Miquelon Canada 49°25N 76°27W 344 C4
Miquelon St-P. & M. 47°8N 56°22W 345 C8
Mīr Kūh Iran 26°22N 58°55E 317 E8
Mīr Shahdād Iran 26°15N 58°29E 317 E8
Mira Italy 45°26N 12°8E 294 B5
Mira por vos Cay Bahamas 22°9N 74°30W 361 B5
Mirabello, Kolpos Greece 35°10N 25°50E 297 D7
Mirador-Río Azul △ Guatemala 17°45N 89°50W 360 C2
Miraj India 16°50N 74°45E 312 L9
Miram Shah Pakistan 33°0N 70°2E 314 C4
Miramar Argentina 38°15S 57°50W 366 D4
Miramar Mozam. 23°50S 35°35E 329 C6
Miramichi Canada 47°2N 65°28W 345 C6
Miramichi B. Canada 47°15N 65°0W 345 C7
Miranda Brazil 20°10S 56°15W 365 H7
Miranda → Brazil 19°25S 57°20W 364 G7
Miranda de Ebro Spain 42°41N 2°57W 293 A4
Miranda do Douro Portugal 41°30N 6°16W 293 B2
Mirandópolis Brazil 21°9S 51°6W 367 A5
Mirango Malawi 13°32S 34°58E 327 E3
Mirani Australia 21°8S 148°53E 334 K6
Mirassol Brazil 20°46S 49°28W 367 A6
Mirbāṭ Oman 17°0N 54°45E 319 D5
Mires Greece 35°4N 24°56E 297 D6
Miri Malaysia 4°23N 113°59E 308 D4
Miriam Vale Australia 24°20S 151°33E 334 C5
Mirim, L. S. Amer. 32°45S 52°50W 367 C5
Mirnyy Antarctica 66°50S 92°30E 277 C14
Mirnyy Russia 62°33N 113°53E 301 C12
Mirokhan Pakistan 27°46N 68°6E 314 F3
Mirond L. Canada 55°6N 102°47W 343 B8
Mirpur Pakistan 33°32N 73°56E 315 C5
Mirpur Batoro Pakistan 24°44N 68°16E 314 G3
Mirpur Bibiwari Pakistan 28°33N 67°44E 314 E2
Mirpur Khas Pakistan 25°30N 69°0E 314 G3
Mirpur Sakro Pakistan 24°33N 67°41E 314 G2
Mirs Bay = Tai Pang Wan China 22°33N 114°24E 305 F11
Mirtağ Turkey 38°23N 41°56E 316 B4
Mirtoo Sea Greece 37°0N 23°20E 295 F10
Miryang S. Korea 35°31N 128°44E 307 G15
Mirzapur India 25°10N 82°34E 315 G10
Mirzapur-cum-Vindhyachal = Mirzapur India 25°10N 82°34E 315 G10
Misantla Mexico 19°56N 96°50W 359 D5
Misawa Japan 40°41N 141°24E 302 D10
Miscou I. Canada 47°57N 64°31W 345 C7
Mish'āb, Ra's al Si. Arabia 28°15N 48°43E 317 D6
Mishan China 45°37N 131°48E 305 B8
Mishawaka U.S.A. 41°40N 86°11W 352 E10
Mishima Japan 35°10N 138°52E 303 G9
Misión Mexico 32°6N 116°53W 351 N10
Misiones ☐ Argentina 27°0S 55°0W 367 B5
Misiones ☐ Paraguay 27°0S 56°0W 366 B4
Miskah Si. Arabia 24°49N 42°56E 316 E4
Miskitos, Cayos Nic. 14°26N 82°50W 360 D3
Miskolc Hungary 48°7N 20°50E 289 D11
Misoke Dem. Rep. of the Congo 0°42S 28°2E 326 C2
Misool Indonesia 1°52S 130°10E 309 E8
Mişr = Egypt ■ Africa 28°0N 31°0E 323 C12
Mişrātah Libya 32°24N 15°3E 323 B9
Missanabie Canada 48°20N 84°6W 344 C3
Missinaibi → Canada 50°43N 81°29W 344 B3
Missinaibi L. Canada 48°23N 83°40W 344 C3
Mission Canada 49°10N 122°15W 342 D4
Mission S. Dak., U.S.A. 43°18N 100°39W 352 D3
Mission Tex., U.S.A. 26°13N 98°20W 356 H5
Mission Beach Australia 17°53S 146°6E 334 B4
Mission Viejo U.S.A. 33°36N 117°40W 351 M9
Missisa L. Canada 52°20N 85°7W 344 B2
Missisicabi → Canada 51°14N 79°31W 344 B4
Mississagi → Canada 46°15N 83°9W 344 C3
Mississauga Canada 43°32N 79°35W 354 C5
Mississippi ☐ U.S.A. 33°0N 90°0W 357 E10
Mississippi → U.S.A. 29°9N 89°15W 357 G10
Mississippi L. Canada 45°5N 76°10W 355 A8
Mississippi River Delta U.S.A. 29°10N 89°15W 357 G10
Mississippi Sd. U.S.A. 30°20N 89°0W 357 F10
Missoula U.S.A. 46°52N 114°1W 348 C6
Missouri ☐ U.S.A. 38°25N 92°30W 352 F7
Missouri → U.S.A. 38°49N 90°7W 352 F8
Missouri City U.S.A. 29°37N 95°32W 356 G7
Missouri Valley U.S.A. 41°34N 95°53W 352 E6
Mist U.S.A. 45°59N 123°15W 350 E3
Mistassibi → Canada 48°53N 72°13W 345 B5
Mistassini → Canada 48°42N 72°20W 345 C5
Mistassini, L. Canada 51°0N 73°30W 344 B5
Mistastin L. Canada 55°57N 63°20W 345 A7
Mistinibi, L. Canada 55°56N 64°17W 345 A7
Mistissini Canada 48°53N 72°12W 345 C5
Misty L. Canada 58°53N 101°40W 343 B8
Misurata = Mişrātah Libya 32°24N 15°3E 323 B9
Mitchell Australia 26°29S 147°58E 335 D4
Mitchell Canada 43°28N 81°12W 354 C3
Mitchell Nebr., U.S.A. 41°57N 103°49W 352 E2
Mitchell Oreg., U.S.A. 44°34N 120°9W 348 D3
Mitchell S. Dak., U.S.A. 43°43N 98°2W 352 D4
Mitchell → Australia 15°12S 141°35E 334 B3
Mitchell, Mt. U.S.A. 35°46N 82°16W 357 D13
Mitchell-Alice Rivers △ Australia 15°28S 142°5E 334 B3
Mitchell Ra. Australia 12°49S 135°36E 334 A2
Mitchelstown Ireland 52°15N 8°16W 282 D3
Mitha Tiwana Pakistan 32°13N 72°6E 314 C5
Mithi Pakistan 24°44N 69°48E 314 G3
Mithrao Pakistan 27°28N 69°40E 314 F3
Mitilini Greece 39°6N 26°35E 295 E12
Mito Japan 36°20N 140°30E 303 F10
Mitrovica = Kosovska Mitrovica Serbia 42°54N 20°52E 295 C9
Mitsamiouli Comoros Is. 11°20S 43°16E 325 a
Mitsinjo Madag. 16°1S 45°52E 329 B8
Mitsiwa Eritrea 15°35N 39°25E 319 D2
Mitsukaidō Japan 36°1N 139°59E 303 F9
Mittagong Australia 34°28S 150°29E 335 E5
Mittimatalik = Pond Inlet Canada 72°40N 77°0W 341 B12
Mitú Colombia 1°15N 70°13W 364 C4
Mitumba Tanzania 7°8S 31°2E 326 D3
Mitumba, Mts. Dem. Rep. of the Congo 7°0S 27°30E 326 D2
Mitwaba Dem. Rep. of the Congo 8°2S 27°17E 327 D2
Mityana Uganda 0°23N 32°2E 326 B3
Mixteco → Mexico 18°11N 98°30W 359 D5
Miyagi ☐ Japan 38°15N 140°45E 302 E10
Miyāh, W. el → Syria 34°44N 39°57E 316 C3
Miyake-Jima Japan 34°5N 139°30E 303 G9
Miyako Japan 39°40N 141°59E 302 E10
Miyako-Jima Japan 24°45N 125°20E 303 M2
Miyako-Rettō Japan 24°24N 125°0E 303 M2
Miyakonojō Japan 31°40N 131°5E 303 J5
Miyani India 21°50N 69°26E 314 J3
Miyanoura-Dake Japan 30°20N 130°31E 303 J5
Miyazaki Japan 31°56N 131°30E 303 J5
Miyazaki ☐ Japan 32°30N 131°30E 303 H5
Miyazu Japan 35°35N 135°10E 303 G7
Miyet, Bahr el = Dead Sea Asia 31°30N 35°30E 318 D4
Miyoshi Japan 34°48N 132°51E 303 G6
Miyun China 40°28N 116°50E 306 D9
Miyun Shuiku China 40°30N 117°0E 307 D9
Mizdah Libya 31°30N 13°0E 323 B8
Mizen Hd. Cork, Ireland 51°27N 9°50W 282 E2
Mizen Hd. Wicklow, Ireland 52°51N 6°4W 282 D5
Mizhi China 37°47N 110°12E 306 F6
Mizoram ☐ India 23°30N 92°40E 313 H18
Mizpe Ramon Israel 30°34N 34°49E 318 E3
Mizuho Antarctica 70°30S 41°0E 277 D5
Mizusawa Japan 39°8N 141°8E 302 E10
Mjölby Sweden 58°20N 15°10E 281 G16
Mjøsa Norway 60°40N 11°0E 280 F14
Mkata Tanzania 5°45S 38°20E 326 D4
Mkhaya ⌓ Swaziland 26°34S 31°45E 329 D5
Mkhuze ⌓ S. Africa 29°27S 29°30E 329 D4
Mkokotoni Tanzania 5°55S 39°15E 326 D4
Mkomazi Tanzania 4°40S 38°7E 326 C4
Mkomazi → S. Africa 30°12S 30°50E 329 E5
Mkomazi ⌓ Tanzania 4°4S 30°2E 326 C3
Mkulwe Tanzania 8°37S 32°20E 327 D3
Mkumbi, Ras Tanzania 7°38S 39°55E 326 D4
Mkushi Zambia 14°25S 29°15E 327 E2
Mkushi River Zambia 13°32S 29°45E 327 E2
Mkuze S. Africa 27°10S 32°0E 329 D5
Mladá Boleslav Czech Rep. 50°27N 14°53E 288 C8
Mlala Hills Tanzania 6°50S 31°40E 326 D3
Mlange = Mulanje Malawi 16°2S 35°33E 327 F4
Mława Poland 53°9N 20°25E 289 B11
Mlawula ⌓ Swaziland 26°12S 32°2E 329 D5
Mljet Croatia 42°43N 17°30E 294 C7
Mmabatho S. Africa 25°49S 25°30E 328 D4
Mo i Rana Norway 66°20N 14°7E 280 C16
Moa Cuba 20°40N 74°56W 361 B4
Moa Indonesia 8°0S 128°0E 309 F7
Moa → S. Leone 6°59N 11°36W 322 G3
Moab U.S.A. 38°35N 109°33W 348 G9
Moala Fiji 18°36S 179°53E 331 a
Moama Australia 36°7S 144°46E 335 F3
Moamba Mozam. 25°36S 32°15E 329 D5
Moapa U.S.A. 36°40N 114°37W 351 J12
Moate Ireland 53°24N 7°44W 282 C4
Moba Dem. Rep. of the Congo 7°0S 29°48E 326 D2
Mobārakābād Iran 28°24N 53°20E 317 D7
Mobaye C.A.R. 4°25N 21°5E 324 D4
Mobayi Dem. Rep. of the Congo 4°15N 21°8E 324 D4
Moberly Lake Canada 55°50N 121°44W 342 B4
Moberly U.S.A. 39°25N 92°26W 352 F7
Mobile U.S.A. 30°41N 88°3W 357 F10
Mobile B. U.S.A. 30°30N 88°0W 357 F11
Mobridge U.S.A. 45°32N 100°26W 352 C3
Moc Chau Vietnam 20°50N 104°38E 310 B5
Moc Hoa Vietnam 10°46N 105°56E 311 G5
Mocabe Kasari Dem. Rep. of the Congo 9°58S 26°12E 327 D2
Moçambique = Mozambique ■ Africa 19°0S 35°0E 327 F4
Moçambique Mozam. 15°3S 40°42E 327 F5
Mocanaqua U.S.A. 41°9N 76°8W 355 E8
Moce Fiji 18°40S 178°29W 331 a
Mochima △ Venezuela 10°30N 64°5W 361 D7
Mochos Greece 35°16N 25°27E 297 D7
Mochudi Botswana 24°27S 26°7E 328 C4
Mocimboa da Praia Mozam. 11°25S 40°20E 327 E5
Moclips U.S.A. 47°14N 124°13W 350 C2
Mocoa Colombia 1°7N 76°35W 364 C3
Mococa Brazil 21°28S 47°0W 367 A6
Mocorito Mexico 25°29N 107°55W 358 B3
Moctezuma Mexico 29°48N 109°42W 358 B3
Moctezuma → Mexico 21°59N 98°34W 359 C5
Mocuba Mozam. 16°54S 36°57E 327 F4
Modane France 45°12N 6°40E 292 D7
Modasa India 23°30N 73°21E 314 H5
Modder → S. Africa 29°2S 24°37E 328 D3
Modderrivier S. Africa 29°2S 24°38E 328 D3
Módena Italy 44°40N 10°55E 294 B4
Modena U.S.A. 37°48N 113°56W 349 H7
Modesto U.S.A. 37°39N 121°0W 350 H6
Módica Italy 36°52N 14°46E 294 F6
Modimolle S. Africa 24°42S 28°22E 329 C4
Modjadjiskloof S. Africa 23°42S 30°10E 329 C5
Moe Australia 38°12S 146°19E 335 F4
Moebase Mozam. 17°3S 38°41E 327 F4
Moengo Suriname 5°45N 54°20W 365 B8
Moffat U.K. 55°21N 3°27W 283 F5
Moga India 30°48N 75°8E 314 D6
Mogadishu = Muqdisho Somali Rep. 2°2N 45°25E 319 G4
Mogador = Essaouira Morocco 31°32N 9°42W 322 B4
Mogalakwena → S. Africa 22°38S 28°40E 329 C4
Mogami-Gawa → Japan 38°45N 140°0E 302 E10
Mogán Canary Is. 27°53N 15°43W 296 G4
Mogaung Burma 25°20N 97°0E 313 G20
Mogi das Cruzes Brazil 23°31S 46°11W 367 A6
Mogi-Guaçu → Brazil 20°53S 48°10W 367 A6
Mogi-Mirim Brazil 22°29S 47°0W 367 A6
Mogilev = Mahilyow Belarus 53°55N 30°18E 289 B16
Mogilev-Podolskiy = Mohyliv-Podilskyy Ukraine 48°26N 27°48E 289 D14
Mogincual Mozam. 15°35S 40°25E 327 F5
Mogocha Russia 53°40N 119°50E 301 D12
Mogok Burma 23°0N 96°40E 313 H20
Mogollon Rim U.S.A. 34°10N 110°50W 349 J8
Mogumber Australia 31°2S 116°3E 333 F2
Mohács Hungary 45°58N 18°41E 289 F10
Mohales Hoek Lesotho 30°7S 27°26E 328 E4
Mohall U.S.A. 48°46N 101°31W 352 A3
Moḥammadābād Iran 37°52N 59°5E 317 B8
Mohammedia Morocco 33°44N 7°21W 322 B4
Mohana → India 24°43N 85°0E 315 G11
Mohanlalganj India 26°41N 80°58E 315 F9
Mohave, L. U.S.A. 35°12N 114°34W 351 K12
Mohawk → U.S.A. 42°47N 73°41W 355 D11
Mohéli Comoros Is. 12°20S 43°40E 325 a
Mohenjodaro Pakistan 27°19N 68°7E 314 F3
Moher, Cliffs of Ireland 52°58N 9°27W 282 D2
Mohicanville Res. U.S.A. 40°45N 82°9W 354 F2
Mohns Ridge Arctic 72°30N 5°0W 276 B7
Mohoro Tanzania 8°6S 39°8E 326 D4
Mohyliv-Podilskyy Ukraine 48°26N 27°48E 289 D14
Moidart, L. U.K. 56°47N 5°52W 283 E3
Moira → Canada 44°21N 77°24W 354 B7
Mõisaküla Estonia 58°3N 25°12E 281 G21
Moisie Canada 50°12N 66°1W 345 B6
Moisie → Canada 50°14N 66°5W 345 B6
Mojave U.S.A. 35°3N 118°10W 351 K8
Mojave ⌓ U.S.A. 35°7N 115°32W 351 K11
Mojave Desert U.S.A. 35°0N 116°30W 351 L10
Mojo Bolivia 21°48S 65°33W 366 A2
Mojokerto Indonesia 7°28S 112°26E 309 G15
Mokai N.Z. 38°32S 175°56E 331 C5
Mokambo Dem. Rep. of the Congo 12°25S 28°20E 327 E2
Mokameh India 25°24N 85°55E 315 G11
Mokau N.Z. 38°42S 174°39E 331 C5
Mokelumne → U.S.A. 38°13N 121°28W 350 G5
Mokelumne Hill U.S.A. 38°18N 120°43W 350 G6
Mokhotlong Lesotho 29°22S 29°2E 329 D4
Mokokchung India 26°15N 94°30E 313 F19
Mokolo → S. Africa 23°14S 27°43E 329 C4
Mokopane S. Africa 24°10S 28°55E 329 C4
Mokpo S. Korea 34°50N 126°25E 307 G14
Mokra Gora Europe 42°50N 20°30E 295 C9
Mol Belgium 51°11N 5°5E 287 C5
Molchanovo Russia 57°40N 83°50E 300 D9
Mold U.K. 53°9N 3°8W 284 D4
Moldavia = Moldova ■ Europe 47°0N 28°0E 289 E15
Moldavia Romania 46°30N 27°0E 289 E14
Molde Norway 62°45N 7°9E 280 E12
Moldova ■ Europe 47°0N 28°0E 289 E15
Moldoveanu, Vf. Romania 45°36N 24°45E 289 F13
Mole → U.K. 51°24N 0°21W 285 F7
Mole Creek Australia 41°34S 146°24E 335 G4
Molepolole Botswana 24°28S 25°28E 328 C4
Molfetta Italy 41°12N 16°36E 294 D7
Moline U.S.A. 41°30N 90°31W 352 E8
Molinos Argentina 25°28S 66°15W 366 B2
Moliro Dem. Rep. of the Congo 8°12S 30°30E 326 D3
Mollendo Peru 17°0S 72°0W 364 G4
Mollerin, L. Australia 30°30S 117°35E 333 F2
Molo Kenya 0°15S 35°44E 326 C4
Molodechno = Maladzyechna Belarus 54°20N 26°50E 289 A14
Molodezhnaya Antarctica 67°40S 45°51E 277 C9
Moloka'i U.S.A. 21°8N 157°0W 346 b
Molokai Fracture Zone Pac. Oc. 28°0N 125°0W 337 E15
Molong Australia 33°5S 148°54E 335 E4
Molopo → Africa 28°30S 20°12E 328 D3
Molson L. Canada 54°22N 96°40W 343 C9
Molteno S. Africa 31°22S 26°22E 328 E4
Molu Indonesia 6°45S 131°40E 309 F8
Molucca Sea Indonesia 0°0 125°0E 309 E6
Moluccas = Maluku Indonesia 1°0S 127°0E 309 E7
Moma Dem. Rep. of the Congo 1°35S 23°52E 326 C1
Moma Mozam. 16°47S 39°4E 327 F4
Mombasa Kenya 4°3S 39°40E 326 C4
Mombetsu Japan 44°21N 143°22E 302 B11
Momchilgrad Bulgaria 41°33N 25°23E 295 D11
Momi Dem. Rep. of the Congo 1°42S 27°0E 326 C2
Mompós Colombia 9°14N 74°26W 364 B4
Møn Denmark 54°57N 12°20E 281 J15
Mon ☐ Burma 16°0N 97°30E 313 L20
Mona, Canal de la = Mona Passage W. Indies 18°30N 67°45W 361 C6
Mona, Isla Puerto Rico 18°5N 67°54W 361 C6
Mona, Pta. Costa Rica 9°37N 82°36W 360 E3
Mona Passage W. Indies 18°30N 67°45W 361 C6
Monaca U.S.A. 40°41N 80°17W 354 F4
Monaco ■ Europe 43°46N 7°23E 292 E7
Monadhliath Mts. U.K. 57°10N 4°4W 283 D4
Monadnock, Mt. U.S.A. 42°52N 72°7W 355 D12
Monaghan Ireland 54°15N 6°57W 282 B5
Monaghan ☐ Ireland 54°11N 6°56W 282 B5
Monahans U.S.A. 31°36N 102°54W 356 F3
Monapo Mozam. 14°56S 40°19E 327 E5
Monar, L. U.K. 57°26N 5°8W 283 D3
Monarch Mt. Canada 51°55N 125°57W 342 C3
Monashee Mts. Canada 51°0N 118°43W 342 C5
Monasterevin Ireland 53°8N 7°4W 282 C4
Monastir = Bitola Macedonia 41°1N 21°20E 295 D9
Monastir Tunisia 35°50N 10°49E 323 A8
Moncayo, Sierra del Spain 41°48N 1°50W 293 B5
Monchegorsk Russia 67°54N 32°58E 280 C25
Mönchengladbach Germany 51°11N 6°27E 288 C4
Monchique Portugal 37°19N 8°38W 293 D1
Moncks Corner U.S.A. 33°12N 80°1W 357 E14
Monclova Mexico 26°54N 101°25W 358 B4
Moncton Canada 46°7N 64°51W 345 C7
Mondego → Portugal 40°9N 8°52W 293 B1
Mondeodo Indonesia 3°34S 122°9E 309 E6
Mondovì Italy 44°23N 7°49E 292 D7
Mondrain I. Australia 34°9S 122°14E 333 F3
Moneague Jamaica 18°16N 77°7W 360 a
Moneron, Ostrov Russia 46°15N 141°16E 302 A10
Monessen U.S.A. 40°9N 79°54W 354 F5
Monett U.S.A. 36°55N 93°55W 352 G7
Moneymore U.K. 54°41N 6°40W 282 B5
Monforte de Lemos Spain 42°31N 7°33W 293 A2
Mong Cai Vietnam 21°27N 107°54E 310 B6
Mong Hsu Burma 21°54N 98°30E 313 J21
Mong Kung Burma 21°35N 97°35E 313 J20
Mong Nai Burma 20°32N 97°46E 313 J20
Mong Pawk Burma 22°4N 99°16E 313 H21
Mong Ton Burma 20°17N 98°45E 313 J21
Mong Wa Burma 21°26N 100°27E 313 J22
Mong Yai Burma 22°21N 98°3E 313 H21
Mongalla Sudan 5°8N 31°42E 323 G12
Mongers, L. Australia 29°25S 117°5E 333 E2
Monghyr = Munger India 25°23N 86°30E 315 G12
Mongibello = Etna Italy 37°50N 14°55E 294 F6
Mongo Chad 12°14N 18°43E 323 F9
Mongolia ■ Asia 47°0N 103°0E 304 B5
Mongolia, Plateau of Asia 45°0N 105°0E 298 D12
Mongu Zambia 15°16S 23°12E 325 H4
Mônguà Angola 16°43S 15°20E 328 B2
Monifieth U.K. 56°30N 2°48W 283 E6
Monkey Bay Malawi 14°7S 35°1E 327 E4
Monkey Mia Australia 25°48S 113°43E 333 E1
Monkey River Belize 16°22N 88°29W 359 D7
Monkoto Dem. Rep. of the Congo 1°38S 20°35E 324 E4
Monkton Canada 43°35N 81°5W 354 C3
Monmouth U.K. 51°48N 2°42W 285 F5
Monmouth Ill., U.S.A. 40°55N 90°39W 352 E8
Monmouth Oreg., U.S.A. 44°51N 123°14W 348 D2
Monmouthshire ☐ U.K. 51°48N 2°54W 285 F5
Mono L. U.S.A. 38°1N 119°1W 350 H7
Monolith U.S.A. 35°7N 118°22W 351 K8
Monolithos Greece 36°7N 27°45E 297 C9
Monongahela U.S.A. 40°12N 79°56W 354 F5
Monópoli Italy 40°57N 17°18E 294 D7
Monos I. Trin. & Tob. 10°42N 61°44W 365 K15
Monroe Ga., U.S.A. 33°47N 83°43W 357 E13
Monroe La., U.S.A. 32°30N 92°7W 356 E8
Monroe Mich., U.S.A. 41°55N 83°24W 353 E12
Monroe N.C., U.S.A. 34°59N 80°33W 357 D14
Monroe N.Y., U.S.A. 41°20N 74°11W 355 E10
Monroe Utah, U.S.A. 38°38N 112°7W 348 G7
Monroe Wash., U.S.A. 47°51N 121°58W 350 C5
Monroe Wis., U.S.A. 42°36N 89°38W 352 D9
Monroe City U.S.A. 39°39N 91°44W 352 F8
Monroeton U.S.A. 41°43N 76°29W 355 E8
Monroeville Ala., U.S.A. 31°31N 87°20W 357 F11
Monroeville Pa., U.S.A. 40°26N 79°45W 354 F5
Monrovia Liberia 6°18N 10°47W 322 G3
Mons Belgium 50°27N 3°58E 287 D3
Monse Indonesia 4°7S 123°15E 309 E6
Mont-de-Marsan France 43°54N 0°31W 292 E3
Mont-Joli Canada 48°37N 68°10W 345 C6
Mont-Laurier Canada 46°35N 75°30W 344 C4
Mont-Louis Canada 49°15N 65°44W 345 C6
Mont-St-Michel, Le France 48°40N 1°30W 292 B3
Mont-Tremblant ⌓ Canada 46°30N 74°30W 344 C5
Montagne d'Ambre △ Madag. 12°37S 49°8E 329 A8
Montagu S. Africa 33°45S 20°8E 328 E3
Montagu I. Antarctica 58°25S 26°20W 277 B1
Montague Canada 46°10N 62°39W 345 C7
Montague, I. Mexico 31°45N 114°48W 358 A2
Montague Ra. Australia 27°15S 119°30E 333 E2
Montague Sd. Australia 14°28S 125°20E 332 B4
Montalbán Spain 40°50N 0°45W 293 B5
Montalvo U.S.A. 34°15N 119°12W 351 L7
Montana Bulgaria 43°27N 23°16E 295 C10
Montaña Peru 6°0S 73°0W 364 E4
Montana ☐ U.S.A. 47°0N 110°0W 348 C9
Montaña Clara, I. Canary Is. 29°17N 13°33W 296 E6
Montargis France 47°59N 2°43E 292 C5
Montauban France 44°2N 1°21E 292 D4
Montauk U.S.A. 41°3N 71°57W 355 E13
Montauk Pt. U.S.A. 41°4N 71°51W 355 E13
Montbéliard France 47°31N 6°48E 292 C7
Montceau-les-Mines France 46°40N 4°23E 292 C6
Montclair U.S.A. 40°49N 74°12W 355 F10
Monte Albán Mexico 17°2N 96°46W 359 D5
Monte Alegre Brazil 2°0S 54°0W 365 D8
Monte Azul Brazil 15°9S 42°53W 365 G10
Monte-Carlo Monaco 43°44N 7°25E 292 E7
Monte Caseros Argentina 30°10S 57°50W 366 C4
Monte Comán Argentina 34°40S 67°53W 366 C2
Monte Crísti Dom. Rep. 19°52N 71°39W 361 C5

Monte Lindo → *Paraguay* 23°56S 57°12W 366 A4
Monte Patria *Chile* 30°42S 70°58W 366 C1
Monte Quemado *Argentina* 25°53S 62°41W 366 B3
Monte Rio *U.S.A.* 38°28N 123°0W 350 G4
Monte Santu, C. di *Italy* 40°5N 9°44E 294 D3
Monte Vista *U.S.A.* 37°35N 106°9W 349 H10
Monteagudo *Argentina* 27°14S 54°8W 367 B5
Montebello *Canada* 45°40N 74°55W 344 C5
Montebello Is. *Australia* 20°30S 115°45E 332 D2
Montecito *U.S.A.* 34°26N 119°40W 351 L7
Montecristo *Italy* 42°20N 10°19E 294 C4
Montego Bay *Jamaica* 18°28N 77°55W 360 a
Montélimar *France* 44°33N 4°45E 292 D6
Montello *U.S.A.* 43°48N 89°20W 352 D9
Montemorelos *Mexico* 25°12N 99°49W 359 B5
Montenegro *Brazil* 29°39S 51°29W 367 B5
Montenegro ■ *Europe* 42°40N 19°20E 295 C8
Montepuez *Mozam.* 13°8S 38°59E 327 E4
Montepuez → *Mozam.* 12°32S 40°27E 327 E5
Monterey *U.S.A.* 36°37N 121°55W 350 J5
Monterey B. *U.S.A.* 36°45N 122°0W 350 J5
Montería *Colombia* 8°46N 75°53W 364 B3
Monteros *Argentina* 27°11S 65°30W 366 B2
Monterrey *Mexico* 25°40N 100°19W 358 B4
Montes Azules ⌂ *Mexico* 16°21N 91°3W 359 D6
Montes Claros *Brazil* 16°30S 43°50W 365 G10
Montesano *U.S.A.* 46°59N 123°36W 350 D3
Montesilvano *Italy* 42°29N 14°8E 294 C6
Montevideo *Uruguay* 34°50S 56°11W 367 C4
Montevideo *U.S.A.* 44°57N 95°43W 352 C6
Montezuma *U.S.A.* 41°35N 92°32W 352 E7
Montezuma Castle ⌂ *U.S.A.* 34°39N 111°45W 349 J8
Montgomery *U.K.* 52°34N 3°8W 285 E4
Montgomery *Ala., U.S.A.* 32°23N 86°19W 357 E11
Montgomery *Pa., U.S.A.* 41°10N 76°53W 354 E8
Montgomery *W. Va., U.S.A.* 38°11N 81°19W 353 F13
Montgomery City *U.S.A.* 38°59N 91°30W 352 F8
Monticello *Ark., U.S.A.* 33°38N 91°47W 356 E9
Monticello *Fla., U.S.A.* 30°33N 83°52W 357 F13
Monticello *Ind., U.S.A.* 40°45N 86°46W 352 E10
Monticello *Iowa, U.S.A.* 42°15N 91°12W 352 D8
Monticello *Ky., U.S.A.* 36°50N 84°51W 353 G11
Monticello *Minn., U.S.A.* 45°18N 93°48W 352 C7
Monticello *Miss., U.S.A.* 31°33N 90°7W 357 F9
Monticello *N.Y., U.S.A.* 41°39N 74°42W 355 E10
Monticello *Utah, U.S.A.* 37°52N 109°21W 349 H9
Montijo *Portugal* 38°41N 8°54W 293 C1
Montilla *Spain* 37°36N 4°40W 293 D3
Montluçon *France* 46°22N 2°36E 292 C5
Montmagny *Canada* 46°58N 70°34W 345 C5
Montmartre *Canada* 50°14N 103°27W 343 C8
Montmorillon *France* 46°26N 0°50E 292 C4
Monto *Australia* 24°52S 151°6E 334 C5
Montongbuwoh *Indonesia* 8°33S 116°4E 309 K19
Montoro *Spain* 38°1N 4°27W 293 C3
Montour Falls *U.S.A.* 42°21N 76°51W 354 D8
Montoursville *U.S.A.* 41°15N 76°55W 354 E8
Montpelier *Idaho, U.S.A.* 42°19N 111°18W 348 E8
Montpelier *Vt., U.S.A.* 44°16N 72°35W 355 B12
Montpellier *France* 43°37N 3°52E 292 E5
Montréal *Canada* 45°30N 73°33W 355 A11
Montreal → *Canada* 47°14N 84°39W 344 C3
Montreal L. *Canada* 54°20N 105°45W 343 C7
Montreal Lake *Canada* 54°3N 105°46W 343 C7
Montreux *Switz.* 46°26N 6°55E 292 C7
Montrose *U.K.* 56°44N 2°27W 283 E6
Montrose *Colo., U.S.A.* 38°29N 107°53W 348 G10
Montrose *Pa., U.S.A.* 41°50N 75°53W 355 E9
Monts, Pte. des *Canada* 49°20N 67°12W 345 C6
Montserrat ☑ *W. Indies* 16°40N 62°10W 361 C7
Montuiri *Spain* 39°34N 2°59E 296 B9
Monywa *Burma* 22°7N 95°11E 313 H19
Monza *Italy* 45°35N 9°16E 292 D8
Monze *Zambia* 16°17S 27°29E 327 F2
Monze, C. *Pakistan* 24°47N 66°37E 314 G2
Monzón *Spain* 41°52N 0°10E 293 B6
Mooers *U.S.A.* 44°58N 73°35W 355 B11
Mooi → *S. Africa* 28°45S 30°34E 329 D5
Mooi River *S. Africa* 29°13S 29°50E 329 D4
Moonah → *Australia* 22°3S 138°33E 334 C2
Moonda, L. *Australia* 25°52S 140°25E 334 D3
Moonie *Australia* 27°46S 150°20E 335 D5
Moonie → *Australia* 29°19S 148°43E 335 D4
Moonta *Australia* 34°6S 137°32E 335 E2
Moora *Australia* 30°37S 115°58E 333 F2
Moorcroft *U.S.A.* 44°16N 104°57W 348 D11
Moore → *Australia* 31°22S 115°30E 333 F2
Moore, L. *Australia* 29°50S 117°35E 333 E2
Moore Park *Australia* 24°43S 152°17E 334 C5
Moore Res. *U.S.A.* 44°20N 71°53W 355 B13
Moore River △ *Australia* 31°7S 115°39E 333 F2
Moorea *French Polynesia* 17°30S 149°50W 331 d
Moorefield *U.S.A.* 39°4N 78°58W 353 F14
Moorfoot Hills *U.K.* 55°44N 3°8W 283 F5
Moorhead *U.S.A.* 46°53N 96°45W 352 B5
Moorpark *U.S.A.* 34°17N 118°53W 351 L8
Moorreesburg *S. Africa* 33°6S 18°38E 328 E2
Moorrinya △ *Australia* 21°42S 144°58E 334 C3
Moose → *Canada* 51°20N 80°25W 344 B3
Moose → *U.S.A.* 43°38N 75°24W 355 C9
Moose Creek *Canada* 45°15N 74°58W 355 A10
Moose Factory *Canada* 51°16N 80°32W 344 B3
Moose Jaw *Canada* 50°24N 105°30W 343 C7
Moose Jaw → *Canada* 50°34N 105°18W 343 C7
Moose Lake *Canada* 53°46N 100°8W 343 C8
Moose Lake *U.S.A.* 46°27N 92°46W 352 B7
Moose Mountain ⌂ *Canada* 49°48N 102°25W 343 D8
Moosehead L. *U.S.A.* 45°38N 69°40W 353 C19
Mooselookmeguntic L. *U.S.A.* 44°55N 70°49W 355 B14
Moosilauke, Mt. *U.S.A.* 44°3N 71°40W 355 B13
Moosomin *Canada* 50°9N 101°40W 343 C8
Moosonee *Canada* 51°17N 80°39W 344 B3
Moosup *U.S.A.* 41°43N 71°53W 355 E13
Mopane *S. Africa* 22°37S 29°52E 329 C4
Mopeia Velha *Mozam.* 17°30S 35°40E 327 F4
Mopipi *Botswana* 21°6S 24°55E 328 C3
Mopoi *C.A.R.* 5°6N 26°54E 326 A2
Mopti *Mali* 14°30N 4°0W 322 F5
Moqor *Afghan.* 32°50N 67°42E 314 C2
Moquegua *Peru* 17°15S 70°46W 364 G4
Mora *Sweden* 61°2N 14°38E 280 F16
Mora *Minn., U.S.A.* 45°53N 93°18W 352 C7
Mora *N. Mex., U.S.A.* 35°58N 105°20W 349 J11
Moradabad *India* 28°50N 78°50E 315 E8
Morafenobe *Madag.* 17°50S 44°53E 329 B7
Moramanga *Madag.* 18°56S 48°12E 329 B8
Moran *Kans., U.S.A.* 37°55N 95°10W 352 G6
Moran *Wyo., U.S.A.* 43°50N 110°31W 348 E8
Moranbah *Australia* 22°1S 148°6E 334 C4
Morant Bay *Jamaica* 17°53N 76°25W 360 a
Morant Cays *Jamaica* 17°22N 76°0W 360 C4
Morant Pt. *Jamaica* 17°55N 76°12W 360 a
Morar *India* 26°14N 78°14E 314 F8
Morar, L. *U.K.* 56°57N 5°40W 283 E3
Moratuwa *Sri Lanka* 6°45N 79°55E 312 R11
Morava → *Serbia* 44°36N 21°4E 295 B9
Morava → *Slovak Rep.* 48°10N 16°59E 289 D9
Moravia *U.S.A.* 42°43N 76°25W 355 D8
Moravian Hts. = Českomoravská Vrchovina *Czech Rep.* 49°30N 15°40E 288 D8
Morawa *Australia* 29°13S 116°0E 333 E2
Morawhanna *Guyana* 8°30N 59°40W 364 B7
Moray □ *U.K.* 57°31N 3°18W 283 D5
Moray Firth *U.K.* 57°40N 3°52W 283 D5
Morbi *India* 22°50N 70°42E 314 H4
Morden *Canada* 49°15N 98°10W 343 D9
Mordovian Republic = Mordvinia □ *Russia* 54°20N 44°30E 290 D7
Mordvinia □ *Russia* 54°20N 44°30E 290 D7
Morea *Greece* 37°45N 22°10E 278 H10
Moreau → *U.S.A.* 45°18N 100°43W 352 C3
Morebeng *S. Africa* 23°30S 29°55E 329 C4
Morecambe *U.K.* 54°5N 2°52W 284 C5
Morecambe B. *U.K.* 54°7N 3°0W 284 C5
Moree *Australia* 29°28S 149°54E 335 D4
Morehead *U.S.A.* 38°11N 83°26W 353 F12
Morehead City *U.S.A.* 34°43N 76°43W 357 D16
Morel → *India* 26°13N 76°36E 314 F7
Morelia *Mexico* 19°42N 101°7W 358 D4
Morella *Australia* 23°0S 143°52E 334 C3
Morella *Spain* 40°35N 0°5W 293 B5
Morelos *Mexico* 26°42N 107°40W 358 B3
Morelos □ *Mexico* 18°45N 99°0W 359 D5
Moremi ⌂ *Botswana* 19°18S 23°10E 328 B3
Morena *India* 26°30N 78°4E 314 F8
Morena, Sierra *Spain* 38°20N 4°0W 293 C3
Moreno Valley *U.S.A.* 33°56N 117°14W 351 M10
Moresby I. *Canada* 52°30N 131°40W 342 C2
Moreton I. *Australia* 27°10S 153°25E 335 D5
Moreton Island △ *Australia* 27°2S 153°24E 335 D5
Morey *Spain* 39°44N 3°20E 296 B10
Morgan *U.S.A.* 41°2N 111°41W 348 F8
Morgan City *U.S.A.* 29°42N 91°12W 356 G9
Morgan Hill *U.S.A.* 37°8N 121°39W 350 H5
Morganfield *U.S.A.* 37°41N 87°55W 352 G10
Morganton *U.S.A.* 35°45N 81°41W 357 D14
Morgantown *U.S.A.* 39°38N 79°57W 353 F14
Morgenzon *S. Africa* 26°45S 29°36E 329 D4
Morghak *Iran* 29°7N 57°54E 317 D8
Morhar → *India* 25°29N 85°11E 315 G11
Mori *Japan* 42°6N 140°35E 302 C10
Moriarty *U.S.A.* 34°59N 106°3W 349 J10
Morice L. *Canada* 53°50N 127°40W 342 C3
Morinville *Canada* 53°49N 113°41W 342 C6
Morioka *Japan* 39°45N 141°8E 302 E10
Moris *Mexico* 28°10N 108°32W 358 B3
Morlaix *France* 48°36N 3°52W 292 B2
Mornington *Australia* 38°15S 145°5E 335 F4
Mornington, I. *Chile* 49°50S 75°30W 368 F1
Mornington I. *Australia* 16°30S 139°30E 334 B2
Moro *Pakistan* 26°40N 68°0E 314 F2
Moro → *Pakistan* 29°42N 67°22E 314 E2
Moro G. *Phil.* 6°30N 123°0E 309 C6
Morocco ■ *N. Afr.* 32°0N 5°50W 322 B4
Morogoro *Tanzania* 6°50S 37°40E 326 D4
Morogoro □ *Tanzania* 8°0S 37°0E 326 D4
Moroleón *Mexico* 20°8N 101°12W 358 C4
Morombe *Madag.* 21°45S 43°22E 329 C7
Moron *Argentina* 34°39S 58°37W 366 C4
Morón *Cuba* 22°8N 78°39W 360 B4
Morón de la Frontera *Spain* 37°6N 5°28W 293 D3
Morona → *Peru* 4°40S 77°10W 364 D3
Morondava *Madag.* 20°17S 44°17E 329 C7
Morongo Valley *U.S.A.* 34°3N 116°37W 351 L10
Moroni *Comoros Is.* 11°40S 43°16E 325 a
Moroni *U.S.A.* 39°32N 111°35W 348 G8
Morotai *Indonesia* 2°10N 128°30E 309 D7
Moroto *Uganda* 2°28N 34°42E 326 B3
Moroto, Mt. *Uganda* 2°30N 34°43E 326 B3
Morpeth *U.K.* 55°10N 1°41W 284 B6
Morphou *Cyprus* 35°12N 32°59E 297 D11
Morphou Bay *Cyprus* 35°15N 32°50E 297 D11
Morrilton *U.S.A.* 35°9N 92°44W 356 D8
Morrinhos *Brazil* 17°45S 49°10W 365 G9
Morrinsville *N.Z.* 37°40S 175°32E 331 B5
Morris *Canada* 49°25N 97°22W 343 D9
Morris *Ill., U.S.A.* 41°22N 88°26W 352 E9
Morris *Minn., U.S.A.* 45°35N 95°55W 352 C6
Morris *N.Y., U.S.A.* 42°33N 75°15W 355 D9
Morris *Pa., U.S.A.* 41°35N 77°17W 354 E7
Morris, Mt. *Australia* 26°9S 131°4E 333 E5
Morris Jesup, Kap *Greenland* 83°40N 34°0W 338 A16
Morrisburg *Canada* 44°55N 75°7W 355 B9
Morristown *Ariz., U.S.A.* 33°51N 112°37W 349 K7
Morristown *N.J., U.S.A.* 40°48N 74°29W 355 F10
Morristown *N.Y., U.S.A.* 44°35N 75°39W 355 B9
Morristown *Tenn., U.S.A.* 36°13N 83°18W 357 C13
Morrisville *N.Y., U.S.A.* 42°53N 75°35W 355 D9
Morrisville *Pa., U.S.A.* 40°13N 74°47W 355 F10
Morrisville *Vt., U.S.A.* 44°34N 72°36W 355 B12
Morro, Pta. *Chile* 27°6S 71°0W 366 B1
Morro Bay *U.S.A.* 35°22N 120°51W 350 K6
Morro del Jable *Canary Is.* 28°3N 14°23W 296 F5
Morro Jable, Pta. de *Canary Is.* 28°2N 14°20W 296 F5
Morrocoy △ *Venezuela* 10°48N 68°13W 361 D6
Morrosquillo, G. de *Colombia* 9°35N 75°40W 360 E4
Morrumbene *Mozam.* 23°31S 35°16E 329 C6
Morshansk *Russia* 53°28N 41°50E 290 D7
Morteros *Argentina* 30°50S 62°0W 366 C3
Mortlach *Canada* 50°27N 106°4W 343 C7
Mortlake *Australia* 38°5S 142°50E 335 F3
Morton *Tex., U.S.A.* 33°44N 102°46W 356 E3
Morton *Wash., U.S.A.* 46°34N 122°17W 350 D4
Moruga *Trin. & Tob.* 10°4N 61°16W 365 K15
Morundah *Australia* 34°57S 146°19E 335 E4
Moruya *Australia* 35°58S 150°3E 335 F5
Morvan *France* 47°5N 4°3E 292 C6
Morven *Australia* 26°22S 147°5E 335 D4
Morvern *U.K.* 56°38N 5°44W 283 E3
Morwell *Australia* 38°10S 146°22E 335 F4
Morzhovets, Ostrov *Russia* 66°44N 42°35E 290 A7
Moscos Is. *Burma* 14°0N 97°30E 310 E1
Moscow = Moskva *Russia* 55°45N 37°37E 290 C6
Moscow *Idaho, U.S.A.* 46°44N 117°0W 348 C5
Moscow *Pa., U.S.A.* 41°20N 75°31W 355 E9
Mosel → *Europe* 50°22N 7°36E 292 A7
Moselle = Mosel → *Europe* 50°22N 7°36E 292 A7
Moses Lake *U.S.A.* 47°8N 119°17W 348 C4
Mosgiel *N.Z.* 45°53S 170°21E 331 F3
Moshaweng → *S. Africa* 26°35S 22°50E 328 D3
Moshchnyy, Ostrov *Russia* 60°1N 27°50E 281 F22
Moshi *Tanzania* 3°22S 37°18E 326 C4
Moshupa *Botswana* 24°46S 25°29E 328 C4
Mosjøen *Norway* 65°51N 13°12E 280 D15
Moskenesøya *Norway* 67°58N 13°0E 280 C15
Moskenstraumen *Norway* 67°47N 12°45E 280 C15
Moskva *Russia* 55°45N 37°37E 290 C6
Mosomane *Botswana* 24°2S 26°19E 328 C4
Mosonmagyaróvár *Hungary* 47°52N 17°18E 289 E9
Mosquera *Colombia* 2°35N 78°24W 364 C3
Mosquero *U.S.A.* 35°47N 103°58W 349 J12
Mosquitia *Honduras* 15°20N 84°10W 360 C3
Mosquito Coast = Mosquitia *Honduras* 15°20N 84°10W 360 C3
Mosquito Creek L. *U.S.A.* 41°18N 80°46W 354 E4
Mosquito L. *Canada* 62°35N 103°20W 343 A8
Mosquitos, G. de los *Panama* 9°15N 81°10W 360 E3
Moss *Norway* 59°27N 10°40E 281 G14
Moss Vale *Australia* 34°32S 150°25E 335 E5
Mossaka *Congo* 1°15S 16°45E 324 E3
Mossbank *Canada* 49°56N 105°56W 343 D7
Mossburn *N.Z.* 45°41S 168°15E 331 F2
Mosselbaai *S. Africa* 34°11S 22°8E 328 E3
Mossendjo *Congo* 2°55S 12°42E 324 E2
Mossgiel *Australia* 33°15S 144°5E 335 E3
Mossman *Australia* 16°21S 145°15E 334 B4
Mossoró *Brazil* 5°10S 37°15W 365 E11
Mossuril *Mozam.* 14°58S 40°42E 327 E5
Most *Czech Rep.* 50°31N 13°38E 288 C7
Mosta *Malta* 35°55N 14°26E 297 D1
Mostaganem *Algeria* 35°54N 0°5E 322 A6
Mostar *Bos.-H.* 43°22N 17°50E 295 C7
Mostardas *Brazil* 31°2S 50°51W 367 C5
Mostiska = Mostyska *Ukraine* 49°48N 23°4E 289 D12
Mosty = Masty *Belarus* 53°27N 24°38E 289 B13
Mostyska *Ukraine* 49°48N 23°4E 289 D12
Mosul = Al Mawṣil *Iraq* 36°15N 43°5E 316 B4
Motagua → *Guatemala* 15°44N 88°14W 360 C2
Motala *Sweden* 58°32N 15°1E 281 G16
Motaze *Mozam.* 24°48S 32°52E 329 C5
Moth *India* 25°43N 78°57E 315 G8
Motherwell *U.K.* 55°47N 3°58W 283 F5
Motihari *India* 26°30N 84°55E 315 F11
Motozintla de Mendoza *Mexico* 15°22N 92°14W 359 D6
Motril *Spain* 36°31N 3°37W 293 D4
Mott *U.S.A.* 46°23N 102°20W 352 B2
Motueka *N.Z.* 41°7S 173°1E 331 D4
Motueka → *N.Z.* 41°5S 173°1E 331 D4
Motul *Mexico* 21°6N 89°17W 359 C7
Mouchalagane → *Canada* 50°56N 68°41W 345 B6
Moudros *Greece* 39°50N 25°18E 295 E11
Mouila *Gabon* 1°50S 11°0E 324 E2
Moulamein *Australia* 35°3S 144°1E 335 F3
Moule à Chique, C. *St. Lucia* 13°43N 60°57W 361 f
Mouliana *Greece* 35°10N 25°59E 297 D7
Moulins *France* 46°35N 3°19E 292 C5
Moulmein *Burma* 16°30N 97°40E 313 L20
Moulouya, O. → *Morocco* 35°5N 2°25W 322 B5
Moultrie *U.S.A.* 31°11N 83°47W 357 F13
Moultrie, L. *U.S.A.* 33°20N 80°5W 357 E14
Mound City *Mo., U.S.A.* 40°7N 95°14W 352 E6
Mound City *S. Dak., U.S.A.* 45°44N 100°4W 352 C3
Moundou *Chad* 8°40N 16°10E 323 G9
Moundsville *U.S.A.* 39°55N 80°44W 354 G4
Moung *Cambodia* 12°46N 103°27E 310 F4
Mount Airy *U.S.A.* 36°31N 80°37W 357 C14
Mount Albert *Canada* 44°8N 79°19W 354 B5
Mount Aspiring △ *N.Z.* 44°19S 168°47E 331 F2
Mount Barker *S. Austral., Australia* 35°5S 138°52E 335 F2
Mount Barker *W. Austral., Australia* 34°38S 117°40E 333 F2
Mount Bellew Bridge *Ireland* 53°28N 8°31W 282 C3
Mount Brydges *Canada* 42°54N 81°29W 354 D3
Mount Burr *Australia* 37°34S 140°26E 335 F3
Mount Carmel = Ha Karmel △ *Israel* 32°45N 35°5E 318 C4
Mount Carmel *Ill., U.S.A.* 38°25N 87°46W 352 F10
Mount Carmel *Pa., U.S.A.* 40°47N 76°26W 355 F8
Mount Clemens *U.S.A.* 42°35N 82°53W 354 D2
Mount Coolon *Australia* 21°25S 147°25E 334 C4
Mount Darwin *Zimbabwe* 16°47S 31°38E 327 F3
Mount Desert I. *U.S.A.* 44°21N 68°20W 353 C19
Mount Dora *U.S.A.* 28°48N 81°38W 357 G14
Mount Edziza ⌂ *Canada* 57°30N 130°45W 342 B2
Mount Elgon △ *E. Afr.* 1°4N 34°42E 326 B3
Mount Field △ *Australia* 42°39S 146°35E 335 G4
Mount Fletcher *S. Africa* 30°40S 28°30E 329 E4
Mount Forest *Canada* 43°59N 80°43W 354 C4
Mount Frankland △ *Australia* 31°47S 116°37E 332 F2
Mount Gambier *Australia* 37°50S 140°46E 335 F3
Mount Garnet *Australia* 17°37S 145°6E 334 B4
Mount Holly *U.S.A.* 39°59N 74°47W 355 G10
Mount Holly Springs *U.S.A.* 40°7N 77°12W 354 F7
Mount Hope *N.S.W., Australia* 32°51S 145°51E 335 E4
Mount Hope *S. Austral., Australia* 34°7S 135°23E 335 E2
Mount Isa *Australia* 20°42S 139°26E 334 C2
Mount Jewett *U.S.A.* 41°44N 78°39W 354 E6
Mount Kaputar △ *Australia* 30°16S 150°10E 335 E5
Mount Kenya △ *Kenya* 0°7S 37°21E 326 C4
Mount Kilimanjaro △ *Tanzania* 3°2S 37°19E 326 C4
Mount Kisco *U.S.A.* 41°12N 73°44W 355 E11
Mount Laguna *U.S.A.* 32°52N 116°25W 351 N10
Mount Larcom *Australia* 23°48S 150°59E 334 C5
Mount Lofty Ranges *Australia* 34°35S 139°5E 335 E2
Mount Magnet *Australia* 28°2S 117°47E 333 E2
Mount Maunganui *N.Z.* 37°40S 176°14E 331 B6
Mount Molloy *Australia* 16°42S 145°20E 334 B4
Mount Morgan *Australia* 23°40S 150°25E 334 C5
Mount Morris *U.S.A.* 42°44N 77°52W 354 D7
Mount Pearl *Canada* 47°31N 52°47W 345 C9
Mount Penn *U.S.A.* 40°20N 75°54W 355 F9
Mount Perry *Australia* 25°13S 151°42E 335 D5
Mount Pleasant *Iowa, U.S.A.* 40°58N 91°33W 352 E8
Mount Pleasant *Mich., U.S.A.* 43°36N 84°46W 353 D11
Mount Pleasant *Pa., U.S.A.* 40°9N 79°33W 354 F5
Mount Pleasant *S.C., U.S.A.* 32°47N 79°52W 357 E15
Mount Pleasant *Tenn., U.S.A.* 35°32N 87°12W 357 D11
Mount Pleasant *Tex., U.S.A.* 33°9N 94°58W 356 E7
Mount Pleasant *Utah, U.S.A.* 39°33N 111°27W 348 G8
Mount Pocono *U.S.A.* 41°7N 75°22W 355 E9
Mount Rainier △ *U.S.A.* 46°55N 121°50W 350 D5
Mount Revelstoke △ *Canada* 51°5N 118°30W 342 C5
Mount Robson ⌂ *Canada* 53°0N 119°0W 342 C5
Mount St. Helens ⌂ *U.S.A.* 46°14N 122°11W 350 D4
Mount Selinda *Zimbabwe* 20°24S 32°43E 329 C5
Mount Shasta *U.S.A.* 41°19N 122°19W 348 F2
Mount Signal *U.S.A.* 32°39N 115°37W 351 N11
Mount Sterling *Ill., U.S.A.* 39°59N 90°45W 352 F8
Mount Sterling *Ky., U.S.A.* 38°4N 83°56W 353 F12
Mount Surprise *Australia* 18°10S 144°17E 334 B3
Mount Union *U.S.A.* 40°23N 77°53W 354 F7
Mount Upton *U.S.A.* 42°26N 75°23W 355 D9
Mount Vernon *Ill., U.S.A.* 38°19N 88°55W 352 F9
Mount Vernon *Ind., U.S.A.* 37°56N 87°54W 352 G10
Mount Vernon *N.Y., U.S.A.* 40°54N 73°49W 355 F11
Mount Vernon *Ohio, U.S.A.* 40°23N 82°29W 354 F2
Mount Vernon *Wash., U.S.A.* 48°25N 122°20W 350 B4
Mount William △ *Australia* 40°56S 148°14E 335 G4
Mountain Ash *U.K.* 51°40N 3°23W 285 F4
Mountain Center *U.S.A.* 33°42N 116°44W 351 M10
Mountain City *Nev., U.S.A.* 41°50N 115°58W 348 F6
Mountain City *Tenn., U.S.A.* 36°29N 81°48W 357 C14
Mountain Dale *U.S.A.* 41°41N 74°32W 355 E10
Mountain Grove *U.S.A.* 37°8N 92°16W 352 G7
Mountain Home *Ark., U.S.A.* 36°20N 92°23W 356 C8
Mountain Home *Idaho, U.S.A.* 43°8N 115°41W 348 E6
Mountain Iron *U.S.A.* 47°32N 92°37W 352 B7
Mountain Pass *U.S.A.* 35°29N 115°35W 351 K11
Mountain View *Ark., U.S.A.* 35°52N 92°7W 356 D8
Mountain View *Calif., U.S.A.* 37°23N 122°5W 350 H4
Mountain View *Hawai'i, U.S.A.* 19°33N 155°7W 346 b
Mountain Zebra △ *S. Africa* 32°14S 25°27E 328 E4
Mountainair *U.S.A.* 34°31N 106°15W 349 J10
Mountlake Terrace *U.S.A.* 47°47N 122°18W 350 C4
Mountmellick *Ireland* 53°7N 7°20W 282 C4
Mountrath *Ireland* 53°0N 7°28W 282 D4
Moura *Australia* 24°35S 149°58E 334 C4
Moura *Brazil* 1°32S 61°38W 364 D6
Moura *Portugal* 38°7N 7°30W 293 C2
Mourdi, Dépression du *Chad* 18°10N 23°0E 323 E10
Mourilyan *Australia* 17°35S 146°3E 334 B4
Mourne → *U.K.* 54°52N 7°26W 282 B4
Mourne Mts. *U.K.* 54°10N 6°0W 282 B5
Mournies *Greece* 35°29N 24°1E 297 D6
Mouscron *Belgium* 50°45N 3°12E 287 D3
Moussoro *Chad* 13°41N 16°35E 323 F9
Moutong *Indonesia* 0°28N 121°13E 309 D6
Movas *Mexico* 28°10N 109°25W 358 B3
Moville *Ireland* 55°11N 7°3W 282 A4
Mowandjum *Australia* 17°22S 123°40E 332 C3
Moy → *Ireland* 54°8N 9°8W 282 B2
Moya *Comoros Is.* 12°18S 44°18E 325 a
Moyale *Kenya* 3°30N 39°0E 326 B4
Moyen Atlas *Morocco* 33°0N 5°0W 322 B4
Moyne, L. Le *Canada* 56°45N 68°47W 345 A6
Moyo *Indonesia* 8°10S 117°40E 308 F5
Moyobamba *Peru* 6°0S 77°0W 364 E3
Moyyero → *Russia* 68°44N 103°42E 301 C11
Moyynqum *Kazakhstan* 44°12N 71°0E 300 E8
Moyynty *Kazakhstan* 47°10N 73°18E 300 E8
Mozambique = Moçambique *Mozam.* 15°3S 40°42E 327 F5
Mozambique ■ *Africa* 19°0S 35°0E 327 F4
Mozambique Chan. *Africa* 17°30S 42°30E 329 B7
Mozdok *Russia* 43°45N 44°48E 291 F7
Mozdūrān *Iran* 36°9N 60°35E 317 B9
Mozhnābād *Iran* 34°7N 60°6E 317 C9
Mozyr = Mazyr *Belarus* 51°59N 29°15E 289 B15
Mpanda *Tanzania* 6°23S 31°1E 326 D3
Mphoengs *Zimbabwe* 21°10S 27°51E 329 C4
Mpika *Zambia* 11°51S 31°25E 327 E3
Mpulungu *Zambia* 8°51S 31°5E 327 D3
Mpumalanga *S. Africa* 29°50S 30°33E 329 D5
Mpumalanga □ *S. Africa* 26°0S 30°0E 329 D5
Mpwapwa *Tanzania* 6°23S 36°30E 326 D4
Mqanduli *S. Africa* 31°49S 28°45E 329 E4
Msaken *Tunisia* 35°49N 10°33E 323 A8
Msambansovu *Zimbabwe* 15°50S 30°3E 327 F3
M'sila → *Algeria* 35°30N 4°29E 322 A6
Msoro *Zambia* 13°35S 31°50E 327 E3
Mstislavl = Mstsislaw *Belarus* 54°0N 31°50E 289 A16
Mstsislaw *Belarus* 54°0N 31°50E 289 A16
Mtama *Tanzania* 10°17S 39°21E 327 E4
Mtamvuna → *S. Africa* 31°6S 30°12E 329 E5
Mthatha *S. Africa* 31°36S 28°49E 329 E4
Mtilikwe → *Zimbabwe* 21°9S 31°30E 327 G3
Mtito Andei *Kenya* 2°41S 38°10E 326 C4
Mtubatuba *S. Africa* 28°30S 32°8E 329 D5
Mtwalume *S. Africa* 30°30S 30°38E 329 E5
Mtwara-Mikindani *Tanzania* 10°20S 40°20E 327 E5
Mu Gia, Deo *Vietnam* 17°40N 105°47E 310 D5
Mu Ko Chang △ *Thailand* 11°59N 102°22E 311 G4
Mu Us Shamo *China* 39°0N 109°0E 306 E5
Muang Chiang Rai = Chiang Rai *Thailand* 19°52N 99°50E 310 C2
Muang Khong *Laos* 14°7N 105°51E 310 E5
Muang Lamphun *Thailand* 18°40N 99°2E 310 C2
Muang Mai *Thailand* 8°5N 98°21E 311 a
Muang Pak Beng *Laos* 19°54N 101°8E 310 C3
Muar *Malaysia* 2°3N 102°34E 311 L4
Muarabungo *Indonesia* 1°28S 102°52E 308 E2
Muaraenim *Indonesia* 3°40S 103°50E 308 E2

Muarajuloi Indonesia 0°12S 114°3E 308 E4
Muarakaman Indonesia 0°2S 116°45E 308 E5
Muaratebo Indonesia 1°30S 102°26E 308 E2
Muaratembesi Indonesia 1°42S 103°8E 308 E2
Muaratewe Indonesia 0°58S 114°52E 308 E4
Mubarakpur India 26°6N 83°18E 315 F10
Mubarraz = Al Mubarraz Si. Arabia 25°30N 49°40E 317 E6
Mubende Uganda 0°33N 31°22E 326 B3
Mubi Nigeria 10°18N 13°16E 323 F8
Mucajaí → Brazil 2°25N 60°52W 364 C6
Muchachos, Roque de los Canary Is. 28°44N 17°52W 296 F2
Muchinga Mts. Zambia 11°30S 31°30E 327 E3
Muck U.K. 56°50N 6°15W 283 E2
Muckadilla Australia 26°35S 148°23E 335 D4
Muckle Flugga U.K. 60°51N 0°54W 283 A8
Mucuri Brazil 18°0S 39°36W 365 G11
Mucusso Angola 18°1S 21°25E 328 B3
Muda Canary Is. 28°34N 13°57W 296 F6
Mudanjiang China 44°38N 129°30E 307 B15
Mudanya Turkey 40°25N 28°50E 295 D13
Muddy Cr. → U.S.A. 38°24N 110°42W 348 G8
Mudgee Australia 32°32S 149°31E 335 E4
Mudjatik → Canada 56°1N 107°36W 343 B7
Muecate Mozam. 14°55S 39°40E 327 E4
Mueda Mozam. 11°36S 39°28E 327 E4
Mueller Ranges Australia 18°18S 126°46E 332 C4
Muende Mozam. 14°28S 33°0E 327 E3
Muerto, Mar Mexico 16°10N 94°10W 359 D6
Mufulira Zambia 12°32S 28°15E 327 E2
Mufumbiro Range Africa 1°25S 29°30E 326 C2
Mughal Sarai India 25°18N 83°7E 315 G10
Mughayrā' Si. Arabia 29°17N 37°41E 316 D3
Mugi Japan 33°40N 134°25E 303 H7
Mugila, Mts. Dem. Rep. of the Congo 7°0S 28°50E 326 D2
Muğla Turkey 37°15N 28°22E 295 F13
Mugu Nepal 29°45N 82°30E 315 E10
Muhammad, Râs Egypt 27°44N 34°16E 316 E2
Muhammad Qol Sudan 20°53N 37°9E 323 D13
Muhammadabad India 26°4N 83°25E 315 F10
Muhesi → Tanzania 7°0S 35°20E 326 D4
Mühlhausen Germany 51°12N 10°27E 288 C6
Mühlig Hofmann fjell Antarctica 72°30S 5°0E 277 D3
Muhos Finland 64°47N 25°59E 280 D21
Muhu Estonia 58°36N 23°11E 281 G20
Muhutwe Tanzania 1°35S 31°45E 326 C3
Mui Wo China 22°16N 113°59E 305 G10
Muine Bheag Ireland 52°42N 6°58W 282 D5
Muir, L. Australia 34°30S 116°40E 333 F2
Muir of Ord U.K. 57°32N 4°28W 283 D4
Mujnak = Muynak Uzbekistan 43°44N 59°10E 300 E6
Muka, Tanjung Malaysia 5°28N 100°11E 311 c
Mukacheve Ukraine 48°27N 22°45E 289 D12
Mukachevo = Mukacheve Ukraine 48°27N 22°45E 289 D12
Mukah Malaysia 2°55N 112°5E 308 D4
Mukandwara India 24°49N 75°59E 314 G6
Mukdahan Thailand 16°32N 104°43E 310 D5
Mukden = Shenyang China 41°48N 123°27E 307 D12
Mukerian India 31°57N 75°37E 314 D6
Mukinbudin Australia 30°55S 118°5E 333 F2
Mukishi Dem. Rep. of the Congo 8°30S 24°44E 327 D1
Mukomuko Indonesia 2°30S 101°10E 308 E2
Mukomwenze Dem. Rep. of the Congo 6°49S 27°15E 326 D2
Muktsar India 30°30N 74°30E 314 D6
Mukur = Moqor Afghan. 32°50N 67°42E 314 C2
Mukutawa → Canada 53°10N 97°24W 343 C9
Mukwela Zambia 17°0S 26°40E 327 F2
Mula Spain 38°3N 1°33W 293 C5
Mula → Pakistan 27°57N 67°36E 314 F2
Mulange Dem. Rep. of the Congo 3°40S 27°10E 326 C2
Mulanje Malawi 16°2S 35°33E 327 F4
Mulanje, Mt. Malawi 16°0S 35°30E 327 F4
Mulchén Chile 37°45S 72°20W 366 D1
Mulde → Germany 51°53N 12°15E 288 C7
Mule Creek Junction U.S.A. 43°23N 104°13W 348 E11
Muleba Tanzania 1°50S 31°37E 326 C3
Mulegé Mexico 26°53N 111°59W 358 B2
Muleshoe U.S.A. 34°13N 102°43W 356 D3
Mulgrave Canada 45°38N 61°31W 345 C7
Mulhacén Spain 37°4N 3°20W 293 D4
Mulhouse France 47°40N 7°20E 292 C7
Mulifanua Samoa 13°50S 171°59W 331 b
Muling China 44°35N 130°10E 307 B16
Mull U.K. 56°25N 5°56W 283 E3
Mull, Sound of U.K. 56°30N 5°50W 283 E3
Mullaittivu Sri Lanka 9°15N 80°49E 312 Q12
Mullen U.S.A. 42°3N 101°1W 352 D3
Mullens U.S.A. 37°35N 81°23W 353 G13
Muller, Pegunungan Indonesia 0°30N 113°30E 308 D4
Mullet Pen. Ireland 54°13N 10°2W 282 B1
Mullewa Australia 28°29S 115°30E 333 E2
Mulligan → Australia 25°0S 139°0E 334 D2
Mullingar Ireland 53°31N 7°21W 282 C4
Mullins U.S.A. 34°12N 79°15W 357 D15
Mullumbimby Australia 28°30S 153°30E 335 D5
Mulobezi Zambia 16°45S 25°7E 327 F2
Mulonga Plain Zambia 16°20S 22°40E 325 H4
Mulroy B. Ireland 55°15N 7°46W 282 A4
Multan Pakistan 30°15N 71°36E 314 D4
Mulumbe, Mts. Dem. Rep. of the Congo 8°40S 27°30E 327 D2
Mulungushi Dam Zambia 14°48S 28°48E 327 E2
Mulvane U.S.A. 37°29N 97°15W 352 G5
Mumbai India 18°56N 72°50E 312 K8
Mumbwa Zambia 15°0S 27°0E 327 F2
Mumias Kenya 0°20N 34°29E 326 C4
Mun → Thailand 15°19N 105°30E 310 E5
Muna Indonesia 5°0S 122°30E 309 F6
Munabao India 25°45N 70°17E 314 G4
Munamagi Estonia 57°43N 27°4E 281 H22
Muncan Indonesia 8°34S 115°11E 309 K18
Muncar Indonesia 8°26S 114°20E 309 J17
München Germany 48°8N 11°34E 288 D6
Munchen-Gladbach = Mönchengladbach Germany 51°11N 6°27E 288 C4
Muncho Lake Canada 59°0N 125°50W 342 B3
Munch'ŏn N. Korea 39°14N 127°19E 307 E14
Muncie U.S.A. 40°12N 85°23W 353 E11
Muncoonie L. West Australia 25°12S 138°40E 334 D2
Mundabbera Australia 25°36S 151°18E 335 D5
Munday U.S.A. 33°27N 99°38W 356 E5
Münden Germany 51°25N 9°38E 288 C5
Mundiwindi Australia 23°47S 120°9E 332 D3
Mundo Novo Brazil 11°50S 40°29W 365 F10
Mundra India 22°54N 69°48E 314 H3
Mundrabilla Australia 31°52S 127°51E 333 F4
Mungallala Australia 26°28S 147°34E 335 D4
Mungallala Cr. → Australia 28°53S 147°5E 335 D4
Mungana Australia 17°8S 144°27E 334 B3
Mungaoli India 24°24N 78°7E 314 G8
Mungari Mozam. 17°12S 33°30E 327 F3
Mungbere Dem. Rep. of the Congo 2°36N 28°28E 326 B2
Mungeli India 22°4N 81°41E 315 H9
Munger India 25°23N 86°30E 315 G12
Mungkan Kandju △ Australia 13°35S 142°52E 334 A3
Munich = München Germany 48°8N 11°34E 288 D6
Munising U.S.A. 46°25N 86°40W 352 B10
Munku-Sardyk Russia 51°45N 100°20E 301 D11
Muñoz Gamero, Pen. Chile 52°30S 73°5W 368 G2
Munroe L. Canada 59°13N 98°35W 343 B9
Munsan S. Korea 37°51N 126°48E 307 F14
Münster Germany 51°58N 7°37E 288 C4
Munster □ Ireland 52°18N 8°44W 282 D3
Muntadgin Australia 31°45S 118°33E 333 F2
Muntok Indonesia 2°5S 105°10E 308 E3
Munyama Zambia 16°5S 28°31E 327 F2
Muong Beng Laos 20°23N 101°46E 310 B3
Muong Boum Vietnam 22°24N 102°49E 310 A4
Muong Et Laos 20°49N 104°1E 310 B5
Muong Hai Laos 21°3N 101°49E 310 B3
Muong Hiem Laos 20°5N 103°22E 310 B4
Muong Houn Laos 20°8N 101°23E 310 B3
Muong Hung Vietnam 20°56N 103°53E 310 B4
Muong Kau Laos 15°6N 105°47E 310 E5
Muong Khao Laos 19°38N 103°32E 310 C4
Muong Khoua Laos 21°5N 102°31E 310 B4
Muong Liep Laos 18°29N 101°40E 310 C3
Muong May Laos 14°49N 106°56E 310 E6
Muong Ngeun Laos 20°36N 101°3E 310 B3
Muong Ngoi Laos 20°43N 102°41E 310 B4
Muong Nhie Vietnam 22°12N 102°28E 310 A4
Muong Nong Laos 16°22N 106°30E 310 D6
Muong Ou Tay Laos 22°7N 101°48E 310 A3
Muong Oua Laos 18°18N 101°20E 310 C3
Muong Peun Laos 20°13N 103°52E 310 B4
Muong Phalane Laos 16°39N 105°34E 310 D5
Muong Phieng Laos 19°6N 101°32E 310 C3
Muong Phine Laos 16°32N 106°2E 310 D6
Muong Sai Laos 20°42N 101°59E 310 B3
Muong Saiapoun Laos 18°24N 101°31E 310 C3
Muong Sen Vietnam 19°24N 104°8E 310 C5
Muong Sing Laos 21°11N 101°9E 310 B3
Muong Son Laos 20°27N 103°19E 310 B4
Muong Soui Laos 19°33N 102°52E 310 C4
Muong Va Laos 21°53N 102°19E 310 B4
Muong Xia Vietnam 20°19N 104°50E 310 B5
Muonio Finland 67°57N 23°40E 280 C20
Muonio älv = Muonionjoki → Finland 67°11N 23°34E 280 C20
Muonioälven = Muonionjoki → Finland 67°11N 23°34E 280 C20
Muonionjoki → Finland 67°11N 23°34E 280 C20
Muping China 37°22N 121°36E 307 F11
Muqdisho Somali Rep. 2°2N 45°25E 319 G4
Mur → Austria 46°18N 16°52E 289 E9
Murakami Japan 38°14N 139°29E 302 E9
Murallón, Cerro Chile 49°48S 73°30W 368 F2
Muranda Rwanda 1°52S 29°20E 326 C2
Murang'a Kenya 0°45S 37°9E 326 C4
Murashi Russia 59°30N 49°0E 290 C8
Murat → Turkey 38°46N 40°0E 291 G7
Muratlı Turkey 41°10N 27°29E 295 D12
Murayama Japan 38°30N 140°25E 302 E10
Murchison → Australia 27°45S 114°0E 333 E1
Murchison, Mt. Antarctica 73°25S 166°20E 277 D11
Murchison Falls Uganda 2°15N 31°30E 326 B3
Murchison Falls △ Uganda 2°17N 31°48E 326 B3
Murchison Ra. Australia 20°0S 134°10E 334 C1
Murchison Rapids Malawi 15°55S 34°35E 327 F3
Murcia Spain 38°5N 1°10W 293 D5
Murcia □ Spain 37°50N 1°30W 293 D5
Murdo U.S.A. 43°53N 100°43W 352 D3
Murdoch Pt. Australia 14°37S 144°55E 334 A3
Mureș → Romania 46°15N 20°13E 289 E11
Mureșul = Mureș → Romania 46°15N 20°13E 289 E11
Murewa Zimbabwe 17°39S 31°47E 329 B5
Murfreesboro N.C., U.S.A. 36°27N 77°6W 357 C16
Murfreesboro Tenn., U.S.A. 35°51N 86°24W 357 D11
Murgap Tajikistan 38°10N 74°2E 300 F8
Murgap → Turkmenistan 38°18N 61°12E 317 B9
Murgenella Australia 11°34S 132°56E 332 B5
Murgha Kibzai Pakistan 30°44N 69°25E 314 D3
Murghob = Murgap Tajikistan 38°10N 74°2E 300 F8
Murgon Australia 26°15S 151°54E 335 D5
Muri India 23°22N 85°52E 315 H11
Muria Indonesia 6°36S 110°53E 309 G14
Muriaé Brazil 21°8S 42°23W 367 A7
Muriel Mine Zimbabwe 17°14S 30°40E 327 F3
Müritz Germany 53°25N 12°42E 288 B7
Murliganj India 25°54N 86°59E 315 G12
Murmansk Russia 68°57N 33°10E 280 B25
Murmashi Russia 68°47N 32°42E 280 B25
Muro Spain 39°44N 3°3E 296 B10
Murom Russia 55°35N 42°3E 290 C7
Muroran Japan 42°25N 141°0E 302 C10
Muroto Japan 33°18N 134°9E 303 H7
Muroto-Misaki Japan 33°15N 134°10E 303 H7
Murphy U.S.A. 43°13N 116°33W 348 E5
Murphys U.S.A. 38°8N 120°28W 350 G6
Murray Ky., U.S.A. 36°37N 88°19W 352 G9
Murray Utah, U.S.A. 40°40N 111°53W 348 F8
Murray → Australia 35°20S 139°22E 335 F2
Murray, L. U.S.A. 34°3N 81°13W 357 D14
Murray Bridge Australia 35°6S 139°14E 335 F2
Murray Fracture Zone Pac. Oc. 35°0N 130°0W 337 D14
Murray Harbour Canada 46°0N 62°28W 345 C7
Murray River △ Australia 34°23S 140°32E 335 E3
Murraysburg S. Africa 31°58S 23°47E 328 E3
Murree Pakistan 33°56N 73°28E 314 C5
Murrieta U.S.A. 33°33N 117°13W 351 M9
Murrumbidgee → Australia 34°43S 143°12E 335 E3
Murrumburrah Australia 34°32S 148°22E 335 E4
Murrurundi Australia 31°42S 150°51E 335 E5
Murshidabad India 24°11N 88°19E 315 G13
Murtle L. Canada 52°8N 119°38W 342 C5
Murtoa Australia 36°35S 142°28E 335 F3
Murungu Tanzania 4°12S 31°10E 326 C3
Mururoa French Polynesia 21°52S 138°55W 337 K14
Murwara India 23°46N 80°28E 315 H9
Murwillumbah Australia 28°18S 153°27E 335 D5
Mürzzuschlag Austria 47°36N 15°41E 288 E8
Muş Turkey 38°45N 41°30E 316 B4
Mûsa, Gebel Egypt 28°33N 33°59E 316 D2
Musa Khel Pakistan 30°59N 69°52E 314 D3
Mūsa Qal'eh Afghan. 32°20N 64°50E 312 C4
Musafirkhana India 26°22N 81°48E 315 F9
Musala Bulgaria 42°13N 23°37E 295 C10
Musala Indonesia 1°41N 98°28E 308 D1
Musan N. Korea 42°12N 129°12E 307 C15
Musangu Dem. Rep. of the Congo 10°28S 23°55E 327 E1
Musasa Tanzania 3°25S 31°30E 326 C3
Musay'īd Qatar 25°0N 51°33E 317 E6
Muscat = Masqat Oman 23°37N 58°36E 319 C6
Muscatine U.S.A. 41°25N 91°3W 352 E8
Muscle Shoals U.S.A. 34°45N 87°40W 357 D11
Musengezi = Unsengedsi → Zimbabwe 15°43S 31°14E 327 F3
Musgrave Harbour Canada 49°27N 53°58W 345 C9
Musgrave Ranges Australia 26°0S 132°0E 333 E5
Mushie Dem. Rep. of the Congo 2°56S 16°55E 324 E3
Musi → Indonesia 2°20S 104°56E 308 E2
Musina S. Africa 22°20S 30°5E 329 C5
Muskeg → Canada 60°20N 123°20W 342 A4
Muskegon U.S.A. 43°14N 86°16W 352 D10
Muskegon → U.S.A. 43°14N 86°21W 352 D10
Muskegon Heights U.S.A. 43°12N 86°16W 352 D10
Muskogee U.S.A. 35°45N 95°22W 356 D7
Muskoka, L. Canada 45°0N 79°25W 354 B5
Muskwa → Canada 58°47N 122°48W 342 B4
Muslīmiyah Syria 36°19N 37°12E 316 B3
Musofu Zambia 13°30S 29°0E 327 E2
Musoma Tanzania 1°30S 33°48E 326 C3
Musquaro, L. Canada 50°38N 61°5W 345 B7
Musquodoboit Harbour Canada 44°50N 63°9W 345 D7
Musselburgh U.K. 55°57N 3°2W 283 F5
Musselshell → U.S.A. 47°21N 107°57W 348 C10
Mussende Angola 10°32S 16°5E 324 G3
Mussoorie India 30°27N 78°6E 314 D8
Mussuco Angola 17°2S 19°3E 328 B2
Mustafakemalpaşa Turkey 40°2N 28°24E 295 D13
Mustang Nepal 29°10N 83°55E 315 E10
Musters, L. Argentina 45°20S 69°25W 368 F3
Musudan N. Korea 40°50N 129°43E 307 D15
Muswellbrook Australia 32°16S 150°56E 335 E5
Mût Egypt 25°28N 28°58E 323 C11
Mut Turkey 36°40N 33°28E 316 B2
Mutanda Mozam. 21°0S 33°34E 329 C5
Mutanda Zambia 12°24S 26°13E 327 E2
Mutare Zimbabwe 18°58S 32°38E 327 F3
Mutawintji △ Australia 31°10S 142°30E 335 E3
Mutha Kenya 1°48S 38°26E 326 C4
Muting Indonesia 7°23S 140°20E 309 F10
Mutki = Mirtağ Turkey 38°23N 41°56E 316 B4
Mutoko Zimbabwe 17°24S 32°13E 329 B5
Mutomo Kenya 1°51S 38°12E 326 C4
Mutoray Russia 60°56N 101°0E 301 C11
Mutsamudu Comoros Is. 12°10S 44°25E 325 a
Mutshatsha Dem. Rep. of the Congo 10°35S 24°20E 327 E1
Mutsu Japan 41°5N 140°55E 302 D10
Mutsu-Wan Japan 41°5N 140°55E 302 D10
Muttaburra Australia 22°38S 144°29E 334 C3
Mutton I. Ireland 52°49N 9°32W 282 D2
Mutuáli Mozam. 14°55S 37°0E 327 E4
Muweilih Egypt 30°42N 34°19E 318 E3
Muy Muy Nic. 12°39N 85°36W 360 D2
Muyinga Burundi 3°14S 30°33E 326 C3
Muynak Uzbekistan 43°44N 59°10E 300 E6
Muyunkum, Peski = Moyynqum Kazakhstan 44°12N 71°0E 300 E8
Muz Tag China 36°25N 87°25E 304 C3
Muzaffarabad Pakistan 34°25N 73°30E 315 B5
Muzaffargarh Pakistan 30°5N 71°14E 314 D4
Muzaffarnagar India 29°26N 77°40E 314 E7
Muzaffarpur India 26°7N 85°23E 315 F11
Muzafirpur Pakistan 30°58N 69°9E 314 D3
Muzhi Russia 65°25N 64°40E 290 A11
Muztagh-Ata China 38°17N 75°7E 304 C2
Mvuma Zimbabwe 19°16S 30°30E 327 F3
Mvurwi Zimbabwe 17°0S 30°57E 327 F3
Mwabvi ⌂ Malawi 16°42S 35°0E 327 F3
Mwadui Tanzania 3°26S 33°32E 326 C3
Mwali = Mohéli Comoros Is. 12°20S 43°40E 325 a
Mwambo Tanzania 10°30S 40°22E 327 E5
Mwandi Zambia 17°30S 24°51E 327 F1
Mwanza Dem. Rep. of the Congo 7°55S 26°43E 326 D2
Mwanza Tanzania 2°30S 32°58E 326 C3
Mwanza Zambia 16°58S 24°28E 327 F1
Mwanza □ Tanzania 2°0S 33°0E 326 C3
Mwaya Tanzania 9°32S 33°55E 327 D3
Mweelrea Ireland 53°39N 9°49W 282 C2
Mweka Dem. Rep. of the Congo 4°50S 21°34E 324 E4
Mwene-Ditu Dem. Rep. of the Congo 6°35S 22°27E 324 F4
Mwenezi Zimbabwe 21°15S 30°48E 327 G3
Mwenezi → Mozam. 22°40S 31°50E 327 G3
Mwenga Dem. Rep. of the Congo 3°1S 28°28E 326 C2
Mweru, L. Zambia 9°0S 28°40E 327 D2
Mweru Wantipa △ Zambia 8°39S 29°25E 327 D2
Mweza Range Zimbabwe 21°0S 30°0E 327 G3
Mwilambwe Dem. Rep. of the Congo 8°7S 25°5E 326 D2
Mwimbi Tanzania 8°38S 31°39E 327 D3
Mwingi Kenya 0°56S 38°4E 326 C4
Mwinilunga Zambia 11°43S 24°25E 327 E1
My Tho Vietnam 10°29N 106°23E 311 G6
Myajlar India 26°15N 70°20E 314 F4
Myanaung Burma 18°18N 95°22E 313 K19
Myanmar = Burma ■ Asia 21°0N 96°30E 313 J20
Myaungmya Burma 16°30N 94°40E 313 L19
Mycenæ = Mikines Greece 37°43N 22°46E 295 F10
Myeik Kyunzu Burma 11°30N 97°30E 311 G1
Myerstown U.S.A. 40°22N 76°19W 355 F8
Myingyan Burma 21°30N 95°20E 313 J19
Myitkyina Burma 25°24N 97°26E 313 G20
Mykines Færoe Is. 62°7N 7°35W 280 E9
Mykolayiv Ukraine 46°58N 32°0E 291 E5
Mykonos Greece 37°30N 25°25E 295 F11
Mymensingh Bangla. 24°45N 90°24E 313 G17
Mynydd Du U.K. 51°52N 3°50W 285 F4
Mýrdalsjökull Iceland 63°40N 19°6W 280 E4
Myrtle Beach U.S.A. 33°42N 78°53W 357 E15
Myrtle Creek U.S.A. 43°1N 123°17W 348 E2
Myrtle Point U.S.A. 43°4N 124°8W 348 E1
Myrtou Cyprus 35°18N 33°4E 297 D12
Mysia Turkey 39°50N 27°0E 295 E12
Mysore = Karnataka □ India 13°15N 77°0E 312 N10
Mysore India 12°17N 76°41E 312 N10
Mystic U.S.A. 41°21N 71°58W 355 E13
Myszków Poland 50°45N 19°22E 289 C10
Mytishchi Russia 55°50N 37°50E 290 C6
Mývatn Iceland 65°36N 17°0W 280 D5
Mzimba Malawi 11°55S 33°39E 327 E3
Mzimkulu → S. Africa 30°44S 30°28E 329 E5
Mzimvubu → S. Africa 31°38S 29°33E 329 E4
Mzuzu Malawi 11°30S 33°55E 327 E3

N

Na Hearadh = Harris U.K. 57°50N 6°55W 283 D2
Na Noi Thailand 18°19N 100°43E 310 C3
Na Phao Laos 17°35N 105°44E 310 D5
Na Sam Vietnam 22°3N 106°37E 310 A6
Na San Vietnam 21°12N 104°2E 310 B5
Na Thon Thailand 9°32N 99°56E 311 b
Naab → Germany 49°1N 12°2E 288 D6
Naantali Finland 60°29N 22°2E 281 F20
Naas Ireland 53°12N 6°40W 282 C5
Nababeep S. Africa 29°36S 17°46E 328 D2
Nabadwip = Navadwip India 23°34N 88°20E 315 H13
Nabawa Australia 28°30S 114°48E 333 E1
Nabberu, L. Australia 25°50S 120°30E 333 E3
Naberezhnyye Chelny Russia 55°42N 52°19E 290 C9
Nabeul Tunisia 36°30N 10°44E 323 A8
Nabha India 30°26N 76°14E 314 D7
Nabīd Iran 29°40N 57°38E 317 D8
Nabire Indonesia 3°15S 135°26E 309 E9
Nabisar Pakistan 25°8N 69°40E 314 G3
Nabisipi → Canada 50°14N 62°13W 345 B7
Nabiswera Uganda 1°27N 32°15E 326 B3
Nāblus = Nābulus West Bank 32°14N 35°15E 318 C4
Naboomspruit S. Africa 24°32S 28°40E 329 C4
Nabouwalu Fiji 17°0S 178°45E 331 a
Nābulus West Bank 32°14N 35°15E 318 C4
Nacala Mozam. 14°31S 40°34E 327 E5
Nacala-Velha Mozam. 14°32S 40°34E 327 E5
Nacaome Honduras 13°31N 87°30W 360 D2
Nacaroa Mozam. 14°22S 39°56E 327 E4
Naches U.S.A. 46°44N 120°42W 348 C3
Naches → U.S.A. 46°38N 120°31W 350 D6
Nachicapau, L. Canada 56°40N 68°5W 345 A6
Nachingwea Tanzania 10°23S 38°49E 327 E4
Nachna India 27°34N 71°41E 314 F4
Nacimiento, L. U.S.A. 35°46N 120°53W 350 K6
Naco Mexico 31°19N 109°56W 358 A3
Nacogdoches U.S.A. 31°36N 94°39W 356 F7
Nácori Chico Mexico 29°40N 108°57W 358 B3
Nacozari de García Mexico 30°25N 109°38W 358 A3
Nacula Fiji 16°54S 177°27E 331 a
Nådendal = Naantali Finland 60°29N 22°2E 281 F20
Nadi Fiji 17°42S 177°20E 331 a
Nadiad India 22°41N 72°56E 314 H5
Nador Morocco 35°14N 2°58W 322 B5
Nadur Malta 36°2N 14°18E 297 C1
Nadūshan Iran 32°2N 53°35E 317 C7
Nadvirna Ukraine 48°37N 24°30E 289 D13
Nadvoitsy Russia 63°52N 34°14E 290 B5
Nadvornaya = Nadvirna Ukraine 48°37N 24°30E 289 D13
Nadym Russia 65°35N 72°42E 300 C8
Nadym → Russia 66°12N 72°0E 300 C8
Nærbø Norway 58°40N 5°39E 281 G11
Næstved Denmark 55°13N 11°44E 281 J14
Nafpaktos Greece 38°24N 21°50E 295 E9
Nafplio Greece 37°33N 22°50E 295 F10
Naft-e Safīd Iran 31°40N 49°17E 317 D6
Naftshahr Iran 34°0N 45°30E 316 C5
Nafud Desert = An Nafūd Si. Arabia 28°15N 41°0E 316 D4
Naga Phil. 13°38N 123°15E 309 B6
Nagagami Canada 50°23N 84°20W 344 B3
Nagahama Japan 35°23N 136°16E 303 G8
Nagai Japan 38°6N 140°2E 302 E10
Nagaland □ India 26°0N 94°30E 313 G19
Nagano Japan 36°40N 138°10E 303 F9
Nagano □ Japan 36°15N 138°0E 303 F9
Nagaoka Japan 37°27N 138°51E 303 F9
Nagappattinam India 10°46N 79°51E 312 P11
Nagar → Bangla. 24°27N 89°12E 315 G13
Nagar Parkar Pakistan 24°28N 70°46E 314 G4
Nagasaki Japan 32°47N 129°50E 303 H4
Nagasaki □ Japan 32°50N 129°40E 303 H4
Nagato Japan 34°19N 131°5E 303 G5
Nagaur India 27°15N 73°45E 314 F5
Nagda India 23°27N 75°25E 314 H6
Nagercoil India 8°12N 77°26E 312 Q10
Nagina India 29°30N 78°30E 315 E8
Nagīneh Iran 34°20N 57°15E 317 C8
Nagir Pakistan 36°12N 74°42E 315 A6
Nagles Mts. Ireland 52°8N 8°30W 282 D3
Nagod India 24°34N 80°36E 315 G9
Nagoorin Australia 24°17S 151°15E 334 C5
Nagorno-Karabakh □ Azerbaijan 39°55N 46°45E 316 B5
Nagornyy Russia 55°58N 124°57E 301 D13
Nagoya Japan 35°10N 136°50E 303 G8
Nagpur India 21°8N 79°10E 312 J11
Nagua Dom. Rep. 19°23N 69°50W 361 C6
Naguabo Puerto Rico 18°13N 65°44W 361 d
Nagykanizsa Hungary 46°28N 17°0E 289 E9
Nagykőrös Hungary 47°5N 19°48E 289 E10
Naha Japan 26°13N 127°42E 303 L3
Nahan India 30°33N 77°18E 314 D7
Nahanni △ Canada 61°36N 125°41W 342 A4
Nahanni Butte Canada 61°2N 123°31W 342 A4
Nahargarh Mad. P., India 24°10N 75°14E 314 G6
Nahargarh Raj., India 24°55N 76°50E 314 G7
Nahariyya Israel 33°1N 35°5E 316 C2
Nahāvand Iran 34°10N 48°22E 317 C6
Nahuel Huapi, L. Argentina 41°0S 71°32W 368 E2
Nahuelbuta △ Chile 37°44S 72°57W 366 D1
Nai Yong Thailand 8°14N 98°22E 311 a
Naicá Mexico 27°53N 105°31W 358 B3
Naicam Canada 52°30N 104°30W 343 C8
Naikoon ⌂ Canada 53°55N 131°55W 342 C2
Naimisharanya India 27°21N 80°30E 315 F9
Nain Canada 56°34N 61°40W 345 A7
Nā'īn Iran 32°54N 53°0E 317 C7
Naini Tal India 29°30N 79°30E 315 E8
Nainpur India 22°30N 80°10E 315 H9
Nainwa India 25°46N 75°51E 314 G6
Nairai Fiji 17°49S 179°15E 331 a
Nairn U.K. 57°35N 3°53W 283 D5
Nairobi Kenya 1°17S 36°48E 326 C4
Nairobi △ Kenya 1°22S 36°50E 326 C4
Naissaar Estonia 59°34N 24°29E 281 G21
Naitaba Fiji 17°0S 179°16W 331 a
Naivasha Kenya 0°40S 36°30E 326 C4
Naivasha, L. Kenya 0°48S 36°20E 326 C4
Najaf = An Najaf Iraq 32°3N 44°15E 316 C5
Najafābād Iran 32°40N 51°15E 317 C6
Najd Si. Arabia 26°30N 42°0E 319 B3
Najibabad India 29°40N 78°20E 314 E8
Najin N. Korea 42°12N 130°15E 307 C16
Najmah Si. Arabia 26°42N 50°6E 317 E6
Najrān Si. Arabia 17°34N 44°18E 319 D3
Naju S. Korea 35°3N 126°43E 307 G14
Nakadōri-Shima Japan 32°57N 129°4E 303 H4
Nakalagba Dem. Rep. of the Congo 2°50N 27°58E 326 B2
Nakaminato Japan 36°21N 140°36E 303 F10
Nakamura Japan 32°59N 132°56E 303 H6
Nakano Japan 36°45N 138°22E 303 F9
Nakano-Shima Japan 29°51N 129°52E 303 K4
Nakashibetsu Japan 43°33N 144°59E 302 C12
Nakfa Eritrea 16°40N 38°32E 319 D2
Nakha Yai, Ko Thailand 8°3N 98°28E 311 a

Nakhichevan = Naxçıvan Azerbaijan 39°12N 45°15E 316 B5
Nakhichevan Rep. = Naxçıvan □ Azerbaijan 39°25N 45°26E 316 B5
Nakhl Egypt 29°55N 33°43E 318 F2
Nakhl-e Taqī Iran 27°28N 52°36E 317 E7
Nakhodka Russia 42°53N 132°54E 302 C6
Nakhon Nayok Thailand 14°12N 101°13E 310 E3
Nakhon Pathom Thailand 13°49N 100°3E 310 F3
Nakhon Phanom Thailand 17°23N 104°43E 310 D5
Nakhon Ratchasima Thailand 14°59N 102°12E 310 E4
Nakhon Sawan Thailand 15°35N 100°10E 310 E3
Nakhon Si Thammarat Thailand 8°29N 100°0E 311 H3
Nakhon Thai Thailand 17°5N 100°44E 310 D3
Nakhtarana India 23°20N 69°15E 314 H3
Nakina Canada 50°10N 86°40W 344 B2
Nakodar India 31°8N 75°31E 314 D6
Naktong → S. Korea 35°7N 128°57E 307 G15
Nakuru Kenya 0°15S 36°4E 326 C4
Nakuru, L. Kenya 0°23S 36°5E 326 C4
Nakusp Canada 50°20N 117°45W 342 C5
Nal Pakistan 27°40N 66°12E 314 F2
Nal → Pakistan 25°20N 65°30E 314 G1
Nalázi Mozam. 24°3S 33°20E 329 C5
Nalchik Russia 43°30N 43°33E 291 F7
Nalgonda India 17°6N 79°15E 312 L11
Nalhati India 24°17N 87°52E 315 G12
Naliya India 23°16N 68°50E 314 H3
Nallamalai Hills India 15°30N 78°50E 312 M11
Nalubaale Dam Uganda 0°30N 33°5E 326 B3
Nam Can Vietnam 8°46N 104°59E 311 H5
Nam-ch'on N. Korea 38°15N 126°26E 307 E14
Nam Co China 30°30N 90°45E 304 C4
Nam Dinh Vietnam 20°25N 106°5E 310 B6
Nam Du, Hon Vietnam 9°41N 104°21E 311 H5
Nam Nao △ Thailand 16°44N 101°32E 310 D3
Nam Ngum Res. Laos 18°35N 102°34E 310 C4
Nam-Phan Vietnam 10°30N 106°0E 311 G6
Nam Phong Thailand 16°42N 102°52E 310 D4
Nam Tha Laos 20°58N 101°30E 310 B3
Nam Tok Thailand 14°21N 99°4E 310 E2
Namacunde Angola 17°18S 15°50E 328 B2
Namacurra Mozam. 17°30S 36°50E 329 B6
Namak, Daryācheh-ye Iran 34°30N 52°0E 317 C7
Namak, Kavir-e Iran 34°30N 57°30E 317 C8
Namakzār, Daryācheh-ye Iran 34°0N 60°30E 317 C9
Namaland Namibia 26°0S 17°0E 328 C2
Namanga Kenya 2°33S 36°47E 326 C4
Namangan Uzbekistan 41°0N 71°40E 300 E8
Namapa Mozam. 13°43S 39°50E 327 E4
Namaqualand S. Africa 30°0S 17°25E 328 E2
Namasagali Uganda 1°2N 33°0E 326 B3
Namber Indonesia 1°2S 134°49E 309 E8
Nambour Australia 26°32S 152°58E 335 D5
Nambouwalu = Nabouwalu Fiji 17°0S 178°45E 331 a
Nambucca Heads Australia 30°37S 153°0E 335 E5
Nambung △ Australia 30°30S 115°5E 333 F2
Namcha Barwa China 29°40N 95°10E 304 D4
Namche Bazar Nepal 27°51N 86°47E 315 F12
Namchonjŏm = Nam-ch'on N. Korea 38°15N 126°26E 307 E14
Namecunda Mozam. 14°54S 37°37E 327 E4
Namenalala Fiji 17°8S 179°9E 331 a
Nameponda Mozam. 15°50S 39°50E 327 F4
Nametil Mozam. 15°40S 39°21E 327 F4
Namew L. Canada 54°14N 101°56W 343 C8
Namgia India 31°48N 78°40E 315 D8
Namib Desert Namibia 22°30S 15°0E 328 C2
Namib-Naukluft ⌂ Namibia 24°40S 15°16E 328 C2
Namibe Angola 15°7S 12°11E 325 H2
Namibe □ Angola 16°35S 12°30E 328 B1
Namibia ■ Africa 22°0S 18°9E 328 C2
Namibwoestyn = Namib Desert Namibia 22°30S 15°0E 328 C2
Namlea Indonesia 3°18S 127°5E 309 E7
Namoi → Australia 30°12S 149°30E 335 E4
Nampa U.S.A. 43°34N 116°34W 348 E5
Namp'o N. Korea 38°52N 125°10E 307 E13
Nampō-Shotō Japan 32°0N 140°0E 303 J10
Nampula Mozam. 15°6S 39°15E 327 F4
Namrole Indonesia 3°46S 126°46E 309 E7
Namse Shankou China 30°0N 82°25E 315 E10
Namsen → Norway 64°28N 11°37E 280 D14
Namsos Norway 64°29N 11°30E 280 D14
Namtok Chat Trakan △ Thailand 17°17N 100°40E 310 D3
Namtok Mae Surin △ Thailand 18°55N 98°2E 310 C2
Namtsy Russia 62°43N 129°37E 301 C13
Namtu Burma 23°5N 97°28E 313 H20
Namtumbo Tanzania 10°30S 36°4E 327 E4
Namu Canada 51°52N 127°50W 342 C3
Namuka-i-Lau Fiji 18°53S 178°37W 331 a
Namur Belgium 50°27N 4°52E 287 D4
Namur □ Belgium 50°17N 5°0E 287 D4
Namuruputh Kenya 4°34N 35°57E 326 B4
Namutoni Namibia 18°49S 16°55E 328 B2
Namwala Zambia 15°44S 26°30E 327 F2
Namwon S. Korea 35°23N 127°23E 307 G14
Namyang N. Korea 42°57N 129°52E 307 C15
Nan Thailand 18°48N 100°46E 310 C3
Nan → Thailand 15°42N 100°9E 310 E3
Nan-ch'ang = Nanchang China 28°42N 115°55E 305 D6
Nanaimo Canada 49°10N 124°0W 342 D4
Nanam N. Korea 41°44N 129°40E 307 D15
Nanango Australia 26°40S 152°0E 335 D5
Nanao Japan 37°0N 137°0E 303 F8
Nanchang China 28°42N 115°55E 305 D6
Nanching = Nanjing China 32°2N 118°47E 305 C6
Nanchong China 30°43N 106°2E 304 C5
Nancy France 48°42N 6°12E 292 B7
Nanda Devi India 30°23N 79°59E 315 D8
Nanda Devi △ India 30°30N 79°50E 315 D8
Nanda Kot India 30°17N 80°5E 315 D9
Nandan Japan 34°10N 134°42E 303 G7
Nanded India 19°10N 77°20E 312 K10
Nandewar Ra. Australia 30°15S 150°35E 335 E5
Nandi = Nadi Fiji 17°42S 177°20E 331 a
Nandigram India 22°1N 87°58E 315 H12
Nandurbar India 21°20N 74°15E 312 J9
Nandyal India 15°30N 78°30E 312 M11
Nanga-Eboko Cameroon 4°41N 12°22E 324 D2
Nanga Parbat Pakistan 35°10N 74°35E 315 B6
Nangade Mozam. 11°5S 39°36E 327 E4
Nangapinoh Indonesia 0°20S 111°44E 308 E4
Nangarhār □ Afghan. 34°20N 70°0E 312 B7
Nangatayap Indonesia 1°32S 110°34E 308 E4
Nangeya Mts. Uganda 3°30N 33°30E 326 B3
Nangong China 37°23N 115°22E 306 F8
Nanhuang China 36°58N 121°48E 307 F11
Nanjeko Zambia 15°31S 23°30E 327 F1
Nanjing China 32°2N 118°47E 305 C6
Nanjirinji Tanzania 9°41S 39°5E 327 D4
Nankana Sahib Pakistan 31°27N 73°38E 314 D5
Nanking = Nanjing China 32°2N 118°47E 305 C6
Nankoku Japan 33°39N 133°44E 303 H6
Nanlang China 22°30N 113°32E 305 G10
Nanning China 22°48N 108°20E 304 D5
Nannup Australia 33°59S 115°48E 333 F2
Nanpara India 27°52N 81°33E 315 F9
Nanpi China 38°2N 116°45E 306 E9
Nanping China 26°38N 118°10E 305 D6
Nanripe Mozam. 13°52S 38°52E 327 E4
Nansei-Shotō = Ryūkyū-rettō Japan 26°0N 126°0E 303 M3
Nansen Basin Arctic 84°0N 50°0E 276 A10
Nansen Sd. Canada 81°0N 91°0W 341 A10
Nansha China 22°45N 113°34E 305 F10
Nanshan I. S. China Sea 10°45N 115°49E 308 B5
Nansio Tanzania 2°3S 33°4E 326 C3
Nantes France 47°12N 1°33W 292 C3
Nanticoke U.S.A. 41°12N 76°0W 355 E8
Nanton Canada 50°21N 113°46W 342 C6
Nantong China 32°1N 120°52E 305 C7
Nantou China 22°32N 113°55E 305 F10
Nantucket I. U.S.A. 41°16N 70°5W 353 E18
Nantwich U.K. 53°4N 2°31W 284 D5
Nanty Glo U.S.A. 40°28N 78°50W 354 F6
Nanuku Passage Fiji 16°45S 179°15W 331 a
Nanuque Brazil 17°50S 40°21W 365 G10
Nanusa, Kepulauan Indonesia 4°45N 127°1E 309 D7
Nanutarra Roadhouse Australia 22°32S 115°30E 332 D2
Nanyang China 33°11N 112°30E 306 H7
Nanyuki Kenya 0°2N 37°4E 326 B4
Nao, C. de la Spain 38°44N 0°14E 293 C6
Naococane, L. Canada 52°50N 70°45W 345 B5
Napa U.S.A. 38°18N 122°17W 350 G4
Napa → U.S.A. 38°10N 122°19W 350 G4
Napanee Canada 44°15N 77°0W 354 B8
Napanoch U.S.A. 41°44N 74°22W 355 E10
Nape Laos 18°18N 105°6E 310 C5
Nape Pass = Keo Neua, Deo Vietnam 18°23N 105°10E 310 C5
Napier N.Z. 39°30S 176°56E 331 C6
Napier Broome B. Australia 14°2S 126°37E 332 B4
Napier Pen. Australia 12°4S 135°43E 334 A2
Napierville Canada 45°11N 73°25W 355 A11
Naples = Nápoli Italy 40°50N 14°15E 294 D6
Naples U.S.A. 26°8N 81°48W 357 H14
Napo → Peru 3°20S 72°40W 364 D4
Napoleon N. Dak., U.S.A. 46°30N 99°46W 352 B4
Napoleon Ohio, U.S.A. 41°23N 84°8W 353 E11
Nápoli Italy 40°50N 14°15E 294 D6
Napopo Dem. Rep. of the Congo 4°15N 28°0E 326 B2
Naqb, Ra's an Jordan 29°48N 35°44E 318 F4
Naqqāsh Iran 35°40N 49°6E 317 C6
Nara Japan 34°40N 135°49E 303 G7
Nara Mali 15°10N 7°20W 322 E4
Nara □ Japan 34°30N 136°0E 303 G8
Nara Canal Pakistan 24°30N 69°20E 314 G3
Nara Visa U.S.A. 35°37N 103°6W 349 J12
Naracoorte Australia 36°58S 140°45E 335 F3
Naradhan Australia 33°34S 146°17E 335 E4
Naraini India 25°11N 80°29E 315 G9
Naranjos Mexico 21°21N 97°41W 359 C5
Narasapur India 16°26N 81°40E 313 L12
Narathiwat Thailand 6°30N 101°48E 311 J3
Narayanganj Bangla. 23°40N 90°33E 313 H17
Narayanpet India 16°45N 77°30E 312 L10
Narberth U.K. 51°47N 4°44W 285 F3
Narbonne France 43°11N 3°0E 292 E5
Nardīn Iran 37°3N 55°59E 317 B7
Nardò Italy 40°11N 18°2E 295 D8
Narembeen Australia 32°7S 118°24E 333 F2
Narendranagar India 30°10N 78°18E 314 D8
Nares Str. Arctic 80°0N 70°0W 338 A13
Naretha Australia 31°0S 124°45E 333 F3
Narew → Poland 52°26N 20°41E 289 B11
Nari → Pakistan 28°0N 67°40E 314 F2
Narin Afghan. 36°5N 69°0E 312 A6
Narindra, Helodranon' i Madag. 14°55S 47°30E 329 A8
Narita Japan 35°47N 140°19E 303 G10
Nariva Swamp Trin. & Tob. 10°26N 61°4W 365 K15
Narmada → India 21°38N 72°36E 314 J5
Narnaul India 28°5N 76°11E 314 E7
Narodnaya Russia 65°5N 59°58E 290 A10
Narok Kenya 1°55S 35°52E 326 C4
Narooma Australia 36°14S 150°4E 335 F5
Narowal Pakistan 32°6N 74°52E 314 C6
Narrabri Australia 30°19S 149°46E 335 E4
Narran → Australia 28°37S 148°12E 335 D4
Narrandera Australia 34°42S 146°31E 335 E4
Narrogin Australia 32°58S 117°14E 333 F2
Narromine Australia 32°12S 148°12E 335 E4
Narrow Hills ⌂ Canada 54°0N 104°37W 343 C8
Narsimhapur India 22°54N 79°14E 315 H8
Narsinghgarh India 23°45N 76°40E 314 H7
Naruto Japan 34°11N 134°37E 303 G7
Narva Estonia 59°23N 28°12E 290 C4
Narva → Russia 59°27N 28°2E 281 G23
Narva Bay = Narva Laht Estonia 59°35N 27°35E 281 G22
Narva Laht Estonia 59°35N 27°35E 281 G22
Narvik Norway 68°28N 17°26E 280 B17
Narwana India 29°39N 76°6E 314 E7
Naryan-Mar Russia 67°42N 53°12E 290 A9
Narym Russia 59°0N 81°30E 300 D9
Naryn Kyrgyzstan 41°26N 75°58E 300 E8
Nasa Norway 66°29N 15°23E 280 C16
Nasau Fiji 17°19S 179°27E 331 a
Nasca = Nazca Peru 14°50S 74°57W 364 F4
Naseby N.Z. 45°1S 170°10E 331 F3
Naselle U.S.A. 46°22N 123°49W 350 D3
Naser, Buheirat en Egypt 23°0N 32°30E 323 D12
Nashua Mont., U.S.A. 48°8N 106°22W 348 B10
Nashua N.H., U.S.A. 42°45N 71°28W 355 D13
Nashville Ark., U.S.A. 33°57N 93°51W 356 E8
Nashville Ga., U.S.A. 31°12N 83°15W 357 F13
Nashville Tenn., U.S.A. 36°10N 86°47W 357 C11
Nasik India 19°58N 73°50E 312 K8
Nasirabad India 26°15N 74°45E 314 F6
Nasirabad Pakistan 28°23N 68°24E 314 E3
Nasiriyah = An Nāşirīyah Iraq 31°0N 46°15E 316 D5
Naskaupi → Canada 53°47N 60°51W 345 B7
Naşrābād Iran 34°8N 51°26E 317 C6
Naşriān-e Pā'īn Iran 32°52N 46°52E 316 C5
Nass → Canada 55°0N 129°40W 342 C3
Nassau Bahamas 25°5N 77°20W 360 A4
Nassau U.S.A. 42°31N 73°37W 355 D11
Nassau, B. Chile 55°20S 68°0W 368 H3
Nasser, L. = Naser, Buheirat en Egypt 23°0N 32°30E 323 D12
Nässjö Sweden 57°39N 14°42E 281 H16
Nastapoka → Canada 56°55N 76°33W 344 A4
Nastapoka, Is. Canada 56°55N 76°50W 344 A4
Nata Botswana 20°12S 26°12E 328 C4
Nata → Botswana 20°14S 26°10E 328 C4
Natal Brazil 5°47S 35°13W 365 E11
Natal Indonesia 0°35N 99°7E 308 D1
Natal Drakensberg ⌂ S. Africa 29°27S 29°30E 329 D4
Naţanz Iran 33°30N 51°55E 317 C6
Natashquan Canada 50°14N 61°46W 345 B7
Natashquan → Canada 50°7N 61°50W 345 B7
Natchez U.S.A. 31°34N 91°24W 356 F9
Natchitoches U.S.A. 31°46N 93°5W 356 F8
Natewa B. Fiji 16°35S 179°40E 331 a
Nathalia Australia 36°1S 145°13E 335 F4
Nathdwara India 24°55N 73°50E 314 G5
Nati, Pta. Spain 40°3N 3°50E 296 A10
Natimuk Australia 36°42S 142°0E 335 F3
Nation → Canada 55°30N 123°32W 342 B4
National City U.S.A. 32°40N 117°5W 351 N9
Natitingou Benin 10°20N 1°26E 322 F6
Natividad, I. Mexico 27°52N 115°11W 358 B1
Natkyizin Burma 14°57N 97°59E 310 E1
Natron, L. Tanzania 2°20S 36°0E 326 C4
Natrona Heights U.S.A. 40°37N 79°44W 354 F5
Natukanaoka Pan Namibia 18°40S 15°45E 328 B2
Natuna Besar, Kepulauan Indonesia 4°0N 108°15E 308 D3
Natuna Is. = Natuna Besar, Kepulauan Indonesia 4°0N 108°15E 308 D3
Natuna Selatan, Kepulauan Indonesia 2°45N 109°0E 308 D3
Natural Bridge U.S.A. 44°5N 75°30W 355 B9
Natural Bridges ⌂ U.S.A. 37°36N 110°0W 349 H9
Naturaliste, C. Tas., Australia 40°50S 148°15E 335 G4
Naturaliste, C. W. Austral., Australia 33°32S 115°0E 330 E4
Naturaliste Plateau Ind. Oc. 34°0S 112°0E 336 L3
Nau Qala Afghan. 34°5N 68°5E 314 B3
Naugatuck U.S.A. 41°30N 73°3W 355 E11
Naujaat = Repulse Bay Canada 66°30N 86°30W 341 C11
Naumburg Germany 51°9N 11°47E 288 C6
Nauru ■ Pac. Oc. 1°0S 166°0E 330 B9
Naushahra = Nowshera Pakistan 34°0N 72°0E 312 C8
Naushahro Pakistan 26°50N 68°7E 314 F3
Naushon I. U.S.A. 41°29N 70°45W 355 E14
Nausori Fiji 18°2S 178°32E 331 a
Nauta Peru 4°31S 73°35W 364 D4
Nautanwa India 27°20N 83°25E 315 F10
Naute ⌂ Namibia 26°55S 17°57E 328 D2
Nautla Mexico 20°13N 96°47W 359 C5
Nava Mexico 28°25N 100°45W 358 B4
Navadwip India 23°34N 88°20E 315 H13
Navahrudak Belarus 53°40N 25°50E 289 B13
Navajo Res. U.S.A. 36°48N 107°36W 349 H10
Navalmoral de la Mata Spain 39°52N 5°33W 293 C3
Navan = An Uaimh Ireland 53°39N 6°41W 282 C5
Navarin, Mys Russia 62°15N 179°5E 276 C16
Navarino, I. Chile 55°0S 67°40W 368 H3
Navarra □ Spain 42°40N 1°40W 293 A5
Navarre U.S.A. 40°43N 81°31W 354 F3
Navarro → U.S.A. 39°11N 123°45W 350 F3
Navasota U.S.A. 30°23N 96°5W 356 F6
Navassa I. W. Indies 18°30N 75°0W 361 C5
Naver → U.K. 58°32N 4°14W 283 C4
Navibandar India 21°26N 69°48E 314 J3
Navidad Chile 33°57S 71°50W 366 C1
Naviraí Brazil 23°8S 54°13W 367 A5
Naviti Fiji 17°7S 177°15E 331 a
Navlakhi India 22°58N 70°28E 314 H4
Năvodari Romania 44°19N 28°36E 289 F15
Navoi = Nawoiy Uzbekistan 40°9N 65°22E 300 E7
Navojoa Mexico 27°6N 109°26W 358 B3
Navolato Mexico 24°47N 107°42W 358 C3
Navsari India 20°57N 72°59E 312 J8
Navua Fiji 18°12S 178°11E 331 a
Nawa Kot Pakistan 28°21N 71°24E 314 E4
Nawab Khan Pakistan 30°17N 69°12E 314 D3
Nawabganj Ut. P., India 26°56N 81°14E 315 F9
Nawabganj Ut. P., India 28°32N 79°40E 315 E8
Nawabshah Pakistan 26°15N 68°25E 314 F3
Nawada India 24°50N 85°33E 315 G11
Nawakot Nepal 27°55N 85°10E 315 F11
Nawalgarh India 27°50N 75°15E 314 F6
Nawanshahr India 32°33N 74°48E 315 C6
Nawar, Dasht-i- Afghan. 33°52N 68°0E 314 C3
Nawoiy Uzbekistan 40°9N 65°22E 300 E7
Naxçıvan Azerbaijan 39°12N 45°15E 316 B5
Naxçıvan □ Azerbaijan 39°25N 45°26E 316 B5
Naxos Greece 37°8N 25°25E 295 F11
Nay, Mui Vietnam 12°55N 109°23E 308 B3
Nāy Band Būshehr, Iran 27°20N 52°40E 317 E7
Nāy Band Khorāsān, Iran 32°20N 57°34E 317 C8
Nayakhan Russia 61°56N 159°0E 301 C16
Nayarit □ Mexico 22°0N 105°0W 358 C4
Nayau Fiji 18°6S 178°10E 331 a
Nayoro Japan 44°21N 142°28E 302 B11
Nayyāl, W. → Si. Arabia 28°35N 39°4E 316 D3
Nazaré Brazil 13°2S 39°0W 365 F11
Nazareth = Nazerat Israel 32°42N 35°17E 318 C4
Nazareth U.S.A. 40°44N 75°19W 355 F9
Nazas Mexico 25°14N 104°8W 358 B4
Nazas → Mexico 25°12N 104°12W 358 B4
Nazca Peru 14°50S 74°57W 364 F4
Nazca Ridge Pac. Oc. 20°0S 80°0W 337 K19
Naze Japan 28°22N 129°27E 303 K4
Naze, The U.K. 51°53N 1°18E 285 F9
Nazerat Israel 32°42N 35°17E 318 C4
Nāzīk Iran 39°1N 45°4E 316 B5
Nazilli Turkey 37°55N 28°15E 295 F13
Nazko Canada 53°1N 123°37W 342 C4
Nazko → Canada 53°7N 123°34W 342 C4
Nazret Ethiopia 8°32N 39°22E 319 F2
Nchanga Zambia 12°30S 27°49E 327 E2
Ncheu Malawi 14°50S 34°47E 327 E3
Ndala Tanzania 4°45S 33°15E 326 C3
Ndalatando Angola 9°12S 14°48E 324 F2
Ndareda Tanzania 4°12S 35°30E 326 C4
Ndélé C.A.R. 8°25N 20°36E 324 C4
Ndjamena Chad 12°10N 14°59E 323 F8
Ndola Zambia 13°0S 28°34E 327 E2
Ndomo ⌂ S. Africa 26°52S 32°15E 329 D5
Ndoto Mts. Kenya 2°0N 37°0E 326 B4
Nduguti Tanzania 4°18S 34°41E 326 C3
Neagh, Lough U.K. 54°37N 6°25W 282 B5
Neah Bay U.S.A. 48°22N 124°37W 350 B2
Neale, L. Australia 24°15S 130°0E 332 D5
Neales → Australia 28°8S 136°47E 335 D2
Neapoli Greece 35°15N 25°37E 297 D7
Near Is. U.S.A. 52°30N 174°0E 346 a
Neath U.K. 51°39N 3°48W 285 F4
Neath Port Talbot □ U.K. 51°42N 3°45W 285 F4
Nebine Cr. → Australia 29°27S 146°56E 335 D4
Nebitdag = Balkanabat Turkmenistan 39°30N 54°22E 317 B7
Nebo Australia 21°42S 148°42E 334 C4
Nebraska □ U.S.A. 41°30N 99°30W 352 E4
Nebraska City U.S.A. 40°41N 95°52W 352 E6
Nébrodi, Monti Italy 37°54N 14°35E 294 F6
Necedah U.S.A. 44°2N 90°4W 352 C8
Nechako → Canada 53°55N 122°42W 342 C4
Neches → U.S.A. 29°58N 93°51W 356 G8
Neckar → Germany 49°27N 8°29E 288 D5
Necochea Argentina 38°30S 58°50W 366 D4
Nederland = Netherlands ■ Europe 52°0N 5°30E 287 C5
Needles Canada 49°53N 118°7W 342 D5
Needles U.S.A. 34°51N 114°37W 351 L12
Needles, The U.K. 50°39N 1°35W 285 G6
Ñeembucú □ Paraguay 27°0S 58°0W 366 B4
Neemuch = Nimach India 24°30N 74°56E 314 G6
Neenah U.S.A. 44°11N 88°28W 352 C9
Neepawa Canada 50°15N 99°30W 343 C9
Neftçala Azerbaijan 39°19N 49°12E 317 B6
Neftekumsk Russia 44°46N 44°50E 291 F7
Nefyn U.K. 52°56N 4°31W 284 E3
Negapatam = Nagappattinam India 10°46N 79°51E 312 P11
Negara Indonesia 8°22S 114°37E 309 J17
Negaunee U.S.A. 46°30N 87°36W 352 B10
Negele Ethiopia 5°20N 39°36E 319 F2
Negev Desert = Hanegev Israel 30°50N 35°0E 318 E4
Negombo Sri Lanka 7°12N 79°50E 312 R11
Negotin Serbia 44°16N 22°37E 295 B10
Negra, Pta. Mauritania 22°54N 16°18W 322 D2
Negra, Pta. Peru 6°6S 81°10W 364 E2
Negrais, C. = Maudin Sun Burma 16°0N 94°30E 313 M19
Negril Jamaica 18°22N 78°20W 360 a
Negro → Argentina 41°2S 62°47W 368 E4
Negro → Brazil 3°0S 60°0W 364 D7
Negro → Uruguay 33°24S 58°22W 366 C4
Negros Phil. 9°30N 122°40E 309 C6
Neguac Canada 47°15N 65°5W 345 C6
Nehalem → U.S.A. 45°40N 123°56W 350 E3
Nehāvand Iran 35°56N 49°31E 317 C6
Nehbandān Iran 31°35N 60°5E 317 D9
Nei Monggol Zizhiqu □ China 42°0N 112°0E 306 D7
Neiafu Tonga 18°39S 173°59W 331 c
Neiges, Piton des Réunion 21°5S 55°29E 325 c
Neijiang China 29°35N 104°55E 304 D5
Neilingding Dao China 22°25N 113°48E 305 G10
Neillsville U.S.A. 44°34N 90°36W 352 C8
Neilton U.S.A. 47°25N 123°53W 348 C2
Neiqiu China 37°15N 114°30E 306 F8
Neiva Colombia 2°56N 75°18W 364 C3
Neixiang China 33°10N 111°52E 306 H6
Nejanilini L. Canada 59°33N 97°48W 343 B9
Nejd = Najd Si. Arabia 26°30N 42°0E 319 B3
Nekā Iran 36°39N 53°19E 317 B7
Nekemte Ethiopia 9°4N 36°30E 319 F2
Neksø Denmark 55°4N 15°8E 281 J16
Nelia Australia 20°39S 142°12E 334 C3
Neligh U.S.A. 42°8N 98°2W 352 D4
Nelkan Russia 57°40N 136°4E 301 D14
Nellore India 14°27N 79°59E 312 M11
Nelson Canada 49°30N 117°20W 342 D5
Nelson N.Z. 41°18S 173°16E 331 D4
Nelson U.K. 53°50N 2°13W 284 D5
Nelson Ariz., U.S.A. 35°31N 113°19W 349 J7
Nelson Nev., U.S.A. 35°42N 114°49W 351 K12
Nelson → Canada 54°33N 98°2W 343 C9
Nelson, C. Australia 38°26S 141°32E 335 F3
Nelson, Estrecho Chile 51°30S 75°0W 368 G2
Nelson Forks Canada 59°30N 124°0W 342 B4
Nelson House Canada 55°47N 98°51W 343 B9
Nelson L. Canada 55°48N 100°7W 343 B8
Nelson Lakes △ N.Z. 41°55S 172°44E 331 D4
Nelspoort S. Africa 32°7S 23°0E 328 E3
Nelspruit S. Africa 25°29S 30°59E 329 D5
Néma Mauritania 16°40N 7°15W 322 E4
Neman = Nemunas → Lithuania 55°25N 21°10E 281 J19
Nemeiben L. Canada 55°20N 105°20W 343 B7
Nemiscau Canada 51°18N 76°54W 344 B4
Nemiscau, L. Canada 51°25N 76°40W 344 B4
Nemunas → Lithuania 55°25N 21°10E 281 J19
Nemuro Japan 43°20N 145°35E 302 C12
Nemuro-Kaikyō Japan 43°30N 145°30E 302 C12
Nen Jiang → China 45°28N 124°30E 307 B13
Nenagh Ireland 52°52N 8°11W 282 D3
Nenasi Malaysia 3°9N 103°23E 311 L4
Nene → U.K. 52°49N 0°11E 285 E8
Nenjiang China 49°10N 125°10E 305 B7
Neno Malawi 15°25S 34°40E 327 F3
Neodesha U.S.A. 37°25N 95°41W 352 G6
Neora Valley △ India 27°0N 88°45E 315 F13
Neosho U.S.A. 36°52N 94°22W 352 G6
Neosho → U.S.A. 36°48N 95°18W 356 C7
Nepal ■ Asia 28°0N 84°30E 315 F11
Nepalganj Nepal 28°5N 81°40E 315 E9
Nepalganj Road India 28°1N 81°41E 315 E9
Nephi U.S.A. 39°43N 111°50W 348 G8
Nephin Ireland 54°1N 9°22W 282 B2
Nephin Beg Range Ireland 54°0N 9°40W 282 C2
Neptune U.S.A. 40°13N 74°2W 355 F10
Nerang Australia 27°58S 153°20E 335 D5
Nerastro, Sarīr Libya 24°20N 20°37E 323 D10
Nerchinsk Russia 52°0N 116°39E 301 D12
Néret, L. Canada 54°45N 70°44W 345 B5
Neretva → Croatia 43°1N 17°27E 295 C7
Neringa Lithuania 55°20N 21°5E 281 J19
Neris → Lithuania 55°8N 24°16E 281 J21
Neryungri Russia 57°38N 124°28E 301 D13
Nescopeck U.S.A. 41°3N 76°12W 355 E8
Ness, L. U.K. 57°15N 4°32W 283 D4
Ness City U.S.A. 38°27N 99°54W 352 F4
Nesterov Ukraine 50°4N 23°58E 289 C12
Nesvizh = Nyasvizh Belarus 53°14N 26°38E 289 B14
Netanya Israel 32°20N 34°51E 318 C3
Netarhat India 23°29N 84°16E 315 H11
Nete → Belgium 51°7N 4°14E 287 C4
Netherdale Australia 21°10S 148°33E 334 K6
Netherlands ■ Europe 52°0N 5°30E 287 C5
Netherlands Antilles ☑ W. Indies 12°15N 69°0W 364 A5
Netrang India 21°39N 73°21E 314 J5
Nettilling L. Canada 66°30N 71°0W 341 C12
Netzahualcóyotl, Presa Mexico 17°8N 93°35W 359 D6
Neubrandenburg Germany 53°33N 13°15E 288 B7
Neuchâtel Switz. 47°0N 6°55E 292 C7
Neuchâtel, Lac de Switz. 46°53N 6°50E 292 C7
Neufchâteau Belgium 49°50N 5°25E 287 E5
Neumayer Antarctica 71°0S 68°30W 277 D17
Neumünster Germany 54°4N 9°58E 288 A5
Neunkirchen Germany 49°20N 7°9E 288 D4
Neuquén Argentina 38°55S 68°0W 368 D3
Neuquén □ Argentina 38°0S 69°50W 366 D2
Neuruppin Germany 52°55N 12°48E 288 B7
Neuse → U.S.A. 35°6N 76°29W 357 D16
Neusiedler See Austria 47°50N 16°47E 289 E9
Neustrelitz Germany 53°21N 13°4E 288 B7
Neva → Russia 59°56N 30°20E 290 C5
Nevada Iowa, U.S.A. 42°1N 93°27W 352 D7
Nevada Mo., U.S.A. 37°51N 94°22W 352 G6
Nevada □ U.S.A. 39°0N 117°0W 348 G5
Nevada City U.S.A. 39°16N 121°1W 350 F6
Nevado, Cerro Argentina 35°30S 68°32W 366 D2
Nevado de Colima = Volcán de Colima △ Mexico 19°30N 103°40W 358 D4

Nevado de Tres Cruces △ Chile 27°13S 69°5W 366 B2
Nevel Russia 56°0N 29°55E 290 C4
Nevers France 47°0N 3°9E 292 C5
Nevertire Australia 31°50S 147°44E 335 E4
Neville Canada 49°58N 107°39W 343 D7
Nevinnomyssk Russia 44°40N 42°0E 291 F7
Nevis St. Kitts & Nevis 17°0N 62°30W 361 C7
Nevşehir Turkey 38°33N 34°40E 316 B2
Nevyansk Russia 57°30N 60°13E 290 C11
New → U.S.A. 38°10N 81°12W 353 F13
New Aiyansh Canada 55°12N 129°4W 342 B3
New Albany Ind., U.S.A. 38°18N 85°49W 353 F11
New Albany Miss., U.S.A. 34°29N 89°0W 357 D10
New Albany Pa., U.S.A. 41°36N 76°27W 355 E8
New Amsterdam Guyana 6°15N 57°36W 364 B7
New Angledool Australia 29°5S 147°55E 335 D4
New Baltimore U.S.A. 42°41N 82°44W 354 D2
New Bedford U.S.A. 41°38N 70°56W 355 E14
New Berlin N.Y., U.S.A. 42°37N 75°20W 355 D9
New Berlin Pa., U.S.A. 40°50N 76°57W 354 F8
New Bern U.S.A. 35°7N 77°3W 357 D16
New Bethlehem U.S.A. 41°0N 79°20W 354 F5
New Bloomfield U.S.A. 40°25N 77°11W 354 F7
New Boston U.S.A. 33°28N 94°25W 356 E7
New Braunfels U.S.A. 29°42N 98°8W 356 G5
New Brighton N.Z. 43°29S 172°43E 331 E4
New Brighton U.S.A. 40°42N 80°19W 354 F4
New Britain Papua N. G. 5°50S 150°20E 330 B8
New Britain U.S.A. 41°40N 72°47W 355 E12
New Brunswick U.S.A. 40°30N 74°27W 355 F10
New Brunswick □ Canada 46°50N 66°30W 345 C6
New Caledonia ⊠ Pac. Oc. 21°0S 165°0E 330 D9
New Caledonia Trough Pac. Oc. 30°0S 165°0E 336 L8
New Castile = Castilla-La Mancha □ Spain 39°30N 3°30W 293 C4
New Castle Ind., U.S.A. 39°55N 85°22W 353 F11
New Castle Pa., U.S.A. 41°0N 80°21W 354 F4
New City U.S.A. 41°9N 73°59W 355 E11
New Concord U.S.A. 39°59N 81°54W 354 G3
New Cumberland U.S.A. 40°30N 80°36W 354 F4
New Cuyama U.S.A. 34°57N 119°38W 351 L7
New Delhi India 28°36N 77°11E 314 E7
New Denver Canada 50°0N 117°25W 342 D5
New Don Pedro Res. U.S.A. 37°43N 120°24W 350 H6
New England U.S.A. 43°0N 71°0W 347 B12
New England N. Dak., U.S.A. 46°32N 102°52W 352 B2
New England Ra. Australia 30°20S 151°45E 335 E5
New Forest △ U.K. 50°53N 1°34W 285 G6
New Galloway U.K. 55°5N 4°9W 283 F4
New Glasgow Canada 45°35N 62°36W 345 C7
New Guinea Oceania 4°0S 136°0E 330 B6
New Hamburg Canada 43°23N 80°42W 354 C4
New Hampshire □ U.S.A. 44°0N 71°30W 355 C13
New Hampton U.S.A. 43°3N 92°19W 352 D7
New Hanover S. Africa 29°22S 30°31E 329 D5
New Hartford U.S.A. 43°4N 75°18W 355 C9
New Haven Conn., U.S.A. 41°18N 72°55W 355 E12
New Haven Mich., U.S.A. 42°44N 82°48W 354 D2
New Hazelton Canada 55°20N 127°30W 342 B3
New Hebrides = Vanuatu ■ Pac. Oc. 15°0S 168°0E 330 C9
New Holland U.S.A. 40°6N 76°5W 355 F8
New Iberia U.S.A. 30°1N 91°49W 356 F9
New Ireland Papua N. G. 3°20S 151°50E 330 B8
New Jersey □ U.S.A. 40°0N 74°30W 353 F16
New Kensington U.S.A. 40°34N 79°46W 354 F5
New Lexington U.S.A. 39°43N 82°13W 353 F12
New Liskeard Canada 47°31N 79°41W 344 C4
New London Conn., U.S.A. 41°22N 72°6W 355 E12
New London Ohio, U.S.A. 41°5N 82°24W 354 E2
New London Wis., U.S.A. 44°23N 88°45W 352 C9
New Madrid U.S.A. 36°36N 89°32W 352 G9
New Martinsville U.S.A. 39°39N 80°52W 353 F13
New Meadows U.S.A. 44°58N 116°18W 348 D5
New Melones L. U.S.A. 37°57N 120°31W 350 H6
New Mexico □ U.S.A. 34°30N 106°0W 349 J11
New Milford Conn., U.S.A. 41°35N 73°25W 355 E11
New Milford Pa., U.S.A. 41°52N 75°44W 355 E9
New Norcia Australia 30°57S 116°13E 333 F2
New Norfolk Australia 42°46S 147°2E 335 G4
New Orleans U.S.A. 29°57N 90°4W 357 G9
New Philadelphia U.S.A. 40°30N 81°27W 354 F3
New Plymouth N.Z. 39°4S 174°5E 331 C5
New Plymouth U.S.A. 43°58N 116°49W 348 E5
New Port Richey U.S.A. 28°16N 82°43W 357 G13
New Providence Bahamas 25°25N 78°35W 360 A4
New Quay U.K. 52°13N 4°21W 285 E3
New Radnor U.K. 52°15N 3°9W 285 E4
New Richmond Canada 48°15N 65°45W 345 C6
New Richmond U.S.A. 45°7N 92°32W 352 C7
New River Gorge ⌓ U.S.A. 37°53N 81°5W 353 G13
New Roads U.S.A. 30°42N 91°26W 356 F9
New Rochelle U.S.A. 40°55N 73°46W 355 F11
New Rockford U.S.A. 47°41N 99°8W 352 B4
New Romney U.K. 50°59N 0°57E 285 G8
New Ross Ireland 52°23N 6°57W 282 D5
New Salem U.S.A. 46°51N 101°25W 352 B3
New Scone = Scone U.K. 56°25N 3°24W 283 E5
New Siberian I. = Novaya Sibir, Ostrov Russia 75°10N 150°0E 301 B16
New Siberian Is. = Novosibirskiye Ostrova Russia 75°0N 142°0E 301 B15
New Smyrna Beach U.S.A. 29°1N 80°56W 357 G14
New South Wales □ Australia 33°0S 146°0E 335 E4
New Tecumseth Canada 44°9N 79°52W 354 B5
New Town U.S.A. 47°59N 102°30W 352 B2
New Tredegar U.K. 51°44N 3°16W 285 F4
New Ulm U.S.A. 44°19N 94°28W 352 C6
New Waterford Canada 46°13N 60°4W 345 C7
New-Wes-Valley Canada 49°8N 53°36W 345 C9
New Westminster Canada 49°13N 122°55W 350 A4
New York U.S.A. 40°43N 74°0W 355 F11
New York □ U.S.A. 43°0N 75°0W 355 D9
New York J.F. Kennedy Int. ✈ (JFK) U.S.A. 40°38N 73°47W 355 F11
New Zealand ■ Oceania 40°0S 176°0E 331 D6
Newaj → India 24°24N 76°49E 314 G7
Newala Tanzania 10°58S 39°18E 327 E4
Newark Del., U.S.A. 39°41N 75°46W 353 F16
Newark N.J., U.S.A. 40°44N 74°10W 355 F10
Newark N.Y., U.S.A. 43°3N 77°6W 354 C7
Newark Ohio, U.S.A. 40°3N 82°24W 354 F2
Newark Liberty Int. ✈ (EWR) U.S.A. 40°42N 74°10W 355 F10
Newark-on-Trent U.K. 53°5N 0°48W 284 D7
Newark Valley U.S.A. 42°14N 76°11W 355 D8
Newberg U.S.A. 45°18N 122°58W 348 D2
Newberry Mich., U.S.A. 46°21N 85°30W 353 B11
Newberry S.C., U.S.A. 34°17N 81°37W 357 D14
Newberry Springs U.S.A. 34°50N 116°41W 351 L10
Newboro L. Canada 44°38N 76°20W 355 B8
Newbridge = Droichead Nua Ireland 53°11N 6°48W 282 C5
Newburgh Canada 44°19N 76°52W 354 B8
Newburgh U.S.A. 41°30N 74°1W 355 E10
Newbury U.K. 51°24N 1°20W 285 F6
Newbury N.H., U.S.A. 43°19N 72°3W 355 B12
Newbury Vt., U.S.A. 44°5N 72°4W 355 B12
Newburyport U.S.A. 42°49N 70°53W 355 D14
Newcastle Australia 33°0S 151°46E 335 E5
Newcastle N.B., Canada 47°1N 65°38W 345 C6
Newcastle Ont., Canada 43°55N 78°35W 344 D4
Newcastle S. Africa 27°45S 29°58E 329 D4
Newcastle U.K. 54°13N 5°54W 282 B6
Newcastle Calif., U.S.A. 38°53N 121°8W 350 G5
Newcastle Wyo., U.S.A. 43°50N 104°11W 348 E11
Newcastle Emlyn U.K. 52°2N 4°28W 285 E3
Newcastle Ra. Australia 15°45S 130°15E 332 C5
Newcastle-under-Lyme U.K. 53°1N 2°14W 284 D5
Newcastle-upon-Tyne U.K. 54°58N 1°36W 284 C6
Newcastle Waters Australia 17°30S 133°28E 334 B1
Newcastle West Ireland 52°27N 9°3W 282 D2
Newcomb U.S.A. 43°58N 74°10W 355 C10
Newcomerstown U.S.A. 40°16N 81°36W 354 F3
Newdegate Australia 33°6S 119°0E 333 F2
Newell Australia 16°20S 145°16E 334 B4
Newell U.S.A. 44°43N 103°25W 352 C2
Newfane U.S.A. 43°17N 78°43W 354 C6
Newfield U.S.A. 42°18N 76°33W 355 D8
Newfound L. U.S.A. 43°40N 71°47W 355 C13
Newfoundland Canada 49°0N 55°0W 345 C8
Newfoundland U.S.A. 41°18N 75°19W 355 E9
Newfoundland & Labrador □ Canada 53°0N 58°0W 345 B8
Newhaven U.K. 50°47N 0°3E 285 G8
Newkirk U.S.A. 36°53N 97°3W 356 C6
Newlyn U.K. 50°6N 5°34W 285 G2
Newman Australia 23°18S 119°45E 332 D2
Newman U.S.A. 37°19N 121°1W 350 H5
Newmarket Canada 44°3N 79°28W 354 B5
Newmarket Ireland 52°13N 9°0W 282 D2
Newmarket U.K. 52°15N 0°25E 285 E8
Newmarket U.S.A. 43°5N 70°56W 355 C14
Newnan U.S.A. 33°23N 84°48W 357 E12
Newport Ireland 53°53N 9°33W 282 C2
Newport I. of W., U.K. 50°42N 1°17W 285 G6
Newport Newport, U.K. 51°35N 3°0W 285 F5
Newport Ark., U.S.A. 35°37N 91°16W 356 D9
Newport Ky., U.S.A. 39°5N 84°29W 353 F11
Newport N.H., U.S.A. 43°22N 72°10W 355 C12
Newport N.Y., U.S.A. 43°11N 75°1W 355 C9
Newport Oreg., U.S.A. 44°39N 124°3W 348 D1
Newport Pa., U.S.A. 40°29N 77°8W 354 F7
Newport R.I., U.S.A. 41°29N 71°19W 355 E13
Newport Tenn., U.S.A. 35°58N 83°11W 357 D13
Newport Vt., U.S.A. 44°56N 72°13W 355 B12
Newport Wash., U.S.A. 48°11N 117°3W 348 B5
Newport □ U.K. 51°33N 3°1W 285 F4
Newport Beach U.S.A. 33°37N 117°56W 351 M9
Newport News U.S.A. 36°58N 76°25W 353 G15
Newport Pagnell U.K. 52°5N 0°43W 285 E7
Newquay U.K. 50°25N 5°6W 285 G2
Newry U.K. 54°11N 6°21W 282 B5
Newton Ill., U.S.A. 38°59N 88°10W 352 F9
Newton Iowa, U.S.A. 41°42N 93°3W 352 E7
Newton Kans., U.S.A. 38°3N 97°21W 352 F5
Newton Mass., U.S.A. 42°21N 71°12W 355 D13
Newton Miss., U.S.A. 32°19N 89°10W 357 E10
Newton N.C., U.S.A. 35°40N 81°13W 357 D14
Newton N.J., U.S.A. 41°3N 74°45W 355 E10
Newton Tex., U.S.A. 30°51N 93°46W 356 F8
Newton Abbot U.K. 50°32N 3°37W 285 G4
Newton Aycliffe U.K. 54°37N 1°34W 284 C6
Newton Falls U.S.A. 41°11N 80°59W 354 E4
Newton Stewart U.K. 54°57N 4°30W 283 G4
Newtonmore U.K. 57°4N 4°8W 283 D4
Newtown U.K. 52°31N 3°19W 285 E4
Newtownabbey U.K. 54°40N 5°56W 282 B6
Newtownards U.K. 54°36N 5°42W 282 B6
Newtownbarry = Bunclody Ireland 52°39N 6°40W 282 D5
Newtownstewart U.K. 54°43N 7°23W 282 B4
Newville U.S.A. 40°10N 77°24W 354 F7
Neya Russia 58°21N 43°49E 290 C7
Neyrīz Iran 29°15N 54°19E 317 D7
Neyshābūr Iran 36°10N 58°50E 317 B8
Nezhin = Nizhyn Ukraine 51°5N 31°55E 291 D5
Nezperce U.S.A. 46°14N 116°14W 348 C5
Ngabang Indonesia 0°23N 109°55E 308 D3
Ngabordamlu, Tanjung Indonesia 6°56S 134°11E 309 F8
N'Gage Angola 7°46S 15°15E 324 F3
Ngami Depression Botswana 20°30S 22°46E 328 C3
Ngamo Zimbabwe 19°3S 27°32E 327 F2
Nganglong Kangri China 33°0N 81°0E 315 C9
Ngao Thailand 18°46N 99°59E 310 C2
Ngaoundéré Cameroon 7°15N 13°35E 324 C2
Ngapara N.Z. 44°57S 170°46E 331 F3
Ngara Tanzania 2°29S 30°40E 326 C3
Ngawi Indonesia 7°24S 111°26E 309 G14
Ngcobo S. Africa 31°37S 28°0E 329 E4
Nghia Lo Vietnam 21°33N 104°28E 310 B5
Ngoma Malawi 13°8S 33°45E 327 E3
Ngomahura Zimbabwe 20°26S 30°43E 327 G3
Ngomba Tanzania 8°20S 32°53E 327 D3
Ngomeni, Ras Kenya 2°59S 40°14E 326 C5
Ngong Kenya 1°22S 36°39E 326 C4
Ngoring Hu China 34°55N 97°5E 304 C4
Ngorongoro Tanzania 3°11S 35°32E 326 C4
Ngorongoro ⌓ Tanzania 2°40S 35°30E 326 C4
Ngozi Burundi 2°54S 29°50E 326 C2
Ngudu Tanzania 2°58S 33°25E 326 C3
Nguigmi Niger 14°20N 13°20E 323 F8
Nguiu Australia 11°46S 130°38E 332 B5
Ngukurr Australia 14°44S 134°44E 334 A1
Ngunga Tanzania 3°37S 33°37E 326 C3
Nguru Nigeria 12°56N 10°29E 323 F8
Nguru Mts. Tanzania 6°0S 37°30E 326 D4
Ngusi Malawi 14°0S 34°50E 327 E3
Nguyen Binh Vietnam 22°39N 105°56E 310 A5
Nha Trang Vietnam 12°16N 109°10E 311 F7
Nhacoongo Mozam. 24°18S 35°14E 329 C6
Nhamaabué Mozam. 17°25S 35°5E 327 F4
Nhamundá → Brazil 2°12S 56°41W 365 D7
Nhangulaze, L. Mozam. 24°0S 34°30E 329 C5
Nhill Australia 36°18S 141°40E 335 F3
Nho Quan Vietnam 20°18N 105°45E 310 B5
Nhulunbuy Australia 12°10S 137°20E 334 A2
Nia-nia Dem. Rep. of the Congo 1°30N 27°40E 326 B2
Niagara Falls Canada 43°7N 79°5W 354 C5
Niagara Falls U.S.A. 43°5N 79°4W 354 C6
Niagara-on-the-Lake Canada 43°15N 79°4W 354 C5
Niah Malaysia 3°58N 113°46E 308 D4
Niamey Niger 13°27N 2°6E 322 F6
Niangara Dem. Rep. of the Congo 3°42N 27°50E 326 B2
Niantic U.S.A. 41°20N 72°11W 355 E12
Nias Indonesia 1°0N 97°30E 308 D1
Niassa □ Mozam. 13°30S 36°0E 327 E4
Niassa ⌓ Mozam. 12°4S 36°57E 327 E4
Nibāk Si. Arabia 24°25N 50°50E 317 E7
Nicaragua ■ Cent. Amer. 11°40N 85°30W 360 D2
Nicaragua, L. de Nic. 12°0N 85°30W 360 D2
Nicastro Italy 38°59N 16°19E 294 E7
Nice France 43°42N 7°14E 292 E7
Niceville U.S.A. 30°31N 86°30W 357 F11
Nichicun, L. Canada 53°5N 71°0W 345 B5
Nichinan Japan 31°38N 131°23E 303 J5
Nicholás, Canal W. Indies 23°30N 80°5W 360 B3
Nicholasville U.S.A. 37°53N 84°34W 353 G11
Nichols U.S.A. 42°1N 76°22W 355 D8
Nicholson Australia 18°2S 128°54E 332 C4
Nicholson U.S.A. 41°37N 75°47W 355 E9
Nicholson → Australia 17°31S 139°36E 334 B2
Nicholson L. Canada 62°40N 102°40W 343 A8
Nicholson Ra. Australia 27°15S 116°45E 333 E2
Nicholville U.S.A. 44°41N 74°39W 355 B10
Nicobar Is. Ind. Oc. 8°0N 93°30E 275 D14
Nicola Canada 50°12N 120°40W 342 C4
Nicolls Town Bahamas 25°8N 78°0W 360 A4
Nicosia Cyprus 35°10N 33°25E 297 D12
Nicoya Costa Rica 10°9N 85°27W 360 D2
Nicoya, G. de Costa Rica 10°0N 85°0W 360 E3
Nicoya, Pen. de Costa Rica 9°45N 85°40W 360 E2
Nidd → U.K. 53°59N 1°23W 284 D6
Niedersachsen □ Germany 52°50N 9°0E 288 B5
Niekerkshoop S. Africa 29°19S 22°51E 328 D3
Niemba Dem. Rep. of the Congo 5°58S 28°24E 326 D2
Niemen = Nemunas → Lithuania 55°25N 21°10E 281 J19
Nienburg Germany 52°39N 9°13E 288 B5
Nieu Bethesda S. Africa 31°51S 24°34E 328 E3
Nieuw Amsterdam Suriname 5°53N 55°5W 365 B7
Nieuw Nickerie Suriname 6°0N 56°59W 365 B7
Nieuwoudtville S. Africa 31°23S 19°7E 328 E2
Nieuwpoort Belgium 51°8N 2°45E 287 C2
Nieves, Pico de las Canary Is. 27°57N 15°35W 296 G4
Niğde Turkey 37°58N 34°40E 316 B2
Nigel S. Africa 26°27S 28°25E 329 D4
Niger ■ W. Afr. 17°30N 10°0E 322 E7
Niger → W. Afr. 5°33N 6°33E 322 G7
Nigeria ■ W. Afr. 8°30N 8°0E 322 G7
Nighasin India 28°14N 80°52E 315 E9
Nightcaps N.Z. 45°57S 168°2E 331 F2
Nihon = Japan ■ Asia 36°0N 136°0E 303 G8
Nii-Jima Japan 34°20N 139°15E 303 G9
Niigata Japan 37°58N 139°0E 302 F9
Niigata □ Japan 37°15N 138°45E 303 F9
Niihama Japan 33°55N 133°16E 303 H6
Ni'ihau U.S.A. 21°54N 160°9W 346 b
Niimi Japan 34°59N 133°28E 303 G6
Niitsu Japan 37°48N 139°7E 302 F9
Nijil Jordan 30°32N 35°33E 318 E4
Nijkerk Neths. 52°13N 5°30E 287 B5
Nijmegen Neths. 51°50N 5°52E 287 C5
Nijverdal Neths. 52°22N 6°28E 287 B6
Nīk Pey Iran 36°50N 48°10E 317 B6
Nikel Russia 69°24N 30°13E 280 B24
Nikiniki Indonesia 9°49S 124°30E 309 F6
Nikkō Japan 36°45N 139°35E 303 F9
Nikkō △ Japan 36°56N 139°37E 303 F9
Nikolayev = Mykolayiv Ukraine 46°58N 32°0E 291 E5
Nikolayevsk Russia 50°0N 45°35E 291 E8
Nikolayevsk-na-Amur Russia 53°8N 140°44E 301 D15
Nikolskoye Russia 55°12N 166°0E 301 D17
Nikopol Ukraine 47°35N 34°25E 291 E5
Nīkshahr Iran 26°15N 60°10E 317 E9
Nikšić Montenegro 42°50N 18°57E 295 C8
Nîl, Nahr en → Africa 30°10N 31°6E 323 B12
Nîl el Abyad → Sudan 15°38N 32°31E 323 E12
Nîl el Azraq → Sudan 15°38N 32°31E 323 E12
Nila Indonesia 6°44S 129°31E 309 F7
Niland U.S.A. 33°14N 115°31W 351 M11
Nile = Nîl, Nahr en → Africa 30°10N 31°6E 323 B12
Niles Mich., U.S.A. 41°50N 86°15W 352 E10
Niles Ohio, U.S.A. 41°11N 80°46W 354 E4
Nim Ka Thana India 27°44N 75°48E 314 F6
Nimach India 24°30N 74°56E 314 G6
Nimbahera India 24°37N 74°45E 314 G6
Nîmes France 43°50N 4°23E 292 E6
Nimfaíon, Ákra = Pines, Akra Greece 40°5N 24°20E 295 D11
Nimmitabel Australia 36°29S 149°15E 335 F4
Nīnawá Iraq 36°25N 43°10E 316 B4
Nīnawá □ Iraq 36°15N 43°0E 316 B4
Nindigully Australia 28°21S 148°50E 335 D4
Ninepin Group China 22°16N 114°21E 305 G11
Nineveh = Nīnawá Iraq 36°25N 43°10E 316 B4
Ning Xian China 35°30N 107°58E 306 G4
Ningaloo ⌓ Australia 22°23S 113°32E 332 D1
Ning'an China 44°22N 129°20E 307 B15
Ningbo China 29°51N 121°28E 305 D7
Ningcheng China 41°32N 119°53E 307 D10
Ningjin China 37°35N 114°57E 306 F8
Ningjing Shan China 30°0N 98°20E 304 C4
Ningling China 34°25N 115°22E 306 G8
Ningpo = Ningbo China 29°51N 121°28E 305 D7
Ningqiang China 32°47N 106°15E 306 H4
Ningshan China 33°21N 108°21E 306 H5
Ningsia Hui A.R. = Ningxia Huizu Zizhiqu □ China 38°0N 106°0E 306 F4
Ningwu China 39°0N 112°18E 306 E7
Ningxia Huizu Zizhiqu □ China 38°0N 106°0E 306 F4
Ningyang China 35°47N 116°45E 306 G9
Ninh Binh Vietnam 20°15N 105°55E 310 B5
Ninh Giang Vietnam 20°44N 106°24E 310 B6
Ninh Hoa Vietnam 12°30N 109°7E 310 F7
Ninh Ma Vietnam 12°48N 109°21E 310 F7
Ninove Belgium 50°51N 4°2E 287 D4
Nioaque Brazil 21°5S 55°50W 367 A4
Niobrara U.S.A. 42°45N 98°2W 352 D4
Niobrara → U.S.A. 42°46N 98°3W 352 D4
Nioro du Sahel Mali 15°15N 9°30W 322 E4
Niort France 46°19N 0°29W 292 C3
Nipawin Canada 53°20N 104°0W 343 C8
Nipigon Canada 49°0N 88°17W 344 C2
Nipigon, L. Canada 49°50N 88°30W 344 C2
Nipishish L. Canada 54°12N 60°45W 345 B7
Nipissing, L. Canada 46°20N 80°0W 344 C4
Nipomo U.S.A. 35°3N 120°29W 351 K6
Nippon = Japan ■ Asia 36°0N 136°0E 303 G8
Nipton U.S.A. 35°28N 115°16W 351 K11
Niquelândia Brazil 14°33S 48°23W 365 F9
Nīr Iran 38°2N 47°59E 316 B5
Nirasaki Japan 35°42N 138°27E 303 G9
Nirmal India 19°3N 78°20E 312 K11
Nirmali India 26°20N 86°35E 315 F12
Niš Serbia 43°19N 21°58E 295 C9
Nişāb Si. Arabia 29°11N 44°43E 316 D5
Nişāb Yemen 14°25N 46°29E 319 E4
Nishinomiya Japan 34°45N 135°20E 303 G7
Nishino'omote Japan 30°43N 130°59E 303 J5
Nishiwaki Japan 34°59N 134°58E 303 G7
Niskibi → Canada 56°29N 88°9W 344 A2
Nisqually → U.S.A. 47°7N 122°42W 350 C4
Nissaki Greece 39°43N 19°52E 297 A3
Nissum Bredning Denmark 56°40N 8°20E 281 H13
Nistru = Dnister → Europe 46°18N 30°17E 289 E16
Nisutlin → Canada 60°14N 132°34W 342 A2
Nitchequon Canada 53°10N 70°58W 345 B5
Niterói Brazil 22°53S 43°7W 367 A7
Nith → Canada 43°12N 80°23W 354 C4
Nith → U.K. 55°14N 3°33W 283 F5
Nitmiluk △ Australia 14°6S 132°15E 332 B5
Nitra Slovak Rep. 48°19N 18°4E 289 D10
Nitra → Slovak Rep. 47°46N 18°10E 289 E10
Niue Cook Is. 19°2S 169°54W 337 J11
Niut Indonesia 0°55N 110°6E 308 D4
Niuzhuang China 40°58N 122°28E 307 D12
Nivala Finland 63°56N 24°57E 280 E21
Nivelles Belgium 50°35N 4°20E 287 D4
Nivernais France 47°15N 3°30E 292 C5
Niverville Canada 49°36N 97°3W 343 D9
Niwas India 23°3N 80°26E 315 H9
Nixa U.S.A. 37°3N 93°18W 352 G7
Nixon U.S.A. 29°16N 97°46W 356 G6
Nizamabad India 18°45N 78°7E 312 K11
Nizamghat India 28°20N 95°45E 313 E19
Nizhne Kolymsk Russia 68°34N 160°55E 301 C17
Nizhneangarsk Russia 55°47N 109°30E 301 D11
Nizhnekamsk Russia 55°38N 51°49E 290 C9
Nizhneudinsk Russia 54°54N 99°3E 301 D10
Nizhnevartovsk Russia 60°56N 76°38E 300 C8
Nizhniy Novgorod Russia 56°20N 44°0E 290 C7
Nizhniy Tagil Russia 57°55N 59°57E 290 C10
Nizhyn Ukraine 51°5N 31°55E 291 D5
Nizip Turkey 37°5N 37°50E 316 B3
Nízké Tatry Slovak Rep. 48°55N 19°30E 289 D10
Nizwá Oman 22°56N 57°32E 319 C6
Njakwa Malawi 11°1S 33°56E 327 E3
Njanji Zambia 14°25S 31°46E 327 E3
Njazidja = Grande Comore Comoros Is. 11°35S 43°20E 325 a
Njinjo Tanzania 8°48S 38°54E 327 D4
Njombe Tanzania 9°20S 34°50E 327 D3
Njombe → Tanzania 6°56S 35°6E 326 D4
Nkana Zambia 12°50S 28°8E 327 E2
Nkandla S. Africa 28°37S 31°5E 329 D5
Nkawkaw Ghana 6°36N 0°49W 322 G5
Nkayi Zimbabwe 19°41S 29°20E 327 F2
Nkhotakota Malawi 12°56S 34°15E 327 E3
Nkhotakota ⌓ Malawi 12°50S 34°0E 327 E3
Nkongsamba Cameroon 4°55N 9°55E 324 D1
Nkurenkuru Namibia 17°42S 18°32E 328 B2
Nmai → Burma 25°30N 97°25E 313 G20
Noakhali = Maijdi Bangla. 22°48N 91°10E 313 H17
Nobel Canada 45°25N 80°6W 354 A4
Nobeoka Japan 32°36N 131°41E 303 H5
Noblesville U.S.A. 40°3N 86°1W 352 E10
Noboribetsu Japan 42°24N 141°6E 302 C10
Noccundra Australia 27°50S 142°36E 335 D3
Nocera Inferiore Italy 40°44N 14°38E 294 D6
Nocona U.S.A. 33°47N 97°44W 356 E6
Noda Japan 35°56N 139°52E 303 G9
Nogales Mexico 31°19N 110°56W 358 A2
Nogales U.S.A. 31°21N 110°56W 349 L8
Nōgata Japan 33°48N 130°44E 303 H5
Noggerup Australia 33°32S 116°5E 333 F2
Noginsk Russia 64°30N 90°50E 301 C10
Nogoa → Australia 23°40S 147°55E 334 C4
Nogoyá Argentina 32°24S 59°48W 366 C4
Nohar India 29°11N 74°49E 314 E6
Nohta India 23°40N 79°34E 315 H8
Noires, Mts. France 48°11N 3°40W 292 B2
Noirmoutier, Î. de France 46°58N 2°10W 292 C2
Nojane Botswana 23°15S 20°14E 328 C3
Nojima-Zaki Japan 34°54N 139°53E 303 G9
Nok Kundi Pakistan 28°50N 62°45E 312 E3
Nok Ta Phao, Ko Thailand 9°23N 99°40E 311 b
Nokaneng Botswana 19°40S 22°17E 328 B3
Nokia Finland 61°30N 23°30E 280 F20
Nokomis Canada 51°35N 105°0W 343 C8
Nokomis L. Canada 57°0N 103°0W 343 B8
Nola C.A.R. 3°35N 16°4E 324 D3
Noma Omuramba → Namibia 18°52S 20°53E 328 B3
Nombre de Dios Panama 9°34N 79°28W 360 E4
Nome U.S.A. 64°30N 165°25W 346 a
Nomo-Zaki Japan 32°35N 129°44E 303 H4
Nomuka Tonga 20°17S 174°48W 331 c
Nomuka Group Tonga 20°20S 174°48W 331 c
Nonacho L. Canada 61°42N 109°40W 343 A7
Nonda Australia 20°40S 142°28E 334 C3
Nong Chang Thailand 15°23N 99°51E 310 E2
Nong Het Laos 19°29N 103°59E 310 C4
Nong Khai Thailand 17°50N 102°46E 310 D4
Nong'an China 44°25N 125°5E 307 B13
Nongoma S. Africa 27°58S 31°35E 329 D5
Nongsa Indonesia 1°11N 104°8E 311 d
Nonoava Mexico 27°28N 106°44W 358 B3
Nonsan S. Korea 36°12N 127°5E 307 F14
Nonthaburi Thailand 13°50N 100°29E 310 F3
Noonamah Australia 12°40S 131°4E 332 B5
Noondie, L. Australia 28°30S 119°30E 333 E2
Noord Brabant □ Neths. 51°40N 5°0E 287 C5
Noord Holland □ Neths. 52°30N 4°45E 287 B4
Noordbeveland Neths. 51°35N 3°50E 287 C3
Noordoostpolder Neths. 52°45N 5°45E 287 B5
Noordwijk Neths. 52°14N 4°26E 287 B4
Noosa Heads Australia 26°25S 153°6E 335 D5
Nootka I. Canada 49°32N 126°42W 342 D3
Nopiming ⌓ Canada 50°30N 95°37W 343 C9
Noralee Canada 53°59N 126°26W 342 C3
Noranda = Rouyn-Noranda Canada 48°20N 79°0W 344 C4
Norco U.S.A. 33°56N 117°33W 351 M9
Nord-Kivu □ Dem. Rep. of the Congo 1°0S 29°0E 326 C2
Nord-Ostsee-Kanal Germany 54°12N 9°32E 288 A5
Nordaustlandet Svalbard 79°14N 23°0E 276 B9
Nordegg Canada 52°29N 116°5W 342 C5
Norderney Germany 53°42N 7°9E 288 B4
Norderstedt Germany 53°42N 10°1E 288 B5
Nordfjord Norway 61°55N 5°30E 280 F11
Nordfriesische Inseln Germany 54°40N 8°20E 288 A5
Nordhausen Germany 51°30N 10°47E 288 C6
Norðoyar Færoe Is. 62°17N 6°35W 280 E9

Nordkapp *Norway* 71°10N 25°50E **280** A21
Nordkapp *Svalbard* 80°31N 20°0E **276** A9
Nordkinnhalvøya *Norway* 70°55N 27°40E **280** A22
Nordrhein-Westfalen □ *Germany* 51°45N 7°30E **288** C4
Nordvik *Russia* 74°2N 111°32E **301** B12
Nore → *Ireland* 52°25N 6°58W **282** D4
Norfolk *Canada* 42°50N 80°23W **354** D4
Norfolk *Nebr., U.S.A.* 42°2N 97°25W **352** D5
Norfolk *Va., U.S.A.* 36°50N 76°17W **353** G15
Norfolk □ *U.K.* 52°39N 0°54E **285** E8
Norfolk Broads △ *U.K.* 52°45N 1°30E **285** E9
Norfolk I. *Pac. Oc.* 28°58S 168°3E **330** D9
Norfolk Ridge *Pac. Oc.* 29°0S 168°0E **336** K8
Norfork L. *U.S.A.* 36°15N 92°14W **356** C8
Norge = Norway ■ *Europe* 63°0N 11°0E **280** E14
Norilsk *Russia* 69°20N 88°6E **301** C9
Norma, Mt. *Australia* 20°55S 140°42E **334** C3
Normal *U.S.A.* 40°31N 88°59W **352** E9
Norman *U.S.A.* 35°13N 97°26W **356** D6
Norman → *Australia* 19°18S 141°51E **334** B3
Norman Wells *Canada* 65°17N 126°51W **340** C7
Normanby → *Australia* 14°23S 144°10E **334** A3
Normandie *France* 48°45N 0°10E **292** B4
Normandin *Canada* 48°49N 72°31W **344** C5
Normandy = Normandie *France* 48°45N 0°10E **292** B4
Normanhurst, Mt. *Australia* 25°4S 122°30E **333** E3
Normanton *Australia* 17°40S 141°10E **334** B3
Normétal *Canada* 49°0N 79°22W **344** C4
Norquay *Canada* 51°53N 102°5W **343** C8
Norquinco *Argentina* 41°51S 70°55W **368** E2
Norrbottens län □ *Sweden* 66°50N 20°0E **280** C19
Norris Point *Canada* 49°31N 57°53W **345** C8
Norristown *U.S.A.* 40°7N 75°21W **355** F9
Norrköping *Sweden* 58°37N 16°11E **281** G17
Norrland *Sweden* 62°15N 15°45E **280** E16
Norrtälje *Sweden* 59°46N 18°42E **281** G18
Norseman *Australia* 32°8S 121°43E **333** F3
Norsk *Russia* 52°30N 130°5E **301** D14
Norte, Pta. del *Canary Is.* 27°51N 17°57W **296** G2
Norte, Serra do *Brazil* 11°20S 59°0W **364** F7
North, C. *Canada* 47°2N 60°20W **345** C7
North Adams *U.S.A.* 42°42N 73°7W **355** D11
North America 40°0N 100°0W **338** F10
North Arm *Canada* 62°0N 114°30W **342** A5
North Augusta *U.S.A.* 33°30N 81°59W **357** E14
North Australian Basin *Ind. Oc.* 14°30S 116°30E **336** J3
North Ayrshire □ *U.K.* 55°45N 4°44W **283** F4
North Bass I. *U.S.A.* 41°40N 82°56W **354** E2
North Battleford *Canada* 52°50N 108°17W **343** C7
North Bay *Canada* 46°20N 79°30W **344** C4
North Belcher Is. *Canada* 56°50N 79°50W **344** A4
North Bend *Oreg., U.S.A.* 43°24N 124°14W **348** E1
North Bend *Pa., U.S.A.* 41°20N 77°42W **354** E7
North Bend *Wash., U.S.A.* 47°30N 121°47W **350** C5
North Bennington *U.S.A.* 42°56N 73°15W **355** D11
North Berwick *U.K.* 56°4N 2°42W **283** E6
North Berwick *U.S.A.* 43°18N 70°44W **355** C14
North C. *Canada* 47°5N 64°0W **345** C7
North C. *N.Z.* 34°23S 173°4E **331** A4
North Canadian → *U.S.A.* 35°22N 95°37W **356** D7
North Canton *U.S.A.* 40°53N 81°24W **354** F3
North Cape = Nordkapp *Norway* 71°10N 25°50E **280** A21
North Caribou L. *Canada* 52°50N 90°40W **344** B1
North Carolina □ *U.S.A.* 35°30N 80°0W **357** D15
North Cascades △ *U.S.A.* 48°45N 121°10W **348** B3
North Channel *Canada* 46°0N 83°0W **344** C3
North Channel *U.K.* 55°13N 5°52W **283** F3
North Charleston *U.S.A.* 32°53N 79°58W **357** E15
North Chicago *U.S.A.* 42°19N 87°51W **352** D10
North Creek *U.S.A.* 43°42N 73°59W **355** C11
North Dakota □ *U.S.A.* 47°30N 100°15W **352** B3
North Downs *U.K.* 51°19N 0°21E **285** F8
North East *U.S.A.* 42°13N 79°50W **354** D5
North East Frontier Agency = Arunachal Pradesh □ *India* 28°0N 95°0E **313** F19
North East Lincolnshire □ *U.K.* 53°34N 0°2W **284** D7
North Eastern □ *Kenya* 1°30N 40°0E **326** B5
North Esk → *U.K.* 56°46N 2°24W **283** E6
North European Plain *Europe* 55°0N 25°0E **278** E10
North Foreland *U.K.* 51°22N 1°28E **285** F9
North Fork *U.S.A.* 37°14N 119°21W **350** H7
North Fork American → *U.S.A.* 38°57N 120°59W **350** G5
North Fork Feather → *U.S.A.* 38°33N 121°30W **350** F5
North Fork Grand → *U.S.A.* 45°47N 102°16W **352** C2
North Fork Red → *U.S.A.* 34°24N 99°14W **356** D5
North Frisian Is. = Nordfriesische Inseln *Germany* 54°40N 8°20E **288** A5
North Gower *Canada* 45°8N 75°43W **355** A9
North Hd. *Australia* 30°14S 114°59E **333** F1
North Henik L. *Canada* 61°45N 97°40W **343** A9
North Highlands *U.S.A.* 38°40N 121°23W **350** G5
North Horr *Kenya* 3°20N 37°8E **326** B4
North I. *Kenya* 4°5N 36°5E **326** B4
North I. *N.Z.* 38°0S 175°0E **331** C5
North I. *Seychelles* 4°25S 55°13E **325** b
North Kingsville *U.S.A.* 41°54N 80°42W **354** E4
North Kitui ⌓ *Kenya* 0°15S 38°29E **326** C4
North Knife → *Canada* 58°53N 94°45W **343** B10
North Koel → *India* 24°45N 83°50E **315** G10
North Korea ■ *Asia* 40°0N 127°0E **307** E14
North Lakhimpur *India* 27°14N 94°7E **313** F19
North Lanarkshire □ *U.K.* 55°52N 3°56W **283** F5
North Las Vegas *U.S.A.* 36°11N 115°7W **351** J11
North Lincolnshire □ *U.K.* 53°36N 0°30W **284** D7
North Little Rock *U.S.A.* 34°45N 92°16W **356** D8
North Loup → *U.S.A.* 41°17N 98°24W **352** E4
North Luangwa △ *Zambia* 11°49S 32°9E **327** E3
North Magnetic Pole *Canada* 82°42N 114°24W **341** B9
North Mankato *U.S.A.* 44°10N 94°2W **352** C6
North Minch *U.K.* 58°5N 5°55W **283** C3
North Moose L. *Canada* 54°4N 100°12W **343** C8
North Myrtle Beach *U.S.A.* 33°48N 78°42W **357** E15
North Nahanni → *Canada* 62°15N 123°20W **342** A4
North Olmsted *U.S.A.* 41°25N 81°56W **354** E3
North Ossetia □ *Russia* 43°30N 44°30E **291** F7
North Pagai, I. = Pagai Utara, Pulau *Indonesia* 2°35S 100°0E **308** E2
North Palisade *U.S.A.* 37°6N 118°31W **350** H8
North Platte *U.S.A.* 41°8N 100°46W **352** E3
North Platte → *U.S.A.* 41°7N 100°42W **352** E3
North Pole *Arctic* 90°0N 0°0 **276** A
North Portal *Canada* 49°0N 102°33W **343** D8
North Powder *U.S.A.* 45°2N 117°55W **348** D5
North Pt. *Barbados* 13°20N 59°37W **361** g
North Pt. *Trin. & Tob.* 11°21N 60°31W **365** J16
North Pt. *U.S.A.* 45°2N 83°16W **354** A1
North Rhine Westphalia = Nordrhein-Westfalen □ *Germany* 51°45N 7°30E **288** C4
North River *Canada* 53°49N 57°6W **345** B8
North Ronaldsay *U.K.* 59°22N 2°26W **283** B6
North Saskatchewan → *Canada* 53°15N 105°5W **343** C7
North Sea *Europe* 56°0N 4°0E **278** D6
North Seal → *Canada* 58°50N 98°7W **343** B9
North Somerset □ *U.K.* 51°24N 2°45W **285** F5
North Sporades = Vories Sporades *Greece* 39°15N 23°30E **295** E10
North Sydney *Canada* 46°12N 60°15W **345** C7
North Syracuse *U.S.A.* 43°8N 76°7W **355** C8
North Taranaki Bight *N.Z.* 38°50S 174°15E **331** C5
North Thompson → *Canada* 50°40N 120°20W **342** C4
North Tonawanda *U.S.A.* 43°2N 78°53W **354** C6
North Troy *U.S.A.* 45°0N 72°24W **355** B12
North Twin I. *Canada* 53°20N 80°0W **344** B4
North Tyne → *U.K.* 55°0N 2°8W **284** B5
North Uist *U.K.* 57°40N 7°15W **283** D1
North Vancouver *Canada* 49°19N 123°4W **350** A3
North Vernon *U.S.A.* 39°0N 85°38W **353** F11
North Wabasca L. *Canada* 56°0N 113°55W **342** B6
North Walsham *U.K.* 52°50N 1°22E **284** E9
North West = Severo-Zapadnyy □ *Russia* 65°0N 40°0E **300** C4
North-West □ *S. Africa* 27°0S 25°0E **328** D4
North West C. *Australia* 21°45S 114°9E **332** D1
North West Frontier □ *Pakistan* 34°0N 72°0E **314** C4
North West Highlands *U.K.* 57°33N 4°58W **283** D4
North West River *Canada* 53°30N 60°10W **345** B7
North Western □ *Zambia* 13°30S 25°30E **327** E2
North Wildwood *U.S.A.* 39°0N 74°48W **353** F16
North York Moors *U.K.* 54°23N 0°53W **284** C7
North York Moors △ *U.K.* 54°27N 0°51W **284** C7
North Yorkshire □ *U.K.* 54°15N 1°25W **284** C6
Northallerton *U.K.* 54°20N 1°26W **284** C6
Northam *Australia* 31°35S 116°42E **333** F2
Northam *S. Africa* 24°56S 27°18E **328** C4
Northampton *Australia* 28°27S 114°33E **333** E1
Northampton *U.K.* 52°15N 0°53W **285** E7
Northampton *Mass., U.S.A.* 42°19N 72°38W **355** D12
Northampton *Pa., U.S.A.* 40°41N 75°30W **355** F9
Northamptonshire □ *U.K.* 52°16N 0°55W **285** E7
Northbridge *U.S.A.* 42°9N 71°39W **355** D13
Northcliffe *Australia* 34°39S 116°7E **333** F2
Northeast Pacific Basin *Pac. Oc.* 32°0N 145°0W **337** D13
Northeast Providence Chan. *W. Indies* 26°0N 76°0W **360** A4
Northern = Limpopo □ *S. Africa* 24°5S 29°0E **329** C4
Northern □ *Malawi* 11°0S 34°0E **327** E3
Northern □ *Zambia* 10°30S 31°0E **327** E3
Northern Areas □ *Pakistan* 36°30N 73°0E **315** A5
Northern Cape □ *S. Africa* 30°0S 20°0E **328** D3
Northern Circars *India* 17°30N 82°30E **313** L13
Northern Indian L. *Canada* 57°20N 97°20W **343** B9
Northern Ireland □ *U.K.* 54°45N 7°0W **282** B5
Northern Lau Group *Fiji* 17°30S 178°59W **331** a
Northern Light L. *Canada* 48°15N 90°39W **344** C1
Northern Marianas ◪ *Pac. Oc.* 17°0N 145°0E **336** F6
Northern Province □ *S. Africa* 24°0S 29°0E **329** C4
Northern Range *Trin. & Tob.* 10°46N 61°15W **365** K15
Northern Territory □ *Australia* 20°0S 133°0E **332** D5
Northfield *Minn., U.S.A.* 44°27N 93°9W **352** C7
Northfield *Vt., U.S.A.* 44°9N 72°40W **355** B12
Northland □ *N.Z.* 35°30S 173°30E **331** A4
Northome *U.S.A.* 47°52N 94°17W **352** B6
Northport *Ala., U.S.A.* 33°14N 87°35W **357** E11
Northport *Wash., U.S.A.* 48°55N 117°48W **348** B5
Northumberland □ *U.K.* 55°12N 2°0W **284** B6
Northumberland, C. *Australia* 38°5S 140°40E **335** F3
Northumberland Is. *Australia* 21°30S 149°50E **334** C4
Northumberland Str. *Canada* 46°20N 64°0W **345** C7
Northville *U.S.A.* 43°13N 74°11W **355** C10
Northwest Pacific Basin *Pac. Oc.* 32°0N 165°0E **336** D8
Northwest Providence Channel *W. Indies* 26°0N 78°0W **360** A4
Northwest Territories □ *Canada* 63°0N 118°0W **340** C8
Northwich *U.K.* 53°15N 2°31W **284** D5
Northwood *Iowa, U.S.A.* 43°27N 93°13W **352** D7
Northwood *N. Dak., U.S.A.* 47°44N 97°34W **352** B5
Norton *U.S.A.* 39°50N 99°53W **352** F4
Norton *Zimbabwe* 17°52S 30°40E **327** F3
Norton Sd. *U.S.A.* 63°50N 164°0W **346** a
Norwalk *Calif., U.S.A.* 33°54N 118°4W **351** M8
Norwalk *Conn., U.S.A.* 41°7N 73°22W **355** E11
Norwalk *Iowa, U.S.A.* 41°29N 93°41W **352** E7
Norwalk *Ohio, U.S.A.* 41°15N 82°37W **354** E2
Norway *Maine, U.S.A.* 44°13N 70°32W **353** C18
Norway *Mich., U.S.A.* 45°47N 87°55W **352** C10
Norway ■ *Europe* 63°0N 11°0E **280** E14
Norway House *Canada* 53°59N 97°50W **343** C9
Norwegian B. *Canada* 77°30N 90°0W **341** B11
Norwegian Basin *Atl. Oc.* 68°0N 2°0W **276** C7
Norwegian Sea *Atl. Oc.* 66°0N 1°0E **278** B6
Norwich *Canada* 42°59N 80°36W **354** D4
Norwich *U.K.* 52°38N 1°18E **285** E9
Norwich *Conn., U.S.A.* 41°31N 72°5W **355** E12
Norwich *N.Y., U.S.A.* 42°32N 75°32W **355** D9
Norwood *Canada* 44°23N 77°59W **354** B7
Norwood *U.S.A.* 44°45N 75°0W **355** B10
Nosappu-Misaki *Japan* 45°26N 141°39E **302** C12
Noshiro *Japan* 40°12N 140°0E **302** D10
Noşratābād *Iran* 29°55N 60°0E **317** D8
Noss Hd. *U.K.* 58°28N 3°3W **283** C5
Nossob → *S. Africa* 26°55S 20°45E **328** D3
Nosy Barren *Madag.* 18°25S 43°40E **325** H8
Nosy Bé *Madag.* 13°25S 48°15E **325** G9
Nosy Boraha *Madag.* 16°50S 49°55E **329** B8
Nosy Lava *Madag.* 14°33S 47°36E **329** A8
Nosy Varika *Madag.* 20°35S 48°32E **329** C8
Noteć → *Poland* 52°44N 15°26E **288** B8
Notikewin → *Canada* 57°2N 117°38W **342** B5
Notodden *Norway* 59°35N 9°17E **281** G13
Notre Dame B. *Canada* 49°45N 55°30W **345** C8
Notre-Dame-de-Koartac = Quaqtaq *Canada* 60°55N 69°40W **341** C13
Notre-Dame-des-Bois *Canada* 45°24N 71°4W **355** A13
Notre-Dame-d'Ivugivic = Ivujivik *Canada* 62°24N 77°55W **341** C12
Notre-Dame-du-Nord *Canada* 47°36N 79°30W **344** C4
Nottawasaga B. *Canada* 44°35N 80°15W **354** B4
Nottaway → *Canada* 51°22N 78°55W **344** B4
Nottingham *U.K.* 52°58N 1°10W **284** E6
Nottingham, City of □ *U.K.* 52°58N 1°10W **284** E6
Nottingham I. *Canada* 63°20N 77°55W **341** C12
Nottinghamshire □ *U.K.* 53°10N 1°3W **284** D6
Nottoway → *U.S.A.* 36°33N 76°55W **353** G15
Notwane → *Botswana* 23°35S 26°58E **328** C4
Nouâdhibou *Mauritania* 20°54N 17°0W **322** D2
Nouâdhibou, Ras *Mauritania* 20°50N 17°0W **322** D2
Nouakchott *Mauritania* 18°9N 15°58W **322** E2
Nouméa *N. Cal.* 22°17S 166°30E **330** D9
Noupoort *S. Africa* 31°10S 24°57E **328** E3
Nouveau Comptoir = Wemindji *Canada* 53°0N 78°49W **344** B4
Nouvelle Amsterdam, Î. *Ind. Oc.* 38°30S 77°30E **275** F13
Nouvelle-Calédonie = New Caledonia ◪ *Pac. Oc.* 21°0S 165°0E **330** D9
Nova Casa Nova *Brazil* 9°25S 41°5W **365** E10
Nova Esperança *Brazil* 23°8S 52°24W **367** A5
Nova Friburgo *Brazil* 22°16S 42°30W **367** A7
Nova Iguaçu *Brazil* 22°45S 43°28W **367** A7
Nova Iorque *Brazil* 7°0S 44°5W **365** E10
Nova Lamego *Guinea-Biss.* 12°19N 14°11W **322** F3
Nova Lima *Brazil* 19°59S 43°51W **367** A7
Nova Lusitânia *Mozam.* 19°50S 34°34E **327** F3
Nova Mambone *Mozam.* 21°0S 35°3E **329** C6
Nova Scotia □ *Canada* 45°10N 63°0W **345** C7
Nova Sofala *Mozam.* 20°7S 34°42E **329** C5
Nova Venécia *Brazil* 18°45S 40°24W **365** G10
Nova Zagora *Bulgaria* 42°32N 26°1E **295** C11
Novar *Canada* 45°27N 79°15W **354** A5
Novara *Italy* 45°28N 8°38E **292** D8
Novato *U.S.A.* 38°6N 122°35W **350** G4
Novaya Ladoga *Russia* 60°7N 32°16E **290** B5
Novaya Lyalya *Russia* 59°4N 60°45E **290** C11
Novaya Sibir, Ostrov *Russia* 75°10N 150°0E **301** B16
Novaya Zemlya *Russia* 75°0N 56°0E **300** B6
Nové Zámky *Slovak Rep.* 48°2N 18°8E **289** D10
Novgorod *Russia* 58°30N 31°25E **290** C5
Novgorod-Severskiy = Novhorod-Siverskyy *Ukraine* 52°2N 33°10E **290** D5
Novhorod-Siverskyy *Ukraine* 52°2N 33°10E **290** D5
Novi Lígure *Italy* 44°46N 8°47E **292** D8
Novi Pazar *Serbia* 43°12N 20°28E **295** C9
Novi Sad *Serbia* 45°18N 19°52E **295** B8
Novo Hamburgo *Brazil* 29°37S 51°7W **367** B5
Novo Mesto *Slovenia* 45°47N 15°12E **294** B6
Novo Remanso *Brazil* 9°41S 42°4W **365** E10
Novoaltaysk *Russia* 53°30N 84°0E **300** D9
Novocherkassk *Russia* 47°27N 40°15E **291** E7
Novogrudok = Navahrudak *Belarus* 53°40N 25°50E **289** B13
Novohrad-Volynskyy *Ukraine* 50°34N 27°35E **289** C14
Novokachalinsk *Russia* 45°5N 132°0E **302** B5
Novokuybyshevsk *Russia* 53°7N 49°58E **290** D8
Novokuznetsk *Russia* 53°45N 87°10E **300** D9
Novolazarevskaya *Antarctica* 71°0S 12°0E **277** D3
Novomoskovsk *Russia* 54°5N 38°15E **290** D6
Novorossiysk *Russia* 44°43N 37°46E **291** F6
Novorybnoye *Russia* 72°50N 105°50E **301** B11
Novoselytsya *Ukraine* 48°14N 26°15E **289** D14
Novoshakhtinsk *Russia* 47°46N 39°58E **291** E6
Novosibirsk *Russia* 55°0N 83°5E **300** D9
Novosibirskiye Ostrova *Russia* 75°0N 142°0E **301** B15
Novotroitsk *Russia* 51°10N 58°15E **290** D10
Novouzensk *Russia* 50°32N 48°17E **291** D8
Novovolynsk *Ukraine* 50°45N 24°4E **289** C13
Novska *Croatia* 45°19N 17°0E **294** B7
Novvy Urengoy *Russia* 65°48N 76°52E **300** C8
Novyy Bor *Russia* 66°43N 52°19E **290** A9
Novyy Port *Russia* 67°40N 72°30E **300** C8
Now Shahr *Iran* 36°40N 51°30E **317** B6
Nowa Sól *Poland* 51°48N 15°44E **288** C8
Nowata *U.S.A.* 36°42N 95°38W **356** C7
Nowbarān *Iran* 35°8N 49°42E **317** C6
Nowghāb *Iran* 33°53N 59°4E **317** C8
Nowgong *Assam, India* 26°20N 92°50E **313** F18
Nowgong *Mad. P., India* 25°4N 79°27E **315** G8
Nowra *Australia* 34°53S 150°35E **335** E5
Nowshera *Pakistan* 34°0N 72°0E **312** C8
Nowy Sącz *Poland* 49°40N 20°41E **289** D11
Nowy Targ *Poland* 49°29N 20°2E **289** D11
Nowy Tomyśl *Poland* 52°19N 16°10E **288** B9
Noxen *U.S.A.* 41°25N 76°4W **355** E8
Noyabr'sk *Russia* 64°34N 76°21E **300** C8
Noyon *France* 49°34N 2°59E **292** B5
Noyon *Mongolia* 43°2N 102°4E **306** C2
Nqutu *S. Africa* 28°13S 30°32E **329** D5
Nsanje *Malawi* 16°55S 35°12E **327** F4
Nsawam *Ghana* 5°50N 0°24W **322** G5
Nsomba *Zambia* 10°45S 29°51E **327** E2
Nu Jiang → *China* 29°58N 97°25E **304** D4
Nu Shan *China* 26°0N 99°20E **304** D4
Nuba Mts. = Nubah, Jibalan *Sudan* 12°0N 31°0E **323** F12
Nubah, Jibalan *Sudan* 12°0N 31°0E **323** F12
Nubia *Africa* 21°0N 32°0E **320** D7
Nubian Desert = Nûbîya, Es Sahrâ en *Sudan* 21°30N 33°30E **323** D12
Nûbîya, Es Sahrâ en *Sudan* 21°30N 33°30E **323** D12
Nuboai *Indonesia* 2°10S 136°30E **309** E9
Nubra → *India* 34°35N 77°35E **315** B7
Nueces → *U.S.A.* 27°51N 97°30W **356** H6
Nueltin L. *Canada* 60°30N 99°30W **343** A9
Nueva Ciudad Guerrero *Mexico* 26°34N 99°12W **359** B5
Nueva Gerona *Cuba* 21°53N 82°49W **360** B3
Nueva Palmira *Uruguay* 33°52S 58°20W **366** C4
Nueva Rosita *Mexico* 27°57N 101°13W **358** B4
Nueva San Salvador *El Salv.* 13°40N 89°18W **360** D2
Nuéve de Julio *Argentina* 35°30S 61°0W **366** D3
Nuevitas *Cuba* 21°30N 77°20W **360** B4
Nuevo, G. *Argentina* 43°0S 64°30W **368** E4
Nuevo Casas Grandes *Mexico* 30°25N 107°55W **358** A3
Nuevo Laredo *Mexico* 27°30N 99°31W **359** B5
Nuevo León □ *Mexico* 25°20N 100°0W **358** C5
Nuevo Rocafuerte *Ecuador* 0°55S 75°27W **364** D3
Nugget Pt. *N.Z.* 46°27S 169°50E **331** G2
Nuhaka *N.Z.* 39°3S 177°45E **331** C6
Nukey Bluff *Australia* 32°26S 135°29E **335** E2
Nukhayb *Iraq* 32°4N 42°3E **316** C4
Nuku Hiva *French Polynesia* 8°54S 140°6W **337** H13
Nuku'alofa *Tonga* 21°10S 175°12W **331** c
Nukus *Uzbekistan* 42°27N 59°41E **300** E6
Nullagine *Australia* 21°53S 120°7E **332** D3
Nullagine → *Australia* 21°20S 120°20E **332** D3
Nullarbor *Australia* 31°28S 130°55E **333** F5
Nullarbor △ *Australia* 32°39S 130°0E **333** F2
Nullarbor Plain *Australia* 31°10S 129°0E **333** F4
Numalla, L. *Australia* 28°43S 144°20E **335** D3
Numan *Nigeria* 9°29N 12°3E **323** G8
Numata *Japan* 36°45N 139°4E **303** F9
Numaykoos Lake ⌓ *Canada* 57°52N 95°58W **343** B9
Numazu *Japan* 35°7N 138°51E **303** G9
Numbulwar *Australia* 14°15S 135°45E **334** A2
Numfoor *Indonesia* 1°0S 134°50E **309** E8
Numurkah *Australia* 36°5S 145°26E **335** F4
Nunaksaluk I. *Canada* 55°49N 60°20W **345** A7
Nunap Isua *Greenland* 59°48N 43°55W **338** D15
Nunavut □ *Canada* 66°0N 85°0W **341** C11
Nunda *U.S.A.* 42°35N 77°56W **354** D7
Nuneaton *U.K.* 52°32N 1°27W **285** E6
Nungarin *Australia* 31°12S 118°6E **333** F2
Nungo *Mozam.* 13°23S 37°43E **327** E4
Nungwe *Tanzania* 2°48S 32°2E **326** C3
Nunivak I. *U.S.A.* 60°10N 166°30W **346** a
Nunkun *India* 33°57N 76°2E **315** C7
Nùoro *Italy* 40°20N 9°20E **294** D3
Nūrābād *Iran* 27°47N 57°12E **317** E8
Nuremberg = Nürnberg *Germany* 49°27N 11°3E **288** D6
Nuri *Mexico* 28°5N 109°22W **358** B3
Nuriootpa *Australia* 34°27S 139°0E **335** E2
Nuristān □ *Afghan.* 35°20N 71°0E **312** B7
Nurmes *Finland* 63°33N 29°10E **280** E23
Nürnberg *Germany* 49°27N 11°3E **288** D6
Nurpur *Pakistan* 31°53N 71°54E **314** D4
Nurran, L. = Terewah, L. *Australia* 29°52S 147°35E **335** D4
Nurrari Lakes *Australia* 29°1S 130°5E **333** E5
Nusa Barung *Indonesia* 8°30S 113°30E **309** H15
Nusa Dua *Indonesia* 8°48S 115°14E **309** K18
Nusa Kambangan *Indonesia* 7°40S 108°10E **309** G13
Nusa Tenggara Barat □ *Indonesia* 8°50S 117°30E **308** F5
Nusa Tenggara Timur □ *Indonesia* 9°30S 122°0E **309** F6
Nusaybin *Turkey* 37°3N 41°10E **291** G7
Nushki *Pakistan* 29°35N 66°0E **314** E2
Nuuk *Greenland* 64°10N 51°35W **339** C14
Nuupere, Pte. *Moorea* 17°36S 149°47W **331** d
Nuwakot *Nepal* 28°10N 83°55E **315** E10
Nuwayb'ī, W. an → *Si. Arabia* 29°18N 34°57E **318** F3
Nuweiba' *Egypt* 28°59N 34°39E **316** D2
Nuwerus *S. Africa* 31°8S 18°24E **328** E2
Nuweveldberge *S. Africa* 32°10S 21°45E **328** E3
Nuyts, Pt. *Australia* 35°4S 116°38E **333** G2
Nuyts Arch. *Australia* 32°35S 133°20E **335** E1
Nxai Pan △ *Botswana* 19°50S 24°46E **328** B3
Nxau-Nxau *Botswana* 18°57S 21°4E **328** B3
Nyabing *Australia* 33°33S 118°9E **333** F2
Nyack *U.S.A.* 41°5N 73°55W **355** E11
Nyagan *Russia* 62°30N 65°38E **300** C7
Nyahanga *Tanzania* 2°20S 33°37E **326** C3
Nyahua *Tanzania* 5°25S 33°23E **326** D3
Nyahururu *Kenya* 0°2N 36°27E **326** B4
Nyainqentanglha Shan *China* 30°0N 90°0E **304** D3
Nyakanazi *Tanzania* 3°2S 31°10E **326** C3
Nyâlâ *Sudan* 12°2N 24°58E **323** F10
Nyamandhlovu *Zimbabwe* 19°55S 28°16E **327** F2
Nyambiti *Tanzania* 2°48S 33°27E **326** C3
Nyamira *Kenya* 0°36S 34°52E **326** B4
Nyamwaga *Tanzania* 1°27S 34°33E **326** C3
Nyandekwa *Tanzania* 3°57S 32°32E **326** C3
Nyandoma *Russia* 61°40N 40°12E **290** B7
Nyanga △ *Zimbabwe* 18°17S 32°46E **327** F3
Nyangana *Namibia* 18°0S 20°40E **328** B3
Nyanguge *Tanzania* 2°30S 33°12E **326** C3
Nyanza *Rwanda* 2°20S 29°42E **326** C2
Nyanza □ *Kenya* 0°10S 34°15E **326** C3
Nyanza-Lac *Burundi* 4°21S 29°36E **326** C2
Nyasa, L. = Malawi, L. *Africa* 12°30S 34°30E **327** E3
Nyasvizh *Belarus* 53°14N 26°38E **289** B14
Nyazepetrovsk *Russia* 56°3N 59°36E **290** C10
Nyazura *Zimbabwe* 18°40S 32°16E **327** F3
Nyazwidzi → *Zimbabwe* 20°0S 31°17E **327** G3
Nybro *Sweden* 56°44N 15°55E **281** H16
Nyda *Russia* 66°40N 72°58E **300** C8
Nyeri *Kenya* 0°23S 36°56E **326** C4
Nyika △ *Malawi* 10°30S 33°53E **327** E3
Nyíregyháza *Hungary* 47°58N 21°47E **289** E11
Nyiru, Mt. *Kenya* 2°8N 36°50E **326** B4
Nykarleby = Uusikaarlepyy *Finland* 63°32N 22°31E **280** E20
Nykøbing *Nordjylland, Denmark* 56°48N 8°51E **281** H13
Nykøbing *Sjælland, Denmark* 54°56N 11°52E **281** J14
Nykøbing *Sjælland, Denmark* 55°55N 11°40E **281** J14
Nyköping *Sweden* 58°45N 17°1E **281** G17
Nylstroom = Modimolle *S. Africa* 24°42S 28°22E **329** C4
Nymagee *Australia* 32°7S 146°20E **335** E4
Nymboida △ *Australia* 29°38S 152°26E **335** D5
Nynäshamn *Sweden* 58°54N 17°57E **281** G17
Nyngan *Australia* 31°30S 147°8E **335** E4
Nyoma Rap *India* 33°10N 78°40E **315** C8
Nyoman = Nemunas → *Lithuania* 55°25N 21°10E **281** J19
Nysa *Poland* 50°30N 17°22E **289** C9
Nysa → *Europe* 52°4N 14°46E **288** B8
Nyslott = Savonlinna *Finland* 61°52N 28°53E **280** F23
Nyssa *U.S.A.* 43°53N 117°0W **348** E5
Nystad = Uusikaupunki *Finland* 60°47N 21°25E **280** F19
Nyunzu *Dem. Rep. of the Congo* 5°57S 27°58E **326** D2
Nyurba *Russia* 63°17N 118°28E **301** C12
Nzega *Tanzania* 4°10S 33°12E **326** C3

Nzérékoré *Guinea* 7°49N 8°48W **322 G4**
Nzeto *Angola* 7°10S 12°52E **324 F2**
Nzilo, Chutes de
Dem. Rep. of the Congo 10°18S 25°27E **327 E2**
Nzubuka *Tanzania* 4°45S 32°50E **326 C3**
Nzwani = Anjouan
Comoros Is. 12°15S 44°20E **325 a**

O

O Le Pupū Pu'e △
Samoa 13°59S 171°43W **331 b**
Ō-Shima *Hokkaidō,*
Japan 41°30N 139°22E **302 D9**
Ō-Shima *Shizuoka,*
Japan 34°44N 139°24E **303 G9**
Oa, Mull of *U.K.* 55°35N 6°20W **283 F2**
Oacoma *U.S.A.* 43°48N 99°24W **352 D4**
Oahe, L. *U.S.A.* 44°27N 100°24W **352 C3**
Oahe Dam *U.S.A.* 44°27N 100°24W **352 C3**
O'ahu *U.S.A.* 21°28N 157°58W **346 b**
Oak Harbor *U.S.A.* 48°18N 122°39W **350 B4**
Oak Hill *U.S.A.* 37°59N 81°9W **353 G13**
Oak Island *U.S.A.* 33°55N 78°10W **357 E15**
Oak Ridge *U.S.A.* 36°1N 84°16W **357 C12**
Oak View *U.S.A.* 34°24N 119°18W **351 L7**
Oakan-Dake *Japan* 43°27N 144°10E **302 C12**
Oakdale *Calif., U.S.A.* 37°46N 120°51W **350 H6**
Oakdale *La., U.S.A.* 30°49N 92°40W **356 F8**
Oakes *U.S.A.* 46°8N 98°6W **352 B4**
Oakesdale *U.S.A.* 47°8N 117°15W **348 C5**
Oakey *Australia* 27°25S 151°43E **335 D5**
Oakfield *U.S.A.* 43°4N 78°16W **354 C6**
Oakham *U.K.* 52°40N 0°43W **285 E7**
Oakhurst *U.S.A.* 37°19N 119°40W **350 H7**
Oakland *U.S.A.* 37°48N 122°18W **350 H4**
Oakley *Idaho, U.S.A.* 42°15N 113°53W **348 E7**
Oakley *Kans., U.S.A.* 39°8N 100°51W **352 F3**
Oakover → *Australia* 21°0S 120°40E **332 D3**
Oakridge *U.S.A.* 43°45N 122°28W **348 E2**
Oakville *Canada* 43°27N 79°41W **354 C5**
Oakville *U.S.A.* 46°51N 123°14W **350 D3**
Oamaru *N.Z.* 45°5S 170°59E **331 F3**
Oasis *Calif., U.S.A.* 37°29N 117°55W **350 H9**
Oasis *Calif., U.S.A.* 33°28N 116°6W **351 M10**
Oates Land *Antarctica* 69°0S 160°0E **277 C11**
Oatlands *Australia* 42°17S 147°21E **335 G4**
Oatman *U.S.A.* 35°1N 114°19W **351 K12**
Oaxaca *Mexico* 17°3N 96°43W **359 D5**
Oaxaca □ *Mexico* 17°0N 96°30W **359 D5**
Ob → *Russia* 66°45N 69°30E **300 C7**
Oba *Canada* 49°4N 84°7W **344 C3**
Obama *Japan* 35°30N 135°45E **303 G7**
Oban *U.K.* 56°25N 5°29W **283 E3**
Obbia *Somali Rep.* 5°25N 48°30E **319 F4**
Obera *Argentina* 27°21S 55°2W **367 B4**
Oberhausen *Germany* 51°28N 6°51E **288 C4**
Oberlin *Kans., U.S.A.* 39°49N 100°32W **352 F3**
Oberlin *La., U.S.A.* 30°37N 92°46W **356 F8**
Oberlin *Ohio, U.S.A.* 41°18N 82°13W **354 E2**
Oberon *Australia* 33°45S 149°52E **335 E4**
Obi, Kepulauan
Indonesia 1°23S 127°45E **309 E7**
Óbidos *Brazil* 1°50S 55°30W **365 D7**
Obihiro *Japan* 42°56N 143°12E **302 C11**
Obilatu *Indonesia* 1°25S 127°20E **309 E7**
Obluchye *Russia* 49°1N 131°4E **301 E14**
Obo *C.A.R.* 5°20N 26°32E **326 A2**
Oboa, Mt. *Uganda* 1°45N 34°45E **326 B3**
Oboyan *Russia* 51°15N 36°21E **300 D4**
Obozerskaya = Obozerskiy
Russia 63°34N 40°21E **290 B7**
Obozerskiy *Russia* 63°34N 40°21E **290 B7**
Observatory Inlet
Canada 55°10N 129°54W **342 B3**
Obshchi Syrt *Russia* 52°0N 53°0E **278 E16**
Obskaya Guba *Russia* 69°0N 73°0E **300 C8**
Obuasi *Ghana* 6°17N 1°40W **322 G5**
Ocala *U.S.A.* 29°11N 82°8W **357 G13**
Ocampo *Chihuahua,*
Mexico 28°11N 108°23W **358 B3**
Ocampo *Tamaulipas,*
Mexico 22°50N 99°20W **359 C5**
Ocaña *Spain* 39°55N 3°30W **293 C4**
Occidental, Cordillera
Colombia 5°0N 76°0W **364 C3**
Occidental, Grand Erg
Algeria 30°20N 1°0E **322 B6**
Ocean City *Md., U.S.A.* 38°20N 75°5W **353 F16**
Ocean City *N.J., U.S.A.* 39°17N 74°35W **353 F16**
Ocean City *Wash.,*
U.S.A. 47°4N 124°10W **350 C2**
Ocean Falls *Canada* 52°18N 127°48W **342 C3**
Ocean I. = Banaba
Kiribati 0°45S 169°50E **336 H8**
Ocean Park *U.S.A.* 46°30N 124°3W **350 D2**
Oceano *U.S.A.* 35°6N 120°37W **351 K6**
Oceanport *U.S.A.* 40°19N 74°3W **355 F10**
Oceanside *U.S.A.* 33°12N 117°23W **351 M9**
Ochil Hills *U.K.* 56°14N 3°40W **283 E5**
Ocho Rios *Jamaica* 18°24N 77°6W **360 a**
Ocilla *U.S.A.* 31°36N 83°15W **357 F13**
Ocmulgee → *U.S.A.* 31°58N 82°33W **357 F13**
Ocniţa *Moldova* 48°25N 27°30E **289 D14**
Oconee → *U.S.A.* 31°58N 82°33W **357 F13**
Oconomowoc *U.S.A.* 43°7N 88°30W **352 D9**
Oconto *U.S.A.* 44°53N 87°52W **352 C10**
Oconto Falls *U.S.A.* 44°52N 88°9W **352 C9**
Ocosingo *Mexico* 16°53N 92°6W **359 D6**
Ocotal *Nic.* 13°41N 86°31W **360 D2**
Ocotlán *Jalisco, Mexico* 20°21N 102°46W **358 C4**
Ocotlán *Oaxaca, Mexico* 16°48N 96°40W **359 D5**
Ōda *Japan* 35°11N 132°30E **303 G6**
Ódáðahraun *Iceland* 65°5N 17°0W **280 D5**
Ŏdaejin *N. Korea* 41°34N 129°40E **307 D15**
Odate *Japan* 40°16N 140°34E **302 D10**
Odawara *Japan* 35°20N 139°6E **303 G9**
Odda *Norway* 60°3N 6°35E **281 F12**
Odei → *Canada* 56°6N 96°54W **343 B9**
Ödemiş *Turkey* 38°15N 28°0E **295 E13**
Odendaalsrus *S. Africa* 27°48S 26°45E **328 D4**
Odense *Denmark* 55°22N 10°23E **281 J14**
Oder → *Europe* 53°33N 14°38E **288 B8**
Odesa *Ukraine* 46°30N 30°45E **291 E5**
Odessa = Odesa *Ukraine* 46°30N 30°45E **291 E5**
Odessa *Canada* 44°17N 76°43W **355 B8**
Odessa *Tex., U.S.A.* 31°52N 102°23W **356 F3**
Odessa *Wash., U.S.A.* 47°20N 118°41W **348 C4**
Odiakwe *Botswana* 20°12S 25°17E **328 C4**
Odienné *Ivory C.* 9°30N 7°34W **322 G4**
Odintsovo *Russia* 55°40N 37°16E **290 C6**
O'Donnell *U.S.A.* 32°58N 101°50W **356 E4**
Odorheiu Secuiesc
Romania 46°21N 25°21E **289 E13**
Odra = Oder → *Europe* 53°33N 14°38E **288 B8**
Odzi *Zimbabwe* 19°0S 32°20E **329 B5**
Odzi → *Zimbabwe* 19°45S 32°23E **329 B5**
Oeiras *Brazil* 7°0S 42°8W **365 E10**
Oelrichs *U.S.A.* 43°11N 103°14W **352 D2**
Oelwein *U.S.A.* 42°41N 91°55W **352 D8**
Oeno I. *Pac. Oc.* 24°0S 131°0W **337 K14**
Oenpelli = Gunbalanya
Australia 12°20S 133°4E **332 B5**
Ofanto → *Italy* 41°22N 16°13E **294 D7**
Offa *Nigeria* 8°13N 4°42E **322 G6**
Offaly □ *Ireland* 53°15N 7°30W **282 C4**
Offenbach *Germany* 50°6N 8°44E **288 C5**
Offenburg *Germany* 48°28N 7°56E **288 D4**
Officer Cr. → *Australia* 27°46S 132°30E **333 E5**
Ofolanga *Tonga* 19°38S 174°27W **331 c**
Ofotfjorden *Norway* 68°27N 17°0E **280 B17**
Ofu *Amer. Samoa* 14°11S 169°41W **331 b**
Ōfunato *Japan* 39°4N 141°43E **302 E10**
Oga *Japan* 39°55N 139°50E **302 E9**
Oga-Hantō *Japan* 39°58N 139°47E **302 E9**
Ogaden *Ethiopia* 7°30N 45°30E **319 F3**
Ōgaki *Japan* 35°21N 136°37E **303 G8**
Ogallala *U.S.A.* 41°8N 101°43W **352 E3**
Ogasawara Gunto
Pac. Oc. 27°0N 142°0E **336 E6**
Ogbomosho *Nigeria* 8°1N 4°11E **322 G6**
Ogden *U.S.A.* 41°13N 111°58W **348 F8**
Ogdensburg *U.S.A.* 44°42N 75°30W **355 B9**
Ogea Driki *Fiji* 19°12S 178°27W **331 a**
Ogea Levu *Fiji* 19°8S 178°24W **331 a**
Ogeechee → *U.S.A.* 31°50N 81°3W **357 F14**
Ogilby *U.S.A.* 32°49N 114°50W **351 N12**
Oglio → *Italy* 45°2N 10°39E **294 B4**
Ogmore *Australia* 22°37S 149°35E **334 C4**
Ogoki *Canada* 51°38N 85°58W **344 B2**
Ogoki → *Canada* 51°38N 85°57W **344 B2**
Ogoki L. *Canada* 50°50N 87°10W **344 B2**
Ogoki Res. *Canada* 50°45N 88°15W **344 B2**
Ogooué → *Gabon* 1°0S 9°0E **324 E1**
Ogowe = Ogooué → *Gabon* 1°0S 9°0E **324 E1**
Ogre *Latvia* 56°49N 24°36E **281 H21**
Ogurchinskiy, Ostrov
Turkmenistan 38°55N 53°2E **317 B7**
Ohai *N.Z.* 45°55S 168°0E **331 F2**
Ohakune *N.Z.* 39°24S 175°24E **331 C5**
Ohata *Japan* 41°24N 141°10E **302 D10**
Ohau, L. *N.Z.* 44°15S 169°53E **331 F2**
Ohio □ *U.S.A.* 40°15N 82°45W **354 F2**
Ohio → *U.S.A.* 36°59N 89°8W **352 G9**
Ohře → *Czech Rep.* 50°30N 14°10E **288 C8**
Ohrid *Macedonia* 41°8N 20°52E **295 D9**
Ohridsko Jezero
Macedonia 41°8N 20°52E **295 D9**
Ohrigstad *S. Africa* 24°39S 30°36E **329 C5**
Oiapoque *Brazil* 3°50N 51°50W **365**
Oikou *China* 38°35N 117°42E **307 E9**
Oil City *U.S.A.* 41°26N 79°42W **354 E5**
Oil Springs *Canada* 42°47N 82°7W **354 D2**
Oildale *U.S.A.* 35°25N 119°1W **351 K7**
Oise → *France* 49°0N 2°4E **292 B5**
Oistins *Barbados* 13°4N 59°33W **361 g**
Oistins B. *Barbados* 13°4N 59°33W **361 g**
Ōita *Japan* 33°14N 131°36E **303 H5**
Ōita □ *Japan* 33°15N 131°30E **303 H5**
Oiticica *Brazil* 5°3S 41°5W **365 E10**
Ojai *U.S.A.* 34°27N 119°15W **351 L7**
Ojinaga *Mexico* 29°34N 104°25W **358 B4**
Ojiya *Japan* 37°18N 138°48E **303 F9**
Ojo Caliente *Mexico* 21°53N 102°15W **358 C4**
Ojos del Salado, Cerro
Argentina 27°0S 68°40W **366 B2**
Oka → *Russia* 56°20N 43°59E **290 C7**
Okaba *Indonesia* 8°6S 139°42E **309 F9**
Okahandja *Namibia* 22°0S 16°59E **328 C2**
Okanagan L. *Canada* 50°0N 119°30W **342 D5**
Okandja *Gabon* 0°35S 13°45E **324 E2**
Okanogan *U.S.A.* 48°22N 119°35W **348 B4**
Okanogan → *U.S.A.* 48°6N 119°44W **348 B4**
Okanogan Range
N. Amer. 49°0N 119°55W **342 D5**
Okapi △
Dem. Rep. of the Congo 2°30N 27°20E **326 B2**
Okaputa *Namibia* 20°5S 17°0E **328 C2**
Okara *Pakistan* 30°50N 73°31E **314 D5**
Okaukuejo *Namibia* 19°10S 16°0E **328 B2**
Okavango Delta
Botswana 18°45S 22°45E **328 B3**
Okavango Swamp = Okavango
Delta *Botswana* 18°45S 22°45E **328 B3**
Okaya *Japan* 36°5N 138°10E **303 F9**
Okayama *Japan* 34°40N 133°54E **303 G6**
Okayama □ *Japan* 35°0N 133°50E **303 G6**
Okazaki *Japan* 34°57N 137°10E **303 G8**
Okeechobee *U.S.A.* 27°15N 80°50W **357 H14**
Okeechobee, L. *U.S.A.* 27°0N 80°50W **357 H14**
Okefenokee ⌓ *U.S.A.* 30°45N 82°18W **357 F13**
Okefenokee Swamp
U.S.A. 30°40N 82°20W **357 F13**
Okehampton *U.K.* 50°44N 4°0W **285 G4**
Okha *India* 22°27N 69°4E **314 H3**
Okha *Russia* 53°40N 143°0E **301 D15**
Okhotsk *Russia* 59°20N 143°10E **301 D15**
Okhotsk, Sea of *Asia* 55°0N 145°0E **301 D15**
Okhotskiy Perevoz
Russia 61°52N 135°35E **301 C14**
Okhtyrka *Ukraine* 50°25N 35°0E **291 D5**
Oki-Shotō *Japan* 36°5N 133°15E **303 F6**
Okiep *S. Africa* 29°39S 17°53E **328 D2**
Okinawa *Japan* 26°19N 127°46E **303 L3**
Okinawa □ *Japan* 26°40N 128°0E **303 L4**
Okinawa-Guntō *Japan* 26°40N 128°0E **303 L4**
Okinawa-Jima *Japan* 26°32N 128°0E **303 L4**
Okino-erabu-Shima
Japan 27°21N 128°33E **303 L4**
Oklahoma □ *U.S.A.* 35°20N 97°30W **356 D6**
Oklahoma City *U.S.A.* 35°30N 97°30W **356 D6**
Okmulgee *U.S.A.* 35°37N 95°58W **356 D7**
Oknitsa = Ocniţa
Moldova 48°25N 27°30E **289 D14**
Okolo *Uganda* 2°37N 31°8E **326 B3**
Okolona *U.S.A.* 34°0N 88°45W **357 E10**
Okombahe *Namibia* 21°23S 15°22E **328 C2**
Okotoks *Canada* 50°43N 113°58W **342 C6**
Oksibil *Indonesia* 4°59S 140°35E **309 E10**
Oksovskiy *Russia* 62°33N 39°57E **290 B6**
Oktabrsk = Oktyabrsk
Kazakhstan 49°28N 57°25E **291 E10**
Oktyabrsk *Kazakhstan* 49°28N 57°25E **291 E10**
Oktyabrskiy = Aktsyabrski
Belarus 52°38N 28°53E **289 B15**
Oktyabrskiy *Russia* 54°28N 53°28E **290 D9**
Oktyabrskoy Revolyutsii, Ostrov
Russia 79°30N 97°0E **301 B10**
Okuru *N.Z.* 43°55S 168°55E **331 E2**
Okushiri-Tō *Japan* 42°15N 139°30E **302 C9**
Okwa → *Botswana* 22°30S 23°0E **328 C3**
Ola *U.S.A.* 35°2N 93°13W **356 D8**
Ólafsfjörður *Iceland* 66°4N 18°39W **280 C4**
Ólafsvík *Iceland* 64°53N 23°43W **280 D2**
Olancha *U.S.A.* 36°17N 118°1W **351 J8**
Olancha Pk. *U.S.A.* 36°16N 118°7W **351 J8**
Olanchito *Honduras* 15°30N 86°30W **360 C2**
Öland *Sweden* 56°45N 16°38E **281 H17**
Olary *Australia* 32°18S 140°19E **335 E3**
Olascoaga *Argentina* 35°15S 60°39W **366 D3**
Olathe *U.S.A.* 38°53N 94°49W **352 F6**
Olavarría *Argentina* 36°55S 60°20W **366 D3**
Oława *Poland* 50°57N 17°20E **289 C9**
Ólbia *Italy* 40°55N 9°31E **294 D3**
Olcott *U.S.A.* 43°20N 78°42W **354 C6**
Old Bahama Chan. = Bahama,
Canal Viejo de
W. Indies 22°10N 77°30W **360 B4**
Old Baldy Pk. = San Antonio, Mt.
U.S.A. 34°17N 117°38W **351 L9**
Old Bridge *U.S.A.* 40°25N 74°22W **355 F10**
Old Castile = Castilla y Leon □
Spain 42°0N 5°0W **293 B3**
Old Crow *Canada* 67°30N 139°55W **340 C6**
Old Dale *U.S.A.* 34°8N 115°47W **351 L11**
Old Forge *N.Y., U.S.A.* 43°43N 74°58W **355 C10**
Old Forge *Pa., U.S.A.* 41°22N 75°45W **355 E9**
Old Perlican *Canada* 48°5N 53°1W **345 C9**
Old Shinyanga *Tanzania* 3°33S 33°27E **326 C3**
Old Speck Mt. *U.S.A.* 44°34N 70°57W **355 B14**
Old Town *U.S.A.* 44°56N 68°39W **353 C19**
Old Washington *U.S.A.* 40°2N 81°27W **354 F3**
Old Wives L. *Canada* 50°5N 106°0W **343 C7**
Oldbury *U.K.* 51°38N 2°33W **285 F5**
Oldcastle *Ireland* 53°46N 7°10W **282 C4**
Oldeani *Tanzania* 3°22S 35°35E **326 C4**
Oldenburg *Germany* 53°9N 8°13E **288 B5**
Oldenzaal *Neths.* 52°19N 6°53E **287 B6**
Oldham *U.K.* 53°33N 2°7W **284 D5**
Oldman → *Canada* 49°57N 111°42W **342 D6**
Oldmeldrum *U.K.* 57°20N 2°19W **283 D6**
Olds *Canada* 51°50N 114°10W **342 C6**
Olduvai Gorge *Tanzania* 2°57S 35°23E **326 C4**
Oldziyt *Mongolia* 44°40N 109°1E **306 B5**
Olean *U.S.A.* 42°5N 78°26W **354 D6**
Olekma → *Russia* 60°22N 120°42E **301 C13**
Olekminsk *Russia* 60°25N 120°30E **301 C13**
Oleksandriya *Ukraine* 50°37N 26°19E **289 C14**
Olema *U.S.A.* 38°3N 122°47W **350 G4**
Olenegorsk *Russia* 68°9N 33°18E **280 B25**
Olenek *Russia* 68°28N 112°18E **301 C12**
Olenek → *Russia* 73°0N 120°10E **301 B13**
Oléron, Î. d' *France* 45°55N 1°15W **292 D3**
Oleśnica *Poland* 51°13N 17°22E **289 C9**
Olevsk *Ukraine* 51°12N 27°39E **289 C14**
Olga *Russia* 43°50N 135°14E **301 E14**
Olga, L. *Canada* 49°47N 77°15W **344 C4**
Olgas, The = Kata Tjuta
Australia 25°20S 130°50E **333 E5**
Ölgiy *Mongolia* 48°56N 89°57E **304 B3**
Olhão *Portugal* 37°3N 7°48W **293 D2**
Olifants = Elefantes →
Africa 24°10S 32°40E **329 C5**
Olifants → *Namibia* 25°30S 19°30E **328 C2**
Olifantshoek *S. Africa* 27°57S 22°42E **328 D3**
Ólimbos, Óros = Olymbos Oros
Greece 40°6N 22°23E **295 D10**
Olímpia *Brazil* 20°44S 48°54W **367 A6**
Olinda *Brazil* 8°1S 34°51W **365 E12**
Oliva *Argentina* 32°0S 63°38W **366 C3**
Olive Branch *U.S.A.* 34°57N 89°49W **357 D10**
Olivehurst *U.S.A.* 39°6N 121°34W **350 F5**
Olivenza *Spain* 38°41N 7°9W **293 C2**
Oliver *Canada* 49°13N 119°37W **342 D5**
Oliver L. *Canada* 56°56N 103°22W **343 B8**
Ollagüe *Chile* 21°15S 68°10W **366 A2**
Olney *Ill., U.S.A.* 38°44N 88°5W **352 F9**
Olney *Tex., U.S.A.* 33°22N 98°45W **356 E5**
Oloitokitok *Kenya* 2°56S 37°30E **326 C4**
Olomane → *Canada* 50°14N 60°37W **345 B7**
Olomouc *Czech Rep.* 49°38N 17°12E **289 D9**
Olonets *Russia* 61°0N 32°54E **290 B5**
Olongapo *Phil.* 14°50N 120°18E **309 B6**
Olosega *Amer. Samoa* 14°10S 169°37W **331 b**
Olosenga = Swains I.
Amer. Samoa 11°11S 171°4W **337 J11**
Olot *Spain* 42°11N 2°30E **293 A7**
Olovyannaya *Russia* 50°58N 115°35E **301 D12**
Oloy → *Russia* 66°29N 159°29E **301 C16**
Olsztyn *Poland* 53°48N 20°29E **289 B11**
Olt → *Romania* 43°43N 24°51E **289 G13**
Olteniţa *Romania* 44°7N 26°42E **289 F14**
Olton *U.S.A.* 34°11N 102°8W **356 D3**
Olymbos *Cyprus* 35°21N 33°45E **297 D12**
Olymbos Oros *Greece* 40°6N 22°23E **295 D10**
Olympia *Greece* 37°39N 21°39E **295 F9**
Olympia *U.S.A.* 47°3N 122°53W **350 D4**
Olympic △ *U.S.A.* 47°45N 123°43W **350 C3**
Olympic Dam *Australia* 30°30S 136°55E **335 E2**
Olympic Mts. *U.S.A.* 47°55N 123°45W **350 C3**
Olympus *Cyprus* 34°56N 32°52E **297 E11**
Olympus, Mt. = Olymbos Oros
Greece 40°6N 22°23E **295 D10**
Olympus, Mt. = Uludağ
Turkey 40°4N 29°13E **295 D13**
Olympus, Mt. *U.S.A.* 47°48N 123°43W **350 C3**
Olyphant *U.S.A.* 41°27N 75°36W **355 E9**
Om → *Russia* 54°59N 73°22E **300 D8**
Om Koi *Thailand* 17°48N 98°22E **310 D2**
Ōma *Japan* 41°45N 141°5E **302 D10**
Ōmachi *Japan* 36°30N 137°50E **303 F8**
Omae-Zaki *Japan* 34°36N 138°14E **303 G9**
Ōmagari *Japan* 39°27N 140°29E **302 E10**
Omagh *U.K.* 54°36N 7°19W **282 B4**
Omagh □ *U.K.* 54°35N 7°15W **282 B4**
Omaha *U.S.A.* 41°17N 95°58W **352 E6**
Omak *U.S.A.* 48°25N 119°31W **348 B4**
Omalos *Greece* 35°19N 23°55E **297 D5**
Oman ■ *Asia* 23°0N 58°0E **319 C6**
Oman, G. of *Asia* 24°30N 58°30E **317 E8**
Omaruru *Namibia* 21°26S 16°0E **328 C2**
Omaruru → *Namibia* 22°7S 14°15E **328 C1**
Omate *Peru* 16°45S 71°0W **364 G4**
Ombai, Selat *Indonesia* 8°30S 124°50E **309 F6**
Omboué *Gabon* 1°35S 9°15E **324 E1**
Ombrone → *Italy* 42°42N 11°5E **294 C4**
Omdurmân *Sudan* 15°40N 32°28E **323 E12**
Omemee *Canada* 44°18N 78°33W **354 B6**
Omeonga
Dem. Rep. of the Congo 3°40S 24°22E **326 C1**
Ometepe, I. de *Nic.* 11°32N 85°35W **360 D2**
Ometepec *Mexico* 16°41N 98°25W **359 D5**
Ominato *Japan* 41°17N 141°10E **302 D10**
Omineca → *Canada* 56°3N 124°16W **342 B4**
Omineca Mts. *Canada* 56°30N 125°30W **342 B3**
Omitara *Namibia* 22°16S 18°2E **328 C2**
Ōmiya = Saitama
Japan 35°54N 139°38E **303 G9**
Ommen *Neths.* 52°31N 6°26E **287 B6**
Ömnögovĭ □ *Mongolia* 43°15N 104°0E **306 C3**
Omo → *Ethiopia* 6°25N 36°10E **319 F2**
Omodhos *Cyprus* 34°51N 32°48E **297 E11**
Omolon → *Russia* 68°42N 158°36E **301 C16**
Omono-Gawa →
Japan 39°46N 140°3E **302 E10**
Omsk *Russia* 55°0N 73°12E **300 D8**
Omsukchan *Russia* 62°32N 155°48E **301 C16**
Ōmu *Japan* 44°34N 142°58E **302 B11**
Omul, Vf. *Romania* 45°27N 25°29E **289 F13**
Ōmura *Japan* 32°56N 129°57E **303 H4**
Omuramba Omatako →
Namibia 17°45S 20°25E **328 B2**
Omuramba Ovambo →
Namibia 18°45S 16°59E **328 B2**
Ōmuta *Japan* 33°5N 130°26E **303 H5**
Onaga *U.S.A.* 39°29N 96°10W **352 F5**
Onalaska *U.S.A.* 43°53N 91°14W **352 D8**
Onancock *U.S.A.* 37°43N 75°45W **353 G16**
Onang *Indonesia* 3°2S 118°49E **309 E5**
Onangue, L. *Gabon* 0°57S 10°4E **324 E2**
Onaping L. *Canada* 47°3N 81°30W **344 C3**
Onavas *Mexico* 28°31N 109°35W **358 B3**
Onawa *U.S.A.* 42°2N 96°6W **352 D5**
Oncócua *Angola* 16°30S 13°25E **328 B1**
Onda *Spain* 39°55N 0°17W **293 C5**
Ondangwa *Namibia* 17°57S 16°4E **328 B2**
Ondjiva *Angola* 16°48S 15°50E **328 B2**
Öndörshil *Mongolia* 45°13N 108°5E **306 B5**
Öndverðarnes *Iceland* 64°52N 24°0W **280 D2**
One Tree *Australia* 34°11S 144°43E **335 E3**
Oneata *Fiji* 18°26S 178°25W **331 a**
Onega *Russia* 64°0N 38°10E **290 B6**
Onega → *Russia* 63°58N 38°2E **290 B6**
Onega, G. of = Onezhskaya Guba
Russia 64°24N 36°38E **290 B6**
Onega, L. = Onezhskoye Ozero
Russia 61°44N 35°22E **290 B6**
Oneida *U.S.A.* 43°6N 75°39W **355 C9**
Oneida L. *U.S.A.* 43°12N 75°54W **355 C9**
O'Neill *U.S.A.* 42°27N 98°39W **352 D4**
Onekotan, Ostrov
Russia 49°25N 154°45E **301 E16**
Onema
Dem. Rep. of the Congo 4°35S 24°30E **326 C1**
Oneonta *U.S.A.* 42°27N 75°4W **355 D9**
Oneşti *Romania* 46°17N 26°47E **289 E14**
Onezhskaya Guba
Russia 64°24N 36°38E **290 B6**
Onezhskoye Ozero
Russia 61°44N 35°22E **290 B6**
Ongarue *N.Z.* 38°42S 175°19E **331 C5**
Ongea Levu = Ogea Levu
Fiji 19°8S 178°24W **331 a**
Ongers → *S. Africa* 31°4S 23°13E **328 E3**
Ongerup *Australia* 33°58S 118°28E **333 F2**
Ongjin *N. Korea* 37°56N 125°21E **307 F13**
Ongkharak *Thailand* 14°8N 101°1E **310 E3**
Ongniud Qi *China* 43°0N 118°38E **307 C10**
Ongoka
Dem. Rep. of the Congo 1°20S 26°0E **326 C2**
Ongole *India* 15°33N 80°2E **312 M12**
Ongon = Havirga
Mongolia 45°41N 113°5E **306 B7**
Onida *U.S.A.* 44°42N 100°4W **352 C3**
Onilahy → *Madag.* 23°34S 43°45E **329 C7**
Onitsha *Nigeria* 6°6N 6°42E **322 G7**
Ono *Fiji* 18°55S 178°29E **331 a**
Onoda *Japan* 33°59N 131°11E **303 G5**
Onslow *Australia* 21°40S 115°12E **332 D2**
Onslow B. *U.S.A.* 34°20N 77°15W **357 D16**
Ontake-San *Japan* 35°53N 137°29E **303 G8**
Ontario *Calif., U.S.A.* 34°4N 117°39W **351 L9**
Ontario *Oreg., U.S.A.* 44°2N 116°58W **348 D5**
Ontario □ *Canada* 48°0N 83°0W **344 B2**
Ontario, L. *N. Amer.* 43°20N 78°0W **354 C7**
Ontonagon *U.S.A.* 46°52N 89°19W **352 B9**
Onyx *U.S.A.* 35°41N 118°14W **351 K8**
Oodnadatta *Australia* 27°33S 135°30E **335 D2**
Ooldea *Australia* 30°27S 131°50E **333 F5**
Oombulgurri *Australia* 15°15S 127°45E **332 C4**
Oorindi *Australia* 20°40S 141°1E **334 C3**
Oost-Vlaanderen □
Belgium 51°5N 3°50E **287 C3**
Oostende *Belgium* 51°15N 2°54E **287 C2**
Oosterhout *Neths.* 51°39N 4°47E **287 C4**
Oosterschelde → *Neths.* 51°33N 4°0E **287 C4**
Oosterwolde *Neths.* 53°0N 6°17E **287 B6**
Ootacamund = Udagamandalam
India 11°30N 76°44E **312 P10**
Ootsa L. *Canada* 53°50N 126°2W **342 C3**
Op Luang △ *Thailand* 18°12N 98°32E **310 C2**
Opala
Dem. Rep. of the Congo 0°40S 24°20E **326 C1**
Opanake *Sri Lanka* 6°35N 80°40E **312 R12**
Opasatika *Canada* 49°30N 82°50W **344 C3**
Opasquia ⌓ *Canada* 53°33N 93°5W **344 B1**
Opava *Czech Rep.* 49°57N 17°58E **289 D9**
Opelika *U.S.A.* 32°39N 85°23W **357 E12**
Opelousas *U.S.A.* 30°32N 92°5W **356 F8**
Opémisca, L. *Canada* 49°56N 74°52W **344 C5**
Opheim *U.S.A.* 48°51N 106°24W **348 B10**
Ophthalmia Ra.
Australia 23°15S 119°30E **332 D2**
Opinaca → *Canada* 52°15N 78°2W **344 B4**
Opinaca, Rés. *Canada* 52°39N 76°20W **344 B4**
Opinnagau → *Canada* 54°12N 82°25W **344 B3**
Opiscotéo, L. *Canada* 53°10N 68°10W **345 B6**
Opobo *Nigeria* 4°35N 7°34E **322 H7**
Opole *Poland* 50°42N 17°58E **289 C9**
Opononо L. *Namibia* 18°8S 15°45E **328 B2**
Oporto = Porto *Portugal* 41°8N 8°40W **293 B1**
Opotiki *N.Z.* 38°1S 177°19E **331 C6**
Opp *U.S.A.* 31°17N 86°16W **357 F11**
Oppdal *Norway* 62°35N 9°41E **280 E13**
Opportunity *U.S.A.* 47°39N 117°15W **348 C5**
Opua *N.Z.* 35°19S 174°9E **331 A5**
Opunake *N.Z.* 39°26S 173°52E **331 C4**
Opuwo *Namibia* 18°3S 13°45E **328 B1**
Ora *Cyprus* 34°51N 33°12E **297 E12**
Oracle *U.S.A.* 32°37N 110°46W **349 K8**
Oradea *Romania* 47°2N 21°58E **289 E11**
Öræfajökull *Iceland* 64°2N 16°39W **280 D5**
Orai *India* 25°58N 79°30E **315 G8**
Oral = Zhayyq →
Kazakhstan 47°0N 51°48E **291 E9**
Oral *Kazakhstan* 51°20N 51°20E **291 D9**
Oran *Algeria* 35°45N 0°39W **322 A5**
Orange *Australia* 33°15S 149°7E **335 E4**
Orange *France* 44°8N 4°47E **292 D6**
Orange *Calif., U.S.A.* 33°47N 117°51W **351 M9**
Orange *Mass., U.S.A.* 42°35N 72°19W **355 D12**
Orange *Tex., U.S.A.* 30°6N 93°44W **356 F8**
Orange *Va., U.S.A.* 38°15N 78°7W **353 F14**
Orange → *S. Africa* 28°41S 16°28E **328 D2**
Orange, C. *Brazil* 4°20N 51°30W **365 C8**
Orange Cove *U.S.A.* 36°38N 119°19W **350 J7**
Orange Free State = Free State □
S. Africa 28°30S 27°0E **328 D4**
Orange Grove *U.S.A.* 27°58N 97°56W **356 H6**
Orange Walk *Belize* 18°6N 88°33W **359 D7**
Orangeburg *U.S.A.* 33°30N 80°52W **357 E14**
Orangeville *Canada* 43°55N 80°5W **354 C4**
Orango *Guinea-Biss.* 11°5N 16°0W **322 F2**
Oranienburg *Germany* 52°45N 13°14E **288 B7**
Oranje = Orange →
S. Africa 28°41S 16°28E **328 D2**
Oranjemund *Namibia* 28°38S 16°29E **328 D2**
Oranjerivier *S. Africa* 29°40S 24°12E **328 D3**
Oranjestad *Aruba* 12°32N 70°2W **361 D5**
Orapa *Botswana* 21°15S 25°30E **325 J5**
Oras *Phil.* 12°9N 125°28E **309 B7**
Orbetello *Italy* 42°27N 11°13E **294 C4**
Orbisonia *U.S.A.* 40°15N 77°54W **354 F7**
Orbost *Australia* 37°40S 148°29E **335 F4**
Orcadas *Antarctica* 60°44S 44°37W **277 C18**
Orcas I. *U.S.A.* 48°42N 122°56W **350 B4**
Orchard City *U.S.A.* 38°50N 107°58W **348 G10**
Orchard Homes *U.S.A.* 46°55N 114°4W **348 C6**
Orchila, I. *Venezuela* 11°48N 66°10W **361 D6**
Orchilla, Pta. *Canary Is.* 27°42N 18°10W **296 G1**
Orcutt *U.S.A.* 34°52N 120°27W **351 L6**
Ord *U.S.A.* 41°36N 98°56W **352 E4**
Ord → *Australia* 15°33S 128°15E **332 C4**
Ord, Mt. *Australia* 17°20S 125°34E **332 C4**
Ord Mts. *U.S.A.* 34°39N 116°45W **351 L10**
Orderville *U.S.A.* 37°17N 112°38W **349 H7**
Ordos = Mu Us Shamo
China 39°0N 109°0E **306 E5**
Ordu *Turkey* 40°55N 37°53E **291 F6**
Ordway *U.S.A.* 38°13N 103°46W **348 G12**
Ore *Dem. Rep. of the Congo* 3°17N 29°30E **326 B2**
Ore Mts. = Erzgebirge
Germany 50°27N 12°55E **288 C7**
Örebro *Sweden* 59°20N 15°18E **281 G16**
Oregon *U.S.A.* 42°1N 89°20W **352 D9**
Oregon □ *U.S.A.* 44°0N 121°0W **348 E3**
Oregon City *U.S.A.* 45°21N 122°36W **350 E4**
Oregon Dunes ⌓
U.S.A. 43°40N 124°10W **348 E1**

Orekhovo-Zuyevo *Russia* 55°50N 38°55E **290** C6
Orel *Russia* 52°57N 36°3E **290** D6
Orem *U.S.A.* 40°19N 111°42W **348** F8
Ören *Turkey* 37°3N 27°57E **295** F12
Orenburg *Russia* 51°45N 55°6E **290** D10
Orense = Ourense *Spain* 42°19N 7°55W **293** A2
Orepuki *N.Z.* 46°19S 167°46E **331** G1
Orestes Pereyra *Mexico* 26°30N 105°39W **358** B3
Orestiada *Greece* 41°30N 26°33E **295** D12
Orfanos Kolpos *Greece* 40°33N 24°0E **295** D11
Orford Ness *U.K.* 52°5N 1°35E **285** E9
Organ Pipe Cactus ⌂ *U.S.A.* 32°0N 112°52W **349** K7
Organos, Pta. de los *Canary Is.* 28°12N 17°17W **296** F2
Orgaz *Spain* 39°39N 3°53W **293** C4
Orgeyev = Orhei *Moldova* 47°24N 28°50E **289** E15
Orhaneli *Turkey* 39°54N 28°59E **295** E13
Orhangazi *Turkey* 40°29N 29°18E **295** D13
Orhei *Moldova* 47°24N 28°50E **289** E15
Orhon Gol → *Mongolia* 50°21N 106°0E **304** A5
Oriental, Cordillera *Colombia* 6°0N 73°0W **364** B4
Oriental, Grand Erg *Algeria* 30°0N 6°30E **322** B7
Orientale □ *Dem. Rep. of the Congo* 2°20N 26°0E **326** B2
Oriente *Argentina* 38°44S 60°37W **366** D3
Orihuela *Spain* 38°7N 0°55W **293** C5
Orillia *Canada* 44°40N 79°24W **354** B5
Orinoco → *Venezuela* 9°15N 61°30W **364** B6
Orion *Canada* 49°27N 110°49W **343** D6
Oriskany *U.S.A.* 43°10N 75°20W **355** C9
Orissa □ *India* 20°0N 84°0E **313** K14
Orissaare *Estonia* 58°34N 23°5E **281** G20
Oristano *Italy* 39°54N 8°36E **294** E3
Oristano, G. di *Italy* 39°50N 8°29E **294** E3
Orizaba *Mexico* 18°51N 97°6W **359** D5
Orizaba, Pico de *Mexico* 18°58N 97°15W **359** D5
Orkanger *Norway* 63°18N 9°52E **280** E13
Orkla → *Norway* 63°18N 9°51E **280** E13
Orkney *S. Africa* 26°58S 26°40E **328** D4
Orkney □ *U.K.* 59°2N 3°13W **283** B5
Orkney Is. *U.K.* 59°0N 3°0W **283** B6
Orland *U.S.A.* 39°45N 122°12W **350** F4
Orlando *U.S.A.* 28°32N 81°22W **357** G14
Orléanais *France* 48°0N 2°0E **292** C5
Orléans *France* 47°54N 1°52E **292** C4
Orleans *U.S.A.* 44°49N 72°12W **355** B12
Orléans, Î. d' *Canada* 46°54N 70°58W **345** C5
Ormara *Pakistan* 25°16N 64°33E **312** G4
Ormoc *Phil.* 11°0N 124°37E **309** B6
Ormond *N.Z.* 38°33S 177°56E **331** C6
Ormond Beach *U.S.A.* 29°17N 81°3W **357** G14
Ormskirk *U.K.* 53°35N 2°54W **284** D5
Ormstown *Canada* 45°8N 74°0W **355** A11
Örnsköldsvik *Sweden* 63°17N 18°40E **280** E18
Oro *N. Korea* 40°1N 127°27E **307** D14
Oro → *Mexico* 25°35N 105°2W **358** B3
Oro Grande *U.S.A.* 34°36N 117°20W **351** L9
Oro Valley *U.S.A.* 32°26N 110°58W **349** K8
Orocué *Colombia* 4°48N 71°20W **364** C4
Orofino *U.S.A.* 46°29N 116°15W **348** C5
Orohena, Mt. *Tahiti* 17°37S 149°28W **331** d
Orol Dengizi = Aral Sea *Asia* 44°30N 60°0E **300** E7
Oromocto *Canada* 45°54N 66°29W **345** C6
Orono *Canada* 43°59N 78°37W **354** C6
Orono *U.S.A.* 44°53N 68°40W **353** C19
Oronsay *U.K.* 56°1N 6°15W **283** E2
Oroqen Zizhiqi *China* 50°34N 123°43E **305** A7
Oroquieta *Phil.* 8°32N 123°44E **309** C6
Orosei *Italy* 40°23N 9°42E **294** D3
Orosháza *Hungary* 46°32N 20°42E **289** E11
Orotukan *Russia* 62°16N 151°42E **301** C16
Oroville *Calif., U.S.A.* 39°31N 121°33W **350** F5
Oroville *Wash., U.S.A.* 48°56N 119°26W **348** B4
Oroville, L. *U.S.A.* 39°33N 121°29W **350** F5
Orroroo *Australia* 32°43S 138°38E **335** E2
Orrville *U.S.A.* 40°50N 81°46W **354** F3
Orsha *Belarus* 54°30N 30°25E **290** D5
Orsk *Russia* 51°12N 58°34E **300** D6
Orşova *Romania* 44°41N 22°25E **289** F12
Ortaca *Turkey* 36°49N 28°45E **295** F13
Ortegal, C. *Spain* 43°43N 7°52W **293** A2
Orthez *France* 43°29N 0°48W **292** E3
Ortigueira *Spain* 43°40N 7°50W **293** A2
Orting *U.S.A.* 47°6N 122°12W **350** C4
Ortles *Italy* 46°31N 10°33E **292** C9
Ortón → *Bolivia* 10°50S 67°0W **364** F5
Ortonville *U.S.A.* 45°19N 96°27W **352** C5
Orūmīyeh *Iran* 37°40N 45°0E **316** B5
Orūmīyeh, Daryācheh-ye *Iran* 37°50N 45°30E **316** B5
Oruro *Bolivia* 18°0S 67°9W **364** G5
Orust *Sweden* 58°10N 11°40E **281** G14
Oruzgān □ *Afghan.* 33°0N 66°0E **312** C5
Orvieto *Italy* 42°43N 12°7E **294** C5
Orwell *N.Y., U.S.A.* 43°35N 75°50W **355** C9
Orwell *Ohio, U.S.A.* 41°32N 80°52W **354** E4
Orwell → *U.K.* 51°59N 1°18E **285** F9
Orwigsburg *U.S.A.* 40°38N 76°6W **355** F8
Oryakhovo *Bulgaria* 43°40N 23°57E **295** C10
Osa *Russia* 57°17N 55°26E **290** C10
Osa, Pen. de *Costa Rica* 8°0N 84°0W **360** E3
Osage *U.S.A.* 43°17N 92°49W **352** D7
Osage → *U.S.A.* 38°36N 91°57W **352** F8
Osage City *U.S.A.* 38°38N 95°50W **352** F6
Ōsaka *Japan* 34°42N 135°30E **303** G7
Osan *S. Korea* 37°11N 127°4E **307** F14
Osawatomie *U.S.A.* 38°31N 94°57W **352** F6
Osborne *U.S.A.* 39°26N 98°42W **352** F4
Osceola *Ark., U.S.A.* 35°42N 89°58W **357** D10
Osceola *Iowa, U.S.A.* 41°2N 93°46W **352** E7
Oscoda *U.S.A.* 44°26N 83°20W **354** B1
Ösel = Saaremaa *Estonia* 58°30N 22°30E **281** G20
Osgoode *Canada* 45°8N 75°36W **355** A9
Osh *Kyrgyzstan* 40°37N 72°49E **300** E8
Oshakati *Namibia* 17°45S 15°40E **325** H3
Oshawa *Canada* 43°50N 78°50W **354** C6
Oshigambo *Namibia* 17°45S 16°5E **328** B2
Oshkosh *Nebr., U.S.A.* 41°24N 102°21W **352** E2
Oshkosh *Wis., U.S.A.* 44°1N 88°33W **352** C9
Oshmyany = Ashmyany *Belarus* 54°26N 25°52E **289** A13
Oshnovīyeh *Iran* 37°2N 45°6E **316** B5
Oshogbo *Nigeria* 7°48N 4°37E **322** G6
Oshtorīnān *Iran* 34°1N 48°38E **317** C6
Oshwe *Dem. Rep. of the Congo* 3°25S 19°28E **324** E3
Osijek *Croatia* 45°34N 18°41E **295** B8
Osipovichi = Asipovichy *Belarus* 53°19N 28°33E **289** B15
Osiyan *India* 26°43N 72°55E **314** F5
Osizweni *S. Africa* 27°49S 30°7E **329** D5
Oskaloosa *U.S.A.* 41°18N 92°39W **352** E7
Oskarshamn *Sweden* 57°15N 16°27E **281** H17
Oskélanéo *Canada* 48°5N 75°15W **344** C4
Öskemen *Kazakhstan* 50°0N 82°36E **300** E9
Oslo *Norway* 59°54N 10°43E **281** G14
Oslofjorden *Norway* 59°20N 10°35E **281** G14
Osmanabad *India* 18°5N 76°10E **312** K10
Osmaniye *Turkey* 37°5N 36°10E **316** B3
Osnabrück *Germany* 52°17N 8°3E **288** B5
Osório *Brazil* 29°53S 50°17W **367** B5
Osorno *Chile* 40°25S 73°0W **368** E2
Osorno, Vol. *Chile* 41°0S 72°30W **368** D2
Osoyoos *Canada* 49°0N 119°30W **342** D5
Osøyro *Norway* 60°9N 5°30E **280** F11
Ospika → *Canada* 56°20N 124°0W **342** B4
Osprey Reef *Australia* 13°52S 146°36E **334** A4
Oss *Neths.* 51°46N 5°32E **287** C5
Ossa, Mt. *Australia* 41°52S 146°3E **335** G4
Ossa, Oros *Greece* 39°47N 22°42E **295** E10
Ossabaw I. *U.S.A.* 31°50N 81°5W **357** F14
Ossining *U.S.A.* 41°10N 73°55W **355** E11
Ossipee *U.S.A.* 43°41N 71°7W **355** C13
Ossokmanuan L. *Canada* 53°25N 65°0W **345** B7
Ossora *Russia* 59°20N 163°13E **301** D17
Ostend = Oostende *Belgium* 51°15N 2°54E **287** C2
Oster *Ukraine* 50°57N 30°53E **289** C16
Österbotten = Pohjanmaa *Finland* 62°58N 22°50E **280** E20
Osterburg *U.S.A.* 40°16N 78°31W **354** F6
Österdalälven *Sweden* 61°30N 13°45E **280** F15
Østerdalen *Norway* 61°40N 10°50E **280** F14
Östermyra = Seinäjoki *Finland* 62°40N 22°51E **280** E20
Österreich = Austria ■ *Europe* 47°0N 14°0E **288** E8
Östersund *Sweden* 63°10N 14°38E **280** E16
Ostfriesische Inseln *Germany* 53°42N 7°0E **288** B4
Ostrava *Czech Rep.* 49°51N 18°18E **289** D10
Ostróda *Poland* 53°42N 19°58E **289** B10
Ostroh *Ukraine* 50°20N 26°30E **289** C14
Ostrołęka *Poland* 53°4N 21°32E **289** B11
Ostrów Mazowiecka *Poland* 52°50N 21°51E **289** B11
Ostrów Wielkopolski *Poland* 51°36N 17°44E **289** C9
Ostrowiec-Świętokrzyski *Poland* 50°55N 21°22E **289** C11
Ostuni *Italy* 40°44N 17°35E **295** D7
Ōsumi-Kaikyō *Japan* 30°55N 131°0E **303** J5
Ōsumi-Shotō *Japan* 30°30N 130°0E **303** J5
Osuna *Spain* 37°14N 5°8W **293** D3
Oswegatchie → *U.S.A.* 44°42N 75°30W **355** B9
Oswego *U.S.A.* 43°27N 76°31W **355** C8
Oswego → *U.S.A.* 43°27N 76°30W **355** C8
Oswestry *U.K.* 52°52N 3°3W **284** E4
Oświęcim *Poland* 50°2N 19°11E **289** C10
Otago □ *N.Z.* 45°15S 170°0E **331** F2
Otago Harbour *N.Z.* 45°47S 170°42E **331** F3
Otaheite B. *Trin. & Tob.* 10°15N 61°30W **365** K15
Ōtake *Japan* 34°12N 132°13E **303** G6
Otaki *N.Z.* 40°45S 175°10E **331** D5
Otaru *Japan* 43°10N 141°0E **302** C10
Otaru-Wan = Ishikari-Wan *Japan* 43°25N 141°1E **302** C10
Otavalo *Ecuador* 0°13N 78°20W **364** C3
Otavi *Namibia* 19°40S 17°24E **328** B2
Otchinjau *Angola* 16°30S 13°56E **328** B1
Otelnuk, L. *Canada* 56°9N 68°12W **345** A6
Othello *U.S.A.* 46°50N 119°10W **348** C4
Otjiwarongo *Namibia* 20°30S 16°33E **328** C2
Oto Tolu Group *Tonga* 20°21S 174°32W **331** c
Otoineppu *Japan* 44°44N 142°16E **302** B11
Otorohanga *N.Z.* 38°12S 175°14E **331** C5
Otoskwin → *Canada* 52°13N 88°6W **344** B2
Otra → *Norway* 58°9N 8°1E **281** G13
Otranto *Italy* 40°9N 18°28E **295** D8
Otranto, C. d' *Italy* 40°7N 18°30E **295** D8
Otranto, Str. of *Italy* 40°15N 18°40E **295** D8
Otse *S. Africa* 25°2S 25°45E **328** D4
Ōtsu *Japan* 35°0N 135°50E **303** G7
Ōtsuki *Japan* 35°36N 138°57E **303** G9
Ottawa = Outaouais → *Canada* 45°27N 74°8W **344** C5
Ottawa *Canada* 45°26N 75°42W **355** A9
Ottawa *Ill., U.S.A.* 41°21N 88°51W **352** E9
Ottawa *Kans., U.S.A.* 38°37N 95°16W **352** F6
Ottawa Is. *Canada* 59°35N 80°10W **341** D11
Otter Cr. → *U.S.A.* 44°13N 73°17W **355** B11
Otter L. *Canada* 55°35N 104°39W **343** B8
Otterville *Canada* 42°55N 80°36W **354** D4
Ottery St. Mary *U.K.* 50°44N 3°17W **285** G4
Otto Beit Bridge *Zimbabwe* 15°59S 28°56E **327** F2
Ottosdal *S. Africa* 26°46S 25°59E **328** D4
Ottumwa *U.S.A.* 41°1N 92°25W **352** E7
Oturkpo *Nigeria* 7°16N 8°8E **322** G7
Otway, B. *Chile* 53°30S 74°0W **368** G2
Otway, C. *Australia* 38°52S 143°30E **335** F3
Otwock *Poland* 52°5N 21°20E **289** B11
Ou → *Laos* 20°4N 102°13E **310** B4
Ou Neua *Laos* 22°18N 101°48E **310** A3
Ou-Sammyaku *Japan* 39°20N 140°35E **302** E10
Ouachita → *U.S.A.* 31°38N 91°49W **356** F9
Ouachita, L. *U.S.A.* 34°34N 93°12W **356** D8
Ouachita Mts. *U.S.A.* 34°30N 94°30W **356** D7
Ouagadougou *Burkina Faso* 12°25N 1°30W **322** F5
Ouahigouya *Burkina Faso* 13°31N 2°25W **322** F5
Ouahran = Oran *Algeria* 35°45N 0°39W **322** A5
Ouallene *Algeria* 24°41N 1°11E **322** D6
Ouargla *Algeria* 31°59N 5°16E **322** B7
Ouarra → *C.A.R.* 5°5N 24°26E **324** C4
Ouarzazate *Morocco* 30°55N 6°50W **322** B4
Oubangi → *Dem. Rep. of the Congo* 0°30S 17°50E **324** E3
Ouddorp *Neths.* 51°50N 3°57E **287** C3
Oude Rijn → *Neths.* 52°12N 4°24E **287** B4
Oudenaarde *Belgium* 50°50N 3°37E **287** D3
Oudtshoorn *S. Africa* 33°35S 22°14E **328** E3
Ouessant, Î. d' *France* 48°28N 5°6W **292** B1
Ouesso *Congo* 1°37N 16°5E **324** D3
Ouest, Pte. de l' *Canada* 49°52N 64°40W **345** C7
Ouezzane *Morocco* 34°51N 5°35W **322** B4
Oughter, L. *Ireland* 54°1N 7°28W **282** B4
Oughterard *Ireland* 53°26N 9°18W **282** C2
Ouidah *Benin* 6°25N 2°0E **322** G6
Oujda *Morocco* 34°41N 1°55W **322** B5
Oulainen *Finland* 64°17N 24°47E **280** D21
Oulu *Finland* 65°1N 25°29E **280** D21
Oulujärvi *Finland* 64°25N 27°15E **280** D22
Oulujoki → *Finland* 65°1N 25°30E **280** D21
Oum Chalouba *Chad* 15°48N 20°46E **323** E10
Oum Hadjer *Chad* 13°18N 19°41E **323** F9
Ounasjoki → *Finland* 66°31N 25°40E **280** C21
Ounguati *Namibia* 22°0S 15°46E **328** C2
Ounianga Sérir *Chad* 18°54N 20°51E **323** E10
Our → *Lux.* 49°55N 6°5E **287** E6
Ouray *U.S.A.* 38°1N 107°40W **349** G10
Ourense *Spain* 42°19N 7°55W **293** A2
Ouricuri *Brazil* 7°53S 40°5W **365** E10
Ourinhos *Brazil* 23°0S 49°54W **367** A6
Ouro Fino *Brazil* 22°16S 46°25W **367** A6
Ouro Prêto *Brazil* 20°20S 43°30W **367** A7
Ourthe → *Belgium* 50°29N 5°35E **287** D5
Ouse → *E. Sussex, U.K.* 50°47N 0°4E **285** G8
Ouse → *N. Yorks., U.K.* 53°44N 0°55W **284** D7
Outaouais → *Canada* 45°27N 74°8W **344** C5
Outardes → *Canada* 49°24N 69°30W **345** C6
Outer Hebrides *U.K.* 57°30N 7°40W **283** D1
Outjo *Namibia* 20°5S 16°7E **328** C2
Outlook *Canada* 51°30N 107°0W **343** C7
Outokumpu *Finland* 62°43N 29°1E **280** E23
Ouyen *Australia* 35°1S 142°22E **335** F3
Ovalau *Fiji* 17°40S 178°48E **331** a
Ovalle *Chile* 30°33S 71°18W **366** C1
Ovamboland *Namibia* 18°30S 16°0E **328** B2
Overflakkee *Neths.* 51°44N 4°10E **287** C4
Overijssel □ *Neths.* 52°25N 6°35E **287** B6
Overland Park *U.S.A.* 38°58N 94°40W **352** F6
Overton *U.S.A.* 36°33N 114°27W **351** J12
Övertorneå *Sweden* 66°23N 23°38E **280** C20
Ovid *U.S.A.* 42°41N 76°49W **355** D8
Oviedo *Spain* 43°25N 5°50W **293** A3
Oviši *Latvia* 57°33N 21°44E **281** H19
Ovoot *Mongolia* 45°21N 113°45E **306** B7
Övör Hangay □ *Mongolia* 45°0N 102°30E **306** B2
Øvre Årdal *Norway* 61°19N 7°48E **280** F12
Ovruch *Ukraine* 51°25N 28°45E **289** C15
Owaka *N.Z.* 46°27S 169°40E **331** G2
Owambo = Ovamboland *Namibia* 18°30S 16°0E **328** B2
Owasco L. *U.S.A.* 42°50N 76°31W **355** D8
Owase *Japan* 34°7N 136°12E **303** G8
Owatonna *U.S.A.* 44°5N 93°14W **352** C7
Owbeh *Afghan.* 34°28N 63°10E **312** B3
Owego *U.S.A.* 42°6N 76°16W **355** D8
Owen Falls Dam = Nalubaale Dam *Uganda* 0°30N 33°5E **326** B3
Owen Sound *Canada* 44°35N 80°55W **354** B4
Owen Stanley Ra. *Papua N. G.* 8°30S 147°0E **330** B7
Oweniny → *Ireland* 54°8N 9°34W **282** B2
Owens → *U.S.A.* 36°32N 117°59W **350** J9
Owens L. *U.S.A.* 36°26N 117°57W **351** J9
Owensboro *U.S.A.* 37°46N 87°7W **352** G10
Owl → *Canada* 57°51N 92°44W **343** B10
Owo *Nigeria* 7°10N 5°39E **322** G7
Owosso *U.S.A.* 43°0N 84°10W **353** D11
Owyhee *U.S.A.* 41°57N 116°6W **348** F5
Owyhee → *U.S.A.* 43°49N 117°2W **348** E5
Owyhee, L. *U.S.A.* 43°38N 117°14W **348** E5
Ox Mts. = Slieve Gamph *Ireland* 54°6N 9°0W **282** B3
Öxarfjörður *Iceland* 66°15N 16°45W **280** C5
Oxbow *Canada* 49°14N 102°10W **343** D8
Oxelösund *Sweden* 58°43N 17°5E **281** G17
Oxford *N.Z.* 43°18S 172°11E **331** E4
Oxford *U.K.* 51°46N 1°15W **285** F6
Oxford *Mass., U.S.A.* 42°7N 71°52W **355** D13
Oxford *Miss., U.S.A.* 34°22N 89°31W **357** D10
Oxford *N.C., U.S.A.* 36°19N 78°35W **357** C15
Oxford *N.Y., U.S.A.* 42°27N 75°36W **355** D9
Oxford *Ohio, U.S.A.* 39°31N 84°45W **353** F11
Oxford L. *Canada* 54°51N 95°37W **343** C9
Oxfordshire □ *U.K.* 51°48N 1°16W **285** F6
Oxnard *U.S.A.* 34°12N 119°11W **351** L7
Oxus = Amudarya → *Uzbekistan* 43°58N 59°34E **300** E6
Oya *Malaysia* 2°55N 111°55E **308** D4
Oyama *Japan* 36°18N 139°48E **303** F9
Oyem *Gabon* 1°34N 11°31E **324** D2
Oyen *Canada* 51°22N 110°28W **343** C6
Oykel → *U.K.* 57°56N 4°26W **283** D4
Oymyakon *Russia* 63°25N 142°44E **301** C15
Oyo *Nigeria* 7°46N 3°56E **322** G6
Oyster Bay *U.S.A.* 40°52N 73°32W **355** F11
Ōyübari *Japan* 43°1N 142°5E **302** C11
Ozamiz *Phil.* 8°15N 123°50E **309** C6
Ozark *Ala., U.S.A.* 31°28N 85°39W **357** F12
Ozark *Ark., U.S.A.* 35°29N 93°50W **356** D8
Ozark *Mo., U.S.A.* 37°1N 93°12W **352** G7
Ozark Plateau *U.S.A.* 37°20N 91°40W **352** G8
Ozarks, L. of the *U.S.A.* 38°12N 92°38W **352** F7
Ózd *Hungary* 48°14N 20°15E **289** D11
Ozette, L. *U.S.A.* 48°6N 124°38W **350** B2
Ozieri *Italy* 40°35N 9°0E **294** D3
Ozona *U.S.A.* 30°43N 101°12W **356** F4
Ozuluama *Mexico* 21°40N 97°51W **359** C5

P

Pa-an *Burma* 16°51N 97°40E **313** L20
Pa Mong Dam *Thailand* 18°0N 102°22E **310** D4
Pa Sak → *Thailand* 15°30N 101°0E **310** E3
Paamiut *Greenland* 62°0N 49°43W **276** C5
Paarl *S. Africa* 33°45S 18°56E **328** E2
Pab Hills *Pakistan* 26°30N 66°45E **314** F2
Pabbay *U.K.* 57°46N 7°14W **283** D1
Pabianice *Poland* 51°40N 19°20E **289** C10
Pabna *Bangla.* 24°1N 89°18E **313** G16
Pabo *Uganda* 3°1N 32°10E **326** B3
Pacaja → *Brazil* 1°56S 50°50W **365** D8
Pacaraima, Sa. *S. Amer.* 4°0N 62°30W **364** C6
Pacasmayo *Peru* 7°20S 79°35W **364** E3
Pachhar *India* 24°40N 77°42E **314** G7
Pachitea → *Peru* 8°46S 74°33W **364** E4
Pachmarhi *India* 22°28N 78°26E **315** H8
Pachnes *Greece* 35°16N 24°4E **297** D6
Pachpadra *India* 25°58N 72°10E **314** G5
Pachuca *Mexico* 20°7N 98°44W **359** C5
Pacific Antarctic Ridge *Pac. Oc.* 43°0S 115°0W **277** B13
Pacific Grove *U.S.A.* 36°38N 121°56W **350** J5
Pacific Ocean 10°0N 140°0W **337** G14
Pacific Rim △ *Canada* 48°40N 124°45W **350** B2
Pacifica *U.S.A.* 37°37N 122°29W **350** H4
Pacitan *Indonesia* 8°12S 111°7E **309** H14
Packwood *U.S.A.* 46°36N 121°40W **350** D5
Padaido, Kepulauan *Indonesia* 1°15S 136°30E **309** E9
Padang *Indonesia* 1°0S 100°20E **308** E2
Padang Endau *Malaysia* 2°40N 103°38E **311** L4
Padangpanjang *Indonesia* 0°40S 100°20E **308** E2
Padangsidempuan *Indonesia* 1°30N 99°15E **308** D1
Paddle Prairie *Canada* 57°57N 117°29W **342** B5
Paddockwood *Canada* 53°30N 105°30W **343** C7
Paderborn *Germany* 51°42N 8°45E **288** C5
Padma *India* 24°12N 85°22E **315** G11
Pádova *Italy* 45°25N 11°53E **294** B4
Padra *India* 22°15N 73°7E **314** H5
Padrauna *India* 26°54N 83°59E **315** F10
Padre I. *U.S.A.* 27°10N 97°25W **356** H6
Padre Island ⌂ *U.S.A.* 27°0N 97°25W **356** H6
Padstow *U.K.* 50°33N 4°58W **285** G3
Padua = Pádova *Italy* 45°25N 11°53E **294** B4
Paducah *Ky., U.S.A.* 37°5N 88°37W **352** G9
Paducah *Tex., U.S.A.* 34°1N 100°18W **356** D4
Paea *Tahiti* 17°41S 149°35W **331** d
Paeroa *N.Z.* 37°23S 175°41E **331** B5
Pafúri *Mozam.* 22°28S 31°17E **329** C5
Pag *Croatia* 44°25N 15°3E **288** F8
Pagadian *Phil.* 7°55N 123°30E **309** C6
Pagai Selatan, Pulau *Indonesia* 3°0S 100°15E **308** E2
Pagai Utara, Pulau *Indonesia* 2°35S 100°0E **308** E2
Pagalu = Annobón *Atl. Oc.* 1°25S 5°36E **321** G4
Pagara *India* 24°22N 80°1E **315** G9
Pagastikos Kolpos *Greece* 39°15N 23°0E **295** E10
Pagatan *Indonesia* 3°33S 115°59E **308** E5
Page *U.S.A.* 36°57N 111°27W **349** H8
Pago Pago *Amer. Samoa* 14°16S 170°43W **331** b
Pagosa Springs *U.S.A.* 37°16N 107°1W **349** H10
Pagwa River *Canada* 50°2N 85°14W **344** B2
Pāhala *U.S.A.* 19°12N 155°29W **346** b
Pahang → *Malaysia* 3°30N 103°9E **311** L4
Pahiatua *N.Z.* 40°27S 175°50E **331** D5
Pahokee *U.S.A.* 26°50N 80°40W **357** H14
Pahrump *U.S.A.* 36°12N 115°59W **351** J11
Pahute Mesa *U.S.A.* 37°20N 116°45W **350** H10
Pai *Thailand* 19°19N 98°27E **310** C2
Paicines *U.S.A.* 36°44N 121°17W **350** J5
Paide *Estonia* 58°53N 25°33E **281** G21
Paignton *U.K.* 50°26N 3°35W **285** G4
Päijänne *Finland* 61°30N 25°30E **280** F21
Pailani *India* 25°45N 80°26E **315** G9
Pailin *Cambodia* 12°46N 102°36E **310** F4
Painan *Indonesia* 1°21S 100°34E **308** E2
Painesville *U.S.A.* 41°43N 81°15W **354** E3
Paint Hills = Wemindji *Canada* 53°0N 78°49W **344** B4
Paint L. *Canada* 55°28N 97°57W **343** B9
Painted Desert *U.S.A.* 36°0N 111°0W **349** J8
Paintsville *U.S.A.* 37°49N 82°48W **353** G12
País Vasco □ *Spain* 42°50N 2°45W **293** A4
Paisley *Canada* 44°18N 81°16W **354** B3
Paisley *U.K.* 55°50N 4°25W **283** F4
Paisley *U.S.A.* 42°42N 120°32W **348** E3
Paita *Peru* 5°11S 81°9W **364** E2
Pajares, Puerto de *Spain* 42°58N 5°46W **293** A3
Pak Lay *Laos* 18°15N 101°27E **310** C3
Pak Phanang *Thailand* 8°21N 100°12E **311** H3
Pak Sane *Laos* 18°22N 103°39E **310** C4
Pak Song *Laos* 15°11N 106°14E **310** E6
Pak Suong *Laos* 19°58N 102°15E **310** C4
Pak Tam Chung *China* 22°24N 114°19E **305** G11
Pakaur *India* 24°38N 87°51E **315** G12
Pakch'ŏn *N. Korea* 39°44N 125°35E **307** E13
Pakenham *Canada* 45°18N 76°18W **355** A8
Pakhuis *S. Africa* 32°9S 19°5E **328** E2
Pakistan ■ *Asia* 30°0N 70°0E **314** E4
Pakkading *Laos* 18°19N 103°59E **310** C4
Pakokku *Burma* 21°20N 95°0E **313** J19
Pakowki L. *Canada* 49°20N 111°0W **343** D6
Pakpattan *Pakistan* 30°25N 73°27E **314** D5
Paktīā □ *Afghan.* 33°30N 69°15E **312** C6
Paktīkā □ *Afghan.* 32°30N 69°0E **312** C6
Pakwach *Uganda* 2°28N 31°27E **326** B3
Pakxe *Laos* 15°5N 105°52E **310** E5
Pal Lahara *India* 21°27N 85°11E **315** J11
Pala *Chad* 9°25N 15°5E **323** G9
Pala *Dem. Rep. of the Congo* 6°45S 29°30E **326** D2
Pala *U.S.A.* 33°22N 117°5W **351** M9
Palabek *Uganda* 3°22N 32°33E **326** B3
Palacios *U.S.A.* 28°42N 96°13W **356** G6
Palagruža *Croatia* 42°24N 16°15E **294** C7
Palam *India* 19°0N 77°0E **312** K10
Palampur *India* 32°10N 76°30E **314** C7
Palana *Australia* 39°45S 147°55E **335** F4
Palana *Russia* 59°10N 159°59E **301** D16
Palanan *Phil.* 17°8N 122°29E **309** A6
Palanan Pt. *Phil.* 17°17N 122°30E **309** A6
Palandri *Pakistan* 33°42N 73°40E **315** C5
Palanga *Lithuania* 55°58N 21°3E **281** J19
Palangkaraya *Indonesia* 2°16S 113°56E **308** E4
Palani Hills *India* 10°14N 77°33E **312** P10
Palanpur *India* 24°10N 72°25E **314** G5
Palapye *Botswana* 22°30S 27°7E **328** C4
Palas *Pakistan* 35°4N 73°14E **315** B5
Palashi *India* 23°47N 88°15E **315** H13
Palasponga *India* 21°47N 85°34E **315** J11
Palatka *Russia* 60°6N 150°54E **301** C16
Palatka *U.S.A.* 29°39N 81°38W **357** G14
Palau ■ *Palau* 7°30N 134°30E **330** A6
Palauk *Burma* 13°10N 98°40E **310** F2
Palawan *Phil.* 9°30N 118°30E **308** C5
Palayankottai *India* 8°45N 77°45E **312** Q10
Paldiski *Estonia* 59°23N 24°9E **281** G21
Palekastro *Greece* 35°12N 26°15E **297** D8
Paleleh *Indonesia* 1°10N 121°50E **309** D6
Palembang *Indonesia* 3°0S 104°50E **308** E2
Palencia *Spain* 42°1N 4°34W **293** A3
Palenque *Mexico* 17°29N 92°1W **359** D6
Paleochora *Greece* 35°16N 23°39E **297** D5
Paleokastritsa *Greece* 39°40N 19°41E **297** A3
Paleometokho *Cyprus* 35°7N 33°11E **297** D12
Palermo *Italy* 38°7N 13°22E **294** E5
Palermo *U.S.A.* 39°26N 121°33W **348** G3
Palestina *Chile* 23°50S 69°47W **368** A3
Palestine *Asia* 32°0N 35°0E **318** D4
Palestine *U.S.A.* 31°46N 95°38W **356** F7
Paletwa *Burma* 21°10N 92°50E **313** J18
Palghat *India* 10°46N 76°42E **312** P10
Palgrave, Mt. *Australia* 23°22S 115°58E **332** D2
Pali *India* 25°50N 73°20E **314** G5
Palikir *Micronesia* 6°55N 158°9E **336** G7
Paliouri, Akra *Greece* 39°57N 23°45E **295** E10
Palisades Res. *U.S.A.* 43°20N 111°12W **348** E8
Paliseul *Belgium* 49°54N 5°8E **287** E5
Palitana *India* 21°32N 71°49E **314** J4
Palizada *Mexico* 18°15N 92°5W **359** D6
Palk Bay *Asia* 9°30N 79°15E **312** Q11
Palk Strait *Asia* 10°0N 79°45E **312** Q11
Palkānah *Iraq* 35°49N 44°26E **316** C5
Palkot *India* 22°53N 84°39E **315** H11
Pallanza = Verbánia *Italy* 45°56N 8°33E **292** D8
Pallarenda *Australia* 19°12S 146°46E **334** B4
Pallinup → *Australia* 34°27S 118°50E **333** F2
Pallisa *Uganda* 1°12N 33°43E **326** B3
Pallu *India* 28°59N 74°14E **314** E6
Palm Bay *U.S.A.* 28°2N 80°35W **357** G14
Palm Beach *U.S.A.* 26°43N 80°2W **357** H14
Palm Coast *U.S.A.* 29°35N 81°12W **357** G14
Palm Desert *U.S.A.* 33°43N 116°22W **351** M10
Palm Is. *Australia* 18°40S 146°35E **334** B4
Palm Springs *U.S.A.* 33°50N 116°33W **351** M10
Palma *Mozam.* 10°46S 40°29E **327** E5
Palma, B. de *Spain* 39°30N 2°39E **296** B9
Palma de Mallorca *Spain* 39°35N 2°39E **296** B9
Palma Soriano *Cuba* 20°15N 76°0W **360** B4
Palmares *Brazil* 8°41S 35°28W **365** E11
Palmas *Brazil* 26°29S 52°0W **367** B5
Palmas, C. *Liberia* 4°27N 7°46W **322** H4
Pálmas, G. di *Italy* 39°0N 8°30E **294** E3
Palmdale *U.S.A.* 34°35N 118°7W **351** L8
Palmeira das Missões *Brazil* 27°55S 53°17W **367** B5
Palmeira dos Índios *Brazil* 9°25S 36°37W **365** E11
Palmer *Antarctica* 64°35S 65°0W **277** C17
Palmer *U.S.A.* 61°36N 149°7W **340** C5
Palmer → *Australia* 16°0S 142°26E **334** B3
Palmer Arch. *Antarctica* 64°15S 65°0W **277** C17
Palmer Lake *U.S.A.* 39°7N 104°55W **348** G11
Palmer Land *Antarctica* 73°0S 63°0W **277** D18
Palmerston *Australia* 12°31S 130°59E **332** B5
Palmerston *Canada* 43°50N 80°51W **354** C4
Palmerston *N.Z.* 45°29S 170°43E **331** F3
Palmerston North *N.Z.* 40°21S 175°39E **331** D5
Palmerton *U.S.A.* 40°48N 75°37W **355** F9
Palmetto *U.S.A.* 27°31N 82°34W **357** H13
Palmi *Italy* 38°21N 15°51E **294** E6
Palmira *Argentina* 32°59S 68°34W **366** C2
Palmira *Colombia* 3°32N 76°16W **364** C3
Palmyra = Tudmur *Syria* 34°36N 38°15E **316** C3
Palmyra *Mo., U.S.A.* 39°48N 91°32W **352** F8
Palmyra *N.J., U.S.A.* 40°0N 75°1W **355** F9
Palmyra *N.Y., U.S.A.* 43°5N 77°18W **354** C7
Palmyra *Pa., U.S.A.* 40°18N 76°36W **355** F8

Palmyra Is. Pac. Oc. 5°52N 162°5W 337 G11
Palo Alto U.S.A. 37°27N 122°10W 350 H4
Palo Seco Trin. & Tob. 10°4N 61°36W 365 K15
Palo Verde U.S.A. 33°26N 114°44W 351 M12
Palo Verde △ Costa Rica 10°21N 85°21W 360 D2
Palomar Mt. U.S.A. 33°22N 116°50W 351 M10
Palopo Indonesia 3°0S 120°16E 309 E6
Palos, C. de Spain 37°38N 0°40W 293 D5
Palos Verdes, Pt. U.S.A. 33°46N 118°25W 351 M8
Palos Verdes Estates U.S.A. 33°48N 118°23W 351 M8
Palu Indonesia 1°0S 119°52E 309 E5
Palu Turkey 38°45N 40°0E 316 B3
Palwal India 28°8N 77°19E 314 E7
Pamanukan Indonesia 6°16S 107°49E 309 G12
Pamekasan Indonesia 7°10S 113°28E 309 G15
Pamenang Indonesia 8°24S 116°6E 309 J19
Pamiers France 43°7N 1°39E 292 E4
Pamir Tajikistan 37°40N 73°0E 300 F8
Pamlico → U.S.A. 35°20N 76°28W 357 D16
Pamlico Sd. U.S.A. 35°20N 76°0W 357 D17
Pampa U.S.A. 35°32N 100°58W 356 D4
Pampa de las Salinas Argentina 32°1S 66°58W 366 C2
Pampanua Indonesia 4°16S 120°8E 309 E6
Pampas Argentina 35°0S 63°0W 366 D3
Pampas Peru 12°20S 74°50W 364 F4
Pamplona Colombia 7°23N 72°39W 364 B4
Pamplona Spain 42°48N 1°38W 293 A5
Pampoenpoort S. Africa 31°3S 22°40E 328 E3
Pan de Azúcar △ Chile 26°0S 70°40W 366 B1
Pana U.S.A. 39°23N 89°5W 352 F9
Panaca U.S.A. 37°47N 114°23W 349 H6
Panaitan Indonesia 6°36S 105°12E 309 G11
Panaji India 15°25N 73°50E 312 M8
Panamá Panama 9°0N 79°25W 360 E4
Panama ■ Cent. Amer. 8°48N 79°55W 360 E4
Panamá, G. de Panama 8°4N 79°20W 360 E4
Panama, Isthmus of Cent. Amer. 9°0N 79°0W 338 J12
Panama Basin Pac. Oc. 5°0N 83°30W 337 G19
Panama Canal Panama 9°10N 79°37W 360 E4
Panama City U.S.A. 30°10N 85°40W 357 F12
Panamint Range U.S.A. 36°20N 117°20W 351 J9
Panamint Springs U.S.A. 36°20N 117°28W 351 J9
Panão Peru 9°55S 75°55W 364 E3
Panare Thailand 6°51N 101°30E 311 J3
Panay Phil. 11°10N 122°30E 309 B6
Panay, G. Phil. 11°0N 122°30E 309 B6
Pančevo Serbia 44°52N 20°41E 295 B9
Panda Mozam. 24°2S 34°45E 329 C5
Pandan Malaysia 1°32N 103°46E 311 d
Pandan Phil. 11°45N 122°10E 309 B6
Pandan, Selat Singapore 1°15N 103°44E 311 d
Pandan Tampoi = Tampoi Malaysia 1°30N 103°39E 311 d
Pandegelang Indonesia 6°25S 106°5E 309 G12
Pandhana India 21°42N 76°13E 314 J7
Pandharpur India 17°41N 75°20E 312 L9
Pando Uruguay 34°44S 56°0W 367 C4
Pando, L. = Hope, L. Australia 28°24S 139°18E 335 D2
Pandokratoras Greece 39°45N 19°50E 297 A3
Pandora Costa Rica 9°43N 83°3W 360 E3
Panevėžys Lithuania 55°42N 24°25E 281 J21
Pang-Long Burma 23°11N 98°45E 313 H21
Pang Sida △ Thailand 14°5N 102°17E 310 E4
Pang-Yang Burma 22°7N 98°48E 313 H21
Panga Dem. Rep. of the Congo 1°52N 26°18E 326 B2
Pangalanes, Canal des = Ampangalana, Lakandranon' Madag. 22°48S 47°50E 329 C8
Pangani Tanzania 5°25S 38°58E 326 D4
Pangani → Tanzania 5°26S 38°58E 326 D4
Pangfou = Bengbu China 32°58N 117°20E 307 H9
Pangil Dem. Rep. of the Congo 3°10S 26°35E 326 C2
Pangkah, Tanjung Indonesia 6°51S 112°33E 309 G15
Pangkajene Indonesia 4°46S 119°34E 309 E5
Pangkalanbrandan Indonesia 4°1N 98°20E 308 D1
Pangkalanbuun Indonesia 2°41S 111°37E 308 E4
Pangkalpinang Indonesia 2°0S 106°0E 308 E3
Pangnirtung Canada 66°8N 65°43W 341 C13
Pangong Tso India 34°40N 78°40E 314 B8
Panguitch U.S.A. 37°50N 112°26W 349 H7
Pangutaran Group Phil. 6°18N 120°34E 309 C6
Panhandle U.S.A. 35°21N 101°23W 356 D4
Pani Mines India 22°29N 73°50E 314 H5
Pania-Mutombo Dem. Rep. of the Congo 5°11S 23°51E 326 D1
Panikota I. India 20°46N 71°21E 314 J4
Panipat India 29°25N 77°2E 314 E7
Panjal Range = Pir Panjal Range India 32°30N 76°50E 314 C7
Panjang, Hon Vietnam 9°20N 103°28E 311 H4
Panjgur Pakistan 27°0N 64°5E 312 F4
Panjim = Panaji India 15°25N 73°50E 312 M8
Panjin China 41°3N 122°2E 307 D12
Panjnad → Pakistan 28°57N 70°30E 314 E4
Panjnad Barrage Pakistan 29°22N 71°15E 314 E4
Panjwai Afghan. 31°26N 65°27E 314 D1
Panmunjŏm N. Korea 37°59N 126°38E 307 F14
Panna India 24°40N 80°15E 315 G9
Panna △ India 24°40N 80°0E 315 G8
Panna Hills India 24°40N 81°15E 315 G9
Pannawonica Australia 21°39S 116°19E 332 D2
Pannga, Tanjung Indonesia 8°54S 116°2E 309 K19
Pannirtuuq = Pangnirtung Canada 66°8N 65°43W 341 C13
Pano Akil Pakistan 27°51N 69°7E 314 F3
Pano Lefkara Cyprus 34°53N 33°20E 297 E12
Pano Panayia Cyprus 34°55N 32°38E 297 E11
Panorama Brazil 21°21S 51°51W 367 A5
Panormos Greece 35°25N 24°41E 297 D6
Pansemal India 21°39N 74°42E 314 J6
Panshan = Panjin China 41°3N 122°2E 307 D12
Panshi China 42°58N 126°5E 307 C14
Pantanal Brazil 17°30S 57°40W 364 H7
Pantanos de Centla ⌓ Mexico 18°25N 92°25W 359 D6
Pantar Indonesia 8°28S 124°10E 309 F6
Pante Macassar E. Timor 9°30S 123°58E 309 F6
Pante Makasar = Pante Macassar E. Timor 9°30S 123°58E 309 F6
Pantelleria Italy 36°50N 11°57E 294 F4
Pánuco Mexico 22°3N 98°10W 359 C5
Panzhihua China 26°33N 101°44E 304 D5
Paola Malta 35°52N 14°30E 297 D2
Paola U.S.A. 38°35N 94°53W 352 F6
Paonia U.S.A. 38°52N 107°36W 348 G10
Paopao Moorea 17°30S 149°49W 331 d
Paoting = Baoding China 38°50N 115°28E 306 E8
Paot'ou = Baotou China 40°32N 110°2E 306 D6
Paoua C.A.R. 7°9N 16°20E 324 C3
Pápa Hungary 47°22N 17°30E 289 E9
Papa Stour U.K. 60°20N 1°42W 283 A7
Papa Westray U.K. 59°20N 2°55W 283 B6
Papagayo → Mexico 16°46N 99°43W 359 D5
Papagayo, G. de Costa Rica 10°30N 85°50W 360 D2
Papakura N.Z. 37°4S 174°59E 331 B5
Papantla Mexico 20°27N 97°19W 359 C5
Papar Malaysia 5°45N 116°0E 308 C5
Papara Tahiti 17°43S 149°31W 331 d
Paparoa △ N.Z. 42°7S 171°26E 331 E3
Papeete Tahiti 17°32S 149°34W 331 d
Papenoo Tahiti 17°30S 149°25W 331 d
Papenoo → Tahiti 17°30S 149°25W 331 d
Papetoai Moorea 17°29S 149°52W 331 d
Paphos Cyprus 34°46N 32°25E 297 E11
Paposo Chile 25°0S 70°30W 366 B1
Papoutsa Cyprus 34°54N 33°4E 297 E12
Papua □ Indonesia 4°0S 137°0E 309 E9
Papua, G. of Papua N. G. 9°0S 144°50E 330 B7
Papua New Guinea ■ Oceania 8°0S 145°0E 330 B7
Papudo Chile 32°29S 71°27W 366 C1
Papun Burma 18°2N 97°30E 313 K20
Papunya Australia 23°15S 131°54E 332 D5
Pará = Belém Brazil 1°20S 48°30W 365 D9
Pará □ Brazil 3°20S 52°0W 365 D8
Paraburdoo Australia 23°14S 117°32E 332 D2
Paracatu Brazil 17°10S 46°50W 365 G9
Paracel Is. S. China Sea 15°50N 112°0E 308 A4
Parachilna Australia 31°10S 138°21E 335 E2
Parachinar Pakistan 33°55N 70°5E 314 C4
Paradip India 20°15N 86°35E 313 J15
Paradise Calif., U.S.A. 39°46N 121°37W 350 F5
Paradise Nev., U.S.A. 36°5N 115°8W 351 J11
Paradise → Canada 53°27N 57°19W 345 B8
Paradise Hill Canada 53°32N 109°28W 343 C7
Paradise River Canada 53°27N 57°17W 345 B8
Paradise Valley U.S.A. 41°30N 117°32W 348 F5
Paradisi Greece 36°18N 28°7E 297 C10
Parado Indonesia 8°42S 118°30E 309 F5
Paragould U.S.A. 36°3N 90°29W 357 C9
Paragua → Venezuela 6°55N 62°55W 364 B6
Paraguaçu → Brazil 12°45S 38°54W 365 F11
Paraguaçu Paulista Brazil 22°22S 50°35W 367 A5
Paraguaná, Pen. de Venezuela 12°0N 70°0W 364 A5
Paraguarí Paraguay 25°36S 57°0W 366 B4
Paraguarí □ Paraguay 26°0S 57°10W 366 B4
Paraguay ■ S. Amer. 23°0S 57°0W 366 A4
Paraguay → Paraguay 27°18S 58°38W 366 B4
Paraíba = João Pessoa Brazil 7°10S 34°52W 365 E12
Paraíba □ Brazil 7°0S 36°0W 365 E11
Paraíba do Sul → Brazil 21°37S 41°3W 367 A7
Parainen Finland 60°18N 22°18E 281 F20
Paraíso Mexico 18°24N 93°14W 359 D6
Parak Iran 27°38N 52°25E 317 E7
Parakou Benin 9°25N 2°40E 322 G6
Paralimni Cyprus 35°2N 33°58E 297 D12
Paramaribo Suriname 5°50N 55°10W 365 B7
Páramos del Batallón y La Negra △ Venezuela 8°2N 71°55W 361 E5
Paramushir, Ostrov Russia 50°24N 156°0E 301 D16
Paran → Israel 30°20N 35°10E 318 E4
Paraná Argentina 31°45S 60°30W 366 C3
Paranã Brazil 12°30S 47°48W 365 F9
Paraná □ Brazil 24°30S 51°0W 367 A5
Paraná → Argentina 33°43S 59°15W 366 C4
Paranaguá Brazil 25°30S 48°30W 367 B6
Paranaíba Brazil 19°40S 51°11W 365 G8
Paranaíba → Brazil 20°6S 51°4W 365 H8
Paranapanema → Brazil 22°40S 53°9W 367 A5
Paranapiacaba, Serra do Brazil 24°31S 48°35W 367 A6
Paranavaí Brazil 23°4S 52°56W 367 A5
Parang Maguindanao, Phil. 7°23N 124°16E 309 C6
Parang Sulu, Phil. 5°55N 120°54E 309 C6
Parângul Mare, Vf. Romania 45°20N 23°37E 289 F12
Paraparaumu N.Z. 40°57S 175°3E 331 D5
Parbati → Mad. P., India 25°50N 76°30E 314 G7
Parbati → Raj., India 26°54N 77°53E 314 F7
Parbhani India 19°8N 76°52E 312 K10
Parchim Germany 53°26N 11°52E 288 B6
Pardes Hanna-Karkur Israel 32°28N 34°57E 318 C3
Pardo → Bahia, Brazil 15°40S 39°0W 365 G11
Pardo → Mato Grosso, Brazil 21°46S 52°9W 367 A5
Pardoo Roadhouse Australia 20°6S 119°3E 332 D2
Pardubice Czech Rep. 50°3N 15°45E 288 C8
Pare Indonesia 7°43S 112°12E 309 G15
Pare Mts. Tanzania 4°0S 37°45E 326 C4
Parecis, Serra dos Brazil 13°0S 60°0W 364 F7
Paren Russia 62°30N 163°15E 301 C17
Parent Canada 47°55N 74°35W 344 C5
Parent, L. Canada 48°31N 77°1W 344 C4
Parepare Indonesia 4°0S 119°40E 309 E5
Parga Greece 39°15N 20°29E 295 E9
Pargas = Parainen Finland 60°18N 22°18E 281 F20
Pargo, Pta. do Madeira 32°49N 17°17W 296 D2
Paria → U.S.A. 36°52N 111°36W 349 H8
Paria, G. de Venezuela 10°20N 62°0W 365 K14
Pariaguán Venezuela 8°51N 64°34W 364 B6
Paricutín, Cerro Mexico 19°28N 102°15W 358 D4
Parigi Indonesia 0°50S 120°5E 309 E6
Parika Guyana 6°50N 58°20W 364 B7
Parikkala Finland 61°33N 29°31E 280 F23
Parima, Serra Brazil 2°30N 64°0W 364 C6
Parinari Peru 4°35S 74°25W 364 D4
Pariñas, Pta. S. Amer. 4°30S 82°0W 362 D2
Parintins Brazil 2°40S 56°50W 365 D7
Pariparit Kyun Burma 14°55N 93°45E 313 M18
Paris Canada 43°12N 80°25W 354 C4
Paris France 48°53N 2°20E 292 B5
Paris Idaho, U.S.A. 42°14N 111°24W 348 E8
Paris Ky., U.S.A. 38°13N 84°15W 353 F11
Paris Tenn., U.S.A. 36°18N 88°19W 357 C10
Paris Tex., U.S.A. 33°40N 95°33W 356 E7
Parish U.S.A. 43°25N 76°8W 355 C8
Parishville U.S.A. 44°38N 74°49W 355 B10
Park U.S.A. 48°45N 122°18W 350 B4
Park City U.S.A. 37°48N 97°20W 352 G5
Park Falls U.S.A. 45°56N 90°27W 352 C8
Park Head Canada 44°36N 81°9W 354 B3
Park Hills U.S.A. 37°51N 90°51W 352 G8
Park Range U.S.A. 40°41N 106°41W 348 F10
Park Rapids U.S.A. 46°55N 95°4W 352 B6
Park River U.S.A. 48°24N 97°45W 352 A5
Park Rynie S. Africa 30°25S 30°45E 329 E5
Parkā Bandar Iran 25°55N 59°35E 317 E8
Parkano Finland 62°1N 23°0E 280 E20
Parker Ariz., U.S.A. 34°9N 114°17W 351 L12
Parker Pa., U.S.A. 41°5N 79°41W 354 E5
Parker Dam U.S.A. 34°18N 114°8W 351 L12
Parkersburg U.S.A. 39°16N 81°34W 353 F13
Parkes Australia 33°9S 148°11E 335 E4
Parkfield U.S.A. 35°54N 120°26W 350 K6
Parkhill Canada 43°15N 81°38W 354 C3
Parkland U.S.A. 47°9N 122°26W 350 C4
Parkston U.S.A. 43°24N 97°59W 352 D5
Parksville Canada 49°20N 124°21W 342 D4
Parkway U.S.A. 38°32N 121°26W 350 G5
Parla Spain 40°14N 3°46W 293 B4
Parma Italy 44°48N 10°20E 292 D9
Parma Idaho, U.S.A. 43°47N 116°57W 348 E5
Parma Ohio, U.S.A. 41°24N 81°43W 354 E3
Parnaguá Brazil 10°10S 44°38W 365 F10
Parnaíba Brazil 2°54S 41°47W 365 D10
Parnaíba → Brazil 3°0S 41°50W 365 D10
Parnassos Greece 38°35N 22°30E 295 E10
Pärnu Estonia 58°28N 24°33E 281 G21
Paro Dzong Bhutan 27°32N 89°53E 315 F13
Paroo → Australia 31°28S 143°32E 335 E3
Paroo-Darling △ Australia 31°32S 144°0E 335 E3
Paros Greece 37°5N 25°12E 295 F11
Parowan U.S.A. 37°51N 112°50W 349 H7
Parral Chile 36°10S 71°52W 366 D1
Parras Mexico 25°25N 102°11W 358 B4
Parrett → U.K. 51°12N 3°1W 285 F4
Parris I. U.S.A. 32°20N 80°41W 357 E14
Parrsboro Canada 45°30N 64°25W 345 C7
Parry I. Canada 45°18N 80°10W 354 A4
Parry Is. Canada 77°0N 110°0W 341 B9
Parry Sound Canada 45°20N 80°0W 354 A5
Parsaloi Kenya 1°16N 36°51E 326 B4
Parsnip → Canada 55°10N 123°2W 342 B4
Parsons U.S.A. 37°20N 95°16W 352 G6
Parsons Ra. Australia 13°30S 135°15E 334 A2
Partinico Italy 38°3N 13°7E 294 E5
Partizansk Russia 43°8N 133°9E 302 C6
Partridge I. Canada 55°59N 87°37W 344 A2
Partry Mts. Ireland 53°40N 9°28W 282 C2
Paru → Brazil 1°33S 52°38W 365 D8
Parvān □ Afghan. 35°0N 69°0E 312 B6
Parvatipuram India 18°50N 83°25E 313 K13
Parvatsar India 26°52N 74°49E 314 F6
Parys S. Africa 26°52S 27°29E 328 D4
Pas, Pta. des Spain 38°46N 1°26E 296 C7
Pas, The Canada 53°45N 101°15W 343 C8
Pasadena Canada 49°1N 57°36W 345 C8
Pasadena Calif., U.S.A. 34°9N 118°8W 351 L8
Pasadena Tex., U.S.A. 29°43N 95°13W 356 G7
Pasaje → Argentina 25°39S 63°56W 366 B3
Pasar Indonesia 8°27S 114°54E 309 J17
Pascagoula U.S.A. 30°21N 88°33W 357 F10
Pascagoula → U.S.A. 30°23N 88°37W 357 F10
Paşcani Romania 47°14N 26°45E 289 E14
Pasco U.S.A. 46°14N 119°6W 348 C4
Pasco, Cerro de Peru 10°45S 76°10W 364 F3
Pasco I. Australia 20°57S 115°20E 332 D2
Pascoag U.S.A. 41°57N 71°42W 355 E13
Pascua, I. de Chile 27°7S 109°23W 337 K17
Pasfield L. Canada 58°24N 105°20W 343 B7
Pasir Mas Malaysia 6°2N 102°8E 311 J4
Pasir Panjang Singapore 1°18N 103°46E 311 d
Pasir Putih Malaysia 5°50N 102°24E 311 K4
Pasirian Indonesia 8°13S 113°8E 309 H15
Pasirkuning Indonesia 0°30S 104°33E 308 E2
Paskūh Iran 27°34N 61°39E 317 E9
Pasley, C. Australia 33°52S 123°35E 333 F3
Pašman Croatia 43°58N 15°20E 288 G8
Pasni Pakistan 25°15N 63°27E 312 G3
Paso Cantinela Mexico 32°33N 115°47W 351 N11
Paso de Indios Argentina 43°55S 69°0W 368 E3
Paso de los Libres Argentina 29°44S 57°10W 366 B4
Paso de los Toros Uruguay 32°45S 56°30W 366 C4
Paso Robles U.S.A. 35°38N 120°41W 350 K6
Paspébiac Canada 48°3N 65°17W 345 C6
Pasrur Pakistan 32°16N 74°43E 314 C6
Passage East Ireland 52°14N 7°0W 282 D5
Passage West Ireland 51°52N 8°21W 282 E3
Passaic U.S.A. 40°51N 74°7W 355 F10
Passau Germany 48°34N 13°28E 288 D7
Passero, C. Italy 36°41N 15°10E 294 F6
Passo Fundo Brazil 28°10S 52°20W 367 B5
Passos Brazil 20°45S 46°37W 365 H9
Pastavy Belarus 55°4N 26°50E 281 J22
Pastaza → Peru 4°50S 76°52W 364 D3
Pasto Colombia 1°13N 77°17W 364 C3
Pasuruan Indonesia 7°40S 112°44E 309 G15
Patagonia Argentina 45°0S 69°0W 368 F3
Patagonia U.S.A. 31°33N 110°45W 349 L8
Patambar Iran 29°45N 60°17E 317 D9
Patan = Lalitapur Nepal 27°40N 85°20E 315 F11
Patan India 23°54N 72°14E 314 H5
Patani Indonesia 0°20N 128°50E 309 D7
Pataudi India 28°18N 76°48E 314 E7
Patchewollock Australia 35°22S 142°12E 335 F3
Patchogue U.S.A. 40°46N 73°1W 355 F11
Pate Kenya 2°10S 41°0E 326 C5
Patea N.Z. 39°45S 174°30E 331 C5
Patensie S. Africa 33°46S 24°49E 328 E3
Paternò Italy 37°34N 14°54E 294 F6
Pateros U.S.A. 48°3N 119°54W 348 B4
Paterson U.S.A. 40°54N 74°9W 355 F10
Paterson Ra. Australia 21°45S 122°10E 332 D3
Pathankot India 32°18N 75°45E 314 C6
Pathein = Bassein Burma 16°45N 94°30E 313 L19
Pathfinder Res. U.S.A. 42°28N 106°51W 348 E10
Pathiu Thailand 10°42N 99°19E 311 G2
Pathum Thani Thailand 14°1N 100°32E 310 E3
Pati Indonesia 6°45S 111°1E 309 G14
Patía → Colombia 2°13N 78°40W 364 C3
Patiala Punjab, India 30°23N 76°26E 314 D7
Patiala Ut. P., India 27°43N 79°1E 315 F8
Patkai Bum India 27°0N 95°30E 313 F19
Patmos Greece 37°21N 26°36E 295 F12
Patna India 25°35N 85°12E 315 G11
Pato Branco Brazil 26°13S 52°40W 367 B5
Patong, Ao Thailand 7°54N 98°17E 311 a
Patonga Uganda 2°45N 33°15E 326 B3
Patos Brazil 6°55S 37°16W 365 E11
Patos, L. dos Brazil 31°20S 51°0W 367 C5
Patos, Río de los → Argentina 31°18S 69°25W 366 C2
Patos de Minas Brazil 18°35S 46°32W 365 G9
Patquía Argentina 30°2S 66°55W 366 C2
Patra Greece 38°14N 21°47E 295 E9
Patraikos Kolpos Greece 38°17N 21°30E 295 E9
Patras = Patra Greece 38°14N 21°47E 295 E9
Patriot Hills Antarctica 82°20S 81°25W 277 E16
Patrocínio Brazil 18°57S 47°0W 365 G9
Pattani Thailand 6°48N 101°15E 311 J3
Pattaya Thailand 12°52N 100°55E 310 F3
Patten U.S.A. 46°0N 68°38W 353 B19
Patterson Calif., U.S.A. 37°28N 121°8W 350 H5
Patterson La., U.S.A. 29°42N 91°18W 356 G9
Patterson, Mt. U.S.A. 38°29N 119°20W 350 G7
Patti Punjab, India 31°17N 74°54E 314 D6
Patti Ut. P., India 25°55N 82°12E 315 G10
Pattoki Pakistan 31°5N 73°52E 314 D5
Patton U.S.A. 40°38N 78°39W 354 F6
Patuakhali Bangla. 22°20N 90°25E 313 H17
Patuanak Canada 55°55N 107°43W 343 B7
Patuca → Honduras 15°50N 84°18W 360 C3
Patuca, Punta Honduras 15°49N 84°14W 360 C3
Patuca △ Honduras 14°30N 85°30W 360 D2
Patvinsuo △ Finland 63°7N 30°45E 280 E24
Pátzcuaro Mexico 19°31N 101°38W 358 D4
Pau France 43°19N 0°25W 292 E3
Pauk Burma 21°27N 94°30E 313 J19
Paul I. Canada 56°30N 61°20W 345 A7
Paul Smiths U.S.A. 44°26N 74°15W 355 B10
Paulatuk Canada 69°25N 124°0W 340 C7
Paulistana Brazil 8°9S 41°9W 365 E10
Paulo Afonso Brazil 9°21S 38°15W 365 E11
Paulpietersburg S. Africa 27°23S 30°50E 329 D5
Pauls Valley U.S.A. 34°44N 97°13W 356 D6
Pauma Valley U.S.A. 33°16N 116°58W 351 M10
Pauri India 30°9N 78°47E 315 D8
Pāveh Iran 35°3N 46°22E 316 C5
Pavia Italy 45°7N 9°8E 292 D8
Pavilion U.S.A. 42°52N 78°1W 354 D6
Pāvilosta Latvia 56°53N 21°14E 281 H19
Pavlodar Kazakhstan 52°33N 77°0E 300 D8
Pavlograd = Pavlohrad Ukraine 48°30N 35°52E 291 E6
Pavlohrad Ukraine 48°30N 35°52E 291 E6
Pavlovo Russia 55°58N 43°5E 290 C7
Pavlovsk Russia 50°26N 40°5E 291 D7
Pavlovskaya Russia 46°17N 39°47E 291 E6
Pawai, Pulau Singapore 1°11N 103°44E 311 d
Pawayan India 28°4N 80°6E 315 E9
Pawhuska U.S.A. 36°40N 96°20W 356 C6
Pawling U.S.A. 41°34N 73°36W 355 E11
Pawnee U.S.A. 36°20N 96°48W 356 C6
Pawnee City U.S.A. 40°7N 96°9W 352 E5
Pawtucket U.S.A. 41°53N 71°23W 355 E13
Paxi Greece 39°14N 20°12E 295 E9
Paximadia Greece 35°0N 24°35E 297 E6
Paxton U.S.A. 40°27N 88°6W 352 E9
Payakumbuh Indonesia 0°20S 100°35E 308 E2
Payette U.S.A. 44°5N 116°56W 348 D5
Payne Bay = Kangirsuk Canada 60°0N 70°0W 341 D13
Payne L. Canada 59°30N 74°30W 341 D12
Paynes Find Australia 29°15S 117°42E 333 E2
Paynesville U.S.A. 45°23N 94°43W 352 C6
Paysandú Uruguay 32°19S 58°8W 366 C4
Payson Ariz., U.S.A. 34°14N 111°20W 349 J8
Payson Utah, U.S.A. 40°3N 111°44W 348 F8
Paz → Guatemala 13°44N 90°10W 360 D1
Paz, B. de la Mexico 24°9N 110°25W 358 C2
Pāzanān Iran 30°35N 49°59E 317 D6
Pazardzhik Bulgaria 42°12N 24°20E 295 C11
Pe Ell U.S.A. 46°34N 123°18W 350 D3
Peabody U.S.A. 42°31N 70°56W 355 D14
Peace → Canada 59°0N 111°25W 342 B6
Peace Point Canada 59°7N 112°27W 342 B6
Peace River Canada 56°15N 117°18W 342 B5
Peach Springs U.S.A. 35°32N 113°25W 349 J7
Peachland Canada 49°47N 119°45W 342 D5
Peachtree City U.S.A. 33°25N 84°35W 357 E12
Peak, The = Kinder Scout U.K. 53°24N 1°52W 284 D6
Peak Charles △ Australia 32°42S 121°10E 333 F3
Peak District △ U.K. 53°24N 1°46W 284 D6
Peak Hill N.S.W., Australia 32°47S 148°11E 335 E4
Peak Hill W. Austral., Australia 25°35S 118°43E 333 E2
Peak Ra. Australia 22°50S 148°20E 334 C4
Peake Cr. → Australia 28°2S 136°7E 335 D2
Peale, Mt. U.S.A. 38°26N 109°14W 348 G9
Pearblossom U.S.A. 34°30N 117°55W 351 L9
Pearl → U.S.A. 30°11N 89°32W 357 F10
Pearl City U.S.A. 21°24N 157°59W 346 b
Pearl Harbor U.S.A. 21°21N 157°57W 346 b
Pearl River U.S.A. 41°4N 74°2W 355 E10
Pearsall U.S.A. 28°54N 99°6W 356 G5
Pearson Int. Toronto ✕ (YYZ) Canada 43°46N 79°35W 354 C5
Peary Land Greenland 82°40N 33°0W 276 A6
Pease → U.S.A. 34°12N 99°2W 356 D5
Peawanuck Canada 55°15N 85°12W 341 D11
Pebane Mozam. 17°10S 38°8E 327 F4
Pebas Peru 3°10S 71°46W 364 D4
Pebble Beach U.S.A. 36°34N 121°57W 350 J5
Peć Serbia 42°40N 20°17E 295 C9
Pechenga Russia 69°29N 31°4E 280 B24
Pechenizhyn Ukraine 48°30N 24°48E 289 D13
Pechiguera, Pta. Canary Is. 28°51N 13°53W 296 F6
Pechora Russia 65°10N 57°11E 290 A10
Pechora → Russia 68°13N 54°15E 290 A9
Pechorskaya Guba Russia 68°40N 54°0E 290 A9
Pechory Russia 57°48N 27°40E 281 H22
Pecos N. Mex., U.S.A. 35°35N 105°41W 349 J11
Pecos Tex., U.S.A. 31°26N 103°30W 356 F3
Pecos → U.S.A. 29°42N 101°22W 356 G4
Pécs Hungary 46°5N 18°15E 289 E10
Pedder, L. Australia 42°55S 146°10E 335 G4
Peddie S. Africa 33°14S 27°7E 329 E4
Pedernales Dom. Rep. 18°2N 71°44W 361 C5
Pedieos → Cyprus 35°10N 33°54E 297 D12
Pedirka Australia 26°40S 135°14E 335 D2
Pedra Azul Brazil 16°2S 41°17W 365 G10
Pedra Lume C. Verde Is. 16°40N 22°52W 322 b
Pedreiras Brazil 4°32S 44°40W 365 D10
Pedro Afonso Brazil 9°0S 48°10W 365 E9
Pedro Cays Jamaica 17°5N 77°48W 360 C4
Pedro de Valdivia Chile 22°55S 69°38W 366 A2
Pedro Juan Caballero Paraguay 22°30S 55°40W 367 A4
Pee Dee = Great Pee Dee → U.S.A. 33°21N 79°10W 357 E15
Peebinga Australia 34°52S 140°57E 335 E3
Peebles U.K. 55°40N 3°11W 283 F5
Peekskill U.S.A. 41°17N 73°55W 355 E11
Peel I. of Man 54°13N 4°40W 284 C3
Peel → Australia 30°50S 150°29E 335 E5
Peel → Canada 67°0N 135°0W 340 C6
Peel Sd. Canada 73°0N 96°0W 340 B10
Peera Peera Poolanna L. Australia 26°30S 138°0E 335 D2
Peerless Lake Canada 56°37N 114°40W 342 B6
Peers Canada 53°40N 116°0W 342 C5
Pegasus Bay N.Z. 43°20S 173°10E 331 E4
Pegu Burma 17°20N 96°29E 313 L20
Pegu Yoma Burma 19°0N 96°0E 313 K20
Pehuajó Argentina 35°45S 62°0W 366 D3
Pei Xian = Pizhou China 34°44N 116°55E 306 G9
Peine Chile 23°45S 68°8W 366 A2
Peine Germany 52°19N 10°14E 288 B6
Peip'ing = Beijing China 39°53N 116°21E 306 E9
Peipus, L. = Chudskoye, Ozero Russia 58°13N 27°30E 281 G22
Peixe Brazil 12°0S 48°40W 365 F9
Peixe → Brazil 21°31S 51°58W 365 H8
Pekalongan Indonesia 6°53S 109°40E 308 F3
Pekan Malaysia 3°30N 103°25E 311 L4
Pekan Nenas Malaysia 1°31N 103°31E 311 d
Pekanbaru Indonesia 0°30N 101°15E 308 D2
Pekin U.S.A. 40°35N 89°40W 352 E9
Peking = Beijing China 39°53N 116°21E 306 E9
Pekutatan Indonesia 8°25S 114°49E 309 J17
Pelabuhan Klang Malaysia 3°0N 101°23E 311 L3

Pelabuhan Ratu, Teluk Indonesia 7°5S 106°32E 309 G12
Pelabuhanratu Indonesia 7°0S 106°32E 309 G12
Pelagie, Is. Italy 35°39N 12°33E 294 G5
Pelaihari Indonesia 3°55S 114°45E 308 E4
Peleaga, Vf. Romania 45°22N 22°55E 289 F12
Pelée, Mt. Martinique 14°48N 61°10W 360 c
Pelee, Pt. Canada 41°54N 82°31W 344 D3
Pelee I. Canada 41°47N 82°40W 354 E2
Pelekech Kenya 3°52N 35°8E 326 B4
Peleng Indonesia 1°20S 123°30E 309 E6
Pelentong Malaysia 1°32N 103°49E 311 d
Pelican U.S.A. 57°58N 136°14W 342 B1
Pelican L. Canada 52°28N 100°20W 343 C8
Pelican Narrows Canada 55°10N 102°56W 343 B8
Pelješac Croatia 42°55N 17°25E 294 C7
Pelkosenniemi Finland 67°6N 27°28E 280 C22
Pella S. Africa 29°1S 19°6E 328 D2
Pella U.S.A. 41°25N 92°55W 352 E7
Pello Finland 66°47N 23°59E 280 C20
Pelly → Canada 62°47N 137°19W 342 A1
Pelly Bay Canada 68°38N 89°50W 341 C11
Peloponnese □ Greece 37°10N 22°0E 295 F10
Pelorus Sd. N.Z. 40°59S 173°59E 331 D4
Pelotas Brazil 31°42S 52°23W 367 C5
Pelotas → Brazil 27°28S 51°55W 367 B5
Pelvoux, Massif du France 44°52N 6°20E 292 D7
Pemalang Indonesia 6°53S 109°23E 309 G13
Pemanggil, Pulau Malaysia 2°37N 104°21E 311 L5
Pematangsiantar Indonesia 2°57N 99°5E 308 D1
Pemba Mozam. 12°58S 40°30E 327 E5
Pemba Zambia 16°30S 27°28E 327 F2
Pemba Channel Tanzania 5°0S 39°37E 326 D4
Pemba I. Tanzania 5°0S 39°45E 326 D4
Pemberton Australia 34°30S 116°0E 333 F2
Pemberton Canada 50°25N 122°50W 342 C4
Pembina → Canada 54°45N 114°17W 342 C6
Pembroke Canada 45°50N 77°7W 344 C4
Pembroke U.K. 51°41N 4°55W 285 F3
Pembrokeshire □ U.K. 51°52N 4°56W 285 F3
Pembrokeshire Coast △ U.K. 51°50N 5°2W 285 F2
Pen-y-Ghent U.K. 54°10N 2°14W 284 C5
Penal Trin. & Tob. 10°9N 61°29W 365 K15
Penang = Pinang Malaysia 5°25N 100°15E 311 c
Penápolis Brazil 21°30S 50°0W 367 A6
Peñarroya-Pueblonuevo Spain 38°19N 5°16W 293 C3
Penarth U.K. 51°26N 3°11W 285 F4
Peñas, C. de Spain 43°42N 5°52W 293 A3
Penas, G. de Chile 47°0S 75°0W 368 F2
Peñas del Chache Canary Is. 29°6N 13°33W 296 E6
Pench △ India 21°45N 79°20E 315 J8
Pench'i = Benxi China 41°20N 123°48E 307 D12
Pend Oreille → U.S.A. 49°4N 117°37W 348 B5
Pend Oreille, L. U.S.A. 48°10N 116°21W 348 B5
Pendembu S. Leone 9°7N 11°14W 322 G3
Pender B. Australia 16°45S 122°42E 332 C3
Pendleton U.S.A. 45°40N 118°47W 348 D4
Pendra India 22°46N 81°57E 315 H9
Penedo Brazil 10°15S 36°36W 365 F11
Penelokan Indonesia 8°17S 115°22E 309 J18
Penetanguishene Canada 44°50N 79°55W 354 B5
Penfield U.S.A. 41°13N 78°35W 354 E6
Peng Chau China 22°17N 114°2E 305 G11
Pengalengan Indonesia 7°9S 107°30E 309 G12
Penge Kasai-Or., Dem. Rep. of the Congo 5°30S 24°33E 326 D1
Penge Sud-Kivu, Dem. Rep. of the Congo 4°27S 28°25E 326 C2
Penglai China 37°48N 120°42E 307 F11
Penguin Australia 41°8S 146°6E 335 G4
Penhalonga Zimbabwe 18°52S 32°40E 327 F3
Peniche Portugal 39°19N 9°22W 293 C1
Penicuik U.K. 55°50N 3°13W 283 F5
Penida, Nusa Indonesia 8°45S 115°30E 308 F5
Peninsular Malaysia □ Malaysia 4°0N 102°0E 311 L4
Penitente, Serra do Brazil 8°45S 46°20W 365 E9
Penkridge U.K. 52°44N 2°6W 284 E5
Penmarch, Pte. de France 47°48N 4°22W 292 C1
Penn Hills U.S.A. 40°28N 79°52W 354 F5
Penn Yan U.S.A. 42°40N 77°3W 354 D7
Pennant Canada 50°32N 108°14W 343 C7
Penner → India 14°35N 80°10E 312 M12
Pennines U.K. 54°45N 2°27W 284 C5
Pennington U.S.A. 39°15N 121°47W 350 F5
Pennsburg U.S.A. 40°23N 75°29W 355 F9
Pennsylvania □ U.S.A. 40°45N 77°30W 353 E15
Penny Canada 53°51N 121°20W 342 C4
Penny Str. Canada 76°30N 97°0W 341 B8
Penobscot → U.S.A. 44°30N 68°48W 353 C19
Penobscot B. U.S.A. 44°35N 68°50W 353 C19
Penola Australia 37°25S 140°48E 335 F3
Penong Australia 31°56S 133°1E 333 F5
Penonomé Panama 8°31N 80°21W 360 E3
Penrhyn Cook Is. 9°0S 158°0W 337 H12
Penrith Australia 33°43S 150°38E 335 E5
Penrith U.K. 54°40N 2°45W 284 C5
Penryn U.K. 50°9N 5°7W 285 G2
Pensacola U.S.A. 30°25N 87°13W 357 F11
Pensacola Mts. Antarctica 84°0S 40°0W 277 E1
Pense Canada 50°25N 104°59W 343 C8
Penshurst Australia 37°49S 142°20E 335 F3
Penticton Canada 49°30N 119°38W 342 D5
Pentland Australia 20°32S 145°25E 334 C4
Pentland Firth U.K. 58°43N 3°10W 283 C5
Pentland Hills U.K. 55°48N 3°25W 283 F5
Pentland Hills ⌓ U.K. 55°50N 3°20W 283 F5
Penza Russia 53°15N 45°5E 290 D8
Penzance U.K. 50°7N 5°33W 285 G2
Penzhino Russia 63°30N 167°55E 301 C17
Penzhinskaya Guba Russia 61°30N 163°0E 301 C17
Peoria Ariz., U.S.A. 33°43N 112°14W 349 K7
Peoria Ill., U.S.A. 40°42N 89°36W 352 E9
Pepacton Res. U.S.A. 42°5N 74°58W 355 D10
Pepani → S. Africa 25°49S 22°47E 328 D3
Pera Hd. Australia 12°55S 141°37E 334 A3
Perabumulih Indonesia 3°27S 104°15E 308 E2
Perak → Malaysia 4°0N 100°50E 311 K3
Perama Kerkyra, Greece 39°34N 19°54E 297 A3
Perama Kriti, Greece 35°20N 24°40E 297 D6
Perancak Indonesia 8°24S 114°37E 309 J17
Peräpohjola Finland 66°16N 26°10E 280 C22
Percé Canada 48°31N 64°13W 345 C7
Perche, Collines du France 48°30N 0°40E 292 B4
Percival Lakes Australia 21°25S 125°0E 332 D4
Percy Is. Australia 21°39S 150°16E 334 C5
Perdido, Mte. Spain 42°40N 0°5E 293 A6
Perdu, Mt. = Perdido, Mte. Spain 42°40N 0°5E 293 A6
Pereira Colombia 4°49N 75°43W 364 C3
Perenjori Australia 29°26S 116°16E 333 E2
Pereyaslav-Khmelnytskyy Ukraine 50°3N 31°28E 291 D5
Pérez, I. Mexico 22°24N 89°42W 359 C7
Pergamino Argentina 33°52S 60°30W 366 C3
Pergau → Malaysia 5°23N 102°2E 311 K3
Perham U.S.A. 46°36N 95°34W 352 B6
Perhentian, Kepulauan Malaysia 5°54N 102°42E 311 K4
Péribonka → Canada 48°45N 72°5W 345 C5
Péribonka, L. Canada 50°1N 71°10W 345 B5
Perico Argentina 24°20S 65°5W 366 A2
Pericos Mexico 25°3N 107°42W 358 B3
Périgueux France 45°10N 0°42E 292 D4
Perijá, Sierra de Colombia 9°30N 73°3W 364 B4
Perijá △ Venezuela 9°30N 72°55W 361 E5
Peristerona → Cyprus 35°8N 33°5E 297 D12
Perito Moreno Argentina 46°36S 70°56W 368 F2
Perkasie U.S.A. 40°22N 75°18W 355 F9
Perlas, Arch. de las Panama 8°41N 79°7W 360 E4
Perlas, Punta de Nic. 12°30N 83°30W 360 D3
Perm Russia 58°0N 56°10E 290 C10
Pernambuco = Recife Brazil 8°0S 35°0W 365 E12
Pernambuco □ Brazil 8°0S 37°0W 365 E11
Pernatty Lagoon Australia 31°30S 137°12E 335 E2
Pernik Bulgaria 42°35N 23°2E 295 C10
Peron Is. Australia 13°9S 130°4E 332 B5
Peron Pen. Australia 26°0S 113°10E 333 E1
Perow Canada 54°35N 126°10W 342 C3
Perpignan France 42°42N 2°53E 292 E5
Perris U.S.A. 33°47N 117°14W 351 M9
Perry Fla., U.S.A. 30°7N 83°35W 357 F13
Perry Ga., U.S.A. 32°28N 83°44W 357 E13
Perry Iowa, U.S.A. 41°51N 94°6W 352 E6
Perry Okla., U.S.A. 36°17N 97°14W 356 C6
Perryton U.S.A. 36°24N 100°48W 356 C4
Perryville U.S.A. 37°43N 89°52W 352 G9
Persepolis Iran 29°55N 52°50E 317 D7
Pershotravensk Ukraine 50°13N 27°40E 289 C14
Persia = Iran ■ Asia 33°0N 53°0E 317 C7
Persian Gulf Asia 27°0N 50°0E 317 E6
Perth Australia 31°57S 115°52E 333 F2
Perth Canada 44°55N 76°15W 355 B8
Perth U.K. 56°24N 3°26W 283 E5
Perth & Kinross □ U.K. 56°45N 3°55W 283 E5
Perth Amboy U.S.A. 40°30N 74°15W 355 F10
Perth-Andover Canada 46°44N 67°42W 345 C6
Perth Basin Ind. Oc. 30°0S 108°0E 336 L2
Peru Ind., U.S.A. 40°45N 86°4W 352 E10
Peru N.Y., U.S.A. 44°35N 73°32W 355 B11
Peru ■ S. Amer. 4°0S 75°0W 364 D4
Peru Basin Pac. Oc. 20°0S 95°0W 337 J18
Peru-Chile Trench Pac. Oc. 20°0S 72°0W 364 G3
Perúgia Italy 43°7N 12°23E 294 C5
Pervomaysk Ukraine 48°10N 30°46E 291 E5
Pervouralsk Russia 56°59N 59°59E 290 C10
Pésaro Italy 43°54N 12°55E 294 C5
Pescara Italy 42°28N 14°13E 294 C6
Peshawar Pakistan 34°2N 71°37E 314 B4
Peshkopi Albania 41°41N 20°25E 295 D9
Peshtigo U.S.A. 45°3N 87°45W 352 C10
Pesqueira Brazil 8°20S 36°42W 365 E11
Petah Tiqwa Israel 32°6N 34°53E 318 C3
Petaling Jaya Malaysia 3°4N 101°42E 311 L3
Petaloudes Greece 36°18N 28°5E 297 C10
Petaluma U.S.A. 38°14N 122°39W 350 G4
Pétange Lux. 49°33N 5°55E 287 E5
Petaro Pakistan 25°31N 68°18E 314 G3
Petatlán Mexico 17°31N 101°16W 358 D4
Petauke Zambia 14°14S 31°20E 327 E3
Petawawa Canada 45°54N 77°17W 344 C4
Petén Itzá, L. Guatemala 16°58N 89°50W 360 C2
Peter I. Br. Virgin Is. 18°22N 64°35W 361 e
Peter I. Øy Antarctica 69°0S 91°0W 277 C16
Peter Pond L. Canada 55°55N 108°44W 343 B7
Peterbell Canada 48°36N 83°21W 344 C3
Peterborough Australia 32°58S 138°51E 335 E2
Peterborough Canada 44°20N 78°20W 354 B6
Peterborough U.K. 52°35N 0°15W 285 E7
Peterborough U.S.A. 42°53N 71°57W 355 D13
Peterborough □ U.K. 52°35N 0°15W 285 E7
Peterculter U.K. 57°6N 2°16W 283 D6
Peterhead U.K. 57°31N 1°48W 283 D7
Peterlee U.K. 54°47N 1°20W 284 C6
Petermann Ranges Australia 26°0S 130°30E 333 E5
Petersburg Alaska, U.S.A. 56°48N 132°58W 346 a
Petersburg Pa., U.S.A. 40°34N 78°3W 354 F6
Petersburg Va., U.S.A. 37°14N 77°24W 353 G15
Petersburg W. Va., U.S.A. 39°1N 79°5W 353 F14
Petersfield U.K. 51°1N 0°56W 285 F7
Petit-Canal Guadeloupe 16°25N 61°31W 360 b
Petit Goâve Haiti 18°27N 72°51W 361 C5
Petit Jardin Canada 48°28N 59°14W 345 C8
Petit Lac Manicouagan Canada 51°25N 67°40W 345 B6
Petit-Mécatina → Canada 50°40N 59°30W 345 B8
Petit-Mécatina, Î. du Canada 50°30N 59°25W 345 B8
Petit Piton St. Lucia 13°51N 61°5W 361 f
Petit-Saguenay Canada 48°15N 70°4W 345 C5
Petitcodiac Canada 45°57N 65°11W 345 C6
Petite Terre, Îles de la Guadeloupe 16°13N 61°9W 360 b
Petitot → Canada 60°14N 123°29W 342 A4
Petitsikapau L. Canada 54°37N 66°25W 345 B6
Petlad India 22°30N 72°45E 314 H5
Peto Mexico 20°8N 88°55W 359 C7
Petone N.Z. 41°13S 174°53E 331 D5
Petorca Chile 32°15S 70°56W 366 C1
Petoskey U.S.A. 45°22N 84°57W 353 C11
Petra Jordan 30°20N 35°22E 318 E4
Petra Spain 39°37N 3°6E 296 B10
Petra, Ostrova Russia 76°15N 118°30E 276 B13
Petra Velikogo, Zaliv Russia 42°40N 132°0E 302 C6
Petrich Bulgaria 41°24N 23°13E 295 D10
Petrified Forest △ U.S.A. 35°0N 109°30W 349 J9
Petrikov = Pyetrikaw Belarus 52°11N 28°29E 289 B15
Petrolândia Brazil 9°5S 38°20W 365 E11
Petrolia Canada 42°54N 82°9W 354 D2
Petrolina Brazil 9°24S 40°30W 365 E10
Petropavl Kazakhstan 54°53N 69°13E 300 D7
Petropavlovsk = Petropavl Kazakhstan 54°53N 69°13E 300 D7
Petropavlovsk-Kamchatskiy Russia 53°3N 158°43E 301 D16
Petrópolis Brazil 22°33S 43°9W 367 A7
Petroşani Romania 45°28N 23°20E 289 F12
Petrovaradin Serbia 45°16N 19°55E 295 B8
Petrovsk Russia 52°22N 45°19E 290 D8
Petrovsk-Zabaykalskiy Russia 51°20N 108°55E 301 D11
Petrozavodsk Russia 61°41N 34°20E 290 B5
Petrus Steyn S. Africa 27°38S 28°8E 329 D4
Petrusburg S. Africa 29°4S 25°26E 328 D4
Peumo Chile 34°21S 71°12W 366 C1
Peureulak Indonesia 4°48N 97°45E 308 D1
Pevek Russia 69°41N 171°19E 301 C18
Pforzheim Germany 48°52N 8°41E 288 D5
Pha Taem △ Thailand 15°32N 105°30E 310 E5
Phaestos Greece 35°2N 24°50E 297 D6
Phagwara India 31°10N 75°40E 314 D6
Phala Botswana 23°45S 26°50E 328 C4
Phalera = Phulera India 26°52N 75°16E 314 F6
Phalodi India 27°12N 72°24E 314 F5
Phaluai, Ko Thailand 9°32N 99°41E 311 b
Phan Thailand 19°28N 99°43E 310 C2
Phan Rang Vietnam 11°34N 109°0E 311 G7
Phan Ri = Hoa Da Vietnam 11°16N 108°40E 311 G7
Phan Thiet Vietnam 11°1N 108°9E 311 G7
Phanat Nikhom Thailand 13°27N 101°11E 310 F3
Phangan, Ko Thailand 9°45N 100°0E 311 H3
Phangnga Thailand 8°28N 98°30E 311 H2
Phangnga, Ao Thailand 8°16N 98°33E 311 a
Phanom Sarakham Thailand 13°45N 101°21E 310 F3
Phaphund India 26°36N 79°28E 315 F8
Pharenda India 27°5N 83°17E 315 F10
Pharr U.S.A. 26°12N 98°11W 356 H5
Phatthalung Thailand 7°39N 100°6E 311 J3
Phayao Thailand 19°11N 99°55E 310 C2
Phelps U.S.A. 42°58N 77°3W 354 D7
Phelps L. Canada 59°15N 103°15W 343 B8
Phenix City U.S.A. 32°28N 85°0W 357 E12
Phet Buri Thailand 13°1N 99°55E 310 F2
Phetchabun Thailand 16°25N 101°8E 310 D3
Phetchabun, Thiu Khao Thailand 16°0N 101°20E 310 E3
Phetchaburi = Phet Buri Thailand 13°1N 99°55E 310 F2
Phi Phi, Ko Thailand 7°45N 98°46E 311 J2
Phiafay Laos 14°48N 106°0E 310 E6
Phibun Mangsahan Thailand 15°14N 105°14E 310 E5
Phichai Thailand 17°22N 100°10E 310 D3
Phichit Thailand 16°26N 100°22E 310 D3
Philadelphia Miss., U.S.A. 32°46N 89°7W 357 E10
Philadelphia N.Y., U.S.A. 44°9N 75°43W 355 B9
Philadelphia Pa., U.S.A. 39°57N 75°9W 355 G9
Philip U.S.A. 44°2N 101°40W 352 C3
Philippeville Belgium 50°12N 4°33E 287 D4
Philippi U.S.A. 39°9N 80°3W 353 F13
Philippi L. Australia 24°20S 138°55E 334 C2
Philippine Basin Pac. Oc. 17°0N 132°0E 336 F5
Philippine Sea Pac. Oc. 18°0N 125°0E 336 F4
Philippine Trench = Mindanao Trench Pac. Oc. 12°0N 126°6E 309 B7
Philippines ■ Asia 12°0N 123°0E 309 B6
Philippolis S. Africa 30°15S 25°16E 328 E4
Philippopolis = Plovdiv Bulgaria 42°8N 24°44E 295 C11
Philipsburg Canada 45°2N 73°5W 355 A11
Philipsburg Mont., U.S.A. 46°20N 113°18W 348 C7
Philipsburg Pa., U.S.A. 40°54N 78°13W 354 F6
Philipstown = Daingean Ireland 53°18N 7°17W 282 C4
Philipstown S. Africa 30°28S 24°30E 328 E3
Phillip I. Australia 38°30S 145°12E 335 F4
Phillips U.S.A. 45°42N 90°24W 352 C8
Phillipsburg Kans., U.S.A. 39°45N 99°19W 352 F4
Phillipsburg N.J., U.S.A. 40°42N 75°12W 355 F9
Philmont U.S.A. 42°15N 73°39W 355 D11
Philomath U.S.A. 44°32N 123°22W 348 D2
Phimai Thailand 15°13N 102°30E 310 E4
Phitsanulok Thailand 16°50N 100°12E 310 D3
Phnom Dangrek Thailand 14°20N 104°0E 310 E5
Phnom Penh Cambodia 11°33N 104°55E 311 G5
Phnum Penh = Phnom Penh Cambodia 11°33N 104°55E 311 G5
Phoenicia U.S.A. 42°5N 74°14W 355 D10
Phoenix Mauritius 20°17S 57°30E 325 d
Phoenix Ariz., U.S.A. 33°26N 112°4W 349 K7
Phoenix N.Y., U.S.A. 43°14N 76°18W 355 C8
Phoenix Is. Kiribati 3°30S 172°0W 336 H10
Phoenixville U.S.A. 40°8N 75°31W 355 F9
Phon Thailand 15°49N 102°36E 310 E4
Phon Tiou Laos 17°53N 104°37E 310 D5
Phong → Thailand 16°23N 102°56E 310 D4
Phong Saly Laos 21°42N 102°9E 310 B4
Phong Tho Vietnam 22°32N 103°21E 310 A4
Phonhong Laos 18°30N 102°25E 310 C4
Phonum Thailand 8°49N 98°48E 311 H2
Phosphate Hill Australia 21°53S 139°58E 334 C2
Photharam Thailand 13°41N 99°51E 310 F2
Phra Nakhon Si Ayutthaya Thailand 14°25N 100°30E 310 E3
Phra Thong, Ko Thailand 9°5N 98°17E 311 H2
Phrae Thailand 18°7N 100°9E 310 C3
Phrom Phiram Thailand 17°2N 100°12E 310 D3
Phu Bia Laos 19°10N 103°0E 310 C4
Phu Chong-Na Yoi △ Thailand 14°25N 105°30E 310 E5
Phu Dien Vietnam 18°58N 105°31E 310 C5
Phu Hin Rang Kla △ Thailand 17°0N 100°59E 310 D3
Phu Kradung △ Thailand 17°2N 101°44E 310 D3
Phu Loi Laos 20°14N 103°14E 310 B4
Phu Luang △ Thailand 17°15N 101°29E 310 D3
Phu Ly Vietnam 20°35N 105°50E 310 B5
Phu Phan △ Thailand 17°0N 103°56E 310 D4
Phu Quoc, Dao Vietnam 10°20N 104°0E 311 G4
Phu Tho Vietnam 21°24N 105°13E 310 B5
Phuc Yen Vietnam 21°16N 105°45E 310 B5
Phuket Thailand 7°53N 98°24E 311 a
Phuket, Ko Thailand 8°0N 98°22E 311 a
Phul India 30°19N 75°14E 314 D6
Phulad India 25°38N 73°49E 314 G5
Phulchari Bangla. 25°11N 89°37E 315 G13
Phulera India 26°52N 75°16E 314 F6
Phulpur India 25°31N 82°49E 315 G10
Phun Phin Thailand 9°7N 99°12E 311 H2
Piacenza Italy 45°1N 9°40E 292 D8
Piai, Tanjung Malaysia 1°17N 103°30E 311 d
Pian Cr. → Australia 30°2S 148°12E 335 E4
Pian-Upe ⌓ Uganda 1°44N 34°20E 326 B3
Pianosa Italy 42°35N 10°5E 294 C4
Piapot Canada 49°59N 109°8W 343 D7
Piatra Neamţ Romania 46°56N 26°21E 289 E14
Piauí □ Brazil 7°0S 43°0W 365 E10
Piauí → Brazil 6°38S 42°42W 365 E10
Piave → Italy 45°32N 12°44E 294 B5
Pibor Post Sudan 6°47N 33°3E 323 G12
Picardie □ France 49°50N 3°0E 292 B5
Picardy = Picardie □ France 49°50N 3°0E 292 B5
Picayune U.S.A. 30°32N 89°41W 357 F10
Pichhor India 25°58N 78°20E 315 G8
Pichilemu Chile 34°22S 72°0W 366 C1
Pichor India 25°11N 78°11E 314 G8
Pickerel L. Canada 48°40N 91°25W 344 C1
Pickering U.K. 54°15N 0°46W 284 C7
Pickering, Vale of U.K. 54°14N 0°45W 284 C7
Pickle Lake Canada 51°30N 90°12W 344 B1
Pickwick L. U.S.A. 35°4N 88°15W 357 D10
Pico Azores 38°28N 28°20W 322 a
Pico Bonito △ Honduras 15°34N 86°48W 360 C2
Pico Truncado Argentina 46°40S 68°0W 368 F3
Picos Brazil 7°5S 41°28W 365 E10
Picton Australia 34°12S 150°34E 335 E5
Picton Canada 44°1N 77°9W 354 B7
Picton N.Z. 41°18S 174°3E 331 D5
Pictou Canada 45°41N 62°42W 345 C7
Picture Butte Canada 49°55N 112°45W 342 D6
Pictured Rocks ⌓ U.S.A. 46°30N 86°30W 352 B10
Picún Leufú Argentina 39°30S 69°5W 368 D3
Pidurutalagala Sri Lanka 7°10N 80°50E 312 R12
Piedmont = Piemonte □ Italy 45°0N 8°0E 292 D7
Piedmont Ala., U.S.A. 33°55N 85°37W 357 E12
Piedmont S.C., U.S.A. 34°42N 82°28W 347 D10
Piedras Negras Mexico 28°42N 100°31W 358 B4
Pieksämäki Finland 62°18N 27°10E 280 E22
Pielinen Finland 63°15N 29°40E 280 E23
Piemonte □ Italy 45°0N 8°0E 292 D7
Pienaarsrivier S. Africa 25°15S 28°18E 329 D4
Piercefield U.S.A. 44°13N 74°35W 355 B10
Pierceland Canada 54°20N 109°46W 343 C7
Pierpont U.S.A. 41°45N 80°34W 354 E4
Pierre U.S.A. 44°22N 100°21W 352 C3
Pierreville Trin. & Tob. 10°16N 61°0W 365 K16
Piet Retief S. Africa 27°1S 30°50E 329 D5
Pietarsaari Finland 63°40N 22°43E 280 E20
Pietermaritzburg S. Africa 29°35S 30°25E 329 D5
Pietersburg = Polokwane S. Africa 23°54S 29°25E 329 C4
Pietrosul, Vf. Maramureş, Romania 47°35N 24°43E 289 E13
Pietrosul, Vf. Suceava, Romania 47°12N 25°18E 289 E13
Pigeon L. Canada 44°27N 78°30W 354 B6
Piggott U.S.A. 36°23N 90°11W 357 C9
Pigüe Argentina 37°36S 62°25W 366 D3
Pihani India 27°36N 80°15E 315 F9
Pihlajavesi Finland 61°45N 28°45E 280 F23
Pijijiapan Mexico 15°42N 93°14W 359 D6
Pikangikum Canada 51°49N 94°0W 343 C10
Pikes Peak U.S.A. 38°50N 105°3W 348 G11
Piketberg S. Africa 32°55S 18°40E 328 E2
Pikeville U.S.A. 37°29N 82°31W 353 G12
Pikou China 39°18N 122°22E 307 E12
Pikwitonei Canada 55°35N 97°9W 343 B9
Piła Poland 53°10N 16°48E 289 B9
Pilanesberg △ S. Africa 25°15S 27°4E 328 D4
Pilani India 28°22N 75°33E 314 E6
Pilar Paraguay 26°50S 58°20W 366 B4
Pilaya → Bolivia 20°55S 64°4W 364 H6
Pilbara Australia 23°35S 117°25E 332 D2
Pilcomayo → Paraguay 25°21S 57°42W 366 B4
Pilgrim's Rest S. Africa 24°55S 30°44E 329 C5
Pilibhit India 28°40N 79°50E 315 E8
Pilica → Poland 51°52N 21°17E 289 C11
Pilipinas = Philippines ■ Asia 12°0N 123°0E 309 B6
Pilkhawa India 28°43N 77°42E 314 E7
Pilliga Australia 30°21S 148°54E 335 E4
Pilos Greece 36°55N 21°42E 295 F9
Pilot Mound Canada 49°15N 98°54W 343 D9
Pilot Point U.S.A. 33°24N 96°58W 356 E6
Pilot Rock U.S.A. 45°29N 118°50W 348 D4
Pima U.S.A. 32°54N 109°50W 349 K9
Pimba Australia 31°18S 136°46E 335 E2
Pimenta Bueno Brazil 11°35S 61°10W 364 F6
Pimentel Peru 6°45S 79°55W 364 E3
Pin Valley △ India 31°50N 77°50E 314 D7
Pinang Malaysia 5°25N 100°15E 311 c
Pinar, C. des Spain 39°53N 3°12E 296 B10
Pinar del Río Cuba 22°26N 83°40W 360 B3
Pınarhisar Turkey 41°37N 27°30E 295 D12
Pinatubo, Mt. Phil. 15°8N 120°21E 309 A6
Pinawa Canada 50°9N 95°50W 343 C9
Pincher Creek Canada 49°30N 113°57W 342 D6
Pinchi L. Canada 54°38N 124°30W 342 C4
Pinckneyville U.S.A. 38°5N 89°23W 352 F9
Pińczów Poland 50°32N 20°32E 289 C11
Pindar Australia 28°30S 115°47E 333 E2
Pindi Gheb Pakistan 33°14N 72°21E 314 C5
Pindos Oros Greece 40°0N 21°0E 295 E9
Pindus Mts. = Pindos Oros Greece 40°0N 21°0E 295 E9
Pine → B.C., Canada 56°8N 120°43W 342 B4
Pine → Sask., Canada 58°50N 105°38W 343 B7
Pine, C. Canada 46°37N 53°32W 345 C9
Pine Bluff U.S.A. 34°13N 92°1W 356 D8
Pine Bluffs U.S.A. 41°11N 104°4W 348 F11
Pine City U.S.A. 45°50N 92°59W 352 C7
Pine Cr. → U.S.A. 41°10N 77°16W 354 E7
Pine Creek Australia 13°50S 131°50E 332 B5
Pine Falls Canada 50°34N 96°11W 343 C9
Pine Flat L. U.S.A. 36°50N 119°20W 350 J7
Pine Grove U.S.A. 40°33N 76°23W 355 F8
Pine Hill Australia 23°38S 146°57E 334 C4
Pine Pass Canada 55°25N 122°42W 342 B4
Pine Point Canada 60°50N 114°28W 342 A6
Pine Ridge U.S.A. 43°2N 102°33W 352 D2
Pine River Canada 51°45N 100°30W 343 C8
Pine River U.S.A. 46°43N 94°24W 352 B6
Pine Valley U.S.A. 32°50N 116°32W 351 N10
Pinecrest U.S.A. 38°12N 120°1W 350 G6
Pinedale Calif., U.S.A. 36°50N 119°48W 350 J7
Pinedale Wyo., U.S.A. 42°52N 109°52W 348 E9
Pinega → Russia 64°30N 44°19E 290 B8
Pinehouse L. Canada 55°32N 106°35W 343 B7
Pineimuta → Canada 52°8N 88°33W 344 B1
Pinerolo Italy 44°53N 7°21E 292 D7
Pines, Akra Greece 40°5N 24°20E 295 D11
Pinetop-Lakeside U.S.A. 34°9N 109°58W 349 J9
Pinetown S. Africa 29°48S 30°54E 329 D5
Pineville U.S.A. 31°19N 92°26W 356 F8
Ping → Thailand 15°42N 100°9E 310 E3
Pingaring Australia 32°40S 118°32E 333 F2
Pingding China 37°47N 113°38E 306 F7
Pingdingshan China 33°43N 113°27E 306 H7
Pingdong Taiwan 22°39N 120°30E 305 D7
Pingdu China 36°42N 119°59E 307 F10
Pingelly Australia 32°32S 117°5E 333 F2
Pingliang China 35°35N 106°31E 306 G4
Pinglu China 39°31N 112°30E 306 E7
Pingluo China 38°52N 106°30E 306 E4
Pingquan China 41°1N 118°37E 307 D10
Pingrup Australia 33°32S 118°29E 333 F2
P'ingtung Taiwan 22°38N 120°30E 305 D7
Pingwu China 32°25N 104°30E 306 H3
Pingxiang China 22°6N 106°46E 304 D5
Pingyao China 37°12N 112°10E 306 F7
Pingyi China 35°30N 117°35E 307 G9
Pingyin China 36°20N 116°25E 306 F9
Pingyuan China 37°10N 116°22E 306 F9
Pinhal Brazil 22°10S 46°46W 367 A6
Pinheiro Brazil 2°31S 45°5W 365 D9
Pinheiro Machado Brazil 31°34S 53°23W 367 C5
Pinhel Portugal 40°50N 7°1W 293 B2
Pini Indonesia 0°10N 98°40E 308 D1
Pinios → Greece 39°55N 22°41E 295 E10
Pinjarra Australia 32°37S 115°52E 333 F2
Pink Mountain Canada 57°3N 122°52W 342 B4
Pinnacles ⌓ U.S.A. 36°25N 121°12W 350 J5
Pinnaroo Australia 35°17S 140°53E 335 F3

Pinon Hills U.S.A. 34°26N 117°39W 351 L9
Pinos Mexico 22°18N 101°34W 358 C4
Pinos, Mt. U.S.A. 34°49N 119°8W 351 L7
Pinos Pt. U.S.A. 36°38N 121°57W 349 H3
Pinrang Indonesia 3°46S 119°41E 309 E5
Pins, Pte. aux Canada 42°15N 81°51W 354 D3
Pinsk Belarus 52°10N 26°1E 289 B14
Pintados Chile 20°35S 69°40W 364 H5
Pinyug Russia 60°5N 48°0E 290 B8
Pioche U.S.A. 37°56N 114°27W 349 H6
Piombino Italy 42°55N 10°32E 294 C4
Pioner, Ostrov Russia 79°50N 92°0E 301 B10
Piopiotaki = Milford Sd. N.Z. 44°41S 167°47E 331 F1
Piorini, L. Brazil 3°15S 62°35W 364 D6
Piotrków Trybunalski Poland 51°23N 19°43E 289 C10
Pīp Iran 26°45N 60°10E 317 E9
Pipar India 26°25N 73°31E 314 F5
Pipar Road India 26°27N 73°27E 314 F5
Piparia Mad. P., India 22°45N 78°23E 314 H8
Piparia Mad. P., India 21°49N 77°37E 314 J7
Pipestone U.S.A. 44°0N 96°19W 352 D5
Pipestone → Canada 52°53N 89°23W 344 B2
Pipestone Cr. → Canada 49°38N 100°15W 343 D8
Piplan Pakistan 32°17N 71°21E 314 C4
Piploda India 23°37N 74°56E 314 H6
Pipmuacan, Rés. Canada 49°45N 70°30W 345 C5
Pippingarra Australia 20°27S 118°42E 332 D2
Piqua U.S.A. 40°9N 84°15W 353 E11
Piquiri → Brazil 24°3S 54°14W 367 A5
Pir Panjal Range India 32°30N 76°50E 314 C7
Pīr Sohrāb Iran 25°44N 60°54E 317 E9
Piracicaba Brazil 22°45S 47°40W 367 A6
Piracuruca Brazil 3°50S 41°50W 365 D10
Pirae Tahiti 17°31S 149°32W 331 d
Piræus = Pireas Greece 37°57N 23°42E 295 F10
Piraiévs = Pireas Greece 37°57N 23°42E 295 F10
Pirajuí Brazil 21°59S 49°29W 367 A6
Piram I. India 21°36N 72°21E 314 J5
Pirané Argentina 25°42S 59°6W 366 B4
Pirapora Brazil 17°20S 44°56W 365 G10
Pirawa India 24°10N 76°2E 314 G7
Pireas Greece 37°57N 23°42E 295 F10
Pirgos Greece 37°40N 21°27E 295 F9
Piribebuy Paraguay 25°26S 57°2W 366 B4
Pirimapun Indonesia 6°20S 138°24E 309 F9
Pirin Planina Bulgaria 41°40N 23°30E 295 D10
Pírineos = Pyrénées Europe 42°45N 0°18E 292 E4
Piripiri Brazil 4°15S 41°46W 365 D10
Pirlangimpi Australia 11°24S 130°26E 332 B5
Pirmasens Germany 49°12N 7°36E 288 D4
Pirot Serbia 43°9N 22°33E 295 C10
Piru Indonesia 3°4S 128°12E 309 E7
Piru U.S.A. 34°25N 118°48W 351 L8
Pisa Italy 43°43N 10°23E 294 C4
Pisagua Chile 19°40S 70°15W 364 G4
Pisco Peru 13°50S 76°12W 364 F3
Písek Czech Rep. 49°19N 14°10E 288 D8
Pishan China 37°30N 78°33E 304 C2
Pīshīn Iran 26°6N 61°47E 317 E9
Pishin Pakistan 30°35N 67°0E 314 D2
Pishin Lora → Pakistan 29°9N 64°5E 314 E1
Pising Indonesia 5°8S 121°53E 309 F6
Pismo Beach U.S.A. 35°9N 120°38W 351 K6
Pissis, Cerro Argentina 27°45S 68°48W 366 B2
Pissouri Cyprus 34°40N 32°42E 297 E11
Pistóia Italy 43°55N 10°54E 294 C4
Pistol B. Canada 62°25N 92°37W 343 A10
Pisuerga → Spain 41°33N 4°52W 293 B3
Pit → U.S.A. 40°47N 122°6W 348 F2
Pitarpunga, L. Australia 34°24S 143°30E 335 E3
Pitcairn I. Pac. Oc. 25°5S 130°5W 337 K14
Pitch L. Trin. & Tob. 10°12N 61°39W 365 K15
Piteå Sweden 65°20N 21°25E 280 D19
Piteälven → Sweden 65°20N 21°25E 280 D19
Pitești Romania 44°52N 24°54E 289 F13
Pithapuram India 17°10N 82°15E 313 L13
Pithara Australia 30°20S 116°35E 333 F2
Pithoragarh India 29°35N 80°13E 315 E9
Pithoro Pakistan 25°31N 69°23E 314 G3
Pitlochry U.K. 56°42N 3°44W 283 E5
Pitsilia Cyprus 34°55N 33°0E 297 E12
Pitt I. Canada 53°30N 129°50W 342 C3
Pittsburg Calif., U.S.A. 38°2N 121°53W 350 G5
Pittsburg Kans., U.S.A. 37°25N 94°42W 352 G6
Pittsburg Tex., U.S.A. 33°0N 94°59W 356 E7
Pittsburgh U.S.A. 40°26N 79°58W 354 F5
Pittsfield Ill., U.S.A. 39°36N 90°49W 352 F8
Pittsfield Maine, U.S.A. 44°47N 69°23W 353 C19
Pittsfield Mass., U.S.A. 42°27N 73°15W 355 D11
Pittsfield N.H., U.S.A. 43°18N 71°20W 355 C13
Pittston U.S.A. 41°19N 75°47W 355 E9
Pittsworth Australia 27°41S 151°37E 335 D5
Pituri → Australia 22°35S 138°30E 334 C2
Piura Peru 5°15S 80°38W 364 E2
Pixley U.S.A. 35°58N 119°18W 350 K7
Pizhou China 34°44N 116°55E 306 G9
Placentia Canada 47°20N 54°0W 345 C9
Placentia B. Canada 47°0N 54°40W 345 C9
Placerville U.S.A. 38°44N 120°48W 350 G6
Placetas Cuba 22°15N 79°44W 360 B4
Plainfield N.J., U.S.A. 40°37N 74°25W 355 F10
Plainfield Ohio, U.S.A. 40°13N 81°43W 354 F3
Plainfield Vt., U.S.A. 44°17N 72°26W 355 B12
Plains Mont., U.S.A. 47°28N 114°53W 348 C6
Plains Tex., U.S.A. 33°11N 102°50W 356 E3
Plainview Nebr., U.S.A. 42°21N 97°47W 352 D5
Plainview Tex., U.S.A. 34°11N 101°43W 356 D4
Plainwell U.S.A. 42°27N 85°38W 353 D11
Plaistow U.S.A. 42°50N 71°6W 355 D13
Plaka, Akra Greece 35°11N 26°19E 297 D8
Plana Cays Bahamas 22°38N 73°30W 361 B5
Planada U.S.A. 37°16N 120°19W 350 H6
Plano U.S.A. 33°1N 96°42W 356 E6
Plant City U.S.A. 28°1N 82°7W 357 G13
Plaquemine U.S.A. 30°17N 91°14W 356 F9
Plasencia Spain 40°3N 6°8W 293 B2
Plaster City U.S.A. 32°47N 115°51W 351 N11
Plaster Rock Canada 46°53N 67°22W 345 C6
Plastun Russia 44°45N 136°19E 302 B8
Plata, Río de la → S. Amer. 34°45S 57°30W 366 C4
Plátani → Italy 37°23N 13°16E 294 F5
Platanos Greece 35°28N 23°33E 297 D5
Platte U.S.A. 43°23N 98°51W 352 D4
Platte → Mo., U.S.A. 39°16N 94°50W 352 F6
Platte → Nebr., U.S.A. 41°4N 95°53W 352 E6
Platteville U.S.A. 42°44N 90°29W 352 D8
Plattsburgh U.S.A. 44°42N 73°28W 355 B11
Plattsmouth U.S.A. 41°1N 95°53W 352 E6
Plauen Germany 50°30N 12°8E 288 C7
Plavinas Latvia 56°35N 25°46E 281 H21
Playa Blanca Canary Is. 28°55N 13°37W 296 F6
Playa Blanca Sur Canary Is. 28°51N 13°50W 296 F6
Playa de las Americas Canary Is. 28°5N 16°43W 296 F3
Playa de Mogán Canary Is. 27°48N 15°47W 296 G4
Playa del Carmen Mexico 20°37N 87°4W 359 C7
Playa del Inglés Canary Is. 27°45N 15°33W 296 G4
Playa Esmerelda Canary Is. 28°8N 14°16W 296 F5
Playgreen L. Canada 54°0N 98°15W 343 C9
Pleasant Bay Canada 46°51N 60°48W 345 C7
Pleasant Hill U.S.A. 37°57N 122°4W 350 H4
Pleasant Mount U.S.A. 41°44N 75°26W 355 E9
Pleasanton Calif., U.S.A. 37°39N 121°52W 350 H5
Pleasanton Tex., U.S.A. 28°58N 98°29W 356 G5
Pleasantville N.J., U.S.A. 39°24N 74°32W 353 F16
Pleasantville Pa., U.S.A. 41°35N 79°34W 354 E5
Plei Ku Vietnam 13°57N 108°0E 310 F7
Plenty → Australia 23°25S 136°31E 334 C2
Plenty, B. of N.Z. 37°45S 177°0E 331 B6
Plentywood U.S.A. 48°47N 104°34W 348 B11
Plesetsk Russia 62°43N 40°20E 290 B7
Plessisville Canada 46°14N 71°47W 345 C5
Plétipi, L. Canada 51°44N 70°6W 345 B5
Pleven Bulgaria 43°26N 24°37E 295 C11
Plevlja Montenegro 43°21N 19°21E 295 C8
Plevna Canada 44°58N 76°59W 354 B8
Płock Poland 52°32N 19°40E 289 B10
Plöckenstein Germany 48°46N 13°51E 288 D7
Ploiești Romania 44°57N 26°5E 289 F14
Plonge, Lac la Canada 55°8N 107°20W 343 B7
Plovdiv Bulgaria 42°8N 24°44E 295 C11
Plover Cove Res. China 22°28N 114°15E 305 G11
Plum U.S.A. 40°29N 79°47W 354 F5
Plum I. U.S.A. 41°11N 72°12W 355 E12
Plumas U.S.A. 39°45N 120°4W 350 F6
Plummer U.S.A. 47°20N 116°53W 348 C5
Plumtree Zimbabwe 20°27S 27°55E 327 G2
Plungė Lithuania 55°53N 21°59E 281 J19
Plymouth Trin. & Tob. 11°14N 60°48W 365 J16
Plymouth U.K. 50°22N 4°10W 285 G3
Plymouth Calif., U.S.A. 38°29N 120°51W 350 G6
Plymouth Ind., U.S.A. 41°21N 86°19W 352 E10
Plymouth Mass., U.S.A. 41°57N 70°40W 355 E14
Plymouth N.C., U.S.A. 35°52N 76°43W 357 D16
Plymouth N.H., U.S.A. 43°46N 71°41W 355 C13
Plymouth Pa., U.S.A. 41°14N 75°57W 355 E9
Plymouth Wis., U.S.A. 43°45N 87°59W 352 D10
Plympton-Wyoming Canada 42°57N 82°7W 354 D2
Plynlimon = Pumlumon Fawr U.K. 52°28N 3°46W 285 E4
Plyussa Russia 58°28N 29°27E 281 G23
Plzeň Czech Rep. 49°45N 13°22E 288 D7
Po → Italy 44°57N 12°4E 294 B5
Po Hai = Bo Hai China 39°0N 119°0E 307 E10
Po Toi China 22°10N 114°16E 305 G11
Pobeda Russia 65°12N 146°12E 301 C15
Pobedy, Pik Kyrgyzstan 42°0N 79°58E 304 B2
Pocahontas U.S.A. 42°44N 94°40W 352 D6
Pocatello U.S.A. 42°52N 112°27W 348 E7
Pocomoke City U.S.A. 38°5N 75°34W 353 F16
Poços de Caldas Brazil 21°50S 46°33W 367 A6
Podgorica Montenegro 42°30N 19°19E 295 C8
Podilska Vysochyna Ukraine 49°0N 28°0E 289 D14
Podolsk Russia 55°25N 37°30E 290 C6
Podporozhye Russia 60°55N 34°2E 290 B5
Pofadder S. Africa 29°10S 19°22E 328 D2
Pogranichnyy Russia 44°25N 131°24E 302 B5
Poh Indonesia 0°46S 122°51E 309 E6
Pohang S. Korea 36°1N 129°23E 307 F15
Pohjanmaa Finland 62°58N 22°50E 280 E20
Pohnpei Micronesia 6°55N 158°10E 336 G7
Pohri India 25°32N 77°22E 314 G6
Poinsett, C. Antarctica 65°42S 113°18E 277 C8
Point Arena U.S.A. 38°55N 123°41W 350 G3
Point Baker U.S.A. 56°21N 133°37W 342 B2
Point Edward Canada 43°0N 82°30W 344 D3
Point Fortin Trin. & Tob. 10°10N 61°42W 365 K15
Point Hope U.S.A. 68°21N 166°47W 346 a
Point L. Canada 65°15N 113°4W 340 C8
Point Lisas Industrial Estate Trin. & Tob. 10°24N 61°29W 365 K15
Point Pedro Sri Lanka 9°50N 80°15E 312 Q12
Point Pelee △ Canada 41°57N 82°31W 354 E2
Point Pleasant N.J., U.S.A. 40°5N 74°4W 355 F10
Point Pleasant W. Va., U.S.A. 38°51N 82°8W 353 F12
Point Reyes ⌂ U.S.A. 38°10N 122°55W 350 G2
Pointe-à-Pitre Guadeloupe 16°10N 61°32W 360 b
Pointe-au-Pic = La Malbaie Canada 47°40N 70°10W 345 C5
Pointe-Claire Canada 45°26N 73°50W 355 A11
Pointe-Gatineau Canada 45°27N 75°41W 355 A9
Pointe-Noire Congo 4°48S 11°53E 324 E2
Pointe-Noire Guadeloupe 16°14N 61°47W 360 b
Poisonbush Ra. Australia 22°30S 121°30E 332 D3
Poissonnier Pt. Australia 19°57S 119°10E 332 C2
Poitiers France 46°35N 0°20E 292 C4
Poitou France 46°40N 0°10W 292 C3
Pojoaque U.S.A. 35°54N 106°1W 349 J10
Pokaran India 27°0N 71°50E 314 F4
Pokataroo Australia 29°30S 148°36E 335 D4
Pokhara Nepal 28°14N 83°58E 315 E10
Poko Dem. Rep. of the Congo 3°7N 26°52E 326 B2
Pokrovsk Russia 61°29N 129°0E 301 C13
Pola = Pula Croatia 44°54N 13°57E 288 F7
Polacca U.S.A. 35°50N 110°23W 349 J8
Polan Iran 25°30N 61°10E 317 E9
Poland ■ Europe 52°0N 20°0E 289 C10
Polar Bear ⌂ Canada 55°0N 83°45W 344 A2
Polatsk Belarus 55°30N 28°50E 281 J23
Polcura Chile 37°17S 71°43W 366 D1
Polesye = Pripet Marshes Europe 52°10N 28°10E 289 B15
Polevskoy Russia 56°26N 60°11E 290 C11
Police Poland 53°33N 14°33E 288 B8
Police, Pte. Seychelles 4°51S 55°32E 325 b
Poligiros Greece 40°23N 23°25E 295 D10
Polillo Is. Phil. 14°56N 122°0E 309 B6
Polis Cyprus 35°2N 32°26E 297 D11
Polk U.S.A. 41°22N 79°56W 354 E5
Pollachi India 10°35N 77°0E 312 P10
Pollença Spain 39°54N 3°1E 296 B10
Pollença, B. de Spain 39°53N 3°8E 296 B10
Polnovat Russia 63°50N 65°54E 300 C7
Polokwane S. Africa 23°54S 29°25E 329 C4
Polonne Ukraine 50°6N 27°30E 289 C14
Polonnoye = Polonne Ukraine 50°6N 27°30E 289 C14
Polson U.S.A. 47°41N 114°9W 348 C6
Poltava Ukraine 49°35N 34°35E 291 E5
Põltsamaa Estonia 58°39N 25°58E 281 G21
Polunochnoye Russia 60°52N 60°25E 300 C7
Põlva Estonia 58°3N 27°3E 281 G22
Polyarny Russia 69°8N 33°20E 280 B25
Polyarnyye Zori Russia 67°22N 32°30E 280 C25
Polynesia Pac. Oc. 10°0S 162°0W 337 F11
Polynésie française = French Polynesia ☑ Pac. Oc. 20°0S 145°0W 337 J13
Pombal Portugal 39°55N 8°40W 293 C1
Pombia Greece 35°0N 24°51E 297 E6
Pomene Mozam. 22°53S 35°33E 329 C6
Pomeroy Ohio, U.S.A. 39°2N 82°2W 353 F12
Pomeroy Wash., U.S.A. 46°28N 117°36W 348 C5
Pomézia Italy 41°40N 12°30E 294 D5
Pomona Australia 26°22S 152°52E 335 D5
Pomona U.S.A. 34°4N 117°45W 351 L9
Pomorskie, Pojezierze Poland 53°40N 16°37E 289 B9
Pomos Cyprus 35°9N 32°33E 297 D11
Pomos, C. Cyprus 35°10N 32°33E 297 D11
Pompano Beach U.S.A. 26°14N 80°7W 357 H14
Pompeys Pillar U.S.A. 45°59N 107°57W 348 D10
Pompeys Pillar ⌂ U.S.A. 46°0N 108°0W 348 D10
Pompton Lakes U.S.A. 41°0N 74°17W 355 F10
Ponape = Pohnpei Micronesia 6°55N 158°10E 336 G7
Ponask L. Canada 54°0N 92°41W 344 B1
Ponca U.S.A. 42°34N 96°43W 352 D5
Ponca City U.S.A. 36°42N 97°5W 356 C6
Ponce Puerto Rico 18°1N 66°37W 361 d
Ponchatoula U.S.A. 30°26N 90°26W 357 F9
Poncheville, L. Canada 50°10N 76°55W 344 B4
Pond U.S.A. 35°43N 119°20W 351 K7
Pond Inlet Canada 72°40N 77°0W 341 B12
Pondicherry India 11°59N 79°50E 312 P11
Ponds, I. of Canada 53°27N 55°52W 345 B8
Ponferrada Spain 42°32N 6°35W 293 A2
Ponnani India 10°45N 75°59E 312 P9
Ponoka Canada 52°42N 113°40W 342 C6
Ponorogo Indonesia 7°52S 111°27E 309 G14
Ponoy Russia 67°0N 41°13E 290 A7
Ponoy → Russia 66°59N 41°17E 290 A7
Ponta Delgada Azores 37°44N 25°40W 322 a
Ponta do Sol Madeira 32°42N 17°7W 296 D2
Ponta Grossa Brazil 25°7S 50°10W 367 B5
Ponta Pora Brazil 22°20S 55°35W 367 A4
Pontarlier France 46°54N 6°20E 292 C7
Pontchartrain, L. U.S.A. 30°5N 90°5W 357 F9
Ponte do Pungué Mozam. 19°30S 34°33E 327 F3
Ponte Nova Brazil 20°25S 42°54W 367 A7
Ponteix Canada 49°46N 107°29W 343 D7
Pontevedra Spain 42°26N 8°40W 293 A1
Pontiac Ill., U.S.A. 40°53N 88°38W 352 E9
Pontiac Mich., U.S.A. 42°38N 83°18W 353 D12
Pontian Kechil Malaysia 1°29N 103°23E 311 d
Pontianak Indonesia 0°3S 109°15E 308 E3
Pontine Is. = Ponziane, Ísole Italy 40°55N 12°57E 294 D5
Pontine Mts. = Kuzey Anadolu Dağları Turkey 41°0N 36°45E 291 F6
Pontivy France 48°5N 2°58W 292 B2
Pontoise France 49°3N 2°5E 292 B5
Ponton → Canada 58°27N 116°11W 342 B5
Pontypool Canada 44°6N 78°38W 354 B6
Pontypool U.K. 51°42N 3°2W 285 F4
Ponziane, Ísole Italy 40°55N 12°57E 294 D5
Poochera Australia 32°43S 134°51E 335 E1
Poole U.K. 50°43N 1°59W 285 G6
Poole □ U.K. 50°43N 1°59W 285 G6
Poona = Pune India 18°29N 73°57E 312 K8
Pooncarie Australia 33°22S 142°31E 335 E3
Poopelloe L. Australia 31°40S 144°0E 335 E3
Poopó, L. de Bolivia 18°30S 67°35W 364 G5
Popayán Colombia 2°27N 76°36W 364 C3
Poperinge Belgium 50°51N 2°42E 287 D2
Popiltah L. Australia 33°10S 141°42E 335 E3
Popio L. Australia 33°10S 141°52E 335 E3
Poplar U.S.A. 48°7N 105°12W 348 B11
Poplar → Canada 53°0N 97°19W 343 C9
Poplar Bluff U.S.A. 36°46N 90°24W 352 G8
Poplarville U.S.A. 30°51N 89°32W 357 F10
Popocatépetl, Volcán Mexico 19°2N 98°38W 359 D5
Popokabaka Dem. Rep. of the Congo 5°41S 16°40E 324 F3
Poprad Slovak Rep. 49°3N 20°18E 289 D11
Porali → Pakistan 25°58N 66°26E 314 G2
Porbandar India 21°44N 69°43E 314 J3
Porcher I. Canada 53°50N 130°30W 342 C2
Porcupine → Canada 59°11N 104°46W 343 B8
Porcupine → U.S.A. 66°34N 145°19W 346 a
Porcupine Gorge △ Australia 20°22S 144°26E 334 C3
Pordenone Italy 45°57N 12°39E 294 B5
Pori Finland 61°29N 21°48E 280 F19
Porkhov Russia 57°45N 29°38E 281 H23
Porlamar Venezuela 10°57N 63°51W 364 A6
Pormpuraaw Australia 14°59S 141°26E 334 A3
Poronaysk Russia 49°13N 143°0E 301 E15
Poroshiri-Dake Japan 42°41N 142°52E 302 C11
Poroto Mts. Tanzania 9°0S 33°30E 327 D3
Porpoise B. Antarctica 66°0S 127°0E 277 C9
Porreres Spain 39°31N 3°2E 296 B10
Porsangerfjorden Norway 70°40N 25°40E 280 A21
Porsgrunn Norway 59°10N 9°40E 281 G13
Port Alberni Canada 49°14N 124°50W 342 D4
Port Alfred S. Africa 33°36S 26°55E 328 E4
Port Alice Canada 50°20N 127°25W 342 C3
Port Allegany U.S.A. 41°48N 78°17W 354 E6
Port Allen U.S.A. 30°27N 91°12W 356 F9
Port Alma Australia 23°38S 150°53E 334 C5
Port Angeles U.S.A. 48°7N 123°27W 350 B3
Port Antonio Jamaica 18°10N 76°26W 360 a
Port Aransas U.S.A. 27°50N 97°4W 356 H6
Port Arthur Australia 43°7S 147°50E 335 G4
Port Arthur U.S.A. 29°54N 93°56W 356 G8
Port au Choix Canada 50°43N 57°22W 345 B8
Port au Port B. Canada 48°40N 58°50W 345 C8
Port-au-Prince Haiti 18°40N 72°20W 361 C5
Port Augusta Australia 32°30S 137°50E 335 E2
Port Austin U.S.A. 44°3N 83°1W 354 B2
Port Bell Uganda 0°18N 32°35E 326 B3
Port Bergé Vaovao Madag. 15°33S 47°40E 329 B8
Port Blandford Canada 48°20N 54°10W 345 C9
Port Bradshaw Australia 12°30S 137°20E 334 A2
Port Broughton Australia 33°37S 137°56E 335 E2
Port Burwell Canada 42°40N 80°48W 354 D4
Port Canning India 22°23N 88°40E 315 H13
Port-Cartier Canada 50°2N 66°50W 345 B6
Port Chalmers N.Z. 45°49S 170°30E 331 F3
Port Charlotte U.S.A. 26°59N 82°6W 357 H13
Port Chester U.S.A. 41°0N 73°40W 355 F11
Port Clements Canada 53°40N 132°10W 342 C2
Port Clinton U.S.A. 41°31N 82°56W 353 E12
Port Colborne Canada 42°50N 79°10W 354 D5
Port Coquitlam Canada 49°15N 122°45W 350 A4
Port Credit Canada 43°33N 79°35W 354 C5
Port Curtis Australia 23°57S 151°20E 334 C5
Port d'Alcúdia Spain 39°50N 3°7E 296 B10
Port Dalhousie Canada 43°13N 79°16W 354 C5
Port d'Andratx Spain 39°32N 2°23E 296 B9
Port Darwin Australia 12°24S 130°45E 332 B5
Port Darwin Falk. Is. 51°50S 59°0W 368 G5
Port Davey Australia 43°16S 145°55E 335 G4
Port-de-Paix Haiti 19°50N 72°50W 361 C5
Port de Pollença Spain 39°54N 3°4E 296 B10
Port de Sóller Spain 39°48N 2°42E 296 B9
Port Dickson Malaysia 2°30N 101°49E 311 L3
Port Douglas Australia 16°30S 145°30E 334 B4
Port Dover Canada 42°47N 80°12W 354 D4
Port Edward Canada 54°12N 130°10W 342 C2
Port Elgin Canada 44°25N 81°25W 354 B3
Port Elizabeth S. Africa 33°58S 25°40E 328 E4
Port Ellen U.K. 55°38N 6°11W 283 F2
Port Erin I. of Man 54°5N 4°45W 284 C3
Port Essington Australia 11°15S 132°10E 332 B5
Port Ewen U.S.A. 41°54N 73°59W 355 E11
Port Fairy Australia 38°22S 142°12E 335 F3
Port Gamble U.S.A. 47°51N 122°34W 350 C4
Port-Gentil Gabon 0°40S 8°50E 324 E1
Port Germein Australia 33°1S 138°1E 335 E2
Port Gibson U.S.A. 31°58N 90°59W 356 F9
Port Glasgow U.K. 55°56N 4°41W 283 F4
Port Harcourt Nigeria 4°40N 7°10E 322 H7
Port Hardy Canada 50°41N 127°30W 342 C3
Port Harrison = Inukjuak Canada 58°25N 78°15W 341 D12
Port Hawkesbury Canada 45°36N 61°22W 345 C7
Port Hedland Australia 20°25S 118°35E 332 D2
Port Henry U.S.A. 44°3N 73°28W 355 B11
Port Hood Canada 46°0N 61°32W 345 C7
Port Hope Canada 43°56N 78°20W 354 C6
Port Hope U.S.A. 43°57N 82°43W 354 C2
Port Hope Simpson Canada 52°33N 56°18W 345 B8
Port Hueneme U.S.A. 34°7N 119°12W 351 L7
Port Huron U.S.A. 42°58N 82°26W 354 D2
Port Jefferson U.S.A. 40°57N 73°3W 355 F11
Port Jervis U.S.A. 41°22N 74°41W 355 E10
Port Kelang = Pelabuhan Klang Malaysia 3°0N 101°23E 311 L3
Port Kenny Australia 33°10S 134°41E 335 E1
Port Lairge = Waterford Ireland 52°15N 7°8W 282 D4
Port Laoise Ireland 53°2N 7°18W 282 C4
Port Lavaca U.S.A. 28°37N 96°38W 356 G6
Port Leyden U.S.A. 43°35N 75°21W 355 C9
Port Lincoln Australia 34°42S 135°52E 335 E2
Port Loko S. Leone 8°48N 12°46W 322 G3
Port-Louis Guadeloupe 16°28N 61°32W 360 b
Port Louis Mauritius 20°10S 57°30E 325 d
Port MacDonnell Australia 38°5S 140°48E 335 F3
Port McNeill Canada 50°35N 127°6W 342 C3
Port Macquarie Australia 31°25S 152°25E 335 E5
Port Maria Jamaica 18°22N 76°54W 360 a
Port Matilda U.S.A. 40°48N 78°3W 354 F6
Port Mellon Canada 49°32N 123°31W 342 D4
Port-Menier Canada 49°51N 64°15W 345 C7
Port Moody Canada 49°17N 122°51W 350 A4
Port Morant Jamaica 17°54N 76°19W 360 a
Port Moresby Papua N. G. 9°24S 147°8E 330 B7
Port Musgrave Australia 11°55S 141°50E 334 A3
Port Neches U.S.A. 30°0N 93°59W 356 G8
Port Nolloth S. Africa 29°17S 16°52E 328 D2
Port Nouveau-Québec = Kangiqsualujjuaq Canada 58°30N 65°59W 341 D13
Port of Spain Trin. & Tob. 10°40N 61°31W 361 D7
Port Orange U.S.A. 29°9N 80°59W 357 G14
Port Orchard U.S.A. 47°32N 122°38W 350 C4
Port Orford U.S.A. 42°45N 124°30W 348 E1
Port Pegasus N.Z. 47°12S 167°41E 331 G1
Port Perry Canada 44°6N 78°56W 354 B6
Port Phillip B. Australia 38°10S 144°50E 335 F3
Port Pirie Australia 33°10S 138°1E 335 E2
Port Renfrew Canada 48°30N 124°20W 350 B2
Port Roper Australia 14°45S 135°25E 334 A2
Port Rowan Canada 42°40N 80°30W 354 D4
Port Safaga = Bûr Safâga Egypt 26°43N 33°57E 316 E2
Port Said = Bûr Sa'îd Egypt 31°16N 32°18E 323 B12
Port St. Joe U.S.A. 29°49N 85°18W 357 G12
Port St. Johns = Umzimvubu S. Africa 31°38S 29°33E 329 E4
Port St. Lucie U.S.A. 27°18N 80°21W 357 H14
Port Sanilac U.S.A. 43°26N 82°33W 354 C2
Port Severn Canada 44°48N 79°43W 354 B5
Port Shepstone S. Africa 30°44S 30°28E 329 E5
Port Simpson Canada 54°30N 130°20W 342 C2
Port Stanley = Stanley Falk. Is. 51°40S 59°51W 368 G5
Port Stanley Canada 42°40N 81°10W 354 D3
Port Sudan = Bûr Sûdân Sudan 19°32N 37°9E 323 E13
Port Sulphur U.S.A. 29°29N 89°42W 357 G10
Port Talbot U.K. 51°35N 3°47W 285 F4
Port Townsend U.S.A. 48°7N 122°45W 350 B4
Port-Vendres France 42°32N 3°8E 292 E5
Port Vila Vanuatu 17°45S 168°18E 330 C9
Port Vladimir Russia 69°25N 33°6E 280 B25
Port Wakefield Australia 34°12S 138°10E 335 E2
Port Washington U.S.A. 43°23N 87°53W 352 D10
Porta Orientalis Romania 45°6N 22°18E 289 F12
Portacloy Ireland 54°20N 9°46W 282 B2
Portadown U.K. 54°25N 6°27W 282 B5
Portaferry U.K. 54°23N 5°33W 282 B6
Portage Pa., U.S.A. 40°23N 78°41W 354 F6
Portage Wis., U.S.A. 43°33N 89°28W 352 D9
Portage la Prairie Canada 49°58N 98°18W 343 D9
Portageville U.S.A. 36°26N 89°42W 352 G9
Portalegre Portugal 39°19N 7°25W 293 C2
Portales U.S.A. 34°11N 103°20W 349 J12
Portarlington Ireland 53°9N 7°14W 282 C4
Portbou Spain 42°25N 3°9E 293 A7
Porter L. N.W.T., Canada 61°41N 108°5W 343 A7
Porter L. Sask., Canada 56°20N 107°20W 343 B7
Porterville S. Africa 33°0S 19°0E 328 E2
Porterville U.S.A. 36°4N 119°1W 350 J8
Porthcawl U.K. 51°29N 3°42W 285 F4
Porthill U.S.A. 48°59N 116°30W 348 B5
Porthmadog U.K. 52°55N 4°8W 284 E3
Portile de Fier Europe 44°44N 22°30E 289 F12
Portimão Portugal 37°8N 8°32W 293 D1
Portishead U.K. 51°29N 2°46W 285 F5
Portknockie U.K. 57°42N 2°51W 283 D6
Portland N.S.W., Australia 33°20S 150°0E 335 E5
Portland Vic., Australia 38°20S 141°35E 335 F3
Portland Canada 44°42N 76°12W 355 B8
Portland Conn., U.S.A. 41°34N 72°38W 355 E12
Portland Maine, U.S.A. 43°39N 70°16W 353 D18
Portland Mich., U.S.A. 42°52N 84°54W 353 D11
Portland Oreg., U.S.A. 45°32N 122°37W 350 E4
Portland Pa., U.S.A. 40°55N 75°6W 355 F9
Portland Tex., U.S.A. 27°53N 97°20W 356 H6
Portland, I. of U.K. 50°33N 2°26W 285 G5
Portland B. Australia 38°15S 141°45E 335 F3
Portland Bight Jamaica 17°52N 77°5W 360 a
Portland Bill U.K. 50°31N 2°28W 285 G5
Portland Canal U.S.A. 55°56N 130°0W 342 B2
Portland Int. ✕ (PDX) U.S.A. 45°35N 122°36W 350 E4
Portland Pt. Jamaica 17°42N 77°11W 360 a

Portmadoc = Porthmadog U.K. 52°55N 4°8W 284 E3
Portmore Jamaica 17°53N 77°53W 360 a
Porto France 42°16N 8°42E 292 E8
Porto Portugal 41°8N 8°40W 293 B1
Pôrto Alegre Brazil 30°5S 51°10W 367 C5
Porto Cristo Spain 39°33N 3°20E 296 B10
Pôrto de Móz Brazil 1°41S 52°13W 365 D8
Porto Empédocle Italy 37°17N 13°32E 294 F5
Pôrto Esperança Brazil 19°37S 57°29W 364 G7
Pôrto Franco Brazil 6°20S 47°24W 365 E9
Porto Inglês C. Verde Is. 15°21N 23°10W 322 b
Pôrto Mendes Brazil 24°30S 54°15W 367 A5
Porto Moniz Madeira 32°52N 17°11W 296 D2
Pôrto Murtinho Brazil 21°45S 57°55W 364 H7
Pôrto Nacional Brazil 10°40S 48°30W 365 F9
Porto-Novo Benin 6°23N 2°42E 322 G6
Porto Petro Spain 39°22N 3°13E 296 B10
Porto Santo, I. de Madeira 33°45N 16°25W 322 B2
Pôrto São José Brazil 22°43S 53°10W 367 A5
Pôrto Seguro Brazil 16°26S 39°5W 365 G11
Porto Tórres Italy 40°50N 8°24E 294 D3
Pôrto União Brazil 26°10S 51°10W 367 B5
Pôrto Válter Brazil 8°15S 72°40W 364 E4
Porto-Vecchio France 41°35N 9°16E 292 F8
Pôrto Velho Brazil 8°46S 63°54W 364 E6
Portobelo Panama 9°35N 79°42W 360 E4
Portoferráio Italy 42°48N 10°20E 294 C4
Portola U.S.A. 39°49N 120°28W 350 F6
Portoscuso Italy 39°12N 8°24E 294 E3
Portoviejo Ecuador 1°7S 80°28W 364 D2
Portpatrick U.K. 54°51N 5°7W 283 G3
Portree U.K. 57°25N 6°12W 283 D2
Portrush U.K. 55°12N 6°40W 282 A5
Portsmouth Dominica 15°34N 61°27W 361 C7
Portsmouth U.K. 50°48N 1°6W 285 G6
Portsmouth N.H., U.S.A. 43°5N 70°45W 355 C14
Portsmouth Ohio, U.S.A. 38°44N 82°57W 353 F12
Portsmouth R.I., U.S.A. 41°36N 71°15W 355 E13
Portsmouth Va., U.S.A. 36°58N 76°23W 353 G15
Portsmouth □ U.K. 50°48N 1°6W 285 G6
Portsoy U.K. 57°41N 2°41W 283 D6
Portstewart U.K. 55°11N 6°43W 282 A5
Porttipahdan tekojärvi Finland 68°5N 26°40E 280 B22
Portugal ■ Europe 40°0N 8°0W 293 C1
Portumna Ireland 53°6N 8°14W 282 C3
Portville U.S.A. 42°3N 78°20W 354 D6
Porvenir Chile 53°10S 70°16W 368 G2
Posadas Argentina 27°30S 55°50W 367 B4
Posht-e Badam Iran 33°2N 55°23E 317 C7
Poso Indonesia 1°20S 120°55E 309 E6
Posse Brazil 14°4S 46°18W 365 F9
Possession I. Antarctica 72°4S 172°0E 277 D11
Possum Kingdom L. U.S.A. 32°52N 98°26W 356 E5
Post U.S.A. 33°12N 101°23W 356 E4
Post Falls U.S.A. 47°43N 116°57W 348 C5
Postavy = Pastavy Belarus 55°4N 26°50E 281 J22
Poste-de-la-Baleine = Kuujjuarapik Canada 55°20N 77°35W 344 A4
Postmasburg S. Africa 28°18S 23°5E 328 D3
Postojna Slovenia 45°46N 14°12E 288 F8
Poston U.S.A. 34°0N 114°24W 351 M12
Postville Canada 54°54N 59°47W 345 B8
Potchefstroom S. Africa 26°41S 27°7E 328 D4
Poteau U.S.A. 35°3N 94°37W 356 D7
Poteet U.S.A. 29°2N 98°35W 356 G5
Potenza Italy 40°38N 15°48E 294 D6
Poteriteri, L. N.Z. 46°5S 167°10E 331 G1
Potgietersrus = Mokopane S. Africa 24°10S 28°55E 329 C4
Poti Georgia 42°10N 41°38E 291 F7
Potiskum Nigeria 11°39N 11°2E 323 F8
Potomac → U.S.A. 38°0N 76°23W 353 F14
Potosí Bolivia 19°38S 65°50W 364 G5
Potosi Mt. U.S.A. 35°57N 115°29W 351 K11
Pototan Phil. 10°54N 122°38E 309 B6
Potrerillos Chile 26°30S 69°30W 366 B2
Potsdam Germany 52°23N 13°3E 288 B7
Potsdam U.S.A. 44°40N 74°59W 355 B10
Pottersville U.S.A. 43°43N 73°50W 355 C11
Pottstown U.S.A. 40°15N 75°39W 355 F9
Pottsville U.S.A. 40°41N 76°12W 355 F8
Pottuvil Sri Lanka 6°55N 81°50E 312 R12
Pouce Coupé Canada 55°40N 120°10W 342 B4
Poughkeepsie U.S.A. 41°42N 73°56W 355 E11
Poulaphouca Res. Ireland 53°8N 6°30W 282 C5
Poulsbo U.S.A. 47°44N 122°38W 350 C4
Poultney U.S.A. 43°31N 73°14W 355 C11
Poulton-le-Fylde U.K. 53°51N 2°58W 284 D5
Pouso Alegre Brazil 22°14S 45°57W 367 A6
Pouthisat Cambodia 12°34N 103°50E 310 F4
Považská Bystrica Slovak Rep. 49°8N 18°27E 289 D10
Povenets Russia 62°50N 34°50E 290 B5
Poverty B. N.Z. 38°43S 178°2E 331 C7
Póvoa de Varzim Portugal 41°25N 8°46W 293 B1
Povungnituk = Puvirnituq Canada 60°2N 77°10W 341 C12
Powassan Canada 46°5N 79°25W 344 C4
Poway U.S.A. 32°58N 117°2W 351 N9
Powder → U.S.A. 46°45N 105°26W 348 C11
Powder River U.S.A. 43°2N 106°59W 348 E10
Powell U.S.A. 44°45N 108°46W 348 D9
Powell, L. U.S.A. 36°57N 111°29W 349 H8
Powell River Canada 49°50N 124°35W 342 D4
Powers U.S.A. 45°41N 87°32W 352 C10
Powys □ U.K. 52°20N 3°20W 285 E4
Poyang Hu China 29°5N 116°20E 305 D6
Poyarkovo Russia 49°36N 128°41E 301 E13
Poza Rica Mexico 20°33N 97°27W 359 C5
Požarevac Serbia 44°35N 21°18E 295 B9
Poznań Poland 52°25N 16°55E 289 B9
Pozo U.S.A. 35°20N 120°24W 351 K6
Pozo Almonte Chile 20°10S 69°50W 364 H5
Pozo Colorado Paraguay 23°30S 58°45W 366 A4
Pozoblanco Spain 38°23N 4°51W 293 C3
Pozzuoli Italy 40°49N 14°7E 294 D6
Prachin Buri Thailand 14°0N 101°25E 310 E3
Prachuap Khiri Khan Thailand 11°49N 99°48E 311 G2
Prado Brazil 17°20S 39°13W 365 G11
Prague = Praha Czech Rep. 50°4N 14°25E 288 C8
Praha Czech Rep. 50°4N 14°25E 288 C8
Praia C. Verde Is. 15°2N 23°34W 322 b
Prainha Amazonas, Brazil 7°10S 60°30W 364 E6
Prainha Pará, Brazil 1°45S 53°30W 365 D8
Prairie Australia 20°50S 144°35E 334 C3
Prairie City U.S.A. 44°28N 118°43W 348 D4
Prairie Dog Town Fork Red → U.S.A. 34°34N 99°58W 356 D5
Prairie du Chien U.S.A. 43°3N 91°9W 352 D8
Prairies, L. of the Canada 51°16N 101°32W 343 C8
Pran Buri Thailand 12°23N 99°55E 310 F2
Prapat Indonesia 2°41N 98°58E 308 D1
Praslin Seychelles 4°18S 55°45E 325 b
Praso, Akra Greece 35°42N 27°46E 297 D9
Prata Brazil 19°25S 48°54W 365 G9
Pratabpur India 23°28N 83°15E 315 H10
Pratapgarh Raj., India 24°2N 74°40E 314 G6
Pratapgarh Ut. P., India 25°56N 81°59E 315 G9
Prato Italy 43°53N 11°6E 294 C4
Pratt U.S.A. 37°39N 98°44W 352 G4
Prattville U.S.A. 32°28N 86°29W 357 E11
Pravia Spain 43°30N 6°12W 293 A2
Praya Indonesia 8°39S 116°17E 308 F5
Precipice △ Australia 25°18S 150°5E 335 D5
Precordillera Argentina 30°0S 69°1W 366 C2
Preeceville Canada 51°57N 102°40W 343 C8
Preiļi Latvia 56°18N 26°43E 281 H22
Premont U.S.A. 27°22N 98°7W 356 H5
Prentice U.S.A. 45°33N 90°17W 352 C8
Preobrazheniye Russia 42°54N 133°54E 302 C6
Preparis North Channel Ind. Oc. 15°27N 94°5E 313 M18
Preparis South Channel Ind. Oc. 14°33N 93°30E 313 M18
Přerov Czech Rep. 49°28N 17°27E 289 D9
Prescott Canada 44°45N 75°30W 355 B9
Prescott Ariz., U.S.A. 34°33N 112°28W 349 J7
Prescott Ark., U.S.A. 33°48N 93°23W 356 E8
Prescott Valley U.S.A. 34°40N 112°18W 349 J7
Preservation Inlet N.Z. 46°8S 166°35E 331 G1
Presho U.S.A. 43°54N 100°3W 352 D3
Presidencia de la Plaza Argentina 27°0S 59°50W 366 B4
Presidencia Roque Saenz Peña Argentina 26°45S 60°30W 366 B3
Presidente Epitácio Brazil 21°56S 52°6W 365 H8
Presidente Hayes □ Paraguay 24°0S 59°0W 366 A4
Presidente Prudente Brazil 22°5S 51°25W 367 A5
Presidio Mexico 29°29N 104°23W 358 B4
Presidio U.S.A. 29°34N 104°22W 356 G2
Prešov Slovak Rep. 49°0N 21°15E 289 D11
Prespa, L. = Prespansko Jezero Macedonia 40°55N 21°0E 295 D9
Prespansko Jezero Macedonia 40°55N 21°0E 295 D9
Presque I. U.S.A. 42°10N 80°6W 354 D4
Presque Isle U.S.A. 46°41N 68°1W 353 B19
Prestatyn U.K. 53°20N 3°24W 284 D4
Presteigne U.K. 52°17N 3°0W 285 E5
Preston Canada 43°23N 80°21W 354 C4
Preston U.K. 53°46N 2°42W 284 D5
Preston Idaho, U.S.A. 42°6N 111°53W 348 E8
Preston Minn., U.S.A. 43°40N 92°5W 352 D7
Preston, C. Australia 20°51S 116°12E 332 D2
Prestonsburg U.S.A. 37°40N 82°47W 353 G12
Prestwick U.K. 55°29N 4°37W 283 F4
Pretoria S. Africa 25°44S 28°12E 329 D4
Preveza Greece 38°57N 20°45E 295 E9
Prey Veng Cambodia 11°35N 105°29E 311 G5
Pribilof Is. U.S.A. 57°0N 170°0W 346 a
Příbram Czech Rep. 49°41N 14°2E 288 D8
Price U.S.A. 39°36N 110°49W 348 G8
Price I. Canada 52°23N 128°41W 342 C3
Prichard U.S.A. 30°44N 88°5W 357 F10
Priekule Latvia 56°26N 21°35E 281 H19
Prienai Lithuania 54°38N 23°57E 281 J20
Prieska S. Africa 29°40S 22°42E 328 D3
Priest L. U.S.A. 48°35N 116°52W 348 B5
Priest River U.S.A. 48°11N 116°55W 348 B5
Priest Valley U.S.A. 36°10N 120°39W 350 J6
Prievidza Slovak Rep. 48°46N 18°36E 289 D10
Prikaspiyskaya Nizmennost = Caspian Depression Eurasia 47°0N 48°0E 291 E8
Prilep Macedonia 41°21N 21°32E 295 D9
Priluki = Pryluky Ukraine 50°30N 32°24E 291 D5
Prime Seal I. Australia 40°3S 147°43E 335 G4
Primo Tapia Mexico 32°16N 116°54W 351 N10
Primrose L. Canada 54°55N 109°45W 343 C7
Prince Albert Canada 53°15N 105°50W 343 C7
Prince Albert S. Africa 33°12S 22°2E 328 E3
Prince Albert △ Canada 54°0N 106°25W 343 C7
Prince Albert Mts. Antarctica 76°0S 161°30E 277 D11
Prince Albert Pen. Canada 72°30N 116°0W 340 B8
Prince Albert Sd. Canada 70°25N 115°0W 340 B8
Prince Alfred, C. Canada 74°20N 124°40W 341 B7
Prince Charles I. Canada 67°47N 76°12W 341 C12
Prince Charles Mts. Antarctica 72°0S 67°0E 277 D6
Prince Edward Fracture Zone Ind. Oc. 46°0S 35°0E 277 A4
Prince Edward I. □ Canada 46°20N 63°20W 345 C7
Prince Edward Is. Ind. Oc. 46°35S 38°0E 275 G11
Prince Edward Pt. Canada 43°56N 76°52W 354 C8
Prince George Canada 53°55N 122°50W 342 C4
Prince Gustaf Adolf Sea Canada 78°30N 107°0W 341 B9
Prince of Wales, C. U.S.A. 65°36N 168°5W 338 C3
Prince of Wales I. Australia 10°40S 142°10E 334 A3
Prince of Wales I. Canada 73°0N 99°0W 340 B10
Prince of Wales I. U.S.A. 55°47N 132°50W 340 D6
Prince Patrick I. Canada 77°0N 120°0W 341 B8
Prince Regent Inlet Canada 73°0N 90°0W 276 B3
Prince Rupert Canada 54°20N 130°20W 342 C2
Princes Town Trin. & Tob. 10°16N 61°23W 365 K15
Princess Charlotte B. Australia 14°25S 144°0E 334 A3
Princess Elizabeth Trough S. Ocean 64°10S 83°0E 277 C7
Princess May Ranges Australia 15°30S 125°30E 332 C4
Princess Royal I. Canada 53°0N 128°40W 342 C3
Princeton Canada 49°27N 120°30W 342 D4
Princeton Calif., U.S.A. 39°24N 122°1W 350 F4
Princeton Ill., U.S.A. 41°23N 89°28W 352 E9
Princeton Ind., U.S.A. 38°21N 87°34W 352 F10
Princeton Ky., U.S.A. 37°7N 87°53W 352 G10
Princeton Mo., U.S.A. 40°24N 93°35W 352 E7
Princeton N.J., U.S.A. 40°21N 74°39W 355 F10
Princeton W. Va., U.S.A. 37°22N 81°6W 353 G13
Principe, I. de Atl. Oc. 1°37N 7°27E 320 F4
Principe da Beira Brazil 12°20S 64°30W 364 F6
Prineville U.S.A. 44°18N 120°51W 348 D3
Prins Harald Kyst Antarctica 70°0S 35°1E 277 D4
Prinsesse Astrid Kyst Antarctica 70°45S 12°30E 277 D3
Prinsesse Ragnhild Kyst Antarctica 70°15S 27°30E 277 D4
Prinzapolca Nic. 13°20N 83°35W 360 D3
Priozersk Russia 61°2N 30°7E 280 F24
Pripet = Prypyat → Europe 51°20N 30°15E 289 C16
Pripet Marshes Europe 52°10N 28°10E 289 B15
Pripyat Marshes = Pripet Marshes Europe 52°10N 28°10E 289 B15
Pripyats = Prypyat → Europe 51°20N 30°15E 289 C16
Priština Serbia 42°40N 21°13E 295 C9
Privas France 44°45N 4°37E 292 D6
Privolzhskaya Vozvyshennost Russia 51°0N 46°0E 291 D8
Privolzhskiy □ Russia 56°0N 50°0E 300 D6
Prizren Serbia 42°13N 20°45E 295 C9
Probolinggo Indonesia 7°46S 113°13E 309 G15
Proctor U.S.A. 43°40N 73°2W 355 C11
Proddatur India 14°45N 78°30E 312 M11
Prodhromos Cyprus 34°57N 32°50E 297 E11
Profondeville Belgium 50°23N 4°52E 287 D4
Progreso Coahuila, Mexico 27°28N 100°59W 358 B4
Progreso Yucatán, Mexico 21°20N 89°40W 359 C7
Progress Antarctica 66°22S 76°22E 277 C12
Prokopyevsk Russia 54°0N 86°45E 300 D9
Prokuplje Serbia 43°16N 21°36E 295 C9
Prome Burma 18°49N 95°13E 313 K19
Prophet → Canada 58°48N 122°40W 342 B4
Prophet River Canada 58°6N 122°43W 342 B4
Propriá Brazil 10°13S 36°51W 365 F11
Propriano France 41°41N 8°52E 292 F8
Proserpine Australia 20°21S 148°36E 334 J6
Prosna → Poland 52°6N 17°44E 289 B9
Prospect U.S.A. 43°18N 75°9W 355 C9
Prosser U.S.A. 46°12N 119°46W 348 C4
Prostějov Czech Rep. 49°30N 17°9E 289 D9
Proston Australia 26°8S 151°32E 335 D5
Provence France 43°40N 5°46E 292 E6
Providence Ky., U.S.A. 37°24N 87°46W 352 G10
Providence R.I., U.S.A. 41°49N 71°24W 355 E13
Providence Bay Canada 45°41N 82°15W 344 C3
Providence Mts. U.S.A. 35°10N 115°15W 351 K11
Providencia, I. de Colombia 13°25N 81°26W 360 D3
Provideniya Russia 64°23N 173°18W 301 C19
Provins France 48°33N 3°15E 292 B5
Provo U.S.A. 40°14N 111°39W 348 F8
Provost Canada 52°25N 110°20W 343 C6
Prudhoe Bay U.S.A. 70°18N 148°22W 346 a
Prudhoe I. Australia 21°19S 149°41E 334 C4
Prud'homme Canada 52°20N 105°54W 343 C7
Pruszków Poland 52°9N 20°49E 289 B11
Prut → Romania 45°28N 28°10E 289 F15
Pruzhany Belarus 52°33N 24°28E 289 B13
Prydz B. Antarctica 69°0S 74°0E 277 C6
Pryluky Ukraine 50°30N 32°24E 291 D5
Pryor U.S.A. 36°19N 95°19W 356 C7
Prypyat → Europe 51°20N 30°15E 289 C16
Przemyśl Poland 49°50N 22°45E 289 D12
Przhevalsk = Karakol Kyrgyzstan 42°30N 78°20E 300 E8
Psara Greece 38°37N 25°38E 295 E11
Psiloritis, Oros Greece 35°15N 24°45E 297 D6
Psira Greece 35°12N 25°52E 297 D7
Pskov Russia 57°50N 28°25E 281 H23
Ptich = Ptsich → Belarus 52°9N 28°52E 289 B15
Ptichia = Vido Greece 39°38N 19°55E 297 A3
Ptolemaida Greece 40°30N 21°43E 295 D9
Ptsich → Belarus 52°9N 28°52E 289 B15
Pu Xian China 36°24N 111°6E 306 F6
Pua Thailand 19°11N 100°55E 310 C3
Puán Argentina 37°30S 62°45W 366 D3
Pu'apu'a Samoa 13°34S 172°9W 331 b
Pucallpa Peru 8°25S 74°30W 364 E4
Puch'on = Bucheon S. Korea 37°28N 126°45E 307 F14
Pudasjärvi Finland 65°23N 26°53E 280 D22
Pudozh Russia 61°48N 36°32E 290 B6
Puducherry = Pondicherry India 11°59N 79°50E 312 P11
Pudukkottai India 10°28N 78°47E 312 P11
Puebla Mexico 19°3N 98°12W 359 D5
Puebla □ Mexico 18°50N 98°0W 359 D5
Pueblo U.S.A. 38°16N 104°37W 348 G11
Pueblo Hundido Chile 26°20S 70°5W 366 B1
Puelches Argentina 38°5S 65°51W 366 D2
Puelén Argentina 37°32S 67°38W 366 D2
Puente Alto Chile 33°32S 70°35W 366 C1
Puente-Genil Spain 37°22N 4°47W 293 D3
Puerca, Pta. Puerto Rico 18°13N 65°36W 361 d
Puerco → U.S.A. 34°22N 107°50W 349 J10
Puerto Aisén Chile 45°27S 73°0W 368 F2
Puerto Ángel Mexico 15°40N 96°29W 359 D5
Puerto Arista Mexico 15°56N 93°48W 359 D6
Puerto Armuelles Panama 8°20N 82°51W 360 E3
Puerto Ayacucho Venezuela 5°40N 67°35W 364 B5
Puerto Barrios Guatemala 15°40N 88°32W 360 C2
Puerto Bermejo Argentina 26°55S 58°34W 366 B4
Puerto Bermúdez Peru 10°20S 74°58W 364 F4
Puerto Bolívar Ecuador 3°19S 79°55W 364 D3
Puerto Cabello Venezuela 10°28N 68°1W 364 A5
Puerto Cabezas Nic. 14°0N 83°30W 360 D3
Puerto Cabo Gracias á Dios Nic. 15°0N 83°10W 360 D3
Puerto Carreño Colombia 6°12N 67°22W 364 B5
Puerto Castilla Honduras 16°0N 86°0W 360 C2
Puerto Chicama Peru 7°45S 79°20W 364 E3
Puerto Coig Argentina 50°54S 69°15W 368 G3
Puerto Cortés Costa Rica 8°55N 84°0W 360 E3
Puerto Cortés Honduras 15°51N 88°0W 360 C2
Puerto Cumarebo Venezuela 11°29N 69°30W 364 A5
Puerto de Alcudia = Port d'Alcúdia Spain 39°50N 3°7E 296 B10
Puerto de Cabrera Spain 39°8N 2°56E 296 B9
Puerto de Gran Tarajal Canary Is. 28°13N 14°1W 296 F5
Puerto de la Cruz Canary Is. 28°24N 16°32W 296 F3
Puerto de los Angeles ⌂ Mexico 23°39N 105°45W 358 C3
Puerto de Pozo Negro Canary Is. 28°19N 13°55W 296 F6
Puerto de Sóller = Port de Sóller Spain 39°48N 2°42E 296 B9
Puerto del Carmen Canary Is. 28°55N 13°38W 296 F6
Puerto del Rosario Canary Is. 28°30N 13°52W 296 F6
Puerto Deseado Argentina 47°55S 66°0W 368 F3
Puerto Escondido Mexico 15°50N 97°3W 359 D5
Puerto Heath Bolivia 12°34S 68°39W 364 F5
Puerto Inírida Colombia 3°53N 67°52W 364 C5
Puerto Juárez Mexico 21°11N 86°49W 359 C7
Puerto La Cruz Venezuela 10°13N 64°38W 364 A6
Puerto Leguízamo Colombia 0°12S 74°46W 364 D4
Puerto Libertad Mexico 29°55N 112°43W 358 B2
Puerto Limón Colombia 3°23N 73°30W 364 C4
Puerto Lobos Argentina 42°0S 65°3W 368 E3
Puerto Madryn Argentina 42°48S 65°4W 368 E3
Puerto Maldonado Peru 12°30S 69°10W 364 F5
Puerto Manatí Cuba 21°22N 76°50W 360 B4
Puerto Montt Chile 41°28S 73°0W 368 E2
Puerto Morazán Nic. 12°51N 87°11W 360 D2
Puerto Morelos Mexico 20°50N 86°52W 359 C7
Puerto Natales Chile 51°45S 72°15W 368 G2
Puerto Padre Cuba 21°13N 76°35W 360 B4
Puerto Páez Venezuela 6°13N 67°28W 364 B5
Puerto Peñasco Mexico 31°20N 113°33W 358 A2
Puerto Pinasco Paraguay 22°36S 57°50W 366 A4
Puerto Plata Dom. Rep. 19°48N 70°45W 361 C5
Puerto Pollensa = Port de Pollença Spain 39°54N 3°4E 296 B10
Puerto Princesa Phil. 9°46N 118°45E 309 C5
Puerto Quepos Costa Rica 9°29N 84°6W 360 E3
Puerto Rico Canary Is. 27°47N 15°42W 296 G4
Puerto Rico ☑ W. Indies 18°15N 66°45W 361 d
Puerto Rico Trench Atl. Oc. 19°50N 66°0W 361 C6
Puerto San Julián Argentina 49°18S 67°43W 368 F3
Puerto Sastre Paraguay 22°2S 57°55W 366 A4
Puerto Suárez Bolivia 18°58S 57°52W 364 G7
Puerto Vallarta Mexico 20°37N 105°15W 358 C3
Puerto Varas Chile 41°19S 72°59W 368 E2
Puerto Wilches Colombia 7°21N 73°54W 364 B4
Puertollano Spain 38°43N 4°7W 293 C3
Pueu Tahiti 17°44S 149°13W 331 d
Pueyrredón, L. Argentina 47°20S 72°0W 368 F2
Puffin I. Ireland 51°50N 10°24W 282 E1
Pugachev Russia 52°0N 48°49E 290 D8
Pugal India 28°30N 72°48E 314 E5
Puge Tanzania 4°45S 33°11E 326 C3
Puget Sound U.S.A. 47°50N 122°30W 348 C2
Pugŏdong N. Korea 42°5N 130°0E 307 C16
Pugu Tanzania 6°55S 39°4E 326 D4
Pūgūnzī Iran 25°49N 59°10E 317 E8
Puig Major Spain 39°48N 2°47E 296 B9
Puigcerdà Spain 42°24N 1°50E 293 A6
Puigpunyent Spain 39°38N 2°32E 296 B9
Pujon-ho N. Korea 40°35N 127°35E 307 D14
Pukaki, L. N.Z. 44°4S 170°1E 331 F3
Pukapuka Cook Is. 10°53S 165°49W 337 J11
Pukaskwa △ Canada 48°20N 86°0W 344 C2
Pukatawagan Canada 55°45N 101°20W 343 B8
Pukchin N. Korea 40°12N 125°45E 307 D13
Pukch'ŏng N. Korea 40°14N 128°10E 307 D15
Pukekohe N.Z. 37°12S 174°55E 331 B5
Pukhrayan India 26°14N 79°51E 315 F8
Pula Croatia 44°54N 13°57E 288 F7
Pulacayo Bolivia 20°25S 66°41W 364 H5
Pulai Malaysia 1°20N 103°31E 311 d
Pulandian China 39°25N 121°58E 307 E11
Pulaski N.Y., U.S.A. 43°34N 76°8W 355 C8
Pulaski Tenn., U.S.A. 35°12N 87°2W 357 D11
Pulaski Va., U.S.A. 37°3N 80°47W 353 G13
Pulau → Indonesia 5°50S 138°15E 309 F9
Puławy Poland 51°23N 21°59E 289 C11
Pulga U.S.A. 39°48N 121°29W 350 F5
Pulicat L. India 13°40N 80°15E 312 N12
Pullman U.S.A. 46°44N 117°10W 348 C5
Pulog, Mt. Phil. 16°40N 120°50E 309 A6
Pułtusk Poland 52°43N 21°6E 289 B11
Pumlumon Fawr U.K. 52°28N 3°46W 285 E4
Puná, I. Ecuador 2°55S 80°5W 364 D2
Punaauia Tahiti 17°37S 149°34W 331 d
Punakaiki N.Z. 42°7S 171°20E 331 E3
Punakha Dzong Bhutan 27°42N 89°52E 313 F16
Punasar India 27°6N 73°6E 314 F5
Punata Bolivia 17°32S 65°50W 364 G5
Punch India 33°48N 74°4E 315 C6
Punch → Pakistan 33°12N 73°40E 314 C5
Punda Maria S. Africa 22°40S 31°5E 329 C5
Pune India 18°29N 73°57E 312 K8
P'ungsan N. Korea 40°50N 128°9E 307 D15
Pungue, Ponte de Mozam. 19°0S 34°0E 327 F3
Punjab □ India 31°0N 76°0E 314 D7
Punjab □ Pakistan 32°0N 72°30E 314 E6
Puno Peru 15°55S 70°3W 364 G4
Punpun → India 25°31N 85°18E 315 G11
Punta, Cerro de Puerto Rico 18°10N 66°37W 361 d
Punta Alta Argentina 38°53S 62°4W 368 D4
Punta Arenas Chile 53°10S 71°0W 368 G2
Punta de Díaz Chile 28°0S 70°45W 366 B1
Punta del Hidalgo Canary Is. 28°33N 16°19W 296 F3
Punta Gorda Belize 16°10N 88°45W 359 D7
Punta Gorda U.S.A. 26°56N 82°3W 357 H13
Punta Prieta Mexico 28°58N 114°17W 358 B2
Punta Prima Spain 39°48N 4°16E 296 B11
Puntarenas Costa Rica 10°0N 84°50W 360 E3
Punto Fijo Venezuela 11°50N 70°13W 364 A4
Punxsatawney U.S.A. 40°57N 78°59W 354 F6
Pupuan Indonesia 8°19S 115°0E 309 J18
Puquio Peru 14°45S 74°10W 364 F4
Pur → Russia 67°31N 77°55E 300 C8
Puracé, Vol. Colombia 2°21N 76°23W 364 C3
Puralia = Puruliya India 23°17N 86°24E 315 H12
Puranpur India 28°31N 80°9E 315 E9
Purbeck, Isle of U.K. 50°39N 1°59W 285 G5
Purcell U.S.A. 35°1N 97°22W 356 D6
Purcell Mts. Canada 49°55N 116°15W 342 D5
Puri India 19°50N 85°58E 313 K14
Purmerend Neths. 52°32N 4°58E 287 B4
Purnia India 25°45N 87°31E 315 G12
Purnululu △ Australia 17°20S 128°20E 332 C4
Pursat = Pouthisat Cambodia 12°34N 103°50E 310 F4
Purukcahu Indonesia 0°35S 114°35E 308 E4
Puruliya India 23°17N 86°24E 315 H12
Purus → Brazil 3°42S 61°28W 364 D6
Puruvesi Finland 61°50N 29°30E 280 F23
Purvis U.S.A. 31°9N 89°25W 357 F10
Purwa India 26°28N 80°47E 315 F9
Purwakarta Indonesia 6°35S 107°29E 309 G12
Purwo, Tanjung Indonesia 8°44S 114°21E 309 K18
Purwodadi Indonesia 7°7S 110°55E 309 G14
Purwokerto Indonesia 7°25S 109°14E 309 G13
Puryŏng N. Korea 42°5N 129°43E 307 C15
Pusa India 25°59N 85°41E 315 G11
Pusan = Busan S. Korea 35°5N 129°0E 307 G15
Pushkin Russia 59°45N 30°25E 281 G24
Pushkino Russia 51°16N 47°0E 291 D8
Putahow L. Canada 59°54N 100°40W 343 B8
Putao Burma 27°28N 97°30E 313 F20
Putaruru N.Z. 38°2S 175°50E 331 C5
Putignano Italy 40°51N 17°7E 294 D7
Puting, Tanjung Indonesia 3°31S 111°46E 308 E4
Putnam U.S.A. 41°55N 71°55W 355 E13
Putorana, Gory Russia 69°0N 95°0E 301 C10
Putrajaya Malaysia 2°55N 101°40E 311 L3
Puttalam Sri Lanka 8°1N 79°55E 312 Q11

Puttgarden Germany 54°30N 11°10E 288 A6
Putumayo → S. Amer. 3°7S 67°58W 364 D5
Putussibau Indonesia 0°50N 112°56E 308 D4
Puvirnituq Canada 60°2N 77°10W 341 C12
Puy-de-Dôme France 45°46N 2°57E 292 D5
Puyallup U.S.A. 47°12N 122°18W 350 C4
Puyang China 35°40N 115°1E 306 G8
Pūzeh Rīg Iran 27°20N 58°40E 317 E8
Pwani □ Tanzania 7°0S 39°0E 326 D4
Pweto Dem. Rep. of the Congo 8°25S 28°51E 327 D2
Pwllheli U.K. 52°53N 4°25W 284 E3
Pya-ozero Russia 66°5N 30°58E 280 C24
Pyapon Burma 16°20N 95°40E 313 L19
Pyasina → Russia 73°30N 87°0E 301 B9
Pyatigorsk Russia 44°2N 43°6E 291 F7
Pyè = Prome Burma 18°49N 95°13E 313 K19
Pyeongtaek S. Korea 37°1N 127°4E 307 F14
Pyetrikaw Belarus 52°11N 28°29E 289 B15
Pyhäjoki Finland 64°28N 24°14E 280 D21
Pyinmana Burma 19°45N 96°12E 313 K20
Pyla, C. Cyprus 34°56N 33°51E 297 E12
Pymatuning Res. U.S.A. 41°30N 80°28W 354 E4
Pyŏktong N. Korea 40°50N 125°50E 307 D13
Pyŏnggang N. Korea 38°24N 127°17E 307 E14
P'yŏngsong N. Korea 39°14N 125°52E 307 E13
P'yŏngyang N. Korea 39°0N 125°30E 307 E13
Pyote U.S.A. 31°32N 103°8W 356 F3
Pyramid L. U.S.A. 40°1N 119°35W 348 F4
Pyramid Pk. U.S.A. 36°25N 116°37W 351 J10
Pyramids Egypt 29°58N 31°9E 323 C12
Pyrénées Europe 42°45N 0°18E 292 E4
Pyu Burma 18°30N 96°28E 313 K20

Q

Qaanaaq Greenland 77°40N 69°0W 276 B4
Qachasnek S. Africa 30°6S 28°42E 329 E4
Qa'el Jafr Jordan 30°20N 36°25E 318 E5
Qa'emābād Iran 31°44N 60°2E 317 D9
Qā'emshahr Iran 36°30N 52°53E 317 B7
Qagan Nur China 43°30N 114°55E 306 C8
Qahar Youyi Zhongqi China 41°12N 112°40E 306 D7
Qahremānshahr = Kermānshāh Iran 34°23N 47°0E 316 C5
Qaidam Pendi China 37°0N 95°0E 304 C4
Qajarīyeh Iran 31°1N 48°22E 317 D6
Qala, Ras il Malta 36°2N 14°20E 297 C1
Qala-i-Jadid = Spīn Būldak Afghan. 31°1N 66°25E 314 D2
Qala Point = Qala, Ras il Malta 36°2N 14°20E 297 C1
Qala Viala Pakistan 30°49N 67°17E 314 D2
Qala Yangi Afghan. 34°20N 66°30E 314 B2
Qal'at al Akhḍar Si. Arabia 28°4N 37°9E 316 E3
Qal'at Dīzah Iraq 36°11N 45°7E 316 B5
Qal'at Ṣāliḥ Iraq 31°31N 47°16E 316 D5
Qal'at Sukkar Iraq 31°51N 46°5E 316 D5
Qamani'tuaq = Baker Lake Canada 64°20N 96°3W 340 C10
Qamdo China 31°15N 97°6E 304 C4
Qamea Fiji 16°45S 179°45W 331 a
Qamruddin Karez Pakistan 31°45N 68°20E 314 D3
Qandahār = Kandahār Afghan. 31°32N 65°43E 312 D4
Qandahār = Kandahār □ Afghan. 31°0N 65°0E 312 D4
Qapān Iran 37°40N 55°47E 317 B7
Qapshaghay Kazakhstan 43°51N 77°14E 300 E8
Qaqortoq Greenland 60°43N 46°0W 276 C5
Qara Qash → China 35°0N 78°30E 315 B8
Qarabutaq Kazakhstan 49°59N 60°14E 300 E7
Qaraghandy Kazakhstan 49°50N 73°10E 300 E8
Qaraghayly Kazakhstan 49°26N 76°0E 300 E8
Qārah Si. Arabia 29°55N 40°3E 316 D4
Qarataū Kazakhstan 43°30N 69°30E 300 E7
Qarataū Zhambyl, Kazakhstan 43°10N 70°28E 300 E8
Qarazhal Kazakhstan 48°2N 70°49E 300 E8
Qardho = Gardo Somali Rep. 9°30N 49°6E 319 F4
Qareh → Iran 39°25N 47°22E 316 B5
Qareh Tekān Iran 36°38N 49°29E 317 B6
Qarnein U.A.E. 24°56N 52°52E 317 E7
Qarqan He → China 39°30N 88°30E 304 C3
Qarqaraly Kazakhstan 49°26N 75°30E 300 E8
Qarshi Uzbekistan 38°53N 65°48E 300 F7
Qartabā Lebanon 34°4N 35°50E 318 A4
Qaryat al Gharab Iraq 31°27N 44°48E 316 D5
Qaryat al 'Ulyā Si. Arabia 27°33N 47°42E 316 E5
Qasr 'Amra Jordan 31°48N 36°35E 316 D3
Qaṣr-e Qand Iran 26°15N 60°45E 317 E9
Qasr-e Shīrīn Iran 34°31N 45°35E 316 C5
Qasr Farâfra Egypt 27°0N 28°1E 323 C11
Qatanā Syria 33°26N 36°4E 318 B5
Qatar ■ Asia 25°30N 51°15E 317 E6
Qatlīsh Iran 37°50N 57°19E 317 B8
Qattâra, Munkhafed el Egypt 29°30N 27°30E 323 C11
Qattâra Depression = Qattâra, Munkhafed el Egypt 29°30N 27°30E 323 C11
Qausuittuq = Resolute Canada 74°42N 94°54W 341 B10
Qawām al Ḥamzah = Al Ḥamzah Iraq 31°43N 44°58E 316 D5
Qāyen Iran 33°40N 59°10E 317 C8
Qazaqstan = Kazakhstan ■ Asia 50°0N 70°0E 300 E7
Qazimämmäd Azerbaijan 40°3N 49°0E 317 A6
Qazvīn Iran 36°15N 50°0E 317 B6
Qazvīn □ Iran 36°20N 50°0E 317 B6
Qena Egypt 26°10N 32°43E 323 C12
Qeqertarsuaq Greenland 69°15N 53°38W 276 C5
Qeqertarsuaq Greenland 69°45N 53°30W 338 C14
Qeshlāq Iran 34°55N 46°28E 316 C5
Qeshm Iran 26°55N 56°10E 317 E8
Qeys Iran 26°32N 53°58E 317 E7
Qezel Owzen → Iran 36°45N 49°22E 317 B6
Qezi'ot Israel 30°52N 34°26E 318 E3
Qi Xian China 34°40N 114°48E 306 G8
Qian Gorlos China 45°5N 124°42E 307 B13
Qian Hai China 22°32N 113°54E 305 F10
Qian Xian China 34°31N 108°15E 306 G5
Qianshan China 22°15N 113°31E 305 G10
Qianyang China 34°40N 107°8E 306 G4
Qi'ao China 22°25N 113°39E 305 G10
Qi'ao Dao China 22°25N 113°38E 305 G10
Qiemo China 38°8N 85°32E 304 C3
Qijiaojing China 43°28N 91°36E 304 B4
Qikiqtarjuaq Canada 67°33N 63°0W 341 C13
Qila Saifullāh Pakistan 30°45N 68°17E 314 D3
Qilian Shan China 38°30N 96°0E 304 C4
Qin He → China 35°1N 113°22E 306 G7
Qin Ling = Qinling Shandi China 33°50N 108°10E 306 H5
Qin'an China 34°48N 105°40E 306 G3
Qing Xian China 38°35N 116°45E 306 E9
Qingcheng China 37°15N 117°40E 307 F9
Qingdao China 36°5N 120°20E 307 F11
Qingfeng China 35°52N 115°8E 306 G8
Qinghai □ China 36°0N 98°0E 304 C4
Qinghai Hu China 36°40N 100°10E 304 C5
Qinghecheng China 41°28N 124°15E 307 D13
Qinghemen China 41°48N 121°25E 307 D11
Qingjian China 37°8N 110°8E 306 F6
Qingjiang = Huaiyin China 33°30N 119°2E 307 H10
Qingshui China 34°48N 106°8E 306 G4
Qingshuihe China 39°55N 111°35E 306 E6
Qingtongxia Shuiku China 37°50N 105°58E 306 F3
Qingxu China 37°34N 112°22E 306 F7
Qingyang China 36°2N 107°55E 306 F4
Qingyuan China 42°10N 124°55E 307 C13
Qingyun China 37°45N 117°20E 307 F9
Qinhuangdao China 39°56N 119°30E 307 E10
Qinling Shandi China 33°50N 108°10E 306 H5
Qinshui China 35°40N 112°8E 306 G7
Qinyang = Jiyuan China 35°7N 112°57E 306 G7
Qinyuan China 36°29N 112°20E 306 F7
Qinzhou China 21°58N 108°38E 304 D5
Qionghai China 19°15N 110°26E 310 C8
Qiongzhou Haixia China 20°10N 110°15E 310 B8
Qiqihar China 47°26N 124°0E 305 B7
Qira China 37°0N 80°48E 304 C3
Qiraîya, W. → Egypt 30°27N 34°0E 318 E3
Qiryat Ata Israel 32°47N 35°6E 318 C4
Qiryat Gat Israel 31°32N 34°46E 318 D3
Qiryat Mal'akhi Israel 31°44N 34°44E 318 D3
Qiryat Shemona Israel 33°13N 35°35E 318 B4
Qiryat Yam Israel 32°51N 35°4E 318 C4
Qishan China 34°25N 107°38E 306 G4
Qitai China 44°2N 89°35E 304 B3
Qixia China 37°17N 120°52E 307 F11
Qızılağac Körfäzi Azerbaijan 39°9N 49°0E 317 B6
Qojūr Iran 36°12N 47°55E 316 B5
Qom Iran 34°40N 51°0E 317 C6
Qom □ Iran 34°40N 51°0E 317 C6
Qomolangma Feng = Everest, Mt. Nepal 28°5N 86°58E 315 E12
Qomsheh Iran 32°0N 51°55E 317 D6
Qoqon = Qŭqon Uzbekistan 40°31N 70°56E 300 E8
Qoraqalpoghistan □ Uzbekistan 43°0N 58°0E 300 E6
Qostanay Kazakhstan 53°10N 63°35E 300 D7
Quabbin Res. U.S.A. 42°20N 72°20W 355 D12
Quairading Australia 32°0S 117°21E 333 F2
Quakertown U.S.A. 40°26N 75°21W 355 F9
Qualicum Beach Canada 49°22N 124°26W 342 D4
Quambatook Australia 35°49S 143°34E 335 F3
Quambone Australia 30°57S 147°53E 335 E4
Quamby Australia 20°22S 140°17E 334 C3
Quan Long = Ca Mau Vietnam 9°7N 105°8E 311 H5
Quanah U.S.A. 34°18N 99°44W 356 D5
Quang Ngai Vietnam 15°13N 108°58E 310 E7
Quang Tri Vietnam 16°45N 107°13E 310 D6
Quang Yen Vietnam 20°56N 106°52E 310 B6
Quantock Hills U.K. 51°8N 3°10W 285 F4
Quanzhou China 24°55N 118°34E 305 D6
Qu'Appelle → Canada 50°33N 103°53W 343 C8
Quaqtaq Canada 60°55N 69°40W 341 C13
Quaraí Brazil 30°15S 56°20W 366 C4
Quartu Sant'Élena Italy 39°15N 9°10E 294 E3
Quartzsite U.S.A. 33°40N 114°13W 351 M12
Quatre Bornes Mauritius 20°15S 57°28E 325 d
Quatsino Sd. Canada 50°25N 127°58W 342 C3
Quba Azerbaijan 41°21N 48°32E 291 F8
Qūchān Iran 37°10N 58°27E 317 B8
Queanbeyan Australia 35°17S 149°14E 335 F4
Québec Canada 46°52N 71°13W 345 C5
Québec □ Canada 48°0N 74°0W 345 C6
Quebrada del Condorito △ Argentina 31°49S 64°40W 366 C3
Queen Alexandra Ra. Antarctica 85°0S 170°0E 277 E11
Queen Charlotte City Canada 53°15N 132°2W 342 C2
Queen Charlotte Is. Canada 53°20N 132°10W 342 C2
Queen Charlotte Sd. Canada 51°0N 128°0W 342 C3
Queen Charlotte Strait Canada 50°45N 127°10W 342 C3
Queen Elizabeth △ Uganda 0°0 30°0E 326 C3
Queen Elizabeth ⌂ U.K. 56°7N 4°30W 283 E4
Queen Elizabeth Is. Canada 76°0N 95°0W 341 B10
Queen Mary Land Antarctica 70°0S 95°0E 277 D7
Queen Maud G. Canada 68°15N 102°30W 340 C9
Queen Maud Land = Dronning Maud Land Antarctica 72°30S 12°0E 277 D3
Queen Maud Mts. Antarctica 86°0S 160°0W 277 E13
Queens Chan. Australia 15°0S 129°30E 332 C4
Queenscliff Australia 38°16S 144°39E 335 F3
Queensland □ Australia 22°0S 142°0E 334 C3
Queenstown Australia 42°4S 145°35E 335 G4
Queenstown N.Z. 45°1S 168°40E 331 F2
Queenstown Singapore 1°18N 103°48E 311 d
Queenstown S. Africa 31°52S 26°52E 328 E4
Queets U.S.A. 47°32N 124°19W 350 C2
Queguay Grande → Uruguay 32°9S 58°9W 366 C4
Queimadas Brazil 11°0S 39°38W 365 F11
Quelimane Mozam. 17°53S 36°58E 327 F4
Quellón Chile 43°7S 73°37W 368 E2
Quelpart = Jeju-do S. Korea 33°29N 126°34E 307 H14
Quemado N. Mex., U.S.A. 34°20N 108°30W 349 J9
Quemado Tex., U.S.A. 28°56N 100°37W 356 G4
Quemú-Quemú Argentina 36°3S 63°36W 366 D3
Quequén Argentina 38°30S 58°30W 366 D4
Querétaro Mexico 20°36N 100°23W 358 C4
Querétaro □ Mexico 21°0N 99°55W 358 C5
Queshan China 32°55N 114°2E 306 H8
Quesnel Canada 53°0N 122°30W 342 C4
Quesnel → Canada 52°58N 122°29W 342 C4
Quesnel L. Canada 52°30N 121°20W 342 C4
Questa U.S.A. 36°42N 105°36W 349 H11
Quetico ⌂ Canada 48°30N 91°45W 344 C1
Quetta Pakistan 30°15N 66°55E 314 D2
Quezaltenango Guatemala 14°50N 91°30W 360 D1
Quezon City Phil. 14°37N 121°2E 309 B6
Qufār Si. Arabia 27°26N 41°37E 316 E4
Qui Nhon Vietnam 13°40N 109°13E 310 F7
Quibala Angola 10°46S 14°59E 324 G2
Quibaxe Angola 8°24S 14°27E 324 F2
Quibdo Colombia 5°42N 76°40W 364 B3
Quiberon France 47°29N 3°9W 292 C2
Quiet L. Canada 61°5N 133°5W 342 A2
Quiindy Paraguay 25°58S 57°14W 366 B4
Quilá Mexico 24°23N 107°13W 358 C3
Quilán, C. Chile 43°15S 74°30W 368 E2
Quilcene U.S.A. 47°49N 122°53W 350 C4
Quilimarí Chile 32°5S 71°30W 366 C1
Quilino Argentina 30°14S 64°29W 366 C3
Quill Lakes Canada 51°55N 104°13W 343 C8
Quillabamba Peru 12°50S 72°50W 364 F4
Quillagua Chile 21°40S 69°40W 366 A2
Quillaicillo Chile 31°17S 71°40W 366 C1
Quillota Chile 32°54S 71°16W 366 C1
Quilmes Argentina 34°43S 58°15W 366 C4
Quilon India 8°50N 76°38E 312 Q10
Quilpie Australia 26°35S 144°11E 335 D3
Quilpué Chile 33°5S 71°33W 366 C1
Quilua Mozam. 16°17S 39°54E 327 F4
Quimilí Argentina 27°40S 62°30W 366 B3
Quimper France 48°0N 4°9W 292 B1
Quimperlé France 47°53N 3°33W 292 C2
Quinault → U.S.A. 47°21N 124°18W 350 C2
Quincy Calif., U.S.A. 39°56N 120°57W 350 F6
Quincy Fla., U.S.A. 30°35N 84°34W 357 F12
Quincy Ill., U.S.A. 39°56N 91°23W 352 F8
Quincy Mass., U.S.A. 42°14N 71°0W 355 D14
Quincy Wash., U.S.A. 47°14N 119°51W 348 C4
Quines Argentina 32°13S 65°48W 366 C2
Quinga Mozam. 15°49S 40°15E 327 F5
Quintana Roo □ Mexico 19°40N 88°30W 359 D7
Quintanar de la Orden Spain 39°36N 3°5W 293 C4
Quinte West Canada 44°10N 77°34W 354 B7
Quintero Chile 32°45S 71°30W 366 C1
Quirihue Chile 36°15S 72°35W 366 D1
Quirindi Australia 31°28S 150°40E 335 E5
Quirinópolis Brazil 18°32S 50°30W 365 G8
Quissanga Mozam. 12°24S 40°28E 327 E5
Quissico Mozam. 24°42S 34°44E 329 C5
Quitilipi Argentina 26°50S 60°13W 366 B3
Quitman U.S.A. 30°47N 83°34W 357 F13
Quito Ecuador 0°15S 78°35W 364 D3
Quixadá Brazil 4°55S 39°0W 365 D11
Quixaxe Mozam. 15°17S 40°4E 327 F5
Qulan Kazakhstan 42°55N 72°43E 300 E8
Qul'ân, Jazâ'ir Egypt 24°22N 35°31E 316 E2
Qumbu S. Africa 31°10S 28°48E 329 E4
Quneitra Syria 33°7N 35°48E 318 B4
Qŭnghirot Uzbekistan 43°2N 58°50E 300 E6
Quoin I. Australia 14°54S 129°32E 332 B4
Quoin Pt. S. Africa 34°46S 19°37E 328 E2
Quorn Australia 32°25S 138°5E 335 E2
Qŭqon Uzbekistan 40°31N 70°56E 300 E8
Qurnat as Sawdā' Lebanon 34°18N 36°6E 318 A5
Quşaybā' Si. Arabia 26°53N 43°35E 316 E4
Qusaybah Iraq 34°24N 40°59E 316 C4
Quseir Egypt 26°7N 34°16E 316 E2
Qūshchī Iran 37°59N 45°3E 316 B5
Quthing Lesotho 30°25S 27°36E 329 E4
Qūṭīābād Iran 35°47N 48°30E 317 C6
Quwo China 35°38N 111°25E 306 G6
Quyang China 38°35N 114°40E 306 E8
Quynh Nhai Vietnam 21°49N 103°33E 310 B4
Quyon Canada 45°31N 76°14W 355 A8
Quzhou China 28°57N 118°54E 305 D6
Quzi China 36°20N 107°20E 306 F4
Qyzylorda Kazakhstan 44°48N 65°28E 300 E7

R

Ra, Ko Thailand 9°13N 98°16E 311 H2
Raahe Finland 64°40N 24°28E 280 D21
Raalte Neths. 52°23N 6°16E 287 B6
Raasay U.K. 57°25N 6°4W 283 D2
Raasay, Sd. of U.K. 57°30N 6°8W 283 D2
Raba Indonesia 8°36S 118°55E 309 F5
Rába → Hungary 47°38N 17°38E 289 E9
Rabai Kenya 3°50S 39°31E 326 C4
Rabat = Victoria Malta 36°3N 14°14E 297 C1
Rabat Malta 35°53N 14°24E 297 D1
Rabat Morocco 34°2N 6°48W 322 B4
Rabaul Papua N. G. 4°24S 152°18E 330 B8
Rabi Fiji 16°30S 179°59W 331 a
Rābigh Si. Arabia 22°50N 39°5E 319 C2
Răbniţa Moldova 47°45N 29°0E 289 E15
Rābor Iran 29°17N 56°55E 317 D8
Race, C. Canada 46°40N 53°5W 345 C9
Rach Gia Vietnam 10°5N 105°5E 311 G5
Rachid Mauritania 18°45N 11°35W 322 E3
Racibórz Poland 50°7N 18°18E 289 C10
Racine U.S.A. 42°44N 87°47W 352 D10
Rackerby U.S.A. 39°26N 121°22W 350 F5
Radama, Nosy Madag. 14°0S 47°47E 329 A8
Radama, Saikanosy Madag. 14°16S 47°53E 329 A8
Rădăuţi Romania 47°50N 25°59E 289 E13
Radcliff U.S.A. 37°51N 85°57W 353 G11
Radekhiv Ukraine 50°25N 24°32E 289 C13
Radekhov = Radekhiv Ukraine 50°25N 24°32E 289 C13
Radford U.S.A. 37°8N 80°34W 353 G13
Radhanpur India 23°50N 71°38E 314 H4
Radhwa, Jabal Si. Arabia 24°34N 38°18E 316 E3
Radisson Qué., Canada 53°47N 77°37W 344 B4
Radisson Sask., Canada 52°30N 107°20W 343 C7
Radium Hot Springs Canada 50°35N 116°2W 342 C5
Radnor Forest U.K. 52°17N 3°10W 285 E4
Radom Poland 51°23N 21°12E 289 C11
Radomsko Poland 51°5N 19°28E 289 C10
Radomyshl Ukraine 50°30N 29°12E 289 C15
Radstock, C. Australia 33°12S 134°20E 335 E1
Radviliškis Lithuania 55°49N 23°33E 281 J20
Radville Canada 49°30N 104°15W 343 D8
Rae Canada 62°50N 116°3W 342 A5
Rae Bareli India 26°18N 81°20E 315 F9
Rae Isthmus Canada 66°40N 87°30W 341 C11
Raeren Belgium 50°41N 6°7E 287 D6
Raeside, L. Australia 29°20S 122°0E 333 E3
Raetihi N.Z. 39°25S 175°17E 331 C5
Rafaela Argentina 31°10S 61°30W 366 C3
Rafah Gaza Strip 31°18N 34°14E 318 D3
Rafai C.A.R. 4°59N 23°58E 326 B1
Rafḥā Si. Arabia 29°35N 43°35E 316 D4
Rafsanjān Iran 30°30N 56°5E 317 D8
Raft Pt. Australia 16°4S 124°26E 332 C3
Râgâ Sudan 8°28N 25°41E 323 G11
Ragachow Belarus 53°8N 30°5E 289 B16
Ragama Sri Lanka 7°0N 79°50E 312 R11
Ragged, Mt. Australia 33°27S 123°25E 333 F3
Ragged Pt. Barbados 13°10N 59°26W 361 g
Raghunathpalli India 22°14N 84°48E 315 H11
Raghunathpur India 23°33N 86°40E 315 H12
Raglan N.Z. 37°55S 174°55E 331 B5
Ragusa Italy 36°55N 14°44E 294 F6
Raha Indonesia 4°55S 123°0E 309 E6
Rahaeng = Tak Thailand 16°52N 99°8E 310 D2
Rahatgarh India 23°47N 78°22E 315 H8
Rahimyar Khan Pakistan 28°30N 70°25E 314 E4
Rāhjerd Iran 34°22N 50°22E 317 C6
Rahole ⌂ Kenya 0°5N 38°57E 326 B4
Rahon India 31°3N 76°7E 314 D7
Raiatéa, Î. French Polynesia 16°50S 151°25W 337 J12
Raichur India 16°10N 77°20E 312 L10
Raiganj India 25°37N 88°10E 315 G13
Raigarh India 21°56N 83°25E 313 J13
Raijua Indonesia 10°37S 121°36E 309 F6
Raikot India 30°41N 75°42E 314 D6
Railton Australia 41°25S 146°28E 335 G4
Rainbow Bridge ⌂ U.S.A. 37°5N 110°58W 349 H8
Rainbow Lake Canada 58°30N 119°23W 342 B5
Rainier U.S.A. 46°53N 122°41W 350 D4
Rainier, Mt. U.S.A. 46°52N 121°46W 350 D5
Rainy L. Canada 48°42N 93°10W 343 D10
Rainy River Canada 48°43N 94°29W 343 D10
Raippaluoto Finland 63°13N 21°14E 280 E19
Raipur India 21°17N 81°45E 313 J12
Raisen India 23°20N 77°48E 314 H8
Raisio Finland 60°28N 22°11E 281 F20
Raj Nandgaon India 21°5N 81°5E 313 J12
Raj Nilgiri India 21°28N 86°46E 315 J12
Raja, Ujung Indonesia 3°40N 96°25E 308 D1
Raja Ampat, Kepulauan Indonesia 0°30S 130°0E 309 E7
Rajahmundry India 17°1N 81°48E 313 L12
Rajaji △ India 30°10N 78°20E 314 D8
Rajang → Malaysia 2°30N 112°0E 308 D4
Rajanpur Pakistan 29°6N 70°19E 314 E4
Rajapalaiyam India 9°25N 77°35E 312 Q10
Rajasthan □ India 26°45N 73°30E 314 F5
Rajasthan Canal = Indira Gandhi Canal India 28°0N 72°0E 314 F5
Rajauri India 33°25N 74°21E 315 C6
Rajgarh Mad. P., India 24°2N 76°45E 314 G7
Rajgarh Raj., India 27°14N 76°38E 314 F7
Rajgarh Raj., India 28°40N 75°25E 314 E6
Rajgir India 25°2N 85°25E 315 G11
Rajkot India 22°15N 70°56E 314 H4
Rajmahal Hills India 24°30N 87°30E 315 G12
Rajpipla India 21°50N 73°30E 312 J8
Rajpur India 22°18N 74°21E 314 H6
Rajpura India 30°25N 76°32E 314 D7
Rajshahi Bangla. 24°22N 88°39E 313 G16
Rajshahi □ Bangla. 25°0N 89°0E 315 G13
Rajula India 21°3N 71°26E 314 J4
Rakaia N.Z. 43°45S 172°1E 331 E4
Rakaia → N.Z. 43°36S 172°15E 331 E4
Rakan, Ra's Qatar 26°10N 51°20E 317 E6
Rakaposhi Pakistan 36°10N 74°25E 315 A6
Rakata, Pulau Indonesia 6°10S 105°20E 308 F3
Rakhiv Ukraine 48°3N 24°12E 289 D13
Rakhni Pakistan 30°4N 69°56E 314 D3
Rakhni → Pakistan 29°31N 69°36E 314 E3
Rakiraki Fiji 17°22S 178°11E 331 a
Rakitnoye Russia 45°36N 134°17E 302 B7
Rakiura △ N.Z. 47°0S 167°50E 331 G1
Rakops Botswana 21°1S 24°28E 328 C3
Rakvere Estonia 59°20N 26°25E 281 G22
Raleigh U.S.A. 35°47N 78°39W 357 D15
Ralik Chain Pac. Oc. 8°0N 168°0E 336 G8
Ralls U.S.A. 33°41N 101°24W 356 E4
Ralston U.S.A. 41°30N 76°57W 354 E8
Ram → Canada 62°1N 123°41W 342 A4
Rām Allāh West Bank 31°55N 35°10E 318 D4
Rama Nic. 12°9N 84°15W 360 D3
Ramakona India 21°43N 78°50E 315 J8
Rāmallāh = Rām Allāh West Bank 31°55N 35°10E 318 D4
Raman Thailand 6°29N 101°18E 311 J3
Ramanathapuram India 9°25N 78°55E 312 Q11
Ramanetaka, B. de Madag. 14°13S 47°52E 329 A8
Ramanujganj India 23°48N 83°42E 315 H10
Ramat Gan Israel 32°4N 34°48E 318 C3
Ramatlhabama S. Africa 25°37S 25°33E 328 D4
Ramban India 33°14N 75°12E 315 C6
Rambi = Rabi Fiji 16°30S 179°59W 331 a
Rambipuji Indonesia 8°12S 113°37E 309 H15
Rame Hd. Australia 37°47S 149°30E 335 F4
Ramechhap Nepal 27°25N 86°10E 315 F12
Ramganga → India 27°5N 79°58E 315 F8
Ramgarh Jharkhand, India 23°40N 85°35E 315 H11
Ramgarh Raj., India 27°16N 75°14E 314 F6
Ramgarh Raj., India 27°30N 70°36E 314 F4
Rāmhormoz Iran 31°15N 49°35E 317 D6
Ramīān Iran 37°3N 55°16E 317 B7
Ramingining Australia 12°19S 135°3E 334 A2
Ramla Israel 31°55N 34°52E 318 D3
Ramm = Rum Jordan 29°39N 35°26E 318 F4
Ramm, Jabal Jordan 29°35N 35°24E 318 F4
Ramnad = Ramanathapuram India 9°25N 78°55E 312 Q11
Ramnagar Jammu & Kashmir, India 32°47N 75°18E 315 C6
Ramnagar Uttaranchal, India 29°24N 79°7E 315 E8
Râmnicu Sărat Romania 45°26N 27°3E 289 F14
Râmnicu Vâlcea Romania 45°9N 24°21E 289 F13
Ramona U.S.A. 33°2N 116°52W 351 M10
Ramore Canada 48°30N 80°25W 344 C3
Ramotswa Botswana 24°50S 25°52E 328 C4
Rampur H.P., India 31°26N 77°43E 314 D7
Rampur Mad. P., India 23°25N 73°53E 314 H5
Rampur Ut. P., India 28°50N 79°5E 315 E8
Rampur Hat India 24°10N 87°50E 315 G12
Rampura India 24°30N 75°27E 314 G6
Ramrama Tola India 21°52N 79°55E 315 J8
Ramree I. Burma 19°0N 93°40E 313 K19
Rāmsar Iran 36°53N 50°41E 317 B6
Ramsey I. of Man 54°20N 4°22W 284 C3
Ramsey U.S.A. 41°4N 74°9W 355 E10
Ramsey L. Canada 47°13N 82°15W 344 C3
Ramsgate U.K. 51°20N 1°25E 285 F9
Ramtek India 21°20N 79°15E 312 J11
Ramu Kenya 3°55N 41°10E 326 B5
Rana Pratap Sagar Dam India 24°58N 75°38E 314 G6
Ranaghat India 23°15N 88°35E 315 H13
Ranahu Pakistan 25°55N 69°45E 314 G3
Ranau Malaysia 6°2N 116°40E 308 C5
Rancagua Chile 34°10S 70°50W 366 C1
Rancheria → Canada 60°13N 129°7W 342 A3
Ranchester U.S.A. 44°54N 107°10W 348 D10
Ranchi India 23°19N 85°27E 315 H11
Rancho Cordova U.S.A. 38°36N 121°18W 350 G5
Rancho Cucamonga U.S.A. 34°10N 117°30W 351 L9
Randalstown U.K. 54°45N 6°19W 282 B5
Randers Denmark 56°29N 10°1E 281 H14
Randfontein S. Africa 26°8S 27°45E 329 D4
Randle U.S.A. 46°32N 121°57W 350 D5
Randolph Mass., U.S.A. 42°10N 71°2W 355 D13
Randolph N.Y., U.S.A. 42°10N 78°59W 354 D6
Randolph Utah, U.S.A. 41°40N 111°11W 348 F8
Randolph Vt., U.S.A. 43°55N 72°40W 355 C12
Randsburg U.S.A. 35°22N 117°39W 351 K9
Rånealven → Sweden 65°50N 22°20E 280 D20
Rangae Thailand 6°19N 101°44E 311 J3
Rangaunu B. N.Z. 34°51S 173°15E 331 A4
Range, The Zimbabwe 19°2S 31°2E 327 F3
Rangeley U.S.A. 44°58N 70°39W 355 B14
Rangeley L. U.S.A. 44°55N 70°43W 355 B14
Rangely U.S.A. 40°5N 108°48W 348 F9
Ranger U.S.A. 32°28N 98°41W 356 E5
Rangia India 26°28N 91°38E 313 F17
Rangiora N.Z. 43°19S 172°36E 331 E4
Rangitaiki → N.Z. 37°54S 176°49E 331 B6
Rangitata → N.Z. 43°45S 171°15E 331 E3
Rangitoto ke te tonga = D'Urville I. N.Z. 40°50S 173°55E 331 D4
Rangkasbitung Indonesia 6°21S 106°15E 309 G12
Rangon → Burma 16°28N 96°40E 313 L20
Rangoon Burma 16°45N 96°20E 313 L20
Rangpur Bangla. 25°42N 89°22E 313 G16
Rangsit Thailand 13°59N 100°37E 310 F3
Ranibennur India 14°35N 75°30E 312 M9

Raniganj Ut. P., India 27°3N 82°13E 315 F9
Raniganj W. Bengal, India 23°40N 87°5E 313 H15
Ranikhet India 29°39N 79°25E 315 E8
Raniwara India 24°50N 72°10E 314 G5
Rāniyah Iraq 36°15N 44°53E 316 B5
Ranka India 23°59N 83°47E 315 H10
Ranken → Australia 20°31S 137°36E 334 C2
Rankin U.S.A. 31°13N 101°56W 356 F4
Rankin Inlet Canada 62°30N 93°0W 340 C10
Rankins Springs Australia 33°49S 146°14E 335 E4
Rannoch, L. U.K. 56°41N 4°20W 283 E4
Rannoch Moor U.K. 56°38N 4°48W 283 E4
Ranobe, Helodranon' i Madag. 23°3S 43°33E 329 C7
Ranohira Madag. 22°29S 45°24E 329 C8
Ranomafana Toamasina, Madag. 18°57S 48°50E 329 B8
Ranomafana Toliara, Madag. 24°34S 47°0E 329 C8
Ranomafana △ Madag. 21°16S 47°25E 329 C8
Ranomena Madag. 23°25S 47°17E 329 C8
Ranong Thailand 9°56N 98°40E 311 H2
Ranotsara Nord Madag. 22°48S 46°36E 329 C8
Rānsa Iran 33°39N 48°18E 317 C6
Ransiki Indonesia 1°30S 134°10E 309 E8
Rantabe Madag. 15°42S 49°39E 329 B8
Rantauprapat Indonesia 2°15N 99°50E 308 D1
Rantemario Indonesia 3°15S 119°57E 309 E5
Ranthambore △ India 26°10N 76°30E 314 F7
Rantoul U.S.A. 40°19N 88°9W 352 E9
Raoyang China 38°15N 115°45E 306 E8
Rap, Ko Thailand 9°19N 99°58E 311 b
Rapa French Polynesia 27°35S 144°20W 337 K13
Rapa Nui = Pascua, I. de Chile 27°7S 109°23W 337 K17
Rapallo Italy 44°21N 9°14E 292 D8
Rapar India 23°34N 70°38E 314 H4
Rāpch Iran 25°40N 59°15E 317 E8
Raper, C. Canada 69°44N 67°6W 341 C13
Rapid City U.S.A. 44°5N 103°14W 352 C2
Rapid River U.S.A. 45°55N 86°58W 352 C10
Rapla Estonia 59°1N 24°52E 281 G21
Rapti → India 26°18N 83°41E 315 F10
Raquette → U.S.A. 45°0N 74°42W 355 B10
Raquette Lake U.S.A. 43°49N 74°40W 355 C10
Rara △ Nepal 29°30N 82°10E 315 E10
Rarotonga Cook Is. 21°30S 160°0W 337 K12
Ra's al 'Ayn Syria 36°45N 40°12E 316 B4
Ra's al Khaymah U.A.E. 25°50N 55°59E 317 E7
Rasca, Pta. de la Canary Is. 27°59N 16°41W 296 G3
Raseiniai Lithuania 55°25N 23°5E 281 J20
Rashmi India 25°4N 74°22E 314 G6
Rasht Iran 37°20N 49°40E 317 B6
Rasi Salai Thailand 15°20N 104°9E 310 E5
Rason L. Australia 28°45S 124°25E 333 E3
Rasra India 25°50N 83°50E 315 G10
Rasul Pakistan 32°42N 73°34E 314 C5
Rat → Canada 49°35N 97°10W 343 D9
Rat Buri Thailand 13°30N 99°54E 310 F2
Rat Islands U.S.A. 52°0N 178°0E 346 a
Rat L. Canada 56°10N 99°40W 343 B9
Ratak Chain Pac. Oc. 1°0N 170°0E 336 G8
Ratangarh India 28°5N 74°35E 314 E6
Raṭāwī Iraq 30°38N 47°13E 316 D5
Rath India 25°36N 79°37E 315 G8
Rath Luirc Ireland 52°21N 8°40W 282 D3
Rathangan Ireland 53°13N 7°1W 282 C4
Rathdrum Ireland 52°56N 6°14W 282 D5
Rathenow Germany 52°37N 12°19E 288 B7
Rathkeale Ireland 52°32N 8°56W 282 D3
Rathlin I. U.K. 55°18N 6°14W 282 A5
Rathmelton Ireland 55°2N 7°38W 282 A4
Ratibor = Racibórz Poland 50°7N 18°18E 289 C10
Ratlam India 23°20N 75°0E 314 H6
Ratnagiri India 16°57N 73°18E 312 L8
Ratodero Pakistan 27°48N 68°18E 314 F3
Raton U.S.A. 36°54N 104°24W 349 H11
Rattaphum Thailand 7°8N 100°16E 311 J3
Rattray Hd. U.K. 57°38N 1°50W 283 D7
Ratz, Mt. Canada 57°23N 132°12W 342 B2
Raub Malaysia 3°47N 101°52E 311 L3
Rauch Argentina 36°45S 59°5W 366 D4
Raudales Mexico 17°27N 93°39W 359 D6
Raufarhöfn Iceland 66°27N 15°57W 280 C6
Raufoss Norway 60°44N 10°37E 280 F14
Raukumara Ra. N.Z. 38°5S 177°55E 331 C6
Rauma Finland 61°10N 21°30E 280 F19
Raumo = Rauma Finland 61°10N 21°30E 280 F19
Raung, Gunung Indonesia 8°8S 114°3E 309 J17
Raurkela India 22°14N 84°50E 315 H11
Rausu-Dake Japan 44°4N 145°7E 302 B12
Rava-Ruska Ukraine 50°15N 23°42E 289 C12
Rava Russkaya = Rava-Ruska Ukraine 50°15N 23°42E 289 C12
Ravalli U.S.A. 47°17N 114°11W 348 C6
Ravānsar Iran 34°43N 46°40E 316 C5
Rāvar Iran 31°20N 56°51E 317 D8
Ravena U.S.A. 42°28N 73°49W 355 D11
Ravenna Italy 44°25N 12°12E 294 B5
Ravenna Nebr., U.S.A. 41°1N 98°55W 352 E4
Ravenna Ohio, U.S.A. 41°9N 81°15W 354 E3
Ravensburg Germany 47°46N 9°36E 288 E5
Ravenshoe Australia 17°37S 145°29E 334 B4
Ravensthorpe Australia 33°35S 120°2E 333 F3
Ravenswood Australia 20°6S 146°54E 334 C4
Ravenswood U.S.A. 38°57N 81°46W 353 F13
Ravi → Pakistan 30°35N 71°49E 314 D4
Rawalpindi Pakistan 33°38N 73°8E 314 C5
Rawāndūz Iraq 36°40N 44°30E 316 B5
Rawang Malaysia 3°20N 101°35E 311 L3
Rawene N.Z. 35°25S 173°32E 331 A4
Rawlinna Australia 30°58S 125°28E 333 F4
Rawlins U.S.A. 41°47N 107°14W 348 F10
Rawlinson Ra. Australia 24°40S 128°30E 333 D4
Rawson Argentina 43°15S 65°5W 368 E3
Raxaul India 26°59N 84°51E 315 F11
Ray U.S.A. 48°21N 103°10W 352 A2
Ray, C. Canada 47°33N 59°15W 345 C8
Raya Ring, Ko Thailand 8°18N 98°29E 311 a
Rayadurg India 14°40N 76°50E 312 M10
Rayagada India 19°15N 83°20E 313 K13
Raychikhinsk Russia 49°46N 129°25E 301 E13
Rāyen Iran 29°34N 57°26E 317 D8
Rayleigh U.K. 51°36N 0°37E 285 F8
Raymond Canada 49°30N 112°35W 342 D6
Raymond Calif., U.S.A. 37°13N 119°54W 350 H7
Raymond N.H., U.S.A. 43°2N 71°11W 355 C13
Raymond Wash., U.S.A. 46°41N 123°44W 350 D3
Raymondville U.S.A. 26°29N 97°47W 356 H6
Raymore Canada 51°25N 104°31W 343 C8
Rayón Mexico 29°43N 110°35W 358 B2
Rayong Thailand 12°40N 101°20E 310 F3
Rayville U.S.A. 32°29N 91°46W 356 E9
Raz, Pte. du France 48°2N 4°47W 292 C1
Razan Iran 35°23N 49°2E 317 C6
Razāzah, Buḩayrat ar Iraq 32°40N 43°35E 316 C4
Razazah, L. = Razāzah, Buḩayrat ar Iraq 32°40N 43°35E 316 C4
Razdel'naya = Rozdilna Ukraine 46°50N 30°2E 289 E16
Razdolnoye Russia 43°30N 131°52E 302 C5
Razeh Iran 32°47N 48°9E 317 C6
Razgrad Bulgaria 43°33N 26°34E 295 C12
Razim, Lacul Romania 44°50N 29°0E 289 F15
Razmak Pakistan 32°45N 69°50E 314 C3
Ré, Î. de France 46°12N 1°30W 292 C3
Reading U.K. 51°27N 0°58W 285 F7
Reading U.S.A. 40°20N 75°56W 355 F9
Reading □ U.K. 51°27N 0°58W 285 F7
Realicó Argentina 35°0S 64°15W 366 D3
Ream Cambodia 10°34N 103°39E 311 G4
Reay Forest U.K. 58°22N 4°55W 283 C4
Rebi Indonesia 6°23S 134°7E 309 F8
Rebiana Libya 24°12N 22°10E 323 D10
Rebiana, Sahrâ' Libya 24°30N 21°0E 323 D10
Reboly Russia 63°49N 30°47E 280 E24
Rebun-Tō Japan 45°23N 141°2E 302 B10
Recherche, Arch. of the Australia 34°15S 122°50E 333 F3
Rechna Doab Pakistan 31°35N 73°30E 314 D5
Rechytsa Belarus 52°21N 30°24E 289 B16
Recife Brazil 8°0S 35°0W 365 E12
Recife Seychelles 4°36S 55°42E 325 b
Recklinghausen Germany 51°37N 7°12E 287 C7
Reconquista Argentina 29°10S 59°45W 366 B4
Recreo Argentina 29°25S 65°10W 366 B2
Red → U.S.A. 31°1N 91°45W 356 F9
Red Bank U.S.A. 40°21N 74°5W 355 F10
Red Bay Canada 51°44N 56°25W 345 B8
Red Bluff U.S.A. 40°11N 122°15W 348 F2
Red Bluff Res. U.S.A. 31°54N 103°55W 349 L12
Red Cliffs Australia 34°19S 142°11E 335 E3
Red Cloud U.S.A. 40°5N 98°32W 352 E4
Red Creek U.S.A. 43°14N 76°45W 355 C8
Red Deer Canada 52°20N 113°50W 342 C6
Red Deer → Alta., Canada 50°58N 110°0W 343 C7
Red Deer → Man., Canada 52°53N 101°1W 343 C8
Red Deer L. Canada 52°55N 101°20W 343 C8
Red Hook U.S.A. 41°55N 73°53W 355 E11
Red Indian L. Canada 48°35N 57°0W 345 C8
Red L. Canada 51°3N 93°49W 343 C10
Red Lake Canada 51°3N 93°49W 343 C10
Red Lake Falls U.S.A. 47°53N 96°16W 352 B5
Red Lake Road Canada 49°59N 93°25W 343 C10
Red Lodge U.S.A. 45°11N 109°15W 348 D9
Red Mountain U.S.A. 35°37N 117°38W 351 K9
Red Oak U.S.A. 41°1N 95°14W 352 E6
Red River of the North → N. Amer. 49°0N 97°15W 352 A5
Red Rock Canada 48°55N 88°15W 344 C2
Red Rock, L. U.S.A. 41°22N 92°59W 352 E7
Red Rocks Pt. Australia 32°13S 127°32E 333 F4
Red Sea Asia 25°0N 36°0E 319 C2
Red Slate Mt. U.S.A. 37°31N 118°52W 350 H8
Red Sucker L. Canada 54°9N 93°40W 344 B1
Red Tower Pass = Turnu Roşu, P. Romania 45°33N 24°17E 289 F13
Red Wing U.S.A. 44°34N 92°31W 352 C7
Redang Malaysia 5°49N 103°2E 311 K4
Redange Lux. 49°46N 5°52E 287 E5
Redcar U.K. 54°37N 1°4W 284 C6
Redcar & Cleveland □ U.K. 54°29N 1°0W 284 C7
Redcliff Canada 50°10N 110°50W 348 A8
Redcliffe Australia 27°12S 153°0E 335 D5
Redcliffe, Mt. Australia 28°30S 121°30E 333 E3
Reddersburg S. Africa 29°41S 26°10E 328 D4
Redding U.S.A. 40°35N 122°24W 348 F2
Redditch U.K. 52°18N 1°55W 285 E6
Redfield U.S.A. 44°53N 98°31W 352 C4
Redford U.S.A. 44°38N 73°48W 355 B11
Redhead Trin. & Tob. 10°44N 60°58W 365 K16
Redlands U.S.A. 34°4N 117°11W 351 M9
Redmond Oreg., U.S.A. 44°17N 121°11W 348 D3
Redmond Wash., U.S.A. 47°40N 122°7W 350 C4
Redon France 47°40N 2°6W 292 C2
Redonda Antigua & B. 16°58N 62°19W 361 C7
Redondela Spain 42°15N 8°38W 293 A1
Redondo Beach U.S.A. 33°50N 118°23W 351 M8
Redruth U.K. 50°14N 5°14W 285 G2
Redvers Canada 49°35N 101°40W 343 D8
Redwater Canada 53°55N 113°6W 342 C6
Redwood U.S.A. 44°18N 75°48W 355 B9
Redwood △ U.S.A. 41°40N 124°5W 348 F1
Redwood City U.S.A. 37°30N 122°15W 350 H4
Redwood Falls U.S.A. 44°32N 95°7W 352 C6
Ree, L. Ireland 53°35N 8°0W 282 C3
Reed City U.S.A. 43°53N 85°31W 353 D11
Reed L. Canada 54°38N 100°30W 343 C8
Reedley U.S.A. 36°36N 119°27W 350 J7
Reedsburg U.S.A. 43°32N 90°0W 352 D8
Reedsport U.S.A. 43°42N 124°6W 348 E1
Reedsville U.S.A. 40°39N 77°35W 354 F7
Reefton N.Z. 42°6S 171°51E 331 E3
Reese → U.S.A. 40°48N 117°4W 348 F5
Refugio U.S.A. 28°18N 97°17W 356 G6
Regensburg Germany 49°1N 12°6E 288 D7
Reggâne = Zaouiet Reggâne Algeria 26°32N 0°3E 322 C6
Réggio di Calábria Italy 38°6N 15°39E 294 E6
Réggio nell'Emília Italy 44°43N 10°36E 294 B4
Reghin Romania 46°46N 24°42E 289 E13
Regina Canada 50°27N 104°35W 343 C8
Regina Beach Canada 50°47N 105°0W 343 C8
Registro Brazil 24°29S 47°49W 367 A6
Rehar → India 23°55N 82°40E 315 H10
Rehli India 23°38N 79°5E 315 H8
Rehoboth Namibia 23°15S 17°4E 328 C2
Rehovot Israel 31°54N 34°48E 318 D3
Reichenbach Germany 50°37N 12°17E 288 C7
Reid Australia 30°49S 128°26E 333 F4
Reidsville U.S.A. 36°21N 79°40W 357 C15
Reigate U.K. 51°14N 0°12W 285 F7
Reims France 49°15N 4°1E 292 B6
Reina Adelaida, Arch. Chile 52°20S 74°0W 368 G2
Reina Sofia, Tenerife ✕ (TFS) Canary Is. 28°3N 16°33W 296 F3
Reindeer → Canada 55°36N 103°11W 343 B8
Reindeer I. Canada 52°30N 98°0W 343 C9
Reindeer L. Canada 57°15N 102°15W 343 B8
Reinga, C. N.Z. 34°25S 172°43E 331 A4
Reinosa Spain 43°2N 4°15W 293 A3
Reitz S. Africa 27°48S 28°29E 329 D4
Reivilo S. Africa 27°36S 24°8E 328 D3
Reliance Canada 63°0N 109°20W 343 A7
Remarkable, Mt. Australia 32°48S 138°10E 335 E2
Rembang Indonesia 6°42S 111°21E 309 G14
Remedios Panama 8°15N 81°50W 360 E3
Remeshk Iran 26°55N 58°50E 317 E8
Remich Lux. 49°32N 6°22E 287 E6
Remscheid Germany 51°11N 7°12E 287 C7
Ren Xian China 37°8N 114°40E 306 F8
Rendang Indonesia 8°26S 115°25E 309 J18
Rendsburg Germany 54°17N 9°39E 288 A5
Renfrew Canada 45°30N 76°40W 355 A8
Renfrewshire □ U.K. 55°49N 4°38W 283 F4
Rengat Indonesia 0°30S 102°45E 308 E2
Rengo Chile 34°24S 70°50W 366 C1
Reni Ukraine 45°28N 28°15E 289 F15
Renmark Australia 34°11S 140°43E 335 E3
Rennell Sd. Canada 53°23N 132°35W 342 C2
Renner Springs Australia 18°20S 133°47E 334 B1
Rennes France 48°7N 1°41W 292 B3
Rennick Glacier Antarctica 70°30S 161°45E 277 D21
Rennie L. Canada 61°32N 105°35W 343 A7
Reno U.S.A. 39°31N 119°48W 350 F7
Reno → Italy 44°38N 12°16E 294 B5
Renovo U.S.A. 41°20N 77°45W 354 E7
Renqiu China 38°43N 116°5E 306 E9
Rensselaer Ind., U.S.A. 40°57N 87°9W 352 E10
Rensselaer N.Y., U.S.A. 42°38N 73°45W 355 D11
Rentería Spain 43°19N 1°54W 293 A5
Renton U.S.A. 47°28N 122°12W 350 C4
Reotipur India 25°33N 83°45E 315 G10
Republic Mo., U.S.A. 37°7N 93°29W 352 G7
Republic Wash., U.S.A. 48°39N 118°44W 348 B4
Republican → U.S.A. 39°4N 96°48W 352 F5
Repulse B. Australia 20°35S 148°46E 334 J6
Repulse Bay Canada 66°30N 86°30W 341 C11
Requena Peru 5°5S 73°52W 364 E4
Requena Spain 39°30N 1°4W 293 C5
Reşadiye = Datça Turkey 36°46N 27°40E 295 F12
Reserve U.S.A. 33°43N 108°45W 349 K9
Resht = Rasht Iran 37°20N 49°40E 317 B6
Resistencia Argentina 27°30S 59°0W 366 B4
Reşiţa Romania 45°18N 21°53E 289 F11
Reso = Raisio Finland 60°28N 22°11E 281 F20
Resolute Canada 74°42N 94°54W 341 B10
Resolution I. Canada 61°30N 65°0W 341 C13
Resolution I. N.Z. 45°40S 166°40E 331 F1
Ressano Garcia Mozam. 25°25S 32°0E 329 D5
Reston Canada 49°33N 101°6W 343 D8
Retalhuleu Guatemala 14°33N 91°46W 360 D1
Retenue, L. de Dem. Rep. of the Congo 11°0S 27°0E 327 E2
Retford U.K. 53°19N 0°56W 284 D7
Rethimno Greece 35°18N 24°30E 297 D6
Rethimno □ Greece 35°23N 24°28E 297 D6
Reti Pakistan 28°5N 69°48E 314 E3
Réunion ⧄ Ind. Oc. 21°0S 56°0E 325 c
Reus Spain 41°10N 1°5E 293 B6
Reutlingen Germany 48°29N 9°12E 288 D5
Reval = Tallinn Estonia 59°22N 24°48E 281 G21
Revda Russia 56°48N 59°57E 290 C10
Revelganj India 25°50N 84°40E 315 G11
Revelstoke Canada 51°0N 118°10W 342 C5
Reventazón Peru 6°10S 80°58W 364 E2
Revillagigedo, Is. de Pac. Oc. 18°40N 112°0W 358 D2
Revuè → Mozam. 19°50S 34°0E 327 F3
Rewa India 24°33N 81°25E 315 G9
Rewari India 28°15N 76°40E 314 E7
Rexburg U.S.A. 43°49N 111°47W 348 E8
Rey Iran 35°35N 51°25E 317 C6
Rey, I. del Panama 8°20N 78°30W 360 E4
Rey, L. del Mexico 27°1N 103°26W 358 B4
Rey Malabo Eq. Guin. 3°45N 8°50E 324 D1
Reyðarfjörður Iceland 65°2N 14°13W 280 D6
Reyes, Pt. U.S.A. 38°0N 123°0W 350 H3
Reykjahlíð Iceland 65°40N 16°55W 280 D5
Reykjanes Iceland 63°48N 22°40W 280 E2
Reykjavík Iceland 64°10N 21°57W 280 D3
Reynolds Ra. Australia 22°30S 133°0E 332 D5
Reynoldsville U.S.A. 41°6N 78°53W 354 E6
Reynosa Mexico 26°7N 98°18W 359 B5
Rēzekne Latvia 56°30N 27°17E 281 H22
Rezvān Iran 27°34N 56°6E 317 E8
Rhayader U.K. 52°18N 3°29W 285 E4
Rhein → Europe 51°52N 6°2E 287 C6
Rhein-Main-Donau-Kanal Germany 49°1N 11°27E 288 D6
Rheine Germany 52°17N 7°26E 288 B4
Rheinland-Pfalz □ Germany 50°0N 7°0E 288 C4
Rhin = Rhein → Europe 51°52N 6°2E 287 C6
Rhine = Rhein → Europe 51°52N 6°2E 287 C6
Rhinebeck U.S.A. 41°56N 73°55W 355 E11
Rhineland-Palatinate = Rheinland-Pfalz □ Germany 50°0N 7°0E 288 C4
Rhinelander U.S.A. 45°38N 89°25W 352 C9
Rhinns Pt. U.K. 55°40N 6°29W 283 F2
Rhino Camp Uganda 3°0N 31°22E 326 B3
Rhir, Cap Morocco 30°38N 9°54W 322 B4
Rhode Island □ U.S.A. 41°40N 71°30W 355 E13
Rhodes Greece 36°15N 28°10E 297 C10
Rhodope Mts. = Rhodopi Planina Bulgaria 41°40N 24°20E 295 D11
Rhodopi Planina Bulgaria 41°40N 24°20E 295 D11
Rhön Germany 50°24N 9°58E 288 C5
Rhondda U.K. 51°39N 3°31W 285 F4
Rhondda Cynon Taff □ U.K. 51°42N 3°27W 285 F4
Rhône → France 43°28N 4°42E 292 E6
Rhum U.K. 57°0N 6°20W 283 E2
Rhyl U.K. 53°20N 3°29W 284 D4
Riachão Brazil 7°20S 46°37W 365 E9
Riasi India 33°10N 74°50E 315 C6
Riau □ Indonesia 0°0 102°35E 308 D2
Riau, Kepulauan Indonesia 0°30N 104°20E 308 D2
Riau Arch. = Riau, Kepulauan Indonesia 0°30N 104°20E 308 D2
Ribadeo Spain 43°35N 7°5W 293 A2
Ribas do Rio Pardo Brazil 20°27S 53°46W 365 H8
Ribauè Mozam. 14°57S 38°17E 327 E4
Ribble → U.K. 53°52N 2°25W 284 D5
Ribe Denmark 55°19N 8°44E 281 J13
Ribeira Brava Madeira 32°41N 17°4W 296 D2
Ribeira Grande C. Verde Is. 17°0N 25°4W 322 b
Ribeirão Prêto Brazil 21°10S 47°50W 367 A6
Riberalta Bolivia 11°0S 66°0W 364 F5
Riccarton N.Z. 43°32S 172°37E 331 E4
Rice U.S.A. 34°5N 114°51W 351 L12
Rice L. Canada 44°12N 78°10W 354 B6
Rice Lake U.S.A. 45°30N 91°44W 352 C8
Rich, C. Canada 44°43N 80°38W 354 B4
Richards Bay S. Africa 28°48S 32°6E 329 D5
Richardson → Canada 58°25N 111°14W 343 B6
Richardson Lakes U.S.A. 44°46N 70°58W 353 C18
Richardson Springs U.S.A. 39°51N 121°46W 350 F5
Riche, C. Australia 34°36S 118°47E 333 F2
Richey U.S.A. 47°39N 105°4W 348 C11
Richfield U.S.A. 38°46N 112°5W 348 G7
Richfield Springs U.S.A. 42°51N 74°59W 355 D10
Richford U.S.A. 45°0N 72°40W 355 B12
Richibucto Canada 46°42N 64°54W 345 C7
Richland Ga., U.S.A. 32°5N 84°40W 357 E12
Richland Wash., U.S.A. 46°17N 119°18W 348 C4
Richland Center U.S.A. 43°21N 90°23W 352 D8
Richlands U.S.A. 37°6N 81°48W 353 G13
Richmond Australia 20°43S 143°8E 334 C3
Richmond N.Z. 41°20S 173°12E 331 D4
Richmond U.K. 54°25N 1°43W 284 C6
Richmond Calif., U.S.A. 37°56N 122°21W 350 H4
Richmond Ind., U.S.A. 39°50N 84°53W 353 F11
Richmond Ky., U.S.A. 37°45N 84°18W 353 G11
Richmond Mich., U.S.A. 42°49N 82°45W 354 D2
Richmond Mo., U.S.A. 39°17N 93°58W 352 F7
Richmond Tex., U.S.A. 29°35N 95°46W 356 G7
Richmond Utah, U.S.A. 41°56N 111°48W 348 F8
Richmond Va., U.S.A. 37°33N 77°27W 353 G15
Richmond Vt., U.S.A. 44°24N 72°59W 355 B12
Richmond Hill Canada 43°52N 79°27W 354 C5
Richmond Ra. Australia 29°0S 152°45E 335 D5
Richtersveld △ S. Africa 28°15S 17°10E 328 D2
Richwood U.S.A. 38°14N 80°32W 353 F13
Ridder = Leninogorsk Kazakhstan 50°20N 83°30E 300 D9
Riddlesburg U.S.A. 40°9N 78°15W 354 F6
Ridgecrest U.S.A. 35°38N 117°40W 351 K9
Ridgefield Conn., U.S.A. 41°17N 73°30W 355 E11
Ridgefield Wash., U.S.A. 45°49N 122°45W 350 E4
Ridgeland Miss., U.S.A. 32°26N 90°8W 357 E9
Ridgeland S.C., U.S.A. 32°29N 80°59W 357 E14
Ridgetown Canada 42°26N 81°52W 354 D3
Ridgewood U.S.A. 40°59N 74°7W 355 F10
Ridgway U.S.A. 41°25N 78°44W 354 E6
Riding Mountain △ Canada 50°50N 100°0W 343 C9
Ridley, Mt. Australia 33°12S 122°7E 333 F3
Riebeek-Oos S. Africa 33°10S 26°10E 328 E4
Ried Austria 48°14N 13°30E 288 D7
Riesa Germany 51°17N 13°17E 288 C7
Riet → S. Africa 29°0S 23°54E 328 D3
Rietbron S. Africa 32°54S 23°10E 328 E3
Rietfontein Namibia 21°58S 20°58E 328 C3
Rieti Italy 42°24N 12°51E 294 C5
Rif = Er Rif Morocco 35°1N 4°1W 322 A5
Riffe L. U.S.A. 46°32N 122°26W 350 D4
Rifle U.S.A. 39°32N 107°47W 348 G10
Rift Valley Africa 7°0N 30°0E 320 G7
Rift Valley □ Kenya 0°20N 36°0E 326 B4
Rīga Latvia 56°53N 24°8E 281 H21
Riga, G. of Latvia 57°40N 23°45E 281 H20
Rīgān Iran 28°37N 58°58E 317 D8
Rīgas Jūras Līcis = Riga, G. of Latvia 57°40N 23°45E 281 H20
Rigaud Canada 45°29N 74°18W 355 A10
Rigby U.S.A. 43°40N 111°55W 348 E8
Rīgestān Afghan. 30°15N 65°0E 312 D4
Riggins U.S.A. 45°25N 116°19W 348 D5
Rigolet Canada 54°10N 58°23W 345 B8
Rihand Dam India 24°9N 83°2E 315 G10
Riihimäki Finland 60°45N 24°48E 280 F21
Riiser-Larsen-halvøya Antarctica 68°0S 35°0E 277 C4
Rijeka Croatia 45°20N 14°21E 288 F8
Rijssen Neths. 52°19N 6°31E 287 B6
Rikuchū-Kaigan △ Japan 39°20N 142°0E 302 E11
Rikuzentakada Japan 39°0N 141°40E 302 E10
Riley U.S.A. 43°32N 119°28W 348 E4
Rima → Nigeria 13°4N 5°10E 322 F7
Rimah, Wadi ar → Si. Arabia 26°5N 41°30E 316 E4
Rimau, Pulau Malaysia 5°15N 100°16E 311 c
Rimbey Canada 52°35N 114°15W 342 C6
Rimersburg U.S.A. 41°3N 79°30W 354 E5
Rímini Italy 44°3N 12°33E 294 B5
Rimouski Canada 48°27N 68°30W 345 C6
Rimrock U.S.A. 46°40N 121°7W 350 D5
Rinca Indonesia 8°45S 119°35E 309 F5
Rincón de Romos Mexico 22°14N 102°18W 358 C4
Rinconada Argentina 22°26S 66°10W 366 A2
Rind → India 25°53N 80°33E 315 G9
Ringas India 27°21N 75°34E 314 F6
Ringgold Is. Fiji 16°15S 179°25W 331 a
Ringkøbing Denmark 56°5N 8°15E 281 H13
Ringvassøya Norway 69°56N 19°15E 280 B18
Ringwood U.S.A. 41°7N 74°15W 355 E10
Rinjani Indonesia 8°24S 116°28E 308 F5
Rio Branco Brazil 9°58S 67°49W 364 E5
Río Branco Uruguay 32°40S 53°40W 367 C5
Río Bravo Mexico 25°59N 98°6W 359 B5
Río Bravo ⌓ N. Amer. 29°2N 102°45W 358 B4
Río Bravo del Norte → Mexico 25°57N 97°9W 359 B5
Rio Brilhante Brazil 21°48S 54°33W 367 A5
Rio Claro Brazil 22°19S 47°35W 367 A6
Rio Claro Trin. & Tob. 10°20N 61°25W 361 D7
Río Colorado Argentina 39°0S 64°0W 368 D4
Río Cuarto Argentina 33°10S 64°25W 366 C3
Rio das Pedras Mozam. 23°8S 35°28E 329 C6
Rio de Janeiro Brazil 22°54S 43°12W 367 A7
Rio de Janeiro □ Brazil 22°50S 43°0W 367 A7
Rio do Sul Brazil 27°13S 49°37W 367 B6
Río Dulce △ Guatemala 15°43N 88°50W 360 C2
Río Gallegos Argentina 51°35S 69°15W 368 G3
Río Grande Argentina 53°50S 67°45W 368 G3
Rio Grande Brazil 32°0S 52°20W 367 C5
Río Grande Mexico 23°50N 103°2W 358 C4
Río Grande Nic. 12°54N 83°33W 360 D3
Río Grande Puerto Rico 18°23N 65°50W 361 d
Rio Grande → N. Amer. 25°58N 97°9W 356 J6
Rio Grande City U.S.A. 26°23N 98°49W 356 H5
Río Grande de Santiago → Mexico 21°36N 105°26W 358 C3
Rio Grande do Norte □ Brazil 5°40S 36°0W 365 E11
Rio Grande do Sul □ Brazil 30°0S 53°0W 367 C5
Río Hato Panama 8°22N 80°10W 360 E3
Río Lagartos Mexico 21°36N 88°10W 359 C7
Rio Largo Brazil 9°28S 35°50W 365 E11
Río Mulatos Bolivia 19°40S 66°50W 364 G5
Río Muni □ Eq. Guin. 1°30N 10°0E 324 D2
Rio Negro Brazil 26°0S 49°55W 367 B6
Rio Pardo Brazil 30°0S 52°30W 367 C5
Río Pilcomayo △ Argentina 25°5S 58°5W 366 B4
Río Platano ⌓ Honduras 15°45N 85°0W 360 C3
Rio Rancho U.S.A. 35°14N 106°41W 349 J10
Río Segundo Argentina 31°40S 63°59W 366 C3
Río Tercero Argentina 32°15S 64°8W 366 C3
Rio Verde Brazil 17°50S 51°0W 365 G8
Río Verde Mexico 21°56N 99°59W 359 C5
Rio Vista U.S.A. 38°10N 121°42W 350 G5
Riobamba Ecuador 1°50S 78°45W 364 D3
Riohacha Colombia 11°33N 72°55W 364 A4
Riosucio Colombia 7°27N 77°7W 364 B3
Riou L. Canada 59°7N 106°25W 343 B7
Ripley Canada 44°4N 81°35W 354 B3
Ripley Calif., U.S.A. 33°32N 114°39W 351 M12
Ripley N.Y., U.S.A. 42°16N 79°43W 354 D5
Ripley Tenn., U.S.A. 35°45N 89°32W 357 D10
Ripley W. Va., U.S.A. 38°49N 81°43W 353 F13
Ripon U.K. 54°9N 1°31W 284 C6
Ripon Calif., U.S.A. 37°44N 121°7W 350 H5
Ripon Wis., U.S.A. 43°51N 88°50W 352 D9
Rishā', W. ar → Si. Arabia 25°33N 44°5E 316 E5
Rishiri-Rebun-Sarobetsu △ Japan 45°26N 141°30E 302 B10
Rishiri-Tō Japan 45°11N 141°15E 302 B10
Rishon le Ẕiyyon Israel 31°58N 34°48E 318 D3
Rison U.S.A. 33°58N 92°11W 356 E8
Risør Norway 58°43N 9°13E 281 G13
Rita Blanca Cr. → U.S.A. 35°40N 102°29W 356 D3

Ritter, Mt. U.S.A. 37°41N 119°12W 350 H7
Rittman U.S.A. 40°58N 81°47W 354 F3
Ritzville U.S.A. 47°8N 118°23W 348 C4
Riva del Garda Italy 45°53N 10°50E 294 B4
Rivadavia B. Aires, Argentina 35°29S 62°59W 366 D3
Rivadavia Mendoza, Argentina 33°13S 68°30W 366 C2
Rivadavia Salta, Argentina 24°5S 62°54W 366 A3
Rivadavia Chile 29°57S 70°35W 366 B1
Rivas Nic. 11°30N 85°50W 360 D2
River Cess Liberia 5°30N 9°32W 322 G4
River Jordan Canada 48°26N 124°3W 350 B2
Rivera Argentina 37°12S 63°14W 366 D3
Rivera Uruguay 31°0S 55°50W 367 C4
Riverbank U.S.A. 37°44N 120°56W 350 H6
Riverdale U.S.A. 36°26N 119°52W 350 J7
Riverhead U.S.A. 40°55N 72°40W 355 F12
Riverhurst Canada 50°55N 106°50W 343 C7
Rivers Canada 50°2N 100°14W 343 C8
Rivers Inlet Canada 51°42N 127°15W 342 C3
Riversdale S. Africa 34°7S 21°15E 328 E3
Riverside U.S.A. 33°59N 117°22W 351 M9
Riverton Australia 34°10S 138°46E 335 E2
Riverton Canada 51°1N 97°0W 343 C9
Riverton N.Z. 46°21S 168°0E 331 G2
Riverton U.S.A. 43°2N 108°23W 348 E9
Riviera U.S.A. 35°4N 114°35W 351 K12
Riviera di Levante Italy 44°15N 9°30E 292 D8
Riviera di Ponente Italy 44°10N 8°20E 292 D8
Rivière-au-Renard Canada 48°59N 64°23W 345 C7
Rivière-du-Loup Canada 47°50N 69°30W 345 C6
Rivière-Pentecôte Canada 49°57N 67°1W 345 C6
Rivière-Pilote Martinique 14°26N 60°53W 360 c
Rivière St-Paul Canada 51°28N 57°45W 345 B8
Rivière-Salée Martinique 14°31N 61°0W 360 c
Rivne Ukraine 50°40N 26°10E 289 C14
Rívoli Italy 45°3N 7°31E 292 D7
Rivoli B. Australia 37°32S 140°3E 335 F3
Riyadh = Ar Riyāḍ Si. Arabia 24°41N 46°42E 316 E5
Riyadh al Khabrā' Si. Arabia 26°2N 43°33E 316 E4
Rize Turkey 41°0N 40°30E 291 F7
Rizhao China 35°25N 119°30E 307 G10
Rizokarpaso Cyprus 35°36N 34°23E 297 D13
Rizzuto, C. Italy 38°53N 17°5E 294 E7
Rjukan Norway 59°54N 8°33E 281 G13
Road Town Br. Virgin Is. 18°27N 64°37W 361 e
Roan Plateau U.S.A. 39°20N 109°20W 348 G9
Roanne France 46°3N 4°4E 292 C6
Roanoke Ala., U.S.A. 33°9N 85°22W 357 E12
Roanoke Va., U.S.A. 37°16N 79°56W 353 G14
Roanoke → U.S.A. 35°57N 76°42W 357 D16
Roanoke I. U.S.A. 35°53N 75°39W 357 D17
Roanoke Rapids U.S.A. 36°28N 77°40W 357 C16
Roatán Honduras 16°18N 86°35W 360 C2
Robāt Sang Iran 35°35N 59°10E 317 C8
Robāṭkarīm Iran 35°25N 50°59E 317 C6
Robāṭkarīm ☐ Iran 35°26N 50°59E 317 B6
Robbins I. Australia 40°42S 145°0E 335 G4
Robe → Australia 21°42S 116°15E 332 D2
Robert Lee U.S.A. 31°54N 100°29W 356 F4
Robertsdale U.S.A. 40°11N 78°6W 354 F6
Robertsganj India 24°44N 83°4E 315 G10
Robertson S. Africa 33°46S 19°50E 328 E2
Robertson I. Antarctica 65°15S 59°30W 277 C18
Robertson Ra. Australia 23°15S 121°0E 332 D3
Robertstown Australia 33°58S 139°5E 335 E2
Roberval Canada 48°32N 72°15W 345 C5
Robeson Chan. N. Amer. 82°0N 61°30W 276 A4
Robesonia U.S.A. 40°21N 76°8W 355 F8
Robinson U.S.A. 39°0N 87°44W 352 F10
Robinson → Australia 16°3S 137°16E 334 B2
Robinson Ra. Australia 25°40S 119°0E 333 E2
Robinvale Australia 34°40S 142°45E 335 E3
Roblin Canada 51°14N 101°21W 343 C8
Roboré Bolivia 18°10S 59°45W 364 G7
Robson Canada 49°20N 117°41W 342 D5
Robson, Mt. Canada 53°10N 119°10W 342 C5
Robstown U.S.A. 27°47N 97°40W 356 H6
Roca, C. da Portugal 38°40N 9°31W 293 C1
Roca Partida, I. Mexico 19°1N 112°2W 358 D2
Rocas, I. Brazil 4°0S 34°1W 365 D12
Rocha Uruguay 34°30S 54°25W 367 C5
Rochdale U.K. 53°38N 2°9W 284 D5
Rochefort Belgium 50°9N 5°12E 287 D5
Rochefort France 45°56N 0°57W 292 D3
Rochelle U.S.A. 41°56N 89°4W 352 E9
Rocher River Canada 61°23N 112°44W 342 A6
Rochester U.K. 51°23N 0°31E 285 F8
Rochester Ind., U.S.A. 41°4N 86°13W 352 E10
Rochester Minn., U.S.A. 44°1N 92°28W 352 C7
Rochester N.H., U.S.A. 43°18N 70°59W 355 C14
Rochester N.Y., U.S.A. 43°10N 77°37W 354 C7
Rock → Canada 60°7N 127°7W 342 A3
Rock, The Australia 35°15S 147°2E 335 F4
Rock Creek U.S.A. 41°40N 80°52W 354 E4
Rock Falls U.S.A. 41°47N 89°41W 352 E9
Rock Hill U.S.A. 34°56N 81°1W 357 D14
Rock Island U.S.A. 41°30N 90°34W 352 E8
Rock Port U.S.A. 40°25N 95°31W 352 E6
Rock Rapids U.S.A. 43°26N 96°10W 352 D5
Rock Sound Bahamas 24°54N 76°12W 360 B4
Rock Springs Mont., U.S.A. 46°49N 106°15W 348 C10
Rock Springs Wyo., U.S.A. 41°35N 109°14W 348 F9
Rock Valley U.S.A. 43°12N 96°18W 352 D5
Rockall Atl. Oc. 57°37N 13°42W 278 D3
Rockdale Tex., U.S.A. 30°39N 97°0W 356 F6
Rockdale Wash., U.S.A. 47°22N 121°28W 350 C5
Rockeby = Mungkan Kandju △ Australia 13°35S 142°52E 334 A3
Rockefeller Plateau Antarctica 76°0S 130°0W 277 E14
Rockford U.S.A. 42°16N 89°6W 352 D9
Rockglen Canada 49°11N 105°57W 343 D7
Rockhampton Australia 23°22S 150°32E 334 C5
Rockingham Australia 32°15S 115°38E 333 F2
Rockingham N.C., U.S.A. 34°57N 79°46W 357 D15
Rockingham Vt., U.S.A. 43°11N 72°29W 355 C12
Rockingham B. Australia 18°5S 146°10E 334 B4
Rocklake U.S.A. 48°47N 99°15W 352 A4
Rockland Canada 45°33N 75°17W 355 A9
Rockland Idaho, U.S.A. 42°34N 112°53W 348 E7
Rockland Maine, U.S.A. 44°6N 69°7W 353 C19
Rockland Mich., U.S.A. 46°44N 89°11W 352 B9
Rocklin U.S.A. 38°48N 121°14W 350 G5
Rockly B. Trin. & Tob. 11°9N 60°46W 365 J16
Rockmart U.S.A. 34°0N 85°3W 357 D12
Rockport Mass., U.S.A. 42°39N 70°37W 355 D14
Rockport Tex., U.S.A. 28°2N 97°3W 356 G6
Rocksprings U.S.A. 30°1N 100°13W 356 F4
Rockville Conn., U.S.A. 41°52N 72°28W 355 E12
Rockville Md., U.S.A. 39°5N 77°9W 353 F15
Rockwall U.S.A. 32°56N 96°28W 356 E6
Rockwell City U.S.A. 42°24N 94°38W 352 D6
Rockwood Canada 43°37N 80°8W 354 C4
Rockwood Maine, U.S.A. 45°41N 69°45W 353 C19
Rockwood Tenn., U.S.A. 35°52N 84°41W 357 D12
Rocky Ford U.S.A. 38°3N 103°43W 348 G12
Rocky Gully Australia 34°30S 116°57E 333 F2
Rocky Harbour Canada 49°36N 57°55W 345 C8
Rocky Island L. Canada 46°55N 83°0W 344 C3
Rocky Lane Canada 58°31N 116°22W 342 B5
Rocky Mount U.S.A. 35°57N 77°48W 357 D16
Rocky Mountain △ U.S.A. 40°25N 105°45W 348 F11
Rocky Mountain House Canada 52°22N 114°55W 342 C6
Rocky Mts. N. Amer. 49°0N 115°0W 348 B6
Rocky Point Namibia 19°3S 12°30E 328 B2
Rod Pakistan 28°10N 63°5E 312 E3
Roda Greece 39°48N 19°46E 297 A3
Rødbyhavn Denmark 54°39N 11°22E 281 J14
Roddickton Canada 50°51N 56°8W 345 B8
Rodez France 44°21N 2°33E 292 D5
Ródhos = Rhodes Greece 36°15N 28°10E 297 C10
Rodia Greece 35°22N 25°1E 297 D7
Rodney Canada 42°34N 81°41W 354 D3
Rodney, C. N.Z. 36°17S 174°50E 331 B5
Rodopos Greece 35°34N 23°45E 297 D5
Rodriguez Ind. Oc. 19°45S 63°20E 275 E13
Roe → U.K. 55°6N 6°59W 282 A5
Roebling U.S.A. 40°7N 74°47W 355 F10
Roebourne Australia 20°44S 117°9E 332 D2
Roebuck B. Australia 18°5S 122°20E 332 C3
Roermond Neths. 51°12N 6°0E 287 C6
Roes Welcome Sd. Canada 65°0N 87°0W 341 C11
Roeselare Belgium 50°57N 3°7E 287 D3
Rogachev = Ragachow Belarus 53°8N 30°5E 289 B16
Rogagua, L. Bolivia 13°43S 66°50W 364 F5
Rogatyn Ukraine 49°24N 24°36E 289 D13
Rogers U.S.A. 36°20N 94°7W 356 C7
Rogers City U.S.A. 45°25N 83°49W 353 C12
Rogersville Canada 46°44N 65°26W 345 C6
Roggan → Canada 54°24N 79°25W 344 B4
Roggan L. Canada 54°8N 77°50W 344 B4
Roggeveen Basin Pac. Oc. 31°30S 95°30W 337 L18
Roggeveldberge S. Africa 32°10S 20°10E 328 E3
Rogoaguado, L. Bolivia 13°0S 65°30W 364 F5
Rogojampi Indonesia 8°19S 114°17E 309 J17
Rogue → U.S.A. 42°26N 124°26W 348 E1
Rohnert Park U.S.A. 38°16N 122°40W 350 G4
Rohri Pakistan 27°45N 68°51E 314 F3
Rohri Canal Pakistan 26°15N 68°27E 314 F3
Rohtak India 28°55N 76°43E 314 E7
Roi Et Thailand 16°4N 103°40E 310 D4
Roja Latvia 57°29N 22°43E 281 H20
Rojas Argentina 34°10S 60°45W 366 C3
Rojo, C. Mexico 21°33N 97°20W 359 C5
Rokan → Indonesia 2°0N 100°50E 308 D2
Rokiškis Lithuania 55°55N 25°35E 281 J21
Rolândia Brazil 23°18S 51°23W 367 A5
Rolla Mo., U.S.A. 37°57N 91°46W 352 G8
Rolla N. Dak., U.S.A. 48°52N 99°37W 352 A4
Rolleston Australia 24°28S 148°35E 334 C4
Rollingstone Australia 19°2S 146°24E 334 B4
Roma Australia 26°32S 148°49E 335 D4
Roma Italy 41°54N 12°28E 294 D5
Roma Sweden 57°32N 18°26E 281 H18
Roma-Los Saenz U.S.A. 26°24N 99°1W 356 H5
Romain, C. U.S.A. 33°0N 79°22W 357 E15
Romaine → Canada 50°18N 63°47W 345 B7
Roman Romania 46°57N 26°55E 289 E14
Romang Indonesia 7°30S 127°20E 309 F7
Românî Egypt 30°59N 32°38E 318 E1
Romania ■ Europe 46°0N 25°0E 289 F12
Romano, Cayo Cuba 22°0N 77°30W 360 B4
Romans-sur-Isère France 45°3N 5°3E 292 D6
Romblon Phil. 12°33N 122°17E 309 B6
Rome = Roma Italy 41°54N 12°28E 294 D5
Rome Ga., U.S.A. 34°15N 85°10W 357 D12
Rome N.Y., U.S.A. 43°13N 75°27W 355 C9
Rome Pa., U.S.A. 41°51N 76°21W 355 E8
Romney U.S.A. 39°21N 78°45W 353 F14
Romney Marsh U.K. 51°2N 0°54E 285 F8
Rømø Denmark 55°10N 8°30E 281 J13
Romorantin-Lanthenay France 47°21N 1°45E 292 C4
Romsdalen Norway 62°25N 7°52E 280 E12
Romsey U.K. 51°0N 1°29W 285 G6
Ron Vietnam 17°53N 106°27E 310 D6
Rona U.K. 57°34N 5°59W 283 D3
Ronan U.S.A. 47°32N 114°6W 348 C6
Roncador, Cayos Colombia 13°32N 80°4W 360 D3
Roncador, Serra do Brazil 12°30S 52°30W 365 F8
Ronda Spain 36°46N 5°12W 293 D3
Rondane Norway 61°57N 9°50E 280 F13
Rondônia ☐ Brazil 11°0S 63°0W 364 F6
Rondonópolis Brazil 16°28S 54°38W 365 G8
Rong, Koh Cambodia 10°45N 103°15E 311 G4
Ronge, L. la Canada 55°6N 105°17W 343 B7
Rønne Denmark 55°6N 14°43E 281 J16
Ronne Ice Shelf Antarctica 77°30S 60°0W 277 D18
Ronsard, C. Australia 24°46S 113°10E 333 D1
Ronse Belgium 50°45N 3°35E 287 D3
Roodepoort S. Africa 26°11S 27°54E 329 D4
Roof Butte U.S.A. 36°28N 109°5W 349 H9
Rooiboklaagte → Namibia 20°50S 21°0E 328 C3
Rooniu, Mt. Tahiti 17°49S 149°12W 331 d
Roorkee India 29°52N 77°59E 314 E7
Roosendaal Neths. 51°32N 4°29E 287 C4
Roosevelt U.S.A. 40°18N 109°59W 348 F9
Roosevelt → Brazil 7°35S 60°20W 364 E6
Roosevelt, Mt. Canada 58°26N 125°20W 342 B3
Roosevelt I. Antarctica 79°30S 162°0W 277 D12
Roper → Australia 14°43S 135°27E 334 A2
Roper Bar Australia 14°44S 134°44E 334 A1
Roque Pérez Argentina 35°25S 59°24W 366 D4
Roquetas de Mar Spain 36°46N 2°36W 293 D4
Roraima ☐ Brazil 2°0N 61°30W 364 C6
Roraima, Mt. Venezuela 5°10N 60°40W 364 B6
Røros Norway 62°35N 11°23E 280 E14
Rosa Zambia 9°33S 31°15E 327 D3
Rosa, L. Bahamas 21°0N 73°30W 361 B5
Rosa, Monte Europe 45°57N 7°53E 292 D7
Rosalia U.S.A. 47°14N 117°22W 348 C5
Rosamond U.S.A. 34°52N 118°10W 351 L8
Rosario Argentina 33°0S 60°40W 366 C3
Rosário Brazil 3°0S 44°15W 365 D10
Rosario Baja Calif., Mexico 30°0N 115°50W 358 B1
Rosario Sinaloa, Mexico 22°58N 105°53W 358 C3
Rosario Paraguay 24°30S 57°35W 366 A4
Rosario de la Frontera Argentina 25°50S 65°0W 366 B3
Rosario de Lerma Argentina 24°59S 65°35W 366 A2
Rosario del Tala Argentina 32°20S 59°10W 366 C4
Rosário do Sul Brazil 30°15S 54°55W 367 C5
Rosarito Mexico 32°20N 117°2W 351 N9
Roscoe U.S.A. 41°56N 74°55W 355 E10
Roscommon Ireland 53°38N 8°11W 282 C3
Roscommon ☐ Ireland 53°49N 8°23W 282 C3
Roscrea Ireland 52°57N 7°49W 282 D4
Rose → Australia 14°16S 135°45E 334 A2
Rose Belle Mauritius 20°24S 57°36E 325 d
Rose Blanche-Harbour Le Cou Canada 47°38N 58°45W 345 C8
Rose Hill Mauritius 20°14S 57°27E 325 d
Rose Pt. Canada 54°11N 131°39W 342 C2
Rose Valley Canada 52°19N 103°49W 343 C8
Roseau Dominica 15°17N 61°24W 361 C7
Roseau U.S.A. 48°51N 95°46W 352 A6
Rosebery Australia 41°46S 145°33E 335 G4
Rosebud S. Dak., U.S.A. 43°14N 100°51W 352 D3
Rosebud Tex., U.S.A. 31°4N 96°59W 356 F6
Roseburg U.S.A. 43°13N 123°20W 348 E2
Rosehearty U.K. 57°42N 2°7W 283 D6
Roseires Res. Sudan 11°51N 34°23E 323 F12
Roseland U.S.A. 38°25N 122°43W 350 G4
Rosemary Canada 50°46N 112°5W 342 C6
Rosenberg U.S.A. 29°34N 95°49W 356 G7
Rosenheim Germany 47°51N 12°7E 288 E7
Roses, G. de Spain 42°10N 3°15E 293 A7
Rosetown Canada 51°35N 107°59W 343 C7
Roseville Calif., U.S.A. 38°45N 121°17W 350 G5
Roseville Mich., U.S.A. 42°30N 82°56W 354 D2
Rosewood Australia 27°38S 152°36E 335 D5
Roshkhvār Iran 34°58N 59°37E 317 C8
Rosignano Maríttimo Italy 43°24N 10°28E 294 C4
Rosignol Guyana 6°15N 57°30W 364 B7
Roşiori de Vede Romania 44°9N 25°0E 289 F13
Roskilde Denmark 55°38N 12°3E 281 J15
Roslavl Russia 53°57N 32°55E 290 D5
Rosmead S. Africa 31°29S 25°8E 328 E4
Ross Australia 42°2S 147°30E 335 G4
Ross N.Z. 42°53S 170°49E 331 E3
Ross Dependency Antarctica 76°0S 170°0W 277 D12
Ross I. Antarctica 77°30S 168°0E 277 D11
Ross Ice Shelf Antarctica 80°0S 180°0E 277 E12
Ross L. U.S.A. 48°44N 121°4W 348 B3
Ross-on-Wye U.K. 51°54N 2°34W 285 F5
Ross River Australia 23°44S 134°30E 334 C1
Ross River Canada 62°30N 131°30W 342 A2
Ross Sea Antarctica 74°0S 178°0E 277 D11
Rossall Pt. U.K. 53°55N 3°3W 284 D4
Rossan Pt. Ireland 54°42N 8°47W 282 B3
Rossano Italy 39°36N 16°39E 294 E7
Rossburn Canada 50°40N 100°49W 343 C8
Rosseau Canada 45°16N 79°39W 354 A5
Rosseau, L. Canada 45°10N 79°35W 354 A5
Rosses, The Ireland 55°2N 8°20W 282 A3
Rossignol, L. Canada 52°43N 73°40W 344 B5
Rossignol L. Canada 44°12N 65°10W 345 D6
Rossiya = Russia ■ Eurasia 62°0N 105°0E 301 C11
Rossland Canada 49°6N 117°50W 342 D5
Rosslare Ireland 52°17N 6°24W 282 D5
Rosslare Harbour Ireland 52°15N 6°20W 282 D5
Rosso Mauritania 16°40N 15°45W 322 E2
Rossosh Russia 50°15N 39°28E 291 D6
Røssvatnet Norway 65°45N 14°5E 280 D16
Røst Norway 67°32N 12°0E 280 C15
Rosthern Canada 52°40N 106°20W 343 C7
Rostock Germany 54°5N 12°8E 288 A7
Rostov Don, Russia 47°15N 39°45E 291 E6
Rostov Sverdlovsk, Russia 57°14N 39°25E 290 C6
Roswell Ga., U.S.A. 34°2N 84°22W 357 D12
Roswell N. Mex., U.S.A. 33°24N 104°32W 349 K11
Rotan U.S.A. 32°51N 100°28W 356 E4
Rother → U.K. 50°59N 0°45E 285 G8
Rothera Antarctica 67°20S 63°0W 277 C17
Rotherham U.K. 53°26N 1°20W 284 D6
Rothes U.K. 57°32N 3°13W 283 D5
Rothesay Canada 45°23N 66°0W 345 C6
Rothesay U.K. 55°50N 5°3W 283 F3
Roti Indonesia 10°50S 123°0E 309 F6
Roto Australia 33°0S 145°30E 335 E4
Rotondo, Mte. France 42°14N 9°8E 292 E8
Rotoroa, L. N.Z. 41°55S 172°39E 331 D4
Rotorua N.Z. 38°9S 176°16E 331 C6
Rotorua, L. N.Z. 38°5S 176°18E 331 C6
Rotterdam Neths. 51°55N 4°30E 287 C4
Rotterdam U.S.A. 42°48N 74°1W 355 D10
Rottnest I. Australia 32°0S 115°27E 333 F2
Rottumeroog Neths. 53°33N 6°34E 287 A6
Rottweil Germany 48°9N 8°37E 288 D5
Rotuma Fiji 12°25S 177°5E 330 C10
Roubaix France 50°40N 3°10E 292 A5
Rouen France 49°27N 1°4E 292 B4
Rouleau Canada 50°10N 104°56W 343 C8
Round I. Mauritius 19°51S 57°45E 325 d
Round Mountain U.S.A. 38°43N 117°4W 348 G5
Round Mt. Australia 30°26S 152°16E 335 E5
Round Rock U.S.A. 30°31N 97°41W 356 F6
Roundup U.S.A. 46°27N 108°33W 348 C9
Rousay U.K. 59°10N 3°2W 283 B5
Rouses Point U.S.A. 44°59N 73°22W 355 B11
Rouseville U.S.A. 41°28N 79°42W 354 E5
Rousse = Ruse Bulgaria 43°48N 25°59E 295 C12
Roussillon France 42°30N 2°35E 292 E5
Rouxville S. Africa 30°25S 26°50E 328 E4
Rouyn-Noranda Canada 48°20N 79°0W 344 C4
Rovaniemi Finland 66°29N 25°41E 280 C21
Rovereto Italy 45°53N 11°3E 294 B4
Rovigo Italy 45°4N 11°47E 294 B4
Rovinj Croatia 45°5N 13°40E 288 F7
Rovno = Rivne Ukraine 50°40N 26°10E 289 C14
Rovuma = Ruvuma → Tanzania 10°29S 40°28E 327 E5
Row'ān Iran 35°8N 48°51E 317 C6
Rowena Australia 29°48S 148°55E 335 D4
Rowley Shoals Australia 17°30S 119°0E 332 C2
Roxas Phil. 11°36N 122°49E 309 B6
Roxboro U.S.A. 36°24N 78°59W 357 C15
Roxborough Trin. & Tob. 11°15N 60°35W 365 J16
Roxburgh N.Z. 45°33S 169°19E 331 F2
Roxbury U.S.A. 40°6N 77°39W 354 F7
Roxby Downs Australia 30°43S 136°46E 335 E2
Roy Mont., U.S.A. 47°20N 108°58W 348 C9
Roy N. Mex., U.S.A. 35°57N 104°12W 349 J11
Roy Utah, U.S.A. 41°10N 112°2W 348 F7
Royal Bardia △ Nepal 28°20N 81°20E 315 E9
Royal Canal Ireland 53°30N 7°13W 282 C4
Royal Chitawan △ Nepal 26°30N 84°30E 315 F11
Royal Leamington Spa U.K. 52°18N 1°31W 285 E6
Royal Natal △ S. Africa 28°43S 28°51E 329 D4
Royal Tunbridge Wells U.K. 51°7N 0°16E 285 F8
Royale, Isle U.S.A. 48°0N 88°54W 352 B9
Royan France 45°37N 1°2W 292 D3
Royston U.K. 52°3N 0°0 285 E7
Rozdilna Ukraine 46°50N 30°2E 289 E16
Rozhyshche Ukraine 50°54N 25°15E 289 C13
Rtishchevo Russia 52°18N 43°46E 290 D7
Ruacaná Namibia 17°27S 14°21E 328 B1
Ruaha △ Tanzania 7°41S 34°30E 326 D3
Ruahine Ra. N.Z. 39°55S 176°2E 331 C6
Ruapehu N.Z. 39°17S 175°35E 331 C5
Ruapuke I. N.Z. 46°46S 168°31E 331 G2
Ruâq, W. → Egypt 30°0N 33°49E 318 F2
Rub' al Khālī Si. Arabia 19°0N 48°0E 319 D4
Rubeho Mts. Tanzania 6°50S 36°25E 326 D4
Rubh a' Mhail U.K. 55°56N 6°8W 283 F2
Rubha Hunish U.K. 57°42N 6°20W 283 D2
Rubha Robhanais = Lewis, Butt of U.K. 58°31N 6°16W 283 C2
Rubicon → U.S.A. 38°53N 121°4W 350 G5
Rubio Venezuela 7°43N 72°22W 364 B4
Rubondo △ Tanzania 2°18S 31°58E 326 C3
Rubtsovsk Russia 51°30N 81°10E 300 D9
Ruby L. U.S.A. 40°10N 115°28W 348 F6
Ruby Mts. U.S.A. 40°30N 115°20W 348 F6
Rubyvale Australia 23°25S 147°42E 334 C4
Rūd Sar Iran 37°8N 50°18E 317 B6
Rudall Australia 33°43S 136°17E 335 E2
Rudall → Australia 22°34S 122°13E 332 D3
Rudall River △ Australia 22°38S 122°30E 332 D3
Rudewa Tanzania 10°7S 34°40E 327 E3
Rudnyy Kazakhstan 52°57N 63°7E 300 D7
Rudolfa, Ostrov Russia 81°45N 58°30E 300 A6
Rudyard U.S.A. 46°14N 84°36W 353 B11
Ruenya → Africa 16°24S 33°48E 327 F3
Ruffling Pt. Br. Virgin Is. 18°44N 64°27W 361 e
Rufiji → Tanzania 7°50S 39°15E 326 D4
Rufino Argentina 34°20S 62°50W 366 C3
Rufunsa Zambia 15°4S 29°34E 327 F2
Rugby U.K. 52°23N 1°16W 285 E6
Rugby U.S.A. 48°22N 100°0W 352 A4
Rügen Germany 54°22N 13°24E 288 A7
Ruhengeri Rwanda 1°30S 29°36E 326 C2
Ruhnu Estonia 57°48N 23°15E 281 H20
Ruhr → Germany 51°27N 6°43E 288 C4
Ruhuhu → Tanzania 10°31S 34°34E 327 E3
Ruidoso U.S.A. 33°20N 105°41W 349 K11
Ruivo, Pico Madeira 32°45N 16°56W 296 D3
Rujm Tal'at al Jamā'ah Jordan 30°24N 35°30E 318 E4
Ruk Pakistan 27°50N 68°42E 314 F3
Rukhla Pakistan 32°27N 71°57E 314 C4
Ruki → Dem. Rep. of the Congo 0°5N 18°17E 324 E3
Rukwa ☐ Tanzania 7°0S 31°30E 326 D3
Rukwa, L. Tanzania 8°0S 32°20E 326 D3
Rulhieres, C. Australia 13°56S 127°22E 332 B4
Rum = Rhum U.K. 57°0N 6°20W 283 E2
Rum Jordan 29°39N 35°26E 318 F4
Rum Cay Bahamas 23°40N 74°58W 361 B5
Rum Jungle Australia 13°0S 130°59E 332 B5
Ruma △ Kenya 0°39S 34°18E 326 C3
Rumāḥ Si. Arabia 25°29N 47°10E 316 E5
Rumania = Romania ■ Europe 46°0N 25°0E 289 F12
Rumaylah Iraq 30°47N 47°37E 316 D5
Rumbêk Sudan 6°54N 29°37E 323 G11
Rumford U.S.A. 44°33N 70°33W 355 B14
Rumia Poland 54°37N 18°25E 289 A10
Rumoi Japan 43°56N 141°39E 302 C10
Rumonge Burundi 3°59S 29°26E 326 C2
Rumson U.S.A. 40°23N 74°0W 355 F11
Rumuruti Kenya 0°17N 36°32E 326 B4
Runan China 33°0N 114°30E 306 H8
Runanga N.Z. 42°25S 171°15E 331 E3
Runaway, C. N.Z. 37°32S 177°59E 331 B6
Runaway Bay Jamaica 18°27N 77°20W 360 a
Runcorn U.K. 53°21N 2°44W 284 D5
Rundu Namibia 17°52S 19°43E 328 B2
Rungwa Tanzania 6°55S 33°32E 326 D3
Rungwa → Tanzania 7°36S 31°50E 326 D3
Rungwa ⌓ Tanzania 6°53S 34°2E 326 D3
Rungwe Tanzania 9°11S 33°32E 327 D3
Rungwe, Mt. Tanzania 9°8S 33°40E 324 F6
Runton Ra. Australia 23°31S 123°6E 332 D3
Ruokolahti Finland 61°17N 28°50E 280 F23
Ruoqiang China 38°55N 88°10E 304 C3
Rupa India 27°15N 92°21E 313 F18
Rupar India 31°2N 76°38E 314 D7
Rupat Indonesia 1°45N 101°40E 308 D2
Rupen → India 23°28N 71°31E 314 H4
Rupert U.S.A. 42°37N 113°41W 348 E7
Rupert → Canada 51°29N 78°45W 344 B4
Rupert B. Canada 51°35N 79°0W 344 B4
Rupert House = Waskaganish Canada 51°30N 78°40W 344 B4
Rupsa India 21°37N 87°1E 315 J12
Rurrenabaque Bolivia 14°30S 67°32W 364 F5
Rusambo Zimbabwe 16°30S 32°4E 327 F3
Rusape Zimbabwe 18°35S 32°8E 327 F3
Ruschuk = Ruse Bulgaria 43°48N 25°59E 295 C12
Ruse Bulgaria 43°48N 25°59E 295 C12
Rush Ireland 53°31N 6°6W 282 C5
Rushan China 36°56N 121°30E 307 F11
Rushden U.K. 52°18N 0°35W 285 E7
Rushmore, Mt. U.S.A. 43°53N 103°28W 352 D2
Rushville Ill., U.S.A. 40°7N 90°34W 352 E8
Rushville Ind., U.S.A. 39°37N 85°27W 353 F11
Rushville Nebr., U.S.A. 42°43N 102°28W 352 D2
Russas Brazil 4°55S 37°50W 365 D11
Russell Canada 50°50N 101°20W 343 C8
Russell Kans., U.S.A. 38°54N 98°52W 352 F4
Russell N.Y., U.S.A. 44°27N 75°9W 355 B9
Russell Pa., U.S.A. 41°56N 79°8W 354 E5
Russell Cave ⌓ U.S.A. 34°59N 85°49W 357 D12
Russell L. Man., Canada 56°15N 101°30W 343 B8
Russell L. N.W.T., Canada 63°5N 115°44W 342 A5
Russellkonda India 19°57N 84°42E 313 K14
Russellville Ala., U.S.A. 34°30N 87°44W 357 D11
Russellville Ark., U.S.A. 35°17N 93°8W 356 D8
Russellville Ky., U.S.A. 36°51N 86°53W 352 G10
Russia ■ Eurasia 62°0N 105°0E 301 C11
Russian → U.S.A. 38°27N 123°8W 350 G3
Russkoye Ustie Russia 71°0N 149°0E 276 B15
Rustam Pakistan 34°25N 72°13E 314 B5
Rustam Shahr Pakistan 26°58N 66°6E 314 F2
Rustavi Georgia 41°30N 45°0E 291 F8
Rustenburg S. Africa 25°41S 27°14E 328 D4
Ruston U.S.A. 32°32N 92°38W 356 E8
Rutana Burundi 3°55S 30°0E 326 C3
Ruteng Indonesia 8°35S 120°30E 309 F6
Ruth U.S.A. 43°42N 82°45W 354 C2
Rutherford U.S.A. 38°26N 122°24W 350 G4
Rutland U.S.A. 43°37N 72°58W 355 C12
Rutland ☐ U.K. 52°38N 0°40W 285 E7
Rutland Water U.K. 52°39N 0°38W 285 E7
Rutledge → Canada 61°4N 112°0W 343 A6
Rutledge L. Canada 61°33N 110°47W 343 A6
Rutog China 33°27N 79°42E 304 C2
Rutshuru Dem. Rep. of the Congo 1°13S 29°25E 326 C2
Ruvu Tanzania 6°49S 38°43E 326 D4
Ruvu → Tanzania 6°23S 38°52E 326 D4
Ruvuba △ Burundi 3°3S 29°33E 326 C2
Ruvuma ☐ Tanzania 10°20S 36°0E 327 E4
Ruvuma → Tanzania 10°29S 40°28E 327 E5
Ruwais U.A.E. 24°5N 52°50E 317 E7
Ruwenzori Africa 0°30N 29°55E 326 B2
Ruwenzori △ Uganda 0°20N 30°0E 326 B2
Ruya → Zimbabwe 16°27S 32°5E 329 B5
Ruyigi Burundi 3°29S 30°15E 326 C3
Ružomberok Slovak Rep. 49°3N 19°17E 289 D10
Rwanda ■ Africa 2°0S 30°0E 326 C3

Ryan, L. *U.K.* 55°0N 5°2W **283** G3
Ryazan *Russia* 54°40N 39°40E **290** D6
Ryazhsk *Russia* 53°45N 40°3E **290** D7
Rybachiy Poluostrov *Russia* 69°43N 32°0E **280** B25
Rybinsk *Russia* 58°5N 38°50E **290** C6
Rybinskoye Vdkhr. *Russia* 58°30N 38°25E **290** C6
Rybnitsa = Râbniţa *Moldova* 47°45N 29°0E **289** E15
Rycroft *Canada* 55°45N 118°40W **342** B5
Ryde *U.K.* 50°43N 1°9W **285** G6
Ryderwood *U.S.A.* 46°23N 123°3W **350** D3
Rye *U.K.* 50°57N 0°45E **285** G8
Rye → *U.K.* 54°11N 0°44W **284** C7
Rye Bay *U.K.* 50°52N 0°49E **285** G8
Rye Patch Res. *U.S.A.* 40°28N 118°19W **348** F4
Ryegate *U.S.A.* 46°18N 109°15W **348** C9
Ryley *Canada* 53°17N 112°26W **342** C6
Rylstone *Australia* 32°46S 149°58E **335** E4
Ryōtsu *Japan* 38°5N 138°26E **302** E9
Rypin *Poland* 53°3N 19°25E **289** B10
Ryūgasaki *Japan* 35°54N 140°11E **303** G10
Ryukyu Is. = Ryūkyū-rettō *Japan* 26°0N 126°0E **303** M3
Ryūkyū-rettō *Japan* 26°0N 126°0E **303** M3
Rzeszów *Poland* 50°5N 21°58E **289** C11
Rzhev *Russia* 56°20N 34°20E **290** C5

S

Sa *Thailand* 18°34N 100°45E **310** C3
Sa Canal *Spain* 38°51N 1°23E **296** C7
Sa Conillera *Spain* 38°59N 1°13E **296** C7
Sa Dec *Vietnam* 10°20N 105°46E **311** G5
Sa Dragonera *Spain* 39°35N 2°19E **296** B9
Sa Mesquida *Spain* 39°55N 4°16E **296** B11
Sa Savina *Spain* 38°44N 1°25E **296** C7
Sa'ādatābād *Fārs, Iran* 30°10N 53°5E **317** D7
Sa'ādatābād *Hormozgān, Iran* 28°3N 55°53E **317** D7
Sa'ādatābād *Kermān, Iran* 29°40N 55°51E **317** D7
Saale → *Germany* 51°56N 11°54E **288** C6
Saalfeld *Germany* 50°38N 11°21E **288** C6
Saanich *Canada* 48°29N 123°26W **350** B3
Saar → *Europe* 49°41N 6°32E **287** E6
Saarbrücken *Germany* 49°14N 6°59E **288** D4
Saaremaa *Estonia* 58°30N 22°30E **281** G20
Saarijärvi *Finland* 62°43N 25°16E **280** E21
Saariselkä *Finland* 68°16N 28°15E **280** B23
Sab 'Ābar *Syria* 33°46N 37°41E **316** C3
Saba *W. Indies* 17°38N 63°14W **361** C7
Šabac *Serbia* 44°48N 19°42E **295** B8
Sabadell *Spain* 41°28N 2°7E **293** B7
Sabah □ *Malaysia* 6°0N 117°0E **308** C5
Sabak Bernam *Malaysia* 3°46N 100°58E **311** L3
Sabalān, Kūhhā-ye *Iran* 38°15N 47°45E **316** B5
Sabalana, Kepulauan *Indonesia* 6°45S 118°50E **309** F5
Sábana de la Mar *Dom. Rep.* 19°7N 69°24W **361** C6
Sábanalarga *Colombia* 10°38N 74°55W **364** A4
Sabang *Indonesia* 5°50N 95°15E **308** C1
Sabará *Brazil* 19°55S 43°46W **365** G10
Sabarmati → *India* 22°18N 72°22E **314** H5
Sabattis *U.S.A.* 44°6N 74°40W **355** B10
Saberania *Indonesia* 2°5S 138°18E **309** E9
Sabhā *Libya* 27°9N 14°29E **323** C8
Sabi → *India* 28°29N 76°44E **314** E7
Sabie *S. Africa* 25°10S 30°48E **329** D5
Sabinal *Mexico* 30°57N 107°30W **358** A3
Sabinal *U.S.A.* 29°19N 99°28W **356** G5
Sabinas *Mexico* 27°51N 101°7W **358** B4
Sabinas → *Mexico* 27°37N 100°42W **358** B4
Sabinas Hidalgo *Mexico* 26°30N 100°10W **358** B4
Sabine → *U.S.A.* 29°59N 93°47W **356** G8
Sabine L. *U.S.A.* 29°53N 93°51W **356** G8
Sabine Pass *U.S.A.* 29°44N 93°54W **356** G8
Sabinsville *U.S.A.* 41°52N 77°31W **354** E7
Sablayan *Phil.* 12°50N 120°50E **309** B6
Sable *Canada* 55°30N 68°21W **345** A6
Sable, C. *Canada* 43°29N 65°38W **345** D6
Sable, C. *U.S.A.* 25°9N 81°8W **360** A3
Sable I. *Canada* 44°0N 60°0W **345** D8
Sabrina Coast *Antarctica* 68°0S 120°0E **277** C9
Sabulubbek *Indonesia* 1°36S 98°40E **308** E1
Sabzevār *Iran* 36°15N 57°40E **317** B8
Sabzvārān *Iran* 28°45N 57°50E **317** D8
Sac City *U.S.A.* 42°25N 95°0W **352** D6
Săcele *Romania* 45°37N 25°41E **289** F13
Sacheon *S. Korea* 35°0N 128°6E **307** G15
Sachigo → *Canada* 55°6N 88°58W **344** A2
Sachigo, L. *Canada* 53°50N 92°12W **344** B1
Sachimbo *Angola* 9°14S 20°16E **324** F4
Sachsen □ *Germany* 50°55N 13°10E **288** C7
Sachsen-Anhalt □ *Germany* 52°0N 12°0E **288** C7
Sackets Harbor *U.S.A.* 43°57N 76°7W **355** C8
Sackville *Canada* 45°54N 64°22W **345** C7
Saco *Maine, U.S.A.* 43°30N 70°27W **355** C14
Saco *Mont., U.S.A.* 48°28N 107°21W **348** B10
Sacramento *U.S.A.* 38°35N 121°29W **350** G5
Sacramento → *U.S.A.* 38°3N 121°56W **350** G5
Sacramento Mts. *U.S.A.* 32°30N 105°30W **349** K11
Sacramento Valley *U.S.A.* 39°30N 122°0W **350** G5
Sada-Misaki *Japan* 33°20N 132°5E **303** H6
Sadabad *India* 27°27N 78°3E **314** F8
Sadani *Tanzania* 5°58S 38°35E **326** D4
Sadao *Thailand* 6°38N 100°26E **311** J3
Sadd el Aali *Egypt* 23°54N 32°54E **323** D12
Saddle Mt. *U.S.A.* 45°58N 123°41W **350** E3
Sadimi *Dem. Rep. of the Congo* 9°25S 23°32E **327** D1
Sado *Japan* 38°0N 138°25E **302** F9
Sadra *India* 23°21N 72°43E **314** H5
Sadri *India* 25°11N 73°26E **314** G5
Sæby *Denmark* 57°21N 10°30E **281** H14
Saegertown *U.S.A.* 41°43N 80°9W **354** E4
Şafājah *Si. Arabia* 26°25N 39°0E **316** E3
Safata B. *Samoa* 14°0S 171°50W **331** b
Säffle *Sweden* 59°8N 12°55E **281** G15
Safford *U.S.A.* 32°50N 109°43W **349** K9
Saffron Walden *U.K.* 52°1N 0°16E **285** E8
Safi *Morocco* 32°18N 9°20W **322** B4
Şafīābād *Iran* 36°45N 57°58E **317** B8
Safīd Dasht *Iran* 33°27N 48°11E **317** C6
Safīd Kūh *Afghan.* 34°45N 63°0E **312** B3
Safīd Rūd → *Iran* 37°23N 50°11E **317** B6
Safipur *India* 26°44N 80°21E **315** F9
Şāfitā *Syria* 34°48N 36°7E **316** C3
Safune *Samoa* 13°25S 172°21W **331** b
Şafwān *Iraq* 30°7N 47°43E **316** D5
Sag Harbor *U.S.A.* 41°0N 72°18W **355** F12
Saga *Japan* 33°15N 130°16E **303** H5
Saga □ *Japan* 33°15N 130°20E **303** H5
Sagae *Japan* 38°22N 140°17E **302** E10
Sagaing *Burma* 21°52N 95°59E **313** J19
Sagamore *U.S.A.* 40°46N 79°14W **354** F5
Saganaga L. *Canada* 48°14N 90°52W **352** A8
Sagar *Karnataka, India* 14°14N 75°6E **312** M9
Sagar *Mad. P., India* 23°50N 78°44E **315** H8
Sagara, L. *Tanzania* 5°20S 31°0E **326** D3
Sagarmatha = Everest, Mt. *Nepal* 28°5N 86°58E **315** E12
Sagarmatha △ *Nepal* 27°55N 86°45E **315** F12
Saginaw *U.S.A.* 43°26N 83°56W **353** D12
Saginaw B. *U.S.A.* 43°50N 83°40W **353** D12
Saglouc = Salluit *Canada* 62°14N 75°38W **341** C12
Sagone *France* 42°7N 8°42E **292** E8
Sagua la Grande *Cuba* 22°50N 80°10W **360** B3
Saguache *U.S.A.* 38°5N 106°8W **348** G10
Saguaro △ *U.S.A.* 32°12N 110°38W **349** K8
Saguenay → *Canada* 48°22N 71°0W **345** C5
Sagunt *Spain* 39°42N 0°18W **293** C5
Sagunto = Sagunt *Spain* 39°42N 0°18W **293** C5
Sagwara *India* 23°41N 74°1E **314** H6
Sahagún *Spain* 42°18N 5°2W **293** A3
Saḩam al Jawlān *Syria* 32°45N 35°55E **318** C4
Sahamandrevo *Madag.* 23°15S 45°35E **329** C8
Sahand, Kūh-e *Iran* 37°44N 46°27E **316** B5
Sahara *Africa* 23°0N 5°0E **322** D6
Saharan Atlas = Saharien, Atlas *Algeria* 33°30N 1°0E **322** B6
Saharanpur *India* 29°58N 77°33E **314** E7
Saharien, Atlas *Algeria* 33°30N 1°0E **322** B6
Saharsa *India* 25°53N 86°36E **315** G12
Sahasinaka *Madag.* 21°49S 47°49E **329** C8
Sahaswan *India* 28°5N 78°45E **315** E8
Saheira, W. el → *Egypt* 30°5N 33°25E **318** E2
Sahel *Africa* 12°0N 8°0W **320** E3
Sahel *Africa* 16°0N 5°0E **322** E5
Sahibganj *India* 25°12N 87°40E **315** G12
Sāḩilīyah *Iraq* 33°43N 42°42E **316** C4
Sahiwal *Pakistan* 30°45N 73°8E **314** D5
Şaḩneh *Iran* 34°29N 47°41E **316** C5
Sahrawi = Western Sahara ■ *Africa* 25°0N 13°0W **322** D3
Sahuaripa *Mexico* 29°3N 109°14W **358** B3
Sahuarita *U.S.A.* 31°57N 110°58W **349** L8
Sahuayo de Díaz *Mexico* 20°4N 102°43W **358** C4
Sai → *India* 25°39N 82°47E **315** G10
Sai Buri *Thailand* 6°43N 101°45E **311** J3
Sai Kung *China* 22°23N 114°16E **305** G11
Sa'id Bundâs *Sudan* 8°24N 24°48E **323** G10
Sa'īdābād = Sīrjān *Iran* 29°30N 55°45E **317** D7
Sa'īdābād *Iran* 36°8N 54°11E **317** B7
Sa'īdīyeh *Iran* 36°20N 48°55E **317** B6
Saidpur *Bangla.* 25°48N 89°0E **313** G16
Saidpur *India* 25°33N 83°11E **315** G10
Saidu Sharif *Pakistan* 34°43N 72°24E **315** B5
Saigō *Japan* 36°12N 133°20E **303** F6
Saigon = Thanh Pho Ho Chi Minh *Vietnam* 10°58N 106°40E **311** G6
Saijō *Japan* 33°55N 133°11E **303** H6
Saikai △ *Japan* 33°12N 129°36E **303** H4
Saikanosy Masoala *Madag.* 15°45S 50°10E **329** B9
Saikhoa Ghat *India* 27°50N 95°40E **313** F19
Saiki *Japan* 32°58N 131°51E **303** H5
Sailana *India* 23°28N 74°55E **314** H6
Sailolof *Indonesia* 1°15S 130°46E **309** E8
Saimaa *Finland* 61°15N 28°15E **280** F23
Saimen = Saimaa *Finland* 61°15N 28°15E **280** F23
Şa'in Dezh *Iran* 36°40N 46°25E **316** B5
St. Abb's Head *U.K.* 55°55N 2°8W **283** F6
St. Alban's *Canada* 47°51N 55°50W **345** C8
St. Albans *U.K.* 51°45N 0°19W **285** F7
St. Albans *Vt., U.S.A.* 44°49N 73°5W **355** B11
St. Albans *W. Va., U.S.A.* 38°23N 81°50W **353** F13
St. Alban's Head *U.K.* 50°34N 2°4W **285** G5
St. Albert *Canada* 53°37N 113°32W **342** C6
St-André *Réunion* 20°57S 55°39E **325** c
St. Andrew's *Canada* 47°45N 59°15W **345** C8
St. Andrews *U.K.* 56°20N 2°47W **283** E6
St-Anicet *Canada* 45°8N 74°22W **355** A10
St. Annes *Canada* 49°40N 96°39W **343** D9
St. Anns B. *Canada* 46°22N 60°25W **345** C7
St. Ann's Bay *Jamaica* 18°26N 77°12W **360** a
St. Anthony *Canada* 51°22N 55°35W **345** B8
St. Anthony *U.S.A.* 43°58N 111°41W **348** E8
St-Antoine *Canada* 46°22N 64°45W **345** C7
St. Arnaud *Australia* 36°40S 143°16E **335** F3
St-Augustin *Canada* 51°13N 58°38W **345** B8
St-Augustin → *Canada* 51°16N 58°40W **345** B8
St. Augustine *U.S.A.* 29°54N 81°19W **357** G14
St. Austell *U.K.* 50°20N 4°47W **285** G3
St. Barbe *Canada* 51°12N 56°46W **345** B8
St-Barthélemy *W. Indies* 17°50N 62°50W **361** C7
St. Bees Hd. *U.K.* 54°31N 3°38W **284** C4
St. Bees I. *Australia* 20°56S 149°26E **334** J7
St-Benoît *Réunion* 21°2S 55°43E **325** c
St. Bride's *Canada* 46°56N 54°10W **345** C9
St. Brides B. *U.K.* 51°49N 5°9W **285** F2
St-Brieuc *France* 48°30N 2°46W **292** B2
St. Catharines *Canada* 43°10N 79°15W **354** C5
St. Catherines I. *U.S.A.* 31°40N 81°10W **357** F14
St. Catherine's Pt. *U.K.* 50°34N 1°18W **285** G6
St-Chamond *France* 45°28N 4°31E **292** D6
St. Charles *Ill., U.S.A.* 41°54N 88°19W **352** E9
St. Charles *Md., U.S.A.* 38°36N 76°56W **353** F15
St. Charles *Mo., U.S.A.* 38°47N 90°29W **352** F8
St. Charles *Va., U.S.A.* 36°48N 83°4W **353** G12
St. Christopher-Nevis = St. Kitts & Nevis ■ *W. Indies* 17°20N 62°40W **361** C7
St. Clair *Mich., U.S.A.* 42°50N 82°30W **354** D2
St. Clair *Pa., U.S.A.* 40°43N 76°12W **355** F8
St. Clair → *U.S.A.* 42°38N 82°31W **354** D2
St. Clair, L. *N. Amer.* 42°27N 82°39W **354** D2
St. Clairsville *U.S.A.* 40°5N 80°54W **354** F4
St. Claude *Canada* 49°40N 98°20W **343** D9
St. Clears *U.K.* 51°49N 4°31W **285** F3
St-Clet *Canada* 45°21N 74°13W **355** A10
St. Cloud *Fla., U.S.A.* 28°15N 81°17W **357** G14
St. Cloud *Minn., U.S.A.* 45°34N 94°10W **352** C6
St. Cricq, C. *Australia* 25°17S 113°6E **333** E1
St. Croix *U.S. Virgin Is.* 17°45N 64°45W **361** C7
St. Croix → *U.S.A.* 44°45N 92°48W **352** C7
St. Croix Falls *U.S.A.* 45°24N 92°38W **352** C7
St. David's *Canada* 48°12N 58°52W **345** C8
St. David's *U.K.* 51°53N 5°16W **285** F2
St. David's Head *U.K.* 51°54N 5°19W **285** F2
St-Denis *France* 48°56N 2°20E **292** B5
St-Denis *Réunion* 20°52S 55°27E **325** c
St-Denis ✕ (RUN) *Réunion* 20°53S 55°32E **325** c
St-Dizier *France* 48°38N 4°56E **292** B6
St. Elias, Mt. *U.S.A.* 60°18N 140°56W **340** C5
St. Elias Mts. *N. Amer.* 60°33N 139°28W **342** A1
St-Étienne *France* 45°27N 4°22E **292** D6
St. Eugène *Canada* 45°30N 74°28W **355** A10
St. Eustatius *W. Indies* 17°20N 63°0W **361** C7
St-Félicien *Canada* 48°40N 72°25W **344** C5
St-Flour *France* 45°2N 3°6E **292** D5
St. Francis *U.S.A.* 39°47N 101°48W **352** F3
St. Francis → *U.S.A.* 34°38N 90°36W **357** D9
St. Francis, C. *S. Africa* 34°14S 24°49E **328** E3
St. Francisville *U.S.A.* 30°47N 91°23W **356** F9
St-François, L. *Canada* 45°10N 74°22W **355** A10
St-Gabriel *Canada* 46°17N 73°24W **344** C5
St. Gallen = Sankt Gallen *Switz.* 47°26N 9°22E **292** C8
St-Gaudens *France* 43°6N 0°44E **292** E4
St. George *Australia* 28°1S 148°30E **335** D4
St. George *Canada* 45°11N 66°50W **345** C6
St. George *S.C., U.S.A.* 33°11N 80°35W **357** E14
St. George *Utah, U.S.A.* 37°6N 113°35W **349** H7
St. George, C. *Canada* 48°30N 59°16W **345** C8
St. George, C. *U.S.A.* 29°40N 85°5W **357** G12
St. George Ra. *Australia* 18°40S 125°0E **332** C4
St. George's *Canada* 48°26N 58°31W **345** C8
St-Georges *Canada* 46°8N 70°40W **345** C5
St. George's *Grenada* 12°5N 61°43W **361** D7
St. George's B. *Canada* 48°24N 58°53W **345** C8
St. Georges Basin *N.S.W., Australia* 35°7S 150°36E **335** F5
St. Georges Basin *W. Austral., Australia* 15°23S 125°2E **332** C4
St. George's Channel *Europe* 52°0N 6°0W **282** E6
St. Georges Hd. *Australia* 35°12S 150°42E **335** F5
St. Gotthard P. = San Gottardo, P. del *Switz.* 46°33N 8°33E **292** C8
St. Helena *Atl. Oc.* 15°58S 5°42W **320** H3
St. Helena *U.S.A.* 38°30N 122°28W **348** G2
St. Helena, Mt. *U.S.A.* 38°40N 122°36W **350** G4
St. Helena B. *S. Africa* 32°40S 18°10E **328** E2
St. Helens *Australia* 41°20S 148°15E **335** G4
St. Helens *U.K.* 53°27N 2°44W **284** D5
St. Helens *U.S.A.* 45°52N 122°48W **350** E4
St. Helens, Mt. *U.S.A.* 46°12N 122°12W **350** D4
St. Helier *U.K.* 49°10N 2°7W **285** H5
St-Hubert *Belgium* 50°2N 5°23E **287** D5
St-Hyacinthe *Canada* 45°40N 72°58W **344** C5
St. Ignace *U.S.A.* 45°52N 84°44W **353** C11
St. Ignace I. *Canada* 48°45N 88°0W **344** C2
St. Ignatius *U.S.A.* 47°19N 114°6W **348** C6
St. Ives *Cambs., U.K.* 52°20N 0°4W **285** E7
St. Ives *Corn., U.K.* 50°12N 5°30W **285** G2
St. James *U.S.A.* 43°59N 94°38W **352** D6
St-Jean → *Canada* 50°17N 64°20W **345** B7
St-Jean, L. *Canada* 48°40N 72°0W **345** C5
St-Jean-Port-Joli *Canada* 47°15N 70°13W **345** C5
St-Jean-sur-Richelieu *Canada* 45°20N 73°20W **355** A11
St-Jérôme *Canada* 45°47N 74°0W **344** C5
St. John *Canada* 45°20N 66°8W **345** C6
St. John *U.S.A.* 38°0N 98°46W **352** F4
St. John → *N. Amer.* 45°12N 66°5W **353** C20
St. John, C. *Canada* 50°0N 55°32W **345** C8
St. John I. *U.S. Virgin Is.* 18°20N 64°42W **361** e
St. John's *Antigua & B.* 17°6N 61°51W **361** C7
St. John's *Canada* 47°35N 52°40W **345** C9
St. Johns *Ariz., U.S.A.* 34°30N 109°22W **349** J9
St. Johns *Mich., U.S.A.* 43°0N 84°33W **353** D11
St. Johns → *U.S.A.* 30°24N 81°24W **357** F14
St. John's Pt. *Ireland* 54°34N 8°27W **282** B3
St. Johnsbury *U.S.A.* 44°25N 72°1W **355** B12
St. Johnsville *U.S.A.* 43°0N 74°43W **355** C10
St-Joseph *Martinique* 14°39N 61°4W **360** c
St-Joseph *Réunion* 21°22S 55°37E **325** c
St. Joseph *La., U.S.A.* 31°55N 91°14W **356** F9
St. Joseph *Mo., U.S.A.* 39°46N 94°50W **352** F6
St. Joseph → *U.S.A.* 42°7N 86°29W **352** D10
St. Joseph, I. *Canada* 46°12N 83°58W **344** C3
St. Joseph, L. *Canada* 51°10N 90°35W **344** B1
St-Jovite *Canada* 46°8N 74°38W **344** C5
St. Kilda *U.K.* 57°49N 8°34W **286** C2
St. Kitts & Nevis ■ *W. Indies* 17°20N 62°40W **361** C7
St. Laurent *Canada* 50°25N 97°58W **343** C9
St. Lawrence *Australia* 22°16S 149°31E **334** C4
St. Lawrence *Canada* 46°54N 55°23W **345** C8
St. Lawrence → *Canada* 49°30N 66°0W **345** C6
St. Lawrence, Gulf of *Canada* 48°25N 62°0W **345** C7
St. Lawrence I. *U.S.A.* 63°30N 170°30W **346** a
St. Lawrence Islands △ *Canada* 44°27N 75°52W **355** B9
St. Leonard *Canada* 47°12N 67°58W **345** C6
St-Leu *Réunion* 21°9S 55°18E **325** c
St. Lewis → *Canada* 52°26N 56°11W **345** B8
St-Lô *France* 49°7N 1°5W **292** B3
St-Louis *Guadeloupe* 15°56N 61°19W **360** b
St-Louis *Réunion* 21°16S 55°25E **325** c
St. Louis *Senegal* 16°8N 16°27W **322** E2
St. Louis *U.S.A.* 38°37N 90°11W **352** F8
St. Louis → *U.S.A.* 46°44N 92°9W **352** B7
St. Lucia ■ *W. Indies* 14°0N 60°57W **361** f
St. Lucia, L. *S. Africa* 28°5S 32°30E **329** D5
St. Lucia Channel *W. Indies* 14°15N 61°0W **361** D7
St. Maarten ☒ *W. Indies* 18°0N 63°5W **361** C7
St. Magnus B. *U.K.* 60°25N 1°35W **283** A7
St-Malo *France* 48°39N 2°1W **292** B2
St-Marc *Haiti* 19°10N 72°41W **361** C5
St. Maries *U.S.A.* 47°19N 116°35W **348** C5
St-Martin ☒ *W. Indies* 18°0N 63°0W **361** C7
St-Martin, C. *Martinique* 14°52N 61°14W **360** c
St. Martin, L. *Canada* 51°40N 98°30W **343** C9
St. Martins *Barbados* 13°5N 59°28W **361** g
St. Mary Pk. *Australia* 31°32S 138°34E **335** E2
St. Marys *Australia* 41°35S 148°11E **335** G4
St. Marys *Canada* 43°20N 81°10W **354** C3
St. Mary's *Corn., U.K.* 49°55N 6°18W **285** H1
St. Mary's *Orkney, U.K.* 58°54N 2°54W **283** C6
St. Marys *Ga., U.S.A.* 30°44N 81°33W **357** F14
St. Marys *Pa., U.S.A.* 41°26N 78°34W **354** E6
St. Mary's, C. *Canada* 46°50N 54°12W **345** C9
St. Mary's B. *Canada* 46°50N 53°50W **345** C9
St. Marys Bay *Canada* 44°25N 66°10W **345** D6
St-Mathieu, Pte. *France* 48°20N 4°45W **292** B1
St. Matthew I. *U.S.A.* 60°24N 172°42W **346** a
St-Maurice → *Canada* 46°21N 72°31W **344** C5
St. Mawes *U.K.* 50°10N 5°2W **285** G2
St-Nazaire *France* 47°17N 2°12W **292** C2
St. Neots *U.K.* 52°14N 0°15W **285** E7
St-Niklaas *Belgium* 51°10N 4°8E **287** C4
St-Omer *France* 50°45N 2°15E **292** A5
St-Pamphile *Canada* 46°58N 69°48W **345** C6
St-Pascal *Canada* 47°32N 69°48W **345** C6
St. Paul *Canada* 54°0N 111°17W **342** C6
St-Paul *Réunion* 20°59S 55°17E **325** c
St. Paul *Minn., U.S.A.* 44°56N 93°5W **352** C7
St. Paul *Nebr., U.S.A.* 41°13N 98°27W **352** E4
St-Paul → *Canada* 51°27N 57°42W **345** B8
St. Paul, Î. *Ind. Oc.* 38°55S 77°34E **275** F13
St. Paul I. *Canada* 47°12N 60°9W **345** C7
St. Peter *U.S.A.* 44°20N 93°57W **352** C7
St. Peter Port *U.K.* 49°26N 2°33W **285** H5
St. Peters *N.S., Canada* 45°40N 60°53W **345** C7
St. Peters *P.E.I., Canada* 46°25N 62°35W **345** C7
St. Petersburg = Sankt-Peterburg *Russia* 59°55N 30°20E **281** G24
St. Petersburg *U.S.A.* 27°46N 82°40W **357** H13
St-Phillippe *Réunion* 21°21S 55°44E **325** c
St-Pie *Canada* 45°30N 72°54W **355** A12
St-Pierre *Martinique* 14°45N 61°10W **360** c
St-Pierre *Réunion* 21°19S 55°28E **325** c
St-Pierre *St-P. & M.* 46°46N 56°12W **345** C8
St-Pierre, L. *Canada* 46°12N 72°52W **344** C5
St-Pierre-et-Miquelon ☒ *N. Amer.* 46°55N 56°10W **345** C8
St-Quentin *Canada* 47°30N 67°23W **345** C6
St-Quentin *France* 49°50N 3°16E **292** B5
St. Regis *U.S.A.* 47°18N 115°6W **348** C6
St. Sebastien, Tanjon' i *Madag.* 12°26S 48°44E **329** A8
St-Siméon *Canada* 47°51N 69°54W **345** C6
St. Simons I. *U.S.A.* 31°12N 81°15W **357** F14
St. Simons Island *U.S.A.* 31°9N 81°22W **357** F14
St. Stephen *Canada* 45°16N 67°17W **345** C6
St. Thomas *Canada* 42°45N 81°10W **354** D3
St. Thomas I. *U.S. Virgin Is.* 18°20N 64°55W **361** e
St-Tite *Canada* 46°45N 72°34W **344** C5
St-Tropez *France* 43°17N 6°38E **292** E7
St-Troud = St. Truiden *Belgium* 50°48N 5°10E **287** D5
St. Truiden *Belgium* 50°48N 5°10E **287** D5
St. Vincent = São Vicente *C. Verde Is.* 17°0N 25°0W **322** b
St. Vincent, G. *Australia* 35°0S 138°0E **335** F2
St. Vincent & the Grenadines ■ *W. Indies* 13°0N 61°10W **361** D7
St. Vincent Passage *W. Indies* 13°30N 61°0W **361** D7
St-Vith *Belgium* 50°17N 6°9E **287** D6
St. Walburg *Canada* 53°39N 109°12W **343** C7
Ste-Agathe-des-Monts *Canada* 46°3N 74°17W **344** C5
Ste-Anne *Guadeloupe* 16°13N 61°24W **360** b
Ste-Anne *Seychelles* 4°36S 55°31E **325** b
Ste-Anne, L. *Canada* 50°0N 67°42W **345** B6
Ste-Anne-des-Monts-Tourelle *Canada* 49°8N 66°30W **345** C6
Ste. Genevieve *U.S.A.* 37°59N 90°2W **352** G8
Ste-Marguerite → *Canada* 50°9N 66°36W **345** B6
Ste-Marie *Canada* 46°26N 71°0W **345** C5
Ste-Marie *Martinique* 14°48N 61°1W **360** c
Ste-Marie *Réunion* 20°53S 55°33E **325** c
Ste-Marie, Ile = Nosy Boraha *Madag.* 16°50S 49°55E **329** B8
Ste-Rose *Guadeloupe* 16°20N 61°45W **360** b
Ste-Rose *Réunion* 21°8S 55°45E **325** c
Ste. Rose du Lac *Canada* 51°4N 99°30W **343** C9
Saintes *France* 45°45N 0°37W **292** D3
Saintes, Îs. des *Guadeloupe* 15°50N 61°35W **360** b
Saintfield *U.K.* 54°28N 5°49W **282** B6
Saintonge *France* 45°40N 0°50W **292** D3
Saipan *N. Marianas* 15°12N 145°45E **336** F6
Sairang *India* 23°50N 92°45E **313** H18
Sairecábur, Cerro *Bolivia* 22°43S 67°54W **366** A2
Saitama *Japan* 35°54N 139°38E **303** G9
Saitama □ *Japan* 36°25N 139°30E **303** F9
Saiyid *Pakistan* 33°7N 73°2E **314** C5
Sajama *Bolivia* 18°7S 69°0W **364** G5
Sajószentpéter *Hungary* 48°12N 20°44E **289** D11
Sajum *India* 33°20N 79°0E **315** C8
Sak → *S. Africa* 30°52S 20°25E **328** E3
Saka *Kenya* 0°9S 39°20E **326** B4
Sakai *Japan* 34°34N 135°27E **303** G7
Sakaide *Japan* 34°19N 133°50E **303** G6
Sakaiminato *Japan* 35°38N 133°11E **303** G6
Sakākah *Si. Arabia* 30°0N 40°8E **316** D4
Sakakawea, L. *U.S.A.* 47°30N 101°25W **352** B3
Sakami → *Canada* 53°40N 76°40W **344** B4
Sakami, L. *Canada* 53°15N 77°0W **344** B4
Sakania *Dem. Rep. of the Congo* 12°43S 28°30E **327** E2
Sakaraha *Madag.* 22°55S 44°32E **329** C7
Sakartvelo = Georgia ■ *Asia* 42°0N 43°0E **291** F7
Sakarya *Turkey* 40°48N 30°25E **291** F5
Sakashima-Guntō *Japan* 24°46N 124°0E **303** M2
Sakata *Japan* 38°55N 139°50E **302** E9
Sakchu *N. Korea* 40°23N 125°2E **307** D13
Sakeny → *Madag.* 20°0S 45°25E **329** C8
Sakha □ *Russia* 66°0N 130°0E **301** C13
Sakhalin *Russia* 51°0N 143°0E **301** D15
Sakhalinskiy Zaliv *Russia* 54°0N 141°0E **301** D15
Šakiai *Lithuania* 54°59N 23°2E **281** J20
Sakon Nakhon *Thailand* 17°10N 104°9E **310** D5
Sakrand *Pakistan* 26°10N 68°15E **314** F3
Sakri *India* 26°13N 86°5E **315** F12
Sakrivier *S. Africa* 30°54S 20°28E **328** E3
Sakti *India* 22°2N 82°58E **315** H10
Sakuma *Japan* 35°3N 137°49E **303** G8
Sakurai *Japan* 34°30N 135°51E **303** G7
Sal *C. Verde Is.* 16°45N 22°55W **322** b
Sal Rei *C. Verde Is.* 16°11N 22°53W **322** b
Sala *Sweden* 59°58N 16°35E **281** G17
Sala Consilina *Italy* 40°23N 15°36E **294** D6
Sala-y-Gómez *Pac. Oc.* 26°28S 105°28W **337** K17
Sala y Gómez Ridge *Pac. Oc.* 25°0S 98°0W **337** K18
Salaberry-de-Valleyfield *Canada* 45°15N 74°8W **355** A10
Salada, L. *Mexico* 32°20N 115°40W **349** K6
Saladas *Argentina* 28°15S 58°40W **366** B4
Saladillo *Argentina* 35°40S 59°55W **366** D4
Salado → *B. Aires, Argentina* 35°44S 57°22W **366** D4
Salado → *La Pampa, Argentina* 37°30S 67°0W **368** D3
Salado → *Santa Fe, Argentina* 31°40S 60°41W **366** C3
Salado → *Mexico* 26°52N 99°19W **356** H5
Salaga *Ghana* 8°31N 0°31W **322** G5
Sālah *Syria* 32°40N 36°45E **318** C5
Şalāḩ ad Dīn □ *Iraq* 34°35N 43°35E **316** C4
Salakos *Greece* 36°17N 27°57E **297** C9
Salālah *Oman* 16°56N 53°59E **319** D5
Salamanca *Chile* 31°46S 70°59W **366** C1
Salamanca *Spain* 40°58N 5°39W **293** B3
Salamanca *U.S.A.* 42°10N 78°43W **354** D6
Salāmatābād *Iran* 35°39N 47°50E **316** C5
Salamina *Greece* 37°56N 23°30E **295** F10
Salamis *Cyprus* 35°11N 33°54E **297** D12
Salar de Atacama *Chile* 23°30S 68°25W **366** A2
Salar de Uyuni *Bolivia* 20°30S 67°45W **364** H5
Salatiga *Indonesia* 7°19S 110°30E **309** G14
Salavat *Russia* 53°21N 55°55E **290** D10
Salaverry *Peru* 8°15S 79°0W **364** E3
Salawati *Indonesia* 1°7S 130°52E **309** E8
Salaya *India* 22°19N 69°35E **314** H3
Salayar *Indonesia* 6°7S 120°30E **309** F6
Salcombe *U.K.* 50°14N 3°47W **285** G4
Saldanha *S. Africa* 33°0S 17°58E **328** E2
Saldanha B. *S. Africa* 33°6S 18°0E **328** E2
Saldus *Latvia* 56°38N 22°30E **281** H20
Sale *Australia* 38°6S 147°6E **335** F4
Salé *Morocco* 34°3N 6°48W **322** B4
Sale *U.K.* 53°26N 2°19W **284** D5
Salekhard *Russia* 66°30N 66°35E **300** C7
Salelologa *Samoa* 13°41S 172°11W **331** b
Salem *India* 11°40N 78°11E **312** P11
Salem *Ill., U.S.A.* 38°38N 88°57W **352** F9
Salem *Ind., U.S.A.* 38°36N 86°6W **352** F10
Salem *Mass., U.S.A.* 42°31N 70°53W **355** D14
Salem *Mo., U.S.A.* 37°39N 91°32W **352** G8
Salem *N.H., U.S.A.* 42°45N 71°12W **355** D13
Salem *N.J., U.S.A.* 39°34N 75°28W **353** F16
Salem *N.Y., U.S.A.* 43°10N 73°20W **355** C11
Salem *Ohio, U.S.A.* 40°54N 80°52W **354** F4
Salem *Oreg., U.S.A.* 44°56N 123°2W **348** D2
Salem *S. Dak., U.S.A.* 43°44N 97°23W **352** D5
Salem *Va., U.S.A.* 37°18N 80°3W **353** G13
Salerno *Italy* 40°41N 14°47E **294** D6
Salford *U.K.* 53°30N 2°18W **284** D5

Salgótarján *Hungary* 48°5N 19°47E **289** D10
Salgueiro *Brazil* 8°4S 39°6W **365** E11
Salibabu *Indonesia* 3°51N 126°40E **309** D7
Salibea = Salybia
Trin. & Tob. 10°43N 61°2W **365** K15
Salida *U.S.A.* 38°32N 106°0W **346** C5
Salihli *Turkey* 38°28N 28°8E **295** E13
Salihorsk *Belarus* 52°51N 27°27E **289** B14
Salima *Malawi* 13°47S 34°28E **325** G6
Salina *Italy* 38°34N 14°50E **294** E6
Salina *Kans., U.S.A.* 38°50N 97°37W **352** F5
Salina *Utah, U.S.A.* 38°58N 111°51W **348** G8
Salina Cruz *Mexico* 16°10N 95°12W **359** D5
Salinas *Brazil* 16°10S 42°10W **365** G10
Salinas *Chile* 23°31S 69°29W **366** A2
Salinas *Ecuador* 2°10S 80°58W **364** D2
Salinas *U.S.A.* 36°40N 121°39W **350** J5
Salinas → *Guatemala* 16°28N 90°31W **359** D6
Salinas → *U.S.A.* 36°45N 121°48W **350** J5
Salinas, B. de *Nic.* 11°4N 85°45W **360** D2
Salinas, Pampa de las
Argentina 31°58S 66°42W **366** C2
Salinas Ambargasta
Argentina 29°0S 65°0W **366** B3
Salinas de Hidalgo
Mexico 22°38N 101°43W **358** C4
Salinas Grandes *Argentina* 30°0S 65°0W **366** C3
Salinas Pueblo Missions ⌂
U.S.A. 34°6N 106°4W **349** J10
Salinas Valley *U.S.A.* 36°15N 121°15W **350** J5
Saline → *Ark., U.S.A.* 33°10N 92°8W **356** E8
Saline → *Kans., U.S.A.* 38°52N 97°30W **352** F5
Salines, C. de ses *Spain* 39°16N 3°4E **296** B10
Salinópolis *Brazil* 0°40S 47°20W **365** D9
Salisbury *Australia* 34°46S 138°38E **335** E2
Salisbury *U.K.* 51°4N 1°47W **285** F6
Salisbury *Md., U.S.A.* 38°22N 75°36W **353** F16
Salisbury *N.C., U.S.A.* 35°40N 80°29W **357** D14
Salisbury I. *Canada* 63°30N 77°0W **341** C12
Salisbury Plain *U.K.* 51°14N 1°55W **285** F6
Şalkhad *Syria* 32°29N 36°43E **318** C5
Salla *Finland* 66°50N 28°49E **280** C23
Salliq = Coral Harbour
Canada 64°8N 83°10W **341** C11
Sallisaw *U.S.A.* 35°28N 94°47W **356** D7
Salluit *Canada* 62°14N 75°38W **341** C12
Salmās *Iran* 38°11N 44°47E **316** B5
Salmo *Canada* 49°10N 117°20W **342** D5
Salmon *U.S.A.* 45°11N 113°54W **348** D7
Salmon → *Canada* 54°3N 122°40W **342** C4
Salmon → *U.S.A.* 45°51N 116°47W **348** D5
Salmon Arm *Canada* 50°40N 119°15W **342** C5
Salmon Gums *Australia* 32°59S 121°38E **333** F3
Salmon River Mts.
U.S.A. 44°50N 115°30W **348** D6
Salo *Finland* 60°22N 23°10E **281** F20
Salome *U.S.A.* 33°47N 113°37W **351** M13
Salon *India* 26°2N 81°27E **315** F9
Salon-de-Provence *France* 43°39N 5°6E **292** E6
Salonica = Thessaloniki
Greece 40°38N 22°58E **295** D10
Salonta *Romania* 46°49N 21°42E **289** E11
Salpausselkä *Finland* 61°3N 26°15E **280** F22
Salsacate *Argentina* 31°20S 65°5W **366** C2
Salsk *Russia* 46°28N 41°30E **291** E7
Salso → *Italy* 37°6N 13°57E **294** F5
Salt → *Canada* 60°0N 112°25W **342** B6
Salt → *U.S.A.* 33°23N 112°19W **349** K7
Salt Fork Red →
U.S.A. 34°27N 99°21W **356** D5
Salt L. *Australia* 30°6S 142°8E **335** E3
Salt Lake City *U.S.A.* 40°45N 111°53W **348** F8
Salt Range *Pakistan* 32°30N 72°25E **314** C5
Salta *Argentina* 24°57S 65°25W **366** A2
Salta □ *Argentina* 24°48S 65°30W **366** A2
Saltash *U.K.* 50°24N 4°14W **285** G3
Saltburn by the Sea
U.K. 54°35N 0°58W **284** C7
Saltcoats *U.K.* 55°38N 4°47W **283** F4
Saltee Is. *Ireland* 52°7N 6°37W **282** D5
Saltfjellet *Norway* 66°40N 15°15E **280** C16
Saltfjorden *Norway* 67°15N 14°10E **280** C16
Saltillo *Mexico* 25°25N 101°0W **358** B4
Salto *Argentina* 34°20S 60°15W **366** C3
Salto *Uruguay* 31°27S 57°50W **366** C4
Salto → *Italy* 42°26N 12°25E **294** C5
Salto del Guaíra
Paraguay 24°3S 54°17W **367** A5
Salton City *U.S.A.* 33°18N 115°57W **351** M11
Salton Sea *U.S.A.* 33°15N 115°45W **351** M11
Saltsburg *U.S.A.* 40°29N 79°27W **354** F5
Saluda → *U.S.A.* 34°1N 81°4W **357** D14
Salûm *Egypt* 31°31N 25°7E **323** B11
Salur *India* 18°27N 83°18E **313** K13
Salvador *Brazil* 13°0S 38°30W **365** F11
Salvador *Canada* 52°10N 109°32W **343** C7
Salvador, El ■
Cent. Amer. 13°50N 89°0W **360** D2
Salvador, L. *U.S.A.* 29°43N 90°15W **357** G9
Salween → *Burma* 16°31N 97°37E **313** L20
Salyan *Azerbaijan* 39°33N 48°59E **291** G8
Salybia *Trin. & Tob.* 10°43N 61°2W **365** K15
Salzach → *Austria* 48°12N 12°56E **288** D7
Salzburg *Austria* 47°48N 13°2E **288** E7
Salzgitter *Germany* 52°9N 10°19E **288** B6
Salzwedel *Germany* 52°52N 11°10E **288** B6
Sam *India* 26°50N 70°31E **314** F4
Sam Neua *Laos* 20°29N 104°5E **310** B5
Sam Ngao *Thailand* 17°18N 99°0E **310** D2
Sam Rayburn Res. *U.S.A.* 31°4N 94°5W **356** F7
Sam Son *Vietnam* 19°44N 105°54E **310** C5
Sam Teu *Laos* 19°59N 104°38E **310** C5
Sama de Langreo = Langreo
Spain 43°18N 5°40W **293** A3
Samagaltay *Russia* 50°36N 95°3E **301** D10
Samales Group *Phil.* 6°0N 122°0E **309** C6
Samana *India* 30°10N 76°13E **314** D7
Samana Cay *Bahamas* 23°3N 73°45W **361** B5
Samanga *Tanzania* 8°20S 39°13E **327** D4
Samangān □ *Afghan.* 36°15N 68°3E **312** B5
Samangwa
Dem. Rep. of the Congo 4°23S 24°10E **326** C1
Samani *Japan* 42°7N 142°56E **302** C11
Samar *Phil.* 12°0N 125°0E **309** B7
Samara *Russia* 53°8N 50°6E **290** D9
Samaria = Shōmrōn
West Bank 32°15N 35°13E **318** C4
Samaria *Greece* 35°17N 23°58E **297** D5
Samarinda *Indonesia* 0°30S 117°9E **308** E5
Samarkand = Samarqand
Uzbekistan 39°40N 66°55E **300** F7
Samarqand *Uzbekistan* 39°40N 66°55E **300** F7
Sāmarrā' *Iraq* 34°12N 43°52E **316** C4
Samastipur *India* 25°50N 85°50E **315** G11
Samba
Dem. Rep. of the Congo 4°38S 26°22E **326** C2
Samba *India* 32°32N 75°10E **315** C6
Sambalpur *India* 21°28N 84°4E **313** J14
Sambar, Tanjung
Indonesia 2°59S 110°19E **308** E4
Sambas *Indonesia* 1°20N 109°20E **308** D3
Sambava *Madag.* 14°16S 50°10E **329** A9
Sambawizi *Zimbabwe* 18°24S 26°13E **327** F2
Sambhal *India* 28°35N 78°37E **315** E8
Sambhar *India* 26°52N 75°6E **314** F6
Sambhar L. *India* 26°55N 75°12E **314** F6
Sambiase *Italy* 38°58N 16°17E **294** E7
Sambir *Ukraine* 49°30N 23°10E **289** D12
Sambor *Cambodia* 12°46N 106°0E **310** F6
Samborombón, B.
Argentina 36°5S 57°20W **366** D4
Samburu ⌂ *Kenya* 0°37N 37°31E **326** B4
Samcheok *S. Korea* 37°30N 129°10E **307** F15
Same *Tanzania* 4°2S 37°38E **326** C4
Samfya *Zambia* 11°22S 29°31E **327** E2
Samnah *Si. Arabia* 25°10N 37°15E **316** E3
Samo Alto *Chile* 30°22S 71°0W **366** C1
Samoa ■ *Pac. Oc.* 14°0S 172°0W **331** b
Samokov *Bulgaria* 42°18N 23°35E **295** C10
Samos *Greece* 37°45N 26°50E **295** F12
Samothráki = Mathraki
Greece 39°48N 19°31E **297** A3
Samothraki *Greece* 40°28N 25°28E **295** D11
Sampacho *Argentina* 33°20S 64°50W **366** C3
Sampalan *Indonesia* 8°41S 115°34E **309** K18
Sampang *Indonesia* 7°11S 113°13E **309** G15
Sampit *Indonesia* 2°34S 113°0E **308** E4
Sampit, Teluk *Indonesia* 3°5S 113°3E **308** E4
Samrong *Cambodia* 14°15N 103°30E **310** E4
Samrong *Thailand* 15°10N 100°40E **310** E3
Samsø *Denmark* 55°50N 10°35E **281** J14
Samsun *Turkey* 41°15N 36°22E **291** F6
Samui, Ko *Thailand* 9°30N 100°0E **311** b
Samusole
Dem. Rep. of the Congo 10°2S 24°0E **327** E1
Samut Prakan *Thailand* 13°32N 100°40E **310** F3
Samut Songkhram
Thailand 13°24N 100°1E **310** F3
Samwari *Pakistan* 28°30N 66°46E **314** E2
San *Mali* 13°15N 4°57W **322** F5
San → *Cambodia* 13°32N 105°57E **310** F5
San → *Poland* 50°45N 21°51E **289** C11
San Agustin, C. *Phil.* 6°20N 126°13E **309** C7
San Agustín de Valle Fértil
Argentina 30°35S 67°30W **366** C2
San Ambrosio *Pac. Oc.* 26°28S 79°53W **362** F3
San Andreas *U.S.A.* 38°12N 120°41W **350** G6
San Andrés, I. de
Caribbean 12°42N 81°46W **360** D3
San Andres Mts.
U.S.A. 33°0N 106°30W **349** K10
San Andrés Tuxtla
Mexico 18°27N 95°13W **359** D5
San Angelo *U.S.A.* 31°28N 100°26W **356** F4
San Anselmo *U.S.A.* 37°59N 122°34W **350** H4
San Antonio *Belize* 16°15N 89°2W **359** D7
San Antonio *Chile* 33°40S 71°40W **366** C1
San Antonio *N. Mex.,*
U.S.A. 33°55N 106°52W **349** K10
San Antonio *Tex.,*
U.S.A. 29°25N 98°29W **356** G5
San Antonio → *U.S.A.* 28°30N 96°54W **356** G6
San Antonio, C.
Argentina 36°15S 56°40W **366** D4
San Antonio, C. de
Cuba 21°50N 84°57W **360** B3
San Antonio, Mt.
U.S.A. 34°17N 117°38W **351** L9
San Antonio de los Baños
Cuba 22°54N 82°31W **360** B3
San Antonio de los Cobres
Argentina 24°10S 66°17W **366** A2
San Antonio Oeste
Argentina 40°40S 65°0W **368** E4
San Ardo *U.S.A.* 36°1N 120°54W **350** J6
San Augustín
Canary Is. 27°47N 15°32W **296** G4
San Augustine *U.S.A.* 31°32N 94°7W **356** F7
San Bartolomé
Canary Is. 28°59N 13°37W **296** F6
San Bartolomé de Tirajana
Canary Is. 27°54N 15°34W **296** G4
San Benedetto del Tronto
Italy 42°57N 13°53E **294** C5
San Benedicto, I.
Mexico 19°18N 110°49W **358** D2
San Benito *U.S.A.* 26°8N 97°38W **356** H6
San Benito → *U.S.A.* 36°53N 121°34W **350** J5
San Benito Mt. *U.S.A.* 36°22N 120°37W **350** J6
San Bernardino *U.S.A.* 34°7N 117°19W **351** L9
San Bernardino Mts.
U.S.A. 34°10N 116°45W **351** L10
San Bernardino Str. *Phil.* 13°0N 125°0E **309** B6
San Bernardo *Chile* 33°40S 70°50W **366** C1
San Bernardo, I. de
Colombia 9°45N 75°50W **364** B3
San Blas *Mexico* 26°5N 108°46W **358** B3
San Blas, Arch. de
Panama 9°50N 78°31W **360** E4
San Blas, C. *U.S.A.* 29°40N 85°21W **357** G12
San Borja *Bolivia* 14°50S 66°52W **364** F5
San Buenaventura = Ventura
U.S.A. 34°17N 119°18W **351** L7
San Buenaventura
Mexico 27°5N 101°32W **358** B4
San Carlos = Sant Carles
Spain 39°3N 1°34E **296** B8
San Carlos *Argentina* 33°50S 69°0W **366** C2
San Carlos *Chile* 36°10S 72°0W **366** D1
San Carlos *Baja Calif. S.,*
Mexico 24°47N 112°7W **358** C2
San Carlos *Coahuila,*
Mexico 29°1N 100°51W **358** B4
San Carlos *Nic.* 11°12N 84°50W **360** D3
San Carlos *Phil.* 10°29N 123°25E **309** B6
San Carlos *Uruguay* 34°46S 54°58W **367** C5
San Carlos *U.S.A.* 33°21N 110°27W **349** K8
San Carlos *Venezuela* 9°40N 68°36W **364** B5
San Carlos de Bariloche
Argentina 41°10S 71°25W **368** E2
San Carlos de Bolívar
Argentina 36°15S 61°6W **368** D4
San Carlos del Zulia
Venezuela 9°1N 71°55W **364** B4
San Carlos L. *U.S.A.* 33°11N 110°32W **349** K8
San Clemente *Chile* 35°30S 71°29W **366** D1
San Clemente *U.S.A.* 33°26N 117°37W **351** M9
San Clemente I.
U.S.A. 32°53N 118°29W **351** N8
San Cristóbal = Es Migjorn Gran
Spain 39°57N 4°3E **296** B11
San Cristóbal *Argentina* 30°20S 61°10W **366** C3
San Cristóbal *Dom. Rep.* 18°25N 70°6W **361** C5
San Cristóbal *Solomon Is.* 10°30S 161°0E **330** C9
San Cristóbal *Venezuela* 7°46N 72°14W **364** B4
San Cristóbal de las Casas
Mexico 16°45N 92°38W **359** D6
San Diego *Calif., U.S.A.* 32°42N 117°9W **351** N9
San Diego *Tex., U.S.A.* 27°46N 98°14W **356** H5
San Diego, C. *Argentina* 54°40S 65°10W **368** G3
San Diego de la Unión
Mexico 21°28N 100°52W **358** C4
San Diego Int. ✈ (SAN)
U.S.A. 32°44N 117°11W **351** N9
San Dimitri, Ras *Malta* 36°4N 14°11E **297** C1
San Dimitri Point = San Dimitri,
Ras *Malta* 36°4N 14°11E **297** C1
San Estanislao
Paraguay 24°39S 56°26W **366** A4
San Felipe *Chile* 32°43S 70°42W **366** C1
San Felipe *Mexico* 31°1N 114°52W **358** A2
San Felipe *Venezuela* 10°20N 68°44W **364** A5
San Felipe → *U.S.A.* 33°10N 115°49W **351** M11
San Félix *Chile* 28°56S 70°28W **366** B1
San Félix *Pac. Oc.* 26°23S 80°0W **362** F2
San Fernando = Sant Ferran
Spain 38°42N 1°28E **296** C7
San Fernando *Chile* 34°30S 71°0W **366** C1
San Fernando *Mexico* 24°51N 98°10W **359** C5
San Fernando *La Union,*
Phil. 16°40N 120°23E **309** A6
San Fernando *Pampanga,*
Phil. 15°5N 120°37E **309** A6
San Fernando *Spain* 36°28N 6°17W **293** D2
San Fernando
Trin. & Tob. 10°16N 61°28W **361** D7
San Fernando *U.S.A.* 34°17N 118°26W **351** L8
San Fernando de Apure
Venezuela 7°54N 67°15W **364** B5
San Fernando de Atabapo
Venezuela 4°3N 67°42W **364** C5
San Francisco *Argentina* 31°30S 62°5W **366** C3
San Francisco *U.S.A.* 37°46N 122°23W **350** H4
San Francisco →
U.S.A. 32°59N 109°22W **349** K9
San Francisco, C. de
Colombia 6°18N 77°29W **362** C3
San Francisco, Paso de
S. Amer. 27°0S 68°0W **366** B2
San Francisco de Macorís
Dom. Rep. 19°19N 70°15W **361** C5
San Francisco del Monte de Oro
Argentina 32°36S 66°8W **366** C2
San Francisco del Oro
Mexico 26°52N 105°51W **358** B3
San Francisco Int. ✈ (SFO)
U.S.A. 37°37N 122°22W **350** H4
San Francisco Javier = Sant
Francesc de Formentera
Spain 38°42N 1°26E **296** C7
San Gabriel *Chile* 33°47S 70°15W **366** C1
San Gabriel Chilac
Mexico 18°19N 97°21W **359** D5
San Gabriel Mts.
U.S.A. 34°17N 117°38W **351** L9
San Gavino Monreale
Italy 39°33N 8°47E **294** E3
San German *Puerto Rico* 18°4N 67°4W **361** d
San Gorgonio Mt.
U.S.A. 34°6N 116°50W **351** L10
San Gottardo, P. del
Switz. 46°33N 8°33E **292** C8
San Gregorio *Uruguay* 32°37S 55°40W **367** C4
San Gregorio *U.S.A.* 37°20N 122°23W **350** H4
San Ignacio *Belize* 17°10N 89°5W **359** D7
San Ignacio *Bolivia* 16°20S 60°55W **364** G6
San Ignacio *Mexico* 27°27N 112°51W **358** B2
San Ignacio *Paraguay* 26°52S 57°3W **366** B4
San Ignacio, L. *Mexico* 26°54N 113°13W **358** B2
San Ildefonso, C. *Phil.* 16°0N 122°1E **309** A6
San Isidro *Argentina* 34°29S 58°31W **366** C4
San Jacinto *U.S.A.* 33°47N 116°57W **351** M10
San Jaime = Sant Jaume
Spain 39°54N 4°4E **296** B11
San Javier *Misiones,*
Argentina 27°55S 55°5W **367** B4
San Javier *Santa Fe,*
Argentina 30°40S 59°55W **366** C4
San Javier *Bolivia* 16°18S 62°30W **364** G6
San Javier *Chile* 35°40S 71°45W **366** D1
San Jerónimo Taviche
Mexico 16°44N 96°35W **359** D5
San Joaquin *U.S.A.* 36°36N 120°11W **350** J6
San Joaquin → *U.S.A.* 38°4N 121°51W **350** G5
San Joaquin Valley
U.S.A. 37°20N 121°0W **350** J6
San Jon *U.S.A.* 35°6N 103°20W **349** J12
San Jordi = Sant Jordi
Spain 39°33N 2°46E **296** B9
San Jorge *Argentina* 31°54S 61°50W **366** C3
San Jorge, B. *Mexico* 31°20N 113°20W **358** A2
San Jorge, G. *Argentina* 46°0S 66°0W **368** F3
San José = San Josep
Spain 38°55N 1°18E **296** C7
San José *Costa Rica* 9°55N 84°2W **360** E3
San José *Guatemala* 14°0N 90°50W **360** D1
San Jose *Mind. Occ., Phil.* 12°27N 121°4E **309** B6
San Jose *Nueva Ecija,*
Phil. 15°45N 120°55E **309** A6
San Jose *U.S.A.* 37°20N 121°53W **350** H5
San Jose → *U.S.A.* 34°25N 106°45W **349** J10
San José, I. *Mexico* 25°0N 110°38W **358** C2
San Jose de Buenavista
Phil. 10°45N 121°56E **309** B6
San José de Chiquitos
Bolivia 17°53S 60°50W **364** G6
San José de Feliciano
Argentina 30°26S 58°46W **366** C4
San José de Jáchal
Argentina 30°15S 68°46W **366** C2
San José de Mayo
Uruguay 34°27S 56°40W **366** C4
San José del Cabo
Mexico 23°3N 109°41W **358** C3
San José del Guaviare
Colombia 2°35N 72°38W **364** C4
San Josep *Spain* 38°55N 1°18E **296** C7
San Juan *Argentina* 31°30S 68°30W **366** C2
San Juan *Puerto Rico* 18°28N 66°7W **361** d
San Juan *Trin. & Tob.* 10°39N 61°29W **365** K15
San Juan □ *Argentina* 31°9S 69°0W **366** C2
San Juan → *Argentina* 32°20S 67°25W **366** C2
San Juan → *Nic.* 10°56N 83°42W **360** D3
San Juan → *U.S.A.* 37°16N 110°26W **349** H8
San Juan Bautista = Sant Joan de
Labritja *Spain* 39°5N 1°31E **296** B8
San Juan Bautista
Paraguay 26°37S 57°6W **366** B4
San Juan Bautista
U.S.A. 36°51N 121°32W **350** J5
San Juan Capistrano
U.S.A. 33°30N 117°40W **351** M9
San Juan Cr. →
U.S.A. 35°40N 120°22W **350** J5
San Juan de Guadelupe
Mexico 24°38N 102°44W **358** C4
San Juan de la Costa
Mexico 24°20N 110°41W **358** C2
San Juan de los Lagos
Mexico 21°15N 102°18W **358** C4
San Juan de los Morros
Venezuela 9°55N 67°21W **364** B5
San Juan del Norte *Nic.* 10°58N 83°40W **360** D3
San Juan del Norte, B. de
Nic. 11°0N 83°40W **360** D3
San Juan del Río
Mexico 20°23N 100°0W **359** C5
San Juan del Sur *Nic.* 11°20N 85°51W **360** D2
San Juan I. *U.S.A.* 48°32N 123°5W **350** B3
San Juan Island ⌂
U.S.A. 48°35N 123°8W **350** B4
San Juan Mts. *U.S.A.* 37°30N 107°0W **349** H10
San Justo *Argentina* 30°47S 60°30W **366** C3
San Kamphaeng
Thailand 18°45N 99°8E **310** C2
San Lázaro, C. *Mexico* 24°50N 112°18W **358** C2
San Leandro *U.S.A.* 37°42N 122°9W **350** H4
San Lorenzo = Sant Llorenç des
Cardassar *Spain* 39°37N 3°17E **296** B10
San Lorenzo *Argentina* 32°45S 60°45W **366** C3
San Lorenzo *Ecuador* 1°15N 78°50W **364** C3
San Lorenzo *Paraguay* 25°20S 57°32W **366** B4
San Lorenzo →
Mexico 24°15N 107°24W **358** C3
San Lorenzo, I. *Mexico* 28°38N 112°51W **358** B2
San Lorenzo, Mte.
Argentina 47°40S 72°20W **368** F2
San Lucas = Cabo San Lucas
Mexico 22°53N 109°54W **358** C3
San Lucas *Bolivia* 20°5S 65°7W **364** H5
San Lucas *Mexico* 27°10N 112°14W **358** B2
San Lucas *U.S.A.* 36°8N 121°1W **350** J5
San Lucas, C. *Mexico* 22°52N 109°53W **358** C3
San Luis *Argentina* 33°20S 66°20W **366** C2
San Luis *Cuba* 22°17N 83°46W **360** B3
San Luis *Guatemala* 16°14N 89°27W **360** C2
San Luis *Ariz., U.S.A.* 32°29N 114°47W **349** K6
San Luis *Colo., U.S.A.* 37°12N 105°25W **349** H11
San Luis □ *Argentina* 34°0S 66°0W **366** C2
San Luis, I. *Mexico* 29°58N 114°26W **358** B2
San Luis, Sierra de
Argentina 32°30S 66°10W **366** C2
San Luis de la Paz
Mexico 21°18N 100°31W **358** C4
San Luis Obispo
U.S.A. 35°17N 120°40W **351** K6
San Luis Potosí *Mexico* 22°9N 100°59W **358** C4
San Luis Potosí □
Mexico 23°0N 101°0W **358** C4
San Luis Res. *U.S.A.* 37°4N 121°5W **350** H5
San Luis Río Colorado
Mexico 32°29N 114°58W **358** A2
San Manuel *U.S.A.* 32°36N 110°38W **349** K8
San Marcos *Guatemala* 14°59N 91°52W **360** D1
San Marcos *Calif.,*
U.S.A. 33°9N 117°10W **351** M9
San Marcos *Tex., U.S.A.* 29°53N 97°56W **356** G6
San Marcos, I. *Mexico* 27°13N 112°6W **358** B2
San Marino *San Marino* 43°55N 12°30E **288** G7
San Marino ■ *Europe* 43°56N 12°25E **294** C5
San Martín *Antarctica* 68°11S 67°0W **277** C17
San Martín *Argentina* 33°5S 68°28W **366** C2
San Martín → *Bolivia* 13°8S 63°43W **364** F6
San Martín, L.
Argentina 48°50S 72°50W **368** F2
San Martín de los Andes
Argentina 40°10S 71°20W **368** E2
San Mateo = Sant Mateu
Spain 39°3N 1°23E **296** B7
San Mateo *U.S.A.* 37°34N 122°19W **350** H4
San Matías *Bolivia* 16°25S 58°20W **364** G7
San Matías, G. *Argentina* 41°30S 64°0W **368** E4
San Miguel = Sant Miguel
Spain 39°3N 1°26E **296** B7
San Miguel *El Salv.* 13°30N 88°12W **360** D2
San Miguel *Panama* 8°27N 78°55W **360** E4
San Miguel *U.S.A.* 35°45N 120°42W **350** K6
San Miguel → *Bolivia* 13°52S 63°56W **364** F6
San Miguel de Tucumán
Argentina 26°50S 65°20W **366** B2
San Miguel del Monte
Argentina 35°23S 58°50W **366** D4
San Miguel I. *U.S.A.* 34°2N 120°23W **351** L6
San Nicolás *Canary Is.* 27°58N 15°47W **296** G4
San Nicolás de los Arroyas
Argentina 33°25S 60°10W **366** C3
San Nicolas I. *U.S.A.* 33°15N 119°30W **351** M7
San Onofre *U.S.A.* 33°22N 117°34W **351** M9
San Pablo *Bolivia* 21°43S 66°38W **366** A2
San Pablo *U.S.A.* 37°58N 122°21W **350** H4
San Pedro *B. Aires,*
Argentina 33°40S 59°40W **366** C4
San Pedro *Misiones,*
Argentina 26°30S 54°10W **367** B5
San Pedro *Chile* 33°54S 71°28W **366** C1
San Pédro *Ivory C.* 4°50N 6°33W **322** H4
San Pedro *Mexico* 23°55N 110°17W **358** C2
San Pedro □ *Paraguay* 24°0S 57°0W **366** A4
San Pedro → *Chihuahua,*
Mexico 28°20N 106°10W **358** B3
San Pedro → *Nayarit,*
Mexico 21°45N 105°30W **358** C3
San Pedro → *U.S.A.* 32°59N 110°47W **349** K8
San Pedro, Pta. *Chile* 25°30S 70°38W **366** B1
San Pedro Channel
U.S.A. 33°30N 118°25W **351** M8
San Pedro de Atacama
Chile 22°55S 68°15W **366** A2
San Pedro de Jujuy
Argentina 24°12S 64°55W **366** A3
San Pedro de las Colonias
Mexico 25°45N 102°59W **358** B4
San Pedro de Macorís
Dom. Rep. 18°30N 69°18W **361** C6
San Pedro del Norte *Nic.* 13°4N 84°33W **360** D3
San Pedro del Paraná
Paraguay 26°43S 56°13W **366** B4
San Pedro Mártir, Sierra
Mexico 31°0N 115°30W **358** A1
San Pedro Mártir △
Mexico 31°0N 115°21W **358** A1
San Pedro Ocampo = Melchor
Ocampo *Mexico* 24°51N 101°39W **358** C4
San Pedro Pochutla
Mexico 15°44N 96°28W **359** D5
San Pedro Sula
Honduras 15°30N 88°0W **360** C2
San Pedro Tututepec
Mexico 16°9N 97°38W **359** D5
San Pietro *Italy* 39°8N 8°17E **294** E3
San Rafael *Argentina* 34°40S 68°21W **366** C2
San Rafael *Calif.,*
U.S.A. 37°58N 122°32W **350** H4
San Rafael *N. Mex.,*
U.S.A. 35°7N 107°53W **349** J10
San Rafael Mt. *U.S.A.* 34°41N 119°52W **351** L7
San Rafael Mts. *U.S.A.* 34°40N 119°50W **351** L7
San Ramón de la Nueva Orán
Argentina 23°10S 64°20W **366** A3
San Remo *Italy* 43°49N 7°46E **292** E7
San Roque *Argentina* 28°25S 58°45W **366** B4
San Roque *Spain* 36°17N 5°21W **293** D3
San Rosendo *Chile* 37°16S 72°43W **366** D1
San Saba *U.S.A.* 31°12N 98°43W **356** F5
San Salvador *El Salv.* 13°40N 89°10W **360** D2
San Salvador *Spain* 39°27N 3°11E **296** B10
San Salvador de Jujuy
Argentina 24°10S 64°48W **366** A3
San Salvador I. *Bahamas* 24°0N 74°40W **361** B5
San Sebastián = Donostia-San
Sebastián *Spain* 43°17N 1°58W **293** A5
San Sebastián *Argentina* 53°10S 68°30W **368** G3
San Sebastián
Puerto Rico 18°20N 66°59W **361** d
San Sebastián de la Gomera
Canary Is. 28°5N 17°7W **296** F2
San Serra = Son Serra
Spain 39°43N 3°13E **296** B10
San Severo *Italy* 41°41N 15°23E **294** D6
San Simeon *U.S.A.* 35°39N 121°11W **350** K5
San Simon *U.S.A.* 32°16N 109°14W **349** K9
San Telmo = Sant Elm
Spain 39°35N 2°21E **296** B9
San Telmo *Mexico* 30°58N 116°6W **358** A1
San Tiburcio *Mexico* 24°8N 101°32W **358** C4
San Valentin, Mte.
Chile 46°30S 73°30W **368** F2
San Vicente de la Barquera
Spain 43°23N 4°29W **293** A3
San Vito *Costa Rica* 8°50N 82°58W **360** E3

Sana‘ Yemen 15°27N 44°12E 319 D3
Sana → Bos.-H. 45°3N 16°23E 288 F9
Sanae IV Antarctica 70°20S 9°0W 277 D2
Sanaga → Cameroon 3°35N 9°38E 324 D1
Sanaloa, Presa Mexico 24°50N 107°20W 358 C3
Sanana Indonesia 2°4S 125°58E 309 E7
Sanand India 22°59N 72°25E 314 H5
Sanandaj Iran 35°18N 47°1E 316 C5
Sanandita Bolivia 21°40S 63°45W 366 A3
Sanawad India 22°11N 76°5E 314 H7
Sancellas = Sencelles Spain 39°39N 2°54E 296 B9
Sanchahe China 44°50N 126°2E 307 B14
Sánchez Dom. Rep. 19°15N 69°36W 361 C6
Sanchor India 24°45N 71°55E 314 G4
Sancti Spíritus Cuba 21°52N 79°33W 360 B4
Sancy, Puy de France 45°32N 2°50E 292 D5
Sand → S. Africa 22°25S 30°5E 329 C5
Sand Hills U.S.A. 42°10N 101°30W 352 D3
Sand Lakes ⌓ Canada 57°51N 98°32W 343 B9
Sand Springs U.S.A. 36°9N 96°7W 356 C6
Sanda Japan 34°53N 135°14E 303 G7
Sandakan Malaysia 5°53N 118°4E 308 C5
Sandan = Sambor Cambodia 12°46N 106°0E 310 F6
Sandanski Bulgaria 41°35N 23°16E 295 D10
Sanday U.K. 59°16N 2°31W 283 B6
Sandefjord Norway 59°10N 10°15E 281 G14
Sanders U.S.A. 35°13N 109°20W 349 J9
Sanderson U.S.A. 30°9N 102°24W 356 F3
Sandersville U.S.A. 32°59N 82°48W 357 E13
Sandfire Roadhouse Australia 19°45S 121°15E 332 C3
Sandfly L. Canada 55°43N 106°6W 343 B7
Sandfontein Namibia 23°48S 19°1E 328 C2
Sandheads, The India 21°10N 88°20E 315 J13
Sandía Peru 14°10S 69°30W 364 F5
Sandila India 27°5N 80°31E 315 F9
Sandnes Norway 58°50N 5°45E 281 G11
Sandnessjøen Norway 66°2N 12°38E 280 C15
Sandoa Dem. Rep. of the Congo 9°41S 23°0E 324 F4
Sandomierz Poland 50°40N 21°43E 289 C11
Sandover → Australia 21°43S 136°32E 334 C2
Sandoway = Thandwe Burma 18°20N 94°30E 313 K19
Sandoy Færoe Is. 61°52N 6°46W 280 F9
Sandpoint U.S.A. 48°17N 116°33W 348 B5
Sandray U.K. 56°53N 7°31W 283 E1
Sandringham U.K. 52°51N 0°31E 284 E8
Sandstone Australia 27°59S 119°16E 333 E2
Sandusky Mich., U.S.A. 43°25N 82°50W 354 C2
Sandusky Ohio, U.S.A. 41°27N 82°42W 354 E2
Sandveld Namibia 21°25S 20°0E 328 C3
Sandviken Sweden 60°38N 16°46E 280 F17
Sandwich, C. Australia 18°14S 146°18E 334 B4
Sandwich B. Canada 53°40N 57°15W 345 B8
Sandwich B. Namibia 23°25S 14°20E 328 C1
Sandy Oreg., U.S.A. 45°24N 122°16W 350 E4
Sandy Pa., U.S.A. 41°6N 78°46W 354 E6
Sandy Utah, U.S.A. 40°32N 111°50W 348 F8
Sandy Bay Canada 55°31N 102°19W 343 B8
Sandy Bight Australia 33°50S 123°20E 333 F3
Sandy C. Queens., Australia 24°42S 153°15E 334 C5
Sandy C. Tas., Australia 41°25S 144°45E 335 G3
Sandy Cay Bahamas 23°13N 75°18W 361 B4
Sandy Cr. → U.S.A. 41°51N 109°47W 348 F9
Sandy L. Canada 53°2N 93°0W 344 B1
Sandy Lake Canada 53°0N 93°15W 344 B1
Sandy Valley U.S.A. 35°49N 115°38W 351 K11
Sanford Fla., U.S.A. 28°48N 81°16W 357 G14
Sanford Maine, U.S.A. 43°27N 70°47W 355 C14
Sanford N.C., U.S.A. 35°29N 79°10W 357 D15
Sanford → Australia 27°22S 115°53E 333 E2
Sanford, Mt. U.S.A. 62°13N 144°8W 340 C5
Sang-i-Masha Afghan. 33°8N 67°27E 314 C2
Sanga Mozam. 12°22S 35°21E 327 E4
Sanga → Congo 1°5S 17°0E 324 E3
Sangamner India 19°37N 74°15E 312 K9
Sangar Afghan. 32°56N 65°30E 314 C1
Sangar Russia 64°2N 127°31E 301 C13
Sangar Sarai Afghan. 34°27N 70°35E 314 B4
Sangarh → Pakistan 30°43N 70°44E 314 D4
Sangay Ecuador 2°0S 78°20W 364 D3
Sange Dem. Rep. of the Congo 6°58S 28°21E 326 D2
Sangeang Indonesia 8°12S 119°6E 309 F5
Sanger U.S.A. 36°42N 119°33W 350 J7
Sangerhausen Germany 51°28N 11°18E 288 C6
Sanggan He → China 38°12N 117°15E 306 E9
Sanggau Indonesia 0°5N 110°30E 308 D4
Sanghar Pakistan 26°2N 68°57E 314 F3
Sangihe, Kepulauan Indonesia 3°0N 125°30E 309 D7
Sangihe, Pulau Indonesia 3°35N 125°30E 309 D7
Sangju S. Korea 36°25N 128°10E 307 F15
Sangkapura Indonesia 5°52S 112°40E 308 F4
Sangkhla Thailand 14°57N 98°28E 310 E2
Sangkulirang Indonesia 0°59N 117°58E 308 D5
Sangla Pakistan 31°43N 73°23E 314 D5
Sangli India 16°55N 74°33E 312 L9
Sangmélima Cameroon 2°57N 12°1E 324 D2
Sangod India 24°55N 76°17E 314 G7
Sangre de Cristo Mts. U.S.A. 37°30N 105°20W 349 H11
Sangre Grande Trin. & Tob. 10°35N 61°8W 365 K15
Sangrur India 30°14N 75°50E 314 D6
Sangudo Canada 53°50N 114°54W 342 C6
Sangue → Brazil 11°1S 58°39W 364 F7
Sanibel U.S.A. 26°27N 82°1W 357 H13
Sanikiluaq Canada 56°32N 79°14W 344 A4
Sanin-Kaigan △ Japan 35°39N 134°37E 303 G7
Sanirajak Canada 68°46N 81°12W 341 C11
Sanjawi Pakistan 30°17N 68°21E 314 D3
Sanje Uganda 0°49S 31°30E 326 C3
Sanjo Japan 37°37N 138°57E 302 F9
Sankh → India 22°15N 84°48E 315 H11
Sankt Gallen Switz. 47°26N 9°22E 292 C8
Sankt Michel = Mikkeli Finland 61°43N 27°15E 280 F22
Sankt Moritz Switz. 46°30N 9°51E 292 C8
Sankt-Peterburg Russia 59°55N 30°20E 281 G24
Sankt Pölten Austria 48°12N 15°38E 288 D8
Sankuru → Dem. Rep. of the Congo 4°17S 20°25E 324 E4
Sanliurfa Turkey 37°12N 38°50E 316 B3
Sanlúcar de Barrameda Spain 36°46N 6°21W 293 D2
Sanmenxia China 34°47N 111°12E 306 G6
Sanming China 26°15N 117°40E 305 D6
Sannaspos S. Africa 29°6S 26°34E 328 D4
Sannicandro Gargánico Italy 41°50N 15°34E 294 D6
Sânnicolau Mare Romania 46°5N 20°39E 289 E11
Sannieshof S. Africa 26°30S 25°47E 328 D4
Sannīn, J. Lebanon 33°57N 35°52E 318 B4
Sanniquellie Liberia 7°19N 8°38W 322 G4
Sanok Poland 49°35N 22°10E 289 D12
Sanquhar U.K. 55°22N 3°54W 283 F5
Sans Souci Trin. & Tob. 10°50N 61°0W 365 K16
Sant Antoni de Portmany Spain 38°59N 1°19E 296 C7
Sant Carles Spain 39°3N 1°34E 296 B8
Sant Elm Spain 39°35N 2°21E 296 B9
Sant Feliu de Guíxols Spain 41°45N 3°1E 293 B7
Sant Ferran Spain 38°42N 1°28E 296 C7
Sant Francesc de Formentera Spain 38°42N 1°26E 296 C7
Sant Jaume Spain 39°54N 4°4E 296 B11
Sant Joan de Labritja Spain 39°5N 1°31E 296 B8
Sant Jordi Ibiza, Spain 38°53N 1°24E 296 C7
Sant Jordi Mallorca, Spain 39°33N 2°46E 296 B9
Sant Jordi, G. de Spain 40°53N 1°2E 293 B6
Sant Llorenç des Cardassar Spain 39°37N 3°17E 296 B10
Sant Mateu Spain 39°3N 1°23E 296 B7
Sant Miquel Spain 39°3N 1°26E 296 B7
Santa Agnés Spain 39°3N 1°21E 296 B7
Santa Ana Bolivia 13°50S 65°40W 364 F5
Santa Ana El Salv. 14°0N 89°31W 360 D2
Santa Ana Mexico 30°33N 111°7W 358 A2
Santa Ana U.S.A. 33°46N 117°52W 351 M9
Sant' Antíoco Italy 39°4N 8°27E 294 E3
Santa Bárbara Chile 37°40S 72°1W 366 D1
Santa Bárbara Honduras 14°53N 88°14W 360 D2
Santa Bárbara Mexico 26°48N 105°49W 358 B3
Santa Barbara U.S.A. 34°25N 119°42W 351 L7
Santa Barbara Channel U.S.A. 34°15N 120°0W 351 L7
Santa Barbara I. U.S.A. 33°29N 119°2W 351 M7
Santa Catalina, Gulf of U.S.A. 33°10N 117°50W 351 N9
Santa Catalina, I. Mexico 25°40N 110°47W 358 B2
Santa Catalina I. U.S.A. 33°23N 118°25W 351 M8
Santa Catarina □ Brazil 27°25S 48°30W 367 B6
Santa Catarina, I. de Brazil 27°30S 48°40W 367 B6
Santa Cecília Brazil 26°56S 50°18W 367 B5
Santa Clara Cuba 22°20N 80°0W 360 B4
Santa Clara Calif., U.S.A. 37°21N 121°57W 350 H5
Santa Clara Utah, U.S.A. 37°8N 113°39W 349 H7
Santa Clara de Olimar Uruguay 32°50S 54°54W 367 C5
Santa Clara Valley U.S.A. 36°50N 121°30W 350 J5
Santa Clarita U.S.A. 34°24N 118°33W 351 L8
Santa Clotilde Peru 2°33S 73°45W 364 D4
Santa Coloma de Gramenet Spain 41°27N 2°13E 293 B7
Santa Cruz Argentina 50°0S 68°32W 368 G3
Santa Cruz Bolivia 17°43S 63°10W 364 G6
Santa Cruz Chile 34°38S 71°27W 366 C1
Santa Cruz Costa Rica 10°15N 85°35W 360 D2
Santa Cruz Madeira 32°42N 16°46W 296 D3
Santa Cruz Phil. 14°20N 121°24E 309 B6
Santa Cruz U.S.A. 36°58N 122°1W 350 J4
Santa Cruz → Argentina 50°10S 68°20W 368 G3
Santa Cruz de la Palma Canary Is. 28°41N 17°46W 296 F2
Santa Cruz de la Palma ✕ (SPC) Canary Is. 28°40N 17°45W 296 F2
Santa Cruz de Tenerife Canary Is. 28°28N 16°15W 296 F3
Santa Cruz del Norte Cuba 23°9N 81°55W 360 B3
Santa Cruz del Sur Cuba 20°44N 78°0W 360 B4
Santa Cruz do Rio Pardo Brazil 22°54S 49°37W 367 A6
Santa Cruz do Sul Brazil 29°42S 52°25W 367 B5
Santa Cruz I. U.S.A. 34°1N 119°43W 351 M7
Santa Cruz Is. Solomon Is. 10°30S 166°0E 330 C9
Santa Cruz Mts. Jamaica 17°58N 77°43W 360 a
Santa Domingo, Cay Bahamas 21°25N 75°15W 360 B4
Santa Elena Argentina 30°58S 59°47W 366 C4
Santa Elena, C. Costa Rica 10°54N 85°56W 360 D2
Santa Eulària des Riu Spain 38°59N 1°32E 296 C8
Santa Fé Argentina 31°35S 60°41W 366 C3
Santa Fe U.S.A. 35°41N 105°57W 349 J11
Santa Fé □ Argentina 31°50S 60°55W 366 C3
Santa Fé do Sul Brazil 20°13S 50°56W 365 H8
Santa Filomena Brazil 9°6S 45°50W 365 E9
Santa Gertrudis Spain 39°0N 1°26E 296 C7
Santa Inês Brazil 13°17S 39°48W 365 F11
Santa Inés, I. Chile 54°0S 73°0W 368 G2
Santa Isabel Argentina 36°10S 66°54W 366 D2
Santa Isabel do Morro Brazil 11°34S 50°40W 365 F8
Santa Lucía Corrientes, Argentina 28°58S 59°5W 366 B4
Santa Lucía San Juan, Argentina 31°30S 68°30W 366 C2
Santa Lucía Uruguay 34°27S 56°24W 366 C4
Santa Lucia Range U.S.A. 36°0N 121°20W 350 K5
Santa Luzia C. Verde Is. 16°50N 24°35W 322 b
Santa Margalida Spain 39°42N 3°6E 296 B10
Santa Margarita Argentina 38°28S 61°35W 366 D3
Santa Margarita U.S.A. 35°23N 120°37W 350 K6
Santa Margarita → U.S.A. 33°13N 117°23W 351 M9
Santa Margarita, I. Mexico 24°27N 111°50W 358 C2
Santa María Argentina 26°40S 66°0W 366 B2
Santa Maria Azores 36°58N 25°6W 322 a
Santa Maria Brazil 29°40S 53°48W 367 B5
Santa Maria C. Verde Is. 16°31N 22°53W 322 b
Santa Maria U.S.A. 34°57N 120°26W 351 L6
Santa María → Mexico 31°0N 107°14W 358 A3
Santa María, B. de Mexico 25°4N 108°6W 358 B3
Santa Maria da Vitória Brazil 13°24S 44°12W 365 F10
Santa María del Camí Spain 39°38N 2°47E 296 B9
Santa Maria di Léuca, C. Italy 39°47N 18°22E 295 E8
Santa Marta Colombia 11°15N 74°13W 364 A4
Santa Marta, Sierra Nevada de Colombia 10°55N 73°50W 364 A4
Santa Marta Grande, C. Brazil 28°43S 48°50W 367 B6
Santa Maura = Lefkada Greece 38°40N 20°43E 295 E9
Santa Monica U.S.A. 34°1N 118°29W 351 M8
Santa Monica Mts. ⌓ U.S.A. 34°4N 118°44W 351 L8
Santa Paula U.S.A. 34°21N 119°4W 351 L7
Santa Ponça Spain 39°30N 2°28E 296 B9
Santa Rosa La Pampa, Argentina 36°40S 64°17W 366 D3
Santa Rosa San Luis, Argentina 32°21S 65°10W 366 C2
Santa Rosa Brazil 27°52S 54°29W 367 B5
Santa Rosa Calif., U.S.A. 38°26N 122°43W 350 G4
Santa Rosa N. Mex., U.S.A. 34°57N 104°41W 349 J11
Santa Rosa and San Jacinto Mts. ⌓ U.S.A. 33°28N 116°20W 351 M10
Santa Rosa de Copán Honduras 14°47N 88°46W 360 D2
Santa Rosa de Río Primero Argentina 31°8S 63°20W 366 C3
Santa Rosa del Sara Bolivia 17°7S 63°35W 364 G6
Santa Rosa I. Calif., U.S.A. 33°58N 120°6W 351 M6
Santa Rosa I. Fla., U.S.A. 30°20N 86°50W 357 F11
Santa Rosa Range U.S.A. 41°45N 117°40W 348 F5
Santa Rosalía Mexico 27°19N 112°17W 358 B2
Santa Sylvina Argentina 27°50S 61°10W 366 B3
Santa Tecla = Nueva San Salvador El Salv. 13°40N 89°18W 360 D2
Santa Teresa Argentina 33°25S 60°47W 366 C3
Santa Teresa Australia 24°8S 134°22E 334 C1
Santa Teresa Mexico 25°17N 97°51W 359 B5
Santa Teresa △ Uruguay 33°57S 53°31W 367 C5
Santa Vitória do Palmar Brazil 33°32S 53°25W 367 C5
Santa Ynez → U.S.A. 34°41N 120°36W 351 L6
Santa Ynez Mts. U.S.A. 34°30N 120°0W 351 L6
Santa Ysabel U.S.A. 33°7N 116°40W 351 M10
Santai China 31°5N 104°58E 304 C5
Santana Madeira 32°48N 16°52W 296 D3
Santana, Coxilha de Brazil 30°50S 55°35W 367 C4
Santana do Livramento Brazil 30°55S 55°30W 367 C4
Santander Spain 43°27N 3°51W 293 A4
Santander Jiménez Mexico 24°13N 98°28W 359 C5
Santanilla, Is. Honduras 17°22N 83°57W 360 C3
Santanyí Spain 39°20N 3°5E 296 B10
Santaquin U.S.A. 39°59N 111°47W 348 G8
Santarém Brazil 2°25S 54°42W 365 D8
Santarém Portugal 39°12N 8°42W 293 C1
Santaren Channel W. Indies 24°0N 79°30W 360 B4
Santee U.S.A. 32°50N 116°58W 351 N10
Santee → U.S.A. 33°7N 79°17W 357 E15
Santiago = São Tiago C. Verde Is. 15°0N 23°40W 322 b
Santiago Brazil 29°11S 54°52W 367 B5
Santiago Canary Is. 28°2N 17°12W 296 F2
Santiago Chile 33°26S 70°40W 366 C1
Santiago Panama 8°0N 81°0W 360 E3
Santiago □ Chile 33°30S 70°50W 366 C1
Santiago → Mexico 25°11N 105°26W 338 G9
Santiago → Peru 4°27S 77°38W 364 D3
Santiago de Compostela Spain 42°52N 8°37W 293 A1
Santiago de Cuba Cuba 20°0N 75°49W 360 C4
Santiago de los Caballeros Dom. Rep. 19°30N 70°40W 361 C5
Santiago del Estero Argentina 27°50S 64°15W 366 B3
Santiago del Estero □ Argentina 27°40S 63°15W 366 B3
Santiago del Teide Canary Is. 28°17N 16°48W 296 F3
Santiago Ixcuintla Mexico 21°49N 105°13W 358 C3
Santiago Jamiltepec Mexico 16°17N 97°49W 359 D5
Santiago Papasquiaro Mexico 25°3N 105°25W 358 C3
Santiago Pinotepa Nacional Mexico 16°19N 98°1W 359 D5
Santiaguillo, L. de Mexico 24°48N 104°48W 358 C4
Santo Amaro Brazil 12°30S 38°43W 365 F11
Santo Anastácio Brazil 21°58S 51°39W 367 A5
Santo André Brazil 23°39S 46°29W 367 A6
Santo Ângelo Brazil 28°15S 54°15W 367 B5
Santo Antão C. Verde Is. 16°52N 25°10W 322 b
Santo Antônio do Içá Brazil 3°5S 67°57W 364 D5
Santo Antônio do Leverger Brazil 15°52S 56°5W 365 G7
Santo Domingo Dom. Rep. 18°30N 69°59W 361 C6
Santo Domingo Baja Calif., Mexico 30°43N 116°2W 358 A1
Santo Domingo Baja Calif. S., Mexico 25°29N 111°55W 358 B2
Santo Domingo Nic. 12°14N 84°59W 360 D3
Santo Domingo de los Colorados Ecuador 0°15S 79°9W 364 D3
Santo Domingo Pueblo U.S.A. 35°31N 106°22W 349 J10
Santo Tomás Mexico 31°33N 116°24W 358 A1
Santo Tomás Peru 14°26S 72°8W 364 F4
Santo Tomé Argentina 28°40S 56°5W 367 B4
Santo Tomé de Guayana = Ciudad Guayana Venezuela 8°0N 62°30W 364 B6
Santoña Spain 43°29N 3°27W 293 A4
Santorini Greece 36°23N 25°27E 295 F11
Santos Brazil 24°0S 46°20W 367 A6
Santos Dumont Brazil 22°55S 43°10W 367 A7
Sanur Indonesia 8°41S 115°15E 309 K18
Sanwer India 22°59N 75°50E 314 H6
Sanxiang China 22°21N 113°25E 305 G9
Sanya China 18°14N 109°29E 310 C7
Sanyuan China 34°35N 108°58E 306 G5
São Bernardo do Campo Brazil 23°45S 46°34W 367 A6
São Borja Brazil 28°39S 56°0W 367 B4
São Carlos Brazil 22°0S 47°50W 367 A6
São Cristóvão Brazil 11°1S 37°15W 365 F11
São Domingos Brazil 13°25S 46°19W 365 F9
São Filipe C. Verde Is. 15°2N 24°30W 322 b
São Francisco Brazil 16°0S 44°50W 365 G10
São Francisco → Brazil 10°30S 36°24W 365 F11
São Francisco do Sul Brazil 26°15S 48°36W 367 B6
São Gabriel Brazil 30°20S 54°20W 367 C5
São Gonçalo Brazil 22°48S 43°5W 367 A7
Sao Hill Tanzania 8°20S 35°12E 327 D4
São João da Boa Vista Brazil 22°0S 46°52W 367 A6
São João da Madeira Portugal 40°54N 8°30W 293 B1
São João del Rei Brazil 21°8S 44°15W 367 A7
São João do Araguaia Brazil 5°23S 48°46W 365 E9
São João do Piauí Brazil 8°21S 42°15W 365 E10
São Joaquim Brazil 28°18S 49°56W 367 B6
São Joaquim △ Brazil 28°12S 49°37W 367 B6
São Jorge Azores 38°38N 28°3W 322 a
São Jorge, Pta. de Madeira 32°50N 16°53W 296 D3
São José Brazil 27°38S 48°39W 367 B5
São José do Norte Brazil 32°1S 52°3W 367 C5
São José do Rio Prêto Brazil 20°50S 49°20W 367 A6
São José dos Campos Brazil 23°7S 45°52W 367 A6
São Leopoldo Brazil 29°50S 51°10W 367 B5
São Lourenço Brazil 22°7S 45°3W 367 A6
São Lourenço → Brazil 17°53S 57°27W 365 G7
São Lourenço, Pta. de Madeira 32°44N 16°39W 296 D3
São Lourenço do Sul Brazil 31°22S 51°58W 367 C5
São Luís Brazil 2°39S 44°15W 365 D10
São Luís Gonzaga Brazil 28°25S 55°0W 367 B5
São Marcos → Brazil 18°15S 47°37W 365 G9
São Marcos, B. de Brazil 2°0S 44°0W 365 D10
São Mateus Brazil 18°44S 39°50W 365 G11
São Mateus do Sul Brazil 25°52S 50°23W 367 B5
São Miguel Azores 37°47N 25°30W 322 a
São Miguel do Oeste Brazil 26°45S 53°34W 367 B5
São Nicolau C. Verde Is. 16°20N 24°20W 322 b
São Paulo Brazil 23°32S 46°38W 367 A6
São Paulo □ Brazil 22°0S 49°0W 367 A6
São Paulo de Olivença Brazil 3°27S 68°48W 364 D5
São Roque Madeira 32°46N 16°48W 296 D3
São Roque, C. de Brazil 5°30S 35°16W 365 E11
São Sebastião, I. de Brazil 23°50S 45°18W 367 A6
São Sebastião do Paraíso Brazil 20°54S 46°59W 367 A6
São Tiago C. Verde Is. 15°0N 23°40W 322 b
São Tomé São Tomé & Príncipe 0°10N 6°39E 320 F4
São Tomé, C. de Brazil 22°0S 40°59W 367 A7
São Tomé & Príncipe ■ Africa 0°12N 6°39E 321 F4
São Vicente Brazil 23°57S 46°23W 367 A6
São Vicente C. Verde Is. 17°0N 25°0W 322 b
São Vicente Madeira 32°48N 17°3W 296 D2
São Vicente, C. de Portugal 37°0N 9°0W 293 D1
Saona, I. Dom. Rep. 18°10N 68°40W 361 C6
Saône → France 45°44N 4°50E 292 D6
Saonek Indonesia 0°22S 130°55E 309 E8
Sapam, Ao Thailand 8°0N 98°26E 311 a
Saparua Indonesia 3°33S 128°40E 309 E7
Sapele Nigeria 5°50N 5°40E 322 G7
Sapelo I. U.S.A. 31°25N 81°12W 357 F14
Sapi ⌓ Zimbabwe 15°48S 29°42E 327 F2
Saposoa Peru 6°55S 76°45W 364 E3
Sapphire Australia 23°28S 147°43E 334 C4
Sappho U.S.A. 48°4N 124°16W 350 B2
Sapporo Japan 43°0N 141°21E 302 C10
Sapulpa U.S.A. 35°59N 96°5W 356 D6
Saqqez Iran 36°15N 46°20E 316 B5
Sar Dasht Iran 32°32N 48°52E 317 C6
Sar-e Pol □ Afghan. 36°20N 65°50E 312 B4
Sar Gachīneh = Yāsūj Iran 30°31N 51°31E 317 D6
Sar Planina Macedonia 42°0N 21°0E 295 C9
Sara Buri = Saraburi Thailand 14°30N 100°55E 310 E3
Sarāb Iran 37°55N 47°40E 316 B5
Sarabadi Iraq 33°1N 44°48E 316 C5
Saraburi Thailand 14°30N 100°55E 310 E3
Saradiya India 21°34N 70°2E 314 J4
Saragossa = Zaragoza Spain 41°39N 0°53W 293 B5
Saraguro Ecuador 3°35S 79°16W 364 D3
Sarahs Turkmenistan 36°32N 61°13E 317 B9
Sarai Naurang Pakistan 32°50N 70°47E 314 C4
Saraikela India 22°42N 85°56E 315 H11
Sarajevo Bos.-H. 43°52N 18°26E 295 C8
Sarakhs = Sarahs Turkmenistan 36°32N 61°13E 317 B9
Saran, Gunung Indonesia 0°30S 111°25E 308 E4
Saranac Lake U.S.A. 44°20N 74°10W 355 B10
Saranac Lakes U.S.A. 44°20N 74°28W 355 B10
Saranda Tanzania 5°45S 34°59E 326 D3
Sarandí del Yi Uruguay 33°18S 55°38W 367 C4
Sarandí Grande Uruguay 33°44S 56°20W 366 C4
Sarangani B. Phil. 6°0N 125°13E 309 C7
Sarangani Is. Phil. 5°25N 125°25E 309 C7
Sarangarh India 21°30N 83°5E 313 J13
Saransk Russia 54°10N 45°10E 290 D8
Sarapul Russia 56°28N 53°48E 290 C9
Sarasota U.S.A. 27°20N 82°32W 357 H13
Saratoga Calif., U.S.A. 37°16N 122°2W 350 H4
Saratoga Wyo., U.S.A. 41°27N 106°49W 348 F10
Saratoga ⌓ U.S.A. 43°0N 73°38W 355 D11
Saratoga Springs U.S.A. 43°5N 73°47W 355 C11
Saratok Malaysia 1°55N 111°17E 308 D4
Saratov Russia 51°30N 46°2E 291 D8
Sarāvān Iran 27°25N 62°15E 317 E9
Saravane Laos 15°43N 106°25E 310 E6
Sarawak □ Malaysia 2°0N 113°0E 308 D4
Saray Turkey 41°26N 27°55E 295 D12
Sarayköy Turkey 37°55N 28°54E 295 F13
Sarbāz Iran 26°38N 61°19E 317 E9
Sarbīsheh Iran 32°30N 59°40E 317 C8
Sarda → India 27°21N 81°23E 315 F9
Sardarshahr India 28°30N 74°29E 314 E6
Sardegna □ Italy 40°0N 9°0E 294 D3
Sardhana India 29°9N 77°39E 314 E7
Sardina, Pta. Canary Is. 28°9N 15°44W 296 F4
Sardinia = Sardegna □ Italy 40°0N 9°0E 294 D3
Sardis Turkey 38°28N 27°58E 295 E12
Sārdūīyeh = Dar Mazār Iran 29°14N 57°20E 317 D8
Saren Indonesia 8°26S 115°34E 309 J18
S'Arenal Spain 39°30N 2°45E 296 B9
Sarera, G. of Indonesia 2°0S 135°0E 330 B6
Sargasso Sea Atl. Oc. 27°0N 72°0W 338 G13
Sargodha Pakistan 32°10N 72°40E 314 C5
Sarh Chad 9°5N 18°23E 323 G9
Sārī Iran 36°30N 53°4E 317 B7
Saria India 21°38N 83°22E 315 J10
Sariab Pakistan 30°6N 66°59E 314 D2
Sarıgöl Turkey 38°14N 28°41E 295 E13
Sarikei Malaysia 2°8N 111°30E 308 D4
Sarila India 25°46N 79°41E 315 G8
Sarina Australia 21°22S 149°13E 334 C4
Sarita U.S.A. 27°13N 97°47W 356 H6
Sariwŏn N. Korea 38°31N 125°46E 307 E13
Sarju → India 27°21N 81°23E 315 F9
Sark U.K. 49°25N 2°22W 285 H5
Sarkari Tala India 27°39N 70°52E 314 F4
Şarköy Turkey 40°36N 27°6E 295 D12
Sarlat-la-Canéda France 44°54N 1°13E 292 D4
Sarmi Indonesia 1°49S 138°44E 309 E9
Sarmiento Argentina 45°35S 69°5W 368 F3
Särna Sweden 61°41N 13°8E 280 F15
Sarnia Canada 42°58N 82°23W 354 D2
Sarolangun Indonesia 2°19S 102°42E 308 E2
Saronikos Kolpos Greece 37°45N 23°45E 295 F10
Saros Körfezi Turkey 40°30N 26°15E 295 D12
Sarpsborg Norway 59°16N 11°7E 281 G14
Sarqan Kazakhstan 45°24N 79°55E 300 E8
Sarre = Saar → Europe 49°41N 6°32E 287 E6
Sarreguemines France 49°5N 7°4E 292 B7
Sarthe → France 47°33N 0°31W 292 C3
Saruna → Pakistan 26°31N 67°7E 314 F2
Sarvar India 26°4N 75°0E 314 F6
Sarvestān Iran 29°20N 53°10E 317 D7
Sary-Tash Kyrgyzstan 39°44N 73°15E 300 F8

Saryshaghan Kazakhstan 46°12N 73°38E 300 E8
Sasan Gir India 21°10N 70°36E 314 J4
Sasaram India 24°57N 84°5E 315 G11
Sasebo Japan 33°10N 129°43E 303 H4
Saser India 34°50N 77°50E 315 B7
Saskatchewan □ Canada 54°40N 106°0W 343 C7
Saskatchewan → Canada 53°37N 100°40W 343 C8
Saskatoon Canada 52°10N 106°38W 343 C7
Saskylakh Russia 71°55N 114°1E 301 B12
Saslaya △ Nic. 13°45N 85°4W 360 D2
Sasolburg S. Africa 26°46S 27°49E 329 D4
Sasovo Russia 54°25N 41°55E 290 D7
Sassandra Ivory C. 4°55N 6°8W 322 H4
Sassandra → Ivory C. 4°58N 6°5W 322 H4
Sássari Italy 40°43N 8°34E 294 D3
Sassnitz Germany 54°29N 13°39E 288 A7
Sassuolo Italy 44°33N 10°47E 294 B4
Sasyk, Ozero Ukraine 45°45N 29°20E 289 F15
Sata-Misaki Japan 31°0N 130°40E 303 J5
Satadougou Mali 12°25N 11°25W 322 F3
Satakunda = Satakunta Finland 61°45N 23°0E 280 F20
Satakunta Finland 61°45N 23°0E 280 F20
Satara India 17°44N 73°58E 312 L8
Satara S. Africa 24°29S 31°47E 329 C5
Satbarwa India 23°55N 84°16E 315 H11
Satevó Mexico 27°57N 106°7W 358 B3
Satilla → U.S.A. 30°59N 81°29W 357 F14
Satka Russia 55°3N 59°1E 290 C10
Satmala Hills Andhra Pradesh, India 19°45N 78°45E 312 K11
Satmala Hills Maharashtra, India 20°15N 74°40E 312 J9
Satna India 24°35N 80°50E 315 G9
Sátoraljaújhely Hungary 48°25N 21°41E 289 D11
Satpura △ India 22°40N 78°15E 314 H8
Satpura Ra. India 21°25N 76°10E 312 J10
Satsuna-Shotō Japan 30°0N 130°0E 303 K5
Sattahip Thailand 12°41N 100°54E 310 F3
Satu Mare Romania 47°46N 22°55E 289 E12
Satui Indonesia 3°50S 115°27E 308 E5
Satun Thailand 6°43N 100°2E 311 J3
Satupa'itea Samoa 13°45S 172°18W 331 b
Saturnina → Brazil 12°15S 58°10W 364 F7
Sauce Argentina 30°5S 58°46W 366 C4
Sauceda Mexico 25°46N 101°19W 358 B4
Saucillo Mexico 28°1N 105°17W 358 B3
Sauda Norway 59°40N 6°20E 281 G12
Sauðarkrókur Iceland 65°45N 19°40W 280 D4
Saudi Arabia ■ Asia 26°0N 44°0E 316 B3
Sauerland Germany 51°12N 7°59E 288 C4
Saugeen → Canada 44°30N 81°22W 354 B3
Saugerties U.S.A. 42°5N 73°57W 355 D11
Saugus U.S.A. 34°25N 118°32W 351 L8
Sauk Centre U.S.A. 45°44N 94°57W 352 C6
Sauk Rapids U.S.A. 45°35N 94°10W 352 C6
Sault Ste. Marie Canada 46°30N 84°20W 344 C3
Sault Ste. Marie U.S.A. 46°30N 84°21W 353 B11
Saumlaki Indonesia 7°55S 131°20E 309 F8
Saumur France 47°15N 0°5W 292 C3
Saunders, C. N.Z. 45°53S 170°45E 331 F3
Saunders I. Antarctica 57°48S 26°28W 277 B1
Saunders Pt. Australia 27°52S 125°38E 333 E4
Saurimo Angola 9°40S 20°12E 324 F4
Sausalito U.S.A. 37°51N 122°29W 350 H4
Savá Honduras 15°32N 86°15W 360 C2
Sava → Serbia 44°50N 20°26E 295 B9
Savage U.S.A. 47°27N 104°21W 348 C11
Savage I. = Niue Cook Is. 19°2S 169°54W 337 J11
Savage River Australia 41°31S 145°14E 335 G4
Savai'i Samoa 13°28S 172°24W 331 b
Savalou Benin 7°57N 1°58E 322 G6
Savane Mozam. 19°37S 35°8E 327 F4
Savanna U.S.A. 42°5N 90°8W 352 D8
Savanna-la-Mar Jamaica 18°10N 78°10W 360 a
Savannah Ga., U.S.A. 32°5N 81°6W 357 E14
Savannah Mo., U.S.A. 39°56N 94°50W 352 F6
Savannah Tenn., U.S.A. 35°14N 88°15W 357 D10
Savannah → U.S.A. 32°2N 80°53W 357 E14
Savannakhet Laos 16°30N 104°49E 310 D5
Savant L. Canada 50°16N 90°44W 344 B1
Savant Lake Canada 50°14N 90°40W 344 B1
Save → Mozam. 21°16S 34°0E 329 C5
Sāveh Iran 35°2N 50°20E 317 C6
Savelugu Ghana 9°38N 0°54W 322 G5
Savo Finland 62°45N 27°30E 280 E22
Savoie □ France 45°26N 6°25E 292 D7
Savolax = Savo Finland 62°45N 27°30E 280 E22
Savona Italy 44°17N 8°30E 292 D8
Savona U.S.A. 42°17N 77°13W 354 D7
Savonlinna Finland 61°52N 28°53E 280 F23
Savoy = Savoie □ France 45°26N 6°25E 292 D7
Savur Turkey 37°34N 40°53E 316 B4
Savusavu Fiji 16°34S 179°15E 331 a
Savusavu B. Fiji 16°45S 179°15E 331 a
Sawahlunto Indonesia 0°40S 100°52E 308 E2
Sawai Indonesia 3°0S 129°5E 309 E7
Sawai Madhopur India 26°0N 76°25E 314 G7
Sawaleke Fiji 17°59S 179°18E 331 a
Sawang Daen Din Thailand 17°28N 103°28E 310 D4
Sawankhalok Thailand 17°19N 99°50E 310 D2
Sawara Japan 35°55N 140°30E 303 G10
Sawatch Range U.S.A. 39°0N 106°30W 348 G10
Sawel Mt. U.K. 54°50N 7°2W 282 B4
Sawi Thailand 10°14N 99°5E 311 G2
Sawmills Zimbabwe 19°30S 28°2E 327 F2
Sawtooth ⌂ U.S.A. 44°0N 114°50W 348 D6
Sawtooth Range U.S.A. 44°3N 114°58W 348 D6
Sawu Indonesia 10°35S 121°50E 309 F6
Sawu Sea Indonesia 9°30S 121°50E 309 F6
Saxby → Australia 18°25S 140°53E 334 B3
Saxmundham U.K. 52°13N 1°30E 285 E9
Saxony = Sachsen □ Germany 50°55N 13°10E 288 C7
Saxony, Lower = Niedersachsen □ Germany 52°50N 9°0E 288 B5
Saxton U.S.A. 40°13N 78°15W 354 F6
Sayabec Canada 48°35N 67°41W 345 C6
Sayaboury Laos 19°15N 101°45E 310 C3
Sayán Peru 11°8S 77°12W 364 F3
Sayan, Vostochnyy Russia 54°0N 96°0E 301 D10
Sayan, Zapadnyy Russia 52°30N 94°0E 301 D10
Saydā Lebanon 33°35N 35°25E 318 B4
Sayhandulaan = Oldziyt Mongolia 44°40N 109°1E 306 B5
Sayḥūt Yemen 15°12N 51°10E 319 D5
Saylac = Zeila Somali Rep. 11°21N 43°30E 319 E3
Saynshand = Buyant-Uhaa Mongolia 44°55N 110°11E 305 B6
Sayre Okla., U.S.A. 35°18N 99°38W 356 D5
Sayre Pa., U.S.A. 41°59N 76°32W 355 E8
Sayreville U.S.A. 40°28N 74°22W 355 F10
Sayula Mexico 19°52N 103°36W 358 D4
Sayward Canada 50°21N 125°55W 342 C3
Sazanit Albania 40°30N 19°20E 295 D8
Sázava → Czech Rep. 49°53N 14°24E 288 D8
Sazin Pakistan 35°35N 73°30E 315 B5
Scafell Pike U.K. 54°27N 3°14W 284 C4
Scalloway U.K. 60°9N 1°17W 283 A7
Scalpay U.K. 57°18N 6°0W 283 D3
Scandia Canada 50°20N 112°2W 342 C6
Scandicci Italy 43°45N 11°11E 294 C4
Scandinavia Europe 64°0N 12°0E 280 E15
Scapa Flow U.K. 58°53N 3°3W 283 C5
Scappoose U.S.A. 45°45N 122°53W 350 E4
Scarba U.K. 56°11N 5°43W 283 E3
Scarborough Trin. & Tob. 11°11N 60°42W 361 D7
Scarborough U.K. 54°17N 0°24W 284 C7
Scariff I. Ireland 51°44N 10°15W 282 E1
Scarp U.K. 58°1N 7°8W 283 C1
Scebeli, Wabi → Somali Rep. 2°0N 44°0E 319 G3
Schaffhausen Switz. 47°42N 8°39E 292 C8
Schagen Neths. 52°49N 4°48E 287 B4
Schaghticoke U.S.A. 42°54N 73°35W 355 D11
Schefferville = Kawawachikamach Canada 54°48N 66°50W 345 B6
Schelde → Belgium 51°15N 4°16E 287 C4
Schell Creek Ra. U.S.A. 39°25N 114°40W 348 G6
Schellsburg U.S.A. 40°3N 78°39W 354 F6
Schenectady U.S.A. 42°49N 73°57W 355 D11
Schenevus U.S.A. 42°33N 74°50W 355 D10
Schiedam Neths. 51°55N 4°25E 287 C4
Schiermonnikoog Neths. 53°30N 6°15E 287 A6
Schio Italy 45°43N 11°21E 294 B4
Schiphol, Amsterdam ✕ (AMS) Neths. 52°18N 4°45E 287 B4
Schleswig Germany 54°31N 9°34E 288 A5
Schleswig-Holstein □ Germany 54°30N 9°30E 288 A5
Schœlcher Martinique 14°36N 61°7W 360 c
Schoharie U.S.A. 42°40N 74°19W 355 D10
Schoharie Cr. → U.S.A. 42°57N 74°18W 355 D10
Scholls U.S.A. 45°24N 122°56W 350 E4
Schouten I. Australia 42°20S 148°20E 335 G4
Schouten Is. = Supiori Indonesia 1°0S 136°0E 309 E9
Schouwen Neths. 51°43N 3°45E 287 C3
Schreiber Canada 48°45N 87°20W 344 C2
Schroffenstein Namibia 27°11S 18°42E 328 D2
Schroon Lake U.S.A. 43°50N 73°46W 355 C11
Schuler Canada 50°20N 110°6W 343 C6
Schumacher Canada 48°30N 81°16W 344 C3
Schurz U.S.A. 38°57N 118°49W 348 G4
Schuyler U.S.A. 41°27N 97°4W 352 E5
Schuylerville U.S.A. 43°6N 73°35W 355 C11
Schuylkill → U.S.A. 39°53N 75°12W 355 G9
Schuylkill Haven U.S.A. 40°37N 76°11W 355 F8
Schwäbische Alb Germany 48°20N 9°30E 288 D5
Schwaner, Pegunungan Indonesia 1°0S 112°30E 308 E4
Schwarzrand Namibia 25°37S 16°50E 328 D2
Schwarzwald Germany 48°30N 8°20E 288 D5
Schwedt Germany 53°3N 14°16E 288 B8
Schweinfurt Germany 50°3N 10°14E 288 C6
Schweiz = Switzerland ■ Europe 46°30N 8°0E 292 C8
Schweizer-Reneke S. Africa 27°11S 25°18E 328 D4
Schwenningen = Villingen-Schwenningen Germany 48°3N 8°26E 288 D5
Schwerin Germany 53°36N 11°22E 288 B6
Schwyz Switz. 47°2N 8°39E 292 C8
Sciacca Italy 37°31N 13°3E 294 F5
Scilla Italy 38°15N 15°43E 294 E6
Scilly, Isles of U.K. 49°56N 6°22W 285 H1
Scioto → U.S.A. 38°44N 83°1W 353 F12
Scituate U.S.A. 42°12N 70°44W 355 D14
Scobey U.S.A. 48°47N 105°25W 348 B11
Scone Australia 32°5S 150°52E 335 E5
Scone U.K. 56°25N 3°24W 283 E5
Scoresbysund = Ittoqqortoormiit Greenland 70°20N 23°0W 276 B6
Scotia Calif., U.S.A. 40°29N 124°6W 348 F1
Scotia N.Y., U.S.A. 42°50N 73°58W 355 D11
Scotia Sea Antarctica 56°5S 56°0W 277 B18
Scotland Canada 43°1N 80°22W 354 C4
Scotland □ U.K. 57°0N 4°0W 283 E5
Scott Antarctica 77°0S 165°0E 277 D11
Scott, C. Australia 13°30S 129°49E 332 B4
Scott City U.S.A. 38°29N 100°54W 352 F3
Scott Glacier Antarctica 66°15S 100°5E 277 C8
Scott I. Antarctica 67°0S 179°0E 277 C11
Scott Is. Canada 50°48N 128°40W 342 C3
Scott L. Canada 59°55N 106°18W 343 B7
Scott Reef Australia 14°0S 121°50E 332 B3
Scottburgh S. Africa 30°15S 30°47E 329 E5
Scottdale U.S.A. 40°6N 79°35W 354 F5
Scottish Borders □ U.K. 55°35N 2°50W 283 F6
Scotts Valley U.S.A. 37°3N 122°1W 350 H4
Scottsbluff U.S.A. 41°52N 103°40W 352 E2
Scottsboro U.S.A. 34°40N 86°2W 357 D11
Scottsburg U.S.A. 38°41N 85°47W 353 F11
Scottsdale Australia 41°9S 147°31E 335 G4
Scottsdale U.S.A. 33°40N 111°53W 349 K8
Scottsville Ky., U.S.A. 36°45N 86°11W 352 G10
Scottsville N.Y., U.S.A. 43°2N 77°47W 354 C7
Scottville U.S.A. 43°58N 86°17W 352 D10
Scranton U.S.A. 41°25N 75°40W 355 E9
Scugog, L. Canada 44°10N 78°55W 354 B6
Scunthorpe U.K. 53°36N 0°39W 284 D7
Scutari = Shkodër Albania 42°4N 19°32E 295 C8
Sea Is. U.S.A. 31°30N 81°7W 357 F14
Seabrook, L. Australia 30°55S 119°40E 333 F2
Seaford U.K. 50°47N 0°7E 285 G8
Seaford U.S.A. 38°39N 75°37W 353 F16
Seaforth Australia 20°55S 148°57E 334 J6
Seaforth Canada 43°35N 81°25W 354 C3
Seaforth, L. U.K. 57°52N 6°36W 283 D2
Seagraves U.S.A. 32°57N 102°34W 356 E3
Seaham U.K. 54°50N 1°20W 284 C6
Seal → Canada 59°4N 94°48W 343 B10
Seal L. Canada 54°20N 61°30W 345 B7
Sealy U.S.A. 29°47N 96°9W 356 G6
Searchlight U.S.A. 35°28N 114°55W 351 K12
Searcy U.S.A. 35°15N 91°44W 356 D9
Searles L. U.S.A. 35°44N 117°21W 351 K9
Seascale U.K. 54°24N 3°29W 284 C4
Seaside Calif., U.S.A. 36°37N 121°50W 350 J5
Seaside Oreg., U.S.A. 46°0N 123°56W 350 E3
Seaspray Australia 38°25S 147°15E 335 F4
Seattle U.S.A. 47°36N 122°19W 350 C4
Seattle-Tacoma Int. ✕ (SEA) U.S.A. 47°27N 122°18W 350 C4
Seaview Ra. Australia 18°40S 145°45E 334 B4
Sebago L. U.S.A. 43°52N 70°34W 355 C14
Sebago Lake U.S.A. 43°51N 70°34W 355 C14
Sebastián Vizcaíno, B. Mexico 28°0N 114°30W 358 B2
Sebastopol = Sevastopol Ukraine 44°35N 33°30E 291 F5
Sebastopol U.S.A. 38°24N 122°49W 350 G4
Sebewaing U.S.A. 43°44N 83°27W 353 D12
Sebha = Sabhā Libya 27°9N 14°29E 323 C8
Şebinkarahisar Turkey 40°22N 38°28E 291 F6
Sebring Fla., U.S.A. 27°30N 81°27W 357 H14
Sebring Ohio, U.S.A. 40°55N 81°2W 354 F3
Sebringville Canada 43°24N 81°4W 354 C3
Sebta = Ceuta N. Afr. 35°52N 5°18W 293 E3
Sebuku Indonesia 3°30S 116°25E 308 E5
Sebuku, Teluk Malaysia 4°0N 118°10E 308 D5
Sechelt Canada 49°25N 123°42W 342 D4
Sechura, Desierto de Peru 6°0S 80°30W 364 E2
Secretary I. N.Z. 45°15S 166°56E 331 F1
Secunderabad India 17°28N 78°30E 312 L11
Security U.S.A. 38°45N 104°45W 348 G11
Sedalia U.S.A. 38°42N 93°14W 352 F7
Sedan France 49°43N 4°57E 292 B6
Sedan U.S.A. 37°8N 96°11W 352 G5
Sedbergh U.K. 54°20N 2°31W 284 C5
Seddon N.Z. 41°40S 174°7E 331 D5
Seddonville N.Z. 41°33S 172°1E 331 D4
Sedé Boqér Israel 30°52N 34°47E 318 E3
Sedeh Fārs, Iran 30°45N 52°11E 317 D7
Sedeh Khorāsān, Iran 33°20N 59°14E 317 C8
Sederot Israel 31°32N 34°37E 318 D3
Sédhiou Senegal 12°44N 15°30W 322 F2
Sedley Canada 50°10N 104°0W 343 C8
Sedona U.S.A. 34°52N 111°46W 349 J8
Sedova, Pik Russia 73°29N 54°58E 300 B6
Sedro-Woolley U.S.A. 48°30N 122°14W 350 B4
Seeheim Namibia 26°50S 17°45E 328 D2
Seeis Namibia 22°29S 17°39E 328 C2
Seekoei → S. Africa 30°18S 25°1E 328 E4
Seeley's Bay Canada 44°29N 76°14W 355 B8
Seferihisar Turkey 38°10N 26°50E 295 E12
Seg-ozero Russia 63°20N 33°46E 290 B5
Segamat Malaysia 2°30N 102°50E 311 L4
Segesta Italy 37°56N 12°50E 294 F5
Seget Indonesia 1°24S 130°58E 309 E8
Segezha Russia 63°44N 34°19E 290 B5
Ségou Mali 13°30N 6°16W 322 F4
Segovia = Coco → Cent. Amer. 15°0N 83°8W 360 D3
Segovia Spain 40°57N 4°10W 293 B3
Segre → Spain 41°40N 0°43E 293 B6
Séguéla Ivory C. 7°55N 6°40W 322 G4
Seguin U.S.A. 29°34N 97°58W 356 G6
Segundo → Argentina 30°53S 62°44W 366 C3
Segura → Spain 38°3N 0°44W 293 C5
Seh Konj, Kūh-e Iran 30°6N 57°30E 317 D8
Seh Qal'eh Iran 33°40N 58°24E 317 C8
Sehitwa Botswana 20°30S 22°30E 328 C3
Sehlabathebe △ Lesotho 29°53S 29°7E 329 D4
Sehore India 23°10N 77°5E 314 H7
Sehwan Pakistan 26°28N 67°53E 314 F2
Seil U.K. 56°18N 5°38W 283 E3
Seiland Norway 70°25N 23°15E 280 A20
Seiling U.S.A. 36°9N 98°56W 356 C5
Seinäjoki Finland 62°40N 22°51E 280 E20
Seine → France 49°26N 0°26E 292 B4
Seistan = Sīstān Asia 30°50N 61°0E 317 D9
Seistan, Daryācheh-ye = Sīstān, Daryācheh-ye Iran 31°0N 61°0E 317 D9
Sekayu Indonesia 2°51S 103°51E 308 E2
Seke Tanzania 3°20S 33°31E 326 C3
Sekenke Tanzania 4°18S 34°11E 326 C3
Sekondi-Takoradi Ghana 4°58N 1°45W 322 H5
Sekudai Malaysia 1°32N 103°39E 311 d
Sekuma Botswana 24°36S 23°50E 328 C3
Selah U.S.A. 46°39N 120°32W 348 C3
Selama Malaysia 5°12N 100°42E 311 K3
Selaru Indonesia 8°9S 131°0E 309 F8
Selatan, Selat Malaysia 5°15N 100°20E 311 c
Selby U.K. 53°47N 1°5W 284 D6
Selby U.S.A. 45°31N 100°2W 352 C3
Selçuk Turkey 37°56N 27°22E 295 F12
Selden U.S.A. 39°33N 100°34W 352 F3
Sele → Italy 40°29N 14°56E 294 D6
Selebi-Pikwe Botswana 21°58S 27°48E 329 C4
Selemdzha → Russia 51°42N 128°53E 301 D13
Selenga = Selenge Mörön → Asia 52°16N 106°16E 304 A5
Selenge Mörön → Asia 52°16N 106°16E 304 A5
Seletan, Tanjung Indonesia 4°10S 114°40E 308 E4
Sélibabi Mauritania 15°10N 12°15W 322 E3
Seligman U.S.A. 35°20N 112°53W 349 J7
Selîma, El Wâhât el Sudan 21°22N 29°19E 323 D11
Selinda Spillway → Botswana 18°35S 23°10E 328 B3
Selinsgrove U.S.A. 40°48N 76°52W 354 F8
Selkirk Canada 50°10N 96°55W 343 C9
Selkirk U.K. 55°33N 2°50W 283 F6
Selkirk I. = Horse I. Canada 53°20N 99°6W 343 C9
Selkirk Mts. Canada 51°15N 117°40W 340 D8
Sellafield U.K. 54°25N 3°29W 284 C4
Sellia Greece 35°12N 24°23E 297 D6
Sells U.S.A. 31°55N 111°53W 349 L8
Selma Ala., U.S.A. 32°25N 87°1W 357 E11
Selma Calif., U.S.A. 36°34N 119°37W 350 J7
Selma N.C., U.S.A. 35°32N 78°17W 357 D15
Selmer U.S.A. 35°10N 88°36W 357 D10
Selous ⌂ Tanzania 8°37S 37°42E 327 D4
Selowandoma Falls Zimbabwe 21°15S 31°50E 327 G3
Selpele Indonesia 0°1S 130°5E 309 E8
Selsey Bill U.K. 50°43N 0°47W 285 G7
Seltso Russia 53°22N 34°4E 290 D5
Selu Indonesia 7°32S 130°55E 309 F8
Selva Argentina 29°50S 62°0W 366 B3
Selva Lancandona = Montes Azules ⌂ Mexico 16°21N 91°3W 359 D6
Selvas Brazil 6°30S 67°0W 364 E5
Selwyn L. Canada 60°0N 104°30W 343 B8
Selwyn Mts. Canada 63°0N 130°0W 340 C6
Selwyn Ra. Australia 21°10S 140°0E 334 C3
Seman → Albania 40°47N 19°30E 295 D8
Semarang Indonesia 7°0S 110°26E 308 F4
Sembabule Uganda 0°4S 31°25E 326 C3
Sembawang Singapore 1°27N 103°50E 311 d
Sembung Indonesia 8°28S 115°11E 309 J18
Semenanjung Blambangan Indonesia 8°42S 114°29E 309 K17
Semeru Indonesia 8°4S 112°55E 309 H15
Semey Kazakhstan 50°30N 80°10E 300 D9
Seminoe Res. U.S.A. 42°9N 106°55W 348 E10
Seminole Okla., U.S.A. 35°14N 96°41W 356 D6
Seminole Tex., U.S.A. 32°43N 102°39W 356 E3
Seminole Draw → U.S.A. 32°27N 102°20W 356 E3
Semipalatinsk = Semey Kazakhstan 50°30N 80°10E 300 D9
Semirara Is. Phil. 12°0N 121°20E 309 B6
Semitau Indonesia 0°29N 111°57E 308 D4
Semiyarka Kazakhstan 50°55N 78°23E 300 D8
Semiyarskoye = Semiyarka Kazakhstan 50°55N 78°23E 300 D8
Semmering P. Austria 47°41N 15°45E 288 E8
Semnān Iran 35°40N 53°23E 317 C7
Semnān □ Iran 36°0N 54°0E 317 C7
Semporna Malaysia 4°30N 118°33E 309 D5
Semuda Indonesia 2°51S 112°58E 308 E4
Sen → Cambodia 12°32N 104°28E 310 F5
Senā Iran 28°27N 51°36E 317 D6
Sena Mozam. 17°25S 35°0E 327 F4
Sena Madureira Brazil 9°5S 68°45W 364 E5
Senador Pompeu Brazil 5°40S 39°20W 365 E11
Senang, Pulau Singapore 1°11N 103°52E 311 d
Senanga Zambia 16°7S 23°16E 325 H4
Senatobia U.S.A. 34°37N 89°58W 357 D10
Sencelles Spain 39°39N 2°54E 296 B9
Sendai Kagoshima, Japan 31°50N 130°20E 303 J5
Sendai Miyagi, Japan 38°15N 140°53E 302 E10
Sendai-Wan Japan 38°15N 141°0E 302 E10
Sendhwa India 21°41N 75°6E 314 J6
Seneca U.S.A. 34°41N 82°57W 357 D13
Seneca Falls U.S.A. 42°55N 76°48W 355 D8
Seneca L. U.S.A. 42°40N 76°54W 354 D8
Senecaville L. U.S.A. 39°55N 81°25W 354 G3
Senegal ■ W. Afr. 14°30N 14°30W 322 F3
Sénégal → W. Afr. 15°48N 16°32W 322 E2
Senegambia Africa 12°45N 12°0W 320 E2
Senekal S. Africa 28°20S 27°36E 329 D4
Senga Hill Zambia 9°19S 31°11E 327 D3
Senge Khambab = Indus → Pakistan 24°20N 67°47E 314 G2
Sengua → Zimbabwe 17°7S 28°5E 327 F2
Senhor-do-Bonfim Brazil 10°30S 40°10W 365 F10
Senigállia Italy 43°43N 13°13E 294 C5
Senj Croatia 45°0N 14°58E 288 F8
Senja Norway 69°25N 17°30E 280 B17
Senkaku-Shotō E. China Sea 25°45N 123°30E 303 M1
Senkuang Indonesia 1°11N 104°2E 311 d
Senlis France 49°13N 2°35E 292 B5
Senmonorom Cambodia 12°27N 107°12E 310 F6
Senneterre Canada 48°25N 77°15W 344 C4
Seno Laos 16°35N 104°50E 310 D5
Sens France 48°11N 3°15E 292 B5
Senta Serbia 45°55N 20°3E 295 B9
Sentani Indonesia 2°36S 140°37E 309 E10
Sentery = Lubao Dem. Rep. of the Congo 5°17S 25°42E 326 D2
Sentinel U.S.A. 32°52N 113°13W 349 K7
Sentosa Singapore 1°16N 103°50E 311 d
Seo de Urgel = La Seu d'Urgell Spain 42°22N 1°23E 293 A6
Seogwipo S. Korea 33°13N 126°34E 307 H14
Seohara India 29°15N 78°33E 315 E8
Seonath → India 21°44N 82°28E 315 J10
Seondha India 26°9N 78°48E 315 F8
Seongnam S. Korea 37°26N 127°8E 307 F14
Seoni India 22°5N 79°30E 315 H8
Seoni Malwa India 22°27N 77°28E 314 H8
Seonsan S. Korea 36°14N 128°17E 307 F15
Seosan S. Korea 36°47N 126°27E 307 F14
Seoul S. Korea 37°31N 126°58E 307 F14
Sepīdān Iran 30°20N 52°5E 317 D7
Sep'o N. Korea 38°57N 127°25E 307 E14
Sepone Laos 16°45N 106°13E 310 D6
Sept-Îles Canada 50°13N 66°22W 345 B6
Sequim U.S.A. 48°5N 123°6W 350 B3
Sequoia △ U.S.A. 36°30N 118°30W 350 J8
Seraing Belgium 50°35N 5°32E 287 D5
Serakhis → Cyprus 35°13N 32°55E 297 D11
Seram Indonesia 3°10S 129°0E 309 E7
Seram Sea Indonesia 2°30S 128°30E 309 E7
Seranantsara Madag. 18°30S 49°5E 329 B8
Serang Indonesia 6°8S 106°10E 309 G12
Serangoon Singapore 1°23N 103°54E 311 d
Serasan Indonesia 2°29N 109°4E 308 D3
Serbia □ Serbia 43°30N 21°0E 295 C9
Serbia ■ Europe 43°20N 20°0E 295 B9
Serdar Turkmenistan 39°4N 56°23E 317 B8
Serdobsk Russia 52°28N 44°10E 290 D7
Seremban Malaysia 2°43N 101°53E 311 L3
Serengeti △ Tanzania 2°11S 35°0E 326 C3
Serengeti Plain Tanzania 2°40S 35°0E 326 C4
Serenje Zambia 13°14S 30°15E 327 E3
Sereth = Siret → Romania 45°24N 28°1E 289 F14
Sergino Russia 62°25N 65°12E 300 C7
Sergipe □ Brazil 10°30S 37°30W 365 F11
Sergiyev Posad Russia 56°20N 38°10E 290 C6
Serhetabat Turkmenistan 35°20N 62°18E 317 C9
Seria Brunei 4°37N 114°23E 308 D4
Serian Malaysia 1°10N 110°31E 308 D4
Seribu, Kepulauan Indonesia 5°36S 106°33E 308 F3
Sericho Kenya 1°5N 39°5E 326 B4
Serifos Greece 37°9N 24°30E 295 F11
Sérigny → Canada 56°47N 66°0W 345 A6
Seringapatam Reef Australia 13°38S 122°5E 332 B3
Seririt Indonesia 8°12S 114°56E 309 J17
Sermata Indonesia 8°15S 128°50E 309 F7
Sermersuaq Greenland 79°30N 62°0W 276 B4
Serov Russia 59°29N 60°35E 290 C11
Serowe Botswana 22°25S 26°43E 328 C4
Serpentine Lakes Australia 28°30S 129°10E 333 E4
Serpent's Mouth = Sierpe, Bocas de la Venezuela 10°0N 61°30W 365 L15
Serpukhov Russia 54°55N 37°28E 290 D6
Serra do Navio Brazil 0°59N 52°3W 365 C8
Serranía San Luís △ Paraguay 22°35S 57°22W 366 A4
Serres Greece 41°5N 23°31E 295 D10
Serrezuela Argentina 30°40S 65°20W 366 C2
Serrinha Brazil 11°39S 39°0W 365 F11
Sertanópolis Brazil 23°4S 51°2W 367 A5
Serua Indonesia 6°18S 130°1E 309 F8
Serui Indonesia 1°53S 136°10E 309 E9
Serule Botswana 21°57S 27°20E 328 C4
Ses Salines Spain 39°21N 3°3E 296 B10
Sese Is. Uganda 0°20S 32°20E 326 C3
Sesepe Indonesia 1°30S 127°59E 309 E7
Sesfontein Namibia 19°7S 13°39E 328 B1
Sesheke Zambia 17°29S 24°13E 328 B3
S'Espalmador Spain 38°47N 1°26E 296 C7
S'Espardell Spain 38°48N 1°29E 296 C7
S'Estanyol Spain 39°22N 2°54E 296 B9
Setana Japan 42°26N 139°51E 302 C9
Sète France 43°25N 3°42E 292 E5
Sete Lagôas Brazil 19°27S 44°16W 365 G10
Sétif Algeria 36°9N 5°26E 322 A7
Seto Japan 35°14N 137°6E 303 G8
Setonaikai Japan 34°20N 133°30E 303 G6
Setonaikai △ Japan 34°15N 133°15E 303 G6
Settat Morocco 33°0N 7°40W 322 B4
Setting L. Canada 55°0N 98°38W 343 C9
Settle U.K. 54°5N 2°16W 284 C5
Settlement, The Br. Virgin Is. 18°43N 64°22W 361 e
Settlers S. Africa 25°2S 28°30E 329 C4
Setúbal Portugal 38°30N 8°58W 293 C1
Setúbal, B. de Portugal 38°40N 8°56W 293 C1
Seul, Lac Canada 50°20N 92°30W 344 B1
Sevan, Ozero = Sevana Lich Armenia 40°30N 45°20E 316 A5
Sevana Lich Armenia 40°30N 45°20E 316 A5
Sevastopol Ukraine 44°35N 33°30E 291 F5
Seven Sisters Canada 54°56N 128°10W 342 C3
Severn → Canada 56°2N 87°36W 344 A2
Severn → U.K. 51°35N 2°40W 285 F5
Severn L. Canada 53°54N 90°48W 344 B1
Severnaya Zemlya Russia 79°0N 100°0E 301 B10
Severnyye Uvaly Russia 60°0N 50°0E 290 C8
Severo-Kurilsk Russia 50°40N 156°8E 301 D16
Severo-Yeniseyskiy Russia 60°22N 93°1E 301 C10

Severo-Zapadnyy □ Russia 65°0N 40°0E 300 C4
Severodvinsk Russia 64°27N 39°58E 290 B6
Severomorsk Russia 69°5N 33°27E 280 B25
Severouralsk Russia 60°9N 59°57E 290 B10
Sevier → U.S.A. 39°4N 113°6W 348 G7
Sevier Desert U.S.A. 39°40N 112°45W 348 G7
Sevier L. U.S.A. 38°54N 113°9W 348 G7
Sevilla Spain 37°23N 5°58W 293 D2
Seville = Sevilla Spain 37°23N 5°58W 293 D2
Sevlievo Bulgaria 43°2N 25°6E 295 C11
Sewani India 28°58N 75°39E 314 E6
Seward Alaska, U.S.A. 60°7N 149°27W 346 a
Seward Nebr., U.S.A. 40°55N 97°6W 352 E5
Seward Pa., U.S.A. 40°25N 79°1W 354 F5
Seward Peninsula U.S.A. 65°30N 166°0W 346 a
Sewell Chile 34°10S 70°23W 366 C1
Sewer Indonesia 5°53S 134°40E 309 F8
Sewickley U.S.A. 40°32N 80°12W 354 F4
Sexsmith Canada 55°21N 118°47W 342 B5
Seychelles ■ Ind. Oc. 5°0S 56°0E 325 b
Seyðisfjörður Iceland 65°16N 13°57W 280 D7
Seydişehir Turkey 37°25N 31°51E 291 G5
Seydvān Iran 38°34N 45°2E 316 B5
Seyhan → Turkey 36°43N 34°53E 316 B2
Seym → Ukraine 51°27N 32°34E 291 D5
Seymour Australia 37°2S 145°10E 335 F4
Seymour S. Africa 32°33S 26°46E 329 E4
Seymour Conn., U.S.A. 41°24N 73°4W 355 E11
Seymour Ind., U.S.A. 38°58N 85°53W 353 F11
Seymour Tex., U.S.A. 33°35N 99°16W 356 E5
Sfântu Gheorghe Romania 45°52N 25°48E 289 F13
Sfax Tunisia 34°49N 10°48E 323 B8
Sha Tau Kok China 22°33N 114°13E 305 F11
Sha Tin China 22°23N 114°12E 305 G11
Shaanxi □ China 35°0N 109°0E 306 G5
Shaba = Katanga □ Dem. Rep. of the Congo 8°0S 25°0E 326 D2
Shaba △ Kenya 0°38N 37°48E 326 B4
Shaballe = Scebeli, Wabi → Somali Rep. 2°0N 44°0E 319 G3
Shabogamo L. Canada 53°15N 66°30W 345 B6
Shabunda Dem. Rep. of the Congo 2°40S 27°16E 326 C2
Shache China 38°20N 77°10E 304 C2
Shackleton Fracture Zone S. Ocean 60°0S 60°0W 277 B18
Shackleton Ice Shelf Antarctica 66°0S 100°0E 277 C8
Shackleton Inlet Antarctica 83°0S 160°0E 277 E11
Shādegān Iran 30°40N 48°38E 317 D6
Shadi India 33°24N 77°14E 315 C7
Shadrinsk Russia 56°5N 63°32E 300 D7
Shadyside U.S.A. 39°58N 80°45W 354 G4
Shafter U.S.A. 35°30N 119°16W 351 K7
Shaftesbury U.K. 51°0N 2°11W 285 F5
Shagram Pakistan 36°24N 72°20E 315 A5
Shah Alizai Pakistan 29°25N 66°33E 314 E2
Shah Bunder Pakistan 24°13N 67°56E 314 G2
Shahabad Punjab, India 30°10N 76°55E 314 D7
Shahabad Raj., India 25°15N 77°11E 314 G7
Shahabad Ut. P., India 27°36N 79°56E 315 F8
Shahadpur Pakistan 25°55N 68°35E 314 G3
Shahbā' Syria 32°52N 36°38E 318 C5
Shahdād Iran 30°30N 57°40E 317 D8
Shahdād, Namakzār-e Iran 30°20N 58°20E 317 D8
Shahdadkot Pakistan 27°50N 67°55E 314 F2
Shahdol India 23°19N 81°26E 315 H9
Shahe China 37°0N 114°32E 306 F8
Shahganj India 26°3N 82°44E 315 F10
Shahgarh India 27°15N 69°50E 314 F3
Shahjahanpur India 27°54N 79°57E 315 F8
Shahpur India 22°12N 77°58E 314 H7
Shahpur Baluchistan, Pakistan 28°46N 68°27E 314 E3
Shahpur Punjab, Pakistan 32°17N 72°26E 314 C5
Shahpur Chakar Pakistan 26°9N 68°39E 314 F3
Shahpura Mad. P., India 23°10N 80°45E 315 H9
Shahpura Raj., India 25°38N 74°56E 314 G6
Shahr-e Bābak Iran 30°7N 55°9E 317 D7
Shahr-e Kord Iran 32°15N 50°55E 317 C6
Shāhrakht Iran 33°38N 60°16E 317 C9
Shahrig Pakistan 30°15N 67°40E 314 D2
Shahukou China 40°20N 112°18E 306 D7
Shaikhabad Afghan. 34°2N 68°45E 314 B3
Shajapur India 23°27N 76°21E 314 H7
Shajing China 22°44N 113°48E 305 F10
Shakargarh Pakistan 32°17N 75°10E 314 C6
Shakawe Botswana 18°28S 21°49E 328 B3
Shaker Heights U.S.A. 41°28N 81°32W 354 E3
Shakhty Russia 47°40N 40°16E 291 E7
Shakhunya Russia 57°40N 46°46E 290 C8
Shaki Nigeria 8°41N 3°21E 322 G6
Shaksam Valley Asia 36°0N 76°20E 315 A7
Shallow Lake Canada 44°36N 81°5W 354 B3
Shalqar Kazakhstan 47°48N 59°39E 300 E6
Shaluli Shan China 30°40N 99°55E 304 C4
Shām Iran 26°39N 57°21E 317 E8
Shām, Bādiyat ash Asia 32°0N 40°0E 316 C3
Shamâl Sînî □ Egypt 30°30N 33°30E 318 E2
Shamattawa Canada 55°51N 92°5W 344 A1
Shamattawa → Canada 55°1N 85°23W 344 A2
Shamīl Iran 27°30N 56°55E 317 E8
Shamkūh Iran 35°47N 57°50E 317 C8
Shamli India 29°32N 77°18E 314 E7
Shammar, Jabal Si. Arabia 27°40N 41°0E 316 E4
Shamo = Gobi Asia 44°0N 110°0E 306 C6
Shamo, L. Ethiopia 5°45N 37°30E 319 F2
Shamokin U.S.A. 40°47N 76°34W 355 F8
Shamrock U.S.A. 35°13N 100°15W 356 D4
Shamva Zimbabwe 17°20S 31°32E 327 F3
Shan □ Burma 21°30N 98°30E 313 J21
Shan Xian China 34°50N 116°5E 306 G9
Shanchengzhen China 42°20N 125°20E 307 C13
Shāndak Iran 28°28N 60°27E 317 D9
Shandon U.S.A. 35°39N 120°23W 350 K6
Shandong □ China 36°0N 118°0E 307 G10
Shandong Bandao China 37°0N 121°0E 307 F11
Shang Xian = Shangzhou China 33°50N 109°58E 306 H5
Shanga Nigeria 11°12N 4°33E 322 F6
Shangalowe Dem. Rep. of the Congo 10°50S 26°30E 327 E2
Shangani Zimbabwe 19°41S 29°20E 329 B4
Shangani → Zimbabwe 18°41S 27°10E 327 F2
Shangbancheng China 40°50N 118°1E 307 D10
Shangdu China 41°30N 113°30E 306 D7
Shanghai China 31°15N 121°26E 305 C7
Shanghe China 37°20N 117°10E 307 F9
Shangnan China 33°32N 110°50E 306 H6
Shangqiu China 34°26N 115°36E 306 G8
Shangrao China 28°25N 117°59E 305 D6
Shangshui China 33°42N 114°35E 305 C6
Shangzhi China 45°22N 127°56E 307 B14
Shangzhou China 33°50N 109°58E 306 H5
Shanhetun China 44°33N 127°15E 307 B14
Shanklin U.K. 50°38N 1°11W 285 G6
Shannon N.Z. 40°33S 175°25E 331 D5
Shannon → Ireland 52°35N 9°30W 282 D2
Shannon ✕ (SNN) Ireland 52°42N 8°57W 282 D3
Shannon, Mouth of the Ireland 52°30N 9°55W 282 D2
Shannon △ Australia 34°35S 116°25E 333 F2
Shannonbridge Ireland 53°17N 8°3W 282 C3
Shansi = Shanxi □ China 37°0N 112°0E 306 F7
Shantar, Ostrov Bolshoy Russia 55°9N 137°40E 301 D14
Shantipur India 23°17N 88°25E 315 H13
Shantou China 23°18N 116°40E 305 D6
Shantung = Shandong □ China 36°0N 118°0E 307 G10
Shanxi □ China 37°0N 112°0E 306 F7
Shanyang China 33°31N 109°55E 306 H5
Shanyin China 39°25N 112°56E 306 E7
Shaoguan China 24°48N 113°35E 305 D6
Shaoxing China 30°0N 120°35E 305 D7
Shaoyang China 27°14N 111°25E 305 D6
Shap U.K. 54°32N 2°40W 284 C5
Shapinsay U.K. 59°3N 2°51W 283 B6
Shaqra' Si. Arabia 25°15N 45°16E 316 E5
Shaqrā' Yemen 13°22N 45°44E 319 E4
Sharafkhāneh Iran 38°11N 45°29E 316 B5
Sharbot Lake Canada 44°46N 76°41W 355 B8
Shari Japan 43°55N 144°40E 302 C12
Sharjah = Ash Shāriqah U.A.E. 25°23N 55°26E 317 E7
Shark B. Australia 25°30S 113°32E 333 E1
Shark Bay △ Australia 25°30S 113°30E 333 E1
Sharm el Sheikh Egypt 27°53N 34°18E 323 C12
Sharon Mass., U.S.A. 42°7N 71°11W 355 D13
Sharon Pa., U.S.A. 41°14N 80°31W 354 E4
Sharon Springs Kans., U.S.A. 38°54N 101°45W 352 F3
Sharon Springs N.Y., U.S.A. 42°48N 74°37W 355 D10
Sharp Pt. Australia 10°58S 142°43E 334 A3
Sharpe L. Canada 54°24N 93°40W 344 B1
Sharpsville U.S.A. 41°15N 80°29W 354 E4
Sharqi, Al Jabal ash Lebanon 33°40N 36°10E 318 B5
Sharya Russia 58°22N 45°20E 290 C8
Shashemene Ethiopia 7°13N 38°33E 319 F2
Shashi Botswana 21°15S 27°27E 329 C4
Shashi China 30°25N 112°14E 305 C6
Shashi → Africa 21°14S 29°20E 327 G2
Shasta, Mt. U.S.A. 41°25N 122°12W 348 F2
Shasta L. U.S.A. 40°43N 122°25W 348 F2
Shatsky Rise Pac. Oc. 34°0N 157°0E 336 D7
Shatt al Arab Asia 29°57N 48°34E 317 D6
Shaunavon Canada 49°35N 108°25W 343 D7
Shaver L. U.S.A. 37°9N 119°18W 350 H7
Shaw → Australia 20°21S 119°17E 332 D2
Shaw I. Australia 20°30S 149°2E 334 J7
Shawanaga Canada 45°31N 80°17W 354 A4
Shawangunk Mts. U.S.A. 41°35N 74°30W 355 E10
Shawano U.S.A. 44°47N 88°36W 352 C9
Shawinigan Canada 46°35N 72°50W 344 C5
Shawmari, J. ash Jordan 30°35N 36°35E 318 E5
Shawnee U.S.A. 35°20N 96°55W 356 D6
Shay Gap Australia 20°30S 120°10E 332 D3
Shaybārā Si. Arabia 25°26N 36°47E 316 E3
Shaykh, J. ash Lebanon 33°25N 35°50E 318 B4
Shaykh Miskīn Syria 32°49N 36°9E 318 C5
Shaykh Sa'īd Iraq 32°34N 46°17E 316 C5
Shchūchīnsk Kazakhstan 52°56N 70°12E 300 D8
She Xian China 36°30N 113°40E 306 F7
Shebele = Scebeli, Wabi → Somali Rep. 2°0N 44°0E 319 G3
Sheboygan U.S.A. 43°46N 87°45W 352 D10
Shediac Canada 46°14N 64°32W 345 C7
Sheelin, L. Ireland 53°48N 7°20W 282 C4
Sheep Haven Ireland 55°11N 7°52W 282 A4
Sheep Range U.S.A. 36°35N 115°15W 351 J11
Sheerness U.K. 51°26N 0°47E 285 F8
Sheet Harbour Canada 44°56N 62°31W 345 D7
Sheffield U.K. 53°23N 1°28W 284 D6
Sheffield Ala., U.S.A. 34°46N 87°41W 357 D11
Sheffield Mass., U.S.A. 42°5N 73°21W 355 D11
Sheffield Pa., U.S.A. 41°42N 79°3W 354 E5
Sheikhpura India 25°9N 85°53E 315 G11
Shekhupura Pakistan 31°42N 73°58E 314 D5
Shekou China 22°30N 113°55E 305 G10
Shelburne N.S., Canada 43°47N 65°20W 345 D6
Shelburne Ont., Canada 44°4N 80°15W 354 B4
Shelburne U.S.A. 44°23N 73°14W 355 B11
Shelburne B. Australia 11°50S 142°50E 334 A3
Shelburne Falls U.S.A. 42°36N 72°45W 355 D12
Shelby Mich., U.S.A. 43°37N 86°22W 352 D10
Shelby Mont., U.S.A. 48°30N 111°51W 348 B8
Shelby N.C., U.S.A. 35°17N 81°32W 357 D14
Shelby Ohio, U.S.A. 40°53N 82°40W 354 F2
Shelbyville Ill., U.S.A. 39°24N 88°48W 352 F9
Shelbyville Ind., U.S.A. 39°31N 85°47W 353 F11
Shelbyville Ky., U.S.A. 38°13N 85°14W 353 F11
Shelbyville Tenn., U.S.A. 35°29N 86°28W 357 D11
Sheldon U.S.A. 43°11N 95°51W 352 D6
Sheldrake Canada 50°20N 64°51W 345 B7
Shelikhova, Zaliv Russia 59°30N 157°0E 301 D16
Shell Lakes Australia 29°20S 127°30E 333 E4
Shellbrook Canada 53°13N 106°24W 343 C7
Shellharbour Australia 34°31S 150°51E 335 E5
Shelter I. U.S.A. 41°4N 72°20W 355 E12
Shelton Conn., U.S.A. 41°19N 73°5W 355 E11
Shelton Wash., U.S.A. 47°13N 123°6W 350 C3
Shen Xian China 36°15N 115°40E 306 F8
Shenandoah Iowa, U.S.A. 40°46N 95°22W 352 E6
Shenandoah Pa., U.S.A. 40°49N 76°12W 355 F8
Shenandoah Va., U.S.A. 38°29N 78°37W 353 F14
Shenandoah → U.S.A. 39°19N 77°44W 353 F15
Shenandoah △ U.S.A. 38°35N 78°22W 353 F14
Shenchi China 39°8N 112°10E 306 E7
Shendam Nigeria 8°49N 9°30E 322 G7
Shendî Sudan 16°46N 33°22E 323 E12
Shengfang China 39°3N 116°42E 306 E9
Shenjingzi China 44°40N 124°30E 307 B13
Shenmu China 38°50N 110°29E 306 E6
Shenqiu China 33°25N 115°5E 306 H8
Shensi = Shaanxi □ China 35°0N 109°0E 306 G5
Shenyang China 41°48N 123°27E 307 D12
Shenzhen China 22°32N 114°5E 305 F10
Shenzhen ✕ (SZX) China 22°41N 113°49E 305 F10
Shenzhen Shuiku China 22°34N 114°8E 305 F11
Shenzhen Wan China 22°27N 113°55E 305 G10
Sheo India 26°11N 71°15E 314 F4
Sheopur Kalan India 25°40N 76°40E 314 G7
Shepetivka Ukraine 50°10N 27°10E 289 C14
Shepetovka = Shepetivka Ukraine 50°10N 27°10E 289 C14
Shepparton Australia 36°23S 145°26E 335 F4
Sheppey, I. of U.K. 51°25N 0°48E 285 F8
Shepton Mallet U.K. 51°11N 2°33W 285 F5
Sheqi China 33°12N 112°57E 306 H7
Sher Qila Pakistan 36°7N 74°2E 315 A6
Sherborne U.K. 50°57N 2°31W 285 G5
Sherbro I. S. Leone 7°30N 12°40W 322 G3
Sherbrooke N.S., Canada 45°8N 61°59W 345 C7
Sherbrooke Qué., Canada 45°28N 71°57W 355 A13
Sherburne U.S.A. 42°41N 75°30W 355 D9
Shergarh India 26°20N 72°18E 314 F5
Sherghati India 24°34N 84°47E 315 G11
Sheridan Ark., U.S.A. 34°19N 92°24W 356 D8
Sheridan Wyo., U.S.A. 44°48N 106°58W 348 D10
Sheringham U.K. 52°56N 1°13E 284 E9
Sherkin I. Ireland 51°28N 9°26W 282 E2
Sherkot India 29°22N 78°35E 315 E8
Sherman U.S.A. 33°38N 96°36W 356 E6
Sherpur India 25°34N 83°47E 315 G10
Sherridon Canada 55°8N 101°5W 343 B8
Sherwood Forest U.K. 53°6N 1°7W 284 D6
Sherwood Park Canada 53°31N 113°19W 342 C6
Sheslay → Canada 58°48N 132°5W 342 B2
Shethanei L. Canada 58°48N 97°50W 343 B9
Shetland □ U.K. 60°30N 1°30W 283 A7
Shetland Is. U.K. 60°30N 1°30W 283 A7
Shetrunji → India 21°19N 72°7E 314 J5
Sheung Shui China 22°31N 114°7E 305 F11
Shey-Phoksundo △ Nepal 29°30N 82°45E 315 E10
Sheyenne → U.S.A. 47°2N 96°50W 352 B5
Shibām Yemen 15°59N 48°36E 319 D4
Shibata Japan 37°57N 139°20E 302 F9
Shibecha Japan 43°17N 144°36E 302 C12
Shibetsu Japan 44°10N 142°23E 302 B11
Shibogama L. Canada 53°35N 88°15W 344 B2
Shibushi Japan 31°25N 131°8E 303 J5
Shickshinny U.S.A. 41°9N 76°9W 355 E8
Shickshock Mts. = Chic-Chocs, Mts. Canada 48°55N 66°0W 345 C6
Shidao China 36°50N 122°25E 307 F12
Shido Japan 34°19N 134°10E 303 G7
Shiel, L. U.K. 56°48N 5°34W 283 E3
Shield, C. Australia 13°20S 136°20E 334 A2
Shīeli Kazakhstan 44°20N 66°15E 300 E7
Shiga □ Japan 35°20N 136°0E 303 G8
Shiguaigou China 40°52N 110°15E 306 D6
Shihchiachuangi = Shijiazhuang China 38°2N 114°28E 306 E8
Shihezi China 44°15N 86°2E 304 B3
Shijiazhuang China 38°2N 114°28E 306 E8
Shikarpur India 28°17N 78°7E 314 E8
Shikarpur Pakistan 27°57N 68°39E 314 F3
Shikohabad India 27°6N 78°36E 315 F8
Shikoku □ Japan 33°30N 133°30E 303 H6
Shikoku-Sanchi Japan 33°30N 133°30E 303 H6
Shikotsu-Ko Japan 42°45N 141°25E 302 C10
Shikotsu-Tōya △ Japan 44°4N 145°8E 302 C10
Shiliguri India 26°45N 88°25E 313 F16
Shiliu = Changjiang China 19°20N 108°55E 310 C7
Shilka Russia 52°0N 115°55E 301 D12
Shilka → Russia 53°20N 121°26E 301 D13
Shillelagh Ireland 52°45N 6°32W 282 D5
Shillington U.S.A. 40°18N 75°58W 355 F9
Shillong India 25°35N 91°53E 313 G17
Shilo West Bank 32°4N 35°18E 318 C4
Shilou China 37°0N 110°48E 306 F6
Shimabara Japan 32°48N 130°20E 303 H5
Shimada Japan 34°49N 138°10E 303 G9
Shimane □ Japan 35°0N 132°30E 303 G6
Shimanovsk Russia 52°15N 127°30E 301 D13
Shimba Hills △ Kenya 4°14S 39°25E 326 C4
Shimizu Japan 35°0N 138°30E 303 G9
Shimla India 31°2N 77°9E 314 D7
Shimodate Japan 36°20N 139°55E 303 F9
Shimoga India 13°57N 75°32E 312 N9
Shimoni Kenya 4°38S 39°20E 326 C4
Shimonoseki Japan 33°58N 130°55E 303 H5
Shimpuru Rapids Namibia 17°45S 19°55E 328 B2
Shin, L. U.K. 58°5N 4°30W 283 C4
Shinano-Gawa → Japan 36°50N 138°30E 303 F9
Shināş Oman 24°46N 56°28E 317 E8
Shīndand Afghan. 33°12N 62°8E 312 C3
Shinglehouse U.S.A. 41°58N 78°12W 354 E6
Shingū Japan 33°40N 135°55E 303 H7
Shingwidzi S. Africa 23°5S 31°25E 329 C5
Shinjō Japan 38°46N 140°18E 302 E10
Shinkolobwe Dem. Rep. of the Congo 11°10S 26°40E 324 G5
Shinshār Syria 34°36N 36°43E 318 A5
Shinyanga Tanzania 3°45S 33°27E 326 C3
Shinyanga □ Tanzania 3°50S 34°0E 326 C3
Shio-no-Misaki Japan 33°25N 135°45E 303 H7
Shiogama Japan 38°19N 141°1E 302 E10
Shiojiri Japan 36°6N 137°58E 303 F8
Shipchenski Prokhod Bulgaria 42°45N 25°15E 295 C11
Shiping China 23°45N 102°23E 304 D5
Shippagan Canada 47°45N 64°45W 345 C7
Shippensburg U.S.A. 40°3N 77°31W 354 F7
Shippenville U.S.A. 41°15N 79°28W 354 E5
Shiprock U.S.A. 36°47N 108°41W 349 H9
Shiqma, N. → Israel 31°37N 34°30E 318 D3
Shiquan China 33°5N 108°15E 306 H5
Shiquan He = Indus → Pakistan 24°20N 67°47E 314 G2
Shīr Kūh Iran 31°39N 54°3E 317 D7
Shiragami-Misaki Japan 41°24N 140°12E 302 D10
Shirakawa Fukushima, Japan 37°7N 140°13E 303 F10
Shirakawa Gifu, Japan 36°17N 136°56E 303 F8
Shirane-San Gumma, Japan 36°48N 139°22E 303 F9
Shirane-San Yamanashi, Japan 35°42N 138°9E 303 G9
Shiraoi Japan 42°33N 141°21E 302 C10
Shīrāz Iran 29°42N 52°30E 317 D7
Shire → Africa 17°42S 35°19E 327 F4
Shiretoko-Misaki Japan 44°21N 145°20E 302 B12
Shirinab → Pakistan 30°15N 66°28E 314 D2
Shiriya-Zaki Japan 41°25N 141°30E 302 D10
Shiroishi Japan 38°0N 140°37E 302 F10
Shirshov Ridge Pac. Oc. 58°0N 170°0E 336 B8
Shīrvān Iran 37°30N 57°50E 317 B8
Shirwa, L. = Chilwa, L. Malawi 15°15S 35°40E 327 F4
Shivpuri India 25°26N 77°42E 314 G7
Shixian China 43°5N 129°50E 307 C15
Shiyan China 22°42N 113°56E 305 F10
Shiyan Shuiku China 22°42N 113°54E 305 F10
Shizuishan China 39°15N 106°50E 306 E4
Shizuoka Japan 34°57N 138°24E 303 G9
Shizuoka □ Japan 35°15N 138°40E 303 G9
Shklov = Shklow Belarus 54°16N 30°15E 289 A16
Shklow Belarus 54°16N 30°15E 289 A16
Shkodër Albania 42°4N 19°32E 295 C8
Shkumbini → Albania 41°2N 19°31E 295 D8
Shmidta, Ostrov Russia 81°0N 91°0E 301 A10
Shō-Gawa → Japan 36°47N 137°4E 303 F8
Shoal L. Canada 49°33N 95°1W 343 D9
Shoal Lake Canada 50°30N 100°35W 343 C8
Shōdo-Shima Japan 34°30N 134°15E 303 G7
Sholapur = Solapur India 17°43N 75°56E 312 L9
Shōmrōn West Bank 32°15N 35°13E 318 C4
Shoreham by Sea U.K. 50°50N 0°16W 285 G7
Shori → Pakistan 28°29N 69°44E 314 E3
Shorkot Road Pakistan 30°47N 72°15E 314 D5
Shoshone Calif., U.S.A. 35°58N 116°16W 351 K10
Shoshone Idaho, U.S.A. 42°56N 114°25W 348 E6
Shoshone L. U.S.A. 44°22N 110°43W 348 D8
Shoshone Mts. U.S.A. 39°20N 117°25W 348 G5
Shoshong Botswana 22°56S 26°31E 328 C4
Shoshoni U.S.A. 43°14N 108°7W 348 E9
Shouguang China 37°52N 118°45E 307 F10
Shouyang China 37°54N 113°8E 306 F7
Show Low U.S.A. 34°15N 110°2W 349 J8
Shqipëria = Albania ■ Europe 41°0N 20°0E 295 D9
Shreveport U.S.A. 32°31N 93°45W 356 E8
Shrewsbury U.K. 52°43N 2°45W 285 E5
Shri Mohangarh India 27°17N 71°18E 314 F4
Shrirampur India 22°44N 88°21E 315 H13
Shropshire □ U.K. 52°36N 2°45W 285 E5
Shū Kazakhstan 43°36N 73°42E 300 E8
Shuangcheng China 45°20N 126°15E 307 B14
Shuanggou China 34°2N 117°30E 307 G9
Shuangliao China 43°29N 123°30E 307 C12
Shuangshanzi China 40°20N 119°8E 307 D10
Shuangyang China 43°28N 125°40E 307 C13
Shuangyashan China 46°28N 131°5E 305 B8
Shuguri Falls Tanzania 8°33S 37°22E 327 D4
Shuiye China 36°7N 114°8E 306 F8
Shujalpur India 23°18N 76°46E 314 H7
Shukpa Kunzang India 34°22N 78°22E 315 B8
Shulan China 44°28N 127°0E 307 B14
Shule China 39°25N 76°3E 304 C2
Shumagin Is. U.S.A. 55°7N 160°30W 346 a
Shumen Bulgaria 43°18N 26°55E 295 C12
Shumikha Russia 55°10N 63°15E 300 D7
Shuo Xian = Shuozhou China 39°20N 112°33E 306 E7
Shuozhou China 39°20N 112°33E 306 E7
Shūr → Fārs, Iran 28°30N 55°0E 317 D7
Shūr → Kermān, Iran 30°52N 57°37E 317 D8
Shūr → Yazd, Iran 31°45N 55°15E 317 D7
Shūr Āb Iran 34°23N 51°11E 317 C6
Shūr Gaz Iran 29°10N 59°20E 317 D8
Shūrāb Iran 33°43N 56°29E 317 C8
Shūrjestān Iran 31°24N 52°25E 317 D7
Shurugwi Zimbabwe 19°40S 30°0E 327 F3
Shūsf Iran 31°50N 60°5E 317 D9
Shūshtar Iran 32°0N 48°50E 317 D6
Shuswap L. Canada 50°55N 119°3W 342 C5
Shuyang China 34°10N 118°42E 307 G10
Shūzū Iran 29°52N 54°30E 317 D7
Shwebo Burma 22°30N 95°45E 313 H19
Shwegu Burma 24°15N 96°26E 313 G20
Shweli → Burma 23°45N 96°45E 313 H20
Shymkent Kazakhstan 42°18N 69°36E 300 E7
Shyok India 34°13N 78°12E 315 B8
Shyok → Pakistan 35°13N 75°53E 315 B6
Si Chon Thailand 9°0N 99°54E 311 H2
Si Kiang = Xi Jiang → China 22°5N 113°20E 305 D6
Si Lanna △ Thailand 19°17N 99°12E 310 C2
Si-ngan = Xi'an China 34°15N 109°0E 306 G5
Si Prachan Thailand 14°37N 100°9E 310 E3
Si Racha Thailand 13°10N 100°48E 310 F3
Si Xian China 33°30N 117°50E 307 H9
Siachen Glacier Asia 35°20N 77°30E 315 B7
Siahaf → Pakistan 29°3N 68°57E 314 E3
Siahan Range Pakistan 27°30N 64°40E 312 F4
Siaksriindrapura Indonesia 0°51N 102°0E 308 D2
Sialkot Pakistan 32°32N 74°30E 314 C6
Siam = Thailand ■ Asia 16°0N 102°0E 310 E4
Sian = Xi'an China 34°15N 109°0E 306 G5
Sian Ka'an △ Mexico 19°35N 87°40W 359 D7
Siantan Indonesia 3°10N 106°15E 308 D3
Sīāreh Iran 28°5N 60°14E 317 D9
Siargao I. Phil. 9°52N 126°3E 309 C7
Siari Pakistan 34°55N 76°40E 315 B7
Siasi Phil. 5°34N 120°50E 309 C6
Siau Indonesia 2°50N 125°25E 309 D7
Šiauliai Lithuania 55°56N 23°15E 281 J20
Sibâi, Gebel el Egypt 25°45N 34°10E 316 E2
Sibang Indonesia 8°34S 115°13E 309 K18
Sibay Russia 52°42N 58°39E 290 D10
Sibayi, L. S. Africa 27°20S 32°45E 329 D5
Šibenik Croatia 43°48N 15°54E 294 C6
Siberia = Sibirskiy □ Russia 58°0N 90°0E 301 D10
Siberia Russia 60°0N 100°0E 276 D13
Siberut Indonesia 1°30S 99°0E 308 E1
Sibi Pakistan 29°30N 67°54E 314 E2
Sibil = Oksibil Indonesia 4°59S 140°35E 309 E10
Sibiloi △ Kenya 4°0N 36°20E 326 B4
Sibirskiy □ Russia 58°0N 90°0E 301 D10
Sibirtsevo Russia 44°12N 132°26E 302 B5
Sibiti Congo 3°38S 13°19E 324 E2
Sibiu Romania 45°45N 24°9E 289 F13
Sibley U.S.A. 43°24N 95°45W 352 D6
Sibolga Indonesia 1°42N 98°45E 308 D1
Sibsagar India 27°0N 94°36E 313 F19
Sibu Malaysia 2°18N 111°49E 308 D4
Sibuco Phil. 7°20N 122°10E 309 C6
Sibuguey B. Phil. 7°50N 122°45E 309 C6
Sibut C.A.R. 5°46N 19°10E 324 C3
Sibutu Phil. 4°45N 119°30E 309 D5
Sibutu Passage E. Indies 4°50N 120°0E 309 D5
Sibuyan I. Phil. 12°25N 122°40E 309 B6
Sibuyan Sea Phil. 12°30N 122°20E 309 B6
Sicamous Canada 50°49N 119°0W 342 C5
Siccus → Australia 31°55S 139°17E 335 E2
Sichuan □ China 30°30N 103°0E 304 C5
Sicilia Italy 37°30N 14°30E 294 F6
Sicily = Sicilia Italy 37°30N 14°30E 294 F6
Sicily, Str. of 37°35N 11°56E 294 F4
Sicuani Peru 14°21S 71°10W 364 F4
Sidari Greece 39°47N 19°41E 297 A3
Siddhapur India 23°56N 72°25E 314 H5
Siddipet India 18°5N 78°51E 312 K11
Sideros, Akra Greece 35°19N 26°19E 297 D8
Sidhauli India 27°17N 80°50E 315 F9
Sidhi India 24°25N 81°53E 315 G9
Sidi-bel-Abbès Algeria 35°13N 0°39W 322 A5
Sidi Ifni Morocco 29°29N 10°12W 322 C3
Sidlaw Hills U.K. 56°32N 3°2W 283 E5
Sidley, Mt. Antarctica 77°2S 126°2W 277 D14
Sidmouth U.K. 50°40N 3°15W 285 G4
Sidmouth, C. Australia 13°25S 143°36E 334 A3
Sidney Canada 48°39N 123°24W 350 B3
Sidney Mont., U.S.A. 47°43N 104°9W 348 C11
Sidney N.Y., U.S.A. 42°19N 75°24W 355 D9
Sidney Nebr., U.S.A. 41°8N 102°59W 352 E2
Sidney Ohio, U.S.A. 40°17N 84°9W 353 E11
Sidney Lanier, L. U.S.A. 34°10N 84°4W 357 D12
Sidoarjo Indonesia 7°27S 112°43E 309 G15
Sidon = Saydā Lebanon 33°35N 35°25E 318 B4
Sidra, G. of = Surt, Khalīj Libya 31°40N 18°30E 323 B9
Siedlce Poland 52°10N 22°20E 289 B12
Sieg → Germany 50°46N 7°6E 288 C4
Siegen Germany 50°51N 8°0E 288 C5
Siem Pang Cambodia 14°7N 106°23E 310 E4
Siem Reap = Siemreab Cambodia 13°20N 103°52E 310 F4
Siemreab Cambodia 13°20N 103°52E 310 F4
Siena Italy 43°19N 11°21E 294 C4
Sieradz Poland 51°37N 18°41E 289 C10

Sierpe, Bocas de la
Venezuela 10°0N 61°30W **365** L15
Sierra Blanca *U.S.A.* 31°11N 105°22W **356** F2
Sierra Blanca Peak
U.S.A. 33°23N 105°49W **349** K11
Sierra City *U.S.A.* 39°34N 120°38W **350** F6
Sierra Colorada
Argentina 40°35S 67°50W **368** E3
Sierra de Bahoruco △
Dom. Rep. 18°10N 71°25W **361** C5
Sierra de La Culata △
Venezuela 8°45N 71°10W **361** E5
Sierra de Lancandón △
Guatemala 16°59N 90°23W **360** C1
Sierra de las Quijadas △
Argentina 32°29S 67°5W **366** C2
Sierra de San Luis △
Venezuela 11°20N 69°43W **361** D6
Sierra de San Pedro Mártir, Parque Nacional △
Mexico 31°10N 115°30W **358** A1
Sierra Gorda *Chile* 22°50S 69°15W **366** A2
Sierra Leone ■ *W. Afr.* 9°0N 12°0W **322** G3
Sierra Madre *Mexico* 16°0N 93°0W **359** D6
Sierra Madre Occidental
Mexico 27°0N 107°0W **358** B3
Sierra Madre Oriental
Mexico 25°0N 100°0W **358** C5
Sierra Mojada *Mexico* 27°18N 103°41W **358** B4
Sierra Nevada *Spain* 37°3N 3°15W **293** D4
Sierra Nevada *U.S.A.* 39°0N 120°30W **350** H8
Sierra Nevada △
Venezuela 8°35N 70°45W **361** E5
Sierra Nevada de Santa Marta △
Colombia 10°56N 73°36W **361** D5
Sierra Vista *U.S.A.* 31°33N 110°18W **349** L8
Sierraville *U.S.A.* 39°36N 120°22W **350** F6
Sífnos *Greece* 37°0N 24°45E **295** F11
Sifton *Canada* 51°21N 100°8W **343** C8
Sifton Pass *Canada* 57°52N 126°15W **342** B3
Sig *Algeria* 35°32N 0°12W **322** A5
Sigatoka *Fiji* 18°8S 177°32E **331** a
Sighetu-Marmației
Romania 47°57N 23°52E **289** E12
Sighișoara *Romania* 46°12N 24°50E **289** E13
Sigli *Indonesia* 5°25N 96°0E **308** C1
Siglufjörður *Iceland* 66°12N 18°55W **280** C4
Signal de Botrang *Belgium* 50°29N 6°4E **287** D6
Signal Pk. *U.S.A.* 33°20N 114°2W **351** M12
Signy I. *Antarctica* 60°45S 45°56W **277** C18
Sigsig *Ecuador* 3°0S 78°50W **364** D3
Sigüenza *Spain* 41°3N 2°40W **293** B4
Siguiri *Guinea* 11°31N 9°10W **322** F4
Sigulda *Latvia* 57°10N 24°55E **281** H21
Sihora *India* 23°29N 80°6E **315** H9
Siikajoki → *Finland* 64°50N 24°43E **280** D21
Siilinjärvi *Finland* 63°4N 27°39E **280** E22
Sijarira Ra. = Chizarira
Zimbabwe 17°36S 27°45E **327** F2
Sika *India* 22°26N 69°47E **314** H3
Sikanni Chief →
Canada 57°47N 122°15W **342** B4
Sikao *Thailand* 7°34N 99°21E **311** J2
Sikar *India* 27°33N 75°10E **314** F6
Sikasso *Mali* 11°18N 5°35W **322** F4
Sikeston *U.S.A.* 36°53N 89°35W **352** G9
Sikhote Alin, Khrebet
Russia 45°0N 136°0E **302** B8
Sikhote Alin Ra. = Sikhote Alin, Khrebet *Russia* 45°0N 136°0E **302** B8
Sikinos *Greece* 36°40N 25°8E **295** F11
Sikkim □ *India* 27°50N 88°30E **313** F16
Sil → *Spain* 42°27N 7°43W **293** A2
Silacayoapan *Mexico* 17°30N 98°9W **359** D5
Silawad *India* 21°54N 74°54E **314** J6
Silchar *India* 24°49N 92°48E **313** G18
Siler City *U.S.A.* 35°44N 79°28W **357** D15
Silesia = Śląsk *Poland* 51°0N 16°30E **288** C9
Silgarhi Doti *Nepal* 29°15N 81°0E **315** E9
Silghat *India* 26°35N 93°0E **313** F18
Silhouette *Seychelles* 4°29S 55°12E **325** b
Silifke *Turkey* 36°22N 33°58E **316** B2
Siliguri = Shiliguri
India 26°45N 88°25E **313** F16
Siling Co *China* 31°50N 89°20E **304** C3
Silistra *Bulgaria* 44°6N 27°19E **295** B12
Silivri *Turkey* 41°4N 28°14E **295** D13
Siljan *Sweden* 60°55N 14°45E **280** F16
Silkeborg *Denmark* 56°10N 9°32E **281** H13
Silkwood *Australia* 17°45S 146°2E **334** B4
Sillajhuay, Cordillera
Chile 19°46S 68°40W **364** G5
Sillamäe *Estonia* 59°24N 27°45E **281** G22
Silloth *U.K.* 54°52N 3°23W **284** C4
Siloam Springs *U.S.A.* 36°11N 94°32W **356** C7
Silsbee *U.S.A.* 30°21N 94°11W **356** F7
Šilutė *Lithuania* 55°21N 21°33E **281** J19
Silvani *India* 23°18N 78°25E **315** H8
Silver City *U.S.A.* 32°46N 108°17W **349** K9
Silver Cr. → *U.S.A.* 43°16N 119°13W **348** E4
Silver Creek *U.S.A.* 42°33N 79°10W **354** D5
Silver L. *U.S.A.* 38°39N 120°6W **350** G6
Silver Lake *Calif.,*
U.S.A. 35°21N 116°7W **351** K10
Silver Lake *Oreg., U.S.A.* 43°8N 121°3W **348** E3
Silvermine Mts. *Ireland* 52°47N 8°15W **282** D3
Silverton *Colo., U.S.A.* 37°49N 107°40W **349** H10
Silverton *Tex., U.S.A.* 34°28N 101°19W **356** D4
Silvies → *U.S.A.* 43°34N 119°2W **348** E4
Simaltala *India* 24°43N 86°33E **315** G12
Simanggang = Sri Aman
Malaysia 1°15N 111°32E **308** D4
Simard, L. *Canada* 47°40N 78°40W **344** C4
Simav *Turkey* 39°4N 28°58E **295** E13
Simba *Tanzania* 2°10S 37°36E **326** C4
Simbirsk *Russia* 54°20N 48°25E **290** D8
Simbo *Tanzania* 4°51S 29°41E **326** C2
Simcoe *Canada* 42°50N 80°20W **344** D3
Simcoe, L. *Canada* 44°25N 79°20W **354** B5
Simdega *India* 22°37N 84°31E **315** H11
Simeria *Romania* 45°51N 23°1E **289** F12
Simeulue *Indonesia* 2°45N 95°45E **308** D1
Simferopol *Ukraine* 44°55N 34°3E **291** F5
Simi *Greece* 36°35N 27°50E **295** F12
Simi Valley *U.S.A.* 34°16N 118°47W **351** L8
Simikot *Nepal* 30°0N 81°50E **315** E9
Simla = Shimla *India* 31°2N 77°9E **314** D7
Simlipal △ *India* 21°45N 86°30E **315** J12
Simmie *Canada* 49°56N 108°6W **343** D7
Simmler *U.S.A.* 35°21N 119°59W **351** K7
Simo älv = Simojoki →
Finland 65°35N 25°1E **280** D21
Simojoki → *Finland* 65°35N 25°1E **280** D21
Simojovel *Mexico* 17°12N 92°38W **359** D6
Simonette → *Canada* 55°9N 118°15W **342** B5
Simonstown *S. Africa* 34°14S 18°26E **328** E2
Simpang Empat *Malaysia* 5°27N 100°29E **311** c
Simplonpass *Switz.* 46°15N 8°3E **292** C8
Simpson Desert *Australia* 25°0S 137°0E **334** D2
Simpson Desert △
Australia 24°59S 138°21E **334** C2
Simpson Pen. *Canada* 68°34N 88°45W **341** C11
Simrishamn *Sweden* 55°33N 14°22E **281** J16
Simsbury *U.S.A.* 41°53N 72°48W **355** E12
Simushir, Ostrov
Russia 46°50N 152°30E **301** E16
Sin Cowe I. *S. China Sea* 9°53N 114°19E **308** C4
Sinabang *Indonesia* 2°30N 96°24E **308** D1
Sinadogo *Somali Rep.* 5°50N 47°0E **319** F4
Sinai = Es Sînâ' *Egypt* 29°0N 34°0E **318** F3
Sinai, Mt. = Mûsa, Gebel
Egypt 28°33N 33°59E **316** D2
Sinaloa □ *Mexico* 25°0N 107°30W **358** C3
Sinaloa de Leyva
Mexico 25°50N 108°14W **358** B3
Sinarades *Greece* 39°34N 19°51E **297** A3
Sincelejo *Colombia* 9°18N 75°24W **364** B3
Sinch'ang *N. Korea* 40°7N 128°28E **307** D15
Sinch'ŏn *N. Korea* 38°17N 125°21E **307** E13
Sinclair *U.S.A.* 41°47N 107°7W **348** F10
Sinclair Mills *Canada* 54°5N 121°40W **342** C4
Sinclair's B. *U.K.* 58°31N 3°5W **283** C5
Sinclairville *U.S.A.* 42°16N 79°16W **354** D5
Sincorá, Serra do *Brazil* 13°30S 41°0W **365** F10
Sind = Sindh □ *Pakistan* 26°0N 69°0E **314** G3
Sind *Pakistan* 26°0N 68°30E **314** G3
Sind → *Jammu & Kashmir,*
India 34°18N 74°45E **315** B6
Sind → *Mad. P., India* 26°26N 79°13E **315** F8
Sind Sagar Doab
Pakistan 32°0N 71°30E **314** D4
Sindangan *Phil.* 8°10N 123°5E **309** C6
Sindangbarang
Indonesia 7°27S 107°1E **309** G12
Sinde *Zambia* 17°28S 25°51E **327** F2
Sindh □ *Pakistan* 26°0N 69°0E **314** G3
Sindri *India* 23°45N 86°42E **315** H12
Sines *Portugal* 37°56N 8°51W **293** D1
Sines, C. de *Portugal* 37°58N 8°53W **293** D1
Sineu *Spain* 39°38N 3°1E **296** B10
Sing Buri *Thailand* 14°53N 100°25E **310** E3
Singa *Sudan* 13°10N 33°57E **323** F12
Singalila △ *India* 27°10N 88°5E **315** F13
Singapore ■ *Asia* 1°17N 103°51E **311** d
Singapore, Straits of *Asia* 1°15N 104°0E **311** d
Singapore Changi ✕ **(SIN)**
Singapore 1°23N 103°59E **311** M4
Singaraja *Indonesia* 8°7S 115°6E **308** F5
Singatoka = Sigatoka
Fiji 18°8S 177°32E **331** a
Singida *Tanzania* 4°49S 34°48E **326** C3
Singida □ *Tanzania* 6°0S 34°30E **326** D3
Singkaling Hkamti
Burma 26°0N 95°39E **313** G19
Singkang *Indonesia* 4°8S 120°1E **309** E6
Singkawang *Indonesia* 1°0N 108°57E **308** D3
Singkep *Indonesia* 0°30S 104°25E **308** E2
Singleton *Australia* 32°33S 151°0E **335** E5
Singleton, Mt. *N. Terr.,*
Australia 22°0S 130°46E **332** D5
Singleton, Mt. *W. Austral.,*
Australia 29°27S 117°15E **333** E2
Singoli *India* 25°0N 75°22E **314** G6
Singora = Songkhla
Thailand 7°13N 100°37E **311** J3
Sinhŭng *N. Korea* 40°11N 127°34E **307** D14
Siniscóla *Italy* 40°34N 9°41E **294** D3
Sinjai *Indonesia* 5°7S 120°20E **309** F6
Sinjār *Iraq* 36°19N 41°52E **316** B4
Sinkat *Sudan* 18°55N 36°49E **323** E13
Sinkiang = Xinjiang Uygur Zizhiqu □ *China* 42°0N 86°0E **304** C3
Sinmak *N. Korea* 38°25N 126°14E **307** E14
Sinmi-do *N. Korea* 39°33N 124°53E **307** E13
Sinnamary *Fr. Guiana* 5°25N 53°0W **365** B8
Sinni → *Italy* 40°8N 16°41E **294** D7
Sinop *Turkey* 42°1N 35°11E **291** F6
Sinor *India* 21°55N 73°20E **314** J5
Sinp'o *N. Korea* 40°0N 128°13E **307** E15
Sinsk *Russia* 61°8N 126°48E **301** C13
Sintang *Indonesia* 0°5N 111°35E **308** D4
Sinton *U.S.A.* 28°2N 97°31W **356** G6
Sintra *Portugal* 38°47N 9°25W **293** C1
Sinŭiju *N. Korea* 40°5N 124°24E **307** D13
Siocon *Phil.* 7°40N 122°10E **309** C6
Siófok *Hungary* 46°54N 18°3E **289** E10
Sion *Switz.* 46°14N 7°20E **292** C7
Sion Mills *U.K.* 54°48N 7°29W **282** B4
Sioux Center *U.S.A.* 43°5N 96°11W **352** D5
Sioux City *U.S.A.* 42°30N 96°24W **352** D5
Sioux Falls *U.S.A.* 43°33N 96°44W **352** D5
Sioux Lookout *Canada* 50°10N 91°50W **344** B1
Sioux Narrows *Canada* 49°25N 94°10W **343** D10
Sipadan *Malaysia* 7°6N 118°38E **309** D5
Siparia *Trin. & Tob.* 10°8N 61°31W **365** K15
Siping *China* 43°8N 124°21E **307** C13
Sipiwesk L. *Canada* 55°5N 97°35W **343** B9
Siple *Antarctica* 75°0S 74°0W **277** D7
Sipra → *India* 23°55N 75°28E **314** H6
Sipura *Indonesia* 2°18S 99°40E **308** E1
Siquia → *Nic.* 12°10N 84°20W **360** D3
Siquijor *Phil.* 9°12N 123°35E **309** C6
Siquirres *Costa Rica* 10°6N 83°30W **360** D3
Şīr Abu Nu'ayr *U.A.E.* 25°20N 54°20E **317** E7
Şīr Banī Yās *U.A.E.* 24°19N 52°37E **317** E7
Sir Edward Pellew Group
Australia 15°40S 137°10E **334** B2
Sir Graham Moore Is.
Australia 13°53S 126°34E **332** B4
Sir James MacBrien, Mt.
Canada 62°7N 127°41W **340** C7
Sira → *Norway* 58°23N 6°34E **281** G12
Siracusa *Italy* 37°4N 15°17E **294** F6
Sirajganj *Bangla.* 24°25N 89°47E **315** G13
Sirathu *India* 25°39N 81°19E **315** G9
Sīrdān *Iran* 36°39N 49°12E **317** B6
Siren *U.S.A.* 45°47N 92°24W **352** C7
Sirer *Spain* 38°56N 1°22E **296** C7
Siret → *Romania* 45°24N 28°1E **289** F14
Sirghāyā *Syria* 33°51N 36°8E **318** B5
Sirinath △ *Thailand* 8°6N 98°17E **311** a
Sīrjān *Iran* 29°30N 55°45E **317** D7
Sirmaur *India* 24°51N 81°23E **315** G9
Sirohi *India* 24°52N 72°53E **314** G5
Sironj *India* 24°5N 77°39E **314** G7
Síros = Syros *Greece* 37°28N 24°57E **295** F11
Sirretta Pk. *U.S.A.* 35°56N 118°19W **351** K8
Sīrrī *Iran* 25°55N 54°32E **317** E7
Sirsa *India* 29°33N 75°4E **314** E6
Sirsa → *India* 26°51N 79°4E **315** F8
Sisak *Croatia* 45°30N 16°21E **288** F9
Sisaket *Thailand* 15°8N 104°23E **310** E5
Sishen *S. Africa* 27°47S 22°59E **328** D3
Sishui *Henan, China* 34°48N 113°15E **306** G7
Sishui *Shandong, China* 35°42N 117°18E **307** G9
Sisipuk L. *Canada* 55°45N 101°50W **343** B8
Sisophon *Cambodia* 13°38N 102°59E **310** F4
Sisseton *U.S.A.* 45°40N 97°3W **352** C5
Sīstān *Asia* 30°50N 61°0E **317** D9
Sīstān, Daryācheh-ye
Iran 31°0N 61°0E **317** D9
Sīstān va Balūchestān □
Iran 27°0N 62°0E **317** E9
Sisters *U.S.A.* 44°18N 121°33W **348** D3
Sisters, The *Seychelles* 4°16S 55°52E **325** b
Siswa Bazar *India* 27°9N 83°46E **315** F10
Sitamarhi *India* 26°37N 85°30E **315** F11
Sitampiky *Madag.* 16°41S 46°6E **329** B8
Sitapur *India* 27°38N 80°45E **315** F9
Siteki *Swaziland* 26°32S 31°58E **329** D5
Sitges *Spain* 41°17N 1°47E **293** B6
Sitia *Greece* 35°13N 26°6E **297** D8
Sitito-Ozima Ridge
Pac. Oc. 23°0N 143°0E **336** E6
Sitka *U.S.A.* 57°3N 135°20W **342** B1
Sitoti *Botswana* 23°15S 23°40E **328** C3
Sittang Myit → *Burma* 17°20N 96°45E **313** L20
Sittard *Neths.* 51°0N 5°52E **287** C5
Sittingbourne *U.K.* 51°21N 0°45E **285** F8
Sittoung = Sittang Myit →
Burma 17°20N 96°45E **313** L20
Sittwe *Burma* 20°18N 92°45E **313** J18
Situbondo *Indonesia* 7°42S 114°0E **309** G16
Si'umu *Samoa* 14°1S 171°48W **331** b
Siuna *Nic.* 13°37N 84°45W **360** D3
Siuri *India* 23°50N 87°34E **315** H12
Sīvand *Iran* 30°5N 52°55E **317** D7
Sivas *Turkey* 39°43N 36°58E **316** B3
Siverek *Turkey* 37°50N 39°19E **316** B3
Sivomaskinskiy *Russia* 66°40N 62°35E **290** A11
Sivrihisar *Turkey* 39°30N 31°35E **291** G5
Sīwa *Egypt* 29°11N 25°31E **323** C11
Sīwa, El Wâhât es *Egypt* 29°10N 25°30E **320** D6
Siwa Oasis = Sīwa, El Wâhât es
Egypt 29°10N 25°30E **320** D6
Siwalik Range *Nepal* 28°0N 83°0E **315** F10
Siwan *India* 26°13N 84°21E **315** F11
Siwana *India* 25°38N 72°25E **314** G5
Six Cross Roads *Barbados* 13°7N 59°28W **361** g
Sixmilebridge *Ireland* 52°44N 8°46W **282** D3
Sixth Cataract *Sudan* 16°20N 32°42E **323** E12
Siziwang Qi *China* 41°25N 111°40E **306** D6
Sjælland *Denmark* 55°30N 11°30E **281** J14
Sjumen = Shumen
Bulgaria 43°18N 26°55E **295** C12
Skadarsko Jezero
Europe 42°10N 19°20E **295** C8
Skaftafell *Iceland* 64°1N 17°0W **280** D5
Skaftafell △ *Iceland* 64°9N 16°50W **280** D5
Skagafjörður *Iceland* 65°54N 19°35W **280** D4
Skagastølstindane
Norway 61°28N 7°52E **280** F12
Skagaströnd *Iceland* 65°50N 20°19W **280** D3
Skagen *Denmark* 57°43N 10°35E **281** H14
Skagerrak *Denmark* 57°30N 9°0E **281** H13
Skagit → *U.S.A.* 48°23N 122°22W **350** B4
Skagway *U.S.A.* 59°28N 135°19W **346** a
Skala-Podilska *Ukraine* 48°50N 26°15E **289** D14
Skala Podolskaya = Skala-Podilska *Ukraine* 48°50N 26°15E **289** D14
Skalat *Ukraine* 49°23N 25°55E **289** D13
Skåne *Sweden* 55°59N 13°30E **281** J15
Skaneateles *U.S.A.* 42°57N 76°26W **355** D8
Skaneateles L. *U.S.A.* 42°51N 76°22W **355** D8
Skardu *Pakistan* 35°20N 75°44E **315** B6
Skarżysko-Kamienna
Poland 51°7N 20°52E **289** C11
Skeena → *Canada* 54°9N 130°5W **342** C2
Skeena Mts. *Canada* 56°40N 128°30W **342** B3
Skegness *U.K.* 53°9N 0°20E **284** D8
Skeldon = Corriverton
Guyana 5°55N 57°20W **364** B7
Skeleton Coast *Namibia* 20°0S 13°0E **325** J2
Skeleton Coast ⌂
Namibia 20°0S 13°20E **328** C1
Skellefteå *Sweden* 64°45N 20°50E **280** D19
Skellefteälven →
Sweden 64°45N 21°10E **280** D19
Skelleftehamn *Sweden* 64°40N 21°9E **280** D19
Skerries, The *U.K.* 53°25N 4°36W **284** D3
Ski *Norway* 59°43N 10°52E **281** G14
Skiathos *Greece* 39°12N 23°30E **295** E10
Skibbereen *Ireland* 51°33N 9°16W **282** E2
Skiddaw *U.K.* 54°39N 3°9W **284** C4
Skidegate *Canada* 53°15N 132°1W **342** C2
Skien *Norway* 59°12N 9°35E **281** G13
Skierniewice *Poland* 51°58N 20°10E **289** C11
Skikda *Algeria* 36°50N 6°58E **322** A7
Skilloura *Cyprus* 35°14N 33°10E **297** D12
Skipton *U.K.* 53°58N 2°3W **284** D5
Skirmish Pt. *Australia* 11°59S 134°17E **334** A1
Skiros *Greece* 38°55N 24°34E **295** E11
Skive *Denmark* 56°33N 9°2E **281** H13
Skjálfandafljót →
Iceland 65°59N 17°25W **280** D5
Skjálfandi *Iceland* 66°5N 17°30W **280** C5
Skole *Ukraine* 49°3N 23°30E **289** D12
Skopelos *Greece* 39°9N 23°47E **295** E10
Skopi *Greece* 35°11N 26°2E **297** D8
Skopje *Macedonia* 42°1N 21°26E **295** C9
Skövde *Sweden* 58°24N 13°50E **281** G15
Skovorodino *Russia* 54°0N 124°0E **301** D13
Skowhegan *U.S.A.* 44°46N 69°43W **353** C19
Skull *Ireland* 51°32N 9°34W **282** E2
Skunk → *U.S.A.* 40°42N 91°7W **352** E8
Skuodas *Lithuania* 56°16N 21°33E **281** H19
Skvyra *Ukraine* 49°44N 29°40E **289** D15
Skye *U.K.* 57°15N 6°10W **283** D2
Skykomish *U.S.A.* 47°42N 121°22W **348** C3
Skyros = Skiros *Greece* 38°55N 24°34E **295** E11
Slade Pt. *Australia* 21°5S 149°13E **334** K7
Slættaratindur *Færoe Is.* 62°18N 7°1W **280** E9
Slagelse *Denmark* 55°23N 11°19E **281** J14
Slamet *Indonesia* 7°16S 109°8E **309** G13
Slane *Ireland* 53°42N 6°33W **282** C5
Slaney → *Ireland* 52°26N 6°33W **282** D5
Slangberge *S. Africa* 31°32S 20°48E **328** E3
Śląsk *Poland* 51°0N 16°30E **288** C9
Slate Is. *Canada* 48°40N 87°0W **344** C2
Slatina *Romania* 44°28N 24°22E **289** F13
Slatington *U.S.A.* 40°45N 75°37W **355** F9
Slaton *U.S.A.* 33°26N 101°39W **356** E4
Slave → *Canada* 61°18N 113°39W **342** A6
Slave Coast *W. Afr.* 6°0N 2°30E **322** G6
Slave Lake *Canada* 55°17N 114°43W **342** B6
Slave Pt. *Canada* 61°11N 115°56W **342** A5
Slavgorod *Russia* 53°1N 78°37E **300** D8
Slavonski Brod *Croatia* 45°11N 18°1E **295** B8
Slavuta *Ukraine* 50°15N 27°2E **289** C14
Slavyanka *Russia* 42°53N 131°21E **302** C5
Slavyansk = Slovyansk
Ukraine 48°55N 37°36E **291** E6
Slawharad *Belarus* 53°27N 31°0E **289** B16
Sleaford *U.K.* 53°0N 0°24W **284** D7
Sleaford B. *Australia* 34°55S 135°45E **335** E2
Sleat, Sd. of *U.K.* 57°5N 5°47W **283** D3
Sleeper Is. *Canada* 58°30N 81°0W **341** D11
Sleeping Bear Dunes ⌂
U.S.A. 44°50N 86°5W **352** C10
Sleepy Eye *U.S.A.* 44°18N 94°43W **352** C6
Slemon L. *Canada* 63°13N 116°4W **342** A5
Slide Mt. *U.S.A.* 42°0N 74°25W **355** E10
Slidell *U.S.A.* 30°17N 89°47W **357** F10
Sliema *Malta* 35°55N 14°30E **297** D2
Slieve Aughty *Ireland* 53°4N 8°30W **282** C3
Slieve Bloom *Ireland* 53°4N 7°40W **282** C4
Slieve Donard *U.K.* 54°11N 5°55W **282** B6
Slieve Gamph *Ireland* 54°6N 9°0W **282** B3
Slieve Gullion *U.K.* 54°7N 6°26W **282** B5
Slieve League *Ireland* 54°40N 8°42W **282** B3
Slieve Mish *Ireland* 52°12N 9°50W **282** D2
Slievenamon *Ireland* 52°25N 7°34W **282** D4
Sligeach = Sligo *Ireland* 54°16N 8°28W **282** B3
Sligo *Ireland* 54°16N 8°28W **282** B3
Sligo *U.S.A.* 41°6N 79°29W **354** E5
Sligo □ *Ireland* 54°8N 8°42W **282** B3
Sligo B. *Ireland* 54°18N 8°40W **282** B3
Slippery Rock *U.S.A.* 41°4N 80°3W **354** E4
Slite *Sweden* 57°42N 18°48E **281** H18
Sliven *Bulgaria* 42°42N 26°19E **295** C12
Sloan *U.S.A.* 35°57N 115°13W **351** K11
Sloansville *U.S.A.* 42°45N 74°22W **355** D10
Slobodskoy *Russia* 58°40N 50°6E **290** C9
Slobozia *Romania* 44°34N 27°23E **289** F14
Slocan *Canada* 49°48N 117°28W **342** D5
Slonim *Belarus* 53°4N 25°19E **289** B13
Slough *U.K.* 51°30N 0°36W **285** F7
Slough □ *U.K.* 51°30N 0°36W **285** F7
Sloughhouse *U.S.A.* 38°26N 121°12W **350** G5
Slovak Rep. ■ *Europe* 48°30N 20°0E **289** D10
Slovakia = Slovak Rep. ■
Europe 48°30N 20°0E **289** D10
Slovakian Ore Mts. = Slovenské Rudohorie *Slovak Rep.* 48°45N 20°0E **289** D10
Slovenia ■ *Europe* 45°58N 14°30E **288** F8
Slovenija = Slovenia ■
Europe 45°58N 14°30E **288** F8
Slovenska = Slovak Rep. ■
Europe 48°30N 20°0E **289** D10
Slovenské Rudohorie
Slovak Rep. 48°45N 20°0E **289** D10
Slovyansk *Ukraine* 48°55N 37°36E **291** E6
Sluch → *Ukraine* 51°37N 26°38E **289** C14
Sluis *Neths.* 51°18N 3°23E **287** C3
Słupsk *Poland* 54°30N 17°3E **289** A9
Slurry *S. Africa* 25°49S 25°42E **328** D4
Slutsk *Belarus* 53°2N 27°31E **289** B14
Slyne Hd. *Ireland* 53°25N 10°10W **282** C1
Slyudyanka *Russia* 51°40N 103°40E **301** D11
Småland *Sweden* 57°15N 15°25E **281** H16
Smalltree L. *Canada* 61°0N 105°0W **343** A8
Smallwood Res. *Canada* 54°5N 64°30W **345** B7
Smarhon *Belarus* 54°20N 26°24E **289** A14
Smartt Syndicate Dam
S. Africa 30°45S 23°10E **328** E3
Smartville *U.S.A.* 39°13N 121°18W **350** F5
Smeaton *Canada* 53°30N 104°49W **343** C8
Smederevo *Serbia* 44°40N 20°57E **295** B9
Smerwick Harbour
Ireland 52°12N 10°23W **282** D1
Smethport *U.S.A.* 41°49N 78°27W **354** E6
Smidovich *Russia* 48°36N 133°49E **301** E14
Smith *Canada* 55°10N 114°0W **342** B6
Smith Center *U.S.A.* 39°47N 98°47W **352** F4
Smith River ⌂ *U.S.A.* 41°55N 124°0W **348** F2
Smithburne →
Australia 17°3S 140°57E **334** B3
Smithers *Canada* 54°45N 127°10W **342** C3
Smithfield *S. Africa* 30°9S 26°30E **329** E4
Smithfield *N.C., U.S.A.* 35°31N 78°21W **357** D15
Smithfield *Utah, U.S.A.* 41°50N 111°50W **348** F8
Smiths Falls *Canada* 44°55N 76°0W **355** B9
Smithton *Australia* 40°53S 145°6E **335** G4
Smithville *Canada* 43°6N 79°33W **354** C5
Smithville *U.S.A.* 30°1N 97°10W **356** F6
Smoky → *Canada* 56°10N 117°21W **342** B5
Smoky Bay *Australia* 32°22S 134°13E **335** E1
Smoky Hill → *U.S.A.* 39°4N 96°48W **352** F5
Smoky Hills *U.S.A.* 39°15N 99°30W **352** F4
Smoky Lake *Canada* 54°10N 112°30W **342** C6
Smøla *Norway* 63°23N 8°3E **280** E13
Smolensk *Russia* 54°45N 32°5E **290** D5
Smolikas, Oros *Greece* 40°9N 20°58E **295** D9
Smolyan *Bulgaria* 41°36N 24°38E **295** D11
Smooth Rock Falls
Canada 49°17N 81°37W **344** C3
Smoothstone L.
Canada 54°40N 106°50W **343** C7
Smorgon = Smarhon
Belarus 54°20N 26°24E **289** A14
Smyrna = İzmir *Turkey* 38°25N 27°8E **295** E12
Smyrna *U.S.A.* 39°18N 75°36W **353** F16
Snæfell *Iceland* 64°48N 15°34W **280** D6
Snaefell *I. of Man* 54°16N 4°27W **284** C3
Snæfellsjökull *Iceland* 64°49N 23°46W **280** D2
Snake → *U.S.A.* 46°12N 119°2W **348** C4
Snake I. *Australia* 38°47S 146°33E **335** F4
Snake Range *U.S.A.* 39°0N 114°20W **348** G6
Snake River Plain
U.S.A. 42°50N 114°0W **348** E7
Snåsavatnet *Norway* 64°12N 12°0E **280** D15
Sneek *Neths.* 53°2N 5°40E **287** A5
Sneem *Ireland* 51°50N 9°54W **282** E2
Sneeuberge *S. Africa* 31°46S 24°20E **328** E3
Snelling *U.S.A.* 37°31N 120°26W **350** H6
Sněžka *Europe* 50°41N 15°50E **288** C8
Snizort, L. *U.K.* 57°33N 6°28W **283** D2
Snøhetta *Norway* 62°19N 9°16E **280** E13
Snohomish *U.S.A.* 47°55N 122°6W **350** C4
Snoqualmie Pass
U.S.A. 47°25N 121°25W **350** C5
Snoul *Cambodia* 12°4N 106°26E **311** F6
Snow Hill *U.S.A.* 38°11N 75°24W **353** F16
Snow Lake *Canada* 54°52N 100°3W **343** C8
Snow Mt. *Calif., U.S.A.* 39°23N 122°45W **350** F4
Snow Mt. *Maine,*
U.S.A. 45°18N 70°48W **355** A14
Snow Shoe *U.S.A.* 41°2N 77°57W **354** E7
Snowbird L. *Canada* 60°45N 103°0W **343** A8
Snowdon *U.K.* 53°4N 4°5W **284** D3
Snowdonia △ *U.K.* 53°7N 3°59W **284** D4
Snowdrift = Łutselk'e
Canada 62°24N 110°44W **343** A6
Snowdrift → *Canada* 62°24N 110°44W **343** A6
Snowflake *U.S.A.* 34°30N 110°5W **349** J8
Snowshoe Pk. *U.S.A.* 48°13N 115°41W **348** B6
Snowtown *Australia* 33°46S 138°14E **335** E2
Snowville *U.S.A.* 41°58N 112°43W **348** F7
Snowy → *Australia* 37°46S 148°30E **335** F4
Snowy Mt. *U.S.A.* 43°42N 74°23W **355** C10
Snowy Mts. *Australia* 36°30S 148°20E **335** F4
Snug Corner *Bahamas* 22°33N 73°52W **361** B5
Snyatyn *Ukraine* 48°27N 25°38E **289** D13
Snyder *Okla., U.S.A.* 34°40N 98°57W **356** D5
Snyder *Tex., U.S.A.* 32°44N 100°55W **356** E4
Soahanina *Madag.* 18°42S 44°13E **329** B7
Soalala *Madag.* 16°6S 45°20E **329** B8
Soaloka *Madag.* 18°32S 45°15E **329** B8
Soamanonga *Madag.* 23°52S 44°47E **329** C7
Soan → *Pakistan* 33°1N 71°44E **314** C4
Soanierana-Ivongo
Madag. 16°55S 49°35E **329** B8
Soanindraniny *Madag.* 19°54S 47°14E **329** B8
Soavina *Madag.* 20°23S 46°56E **329** C8
Soavinandriana *Madag.* 19°9S 46°45E **329** B8
Sobat, Nahr → *Sudan* 9°22N 31°33E **323** G12
Sobhapur *India* 22°47N 78°17E **314** H8
Sobradinho, Reprêsa de
Brazil 9°30S 42°0W **365** E10
Sobral *Brazil* 3°50S 40°20W **365** D10
Soc Giang *Vietnam* 22°54N 106°1E **310** A6
Soc Trang *Vietnam* 9°37N 105°50E **311** H5
Socastee *U.S.A.* 33°41N 78°59W **357** E15
Soch'e = Shache *China* 38°20N 77°10E **304** C2
Sochi *Russia* 43°35N 39°40E **291** F6
Société, Îs. de la
French Polynesia 17°0S 151°0W **337** J12
Society Is. = Société, Îs. de la
French Polynesia 17°0S 151°0W **337** J12
Socompa, Portezuelo de
Chile 24°27S 68°18W **366** A2
Socorro *N. Mex., U.S.A.* 34°4N 106°54W **349** J10
Socorro *Tex., U.S.A.* 31°39N 106°18W **356** F1
Socorro, I. *Mexico* 18°45N 110°58W **358** D2
Socotra *Yemen* 12°30N 54°0E **319** E5
Soda L. *U.S.A.* 35°10N 116°4W **349** J5
Soda Plains *India* 35°30N 79°0E **315** B8
Soda Springs *U.S.A.* 42°39N 111°36W **348** E8
Sodankylä *Finland* 67°29N 26°40E **280** C22

Soddy-Daisy U.S.A. 35°17N 85°10W 357 D12
Söderhamn Sweden 61°18N 17°10E 280 F17
Söderköping Sweden 58°31N 16°20E 281 G17
Södermanland Sweden 58°56N 16°55E 281 G17
Södertälje Sweden 59°12N 17°39E 281 G17
Sodiri Sudan 14°27N 29°0E 323 F11
Sodus U.S.A. 43°14N 77°4W 354 C7
Sodwana Bay △ S. Africa 27°35S 32°43E 329 D5
Soekmekaar = Morebeng S. Africa 23°30S 29°55E 329 C4
Soest Neths. 52°9N 5°19E 287 B5
Sofala □ Mozam. 19°30S 34°30E 329 B5
Sofia = Sofiya Bulgaria 42°45N 23°20E 295 C10
Sofia → Madag. 15°27S 47°23E 329 B8
Sofiya Bulgaria 42°45N 23°20E 295 C10
Sōfu-Gan Japan 29°49N 140°21E 303 K10
Sogamoso Colombia 5°43N 72°56W 364 B4
Sogār Iran 25°53N 58°6E 317 E8
Sogndalsfjøra Norway 61°14N 7°5E 280 F12
Søgne Norway 58°5N 7°48E 281 G12
Sognefjorden Norway 61°10N 5°50E 280 F11
Soh Iran 33°26N 51°27E 317 C6
Sohâg Egypt 26°33N 31°43E 323 C12
Sohagpur India 22°42N 78°12E 314 H8
Soignies Belgium 50°35N 4°5E 287 D4
Soissons France 49°25N 3°19E 292 B5
Sōja Japan 34°40N 133°45E 303 G6
Sojat India 25°55N 73°45E 314 G5
Sokal Ukraine 50°31N 24°15E 289 C13
Sokcho S. Korea 38°12N 128°36E 307 E15
Söke Turkey 37°48N 27°28E 295 F12
Sokelo Dem. Rep. of the Congo 9°55S 24°36E 327 D1
Sokhumi Georgia 43°0N 41°0E 291 F7
Soko Is. China 22°10N 113°54E 305 G10
Sokodé Togo 9°0N 1°11E 322 G6
Sokol Russia 59°30N 40°5E 290 C7
Sokółka Poland 53°25N 23°30E 289 B12
Sokołów Podlaski Poland 52°25N 22°15E 289 B12
Sokoto Nigeria 13°2N 5°16E 322 F7
Sol Iletsk Russia 51°10N 55°0E 290 D10
Solai Kenya 0°2N 36°12E 326 B4
Solan India 30°55N 77°7E 314 D7
Solana Beach U.S.A. 32°58N 117°16W 351 N9
Solander I. N.Z. 46°34S 166°54E 331 G1
Solano Phil. 16°31N 121°15E 309 A6
Solapur India 17°43N 75°56E 312 L9
Soldotna U.S.A. 60°29N 151°3W 340 C4
Soléa Cyprus 35°5N 33°4E 297 D12
Soledad Colombia 10°55N 74°46W 364 A4
Soledad U.S.A. 36°26N 121°20W 350 J5
Soledad Venezuela 8°10N 63°34W 364 B6
Solent, The U.K. 50°45N 1°25W 285 G6
Solfonntaggen Norway 60°2N 6°57E 281 F12
Solhan Turkey 38°57N 41°3E 316 B4
Soligalich Russia 59°5N 42°10E 290 C7
Soligorsk = Salihorsk Belarus 52°51N 27°27E 289 B14
Solihull U.K. 52°26N 1°47W 285 E6
Solikamsk Russia 59°38N 56°50E 290 C10
Solila Madag. 21°25S 46°37E 329 C8
Solimões = Amazonas → S. Amer. 0°5S 50°0W 365 D8
Solingen Germany 51°10N 7°5E 288 C4
Sollefteå Sweden 63°12N 17°20E 280 E17
Sóller Spain 39°46N 2°43E 296 B9
Solo → Indonesia 6°47S 112°22E 309 G15
Sologne France 47°40N 1°45E 292 C4
Solok Indonesia 0°45S 100°40E 308 E2
Sololá Guatemala 14°49N 91°10W 360 D1
Sololo Kenya 3°33N 38°39E 326 B4
Solomon, N. Fork → U.S.A. 39°29N 98°26W 352 F4
Solomon, S. Fork → U.S.A. 39°25N 99°12W 352 F4
Solomon Is. ■ Pac. Oc. 6°0S 155°0E 330 B8
Solomon Rise Pac. Oc. 1°0N 157°0E 336 G7
Solon China 46°32N 121°10E 305 B7
Solon Springs U.S.A. 46°22N 91°49W 352 B8
Solor Indonesia 8°27S 123°0E 309 F6
Solothurn Switz. 47°13N 7°32E 292 C7
Šolta Croatia 43°24N 16°15E 294 C7
Solṭānābād Khorāsān, Iran 34°13N 59°58E 317 C8
Solṭānābād Khorāsān, Iran 36°29N 58°5E 317 B8
Solunska Glava Macedonia 41°44N 21°31E 295 D9
Solvang U.S.A. 34°36N 120°8W 351 L6
Solvay U.S.A. 43°3N 76°13W 355 C8
Sölvesborg Sweden 56°5N 14°35E 281 H16
Solvychegodsk Russia 61°21N 46°56E 290 B8
Solway Firth U.K. 54°49N 3°35W 284 C4
Solwezi Zambia 12°11S 26°21E 327 E2
Sōma Japan 37°40N 140°50E 302 F10
Soma Turkey 39°10N 27°35E 295 E12
Somabhula Zimbabwe 19°42S 29°40E 329 B4
Somali Pen. Africa 7°0N 46°0E 320 F8
Somali Rep. ■ Africa 7°0N 47°0E 319 F4
Somalia = Somali Rep. ■ Africa 7°0N 47°0E 319 F4
Somaliland □ Somali Rep. 9°0N 46°0E 319 F4
Sombor Serbia 45°46N 19°9E 295 B8
Sombra Canada 42°43N 82°29W 354 D2
Sombrerete Mexico 23°38N 103°39W 358 C4
Sombrero Anguilla 18°37N 63°30W 361 C7
Somdari India 25°47N 72°38E 314 G5
Somers U.S.A. 48°5N 114°13W 348 B6
Somerset Ky., U.S.A. 37°5N 84°36W 353 G11
Somerset Mass., U.S.A. 41°47N 71°8W 355 E13
Somerset Pa., U.S.A. 40°1N 79°5W 354 F5
Somerset □ U.K. 51°9N 3°0W 285 F5
Somerset East S. Africa 32°42S 25°35E 328 E4
Somerset I. Canada 73°30N 93°0W 340 B10
Somerset West S. Africa 34°8S 18°50E 328 E2
Somersworth U.S.A. 43°16N 70°52W 355 C14
Somerton U.S.A. 32°36N 114°43W 349 K6
Somerville U.S.A. 40°35N 74°38W 355 F10
Someş → Romania 47°49N 22°43E 289 D12
Somme → France 50°11N 1°38E 292 A4
Somnath India 20°53N 70°22E 314 J4
Somosierra, Puerto de Spain 41°4N 3°35W 293 B4
Somosomo Fiji 16°47S 179°58W 331 a
Somosomo Str. Fiji 16°0S 180°0E 331 a
Somoto Nic. 13°28N 86°37W 360 D2
Somport, Puerto de Spain 42°48N 0°31W 292 E3
Son → India 25°42N 84°52E 315 G11
Son Ha Vietnam 15°3N 108°34E 310 E7
Son Hoa Vietnam 13°2N 108°58E 310 F7
Son La Vietnam 21°20N 103°50E 310 B4
Son Serra Spain 39°43N 3°13E 296 B10
Son Tay Vietnam 21°8N 105°30E 310 B5
Soná Panama 8°0N 81°20W 360 E3
Sonamarg India 34°18N 75°21E 315 B6
Sonamukhi India 23°18N 87°27E 315 H12
Sonar → India 24°24N 79°56E 315 G8
Sŏnch'ŏn N. Korea 39°48N 124°55E 307 E13
Sondags → S. Africa 33°44S 25°51E 328 E4
Sondar India 33°28N 75°56E 315 C6
Sønderborg Denmark 54°55N 9°49E 281 J13
Sóndrio Italy 46°10N 9°52E 292 C8
Sone Mozam. 17°23S 34°55E 327 F3
Sonepur India 20°55N 83°50E 313 J13
Song Thailand 18°28N 100°11E 310 C3
Song Cau Vietnam 13°27N 109°18E 310 F7
Song Xian China 34°12N 112°8E 306 G7
Songan Indonesia 8°13S 115°24E 309 J18
Songea Tanzania 10°40S 35°40E 327 E4
Songgang China 22°46N 113°50E 305 F10
Songhua Hu China 43°35N 126°50E 307 C14
Songhua Jiang → China 47°45N 132°30E 305 B8
Songimvelo ⌓ S. Africa 25°50S 31°2E 329 D5
Sŏngjin = Kimch'aek N. Korea 40°40N 129°10E 307 D15
Songkhla Thailand 7°13N 100°37E 311 J3
Songnim N. Korea 38°45N 125°39E 307 E13
Songo Mozam. 15°34S 32°38E 325 H6
Songo Sudan 9°47N 24°21E 323 G10
Songpan China 32°40N 103°30E 304 C5
Songwe Dem. Rep. of the Congo 3°20S 26°16E 326 C2
Songwe → Africa 9°44S 33°58E 327 D3
Sonhat India 23°29N 82°31E 315 H10
Sonid Youqi China 42°45N 112°48E 306 C7
Sonipat India 29°0N 77°5E 314 E7
Sonkach India 22°59N 76°21E 314 H7
Sonmiani Pakistan 25°25N 66°40E 314 G2
Sonmiani B. Pakistan 25°15N 66°30E 314 G2
Sono → Brazil 9°58S 48°11W 365 E9
Sonoma U.S.A. 38°18N 122°28W 350 G4
Sonora Calif., U.S.A. 37°59N 120°23W 350 H6
Sonora Tex., U.S.A. 30°34N 100°39W 356 F4
Sonora □ Mexico 29°20N 110°40W 358 B2
Sonora → Mexico 29°5N 110°55W 358 B2
Sonoran Desert U.S.A. 33°40N 113°30W 351 L12
Sonoyta Mexico 31°51N 112°50W 358 A2
Sonsonate El Salv. 13°43N 89°44W 360 D2
Soochow = Suzhou China 31°19N 120°38E 305 C7
Sooke Canada 48°13N 123°43W 350 B3
Soomaaliya = Somali Rep. ■ Africa 7°0N 47°0E 319 F4
Sop Hao Laos 20°33N 104°27E 310 B5
Sop Prap Thailand 17°53N 99°20E 310 D2
Sopi Indonesia 2°34N 128°28E 309 D7
Sopot Poland 54°27N 18°31E 289 A10
Sopron Hungary 47°45N 16°32E 289 E9
Sopur India 34°18N 74°27E 315 B6
Sør-Rondane Antarctica 72°0S 25°0E 277 D4
Sorah Pakistan 27°13N 68°56E 314 F3
Soraon India 25°37N 81°51E 315 G9
Sorel-Tracy Canada 46°0N 73°10W 344 C5
Sórgono Italy 40°1N 9°6E 294 D3
Soria Spain 41°43N 2°32W 293 B4
Soriano Uruguay 33°24S 58°19W 366 C4
Sorkh, Kuh-e Iran 35°40N 58°30E 317 C8
Soroca Moldova 48°8N 28°12E 289 D15
Sorocaba Brazil 23°31S 47°27W 367 A6
Sorochinsk Russia 52°26N 53°10E 290 D9
Soroki = Soroca Moldova 48°8N 28°12E 289 D15
Sorong Indonesia 0°55S 131°15E 309 E8
Soroni Greece 36°21N 28°1E 297 C10
Soroti Uganda 1°43N 33°35E 326 B3
Sørøya Norway 70°40N 22°30E 280 A20
Sørøysundet Norway 70°25N 23°0E 280 A20
Sorrell Australia 42°47S 147°34E 335 G4
Sorrento Italy 40°37N 14°22E 294 D6
Sorsele Sweden 65°31N 17°30E 280 D17
Sorsogon Phil. 13°0N 124°0E 309 B6
Sortavala Russia 61°42N 30°41E 280 F24
Sortland Norway 68°42N 15°25E 280 B16
Soscumica, L. Canada 50°15N 77°27W 344 B4
Sosnogorsk Russia 63°37N 53°51E 290 B9
Sosnowiec Poland 50°20N 19°10E 289 C10
Sossus Vlei Namibia 24°40S 15°23E 328 C2
Sŏsura N. Korea 42°16N 130°36E 307 C16
Sot → India 27°27N 79°37E 315 F8
Sotavento C. Verde Is. 15°0N 25°0W 322 b
Sotik Kenya 0°41S 35°7E 326 C4
Sotkamo Finland 64°8N 28°23E 280 D23
Soto la Marina Mexico 23°46N 98°13W 359 C5
Soto la Marina → Mexico 23°45N 97°45W 359 C5
Sotuta Mexico 20°36N 89°1W 359 C7
Souanké Congo 2°10N 14°3E 324 D2
Souda Greece 35°29N 24°4E 297 D6
Soudas, Ormos Greece 35°25N 24°10E 297 D6
Souderton U.S.A. 40°19N 75°19W 355 F9
Soufrière Guadeloupe 16°5N 61°40W 360 b
Soufrière St. Lucia 13°51N 61°3W 361 f
Soufrière Bay Dominica 15°13N 61°22W 361 f
Soukhouma Laos 14°38N 105°48E 310 E5
Sŏul = Seoul S. Korea 37°31N 126°58E 307 F14
Sound, The U.K. 50°20N 4°10W 285 G3
Sources, Mt. aux Lesotho 28°45S 28°50E 329 D4
Soure Brazil 0°35S 48°30W 365 D9
Souris Man., Canada 49°40N 100°20W 343 D8
Souris P.E.I., Canada 46°21N 62°15W 345 C7
Souris → N. Amer. 49°40N 99°34W 352 A4
Sousa Brazil 6°45S 38°10W 365 E11
Sousse Tunisia 35°50N 10°38E 323 A8
Sout → S. Africa 31°35S 18°24E 328 E2
South Africa ■ Africa 32°0S 23°0E 328 E3
South America 10°0S 60°0W 362 E5
South Aulatsivik I. Canada 56°45N 61°30W 345 A7
South Australia □ Australia 32°0S 139°0E 335 E2
South Australian Basin Ind. Oc. 38°0S 126°0E 336 L4
South Ayrshire □ U.K. 55°18N 4°41W 283 F4
South Baldy Pk. U.S.A. 34°6N 107°11W 349 J10
South Bass I. U.S.A. 41°39N 82°49W 354 E2
South Bend Ind., U.S.A. 41°41N 86°15W 352 E10
South Bend Wash., U.S.A. 46°40N 123°48W 350 D3
South Boston U.S.A. 36°42N 78°54W 353 G14
South Branch Canada 47°55N 59°2W 345 C8
South Brook Canada 49°26N 56°5W 345 C8
South Bruny I. Australia 43°20S 147°15E 335 G4
South C. Australia 43°39S 146°42E 330 F7
South Carolina □ U.S.A. 34°0N 81°0W 357 E14
South Charleston U.S.A. 38°22N 81°44W 353 F13
South China Sea Asia 10°0N 113°0E 308 C4
South Cumberland Is. △ Australia 20°42S 149°11E 334 J7
South Dakota □ U.S.A. 44°15N 100°0W 352 C4
South Deerfield U.S.A. 42°29N 72°37W 355 D12
South Downs U.K. 50°52N 0°25W 285 G7
South East C. Australia 43°40S 146°50E 335 G4
South East Is. Australia 34°17S 123°30E 333 F3
South Esk → U.K. 56°43N 2°31W 283 E6
South Fiji Basin Pac. Oc. 26°0S 175°0E 336 K9
South Foreland U.K. 51°8N 1°24E 285 F9
South Fork American → U.S.A. 38°57N 120°59W 350 G5
South Fork Feather → U.S.A. 39°17N 121°36W 350 F5
South Fork Grand → U.S.A. 45°43N 102°17W 352 C2
South Fork Milk → U.S.A. 48°4N 106°19W 348 B10
South Fork Republican → U.S.A. 40°3N 101°31W 352 E3
South Georgia Antarctica 54°30S 37°0W 368 G9
South Gloucestershire □ U.K. 51°32N 2°28W 285 F5
South Hadley U.S.A. 42°16N 72°35W 355 D12
South Haven U.S.A. 42°24N 86°16W 352 D10
South Henik L. Canada 61°30N 97°20W 343 A9
South Horr Kenya 2°12N 36°56E 326 B4
South I. Kenya 2°35N 36°35E 326 B4
South I. N.Z. 44°0S 170°0E 331 F3
South Indian Lake Canada 56°47N 98°56W 343 B9
South Invercargill N.Z. 46°26S 168°23E 331 G2
South Island △ Kenya 2°39N 36°35E 326 B4
South Kitui ⌓ Kenya 1°48S 38°46E 326 C4
South Knife → Canada 58°55N 94°37W 343 B10
South Koel → India 22°32N 85°14E 315 H11
South Korea ■ Asia 36°0N 128°0E 307 G15
South Lake Tahoe U.S.A. 38°57N 119°59W 350 G6
South Lanarkshire □ U.K. 55°37N 3°53W 283 F5
South Loup → U.S.A. 41°4N 98°39W 352 E4
South Luangwa △ Zambia 13°0S 31°20E 327 E3
South Magnetic Pole Antarctica 64°8S 138°8E 277 C9
South Milwaukee U.S.A. 42°55N 87°52W 352 D10
South Molton U.K. 51°1N 3°51W 285 F4
South Moose L. Canada 53°49N 100°1W 343 C8
South Nahanni → Canada 61°3N 123°21W 342 A4
South Nation → Canada 45°34N 75°6W 355 A9
South Natuna Is. = Natuna Selatan, Kepulauan Indonesia 2°45N 109°0E 308 D3
South Negril Pt. Jamaica 18°16N 78°22W 360 a
South Orkney Is. Antarctica 63°0S 45°0W 277 C18
South Ossetia □ Georgia 42°21N 44°2E 291 F7
South Pagai, I. = Pagai Selatan, Pulau Indonesia 3°0S 100°15E 308 E2
South Paris U.S.A. 44°14N 70°31W 355 B14
South Pittsburg U.S.A. 35°1N 85°42W 357 D12
South Platte → U.S.A. 41°7N 100°42W 352 E3
South Pole Antarctica 90°0S 0°0 277 E
South Porcupine Canada 48°30N 81°12W 344 C3
South Portland U.S.A. 43°38N 70°15W 353 D18
South Pt. Barbados 13°2N 59°32W 361 g
South Pt. U.S.A. 44°52N 83°19W 354 B1
South River Canada 45°52N 79°23W 344 C4
South River U.S.A. 40°27N 74°23W 355 F10
South Ronaldsay U.K. 58°48N 2°58W 283 C6
South Sandwich Is. Antarctica 57°0S 27°0W 277 B1
South Sandwich Trench Atl. Oc. 56°0S 24°0W 277 B1
South Saskatchewan → Canada 53°15N 105°5W 343 C7
South Seal → Canada 58°48N 98°8W 343 B9
South Shetland Is. Antarctica 62°0S 59°0W 277 C18
South Shields U.K. 55°0N 1°25W 284 C6
South Sioux City U.S.A. 42°28N 96°24W 352 D5
South Sister U.S.A. 44°4N 121°51W 348 D3
South Taranaki Bight N.Z. 39°40S 174°5E 331 C5
South Tasman Rise S. Ocean 48°0S 146°0E 277 A10
South Thompson → Canada 50°40N 120°20W 342 C4
South Twin I. Canada 53°7N 79°52W 344 B4
South Tyne → U.K. 54°59N 2°8W 284 C5
South Uist U.K. 57°20N 7°15W 283 D1
South Valley U.S.A. 35°1N 106°41W 349 J10
South Wellesley Is. Australia 16°58S 139°17E 334 B2
South West C. Australia 43°34S 146°3E 335 G4
South West C. N.Z. 47°17S 167°28E 331 G1
South Williamsport U.S.A. 41°13N 77°0W 354 E8
South Yorkshire □ U.K. 53°27N 1°36W 284 D6
Southampton Canada 44°30N 81°25W 354 B3
Southampton U.K. 50°54N 1°23W 285 G6
Southampton U.S.A. 40°53N 72°23W 355 F12
Southampton □ U.K. 50°54N 1°23W 285 G6
Southampton I. Canada 64°30N 84°0W 341 C11
Southaven U.S.A. 34°59N 90°0W 357 D9
Southbank Canada 54°2N 125°46W 342 C3
Southbridge N.Z. 43°48S 172°16E 331 E4
Southbridge U.S.A. 42°5N 72°2W 355 D12
Southend Canada 56°19N 103°22W 343 B8
Southend-on-Sea U.K. 51°32N 0°44E 285 F8
Southend-on-Sea □ U.K. 51°32N 0°44E 285 F8
Southern = Yuzhnyy □ Russia 44°0N 40°0E 300 E5
Southern □ Malawi 15°0S 35°0E 327 F4
Southern □ Zambia 16°20S 26°20E 327 F2
Southern Alps N.Z. 43°41S 170°11E 331 E3
Southern Cross Australia 31°12S 119°15E 333 F2
Southern Indian L. Canada 57°10N 98°30W 343 B9
Southern Lau Group Fiji 18°40S 178°40W 331 a
Southern Ocean Antarctica 62°0S 60°0E 277 C6
Southern Pines U.S.A. 35°11N 79°24W 357 D15
Southern Uplands U.K. 55°28N 3°52W 283 F5
Southington U.S.A. 41°36N 72°53W 355 E12
Southland □ N.Z. 45°30S 168°0E 331 F1
Southold U.S.A. 41°4N 72°26W 355 E12
Southport Australia 27°58S 153°25E 335 D5
Southport U.K. 53°39N 3°0W 284 D4
Southport U.S.A. 42°3N 76°49W 354 D8
Southwest △ Australia 43°8S 146°5E 335 G4
Southwest Pacific Basin Pac. Oc. 40°0S 140°0W 277 A12
Southwold U.K. 52°20N 1°41E 285 E9
Southwood △ Australia 27°48S 150°8E 335 D5
Soutpansberg S. Africa 23°0S 29°30E 329 C4
Sovetsk Kaliningrad, Russia 55°6N 21°50E 281 J19
Sovetsk Kirov, Russia 57°38N 48°53E 290 C8
Sovetskaya Gavan = Vanino Russia 48°50N 140°5E 301 E15
Soweto S. Africa 26°14S 27°52E 329 D4
Sōya-Kaikyō = La Perouse Str. Asia 45°40N 142°0E 302 B11
Sōya-Misaki Japan 45°30N 141°55E 302 B10
Soyo Angola 6°13S 12°20E 324 F2
Sozh → Belarus 51°57N 30°48E 289 B16
Spa Belgium 50°29N 5°53E 287 D5
Spain ■ Europe 39°0N 4°0W 293 B4
Spalding Australia 33°30S 138°37E 335 E2
Spalding U.K. 52°48N 0°9W 284 E7
Spanaway U.S.A. 47°6N 122°26W 350 C4
Spangler U.S.A. 40°39N 78°48W 354 F6
Spanish Canada 46°12N 82°20W 344 C3
Spanish Fork U.S.A. 40°7N 111°39W 348 F8
Spanish Town Br. Virgin Is. 17°43N 64°26W 361 e
Spanish Town Jamaica 18°0N 76°57W 360 a
Sparks U.S.A. 39°32N 119°45W 350 F7
Sparta = Sparti Greece 37°5N 22°25E 295 F10
Sparta Mich., U.S.A. 43°10N 85°42W 353 D11
Sparta N.J., U.S.A. 41°2N 74°38W 355 E10
Sparta Wis., U.S.A. 43°56N 90°49W 352 D8
Spartanburg U.S.A. 34°56N 81°57W 357 D14
Spartansburg U.S.A. 41°49N 79°41W 354 E5
Sparti Greece 37°5N 22°25E 295 F10
Spartivento, C. Calabria, Italy 37°55N 16°4E 294 F7
Spartivento, C. Sard., Italy 38°53N 8°50E 294 E3
Sparwood Canada 49°44N 114°53W 342 D6
Spassk Dalniy Russia 44°40N 132°48E 302 B6
Spatha, Akra Greece 35°42N 23°43E 297 D5
Spatsizi → Canada 57°42N 128°7W 342 B3
Spatsizi Plateau Wilderness ⌓ Canada 57°40N 128°0W 342 B3
Spean → U.K. 56°55N 4°59W 283 E4
Spearfish U.S.A. 44°30N 103°52W 352 C2
Spearman U.S.A. 36°12N 101°12W 356 C4
Speculator U.S.A. 43°30N 74°22W 355 C10
Speightstown Barbados 13°15N 59°39W 361 g
Speke Gulf Tanzania 2°20S 32°50E 326 C3
Spence Bay = Taloyoak Canada 69°32N 93°32W 340 C10
Spencer Idaho, U.S.A. 44°22N 112°11W 348 D7
Spencer Iowa, U.S.A. 43°9N 95°9W 352 D6
Spencer N.Y., U.S.A. 42°13N 76°30W 355 D8
Spencer Nebr., U.S.A. 42°53N 98°42W 352 D4
Spencer, C. Australia 35°20S 136°53E 335 F2
Spencer B. Namibia 25°30S 14°47E 328 D1
Spencer G. Australia 34°0S 137°20E 335 E2
Spencerville Canada 44°51N 75°33W 355 B9
Spences Bridge Canada 50°25N 121°20W 342 C4
Spennymoor U.K. 54°42N 1°36W 284 C6
Spenser Mts. N.Z. 42°15S 172°45E 331 E4
Sperrin Mts. U.K. 54°50N 7°0W 282 B5
Spey → U.K. 57°40N 3°6W 283 D5
Speyer Germany 49°29N 8°25E 288 D5
Spezand Pakistan 29°59N 67°0E 314 E2
Spiddle Ireland 53°15N 9°18W 282 C2
Spili Greece 35°13N 24°31E 297 D6
Spīn Būldak Afghan. 31°1N 66°25E 314 D2
Spinalonga Greece 35°18N 25°44E 297 D7
Spirit Lake U.S.A. 46°15N 122°9W 350 D4
Spirit River Canada 55°45N 118°50W 342 B5
Spiritwood Canada 53°24N 107°33W 343 C7
Spithead U.K. 50°45N 1°10W 285 G6
Spitzbergen = Svalbard Arctic 78°0N 17°0E 276 B8
Spjelkavik Norway 62°28N 6°22E 280 E12
Split Croatia 43°31N 16°26E 294 C7
Split L. Canada 56°8N 96°15W 343 B9
Split Lake Canada 56°8N 96°15W 343 B9
Spofford U.S.A. 29°10N 100°25W 356 G4
Spokane U.S.A. 47°40N 117°24W 348 C5
Spoleto Italy 42°44N 12°44E 294 C5
Spooner U.S.A. 45°50N 91°53W 352 C8
Sporyy Navolok, Mys Russia 75°50N 68°40E 300 B7
Sprague U.S.A. 47°18N 117°59W 348 C5
Spratly I. S. China Sea 8°38N 111°55E 308 C4
Spratly Is. S. China Sea 8°20N 112°0E 308 C4
Spray U.S.A. 44°50N 119°48W 348 D4
Spree → Germany 52°32N 13°12E 288 B7
Sprengisandur Iceland 64°52N 18°7W 280 D4
Spring City U.S.A. 40°11N 75°33W 355 F9
Spring Creek U.S.A. 40°44N 115°35W 348 F6
Spring Garden U.S.A. 39°52N 120°47W 350 F6
Spring Hall Barbados 13°18N 59°36W 361 g
Spring Hill U.S.A. 28°27N 82°41W 357 G13
Spring Mts. U.S.A. 36°0N 115°45W 351 J11
Spring Valley Calif., U.S.A. 32°44N 116°59W 351 N10
Spring Valley Nev., U.S.A. 36°6N 115°14W 351 J11
Springbok S. Africa 29°42S 17°54E 328 D2
Springboro U.S.A. 41°48N 80°22W 354 E4
Springdale Canada 49°30N 56°6W 345 C8
Springdale U.S.A. 36°11N 94°8W 356 C7
Springer U.S.A. 36°22N 104°36W 349 H11
Springerville U.S.A. 34°8N 109°17W 349 J9
Springfield Canada 42°50N 80°56W 354 D4
Springfield N.Z. 43°19S 171°56E 331 E3
Springfield Colo., U.S.A. 37°24N 102°37W 349 H12
Springfield Ill., U.S.A. 39°48N 89°39W 352 F9
Springfield Mass., U.S.A. 42°6N 72°35W 355 D12
Springfield Mo., U.S.A. 37°13N 93°17W 352 G7
Springfield Ohio, U.S.A. 39°55N 83°49W 353 F12
Springfield Oreg., U.S.A. 44°3N 123°1W 348 D2
Springfield Tenn., U.S.A. 36°31N 86°53W 357 C11
Springfield Vt., U.S.A. 43°18N 72°29W 355 C12
Springfontein S. Africa 30°15S 25°40E 328 E4
Springhill Canada 45°40N 64°4W 345 C7
Springhill U.S.A. 33°0N 93°28W 356 E8
Springhouse Canada 51°56N 122°7W 342 C4
Springs S. Africa 26°13S 28°25E 329 D4
Springsure Australia 24°8S 148°6E 334 C4
Springvale U.S.A. 43°28N 70°48W 355 C14
Springville Calif., U.S.A. 36°8N 118°49W 350 J8
Springville N.Y., U.S.A. 42°31N 78°40W 354 D6
Springville Utah, U.S.A. 40°10N 111°37W 348 F8
Springwater U.S.A. 42°38N 77°35W 354 D7
Spruce-Creek U.S.A. 40°36N 78°9W 354 F6
Spruce Knob-Seneca Rocks ⌓ U.S.A. 38°50N 79°30W 353 F14
Spruce Mt. U.S.A. 44°12N 72°19W 355 B12
Spur U.S.A. 33°28N 100°52W 356 E4
Spurn Hd. U.K. 53°35N 0°8E 284 D8
Spuzzum Canada 49°37N 121°23W 342 D4
Squam L. U.S.A. 43°45N 71°32W 355 C13
Squamish Canada 49°45N 123°10W 342 D4
Square Islands Canada 52°47N 55°47W 345 B8
Squires, Mt. Australia 26°14S 127°28E 333 E4
Srbija = Serbia ■ Europe 43°20N 20°0E 295 B9
Sre Ambel Cambodia 11°8N 103°46E 311 G4
Sre Khtum Cambodia 12°10N 106°52E 311 F6
Sre Umbell = Sre Ambel Cambodia 11°8N 103°46E 311 G4
Srebrenica Bos.-H. 44°6N 19°18E 295 B8
Sredinny Ra. = Sredinnyy Khrebet Russia 57°0N 160°0E 301 D16
Sredinnyy Khrebet Russia 57°0N 160°0E 301 D16
Srednekolymsk Russia 67°27N 153°40E 301 C16
Śrem Poland 52°6N 17°2E 289 B9
Sremska Mitrovica Serbia 44°59N 19°38E 295 B8
Srepok → Cambodia 13°33N 106°16E 310 F6
Sretensk Russia 52°10N 117°40E 301 D12
Sri Aman Malaysia 1°15N 111°32E 308 D4
Sri Lanka ■ Asia 7°30N 80°50E 312 R12
Srikakulam India 18°14N 83°58E 313 K13
Srinagar India 34°5N 74°50E 315 B6
Srinagarind Res. Thailand 14°35N 99°0E 310 E2
Srono Indonesia 8°24S 114°16E 309 J17
Staaten → Australia 16°24S 141°17E 334 B3
Staaten River △ Australia 16°15S 142°40E 334 B3
Stade Germany 53°35N 9°29E 288 B5
Stadskanaal Neths. 53°4N 6°55E 287 A6

Staffa U.K. 56°27N 6°21W 283 E2
Stafford U.K. 52°49N 2°7W 284 E5
Stafford U.S.A. 37°58N 98°36W 352 G4
Stafford Springs U.S.A. 41°57N 72°18W 355 E12
Staffordshire □ U.K. 52°53N 2°10W 284 E5
Staines U.K. 51°26N 0°29W 285 F7
Stakhanov Ukraine 48°35N 38°40E 291 E6
Stalida Greece 35°17N 25°25E 297 D7
Stalowa Wola Poland 50°34N 22°3E 289 C12
Stalybridge U.K. 53°28N 2°3W 284 D5
Stamford Australia 21°15S 143°46E 334 C3
Stamford U.K. 52°39N 0°29W 285 E7
Stamford Conn., U.S.A. 41°3N 73°32W 355 E11
Stamford N.Y., U.S.A. 42°25N 74°38W 355 D10
Stamford Tex., U.S.A. 32°57N 99°48W 356 E5
Stampriet Namibia 24°20S 18°28E 328 C2
Stamps U.S.A. 33°22N 93°30W 356 E8
Standerton S. Africa 26°55S 29°7E 329 D4
Standish U.S.A. 43°59N 83°57W 353 D12
Stanford S. Africa 34°26S 19°29E 328 E2
Stanford U.S.A. 47°9N 110°13W 348 C8
Stanger S. Africa 29°27S 31°14E 329 D5
Stängselåsen = Salpausselkä Finland 61°3N 26°15E 280 F22
Stanislaus → U.S.A. 37°40N 121°14W 350 H5
Stanke Dimitrov Bulgaria 42°17N 23°9E 295 C10
Stanley Australia 40°46S 145°19E 335 G4
Stanley China 22°13N 114°12E 305 G11
Stanley Falk. Is. 51°40S 59°51W 368 G5
Stanley U.K. 54°53N 1°41W 284 C6
Stanley Idaho, U.S.A. 44°13N 114°56W 348 D6
Stanley N. Dak., U.S.A. 48°19N 102°23W 352 A2
Stanley N.Y., U.S.A. 42°48N 77°6W 354 D7
Stanley Mission Canada 55°25N 104°33W 343 B8
Stanovoy Khrebet Russia 55°0N 130°0E 301 D13
Stanovoy Ra. = Stanovoy Khrebet Russia 55°0N 130°0E 301 D13
Stansmore Ra. Australia 21°23S 128°33E 332 D4
Stansted, London ✕ (STN) U.K. 51°54N 0°14E 285 F8
Stanthorpe Australia 28°36S 151°59E 335 D5
Stanton U.S.A. 32°8N 101°48W 356 E4
Stanwood U.S.A. 48°15N 122°23W 350 B4
Staples U.S.A. 46°21N 94°48W 352 B6
Stapleton U.S.A. 41°29N 100°31W 352 E3
Star City Canada 52°50N 104°20W 343 C8
Star Lake U.S.A. 44°10N 75°2W 355 B9
Stara Planina Bulgaria 43°15N 23°0E 295 C10
Stara Zagora Bulgaria 42°26N 25°39E 295 C11
Starachowice Poland 51°3N 21°2E 289 C11
Staraya Russa Russia 57°58N 31°23E 290 C5
Starbuck I. Kiribati 5°37S 155°55W 337 H12
Starcke △ Australia 14°56S 145°2E 334 A4
Stargard Szczeciński Poland 53°20N 15°0E 288 B8
Staritsa Russia 56°33N 34°55E 290 C5
Starke U.S.A. 29°57N 82°7W 357 G13
Starkville U.S.A. 33°28N 88°49W 357 E10
Starogard Gdański Poland 53°59N 18°30E 289 B10
Starokonstantinov = Starokonstyantyniv Ukraine 49°48N 27°10E 289 D14
Starokonstyantyniv Ukraine 49°48N 27°10E 289 D14
Start Pt. U.K. 50°13N 3°39W 285 G4
Staryy Chartoriysk Ukraine 51°15N 25°54E 289 C13
Staryy Oskol Russia 51°19N 37°55E 291 D6
State College U.S.A. 40°48N 77°52W 354 F7
Stateline U.S.A. 38°57N 119°56W 350 G7
Staten, I. = Estados, I. de Los Argentina 54°40S 64°30W 368 G4
Staten I. U.S.A. 40°35N 74°9W 355 F10
Statesboro U.S.A. 32°27N 81°47W 357 E14
Statesville U.S.A. 35°47N 80°53W 357 D14
Statia = St. Eustatius W. Indies 17°20N 63°0W 361 C7
Stauffer U.S.A. 34°45N 119°3W 351 L7
Staunton Ill., U.S.A. 39°1N 89°47W 352 F9
Staunton Va., U.S.A. 38°9N 79°4W 353 F14
Stavanger Norway 58°57N 5°40E 281 G11
Staveley N.Z. 43°40S 171°32E 331 E3
Stavelot Belgium 50°23N 5°55E 287 D5
Stavern Norway 59°0N 10°1E 281 G14
Stavoren Neths. 52°53N 5°22E 287 B5
Stavropol Russia 45°5N 42°0E 291 E7
Stavros Cyprus 35°1N 32°38E 297 D11
Stavros Greece 35°12N 24°45E 297 D6
Stavros, Akra Greece 35°26N 24°58E 297 D6
Stawell Australia 37°5S 142°47E 335 F3
Stawell → Australia 20°20S 142°55E 334 C3
Stayner Canada 44°25N 80°5W 354 B4
Stayton U.S.A. 44°48N 122°48W 348 D2
Steamboat Springs U.S.A. 40°29N 106°50W 348 F10
Steele U.S.A. 46°51N 99°55W 352 B4
Steelton U.S.A. 40°14N 76°50W 354 F8
Steen River Canada 59°40N 117°12W 342 B5
Steens Mt. U.S.A. 42°35N 118°40W 348 E4
Steenwijk Neths. 52°47N 6°7E 287 B6
Steep Pt. Australia 26°8S 113°8E 333 E1
Steep Rock Canada 51°30N 98°48W 343 C9
Stefanie L. = Chew Bahir Ethiopia 4°40N 36°50E 319 G2
Stefansson Bay Antarctica 67°20S 59°8E 277 C5
Steiermark □ Austria 47°26N 15°0E 288 E8
Steilacoom U.S.A. 47°10N 122°36W 350 C4
Steilrandberge Namibia 17°45S 13°20E 328 B1
Steinbach Canada 49°32N 96°40W 343 D9
Steinhausen Namibia 21°49S 18°20E 328 C2
Steinkjer Norway 64°1N 11°31E 280 D14
Steinkopf S. Africa 29°18S 17°43E 328 D2
Stellarton Canada 45°32N 62°30W 345 C7
Stellenbosch S. Africa 33°58S 18°50E 328 E2
Stendal Germany 52°36N 11°53E 288 B6
Steornabhaigh = Stornoway U.K. 58°13N 6°23W 283 C2
Stepanakert = Xankändi Azerbaijan 39°52N 46°49E 316 B5
Stephens Creek Australia 31°50S 141°30E 335 E3
Stephens I. Canada 54°10N 130°45W 342 C2
Stephens L. Canada 56°32N 95°0W 343 B9
Stephenville Canada 48°31N 58°35W 345 C8
Stephenville U.S.A. 32°13N 98°12W 356 E5
Steppe Asia 50°0N 50°0E 298 C7
Sterkstroom S. Africa 31°32S 26°32E 328 E4
Sterling Colo., U.S.A. 40°37N 103°13W 348 F12
Sterling Ill., U.S.A. 41°48N 89°42W 352 E9
Sterling Kans., U.S.A. 38°13N 98°12W 352 F4
Sterling City U.S.A. 31°51N 101°0W 356 F4
Sterling Heights U.S.A. 42°35N 83°2W 353 D12
Sterling Run U.S.A. 41°25N 78°12W 354 E6
Sterlitamak Russia 53°40N 56°0E 290 D10
Sternes Greece 35°30N 24°9E 297 D6
Stettin = Szczecin Poland 53°27N 14°27E 288 B8
Stettiner Haff Germany 53°47N 14°15E 288 B8
Stettler Canada 52°19N 112°40W 342 C6
Steubenville U.S.A. 40°22N 80°37W 354 F4
Stevenage U.K. 51°55N 0°13W 285 F7
Stevens Point U.S.A. 44°31N 89°34W 352 C9
Stevenson U.S.A. 45°42N 121°53W 350 E5
Stevenson → Australia 27°6S 135°33E 335 D2
Stevenson L. Canada 53°55N 96°0W 343 C9
Stevensville U.S.A. 46°30N 114°5W 348 C6
Stewart Canada 55°56N 129°57W 342 B3
Stewart U.S.A. 39°5N 119°46W 350 F7
Stewart → Canada 63°19N 139°26W 340 C6
Stewart, C. Australia 11°57S 134°56E 334 A1
Stewart, I. Chile 54°50S 71°15W 368 G2
Stewart I. N.Z. 46°58S 167°54E 331 G1
Stewarts Point U.S.A. 38°39N 123°24W 350 G3
Stewartville U.S.A. 43°51N 92°29W 352 D7
Stewiacke Canada 45°9N 63°22W 345 C7
Steynsburg S. Africa 31°15S 25°49E 328 E4
Steyr Austria 48°3N 14°25E 288 D8
Steytlerville S. Africa 33°17S 24°19E 328 E3
Stigler U.S.A. 35°15N 95°8W 356 D7
Stikine → Canada 56°40N 132°30W 342 B2
Stilfontein S. Africa 26°51S 26°50E 328 D4
Stillwater N.Z. 42°27S 171°20E 331 E3
Stillwater N.Y., U.S.A. 42°55N 73°41W 355 D11
Stillwater Okla., U.S.A. 36°7N 97°4W 356 C6
Stillwater Range U.S.A. 39°50N 118°5W 348 G4
Stillwater Res. U.S.A. 43°54N 75°3W 355 C9
Stilwell U.S.A. 35°49N 94°38W 356 D7
Stînga Nistrului □ Moldova 47°20N 29°15E 289 E15
Štip Macedonia 41°42N 22°10E 295 D10
Stirling Canada 44°18N 77°33W 354 B7
Stirling U.K. 56°8N 3°57W 283 E5
Stirling □ U.K. 56°12N 4°18W 283 E4
Stirling Ra. Australia 34°23S 118°0E 333 F2
Stirling Range △ Australia 34°26S 118°20E 333 F2
Stittsville Canada 45°15N 75°55W 355 A9
Stjernøya Norway 70°20N 22°40E 280 A20
Stjørdalshalsen Norway 63°29N 10°51E 280 E14
Stockerau Austria 48°24N 16°12E 288 D9
Stockholm Sweden 59°19N 18°4E 281 G18
Stockport U.K. 53°25N 2°9W 284 D5
Stocksbridge U.K. 53°29N 1°35W 284 D6
Stockton Calif., U.S.A. 37°58N 121°17W 350 H5
Stockton Kans., U.S.A. 39°26N 99°16W 352 F4
Stockton Mo., U.S.A. 37°42N 93°48W 352 G7
Stockton-on-Tees U.K. 54°35N 1°19W 284 C6
Stockton-on-Tees □ U.K. 54°35N 1°19W 284 C6
Stockton Plateau U.S.A. 30°30N 102°30W 356 F3
Stoeng Treng Cambodia 13°31N 105°58E 310 F5
Stoer, Pt. of U.K. 58°16N 5°23W 283 C3
Stoke-on-Trent U.K. 53°1N 2°11W 284 D5
Stoke-on-Trent □ U.K. 53°1N 2°11W 284 D5
Stokes △ Australia 33°45S 121°11E 333 F3
Stokes Pt. Australia 40°10S 143°56E 335 G3
Stokes Ra. Australia 15°50S 130°50E 332 C5
Stokksnes Iceland 64°14N 14°58W 280 D6
Stokmarknes Norway 68°34N 14°54E 280 B16
Stolac Bos.-H. 43°5N 17°59E 295 C7
Stolbovoy, Ostrov Russia 74°44N 135°14E 301 B14
Stolbtsy = Stowbtsy Belarus 53°30N 26°43E 289 B14
Stolin Belarus 51°53N 26°50E 289 C14
Stomio Greece 35°21N 23°32E 297 D5
Stone U.K. 52°55N 2°9W 284 E5
Stoneboro U.S.A. 41°20N 80°7W 354 E4
Stonehaven U.K. 56°59N 2°12W 283 E6
Stonehenge Australia 24°22S 143°17E 334 C3
Stonehenge U.K. 51°9N 1°45W 285 F6
Stonewall Canada 50°10N 97°19W 343 C9
Stony L. Man., Canada 58°51N 98°40W 343 B9
Stony L. Ont., Canada 44°30N 78°5W 354 B6
Stony Point U.S.A. 41°14N 73°59W 355 E11
Stony Pt. U.S.A. 43°50N 76°18W 355 C8
Stony Rapids Canada 59°16N 105°50W 343 B7
Stony Tunguska = Tunguska, Podkamennaya → Russia 61°50N 90°13E 301 C10
Stonyford U.S.A. 39°23N 122°33W 350 F4
Stora Lulevatten Sweden 67°10N 19°30E 280 C18
Storavan Sweden 65°45N 18°10E 280 D18
Stord Norway 59°52N 5°23E 281 G11
Store Bælt Denmark 55°20N 11°0E 281 J14
Storm B. Australia 43°10S 147°30E 335 G4
Storm Lake U.S.A. 42°39N 95°13W 352 D6
Stormberge S. Africa 31°16S 26°17E 328 E4
Stormsrivier S. Africa 33°59S 23°52E 328 E3
Stornoway U.K. 58°13N 6°23W 283 C2
Storozhinets = Storozhynets Ukraine 48°14N 25°45E 289 D13
Storozhynets Ukraine 48°14N 25°45E 289 D13
Storrs U.S.A. 41°49N 72°15W 355 E12
Storsjön Sweden 63°9N 14°30E 280 E16
Storuman Sweden 65°5N 17°10E 280 D17
Storuman, L. Sweden 65°13N 16°50E 280 D17
Stouffville Canada 43°58N 79°15W 354 C5
Stoughton Canada 49°40N 103°0W 343 D8
Stour → Dorset, U.K. 50°43N 1°47W 285 G6
Stour → Kent, U.K. 51°18N 1°22E 285 F9
Stour → Suffolk, U.K. 51°57N 1°4E 285 F9
Stourbridge U.K. 52°28N 2°8W 285 E5
Stout L. Canada 52°0N 94°40W 343 C10
Stove Pipe Wells Village U.S.A. 36°35N 117°11W 351 J9
Stow U.S.A. 41°10N 81°27W 354 E3
Stowbtsy Belarus 53°30N 26°43E 289 B14
Stowmarket U.K. 52°12N 1°0E 285 E9
Strabane U.K. 54°50N 7°27W 282 B4
Strahan Australia 42°9S 145°20E 335 G4
Stralsund Germany 54°18N 13°4E 288 A7
Strand S. Africa 34°9S 18°48E 328 E2
Stranda Møre og Romsdal, Norway 62°19N 6°58E 280 E12
Stranda Nord-Trøndelag, Norway 63°33N 10°14E 280 E14
Strangford L. U.K. 54°30N 5°37W 282 B6
Stranorlar Ireland 54°48N 7°46W 282 B4
Stranraer U.K. 54°54N 5°1W 283 G3
Strasbourg Canada 51°4N 104°55W 343 C8
Strasbourg France 48°35N 7°42E 292 B7
Stratford Canada 43°23N 81°0W 354 C4
Stratford N.Z. 39°20S 174°19E 331 C5
Stratford Calif., U.S.A. 36°11N 119°49W 350 J7
Stratford Conn., U.S.A. 41°12N 73°8W 355 E11
Stratford Tex., U.S.A. 36°20N 102°4W 356 C3
Stratford-upon-Avon U.K. 52°12N 1°42W 285 E6
Strath Spey U.K. 57°9N 3°49W 283 D5
Strathalbyn Australia 35°13S 138°53E 335 F2
Strathaven U.K. 55°40N 4°5W 283 F4
Strathcona ⌓ Canada 49°38N 125°40W 342 D3
Strathmore Canada 51°5N 113°18W 342 C6
Strathmore U.K. 56°37N 3°7W 283 E5
Strathmore U.S.A. 36°9N 119°4W 350 J7
Strathnaver Canada 53°20N 122°33W 342 C4
Strathpeffer U.K. 57°35N 4°32W 283 D4
Strathroy Canada 42°58N 81°38W 354 D3
Strathy Pt. U.K. 58°36N 4°1W 283 C4
Strattanville U.S.A. 41°12N 79°19W 354 E5
Stratton U.S.A. 45°8N 70°26W 355 A14
Stratton Mt. U.S.A. 43°4N 72°55W 355 C12
Straubing Germany 48°52N 12°34E 288 D7
Straumnes Iceland 66°26N 23°8W 280 C2
Strawberry → U.S.A. 40°10N 110°24W 348 F8
Streaky B. Australia 32°48S 134°13E 335 E1
Streaky Bay Australia 32°51S 134°18E 335 E1
Streator U.S.A. 41°8N 88°50W 352 E9
Streetsboro U.S.A. 41°14N 81°21W 354 E3
Streetsville Canada 43°35N 79°42W 354 C5
Strelka Russia 58°5N 93°3E 301 D10
Streng → Cambodia 13°12N 103°37E 310 F4
Streymoy Færoe Is. 62°8N 7°5W 280 E9
Strezhevoy Russia 60°42N 77°34E 300 C8
Strimonas → Greece 40°46N 23°51E 295 D10
Strokestown Ireland 53°46N 8°7W 282 C3
Stroma U.K. 58°41N 3°7W 283 C5
Strómboli Italy 38°47N 15°13E 294 E6
Stromeferry U.K. 57°21N 5°33W 283 D3
Stromness U.K. 58°58N 3°17W 283 C5
Stromsburg U.S.A. 41°7N 97°36W 352 E5
Strömstad Sweden 58°56N 11°10E 281 G14
Strömsund Sweden 63°51N 15°33E 280 E16
Strongsville U.S.A. 41°19N 81°50W 354 E3
Stronsay U.K. 59°7N 2°35W 283 B6
Stroud U.K. 51°45N 2°13W 285 F5
Stroud Road Australia 32°18S 151°57E 335 E5
Stroudsburg U.S.A. 40°59N 75°12W 355 F9
Stroumbi Cyprus 34°53N 32°29E 297 E11
Struer Denmark 56°30N 8°35E 281 H13
Strugi Krasnyye Russia 58°21N 29°1E 281 G23
Strumica Macedonia 41°28N 22°41E 295 D10
Struthers Canada 48°41N 85°51W 344 C2
Struthers U.S.A. 41°4N 80°39W 354 E4
Stryker U.S.A. 48°41N 114°46W 348 B6
Stryy Ukraine 49°16N 23°48E 289 D12
Strzelecki Cr. → Australia 29°37S 139°59E 335 D2
Strzelecki Desert Australia 29°30S 140°0E 335 D3
Stuart Fla., U.S.A. 27°12N 80°15W 357 H14
Stuart Nebr., U.S.A. 42°36N 99°8W 352 D4
Stuart → Canada 54°0N 123°35W 342 C4
Stuart Bluff Ra. Australia 22°50S 131°52E 332 D5
Stuart L. Canada 54°30N 124°30W 342 C4
Stuart Ra. Australia 29°10S 134°56E 335 D1
Stull L. Canada 54°24N 92°34W 344 B1
Stung Treng = Stoeng Treng Cambodia 13°31N 105°58E 310 F5
Stupart → Canada 56°0N 93°25W 344 A1
Sturgeon B. Canada 52°0N 97°50W 343 C9
Sturgeon Bay U.S.A. 44°50N 87°23W 352 C10
Sturgeon Falls Canada 46°25N 79°57W 344 C4
Sturgeon L. Alta., Canada 55°6N 117°32W 342 B5
Sturgeon L. Ont., Canada 50°0N 90°45W 344 C1
Sturgeon L. Ont., Canada 44°28N 78°43W 354 B6
Sturgis Canada 51°56N 102°36W 343 C8
Sturgis Mich., U.S.A. 41°48N 85°25W 353 E11
Sturgis S. Dak., U.S.A. 44°25N 103°31W 352 C2
Sturt △ Australia 27°17S 141°37E 335 D3
Sturt Cr. → Australia 19°8S 127°50E 332 C4
Sturt Stony Desert Australia 28°30S 141°0E 335 D3
Stutterheim S. Africa 32°33S 27°28E 328 E4
Stuttgart Germany 48°48N 9°11E 288 D5
Stuttgart U.S.A. 34°30N 91°33W 356 D9
Stuyvesant U.S.A. 42°23N 73°45W 355 D11
Stykkishólmur Iceland 65°2N 22°40W 280 D2
Styria = Steiermark □ Austria 47°26N 15°0E 288 E8
Su Xian = Suzhou China 33°41N 116°59E 306 H9
Suakin Sudan 19°8N 37°20E 323 E13
Suan N. Korea 38°42N 126°22E 307 E14
Suar India 29°2N 79°3E 315 E8
Subang Indonesia 6°34S 107°45E 309 G12
Subansiri → India 26°48N 93°50E 313 F18
Subarnarekha → India 22°34N 87°24E 315 H12
Subayhah Si. Arabia 30°2N 38°50E 316 D3
Subi Indonesia 2°58N 108°50E 308 D3
Subotica Serbia 46°6N 19°39E 295 A8
Suceava Romania 47°38N 26°16E 289 E14
Suchan = Partizansk Russia 43°8N 133°9E 302 C6
Suchil Mexico 23°38N 103°55W 358 C4
Suchitoto El Salv. 13°56N 89°0W 360 D2
Suchou = Suzhou China 31°19N 120°38E 305 C7
Süchow = Xuzhou China 34°18N 117°10E 307 G9
Suck → Ireland 53°17N 8°3W 282 C3
Sucre Bolivia 19°0S 65°15W 364 G5
Sucuriú → Brazil 20°47S 51°38W 365 H8
Sud, Pte. du Canada 49°3N 62°14W 345 C7
Sud-Kivu □ Dem. Rep. of the Congo 3°0S 28°30E 326 C2
Sud-Ouest, Pte. Canada 49°23N 63°36W 345 C7
Sud-Ouest, Pte. Mauritius 20°28S 57°18E 325 d
Sudan U.S.A. 34°4N 102°31W 356 D3
Sudan ■ Africa 15°0N 30°0E 323 E11
Sudbury Canada 46°30N 81°0W 344 C3
Sudbury U.K. 52°2N 0°45E 285 E8
Sûdd Sudan 8°20N 30°0E 323 G12
Sudeten Mts. = Sudety Europe 50°20N 16°45E 289 C9
Sudety Europe 50°20N 16°45E 289 C9
Suðuroy Færoe Is. 61°32N 6°50W 280 F9
Sudi Tanzania 10°11S 39°57E 327 E4
Sudirman, Pegunungan Indonesia 4°30S 137°0E 309 E9
Sudong, Pulau Singapore 1°13N 103°44E 311 d
Sueca Spain 39°12N 0°21W 293 C5
Suemez I. U.S.A. 55°15N 133°20W 342 B2
Suez = El Suweis Egypt 29°58N 32°31E 323 C12
Suez, G. of = Suweis, Khalîg el Egypt 28°40N 33°0E 323 C12
Suez Canal = Suweis, Qanâ es Egypt 31°0N 32°20E 323 B12
Suffield Canada 50°12N 111°10W 342 C6
Suffolk U.S.A. 36°44N 76°35W 353 G15
Suffolk □ U.K. 52°16N 1°0E 285 E9
Sugar Grove U.S.A. 41°59N 79°20W 354 E5
Sugarive → India 26°16N 86°24E 315 F12
Sugluk = Salluit Canada 62°14N 75°38W 341 C12
Şuḩār Oman 24°20N 56°40E 317 E8
Sühbaatar □ Mongolia 45°30N 114°0E 306 B8
Suhl Germany 50°36N 10°42E 288 C6
Sui Pakistan 28°37N 69°19E 314 E3
Sui Xian China 34°25N 115°2E 306 G8
Suide China 37°30N 110°12E 306 F6
Suifenhe China 44°25N 131°10E 307 B16
Suihua China 46°32N 126°55E 305 B7
Suining Jiangsu, China 33°56N 117°58E 307 H9
Suining Sichuan, China 30°26N 105°35E 304 C5
Suiping China 33°10N 113°59E 306 H7
Suir → Ireland 52°16N 7°9W 282 D4
Suisse = Switzerland ■ Europe 46°30N 8°0E 292 C8
Suisun City U.S.A. 38°15N 122°2W 350 G4
Suiyang China 44°30N 130°56E 307 B16
Suizhong China 40°21N 120°20E 307 D11
Sujangarh India 27°42N 74°31E 314 F6
Sukabumi Indonesia 6°56S 106°50E 309 G12
Sukadana Indonesia 1°10S 110°0E 308 E3
Sukagawa Japan 37°17N 140°23E 303 F10
Sukaraja Indonesia 2°28S 110°25E 308 E4
Sukawati Indonesia 8°35S 115°17E 309 K18
Sukch'ŏn N. Korea 39°22N 125°35E 307 E13
Sukhona → Russia 61°15N 46°39E 290 C6
Sukhothai Thailand 17°1N 99°49E 310 D2
Sukhumi = Sokhumi Georgia 43°0N 41°0E 291 F7
Sukkur Pakistan 27°42N 68°54E 314 F3
Sukkur Barrage Pakistan 27°40N 68°50E 314 F3
Sukri → India 25°4N 71°43E 314 G4
Sukumo Japan 32°56N 132°44E 303 H6
Sukunka → Canada 55°45N 121°15W 342 B4
Sula, Kepulauan Indonesia 1°45S 125°0E 309 E7
Sulaco → Honduras 15°2N 87°44W 360 C2
Sulaiman Range Pakistan 30°30N 69°50E 314 D3
Sūlār Iran 31°53N 51°54E 317 D6
Sulawesi Barat □ Indonesia 3°0S 119°0E 309 E5
Sulawesi Sea = Celebes Sea Indonesia 3°0N 123°0E 309 D6
Sulawesi Selatan □ Indonesia 2°30S 120°0E 309 E6
Sulawesi Tengah □ Indonesia 1°30S 121°0E 309 E6
Sulawesi Tenggara □ Indonesia 3°50S 122°0E 309 E6
Sulawesi Utara □ Indonesia 1°0N 124°0E 309 D6
Sulima S. Leone 6°58N 11°32W 322 G3
Sulina Romania 45°10N 29°40E 289 F15
Sulitjelma Norway 67°9N 16°3E 280 C17
Sullana Peru 4°52S 80°39W 364 D2
Sullivan Ill., U.S.A. 39°36N 88°37W 352 F9
Sullivan Ind., U.S.A. 39°6N 87°24W 352 F10
Sullivan Mo., U.S.A. 38°13N 91°10W 352 F8
Sullivan Bay Canada 50°55N 126°50W 342 C3
Sullivan I. = Lanbi Kyun Burma 10°50N 98°20E 311 G2
Sullom Voe U.K. 60°27N 1°20W 283 A7
Sulphur La., U.S.A. 30°14N 93°23W 356 F8
Sulphur Okla., U.S.A. 34°31N 96°58W 356 D6
Sulphur Pt. Canada 60°56N 114°48W 342 A6
Sulphur Springs U.S.A. 33°8N 95°36W 356 E7
Sultan Canada 47°36N 82°47W 344 C3
Sultan U.S.A. 47°52N 121°49W 350 C5
Sultan Hamud Kenya 2°1S 37°22E 326 C4
Sultanpur Mad. P., India 23°9N 77°56E 314 H8
Sultanpur Punjab, India 31°13N 75°11E 314 D6
Sultanpur Ut. P., India 26°18N 82°4E 315 F10
Sulu Arch. Phil. 6°0N 121°0E 309 C6
Sulu Sea E. Indies 8°0N 120°0E 309 C6
Suluq Libya 31°44N 20°14E 323 B10
Sulzberger Ice Shelf Antarctica 78°0S 150°0W 277 E13
Sumalata Indonesia 1°0N 122°31E 309 D6
Sumampa Argentina 29°25S 63°29W 366 B3
Sumatera Indonesia 0°40N 100°20E 308 D2
Sumatera Barat □ Indonesia 1°0S 101°0E 308 E2
Sumatera Utara □ Indonesia 2°30N 98°0E 308 D1
Sumatra = Sumatera Indonesia 0°40N 100°20E 308 D2
Sumba Indonesia 9°45S 119°35E 309 F5
Sumba, Selat Indonesia 9°0S 118°40E 309 F5
Sumbawa Indonesia 8°26S 117°30E 308 F5
Sumbawa Besar Indonesia 8°30S 117°26E 308 F5
Sumbawanga □ Tanzania 8°0S 31°30E 324 F6
Sumbe Angola 11°10S 13°48E 324 G2
Sumbu △ Zambia 8°43S 30°22E 327 D3
Sumburgh Hd. U.K. 59°52N 1°17W 283 B7
Sumdeo India 31°26N 78°44E 315 D8
Sumdo China 35°6N 78°41E 315 B8
Sumedang Indonesia 6°52S 107°55E 309 G12
Šumen = Shumen Bulgaria 43°18N 26°55E 295 C12
Sumenep Indonesia 7°1S 113°52E 309 G15
Sumgait = Sumqayıt Azerbaijan 40°34N 49°38E 291 F8
Summer L. U.S.A. 42°50N 120°45W 348 E3
Summerland Canada 49°32N 119°41W 342 D5
Summerside Canada 46°24N 63°47W 345 C7
Summersville U.S.A. 38°17N 80°51W 353 F13
Summerville Ga., U.S.A. 34°29N 85°21W 357 D12
Summerville S.C., U.S.A. 33°1N 80°11W 357 E14
Summit Lake Canada 54°20N 122°40W 342 C4
Summit Peak U.S.A. 37°21N 106°42W 349 H10
Sumner Iowa, U.S.A. 42°51N 92°6W 352 D7
Sumner Wash., U.S.A. 47°12N 122°14W 350 C4
Sumoto Japan 34°21N 134°54E 303 G7
Šumperk Czech Rep. 49°59N 16°59E 289 D9
Sumqayıt Azerbaijan 40°34N 49°38E 291 F8
Sumter U.S.A. 33°55N 80°21W 357 E14
Sumy Ukraine 50°57N 34°50E 291 D5
Sun City S. Africa 25°17S 27°3E 328 D4
Sun City Ariz., U.S.A. 33°35N 112°16W 349 K7
Sun City Calif., U.S.A. 33°42N 117°11W 351 M9
Sun City Center U.S.A. 27°43N 82°21W 357 H13
Sun Lakes U.S.A. 33°10N 111°52W 349 K8
Sun Valley U.S.A. 43°42N 114°21W 348 E6
Sunagawa Japan 43°29N 141°55E 302 C10
Sunan N. Korea 39°15N 125°40E 307 E13
Sunart, L. U.K. 56°42N 5°43W 283 E3
Sunburst U.S.A. 48°53N 111°55W 348 B8
Sunbury Australia 37°35S 144°44E 335 F3
Sunbury U.S.A. 40°52N 76°48W 355 F8
Sunchales Argentina 30°58S 61°35W 366 C3
Suncheon S. Korea 34°52N 127°31E 307 G14
Suncho Corral Argentina 27°55S 63°27W 366 B3
Sunch'on N. Korea 39°25N 125°56E 307 E13
Suncook U.S.A. 43°8N 71°27W 355 C13
Sunda, Selat Indonesia 6°20S 105°30E 308 F3
Sunda Is. Indonesia 5°0S 105°0E 336 H2
Sunda Str. = Sunda, Selat Indonesia 6°20S 105°30E 308 F3
Sunda Trench = Java Trench Ind. Oc. 9°0S 105°0E 308 F3
Sundance Canada 56°32N 94°4W 343 B10
Sundance U.S.A. 44°24N 104°23W 348 D11
Sundar Nagar India 31°32N 76°53E 314 D7
Sundarbans Asia 22°0N 89°0E 313 J16
Sundarbans △ India 22°0N 88°45E 315 J13
Sundargarh India 22°4N 84°5E 313 H14
Sundays = Sondags → S. Africa 33°44S 25°51E 328 E4
Sunderland Canada 44°16N 79°4W 354 B5
Sunderland U.K. 54°55N 1°23W 284 C6
Sundown △ Australia 28°49S 151°38E 335 D5
Sundre Canada 51°49N 114°38W 342 C6
Sundsvall Sweden 62°23N 17°17E 280 E17
Sung Hei Vietnam 10°20N 106°2E 311 G6
Sungai Acheh Malaysia 5°8N 100°30E 311 c
Sungai Kolok Thailand 6°2N 101°58E 311 J3
Sungai Lembing Malaysia 3°55N 103°3E 311 L4
Sungai Petani Malaysia 5°37N 100°30E 311 K3
Sungaigerong Indonesia 2°59S 104°52E 308 E2
Sungailiat Indonesia 1°51S 106°8E 308 E3
Sungaipenuh Indonesia 2°1S 101°20E 308 E2
Sungari = Songhua Jiang →

China 47°45N 132°30E 305 B8
Sunghua Chiang = Songhua Jiang → China 47°45N 132°30E 305 B8
Sunland Park U.S.A. 31°50N 106°40W 349 L10
Sunndalsøra Norway 62°40N 8°33E 280 E13
Sunnyside U.S.A. 46°20N 120°0W 348 C4
Sunnyvale U.S.A. 37°23N 122°2W 350 H4
Sunrise Manor U.S.A. 36°12N 115°4W 351 J11
Suntar Russia 62°15N 117°30E 301 C12
Suomenselkä Finland 62°52N 24°0E 280 E21
Suomi = Finland ■ Europe 63°0N 27°0E 280 E22
Suomussalmi Finland 64°54N 29°10E 280 D23
Suoyarvi Russia 62°3N 32°20E 290 B5
Supai U.S.A. 36°15N 112°41W 349 H7
Supaul India 26°10N 86°40E 315 F12
Superior Ariz., U.S.A. 33°18N 111°6W 349 K8
Superior Mont., U.S.A. 47°12N 114°53W 348 C6
Superior Nebr., U.S.A. 40°1N 98°4W 352 E4
Superior Wis., U.S.A. 46°44N 92°6W 352 B7
Superior, L. N. Amer. 47°0N 87°0W 344 C2
Suphan Buri Thailand 14°14N 100°10E 310 E3
Suphan Dağı Turkey 38°54N 42°48E 316 B4
Supiori Indonesia 1°0S 136°0E 309 E9
Supung Shuiku China 40°35N 124°50E 307 D13
Sūq Suwayq Si. Arabia 24°23N 38°27E 316 E3
Suqian China 33°54N 118°8E 307 H10
Suquṭra = Socotra Yemen 12°30N 54°0E 319 E5
Sūr Lebanon 33°19N 35°16E 318 B4
Şūr Oman 22°34N 59°32E 319 C6
Sur, Pt. U.S.A. 36°18N 121°54W 350 J5
Sura → Russia 56°6N 46°0E 290 C8
Surab Pakistan 28°25N 66°15E 314 E2
Surabaja = Surabaya Indonesia 7°17S 112°45E 308 F4
Surabaya Indonesia 7°17S 112°45E 308 F4
Surakarta Indonesia 7°35S 110°48E 308 F4
Surat Australia 27°10S 149°6E 335 D4
Surat India 21°12N 72°55E 312 J8
Surat Thani Thailand 9°6N 99°20E 311 H2
Suratgarh India 29°18N 73°55E 314 E5
Surendranagar India 22°45N 71°40E 314 H4
Surf U.S.A. 34°41N 120°36W 351 L6
Surfers Paradise Australia 28°0S 153°25E 335 D5
Surgut Russia 61°14N 73°20E 300 C8
Suriapet India 17°10N 79°40E 312 L11
Surigao Phil. 9°47N 125°29E 309 C7
Surin Thailand 14°50N 103°34E 310 E4
Surin Nua, Ko Thailand 9°30N 97°55E 311 H1
Surinam = Suriname ■ S. Amer. 4°0N 56°0W 365 C7
Suriname ■ S. Amer. 4°0N 56°0W 365 C7
Suriname → Suriname 5°50N 55°15W 365 B7
Sūrmaq Iran 31°3N 52°48E 317 D7
Surrey Canada 49°7N 122°45W 350 A4
Surrey □ U.K. 51°15N 0°31W 285 F7
Sursand India 26°39N 85°43E 315 F11
Sursar → India 26°14N 87°3E 315 F12
Surt Libya 31°11N 16°39E 323 B9
Surt, Khalīj Libya 31°40N 18°30E 323 B9
Surtanahu Pakistan 26°22N 70°0E 314 F4
Surtsey Iceland 63°20N 20°30W 280 E3
Suruga-Wan Japan 34°45N 138°30E 303 G9
Susaki Japan 33°22N 133°17E 303 H6
Sūsangerd Iran 31°35N 48°6E 317 D6
Susanville U.S.A. 40°25N 120°39W 348 F3
Susner India 23°57N 76°5E 314 H7
Susquehanna U.S.A. 41°57N 75°36W 355 E9
Susquehanna → U.S.A. 39°33N 76°5W 355 G8
Susques Argentina 23°35S 66°25W 366 A2
Sussex Canada 45°45N 65°37W 345 C6
Sussex U.S.A. 41°13N 74°37W 355 E10
Sussex, E. □ U.K. 51°0N 0°20E 285 G8
Sussex, W. □ U.K. 51°0N 0°30W 285 G7
Sustut → Canada 56°20N 127°30W 342 B3
Susuman Russia 62°47N 148°10E 301 C15
Susunu Indonesia 3°7S 133°39E 309 E8
Susurluk Turkey 39°54N 28°8E 295 E13
Sutherland S. Africa 32°24S 20°40E 328 E3
Sutherland U.K. 58°12N 4°50W 283 C4
Sutherland U.S.A. 41°10N 101°8W 352 E3
Sutherland Falls N.Z. 44°48S 167°46E 331 F1
Sutherlin U.S.A. 43°23N 123°19W 348 E2
Suthri India 23°3N 68°55E 314 H3
Sutlej → Pakistan 29°23N 71°3E 314 E4
Sutter U.S.A. 39°10N 121°45W 350 F5
Sutter Buttes U.S.A. 39°12N 121°49W 350 F5
Sutter Creek U.S.A. 38°24N 120°48W 350 G6
Sutton Canada 45°6N 72°37W 355 A12
Sutton Nebr., U.S.A. 40°36N 97°52W 352 E5
Sutton W. Va., U.S.A. 38°40N 80°43W 353 F13
Sutton → Canada 55°15N 83°45W 344 A3
Sutton Coldfield U.K. 52°35N 1°49W 285 E6
Sutton in Ashfield U.K. 53°8N 1°16W 284 D6
Sutton L. Canada 54°15N 84°42W 344 B3
Suttor → Australia 21°36S 147°2E 334 C4
Suttsu Japan 42°48N 140°14E 302 C10
Suva Fiji 18°6S 178°30E 331 a
Suva Planina Serbia 43°10N 22°5E 295 C10
Suvorov Is. = Suwarrow Is. Cook Is. 13°15S 163°5W 337 J11
Suwałki Poland 54°8N 22°59E 289 A12
Suwana Indonesia 8°44S 115°36E 309 K18
Suwannaphum Thailand 15°33N 103°47E 310 E4
Suwannee → U.S.A. 29°17N 83°10W 357 G13
Suwanose-Jima Japan 29°38N 129°43E 303 K4
Suwarrow Is. Cook Is. 13°15S 163°5W 337 J11
Suwayq aş Şuqban Iraq 31°32N 46°7E 316 D5
Suweis, Khalîg el Egypt 28°40N 33°0E 323 C12
Suweis, Qanâ es Egypt 31°0N 32°20E 323 B12
Suwon S. Korea 37°17N 127°1E 307 F14
Suzdal Russia 56°29N 40°26E 290 C7
Suzhou Anhui, China 33°41N 116°59E 306 H9
Suzhou Jiangsu, China 31°19N 120°38E 305 C7
Suzu Japan 37°25N 137°17E 303 F8
Suzu-Misaki Japan 37°31N 137°21E 303 F8
Suzuka Japan 34°55N 136°36E 303 G8
Svalbard Arctic 78°0N 17°0E 276 B8
Svalbard Radio = Longyearbyen Svalbard 78°13N 15°40E 276 B8
Svappavaara Sweden 67°40N 21°3E 280 C19
Svartisen Norway 66°40N 13°59E 280 C15
Svay Chek Cambodia 13°48N 102°58E 310 F4
Svay Rieng Cambodia 11°9N 105°45E 311 G5
Svealand □ Sweden 60°20N 15°0E 281 F16
Sveg Sweden 62°2N 14°21E 280 E16
Svendborg Denmark 55°4N 10°35E 281 J14
Sverdrup Chan. Canada 79°56N 96°25W 341 B10
Sverdrup Is. Canada 79°0N 97°0W 341 B10
Sverige = Sweden ■ Europe 57°0N 15°0E 281 H16
Svetlaya Russia 46°33N 138°18E 302 A9
Svetlogorsk = Svyetlahorsk Belarus 52°38N 29°46E 289 B15
Svir → Russia 60°30N 32°48E 290 B5
Svishtov Bulgaria 43°36N 25°23E 295 C11
Svislach Belarus 53°3N 24°2E 289 B13
Svizzera = Switzerland ■ Europe 46°30N 8°0E 292 C8
Svobodnyy Russia 51°20N 128°0E 301 D13
Svolvær Norway 68°15N 14°34E 280 B16
Svyetlahorsk Belarus 52°38N 29°46E 289 B15
Swabian Alps = Schwäbische Alb Germany 48°20N 9°30E 288 D5
Swaffham U.K. 52°39N 0°42E 285 E8
Swains I. Amer. Samoa 11°11S 171°4W 337 J11
Swainsboro U.S.A. 32°36N 82°20W 357 E13
Swakop → Namibia 22°38S 14°36E 328 C2
Swakopmund Namibia 22°37S 14°30E 328 C1
Swale → U.K. 54°5N 1°20W 284 C6
Swan → Australia 32°3S 115°45E 333 F2
Swan → Canada 52°30N 100°45W 343 C8
Swan Hill Australia 35°20S 143°33E 335 F3
Swan Hills Canada 54°43N 115°24W 342 C5
Swan Is. = Santanilla, Is. Honduras 17°22N 83°57W 360 C3
Swan L. Canada 52°30N 100°40W 343 C8
Swan Ra. U.S.A. 48°0N 113°45W 348 C7
Swan River Canada 52°10N 101°16W 343 C8
Swanage U.K. 50°36N 1°58W 285 G6
Swansea Australia 42°8S 148°4E 335 G4
Swansea Canada 43°38N 79°28W 354 C5
Swansea U.K. 51°37N 3°57W 285 F4
Swansea □ U.K. 51°38N 4°3W 285 F3
Swar → Pakistan 34°40N 72°5E 315 B5
Swartberge S. Africa 33°20S 22°0E 328 E3
Swartmodder S. Africa 28°1S 20°32E 328 D3
Swartnossob → Namibia 23°8S 18°42E 328 C2
Swartruggens S. Africa 25°39S 26°42E 328 D4
Swastika Canada 48°7N 80°6W 344 C3
Swatow = Shantou China 23°18N 116°40E 305 D6
Swaziland ■ Africa 26°30S 31°30E 329 D5
Sweden ■ Europe 57°0N 15°0E 281 H16
Sweet Grass U.S.A. 48°59N 111°58W 348 B8
Sweet Home U.S.A. 44°24N 122°44W 348 D2
Sweetwater Nev., U.S.A. 38°27N 119°9W 350 G7
Sweetwater Tenn., U.S.A. 35°36N 84°28W 357 D12
Sweetwater Tex., U.S.A. 32°28N 100°25W 356 E4
Sweetwater → U.S.A. 42°31N 107°2W 348 E10
Swellendam S. Africa 34°1S 20°26E 328 E3
Świdnica Poland 50°50N 16°30E 289 C9
Świdnik Poland 51°13N 22°39E 289 C12
Świebodzin Poland 52°15N 15°31E 288 B8
Świecie Poland 53°25N 18°30E 289 B10
Swift Current Canada 50°20N 107°45W 343 C7
Swiftcurrent → Canada 50°38N 107°44W 343 C7
Swilly, L. Ireland 55°12N 7°33W 282 A4
Swindon U.K. 51°34N 1°46W 285 F6
Swindon □ U.K. 51°34N 1°46W 285 F6
Swinemünde = Świnoujście Poland 53°54N 14°16E 288 B8
Swinford Ireland 53°57N 8°58W 282 C3
Świnoujście Poland 53°54N 14°16E 288 B8
Switzerland ■ Europe 46°30N 8°0E 292 C8
Swords Ireland 53°28N 6°13W 282 C5
Swoyerville U.S.A. 41°18N 75°53W 355 E9
Sydenham → Canada 42°33N 82°25W 354 D2
Sydney Australia 33°52S 151°12E 335 E5
Sydney Canada 46°7N 60°7W 345 C7
Sydney L. Canada 50°41N 94°25W 343 C10
Sydney Mines Canada 46°18N 60°15W 345 C7
Sydprøven = Alluitsup Paa Greenland 60°30N 45°35W 276 C5
Sydra, G. of = Surt, Khalīj Libya 31°40N 18°30E 323 B9
Sykesville U.S.A. 41°3N 78°50W 354 E6
Syktyvkar Russia 61°45N 50°40E 290 B9
Sylacauga U.S.A. 33°10N 86°15W 357 E11
Sylarna Sweden 63°2N 12°13E 280 E15
Sylhet Bangla. 24°54N 91°52E 313 G17
Sylhet □ Bangla. 24°50N 91°50E 313 G17
Sylt Germany 54°54N 8°22E 288 A5
Sylvan Beach U.S.A. 43°12N 75°44W 355 C9
Sylvan Lake Canada 52°20N 114°3W 342 C6
Sylvania Ga., U.S.A. 32°45N 81°38W 357 E14
Sylvania Ohio, U.S.A. 41°43N 83°42W 353 E12
Sylvester U.S.A. 31°32N 83°50W 357 F13
Sym Russia 60°20N 88°18E 300 C9
Synnot Ra. Australia 16°30S 125°20E 332 C4
Syowa Antarctica 68°50S 12°0E 277 C5
Syracuse Kans., U.S.A. 37°59N 101°45W 352 G3
Syracuse N.Y., U.S.A. 43°3N 76°9W 355 C8
Syracuse Nebr., U.S.A. 40°39N 96°11W 352 E5
Syrdarya → Kazakhstan 46°3N 61°0E 300 E7
Syria ■ Asia 35°0N 38°0E 316 C3
Syrian Desert = Shām, Bādiyat ash Asia 32°0N 40°0E 316 C3
Syros Greece 37°28N 24°57E 295 F11
Syzran Russia 53°12N 48°30E 290 D8
Szczecin Poland 53°27N 14°27E 288 B8
Szczecinek Poland 53°43N 16°41E 289 B9
Szczeciński, Zalew = Stettiner Haff Germany 53°47N 14°15E 288 B8
Szczytno Poland 53°33N 21°0E 289 B11
Szechwan = Sichuan □ China 30°30N 103°0E 304 C5
Szeged Hungary 46°16N 20°10E 289 E11
Székesfehérvár Hungary 47°15N 18°25E 289 E10
Szekszárd Hungary 46°22N 18°42E 289 E10
Szentes Hungary 46°39N 20°21E 289 E11
Szolnok Hungary 47°10N 20°15E 289 E11
Szombathely Hungary 47°14N 16°38E 289 E9

T

Ta Khli Khok Thailand 15°18N 100°20E 310 E3
Ta Lai Vietnam 11°24N 107°23E 311 G6
Tabacal Argentina 23°15S 64°15W 366 A3
Tabaco Phil. 13°22N 123°44E 309 B6
Ţābah Si. Arabia 26°55N 42°38E 316 E4
Tabanan Indonesia 8°32S 115°8E 309 K18
Ţabas Khorāsān, Iran 32°48N 60°12E 317 C9
Ţabas Yazd, Iran 33°35N 56°55E 317 C8
Tabasará, Serranía de Panama 8°35N 81°40W 360 E3
Tabasco □ Mexico 18°0N 92°40W 359 D6
Tabāsīn Iran 31°12N 57°54E 317 D8
Tabatinga, Serra da Brazil 10°30S 44°0W 365 F10
Taber Canada 49°47N 112°8W 342 D6
Taberg U.S.A. 43°18N 75°37W 355 C9
Tablas Phil. 12°25N 122°2E 309 B6
Table, Pte. de la Réunion 21°14S 55°48E 325 c
Table B. Canada 53°40N 56°25W 345 B8
Table B. S. Africa 33°35S 18°25E 328 E2
Table Mt. S. Africa 33°58S 18°26E 328 E2
Table Rock L. U.S.A. 36°36N 93°19W 352 G7
Tabletop, Mt. Australia 23°24S 147°11E 334 C4
Tábor Czech Rep. 49°25N 14°39E 288 D8
Tabora Tanzania 5°2S 32°50E 326 D3
Tabora □ Tanzania 5°0S 33°0E 326 D3
Tabou Ivory C. 4°30N 7°20W 322 H4
Tabrīz Iran 38°7N 46°20E 316 B5
Tabuaeran Kiribati 3°51N 159°22W 337 G12
Tabūk Si. Arabia 28°23N 36°36E 316 D3
Tabūk □ Si. Arabia 27°40N 36°50E 316 E3
Tacámbaro de Codallos Mexico 19°14N 101°28W 358 D4
Tacheng China 46°40N 82°58E 304 B3
Tach'ing Shan = Daqing Shan China 40°40N 111°0E 306 D6
Tacloban Phil. 11°15N 124°58E 309 B6
Tacna Peru 18°0S 70°20W 364 G4
Tacoma U.S.A. 47°14N 122°26W 350 C4
Tacuarembó Uruguay 31°45S 56°0W 367 C4
Tademaït, Plateau du Algeria 28°30N 2°30E 322 C6
Tadjoura Djibouti 11°50N 42°55E 319 E3
Tadmor N.Z. 41°27S 172°45E 331 D4
Tadoule L. Canada 58°36N 98°20W 343 B9
Tadoussac Canada 48°11N 69°42W 345 C6
Tadzhikistan = Tajikistan ■ Asia 38°30N 70°0E 300 F8
Taegu = Daegu S. Korea 35°50N 128°37E 307 G15
Taegwan N. Korea 40°13N 125°12E 307 D13
Taejŏn = Daejeon S. Korea 36°20N 127°28E 307 F14
Taen, Ko Thailand 9°22N 99°57E 311 b
Tafalla Spain 42°30N 1°41W 293 A5
Tafelbaai = Table B. S. Africa 33°35S 18°25E 328 E2
Tafermaar Indonesia 6°47S 134°10E 309 F8
Tafí Viejo Argentina 26°43S 65°17W 366 B2
Tafīhān Iran 29°25N 52°39E 317 D7
Tafresh Iran 34°45N 49°57E 317 C6
Taft Iran 31°45N 54°14E 317 D7
Taft Phil. 11°57N 125°30E 309 B7
Taft U.S.A. 35°8N 119°28W 351 K7
Taftan Pakistan 29°0N 61°30E 312 E2
Taftān, Kūh-e Iran 28°40N 61°0E 317 D9
Taga Samoa 13°46S 172°28W 331 b
Taga Dzong Bhutan 27°5N 89°55E 313 F16
Taganrog Russia 47°12N 38°50E 291 E6
Tagbilaran Phil. 9°39N 123°51E 309 C6
Tagish Canada 60°19N 134°16W 342 A2
Tagish L. Canada 60°10N 134°20W 342 A2
Tagliamento → Italy 45°38N 13°6E 294 B5
Tagomago Spain 39°2N 1°39E 296 B8
Taguatinga Brazil 12°27S 46°22W 365 F10
Tagum Phil. 7°33N 125°53E 309 C7
Tagus = Tejo → Europe 38°40N 9°24W 293 C1
Tahakopa N.Z. 46°30S 169°23E 331 G2
Tahan, Gunung Malaysia 4°34N 102°17E 311 K4
Tahat Algeria 23°18N 5°33E 322 D7
Tāherī Iran 27°43N 52°20E 317 E7
Tahiti French Polynesia 17°37S 149°27W 331 d
Tahiti, I. Tahiti 17°37S 149°27W 331 d
Tahlequah U.S.A. 35°55N 94°58W 356 D7
Tahoe, L. U.S.A. 39°6N 120°2W 350 G6
Tahoe City U.S.A. 39°10N 120°9W 350 F6
Tahoka U.S.A. 33°10N 101°48W 356 E4
Taholah U.S.A. 47°21N 124°17W 350 C2
Tahoua Niger 14°57N 5°16E 322 F7
Tahrūd Iran 29°26N 57°49E 317 D8
Tahsis Canada 49°55N 126°40W 342 D3
Tahta Egypt 26°44N 31°32E 323 C12
Tahulandang Indonesia 2°27N 125°23E 309 D7
Tahuna Indonesia 3°38N 125°30E 309 D7
Tai Au Mun China 22°18N 114°17E 305 G11
Tai Mo Shan China 22°25N 114°7E 305 G11
Tai O China 22°15N 113°52E 305 G10
Tai Pang Wan China 22°33N 114°24E 305 F11
Tai Po China 22°27N 114°10E 305 G11
Tai Rom Yen △ Thailand 8°45N 99°30E 311 H2
Tai Shan China 36°25N 117°20E 307 F9
Tai Yue Shan = Lantau I. China 22°15N 113°56E 305 G10
Tai'an China 36°12N 117°8E 307 F9
Taiarapu, Presqu'île de Tahiti 17°47S 149°14W 331 d
Taibei = T'aipei Taiwan 25°4N 121°29E 305 D7
Taibique Canary Is. 27°42N 17°58W 296 G2
Taibus Qi China 41°54N 115°22E 306 D8
T'aichung Taiwan 24°9N 120°37E 305 D7
Taieri → N.Z. 46°3S 170°12E 331 G3
Taigu China 37°28N 112°30E 306 F7
Taihang Shan China 36°0N 113°30E 306 G7
Taihape N.Z. 39°41S 175°48E 331 C5
Taihe China 33°20N 115°42E 306 H8
Taikang China 34°5N 114°50E 306 G8
Tailem Bend Australia 35°12S 139°29E 335 F2
Taimyr Peninsula = Taymyr, Poluostrov Russia 75°0N 100°0E 301 B11
Tain U.K. 57°49N 4°4W 283 D4
T'ainan Taiwan 23°0N 120°10E 305 D7
Taipa China 22°10N 113°35E 305 G10
T'aipei Taiwan 25°4N 121°29E 305 D7
Taiping Malaysia 4°51N 100°44E 311 K3
Taipingzhen China 33°35N 111°42E 306 H6
Tairbeart = Tarbert U.K. 57°54N 6°49W 283 D2
Taita Hills Kenya 3°25S 38°15E 326 C4
Taitao, Pen. de Chile 46°30S 75°0W 368 F2
T'aitung Taiwan 22°43N 121°4E 305 D7
Taivalkoski Finland 65°33N 28°12E 280 D23
Taiwan ■ Asia 23°30N 121°0E 305 D7
Taiyiba Israel 32°36N 35°27E 318 C4
Taiyuan China 37°52N 112°33E 306 F7
Taizhong = T'aichung Taiwan 24°9N 120°37E 305 D7
Ta'izz Yemen 13°35N 44°2E 319 E3
Tājābād Iran 30°2N 54°24E 317 D7
Tajikistan ■ Asia 38°30N 70°0E 300 F8
Tajima Japan 37°12N 139°46E 303 F9
Tajo = Tejo → Europe 38°40N 9°24W 293 C1
Tajrīsh Iran 35°48N 51°25E 317 C6
Tak Thailand 16°52N 99°8E 310 D2
Takāb Iran 36°24N 47°7E 316 B5
Takachiho Japan 32°42N 131°18E 303 H5
Takachu Botswana 22°37S 21°58E 328 C3
Takada Japan 37°7N 138°15E 303 F9
Takahagi Japan 36°43N 140°45E 303 F10
Takaka N.Z. 40°51S 172°50E 331 D4
Takamaka Seychelles 4°50S 55°30E 325 b
Takamatsu Japan 34°20N 134°5E 303 G7
Takaoka Japan 36°47N 137°0E 303 F8
Takapuna N.Z. 36°47S 174°47E 331 B5
Takasaki Japan 36°20N 139°0E 303 F9
Takatsuki Japan 34°51N 135°37E 303 G7
Takaungu Kenya 3°38S 39°52E 326 C4
Takayama Japan 36°18N 137°11E 303 F8
Take-Shima Japan 30°49N 130°26E 303 J5
Takefu Japan 35°50N 136°10E 303 G8
Takengon Indonesia 4°45N 96°50E 308 D1
Takeo Japan 33°12N 130°1E 303 H5
Takeshima = Tok-do Asia 37°15N 131°52E 303 F5
Tākestān Iran 36°0N 49°40E 317 C6
Taketa Japan 32°58N 131°24E 303 H5
Takev Cambodia 10°59N 104°47E 311 G5
Takh India 33°6N 77°32E 315 C7
Takht-Sulaiman Pakistan 31°40N 69°58E 314 D3
Takikawa Japan 43°33N 141°54E 302 C10
Takla L. Canada 55°15N 125°45W 342 B3
Takla Landing Canada 55°30N 125°50W 342 B3
Takla Makan China 38°0N 83°0E 304 C3
Taklamakan Shamo = Takla Makan China 38°0N 83°0E 304 C3
Taku → Canada 58°30N 133°50W 342 B2
Takua Thung Thailand 8°24N 98°27E 311 a
Tal Halāl Iran 28°54N 55°1E 317 D7
Tala Uruguay 34°21S 55°46W 367 C4
Talagang Pakistan 32°55N 72°25E 314 C5
Talagante Chile 33°40S 70°50W 366 C1
Talamanca, Cordillera de Cent. Amer. 9°20N 83°20W 360 E3
Talara Peru 4°38S 81°18W 364 D2
Talas Kyrgyzstan 42°30N 72°13E 300 E8
Talâta Egypt 30°36N 32°20E 318 E1
Talaud, Kepulauan Indonesia 4°30N 126°50E 309 D7
Talaud Is. = Talaud, Kepulauan Indonesia 4°30N 126°50E 309 D7
Talavera de la Reina Spain 39°55N 4°46W 293 C3
Talayan Phil. 6°52N 124°24E 309 C6
Talbandh India 22°3N 86°20E 315 H12
Talbot, C. Australia 13°48S 126°43E 332 B4
Talbragar → Australia 32°12S 148°37E 335 E4
Talca Chile 35°28S 71°40W 366 D1
Talcahuano Chile 36°40S 73°10W 366 D1
Talcher India 21°0N 85°18E 313 J14
Taldy Kurgan = Taldyqorghan Kazakhstan 45°10N 78°45E 300 E8
Taldyqorghan Kazakhstan 45°10N 78°45E 300 E8
Tālesh Iran 37°58N 48°58E 317 B6
Tālesh, Kūhhā-ye Iran 37°42N 48°55E 317 B6
Tali Post Sudan 5°55N 30°44E 323 G12
Taliabu Indonesia 1°50S 125°0E 309 E6
Talibon Phil. 10°9N 124°20E 309 B6
Talibong, Ko Thailand 7°15N 99°23E 311 J2
Talihina U.S.A. 34°45N 95°3W 356 D7
Taliwang Indonesia 8°50S 116°55E 308 F5
Tall 'Afar Iraq 36°22N 42°27E 316 B4
Tall Kalakh Syria 34°41N 36°15E 318 A5
Talladega U.S.A. 33°26N 86°6W 357 E11
Tallahassee U.S.A. 30°27N 84°17W 357 F12
Tallangatta Australia 36°15S 147°19E 335 F4
Tallering Pk. Australia 28°6S 115°37E 333 E2
Talli Pakistan 29°32N 68°8E 314 E3
Tallinn Estonia 59°22N 24°48E 281 G21
Tallmadge U.S.A. 41°6N 81°27W 354 E3
Tallulah U.S.A. 32°25N 91°11W 356 E9
Taloyoak Canada 69°32N 93°32W 340 C10
Talpa de Allende Mexico 20°23N 104°51W 358 C4
Talparo Trin. & Tob. 10°30N 61°17W 365 K15
Talsi Latvia 57°10N 22°30E 281 H20
Taltal Chile 25°23S 70°33W 366 B1
Taltson → Canada 61°24N 112°46W 342 A6
Talwood Australia 28°29S 149°29E 335 D4
Talyawalka Cr. → Australia 32°28S 142°22E 335 E3
Tam Ky Vietnam 15°34N 108°29E 310 E7
Tam Quan Vietnam 14°35N 109°3E 310 E7
Tama U.S.A. 41°58N 92°35W 352 E7
Tamale Ghana 9°22N 0°50W 322 G5
Taman Negara △ Malaysia 4°38N 102°26E 311 K4
Tamano Japan 34°29N 133°59E 303 G6
Tamanrasset Algeria 22°50N 5°30E 322 D7
Tamaqua U.S.A. 40°48N 75°58W 355 F9
Tamar → U.K. 50°27N 4°15W 285 G3
Tamarin Mauritius 20°19S 57°20E 325 d
Tamarinda Spain 39°55N 3°49E 296 B10
Tamashima Japan 34°32N 133°40E 303 G6
Tamatave = Toamasina Madag. 18°10S 49°25E 329 B8
Tamaulipas □ Mexico 24°0N 98°45W 359 C5
Tamaulipas, Sierra de Mexico 23°30N 98°20W 359 C5
Tamazula Mexico 24°57N 106°57W 358 C3
Tamazunchale Mexico 21°16N 98°47W 359 C5
Tambach Kenya 0°36N 35°31E 326 B4
Tambacounda Senegal 13°45N 13°40W 322 F3
Tambelan, Kepulauan Indonesia 1°0N 107°30E 308 D3
Tambellup Australia 34°4S 117°37E 333 F2
Tambo Australia 24°54S 146°14E 334 C4
Tambo de Mora Peru 13°30S 76°8W 364 F3
Tambohorano Madag. 17°30S 43°58E 329 B7
Tambora Indonesia 8°12S 118°5E 308 F5
Tambov Russia 52°45N 41°28E 290 D7
Tambuku Indonesia 7°8S 113°40E 309 G15
Tâmega → Portugal 41°5N 8°21W 293 B1
Tamenglong India 25°0N 93°35E 313 G18
Tamiahua, L. de Mexico 21°35N 97°35W 359 C5
Tamil Nadu □ India 11°0N 77°0E 312 P10
Tamluk India 22°18N 87°58E 315 H12
Tammerfors = Tampere Finland 61°30N 23°50E 280 F20
Tammisaari Finland 60°0N 23°26E 281 G20
Tamo Abu, Banjaran Malaysia 3°10N 115°5E 308 D5
Tampa U.S.A. 27°56N 82°27W 357 H13
Tampa, Tanjung Indonesia 8°55S 116°12E 309 K19
Tampa B. U.S.A. 27°50N 82°30W 357 H13
Tampere Finland 61°30N 23°50E 280 F20
Tampico Mexico 22°13N 97°51W 359 C5
Tampin Malaysia 2°28N 102°13E 311 L4
Tampoi Malaysia 1°30N 103°39E 311 d
Tamu Burma 24°13N 94°12E 313 G19
Tamworth Australia 31°7S 150°58E 335 E5
Tamworth Canada 44°29N 77°0W 354 B8
Tamworth U.K. 52°39N 1°41W 285 E6
Tan An Vietnam 10°32N 106°25E 311 G6
Tan Chau Vietnam 10°48N 105°12E 311 G5
Tan-Tan Morocco 28°29N 11°1W 322 C3
Tana → Kenya 2°32S 40°31E 326 C5
Tana → Norway 70°30N 28°14E 280 A23
Tana, L. Ethiopia 13°5N 37°30E 319 E2
Tana River Primate ⌂ Kenya 1°55S 40°7E 326 C5
Tanabe Japan 33°44N 135°22E 303 H7
Tanafjorden Norway 70°45N 28°25E 280 A23
Tanahbala Indonesia 0°30S 98°30E 308 E1
Tanahgrogot Indonesia 1°55S 116°15E 308 E5
Tanahjampea Indonesia 7°10S 120°35E 309 F6
Tanahmasa Indonesia 0°12S 98°39E 308 E1
Tanahmerah Indonesia 6°5S 140°16E 309 F10
Tanakpur India 29°5N 80°7E 315 E9
Tanakura Japan 37°10N 140°20E 303 F10
Tanami Desert Australia 18°50S 132°0E 332 C5
Tanami Mine Australia 19°59S 129°43E 332 C4
Tananarive = Antananarivo Madag. 18°55S 47°31E 329 B8
Tánaro → Italy 44°55N 8°40E 292 D8
Tancheng China 34°25N 118°20E 307 G10
Tanch'ŏn N. Korea 40°27N 128°54E 307 D15
Tanda Ut. P., India 26°33N 82°35E 315 F10
Tanda Ut. P., India 28°57N 78°56E 315 E8
Tandag Phil. 9°4N 126°9E 309 C7
Tandaia Tanzania 9°25S 34°15E 327 D3
Tandaué Angola 16°58S 18°5E 328 B2
Tandil Argentina 37°15S 59°6W 366 D4
Tandil, Sa. del Argentina 37°30S 59°0W 366 D4
Tandlianwala Pakistan 31°3N 73°9E 314 D5
Tando Adam Pakistan 25°45N 68°40E 314 G3
Tando Allahyar Pakistan 25°28N 68°43E 314 G3
Tando Bago Pakistan 24°47N 68°58E 314 G3
Tando Mohommed Khan Pakistan 25°8N 68°32E 314 G3
Tandou L. Australia 32°40S 142°5E 335 E3
Tandoureh △ Iran 37°50N 59°0E 316 B8
Tandragee U.K. 54°21N 6°24W 282 B5
Tane-ga-Shima Japan 30°30N 131°0E 303 J5
Taneatua N.Z. 38°4S 177°1E 331 C6
Tanen Tong Dan = Dawna Ra. Burma 16°30N 98°30E 310 D2
Tanezrouft Algeria 23°9N 0°11E 322 D6
Tang, Koh Cambodia 10°16N 103°7E 311 G4
Tang, Ra's-e Iran 25°21N 59°52E 317 E8

Tang Krasang Cambodia 12°34N 105°3E 310 F5
Tanga Tanzania 5°5S 39°2E 326 D4
Tanga □ Tanzania 5°20S 38°0E 326 D4
Tanganyika, L. Africa 6°40S 30°0E 326 D3
Tanger Morocco 35°50N 5°49W 322 A4
Tangerang Indonesia 6°11S 106°37E 309 G12
Tanggu China 39°2N 117°40E 307 E9
Tanggula Shan China 32°40N 92°10E 304 C4
Tanghe China 32°47N 112°50E 306 H7
Tanghla Range = Tanggula Shan China 32°40N 92°10E 304 C4
Tangier = Tanger Morocco 35°50N 5°49W 322 A4
Tangjia China 22°22N 113°35E 305 G10
Tangjia Wan China 22°21N 113°36E 305 G10
Tangorin Australia 21°47S 144°12E 334 C3
Tangorombohitr'i Makay Madag. 21°0S 45°15E 329 C8
Tangshan China 39°38N 118°10E 307 E10
Tangtou China 35°28N 118°30E 307 G10
Tanimbar, Kepulauan Indonesia 7°30S 131°30E 309 F8
Tanimbar Is. = Tanimbar, Kepulauan Indonesia 7°30S 131°30E 309 F8
Taninthari = Tenasserim Burma 12°6N 99°3E 311 F2
Tanjay Phil. 9°30N 123°5E 309 C6
Tanjong Malim Malaysia 3°42N 101°31E 311 L3
Tanjong Pelepas Malaysia 1°21N 103°33E 311 d
Tanjore = Thanjavur India 10°48N 79°12E 312 P11
Tanjung Indonesia 8°21S 116°9E 309 J19
Tanjung Phil. 2°10S 115°25E 308 E5
Tanjung Tokong Malaysia 5°28N 100°18E 311 c
Tanjungbalai Indonesia 2°55N 99°44E 308 D1
Tanjungbatu Indonesia 2°23N 118°3E 308 D5
Tanjungkarang Telukbetung Indonesia 5°20S 105°10E 308 F3
Tanjungpandan Indonesia 2°43S 107°38E 308 E3
Tanjungpinang Indonesia 1°5N 104°30E 308 D2
Tanjungredeb Indonesia 2°9N 117°29E 308 D5
Tanjungselor Indonesia 2°55N 117°25E 308 D5
Tank Pakistan 32°14N 70°25E 314 C4
Tankhala India 21°58N 73°47E 314 J5
Tankwa-Karoo △ S. Africa 32°14S 19°50E 328 E2
Tannersville U.S.A. 41°3N 75°18W 355 E9
Tannu Ola Asia 51°0N 94°0E 301 D10
Tannum Sands Australia 23°57S 151°22E 334 C5
Tanout Niger 14°50N 8°55E 322 F7
Tanta Egypt 30°45N 30°57E 323 B12
Tantoyuca Mexico 21°21N 98°14W 359 C5
Tantung = Dandong China 40°10N 124°20E 307 D13
Tanunda Australia 34°30S 139°0E 335 E2
Tanzania ■ Africa 6°0S 34°0E 326 D3
Tanzhou China 22°16N 113°28E 305 G9
Tanzilla → Canada 58°8N 130°43W 342 B2
Tao, Ko Thailand 10°5N 99°52E 311 G2
Tao'an = Taonan China 45°22N 122°40E 307 B12
Tao'er He → China 45°45N 124°5E 307 B13
Taolanaro Madag. 25°2S 47°0E 329 D8
Taole China 38°48N 106°40E 306 E4
Taonan China 45°22N 122°40E 307 B12
Taos U.S.A. 36°24N 105°35W 349 H11
Taoudenni Mali 22°40N 3°55W 322 D5
Tapa Estonia 59°15N 25°50E 281 G21
Tapa Shan = Daba Shan China 32°0N 109°0E 305 C5
Tapachula Mexico 14°54N 92°17W 359 E6
Tapah Malaysia 4°12N 101°15E 311 K3
Tapajós → Brazil 2°24S 54°41W 365 D8
Tapaktuan Indonesia 3°15N 97°10E 308 D1
Tapanahoni → Suriname 4°20N 54°25W 365 C8
Tapanui N.Z. 45°56S 169°18E 331 F2
Tapauá → Brazil 5°40S 64°21W 364 E6
Tapes Brazil 30°40S 51°23W 367 C5
Tapeta Liberia 6°29N 8°52W 322 G4
Taphan Hin Thailand 16°13N 100°26E 310 D3
Tapirapecó, Serra Venezuela 1°10N 65°0W 364 C6
Tapo-Capara △ Venezuela 7°55N 71°15W 361 E5
Tapti → India 21°8N 72°41E 312 J8
Tapuae-o-Uenuku N.Z. 42°0S 173°39E 331 E4
Tapul Group Phil. 5°35N 120°50E 309 C6
Tapurucuará Brazil 0°24S 65°2W 364 D5
Ţaqtaq Iraq 35°53N 44°35E 316 C5
Taquara Brazil 29°36S 50°46W 367 B5
Taquari → Brazil 19°15S 57°17W 364 G7
Tara Australia 27°17S 150°31E 335 D5
Tara Canada 44°28N 81°9W 354 B3
Tara Russia 56°55N 74°24E 300 D8
Tara Zambia 16°58S 26°45E 327 F2
Tara → Montenegro 43°21N 18°51E 295 C8
Tarābulus Lebanon 34°31N 35°50E 318 A4
Tarābulus Libya 32°49N 13°7E 323 B8
Taradehi India 23°18N 79°21E 315 H8
Tarajalejo Canary Is. 28°12N 14°7W 296 F5
Tarakan Indonesia 3°20N 117°35E 308 D5
Tarakit, Mt. Kenya 2°2N 35°10E 326 B4
Tarama-Jima Japan 24°39N 124°42E 303 M2
Taran, Mys Russia 54°56N 19°59E 281 J18
Taranagar India 28°43N 74°50E 314 E6
Taranaki □ N.Z. 39°25S 174°30E 331 C5
Taranaki, Mt. N.Z. 39°17S 174°5E 331 C5
Tarancón Spain 40°1N 3°1W 293 B4
Tarangire △ Tanzania 4°21S 36°7E 326 C4
Taransay U.K. 57°54N 7°0W 283 D1
Táranto Italy 40°28N 17°14E 294 D7
Táranto, G. di Italy 40°8N 17°20E 294 D7
Tarapacá Colombia 2°56S 69°46W 364 D5
Tarapacá □ Chile 20°45S 69°30W 366 A2
Tarapoto Peru 6°30S 76°20W 364 E3
Tararua Ra. N.Z. 40°45S 175°25E 331 D5
Tarashcha Ukraine 49°30N 30°31E 289 D16
Tarauacá Brazil 8°6S 70°48W 364 E4
Tarauacá → Brazil 6°42S 69°48W 364 E5
Taravao Tahiti 17°43S 149°18W 331 d
Taravao, Isthme de Tahiti 17°43S 149°19W 331 d
Tarawa Kiribati 1°30N 173°0E 336 G9
Tarawera N.Z. 39°2S 176°36E 331 C6
Tarawera, L. N.Z. 38°13S 176°27E 331 C6
Taraz Kazakhstan 42°54N 71°22E 300 E8
Tarazona Spain 41°55N 1°43W 293 B5
Tarbagatay, Khrebet Kazakhstan 48°0N 83°0E 300 E9
Tarbat Ness U.K. 57°52N 3°47W 283 D5
Tarbela Dam Pakistan 34°8N 72°52E 314 B5
Tarbert Ireland 52°34N 9°22W 282 D2
Tarbert Argyll & Bute, U.K. 55°52N 5°25W 283 F3
Tarbert W. Isles, U.K. 57°54N 6°49W 283 D2
Tarbes France 43°15N 0°3E 292 E4
Tarboro U.S.A. 35°54N 77°32W 357 D16
Tarcoola Australia 30°44S 134°36E 335 E1
Tarcoon Australia 30°15S 146°43E 335 E4
Taree Australia 31°50S 152°30E 335 E5
Tarfaya Morocco 27°55N 12°55W 322 C3
Târgovişte Romania 44°55N 25°27E 289 F13
Târgu-Jiu Romania 45°5N 23°19E 289 F12
Târgu Mureş Romania 46°31N 24°38E 289 E13
Ţarif U.A.E. 24°3N 53°46E 317 E7
Tarifa Spain 36°1N 5°36W 293 D3
Tarija Bolivia 21°30S 64°40W 366 A3
Tarija □ Bolivia 21°30S 63°30W 366 A3
Tariku → Indonesia 2°55S 138°26E 309 E9
Tarim Basin = Tarim Pendi China 40°0N 84°0E 304 B3
Tarim He → China 39°30N 88°30E 304 C3
Tarim Pendi China 40°0N 84°0E 304 B3
Taritatu → Indonesia 2°54S 138°27E 309 E9
Tarka → S. Africa 32°10S 26°0E 328 E4
Tarka La Bhutan 27°12N 89°44E 315 F13
Tarkastad S. Africa 32°0S 26°16E 328 E4
Tarkhankut, Mys Ukraine 45°25N 32°30E 291 E5
Tarko Sale Russia 64°55N 77°50E 300 C8
Tarkwa Ghana 5°20N 2°0W 322 G5
Tarlac Phil. 15°29N 120°35E 309 A6
Tarma Peru 11°25S 75°45W 364 F3
Tarn → France 44°5N 1°6E 292 E4
Târnăveni Romania 46°19N 24°13E 289 E13
Tarnobrzeg Poland 50°35N 21°41E 289 C11
Tarnów Poland 50°3N 21°0E 289 C11
Tarnowskie Góry Poland 50°27N 18°54E 289 C10
Ţārom Iran 28°11N 55°46E 317 D7
Taroom Australia 25°36S 149°48E 335 D4
Taroudannt Morocco 30°30N 8°52W 322 B4
Tarpon Springs U.S.A. 28°9N 82°45W 357 G13
Tarrafal C. Verde Is. 15°18N 23°39W 322 b
Tarragona Spain 41°5N 1°17E 293 B6
Tarraleah Australia 42°17S 146°26E 335 G4
Tarrasa = Terrassa Spain 41°34N 2°1E 293 B7
Tarrytown U.S.A. 41°4N 73°52W 355 E11
Tarshiha = Me'ona Israel 33°1N 35°15E 318 B4
Tarsus Turkey 36°58N 34°55E 316 B2
Tartagal Argentina 22°30S 63°50W 366 A3
Tartu Estonia 58°20N 26°44E 281 G22
Ţarţūs Syria 34°55N 35°55E 316 C2
Tarumizu Japan 31°29N 130°42E 303 J5
Tarutao = Ko Tarutao △ Thailand 6°31N 99°26E 311 J2
Tarutao, Ko Thailand 6°33N 99°40E 311 J2
Tarutung Indonesia 2°0N 98°54E 308 D1
Taseko → Canada 52°8N 123°45W 342 C4
Tash-Kömür Kyrgyzstan 41°40N 72°10E 300 E8
Tash-Kumyr = Tash-Kömür Kyrgyzstan 41°40N 72°10E 300 E8
Tashauz = Dashoguz Turkmenistan 41°49N 59°58E 300 E6
Tashi Chho Dzong = Thimphu Bhutan 27°31N 89°45E 313 F16
Ţashk, Daryācheh-ye Iran 29°45N 53°35E 317 D7
Tashkent = Toshkent Uzbekistan 41°20N 69°10E 300 E7
Tashtagol Russia 52°47N 87°53E 300 D9
Tasiilaq Greenland 65°40N 37°20W 276 C6
Tasik Kenyir Malaysia 5°5N 102°45E 311 K4
Tasikmalaya Indonesia 7°18S 108°12E 309 G13
Tåsjön Sweden 64°15N 15°40E 280 D16
Taskan Russia 62°59N 150°20E 301 C16
Tasman B. N.Z. 40°59S 173°25E 331 D4
Tasman Basin Pac. Oc. 46°0S 158°0E 336 M7
Tasman Mts. N.Z. 41°3S 172°25E 331 D4
Tasman Pen. Australia 43°10S 148°0E 335 G4
Tasman Sea Pac. Oc. 36°0S 160°0E 330 E9
Tasmania □ Australia 42°0S 146°30E 335 G4
Tasmanian Wilderness World Heritage Area △ Australia 43°0S 146°0E 335 G4
Tassili n'Ajjer Algeria 25°47N 8°1E 322 C7
Tassili-Oua-n-Ahaggar Algeria 20°41N 5°30E 322 D7
Tata Morocco 29°46N 7°56W 322 C4
Tatabánya Hungary 47°32N 18°25E 289 E10
Tatahouine Tunisia 32°56N 10°27E 323 B8
Tataouine Tunisia 32°57N 10°29E 323 B8
Tatar Republic = Tatarstan □ Russia 55°30N 51°30E 290 C9
Tatarbunary Ukraine 45°50N 29°39E 289 F15
Tatarsk Russia 55°14N 76°0E 300 D8
Tatarstan □ Russia 55°30N 51°30E 290 C9
Tatatua, Pte. Tahiti 17°44S 149°8W 331 d
Tateyama Japan 35°0N 139°50E 303 G9
Tathlina L. Canada 60°33N 117°39W 342 A5
Tathra Australia 36°44S 149°59E 335 F4
Tatinnai L. Canada 60°55N 97°40W 343 A9
Tatla Lake Canada 52°0N 124°20W 342 C4
Tatnam, C. Canada 57°16N 91°0W 343 B10
Tatra = Tatry Slovak Rep. 49°20N 20°0E 289 D11
Tatry Slovak Rep. 49°20N 20°0E 289 D11
Tatshenshini → Canada 59°28N 137°45W 342 B1
Tatsuno Japan 34°52N 134°33E 303 G7
Tatta Pakistan 24°42N 67°55E 314 G2
Tatuí Brazil 23°25S 47°53W 367 A6
Tatum U.S.A. 33°16N 103°19W 349 K12
Tat'ung = Datong China 40°6N 113°18E 306 D7
Tatvan Turkey 38°31N 42°15E 316 B4
Ta'ū Amer. Samoa 14°15S 169°30W 331 b
Taubaté Brazil 23°0S 45°36W 367 A6
Tauern Austria 47°15N 12°40E 288 E7
Taumarunui N.Z. 38°53S 175°15E 331 C5
Taumaturgo Brazil 8°54S 72°51W 364 E4
Taung S. Africa 27°33S 24°47E 328 D3
Taungdwingyi Burma 20°1N 95°40E 313 J19
Taunggyi Burma 20°50N 97°0E 313 J20
Taungup Burma 18°51N 94°14E 313 K19
Taunsa Pakistan 30°42N 70°39E 314 D4
Taunsa Barrage Pakistan 30°42N 70°50E 314 D4
Taunton U.K. 51°1N 3°5W 285 F4
Taunton U.S.A. 41°54N 71°6W 355 E13
Taunus Germany 50°13N 8°34E 288 C5
Taupo N.Z. 38°41S 176°7E 331 C6
Taupo, L. N.Z. 38°46S 175°55E 331 C5
Tauragė Lithuania 55°14N 22°16E 281 J20
Tauranga N.Z. 37°42S 176°11E 331 B6
Tauranga Harb. N.Z. 37°30S 176°5E 331 B6
Taureau, Rés. Canada 46°46N 73°50W 344 C5
Taurianova Italy 38°21N 16°1E 294 E7
Taurus Mts. = Toros Dağları Turkey 37°0N 32°30E 316 B2
Tautira Tahiti 17°44S 149°9W 331 d
Tavan Bogd Uul Mongolia 49°10N 87°49E 304 B3
Tavastehus = Hämeenlinna Finland 61°0N 24°28E 280 F21
Tavda Russia 58°7N 65°8E 300 D7
Tavda → Russia 57°47N 67°18E 300 D7
Taveta Kenya 3°23S 37°37E 326 C4
Taveuni Fiji 16°51S 179°58W 331 a
Tavira Portugal 37°8N 7°40W 293 D2
Tavistock Canada 43°19N 80°50W 354 C4
Tavistock U.K. 50°33N 4°9W 285 G3
Tavoy Burma 14°2N 98°12E 310 E2
Tavua Fiji 17°37S 177°5E 331 a
Tavuki Fiji 19°7S 178°8E 331 a
Taw → U.K. 51°4N 4°4W 285 F3
Tawa → India 22°48N 77°48E 314 H8
Tawas City U.S.A. 44°16N 83°31W 353 C12
Tawau Malaysia 4°20N 117°55E 308 D5
Tawi-Tawi Phil. 5°10N 120°15E 309 B6
Taxco Mexico 18°33N 99°36W 359 D5
Taxila Pakistan 33°42N 72°52E 314 C5
Taxkorgan Tajik Zizhixian China 37°49N 75°14E 304 C2
Tay → U.K. 56°37N 3°38W 283 E5
Tay, Firth of U.K. 56°25N 3°8W 283 E5
Tay, L. Australia 32°55S 120°48E 333 F3
Tay, L. U.K. 56°32N 4°8W 283 E4
Tay ⌓ U.K. 56°43N 3°59W 283 E5
Tay Ninh Vietnam 11°20N 106°5E 311 G6
Tayabamba Peru 8°15S 77°16W 364 E3
Taygetos Oros Greece 37°0N 22°23E 295 F10
Taylakova Russia 59°13N 74°0E 300 D8
Taylakovy = Taylakova Russia 59°13N 74°0E 300 D8
Taylor Canada 56°13N 120°40W 342 B4
Taylor Nebr., U.S.A. 41°46N 99°23W 352 E4
Taylor Pa., U.S.A. 41°23N 75°43W 355 E9
Taylor Tex., U.S.A. 30°34N 97°25W 356 F6
Taylor, Mt. U.S.A. 35°14N 107°37W 349 J10
Taylorville U.S.A. 39°33N 89°18W 352 F9
Taymā Si. Arabia 27°35N 38°45E 316 E3
Taymyr, Oz. Russia 74°20N 102°0E 301 B11
Taymyr, Poluostrov Russia 75°0N 100°0E 301 B11
Tayport U.K. 56°27N 2°52W 283 E6
Tayrona △ Colombia 11°20N 74°2W 361 D5
Tayshet Russia 55°58N 98°1E 301 D10
Taytay Phil. 10°45N 119°30E 309 B5
Tāyyebād Iran 34°45N 60°45E 317 C9
Tāyyebād □ Iran 34°44N 60°44E 317 C9
Taz → Russia 67°32N 78°40E 300 C8
Taza Morocco 34°16N 4°6W 322 B5
Tāza Khurmātū Iraq 35°18N 44°20E 316 C5
Tazawa-Ko Japan 39°43N 140°40E 302 E10
Tazin → Canada 59°48N 109°55W 343 B7
Tazin L. Canada 59°44N 108°42W 343 B7
Tazovskiy Russia 67°30N 78°44E 300 C8
Tbilisi Georgia 41°43N 44°50E 291 F7
Tchad = Chad ■ Africa 15°0N 17°15E 323 F8
Tchad, L. Chad 13°30N 14°30E 323 F8
Tch'eng-tou = Chengdu China 30°38N 104°2E 304 C5
Tchentlo L. Canada 55°15N 125°0W 342 B4
Tchibanga Gabon 2°45S 11°0E 324 E2
Tch'ong-k'ing = Chongqing China 29°35N 106°25E 304 D5
Tczew Poland 54°8N 18°50E 289 A10
Te Anau, L. N.Z. 45°15S 167°45E 331 F1
Te Aroha N.Z. 37°32S 175°44E 331 B5
Te Awamutu N.Z. 38°1S 175°20E 331 C5
Te Ika a Maui = North I. N.Z. 38°0S 175°0E 331 C5
Te Kuiti N.Z. 38°20S 175°11E 331 C5
Te Puke N.Z. 37°46S 176°22E 331 B6
Te Waewae B. N.Z. 46°13S 167°33E 331 G1
Te Wai Pounamu = South I. N.Z. 44°0S 170°0E 331 F3
Teague U.S.A. 31°38N 96°17W 356 F6
Teahupoo Tahiti 17°50S 149°16W 331 d
Teapa Mexico 17°33N 92°57W 359 D6
Tebakang Malaysia 1°6N 110°30E 308 D4
Teberu Malaysia 1°30N 103°42E 311 d
Tébessa Algeria 35°22N 8°8E 322 A7
Tebicuary → Paraguay 26°36S 58°16W 366 B4
Tebingtinggi Riau, Indonesia 1°0N 102°45E 308 E2
Tebingtinggi Sumatera Utara, Indonesia 3°20N 99°9E 308 D1
Tecate Mexico 32°34N 116°38W 351 N10
Tecka Argentina 43°29S 70°48W 368 E2
Tecomán Mexico 18°55N 103°53W 358 D4
Tecopa U.S.A. 35°51N 116°13W 351 K10
Tecoripa Mexico 28°37N 109°57W 358 B3
Tecuala Mexico 22°23N 105°27W 358 C3
Tecuci Romania 45°51N 27°27E 289 F14
Tecumseh Canada 42°19N 82°54W 354 D2
Tecumseh Mich., U.S.A. 42°0N 83°57W 353 D12
Tecumseh Okla., U.S.A. 35°15N 96°56W 356 D6
Tedzhen = Tejen Turkmenistan 37°23N 60°31E 300 F7
Tees → U.K. 54°37N 1°10W 284 C6
Tees B. U.K. 54°40N 1°9W 284 C6
Teeswater Canada 43°59N 81°17W 354 C3
Tefé Brazil 3°25S 64°50W 364 D6
Tegal Indonesia 6°52S 109°8E 308 F3
Tegallalang Indonesia 8°27S 115°17E 309 J18
Tegalsari Indonesia 8°25S 114°8E 309 J17
Tegid, L. = Bala, L. U.K. 52°53N 3°37W 284 E4
Tegucigalpa Honduras 14°5N 87°14W 360 D2
Tehachapi U.S.A. 35°8N 118°27W 351 K8
Tehachapi Mts. U.S.A. 35°0N 118°30W 351 L8
Teheran = Tehrān Iran 35°41N 51°25E 317 C6
Tehoru Indonesia 3°23S 129°30E 309 E7
Tehrān Iran 35°41N 51°25E 317 C6
Tehrān □ Iran 35°30N 51°30E 317 C6
Tehri India 30°23N 78°29E 315 D8
Tehuacán Mexico 18°27N 97°23W 359 D5
Tehuantepec Mexico 16°21N 95°13W 359 D5
Tehuantepec, G. de Mexico 15°50N 95°12W 359 D5
Tehuantepec, Istmo de Mexico 17°15N 94°30W 359 D6
Teide, Pico de Canary Is. 28°15N 16°38W 296 F3
Teifi → U.K. 52°5N 4°41W 285 E3
Teign → U.K. 50°32N 3°32W 285 G4
Teignmouth U.K. 50°33N 3°31W 285 G4
Tejakula Indonesia 8°8S 115°20E 309 J18
Tejam India 29°57N 80°11E 315 E9
Tejen Turkmenistan 37°23N 60°31E 300 F7
Tejen → Turkmenistan 37°24N 60°38E 317 B9
Tejo → Europe 38°40N 9°24W 293 C1
Tejon Pass U.S.A. 34°49N 118°53W 351 L8
Tekamah U.S.A. 41°47N 96°13W 352 E5
Tekapo, L. N.Z. 43°53S 170°33E 331 E3
Tekax Mexico 20°12N 89°17W 359 C7
Tekeli Kazakhstan 44°50N 79°0E 300 E8
Tekirdağ Turkey 40°58N 27°30E 295 D12
Tekkali India 18°37N 84°15E 313 K14
Tekoa U.S.A. 47°14N 117°4W 348 C5
Tekong Besar, Pulau Singapore 1°25N 104°3E 311 d
Tel Aviv ✗ (TLV) Israel 32°5N 34°49E 318 C3
Tel Aviv-Yafo Israel 32°4N 34°48E 318 C3
Tel Lakhish Israel 31°34N 34°51E 318 D3
Tel Megiddo Israel 32°35N 35°11E 318 C4
Tela Honduras 15°40N 87°28W 360 C2
Telanaipura = Jambi Indonesia 1°38S 103°30E 308 E2
Telavi Georgia 42°0N 45°30E 291 F8
Telde Canary Is. 27°59N 15°25W 296 G4
Telegraph Creek Canada 58°0N 131°10W 342 B2
Telekhany = Tsyelyakhany Belarus 52°30N 25°46E 289 B13
Telemark Norway 59°15N 7°40E 281 G12
Telén Argentina 36°15S 65°31W 366 D2
Teleng Iran 25°47N 61°3E 317 E9
Teles Pires → Brazil 7°21S 58°3W 364 E7
Telescope Pk. U.S.A. 36°10N 117°5W 351 J9
Telfer Mine Australia 21°40S 122°12E 332 C3
Telford U.K. 52°40N 2°27W 285 E5
Telford and Wrekin □ U.K. 52°45N 2°27W 284 E5
Telkwa Canada 54°41N 127°5W 342 C3
Tell City U.S.A. 37°57N 86°46W 352 G10
Tellicherry India 11°45N 75°30E 312 P9
Telluride U.S.A. 37°56N 107°49W 349 H10
Teloloapán Mexico 18°21N 99°51W 359 D5
Telpos Iz Russia 63°16N 59°13E 290 B10
Telsen Argentina 42°30S 66°50W 368 E3
Telšiai Lithuania 55°59N 22°14E 281 J20
Teluk Anson = Teluk Intan Malaysia 4°3N 101°0E 311 K3
Teluk Bahang Malaysia 5°28N 100°13E 311 c
Teluk Betung = Tanjungkarang Telukbetung Indonesia 5°20S 105°10E 308 F3
Teluk Intan Malaysia 4°3N 101°0E 311 K3
Teluk Kumbar Malaysia 5°18N 100°14E 311 c
Telukbutun Indonesia 4°13N 108°12E 308 D3
Telukdalem Indonesia 0°33N 97°50E 308 D1
Tema Ghana 5°41N 0°0 322 G5
Temagami, L. Canada 47°0N 80°10W 344 C3
Temax Mexico 21°9N 88°56W 359 C7
Temba S. Africa 25°20S 28°17E 329 D4
Tembagapura Indonesia 4°20S 137°0E 309 E9
Tembe Dem. Rep. of the Congo 0°16S 28°14E 326 C2
Tembe ⌓ S. Africa 26°51S 32°24E 329 D5
Temblor Range U.S.A. 35°20N 119°50W 351 K7
Teme → U.K. 52°11N 2°13W 285 E5
Temecula U.S.A. 33°30N 117°9W 351 M9
Temerloh Malaysia 3°27N 102°25E 308 D2
Teminabuan Indonesia 1°26S 132°1E 309 E8
Temir Kazakhstan 49°1N 57°14E 291 E10
Temirtau Kazakhstan 50°5N 72°56E 300 D8
Temirtau Russia 53°10N 87°30E 300 D9
Témiscamie → Canada 50°59N 73°5W 345 B5
Témiscaming Canada 46°44N 79°5W 344 C4
Témiscamingue, L. Canada 47°10N 79°25W 344 C4
Temosachic Mexico 28°57N 107°51W 358 B3
Tempe U.S.A. 33°24N 111°54W 349 K8
Tempiute U.S.A. 37°39N 115°38W 350 H11
Temple U.S.A. 31°6N 97°21W 356 F6
Temple B. Australia 12°15S 143°3E 334 A3
Templemore Ireland 52°47N 7°51W 282 D4
Templeton U.S.A. 35°33N 120°42W 350 K6
Templeton → Australia 21°0S 138°40E 334 C2
Tempoal de Sánchez Mexico 21°31N 98°23W 359 C5
Temuco Chile 38°45S 72°40W 368 D2
Temuka N.Z. 44°14S 171°17E 331 F3
Tenabo Mexico 20°3N 90°14W 359 C6
Tenaha U.S.A. 31°57N 94°15W 356 F7
Tenakee Springs U.S.A. 57°47N 135°13W 342 B1
Tenali India 16°15N 80°35E 313 L12
Tenancingo de Degollado Mexico 18°58N 99°36W 359 D5
Tenango del Valle Mexico 19°7N 99°33W 359 D5
Tenaro, Akra Greece 36°22N 22°27E 295 F10
Tenasserim Burma 12°6N 99°3E 311 F2
Tenasserim □ Burma 14°0N 98°30E 310 F2
Tenby U.K. 51°40N 4°42W 285 F3
Tenda, Colle di France 44°7N 7°36E 292 D7
Tendaho Ethiopia 11°48N 40°54E 319 E3
Tendukhera India 23°24N 79°33E 315 H8
Teneguía, Volcanes de Canary Is. 28°28N 17°51W 296 F2
Tenerife Canary Is. 28°15N 16°35W 296 F3
Tenerife, Pico Canary Is. 27°43N 18°1W 296 G1
Tenerife Norte ✗ (TFN) Canary Is. 28°28N 16°17W 296 F3
Tenerife Sur ✗ (TFS) Canary Is. 28°3N 16°33W 296 F3
Teng Xian China 35°5N 117°10E 307 G9
Tengah, Kepulauan Indonesia 7°5S 118°15E 308 F5
Tengchong China 25°0N 98°28E 304 D4
Tengchowfu = Penglai China 37°48N 120°42E 307 F11
Tenggarong Indonesia 0°24S 116°58E 308 E5
Tengger Shamo China 38°0N 104°0E 304 C5
Tenggol, Pulau Malaysia 4°48N 103°41E 311 K4
Tengiz Köli Kazakhstan 50°30N 69°0E 300 D7
Teniente Enciso △ Paraguay 21°5S 61°8W 366 A3
Teniente Rodolfo Marsh Antarctica 62°30S 58°0W 277 C18
Tenino U.S.A. 46°51N 122°51W 350 D4
Tenkasi India 8°55N 77°20E 312 Q10
Tenke Katanga, Dem. Rep. of the Congo 11°22S 26°40E 327 E2
Tenke Katanga, Dem. Rep. of the Congo 10°32S 26°7E 327 E2
Tennant Creek Australia 19°30S 134°15E 334 B1
Tennessee □ U.S.A. 36°0N 86°30W 357 D11
Tennessee → U.S.A. 37°4N 88°34W 357 C10
Teno, Pta. de Canary Is. 28°21N 16°55W 296 F3
Tenom Malaysia 5°4N 115°57E 308 C5
Tenosique Mexico 17°29N 91°26W 359 D6
Tenryū-Gawa → Japan 35°39N 137°48E 303 G8
Tenterden U.K. 51°4N 0°42E 285 F8
Tenterfield Australia 29°0S 152°0E 335 D5
Teófilo Otoni Brazil 17°50S 41°30W 365 G10
Tepa Indonesia 7°52S 129°31E 309 F7
Tepalcatepec → Mexico 18°35N 101°59W 358 D4
Tepehuanes Mexico 25°21N 105°44W 358 B3
Tepetongo Mexico 22°28N 103°9W 358 C4
Tepic Mexico 21°30N 104°54W 358 C4
Teplice Czech Rep. 50°40N 13°48E 288 C7
Tepoca, C. Mexico 30°20N 112°25W 358 A2
Tequila Mexico 20°54N 103°47W 358 C4
Ter → Spain 42°2N 3°12E 293 A7
Ter Apel Neths. 52°53N 7°5E 287 B7
Téra Niger 14°0N 0°45E 322 F6
Teraina Kiribati 4°43N 160°25W 337 G12
Téramo Italy 42°39N 13°42E 294 C5
Terang Australia 38°15S 142°55E 335 F3
Terang, Teluk Indonesia 8°44S 116°0E 309 K19
Terceira Azores 38°43N 27°13W 322 a
Tercero → Argentina 32°58S 61°47W 366 C3
Terebovlya Ukraine 49°18N 25°44E 289 D13
Terek → Russia 44°0N 47°30E 291 F8
Terepaima △ Venezuela 9°58N 69°17W 361 E6
Teresina Brazil 5°9S 42°45W 365 E10
Terewah, L. Australia 29°52S 147°35E 335 D4
Teridgerie Cr. → Australia 30°25S 148°50E 335 E4
Termez = Termiz Uzbekistan 37°15N 67°15E 300 F7
Términi Imerese Italy 37°59N 13°42E 294 F5
Términos, L. de Mexico 18°37N 91°33W 359 D6
Termiz Uzbekistan 37°15N 67°15E 300 F7
Térmoli Italy 42°0N 15°0E 294 C6
Ternate Indonesia 0°45N 127°25E 309 D7
Terneuzen Neths. 51°20N 3°50E 287 C3
Terney Russia 45°3N 136°37E 302 B8
Terni Italy 42°34N 12°37E 294 C5
Ternopil Ukraine 49°30N 25°40E 289 D13
Ternopol = Ternopil Ukraine 49°30N 25°40E 289 D13
Terowie Australia 33°8S 138°55E 335 E2
Terra Bella U.S.A. 35°58N 119°3W 351 K7
Terra Nova △ Canada 48°33N 53°55W 345 C9
Terrace Canada 54°30N 128°35W 342 C3

Terrace Bay *Canada* 48°47N 87°5W **344** C2
Terracina *Italy* 41°17N 13°15E **294** D5
Terralba *Italy* 39°43N 8°39E **294** E3
Terrassa *Spain* 41°34N 2°1E **293** B7
Terre Haute *U.S.A.* 39°28N 87°25W **352** F10
Terrebonne B. *U.S.A.* 29°5N 90°35W **357** G9
Terrell *U.S.A.* 32°44N 96°17W **356** E6
Terrenceville *Canada* 47°40N 54°44W **345** C9
Terry *U.S.A.* 46°47N 105°19W **348** C11
Terryville *U.S.A.* 41°41N 73°3W **355** E11
Terschelling *Neths.* 53°25N 5°20E **287** A5
Teruel *Spain* 40°22N 1°8W **293** B5
Tervola *Finland* 66°6N 24°49E **280** C21
Teryaweynya L. *Australia* 32°18S 143°22E **335** E3
Teshio *Japan* 44°53N 141°44E **302** B10
Teshio-Gawa → *Japan* 44°53N 141°45E **302** B10
Tesiyn Gol → *Mongolia* 50°40N 93°20E **304** A4
Teslin *Canada* 60°10N 132°43W **342** A2
Teslin → *Canada* 61°34N 134°35W **342** A2
Teslin L. *Canada* 60°15N 132°57W **342** A2
Tessalit *Mali* 20°12N 1°0E **322** D6
Tessaoua *Niger* 13°47N 7°56E **322** F7
Test → *U.K.* 50°56N 1°29W **285** G6
Testigos, Is. Los *Venezuela* 11°23N 63°7W **361** D7
Tetachuck L. *Canada* 53°18N 125°55W **342** C3
Tetas, Pta. *Chile* 23°31S 70°38W **366** A1
Tete *Mozam.* 16°13S 33°33E **327** F3
Tete □ *Mozam.* 15°15S 32°40E **327** F3
Teterev → *Ukraine* 51°1N 30°5E **289** C16
Teteven *Bulgaria* 42°58N 24°17E **295** C11
Tethul → *Canada* 60°35N 112°12W **342** A6
Tetiyev *Ukraine* 49°22N 29°38E **289** D15
Teton → *U.S.A.* 47°56N 110°31W **348** C8
Tétouan *Morocco* 35°35N 5°21W **322** A4
Tetovo *Macedonia* 42°1N 20°59E **295** C9
Tetufera, Mt. *Tahiti* 17°40S 149°26W **331** d
Teuco → *Argentina* 25°35S 60°11W **366** B3
Teulon *Canada* 50°23N 97°16W **343** C9
Teun *Indonesia* 6°59S 129°8E **309** F7
Teuri-Tō *Japan* 44°26N 141°19E **302** B10
Teutoburger Wald *Germany* 52°5N 8°22E **288** B5
Tevere → *Italy* 41°44N 12°14E **294** D5
Teverya *Israel* 32°47N 35°32E **318** C4
Teviot → *U.K.* 55°29N 2°38W **283** F6
Tewantin *Australia* 26°27S 153°3E **335** D5
Tewkesbury *U.K.* 51°59N 2°9W **285** F5
Texada I. *Canada* 49°40N 124°25W **342** D4
Texarkana *Ark., U.S.A.* 33°26N 94°2W **356** E7
Texarkana *Tex., U.S.A.* 33°26N 94°3W **356** E7
Texas *Australia* 28°49S 151°9E **335** D5
Texas □ *U.S.A.* 31°40N 98°30W **356** F5
Texas City *U.S.A.* 29°24N 94°54W **356** G7
Texel *Neths.* 53°5N 4°50E **287** A4
Texline *U.S.A.* 36°23N 103°2W **356** C3
Texoma, L. *U.S.A.* 33°50N 96°34W **356** E6
Teyateyaneng *Lesotho* 29°7S 27°34E **325** K5
Tezin *Afghan.* 34°24N 69°30E **314** B3
Teziutlán *Mexico* 19°49N 97°21W **359** D5
Tezpur *India* 26°40N 92°45E **313** F18
Tezzeron L. *Canada* 54°43N 124°30W **342** C4
Tha-anne → *Canada* 60°31N 94°37W **343** A10
Tha Deua *Laos* 17°57N 102°53E **310** D4
Tha Deua *Laos* 19°26N 101°50E **310** C3
Tha Pla *Thailand* 17°48N 100°32E **310** D3
Tha Rua *Thailand* 14°34N 100°44E **310** E3
Tha Sala *Thailand* 8°40N 99°56E **311** H2
Tha Song Yang *Thailand* 17°34N 97°55E **310** D1
Thaba Putsoa *Lesotho* 29°45S 28°0E **329** D4
Thabana Ntlenyana *Lesotho* 29°30S 29°16E **329** D4
Thabazimbi *S. Africa* 24°40S 27°21E **329** C4
Thādiq *Si. Arabia* 25°18N 45°52E **316** E5
Thai Binh *Vietnam* 20°35N 106°1E **310** B6
Thai Muang *Thailand* 8°24N 98°16E **311** H2
Thai Nguyen *Vietnam* 21°35N 105°55E **310** B5
Thailand ■ *Asia* 16°0N 102°0E **310** E4
Thailand, G. of *Asia* 11°30N 101°0E **311** G3
Thakhek *Laos* 17°25N 104°45E **310** D5
Thal *Pakistan* 33°28N 70°33E **314** C4
Thal Desert *Pakistan* 31°10N 71°30E **314** D4
Thala La = Hkakabo Razi *Burma* 28°25N 97°23E **313** E20
Thalabarivat *Cambodia* 13°33N 105°57E **310** F5
Thallon *Australia* 28°39S 148°49E **335** D4
Thalu, Ko *Thailand* 9°26N 99°54E **311** b
Thames *N.Z.* 37°7S 175°34E **331** B5
Thames → *Canada* 42°20N 82°25W **354** D2
Thames → *U.K.* 51°29N 0°34E **285** F8
Thames → *U.S.A.* 41°18N 72°5W **355** E12
Thames Estuary *U.K.* 51°29N 0°52E **285** F8
Thamesford *Canada* 43°4N 81°0W **354** C4
Thamesville *Canada* 42°33N 81°59W **354** D3
Than *India* 22°34N 71°11E **314** H4
Than Uyen *Vietnam* 22°0N 103°54E **310** B4
Thana Gazi *India* 27°25N 76°19E **314** F7
Thandla *India* 23°0N 74°34E **314** H6
Thandwe *Burma* 18°20N 94°30E **313** K19
Thane *India* 19°12N 72°59E **312** K8
Thanesar *India* 30°1N 76°52E **314** D7
Thanet, I. of *U.K.* 51°21N 1°20E **285** F9
Thangool *Australia* 24°38S 150°42E **334** C5
Thanh Hoa *Vietnam* 19°48N 105°46E **310** C5
Thanh Hung *Vietnam* 9°55N 105°43E **311** H5
Thanh Pho Ho Chi Minh *Vietnam* 10°58N 106°40E **311** G6
Thanh Thuy *Vietnam* 22°55N 104°51E **310** A5
Thanjavur *India* 10°48N 79°12E **312** P11
Thano Bula Khan *Pakistan* 25°22N 67°50E **314** G2
Thaolintoa L. *Canada* 61°30N 96°25W **343** A9
Thap Lan △ *Thailand* 14°15N 102°16E **310** E4
Thap Sakae *Thailand* 11°30N 99°37E **311** G2
Thap Than *Thailand* 15°27N 99°54E **310** E2
Thar Desert *India* 28°0N 72°0E **314** F5
Tharad *India* 24°30N 71°44E **314** G4
Thargomindah *Australia* 27°58S 143°46E **335** D3
Tharp Fracture Zone *S. Ocean* 54°0S 135°0W **277** B14
Tharrawaddy *Burma* 17°38N 95°48E **313** L19
Tharthār, Buḩayrat ath *Iraq* 34°0N 43°15E **316** C4
Tharthar, L. = Tharthār, Buḩayrat ath *Iraq* 34°0N 43°15E **316** C4
Tharthār, W. ath → *Iraq* 34°32N 43°4E **316** C4
Thasos *Greece* 40°40N 24°40E **295** D11
That Khe *Vietnam* 22°16N 106°28E **310** A6
Thatcher *Ariz., U.S.A.* 32°51N 109°46W **349** K9
Thatcher *Colo., U.S.A.* 37°33N 104°7W **349** H11
Thaton *Burma* 16°55N 97°22E **313** L20
Thaungdut *Burma* 24°30N 94°40E **313** G19
Thayer *U.S.A.* 36°31N 91°33W **352** G8
Thayetmyo *Burma* 19°20N 95°10E **313** K19
Thazi *Burma* 21°0N 96°5E **313** J20
The Broads *U.K.* 52°45N 1°30E **284** E9
The Everglades *U.S.A.* 25°50N 81°0W **357** J14
The Gulf = Persian Gulf *Asia* 27°0N 50°0E **317** E6
The Hague = 's-Gravenhage *Neths.* 52°7N 4°17E **287** B4
The Pas *Canada* 53°45N 101°15W **343** C8
The Wash *U.K.* 52°58N 0°20E **284** E8
The Weald *U.K.* 51°4N 0°20E **285** F8
Thebes = Thiva *Greece* 38°19N 23°19E **295** E10
Thebes *Egypt* 25°40N 32°35E **323** C12
Thedford *U.S.A.* 41°59N 100°35W **352** E3
Theebine *Australia* 25°57S 152°34E **335** D5
Thekulthili L. *Canada* 61°3N 110°0W **343** A7
Thelon → *Canada* 64°16N 96°4W **343** A8
Theodore *Australia* 24°55S 150°3E **334** C5
Theodore *Canada* 51°26N 102°55W **343** C8
Theodore *U.S.A.* 30°33N 88°10W **357** F10
Theodore Roosevelt △ *U.S.A.* 47°0N 103°25W **352** B2
Theodore Roosevelt L. *U.S.A.* 33°40N 111°10W **349** K8
Thepha *Thailand* 6°52N 100°58E **311** J3
Theresa *U.S.A.* 44°13N 75°48W **355** B9
Thermopiles *Greece* 38°48N 22°35E **295** E10
Thermopolis *U.S.A.* 43°39N 108°13W **348** E9
Thermopylae P. = Thermopiles *Greece* 38°48N 22°35E **295** E10
Thessalon *Canada* 46°20N 83°30W **344** C3
Thessaloniki *Greece* 40°38N 22°58E **295** D10
Thessaloníki, Gulf of = Thessaloniki Kolpos *Greece* 40°15N 22°45E **295** D10
Thessaloniki Kolpos *Greece* 40°15N 22°45E **295** D10
Thetford *U.K.* 52°25N 0°45E **285** E8
Thetford Mines *Canada* 46°8N 71°18W **345** C5
Theun → *Laos* 18°19N 104°0E **310** C5
Theunissen *S. Africa* 28°26S 26°43E **328** D4
Thevenard *Australia* 32°9S 133°38E **335** E1
Thicket Portage *Canada* 55°19N 97°42W **343** B9
Thief River Falls *U.S.A.* 48°7N 96°10W **352** A5
Thiel Mts. *Antarctica* 85°15S 91°0W **277** E16
Thiers *France* 45°52N 3°33E **292** D5
Thiès *Senegal* 14°50N 16°51W **322** F2
Thika *Kenya* 1°1S 37°5E **326** C4
Thimphu *Bhutan* 27°31N 89°45E **313** F16
Thina → *S. Africa* 31°18S 29°13E **329** E4
Þingvallavatn *Iceland* 64°11N 21°9W **280** D3
Thionville *France* 49°20N 6°10E **292** B7
Thira = Santorini *Greece* 36°23N 25°27E **295** F11
Third Cataract *Sudan* 19°42N 30°20E **323** E12
Thirsk *U.K.* 54°14N 1°19W **284** C6
Thiruvananthapuram = Trivandrum *India* 8°41N 77°0E **312** Q10
Thisted *Denmark* 56°58N 8°40E **281** H13
Thistle I. *Australia* 35°0S 136°8E **335** F2
Thithia = Cicia *Fiji* 17°45S 179°18W **331** a
Thiva *Greece* 38°19N 23°19E **295** E10
Þjórsá → *Iceland* 63°47N 20°48W **280** E3
Thlewiaza → *Canada* 60°29N 94°40W **343** A10
Thmar Puok *Cambodia* 13°57N 103°4E **310** F4
Tho Vinh *Vietnam* 19°16N 105°42E **310** C5
Thoa → *Canada* 60°31N 109°47W **343** A7
Thoen *Thailand* 17°43N 99°12E **310** D2
Thoeng *Thailand* 19°41N 100°12E **310** C3
Thohoyandou *S. Africa* 22°58S 30°29E **325** J6
Tholdi *Pakistan* 35°5N 76°6E **315** B7
Thomas *U.S.A.* 35°45N 98°45W **356** D5
Thomas, L. *Australia* 26°4S 137°58E **335** D2
Thomaston *U.S.A.* 32°53N 84°20W **357** E12
Thomasville *Ala., U.S.A.* 31°55N 87°44W **357** F11
Thomasville *Ga., U.S.A.* 30°50N 83°59W **357** F13
Thomasville *N.C., U.S.A.* 35°53N 80°5W **357** D14
Thompson *Canada* 55°45N 97°52W **343** B9
Thompson *U.S.A.* 41°52N 75°31W **355** E9
Thompson → *Canada* 50°15N 121°24W **342** C4
Thompson → *U.S.A.* 39°46N 93°37W **352** F7
Thompson Falls *U.S.A.* 47°36N 115°21W **348** C6
Thompson Pk. *U.S.A.* 41°0N 123°2W **348** F2
Thompson Springs *U.S.A.* 38°58N 109°43W **348** G9
Thompsontown *U.S.A.* 40°33N 77°14W **354** F7
Thomson *U.S.A.* 33°28N 82°30W **357** E13
Thomson → *Australia* 25°11S 142°53E **334** C3
Thong Yang *Thailand* 9°28N 99°56E **311** b
Þórisvatn *Iceland* 64°20N 18°55W **280** D4
Thornaby on Tees *U.K.* 54°33N 1°18W **284** C6
Thornbury *Canada* 44°34N 80°26W **354** B4
Thorne *U.K.* 53°37N 0°57W **284** D7
Thornhill *Canada* 54°31N 128°32W **342** C3
Thornton *U.S.A.* 39°52N 104°58W **348** G11
Thorold *Canada* 43°7N 79°12W **354** C5
Þórshöfn *Iceland* 66°12N 15°20W **280** C6
Thouin, C. *Australia* 20°20S 118°10E **332** D2
Thousand Oaks *U.S.A.* 34°10N 118°50W **351** L8
Thrace *Turkey* 41°0N 27°0E **295** D12
Three Forks *U.S.A.* 45°54N 111°33W **348** D8
Three Hills *Canada* 51°43N 113°15W **342** C6
Three Hummock I. *Australia* 40°25S 144°55E **335** G3
Three Pagodas Pass *Asia* 15°20N 98°30E **310** E2
Three Points, C. *Ghana* 4°42N 2°6W **322** H5
Three Rivers *Calif., U.S.A.* 36°26N 118°54W **350** J8
Three Rivers *Tex., U.S.A.* 28°28N 98°11W **356** G5
Three Springs *Australia* 29°32S 115°45E **333** E2
Throssell, L. *Australia* 27°33S 124°10E **333** E3
Throssell Ra. *Australia* 22°3S 121°43E **332** D3
Thrushton △ *Australia* 27°47S 147°40E **335** D4
Thua → *Kenya* 1°31S 39°30E **326** C4
Thuan Hoa *Vietnam* 8°58N 105°30E **311** H5
Thubun Lakes *Canada* 61°30N 112°0W **343** A6
Thuin *Belgium* 50°20N 4°17E **287** D4
Thule = Qaanaaq *Greenland* 77°40N 69°0W **276** B4
Thule Air Base = Uummannaq *Greenland* 77°28N 69°13W **276** B4
Thun *Switz.* 46°45N 7°38E **292** C7
Thunder B. *U.S.A.* 45°0N 83°20W **354** B1
Thunder Bay *Canada* 48°20N 89°15W **344** C2
Thung Salaeng Luang △ *Thailand* 16°43N 100°50E **310** D3
Thung Song *Thailand* 8°10N 99°40E **311** H2
Thunkar *Bhutan* 27°55N 91°0E **313** F17
Thuong Tra *Vietnam* 16°2N 107°42E **310** D6
Thüringer Wald *Germany* 50°35N 11°0E **288** C6
Thurles *Ireland* 52°41N 7°49W **282** D4
Thurrock □ *U.K.* 51°31N 0°23E **285** F8
Thursday I. *Australia* 10°30S 142°3E **334** A3
Thurso *Canada* 45°36N 75°15W **344** C4
Thurso *U.K.* 58°36N 3°32W **283** C5
Thurso → *U.K.* 58°36N 3°32W **283** C5
Thurston I. *Antarctica* 72°0S 100°0W **277** D16
Thutade L. *Canada* 57°0N 126°55W **342** B3
Thyolo *Malawi* 16°7S 35°5E **327** F4
Ti-Tree *Australia* 22°5S 133°22E **334** C1
Tian Shan *Asia* 40°30N 76°0E **304** B3
Tianjin *China* 39°7N 117°12E **307** E9
Tianshifu *China* 41°17N 124°22E **307** D13
Tianshui *China* 34°32N 105°40E **306** G3
Tianyar *Indonesia* 8°12S 115°30E **309** J18
Tianzhen *China* 40°24N 114°5E **306** D8
Tianzhuangtai *China* 40°43N 122°5E **307** D12
Tiarei *Tahiti* 17°32S 149°20W **331** d
Tiaret *Algeria* 35°20N 1°21E **322** A6
Tibagi *Brazil* 24°30S 50°24W **367** A5
Tibagi → *Brazil* 22°47S 51°1W **367** A5
Tibastī, Sarīr *Libya* 22°50N 18°30E **323** D9
Tibati *Cameroon* 6°22N 12°30E **324** C2
Tiber = Tevere → *Italy* 41°44N 12°14E **294** D5
Tiber Res. *U.S.A.* 48°19N 111°6W **348** B8
Tiberias = Teverya *Israel* 32°47N 35°32E **318** C4
Tiberias, L. = Yam Kinneret *Israel* 32°45N 35°35E **318** C4
Tibesti *Chad* 21°0N 17°30E **323** D9
Tibet = Xizang Zizhiqu □ *China* 32°0N 88°0E **304** C3
Tibet, Plateau of *Asia* 32°0N 86°0E **298** E10
Tibnī *Syria* 35°36N 39°50E **316** C3
Tibooburra *Australia* 29°26S 142°1E **335** D3
Tiburón, I. *Mexico* 29°0N 112°25W **358** B2
Ticino → *Italy* 45°9N 9°14E **292** D8
Ticonderoga *U.S.A.* 43°51N 73°26W **355** C11
Ticul *Mexico* 20°24N 89°32W **359** C7
Tidaholm *Sweden* 58°12N 13°58E **281** G15
Tiddim *Burma* 23°28N 93°45E **313** H18
Tidioute *U.S.A.* 41°41N 79°24W **354** E5
Tidjikja *Mauritania* 18°29N 11°35W **322** E3
Tidore *Indonesia* 0°40N 127°25E **309** D7
Tiefa *China* 42°28N 123°26E **307** C12
Tiegang Shuiku *China* 22°37N 113°53E **305** F10
Tiel *Neths.* 51°53N 5°26E **287** C5
Tieling *China* 42°20N 123°55E **307** C12
Tielt *Belgium* 51°0N 3°20E **287** C3
Tien Shan = Tian Shan *Asia* 40°30N 76°0E **304** B3
Tien-tsin = Tianjin *China* 39°7N 117°12E **307** E9
Tien Yen *Vietnam* 21°20N 107°24E **310** B6
T'ienching = Tianjin *China* 39°7N 117°12E **307** E9
Tienen *Belgium* 50°48N 4°57E **287** D4
Tientsin = Tianjin *China* 39°7N 117°12E **307** E9
Tieri *Australia* 23°2S 148°21E **334** C4
Tierra Amarilla *Chile* 27°28S 70°18W **366** B1
Tierra Amarilla *U.S.A.* 36°42N 106°33W **349** H10
Tierra Colorada *Mexico* 17°11N 99°32W **359** D5
Tierra de Campos *Spain* 42°10N 4°50W **293** A3
Tierra del Fuego, I. Gr. de *Argentina* 54°0S 69°0W **368** G3
Tiétar → *Spain* 39°50N 6°1W **293** C3
Tieté → *Brazil* 20°40S 51°35W **367** A5
Tiffin *U.S.A.* 41°7N 83°11W **353** E12
Tifton *U.S.A.* 31°27N 83°31W **357** F13
Tifu *Indonesia* 3°39S 126°24E **309** E7
Tighina *Moldova* 46°50N 29°30E **289** E15
Tigil *Russia* 57°49N 158°40E **301** D16
Tignish *Canada* 46°58N 64°2W **345** C7
Tigre → *Peru* 4°30S 74°10W **364** D4
Tigre → *Venezuela* 9°20N 62°30W **364** B6
Tigris = Dijlah, Nahr → *Asia* 31°0N 47°25E **316** D5
Tigyaing *Burma* 23°45N 96°10E **313** H20
Tijara *India* 27°56N 76°31E **314** F7
Tijuana *Mexico* 32°32N 117°1W **351** N9
Tikal *Guatemala* 17°13N 89°24W **360** C2
Tikal △ *Guatemala* 17°23N 89°34W **360** C2
Tikamgarh *India* 24°44N 78°50E **315** G8
Tikhoretsk *Russia* 45°56N 40°5E **291** E7
Tikhvin *Russia* 59°35N 33°30E **290** C5
Tikiraqjuaq = Whale Cove *Canada* 62°10N 92°34W **343** A10
Tikrīt *Iraq* 34°35N 43°37E **316** C4
Tiksi *Russia* 71°40N 128°45E **301** B13
Tilamuta *Indonesia* 0°32N 122°23E **309** D6
Tilburg *Neths.* 51°31N 5°6E **287** C5
Tilbury *Canada* 42°17N 82°23W **354** D2
Tilbury *U.K.* 51°27N 0°22E **285** F8
Tilcara *Argentina* 23°36S 65°23W **366** A2
Tilden *U.S.A.* 42°3N 97°50W **352** D5
Tilhar *India* 28°0N 79°45E **315** F8
Tilichiki *Russia* 60°27N 166°5E **301** C17
Tilissos *Greece* 35°20N 25°1E **297** D7
Till → *U.K.* 55°41N 2°13W **284** B5
Tillamook *U.S.A.* 45°27N 123°51W **348** D2
Tillsonburg *Canada* 42°53N 80°44W **354** D4
Tillyeria *Cyprus* 35°6N 32°40E **297** D11
Tilos *Greece* 36°27N 27°27E **295** F12
Tilpa *Australia* 30°57S 144°24E **335** E3
Tilt → *U.K.* 56°46N 3°51W **283** E5
Tilton *U.S.A.* 43°27N 71°36W **355** C13
Tiltonsville *U.S.A.* 40°10N 80°41W **354** F4
Timanfaya △ *Canary Is.* 29°0N 13°46W **296** F6
Timanskiy Kryazh *Russia* 65°58N 50°5E **290** A9
Timaru *N.Z.* 44°23S 171°14E **331** F3
Timau *Kenya* 0°4N 37°15E **326** B4
Timbaki *Greece* 35°4N 24°45E **297** D6
Timber Creek *Australia* 15°40S 130°29E **332** C5
Timber Lake *U.S.A.* 45°26N 101°5W **352** C3
Timber Mt. *U.S.A.* 37°6N 116°28W **350** H10
Timbuktu = Tombouctou *Mali* 16°50N 3°0W **322** E5
Timi *Cyprus* 34°44N 32°31E **297** E11
Timimoun *Algeria* 29°14N 0°16E **322** C6
Timiris, Râs *Mauritania* 19°21N 16°30W **322** E2
Timiskaming, L. = Témiscamingue, L. *Canada* 47°10N 79°25W **344** C4
Timişoara *Romania* 45°43N 21°15E **289** F11
Timmins *Canada* 48°28N 81°25W **344** C3
Timok → *Serbia* 44°10N 22°40E **295** B10
Timoleague *Ireland* 51°39N 8°46W **282** E3
Timor *Asia* 9°0S 125°0E **309** F7
Timor Leste = East Timor ■ *Asia* 8°50S 126°0E **309** F7
Timor Sea *Ind. Oc.* 12°0S 127°0E **332** B4
Tin Can Bay *Australia* 25°56S 153°0E **335** D5
Tin Mt. *U.S.A.* 36°50N 117°10W **350** J9
Tina = Thina → *S. Africa* 31°18S 29°13E **329** E4
Tîna, Khalîg el *Egypt* 31°10N 32°40E **318** D1
Tinaca Pt. *Phil.* 5°30N 125°25E **309** C7
Tinajo *Canary Is.* 29°4N 13°42W **296** E6
Tindal *Australia* 14°31S 132°22E **332** B5
Tindouf *Algeria* 27°42N 8°10W **322** C4
Tinfunque △ *Paraguay* 23°55S 60°17W **366** A3
Tinggi, Pulau *Malaysia* 2°18N 104°7E **311** L5
Tingo Maria *Peru* 9°10S 75°54W **364** E3
Tingrela *Ivory C.* 10°27N 6°25W **322** F4
Tinh Bien *Vietnam* 10°36N 104°57E **311** G5
Tinian *N. Marianas* 15°0N 145°38E **336** F6
Tinnevelly = Tirunelveli *India* 8°45N 77°45E **312** Q10
Tinogasta *Argentina* 28°5S 67°32W **366** B2
Tinos *Greece* 37°33N 25°8E **295** F11
Tinpahar *India* 24°59N 87°44E **315** G12
Tintina *Argentina* 27°2S 62°45W **366** B3
Tintinara *Australia* 35°48S 140°2E **335** F3
Tioga *N. Dak., U.S.A.* 48°24N 102°56W **352** A2
Tioga *Pa., U.S.A.* 41°55N 77°8W **354** E7
Tioman, Pulau *Malaysia* 2°50N 104°10E **311** L5
Tionesta *U.S.A.* 41°30N 79°28W **354** E5
Tipperary *Ireland* 52°28N 8°10W **282** D3
Tipperary □ *Ireland* 52°37N 7°55W **282** D4
Tipton *Calif., U.S.A.* 36°4N 119°19W **350** J7
Tipton *Iowa, U.S.A.* 41°46N 91°8W **352** E8
Tipton Mt. *U.S.A.* 35°32N 114°12W **351** K12
Tiptonville *U.S.A.* 36°23N 89°29W **357** C10
Tīrān *Iran* 32°45N 51°8E **317** C6
Tiranë *Albania* 41°18N 19°49E **295** D8
Tirari Desert *Australia* 28°22S 138°7E **335** D2
Tiraspol *Moldova* 46°55N 29°35E **289** E15
Tire *Turkey* 38°5N 27°45E **295** E12
Tirebolu *Turkey* 40°58N 38°45E **291** F6
Tiree *U.K.* 56°31N 6°55W **283** E2
Tiree, Passage of *U.K.* 56°30N 6°30W **283** E2
Tîrgovişte = Târgovişte *Romania* 44°55N 25°27E **289** F13
Tîrgu-Jiu = Târgu-Jiu *Romania* 45°5N 23°19E **289** F12
Tîrgu Mureş = Târgu Mureş *Romania* 46°31N 24°38E **289** E13
Tirich Mir *Pakistan* 36°15N 71°55E **312** A7
Tiritiri o te Moana = Southern Alps *N.Z.* 43°41S 170°11E **331** E3
Tirnavos *Greece* 39°45N 22°18E **295** E10
Tirodi *India* 21°40N 79°44E **312** J11
Tirol □ *Austria* 47°3N 10°43E **288** E6
Tirso → *Italy* 39°53N 8°32E **294** E3
Tiruchchirappalli *India* 10°45N 78°45E **312** P11
Tirunelveli *India* 8°45N 77°45E **312** Q10
Tirupati *India* 13°39N 79°25E **312** N11
Tiruppur *India* 11°5N 77°22E **312** P10
Tiruvannamalai *India* 12°15N 79°5E **312** N11
Tisa *India* 32°50N 76°9E **314** C7
Tisa → *Serbia* 45°15N 20°17E **295** B9
Tisdale *Canada* 52°50N 104°0W **343** C8
Tishomingo *U.S.A.* 34°14N 96°41W **356** D6
Tisza = Tisa → *Serbia* 45°15N 20°17E **295** B9
Tit-Ary *Russia* 71°55N 127°2E **301** B13
Tithwal *Pakistan* 34°21N 73°50E **315** B5
Titicaca, L. *S. Amer.* 15°30S 69°30W **364** G5
Titiwa *Nigeria* 12°14N 12°53E **323** F8
Titule *Dem. Rep. of the Congo* 3°15N 25°31E **326** B2
Titusville *Fla., U.S.A.* 28°37N 80°49W **357** G14
Titusville *Pa., U.S.A.* 41°38N 79°41W **354** E5
Tivaouane *Senegal* 14°56N 16°45W **322** F2
Tiverton *U.K.* 50°54N 3°29W **285** G4
Tívoli *Italy* 41°58N 12°45E **294** D5
Tizi-Ouzou *Algeria* 36°42N 4°3E **322** A6
Tizimín *Mexico* 21°9N 88°9W **359** C7
Tiznit *Morocco* 29°48N 9°45W **322** C4
Tjeggelvas *Sweden* 66°37N 17°45E **280** C17
Tjieggelvas = Tjeggelvas *Sweden* 66°37N 17°45E **280** C17
Tjirebon = Cirebon *Indonesia* 6°45S 108°32E **308** F3
Tjluring *Indonesia* 8°25S 114°13E **309** J17
Tjörn *Sweden* 58°0N 11°35E **281** H14
Tlacotalpan *Mexico* 18°37N 95°40W **359** D5
Tlahualilo de Zaragoza *Mexico* 26°7N 103°27W **358** B4
Tlaquepaque *Mexico* 20°39N 103°19W **358** C4
Tlaxcala *Mexico* 19°19N 98°14W **359** D5
Tlaxcala □ *Mexico* 19°25N 98°10W **359** D5
Tlaxiaco *Mexico* 17°25N 97°35W **359** D5
Tlemcen *Algeria* 34°52N 1°21W **322** B5
To Bong *Vietnam* 12°45N 109°16E **310** F7
Toa Payoh *Singapore* 1°20N 103°51E **311** d
Toad → *Canada* 59°25N 124°57W **342** B4
Toad River *Canada* 58°51N 125°14W **342** B3
Toamasina *Madag.* 18°10S 49°25E **329** B8
Toamasina □ *Madag.* 18°0S 49°0E **329** B8
Toay *Argentina* 36°43S 64°38W **366** D3
Toba *Japan* 34°30N 136°51E **303** G8
Toba, Danau *Indonesia* 2°30N 97°30E **308** D1
Toba Kakar *Pakistan* 31°30N 69°0E **314** D3
Toba Tek Singh *Pakistan* 30°55N 72°25E **314** D5
Tobago *Trin. & Tob.* 11°10N 60°30W **361** D7
Tobelo *Indonesia* 1°45N 127°56E **309** D7
Tobermory *Canada* 45°12N 81°40W **354** A3
Tobermory *U.K.* 56°38N 6°5W **283** E2
Tobi *Pac. Oc.* 2°40N 131°10E **309** D8
Tobi-Shima *Japan* 41°12N 139°34E **302** D9
Tobin, L. *Australia* 21°45S 125°49E **332** D4
Tobin L. *Canada* 53°35N 103°30W **343** C8
Toboali *Indonesia* 3°0S 106°25E **308** E3
Tobol → *Russia* 58°10N 68°12E **300** D7
Toboli *Indonesia* 0°38S 120°5E **309** E6
Tobolsk *Russia* 58°15N 68°10E **300** D7
Tobruk = Tubruq *Libya* 32°7N 23°55E **323** B10
Tobyhanna *U.S.A.* 41°11N 75°25W **355** E9
Tobyl = Tobol → *Russia* 58°10N 68°12E **300** D7
Tocantinópolis *Brazil* 6°20S 47°25W **365** E9
Tocantins □ *Brazil* 10°0S 48°0W **365** F9
Tocantins → *Brazil* 1°45S 49°10W **365** D9
Toccoa *U.S.A.* 34°35N 83°19W **357** D13
Tochi → *Pakistan* 32°49N 70°41E **314** C4
Tochigi *Japan* 36°25N 139°45E **303** F9
Tochigi □ *Japan* 36°45N 139°45E **303** F9
Toco *Trin. & Tob.* 10°49N 60°57W **365** K16
Toconao *Chile* 23°11S 68°1W **366** A2
Tocopilla *Chile* 22°5S 70°10W **366** A1
Tocumwal *Australia* 35°51S 145°31E **335** F4
Tocuyo → *Venezuela* 11°3N 68°23W **364** A5
Todd → *Australia* 24°52S 135°48E **334** C2
Todeli *Indonesia* 1°40S 124°29E **309** E6
Todenyang *Kenya* 4°35N 35°56E **326** B4
Todgarh *India* 25°42N 73°58E **314** G5
Todos os Santos, B. de *Brazil* 12°48S 38°38W **365** F11
Todos Santos *Mexico* 23°26N 110°13W **358** C2
Toe Hd. *U.K.* 57°50N 7°8W **283** D1
Tofield *Canada* 53°25N 112°40W **342** C6
Tofino *Canada* 49°11N 125°55W **342** D3
Tofua *Tonga* 19°45S 175°5W **331** c
Tōgane *Japan* 35°33N 140°22E **303** G10
Togian, Kepulauan *Indonesia* 0°20S 121°50E **309** E6
Togliatti *Russia* 53°32N 49°24E **290** D8
Togo ■ *W. Afr.* 8°30N 1°35E **322** G6
Togtoh *China* 40°15N 111°10E **306** D6
Tohiea, Mt. *Moorea* 17°33S 149°49W **331** d
Tōhoku □ *Japan* 39°50N 141°45E **302** E10
Töhöm *Mongolia* 44°27N 108°2E **306** B5
Toinya *Sudan* 6°17N 29°46E **323** G11
Toiyabe Range *U.S.A.* 39°30N 117°0W **348** G5
Tojikiston = Tajikistan ■ *Asia* 38°30N 70°0E **300** F8
Tojo *Indonesia* 1°20S 121°15E **309** E6
Tōjō *Japan* 34°53N 133°16E **303** G6
Tok *U.S.A.* 63°20N 142°59W **346** a
Tok-do *Asia* 37°15N 131°52E **303** F5
Tokachi-Dake *Japan* 43°17N 142°5E **302** C11
Tokachi-Gawa → *Japan* 42°44N 143°42E **302** C11
Tokala *Indonesia* 1°30S 121°40E **309** E6
Tōkamachi *Japan* 37°8N 138°43E **303** F9
Tokanui *N.Z.* 46°34S 168°56E **331** G2
Tokara-Rettō *Japan* 29°37N 129°43E **303** K4
Tokarahi *N.Z.* 44°56S 170°39E **331** F3
Tokashiki-Shima *Japan* 26°11N 127°21E **303** L3
Tokat *Turkey* 40°22N 36°35E **291** F6
Tŏkch'ŏn *N. Korea* 39°45N 126°18E **307** E14
Tokeland *U.S.A.* 46°42N 123°59W **350** D3
Tokelau Is. *Pac. Oc.* 9°0S 171°45W **336** H10
Tokmak *Kyrgyzstan* 42°49N 75°15E **300** E8
Toko Ra. *Australia* 23°5S 138°20E **334** C2
Tokoro-Gawa → *Japan* 44°7N 144°5E **302** B12
Toku *Tonga* 18°10S 174°11W **331** c
Tokuno-Shima *Japan* 27°56N 128°55E **303** L4
Tokushima *Japan* 34°4N 134°34E **303** G7
Tokushima □ *Japan* 33°55N 134°0E **303** H7
Tokuyama *Japan* 34°3N 131°50E **303** G5

Tōkyō Japan 35°43N 139°45E 303 G9
Tolaga Bay N.Z. 38°21S 178°20E 331 C7
Tolbukhin = Dobrich Bulgaria 43°37N 27°49E 295 C12
Toledo Brazil 24°44S 53°45W 367 A5
Toledo Spain 39°50N 4°2W 293 C3
Toledo Ohio, U.S.A. 41°39N 83°33W 353 E12
Toledo Oreg., U.S.A. 44°37N 123°56W 348 D2
Toledo Wash., U.S.A. 46°26N 122°51W 348 C2
Toledo, Montes de Spain 39°33N 4°20W 293 C3
Toledo Bend Res. U.S.A. 31°11N 93°34W 356 F8
Tolga Australia 17°15S 145°29E 334 B4
Toliara Madag. 23°21S 43°40E 329 C7
Toliara □ Madag. 21°0S 45°0E 329 C8
Tolima Colombia 4°40N 75°19W 364 C3
Tolitoli Indonesia 1°5N 120°50E 309 D6
Tollhouse U.S.A. 37°1N 119°24W 350 H7
Tolmachevo Russia 58°56N 29°51E 281 G23
Tolo, Teluk Indonesia 2°20S 122°10E 309 E6
Tolo Harbour China 22°27N 114°12E 305 G11
Toluca Mexico 19°17N 99°40W 359 D5
Tom Burke S. Africa 23°5S 28°0E 329 C4
Tom Price Australia 22°40S 117°48E 332 D2
Tomah U.S.A. 43°59N 90°30W 352 D8
Tomahawk U.S.A. 45°28N 89°44W 352 C9
Tomakomai Japan 42°38N 141°36E 302 C10
Tomales U.S.A. 38°15N 122°53W 350 G4
Tomales B. U.S.A. 38°15N 123°58W 350 G3
Tomanivi Fiji 17°37S 178°1E 331 a
Tomar Portugal 39°36N 8°25W 293 C1
Tomaszów Mazowiecki Poland 51°30N 20°2E 289 C10
Tomatlán Mexico 19°56N 105°15W 358 D3
Tombador, Serra do Brazil 12°0S 58°0W 364 F7
Tombigbee → U.S.A. 31°8N 87°57W 357 F11
Tombouctou Mali 16°50N 3°0W 322 E5
Tombstone U.S.A. 31°43N 110°4W 349 L8
Tombua Angola 15°55S 11°55E 328 B1
Tomé Chile 36°36S 72°57W 366 D1
Tomelloso Spain 39°10N 3°2W 293 C4
Tomini Indonesia 0°30N 120°30E 309 D6
Tomini, Teluk Indonesia 0°10S 121°0E 309 E6
Tomintoul U.K. 57°15N 3°23W 283 D5
Tomkinson Ranges Australia 26°11S 129°5E 333 E4
Tommot Russia 59°4N 126°20E 301 D13
Tomnop Ta Suos Cambodia 11°20N 104°15E 311 G5
Tomo → Colombia 5°20N 67°48W 364 B5
Toms Place U.S.A. 37°34N 118°41W 350 H8
Toms River U.S.A. 39°58N 74°12W 355 G10
Tomsk Russia 56°30N 85°5E 300 D9
Tonalá Chiapas, Mexico 16°4N 93°45W 359 D6
Tonalá Jalisco, Mexico 20°37N 103°14W 358 C4
Tonantins Brazil 2°45S 67°45W 364 D5
Tonasket U.S.A. 48°42N 119°26W 348 B4
Tonawanda U.S.A. 43°1N 78°53W 354 D6
Tonb Iran 26°15N 55°15E 317 E7
Tonbridge U.K. 51°11N 0°17E 285 F8
Tondano Indonesia 1°35N 124°54E 309 D6
Tondoro Namibia 17°45S 18°50E 328 B2
Tone → Australia 34°25S 116°25E 333 F2
Tone-Gawa → Japan 35°44N 140°51E 303 F9
Tonekābon Iran 36°45N 51°12E 317 B6
Tong Xian China 39°55N 116°35E 306 E9
Tong-Yeong S. Korea 34°50N 128°20E 307 G15
Tonga ■ Pac. Oc. 19°50S 174°30W 331 c
Tonga Trench Pac. Oc. 18°0S 173°0W 336 J10
Tongaat S. Africa 29°33S 31°9E 329 D5
Tongareva = Penrhyn Cook Is. 9°0S 158°0W 337 H12
Tongariro △ N.Z. 39°8S 175°33E 331 C5
Tongatapu Tonga 21°10S 175°10W 331 c
Tongatapu Group Tonga 21°0S 175°0W 331 c
Tongchuan China 35°6N 109°3E 306 G5
Tongeren Belgium 50°47N 5°28E 287 D5
Tonggu Jiao China 22°22N 113°37E 305 G10
Tongguan China 34°40N 110°25E 306 G6
Tonghua China 41°42N 125°58E 307 D13
Tongjosŏn Man N. Korea 39°30N 128°0E 307 E15
Tongking, G. of = Tonkin, G. of Asia 20°0N 108°0E 310 B7
Tongliao China 43°38N 122°18E 307 C12
Tongling China 30°55N 117°48E 305 C6
Tongobory Madag. 23°32S 44°20E 329 C7
Tongoy Chile 30°16S 71°31W 366 C1
Tongres = Tongeren Belgium 50°47N 5°28E 287 D5
Tongsa Dzong Bhutan 27°31N 90°31E 313 F17
Tongshi China 18°30N 109°20E 310 C7
Tongue U.K. 58°29N 4°25W 283 C4
Tongue → U.S.A. 46°25N 105°52W 348 C11
Tongwei China 35°0N 105°5E 306 G3
Tongxin China 36°59N 105°58E 306 F3
Tongyang N. Korea 39°9N 126°53E 307 E14
Tongyu China 44°45N 123°4E 307 B12
Tonj Sudan 7°20N 28°44E 323 G11
Tonk India 26°6N 75°54E 314 F6
Tonkawa U.S.A. 36°41N 97°18W 356 C6
Tonkin = Bac Phan Vietnam 22°0N 105°0E 310 B5
Tonkin, G. of Asia 20°0N 108°0E 310 B7
Tonle Sap Cambodia 13°0N 104°0E 311 F5
Tono Japan 39°19N 141°32E 302 E10
Tonopah U.S.A. 38°4N 117°14W 349 G5
Tonosí Panama 7°20N 80°20W 360 E3
Tons → Haryana, India 30°30N 77°39E 314 D7
Tons → Ut. P., India 26°1N 83°33E 315 F10
Tønsberg Norway 59°19N 10°25E 281 G14
Tonto △ U.S.A. 33°39N 111°7W 349 K8
Tonumea Tonga 20°30S 174°30W 331 c
Toobanna Australia 18°42S 146°9E 334 B4
Toodyay Australia 31°34S 116°28E 333 F2
Tooele U.S.A. 40°32N 112°18W 348 F7
Toompine Australia 27°15S 144°19E 335 D3
Toora Australia 38°39S 146°23E 335 F4
Toora-Khem Russia 52°28N 96°17E 301 D10
Toowoomba Australia 27°32S 151°56E 335 D5
Top-ozero Russia 65°35N 32°0E 280 D25
Top Springs Australia 16°37S 131°51E 332 C5
Topaz U.S.A. 38°41N 119°30W 350 G7
Topeka U.S.A. 39°3N 95°40W 352 F6
Topley Canada 54°49N 126°18W 342 C3
Topocalma, Pta. Chile 34°10S 72°2W 366 C1
Topock U.S.A. 34°46N 114°29W 351 L12
Topol'čany Slovak Rep. 48°35N 18°12E 289 D10
Topolobampo Mexico 25°36N 109°3W 358 B3
Toppenish U.S.A. 46°23N 120°19W 348 C3
Toraka Vestale Madag. 16°20S 43°58E 329 B7
Torata Peru 17°23S 70°1W 364 G4
Torbalı Turkey 38°10N 27°21E 295 E12
Torbat-e Heydārīyeh Iran 35°15N 59°12E 317 C8
Torbat-e Jām Iran 35°16N 60°35E 317 C9
Torbay Canada 47°40N 52°42W 345 C9
Torbay □ U.K. 50°26N 3°31W 285 G4
Tordesillas Spain 41°30N 5°0W 293 B3
Torfaen □ U.K. 51°43N 3°3W 285 F4
Torgau Germany 51°34N 13°0E 288 C7
Torhout Belgium 51°5N 3°7E 287 C3
Tori-Shima Japan 30°29N 140°19E 303 J10
Torino Italy 45°3N 7°40E 292 D7
Torit Sudan 4°27N 32°31E 323 H12
Torkamān Iran 37°35N 47°23E 316 B5
Tormes → Spain 41°18N 6°29W 293 B2
Tornado Mt. Canada 49°55N 114°40W 342 D6
Torneå = Tornio Finland 65°50N 24°12E 280 D21
Torneälven → Europe 65°50N 24°12E 280 D21
Torneträsk Sweden 68°24N 19°15E 280 B18
Tornio Finland 65°50N 24°12E 280 D21
Tornionjoki = Torneälven → Europe 65°50N 24°12E 280 D21
Tornquist Argentina 38°8S 62°15W 366 D3
Toro Spain 39°59N 4°8E 296 B11
Toro, Cerro del Chile 29°10S 69°50W 366 B2
Toro △ Uganda 1°5N 30°22E 326 C3
Toro Pk. U.S.A. 33°34N 116°24W 351 M10
Toronto Canada 43°39N 79°20W 354 C5
Toronto U.S.A. 40°28N 80°36W 354 F4
Toronto Lester B. Pearson Int. ✕ (YYZ) Canada 43°46N 79°35W 354 C5
Toropets Russia 56°30N 31°40E 290 C5
Tororo Uganda 0°45N 34°12E 326 B3
Toros Dağları Turkey 37°0N 32°30E 316 B2
Torpa India 22°57N 85°6E 315 H11
Torquay U.K. 50°27N 3°32W 285 G4
Torrance U.S.A. 33°50N 118°20W 351 M8
Torre de Moncorvo Portugal 41°12N 7°8W 293 B2
Torre del Greco Italy 40°47N 14°22E 294 D6
Torrejón de Ardoz Spain 40°27N 3°29W 293 B4
Torrelavega Spain 43°20N 4°5W 293 A3
Torremolinos Spain 36°38N 4°30W 293 D3
Torrens, L. Australia 31°0S 137°50E 335 E2
Torrens Cr. → Australia 22°23S 145°9E 334 C4
Torrens Creek Australia 20°48S 145°3E 334 C4
Torrent Spain 39°27N 0°28W 293 C5
Torreón Mexico 25°33N 103°26W 358 B4
Torres Brazil 29°21S 49°44W 367 B5
Torres Mexico 28°46N 110°47W 358 B2
Torres Strait Australia 9°50S 142°20E 330 B7
Torres Vedras Portugal 39°5N 9°15W 293 C1
Torrevieja Spain 37°59N 0°42W 293 D5
Torrey U.S.A. 38°18N 111°25W 348 G8
Torridge → U.K. 51°0N 4°13W 285 G3
Torridon, L. U.K. 57°35N 5°50W 283 D3
Torrington Conn., U.S.A. 41°48N 73°7W 355 E11
Torrington Wyo., U.S.A. 42°4N 104°11W 348 E11
Tórshavn Færoe Is. 62°5N 6°56W 280 E9
Tortola Br. Virgin Is. 18°19N 64°45W 361 e
Tortosa Spain 40°49N 0°31E 293 B6
Tortosa, C. Spain 40°41N 0°52E 293 B6
Tortue, Î. de la Haiti 20°5N 72°57W 361 B5
Tortuguero △ Costa Rica 10°31N 83°29W 360 D3
Ţorūd Iran 35°25N 55°5E 317 C7
Toruń Poland 53°2N 18°39E 289 B10
Tory I. Ireland 55°16N 8°14W 282 A3
Tosa Japan 33°24N 133°23E 303 H6
Tosa-Shimizu Japan 32°52N 132°58E 303 H6
Tosa-Wan Japan 33°15N 133°30E 303 H6
Toscana □ Italy 43°25N 11°0E 294 C4
Toshka Lakes Egypt 22°50N 31°0E 323 D12
Toshkent Uzbekistan 41°20N 69°10E 300 E7
Tostado Argentina 29°15S 61°50W 366 B3
Tostón, Pta. de Canary Is. 28°42N 14°2W 296 F5
Tosu Japan 33°22N 130°31E 303 H5
Toteng Botswana 20°22S 22°58E 328 C3
Totma Russia 60°0N 42°40E 290 C7
Totnes U.K. 50°26N 3°42W 285 G4
Totness Suriname 5°53N 56°19W 365 B7
Totonicapán Guatemala 14°58N 91°12W 360 D1
Totoya, I. Fiji 18°57S 179°50W 331 a
Totten Glacier Antarctica 66°45S 116°10E 277 C8
Tottenham Australia 32°14S 147°21E 335 E4
Tottenham Canada 44°1N 79°49W 354 B5
Tottori Japan 35°30N 134°15E 303 G7
Tottori □ Japan 35°30N 134°12E 303 G7
Toubkal, Djebel Morocco 31°0N 8°0W 322 B4
Tougan Burkina Faso 13°11N 2°58W 322 F5
Touggourt Algeria 33°6N 6°4E 322 B7
Toul France 48°40N 5°53E 292 B6
Toulon France 43°10N 5°55E 292 E6
Toulouse France 43°37N 1°27E 292 E4
Toummo Niger 22°45N 14°8E 323 D8
Toungoo Burma 19°0N 96°30E 313 K20
Touraine France 47°20N 0°30E 292 C4
Tourcoing France 50°42N 3°10E 292 A5
Touriñán, C. Spain 43°3N 9°18W 293 A1
Tournai Belgium 50°35N 3°25E 287 D3
Tournon-sur-Rhône France 45°4N 4°50E 292 D6
Tours France 47°22N 0°40E 292 C4
Toussora, Mt. C.A.R. 9°7N 23°14E 324 C4
Touws → S. Africa 33°45S 21°11E 328 E3
Touwsrivier S. Africa 33°20S 20°2E 328 E3
Towada Japan 40°37N 141°13E 302 D10
Towada-Hachimantai △ Japan 40°20N 140°55E 302 D10
Towada-Ko Japan 40°28N 140°55E 302 D10
Towanda U.S.A. 41°46N 76°27W 355 E8
Tower U.S.A. 47°48N 92°17W 352 B7
Towerhill Cr. → Australia 22°28S 144°35E 334 C3
Towner U.S.A. 48°21N 100°25W 352 A3
Townsend U.S.A. 46°19N 111°31W 348 C8
Townshend I. Australia 22°10S 150°31E 334 C5
Townsville Australia 19°15S 146°45E 334 B4
Towraghondī Afghan. 35°13N 62°16E 312 B3
Towson U.S.A. 39°24N 76°36W 353 F15
Towuti, Danau Indonesia 2°45S 121°32E 309 E6
Toya-Ko Japan 42°35N 140°51E 302 C10
Toyama Japan 36°40N 137°15E 303 F8
Toyama □ Japan 36°45N 137°30E 303 F8
Toyama-Wan Japan 37°0N 137°30E 303 F8
Toyapakeh Indonesia 8°41S 115°29E 309 K18
Toyohashi Japan 34°45N 137°25E 303 G8
Toyokawa Japan 34°48N 137°27E 303 G8
Toyonaka Japan 34°46N 135°28E 303 G7
Toyooka Japan 35°35N 134°48E 303 G7
Toyota Japan 35°3N 137°7E 303 G8
Tozeur Tunisia 33°56N 8°8E 322 B7
Tozkhurmato Iraq 34°56N 44°38E 316 C5
Trá Li = Tralee Ireland 52°16N 9°42W 282 D2
Tra On Vietnam 9°58N 105°55E 311 H5
Trabzon Turkey 41°0N 39°45E 291 F6
Tracadie-Sheila Canada 47°30N 64°55W 345 C7
Tracy Calif., U.S.A. 37°44N 121°26W 350 H5
Tracy Minn., U.S.A. 44°14N 95°37W 352 C6
Trafalgar, C. Spain 36°10N 6°2W 293 D2
Trail Canada 49°5N 117°40W 342 D5
Trainor L. Canada 60°24N 120°17W 342 A4
Trakai △ Lithuania 54°30N 25°10E 281 J21
Trákhonas Cyprus 35°12N 33°21E 297 D12
Tralee Ireland 52°16N 9°42W 282 D2
Tralee B. Ireland 52°17N 9°55W 282 D2
Tramore Ireland 52°10N 7°10W 282 D4
Tramore B. Ireland 52°9N 7°10W 282 D4
Tran Ninh, Cao Nguyen Laos 19°30N 103°10E 310 C4
Tranås Sweden 58°3N 14°59E 281 G16
Trancas Argentina 26°11S 65°20W 366 B2
Trang Thailand 7°33N 99°38E 311 J2
Trangahy Madag. 19°7S 44°31E 329 B7
Trangan Indonesia 6°40S 134°20E 309 F8
Trangie Australia 32°4S 148°0E 335 E4
Trani Italy 41°17N 16°25E 294 D7
Tranoroa Madag. 24°42S 45°4E 329 C8
Tranqueras Uruguay 31°13S 55°45W 367 C4
Transantarctic Mts. Antarctica 85°0S 170°0W 277 E12
Transilvania Romania 46°30N 24°0E 289 E12
Transilvanian Alps = Carpaţii Meridionali Romania 45°30N 25°0E 289 F13
Transnistria = Stînga Nistrului □ Moldova 47°20N 29°15E 289 E15
Transylvania = Transilvania Romania 46°30N 24°0E 289 E12
Trápani Italy 38°1N 12°29E 294 E5
Trapper Pk. U.S.A. 45°54N 114°18W 348 D6
Traralgon Australia 38°12S 146°34E 335 F4
Trasimeno, L. Italy 43°8N 12°6E 294 C5
Trat Thailand 12°14N 102°33E 311 F4
Tratani → Pakistan 29°19N 68°20E 314 E3
Traun Austria 48°14N 14°15E 288 D8
Traveller's L. Australia 33°20S 142°0E 335 E3
Travemünde Germany 53°57N 10°52E 288 B6
Travers, Mt. N.Z. 42°1S 172°45E 331 E4
Traverse City U.S.A. 44°46N 85°38W 353 C11
Travis, L. U.S.A. 30°24N 97°55W 356 F6
Travnik Bos.-H. 44°17N 17°39E 295 B7
Trawbreaga B. Ireland 55°20N 7°25W 282 A4
Trébbia → Italy 45°4N 9°41E 292 D8
Třebíč Czech Rep. 49°14N 15°55E 288 D8
Trebinje Bos.-H. 42°44N 18°22E 295 C8
Trebonne Australia 18°37S 146°5E 334 B4
Tregaron U.K. 52°14N 3°56W 285 E4
Tregrosse Is. Australia 17°41S 150°43E 334 B5
Treherne Canada 49°38N 98°42W 343 D9
Treinta y Tres Uruguay 33°16S 54°17W 367 C5
Trelawney Zimbabwe 17°30S 30°30E 329 B5
Trelew Argentina 43°10S 65°20W 368 E3
Trelleborg Sweden 55°20N 13°10E 281 J15
Tremadog Bay U.K. 52°51N 4°18W 284 E3
Tremonton U.S.A. 41°43N 112°10W 348 F7
Tremp Spain 42°10N 0°52E 293 A6
Trenche → Canada 47°46N 72°53W 344 C5
Trenčín Slovak Rep. 48°52N 18°4E 289 D10
Trenggalek Indonesia 8°3S 111°43E 309 H14
Trenque Lauquen Argentina 36°5S 62°45W 366 D3
Trent → Canada 44°6N 77°34W 354 B7
Trent → U.K. 53°41N 0°42W 284 D7
Trento Italy 46°4N 11°8E 294 A4
Trenton = Quinte West Canada 44°10N 77°34W 354 B7
Trenton Mo., U.S.A. 40°5N 93°37W 352 E7
Trenton N.J., U.S.A. 40°14N 74°46W 355 F10
Trenton Nebr., U.S.A. 40°11N 101°1W 352 E3
Trepassey Canada 46°43N 53°25W 345 C9
Tres Arroyos Argentina 38°26S 60°20W 366 D3
Três Corações Brazil 21°44S 45°15W 367 A6
Três Lagoas Brazil 20°50S 51°43W 365 H8
Tres Lomas Argentina 36°27S 62°51W 366 D3
Tres Montes, C. Chile 46°50S 75°30W 368 F1
Tres Pinos U.S.A. 36°48N 121°19W 350 J5
Três Pontas Brazil 21°23S 45°29W 367 A6
Tres Puentes Chile 27°50S 70°15W 366 B1
Tres Puntas, C. Argentina 47°0S 66°0W 368 F3
Três Rios Brazil 22°6S 43°15W 367 A7
Tres Valles Mexico 18°15N 96°8W 359 D5
Tresco U.K. 49°57N 6°20W 285 H1
Treviso Italy 45°40N 12°15E 294 B5
Triabunna Australia 42°30S 147°55E 335 G4
Trianda Greece 36°25N 28°10E 297 C10
Triangle Zimbabwe 21°2S 31°28E 329 C5
Tribal Areas □ Pakistan 33°0N 70°0E 314 C4
Tribulation, C. Australia 16°5S 145°29E 334 B4
Tribune U.S.A. 38°28N 101°45W 352 F3
Trichinopoly = Tiruchchirappalli India 10°45N 78°45E 312 P11
Trichur India 10°30N 76°18E 312 P10
Trida Australia 33°1S 145°1E 335 E4
Trier Germany 49°45N 6°38E 288 D4
Trieste Italy 45°40N 13°46E 294 B5
Triglav Slovenia 46°21N 13°50E 288 E7
Trikala Greece 39°34N 21°47E 295 E9
Trikomo Cyprus 35°17N 33°52E 297 D12
Trikora, Puncak Indonesia 4°15S 138°45E 309 E9
Trim Ireland 53°33N 6°48W 282 C5
Trimmu Dam Pakistan 31°10N 72°8E 314 D5
Trincomalee Sri Lanka 8°38N 81°15E 312 Q12
Trindade Brazil 16°40S 49°30W 365 G9
Trindade, I. Atl. Oc. 20°20S 29°50W 274 F8
Trinidad Bolivia 14°46S 64°50W 364 F6
Trinidad Cuba 21°48N 80°0W 360 B4
Trinidad Trin. & Tob. 10°30N 61°15W 361 D7
Trinidad Uruguay 33°30S 56°50W 366 C4
Trinidad U.S.A. 37°10N 104°31W 349 H11
Trinidad → Mexico 17°49N 95°9W 359 D5
Trinidad & Tobago ■ W. Indies 10°30N 61°20W 361 D7
Trinity Canada 48°59N 53°55W 345 C9
Trinity U.S.A. 30°57N 95°22W 356 F7
Trinity → Calif., U.S.A. 41°11N 123°42W 348 F2
Trinity → Tex., U.S.A. 29°45N 94°43W 356 G7
Trinity B. Canada 48°20N 53°10W 345 C9
Trinity Hills Trin. & Tob. 10°7N 61°7W 365 K15
Trinity Is. U.S.A. 56°33N 154°25W 346 a
Trinity Range U.S.A. 40°10N 118°40W 348 F4
Trinkitat Sudan 18°45N 37°51E 323 E13
Trinway U.S.A. 40°9N 82°1W 354 F2
Triolet Mauritius 20°4S 57°32E 325 d
Tripoli = Tarābulus Lebanon 34°31N 35°50E 318 A4
Tripoli = Tarābulus Libya 32°49N 13°7E 323 B8
Tripoli Greece 37°31N 22°25E 295 F10
Tripolitania N. Afr. 31°0N 13°0E 323 B8
Tripura □ India 24°0N 92°0E 313 H18
Tripylos Cyprus 34°59N 32°41E 297 E11
Tristan da Cunha Atl. Oc. 37°6S 12°20W 321 K2
Trisul India 30°19N 79°47E 315 D8
Trivandrum India 8°41N 77°0E 312 Q10
Trnava Slovak Rep. 48°23N 17°35E 289 D9
Trochu Canada 51°50N 113°13W 342 C6
Trodely I. Canada 52°15N 79°26W 344 B4
Troglav Croatia 43°56N 16°36E 294 C7
Troilus, L. Canada 50°50N 74°35W 344 B5
Trois-Pistoles Canada 48°5N 69°10W 345 C6
Trois-Rivières Canada 46°25N 72°34W 344 C5
Trois-Rivières Guadeloupe 15°57N 61°40W 360 b
Troitsk Russia 54°10N 61°35E 300 D7
Troitsko Pechorsk Russia 62°40N 56°10E 290 B10
Trölladyngja Iceland 64°54N 17°16W 280 D5
Trollhättan Sweden 58°17N 12°20E 281 G15
Trollheimen Norway 62°46N 9°1E 280 E13
Trombetas → Brazil 1°55S 55°35W 365 D7
Tromsø Norway 69°40N 18°56E 280 B18
Trona U.S.A. 35°46N 117°23W 351 K9
Tronador, Mte. Argentina 41°10S 71°50W 368 E2
Trøndelag Norway 64°17N 11°50E 280 D14
Trondheim Norway 63°36N 10°25E 280 E14
Trondheimsfjorden Norway 63°35N 10°30E 280 E14
Troodos Cyprus 34°55N 32°52E 297 E11
Troon U.K. 55°33N 4°39W 283 F4
Tropic U.S.A. 37°37N 112°5W 349 H7
Trostan U.K. 55°3N 6°10W 282 A5
Trou Gras Pt. St. Lucia 13°51N 60°53W 361 f
Trout → Canada 61°19N 119°51W 342 A5
Trout L. N.W.T., Canada 60°40N 121°14W 342 A4
Trout L. Ont., Canada 51°20N 93°15W 343 C10
Trout Lake Canada 56°30N 114°32W 342 B6
Trout Lake U.S.A. 46°0N 121°32W 350 E5
Trout River Canada 49°29N 58°8W 345 C8
Trout Run U.S.A. 41°23N 77°3W 354 E7
Trouville-sur-Mer France 49°21N 0°5E 292 B4
Trowbridge U.K. 51°18N 2°12W 285 F5
Troy Turkey 39°57N 26°12E 295 E12
Troy Ala., U.S.A. 31°48N 85°58W 357 F12
Troy Kans., U.S.A. 39°47N 95°5W 352 F6
Troy Mo., U.S.A. 38°59N 90°59W 352 F8
Troy Mont., U.S.A. 48°28N 115°53W 348 B6
Troy N.Y., U.S.A. 42°44N 73°41W 355 D11
Troy Ohio, U.S.A. 40°2N 84°12W 353 E11
Troy Pa., U.S.A. 41°47N 76°47W 355 E8
Troyes France 48°19N 4°3E 292 B6
Truchas Pk. U.S.A. 35°58N 105°39W 349 J11
Trucial States = United Arab Emirates ■ Asia 23°50N 54°0E 317 F7
Truckee U.S.A. 39°20N 120°11W 350 F6
Trudovoye Russia 43°17N 132°5E 302 C6
Trujillo Honduras 16°0N 86°0W 360 C2
Trujillo Peru 8°6S 79°0W 364 E3
Trujillo Spain 39°28N 5°55W 293 C3
Trujillo U.S.A. 35°32N 104°42W 349 J11
Trujillo Venezuela 9°22N 70°38W 364 B4
Truk Micronesia 7°25N 151°46E 336 G7
Trumann U.S.A. 35°41N 90°31W 357 D9
Trumansburg U.S.A. 42°33N 76°40W 355 D8
Trumbull, Mt. U.S.A. 36°25N 113°19W 349 H7
Trundle Australia 32°53S 147°35E 335 E4
Trung-Phan = Annam Vietnam 16°0N 108°0E 310 E7
Truro Canada 45°21N 63°14W 345 C7
Truro U.K. 50°16N 5°4W 285 G2
Truskavets Ukraine 49°17N 23°30E 289 D12
Trutch Canada 57°44N 122°57W 342 B4
Truth or Consequences U.S.A. 33°8N 107°15W 349 K10
Trutnov Czech Rep. 50°37N 15°54E 288 C8
Truxton U.S.A. 42°45N 76°2W 355 D8
Tryonville U.S.A. 41°42N 79°48W 354 E5
Tsandi Namibia 17°42S 14°50E 328 B1
Tsaratanana Madag. 16°47S 47°39E 329 B8
Tsaratanana, Mt. de = Maromokotro Madag. 14°0S 49°0E 329 A8
Tsaratanana △ Madag. 13°57S 48°52E 329 A8
Tsau Botswana 20°8S 22°22E 328 C3
Tsavo Kenya 2°59S 38°28E 326 C4
Tsavo East △ Kenya 2°44S 38°47E 326 C4
Tsavo West △ Kenya 3°19S 37°57E 326 C4
Tsentralnyy □ Russia 52°0N 40°0E 300 D4
Tses Namibia 25°58S 18°8E 328 D2
Tsetserleg Mongolia 47°36N 101°32E 304 B5
Tsévié Togo 6°25N 1°20E 322 G6
Tshabong Botswana 26°2S 22°29E 328 D3
Tshane Botswana 24°5S 21°54E 328 C3
Tshela Dem. Rep. of the Congo 4°57S 13°4E 324 E2
Tshesebe Botswana 21°51S 27°32E 329 C4
Tshibeke Dem. Rep. of the Congo 2°40S 28°35E 326 C2
Tshibinda Dem. Rep. of the Congo 2°23S 28°43E 326 C2
Tshikapa Dem. Rep. of the Congo 6°28S 20°48E 324 F4
Tshilenge Dem. Rep. of the Congo 6°17S 23°48E 326 D1
Tshinsenda Dem. Rep. of the Congo 12°20S 28°0E 327 E2
Tshofa Dem. Rep. of the Congo 5°13S 25°16E 326 D2
Tshwane = Pretoria S. Africa 25°44S 28°12E 329 D4
Tshwane Botswana 22°24S 22°1E 328 C3
Tsigara Botswana 20°22S 25°54E 328 C4
Tsihombe Madag. 25°10S 45°41E 329 D8
Tsiigehtchic Canada 67°15N 134°0W 340 C6
Ts'il-os △ Canada 51°9N 123°59W 342 C4
Tsimlyansk Res. = Tsimlyanskoye Vdkhr. Russia 48°0N 43°0E 291 E7
Tsimlyanskoye Vdkhr. Russia 48°0N 43°0E 291 E7
Tsinan = Jinan China 36°38N 117°1E 306 F9
Tsineng S. Africa 27°5S 23°5E 328 D3
Tsing Yi China 22°21N 114°6E 305 G11
Tsinghai = Qinghai □ China 36°0N 98°0E 304 C4
Tsingtao = Qingdao China 36°5N 120°20E 307 F11
Tsingy de Bemaraha △ Madag. 18°35S 45°25E 329 B8
Tsingy de Namoroka △ Madag. 16°29S 45°25E 329 B8
Tsinjoarivo Madag. 19°37S 47°40E 329 B8
Tsinjomitondraka Madag. 15°40S 47°8E 329 B8
Tsirigo = Kythira Greece 36°8N 23°0E 295 F10
Tsiroanomandidy Madag. 18°46S 46°2E 329 B8
Tsitondroina Madag. 21°19S 46°0E 329 C8
Tsitsikamma △ S. Africa 34°3S 23°40E 328 E3
Tsivory Madag. 24°4S 46°5E 329 C8
Tskhinvali Georgia 42°14N 44°1E 291 F7
Tsna → Russia 54°55N 41°58E 290 D7
Tso Moriri, L. India 32°50N 78°20E 315 C8
Tsobis Namibia 19°27S 17°30E 328 B2
Tsodilo Hill Botswana 18°49S 21°43E 328 B3
Tsogttsetsiy = Baruunsuu Mongolia 43°43N 105°35E 306 C3
Tsolo S. Africa 31°18S 28°37E 329 E4
Tsomo S. Africa 32°0S 27°42E 329 E4
Tsu Japan 34°45N 136°25E 303 G8
Tsu L. Canada 60°40N 111°52W 342 A6
Tsuchiura Japan 36°5N 140°15E 303 F10
Tsuen Wan China 22°22N 114°6E 305 G11
Tsugaru-Kaikyō Japan 41°35N 141°0E 302 D10
Tsumeb Namibia 19°9S 17°44E 328 B2
Tsumis Namibia 23°39S 17°29E 328 C2
Tsuruga Japan 35°45N 136°2E 303 G8
Tsurugi-San Japan 33°51N 134°6E 303 H7
Tsuruoka Japan 38°44N 139°50E 302 E9
Tsushima Gifu, Japan 35°10N 136°43E 303 G8
Tsushima Nagasaki, Japan 34°20N 129°20E 303 G4
Tsuyama Japan 35°3N 134°0E 303 G7
Tsyelyakhany Belarus 52°30N 25°46E 289 B13
Tual Indonesia 5°38S 132°44E 309 F8
Tualatin U.S.A. 45°23N 122°45W 350 E4
Tuam Ireland 53°31N 8°51W 282 C3
Tuamotu, Îs. French Polynesia 17°0S 144°0W 337 J13
Tuamotu Arch. = Tuamotu, Îs. French Polynesia 17°0S 144°0W 337 J13
Tuamotu Ridge Pac. Oc. 20°0S 138°0W 337 K14
Tuao Phil. 17°55N 121°22E 309 A6
Tuapse Russia 44°5N 39°10E 291 F6
Tuas Singapore 1°19N 103°39E 311 d
Tuatapere N.Z. 46°8S 167°41E 331 G1
Tuba City U.S.A. 36°8N 111°14W 349 H8
Tuban Indonesia 6°54S 112°3E 309 G15
Tubani Botswana 24°46S 24°18E 328 C3
Tubarão Brazil 28°30S 49°0W 367 B6

Tūbās *West Bank* 32°20N 35°22E **318** C4
Tubas → *Namibia* 22°54S 14°35E **328** C2
Tübingen *Germany* 48°31N 9°4E **288** D5
Tubou *Fiji* 18°13S 178°48W **331** a
Tubruq *Libya* 32°7N 23°55E **323** B10
Tubuaï, Îs. *French Polynesia* 25°0S 150°0W **337** K13
Tuc Trung *Vietnam* 11°1N 107°12E **311** G6
Tucacas *Venezuela* 10°48N 68°19W **364** A5
Tuchodi → *Canada* 58°17N 123°42W **342** B4
Tuckanarra *Australia* 27°7S 118°5E **333** E2
Tucson *U.S.A.* 32°13N 110°58W **349** K8
Tucumán □ *Argentina* 26°48S 66°2W **366** B2
Tucumcari *U.S.A.* 35°10N 103°44W **349** J12
Tucupita *Venezuela* 9°2N 62°3W **364** B6
Tucuruí *Brazil* 3°42S 49°44W **365** D9
Tucuruí, Reprêsa de *Brazil* 4°0S 49°30W **365** D9
Tudela *Spain* 42°4N 1°39W **293** A5
Tudmur *Syria* 34°36N 38°15E **316** C3
Tudor, L. *Canada* 55°50N 65°25W **345** A6
Tuen Mun *China* 22°24N 113°59E **305** G10
Tugela → *S. Africa* 29°14S 31°30E **329** D5
Tuguegarao *Phil.* 17°35N 121°42E **309** A6
Tugur *Russia* 53°44N 136°45E **301** D14
Tui *Spain* 42°3N 8°39W **293** A1
Tuineje *Canary Is.* 28°19N 14°3W **296** F5
Tukangbesi, Kepulauan *Indonesia* 6°0S 124°0E **309** F6
Tukarak I. *Canada* 56°15N 78°45W **344** A4
Tukayyid *Iraq* 29°47N 45°36E **316** D5
Tukkae, Ao *Thailand* 7°51N 98°25E **311** a
Tuktoyaktuk *Canada* 69°27N 133°2W **340** C6
Tukums *Latvia* 56°58N 23°10E **281** H20
Tukuyu *Tanzania* 9°17S 33°35E **327** D3
Tula *Hidalgo, Mexico* 20°3N 99°21W **359** C5
Tula *Tamaulipas, Mexico* 23°0N 99°43W **359** C5
Tula *Russia* 54°13N 37°38E **290** D6
Tulancingo *Mexico* 20°5N 98°22W **359** C5
Tulare *U.S.A.* 36°13N 119°21W **350** J7
Tulare Lake Bed *U.S.A.* 36°0N 119°48W **350** K7
Tularosa *U.S.A.* 33°5N 106°1W **349** K10
Tulbagh *S. Africa* 33°16S 19°6E **328** E2
Tulcán *Ecuador* 0°48N 77°43W **364** C3
Tulcea *Romania* 45°13N 28°46E **289** F15
Tulchyn *Ukraine* 48°41N 28°49E **289** D15
Tūleh *Iran* 34°35N 52°33E **317** C7
Tulemalu L. *Canada* 62°58N 99°25W **343** A9
Tuli *Zimbabwe* 21°58S 29°13E **327** G2
Tulia *U.S.A.* 34°32N 101°46W **356** D4
Tulita *Canada* 64°57N 125°30W **340** C7
Ţūlkarm *West Bank* 32°19N 35°2E **318** C4
Tulla *Ireland* 52°53N 8°46W **282** D3
Tullahoma *U.S.A.* 35°22N 86°13W **357** D11
Tullamore *Australia* 32°39S 147°36E **335** E4
Tullamore *Ireland* 53°16N 7°31W **282** C4
Tulle *France* 45°16N 1°46E **292** D4
Tullow *Ireland* 52°49N 6°45W **282** D5
Tully *Australia* 17°56S 145°55E **334** B4
Tully *U.S.A.* 42°48N 76°7W **355** D8
Tulsa *U.S.A.* 36°10N 95°55W **356** C7
Tulsequah *Canada* 58°39N 133°35W **342** B2
Tulua *Colombia* 4°6N 76°11W **364** C3
Tulun *Russia* 54°32N 100°35E **301** D11
Tulungagung *Indonesia* 8°5S 111°54E **309** H14
Tuma → *Nic.* 13°6N 84°35W **360** D3
Tumacacori ⌂ *U.S.A.* 31°35N 111°6W **349** L8
Tumaco *Colombia* 1°50N 78°45W **364** C3
Tumatumari *Guyana* 5°20N 58°55W **364** B7
Tumba *Sweden* 59°12N 17°48E **281** G17
Tumba, L. *Dem. Rep. of the Congo* 0°50S 18°0E **324** E3
Tumbarumba *Australia* 35°44S 148°0E **335** F4
Tumbaya *Argentina* 23°50S 65°26W **366** A2
Tumbes *Peru* 3°37S 80°27W **364** D2
Tumbler Ridge *Canada* 55°8N 121°0W **342** B4
Tumbwe *Dem. Rep. of the Congo* 11°25S 27°15E **327** E2
Tumby Bay *Australia* 34°21S 136°8E **335** E2
Tumd Youqi *China* 40°30N 110°30E **306** D6
Tumen *China* 43°0N 129°50E **307** C15
Tumen Jiang → *China* 42°20N 130°35E **307** C16
Tumeremo *Venezuela* 7°18N 61°30W **364** B6
Tumkur *India* 13°18N 77°6E **312** N10
Tump *Pakistan* 26°7N 62°16E **312** F3
Tumpat *Malaysia* 6°11N 102°10E **311** J4
Tumu *Ghana* 10°56N 1°56W **322** F5
Tumucumaque, Serra *Brazil* 2°0N 55°0W **365** C8
Tumut *Australia* 35°16S 148°13E **335** F4
Tumwater *U.S.A.* 47°1N 122°54W **350** C4
Tuna *India* 22°59N 70°5E **314** H4
Tunapuna *Trin. & Tob.* 10°38N 61°24W **365** K15
Tunas de Zaza *Cuba* 21°39N 79°34W **360** B4
Tunbridge Wells = Royal Tunbridge Wells *U.K.* 51°7N 0°16E **285** F8
Tuncurry *Australia* 32°17S 152°29E **335** E5
Tundla *India* 27°12N 78°17E **314** F8
Tunduru *Tanzania* 11°8S 37°25E **327** E4
Tundzha → *Bulgaria* 41°40N 26°35E **295** C11
Tung Chung *China* 22°17N 113°57E **305** G10
Tung Lung Chau *China* 22°15N 114°17E **305** G11
Tungabhadra → *India* 15°57N 78°15E **312** M11
Tungla *Nic.* 13°24N 84°21W **360** D3
Tungsten *Canada* 61°57N 128°16W **342** A3
Tunguska, Nizhnyaya → *Russia* 65°48N 88°4E **301** C9
Tunguska, Podkamennaya → *Russia* 61°50N 90°13E **301** C10
Tunica *U.S.A.* 34°41N 90°23W **357** D9
Tunis *Tunisia* 36°50N 10°11E **322** A7
Tunisia ■ *Africa* 33°30N 9°10E **323** A7
Tunja *Colombia* 5°33N 73°25W **364** B4
Tunkhannock *U.S.A.* 41°32N 75°57W **355** E9
Tunliu *China* 36°13N 112°52E **306** F7
Tunnel Creek △ *Australia* 17°41S 125°18E **332** C4
Tunnsjøen *Norway* 64°45N 13°25E **280** D15
Tunungayualok I. *Canada* 56°0N 61°0W **345** A7
Tunuyán *Argentina* 33°35S 69°0W **366** C2
Tunuyán → *Argentina* 33°33S 67°30W **366** C2
Tuolumne *U.S.A.* 37°58N 120°15W **350** H6
Tuolumne → *U.S.A.* 37°36N 121°13W **350** H5
Tūp Āghāj *Iran* 36°3N 47°50E **316** B5
Tupã *Brazil* 21°57S 50°28W **367** A5
Tupelo *U.S.A.* 34°16N 88°43W **357** D10
Tupinambaranas *Brazil* 3°0S 58°0W **364** D7
Tupiza *Bolivia* 21°30S 65°40W **366** A2
Tupman *U.S.A.* 35°18N 119°21W **351** K7
Tupper *Canada* 55°32N 120°1W **342** B4
Tupper Lake *U.S.A.* 44°14N 74°28W **355** B10
Tupungato, Cerro *S. Amer.* 33°15S 69°50W **366** C2
Tuquan *China* 45°18N 121°38E **307** B11
Túquerres *Colombia* 1°5N 77°37W **364** C3
Tura *Russia* 64°20N 100°17E **301** C11
Turabah *Si. Arabia* 28°20N 43°15E **316** D4
Tūrān *Iran* 35°39N 56°42E **317** C8
Turan *Russia* 51°55N 94°0E **301** D10
Ţurayf *Si. Arabia* 31°41N 38°39E **316** D3
Turda *Romania* 46°34N 23°47E **289** E12
Turek *Poland* 52°3N 18°30E **289** B10
Turén *Venezuela* 9°17N 69°6W **364** B5
Turfan = Turpan *China* 43°58N 89°10E **304** B3
Turfan Basin = Turpan Pendi *China* 42°40N 89°25E **304** B3
Turfan Depression = Turpan Pendi *China* 42°40N 89°25E **304** B3
Turgeon → *Canada* 50°0N 78°56W **344** C4
Tŭrgovishte *Bulgaria* 43°17N 26°38E **295** C12
Turgutlu *Turkey* 38°30N 27°43E **295** E12
Turgwe → *Zimbabwe* 21°31S 32°15E **329** C5
Turia → *Spain* 39°27N 0°19W **293** C5
Turiaçu *Brazil* 1°40S 45°19W **365** D9
Turiaçu → *Brazil* 1°36S 45°19W **365** D9
Turin = Torino *Italy* 45°3N 7°40E **292** D7
Turkana, L. *Africa* 3°30N 36°5E **326** B4
Turkestan = Türkistan *Kazakhstan* 43°17N 68°16E **300** E7
Turkey ■ *Eurasia* 39°0N 36°0E **291** G6
Turkey Creek = Warmun *Australia* 17°2S 128°12E **332** C4
Türkistan *Kazakhstan* 43°17N 68°16E **300** E7
Türkmenabat *Turkmenistan* 39°6N 63°34E **317** B9
Türkmenbashi *Turkmenistan* 40°5N 53°5E **317** A7
Turkmenistan ■ *Asia* 39°0N 59°0E **300** F6
Turks & Caicos Is. ☑ *W. Indies* 21°20N 71°20W **361** B5
Turks Island Passage *W. Indies* 21°30N 71°30W **361** B5
Turku *Finland* 60°30N 22°19E **281** F20
Turkwel → *Kenya* 3°6N 36°6E **326** B4
Turlock *U.S.A.* 37°30N 120°51W **350** H6
Turnagain → *Canada* 59°12N 127°35W **342** B3
Turnagain, C. *N.Z.* 40°28S 176°38E **331** D6
Turneffe Is. *Belize* 17°20N 87°50W **359** D7
Turner *U.S.A.* 48°51N 108°24W **348** B9
Turner Pt. *Australia* 11°47S 133°32E **334** A1
Turner Valley *Canada* 50°40N 114°17W **342** C6
Turners Falls *U.S.A.* 42°36N 72°33W **355** D12
Turnhout *Belgium* 51°19N 4°57E **287** C4
Turnor L. *Canada* 56°35N 108°35W **343** B7
Tŭrnovo = Veliko Tŭrnovo *Bulgaria* 43°5N 25°41E **295** C11
Turnu Măgurele *Romania* 43°46N 24°56E **289** G13
Turnu Roşu, P. *Romania* 45°33N 24°17E **289** F13
Turpan *China* 43°58N 89°10E **304** B3
Turpan Pendi *China* 42°40N 89°25E **304** B3
Turriff *U.K.* 57°32N 2°27W **283** D6
Tursāq *Iraq* 33°27N 45°47E **316** C5
Turtle Head I. *Australia* 10°56S 142°37E **334** A3
Turtle L. *Canada* 53°36N 108°38W **343** C7
Turtle Lake *U.S.A.* 47°31N 100°53W **352** B3
Turtleford *Canada* 53°23N 108°57W **343** C7
Turuépano △ *Venezuela* 10°34N 62°43W **361** D7
Turukhansk *Russia* 65°21N 88°5E **301** C9
Tuscaloosa *U.S.A.* 33°12N 87°34W **357** E11
Tuscany = Toscana □ *Italy* 43°25N 11°0E **294** C4
Tuscarawas → *U.S.A.* 40°24N 81°25W **354** F3
Tuscarora Mt. *U.S.A.* 40°55N 77°55W **354** F7
Tuscola *Ill., U.S.A.* 39°48N 88°17W **352** F9
Tuscola *Tex., U.S.A.* 32°12N 99°48W **356** E5
Tuscumbia *U.S.A.* 34°44N 87°42W **357** D11
Tuskegee *U.S.A.* 32°25N 85°42W **357** E12
Tuticorin *India* 8°50N 78°12E **312** Q11
Tutóia *Brazil* 2°45S 42°20W **365** D10
Tutong *Brunei* 4°47N 114°40E **308** D4
Tutrakan *Bulgaria* 44°2N 26°40E **295** B12
Tuttle Creek L. *U.S.A.* 39°15N 96°36W **352** F5
Tuttlingen *Germany* 47°58N 8°48E **288** E5
Tutuala *E. Timor* 8°25S 127°15E **309** F7
Tutuila *Amer. Samoa* 14°19S 170°50W **331** b
Tutume *Botswana* 20°30S 27°5E **325** J5
Tuva □ *Russia* 51°30N 95°0E **301** D10
Tuvalu ■ *Pac. Oc.* 8°0S 178°0E **330** B10
Tuvuca *Fiji* 17°40S 178°48W **331** a
Tuxpan *Mexico* 20°57N 97°24W **359** C5
Tuxtla Gutiérrez *Mexico* 16°45N 93°7W **359** D6
Tuy = Tui *Spain* 42°3N 8°39W **293** A1
Tuy An *Vietnam* 13°17N 109°16E **310** F7
Tuy Duc *Vietnam* 12°15N 107°27E **311** F6
Tuy Hoa *Vietnam* 13°5N 109°10E **310** F7
Tuy Phong *Vietnam* 11°14N 108°43E **311** G7
Tuya L. *Canada* 59°7N 130°35W **342** B2
Tuyen Hoa *Vietnam* 17°50N 106°10E **310** D6
Tuyen Quang *Vietnam* 21°50N 105°10E **310** B5
Tūysarkān *Iran* 34°33N 48°27E **317** C6
Tuz Gölü *Turkey* 38°42N 33°18E **291** G5
Ţūz Khurmātū = Tozkhurmato *Iraq* 34°56N 44°38E **316** C5
Tuzigoot △ *U.S.A.* 34°46N 112°2W **349** J7
Tuzla *Bos.-H.* 44°34N 18°41E **295** B8
Tver *Russia* 56°55N 35°55E **290** C6
Twain *U.S.A.* 40°1N 121°3W **350** E5
Twain Harte *U.S.A.* 38°2N 120°14W **350** G6
Tweed *Canada* 44°29N 77°19W **354** B7
Tweed → *U.K.* 55°45N 2°0W **283** F6
Tweed Heads *Australia* 28°10S 153°31E **335** D5
Tweedsmuir ⌂ *Canada* 53°0N 126°20W **342** C3
Twentynine Palms *U.S.A.* 34°8N 116°3W **351** L10
Twillingate *Canada* 49°42N 54°45W **345** C9
Twin Bridges *U.S.A.* 45°33N 112°20W **348** D7
Twin Falls *Canada* 53°30N 64°32W **345** B7
Twin Falls *U.S.A.* 42°34N 114°28W **348** E6
Twin Valley *U.S.A.* 47°16N 96°16W **352** B5
Twinsburg *U.S.A.* 41°19N 81°26W **354** E3
Twitchell Res. *U.S.A.* 34°59N 120°19W **351** L6
Two Harbors *U.S.A.* 47°2N 91°40W **352** B8
Two Hills *Canada* 53°43N 111°52W **342** C6
Two Rivers *U.S.A.* 44°9N 87°34W **352** C10
Two Rocks *Australia* 31°30S 115°35E **333** F2
Twofold B. *Australia* 37°8S 149°59E **335** F4
Tyachiv *Ukraine* 48°1N 23°35E **289** D12
Tychy *Poland* 50°9N 18°59E **289** C10
Tyler *Minn., U.S.A.* 44°17N 96°8W **352** C5
Tyler *Tex., U.S.A.* 32°21N 95°18W **356** E7
Tynda *Russia* 55°10N 124°43E **301** D13
Tyndall *U.S.A.* 43°0N 97°50W **352** D5
Tyne → *U.K.* 54°59N 1°32W **284** C6
Tyne & Wear □ *U.K.* 55°6N 1°17W **284** B6
Tynemouth *U.K.* 55°1N 1°26W **284** B6
Tyre = Sūr *Lebanon* 33°19N 35°16E **318** B4
Tyrifjorden *Norway* 60°2N 10°8E **281** F14
Tyrol = Tirol □ *Austria* 47°3N 10°43E **288** E6
Tyrone *U.S.A.* 40°40N 78°14W **354** F6
Tyrone □ *U.K.* 54°38N 7°11W **282** B4
Tyrrell → *Australia* 35°26S 142°51E **335** F3
Tyrrell, L. *Australia* 35°20S 142°50E **335** F3
Tyrrell L. *Canada* 63°7N 105°27W **343** A7
Tyrrhenian Sea *Medit. S.* 40°0N 12°30E **294** E5
Tysfjorden *Norway* 68°7N 16°25E **280** B17
Tyulgan *Russia* 52°22N 56°12E **290** D10
Tyumen *Russia* 57°11N 65°29E **300** D7
Tywi → *U.K.* 51°48N 4°21W **285** F3
Tywyn *U.K.* 52°35N 4°5W **285** E3
Tzaneen *S. Africa* 23°47S 30°9E **329** C5
Tzermiado *Greece* 35°12N 25°29E **297** D7
Tzukong = Zigong *China* 29°15N 104°48E **304** D5

U

U Taphao *Thailand* 12°35N 101°0E **310** F3
U.S.A. = United States of America ■ *N. Amer.* 37°0N 96°0W **346** C7
U.S. Virgin Is. ☑ *W. Indies* 18°20N 65°0W **361** e
Uanle Uen *Somali Rep.* 2°37N 44°54E **319** G3
Uatumã → *Brazil* 2°26S 57°37W **364** D7
Uaupés *Brazil* 0°8S 67°5W **364** D5
Uaupés → *Brazil* 0°2N 67°16W **364** C5
Uaxactún *Guatemala* 17°25N 89°29W **360** C2
Ubá *Brazil* 21°8S 43°0W **367** A7
Ubaitaba *Brazil* 14°18S 39°20W **365** F11
Ubangi = Oubangi → *Dem. Rep. of the Congo* 0°30S 17°50E **324** E3
Ubauro *Pakistan* 28°15N 69°45E **314** E3
Ubayyiḍ, W. al → *Iraq* 32°34N 43°48E **316** C4
Ube *Japan* 33°56N 131°15E **303** H5
Úbeda *Spain* 38°3N 3°23W **293** C4
Uberaba *Brazil* 19°50S 47°55W **365** G9
Uberlândia *Brazil* 19°0S 48°20W **365** G9
Ubin, Pulau *Singapore* 1°24N 103°57E **311** d
Ubolratna Res. *Thailand* 16°45N 102°30E **310** D4
Ubombo *S. Africa* 27°31S 32°4E **329** D5
Ubon Ratchathani *Thailand* 15°15N 104°50E **310** E5
Ubondo *Dem. Rep. of the Congo* 0°55S 25°42E **326** C2
Ubort → *Belarus* 52°6N 28°30E **289** B15
Ubud *Indonesia* 8°30S 115°16E **309** J18
Ubundu *Dem. Rep. of the Congo* 0°22S 25°30E **326** C2
Ucayali → *Peru* 4°30S 73°30W **364** D4
Uchab *Namibia* 19°47S 17°42E **328** B2
Uchiura-Wan *Japan* 42°25N 140°40E **302** C10
Uchquduq *Uzbekistan* 41°50N 62°50E **300** E7
Uchur → *Russia* 58°48N 130°35E **301** D14
Ucluelet *Canada* 48°57N 125°32W **342** D3
Uda → *Russia* 54°42N 135°14E **301** D14
Udagamandalam *India* 11°30N 76°44E **312** P10
Udainagar *India* 22°33N 76°13E **314** H7
Udaipur *India* 24°36N 73°44E **314** G5
Udaipur Garhi *Nepal* 27°0N 86°35E **315** F12
Udala *India* 21°35N 86°34E **315** J12
Uddevalla *Sweden* 58°21N 11°55E **281** G14
Uddjaure *Sweden* 65°56N 17°49E **280** D17
Uden *Neths.* 51°40N 5°37E **287** C5
Udgir *India* 18°25N 77°5E **312** K10
Udhampur *India* 33°0N 75°5E **315** C6
Údine *Italy* 46°3N 13°14E **294** A5
Udintsev Fracture Zone *S. Ocean* 57°0S 145°0W **277** B13
Udmurtia □ *Russia* 57°30N 52°30E **290** C9
Udon Thani *Thailand* 17°29N 102°46E **310** D4
Udu Pt. *Fiji* 16°9S 179°57W **331** a
Udupi *India* 13°25N 74°42E **312** N9
Udzungwa △ *Tanzania* 7°52S 36°35E **326** D4
Udzungwa Range *Tanzania* 9°30S 35°10E **327** D4
Ueda *Japan* 36°24N 138°16E **303** F9
Uedineniya, Os. *Russia* 78°0N 85°0E **276** B12
Uele → *Dem. Rep. of the Congo* 3°45N 24°45E **324** D4
Uelen *Russia* 66°10N 170°0W **301** C19
Uelzen *Germany* 52°57N 10°32E **288** B6
Ufa *Russia* 54°45N 55°55E **290** D10
Ufa → *Russia* 54°40N 56°0E **290** D10
Ugab → *Namibia* 20°55S 13°30E **328** C1
Ugalla → *Tanzania* 5°8S 30°42E **326** D3
Ugalla River ⌂ *Tanzania* 5°50S 31°54E **326** D3
Uganda ■ *Africa* 2°0N 32°0E **326** B3
Ugie *S. Africa* 31°10S 28°13E **329** E4
Uglegorsk *Russia* 49°5N 142°2E **301** E15
Ugljan *Croatia* 44°12N 15°10E **288** F8
Uhlenhorst *Namibia* 23°45S 17°55E **328** C2
Uhrichsville *U.S.A.* 40°24N 81°21W **354** F3
Uibhist a Deas = South Uist *U.K.* 57°20N 7°15W **283** D1
Uibhist a Tuath = North Uist *U.K.* 57°40N 7°15W **283** D1
Uig *U.K.* 57°35N 6°21W **283** D2
Uíge *Angola* 7°30S 14°40E **324** F2
Uiha *Tonga* 19°54S 174°25W **331** c
Uijeongbu *S. Korea* 37°44N 127°2E **307** F14
Ŭiju *N. Korea* 40°15N 124°35E **307** D13
Uinta Mts. *U.S.A.* 40°45N 110°30W **348** F8
Uis *Namibia* 21°8S 14°49E **328** C1
Uiseong *S. Korea* 36°21N 128°45E **307** F15
Uitenhage *S. Africa* 33°40S 25°28E **328** E4
Uithuizen *Neths.* 53°24N 6°41E **287** A6
Ujh → *India* 32°10N 75°18E **314** C6
Ujhani *India* 28°0N 79°6E **315** F8
Uji-guntō *Japan* 31°15N 129°25E **303** J4
Ujjain *India* 23°9N 75°43E **314** H6
Ujung Pandang *Indonesia* 5°10S 119°20E **309** F5
Uka *Russia* 57°50N 162°0E **301** D17
Ukara I. *Tanzania* 1°50S 33°0E **326** C3
Uke-Shima *Japan* 28°2N 129°14E **303** K4
Ukerewe I. *Tanzania* 2°0S 33°0E **326** C3
Ukhrul *India* 25°10N 94°25E **313** G19
Ukhta *Russia* 63°34N 53°41E **290** B9
Ukiah *U.S.A.* 39°9N 123°13W **350** F3
Ukmergė *Lithuania* 55°15N 24°45E **281** J21
Ukraine ■ *Europe* 49°0N 32°0E **291** E5
Ukwi *Botswana* 23°29S 20°30E **328** C3
Ulaan-Uul *Mongolia* 44°13N 111°10E **306** B6
Ulaanbaatar *Mongolia* 47°55N 106°53E **304** B5
Ulaangom *Mongolia* 50°5N 92°10E **304** A4
Ulaanjirem *Mongolia* 45°5N 105°30E **306** B3
Ulamba *Dem. Rep. of the Congo* 9°3S 23°38E **327** D1
Ulan Bator = Ulaanbaatar *Mongolia* 47°55N 106°53E **304** B5
Ulan Ude *Russia* 51°45N 107°40E **301** D11
Ulaya *Morogoro, Tanzania* 7°3S 36°55E **326** D4
Ulaya *Tabora, Tanzania* 4°25S 33°30E **326** C3
Ulcinj *Montenegro* 41°58N 19°10E **295** D8
Ulco *S. Africa* 28°21S 24°15E **328** D3
Ule älv = Oulujoki → *Finland* 65°1N 25°30E **280** D21
Ule träsk = Oulujärvi *Finland* 64°25N 27°15E **280** D22
Uleåborg = Oulu *Finland* 65°1N 25°29E **280** D21
Ulefoss *Norway* 59°17N 9°16E **281** G13
Ulhasnagar *India* 19°15N 73°10E **312** K8
Uliastay *Mongolia* 47°56N 97°28E **304** B4
Uljin *S. Korea* 36°59N 129°24E **307** F15
Ulladulla *Australia* 35°21S 150°29E **335** F5
Ullapool *U.K.* 57°54N 5°9W **283** D3
Ulleungdo *S. Korea* 37°30N 130°30E **303** F5
Ullswater *U.K.* 54°34N 2°52W **284** C5
Ulm *Germany* 48°23N 9°58E **288** D5
Ulmarra *Australia* 29°37S 153°4E **335** D5
Ulonguè *Mozam.* 14°37S 34°19E **327** E3
Ulricehamn *Sweden* 57°46N 13°26E **281** H15
Ulsan *S. Korea* 35°20N 129°15E **307** G15
Ulsta *U.K.* 60°30N 1°9W **283** A7
Ulster □ *U.K.* 54°35N 6°30W **282** B5
Ulubat Gölü *Turkey* 40°9N 28°35E **295** D13
Uludağ *Turkey* 40°4N 29°13E **295** D13
Uluguru Mts. *Tanzania* 7°15S 37°40E **326** D4
Ulungur He → *China* 47°1N 87°24E **304** B3
Uluru *Australia* 25°23S 131°5E **333** E5
Uluru-Kata Tjuta △ *Australia* 25°19S 131°1E **333** E5
Ulutau *Kazakhstan* 48°39N 67°1E **300** E7
Uluwatu *Indonesia* 8°50S 115°5E **309** K18
Ulva *U.K.* 56°29N 6°13W **283** E2
Ulverston *U.K.* 54°13N 3°5W **284** C4
Ulverstone *Australia* 41°11S 146°11E **335** G4
Ulya *Russia* 59°10N 142°0E **301** D15
Ulyanovsk = Simbirsk *Russia* 54°20N 48°25E **290** D8
Ulyasutay = Uliastay *Mongolia* 47°56N 97°28E **304** B4
Ulysses *U.S.A.* 37°35N 101°22W **352** G3
Umala *Bolivia* 17°25S 68°5W **364** G5
'Umān = Oman ■ *Asia* 23°0N 58°0E **319** C6
Uman *Ukraine* 48°40N 30°12E **289** D16
Umaria *India* 23°35N 80°50E **315** H9
Umarkot *Pakistan* 25°15N 69°40E **314** G3
Umarpada *India* 21°27N 73°30E **314** J5
Umatilla *U.S.A.* 45°55N 119°21W **348** D4
Umba *Russia* 66°42N 34°11E **290** A5
Umbagog L. *U.S.A.* 44°46N 71°3W **355** B13
Umbakumba *Australia* 13°47S 136°50E **334** A2
Umbrella Mts. *N.Z.* 45°35S 169°5E **331** F2
Umeå *Sweden* 63°45N 20°20E **280** E19
Umeälven → *Sweden* 63°45N 20°20E **280** E19
Umera *Indonesia* 0°12S 129°37E **309** E7
Umfuli → *Zimbabwe* 17°30S 29°23E **327** F2
Umfurudzi ⌂ *Zimbabwe* 17°6S 31°40E **327** F3
Umgusa *Zimbabwe* 19°29S 27°52E **327** F2
Umiujaq *Canada* 56°33N 76°33W **344** A4
Umkomaas *S. Africa* 30°13S 30°48E **329** E5
Umlazi *S. Africa* 29°59S 30°54E **325** L6
Umm ad Daraj, J. *Jordan* 32°18N 35°48E **318** C4
Umm al Qaywayn *U.A.E.* 25°30N 55°35E **317** E7
Umm al Qittayn *Jordan* 32°18N 36°40E **318** C5
Umm Bāb *Qatar* 25°12N 50°48E **317** E6
Umm Durman = Omdurmân *Sudan* 15°40N 32°28E **323** E12
Umm el Fahm *Israel* 32°31N 35°9E **318** C4
Umm Keddada *Sudan* 13°33N 26°35E **323** F11
Umm Lajj *Si. Arabia* 25°0N 37°23E **316** E3
Umm Qasr *Iraq* 30°1N 47°58E **316** D5
Umm Ruwaba *Sudan* 12°50N 31°20E **323** F12
Umnak I. *U.S.A.* 53°15N 168°20W **346** a
Umniati → *Zimbabwe* 16°49S 28°45E **327** F2
Umpqua → *U.S.A.* 43°40N 124°12W **348** E1
Umreth *India* 22°41N 73°4E **314** H5
Umtata = Mthatha *S. Africa* 31°36S 28°49E **329** E4
Umuarama *Brazil* 23°45S 53°20W **367** A5
Umvukwe Ra. *Zimbabwe* 16°45S 30°45E **327** F3
Umzimvubu *S. Africa* 31°38S 29°33E **329** E4
Umzingwane → *Zimbabwe* 22°12S 29°56E **327** G2
Umzinto *S. Africa* 30°15S 30°45E **329** E5
Una *India* 20°46N 71°8E **314** J4
Una → *Bos.-H.* 45°0N 16°20E **288** F9
Unadilla *U.S.A.* 42°20N 75°19W **355** D9
Unalakleet *U.S.A.* 63°52N 160°47W **346** a
Unalaska *U.S.A.* 53°53N 166°32W **346** a
Unalaska I. *U.S.A.* 53°35N 166°50W **346** a
'Unayzah *Si. Arabia* 26°6N 43°58E **316** E4
'Unayzah, J. *Asia* 32°12N 39°18E **316** C3
Uncía *Bolivia* 18°25S 66°40W **364** G5
Uncompahgre Peak *U.S.A.* 38°4N 107°28W **348** G10
Uncompahgre Plateau *U.S.A.* 38°20N 108°15W **348** G9
Undara Volcanic △ *Australia* 18°14S 144°41E **334** B3
Underbool *Australia* 35°10S 141°51E **335** F3
Ungarie *Australia* 33°38S 146°56E **335** E4
Ungarra *Australia* 34°12S 136°2E **335** E2
Ungava, Pén. d' *Canada* 60°0N 74°0W **341** D12
Ungava B. *Canada* 59°30N 67°30W **341** D13
Ungeny = Ungheni *Moldova* 47°11N 27°51E **289** E14
Unggi *N. Korea* 42°16N 130°28E **307** C16
Ungheni *Moldova* 47°11N 27°51E **289** E14
Ungwana B. *Kenya* 2°45S 40°20E **326** C5
União da Vitória *Brazil* 26°13S 51°5W **367** B5
Unimak I. *U.S.A.* 54°45N 164°0W **346** a
Union *Miss., U.S.A.* 32°34N 89°7W **357** E10
Union *Mo., U.S.A.* 38°27N 91°0W **352** F8
Union *S.C., U.S.A.* 34°43N 81°37W **357** D14
Union City *Calif., U.S.A.* 37°36N 122°1W **350** H4
Union City *N.J., U.S.A.* 40°45N 74°2W **355** F10
Union City *Pa., U.S.A.* 41°54N 79°51W **354** E5
Union City *Tenn., U.S.A.* 36°26N 89°3W **357** C10
Union Gap *U.S.A.* 46°33N 120°28W **348** C3
Union Springs *U.S.A.* 32°9N 85°43W **357** E12
Uniondale *S. Africa* 33°39S 23°7E **328** E3
Uniontown *U.S.A.* 39°54N 79°44W **353** F14
Unionville *U.S.A.* 40°29N 93°1W **352** E7
United Arab Emirates ■ *Asia* 23°50N 54°0E **317** F7
United Kingdom ■ *Europe* 53°0N 2°0W **286** E6
United States of America ■ *N. Amer.* 37°0N 96°0W **346** C7
Unity *Canada* 52°30N 109°5W **343** C7
University Park *U.S.A.* 32°17N 106°45W **349** K10
University Place *U.S.A.* 47°14N 122°33W **350** C4
Unjha *India* 23°46N 72°24E **314** H5
Unnao *India* 26°35N 80°30E **315** F9
Unsengedsi → *Zimbabwe* 15°43S 31°14E **327** F3
Unst *U.K.* 60°44N 0°53W **283** A8
Unuk → *Canada* 56°5N 131°3W **342** B2
Unzen-Amakusa △ *Japan* 32°15N 130°10E **303** H5
Uozu *Japan* 36°48N 137°24E **303** F8
Upata *Venezuela* 8°1N 62°24W **364** B6
Upemba, L. *Dem. Rep. of the Congo* 8°30S 26°20E **327** D2
Upemba △ *Dem. Rep. of the Congo* 9°0S 26°35E **327** D2
Upernavik *Greenland* 72°49N 56°20W **276** B5
Upington *S. Africa* 28°25S 21°15E **328** D3
Upleta *India* 21°46N 70°16E **314** J4
'Upolu *Samoa* 13°58S 172°0W **331** b
Upper Alkali L. *U.S.A.* 41°47N 120°8W **348** F3
Upper Arrow L. *Canada* 50°30N 117°50W **342** C5
Upper Darby *U.S.A.* 39°55N 75°16W **353** F16
Upper Foster L. *Canada* 56°47N 105°20W **343** B7
Upper Hutt *N.Z.* 41°8S 175°5E **331** D5
Upper Klamath L. *U.S.A.* 42°25N 121°55W **348** E3
Upper Lake *U.S.A.* 39°10N 122°54W **350** F4
Upper Manzanilla *Trin. & Tob.* 10°31N 61°4W **365** K15
Upper Missouri Breaks △ *U.S.A.* 47°50N 109°55W **348** C9
Upper Musquodoboit *Canada* 45°10N 62°58W **345** C7
Upper Red L. *U.S.A.* 48°8N 94°45W **352** A6
Upper Sandusky *U.S.A.* 40°50N 83°17W **353** E12
Upper Volta = Burkina Faso ■ *Africa* 12°0N 1°0W **322** F5
Uppland *Sweden* 59°59N 17°48E **281** G17
Uppsala *Sweden* 59°53N 17°38E **281** G17
Upshi *India* 33°48N 77°52E **315** C7
Upstart, C. *Australia* 19°41S 147°45E **334** B4
Upton *U.S.A.* 44°6N 104°38W **348** D11
Uqsuqtuuq = Gjoa Haven *Canada* 68°38N 95°53W **340** C10
Ur *Iraq* 30°55N 46°25E **316** D5
Urad Qianqi *China* 40°40N 108°30E **306** D5
Urakawa *Japan* 42°9N 142°47E **302** C11
Ural = Uralskiy □ *Russia* 64°0N 70°0E **300** C7

Ural = Zhayyq → Kazakhstan 47°0N 51°48E 291 E9
Ural Australia 33°21S 146°12E 335 E4
Ural Mts. = Uralskie Gory Eurasia 60°0N 59°0E 290 C10
Uralla Australia 30°37S 151°29E 335 E5
Uralsk = Oral Kazakhstan 51°20N 51°20E 291 D9
Uralskie Gory Eurasia 60°0N 59°0E 290 C10
Uralskiy □ Russia 64°0N 70°0E 300 C7
Urambo Tanzania 5°4S 32°0E 326 D3
Urandangi Australia 21°32S 138°14E 334 C2
Uranium City Canada 59°34N 108°37W 343 B7
Uraricoera → Brazil 3°2N 60°30W 364 C6
Urasoe Japan 26°15N 127°43E 303 L3
Urawa = Saitama Japan 35°54N 139°38E 303 G9
Uray Russia 60°5N 65°15E 300 C7
'Uray'irah Si. Arabia 25°57N 48°53E 317 E6
Urbana Ill., U.S.A. 40°7N 88°12W 352 E9
Urbana Ohio, U.S.A. 40°7N 83°45W 353 E12
Urbandale U.S.A. 41°38N 93°43W 352 E7
Urbino Italy 43°43N 12°38E 294 C5
Urbión, Picos de Spain 42°1N 2°52W 293 A4
Urcos Peru 13°40S 71°38W 364 F4
Urdinarrain Argentina 32°37S 58°52W 366 C4
Ure → U.K. 54°5N 1°20W 284 C6
Ures Mexico 29°26N 110°24W 358 B2
Urewera △ N.Z. 38°29S 177°7E 331 C6
Urfa = Sanliurfa Turkey 37°12N 38°50E 316 B3
Urganch Uzbekistan 41°40N 60°41E 300 E7
Urgench = Urganch Uzbekistan 41°40N 60°41E 300 E7
Ürgüp Turkey 38°38N 34°56E 316 B2
Uri India 34°8N 74°2E 315 B6
Uribia Colombia 11°43N 72°16W 364 A4
Uriondo Bolivia 21°41S 64°41W 366 A3
Urique Mexico 27°13N 107°55W 358 B3
Urique → Mexico 26°29N 107°58W 358 B3
Urk Neths. 52°39N 5°36E 287 B5
Urla Turkey 38°20N 26°47E 295 E12
Urmia = Orūmīyeh Iran 37°40N 45°0E 316 B5
Uroševac Kosovo 42°23N 21°10E 295 C9
Uroyan, Montanas de Puerto Rico 18°12N 67°0W 361 d
Uruaçu Brazil 14°30S 49°10W 365 F9
Uruapan Mexico 19°24N 102°3W 358 D4
Urubamba → Peru 10°43S 73°48W 364 F4
Uruçara Brazil 2°32S 57°45W 364 D7
Uruçuí Brazil 7°20S 44°28W 365 E10
Uruguai → Brazil 26°0S 53°30W 367 B5
Uruguaiana Brazil 29°50S 57°0W 366 B4
Uruguay ■ S. Amer. 32°30S 56°30W 366 C4
Uruguay → S. Amer. 34°12S 58°18W 366 C4
Urumchi = Ürümqi China 43°45N 87°45E 304 B3
Ürümqi China 43°45N 87°45E 304 B3
Urup, Ostrov Russia 46°0N 151°0E 301 E16
Ürzhar Kazakhstan 47°5N 81°38E 300 E9
Usa → Russia 66°16N 59°49E 290 A10
Uşak Turkey 38°43N 29°28E 291 G4
Usakos Namibia 21°54S 15°31E 328 C2
Usedom Germany 53°55N 14°2E 288 B8
Useless Loop Australia 26°8S 113°23E 333 E1
Ushakova, Ostrov Russia 82°0N 80°0E 276 A12
Ushant = Ouessant, Î. d' France 48°28N 5°6W 292 B1
Ushashi Tanzania 1°59S 33°57E 326 C3
Ushibuka Japan 32°11N 130°1E 303 H5
Üshtöbe Kazakhstan 45°16N 78°0E 300 E8
Ushuaia Argentina 54°50S 68°23W 368 G3
Ushumun Russia 52°47N 126°32E 301 D13
Usk Canada 54°38N 128°26W 342 C3
Usk → U.K. 51°33N 2°58W 285 F5
Uska India 27°12N 83°7E 315 F10
Usman Russia 52°5N 39°48E 290 D6
Usoke Tanzania 5°8S 32°24E 326 D3
Usolye Sibirskoye Russia 52°48N 103°40E 301 D11
Uspallata, P. de Argentina 32°37S 69°22W 366 C2
Ussuriysk Russia 43°48N 131°59E 302 C5
Ussurka Russia 45°12N 133°31E 302 B6
Ust-Bolsheretsk Russia 52°50N 156°15E 301 D16
Ust-Chaun Russia 68°47N 170°30E 301 C18
Ust-Ilimsk Russia 58°3N 102°39E 301 D11
Ust-Ishim Russia 57°45N 71°10E 300 D8
Ust-Kamchatsk Russia 56°10N 162°28E 301 D17
Ust-Kamenogorsk = Öskemen Kazakhstan 50°0N 82°36E 300 E9
Ust-Khayryuzovo Russia 57°15N 156°45E 301 D16
Ust-Kut Russia 56°50N 105°42E 301 D11
Ust-Kuyga Russia 70°1N 135°43E 301 B14
Ust-Maya Russia 60°30N 134°28E 301 C14
Ust-Mil Russia 59°40N 133°11E 301 D14
Ust-Nera Russia 64°35N 143°15E 301 C15
Ust-Nyukzha Russia 56°34N 121°37E 301 D13
Ust-Olenek Russia 73°0N 120°5E 301 B12
Ust-Omchug Russia 61°9N 149°38E 301 C15
Ust-Port Russia 69°40N 84°26E 300 C9
Ust-Tsilma Russia 65°28N 52°11E 290 A9
Ust Urt = Ustyurt Plateau Asia 44°0N 55°0E 300 E6
Ust-Usa Russia 66°2N 56°57E 290 A10
Ust-Vorkuta Russia 67°24N 64°0E 290 A11
Ústí nad Labem Czech Rep. 50°41N 14°3E 288 C8
Ústica Italy 38°42N 13°11E 294 E5
Ustinov = Izhevsk Russia 56°51N 53°14E 290 C9
Ustyurt Plateau Asia 44°0N 55°0E 300 E6
Usu China 44°27N 84°40E 304 B3
Usuki Japan 33°8N 131°49E 303 H5
Usulután El Salv. 13°25N 88°28W 360 D2
Usumacinta → Mexico 18°24N 92°38W 359 D6
Usumbura = Bujumbura Burundi 3°16S 29°18E 326 C2
Usure Tanzania 4°40S 34°22E 326 C3
Usutuo → Mozam. 26°48S 32°7E 329 D5
Uta Indonesia 4°33S 136°0E 309 E9
Utah □ U.S.A. 39°20N 111°30W 348 G8
Utah L. U.S.A. 40°12N 111°48W 348 F8
Utara, Selat Malaysia 5°28N 100°20E 311 c
Utarni India 26°5N 71°58E 314 F4
Utatlan Guatemala 15°2N 91°11W 360 C1
Ute Creek → U.S.A. 35°21N 103°50W 349 J12
Utena Lithuania 55°27N 25°40E 281 J21
Utete Tanzania 8°0S 38°45E 326 D4
Uthai Thani Thailand 15°22N 100°3E 310 E3
Uthal Pakistan 25°44N 66°40E 314 G2
Utiariti Brazil 13°0S 58°10W 364 F7
Utica N.Y., U.S.A. 43°6N 75°14W 355 C9
Utica Ohio, U.S.A. 40°14N 82°27W 354 F2
Utikuma L. Canada 55°50N 115°30W 342 B5
Utopia Australia 22°14S 134°33E 334 C1
Utraula India 27°19N 82°25E 315 F10
Utrecht Neths. 52°5N 5°8E 287 B5
Utrecht S. Africa 27°38S 30°20E 329 D5
Utrecht □ Neths. 52°6N 5°7E 287 B5
Utrera Spain 37°12N 5°48W 293 D3
Utsjoki → Finland 69°51N 26°59E 280 B22
Utsunomiya Japan 36°30N 139°50E 303 F9
Uttar Pradesh □ India 27°0N 80°0E 315 F9
Uttaradit Thailand 17°36N 100°5E 310 D3
Uttaranchal □ India 30°0N 79°30E 315 D8
Uttoxeter U.K. 52°54N 1°52W 284 E6
Utuado Puerto Rico 18°16N 66°42W 361 d
Uummannaq Greenland 77°28N 69°13W 276 B4
Uummannaq Greenland 70°58N 52°17W 276 B5
Uummannarsuaq = Nunap Isua Greenland 59°48N 43°55W 338 D15
Uusikaarlepyy Finland 63°32N 22°31E 280 E20
Uusikaupunki Finland 60°47N 21°25E 280 F19
Uva Russia 56°59N 52°13E 290 C9
Uvalde U.S.A. 29°13N 99°47W 356 G5
Uvat Russia 59°5N 68°50E 300 D7
Uvinza Tanzania 5°5S 30°24E 326 D3
Uvira Dem. Rep. of the Congo 3°22S 29°3E 326 C2
Uvs Nuur Mongolia 50°20N 92°30E 304 A4
'Uwairidh, Ḥarrat al Si. Arabia 26°50N 38°0E 316 E3
Uwajima Japan 33°10N 132°35E 303 H6
Uwanda ⌂ Tanzania 7°46S 32°0E 326 D3
Uweinat, Jebel Sudan 21°54N 24°58E 323 D10
Uxbridge Canada 44°6N 79°7W 354 B5
Uxin Qi China 38°50N 109°5E 306 E5
Uxmal Mexico 20°22N 89°46W 359 C7
Üydzin Mongolia 44°9N 107°0E 306 B4
Uyo Nigeria 5°1N 7°53E 322 G7
Uyûn Mûsa Egypt 29°53N 32°40E 318 F1
Uyuni Bolivia 20°28S 66°47W 364 H5
Uzbekistan ■ Asia 41°30N 65°0E 300 E7
Uzboy → Turkmenistan 39°30N 55°0E 317 B7
Uzen Kazakhstan 43°29N 52°54E 291 F9
Uzen, Bolshoi = Uzen, Mal → Kazakhstan 49°4N 49°44E 291 E8
Uzen, Mal → Kazakhstan 49°4N 49°44E 291 E8
Uzerche France 45°25N 1°34E 292 D4
Uzh → Ukraine 51°15N 30°12E 289 C16
Uzhgorod = Uzhhorod Ukraine 48°36N 22°18E 289 D12
Uzhhorod Ukraine 48°36N 22°18E 289 D12
Užice Serbia 43°55N 19°50E 295 C8
Uzunköprü Turkey 41°16N 26°43E 295 D12

V

Vaal → S. Africa 29°4S 23°38E 328 D3
Vaal Dam S. Africa 27°0S 28°14E 329 D4
Vaalbos △ S. Africa 28°22S 24°20E 328 D3
Vaalwater S. Africa 24°15S 28°8E 329 C4
Vaasa Finland 63°6N 21°38E 280 E19
Vác Hungary 47°49N 19°10E 289 E10
Vacaria Brazil 28°31S 50°52W 367 B5
Vacata Fiji 17°15S 179°31W 331 a
Vacaville U.S.A. 38°21N 121°59W 350 G5
Vach = Vakh → Russia 60°45N 76°45E 300 C8
Vache, Î. à Haiti 18°2N 73°35W 361 C5
Vacoas Mauritius 20°18S 57°29E 325 d
Vadnagar India 23°47N 72°40E 314 H5
Vadodara India 22°20N 73°10E 314 H5
Vadsø Norway 70°3N 29°50E 280 A23
Vaduz Liech. 47°8N 9°31E 292 C8
Værøy Norway 67°40N 12°40E 280 C15
Vágar Færoe Is. 62°5N 7°15W 280 E9
Vagia, Akra Greece 36°15N 28°11E 297 C10
Vågsfjorden Norway 68°50N 16°50E 280 B17
Váh → Slovak Rep. 47°43N 18°7E 289 D9
Vahsel B. Antarctica 75°0S 35°0W 277 D1
Váhtjer = Gällivare Sweden 67°9N 20°40E 280 C19
Vaï Greece 35°15N 26°18E 297 D8
Vaigach Russia 70°10N 59°0E 300 B6
Vaihiria, L. Tahiti 17°40S 149°25W 331 d
Vail U.S.A. 39°40N 106°20W 346 C5
Vairao Tahiti 17°47S 149°17W 331 d
Vaisali → India 26°28N 78°53E 315 F8
Vaitogi Amer. Samoa 14°24S 170°44W 331 b
Vakh → Russia 60°45N 76°45E 300 C8
Val-d'Or Canada 48°7N 77°47W 344 C4
Val Marie Canada 49°15N 107°45W 343 D7
Valaam Russia 61°22N 30°57E 280 F24
Valahia Romania 44°35N 25°0E 289 F13
Valandovo Macedonia 41°19N 22°34E 295 D10
Valcheta Argentina 40°40S 66°8W 368 E3
Valdai Hills = Valdayskaya Vozvyshennost Russia 57°0N 33°30E 290 C5
Valdayskaya Vozvyshennost Russia 57°0N 33°30E 290 C5
Valdepeñas Spain 38°43N 3°25W 293 C4
Valdés, Pen. Argentina 42°30S 63°45W 368 E4
Valdez U.S.A. 61°7N 146°16W 346 a
Valdivia Chile 39°50S 73°14W 368 D2
Valdivia Abyssal Plain S. Ocean 62°30S 70°0E 277 C6
Valdosta U.S.A. 30°50N 83°17W 357 F13
Valdres Norway 61°5N 9°5E 280 F13
Vale U.S.A. 43°59N 117°15W 348 E5
Vale of Glamorgan □ U.K. 51°28N 3°25W 285 F4
Valemount Canada 52°50N 119°15W 342 C5
Valença Brazil 13°20S 39°5W 365 F11
Valença do Piauí Brazil 6°20S 41°45W 365 E10
Valence France 44°57N 4°54E 292 D6
Valencia Spain 39°27N 0°23W 293 C5
Valencia Trin. & Tob. 10°39N 61°11W 365 K15
Valencia U.S.A. 34°48N 106°43W 349 J10
Valencia Venezuela 10°11N 68°0W 364 A5
Valencia □ Spain 39°20N 0°40W 293 C5
Valencia, G. de Spain 39°30N 0°20E 293 C6
Valencia de Alcántara Spain 39°25N 7°14W 293 C2
Valencia I. Ireland 51°54N 10°22W 282 E1
Valenciennes France 50°20N 3°34E 292 A5
Valentim, Sa. do Brazil 6°0S 43°30W 365 E10
Valentin Russia 43°8N 134°17E 302 C7
Valentine Nebr., U.S.A. 42°52N 100°33W 352 D3
Valentine Tex., U.S.A. 30°35N 104°30W 356 F2
Valera Venezuela 9°19N 70°37W 364 B4
Valga Estonia 57°47N 26°2E 281 H22
Valier U.S.A. 48°18N 112°16W 348 B7
Valjevo Serbia 44°18N 19°53E 295 B8
Valka Latvia 57°46N 26°3E 281 H22
Valkeakoski Finland 61°16N 24°2E 280 F21
Valkenswaard Neths. 51°21N 5°29E 287 C5
Vall de Uxó = La Vall d'Uixó Spain 39°49N 0°15W 293 C5
Valladolid Mexico 20°41N 88°12W 359 C7
Valladolid Spain 41°38N 4°43W 293 B3
Valldemossa Spain 39°43N 2°37E 296 B9
Valle de la Pascua Venezuela 9°13N 66°0W 364 B5
Valle de las Palmas Mexico 32°20N 116°43W 351 N10
Valle de Santiago Mexico 20°23N 101°12W 358 C4
Valle de Zaragoza Mexico 27°25N 105°50W 358 B3
Valle Fértil, Sierra del Argentina 30°20S 68°0W 366 C2
Valle Gran Rey Canary Is. 28°5N 17°20W 296 F2
Valle Hermoso Mexico 25°35N 97°40W 359 B5
Valle Nacional Mexico 17°47N 96°18W 359 D5
Valledupar Colombia 10°29N 73°15W 364 A4
Vallehermoso Canary Is. 28°10N 17°15W 296 F2
Vallejo U.S.A. 38°7N 122°14W 350 G4
Vallenar Chile 28°30S 70°50W 366 B1
Valletta Malta 35°54N 14°31E 297 D2
Valley Center U.S.A. 33°13N 117°2W 351 M9
Valley City U.S.A. 46°55N 98°0W 352 B5
Valley Falls Oreg., U.S.A. 42°29N 120°17W 348 E3
Valley Falls R.I., U.S.A. 41°54N 71°24W 355 E13
Valley of Flowers △ India 30°50N 79°40E 315 D8
Valley Springs U.S.A. 38°12N 120°50W 350 G6
Valley View U.S.A. 40°39N 76°33W 355 F8
Valley Wells U.S.A. 35°27N 115°46W 351 K11
Valleyview Canada 55°5N 117°17W 342 B5
Vallimanca, Arroyo Argentina 35°40S 59°10W 366 D4
Valls Spain 41°18N 1°15E 293 B6
Valmiera Latvia 57°37N 25°29E 281 H21
Valognes France 49°30N 1°28W 292 B3
Valona = Vlorë Albania 40°32N 19°28E 295 D8
Valozhyn Belarus 54°3N 26°30E 289 A14
Valparaíso Chile 33°2S 71°40W 366 C1
Valparaíso Mexico 22°46N 103°34W 358 C4
Valparaiso U.S.A. 41°28N 87°4W 352 E10
Valparaíso □ Chile 33°2S 71°40W 366 C1
Vals → S. Africa 27°23S 26°30E 328 D4
Vals, Tanjung Indonesia 8°26S 137°25E 309 F9
Valsad India 20°40N 72°58E 312 J8
Valverde Canary Is. 27°48N 17°55W 296 G2
Valverde del Camino Spain 37°35N 6°47W 293 D2
Vammala Finland 61°20N 22°54E 280 F20
Vamos Greece 35°24N 24°13E 297 D6
Van Turkey 38°30N 43°20E 316 B4
Van, L. = Van Gölü Turkey 38°30N 43°0E 316 B4
Van Alstyne U.S.A. 33°25N 96°35W 356 E6
Van Blommestein Meer Suriname 4°45N 55°5W 365 C7
Van Buren Canada 47°10N 67°55W 345 C6
Van Buren Ark., U.S.A. 35°26N 94°21W 356 D7
Van Buren Maine, U.S.A. 47°10N 67°58W 353 B20
Van Buren Mo., U.S.A. 37°0N 91°1W 352 G8
Van Canh Vietnam 13°37N 109°0E 310 F7
Van Diemen, C. N. Terr., Australia 11°9S 130°24E 332 B5
Van Diemen, C. Queens., Australia 16°30S 139°46E 334 B2
Van Diemen G. Australia 11°45S 132°0E 332 B5
Van Gölü Turkey 38°30N 43°0E 316 B4
Van Horn U.S.A. 31°3N 104°50W 356 F2
Van Ninh Vietnam 12°42N 109°14E 310 F7
Van Rees, Pegunungan Indonesia 2°35S 138°15E 309 E9
Van Wert U.S.A. 40°52N 84°35W 353 E11
Van Yen Vietnam 21°4N 104°42E 310 B5
Vanadzor Armenia 40°48N 44°30E 291 F7
Vanavara Russia 60°22N 102°16E 301 C11
Vancouver Canada 49°15N 123°7W 350 A3
Vancouver U.S.A. 45°38N 122°40W 350 E4
Vancouver, C. Australia 35°2S 118°11E 333 G2
Vancouver I. Canada 49°50N 126°0W 350 A1
Vancouver Int. ✈ (YVR) Canada 49°10N 123°10W 350 A3
Vanda = Vantaa Finland 60°18N 24°56E 281 F21
Vandalia Ill., U.S.A. 38°58N 89°6W 352 F9
Vandalia Mo., U.S.A. 39°19N 91°29W 352 F8
Vandenberg Village U.S.A. 34°43N 120°28W 351 L6
Vanderbijlpark S. Africa 26°42S 27°54E 329 D4
Vandergrift U.S.A. 40°36N 79°34W 354 F5
Vanderhoof Canada 54°0N 124°0W 342 C4
Vanderkloof Dam S. Africa 30°4S 24°40E 328 E3
Vanderlin I. Australia 15°44S 137°2E 334 B2
Vänern Sweden 58°47N 13°30E 281 G15
Vänersborg Sweden 58°26N 12°19E 281 G15
Vang Vieng Laos 18°58N 102°32E 310 C4
Vanga Kenya 4°35S 39°12E 326 C4
Vangaindrano Madag. 23°21S 47°36E 329 C8
Vanguard Canada 49°55N 107°20W 343 D7
Vanino Russia 48°50N 140°5E 301 E15
Vännäs Sweden 63°58N 19°48E 280 E18
Vannes France 47°40N 2°47W 292 C2
Vannøya Norway 70°6N 19°50E 280 A18
Vanrhynsdorp S. Africa 31°36S 18°44E 328 E2
Vansbro Sweden 60°32N 14°15E 281 F16
Vansittart B. Australia 14°3S 126°17E 332 B4
Vantaa Finland 60°18N 24°56E 281 F21
Vanua Balavu Fiji 17°12S 178°55W 331 a
Vanua Levu Fiji 16°33S 179°15E 331 a
Vanua Vatu Fiji 18°22S 179°15W 331 a
Vanuatu ■ Pac. Oc. 15°0S 168°0E 330 C9
Vanwyksvlei S. Africa 30°18S 21°49E 328 E3
Vanzylsrus S. Africa 26°52S 22°4E 328 D3
Vapnyarka Ukraine 48°32N 28°45E 289 D15
Var → France 43°39N 7°12E 292 E7
Varāmīn Iran 35°20N 51°39E 317 C6
Varāmīn □ Iran 35°18N 51°35E 317 B6
Varanasi India 25°22N 83°0E 315 G10
Varangerfjorden Norway 70°3N 29°25E 280 A23
Varangerhalvøya Norway 70°25N 29°30E 280 A23
Varaždin Croatia 46°20N 16°20E 288 E9
Varberg Sweden 57°6N 12°20E 281 H15
Vardak □ Afghan. 34°0N 68°0E 312 B6
Vardar = Axios → Greece 40°57N 22°35E 295 D10
Varde Denmark 55°38N 8°29E 281 J13
Vardø Norway 70°23N 31°5E 280 A24
Varella, Mui Vietnam 12°54N 109°26E 310 F7
Varėna Lithuania 54°12N 24°30E 281 J21
Varese Italy 45°48N 8°50E 292 D8
Varginha Brazil 21°33S 45°25W 367 A6
Varillas Chile 24°0S 70°10W 366 A1
Varkaus Finland 62°19N 27°50E 280 E22
Varna Bulgaria 43°13N 27°56E 295 C12
Värnamo Sweden 57°10N 14°3E 281 H16
Vars Canada 45°21N 75°21W 355 A9
Varysburg U.S.A. 42°46N 78°19W 354 D6
Varzaneh Iran 32°25N 52°40E 317 C7
Vasa = Vaasa Finland 63°6N 21°38E 280 E19
Vasa Barris → Brazil 11°10S 37°10W 365 F11
Vascongadas = País Vasco □ Spain 42°50N 2°45W 293 A4
Vasht = Khāsh Iran 28°15N 61°15E 317 D9
Vasilevichi Belarus 52°15N 29°50E 289 B15
Vasilkov = Vasylkiv Ukraine 50°7N 30°15E 289 C16
Vaslui Romania 46°38N 27°42E 289 E14
Vassar Canada 49°10N 95°55W 343 D9
Vassar U.S.A. 43°22N 83°35W 353 D12
Västerås Sweden 59°37N 16°38E 281 G17
Västerbotten Sweden 64°36N 20°4E 280 D19
Västerdalälven → Sweden 60°30N 14°7E 280 F16
Västervik Sweden 57°43N 16°33E 281 H17
Västmanland Sweden 59°45N 16°20E 281 G17
Vasto Italy 42°8N 14°40E 294 C6
Vasylkiv Ukraine 50°7N 30°15E 289 C16
Vatersay U.K. 56°55N 7°32W 283 E1
Vatican City ■ Europe 41°54N 12°27E 294 D5
Vatili Cyprus 35°6N 33°40E 297 D12
Vatiu = Atiu Cook Is. 20°0S 158°10W 337 J12
Vatnajökull Iceland 64°30N 16°48W 280 D5
Vatolakkos Greece 35°27N 23°53E 297 D5
Vatoloha Madag. 17°52S 47°48E 329 B8
Vatomandry Madag. 19°20S 48°59E 329 B8
Vatra-Dornei Romania 47°22N 25°22E 289 E13
Vatrak → India 23°9N 73°2E 314 H5
Vättern Sweden 58°25N 14°30E 281 G16
Vatu Vara Fiji 17°26S 179°31W 331 a
Vatulele Fiji 18°33S 177°37E 331 a
Vaudreuil-Dorion Canada 45°23N 74°3W 355 A10
Vaughn Mont., U.S.A. 47°33N 111°33W 348 C8
Vaughn N. Mex., U.S.A. 34°36N 105°13W 349 J11
Vaujours L. Canada 55°27N 74°15W 344 A5
Vaupés = Uaupés → Brazil 0°2N 67°16W 364 C5
Vaupes □ Colombia 1°0N 71°0W 364 C4
Vauxhall Canada 50°5N 112°9W 342 C6
Vav India 24°22N 71°31E 314 G4
Vavatenina Madag. 17°28S 49°12E 329 B8
Vava'u Tonga 18°36S 174°0W 331 c
Vava'u Group Tonga 18°40S 174°0W 331 c
Vawkavysk Belarus 53°9N 24°30E 289 B13
Växjö Sweden 56°52N 14°50E 281 H16
Vaygach, Ostrov Russia 70°0N 60°0E 300 C6
Veaikevárri = Svappavaara Sweden 67°40N 21°3E 280 C19
Vechte → Neths. 52°34N 6°6E 287 B6
Vedea → Romania 43°42N 25°41E 289 G13
Vedia Argentina 34°30S 61°31W 366 C3
Veendam Neths. 53°5N 6°52E 287 A6
Veenendaal Neths. 52°2N 5°34E 287 B5
Vefsna → Norway 65°48N 13°10E 280 D15
Vega Norway 65°40N 11°55E 280 D14
Vega U.S.A. 35°15N 102°26W 356 D3
Vega Baja Puerto Rico 18°27N 66°23W 361 d
Vegreville Canada 53°30N 112°5W 342 C6
Vejer de la Frontera Spain 36°15N 5°59W 293 D3
Vejle Denmark 55°43N 9°30E 281 J13
Velas, C. Costa Rica 10°21N 85°52W 360 D2
Velasco, Sierra de Argentina 29°20S 67°10W 366 B2
Velddrif S. Africa 32°42S 18°11E 328 E2
Velebit Planina Croatia 44°50N 15°20E 288 F8
Veles Macedonia 41°46N 21°47E 295 D9
Vélez-Málaga Spain 36°48N 4°5W 293 D3
Vélez Rubio Spain 37°41N 2°5W 293 D4
Velhas → Brazil 17°13S 44°49W 365 G10
Velika Kapela Croatia 45°10N 15°5E 288 F8
Velikaya → Russia 57°48N 28°10E 290 C4
Velikaya Kema Russia 45°30N 137°12E 302 B8
Veliki Ustyug Russia 60°47N 46°20E 290 B8
Velikiye Luki Russia 56°25N 30°32E 290 C5
Veliko Tŭrnovo Bulgaria 43°5N 25°41E 295 C11
Velikonda Range India 14°45N 79°10E 312 M11
Velletri Italy 41°41N 12°47E 294 D5
Vellore India 12°57N 79°10E 312 N11
Velsk Russia 61°10N 42°5E 290 B7
Veluwezoom △ Neths. 52°5N 6°0E 287 B6
Velva U.S.A. 48°4N 100°56W 352 A3
Venado Mexico 22°56N 101°6W 358 C4
Venado Tuerto Argentina 33°50S 62°0W 366 C3
Vendée □ France 46°50N 1°35W 292 C3
Vendôme France 47°47N 1°3E 292 C4
Venézia Italy 45°27N 12°21E 294 B5
Venézia, G. di Italy 45°15N 13°0E 294 B5
Venezuela ■ S. Amer. 8°0N 66°0W 364 B5
Venezuela, G. de Venezuela 11°30N 71°0W 364 A4
Vengurla India 15°53N 73°45E 312 M8
Venice = Venézia Italy 45°27N 12°21E 294 B5
Venice U.S.A. 27°6N 82°27W 357 H13
Venkatapuram India 18°20N 80°30E 313 K12
Venlo Neths. 51°22N 6°11E 287 C6
Vennesla Norway 58°15N 7°59E 281 G12
Venray Neths. 51°31N 6°0E 287 C6
Ventana, Punta de la Mexico 24°4N 109°48W 358 C3
Ventana, Sa. de la Argentina 38°0S 62°30W 366 D3
Ventersburg S. Africa 28°7S 27°9E 328 D4
Venterstad S. Africa 30°47S 25°48E 328 E4
Ventnor U.K. 50°36N 1°12W 285 G6
Ventoténe Italy 40°47N 13°25E 294 D5
Ventoux, Mt. France 44°10N 5°17E 292 D6
Ventspils Latvia 57°25N 21°32E 281 H19
Ventuarí → Venezuela 3°58N 67°2W 364 C5
Ventucopa U.S.A. 34°50N 119°29W 351 L7
Ventura U.S.A. 34°17N 119°18W 351 L7
Vénus, Pte. Tahiti 17°29S 149°29W 331 d
Venus B. Australia 38°40S 145°42E 335 F4
Venustiano Carranza Mexico 30°25N 115°53W 358 A1
Vera Argentina 29°30S 60°20W 366 B3
Vera Spain 37°15N 1°51W 293 D5
Veracruz Mexico 19°11N 96°8W 359 D5
Veracruz □ Mexico 19°0N 96°15W 359 D5
Veraval India 20°53N 70°27E 314 J4
Verbánia Italy 45°56N 8°33E 292 D8
Vercelli Italy 45°19N 8°25E 292 D8
Verdalsøra Norway 63°48N 11°30E 280 E14
Verde → Argentina 41°56S 65°5W 368 E3
Verde → Goiás, Brazil 18°1S 50°14W 365 G8
Verde → Mato Grosso do Sul, Brazil 21°25S 52°20W 365 H8
Verde → Chihuahua, Mexico 26°29N 107°58W 358 B3
Verde → Oaxaca, Mexico 15°59N 97°50W 359 D5
Verde → Veracruz, Mexico 21°10N 102°50W 358 C4
Verde → Paraguay 23°9S 57°37W 366 A4
Verde → U.S.A. 33°33N 111°40W 346 D4
Verde, Cay Bahamas 23°0N 75°5W 360 B4
Verden Germany 52°55N 9°14E 288 B5
Verdi U.S.A. 39°31N 119°59W 350 F7
Verdun France 49°9N 5°24E 292 B6
Vereeniging S. Africa 26°38S 27°57E 329 D4
Verga, C. Guinea 10°30N 14°10W 322 F3
Vergara Uruguay 32°56S 53°57W 367 C5
Vergemont Cr. → Australia 24°16S 143°16E 334 C3
Vergennes U.S.A. 44°10N 73°15W 355 B11
Veria Greece 40°34N 22°12E 295 D10
Verín Spain 41°57N 7°27W 293 B2
Verkhnetulomskoye Vdkhr. Russia 68°36N 31°12E 280 B24
Verkhnevilyuysk Russia 63°27N 120°18E 301 C13
Verkhniy Baskunchak Russia 48°14N 46°44E 291 E8
Verkhoyansk Russia 67°35N 133°25E 301 C14
Verkhoyansk Ra. = Verkhoyanskiy Khrebet Russia 66°0N 129°0E 301 C13
Verkhoyanskiy Khrebet Russia 66°0N 129°0E 301 C13
Vermilion Canada 53°20N 110°50W 343 C6
Vermilion U.S.A. 41°25N 82°22W 354 E2
Vermilion → Canada 53°22N 110°51W 343 C6
Vermilion B. U.S.A. 29°42N 92°0W 356 G9
Vermilion Bay Canada 49°51N 93°34W 343 D10
Vermilion L. U.S.A. 47°53N 92°26W 352 B7
Vermillion U.S.A. 42°47N 96°56W 352 D5
Vermillion → Canada 47°38N 72°56W 344 C5
Vermont □ U.S.A. 44°0N 73°0W 355 C12
Vernadsky Antarctica 65°0S 64°0W 277 C17
Vernal U.S.A. 40°27N 109°32W 348 F9
Vernalis U.S.A. 37°36N 121°17W 350 H5

Verner *Canada* 46°25N 80°8W 344 C3
Verneukpan *S. Africa* 30°0S 21°0E 328 E3
Vernon *Canada* 50°20N 119°15W 342 C5
Vernon *U.S.A.* 34°9N 99°17W 356 D5
Vernonia *U.S.A.* 45°52N 123°11W 350 E3
Vero Beach *U.S.A.* 27°38N 80°24W 357 H14
Véroia = Veria *Greece* 40°34N 22°12E 295 D10
Verona *Canada* 44°29N 76°42W 355 B8
Verona *Italy* 45°27N 10°59E 294 B4
Versailles *France* 48°48N 2°7E 292 B5
Vert, C. *Senegal* 14°45N 17°30W 322 F2
Verulam *S. Africa* 29°38S 31°2E 329 D5
Verviers *Belgium* 50°37N 5°52E 287 D5
Veselovskoye Vdkhr. *Russia* 46°58N 41°25E 291 E7
Vesoul *France* 47°40N 6°11E 292 C7
Vesterålen *Norway* 68°45N 15°0E 280 B16
Vestfjorden *Norway* 67°55N 14°0E 280 C16
Vestmannaeyjar *Iceland* 63°27N 20°15W 280 E3
Vestspitsbergen *Svalbard* 78°40N 17°0E 276 B8
Vestvågøya *Norway* 68°18N 13°50E 280 B15
Vesuvio *Italy* 40°49N 14°26E 294 D6
Vesuvius, Mt. = Vesuvio *Italy* 40°49N 14°26E 294 D6
Veszprém *Hungary* 47°8N 17°57E 289 E9
Vetlanda *Sweden* 57°24N 15°3E 281 H16
Vetlugu → *Russia* 56°36N 46°4E 290 C8
Vettore, Mte. *Italy* 42°49N 13°16E 294 C5
Veurne *Belgium* 51°5N 2°40E 287 C2
Veys *Iran* 31°30N 49°0E 317 D6
Vezhen *Bulgaria* 42°50N 24°20E 295 C11
Vi Thanh *Vietnam* 9°42N 105°26E 311 H5
Viacha *Bolivia* 16°39S 68°18W 364 G5
Viamão *Brazil* 30°5S 51°0W 367 C5
Viana *Brazil* 3°13S 44°55W 365 D10
Viana do Alentejo *Portugal* 38°17N 7°59W 293 C2
Viana do Castelo *Portugal* 41°42N 8°50W 293 B1
Vianden *Lux.* 49°56N 6°12E 287 E6
Viangchan = Vientiane *Laos* 17°58N 102°36E 310 D4
Vianópolis *Brazil* 16°40S 48°35W 365 G9
Vianos *Greece* 35°2N 25°21E 297 D7
Viaréggio *Italy* 43°52N 10°14E 294 C4
Vibo Valéntia *Italy* 38°40N 16°6E 294 E7
Viborg *Denmark* 56°27N 9°23E 281 H13
Vic *Spain* 41°58N 2°19E 293 B7
Vicenza *Italy* 45°33N 11°33E 294 B4
Vich = Vic *Spain* 41°58N 2°19E 293 B7
Vichada → *Colombia* 4°55N 67°50W 364 C5
Vichy *France* 46°9N 3°26E 292 C5
Vicksburg *U.S.A.* 33°45N 113°45W 351 M13
Victor *India* 21°0N 71°30E 314 J4
Victor *U.S.A.* 42°58N 77°24W 354 D7
Victor Harbor *Australia* 35°30S 138°37E 335 F2
Victoria *Argentina* 32°40S 60°10W 366 C3
Victoria *Canada* 48°30N 123°25W 350 B3
Victoria *Chile* 38°13S 72°20W 368 D2
Victoria *China* 22°17N 114°9E 305 G1
Victoria *Malta* 36°3N 14°14E 297 C1
Victoria *Seychelles* 4°38S 55°28E 325 b
Victoria *Kans., U.S.A.* 38°52N 99°9W 352 F4
Victoria *Tex., U.S.A.* 28°48N 97°0W 356 G6
Victoria □ *Australia* 37°0S 144°0E 335 F3
Victoria → *Australia* 15°10S 129°40E 332 C4
Victoria, Grand L. *Canada* 47°31N 77°30W 344 C4
Victoria, L. *Africa* 1°0S 33°0E 326 C3
Victoria, L. *Australia* 33°57S 141°15E 335 E3
Victoria, Mt. *Burma* 21°14N 93°55E 313 J18
Victoria Beach *Canada* 50°40N 96°35W 343 C9
Victoria de Durango = Durango *Mexico* 24°3N 104°39W 358 C4
Victoria de las Tunas = Las Tunas *Cuba* 20°58N 76°59W 360 B4
Victoria Falls *Zimbabwe* 17°58S 25°52E 327 F2
Victoria Harbour *Canada* 44°45N 79°45W 354 B5
Victoria I. *Canada* 71°0N 111°0W 340 B8
Victoria L. *Canada* 48°20N 57°27W 345 C8
Victoria Ld. *Antarctica* 75°0S 160°0E 277 D11
Victoria Nile → *Uganda* 2°14N 31°26E 326 B3
Victoria River *Australia* 16°25S 131°0E 332 C5
Victoria Str. *Canada* 69°31N 100°30W 340 C9
Victoria West *S. Africa* 31°25S 23°4E 328 E3
Victoriaville *Canada* 46°4N 71°56W 345 C5
Victorica *Argentina* 36°20S 65°30W 366 D2
Victorville *U.S.A.* 34°32N 117°18W 351 L9
Vicuña *Chile* 30°0S 70°50W 366 C1
Vicuña Mackenna *Argentina* 33°53S 64°25W 366 C3
Vidal *U.S.A.* 34°7N 114°31W 351 L12
Vidal Junction *U.S.A.* 34°11N 114°34W 351 L12
Vidalia *U.S.A.* 32°13N 82°25W 357 E13
Vidin *Bulgaria* 43°59N 22°50E 295 C10
Vidisha *India* 23°28N 77°53E 314 H7
Vido *Greece* 39°38N 19°55E 297 A3
Vidzy *Belarus* 55°23N 26°37E 281 J22
Viedma *Argentina* 40°50S 63°0W 368 E4
Viedma, L. *Argentina* 49°30S 72°30W 368 F2
Vielsalm *Belgium* 50°17N 5°54E 287 D5
Vieng Pou Kha *Laos* 20°41N 101°4E 310 B3
Vienna = Wien *Austria* 48°12N 16°22E 288 D9
Vienna *Ill., U.S.A.* 37°25N 88°54W 352 G9
Vienna *Mo., U.S.A.* 38°11N 91°57W 352 F8
Vienne *France* 45°31N 4°53E 292 D6
Vienne → *France* 47°13N 0°5E 292 C4
Vientiane *Laos* 17°58N 102°36E 310 D4
Vientos, Paso de los *Caribbean* 20°0N 74°0W 361 C5
Vieques *Puerto Rico* 18°8N 65°25W 361 d
Vierge Pt. *St. Lucia* 13°49N 60°53W 361 f
Vierzon *France* 47°13N 2°5E 292 C5
Vietnam ■ *Asia* 19°0N 106°0E 310 C6
Vieux Fort *St. Lucia* 13°46N 60°58W 361 f
Vigan *Phil.* 17°35N 120°28E 309 A6
Vigévano *Italy* 45°19N 8°51E 292 D8
Vigia *Brazil* 0°50S 48°5W 365 D9
Víglas, Akra *Greece* 35°54N 27°51E 297 D9
Vigo *Spain* 42°12N 8°41W 293 A1
Vihowa *Pakistan* 31°8N 70°30E 314 D4
Vihowa → *Pakistan* 31°8N 70°41E 314 D4
Vijayawada *India* 16°31N 80°39E 313 L12
Vijosë → *Albania* 40°37N 19°24E 295 D8
Vík *Iceland* 63°25N 19°1W 280 E4
Vikeke = Viqueque *E. Timor* 8°52S 126°23E 309 F7
Viking *Canada* 53°7N 111°50W 342 C6
Vikna *Norway* 64°55N 10°58E 280 D14
Vila da Maganja *Mozam.* 17°18S 37°30E 327 F4
Vila da Ribeira Brava *C. Verde Is.* 16°32N 24°25W 322 b
Vila do Bispo *Portugal* 37°5N 8°53W 293 D1
Vila Franca de Xira *Portugal* 38°57N 8°59W 293 C1
Vila Gamito *Mozam.* 14°12S 33°0E 327 E3
Vila Gomes da Costa *Mozam.* 24°20S 33°37E 329 C5
Vila Machado *Mozam.* 19°15S 34°14E 327 F3
Vila Mouzinho *Mozam.* 14°48S 34°25E 327 E3
Vila Nova de Gaia *Portugal* 41°8N 8°37W 293 B1
Vila Real *Portugal* 41°17N 7°48W 293 B2
Vila-real de los Infantes *Spain* 39°55N 0°3W 293 C5
Vila Real de Santo António *Portugal* 37°10N 7°28W 293 D2
Vila Vasco da Gama *Mozam.* 14°54S 32°14E 327 E3
Vila Velha *Brazil* 20°20S 40°17W 367 A7
Vilagarcía de Arousa *Spain* 42°34N 8°46W 293 A1
Vilaine → *France* 47°30N 2°27W 292 C2
Vilanandro, Tanjona *Madag.* 16°11S 44°27E 329 B7
Vilanculos *Mozam.* 22°1S 35°17E 329 C6
Vilanova i la Geltrú *Spain* 41°13N 1°40E 293 B6
Vilcheka, Zemlya *Russia* 80°30N 60°30E 276 A11
Vileyka *Belarus* 54°30N 26°53E 289 A14
Vilhelmina *Sweden* 64°35N 16°39E 280 D17
Vilhena *Brazil* 12°40S 60°5W 364 F6
Viliya = Neris → *Lithuania* 55°8N 24°16E 281 J21
Viljandi *Estonia* 58°28N 25°30E 281 G21
Vilkitskogo, Proliv *Russia* 78°0N 103°0E 301 B11
Vilkovo = Vylkove *Ukraine* 45°28N 29°32E 289 F15
Villa Abecia *Bolivia* 21°0S 68°18W 366 A2
Villa Ana *Argentina* 28°28S 59°40W 366 B4
Villa Ángela *Argentina* 27°34S 60°45W 366 B3
Villa Bella *Bolivia* 10°25S 65°22W 364 F5
Villa Cañás *Argentina* 34°0S 61°35W 366 C3
Villa Colón *Argentina* 31°38S 68°20W 366 C2
Villa Constitución *Argentina* 33°15S 60°20W 366 C3
Villa de Arriaga *Mexico* 21°56N 101°20W 358 C4
Villa de María *Argentina* 29°55S 63°43W 366 B3
Villa de Méndez *Mexico* 25°7N 98°34W 359 B5
Villa Dolores *Argentina* 31°58S 65°15W 366 C2
Villa Frontera *Mexico* 26°56N 101°27W 358 B4
Villa Guillermina *Argentina* 28°15S 59°29W 366 B4
Villa Hayes *Paraguay* 25°5S 57°20W 366 B4
Villa Hidalgo *Mexico* 24°15N 99°26W 359 C5
Villa Iris *Argentina* 38°12S 63°12W 366 D3
Villa María *Argentina* 32°20S 63°10W 366 C3
Villa Mazán *Argentina* 28°40S 66°30W 366 B2
Villa Montes *Bolivia* 21°10S 63°30W 366 A3
Villa Ocampo *Argentina* 28°30S 59°20W 366 B4
Villa Ocampo *Mexico* 26°27N 105°31W 358 B3
Villa Ojo de Agua *Argentina* 29°30S 63°44W 366 B3
Villa San José *Argentina* 32°12S 58°15W 366 C4
Villa San Martín *Argentina* 28°15S 64°9W 366 B3
Villa Unión *Mexico* 23°12N 106°14W 358 C3
Villacarlos *Spain* 39°53N 4°17E 296 B11
Villacarrillo *Spain* 38°7N 3°3W 293 C4
Villach *Austria* 46°37N 13°51E 288 E7
Villafranca de los Caballeros *Spain* 39°34N 3°25E 296 B10
Villagrán *Mexico* 24°29N 99°29W 359 C5
Villaguay *Argentina* 32°0S 59°0W 366 C4
Villahermosa *Mexico* 17°59N 92°55W 359 D6
Villajoyosa *Spain* 38°30N 0°12W 293 C5
Villalba *Spain* 43°26N 7°40W 293 A2
Villanueva *U.S.A.* 35°16N 105°22W 349 J11
Villanueva de la Serena *Spain* 38°59N 5°50W 293 C3
Villanueva y Geltrú = Vilanova i la Geltrú *Spain* 41°13N 1°40E 293 B6
Villarreal = Vila-real de los Infantes *Spain* 39°55N 0°3W 293 C5
Villarrica *Chile* 39°15S 72°15W 368 D2
Villarrica *Paraguay* 25°40S 56°30W 366 B4
Villarrobledo *Spain* 39°18N 2°36W 293 C4
Villavicencio *Argentina* 32°28S 69°0W 366 C2
Villavicencio *Colombia* 4°9N 73°37W 364 C4
Villaviciosa *Spain* 43°32N 5°27W 293 A3
Villazón *Bolivia* 22°0S 65°35W 366 A2
Ville-Marie *Canada* 47°20N 79°30W 344 C4
Ville Platte *U.S.A.* 30°41N 92°17W 356 F8
Villena *Spain* 38°39N 0°52W 293 C5
Villeneuve-d'Ascq *France* 50°38N 3°9E 292 A5
Villeneuve-sur-Lot *France* 44°24N 0°42E 292 D4
Villiers *S. Africa* 27°2S 28°36E 329 D4
Villingen-Schwenningen *Germany* 48°3N 8°26E 288 D5
Villmanstrand = Lappeenranta *Finland* 61°3N 28°12E 280 F23
Vilna *Canada* 54°7N 111°55W 342 C6
Vilnius *Lithuania* 54°38N 25°19E 281 J21
Vilvoorde *Belgium* 50°56N 4°26E 287 D4
Vilyuy → *Russia* 64°24N 126°26E 301 C13
Vilyuysk *Russia* 63°40N 121°35E 301 C13
Viña del Mar *Chile* 33°0S 71°30W 366 C1
Vinarós *Spain* 40°30N 0°27E 293 B6
Vincennes *U.S.A.* 38°41N 87°32W 352 F10
Vincent *U.S.A.* 34°33N 118°11W 351 L8
Vinchina *Argentina* 28°45S 68°15W 366 B2
Vindelälven → *Sweden* 63°55N 19°50E 280 E18
Vindeln *Sweden* 64°12N 19°43E 280 D18
Vindhya Ra. *India* 22°50N 77°0E 314 H7
Vineland *U.S.A.* 39°29N 75°2W 353 F16
Vinh *Vietnam* 18°45N 105°38E 310 C5
Vinh Linh *Vietnam* 17°4N 107°2E 310 D6
Vinh Long *Vietnam* 10°16N 105°57E 311 G5
Vinh Yen *Vietnam* 21°21N 105°35E 310 B5
Vinita *U.S.A.* 36°39N 95°9W 356 C7
Vinkovci *Croatia* 45°19N 18°48E 295 B8
Vinnitsa = Vinnytsya *Ukraine* 49°15N 28°30E 289 D15
Vinnytsya *Ukraine* 49°15N 28°30E 289 D15
Vinson Massif *Antarctica* 78°35S 85°25W 277 D16
Vinton *Calif., U.S.A.* 39°48N 120°10W 350 F6
Vinton *Iowa, U.S.A.* 42°10N 92°1W 352 D7
Vinton *La., U.S.A.* 30°11N 93°35W 356 F8
Viqueque *E. Timor* 8°52S 126°23E 309 F7
Virac *Phil.* 13°30N 124°20E 309 B6
Virachey *Cambodia* 13°59N 106°49E 310 F6
Virachey △ *Cambodia* 14°14N 106°55E 310 E6
Virago Sd. *Canada* 54°0N 132°30W 342 C2
Viramgam *India* 23°5N 72°0E 314 H5
Viranşehir *Turkey* 37°13N 39°45E 316 B3
Virawah *Pakistan* 24°31N 70°46E 314 G4
Virden *Canada* 49°50N 100°56W 343 D8
Vire *France* 48°50N 0°53W 292 B3
Vírgenes, C. *Argentina* 52°19S 68°21W 368 G3
Virgin → *U.S.A.* 36°28N 114°21W 349 H6
Virgin Gorda *Br. Virgin Is.* 18°30N 64°26W 361 e
Virgin Is. (British) ☑ *W. Indies* 18°30N 64°30W 361 e
Virgin Is. (U.S.) ☑ *W. Indies* 18°20N 65°0W 361 e
Virgin Islands △ *U.S. Virgin Is.* 18°21N 64°43W 361 C7
Virginia *S. Africa* 28°8S 26°55E 328 D4
Virginia *U.S.A.* 47°31N 92°32W 352 B7
Virginia □ *U.S.A.* 37°30N 78°45W 353 G14
Virginia Beach *U.S.A.* 36°44N 76°0W 353 F16
Virginia City *Mont., U.S.A.* 45°18N 111°56W 348 D8
Virginia City *Nev., U.S.A.* 39°19N 119°39W 350 F7
Virginia Falls *Canada* 61°38N 125°42W 342 A3
Virginiatown *Canada* 48°9N 79°36W 344 C4
Viroqua *U.S.A.* 43°34N 90°53W 352 D8
Virovitica *Croatia* 45°51N 17°21E 294 B7
Virpur *India* 21°51N 70°42E 314 J4
Virton *Belgium* 49°35N 5°32E 287 E5
Virudunagar *India* 9°30N 77°58E 312 Q10
Virunga △ *Dem. Rep. of the Congo* 0°5N 29°38E 326 B2
Vis *Croatia* 43°4N 16°10E 294 C7
Visalia *U.S.A.* 36°20N 119°18W 350 J7
Visayan Sea *Phil.* 11°30N 123°30E 309 B6
Visby *Sweden* 57°37N 18°18E 281 H18
Viscount Melville Sd. *Canada* 74°10N 108°0W 341 B9
Visé *Belgium* 50°44N 5°41E 287 D5
Višegrad *Bos.-H.* 43°47N 19°17E 295 C8
Viseu *Brazil* 1°10S 46°5W 365 D9
Viseu *Portugal* 40°40N 7°55W 293 B2
Vishakhapatnam *India* 17°45N 83°20E 313 L13
Visnagar *India* 23°45N 72°32E 314 H5
Viso, Mte. *Italy* 44°38N 7°5E 292 D7
Visokoi I. *Antarctica* 56°43S 27°15W 277 B1
Vista *U.S.A.* 33°12N 117°14W 351 M9
Vistula = Wisła → *Poland* 54°22N 18°55E 289 A10
Vitebsk = Vitsyebsk *Belarus* 55°10N 30°15E 290 C5
Viterbo *Italy* 42°25N 12°6E 294 C5
Viti Levu *Fiji* 17°30S 177°30E 331 a
Vitigudino *Spain* 41°1N 6°26W 293 B2
Vitim *Russia* 59°28N 112°35E 301 D12
Vitim → *Russia* 59°26N 112°34E 301 D12
Vitória *Brazil* 20°20S 40°22W 365 H10
Vitória da Conquista *Brazil* 14°51S 40°51W 365 F10
Vitória de São Antão *Brazil* 8°10S 35°20W 365 E11
Vitoria-Gasteiz *Spain* 42°50N 2°41W 293 A4
Vitsyebsk *Belarus* 55°10N 30°15E 290 C5
Vittória *Italy* 36°57N 14°32E 294 F6
Vittório Véneto *Italy* 45°59N 12°18E 294 B5
Viveiro *Spain* 43°39N 7°38W 293 A2
Vivian *U.S.A.* 32°53N 93°59W 356 E8
Viwa *Fiji* 17°10S 177°58E 331 a
Vizcaíno, Desierto de *Mexico* 27°30N 113°45W 358 B2
Vizcaíno, Sierra *Mexico* 27°30N 114°0W 358 B2
Vize *Turkey* 41°34N 27°45E 295 D12
Vizianagaram *India* 18°6N 83°30E 313 K13
Vlaardingen *Neths.* 51°55N 4°21E 287 C4
Vladikavkaz *Russia* 43°0N 44°35E 291 F7
Vladimir *Russia* 56°15N 40°30E 290 C7
Vladimir Volynskiy = Volodymyr-Volynskyy *Ukraine* 50°50N 24°18E 289 C13
Vladivostok *Russia* 43°10N 131°53E 302 C5
Vlieland *Neths.* 53°16N 4°55E 287 A4
Vlissingen *Neths.* 51°26N 3°34E 287 C3
Vlorë *Albania* 40°32N 19°28E 295 D8
Vltava → *Czech Rep.* 50°21N 14°30E 288 D8
Vo Dat *Vietnam* 11°9N 107°31E 311 G6
Voe *U.K.* 60°21N 1°16W 283 A7
Vogelkop = Doberai, Jazirah *Indonesia* 1°25S 133°0E 309 E8
Vogelsberg *Germany* 50°31N 9°12E 288 C5
Voghera *Italy* 44°59N 9°1E 292 D8
Vohibinany *Madag.* 18°49S 49°4E 329 B8
Vohilava *Madag.* 21°4S 48°0E 329 C8
Vohimarina = Iharana *Madag.* 13°25S 50°0E 329 A9
Vohimena, Tanjon' i *Madag.* 25°36S 45°8E 329 D8
Vohipeno *Madag.* 22°22S 47°51E 329 C8
Voi *Kenya* 3°25S 38°32E 326 C4
Voiron *France* 45°22N 5°35E 292 D6
Voisey B. *Canada* 56°15N 61°50W 345 A7
Vojmsjön *Sweden* 65°0N 16°24E 280 D17
Vojvodina □ *Serbia* 45°20N 20°0E 295 B9
Volborg *U.S.A.* 45°51N 105°41W 348 D11
Volcán de Colima △ *Mexico* 19°30N 103°40W 358 D4
Volcano Is. = Kazan-Rettō *Pac. Oc.* 25°0N 141°0E 336 E6
Volcans △ *Rwanda* 1°30S 29°26E 326 C2
Volda *Norway* 62°9N 6°5E 280 E12
Volga = Privolzhskiy □ *Russia* 56°0N 50°0E 300 D6
Volga → *Russia* 46°0N 48°30E 291 E8
Volga Hts. = Privolzhskaya Vozvyshennost *Russia* 51°0N 46°0E 291 D8
Volgodonsk *Russia* 47°33N 42°5E 291 E7
Volgograd *Russia* 48°40N 44°25E 291 E7
Volgogradskoye Vdkhr. *Russia* 50°0N 45°20E 291 D8
Volkhov → *Russia* 60°8N 32°20E 290 B5
Volkovysk = Vawkavysk *Belarus* 53°9N 24°30E 289 B13
Volksrust *S. Africa* 27°24S 29°53E 329 D4
Volochanka *Russia* 71°0N 94°28E 301 B10
Volodymyr-Volynskyy *Ukraine* 50°50N 24°18E 289 C13
Vologda *Russia* 59°10N 39°45E 290 C6
Volos *Greece* 39°24N 22°59E 295 E10
Volosovo *Russia* 59°27N 29°32E 281 G23
Volovets *Ukraine* 48°43N 23°11E 289 D12
Volozhin = Valozhyn *Belarus* 54°3N 26°30E 289 A14
Volsk *Russia* 52°5N 47°22E 290 D8
Volta → *Ghana* 5°46N 0°41E 320 F4
Volta, L. *Ghana* 7°30N 0°0 322 G6
Volta Redonda *Brazil* 22°31S 44°5W 367 A7
Voltaire, C. *Australia* 14°16S 125°35E 332 B4
Volterra *Italy* 43°24N 10°51E 294 C4
Volturno → *Italy* 41°1N 13°55E 294 D5
Volzhskiy *Russia* 48°56N 44°46E 291 E7
Vomo *Fiji* 17°30S 177°15E 331 a
Vondrozo *Madag.* 22°49S 47°20E 329 C8
Vopnafjörður *Iceland* 65°45N 14°50W 280 D6
Vories Sporades *Greece* 39°15N 23°30E 295 E10
Vorkuta *Russia* 67°48N 64°20E 300 A11
Vormsi *Estonia* 59°1N 23°13E 281 G20
Voronezh *Russia* 51°40N 39°10E 291 D6
Võrts Järv *Estonia* 58°16N 26°3E 281 G22
Võru *Estonia* 57°48N 26°54E 281 H22
Vosges *France* 48°20N 7°10E 292 B7
Voss *Norway* 60°38N 6°26E 280 F12
Vostok *Antarctica* 78°30S 106°50E 277 D8
Vostok I. *Kiribati* 10°5S 152°23W 337 J12
Votkinsk *Russia* 57°0N 53°55E 290 C9
Votkinskoye Vdkhr. *Russia* 57°22N 55°12E 290 C10
Votsuri-Shima *Japan* 25°45N 123°29E 303 M1
Vouga → *Portugal* 40°41N 8°40W 293 B1
Vouxa, Akra *Greece* 35°37N 23°32E 297 D5
Voyageurs △ *U.S.A.* 48°32N 93°0W 352 A7
Voynitsa *Russia* 65°10N 30°20E 280 D24
Vozhe, Ozero *Russia* 60°45N 39°0E 290 B6
Voznesensk *Ukraine* 47°35N 31°21E 291 E5
Voznesenye *Russia* 61°0N 35°28E 290 B6
Vrangelya, Ostrov *Russia* 71°0N 180°0E 301 B19
Vranje *Serbia* 42°34N 21°54E 295 C9
Vratsa *Bulgaria* 43°15N 23°30E 295 C10
Vrbas → *Bos.-H.* 45°8N 17°29E 294 B7
Vrede *S. Africa* 27°24S 29°6E 329 D4
Vredefort *S. Africa* 27°0S 27°22E 328 D4
Vredenburg *S. Africa* 32°56S 18°0E 328 E2
Vredendal *S. Africa* 31°41S 18°35E 328 E2
Vrindavan *India* 27°37N 77°40E 314 F7
Vrisses *Greece* 35°23N 24°13E 297 D6
Vršac *Serbia* 45°8N 21°20E 295 B9
Vryburg *S. Africa* 26°55S 24°45E 328 D3
Vryheid *S. Africa* 27°45S 30°47E 329 D5
Vu Liet *Vietnam* 18°43N 105°23E 310 C5
Vukovar *Croatia* 45°21N 18°59E 295 B8
Vulcan *Canada* 50°25N 113°15W 342 C6
Vulcan *Romania* 45°23N 23°17E 289 F12
Vulcanești *Moldova* 45°41N 28°18E 289 F15
Vulcano *Italy* 38°24N 14°58E 294 E6
Vulkaneshty = Vulcanești *Moldova* 45°41N 28°18E 289 F15
Vunduzi → *Mozam.* 18°56S 34°1E 327 F3
Vung Tau *Vietnam* 10°21N 107°4E 311 G6
Vunidawa *Fiji* 17°50S 178°21E 331 a
Vunisea *Fiji* 19°3S 178°10E 331 a
Vwaza ⌂ *Malawi* 10°58S 33°25E 327 E3
Vyartsilya *Russia* 62°8N 30°45E 280 E24
Vyatka = Kirov *Russia* 58°35N 49°40E 290 C8
Vyatka → *Russia* 55°37N 51°28E 290 C9
Vyatskiye Polyany *Russia* 56°14N 51°5E 290 C9
Vyazemskiy *Russia* 47°32N 134°45E 301 E14
Vyazma *Russia* 55°10N 34°15E 290 C5
Vyborg *Russia* 60°43N 28°47E 280 F23
Vychegda → *Russia* 61°18N 46°36E 290 B8
Vychodné Beskydy *Europe* 49°20N 22°0E 289 D11
Vyg-ozero *Russia* 63°47N 34°29E 290 B5
Vylkove *Ukraine* 45°28N 29°32E 289 F15
Vynohradiv *Ukraine* 48°9N 23°2E 289 D12
Vyrnwy, L. *U.K.* 52°48N 3°31W 284 E4
Vyshniy Volochek *Russia* 57°30N 34°30E 290 C5
Vyshzha = imeni 26 Bakinskikh Komissarov *Turkmenistan* 39°22N 54°10E 317 B7
Vyškov *Czech Rep.* 49°17N 17°0E 289 D9
Vytegra *Russia* 61°0N 36°27E 290 B6

W

W.A.C. Bennett Dam *Canada* 56°2N 122°6W 342 B4
Wa *Ghana* 10°7N 2°25W 322 F5
Waal → *Neths.* 51°37N 5°0E 287 C5
Waalwijk *Neths.* 51°42N 5°4E 287 C5
Wabakimi △ *Canada* 50°43N 89°29W 344 B2
Wabana *Canada* 47°40N 53°0W 345 C9
Wabasca → *Canada* 58°22N 115°20W 342 B5
Wabasca-Desmarais *Canada* 55°57N 113°56W 342 B6
Wabash *U.S.A.* 40°48N 85°49W 353 E11
Wabash → *U.S.A.* 37°48N 88°2W 352 G9
Wabigoon L. *Canada* 49°44N 92°44W 343 D10
Wabowden *Canada* 54°55N 98°38W 343 C9
Wabuk Pt. *Canada* 55°20N 85°5W 344 A2
Wabush *Canada* 52°55N 66°52W 345 B6
Waco *U.S.A.* 31°33N 97°9W 356 F6
Waconichi, L. *Canada* 50°8N 74°0W 344 B5
Wad Hamid *Sudan* 16°30N 32°45E 323 E12
Wad Medanî *Sudan* 14°28N 33°30E 323 F12
Wad Thana *Pakistan* 27°22N 66°23E 314 F2
Wadai *Africa* 12°0N 19°0E 320 E5
Wadayama *Japan* 35°19N 134°52E 303 G7
Waddeneilanden *Neths.* 53°25N 5°10E 287 A5
Waddenzee *Neths.* 53°6N 5°10E 287 A5
Waddington *U.S.A.* 44°52N 75°12W 355 B9
Waddington, Mt. *Canada* 51°23N 125°15W 342 C3
Waddy Pt. *Australia* 24°58S 153°21E 335 C5
Wadebridge *U.K.* 50°31N 4°51W 285 G3
Wadena *Canada* 51°57N 103°47W 343 C8
Wadena *U.S.A.* 46°26N 95°8W 352 B6
Wadeye *Australia* 14°28S 129°52E 332 B4
Wadhams *Canada* 51°30N 127°30W 342 C3
Wādī as Sīr *Jordan* 31°56N 35°49E 318 D4
Wadi Halfa *Sudan* 21°53N 31°19E 323 D12
Wadi Rum △ *Jordan* 29°30N 35°20E 318 F4
Wadsworth *Nev., U.S.A.* 39°38N 119°17W 348 G4
Wadsworth *Ohio, U.S.A.* 41°2N 81°44W 354 E3
Waegwan *S. Korea* 35°59N 128°23E 307 G15
Wafangdian *China* 39°38N 121°58E 307 E11
Wafrah *Si. Arabia* 28°33N 47°56E 316 D5
Wageningen *Neths.* 51°58N 5°40E 287 C5
Wager B. *Canada* 65°26N 88°40W 341 C11
Wagga Wagga *Australia* 35°7S 147°24E 335 F4
Waghete *Indonesia* 4°10S 135°50E 309 E9
Wagin *Australia* 33°17S 117°25E 333 F2
Wagner *U.S.A.* 43°5N 98°18W 352 D4
Wagon Mound *U.S.A.* 36°1N 104°42W 349 H11
Wagoner *U.S.A.* 35°58N 95°22W 356 D7
Wah *Pakistan* 33°45N 72°40E 314 C5
Wahai *Indonesia* 2°48S 129°35E 309 E7
Wahiawā *U.S.A.* 21°30N 158°2W 346 b
Wâhid *Egypt* 30°48N 32°21E 318 E1
Wahnai *Afghan.* 32°40N 65°50E 314 C1
Wahoo *U.S.A.* 41°13N 96°37W 352 E5
Wahpeton *U.S.A.* 46°16N 96°36W 352 B5
Waiau → *N.Z.* 42°47S 173°22E 331 E4
Waibeem *Indonesia* 0°30S 132°59E 309 E8
Waigeo *Indonesia* 0°20S 130°40E 309 E8
Waihi *N.Z.* 37°23S 175°52E 331 B5
Waihou → *N.Z.* 37°15S 175°40E 331 B5
Waika *Dem. Rep. of the Congo* 2°22S 25°42E 326 C2
Waikabubak *Indonesia* 9°45S 119°25E 309 F5
Waikaremoana, L. *N.Z.* 38°49S 177°9E 331 C6
Waikari *N.Z.* 42°58S 172°41E 331 E4
Waikato → *N.Z.* 37°23S 174°43E 331 B5
Waikerie *Australia* 34°9S 140°0E 335 E3
Waikokopu *N.Z.* 39°3S 177°52E 331 C6
Waikouaiti *N.Z.* 45°36S 170°41E 331 F3
Wailingding Dao *China* 22°6N 114°2E 305 G11
Wailuku *U.S.A.* 20°53N 156°30W 346 b
Waimakariri → *N.Z.* 43°24S 172°42E 331 E4
Waimate *N.Z.* 44°45S 171°3E 331 F3
Wainganga → *India* 18°50N 79°55E 312 K11
Waingapu *Indonesia* 9°35S 120°11E 309 F6
Waini → *Guyana* 8°20N 59°50W 364 B7
Wainwright *Canada* 52°50N 110°50W 343 C6
Waiouru *N.Z.* 39°28S 175°41E 331 C5
Waipara *N.Z.* 43°3S 172°46E 331 E4
Waipawa *N.Z.* 39°56S 176°38E 331 C6
Waipiro *N.Z.* 38°2S 178°22E 331 C7
Waipoua Forest *N.Z.* 35°39S 173°33E 331 A4
Waipu *N.Z.* 35°59S 174°29E 331 A5
Waipukurau *N.Z.* 40°1S 176°33E 331 D6
Wairakei *N.Z.* 38°37S 176°6E 331 C6
Wairarapa, L. *N.Z.* 41°14S 175°15E 331 D5
Wairoa *N.Z.* 39°3S 177°25E 331 C6
Waitaki → *N.Z.* 44°56S 171°7E 331 F3
Waitangi *N.Z.* 35°16S 174°5E 331 A5
Waitara *N.Z.* 38°59S 174°15E 331 C5
Waitomo Caves *N.Z.* 38°16S 175°7E 331 C5
Waitsburg *U.S.A.* 46°16N 118°9W 348 C4
Waiuku *N.Z.* 37°15S 174°45E 331 B5
Wajima *Japan* 37°30N 137°0E 303 F8
Wajir *Kenya* 1°42N 40°5E 326 B5
Wakasa *Japan* 35°20N 134°24E 303 G7
Wakasa-Wan *Japan* 35°40N 135°30E 303 G7
Wakatipu, L. *N.Z.* 45°5S 168°33E 331 F2
Wakaw *Canada* 52°39N 105°44W 343 C7
Wakaya *Fiji* 17°37S 179°0E 331 a

Wakayama *Japan* 34°15N 135°15E **303** G7
Wakayama □ *Japan* 33°50N 135°30E **303** H7
Wake Forest *U.S.A.* 35°59N 78°30W **357** D15
Wake I. *Pac. Oc.* 19°18N 166°36E **336** F8
WaKeeney *U.S.A.* 39°1N 99°53W **352** F4
Wakefield *Jamaica* 18°26N 77°42W **360** a
Wakefield *N.Z.* 41°24S 173°5E **331** D4
Wakefield *U.K.* 53°41N 1°29W **284** D6
Wakefield *Mass., U.S.A.* 42°30N 71°5W **355** D13
Wakefield *Mich., U.S.A.* 46°29N 89°56W **352** B9
Wakkanai *Japan* 45°28N 141°35E **302** B10
Wakkerstroom *S. Africa* 27°24S 30°10E **329** D5
Wakool *Australia* 35°28S 144°23E **335** F3
Wakool → *Australia* 35°5S 143°33E **335** F3
Wakre *Indonesia* 0°19S 131°5E **309** E8
Wakuach, L. *Canada* 55°34N 67°32W **345** A6
Walamba *Zambia* 13°30S 28°42E **327** E2
Wałbrzych *Poland* 50°45N 16°18E **288** C9
Walbury Hill *U.K.* 51°21N 1°28W **285** F6
Walcha *Australia* 30°55S 151°31E **335** E5
Walcheren *Neths.* 51°30N 3°35E **287** C3
Walcott *U.S.A.* 41°46N 106°51W **348** F10
Wałcz *Poland* 53°17N 16°27E **288** B9
Waldburg Ra. *Australia* 24°40S 117°35E **333** D2
Walden *Colo., U.S.A.* 40°44N 106°17W **348** F10
Walden *N.Y., U.S.A.* 41°34N 74°11W **355** E10
Waldport *U.S.A.* 44°26N 124°4W **348** D1
Waldron *U.S.A.* 34°54N 94°5W **356** D7
Walebing *Australia* 30°41S 116°13E **333** F2
Wales □ *U.K.* 52°19N 4°43W **285** E3
Walgett *Australia* 30°0S 148°5E **335** E4
Walgreen Coast *Antarctica* 75°15S 105°0W **277** D15
Walker *U.S.A.* 47°6N 94°35W **352** B6
Walker, L. *Canada* 50°20N 67°11W **345** B6
Walker L. *Canada* 54°42N 95°57W **343** C9
Walker L. *U.S.A.* 38°42N 118°43W **348** G4
Walkerston *Australia* 21°11S 149°8E **334** K7
Walkerton *Canada* 44°10N 81°10W **354** B3
Wall *U.S.A.* 44°0N 102°8W **352** C2
Walla Walla *U.S.A.* 46°4N 118°20W **348** C4
Wallace *Idaho, U.S.A.* 47°28N 115°56W **348** C6
Wallace *N.C., U.S.A.* 34°44N 77°59W **357** D16
Wallaceburg *Canada* 42°34N 82°23W **354** D2
Wallachia = Valahia *Romania* 44°35N 25°0E **289** F13
Wallal *Australia* 26°32S 146°7E **335** D4
Wallam Cr. → *Australia* 28°40S 147°20E **335** D4
Wallambin, L. *Australia* 30°57S 117°35E **333** F2
Wallangarra *Australia* 28°56S 151°58E **335** D5
Wallaroo *Australia* 33°56S 137°39E **335** E2
Wallenpaupack, L. *U.S.A.* 41°25N 75°15W **355** E9
Wallingford *U.S.A.* 41°27N 72°50W **355** E12
Wallis & Futuna, Is. *Pac. Oc.* 13°18S 176°10W **330** C11
Wallowa *U.S.A.* 45°34N 117°32W **348** D5
Wallowa Mts. *U.S.A.* 45°20N 117°30W **348** D5
Walls *U.K.* 60°14N 1°33W **283** A7
Walls of Jerusalem △ *Australia* 41°56S 146°15E **335** G4
Wallula *U.S.A.* 46°5N 118°54W **348** C4
Wallumbilla *Australia* 26°33S 149°9E **335** D4
Walmsley L. *Canada* 63°25N 108°36W **343** A7
Walney, I. of *U.K.* 54°6N 3°15W **284** C4
Walnut Canyon ⌂ *U.S.A.* 35°15N 111°20W **349** J8
Walnut Creek *U.S.A.* 37°54N 122°4W **350** H4
Walpole *Australia* 34°58S 116°44E **333** F2
Walpole *U.S.A.* 42°9N 71°15W **355** D13
Walpole-Nornalup △ *Australia* 35°0S 116°45E **332** G2
Walsall *U.K.* 52°35N 1°58W **285** E6
Walsenburg *U.S.A.* 37°38N 104°47W **349** H11
Walsh *U.S.A.* 37°23N 102°17W **349** H12
Walsh → *Australia* 16°31S 143°42E **334** B3
Walter F. George Res. *U.S.A.* 31°38N 85°4W **357** F12
Walterboro *U.S.A.* 32°55N 80°40W **357** E14
Walters *U.S.A.* 34°22N 98°19W **356** D5
Waltham *U.S.A.* 42°23N 71°14W **355** D13
Waltman *U.S.A.* 43°4N 107°12W **348** E10
Walton *U.S.A.* 42°10N 75°8W **355** D9
Walton-on-the-Naze *U.K.* 51°51N 1°17E **285** F9
Walvis Bay *Namibia* 23°0S 14°28E **328** C1
Walvisbaai = Walvis Bay *Namibia* 23°0S 14°28E **328** C1
Wamba *Dem. Rep. of the Congo* 2°10N 27°57E **326** B2
Wamba *Kenya* 0°58N 37°19E **326** B4
Wamego *U.S.A.* 39°12N 96°18W **352** F5
Wamena *Indonesia* 4°4S 138°57E **309** E9
Wamsutter *U.S.A.* 41°40N 107°58W **348** F10
Wamulan *Indonesia* 3°27S 126°7E **309** E7
Wan Xian *China* 38°47N 115°7E **306** E8
Wana *Pakistan* 32°20N 69°32E **314** C3
Wanaaring *Australia* 29°38S 144°9E **335** D3
Wanaka *N.Z.* 44°42S 169°9E **331** F2
Wanaka, L. *N.Z.* 44°33S 169°7E **331** F2
Wanapitei L. *Canada* 46°45N 80°40W **344** C3
Wandel Sea = McKinley Sea *Arctic* 82°0N 0°0 **276** A7
Wanderer *Zimbabwe* 19°36S 30°1E **327** F3
Wandhari *Pakistan* 27°42N 66°48E **314** F2
Wandoan *Australia* 26°5S 149°55E **335** D4
Wanfu *China* 40°8N 122°38E **307** D12
Wang → *Thailand* 17°8N 99°2E **310** D2
Wang Noi *Thailand* 14°13N 100°44E **310** E3
Wang Saphung *Thailand* 17°18N 101°46E **310** D3
Wang Thong *Thailand* 16°50N 100°26E **310** D3
Wanga *Dem. Rep. of the Congo* 2°58N 29°12E **326** B2
Wangal *Indonesia* 6°8S 134°9E **309** F8
Wanganella *Australia* 35°6S 144°49E **335** F3
Wanganui *N.Z.* 39°56S 175°3E **331** C5
Wangaratta *Australia* 36°21S 146°19E **335** F4
Wangary *Australia* 34°35S 135°29E **335** E2
Wangdu *China* 38°40N 115°7E **306** E8
Wangerooge *Germany* 53°47N 7°54E **288** B4
Wangiwangi *Indonesia* 5°22S 123°37E **309** F6
Wangqing *China* 43°12N 129°42E **307** C15
Wankaner *India* 22°35N 71°0E **314** H4
Wanlaweyne = Uanle Uen *Somali Rep.* 2°37N 44°54E **319** G3
Wanless *Canada* 54°11N 101°21W **343** C8
Wanneroo *Australia* 31°42S 115°46E **333** F2
Wanning *China* 18°48N 110°22E **310** C8
Wannoo Billabong Roadhouse *Australia* 27°25S 115°49E **333** E2
Wanon Niwat *Thailand* 17°38N 103°46E **310** D4
Wanqinsha *China* 22°43N 113°33E **305** F10
Wanquan *China* 40°50N 114°40E **306** D8
Wanrong *China* 35°25N 110°50E **306** G6
Wanshan Qundao *China* 21°57N 113°45E **305** G10
Wantage *U.K.* 51°35N 1°25W **285** F6
Wanxian *China* 30°42N 108°20E **304** C5
Wanzai *China* 22°12N 113°31E **305** G10
Wapakoneta *U.S.A.* 40°34N 84°12W **353** E11
Wapato *U.S.A.* 46°27N 120°25W **348** C3
Wapawekka L. *Canada* 54°55N 104°40W **343** C8
Wapikopa L. *Canada* 52°56N 87°53W **344** B2
Wapiti → *Canada* 55°5N 118°18W **342** B5
Wappingers Falls *U.S.A.* 41°36N 73°55W **355** E11
Wapsipinicon → *U.S.A.* 41°44N 90°19W **352** E8
Wapusk △ *Canada* 57°46N 93°22W **343** B10
Warangal *India* 17°58N 79°35E **312** L11
Waraseoni *India* 21°45N 80°2E **315** J9
Waratah *Australia* 41°30S 145°30E **335** G4
Waratah B. *Australia* 38°54S 146°5E **335** F4
Warburton *Vic., Australia* 37°47S 145°42E **335** F4
Warburton *W. Austral., Australia* 26°8S 126°35E **333** E4
Warburton → *Australia* 28°4S 137°28E **335** D2
Warburton Ra. *Australia* 25°55S 126°28E **333** E4
Ward *N.Z.* 41°49S 174°11E **331** D5
Ward → *Australia* 26°28S 146°6E **335** D4
Ward Mt. *U.S.A.* 37°12N 118°54W **350** H8
Warden *S. Africa* 27°50S 29°0E **329** D4
Wardha *India* 20°45N 78°39E **312** J11
Wardha → *India* 19°57N 79°11E **312** K11
Ware *Canada* 57°26N 125°41W **342** B3
Ware *U.K.* 51°49N 0°0 **285** F8
Ware *U.S.A.* 42°16N 72°14W **355** D12
Waregem *Belgium* 50°53N 3°27E **287** D3
Wareham *U.S.A.* 41°46N 70°43W **355** E14
Waremme *Belgium* 50°43N 5°15E **287** D5
Warialda *Australia* 29°29S 150°33E **335** D5
Wariap *Indonesia* 1°30S 134°5E **309** E8
Warin Chamrap *Thailand* 15°12N 104°53E **310** E5
Warkopi *Indonesia* 1°12S 134°9E **309** E8
Warm Springs *U.S.A.* 38°10N 116°20W **349** G5
Warman *Canada* 52°19N 106°30W **343** C7
Warmbad = Bela Bela *S. Africa* 24°51S 28°19E **329** C4
Warmbad *Namibia* 28°25S 18°42E **328** D2
Warminster *U.K.* 51°12N 2°10W **285** F5
Warminster *U.S.A.* 40°12N 75°6W **355** F9
Warmun *Australia* 17°2S 128°12E **332** C4
Warner Mts. *U.S.A.* 41°40N 120°15W **348** F3
Warner Robins *U.S.A.* 32°37N 83°36W **357** E13
Waroona *Australia* 32°50S 115°58E **333** F2
Warracknabeal *Australia* 36°9S 142°26E **335** F3
Warragul *Australia* 38°10S 145°58E **335** F4
Warrego → *Australia* 30°24S 145°21E **335** E4
Warrego Ra. *Australia* 24°58S 146°0E **334** C4
Warren *Australia* 31°42S 147°51E **335** E4
Warren *Ark., U.S.A.* 33°37N 92°4W **356** E8
Warren *Mich., U.S.A.* 42°28N 83°1W **353** D12
Warren *Minn., U.S.A.* 48°12N 96°46W **352** A5
Warren *Ohio, U.S.A.* 41°14N 80°49W **354** E4
Warren *Pa., U.S.A.* 41°51N 79°9W **354** E5
Warrenpoint *U.K.* 54°6N 6°15W **282** B5
Warrensburg *Mo., U.S.A.* 38°46N 93°44W **352** F7
Warrensburg *N.Y., U.S.A.* 43°29N 73°46W **355** C11
Warrenton *S. Africa* 28°9S 24°47E **328** D3
Warrenton *U.S.A.* 46°10N 123°56W **350** D3
Warri *Nigeria* 5°30N 5°41E **322** G7
Warrina *Australia* 28°12S 135°50E **335** D2
Warrington *U.K.* 53°24N 2°35W **284** D5
Warrington *U.S.A.* 30°23N 87°17W **357** F11
Warrington □ *U.K.* 53°24N 2°35W **284** D5
Warrnambool *Australia* 38°25S 142°30E **335** F3
Warroad *U.S.A.* 48°54N 95°19W **352** A6
Warruwi *Australia* 11°36S 133°20E **334** A1
Warsa *Indonesia* 0°47S 135°55E **309** E9
Warsak Dam *Pakistan* 34°11N 71°19E **314** B4
Warsaw = Warszawa *Poland* 52°14N 21°0E **289** B11
Warsaw *Ind., U.S.A.* 41°14N 85°51W **353** E11
Warsaw *N.Y., U.S.A.* 42°45N 78°8W **354** D6
Warsaw *Ohio, U.S.A.* 40°20N 82°0W **354** F3
Warszawa *Poland* 52°14N 21°0E **289** B11
Warta → *Poland* 52°35N 14°39E **288** B8
Warthe = Warta → *Poland* 52°35N 14°39E **288** B8
Waru *Indonesia* 3°30S 130°36E **309** E8
Warwick *Australia* 28°10S 152°1E **335** D5
Warwick *U.K.* 52°18N 1°35W **285** E6
Warwick *N.Y., U.S.A.* 41°16N 74°22W **355** E10
Warwick *R.I., U.S.A.* 41°42N 71°28W **355** E13
Warwickshire □ *U.K.* 52°14N 1°38W **285** E6
Wasaga Beach *Canada* 44°31N 80°1W **354** B4
Wasagaming *Canada* 50°39N 99°58W **343** C9
Wasatch Ra. *U.S.A.* 40°0N 111°30W **348** F8
Wasbank *S. Africa* 28°15S 30°9E **329** D5
Wasco *Calif., U.S.A.* 35°36N 119°20W **351** K7
Wasco *Oreg., U.S.A.* 45°36N 120°42W **348** D3
Waseca *U.S.A.* 44°5N 93°30W **352** C7
Wasekamio L. *Canada* 56°45N 108°45W **343** B7
Wash, The *U.K.* 52°58N 0°20E **284** E8
Washago *Canada* 44°45N 79°20W **354** B5
Washburn *N. Dak., U.S.A.* 47°17N 101°2W **352** B3
Washburn *Wis., U.S.A.* 46°40N 90°54W **352** B8
Washim *India* 20°3N 77°0E **312** J10
Washington *U.K.* 54°55N 1°30W **284** C6
Washington *D.C., U.S.A.* 38°53N 77°2W **353** F15
Washington *Ga., U.S.A.* 33°44N 82°44W **357** E13
Washington *Ind., U.S.A.* 38°40N 87°10W **352** F10
Washington *Iowa, U.S.A.* 41°18N 91°42W **352** E8
Washington *Mo., U.S.A.* 38°33N 91°1W **352** F8
Washington *N.C., U.S.A.* 35°33N 77°3W **357** D16
Washington *N.J., U.S.A.* 40°46N 74°59W **355** F10
Washington *Pa., U.S.A.* 40°10N 80°15W **354** F4
Washington *Utah, U.S.A.* 37°8N 113°31W **349** H7
Washington □ *U.S.A.* 47°30N 120°30W **348** C3
Washington, Mt. *U.S.A.* 44°16N 71°18W **355** B13
Washington Court House *U.S.A.* 39°32N 83°26W **353** F12
Washington I. *U.S.A.* 45°23N 86°54W **352** C10
Washougal *U.S.A.* 45°35N 122°21W **350** E4
Washpool △ *Australia* 29°22S 152°20E **335** D5
Wasian *Indonesia* 1°47S 133°19E **309** E8
Wasilla *U.S.A.* 61°35N 149°26W **340** C5
Wasior *Indonesia* 2°43S 134°30E **309** E8
Wāsiṭ □ *Iraq* 32°50N 45°50E **316** C5
Waskaganish *Canada* 51°30N 78°40W **344** B4
Waskaiowaka L. *Canada* 56°33N 96°23W **343** B9
Waskesiu Lake *Canada* 53°55N 106°5W **343** C7
Wasserkuppe *Germany* 50°29N 9°55E **288** C5
Waswanipi *Canada* 49°40N 76°29W **344** C4
Waswanipi, L. *Canada* 49°35N 76°40W **344** C4
Watampone *Indonesia* 4°29S 120°25E **309** E6
Watamu *Kenya* 3°23S 40°0E **326** C5
Watarrka △ *Australia* 24°20S 131°30E **332** D5
Water Park Pt. *Australia* 22°56S 150°47E **334** C5
Water Valley *U.S.A.* 34°10N 89°38W **357** D10
Waterberg Plateau ⌂ *Namibia* 20°25S 17°18E **328** C2
Waterberge *S. Africa* 24°10S 28°0E **329** C4
Waterbury *Conn., U.S.A.* 41°33N 73°3W **355** E11
Waterbury *Vt., U.S.A.* 44°20N 72°46W **355** B12
Waterbury L. *Canada* 58°10N 104°22W **343** B8
Waterdown *Canada* 43°20N 79°53W **354** C5
Waterford *Canada* 42°56N 80°17W **354** D4
Waterford *Ireland* 52°15N 7°8W **282** D4
Waterford *Calif., U.S.A.* 37°38N 120°46W **350** H6
Waterford *Pa., U.S.A.* 41°57N 79°59W **354** E5
Waterford □ *Ireland* 52°10N 7°40W **282** D4
Waterford Harbour *Ireland* 52°8N 6°58W **282** D5
Waterhen L. *Canada* 52°10N 99°40W **343** C9
Waterloo *Belgium* 50°43N 4°25E **287** D4
Waterloo *Ont., Canada* 43°30N 80°32W **354** C4
Waterloo *Qué., Canada* 45°22N 72°32W **355** A12
Waterloo *Ill., U.S.A.* 38°20N 90°9W **352** F8
Waterloo *Iowa, U.S.A.* 42°30N 92°21W **352** D7
Waterloo *N.Y., U.S.A.* 42°54N 76°52W **354** D8
Watersmeet *U.S.A.* 46°16N 89°11W **352** B9
Waterton Lakes △ *Canada* 48°45N 115°0W **342** D6
Watertown *Conn., U.S.A.* 41°36N 73°7W **355** E11
Watertown *N.Y., U.S.A.* 43°59N 75°55W **355** C9
Watertown *S. Dak., U.S.A.* 44°54N 97°7W **352** C5
Watertown *Wis., U.S.A.* 43°12N 88°43W **352** D9
Waterval-Boven *S. Africa* 25°40S 30°18E **329** D5
Waterville *Canada* 45°16N 71°54W **355** A13
Waterville *Maine, U.S.A.* 44°33N 69°38W **353** C19
Waterville *N.Y., U.S.A.* 42°56N 75°23W **355** D9
Waterville *Pa., U.S.A.* 41°19N 77°21W **354** E7
Waterville *Wash., U.S.A.* 47°39N 120°4W **348** C3
Watervliet *U.S.A.* 42°44N 73°42W **355** D11
Wates *Indonesia* 7°51S 110°10E **309** G14
Watford *Canada* 42°57N 81°53W **354** D3
Watford *U.K.* 51°40N 0°24W **285** F7
Watford City *U.S.A.* 47°48N 103°17W **352** B2
Wathaman → *Canada* 57°16N 102°59W **343** B8
Wathaman L. *Canada* 56°58N 103°44W **343** B8
Watheroo *Australia* 30°15S 116°5E **333** F2
Watheroo △ *Australia* 30°19S 115°48E **333** F2
Wating *China* 35°40N 106°38E **306** G4
Watkins Glen *U.S.A.* 42°23N 76°52W **354** D8
Watling I. = San Salvador I. *Bahamas* 24°0N 74°40W **361** B5
Watonga *U.S.A.* 35°51N 98°25W **356** D5
Watrous *Canada* 51°40N 105°25W **343** C7
Watrous *U.S.A.* 35°48N 104°59W **349** J11
Watsa *Dem. Rep. of the Congo* 3°4N 29°30E **326** B2
Watseka *U.S.A.* 40°47N 87°44W **352** E10
Watson *Canada* 52°10N 104°30W **343** C8
Watson Lake *Canada* 60°6N 128°49W **342** A3
Watsontown *U.S.A.* 41°5N 76°52W **354** E8
Watsonville *U.S.A.* 36°55N 121°45W **350** J5
Wattiwarriganna Cr. → *Australia* 28°57S 136°10E **335** D2
Watuata = Batuata *Indonesia* 6°12S 122°42E **309** F6
Watubela, Kepulauan *Indonesia* 4°28S 131°35E **309** E8
Watubela Is. = Watubela, Kepulauan *Indonesia* 4°28S 131°35E **309** E8
Wau = Wâw *Sudan* 7°45N 28°1E **323** G11
Waubamik *Canada* 45°27N 80°1W **354** A4
Waubay *U.S.A.* 45°20N 97°18W **352** C5
Wauchope *N.S.W., Australia* 31°28S 152°45E **335** E5
Wauchope *N. Terr., Australia* 20°36S 134°15E **334** C1
Wauchula *U.S.A.* 27°33N 81°49W **357** H14
Waukarlycarly, L. *Australia* 21°18S 121°56E **332** D3
Waukegan *U.S.A.* 42°22N 87°50W **352** D10
Waukesha *U.S.A.* 43°1N 88°14W **352** D9
Waukon *U.S.A.* 43°16N 91°29W **352** D8
Waupaca *U.S.A.* 44°21N 89°5W **352** C9
Waupun *U.S.A.* 43°38N 88°44W **352** D9
Waurika *U.S.A.* 34°10N 98°0W **356** D6
Wausau *U.S.A.* 44°58N 89°38W **352** C9
Wautoma *U.S.A.* 44°4N 89°18W **352** C9
Wauwatosa *U.S.A.* 43°2N 88°0W **352** D9
Waveney → *U.K.* 52°35N 1°39E **285** E9
Waverley *N.Z.* 39°46S 174°37E **331** C5
Waverly *Iowa, U.S.A.* 42°44N 92°29W **352** D7
Waverly *N.Y., U.S.A.* 42°1N 76°32W **355** E8
Wavre *Belgium* 50°43N 4°38E **287** D4
Wâw *Sudan* 7°45N 28°1E **323** G11
Wāw al Kabīr *Libya* 25°20N 16°43E **323** C9
Wawa *Canada* 47°59N 84°47W **344** C3
Wawanesa *Canada* 49°36N 99°40W **343** D9
Wawona *U.S.A.* 37°32N 119°39W **350** H7
Waxahachie *U.S.A.* 32°24N 96°51W **356** E6
Way, L. *Australia* 26°45S 120°16E **333** E3
Waya *Fiji* 17°19S 177°10E **331** a
Waycross *U.S.A.* 31°13N 82°21W **357** F13
Wayland *U.S.A.* 42°34N 77°35W **354** D7
Wayne *Nebr., U.S.A.* 42°14N 97°1W **352** D5
Wayne *W. Va., U.S.A.* 38°13N 82°27W **353** F12
Waynesboro *Ga., U.S.A.* 33°6N 82°1W **357** E13
Waynesboro *Miss., U.S.A.* 31°40N 88°39W **357** F10
Waynesboro *Pa., U.S.A.* 39°45N 77°35W **353** F15
Waynesboro *Va., U.S.A.* 38°4N 78°53W **353** F14
Waynesburg *U.S.A.* 39°54N 80°11W **353** F13
Waynesville *U.S.A.* 35°28N 82°58W **357** D13
Waynoka *U.S.A.* 36°35N 98°53W **356** C5
Wazirabad *Pakistan* 32°30N 74°8E **314** C6
We *Indonesia* 5°51N 95°18E **308** C1
Weald, The *U.K.* 51°4N 0°20E **285** F8
Wear → *U.K.* 54°55N 1°23W **284** C6
Weatherford *Okla., U.S.A.* 35°32N 98°43W **356** D5
Weatherford *Tex., U.S.A.* 32°46N 97°48W **356** E6
Weaverville *U.S.A.* 40°44N 122°56W **348** F2
Webb City *U.S.A.* 37°9N 94°28W **352** G6
Webequie *Canada* 52°59N 87°21W **344** B2
Webster *Mass., U.S.A.* 42°3N 71°53W **355** D13
Webster *N.Y., U.S.A.* 43°13N 77°26W **354** C7
Webster *S. Dak., U.S.A.* 45°20N 97°31W **352** C5
Webster City *U.S.A.* 42°28N 93°49W **352** D7
Webster Springs *U.S.A.* 38°29N 80°25W **353** F13
Weda *Indonesia* 0°21N 127°50E **309** D7
Weda, Teluk *Indonesia* 0°20N 128°0E **309** D7
Weddell Abyssal Plain *S. Ocean* 65°0S 20°0W **277** C2
Weddell I. *Falk. Is.* 51°50S 61°0W **368** G4
Weddell Sea *Antarctica* 72°30S 40°0W **277** D1
Wedderburn *Australia* 36°26S 143°33E **335** F3
Wedgeport *Canada* 43°44N 65°59W **345** D6
Wedza *Zimbabwe* 18°40S 31°33E **327** F3
Wee Waa *Australia* 30°11S 149°26E **335** E4
Weed *U.S.A.* 41°25N 122°23W **348** F2
Weed Heights *U.S.A.* 38°59N 119°13W **350** G7
Weedsport *U.S.A.* 43°3N 76°34W **355** C8
Weedville *U.S.A.* 41°17N 78°30W **354** E6
Weenen *S. Africa* 28°48S 30°7E **329** D5
Weert *Neths.* 51°15N 5°43E **287** C5
Wei He → *Hebei, China* 36°10N 115°45E **306** F8
Wei He → *Shaanxi, China* 34°38N 110°15E **306** G6
Weichang *China* 41°58N 117°49E **307** D9
Weichuan *China* 34°20N 113°59E **306** G7
Weiden *Germany* 49°41N 12°10E **288** D7
Weifang *China* 36°44N 119°7E **307** F10
Weihai *China* 37°30N 122°6E **307** F12
Weimar *Germany* 50°58N 11°19E **288** C6
Weinan *China* 34°31N 109°29E **306** G5
Weipa *Australia* 12°40S 141°50E **334** A3
Weir → *Australia* 28°20S 149°50E **335** D4
Weir → *Canada* 56°54N 93°21W **343** B10
Weir River *Canada* 56°49N 94°6W **343** B10
Weirton *U.S.A.* 40°24N 80°35W **354** F4
Weiser *U.S.A.* 44°15N 116°58W **348** D5
Weishan *China* 34°47N 117°5E **307** G9
Weiyuan *China* 35°7N 104°10E **306** G3
Wejherowo *Poland* 54°35N 18°12E **289** A10
Wekusko L. *Canada* 54°40N 99°50W **343** C9
Welch *U.S.A.* 37°26N 81°35W **353** G13
Welford △ *Australia* 25°5S 143°16E **334** D3
Welkom *S. Africa* 28°0S 26°46E **328** D4
Welland *Canada* 43°0N 79°15W **354** D5
Welland → *U.K.* 52°51N 0°5W **285** E7
Wellesley Is. *Australia* 16°42S 139°30E **334** B2
Wellingborough *U.K.* 52°19N 0°41W **285** E7
Wellington *Australia* 32°35S 148°59E **335** E4
Wellington *Canada* 43°57N 77°20W **354** C7
Wellington *N.Z.* 41°19S 174°46E **331** D5
Wellington *S. Africa* 33°38S 19°1E **328** E2
Wellington *Somst., U.K.* 50°58N 3°13W **285** G4
Wellington *Telford & Wrekin, U.K.* 52°42N 2°30W **285** E5
Wellington *Colo., U.S.A.* 40°42N 105°0W **348** F11
Wellington *Kans., U.S.A.* 37°16N 97°24W **352** G5
Wellington *Nev., U.S.A.* 38°45N 119°23W **350** G7
Wellington *Ohio, U.S.A.* 41°10N 82°13W **354** E2
Wellington *Tex., U.S.A.* 34°51N 100°13W **356** D4
Wellington, I. *Chile* 49°30S 75°0W **368** F2
Wellington, L. *Australia* 38°6S 147°20E **335** F4
Wellington Chan. *Canada* 75°0N 93°0W **341** B10
Wells *U.K.* 51°13N 2°39W **285** F5
Wells *Maine, U.S.A.* 43°20N 70°35W **355** C14
Wells *N.Y., U.S.A.* 43°24N 74°17W **355** C10
Wells *Nev., U.S.A.* 41°7N 114°58W **348** F6
Wells, L. *Australia* 26°44S 123°15E **333** E3
Wells, Mt. *Australia* 17°25S 127°8E **332** C4
Wells Gray ⌂ *Canada* 52°30N 120°15W **342** C4
Wells-next-the-Sea *U.K.* 52°57N 0°51E **284** E8
Wells River *U.S.A.* 44°9N 72°4W **355** B12
Wellsboro *U.S.A.* 41°45N 77°18W **354** E7
Wellsburg *U.S.A.* 40°16N 80°37W **354** F4
Wellsville *N.Y., U.S.A.* 42°7N 77°57W **354** D7
Wellsville *Ohio, U.S.A.* 40°36N 80°39W **354** F4
Wellsville *Utah, U.S.A.* 41°38N 111°56W **348** F8
Wellton *U.S.A.* 32°40N 114°8W **349** K6
Wels *Austria* 48°9N 14°1E **288** D8
Welshpool *U.K.* 52°39N 3°8W **285** E4
Welwyn Garden City *U.K.* 51°48N 0°12W **285** F7
Wem *U.K.* 52°52N 2°44W **284** E5
Wembere → *Tanzania* 4°10S 34°15E **326** C3
Wemindji *Canada* 53°0N 78°49W **344** B4
Wen Xian *China* 34°55N 113°5E **306** G7
Wenatchee *U.S.A.* 47°25N 120°19W **348** C3
Wenchang *China* 19°38N 110°42E **310** C8
Wenchi *Ghana* 7°46N 2°8W **322** G5
Wenchow = Wenzhou *China* 28°0N 120°38E **305** D7
Wenden *U.S.A.* 33°49N 113°33W **351** M13
Wendeng *China* 37°15N 122°5E **307** F12
Wendesi *Indonesia* 2°30S 134°17E **309** E8
Wendover *U.S.A.* 40°44N 114°2W **348** F6
Wenlock → *Australia* 12°2S 141°55E **334** A3
Wenshan *China* 23°20N 104°18E **304** D5
Wenshang *China* 35°45N 116°30E **306** G9
Wenshui *China* 37°26N 112°1E **306** F7
Wensleydale *U.K.* 54°17N 2°0W **284** C6
Wensu *China* 41°15N 80°10E **304** B3
Wensum → *U.K.* 52°40N 1°15E **284** E8
Wentworth *Australia* 34°2S 141°54E **335** E3
Wentzel L. *Canada* 59°2N 114°28W **342** B6
Wenut *Indonesia* 3°11S 133°19E **309** E8
Wenxi *China* 35°20N 111°10E **306** G6
Wenxian *China* 32°43N 104°36E **306** H3
Wenzhou *China* 28°0N 120°38E **305** D7
Weott *U.S.A.* 40°20N 123°55W **348** F2
Wepener *S. Africa* 29°42S 27°3E **328** D4
Werda *Botswana* 25°24S 23°15E **328** D3
Weri *Indonesia* 3°10S 132°38E **309** E8
Werra → *Germany* 51°24N 9°39E **288** C5
Werrimull *Australia* 34°25S 141°38E **335** E3
Werris Creek *Australia* 31°18S 150°38E **335** E5
Weser → *Germany* 53°36N 8°28E **288** B5
Wesiri *Indonesia* 7°30S 126°30E **309** F7
Weslaco *U.S.A.* 26°10N 97°58W **356** H6
Weslemkoon L. *Canada* 45°2N 77°25W **354** A7
Wesleyville *U.S.A.* 42°9N 80°0W **354** D4
Wessel, C. *Australia* 10°59S 136°46E **334** A2
Wessel Is. *Australia* 11°10S 136°45E **334** A2
Wessington Springs *U.S.A.* 44°5N 98°34W **352** C4
West *U.S.A.* 31°48N 97°6W **356** F6
West → *U.S.A.* 42°52N 72°33W **355** D12
West Allis *U.S.A.* 43°1N 88°0W **352** D9
West Antarctica *Antarctica* 80°0S 90°0W **277** D15
West Baines → *Australia* 15°38S 129°59E **332** C4
West Bank ■ *Asia* 32°6N 35°13E **318** C4
West Bend *U.S.A.* 43°25N 88°11W **352** D9
West Bengal □ *India* 23°0N 88°0E **315** H13
West Berkshire □ *U.K.* 51°25N 1°17W **285** F6
West Beskids = Západné Beskydy *Europe* 49°30N 19°0E **289** D10
West Branch *U.S.A.* 44°17N 84°14W **353** C11
West Branch Susquehanna → *U.S.A.* 40°53N 76°48W **355** F8
West Bromwich *U.K.* 52°32N 1°59W **285** E6
West Burra *U.K.* 60°5N 1°21W **283** A7
West Canada Cr. → *U.S.A.* 43°1N 74°58W **355** C10
West Caroline Basin *Pac. Oc.* 4°0N 138°0E **336** G5
West Chazy *U.S.A.* 44°49N 73°28W **355** B11
West Chester *U.S.A.* 39°58N 75°36W **355** G9
West Coast ⌂ *Namibia* 21°53S 14°14E **328** C1
West Coast △ *S. Africa* 33°13S 18°0E **328** E2
West Columbia *U.S.A.* 29°9N 95°39W **356** G7
West Covina *U.S.A.* 34°4N 117°54W **351** L9
West Des Moines *U.S.A.* 41°35N 93°43W **352** E7
West Dunbartonshire □ *U.K.* 55°59N 4°30W **283** F4
West End *Bahamas* 26°41N 78°58W **360** A4
West Falkland *Falk. Is.* 51°40S 60°0W **368** G4
West Fargo *U.S.A.* 46°52N 96°54W **352** B5
West Farmington *U.S.A.* 41°23N 80°58W **354** E4
West Fiji Basin *Pac. Oc.* 17°0S 173°0E **336** J9
West Fjord = Vestfjorden *Norway* 67°55N 14°0E **280** C16
West Fork Trinity →

U.S.A. 32°48N 96°54W 356 E6
West Frankfort U.S.A. 37°54N 88°55W 352 G9
West Grand L. U.S.A. 45°14N 67°51W 353 C20
West Hartford U.S.A. 41°45N 72°44W 355 E12
West Haven U.S.A. 41°17N 72°57W 355 E12
West Hazleton U.S.A. 40°58N 76°0W 355 F9
West Helena U.S.A. 34°33N 90°38W 357 D9
West Hurley U.S.A. 41°59N 74°7W 355 E10
West Ice Shelf Antarctica 67°0S 85°0E 277 C7
West Indies Cent. Amer. 15°0N 65°0W 361 D7
West Jordan U.S.A. 40°36N 111°56W 348 F8
West Lamma Channel China 22°14N 114°4E 305 G11
West Linn U.S.A. 45°21N 122°36W 350 E4
West Lorne Canada 42°36N 81°36W 354 D3
West Lothian □ U.K. 55°54N 3°36W 283 F5
West Lunga → Zambia 13°6S 24°39E 327 E1
West MacDonnell △ Australia 23°38S 132°59E 332 D5
West Mariana Basin Pac. Oc. 15°0N 137°0E 336 F5
West Memphis U.S.A. 35°8N 90°11W 357 D9
West Midlands □ U.K. 52°26N 2°0W 285 E6
West Mifflin U.S.A. 40°21N 79°52W 354 F5
West Milford U.S.A. 41°8N 74°22W 355 E10
West Milton U.S.A. 41°1N 76°50W 354 E8
West Monroe U.S.A. 32°31N 92°9W 356 E8
West Newton U.S.A. 40°14N 79°46W 354 F5
West Nicholson Zimbabwe 21°2S 29°20E 327 G2
West Odessa U.S.A. 31°50N 102°30W 356 F3
West Palm Beach U.S.A. 26°43N 80°3W 357 H14
West Plains U.S.A. 36°44N 91°51W 352 G8
West Point Miss., U.S.A. 33°36N 88°39W 357 E10
West Point N.Y., U.S.A. 41°24N 73°58W 355 E11
West Point Nebr., U.S.A. 41°51N 96°43W 352 E5
West Point Va., U.S.A. 37°32N 76°48W 353 G15
West Point L. U.S.A. 33°8N 85°0W 357 E12
West Pt. = Ouest, Pte. de l' Canada 49°52N 64°40W 345 C7
West Pt. Australia 35°1S 135°56E 335 F2
West Road → Canada 53°18N 122°53W 342 C4
West Rutland U.S.A. 43°36N 73°3W 355 C11
West Schelde = Westerschelde → Neths. 51°25N 3°25E 287 C3
West Seneca U.S.A. 42°51N 78°48W 354 D6
West Siberian Plain Russia 62°0N 75°0E 298 B9
West Sussex □ U.K. 50°55N 0°30W 285 G7
West-Terschelling Neths. 53°22N 5°13E 287 A5
West Valley City U.S.A. 40°42N 111°58W 348 F8
West Virginia □ U.S.A. 38°45N 80°30W 353 F13
West-Vlaanderen □ Belgium 51°0N 3°0E 287 D2
West Walker → U.S.A. 38°54N 119°9W 350 G7
West Wyalong Australia 33°56S 147°10E 335 E4
West Yellowstone U.S.A. 44°40N 111°6W 348 D8
West Yorkshire □ U.K. 53°45N 1°40W 284 D6
Westall, Pt. Australia 32°55S 134°4E 335 E1
Westbrook U.S.A. 43°41N 70°22W 353 D18
Westbury Australia 41°30S 146°51E 335 G4
Westby U.S.A. 48°52N 104°3W 348 B11
Westend U.S.A. 35°42N 117°24W 351 K9
Westerland Germany 54°54N 8°17E 288 A5
Westerly U.S.A. 41°22N 71°50W 355 E13
Western □ Kenya 0°30N 34°30E 326 B3
Western □ Zambia 15°0S 24°4E 327 F1
Western Australia □ Australia 25°0S 118°0E 333 E2
Western Cape □ S. Africa 34°0S 20°0E 328 E3
Western Dvina = Daugava → Latvia 57°4N 24°3E 281 H21
Western Ghats India 14°0N 75°0E 312 N9
Western Isles □ U.K. 57°30N 7°10W 283 D1
Western Sahara ■ Africa 25°0N 13°0W 322 D3
Western Samoa = Samoa ■ Pac. Oc. 14°0S 172°0W 331 b
Western Sierra Madre = Madre Occidental, Sierra Mexico 27°0N 107°0W 358 B3
Westernport U.S.A. 39°29N 79°3W 353 F14
Westerschelde → Neths. 51°25N 3°25E 287 C3
Westerwald Germany 50°38N 7°56E 288 C4
Westfield Mass., U.S.A. 42°7N 72°45W 355 D12
Westfield N.Y., U.S.A. 42°20N 79°35W 354 D5
Westfield Pa., U.S.A. 41°55N 77°32W 354 E7
Westhill U.K. 57°9N 2°19W 283 D6
Westhope U.S.A. 48°55N 101°1W 352 A3
Westland △ N.Z. 43°16S 170°16E 331 E2
Westland Bight N.Z. 42°55S 170°5E 331 E3
Westlock Canada 54°9N 113°55W 342 C6
Westmar Australia 27°55S 149°44E 335 D4
Westmeath □ Ireland 53°33N 7°34W 282 C4
Westminster Calif., U.S.A. 33°45N 118°0W 351 M8
Westminster Colo., U.S.A. 39°50N 105°2W 348 G11
Westminster Md., U.S.A. 39°34N 76°59W 353 F15
Westmont U.S.A. 40°19N 78°58W 354 F6
Westmoreland Barbados 13°13N 59°37W 361 g
Westmorland U.S.A. 33°2N 115°37W 351 M11
Weston Oreg., U.S.A. 45°49N 118°26W 348 D4
Weston W. Va., U.S.A. 39°2N 80°28W 353 F13
Weston I. Canada 52°33N 79°36W 344 B4
Weston-super-Mare U.K. 51°21N 2°58W 285 F5
Westover U.S.A. 40°45N 78°40W 354 F6
Westport Canada 44°40N 76°25W 355 B8
Westport Ireland 53°48N 9°31W 282 C2
Westport N.Z. 41°46S 171°37E 331 D3
Westport N.Y., U.S.A. 44°11N 73°26W 355 B11
Westport Oreg., U.S.A. 46°8N 123°23W 350 D3
Westport Wash., U.S.A. 46°53N 124°6W 350 D2
Westray Canada 53°36N 101°24W 343 C8
Westray U.K. 59°18N 3°0W 283 B5
Westree Canada 47°26N 81°34W 344 C3
Westville U.S.A. 39°8N 120°42W 350 F6
Westwood U.S.A. 40°18N 121°0W 348 F3
Wetar Indonesia 7°48S 126°30E 309 F7
Wetaskiwin Canada 52°55N 113°24W 342 C6
Wete Tanzania 5°4S 39°43E 324 F7
Wetherby U.K. 53°56N 1°23W 284 D6
Wethersfield U.S.A. 41°42N 72°40W 355 E12
Wetteren Belgium 51°0N 3°53E 287 D3
Wetzlar Germany 50°32N 8°31E 288 C5
Wewoka U.S.A. 35°9N 96°30W 356 D6
Wexford Ireland 52°20N 6°28W 282 D5
Wexford □ Ireland 52°20N 6°25W 282 D5
Wexford Harbour Ireland 52°20N 6°25W 282 D5
Weyburn Canada 49°40N 103°50W 343 D8
Weymouth Canada 44°30N 66°1W 345 D6
Weymouth U.K. 50°37N 2°28W 285 G5
Weymouth U.S.A. 42°13N 70°58W 355 D14
Weymouth, C. Australia 12°37S 143°27E 334 A3
Wha Ti Canada 63°8N 117°16W 340 C8
Whakaari = White I. N.Z. 37°30S 177°13E 331 B6
Whakatane N.Z. 37°57S 177°1E 331 B6
Whale → Canada 58°15N 67°40W 345 A6
Whale Cove Canada 62°10N 92°34W 343 A10
Whales, B. of Antarctica 78°0S 160°0W 277 D12
Whalsay U.K. 60°22N 0°59W 283 A8
Whangamata N.Z. 37°12S 175°53E 331 B5
Whangamomona N.Z. 39°8S 174°44E 331 C5
Whanganui △ N.Z. 39°17S 174°53E 331 C5
Whangarei N.Z. 35°43S 174°21E 331 A5
Whangarei Harb. N.Z. 35°45S 174°28E 331 A5
Wharekauri = Chatham Is. Pac. Oc. 44°0S 176°40W 336 M10
Wharfe → U.K. 53°51N 1°9W 284 D6
Wharfedale U.K. 54°6N 2°1W 284 C5
Wharton N.J., U.S.A. 40°54N 74°35W 355 F10
Wharton Pa., U.S.A. 41°31N 78°1W 354 E6
Wharton Tex., U.S.A. 29°19N 96°6W 356 G6
Wharton Basin Ind. Oc. 22°0S 92°0E 336 J2
Wheatland Calif., U.S.A. 39°1N 121°25W 350 F5
Wheatland Wyo., U.S.A. 42°3N 104°58W 348 E11
Wheatley Canada 42°6N 82°27W 354 D2
Wheaton Md., U.S.A. 39°3N 77°3W 353 F15
Wheaton Minn., U.S.A. 45°48N 96°30W 352 C5
Wheelbarrow Pk. U.S.A. 37°26N 116°5W 350 H10
Wheeler Oreg., U.S.A. 45°41N 123°53W 348 D2
Wheeler Tex., U.S.A. 35°27N 100°16W 356 D4
Wheeler → Canada 57°2N 67°13W 345 A6
Wheeler L. U.S.A. 34°48N 87°23W 357 D11
Wheeler Pk. N. Mex., U.S.A. 36°34N 105°25W 349 H11
Wheeler Pk. Nev., U.S.A. 38°57N 114°15W 348 G6
Wheeler Ridge U.S.A. 35°0N 118°57W 351 L8
Wheelersburg U.S.A. 38°44N 82°51W 353 F12
Wheeling U.S.A. 40°4N 80°43W 354 F4
Whernside U.K. 54°14N 2°24W 284 C5
Whiddy I. Ireland 51°41N 9°31W 282 E2
Whiskey Jack L. Canada 58°23N 101°55W 343 B8
Whiskeytown-Shasta-Trinity ⌂ U.S.A. 40°45N 122°15W 348 F2
Whistleduck Cr. → Australia 20°15S 135°18E 334 C2
Whistler Canada 50°7N 122°58W 342 C4
Whitby Canada 43°52N 78°56W 354 C6
Whitby U.K. 54°29N 0°37W 284 C7
White → Ark., U.S.A. 33°57N 91°5W 356 E9
White → Ind., U.S.A. 38°25N 87°45W 352 F10
White → S. Dak., U.S.A. 43°42N 99°27W 352 D4
White → Tex., U.S.A. 33°14N 100°56W 356 E4
White → Utah, U.S.A. 40°4N 109°41W 348 F9
White → Vt., U.S.A. 43°37N 72°20W 355 C12
White → Wash., U.S.A. 47°12N 122°15W 350 C4
White, L. Australia 21°9S 128°56E 332 D4
White B. Canada 50°0N 56°35W 345 C8
White Bird U.S.A. 45°46N 116°18W 348 D5
White Butte U.S.A. 46°23N 103°18W 352 B2
White City U.S.A. 42°26N 122°51W 348 E2
White Cliffs Australia 30°50S 143°10E 335 E3
White Hall U.S.A. 39°26N 90°24W 352 F8
White Haven U.S.A. 41°4N 75°47W 355 E9
White Horse, Vale of U.K. 51°37N 1°30W 285 F6
White I. N.Z. 37°30S 177°13E 331 B6
White L. Canada 45°18N 76°31W 355 A8
White L. U.S.A. 29°44N 92°30W 356 G8
White Mountain Peak U.S.A. 37°38N 118°15W 349 H4
White Mts. Calif., U.S.A. 37°30N 118°15W 350 H8
White Mts. N.H., U.S.A. 44°15N 71°15W 355 B13
White Mts. △ Australia 20°43S 145°12E 334 C4
White Nile = Nîl el Abyad → Sudan 15°38N 32°31E 323 E12
White Otter L. Canada 49°5N 91°55W 344 C1
White Pass U.S.A. 46°38N 121°24W 350 D5
White Plains U.S.A. 41°2N 73°46W 355 E11
White River Canada 48°35N 85°20W 344 C2
White River S. Africa 25°20S 31°0E 329 D5
White River U.S.A. 43°34N 100°45W 352 D3
White Rock Canada 49°2N 122°48W 350 A4
White Rock U.S.A. 35°50N 106°12W 349 J10
White Russia = Belarus ■ Europe 53°30N 27°0E 289 B14
White Sands ⌂ U.S.A. 32°46N 106°20W 349 K10
White Sea = Beloye More Russia 66°30N 38°0E 280 C25
White Sulphur Springs Mont., U.S.A. 46°33N 110°54W 348 C8
White Sulphur Springs W. Va., U.S.A. 37°48N 80°18W 353 G13
White Swan U.S.A. 46°23N 120°44W 350 D6
Whitecliffs N.Z. 43°26S 171°55E 331 E3
Whitecourt Canada 54°10N 115°45W 342 C5
Whiteface Mt. U.S.A. 44°22N 73°54W 355 B11
Whitefield U.S.A. 44°23N 71°37W 355 B13
Whitefish U.S.A. 48°25N 114°20W 348 B6
Whitefish B. U.S.A. 46°40N 84°55W 344 C3
Whitefish L. Canada 62°41N 106°48W 343 A7
Whitefish Pt. U.S.A. 46°45N 84°59W 353 B11
Whitegull, L. = Goélands, L. aux Canada 55°27N 64°17W 345 A7
Whitehall Mich., U.S.A. 43°24N 86°21W 352 D10
Whitehall Mont., U.S.A. 45°52N 112°6W 348 D7
Whitehall N.Y., U.S.A. 43°33N 73°24W 355 C11
Whitehall Wis., U.S.A. 44°22N 91°19W 352 C8
Whitehaven U.K. 54°33N 3°35W 284 C4
Whitehorse Canada 60°43N 135°3W 342 A1
Whitemark Australia 40°7S 148°3E 335 G4
Whiteriver U.S.A. 33°50N 109°58W 349 K9
Whitesand → Canada 60°9N 115°45W 342 A5
Whitesands S. Africa 34°23S 20°50E 328 E3
Whitesboro N.Y., U.S.A. 43°7N 75°18W 355 C9
Whitesboro Tex., U.S.A. 33°39N 96°54W 356 E6
Whiteshell ⌂ Canada 50°0N 95°40W 343 D9
Whitesville U.S.A. 42°2N 77°46W 354 D7
Whiteville U.S.A. 34°20N 78°42W 357 D15
Whitewater U.S.A. 42°50N 88°44W 352 D9
Whitewater Baldy U.S.A. 33°20N 108°39W 349 K9
Whitewater L. Canada 50°50N 89°10W 344 B2
Whitewood Australia 21°28S 143°30E 334 C3
Whitewood Canada 50°20N 102°20W 343 C8
Whithorn U.K. 54°44N 4°26W 283 G4
Whitianga N.Z. 36°47S 175°41E 331 B5
Whitman U.S.A. 42°5N 70°56W 355 D14
Whitney Canada 45°31N 78°14W 354 A6
Whitney, Mt. U.S.A. 36°35N 118°18W 350 J8
Whitney Point U.S.A. 42°20N 75°58W 355 D9
Whitstable U.K. 51°21N 1°3E 285 F9
Whitsunday I. Australia 20°15S 149°4E 334 J7
Whitsunday Islands △ Australia 20°15S 149°0E 334 J7
Whitsunday Passage Australia 20°16S 148°51E 334 J6
Whittier U.S.A. 33°58N 118°2W 351 M8
Whittlesea Australia 37°27S 145°9E 335 F4
Wholdaia L. Canada 60°43N 104°20W 343 A8
Whyalla Australia 33°2S 137°30E 335 E2
Wiang Kosai △ Thailand 17°54N 99°29E 310 D2
Wiarton Canada 44°40N 81°10W 354 B3
Wiay U.K. 57°24N 7°13W 283 D1
Wibaux U.S.A. 46°59N 104°11W 348 C11
Wichian Buri Thailand 15°39N 101°7E 310 E3
Wichita U.S.A. 37°42N 97°20W 352 G5
Wichita Falls U.S.A. 33°54N 98°30W 356 E5
Wick U.K. 58°26N 3°5W 283 C5
Wicked Pt. Canada 43°52N 77°15W 354 C7
Wickenburg U.S.A. 33°58N 112°44W 349 K7
Wickepin Australia 32°50S 117°30E 333 F2
Wickham Australia 20°42S 117°11E 332 D2
Wickham, C. Australia 39°35S 143°57E 335 F3
Wickliffe U.S.A. 41°36N 81°28W 354 E3
Wicklow Ireland 52°59N 6°3W 282 D5
Wicklow □ Ireland 52°57N 6°25W 282 D5
Wicklow Hd. Ireland 52°58N 6°0W 282 D6
Wicklow Mts. Ireland 52°58N 6°26W 282 C5
Wicklow Mts. △ Ireland 53°6N 6°21W 282 C5
Widgeegoara Cr. → Australia 28°51S 146°34E 335 D4
Widgiemooltha Australia 31°30S 121°34E 333 F3
Widnes U.K. 53°23N 2°45W 284 D5
Wieluń Poland 51°15N 18°34E 289 C10
Wien Austria 48°12N 16°22E 288 D9
Wiener Neustadt Austria 47°49N 16°16E 288 E9
Wiesbaden Germany 50°4N 8°14E 288 C5
Wigan U.K. 53°33N 2°38W 284 D5
Wiggins Colo., U.S.A. 40°14N 104°4W 348 F11
Wiggins Miss., U.S.A. 30°51N 89°8W 357 F10
Wight, I. of U.K. 50°41N 1°17W 285 G6
Wigston U.K. 52°35N 1°6W 285 E6
Wigton U.K. 54°50N 3°10W 284 C4
Wigtown U.K. 54°53N 4°27W 283 G4
Wigtown B. U.K. 54°46N 4°15W 283 G4
Wilber U.S.A. 40°29N 96°58W 352 E5
Wilberforce Canada 45°2N 78°13W 354 A6
Wilberforce, C. Australia 11°54S 136°35E 334 A2
Wilburton U.S.A. 34°55N 95°19W 356 D7
Wilcannia Australia 31°30S 143°26E 335 E3
Wilcox U.S.A. 41°35N 78°41W 354 E6
Wildrose U.S.A. 36°14N 117°11W 351 J9
Wildspitze Austria 46°53N 10°53E 288 E6
Wilge → S. Africa 27°3S 28°20E 329 D4
Wilhelm II Coast Antarctica 68°0S 90°0E 277 C7
Wilhelmshaven Germany 53°31N 8°7E 288 B5
Wilhelmstal Namibia 21°58S 16°21E 328 C2
Wilkes-Barre U.S.A. 41°15N 75°53W 355 E9
Wilkes Land Antarctica 69°0S 120°0E 277 D9
Wilkie Canada 52°27N 108°42W 343 C7
Wilkinsburg U.S.A. 40°26N 79°52W 354 F5
Wilkinson Lakes Australia 29°40S 132°39E 333 E5
Willandra Creek → Australia 33°22S 145°52E 335 E4
Willapa B. U.S.A. 46°40N 124°0W 348 C1
Willapa Hills U.S.A. 46°35N 123°25W 350 D3
Willard N.Y., U.S.A. 42°40N 76°50W 354 D8
Willard Ohio, U.S.A. 41°3N 82°44W 354 E2
Willcox U.S.A. 32°15N 109°50W 349 K9
Willemstad Neth. Ant. 12°5N 68°55W 361 D6
Willet U.S.A. 42°28N 75°55W 355 D9
William → Canada 59°8N 109°19W 343 B7
William 'Bill' Dannelly Res. U.S.A. 32°6N 87°24W 357 E11
William Creek Australia 28°58S 136°22E 335 D2
Williams Australia 33°2S 116°52E 333 F2
Williams Ariz., U.S.A. 35°15N 112°11W 349 J7
Williams Calif., U.S.A. 39°9N 122°9W 350 F4
Williams Harbour Canada 52°33N 55°47W 345 B8
Williams Lake Canada 52°10N 122°10W 342 C4
Williamsburg Ky., U.S.A. 36°44N 84°10W 353 G11
Williamsburg Pa., U.S.A. 40°28N 78°12W 354 F6
Williamsburg Va., U.S.A. 37°16N 76°43W 353 G15
Williamson N.Y., U.S.A. 43°14N 77°11W 354 C7
Williamson W. Va., U.S.A. 37°41N 82°17W 353 G12
Williamsport U.S.A. 41°15N 77°1W 354 E7
Williamston U.S.A. 35°51N 77°4W 357 D16
Williamstown Australia 37°51S 144°52E 335 F3
Williamstown Ky., U.S.A. 38°38N 84°34W 353 F11
Williamstown Mass., U.S.A. 42°43N 73°12W 355 D11
Williamstown N.Y., U.S.A. 43°26N 75°53W 355 C9
Willimantic U.S.A. 41°43N 72°13W 355 E12
Willingboro U.S.A. 40°3N 74°54W 353 E16
Williston S. Africa 31°20S 20°53E 328 E3
Williston Fla., U.S.A. 29°23N 82°27W 357 G13
Williston N. Dak., U.S.A. 48°9N 103°37W 352 A2
Williston L. Canada 56°0N 124°0W 342 B4
Willits U.S.A. 39°25N 123°21W 348 G2
Willmar U.S.A. 45°7N 95°3W 352 C6
Willmore Wilderness ⌂ Canada 53°45N 119°30W 342 C5
Willoughby U.S.A. 41°39N 81°24W 354 E3
Willow Bunch Canada 49°20N 105°35W 343 D7
Willow L. Canada 62°10N 119°8W 342 A5
Willow Wall, The China 42°10N 122°0E 307 C12
Willowick U.S.A. 41°38N 81°28W 354 E3
Willowlake → Canada 62°42N 123°8W 342 A4
Willowmore S. Africa 33°15S 23°30E 328 E3
Willows U.S.A. 39°31N 122°12W 350 F4
Willowvale = Gatyana S. Africa 32°16S 28°31E 329 E4
Wills, L. Australia 21°25S 128°51E 332 D4
Wills Cr. → Australia 22°43S 140°2E 334 C3
Willsboro U.S.A. 44°21N 73°24W 355 B11
Willunga Australia 35°15S 138°30E 335 F2
Wilmette U.S.A. 42°4N 87°42W 352 D10
Wilmington Australia 32°39S 138°7E 335 E2
Wilmington Del., U.S.A. 39°45N 75°33W 353 F16
Wilmington N.C., U.S.A. 34°14N 77°55W 357 D16
Wilmington Ohio, U.S.A. 39°27N 83°50W 353 F12
Wilmington Vt., U.S.A. 42°52N 72°52W 355 D12
Wilmslow U.K. 53°19N 2°13W 284 D5
Wilpena Cr. → Australia 31°25S 139°29E 335 E2
Wilsall U.S.A. 45°59N 110°38W 348 D8
Wilson N.C., U.S.A. 35°44N 77°55W 357 D16
Wilson N.Y., U.S.A. 43°19N 78°50W 354 C6
Wilson Pa., U.S.A. 40°41N 75°15W 355 F9
Wilson → Australia 16°48S 128°16E 332 C4
Wilson Bluff Australia 31°41S 129°0E 333 F4
Wilson Inlet Australia 35°0S 117°22E 333 G2
Wilsons Promontory Australia 38°59S 146°23E 335 F4
Wilton U.S.A. 47°10N 100°47W 352 B3
Wilton → Australia 14°45S 134°33E 334 A1
Wiltshire □ U.K. 51°18N 1°53W 285 F6
Wiltz Lux. 49°57N 5°55E 287 E5
Wiluna Australia 26°36S 120°14E 333 E3
Wimborne Minster U.K. 50°48N 1°59W 285 G6
Wimmera → Australia 36°8S 141°56E 335 F3
Winam G. Kenya 0°20S 34°15E 326 C3
Winburg S. Africa 28°30S 27°2E 328 D4
Winchendon U.S.A. 42°41N 72°3W 355 D12
Winchester U.K. 51°4N 1°18W 285 F6
Winchester Conn., U.S.A. 41°53N 73°9W 355 E11
Winchester Idaho, U.S.A. 46°14N 116°38W 348 C5
Winchester Ind., U.S.A. 40°10N 84°59W 353 E11
Winchester Ky., U.S.A. 37°59N 84°11W 353 G11
Winchester N.H., U.S.A. 42°46N 72°23W 355 D12
Winchester Nev., U.S.A. 36°7N 115°7W 351 J11
Winchester Tenn., U.S.A. 35°11N 86°7W 357 D11
Winchester Va., U.S.A. 39°11N 78°10W 353 F14
Wind → U.S.A. 43°12N 108°12W 348 E9
Wind Cave △ U.S.A. 43°32N 103°17W 352 D2
Wind River Range U.S.A. 43°0N 109°30W 348 E9
Windau = Ventspils Latvia 57°25N 21°32E 281 H19
Windber U.S.A. 40°14N 78°50W 354 F6
Winder U.S.A. 34°0N 83°45W 357 D13
Windermere U.K. 54°23N 2°55W 284 C5
Windhoek Namibia 22°35S 17°4E 328 C2
Windjana Gorge △ Australia 17°51S 125°0E 332 C3
Windom U.S.A. 43°52N 95°7W 352 D6
Windorah Australia 25°24S 142°36E 334 D3
Window Rock U.S.A. 35°41N 109°3W 349 J9
Windrush → U.K. 51°43N 1°24W 285 F6
Windsor Australia 33°37S 150°50E 335 E5
Windsor N.S., Canada 44°59N 64°5W 345 D7
Windsor Ont., Canada 42°18N 83°0W 354 D2
Windsor U.K. 51°29N 0°36W 285 F7
Windsor Calif., U.S.A. 38°33N 122°49W 348 G2
Windsor Colo., U.S.A. 40°29N 104°54W 348 F11
Windsor Conn., U.S.A. 41°50N 72°39W 355 E12
Windsor Mo., U.S.A. 38°32N 93°31W 352 F7
Windsor N.Y., U.S.A. 42°5N 75°37W 355 D9
Windsor Vt., U.S.A. 43°29N 72°24W 355 C12
Windsor & Maidenhead □ U.K. 51°29N 0°40W 285 F7
Windsorton S. Africa 28°16S 24°44E 328 D3
Windward Is. W. Indies 13°0N 61°0W 361 D7
Windward Passage = Vientos, Paso de los Caribbean 20°0N 74°0W 361 C5
Winefred L. Canada 55°30N 110°30W 343 B6
Winfield U.S.A. 37°15N 96°59W 352 G5
Wingate Mts. Australia 14°25S 130°40E 332 B5
Wingham Australia 31°48S 152°22E 335 E5
Wingham Canada 43°55N 81°20W 354 C3
Winisk Canada 55°20N 85°15W 344 A2
Winisk → Canada 55°17N 85°5W 344 A2
Winisk L. Canada 52°55N 87°22W 344 B2
Wink U.S.A. 31°45N 103°9W 356 F3
Winkler Canada 49°10N 97°56W 343 D9
Winlock U.S.A. 46°30N 122°56W 350 D4
Winneba Ghana 5°25N 0°36W 322 G5
Winnebago, L. U.S.A. 44°0N 88°26W 352 D9
Winnecke Cr. → Australia 18°35S 131°34E 332 C5
Winnemucca U.S.A. 40°58N 117°44W 348 F5
Winnemucca L. U.S.A. 40°7N 119°21W 348 F4
Winner U.S.A. 43°22N 99°52W 352 D4
Winnett U.S.A. 47°0N 108°21W 348 C9
Winnfield U.S.A. 31°56N 92°38W 356 F8
Winnibigoshish, L. U.S.A. 47°27N 94°13W 352 B6
Winnipeg Canada 49°54N 97°9W 343 D9
Winnipeg → Canada 50°38N 96°19W 343 C9
Winnipeg, L. Canada 52°0N 97°0W 343 C9
Winnipeg Beach Canada 50°30N 96°58W 343 C9
Winnipegosis Canada 51°39N 99°55W 343 C9
Winnipegosis L. Canada 52°30N 100°0W 343 C9
Winnipesaukee, L. U.S.A. 43°38N 71°21W 355 C13
Winnisquam L. U.S.A. 43°33N 71°31W 355 C13
Winnsboro La., U.S.A. 32°10N 91°43W 356 E9
Winnsboro S.C., U.S.A. 34°23N 81°5W 357 D14
Winnsboro Tex., U.S.A. 32°58N 95°17W 356 E7
Winokapau, L. Canada 53°15N 62°50W 345 B7
Winona Minn., U.S.A. 44°3N 91°39W 352 C8
Winona Miss., U.S.A. 33°29N 89°44W 357 E10
Winooski U.S.A. 44°29N 73°11W 355 B11
Winooski → U.S.A. 44°32N 73°17W 355 B11
Winschoten Neths. 53°9N 7°3E 287 A7
Winsford U.K. 53°12N 2°31W 284 D5
Winslow = Bainbridge Island U.S.A. 47°38N 122°32W 350 C4
Winslow U.S.A. 35°2N 110°42W 349 J8
Winsted U.S.A. 41°55N 73°4W 355 E11
Winston-Salem U.S.A. 36°6N 80°15W 357 C14
Winter Garden U.S.A. 28°34N 81°35W 357 G14
Winter Haven U.S.A. 28°1N 81°44W 357 G14
Winter Park U.S.A. 28°36N 81°20W 357 G14
Winterhaven U.S.A. 32°44N 114°38W 351 N12
Winters U.S.A. 38°32N 121°58W 350 G5
Winterset U.S.A. 41°20N 94°1W 352 E6
Wintersville U.S.A. 40°23N 80°42W 354 F4
Winterswijk Neths. 51°58N 6°43E 287 C6
Winterthur Switz. 47°30N 8°44E 292 C8
Winthrop U.S.A. 48°28N 120°10W 348 B3
Winton Australia 22°24S 143°3E 334 C3
Winton N.Z. 46°8S 168°20E 331 G2
Wirrulla Australia 32°24S 134°31E 335 E1
Wisbech U.K. 52°41N 0°9E 285 E8
Wisconsin □ U.S.A. 44°45N 89°30W 352 C9
Wisconsin → U.S.A. 43°0N 91°15W 352 D8
Wisconsin Rapids U.S.A. 44°23N 89°49W 352 C9
Wisdom U.S.A. 45°37N 113°27W 348 D7
Wishaw U.K. 55°46N 3°54W 283 F5
Wishek U.S.A. 46°16N 99°33W 352 B4
Wisła → Poland 54°22N 18°55E 289 A10
Wismar Germany 53°54N 11°29E 288 B6
Wisner U.S.A. 41°59N 96°55W 352 E5
Witbank S. Africa 25°51S 29°14E 329 D4
Witdraai S. Africa 26°58S 20°48E 328 D3
Witham U.K. 51°48N 0°40E 285 F8
Witham → U.K. 52°59N 0°2W 284 E7
Withernsea U.K. 53°44N 0°1E 284 D8
Witjira △ Australia 26°22S 135°37E 335 D2
Witless Bay Canada 47°17N 52°50W 345 C9
Witney U.K. 51°48N 1°28W 285 F6
Witnossob → Namibia 23°55S 18°45E 328 D3
Wittenberge Germany 53°0N 11°45E 288 B6
Wittenoom Australia 22°15S 118°20E 332 D2
Witu Kenya 2°23S 40°26E 326 C5
Witvlei Namibia 22°23S 18°32E 328 C2
Wiwon N. Korea 40°54N 126°3E 307 D14
Wkra → Poland 52°27N 20°44E 289 B11
Wlingi Indonesia 8°5S 112°25E 309 H15
Włocławek Poland 52°40N 19°3E 289 B10
Włodawa Poland 51°33N 23°31E 289 C12
Woburn U.S.A. 42°29N 71°9W 355 D13
Wodian China 32°50N 112°35E 306 H7
Wodonga Australia 36°5S 146°50E 335 F4
Wokam Indonesia 5°45S 134°28E 309 F8
Woking U.K. 51°19N 0°34W 285 F7
Wokingham U.K. 51°24N 0°49W 285 F7
Wokingham □ U.K. 51°25N 0°51W 285 F7
Wolf → Canada 60°17N 132°33W 342 A2
Wolf Creek U.S.A. 47°0N 112°4W 348 C7
Wolf L. Canada 60°24N 131°40W 342 A2

Wolf Point *U.S.A.* 48°5N 105°39W **348** B11
Wolfe I. *Canada* 44°7N 76°20W **355** B8
Wolfeboro *U.S.A.* 43°35N 71°13W **355** C13
Wolfsberg *Austria* 46°50N 14°52E **288** E8
Wolfsburg *Germany* 52°25N 10°48E **288** B6
Wolin *Poland* 53°50N 14°37E **288** B8
Wollaston, Is. *Chile* 55°40S 67°30W **368** H3
Wollaston L. *Canada* 58°7N 103°10W **343** B8
Wollaston Lake *Canada* 58°3N 103°33W **343** B8
Wollaston Pen. *Canada* 69°30N 115°0W **340** C8
Wollongong *Australia* 34°25S 150°54E **335** E5
Wolmaransstad *S. Africa* 27°12S 25°59E **328** D4
Wolseley *S. Africa* 33°26S 19°7E **328** E2
Wolsey *U.S.A.* 44°25N 98°28W **352** C4
Wolstenholme, C. *Canada* 62°35N 77°30W **338** C12
Wolvega *Neths.* 52°52N 6°0E **287** B6
Wolverhampton *U.K.* 52°35N 2°7W **285** E5
Wondai *Australia* 26°20S 151°49E **335** D5
Wongalarroo L. *Australia* 31°32S 144°0E **335** E3
Wongan Hills *Australia* 30°51S 116°37E **333** F2
Wonju *S. Korea* 37°22N 127°58E **307** F14
Wonosari *Indonesia* 7°58S 110°36E **309** G14
Wonosobo *Indonesia* 7°22S 109°54E **309** G13
Wonowon *Canada* 56°44N 121°48W **342** B4
Wŏnsan *N. Korea* 39°11N 127°27E **307** E14
Wonthaggi *Australia* 38°37S 145°37E **335** F4
Wood Buffalo △ *Canada* 59°0N 113°41W **342** B6
Wood Is. *Australia* 16°24S 123°19E **332** C3
Wood L. *Canada* 55°17N 103°17W **343** B8
Woodah, I. *Australia* 13°27S 136°10E **334** A2
Woodbourne *U.S.A.* 41°46N 74°36W **355** E10
Woodbridge *Canada* 43°47N 79°36W **354** C5
Woodbridge *U.K.* 52°6N 1°20E **285** E9
Woodburn *U.S.A.* 45°9N 122°51W **348** D2
Woodenbong *Australia* 28°24S 152°39E **335** D5
Woodend *Australia* 37°20S 144°33E **335** F3
Woodford *Australia* 26°58S 152°47E **335** D5
Woodfords *U.S.A.* 38°47N 119°50W **350** G7
Woodlake *U.S.A.* 36°25N 119°6W **350** J7
Woodland *Calif., U.S.A.* 38°41N 121°46W **350** G5
Woodland *Maine, U.S.A.* 45°9N 67°25W **353** C20
Woodland *Pa., U.S.A.* 41°0N 78°21W **354** F6
Woodland *Wash., U.S.A.* 45°54N 122°45W **350** E4
Woodland Caribou ⌂ *Canada* 51°0N 94°45W **343** C10
Woodlands *Singapore* 1°26N 103°46E **311** d
Woodlands, The *U.S.A.* 30°9N 95°29W **356** F7
Woodonga *Australia* 36°10S 146°50E **335** F4
Woodridge *Canada* 49°20N 96°9W **343** D9
Woodroffe, Mt. *Australia* 26°20S 131°45E **333** E5
Woods, L. *Australia* 17°50S 133°30E **334** B1
Woods, L. of the *Canada* 49°15N 94°45W **343** D10
Woodstock *Australia* 19°35S 146°50E **334** B4
Woodstock *N.B., Canada* 46°11N 67°37W **345** C6
Woodstock *Ont., Canada* 43°10N 80°45W **354** C4
Woodstock *U.K.* 51°51N 1°20W **285** F6
Woodstock *Ill., U.S.A.* 42°19N 88°27W **352** D9
Woodstock *Vt., U.S.A.* 43°37N 72°31W **355** C12
Woodsville *U.S.A.* 44°9N 72°2W **355** B13
Woodville *N.Z.* 40°20S 175°53E **331** D5
Woodville *Miss., U.S.A.* 31°6N 91°18W **356** F9
Woodville *Tex., U.S.A.* 30°47N 94°25W **356** F7
Woodward *U.S.A.* 36°26N 99°24W **356** C5
Woody *U.S.A.* 35°42N 118°50W **351** K8
Woody → *Canada* 52°31N 100°51W **343** C8
Woolacombe *U.K.* 51°10N 4°13W **285** F3
Woolamai, C. *Australia* 38°30S 145°23E **335** F4
Wooler *U.K.* 55°33N 2°1W **284** B5
Woolgoolga *Australia* 30°6S 153°11E **335** E5
Woomera *Australia* 31°5S 136°50E **335** E2
Woonsocket *R.I., U.S.A.* 42°0N 71°31W **355** E13
Woonsocket *S. Dak., U.S.A.* 44°3N 98°17W **352** C4
Wooramel → *Australia* 25°47S 114°10E **333** E1
Wooramel Roadhouse *Australia* 25°45S 114°17E **333** E1
Wooroonooran △ *Australia* 16°25S 146°1E **334** B4
Wooster *U.S.A.* 40°48N 81°56W **354** F3
Worcester *S. Africa* 33°39S 19°27E **328** E2
Worcester *U.K.* 52°11N 2°12W **285** E5
Worcester *Mass., U.S.A.* 42°16N 71°48W **355** D13
Worcester *N.Y., U.S.A.* 42°36N 74°45W **355** D10
Worcestershire □ *U.K.* 52°13N 2°10W **285** E5
Workington *U.K.* 54°39N 3°33W **284** C4
Worksop *U.K.* 53°18N 1°7W **284** D6
Workum *Neths.* 52°59N 5°26E **287** B5
Worland *U.S.A.* 44°1N 107°57W **348** D10
Worms *Germany* 49°37N 8°21E **288** D5
Worsley *Canada* 56°31N 119°8W **342** B5
Wortham *U.S.A.* 31°47N 96°28W **356** F6
Worthing *Barbados* 13°5N 59°35W **361** g
Worthing *U.K.* 50°49N 0°21W **285** G7
Worthington *Minn., U.S.A.* 43°37N 95°36W **352** D6
Worthington *Pa., U.S.A.* 40°50N 79°38W **354** F5
Wosi *Indonesia* 0°15S 128°0E **309** E7
Wote *Kenya* 1°47S 37°38E **326** C4
Wou-han = Wuhan *China* 30°31N 114°18E **305** C6
Wousi = Wuxi *China* 31°33N 120°18E **305** C7
Wowoni *Indonesia* 4°5S 123°5E **309** E6
Wrangel I. = Vrangelya, Ostrov *Russia* 71°0N 180°0E **301** B19
Wrangell *U.S.A.* 56°28N 132°23W **342** B2
Wrangell Mts. *U.S.A.* 61°30N 142°0W **340** C5
Wrath, C. *U.K.* 58°38N 5°1W **283** C3
Wray *U.S.A.* 40°5N 102°13W **348** F12
Wrekin, The *U.K.* 52°41N 2°32W **285** E5
Wrens *U.S.A.* 33°12N 82°23W **357** E13
Wrexham *U.K.* 53°3N 3°0W **284** D4
Wrexham □ *U.K.* 53°1N 2°58W **284** D5
Wright *Fla., U.S.A.* 30°27N 86°38W **357** F11
Wright *Wyo., U.S.A.* 43°45N 105°28W **348** E11
Wright Pt. *Canada* 43°48N 81°44W **354** C3
Wrightson, Mt. *U.S.A.* 31°42N 110°51W **349** L8
Wrightwood *U.S.A.* 34°22N 117°38W **351** L9
Wrigley *Canada* 63°16N 123°37W **340** C7
Wrocław *Poland* 51°5N 17°5E **289** C9
Września *Poland* 52°21N 17°36E **289** B9
Wu Jiang → *China* 29°40N 107°20E **304** D5
Wu Kau Tang *China* 22°30N 114°14E **305** F11
Wu'an *China* 36°40N 114°15E **306** F8
Wubin *Australia* 30°6S 116°37E **333** F2
Wubu *China* 37°28N 110°42E **306** F6
Wuchang *China* 44°55N 127°5E **307** B14
Wucheng *China* 37°12N 116°20E **306** F9
Wuchuan *China* 41°5N 111°28E **306** D6
Wudi *China* 37°40N 117°35E **307** F9
Wuding He → *China* 37°2N 110°23E **306** F6
Wudinna *Australia* 33°0S 135°22E **335** E2
Wudu *China* 33°22N 104°54E **306** H3
Wuguishan *China* 22°25N 113°25E **305** G9
Wuhai *China* 39°47N 106°52E **304** C5
Wuhan *China* 30°31N 114°18E **305** C6
Wuhe *China* 33°10N 117°50E **307** H9
Wuhsi = Wuxi *China* 31°33N 120°18E **305** C7
Wuhu *China* 31°22N 118°21E **305** C6
Wukari *Nigeria* 7°51N 9°42E **322** G7
Wulajie *China* 44°6N 126°33E **307** B14
Wulanbulang *China* 41°5N 110°55E **306** D6
Wular L. *India* 34°20N 74°30E **315** B6
Wulian *China* 35°40N 119°12E **307** G10
Wuliaru *Indonesia* 7°27S 131°0E **309** F8
Wulumuchi = Ürümqi *China* 43°45N 87°45E **304** B3
Wundanyi *Kenya* 3°24S 38°22E **326** C4
Wunnummin L. *Canada* 52°55N 89°10W **344** B2
Wuntho *Burma* 23°55N 95°45E **313** H19
Wupatki ⌂ *U.S.A.* 35°35N 111°20W **349** J8
Wuppertal *Germany* 51°16N 7°12E **288** C4
Wuppertal *S. Africa* 32°13S 19°12E **328** E2
Wuqing *China* 39°23N 117°4E **307** E9
Wurtsboro *U.S.A.* 41°35N 74°29W **355** E10
Würzburg *Germany* 49°46N 9°55E **288** D5
Wushan *China* 34°43N 104°53E **306** G3
Wushi *China* 41°9N 79°13E **304** B2
Wutai *China* 38°40N 113°12E **306** E7
Wuting = Huimin *China* 37°27N 117°28E **307** F9
Wutonghaolai *China* 42°50N 120°5E **307** C11
Wutongqiao *China* 29°22N 103°50E **304** D5
Wuwei *China* 37°57N 102°34E **304** C5
Wuxi *China* 31°33N 120°18E **305** C7
Wuxiang *China* 36°49N 112°50E **306** F7
Wuyang *China* 33°25N 113°35E **306** H7
Wuyi *China* 37°46N 115°56E **306** F8
Wuyi Shan *China* 27°0N 117°0E **305** D6
Wuyuan *China* 41°2N 108°20E **306** D5
Wuzhai *China* 38°54N 111°48E **306** E6
Wuzhi Shan *China* 18°45N 109°45E **310** C7
Wuzhong *China* 38°2N 106°12E **306** E4
Wuzhou *China* 23°30N 111°18E **305** D6
Wyaaba Cr. → *Australia* 16°27S 141°35E **334** B3
Wyalkatchem *Australia* 31°8S 117°22E **333** F2
Wyalusing *U.S.A.* 41°40N 76°16W **355** E8
Wyandotte *U.S.A.* 42°12N 83°9W **353** D12
Wyandra *Australia* 27°12S 145°56E **335** D4
Wyangala, L. *Australia* 33°54S 149°0E **335** E4
Wyara, L. *Australia* 28°42S 144°14E **335** D3
Wycheproof *Australia* 36°5S 143°17E **335** F3
Wycliffe Well *Australia* 20°48S 134°14E **334** C1
Wye → *U.K.* 51°38N 2°40W **285** F5
Wyemandoo *Australia* 28°28S 118°29E **333** E2
Wymondham *U.K.* 52°35N 1°7E **285** E9
Wymore *U.S.A.* 40°7N 96°40W **352** E5
Wyndham *Australia* 15°33S 128°3E **332** C4
Wyndham *N.Z.* 46°20S 168°51E **331** G2
Wynyard *Australia* 41°5S 145°44E **335** G4
Wynyard *Canada* 51°45N 104°10W **343** C8
Wyola L. *Australia* 29°8S 130°17E **333** E5
Wyoming = Plympton-Wyoming *Canada* 42°57N 82°7W **354** D2
Wyoming □ *U.S.A.* 43°0N 107°30W **348** E10
Wyomissing *U.S.A.* 40°20N 75°59W **355** F9
Wyong *Australia* 33°14S 151°24E **335** E5
Wytheville *U.S.A.* 36°57N 81°5W **353** G13

X

Xaafuun *Somali Rep.* 10°25N 51°16E **319** E5
Xaafuun, Ras *Somali Rep.* 10°27N 51°24E **319** E5
Xaçmaz *Azerbaijan* 41°31N 48°42E **291** F8
Xai-Xai *Mozam.* 25°6S 33°31E **329** D5
Xainza *China* 30°58N 88°35E **304** C3
Xalapa *Mexico* 19°32N 96°55W **359** D5
Xangongo *Angola* 16°45S 15°5E **328** B2
Xankändi *Azerbaijan* 39°52N 46°49E **316** B5
Xanthi *Greece* 41°10N 24°58E **295** D11
Xanxerê *Brazil* 26°53S 52°23W **367** B5
Xapuri *Brazil* 10°35S 68°35W **364** F5
Xar Moron He → *China* 43°25N 120°35E **307** C11
Xátiva *Spain* 38°59N 0°32W **293** C5
Xau, L. *Botswana* 21°15S 24°44E **328** C3
Xavantina *Brazil* 21°15S 52°48W **367** A5
Xenia *U.S.A.* 39°41N 83°56W **353** F12
Xeropotamos → *Cyprus* 34°42N 32°33E **297** E11
Xhora *S. Africa* 31°55S 28°38E **329** E4
Xhumo *Botswana* 21°7S 24°35E **328** C3
Xi Jiang → *China* 22°5N 113°20E **305** D6
Xi Xian *China* 36°41N 110°58E **306** F6
Xia Xian *China* 35°8N 111°12E **306** G6
Xiachengzi *China* 44°40N 130°18E **307** B16
Xiaguan *China* 25°32N 100°16E **304** D5
Xiajin *China* 36°56N 116°0E **306** F9
Xiamen *China* 24°25N 118°4E **305** D6
Xi'an *China* 34°15N 109°0E **306** G5
Xian Xian *China* 38°12N 116°6E **306** E9
Xiang Jiang → *China* 28°55N 112°50E **305** D6
Xiangcheng *Henan, China* 33°29N 114°52E **306** H8
Xiangcheng *Henan, China* 33°50N 113°27E **306** H7
Xiangfan *China* 32°2N 112°8E **305** C6
Xianggang = Hong Kong □ *China* 22°11N 114°14E **305** G11
Xianghuang Qi *China* 42°2N 113°50E **306** C7
Xiangning *China* 35°58N 110°50E **306** G6
Xiangquan *China* 36°30N 113°1E **306** F7
Xiangquan He = Sutlej → *Pakistan* 29°23N 71°3E **314** E4
Xiangshui *China* 34°12N 119°33E **307** G10
Xiangtan *China* 27°51N 112°54E **305** D6
Xianyang *China* 34°20N 108°40E **306** G5
Xiao Hinggan Ling *China* 49°0N 127°0E **305** B7
Xiao Xian *China* 34°15N 116°55E **306** G9
Xiaoyi *China* 37°8N 111°48E **306** F6
Xiawa *China* 42°35N 120°38E **307** C11
Xiayi *China* 34°15N 116°10E **306** G9
Xichang *China* 27°51N 102°19E **304** D5
Xichuan *China* 33°0N 111°30E **306** H6
Xieng Khouang *Laos* 19°17N 103°25E **310** C4
Xifei He → *China* 32°45N 116°40E **306** H9
Xifeng *Gansu, China* 35°40N 107°40E **306** G4
Xifeng *Liaoning, China* 42°42N 124°45E **307** C13
Xifengzhen = Xifeng *China* 35°40N 107°40E **306** G4
Xigazê *China* 29°5N 88°45E **304** D3
Xihe *China* 34°2N 105°20E **306** G3
Xihua *China* 33°45N 114°30E **306** H8
Xili Shuiku *China* 22°36N 113°57E **305** F10
Xiliao He → *China* 43°32N 123°35E **307** C12
Ximana *Mozam.* 19°24S 33°58E **327** F3
Xin Xian = Xinzhou *China* 38°22N 112°46E **306** E7
Xinavane *Mozam.* 25°2S 32°47E **329** D5
Xinbin *China* 41°40N 125°2E **307** D13
Xincun *China* 38°15N 117°45E **307** E9
Xing Xian *China* 38°27N 111°7E **306** E6
Xing'an *China* 25°38N 110°40E **305** D6
Xingcheng *China* 40°40N 120°45E **307** D11
Xinghe *China* 40°55N 113°55E **306** D7
Xinghua *China* 32°58N 119°48E **307** H10
Xinglong *China* 40°25N 117°30E **307** D9
Xingping *China* 34°20N 108°28E **306** G5
Xingtai *China* 37°3N 114°32E **306** F8
Xingu → *Brazil* 1°30S 51°53W **365** D8
Xingyang *China* 34°45N 112°52E **306** G7
Xinhe *China* 37°30N 115°15E **306** F8
Xining *China* 36°34N 101°40E **304** C5
Xinjiang *China* 35°34N 111°11E **306** G6
Xinjiang Uygur Zizhiqu □ *China* 42°0N 86°0E **304** C3
Xinjin = Pulandian *China* 39°25N 121°58E **307** E11
Xinkai He → *China* 43°32N 123°35E **307** C12
Xinken *China* 22°39N 113°36E **305** F10
Xinle *China* 38°25N 114°40E **306** E8
Xinlitun *China* 42°0N 122°8E **307** D12
Xinmin *China* 41°59N 122°50E **307** D12
Xintai *China* 35°55N 117°45E **307** G9
Xinwan *China* 22°47N 113°40E **305** F10
Xinxiang *China* 35°18N 113°50E **306** G7
Xinzhan *China* 43°50N 127°18E **307** C14
Xinzheng *China* 34°20N 113°45E **306** G7
Xinzhou *Hainan, China* 19°43N 109°17E **310** C7
Xinzhou *Shanxi, China* 38°22N 112°46E **306** E7
Xiongyuecheng *China* 40°12N 122°5E **307** D12
Xiping *Henan, China* 33°22N 114°5E **306** H8
Xiping *Henan, China* 33°25N 111°8E **306** H6
Xique-Xique *Brazil* 10°50S 42°40W **365** F10
Xisha Qundao = Paracel Is. *S. China Sea* 15°50N 112°0E **308** A4
Xiuyan *China* 40°18N 123°11E **307** D12
Xixabangma Feng *China* 28°20N 85°40E **315** E11
Xixia *China* 33°25N 111°29E **306** H6
Xixiang *China* 33°0N 107°44E **306** H4
Xixón = Gijón *Spain* 43°32N 5°42W **293** A3
Xiyang *China* 37°38N 113°38E **306** F7
Xizang Zizhiqu □ *China* 32°0N 88°0E **304** C3
Xlendi *Malta* 36°1N 14°12E **297** C1
Xochob *Mexico* 19°21N 89°48W **359** D7
Xuan Loc *Vietnam* 10°56N 107°14E **311** G6
Xuanhua *China* 40°40N 115°2E **306** D8
Xuchang *China* 34°2N 113°48E **306** G7
Xun Xian *China* 35°42N 114°33E **306** G8
Xunyang *China* 32°48N 109°22E **306** H5
Xunyi *China* 35°8N 108°20E **306** G5
Xúquer → *Spain* 39°5N 0°10W **293** C5
Xushui *China* 39°2N 115°40E **306** E8
Xuyen Moc *Vietnam* 10°34N 107°25E **311** G6
Xuzhou *China* 34°18N 117°10E **307** G9
Xylophagou *Cyprus* 34°54N 33°51E **297** E12

Y

Ya Xian = Sanya *China* 18°14N 109°29E **310** C7
Yaamba *Australia* 23°8S 150°22E **334** C5
Yaapeet *Australia* 35°45S 142°3E **335** F3
Yablonovyy Khrebet *Russia* 53°0N 114°0E **301** D12
Yablonovyy Ra. = Yablonovyy Khrebet *Russia* 53°0N 114°0E **301** D12
Yabrai Shan *China* 39°40N 103°0E **306** E2
Yabrūd *Syria* 33°58N 36°39E **318** B5
Yabucoa *Puerto Rico* 18°3N 65°53W **361** d
Yacambú △ *Venezuela* 9°42N 69°27W **361** E6
Yacheng *China* 18°22N 109°6E **310** C7
Yacuiba *Bolivia* 22°0S 63°43W **366** A3
Yacuma → *Bolivia* 13°38S 65°23W **364** F5
Yadgir *India* 16°45N 77°5E **312** L10
Yadkin → *U.S.A.* 35°23N 80°4W **357** D14
Yadua *Fiji* 16°49S 178°18E **331** a
Yaeyama-Rettō *Japan* 24°30N 123°40E **303** M1
Yagasa Cluster *Fiji* 18°57S 178°28W **331** a
Yagodnoye *Russia* 62°33N 149°40E **301** C15
Yahila *Dem. Rep. of the Congo* 0°13N 24°28E **326** B1
Yahk *Canada* 49°6N 116°10W **342** D5
Yahuma *Dem. Rep. of the Congo* 1°0N 23°10E **324** D4
Yaita *Japan* 36°48N 139°56E **303** F9
Yaiza *Canary Is.* 28°57N 13°46W **296** F6
Yakima *U.S.A.* 46°36N 120°31W **348** C3
Yakima → *U.S.A.* 46°15N 119°14W **348** C4
Yakishiri-Jima *Japan* 44°26N 141°25E **302** B10
Yakobi I. *U.S.A.* 58°0N 136°30W **342** B1
Yakovlevka *Russia* 44°26N 133°28E **302** B6
Yaku-Shima *Japan* 30°20N 130°30E **303** J5
Yakumo *Japan* 42°15N 140°16E **302** C10
Yakutat *U.S.A.* 59°33N 139°44W **340** D6
Yakutia = Sakha □ *Russia* 66°0N 130°0E **301** C13
Yakutsk *Russia* 62°5N 129°50E **301** C13
Yala *Thailand* 6°33N 101°18E **311** J3
Yalboroo *Australia* 20°50S 148°40E **334** J6
Yale *U.S.A.* 43°8N 82°48W **354** C2
Yalgoo *Australia* 28°16S 116°39E **333** E2
Yalgorup △ *Australia* 32°39S 115°38E **333** F2
Yalinga *C.A.R.* 6°33N 23°10E **324** C4
Yalkabul, Pta. *Mexico* 21°32N 88°37W **359** C7
Yalleroi *Australia* 24°3S 145°42E **334** C4
Yalobusha → *U.S.A.* 33°33N 90°10W **357** E9
Yalong Jiang → *China* 26°40N 101°55E **304** D5
Yalova *Turkey* 40°41N 29°15E **295** D13
Yalta *Ukraine* 44°30N 34°10E **291** F5
Yalu Jiang → *China* 39°55N 124°19E **307** E13
Yam Ha Melaḥ = Dead Sea *Asia* 31°30N 35°30E **318** D4
Yam Kinneret *Israel* 32°45N 35°35E **318** C4
Yamada *Japan* 33°33N 130°49E **303** H5
Yamagata *Japan* 38°15N 140°15E **302** E10
Yamagata □ *Japan* 38°30N 140°0E **302** E10
Yamaguchi *Japan* 34°10N 131°32E **303** G5
Yamaguchi □ *Japan* 34°20N 131°40E **303** G5
Yamal, Poluostrov *Russia* 71°0N 70°0E **300** B8
Yamal Pen. = Yamal, Poluostrov *Russia* 71°0N 70°0E **300** B8
Yamanashi □ *Japan* 35°40N 138°40E **303** G9
Yamanie Falls △ *Australia* 18°29S 146°9E **334** B4
Yamantau, Gora *Russia* 54°15N 58°6E **290** D10
Yamato Ridge *Sea of Japan* 39°20N 135°0E **302** E7
Yamba *Australia* 29°26S 153°23E **335** D5
Yambarran Ra. *Australia* 15°10S 130°25E **332** C5
Yâmbiô *Sudan* 4°35N 28°16E **323** H11
Yambol *Bulgaria* 42°30N 26°30E **295** C12
Yamdena *Indonesia* 7°45S 131°20E **309** F8
Yame *Japan* 33°13N 130°35E **303** H5
Yamethin *Burma* 20°29N 96°18E **313** J20
Yamma Yamma, L. *Australia* 26°16S 141°20E **335** D3
Yamoussoukro *Ivory C.* 6°49N 5°17W **322** G4
Yampa → *U.S.A.* 40°32N 108°59W **348** F9
Yampi Sd. *Australia* 16°8S 123°38E **332** C3
Yampil *Moldova* 48°15N 28°15E **289** D15
Yampol = Yampil *Moldova* 48°15N 28°15E **289** D15
Yamuna → *India* 25°30N 81°53E **315** G9
Yamunanagar *India* 30°7N 77°17E **314** D7
Yamzho Yumco *China* 28°48N 90°35E **304** D4
Yana → *Russia* 71°30N 136°0E **301** B14
Yanagawa *Japan* 33°10N 130°24E **303** H5
Yanai *Japan* 33°58N 132°7E **303** H6
Yan'an *China* 36°35N 109°26E **306** F5
Yanaul *Russia* 56°25N 55°0E **290** C10
Yanbu 'al Baḥr *Si. Arabia* 24°0N 38°5E **316** F3
Yanchang *China* 36°43N 110°1E **306** F6
Yancheng *Henan, China* 33°35N 114°0E **306** H8
Yancheng *Jiangsu, China* 33°23N 120°8E **307** H11
Yanchep *Australia* 31°33S 115°37E **333** F2
Yanchi *China* 37°48N 107°20E **306** F4
Yanchuan *China* 36°51N 110°10E **306** F6
Yanco Cr. → *Australia* 35°14S 145°35E **335** F4
Yandicoogina *Australia* 22°49S 119°12E **332** D2
Yandoon *Burma* 17°0N 95°40E **313** L19
Yang Xian *China* 33°15N 107°30E **306** H4
Yang-yang *S. Korea* 38°4N 128°38E **307** E15
Yangambi *Dem. Rep. of the Congo* 0°47N 24°24E **326** B1
Yangcheng *China* 35°28N 112°22E **306** G7
Yangch'ü = Taiyuan *China* 37°52N 112°33E **306** F7
Yanggao *China* 40°21N 113°55E **306** D7
Yanggu *China* 36°8N 115°43E **306** F8
Yangliuqing *China* 39°2N 117°5E **307** E9
Yangon = Rangoon *Burma* 16°45N 96°20E **313** L20
Yangpingguan *China* 32°58N 106°5E **306** H4
Yangquan *China* 37°58N 113°31E **306** F7
Yangtse = Chang Jiang → *China* 31°48N 121°10E **305** C7
Yangtze Kiang = Chang Jiang → *China* 31°48N 121°10E **305** C7
Yangyuan *China* 40°1N 114°10E **306** D8
Yangzhou *China* 32°21N 119°26E **305** C6
Yanji *China* 42°59N 129°30E **307** C15
Yankton *U.S.A.* 42°53N 97°23W **352** D5
Yanonge *Dem. Rep. of the Congo* 0°35N 24°38E **326** B1
Yanqi *China* 42°5N 86°35E **304** B3
Yanqing *China* 40°30N 115°58E **306** D8
Yanshan *China* 38°4N 117°22E **307** E9
Yanshou *China* 45°28N 128°22E **307** B15
Yantabulla *Australia* 29°21S 145°0E **335** D4
Yantai *China* 37°34N 121°22E **307** F11
Yantian *China* 22°35N 114°16E **305** F11
Yanuca *Fiji* 18°24S 178°0E **331** a
Yanzhou *China* 35°35N 116°49E **306** G9
Yao Noi, Ko *Thailand* 8°7N 98°37E **311** a
Yao Xian *China* 34°55N 108°59E **306** G5
Yao Yai, Ko *Thailand* 8°0N 98°35E **311** a
Yaoundé *Cameroon* 3°50N 11°35E **324** D2
Yaowan *China* 34°15N 118°3E **307** G10
Yap *Pac. Oc.* 9°30N 138°10E **336** G5
Yapen *Indonesia* 1°50S 136°0E **309** E9
Yapen, Selat *Indonesia* 1°20S 136°10E **309** E9
Yapero *Indonesia* 4°59S 137°11E **309** E9
Yappar → *Australia* 18°22S 141°16E **334** B3
Yaqaga *Fiji* 16°35S 178°36E **331** a
Yaqui → *Mexico* 27°37N 110°39W **358** B2
Yar-Sale *Russia* 66°50N 70°50E **300** C8
Yaraka *Australia* 24°53S 144°3E **334** C3
Yaransk *Russia* 57°22N 47°49E **290** C8
Yare → *U.K.* 52°35N 1°38E **285** E9
Yaremcha *Ukraine* 48°27N 24°33E **289** D13
Yarensk *Russia* 62°11N 49°15E **290** B8
Yarí → *Colombia* 0°20S 72°20W **364** D4
Yarkand = Shache *China* 38°20N 77°10E **304** C2
Yarkant He → *China* 40°26N 80°59E **304** B3
Yarker *Canada* 44°23N 76°46W **355** B8
Yarkhun → *Pakistan* 36°17N 72°30E **315** A5
Yarlung Ziangbo Jiang = Brahmaputra → *Asia* 23°40N 90°35E **315** H13
Yarmouth *Canada* 43°50N 66°7W **345** D6
Yarmūk → *Syria* 32°42N 35°40E **318** C4
Yaroslavl *Russia* 57°35N 39°55E **290** C6
Yarqa, W. → *Egypt* 30°0N 33°49E **318** F2
Yarra Yarra Lakes *Australia* 29°40S 115°45E **333** E2
Yarram *Australia* 38°29S 146°39E **335** F4
Yarraman *Australia* 26°50S 152°0E **335** D5
Yarras *Australia* 31°25S 152°20E **335** E5
Yartsevo *Russia* 60°20N 90°0E **301** C10
Yarumal *Colombia* 6°58N 75°24W **364** B3
Yasawa *Fiji* 16°47S 177°31E **331** a
Yasawa Group *Fiji* 17°0S 177°23E **331** a
Yaselda *Belarus* 52°7N 26°28E **289** B14
Yasin *Pakistan* 36°24N 73°23E **315** A5
Yasinski, L. *Canada* 53°16N 77°35W **344** B4
Yasinya *Ukraine* 48°16N 24°21E **289** D13
Yasothon *Thailand* 15°50N 104°10E **310** E5
Yass *Australia* 34°49S 148°54E **335** E4
Yāsūj *Iran* 30°31N 51°31E **317** D6
Yatağan *Turkey* 37°20N 28°10E **295** F13
Yates Center *U.S.A.* 37°53N 95°44W **352** G6
Yathkyed L. *Canada* 62°40N 98°0W **343** A9
Yatsushiro *Japan* 32°30N 130°40E **303** H5
Yatta Plateau *Kenya* 2°0S 38°0E **326** C4
Yauco *Puerto Rico* 18°2N 66°51W **361** d
Yavari → *Peru* 4°21S 70°2W **364** D4
Yávaros *Mexico* 26°42N 109°31W **358** B3
Yavatmal *India* 20°20N 78°15E **312** J11
Yavne *Israel* 31°52N 34°45E **318** D3
Yavoriv *Ukraine* 49°55N 23°20E **289** D12
Yavorov = Yavoriv *Ukraine* 49°55N 23°20E **289** D12
Yawatahama *Japan* 33°27N 132°24E **303** H6
Yawri B. *S. Leone* 8°22N 13°0W **322** G3
Yaxian = Sanya *China* 18°14N 109°29E **310** C7
Yazd *Iran* 31°55N 54°27E **317** D7
Yazd □ *Iran* 32°0N 55°0E **317** D7
Yazd-e Khvāst *Iran* 31°31N 52°7E **317** D7
Yazman *Pakistan* 29°8N 71°45E **314** E4
Yazoo City *U.S.A.* 32°51N 90°25W **357** E9
Ybycuí △ *Paraguay* 26°5S 56°46W **366** B4
Ybytyruzú △ *Paraguay* 25°51S 56°11W **367** B4
Yding Skovhøj *Denmark* 55°59N 9°46E **281** J13
Ye *Burma* 15°15N 97°15E **310** E1
Ye Xian *China* 33°35N 113°25E **306** H7
Yebyu *Burma* 14°15N 98°13E **310** E2
Yecheng *China* 37°54N 77°26E **304** C2
Yecheon *S. Korea* 36°39N 128°27E **307** F15
Yecla *Spain* 38°35N 1°5W **293** C5
Yécora *Mexico* 28°20N 108°58W **358** B3
Yedintsy = Edineţ *Moldova* 48°9N 27°18E **289** D14
Yegros *Paraguay* 26°20S 56°25W **366** B4
Yehbuah *Indonesia* 8°23S 114°45E **309** J17
Yehuda, Midbar *Israel* 31°35N 35°15E **318** D4
Yei *Sudan* 4°9N 30°40E **323** H12
Yekaterinburg *Russia* 56°50N 60°30E **279** D18
Yelarbon *Australia* 28°33S 150°38E **335** D5
Yelets *Russia* 52°40N 38°30E **290** D6
Yelizavetgrad = Kirovohrad *Ukraine* 48°35N 32°20E **291** E5
Yell *U.K.* 60°35N 1°5W **283** A7
Yell Sd. *U.K.* 60°33N 1°15W **283** A7
Yellow Sea *China* 35°0N 123°0E **307** G12
Yellowhead Pass *Canada* 52°53N 118°25W **342** C5
Yellowknife *Canada* 62°27N 114°29W **342** A6
Yellowknife → *Canada* 62°31N 114°19W **342** A6
Yellowstone → *U.S.A.* 47°59N 103°59W **348** C12
Yellowstone △ *U.S.A.* 44°40N 110°30W **348** D8
Yellowstone L. *U.S.A.* 44°27N 110°22W **348** D8
Yelsk *Belarus* 51°50N 29°10E **289** C15
Yemen ■ *Asia* 15°0N 44°0E **319** E3
Yen Bai *Vietnam* 21°42N 104°52E **310** B5
Yenangyaung *Burma* 20°30N 95°0E **313** J19
Yenbo = Yanbu 'al Baḥr *Si. Arabia* 24°0N 38°5E **316** F3
Yenda *Australia* 34°13S 146°14E **335** E4